The
ENCYCLOPEDIA
OF FOOTBALL

THIRTEENTH REVISED EDITION

The
ENCYCLOPEDIA
OF FOOTBALL

By ROGER TREAT

Revisions Edited by Pete Palmer

THIRTEENTH REVISED EDITION

South Brunswick and New York: A. S. Barnes and Company
London: Thomas Yoseloff Ltd

Library of Congress Catalogue Card Number: 74-30970

A. S. Barnes and Co., Inc.
Cranbury, New Jersey 08512

Thomas Yoseloff Ltd
108 New Bond St.
London W1Y OQX, England

ISBN 0-498-01717-6
Printed in the United States of America

Foreword
by Pete Rozelle

For their efforts in producing and now revising and republishing *The Encyclopedia of Football,* A. S. Barnes and Company deserve the thanks and congratulations of everyone associated with the National Football League.

Roger Treat, as editor, and his associates have brought forth a monumental amount of information about major league football that will be a welcome addition to the book shelves of all sports-loving Americans.

The painstaking manner in which the names of players, clubs and coaches; the history of the game, individual and team statistics and other information was collected, edited and placed in this volume is evident in each of its pages. It was truly a tremendous task.

We of the National Football League are proud of this book. It bears witness to the sound growth of the sport that had its inception in 1895. Along the way to its present position, it once numbered among its believers "Mr. Baseball," Connie Mack, who guided a professional team in 1902.

From the formation of the American Professional Football League in 1920, until today, the growth has been phenomenal. The problems of development created many failures, caused many heartbreaks, but they also served to make more determined those who saw ahead the brilliant future of professional football.

Whatever success the National Football League has had is due, in no small measure, to the wholehearted support it has received through the years from newspapermen, radio announcers and commentators, and, more recently, television announcers and commentators.

To the spectator whose passage through the turnstiles brought the wherewithal to make it possible to continue, we owe a special tribute. The fan, whose loyalty, year in and year out, has contributed his support to our teams, calls for the gratitude of all who are interested in this great game.

The Encyclopedia of Football is, in itself, a tribute to all those who have, in small or large measure, played a part in making major league football one of the nation's most popular sports.

Preface

"It's like a lightning-fast chess game with pawns weighing 250 pounds. I make my gambit; the defense makes the counter-play. If all my pawns, castles, knights and bishops do what they are supposed to do, my king—that's the ball carrier—goes over for a touchdown. The tiniest mistake means disaster. A guard shifts his feet and gives the play away. A halfback takes a peek at the defensive end and tells him, 'Here I come, brother, get ready.' Brains win in this league; brains and psychology."

That, to a veteran quarterback in the National Football League, is major league football, a kingdom where men of intense competitive fire play the game for pay, but would play it for free if no salary were forthcoming. They deny this, but this ancient observer, who knows them well, would bet on it.

For these men are a race apart. Football is as essential to them as breathing. Their *esprit de corps* is tremendous; their personal valor is majestic. The painful, blue-black bruises they carry from August to December, the shoulder separations, the twisted bone-joints and mangled muscles are minor annoyances to be overcome each Sunday afternoon with gallons of novocaine.

Through many seasons the writer has known these players. In the dressing rooms before and after victory and defeat; at the training camps where the All America rookie learns with dramatic suddenness that he knows very little about football; through the long train rides from coast to coast; in their homes with their wives and children; in the hospitals where they mend their broken bones. His admiration grew until it had to pour out on paper.

Thus this history.

Who were (and are) they? What did they do? Who taught them how to do it? These were the simple questions proposed by A. S. Barnes and Company, as the project started.

It was decided to begin the formal listing of statistics with the season of 1919. But the league itself kept no records until 1933. After that the material was available and the collecting of it routine. Before that was a sixteen-year void that had to be filled through excavations and research which might not have bewildered the FBI but were certainly a catastrophic experience for an amateur sleuth.

A card system was created to pick up the playing records of each man. One by one these entries were gleaned from flaky, old programs, brittle newspaper clippings, micro-films, record books and the memories of many men until nearly fifty thousand individual "years played" were accumulated.

Without monumental help from many sources, this volume could never have been completed. The list of contributors follows, and if any have been shuffled aside in the confusion of ceiling-high piles of data, an apology is offered in advance.

An SOS was broadcast in all directions, endorsed by the late Commissioner Bert Bell of the NFL. The response was heart-warming. George Calhoun of Green Bay, Wisconsin, forwarded his precious, and massive, files and proved to be a true triple-threat on digging up facts which once seemed as inaccessible as the vital statistics on the population of Mars. Edward Caswell checked in from Buffalo, New York, with proof that he had been a major league football fanatic for years and years, keeping records and files of his own just for the fun of it. These two men were the main sources of supply, the arsenals of difficult data. They were both fervent football fanatics and the writer is eternally grateful for the hours of work they have contributed to this production.

The office of the Commissioner of the National Football League has been drained of its records. Commissioner Bert Bell himself, later Commissioner "Pete" Rozelle; Joe Labrum, his assistant; the office staff, all have been loyal co-workers.

Several who were active in the league in by-gone days have contributed. Robert Haines of the old Frankford Yellowjackets; Val Ness of the Minneapolis Maroons; Ed Simandl of Orange and Newark; Ole Haugsrud of Duluth in the days of the Eskimos; Ned Kornaus of Chicago, another statistical maniac; Carroll Sollars of Mansfield, Ohio; Jim Schlemmer, Akron, Ohio, sports editor, an expert on the times when Canton, Dayton, Columbus, Hammond, Racine and Rock Island fielded their teams; Eddie Cook, once a frantic assistant in the Sports Department of the Washington *Daily News,* who found himself working once more for his old boss.

Jim Conzelman, the "Mad Genius" of the Chicago Cardinals' days of glory spearheaded by the "Dream Backfield" of a few years ago, dug into his memory of less abundant years with the Rock Island Independents, the Milwaukee Badgers, the Detroit Panthers, the Providence Steamrollers and the original Chicago (Staley) Bears, to fill in many gaps in the records. All the charter members, such as Steve Owen, Curly Lambeau, George Halas and Paddy Driscoll, who took their lumps before the days of novocaine, did their share as co-editors.

From the shadows of the early days, old players popped up to add information on themselves and teammates. Frank Lane, the frantic major league baseball trader, who was a guard for Cincinnati in 1921; Dr. George Munns (retired), who played on the same team to finance his medical education; John Bonadies of Hartford and Dr. Vincent LaCava, who managed the Hartford Blues; Joseph LaBissoniere of Hammond; Dr. Joseph Alexander of the early Giants, Rochester and Milwaukee; Rudolph Tersch of Minneapolis; Ben Friedman of Cleveland, Detroit, New York and Brooklyn; Barlow Irvin of Buffalo and Tommy Hughitt of the same team; Oliver Kraehe of the 1923 St. Louis team; Wilfrid Smith, sports editor of the Chicago *Tribune,* who played with Hammond and the Chicago Cardinals; John "Bunny" Barrett of Akron, Detroit and the Pottsville Maroons; Fred Putzier of Minneapolis; Walter Flanagan of the Rock Island years of glory, and "Mike" Wilson of the same team, later boss of NFL officials; John Lee Snoots, teammate of the fabulous Nesser brothers of Columbus Panhandle years, before the NFL was born. Al Nesser himself; Marty Beck, Dick Stahlman and dozens more from the 1920 era. Tom Watkins, collector of Louisville history added his share, Ed Healey, giant Chicago Bear tackle and one of the first to enter the Hall of Fame, solved many difficult problems.

Others did their share, like Homer Ruh of Columbus; Ray Witter of Rochester; Oscar "Oc" Anderson of Buffalo; Edward Hunt of the Hartford Blues; Milton Ghee of Canton and Hammond; Frank Bucher of Pottsville and Detroit; David Reese of Dayton; Gale Bullman of Columbus; Francis Matteo of Rochester, and Leo Lyons, who managed the team; Andy Nemecek of Columbus; Arda Bowser of Canton and Cleveland; Adrian Baril of Milwaukee and Minneapolis; Roman Brumm of Milwaukee and Racine; Francis Bacon of Dayton and Ken Huffine of the same team.

One of the most helpful, to whom must go special gratitude, was Jack R. Brown of the old Dayton Triangles, athletic director of the University of Dayton, which has always turned out a fine crop of pro players; and to E. Paul "Deke" Lynch of Columbus; Aaron Hertzman of Louisville, one of the pioneers and manager of early Louisville teams; Fred Heinisch of Racine; W. Roy "Link" Lyman of the old Bears; Edward Carroll of Canton, and fans like Richard Geisler of Washington, John Crelli of Pittsburgh and Walter Farquhar of Pottsville, who like to relive the colorful, older days in the welcome letters.

High on the list for dedicated help are Fr. Michael J. O'Donnell of Villanova University; Ed Black of the 1926 Newark Bears of the "Red Grange" league; Carl Etelman, star quarterback of the Boston Braves in the same league; Vic Frolund of Youngstown, veteran fan; Ed Pavlick of Milwaukee, another of the same. The efforts of N. H. "Hal" Richter of Massillon, vagabond player of the 1920s and permanent enthusiast, were most valuable.

The story and statistics of the All America Football Conference came by courtesy of Joe Petritz, former publicity director of Notre Dame and the AAFC. To the late Arch Ward, sports editor, and Ed Prell, major league football writer, of the Chicago *Tribune*, and to Wilfrid Smith, present sports editor, my thanks for the story of the All Star games at Chicago.

Al Ward, publicity director of the American Football League, helped keep those records straight.

The owners, publicity directors, coaches and other officials of the active clubs were harassed with inquiries, bombarded with questionnaires. They responded as nobly from the front office as their more muscular co-workers do on the playing fields.

To the registrars of more than five hundred colleges who searched their records for minor facts and reported them promptly, a salute.

Finally, for countless hours of clerical drudgery, reshuffling of lists, addressing of hundreds of envelopes, thanks to my own personal "staff": my late mother, Mrs. Esther Treat Mills; my wife, Gerda Dahl Treat, my two sons, John and Peter Treat; Suzanne Treat, who all contributed many hours.

With the death of Roger Treat in 1969, revisions were taken over by Suzanne Treat. Pete Palmer assumed the editorship in 1970. He was assisted in revising this thirteenth edition by Don Weiss of the NFL in New York, Don Smith of the Hall of Fame in Canton, Ohio, and Denny Lynch of the New England Patriots.

Contents

11

The

ENCYCLOPEDIA
OF FOOTBALL

THIRTEENTH REVISED EDITION

1 The Story of the Game

THE EVOLUTION OF FOOTBALL

The celestial spirit of an unknown Dane who died in England soon after the year 1,000 A.D. may be strutting around the universe at this moment claiming that he is responsible for the game of football. He never played any version of the game as it is known today and the credit due him stems from an episode in which others used his head.

This Dane, whose name, under the circumstances, could not have been recorded for posterity, was a member of the armed forces of the "dastardly aggressor" of the moment. England was occupied by the victorious Danes, a condition which lasted from 1016 to 1042, and during that period, this unknown father of football died, and was buried on the battlefield. Time passed. The British rose again to drive the aggressors into the sea and the unknown Danish GI mouldered in his grave.

Some time later, an Englishman, digging in the old battlefield, unearthed the skull of this Dane, and, muttering about unpleasant memories of the days of the occupation, proceeded to kick the skull around the pasture. Other Englishmen joined in the fun and some youngsters, watching this new pastime, dug farther, until other Danish skulls were found. Soon, everyone in the township was kicking a skull and this sport continued until toes became more painful than the smoldering hatred of the Danes. It was not long before some minor inventive genius of the time produced the inflated bladder of a cow to take the place of the skulls, and thus the head of the unknown Dane had been used to create the embryo of football. There was a long road to travel from that pasture pastime to the passing skill of Redskin Sam Baugh, the elusive wizardry of Packer Don Hutson and the devastating black magic of T-formations. It would take nearly a thousand years to produce the lightning thrusts and bewildering deception of American Professional Football, but an ever-increasing multitude of major league fans in the United States of America is fanatically grateful that an unnamed Englishman did unearth a certain skull and did proceed to boot it for that first field goal attempt in history.

As if to set the pattern for later days, or perhaps to prove that there is nothing new, ever, anywhere, "Over-emphasis" blossomed within the first century of football history. Those who lately howled that football must be abolished to preserve the good way of life, merely parroted the words of King Henry II (1159–1189), who not only threatened banishment of the sport, but did indeed ban it forever during his reign.

The ban followed a national craze which had developed over the joys of booting the inflated bladders in contests which were a combination of soccer, vandalism and mass modified-homicide. For the "big game" of those days was played in no stadium, but around, over and through two townships. The entire population of each contestant met at a point between the towns, the bladder was tossed in the middle, and chaos broke loose. The touchdown was scored when the ball was kicked into the center of the opposing town and there were no further rules to confuse the issue. If children, gentle old ladies and valuable livestock were trampled in the process, there were no referees to step off penalties. Gardens, crops, fences and even dwellings were flattened as the valiant athletes gave it the "old college try." Nor were there any gate receipts; the fans

15

were taking part in the game. It would have been a glorious spectacle for television with no one to dictate restrictions. The celebrations which took place in the conquered village formed a pattern for American Legion conventions of later years and King Henry soon learned that the Danish occupation had been less devastating than one season of "futballe" as it was then called.

Futballe brought on its own banishment for still another reason. National preparedness in those days required each male citizen to put in a certain number of hours of archery practice, even as his descendants would practice running into burrows to escape the weapons of the future. When King Henry found that his soldiers were too busy playing futballe to tend to their bow and arrow exercises he blew the whistle. "No more futballe," he said. "We must build our national security with such a formidable fighting force that no aggressor will dare attack."

Futballe immediately "went underground" and was played only in those communities where the big-shot hoodlums of the time were able to corrupt the local police.

This condition prevailed for the next four hundred years.

The invention of firearms bailed futballe out of official disgrace early in the sixteenth century, and James I revoked the ban at the request of thousands of sportsmen who had been playing all the time anyway, but wanted to make the game respectable. The game spread to all sections of the British Isles, and, unlike its namesake of modern times, it was a sport concerning a foot and a ball. There was no running with the ball; there was no forward passing. The previous assaults between townships were now confined to a standard-sized playing field and points were scored for driving the ball across the opponent's goal. Later refinements produced goal posts and restrictions of the number of players. Eventually, this game became known as "Association Football" to distinguish it from other varieties. This designation was shortened to "Assoc." and, through slang, to "soccer," which it is called today.

In this same period, futballe drifted over into Ireland, where it was immediately condemned as a sissy game, sorely in need of a strong injection of manliness, Irish style. The denizens of Ireland added some features of their own, mainly punching with the fists. This punching was supposedly aimed at the ball with intent to propel it toward the goal-line, but it was so much more satisfying to miss the ball and punch the opponent in the head that Gaelic football, as it is played today, is still a cross between boxing and soccer with emphasis on the former. It has changed little in nearly six hundred years.

The first variation from soccer, which pointed the way to the pattern of American football, took place at Rugby College in England in 1823. During an inter-class game of soccer, a player named William Ellis, discouraged with his lack of success at kicking the ball, was inspired to pick it up in his hands and run with it, thus scoring the first touchdown in history. Ellis was temporarily disgraced by his breach of sportsmanship, but soon, more adventurous souls decided to change the rules to permit running with the ball—and thus the game of Rugby was born.

In the ranks of the Pilgrim Fathers there were plenty of soccer players. There may even have been a few soccer balls, as well as cricket equipment, on the *Mayflower* when she made her momentous trip to these shores. But, strangely enough, there is no sign that any of the early immigrants to this country were Rugby players. The game was apparently unknown, or little appreciated, until 1875, when Harvard College, feeling its muscles at soccer, and unable to find a contender among the other American colleges, challenged McGill University to come down from Montreal to play a match of football. McGill came, but, unfortunately it was a Rugby team which showed up. A compromise was reached by playing half the game under soccer rules, half under Rugby, and the American boys liked the foreign game so much that they forgot all about soccer.

The next year Harvard sold the idea of playing Rugby to Yale to start a rivalry which is still renewed annually. Six years before, Rutgers had played Princeton in a football (soccer) game, enabling these universities to lay claim to being the pioneers of intercollegiate gridiron warfare, which was to be periodically accused of over-emphasis, and also periodically forgiven by the American public which loved the game.

For many years, Yale, Harvard and Princeton, then called "The Big Three," dominated the collegiate game, with the balance of the present members of the Ivy League assuming the secondary roles. It was not until well after World War I that the public became aware that football was not the exclusive property of the Eastern seaboard.

Early All America teams were dominated by the Big Three. Occasionally a West Point player, or a member of the Carlisle Indians, would get his name on the list, but seldom.

In present times there are nearly as many "All" teams as there were players in the early days of American football. Even now these mythical line-ups seldom include the first college rookies to be selected by the major league clubs when it comes to the annual player drafts. As many big stars in the major leagues have come from such unlikely campuses as Western Michigan State, Abilene Christian, St. Anselm's, Grambling and West Louisiana Teachers as have checked in from the Big Ten and similar highly publicized collegiate leagues.

Scoring originally paid off most highly on the field goal, which counted 5 against 1 for a touchdown. As late as 1884, a safety was 1 point, a touchdown 2, a point-after-touchdown 4, and a field goal 5. Later a touchdown was awarded 5 points, the same as a field goal, with the point-after-touchdown dropping to 1 and the safety becoming 2. Finally, in 1910 the field goal was dropped to 3 points, and, in 1912 the touchdown became 6 to set up the entire scoring routine as it is today. Recently there was a movement led by Commissioner Bert Bell of the National Football League to make the touchdown equal to 7 points, to eliminate the point-after-touchdown altogether, and to provide for a sudden-death play-off in case of a tie. Bell believed that the point-after-touchdown is an unnatural sideline of football which depends too much on the skill of a few players, and that the fans deserve a decision at the end of any football game—as well as the players, owners and coaches.

The pattern of football strategy has progressed rapidly within seventy-five years from an offense which consisted mostly of "grab-it-and-run" to the intricate refinements of T-formation which can produce upward of ten thousand variations, counting individual blocking assignments, flankers, decoys and men-in-motion.

The first dramatic innovation was the so-called "flying-wedge," in which a phalanx of blocking linemen hung on to suitcase handles sewed to the pants of the man in front, and thundered down the field thus tied together with the ball carrier flitting along behind waiting for the opposition to be rolled up in a broken heap along the way.

This led to so many serious injuries—and deaths—and brought on such a savage game that President Teddy Roosevelt threatened to send football to Siberia if adequate safety precautions were not taken. In 1905, a gigantic Swarthmore tackle named Bob Maxwell, apparently the key-man in Swarthmore's defense, was seriously manhandled by the little gentlemen from Pennsylvania. A photograph of the bleeding Maxwell leaving the field incensed President Roosevelt and it was then that he waved the big stick at collegiate football.

The next year (1906) the forward pass was legalized in an effort to open up the game, the flying wedge was banished, and football had entered its next phase of growth.

It was not until 1913, however, that Gus Dorais (later to be coach of the Detroit Lions) and Knute Rockne, as Notre Dame players, brought the forward pass into a game with West Point and scored a sensational triumph. From that moment until the mid-1930's, the forward pass was something that a daring quarterback might demand on third down or when a game was hopelessly lost. It was a desperation measure for extreme circumstances.

And then, at little-known (at the time) Texas Christian University, there appeared a halfback named Samuel Adrian Baugh, and football, particularly the professional game, was about to make the most revolutionary change in its format to date. For Baugh, easily the most sensational passer of record, made the forward pass a routine offensive performance, a natural development of football warfare. Parenthetically, Baugh began to strike through the air at the same time that aircraft became the dominant factor of the bigger game known as "war," a fact that may have deeper meaning to deeper thinkers. This innovation led to further ramifications of football, until, in current times, roughly half of all offensive football is the forward pass.

Other changes have concerned themselves with offensive backfield formations: the single-wing, double-wing, punt, short-punt, Notre Dame box, the A and double A, and, finally and most important, the T.

The origin of the T is not entirely clear. It existed as far back as 1920, probably before that. But its devastating deception and all-around possibilities were not fully realized until George Halas, owner-coach of the Chicago Bears, and Clark Shaughnessy went to work on it in the late 1930's with the immortal Sidney Luckman as T quarterback. It was Halas who realized fully the possibilities of creating another effective blocker in the forward line by the almost too simple device of permitting the center to hand back the ball while he kept his eyes on his opponent, not looking back between his own legs. It was Halas—and Luckman—who worked out the pantomime of hand-faking that is now routine to the expert T quarterbacks. It was Halas who developed more plays now used by the other professional teams, as well as hundreds of college squads, than any other coach. Halas now claims that the Bears can call more than ten thousand different plays—and that there are still many realms in the higher strata of T-formation that he has not had time to develop as yet.

The man-in-motion, and the flankers were developed in the National Football League and their deadly possibilities have loosened up the defense so that football has become a whirlwind operation of speed combined with crushing power.

At the same time defense has been catching up with the T, and now it is almost mandatory for a professional team to have an offense which combines wing formations, short-punts, and other variations, with the T, so that the fan reaps a full menu of offensive fireworks whenever two of the major league teams tangle their talents in a showdown.

The result of this development has been higher, faster scoring. It is not unusual for a team to score more points in one game (the record of 72 is held by the Washington Redskins) than some teams scored in an entire season not many years ago. (The Philadelphia Eagles scored 51 points in 12 games in 1936.) Through statistical studies, training of officials and other innovations the National Football League has speeded up its game.

Steadily increasing attendance figures, despite the drain-off to television, radio, and the ever-present problem of bad weather in late fall, prove that major league football is the healthiest young sport in America. More and more fans are realizing each year that big league football, so far as skill and ability is concerned, bears the same relation to the college game that big league baseball does to minor league baseball.

With its rosters a listing of the finest players the thousands of colleges can produce, it is a tornado of touchdown thrills.

THE BEGINNING ERA

The first professional football team to be recognized as such played in the township of Latrobe, in Westmoreland County, Pennsylvania, forty miles southeast of Pittsburgh. It was sponsored by the local YMCA. Latrobe made its artistic debut on August 31, 1895.

by defeating Jeannette, another township ten miles away, by the impressive score of 12–0. For the next ten years, Latrobe fielded a powerful team which played wherever and whenever it could, for whatever cash it could get.

Dr. John Brallier, who was to become a dentist in Latrobe, is awarded the distinction of having become one of the first "confessed" professionals when he deserted the University of West Virginia team to play for Latrobe. Fielding Yost, who later denounced professional football, played for Greensburg; and "Doggie" Trenchard of Princeton, Walter Okeson of Lehigh, Walter Howard of Cornell were a few of the early college stars to join the early rampages. In 1897, the entire Lafayette backfield (Best, Barclay, Bray and Walbridge) played for Greensburg.

During the next few years, other professional teams began to appear. The city of Pittsburgh developed the Duquesne County and Athletic Club, and its rosters listed some of the finest collegiate players of the time. Arthur Poe of Princeton, "Pudge" Heffelfinger of Yale; Bemus and Hawey Pierce, the two magnificent Indians from Carlisle; G. H. Brooke and P. D. Overfield of Pennsylvania, Fred Crolius of Dartmouth, all as prominent then as the current swarms of All Americans are now, played with the Pittsburgh club.

Upper New York State followed Pennsylvania into the joys of professional football soon after the turn of the century. Teams existed in Buffalo, Syracuse, Watertown, Auburn, Corinth, Clayton, Oswego, Alexandria Bay and Ogdensburg. One of the outstanding players for Watertown and Syracuse was Phil Draper, former miracle-man back of Williams College, another great player who was born fifty years too soon to reap the gold and glory that would have been his today.

On December 28, 1902, Syracuse, with Draper, Glenn "Pop" Warner, and his brother Bill, along with the peripatetic Pierce brothers, Bemus and Hawey, played the Phila-delphia Nationals to a 6–0 defeat in Madison Square Garden, New York. The officials worked in full dress, including high silk hats and white gloves. Thirty years later, the Chicago Bears defeated the Portsmouth Spartans, 9-0, indoors at Chicago Stadium. That, up to 1958, was the end of indoor football.

Also in 1902, Connie Mack organized a football team which he named the "Athletics." He put the spectacular playboy pitcher, Rube Waddell, in the line-up, much to the Rube's confusion, and claimed the championship of the world after beating Pittsburgh, which had a fullback by the name of Christy Mathewson who had once been a line-crasher at Bucknell. The Indian Pierces played for Mack—and for almost everybody else.

Starting in 1904, and lasting until 1920 when the American Professional Football Association, the father of the National Football League, was formed, Ohio was the battleground, and the nursery, for major league football. Canton, Massillon, Akron, Columbus and Dayton contained many violent and valiant men, ever ready for some periodic bloodletting against any team which cared to show up. It was at Canton that Jim Thorpe first appeared to play for many years until he finished his career with the New York Giants in 1925.

When Billy Heston, an all-time Michigan backfield ace, expressed a willingness to pick up some pocket money after finishing his college career in 1904, Canton, Massillon and Akron got themselves into a bidding auction for his services. Heston, believing he had the three teams over a barrel, lifted his demands to the point where all three rebelled and refused to hire him at any price. A year later, Heston did play one game for Canton for a fabulous $600, was massacred on the first play by the Massillon defense and never gained another inch. He played one more game in Chicago, collected a broken leg early in the game, and that was the end of his professional career.

Charlie Moran, major league umpire of renown, was a great back for Massillon in the same era. From the Carlisle Indian school came the Pierce brothers, Bemus and Hawey, and the great players called Frank Mt. Pleasant and Albert Exendine. Later, Jim Thorpe organized an entire team of Indians, who called themselves the "Oorang Indians" and played in the NFL in 1922 and 1923, sometimes representing Marion, Ohio. Before that, Jim went through the glory, and the heartbreak, of his experiences at the 1912 Olympic games at Stockholm, where he and George Patton of West Point dominated the scene.

As time went on, Columbus and Shelby in Ohio had teams. The Columbus Panhandles, managed by Joe Carr, who later became president of the National Football League (from 1921 until his death in 1939), had the distinction of fielding one of the strangest line-ups in football history. In 1906, six of its eleven positions were filled by brothers named "Nesser." None of them had ever accepted any of the offers made by many colleges. They played with many teams for many years, brother Al finally writing an end to the family saga with the Cleveland team in 1931.

In the late teens, Knute Rockne and Charles "Gus" Dorais, whose forward-passing act had recently flabbergasted a highly touted West Point team, moved into professional football. They played with so many teams, jumping from one high bidder to another, that it would be impossible to trace their careers with any degree of accuracy. It is reported that the Columbus team found itself facing Rockne in six different uniforms during one season. Dorais later became coach of the Detroit Lions from 1943 through 1947.

Men who were destined to make their fame as coaches, rather than players, appeared in the Canton-Massillon line-ups of 1919. "Tuss" McLaughry, later of Dartmouth; and the late "Jock" Sutherland and Earle "Greasy" Neale took part in those bitter struggles. Charlie Brinkley, the great Harvard drop-kicker, tried it for a while with little success. "Fido" Kempton, a tiny quarterback from Yale, joined Canton for a few games in 1921.

War must be given some credit for the birth, or at least the conception, of what is now known as the National Football League. For, in 1918, the team representing the Great Lakes Naval Training Station was chosen to play in the Rose Bowl, where it proceeded to wallop the Mare Island squad. On that Great Lakes team were the men who would mold and nurse major league football to its present prosperity. George Halas, fresh from the University of Illinois, was its brilliant end. Jim Conzelman, John "Paddy" Driscoll, Harold Erickson were in its backfield. Hugh Blacklock, a fine Bear tackle to be, was there, as were two excellent guards from Notre Dame, Jerry Jones and Emmett Keefe, who would play in the league to come.

There were many truly magnificent players in this early era of growth, many almost unknown to current fans who have been conditioned to believe that major league football "began" with the spectacular unveiling of Harold "Red" Grange in 1925. Only the name of Jim Thorpe seems to carry over from those dark days of guerrilla warfare on the fields of Pennsylvania, Ohio and upper New York, although the eyes of the old-timers will light up with a strange fire when they talk of these "good, old days" when each man either played the sixty minutes or was carried off on a stretcher. Not for them are the tactics of specialists and platoons.

Thorpe was, without doubt, a superlative back who could kick, crash or run in the open. He was a physical freak, who could, like Babe Ruth, Walter Hagen and Harry Greb, ignore all the rules in the fitness manuals and still perform at a peak efficiency beyond the reach of lesser athletes. Thorpe used an open field running technique all his own, not dodging violently, but moving with a deceptive hip-twist that seemed to make him almost impossible to drop. Jim himself explained it thus: "I gave them a leg for a second, then took it away." Another weapon Thorpe used in the early days was an illegal, and decidedly lethal, shoulder-pad which had an outer covering of sheet metal concealed under his uniform jersey. When he crashed into optimistic tacklers with this device, devastation set in. Not until he joined the New York Giants in 1925 did anyone persuade Jim that he was not allowed to carry such murderous concealed weapons onto a football field. It is generally conceded by all the deeper thinkers of the current National Football League that, if Jim Thorpe were now coming out of college, he would undoubtedly be the highest-paid rookie the league had ever known, and, perhaps, its greatest star.

All these warriors of old, many gone on to the gridirons of Valhalla, were the pioneers of America's most exciting sport. They would have played for nothing if they had to—and often did, even as "professionals." The dynamic drive of these men, joined with that of other men of similar courage and aggressiveness, made the league what it is today, and pointed the way toward the greater triumphs of the future.

2 Year-by-Year History from 1919 to the Present

1919

The National Football League was conceived in July, 1919, in Canton, Ohio. It was a predictable act of growth from the dozens of professional teams that had developed in the midwest and in upper New York state.

Five teams signed up that day and all of them remained in the league until 1925, some longer. These were the pioneers: Akron (Frank Neid), Canton (Ralph Hays, in whose auto agency the meeting was held), Columbus (Joe Carr, who would become league president from 1921-39), Dayton (Carl Storck) and Rochester (Leo Lyons). They called it the American Professional Football Association. Franchise cost was $25.

There were plenty of top level players on these five rosters; many men who would have been big bonus rookies if they could have delayed their birth a half-century. There was no planned schedule of games, nor would there be for the next 15 years. Games were set up where there was a possibility of gate receipts; travel was difficult; players jumped from one team to another for an extra payday.

At the end of the season, the Canton Bulldogs claimed the championship. The Massillon Tigers, manned by names that would be prominent through football history, were strong contenders.

However, in the showdown game at the end of the season, Canton beat Massillon, 3-0, on a field goal by Jim Thorpe. Forty years later, Thorpe would be one of the first group enshrined in pro football's Hall of Fame located in Canton, only a few hundred yards from the site of the 1919 game.

1919 AKRON PROS
COACH- Elgie Tobin

Brown, George - B	Kester, Walt - G
Bryant, Jim - Q	Maloney, "Jackie" - C
Cobb, Al - T	Martin, Roy - B
Copley, Charley - T	Munns, George - B
Crawford, Ken - B	Nesser, Al - G
Crisp, Park - G	Pollard, "Fritz" - B
Cusack, Bill - E	Purdy, Clair - Q
Deibel, Art - C	Scott, John - B
Dobbins, John - B	Sefton, Fred - E
Druesbach, Ollie - G	Sweeney, - E
Francis - G	Tobin, Elgie - B
Gaskeen, Harry - E	Waldsmith, Ralph - C
Gillette, - B	Wall, Pete - B
Hollenback, Oscar - G	Welch, Howard - E
Johnson, Frank - B	White, Harold - G
Joy, Bill - B	Ziegler, "Gus" - G

1919 CANTON BULLDOGS
COACH - Jim Thorpe

Barron, Jim - T	Kelly, - B
Bolen, Charles - E	Lowe, "Bull" - T
Buck, "Cub" - T	McClelland, Bill - Q
Calac, Pete - B	McGregor, John - C
Corcoran, Art - E	Martin, Roy - B
Chamberlin, Guy - E	O'Connor, Dan - G
Devlin, Mark - B	Pierce, George - G
Edwards, Gene - G	Rehor, Fred - G
Feeney, Al - C	Seidel, Fred - G
Gormley, Tom - T	Spears, Clarence - T
Grigg, Cecil - B	Speck, "Dutch" - G
Guyon, Joe - B	Telfer, Alex - E
Jackson - B	Thorpe, Jim - B
Keady, Jim - B	Turner, John - C
Kellison, John - T	Whelan, Tom - E

1919 CLEVELAND INDIANS
COACH - Ed Green

Allshouse, Charles - E	Brown, Matt - B
Allshouse, George - G	Carlson, "Red" - E
Brickley, George - B	Cartwright, - B

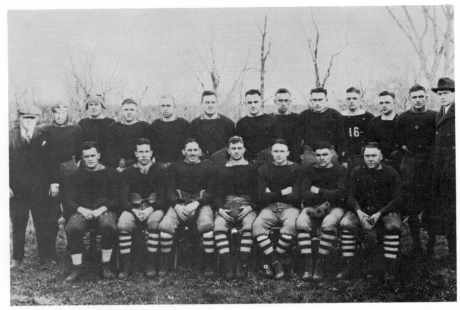

The 1919 Triangles. *Standing:* **Stork, Mgr., Roudebush, Reese, Albers, Clark, Winston, Thiele, Cutler, Stoecklein, Hauser, Dellinger, Partlow, Talbott, Coach.** *Sitting:* **Bacon, Yerger, Abrell, Mahrt, Captain, Fenner, Kinderdine, Tidd. Record for the year: Triangles 51, Nordyke-Marmon 0; Triangles 26, Pitcairn Quakers 0; Triangles 14, Cleveland Panthers 19; Triangles 26, Cincinnati Celts 0; Triangles 0, Panhandles 6; Triangles 20, Pine Village 0; Triangles 0, Massillon 0, and Triangles 21, Panhandles 0.**

Clark, Les - B	Mattern, Joe - B
Connell, Jackson - B	Miles, Mark - T
Cody, Leo - B	Murphy, Joe - G
Denaple, Ed - B	Pauxtis, Simon - B
Doane, Joe - B	Perlman, Les - T
Drummy, Jim - Q	Pierotti, Al - C
Ducote, "Moon" - B	Scheule, Norman - B
Gaffney - T	Scott, Jim - E
Gordon, Ralph - B	Seidel, Fred - T
Graham, Sam - T	Sheehan - T
Haggerty, John - G	Solon, Lorin - B
Hanley, Ed - B	Stahl, Ed - G
Hicks, - B	Sweetland, Fred - B
Kane, - T	Tallman, Charles - T
Kerr, George - T	Telfer, Alex - E
Kesner, Jim - Q	Thomas, Carl - T
Lowe, "Bulger" - E	Trowbridge, Ray - F
Lyons, - G	Ziegler, "Gus" - G

1919 COLUMBUS PANHANDLES
COACH - Ted Nesser

Beckwith, - G	Nesser, Phil - G
Brigham, Hiram - C	Nesser, Ted - B
Davis, - E	Rogers, Walter - B
Davis, John - E	Ruh, Emmett - E
Gaulke, Hal - B	Ruh, Homer - E
Kuehner, Oscar - T	Snoots, Lee - B
Mulbarger, Joe - T	Waite, Will - B
Nesser, Fred - G	Walters, - G
Nesser, John - Q	Wolford, Oscar - G

1919 DAYTON TRIANGLES
COACH - Nelson Talbott

Abrell, Dick - B	Partlow, Lou - B
Bacon, Francis - B	Reese, Dave - E
Clark, Harold - E	Roudebush, George - B
Cutler, Harry - T	Stoecklein, Earl - T
Dellinger, Larry - G	Thiele, Carl - E
Fenner, Lee - E	Tidd, Glenn - T
Hauser, Earl - E	Winston, Charles - G
Kinderdine, George - C	Yerger, Howard - B
Mahrt, Al - B	

1919 DETROIT HERALDS
COACH - Billy Marshall

Braden, - T	Horning, "Steamer" - T
Carman, Charles - G	Kelly, Jim - B
Carleton, Art - G	Kreuz, Lou - Q
Carpenter, Walker - T	Lenahan, "Nig" - B
Costello, Harry - Q	Miller, W. Blake - E
Dunne, "Pat" - B	Sacksteder, Norb - B
Finsterwald, Russ - B	Straight, Herbert - G
Gardner, Milt - T	Talman, Howard - T
Guy, Charles - C	Tandy, George - G
Hays, - B	Whipple, Ray - E
Holden, - T	Wyman, Arnold - E

1919 HAMMOND PROS
COACH -

Barrett, John - B	Bergman, Alfred - Q
Baston, Al - E	Blacklock, Hugh - T

Brickley, George - B
Cole, M. - E
DesJardien, Paul - C
Falcon, Gil - B
Falcon, Dick - C
Ghee, Milt - Q
Halas, George - E
Howard, W. - B

Jones, Jerry - G
Keefe, Emmett - G
King, Dick - B
McLaughlin, Gene - T
Rydzewski, Frank - T
Seliger, - G
Wyman, Arnold - B

1919 MASSILLON TIGERS
COACHES - Bob Nash & Tom Keady

Barrett, Charles - B
Baujan, Harry - E
Cheetah, Jim - T
Cofall, Stan - Q
Conn, "Tuffy" - B
Cubbage, Ben - G
Derr, Ben - B
Dorais, "Gus" - Q
Garrett, Al - T
Gougler, Roscoe - B
Herron, "Pat" - E
Hess, Walt - B
Higgins, Bob - E
Johnson, Frank - G
Jones, Jerry - G
Keady, Jim - B
Kester, Walter - B
Lingrell, Roy - B
Little Lou - B
McLaren, George - B
Mackert, Bob - G
Maginnis, W. Davis - B

Miller, "Shorty" - Q
Miller, "Heinie" - E
Miller, John - B
Nash, Bob - E
Peck, Bob - C
Rambaud, Carl - T
Rockne, Knute - E
Rydzewski, Frank - T
Scott, Jim - B
Sies, Dale - T
Smith "Pat" - B
Spagna, Joe - C
Sutherland, "Jock" - G
Talman, Howard - B
Thornhill, "Tiny" - T
Tressel, John - E
Wesbecher, Al - G
Whalen, Bill - B
Wimberly, Byron - G
Wray, Lud - C
Zemen, Ladimir - E

1919 ROCHESTER JEFFERSONS
COACH - Leo Lyons

Argus, Bob - B
Bachmaier, Joe - G
Barsha, John - B
Brown, Ray - B
Connors, Hamilton - E
DuMoe, Joe - E
DuMoe, Bill - B
Erwig, Bill - B

Forsyth, Ben - C
Lyons, Leo - E
Purdy, Clair - B
Rafter, Bill - B
Witter, Ray - E
Witter, Bob - B
Wood, Jim - G

1919 ROCK ISLAND
INDEPENDENTS
COACH - "Rube" Ursella
& John Roche

Buland, Walt - T
Chicken, Fred - B
Fitzgerald, Freeman - C
Fosdick, Bob - G
Henry, Tom - B
Hunzelman, Harry - G
Lyle, Dewey - T
Mansfield, Jerry - B

Marshall, Robert - E
Novak, Ed - B
Quinn, George - B
Robb, Loyal - B
Smith, Frank - G
Smith, Okla - E
Ursella, "Rube" - Q
Wyland, Guido - G

1919 TOLEDO MAROONS
COACH -

Baxter, Jim - E
Brown, Tom - T
Detray, - B
Hackett, Hugh - E
Lutz, Rudy - E
McLean, Ray - B
Marshall, Bill - Q
Mauder, "Dutch" - G
Miller, "Shorty" - Q

Neitzski, - B
Nichols, Charles - B
Schimmel, John - G
Schultz, - C
Heibert, Harry - B
Sheeks, Paul - Q
Turnquist, - T
Weiss, Jules - C

1919 WHEELING
COACH -

Abbott, - E
Becker, - G
Fausch, Frank - B
Fesit, - C
Fleischman, - T
Gasteen, - E
Mallaney, - Q

Munson, - B
O'Connell, - B
Sloan, - T
Stone, - B
Strobel, - E
Stump, - T
Thomas, Carl - G

1920

The five original teams were ready for action again in 1920 and several more scraped up $100, the new price, to join the league. Among them were the Decatur Staleys and the Racine Cardinals of Chicago. These two, as the Chicago Bears and Chicago-St. Louis Cardinals, would be the only survivors 50 years later. The Green Bay Packers, playing non-league ball in 1920, would join in 1922.

Massillon and Muncie (Ind.) were represented at this meeting but never could get teams on the field. Hammond (Ind.) and Rock Island (Ill.), did play this and several other seasons.

Buffalo, Detroit and the Chicago Tigers were not represented at the meeting but played enough games against the others to be credited with being part of the loose operation that was 1920.

Jim Thorpe was elected president of the league, then called the American Professional Football Association.

At the end of the year, undefeated after finishing the season with a scoreless tie against Buffalo and another scoreless tie with the Decatur Staleys, Akron could claim the best record. No one scored on them in 13 games.

In later years, the Chicago Bears, who descended from the Decatur Staleys, claimed a tie for the 1920 title on the record of the one scoreless game with Akron. For this contest, the Staley's wisely enlisted the help of the sensational halfback-punter-dropkicker John "Paddy" Driscoll, who, as a member of his regular team, the Racine-Chicago Cardinals, had beaten the Staleys almost single-handedly for their only defeat. "Paddy" was on his way to the Hall of Fame.

It was a busy time for some players. The Buffalo All Americans, with some of the

The Dayton Triangles fielded teams from 1920 through 1929. This was the 1920 squad. *Back row from left:* **Carl Storck, manager and later league president; Cutler, asst. coach; Paul Davis, guard; Winston; Francis Bacon, back; Earley; Stoecklein; Edward Sauer, tackle; Hauser; Fred Slackford, back; Lawrence Dellinger, guard; George Roudebush, back; Carl Thiele, end; Russell Hathaway, tackle; Talbot, coach;** *middle row:* **Helvie, end; Glenn Tidd, tackle; George Kinderdine, center; Alphonse Mahrt, back; Louis Partlow, back; David Reese, end; Norbert Sacksteder, back;** *front row:* **Clark; Lee Fenner, end; Abrell.**

most famous college players of all time in the lineup, played on Sundays. The same squad played as the Philadelphia Quakers on Saturdays.

Joe Guyon, Canton Bulldog back who would be selected for the Hall of Fame in 1966, punted 95-yards against the Chicago Tigers on Nov. 14. This kick was a yard longer than the 94-yarder by Wilbur Henry recognized as the longest in the NFL record book.

Frank Moran, who, in 1913, had boxed Jess Willard for the heavyweight title, played with the Akron Pros.

No history of professional football could be complete without an early salute to George Stanley Halas, who joined the league in 1920 with his Decatur Staleys team. For the next half century as player-coach-owner he would be, more than any other man, the force that kept pro football going on the road to prosperity.

As a graduating football star at the University of Illinois in 1918, he had heard his coach, Bob Zuppke, say: "Why is it that just when you men are ready to learn something about playing football your career is ended? You have learned only the beginning in college. There is so much more."

Halas took this thought with him and, 50 years later, nearly 30 prosperous pro teams would be fascinating 50 million fans every autumn Sunday.

1920 AKRON PROS
COACH - Elgie Tobin

Bailey, Russ - C	Miles, Mark - T
Bierce, Bruce - E	Moran, Frank - G
Brown, George - G	Nash, Bob = E
Cobb, Al - G	Nesser, Al - G
Conn, George - B	Pierce, Bemus - B
Copley, Charles - T	Pollard, "Fritz" - B
Crawford, Ken - G	Preston, - T
Garrett, Al - E	Rendall, Den - B
Harris, Harry - Q	Robeson, Paul - E
Holleran, Tom - B	Sweetland, Fred - B
Johnson, Frank - T	Tobin, Elgie - B
King, Andy - B	Tomlin, Brad - G
McCormick, Frank - B	

The Akron Pros of 1920 were unbeaten in 10 games and gave 13 straight opponents zero points. In 1921, the team shown above continued the streak through five more games and were beaten in the 19th game by a field goal. From the left, *top row:* **"Fritz" Pollard, Marty Beck, Marchall Jones, Leo Tobin, Jim Flowers, Paul Robeson, "Rip" King, Al Nesser, Charley Copley, Miss Thomas;** *bottom row:* **Elgie Tobin, Russ Bailey, "Pike" Johnson, Brad Tomlin, "Scotty" Bierce, Roy Ratican, Carl Kramer, owners Art Ranney and Frank Neid.**

1920 BUFFALO ALL AMERICANS
COACH - Barney Lepper

Anderson, "Ockie" - B	Miller, "Heinie" - E
Baston, Bert - E	Mills, Charles - B
Brace, Bill - G	Nash, Bob = T
Brick, Shirley - B	Oliphant, Elmer - B
Casey, Eddie - B	Potteiger, Earl - Q
Fletcher, Andy - B	Rupp, john - G
Gavin, "Buck" - B	Scott, John - B
Gillo, "Hank" - B	Shelton, Murray - E
Goetz, Angus - T	Smith, "Pat" - B
Gormley, Tom - T	Spagna, Joe - G
Hillhouse, Andy - B	Thielscher, Karl - B
Horning, "Steamer" - T	Thornhill, "Tiny" - T
Hughitt, "Tommy" - Q	Weldon, John - B
Laird, Jim - B	Werder, Gerry - B
Lepper, Barney - T	Wray, Lud - C
Little, Lou - T	Youngstrom, Adolph - G

1920 CANTON BULLDOGS
COACH - Jim Thorpe

Buck, "Cub" - T	Hendren, John - B
Calac, Pete - B	Henry, "Fats" - T
Corcoran, Art - B	Higgins, Bob - E
Dadmun, Harrie - G	Kellison, John - T
Devlin, Mark - B	Lowe, "Bull" - E
Edwards, Gene - G	Martin, Roy - B
Feeney, Al - C	O'Connor, Dan - G
Gilroy, John - B	Petty, Ross - G
Gormley, Tom - T	Smythe, Lou - B
Green, Larry - E	Speck, "Dutch" - G
Grigg, Cecil - B	Thorpe, Jim - B
Guyon, Joe - B	Whelan, Tom - T
Haggerty, John - G	

1920 CHICAGO CARDINALS
COACH - Marshall Smith

Buckeye, Garland - G	Gillies, Fred - T
Brennan, Willis - T	Halstrom, Bernie - B
Carey, Joe - G	Knight, Charles - C
Clark, Bill - G	LaRosa, Paul - E
Curran, Harry - B	**McInerny, Arnold** - C
DesJardiens, Paul - G	O'Connor, Dan - G
Driscoll, "Paddy" - B	Sachs, Len - E
Egan, Dick - E	Whalen, Bill - T
Florence, Paul - E	Zoia, Clyde - G

1920 CHICAGO TIGERS
COACH - Paul DesJardiens

Annan, Dunc - B	Knop, Oscar - B
Barrett, John - B	Malone, Grover - B
Bennett, Joe - T	Mathews, Neilson - T
Buckey, Garland - G	Meagher, Jack - E
Derr, Ben - B	Mumgavin, "Jock" - T
DesJardiens, Paul - C	Pierce, George - G
Falcon, Gil - B	Reeve, Lew - T
Falcon, Dick - B	Rydzewski, Frank - T
Ghee, Milt - Q	Voight, - G
Keefe, Emmett - G	Young, Ralph

1920 CLEVELAND PANTHERS
COACH - Stan Cofall & Jim O'Donnell

Baston, Bert - E	Conn, George - B
Baujan, Harry - E	Cramer, Carl - B
Brickley, George - B	Devlin, Mark - B
Bryant, Jim - B	Doane, Joe - B
Cofall, Stan - B	Ducote, "Moon" - B

Garrett, Al - E
Gilroy, John - B
Ghee, Milt - Q
Gordon, Ralph - B
Gormley, Tom - T
Haggerty, John - G
Hastings, Charles - B
Herron, "Pat" - E
Kerr, George - T
Marshall, Bob - E
Mattern, Joe - B
Miles, Mark - T
O'Connor, Dan - G

O'Hearn, John - B
Perlman, Les - G
Petrie, Elmer - B
Pierotti, Al - C
Rydzewski, Frank - T
Schuele, Norman - B
Sies, Dale - G
Spagna, Joe - G
Stahl, Ed - T
Sweetland, Fred - B
Thornhill, "Tiny" - T
Trowbridge, Ray - E
Wesbecher, Al - T

1920 HAMMOND PROS
COACH - Gil Falcon

Barsha, John - T
Blocker, Frank - C
Cole, M. - E
Davis, Ed - G
Dietz, - G
Falcon, Gil - B
Gillo, "Hank" - B
Johnson, Frank - T
Kolls, Lou - C

Mathews, Neilson - T
Mayers, Paul - E
Pliska, Joe - B
Roberts, Mace - B
Robeson, Paul - E
Rydzewski, Frank - G
Speck, "Dutch" - G
Ward, - Q
Warren, - B

1920 COLUMBUS PANHANDLES
COACH - Ted Nesser

Brighan, Hiram - C
Davis, John - B
Gaulke, Hal - B
Hawk - G
Kuehner, Oscar - G
Lone Star - T
Moody, Wilkie - B
Mulbarger, Joe - T
Nesser, Frank - B

Nesser, Ted - G
Peabody, Dwight - E
Reeve, Lew - T
Ruh, Homer - E
Snoots, Lee - B
Schneider, John - B
Waite, Will - G
Wolford, Oscar - C

1920 ROCHESTER JEFFERSONS
COACH - Leo Lyons

Argus, Bob - B
Bachmaier, Joe - G
Carroll, Bart - C
Clark, "Babe" - E
Clime, Ben - T
DuMoe, Joe - E
Erwig, Bill - B
Forsyth, Ben - C
Irwin, Jim - B
King, Dick - B

Laird, Jim - B
Lowery, Darby - T
Oliphant, Elmer - B
Purdy, Clair - Q
Quigley, "Red" - B
Smith, "Hank" - C
Thomas, Carl - G
Usher, Lou - T
Webb, Art - T
Witter, Ray - B

1920 DAYTON TRIANGLES
COACH - Nelson Talbott

Abrel, Dick - E
Bacon, Francis - B
Clark, "Fuss" - E
Cutler, Harry - T
Davis, Ed - G
Dellinger, Larry - G
Early, Guy - G
Fenner, Lee - E
Hathaway, Russ - T
Hauser, Earl - E
Helvie, "Chuck" - E
Kinderdine, George - C
Mahrt, Al - B

O'Connor, Dan - G
Partlow, Lou - B
Reese, Dave - E
Roudebush, George - B
Sacksteder, Norb - B
Sauer, Ed - T
Slackford, Fred - B
Stoecklein, Earl - T
Thiele, Carl - E
Tidd, Glenn - T
Turner, John - G
Winston, Charles - G

1920 ROCK ISLAND INDEPENDENTS
COACH - "Rube" Ursella

Buland, Walt - T
Chicken, Fred - B
Denfield, Fred - G
Fitzgerald, Freeman - C
Gunderson, Borge - C
Healey, Ed - T
Kuehl, Walt - Q
Lyle, Dewey - G
Mansfield, Jerry - B
Marshall, "Rube" - E
Mockmore, Charles - G

Nichols, Sid - Q
Novak, Ed - B
Quinn, George - B
Shaw, Ed - B
Synhorst, John - T
Smith, Okla - E
Ursella, "Rube" - B
Webber, Harry - E
Wenig, Obe - E
Wyland, Guido - G
Wyman, Arnold - B

1920 DECATUR STALEYS
COACH - George Halas

Adkins, Roy - G
Blacklock, Hugh - T
Chamberlin, Guy - E
Clark, Bill - G
Conzelman, Jim - Q
Dressen, Charley - Q
Driscoll, "Paddy" - B
Englund, Harry - E
Feichtinger, Andy - E
Gepford, Sid - B
Halas, George - E
High, Len - B
Ingwerson, Bert - T
Johnson, Leo - B
Jones, Jerry - G
Keefe, Jerry - G

Koehler, Bob - B
LaForest, W. - B
Lanum, Ralph - B
MacWherter, Kyle - B
May, Walter - G
Mintun, John - C
Pearce, "Pard" - Q
Petty, Ross - G
Shank, Henry - B
Shoemake, Hub - G
Sternaman, Ed - B
Taylor, John - T
Trafton, George - C
Veach, Walter - B
Young, Randy - T

1920 DETROIT HERALDS
COACH - "Tillie" Voss

Applegran, Clarence - G
Dunne, "Pat" - B
Fitzgerald, Freeman - T
Guy, Charles - C
Hanley, Ed - B
Horning, "Steamer" - G
Jacobs, - B

Krinther, - B
Lowery, Darby - T
Maher, -
Runkle, Gil - C
Shanley, - B
Wilson, "Shorty" - Q

1921

	W	L	T	Pct.
Chicago Bears*	10	1	1	.909
Buffalo	9	1	2	.900
Akron	7	2	1	.778
Green Bay	6	2	2	.750
Canton	4	3	3	.571
Dayton	4	3	1	.571
Rock Island	5	4	1	.556
Chicago Cards	2	3	2	.400
Cleveland	2	6	0	.250
Rochester	2	6	0	.250
Detroit	1	7	1	.125
Columbus	0	6	0	.000
Cincinnati	0	8	0	.000

* Staleys

The first uproar over the NFL title (it was still the APFA) developed after the 1921 season. Nearly 50 years later survivors of the Buffalo team were still protesting that they had won the title when they beat the Chicago Staleys, 7-6, after both teams had ended the season unbeaten. However, they had then gone to Chicago for a "post-season" rematch with the Staleys and had lost, 10-7.

The Staleys (Bears the next season) then claimed the title and have been claiming it successfully ever since. The Buffalo players got gold championship footballs but official silence from the league office on all their pleas.

The league standing printed above is the official listing from modern NFL records, as are all others which follow. However, it is incomplete and inaccurate. Five teams—Evansville, Hammond, Louisville, Minneapolis and Muncie—played league games early in the season but failed to finish. After the first two games, Evansville was leading the league in a tie with Green Bay, Decatur and Akron (2-0).

The inaccuracy of these league standings from 1921 through 1933, still offered as "official" is emphasized by a breakdown of the 1921 Green Bay record (6-2-2).

Green Bay opened the season with victories over the Chicago Boosters, Rockford, the Chicago Cornhuskers and Beloit, none of whom was ever considered more than a sand lot team. The Packers then lost to Rock Island, a league team, triumphed over Minneapolis, Evansville and Hammond, all actually in the league but not recognized in current NFL standings. A tie with the Cardinals followed, then a loss to Decatur and another tie, this one with Racine, not yet in the league.

Thus, Green Bay's actual record was 3-2-1, unless it is judged by present league policy of ignoring Minneapolis, Evansville and Hammond. With that in mind, the final Packer standing is 0-2-1.

Joe E. Carr, manager of the Columbus team, and an experienced sports promoter, was elected president of the league, replacing Jim Thorpe. Carr would serve until 1939 and was the first of the fine commissioners the NFL would select.

Through this period of 1919 through 1927, six brothers, the Nessers of Columbus (Alfred, Frank, Fred, John, Phil, Ted) played on the Columbus team—and others. They were all top level players who would have been stars in any generation.

1921 AKRON PROS
COACH - Elgie Tobin
3rd 7-2-1

Bailey, Russ - C	King, Andy - B
Beck, Marty - B	McCormick, Frank - B & T
Bierce, Bruce - E	Nesser, Al - E & G
Cobb, Alfred - G	Pollard, "Fritz" - B
Copley, Charles - T	Ratekin, Roy - E
Corcoran, Art - E & B	Read, - G
Cramer, Carl - B	Robeson, Paul - E
Dasstling, Dane - T	Sheeks, Paul - Q
Flower, Jim - T	Tobin, Elgie - E & B
Haas, Bruno - B	Tobin, Leo - G
Johnson, Frank - T	Tomlin, "Tom" - 6
Jones, Marchall - B	

1921 BUFFALO ALL AMERICANS
COACH - "Tommy" Hughitt
1st or 2nd (title disputed) 9-1-2

Anderson, "Ock" - B	Oliphant, Elmer - B
Beck, Carl - B	Scott, John - B
Brace, Bill - G	Shelton, Murray - E
Gardner, Milt - G	Smith, "Pat" - B
Guy, Charles - C	Spagna, Joe - G
Hillhouse, Andy - B	Stein, Herb - T
Horning, "Steamer" - T	Sullivan, John - B
Hughitt, "Tommy" - Q	Urban, Luke - E
Kuehl, Walt - B	Usher, Ed - B
Laird, Jim - B	Voss, Walter - E
Little, Lou - T	Ward, Bill - G
Miller, Henry - E	Weldon, John - B
Nash, Bob - T	Wray, Lud - C
O'Hearn, John - B & E	Youngstrom, Adolph - G

1921 CANTON BULLDOGS
COACH - Eugene Edwards
5th 4-3-3

Carroll, Elmer - E	Osborn, Bob - G
Conover, Larry - C	Robb, Harry - Q
Edwards, Gene - G	Sauer, Ed - T
Falcon, Gil - B	Seidel, Fred - G
Feeney, Al - C	Slackford, Fred - B
Griffiths, Paul - G	Smythe, Lou - B
Grigg, Cecil - B	Speck, "Dutch" - G
Henry "Fats" - T	Steele, "Red" - E
Higgins, Bob - E	Way, Charles - B
Kellison, John - T	West, D. Belford - T
Kempton, "Fido" - Q	Williams, "Inky" - E
Morrow, Jim - B	Youngstrom, Adolph - G

1921 CHICAGO STALEYS
COACH - George Halas
1st 10-1-1 (Disputed by Buffalo)

Adkins, Roy - G	Bolan, George - B
Barker, Dick - G	Chamberlin, Guy - E
Blacklock, Hugh - T	Englund, Harry - E

Feichtinger, Andy - E
Halas, George - E
Harley, "Chic" - B
Huffine, Ken - B
Ingwerson, Bert - G
Jones, Jerry - T
Koehler, Bob - B
Lanum, Ralph - B
Mintun, John - C
Pearce, Walt - Q

Rupp, Nelson - Q
Scott, Ralph - T
Shoemake, Hub - G
Smith, Russ - G
Sternaman, Ed - B
Stinchcomb, Gaylord - Q
Taylor, John - T
Trafton, George - C
Usher, Lou - T

Mulbarger, Joe - T
Murtha, Paul - B
Nesser, Frank - B & G
Nesser, Fred - G
Nesser, John - Q
Nesser, Phil - G
Nesser, Ted - C

Rauch, Dick - G
Ruh, Emmett - B
Ruh, Homer - E
Snoots, Lee - B
Waite, Will - G
Wolford, Oscar - T & C

1921 CHICAGO CARDINALS
COACH - "Paddy" Driscoll
7th 2-3-2-

Barry, Norm - Q
Brennan, Willis - G
Buckeye, Garland - G
Charpier, Len - B
Curran, Harry - B
Driscoll, "Paddy" - B
Egan, Dick - E
Gillies, Fred - T
Halstrom, Bernie - B
Horween, Arnold - B
Horween, Ralph - B
Knight, Charles - C

Koehler, Bob - B
LaRosa, Paul - E
McInerny, Arnie - C
Marquardt, John - E
O'Connor, Dan - G
Potteiger, Earl - Q
Rydzewski, Frank - T
Sachs, Len - E
Scanlon, John - B
Steger, Pete - B
Whalen, Bill - G
Zoia, Clyde - G

1921 DAYTON TRIANGLES
COACH - Nelson Talbott &
Frank Hinkey
6th 4-3-1

Abbott, Fay - B
Bacon, Francis - B
Davis, Ed - G
Dellinger, Larry - G
Fenner, Lee - E
Hathaway, Russ - T
Kinderdine, George - C
King, Paul, B & E
Mahrt, Al - B
Mohardt, John - B
Partlow, Lou - B

Redmond, "Gus" - G & B
Reese, Dave - E
Roudebush, George - B
Rupp, Nelson - Q
Sampson, Art - G
Sauer, Ed - T
Sies, Dale - G
Stahl, Ed - T
Thiele, Carl - E
Tidd, Glenn - T
Tschappatt, Chalmers - T

1921 CINCINNATI CELTS
COACH -
13th 0-8-0

Beekley, Ferris - G
Costello, Harry - Q
Costello, Rory - C
Crawford, Ken - B & G
Dasstling, Dane - T
Doherty, Bill - C
Early, Guy - G
Fortmyer, Al - B
Fritsch, Louis - B
Hauser, Earl - E
King, Paul - B
Knabb, Chet - B

Krueck, Ed - B & E
Lane, Frank - G
Lewis, Art - T
McMahan, - B
Melvin, - E
Munns, George - Q
Orth, Henry - G
Schuessler, Erwin - T
Schupp, Walt - T
Thompson, Dave - B
Volz, Pete - E

1921 DETROIT PANTHERS
COACH - "Tillie" Voss
11th 1-7-1

Brandau, - B
Carman, Ed - T
Clago, Walt - E
Coughlin, Frank - T
DaPrato, Neno - B
DeGree, Walt - G
Dunn, "Pat" - B
Gardner, Milt - G
Gavin, "Buck" - B
Guy, Charles - C

Horning, "Steamer" - T
Krieger, Earl - B
Kuehl, Walt - B
Miller, W. Blake - E
Moegler, Ed - B
Sacksteder, Norb - B
Stobbs, Bill - B
Voss, "Tillie" - Q
Williams, - G

1921 EVANSVILLE CRIMSON GIANTS
COACH - Frank Fausch

Anderson, - B
Bondurant, Bourbon - G
Fausch, Frank - B
Fishman, Abe - G
Fishman, Alex - T
Fritsch, Lou - B
Garnjorst, Don - G
Goldsmith, Earl - E
Gorman, Earl - T
Henderson, Herb - B
Ingle, - B
Jackson, Colville - E
Lauer, Alfred - B
Lensing, Vince - G
Lindsey, Menzies - Q
McDonald, John - T

Morrison, - B
Rosenberger, "Tubby" -
Noreen, Olaf - B
O'Neil, Bill - E
Runsey, Roy - T
Spain, Dick - G
Speck, "Dutch" - G
Spiegel, Clarence - B &
Strone, - B
Tally,
Warweg,
Whitehead, Walker - B
Williams, Travis - B
Windbiele, Joe - C
Zeller, Jerry - B

1921 CLEVELAND INDIANS
COACH -
9th 2-6-0

Baston, Al - E
Baujan, Harry - E
Dower, J. Philip - B
Brawley, Edward - G
Brewer, Brooke - B
Calac, Pete - B
Corcoran, Art - E
Ghee, Milt - Q
Guyon, Joe - B
Haas, Bruno - B

Hendren, John - B
Lowe, "Bull" - E & B
Murphy, Joe - B
O'Connor, Dan - G
Patterson, - Q
Perlman, Les - G
Tandy, George - C
Thorpe, Jim - B
Waldsmith, Ralph - G
Whelan, Tom - T

1921 GREEN BAY PACKERS
COACH - "Curly" Lambeau
4th 6-2-2

Abrams, Nate - E
Barry, Norm - Q
Buck, "Cub" - T
Carey, Joe - G
Cook, Jim - G
Coughlin, Frank - T

DeMoe, "Gus" - E
Douglas, George - C
Elliot, Burt - B
Gavin, Fritz - E
Glick, Ed - B
Hayes, Dave - E

1921 COLUMBUS PANHANDLES
COACH - Ted Nesser
12th 0-6-0

Bliss, Harry - Q
Davis, Ed - G
Gaulke, Hal - B
Glassman, Morris - E

Hopkins, Ted - E
Houck, Joe - G
Karch, Bob - T
Kuehner, Oscar - G

Rauch, Dick - G
Roberts, Jim - B & E
Saunders, - B
Simpson, Felix - Q
Stein, Herb - C

Stein, Russ - T
Tanner, John - E
Tierney, Festus - G
Watson, Grady - B
White, Wilbur - E

1923

	W	L	T	Pct.
Canton	11	0	1	1.000
Chicago Bears	9	2	1	.818
Green Bay	7	2	1	.778
Milwaukee	7	2	3	.778
Cleveland	3	1	3	.750
Chicago Cards	8	4	0	.667
Duluth	4	3	0	.571
Columbus	5	4	1	.556
Buffalo	5	4	3	.556
Racine	4	4	2	.500
Toledo	2	3	2	.400
Rock Island	2	3	3	.400
Minneapolis	2	5	2	.286
St. Louis	1	4	2	.200
Hammond	1	5	1	.167
Dayton	1	6	1	.143
Akron	1	6	0	.143
Marion	1	10	0	.091
Rochester	0	2	0	.000
Louisville	0	3	0	.000

It was a 20-team league in 1923. Evansville had dropped off for good, but the rest of the 1922 list hung on and there were new entries from Duluth and St. Louis. Cleveland came back with new owners.

Canton was still unbeatable and finished at 11-0-1, which gave them a two-year record of 21 victories, three ties and no losses. The Chicago Bears, 9-2-1, were second again, with Green Bay moving up to third place.

George Halas, Chicago Bear end, recovered a fumble of the Oorang Indians and ran 98-yards (TD), a record, Nov. 4.

Wilbur "Fats" Henry, Canton tackle, punted 94 yards against Akron, Oct. 28. The NFL recognizes this as a record despite Joe Guyon's punt of 95 yards in 1920.

1923 AKRON PROS
COACH - Wayne Brenkert
17th 1-6-0

Brenkert, Wayne - B
Brown, George - G
Cramer, Carl - B
Daum, Carl - E
Edgar, Alex - B & G
Flower, Jim - T
Haley, Arthur - B
Hardy, Isham - G
Hendrian, "Dutch" - Q
LeJeune, Walt - G
Malone, Grover - B & E

Michaels, Alton - B
Mills, Joe - C
Nesser, Al - E & G
Roberts, Jim - E
Scott, Gene - G
Shaw, Ed - B
Sprinkle, Hubert - T
Stewart, Charles - G
Wallace, Fred - G
Wilson, Milton - T

1923 BUFFALO ALL AMERICANS
COACH - "Tommy" Hughitt
9th 5-4-3

Carberry, Glenn - E
Connors, Stafford -B
Corcoran, Art - E
Culver, Frank - C
Edgar, Alex - B & G
Flavin, John - B
Foster, Fred - B
Gregory, Frank - B
Gulian, Mike - T
Holleran, Tom - B
Hughitt, "Tommy" - Q
Kelly, "Clancy" - G
McCormick, Elmer - G

Mahoney, John - B
Martineau, Roy - G & B
Morrissey, Frank - T
Mulvey, Vince - B
Nash, Bob - T
Roderick, Ben - B
Scott, John - B
Smith, "Pat" - B
Thomas, Carl - G
Traynor, Mike - B
Urban, Luke - E
Youngstrom, Adolph - G

1923 CANTON BULLDOGS
COACH - Guy Chamberlin
1st 11-0-1

Carroll, Elmer - E
Chamberlin, Guy - E
Comstock, Rudy - G
Conover, Larry - C
Culver, Frank - C
Elliott, Wallace - B
Grigg, Cecil - B
Hendrian, "Dutch" - Q
Henry, "Fats" - T
Jones, Ben - B
Lyman, "Link" - T

Mullen, Verne - E
Osborn, "Duke" - G
Robb, Harry - Q
Roberts, Walcott, - B
Roderick, Ben - B
Shaw, Ed - B
Smith, Russ - T
Smythe, Lou - B
Speck, "Dutch" - G
Williams, Joe - G

1923 CHICAGO BEARS
COACH - George Halas
2nd 9-2-1

Anderson, Ed - E
Anderson, "Hunk" - G
Blacklock, Hugh - T
Bolan, George - B
Bryan, John - Q
Fetz, "Gus" - B
Flaherty, Jim - E
Garvey, "Hec" - E
Halas, George - E
Hanny, Frank - E
Healey, Ed - T

Knop, Oscar - B
LaFleur, Joe - B & G
Lanum, Ralph - B
Rydzewski, Frank - T
Scott, Ralph - T
Sigmund, Art - G
Sternaman, Ed - B
Sternaman, Joe - Q
Trafton, George - C
Usher, Lou - T
Walquist, Laurie - Q

1923 CHICAGO CARDINALS
COACH - Arnold Horween
6th 8-4-0

Anderson, Ed - E
Brennan, Willis - G
Buckeye, Garland - G
Crangle, John - B
Driscoll, "Paddy" - B
Egan, Dick - E
Folz, Art - Q
Gillies, Fred - T
Horween, Arnold - Q
Horween, Ralph - B
Kiley, Roger - E
King, Andy - B

Koehler, Bob - B
Leonard, John - T
McInerny, Arnie - C
McMahon, Byron - G
Mohardt, John - B
Montgomery, Ralph - T
O'Connor, Dan - G
Sachs, Len - E
Smith, Russ - G
Smith, Wilfred - E
Whalen, Bill - G
Zola, Clyde - G

1923 CLEVELAND INDIANS
COACH
5th 3-1-3

Anderson, Will B & G
Bahan, Len - B
Bierce, Bruce - E
Bowser, Arda - B
Civiletto, Frank - B
Cobb, Al - G

Ebersole, Hal - G & C
Edler, Bob - B
Edwards, Gene - G
Gardner, George - E
Guy, Charles - C
Huffman, Iolas - T

Canton's Bulldogs were league champions in 1922 and 1923, then moved to Cleveland where they again won the title in 1924. This is the 1923 squad, *top row from left:* **Oscar Hendrian, back; Harry Robb, quarterback; Ben Jones, back, Louis Smythe, center; Cecil Griggs, back; Wallace Elliott, back; Walcott Roberts, back;** *middle row:* **Elmer Carroll, end; Wilbur Henry, tackle; Robert Osborne, guard; Lawrence Conover, center; Roudolph Comstock, guard; Roy Lyman, tackle; Guy Chamberlain, end;** *bottom row:* **Norman Speck, guard; Herman Smith, trainer; Joseph Williams, tackle.**

Johns, Jim - G
Keck, Stan - T
Kyle, John - B
McMillin, "Bo" - Q
Myers, Cy - E
Partlow, Gene - B
Roby, Doug - B
Rosatti, Roman - T

Setron, Joe - G
Stinchcomb, "Pete" - Q
Tanner, John - E
Vince, Ralph - G
Weinberg, Saul - T
Wolf, Dick - B
Work, Joe - B

1923 COLUMBUS TIGERS
COACH - "Gus" Tebell &
"Pete" Stinchcomb
8th 5-4-1

Bonowitz, Elliott - G
Goebel, Paul - E
Goetz, Angus - T
Hanson, Ray - B
Heldt, John - C
Isabel, Wilmer - B
Mulbarger, Joe - T
Nemecek, Andy - G
Passuelo, Bill - G
Randolph, Harry - B

Rapp, "Goldie" - B
Ruh, Emmett - B
Ruh, Homer - E
Sack, John - G
Snoots, Lee - B
Sonnenberg, "Gus" - G
Stinchcomb, "Pete" - Q
Tebell, "Gus" - E
Weaver, Jim - C
Winters, Lin - B

1923 DAYTON TRIANGLES
COACH - Carl Storck
16th 1-6-1

Abbott, Fay - B
Bacon, Frank - B
Beasley, John - G
Berns, Bill - G
Burgner, Earl - B
Crawford, Ken - B & G
Dellinger, Larry - G
Fenner, Lee - E
Hathaway, Russ - T
Huffine, Ken - B
Jolley, Al - T

Kinderdine, George - C
Kinderdine, Walt - B
Lauer, Hal - B
Mahrt, Al - Q
Partlow, Lou - B
Reese, Dave - E
Sauer, Ed - T
Thiele, Carl - E
Tidd, Glenn - T
Ward, Gil - T

1923 DULUTH KELLEYS
COACH -
7th 4-3-0

Dunn, Rod - G
Gilbert, Walt - B
Harris, Ken - B
Haven, John - E

Johnson, Art - T
Kelly, Charles _ B
Kieley, Howard _ T
McDonnell, "Mickey" - B

Madigan, John - C
Marshall, Bob - E
Method, Russ - B
Morse, "Red" - G
O'Donnell, Dick - E
Rooney, "Cobb" - Q
Rooney, Joe - E

Rooney, Bill - B & C
Rundquist, Harry - T
Stein, Bill - G
Sternaman, Joe - B
Strand, Lief - C
Vexall, Roy - B
Williams, Dan - G

1923 GREEN BAY PACKERS
COACH - "Curly" Lambeau
3rd 7-2-1

Basing, Myrt - B & E
Buck "Cub" - T
Earpe, "Jug" - T
Erickson, Hal - B
Gardner, Milt - G
Gavin, Fritz - E & B
Gray, D. - E
Hanson, Roy - B
Hayes, Norb - E
Kenyon, Crowell - G

Lambeau, "Curly" - B
Leaper, Wes - E
Lyle, Dewey - E
Mathys, Charles - Q
Mills, Tom - B
Murray, Dick - T
Niemann, Walt - C
Smith, Earl - G
Wheeler, Kyle - E
Woodin, Howie - G

1923 HAMMOND PROS
COACH - "Fritz" Pollard
15th 1-5-1

Annan, Dunc - Q
Barrett, John - B
Berry, George - G & C
Butler, Sol - B
Butler, Bill - B
Cearing, Lloyd - B
Detwiler, John - B
Ghee, Milt - Q
Hanke, Carl - E
Hess, Walt - B
Knop, Oscar - B
Kovascy, Bill - T
Larson, - B

Neal, Bob - G
Noonan, George - B
Oltz, Russ - C & T
Pollard, "Fritz" - B
Risley, Elliott - T
Robinson, Ed - B
Rydzewski, Frank - T
Siebert, Ed - G
Smith, - G
Sullivan, Steve - Q
Tallant, Dave - T
Usher, Lou - T
Williams, "Inky" - E

1923 LOUISVILLE BRECKS
COACH - Jim Kendrick
19th -0-3-0

Anderson, Chet - T
Boldt, Chase - B & E
Borntraeger, Bill - B
Brunklacher, Austin - G
Broderick, Ted - B
Espie, Al - T
Ford, Salem - B
Gibson, Dick - T & G
Grabfelder, Earl - B
Gruber, Herb - B
Guigliano, Patsy - B
Higgins, Austin - C
Irwin, Jim - B
Karch, Bob - T
Kendrick, Jim - B

Lanham, Charles - T
McGehean, Bob - B
Meredith, Russ - G
Miller, Lloyd - B
Olmstead, Larry - G & T
Otto, Alvin - C & G
Quast, John - E & B
Reiser, Earl - E & B
Rowan, John - B & E
VanDyke, Jim - B
Wanless, George - E & G
White, Bob - E
Wiggs, Hubert - B

1923 MILWAUKEE BADGERS
COACH - Jim Conzelman
4th 7-2-3

Blailock, Russ - T
Conzelman, Jim - Q
Doane, Joe - B
Dooley, John - G
Erickson, Hal - B
Larson, Fred - C
McGinnis, Larry - G
McMillin, "Bo" - Q
Mattox, Marv - B
Meadows, Eric - B
Milton, Tom - E
Mooney, George - B & E
Nadolney, Romanus - G

Pierotti, Al - C
Rate, Ed - B
Reichle, Dick - E
Sachs, Len - E
Smith, Russ - G
Strickland, Bill - G
Turner, Jim - B
Underwood, John - G
Usher, Lou - T
Vassau, Roy - T
Wenke, Adolph - T
Widerquist, Chet - T
Winkelman, Ben - E

1923 MINNEAPOLIS MARINES
COACH -
13th 2-5-2

Baril, Adrian - T
Chicken, Fred - B
Christenson, Oscar - E
Cleve, Einer - B
Coughlin, Frank - T
Flynn, Paul - E
Fortune, Burnell - G
Fosdick, Bob - G
Gaustad, Art - G
Gunderson, Harry - C & G
Hanson, Roy - B
Hudson, Dick - B

Irgens, Einar - E
Jonasen, Charles - B
Kaplan, Sid - B
Kramer, George - T
Marshall, Bob - E
Mehre, Harry - C
Mohs, Lou = E
Pahl, Lou - B
Simpson, Eber - B
Tersch, Rudy - T
Tierney, Festus - G
Williams, Rolland - B

1923 OORANG INDIANS
(Played for Marion, Ohio)
COACH - Jim Thorpe
18th 1-10-0

Arrowhead - E
Barrell - C
Big Bear - T
Black Bear - E
Boutwell, Leon - Q
Buffalo - G
Busch, Elmer - G
Calac, Pete - B
Deadeye - T
Eagle Feather - B
Gray Horse - B
Guyon, Joe - B
Lassa, Nick - T & C

Little Twig, Joe - E
Lone Wolf - G
McLemore, Emmett - B
Pierce, Bemus - B
Powell, Stancil - G
Red Fang - T
Red Foot - E
Red Fox - B
Running Deer - E
Thorpe, Jack - G
Thorpe, Jim - B
Tomahawk - B
Welmus, Woodchuck - E

1923 RACINE LEGION
COACH -
10th 4-4-2

Barr, Wally - B
Baxter, Ernie - B
Braman, Bill - T
Dressen, Charley - Q
Elliott, Al - B
Foster, Bob - B
Gillo, "Hank" - B
Gorman, Earl - G
Halladay, Dick - E
Hartong, George - G
Heinisch, Fred - B
Hueller, John - G
Langhoff, Irv - B
Long, - G

Lunde, Les - G
McCaw, Bill - E
Mauer, Jake - G
Meyers, Paul - E
Miller, Ray - E
Mintun, "Jake" - C
Murry, Don - T
Roessler, Fritz - E
Romney, Milt - Q
Smith, Len - E
Stark, Howie - T
Strickland, Bill - T
Williams, Rolland - B

1923 ROCHESTER JEFFERSONS
COACH - Leo Lyons
19th -0-2-0

Argus, Bob - B
Bachmaier, Joe - G
Bancroft, Hugh - E
Carroll, Bart - C
Clark, Hal - E
Dooley, John - G
Foster, Fred - B
Gavigan, Mike - B
Kasper, Tom - B
Keck, Stan - T
Leonard, Jim - T
Lowery, Darby - T

McShea, Joe - G
Martineau, Roy - G
Matteo, Frank - T
Noonan, Gerry - B
Peyton, Leo - B
Roy, Elmer - E
Sheard, Al - B
Smith, "Hank" - C
Wallace, Gordon - B
Welsh, Jim - G
Witter, Ray - E
Wood, Jim - G

**1923 ROCK ISLAND
INDEPENDENTS
COACH -
12th 2-3-3**

Amstrong, John - Q	Lowe, "Bull" - E
Bernstein. Joe - G	Lundgren, Charley - B
Butler, "Sol" - B	Phelan, Bob - B
Cotton, Forrest - T	Sies, Dale - G
DeClerk, Frank - C	Slater, "Duke" - T
Giaver, Bill - B	Smith, Earl - T
Gorgal, Alex - B	Thompson, George - G
Kadesky, Max - E	Thompson, Alvie - T
Kolls, Lou - C	Wilson, "Mike" - E
Kuehl, Walt - B	

**1923 ST. LOUIS BROWNS
COACH - Leroy Andrews
14th 1-4-2**

Andrews, LeRoy - G	Moran, - B
Cardwell, John - B	Murrah, Bill - T
Casey, Al - B	Siegfried, Orville - B & T
Finnegan, Jim - E	Simpson, Eber - Q
Gray, D. - E	Travis, Ed - T
King, Dick - B	Weller, Ray - T
Kraehe, Ollie - G	Werner, Sox - B
Kreinheder, Walt - C	Wilder, Hal - G & E
Meinhardt, George - G	Windburn, Ernie - E
Meese, Ward - E	Wycoff, Lee - B & T
Milton, Thomas - E	

**1923 TOLEDO MAROONS
COACHES - Gil Falcon &
George Johnson**

Batcheller, Don - T	Lauer, Hal - B
Conrad, Marty - C	McNamara, Tom - G
Falcon, Gil - B	O'Neill, Gerry - B
Fitzgerald, Francis - B	Seyfrit, Mike - E
Gillis, Joe - T	Strauss, Art - B
Hill, Harry - B	Thorpe, Jim - B
Horning, "Steamer" - T	Voss, "Tillie" - E
Hunt, Ben - T	Watson, Grady - B
Jones, Jerry - G	White, Wilbur - E
Kirkgard, - B	

1924

	W	L	T	Pct.
Cleveland	7	1	1	.875
Chicago Bears	6	1	4	.856
Frankford	11	2	1	.846
Duluth	4	1	0	.800
Rock Island	6	2	2	.750
Green Bay	7	4	0	.636
Racine	5	3	2	.625
Buffalo	6	4	4	.600
Chicago Cardinals	5	5	0	.500
Columbus	4	4	1	.500
Hammond	2	2	0	.500
Milwaukee	5	8	0	.385
Dayton	2	6	0	.250
Kansas City	2	7	0	.222
Akron	1	6	0	.143
Kenosha	0	5	1	.000
Minneapolis	0	6	0	.000
Rochester	0	7	0	.000

The NFL dropped two to 18 teams in 1924, and there had been several changes. Toledo, St. Louis, Louisville and the Marion-Oorang Indians were gone. The Indian players went to other teams—Jim Thorpe played with Rock Island and so did Joe Guyon; Pete Calac went with Buffalo. New teams were formed in Frankford, a suburb of Philadelphia, and in Kenosha, Wis.

Canton had no team in the NFL in 1924. The players had gone to Cleveland to play there as the Bulldogs and to win the title for the third time with 7-1-1.

Once more the Chicago Bears were second, only a half game behind and the surprising, new Frankford Yellowjackets were next with 11-2-1.

"Paddy" Driscoll, Chi-Card halfback contributed a 50-yard dropkick field goal against Milwaukee, tying Henry's record, Oct. 11.

**1924 AKRON PROS
COACH - Jim Robertson
15th 1-6-0**

Barrett, John - T	Mills, Stan - E
Beck, Marty - B	Nesser, Al - E & G
Berry, George - C	Newman, Howard - T
Brenkert, Wayne - B	Robertson, Jim - Q
Butler, "Sol" - B	Sechrist, Walt - G
Cardarelli, Carl - C	Speck, "Dutch" - G
Cramer, Carl - B	Sprinkle, Hubert - T
Daum, Carl - E	Stahlman, Dick - E
Flower, Jim - T	Wallace, Fred - G
Hogan, Paul - B	West, Charles - B
Hogue, Frank - B	Wilson, Milton - T
Michaels, Alton - B	Zimmerman, Giff - B
Mills, Joe - C	

**1924 BUFFALO BISONS
COACH - "Tommy" Hughitt
8th 6-4-4**

Ailinger, Jim - G	Hughitt, "Tommy" - Q
Boynton, Ben - Q	Jones, Ken - B
Calac, Pete - B	Kaw, Ed - B
Carberry, Glenn - E	Kraus, Frank - T
Collins, Harry - G	McCormick, Elmer - G
Connors, Stafford - B	Mitchell, Al - T
Culver, Frank - C	Morrissey, Frank - T
Feist, Lou - T & E	Traynor, Mike - B
Flavin, John - B	Urban, Luke - E
Gregory, Frank - B	Watters, Len - E
Guarnieri, Al - Q & E	Youngstrom, Adolph - G
Huffman, Iolas - T	

**1924 CHICAGO BEARS
COACH - George Halas
2nd 6-1-4**

Anderson, "Hunk" - G	Englund, Harry - E
Blacklock, Hugh - T	Garvey, "Hec" - E
Bolan, George - B	Greenwood, Glen - B
Bryan, John - B	Halas, George - E

Hanny, Frank - T & E
Healey, Ed - T
Hurst, Bill - G
Johnson, O. G. - B
Kendrick, Jim - B & E
Knop, Oscar - B
LaFleur, Joe - B & G
Lanum, Ralph - B
Leonard, Jim - T
McMillen, Jim - G
Mullen, Verne - E

Murray, Dick - T
O'Connell, Harry - C
Romney, Milt - B
Scott, Ralph - T
Sternaman, Ed - B
Sternaman, Joe - Q
Taft, Merrill - B
Trafton, George - C
Walquist, Laurie - Q
White, Roy - B

Kuehl, Walt - B
Mahrt, Armin - B
Muirhead, Stan - G
Partlow, Lou - B
Redmond, "Gus" - G & B

Sauer, Ed - T
Sies, Dale - G
Tidd, Glenn - T
Williams, "Inky" - E

1924 CHICAGO CARDINALS
COACH - Arnold Horween
9th 5-5-0

Anderson, Ed - E
Brennan, Willis - G
Buckeye, Garland - G
Clark, Charles - G
DeStefano, Fred - B
Driscoll, "Paddy" - B
Folz, Art - Q
Gillies, Fred - T
Hanke, Carl - E
Hartong, George - G
Horween, Arnold - B

Hurlburt, John - B
King, Andy - B
Koehler, Bob - B
McElwain, Bill - B
McInerny, Arnie - C
McNulty, Paul - E
O'Connor, Dan - G
Ryan, Jim - B
Smith, Wilfred - T
Whalen, Bill - G

1924 DULUTH KELLEYS
COACH -
4th 4-1-0

Bratt, Joe - E
Carlson, Gene - G
Clow, Herb - B
Cobb, Bill - T
Engstrom, George - G
Gilbert, Walt - B
Harris, Ken - B
Johnson, Art - T
Kelly, Charles - B
Kieley, Howard - T
Koziak, Mike - G
McDonnell, "Mickey" - B
Marshall, Bob - E

Method, Russ - B
O'Toole, Bill - G
Rooney, "Cobb" - Q
Rooney, Joe - E
Rooney, Bill - B
Rundquist, "Porky" - T
Sanford, Jim - T
Stein, Bill - G & C
Strand, Lief - C
Underwood, John - E & G
Vexall, Roy - B
Williams, Dan - G

1924 CLEVELAND BULLDOGS
COACH - Guy Chamberlin
1st 7-1-1

Ault, Chalmers - T
Bierce, Bruce - E
Chamberlin, Guy - E
Cobb, Alf - G
Comstock Rudy - G
Edwards, Gene - G
Elliott, Wally - B
Honaker, Charles - E
Johns, Jim - G
Jones, Ben - B
Jones, Jerry - T
Lyman, "Link" - T
Muirhead, Stan - G

Newman, Howard - T
Noble, Dave - B
Nugent, Clem - B
Osborn, "Duke" - C
Partlow, Gene - B
Roberts, Walcott - B
Smith, Olin - T
Smith, Russ - G
Tanner, John - E & B
Vince, Ralph - G
Wolf, Dick - B
Work, Joe - B
Workman, 'Hoge" - B

1924 FRANKFORD
YELLOWJACKETS
COACH - Bob Berryman
6th 11-2-1

Bednar, Al - G
Behman, "Bull" - T
Berryman, Bob - B
Dayhoff, Harry - B
Doyle, Ed - E
Finn, John - B
Gulian, Mike - T
Hamer, Ernie - B
Haws, Harve - Q
Hoffman, Bill - G
Jamieson, Bob - C
Kellogg, Bill - B
Lowe, " Bull" - E

Miller, "Heinie" - E
O'Connell, Milt - E
Scott, John - B
Smith, "Pat" - B
Spagna, Joe - G
Stein, Herb - C
Stein, Russ - T
Storer, John - B
Sullivan, George - B
Thomas, Bill - B & E
Way, Charles - B
Welsh, Jim - G

1924 COLUMBUS TIGERS
COACH - "Red" Weaver
10th 4-4-1

Duvall, Earl - G
Ellis, Walt - T
Goebel, Paul - E
Halleck, Neil - B
Hanson, Ray - B
Isabel, Wilmer - B
Layport, John - G
Mantell, Joe - G
Moody, Wilkie - B
Mulbarger, Joe - T
Nemecek, Andy - G

Petcoff, Boni - T
Rapp, "Goldie" - B
Ruh, Homer - E
Schell, Herb - B
Snoots, Lee - B
Stock, Herb - B
Tebell, "Gus" - E
Tynes, Dave - B
Winters, Lin - B
Wolford, Oscar - C

1924 GREEN BAY PACKERS
COACH - "Curly" Lambeau
6th 7-4-0

Basing, Myrt, - B & E
Beasey, John - B
Buck, "Cub" - T
Buland, Walt - T
Duford, Wilford - B
Earpe, "Jug" - T & C
Gardner, "Moose" - G
Hearden, Len - B & E
Hendrian, "Dutch" - Q
Lambeau, "Curly" - B

Lewellen, Verne - B
Ludtke, Norm - G
Mathys, Charles - Q
Milton, Tom - E
Murray, Dick - T
Niemann, Walt - C
O'Donnell, Dick - E
Rosatti, Roman - T
Voss, "Tillie" - E
Woodin, Howie - G

1924 DAYTON TRIANGLES
COACH - Carl Storck
13th 2-6-0

Abbott, Fay - B
Bacon, Francis - B
Beeming, - G
Berns, Bill - B
Bonowitz, Elliott - G
Egan, Dick - E
Faust, Dick - T

Fenner, Lee - E
Hathaway, Russ - T
Huffine, Ken - B
Jones, Ben - B
Kinderdine, George - C
Kinderdine, Jim - G
Kinderdine, Walt - B

1924 HAMMOND PROS
COACH - "Fritz" Pollard
11th 2-2-0

Annan, Dunc - Q
Berry, George - G & C
Bernstein, Joe - G
Butler, "Sol" - B
Detwiler, John - B
Falcon, Gil - B
Fortune, Burnell -G
Hess, Walt - B
Neal, Bob - G
Oltz, Russ - C & T
Pollard, "Fritz" - B

Roberts, Mace - B & E
Robinson, Ed - T
Rydzewski, Frank - T & C
Sachs, Len - E
Seyfrit, Mike - E
Stahlman, Dick - T
Sullivan, Steve - Q
Tallant, Dave - T
Usher, Lou - T
Watson, Grady - B
Williams, "Inky" - E

1924 KANSAS CITY COWBOYS
COACH - Leroy Andrews
14th 2-7-0

Anderson, Tom - B	McLemore, Emmett - B
Andrews, Roy - B & G	Milan, Joe - E
Ashbaugh, Bill - B	Milton, John - E
Bassett, Henry - T	Mintun, John - C
Berquist, Jay - G	Owen, Steve - T
Bradshaw, Jim - Q	Peterson, Len - E & G
Bristow, Obie - B	Quinn, Ivan - G
Choate - G	Rehnquist, Milt - G & C
Corgan, Charles - E & B	Sears, Dick - B
DeWitz, Rufus - B	Strauss, Art - B
Guyon, Joe - B	Tays, Jim - B
Hill, Charley - B	Thompson, Al - T
Hill, Harry - B	Usher, Ed - B
Howard, Bob - G	Webber, Howie - E
Krueger, Al - T	White, Phil - B
Lane, Lew - Q	Wiedich, Ralph - T

1924 KENOSHA MAROONS
COACH - Earl Potteiger
16th 0-5-1

Baxter, Ernie - B	Pattison, Roger - G
Carlson, Irv - G	Pearce, "Pard" - Q
Cassidy, Bill - E	Potteiger, Earl - Q & E
Conrad, Marty - C	Seasholtz, George - B
Dahlgren, George - G & C	Sies, Dale - G
Egan, Dick - E	Simpson, T. Felix - B
Fortune, Burnell - G	Stahlman, Dick - E
Gardner, "Moose" - G & T	Usher, Lou - T
Gorman, Earl - G &T	Vick, Dick - Q
Heinisch, Fred - B & E	Walters, - B
Hess, Walt - B	Watson, Grady - B
Hurst, Bill - G	Williams, "Inky" - E
Meese, Ward - E	Wood, Marvin - G
Oberbroekling, Ray - T	

1924 MILWAUKEE BADGERS
COACH - Jim Conzelman
12th 5-8-0

Berger, Walt - T	Nadolney, Romanus - G
Conzelman, Jim - Q	Neacy, Clem - E
Coyle, Frank - E	Pierotti, Al - C
Doane, Joe - B	Sachs, Len - E
Dunn, "Red" - Q	Smith, Russ - G
Erickson, Hal - B	Swanson, Evar - E
Foster, Bob - B	Taugher, Claude - B
Larson, "Ojay" - C	Usher, Lou - T
LeJeune, Walt - G	Weller, Ray - T
McGinnis, Larry - G	Widerquist, Chet - T
Mooney, George - B & E	Winkleman, Ben - E & B
Morrissey, Frank - T	

1924 MINNEAPOLIS MARINES
COACH -
16th -0-6-0

Baril, Adrian - T	Maynaugh, Roland - G
Chicken, Fred - B	Mehre, Harry - C
Christenson, Oscar - E	Mohs, Lou - E
Cleve, Einar - B	Norton, Marty - B
Dunnigan, Mert - T	Novak, Ed - B
Eberts, "Beanie" - G	Pahl, Lou - B
Fosdick, Bob - G	Putzier, Fred - B
Houle, Wilfred - B	Scott, Gene - G
Irgens, Einar - E	Simon, John - E
Johns, Jim - G	Simpson, Eber - B
Kramer, George - T	Tersch, Rudy - T
Madigan, John - C	Tierney, Festus - G
Marshall, Bob - E	

1924 RACINE LEGION
COACH -
7th 5-3-2

Barr, Wally - B	King, Ralph - T
Bentzien, Al - B	Lunde, Les - G
Brumm, Roman - T	Mintun, John -C
Croft, Jack - G	Mohardt, John - B
Elliott, Al - B	Murry, Don - T
Giaver, Bill - B & E	Oltz, Russ - C & T
Gillo, "Hank" - B	Palmer, Charley - B
Halladay, Dick - E	Roessler, Fritz - E
Hanley, Dick - B	Romney, Milt - B
Hartong, George - G	Smith, Len - T
Heinisch, Fred - B & E	Webster, Fred - B
Hueller, John - G	

1924 ROCHESTER JEFFERSONS
COACH - Cecil Grigg
16th 0-7-0

Adams, Joe - T	Martineau, Roy - G
Anderson, Will - E & B	Matteo, Frank - T
Argus, Bob = B	Noonan, Gerry - B
Bachmaier, Joe - G	Perlman, Les - G
Baysinger, Reeves - T	Peyton, Leo - B
Clark, Hal - E	Rafter Bill - B
Coaker, John - T	Roy, Elmer - E
Culver, Frank - C	Sheard, Al - B
Dooley, John - G	Smith, "Hank" - C
Foster, Fred - B	Smythe, Lou - B
Grigg, Cecil - Q	Thomas, Carl - G
Kelly, "Clancy" - G	Wood, Jim - G
Lowery, Darby - T	

1924 ROCK ISLAND INDEPENDENTS
COACH - John Armstrong
5th 6-2-2

Armstrong, John - Q	Little Twig, Joe - T & E
Ashbaugh, Bill - B	Lyle, Dewey - E & G
Bernstein, Joe - G	McCarthy, Vince - Q
Bradshaw, Wes - B	Novak, Ed - B
Buland, Walt - T	Phelan, Bob - B
Burton, Lyle - G	Roberts, Walcott - B
Cotton, Forrest - T	Rooney, Joe - E
Coyle, Frank - E	Ryan, Jim - B
DeClerk, Frank - C	Scott, Ed - G
Earpe, Francis - G	Slater, "Duke" - T
Fosdick, Bob - G	Thompson, Fred - E
Gavin, "Buck" - B	Thompson, George - G
Guyon, Joe - B	Thorpe, Jim - B
Kolls, Lou - C & T	Ursella, "Rube" - B
Kraker, Joe - G	Wilson, "Mike" - E

1925

	W	L	T	Pct.
Chicago Cards	11	2	1	.846
Pottsville	10	2	0	.833
Detroit	8	2	2	.800
New York	8	4	0	.667
Akron	4	2	2	.667
Frankford	13	7	0	.650
Chicago Bears	9	5	3	.643
Rock Island	5	3	3	.625
Green Bay	8	5	0	.615
Providence	6	5	1	.545
Canton	4	4	0	.500

Cleveland	5	8	1	.392
Kansas City	2	5	1	.286
Hammond	1	3	0	.250
Buffalo	1	6	2	.143
Duluth	0	3	0	.000
Rochester	0	6	1	.000
Milwaukee	0	6	0	.000
Dayton	0	7	1	.000
Columbus	0	9	0	.000

There were all kinds of explosions around the NFL in 1925, some of them still vibrating a half-century later.

The Pottsville (Pa.) Maroons, a veteran independent team new in the NFL, won the title then lost it, not on the field but by orders of league president Joe Carr.

Harold "Red" Grange came out of college in late November, joined the Chicago Bears and pulled swarms of customers through the ticket gates.

Tim Mara bought a New York franchise for $500 and named it the Giants.

There were again 20 teams in the league, with new ones at New York, Pottsville, Detroit, Providence and back at Canton, which had lost its squad to Cleveland the year before. Racine, Kenosha and Minneapolis had dropped out.

Grange pulled 36,000 fans in his first pro game in Wrigley Field, Chicago, against the Cardinals; a week later 28,000 came to see him go against Columbus. The Bears then went on tour to play seven games in 11 days at St. Louis, at Philadelphia (35,000), at New York (73,000), and from there through the South and on to the West Coast.

While Grange was spreading good will and interest through the U.S., and putting a fat pile of money in the treasury of all the other teams, especially the New York Giants, things were happening back at Chicago.

The Pottsville Maroons were invited to play the Cardinals "for the title". They played and Pottsville won, 21-7, with Walter French of West Point starring for the Pennsylvania team.

A week later, the championship celebration still in force, Pottsville played a Notre Dame All-Star team, including the 4 Horsemen, in a post season exhibition game at Philadelphia.

Not before, but after the game, the Frankford Yellowjackets protested, claiming an invasion of their territorial rights. President Joe Carr supported this claim and told the Chicago Cardinals to play another game or two. The Cardinals arranged a game against the disrupted Milwaukee squad, which had disbanded for the season. The Cards won and now their record 11-2-1 was better than Pottsville's 10-2-0.

The Cardinals then claimed the title and have successfully defended that claim ever since despite an annual protest from the Pottsville area.

Soon after the final game it was discovered that the Milwaukee team had used four high school players. Its franchise was cancelled by President Carr, and its manager, Arthur Folz, was suspended "for life", the only man in NFL history to draw that sentence.

"Paddy" Driscoll, Chi-Cards, dropkicked four field goals (23, 18, 50, 35 yards) against Columbus, Oct. 11. The 50-yarder tied the record for distance.

1925 AKRON PROS
COACH - George Berry
5th 4-2-2

Annan, Dunc - Q	Falcon, Gil - B
Barrett, John - T	Henry, Fritz - G
Berry, George - G & C	Michaels, Alton - B
Bierce, Bruce - E	Mills, Joe - E & C
Bissell, Fred - E	Niehaus, Francis - B
Blailock, Russ - T	Nesser, Al - E & G
Caldwell, Cyril - G	Newman, Olin - E
Clements, Chase - G	Pollard, "Fritz" - B
Conrad, Marty - C	Roberston, Jim - B
Cramer, Carl - B	Stahlman, Dick - T
Daum, Carl - E	

1925 BUFFALO BISONS
COACH - Walt Koppisch
15th 1-6-2

Barber, Ben - T	Gwosden, Milo - E
Bruder, Woodie - B	Harvey, Norm - T
Burt, Russ - B	Kendrick, Jim - B & E
Carman, Ed - T	Kennedy, Joe - B
Christman, Floyd - B	Koppisch, Walt - B
Curzon, Harry - B & E	McCormich, Elmer - G
Feist, Lou - T & E	Noble, Jim - E
Fisher, Darrell - B	Reed, Max - C
Foster, Jim - Q	VanDyne, Charles - T
Gay, Chet - T	Youngstrom, Adolph - G

1925 CANTON BULLDOGS
COACHES - Harry Robb &
Wilbur Henry
11th 4-4-0

Brenner, Ray - B	Carroll, Elmer - E
Burt, Hal - G	Comstock, Rudy - G
Calac, Pete - B	Culver, Frank - C

Rochester Jeffersons team 1925. *Bottom row* (left to right): Alfred Sheard, Arnold "Jake" Hoffman, Cecil Grigg. *Middle row:* Edward Lynch, Frank Matteo, Roy Martineau, Henry Smith, Darby Lowery, John Dooley, Eugene Bedford. *Top row:* Harold Clark, Robert Argus, Leo V. Lyons, mgr., Edward Schlegel, treas., Clarence Kelly, Louis Smythe. (Photo by Leo V. Lyons.)

Fisher, Bob - B
Flattery, Wilson - G
Fleming, Wilmer - B
Guanieri, Al - Q
Henry, "Fats" - T
Hogan, Paul - B
Jones, Ben - B
Kyle, Jim - G
Lyman, "Link" - T
McRoberts, Wade - C

Merrilat, Lou - E
Redinger, Otis - B
Robb, Harry - Q
Robb, Stan - E
Roderick, Ben - B
Sacksteder, Norb - B
Schuster, Dick - E & G
Speck, "Dutch" - G
Strasser, Clarence - E
Zimmerman, Giff - B

Smith, Russ - G
Sternaman, Ed - B
Sternaman, Joe - Q

Trafton, George - C
Walquist, Laurie - Q
White, Roy - B

1925 CHICAGO CARDINALS
COACH - Norman Barry
1st 11-2-1
(Disputed by Pottsville)

1925 CHICAGO BEARS
COACH - George Halas
7th 9-5-3

Anderson, "Hunk" - G
Blacklock, Hugh - T
Britton, Earl - B
Bryan, John - B
Crawford, Walt - T
Fleckenstein, Bill - G & C
Garvey, "Hec" - E
Grange, "Red" - B
Halas, George - E
Hanny, Frank - E

Healey, Ed - T
King, Ralph - G
Knop, Oscar - B
McElwain, Bill - B
McMillen, Jim - G
Mohardt, John - B
Mullen, Verne - E
Murry, Don - T
Romney, Milt - Q
Scott, Ralph - T

Anderson, Ed - E
Blumenthal, Morris - B
Blumer, Herb - E & T
Brennan, Willis - G
Claypool, Ralph - C
DeStafano, Fred - B
Driscoll, "Paddy" - Q
Dunn, Joe - Q
Erickson, Hal - B
Evans, Earl - T
Folz, Art - Q
Gillies, Fred - T

Hurlburt, John - B
Koehler, Bob - B
Lunz, Gerry - G
McDonnell, "Mickey" - B
McInerny, Arnie - C
McNulty, Paul - E
Mahoney, "Ike" - B
Sachs, Len - E
Smith, Wilfred - E
Swanson, Evar - E
Tays, Jim - B

Charles Berry *(left)*, Captain of the Pottsville Maroons, greets George Trafton, head man of the Chicago Bears, before a game in 1925. Berry later became a top umpire in major league baseball and an official in the National Football League. (International News Photo.)

1925 CLEVELAND BULLDOGS
COACH -
12th 5-8-1

Ault, Chalmers - G	Carberry, Glenn - E	Eichenlaub, Ray - B	Nardacci, Nick - B
Baldwin, George - E	Cardarelli, Carl - C	Elliott, Wally - B	Nesser, Al - T
Bauer, Herb - T	Cobb, Alf - G	Hadden, Al - B	Noble, Dave - B
Brannon, Phil - E	Conover, Larry - C	Jones, Ben - B	Norton, Ray - B
Broadley, Karl - G	Eckburg, "Gus" - B	Kreinheder, Walt - G	Rehnquist, Milt - G & C
Burt, Hal - G	Edwards, Gene - G	Kutler, Rudy - E	Roberts, Walcott - B
		Loucks, Ed - E	Segal, Maurey - E
		Meredith, Russ - G	Spiers, Bob - T
		Michaels, Al - B	Sprinkle, Hubert - T
		Myers, Cy - E	Stringer, Gene - B

Red Grange, *left*, just out of college in 1925, talks with George Halas, his new boss, owner of the Chicago Bears. Halas was also the coach and played end.

Suchy, Paul - E	Williams, "Inky" - E
Vince, Ralph - G	Wolf, Dick - B
Wallace, Fred - G	Work, Joe - B
Webber, Howie - E	Workman, Harry - B

Guy, Charles - C
Huffine, Ken - B
Joseph, Zern - E & T
Kinderdine, George - C
Kinderdine, Walt - B
Knecht, Bill - T
Layport, John - G

Mahrt, Armin - B
Mahrt, John - E
Mayl, Gene - E
Partlow, Lou - B
Sacksteder, Norb - B
Sauer, Ed - T
Young, Russ - B

1925 COLUMBUS TIGERS
COACH ' "Red" Weaver
20th 0-9-0

Albanese, Don - E	Nemecek, Andy - G &C
Bullman, Gale - E	Nesser, Frank - B & G
Churchman, Charles - B	Petcoff, Boni - T
Davis, Herb - B	Rapp, "Goldie" - B
Duvall, Earl - G	Regan, Jim - Q
Eichenlaub, Ray - B	Rohleder, George - E & T
Ellis, Walt - T	Ruh, Homer - E
Goebel, Paul - E	Runkle, Gil - E
Guy, Charles - C	Sack, John - G
Long, Tom - G	Snoots, Lee - B
Lynch, Paul - B	Stock, Herb - B
Moody, Wilkie - B	Tynes, Dave - B
Mulbarger, Joe - T	

1925 DETROIT PANTHERS
COACH - Jim Conzelman
3rd 8-2-2

Bucher, Frank - E	Lauer, Hal - B & E
Conzelman, Jim - Q	McNamara, Tom - G
Crook, Al - C & T	Marion, Phil - B
Doane, Joe - B	Smith, Russ - G
Ellis, Walt "Speed" - T	Sonnenberg, "Gus" - G
Fleischman, Godfrey - G	Vick, "Ernie" - C
Hadden, Al - B	Vick, Dick - Q
Hogan, Tom - T	Voss, "Tillie" - E
Hultman, Vivian - E	Wimberly, Byron - G

1925 DAYTON TRIANGLES
COACH - Carl Storck
19th 0-7-1

Abbott, Fay - Q	Drayer, Clarence - T
Bacon, Francis - B	Fenner, Lee - E
Bonowitz, Elliott - G	Gabler, John - G
Dobeliet, Dick - B	Graham, Al - B

1925 DULUTH KELLEYS
COACH -
16th 0-3-0

Black, Charley - E	Denfield, Fred - T
Carlson, Gene - G	Gilbert, Walt - B
Cobb, Bill - T	Johnson, Art - T

Kelly, Charles - B
Kieley, Howard - T
Koziak, Mike - G
McDonnell, "Mickey" - B
Marshall, Bob - E
Method, Russ - B
O'Neill, Tom - E
Rooney, "Cobb" - Q

Rooney, Bill - B & C
Rundquist, Harry - T
Stein, Bill - C
Strand, Lief - C
Tobin, Rex - E
Underwood, John - E & G
Vexall, Roy - B
Williams, Dan - G

Owen, Bill - T
Rehnquist, Milt - G & C
Sermon, Ray - Q
Thompson, Al - T

Usher, Ed - B
Webber, Howie - E
White, Phil - B

1925 MILWAUKEE BADGERS
COACH - John Bryant
17th 0-6-0

Baril, Adrian - T
Barr, Wally - B
Brumm, Roman - G
Bryan, John - B
DeLaporte, Darol - B
Dunn, "Red" - Q
Dunnigan, Mert - T
Fahay, John - G
Gillo, "Hank" - B

McNally, John "Blood" - B
Mason, Sam - B
Miller, "Heinie" - E
Nadolney, Romanus - G
Neacy, Clem - E
Roessler, Fritz - E
Rydzewski, Frank - T
Tierney, Festus - G
Traynor, Bernie - C

1925 FRANKFORD YELLOWJACKETS
COACH - Guy Chamberlin
6th 13-7-0

Bednar, Al - G
Behman, "Bull" - T
Bruder, Woodie - B
Burnham, Stan - B
Cartin, Charley - T
Chamberlin, Guy - E
Clement, Alex - B
Craig, Clark - E
Crowther, Rae - E
Crowther, Saville - G
Ernst, Jack - Q
Fitzke, Bob - B
Hamer, Ernie - B
Harms, Art - T
Haws, Harve - Q
Hoffman, Bill - G

Homan, Henry - Q
Jones, Ben - B
Lowe, "Bull" - E
Lyman, "Link" - T
McCormick, Elmer - G & C
Moran, "Hap" - B
O'Connell, Milt - E
Sechrist, Walt - G
Seidelson, Harry - G
Smythe, Lou - B
Spagna, Joe - G & C
Springsteen, Bill - C
Stockton, Houston - B
Sullivan, George - B
Welsh, Jim - G
Wilsbach, Frank - G

1925 NEW YORK GIANTS
COACH - Bob Folwell
4th 8-4-0

Alexander, Joe - C
Bednar, Al - G
Benkert, "Heinie" - B
Bomar, Lynn - E
Brennan, Matt - Q
Carney, Art - G
Frugonne, Jim - B
Haines, "Hinkey" - B
Hendrian, "Dutch" - Q
Hill, Harry - B
Jappe, Paul - E
Kenyon, Bill - B
Koppisch, Walter - B
McBride, Jack - B
McGinley, Ed - T

Milstead, Century - T
Moran, Tom - B
Myers, Tom - B
Nash, Bob - T
Nordstrom, Harry - G
Palm, "Mike" - Q
Parnell, "Babe" - T
Potteiger, Earl - B & E
Reynolds, Owen - E
Rooney, "Cobb" - Q
Thorpe, Jim - B
Tomlin, Bradley - G
Walbridge, Lyman - C
White, Phil - B
Williams, Joe - G

1925 GREEN BAY PACKERS
COACH "Curly" Lambeau
9th 8-5-0

Abramson, George - T
Basing, Myrt - B & E
Buck, "Cub" - T
Crowley, Jim - B
Earpe, "Jug" - T & C
Gardner, Milt - G
Harris, Welton - B
Kotal, Ed - B
Lambeau, "Curly" - B

Larson, "Ojay" - C
LeJeune, Walt - G
Lewellen, Verne - B
Mathys, Charles - Q
Norton, Martin - B
O'Donnell, Dick - E
Vergara, George - E
Wilkins, Ted - E
Woodin, Howie - G

1925 POTTSVILLE MAROONS
COACH - Dick Rauch
2nd 10-2-0
(Pottsville claims title)

Beck, Carl - B
Beck, Clarence - T
Berry, Charley - E
Bihl, Vic - T
Bucher, Frank - E
Chapman, Tom - T
Dayhoff, Harry - B
Doyle, Ed - E
Ernst, Jack - Q
Flanagan, "Hoot" - B
French, Walter - B

Hathaway, Russ - T
Hauptly, Joe - G
Hughes, Denny - C
Latone, Tony - B
Lebengood, "Fungy" - B
Osborn, "Duke" - G
Racis, Frank - G
Rauch, Dick - G
Stein, Herb - C
Stein, Russ - T
Wentz, "Barney" - B

1925 HAMMOND PROS
COACH - "Fritz" Pollard
14th 1-3-0

Annan, Dunc - Q
Carman, Ed - T
Crawford, Ken - B & G
Curzon, Harry - B & E
Dahlgren, George - G
Falcon, Gil - B
Fortune, Burnell - G
Giaver, Bill - B
Hess, Walt - B
Hudson, Dick - B
Hunter, Merle - T & G
Kendrick, Jim - B & E
King, Andy - B

McDonnell, "Mickey" - B
Magnusson, Glenn - C
Meese, Ward - E
Neal, Bob - G
Oltz, Russ - C & T
Pollard, "Fritz" - B
Robinson, Ed - B
Rydzewski, Frank - T
Sachs, Len - E
Tallant, Dave - T
Watson, Grady - B
Williams, "Inky" - E

1925 PROVIDENCE STEAMROLLERS
COACH -
10th 6-5-1

Braney, John - G
Bristow, George - B
Burke, Charley - B
Connors, Stafford - B
Crowley, Jim - B
Eckstein, Adolph - C
Garvey, Francis - E
Golembeske, Tony - E
Gulian, Mike - T
Higgins, Paul - B
Kozlowsky, Joe - T

Laird, Jim - B
Lowe, "Bull" - E
MacPhee, Walt - B
McGoldrick, Hugh - T
McIntosh, Ira - B
Maloney, Gerry - E
Miller, Don - B
Oden, "Curly" - Q
Pearce, "Pard" - Q
Pohlman, John - B
Pollard, "Fritz" - B

1925 KANSAS CITY COWBOYS
COACH - Leroy Andrews
13th 2-5-1

Andrews, Roy - B & G
Ashbaugh, Bill - B
Bloodgood, "Bert" - Q
Bristow, Obie - B
Browning, Bob - Q
Corgan, Charley - E
DeWitz, Rufus - B
Guyon, Joe - B

Hanson, Steve - B & E
Hill, Charley - B
Hill, Harry - B
Howard, "Dosie" - G
Milan, Joe - E
Mintun, John - C
Munn, Lyle - E
Owen, Steve - T

Riopel, Al - B
Share, Nate - G
Sheehan, John - G
Shurtleff, Bert - C & G
Spellman, John - E & T

Sweet, Fred - B
Thomas, Gene - B
Wentworth, Shirley - B
Young, "Sam" - T

1925 ROCHESTER JEFFERSONS
COACH - Cecil Grigg
16th 0-6-1

Argus, Bob - B
Bedford, Bill - E
Clark, Hal - E
Connors, Ham - E
Dooley, John - G
Fivaz, Bill - C & G
Grigg, Cecil - Q
Hoffman, "Jake" - B
Kellogg, Bill - B
Kelly, "Clancy" - G
Lowery, Darby - T

Lynch, Ed - E
Mackert, Bob - T
Martineau, Roy - C
Matteo, Frank - T
Payn, Marshall - C
Peyton, Leo - B
Roy, Elmer - E
Sheard, Al - B
Smith, "Hank" - C
Smythe, Lou - B
Ziff, Dave - E & G

1925 ROCK ISLAND
INDEPENDENTS
COACH - "Rube" Ursella
8th 5-3-3

Armstrong, John - Q
Belding, Les - E
Burton, Lyle - G
Cotton, Forrest - T
Coyle, Frank - E
DeClerk, Frank - C
Elliott, Al - B
Gavin, "Buck" - B
Hendrian, "Dutch" - Q
Herman, Ed - E
Kolls, Lou - C & T
Lamb, Roy - B

Little Twig, Joe - T & E
Lyle, Dewey - G
McCarthy, Vince - Q
Novak, Ed - B
Rooney, Joe - E
Slater, "Duke" - T
Swanson, Evar - E
Thompson, George - G
Ursella, Rube - B
Widerquist, Chet - T
Wilson, "Mike" - E

1926

NATIONAL FOOTBALL LEAGUE

	W	L	T	Pct.
Frankford	14	1	1	.933
Chicago Bears	12	1	3	.923
Pottsville	10	2	1	.833
Kansas City	8	3	0	.727
Green Bay	7	3	3	.700
Los Angeles	6	3	1	.667
New York	8	4	0	.667
Duluth	6	5	2	.545
Buffalo	4	4	2	.500
Chicago Cardinals	5	6	1	.455
Providence	5	7	0	.417
Detroit	4	6	2	.400
Hartford	3	7	0	.300
Brooklyn	3	8	0	.272
Milwaukee	2	7	0	.222
Dayton	1	4	1	.200
Akron	1	4	3	.200
Racine	1	4	0	.200
Columbus	1	6	0	.144
Canton	1	9	3	.100
Louisville	0	4	0	.000
Hammond	0	4	0	.000

AMERICAN FOOTBALL LEAGUE

(1926)

	W	L	T	Pct.
Philadelphia	7	2	0	.778
New York	9	5	0	.643
Cleveland	3	2	0	.600
Los Angeles	6	6	2	.600
Chicago	5	6	3	.455
Boston	2	4	0	.333
Rock Island	2	5	1	.283
Brooklyn	1	3	0	.250
Newark	0	4	2	.000

A lot of people became optimistic in the booming U.S.A. of 1926. The enthusiasm and gate receipts stirred up by Red Grange put 31 pro football teams in action to start this season. The Frankford Yellowjackets won the NFL title with a 14-1-1 record.

There were 22 teams in the NFL and Red himself became a victim of his own sensational rookie record. He and his manager, C. C. Pyle, created the American Football League with Red playing for the New York entry. They placed franchises in Cleveland, Los Angeles, Chicago, Boston, Rock Island, Brooklyn, Newark and Philadelphia, where the Quakers, coached by Century Milstead (who hustled back to the New York Giants the next year) won the title (7-2-0). Not all the AFL teams finished the season but they were all finished when it was over. The League was a financial disaster for all teams.

The New York Giants (NFL) beat the Philadelphia Quakers (AFL), 31-0, in the first interleague playoff, Dec. 12.

The NFL had new teams at Hartford (Conn.), Brooklyn, Racine (Wis.), a road team representing Los Angeles and another road team out of Chicago, which called itself the Louisville Colonels. Rock Island jumped to the AFL, Rochester dropped out for good and Cleveland suspended.

Elbert Bloodgood, Kansas City back, drop-kicked four field goals (35, 32, 20, 25 yds.) against Duluth, Dec. 13.

Rule adopted making all college players ineligible for NFL action until their classes had graduated.

Roster limits made 18 maximum, 15 minimum.

1926 AKRON PROS
COACH - Al Nesser &
"Rube" Ursella
17th 1-4-3

Annan, Dunc - Q	Marks, Larry - Q
Beck, Marty - B	Mills, Joe - E & C
Berry, George - G	Nesser, Al - E
Bissell, Fred - E	Newman, Olin - E
Galdwell, Cyril - T	Pollard, "Fritz" - B
Chase, Ralph - T	Rohleder, George - T & E
Cramer, Carl - B	Running, Wolf - T
Daum, Carl - E	Seidelson, Harry - G
Davis, Carl - T	Ursella, "Rube" - B
Griggs, Haldane - B	Wallace, Fred - G
Little Twig, Joe - E	Wendler, Harold - B
McCombs, Nat - T	

1926 BROOKLYN LIONS
COACH -
14th 3-8-0

Bagby, Herman - Q	Myers, Tom - Q
Blacklock, Hugh - T	Nordstrom, Harry - G
Bond, Jim - G	Plumridge, Ted - C
Brennan, Matt - Q	Reagen, Ed - T
Britton, Earl - B	Reynolds, Owen - E
Connors, Stafford - B	Reynolds, Quentin - T
Douglas, Leo - B	Rooney, Bill - B
Drews, Ted - E	Sheldon, Jim - E
Garvey, "Hec" - T	Snell, George - B
Harrison, Ed - E	Stephens, Bill - C
Howard, Al - G	Stevenson, Art - G
Jappe, Paul - E	Stuhldreyer, Harry - Q
Kobolinski, Stan - C & G	Taylor, John - T
Leith, Al - Q	Thomas, Rex - B
McCullough, Jim - G	Weber, Charles - G
McGrath, Dick - T	Yeager, Jim - T
Morris, Bob - G	Ziff, Dave - E

1926 BUFFALO RANGERS
COACH - Jim Kendrick
9th 4-4-2

Allison, Jim - E	McGilbra, Sanford - T
Bradshaw, Wes - B	Nairan, Roger - E
Caywood, Les - T	Nix, George - T
Dimmick, Don - B	Powell, Roger - E
Edmondson, Van - C	Schwarzer, Ted - G
Fay, Jim - B	Slough, Elmer - B
Feist, Lou - T & E	Swain, Alton - E
Guffey, Roy - E	Vaughn, Bill - B
Hobson, Ben - B	Weathers, Guy - G
Irvin, Barlow - G	Wilcox, John - T
Kendrick, Jim - Q & E	Willson, Joe - G
Kirk, George - C	Wilson, "Fay" - B

1926 CANTON BULLDOGS
COACHES - Harry Robb &
Wilbur Henry

Babcock, Sam - B	Robb, Harry - Q
Butler, "Sol" - B	Robb, Stan - E
Calac, Pete - B	Roberts, Guy - B
Comber, John - B	Roderick, Ben - B
Deibel, Art - T	Sack, John - G
Flattery, Wilson - G	Seeds, Frank - B
Henry, "Fats" - T	Speck, "Dutch" - G
Kyle, Jim - G	Stein, Russ - T & E
Little Twig, Joe - E & T	Thorpe, Jim - B
McRoberts, Wade - C	Vick, Dick - Q
Marker, Cliff - B & E	Wallace, Fred - G
Nelson, Don - C	Zerbe, Harold - E
Nichols, John - G	

1926 CHICAGO BEARS
COACH - George Halas
2nd 12-1-3

Bryan, John - B	Lyman, "Link" - T
Buckler, Bill - G	McMillen, Jim - G
Driscoll, "Paddy" - B	Mullen, Verne - E
Evans, Earl - T	Murry, Don - T
Fleckenstein, Bill - G & C	Romney, Milt - Q
Halas, George - E	Senn, Bill - B
Hanny, Frank - E	Sternaman, Ed - B
Healey, Ed - T	Trafton, George - C
Knop, Oscar - B	Walquist, Laurie - Q
Lemon, Cliff - T	

1926 CHICAGO CARDINALS
COACH - Norman Barry
10th 5-6-1

Blumer, Herb - G & E	Lamb, Roy - B
Brennan, Willis - G	Lunz, Gerry - G
Claypool, Ralph - C	McDonnell, "Mickey" - B
Dunn, Joe - Q	McElwain, Bill - B
Ellis, Walt - T	McInerny, Arnie - E
Erickson, Hal - B	Mahoney, "Ike" - Q
Francis, Gene - B	Slater, "Duke" - T
Gillies, Fred - T	Stuessy, John - T
Greene, Ed - E & G	Swanson, Evar - E
Hogan, Tom - T	Weller, Ray - T
Kellogg, Bill - B	Widerquist, Chet - T
Kieley, Howard - T	Woodruff, Jim - E
Koehler, Bob - B	

1926 COLUMBUS TIGERS
COACH - John Heldt
19th 1-6-1

Barnum, Bob - B	Nesser, Frank - B & G
Berrehsen, Bill - T	Nonnemaker, "Gus" - E
Bertoglio, Jim - B	Pearce, Harley - E
Conley, John - T	Petcoff, Boni - T
Davis, Herb - B	Plank, Earl - E
Duvall, Earl - G	Rapp, "Goldie" - B
Gorrill, Charley - E	Reichle, Lou - C
Heldt, John - C	Richter, Hal - T
Little Twig, Joe - T & E	Ruh, Homer - E
Mulbarger, Joe - T	Woods, Gerry - B
Murphy, Tom - B	

1926 DAYTON TRIANGLES
COACH - Lou Mahrt
16th 1-4-1

Abbott, Fay - B	Guy, Charles - C
Bacon, Frank - B	Huffine, Ken - B
Becker, John - T	Hummon, John - E
Beckley, Art - B	Kinderdine, George - C
Bonowitz, Elliott - G	Knecht, Bill - T
Brown, Jack - C	Layport, John - G
Calhoun, Eric - T	Mahrt, Lou - Q
Dobeliet, Dick - B	Mayl, Gene - E
Drayer, Clarence - T	Partlow, Lou - B
Fenner, Lee - E	Reiter, Wilbur - G
Gabler, John - G	Sauer, Ed - T
Graham, Al - G	Young, Russ - B

1926 DETROIT PANTHERS
COACH - Jim Conzelman
12th 4-6-2

Barrett, John - T & C
Cameron, Ed - G
Carlson, Wes - G
Conzelman, Jim - Q
Crook, Al - C & T
Doane, Joe - B
Edwards, Tom - T
Ellis, Walt - T
Fleischman, Godfrey - G
Gregory, Bruce - B
Grube, Charles - E
Hadden, Al - B
Harvey, Norm - T & E
Hogan, Tom - T
Hultman, Vivian - E
Lauer, Hal - B
Lynch, Ed - E
McDonnell, "Mickey" - B
McNamara, Tom - G
Marion, Phil - B
Scharer, Ed - B
Sonnenberg, "Gus" - G
Vick, Dick - Q

1926 HAMMOND PROS
COACH - Dunc Annan
21st 0-4-0

Annan, Dunc - Q
Barry, George - G & C
Butler, Bill - B
Carr, Lee - B
Curzon, Harry - B & E
Dahlgren, George - G
Fisher, George - T
Gavin, "Buck" - B
Hahn, Ray - E
Hudson, Dick - B
Hunter, Merle - G
McKetes, - B
Nagida, - B
Neal, Bob - G
Rydzewski, Frank - T
Sechrist, Walt - G
Smith, Russ - T
Ursella, "Rube" - B
Usher, Lou - T
Williams, "Inky" - E

1926 DULUTH ESKIMOS
COACH - Ernie Nevers
8th 6-5-2

Buland, Walt - T
Carlson, Gene - G
Cobb, Bill - T
Fitzgibbons, Paul - B
Gayer, "Chet" - T
Gilbert, Walt - B
Heinisch, Fred - B & E
Johnson, Art - T
Kelly, Charles - Q
Kiesling, Walt - G
Larson, Lou - B
McNally, John "Blood" - B
Manion, Jim - G
Marshall, Bob - E
Method, Russ - B
Murphy, Phil - C
Murray, John - E
Nevers, Ernie - B
O'Brien, Charles - E
Quam, "Red" - B
Rooney, "Cobb" - Q
Rooney, Joe - E
Rooney, Bill - B
Rundquist, Harry - T
Scanlon, Dewey - B
Stein, Bill - C & G
Strand, Lief - C
Suess, Ray - T
Sullivan, Hew - T
Underwood, John - E & G
Williams, Dan - G

1926 HARTFORD BLUES
COACH - Dr. John Keough
13th 3-7-0

Barnikow, Ed - B
Bonadies, John - G
Brian, Harry - B
Corgan, Charley - Q & E
Dally, - G
Donlan, Jim - G
Edwards, Bill - B
Flynn, Furlong - T
Foley, Jim - Q
Friedman, "Jake" - E
Garvey, "Hec" - T
Gildea, Denny - C
Halloran, "Dimp" - B
Harris, John - B
Jamerson, "Lefty" = E
Keenan, Ed - G
Lynch, Ed - E
McCann, Ernie - T & E
McCormick, Elmer - C & G
McEvoy, Ed - B
McMahon, Harry - B
Manning, Joe - B
Nichols, Ralph - T
Noble, Dick - G
O'Connell, Grattan - E
O'Connor, Francis - T
O'Neil, Charley - C
Perrin, John - Q
Radzievitch, Vic - Q & G
Santone, Joe - G
Segretta, Rocco - B
Simendinger, Ken - B
Smythe, Lou - B
Thomas, Enid - B
Webber, Howie - E
Werwaiss, Elbert - T
Zehrer, Henry - B

1926 FRANKFORD YELLOWJACKETS
COACH - Guy Chamberlin
1st 14-1-1

Books, Bob - B
Bruder, Woodie - B
Budd, John - T
Carpe, Joe - T
Chamberlin, Guy - E
Comstock, Rudy - G
Conover, Larry - C
Crowther, Rae - E
Douglass, Leo - B
Graham, Fred - E
Hamer, Ernie - B
Hoffman, Bill - G
Hogan, Paul - B
Homan, Henry - Q
Jones, Ben - Q
Lowe, "Bull" - E
Mahan, "Red" - G
Moran, "Hap" - B
Potts, Bob - T
Reed, Max - C
Roberts, Walcott - B
Smythe, Lou - B
Springsteen, Bill - C
Stockton, Houston - B
Weir, Ed - T
Wilcox, Ed - B
Youngstrom, "Swede" - G

1926 KANSAS CITY COWBOYS
COACH - Leroy Andrews
4th 8-3-0

Andrews, Roy - B & G
Bagby, Herm - B
Berquist, Jay - G
Bloodgood, "Bert" - Q
Bristow, Obie - B
Caywood, Les - G
Cobb, Tom - T
Corgan, Charley - E & B
Crook, Al - C & T
DeWitz, Rufus - B
Hill, Charley - B
Hill, Harry - B
Howard, Bob - G
Hummel, Arnie - B
Jacquith, Jim - B
Munn, Lyle - E
Murphy, Tom - B
Owen, Bill - T
Randels, Horace - E
Rehnquist, Milt - G
Smith, Clyde - C
Spear, Glen - B
Thompson, Al - T
Westoupal, Joe - C
Wilson, Fay - B

1926 GREEN BAY PACKERS
COACH - "Curly" Lambeau
5th 7-3-3

Abramson, George - T
Basing, Myrt - B & E
Cahoon, Ivan - T
Carlson, Wes - G
Cyre, Hec - T
Earpe, "Jug" - T & C
Enright, Rex - B
Flaherty, Dick - E
Gardner, Milt - G
Harris, Welton - B & E
Kotal, Ed - B
Kuick, Stan - G
Lambeau, "Curly" - B
LeJeune, Walt - G
Lewellen, Verne - B
Lidberg, Carl - B
MacAuliffe, John - B
McGaw, Walt - G
Mathys, Charles - Q
Norton, Martin - B
O'Donnell, Dick - E
Purdy, Everette - B
Rosatti, Roman - T
Rose, Bob - C
Woodin, Howie - G

1926 LOS ANGELES BUCCANEERS
COACHES - "Brick" Muller
& "Tut" Imlay
6th 6-3-1

Ash, Julian - G
Bangs, Ben - B & E
Beach, Fred - G
Finch, "Bull" - B
Gutteron, Bill - B
Hawkins, John - T
Hufford, Darrell - E
Imlay, "Tut" - Q
McArthur, John - C
Maul, "Tuffy" - B
Muller, "Brick" - E
Newmeyer, Don - T
Nolan, John - G
Sandberg, Arnold - B
Schaffnit, Pete - E & B
Thompson, Don - G
Thurman, John - T
White, Ellery - B
Young, "Al" - B

1926 LOUISVILLE COLONELS
(Chicago road team)
COACH - Bill Harley
21st 0-4-0

Bernoske, Dan - G
Berwick, Ed - C
Bolan, Joe - T
Bush, Ray - E
Carlson, Clarence - E
Curzon, Harry - B & E
Eiden, Jim - T
Flannagan, Bill - T
Giaver, Bill - B
Gansberg, Al - T & E
Golsen, Gene - B
Golsen, Tom - B
Green, J.B.H. - T
Greenwood, Glenn - B
Hanson, Steve - E
Jackson, Larry - C

Kirchner, Adolph - T
Leaf, Garfield - T
McCaw, Bill - G
McDonald, John - T
Metzger, Lou - B
Palmer, Charley - B
Richter, Hal - E & T
Robinson, Ed - B
Sachs, Len - E
Scanlon, John - B
Sechrist, Walt - G
Sherry, Gerry - E
Slagle, George - T
Stinchcomb, "Pete" - Q
Stuckey, Bill - B
Vainowski, Pete - G

1926 MILWAUKEE BADGERS
COACH - John Bryan
15th 2-7-0

Abel, Fred - B
Ashmore, Marion - T
Bergen, Bill - B
Bryan, John - B
Burks, Joe - C
Curtin, Don - B
Dilweg, Lavern - E
Dunnigan, Mert - T
Fischer, Clark - B
Gay, Chet - T
Hallquist, Stone - B

Heimsch, John - B
Hertz, Frank - E & T
Kuick, Stan - G
Lane, Francis - T
McNally, John "Blood" - B
Moran, Art - T
Murphy, Tom - B
Neacy, Clem - E
Orwoll, Ossie - B
Slater, Howie - B

1926 NEW YORK GIANTS
COACH - Joe Alexander
7th 8-4-0

Alexander, John - T
Alexander, Joe - C & G
Bednar, Al - G
Biggs, Riley - C
Bomar, Lynn - E
Carney, Art - E
Grigg, Cecil - Q
Hagerty, Jack - Q
Haines, "Hinkey" - B
Harms, Art - T
Harris, Ollie - E
Hill, Harry - B
Hill, "Kid" - B
Hogan, Paul - B

Killinger, Glenn - B
Koppisch, Walt - B
McBride, Jack - B
Murtaugh, George - C & E
Nesser, Al - G
Owen, Steve - T
Palm, "Mike" - Q
Parnell, "Babe" - T
Potteiger, Earl - B & E
Stevenson, Art - G
Tomlin, Bradley - G
Voss, "Tilly" - E
Webber, Howie - E
Williams, Joe - G

1926 POTTSVILLE MAROONS
COACH - Dick Rauch
3rd 10-2-1

Benkert, "Heinie" - B
Berry, Charley - E
Brown, Jesse - B
Bucher, Frank - E
Ernst, Jack - Q
Flanagan, "Hoot" - B
Hathaway, Russ - T
Jawish, Henry - G
Kenneally, George - E
Kobolinski, Stan - C
Latone, Tony - B

Millman, Bob - B
Neihaus, Frank - B
Oliker, Aaron - E
Osborn, "Duke" - G
Racis, Frank - G
Stein, Herb - C
Welsh, Jim - G
Wentz, Barney - B
Wilton, Craig - E
Wissinger, Zonar - G
Youngfleisch, Francis - C

1926 PROVIDENCE
STEAMROLLERS
COACH -
11th 5-7-0

Braney, John - G
Burke, Charles - B
Donahue, John - T
Eckstein, Adolph - C
Etelman, Carl - B
Forst, Art - B
Garvey, Francis - E
Golembeski, Tony - E
Graham, Fred - E
Gulian, Mike - T
Hagenbuckle, Vernon - E
Hummell, - B
Keefer, Jackson - B
Koplow, Joe - T
Kozlowsky, Joe - T
Laird, Jim - B
Lester, Hal - E
MacPhee, Walt - B
McCrillis, Ed - G

McGlone, Joe - B
McIntosh, Ira - B
Manning, Joe - B
Oden, "Curly" - Q
Sampson, Seneca - B
Sayforth, - B
Scott, Charles - T
Share, Nate - G
Shurtleff, Bert - T
Smythe, Lou - B
Spellman, John - T
Stifler, Jim - E
Sweet, Fred - B
Talbot, John - E
Thomas, Gene - B
Triggs, John - B
Wentworth, Shirley - B
Wesley, Lecil - C
Young, "Sam" - T

1926 RACINE LEGION
COACH - "Hank" Gillo
16th 1-4-0

Barr, Wally - B
Bernard, George - G
Bieberstein, Adolph - G
Boettcher, Ray - B & G
Brumm, Roman - T
Burnsite, George - Q
Curtin, Don - Q
Fahay, John - B & E
Gay, Chet - T
Gillo, "Hank" - B
Glennie, George - G & E
Hardy, Dick - T

Heinisch, Fred - B & E
Hobscheid, Frank - G
Kernwein, Graham - B
Linnan, Francis - T
Longstreet, Roy - C
McIllwain, Wally - B
Matthews, Frank - E
Mintun, John - C
Murphy, Jim - B
Oldham, Jim - B & E
Reichow, Charles - B
Sterr, Gil - Q

1926 BOSTON BULLDOGS (AFL)
COACH - Herb Treat
6th 2-4-0

Coleman, Ed - G & E
Corrigan, Phil - Q
Cronin, Bill - B
Etelman, Carl - Q
Gehrke, Erwin - Q
Gilroy, John - B
Gilroy, Ralph - B
Hagenbuckle, Vernon - E
Johnson, Oscar - B
Lowe, "Bull" - E
McGlone, Joe - Q
McManus, Art - T

Morrison, Charles - E & G
Murphy, Bill - T & E
O'Brien, Tom - T
Patten, Steve - G
Pierotti, Al - C
Ray, Art - G
Smith, Francis - C & G
Stephen, Bill - C & T
Surabian, "Zeke" - G
Treat, Herb - T
Wallis, Jim - Q

1926 BROOKLYN HORSEMEN
(AFL)
COACH - Bob Berryman
8th 1-3-0

Baldwin, George - E & G
Bingham, John - E
Bolger, Jim - B
Brennan, Paul - G & T
Britton, Earl - B
Drews, Ted - E
Fitzgerald, John - Q
Frugonne, Jim - B
Garvey, "Hec" - T
Harrison, Ed - E
Howard, Al - B
Hummell, Charles - T
Hunsinger, Ed - E

Kozlock, - T
Layden, Elmer - B
Nichols, Bob - T
Plumridge, Ted - C
Pollock, Sheldon - C
Prendergast, Leo - T
Sehres, Dave - B
Share, Nate - G
Sheehy, John - C
Smith, Ray - Q
Stuhldreyer, Harry - Q
Taylor, John - G

1926 CHICAGO BULLS (AFL)
COACH - Joe Sternaman
5th 5-6-3

Anderson, Eddie - E
Blackwood, Hal - G
Boyle, John - E
Buckeye, Garland - G
Connell, Ward - B
Crawford, Walt - T
Fahay, John - E
Giaver, Bill - B
Goodman, Audrey - T
Graham, Fred - E
Hall, Harry - Q
Larson, "Ojay" - C
McMullan, John - T

Mahan, "Red" - T & G
Mohardt, John - B
Richerson, Doss - G
Romey, Dick - E
Stahlman, Dick - T
Sternaman, Joe - Q
Strader, "Red" - B
Swenson, Merwin - C
Tays, Jim - B
White, Phil - B
White, Roy - B
Whiteman, Sam - B

1926 CLEVELAND PANTHERS (AFL)
COACH - Ray Watts
3rd 3-2-0

Campbell, Freeman - E
Cunningham, Hal - E
Dean - T
Behm, Norton - B & E
Campbell, Freeman - E
Cunningham, Hal - E
Elliott, Wally - B
Evans, Myles - T
Gribben, Bill - B
Hadden, Al - B
Kregenow, Ed - B
Lehrer, Chris - B
Michaels, Al - B
Nesser, Al - E & G
Noble, Dave - B

Otterbacher, - G
Potter, Charles - G
Red Fox - B
Roberts, Guy - B
Roberts, Jim - B & E & T
Sack, John - G
Scaglione, - T
Sechrist, Walt - G
Spiers, Bob - T
Thornburg, Al - T
Vince, Ralph - G
Virant, Leo - G
Weaver, Jim - C
Winters, Jay - B
Wolf, Dick - B

1926 LOS ANGELES WILDCATS (AFL)
COACH - Jim Clark
4th 6-6-2

Bradshaw, Jim - Q
Bross, Mal - B
Bucklin, Tom - B
Busch, Nick - G
Carey, Dana - G
Clark, Jim - E
Erickson, Walden - T
Flaherty, Ray - E
Illman, Ed - Q
Johnston, Charles - T
Lawson, Jim - E

McRae, Ed - G
Morrison, "Ram" - B
Morrison, "Duke" - B
Reed, Dick - E
Shipkey, Harry - T
Stephens, Les - C
Vesser, John - E
Walters, Chal - C
Wilson, Abe - G
Wilson, George - B

1926 NEW YORK YANKEES (AFL)
COACH - Ralph Scott
2nd 9-5-0

Baker, Roy - B & G
Coglizer, Art - E
Fry, Wes - Q
Garvey, "Hec" - G
Goebel, Paul - E
Goetz, Angus - T
Grange, "Red" - B
Griffen, Hal - C
Hall, Ray - T
Hubert, "Pooley" - Q
Kearney, Frank - T

Kriz, Leo - T
Maloney, "Red" - E
Marks, Larry - B & E
Michalske, "Mike" - G
Minick, Paul - G
Oliver, Bill - G
Otte, Lowell - E
Pease, George - Q
Schimititsch, Steve - G & C
Scott, Ralph - T
Tryon, Ed - B

1926 NEWARK BEARS (AFL)
COACH - Harold Hansen
9th 0-4-2

Black, Ed - E
Brewster, Jim - Q
Clark, Russ - T
Connelly, Vince - B
Davis, Carl - T
Goldstein, Izzy - G
Hansen, Harold - B & G
Johnson, Knute - E
Kerr, - G
King, Ken - E
McManus, Art - T

Manell, Don - G
Maurer, Adrian - B
Murray, John - C
Newton, "Ark" - B
Rice, Olin - C
Rives, Bob - T
Stein, Sam - E
Tursi, Silvio - E
Williams, "Cy" - G
Williams, Ivan - B
Wycoff, Doug - Q

1926 PHILADELPHIA QUAKERS (AFL)
COACH - Bob Folwell
1st 7-2-0

Asplundh, Les - B
Beattie, Bob - T
Behman, "Bull" - T
Cartin, Charles - T
Coleman, Ed - E & G
Crowthers, Saville - G
Dinsmore, Bob - B
Elliott, Wally - B
Fay, Jerry - G
Ford, Adrian - B & E
Gebhard, Lou - B
Johnson, Knute - E

Kostos, Joe - E
Kreuz, Al - B
Marhefka, Joe - B
Milstead, Century - T
Robinson, Karl - C
Scott, John - Q
Spagna, Joe - G & C
Sullivan, George - B
Thomas, Bill - B & E
Tully, George - E
Way, "Pie" - B

1926 ROCK ISLAND INDEPENDENTS
COACH - John Armstrong
7th 2-5-1

Armstrong, John - Q
Biggs, Riley - C & G
Bradshaw, Wes - B
Coyle, Frank - E
Cunningham, Hal - B
Hartzog, Howard - G
Hertz, Frank - E & T
Hill, Harry - B
Jacquith, Jim - Q
Kaplan, Sid - B
Kolls, Lou - C
McCarthy, Vince - B

Norton, Marty - B
Novak, Ed - B
Rohrbaugh, Ray - B
Scarpino, Bill - E
Slater, "Duke" - T
Stahlman, Dick - T
Truckenmiller, Ken - G
Urban, Luke - E
Walker, Homer - E
Widerquist, Chet - G
Wiedich, Ralph - T
Wilson, "Mike" - E

1927

	W	L	T	Pct.
New York Giants	11	1	1	.917
Green Bay	7	2	1	.778
Chicago Bears	9	3	2	.750
Cleveland	8	4	1	.667
Providence	8	5	1	.615
New York Yankees	7	8	1	.467
Frankford	6	9	3	.400
Pottsville	5	8	0	.385
Chicago Cardinals	3	7	1	.300
Dayton	1	6	1	.143
Duluth	1	8	1	.111
Buffalo	0	5	0	.000

Between 1926 and 1927, 19 pro football teams conceded financial defeat, and the NFL was down to 12 active rosters. The American Football League of 1926 was gone.

The National lost Kansas City, Los Angeles, Detroit, Hartford, Brooklyn, Milwaukee, Racine, Louisville. Four legendary midwest teams—Akron, Canton, Columbus and Hammond—dropped out. There was a new team in Cleveland and Grange took his AFL Yanks into the NFL as the New York Yankees, where they finished 7-8-1 in sixth place behind the New York Giants (11-1-1) who won their first league title this season. Most teams played at least 10 games except Buffalo, which lost five, won none. This was the last season in the NFL for Buffalo, but they would be back again—and again.

John Storer, Frankford fullback (1924), died Jan. 15.

McInerny, Arnie - E & C
Mahoney, "Ike" - Q
Moran, Francis - B
Mullen, Verne - E
Risvold, Ray - Q
Roach, Rollin - B
Slater, "Duke" - T

Springsteen, Bill - E & C
Strader, "Red" - B
Swanson, Evar - E
Vesser, John - E
Waldron, Austin - G
Weller, Ray - T
Yeisley, Don - E

1927 CLEVELAND BULLDOGS
COACH - Leroy Andrews
4th 8-4-1

Andrews, Leroy - B & G
Bacchus, Carl - E
Bagby, Herman - B
Bloodgood, "Bert" - Q
Broda, Hal - E
Caywood, Les - G
Cobb, Tom - T
Cunningham, Hal - E
DeWitz, Herb - B
Feather, Elwin - B
Flohr, Les - C
Friedman, Ben - Q
Howard, Bob - G
Kelley, Frank - B

Krysl, Gerry - T
McGee, Harry - G
Munn, Lyle - E
Owen, Bill - T
Peery, Gordon - Q
Randels, Horace - E
Rehnquist, Milt - G & C
Sechrist, Walt - G
Simmons, Jim - B
Smith, Clyde - C
Thomas, Rex - B
Webber, Howard - E
Wiberg, Oscar - B
Wolf, Dick - B

1927 BUFFALO BISONS
COACH - "Dim" Batterson
12th 0-5-0

Allison, Jim - E
Beuthel, Lloyd - G
Bohren, Karl - B
Carr, Harlan - Q
Dimmick, Don - B
Doyle, Ed - G
Harvey, Norm - T
Hathaway, Russ - T
Hauser, Ken - B
Hobson, Ben - Q
Irvin, Barlow - G
McArthur, John - C

McConnell, Felton - G
Minick, Paul - G
Otte, Lowell - E
Roderick, Ben - B
Roy, Elmer - E
Snell, George - B
Underwood, John - G
VanHorne, Charles - B
Vedder, Norton - B
Watson, Grady - B
White, - E
Willson, Joe - G

1927 DAYTON TRIANGLES
COACH - Lou Mahrt
10th 1-6-1

Abbott, Fay - B
Achui, "Sneeze" - B
Becker, John - T
Belanich, Bill - T
Britton, Earl - B
Brown, Jack - C
Cabrinha, "Gus" - B
DeWeese, "Eddy" - G
Fenner, Lee - E
Graham, Al - G
Hippa, Sam - E
Hummon, John - E

Joseph, "Red" - E
Joseph, Zern - E & T
Kinderdine, George - C
Mahrt, Lou - Q
Partlow, Lou - B
Reiter, Wilbur - G & E
Roll, Clayton - E
Seibert, Ed - G
Sillin, Frank - B
Tays, Jim - B
Zimmerman, Carl - G

1927 CHICAGO BEARS
COACH - George Halas
3rd 9-3-2

Ashmore, Marion - T
Buckler, Bill - G
Driscoll, "Paddy" - B
Evans, Earl - T
Fleckenstein, Bill - G
Halas, George - E
Hanny, Frank - E
Healey, Ed - T
Hobscheid, Frank - G
Kassel, Charles - E
Knop, Oscar - B
Lyman, "Link" - T

McMillen, Jim - G
Murry, Don - T
Neacy, Clem - E
Romney, Milt - Q
Senn, Bill - B
Sternaman, Ed - B
Sternaman, Joe - Q
Trafton, George - C
Vick, "Ernie" - C
Voss, "Tillie" - E
Walquist, Laurie - Q
White, Roy - B

1927 DULUTH ESKIMOS
COACH - Ernie Nevers
11th 1-8-1

Ashmore, Marion - T
Belden, "Bunny" - B
Burke, Bob - T
Carlson, Gene - G
Clark, Arthur - Q
Cronin, Francis - E
Gilbert, Walt - B
Goldfein, Jersey - B
Johnson, Art - T
Kiesling, Walt - G
Lang, "Tex" - T
McCarthy, Jim - T
McNally, John "Blood" - B
McNellis, Bill - B
Manion, Jim - G

Marshall, Bob - E
Method, Russ - B
Monelie, Bill - B
Neacy, Clem - E
Nevers, Ernie - B
Rooney, "Cobb" - Q
Rooney, Joe - E
Rooney, Bill - B
Stein, Bill - C
Strand, Lief - C
Suess, Ray - T
Underwood, John - E & G
Warner, Bob - B
Williams, Dan - G

1927 CHICAGO CARDINALS
COACH - Fred Gillies
9th 3-7-1

Berquist, Jay - G
Blumer, Herb - E & T
Brennan, Willis - G
Bucklin, Tom - B
Chamberlin, Guy - E
Ellis, Walt - T
Erickson, Hal - B

Gillies, Fred - T
Goodman, Aubrey - T
Greene, Ed - E & G
Hummel, Arnie - B & G
Jones, Ben - Q
Lamb, Roy - Q
McDonnell, "Mickey" - B

1927 FRANKFORD YELLOWJACKETS
COACH - Charles Moran & Ed Weir
6th 6-9-3

Behman, "Bull" - T
Britton, Earl - B

Carpe, Joe - T
Clark, Art - B

Comstock, Rudy - G
Connaughton, "Babe" - G
Cortemeglia, Chris - B
Dougherity, Russ - B
Davis, Carl - T
Donohoe, Bill - Q
Filak, John - T
Fitzgibbon, Paul - B
Ford, Adrian - B
Grigg, Cecil - Q
Hamer, Ernie - B
Homan, Henry - Q
Kassell, Charley - E
Kostos, Tony - E
Leary, Tom - E
McGrath, Frank - E
Marker, Cliff - B

Maxwell, Joe - E & C
Mercer, Ken - B
Molinet, Lou - B
Montgomery, "Sully" - T
Moran, "Hap" - B
Morrison, Ed - B
Moynihan, Dick - B
Reed, Max - C
Richards, Pete - C
Rogers, Charles - Q
Sieracki, Stan - T
Tully, George - E
Weir, Ed - T
Weir, Joe - E
Wilcox, Ed - B
Youngstrom, "Swede" - G

1927 GREEN BAY PACKERS
COACH - "Curly" Lambeau
2nd 7-2-1

Basing, Myrt - B & E
Cahoon, Ivan - T
Cyre, Hector - T
Darling, Bernie - C
Dilweg, Lavern - E
Dunn, "Red" - Q
Earpe, "Jug" - T & C
Enright, Rex - B
Hearden, Tom - B
Jones, Bruce - G
Kotal, Ed - B
Lambeau, "Curly" - B

Lewellen, Verne - B
Lidberg, Carl - B
Mayer, Frank - G
Norton, Martin - B
O'Donnell, Dick - E
Perry, Claude - T
Purdy, Everett - B
Rosatti, Roman - T
Skeate, Gil - B
Smith, "Red" - G & E
Tuttle, George - E
Woodin, Howie - G

1927 NEW YORK GIANTS
COACH - Earl Potteiger
1st 11-1-1

Alexander, Joe - C & E
Biggs, Riley - C
Caywood, Les - G
Corgan, Charles - E
Garvey, "Hec" - G
Guyon, Joe - B
Hagerty, Jack - Q
Haines, "Hinkey" - Q
Henry, "Fats" - T
Howard, Al - G
Hubbard, "Cal" - T & E
Imlay, "Tut" - Q
Jappe, Paul - E & C

Kendrick, Jim - E & T
McBride, Jack - B
Marker, Cliff - B & E
Milstead, Century - T
Murtagh, George - C
Nesser, Al - G & C
Owen, Steve - T
Parnell, Fred - T
Potteiger, Earl - E
Stahlman, Dick - T & E
White, Phil - B
Wilson, "Fay" - B
Wycoff, Doug - Q

1927 NEW YORK YANKEES
COACH - Ralph Scott
6th 7-8-1

Badgro, "Red" - E
Baker, Roy - B
Bayley, John - T
Beattie, Bob - T
Crawford, Walt - T
Earpe, "Jug" - G
Flaherty, Ray - E
Fry, Wes - Q
Grange, "Red" - B
Hall, Ray - T
Harvey, Norm - T
Kelly, Bill - Q
Kolls, Lou - C & T

Kramer, Fred - G
Lawson, Jim - E
Lewellen, Verne - B
McArthur, John - C
Maloney, Gerry - E
Marks, Larry - Q
Michalske, "Mike" - G
Molenda, "Bo" - B
Oliver, "Bill" - G
Olson, Forrest - G
Scott, Ralph - T
Stephens, Les - C
Tryon, Ed - B

1927 POTTSVILLE MAROONS
COACH - Dick Rauch
8th 5-8-0

Barrett, John - C & T
Budd, John - T
Carpe, Joe - T
Carr, Harlan - B
Caywood, Les - T
Doane, Joe - B
Erickson, Walden - T
Ernst, Jack - Q
Farina, Nick - C
Ford, Adrian - B & E
Henry, "Fats" - T
Hoffman, Bill - G
Hultman, Vivian - E
Kenneally, George - E
Kirkleski, Frank - B

Latone, Tony - B
LeJeune, Walt - G
Mayer, Emil - E
Millman, Bob - B
Moore, Walt - Q
Mullen, Vern - E
Osborn, "Duke" - G
Racis, Frank - G
Rebseamen, Paul - C
Roberts, Guy - B
Scharer, Ed - Q
Underwood, John - E
Wentz, Barney - B
Youngfleisch, Frank - C

1927 PROVIDENCE STEAMROLLERS
COACH - Jim Conzelman
5th 8-5-1

Conzelman, Jim - Q
Cronin, John - B
Cronin, Bill - B
Doane, Joe - B
Donahue, John - T
Fleischman, Godfrey - G
Gulian, Mike - T
Hadden, Al - B
Kozlowsky, Joe - T
Laird, Jim - B & G
Lowe, "Bull" - E
Lynch, Ed - E
Mishel, Dave - B
O'Connell, Grattan - E

Oden, "Curly" - Q
Pierotti, Al - C
Pritchard, Bill - Q
Smith, Orland - T
Sonnenberg, "Gus" - G
Spellman, John - E & T
Stifler, Jim - E
Surabian, "Zeke" - T
Wesley, Lecit - C
Wilson, Abe - G
Wilson, George - B
Young, "Sam" - T
Young, Lester - B

1928

	W	L	T	Pct.
Providence	8	1	2	.888
Frankford	11	3	2	.786
Detroit	7	2	1	.778
Green Bay	6	4	3	.600
Chicago Bears	7	5	1	.583
New York Giants	4	7	2	.364
New York Yankees	4	8	1	.333
Pottsville	2	8	0	.200
Chicago Cardinals	1	5	0	.167
Dayton	0	7	0	.000

There was not much change in the NFL of 1928. Although money was loose and crazy in a booming stock market, none of it seemed ready for pro football.

Cleveland dropped out again. Duluth folded and Buffalo stopped operation.

Detroit came in again in 1928 and a new champion, the Providence Steamrollers, had an 8-1-2 record, nosing out the defending Yellowjackets by a half-game.

1928 CHICAGO BEARS
COACH - George Halas
5th 7-5-1

Buckler, Bill - G
Carlson, Roy - E
Drews, Ted - E
Driscoll, "Paddy" - B
Evans, Earl - T
Fleckenstein, Bill - G
Hadden, Al - B
Halas, George - E
Knop, Oscar - B
Lyman, "Link" - T
McMillen, Jim - G
Murry, Don - T

Romney, Milt - Q
Russell, Reg - E
Senn, Bill - B
Sternaman, Joe - Q
Sturtridge, Dick - Q
Trafton, George - C
Vick, "Ernie" - C
Voss, "Tillie" - E
Wallace, John - E
Walquist, Laurie - Q
White, Roy - B
Wynne, Elmer - B

1928 FRANKFORD YELLOWJACKETS
COACH - Ed Weir
2nd 11-3-2

Behman, "Bull" - T
Comstock, Rudy - G
Diehl, Walt - B & G
Elkins, "Chief" B & G & E
Filak, John - T
Hamer, Ernie - B
Hanson, Hal - G
Homan, Henry - Q
Kassel, Charles - E
Kostos, Tony - E
Leary, Tom - E

Mahoney, Roger - C
Maxwell, Joe - E & C
Mercer, Ken - Q
Oehlrich, Arnold - B
Roepke, John - B
Rogers, Charles - B
Stockton, Houston - B
Waite, Carl - E
Weir, Ed - T
Weller, Ray - T

1928 CHICAGO CARDINALS
COACH - Guy Chamberlin
9th 1-5-0

Allen, Ed - E
Bliss, Homer - G
Blumer, Herb - T
Bradley, Bill - G
Claypool, Ralph - C
Curzon, Harry - B & E
Davidson, Joe - G
Erickson, Hal - B
Fitzgibbon, Paul - B
Flora, Bill - B
Gillies, Fred - T
Grant, Hugh - Q
Illman, Ed - B
Jones, Ben - B

Killiher, - G
McDonnell, "Mickey" - B
Mahoney, "Ike" - Q
Marelli, Ray - G
Murphy, Jim - B
Neacy, Clem - E
Risvold, Ray - B
Slater, "Duke" - T
Springsteen, Bill - C & E
Stein, Bill - C
Strack, Charles - G
Widerquist, Chet - T
Yeisley, Don - E

1928 GREEN BAY PACKERS
COACH - "Curly" Lambeau
4th 6-4-3

Ashmore, Marion - T
Baker, Roy - B & E
Bowdoin, Jim - G
Cahoon, Ivan - T
Darling, Bernie - C & G
Dilweg, Lavern - E
Dunn, "Red" - Q
Earpe, "Jug" - T & C
Estes, Roy - B
Griffen, Hal - C
Hearden, Tom - B
Jones, Bruce - G
Kotal, Ed - B

Lambeau, "Curly" - B
Lewellen, Verne - B
Lidberg, Carl - B
Lollar, George - B
Marks, Larry - Q
Minick, Paul - G
Nash, Tom - E
Norton, Martin - B
O'Boyle, Harry - B
O'Donnell, Dick - E
Perry, Claude - T
Webber, Howard - E
Woodin, Howie - G

1928 DAYTON TRIANGLES
COACH - "Fay" Abbott
10th 0-7-0

Abbott, Fay - B
Achui, "Sneeze" - B
Becker, John - B
Belanich, Bill - T
Bradley, Gerry - B
Britton, Earl - B
Brown, Jack - C
Charles, Win - Q
Cook, Clair - B
DeWeese, "Ebby" - G
Faust, Dick - T
Fenner, Lee - E
Graham, Al - G
Graham, Clarence - B

Hippa, Sam - E
Hummon, John - E
Keefer, Jackson - B
Kinderdine, George - C
Mankat, Carl - T
Matsu, Art - Q
Partlow, Lou - B
Seibert, Ed - G
Sillin, Frank - B
Spencer, Jim - G
Strosnider, Aubrey - G
Zimmerman, Carl - G

1928 NEW YORK GIANTS
COACH - Earl Potteiger
6th 4-7-2

Allison, James "Neely" - E
Bloodgood, "Bert" - Q
Caldwell, Bruce - B
Eckhardt, Oscar - B
Flaherty, Ray - E
Garvey, "Hec" - G & E
Hagerty, Jack - B
Haines, "Hinkey" - B
Hartzog, Howard - T
Hubbard, "Cal" - E
Jappe, Paul - E & G
McBride, Jack - B
Milstead, Century - T

Moran, "Hap" - B
Murtagh, George - C
Nesser, Al - G & E
Owen, Steve - T
Plansky, Tony - B
Potteiger, Earl - Q & E
Reed, Maxwell - C
Rosatti, Roman - T
Schuette, Paul - G
Stahlman, Dick - T
Wesley, "Bull" - C
Wilson, "Fay" - B

1928 DETROIT WOLVERINES
COACH - Leroy Andrews
3rd 7-2-1

Andrews, Leroy - G
Bacchus, Carl - E
Bachor, Ludwig - T
Barrett, John - C & T
Caywood, Les - G
Cobb, Tom - T
Feather, "Tiny" - B
Friedman, Ben - Q
Hogan, Tom - T
Howard, Bob - G
Jackson, Henry - B

Munn, Lyle - E
Owen, Bill - T
Randels, Horace - E
Scharer, Ed - Q
Sedbrook, Len - Q
Thomas, Rex - B
Vick, "Ernie" - C
Westoupal, Joe - C
Wiberg, Oscar - B
Widerquist, Chet - T

1928 NEW YORK YANKEES
COACH - Dick Rauch
7th 4-8-1

Colahan, John - T
Cyre, Hector - T
Ernst, Jack - Q
Flaherty, Ray - E
Gallagher, Ed - T
Grube, Frank - E
Hogue, Murrel - G
Kelly, Bill - Q
Levy, Harve - G & T
McArthur, John - C
McClain, Joe - G

McGrath, Frank - E
Michalske, "Mike" - G
Molenda, "Bo" - B
Pritchard, Bill - B
Racis, Frank - G
Rauch, Dick - G
Rooney, "Cobb" - Q
Salemi, Sam - B
Smith, "Red" - B & E
Stevenson, Art - C & G
Welch, Gil - B

1928 POTTSVILLE MAROONS
COACH - Wilbur "Fats" Henry
8th 2-8-0

Budd, John - T	McNally, John "Blood" - B
Carpe, Joe - T & E	Moran, "Hap" - B
Ernst, Jack - Q	Mullen, Vern - E
Goodwin, Earl - E	Norman, Will - B
Goodwin, Myrl - B	Osborn, "Duke" - G & C
Henry, "Fats" - T & E	Racis, Frank - G
Kenneally, George - E	Rooney, Joe - E
Kiesling, Walt - G	Stein, Herb - C
Kirkleski, Frank - B	Wentz, Barney - B
Latone, Tony - B	

1928 PROVIDENCE
STEAMROLLERS
COACH - Jim Conzelman
1st 8-1-2

Conzelman, Jim - Q	Rehnquist, Milt - C & G
Cronin, John - B & E	Shockley, Arnie - G
Cronin, Bill - B	Simmons, Jim - B
Fleischman, Godfrey - G	Smith, Clyde - C
Hadden, Al - B	Smith, Leo - E
Hanny, Frank - E	Smith, Orland - T
Harvey, Norm - E & T	Sonnenberg, "Gus" - G &
Jackson, Perry - T & E	Spellman, John - E & T
Laird, Jim - G	Williams, Art - B
Longo, Tony - G	Wilson, Abe - G
Oden, "Curly" - Q	Wilson, George - B
Pierotti, Al - C	

1929

	W	L	T	Pct.
Green Bay	12	0	1	1.000
New York	12	1	1	.923
Frankford	9	4	5	.692
Chicago Cardinals	6	6	1	.500
Boston	4	4	0	.500
Stapleton	3	4	3	.429
Orange	3	4	4	.429
Providence	4	6	2	.400
Chicago Bears	4	8	2	.333
Buffalo	1	7	1	.125
Minneapolis	1	9	0	.100
Dayton	0	6	0	.000

"Red" Grange and his New York Yankees dropped out before the 1929 season and so did the Pottsville Maroons and Detroit.

Grange went back to the Chicago Bears and Pottsville started a determined, non-playing campaign to regain the title it had won in 1925 on the field and lost by league office maneuvering later. Joe Zacco, the Maroons manager, and several of his star players were still holding protest meetings 35 years later.

There was a new team at Boston, the Braves; Buffalo tried again; Minneapolis had a new franchise; the Staten Island Stapletons were born and the Orange (N.J.) Tornadoes.

All the new teams were more successful on the field than the weary Dayton Triangles, who had been in the battle since 1919. They completed a 13 games losing streak over two seasons and became part of the inactive history.

The Green Bay Packers won their first title with a 12-0-1 record.

Ernie Nevers, Chi-Card fullback, scored six touchdowns and four extra points (40) against Chicago Bears, Nov. 28, a record unbroken as this edition went to press in 1967.

Shirley Brick, Buffalo end, died in car crash.

Fourth official—field judge—added to regular crews.

1929 BOSTON BRAVES
COACH - Dick Rauch
5th 4-4-0

Carpe, Joe - T	Maloney, "Red" - E
Connor, Bill - T	Marston, Ralph - B
Druehl, Bill - B	Miller, Al - Q
Ernst, Jack - Q	Pierotti, Al - C
Howell, Wilfred - E	Racis, Frank - G
Johnson, Oscar - B	Rauch, Dick - G
Kenneally, George - E	Scholl, Roy - G
Kittredge, Paul - B	Shockley, Arnold - G
Koplow, Joe - T	Shurtleff, "Bert" - T & C
Kozlowsky, Joe - T	Stockton, Houston - B
Latone, Tony - B	Surabian, "Zeke" - T
Lawrence, Ed - B	Towle, Thurston - E
McCrillis, Ed - G	Wentworth, Shirley - B

1929 BUFFALO BISON
COACH - Al Jolley
10th 1-7-1

Big Twig - G	Mahan, Bob - B & E
(also played as Nat McCombs)	Myles, Harry - E
Bizer, Herb - B	Plank, Earl - E
Brewster, Walt - T	Rapp, "Goldie" - B
Comstock, Ed - G	Rodriguez, Jess - B
Coumier, Ulysses - B	Rosen, Stan - B
Dorfman, Art - C	Ryan, Clarence - Q
Glassman, Frank - G	Shurtcliffe, Charles - B
Hagberg, Rudy - C & B	Voss, Walter - E
Jolley, Al - T	Weimer, Howie - Q
McCombs, Nat - T	Woodruff, Jim - E

1929 CHICAGO BEARS
COACH - George Halas
9th 4-8-2

Carlson, Jules - G	Grange, "Red" - B
Cunningham, Hal - E	Halas, George - E
Driscoll, "Paddy" - B	Hearden, Tom - B
Elness, Leland - Q	Holmer, Walt - B
Evans, Earl - T	Johnsos, Luke - E
Fleckenstein, Bill - G	Kopcha, Joe - G
Grange, Garland - E	Long, Harvey - T

Maillard, Ralph - T
Murry, Don - T
Nelson, Ev - T
Pearson, "Bert" - C
Polisky, John - T
Ryan, John - T

Senn, Bill - B
Sternaman, Joe - Q
Sturtridge, Dick - B
Trafton, George - C
Walquist, Laurie - Q
White, Roy - B

McNally, John "Blood" - B
Michalske, "Mike" - G
Minick, Paul - G
Molenda, "Bo" - B
Nash, Tom - E
O'Boyle, Harry - B

O'Donnell, Dick - E
Perry, Claude - T
Smith, "Red" - B & G
Woodin, Howie - G
Young, Bill - G
Zuidmulder, Dave - B

1929 CHICAGO CARDINALS
COACH - Ernie Nevers
4th 6-6-1

Baker, Roy - B
Belden, Charles - Q
Blumer, Herb - E
Britton, Earl - B
Busse, Ellis - B
Butts, Ed - B
Dowling, Pat - E
Elkins, Fait - B
Gibbons, Austin - C & G
Hill, Don - B
Hogue, Murrell - T
Kassel, Charles - E
Kiesling, Walt - G
Lange, Jim - E

Larson, Fred - C
Larson, Lou - B
McDonnell, "Mickey" - B
Method, Russ - B
Nevers, Ernie - B
Rooney, "Cobb" - Q
Rooney, Bill - B & C
Rose, Gene - Q
Slater, "Duke" - T
Stein, Bill - G
Tinsley, Jess - T
Underwood, John - G
Williams, Jake - T

1929 DAYTON TRIANGLES
COACH - "Fay" Abbott
12th 0-6-0

Abbott, Fay - B
Becker, John - T
Belanich, Bill - T
Brewer, John - B
Brown, Jack - C
Buchanan, Steve - Q
Carlson, Roy - E
Depler, John - G
Duffy, Pat - Q
Faust, Dick - T
Fenner, Lee - E
Graham, Al - G
Haas, Bob - B

Kauffman, John - T
Kinderdine, George - C
Mankat, Carl - T
Partlow, Lou - B
Sillin, Frank - B
Singleton, John - B
Spencer, Jim - G
Tolley, Ed - G
Voss, "Tilly" - E
Wallace, John - E
Wynne, Elmer - B
Zimmerman, Carl - G

1929 FRANKFORD YELLOWJACKETS
COACH - "Bull" Behman
3rd 9-4-5

Barna, George - E
Behman, "Bull" - T
Capps, Wilbur - G
Comstock, Rudy - G
Diehl, Walt - B
Elkins, Fait - B
Filak, John - T
Halicki, Ed - B
Hanson, Hal - G
Homan, Henry - Q
James, Ted - G
Kelly, Bill - Q

Kostos, Tony - E
Kostos, Marty - E
Maglisceau, Al - T
Mahoney, Roger - C
Malcolm, Harry - T
Maxwell, Joe - E & C
Mercer, Ken - B
Oehlrich, Arnold - B
Rogers, Charles - B
Thompson, John - T
Wilson, George - B

1929 GREEN BAY PACKERS
COACH - "Curly" Lambeau
1st 12-0-1

Ashmore, Marion - T
Baker, Roy - B
Bowdoin, Jim - G
Cahoon, Ivan - T
Darling, Bernie - C
Dilweg, Lavern - E
Dunn, "Red" - Q
Earpe, "Jug" - T & C
Evans, John - B

Hill, Don - B
Hubbard, "Cal" - T
Kern, Bill - T
Kotal, Ed - B
Laabs, Kermit - B
Lambeau, "Curly" - B
Lewellen, Verne - B
Lidberg, Carl - B
McCrary, Hurdis - Q

1929 MINNEAPOLIS REDJACKETS
COACH - Herb Joesting
11th 1-9-0

Chrape, Joe - G
Erickson, Hal - B
Fahay, John - E
Frantz, Herb - T
Haycraft, Ken - E
Joesting, Herb - B
Kramer, Fred - G
Lovin, Fritz - G
Lundell, Bob - E
Maeder, Al - T

Mehelich, Tom - G
Nydall, Mal - B
Oas, Ben - C & B
O'Brien, John - B
Sandberg, Carl - B
Ursella, "Rube" - B
Widerquist, Chet - T
Willegalle, Henry - B
Wilson, Leland - E
Young, "Sam" - T

1929 NEW YORK GIANTS
COACH - Leroy Andrews
2nd 12-1-1

Ashburn, Cliff - G & E
Campbell, Glenn - E
Caywood, Les - G
Feather, "Tiny" - B
Flaherty, Ray - E
Friedman, Ben - Q
Hagerty, Jack - Q
Howard, Bob - G
Lyon, George - T
McMullen, Dan - G
Mielziner, Saul - C & G & T

Moran, "Hap" - B
Munn, Lyle - E
Murtagh, George - C & B
Owen, Steve - T
Owen, Bill - T
Plansky, Tony - B
Rice, Bill - E
Sedbrook, Len - B
Snyder, Gerry - Q
Westoupal, Joe - C
Wilson, "Fay" - B

1929 ORANGE TORNADOES
COACH - John Depler
7th 3-4-4

Barkman, Ralph - Q
Beattie, Bob - T
Benkert, "Heinie" - Q
Clarkin, Bill - T
Cuneo, Ed - G
Depler, John - C
Dwyer, Bob - B
Feaster, Bill - T
Hamas, Steve - B
Hambacher, Ernie - B & G
Johnson, Leon - E
Kelly, - T
Kerrigan, Tom - G
Kirkleski, Frank - Q
Longua, Paul - E

Lott, John - T
Lyncat - E
McArthur, John - C & G
McCormick, Felix - B
Mitchell, Fred - C
Norman, Will - B
Pease, George - Q
Salata, Andy - G
Scott, Phil - E
Smith, Donald - G
Tomaini, John - E
VanHorn, Charles - B
Waite, Carl - E & B
Yeager, Jim - T

1929 PROVIDENCE STEAMROLLERS
COACH - Jim Conzelman
8th 4-6-2

Conzelman, Jim - Q
Cronin, John - B
Cronin, Bill - B
Fleischman, Godfrey - G
Garvey, "Hec" - T
Golembeske, Tony - E
Hadden, Al - B & E
Hanny, Frank - E
Harvey, Norm - E & T
Jackson, Perry - T & E
Jennings, Lou - E & C
McBride, Jack - B

McGuirk, Warren - T
Oden, "Curly" - Q
Rehnquist, Milt - G
Shockley, Arnie - G
Smith, Clyde - C
Smith, Orland - T
Spellman, John - E & T
Stockton, Houston - B
Welch, Gil - B
Williams, Art - B
Wilson, Abe - G
Wilson, George - B

**1929 STATEN ISLAND
STAPLETONS
COACH - Doug Wycoff
6th 3-4-3**

Briante, Frank - B
Bunyan, John - G
Dunn, Bob - C & T
Godwin, Walt - G
Haines, "Hinkey" - B
Kuczo, Paul - Q
Leary, Tom - E
Lomasney, Tom - E
Lord, John - G
McGee, Harry - C
Martin, Herschel - B

Miller, John - T
Pessalano, Lou - T & E
Riordan, Charles - E & B
Satenstein, Bernie - G & E
Shapiro, John - B
Skudin, Dave - G & E
Stein, Sam - E
Strong, Ken - B
Williams, "Cy" - G
Williams, Ivan - B
Wycoff, Doug - Q

1930

	W	L	T	Pct.
Green Bay	10	3	1	.769
New York	13	4	0	.765
Chicago Bears	9	4	1	.692
Brooklyn	7	4	1	.636
Providence	6	4	1	.600
Stapleton	5	5	2	.500
Chicago Cardinals	5	6	2	.455
Portsmouth	5	6	3	.455
Frankford	4	14	1	.222
Minneapolis	1	7	1	.125
Newark	1	10	1	.091

The NFL dropped only one team in 1930 although the country was now a year deep into the historic depression.

Boston, Buffalo and Dayton were gone. The Orange Tornadoes shifted to Newark, N.J. for one year. There were new teams at Brooklyn and Portsmouth, Ohio.

The Green Bay Packers won their second title with a 10-3-1 record, which was .004 percentage points better than New York at 13-4-0.

The player limit was increased to a maximum of 20 and a minimum of 16. Thirty years later it would be double at 40 and heading higher.

New York Giants raised $115,163 for New York Unemployment fund by beating Notre Dame All-Stars in exhibition game, 21-0, in New York Polo Grounds, Dec. 14.

**1930 BROOKLYN DODGERS
COACH - Al Jolley
4th 7-4-1**

Bleeker, Mal - G
Clark, Myers - Q
Comstock, Ed - G
Crowl, Dick - C

Cuneo, Ed - G
Garvey, "Hec" - T
Getz, Fred - E
Gillson, Bob - G

Greenberg, Ben - B
Hagberg, Rudy - C & B
Hagerty, Loris - B
Haines, "Hoot" - T
Harris, Dud - T
Jolley, Al - T
Kelsch, Matt - E
Kelly, Bill - Q
Lott, John - T
McArthur, John - C & T
McBride, Jack - B
Mahan, Bob - B & E
Mattison, Ralph - G

Miller, Henry - Q
Mooney, Jim - E & Q & T
Plank, Earl - E
Rowan, Ev - E & B
Schieb, Lee - C
Schuber, Jim - B
Stotsbery, Harold - T
Stramiello, Mike - E
Thomas, Rex - Q
Thomason, John - Q
Tomaini, John - E
Weimer, Howard - Q
Worden, Stu - G
Yablok, "Indian" - Q

**1930 CHICAGO BEARS
COACH - Ralph Jones
3rd 9-4-1**

Ashburn, Cliff - G
Blackman, Lennon - B
Brumbaugh, Carl - Q
Carlson, Jules - G
Drury, Lyle - E
Fleckenstein, Bill - G
Franklin, Paul - B
Frump, "Babe" - G
Grange, Garland - E
Grange, "Red" - B
Holmer, Walt - B
Johnsos, Luke - E
Lintzenich, Joe - B
Lyman, "Link" - T

McMullan, Dan - G
Murry, Don - T
Nagurski, Bronko - B
Nesbitt, Dick - B
Pauley, Frank - T
Pearson, "Bert" - C
Savoldi, Joe - B
Schuette, Paul - G
Senn, Bill - B
Steinbach, Larry - T
Sternaman, Joe - Q
Trafton, George - C
Walquist, Laurie - Q

**1930 CHICAGO CARDINALS
COACH - Ernie Nevers
7th 5-6-2**

Baker, Roy - Q
Belden, Charles - Q
Blumer, Herb - T
Bogue, George - B
Boyd, Bill - Q
Diehl, Charles - G
Erickson, "Mickey" - C
Failing, Fred - B
Flenniken, Max - B
Gordon, Lou - T
Handler, Phil - G
Kassel, Charles - E
Kenneally, George - G

Kiesling, Walt - G
McDonnell, "Mickey" - B
Maple, Howard - Q
Nevers, Ernie - B
Pappio, Joe - B & E
Randolph, Clare - C
Rooney, "Cobb" - Q
Rose, Gene - B
Slater, "Duke" - T
Tinsley, Jess - T
Vesser, John - E
Weaver, "Buck" - G
Williams, Jake - T

**1930 FRANKFORD
YELLOWJACKETS
COACHES - "Bull" Behman &
George Gibson
9th 4-14-1**

Barrager, Nate - C
Behman, "Bull" - T
Bollinger, Ed - G
Capps, Wilbur - T
Crabtree, Clyde - Q
Diehl, Walt - B
Ernst, Jack - Q
Gibson, George - G
Goodbread, Royce - B
Halicki, Ed - B
Hanson, Hal - G
Havens, Charles - C
Homan, Henry - Q
Hutton, Leon - E & B
Joesting, Herb - B
Jones, Tom - G
Kostos, Tony - E
Long, Harvey - T
Lunz, Gerry - T
McArthur, John - T

Mahoney, Roger - C
Nydall, Mal - B
Panaccion, Vic - T
Pederson, Jim - E
Pharmer, Art - B
Rengel, Neil - B
Richards, Ray - G
Rodriguez, Kelly - B
Seborg, Henry - Q
Schultz, John - B
Smith, "Gene" - G
Steponovich, Tony - G
Tackwell, "Cookie" - E
Tanner, Bob - E
VanSickle, Clyde - T
Ward, John - T
Watkins, Gordon - T
Wilson, Leland - E
Wright, Al - B

1930 GREEN BAY PACKERS
COACH - "Curly" Lambeau
1st 10-3-1

Bloodgood, "Bert" - Q
Bowdoin, Jim - G
Darling, Bernie - C
Dilweg, Lavern - E
Dunn, "Red" - Q
Earpe, "Jug" - T & C
Engelmann, Wuert - B
Fitzgibbon, Paul - B
Franta, Herb - T
Hanny, Frank - T
Haycroft, Ken - E
Herber, Arnie - Q
Hubbard, "Cal" - T
Kern, Bill - T
Lewellen, Verne - B

Lidberg, Carl - B
McCrary, Hurdis - B
McNally, John "Blood" - B
Michalske, "Mike" - G
Molenda, "Bo" - B
Nash, Tom - E
O'Donnell, Dick - E
Pape, Oran - B
Perry, Claude - T
Radick, Ken - E & T
Sleight, "Red" - T
Wilson, "Fay" - B
Woodin, Howie - G
Zuidmulder, Dave - B
Zuver, Merle - C

1930 MINNEAPOLIS REDJACKETS
COACH - George Gibson
10th 1-7-1

Barrager, Nate - C
Capps, Wilbur - T
Corcoran, John - C
Crabtree, Clyde - Q
Erickson, Hal - B
Franta, Herb - T
Gibson, George - G
Goodbread, Royce - B
Haliki, Ed - B
Hanson, Hal - G
Haycraft, Ken - E
Hogue, Murrel - G
Joesting, Herb - B
Jones, Tom - G
Kakela, Wayne - C
Kostos, Tony - E
Lundell, Bob - E

Mahoney, Roger - C
Miller, Verne - B
Nemzek, Ted - G
Nydall, Mal - B
Oas, Ben - C & B
Pape, Oran - B
Pederson, Jim - Q
Pharmer, Art - Q
Rodriquez, Kelly - B
Seborg, Henry - Q & G
Steponovich, Tony - G & E
Tackwell, "Cookie" - E
Truesdell, Hal - T
Ward, John - T
Watkins, Gordon - T
Wilson, Leland - E
Young, "Sam" - G & E

1930 NEW YORK GIANTS
COACH - Leroy Andrews
2nd 13-4-0

Badgro, "Red" - E
Burnett, Dale - B
Cagle, Chris - B
Campbell, Glenn - E
Caywood, Les - G
Comstock, Rudy - G
Feather, "Tiny" - B
Friedman, Ben - Q
Gibson, Denver - G
Grant, Len - T
Hagerty, Jack - Q
Hilpert, Hal - B & E

Howard, Bob - G
Mielziner, Saul - C & G
Moran, "Hap" - B
Murtagh, George - C & B
Owen, Steve - T
Owen, Bill - T
Sedbrook, Len - B
Stahlman, Dick - T & E
Westoupal, Joe - C
Wiberg, Oscar - B
Wilson, "Fay" - B

1930 NEWARK TORNADOES
COACH - John Depler
11th 1-10-1

Andrulewicz, Ted - B
Barkman, Ralph - Q
Beattie, Bob - T
Benkert, "Heinie" - B
Bogue, George - B
Borelli, Nick - B
Bove, Pete - G
Brennan, Phil - E
Briante, Frank - Q
Clancy, Stu - B
Connor, Bill - T

Cordovano, Sam - G
Davidson, Joe - G & C
Depler, John - C
Dibb, John - T
Ellor, Al - G & E
Feaster, Bill - T
Finn, Bernie - Q
Frank, Paul - B
Grace, Les - E
Hauser, Ken - B & E
Horton, Les - B

Jones, Bruce - G
Kerrigan, Tom - G
Kirkleski, Frank - B
Law, John - T
Leary, Tom - E
Liston, Paul - T
Longua, Paul - B
McArthur, John - C & G
McCormick, Felix - B
McGee, Harry - B
Manfreda, Tony - B
Martin, Herschel - B
Mitchell, Fred - C

Mooney, Jim - T & B
Myles, Henry - E
Salata, Andy - G
Sebo, Sam - B
Smith, Donald - G
Smith, "Red" - B & G
Tays, Jim - B
Tomaini, John - E
Wagner, Ray - E
Waite, Carl - E & B
Webber, Howie - E
Woerner, Erwin - T

1930 PORTSMOUTH SPARTANS
COACH - "Potsy" Clark
8th 5-6-3

Ambrose, Walt - G
Bennett, Charles - Q
Braidwood, Charles - E
Brown, Dick - C
Christensen, Koester - E
DeWeese, "Ebby" - G
Douds, Forrest - T
Eby, Byron - B
Fenner, Lee - E
Fleckenstein, Bill - G & E
Glassgow, Will - B
Graham, Al - G
Grant, Aaron - C
Griffen, Hal - C
Hanny, Frank - E & T
Harris, Dud - T
Hastings, George - T
Jennings, Lou - E
Johnson, Bob - T

Joseph, Chal - E
Kahl, "Cy" - Q
Lewis, Leland - B
Lumpkin, "Father" - Q
Lyon, George - T
McLain, Mayes - Q
Mayer, Emil - E
Meyer, Ernie - G
Novotny, Ray - B
Peters, "Frosty" - B
Ringwalt, Carroll - G & C
Roberts, Fred - T
Ryan, John - T
Schleusner, Vin - T
Shearer, Ron - T
Smith, H. Gene - G
Smith, Ray - C
Weaver, Charles - G
Wesley, Lecil - C

1930 PROVIDENCE STEAMROLLERS
COACH - Jim Conzelman
5th 6-4-1

Cronin, John - B
Douds, Forrest - T
Edwards, Charles - B
Eschbach, Herb - C
Gentry, Weldon - G
Graham, Al - G
Hadden, Al - B
Holm, "Tony" - B
Jackson, Perry - T
Kozlowsky, Joe - T
Kucharski, Ted - E
Latone, Tony - B
McArthur, John - C

McGuirk, Warren - T
Meeker, Herb - Q
Oden, "Curly" - Q
Peters, "Frosty" - B
Racis, Frank - G & E
Rehnquist, Milt - G
Rose, Al - E
Smith, Ray - C
Sonnenberg, "Gus" - G
Spellman, John - E
Webber, Howie - E
Williams, Art - B
Young, Herman - E

1930 STATEN ISLAND STAPLETONS
COACH -
6th 5-5-2

Archoska, Jules - E
Brown, Fred - G
Buckley, Ed - Q
Bunyan, John - G
Demyanovich, John - G
Dryden, - B
Finn, Bernie - Q
Fitzgerald, Don - C
Follet, Beryl - Q
Halpern, Bob - T
Henry, - G
Kloppenberg, Harry - E & T
Lawrence, Ed - B & E
Lundell, Bob - E

Miller, John - T
Myers, Dave - G
Nicely, - T
Rapp, Herb - C
Satenstein, Bernie - G
Snyder, Gerry - B
Stein, Sam - E
Strong, Ken - B
Tays, Jim - B
Wexler, Bill - C
Wilcox, John - T
Williams, "Cy" - G
Wilson, "Fay" - B
Wycoff, Doug - Q

1931

	W	L	T	Pct.
Green Bay	12	2	0	.857
Portsmouth	11	3	0	.786
Chicago Bears	8	4	0	.667
Chicago Cardinals	5	4	0	.556
New York	6	6	1	.500
Providence	4	4	3	.500
Stapleton	4	6	1	.400
Cleveland	2	8	0	.200
Brooklyn	2	12	0	.143
Frankford	1	6	1	.143

The NFL was down to 10 teams in 1931 and it would stay at or below this figure for nearly 20 years. In 1950, when it absorbed the remnants of the All American Football Conference, the count would rise to 13.

Minneapolis was gone and so were the Newark Tornadoes. There was a new team in Cleveland.

The Chicago Bears, Green Bay Packers and Portsmouth Spartans were fined $1,000 each by the league for having players on their roster whose college classes had not been graduated.

Green Bay won its third straight title with 12-2-0 to beat out Portsmouth, 11-3-0, a trick no other would do until the Packers did it again in 1965-67.

1931 BROOKLYN DODGERS
COACH - John Depler
9th 2-12-0

Abbruzini, Frank - E & B - G
Apsit, Marger - B
Bultman, Art - C
Dowler, Tom - B
Fleckenstein, Bill - G & C
Fulton, Ted - G
Gillson, Bob - G
Gordon, Lou - T
Haines, "Hoot" - T
Hanson, Tom - B
Jonas, Marvin - C
Jones, Bruce - G
Kirkleski, Frank - Q
Kloppenberg, Harry - E
Lubratovich, Milo - T
McBride, Jack - B
Mielziner, Saul - C
Mizell, Warner - B
Mooney, Jim - E & T
Myers, Dennis - G
Nemecek, Jerry - E
O'Donnell, Dick - E
Perry, Claude - T
Peters, "Frosty" - Q
Radick, Ken - G & E
Scalzi, John - Q
Senn, Bill - Q
Stramiello, Mike - E
Thomas, Rex - Q
Thomason, John - Q
Tomaini, John - E
Vance, Joe - B
Wagner, Ray - E
Watkins, Gordon - T
Yablok, "Indian" - Q

1931 CHICAGO BEARS
COACH - Ralph Jones
3rd 8-4-0

Brumbaugh, Carl - Q
Buckler, Bill - G
Burdick, Lloyd - T
Carlson, Jules - G
Drury, Lyle - E
Edwards, Charles - B
Flanagan, Latham - E
Franklin, Paul - B
Grange, Garland - E
Grange, "Red" - B
Hibbs, Jesse - T
Jensvold, Leo - B
Joesting, Herb - B
Johnsos, Luke - E
Kawal, Ed - C
Lintzenich, Joe - B

Lyman, "Link" - T
Lyon, George - T
McMullan, Dan - G
Mastrogany, "Gus" - E
Molesworth, Keith - Q
Murry, Don - T
Myers, Dennis - G
Nagurski, Bronco - B
Nesbitt, Dick - B
Pearson, "Bert" - C
Schuette, Paul - G
Senn, Bill - B
Steinbach, Larry - T
Tackwell, "Cookie" - E & T
Trafton, George - C
Walquist, Laurie - Q

1931 CHICAGO CARDINALS
COACHES - Ernie Nevers &
Leroy Andrews
4th 5-4-0

Belden, Charles - Q
Boyd, Bill - B
Caywood, Les - G
Cobb, Tom - T
Creighton, Milan - E
Diehl, Charles - G
Erickson, Mike - C
Flanagan, Latham - E
Glasscow, Willis - B
Gordon, Lou - T
Handler, Phil - G
Hill, Irv - Q
Holmer, Walt - B
Kassel, Charles - E
Kiesling, Walt - G
McNally, Frank - C
Mahoney, "Ike" - Q
Malloy, Les - Q
Nevers, Ernie - B
Rogge, George - E
Rose, Gene - B
Shaw, Jesse - G
Slater, "Duke" - T
Steinbach, Larry - T
Tinsley, Jess - T
Vesser, John - E
Williams, Jake - T

1931 CLEVELAND INDIANS
COACHES - Al Cornsweet &
"Hoge" Workman
8th 2-8-0

Braidwood, Charles - E
Clark, Myers - Q
Cornsweet, Al - B
Critchfield, "Hank" - C
Cullen, Dave - G
Danziger, Fred - B
Elliott, Wally - B
Gregory, Mike - G
Herrin, Houston - C & G
Hurley, John - E
Hutson, Merle - G
Jensvold, Leo - Q
Jessen, Ernie - T
Jolley, Al - T
Joseph, Chal - E
Kriss, Howie - B
Lamme, "Buck" - E
Lee, Hilary - G
Lewis, Leland - B
Lyon, George - T
MacMillan, Stew - C & G
Mishel, Dave - B
Munday, George - T
Nesser, Al - E & G
Novotny, Ray - B
Pignatelli, Carl - B
Ridler, Don - T
Tarr, Jim - E
Vokaty, Otto - B
Waters, Dale - B
Weimer, Howie - B
Wilson, "Drip" - B
Workman, "Hoge" - Q

**1931 FRANKFORD
YELLOWJACKETS**
COACH - "Bull" Behman
10th 1-6-1

Apsit, Marger - Q
Barrager, Nate - C
Behman, "Bull" - T
Brumbaugh, Justin - B
Fleckenstein, Bill - E & T
Joesting, Herb - B
Jones, Tom - G
Kaer, Mort - Q
Koeninger, Art - T & C
Kostos, Tony - E
Leary, Tom - E
McDonnell, "Mickey" - B
Magner, Jim - Q
Mizell, Warner - B
Nydall, Mal - B
Pederson, Jim - B & E
Pharmer, Art - B
Racis, Frank - G
Ringwalt, Carroll - C & G
Seborg, Henry - Q
Tackwell, "Cookie" - E
Wilson, Leland - E

1931 GREEN BAY PACKERS
COACH - "Curly" Lambeau
1st 12-2-0

Baker, Frank - E
Barrager, Nate - C
Bowdoin, Jim - G
Bruder, "Hank" - B

Comstock, Rudy - G
Darling, Bernie - C & G
Davenport, Wayne - B
Dilweg, Lavern - E
Don Carlos, Waldo - C
Dunn, "Red" - Q
Earpe, "Jug" - T & C
Engelmann, Wuert - B
Fitzgibbon, Paul - Q
Gantenbein, Milt - E
Grove, Roger - Q
Herber, Arnie - Q
Hubbard, "Cal" - T
Jenison, Ray - T
Johnston, Art - B

Lewellen, Verne - B
McCrary, Hurdis - B
McNally, John "Blood" - B
Michalske, "Mike" - G
Molenda, "Bo" - B
Nash, Tom - E
Perry, Claude - T
Radick, Ken - E & T
Saunders, Russ - B
Sleight, Elmer - T
Stahlman, Dick - T
Wilson, "Fay" - B
Woodin, Howie - G
Zuidmulder, Dave - B

1931 NEW YORK GIANTS
COACH - Steve Owen
5th 6-6-1

Artman, "Chang" - T
Badgro, "Red" - E
Broadstone, Marion - T
Bucklin, Tom - B & G
Burnett, Dale - B
Cagle, Chris - B
Campbell, Glenn - E
Caywood, Les - G
Feather, "Tiny" - B
Flaherty, Ray - E
Flenniken, Max - B
Friedman, Ben - Q
Gibson, Denver - G
Grant, Len - T

Hein, Mel - C
Kitzmiller, John - B
Moran, "Hap" - B
Munday, George - T
Murtagh, George - C
Owen, Steve - T
Owen, Bill - T
Rehnquist, Milt - G & T
Sark, Harvey - G
Schwab, Ray - B
Sedbrook, Len - B
Smith, "Red" - B & G
Stein, Sam - E & T
Wycoff, Doug - B

1931 PORTSMOUTH SPARTANS
COACH - "Potsy" Clark
2nd 11-3-0

Alford, Gene - Q
Armstrong, Bob - T & C
Bodenger, Morris - G
Cavosie, John - B
Christensen, George - T
Clark, "Dutch" - Q
Douds, Forrest - T
Ebding, Harry - E
Emerson, "Ox" - G
Hastings, George - T
Holm, Bernie - B
Kahl, "Cy" - Q
Lee, Hilary - E
Long, Lou - E
Lumpkin, "Father" - B

McKalip, Bill - E
McLain, Mayes - B
Miller, J. Bob - C
Mitchell, Granville - E & T
Peterson, Les - E & G & C
Presnell, Glenn - Q
Randolph, Clare - C & E
Roberts, Fred - T
Schleusner, Vin - T
Schwartz, Elmer - B
Shelley, Dex - B
Stennett, Fred - B
Wager, John - C & G
Waters, Dale - E & T

1931 PROVIDENCE
STEAMROLLERS
COACH - Ed Robinson
6th 4-4-3

August, Ed - B
Dagata, Fred - B
Edwards, Charles - B
Eschbach, Herb - C
Gentry, Weldon - G
Goodbread, Royce - B
Graham, Al - G
Irvin, "Tex" - T
McArthur, John - C & E
Meeker, Herb - B
Oden, "Curly" - Q
Pape, Oran - B

Pope, Lew - B
Pyne, George - T
Rehnquist, Milt - G
Rose, Al - E
Schein, Joe - T
Shelley, Dex - B
Smith, Ray - C
Sofish, Andy - G
Spellman, John - E
Titmas, Herb - Q
Williams, Art - B
Woodruff, Lee - B

1931 STATEN ISLAND
STAPLETONS
COACH - "Hinkey" Haines
7th 4-6-1

Baker, Roy - Q
Barrabee, Bob - E
Clancy, Stu - B
Comstock, Ed - T
Constantine, Irv - B
Cunningham, Hal - E
Demyanovich, John - G
Feather, "Chief" - B
Fitzgerald, Don - C
Follet, Beryl - Q
Garvey, "Hec" - T
Haines, Harry - T
Haines, "Hinkey" - Q

Hart, Les - Q
Kanya, Al - E & T
Laird, Jim - G
McLain, Mayes - B
Marshall, Cloyd - E
Miller, John - T
Obst, Henry - G
Parkinson, Tom - B
Rapp, Herb - C
Satenstein, Bernie - G
Strong, Ken - B
Taylor, "Jake" - G & C
Yablok, "Indian" - Q

1932

	W	L	T	Pct.
Chicago Bears	7	1	6	.875
Green Bay	10	3	1	.767
Portsmouth	6	2	4	.750
Boston	4	4	2	.500
New York	4	6	2	.400
Brooklyn	3	9	0	.250
Chicago Cardinals	2	6	2	.250
Stapleton	2	7	3	.222

George Preston Marshall, who would go into the Hall of Fame as an owner with the first group so honored, took over the inactive Boston franchise this year and the Redskins were born. His first coach was Lud Wray. Marshall headed a syndicate of Vincent Bendix, Jay O'Brien and M. Dorland Doyle.

The Chicago Bears won the championship, defeating the Portsmouth Spartans, 9-0, indoors at the Chicago Stadium.

LEADERS: Individual leaders for the year: Scoring—Earl "Dutch" Clark (Portsmouth), 39; Rushing—Bob Campiglio, Staten Island) —504 yards; Passing—Arnold Herber (Green Bay); Pass Receiving—Luke Johnsos (Chi-Bears), 24; Field goals—Earl "Dutch" Clark (Portsmouth), 3.

William Seth Oliver, N.Y. Yanks-Yankees guard (1926-27) died, May 1.

1932 BOSTON BRAVES
COACH - Lud Wray
4th 4-4-2

Artman, "Chang" - T
Battles, Cliff - B
Clark, Myers - Q
Collins, Paul - E
Edwards, "Turk" - T
Erickson, Mike - C
Felber, Fred - E

Hughes, Henry - B
Hurley, George - G
Kenneally, George - E
Kresky, Joe - G
MacMurdo, Jim - T
Musick, Jim - Q
Oden, "Curly" - Q

Pape, Oran - B
Peterson, Russ - T
Pinckert, Ernie - B
Plansky, Tony - B
Rehnquist, Milt - C
Roberts, John - Q
Rust, Reg - B
Schmidt, Kermit - E

Schuette, Paul - G
Siano, Tony - C
Spellman, John - E & G
Waters, Dale - E & T
Westfall, Ed - B
Wilderson, Basil - E & T
Woodruff, Lee - Q

1932 BROOKLYN DODGERS
COACH - Ben Friedman
6th 3-9-0

Ambrose, John - C
Bowdoin, Jim - G
Bunyan, John - G
Caywood, Les - G
Cronin, Jerry - E
Eberdt, Jess - C
Ely, Harold - T
Friedman, Ben - Q
Fulton, Ted - G
Greenshields, Donn - T
Grossman, John - Q
Halperin, Bob - Q
Hickman, Herman - G
Jones, Bruce - G
Karcis, John - B
Lubratovich, Milo - T
Lyon, "Babe" - T

McBride, Jack - B
McNeil, Francis - E
Mielziner, Saul - C
Novotny, Ray - Q
Raffel, Bill - E
Riblett, Paul - E
Rowan, Everett - E
Sansen, Ollie - B
Stein, Sam - E
Stramiello, Mike - E
Thomason, "Stumpy" - B
Toscani, Francis - B
Wiberg, Oscar - Q
Williams, Art - B
Williams, "Cy" - G
Worden, Stu - G

1932 CHICAGO BEARS
COACH - Ralph Jones
1st 7-1-6

Bergerson, Gil - T
Brumbaugh, Carl - Q
Buckler, Bill - G
Burdick, Lloyd - T
Carlson, Jules - G
Corbett, George - Q
Culver, Al - T
Doehring, John - B
Ely, Hal - T
Engebretsen, "Tiny" - G
Franklin, Paul - B & E
Grange, "Red" - B
Hewitt, Bill - E
Joesting, Herb - B
Johnsos, Luke - E

Kopcha, Joe - G
Leahy, Bernie - B
Miller, "Ookie" - C
Molesworth, Keith - Q
Moore, Allen - B
Murry, Don - T
Nagurski, Bronko - B
Nesbitt, Dick - B
Pearson, "Bert" - C
Pederson, Jim - E & B
Schuette, Paul - G
Sisk, John - B
Tackwell, "Cookie" - E
Trafton, George - C

1932 CHICAGO CARDINALS
COACH - Jack Chevigny
7th 2-6-2

Braidwood, Charles - E
Creighton, Milan - E
Douds, Forrest - T
Finn, Bernie - B
Gordon, Lou - T
Graham, Al - G
Handler, Phil - G
Hill, Irv - Q
Holm, Bernie - B
Holmer, Walt - B
Kassel, Charles - E
Kiesling, Walt - G
Ledbetter, Homer - B
Lillard, Joe - B
McNally, Frank - C
Malloy, Les - Q
Martin, Glenn - B

Moore, "Bucky" - B
Moynihan, Tim - C
Peters, "Frosty" - B
Risk, Ed - Q
Rogge, George - E
Rose, Gene - B
Scardine, Carmen - B
Schwartz, Elmer - B
Shelley, Dex - B
Simas, Bill - Q
Steinbach, Larry - T
Stennet, Fred - B
Tinsley, Jess - T
Toscani, Frank - B
Wendt, Ken - G
Williams, "Jake" - T

1932 GREEN BAY PACKERS
COACH - "Curly" Lambeau
2nd 10-3-1

Aspit, Marger - B
Barrager, Nate - C
Bruder, "Hank" - Q
Bultman, Art - C
Comstock, Rudy - G
Culver, Al - T
Dilweg, Lavern - E
Earpe, "Jug" - T & C
Engelmann, Wuert - B
Fitzgibbon, Paul - B
Gantenbein, Milt - E
Grove, Roger - Q
Herber, Arnie - Q
Hinkle, Clark - B
Hubbard, "Cal" - T

Lewellen, Verne - B
McCrary, Hurdis - B
McNally, John "Blood" - B
Michalske, "Mike" - G
Molenda, "Bo" - B
Nash, Tom - E
O'Boyle, Harry - B
Perry, Claude - T
Peterson, Les - E & T
Rose, Al - E
Shelley, Dex - B
Stahlman, Dick - T
VanSickle, Clyde - T
Zeller, Joe - G

1932 NEW YORK GIANTS
COACH - Steve Owen
5th 4-6-2

Badgro, "Red" - E
Bowdoin, Jim - G
Burnett, Dale - B
Cagle, Chris - B
Campbell, Glenn - E
Caywood, Les - G
Clancy, Stu - Q
Dubofsky, "Mush" - G
Feather, "Tiny" - B
Flaherty, Ray - E
Gibson, Denver - G
Grant, Len - T
Hagerty, Jack - B
Hein, Mel - C

Irvin, Cecil - T
Jones, Tom - G
Kelly, "Shipwreck" - B
McBride, Jack - B
Molenda, "Bo" - B
Moran, "Hap" - B
Mulleneaux, Lee - B
Munday, George - T
Murtagh, George - C
Owen, Bill - T
Powell, Dick - E
Vokaty, Otto - B
Workman, "Hoge" - B

1932 PORTSMOUTH SPARTANS
COACH - "Potsy" Clark
3rd 6-2-4

Alford, Gene - Q
Armstrong, Bob - E & T
Bodenger, Morris - G
Cavosie, John - B
Christensen, George - T
Clark, "Dutch" - Q
Davis, Ray - G & C
Ebding, Harry - E
Emerson, "Ox" - G
Griffen, Hal - C
Gutowsky, "Ace" - B

Lumpkin, "Father" - B
McKalip, Bill - E
McMullen, Dan - G
Mitchell, Gran - E & T
Presnell, Glenn - Q
Randolph, Clare - C
Rascher, Ambrose - T
Ribble, Loran - G
Roberts, Fred - T
Wager, John - C & T
Wilson, "Fay" - B

1932 STATEN ISLAND
STAPLETONS
COACH - Harold Hanson
8th 2-7-3

Bunyan, John - G
Campiglio, Bob - Q
Clancy, Stu - B
Concannon, Ernie - G
Demas, George - G
Finn, Bernie - B
Frahm, Herald - B
Fry, Harry - E
Grant, Ross - G
Hanson, Tom - B

Hinton, "Grassy" - Q
Intrieri, Marne - G & C
Kamp, Jim - T
Kanya, Al - T & E
Koeninger, Art - C
Ledbetter, Chet - B
McGee, Harry - C
Marshall, Cloyd - E
Maynard. Les - B & E
Norris, John - E

Pape, Oran - B
Peterson, Les - E
Raskowski, Leo - T
Reuter, Vic - C
Roberts, John - B
Satenstein, Bernie - G
Schwab, Ray - E

Stramiello, Mike - E
Strong, Ken - B
Teeter, Al - E
Vance, Bob - B
Wilkerson, Basil - E & T
Wilson, Stu - E & B
Wycoff, Doug - Q

1933

WESTERN DIVISION

Chicago Bears	10	2	1	.833
Portsmouth	6	5	0	.554
Green Bay	5	7	1	.418
Cincinnati	3	6	1	.333
Chicago Cardinals	1	9	1	.100

EASTERN DIVISION

New York	11	3	0	.786
Brooklyn	5	4	1	.556
Boston	5	5	2	.500
Philadelphia	3	5	1	.375
Pittsburgh	3	6	2	.333

TITLE: Chicago Bears beat New York, 23-21, for the championship at Chicago, Dec. 17. It was the first such game between divisional winners, a system proposed by George P. Marshall.

LEADERS: Individual leaders for the year: Scoring—Ken Strong (New York), Glenn Presnell (Portsmouth) (tie), 64; Rushing—Cliff Battles (Boston), 737 yds.; Passing—Harry Newman (New York); Pass Receiving—John Kelly (Brooklyn), 21; Field Goals—Jack Manders (Chicago Bears), Glenn Presnell (Portsmouth), 6 (tie).

COACHES: William "Lone Star" Dietz replaced Lud Wray as head coach at Boston; John McEwan replaced Benny Friedman at Brooklyn; George Halas resumed coaching Chicago Bears, replacing Ralph Jones; Lud Wray coached the new Philadelphia team; Forrest Douds coached the new Pittsburgh Pirates; Paul Schissler replaced Jack Chevigny at Chicago Cardinals.

NOTES: Goal posts returned to goal line and forward pass made legal from anywhere behind line of scrimmage.

Frankford Yellowjackets franchise sold to Bert Bell and Ludlow Wray and moved to Philadelphia; another created for Art Rooney and A. McCool at Pittsburgh.

Gil LeFebvre, Cincinnati back, returned punt 98 yards (TD) against Brooklyn (record) Dec. 3.

TITLE GAME

Jack Manders opened the scoring for the Bears with a 16-yard field goal in the first quarter

Manders pumped another one over from 40 yards in the second period before the Giants' Harry Newman whipped a pass to Red Badgro in the end zone for the Giants' first touchdown. Strong converted and the Giants led, 7-6, at the half.

The reliable Manders banged over another field goal from 28 yards away in the third period but Newman engineered a drive for New York that ended when Max Krause plowed over from the Chicago one and Strong again converted to make it 14-9. The Bears came right back to score again on a pass from Bronko Nagurski to Bill Karr and Manders' extra point put them ahead, 16-14, as the third quarter ended.

In the last period the Giants invented a play to score again. Strong, starting from the Bears' 8-yard line, was trapped for a loss. In desperation, he lateraled to Newman, who recovered from his surprise in time to flee to the opposite side of the field. When he too was trapped he threw the ball in the general direction of the goal line—and there was Strong to catch it for a touchdown. Strong's conversion put the Giants in the lead again, 21-16. But the Bears came back to the Giants' 36. Nagurski lobbed a pass over the line to Bill Hewitt, who lateraled to Bill Karr, who went the distance. Manders' conversion made it 23-21 for the Bears' victory.

Chicago Bears	3	3	10	7—23
New York Giants	0	7	7	7—21

Touchdowns—Karr 2, Badgro, Krause, Strong.
Points after touchdown—Strong 3, Manders 3.
Field goals—Manders 2.

Attendance: 26,000.

Players' Shares: Chicago $210.34; New York $140.22.

1933 BOSTON REDSKINS
COACH - "Lone Star" Dietz
3rd 5-5-2

Aspit, Marger - Q
Battles, Cliff - B
Campiglio, Bob - Q
Cherne, Hal - T
Collins, Paul - E
Crow, Orien - C
Edwards, "Turk" - T
Frankian, "Ike" - E
Hokuf, Steve - E & B
Holmer, Walt - B
Horstmann, Roy - B
Hurley, George - G
Intrieri, Marne - G

Johnson, Larry - C
Kamp, Jim - T
LePresta, Ben - Q
MacMurdo, Jim - T
Musick, Jim - Q
Pinckert, Ernie - B
Riley, John - T
Scafide, John - T
Steponovich, Mike - G
Ward, David - G & E
Waters, Dale - E
Weller, Louis - Q
Westfall, Ed - B

1933 BROOKLYN DODGERS
COACH - John "Cap" McEwan
2nd 5-4-1

Cagle, Chris - B
Chalmers, George - G
Douglas, Ben - B
Ely, Harold - T
Fishel, Dick - Q
Friedman, Ben - Q
Greenshields, Don - T
Hickman, Herman - G
Jones, Bruce - G
Karcis, John - B
Kelly, "Shipwreck" - Q
Kloppenberg, Harry - E
Lubratovich, Milo - T
Lyons, John - E

Mielziner, Saul - C
Morrison, Maynard - C
Nash, Tom - E
Peterson, Les - E
Raskowski, Leo - T
Rayburn, Virgil - E
Rhea, Hugh - G
Riblett, Paul - E
Richards, Dick - B
Sansen, Ollie - Q
Thomason, "Stumpy" - B
Worden, Stu - G
Wright, Ralph - T

1933 CHICAGO BEARS
COACH - George Halas
1st 10-2-1
(Beat New York for title, 23-21)

Bergerson, Gil - T
Brumbaugh, Carl - Q
Buckler, Bill - G
Carlson, Jules - G
Corbett, George - Q
Doehring, John - B
Franklin, Paul - B & E
Grange, "Red" - B
Hewitt, Bill - E
Johnsos, Luke - E
Karr, Bill - E
Kopcha, Joe - G
Lyman, "Link" - T
Manders, Jack - B

Miller, "Ookie" - C
Molesworth, Keith - Q
Musso, George - G
Nagurski, Bronko - B
Nesbitt, Dick - B
Pearson, "Bert" - C
Richards, Ray - G
Ronzani, Gene - B
Sisk, John - B
Smith, Dick - C
Stahlman, Dick - T
Tackwell, "Cookie" - E
Zeller, Joe - G

1933 CHICAGO CARDINALS
COACH - Paul Schissler
5th 1-9-1

Auer, Howard - T
Bausch, Jim - B
Bennett, Charles - Q
Bergerson, Gil - T
Blumer, Herb - T
Creighton, Milan - E
Engebretsen, Paul - G

Gordon, Lou - T
Graham, Al - G
Handler, Phil - G
Hansen, Cliff - B
Hinchman, "Hub" - B
Johnson, - B
Kassel, Charles - E

Kiesling, Walt - G
Koken, Mike - Q
Lainhart, Porter - B
Lamb, Roy - Q
Ledbetter, Homer - B
Lillard, Joe - B
McNally, Frank - C
Malloy, Les - Q
Moe, Hal - B
Moynihan, Tim - C
Nesbitt, Dick - B

Nisbet, Dave - E
Ribble, Loran - G
Rogge, George - E
Simas, Bill - Q
Steinbach, Larry - T
Tinsley, Jess - T
Tipton, Howard - Q & G
Vokaty, Otto - B
Williams, "Jake" - T
Yarr, Tom - C

1933 CINCINNATI REDS
COACHES - Al Jolley & Mike Palm
4th 3-6-1

Abbruzzino, Frank - E & G
Bausch, Jim - B
Berner, Milford - C
Blondin, Tom - G
Braidwood, Charles - E
Burdick, Lloyd - T
Burleson, John - G
Caywood, Les - G
Clark, Myers - Q
Corzine, Les - B
Crakes, Joe - E
Doell, Walt - T
Draveling, Leo - T
Elkins, "Chief" - B
Grant, Ross - G
Hilpert, Hal - B & E

Lee, Hilary - G
LeFebvre, Gil - B
Mooney, Jim - E & T
Moses, Don - Q
Mullennaux, Lee - B
Munday, George - T
Palm, Mike - Q
Pope, Lew - B
Powell, Dick - E
Rogers, John - C
Schmidt, Kermit - E
Senn, Bill - B
Squyres, Seamen - B
Tackwell, "Cookie" - E
Wiberg, Oscar - B
Workman, Blake - B

1933 GREEN BAY PACKERS
COACH - "Curly" Lambeau
3rd 5-7-1

Bettencourt, Larry - C
Bruder, "Hank" - Q
Bultman, Art - C
Comstock, Rudy - G
Dilweg, Lavern - E
Engelmann, Wuert - B
Evans, Lon - G
Gantenbein, Milt - E
Goldenberg, "Buckets" - B
Greeney, Norman - G
Grove, Roger - B
Herber, Arnie - Q
Hinkle, Clark - B
Hubbard, "Cal" - T

Kurth, Joe - T
McCrary, Hurdis - B
McNally, John "Blood" - B
Michalske, "Mike" - G
Monnett, Bob - B
Mott, Norm - B
Perry, Claude - T
Quatse, Jess - T
Rose, Al - E
Sarafiny, Al - C & G
Smith, Ben - E
Van Sickle, Clyde - T
Young, Paul - G

1933 NEW YORK GIANTS
COACH - Steve Owen
1st 11-3-0
(Lost title to Chicago Bears, 23-21)

Badgro, "Red" - E
Burnett, Dale - B
Campbell, Glenn - E
Cannela, John - T & G & C
Clancy, Stu - Q
Feather, "Tiny" - B & E
Flaherty, Ray - E
Gibson, Denver - G
Grant, Len - T
Hein, Mel - C
Irvin, "Tex" - T
Jones, Tom - G
Krause, Max - B
McBride, Jack - B

Molenda, "Bo" - B
Moran, "Hap" - B
Morgan, Bill - T
Newman, Harry - Q
Owen, Steve - T
Owen, Bill - T
Reese, Henry - C
Richards, "Kink" - B
Rovinsky, Tony - B
Russell, "Fay" - B
Satenstein, Bernie - G
Strong, Ken - B
Zapustas, Joe - E
Zyntell, Jim - G

1933 PHILADELPHIA EAGLES
COACH - Lud Wray
4th 3-5-1

Auer, Howie - T	Maynard, Les - B & E
Carpe, Joe - T	O'Boyle, Harry - B
Carter, Joe - T	Obst, Henry - G & E
Cuba, Paul - T	Prisco, Nick - B
Davis, Syl - B	Roberts, John - B
Fencl, Dick - E	Rowan, Ev - E
Gonya, Bob - T	Russell, "Reb" - B
Hanson, Tom - B	Smith, Ray - C
Kenneally, George - E	Smith, Dick - C
Kirkman, Roger - Q	Steinbach, Larry - T & G
Koeninger, Art - C	Thornton, Dick - B
Kresky, Joe - G	Turnbow, Guy - T
Lackman, Dick - B	Whire, John - B
Lainhart, Porter - B	Willson, Osborn - G
Leathers, Milt - G	Woodruff, Lee - B
Lechthaler, Roy - G	Zyntell, Jim - G
Lipski, John - C	

1933 PITTSBURGH PIRATES
COACH - Forrest Douds
5th 3-6-2

Artman, Corwan - T	Lantz, Monty - C
Brovelli, Angie - Q	Letsinger, Jim - G
Burleson, John - G & T	Moore, "Bucky" - B
Clark, Jim - B	Moss, Paul - E
Cooper, Sam - T	Oehler, John - C
Critchfield, Larry - G	Quatse, Jess - T
Dailey, Ted - E	Raskowsky, Leo - T
DeCarbo, Nick - G	Rhodes, Don - T
Douds, "Jap" - T	Robinson, Gil - E
Engebretsen, Paul - G & T	Schwartz, Elmer - B
Holm, Bernie - B	Shaffer, George - Q
Holmer, Walt - B	Sortet, Bill - E
Hood, Frank - B	Tanguay, Bill - B
Janacek, Clarence - G	Tesser, Ray - E
Kelsch, Chris - B	Vaughn, John - Q
Kemp, Ray - T	Westfall, Ed - B
Kottler, Marty - B	Whalen, Tom - B

1933 PORTSMOUTH SPARTANS
COACH - "Potsy" Clark
2nd 6-5-0

Alford, Gene - Q	Emerson, "Ox" - G
Bodenger, Morris - G	Gutowsky, "Ace" - B
Boswell, Ben - T	Hunter, Romney - E
Bowdoin, Jim - G	Lumpkin, "Father" - B
Burleson, John - G	Mitchell, Gran - E & T
Caddell, Ernie - B	Presnell, Glenn - Q
Cavosie, John - B & E	Randolph, Clare - C
Christensen, George - T	Schaake, Elmer - B
Davis, Ray - G	Schneller, John - E
Davis, Syl - B & G	Thayer, Harry - T
Ebding, Harry - E	Wager, John - C
Elser, Earl - T	Wilson, "Fay" - B

1934

EASTERN DIVISION

New York	8	5	0	.615
Boston	6	6	0	.500
Brooklyn	4	7	0	.363
Philadelphia	4	7	0	.363
Pittsburgh	2	10	0	.166

WESTERN DIVISION

Chicago Bears	13	0	0	1.000
Detroit	10	3	0	.769
Green Bay	7	6	0	.538
Chicago Cardinals	5	6	0	.454
St. Louis	1	2	0	.333
Cincinnati	0	8	0	.000

* Franchise transferred to St. Louis, Nov. 5, 1934

New York beat the Chicago Bears, 30-13, for the championship at New York, Dec. 9.

LEADERS: Individual leaders for the season: Scoring—Jack Manders, Chicago Bears, 79; Rushing—Beattie Feathers, Chicago Bears, 1,004 yds., new record, first 1,000-yard season; Passing—Arnold Herber, Green Bay; Pass Receiving—Joe Carter, Philadelphia, 16; Field Goals—Jack Manders, Chicago Bears, 10.

COACHES: Luby DiMelio replaced Forrest Douds as head coach at Pittsburgh.

NOTES: Cincinnati franchise transferred to St. Louis after eight losing games—finished 1-2 for season and dropped out.

Portsmouth franchise bought by G. A. Richards and moved to Detroit.

Chicago Bear held to 0-0 by Collegians in first annual All-Star game sponsored by Tribune Charities at Chicago.

Glenn Presnell, Detroit back, kicked 54-yard field goal against Green Bay (record) Oct. 7.

Beattie Feathers, Chi-Bear back, rushed 1,004 yards for season (record).

TITLE GAME

With the temperature at nine degrees and the Polo Grounds covered with sheet ice, this contest became known as the "Sneaker" game when Steve Owen, New York coach, provided his squad with basketball shoes to open the second half and thus brought about four touchdowns and the rout of the Bears who had beaten the Giants twice during the regular season.

When the game began, the Bears were carrying a thirteen-consecutive-game winning streak and they had completed thirty-three games in a row without defeat. But Beattie Feathers, the sensational halfback, and Joe Kopcha, their brilliant lineman, were injured too severely to play (as was Harry Newman, Giant quarterback). Still the Bears were heavily favored to win.

Ken Strong got the Giants off on top in the first quarter with a 38-yard field goal which was the only score in that period.

The Bears smashed back for their first touchdown on a one-yard plunge by Nagurski. Manders' extra point and a field goal by Manders gave the Bears a 10–3 lead as the half ended.

Manders booted another from the 24-yard line in the third quarter and then the roof fell in for the Bears.

As the last period began, the New York team was getting used to their new footwear. Ed Danowski started the rout with a 28-yard pass to Ike Frankian. Moments later, Ken Strong galloped 42 yards for another score. Then, so rapidly that the Bears were completely lost, Danowski and Strong ran for touchdowns to turn the game into a track meet. Strong cashed three of four conversion attempts and the score ended at 30–13.

New York Giants	3	0	0	27–30
Chicago Bears	0	10	3	0–13

Touchdowns—Nagurski, Frankian, Strong 2, Danowski.
Points after touchdown—Manders, Strong 3.
Field goals—Manders 2, Strong.

Attendance: 35,059.

Players Shares: New York $621.00; Chicago $414.02.

1934 BOSTON REDSKINS
COACH - "Lone Star" Dietz
2nd 6-6-0

Arenz, Arnold - Q
Battles, Cliff - B
Bausch, Frank - C
Boswell, Ben - T
Collins, Paul - E
Concannon, Ernie - G
Crow, Orien - C
Edwards, "Turk" - T
Ellstrom, Marv - B
Hokuf, Steve - Q & E
Intrieri, Marne - G
Johnson, Larry - C
McNamara, Bob - E
McPhail, Harold - B
Malone, Charley - E
O'Brien, Gail - T
Olsson, Les - G
Pinckert, Ernie - B
Rentner, "Pug" - B
Sarboe, Phil - Q
Sinko, Steve - T
Tosi, Flavio - E
Walton, Frank - G
Wright, Ted - Q
Wycoff, Doug - Q

1934 BROOKLYN DODGERS
COACH - John "Cap" McEwan
3rd 4-7-0

Ariail, "Gump" - E
Becker, Wayland - E
Bowdoin, Jim - G
Brodnicki, Chuck - T
Cagle, Chris - Q
Cannella, John - G
Cronkhite, Henry - E
Demas, George - G
Ely, Harold - T
Engebretsen, Paul - G
Friedman, Ben - Q
Grossman, John - B

Hickman, Herman - G
Hugret, Joe - E
Jones, Bruce - G
Karcis, John - B
Kelly, "Shipwreck" - Q
Kercheval, Ralph - B
Kloppenberg, Harry - E
Lubratovich, Milo - T
Mielziner, Saul - C
Montgomery, Cliff - Q
Morrison, Maynard - C
Nash, Tom - E
Nesbitt, Dick - B
Peterson, Phil - E
Riblett, Paul - E
Sansen, Ollie - B
Siano, Tony - C
Stramiello, Mike - E
Thomason, "Stumpy" - B
Worden, Stu - G

1934 CHICAGO BEARS
COACH - George Halas
1st 13-0-0
(Lost title to New York, 30-13)

Aspatore, Ed - T
Becker, Wayland - E
Brumbaugh, Carl - Q
Buss, Art - T
Carlson, Jules - G
Corbett, George - Q
Doehring, John - B
Feathers, Beattie - B
Grange, "Red" - B
Hewitt, Bill - E
Johnsos, Luke - E
Karr, Bill - E
Kawal, Ed - C & T
Kiesling, Walt - G
Kopcha, Joe - G
Lyman, "Link" - T
Manders, Jack - B
Masterson, Bernie - Q
Miller, "Ookie" - C
Molesworth, Keith - Q
Musso, George - G
Nagurski, Bronko - B
Pearson, "Bert" - C
Ronzani, Gene - B
Rosequist, Ted - T
Sisk, John - B
Zeller, Joe - G
Zizak, Vince - T

1934 CHICAGO CARDINALS
COACH - Paul Schissler
4th 4-6-0

Cook, Dave - B
Creighton, Milan - E
Cuppoletti, Bree - G
Duggins, George - E
Field, Harry - T
Gordon, Lou - T
Greene, Frank - Q
Griffith, Homer - B
Handler, Phil - G
Hinchman, "Hub" - B
Horstmann, Roy - B
Hughes, Bernie - C
Isaacson, Ted - T
Krejci, Joe - E
McNally, Frank - C
Mehringer, Pete - T
Mikulak, Mike - B
Murphy, Tom - Q
Neuman, Bob - E
Pardonner, Paul - Q
Russell, Doug - B
Sarboe, Phil - Q
Shenefelt, Paul - T
Smith, Bill - E
Tipton, Howard - B & G
Volok, Bill - G

1934 CINCINNATI REDS
COACHES - Mike Palm & Myers Clark
5th 0-8-0
(To St. Louis after 8 games)

Alford, Gene - Q
Ariail, "Gump" - E
Aspatore, Ed - T
Bushby, Tom - B
Caywood, Les - G
Clark, Myers - Q
Corzine, Les - B
Elser, Earl - T
Feather, "Tiny" - B
Grant, Ross - G
Hanson, Homer - G
Howell, Foster - T
Lay, Russ - G
Lee, Hilary - G
LeFebvre, Gil - B
Lewis, Bill - B
Maples, Talmadge - C
Mooney, Jim - E & T
Moore, Cliff - B
Mott, Norm - B
Mulleneaux, Lee - C & B
Munday, George - T
Parriott, Bill - B
Pope, Lew - Q
Rogers, John - C
Sark, Harvey - G
Saumer, Syl - B
Sohn, "Ben" - B
Steverson, Norris - Q
Tackwell, "Cookie" - E
Vokaty, Otto - B
Wilging, Coleman - E & T
Wilkerson, Basil - E & T
Zunker, Charles - T

1934 DETROIT LIONS
COACH - "Potsy" Clark
2nd 10-3-0

Bernard, Charles - C	Johnson, John - T
Bodenger, Morris - G	Knox, Sam - G
Caddel, Ernie - B	Lay, Russ - G
Christensen, Frank - B	Lumpkin, "Father" - B
Christensen, George - T	McKalip, Bill - E
Clark, "Dutch" - Q	McWilliams, Bill - B
Ebding, Harry - E	Mitchell, Gran - E
Emerick, Bob - T	Presnell, Glen - Q
Emerson, "Ox" - G	Randolph, Clare - C
Gutowsky, "Ace" - B	Richards, Ray - G
Hinchman, "Bert" - B	Rowe, Bob - B
Hupke, Tom - G	Schneller, John - E

1934 GREEN BAY PACKERS
COACH - "Curly" Lambeau
3rd 7-6-0

Barrager, Nate - C	Jones, Bob - G
Bruder, "Hank" - Q	Jorgenson, Carl - T
Bultman, Art - C	Kurth, Joe - T
Butler, Frank - C	Laws, Joe - B
Casper, Charles - B	Michalske, "Mike" - G
Dilweg, Laverne - E	Monnett, Bob - B
Engebretsen, Paul - G	Norgard, Al - E
Evans, Lon - G	Perry, Claude - T
Gantenbein, Milt - E	Peterson, Les - E
Goldenberg, "Buckets" - B	Rose, Al - E
Grove, Roger - Q	Schwammel, Adolph - T
Herber, Arnie - Q	Seibold, Champ - G
Hinkle, Clark - B	Witte, Earl - B
Johnston, Chet - B	Wunsch, Harry - G

1934 NEW YORK GIANTS
COACH - Steve Owen
1st 8-5-0
(Won title from Chicago Bears, 30-13)

Badgro, "Red" - E	Jones, Tom - G
Bellinger, Bob - G	Krause, Max - B
Boyle, Bill - T	McBride, Jack - B
Burnett, Dale - B	Molenda, "Bo" - B
Cannella, John - T & G	Morgan, Bill - T
Clancy, Stu - Q	Newman, Harry - Q
Danowski, Ed - Q	Norby, John - B
DellIsola, John - G & C	Owen, Bill - T
Flaherty, Ray - E	Reese, Henry - C
Frankian, "Ike" - E	Richards, "Kink" - B
Gibson, Denver - G	Scheuer, Abe - T
Grant, Len - T	Smith, Willis - B
Hein, Mel - C	Stafford, Harrison - B
Irvin, "Tex" - T	Strong, Ken - B

1934 PHILADELPHIA EAGLES
COACH - Lud Wray
4th 4-7-0

Barnhart, Dan - B	Kenneally, George - E
Brodnicki, Charles - C & T	Kirkman, Roger - Q
Carter, Joe - E	Knapper, Joe - B
Clark, Myers - Q	Kresky, Joe - G
Cuba, Paul - T	Lackman, Dick - B
Dempsey, John - T	Leonard, Jim - Q
Ellstrom, Marv - B	Lipski, John - C
Gonya, Bob - T & E	MacMurdo, Jim - T
Hajek, Charles - C	Matesic, Ed - B
Hanson, Tom - B	Milam, Barnes - G
Johnson, Lorne - B	Norby, John - B
Kavel, George - B	Pilconis, Joe - E

Poth, Phil - G	Weiner, Al - B
Roberts, John - B	Willson, Osborn - G
Storm, Ed - B	Zizak, Vince - T & G
Turnbow, Guy - T	Zyntell, Jim - G

1934 PITTSBURGH PIRATES
COACH - Luby DiMelio
5th 2-10-0

Brovelli, Angie - Q	Oehler, John - C
Ciccone, Ben - C	Potts, Bill - B
Clark, Jim - B	Quatse, Jess - T
Dempsey, John - T	Rado, Alex - B
Douds, Forrest - T	Rajkovich, Pete - B
Greeney, Norm - G	Ribble, Loran - G
Heller, Warren - B	Roberts, John - B
Kavel, George - B	Saumer, Syl - Q
Kelsch, Chris - B	Skladany, Joe - E
Kvaternik, Zvonimir - G	Smith, Ben - E
Levey, Jim - B	Snyder, Bill - B
McNally, John "Blood" - B	Sortet, Bill - G
Marchi, Basilio - G	Tesser, Ray - E
Marker, Harry - B	Vaughn, John - Q
Mott, "Buster" - B	Weinberg, Henry - T
Niccolai, Armand - T	Zaninelli, Silvio - Q

1934 ST. LOUIS GUNNERS
COACH - Mike Palm
5th 1-2-0
(8 previous games as Cincinnati)

Alford, Gene - Q	McLeod, Russ - C
Andrews, "Jabby" - B	Montgomery, Bill - T
Casper, Charles - B	Moss, Paul - E
Corzine, Les - B	Mulleneaux, Lee - C & B
Diehl, Charles - G	Munday, George - T
Elser, Earl - T	Norby, John - B
Gladden, Jim - E	Rapp, "Manny" - B
Johnston, Chet - B	Reynolds, Homer - G
LaPresta, Ben - Q	Rogge, George - E
Lay, Russ - G	Sandberg, Sig - T
Lyon, George - T	Senn, Bill - B
McGirl, Len - G	Weldin, Hal - C
McLaughlin, Charles - B	Workman, Blake - Q

1935

WESTERN DIVISION

Detroit	7	3	2	.700
Green Bay	8	4	0	.667
Chicago Cardinals	6	4	2	.600
Chicago Bears	6	4	2	.600

EASTERN DIVISION

New York	9	3	0	.750
Brooklyn	5	6	1	.454
Pittsburgh	4	8	0	.333
Boston•	2	8	1	.200
Philadelphia•	2	9	0	.181

* One game cancelled.

TITLE: Detroit beat New York, 26-7, for the championship at Detroit University Stadium, Dec. 15.

LEADERS: Individual leaders for the season: Scoring—Earl "Dutch" Clark (Detroit), 55; Rushing—Douglas Russell (Chi-Cards), 499 yds.; Passing—Ed Danowski (New York); Pass Receiving—Charles "Tod" Goodwin (New York), 26; Field Goals—Armand Niccolai (Pittsburgh), Bill Smith (Chi-Cards), 6 (tie).

COACHES: Eddie Casey replaced William "Lone Star" Dietz as head coach of the Boston Redskins; Paul Schissler replaced John McEwan at Brooklyn; Joe Bach replaced Luby DiMelio at Pittsburgh; Milan Creighton replaced Paul Schissler at Chicago Cardinals.

NOTES: Roster limit increased 4 to 24.

Draft of college players proposed and adopted for 1936, suggested by Bert Bell.

Ralph Kercheval, Brooklyn, punted 86 yards against Chi-Bears, Oct. 20.

Charles Kemmerer, Philadelphia tackle, retired from football to start long career as heavyweight wrestling "champion" under name of "Babe" Sharkey.

"Red" Grange retired, and, in a letter to Arch Ward, sports editor of the Chicago Tribune, made these comments about pro football: "I say that a football player, after three years in college, doesn't know anything about football. Pro football is the difference between the New York Giants baseball team and an amateur nine. College players not only do not know how to play football, but they don't take as much interest in the game as the pros. In college you have studies to make up, lectures to attend, scholastic requirements to satisfy. In pro ball you are free from all this. You have nothing to do but eat, drink and sleep football and that is just what the boys do.

"Pro football is smart. It is so smart you can rarely work the same play twice with the same results. Competition is keen. There are no set-ups in pro football. The big league player knows *football*, not just a theory or system."

TITLE GAME

The power of the Detroit backfield was evident from the first kick-off which the Lions took right back to a touchdown with Leroy "Ace" Gutowsky plowing over from the 2-yard line. Glenn Presnell kicked the extra point.

The Giants were unable to move successfully and Detroit scored again when Earl "Dutch" Clark broke loose for a 40-yard touchdown romp. Clark tried the conversion and missed.

In the second quarter, which was scoreless, the Giants smashed as far as the Detroit 4-yard line but were unable to go any further. The Lions led, 13–0, at the end of the half.

The Giants racked up their only score in the third quarter when Ed Danowski passed from the Detroit 42. Strong caught the ball in full stride on the 30 and went all the way, kicking the conversion to make it 13–7. But that was the end of the Giants.

In the fourth quarter, the Lions took full charge of the game, capitalizing on the New York desperation passes. George Christensen blocked a punt by Danowski and recovered the ball on the New York 26. The Lions drove to the 4 where Ernie Caddel took the ball over on his favorite reverse play. The extra point was missed. Later in the period, Raymond "Buddy" Parker intercepted Danowski's pass attempt on the Giant 32 and fled to the 9. Buddy then smashed the rest of the way for the final score and Clark picked up the extra point to make it 26–7.

Detroit Lions	13	0	0	13–	2(
New York Giants	0	7	0	0–	7

Touchdowns—Strong, Gutowsky, Clark, Caddel, Parker.

Points after touchdown—Strong, Presnell, Clark.

Attendance: 15,000.

Players Shares: Detroit $300.00; New York $200.00.

1935 BOSTON REDSKINS
COACH - Eddie Casey
4th 2-8-1

Baltzell, Dick - B	Collins, Paul - E
Barber, Jim - T	Concannon, Ernie - G
Battles, Cliff - B	Edwards, "Turk" - T
Bausch, Frank - C	Hokuf, Steve - Q & E

Johnson, Larry - C
Kahn, Ed - G
McPhail, Harold - B
Malone, Charley - E
Moran, Jim - G
Musick, Jim - Q
Nott, Doug - Q
O'Brien, Gail - T
Olsson, Les - G

Pinckert, Ernie - B
Rentner, "Pug" - Q
Sebastian, Mike - B
Shepherd, Bill - Q
Siemering, Larry - C
Sinko, Steve - T
Tosi, Flavio - E
Weisenbaugh, Henry - B
Wright, "Ted" - B

1935 BROOKLYN DODGERS
COACH - Paul Schissler
2nd 5-6-1

Becker, Wayland - E
Bergerson, Gil - T
Croft, "Windy" - G
Eagle, Alex - T
Franklin, Norm - B
Fuqua, Ray - E
Grossman, John - Q
Hayduk, Henry - G
Heldt, Carl - T
Hornbeak, Jay - Q
Hubbard, Wes - E
Karcis, John - B
Kercheval, Ralph - B
Kirkland, B'ho - G

Kostka, Stan - B
Lee, Bill - T
Lubratovich, Milo - T
Lumpkin, "Father" - Q
McDonald, Walt - C
Norby, John - B
Oehler, John - C
Riblett, Paul - E
Robinson, John - T
Sansen, Ollie - Q
Stojack, Frank - G
Thomason, "Stumpy" - B
White, Wilbur - Q
Wright, "Ted" - Q

1935 CHICAGO BEARS
COACH - George Halas
4th 6-4-2

Buss, Art - T
Carlson, Jules - G
Corbett, George - Q
Crawford, Fred - E & T
Dunlap, Bob - Q
Feathers, Beattie - B
Grosvenor, George - B
Hewitt, Bill - E
Johnsos, Luke - E
Karr, Bill - E
Kawal, Ed - C
Kopcha, Joe - G
McPherson, "Amy" - G
Manders, Jack - B
Masterson, Bernie - Q

Miller, "Ookie" - C
Miller, Milford - G
Molesworth, Keith - Q
Musso, George - G
Nagurski, Bronko - B
Pollock, Bill - B
Richards, Ray - G
Ronzani, Gene - B
Rosequist, Ted - E & T
Sisk, John - B
Sullivan, Frank - C
Trost, Milt - T
Wetzel, Damon - B
Zeller, Joe - G

1935 CHICAGO CARDINALS
COACH - Milan Creighton
3rd 6-4-2

Berry, Gil - B
Blazine, Tony - T
Cook, Dave - B
Creighton, Milan - E
Cuppoletti, Bree - G
Davis, Ray - E
Deskin, Versil - E
Dowell, "Mule" - B
Field, Harry - T
Gordon, Lou - T
Handler, Phil - G
Hanson, Homer - G
Hughes, Bernie - C
Isaacson, Ted - T
Mehringer, Pete - T

Mikulak, Mike - B
Mooney, Jim - E & T
Neuman, Bob - E
Nichelini, Al - B
Pangle, Hal - Q
Pardonner, Paul - Q
Pearson, "Bert" - C
Peterson, Ken - B
Russell, Doug - B
Sarboe, Phil - Q
Shenefelt, Paul - T
Smith, Bill - E
Tipton, Howard - B & G
Volok, Bill - G
Wilson, Bill - E

1935 DETROIT LIONS
COACH - "Potsy" - Clark
1st 7-3-2

(Won title from New York,
26-7)

Banas, Steve - Q
Caddel, Ernie - B

Christensen, Frank - B
Christensen, George - T

Clark, "Dutch" - Q
Ebding, Harry - E
Emerson, "Ox" - G
Gagnon, Roy - G
Gutowsky, "Ace" - B
Hupke, Tom - G
Johnson, John - T
Kaska, Tony - B
Klewicki, Ed - E
Knox, Sam - G
LeFebvre, Gil - B
Mitchell, Gran - E
Monahan, Regis - G

Morse, Ray - E
Nott, Doug - Q
O'Neill, William - B
Parker, "Buddy" - B
Presnell, Glen - Q
Randolph, Clare - C
Richins, Aldo - B
Schneller, John - E
Sheperd, Bill - Q
Stacy, Jim - T
Steen, Jim - T
Vaughan, Charles - Q
Ward, Elmer - C

1935 GREEN BAY PACKERS
COACH - "Curly" Lambeau
2nd 8-4-0

Barrager, Nate - C
Bruder, "Hank" - Q
Butler, Frank - C
Engebretsen, Paul - G
Evans, Lon - G
Gantenbein, Milt - E
Goldenberg, "Buckets" - Q
Grove, Roger - Q
Herber, Arnie - Q
Hinkle, Clark - B
Hubbard, "Cal" - T & E
Hutson, Don - E
Johnston, Chet - B
Kiesling, Walt - G
Laws, Joe - B

McNally, John "Blood" - B
Maddox, George - T
Michalske, "Mike" - G
Monnett, Bob - B
O'Connor, Bob - G
Perry, Claude - T
Rose, Al - E
Sauer, George - B
Schneidman, Herman - Q
Schwammell, Adolph - T
Seibold, Champ - T
Smith, Ernie - T
Svendsen, George - C
Tenner, Bob - E
Vairo, Dom - E

1935 NEW YORK GIANTS
COACH - Steve Owen
1st 9-3-0
(Lost title to Detroit, 26-7)

Badgro, "Red" - E
Bellinger, Bob - G
Borden, Les - E
Burnett, Dale - B
Clancy, Stu - B
Corzine, Les - B
Danowski, Ed - Q
DellIsola, John - G & C
Flaherty, Ray - E
Frankian, "Ike" - E
Goodwin, "Ted" - E
Grant, Len - T
Hein, Mel - C
Irvin, Cecil - T
Jones, Tom - G

Kaplan, Bernie - G
Krause, Max - B
Mackorell, John - B
Mitchell, Gran - E
Molenda, "Bo" - B
Morgan, Bill - T
Newman, Harry - Q
Owen, Bill - T
Quatse, Jess - T
Richards, "Kink" - B
Sarausky, Tony - B
Shaffer, Leland - Q
Singer, Walt - E
Strong, Ken - B

1935 PHILADELPHIA EAGLES
COACH - Lud Wray
5th 2-9-0

Bailey, Howie - T
Banas, Steve - Q
Benson, Harry - G
Brian, Bill - T
Bushby, Tom - B
Carter, Joe - E
Cuba, Paul - T
Frahm, Herald - B
Graham, Tom - G
Hanson, Homer - G
Hanson, Tom - B
Jorgenson, Carl - T
Kenneally, George - E

Kirkman, Roger - Q
Kresky, Joe - G
Kupcinet, Irv - Q
Lackman, Dick - B
Leonard, Jim - Q
MacMurdo, Jim - T
McPherson, "Amy" - C
Manske, "Eggs" - E
Matesic, Ed - B
Padlow, Max - E
Pitts, "Alabama" - B
Raskowski, Leo - T
Reese, Henry - C

Robison, Burle - E
Rowe, Bob - B
Sebastian, Mike - B
Shaub, Harry - G
Storm, Ed - B
Thomason, "Stumpy" - Q

Weinstock, "Izzy" - B
Williams, Clyde - T
Willson, Osborne - G
Zizak, Vince - T & G
Zyntell, Jim - G

1935 PITTSBURGH PIRATES
COACH - Joe Bach
3rd 4-8-0

Arndt, Al - G
Augusterfer, Gene - Q
Bray, Maury - T
Campbell, Glenn - E
Casper, Charles - B
Ciccone, Ben - C
Doehring, John - B
Doloway, Cliff - E
Ellstrom, Marv - B
Gildea, John - B
Greeney, Norm - G
Hayduk, Henry - G
Heller, Warren - B
Hoel, Bob - G
Kresky, Joe - G
Levey, Jim - B
Malkovich, Joe - C
Mulleneaux, Lee - C
Niccolai, Armand - T

Nixon, Mike - B
Olejniczak, Stan - T & G
Pittman, Mel - C
Rado, George - G
Ribble, Loran - G
Sandberg, Sig - T
Sebastian, Mike - B
Skoronski, Ed - C & G & E
Smith, Ben - E
Snyder, Bill - G
Sortet, Bill - E
Strutt, Art - B
Turley, John - Q
Vidoni, Vic - E & G
Weisenbaugh, Henry - B
Wetzel, Damon - B
Wiehl, Joe - T
Zaninelli, Silvio - Q

LEADERS: Individual leaders for the season: Scoring—Earl "Dutch" Clark (Detroit), 73; Rushing—Alphonse "Tuffy" Leemans (New York), 830 yds.; Passing—Arnold Herber (Green Bay); Pass Receiving—Don Hutson (Green Bay), 34; Field Goals—Jack Manders (Chi-Bears), Armand Niccolai (Pittsburgh), 7 (tie).

COACHES: Ray Flaherty replaced Eddie Casey as head coach of the Boston Redskins; Bert Bell replaced Lud Wray at Philadelphia.

NOTES: Jay Berwanger, University of Chicago halfback was the first player selected (by Philadelphia) in the first NFL player draft. He did not sign. Qback Riley Smith, second, picked by Boston, did sign and played five years.

Roster limit increased one to 25.

Boston Shamrocks won the American Football League title with an 8-3-0 record.

1936

TITLE GAME

WESTERN DIVISION

Green Bay	10	1	1	.909
Chicago Bears	9	3	0	.750
Detroit	8	4	0	.667
Chicago Cardinals	3	8	1	.272

EASTERN DIVISION

Boston	7	5	0	.714
Pittsburgh	6	6	0	.500
New York	5	6	1	.454
Brooklyn	3	8	1	.272
Philadelphia	1	11	0	.084

AMERICAN FOOTBALL LEAGUE
(1936)

	W	L	T	Pct.
Boston	8	3	0	.727
Cleveland	5	2	2	.714
New York	5	3	2	.625
Pittsburgh	3	2	1	.600
Rochester	1	6	0	.143
Brooklyn	0	6	1	.000

TITLE: Green Bay beat the Boston Redskins, 21-6, for the championship at the Polo Grounds in New York. George Marshall, owner of the Redskins, refused to play the title game in Boston because of poor fan support during the season. He moved the team to Washington to start 1937.

Perfect weather and field conditions were in force at the Polo Grounds and the devastating Packer attack was running at full throttle.

Immediately after the kick-off, Lou Gordon recovered Riley Smith's fumble at midfield. Arnold Herber struck through the air at once, heaving a 43-yard touchdown to Don Hutson. Ernie Smith converted to give the Packers a 7-point lead before the game was three minutes old. Right after the next kick-off, the Redskins lost their great halfback, Cliff Battles, who was injured so badly he played no more that day.

The 'Skins got back in the game on the first play of the second period when "Pug" Rentner crashed over from the one-yard line to make it 7-6. Riley Smith missed the conversion.

Herber fired another long one, 52 yards to Johnny "Blood" McNally, to move the Packers to the Boston 8-yard line, and then pitched to Milt Gantenbein in the end zone in the third quarter. Smith converted. The Redskins got a setback in this period when Frank Bausch, their dynamic center, was tossed out of the game for fighting with Frank Butler.

The Packers scored once more in the last period when Monnett went over from the 2 after a Boston punt was blocked. Engebretsen converted to make it 21–6, the final score.

Green Bay Packers	7	0	7	7—21
Boston Redskins	0	6	0	0— 6

Touchdowns—Hutson, Rentner, Gantenbein, Monnett.
Points after touchdown—Ernest Smith 2, Engebretsen.

Attendance: 29,545.

Players' Shares: Green Bay $540.00; Boston $400.00.

1936 BOSTON REDSKINS
COACH - Ray Flaherty
1st 7-5-0
(Lost title to Green Bay, 21-6)

Barber, Jim - T
Battles, Cliff - B
Bausch, Frank - C
Britt, Ed - B
Busick, Sam - E
Carroll, Vic - T
Concannon, Ernie - G
Edwards, "Turk" - T
Irwin, Don - B
Justice, "Chug" - B
Kahn, Ed - G
Karcher, Jim - G
McChesney, Bob - E
Malone, Charley - E
Millner, Wayne - E
Moran, Jim - G
Musick, Jim - Q
O'Brien, Gail - T
Olsson, Les - G
Pickert, Ernie - B
Rentner, "Pug" - Q
Siemering, Larry - C
Sinko, Steve - T
Smith, Ed - B
Smith, Riley - Q
Temple, Mark - B
Tosi, Flavio - E
Weisenbaugh, Henry - B

1936 BROOKLYN DODGERS
COACH - Paul Schissler
4th 3-8-1

Badgro, "Red" - E
Barrett, Jeff - E
Bergerson, Gil - T
Biancone, John - Q
Boyer, Verdi - G
Cook, Dave - B
Crayne, Dick - B
Franklin, Norm - B
Fuqua, Ray - E
Grossman, John - Q
Hartman, Jim - E
Heldt, Carl - T
Jorgenson, Wagner - C
Kaska, Tony - B
Kercheval, Ralph - B
Kirkland, B'ho - G
Krause, "Red" - C
Lee, Bill - T
Lumpkin, "Father" - Q
Maniaci, Joe - B
Oehler, John - C
Riblett, Paul - E
Robinson, John - T
Rukas, Justin - G
Sarboe, Phil - Q
Stojack, Frank - G
Temple, Mark - B
Whately, Jim - T & E
Wilson, Bob - Q
Yezerski, John - T

1936 CHICAGO BEARS
COACH - George Halas
2nd 9-3-0

Allman, Bob - E
Brumbaugh, Carl - Q
Carlson, Jules - G
Corbett, George - Q
Doehring, John - B
Feathers, Beattie - B
Fortman, Dan - G
Grosvenor, George - B
Hewitt, Bill - E
Johnsos, Luke - E
Karr, Bill - E
Kawal, Ed - C

Manders, Jack - B
Masterson, Bernie - Q
Michaels, Ed - G
Miller, "Ookie" - C
Molesworth, Keith - Q
Musso, George - G
Nagurski, Bronko - B
Nolting, Ray - B
Oech, Vern - T
Pollock, Bill - E
Ronzani, Gene - B
Rosequist, Ted - T
Sisk, John - B
Stydahar, Joe - T
Sullivan, Frank - C
Thompson, Russ - T
Trost, Milt - T
Zeller, Joe - G

1936 CHICAGO CARDINALS
COACH - Milan Creighton
4th 3-8-1

Baker, Conway - T
Blazine, Tony - T
Brett, Ed - E
Carter, Ross - G
Cook, Dave - B
Creighton, Milan - E
Cuppoletti, Bree - G
Deskin, Versil - E
Dowell, "Mule" - B
Ellstrom, Marv - B
Field, Harry - T
Grosvenor, George - B
Handler, Phil - G
Hanson, Homer - G
Hughes, Bernie - C
Kellogg, Clarence - B
Lawrence, Jim - B
Lind, Al - C
McBride, Charles - B
Mehringer, Pete - T
Mikulak, Mike - B
Miller, Milford - G
Neuman, Bob - E
Nichelini, Al - B
Pangle, Hal - B
Pearson, "Bert" - C
Robinson, John - T
Russell, Doug - B
Sarboe, Phil - Q
Smith, Bill - E
Tipton, Howard - B & G
Vaughan, Charles - B
Volok, Bill - G
Wilson, Bill - E

1936 DETROIT LIONS
COACH - "Potsy" Clark
3rd 8-4-0

Caddel, Ernie - B
Christensen, Frank - B
Christensen, George - T
Clark, "Dutch" - Q
Ebding, Harry - E
Emerson, "Ox" - G
Gutowsky, "Ace" - B
Hupke, Tom - G
Johnson, John - T
Klewicki, Ed - E
Knox, Sam - G
Kopcha, Joe - G
McKalip, Bill - E
Monahan, Regis - G
Morse, Ray - E
Parker, "Buddy" - B
Peterson, Ken - B
Presnell, Glen - Q
Randolph, Clare - C
Ritchhart, Del - C
Schneller, John - E
Shepherd, Bill - Q
Stacy, Jim - T
Steen, Jim - T
Wagner, Sid - G
White, Wilbur - B

1936 GREEN BAY PACKERS
COACH - "Curly" Lambeau
1st 10-1-1
(Beat Boston for title, 21-6)

Becker, Wayland - E
Bruder, "Hank" - Q
Butler, Frank - C
Clemens, Cal - Q
Engebretsen, Paul - G
Evans, Lon - T
Gantenbein, Milt - E
Goldenberg, "Buckets" - Q&G
Gordon, Lou - T
Herber, Arnie - Q
Hinkle, Clark - B
Hutson, Don - E
Johnston, Chet - B
Kiesling, Walt - G
Laws, Joe - B
Letlow, Russ - G
McNally, John "Blood" - B
Mattos, Harry - B
Miller, Paul - B
Monnett, Bob - Q
Paulekas, Tony - C
Rose, Al - E
Sauer, George - B
Scherer, Bernie - E
Schneidmann, Herman - B&E
Schwammel, Adolph - T
Seibold, Champ - T
Smith, Ernie - T
Svendsen, George - C

1936 NEW YORK GIANTS
COACH - Steve Owen
3rd 5-6-1

Anderson, Winston - E
Burnett, Dale - B
Corzine, Les - B
Danowski, Ed - Q
Davis, Gaines - G
Dell Isola, John - C & G
Dugan, Len - C
Dunlap, Bob - Q
Goodwin, "Tod" - E
Grant, Len - T
Haden, John - T
Hein, Mel - C
Hubbard, "Cal" - T
Johnson, Larry - C
Jones, Tom - G

Kaplan, Bernie - G
Krause, Max - B
Leemans, "Tuffy" - B
Lewis, Art - T & G
Manton, "Tillie" - E
Mitchell, Gran - E
Morgan, Bill - T
Owen, Bill - T
Phillips, Ewell - G
Richards, "Kink" - B
Rose, Roy - E
Sarausky, Tony - B
Shaffer, Leland - Q
Singer, Walt - E
Tarrant, Bob - E

1936 PHILADELPHIA EAGLES
COACH - Bert Bell
5th 1-11-0

Bassman, Herm - B
Brian, Bill - T
Buss, Art - T
Carter, Joe - E
Frey, Glenn - B
Golomb, Rudy - G
Hanson, Tom - B
Jackson, Don - B
Kane, Carl - B
Kusko, John - B
Leonard, Jim - Q
MacMurdo, Jim - T
McPherson, "Amy" - G

Manske, "Eggs" - E
Masters, Walt - Q
Mulligan, George - E
Padlow, Max - E
Pilconis, Joe - E
Pivarnik, Joe - G
Reese, Henry - C
Russell, Him - T & G
Smukler, Dave - B
Stevens, Pete - C
Thomason, "Stumpy" - Q
Zizak, Vince - T & G

1936 PITTSBURGH PIRATES
COACH - Joe Bach
2nd 6-6-0

Bray, Maury - T
Brett, Ed - E
Croft, Win - G
Fiske, Max - B
Gildea, John - Q
Heller, Warren - B
Hubbard, "Cal" - T & E
Kakasic, George - G
Karcis, John - B
Karpowich, Ed - T
Lajousky, Bill - G
Levey, Jim - B
McDonald, Ed - B
Matesic, Ed - B

Mayhew, Hayden - G
Mulleneaux, Lee - C
Niccolai, Armand - T
Raborn, Carroll - C
Rado, George - G
Sandberg, Sig - T
Sandefur, Wayne - B
Sites, Vin - E
Skoronski, Ed - C & E & T
Sortet, Bill - E
Strutt, Art - B
Turley, John - Q
Vidoni, Vic - E
Zaninelli, Silvio - Q

1936 BOSTON SHAMROCKS (AFL)
COACH - George Kenneally
1st 8-3-0

Bartlett, Earl - B
Blanchard, Don - B
Booker, Pete - B
Cipra, Ernie - C
Ellstrom, Marv - B
Elser, Don - B
Elser, Earl - T
Flanagan, Phil - G
Fleming, Frank - E
Hinckle, Bernie - B
Kepler, Bob - B
Morandos, Tony - C
Morris, Nick - B
Mulligan, George - E

Nunn, Hal - E
O'Donnell, Tom - E
Rustich, Frank - B
Sarno, Amerino - T
Soar, "Hank" - B
Swan, Pat - T
Sieck, "Red" - G
Tarrant, Bob - E
Uzdvanis, Walt - E & T
Warwick, Ed - B
Wolfendale, Ralph - G
Zapustas, Joe - Q
Zyntell, Jim - G

1936 BROOKLYN TIGERS (AFL)
COACH - Mike Palm
6th 0-6-1

Baker, Charles - G
Begelman, John - B
Dailey, Don - E
Dodyns, Bob - T
Endler, Hal - E
Frahm, Herald - B
Gladden, Jim - E
Harrison, "Pat" - T
Helmer, Clare - T
Hughes, Frank - E
Kaplan, Lou - G
Lochiner, Art - B

Lyon, George - T
Machlowitz, Nate - B
Munday, George - T
Newman, Harry - Q
Oliver, Dick - B
O'Neill, Bill - B
Rhea, Hugh - G
Rogers, John - C
Thompson, Bill - C
Williams, Clyde - G
Zuk, Stan - B

1926 CLEVELAND RAMS (AFL)
COACH - Damon Wetzel
2nd 5-2-2

Allmen, Stan - G
Andrusking, Sig - G
Cavosie, Joe - B
Ciccone, Ben - C
Cooper, Bill - B
Cox, Budd - E
Cox, Bob - E
Detzel, Art - T
Elduayan, Nebb - G
Gaul, Francis - Q
Gillman, Sid - E
Harre, Gil - T
Jones, Gomer - C

Joyce, Emmett - G
Kepler, Bob - B
McIntosh, Jay - G
Mattos, Harry - B
Novotny, Ray - B
O'Keefe, Declan - T
Padlow, Max - E
Pincura, Stan - Q
Rhodes, Don - T
Sadowsky, Len - B
Sebastian, Mike - B
Sweeney, Bill - G
Wetzel, Damon - B

1936 NEW YORK YANKS (AFL)
COACH - Jack McBride
3rd 5-3-2

Abee, Bill - B
Armstrong, Ellsworth - T
Baltzell, Vic - B
Bodenger, Morrie - G
Bogacki, Henry - C
Borden, Les - E
Clancy, Stu - B
Concannon, Ernie - G
Davis, Kermit - E
Dubilier, - C
Emerick, Bob - T
Farrar, "Vinnie" - B & G
Flenthorpe, Don - G
Floyd, Al - E
Ford, Duane - G
Fraley, Jim - B
Irwin, Don - B
Johnson, Larry - C
Kaufman, Les - B

Klein, Irv - E
Mooney, Jim - E
Nesmith, Ole - B
Newman, Harry - Q
Obst, Henry - G
Ossowski, Marty - T
Peterson, John - B
Pike, John - G
Rose, Al - E
Rustich, Frank - B
Siegal, Charles - B
Strong, Ken - Q
Thompson, Bill - C
Temple, Harry - B
Updike, Hal - T
Waleski, Stan - B
White, Wilbur - B
Wilder, Newell - C
Wycoff, Doug - Q

1936 PITTSBURGH AMERICANS (AFL)
COACH - Rudy Comstock
4th 3-2-1

Beltz, Dick - B
Bender, Ed - G
Davis, Ray - E
Draginis, Pete - Q
Dreiling, Frank - G
Fife, Jim - E
Gilbert, Homer - T
Gruver, Grover - E
Keeble, Joe - Q
Long, Leon - B
Perry, Claude - T

Platukis, Vin - B
Poilek, Joe - B
Potts, Bill - B
Quatse, Jess - T
Ribble, Loran - G & C
Skulos, Mike - G
Smith, Ben - E
Snyder, Bob - Q
Turner, Jim - C
Tyson, Ed - G

1936 ROCHESTER TIGERS (AFL)
(Played at Syracuse to Oct. 25)
COACHES - "Red" Badgro &
Don Irwin
5th 1-6-0

Andorka, Del - T	Ginsberg, Izzy - E
Badgro, "Red" - E	Hale, Russ - G
Bogacki, "Hank" - C	Hein, Floyd - B
Clancy, Paul - E	Hughes, Frank - E
Clark, Jim - B	Inabinet, Clarence - G
Davis, Kermit - E	Irwin, Don - B
Demyanovich, Joe - B	Kramer, "Sol" - B
Egan, "Red" - B	McBride, Charles - B
Ellstrom, Marv - B	McNeese, Tom - B
Fillingham, - T	Pillsbury, Gordon - C
Floyd, Al - E	Saussele, Ted - B
Franklyn, John - T	Schaub, George - G
Garland, Ed - T	VanCleef, - B
Gavin, Francis - E	Wasicek, Charles - T

1937

EASTERN DIVISION

Washington	8	3	0	.727
New York	6	3	2	.667
Pittsburgh	4	7	0	.364
Brooklyn	3	7	1	.300
Philadelphia	2	8	1	.200

WESTERN DIVISION

Chicago Bears	9	1	1	.900
Green Bay	7	4	0	.636
Detroit	7	4	0	.636
Chicago Cardinals	5	5	1	.500
Cleveland	1	10	0	.091

AMERICAN FOOTBALL LEAGUE
(1937)

	W	L	T	Pct.
Los Angeles	8	0	0	1.000
Rochester	3	3	1	.500
New York	2	3	1	.400
Cincinnati	2	3	2	.400
Boston	2	5	0	.286
Pittsburgh	0	3	0	.000

TITLES: Washington beat the Chicago Bears, 28-21, for the championship at Chicago, Dec. 12.

LEADERS: Individual leaders for the season: Scoring—Jack Manders (Chi-Bears), 69; Rushing—Cliff Battles (Washington), 874 yds.; Passing—Sam Baugh (Washington); Pass Receiving—Don Hutson (Green Bay), 41; Field Goals—Jack Manders (Chi-Bears), 8.

FIRST DRAFT: Harrison "Sam" Francis (Nebraska)—Back—by Philadelphia.

COACHES: George "Potsy" Clark replaced Paul Schissler as head coach at Brooklyn; Hugo Bezdek started as head coach at Cleveland; Earl "Dutch" Clark replaced "Potsy" Clark at Detroit; John "Blood" McNally replaced Joe Bach at Pittsburgh.

NOTES: Boston Redskin franchise transferred to Washington; Homer Marshman granted franchise for Cleveland.

James "Pat" Coffee, Chi-Cards, passed 97-yards to Gaynell Tinsley (TD) against Chicago Bears, Dec. 5.

Vern Huffman, Detroit, ran 100 yards with interception (TD) against Brooklyn, Oct. 12.

Joe "Little Twig" Johnson of Oorang Indians, Akron, Rock Island, Canton, tackle, died.

Los Angeles Bulldogs won the American Football League title with an 8-0-0 record.

TITLE GAME

The Bears bumped into a young rookie by the name of Sam Baugh on this ice-covered field. He immediately began to give them nightmares, and continued to do so for the rest of his career.

Cliff Battles racked up the first Redskin touchdown in the first period, scoring on a 10-yard romp through tackle. Riley Smith's conversion made it 7–0. Jack Manders pounded over for the Bears from 10 yards out and converted to tie the score.

In the second quarter, Bernie Masterson passed 20 yards to Manders for another six-pointer and Manders again converted to give the Bears a 14–7 lead at the rest period.

Baugh went through the air to Wayne Millner for 55 yards and a touchdown early in the third quarter and Smith kicked the extra point. Masterson passed 3 yards to Manske and Manders converted to put the Bears back in the lead.

The fourth quarter was all Baugh. He passed for a seventy-eight yarder to Wayne Millner for one touchdown and then to Ed Justice for 35 yards on another. Smith kicked both extra points for a final score of 28–21 to take the title to Washington.

Washington Redskins	7	0	7	14—28
Chicago Bears	7	7	7	0—21

Touchdowns—Battles, Millner 2, Justice, Manders 2, Manske.

Points after touchdown—Manders 3, Riley Smith 4.

Attendance: 15,870.

Players' Shares: Washington $300.00; Chicago $250.00.

1937 BROOKLYN DODGERS
COACH - "Potsy" Clark
4th 3-7-1

Albanese, Vannie - B	Kelly, John - Q
Andrusking, Sig - G	Kercheval, Ralph - Q
Austin, Jim - E	King, Fred - B
Barrett, Jeff - E	Krause, "Red" - C
Brumbaugh, Boyd - B	Lee, Bill - T
Cooper, Norm - C	Leisk, Wardell - G
Crayne, Dick - B	Lumpkin, "Father" - B
Cumiskey, Frank - E	Maniaci, Joe - B
Daniell, Averell - T	Mitchell, Gran - E
Franklin, Norm - B	Nelson, Don - G
Goddard, Ed - Q	Nori, Reino - Q
Golemgeske, John - T	Parker, "Ace" - Q
Harrison, "Pat" - T	Reckmack, Ray - B & E
Ilowit, Roy - T	Sandberg, Sig - T
Johnson, Albert - B	Skoronski, Ed - G & E
Jorgenson, Wagner - C	Whately, Jim - T & E
Kaska, Tony - B	

1937 CHICAGO BEARS
COACH - George Halas
1st 9-1-1
(Lost title to Washington, 28-21)

Bausch, Frank - C	Manske, "Eggs" - E
Bell, Kay - T	Masterson, Bernie - Q
Bettridge, John - B	Molesworth, Keith - Q
Bjork, Del - T	Musso, George - G
Buivid, Ray - B	Nagurski, Bronko - B
Conkright, "Red" - C	Nolting, Ray - B
Corbett, George - Q	Plasman, Dick - E
Doehring, John - B	Rentner, "Pug" - B
Feathers, Beattie - B	Ronzani, Gene - B
Fortman, Dan - G	Stydahar, Joe - T
Francis, "Sam" - B	Sullivan, Frank - C
Hammond, Henry - E	Thompson, Russ - T
Karr, Bill - E	Trost, Milt - T
McDonald, Les - E	Wilson, George - E
Manders, Jack - B	Zeller, Joe - G

1937 CHICAGO CARDINALS
COACH - Milan Creighton
4th 5-5-1

Baker, Conway - T	Miller, Milford - G
Blazine, Tony - T	Morrow, John - G
Carlson, Hal - G	Muellner, Bill - E
Carter, Ross - G	Nolan, Earl - T
Coffee, "Pat" - Q	Pangle, Hal - B
Crass, Bill - B	Parker, "Buddy" - B
Creighton, Milan - E	Reed, Joe - B
Cuppoletti, Bree - G	Reynolds, John - C
Deskin, Versil - E	Robinson, John - T
Dugan, Len - C	Russell, Doug - B
Fiske, Max - B	Smith, Bill - E
Grosvenor, George - B	Tinsley, Gaynell - E
Harmon, "Ham" - C	Tipton, Howie - Q & G
Hoel, Bob - G	Tyler, Pete - B
Lawrence, Jim - B	Volok, Bill - G
May, Bill - Q	Wilson, Bill - E

1937 CLEVELAND RAMS
COACH - Hugo Bezdek
5th 1-10-0

Alfonse, Jules - Q	Mattos, Harry - B
Barber, Mark - B	Miller, "Ookie" - C
Bettridge, John - B	Miller, Ralph - T
Brumbaugh, Carl - Q	O'Neill, Bill - B
Bucklew, Phil - E	Pincura, Stan - Q
Burmeister, Forrest - G	Prather, Dale - E & T
Busich, Sam - E	Rosequist, Ted - T
Cherundolo, Chuck - C	Savatsky, Ollie - E
Cooper, Bill - Q	Sebastian, Mike - B
Drake, John - B	Skoronski, Ed - C & G & E
Emerick, Bob - T	Snyder, Bob - Q
Gift, Wayne - B	Turner, Jim - C
Goddard, Ed - B	Underwood, Forrest - T
Halleck, Paul - E	Uzdvanis, Walt - E & T
Isselhardt, Ralph - T	Williams, Joe - B
Johnson, Ray - B	Zoll, Dick - G
Keeble, Joe - B	
Livingston, Ted - T	

1937 DETROIT LIONS
COACH - "Dutch" Clark
3rd 7-4-0

Caddel, Ernie - B	Isselhardt, Ralph - G
Cardwell, Lloyd - B	Johnson, John - T
Christensen, Frank - B	Kizzire, Lee - B
Christensen, George - T	Klewicki, Ed - E
Clark, "Dutch" - Q	Monahan, Regis - G
Cooper, Hal - G	Morse, Ray - E
Ebding, Harry - E	Payne, Charley - B
Emerson, "Ox" - G	Reckmack, Ray - B & E
Feldhaus, Bill - G	Reynolds, Bob - T
Fena, Tom - G	Ritchhart, Del - C
Gutowsky, "Ace" - B	Shepherd, Bill - B
Hanneman, Charles - E	Stacy, Jim - T
Huffman, Vern - Q	Stokes, Lee - C
Hupke, Tom - G	Wagner, Sid - G

1937 GREEN BAY PACKERS
COACH "Curly" Lambeau
2nd 7-4-0

Banet, Herb - B	Lester, Darrell - C
Becker, Wayland - E	Letlow, Russ - G
Bruder, "Hank" - Q	Michalske, "Mike" - G
Daniell, Averell - T	Miller, Paul - E & B
Engebretsen, Paul - G	Monnett, Bob - Q
Evans, Lon - G	Peterson, Ray - B
Gantenbein, Milt - E	Sauer, George - B
Goldenberg, "Buckets" Q & G	Schammel, Francis - G
Gordon, Lou - T	Scherer, Bernie - E
Herber, Arnie - Q	Schneidmann, Herm - B
Hinkle, Clark - B	Seibold, Champ - T
Hutson, Don - E	Smith, Ed - B
Jankowski, Ed - B	Smith, Ernie - T
Johnston, Chet - B	Sturgeon, Lyle - T
Laws, Joe - B	Sevendsen, Earl - C
Lee, Bill - T	Svendsen, George - C

1937 NEW YORK GIANTS
COACH - Steve Owen
2nd 6-3-2

Burnett, Dale - B	Haden, John - T
Cole, Peter - G	Hanken, Ray - E
Corzine, Les - B	Hein, Mel - C
Cuff, Ward - B	Howell, Jim Lee - E
Danowski, Ed - Q	Johnson, Larry - C
Dell Isola, John - G	Kobrosky, Milt - B
Dennerlein, Gerry - T	Leemans, "Tuffy" - B
Galazin, Stan - C	Lunday, Ken - G
Gelatka, Chuck - E	Manton, "Tillie" - B
Grant, Len - T	Neill, Jim - B

Parry, Owen - T
Poole, Jim - E
Richards, "Kink" - B
Sarausky, Tony - B
Shaffer, Leland - Q

Soar, "Hank" - B
Tuttle, Orville - G
Walls, Will - E
White, "Tarzan" - G
Widseth, Ed - T

1937 PHILADELPHIA EAGLES
COACH - Bert Bell
5th 2-8-1

Arnold, Jay - Q
Baze, Win - B
Buss, Art - T
Carter, Joe - E
Dempsey, John - T
Ferko, John - T
Frey, Glenn - B
Hanson, Tom - B
Harper, Maury - C
Hewitt, Bill - E
Holcomb, Bill -T
Hughes, Bill - G & C
Keen, "Rabbit" - B
Knox, Charles - T
Kusko, John - B

Leonard, Jim - Q
MacMurdo, Jim - T
McPherson, "Amy" - G
Masters, Bob - B
Mortell, Emmett - Q
Pilconis, Joe - E
Rado, George - G & E
Reese, Henry - C
Roton, Herb - E
Russell, Jim - T & G
Smukler, Dave - B
Spillers, Ray - T
Stockton, Herschel - G
Zizak, Vince - G

1937 PITTSBURGH PIRATES
COACH - John "Blood" McNally
3rd 4-7-0

Basrak, Mike - C
Billock, Frank - T
Breedon, Bill - B & E
Brett, Ed - E
Cara, Dom - E
Cardwell, Joe - T & E
Davidson, Bill - B
Fiske, Max - B
Gentry, Byron - G
Gildea, John - B
Haines, Byron - B
Harris, Bill - E
Holcomb, Bill - T
Kakasic, George - G
Karcis, John - B
Karpowich, Ed - T

Kiesling, Walt - G
McNally, John "Blood" - B
Mayhew, Hayden - G
Niccolai, Armand - T
Perko, John - G
Raborn, Carroll - C
Rado, George - G
Sandberg, Sig - T
Sandefur, Wayne - B
Sites, Vin - E
Smith, Stu = B & E
Sortet, Bill - E
Thompson, Clarence - B & E
Weinstock, Izzy - Q
Zaninelli, Silvio - Q

1937 WASHINGTON REDSKINS
COACH - Ray Flaherty
1st 8-3-0
(Beat Chicago Bears for the title,
28-21)

Barber, Jim - T
Bassi, Dick - G
Battles, Cliff - B
Baugh, Sam - B
Bond, Chuck - T
Britt, Ed - B
Carroll, Vic - G
Edwards, "Turk" - T
Howell, Millard - B
Irwin, Don - B
Justice, Ed - B
Kahn, Ed - G
Karcher, Jim - G
Kawal, Ed - C

Krause, "Red" - C
Krause, Max - B
McChesney, Bob - E
Malone, Charley - E
Michaels, Ed - G
Millner, Wayne - E
Olsson, Les - G
Peterson, Nelson - B
Pinckert, Ernie - B
Smith, Ben - E
Smith, George - C
Smith, Riley - Q
Young, Bill - T

1937 BOSTON SHAMROCKS (AFL)
COACH - George Kenneally
5th 2-5-0

Bartlett, Earl - B
Blanchard, Don - B & G

Brewin, John - E
Cipra, Ernie - C

Concannon, Ernie - G
Davis, Kermit - E
Draginis, Pete - Q
Dulkie, Joe - B
Ellstrom, Marv - B
Fleming, Frank - E
Harris, Bill - E
Hinckle, Bernie - Q
Kelley, Larry - E
McNeese, Tom - B
Mittrick, Jim - B

Morandos, Tony - C
Morris, Nick - B
Pendergast, Bill - B
Prather, Dale - E & T
Sarno, Amerino - T
Swan, Joe - T
Swan, Pat - T
Warwick, Ed - B
Zapustas, Joe - Q
Zyntell, Jim - G

1937 CINCINNATI BENGALS (AFL)
COACH - Hal Pennington
4th 2-3-2

Antonini, Ettore - E
Burch, Bill - B
Cavosie, Joe - B
Ciccone, Ben - C
Coleman, Jim - G
Cooper, Bill - Q
Dye, Bill - B
Geyer, Don - B
Glassford, Bill - G
Harrison, "Pat" - T
Lightner, Harry - C
McAfee, John - B
McPhail, Hal - B
Mattos, Harry - B
Mulleneaux, Lee - C & B
Muellner, Bill - E

O'Keefe, Declan - T
Padlow, Max - E
Potter, Lexie - T
Reynolds, Homer - G
Schwarzberg, Bill - B
Sebastian, Mike - B
Shelton, Al - E
Sites, Vince - E
Sigillo, Dom - T
Smith, Inwood - G
Steinkemper, Bill - T
Sweeney, Russ - E
Underwood, Forrest - T
Wagner, Sheldon - G
Wilke, Bob - B
Wunderlich, Fred - Q

1937 LOS ANGELES BULLDOGS (AFL)
COACH - "Gus" Henderson
1st 8-0-0

Austin, Jim - E
Barnhart, Dan - B
Beatty, Homer - B
Boyer, Verdi - G
Clemens, Cal - Q
Clemons, Ray - G
Davis, Dave - B
Donnell, "Gerry" - B & G
Field, Harry - T
Frankian, "Ike" - E
Gentry, Byron - G
Gore, Gordon - B
Howard, Bill - B
Hughes, Bernie - C

Karpus, Andy - B
Mehringer, Pete - T
Miller, "Pot" - Q
Moore, Bill - E
Muellner, Bill - E
Nichelini, Al - B
O'Brien, Gail - T
Pearson, "Bert" - C
Phillips, Ewell - G
Richards, Ray - G
Sinko, Steve - T
Stark, Ed - B
Waller, Bill - E
Wickersham, Hal - Q

1937 NEW YORK YANKS (AFL)
COACH - Jim Mooney
3rd 2-3-1

Abee, Bill - B
Andrusking, Sig - G
Bobrowsky, Pete - E
Buivid, Ray - B
Carlson, Hal - T
Dobbs, Ben - E
Douglas, Bob - B
Drobnitch, Alex - G
Funk, Fred - B
Grillo, Al - T
Hambright, Fred - B
Hewes, "Bo" - B
Hunt, "Zeke" - C
Jones, Tom - G
Karpus, Andy - B

Keeble, Joe - B
Klein, Irv - E & T
Kuhn, Gil - C
McCarthy, Bill - E
Mooney, Jim - E
Muellner, Bill - E
Nesmith, Ole - B
Ossowski, Marty - T
Paquin, Leo - E & C
Parker, Bernie - B
Sleck, "Red" - G
Strong, Ken - Q
Wieczorek, John - B
Wolcuff, Nick - T

1937 PITTSBURGH AMERICANS (AFL)
COACH - Jess Quatse
6th 0-3-0

Bardes, Howie - Q	Perry, Claude - T
Bender, Ed - T	Platukis, Vin - B
Capatelli, Jerry - G	Quatse, Jess - T
Cassidy, Joe - B	Reissig, Bill - B & E
Darnell, Larry - G	Ribble, Loran - G
Dobbs, Ben - E	Rutherford - B
Douglas, Bob - B	Saulis, Joe - B
Dreiling, Frank - C	Skulos, Mike - G
East, Vernon - B	Spinosa, Al - C
Fife, Jim - E	Tyson, Ed - G
Krumenacher, Paul - E	Van Horne, - C
Matesic, Ed - B	Wagner, Harry - B

1937 ROCHESTER TIGERS (AFL)
COACH - Mike Palm
2nd 3-3-1

Brochmann, Art - T	Ohrt, John - B
Capatelli, Jerry - G	O'Neill, Bill - B
Crotty, Dave - G	Popadak, John - T
Endler, Hal - E	Poste, Les - B
Farrar, "Vinnie" - B & G	Sandefur, Wayne - B
Ganaposki, Ed - C	Savatsky, Ollie - E
Harrison, "Pat" - T	Sebastian, Mike - B
Kaplan, Lou - G	Showalter, Frank - T
LeFebvre, Gil - B	Stidham, Ernie - C
Lochiner, Art - B	Stulgate, Jerry - E
Newman, Harry - Q	Zizak, Charles - T & G

1938

EASTERN DIVISION

New York	8	2	1	.800
Washington	6	3	2	.667
Brooklyn	4	4	3	.500
Philadelphia	5	6	0	.455
Pittsburgh	2	9	0	.182

WESTERN DIVISION

Green Bay	8	3	0	.727
Detroit	7	4	0	.636
Chicago Bears	6	5	0	.545
Cleveland	4	7	0	.364
Chicago Cardinals	2	9	0	.182

TITLE: The New York Giants beat Green Bay for the championship, 23-17, in New York, Dec. 11.

LEADERS: Individual leaders for the season: Scoring—Clark Hinkle (Green Bay), 58; Rushing—Byron "Whizzer" White (Pittsburgh), 567 yds.; Passing—Ed Danowski (New York); Pass Receiving—Gaynell Tinsley (Chi-Cards), 41; Field Goals—Ward Cuff (New York), Ralph Kercheval (Brooklyn), 5 (tie).

FIRST DRAFT: Corbett Davis (Indiana) —Back—by Cleveland.

COACHES: Art Lewis replaced Hugo Bezdek as head coach at Cleveland after 4 games.

NOTES: Roster limit increased 5 to 30.

Doug Russell, Chi-Cards, passed 98 yards to Gaynell Tinsley (TD) against Cleveland, Nov. 27.

Jim Sanford, Duluth tackle, died April 7.

TITLE GAME

A real slam-bang, bruising thriller was staged for the largest crowd to turn out for a professional championship game up to that time. The entire league had played to a new high in attendance records, the average being up more than 15 percent above previous marks. The victorious Giants became the first team since 1933 (when the league was split into two divisions) to win the championship twice.

The Giants were off on top when two Green Bay punts were blocked early in the game. Ward Cuff cashed one of these for a 13-yard field goal. Tuffy Leemans smashed over from the 6 for a touchdown on the other. Gildea missed the conversion and the Giants led, 9–0, at the end of the period.

Arnie Herber launched a 50-yard pass to Karl Mulleneaux for a TD early in the second quarter and Engebretsen kicked the conversion. The Giants made it 16-7 when Ed Danowski passed 20 yards to Hap Barnard in the end zone and Ward Cuff obliged with the extra point. Clark Hinkle smashed over from the 6 to lead to another conversion by Engebretsen and the Giants led, 16-14, at the half.

The Packers took the second half kick-off back to the Giant 15, where Engebretsen hoisted a field goal. The Giants stormed back to the Packer 23 from where Danowski passed to Hank Soar on the 2 and Soar plowed over for the TD. Cuff added the extra and the score was 23–17. There was no further scoring in this period nor in the next.

New York Giants	9	7	7	0—23
Green Bay Packers	0	14	3	0—17

Touchdowns—Leemans, Barnard, Soar, C. Mulleneaux, Hinkle.

Points after touchdown—Cuff 2, Engebretsen 2.

Field Goals: Engebretsen, Cuff.

Attendance: 48,120.

Players' Shares: New York $900.00;
Green Bay $700.00.

1938 BROOKLYN DODGERS
COACH - "Potsy" Clark
3rd 4-4-3

Albanese, "Vannie" - B	Kercheval, Ralph - B
Austin, Jim - E	Kinard, "Bruiser" - T
Barrett, Jeff - E	Kosel, Stan - B
Britt, Ed - B	Maniaci, Joe - B
Brumbaugh, Boyd - Q	Mark, Lou - C
Butcher, Wen - B	Merlin, Ed - G
Cooper, Norm - C	Moore, Gene - C
Disend, Leo - T	Noyes, Len - G
Druze, John - E	Parker, "Ace" - Q
Emerson, "Ox" - G	Reissig, Bill - B & E
Farrell, Ed - B	Sarausky, Tony - Q
Feathers, Beattie - B	Schwartz, Perry - E
Golemgeske, John - T	Sivell, Jim - G
Hill, Harold - E	Waller, Bill - E
Kaska, Tony - B	Whately, Jim - T

1938 CHICAGO BEARS
COACH - George Halas
3rd 6-5-0

Bassi, Dick - G	Manske, "Eggs" - E
Bausch, Frank - C	Masterson, Bernie - Q
Bjork, Del - T	Musso, George - G
Brumbaugh, Carl - Q	Nolting, Ray - B
Buivid, Ray - B	Nori, Reino - B
Conkright, Bill - C	Oelerich, John - B
Corbett, George - Q	Plasman, Dick - E
Corzine, Les - B	Ronzani, Gene - B
Draher, Ferd - E	Schweidler, Dick - B
Famiglietti, Gary - B	Stydahar, Joe - T
Fortman, Dan - G	Sullivan, Frank - C
Francis, Sam - B	Swisher, Bob - B
Gordon, Lou - T	Thompson, Russ - T
Johnson, Albert - B	Trost, Milt - T
Karr, Bill - E	Wilson, George - E
McDonald, Les - E	Zarnas, "Gus" - G
Manders, Jack - B	Zeller, Joe - G
Maniaci, Joe - B	

1938 CHICAGO CARDINALS
COACH - Milan Creighton
5th 2-9-0

Agee, Sam - B	Lawrence, Jim - B
Babartsky, Al - T	McGee, Bob - T
Baker, Conway - T	May, Bill - Q
Bilbo, Jon - T	Morrow, John - G
Blazine, Tony - T	Mulleneaux, Lee - C
Bradley, Hal - E	Nolan, Earl - T
Burnett, Ray - B	Pangle, Hal - Q
Carter, Ross - G	Parker, "Buddy" - B
Cherry, Ed - B	Patrick, Frank - Q
Coffee, "Pat" - Q	Popovich, Milt - B
Cuppoletti, Bree - G	Robbins, John - Q
Deskin, Versil - E	Russell, Doug - B
Dougherty, Phil - C	Sloan, Dwight - Q
Dugan, Len - C	Smith, Bill - E
Dunstan, Elwyn - T	Tinsley, Gaynell - E
Fisher, Ev - E & B	Tyler, Pete - Q
Hoel, Bob - G	Volok, Bill - G

1938 CLEVELAND RAMS
COACHES - Hugo Bezdek
& Art Lewis
4th 4-7-0

Alfonse, Jules - Q	Littlefield, Carl - B
Benton, Jim - E	Livingston, Ted - T
Brazell, Carl - Q	Markov, Vic - G
Cherundolo, Chuck - C	May, Jack - C
Chesbro, "Red" - G	Miller, Ralph - T
Conlee, Gerry - C	Peterson, Nelson - B
Davis, "Corby" - B	Pincura, Stan - Q
Davis, Bob - B	Prather, Dale - E
Drake, John - B	Ragazzo, Phil - G
Giannoni, John - E	Ream, Charley - T
Goddard, Ed - B	Robinson, John - T
Hamilton, Ray - E	Snyder, Bob - Q
Hupke, Tom - G	Spadaccini, Vic - Q
Johnson, Ray - B	Stephens, John - E
Kovatch, John - E	Tuckey, Dick - B
Krause, Bill - T	Zoll, Dick - G & T
Lewis, Art - T	

1938 DETROIT LIONS
COACH - "Dutch" Clark
2nd 7-4-0

Barle, Lou - Q	Monahan, Regis - G
Caddel, Ernie - B	Morse, Ray - E
Cardwell, Lloyd - B	Moscrip, Jim - E
Christensen, George - T	Nardi, Dick - B
Clark, "Dutch" - Q	Patt, Maurice - E
Feldhaus, Bill - G	Radovich, Bill - G
Graham, Les - G	Reynolds, Bob - T
Gutowsky, "Ace" - B	Rogers, Bill - T
Hanneman, Charles - E	Ryan, Kent - B
Huffman, Vern - Q	Shepherd, Bill - Q
Johnson, John - T	Stokes, Lee - C
Klewicki, Ed - E	Szakash, Paul - Q
McDonald, Jim - Q	Vanzo, Fred - Q
Mackenroth, John - C	Wagner, Sid - G
Matisi, Tony - T	Wojciechowicz, Alex - C

1938 GREEN BAY PACKERS
COACH - "Curly" Lambeau
1st 8-3-0
(Lost title to New York, 23-17)

Becker, Wayland - E	Lee, Bill - T
Borak, Tony - E	Lester, Darrell - C
Bruder, "Hank" - Q	Letlow, Russ - G
Butler, Frank - T	Miller, Charles - C
Engebretsen, Paul - G	Miller, Paul - B
Gantenbein, Milt - E	Monnett, Bob - B
Goldenberg, "Buckets" - G	Mulleneaux, Carl - E
Herber, Arnie - Q	Mulleneaux, Lee - C
Hinkle, Clark - B	Ray, "Baby" - T
Howell, John - B	Scherer, Bernie - E
Hutson, Don - E	Schneidman, Herman - Q
Isbell, Cecil - Q	Schoemann, Leroy - C
Jankowski, Ed - B	Seibold, Champ - T
Johnston, Chet - B	Tinsley, Pete - G
Jones, Tom - G	Uram, Andy - B
Katalinas, Leo - T	Weisgerber, Dick - Q
Laws, Joe - B	

1938 NEW YORK GIANTS
COACH - Steve Owen
1st 8-2-1
(Beat Green Bay for title, 23-17)

Barnard, "Hap" - E	Burnett, Dale B
Barnum, Len - Q	Cole, Peter - G

Cope, Frank - T
Cuff, Ward - B
Danowski, Ed - Q
Dell Isola, John - G
Falaschi, Nello - Q
Galazin, Stan - C
Gelatka, Charles - E
Gildea, John - B
Haden, John - T
Hanken, Ray - E
Hein, Mel - C
Howell, Jim Lee - E
Johnson, Larry - C
Karcis, John - B

Leemans, "Tuffy" - B
Lunday, Ken - G
Manton, "Tillie" - B
Mellus, John - T
Parry, Owen - T
Poole, Jim - E
Richards, "Kink" - B
Shaffer, Leland - Q
Soar, "Hank" - B
Tuttle, Orville - G
Walls, Will - E
White, "Tarzan" - G
Widseth, Ed - T
Wolfe, Hugh - B

Manton, "Tillie" - B
Masterson, Bob - E
Millner, Wayne - E
Olsson, Les - G
Parks, Ed - C
Pinckert, Ernie - B
Smith, Riley - Q

Stralka, Clem - G
Tuckey, Dick - B
Turner, Jay - B
Wilkin, Willie - T
Young, Roy - T
Young, Bill - T

1939

WESTERN DIVISION

Green Bay	9	2	0	.818
Chicago Bears	8	3	0	.727
Detroit	6	5	0	.545
Cleveland	5	5	1	.500
Chicago Cardinals	1	10	0	.091

EASTERN DIVISION

New York	9	1	1	.900
Washington	8	2	1	.800
Brooklyn	4	6	1	.400
Philadelphia	1	9	1	.100
Pittsburgh	1	9	1	.100

1938 PHILADELPHIA EAGLES
COACH - Bert Bell
4th 5-6-0

Arnold, Jay - B
Bukant, Joe - B
Burnette, Tom - B
Carter, Joe - E
Cole, John - B
Dow, Elwood - Q
Ellis, Drew - T
Ferko, John - T
Fiedler, Bill - G
Giddens, Herschel - T
Harper, Maury - C
Hewitt, Bill - E
Hughes, Bill - G
Keeling, Ray - T
Keen, Allen - B

Kusko, John - B
Lee, Bernie - B
Masters, Bob - Q
Mortell, Emmett - B
Pylman, Bob - T
Rado, George - G & E
Ramsey, Herschel - E
Reese, Henry - C
Riffle, Dick - B
Schmitt, Ted - G
Smukler, Dave - B
Stockton, Herschel - G
Wilson, Bill - E
Woltman, Clem - T

1938 PITTSBURGH PIRATES
COACH - John "Blood" McNally
5th 2-9-0

Basrak, Mike - C
Burnette, Tom - B
Cara, Dom - E
Cardwell, Joe - T
Davidson, Bill - B & E
Douglas, Bob - B
Doyle, Ted - T
Farrar, "Vince" - B & G
Farrell, Ed - B
Farroh, Shipley - G
Filchock, Frank - Q
Fiske, Max - B
Gentry, Byron - G
Hanson, Tom - B
Kakasic, George - G
Karcis, John - B
Karpowich, Ed - T
Kiesling, Walt - G
Lassahn, Lou - E & T
Lee, Bernie - B
McDade, Karl - C
McDonough, Paul - E

McNally, John "Blood" - B
Manske, "Egge" - E
Maras, Joe - C & T
Mayhew, Hayden - G
Niccolai, Armond - T
Nosich, John - T
Oelerich, John - B
Perko, John - G
Platukis, George - E
Robinson, John - T
Rorison, Jim - T
Smith, Stu - Q
Sortet, Bill - E
Tatum, Jess - E
Thompson, Clarence - B
Tommerson, Clarence - B
Tsoutsouvas, Lou - C
Weinstock, Izzy - Q
White, "Whizzer" - B
Wilson, Bill - E

1938 WASHINGTON REDSKINS
COACH - Ray Flaherty
2nd 6-3-2

Barber, Jim - T
Bartos, Henry - G
Baugh, Sam - Q
Bond, Charles - T
Bond, Randall - B
Bradley, Harold - B
Carroll, Vic - T & C
Edwards, "Turk" - T
Erickson, Carl - C
Farkas, Andy - B

Filchock, Frank - Q
Hartman, Bill - Q
Irwin, Don - B
Justice, Ed - B
Karamatic, George - B
Karcher, Jim - G
Krause, "Red" - C
Krause, Max - B
McChesney, Bob - E
Malone, Charley - E

TITLE: Green Bay beat New York, 27-0, for the championship at Milwaukee, Dec. 10.

LEADERS: Individual leaders for the season: Scoring—Andy Farkas (Washington), 68; Rushing—Bill Osmanski (Chi-Bears), 699 yds.; Passing—Parker Hall (Cleveland); Pass Receiving—Don Hutson (Green Bay), 34; Field Goals—Ward Cuff (New York), 7; Punting—John Pingel (Detroit), 43.0 yds.

FIRST DRAFT: Charles "Ki" Aldrich (TCU)—Center—by Chi-Cards.

COACHES: Earl "Dutch" Clark replaced Art Lewis as head coach of Cleveland Rams; Gus Henderson replaced "Dutch" Clark at Detroit; Walt Kiesling replaced John "Blood" McNally after three games at Pittsburgh; Ernie Nevers replaced Milan Creighton at Chicago Cardinals.

NOTES: Joe E. Carr, NFL president since 1921, died May 20; Carl L. Storck named president.

John "Blood" McNally (Milwaukee, Duluth, Pottsville, Green Bay, Pittsburgh halfback) retired after 15 years.

Andy Uram, Green Bay back, ran 97 yards for TD against Chi-Cards (record) Oct. 8.

Frank Filchock, Washington qback, passed for 99 yards (TD) to Andy Farkas against Pittsburgh, Oct. 15.

TITLE GAME

This game, played on dry ground but with a chill 35-mph wind brought sweet revenge to Green Bay, who had lost the title to the Giants the previous year.

Arnie Herber tossed a 7-yard pass to Milt Gantenbein in the end zone and Engebretsen cashed the conversion in the first period. There was no further scoring and the Packers led, 7-0, at the half.

Engebretsen continued his scoring with a 29-yard field goal in the third period. Joe Laws then caught Cecil Isbell's 20-yard pass on the Giant 7 and scooted across. Engebretsen again converted to make it 17-0

Late in the fourth quarter, Ernie Smith kicked a 42-yard field goal. A few plays later an interception led the Packers to the Giant 12. From there, on a double reverse, Jacunski carried to the one and, on the next play, Jankowski took it over. Smith converted and it was 27-0, the final score.

Green Bay Packers	7	0	10	10—27
New York Giants	0	0	0	0— 0

Touchdowns—Gantenbein, Laws, Jankowski.
Points after touchdown—Engebretsen 2, Smith.
Field goals—Engebretsen, Smith.

Attendance: 32,279.
Players' Shares: Green Bay $850.00; New York $650.00.

1939 BROOKLYN DODGERS
COACH - "Potsy" Clark
3rd 4-6-1

Brumbaugh, Boyd - B
Butcher, Wen - Q
Carnelly, Ray - Q
Disend, Leo - T
Farrell, Ed - B
Feathers, Beattie - B
Folk, Dick - B
Francis, "Sam" - B
Golemgeske, John - T
Gutowsky, "Ace" - B
Haak, Bob - T
Heikkinen, Ralph - G
Hill, Harold - E
Hodges, Herman - E
Humphrey, Paul - C
Janiak, Len - B
Kaplanoff, Carl - T
Kercheval, Ralph - B
Kinard, "Bruiser" - T
Kosel, Stan - B
Lane, Les - T
Leckonby, Bill - B
Lenc, George - E
Manders, "Pug" - B

Mark, Lou - C
Merlin, Ed - G
Nardi, Dick - B
Parker, "Ace" - Q
Ratica, Joe - C
Reissig, Bill - B & E
Schwartz, Perry - E
Shellogg, Alec - T
Sivell, Jim - G
Tosi, John - G
Young, Walt - E
Zarnas, "Gus" - G

1939 CHICAGO BEARS
COACH - George Halas
2nd 8-3-0

Apolskis, Chuck - E
Bassi, Dick - G
Bausch, Frank - C
Bray, Ray - G
Chesney, Chet - C
Famiglietti, Gary - B
Forte, Aldo - G
Fortman, Dan - G
Heileman, Charles - E
Johnson, Albert - B
Luckman, Sid - Q
MacLeod, Bob - B
McDonald, Les - E
Manders, Jack - B
Maniaci, Joe - B
Manske, "Eggs" - E
Masterson, Bernie - Q
Musso, George - G
Nolting, Ray - B
Osmanski, Bill - B
Patterson, Bill - B
Plasman, Dick - E
Schweidler, Dick - B
Shellogg, Alec - T
Sherman, "Solly" - Q
Siegel, John - E
Snyder, Bob - Q
Stolfa, Anton - B
Stydahar, Joe - T
Sullivan, Frank - C
Swisher, Bob - B
Thompson, Russ - T
Torrance, John - T
Trost, Milt - T
Wilson, George - E

1939 CHICAGO CARDINALS
COACH - Ernie Nevers
5th 1-10-0

Adams, Henry - C
Agee, Sam - B
Aldrich, "Ki" - C
Babartsky, Al - T
Baker, Conway - T
Bilbo, Jon - T
Birlem, Keith - B & E
Blazine, Tony - T
Bradley, Hal - E
Carter, Ross - G
Cherry, Ed - B
Cosner, Don - B
Crowder, Earl - Q
Deskin, Versil - E
Dugan, Len - C
Dunstan, Elwyn - T
Faust, George - Q
Fisher, Ev - Q
Gainor, Charles - E
Goldberg, "Biggie" - B
Huffman, Frank - G
Johnson, Albert - B
Klumb, John - E
Kochel, Mike - G
Lawrence, Jim - B
McDonough, Coley - B
Mason, Joel - E
Monahan, Regis - G
Neill, Jim - B
Parker, "Buddy" - B
Patrick, Frank - Q
Popovich, Milt - B
Reed, Joe - B
Robbins, John - Q
Rogers, Glynn - G
Russell, Doug - B
Sabados, Andy - G & C
Smith, Bill - E
Thomas, Jim - G
Volok, Bill - G
Wheeler, Ernie - B
Zelencik, Frank - T

1939 CLEVELAND RAMS
COACH - "Dutch" Clark
4th 5-5-1

Adams, Chet - T
Atty, Alex - G
Barle, Lou - Q
Benton, Jim - E
Bostick, Lew - G
Cherundolo, Chuck — C
Conkright, Bill - C
Davis, "Corby" - B
Dowd, Gerry - C
Drake, John - B
Dunstan, Elwyn - T
Friend, Ben - T
Hall, Parker - Q
Hitt, Joel - E
Hupke, Tom - G
Lazetich, Bill - B
Lewis, Art - T
Livingston, Ted - T
McDonough, Paul - E
McGarry, "Barney" - G
McRaven, Bill - B
Matheson, Riley - G
Moan, "Kelly" - B
Neihaus, Ralph - T
Patt, Maurey - E
Perrie, Mike - B
Ragazzo, Phil - G
Rodak, Mike - E & B
Russell, Doug - B
Schenker, Nate - T

Slovak, Marty - B
Smilanich, Bronko - B
Smith, Gaylon - B

Spadaccini, Vic - Q
Wilson, John - E

1939 PHILADELPHIA EAGLES
COACH - Bert Bell
4th 1-9-1

Arnold, Jay - B
Britt, Rankin - E
Bukant, Joe - B
Carter, Joe - E
Coston, Fred - C
Cuppoletti, Bree - G
Dow, Elwood - Q
Ellis, Drew - T
Harper, Maury - C
Hewitt, Bill - E
Hughes, Bill - G
Keeling, Ray - T
Kolberg, Elmer - E & B
Kriel, Emmett - G

Mortell, Emmett - B
Murray, Francis - B
Newton, Charles - B
O'Brien, Davey - Q
Pylman, Bob - T
Ramsay, Herschel - E
Reese, Henry - C
Riffle, Dick - B
Schmitt, Ted - G
Schuehle, Carl - B
Smukler, Dave - B
Somers, George - T
White, "Allie" - G
Woltman, Clem - T

1939 DETROIT LIONS
COACH - "Gus" Henderson
3rd 6-5-0

Austin, Jim - E
Berry, Connie Mack - E
Brill, Hal - B
Calvelli, Tony - C
Cardwell, Lloyd - B
Clemons, Ray - G
Diehl, Dave - E
Feldhaus, Bill - G
George, Ray - T
Gore, Gordon - B
Hamilton, Ray - E
Hanneman, Charles - E
Hutchinson, Elvin - B
Johnson, John - T
McDonald, Jim - Q
Maronic, Steve - T
Martinovich, Phil - G
Moore, Bill - E

Moscrip, Jim - E
Pingel, John - Q
Radovich, Bill - G
Rogers, Bill - T
Ryan, Kent - B
Shepherd, Bill - Q
Sloan, Dwight - Q
Stokes, Lee - C
Szakash, Paul - Q
Thomas, Cal - G
Tonelli, Amerigo - C
Tully, Darrell - Q
Vanzo, Fred - B
Weiss, Howie - B
Wiatrak, John - C
Wiethe, John - G
Wojciechowicz, Alex - C

1939 PITTSBURGH STEELERS
COACHES - John "Blood" McNally &
Walt Kiesling
5th 1-9-1

Bartlett, Earl - B
Becker, Wayland - E
Bond, Randall - Q
Boyd, Sam - E
Brumbaugh, Boyd - B
Campbell, Don - T
Cherry, Ed - B
Davidson, Bill - B
Doyle, Ted - T
Dugan, Len - C
Farrar, "Vinnie" - B & G
Fiske, Max - E & B
Francis, "Sam" - B
Gentry, Byron - G
Grabinski, Thad - C
Johnston, Chet - B
Kakasic, George - G
Karpowich, Ed - T
Lee, John - B
Littlefield, Carl - B

McCullough, Hugh - B
McDonough, Coley - Q
McNally, John "Blood" - B
Maras, Joe - C & T
Masters, Bob - B
Midler, Lou - G
Nardi, Dick - B
Niccolai, Armand - T
Pavkov, Stonko - G
Perko, John - G
Platukis, George - E
Scherer, Bernie - E
Schuelke, Karl - B
Sortet, Bill - E
Souchak, Frank - E
Tomasetti, Lou - B
Tommerson, Clarence - B
Tosi, John - C & G
Wheeler, Ernie - B
Williams, Joe - B

1939 GREEN BAY PACKERS
COACH - "Curly" Lambeau
1st 9-2-0
(Beat New York for title, 27-0)

Balaz, Frank - B
Biolo, John - G
Brennan, John - G
Brock, Charles - C
Bruder, "Hank" - Q
Buhler, Larry - Q
Craig, Larry - B
Engebretsen, Paul - G
Gantenbein, Milt - E
Goldenberg, "Buckets" - G
Greenfield, Tom - C
Herber, Arnie - Q
Hinkle, Clark - B
Hutson, Don - E
Isbell, Cecil - Q
Jacunski, Harry - E
Jankowski, Ed - B
Kell, Paul - T

Kilbourne, Warren - T
Lawrence, Jim - B
Laws, Joe - B
Lee, Bill - T
Letlow, Russ - G
Moore, Al - E
Mulleneaux, Carl - E
Ray, "Baby" - T
Schultz, Charles - T
Smith, Ernie - T
Steen, Frank - E
Svendsen, Earl - C
Thompson, Clarence - B
Tinsley, Pete - G
Twedell, Francis - G
Uram, Andy - B
Weisgerber, Dick - Q
Zarnas, "Gus" - G

1939 WASHINGTON REDSKINS
COACH - Ray Flaherty
2nd 8-2-1

Barber, Jim - T
Baugh, Sam - Q
Birlem, Keith - B
Bradley, Harold - E
Carroll, Vic - T & C
Edwards, "Turk" - T
Erickson, Carl - C
Farkas, Andy - B
Farman, Dick - G
Filchock, Frank - Q
German, Jim - B
Irwin, Don - B
Johnston, Jim - B
Justice, Ed - B
Karcher, Jim - G
Krause, Max - B
McChesney, Bob - E
Malone, Charley - E

Masterson, Bob - E
Meade, Jim - B
Millner, Wayne - E
Moore, Wilbur - B
Morgan, Boyd - B
Parks, Ed - C
Pinckert, Ernie - B
Russell, Torrance - T
Shugart, Clyde - G
Slivinski, Steve - G
Spirida, John - E
Stralka, Clem - G
Todd, Dick - B
Turner, Jay - B
Uhrinyak, Steve - G
Wilkin, Willie - T
Young, Bill - T

1939 NEW YORK GIANTS
COACH - Steve Owen
1st 9-1-1
(Lost to Green Bay for title,
27-0)

Barnum, Len - B
Burnett, Dale - B
Cole, Pete - G
Cope, Frank - T
Cuff, Ward - B
Danowski, Ed - Q
Dell Isola, John - G
Falaschi, Nello - Q
Galazin, Stan - C
Gelatka, Charles - E
Hein, Mel - C
Howell, Jim Lee - E
Johnson, Larry - C
Karcis, John - B
Kline, Harry - E
Leemans, "Tuffy" - B

Lunday, Ken - G & C
Mellus, John - T
Miller, Ed - Q
Oldershaw, Doug - G
Owen, Alton - B
Parry, "Ox" - T
Poole, Jim - E
Richards, "Kink" - B
Shaffer, Leland - Q & E
Soar, "Hank" - B
Strong, Ken - B
Tuttle, Orville - G
Walls, Will - E
White, "Tarzan" - G
Widseth, Ed - T

1940

1940
WESTERN DIVISION
Chicago Bears   8   3   0   .727

	W	L	T	Pct.
Green Bay	6	4	1	.600
Detroit	5	5	1	.500
Cleveland	4	6	1	.400
Chicago Cardinals	2	7	2	.222

EASTERN DIVISION

	W	L	T	Pct.
Washington	9	2	0	.818
Brooklyn	8	3	0	.727
New York	6	4	1	.600
Pittsburgh	2	7	2	.222
Philadelphia	1	10	0	.091

AMERICAN FOOTBALL LEAGUE (1940)

	W	L	T	Pct.
Columbus	8	1	1	.888
Milwaukee	7	2	0	.777
Boston	5	4	1	.555
New York	4	5	0	.445
Buffalo	2	8	0	.200
Cincinnati	1	7	0	.125

TITLE: Chicago Bears beat Washington, 73-0, for the championship at Washington, Dec. 8.

LEADERS: Individual leaders for the season: Scoring—Don Hutson (Green Bay), 57; Rushing—Byron "Whizzer" White (Detroit), 514 yds.; Passing—Sam Baugh (Washington); Pass Receiving—Don Looney (Philadelphia), 58; Field Goals—Clark Hinkle (Green Bay), 9; Punting—Sam Baugh (Washington), 51.0 yds.; league record.

FIRST DRAFT: George Cafego (Tennessee)—Qback—by Chi-Cards.

COACHES: "Jock" Sutherland replaced "Potsy" Clark as head coach at Brooklyn; "Potsy" Clark replaced Gus Henderson at Detroit; Jim Conzelman replaced Ernie Nevers at Chicago Cardinals.

NOTES: Roster limited increased 3 to 33.

Detroit fined $5,000 for "tampering" with "Bulldog" Turner, drafted by Chicago Bears.

Fred L. Mandel Jr. bought Detroit Lions from G. A. Richards; Alexis Thompson bought Pittsburgh Steelers from Art Rooney who then bought half-interest in Philadelphia Eagles.

Robert "Davey" O'Brien, Philadelphia, attempted 60 passes, record, completed 33 against Washington, Dec. 1.

The Columbus Bullies of the new AFL won the league title with an 8-1-1 record.

TITLE GAME

The most fantastic exhibition of sheer football power and genius, combined with perfect timing and good luck, fashioned this championship game into one that will be mentioned with awe as long as football is played. Washington was far from an outclassed team. In fact their seasonal record was better (9 wins, 2 losses) than the Bears' (8 wins, 3 losses). They were expected to triumph. Baugh had been having his best year to date—the team was ready.

The Bears received and, on the second play, Bill Osmanski sped around his left end for 68 yards and a touchdown. Jack Manders converted. Sid Luckman scored the next with a one-yard plunge after driving the team 80 yards. Bob Snyder kicked the extra point. Joe Maniaci followed Osmanski's trail around left end for 42 yards and a TD, and Phil Martinovich cashed the conversion to make it 21–0 at the end of the quarter.

The second period was fairly quiet; the only scoring was Luckman's 30-yard pass to Ken Kavanaugh in the end zone and Snyder's second conversion.

Hampton Pool intercepted a Baugh pass to open the second half and ran 19 yards for a touchdown with Dick Plasman converting. Ray Nolting blasted for 23 yards and another score and this time Plasman missed the conversion. George McAfee then intercepted Roy Zimmerman's pass and returned 34 yards for a TD and Joe Stydahar kicked the extra point. Clyde Turner got into the act by intercepting another Zimmerman throw and going 21 yards over the goal. The Redskins blocked Maniaci's conversion attempt. This made it 54-0 as the third quarter ended.

Harry Clark went around his right end for 44 yards and a TD and Gary Famiglietti missed the conversion. A few minutes later, Famiglietti atoned by smashing over from the 2 after Bulldog Turner had recovered Frank Filchock's fumble. This time, Sollie Sherman passed to Maniaci for the extra point. Clark scored the final TD from the one-yard line but the Sherman-

Maniaci pass-for-conversion attempt went wild.

Ten different Bears had scored eleven touchdowns; six different players had scored seven conversions.

Chicago Bears	21	7 26	19—73	
Washington Redskins	0	0 0	0— 0	

Touchdowns—Osmanski, Luckman, Maniaci, Kavanaugh, Turner, Pool, Nolting, McAfee, Clark 2, Famiglietti.

Points after touchdown—Manders, Snyder 2, Martinovich, Plasman, Stydahar, Maniaci.

Attendance: 36,034.

Players' Shares: Chicago $873.99; Washington $606.25.

1940 BROOKLYN DODGERS
COACH - "Jock" Sutherland
2nd 8-3-0

Bailey, "Bill" - E	Kristufek, Frank - T
Busby, Sherrill - E	Leckonby, Bill - B
Butcher, Wen - B	McFadden, Banks - B
Cafego, George - Q	Manders, "Pug" - B
Cassiano, Dick - B	Mark, Lou - C
Coon, "Ty" - G	Merrill, Walt - T
Francis, "Sam" - B	Parker, 'Ace" - Q
Golemgeske, John - T	Petro, Steve - G
Gussie, Mike - G	Schwartz, Perry - E
Heater, Bill - T	Shetley, Rhoten - Q
Hill, Harold - E	Sivell, Jim - G
Hodges, Herman - E	Svendsen, Earl - C & G
Jocher, Art - G	Titus, Silas - E & C
Kercheval, Ralph - B	Winslow, Bob - E
Kinard, "Bruiser" - T	Young, Walt - E
Kish, Ben - Q	Zadworney, Frank - B
Kober, Matt - G	

1940 CHICAGO BEARS
COACH - George Halas
1st 8-3-0
(Best Washington for title, 73-0)

Artoe, Lee - T	Martinovich, Phil - G
Baisi, Al - G	Masterson, Bernie - Q
Bausch, Frank - C	Mihal, Joe - T
Bray, Ray - G	Musso, George - G
Bussey, Young - Q	Nolting, Ray - B
Chesney, Chet - C	Nowaskey, Bob - E
Clark, Harry - B	Osmanski, Bill - B
Famiglietti, Gary - B	Plasman, Dick - E
Forte, Aldo - G	Pool, Hamp - E
Fortmann, Dan - G	Sherman, "Solly" - Q
Kavanaugh, Ken - E	Siegel, John - E
Kolman, Ed - T	Snyder, Bob - Q
Luckman, Sid - Q	Stydahar, Joe - T
McAfee, George - B	Swisher, Bob - B
McLean, Ray - B	Torrance, John - T
Manders, Jack - B	Turner, "Bulldog" - C
Maniaci, Joe - B	Wilson, George - E
Manske, "Eggs" - E	

1940 CHICAGO CARDINALS
COACH - Jim Conzelman
5th 2-7-2

Aldrich, "Ki" - C	Kellogg, Bob - B
Baker, Conway - G	Klumb, John - E
Beinor, Ed - E	Kuharich, Joe - G
Blazine, Tony - T	McCullough, Hugh - B
Busler, Ray - T	Madden, Lloyd - B
Chisick, Andy - C	Murphy, Bill - G
Christenson, Marty - B	Parker, "Buddy" - Q
Clark, Beryl - B	Pate, Rupert - G
Coppage, Al - E	Popovich, Milt - B
Davis, Bill - T	Ranspot, Keith - E
Dewell, Bill - E	Sabados, Andy - G
Elkins, Ev - B	Schneidman, Herman - Q
German, Jim - B	Shirk, John - E
Goldberg, "Biggie" - B	Tinsley, Gaynell - E
Hall, John - B	Tonelli, Mario - B
Huffman, Frank - G	White, "Tarzan" - G
Ivy, "Pop" - E	Williams, Rex - C
Johnson, Albert - Q	Wood, Bob - T
Johnson, Ray - B	Zontini, Lou - B

1940 CLEVELAND RAMS
COACH - "Dutch" Clark
4th 4-6-1

Adams, Chet - T	Livingston, Ted - T
Anderson, Stan - E & T	McDonough, Paul - E
Benton, Jim - E	McGarry, "Barney" - G
Berry, Connie Mack - E	Magnani, Dante - B
Clay, Boyd - T	Matheson, Riley - G
Conkright, Bill - C	Murphy, Harvey - E
Cordill, Ollie - B	Nix, John - B
Crowder, Earl - Q	Olson, Glen - B
Drake, John - B	Patt, Maurey - E
Dunstan, Elwyn - T	Ragazzo, Phil - G
Gehrke, Fred - B	Rockwell, Henry - C & G
Gillette, Jim - B	Rodak, Mike - E & B
Goolsby, Jim - C	Shirey, Fred - T
Gudauskas, Pete - G	Slovak, Marty - B
Hall, Parker - B	Smith, Gaylon - Q
Haman, John - C	Spadaccini, Vic - Q
Heineman, Ken - B	Stevenson, Ralph - G
Janiak, Len - B	Wilson, John - E
Kinek, Mike - E	

1940 DETROIT LIONS
COACH - "Potsy" Clark
3rd 5-5-1

Callihan, Bill - B	Price, "Cotton" - Q
Calvelli, Tony - C	Radovich, Bill - G
Cardwell, Lloyd - B	Rogers, Bill - T
Crabtree, Clem - T	Rouse, Stillman - E
Diehl, Dave - E	Ryan, Kent - B
Feldhaus, Bill - G	Shepherd, Bill - Q
Fisk, Bill - E	Sloan, Dwight - Q
Furst, Tony - T	Smith, Harry - T
Hackenbruck, John - T	Speelman, Harry - G
Hanneman, Charles - E	Thomas, Cal - G
Johnson, John - T	Tsoutsouvas, John - C
McDonald, Les - E	Vanzo, Fred - B
Maronic, Steve - T	Weiss, Howie - B
Moore, Paul - B	White, "Whizzer" - Q
Morlock, John - B	Wiethe, John - G
Morris, Glen - B	Winslow, Bob - E
Morse, Ray - E	Wojciechowicz, Alex - C

1940 GREEN BAY PACKERS
COACH - "Curly" Lambeau
2nd 6-4-1

Adkins, Bob - E & B	Balaz, Frank - B

Brock, Charley - C
Brock, Lou - B
Buhler, Larry - Q
Craig, Larry - Q
Disend, Leo - T
Engebretsen, Paul - G
Evans, Dick - E
Feathers, Beattie - B
Gantenbein, Milt - E
Goldenberg, "Buckets" - G
Greenfield, Tom - C
Herber, Arnie - B
Hinkle, Clark - B
Hutson, Don - E
Isbell, Cecil - Q
Jacunski, Harry - E
Jankowski, Ed - B
Johnson, Howie - G

Kell, Paul - T
Laws, Joe - B
Lee, Bill - T
Letlow, Russ - G
Midler, Lou - G
Mulleneaux, Carl - E
Ray, "Baby" - T
Riddick, Ray - E
Schultz, Charles - T
Seeman, George - E
Seibold, Champ - T
Shirey, Fred - T
Svendsen, George - C
Tinsley, Pete - G
Uram, Andy - B
Van Every, Hal - B
Weisgerber, Dick - B
Zarnas, "Gus" - G

Patterson, Bill - Q
Pavkov, Stonko - G
Perko, John - G
Pirro, Rocco - G & B
Platukis, George - E
Sanders, John - G
Schmidt, John - C

Sortet, Bill - E
Sullivan, Frank - C
Thompson, "Tommy" - Q
Tomasetti, Lou - B
Woudenberg, John - T
Yurchey, John - B

1940 WASHINGTON REDSKINS
COACH - Ray Flaherty
1st 9-2-0
(Lost to Chicago Bears for
title, 73-0)

Andrako, Steve - C
Barber, Jim - T
Baugh, Sam - Q
Carroll, Vic - T & C
Edwards, "Turk" - T
Farkas, Andy - B
Farman, Dick - G
Filchock, Frank - Q
Fisher, Bob - T
Hare, Ray - B
Hoffman, Bob - B
Johnston, Jim - B
Justice, Ed - B
Krause, Max - B
McChesney, Bob - E
Malone, Charley - E
Masterson, Bob - E

Meade, Jim - B
Millner, Wayne - E
Moore, Wilbur - B
Morgan, Boyd - B
Parks, Ed - C
Pinckert, Ernie - B
Russell, Torrance - T
Sanford, Haywood - E
Seymour, Bob - B
Shugart, Clyde - G
Slivinski, Steve - G
Stralka, Clem - G
Titchenal, Bob - C & E
Todd, Dick - B
Wilkin, Willie - T
Young, Bill - T
Zimmerman, Leroy - Q

1940 NEW YORK GIANTS
COACH - Steve Owen
3rd 6-4-1

Barnum, Len - Q
Cole, Pete - G
Cope, Frank - T
Cuff, Ward - B
Dell Isola, John - G
Dennerlein, Gerald - T
Duggan, Gil - T
Eakin, Kay - B
Edwards, Bill - G
Falaschi, Nello - Q
Gelatka, Charles - E
Goldsmith, Wen - C
Harrison, Max - E
Hein, Mel - C
Hinkle, Jack - Q
Howell, Jim Lee - E
Kline, Harry - E
Lansdell, Granville - B

Leemans, "Tuffy" - B
Lunday, Ken - G & C
McGee, Ed - T
McLaughry, John - B
Mellus, John - T
Miller, Ed - Q
Moore, Ken - G
Nielson, Walter - B
Oldershaw, Doug - G
Owen, Al - B
Perdue, Willard - E
Poole, Jim - E
Principe, Dom - B
Shaffer, Leland - Q
Soar, "Hank" - B
Tomaselli, Carl - E
Tuttle, Orville - G
Widseth, Ed - T

1940 BOSTON BEARS (AFL)
COACH - Eddie Casey
3rd 5-4-1

Ananis, Vito - B
Behan, Fee - E
Cory, Tom - E
Donnell, Gerry - B
Fisher, Thel - B
Holstrom, Bob - B
Kaplanoff, Karl - T
Karpus, Andy - B
Kohler, Morris - B
Lane, Les - T
Lindon, Luther - T
Marino, Vic - G
Mason, Joel - E

Mastriola, Fred - G
Nash, Tom - E
Negri, "Red" - G
Obeck, Vic - T
Padgen, Nick - C
Patrick, Frank - B
Ranspot, Keith - E
Ratica, Joe - C
Shipla, Sterling - G
Slotnick, Leo - B
Wheeler, Ernie - B
Yablonski, Joe - B

1940 PHILADELPHIA EAGLES
COACH - Bert Bell
5th 1-10-0

Arnold, Jay - B
Bassi, Dick - G
Bukant, Joe - B
Carter, Joe - E
Cherundolo, Chuck - C
Cole, John - B
Dow, Elwood - Q
Emmons, Franklin - B
George, Ray - T
Ginney, Jerry - G
Hackney, Elmer - B
Harper, Maury - C
Hughes, Bill - G
Kolberg, Elmer - E & B
Looney, Don - E

McDonald, Les - E
Murray, Francis - B
Newton, Charles - B
O'Brien, Davey - Q
Ragazzo, Phil - T
Ramsay, Herschel - E
Riffle, Dick - B
Schmitt, Ted - G
Schultz, Eberle - G
Somers, George - T
Thompson, Russ - T
Trost, Milt - T
Watkins, Forrest - Q
Wendlick, Joe - E
Woltman, Clem - T

1940 BUFFALO INDIANS (AFL)
COACH - "Red" Sieck
5th 2-8-0

Banas, Steve - Q
Bogacki, Henry - C
Bukovich, Dan - G
Drobnitch, Alex - G
Farris, John - B
Fedorchak, John - Q
Gilbert, Steve - E
Gottlieb, Art - B
Hrycyszyn, Steve - Q & G
Karpowich, Ed - T
Koepsell, Bill - B
Littlefield, Carl - B
McGrath, Maurey - T

Mullin, - B
Nesmith, Ole - B
Padow, Walt - G
Peace, Larry - B
Pegg, Hal - C
Shellogg, Alec - T
Sieck, "Red" - G
Siminski, Ed - E
Snell, Dan - E
Stylianos, John - B
Szur, Joe - B
Wile, Russ - E

1940 PITTSBURGH STEELERS
COACH - Walt Kiesling
4th 2-7-2

Boyd, Sam - E
Bruder, "Hank" - Q
Brumbaugh, Boyd - B
Bykowski, Frank - G
Campbell, Don - T
Condit, Merlin - B
Doyle, Ted - T
Fisher, Ev - B
Goff, Clark - T
Grabinski, Thad - C & G

Ivy, "Pop" - E
Johnston, Chet - B
Kichefski, Walt - E
Kiick, George - B
Klumb, John - E
McDonough, Coley - Q
Maras, Joe - T & C
Nery, Carl - G
Niccolai, Armand - T
Noppenberg, John - Q & E

1940 CINCINNATI BENGALS (AFL)
COACH - Dana King
6th 1-7-0

Balestreri, John - E
Bernard, Dave - B
Blackaby, Inman - B
Bohrer, Bob - C

Carnes, Wilce - B
Gerdes, Bill - T
Leroy, Gene - B
McRaven, Bill - B

Marotti, Lou - G
Mergenthal, Art - T
Metzger, Charles - B
Monday, Oscar - G
Popov, John - B
Popp, Tony - E

Rice, - C
Rogers, John - B
Schmerge, Al - G
Shelton, Al - E
Smith, Inwood - G
Wakeman, Argyle - E

1940 COLUMBUS BULLIES (AFL)
COACH - Phil Bucklew
1st 8-1-1

Aleskus, Joe - C
Alfonse, Jules - Q
Arnold, Jay - B
Balestreri, John - E
Bell, Kay - T
Bogden, Pete - E
Bucklew, Phil - E
Buckley, Russ - B
Cory, Tom - E
Cox, - E
Davis, Bob - B & E
Donnell, Jerry - B
Johnson, Ray - B
Karcher, Jim - T
Kelley, Vince - G
Kohler, Morrie - B

LeBay, John - B
Lindon, Luther - T
Monday, Oscar - G
Mulleneaux, Lee - C
Myers, Glenn - E
Neihaus, Ralph - T
O'Keefe, Declan - T
Peterson, Nelson - B
Pollack, Milt - T
Reupke, Gordon - B
Sigillo, Dom - T
West, Ed - E
Williams, Joe - B
Wunderlich, Fred - Q
Zimmerman, Joe - G

1940 MILWAUKEE CHIEFS (AFL)
COACH - "Tiny" Cahoon
2nd 7-2-0

Akin, Len - G
Barnes, Sherm - E
Beauregard, Dick - B
Beckett, Warren - B
Behan, Fee - E
Blaha, Art - B
Bykowski, Frank - G
Carson, Howie - B
Cole, Ray - B
Doehring, John - B
Eckl, Bob - T
Gould, George - B
Hickey, Bill - B
Hoel, Bob - T
Holstrom, Bob - B
Horkey, Roland - B
Humphrey, Paul - C
Karamatic, George - B

Larsen, Merle - G
Lenich, Bill - C
Maltsch, John - B
Merlin, Ed - G
Murray, Joe - E
Myre, Charles - B
Novakofski, Al - B
Ohlgren, Earl - E
Pederson, Win - T
Perino, Mike - T
Shipla, Sterling - G
Strong, Dave - B
Temple, Bob - E
Vaessen, Matt - G
West, John - C
Wilson, John - B
Yatchet, Vin - B

1940 NEW YORK YANKS (AFL)
COACH - Jack McBride
4th 4-5-0

Albanese, Vin - B
Berry, Connie Mack - E
Bohlman, Frank - T
Britt, Ed - B
DeNisco, Jerry - C & T
Dokas, Bill - E & T
Elkins, Lee - E
Everly, - T
Farris, John - B
Fischer, Les - C
Goodman, Bob - G
Gustafson, Harlan - E
Harte, Charles - G
Hoctor, Joe - B
Hutchinson, Bill - B
Ickes, Lloyd - B

Kilbourne, Warren - T
Kirschner, Herb - G
Lenc, George - E
McGee, Ed - T
Manrodt, Spence - G
Migdal, Joe - B
Novotny, Harry - G
Reese, "Hank" - C
Seabury, George - T
Shamis, Tony - T
Simonovich, - T
Starr, Don - B
Strosser, Walt - B
Urban, John - B
Williams, Rex - C

1941

WESTERN DIVISION

Chicago Bears	10	1	0	.909
Green Bay	10	1	0	.909
Detroit	4	6	1	.400
Chicago Cardinals	3	7	1	.300
Cleveland	2	9	0	.182

EASTERN DIVISION

New York	8	3	0	.727
Brooklyn	7	4	0	.636
Washington	6	5	0	.545
Philadelphia	2	8	1	.200
Pittsburgh	1	9	1	.100

AMERICAN FOOTBALL LEAGUE (1941)

Columbus	5	1	2	.833
New York	5	2	1	.714
Milwaukee	4	3	1	.591
Buffalo	2	6	0	.250
Cincinnati	1	5	2	.167

TITLE: Chicago Bears beat New York, 37-9, for championship at Chicago, Dec. 21. Bears had defeated Green Bay, 33-14, in division tie playoff.

LEADERS: Individual leaders for the season: Scoring—Don Hutson (Green Bay), 95; Rushing—Clarence "Pug" Manders (Brooklyn), 486 yds.; Passing—Cecil Isbell (Green Bay); Pass Receiving—Don Hutson (Green Bay), 58; Field Goals—Clark Hinkle (Green Bay), 6; Punting—Sam Baugh (Washington), 48.7 yds.; Interceptions—Marshall Goldberg (Chi-Cards), 7.

FIRST DRAFT: Tom Harmon (Michigan)—Back—by Philadelphia.

COACHES: Bill Edwards replaced George "Potsy" Clark as head coach at Detroit, replaced by John Karcis after 3 games; "Greasy" Neale replaced Bert Bell at Philadelphia; Bert Bell replaced Walt Kiesling at Pittsburgh, resigned after second game, replaced by Aldo Donelli, who gave way to Walt Kiesling after 7 games.

NOTES: Elmer Layden named commissioner for 5 years, replacing president Carl L. Storck.

Philadelphia and Pittsburgh swapped franchises.

Cleveland franchise sold by Homer Marshman to Dan Reeves and Fred Levy, Jr.

The Columbus Bullies won the American Football League title with a 5-1-2 record.

The NFL sent 638 men into service for World War II.

TITLE GAME

Pearl Harbor Day was only two weeks past when they met for the championship, a factor which kept the attendance down to ridiculous figures as this great Bear team prepared to break up for the duration. Young Bussey, Bear quarterback, would be killed in action before the war was over. And Jack Lummus, New York, would die on Iwo Jima.

Bob Snyder put the Bears in front with a 14-yard field goal in the first quarter, but the Giants led after the whistle ended the period, because Tuffy Leemans had sent a 4-yard pass to George Franck, who galloped 27 more yards for the touchdown. Johnny Siegal blocked Ward Cuff's conversion attempt.

Snyder continued the long-range bombardment in the second quarter, booting a field goal from the 39 and another from the 37. There was no other scoring and the Bears led 9–6 at the half.

Ward Cuff kicked a three-pointer from the 17 to tie the score early in the third period but that was the end of the Giants. Norm Standlee smashed through right tackle for 2 yards and a TD, Snyder kicking the extra, then Standlee hit for another from 7 yards out and Joe Maniaci converted. This made it 23–9 as the fourth period opened. George McAfee then hit the line for 5 yards and another marker with Lee Artoe kicking the conversion successfully. Ken Kavanaugh added the final TD by scooping up a fumbled lateral pass from Hank Soar that was intended for Andy Marefos and racing 42 yards for the touchdown. This time Ray McLean drop-kicked the conversion and it was 37–9.

Chicago Bears	3	6	14	14—37
New York Giants	6	0	3	0— 9

Touchdowns—Franck, Standlee, McAfee, Kavanaugh.
Points after touchdown—Snyder, Maniaci, Artoe, McLean.
Field Goals—Cuff, Snyder 3.

Attendance: 13,341.
Players Shares: Chicago $430.94; New York $288.70.

1941 BROOKLYN DODGERS
COACH - "Jock" Sutherland
2nd 7-4-0

Alfson, Warren - G	Leckonby, Bill - B
Bailey, Ed - E	McAdams, Dean - B
Butcher, Wen - Q	Manders, "Pug" - B
Condit, Merlyn - B	Merrill, Walt - T
Cotton, Russ - B	Parker, "Ace" - Q
Dobrus, Pete - T	Parker, Dave - E
Frick, Ray - C	Peace, Larry - B
Fronczek, Andy - T	Petro, Steve - G
Hodges, Herman - E	Robertson, Tom - C
Jones, Thurman - B	Rucinski, Ed - E
Jurich, Mike - T	Schwartz, Perry - E
Kinard, "Bruiser" - T	Shetley, Rhoten - Q
Kinard, George - G	Sivell, Jim - G
Kish, Ben - Q	Stasica, Leo - B
Koons, Joe - C	Svendsen, Earl - C
Kracum, George - B	Titus, Silas - E & C
Kristufek, Frank - T	Wemple, Don - E

1941 CHICAGO BEARS
COACH - George Halas
1st 10-1-0
(Beat New York for title, 37-9 after beating Green Bay in playoff, 33-14)

Artoe, Lee - T	Maniaci, Joe - B
Baisi, Al - G	Matuza, Al - C
Bray, Ray - G	Mihal, Joe - T
Bussey, Young - Q	Musso, George - G
Clark, Harry - B	Nolting, Ray - B
Famiglietti, Gary - B	Nowaskey, Bob - E
Federovich, John - T	Osmanski, Bill - B
Forte, Aldo - G	Plasman, Dick - E
Fortmann, Dan - G	Pool, Hamp - E
Gallarneau, Hugh - B	Siegel, John - E
Hughes, Bill - C	Snyder, Bob - Q
Kavanaugh, Ken - E	Standlee, Norm - B
Kolman, Ed - T	Stydahar, Joe - T
Lahar, Hal - G	Swisher, Bob - B
Luckman, Sid - Q	Turner, "Bulldog" - C
McAfee, George - B	Wilson, George - E
McLean, Ray - B	

1941 CHICAGO CARDINALS
COACH - Jim Conzelman
4th 3-7-1

Apolskis, Ray - G & C	Johnson, Albert - Q
Babartsky, Al - T	Kuharich, Joe - G
Baker, Conway - G	Kuzman, John - T
Balaz, Frank - B	Lokanc, Joe - G
Beinor, Ed - T	McCullough, Hugh - B
Busler, Ray - T	Mallouf, Ray - Q
Chisick, Andy - C	Martin, John - B
Clement, John - B	Monfort, Avery - B
Coppage, Al - E	Morrow, Bob - B
Daddio, Bill - E	Murphy, Bill - G
Davis, Bill - T	Parker, "Buddy" - Q
Dewell, Bill - E	Popovich, Milt - B & G
Evans, Dick - E	Rankin, Walt - B
Goldberg, "Biggie" - B	Shook, Fred - C
Hall, John - B	Vanzo, Fred - Q
Higgins, John - G	White, "Tarzan" - G
Huffman, Frank - G	Zontini, Lou - B
Ivy, "Pop" - E	

1941 CLEVELAND RAMS
COACH - "Dutch" Clark
5th 2-9-0

Adams, Chet - T	Armstrong, Graham - T
Andersen, Stan - E	Clay, Boyd - T

Sid Luckman, Chicago Bear QB, rips off some yardage up the middle in the title game with the New York Giants in 1941. Bears won, 37-9. (Acme Newspicture.)

Conkright, Bill - C	Magnani, Dante - B	Buccianeri, Amadeo - G	Lee, Bill - T
Davis, "Corby" - Q	Maher, Frank - B	Buhler, Larry - Q	Letlow, Russ - G
Drake, John - B	Matheson, Riley - G	Canadeo, Tony - B	Lyman, Del - T
Dunstan, Elwyn - T	Morris, George - B	Craig, Larry - Q	McLaughlin, Lee - G
Gallovich, Tony - B	Mucha, Rudy - Q & G	Engebretsen, Paul - G	Mulleneaux, Carl - E
Goodnight, Owen - B	Patt, Maurey - E	Frutig, Ed - E	Pannell, Ernie - T
Gregory, John - G	Prochaska, Ray - E	Goldenberg, "Buckets" - G	Paskvan, George - B
Hall, Parker - B	Reith, Bill - C	Greenfield, Tom - C	Ray, "Baby" - T
Haman, John - C	Rockwell, Henry - C & G	Hinkle, Clark - B	Riddick, Ray - E
Hanneman, Charles - E	Seabright, Charles - Q	Hutson, Don - E	Rohrig, Herman - B
Hershey, Kirk - E	Shirey, Fred - T	Isbell, Cecil - Q	Schultz, Charles - T
Hickey, "Red" - E	Simington, Milt - G	Jacunski, Harry - E	Svendsen, George - C
Janiak, Len - B	Slovak, Marty - B	Jankowski, Ed - B	Tinsley, Pete - G
Kostiuk, Mike - G	Smith, Gaylon - B	Johnson, Howie - G	Uram, Andy - B
Lyman, Del - T	Thorpe, Wilfred - G	Johnson, Bill - E	Urban, Alex - E
McDonough, Paul - E	Wilson, Gordon - G	Kuusisto, Bill - G	Van Every, Hal - B
McGarry, Bernie - G	Wilson, John - E	Laws, Joe - B	

1941 DETROIT LIONS
COACH - Bill Edwards
3rd 4-6-1

Andersen, Stan - E & T	Moore, Paul - Q
Batinski, Stan - G	Nelson, Bob - C & T
Belichick, Steve - B	Noppenberg, John - B
Booth, Dick - B	Obee, Dunc - C
Britt, Maurey - E	Parsons, Lloyd - B
Callihan, Bill - Q	Pavelec, Ted - G
Cardwell, Lloyd - B	Piepul, Milt - B
Crabtree, Clem - T	Price, Charley - Q
Fisk, Bill - E	Radovich, Bill - G
Furst, Tony - T	Schibanoff, Alex - T
Hanneman, Charles - E	Szakash, Paul - E & B
Hopp, Harry - Q	Tomasetti, Lou - B
Jefferson, Bill - B	Tripson, John - T
Jett, John - E	Uremovich, Emil - T
Lio, Augie - G	Vanzo, Fred - Q
Logan, Andy - T	White, "Whizzer" - B
Mathews, Ned - B	Wiethe, John - G
Mattiford, John - G	Wojciechowicz, Alex - C

1941 GREEN BAY PACKERS
COACH - "Curly" Lambeau
1st 10-1-0
(Lost playoff to Chicago Bears, 33-14)

Adkins, Bob - B & E	Brock, Charles - C
Balaz, Frank - B	Brock, Lou - Q

1941 NEW YORK GIANTS
COACH - Steve Owen
1st 8-3-0
(Lost title to Chicago Bears, 37-9)

Blazine, Tony - T	McClain, Clint - B
Cope, Frank - T	Marefos, Andy - B
Cuff, Ward - B	Mellus, John - T
Danowski, Ed - Q	Oldershaw, Doug - G
DeFilippo, Lou - C	Pederson, Win - T
Dennery, Vince - E	Poole, Jim - E
Eakin, Kay - B	Principe, Dom - B
Edwards, Bill - G	Pugh, Marion - Q
Eshmont, Len - B	Reagen, Frank - B
Falaschi, Nello - Q	Shaffer, Leland - Q
Franck, George - B	Soar, "Hank" - B
Gladchuck, Chet - C	Sohn, Ben - T
Hein, Mel - C	Tuttle, Orville - G
Horne, Dick - E	Vosberg, Don - E
Howell, Jim Lee - E	Walls, Will - E
Leemans, "Tuffy" - B	Yeager, Howard - B
Lummus, John - E	Younce, Len - G
Lunday, Ken - G	

1941 PHILADELPHIA EAGLES
COACH - "Greasey" Neale
4th 2-8-1

Banta, "Jack" - B	Bartholomew, Sam - B
Barnum, Len - Q	Basca, Mike - B

Clarke Hinkle, Packer fullback, shows the determination which made him one of the all-time greats as he carries the ball for a 12-yard gain against the Chicago Bears in Wrigley Field on December 14, 1941. Hampton Poole, Bear end, comes in to check Hinkle's rush. The Bears won 33-14.

Bausch, Frank - C
Bjorklund, Bob - C
Cabrelli, Larry - E
Castiglia, Jim - B
Cemore, Tony - G
Conti, Enio - G
DeSantis, Dan - B
DiFilippo, Dave - G
Eibner, John - T
Feibish, Bernie - C
Ferrante, Jack - E
Fox, Terry - B
Frank, Joe - T
Fritz, Ralph - G
Gerber, Elwood - G
Ghecas, Lou - B
Gloden, Fred - B
Graham, Lyle - C

Harrison, Gran - E
Hershey, Kirk - E
Humbert, Dick - E
Kreiger, Bob - E
Landsberg, Mort - B
McAfee, Wes - B
Piro, Henry - E
Ragazzo, Phil - T
Sears, Vic - T
Shonk, John - E
Stasica, Leo - B
Sturgeon, Cecil - T
Suffridge, Bob - G
Thompson, "Tommy" - Q
Tomasetti, Lou - B
Watkins, Foster - B
West, Hodges - T

Kolberg, Elmer - E
Looney, Don - E
McDonough, Coley - Q
Maher, Frank - B
Nery, Carl - G
Niccolai, Armand - T
Noppenberg, John – B
Patrick, John - Q
Pirro, Rocco - Q & G
Platukas, George - E

Riffle, Dick - B
Sanders, Joe - G
Schiechl, John - C
Shultz, Elbie - G
Somers, George - T
Starrett, Ben - B
Wendlick, Joe - E
Williams, Don - G
Woudenberg, John - T
Zopetti, Frank - B

1941 WASHINGTON REDSKINS
COACH - Ray Flaherty
3rd 6-5-0

Aguirre, Joe - E
Aldrich, "Ki" - C
Banta, "Jack" - B
Barber, Jim - T
Baugh, Sam - Q
Beinor, Ed - T
Carroll, Vic - T
Cifers, Ed - E
Clair, Frank - E
Davis, Fred - T
Dow, Ken - B
Farkas, Andy - B
Farman, Dick - G
Filchock, Frank - Q
Gentry, Lee - B
Hare, Cecil - B
Hare, Ray - B
Hoffman, Bob - B

Justice, Ed - B & E
Krueger, Al - E & B
McChesney, Bob - E
Masterson, Bob - E
Millner, Wayne - E
Moore, Wilbur - B
Seymour, Bob - B
Shugart, Clyde - G
Slivinski, Steve - G
Smith, George - C
Stralka, Clem - G
Stuart, Jim - T
Titchenal, Bob - E & C
Todd, Dick - B
Wilkin, Willie - T
Young, Bill - T
Zimmerman, Leroy - Q

1941 PITTSBURGH STEELERS
COACHES - Bert Bell, Aldo
Donelli, & Walt Kiesling
5th 1-9-1

Arnold, Jay - Q
Bassi, Dick - G
Brumbaugh, Boyd - B
Cherundulo, Chuck - C
Coomer, Joe - T
Dodson, Les - B
Dolly, Dick - E
Donelli, Allan - B

Doyle, Ted - T
Hackney, Elmer - B
Harper, Maury - C
Hickey, "Red" - E
Hoague, Joe - B
Jones, Art - B
Kahler, Royal - T
Kichefski, Walt - E

1941 BUFFALO TIGERS (AFL)
COACH - "Tiny" Engebretsen
4th 2-6-0

Banas, Steve - Q
Barnes, Sherm - E
Blodzinski, Ed - G
Bogacki, Henry - C
Dahl, Levant - E
Dolan, John - E
Elliott, Ralph - T
Holstrom, Bob - Q
Hrycyszyn, Steve - Q
Hughes, Ed - E
Karpus, Andy - B
Losey, Leon - B
Luebcke, Henry - T
McLain, Mal - B
Mastriola, Fred - G
Morabito, Dan - T
Naughton, Clem - E
Osborne, Merle - B
Ratica, Joe - C
Russell, Roy - B & E
Shellogg, Alec - T
Tolliver, Lou - B
Toth, Nick - G
Wheeler, Ernie - B
Yurkonis, Larry - B

1941 NEW YORK AMERICANS (AFL)
COACH - Jack McBride
2nd 5-2-1

Apolskis, Chuck - E & C
Armstrong, Charles - B
Byrd, Tom - G
Drahos, Nick - T
Drobnitch, Alex - G
Gallagher, Bill - B
Grillo, Al - T
Harmon, Tom - B
Harris, Fred - T
Hinkle, John - B
Hutchinson, Bill - B
Karpus, Andy - B
Keahey, Eulis - T
Kimbrough, John - B
Kohler, Morrie - B
Kopcha, Mike - C
Mason, Joel - E
Martinovich, Phil - G & B
Negri, "Red" - G
Orf, Roland - E
Owen, Al - B
Pate, Rupert - G & B
Ranspot, Keith - E
Saecker, Well - E
Sieck, "Red" - G

1941 CINCINNATI BENGALS (AFL)
COACH - Dana King
5th 1-5-2

Aloia, Henry - B
Benson, Leo - C
Bernard, Dave - Q
Eckl, Bob - T
Garvey, Jim - T
Gerdes, Bill - T
Gudauskas, Pete - G
Kopp, Bill - G
Koprowski, John - B
Kruse, Joe - E
Lass, Dick - B
Lee, Cobbie - B
McGannon, Bill - B
Malesevich, Bronko - B
Millnovich, Joe - B
Morris, Herman - G
Petry, Basil - C
Popov, John - B
Rebol, Ray - T
Rogers, John - B & E
Shelton, Al - E
Slagle, Charles - G
Tornquist, Gene - B
West, Ed - E

1941 COLUMBUS BULLIES (AFL)
COACH - Phil Bucklew
1st 5-1-2

Aleskus, Joe - C
Alfonse, Jules - Q
Becker, Wayland - E
Bell, Kay - T
Bucklew, Phil - E
Buckley, Russ - B
Ciccone, Bill - G
Costell, Carl - E
Davis, Bob - B
Emerson, Ralph - G
Keriosotis, Nick - G
LeBay, John - Q
Livingston, Ted - T
McGannon, Bill - B
Matheny, Bill - B
Mulleneaux, Lee - C
Neihaus, Ralph - T
O'Keefe, Dec - T
Olson, Glenn - B
Padgen, Nick - C
Peterson, Nelson - B
Phillips, Bill - B
Sigillo, Dom - T
Spadaccini, Vic - B
Strausbaugh, Jim - B
Thom, Len - E
Wilson, Gordon - G
Zimmerman, Joe - T & G

1941 MILWAUKEE CHIEFS (AFL)
COACH - "Tiny" Cahoon
3rd 4-3-1

Akin, Len - G
Berry, Connie Mack - E
Bohlman, Fran - T
Bykowski, Frank - G
Carson, Howie - Q
Eckl, Bob - T
Elliott, Ralph - T
Ellis, Vernon - G
Haley, Don - G
Hickey, Bill - B
Hoel, Bob - T
Hughes, Ed - E
Humphrey, Paul - C
Larsen, Merle - G
Lass, Dick - B
Lenich, Bill - C
McClain, Mal - B
Malesevich, Bronko - Q
Maltsch, John - B
Manders, Phil - Q
Merka, Milt - B
Mesec, "Iggy" - B
Novakofski, Al - B
Ohlgren, Earl - E
Patrick, Frank - B
Perkins, Don - B
Pfeffer, Howie - B
Pinczak, John - G
Splinter, Fran - B & E
Stephens, Bob - B & E
Temple, Bob - E
Thompson, Gil - E
Trebbin, John - B
Trost, Milt - T
Weiss, Howie - B

1942

EASTERN DIVISION

Washington	10	1	0	.909
Pittsburgh	7	4	0	.636
New York	5	5	1	.500
Brooklyn	3	8	0	.273
Philadelphia	2	9	0	.182

WESTERN DIVISION

Chicago Bears	11	0	0	1.000
Green Bay	8	2	1	.800
Cleveland	5	6	0	.455
Chicago Cardinals	3	8	0	.273
Detroit	0	11	0	.000

TITLE: Washington beat the Chicago Bears, 14-6, for the championship at Washington, Dec. 13. The Bears had won eleven, lost none during the season.

LEADERS: Individual leaders for the season: Scoring—Don Hutson (Green Bay), 138, a record which would be tops until Hornung's 176 in 1960; Rushing—Bill Dudley (Pittsburgh), 696 yds.; Passing—Cecil Isbell (Green Bay); Pass Receiving—Don Hutson (Green Bay), 74 with record 17 TDs; Field Goals—Bill Daddio (Chi-Cards), 5; Punting—Sam Baugh (Washington), 46.6 yds.; Interceptions—"Bulldog" Turner (Chi-Bears), 8.

FIRST DRAFT: Bill Dudley (Virginia)—Back—by Pittsburgh.

COACHES: Mike Getto replaced "Jock" Sutherland as head coach at Brooklyn; "Hunk" Anderson and Luke Johnsos, as co-coaches, replaced George Halas at Chicago Bears; John Karcis replaced Bill Edwards after third game at Detroit.

NOTES: Cecil Isbell, Green Bay, passed 4 inches (TD) to Don Hutson against Cleveland, Oct. 18.

Don Hutson caught 17 touchdown passes, new record.

NFL raised $680,347 for War Relief charities.

TITLE GAME

The two top passers of the era were at each other's throats in this championship match, for Sam Baugh and Sid Luckman had led their respective teams through their best seasonal records of history. Baugh at this time was still playing halfback in a single-wing formation although the Bears had been shooting the T for three seasons.

The first period was scoreless. In the second, Lee Artoe snatched up a fumbled pass from center and scampered 50 yards for a touchdown but missed the conversion. Baugh sent a 25-yard touchdown toss to Wilbur Moore which led to Bob Masterson's successful conversion for a 7–6 lead, and a half-time score of 7–6, Redskins.

In the third period, Andy Farkas, carrying the ball on ten out of twelve plays, drove for 80 yards and a touchdown, the scoring smash starting from the Bears' one-yard line. Masterson again converted to make it 14–6; the final period was scoreless.

Washington Redskins	0	7	7	0—14
Chicago Bears	0	6	0	0—6

Touchdowns—Artoe, Moore, Farkas. Points after touchdown—Masterson 2.

Attendance: 36,006.

Players' Shares: Washington $965.89; Chicago $637.56.

1942 BROOKLYN DODGERS
COACH - Mike Getto
4th 3-8-0

Butcher, Wen - Q
Condit, Merlyn - B
Courtney, Gerry - B
Deremer, Art - C
Eliason, Don - E
Fedora, Walt - B
Gifford, Bob - B
Hodges, Herman - E
Jefferson, Bill - B
Jeffries, Bob - G
Jocher, Art - G
Jones, Thurman - B
Jurich, Mike - T
Kapitansky, Bernie - G
Keahey, Eulis - T
Kinard, "Bruiser" - T
Kinard, George - G
McAdams, Dean - B
McCullough, Harold - B
Manders, "Pug" - B
Mecham, Curt - B
Merrill, Walt - T
Nixon, Mike - B
Pierce, Don - C

Robertson, Bob - B
Robertson, Tom - C
Rucinski, Ed - E
Schwartz, Perry - E
Shetley, Rhoten - Q
Sivell, Jim - G
Svendsen, Earl - G & C
Titus, Silas - E & C
Tofil, Joe - E & B
Vetter, John - B
Weiner, Bernie - G

1942 CHICAGO BEARS
COACH - George Halas
1st 11-0-0
(Lost title to Washington, 14-6)

Akin, Len - G
Artoe, Lee - T
Berry, Connie Mack - E
Bray, Ray - G
Clark, Harry - B
Clarkson, Stu - C
Drulis, Chuck - G
Famiglietti, Gary - B
Fortmann, Dan - G
Gallarneau, Hugh - B
Geyer, Bill - B
Hempel, Bill - T
Hoptowit, Al - T
Keriosotis, Nick - G
Kissell, Adolph - B
Kolman, Ed - T
Luckman, Sid - Q

McLean, Ray - B
Matuza, Al - C
Maznicki, Frank - B
Morris, Frank - B
Musso, George - G
Nolting, Ray - B
Nowaskey, Bob - E
O'Rourke, Charles - Q
Osmanski, Bill - B
Petty, John - B
Pool, Hamp - E
Siegel, John - E
Stydahar, Joe - T
Turner, "Bulldog" - C
Wager, Clint - E
Wilson, George - E

1942 CHICAGO CARDINALS
COACH - Jim Conzelman
4th 3-8-0

Allton, Joe - T
Apolskis, Ray - C & G
Babartsky, Al - T
Baker, Conway - T
Banonis, Vince - C
Bertagnolli, Libero - G
Bohlman, Frank - G
Bukant, Joe - B
Bulger, Chet - T
Cheatham, Lloyd - Q
Ciccone, Ben - C
Coppage, Al - E
Daddio, Bill - E
Duggan, Gil - T
Ebli, Ray - E
Evans, Dick - E

Fife, Ralph - G
Goldberg, "Biggie" - B
Ivy, "Pop" - E
Knolla, John - B
Lach, Steve - B
Maddock, Bob - G
Martin, John - B
Morrow, Bob - B
Nagel, Ross - T
Olson, Carl - T
Parker, "Buddy" - Q
Popovich, Milt - B
Schwenk, Wilson - Q
Seibold, Champ - T
Wheeler, Ernie - B
Wilson, Gordon - G

1942 CLEVELAND RAMS
COACH - "Dutch" Clark
3rd 5-6-0

Adams, Chet - T
Benton, Jim - E
Boone, Bob - B
Brahm, Larry - G
Clay, Boyd - T
Conkright, Bill - C
Davis, "Corby" - B
Elston, Art - Q
Fawcett, Jake - T
Gibson, Billy Joe - B
Godfrey, Herb - E
Hall, Parker - Q
Hightower, John - E
Jacobs, Jack - B
Janiak, Len - B
Johnson, Don - C
Lazetich, Bill - B
McGarry, "Barney" - G

Magnani, Dante - B
Matheson, Riley - G
Morris, George - B
Pasqua, Joe - T
Patt, Maurey - E
Petchel, John - Q
Platukis, George - E
Plunkett, Warren - Q
Pritchard, "Bosh" - B
Reith, Bill - C
Rockwell, Henry - C & E
Schupbach, O. T. - T
(Played as "Tex" Mooney)
Smith, Gaylon - B
Stuart, Roy - G
Thorpe, Wilfred - G
Wilson, John - E

1942 DETROIT LIONS
COACHES - Bill Edwards &
John Karcis
5th -0-11-0

Arena, Tony - C	Mathews, Ned - B
Banjavic, Emil - B	Pavelec, Ted - G
Behan, Charley - E	Polanski, John - B
Callihan, Bill - Q	Ranspot, Keith - E
Cardwell, Lloyd - B	Sanzotta, Dom - B
Colella, Tom - B	Sartori, Larry - G
Evans, Murray - Q	Schibanoff, Alex - T
Fisk, Bill - E	Schiechl, John - C
Gill, Sloko - G	Scott, Perry - E
Goodmann, Henry - T	Seltzer, Harry - B
Grigonis, Frank - B	Speth, George - T
Hackney, Elmer - B	Stringfellow, Joe - E
Hall, John - B	Szakash, Paul - E & B
Harrison, Gran - E	Uremovich, Emil - T
Hopp, Harry - Q	Wetterlund, Chet - B
Kennedy, Bill - E & G	Wiethe, John - G
Knorr, Larry - E	Wojciechowicz, Alex - C
Lio, Augie - G	Zuzzio, Tony - G

1942 GREEN BAY PACKERS
COACH - "Curly" Lambeau
2nd 8-2-1

Berezney, Paul - T	Kuusisto, Bill - G
Brock, Charley - C	Laws, Joe - B
Brock, Lou - Q	Lee, Bill - T
Canadeo, Tony - B	Letlow, Russ - G
Carter, Joe - E	Mason, Joel - E
Craig, Larry - Q & E	Ohlgren, Earl - E
Croft, "Tiny" - T	Pannell, Ernie - T
Flowers, Bob - C	Ranspot, Keith - E
Fritsch, Ted - B	Ray, "Baby" - T
Goldenberg, "Buckets" - G	Riddick, Ray - E
Hinte, Hale - E	Sample, Charles - B
Hutson, Don - E	Starrett, Ben - B
Ingalls, Bob - C	Stonebraker, John - E
Isbell, Cecil - Q	Tinsley, Pete - G
Jacunski, Harry - E	Uram, Andy - B
Kahler, Bob - B	Van Hull, Fred - G
Kahler, Royal - T	Weisgerber, Dick - Q

1942 NEW YORK GIANTS
COACH - Steve Owen
3rd 5-5-1

Adams, O'Neal - E	Keahey, Eulis - G
Avedisian, Charles - G	Kline, Harry - E
Barrett, Emmett - C	Lascari, John - E
Bell, Kay - T	Lechner, Ed - T
Blozis, Al - T	Leemans, "Tuffy" - B
Buffington, Harry - G	Liebel, Frank - E
Cantor, Leo - B	Lieberum, Don - B
Chickerneo, John - B	Marefos, Andy - B
Cope, Frank - T	Owen, Al - B
Cuff, Ward - B	Principe, Dom - B
Edwards, Bill - G	Sieck, "Red" - G
Hall, Harold - C	Shaffer, Leland - Q
Hapes, Merle - B	Soar, "Hank" - B
Hein, Mel - C	Stenn, Paul - T
Hiemstra, Ed - C	Trocolor, Bob - B
Howell, Jim Lee - E	Walls, Will - E
Hutchinson, Bill - B	

1942 PHILADELPHIA EAGLES
COACH - "Greasey" Neale
5th 2-9-0

Barnum, Len - Q	Conti, Enio - G
Binotti, John - B	Cook, Leon - T
Brennan, Leo - G	Davis, Bob - B
Cabrelli, Larry - E	Donelli, Allan - B
Combs, Bill - E	Eibner, John - T

Erdlitz, Dick - B	Meyer, Fred - E
Frank, Joe - T	Milling, Al - G
Gerber, Elwood - G	Pate, Rupert - G
Graves, Ray - C	Priestly, Bob - E
Hall, Irv - B	Pritchard, "Bosh" - B
Halverson, Bill - T	Sears, Vic - T
Hayden, Ken - C	Smith, John - E
Hrabetin, Frank - T	Stackpool, John - B
Jefferson, Bill - B	Steele, Ernie - B
Johnson, Albert - B	Supulski, Len - E
Kaplan, Bernie - G	Thacker, Al - B
Kasky, Ed - T	Thompson, "Tommy" - Q
Lankas, Jim - B	Tomasetti, Lou - B
Levanitis, Steve - T	Wear, Bob - C
Marchi, Basilio - G	Williams, "Tex" - C
Masters, Bob - B	Williams, Ted - B

1942 PITTSBURGH STEELERS
COACH - Walt Kiesling
2nd 7-4-0

Albrecht, Art - T & C	Mosher, Clure - C
Binotti, John - B	Naioti, John - B
Bova, Tony - E	Niccolai, Armand - T
Brown, Tom - E	Pastin, Frank - G
Cherundolo, Chuck – C	Riffle, Dick - B
Cotton, Russ - Q	Rodak, Mike - B & E & G
Donelli, Allan - B	Sanders, John - G
Doyle, Ted - T	Sandig, Curt - B
Dudley, Bill - B	Schiechl, John - C
Gonda, George - B	Schultz, Elbie - G
Hinte, Hal - E	Simington, Milt - G
Hoague, Joe - B	Sirochman, George - G
Kichefski, Walt - E	Somers, George - T
Lamas, Joe - G	Tomasic, Andy - B
Law, Hubbard - G	Wenzel, Ralph - E
Looney, Don - E	Woudenberg, John - T
Martin, Vernon - Q	

1942 WASHINGTON REDSKINS
COACH - Ray Flaherty
1st 10-1-0
(Beat Chicago Bears for title,
14-6)

Aldrich, "Ki" - C	Malone, Charley - E
Baugh, Sam - Q	Masterson, Bob - E
Beinor, Ed - T	Moore, Wilbur - B
Carroll, Vic - T	Poillon, Dick - B
Cifers, Ed - E	Seymour, Bob - B
Davis, Fred - T	Shugart, Clyde - G
Deal, Rufus - B	Slivinski, Steve - G
Farkas, Andy - B	Smith, George - C
Farman, Dick - G	Stralka, Clem - G
Goodyear, John - B	Titchenal, Bob - E & C
Hare, Cecil - B	Todd, Dick - B
Hare, Ray - B	Watts, George - T
Justice, Ed - B	Whited, Marvin - B & G
Juzwik, Steve - B	Wilkin, Willie - T
Kovatch, John - E	Young, Bill - T
Krueger, Al - E	Zeno, Joe - G
McChesney, Bob - E	Zimmerman, Leroy - Q

1943

WESTERN DIVISION

Chicago Bears	8	1	1	.889
Green Bay	7	2	1	.778
Detroit	3	6	1	.333
Chicago Cardinals	0	10	0	.000

EASTERN DIVISION

Washington	6	3	1	.667
New York	6	3	1	.667
Phil-Pitt	5	4	1	.555
Brooklyn	2	8	0	.200

TITLE: Chicago Bears beat Washington, 41-21, for championship. Washington had beaten New York, 28-0, in division playoff.

LEADERS: Individual leaders for the season: Scoring— Don Hutson (Green Bay), 117; Rushing—Bill Paschal (New York), 572 yds.; Passing—Sam Baugh (Washington); Pass Receiving—Don Hutson (Green Bay), 47; Field Goals—Don Hutson (Green Bay), 3; Punting—Sam Baugh (Washington), 45.9 yds.; Interceptions—Sam Baugh (Washington), 11.

FIRST DRAFT: Frank Sinkwich (Georgia)—Back—by Detroit.

COACHES: Pete Cawthorn replaced Mike Getto as head coach at Brooklyn; "Gus" Dorais replaced John Karcis at Detroit; Phil Handler replaced Jim Conzelman with Chicago Cardinals; "Dutch" Bergman replaced Ray Flaherty at Washington.

NOTES: Philadelphia and Pittsburgh merged for the season with "Greasy" Neale and Walt Kiesling co-coaches; Cleveland Rams suspended operation for one season. Roster limit reduced 2 to 28.

Sid Luckman, Chi-Bears, threw seven touchdown passes (record) against New York, Nov. 14.

TITLE GAME

Although all the teams in the league had been depleted of most of their star players by World War II, Sid Luckman of the Bears and Sam Baugh of the Redskins had kept the fans' interest high with their spectacular passing. Against the Giants, Luckman had thrown for seven touchdowns in one game and Baugh had led the Washington team to a divisional tie with the New York Giants and then to a 28-0 victory in the play-off game.

The Bears, beaten previously by the Redskins during a season game, had lured the aged Bronko Nagurski out of retirement, but it was Luckman's passing that saved the title for the Bears. Baugh received a concussion late in the game which put the Redskins out of contention.

There was no scoring in the first period. The Redskins clicked first when Andy Farkas plowed one yard to start the second quarter and Bob Masterson converted for 7–0. Luckman fired 31 yards to Harry Clark on a screen-pass for a touchdown and Bob Snyder's extra point tied the game. The Bears led, 14–7, at the half following a 3-yard plunge for a touchdown by Nagurski and Snyder's conversion.

Luckman opened the third period with two touchdown passes, the first traveling 36 yards to Dante Magnani, the second again to Magnani for a 66-yard romp from the flat. Snyder kicked the first conversion, missed the second. The Redskins made it 27–14 at the end of the third quarter after Baugh passed 8 yards to Andy Farkas who ran 9 more for the counter. Masterson converted.

Luckman had two more TD's in his guns for the last period. He threw the first 29 yards to Jim Benton in the end zone, the second 16 yards to Harry Clark, who took it on the goal line. Bob Snyder kicked both conversions. Sam Baugh, just before he was injured, passed 26 yards to Joe Aguirre in the end zone, Aguirre kicked the point and the game ended, 41–21.

Chicago Bears	0	14	13	14—41
Washington Redskins	0	7	7	7—21

Touchdowns—Clark 2, Magnani 2, Nagurski, Benton, Farkas 2, Aguirre.
Points after touchdown—Snyder 5, Masterson 2, Aguirre.

Attendance: 34,320.

Players' Share: Chicago $1,146.87; Washington $765.78.

1943 BROOKLYN DODGERS
COACH - "Pete" Cawthorn
4th 2-8-0

Armstrong, Bill - G
Bandura, John - E
Brown, Bill - Q
Cafego, George - Q
Condit, Merlyn - B
Conkright, Bill - C
Davis, Bill - T
Edwards, Marshall - B
Fawcett, Jake - T
Grandinette, George - G

Gutknecht, Al - G
Heineman, Ken - B
Johnson, Cecil - B
Jones, Lewis - G
Kinard, "Bruiser" - T
Kowalski, Andy - E
McAdams, Dean - B
Manders, "Pug" - B
Manton, "Tilly" - Q
Marek, Joe - Q

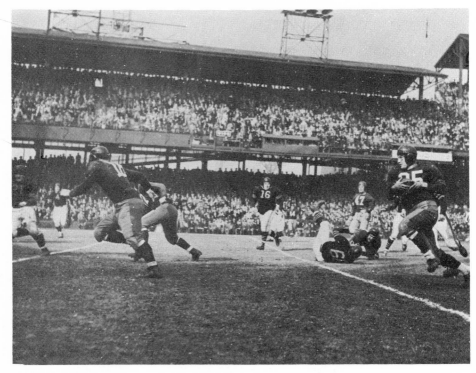

Redskin Wilbur Moore, who made a habit of slaughtering Bears, rolls out from a reverse during game in 1943. Solid blocking forms out in front. (Nate Fine Photo.)

Martin, Frank - B
Matisi, John - T
Owens, Truett - G
Ranspot, Keith - E
Sachse, Frank - B
Schmarr, Herman - E
Schupbach, O.T. - T
(Tex Mooney)

Sergienko, George - T
Setcavage, Joe - Q
Stewart, Vaugh - C
Sevendsen, Earl - C
Swaidon, Phil - G
Webb, George - E
Wehba, Ray - E

1943 CHICAGO BEARS
COACHES - Luke Johnsos &
"Hunk" Anderson
1st 8-1-1
(Beat Washington for title, 41-21)

Babartshy, Al - T
Benton, Jim - E
Berry, Connie Mack - E
Clark, Harry - B
Digris, Bernie - T
Famiglietti, Gary - B
Fortmann, Dan - G
Geyer, Bill - B
Gudauskas, Pete - G
Hoptowit, Al - T
Ippolito, Tony - G
Logan, Jim - G
Luckman, Sid - Q
McEnulty, Doug - B
McLean, Ray - B
Magnani, Dante - B
Masters, Bob - B

Matuza, Al - C
Merkel, Monte - G
Mundee, Fred - C
Musso, George - G
Nagurski, Bronko - B & T
Nolting, Ray - B
Osmanski, Bill - B
Pool, Hamp - E
Siegel, John - E
Sigillo, Dom - T
Snyder, Bob - Q
Steinkemper, Bill - T
Steuber, Bob - B
Turner, "Bulldog" - C
Vodicka, Joe - B
Wilson, George - E

1943 CHICAGO CARDINALS
COACH - Phil Handler
4th 0-10-0

Albrecht, Art - T
Baker, Conway - G
Booth, Clarence - T
Bukant, Joe - B
Bulger, Chet - T
Cahill, Ron - B
Currivan, Don - E
Duggan, Gil - T
Ghersanich, Vernon - G
Goldberg, "Biggie" - B
Grigas, John - B
Hall, John - B
Marotti, Lou - G
Martin, John - B
Masters, Walt - Q

Morrow, Bob - Q
Parker, "Buddy" - Q
Pierce, Don - C
Puplis, Andy - Q
Purdin, Cal - B
Rankin, Walt - B
Rexer, Freeman - E
Rhea, Floyd - G
Robnett, Marshall - G
Rucinski, Ed - E
Smith, George - B
Stewart, Vaughn - C
Stokes, Lee - C
Wager, Clint - E
Wilson, Gordon - G

1943 DETROIT LIONS
COACH - "Gus" Dorais
3rd 3-6-1

Batinski, Stan - G
Busich, Sam - E
Callihan, Bill - Q
Cardwell, Lloyd - B

Colella, Tom - B
Conlee, Gerry - C
Corgan, Mike - B
Evans, Murray - Q

Wilbur Moore of Washington about to catch one of Sam Baugh's passes and go for a touchdown against the Philadelphia Eagles during a 1943 game. The Eagle trying to break it up (7) is Leroy Zimmerman, former Redskin quarterback. (Nate Fine Photo.)

Fenenbock, Chuck - B
Fisk, Bill - E
Hackney, Elmer - B
Hightower, John - E
Hopp, Harry - Q
Kaporch, Alex - T
Keene, Bob - B
Ketzko, Alex - T
Kuczynski, Al - E
Layden, Bob - E
Liles, "Sonny" - G
Lio, Augie - G
Matheson, John - E

Matheson, Riley - G
Mathews, Ned - B
Opalewski, Ed - T
Pavelec, Ted - G
Rockenback, Lyle - G
Rosteck, Ernie - C
Rubino, Tony - G
Sinkwich, Frank - B
Stuart, Roy - G
VanTone, Art - B
Wickett, Lloyd - T
Wojciechowicz, Alex - C

McPherson,"Amy"- T & C
Mason, Joel - E
Perkins, Don - B
Ray, "Baby" - T
Schwammel, Adolph - T

Sorenson, Glenn - G
Starrett, Ben - B
Tinsley, Pete - G
Uram, Andy - B

1943 GREEN BAY PACKERS
COACH - "Curly" Lambeau
2nd 7-2-1

Adams, Chet - T
Berezney, Paul - T
Brock, Charley - C
Brock, Lou - Q
Canadeo, Tony - B
Comp, Irv - Q
Craig, Larry - Q & E
Croft, "Tiny" - T
Evans, Dick - E
Falkenstein, Tony - B

Flowers, Bob - C
Fries, Sherwood - G
Fritsch, Ted - B
Goldenberg,"Buckets"- G
Hutson, Don - E
Jacunski, Harry - E
Kahler, Bob - B
Kuusisto, Bill - G
Lankas, Jim - B
Laws, Joe - B

1943 NEW YORK GIANTS
COACH - Steve Owen
2nd 6-3-1

Adams, O'Neal - E
Adams, Verlin - E & T
Avedisian, Chuck - G
Barker, Hubert - B
Blozis, Al - T
Brown, Dave - B
Carroll, Vic - T
Cope, Frank - T
Cuff, Ward - B
Dubzinski, Walt - G
Hein, Mel - C
Karcis, John - B
Kinscherf, Carl - B
Leemans, "Tuffy" - B
Liebel, Frank - E

Marone, Sal - G
Nix, Emery - Q
Paschal, Bill - B
Piccolo, Bill - C
Pritko, Steve - E
Roberts, Tom - T
Shaffer, Leland - Q
Soar, "Hank" - B
Sulaitis, Joe - B & E
Trocolor, Bob - B
Umont, Frank - T
Visnic, Larry - G
Walls, Will - E
Younce, Len - G

Redskin Sam Baugh intercepts a pass thrown to Green Bay end Nolan Luhn in 1943. Early in his career Baugh was a top defensive back, leading the league in interceptions in 1943. (Nate Fine Photo.)

1943 PHIL-PITT (Merger)
COACHES - "Greasey" Neale &
Walt Kiesling
3rd 5-4-1

Bova, Tony - E	Masters, Bob - B
Butler, John - B	Michaels, Ed - G
Cabrelli, Larry - E	Miller, Tom - E
Canale, Rocco - G	Paschka, Gordon - G
Conti, Enio - G	Reutt, Ray - E
Doyle, Ted - T	Sader, Steve - B
Frank, Joe - T	Schultz, Eberle - G
Cauer, Charley - B & E	Sears, Vic - T
Graves, Ray - C	Sherman, Allie - Q
Hewitt, Bill - E	Steele, Ernie - B
Hinkle, John - B	Steward, Dean - B
Kilroy, Frank - T	Thurbon, Bob - Q
Kish, Ben - Q	Wistert, Al - T
Laux, Ted - Q	Wukits, Al - C
McCullough, Hugh - B	Zimmerman, Leroy - Q

1943 WASHINGTON REDSKINS
COACH - "Dutch" Bergman
1st 6-3-1
(Lost title to Chicago Bears,
41-21, after beating New York
in playoff, 28-0)

Aguirre, Joe - E	Dunn, Coye - B
Akins, Frank - B	Farkas, Andy - B
Baugh, Sam - Q	Farman, Dick - G
Cafego, George - Q	Fiorentino, Al - G
Conkright, Bill - C	Gibson, Billy Joe - B & E

Hare, Ray - B	Rymkus, Lou - T
Hayden, Ken - C	Seno, Frank - B
Jenkins, Jacque - B	Seymour, Bob - B
Lapka, Ted - E	Shugart, Clyde - G
Leon, Tony - G	Slivinski, Steve - G
Masterson, Bob - E	Smith, George - C
Moore, Wilbur - B	Smith, John - E
Pasqua, Joe - T	Stasica, Leo - B
Paternoster, Angelo - G	Wilkin, Willie - T
Piasecky, Alex - E	Zeno, Joe - G
Ribar, Frank - G	

1944

WESTERN DIVISION

Green Bay	8	2	0	.800
Chicago Bears	6	3	1	.667
Detroit	6	3	1	.667
Cleveland	4	6	0	.400
Card-Pitt	0	10	0	.000

EASTERN DIVISION

New York	8	1	1	.889
Philadelphia	7	1	2	.875
Washington	6	3	1	.667
Boston	2	8	0	.200
Brooklyn	0	10	0	.000

TITLE: Green Bay beat New York, 14-7, for the championship at New York, Dec. 17.

LEADERS: Individual leaders for the season: Scoring—Don Hutson (Green Bay), 85; Rushing—Bill Paschal (New York), 737 yds.; Passing—Frank Filchock (Washington); Pass Receiving—Don Hutson (Green Bay), 58; Field Goals—Ken Strong (New York), 6; Punting—Frank Sinkwich (Detroit), 41.0 yds.; Interceptions—Howard Livingston (New York), 9.

FIRST DRAFT: Marlin "Pat" Harder (Wisconsin)—Back—by Chi-Cards.

COACHES: New franchise at Boston, called Yanks, owned by Ted Collins, coached by Herb Kopf; Cleveland Rams returned to action after suspending through 1943 with "Buff" Donelli replacing Earl "Dutch" Clark as head coach; Dudley DeGroot replaced Arthur "Dutch" Bergman at Washington.

NOTES: Chicago Cardinals and Pittsburgh Steelers merged for one year with co-coaches Walt Kiesling and Phil Handler.

Loran Ribble, Pittsburgh, Portsmouth, Chi-Card guard (1932-37) died.

TITLE GAME

After a scoreless first period, Ted Fritsch put the Packers ahead with a 2-yard touchdown plunge and Don Hutson converted to make it 7-0. Later in the period, Irv Comp passed to Ted Fritsch for 26 yards and another TD with Hutson's conversion giving the Green Bay team a 14-0 lead at half-time.

The third period was scoreless, but, at its end, the Giants were on the Packer one-yard line and Ward Cuff plunged across on the first play of the last quarter. Ken Strong kicked the conversion to make it 14-7 and there was no further scoring.

Green Bay Packers	0	14	0	0—14
New York Giants	0	0	0	7— 7

Touchdowns—Fritsch 2, Cuff.
Points after touchdown—Hutson 2, Strong.

Attendance: 46, 016.

Players' Share: Green Bay $1,449.71; New York $814.36.

1944 BOSTON YANKS
COACH - Herb Kopf
4th 2-8-0

Albrecht, Art - T	Magee, Jim - C
Cafego, George - Q	Martin, John - B
Commisa, Vince - G	Morelli, John - G
Crain, Milt - B	Ranspot, Keith - E
Crowley, Joe - E	Rexer, Freeman - E
Davis, Bob - Q	Riggs, Thron - T
Dubzinski, Walt - C	Sanders, Paul - B
Falkenstein, Tony - B	Santora, Frank - B
Franco, Ed - T	Smukler, Dave - B
Gaziano, Frank - G	Stasica, Leo - B
Giddens, Herschel - T	Steinmetz, Ken - B
Goldman, Sam - E	Tiller, Morgan - E
Gudmundson, Scott - Q	Turbert, Francis - B
Harrison, Dick - E	Walker, Bill - G
Korisky, Ed - G	Williams, Ted - B
Lio, Augie - G	Wilson, Gordon - G
McGee, Ed - T	Wynne, Harry - E
McRoberts, Bob - B	

1944 BROOKLYN TIGERS
COACHES - "Pete" Cawthorn,
Ed Kubale & Frank Bridges
5th 0-10-0

Aiello, Tony - B	Marko, Steve - B
Brown, Bill - Q	Martin, Frank - B
Butler, John - Q	Masterson, Bob - E
Carter, Joe - E	Reynolds, Bill - B
Doherty, George - T	Rhea, Floyd - G
Ellis, John - G	Sachse, Frank - B
Falkenstein, Tony - Q	Sergienko, George - T
Fryer, Ken - B	Sivell, Jim - G
Hare, Ray - Q	Smith, George - C
Johnson, Cecil - B	Stewart, Vaughn - C
Kinard, "Bruiser" - T	Strom, Frank - T
Kowalski, Andy - E	Taylor, Charles - Q & G
LaFitte, Bill - E	Trocolor, Bob - B
Leon, Tony - G	Uguccioni, Enrico - E
McDonald, Don - E	Ware, Charles - T
McGibbony, Charles - Q	Weeks, George - E
McMichaels, John - B	Wilson, Gordon - G
Manders, "Pug" - B	

1944 CHICAGO BEARS
COACHES - Luke Johnsos &
"Hunk" Anderson
2nd 6-3-1

Babartsky, Al - T	Margarita, "Hank" - B
Berry, Connie Mack - E	Masters, Bob - B
Burnell, Max - B	Mooney, Bow Tipp - B
Croft, Abe - E	Mundee, Fred - C
Famiglietti, Gary - B	Musso, George - G
Fordham, Jim - B	Plasman, Dick - E
Glenn, Bill - B	Podmajersky, Paul - G
Greenich, Harley - B	Roberts, Tom - T
Gryco, Al - B	Ronzani, Gene - Q
Gudauskas, Pete - G	Sigillo, Dom - T
Hoptowit, Al - T	Smeja, Rudy - E
Kelly, Elmo - E	Sprinkle, Ed - G
Long, John - Q	Sweeney, Jim - T
Luckman, Sid - Q	Turner, "Bulldog" - C
McEnulty, Doug - B	Wilson, George - E
McLean, Ray - B	Zorich, George - G

1944 CARD-PITT (Merger)
COACHES - Phil Handler &
Walt Kiesling
5th 0-10-0

Baker, Conway - T	Booth, Clarence - T
Banonis, Vince - C	Bova, Tony - E & B

Alonzo Stagg, *left*, who has been involved in football for generations, gets his Coach-of-the-Year trophy in 1944 from Otto Graham, who came out of Northwestern University in 1943 to become one of the great quarterbacks in pro history. (Acme Pictures.)

Bulger, Chet - T
Butler, John - B
Currivan, Don - E
Doyle, Ted - T
Duggan, Gil - T
Grigas, John - B
Kichefski, Walt - E
McCarthy, John - Q
McDonough, Coley - Q
Magulick, George - B
Marotti, Lou - G
Martin, John - B

Masters, Walt - Q
Merkovsky, Elmer - T
Perko, John - G
Popovich, John - B
Rankin, Walt - Q
Robnett, Marshall - G & C
Rucinski, Ed - E & B
Schultz, Eberle - G
Semes, Bernie - B
Thurbon, Bob - B
Wager, Clint - E
Wukits, Al - C

1944 CLEVELAND RAMS
COACH - Aldo Donelli
4th 4-6-0

Benton, Jim - E
Bernard, Dave - Q
Carson, Howie - B
Clay, Boyd - T
Colella, Tom - B
Conkright, Bill - C
Corbo, Tom - G
Fawcett, Jake - T
Gibson, Billy Joe - E & C
Gillette, Jim - B
Gutknecht, Al - G
Hamilton, Ray - E
Huggins, Roy - B
Jones, Harvey - Q
Kabealo, Mike - B
Karrs, John - Q

Konetsky, Floyd - E
Lear, Les - G
Lyman, Del - T
Matheson, Riley - G
Olsen, Norm - T
Petchel, John - Q
Pritko, Steve - E
Pudloski, Chet - T
Reisz, Al - B
Rieth, Bill - C
Riffle, Charles - G
Scarry, Mike - C
Skoozen, Stan - B
West, Walt - B
Zontini, Lou - B

1944 DETROIT LIONS
COACH - "Gus" Dorais
3rd 6-3-1

Aiello, Tony - B
Batinski, Stan - G
Blessing, Paul - E
Bouldin, Fred - T
Callihan, Bill - Q
Clark, Wayne - E
Dawley, Fred - B
Diehl, Dave - E
D'Orazio, Joe - T
Eiden, Ed - C
Furst, Tony - T
Greene, John - E
Hackney, Elmer - B
Hansen, Dale - T
Kaporch, Al - T
Keene, Bob - B

Kennedy, Tom - T
Liles, Elvin - G
Lindon, Luther - T
Lowther, Russ - B
Matheson, John - E
Opalewski, Ed - T
Rexer, Freeman - E
Rogers, Bill - T
Rosteck, Ernie - C
Sinkwich, Frank - B
Sirochman, George - G
Trebotich, Ivan - B
VanTone, Art - B
Westfall, Bob - B
Wojciechowicz, Alex - C

1944 GREEN BAY PACKERS
COACH - "Curly" Lambeau
1st 8-2-0
(Beat New York for title, 14-7)

Berezney, Paul - T
Bilda, Dick - B
Brock, Charley - C
Brock, Lou - Q
Bucchianeri, Amadeo - G
Canadeo, Tony - B
Comp, Irv - Q
Craig, Larry - G
Croft, "Tiny" - T
Duhart, Paul - B
Flowers, Bob - C
Fritsch, Ted - B
Goldenberg, "Buckets" - G
Hutson, Don - E
Jacunski, Harry - E
Kahler, Bob - B

Kercher, Bob - E
Kuusisto, Bill - G
Laws, Joe - B
McKay, Roy - B
McPherson, "Amy" - T & C
Mason, Joel - E
Perkins, Don - B
Ray, "Baby" - T
Schwammel, Adolph - T
Sorenson, Glen - G
Starrett, Ben - Q
Tinsley, Pete - G
Tollefson, Charley - G
Urban, Alex - E
Wehba, Ray - E

1944 NEW YORK GIANTS
COACH - Steve Owen
1st 8-1-1
(Lost to Green Bay for title, 14-7)

Adams, O'Neal - E
Adams, Verlin - E
Avedisian, Charles - G
Barker, Hubert - B
Beebe, Keith - B
Blozis, Al - T
Calligaro, Len - Q
Caranci, Roland - T
Carroll, Vic - T
Clay, Roy - B
Cope, Frank - T
Cuff, Ward - B
Hein, Mel - C
Herber, Arnie - Q

Kane, Herb - T
Kinscherf, Carl - B
Liebel, Frank - E
Livingston, Howie - B
Paschal, Bill - B
Petrilas, Bill - E & B
Piccolo, Bill - C
Sivell, Jim - G
Soar, "Hank" - B
Strong, Ken - B
Sulaitis, Joe - B
Umont, Frank - T
Visnic, Larry - G
Weiss, John - E
Younce, Len - G

1944 PHILADELPHIA EAGLES
COACH - "Greasey" Neale
2nd 7-1-2

Banducci, Bruno - G
Banta, "Jack" - B
Bleeker, Mel - B
Cabrelli, Larry - E
Canale, Rocco - G
Conti, Enio - G
Durko, John - E
Eiden, Ed - C
Fagioli, Carl - G
Ferrante, Jack - E
Friedman, Bob - T
Gauer, Charles - E
Hinkle, Jack - B
Jarvi, Toimi - B
Kilroy, "Bucko" - T
Kish, Ben - B

Laux, Ted - Q
Lindskog, Vic - C
McDonald, Don - E
Macioszczyk, Art - B
Mandarino, Mike - T
Manzini, Baptiste - C
Maronic, "Duke" - G
Michaels, Ed - G
Miller, Tom - E
Nowak, Walt - E
Sherman, Allie - Q
Steele, Ernie - B
VanBuren, Steve - B
Wistert, Al - T
Yovicsin, John - E
Zimmerman, Leroy - Q

1944 WASHINGTON REDSKINS
COACH - Dud DeGroot
3rd 6-3-1

Aguirre, Joe - E
Akins, Frank - B
Baugh, Sam - Q
Bedore, Tom - G
Compofreda, Nick - C & T
Dye, Les - E
Farkas, Andy - B
Filchock, Frank - Q
Fiorentino, Al - G
Foltz, Vernon - C
Fuller, Larry - B
Johnson, Larry - C
Keenan, John - G & C
Lapka, Ted - E
Marcus, Peter - E
Merkle, Ed - G
Micka, Mike - B

Monaco, Ray - G
Moore, Wilbur - B
Natowich, Andy - B
North, Jim - T
Piasecky, Alex - E
Seno, Frank - B
Seymour, Bob - B
Sharp, Ev - T
Shugart, Clyde - G
Sneddon, Bob - B
Turley, Doug - E
Ucovich, Mitch - T
Ungerer, Joe - T
Walton, Frank - G
Weldon, Larry - Q
Zeno, Joe - G

1945

WESTERN DIVISION

Cleveland	9	1	0	.900
Detroit	7	3	0	.700
Green Bay	6	4	0	.600

| Chicago Bears | 3 | 7 | 0 | .300 |
| Chicago Cardinals | 1 | 9 | 0 | .100 |

EASTERN DIVISION

Washington	8	2	0	.800
Philadelphia	7	3	0	.700
New York	3	6	1	.333
Boston	3	6	1	.333
Pittsburgh	2	8	0	.200

TITLE: Cleveland beat Washington, 15-14, for the championship at Cleveland, Dec. 16.

LEADERS: Individual leaders for the season: Scoring—Steve VanBuren (Philadelphia), 110; Rushing—Steve VanBuren (Philadelphia), 832 yds.; Passing—Sam Baugh (Washington) (128 completions in 182 passes, 70.3% completions, highest all-time); Pass Receiving—Don Hutson (Green Bay), 47; Field Goals—Joe Aguirre (Washington), 7; Punting—Roy McKay (Green Bay), 41.2 yds.; Interceptions—Leroy Zimmerman (Philadelphia), 7.

FIRST DRAFT: Charles Trippi (Georgia)—Back—by Chi-Cards.

COACHES: Adam Walsh replaced Aldo "Buff" Donelli as head coach at Cleveland; Jim Leonard replaced Walt Kiesling at Pittsburgh.

NOTES: Brooklyn Tigers merged with Boston Yanks.

Roster limit raised 5 to 33.

Mel Hein, New York Giants center, retired after 15 years.

Don Hutson, Green Bay end, scored 29 points in second period (4 TDs, 5 PATs) against Detroit, Oct. 7.

Don Hutson, retired holding scoring record (823).

Jim Benton, Cleveland end, gained 303 yards with 10 passes caught (record) against Detroit, Nov. 22.

TITLE GAME

It was so cold in Cleveland on the day of the game that the musical instruments froze, putting the great Redskin band out of action even before the game started. The field had been covered with mountains of straw but was slippery underfoot. The wind was strong and erratic.

Sam Baugh attempted a pass from his end zone in the first quarter. The wind veered the ball into the goal post for an automatic safety to give the Rams a 2-point lead.

In the second period, Frank Filchock passed 26 yards to Steve Bagarus who ran 12 more for the first touchdown. Joe Aguirre converted to put the Redskins ahead 7-2. Waterfield then passed 25 yards to Jim Benton who added 12 more for a TD and Waterfield's conversion made it 9-7 at the end of the half.

In the third, Waterfield threw 39 yards to Jim Gillette, who then scored from the 14. Waterfield's conversion missed to keep it 15-7.

Filchock passed the 'Skins to within 2 points of the Rams, with an 8-yard pitch to Bob Seymour in the end zone. Aguirre again converted.

The fourth period was scoreless and the game ended 15-14.

| Cleveland Rams | 2 | 7 | 6 | 0—15 |
| Washington Redskins | 0 | 7 | 7 | 0—14 |

Touchdowns—Benton, Gillette, Bagarus, Seymour.
Points after touchdown—Aguirre 2, Waterfield.
Safety—Automatic.

Attendance: 32,178.
Players' Share: Cleveland $1,468.74; Washington $902.47.

1945 BOSTON YANKS
COACH - Herb Kopf
4th 3-6-1

Anderson, Bill - E	Manders, "Pug" - B
Cafego, George - B	Mark, Louis - C & E
Crowley, Joe - E	Marko, Steve - B
Currivan, Don - E	Martin, Frank - B
Davis, Bob - Q	Martin, John - Q
Deeks, Don - T	Masterson, Bob - E
Dimancheff, "Babe" - B	Mathews, Ned - B
Doherty, George - T	Micka, Mike - B
Duhart, Paul - B	Morelli, John - G
Fiorentino, Al - G	Parker, "Ace" - Q
Grigas, John - B	Ranspot, Keith - E
Gudmundson, Scott - Q	Rhea, Floyd - G
Jones, Ellis - G	Sachse, Frank - B
Kowalski, Andy - E	Sachse, John - C
Leon, Tony - G	Sergienko, George - T
Lio, Augie - G	Smith, George - C
McCullough, Hugh - B	Steinmetz, Ken - B
McGee, Ed - T	Walker, Bill - G
Magee, Jim - C	

President Harry S. Truman, happy to get his lifetime NFL pass from Elmer Layden, president of the league, center, and George P. Marshall, owner of the Washington Redskins. (Acme Photo.)

1945 CHICAGO BEARS
COACHES - Luke Johnsos &
"Hunk" Anderson
4th 3-7-0

Artoe, Lee - T
Babartsky, Al - T
Berry, Connie Mack - E
Burgeis, Glen - T
Croft, Abe - E
Daniell, Jim - T
Drulis, Chuck - G
Famiglietti, Gary - B
Fordham, Jim - B
Gallarneau, Hugh - B
Grygo, Al - B
Gudauskas, Pete - G
Hoptowit, Al - T
Hunt, John - B
Jones, Edgar - B
Kavanaugh, Ken - E
Keriosotis, Nick - G
Long, John - Q
Luckman, Sid - Q
McAfee, George - B
McLean, Ray - B
Margarita, "Hank" - B

Masterson, Forrest - C & G
Mitchell, Charley - B
Mooney, Bow Tipp - Q
Morton, John - E
Mucha, Rudy - G
Mundee, Fred - C
Perez, Pete - G
Perkins, Don - B
Ramsey, Frank - T
Roberts, Tom - T
Ronzani, Gene - B
Schiechl, John - C
Smeja, Rudy - E
Sprinkle, Ed - E
Stydahar, Joe - T
Swisher, Bob - B
Turner, "Bulldog" - C
Vodicka, Joe - B
Vucinich, Milt - C
Wilson, George - E
Zorich, George - G

Braden, Dave - G
Bruckner, Les - B
Bulger, Chet - T
Busler, Ray - T
Campbell, Bill - C
Cantor, Leo - B
Carter, Joe - E
Christman, Paul - Q
Collins, Paul - Q
Dewell, Bill - E
Drulis, Al - B
Duggan, Gil - T
Durko, John - E
Eckl, Bob - T
Enich, Steve - G
Fife, Ralph - G
Foster, Ralph - T
Fuller, Larry -B
Ivy, "Pop" - E
Knolla, John - Q
Kuharich, Joe - G
Lindow, Al - B

Maeda, Chet - B
Marotti, Lou - G
Mertes, "Buzz" - Q
Norman, Bob - C
Obeck, Vic - G
Oliver, Vince - Q
Poole, Jim - E
Rankin, Walt - B
Rexer, Freeman, - E
Reynolds, Bill - B
Robl, Hal - B
Robnett, Marshall - G & C
Rucinski, Ed - E
Seno, Frank - B
Speegle, Cliff - C
Tonelli, Mario - B
Ucovich, Mitch - T
Vodicka, Joe - Q
Wager, Clint - E
Watt, Walt - B
Wilson, Gordon - G
Zimny, Bob - T

1945 CHICAGO CARDINALS
COACH - Phil Handler
5th 1-9-0

Apolskis, Ray - C & G
Baker, Conway - T
Balaz, Frank - B

Bertagnolli, Libero - G
Blackwell, Hal - B
Bonelli, Ernie - Q

1945 CLEVELAND RAMS
COACH - Adam Walsh
1st 9-1-0
(Best Washington for title, 15-14)

Armstrong, Graham - T
Benton, Jim - E
Bernard, Dave - Q
Bouley, Gil - T
Colella, Tom - B
DeLauer, Bob - C

Eason, Roger - T
Gehrke, Fred - B
Gillette, Jim - B
Greenwood, Don - B
Hamilton, Ray - E
Harding, Roger - C

General Dwight D. Eisenhower enjoys a Redskin-New York Giant game in Griffith Stadium, Washington, October 28, 1945. (Nate Fine Photo.)

Hickey, "Red" - E
Jacobs, Jack - B
Jones, Harvey - B
Koch, George - B
Konetsky, Floyd - E
Lazetich, Milan - G
Lear, Les - B
Levy, Len - T
Liles, Elvin - G
Matheson, Riley - G
Mergenthal, Art - G
Monaco, Ray - G
Mucha, Rudy - G
Nemeth, Steve - Q

Phillips, George - B
Pritko, Steve - E
Reisz, Al - B
Rieth, Bill - C & G
Ruthstrom, Ralph - B
Scarry, Mike - C
Schultz, Eberle - G
Shaw, Bob - E
Sikich, Rudy - T
Waterfield, Bob - Q
West, Pat - Q
Winkler, Joe - C
Worden, Jim - B
Zirinsky, Walt - B

Price, Charles - Q
Radovich, Bill - G
Roberson, Lake - E
Ryan, Dave - B
Sartori, Larry - G
Sigillo, Dom - T
Sneddon, Bob - B
Szymanski, Frank - C
Tassos, Damon - G

Thomason, Jim - B
Trebotich, Ivan - B
Uremovich, Emil - T
VanTone, Art - B
Weber, Dick - B
Westfall, Bob - B
Williams, Rex - C
Wojciechowicz, Alex - C

1945 GREEN BAY PACKERS
COACH - "Curly" Lambeau
3rd 6-4-0

1945 DETROIT LIONS
COACH - "Gus" Dorais
2nd 7-3-0

Batinski, Stan - G
Booth, Dick - B
Brumley, Bob - B
Callihan, Bill - Q
DeShane, Charles - B
Diehl, Dave - E
Farkas, Andy - B
Fenenbock, Chuck - B
Frutig, Ed - E
Greene, John - E
Grefe, Ted - E
Hackney, Elmer - B
Kaporch, Al - T
Keene, Bob - B

Knorr, Larry - E
Kostiuk, Mike - T
Kring, Frank - B
Krol, Joe - B
Liles, Elvin - G
Lindon, Luther - T
Madarik, Elmer - B
Manzo, Joe - T
Matheson, John - E
Mazza, Vince - B
Mesak, Dick - T
Milano, Arch - E
Mugg, Garvin - T
Nelson, Bob - C

Adkins, Bob - E & G
Barnett, Solon - T
Brock, Charley - C
Brock, Lou - Q
Bucchianeri, Amadeo - G
Comp, Irv - Q
Craig, Larry - Q
Crimmins, Bernie - G
Croft, "Tiny" - T
Flowers, Bob - C
Frankowski, Ray - G
Fritsch, Ted - B
Frutig, Ed - E
Goldenberg, "Buckets" - G
Goodnight, Clyde - E
Hutson, Don - E
Keuper, Ken - Q & E
Kuusisto, Bill - G
Laws, Joe - B

Lipscomb, Paul - T
Luhn, Nolan - E
McKay, Roy - B
McPherson, "Amy" - T & C
Mason, Joel - E
Mosely, Russ - B
Mulleneaux, Carl - E
Neal, "Ed" - T
Pannell, Ernie - T
Perkins, Don - B
Ray, "Baby" - T
Sample, Charles - B
Smith, Bruce - B
Snelling, Ken - B
Sorenson, Glen - G
Starrett, Ben - B
Tinsley, Pete - G
Tollefson, Charles - G
Urban, Alex - E

1945 NEW YORK GIANTS
COACH - Steve Owen
3rd 3-6-1

Adams, Verlin - E & G
Barbour, Elmer - Q
Barker, Hubert - B
Carroll, Vic - T & C
Cope, Frank - T
Cuff, Ward - B
DeFilippo, Lou - C
Doolan, John - B
Eaton, Lou - T
Filipowicz, Steve - B
Fox, Sam - E
Franck, George - B
Garner, Bob - G
Grate, Carl - G
Hein, Mel - C
Herber, Arnie - Q
Hovious, John - B
Kane, Herb - T
Kearns, Tom - T
Klotovich, Mike - B
Liebel, Frank - E
Lindahl, Virgil - G & E
Little, Jim - T

Livingston, Howie - B
Martin, Frank - B
Morrow, Bob - B
Paschal, Bill - B
Pederson, Win - T
Petrilas, Bill - E & B
Piccolo, Bill - C
Poole, Jim - E
Pugh, Marion - Q
Ragazzo, Phil - T
Shaffer, Leland - Q
Shedlosky, Ed - B
Sivell, Jim - G
Springer, Harold - E
Strong, Ken - B
Sulaitis, Joe - B
Tomaini, Army - T
Umont, Frank - T
Visnic, Larry - G
Weiss, John - E
White, "Tarzan" - G
Wynne, Harry - E

1945 PHILADELPHIA EAGLES
COACH - "Greasey" Neale
2nd 7-3-0

Agajanian, Ben - K
Banducci, Bruno - G
Banta, "Jack" - B
Bleeker, Mel - B
Butler, John - B
Cabrelli, Larry - E
Canale, Rocco - G
Castiglia, Jim - B
Conti, Enio - G
Erdlitz, Dick - B
Ferrante, Jack - E
Fox, Terry - B
Fritts, George - T
Gauer, Charles - E
Hinkle, Jack - B
Humbert, Dick - E
Karnofsky, Abe - E
Kilroy, "Bucko" - T
Kish, Ben - B
Lindskog, Vic - C
McDonald, Don - E

Mandarino, Mike - C
Manzini, Baptiste - C
Maronic, "Duke" - G
Meyer, Fred - E
Michaels, Ed - G
Ramsey, Herschel - E
Rogalla, John - B
Sanders, John - G
Sears, Vic - T
Sherman, Allie - Q
Shires, Marshall - T
Smith, John - T
Smith, Milt - E
Steele, Ernie - B
Steinke, Gil - B
Suffridge, Bob - G
Thompson, "Tommy" - Q
VanBuren, Steve - B
Warren, Busit - B
Wistert, Al - T
Zimmerman, Leroy - Q

1945 PITTSBURGH STEELERS
COACH - Jim Leonard
5th 2-8-0

Agajanian, Ben - K
Alberghini, Tom - G
Bova, Tony - E & B
Brandau, Art - C
Brown, Bill - Q
Buda, Carl - G
Chamberlain, Garth - G
Cherundolo, Chuck - C
Cibulas, Joe - T
Coomer, Joe - T
DePascal, Carmine - E
DePaul, Henry - G
Dolly, Dick - E
Doyle, Ted - T
Dudley, Bill - B
Duhart, Paul - B

Foltz, Vernon - C & T
Frketich, Len - T
Itzel, John - B
Jarvi, Toimi - B
Jones, Art - B
Kiick, George - B
Kimble, Frank - E
Kondria, John - T
Koshlap, Jules - B
Law, Hubbard - G
Lowther, Russ - B
Lucente, John - B
McNamara, Ed - T
Merkovsky, Elmer - T
Naioti, John - B
Nichols, Al - B

O'Delli, Mel - B
Olszewski, Al - E
Patrick, John - Q
Pense, Leon - Q & C
Perko, John - G
Petchel, John - Q
Petrella, John - B
Pierre, Joe - E
Popovich, John - B

Postus, Al - B
Sorce, Ross - T
Stofko, Ed - B
Stough, Glen - T
Tiller, Morgan - E
Tinsley, Sid - B
Titus, Silas - E & C
Warren, Busit - B
Wukits, Al - C

1945 WASHINGTON REDSKINS
COACH - Dud DeGroot
1st 8-2-0
(Lost to Cleveland for title,
15-14)

Adams, John - T
Aguirre, Joe - E
Akins, Frank - B
Aldrich, "Ki" - C
Ananis, Vito - B
Audet, Earl - T
Bagarus, Steve - B
Barber, Ernie - C
Baugh, Sam - Q
Condit, Merlyn - B
Davis, Fred - T
DeCorrevont, Bill - B
DeFruiter, Bob - B
DeMao, Al - C
Doolan, John - B
Dye, Les - E
Filchock, Frank - Q
Fuller, Larry - B
Gaffney, Jim - B
Hanna, Elzaphan, - G
Hare, Cecil - B

Keenan, John - G
Koniszewski, John - T
Lennan, Reid - G & C
Lolotai, Al - G
Micka, Mike - B
Miller, Tom - E
Millner, Wayne - E
Moore, Wilbur - B
Piasecky, Alex - E
Pressley, Lee - C & B
Rosato, Sal - B
Seymour, Bob - B
Sharp, Ev - T
Stralka, Clem - G
Todd, Dick - B
Turley, Doug - E
Ungerer, Joe - T
Walton, Frank - G
Watson, Jim - C
Weldon, Larry - Q & E
Whited, Marvin - B & G

1946

NATIONAL FOOTBALL LEAGUE
WESTERN DIVISION

Chicago Bears	8	2	1	.800
Los Angeles	6	4	1	.600
Green Bay	6	5	0	.545
Chicago Cardinals	6	5	0	.545
Detroit	1	10	0	.091

EASTERN DIVISION

New York	7	3	1	.700
Philadelphia	6	5	0	.545
Washington	5	5	1	.500
Pittsburgh	5	5	1	.500
Boston	2	8	1	.200

Chicago Bears   24   New York   14

ALL AMERICA FOOTBALL
CONFERENCE
WESTERN DIVISION

Cleveland	12	2	0	.857
San Francisco	9	5	0	.643
Los Angeles	7	5	2	.583
Chicago	5	6	3	.455

EASTERN DIVISION

New York	10	3	1	.769
Brooklyn	3	10	1	.231
Buffalo	3	10	1	.231
Miami	3	11	0	.154

Championship Game—
Cleveland 14, New York 9

TITLE: The Chicago Bears beat the New York Giants, 24-14, for the championship at New York, Dec. 15. Before the game New York quarterback Frank Filchock and halfback Merle Hapes had been questioned about an attempt by a New York man to fix the game. Hapes was suspended indefinitely and not permitted to play. Filchock played brilliantly but was suspended indefinitely after the game. His suspension was lifted in 1950 and he played briefly with the Baltimore Colts that season. He later coached the AFL Denver Broncos (1960-61).

LEADERS: Individual leaders for the season: Scoring—Ted Fritsch (Green Bay), 100; Rushing—Bill Dudley (Pittsburgh), 604 yds.; Passing—Bob Waterfield (Cleveland); Pass Receiving—Jim Benton (Los Angeles), 63; Field Goals—Ted Fritsch (Green Bay), 9; Punting—Roy McKay (Green Bay), 42.7 yds.; Interceptions—Bill Dudley (Pittsburgh), 10.

AAFC LEADERS: Scoring—Alyn Beals (San Francisco), 73; Rushing—Fletcher Perry (San Francisco), 783 yds.; Passing—Otto Graham (Cleveland); Pass Receiving—Mac Speedie (Cleveland), 40; Field Goals—Howard Johnson (New York), 7.

FIRST DRAFT: Francis Dancewicz (Notre Dame)—Qback—by Boston.

COACHES: George Halas resumed head coaching for Chicago Bears after returning from Navy service, replacing co-coaches Luke Johnson and "Hunk" Anderson; "Jock" Sutherland replaced Jim Leonard at Pittsburgh; Jim Conzelman returned to the Chicago Cardinals, replacing Phil Handler; "Turk" Edwards took over for Dud DeGroot at Washington. First coaches in the new All American Football Conference were: Malcolm Stevens, Tom Scott and Cliff Battles (Brooklyn); Lowell Dawson (Buffalo); Dick Hanley, Bob Dove, Ned Mathews, Willie Wilkin and Pat Boland (Chicago); Paul Brown (Cleveland); Dudley DeGroot (Los Angeles); Jack Meagher, replaced by Hampton Pool in midseason (Miami); Ray Flaherty (New York); Lawrence "Buck" Shaw (San Francisco).

NOTES: Frank Seno, Chi-Cards halfback, returned kickoff 105 yards (TD) against New York Giants, Oct. 20.

The All American Football Conference started play with teams in Brooklyn, Buffalo, Chicago, Cleveland, Los Angeles, Miami, New York and San Francisco.

In the AAFC, the Cleveland Browns won the title game, beating the New York Yankees, 14-9.

The NFL champion Cleveland Rams moved to Los Angeles.

Bert Bell appointed league commissioner, replacing Elmer Layden.

NFL TITLE GAME

The Sid Luckman-to-Ken Kavanaugh pass combination opened the scoring for the Bears in the first period with a 21-yard toss over the goal and Frank Maznicki's conversion made it 7-0. The Bears increased their lead to 14-0 when Dante Magnani intercepted Filchock's pass and raced 19 yards for the TD, then kicked the extra point. The Giants got their first touchdown in the same period when Filchock passed 38 yards to Frank Liebel. Ken Strong converted.

There was no scoring in the second period.

In the third, the Giants pulled even at 14-14 when Filchock passed 5 yards for a TD to Steve Filipowicz and Strong converted.

Sid Luckman fooled the Giants completely with a "keep-it" play in the fourth quarter, running 19 yards for a touchdown and Maznicki converted again. Later in the quarter, Maznicki booted a field goal from the 26 to make the final score 24-14.

Touchdowns—Kavanaugh, Magnani, Luckman, Liebel, Filipowicz.
Points after touchdown—Maznicki 3, Strong 2.

Attendance: 58,346.
Players' Shares: Chicago $1,975.82; New York $1,295.57.

1946 BOSTON YANKS
COACH - Herb Kopf
5th 2-8-1

Abbruzzi, Lou - B	Governali, Paul - Q
Badaczewski, John - G	Grigas, John - B
Bailey, Sam - E	Hoague, Joe - B
Calcagni, Ralph - T	Juster, Reuben - T
Canale, Rocco - G	Karnofsky, Abe - B

Crisler, Hal - E
Currivan, Don - E
Dancewicz, Francis - Q
Davis, Bob - B
Dean, Tom - T
Deeks, Don - T
Dimancheff, "Babe" - B
Domnanovich, Joe - C
Eliason, Don - E
Famiglietti, Gary - B
Gillette, Jim - B
Goldman, Sam - E

Lee, Gene - C
Leon, Tony - G
McGee, Ed - T
Magee, Jim - C
Maley, Howard - B
Micka, Mike - B
Pederson, Win - T
Romboli, Rudy - B
Scollard, Nick - E
Sierocinski, Steve - T
Sulaitis, Joe - B
Zeno, Joe - G

Rubino, Tony - G
Ryan, Dave - B
Sanzotta, Dom - B
Schottel, Ivan - Q
Spangler, Gene - B
Szymanski, Frank - C
Tassos, Damon - G

Thomas, Russ - T
Uremovich, Emil - T
Vezmar, Walt - G
Westfall, Bob - B
Wickett, Lloyd - T
Wilson, "Camp" - B
Wojciechowicz, Alex - C

1946 GREEN BAY PACKERS
COACH - :"Curly" Lambeau
3rd 6-5-0

Aberson, Cliff - B
Barnett, Solon - T & G
Bennett, Earl - G
Brock, Charley - C
Canadeo, Tony - B
Comp, Irv - Q
Craig, Larry - Q
Croft, "Tiny" - T
Flowers, Bob - C
Forte, Bob - B
Fritsch, Ted - B
Gatewood, Les - C
Goodnight, Clyde - E
Keuper, Ken - B
Kuusisto, Bill - G
Lee, Bill - T
Letlow, Russ - G
Lipscomb, Paul - T
Luhn, Nolan - E
McKay, Roy - B

Miller, Ton - E
Mitchell, Charles - B
Mosely, Russ - B
Mulleneaux, Carl - E
Neal, "Ed" - T & G
Nussbaumer, Bob - B
Odson, Urban - T
Pregulman, Merv - G
Prescott, Hal - E
Ray, "Baby" - T
Riddick, Ray - E
Rohrig, Herman - B
Schlinkman, Walt - B
Smith, Bruce - B
Sparlis, Al - G
Tollefson, Charles - G
Wells, Don - E
Wildung, Dick - G
Zupek, Al - B

1946 CHICAGO BEARS
COACH - George Halas
1st 8-2-1
(Beat New York for title, 24-14)

Baisi, Al - G
Berry, Connie Mack - E
Bray, Ray - G
Clarkson, Stu - C
Davis, Fred - T
Drulis, Chuck - G
Farris, Tom - Q
Federovich, John - T
Forte, Aldo - G
Gallarneau, Hugh - B
Geyer, Bill - B
Jarmoluk, Mike - T
Kavanaugh, Ken - E
Keane, Jim - E
Kolman, Ed - T
Lamb, Walt - E
Luckman, Sid - Q
McAfee, George - B

McLean, Ray - B
Magnani, Dante - B
Margarita, "Hank" - B
Maznicki, Frank - B
Mucha, Rudy - G
Mullins, Noah - B
Osmanski, Joe - B
Osmanski, Bill - B
Perkins, Don - B
Preston, Pat - G
Reese, Lloyd - B
Schiechl, John - C
Schweidler, Dick - B
Sprinkle, Ed - E
Stickel, Walt - T
Stydahar, Joe - T
Turner, "Bulldog" - C
Wilson, George - E

1946 LOS ANGELES RAMS
COACH - Adam Walsh
2nd 6-4-1

Banta, "Jack" - B
Benton, Jim - E
Bouley, Gil - T
DeLauer, Bob - C
Eason, Roger - G
Farmer, Tom - B
Fawcett, Jake - T
Gehrke, Fred - B
Hamilton, Ray - E
Harding, Roger - C
Hardy, Jim - Q
Harmon, Tom - B
Hickey, "Red" - E
Hoffman, Bob - B
Holovak, Mike - B
Johnson, Clyde - T
Lazetich, Mike - G

Lear, Les - G
Levy, Len - G
Matheson, Riley - G
Mergenthal, Art - G
Naumetz, Fred - C
Pasqua, Joe - T
Pritko, Steve - E
Reisz, Al - B
Ruthstrom, Ralph - B
Schultz, Eberle - T
Shaw, Bob - E
Strode, Woody - E
Sucic, Steve - B
Washington, Ken - B
Waterfield, Bob - Q
West, Pat - B
Wilson, John - B

1946 CHICAGO CARDINALS
COACH - Jim Conzelman
4th 6-5-0

Angsman, Elmer - B
Apolskis, Ray - G & C
Arms, Lloyd - G
Banonis, Vince - C
Blackburn, Bill - C
Bulger, Chet - T
Campbell, Bill - C
Christman, Paul - Q
Colhouer, Jake - G
Conoly, Bill - G
Cuff, Ward - B
Dewell, Bill - E
Drulis, Al - B
Foster, Ralph - T
Goldberg, "Biggie" - B
Harder, "Pat" - B
Hust, Al - E
Ivy, "Pop" - E

Johnston, Jim - B
Kearns, Tom - T
Kutner, Mal - E
Maddock, Bob - G
Mallouf, Ray - Q
Mauldin, Stan - T
Montgomery, Bill - B
Parker, Joe - E
Plasman, Dick - E
Ramsey, "Buster" - G
Rankin, Walt - B
Rucinski, Ed - E
Sarringhaus, Paul - B
Seno, Frank - B
Strausbuagh, Jim - B
Sutch, George - B
Szot, Walt - T
Zimny, Bob - T

1946 NEW YORK GIANTS
COACH - Steve Owen
1st 7-3-1
(Lost to Chicago Bears for
title, 24-14)

Brown, Dave - B
Byler, Joe - T
Carroll, Vic - T
Cope, Frank - T
Coulter, DeWitt - T
DeFilippo, Lou - C
Dobelstein, Bob - G
Doolan, John - B
Edwards, Bill - G
Filchock, Frank - Q
Filipowicz, Steve - B
Franck, George - B
Gladchuk, Chet - C

Gorgone, Pete - B
Hapes, Merle - B
Hare, Cecil - B
Howell, Jim Lee - E
Liebel, Frank - E
Livingston, Howie - B
Lunday, Ken - G
McCafferty, Don - E
Mead, John - E
Nix, Emery - Q
Palazzi, Lou - C
Paschal, Bill - B
Poole, Jim - E

1946 DETROIT LIONS
COACH - "Gus" Dorais
5th 1-10-0

Batinski, Stan - G
Calahan, Jim - B
Cifers, Bob - Q
Cremer, Ted - E
DeCorrevont, Bill - B
DeShane, Charles - B
Fichman, Leon - T
Forte, Aldo - G
Frutig, Ed - E
Greene, John - E

Hackney, Elmer - B
Helms, John - E
Jones, Jim - B
Jones, Ralph - E
Jurkewicz, Walt - C
McCoy, Joel - B
Madarik, Elmer - B
Matheson, John - E
Mazza, Vince - E
Montgomery, Jim - T

Ragazzo, Phil - T
Reagen, Frank - B
Soar, "Hank" - B
Strong, Ken - B

Tuttle, Orville - G
Weiss, John - E
White, Jim - T
Younce, Len - G

1946 PHILADELPHIA EAGLES
COACH - "Greasey" Neale
2nd 6-5-0

Bleeker, Mel - B
Cabrelli, Larry - E
Castiglia, Jim - B
Craft, Russ - B
Douglas, Otis - T
Eibner, John - T
Ferrante, Jack - E
Friedlund, Bob - E
Graves, Ray - C
Gude, Henry - G
Hinkle, Jack - B
Humbert, Dick - E
Kilroy, "Bucko" - T
Kish, Ben - B
Kmetovic, Pete - B
Krieger, Bob - E
Kuczynski, Al - E
Lindskog, Vic - C
Lio, Augie - G
MacDowell, Jay - E & T

McDonald, Don - E
McDonough, Bob - G
Maronic, "Duke" - G
Michaels, Ed - G
Muha, Joe - B
Ormsbee, Elliott - B
Patton, "Cliff" - G
Pritchard, "Bosh" - B
Sears, Vic - T
Sherman, Allie - Q
Smeja, Rudy - E
Steele, Ernie - B
Steinke, Gil - B
Thompson, "Tommy" - Q
VanBuren, Steve - B
Wistert, Al - T
Wojciechowicz, Alex - C
Wyhonic, John - G
Zimmerman, Leroy - Q

1946 PITTSBURGH STEELERS
COACH - "Jock" Sutherland
4th 5-5-1

Bonelli, Ernie - B
Bova, Tony - E
Brandau, Art - C
Bucek, Felix - G
Cherundolo, Chuck - C
Clement, John - Q
Compagno, Tony - B
Condit, Merlyn - B
Coomer, Joe - T
Davis, Bob - E
Dudley, Bill - B
Dutton, Bill - B
Fife, Ralph - G
Garnaas, Bill - B
Gorinski, Walt - B
Gray, Sam - E
Jansante, Val - E

Kielbasa, Max - B
Klapstein, Earl - T
Lach, Steve - Q
McCaffray, Art - T
Mattioli, Frank - G
Mehelich, Charles - E
Merkovsky, Elmer - T
Patrick, John - Q
Perko, John - G
Repko, Joe - T
Reynolds, Jim - B
Rogers, Cullen - B
Seabright, Charles - Q
Skorich, Nick - G
Titus, George - C
Tomasic, Andy - B
Wiley, John - T

1946 WASHINGTON REDSKINS
COACH - "Turk" Edwards
3rd 5-5-1

Adams, John - T
Akins, Frank - B
Aldrich, "Ki" - C
Avery, Don - T
Bagarus, Steve - B
Baugh, Sam - Q
Britt, Oscar - G
Cifers, Ed - E
Couppee, Al - B & G
DeFruiter, Bob - B
DeMao, Al - C
Ehrhardt, Clyde - C
Gaffney, Jim - B
Jacobs, Jack - Q
Jaffurs, John - G
Jenkins, Jacque - B
Koniszewski, John - T

Kovatch, John - E
Lapka, Ted - E
Lookabaugh, John - E
Moore, Wilbur - B
Peebles, Jim - E
Poillon, Dick - B
Rosato, Sal - B
Saenz, Ed - B
Schilling, Ralph - E
Steber, John - G
Stenn, Paul - T
Straika, Clem - G
Todd, Dick - B
Turley, Doug - E
Ward, Bill - G
Youel, Jim - Q
Young, Bill - T

1946 BROOKLYN DODGERS
(AAFC)
COACHES - Malcolm Stevens,
Cliff Battles & Tom Scott
2nd 3-10-1

Adams, O'Neal - E
Armstrong, Charles - B
Bernhardt, George - G
Billman, George - G
Buffington, Harry - G
Colmer, John - B
Connolly, Harry - B
Daley, Bill - B
Daukas, Nick - T
Davis, Joe - E
Dobbs, Glenn - B
Freeman, John - G
Gafford, Roy - B
Gibson, Billy Joe - C & E
Hrabetin, Frank - T
Jones, "Dub" - B
Judd, Saxon - E
McCain, Bob - E
McCarthy, Jim - E

McDonald, Walt - Q
Maack, Herb - T
Martinovich, Phil - G
Mayne, Lou - B
Mieszkowski, Ed - T
Morrow, Russ - C
Obeck, Vic - G
Paffrath, Bob - Q
Perdue, Will - E
Perpich, George - T
Principe, Dom - B
Purdin, Cal - B
Rudy, Martin - T
Segienko, George - T
Shetley, Rhoten - Q
Tackett, Doyle - B
Timmons, Charles - B
VanTone, Art - B
Warrington, Caleb - C

1946 BUFFALO BISONS
(AAFC)
COACH - Lowell Dawson
2nd 3-10-1

Batorski, John - E
Black, John - B
Brazinsky, Sam - C
Comer, Marty - E
Daddio, Bill - E
Dekdebrun, Al - Q
Doherty, George - G
Dudish, Andy - B
Dugger, John - T
Ebli, Ray - E
Fekete, John - B
Grigg, Forrest - T
Hopp, Harry - Q
Johnston, Pres - B
Jones, Elmer - G
Juzwik, Steve - B
King, "Fay" - E
Klenk, Quentin - T
Klug, Al - T
Klutka, Nick - E
Kostiuk, Mike - T
Kramer, John - T
Kulbitski, Vic - B

Lahar, Hal - G
Lecture, Jim - C
Martinelli, Jim - C
Matisi, John - T
Mutryn, Chet - B
Nelson, Herb - E
Perko, John - G
Pirro, Rocco - G
Prewitt, Felton - C
Pucci, Ben - T
Sandig, Curt - B
Schilling, Ralph - E
Stanley, C. B. - T
Stofer, Ken - Q
Stuart, Roy - G & B
Terlep, George - Q
Thibaut, Jim - B
Thurbon, Bob - B
Tomasetti, Lou - B
Vandeweghe, Al - E
White, Gene - B
Wukits, Al - C
Zontini, Lou - B

1946 CHICAGO ROCKETS
(AAFC)
COACHES - Dick Hanley, Bob
Dove, Ned Mathews, Willie
Wilkin & Pat Boland
4th 5-6-3

Boedecker, Bill - B
Brutz, Jim - T
Clay, Walt - B
Coleman, Herb - C
Cox, Norm - Q
Dove, Bob - E
Griffin, Don - B
Heywood, Ralph - E
Hillenbrand, Billy - Q
Hirsch, Elroy - B
Hoernschemeyer, Bob - B
Huneke, Charles - T
Kellagher, Bill - B
Klenk, Quentin - T
Lahey, Tom - E
Lamana, Pete - C
Lewis, Ernie - B

Mathews, Ned - B
Morris, "Max" - E
Motl, Bob - E
Nemeth, Steve - Q
O'Neal, Jim - G
Parks, Ed - C
Pearcy, Jim - G
Quillen, Frank - E
Ruetz, Joe - G
Schroeder, Bill - Q
Sumpter, Tony - G
Verry, Norm - T
Vogds, Evan - G
Wasserbach, Lloyd - T
Wilkin, Willie - T
Williams, Walt - B

1946 CLEVELAND BROWNS
(AAFC)
COACH - Paul Brown
1st 12-2-0
(Beat New York for title, 14-9)

Adams, Chet - T	Lavelli, Dante - E
Akins, Al - B	Lewis, Cliff - Q
Blandin, Ernie - T	Lund, Bill - B
Cheroke, George - T	Maceau, Mel - C
Colella, Tom - B	Motley, Marion - B
Coppage, Al - E	Rokisky, John - E
Daniell, Jim - T	Rymkus, Lou - T
Evans, Fred - B	Saban, Lou - B
Fekete, Gene - B	Scarry, Mike - C
Gatski, Frank - C	Schwenk, Wilson - Q
Graham, Otto - Q	Smith, Gaylon - B
Greenwood, Don - B	Speedie, Mac - E
Groza, Lou - T	Steuber, Bob - B
Harrington, John - E	Terrell, Ray - B
Houston, Lin - G	Ulinski, Ed - G
Jones, Edgar - B	Willis, Bill - G
Kapter, Alex - G	Yonaker, John - E
Kolesar, Bob - G	Young, George - E

1946 LOS ANGELES DONS
(AAFC)
COACH - Dud DeGroot
3rd 7-5-2

Aguirre, Joe - E	Mitchell, Paul - T
Artoe, Lee - T	Mitchell, Bob - B
Audet, Earl - T	Morton, John - E
Bertelli, Angelo - Q	Nelson, Bob - C
Clark, Harry - B	Nolander, Don - C
Duggan, Gil - T	Nowaskey, Bob - E
Elsey, Earl - B	Nygren, Bernie - B
Fenebock, Chuck - B	O'Rourke, Charley - Q
Frankowski, Ray - G	Polanski, John - B
Gentry, Dale - E	Radovich, Bill - G
Kerr, Bill - E	Reinhard, Bob - T
Kimbrough, John - B	Rockwell, Henry - C & G
Kreuger, Al - E	Seymour, Bob - B
Lolotai, Al - G	Sneddon, Bob - B
McQuary, John - B	Trigilio, Frank - B
Marefos, Andy - B	Vinnola, Paul - B
Mertes, "Buzz" - B	Yokas, Frank - G
Mihal, Joe - T	

1946 MIAMI SEAHAWKS
(AAFC)
COACHES - Jack Meagher &
Hamp Pool
4th 3-11-0

Bell, Ed - G	McDonald, Walt - Q
Berezney, Paul - T	Mitchell, Fondren - B
Blount, Lamar - E	Nelson, Jim - B
Cato, Daryl - C	Olenski, Mitch - T
Daley, Bill - B	Paffrath, Bob - B
Davis, Lamar - E	Pool, Hamp - E
Davis, Bill - T	Prince, Charley - Q
Eakin, Kay - B	Pugh, Marion - Q
Ellenson, Gene - T	Purdin, Cal - B
Erdlitz, Dick - B	Reece, Don - T
Fox, Terry - B	Reynolds, Jim - B
Gafford, Roy - B	Scott, Prince - E
Gloden, Fred - B	Sivell, Ralph - G
Hekkers, George - T	Stasica, Stan - B
Holley, Ken - B	Tarrant, Jim - Q
Hopp, Harry - Q	Tavenor, John - C
Horne, Dick - E	Taylor, Charles - G
Hrabetin, Frank - T	Trigilio, Frank - B
Johnston, Preston - B	Ulrich, Hub - E
Jones, "Dub" - B	Vardian, John - B
Jungmichel, Hal - G	Whitlow, Ken - C
Koslowski, Stan - B	Williams, John - C
Kowalski, Andy - E	Wukits, Al - C & G
Krivonak, Joe - G	Zorich, George - G

1946 NEW YORK YANKEES (AAFC)
COACH - Ray Flaherty
1st 10-3-1
(Lost to Cleveland for title, 14-9)

Alford, Bruce - E	Palmer, Darrell - T
Baldwin, John - C	Parker, "Ace" - Q
Bentz, Roman - T	Perina, Bob - B
Burrus, Harry - B & E	Piskor, Roman - T
Cheatham, Lloyd - Q	Proctor, Dewey - B
Conger, Mel - E	Prokop, Ed - B
Doherty, George - G	Riffle, Charles - G
Hare, Ray - Q	Robertson, Tom - C
Johnson, Harvey - B	Russell, John - E
Johnson, Nate - T	Sanders, "Spec" - B
Karmazin, Mike - G	Schwartz, Perry - E
Kennedy, Bob - B	Sinkwich, Frank - B
Kinard, "Bruiser" - T	Sossamon, Lou - C
Kinard, George - G	Stanton, Henry - E
McCollum, Harley - T	Sweiger, Bob - B
Manders, "Pug" - B	Wagner, Lowell - B
Masterson, Bob - E	Yachanich, Joe - G
Morrow, Bob - B	

1946 SAN FRANCISCO 49ERS
(AAFC)
COACH - "Buck" Shaw
2nd 9-5-0

Albert, Frankie - Q	Hall, Parker - Q
Balatti, Ed - E	Kuzman, John - T
Banducci, Bruno - G	Mathews, Ned - B
Bassi, Dick - G	Mellus, John - T
Beals, Al - E	Norberg, "Hank" - E
Bryant, Bob - T	Parsons, Earle - B
Casenega, Ken - B	Pavlich, Charles - G
Conlee, Gerry - C	Remington, Bill - C
Durdan, Don - B	Renfro, Dick - B
Elston, Art - C	Roskie, Ken - B
Eshmont, Len - B	Standlee, Norm - B
Fisk, Bill - E	Strzykalski, John - B
Forrest, Ed - G	Susoeff, Nick - E
Franceschi, Pete - B	Thornton, Bob - G
Freitas, Jesse - Q	Titchenal, Bob - E
Gregory, Garland - G	Vetrano, Joe - B
Grgich, Visco - G	Woudenberg, John - T

1947

NATIONAL FOOTBALL LEAGUE

WESTERN DIVISION

Chicago Cardinals	9	3	0	.750
Chicago Bears	8	4	0	.667
Green Bay	6	5	1	.545
Los Angeles	6	6	0	.500
Detroit	3	9	0	.250

EASTERN DIVISION

Philadelphia	8	4	0	.667
Pittsburgh	8	4	0	.667
Boston	4	7	1	.364
Washington	4	8	0	.333
New York	2	8	2	.200

ALL AMERICA FOOTBALL CONFERENCE

WESTERN DIVISION

Cleveland	12	1	1	.923
San Francisco	8	4	2	.667
Los Angeles	7	7	0	.500
Chicago	1	13	0	.071

EASTERN DIVISION

New York	11	2	1	.846

Buffalo	8	4	2	.667
Brooklyn	3	10	1	.231
Baltimore	2	11	1	.154

Championship Game—
Cleveland 14, New York 3

TITLE: The Chicago Cardinals beat Philadelphia, 28-21, for the championship. Philadelphia had defeated Pittsburgh, 21-0, in an Eastern Division playoff.

LEADERS: Individual leaders for the season: Scoring—"Pat" Harder (Chi-Cards), 102; Rushing—Steve VanBuren (Philadelphia), 1,008 yds., new record; Passing—Sam Baugh (Washington); Pass Receiving—Jim Keane (Chi-Bears), 64; Field Goals—"Pat" Harder (Chi-Cards), 7; Punting—Jack Jacobs (Green Bay), 43.5 yds.; Interceptions—Frank Reagen (New York), 10. In the AAFC: Scoring—Chet Mutryn (Buffalo), 96; Rushing—Marion Motley (Cleveland), 964 yds.; Passing—Otto Graham (Cleveland); Pass Receiving—Mac Speedie (Cleveland), 58; Field Goals—Rex Grossman (Baltimore), 10.

BONUS PICK: Bob Fenimore, Okla. A. & M. Back, Chicago Bears.

COACHES: Maurice "Clipper" Smith replaced Herb Kopf as head coach at Boston; Bob Snyder replaced Adam Walsh at Los Angeles. In the AAFC, Cecil Isbell was coach of the new Baltimore team; Jim Crowley replaced the combination at Chicago and was replaced by Hampton Pool late in the season; Dudley DeGroot was replaced in midseason by Mel Hein and Ted Shipkey for the L.A. Dons.

NOTES: Fifth official, back judge, used for first time by NFL.

New league rule covers failure to report offer of a bribe to league office, also any attempt to fix a game.

Charles W. Bidwill, owner of Chicago Cardinals died April 19, before his team would win the championship he had dreamed of for many years.

Kenny Washington, Los Angeles Rams back, ran 92 yards from scrimmage (TD) against Chi-Cards, Nov. 2.

Steve Van Buren, Philadelphia back, rushed 1,008 yards for season.

Bob Waterfield, Los Angeles qback, punted 86 yards against Green Bay, Oct. 5.

Jeff Burkett, Chi-Card back, died in airplane crash, Oct. 24.

Bill Hewitt, Chi-Bear, Philadelphia end, killed in automobile, Jan. 14.

Miami dropped out of AAFC and was replaced by Baltimore.

Cleveland beat New York for AAFC title, 14-3.

NFL TITLE GAME

The field was fast and frozen, the weather frigid when they clashed for the championship. The new eight-man-line defense developed by coach Earle "Greasy" Neale, although highly effective all season, backfired in this game.

In the first period, Charlie Trippi squirted through tackle on a quick-opener and went 44 yards for a touchdown. Harder kicked the conversion.

In the second period, Elmer Angsman, on the same play, went 70 yards for the Cardinals' second score and Harder converted. The Eagles came back to make it 14–7 at the half after Tommy Thompson passed 53 yards to Pat McHugh, who ran 17 more to score, with Cliff Patton converting.

Charlie Trippi ran a punt back for 75 yards and a TD in the third period and Harder again converted to make it 21-7, but the Eagles countered with a 73-yard drive, Steve Van Buren scoring from the one-yard line and Patton again converting to make it 21–14.

Again on the quick-opener Elmer Angsman burst loose for his second 70-yard touchdown run in the fourth quarter and Harder converted. And again the Eagles smashed through on the ground with Russ Craft crashing from the one and Patton once more converting to end the scoring at 28–21.

| Chicago Cardinals | 7 | 7 | 7 | 7—28 |
| Philadelphia Eagles | 0 | 7 | 7 | 7—21 |

Touchdowns—Trippi 2, Angsman 2, McHugh, Van Buren, Craft.
Points after touchdown—Harder 4, Patton 3.

Attendance: 30,759.

Players' Shares: Cardinals $1.132; Philadelphia $754.

1947 BOSTON YANKS
COACH - "Clipper" Smith
3rd 4-7-1

Badaczewski, John - G
Barzilauskas, "Fritz" - G
Canale, Rocco - G
Chipley, Bill - E
Collins, Bill - G
Crisler, Hal - E
Currivan, Don - E
Dancewicz, Francis - Q
Dean, Tom - T
Deeks, Don - T
Domnanovich, Joe - C
Fiorentino, Ed - E
Godwin, Bill - C
Golding, Joe - B
Goldman, Sam - E
Governali, Paul - Q
Grigas, John - B
Kennedy, Bill - G
Long, Bob - B

McClure, Bob - G
Maley, Howie - B
Maznicki, Frank - B
Mello, Jim - B
Micka, Mike - B
Paschal, Bill - B
Poto, John - B
Rodgers, Tom - T
Somboli, Rudy - B
Sabasteanski, Joe - C
Scollard, Nick - E
Seno, Frank - B
Sidorik, Alex - T
Sucic, Steve - B
Vogelaar, Carroll - T
Watt, Joe - B
Williams, Walt - B
Wright, Jim - G
Zeno, Joe - G

1947 CHICAGO BEARS
COACH - George Halas
2nd 8-4-0

Allen, Ed - B
Bray, Ray - G
Cifers, Ed - E
Clarkson, Stu - C
Davis, Fred - T
Drulis, Chuck - G
Ecker, Enrique - T
Farris, Tom - Q
Fenimore, Bob - B
Gallarneau, Hugh - B
Garrett, Thurman - G
Gulyancis, George - B
Hartman, Fred - T
Holovak, Mike - B
Jarmoluk, Mike - T
Johnson, Bill - G
Kavanaugh, Ken - E
Keane, Jim - E

Kindt, Don - B
Kolman, Ed - T
Luckman, Sid - Q
McAfee, George - B
McLean, Ray - B
Matheson, John - E
Milner, Bill - G
Minini, Frank - B
Mullins, Noah - B
Osmanski, Joe - B
Osmanski, Bill - B
Preston, Pat - G
Reader, Russ - B
Sacrinty, Nick - Q
Smith, H. Allen - E
Sprinkle, Ed - E
Stickel, Walt - T
Turner, "Bulldog" - C

1947 CHICAGO CARDINALS
COACH - Jim Conzelman
1st 9-3-0
(Beat Philadelphia for title,
28-21)

Andros, Plato - G
Angsman, Elmer - B
Apolskis, Ray - G & C
Arms, Lloyd - G
Banonis, Vince - C
Blackburn, Bill - C
Bulger, Chet - T
Burkett, Jeff - E
Campbell, Bill - C
Christman, Paul - Q
Cochran, "Red" - B
Colhouer, Jake - G
Coomer, Joe - T
DeCorrevont, Bill - B
Dewell, Bill - E
Dimancheff, "Babe" - B
Doolan, John - E
Esser, Clarence - E & T

Goldberg, "Biggie" - B
Harder, "Pat" - B
Ivy, "Pop" - E
Karwales, John - E
Kutner, Mal - E
Mallouf, Ray - Q
Martin, Caleb - T
Mauldin, Stan - T
Nichols, Ham - G
Parker, Joe - E
Plasman, Dick - E & T
Ramsey, "Buster" - G
Rankin, Walt - B
Schwall, Vic - B
Smith, Charles - B
Szot, Walt - T
Trippi, Charley - B
Zimny, Bob - T

1947 DETROIT LIONS
COACH - "Gus" Dorais
5th 3-9-0

Batinski, Stan - G
Chase, Ben - G

Cook, Ted - E
Cremer, Ted - E

DeFruiter, Bob - B
DeShane, Charles - G
Dudley, Bill - B
Dugger, John - T
Fichman, Leon - T
Greene, John - E
Hekkers, George - T
Heywood, Ralph - E
Hillman, Bill - B
Ivory, Bob - G
James, Tom - B
Jones, Elmer - G
Kmetovic, Pete - B
Lear, Les - G
LeForce, Clyde - Q
Madarik, Elmer - B
Margucci, Joe - Q
Mote, Kelly - E
Nelson, Reed - C

O'Brien, Bill - B
Olenski, Mitch - T
Pregulman, Marv - G
Reese, Ken - B
Rhea, Floyd - G
Sanchez, John - T
Souders, Cecil - E
Stacco, Ed - T
Stovall, Dick - C
Sucic, Steve - B
Szymanski, Frank - C
Thomas, Russ - T
Vezmar, Walt - G
Ward, Bill - G
Watt, Joe - B
Westfall, Bob - B
Wiese, Bob - B
Wilson, "Camp" - B
Zimmerman, Leroy - Q

1947 GREEN BAY PACKERS
COACH - "Curly" Lambeau
3rd 6-5-1

Bell, Ed - G
Brock, Charley - C
Canadeo, Tony - B
Clemons, Ray - G
Cody, Ed - B
Comp, Irv - Q
Craig, Larry - E
Croft, "Tiny" - T
Cuff, Ward - B
Davis, Ralph - G
Flowers, Bob - C
Forte, Aldo - G
Forte, Bob - B
Fritsch, Ted - B
Gatewood, Les - C
Gillette, Jim - B
Goodnight, Clyde - E
Jacobs, Jack - Q

Keuper, Ken - B
Kovatch, John - E
Lipscomb, Paul - T
Luhn, Nolan - E
McDougal, Bob - B
McKay, Roy - B
Neal, "Ed" - T & G
Odson, Urban - T
Ray, "Baby" - T
Rohrig, Herman - B
Schlinkman, Walt - B
Skoglund, Bob - E
Smith, Bruce - B
Tassos, Damon - G
Wells, Don - E
Wildung, Dick - G
Wilson, Gene - E

1947 LOS ANGELES RAMS
COACH - Bob Snyder
4th 6-6-0

Bagarus, Steve - B
Banta, "Jack" - B
Benton, Jim - E
Bleeker, Mel - B
Bouley, Gil - T
Champagne, Ed - T
Cowhig, Gerry - B
David, Bob - G
Dean, Hal - G
Eason, Roger - G
Finlay, John - G
Gehrke, Fred - B
Hamilton, Ray - E
Hardy, Jim - Q
Harmon, Tom - B
Hickey, "Red" - E
Hoerner, Dick - B
Hoffman, Bob - B

Horvath, Les - B
Hubbell, Frank - E
Huffman, Dick - T
Johnson, Clyde - T
Ksionzyk, John - Q
Lazetich, Mike - G
Magnani, Dante - B
Martin, John - C
Matheson, Riley - G
Naumetz, Fred - C
Pritko, Steve - E
Schultz, Eberle - T
Smyth, Bill - T
Washington, Ken - B
Waterfield, Bob - Q
West, Pat - B
Wilson, John - B
Zilly, John - E

1947 NEW YORK GIANTS
COACH - Steve Owen
5th 2-8-2

Blumenstock, Jim - B
Brown, Dave - B
Browning, Greg - E
Cannady, John - LB

Carroll, Vic - T & E
Cheverko, George - B
Cope, Frank - T
Coulter, DeWitt - T & E

DeFilippo. Lou - C
Dobelstein, Bob - G
Faircloth, Art - B
Franck, George - B
Gladchuk, Chet - C
Governali, Paul - Q
Hachten, Bill - G
Howell, Jim Lee - E
Iverson, Chris - B
Liebel. Frank - E
Livingston, Howie - B
Lunday, Ken - G
Mead, John - E
Miklich, Bill - B
Niles, Gerry - B

Palazzi, Lou - C
Paschal, Bill - B
Paschka, Gordon - B
Poole, Ray - E
Ragazzo, Phil - T
Reagen, Frank - B
Roberts, "Choo Choo" - B
Schuler, Bill - T
Strong, Ken - B
Sulaitis, Joe - B & E
Tobin, George - G
Weiss, John - E
White, Jim - T
Younce, Len - G

Deeks, Don - T
DeFruiter, Bob - B
DeMao, Al - C
Duckworth, Joe - E
Farmer, Tom - B
Garzoni, Mike - G
Gray, Bill - G
Harris, "Hank" - G
Jenkins, Jacque - B
Jones, Harvey - B
Lookabaugh, John - E
McKee, Paul - E
Mont, Tommy - Q
Nobile, Leo - G
Nussbaumer, Bob - B
Pacewic, Vin - Q

Peebles, Jim - E
Poillon, Dick - B
Rosato, Sal - B
Ruthstrom, Ralph - B
Saenz, Ed - B
Sanchez, John - T
Sommers, John - C
Steber, John - G
Taylor, Hugh - E
Tereshinski, Joe - E
Todd, Dick - B
Turley, Doug - E
Ward, Bill - G
Wilde, George - B
Williamson, Ernie - T
Youel, Jim - Q

1947 PHILADELPHIA EAGLES
COACH - "Greasey" Neale
1st 8-4-0
(Lost to Chicago Cardinals for
title, 28-21, after beating
Pittsburgh in playoff, 21-0)

Armstrong, Neil - E
Baisi, Al - G
Bauman, Alf - T
Cabrelli, Larry - E
Campion, Tom - T
Crafts, Russ - B
Doss, Noble - B
Douglas, Otis - T
Ferrante, Jack - E
Green, John - E
Harding, Roger - C
Hinkle, Jack - B
Humbert, Dick - E
Kekeris, Jim - T
Kilroy, "Bucko" - G
Kish, Ben - B
Lindskog, Vic - C
MacDowell, Jay - T
McHugh. "Pat" - B
Macioszczyk, Art - B

Mackrides, Bill - Q
Maronic, "Duke" - G
Muha, Joe - B
Patton, "Cliff" - G
Pihos, Pete - E
Prescott, Hal - E
Pritchard, "Bosh" - B
Sears, Vic - T
Sherman, Allie - Q
Steele, Ernie - B
Steinke, Gil - B
Talcott, Don - T
Thompson, "Tommy" - Q
Van Buren, Steve - B
Weedon, Don - G
Williams, Boyd - C
Wistert, Al - T
Wojciechowicz, Alex - C
Wyhonic, John - G

1947 BALTIMORE COLTS
(AAFC)
COACH - Cecil Isbell
4th 2-11-1

Baumgartner, Bill - E
Bechtol, "Hub" - E
Black, John - B
Blount, Lamar - B & E
Case, Ernie - Q
Castiglia, Jim - B
Cure, Armand - B
Davis, Lamar - E
Dudish, Andy - B
French, Barry - G
Galvin, John - Q
Getchell, Gorham - E
Grain, Ed - G
Handley, Dick - C
Hekkers, George - T
Higgins, Luke - G
Hillenbrand, Billy - B
Jones, Ralph - E
Kasap, Mike - T
Klug, Al - T
Kobda, Joe - C

Konetsky, Floyd - E
Landrigan, Jim - T
Lio, Augie - G
Madar, Elmer - E
Marino, Vic - G
Mellus, John - T
Mertes, "Buzz" - B
Meyer, Gil - E
Mobley, Rudy - B
Nemeth, Steve- Q
Perpich, George - T
Phillips, Mike - C
Schwenk, Wilson - Q
Sigurdson, Sig - E
Sinkwich, Frank - B
Terrell, Ray - B
Trebotich, Ivan - B
Vardian, John - B
Wright, John - B
Yokas, Frank -G
Zorich, George - G

1947 PITTSBURGH STEELERS
COACH - "Jock" Sutherland
1st 8-4-0
(Lost to Philadelphia in playoff,
21-0)

Bova, Tony - E
Calcagni, Ralph - T
Cherundolo, Chuck – C
Cifers, Bob - Q
Clement, John - Q
Compagno, Tony - B
Cregar, Bill - G
Davis, Paul, - Q
Davis, Bob - E
Drulis, Al - B
Garnaas, Bill - Q
Glamp, Joe - B
Gray, Sam - E
Hornick, Bill - T
Hubka, Gene - B
Jansante, Val - E
Lach, Steve - Q

Mastrangelo, John - G
Meeks, Bryant - C
Mehelich, Charles - E
Moore, Bill - G
Morales, Gonzales - B
Nickel, Elbie - E
Perko, John - G
Repko, Joe - T
Seabright, Charles - Q
Sinkovitz, Frank - C
Skorich, Nick - G
Slater, Walt - B
Stenn, Paul - T
Sullivan, Bob - B
White, Paul - B
Wiley, John - T
Wydo, Frank - T

1947 BROOKLYN DODGERS
(AAFC)
COACH - Cliff Battles
3rd 3=10-1

Adams, O'Neal - E
Akins, Al - B
Benson, George - B
Bernhardt, George - G
Buffington. Harry - G
Colmer, John - B
Conger, Mel - E
Daukas, Lou - C
Daukas, Nick - T
Dobbs, Glenn - B
Gafford, Roy - B
Gibson, Billy Joe - C & E
Gustafson, Ed - C
Harris, Amos - G
Harris, Elmore - B
Hein, Bob - E
Hoernschemeyer, Bob - B
Huneke, Charles - T
Jeffers, Ed - G
Jones, "Dub" - B
Jones, Billie - G

Judd, Saxon - E
Kowalski, Adolph - Q
Laurinaitis, Frank - G
McCarthy, Jim - E
McDonald, Walt - Q
Martinovich, Phil - G
Mieszkowski, Ed - T
Morrow, Russ - C & E
Nelson, Herb - E
Nygren, Bernie - B
Patanelli, Mike – E
Perina, Bob - B
Ruby, Martin - T
Schneider, Leroy - T
Scruggs, Ed - E
Tackett, Doyle - B
Tevis, Leek - B
Thompson, Hal - E
Wacrington, Cabel - C & G
Wetz, Harlan - T
Williams, Garland - T

1947 WASHINGTON REDSKINS
COACH - "Turk" Edwards
4th 4-8-0

Adams, John - T
Aldrich, "Ki" - C
Avery, Don - T

Baugh, Sam - Q
Boensch, Fred - G
Castiglia, Jim - B

1947 BUFFALO BILLS (AAFC)
COACH - Lowell Dawson
2nd 8-4-2

Armstrong, Graham - T
Baldwin, Al - E

Blount, Lamar - B
Carpenter, John - T

Comer, Marty - E
Coppage, Al - E
Corley, Elbert - C
Doherty, George - G
Duggan, Gil - T
Evans, Fred - B
Gibson, Paul - E
Groves, George - G
Haynes, Joe - C
Hirsch, Ed - LB
Juzwik, Steve - B
Kerns, John - T
King, "Fay" - E
Koch, George - B
Kozel, Chet - T
Kuffel, Ray - E
Kulbitski, Vic - B

Lahar, Hal - G
Manders, "Pug" - B
Maskas, John - G
Mazza, Vin - E
Morton, John - E
Mutryn, Chet - B
Pirro, Rocco - G
Prewitt, Felton - C
Pucci, Ben - T
Ratterman, George - Q
Reisz, Al - Q
Rykovich, Julie - B
Scott, Vin - G
Terlep, George - Q
Tomasetti, Lou - B
Wizbicki, Alex - B

1947 LOS ANGELES DONS (AAFC)
COACHES - Dud DeGroot, Mel
Hein & Ted Shipkey
3rd 7-7-0

Agajanian, Ben - K
Agase, Alex - G
Aguirre, Joe - E
Anderson, Ezz - E
Artoe, Lee - T
Audet, Earl - T
Baldwin, Burr - E
Berezney, Pete - T
Brown, John - C
Clark, Harry - B
Clay, Walt - B
Danehe, Dick - T & C
Fenenbock, Chuck - B
Frankowski, Ray - G
Gallagher, Bernie - G
Gentry, Dale - E
Heap, Walt - B
Hopp, Harry - Q
Kelly, Bob - B

Kimbrough, John - B
Landsburg, Mort - B
Lennan, Reid - G
Levy, Len - G
Lolotai, Al - G
Mitchell, Paul - T
Mitchell, Bob - B
Nelson, Bob - C
Nowaskey, Bob - E
O'Rourke, Charley - Q
Pigott, "Bert" - B
Radovich, Bill - G
Reinhard, Bob - T
Reinhard, Bill - Q
Rockwell, Henry - C & G
Smith, Jim - T
Steuber, Bob - B
Titchenal, Bob - E

1947 CHICAGO ROCKETS (AAFC)
COACHES - Jim Crowley &
Hamp Pool
4th 1-13-0

Agase, Alex - G
Bass, Bill - B
Bauman, Alf - T
Berry, Connie Mack - E
Bertilli, Angelo - Q
Billman, John - G
Clay, Walt - B
Coleman, Herb - C
Cox, Norm - B
Daley, Bill - B
Dekdebrun, Al - Q
Dove, Bob - E
Ebli, Ray - E
Evans, Fred - B
Grigg, Forrest - T
Harrington, John - E
Hecht, Al - G
Hirsch, Elroy - B
Hoernschemeyer, Bob - B
Huneke, Charles - T
Kellagher, Bill - B
Kuzman, John - T
Lahey, Tom - E
Lamana, Pete - C

Lewis, Ernie - B
McCollum, Harley - T
Mattingly, Fran - G
Mihal, Joe - T
Morris, "Max" - E
Mulready, Jerry - E
Negus, Fred - C
Niedziela, Bruno - T
O'Neal, Jim - G
Percy, Jim - G
Pucci, Ben - T
Quillen, Frank - E
Ramsey, Ray - B
Rokisky, John - E
Rothrock, Cliff - C
Rotunna, Tony - B
Sanchez, John - T
Scalissi, Ted - B
Schroeder, Bill - B
Sumpter, Tony - G
Vacanti, Sam - Q
Verry, Norm - T
Vogds, Evan - G
Wasserbach, Lloyd - T

1947 NEW YORK YANKEES (AAFC)
COACH - Ray Flaherty
1st 11-2-1
(Lost to Cleveland for title, 14-3)

Alford, Bruce - E
Baldwin, John - C
Barwegan, Dick - G
Bentz, Roman - T
Burrus, Harry - E & B
Cardinal, Fred - B
Cheatham, Lloyd - Q
Davis, Van - E
Duke, Paul - C
Durishan, John - T
Elliott, Charles - T
Grain, Ed - G
Johnson, Harvey - Q
Johnson, Nate - T
Kennedy, Bob - B
Kinard, "Bruiser" - T
Kurrasch, Roy - E
Ossowski, Ted - T
Palmer, Darrell - T

Poole, Ollie - E
Proctor, Dewey - B
Prokop, Ed - B
Raimondi, Ben - Q
Riffle, Charles - G
Rowe, Harmon - B
Ruskusky, Ray - E
Russell, John - E
Sanders, "Spec" - B
Schleich, Vic - T
Sharkey, Ed - G
Sinkwich, Frank - B
Sossamon, Lou - C
Stanton, Henry - E
Stewart, Ralph - C
Sweiger, Bob - B
Sylvester, John - B
Wagner, Lowell - B
Yachanich, Joe - G
Young, "Buddy" - B

1947 CLEVELAND BROWNS (AAFC)
COACH - Paul Brown
1st 12-1-1
(Beat New York for title, 14-3)

1947 SAN FRANCISCO 49ERS (AAFC)
COACH - "Buck" Shaw
2nd 8-4-2

Adamle, Tony - B
Adams, Chet - T
Allen, Ermal - Q
Blandin, Ernie - T
Boedecker, Bill - B
Colella, Tom - B
Cowan, Bob - B
Dellerba, Spiro - B
Dewar, Jim - B
Gatski, Frank - C
Gaudio, Bob - G
Gillom, Horace - E
Graham, Otto - Q
Greenwood, Don - B
Groza, Lou - T
Houston, Lin - G
Humble, Weldon - G
Jones, Edgar - B
Kapter, Alex - G

Lavelli, Dante - E
Lewis, Cliff - Q
Lund, Bill - B
Maceau, Mel - C
Mayne, Lew - B
Motley, Marion - B
Piskor, Roman - T
Rymkus, Lou - T
Saban, Lou - B
Scarry, Mike - C
Shurnas, Marshall - E
Simonetti, Len - T
Speedie, Mac - E
Terrell, Ray - B
Ulinski, Ed - G
Willis, Bill - G
Yonakor, John - E
Young, George - E

Albert, Frank - Q
Balatti, Ed - E
Baldwin, John - C
Banducci, Bruno - G
Bassi, Dick - G
Beals, Al - E
Bryant, Bob - T
Calvelli, Tony - C
Carr, Ed - B
Conlee, Gerry - C
Crowell, Odis - T
Durdan, Don - B
Elston, Art - C
Eshmont, Len - B
Fisk, Bill - E
Forrest, Ed - G
Freitas, Jesse - Q
Gregory, Garland - G

Grgich, Visco - G
Horne, Dick - E
Masini, Len - B
Mathews, Ned - B
Norberg, "Hank" - E
Parsons, Earle - B
Robnett, Ed - B
Satterfield, Al - T
Schiechl, John - C
Smith, George - C
Standlee, Norm - B
Strzykalski, John - B
Susoeff, Nick - E
Thornton, Bob - G
Vetrano, Joe - B
Wallace, Bev - Q
Woudenberg, John - T
Yonamine, Wally - B

1948

NATIONAL FOOTBALL LEAGUE

EASTERN DIVISION

Philadelphia	9	2	1	.818
Washington	7	5	0	.583
New York	4	8	0	.333
Pittsburgh	4	8	0	.333
Boston	3	9	0	.250

WESTERN DIVISION

Chicago Cardinals	11	1	0	.917
Chicago Bears	10	2	0	.833
Los Angeles	6	5	1	.545
Green Bay	3	9	0	.250
Detroit	2	10	0	.167

ALL AMERICA FOOTBALL CONFERENCE

WESTERN DIVISION

Cleveland	14	0	0	1.000
San Francisco	12	2	0	.857
Los Angeles	7	7	0	.500
Chicago	1	13	0	.071

EASTERN DIVISION

Buffalo	8*	7	0	.533
Baltimore	7	8*	0	.467
New York	6	8	0	.429
Brooklyn	2	12	0	.143

* Includes divisional play-off

Championship Game—
 Cleveland 49, Buffalo 7

TITLE: Philadelphia beat the Chicago Cardinals, 7-0, for the championship in Philadelphia, Dec. 19. The field was covered with deep snow, line-markers were invisible and one of the worst storms in Philadelphia history poured more snow on the field all through the game.

LEADERS: Individual leaders for the season: Scoring—"Pat" Harder (Chi-Cards), 110; Rushing—Steve VanBuren (Philadelphia), 945 yds.; Passing—Lurtis "Tommy" Thompson (Philadelphia); Pass Receiving—Tom Fears (Los Angeles), 51; Field Goals—John "Cliff" Patton (Philadelphia), 8; Punting—Joe Muha (Philadelphia), 47.2 yds.; Interceptions—Dan Sandifer (Washington), 13. In the AAFC: Scoring—Orban "Spec" Sanders (New York), 114 (record); Rushing—Orban Sanders (New York), 1,432 yds. (record); Passing—Otto Graham; Pass Receiving—Mac Speedie (Cleveland), 67 (record); Field Goals—Ben Agajanian (Los Angeles), 15 (record).

BONUS PICK: Harry Gilmer, Alabama qback (Washington).

COACHES: Alvin "Bo" McMillin replaced Charles "Gus" Dorais as head coach at Detroit; Clark Shaughnessy replaced Bob Snyder at Los Angeles; John Michelosen replaced "Jock" Sutherland at Pittsburgh. In the AAFC, Carl Voyles replaced Cliff Battles at Brooklyn; Norman "Red" Strader replaced Ray Flaherty at New York in mid-season; Ed McKeever replaced Hampton Pool at Chicago; Jim Phelan replaced Mel Hein and Ted Shipkey at Los Angeles.

NOTES: Roster limit increased one to 35.

Syndicate headed by D. Lyle Fife bought Detroit Lions from Fred Mandel, Jr.

"Jock" Sutherland, coach of Pittsburgh Steelers, died, April 11.

Marlin "Pat" Harder, Chi-Cards fullback, kicked nine extra points (record) against New York Giants, Oct. 17.

Charlie Conerly, N. Y. Giants qback, completed 36 passes (record) against Pittsburgh, attempted 53, Dec. 5.

Dan Sandifer, Washington back, intercepted 13 passes (record).

Bob Waterfield, Los Angeles, punted 88 yards against Green Bay, Oct. 17.

Dick Poillon, Washington, returned intercepted lateral pass 93 yards (TD) (record) against Philadelphia, Nov. 21.

Stan Mauldin, Chi-Card tackle, died of heart attack after game against Philadelphia, Sept. 24.

Cleveland beat Buffalo for AAFC title, 49-7.

NFL TITLE GAME

Referee Ronald Gibbs and his crew did a remarkable job of officiating under almost impossible blizzard conditions.

The 36,309 true fanatics who sat through the game saw the two teams struggle back and forth through the arctic conditions until Frank Kilroy recovered quarterback Ray Mallouf's fumble on the Cardinal 17-yard line in the fourth period after three scoreless sessions. It was now or never for the Eagles and they powered across for the touchdown, Steve Van Buren smashing 5 yards to score. Cliff Patton kicked the extra point.

| Philadelphia Eagles | 0 | 0 | 0 | 7—7 |
| Chicago Cardinals | 0 | 0 | 0 | 0—0 |

Touchdown—Van Buren.
Point after touchdown—Patton.

Attendance: 36,309.

Players' Shares: Philadelphia $1,540.84; Cardinals $874.39.

1948 BOSTON YANKS
COACH - "Clipper" Smith
5th 3-9-0

Badaczewski, John - G
Barzilauskas, "Fritz" - G
Batinski, Stan - G
Chipley, Bill - E
Currivan, Don - E
Dancewicz, Francis - Q
Davis, Bob - T
Dekdebrun, Al - Q
Domnanovich, Joe - C
Godwin, Bill - C
Golding, Joe - B
Hazelhurst, Bob - B
Heywood, Ralph - E
Jarmoluk, Mike - T
McClure, Bob - G
Malinowski, Gene - B
Mancha, Vaughn - C
Micka, Mike - B
Muehlheuser, Frank - B
Nelson, Frank - B
Nolan, John - T
Paschal, Bill - B
Poto, John - B
Pritko, Steve - E
Roman, George - T
Romboli, Rudy - B
Ryan, Dave - B
Sabasteanski, Joe - C
Scollard, Nick - E
Seno, Frank - B
Slosburg, Phil - B
Sullivan, George - E
Tyree, Jim - E
Vogelaar, Carroll - T
Youel, Jim - Q
Zimmerman, Leroy - Q

1948 CHICAGO BEARS
COACH - George Halas
2nd 10-2-0

Abbey, Joe - E
Bauman, Alf - T
Boone, J. R. - B
Bray, Ray - G
Canaday, Jim - B
Cifers, Ed - E
Clarkson, Stu - C
Connor, George - T
Davis, Fred - T
DeCorrevont, Bill - B
Drulis, Chuck - G
Evans, Fred - B
Flanagan, Dick - G
Garrett, Thurman - C
Gulyanics, George - B
Holovak, Mike - B
Kavanaugh, Ken - E
Keane, Jim - E
Kindt, Don - B
Lawler, Al - B
Layne, Bobby - Q
Luckman, Sid - Q
Lujack, John - Q
McAfee, George - B
Milner, Bill - G
Minini, Frank - B
Mullins, Noah - B
Norberg, Henry - E
Osmanski, Joe - B
Preston, Pat - G
Serini, Wash - G
Smith, H. Allen - E
Sprinkle, Ed - E
Stenn, Paul - T
Stickel, Walt - T
Turner, "Bulldog" - C
Venturelli, Fred - K

1948 CHICAGO CARDINALS
COACH - Jim Conzelman
1st 11-1-0
(Lost to Philadelphia for title, 7-0)

Andros, Plato - G
Angsman, Elmer - B
Apolskis, Ray - G & C
Arms, Lloyd - G
Badaczewski, John - G
Banonis, Vince - C
Blackburn, Bill - C
Bulger, Chet - T
Campbell, Bill - C
Christman, Paul - Q
Clatt, Corwin - B
Cochran, "Red" - B
Colhouer, Jake - G
Coomer, Joe - T
Davis, Jerry - B
Dewell, Bill - E
Dimancheff, "Babe" - B
Doolan, John - B & E
Dove, Bob - E
Eikenberg, Charles - Q
Goldberg, "Biggie" - B
Goldman, Sam - E
Hanlon, Bob - B
Harder, "Pat" - B
Jacobs, Marv - T
Kutner, Mal - E
Liebel, Frank - E
Loepfe, Dick - T
Mallouf, Ray - Q
Mauldin, Stan - T
Nichols, Ham - G
Ramsey, "Buster" - G
Ravensberg, Bob - E
Schwall, Vic - B
Szot, Walt - T
Trippi, Charley - B
Wedel, Dick - G
Yablonski, Ventan - B
Zimny, Bob - T

1948 DETROIT LIONS
COACH - "Bo" McMillin
5th 2-10-0

Baumgardner, Max - E
Bingaman, Les - G
Briggs, Paul - T
Brown, Howie - G
DeShane, Charles - G
Dudish, Andy - B
Dudley, Bill - B
Dugger, John - T
Ellis, Larry - B
Enke, Fred - Q
Gillette, Jim - B
Greene, John - E
Grimes, George - B
Groomes, Mel - B
Hansen, Dale - T
Harding, Roger - C
Hekkers, George - T
Jones, Elmer - G
LeForce, Clyde - Q
Mann, Bob - E
Margucci, Joe - Q
Maves, Earl - B
Miklich, Bill - G
Mote, Kelly - E
Pregulman, Merv - C
Roskie, Ken - B
Sarratt, Charley - Q
Sarringhaus, Paul - B
Schottel, Ivan - E
Souders, Cecil - E
Stovall, Dick - G & C
Sucic, Steve - B
Thomas, Russ - T
Ward, Bill - G
Watt, Joe - B
Wiese, Bob - B
Wilson, "Camp" - B

1948 GREEN BAY PACKERS
COACH - "Curly" Lambeau
4th 3-9-0

Baxter, Lloyd - C
Bell, Ed - G
Canadeo, Tony - B
Cody, Ed - B
Comp, Irv - Q
Cook, Ted - E
Craig, Larry - E
Cremer, Ted - E
Davis, Ralph - G
Deeks, Don - T
Earhart, Ralph - B
Flowers, Bob - C
Forte, Bob - B
Fritsch, Ted - B
Girard, "Jug" - B
Goodnight, Clyde - E
Jacobs, Jack - Q
Kekeris, Jim - T
Lipscomb, Paul - T
Luhn, Nolan - E
Moss, Perry - Q
Neal, "Ed" - T
Odson, Urban - T
Olsonoski, Larry - G
Provo, Fred - B
Ray, "Baby" - T
Rhodemyre, Jay - C
Roskie, Ken - B
Schlinkman, Walt - B
Smith, Bruce - B
Smith, Oscar - B
Tassos, Damon - G
Vogds, Evan - G
Wells, Don - E
West, Pat - B
Wildung, Dick - T
Wilson, Gene - E

1948 LOS ANGELES RAMS
COACH - Clark Shaughnessy
3rd 6-5-1

Agler, Bob - B
Banta, "Jack" - B
Bouley, Gil - T
Brink, Larry - E
Champagne, Ed - T
Corn, Joe - B
Cowhig, Gerry - B
Currivan, Don - E
David, Bob - G
Dean, Hal - G
DeFruiter, Bob - B
Eason, Roger - G
Fears, Tom - E
Finlay, John - G
Gehrke, Fred - B
Hardy, Jim - Q
Hickey, "Red" - E
Hoerner, Dick - B
Hoffman, Bob - B
Horvath, Les - B
Hubbell, Frank - E
Huffman, Dick - T
Keane, Tom - B
Lazetich, Mike - G
Magnani, Dante - B
Martin, John - C
Mello, Jim - B
Naumetz, Fred - C

Paul, Don - C
Repko, Joe - T
Rickards, Paul - B
Smith, Bruce - B
Smyth, Bill - E
Sparkman, Al - T

Washington, Ken - B
Waterfield, Bob - Q
West, Pat - B
Yagiello, Ray - G
Zilly, John - E

1948 NEW YORK GIANTS
COACH - Steve Owen
3rd 4-8-0

Atwood, John - B
Beil, Larry - T
Cannady, John - C
Cheverko, George - B
Coates, Ray - B
Conerly, Charley - Q
Coulter, DeWitt - T
Dobelstein, Bob - G
Erickson, Bill - G
Ettinger, Don - G
Faircloth, Art - B
Fennema, Carl - C
Garzoni, Mike - G
Gehrke, Bruce - E
Governali, Paul - Q
Howell, Jim Lee - E
Johnson, Joe - B
Keuper, Ken - B
Miklich, Bill - G

Minisi, Tony - B
Pipkin, Joyce - E
Poole, Ray - E
Reagan, Frank - B
Roberts, "Choo Choo" - B
Royston, Ed - G
Schuler, Bill - T
Scott, Joe - B
Siegel, Jules - B
Sulaitis, Joe - B
Swiacki, Bill - E
Treadaway, John - T
Tunnell, Em - B
Walker, Paul - E
White, Jim - T
Williams, Frank - B
Williamson, Ernie - T
Younce, Len - G

1948 PHILADELPHIA EAGLES
COACH - "Greasey" Neale
1st 9-2-1
(Beat Chicago Cardinals for title,
7-0)

Armstrong, Neil - E
Barnes, "Piggy" - G
Craft, Russ - B
Doss, Noble - B
Douglas, Otis - T
Ferrante, Jack - E
Gianelli, Mario - G
Green, John - E
Hartman, Fred - T
Humbert, Dick - E
Johnson, Alvin - Q
Kilroy, "Bucko" - G
Kish, Ben - B
Lindskog, Vic - C
MacDowell, Jay - T
McHugh, "Pat" - B
Mackrides, Bill - Q
Magee, John - G
Manzini, Baptiste - C

Maronic, "Duke" - G
Muha, Joe - B
Myers, John - B
Palmer, Les - B
Parmer, Jim - B
Patton, "Cliff" - G
Pihos, Pete - E
Prescott, Hal - E
Pritchard, "Bosh" - B
Savitsky, George - T
Sears, Vic - T
Steele, Ernie - B
Steinke, Gil - B
Szymanski, Frank - C
Thompson, "Tommy" - Q
Van Buren, Steve - B
Wistert, Al - T
Wojciechowski, Alex - C

1948 PITTSBURGH STEELERS
COACH - John Michelosen
4th 4-8-0

Cherundolo, Chuck - C
Cifers, Bob - Q
Clement, John - Q
Compagno, Tony - B
Cregar, Bill - G
Davis, Paul - Q
Davis, Bob - E
Evans, Ray - Q
Garnaas, Wilford - B
Gasparella, Joe - Q
Glamp, Joe - B
Jansante, Val - E
Kurrasch, Roy - E
Mastrangelo, John - G
Meeks, Bryant - C
Mehelich, Charles - E

Moore, Bill - G
Morales, Gonzales - B
Mosley, Norman - B
Nickel, Elbie - E
Nobile, Leo - G
Nuzum, Gerry - B
Papach, George - G
Ryan, Ed - E
Samuelson, Carl - T
Seabright, Charley - Q
Shipkey, Gerry - B
Shurtz, Hubert - T
Sinkovitz, Frank - C
Skorich, Nick - G
Suhey, Steve - G
Wiley, John - T
Wydo, Frank - T

1948 WASHINGTON REDSKINS
COACH - "Turk" Edwards
2nd 7-5-0

Adams, John - T
Bagarus, Steve - B
Baugh, Sam - Q
Boensch, Fred - G
Butkus, Carl - T
Castiglia, Jim - B
Cheverko, George - B
Corbitt, Don - C
Crisler, Harold - E
DeMao, Al - C
Edwards, Weldon - T
Ehrhardt, Clyde - C
Farmer, Tom - B
Gilmer, Harry - Q
Gray, Bill - G
Harris, Henry - G
Hartley, Howard - B
Hollar, John - B
Katrishen, Mike - G
Koniszewski, John - T
Livingston, Howie - B

McKee, Paul - E
Macioszczyk, Art - B
Madarik, Elmer - B
Mont, Tom - Q
Nussbaumer, Bob - B
Peebles, Jim - E
Poillon, Dick - B
Quirk, Ed - B
Roussos, Mike - T
Saenz, Ed - B
Sanchez, John - T
Sandifer, Dan - B
Shoener, Herb - E
Stacco, Ed - T
Steber, John - G
Taylor, Hugh - E
Tereshinski, Joe - E
Todd, Dick - B
Turley, Doug - E
Youel, Jim - Q

1948 BALTIMORE COLTS (AAFC)
COACH - Cecil Isbell
1st 7-7-0
(Lost to Buffalo in playoff,
28-17)

Artoe, Lee - T
Barwegan, Dick - G
Bechtol, Hub - E
Berezney, Pete - T
Blandin, Ernie - T
Coleman, Herb - C
Corley, Bert - C
Davis, Lamar - E
Dellerba, Spiro - B
Fowler, Aubrey - B
French, Barry - G
Gambino, Lu - B
Garrett, Bill - G
Grain, Ed - G
Grossman, Rex - B
Groves, George - G
Hillenbrand, Bill - B
Klug, Al - T
Leicht, "Jake" - B
McCormick, Len - C

Maves, Earl - B
Mayne, Lou - B
Mellus, John - T
Mertes, "Bus" - B
North, John - E
Nowaskey, Bob - E
O'Rourke, Charles - Q
Pfohl, Bob - B
Poole, Ollie - E
Sidorik, Alex - T
Simmons, John - G
Smith, Joe - E
Spruill, Jim - T
Stewart, Ralph - C
Sylvester, John - B
Tittle, Y. A. - Q
Vacanti, Sam - Q
Vardian, John - B
Williams, Win - E

1948 BROOKLYN DODGERS (AAFC)
COACH - Carl Voyles
4th 2-12-0

Akins, Al - B
Allen, Carl - B
Bernhardt, George - G
Brown, Hardy - LB
Buffington, Harry - G
Burrus, Harry - E
Camp, Jim - B
Chappuis, Bob - B
Clowes, John - T
Colmer, John - B
Cooper, Jim - C
Dewar, Jim - B
Dudish, Andy - B
Edwards, Dan - E
Foldberg, Hank - E
Forkovitch, Nick - B
Gafford, Roy - B
Gustafson, Ed - C
Harris, Amos - G
Hoernschemeyer, Bob - B
Huneke, Charles - T
Judd, Saxon - E
Klasnic, John - B
Leonetti, Bob - G

McDonald, Walt - Q
Marcolini, Hugo - B
Mikula, Tom - B
Morris, Max - E
Nelson, Herb - E & T
Ramsey, Ray - B
Ruby, Martin - T
Sazio, Ralph - T
Scruggs, Ed - E
Sieradzki, Steve - B
Smith, Jim - B
Smith, Bob - T
Spencer, Joe - T
St. John, Herb - G
Strohmeyer, George - C
Sullivan, Bob - B
Tackett, Doyle - Q
Tervis, Leek - B
Thompson, Hal - E
Warren, Morrie - B
Warrington, Caleb - C & G
Williams, Harlan - T
Wozniak, John - G

1948 BUFFALO BILLS (AAFC)
COACH - Lowell Dawson
1st 7-7-0
(Lost title to Cleveland, 49-7
after beating Baltimore in playoff
28-18)

Akins, Al - B
Armstrong, Graham - T
Balatti, Ed - E
Baldwin, Al - E
Baldwin, John - C
Bumgardner, Rex - B
Callahan, Bob - C
Carpenter, John - T
Comer, Marty - E
Gibson, Paul - E
Gompers, Bill - B
Hirsch, Ed - LB
Kerns, John - T
King, Ed - G
Kisidy, George - E
Kissell, John = T
Kosikowski, Frank - E
Kozel, Chet - T
Kulbitski, Vic - B
Lahar, Hal - G
Leonetti, Bob - T

Maggiolo, "Chick" - B
Mazza, Vin - E
Mutryn, Chet - B
O'Connor, Bill - E
Pirro, Rocco - G
Prewitt, Felton - C
Ratterman, George - Q
Rykovoch, Julie - B
Schneider, Don - B
Schuette, Carl - B
Scott, Vin - G
Smith, Jim - B
Statuto, Art - C
Stefik, Bob - E
Steuber, Bob - B
Still, Jim - Q
Terlep, George - Q
Tomasetti, Lou - B
Whalen, Jerry - G
Wiznicki, Alex - B
Wyhonic, John - G

Saban, Lou - B
Sensenbaugher, Dean - B
Simonetti, Len - T
Speedie, Mac - E
Terlep, George - Q

Ulinski, Ed - G
Willis, Bill - G
Yonaker, John - E
Young, George - E

1948 LOS ANGELES DONS (AAFC)
COACH - Jim Phelan
3rd 7-7-0

Agajanian, Ben - K
Aguirre, Joe - E
Audet, Earl - T
Avery, Don - T
Baldwin, Burr - E
Brown, John - C
Clark, Harry - B
Clay, Walt - B
Danehe, Dick - T
Dobbs, Glenn - B
Durkota, Jeff - B
Fenenbock, Chuck - B
Fisk, Bill - E
Flagerman, John - C
Ford, Len - E
Frankowski, Ray - G
Gentry, Dale - E
Graham, Mike - B
Heap, Walt - Q
Johnson, Clyde - T

Kelly, Bob - B
Kimbrough, John - B
Levy, Len - G
Lolotai, Al - G
Masini, Len - B
Mihajlovich, Lou - E
Mitchell, Paul - T
Mitchell, Bob - Q
Naumu, John - B
Nelson, Bob - C
Ottele, Dick - Q
Perotti, Mike - T
Ramsey, Knox - G
Reinhard, Bob - T
Reinhard, Bill - B
Rockwell, Henry - C & G
Sexton, Lin - B
Smith, Bill - T
Wedemeyer, Herman - B
Winkler, Bernie - T

1948 CHICAGO ROCKETS
(AAFC)
COACH - Ed McKeever
4th 1-13-0

Bernhardt, George - G
Bertelli, Angelo - Q
Brutz, Jim - T
Burrus, Harry - E
Clark, Harry - B
Coleman, Herb - C
Czarobski, "Zyggy" - G
David, Bob - G
Ecker, Enrique - T
Elliott, Charles - T
Evans, Fred - B
Farris, Tom - Q
Fenenbock, "Chuck" - B
Freitas, Jesse - Q
Hirsch, Elroy - B
Jensen, Bob - E
Johnson, Farnham - E
Johnson, Nate - T
Juzwik, Steve - B
Kellagher, Bill - B
King, "Dolly" - E
Kozel, Chet - T

Kuffel, Ray - E
Lamana, Pete - LB & C
Lewis, Ernie - B
Livingston, Bob - B
McCarthy, Jim - E
Mello, Jim - B
Negus, Fred - C
Owens, "Ike" - E
Pearcy, Jim - G
Perina, Bob - B
Piskor, Roman - T
Proctor, Dewey - B
Prokop, Ed - B
Prokop, Joe - B
Rapacz, John - C
Ruetz, Joe - G
Rykovich, Julie - B
Simmons, Floyd - B
Smith, Bill - T
Urban, Gasper - G
Uremovich, Emil - T
Vacanti, Sam - Q

1948 CLEVELAND BROWNS
(AAFC)
COACH - Paul Brown
1st 9-1-2
(Beat Buffalo for title, 49-7)

Adamle, Tony - B
Adams, Chet - T
Agase, Alex - G
Boedecker, Bill - B
Cline, Ollie - B
Colella, Tom - B
Cowan, Bob - B
Gatski, Frank - C
Gaudio, Bob - G
Gillom, Horace - E
Graham, Otto - Q
Grigg, Forrest - T
Groza, Lou - T

Houston, Lin - G
Humble, Weldon - G
James, Tom - B
Jones, Edgar - B
Jones, "Dub" - B
Kosikowski, Frank - E
Lavelli, Dante - E
Lewis, Cliff - Q
Maceau, Mel - C
Motley, Marion - B
Parseghian, Ara - B
Pucci, Ben - T
Rymkus, Lou - T

1948 NEW YORK YANKEES
(AAFC)
COACH - Ray Flaherty &
"Red" Strader
3rd 6-8-0

Alford, Bruce - E
Balatti, Ed - E
Bentz, Roman - T
Butkus, Carl - T
Casey, Tom - B
Chambers, Bill - T
Cheatham, Lloyd - Q
Cleary, Paul - E
Crawford, Denver - T
Daley, Bill - B
Davis, Van - E
Dekdebrun, Al - Q
Garzoni, Mike - G
Greene, Nelson - T
Iverson, "Duke" - B
Johnson, Glenn - T
Johnson, Harvey - Q
Kennedy, Bob - B
Lane, Clayton - T
Layden, Pete - B
McDonald, Don - E
Magliolo, Joe - Q
Mitchell, Paul - T
Nabors, Roland - C

Palmer, Darrell - T
Parker, Howie - B
Perantoni, Frank - C
Riffle, Charley - G
Rokisky, John - E
Rowe, Harmon - B
Russell, John - E
Sanders, "Speed" - B
Schnellbacher, Otto - B
Schwenk, Wilson - Q
Sharkey, Ed - G
Shirley, Marion - T
Sieradski, Steve - B
Signaigo, Joe - G
Sossamon, Lou - C
Stewart, Ralph - C
Sweiger, Bob - B
Tew, Lowell - B
Wagner, Lowell - B
Weinmeister, Arnie - T
Werder, Dick - G
Yachanich, Joe - G
Young, "Buddy" - B

1948 SAN FRANCISCO 49ERS
(AAFC)
COACH - "Buck" Shaw
2nd 12-2-0

Albert, Frankie - Q
Balatti, Ed - E
Banducci, Bruno - G
Beals, Al - E
Bentz, Roman - T
Bruce, Gail - E
Bryant, Bob - T
Carr, Ed - B
Casenega, Ken - B
Cason, Jim - B
Clark, Don - G

Collier, Floyd - T
Cox, Jim - G
Crowe, Paul - B
Elliott, Charles - T
Elston, Art - C
Eshmont, Len - B
Evansen, Paul - G
Grgich, Visco - G
Hall, Forrest - B
Howell, Clarence - E

Johnson, Bill - C
Land, Fred - G
Lillywhite, Verl - B
McCormick, Walt - C
Maloney, Norm - E
Masini, Len - B
Matheson, Riley - G
Mike, Bob - T
Perry, "Joe" - B
Puddy, Hal - T

Shoener, Hal - E
Standlee, Norm - B
Strzykalski, John - B
Sullivan, Bob - B
Susoeff, Nick - E
Vetrano, Joe - B
Wallace, Bev - Q
Williams, Joel - C
Woudenberg, John - T

1949

NATIONAL FOOTBALL LEAGUE

EASTERN DIVISION

Philadelphia	11	1	0	.917
Pittsburgh	6	5	1	.545
New York Giants	6	6	0	.500
Washington	4	7	1	.364
New York Bulldogs	1	10	1	.091

WESTERN DIVISION

Los Angeles	8	2	2	.800
Chicago Bears	9	3	0	.750
Chicago Cardinals	6	5	1	.545
Detroit	4	8	0	.333
Green Bay	2	10	0	.167

ALL AMERICA FOOTBALL CONFERENCE

	W	L	T	Pct.
Cleveland	9	1	2	.900
San Francisco	9	3	0	.750
Bklyn-N.Y.	8	4	0	.667
Buffalo	5	5	2	.500
Chicago	4	8	0	.333
Los Angeles	4	8	0	.333
Baltimore	1	11	0	.083

Championship Game—
Cleveland 21, San Francisco 7

TITLE: Philadelphia beat Los Angeles, 14-0, for the championship at Los Angeles, Dec. 18.

LEADERS: Individual leaders for the season: Scoring—Marlin "Pat" Harder (Chi-Cards), Gene Roberts (N. Y. Giants), 102 (tie); Rushing—Steve VanBuren (Philadelphia), 1,146 yds., new record; Passing—Sam Baugh (Washington); Pass Receiving—Tom Fears (Los Angeles), 77; Field Goals—John Patton (Philadelphia), Bob Waterfield (Los Angeles), 9 (tie); Punting—Mike Boyda (N. Y. Bulldogs), 44.2 yds.; Interceptions—Bob Nussbaumer (Chi-Cards), 12. In the AAFC: Scoring—Lou Groza (Cleveland), 84; Rushing—Orban "Spec" Sanders (New York), 709 yds.; Passing—Glenn Dobbs (Brooklyn-New York), and Otto Graham (Cleveland), tied; Pass Receiving—Dante Lavelli (Cleveland), 40; Field Goals—Lou Groza (Cleveland), 13.

BONUS PICK: Charles Bednarik, Pennsylvania center, Philadelphia.

COACHES: Phil Handler and "Buddy" Parker, as co-coaches, replaced Jim Conzelman at Chicago Cardinals; John Whelchel replaced "Turk" Edwards at Washington, resigned, Nov. 7 and was replaced by Herman Ball. In the AAFC, Walter Driskill replaced Cecil Isbell at Baltimore in midseason; Clem Crowe replaced Lowell Dawson at Buffalo in midseason; Ray Flaherty replaced Ed McKeever at Chicago.

NOTES: The New York Bulldogs, made up of players from the Boston Yanks (1944-48) played one season with Charles Ewart as head coach.

Roster limit dropped 3 to 32; free substitution rule adopted.

Syndicate headed by James P. Clark bought Philadelphia franchise from Alexis Thompson.

Bob Gage, Pittsburgh halfback, ran 97 yards (TD) from scrimmage (tying record) against Chi-Bears, Dec. 4.

Steve Van Buren, Philadelphia, rushed 1,146 yards.

Tony Canadeo, Green Bay, rushed 1,052 yards.

John Lujack, Chi-Bears qback, gained 468 yards passing against Chi-Cards, Dec. 11.

Bob Smith, Detroit back, ran 102 yards with intercepted pass (TD and record) against Chi-Bears, Nov. 24.

Brooklyn and New York Yankees combined in the AAFC and the league played as one division. Cleveland, first with 9-1-2 record, beat San Francisco, second, in a "playoff" game, 21-7.

All American Football Conference abandoned after four years of action. Cleveland, San Francisco and Baltimore moved into NFL. Other players were pooled and drafted by NFL teams.

Alvin Thornburg, Cleveland tackle (1926) died April 20.

Bill Slyker, Evansville end (1922) died Sept. 1.

"Dinger" Doane, Cleveland, Milwaukee, Detroit, Pottsville, Providence fullback (1919-1927) died, June 5.

NFL TITLE GAME

Under drenching rain, the game was scoreless until midway in the second quarter when Tommy Thompson, Eagle quarterback, threw one of his few passes and connected with end Pete Pihos for 31 yards and a touchdown. Cliff Patton converted and the defending champions led 7-0.

Late in the third period, Waterfield, attempting a punt from his own five, slipped, and the kick was blocked by Ed Skladany, who grabbed the loose ball for a touchdown. Patton again converted and this ended the scoring.

Philadelphia Eagles	0	7	7	0—14
Los Angeles Rams	0	0	0	0—0

Touchdowns—Pihos, Skladany.
Points after touchdown—Patton 2.
Attendance: 27,980.
Players' Shares: Philadelphia $1,094.68; Los Angeles $739.66.

1949 CHICAGO BEARS
COACH - George Halas
2nd 9-3-0

Abbey, Joe - E
Bauman, Alf - T
Blanda, George - Q
Boone, J. R. - B
Bray, Ray - G
Canaday, Jim - B
Clarkson, Stu - C
Cody, Ed - B
Connor, George - T
Davis, Fred - T
DeCorrevont, Bill - B
Dreyer, Walt - B
Drulis, Chuck - G
Dugger, John - E
Flanagan, Dick - G
Gulyanics, George - B
Hoffman, John - B
Kavanaugh, Ken - E

Keane, Jim - E
Kindt, Don - B
Luckman, Sid - Q
Lujack, John - Q
McAfee, George - B
Magnani, Dante - B
Milner, Bill - G
Osmanski, Joe - B
Perina, Bob - B
Preston, Pat - G
Rykovich, Julie - B
Serini, Wash - G
Sprinkle, Ed - E
Stenn, Paul - T
Stickel, Walt - T
Szymanski, Frank - C
Turner, "Bulldog" - C

1949 CHICAGO CARDINALS
COACHES - "Buddy" Parker
& Phil Handler
3rd 6-5-1

Andros, Plato - G
Angsman, Elmer - B
Apolskis, Ray - G
Banonis, Vince - C
Blackburn, Bill - C
Bulger, Chet - T
Cain, Jim - E
Campbell, Bill - C
Christman, Paul - Q
Clatt, Corwin - B
Cochran, "Red" - B
Coomer, Joe - T
Davis, Jerry - B
Dewell, Bill - E
Dimancheff, "Babe" - B
Dove, Bob - E
Fischer, Bill - T

Goldsberry, John - T
Harder, "Pat" - B
Hardy, Jim - Q
Kutner, Mal - E
Loepfe, Dick - T
Nichols, Ham - G
Nussbaumer, Bob - B
Petrovich, George - T
Ramsey, "Buster" - G
Ravensberg, Bob - E
Schwall, Vic - B
Self, Clarence - B
Trippi, Charley - B
Wham, Tom - E
Yablonski, Ventan - B
Zimny, Bob - T

1949 DETROIT LIONS
COACH - "Bo" McMillin
4th 4-8-0

Addams, Abe - E
Bingaman, Les - G

Box, Cloyce - B
Brown, Howard - G

DeMarco, Mario - G
DeShane, Charles - G
Doll, Don - B
Dudley, Bill - B
Enke, Fred - Q
Goldman, Sam - E
Greene, John - E
Groomes, Mel. - B
Hafen, Bernie - E
Hekkers, George - T
Hollar, John - B
Karstens, George - C
LeForce, Clyde - Q
Maggioli, "Chick" - B
Mann, Bob - E
Mello, Jim - B

Mote, Kelly - E
Panelli, John - B
Pifferini, Bob - C
Poole, Ollie - E
Prchlik, John - T
Roussos, Mike - T
Russas, Al - T
Simmons, John - G & C
Smith, Jim - B
Souders, Cecil - E & T
Thomas, Russ - T
Treadway, John - T
Triplett, Wally - B
Tripucka, Frank - Q
Ward, Bill - G
Wilson, "Camp" - B

1949 GREEN BAY PACKERS
COACH - "Curly" Lambeau
5th 2-10-0

Bell, Ed - G
Burris, Paul - G
Canadeo, Tony - B
Cifers, Bob - Q
Comp, Irv - Q
Cook, Ted - E
Craig, Larry - E
Earhart, Ralph - B
Eason, Roger - G
Ethridge, Joe - T
Ferry, Lou - T
Flowers, Bob - C
Forte, Bob - B
Fritsch, Ted - B
Girard, "Jug" - B
Harding, Roger - C
Heath, Stan - Q
Jacobs, Jack - Q
Johnson, Glenn - T

Kelley, Bill - E
Kirby, John - B
Krantz, Ken - B
Lipscomb, Paul - T
Luhn, Nolan - E
Neal, "Ed" - T & C
Odson, Urban - T
Olsen, Ralph - E
Olsonoski, Larry - G
Orlich, Dan - E
Pritko, Steve - E
Rhodemyre, Jay - C
Schlinkman, Walt - B
Smith, Oscar - B
Summerhays, Bob - B
Tassos, Damon - G
Vogds, Evan - G
Wells, Don - E
Wildung, Dick - T

1949 LOS ANGELES RAMS
COACH - Clark Shaughnessy
1st 8-2-2
(Lost to Philadelphia for title, 14-0)

Agler, Bob - B
Bouley, Gil - T
Brink, Larry - E
Champagne, Ed - T
Cowhig, Gerry - B
Currivan, Don - E
Dean, Hal - G
Fears, Tom - E
Finlay, John - G
Gehrke, Fred - B
Hirsch, Elroy - B
Hoerner, Dick - B
Hubbell, Frank - E
Huffman, Dick - T
Kalmanir, Tom - B
Keane, Tom - E
Lazetich, Mike - G

Martin, John - C
Naumetz, Fred - C
Paul, Don - C
Repko, Joe - T
Shaw, Bob - E
Sims, George - B
Smith, Verda - B
Smyth, Bill - E
Sparkman, Al - T
Thomason, Bobby - Q
VanBrocklin, Norm - Q
Waterfield, Bob - Q
Williams, Jerry - B
Yagiello, Ray - G
Younger, "Tank" - B
Zilly, John - E

1949 NEW YORK BULLDOGS
COACH - Charley Ewart
5th 1-10-1

Abbey, Joe - E
Barzilauskas, "Fritz" - G
Batinski, Stan - G
Blake, Tom - T
Boyda, Mike - B
Campbell, Bill - B & C
Canady, Jim - C
Chipley, Bill - E
DeMoss, Bob - Q

Domnanovich, Joe - C
Ellis, Herb - C
Gaul, Frank - T
Golding, Joe - B
Harding, Roger - C
Heywood, Ralph - E
Jarmoluk, Mike - T
Layne, Bobby - Q
Muehlheuser, Frank - B

Nelson, Frank - B
Nolan, John - T
Olsonoski, Larry - G
Osmanski, Joe - B
Pregulman, Merv - G
Prescott, Hal - E
Pritko, Steve - E
Rauch, John - Q
Roman, George - T
Sabasteanski, Joe - G
Scollard, Nick - E

Sensenbaugher, Dean - B
Shoults, Paul - B
Slosburg, Phil - B
Smith, Oscar - B
Sponaugle, Bob - E
Tamburo, Sam - E
Vogelaar, Carroll - T
Wade, Jim - B
Watt, Joe - B
Weaver, John - G

1949 NEW YORK GIANTS
COACH - Steve Owen
3rd 6-6-0

Agajanian, Ben - K
Austin, Bill - T
Baker, Jon - G
Butkus, Carl - T
Cannady, John - LB
Coates, Ray - B
Colhouer, "Jake" - G
Conerly, Charley - Q
Doulter, DeWitt - C
Derogatis, Al - T
Duden, Dick - E
Ettinger, Don - G
Fennema, Carl - C
Fischer, Cletus - B
Greenhalgh, Bob - B
Hensley, Dick - E
Hutchinson, Ralph - T

Kershaw, George - E
Kolman, Ed - T
Lovuolo, Frank - E
Mallouf, Ray - Q
Mertes, "Bus" - B
Mullins, Noah - B
Poole, Ray - E
Roberts, "Choo Choo" - B
Royston, Ed - G
Salschneider, John - B
Sanchez, John - T
Scott, Joe - B
Sulaitis, Joe - B
Swiacki, Bill - E
Tunnell, Em - B
White, Jim - T

1949 PHILADELPHIA EAGLES
COACH - "Greasey" Neale
1st 11-1-0
(Beat Los Angeles for title,
14-0)

Armstrong, Neil - E
Barnes, "Piggy" - G
Bednarik, "Chuck" - C
Craft, Russ - B
Douglas, Otis - T
Ferrante, Jack - E
Gianelli, Mario - G
Green, John - E
Humbert, Dick - E
Jarmoluk, Mike - T
Kilroy, "Bucko" - G
Kish, Ben - B
Lindskog, Vic - C
MacDowell, Jay - T
McHugh, "Pat" - B
Mackrides, Bill - Q
Magee, John - G
Maronic, "Duke" - G

Muha, Joe - B
Myers, John - B
Parmer, Jim - B
Patton, "Cliff" - G
Pihos, Pete - E
Prescott, Hal - E
Pritchard, "Bosh" - B
Reagan, Frank - B
Savitsky, George - T
Scott, Clyde - B
Sears, Vic - T
Skladany, Leo - E
Thompson, "Tommy" - Q
Tripucka, Frank - Q
VanBuren, Steve - B
Wistert, Al - T
Wojciechowicz, Alex - C
Ziegler, Frank - B

1949 PITTSBURGH STEELERS
COACH - John Michelosen
2nd 6-5-1

Balog, Bob - C
Barbolak, Pete - T
Davis, Bob - E
Finks, Jim - Q
Gage, Bob - B
Geri, Joe - Q
Glamp, Joe - B
Hanlon, Bob - B
Hartley, Howard - B
Hogan, Darrell - G
Hollingsworth, Joe - B
Jansante, Val - E
Long, Bill - E
McPeak, Bill - E
Mehelich, Charles - E
Minini, Frank - B

Moore, Bill - G
Nickel, Elbie - E
Nobile, Leo - G
Nuzum, Jerry - B
Papach, George - B
Ragunas, Vin - B
Samuel, Don - B
Samuelson, Carl - T
Seabright, Charles - Q
Shipkey, Gerry - B
Sinkovitz, Frank - C
Suhey, Steve - G
Szot, Walt - T
Walsh, Bill - C
Wiley, John - T
Wydo, Frank - T

1949 WASHINGTON REDSKINS
COACHES - John Whelchel &
Herman Ball
4th 4-7-1

Adams, John - T
Badaczewski, John - G
Baugh, Sam - Q
Berrang, Ed - E
Cochran, Tom - B
Crisler, Hal - E
DeMao, Al - C
Dowda, Harry - B
Ehrhardt, Clyde - C
Gilmer, Harry - Q
Goode, Bob - B
Goodnight, Clyde - E
Hendren, Bob - T
Hollar, John - B
Katrishen, Mike - T
Livingston, Howie - B
Mont, Tom - Q
Niemi, Laurie - T

Peebles, Jim - E
Poillon, Dick - B
Quirk, Ed - B
Roussos, Mike - T
Saenz, Ed - B
Sanchez, John - T
Sandifer, Dan - B
Seno, Frank - B
Shoener, Herb - E
Siegert, Herb - G
Soboleski, Joe - G
Steber, John - G
Stout, Pete - B
Stovall, Dick - C
Szafaryn, Len - T
Taylor, Hugh - E
Tereshinski, Joe - E

1949 BALTIMORE COLTS (AAFC)
COACHES - Cecil Isbell &
Walt Driskill
7th 1-11-0

Barwegan, Dick - G
Bechtol, Hub - E
Beson, Warren - C
Blandin, Ernie - T
Cooper, Ken - G
Cowan, Bob - B
Davis, Lamar - E
Dellerba, Spiro - B
French, Barry - G
Gambino, Lu - B
Garrett, Bill - G
Grossman, Rex - B
Jagade, Harry - B
Jenkins, Jon - T
Kelly, Bob - B
Kingery, Wayne - B
Leicht, "Jake" - B

Leonard, Bill - E
Mellus, John - T
North, John - E
Nowaskey, Bob - E
O'Rourke, Charles - Q
Page, Paul - B
Pfohl, Bob - B
Prewitt, Felton - C
Ruthstrom, Ralph - B
Sidorik, Alex - T
Spruill, Jim - T
Stone, Billy - B
Tillman, Al - C
Tittle, Y. A. - Q
Vacanti, Sam - Q
Wedemeyer, Herman - B
Williams, Win - E

1949 BUFFALO BILLS (AAFC)
COACHES - Lowell Dawson &
Clem Crowe
4th 5-5-2

Adams, Chet - T
Baldwin, Al - E
Bumgardner, Rex - B
Carpenter, John - T
Cline, Ollie - B
Colella, Tom - B
Freitas, Jesse - Q
Gibron, Abe - G
Gibson, Paul - E
Herring, Hal - C
Hirsch, Ed - LB
Joe, Larry - B
Kerns, John - T
King, Ed - G
Kissell, John - T
Kissell, Vito - B
Livingstone, Bob - B
Logel, Bob - E
Lukens, Jim - E

Maskas, John - G
Mazza, Vin - E
Mutryn, Chet - B
Oristaglio, Bob - E
Pirro, Rocco - G
Ratterman, George - Q
Schroll, Bill - B
Schuette, Carl - LB & C
Stanton, Bill - E
Statuto, Art - C
Stautzenberger, Odell - G
Still, Jim - Q
Sutton, Joe - B
Tomasetti, Lou - B
Vasicek, Vic - G
Volz, Wilbur - B
Wizbicki, Alex - B
Wyhonic, John - G

1949 CHICAGO HORNETS
(AAFC)
COACH - Ray Flaherty
5th 4-8-0

Aschenbrenner, Frank - B
Bailey, Jim - G
Brown, Hardy - LB
Buksar, George - B
Chappuis, Bob - B
Cleary, Paul - E
Clement, John - Q
Clowes, John - T
Collins, Al - B
Czarobski, "Zyggy" - G
Donaldson, John - B
Edwards, Dan - E
Foldberg, "Hank" - E
Hazelwood, Ted - T
Heck, Bob - E
Hoernschemeyer, Bob - B
Jensen, Bob - E
Johnson, Nate - T
King, "Dolly" - E

Kuffel, Ray - E
Lewis, Ernie - B
Livingstone, Bob - B
McCarthy, Jim - E
McDonald, Walt - Q
Negus, Fred - C
Paine, Homer - T
Patterson, Paul - B
Pearcy, Jim - G
Ramsey, Ray - B
Rapacz, John - C
Richeson, Ray - G
St. John, Herb - G
Smith, Jim - B
Soboleski, Joe - T
Strohmeyer, George - C
Sweiger, Bob - B
Wendell, Marty - G
Williams, Garland - T

Ecklund, Brad - C
Erickson, Bill - G
Garza, Dan - E
Howard, Sherm - B
Iverson, "Duke" - B
Johnson, Gil - B
Johnson, Harvey - Q
Kennedy, Bob - B
Kusserow, Lou - B
Landry, Tom - B
Layden, Pete - B
Mastrangelo, John - G
Mitchell, Paul - T
Panciera, Don - Q
Perantoni, Frank - C

Poole, Barney - E
Proctor, Dewey - B
Prokop, Ed - B
Rowe, Harmon - B
Ruby, Martin - T
Russell, John - E
Schnellbacher, Otto - B
Sharkey, Ed - G
Shirley, Marion - T
Signaigo, Joe - G
Tew, Lowell - B
Weinmeister, Arnie - T
Wozniak, John - G
Young, "Buddy" - B

1949 SAN FRANCISCO 49ERS
(AAFC)
COACH - "Buck" Shaw
2nd 9-3-0
(Lost to Cleveland for title, 21

Albert, Frankie - Q
Banducci, Bruno - G
Beals, Al - E
Bruce, Gail - E
Bryant, Bob - T
Carpenter, John - T
Carr, Ed - B
Cason, Jim - B
Cathcart, Sam - B
Clark, Don - G
Crowe, Paul - B
Eshmont, Len - B
Evans, Ray - T
Garlin, Don - B
Grgich, Visco - G
Hobbs, Domer - G
Hobbs, Homer - G
Johnson, Bill - C

Lillywhite, Verl - B
Maloney, Norm - E
Mike, Bob - T
Morgan, Joe - T
Perry, "Joe" - B
Quilter, Charley - T
Sabuco, Tino - C
Salata, Paul - E
Shoener, Hal - E
Standlee, Norm - B
Strzykalski, John - B
Susoeff, Nick - E
Vetrano, Joe - B
Wagner, Lowell - B
Wallace, Bev - Q
Wisman, Pete - C
Woudenberg, John - T

1949 CLEVELAND BROWNS
(AAFC)
COACH - Paul Brown
1st 9-1-2
(Beat San Francisco for title,
21-7)

Adamle, Tony - B
Agase, Alex - G
Boedecker, Bill - B
Gatski, Frank - C
Gaudio, Bob - G
Gillom, Horace - E
Graham, Otto - Q
Grigg, Forrest - T
Groza, Lou - T
Horvath, Les - B
Houston, Lin - G
Humble, Weldon - G
James, Tom - B
Jones, Edgar - B
Jones, "Dub" - B
Lahr, Warren - B

Lavelli, Dante - E
Lewis, Cliff - Q
Motley, Marion - B
O'Connor, Bill - E
Palmer, Darrell - T
Parseghian, Ara - B
Rymkus, Lou - T
Saban, Lou - B
Speedie, Mac - E
Spencer, Joe - T
Susteric, Ed - B
Thompson, Tommy - C
Ulinski, Ed - G
Willis, Bill - G
Yonaker, John - E
Young, George - E

1950

AMERICAN CONFERENCE

Cleveland	10	2	0	.833
New York Giants	10	2	0	.833
Philadelphia	6	6	0	.500
Pittsburgh	6	6	0	.500
Chicago Cardinals	5	7	0	.417
Washington	3	9	0	.250

NATIONAL CONFERENCE

Los Angeles	9	3	0	.750
Chicago Bears	9	3	0	.750
New York Yanks	7	5	0	.583
Detroit	6	6	0	.500
Green Bay	3	9	0	.250
San Francisco	3	9	0	.250
Baltimore	1	11	0	.083

1949 LOS ANGELES DONS (AAFC)
COACH - Jim Phelan
6th 4-8-0

Aguirre, Joe - E
Baldwin, Burr - E
Brown, John - C
Clay, Walt - B
Crowe, Paul - B
Davis, Harper - B
Dobbs, Glenn - B
Dobelstein, Bob - G
Donaldson, John - B
Dworsky, Dan - Q
Fletcher, Ollie - G
Ford, Len - E
Grimes, Bill - B
Henke, Ed - T
Hoffman, Bob - B
Holder, Lew - E
Howell, Earl - B
Kelley, Ed - T

Kennedy, Bob - B
Lolatai, Al - G
McWilliams, Tom - B
Murphy, George - B
Nelson, Bob - C
Perotti, Make - T
Pipkin, Joyce - Q
Ramsey, Knox - G
Reinhard, Bob - T
Rodgers, Hosea - B
Spavital, Jim - B
Taliaferro, George - B
Tinsley, Bob - T
Whaley, Ben - G
Wilkins, Dick - E
Williamson, Ernie - T
Wimberly, Ab - E
Woodward, Dick - C

TITLE: Cleveland beat Los Angeles for the championship, 30-28 at Cleveland, Dec. 24. In conference tie playoffs, Cleveland had beaten New York, 8-3 and Los Angeles had defeated the Chicago Bears, 24-14. It was Cleveland's first year in the NFL after winning four consecutive titles in the All America Football Conference.

LEADERS: Individual leaders for the season: Scoring—Doak Walker (Detroit), 128;

1949 NEW YORK YANKEES
(AAFC)
(Merged with Brooklyn)
COACH - "Red" Strader
3rd 8-4-0

Alford, Bruce - E
Brown, George - G
Chambers, Bill - T

Colmer, John - B
Davis, Van - E
Doss, Noble - B

Rushing—Marion Motley (Cleveland), 810 yds.; Passing—Norm VanBrocklin (Los Angeles); Pass Receiving—Tom Fears (Los Angeles), 84, new record; Field Goals—Lou Groza (Cleveland), 13; Punting—Fred Morrison (Chi-Bears), 43.3 yds.; Interceptions—Orban Sanders (N. Y. Yankees), 13.

BONUS PICK: Leon Hart, Notre Dame end, Detroit.

COACHES: Clem Crowe replaced Walter Driskill as head coach at Baltimore; Gene Ronzani replaced "Curly" Lambeau at Green Bay; Joe Stydahar replaced Clark Shaughnessy at Los Angeles; "Curly" Lambeau replaced the "Buddy" Parker-Phil Handler combination with the Chicago Cardinals.

NOTES: Cleveland, San Francisco and Baltimore from the AAFC joined the NFL. Other players from the AAFC were selected by NFL teams in a pool-draft. Players from the 1949 New York Bulldogs team were also distributed.

Bob Waterfield, Los Angeles, kicked nine extra points against Baltimore (tied Harder's record) Oct. 22.

Bob Hoernschemeyer, Detroit, ran 96 yards from scrimmage (TD) against N. Y. Yanks, Nov. 23.

Jim Spavital, Baltimore back, ran 96 yards from scrimmage (TD) against Green Bay, Nov. 5.

Jim Hardy, Chi-Cards, had eight passes intercepted by Philadelphia (record), Sept. 24.

Tom Fears, Los Angeles end, caught 84 passes (record) including 18 (record) against Green Bay, Dec. 3.

Cloyce Box, Detroit end, gained 302 yards with 12 passes caught against Baltimore, Dec. 3.

Bob Shaw, Chi-Cards end, caught five touchdown passes (record) against Baltimore, Oct. 12.

Orban "Red" Sanders, N. Y. Yanks back, intercepted 13 passes (tied Sandifer's record).

Bill Dudley, Washington, returned punt 96 yards (TD) against Pittsburgh, Dec. 3.

Los Angeles Rams scored 466 points in 12 games (record) including 70 against Baltimore, Dec.

Carl L. Storck, NFL sec. treas., 1921-39; president 1939-41, died March 13.

TITLE GAME

Only 27 seconds after the kick-oft, Waterfield threw to Glenn Davis for 82 yards and a touchdown and converted for 7–0. Graham came right back with a completion to William "Dub" Jones and Groza converted to tie, 7–7. The Rams went ahead again, 14–7, when Hoerner plunged 3 yards to score and Waterfield converted.

In the second quarter, Graham threw another TD to Dante Lavelli, but the attempt at conversion failed when the pass from center was juggled and the Rams still led, 14–13.

Early in the second half, Graham again passed to Lavelli for a score and Groza's conversion made it 20–14. Dick Hoerner's one-yard plunge and Waterfield's conversion put the Rams ahead 21–20, and, seconds later, Larry Brink picked up Motley's fumble on the Brown 6 to score again. Waterfield converted and it was 28–20.

Graham put the Browns back in the game in the last quarter with a TD pitch to Rex Bumgardner and Groza converted for 28–27. An interception gave the Browns the ball in the closing minutes and, from the 16-yard line, with twenty-eight seconds remaining, Lou Groza booted a 3-pointer to win the game for the Browns 30–28.

| Cleveland Browns | 7 | 6 | 7 | 10–30 |
| Los Angeles Rams | 14 | 0 | 14 | 0–28 |

Touchdowns—Jones, Lavelli 2, Bumgardner, Davis, Hoerner 2, Brink.
Field Goal—Groza.

Points after touchdown—Groza 3, Waterfield 4.

Attendance: 29,751.

Players' Shares: Cleveland $1,113.16; Los Angeles $686.44.

1950 BALTIMORE COLTS
COACH - Clem Crowe
7th 1-11-0

Averno, Sisto - G	Fletcher, Oliver - G
Blanda, George - Q	French, Barry - G
Blandin, Ernest - T	Grossman, Rex - B
Brown, Hardy - LB	Jenkins, Jon - T
Buksar, George - B	Jensen, Bob - E
Burk, Adrian - Q	King, Ed - G
Campbell, Leon - B	Kissell, Vito - B
Collins, Albin - B	Livingston, Bob - B
Colo, Don - T	Maggioli, "Chick" - B
Cooper, Ken - G	Mazzanti, Gino - B
Crisler, Hal - E	Murray, Earl - G
Donovan, Art - T	Mutryn, Chet - B
Filchock, Frank - Q	Nelson, Bob - C

North, John - E
Nowasky, Bob - E
Oristaglio, Bob - E
Owens, Jim - E
Perina, Bob - B
Rich, Herb - B
Salata, Paul - E
Schweder, John - G

Spaniel, Frank - B
Spavital, Jim - B
Spinney, Art - E
Stone, Bill - B
Tittle, Y. A. - Q
Williams, Joel - C
Zalejski, Ernie - B

1950 CHICAGO BEARS
COACH - George Halas
2nd 9-3-0

Barwegan, Dick - G
Bauman, Alf - T
Blanda, George - Q
Boone, J. R. - B
Bradley, Ed - E
Bray, Ray - G
Campana, Al - B
Clarkson, Stu - C
Cody, Ed - B
Connor, George - T
Davis, Fred - T
Davis, Harper - B
Dempsey, Franklin - T
Garrett, Bill - G
Gulyanics, George - B
Hansen, Wayne - G
Hoffman, John - B
Hunsinger, Chuck - B

Kavanaugh, Ken - E
Keane, Jim - E
Kindt, Don - B
Luckman, Sid - Q
Lujack, John - Q
McAfee, George - B
Morrison, "Curly" - B
Negus, Fred - C
O'Quinn, "Red" - E
Reid, Floyd - B
Romanik, Steve - Q
Rykovich, Julie - B
Serini, Wash - G
Sprinkle, Ed - E
Stenn, Paul - T
Turner, "Bulldog" - C
Weatherly, Gerry - C
Wightkin, Bill - E

1950 CHICAGO CARDINALS
COACH - "Curly" Lambeau
5th 5-7-0

Andros, Plato - G
Angle, Bob - B
Angsman, Elmer - B
Apolskis, Ray - G & C
Bagdon, Ed - G
Banonis, Vince - C
Blackburn, Bill - C
Cochran, "Red" - B
Cowhig, Jerry - B
Davis, Jerry - B
Dimancheff, "Babe" - B
Dove, Bob - E
Fischer, Bill - T
Gehrke, Fred - B
Goldsberry, John - T
Harder, "Pat" - B
Hardy, Jim - Q
Hennessey, Jerry - E
Hock, John - T

Jennings, John - T
Kutner, Mal - E
Lipinski, Jim - T
McDermott, Lloyd - T
Nussbaumer, Bob - B
Paul, Don - B
Petrovich, George - T
Polsfoot, Fran - E
Ramsey, "Buster" - G
Ramsey, Knox - G
Ramsey, Ray - B
Schwall, Vic - B
Shaw, Bob - E
Svoboda, Bill - LB
Swistowicz, Mike - B
Trippi, Charley - B
Tripucka, Frank - Q
Wham, Tom - E
Yablonski, Ventan - B

1950 CLEVELAND BROWNS
COACH - Paul Brown
1st 10-2-0
(Beat New York in playoff, 8-3)
(Beat Los Angeles for title,
30-28)

Adamle, Tony - B
Agase, Alex - G
Bumgardner, Rex - B
Carpenter, Ken - B
Cole, Emerson - B
Ford, Len - E
Gatski, Frank - C
Gibron, Abe - G
Gillom, Horace - E
Gorgal, Ken - B
Graham, Otto - Q
Grigg, Forrest - T
Groza, Lou - T
Herring, Hal - C
Houston, Lin - G
Humble, Weldon - G
James, Tom - B

Jones, "Dub" - B
Kissell, John - T
Lahr, Warren - B
Lavelli, Dante - E
Lewis, Cliff - Q
Martin, Jim - G & E
Moselle, Dom - B
Motley, Marion - B
Palmer, Darrell - T
Phelps, Don - B
Rymkus, Lou - T
Sandusky, John - T
Speedie, Mac - E
Thompson, Tom - C
Willis, Bill - G
Young, George - E

1950 DETROIT LIONS
COACH - "Bo" McMillin
4th 6-6-0

Bingaman, Les - G
Box, Cloyce - E
Brown, Howard - G
Bulger, Chet - T
Cain, Jim - E
Cifelli, Gus - T
Cline, Ollie - B
Creekmur, Lou - G
Doll, Don - B
Enke, Fred - Q
Flanagan, Dick - G
Greene, John - E
Grossman, Rex - B
Hafen, Bernie - E
Hart, Leon - E
Hoernschemeyer, Bob - B
Jaszewski, Floyd - T
Krall, Gerry - B
Layne, Bobby - Q

Lininger, Ray - C
McDermott, Floyd - T
McGraw, Thurman - T
Magnani, Dante - B
Panciera, Don - B
Panelli, John - B
Pearson, Lin - B
Frohlik, John - T
Rifenburg, Dick - E
Sandifer, Dan - B
Schroll, Bill - B
Self, Clarence - B
Simmons, John - G & C
Smith, Jim - B
Soboleski, Joe - G
Triplett, Wally - B
Walker, Doak - B
Watson, Joe - C

1950 GREEN BAY PACKERS
COACH - Gene Ronzani
5th 3-9-0

Baldwin, Al - E
Boedeker, Bill - B
Burris, Paul - G
Canadeo, Tony - B
Cannava, Tony - B
Christman, Paul - Q
Cloud, John - B
Cook, Ted - E
Coutre, Larry - B
DiPierro, Ray - G
Dryer, Walt - B
Drulis, Chuck - G
Ecker, Enrique - T
Forte, Bob - B
Fritsch, Ted - B
Girard, "Jug" - B
Grimes, Billy - B
McGeary, Clarence - T

Manley, Bill - G & T
Mann, Bob - E
Neal, "Ed" - C
O'Malley, Bob - B
Orlich, Dan - E
Pritko, Steve - E
Reid, "Breezy" - B
Rote, Tobin - Q
Schuette, Carl - C
Spencer, Joe - T
Stansauk, Don - T
Steiner, "Rebel" - E
Summerhays, Bob - B
Szafaryn, Len - G
Tonnemaker, Clayt - C
Wildung, Dick - T
Wimberly, Ab - E
Wizbicki, Alex - B

1950 LOS ANGELES RAMS
COACH - Joe Stydahar
1st 9-3-0
(Beat Chicago Bears in playoff,
24-14) (Lost title to Cleveland,
30-28)

Barry, Paul - B
Bouley, Gil - T
Boyd, Bob - E
Brink, Larry - E
Champagne, Ed - T
Davis, Glenn - B
Fears, Tom - E
Finlay, John - G
Hirsch, Elroy - B
Hoerner, Dick - B
Huffman, Dick - T
Kalmanir, Tom - B
Keane, Tom - E
Lazetich, "Mike" - G
Lewis, Woodley - B
Naumetz, Fred - C
Pasquariello, Ralph - B

Paul, Don - C
Reinhard, Bob - T
Sims, George - B
Smith, Verda - B
Smyth, Bill - E
Statuto, Art - C
Stephenson, Dave - G
Thompson, Harry - G
Towler, Dan - B
Van Brocklin, Norm - Q
Vasicek, Vic - G
Waterfield, Bob - Q
West, Stan - G
Williams, Jerry - B
Younger, "Tank" - B
Zilly, John - E

1950 NEW YORK GIANTS
COACH - Steve Owen
1st 10-2-0
(Lost playoff to Cleveland, 8-3)

Austin, Bill - G
Baker, Jon - G

Cannady, John - LB & C
Clay, Randall - B

Conerly, Charley - Q
DeRogatis, Al - T
Duncan, Jim - E
Ettinger, Don - G
Griffith, Forrest - B
Jackson, Bob - B
Landry, Tom - B
McChesney, Bob - E
Mastrangelo, John - G
Milner, "Bill" - G
Mote, Kelly - E
Ostendarp, Jim - B
Poole, Ray - E
Price, Ed - B
Rapacz, John - C

Roberts, "Choo Choo" - B
Roman, George - T
Rowe, Harmon - B
Sanchez, John - T
Schnellbacher, Otto - B
Scott, Joe - B
Skladany, Leo - E
Sulaitis, Joe - B & C
Swiacki, Bill - E
Tidwell, Travis - Q
Tunnell, Em - B
Weinmeister, Arnie - T
White, Jim - T
Williams, Ellery - E
Woodward, Dick - C

Seabright, Charley - Q
Shipkey, Gerry - B
Sinkovitz, Frank - C
Smith, Truett - Q
Stautner, Ernie - T

Szot, Walt - T
Tomlinson, Dick - G
Walsh, Bill - C
Wiley, John - T
Wydo, Frank - T

1950 SAN BRANCISCO 49ERS
COACH - "Buck" Shaw
5th 3-9-0

Albert, Frankie - Q
Banducci, Bruno - G
Beals, Al - E
Bruce, Gail - E
Burke, Don - B
Campora, Don - T
Cason, Jim - B
Cathcart, Royal - B
Cathcart, Sam - B
Collins, Ray - T
Dow, Harley - G
Evans, Ray - T
Garlin, Don - B
Gehrke, Fred - B
Grgich, Visco - G
Hobbs, Homer - G
Johnson, Bill - C
Lillywhite, Verl - B

Livingston, Howie - B
Loyd, Ed - E
Matthews, Clay - T
Nix, John - E
Nomellini, Leo - T
Perry, Joe - B
Powers, Jim - Q
Quilter, Charley - T
Salata, Paul - E
Sandifer, Dan - B
Shaw, Charley - G
Shoener, Hal - E
Sitko, Emil - B
Soltau, Gordon - E
Standlee, Norm - B
Strzylkalski, John - B
Wagner, Lowell - B
Wissman, Pete - C

1950 NEW YORK YANKS
COACH - "Red" Strader
3rd 7-5-0

Adams, Chet - T
Aldridge, Ben - B
Alford, Bruce - E
Brown, George - G
Champion, Jim - G
Clowes, John - T
Domnanovich, Joe - C
Ecklund, Brad - C
Edwards, Dan - E
Golding, Joe - B
Howard, Sherm - B
Iverson, Chris - B
Jenkins, Jon - T
Johnson, Nate - T
Kennedy, Bob - B
Kusserow, Lou - B
Layden, Pete - B
Mitchell, Paul - T

Nolan, John - G
Poole, Barney - E
Ratterman, George - Q
Rauch, John - Q
Ruby, Martin - T
Russell, John - E
Sanders, Orban - B
Sharkey, Ed - G
Signaigo, Joe - G
Swistowicz, Mike - B
Taliaferro, George - B
Toth, Zollie - B
Vogelaar, Carroll - T
Weiner, Art - E
Wozniak, John - G
Yonaker, John - E
Young, "Buddy" - B

1950 WASHINGTON REDSKINS
COACH - Herman Ball
6th 3-9-0

Badaczewski, John - G
Bartos, Joe - B
Baugh, Sam - Q
Berrang, Ed - E
Brown, Dan - E
Brown, Hardy - LB
Dale, Roland - E
DeMao, Al - C
Dowda, Harry - B
Drazenovich, Chuck - LB
Dudley, Bill - B
Gilmer, Harry - Q
Goode, Bov - B
Goodnight, Clyde - E
Haynes, Hall - B
Hendren, Bob - T
Houghton, Gerry - T
Justice, "Choo Choo" - B

Karras, Lou - T
Lipscomb, Paul - T
Livingston, Howie - B
Niemi, Laurie - T
Pepper, Gene - G
Quirk, Ed - B & C
Saenz, Ed - B
Sebek, Nick - Q
Siegert, Herb - G
Spaniel Frank - B
Steber, John - G
Stout, Pete - B
Taylor, Hugh - E
Tereshinski, Joe - E
Thomas, George - B
Ulinski, Harry - C
Witucki, Casimir - G

1950 PHILADELPHIA EAGLES
COACH - "Greasy" Neale
3rd 6-6-0

Armstrong, Neil - E
Barnes, "Piggy" - G
Bednarik, "Chuck" - C
Boedecker, Bill - B
Craft, Russ - B
Ferrante, Jack - E
Giannelli, Mario - G
Green, John - E
Hix, Bill - E
Jarmoluk, Mike - T
Kilroy, "Bucko" - G
Ledbetter, Toy - B
Lindskog, Vic - C
MacDowell, Jay - T
McHugh, "Pat" - B
Mackrides, Bill - Q
Magee, John - G
Maronic, "Duke" - G

Muha, George - B
Myers, John - B
Parmer, Jim - B
Patton, "Cliff" - G
Pihos, Pete - E
Reagan, Frank - B
Sandifer, Dan - B
Scott, Clyde - B
Sears, Vic - T
Stickel, Walt - T
Sutton, Joe - B
Thompson, "Tommy" - Q
Van Buren, Steve - B
Willey, Norm "Wildman" - E
Wistert, Al - T
Wojciechowicz, Alex - C
Ziegler, Frank - B

1951

1950 PITTSBURGH STEELERS
COACH - John Michelosen
3rd 6-6-0

Allen, Lou - T
Balog, Bob - C
Chandnois, Lynn - B
Davis, Bob - E
Finks, Jim - Q
Gage, Bob - B
Gasparella, Joe - Q
Geri, Joe - Q
Hartley, Howard - B
Hays, George - E
Hogan, Darrell - G
Hollingsworth, Joe - B

Hughes, George - G
Jansante, Val - E
Long, Bill - E
McPeak, Bill - E
McWilliams, Tom - B
Mehelich, Charley - E
Nickel, Elbie - E
Nicksich, George - G
Nuzum, Gerry - B
Rogel, Fran - B
Samuel, Don - B
Samuelson, Carl - T

NATIONAL CONFERENCE

Los Angeles	8	4	0	.667
Detroit	7	4	1	.636
San Francisco	7	4	1	.636
Chicago Bears	7	5	0	.583
Green Bay	3	9	0	.250
New York Yanks	1	9	2	.100

AMERICAN CONFERENCE

Cleveland	11	1	1	.917
New York Giants	9	2	1	.818
Washington	5	7	0	.417
Pittsburgh	4	7	1	.364
Philadelphia	4	8	0	.333
Chicago Cardinals	3	9	0	.250

Los Angeles   24   Cleveland   17

TITLE: Los Angeles beat Cleveland, 24-17, for the championship in Los Angeles, Dec. 23.

LEADERS: Individual leaders for the season: Scoring—Elroy Hirsch (Los Angeles), 102; Rushing—Eddie Price (N. Y. Giants), 971 yds.; Passing—Bob Waterfield (Los Angeles); Pass Receiving—Elroy Hirsch (Los Angeles), 66; Field Goals—Bob Waterfield (Los Angeles), 13; Punting—Horace Gillom (Cleveland), 45.5 yds.; Interceptions—Otto Schnellbacher (N. Y. Giants), 11.

BONUS PICK: Kyle Rote, SMU back, New York Giants.

COACHES: Raymond "Buddy" Parker replaced Alvin "Bo" McMillin as head coach at Detroit; Jimmy Phelan replaced "Red" Strader with the New York Yanks; "Bo" McMillin replaced Earle "Greasy" Neale at Philadelphia, resigned after the second game and was replaced by Wayne Millner; Herman Ball replaced by Dick Todd in Washington at mid-season.

NOTES: First Pro Bowl game played at Los Angeles.

Roster limit raised one to 33.

1950 Baltimore Colt franchise cancelled and players made available to other teams.

Tackle, guard and center became ineligible for receiving forward pass.

William "Dub" Jones, Cleveland back, scored six touchdowns (36 points) against Chi-Bears, Nov. 25.

Bob Waterfield, L.A. Rams qback, kicked five field goals (17, 40, 25, 20, 39 yds.) against Detroit (tied record) Dec. 9.

Norman Van Brocklin, Los Angeles qback, gained 554 yards passing (41-27) against N. Y. Yanks (record) Sept. 28.

Elroy Hirsch, Los Angeles end, gained 1,495 yards with pass receptions (66), a record, including 17 touchdown passes to tie Hutson's 1942 record.

Jerry Williams, Los Angeles, returned missed field goal 99 yards (TD), record, against Green Bay, Dec. 16.

Cleveland penalized 22 times, 209 yards (record) against Chi-Bears, Nov. 25.

Dr. Tony Ippolitto, Chi-Bear guard (1943) died in train wreck, Nov. 12.

Chris O'Brien, first owner of Chi-Cards, died June 3.

TITLE GAME

The Los Angeles Rams, after losing the last two championship play-offs, finally beat the Browns for the first time to win the title. It was the first time the defending champions had ever lost a championship after four victorious years in the All America Football Conference and one in the NFL.

After a scoreless first period, Waterfield drove the Rams to the Cleveland one-yard line, then gave the ball to Dick Hoerner who plowed over. Waterfield converted.

Cleveland got its first three points from a 52-yard field goal by Lou Groza, the longest in championship history but 4 yards short of the all-time big one of 56 yards kicked by Albert Rechichar. The Browns scored again the second quarter on a 17-yard pass from Graham to William "Dub" Jones and Groza converted to make the score 10-7 at the half.

The Rams went ahead, 14–10 in the third period after Larry Brink's crashing tackle of Graham produced a fumble. The ball was picked up and hurried to the Brown one-yard line by Andy Robustelli. Dan Towler banged over for the touchdown and Waterfield converted.

The Browns pulled even early in the fourth period after Waterfield's 17-yard field goal had put the Rams ahead 17–10. They traveled 70 yards with the last one-yard plunge by Ken Carpenter bagging the vital points. Groza again scored the extra point.

Norman Van Brocklin, quarterbacking the Rams through most of the second half, then fired a long pass to Tom Fears behind the Brown defense for a 73-yard touchdown play which proved to be the winner. Waterfield booted his third extra point and the Rams held solidly against the Brown's frantic efforts to get the game even once more.

| Los Angeles Rams | 0 | 7 | 7 | 10—24 |
| Cleveland Browns | 0 | 10 | 0 | 7—17 |

Touchdowns—Hoerner, Towler, Fears, Jones, Carpenter.
Field Goals—Waterfield, Groza.
Points after touchdown—Waterfield 3, Groza 2.

Attendance: 59,475.

Players' Share: Los Angeles $2,108.44; Cleveland $1,483.12.

1951 CHICAGO BEARS
COACH - George Halas
4th 7-5-0

Barwegan, Dick - G	Morrison, "Curly" - B
Blanda, George - Q	Moser, Bob - C
Boone, J. R. - B	Neal, Ed - T
Bray, Ray - G	O'Quinn, "Red" - E
Campana, Al - B	Romanik, Steve - Q
Clarkson, Stu - C	Rowland, Brad - B
Connor, George - T	Rykovich, Julie - B
Cowan, Les - T	Schroeder, Gene - E
Davis, Fred - T	Serini, Wash - G
Dempsey, Frank - T	Sprinkle, Ed - E
Dottley, John - B	Stautberg, Gerry - G
Gulyanics, George - B	Stenn, Paul - T
Hansen, Wayne - G	Stone, Billy - B
Hoffman, John - B	Turner, "Bulldog" - C
Hunsinger, Chuck - B	White, Wilford - B
Keane, Jim - E	Wightkin, Bill - E
Kindt, Don - B	Williams, Bob - Q
Lujack, John - Q	

1951 CHICAGO CARDINALS
COACH - "Curly" Lambeau
6th 3-9-0

Angsman, Elmer - B	Panelli, John - B
Bagdon, Ed - G	Pasquariello, Ralph - B
Bienemann, Tom - E	Patton, "Cliff" - G
Cross, Bill - B	Paul, Don - B
Davis, Jerry - B	Polsfoot, Fran - E
Dove, Bob - E	Ramsey, "Buster" - G
Ferry, Lou - T	Ramsey, Knox - G
Fischer, Bill - T	Ramsey, Ray - B
Gasparella, Joe - Q	Sanford, Leo - C
Gay, Bill - B	Simmons, John - C
Groom, Jerry - C	Sitko, Emil - B
Hardy, Jim - Q	Stonesifer, Don - E
Hennessey, Jerry - E	Svoboda, Bill - LB
Houghton, Gerry - T	Trippi, Charley - B
Jennings, John - T	Tripucka, Frank - Q
Joyce, Don - T	Wallner, Fred - G
Klimek, Tony - E	Wham, Tom - E
Lauro, Lin - B	Whitman, Laverne - B
Lynch, Lynn - G	Yablonski, Ventan - B
McDermott, Lloyd - T	

1951 CLEVELAND BROWNS
COACH - Paul Brown
1st 11-1-1
(Lost title to Los Angeles, 24-17)

Adamle, Tony - B	Jones, "Dub" - B
Agase, Alex - G	Kissell, John - T
Bumgardner, Rex - B	Lahr, Warren - B
Carpenter, Ken - B	Lavelli, Dante - E
Cole, Emerson - B	Lewis, Cliff - Q
Ford, Len - E	Motley, Marion - B
Gatski, Frank -C	Oristaglio, Bob - E
Gaudio, Bob - G	Palmer, Darrell - T
Gibron, Abe - G	Phelps, Don - B
Gillom, Horace - E	Rymkus, Lou - T
Graham, Otto - Q	Sandusky, John - T
Grigg, Forrest - T	Shula, Don - B
Groza, Lou - T	Speedie, Mac - E
Herring, Hal - C	Taseff, Carl - B
Houston, Lin - G	Thompson, Tom - C
Jagade, Harry - B	Willis, Bill - G
James, Tom - B	Young, George - E

1951 DETROIT LIONS
COACH - "Buddy" Parker
2nd 7-4-1

Banonis, Vince - C	Hoernschemeyer, Bob - B
Berrang, Ed - E	Jaszewski, Floyd - T
Bingaman, Les - G	Layne, Bobby - Q
Christiansen, John - B	Lininger, Ray - C
Cifelli, Gus - T	McGraw, Thurman - T
Cline, Ollis - B	Martin, Jim - E
Clowes, John - T	Momsen, Bob - G
Creekmur, Lou - G	Murakowski, Art - B
D'Alonzo, Pete - B	Pearson, Lin - B
Dibble, Dorne - E	Prchlik, John - T
Doll, Don - B	Rogas, Dan - T
Doran, Jim - E	Self, Clarence - B
Enke, Fred - Q	Smith, Jim - B
Flanagan, Dick - G	Swiacki, Bill - E
French, Barry - G	Torgeson, Lavern - LB & C
Harder, "Pat" - B	Walker, Doak - B
Hart, Leon - E	Womack, Bruce - G
Hill, Jim - B	

1951 GREEN BAY PACKERS
COACH - Gene Ronzani
5th 3-9-0

Afflis, "Dick" - G	Moselle, Dom - B
Burris, Paul - G	Neal, "Ed" - T
Canadeo, Tony - B	Nichols, Ham - G
Cloud, John - B	Nussbaumer, Bob - B
Collins, Al - B	Orlich, Dan - E
Cone, Fred - B	Pelfrey, Ray - B & E
Davis, Harper - B	Reid, "Breezy" - B
DiPierro, Ray - G	Rhodemyre, Jay - C
Ecker, Enrique - T	Rote, Tobin - Q
Elliott, Carleton - E	Ruetz, Howard - T
Felker, Art - E	Schroll, Bill - G
Girard, "Jug" - B	Schuette, Carl - C
Grimes, Billy - B	Spencer, Joe - T
Jansante, Val - E	Stansauk, Don - T
Loomis, Ace - B	Steiner, Roy - E
Manley, Bill - G & T	Stephenson, Dave - G
Mann, Bob - E	Summerhays, Bob - B
Martinkovich, John - E	Thomason, Bob - Q
Michaels, Walt - G	Wildung, Dick - T
Moje, Dick - E	Wimberly, Ab - E

1951 LOS ANGELES RAMS
COACH - Joe Stydahar
1st 8-4-0
(Best Cleveland for title, 24-17)

Boyd, Bob - E & B	McLaughlin, Leon - C
Brink, Larry - E	Paul, Don - LB
Collier, Bob - T	Reid, Joe - C
Dahms, Tom - T	Rich, Herb - B
Dougherty, Dick - G	Robustelli, Andy - E
Davis, Glenn - B	Simensen, Don - T
Fears, Tom - E	Smith, Verda - B
Finlay, John - G	Thompson, Harry - G
Halliday, John - T	Toogood, Charley - T
Hecker, Norb - E & B	Towler, Dan - B
Hirsch, Elroy - E & B	Van Brocklin, Norm - Q
Hoerner, Dick - B	Waterfield, Bob - Q
Johnson, Marv - B	West, Stan - G
Kalmanir, Tom - B	Williams, Jerry - B
Keane, Tom - B & E	Winkler, Jim - T
Lange, Bill - G	Younger, "Tank" - B
Lewis, Woodley - B	Zilly, John - E

1951 NEW YORK GIANTS
COACH - Steve Owen
2nd 9-2-1

Albright, Bill - G	Baker, Jon - G
Amberg, John - B	Barzilauskas, Fritz - G

Cannaday, John - LB & C
Conerly, Charley - Q
Coulter, DeWitt - T
DeRogatis, Al - T
Duncan, Jim - E
Griffith, Forrest - B
Hannah, Herb - T
Hudson Bob - E
Jackson, Bob - B
Krouse, Ray - T
Landry, Tom - B
McChesney, Bob - E
Maronic, "Duke" - G
Mote, Kelly - E
Murray, Earl - G
Ostendarp, Jim - B

Poole, Ray - E
Price, Ed - B
Pritchard, "Bosh" - B
Rapacz, John - C
Rote, Kyle - B
Rowe, Harmon - B
Schnellbacher, Otto - B
Scott, Joe - B
Stribling, "Bill " - E
Sulaitis, Joe - G
Tidwell, Travis - Q
Tunnell, Em - B
Weinmeister, Arnie - T
Wilkinson, Bob - E
Woodward, Dick - C

Levanti, Lou - G
McPeak, Bill - E
Mathews, Ray - B
Mehelich, Charley - E
Minarik, Henry - E
Momsen, Tony - C
Nickel, Elbie - E
Nuzum, Gerry - B
Ortman, Chuck - Q
Rogel, Fran - B

Samuelson, Carl - T
Schweder, John - G
Shipkey, Gerry - B
Sinkovitz, Frank - C
Smith, Truett - Q
Stautner, Ernie - T
Tomlinson, Dick - G
Walsh, Bill - C
Wydo, Frank - T

1951 SAN FRANCISCO 49ERS
COACH - "Buck" Shaw
3rd 7-4-1

1951 NEW YORK YANKS
COACH - "Red" Strader
6th 1-9-2

Albert, Frankie - Q
Arenas, Joe - B
Banducci, Bruno - G
Beals, Al - E
Berry, Rex - B
Brown, Hardy - LB
Bruce, Gail - E
Burke, Don - G
Carapella, Al - T
Cason, Jim - B
Collins, Ray - T
Downs, Bob - G
Feher, Nick - G
Grgich, Visco - G
Henke, Ed - E
Jessup, Bill - E
Johnson, Bill - C

Lillywhite, Verl - B
Monachino, Jim - B
Nomellini, Leo - T
Perry, Joe - B
Powers, Jim - Q
Schabarum, Pete - B
Soltau, Gordon - E
Sparks, Dave - G
Standlee, Norm - B
Strickland, Bish - B
Strzykalski, John - B
Tanner, Hamp - T
Tittle, Y. A. -Q
Wagner, Lowell - B
White, Bob - B
Wilson, Bill - E
Wismann, Pete - C

Aldridge, Ben - B
Alford, Bruce - E
Averno, Sisto - G
Celeri, Bob - Q
Champion, Jim - G
Clowes, John - T
Colo, Don - T
Crowe, Paul - B
Cullom, Jim - G
Domnanovich, Joe - C
Donovan, Art - T
Ecklund, Brad - C
Edwards, Dan - E
Garza, Dan - E
Golding, Joe - B
Griffin, Bob - B
Howard, Sherm - B
Iverson, Chris - B
Johnson, Harvey - B

Kissell, Vito - B
McCormack, Mike - T
Meisenheimer, Darrell - B
Mitchell, Paul - T
Nagel, Ross - T
O'Connor, Bill - E
Pollard, Al - B
Poole, Barney - E
Ratterman, George - Q
Rauch, John - Q
Siegert, Wayne - G
Soboleski, Joe - T
Stroschein, Brock - E
Tait, Art - E
Taliaferro, George - B
Toth, Zollie "Tug Boat" - B
Wallace, Bev - Q
Wozniak, John - G
Young, "Buddy" - B

1951 WASHINGTON REDSKINS
COACH - Herman Ball &
Dick Todd
3rd 5-7-0

1951 PHILADELPHIA EAGLES
COACHES - "Bo" McMillin &
Wayne Millner
5th 4-8-0

Badaczewski, John - G
Baugh, Sam - Q
Berrang, Ed - E
Brito, Gene - E
Brown, Bill - G
Buksar, George - B
Cox, Bill - B
DeMao, Al - C
Dowda, Harry - B
Drazenovich, Chuck - LB
Dudley, Bill - B
Dwyer, John - B
Ferris, Neil - B
Gilmer, Harry - Q
Goode, Bob - B
Heath, Leon - B
Hendren, Bob - T
Karras, Lou - T

Lipscomb, Paul - T
Niemi, Laurie - T
Papit, John - B
Peebles, Jim - E
Pepper, Gene - G
Quirk, Ed - B
Ricca, Jim - G
Saenz, Ed - B
Salem, Ed - B
Siegert, Herb - G
Staton, Jim - T
Taylor, Hugh - E
Tereshinski, Joe - E
Thomas, George - B
Ulinski, Harry - C
Witucki, Casimir - G
Yowarsky, Walt - E

Armstrong, Neil - E
Barnes, "Piggy" - G
Bednarik, "Chuck" - C
Burk, Adrian - Q
Cowhig, Gerry - B
Craft, Russ - B
Farragut, Ken - C
Giannelli, Mario - G
Grant, Harry - E
Green, John - E
Hansen, Roscoe - T
Jarmoluk, Mike - T
Kilroy, "Bucko" - T
Lindskog, Vic - C
MacDowell, Jay - T
McHugh, "Pat" - B
Mackrides, Bill - Q
Magee, John - G
O'Quinn, "Red" - E

Parmer, Jim - B
Pihos, Pete - E
Pollard, Al - B
Pritchard, "Bosh" - B
Rauch, John - Q
Reagan, Frank - B
Romero, Ray - G
Sandifer, Dan - B
Scott, Clyde - B
Sears, Vic - T
Steele, Dick - T
Stickel, Walt - T
Sutton, Joe - B
Van Buren, Ebert - B
Van Buren, Steve - B
Walston, Bob - E
Willey, Norm - E
Wistert, Al - T
Ziegler, Frank - B

1952

1951 PITTSBURGH STEELERS
COACH - John Michelosen
4th 4-7-1

Allen, Lou - T
Butler, Jack - E
Chandnois, Lynn - B
Dodrill, Dale - G
Finks, Jim - Q
Gasparella, Joe - Q
Geri, Joe - Q
Hartley, Howard - B

Hays, George - T
Hendley, Dick - Q
Hogan, Darrell - G
Hollingsworth, Joe - B
Hughes, George - G
Jansante, Val - E
Jelley, Tom - E
Lea, Paul - T

NATIONAL CONFERENCE

Detroit	9	3	0	.750
Los Angeles	9	3	0	.750
San Francisco	7	5	0	.583
Green Bay	6	6	0	.500
Chicago Bears	5	7	0	.417
Dallas	1	11	0	.083

Detroit defeated Los Angeles, 31–21, in conference playoff

AMERICAN CONFERENCE

Cleveland	8	4	0	.667
New York	7	5	0	.583
Philadelphia	7	5	0	.583
Pittsburgh	5	7	0	.417
Chicago Cards	4	8	0	.333
Washington	4	8	0	.333

TITLE: Detroit beat Cleveland, 17-7, for the championship in Cleveland, Dec. 28. Before that, Detroit beat Los Angeles, 31-21, in conference playoff.

LEADERS: Individual leaders for the season: Scoring—Gordon Soltau (San Francisco), 94; Rushing—Dan Towler (Los Angeles), 894 yds.; Passing—Norman Van-Brocklin (Los Angeles); Pass Receiving—Mac Speedie (Cleveland), 62; Field Goals—Lou Groza (Cleveland), 19; Punting—Horace Gillom (Cleveland), 45.7 yds.; Interceptions—Dick Lane (Los Angeles), 14, new record.

BONUS PICK: William Wade, Vanderbilt qback, Los Angeles.

COACHES: New York Yanks franchise moved to Dallas as Texans under new ownership, lasted one year with Jim Phelan as head coach. Hamp Pool replaced Joe Stydahar as head coach at Los Angeles; Jim Trimble replaced Wayne Millner at Philadelphia; Joe Bach replaced John Michelosen at Pittsburgh; Joe Kuharich replaced "Curly" Lambeau at Chicago Cardinals; "Curly" Lambeau replaced Dick Todd at Washington.

NOTES: Samuel Adrian Baugh, Washington qback, retired after 16 years (record). He had led the NFL in passing six years; punting four years; interceptions one year; his four interceptions in one game was a record; his 70.3% pass completions in 1945 was a record; his 51.0 yards punting, including an 85-yarder in 1940 was top; he threw 186 touchdown passes.

Dick Lane; Los Angeles, intercepted 14 passes (record).

Bill Hillman, Detroit back (1947) died.

The Los Angeles Rams, losing to Green Bay, 28-6, with 12 minutes to play on Oct. 13, at Milwaukee, won the game, 30-28. Bob Waterfield, Ram qback, passed for three touchdowns, kicked three extra points and a field goal in one of the most spectacular rallies in history.

TITLE GAME

After a scoreless first period, Layne drove the Lions from midfield early in the second and scored the touchdown himself from the 2-yard line. Harder converted. Groza tried and missed field goals from the 44 and 47 and there was no other scoring in the first half.

Doak Walker broke loose for a 67 yard romp and a touchdown in the third period and Harder's second conversion put Detroit ahead 14-0. Cleveland sent Jagade over on a 7-yard smash and Groza converted to go into the fourth period 14-7. The Browns had been as close as Detroit's 5-yard line but were stopped by a solid defense.

Martin recovered a Cleveland fumble in the fourth and Harder booted a 36 yard field goal for the final score. The Detroit defense again halted the Browns inside the 10 to end the game 17-7.

Detroit Lions	0	7	7	3—17
Cleveland Browns	0	0	7	0— 7

Touchdowns—Layne, Walker (Detroit), Jagade (Cleveland).

Field Goal—Harder (Detroit).

Extra Points—Harder 2 (Detroit); Groza 1 (Cleveland).

Attendance: 50,934.

Players' Share: Detroit $2,274.77; Cleveland $1,712.49.

1952 CHICAGO BEARS
COACH - George Halas
5th 5-7-0

Barwegan, Dick - G
Bishop, Bill - T
Blanda, George - Q
Bradley, Ed - G
Campana, Al - B
Campbell, Leon - B
Clark, Herm - G
Cole, Emerson - B
Connor, George - T
Cross, Bob - T
Dempsey, Frank - T
Dimancheff, "Babe" - B
Dooley, Jim - E
Dottley, John - B
George, Bill - T
Gulyanics, George - B
Hansen, Wayne = G
Hoffman, Jack - E

Hoffman, John - B
Hunsinger, Chuck - B
Kindt, Don - B
Lesane, Jim - B
McColl, Bill - E
Macon, Eddie - B
Morrison, "Curly" - B
Moser, Bob - C
Romanik, Steve - Q
Schroeder, Gene - E
Sprinkle, Ed - E
Stone, Billy - B
Turner, "Bulldog" - C
Weatherly, Gerry - C
White, Wilford - B
Wightkin, Bill - E
Williams, Fred - T
Williams, Bob - Q

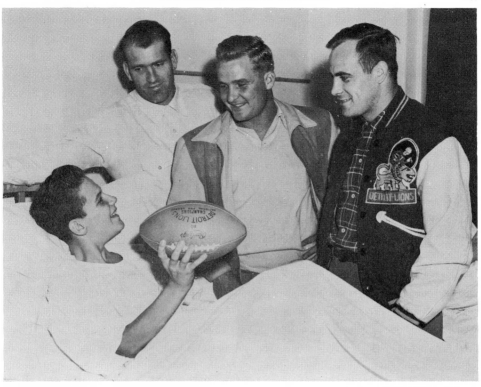

The best treatment. Hospital becomes more cheerful for this youngster, visited by Cloyce Box, *left*, Bobby Layne, *center*, and Bob Hoernschmeyer of Detroit's 1952-53 championship teams.

1952 CHICAGO CARDINALS
COACH - Joe Kuharich
5th 4-8-0

Anderson, Clif - E	Paul, Don - B
Angsman, Elmer - B	Pelfrey, Ray - E
Barni, Roy - B	Peters, Volney - T
Bienemann, Tom - E	Polofsky, Gordon - G
Cross, Bill - B	Polsfoot, Fran - E
Dove, Bob - E	Popa, Eli - B
Fischer, Bill - G	Ramsey, Ray - B
Gay, Bill - B	Sanford, Lee - G & C
Geri, Joe - B	Sikora, Mike - G
Groom, Jerry - T	Simmons, John - C
Jennings, John - T	Sitko, Emil - B
Joyce, Don - T	Stonesifer, Don - E
Karras, John - B	Svoboda, Bill - LB
Klimek, Tony - G	Thomas, Ralph - E
Lipostad, Ed - G	Triplett, Wally - B
Matson, Ollie - B	Trippi, Charley - B
Mergen, Mike - T	Tripucka, Frank - Q
Panciera, Don - Q	Wallner, Fred - G
Panelli, John - B	Whitman, Laverne - B
Pasquariello, Ralph - B	

1952 CLEVELAND BROWNS
COACH - Paul Brown
1st 8-4-0
(Lost title to Detroit, 17-7)

Brewster, "Pete" - E	Cole, Emerson - B
Bumgardner, Rex - B	Ford, Len - E
Carpenter, Ken - B	Groza, Lou - T

Helluin, Jerry - T	Michaels, Walt - B
Herring, Hal - C	Motley, Marion - B
Houston, Lin - G	Palmer, Darrell - T
Howard, Sherm - B	Phelps, Don - B
Jagade, Harry - B	Ratterman, George - Q
James, Tom - B	Rechichar, Bert - B
Jones, "Dub" - B	Renfro, Ray - B
Gain, Bob - T	Sandusky, John - T
Gatski, Frank - C	Sharkey, Ed - G
Gibron, Abe - G	Shula, Don - B
Gillom, Horace - E	Skibinski, Joe - G
Graham, Otto - Q	Speedie, Mac - E
Kissell, John - T	Thompson, Tom - C
Lahr, Warren - B	Willis, Bill - G
Lavelli, Dante - E	Young, George - E

1952 DALLAS TEXANS
COACH - Jimmy Phelan
6th 1-11-0

Averno, Sisto - G	Ecklund, Brad - C
Baggett, Bill - B	Edwards, Dan - E
Campanella, Joe - T	Felker, Gene - E
Cannamella, Pat - G	Flowers, Keith - C
Celeri, Bob - Q	Gandee, "Sonny" - E
Colo, Don - T	Grigg, Forrest - T
Davis, Jerry - B	Hoerner, Dick - B
Donovan, Art - T	Humble, Weldon - G

Jackson, Ken - T
Jankovich, Keever - E
Keane, Tom - B
Lansford, Jim - T
Lauricella, Hank - B
McKissack, Dick - B
Marchetti, Gino - E
Ortman, Chuck - Q
Pelfrey, Ray - E
Petitbon, John - B
Poole, Barney - E
Reid, Joe - C

Robison, George - G
Sherman, Will - B
Soboleski, Joe - G
Tait, Art - E
Taliaferro, George - B
Tanner, Hamp - T
Toth, Zollie - B
Tripucka, Frank - Q
Wilkins, Dick - E
Williams, Stan - E
Wozniak, John - G
Young, "Buddy" - B

Dwyer, John - B
Fears, Tom - E
Hecker, Norb - E & B
Hirsch, Elroy - B & E
Johnson, Marv - B
Klosterman, Don - Q
Lane, Dick - B
Lange, Bill - G
Lewis, Woodley - B
McFadin, "Bud" - G
McLaughlin, Leon - C
Mayes, Carl - B
Myers, John - B
Paul, Don - LB & C
Putnam, Duane - G

Quinlan, Volney - B
Rich, Herb - B
Robustelli, Andy - E
Simensen, Don - T
Smith, Verda - B
Teeuws, Len - T
Thompson, Harry - G
Toogood, Charley - T
Towler, Dan - B
Van Brocklin, Norm - Q
Waterfield, Bob - Q
West, Stan - G
Williams, Jerry - B
Winkler, Jim - T
Younger, "Tank" - B

1952 DETROIT LIONS
COACH - "Buddy" Parker
1st 9-3-0
(Beat Los Angeles in playoff,
31-21) (Beat Cleveland for
title, 17-7)

Bailey, Byron - B
Banonis, Vince - C
Bingaman, Les - G
Box, Cloyce - E
Campbell, Stan - G
Christiansen, John - B
Cifelli, Gus - T
Cline, Ollie - B
Creekmur, Lou - G & T
D'Alonzo, Pete - B
David, Jim - B
Doll, Don - B
Doran, Jim - E
Dublinski, Tom - Q
Earon, Blaine - E
Flanagan, Dick - G
Gandee, "Sonny" - E
Girard, "Jug" - B
Harder, "Pat" - B

Hardy, Jim - Q
Hart, Leon - E
Hill, Jim - B
Hoernschemeyer, Bob - B
Lary, Yale - B
Layne, Bobby - Q
McGraw, Thurman - T
Martin, Jim - G
Miller, Bob - T
Pearson, Lin - B
Prchlik, John - E
Scott, Clyde - B
Smith, Jim - B
Stanfel, Dick - G
Summerall, "Pat" - E
Swiacki, Bill - E
Torgeson, Lavern - LB & C
Walker, Doak - B

1952 NEW YORK GIANTS
COACH - Steve Owen
2nd 7-5-0

Albright, Bill - G
Amberg, John - B
Baker, Jon - G
Beck, Ray - G
Benners, Fred - Q
Cannaday, John - LB & C
Conerly, Charley - Q
Coulter, DeWitt - T & C
DeRogatis, Al - T
Duncan, Jim - E
Gifford, Frank - B
Hudson, Bob - E
Kennard, George - G
Knight, Pat - B
Krouse, Ray - T
Landry, Tom - B
McChesney, Bob - E

Menasco, Don - B
Mitchell, Harold - T
Mote, Kelly - E
Patton, Robert - G
Poole, Ray - E
Price, Ed - B
Rapacz, John - C
Rote, Kyle - B
Rowe, Harmon - B
Scott, Joe - B
Sherrod, Horace - E
Stribling, "Bill" - E
Sulaitis, Joe - G
Thomas, George - B
Tunnell, Em - B
Weinmeister, Arnie - T
Wilkinson, Bob - E
Yelvington, Dick - T

1952 GREEN BAY PACKERS
COACH - Gene Ronzani
4th 6-6-0

Afflis, "Dick" - G
Bray, Ray - G
Canadeo, Tony - B
Cone, Fred - B
Dees, Bob - T
Dillon, Bobby - B
Dowden, Steve - T
Elliott, Carleton - E
Faverty, Hal - E
Floyd, Bobby Jack - B
Forte, Bob - B
Grimes, Billy - B
Hanner, "Dave" - T
Howton, Bill - E
Johnson, Marv - B
Johnson, Tom - T
Keane, Jim - E
Logan, Dick - T
Loomis, Ace - B

Mann, Bob - E
Martinkovich, John - E
Moselle, Dom - B
Parilli, "Babe" - Q
Pearson, Lin - B
Reichardt, Bill - B
Reid, "Breezy" - B
Rhodemyre, Jay - C
Robinson, Bill - B
Rote, Tobin - Q
Ruetz, Howard - T
Ruzich, Steve - G
Sandifer, Dan - B
Schmidt, George - C
Self, Clarence - B
Serini, Wash - G
Stephenson, Dave - G
Teteak, Deral - G
Wimberly, Ab - E

1952 PHILADELPHIA EAGLES
COACH - Jim Trimble
3rd 7-5-0

Bawel, "Bibbles" - B
Bednarik, "Chuck" - C
Brewer, John - B
Burk, Adrian - Q
Craft, Russ - B
Enke, Fred - Q
Farragut, Ken - C
Ferris, Neil - B
Goldston, Ralph - B
Grant, Harry - E
Horrell, Bill - G
Huzvar, John - B
Jarmoluk, Mike - T
Kilroy, "Bucko" - G
Magee, John - G
Nipp, Maurey - G
Oristaglio, Bob - E
Parmer, Jim - B
Pihos, Pete - E

Pollard, Al - B
Ramsey, Knox - G
Restic, Joe - E
Robinson, Wayne - LB & C
Rogas, Dan - G
Scott, Clyde - B
Sears, Vic - T
Snyder, Ken - T
Stevens, Don - B
Stringer, Bob - B
Sutton, Joe - B
Thomason, Bobby - Q
Tyrrell, Joe - G
Van Buren, Ebert - B
Walston, Bob - E
Willey, Norm - E
Wydo, Frank - T
Ziegler, Frank - B
Zilly, John - E

1952 PITTSBURGH STEELERS
COACH - Joe Bach
4th 5-7-0

Andabaker, Rudy - G
Brady, Pat - Q
Brandt, Jim - B
Butler, Jack - E
Calvin, Tom - B
Chandnois, Lynn - B
Dodrill, Dale - G
Ferry, Lou - T
Finks, Jim - Q

Fugler, Dick - T
Hartley, Howard - B
Hays, George - E & T
Hensley, Dick - E
Hipps, Claude - B
Hogan, Darrell - G
Hughes, George - G
Kerkorian, Gary - Q
Kissell, Ed - Q

1952 LOS ANGELES RAMS
COACH - Hamp Pool
1st 9-3-0
(Lost to Detroit in playoff, 31-21)

Barry, Paul - B
Brink, Larry - E
Carey, Bob - E

Casner, Ken - T
Dahms, Tom - T
Daugherty, Dick - G

Ladygo, Pete - G
Levanti, Lou - C
McPeak, Bill - E
Mathews, Ray - B
Modzelewski, Ed - B
Murray, Earl - G
Nickel, Elbie - E
Rogel, Fran - B

Schweder, John - G
Shipkey, Gerry - B
Sinkovitz, Frank - C
Spinks, Jack - B
Stautner, Ernie - T
Sulima, George - E
Tarasovic, George - E
Walsh, Bill - C

1952 SAN FRANCISCO 49ERS
COACH - "Buck" Shaw
3rd 7-5-0

Albert, Frankie - Q
Aldridge, Ben - B
Arenas, Joe - B
Banducci, Bruno - G
Berry, Rex - B
Boone, J. R. - B
Brown, Hardy - LB
Burke, Don - G
Campora, Don - T
Carapella, Al - T
Cason, Jim - B
Cathcart, Sam - B
Collins, Ray - T
Endriss, Al - E
Feher, Nick - G
Grgich, Visco - G
Henke, Ed - E
Jessup, Bill - E
Johnson, Bill - C

McElhenny, Hugh - B
Meyers, Bob - B
Momsen, Bob - G
Nomellini, Leo - T
O'Donahue, Pat - E
Perry, Joe - B
Powell, Charley - E
Powers, Jim - Q
Smith, Jerry - G
Soltau, Gordon - E
Standlee, Norm - B
Strzykalski, John - B
Tittle, Y. A. - Q
Toneff, Bob - T
Wagner, Lowell - B
White, Bob - B
Wilson, Bill - E
Wismann, Pete - C

1952 WASHINGTON REDSKINS
COACH - "Curly" Lambeau
6th 4-8-0

Alban, Dick - B
Bagdon, Ed - G
Baugh, Sam - Q
Berrang, Ed - E
Brito, Gene - E
Brown, Bill - G
Buksar, George - B
Clark, Jim - G
Cloud, John - B
Cox, Bill - B
Davis, Andy - B
DeMao, Al - C
Dowda, Harry - B
Drazenovich, Chuck - LB
Ecker, Enrique - T
Ferris, Neil - B
Gilmer, Harry - Q
Heath, Leon - B
Hennessey, Jerry - E

Justice, "Choo Choo" - B
LeBaron, Ed - Q
Lipscomb, Paul - T
Momsen, Tony - C
Moss, Joe - T
Niemi, Laurie - T
Papit, John - B
Pepper, Gene - G
Ramsey, Knox - G
Ricca, Jim - G
Rykovich, Julie - B
Sykes, Bob - B
Taylor, Hugh - B
Tereshinski, Joe - E
Venuto, Sam - B
Williams, John - B
Woodward, Dick - C
Yonaker, John - E

1953

WESTERN CONFERENCE

Detroit	10	2	0	.83
San Francisco	9	3	0	.75
Los Angeles	8	3	1	.72
Chicago Bears	3	8	1	.27
Baltimore	3	9	0	.250
Green Bay	2	9	1	.182

EASTERN CONFERENCE

Cleveland	11	1	0	.917
Philadelphia	7	4	1	.636
Washington	6	5	1	.545
Pittsburgh	6	6	0	.500
New York	3	9	0	.250

Chicago Cardinals	1	10	1	.091

Detroit defeated Cleveland, 17-16

TITLE: Detroit beat Cleveland, 17-16, for the championship at Detroit, Dec. 27.

LEADERS: Individual leaders for the season: Scoring—Gordon Soltau (San Francisco), 114; Rushing—Fletcher "Joe" Perry (San Francisco), 1,018 yds.; Passing—Otto Graham (Cleveland); Pass Receiving—Pete Pihos (Philadelphia), 63; Field Goals—Lou Groza (Cleveland), 23, new record; Punting—Pat Brady (Pittsburgh), 46.9 yds.; Interceptions—Jack Christiansen (Detroit), 12.

BONUS PICK: Harry Babcock, Georgia end, San Francisco.

COACHES: Keith Molesworth was head coach of new Baltimore Colts. Joe Stydahar replaced Joe Kuharich as head coach of Chicago Cardinals.

NOTES: Jim Thorpe died, March 28.

Bert Rechichar, Baltimore linebacker, kicked 56-yard field goal against Chi-Bears, breaking Glenn Presnell's 54-yard record. It was the first attempt by Rechichar in a league game.

Joe Perry, San Francisco, rushed 1,018 yards.

Bobby Layne, Detroit qback, passed to Cloyce Box for 97 yards (TD) against Green Bay, Nov. 26.

"Buddy" Young, Baltimore, returned kickoff 104 yards (TD) against Philadelphia, Nov. 15.

Frank Blocker, Hammond center (1920) died, Dec. 5.

TITLE GAME

LaVern Torgeson of Detroit knocked the ball out of the hands of Otto Graham early in the first period. Bingaman recovered for Detroit on the Cleveland 13 and Doak Walker scored from the one. Walker added the extra point. In the second period Groza kicked a 13-yard field goal for Cleveland and Walker booted one for Detroit from the 23. The Lions led, 10-3 at the half.

Harry Jagade scored Cleveland's only touchdown from nine yards out in the third period and Groza added the extra point to tie the game. Groza kicked two more field goals in the fourth period, from the 15 and 43 yard lines and Cleveland was winning, 16–10, with 2½ minutes to play. Layne then hit four of six passes, the last a 33-yarder to Jim Doran for the touchdown. Walker's conversion put the Lions ahead, 17–16. Karilivacz intercepted Graham's first pass after the kickoff and the Lions ran out the clock for the victory.

Detroit Lions	7	3	0	7—17
Cleveland Browns	0	3	7	6—16

Touchdowns—Walker, Doran (Detroit), Jagade (Cleveland).

Conversions—Walker 2 (Detroit), Groza (Cleveland).

Field Goals—Walker (Detroit), Groza 3 (Cleveland).

Attendance: 54,577.

Players' Share: Detroit $2,424.10; Cleveland $1,654.26.

1953 BALTIMORE COLTS
COACH - Keith Molesworth
5th 3-9-0

Agase, Alex - G
Averno, Sisto - G
Barwegan, Dick - G
Blandin, Ernest - T
Brethauer, Monte - E
Campanella, Joseph - T
Coutre, Larry - B
Del Bello, John - B
Donovan, Art - T
Ecklund, Brad - C
Edwards, Dan - E
Embree, Mel - E
Enke, Fred - Q
Finnin, Tom - T
Flowers, Dick - Q
Huzvar, John - B
Jackson, Ken - T
Kalmanir, Tom - B

Keane, Tom - B
Lange, Bill - G
Little, John - T
McPhail, "Buck" - B
Marchetti, Gino - E
Mioduszewski, Ed - B
Pellington, Bill - LB
Poole, Barney - E
Rechichar, Bert - LB
Sharkey, Ed - G
Shula, Don - B
Spinney, Art - E
Taliaferro, George - B
Taseff, Carl - B
Wingate, Elmer - E
Winkler, Jim - T
Young, "Buddy" - B

1953 CHICAGO BEARS
COACH - George Halas
4th 3-8-1

Anderson, Bill - B
Autrey, Bill - C
Badaczewski, John - G
Bishop, Bill - T
Blanda, George - Q
Campbell, Leon - B
Connor, George - T
Davis, Art - T
Dempsey, Frank - T
Dooley, Jim - E
Dottley, John - B
Figner, George - B
Floyd, Bobby Jack - B
George, Bill - G
Gilbert, Kline - T
Hansen, Wayne - G
Hatley, John - G
Helwig, John - E & G
Hensley, Dick - E
Hoffman, John - B

Kindt, Don - B
Kreamcheck, John - T
Livingston, Howard - B
Lowe, Lloyd - B
McColl, Bill - E
Macon, Eddie - B
Morrison, "Curly" - B
Moser, Bob - C
O'Connell, Tom - Q
Proctor, Rex - B
Romanik, Steve - Q
Shipkey, Gerry - B
Sprinkle, Ed - E
Stone, Billy - B
Thrower, Willie - Q
Weatherly, Gerry - C
Whitman, Laverne - B
Wightkin, Bill - E
Williams, Fred - T

1953 CHICAGO CARDINALS
COACH - Joe Stydahar
6th 1-10-1

Anderson, Clif - E
Barni, Roy - B
Bienemann, Tom - E
Campana, Al - B
Carter, Willie - B
Chickillo, Nick - G
Cross, Bill - B
Curcillo, Tony - B
Dove, Bob - E
Fischer, Bill - G
Gilchrist, George - T
Groom, Jerry - T
Higgins, Tom - T
Husmann, Ed - G
Jankovich, Keever - E
Jennings, John - T
Joyce, Don - T
Nagel, Ray - B
Nagler, Gern - E
Olszewski, John - B
Panelli, John - B

Paul, Don - B
Peters, Volney - T
Polofsky, Gordon - G
Psaltis, Jim - B
Ramsey, Ray - E
Romanik, Steve - Q
Root, Jim - Q
Sandifer, Dan - B
Sanford, Leo - G & C
Schmidt, George - E
Simmons, John - C
Spinks, Jack - G
Stonesifer, Don - E
Suminski, Dave - G
Summerall, "Pat" - E & K
Svoboda, Bill - LB
Triplett, Wally - B
Trippi, Charley - B
Watford, Gerry - G
Whitman, Laverne - B

1953 CLEVELAND BROWNS
COACH - Paul Brown
1st 11-1-0
(Lost title to Detroit, 17-16)

Atkins, Doug - E
Brewster, "Pete" - E
Carpenter, Ken - B
Catlin, Tom - LB & C
Colo, Don - T
Donaldson, Gene - G
Ford, Len - E
Gatski, Frank - C
Gibron, Abe - G
Gillom, Horace - E
Gorgal, Ken - B
Graham, Otto - Q
Groza, Lou - T
Helluin, Jerry - T
Houston, Lin - G
Howard, Sherm - B
Jagade, Harry - B

James, Tom - B
Jones, "Dub" - B
Konz, Ken - B
Lahr, Warren - B
Lavelli, Dante - E
Michaels, Walt - LB
Motley, Marion - B
Noll, Chuck - G
Palmer, Darrell - T
Ratterman, George - Q
Renfro, Ray - B
Reynolds, Bill - B
Sandusky, John - T
Steinbrunner, Don - T
Thompson, Tom - C
Willis, Bill - G
Young, George - E

1953 DETROIT LIONS
COACH - "Buddy" Parker
1st 10-2-0
(Beat Cleveland for title, 17-16)

Ane, Charley - T & C
Bailey, Byron - B
Banonis, Vince - C
Bingaman, Les - G
Box, Cloyce - E
Cain, Jim - E
Carpenter, Lew - B
Christiansen, John - B
Cline, Ollie - B
Creekmur, Lou - T
David, Jim - B
Dibble, Dorne - E
Doran, Jim - E
Dove, Bob - E
Dublinski, Tom - Q
Earon, Blaine - E
Gandee, "Sonny" - E
Gedman, Gene - B
Girard, "Jug" - B

Harder, "Pat" - B
Hart, Leon - E
Hoernschemeyer, Bob - B
Karilivacz, Carl - B
Lary, Yale - B
Layne, Bobby - Q
McGraw, Thurman - T
Martin, Jim - G
Miller, Bob - T
Prchlik, John - T
Schmidt, Joe - LB
Sewell, Harley - G
Smith, Jim - B
Smith, Bob - B
Spencer, Ollie - G
Stanfel, Dick - G
Torgeson, Lavern - LB & C
Walker, Doak - B

1953 GREEN BAY PACKERS
COACH - Gene Ronzani
7th 2-9-1

Afflis, "Dick" - G
Aldridge, Ben - B
Bailey, Byron - B
Barton, Don - B
Boone, J. R. - B
Brown, Bill - G
Carmichael, Al - B
Cifelli, Gus - T
Cone, Fred - B
Coutre, Larry - B
Dawson, Gil - B
Dillon, Bobby - B
Elliott, Carleton - E
Ferguson, Howie - B
Forester, "Bill" - T
Forte, Bob - B
Hanner, "Dave" - T
Hays, George - E
Howton, Bill - E
Johnson, Marv - B

Logan, Dick - T
Loomis, Ace - B
Mann, Bob - E
Martinkovich, John - E
Papit, John - B
Parilli, "Babe" - Q
Reid, "Breezy" - B
Ringo, Jim - C
Rote, Tobin - Q
Ruetz, Howard - T
Rush, Clive - E
Ruzich, Steve - G
Sandifer, Dan - B
Stephenson, Dave - G
Szafaryn, Len - G
Teteak, Deral - G
Tonnemaker, Clayt - C
Walker, Val Joe - B
Wildung, Dick - T
Zatkoff, Roger - T

1953 LOS ANGELES RAMS
COACH - Hamp Pool
3rd 8-3-1

Agajanian, Ben - K
Boyd, Bob - E
Brink, Larry - E
Bukich, Rudy - Q
Dahms, Tom - T
Daugherty, Dick - G
Dwyer, John - B
Fears, Tom - E
Ferris, Neil - B
Fry, Bob - T
Fuller, Frank - T
Griffin, Bob - C
Hecker, Norb - E & B
Hirsch, Elroy - E & B
Hock, John - G
Lane, Dick - B
Lewis, Woodley - B
Lipscomb, "Daddy" - T
McCormick, Tom - B

McFadin, "Bud" - G
McLaughlin, Leon - C
Myers, Brad - B
Paul, Don - LB & C
Putnam, Duane - G
Quinlan, Volney - B
Rich, Herb - B
Robustelli, Andy - E
Smith, Verda - B
Svare, Harland - LB & G
Teeuws, Len - T
Thompson, Harry - G
Toogood, Charley - T
Towler, Dan - B
Van Brocklin, Norm - Q
West, Stan - G
Younger, "Tank" - B

1953 NEW YORK GIANTS
COACH - Steve Owen
5th 3-9-0

Albright, Bill - G
Anderson, Clif - E
Austin, Bill - G
Avinger, Clarence - B
Brown, Rosie - T
Cannaday, John - LB
Clay, Randall - B
Conerly, Charley - Q
Douglas, Everett - T
Duncan, Jim - E
Galiffa, Arnold - Q
Gifford, Frank - B
Grandelius, "Sonny" - B
Hodel, Merwin - B
Kennard, George - G
Krouse, Ray - T
Lagod, Chet - G
Landry, Tom - B
Long, Buford - B

Mackrides, Bill - Q
Menasco, Don - B
Miles, Leo - B
Pelfrey, Ray - E
Peviani, Bob - G
Price, Ed - B
Ramona, Joe - G
Rapacz, John - C
Rote, Kyle - B
Scott, Joe - E
Stribling, "Bill" - E
Stroud, Jack - G
Sulaitis, Joe - E
Tunnell, Em - B
Weinmeister, Arnie - T
Wietecha, Ray - C
Woodward, Dick - C
Yelvington, Dick - T

1953 PHILADELPHIA EAGLES
COACH - Jim Trimble
2nd 7-4-1

Bednarik, "Chuck" - C
Brewer, John - B
Brookshier, Tom - B
Burk, Adrian - Q
Craft, Russ - B
Farragut, Ken - C
Gambold, Bob - B
Giancanelli, "Skippy" - B
Hudson, Bob - B
Irvin, Bill - E
Jarmoluk, Mike - T
Johnson, Don - B
Kilroy, "Bucko" - G
Ledbetter, Toy - B
Magee, John - G
Michels, John - G
Mrkonic, George - T
Nipp, Maurey - G

Parmer, Jim - B
Pihos, Pete - E
Pollard, Al - B
Richardson, Jess - T
Robinson, Wayne - LB & C
Schnelker, Bob - E
Scott, Tom - E
Sears, Vic - T
Snyder, Ken - T
Stringer, Bob - B
Thomason, Bob - Q
Van Buren, Ebert - B
Walston, Bob - E
Willey, Norm - E
Williams, Jerry - B
Wydo, Frank - T
Ziegler, Frank - B

1953 PITTSBURGH STEELERS
COACH - Joe Bach
4th 6-6-0

Alderton, John - E
Barker, Ed - E
Bolkovac, Nick - T
Brady, Pat - Q
Brandt, Jim - B
Butler, Jack - E
Calvin, Tom - B
Chandnois, Lynn - B
DeCarlo, Art - B
Dodrill, Dale - G
Elter, Leo - B
Ferry, Lou - T
Finks, Jim - Q
Flanagan, Dick - G
Fullerton, Ed - B
Gaona, Bob - T
Hegarty, Bill - T
Hipps, Claude - B

Hogan, Darrell - G
Hughes, George - G
McFadden, Marv - G
McPeak, Bill - E
Mackrides, Bill - Q
Marchibroda, Ted - Q
Mathews, Ray - B
Matuszak, Marv - G
Nickel, Elbie - E
Palmer, Tom - T
Rogel, Fran - B
Schweder, John - G
Stautner, Ernie - T
Sulima, George - E
Tarasovic, George - E
Tepe, Lou - C
Walsh, Bill - C

1953 SAN FRANCISCO 49ERS
COACH - "Buck" Shaw
2nd 9-3-0

Arenas, Joe - B
Babcock, Harry - E
Bahnsen, Ken - B
Banducci, Bruno - G
Berry, Rex - B
Brown, Hardy - LB
Brown, Pete - C
Bruney, Fred - B
Burke, Don - G
Carapella, Al - T
Feher, Nick - G
Hogland, Doug - T
Johnson, Bill - C
Ledyard, Hal - Q
McElhenny, Hugh - B
Manley, Joe - C
Matthews, Clay - E
Michalik, Art - G

Miller, Hal - T
Mixon, Bill - B
Monachino, Jim - B
Morton, John - B
Nomellini, Leo - T
Perry, Joe - B
Powell, Charley - E
Powers, Jim - Q
St. Clair, Bob - T
Schabarum, Pete - B
Smith, Jerry - G
Soltau, Gordon - E
Tittle, Y. A. - Q
Van Doren, Bob - E
Wagner, Lowell - B
Wilson, Bill - E

1953 WASHINGTON REDSKINS
COACH - "Curly" Lambeau
3rd 6-5-1

Alban, Dick - B
Baker, "Sam" - K & B
Barry, Paul - B
Boll, Don - T
Brito, Gene - E
Campora, Don - T

Clark, Jim - G
Cloud, John - B
Dekker, Paul - E
DeMao, Al - C
Doll, Don - B
Dowda, Harry - B

Drazenovich, Chuck - LB
Dudley, Bill - B
Haynes, Hall - B
Hazelwood, Ted - T
Heath, Leon - B
Hegarty, Bill - T
Hennessey, Jerry - E
Justice, "Choo Choo" - B
Le Baron, Ed - Q
Lipscomb, Paul - T
Modzelewski, Dick - T
Niemi, Laurie - T
Papit, John - B

Pepper, Gene - G
Polsfoot, Fran - E
Ramsey, Knox - G
Ricca, Jim - T
Rykovich, Julie - B
Scarbath, Jack - Q
Suminski, Dave - G
Taylor, Hugh - E
Tereshinski, Joe - E
Ulinski, Harry - C
Williams, John - B
Witucki, Casimir - G

1954

EASTERN CONFERENCE

Cleveland	9	3	0	.750
Philadelphia	7	4	1	.636
New York	7	5	0	.583
Pittsburgh	5	7	0	.417
Washington	3	9	0	.250
Chicago Cardinals	2	10	0	.167

WESTERN CONFERENCE

Detroit	9	2	1	.818
Chicago Bears	8	4	0	.667
San Francisco	7	4	1	.636
Los Angeles	6	5	1	.545
Green Bay	4	8	0	.333
Baltimore	3	9	0	.250

TITLE: Cleveland beat Detroit, 56-10, for the championship at Cleveland, Dec. 26.

LEADERS: Individual leaders for the season: Scoring—Bobby Walston (Philadelphia), 114; Rushing—Fletcher "Joe" Perry (San Francisco), 1,049 yds.; Passing—Norm Van Brocklin (Los Angeles); Pass Receiving —Pete Pihos (Philadelphia), Bill Wilson (San Francisco), 60 (tie); Field Goals— Lou Groza (Cleveland), 16; Punting—Pat Brady (Pittsburgh), 43.2 yds.; Interceptions—Dick Lane (Chi-Cards), 10.

BONUS PICK: Robert Garrett, Stanford back, Cleveland.

COACHES: Wilbur "Weeb" Ewbank replaced Keith Molesworth as head coach at Baltimore; Lisle Blackbourn took over from Gene Ronzani at Green Bay; Jim Lee Howell replaced Steve Owen at New York; Walter Kiesling replaced Joe Bach at Pittsburgh; Joe Kuharich replaced "Curly" Lambeau at Washington.

NOTES: Joe Perry, San Francisco, rushed 1,049 yards.

Adrian Burk, Philadelphia, qback, threw seven touchdown passes against Washington, tying Sid Luckman's record, Oct. 17.

Dave Sparks, Washington tackle, died after game against Cleveland, Dec. 5.

TITLE GAME

Doak Walker kicked a 36-yard field goal to open the scoring. Graham tossed touchdown passes to Renfro and Brewster in the same period and Groza's conversion made it 14-3. Graham scored two more in the second himself and passed to Brewster for another. Groza collected all the extra points. Bowman scored one for Detroit and Walker converted for the Lion's last score. It was 35-10 at the half.

Graham crashed over for another as the third half opened and Morrison plowed 13 yards for the Brown's seventh TD in the third period. In the final period Hanulak scored the final and Groza completed eight conversions.

Cleveland Browns	14	21	14	7—56
Detroit Lions	3	7	0	0—10

Touchdowns—Renfro 2, Brewster, Graham 3, Morrison, Hanulak (Cleveland), Bowman (Detroit).
Conversions—Groza 8 (Cleveland), Walker (Detroit).
Field Goal—Walker (Detroit).

Attendance: 43,827.
Players' Share: Cleveland $2,478.57; Detroit $1,585.63.

1954 BALTIMORE COLTS
COACH - "Weeb" Ewbank
6th 3-9-0

Averno, Sisto - G
Barwegan, Dick - G
Bighead, Jack - E
Campanella, Joseph - G
Cheatham, Ernest - T
Colteryahn, Lloyd - E
Davidson, "Cotton" - Q
Donovan, Art - T
Edwards, Dan - E
Eggers, Doug - LB & G
Enke, Fred - Q
Finnin, Tom - T
Huzvar, John - B
Jackson, Ken - T
Joyce, Don - E
Keane, Tom - B
Kerkorian, Gary - Q
Langas, Bob - E
Leberman, Bob - B
Lesane, Jim - B

Little, John - T
McMillan, Charles - B
Marchetti, Gino - E
Mutscheller, Jim - E
Nutter, "Buzz" - C
Pellington, Bill - LB & G
Pepper, Gene - G
Radosevich, George - C
Raiff, Jim - G
Rechichar, Bert - LB & B
Robinson, Charley - G
Sandusky, Alex - G
Shula, Don - B
Spinney, Art - G
Taliaferro, George - B
Taseff, Carl - B
Toth, Zollie - B
Womble, Royce - B
Young, "Buddy" - B

1954 CHICAGO BEARS
COACH - George Halas
2nd 8-4-0

Anderson, Bill - B
Bishop, Bill - T

Blanda, George - Q
Bratkowski, "Zeke" - Q

Brink, Larry - E
Brown, Ed - Q
Campbell, Leon - B
Clark, Herm - G
Connor, George - T
Daffer, Ted - E
Dooley, Jim - E
George, Bill - G
Gilbert, Kline - T
Hansen, Wayne - G & C
Helwig, John - G
Hill, Harlon - E
Hoffman, John - B
Jagade, Harry - B
Jones, Stan - T
Kindt, Don - B
Kreamcheck, John - T
Lesane, Jim - B

Lipscomb, Paul - T
Lowe, Lloyd - B
McColl, Bill - E
McElroy, "Bucky" - B
Meadows, Ed - E
Moore, McNeil - B
Perini, Evo - B
Schroeder, Gene - E
Smith, Ray - B
Sprinkle, Ed - E
Stone, Billy - B
Strickland, Larry - C
Wallace, Stan - B
Weatherly, Gerry - C
Whitman, Laverne - B
Wightkin, Bill - T
Williams, Fred - T

Dublinski, Tom - Q
Gandee, "Sonny" - E
Girard, "Jug" - B
Hart, Leon - E
Hoernschemeyer, Bob - B
Karilivacz, Carl - B
Kercher, Dick - B
Layne, Bobby - Q
McGraw, Thurman - T
Mains, Gil - T
Martin, Jim - G

Miketa, Andy - C
Miller, Bob - T
Perry, Gerry - T
Schmidt, Joe - LB
Sewell, Harley - G
Smith, Bob - B
Stanfel, Dick - G
Stits, Bill - B
Torgeson, Lavern - LB & C
Turner, Hal - E
Walker, Doak - B

1954 CHICAGO CARDINALS
COACH - Joe Stydahar
6th 2-10-0

Arterburn, Elmer - B
Barry, Paul - B
Bienemann, Tom - E
Brancato, George - B
Bredde, Bill - B
Brosky, Al - B
Crittendon, John - E
Embree, Mel - E
Fanucchi, Ledio - T
Fugler, Dick - T
Goble, Les - B
Groom, Jerry - T
Hatley, John - G
Jennings, John - T
Kinek, George - B
King, Emmett - B
Kingery, Ellsworth - B
Knafelc, Gary - E
Ladd, Jim - E
Lane, Dick - B

Lange, Bill - G
McHan, Lamar - Q
Matson, Ollie - B
Morgan, Bob - T
Oakley, Charley - B
Olszewski, John - B
Polofsky, Gordon - G
Romanik, Steve - Q
Sanford, Leo - C
Sears, Jim - B
Simmons, John - C
Stonesifer, Don - E
Sugar, Leo - E
Summerall, "Pat" - E & K
Teeuws, Len - T
Trippi, Charley - B
Ulrich, Charles - T
Wallner, Fred - G
Watford, Gerry - G

1954 CLEVELAND BROWNS
COACH - Paul Brown
1st 9-3-0
(Beat Detroit for title, 56-10)

Adamle, Tony - B
Atkins, Doug - E
Bassett, Maurice - B
Bradley, Harold - G
Brewster, "Pete" - E
Catlin, Tom - LB & C
Colo, Don - T
Ford, Len - E
Forester, Herschel - G
Gain, Bob - T
Gatski, Frank - C
Gibron, Abe - G
Gillom, Horace - E
Gorgal, Ken - B
Graham, Otto - Q
Groza, Lou - T
Hanulak, Chet - B

James, Tom - B
Jones, "Dub" - B
King, Don - T
Kissell, John - T
Konz, Ken - B
Lahr, Warren - B
Lavelli, Dante - E
McCormack, Mike - T
Massey, Carleton - E
Michaels, Walt - LB
Morrison, Fred - B
Noll, Chuck - G
Paul, Don - B
Ratterman, George - Q
Renfro, Ray - B
Reynolds, Bill - B
Sandusky, John - T

1954 DETROIT LIONS
COACH - "Buddy" Parker
1st 9-2-1
(Lost title to Cleveland, 56-10)

Ane, Charley - T
Bingaman, Les - G
Bowman, Bill - B
Box, Cloyce - E
Cain, Jim - E
Carpenter, Lew - B

Christiansen, John - B
Creekmur, Lou - T
David, Jim - B
Dibble, Dorne - E
Doran, Jim - E
Dove, Bob - E & G

1954 GREEN BAY PACKERS
COACH - Lisle Blackbourn
5th 4-8-0

Afflis, "Dick" - G
Barry, Al - G
Brown, Bill - G
Carmichael, Al - B
Cone, Fred - B
Dillon, Bobby - B
Elliott, Carleton - E
Ferguson, Howie - B
Forester, "Bill" - G
Garrett, Bob - Q
Hanner, "Dave" - T
Helluin, Jerry - T
Howton, Bill - E
Hunter, Art - T
Johnson, "Joe" - B
Knafelc, Gary - E
Knutson, Gene - E

McGee, Max - E
Martinkovich, John - E
Miller, Don - B
Psaltis, Jim - B
Reid, "Breezy" - B
Ringo, Jim - C
Rote, Tobin - Q
Ruzich, Steve - G
Self, Clarence - B
Stephenson, Dave - G & C
Switzer, Veryl - B
Szafaryn, Len - T
Teteak, Deral - G
Tonnemaker, Clayt - C
Walker, Val Joe - B
White, Gene - B
Zatkoff, Roger - T

1954 LOS ANGELES RAMS
COACH - Hamp Pool
4th 6-5-1

Bowers, Bill - B
Boyd, Bob - E
Carey, Bob - E
Cross, Bob - T
Dahms, Tom - T
Doll, Don - B
Dwyer, John - B
Fears, Tom - E
Griffin, Bob - C
Hauser, Art - G
Haynes, Hall - B
Hirsch, Elroy - E
Hughes, Ed - B
Lewis, Woodley - B
Lipscomb, "Daddy" - T
McCormick, Tom - B
McFadin, "Bud" - LG & T

McLaughlin, Leon - C
Miller, Paul - E
Paul, Don - LB & C
Putnam, Duane - G
Quinlan, Volney "Skeet" - B
Richter, Les - LB & G
Robustelli, Andy - E
Sherman, Will - B
Svare, Harland - LB & G
Thompson, Harry - G
Toogood, Charley - T
Towler, Dan - B
Van Brocklin, Norm - Q
Wade, Bill - Q
Wardlow, Duane - E
West, Stan - G
Younger, "Tank" - B

1954 NEW YORK GIANTS
COACH - Jim Lee Howell
3rd 7-5-0

Agajanian, Ben - K
Albright, Bill - G
Austin, Bill - G
Bauer, John - G
Berry, Wayne - B
Brown, Rosie - T
Cannaday, John - LB
Carroccio, Russ - G
Clatterbuck, Bob - Q
Collins, Ray - T
Conerly, Charley - Q
Epps, Bob - B
Gifford, Frank - B
Heinrich, Don - Q
Johnson, Herb - B
Kennard, George - G
Knight, Pat - E
Krouse, Ray - T
Landry, Tom - B

Livingston, Cliff - LB & E
Long, Buford - B
MacAfee, Ken - E
Mangum, Pete - B
Nolan, Dick - B
Poole, Barney - E
Price, Ed - B
Rapacz, John - C
Rich, Herb - B
Rote, Kyle - B
Schnelker, Bob - E
Shipp, Bill - T
Stroud, Jack - G
Svoboda, Bill - LB
Topp, Bob - E
Tunnell, Em - B
Wietecha, Ray - C
Wilkins, Dick - E
Yelvington, Dick - T

1954 PHILADELPHIA EAGLES
COACH - Jim Trimble
2nd 7-4-1

Barni, Roy - B	Miller, Don - B
Bednarik, "Chuck" - C	Moselle, Dom - B
Burk, Adrian - Q	Norton, Gerry - B
Cifelli, Gus - T	Parmer, Jim - B
Dowda, Harry - B	Pihos, Pete - E
Farragut, Ken - C	Richardson, Jess - T
Giancanelli, "Skippy" - B	Robinson, Wayne - LB
Goldston, Ralph - B	Roffler, Bill - B
Higgins, Tom - T	Scott, Tom - E
Hudson, Bob - B	Sharkey, Ed - G
Huxhold, Ken - G	Snyder, Ken - T
Jarmoluk, Mike - T	Stevens, Don - B
Johnson, Don - B	Thomason, John - Q
Kilroy, "Bucko" - G	Walston, Bob - E
Ledbetter, Toy - B	Willey, Norm - E
Luft, Don - E	Williams, Jerry - B
Magee, John - G	Worden, Neil - B
Mavraides, Menil - G	Wydo, Frank - T

1954 WASHINGTON REDSKINS
COACH - Joe Kuharich
5th 3-9-0

Adducci, Nick - B	Menasco, Don - B
Alban, Dick - B	Modzelewski, Dick - T
Atkeson, Dale - B	Morgan, Bob - T
Barfield, Ken - T	Morley, Sam - E
Barker, Ed - E	Ostrowski, Chet - E
Berschet, Marv - G	Peters, Volney - T
Boll, Don - T	Ricca, Jim - T
Carson, John - E	Rosso, George - B
Cudzik, Walt - C	Scarbath, Jack - Q
Dorow, Al - Q	Schrader, Jim - C
Drazenovich, Chuck - LB	Scudero, Joe - B
Felton, Ralph - B	Sparks, Dave - G
Gilmer, Harry - Q	Taylor, Hugh - E
Goode, Bob - B	Tereshinski, Joe - E
Hansen, Ron - G	Ulinski, Harry - C
Janovicz, Vic - B	Wells, Billy - B
Justice, "Choo Choo" - B	Witucki, Casimir - G
Kincaid, Jim - B	Yowarsky, Walt - E
Lipscomb, Paul - T	

1954 PITTSBURGH STEELERS
COACHES - Joe Bach &
Walt Kiesling
4th 5-7-0

Andabaker, Rudy - G	Kissell, Ed - Q
Bolkovac, Nick - T	Ladygo, Pete - G
Brady, Pat - Q	Lattner, John - B
Brandt, Jim - B	McConnell, Dewey - E
Brundage, Dewey, E	McPeak, Bill - E
Butler, Jack - B	Matesic, Joe - T
Calvin, Tom - B	Mathews, Ray - B
Cameron, Paul - B	Nickel, Elbie - E
Chandnois, Lynn - B	O'Brien, John - E
Cheatham, Ernie - T	Palmer, Tom - T
Cifelli, Gus - T	Rogel, Fran - B
Craft, Russ - B	Schweder, John - G
Dodrill, Dale - G	Sheriff, Stan - G
Elter, Leo - B	Shields, Burrel - B
Ferry, Lou - T	Stautner, Ernie - T
Finks, Jim - Q	Sulima, George - E
Flanagan, Dick - G	Tepe, Lou - C
Gaona, Bob - T	Walsh, Bill - C
Held, Paul - Q	Zombek, Joe - E
Hughes, George - G	

1954 SAN FRANCISCO 49ERS
COACH - "Buck" Shaw
3rd 7-4-1

Arenas, Joe - B	Johnson, John Henry - B
Babcock, Harry - E	Johnson, Bill - C
Banducci, Bruno - G	McElhenny, Hugh - B
Berry, Rex - B	Matthews, Clay - E
Brown, Hardy - LB	Michalik, Art - G
Brown, Pete - C	Mixon, Bill - B
Brumfield, Jack - E	Nomellini, Leo - T
Burke, Don - G	Perry, Joe - B
Campbell, Marion - T	Sagely, Floyd - E
Carapella, Al - T	St. Clair, Bob - T
Cason, Jim - B	Schabarum, Pete - B
Cassara, Frank - B	Soltau, Gordon - E
Connolly, Ted - G	Tidwell, Bill - B
Duncan, Maury - Q	Tittle, Y. A. - Q
Feher, Nick - G	Toneff, Bob - T
Galiffa, Arnie - Q	Williams, John - B
Hantla, Bob - G	Wilson, Bill - E
Hogland, Doug - G	Wismann, Pete - C
Jessup, Bill - E	

1955

EASTERN CONFERENCE

Cleveland	9	2	1	.818
Washington	8	4	0	.667
New York	6	5	1	.545
Chicago Cards	4	7	1	.364
Philadelphia	4	7	1	.364
Pittsburgh	4	8	0	.333

WESTERN CONFERENCE

Los Angeles	8	3	1	.727
Chicago Bears	8	4	0	.667
Green Bay	6	6	0	.500
Baltimore	5	6	1	.455
San Francisco	4	8	0	.333
Detroit	3	9	0	.250

TITLE: Cleveland beat Los Angeles, 38-14, for the championship at Los Angeles, Dec. 26.

LEADERS: Individual leaders for the season: Scoring—Doak Walker (Detroit), 96; Rushing—Alan Ameche (Baltimore), 961 yds.; Passing—Otto Graham (Cleveland); Pass Receiving—Pete Pihos (Philadelphia), 62; Field Goals—Fred Cone (Green Bay), 16; Punting—Norm VanBrocklin (Los Angeles), 44.6 yds.; Interceptions—Willard Sherman (Los Angeles), 11.

BONUS PICK: George Shaw, Oregon qback, Baltimore.

COACHES: Sid Gillman replaced Hampton Pool as head coach at Los Angeles; Ray Richards replaced Joe Stydahar with Chicago Cardinals; "Red" Strader took over for "Buck" Shaw at San Francisco.

End of a brilliant career. Otto Graham (14), fine quarterback of the Cleveland Browns for many years, carries against the Los Angeles Rams in the championship game of 1955. Graham tossed touchdown passes to Ray Renfro and Dante Lavelli, and scored two more himself to lead the Browns to the title, 38–14. It was Graham's last game in the NFL. He was voted into the Hall of Fame in 1965.

NOTES: Ogden Compton, Chi-Cards qback, passed to Dick Lane 98 yards (TD) against Green Bay, Nov. 13.

TITLE GAME

Groza's 26-yard field goal was the only scoring in the first quarter. Early in the second, Paul intercepted Van Brocklin's pass and ran 65 yards for a touchdown and Groza made it 10–0. On Los Angeles' second play after the kickoff, Van Brocklin threw a 67-yard touchdown to Quinlan and Richter made it 10–7. Late in the half Graham tossed a 50-yard score to Lavelli and Groza converted.

Graham himself scored two touchdowns for Cleveland in the third period and threw another to Renfro in the fourth. Waller scored Los Angeles final TD on a 4-yard run and Richter made it 38–14, the final score. Cleveland had intercepted six of Van Brocklin's passes.

Cleveland Browns	3	14	14	7–38
Los Angeles	0	7	0	7–14

Touchdowns—Graham 2, Renfro, Paul, Lavelli (Cleveland), Quinlan, Waller (Los Angeles).

Conversions—Groza 5 (Cleveland), Richter 2 (Los Angeles).

Field Goal—Groza (Cleveland).

Attendance: 85,693.

Players' Share: Cleveland $3,508.21; Los Angeles $2,316.26.

1955 BALTIMORE COLTS
COACH - "Weeb" Ewbank
4th 5-6-1

Ameche, Alan - B
Berry, Raymond - E

Brethauer, Monte - E
Bryant, Walter - B

Campanella, Joseph T & G
Chorovich, Dick - T
Colteryahn, Lloyd - E
Donovan, Art - T
Dupre, Louis - B
Eggers, Doug - LB & G
Finnin, Tom - T
Hugasian, Harry - B
Jackson, Ken - T
Joyce, Don - E
Kerkorian, Gary - Q
Marchetti, Gino - E
Mutscheller, Jim - E
Myers, Bob - T
Nutter, "Buzz" - C
Patera, John - T
Pellington, Bill - LB & G

Preas, George - T
Radosevich, George - C
Rechichar, Bert - LB & B
Renfro, Dean - B
Sandusky, Alex - G
Shaw, George - Q
Shields, Burrel - B
Shula, Don - B
Spinney, Art - G
Szymanski, Dick - C
Taseff, Carl - B
Thomas, Jesse - B
White, Bob - B
Womble, Royce - B
Young, "Buddy" - B
Young, Dick - B

Lahr, Warren - B
Lavelli, Dante - E
McCormack, Mike - T
Massey, Carlton - E
Michaels, Walt - LB
Modzelewski, Ed - B
Morrison, Fred - B
Noll, Chuck - G
Palumbo, Sam - C

Paul, Don - B
Perini, Evo - B
Petitbon, John - B
Ratterman, George - Q
Renfro, Ray - B
Sandusky, John - T
Smith, Bob - B
Weber, Chuck - LB
White, Bob - B

1955 DETROIT LIONS
COACH - "Buddy" Parker
6th 3-9-0

Ane, Charley - T
Atkins, George - G
Cain, Jim - E
Campbell, Stan - G
Carpenter, Lew - B
Christiansen, John - B
Creekmur, Lou - T
Cunningham, Leon - C
David, Jim - B
Dibble, Dorne - E
Doran, Jim - E
Fucci, Dom - B
Gandee, "Sonny" - E
Gilmer, Harry - Q
Girard, "Jug" - B
Hart, Leon - E
Hoernschemeyer, Bob - B
Jenkins, Walt - E & T
Karilivacz, Carl - B

Layne, Bobby - Q
Long, Bob - E
McCord, Darris - T
Mains, Gil - T
Martin, Jim - G
Middleton, Dave - B
Miketa, Andy - C
Miller, Bob - T
Ricca, Jim - G
Riley, Leon - B
Salsbury, Jim - G
Schmidt, Joe - LB
Sewell, Harley - G
Stanfel, Dick - G
Stits, Bill - B
Toper, Ted - LB
Walker, Doak - B
Woit, Dick - B
Yowarsky, Walt - E

1955 CHICAGO BEARS
COACH - George Halas
2nd 8-4-0

Atkins, Doug - E
Bishop, Bill - T
Blanda, George - Q
Brown, Ed - Q
Casares, Ric - B
Clark, Herm - G
Connor, George - T
Drzewiecki, Ron - B
Fortunato, Joe - LB
George, Bill - LB & G
Gilbert, Kline - T
Gorgal, Ken - B
Hansen, Wayne - G
Helwig, John - E & G
Hill, Harlon - E
Hoffman, Jack - E
Hoffman, John - B
Hugasian, Harry - B

Jagade, Harry - B
Jecha, Ray - G
Jones, Stan - T
Kindt, Don - B
Kreamcheck, John - G & T
McColl, Bill - E
Mosley, Henry - B
Perini, Evo - B
Schroeder, Gene - E
Smith, Ray - B
Sprinkle, Ed - E
Strickland, Larry - C
Sumner, Charley - B
Watkins, Bob - B
Wightkin, Bill - E & T
Williams, Fred - T
Williams, Bob - Q

1955 GREEN BAY PACKERS
COACH - Lisle Blackbourn
3rd 6-6-0

Bettis, Tom - G
Bookout, Bill - B
Borden, Nate - E
Brackins, Charley - Q
Brown, Bill - G
Bullough, Harry - G
Capuzzi, Jim - Q
Carmichael, Al - B
Clemens, Bob - B
Cone, Fred - B
Dahms, Tom - T
Deschaine, Dick - E
Dillon, Bobby - B
Ferguson, Howie - B
Forester, "Bill" - G
Hanner, "Dave" - T
Held, Paul - Q
Helluin, "Jerry" - T
Howton, Bill - E
Jennings, Jim - E

Johnson, "Joe" - B
Knafelc, Gary - E
Lucky, Bill - T
Martinkovich, John - E
Nix, Doyle - B
O'Donahue, Pat - E
Reid, "Breezy" - B
Ringo, Jim - C
Romine, Al - B
Rote, Tobin - Q
Self, Clarence - B
Skibinski, Joe - G
Spinks, Jack - G
Stephenson, Dave - G & C
Switzer, Veryl - B
Szafaryn, Len - T
Teteak, Deral - G
Timberlake, George - G
Walker, Val Joe - B
Zatkoff, Roger - T

1955 CHICAGO CARDINALS
COACH - Ray Richards
4th 4-7-1

Bernardi, Frank - B
Bienemann, Tom - E
Boydston, Max - E
Brubaker, Dick - E
Carr, Jim - B
Compton, Ogden - Q
Crow, Lindon - B
Delevan, Burt - T
Goble, Les - B
Groom, Jerry - T
Hammack, Mal - B
Hartshong, Larry - G
Hatley, John - G
Hill, Jim - B
Jennings, John - T
Keane, Tom - B
Lane, Dick - B
Lange, Bill - G
Leggett, Dave - Q

McHan, Lamar - Q
McPhee, Frank - E
Mann, Dave - B
Matson, Ollie - B
Nagler, Gern - E
Olszewski, John - B
Pasquesi, Tony - T
Psaltis, Jim - B
Sanford, Leo - C
Simmons, John - C
Stonesifer, Don - E
Sugar, Leo - E
Summerall, "Pat" - E & K
Teeuws, Len - T
Thompson, Harry - G
Trippi, Charley - B
Ulrich, Charles - T
Wallner, Fred - G

1955 LOS ANGELES RAMS
COACH - Sid Gillman
1st 8-3-1
(Lost title to Cleveland, 38-14)

Bighead, Jack - E
Boyd, Bob - E
Burroughs, Don - B
Cason, Jim - B
Cross, Bob - T
Ellena, Jack - G
Fears, Tom - E
Fournet, Sid - G
Fuller, Frank - T
Griffin, Bob - C
Hauser, Art - T
Haynes, Hall - B

Hirsch, Elroy - E
Hock, John - G
Holtzman, Glen - T
Hughes, Ed - B
Lewis, Woodley - B & E
Lipscomb, "Daddy" - T
McCormick, Tom - B
McFadin, "Bud" - T
McLaughlin, Leon - C
Miller, Paul - E
Morris, Larry - LB
Paul, Don - LB & C

1955 CLEVELAND BROWNS
COACH - Paul Brown
1st 9-2-1
(Beat Los Angeles for title, 38-14)

Bassett, Maurice - B
Bradley, Harold - G
Brewster, "Pete" - E
Colo, Don - T
Ford, Henry - B
Ford, Len - E
Forester, Herschel - G
Gain, Bob - T
Gatski, Frank - C

Gibron, Abe - G
Gillom, Horace - E
Graham, Otto - Q
Groza, Lou - T
James, Tom - B
Jones, Tom - T
Jones, "Dub" - B
Kissell, John - T
Konz, Ken - B

Putnam, Duane - G
Quinlan, Volney - B
Richter, Les - LB & G
Robustelli, Andy - E
Sherman, Will - B
Taylor, Cecil - B

Toogood, Charley - T
Towler, Dan - B
Van Brocklin, Norm - Q
Wade, Bill - Q
Waller, Ron - B
Younger, "Tank" - B

1955 NEW YORK GIANTS
COACH - Jim Lee Howell
3rd 6-5-1

Agajanian, Ben - K
Austin, Bill - G
Beck, Ray - G
Boggan, Rex - T
Broussard, Fred - C
Brown, Rosie - T
Carroccio, Russ - G
Clatterbuck, Bob - Q
Conerly, Charley - Q
Epps, Bob - B
Gifford, Frank - B
Grier, Rosey - T
Hall, John - E
Heap, Joe - B
Heinrich, Don - Q
Kennard, George - G
Knight, Pat - E
Krouse, Ray - T
Landry, Tom - B
Livingston, Cliff - LB & E

Long, Buford - B
MacAfee, Ken - E
Nolan, Dick - B
Patton, Jim - B
Price, Ed - B
Rich, Herb - B
Rote, Kyle - B
Schnelker, Bob - E
Stroud, Jack - G
Svare, Harland - LB
Svoboda, Bill - LB
Triplett, Mel - B
Tunnell, Em - B
Weaver, Larrye - B
Webster, Alex - B
West, Stan - G
Wietecha, Ray - C
Yelvington, Dick - T
Yowarsky, Walt - E

1955 PHILADELPHIA EAGLES
COACH - Jim Trimble
5th 4-7-1

Barni, Roy - B
Bawel, "Bibbles" - B
Bednarik, "Chuck" - LB & C
Bell, Ed - B & E
Bielski, Dick - B
Burk, Adrian - Q
Carroccio, Russ - G
Dowda, Harry - B
Giancanelli, "Skippy" - B
Goldston, Ralph - B
Goode, Bob - B
Higgins, Tom - T
Hudson, Bob - B
Huxhold, Ken - G
Jarmoluk, Mike - T
Johnson, Don - B
Kelley, Bob - C
Kilroy, "Bucko" - G & T
Lansford, "Buck" - G & T

Ledbetter, Toy - B
Magee, John - G
Norton, Gerry - B
Parmer, Jim - B
Pihos, Pete - E
Ricca, Jim - T
Richardson, Jess - T
Robinson, Wayne - LB
Scott, Tom - E
Sharkey, Ed - G
Snyder, Ken - T
Stribling, "Bill" - E
Taliaferro, George - B
Thomason, Bob - Q
Walston, Bob - E
Weatherall, Jim - T
Wegert, Ted - B
Willey, Norm - E
Wydo, Frank - T

1955 PITTSBURGH STEELERS
COACH - Walt Kiesling
6th 4-8-0

Bernet, Ed - E
Broussard, Fred - C
Butler, Jack - B
Campbell, Leon - B
Chandnois, Lynn - B
Dodrill, Dale - G
Doyle, Dick - B
Eaton, Vic - Q
Feher, Nick - G
Ferry, Lou - T
Finks, Jim - Q
Flanagan, Dick - G
Gaona, Bob - T
Harkey, Lem - B
Hill, Jim - B
McCabe, Richie - B
McClairen, Jack - E
McClung, Willie - T
McPeak, Bill - E

Marchibroda, Ted - Q
Mathews, Ray - B
Matuszak, Marv - LB & G
Meadows, Ed - E
Michalik, Art - G
Modzelewski, Dick - T
Motley, Marion - B
Nickel, Elbie - E
O'Brien, John - E
O'Malley, Joe - E
Oniskey, Dick - G
Reger, John - LB & G
Rogel, Fran - B
Schweder, John - G
Stautner, Ernie - T
Tepe, Lou - C
Varrichione, Frank - T
Watson, Sid - B
Weed, "Tad" - K

1955 SAN FRANCISCO 49ERS
COACH - "Red" Strader
5th 4-8-0

Arenas, Joe - B
Babcock, Harry - E
Beattie, Ed - C
Berry, Rex - B
Brown, Hardy - LB
Campbell, Marion - T
Carapella, Al - T
Carr, Paul - LB & B
Duncan, Maury - Q
Hantla, Bob - G
Hardy, Carroll - B
Harkey, Lem - B
Hazeltine, Matt - LB
Hogland, Doug - G
Johnson, John Henry - B
Johnson, Bill - C
Kraemer, Eldred - G
Laughlin, Henry - B
Luna, Bob - K & B

McElhenny, Hugh - B
Maderos, George - B
Matthews, Clay - E
Moegle, Dick - B
Nomellini, Leo - T
Palatella, Lou - G
Perry, Joe - B
Powell, Charley - E
St. Clair, Bob - T
Sharkey, Ed - G
Smith, Ernie - B
Soltau, Gordon - E
Stolhandske, Tom - E
Tittle, Y. A. - Q
Toneff, Bob - T
Vaught, Ted - E
Wagner, Lowell - B
Wilson, Bill - E
Youngelman, Sid - T

1955 WASHINGTON REDSKINS
COACH - Joe Kuharich
2nd 8-4-0

Adducci, Nick - B
Alban, Dick - B
Allen, John - C
Atkeson, Dale - B
Barni, Roy - B
Berschet, Marv - G
Boll, Don - T
Brito, Gene - E
Carson, John - E
Cox, Bill - E
Davlin, Mike - T
Dorow, Al - Q
Drazenovich, Chuck - LB
Elter, Leo - B
Felton, Ralph - B
Goode, Bob - B
Guglielmi, Ralph - Q
Hecker, Norbert - B
Houston, Walt - G

Janowicz, Vic - B
Jones, Chuck - E
Kimmel, J. D. - T
LeBaron, Ed - Q
Marciniak, Ron - G
Miller, Fred - T
Monachino, Jim - B
Norman, Jim - T
Norris, Harold - B
Ostrowski, Chet - E
Peters, Volney - T
Scudero, Joe - B
Stephens, "Red" - G
Thomas, Ralph - E
Torgeson, Lavern - LB
Ulinski, Harry - C
Witucki, Casimir - G
Zagers, Bert - B

1956

EASTERN CONFERENCE

New York	8	3	1	.727
Chicago Cards	7	5	0	.583
Washington	6	6	0	.500
Cleveland	5	7	0	.417
Pittsburgh	5	7	0	.417
Philadelphia	3	8	1	.273

WESTERN CONFERENCE

Chicago Bears	9	2	1	.818
Detroit	9	3	0	.750
San Francisco	5	6	1	.455
Baltimore	5	7	0	.417
Green Bay	4	8	0	.333
Los Angeles	4	8	0	.333

TITLE: New York beat the Chicago Bears, 47-7, for the championship at New York, Dec. 30.

LEADERS: Individual leaders for the season: Scoring—Bobby Layne (Detroit), 99; Rushing—Rick Casares (Chi-Bears), 1,126 yds.; Passing—Ed Brown (Chi-Bears); Pass Receiving—Bill Wilson (San Francisco), 60; Field Goals—"Sam" Baker (Washington), 17; Punting—Norman VanBrocklin (Los Angeles), 43.1 yds.; Interceptions—Lindon Crow, 11.

BONUS PICK: Gary Glick, Colorado A&M back, Pittsburgh.

COACHES: "Paddy" Driscoll appointed head coach of Chicago Bears to replace George Halas; Hugh Devore took over for Jim Trimble at Philadelphia; Frankie Albert replaced "Red" Strader at San Francisco.

NOTES: Hugh L. "Shorty" Ray, technical and rules adviser for NFL from 1938-52, died at 72, Sept. 16.

Ric Casares, Chi-Bear fullback, rushed 1,126 yards.

Frank Bernardi, Chi-Cards, returned punt 96 yards (TD) against Washington, Oct. 14.

Al Carmichael, Green Bay, returned kickoff 106 yards (TD) (record) against Chi-Bears, Oct. 7.

Ollie Matson, Chi-Cards, returned kickoff 105 yards (TD) against Washington, Oct. 14.

TITLE GAME

Triplett smashed 17 yards over the icy ground for the first New York touchdown and Agajanian scored the first of five conversions. The Giants recovered Casares fumble on the Bear's 15 and Agajanian kicked the first of two field goals from the 17. He kicked the other still in the first period after Patton intercepted Brown's pass. This one was from the 43 yard line.

In the second period Webster crashed over from the 3 and the Bears got their only touchdown when Casares scored from 9 yards out. Webster racked up another on a one-yard plunge. The Giants made it 34-7 at the half when Moore recovered Brown's punt in the end zone after it was blocked by Beck.

Conerly passed to Rote for a 9-yard touchdowner in the third period and tossed

one 14 yards to Gifford in the final period to complete the scoring, at 47-7.

New York Giants	13	21	6	7—47
Chicago Bears	0	7	0	0— 7

Touchdowns—Webster 2, Triplett, Rote, H. Moore, Gifford (New York), Casares (Chicago).

Conversions—Agajanian 5 (New York), Blanda (Chicago).

Field Goals—Agajanian 2 (New York).

Attendance: 56,836.

Players' Share: New York $3,779.19; Chicago $2,485.16.

1956 BALTIMORE COLTS
COACH - "Weeb" Ewbank
4th 5-7-0

Ameche, Alan - B	Moore, Lenny - B
Berry, Raymond - E	Mutscheller, Jim - E
Campanella, Joseph - G	Nutter, "Buzz" - C
Chorovich, Dick - T	Nyers, Dick - B
Colteryahn, Lloyd - E	Patera, John - G
Donovan, Art - T	Pellington, Bill - LB & G
Dupre, Louis - B	Peterson, Gerry - T
Eggers, Doug - LB & G	Preas, George - T
Feamster, Tom - T	Radosevich, George - C
Finnin, Tom - T	Rechichar, Bert - B & LB
Flowers, Bernie - E	Sandusky, Alex - G
Harness, Jim - B	Shaw, George - Q
Hermann, John - B	Shula, Don - B
Jackson, Ken - T	Spinney, Art - G
James, Tom - B	Taseff, Carl - B
Joyce, Don - E	Thomas, Jesse - B
Kerkorian, Gary - Q	Unitas, John - Q
Koman, Bill - G	Vessels, Bill - B
Lipscomb, "Daddy" - T	Womble, Royce - B
Marchetti, Gino - E	Young, Dick - B

1956 CHICAGO BEARS
COACH - "Paddy" Driscoll
1st 9-2-1
(Lost title to New York, 47-7)

Atkins, Doug - E	Hill, Harlon - E
Bingham, Don - B	Hoffman, Jack - E
Bishop, Bill - T	Hoffman, John - B
Blanda, George - Q	Jeter, Perry - B
Brackett, Martin - T	Jones, Stan - T
Brown, Ed - Q	Klawitter, Dick - C
Carl, Harland - B	McColl, Bill - E
Caroline, J. C. - B	Meadows, Ed - E
Casares, Ric - B	Mellekas, John - T
Castete, Jesse - B	Moore, McNeil - B
Clark, Herm - G	Roggeman, Tom - G
Dooley, Jim - E	Schroeder, Gene - E
Fortunato, Joe - LB	Smith, J. D. - B
George, Bill - LB	Smith, Ray - B
Gilbert, Kline - T	Strickland, Larry - C
Gorgal, Ken - B	Wallace, Stan - B
Haluska, Jim - B	Watkins, Bob - B
Hansen, Wayne - G	Wightkin, Bill - E & T
Helwig, John - E & G	Williams, Fred - T

Mel Triplett, New York Giant fullback, knocked over everything except Yankee Stadium scoring this first touchdown against the Chicago Bears in the 1956 title game. The official here is about to bite the dust (which was frozen solid) as Triplett smashes for 17 yards and a touchdown. The futile Bears are Ray Smith (20), J. C. Caroline (25), and McNeil Moore (29). Alex Webster, Giant halfback (29) in white, goes along for moral support.

1956 CHICAGO CARDINALS
COACH - Ray Richards
2nd 7-5-0

Anderson, Charley - E
Bernardi, Frank - B
Bienemann, Tom - E
Boydston, Max - E
Brettschneider, Carl - LB
Brown, Hardy - LB
Burl, Alex - B
Childress, Joe - B
Crow, Lindon - B
Dahms, Tom - T
Delavan, Burt - G
Dittrich, John - G
Hill, Jim - B
Hogland, Doug - G
Husmann, Ed - G
Jagielski, Harry - T
Jennings, John - T
Konovsky, Bob - G
Lane, Dick - B

Lewis, Woodley - B
McHan, Lamar - Q
Mann, Dave - B
Matson, Ollie - B
Nagler, Gern - E
Olszewski, John - B
Pasquesi, Tony - T
Roach, John - Q
Root, Jim - Q
Sanford, Leo - C
Simmons, John - C
Spence, Julian - B
Stonesifer, Don - E
Sugar, Leo - E
Summerall, "Pat" - K & E
Teeuws, Len - T
Ulrich, Charles - T
Weber, Chuck - LB
West, Stan - G

1956 CLEVELAND BROWNS
COACH - Paul Brown
4th 5-7-0

Bassett, Maurice - B

Bradley, Harold - G

Brewster, "Pete" - E
Carpenter, Pres - B
Colo, Don - T
Fiss, Galen - LB
Ford, Len - E
Forester, Herschel - G
Gain, Bob - T
Gatski, Frank - C
Gibron, Abe - G
Gillom, Horace - E
Goss, Don - T
Groza, Lou - T
Hunter, Art - T & C
Kinard, Bill - B
Kissell, John - T
Konz, Ken - B
Lahr, Warren - B
Lavelli, Dante - E
McCormack, Mike

Macerelli, John - T
Massey, Carleton - E
Michaels, Walt - LB
Modzelewski, Ed - B
Morrison, Fred - B
Noll, Chuck - G
O'Connell, Tom - Q
Palumbo, Sam - C
Parilli, "Babe" - Q
Paul, Don - B
Petitbon, John - B
Quinlan, Volney - B
Ratterman, George - Q
Renfro, Ray - B
Smith, Jim Ray - G
Smith, Bob - B
Weber, Chuck - LB
Wren, Lowe - B

1956 DETROIT LIONS
COACH - "Buddy" Parker
2nd 9-3-0

Ane, Charley - C
Bowman, Bill - B

Campbell, Stan - G
Cassady, Howard - B

Christiansen, John - B
Creekmur, Lou - T
Cronin, Gene - E
David, Jim - B
Dibble, Dorne - E
Doran, Jim - E
Gandee, "Sonny" - E
Gedman, Gene - B
Gilmer, Harry - Q
Girard, "Jug" - B
Hart, Leon - B
Karilivacz, Carl - B
Krouse, Ray - T
Lary, Yale - B
Layne, Bobby - Q
Long, Bob - E

Lusk, Bob - C
McCord, Darris - T
McIlhenny, Don - B
Mains, Gil - T
Martin, Jim - G
Middleton, Dave - E
Miller, Bob - T
Perry, Gerry - T
Reichow, Gerry - B
Salsbury, Jim - G
Schmidt, Joe - LB
Sewell, Harley - G
Spencer, Ollie - T
Stits, Bill - B
Tracy, Tom - B

Burnine, Hal - E
Chandler, Don - K
Clatterbuck, Bob - Q
Conerly, Charley - Q
Filipski, Gene - B
Gifford, Frank - B
Grier, Rosey - T
Heinrich, Don - Q
Hermann, John - B
Huff, "Sam" - LB
Hughes, Ed - B
Huth, Gerry - G
Katcavage, Jim - E
Livingston, Cliff - LB & E
MacAfee, Ken - E
Modzelewski, Dick - T
Moore, Henry - B

Nolan, Dick - B
Patton, Jim - B
Rich, Herb - B
Robustelli, Andy - E
Rote, Kyle - E
Schnelker, Bob - E
Spinks, Jack - G
Stroud, Jack - G
Svare, Harland - LB
Svoboda, Bill - LB
Triplett, Mel - B
Tunnell, Em - B
Webster, Alex - B
Wietecha, Ray - C
Yelvington, Dick - T
Yowarsky, Walt - E

1956 GREEN BAY PACKERS
COACH - Lisle Blackbourn
5th 4-8-0

Barnes, Emery - E
Bettis, Tom - G
Bookout, Bill - B
Borden, Nate - E
Brown, Bill - G
Capuzzi, Jim - Q
Carmichael, Al - B
Cone, Fred - B
Deschaine, Dick - E
Dillon, Bobby - B
Ferguson, Howie - B
Forester, "Bill" - G
Gorgal, Ken - B
Gregg, Forrest - G
Gremminger, Hank - B
Hanner, "Dave" - T
Helluin, "Jerry" - T
Howton, Bill - E
Johnson, "Joe" - B
King, Don - T

Knafelc, Gary - E
Knutson, Gene - E
Lauer, Larry - C
Losch, John - B
Martinkovich, John - E
Reid, "Breezy" - B
Ringo, Jim - C
Roberts, Bill - B
Rote, Tobin - Q
Sandusky, John - T
Skibinski, Joe - G
Skoronski, Bob - T
Smith, Gerry - G
Spinks, Jack - G
Starr, Bart - Q
Szafaryn, Len - T & G
Teteak, Deral - G
Walker, Val Joe - B
Young, Glen - B
Zatkoff, Roger - T

1956 PHILADELPHIA EAGLES
COACH - Hugh Devore
6th 3-8-1

Bawel, "Bibbles" - B
Bednarik, "Chuck" LB & C
Bell, Ed - B
Berzinski, Bill - B
Bielski, Dick - B
Bredice, John - E
Brookshier, Tom - B
Burk, Adrian - Q
Burnine, Hal - E
Campbell, Marion - T
D'Agostino, Frank - G
Dimmick, Tom - G
Giancanelli, "Skippy" - B
Gibron, Abe - G
Huxhold, Ken - G
Keller, Ken - B
Kelley, Bob - C
King, Don - T
Lansford, "Buck" - T
Murley, Dick - T
Nipp, Maurey - G

Norton, Gerry - B
Parmer, Jim - B
Pellegrini, Bob - LB & G
Retlaff, "Pete" - E
Ricca, Jim - T
Richardson, Jess - T
Riley, Lee - B
Robinson, Wayne - LB & C
Ryan, John - B
Schaefer, Don - B
Scott, Tom - LB & E
Smith, Bob - B
Stribling, "Bill" - E
Thomason, Bob - Q
Walston, Bob - E
Weatherall, Jim - T
Wegert, Ted - B
Willey, Norm - E
Wydo, Frank - T
Youngelman, Sid - T

1956 LOS ANGELES RAMS
COACH - Sid Gillman
6th 4-8-0

Boyd, Bob - E
Bukich, Rudy - Q
Burroughs, Don - B
Carey, Bob - E
Cason, Jim - B
Castete, Jesse - B
Clarke, Leon - E
Daugherty, Dick - G
Ellena, Jack - G
Fears, Tom - E
Fournet, Sid - G
Fry, Bob - T
Griffin, Bob - C
Hauser, Art - T
Hirsch, Elroy - E
Hock, John - G
Holladay, Bob - B
Holtzman, Glen - T
Mcfadin, "Bud" - T
Marconi, Joe - B

Miller, Paul - E
Miller, Ron - E
Morris, Larry - LB & C
Morrow, John - G
Myers, Brad - B
Panfil, Ken - T
Pitts, Hugh - LB & C
Putnam, Duane - G
Quinlan, Volney - Q
Richter, Les - LB
Sherman, Will - B
Shiver, Ray - B
Toogood, Charley - T
Van Brocklin, Norm - Q
Wade, Bill - Q
Waller, Ron - B
Wardlow, Duane - E
Whittenton, "Jess" - B
Wilson, Tom - B
Younger, "Tank" - B

1956 PITTSBURGH STEELERS
COACH - Walt Kiesling
5th 5-7-0

Alban, Dick - B
Baldacci, Lou - B
Bruney, Fred - B
Butler, Jack - B
Cenci, John - C
Chandnois, Lynn - B
Davis, Art - B
Dodrill, Dale - G
Ford, Henry - B
Gaona, Bob - T
Glatz, Fred - E
Glick, Gary - B
Jecha, Ray - G
Krupa, Joe - T
McClairen, Jack - E
McClung, Willie - T
McFadden, Marv - G
McPeak, Bill - E
Marchibroda, Ted - Q

Mathews, Ray - E
Matuszak, Marv - LB & G
Michalik, Art - G
Murley, Dick - T
Nickel, Elbie - E
O'Brien, John - E
O'Malley, Joe - E
O'Neil, Bob - G
Perry, Lowell - E
Reger, John - LB & G
Rogel, Fran - B
Scarbath, Jack - Q
Shepard, Charley - B
Stautner, Ernie - T
Stock, John - E
Tarasovic, George - LB & C
Taylor, James - C
Varrichione, Frank - T
Watson, Sid - B

1956 NEW YORK GIANTS
COACH - Jim Lee Howell
1st 8-3-1
(Beat Chicago Bears for title, 47-7)

Agajanian, Ben - K
Austin, Bill - G

Beck, Ray - G
Brown, Rosie - T

1956 SAN FRANCISCO 49ERS
COACH - Frank Albert
3rd 5-6-1

Arenas, Joe - B
Beattie, Ed - C
Berry, Rex - B

Bosley, Bruce - T
Brown, Hardy - LB
Bruney, Fred - B

Carr, Paul - LB
Conner, Clyde - E
Connolly, Ted - G
Cross, Bob - T
Goad, Paul - B
Gonzaga, John - T
Hazeltine, Matt - LB
Henke, Ed - E & T
Herchman, Bill - T
Holladay, Bob - B
Jessup, Bill - E
Johnson, John Henry - B
Johnson, Bill - C
McCormick, Tom - B
McElhenny, Hugh - B
Maderos, George - B
Moegle, Dick - B
Morrall, Earl - Q
Morris, George - C

Nomellini, Leo - T
Palatella, Lou - G
Perry, Joe - B
Powell, Charley - E
Rucka, Leo - C & LB
Sagely, Floyd - E
St. Clair, Bob - T
Sardisco, Tony - G & LB
Sharkey, Ed - G
Sheriff, Stan - LB
Smith, Charley - E
Smith, Ernie - B
Smith, J. D. - B
Smith, Jerry - G
Soltau, Gordon - E
Tittle, Y. A. - Q
Toneff, Bob - T
Wilson, Bill - E

1956 WASHINGTON REDSKINS
COACH - Joe Kuharich
3rd 6-6-0

Allen, John - C
Atkeson, Dale - B
Baker, "Sam" - K
Barni, Roy - B
Boll, Don - T
Brito, Gene - E
Carson, John - E
Christensen, Erik - E
DeCarlo, Art - B
Dorow, Al - Q
Drazenovich, Chuck - LB
Elter, Leo - B
Felton, Ralph - B
Fulcher, Bill - G
Hecker, Norbert - B
Jagielski, Harry - T
James, Dick - B
Kimmel, J. D. - T
LeBaron, Ed - Q
Lowe, Gary - B

Meilinger, Steve - E
Miller, John - T
Norris, Hal - B
Ostrowski, Chet - E
Paluck, John - E
Peters, Volney - T
Planutis, Gerry - B
Runnels, Tom - B
Sardisco, Tony - G
Schrader, Jim - C
Scudero, Joe - B
Stanfel, Dick - G
Stephens, "Red" - G
Thomas, Ralph - E
Torgeson, Lavern - LB
Ulinski, Harry - C
Wells, Billy - B
Witucki, "Casimir" - G
Wyant, Fred - Q

1957

WESTERN CONFERENCE

Detroit	8	4	0	.667
San Francisco	8	4	0	.667
Baltimore	7	5	0	.583
Los Angeles	6	6	0	.500
Chicago Bears	5	7	0	.417
Green Bay	3	9	0	.250

Detroit defeated San Francisco, 31–27, in conference playoff

EASTERN CONFERENCE

Cleveland	9	2	1	.818
New York	7	5	0	.583
Pittsburgh	6	6	0	.500
Washington	5	6	1	.455
Philadelphia	4	8	0	.333
Chicago Cardinals	3	9	0	.250

TITLE: Detroit beat Cleveland, 59-14 for the championship at Detroit, Dec. 29.

Detroit earned the title game by defeating San Francisco, 31-27 in a playoff in the Western Conference.

LEADERS: Individual leaders for the season: Scoring—"Sam" Baker (Washington), Lou Groza (Cleveland), 77 (tie); Rushing—Jim Brown (Cleveland), 942 yds.; Passing—Tom O'Connell (Cleveland); Pass Receiving—Bill Wilson (San Francisco), 52; Field Goals—Lou Groza (Cleveland), 15; Punting—Don Chandler (New York), 44.6 yds.; Interceptions—Milt Davis (Baltimore), Jack Christiansen (Detroit), Jack Butler (Pittsburgh), 10 (tie).

BONUS PICK: Paul Hornung, Notre Dame back, Green Bay.

COACHES: Raymond "Buddy" Parker resigned as head coach of Detroit just before season, was replaced by George Wilson and took over at Pittsburgh, replacing Walt Kiesling.

NOTES: "Tony" Morabito, president of 49ers, died, Oct. 27.

Bill McPeak, Pittsburgh defensive end, retired holding safety record (3).

Jim Brown, Cleveland, rushed 237 yards (31 attempts) breaking own record, against Los Angeles, Nov. 24.

Larry Barnes, San Francisco, punted 86 yards against Chi-Cards, Sept. 26.

Roy Barni, Washington back, shot dead in August.

Harry Randolph, Columbus back (1923) died, Dec. 3.

TITLE GAME

Detroit, playing without quarterback Bobby Layne, whose leg had been broken in a recent game, dominated this contest from start to finish. Martin scored first with a 31-yard field goal. Tobin Rote smashed through center for 1-yard and the first touchdown and Gedman got another in the first period on a one-yard thrust.

Brown raced 17 yards around end early in the second period for the first Cleveland score and Groza converted. However, Detroit came back with two more, the first a 26-yard pass from Rote to Junker on a fake field goal play, the second when Barr intercepted a Plum pass on Cleveland's 19 and raced over. It was 31-7 at the half.

Lew Carpenter got Cleveland's other touchdown in the third quarter and Groza made the extra point. Detroit came back with two more in this period. Rote passed from his own 22 to Doran who went all the way for 78 yards, second longest pass touchdown in championship history.

Rote opened the fourth quarter with a touchdown strike to Middleton over the goal from Cleveland's 23. Later, Reichow, quarterbacking for the Lions, tossed 16 yards to Cassady for Detroit's eighth touchdown. Martin completed all the conversion attempts and the final score was 59–14.

Detroit Lions	17	14	14	14—59
Cleveland Browns	0	7	7	0—14

Touchdowns—Rote, Gedman, Junker 2, Barr, Doran, Middleton, Cassady (Detroit), Brown, L. Carpenter, (Cleveland). Conversions—Martin 8 (Detroit), Groza 2 (Cleveland).
Field Goal—Martin, 31 yards (Detroit).

Attendance: 55,263.

Players' Share: Detroit $4,295.41; Cleveland $2,750.30.

Clark, Herm - G
Damore, John - G
Dooley, Jim - E
Drzewieki, Ron - B
Fortunato, Joe - LB
Galimore, Willie - B
George, Bill - LB
Gilbert, Kline - T
Hansen, Wayne - G & C
Hill, Harlon - E
Hoffman, Jack - E
Jeter, Perry - B
Johnson, Jack - B
Jones, Stan - T
Kilcullen, Bob - T

Knox, Ron - Q
Leggett, Earl - T
McColl, Bill - E
Meadows, Ed - E
Moore, McNeil - B
Roggeman, Tom - G
Schroeder, Gene - E
Smith, Ray - B
Strickland, Larry - C
Wallace, Stan - B
Watkins, Bob - B
Wightkin, Bill - E & T
Williams, Fred - T
Zucco, Vic - B

1957 CHICAGO CARDINALS
COACH - Ray Richards
6th 3-9-0

Bernardi, Frank - B
Bock, Wayne - T
Boydston, Max - E
Brettschneider, Carl - LB
Brubaker, Dick - E
Carr, Jim - B
Childress, Joe - B
Crow, Lindon - B
Finnin, Tom - T
Hammack, Mal - B
Hill, Jim - B
Hogland, Doug - G
Husmann, Ed - G
Jennings, John - T
Konovsky, Bob - G
Lane, Dick - B
Larson, Paul - Q
Lewis, Woodley - B
Lunceford, Dave - T
McHan, Lamar - Q

Mann, Dave - B
Marchibroda, Ted - Q
Matson, Ollie - B
Nagler, Gern - E
Olszewski, John - B
Pasquesi, Tony - T
Putman, Earl - C
Sagely, Floyd - E
Sanford, Leo - G & C
Sears, Jim - B
Sugar, Leo - E
Summerall, "Pat" - K & E
Taylor, Jim - C
Teeuws, Len - T
Toogood, Charley - G
Tubbs, Jerry - LB
Ulrich, Charles - T
Weber, Chuck - LB
West, Stan - G

1957 BALTIMORE COLTS
COACH - "Weeb" Ewbank
3rd 7-5-0

Ameche, Alan - B
Berry, Raymond - E
Braase, Ordell - E
Call, John - B
Campanella, Joseph - T
Davidson, "Cotton" - Q
Davis, Milton - B
DeCarlo, Art - B
Donovan, Art - T
Dupre, Louis - B
Eggers, Doug - LB
Jackson, Ken - T
Joyce, Don - E
Lipscomb, "Daddy" - T
Marchetti, Gino - E
Moore, Henry - B
Moore, Lenny - B
Mutscheller, Jim - E
Myhra, Steve - G

Nelson, Andy - B
Nutter, "Buzz" - C
Nyers, Dick - B
Owens, Luke - T
Parker, Jim - T
Patera, John - G
Pellington, Bill - LB
Preas, George - T
Pricer, Bill - B
Rechichar, Bert - LB & B
Sandusky, Alex - G
Shaw, George - Q
Shinnick, Don - LB
Spinney, Art - G
Szymanski, Dick - C
Taseff, Carl - B
Thomas, Jesse - B
Unitas, John - Q
Womble, Royce - B

1957 CLEVELAND BROWNS
COACH - Paul Brown
1st 9-2-1
(Lost title to Detroit, 59-14)

Amstutz, Joe - C
Borton, John - Q
Brewster, "Pete" - E
Brown, Jim - B
Campbell, Milt - B
Carpenter, Lew - B
Carpenter, Pres - E
Catlin, Tom - LB & C
Clarke, Frank - E
Colo, Don - T
Costello, Vince - LB
Fiss, Galen - LB
Ford, Len - E
Forester, Herschel - G
Freeman, Bob - B
Gain, Bob - T
Groza, Lou - T
Hanulak, Chet - B
Hunter, Art - C

Jordan, Henry - T
Konz, Ken - B
Lahr, Warren - B
McCormack, Mike - T
Michaels, Walt - LB
Modzelewski, Ed - B
Noll, Chuck - G
O'Connell, Tom - Q
Paul, Don - B
Plum, Milt - Q
Quinlan, Bill - E
Renfro, Ray - B
Reynolds, Bill - B
Robison, Fred - G
Sheriff, Stan - LB & G
Smith, Jim Ray - G
Wiggin, Paul - E
Wren, Lowe - B

1957 CHICAGO BEARS
COACH - "Paddy" Driscoll
5th 5-7-0

Atkins, Doug - E
Bishop, Bill - T
Blanda, George - Q
Brackett, Martin - T

Bratkowski, "Zeke" - Q
Brown, Ed - Q
Caroline, J. C. - B
Casares, Ric - B

1957 DETROIT LIONS
COACH - George Wilson
1st 8-4-0
(Best San Francisco in playoff, 31-27)
(Beat Cleveland for title, 59-14)

Ane, Charley - T & C
Barr, Terry - B

Brown, Marv - B
Campbell, Stan - G

Cassady, Howard - B
Christiansen, John - B
Creekmur, Lou - T
Cronin, Gene - E
David, Jim - B
Dibble, Dorne - E
Doran, Jim - E
Gatski, Frank - C
Gedman, Gene - B
Gordy, John - G
Hart, Leon - B
Johnson, John Henry - B
Junker, Steve - E
Karilivacz, Carl - B
Krouse, Ray - T
Lary, Yale - B

Layne, Bobby - Q
Long, Bob - LB
Lowe, Gary - B
McCord, Darris - T
Mains, Gil - T
Martin, Jim - LB
Middleton, Dave - E
Miller, Bob - T
Perry, Gerry - T
Reichow, Gerry - B
Rote, Tobin - Q
Russell, Ken - T
Schmidt, Joe - LB
Sewell, Harley - G
Tracy, Tom - B
Zatkoff, Roger - LB

Martinkovich, John - E
Modzelewski, Dick - T
Nolan, Dick - B
Patton, Jim - B
Robustelli, Andy - E
Rote, Kyle - E
Schnelker, Bob - E
Spinks, Jack - G
Stroud, Jack - G

Svare, Harland - LB
Svoboda, Bill - LB
Triplett, Mel - B
Tunnell, Em - B
Webster, Alex - B
Wietecha, Ray - C
Yelvington, Dick - T
Yowarsky, Walt - E

1957 PHILADELPHIA EAGLES
COACH - Hugh Devore
5th 4-8-0

Barnes, Billy - B
Bednarik, "Chuck" LB & C
Bell, Ed - B
Bielski, Dick - E & B
Brookshire, Tom - B
Burnine, Hal - E
Campbell, Marion - T
Dorow, Al - Q
Gaona, Bob - T
Gibron, Abe - G
Harris, Jim - B
Hudson, Bob - B
Huxhold, Ken - G
Jurgensen, "Sonny" - Q
Keller, Ken - B
Koman, Bill - LB
Lansford, "Buck" - T
McDonald, Tom - B

Mavraides, Menil - G
Norton, Gerry - B
Peaks, Clarence - B
Retzlaff, "Pete" - B
Ryan, John - B
Saidock, Tom - T
Scott, Tom - LB & E
Simerson, John - C
Stribling, "Bill" - E
Szafaryn, Len - T
Thomason, Bob - Q
Walston, Bob - E
Weatherall, Jim - T
Willey, Norm - E
Worden, Neil - B
Wydo, Frank - T
Youngelman, Sid - T

1957 GREEN BAY PACKERS
COACH - Lisle Blackbourn
6th 3-9-0

Amundsen, Norm - G
Barry, Al - G
Bettis, Tom - G
Borden, Nate - E
Carmichael, Al - B
Cone, Fred - B
DanJean, Ernie - G
Deschaine, Dick - E
Dillon, Bobby - B
Ferguson, Howie - B
Forester, "Bill" - G
Gremminger, Hank - B
Hanner, "Dave" - T
Helluin, "Jerry" - T
Hornung, Paul - B
Howton, Bill - E
Johnson, "Joe" - B
Kinard, Billy - B

Knafelc, Gary - E
Kramer, Ron - E
Lauer, Larry - C
McGee, Max - E
McIlhenny, Don - B
Massey, Carleton - E
Masters, Norm - T
Palumbo, Sam - C
Parilli, "Babe" - Q
Petitbon, John - B
Purnell, Frank - B
Ringo, Jim - C
Salsbury, Jim - G
Spencer, Ollie - T
Starr, Bart - Q
Symank, John - B
Temp, Jim - E
Vereen, Carl - T

1957 PITTSBURGH STEELERS
COACH - "Buddy" Parker
3rd 6-6-0

Alban, Dick - B
Beatty, Ed - C
Bowman, Bill - B
Bruney, Fred - B
Butler, Jack - B
Cichowski, Gene - B
Dawson, Len - Q
Derby, Dean - B
Dodrill, Dale - G
Fournet, Sid - G
Girard, "Jug" - E
Glick, Gary - B
Gunderman, Bob - E
Hughes, Dick - B
Kemp, Jack - Q
Krupa, Joe - T
Leahy, Gerry - T
Lee, Herman - T & G
Liddick, Dave - T
McCabe, Richie - B
McClairen, Jack - E

McClung, Willie - T
McPeak, Bill - E
Mathews, Ray - E
Michael, Bill - G
Morrall, Earl - Q
Nickel, Elbie - E
Nisby, John - G
O'Neil, Bob - G
Priatko, Bill - LB
Reger, John - LB
Richards, Perry - E
Rogel, Fran - B
Rozelle, Aubrey - LB
Sandusky, Mike - G
Stautner, Ernie - T
Tarasovic, George - E
Varrichione, Frank - T
Watson, Sid - B
Wells, Billy - B
Young, Dick - B

1957 LOS ANGELES RAMS
COACH - Sid Gillman
4th 6-6-0

Arnett, Jon - B
Boyd, Bob - E
Bravo, Alex - B
Burroughs, Don - B
Castete, Jesse - B
Clarke, Leon - E
Cothren, Paige - K
Daugherty, Dick - C
Dougherty, Bob - LB & E
Fry, Bob - T
Fuller, Frank - T
Griffin, Bob - C
Hauser, Art - T
Hirsch, Elroy - E
Hock, John - G
Holtzman, Glen - T
Houser, John - G
Lundy, Lamar - E

Marconi, Joe - B
Miller, Paul - E
Morris, Larry - LB & C
Panfil, Ken - T
Pardee, John - LB & C
Putnam, Duane - G
Richter, Les - LB & G
Sherman, Will - B
Shofner, Del - B
Smith, Billy Ray - T & E
Strugar, George - T
Taylor, Cecil - B
Van Brocklin, Norm - Q
Wade, Bill - Q
Waller, Ron - B
Whittenton, "Jess" - B
Wilson, Tom - B
Younger, "Tank" - B

1957 SAN FRANCISCO 49ERS
COACH - Frank Albert
1st 8-4-0 (tied)
(Lost playoff to Detroit, 31-27)

Arenas, Joe - B
Babb, Gene - B
Barnes, Larry - B
Bosley, Bruce - G
Brodie, John - Q
Carr, Paul - LB
Connor, Clyde - E
Connolly, Ted - G
Cross, Bob - T
Dahms, Tom - T
Gonzaga, John - T
Hazeltine, Matt - LB

Henke, Ed - E
Herchman, Bill - T
Holladay, Bob - B
Jessup, Bill - E
McElhenny, Hugh - B
Matuszak, Marv - LB
Moegle, Dick - B
Morze, Frank - C
Nomellini, Leo - T
Owens, R. C. - E
Palatella, Lou - G
Perry, Joe - B

1957 NEW YORK GIANTS
COACH - Jim Lee Howell
2nd 7-5-0

Agajanian, Ben - K
Austin, Bill - G
Beck, Ray - G
Bookman, John - B
Brown, Rosie - T
Chandler, Don - K
Clatterbuck, Bob - Q
Conerly, Charley - Q
Crawford, Ed - B

Epps, Bob - B
Filipski, Gene - B
Gifford, Frank - B
Heinrich, Don - Q
Huff, "Sam" - LB
Hughes, Ed - B
Katcavage, Jim - E
Livingston, Cliff - LB & E
MacAfee, Ken - E

Powell, Charley - LB
Ridlon, Jim - B
Rubke, Karl - LB
St. Clair, Bob - T
Sheriff, Stan - LB
Smith, J. D. - B
Soltau, Gordon - E

Spence, Julian - B
Stits, Bill - B
Tittle, Y. A. - Q
Toneff, Bob - T
Walker, Val Joe - B
Wilson, Bill - E

1957 WASHINGTON REDSKINS
COACH - Joe Kuharich
4th 5-6-1

Allen, John - C
Baker, "Sam" - K
Boll, Don - T
Bosseler, Don - B
Braatz, Tom - E
Brito, Gene - E
Bukich, Rudy - Q
Carson, John - E
DeCarlo, Art - B
Dee, Bob - E
Drazenovich, Chuck - LB
Elter, Leo - B
Felton, Ralph - B
Fulcher, Bill - G
Hecker, Norbert - B
James, Dick - B
Khayat, Ed - T
LeBaron, Ed - Q
Lemek, Ray - T

Lowe, Gary - B
Meilinger, Steve - E
Ostrowski, Chet - E
Owens, Don - T
Peters, Volney - T
Podoley, Jim - B
Renfro, Will - T
Runnels, Tom - B
Schrader, Jim - C
Scudero, Joe - B
Shula, Don - B
Stanfel, Dick - G
Stephens, "Red" - G
Sutton, Ed - B
Torgeson, Lavern - LB
Voytek, Ed - G
Walton, Joe - E
Wells, Billy - B
Zagers, Bert - B

1958

EASTERN CONFERENCE

New York	9	3	0	.750
Cleveland	9	3	0	.750
Pittsburgh	7	4	1	.636
Washington	4	7	1	.364
Philadelphia	2	9	1	.182
Chicago Cards	2	9	1	.182

New York defeated Cleveland, 10–0 in conference playoff

WESTERN CONFERENCE

Baltimore	9	3	0	.750
Los Angeles	8	4	0	.667
Chicago Bears	8	4	0	.667
San Francisco	6	6	0	.500
Detroit	4	7	1	.364
Green Bay	1	10	1	.091

TITLE: Baltimore beat New York, 23-17 for the championship in New York, Dec. 28, in the first sudden-death overtime contest in NFL history. New York had previously beaten Cleveland, 10-0, in a playoff for the Eastern conference title.

LEADERS: Individual leaders for the season: Scoring—Jim Brown (Cleveland), 108; Rushing—Jim Brown (Cleveland), 1,527 yds., a new record; Passing—Eddie LeBaron (Washington); Pass Receiving—Raymond Berry (Baltimore), "Pete" Retzlaff (Philadelphia), 56 (tie); Field Goals—Paige Cothren (Los Angeles), Tom Miner (Pittsburgh), 14 (tie); Punting—"Sam" Baker, (Washington), 45.4 yds.; Interceptions—Jim Patton (New York), 11.

BONUS PICK—King Hill, Rice qback, Chicago Cardinals.

COACHES: George Halas resumed as head coach of Bears, replacing "Paddy" Driscoll; Ray "Scooter" McLean took over from Lisle Blackbourn at Green Bay; Lawrence "Buck" Shaw replaced Hugh Devore at Philadelphia; Frank "Pop" Ivy replaced Ray Richards with Chicago Cardinals.

NOTES: Bonus pick eliminated from draft of college players.

Jim Brown, Cleveland, rushed 1,527 yards (record).

TITLE GAME

Half of the opening quarter elapsed before Baltimore registered the game's first first down, via a 60-yard Unitas to Moore pass play to New York's 25. Myhra's fourth-down field goal attempt from the 27 was blocked by Huff.

Gifford's sweep of 38 yards around left end helped move the Giants from their 27 to the Colt's 29. Summerall's fourth-down field goal from the 36 at 12:58 of the first period made it: New York 3, Baltimore 0.

Krouse recovered Gifford's fumble on the New York 20 on the first play of the second quarter. Five consecutive running plays produced a Baltimore touchdown, with Ameche plunging two yards for the score at 2:26. Myhra converted. Baltimore 7, New York 3.

Following Guy's recovery of Simpson's fumble on the Colt's 10, Joyce regained the ball for Baltimore on its 14 by pouncing on Gifford's bobble. Hard running by Moore and Ameche and three Unitas passes for 28 yards advanced the Colts to the Giants' 15. Unitas threw to Berry in the end zone at 13:40. Myhra converted. Baltimore 14, New York 3.

A Baltimore drive of 58 yards in the third quarter was stalled on the Giants' one, New York taking over on its five, where Ameche was stopped by Livingston on fourth down. Three plays later Conerly floated a pass to Rote, who fumbled upon being hit by Nelson on the Colts' 25—Webster scooped up the loose ball and dashed to the one. Triplett banged across for the score on second down at 11:14. Summerall added the extra point. Baltimore 14, New York 10.

New York launched a TD drive the next time it took possession of the ball on its 19. Conerly threw to Schnelker for gains of 17 and 46 yards to Baltimore's 15, then fired to Gifford for the touchdown at 0:53 of the fourth quarter. Summerall kicked the extra point, New York 17, Baltimore 14.

With less than two minutes remaining Taseff made a fair catch of Chandler's punt on Baltimore's 14. Unitas completed four of seven consecutive passes, the last three to Berry for gains of 25, 15 and 22 yards to the Giants' 13. Myhra booted a field goal from the 20 at 14:53. New York 17, Baltimore 17.

New York won the toss to start the National Football League's first sudden-death playoff and elected to receive. After three plays netted nine yards to the New York 29, Chandler punted to Taseff, who returned the ball one yard to Baltimore's 20-yard line. Unitas connected on four of five passes, two to Berry for 33 yards, as Colts surged to Giants' one in 12 plays. Ameche shot through a gaping hole in the right side of his line to score the winning touchdown on the 13th play. No conversion was attempted and the game ended after 8:15 of the sudden-death period.

| Baltimore Colts | 0 | 14 | 0 | 3 | 6—23 |
| New York Giants | 3 | 0 | 7 | 7 | 0—17 |

Touchdowns—Ameche 2, Berry, (Baltimore), Triplett, Gifford, (New York).
Conversions—Myhra 2, (Baltimore), Summerall 2, (New York).
Field Goals—Myhra (20 yards), (Baltimore), Summerall (36 yards), (New York).

Attendance. 64,185.
Players' Share: Baltimore $4,718.77; New York $3,111.33.

1958 BALTIMORE COLTS
COACH - "Weeb" Ewbank
1st 9-3-0
(Beat New York for title, 23-17 Overtime)

Ameche, Alan - B
Berry, Raymond - E
Braase, Ordell - E
Brown, Ray - B
Call, John - B
Davis, Milton - B
DeCarlo, Art - B
Donovan, Art - T
Dupre, Louis - B
Horn, Dick - B
Joyce, Don - E
Krouse, Ray - T
Lipscomb, "Daddy" - T
Lyles, Lenny - B
Marchetti, Gino - E
Moore, Lenny - B
Mutscheller, Jim - E
Myhra, Steve - G
Nelson, Andy - B
Nutter, "Buzz" - C
Parker, Jim - T
Pellington, Bill - LB
Plunkett, Sherm - T
Preas, George - T
Pricer, Bill - B
Rechichar, Bert - LB
Sample, John - B
Sandusky, Alex - G
Sanford, Leo - LB
Shaw, George - Q
Shinnick, Don - LB
Simpson, Jackie - B
Spinney, Art - G
Stone, Avatus - B
Szymanski, Dick - C
Taseff, Carl - B
Thurston, Fred - G
Unitas, John - Q

1958 CHICAGO BEARS
COACH - George Halas
3rd 8-4-0

Anderson, Ralph - B
Atkins, Doug - E
Barnes, Erich - B
Bishop, Bill - T
Blanda, George - Q
Bratkowski, "Zeke" - Q
Brown, Ed - Q
Bukich, Rudy - Q
Carey, Bob - E
Caroline, J. C. - B
Casares, Ric - B
Cooke, Ed - E
Douglas, Merrill - B
Fortunato, Joe - LB
Galimore, Willie - B
George, Bill - LB
Gibron, Abe - G
Hansen, Wayne - G & C
Healy, Michael - G
Hill, Harlon - E
Hoffman, Jack - E
Howley, Chuck - LB
Jewett, Bob - E
Johnson, Jack - B
Jones, Stan - T
Kilcullen, Bob - T
Klein, Dick - T
Lee, Herman - T
Leggett, Earl - T
McColl, Bill - E
Mellekas, John - C
Morris, Johnny - B
Roehnelt, Bill - G
Ryan, John - B & E
Strickland, Larry - C
Sumner, Charley - B
Wallace, Stan - B
Whittenton, "Jess" - B
Williams, Fred - T
Zucco, Vic - B

1958 CHICAGO CARDINALS
COACH - "Pop" Ivy
6th 2-9-1

Boydston, Max - E
Brettschneider, Carl - LB
Childress, Joe - B
Conrad, Bobby Joe - B
Cook, Ed - T
Cross, Bob - T
Crow, John - B
Culpepper, Ed - T
Eggers, Doug - LB
Gillis, Don - C
Gordon, Bob - B
Gray, Ken - G
Hammack, Mal - B
Hill, King - Q
Hogland, Doug - G
Husmann, Ed - B
Jackson, Charley - B
Konovsky, Bob - G
Lander, Lowell - B
Lane, Dick - B
Lewis, Woodley - E
McCusker, Jim - T
McHan, Lamar - Q
Matson, Ollie - B
Meinert, Dale - G
Nagler, Gern - E
Nolan, Dick - B
Owens, Luke - T
Patera, John - LB
Philpott, Dean - B
Reynolds, Mack - Q
Sears, Jim - B
Sugar, Leo - E
Taylor, Jim - LB
Tubbs, Jerry - LB
Ulrich, Charles - T
Watkins, Bob - B
Weber, Chuck - LB

Alan Ameche (35) of the Colts plunges over the Giants' line for the winning touchdown in the 1958 "sudden death" championship game. The final score was 23-17. (Wide World Photo.)

1958 CLEVELAND BROWNS
COACH - Paul Brown
1st 9-3-0
(Lost playoff to New York, 10-0)

Bolden, Leroy - B
Brewster, "Pete" - E
Brown, Jim - B
Carpenter, Lew - B
Carpenter, Pres - E
Catlin, Tom - LB & C
Clarke, Frank - E
Colo, Don - T
Costello, Vince - LB
Davis, Willie - E & T
Deschaine, Dick - E
Fiss, Galen - LB
Freeman, Bob - B
Gain, Bob - T
Groza, Lou - T
Hickerson, Gene - G
Hunter, Art - C
Jordan, Henry - T

Konz, Ken - B
Lahr, Warren - B
McClung, Willie - T
McCormack, Mike - T
Michaels, Walt - LB
Mitchell, Bob - B
Modzelewski, Ed - B
Ninowski, Jim - Q
Noll, Chuck - G
Paul, Don - B
Plum, Milt - Q
Quinlan, Bill - E
Renfro, Ray - B
Shofner, Jim - B
Smith, Jim Ray - G
Wiggin, Paul - E
Wren, Lowe - B

1958 DETROIT LIONS
COACH - George Wilson
5th 4-7-1

Ane, Charley - C & T
Barr, Terry - B

Campbell, Stan - G
Cassady, Howard - B

Christiansen, John - B
Creekmur, Lou - T
Cronin, Gene - E
David, Jim - B
Doran, Jim - E
Gedman, Gene - B
Gibbons, Jim - E
Glass, Bill - G
Hogland, Doug - G
Johnson, John Henry - B
Karras, Alex - T
Koepfer, Karl - G
Lary, Yale - B
Layne, Bobby - Q
Lewis, Dan - B
Long, Bob - LB
Lowe, Gary - B
McCord, Darris - T

Mains, Gil - T
Martin, Jim - LB & K
Middleton, Dave - E
Miller, Bob - T
Morrall, Earl - Q
Perry, Gerry - T
Richards, Perry - E
Rote, Tobin - Q
Russell, Ken - T
Rychlec, Tom - E
Schmidt, Joe - LB
Sewell, Harley - G
Walker, Wayne - LB
Webb, Ken - B
Whitsell, Dave - B
Zatkoff, Roger - LB

1958 GREEN BAY PACKERS
COACH - "Scooter" McLean
6th 1-10-1

Bettis, Tom - LB
Borden, Nate - E
Bullough, Harry - G
Carmichael, Al - B
Currie, Dan - LB
Dillon, Bobby - B
Ferguson, Howie - B
Ford, Len - E

Forester, "Bill" - LB
Francis, Joe - Q
Gregg, Forrest - G
Gremminger, Hank - B
Hanner, "Dave" - T
Hornung, Paul - B
Howton, Bill - E
Johnson, "Joe" - B

Kimmell, J. D. - T
Kinard, Billy - B
Knafelc, Gary - E
Kramer, Gerry - G
McGee, Max - E
McIlhenny, Don - B
Massey, Carleton - E
Masters, Norm - T
Matuszak, Marv - LB
Meilinger, Steve - E
Nitschke, Ray - LB

Parilli, "Babe" - Q
Ringo, Jim - C
Romine, Al - B
Salsbury, Jim - G
Shanley, Jim - B
Spencer, Ollie - T
Starr, Bart - Q
Symank, John - B
Taylor, Jim - B
Temp, Jim - E
Whittenton, "Jess" - B

Norton, Gerry - B
Owens, Don - T
Peaks, Clarence - B
Pellegrini, Bob - LB
Peters, Volney - T
Retzlaff, "Pete" - E
Richardson, Jess - T
Riley, Lee - B
Ryan, John - B

Scott, Tom - LB
Simerson, John - C
Snyder, Ken - T
Szafarny, Len - T
Van Brocklin, Norm - Q
Walston, Bob - E
Wells, Billy - B
Youngelman, Sid - T

1958 LOS ANGELES RAMS
COACH - Sid Gillman
2nd 8-4-0

Arnett, Jon - B
Baker, John - T
Braatz, Tom - E
Bradshaw, Charley - T
Bravo, Alex - B
Bruney, Fred - B
Burroughs, Don - B
Clarke, Leon - E
Cothren, Paige - K
Daugherty, Dick - LB
Fry, Bob - T
Fuller, Frank - T
Harris, Jim - B
Holtzman, Glen - E
Houser, John - G
Iglehart, Floyd - B
Jobko, Bill - LB
Jones, Jim - B
Lansford, "Buck" - G

Lundy, Lamar - E
Marconi, Joe - B
Michaels, Lou - E
Morris, John - B
Morrow, John - C
Panfil, Ken - T
Pardee, John - LB
Phillips, Jim - E
Putnam, Duane - G
Richter, Les - LB
Ryan, Frank - Q
Sherman, Will - B
Shofner, Del - E
Strugar, George - T
Thomas, Clendon - B
Wade, Bill - Q
Waller, Ron - B
Wilkins, Roy - E & LB
Wilson, Tom - B

1958 PITTSBURGH STEELERS
COACH - "Buddy" Parker
3rd 7-4-1

Alban, Dick - B
Beatty, Ed - C
Bishop, Don - E
Butler, Jack - B
Campbell, "Soup" - LB
Christy, Dick - B
Dawson, Len - Q
Derby, Dean - B
Dess, Darrell - T
Dodrill, Dale - G
Dougherty, Bob - LB
Elter, Leo - B
Evans, Jon - E
Glick, Gary - B
Karras, Ted - T
Krisher, Bill - G
Krupa, Joe - T
Krutko, Larry - B
Lasse, Dick - E & LB
Layne, Bobby - Q

Lewis, Joe - T
Lucas, Dick - E
McCabe, Richie - B
McClairen, Jack - E
Mathews, Ray - B & E
Miner, Tom - E
Morrall, Earl - Q
Nisby, John - G
Orr, Jim - E
Reger, John - LB
Reynolds, Billy - B
Sandusky, Mike - G
Simerson, John - C
Smith, Billy Ray - E
Stautner, Ernie - T
Tarasovic, George - E
Tracy, Tom - B
Varrichione, Frank - T
Younger, "Tank" - B

1958 NEW YORK GIANTS
COACH - Jim Lee Howell
1st 9-3-0
(Best Cleveland in playoff, 10-3)
(Lost title to Baltimore, 23-17,
Overtime)

Barry, Al - G
Brackett, Martin - T
Brown, Rosie - T
Chandler, Don - K
Conerly, Charley - Q
Crow, Lindon - B
Dublinski, Tom - Q
Gifford, Frank - B
Grier, Rosey - T
Guy, Mel - T & G
Heinrich, Don - Q
Huff, "Sam" - LB
Hughes, Ed - B
Jelacic, Jon - G
Karilivacz, Carl - B
Katcavage, Jim - E
King, Phil - B
Livingston, Cliff - LB

Lott, Bill - B
MacAfee, Ken - E
Maynard, Don - B
Mischak, Bob - G
Modzelewski, Dick - T
Patton, Jim - B
Robustelli, Andy - E
Rote, Kyle - E
Schnelker, Bob - E
Stroud, Jack - G
Summerall, "Pat" - E
Svare, Harland - LB
Svoboda, Bill - LB
Triplett, Mel - B
Tunnell, Em - B
Webster, Alex - B
Wietecha, Ray - C
Youso, Frank - T

1958 SAN FRANCISCO 49ERS
COACH - Frank Albert
4th 6-6-0

Atkins, Bill - B
Babb, Gene - B
Bosley, Bruce - G
Brodie, John - Q
Connor, Clyde - E
Connolly, Ted - G
Dugan, Fred - E
Gonzaga, John - T
Hazeltine, Matt - LB
Henke, Ed - E
Herchman, Bill - T
Jessup, Bill - E
McElhenny, Hugh - B
Matuszak, Marv - LB
Mertens, Jerry - B
Moegle, Dick - B
Morris, Dennit - LB
Morze, Frank - C
Nomellini, Leo - T

Owens, R. C. - E
Pace, Jim - B
Palatella, Lou - G
Perry, Joe - B
Ridlon, Jim - B
Rubke, Karl - LB
St. Clair, Bob - T
Smith, J. D. - B
Soltau, Gordon - E
Stits, Bill - B
Teresa, Tony - B
Thomas, John - T
Tittle, Y. A. - Q
Toneff, Bob - T
Tubbs, Jery - LB
Wilson, Bill - E
Wittenborn, John - G
Woodson, Abe - B
Yowarsky, Walt - C

1958 PHILADELPHIA EAGLES
COACH - "Buck" Shaw
5th 2-9-1

Barnes, Billy - B
Bednarik, "Chuck" - LB &
Bell, Ed - B
Bielski, Dick - E
Bradley, Hal - G
Brookshier, Tom - B
Campbell, Marion - T
Cooke, Ed - E
Hudson, Bob - B
Huxhold, Ken - G
Jacobs, Proverb - T

Jurgensen, "Sonny" - Q
Khayat, Ed - T
Koman, Bill - LB
Kowalczyk, Walt - B
Laack, Galen - G
Louderback, Tom - LB
McDonald, Tom - B
Meadows, Ed - E
Mitcham, Gene - E
Myers, Brad - B
Nacrelli, Andy - E

1958 WASHINGTON REDSKINS
COACH - Joe Kuharich
4th 4-7-1

Allen, John - C
Anderson, "Bill" - E
Baker, "Sam" - K
Boll, Don - T
Bosseler, Don - B
Braatz, Tom - E
Brito, Gene - E
Brueckman, Charley - C & LB
Bukich, Rudy - Q
Carson, John - E
Cichowski, Gene - B
Dee, Bob - E

Drazenovich, Chuck - LB
Felton, Ralph - LB
Fulcher, Bill - G
Guglielmi, Ralph - Q
James, Dick - B
Kuchta, Frank - C
LeBaron, Ed - Q
Lemek, Ray - T
Lynch, Dick - B
Miller, John - T
Nix, Doyle - B
Olszewski, John - B

Ostrowski, Chet - E
Podoley, Jim - B
Renfro, Will - T
Schrader, Jim - C
Scudero, Joe - B
Sommer, Mike - B
Stanfel, Dick - G
Stephens, "Red" - G

Sutton, Ed - B
Voytek, Ed - G
Walters, Les - B
Walton, Joe - E
Watson, Sid - B
Weatherall, Jim - T
Zagers, Bert - B

1959

EASTERN CONFERENCE

New York	10	2	0	.883
Cleveland	7	5	0	.583
Philadelphia	7	5	0	.583
Pittsburgh	6	5	1	.545
Washington	3	9	0	.250
Chicago Cards	2	10	0	.167

WESTERN CONFERENCE

Baltimore	9	3	0	.750
Chicago Bears	8	4	0	.667
Green Bay	7	5	0	.583
San Francisco	7	5	0	.583
Detroit	3	8	1	.273
Los Angeles	2	10	0	.167

TITLE: Baltimore beat New York, 31-16 for the championship at Baltimore, Dec. 27.

LEADERS: Individual leaders for the season; Scoring—Paul Hornung (Green Bay), 94; Rushing—Jim Brown (Cleveland), 1,329 yds.; Passing—Charley Conerly (New York); Pass Receiving—Raymond Berry (Baltimore), 66; Field Goals—"Pat" Summerall (New York), 20; Punting—Yale Lary (Detroit), 47.1 yds.; Interceptions—Dean Derby (Pittsburgh), Milt Davis (Baltimore), Don Shinnick (Baltimore), 7 (tie).

FIRST DRAFT: Randolph Duncan (Iowa)—Qback—by Green Bay.

COACHES: Vince Lombardi replaced "Scooter" McLean as Green Bay head coach; "Red" Hickey replaced Frankie Albert at San Francisco; Mike Nixon replaced Joe Kuharich at Washington.

NOTES: Player limit raised one to 36. Draft lowered from 30 to 20 selections.

Bert Bell, commissioner since 1946, died at Philadelphia-Pittsburgh game in Philadelphia, Oct. 11. Austin H. Gunsel, treasurer, made acting commissioner for rest of season.

Tim Mara, founder of New York Giants in 1925, died, Feb. 17.

Jim Brown, Cleveland, rushed 1,329 yards.

J. D. Smith, San Francisco, rushed 1,036 yards.

John Unitas, Baltimore, threw 32 touchdown passes (record).

Abe Woodson, San Francisco, returned kickoff 105 yards (TD) against Los Angeles, Nov. 8.

Carl Taseff, Baltimore, returned missed field goal 99 yards (TD), tying record against Los Angeles, Dec. 12.

Galen Laack, Philadelphia guard, killed in car, Jan. 1.

Jake Taylor, Staten Island guard (1931) died, Nov. 2.

TITLE GAME

Baltimore scored from 80 yards out the first time it had the ball, with a 59-yard Unitas to Moore pass ending the drive. Myhra converted to make it 7–0. New York came back in the first period from its own 40 to the Baltimore 23 and Summerail kicked a field goal. It was 7–3 at the end of the first period.

New York moved the score to 7–6 in the second period, during which Summerall's second field goal was the only scoring. It was a 37-yard shot. Myhra of Baltimore missed from the 42.

In the third period New York went ahead 9–7 on Summerall's third field goal, this one from 22 yards out. The New York defense was still making a magnificent stand against the relentless attack of John Unitas and his offensive unit.

Shortly after the fourth quarter started, Unitas put Baltimore ahead with a five-yard touchdown run on a roll-out option play. Myhra's conversion made it Baltimore 14, New York 9. Andrew Nelson intercepted a Conerly pass to set up Baltimore's next score from the New York 14. Unitas passed to Richardson for the touchdown and Myhra again converted to push the lead to 21–9.

With time running out and 12 points needed, Conerly was forced to pass desperately. One of them was picked off by John Sample, defensive back of Baltimore and run back 42 yards for a touchdown. Myhra's kick made it 28–9.

Sample's second interception of a Conerly pass gave Baltimore the ball on New York's 18 and Myhra booted a field goal from the 25 to make the score, 31-9. Bob Schnelker scored for New York on a pass from Conerly covering 32 yards. Summerall's kick made it, 31-16, final.

Baltimore Colts	7	0	0 24—31
New York Giants	3	3	3 .7—16

Touchdowns—Moore, Unitas, Richardson, Sample (Baltimore), Schnelker (New York).
Conversions—Myhra 4 (Baltimore); Summerall (New York).
Field Goals—Myhra (25 yards) (Baltimore); Summerall 3, (23) (37) (22), (New York).

Attendance: 57,545.

Players' Share: Baltimore $4,674.44; New York $3,083.27.

1959 BALTIMORE COLTS
COACH - "Weeb" Ewbank
1st 9-3-0
(Beat New York for title, 31-16)

Ameche, Alan - B
Berry, Raymond - E
Braase, Ordell - E
Brown, Ray - B
Cooke, Edward - E
Davis, Milton - B
DeCarlo, Art - B
Donovan, Art - T
Dupre, Louis - B
Hawkins, Alex - B
Joyce, Don - E
Krouse, Ray - T
Lewis, Hal - B
Lipscomb, "Daddy" - T
Marchetti, Gino - E
Matuszak, Marv - LB
Moore, Lenny - B
Mutscheller, Jim - E
Myhra, Steve - G
Nelson, Andy - B

Nutter, "Buzz" - C
Parker, Jim - T
Pellington, Bill - LB
Plunkett, Sherm - T
Preas, George - T
Pricer, Bill - B
Rechichar, Bert - LB
Richardson, Gerry - E
Sample, John - B
Sandusky, Alex - B
Sherer, Dave - E
Shinnick, Don - LB
Simpson, Jackie - B
Sommer, Mike - B
Spinney, Art - G
Szymanski, Dick - LB & C
Taseff, Carl - B
Unitas, John - Q

1959 CHICAGO BEARS
COACH - George Halas
2nd 8-4-0

Adams, John - B
Atkins, Doug - E
Aveni, John - E
Barnes, Erich - B
Bishop, Don - B
Bishop, Bill - T
Bratkowski, "Zeke" - Q
Brown, Ed - Q
Bukich, Rudy - Q
Caroline, J. C. - B
Casares, Ric - B
Damore, John - G
Dewveall, Bill - E
Dooley, Jim - B
Douglas, Merrill - B

Fortunato, Joe - LB
Galimore, Willie - B
George, Bill - LB
Gibron, Abe - G
Healy, Michael - G
Hill, Harlon - E
Howley, Chuck - LB
Johnson, Jack - B
Johnson, Pete - B
Jones, Stan - G
Klein, Dick - T
Lee, Herman - T
Leggett, Earl - T
McColl, Bill - E

Mellekas, John - C
Morris, Johnny - B
Morris, Larry - LB
Nickla, Ed - T
Petitbon, Rich - B
Roehnelt, Bill - LB

Strickland, Larry - C
Sumner, Charley - B
Taylor, Lionel - E
Williams, Fred - T
Zucco, Vic - B

1959 CHICAGO CARDINALS
COACH - "Pop" Ivy
6th 2-10-0

Bates, Ted - LB
Brettschneider, Carl - LB
Childress, Joe - B
Conrad, Bobby Joe - B
Cook, Ed - T & G
Cross, Bob - T
Crow, John - B
Culpepper, Ed - T
Fuller, Frank - T
Gillis, Don - C
Glick, Fred - B
Gray, Ken - G
Hall, Ken - B
Hammack, Mal - B
Hauser, Art - G
Hickman, Larry - B
Hill, Jim - B
Hill, King - Q
Husmann, Ed - T
Koman, Bill - LB

Lane, Dick - B
Lewis, "Mac" - T
Lewis, Woodley - E
Meinert, Dale - G
Memmelaar, Dale - G
Norton, Jerry - B
Owens, Luke - T
Panfil, Ken - T
Patera, John - LB
Randle, "Sonny" - E
Reynolds, Mack - Q
Richards, Perry - E
Roach, John - Q
Rushing, Marion - LB & E
Schleicher, Maury - LB
Stacy, Billy - B
Sugar, Leo - E
Tracey, John - E
Wagstaff, Jim - B

1959 CLEVELAND BROWNS
COACH - Paul Brown
2nd 7-5-0

Bolden, Leroy - B
Brown, Jim - B
Carpenter, Pres - E
Clarke, Frank - E
Costello, Vince - LB
Davis, Willie - T
Fiss, Galen - LB
Gain, Bob - T
Groza, Lou - B
Hickerson, Gene - G
Howton, Bill - E
Hunter, Art - C
Konz, Ken - B
Kreitling, Rich - E
Lahr, Warren - B
Lloyd, Dave - LB & C
McClung, Willie - T
McCormack, Mike - T

Michaels, Walt - LB
Mitchell, Bob - B
Modzelewski, Ed - B
Ninowski, Jim - Q
Noll, Chuck - G
O'Brien, Fran - T
Parrish, Bernie - B
Peters, Floyd - T
Plum, Milt - Q
Ptacek, Bob - Q
Renfro, Ray - B
Schafrath, Dick - T
Shofner, Jim - B
Smith, Jim Ray - G
Wiggin, Paul - E
Wooten, John - G
Wren, Lowe - B
Youngelman, Sid - T

1959 DETROIT LIONS
COACH - George Wilson
6th 3-8-1

Ane, Charley - C & T
Barr, Terry - B
Cassady, Howard - B
Cook, Gene - E
Creekmur, Lou - T
Cronin, Gene - E
David, Jim - B
Doran, Jim - E
Gibbons, Jim - E
Glass, Bill - E
Gordy, John - G
Grottkau, Bob - G

Johnson, John Henry - B
Junker, Steve - E
Karras, Alex - T
Lary, Yale - B
LeBeau, Dick - B
Lewis, Dan - B
Long, Bob - LB
Lowe, Gary - B
McCord, Darris - T
Mains, Gil - T
Martin, Jim - LB
Middleton, Dave - E

Morrall, Earl - Q
Paolucci, Ben - T
Perry, Gerry - T
Pietrosante, Nick - B
Rabold, Mike - G
Reichow, Gerry - B
Rote, Tobin - Q
Russell, Ken - T

Schmidt, Joe - LB
Sewell, Harley - G
Spencer, Ollie - T
Steffen, Jim - B
Walker, Wayne - LB
Weatherall, Jim - T
Webb, Ken - B
Whitsell, Dave - B

Scott, Tom - LB
Shaw, George - Q
Stits, Bill - B
Stroud, Jack - G
Summerall, "Pat" - E
Sutherin, Don - B

Svare, Harland - LB
Triplett, Mel - B
Webster, Alex - B
Wietecha, Ray - C
Youso, Frank - T

1959 PHILADELPHIA EAGLES
COACH - "Buck" Shaw
3rd 7-5-0

Aschbacher, Darrel - G
Barnes, Billy - B
Bednarik, "Chuck"- LB & C
Bielski, Dick - E
Brookshier, Tom - B
Campbell, Marion - T
Campbell, Stan - G
Carr, Jim - B
Catlin, Tom - LB
Cothren, Paige - K
DeLucca, Gerry - T
Huth, Gerry - G
Johnson, Gene - B
Jurgensen, "Sonny" - Q
Khayat, Ed - E
Kowalczyk, Walt - B
Louderback, Tom - LB
MacAfee, Ken - E
McCusker, Jim - T

McDonald, Tom - B
Nocera, John - LB
Owens, Don - T
Pagliei, Joe - B
Peaks, Clarence - B
Pellegrini, Bob - LB
Powell, Art - B
Retzlaff, "Pete" - E
Richardson, Jess - T
Riley, Lee - B
Robb, Joe - E
Sapp, Theron - B
Smith, Jess - T
Striegel, Bill - G
Van Brocklin, Norm - Q
Walston, Bob - E
Weber, Chuck - LB
Wilson, Jerry - E

1959 GREEN BAY PACKERS
COACH - Vince Lombardi
3rd 7-5-0

Beck, Ken - T
Bettis, Tom - LB
Borden, Nate - E
Brown, Tim - B
Butler, Bill - B
Carpenter, Lew - B
Currie, Dan - LB
Dillon, Bobby - B
Dittrich, John - G
Dowler, Boyd - E
Forester, "Bill" - LB
Francis, Joe - Q
Freeman, Bob - B
Gregg, Forrest - T
Gremminger, Hank - B
Hanner, "Dave" - T
Hornung, Paul - B
Jordan, Henry - T
Knafelc, Gary - E

Kramer, Gerry - G
Kramer, Ron - E
McGee, Max - E
McHan, Lamar - Q
McIlhenny, Don - B
Masters, Norm - T
Nitschke, Ray - LB
Quinlan, Bill - E
Ringo, Jim - C
Skoronski, Bob - T
Starr, Bart - Q
Symank, John - B
Taylor, Jim - B
Temp, Jim - E
Thurston, Fred - G
Tunnell, Em - B
Whittenton, "Jess" - B
Williams, A. D. - E

1959 PITTSBURGH STEELERS
COACH - "Buddy" Parker
4th 6-5-1

Alban, Dick - B
Barnett, Tom - B
Beams, Byron - T
Beatty, Ed - C
Bishop, Don - B
Brewster, "Pete" - E
Butler, Jack - B
Call, John - B
Campbell, "Soup" - LB
Dawson, Len - Q
Derby, Dean - B
Dial, "Buddy" - E
Dodrill, Dale - G
Elter, Leo - B
Fisher, Ray - T
Glick, Gary - B
Hall, Ron - B
Hayes, Dick - LB
Henry, Mike - LB
Karras, Ted - T

Krupa, Joe - T
Krutko, Larry - B
Lasse, Dick - LB
Layne, Bobby - Q
Lewis, Joe - T
Luna, Bob - K
McClairen, Jack - E
Mathews, Ray - E
Nagler, Gern - E
Nisby, John - G
Orr, Jim - E
Reger, John - LB
Sandusky, Mike - G
Smith, Billy Ray - E
Stautner, Ernie - T
Sutherin, Don - B
Tarasovic, George - E
Tracy, Tom - B
Varrichione, Frank - T

1959 LOS ANGELES RAMS
COACH - Sid Gillman
6th 2-10-0

Arnett, Jon - B
Baker, John - E & T
Bradshaw, Charley - T
Brito, Gene - E
Burroughs, Don - B
Clarke, Leon - E
Dickson, Paul - T
Franckhauser, Tom - B
Fry, Bob - T
Guzik, John - LB
Houser, John - G
Humphrey, "Buddy" - Q
Jobko, Bill - LB & C
Karilivacz, Carl - B
Lansford, "Buck" - G
Lovetere, John - T
Lundy, Lamar - E
Marconi, Joe - B
Matson, Ollie - B

Meador, Ed - B
Michaels, Lou - E & T
Morris, John - B
Morrow, John - C
Pardee, John - LB
Phillips, Jim - E
Putnam, Duane - G
Richter, Les - LB
Ryan, Frank - Q
Selawski, Gene - T
Sherman, Will - B
Shofner, Del - E
Strugar, George - T
Thomas, Clendon - B
Wade, Bill - Q
Wilkins, Roy - LB
Williams, Sam - E
Wilson, Tom - B

1959 SAN FRANCISCO 49ERS
COACH - "Red" Hickey
4th 7-5-0

Atkins, Bill - B
Baker, Dave - B
Bosley, Bruce - G
Brodie, John - Q
Clark, Monte - T
Connor, Clyde - E
Connolly, Ted - G
Davis, Tom - K
Dove, Ed - B
Dugan, Fred - E
Gonzaga, John - T
Harrison, Bob - LB
Hazeltine, Matt - LB
Henke, Ed - E
Herchman, Bill - T
Krueger, Charley - E
Lyles, Lenny - B
McElhenny, Hugh - B.
Mertens, Jerry - B

Moegle, Dick - B
Morze, Frank - C
Nomellini, Leo - T
Osborne, "Clancy" - LB
Owens, R. C. - E
Perry, Joe - B
Ridlon, Jim - B
Roberts, Cornelius - B
Rubke, Karl - LB
St. Clair, Bob - T
Schmidt, Henry - T
Smith, J. D. - B
Thomas, John - T
Tittle, Y. A. - Q
Tubbs, Jerry - LB
Wilson, Bill - E
Wittenborn, John - G
Woodson, Abe - B

1959 NEW YORK GIANTS
COACH - Jim Lee Howell
1st 10-2-1
(Lost title to Baltimore, 31-16)

Barry, Al - G
Biscaha, Joe - E
Brown, Rosie - T
Chandler, Don - K
Conerly, Charley - Q
Crow, Lindon - B
Dess, Darrell - G
Gifford, Frank - B
Grier, Rosey - T
Guy, Mel - T & G
Hauser, Art - T
Heinrich, Don - Q
Huff, "Sam" - LB
Katcavage, Jim - E

Kelly, Ellison - G
Kimber, Bill - E
King, Phil - B
Livingston, Cliff - LB
Lynch, Dick - B
Modzelewski, Dick - T
Morrison, Joe - B
Nolan, Dick - B
Patton, Jim - B
Robustelli, Andy - E
Rote, Kyle - E
Schmidt, Bob - T
Schnelker, Bob - E
Scott, George - B

1959 WASHINGTON REDSKINS
COACH - Mike Nixon
5th 3-9-0

Anderson, "Bill" - E	LeBaron, Ed - Q
Baker, "Sam" - K	Lemek, Ray - T
Boll, Don - T	MacAfee, Ken - E
Bosseler, Don - B	McCabe, Dick - B
Braatz, Tom - E	Meadows, Ed - T
Carson, John - E	Miller, John - T
Churchwell, Don - T	Nix, Doyle - B
Cichowski, Gene - B	Olszewski, John - B
Day, "Eagle" - Q	Ostrowski, Chet - E
Drazenovich, Chuck - LB	Paluck, John - E
Felton, Ralph - LB	Podoley, Jim - B
Glick, Gary - B	Renfro, Will - T
Gob, Art - E & G	Schrader, Jim - C
Guglielmi, Ralph - Q	Scotti, Ben - B
Haley, Dick - B	Sommer, Mike - B
Hudson, Bob - G & LB	Stephens, "Red" - G
James, Dick - B	Stits, Bill - B
Karas, Emil - G	Sutton, Ed - B
Kuchta, Frank - C	Toneff, Bob - T
Lawrence, Don - T	Walton, Joe - E

1960

NATIONAL FOOTBALL LEAGUE

EASTERN CONFERENCE

Philadelphia	10	2	0	.833
Cleveland	8	3	1	.727
New York Giants	6	4	2	.600
St. Louis	6	5	1	.545
Pittsburgh	5	6	1	.455
Washington	1	9	2	.100

WESTERN CONFERENCE

Green Bay	8	4	0	.667
Detroit	7	5	0	.583
San Francisco	7	5	0	.583
Baltimore	6	6	0	.500
Chicago	5	6	1	.455
L. A. Rams	4	7	1	.364
Dallas Cowboys	0	11	1	.000

AMERICAN FOOTBALL LEAGUE

EASTERN DIVISION

	W	L	T	Pct.
Houston	10	4	0	.714
N.Y. Titans	7	7	0	.500
Buffalo	5	8	1	.385
Boston	5	9	0	.357

WESTERN DIVISION

	W	L	T	Pct.
L.A. Chargers	10	4	0	.714
Dallas Texans	8	6	0	.571
Oakland	6	8	0	.429
Denver	4	9	1	.308

Championship Game—
Houston 24 L.A. Chargers 16

TITLES: In the NFL, Philadelphia beat Green Bay, 17-13 for the championship at Philadelphia, Dec. 26. In the AFL, Houston beat Los Angeles, 24-16 at Houston, Jan. 1, 1961.

NFL LEADERS: Individual leaders for the season: Scoring—Paul Hornung (Green Bay), 176, a new record; Rushing—Jim Brown (Cleveland), 1,257 yds.; Passing—Milt Plum (Cleveland); Pass Receiving—Raymond Berry (Baltimore), 74; Field Goals—Tom Davis (San Francisco), 19; Punting—Gerry Norton (St. Louis), 45.6 yds.; Interceptions—Gerry Norton (St. Louis), Dave Baker (San Francisco), 10 (tie).

AFL LEADERS: Scoring—Eugene Mingo (Denver), 123; Rushing—Abner Haynes (Dallas)—875 yards; Passing—Jack Kemp (Los Angeles); Pass Receiving—Lionel Taylor (Denver), 92; Field Goals—Eugene Mingo (Denver), 18; Punting—Paul Maguire (Los Angeles), 40.5 yds.; Interceptions—Austin Gonsoulin (Denver), 11.

FIRST DRAFT: NFL—Billy Cannon (LSU)—Back—by Los Angeles (signed with Houston (AFL). AFL—Gerhard Schwedes (Syracuse)—Back—by Boston.

NFL COACHES: Dallas Cowboys played first season in the league as part of the Western Conference with Tom Landry as head coach. Bob Waterfield replaced Sid Gillman as head coach of Los Angeles. In the AFL the first coaches were Lou Saban (Boston); "Buster" Ramsey (Buffalo); Hank Stram (Dallas); Frank Filchock (Denver); Lou Rymkus (Houston); Sid Gillman (Los Angeles); Sam Baugh (New York); Eddie Erdelatz (Oakland).

NOTES: Alvin "Pete" Rozelle elected NFL commissioner.

Chicago Cardinals transferred to St. Louis.

Paul Hornung set scoring record, 176 in 14 games, breaking Don Hutson's 138 in 11 games (1942).

Jim Brown, Cleveland, rushed 1,257 yards.

Jim Taylor, Green Bay, rushed 1,101 yards.

John David Crow, St. Louis, rushed 1,011 yards.

Eddie LeBaron, Dallas, passed 2 inches

to Dick Bielski (TD) against Washington (record), Oct. 9.

The American Football League, the fourth with this name since 1926, started play with eight teams in Boston, Buffalo, Dallas, Denver, Houston, Los Angeles, New York and Oakland.

Ben Agajanian, kicker, and Hardy Brown, linebacker, became the only two men to play in the NFL, the AFL and the AAFC.

DEATHS: Ralph Anderson, L.A. Chargers end, of diabetes attack, Nov. 26.

Howard Glenn, N.Y. Titans back, of broken neck after game at Houston, Oct. 9.

Rudolph Hagberg, Buffalo, Brooklyn center (1929-30), Nov. 25.

Andrew R. Turnbull, first president Green Bay Packers, Oct. 17.

Jerry Mansfield, Rock Island back (1921), Oct. 27.

Lew Reeve, Chi-Tiger, Columbus tackle (1920), May 14.

NFL TITLE GAME

Philadelphia received the kickoff and lost the ball on the first play when Van Brocklin's pass to Barnes in the flat was intercepted by Quinlan on the Eagle 14-yard line. The Packers moved to the six and lost the ball on downs. On the Eagles' third play Dean fumbled and the ball was recovered by Green Bay's Bill Forester on the 22. Philadelphia held on the 13 after six plays and Hornung kicked a field goal from the 20 to put Green Bay ahead 3–0.

Early in the second period Hornung kicked another 3-pointer from the 23 and the Packers led 6–0. Later in the period Philadelphia started from their own 43 following a punt. Van Brocklin passed 22 yards to McDonald and then 35 yards to the same receiver for a touchdown. Walston converted and the Eagles led 7–6. Later in the second period Walston kicked a 15-yard field goal to increase the lead to 10–6. As the half ended Hornung missed a kick from the Eagle 13.

There was no scoring in the third period, but the Packers had a long drive going as the last chapter opened. McGee finally took Starr's seven-yard pass for a

touchdown, and Hornung's conversion put Green Bay ahead, 13–10.

This lead lasted only for one series of downs by the Eagles. Ted Dean, rookie fullback, took Hornung's kickoff on the three and flew to Green Bay's 39 before he was smashed out of bounds. Dean and Barnes pounded to the Green Bay five-yard line and then Van Brocklin sent Dean around left end for the touchdown. Walston's conversion produced the final score 17–13. As the game ended Starr was passing desperately against the clock and Taylor was stopped on the Philadelphia 10 by Bednarik.

Philadelphia Eagles	0	10	0	7–17
Green Bay Packers	3	3	0	7–13

Touchdowns: McDonald, Dean (Philadelphia); McGee (Green Bay).

Conversions: Walston 2 (Philadelphia); Hornung (Green Bay).

Field Goals: Hornung 2 (Green Bay); Walston (Philadelphia).

Attendance: 67,325.
Players' Share: Philadelphia $5,116.55; Green Bay $3,105.14.

1960 AFL TITLE GAME

Ben Agajanian kicked 38 and 22 yard field goals to give the Los Angeles Chargers a 6-0 lead in the first quarter of the first AFL championship game. He added another from 27 yards in the second period, but the Houston Oilers took the halftime lead when Dave Smith scored on George Blanda's 17-yard pass and Blanda kicked the conversion and an 18-yard field goal, to make it 10-9.

Bill Groman scored for Houston on a 7-yard pass from Blanda, who also converted in the third quarter. Paul Lowe scored for Los Angeles with a 2-yard smash and Agajanian added the extra point.

In the final period, Bill Cannon scored on an 88-yard pass from Blanda who kicked the conversion to make the final score 24-16 and give Houston the first AFL title.

Houston	0	10	7	7	24
Los Angeles	6	3	7	0	16

Touchdowns—Smith, Groman, Lowe, Cannon.

Field Goals—Agajanian 3, Blanda.
PAT's—Agajanian, Blanda 3.
    Attendance: 32,183.
    Players' Share: Houston $1,025.73; Los
Angeles $718.61.

1960 BALTIMORE COLTS
COACH - "Webb" Ewbank
4th 6-6-0

Ameche, Alan - B	Parker, Jim - T
Berry, Raymond - E	Pellington, Bill - LB
Boyd, Bob - B	Plunkett, Sherm - T
Braase, Ordell - E	Preas, George - T
Brown, Ray - B	Pricer, Bill - B
Colvin, James - T	Pyle, Palmer - G
Davis, Milton - B	Richardson, Gerry - E
DeCarlo, Art - B	Sample, John - B
Donovan, Art - T	Sandusky, Alex - G
Hawkins, Alex - B	Shields, Lebron - T
Joyce, Don - E	Shinnick, Don - LB
Kovac, Ed - B	Simpson, Jackie - B
Lipscomb, "Daddy" - T	Smith, Roger - E & LB
Marchetti, Gino - E	Sommer, Mike - B
Matuszak, Marv - LB	Spinney, Art - G
Moore, Lenny - B	Szymanski, Dick - LB & C
Mutscheller, Jim - E	Taseff, Carl - B
Myhra, Steve - G	Unitas, John - Q
Nelson, Andy - B	Welch, Jim - B
Nutter, "Buzz" - C	

1960 CHICAGO BEARS
COACH - George Halas
5th 5-6-1

Adams, John - B	Jones, Stan - G
Atkins, Doug - E	Karras, Ted - G
Aveni, John - E	Kilcullen, Bob - T
Barnes, Erich - B	Kirk, Ken - LB & C
Bishop, Bill - T	Konovsky, Bob - G
Bivins, Charley - B	LeClerc, Roger - LB
Bratkowski, "Zeke" - Q	Lee, Herman - T
Brown, Ed - Q	Leggett, Earl - T
Caroline, J. C. - B	Manning, Pete - E
Casares, Ric - B	Mellekas, John - C
Coia, Angie - E	Morris, Johnny - B
Davis, Roger - G	Morris, Larry - LB
Dewveall, Bill - E	Petitbon, Rich - B
Dooley, Jim - E	Rowland, Justin - E
Douglas, Merrill - B	Shaw, Glen - B
Fanning, Stan - T	Sumner, Charley - B
Farrington, "Bo" - E	Wetoska, Bob - T
Fortunato, Joe - LB	Williams, Fred - T
Galimore, Willie - B	Youmans, Maury - T
George, Bill - LB	Zucco, Vic - B
Hill, Harlon - E	

1960 CLEVELAND BROWNS
COACH - Paul Brown
2nd 8-3-1

Baker, "Sam" - K	Houston, Jim - LB
Brown, Jim - B	Kreitling, Rich - E
Caleb, Jamie - B	Lloyd, Dave - LB & C
Clarke, Leon - E	McCormack, Mike - T
Costello, Vince - LB	Marshall, Jim - E
Dawson, Len - Q	Michaels, Walt - LB
Denton, Bob - T	Mitchell, Bob - B
Fichtner, Ross - B	Morrow, John - C
Fiss, Galen - LB	Mostardi, Dick - B
Fleming, Don - B	Murphy, Fred - E
Franklin, Bob - B	Nagler, Gern - E
Gain, Bob - T	Parrish, Bernie - B
Gautt, Prentice - B	Peters, Floyd - T
Hickerson, Gene - G	Plum, Milt - Q

1960 DALLAS COWBOYS
COACH - Tom Landry
7th 0-11-1

Babb, Gene - B	Guy, Mel - G
Bercich, Bob - B	Hansen, Wayne - LB
Bielski, Dick - E	Healy, Don - T
Bishop, Don - B	Heinrich, Don - Q
Borden, Nate - E	Herchmann, Bill - T
Braatz, Tom - LB	Houser, John - T & C
Bradfute, By - T	Howton, Bill - E
Butler, Bill - B	Hussmann, Ed - T
Clarke, Frank - E	Klein, Dick - T
Cone, Fred - B	Kowalczyk, Walt - B
Connelly, Mike - C	LeBaron, Ed - Q
Cronin, Gene - E	Lewis, Woodley - E
Dickson, Paul - T	McIlhenny, Don - B
Doelling, Fred - B	Mathews, Ray - E
Doran, Jim - E	Meredith, Don - Q
Dowdle, Mike - LB	Mooty, Jim - B
Dugan, Fred - E	Patera, John - LB
Dupre, Louis - B	Putnam, Duane - G
Falls, Mike - G	Sherer, Dave - E
Franckhauser, Tom - B	Tubbs, Gerry - LB
Fry, Bob - T	Wisener, Gary - E
Gonzaga, John - E	

1960 DETROIT LIONS
COACH - George Wilson
2nd 7-5-0

Alderman, Grady - G	Maher, Bruce - B
Barr, Terry - B	Mains, Gil - T
Brettschneider, Carl - LB	Martin, Jim - LB & K
Brown, Roger - T	Messner, Max - LB
Cassady, Howard - B	Middleton, Dave - E
Cogdill, Gail - E	Morrall, Earl - Q
Davis, Glenn - E	Ninowski, Jim - Q
Gibbons, Jim - E	Pietrosante, Nick - B
Glass, Bill - E	Rabb, Warren - Q
Gordy, John - G	Schmidt, Joe - LB
Grottkau, Bob - G	Scholtz, Bob - C
Junker, Steve - E	Sewell, Harley - G
Karras, Alex - T	Spencer, Ollie - T
Lane, Dick - B	Steffen, Jim - B
Lary, Yale - B	Walker, Wayne - LB
LeBeau, Dick - B	Weatherall, Jim - T
Lewis, Dan - B	Webb, Ken - B
Lowe, Gary - B	Whitsell, Dave - B
McClung, Willie - T	Williams, Sam - E
McCord, Darris - E	

1960 GREEN BAY PACKERS
COACH - Vince Lombardi
1st 8-4-0
(Lost title to Philadelphia, 17-13)

Beck, Ken - T & E	Iman, Ken - C
Bettis, Tom - LB	Jordan, Henry - T
Carpenter, Lew - B	Knafelc, Gary - E
Currie, Dan - LB	Kramer, Gerry - G
Cvercko, Andy - G	Kramer, Ron - E
Davis, Willie - E	McGee, Max - E
Dowler, Boyd - E	McHan, Lamar - Q
Forester, "Bill" - LB	Masters, Norm - T
Gregg, Forrest - T	Meilinger, Steve - E
Gremminger, Hank - B	Miller, John - T
Hackbart, Dale - B	Moore, Tom - B
Hanner, "Dave" - T	Nitschke, Ray - LB
Hickman, Larry - B	Pesonen, Dick - B
Hornung, Paul - B	Quinlan, Bill - E

Prestel, Jim - T
Renfro, Ray - B
Schafrath, Dick - T
Selawski, Gene - T
Shofner, Jim - B

Smith, Jim Ray - G
Stephens, Larry - T
Wiggin, Paul - E
Williams, A. D. - E
Wooten, John - G

Ringo, Jim - C
Skoronski, Bob - T
Starr, Bart - Q
Symank, John - B
Taylor, Jim - B
Temp, Jim - E

Thurston, Fred - G
Tunnell, Em - B
Whittenton, "Jess" - B
Winslow, Paul - B
Wood, Willie - B

Owens, Don - T
Peaks, Clarence - B
Pellegrini, Bob - LB
Reichow, Gerry - Q & E
Retzlaff, "Pete" - E
Richardson, Jess - T
Robb, Joe - E
Sapp, Theron - B

Smith, Jess - T
Van Brocklin, Norm - Q
Walston, Bob - E
Weber, Chuck - LB
Wilcox, John - T & E
Wilson, Jerry - E
Wittenborn, John - G

1960 LOS ANGELES RAMS
COACH - Bob Waterfield
6th 4-7-1

Arnett, Jon - B
Baker, John - T
Bass, Dick - B
Boeke, Jim - T
Bradshaw, Charley - T
Brito, Gene - E
Britt, Charley - B
Dale, Carroll - E
Ellersick, Don - B
Guzik, John - B
Hord, Roy - G
Humphrey, "Buddy" - Q
Hunter, Art - C
Janerette, Charley - G
Jobko, Bill - LB & C
Karilivacz, Carl - B
Kenerson, John - T
Lansford, "Buck" - G
Long, Bob - LB
Lovetere, John - T

Lundy, Lamar - E
Marconi, Joe - B
Matson, Ollie - B
Meador, Ed - B
Michaels, Lou - E
Morris, John - B
Pardee, John - LB
Phillips, Jim - E
Richter, Les - LB
Ryan, Frank - Q
Sherman, Will - B
Shofner, Del - E
Stalcup, Jerry - G
Strugar, George - T
Thomas, Clendon - B
Valdez, Vernon - B
Villanueva, Dan - K
Wade, Bill - Q
Wilson, Tom - B

1960 NEW YORK GIANTS
COACH - Jim Lee Howell
3rd 6-4-2

Boll, Don - T
Brown, Rosie - T
Chandler, Don - K
Conerly, Charley - Q
Cordileone, Lou - G
Crawford, Bill - G
Crow, Lindon - B
Dess, Darrell - G
Gifford, Frank - B
Grier, Rosey - T
Grosscup, Lee - Q
Huff, "Sam" - LB
Jacobs, Proverb - T
Katcavage, Jim - E
Kimber, Bill - E
King, Phil - B
Leo, Jim - LB
Livingston, Cliff - LB
Lynch, Dick - B
Mazurek, Ed - T

Morrison, Joe - B
Nolan, Dick - B
Patton, Jim - B
Riley, Leon - B
Robustelli, Andy - E
Rote, Kyle - E
Schmidt, Bob - T
Schnelker, Bob - E
Scott, Tom - LB
Shaw, George - Q
Simms, Bob - E
Stits, Bill - B
Stroud, Jack - G
Summerall, "Pat" - E
Sutton, Ed - B
Svare, Harland - LB
Triplett, Mel - B
Webster, Alex - B
Wietecha, Ray - C
Youso, Frank - T

1960 PHILADELPHIA EAGLES
COACH - "Buck" Shaw
1st 10-2-0
(Best Green Bay for title, 17-13)

Barnes, Billy - B
Baughan, Max - LB
Bednarik, "Chuck" - LB & C
Brookshier, Tom - B
Brown, Tim - B
Burroughs, Don - B
Campbell, Marion - T
Campbell, Stan - G
Carr, Jim - B
Dean, Ted - B
Freeman, Bob - B
Gossage, "Gene" - T & E

Gunnels, "Riley" - T
Huth, Gerry - G
Jackson, Bob - B
Johnson, Gene - B
Jurgensen, "Sonny" - Q
Keys, Howie - T & C
Khayat, Ed - T
Lapham, Bill - C
Lucas, Dick - E
McCusker, Jim - T
McDonald, Tom - B
Nocera, John - LB

1960 PITTSBURGH STEELERS
COACH - "Buddy" Parker
5th 5-6-1

Barnett, Tom - B
Beams, Byron - T
Beatty, Ed - C
Brewster, "Pete" - E
Bukich, Rudy - Q
Campbell, "Soup" - LB
Carpenter, Pres - E
Derby, Dean - B
Dial, "Buddy" - E
Green, Bobby Joe - K
Hayes, Dick - LB
Henry, Mike - LB
James, Dan - C
Johnson, John Henry - B
Johnston, Rex - B
Kapele, John - T
Krupa, Joe - T
Krutko, Larry - B
Layne, Bobby - Q
Lewis, Joe - T
Longenecker, Ken - T

McClairen, Jack - E
Moegle, Dick - B
Morris, John - B
Nisby, John - G
Orr, Jim - E
Rechichar, Bert - B
Reger, John - LB
Renfro, Will - T
Sandusky, Mike - G
Scales, Charley - B
Scudero, Joe - B
Smith, Billy Ray - E
Stautner, Ernie - E
Stehouwer, Ron - G
Sutherin, Don - B
Tarasovic, George - E
Tracy, Tom - B
Varrichione, Frank - T
Williamson, Fred - B
Wren, "Junior" - B

1960 ST. LOUIS CARDINALS
COACH - "Pop" Ivy
4th 6-5-1

Bates, Ted - LB
Childress, Joe - B
Conrad, Bobby Joe - B
Cook, Ed - T
Crow, John David - B
Culpepper, Ed - T
Day, Tom - E
Driskill, Joe - B
Ellzey, Charles - LB
Fritsch, Ernie - C
Fuller, Frank - T
Gillis, Don - C
Glick, Fred - B
Gray, Ken - G
Hammack, Mal - B
Hill, Jim - B
Hill, King - Q
Izo, George - Q
Koman, Bill - LB
McGee, Mike - G

McInnis, Hugh - E
Meinert, Dale - LB
Memmelaar, Dale - T & G
Mestnik, Frank - B
Norton, Gerry - B
Owens, Don - T
Owens, Luke - E
Panfil, Ken - T
Perry, Gerry - E
Rabold, Mike - G
Randle, "Sonny" - E
Redmond, Tom - T
Richards, Perry - E
Roach, John - Q
Stacy, Bill - B
Sugar, Leo - E
Towns, Bob - B
Tracey, John - LB
West, Willie - B
Wilson, Larry - B

1960 SAN FRANCISCO 49ERS
COACH - "Red" Hickey
2nd 7-5-0

Baker, Dave - B
Bosley, Bruce - G
Brodie, John - Q
Clark, Monte - T
Colchico, Dan - E
Connor, Clyde - E
Connolly, Ted - G
Davis, Tom - K
Dove, Ed - B
Harrison, Bob - LB
Hazeltine, Matt - LB

Henke, Ed - E
Kelley, Gorden - LB
Krueger, Charley - E
Lyles, Lenny - B
McElhenny, Hugh - B
Mackey, Dee - E
Magac, Mike - G
Mertens, Jerry - B
Morze, Frank - C
Nomellini, Leo - T
Norton, Ray - B

Osborne, "Clancy" - LB
Owens, R. C. - E
Perry, Joe - B
Ridlon, Jim - B
Rohde, Len - E
Roberts, Cornelius - B
Rubke, Karl - LB & C
St. Clair, Bob - T
Schmidt, Henry - T

Smith, J. D. - B
Stickles, Monty - E
Thomas, John - T
Tittle, Y. A. - Q
Waters, Bob - Q
Wilson, Jerry - LB
Wilson, Bill - E
Wittenborn, John - G
Woodson, Abe - B

Ford, Fred - B
Fowler, Willmer - B
Grabosky, Gene - T
Green, John - Q
Harper, Darrell - B
Hergert, Joe - LB
Hoisington, Al - E
Johnson, Jack - B
Kinard, Bill - B
Kulbacki, Joe - B
Laraway, Jack - LB
Lewis, Hal - B
Lucas, Richie - Q
McCabe, Dick - B
McGrew, Dan - C
McMurtry, Chuck - T
Matsos, Archie - LB
Meyer, Ed - T

Moore, Leroy - E
Muelhaupt, Ed - G
O'Connell, Tom - Q
Olson, Hal - T
Palumbo, Sam - G
Remmert, Denny - LB
Rutkowski, Charley - E
Rychlec, Tom - E
Schaffer, Joe - LB
Scott, John - T
Sedlock, Bob - T
Smith, Carl - B
Sorey, Jim - T
Torczon, Laverne - E
Wagstaff, Jim - B
Wegert, Ted - B
Yoho, Mack - E

1960 WASHINGTON REDSKINS
COACH - Mike Nixon
6th 1-9-2

Anderson, "Bill" - E
Bosseler, Don - B
Breedlove, Rod - LB
Brewer, Homer - B
Crotty, Jim - B
Day, "Eagle" - Q
Felton, Ralph - LB
Glick, Gary - B
Gob, Art - B
Guglielmi, Ralph - Q
Haley, Dick - B
Heenan, Pat - E
Horner, Sam - B
James, Dick - B
Khayat, Bob - K
Krouse, Ray - T
Lasse, Dick - LB
Lawrence, Don - T
Lemek, Ray - T

O'Brien, Francis - T
Olszewski, John - B
Osborne, Tom - E
Paluck, John - E
Podoley, Jim - B
Promuto, Vince - G
Reynolds, Mack - Q
Roehnelt, Bill - LB
Schrader, Jim - C
Scotti, Ben - B
Stallings, Don - E
Stephens, "Red" - G
Stynchula, Andy - E
Toneff, Bob - T
Vereb, Ed - B
Walton, Joe - E
Whitlow, Bob - C
Wilkins, Roy - G
Wulff, Jim - B

1960 BOSTON PATRIOTS (AFL)
COACH - Lou Saban
4th 5-9-0

Addison, Tom - LB
Atchason, Jack - E
Beach, Walt - B
Bennett, Phil - LB
Biscaha, Joe - E
Brown, Bill - LB
Bruney, Fred - B
Burton, Ron - B
Cappelletti, Gino - G
Christy, Dick - B
Cohen, Abe - G
Colclough, Jim - E
Crawford, Jim - B
Cross, Bob - T
Crouthamel, "Jake" - B
Crow, Al - T
Cudzik, Walt - C
Danenhauer, Bill - E
Davis, Jack - G
Dee, Bob - E
DeLucca, Gerry - T
Dimitroff, Tom - Q
Discenzo, Tony - T
Garron, Larry - B
Green, Jerry - B
Greene, Tom - Q
Hauser, Art - T
Hunt, Jim - E

Jacobs, Harry - LB
Jagielski, Harry - T
Johnson, "Joe" - B
Larson, Bill - B
Lee, Bob - Q
Leo, Charley - G
Livingston, Walt - B
Lofton, Oscar - E
Long, Mike - E
McComb, Don - E
McGee, George - T
Miller, Al - B
O'Hanley, Ross - B
Richardson, Al - E
Rudolph, John - LB
Sardisco, Tony - LB
Schwedes, Gerhard - B
Shonta, Chuck - B
Smith, Hal - T
Soltis, Bob - B
Songin, "Butch" - Q
Stephens, Tom - B
Striegel, Bill - LB
Washington, Clyde - B
Wells, Billy - B
White, Harve - Q
Yates, Bob - T

1960 BUFFALO BILLS (AFL)
COACH - "Buster" Ramsey
3rd 5-8-1

Atkins, Bill - B
Barrett, Bob - E
Blazer, Phil - G
Brodhead, Bob - Q
Brubaker, Dick - E
Buzynski, Bernie - LB

Carlton, Wray - B
Chamberlain, Dan - E
Chelf, Don - G
Crockett, Monte - E
Discenzo, Tony - T
Dubenion, Elbert - B

1960 DENVER BRONCOS (AFL)
COACH - Frank Filchock
4th 4-9-1

Adamson, Ken - G
Allen, Don - B
Alliston, Vaughan - LB
Bell, Henry - B
Bernardi, Frank - B
Brodnax, John - B
Brown, Hardy - LB
Carmichael, Al - B
Carothers, Don - E
Carpenter, Ken - E
Danenhauer, El - T
Danenhauer, Bill - E
Davis, Jack - G
Day, Al - LB
Doyle, Dick - B
Dublinski, Tom - Q
Epperson, John - E
Gavin, Chuck - B
Gonsoulin, "Goose" - B
Greer, Jim - E
Hatley, John - T
Herring, George - Q
Holtz, Gordie - T

Hudson, Bob - LB
Jessup, Bill - E
King, Don - T
Kuchta, Frank - C
Larpenter, Carl - G
McFadin, "Bud" - T
McNamara, Bob - B
Mangum, "Pete" - LB
Mingo, Gene - B
Nichols, "Mike" - C
Pyeatt, John - B
Rolle, Dave - B
Romine, Al - B
Smith, Hal - T
Smith, Willie - T
Stransky, Bob - B
Strickland, Dave - G
Taylor, Lionel - E
Tripucka, Frank - Q
Wegert, Ted - B
Yelverton, Bill - E
Young, Joe - E

1960 HOUSTON OILERS (AFL)
COACH - Lou Rymkus
1st 10-4-0
(Best Los Angeles for title, 24-16)

Allen, Dalva - E
Atchason, Jack - E
Banfield, "Tony" - B
Belotti, George - C
Blanda, George - Q
Brown, Don - B
Cannon, Billy - B
Carson, John - E
Cline, Doug - LB
Davidson, Pete - T
Dukes, Mike - LB
Floyd, Don - E
Gordon, Bob - B
Greaves, Gary - T
Groman, Bill - E
Hall, Ken - B
Helluin, "Jerry" - T
Hennigan, Charley - E
Jamison, Al - T
Johnston, Mark - B
Kendall, Charley - B

Lanphear, Dan - E
Lee, Jackie - Q
McDaniel, "Wahoo" - G
Michael, Dick - T
Milstead, Charley - Q
Morris, Dennit - LB
Norton, Jim - B
Perlo, Phil - LB
Pitts, Hugh - LB
Shirkey, George - T
Simerson, John - C
Smith, Dave - B
Spence, Julie - B
Talamini, Bob - G
Tolar, Charley - B
Trask, Orville - T
Wallner, Fred - G
Wharton, Hogan - G
White, John - E
White, "Bob" - B
Witcher, Tom - E

1960 DALLAS TEXANS (AFL)
COACH - "Hank" Stram
2nd 8-6-0

Barton, Jim - C	Harris, Jim - B
Bernet, Ed - E	Haynes, Abner - B
Bookman, John - B	Headrick, Sherrill - LB
Boydston, Max - E	Hudson, Bob - LB
Branch, Mel - E	Jackson, Charley - B
Bryant, Bob - E	Johnson, "Curley" - B
Burford, Chris - E	Krisher, Bill - G
Collins, Ray - T	Miller, Paul - E
Corey, Walt - LB	Napier, "Buffalo" - T
Cornelison, Jerry - T	Nunnery, Bob - T
Daniels, Clem - B	Reynolds, Al - G
Davidson, "Cotton" - Q	Robinson, John - B
Diamond, Charley - T	Rochester, Paul - T
Dickinson, "Bo" - B	Spikes, Jack - B
Dimmick, Tom - C	Stone, Jack - T
Enis, Hunter - Q	Stover, "Smokey" - LB
Flynn, Don - B	Swink, Jim - B
Fournet, Sid - G	Terrell, Marv - G
Frey, Dick - E	Webster, Dave - B
Granderson, Rufe - T	Wood, Duane - B
Greene, Ted - LB	Zaruba, Carroll - B

1960 NEW YORK TITANS (AFL)
COACH - Sam Baugh
2nd 7-7-0

Baker, Larry - T	Julian, Fred - B
Barnes, Ernie - T	Katcik, Joe - T
Bell, Ed - B	Klotz, John - T
Bohling, Dewey - B	McMillan, John - G
Burton, Leon - B	Marques, Bob - LB
Callahan, Dan - G	Martin, Blanche - B
Campbell, Ken - E	Mathis, Bill - B
Cockrell, Gene - T	Maynard, Don - B
Cooke, Ed - E	Mischak, Bob - G
Cooper, Thurlow - E	Mumley, Nick - T
D'Agostino, Frank - G	Pagliei, Joe - LB
Dombroski, Leon - LB	Powell, Art - E
Donnahoo, Roger - B	Reifsnyder, Bob - E
Dorow, Al - Q	Ross, Dave - E
Dupre, Charley - B	Ryan, Joe - E
Ellis, Roger - LB	Saidock, Tom - T
Felt, Dick - B	Sapienza, Americo - B
Glenn, Howard - G	Schwedes, Gerhard - B
Grantham, Larry - LB	Scrabis, Bob - Q
Guesman, Dick - T	Shockley, Bill - B
Hart, "Pete" - B	Tharp, Tom - Q
Herndon, Don - B	Wegert, Ted - B
Hudock, Mike - C	Whitley, Hal - LB
Jamieson, Dick - Q	Youngelman, Sid - T

1960 OAKLAND RAIDERS
COACH - Eddie Erdalatz
3rd 6-8-0

Armstrong, Ramon - G	Hoisington, Al - E
Asad, Doug - E	Joyner, L. C. - B
Barbee, Joe - T	Keyes, Bob - B
Barnes, Larry - E	Larscheid, Jack - B
Bravo, Alex - B	Larson, Paul - Q
Cannavino, Joe - B	Locklin, Bill - LB
Cavalli, Carmen - E	Lott, Bill - B
Churchwell, Don - T	Louderback, Tom - LB
Crow, Wayne - B	McFarland, Nyle - B
Deskins, Don - G	Macon, Eddie - B
Dittrich, John - G	Manoukian, Don - G
Dougherty, Bob - LB	Morris, Riley - LB
Fields, George - E	Oglesby, Paul - T
Flores, Tom - Q	Otto, Jim - C
Goldstein, Al - E	Parilli, "Babe" - Q
Hardy, Charley - E	Powell, Charley - E
Harris, John - B	Prebola, Gene - E
Hawkins, Wayne - G	Reynolds, Billy - B

Sabal, Ron - G	Teresa, Tony - B
Smith, Jim - B	Truax, Dalton - T
Striegel, Bill - T	Warzeka, Ron - T

1960 LOS ANGELES CHARGERS (AFL)
COACH - Sid Gillman
1st 10-4-0
(Lost title to Houston, 24-16)

Agajanian, Ben - K	Kocourek, Dave - E
Anderson, Ralph - E	Kompara, John - T
Bansavage, Al - LB	Laraba, Bob - B
Barry, Al - G	Loudd, Rommie - LB
Bobo, Hubert - LB	Lowe, Paul - B
Botchan, Ron - LB	McNeil, Charley - B
Brueckman, Charley - LB	Maguire, Paul - LB
Chorovich, Dick - T	Martin, Blanche - B
Clarke, Howie - E	Mix, Ron - T
Clatterbuck, Bob - Q	Nery, Ron - E
Cole, Fred - G	Nix, Doyle - B
DeLuca, Sam - T	Norris, Trusse - E
Donnell, Ben - E	Norton, Don - E
Ferguson, Howie - B	Peters, Volney - T
Ferrante, Orlando - G	Rogers, Don - C
Finneran, Gary - T	Schleicher, Maury - E
Flowers, Charley - B	Sears, Jim - Q
Ford, Fred - B	Thomas, Jesse - B
Garner, Bob - B	Wallace, Henry - B
Gob, Art - E	Waller, Ron - B
Harris, Dick - B	Womble, Royce - B
Karas, Emil - LB	Wright, Ernie - T
Kemp, Jack - Q	Zeman, Bob - B
Kempinski, Chuck - G	

1961

NATIONAL FOOTBALL LEAGUE
EASTERN CONFERENCE

New York	10	3	1	.769
Philadelphia	10	4	0	.714
Cleveland	8	5	1	.615
St. Louis	7	7	0	.500
Pittsburgh	6	8	0	.429
Dallas	4	9	1	.308
Washington	1	12	1	.077

WESTERN CONFERENCE

Green Bay	11	3	0	.786
Detroit	8	5	1	.715
Chicago	8	6	0	.571
Baltimore	8	6	0	.571
San Francisco	7	6	1	.538
Los Angeles	4	10	0	.286
Minnesota	3	11	0	.214

AMERICAN FOOTBALL LEAGUE
EASTERN DIVISION

	W	L	T	Pct.
Houston	10	3	1	.769
Boston	9	4	1	.692
New York	7	7	0	.500
Buffalo	6	8	0	.429

WESTERN DIVISION

San Diego	12	2	0	.857
Dallas	6	8	0	.429

The wives benefit too. Coach Vince Lombardi of the 1961 Green Bay champions is surrounded by happy Packers who all got mink stoles as part of the celebration. (Life Photo.)

Denver	3	11	0	.214
Oakland	2	12	0	.143

Championship Game
Houston, 10; San Diego, 3

TITLE: In the NFL Green Bay beat New York, 37-0, for the championship at Green Bay, Dec. 31. Detroit beat Cleveland, 17-16 in the inaugural second place playoff at Miami. In the AFL, Houston beat San Diego, 10-3, at San Diego, Dec. 24.

NFL LEADERS: Individual leaders for the season: Scoring—Paul Hornung (Green Bay), 146; Rushing—Jim Brown (Cleveland), 1,408 yds.; Passing—Milt Plum (Cleveland); Pass Receiving—Jim Phillips (Los Angeles), 78; Field Goals—Steve Myhra (Baltimore), 21; Punting—Yale Lary (Detroit), 48.4 yds.; Interceptions—Dick Lynch (New York), 9.

AFL LEADERS: Scoring—Gino Cappaletti (Boston), 147; Rushing—Billy Cannon (Houston); 948 yds.; Passing—George Blanda (Houston); Pass Receiving—Lionel Taylor (Denver), 100; Field Goals—Gino Cappelletti (Boston), 17; Punting—Bill Atkins (Buffalo), 44.5 yds.; Interceptions—Bill Atkins (Buffalo), 10.

FIRST DRAFT: NFL Tommy Mason (Tulane) — Back — by Minnesota. AFL — Bob Gaiters (New Mexico State)—Back—by Denver; signed by New York (NFL).

COACHES: Minnesota Vikings added to league with Norman Van Brocklin as head coach. Alex Sherman replaced Jim Lee Howell as coach of New York; Nick Skorich replaced "Buck" Shaw with champion Philadelphia; Bill McPeak replaced Mike Nixon at Washington. In the AFL, Mike Holovak replaced Lou Saban at Boston after five games; Wally Lemm replaced Lou Rymkus at Houston after five games; Marty Feldman replaced Eddie Erdelatz at Oakland after two games.

NOTES: Arthur B. Modell and associates bought Cleveland franchise.

First million dollar gate in history when Green Bay played New York for title.

Minnesota Vikings added to Western Conference and Dallas switched to Eastern.

The Los Angeles Chargers of the AFL moved to San Diego.

Emlen Tunnell, New York Giants, Green Bay back (1948-61) retired after 14 years holding record most interceptions, 79.

Charley Conerly, N. Y. Giants qback, retired after 14 years.

Paul Hornung scored 33 points one game against Baltimore (3 TD's, 6 PAT's, 3 field goals), Oct. 8.

Roger LeClerc, Chi-Bears, kicked five field goals (12, 30, 12, 32, 15 yards) against Detroit, tying record Dec. 3.

Charlie Kreuger San Francisco tackle, tied safety record, 3.

Jim Brown, Cleveland, rushed 237 yards (34 attempts) against Philadelphia, tying his own record and got 1,408 yards for the season.

Jim Taylor, Green Bay, rushed 1,307 yards.

"Sonny" Jurgensen, Philadelphia qback, gained 3,723 yards passing, record, and threw 32 TD's to tie record of John Unitas (1959).

Bill Wade, Chi-Bear, passed to "Bo" Farrington for 98 yards (TD) against Detroit, Oct. 8.

Erich Barnes, New York, ran 102 yards with interception (TD) tied record, against Dallas, Oct. 22.

Tim Brown, Philadelphia, returned kickoff 105 yards (TD) against Cleveland, Sept. 17. It was opening kickoff of first game.

Jon Arnett, Los Angeles, returned kickoff 105 yards (TD) against Detroit, Oct. 29.

NFL TITLE GAME

A frozen field and frigid winds did not hinder the powerhouse Green Bay team which smashed the New York Giants. The game developed into a one-sided, no-contest affair shortly after the second period began.

Late in the first period the Giants lost a touchdown when Rote dropped Tittle's pass on the Green Bay 10. Rote was in the clear

Hornung punched over the goal on the first play of the second period from the New York 6 and kicked the extra point. Within five minutes, Nitschke intercepted Tittle's pass on the Giant 33. Starr passed 13 yards to Dowler for a touchdown and Hornung scored the conversion.

Gremminger intercepted a Tittle pass on New York's 36 and Starr whipped another touchdown pass to R. Kramer from the 13. Hornung cashed his third PAT.

Conerly replaced Tittle and drove the Giants to the Green Bay 6 but Gaiters failed to get the ball to Rote, again in the open on a fourth down pass, and Green Bay rolled again. Starr, racing the clock, took the Packers to the New York 10 and Hornung tapped over a 17-yard field goal to end the half at 24–0.

In the third quarter, Morrison fumbled Dowler's punt on the New York 21 and Hornung booted another field goal from the 22. Later in the period, Staar pitched a 13-yard touchdown to Kramer who got behind Morrison.

The final three points, Hornung's third field goal, from 19 yards out, came after Whittenton intercepted a Tittle pass on the Green Bay 38.

Green Bay Packers	0	24	10	3—37
New York Giants	0	0	0	0— 0

Touchdowns: Hornung, Dowler, R. Kramer 2.

Field goals: Hornung 3.
Conversions: Hornung 4.

Attendance: 39,029.
Players' Share: Green Bay $5,195.44; New York $3,339.99.

1961 AFL TITLE GAME

A 46-yard field goal by George Blanda gave the Houston Oilers a 3-0 halftime lead over San Diego in this low scoring game. The kick came midway in the second period.

Billy Cannon scored a touchdown on a 35-yard pass from Blanda in the third quarter and Blanda added the conversion.

San Diego avoided a shutout when George Blair kicked a field goal late in the final period to make it 10-3.

Houston	0	3	7	0	10
San Diego	0	0	0	3	3

Touchdowns—Cannon.
Field Goals—Blanda, Blair.
PAT's—Blanda.
Attendance: 29,566.
Players' Share: Houston $1,792.79; San Diego $1,111.81.

1961 BALTIMORE COLTS
COACH - "Weeb" Ewbank
4th 8-6-0

Berry, Raymond - E
Boyd, Bob - B
Braase, Ordell - E
Burkett, Walter - LB
Colvin, James - T
Diehl, John - T
Donovan, Art - T
Feagin, Wiley - G
Gilburg, Tom - T
Glick, Gary - B
Gregory, Ken - E
Harrison, Bob - B
Hawkins, Alex - B
Hill, Jerry - B
Lewis, Joe - T
Linne, Aubrey - E
Lyles, Lenny - B
McHan, Lamar - Q
Mackey, Dee - E
Marchetti, Gino - E
Matte, Tom - B
Matuszak, Marv - LB
Moore, Lenny - B
Mutscheller, Jim - E
Myhra, Steve - G
Nelson, Andy - B
Orr, Jim - E
Parker, Jim - T
Pellington, Bill - LB
Perry, Joe - B
Preas, George - T
Pyle, Palmer - G
Sandusky, Alex - G
Shinnick, Don - LB
Smith, Billy Ray - T
Smolinski, Mark - B
Sommer, Mike - B
Szymanski, Dick - C
Taseff, Carl - B
Unitas, John - Q
Welch, Jim - B

1961 CHICAGO BEARS
COACH - George Halas
3rd 8-6-0

Adams, John - B
Anderson, Art - T
Atkins, Doug - E
Bivins, Charley - B
Brown, Ed - Q
Brown, Bill - B
Caroline, J. C. - B
Casares, Ric - B
Coia, Angie - E
Davis, Roger - G
Ditka, Mike - E
Dooley, Jim - E
Fanning, Stan - T
Farrington, "Bo" - E
Fortunato, Joe - LB
Galimore, Willie - B
George, Bill - LB
Hill, Harlon - E
Jackson, Bob - B
Jones, Stan - G
Karras, Ted - G
Kilcullen, Bob - E
Kirk, Ken - LB & C
LeClerc, Roger - LB
Lee, Herman - T
Manning, Pete - B
Mellekas, John - T
Morris, Johnny - B
Morris, Larry - LB
Mullins, Don - B
Norman, Dick - Q
Petitbon, Rich - B
Pyle, Mike - C
Smith, Jim - B
Taylor, "Rosie" - B
Wade, Bill - Q
Wetoska, Bob - T
Whitsell, Dave - B
Williams, Fred - T
Youmans, Maury - E

1961 CLEVELAND BROWNS
COACH - Paul Brown
3rd 8-5-1

Baker, "Sam" - K
Brewer, John - E
Brown, Jim - B
Clarke, Leon - E
Costello, Vince - LB
Crespino, Bob - B
Dawson, Len - Q
Ferguson, Charles - E
Fichtner, Ross - B
Fiss, Galen - LB
Fleming, Don - B
Franklin, Bob - B
Gain, Bob - T
Groza, Lou - T
Houston, Jim - LB
Kreitling, Rich - E
Linden, Errol - T
Lloyd, Dave - LB & C
McCormack, Mike - T
Michaels, Walt - LB
Mitchell, Bob - B
Morrow, John - C
Nagler, Gern - E
Nutting, Ed - T
Parrish, Bernie - B
Peters, Floyd - T & E
Plum, Milt - Q
Powell, Preston - B
Putnam, Duane - G
Renfro, Ray - B
Schafrath, Dick - T
Shofner, Jim - B
Smith, Jim Ray - G
Stephens, Larry - T
Watkins, Tom - B
Wiggin, Paul - E
Wooten, John - G

1961 DALLAS COWBOYS
COACH - Tom Landry
6th 4-9-1

Babb, Gene - LB & B
Bercich, Bob - B
Bielski, Dick - E
Bishop, Don - B
Borden, Nate - E
Bradfute, By - T
Clarke, Frank - E
Connelly, Mike - C
Cvercko, Andy - G
Davis, Arnold - LB
Doran, Jim - E
Douglas, Merrill - B
Dowdle, Mike - LB
Dupre, Louis - B
Falls, Mike - G
Franckhauser, Tom - B
Frost, Ken - T
Fry, Bob - T
Granger, Charley - T
Green, Allen - K
Gregory, Glynn - E

Grottkau, Bob - G
Harris, Jim - B
Healy, Don - T
Herchmann, Bill - T
Houser, John - G
Howley, Chuck - LB
Howton, Bill - E
Humphrey, "Buddy" - Q
LeBaron, Ed - Q
Lilly, Bob - E
Livingston, Warren - B
Lockett, J. W. - B
McCreary, Bob - T
Marsh, Amos - B
Meredith, Don - Q
Moegle, Dick - B
Murchison, Ola Lee - E
Patera, John - LB
Perkins, Don - B
Tubbs, Gerry - LB

1961 LOS ANGELES RAMS
COACH - Bob Waterfield
6th 4-10-0

Allen, Duane - E
Arnett, Jon - B
Atkins, Pervis - B
Baker, John - E
Bass, Dick - B
Boeke, Jim - T
Bratkowski, "Zeke" - Q
Britt, Charley - B
Cowan, Charley - G
Coyle, Ross - B
Crow, Lindon - B
Dale, Carroll - E
Hall, Alvin - B
Hector, Willie - T
Henry, Urban - T
Hord, Roy - G
Hunter, Art - C
Jobko, Bill - LB & C
Jones, Dave - E
Kimbrough, Elbert - B

Long, Bob - LB
Lovetere, John - T
Lundy, Lamar - E
McKeever, Marlin - LB
Marconi, Joe - B
Matson, Ollie - B
Meador, Ed - B
Pardee, John - LB
Phillips, Jim - E
Richter, Les - LB
Ryan, Frank - Q
Scibelli, Joe - G
Strugar, George - T
Tarbox, Bruce - G
Thomas, Clendon - B
Varrichione, Frank - T
Villanueva, Dan - K
Williams, Frank - B
Wilson, Tom - B

1961 DETROIT LIONS
COACH - George Wilson
2nd 8-5-1

Barr, Terry - B
Brettschneider, Carl - LB
Brown, Roger - T
Cassady, Howard - B
Cogdill, Gail - E
Davis, Glenn - E
Gibbons, Jim - E
Glass, Bill - E
Gonzaga, John - T
Gordy, John - G
Karras, Alex - T
Lane, Dick - B
LaRose, Dan - T
Lary, Yale - B
LeBeau, Dick - B
Lewis, Dan - B
Lowe, Gary - B
McClung, Willie - T
McCord, Darris - E
Maher, Bruce - B

Mains, Gil - T
Martin, Jim - LB
Messner, Max - LB
Mills, Dick - G
Morrall, Earl - Q
Ninowski, Jim - Q
Olszewski, John - B
Pietrosante, Nick - B
Schmidt, Joe - LB
Scholtz, Bob - C
Sewell, Harley - G
Spencer, Ollie - G
Steffen, Jim - B
Studstill, Pat - B
Walker, Wayne - LB
Ward, Paul - T
Webb, Ken - B
Whitlow, Bob - C & G
Williams, Sam - E

1961 MINNESOTA VIKINGS
COACH - Norm Van Brocklin
7th 3-11-0

Alderman, Grady - T
Bishop, Bill - T
Caleb, Jamie - B
Culpepper, Ed - T
Denton, Bob - T
Derby, Dean - B
Dickson, Paul - T
Gault, Bill - B
Grecni, Dick - LB
Haley, Dick - B
Hawkins, "Rip" - LB
Hayes, Ray - B
Huth, Gerry - G
Johnson, Gene - B
Joyce, Don - T
Lapham, Bill - C
Leo, Jim - E
McElhenny, Hugh - B
Marshall, Jim - E
Mason, Tom - B
Mayberry, Doug - B
Mercer, Mike - K

Middleton, Dave - E
Morris, John - B
Mostardi, Rich - B
Murphy, Fred - E
Osborne, "Clancy" - LB
Pesonen, Dick - B
Peterson, Ken - G
Prestel, Jim - T
Rabold, Mike - G
Reichow, Gerry - E
Rowland, Justin - B
Rubke, Karl - LB
Schnelker, Bob - E
Shaw, George - Q
Sherman, Will - B
Shields, Lebron - E
Smith, Gordon - E
Sumner, Charley - B
Tarkenton, Fran - Q
Triplett, Mel - B
Williams, A. D. - E
Youso, Frank - T

1961 GREEN BAY PACKERS
COACH - Vince Lombardi
1st 11-3-0
(Beat New York for title, 37-0)

Adderley, Herb - B
Agajanian, Ben - K
Bettis, Tom - LB
Carpenter, Lew - B
Currie, Dan - LB
Davidson, Ben - E
Davis, Willie - E
Dowler, Boyd - E
Folkins, Lee - E
Forester, "Bill" - LB
Gregg, Forrest - T
Gremminger, Hank - B
Hanner, "Dave" - T
Hornung, Paul - B
Iman, Ken - C
Jordan, Henry - T
Knafelc, Gary - E
Kostelnik, Ron - T
Kramer, Gerry - G

Kramer, Ron - E
McGee, Max - E
Masters, Norm - T
Moore, Tom - B
Nitschke, Ray - LB
Pitts, Elijah - B
Quinlan, Bill - E
Ringo, Jim - C
Roach, John - Q
Skoronski, Bob - T
Starr, Bart - Q
Symank, John - B
Taylor, Jim - B
Thurston, Fred - G
Toburen, Nelson - LB
Tunnell, Em - B
Whittenton, "Jess" - B
Wood, Willie - B

1961 NEW YORK GIANTS
COACH - "Allie" Sherman
1st 10-3-1
(Lost title to Green Bay, 37-0)

Barnes, Erich - B
Brown, Rosie - T
Chandler, Don - K
Conerly, Charley - Q
Dess, Darrell - G
Gaiters, Bob - B
Grier, Rosey - T
Grosscup, Lee - Q
Hall, Peter - E
Hayes, Larry - LB
Huff, "Sam" - LB
Janarette, Chuck - T
Johnson, Gene - B
Katcavage, Jim - E
King, Phil - B
Larson, Greg - T
Livingston, Cliff - LB
Lynch, Dick - B
Modzelewski, Dick - T

Morrison, Joe - B
Nolan, Dick - B
Patton, Jim - B
Robustelli, Andy - E
Rote, Kyle - E
Scott, Tom - LB
Shofner, Del - E
Simms, Bob - LB
Smith, "Zeke" - G
Stits, Bill - B
Stroud, Jack - G
Summerall, "Pat" - E
Tittle, Y. A. - Q
Walker, "Mickey" - G
Walton, Joe - E
Webb, Allen - B
Webster, Alex - B
Wells, Joel - B
Wietecha, Ray - C

1961 PHILADELPHIA EAGLES
COACH - Nick Skorich
2nd 10-4-0

Amerson, Glen - B	Lucas, Dick - E
Barnes, Billy - B	McCusker, Jim - T
Baughan, Max - LB	McDonald, Tom - B
Bednarik,"Chuck"-LB&C	Nocera, John - LB
Brookshier, Tom - B	Oakes, Don - T
Brown, Tim - B	Peaks, Clarence - B
Burroughs, Don - B	Pellegrini, Bob - LB
Campbell, Marion - T	Renfro, Will - E
Campbell, Stan - G	Retzlaff, "Pete" - E
Carr, Jim - B	Richardson, Jess - T
Cross, Irv - B	Sapp, Theron - B
Dean, Ted - B	Smith, Jess - T
Freeman, Bob - B	Sugar, Leo - E
Gossage, "Gene" - E	Taseff, Carl - B
Gunnels, "Riley" - T	Tracey, John - E
Hill, King - Q	Walston, Bob - E
Jurgensen, "Sonny" - Q	Weber, Chuck - LB
Keys, Howie - C & G	Wittenborn, John - G
Khayat, Ed - T	

1961 SAN FRANCISCO 49ERS
COACH - "Red" Hickey
5th 7-6-1

Baker, Dave - B	Lopaskey, Bill - G
Bosley, Bruce - G	McIlhenny, Don - B
Brodie, John - Q	Magac, Mike - G
Casey, Bernie - B	Mertens, Jerry - B
Clark, Monte - T	Messer, Dale - B
Colchico, Dan - E	Morze, Frank - C
Connor, Clyde - E	Nomellini, Leo - T
Connolly, Ted - G	Norton, Ray - B
Cooper, Bill - B	Owens, R. C. - E
Cordileone, Lou - G	Ridlon, Jim - B
Davis, Tom - K	Rohde, Len - T
Dove, Ed - B	Roberts, Cornelius - B
Harrison, Bob - LB	St. Clair, Bob - T
Hazeltine, Matt - LB	Smith, J. D. - B
Johnson, Jim - B	Stickles, Monty - E
Kammerer, Carl - LB	Thomas, Aaron - E
Kelley, Gorden - LB	Thomas, John - T
Kilmer, Bill - Q	Waters, Bob - Q
Krueger, Charley - E	Woodson, Abe - B
Lakes, Roland - E	

1961 PITTSBURGH STEELERS
COACH - "Buddy" Parker
5th 6-8-0

Beatty, Ed - C	Layne, Bobby - Q
Bradshaw, Charley - T	Lipscomb, "Daddy" - T
Bukich, Rudy - Q	Mack, "Red" - B
Burnett, Len - B	Meilinger, Steve - E
Butler, Bill - B	Michaels, Lou - E
Carpenter, Pres - E	Nisby, John - G
Clement, Henry -E	Nofsinger, Terry - Q
Coronado, Bob - E	Nutter, "Buzz" - C
Daniel, Bill - B	Pottios, Myron - LB
Demko, George - T	Reger, John - LB
Derby, Dean - B	Sample, John - B
Dial, "Buddy" - E	Sandusky, Mike - G
Green, Bobby Joe - K	Scales, Charley - B
Haley, Dick - B	Schmitz, Bob - LB
Henry, Mike - LB	Schnelker, Bob - E
Hoak, Dick - B	Scott, Wilbert - LB
James, Dan - T	Simpson, Jackie - B
Johnson, John Henry - B	Stanton, John - B
Kapele, John - E	Stautner, Ernie - E
Keys, Brady - B	Stehouwer, Ron - G
Klein, Dick - T	Tarasovic, George - LB
Krupa, Joe - T	Tracy, Tom - B

1961 WASHINGTON REDSKINS
COACH - Bill McPeak
7th 1-12-1

Anderson, "Bill" - E	Lawrence, Don - T
Aveni, John - K	Lemek, Ray - T
Beatty, Ed - C	Luce, Lew - B
Bosseler, Don - B	Mattson, Riley - T
Breedlove, Rod - LB	O'Brien, Francis - T
Cronin, Gene - E	Osborne, Tom - E
Crotty, Jim - B	Paluck, John - E
Cunningham, Jim - B	Promuto, Vince - G
Darre, Bernie - G	Rutgens, Joe - T
Dugan, Fred - E	Schick, Doyle - LB
Glick, Gary - B	Schrader, Jim - C
Hackbart, Dale - B	Scotti, Ben - B
Hageman, Fred - C	Snead, Norm - Q
Horner, Sam - B	Sommer, Mike - B
Izo, George - Q	Steffen, Jim - B
James, Dick - B	Stynchula, Andy - E
Junker, Steve - E	Toneff, Bob - T
Kerr, Jim - B	Whitlow, Bob - C
Krakoski, Joe - B	Wilkins, Roy - LB
Lasse, Dick - LB	Wulff, Jim - B

1961 ST. LOUIS CARDINALS
COACH - "Pop" Ivy, Chuck
Drulis, Ray Prochaska and
Ray Willsey

Anderson, Taz - E	Koman, Bill - LB
Bates, Ted - LB	Lage, Dick - E
Conrad, Bobby Joe - B	Lee, Monte - LB
Cook, Ed - T	McDole, Roland - T
Crow, John David - B	McGee, Mike - G
DeMarco, Bob - G	McInnis, Hugh - E
Driskill, Joe - B	McMillan, Ernie - T
Ellzey, Charley - LB	Meilinger, Steve - E
Etcheverry, Sam - Q	Meinert, Dale - LB
Fischer, Pat - B	Memmelaar, Dale - T & G
Fuller, Frank - T	Mestnik, Frank - B
Gautt, Prentice - B	Norton, Gerry - B
Gillis, Don - C	Owens, Don - T
Granger, Charley - T	Owens, Luke - T
Gray, Ken - G	Panfil, Ken - T
Griffin, Bob - C	Perry, Gerry - E
Guglielmi, Ralph - Q	Randle, "Sonny" - E
Hall, Ken - B	Redmond, Tom - G
Hammack, Mal - B	Robb, Joe - E
Henke, Ed - E	Stacy, Bill - B
Hill, Jim - B	West, Willie - B
Johnson, Charley - Q	Wilson, Larry - B

1961 BOSTON PATRIOTS (AFL)
COACH - Lou Saban, Mike Holovak
2nd 9-4-1

Addison, Tom - LB	Klein, Dick - T
Antwine, Houston - T	Leo, Charley - G
Beach, Walt - B	Lindquist, Paul - T
Bruney, Fred - B	Long, Charley - T
Burton, Ron - B	Lott, Bill - B
Cappelletti, Gino - E	Loudd, Rommie - LB
Colclough, Jim - E	Moore, Leroy - E
Crawford, Jim - B	O'Hanley, Ross - B
Cudzik, Walt - C	Parilli, "Babe" - Q
Dee, Bob - E	Perkins, Will - G
DeLucca, Gerry - T	Ratkowski, Ray - B
Eisenhauer, Larry - E	Robotti, Frank - LB
Garron, Larry - B	Romine, Al - B
Graham, Milt - T	Sardisco, Tony - G
Hall, Ron - B	Schwedes, Gerhard - B
Hunt, Jim - T	Shonta, Chuck - B
Jacobs, Harry - LB	Simerson, John - T
Jagielski, Harry - T	Soltis, Bob - B
Johnson, "Joe" - E	Songin, "Butch" - Q
Kimber, Bill - E	Stephens, Tom - E

Towns, Bob - B
Washington, Clyde - B
Webb, Don - B

West, Mel - B
Yates, Bob - C
Yewcic, Tom - Q

1961 BUFFALO BILLS (AFL)
COACH - "Buster" Ramsey
4th 6-8-0

Atkins, Bill - B
Baker, Art - B
Barber, Stu - LB
Bass, Glenn - E
Bemiller, Al - C
Bohling, Dewey - B
Brown, Fred - B
Carlton, Wray - B
Chamberlain, Dan - E
Chelf, Don - T
Crockett, Monte - E
Crotty, Jim - B
Day, Tom - E
Dittrich, John - G
Dubenion, Elbert - B
Felton, Ralph - LB
Fowler, Willmer - B
Green, John - Q
Hergert, Joe - LB
Johnson, Jack - B
Letner, Bob - LB
Lucas, Richie - Q

McCabe, Dick - B
McDonald, Don - B
McMurtry, Chuck - T
Majors, Bill - B
Matsos, Archie - LB
Muelhaupt, Ed - G
O'Connell, Tom - Q
Olson, Hal - T
Rabb, Warren - Q
Reynolds, Mack - Q
Rice, Kent - T
Richards, Perry - E
Rychlec, Tom - E
Scott, John - T
Shaw, Bill - G
Shockley, Bill - B
Sorey, Jim - T
Torczon, Laverne - E
Valdez, Vernon - B
Wagstaff, Jim - B
Wolff, Wayne - G
Yoho, Mack - E

1961 DENVER BRONCOS (AFL)
COACH - Frank Filchock
3rd 3-11-0

Adamson, Ken - G
Allen, Elihu - B
Ames, Dave - B
Barton, Jim - C
Bukaty, Fred - B
Carmichael, Al - B
Cash, John - E
Danenhauer, El - T
Eifrid, Jim - LB
Evans, Dale - B
Frazier, Adolphus - B
Gavin, Chuck - E
Gonsoulin, "Goose" - B
Griffin, Bob - G
Guy, "Buzz" - G
Hauser, Art - T
Herring, George - Q
Hill, Jack - B
Holz, Gordie - T
Hudson, Bob - LB
Konovsky, Bob - E
Lamberti, Pat - LB
Larpenter, Carl - G

McDaniel, "Wahoo" - LB
McFadin, "Bud" - T
McMillin, Jim - B
McNamara, Bob - B
Mattox, John - T
Mingo, Gene - B
Nichols, "Mike" - C
Nugent, Phil - B
Prebola, Gene - E
Pyeatt, John - B
Reed, Leo - T
Roehnelt, Bill - LB
Sears, Jim - B
Simpson, Jack - LB
Smith, Dan - B
Stalcup, Jerry - LB
Stinnette, Jim - B
Stone, Don - B
Sturm, Jerry - T
Taylor, Lionel - E
Traynham, Jerry - B
Tripucka, Frank - Q
Young, Joe - E

1961 HOUSTON OILERS (AFL)
COACHES - Lou Rymkus & Wally
Lemm
1st 10-3-1
(Beat San Diego for title, 10-3)

Allen, Dalva - E
Banfield, "Tony" - B
Beams, Byron - T
Belotti, George - C
Blanda, George - Q
Botchan, Ron - LB
Cannon, Billy - B
Cline, Doug - LB
Dewveall, Will - E
Dukes, Mike - LB

Floyd, Don - E
Frey, Dick - E
Glick, Fred - B
Groman, Bill - E
Guy, "Buzz" - G
Guzik, John - LB
Hall, Ken - B
Hennigan, Charley - E
Husmann, Ed - T
Jamison, Al - T

Johnston, Mark - B
Jones, Gene - B
Kelly, Bob - T
King, Claude - B
Laraway, Jack - LB
Lee, Jackie - Q
McLeod, Bob - E
Michael, Dick - T
Milstead, Charley - Q
Morris, Dennit - LB
Norton, Jim - B
Perkins, Will - G

Reed, Leo - G
Schmidt, Bob - C
Shirkey, George - T
Smith, Dave - B
Spence, Julie - B
Talamini, Bob - G
Tolar, Charles - B
Trask, Orville - T
Wharton, Hogan - G
White, John - E
Wisener, Gary - B

1961 DALLAS TEXANS (AFL)
COACH - "Hank" Stram
2nd 6-8-0

Agajanian, Ben - K
Barnes, Charley - E
Boydston, Max - E
Branch, Mel - E
Burford, Chris - E
Cadwell, John - G
Collins, Ray - T
Cornelison, Jerry - T
Davidson, "Cotton" - Q
Diamond, Charley - T
Dickinson, "Bo" - B
Duncan, Randy - Q
Flynn, Don - B
Fournet, Sid - G
Gilliam, Jon - C
Grayson, Dave - B
Greene, Ted - LB
Greene, Tom - Q
Haynes, Abner - B
Headrick, Sherrill - LB
Holub, Emil - LB

Hynes, Paul - B
Jackson, Frank - B
Jeralds, Luther - E
Johnson, Jack - B
Kelley, Ed - B
Krisher, Bill - G
Mays, Gerry - T
Miller, Paul - E
Napier, "Buffalo" - T
Nix, Doyle - B
Pricer, Billy - B
Reynolds, Al - G
Robinson, John - B
Rochester, Paul - T
Romeo, Tony - E
Spikes, Jack - B
Stover, "Smokey" - LB
Terrell, Marv - G
Tyrer, Jim - T
Webster, Dave - B
Wood, Duane - B

1961 NEW YORK TITANS (AFL)
COACH - Sam Baugh
3rd 7-7-0

Allard, Don - Q
Ames, Dave - B
Apple, Jim - B
Bobo, Hubert - LB
Bohling, Dewey - B
Bookman, John - B
Brooks, Bob - B
Budrewicz, Tom - G
Christy, Dick - B
Cockrell, Gene - T
Cooke, Ed - E
Cooper, Thurlow - E
Dorow, Al - Q
Ellis, Roger - LB
Felt, Dick - B
Fields, Jerry - LB
Flynn, Don - B
Furey, Jim - LB
Grantham, Larry - LB
Gray, Mose - T
Guesman, Dick - T
Hudock, Mike - C
Hynes, Paul - B
Jacobs, Proverb - T

Jamieson, Dick - Q
Johnson, "Curley" - B
Klotz, John - T
Lamberti, Pat - LB
McMullan, John - G
Mathis, Bill - B
Maynard, Don - B
Mischak, Bob - G
Mumley, Nick - E
O'Neil, Bob - G
Paulson, Dainard - B
Powell, Art - E
Rechichar, Bert - LB
Reifsnyder, Bob - E
Renn, Bob - B
Riley, Leon - B
Saidock, Tom - T
Scrabis, Bob - Q
Shockley, Bill - B
Walsh, Ed - T
West, Mel - B
Wren, "Junior" - B
Youngelman, Sid - T

1961 OAKLAND RAIDERS (AFL)
COACH - Marty Feldman
4th 2-12-0

Asad, Doug - E
Bansavage, Al - LB

Bravo, Alex - B
Brewington, John - T

Burch, Gerry - E
Cannavino, Joe - B
Coolbaugh, Bob - E
Crow, Wayne - B
Daniels, Clem - B
Dougherty, Bob - LB
Fields, George - T
Finneran, Gary - T
Fleming, George - B
Flores, Tom - Q
Fuller, Charley - B
Garner, Bob - B
Hardy, Charley - E
Harris, John - B
Hawkins, Wayne - G
Jagielski, Harry - T
Jelacic, Jon - E
Jones, Jim - B

Kowalczyk, Walt - B
Larscheid, Jack - B
Louderback, Tom - LB
Miller, Alan - B
Morris, Riley - LB
Otto, Jim - C
Papac, Nick - Q
Peters, Volney - T
Powell, Charley - E
Roberts, Cliff - T
Roedel, Herb - G
Sabal, Ron - T
Smith, Hal - T
Smith, Bill - G
Stone, Jack - T
Voight, Bob - T
Williamson, Fred - B

AMERICAN FOOTBALL LEAGUE

EASTERN DIVISION

	W	L	T	Pct.
Houston	11	3	0	.786
Boston	9	4	1	.692
Buffalo	7	6	1	.538
New York	5	9	0	.357

WESTERN DIVISION

Dallas	11	3	0	.786
Denver	7	7	0	.500
San Diego	4	10	0	.286
Oakland	1	13	0	.071

1961 SAN DIEGO CHARGERS (AFL)
COACH - Sid Gillman
1st 12-2-0
(Lost title to Houston, 10-3)

Allen, Chuck - LB
Barnes, Ernie - G
Belotti, George - C
Blair, George - B
Clark, Howie - E
DeLuca, Sam - T
Enis, Hunter - Q
Faison, Earl - E
Ferrante, Orlando - G
Flowers, Charley - B
Gibson, Claude - B
Harris, Dick - B
Hayes, Luther - E
Hudson, Bill - T
Karas, Emil - LB
Kemp, Jack - Q
Kocourek, Dave - E
Ladd, Ernie - T
Laraba, Bob - LB

Lincoln, Keith - B
Lowe, Paul - B
MacKinnon, Jacque - B
McNeil, Charley - B
Maguire, Paul - LB
Mix, Ron - T
Nery, Ron - E
Norton, Don - E
Plunkett, Sherman - T
Roberson, "Bo" - B
Rogers, Don - C
Scarpitto, Bob - B
Schleicher, Maury - LB
Schmidt, Henry - T
Selawski, Gene - T
Whitehead, "Bud" - B
Wright, Ernie - T
Zeman, Bob - B

1962

NATIONAL FOOTBALL LEAGUE

EASTERN CONFERENCE

New York	12	2	0	.857
Pittsburgh	9	5	0	.643
Cleveland	7	6	1	.538
Washington	5	7	2	.417
Dallas	5	8	1	.385
St. Louis	4	9	1	.308
Philadelphia	3	10	1	.231

WESTERN CONFERENCE

Green Bay	13	1	0	.929
Detroit	11	3	0	.786
Chicago	9	5	0	.643
Baltimore	7	7	0	.500
San Francisco	6	8	0	.429
Minnesota	2	11	1	.154
Los Angeles	1	12	1	.077

Green Bay defeated New York, 16–7

Championship Game
Dallas, 20; Houston, 17
(Won by Brooker's field goal
in second overtime period)

TITLE: In the NFL Green Bay beat New York, 16-7, at New York, Dec. 30. Detroit beat Philadelphia, 38-10 in the second place playoff at Miami. In the AFL, Dallas beat Houston, 20-17 in the second overtime period at Houston, Dec. 23.

NFL LEADERS: Individual leaders for the year: Scoring—Jim Taylor (Green Bay), 114; Rushing—Jim Taylor, 1,474 yds.; Passing—Bryan Starr (Green Bay); Pass Receiving—Bobby Mitchell (Washington), 72; Field Goals—Lou Michaels (Pittsburgh), 26 (new record); Punting—Tom Davis (San Francisco), 45.6 yds.; Interceptions—Willie Wood (Green Bay), 9.

AFL LEADERS: Scoring—Eugene Mingo (Denver), 137; Rushing—"Cookie" Gilchrist (Buffalo), 1,096 yds.; Passing—Len Dawson (Dallas); Pass Receiving—Lionel Taylor (Denver), 77; Field Goals—Eugene Mingo (Denver), 27; (AFL record); Punting—Jim Fraser (Denver), 43.6 yards; Interceptions—Leon Riley (New York), 11.

FIRST DRAFT: NFL—Ernie Davis (Syracuse)—Back—by Washington (traded, preseason to Cleveland and died of leukemia before playing league game). AFL—Roman Gabriel (N. Carolina State)—qback—by Oakland; signed by L.A. Rams (NFL).

COACHES: Harland Svare, who had replaced Bob Waterfield as coach of the Los Angeles Rams in mid-season 1961, was named head coach. Wally Lemm replaced Frank "Pop" Ivy as coach of St. Louis. In the AFL, Lou Saban replaced "Buster" Ramsey at Buffalo; Jack Faulkner replaced Frank

Filchock at Denver; Frank "Pop" Ivy replaced Wally Lemm at Houston; Clyde "Bulldog" Turner replaced Sam Baugh at New York; William "Red" Conkright replaced Marty Feldman at Oakland after five games.

NOTES: Dan Reeves bought enough additional stock to become majority owner of the Los Angeles Rams.

Mrs. Violet Bidwell Wolfner, principal owner of the St. Louis Cardinals, died, Jan. 29.

Walt Kiesling, veteran player-coach, died Mar. 3.

James P. Clark, chairman of the board of the Philadelphia Eagles, died, April 17.

Hall of Fame under construction at Canton, Ohio, Richard McCann director.

Bobby Layne, Chi-Bears, N. Y. Bulldogs, Detroit, Pittsburgh qback, retired after 15 years.

"Chuck" Bednarik, Philadelphia center-linebacker, retired after 14 years.

Fletcher "Joe" Perry, San Francisco, Baltimore fullback, retired after 14 years in NFL, two in AAFC.

Bob Walston, Philadelphia, end-kicker, retired holding alltime scoring record, 881.

Lou Michaels, Pittsburgh, kicked 26 field goals, record.

Ernie Stautner, Pittsburgh tackle, tied safety record, 3.

Roger Brown, Detroit tackle, scored two safeties during season, record.

Jim Taylor, Green Bay, rushed 1,474 yards.

John Henry Johnson, Pittsburgh, rushed 1,141 yards.

Y. A. Tittle, New York, threw seven touchdown passes to tie record and gained 505 yards passing against Washington, Oct. 28.

Y. A. Tittle, New York, threw 33 touchdown passes for season, record.

Richie Petitbon, Chi-Bears, ran 101 yards with interception (TD) against Los Angeles, Dec. 9.

Mike Gaechter, Dallas, ran 100 yards with interception (TD) against Philadelphia, Oct. 14.

Tim Brown, Philadelphia, returned missed field goal 99 yards (TD) tying record, against St. Louis, Sept. 16.

Ron Hatcher, Michigan State back, became first Negro signed by Washington, last NFL team to end color ban.

Bob Laraba, San Diego back, killed in car, Feb. 16.

Ralph Ruthstrom, Los Angeles, Washington back, killed in truck accident, March 29.

NFL TITLE GAME

This was a bonecracking game between two tremendous defensive teams. It was played on a rock-hard frozen field with wind gusting to 40 m.p.h., but the 64,892 fans stayed until the end. It was anybody's game through the first 58 minutes and 10 seconds when Jerry Kramer's third field goal wrapped it up for Green Bay.

The Packers banged out 50 yards the first time they had the ball and settled for a 26-yard field goal by Jerry Kramer.

In the second period, Phil King fumbled on the Giant 28 and Nitschke recovered. Hornung threw a 21-yard pass to Dowler and Jim Taylor smashed over for the touchdown from 7 yards. Kramer kicked the point and there was no more scoring in the first half, which ended 10–0.

The fired-up Giants stopped Green Bay's attack in the early part of the second half. With fourth down on their 15, McGee attempted a punt for the Packers. It was blocked by Erich Barnes, New York defensive back, and recovered over the goal for a touchdown by rookie Jim Collier. Chandler converted.

A few minutes later, after New York had again stopped Green Bay, Sam Horner fumbled a punt by McGee and it resulted in Kramer's second field goal, this one from the 29.

The Giants came on again and moved to the Green Bay 17 through an interference penalty called against defensive back Willie Wood of the Packers, accused of fouling Joe Walton on a pass from Tittle. Wood protested and was ejected from the game. Symank replaced him.

The eager Giants started driving for the go-ahead touchdown but were penalized repeatedly and soon faced a fourth down and 52 yards to go situation. It was their last serious threat but the game was still open until Kramer kicked his third field goal from the 30, making the score 16–7 with less than two minutes to play.

| Green Bay Packers | 3 | 7 | 3 | 3–16 |
| New York Giants | 0 | 0 | 7 | 0– 7 |

Packers—Field goal—J. Kramer, 26 yds.
Packers—Touchdown—Taylor (7-yard run) ; J. Kramer kick.
Giants — Touchdown — Collier recovered blocked punt in end zone; Chandler kick.
Packers—Field goal—J. Kramer, 29 yds.
Packers—Field goal—J. Kramer, 30 yds.

Attendance: 64,892.

Players' Share: Green Bay $5,888.57; New York $4,166.85.

1962 AFL TITLE GAME

This first overtime title game in AFL history was decided with a 25-yard field goal by Tom Brooker after 12 minutes of the second extra period, giving the title to Dallas, 20-17.

Brooker also opened the scoring in the first quarter with a 16 yard field goal. In the second period, Abner Haynes scored on a 28-yard touchdown pass from Len Dawson and a 2-yard smash. Brooker made both conversions and Dallas led, 17-0 at the half.

Houston got seven points in the third on George Blanda's 15-yard toss to Willard Dewveall and Blanda's conversion. The Oilers tied the game in the fourth quarter with a 1-yard touchdown by Charles Tolar, Blanda's extra point and a 31-yard field goal by Blanda.

The first overtime period was scoreless.

| Dallas | 3 | 14 | 0 | 0 | 0 | 3 | 20 |
| Houston | 0 | 0 | 7 | 10 | 0 | 0 | 17 |

Touchdowns—Haynes 2, Dewveall, Tolar.
Field Goals—Brooker 2, Blanda.
PAT's—Brooker 2; Blanda 2.

Attendance: 37,981.

Players' Share: Dallas $2,206.64; Houston $1,471.09.

1962 BALTIMORE COLTS
COACH - "Weeb" Ewbank
4th 7-7-0

Berry, Raymond - E	Orr, Jim - E
Bielski, Dick - E	Owens, Raleigh - E
Boyd, Bob - B	Parker, Jim - T
Braase, Ordell - E	Pellington, Bill - LB
Burkett, Walter - LB	Perry, Joe - B
Clemens, Bob - B	Preas, George - T
Colvin, James - T	Pyle, Palmer - G
Diehl, John - T	Sandusky, Alex - G
Feagin, Wiley - G	Saul, Bill - LB
Gilburg, Tom - T	Shinnick, Don - LB
Harris, Wendell - B	Smith, Billy Ray - T
Hawkins, Alex - B	Smolinski, Mark - B
Kirchiro, Bill - G	Sullivan, Dan - T
Lyles, Lenny - B	Szymanski, Dick - C
McHan, Lamar - Q	Thompson, Don - LB
Mackey, Dee - E	Turner, "Bake" - B
Marchetti, Gino - E	Unitas, John - Q
Matte, Tom - B	Welch, Jim - B
Moore, Lenny - B	Yohn, Dave - LB
Nelson, Andy - B	

1962 CHICAGO BEARS
COACH - George Halas
3rd 9-5-0

Adams, John - E	Kilcullen, Bob - T
Anderson, Art - T	LeClerc, Roger - LB
Atkins, Doug - E	Lee, Herman - T
Bivins, Charley - B	Leggett, Earl - T
Bukich, Rudy - Q	McRae, Ben - B
Bull, Ron - B	Marconi, Joe - B
Cadile, Jim - T	Martin, Bill - B
Caroline, J. C. - B	Morris, Johnny - B
Casares, Ric - B	Morris, Larry - LB
Coia, Angie - E	Mullins, Don - B
Davis, Roger - G	Neck, Tom - B
Ditka, Mike - E	O'Bradovich, Ed - E
Dooley, Jim - E	Petitbon, Rich - B
Fanning, Stan - T	Pyle, Mike - C
Farrington, "Bo" - E	Taylor, "Rosie" - B
Fortunato, Joe - LB	Wade, Bill - Q
Galimore, Willie - B	Wetoska, Bob - T
George, Bill - LB	Whitsell, Dave - B
Green, Bobby Joe - K	Williams, Fred - T
Jones, Stan - G	Youmans, Maury - E
Karras, Ted - G	

1962 CLEVELAND BROWNS
COACH - Paul Brown
3rd 7-6-1

Brewer, John - E	Lucci, Mike - LB
Brown, Jim - B	McCormack, Mike - T
Brown, John - T	Morrow, John - C
Cassady, Howard - B	Morze, Frank - C
Clarke, Leon - E	Ninowski, Jim - Q
Collins, Gary - E	Parker, Frank - T
Costello, Vince - LB	Parrish, Bernie - B
Crespino, Bob - E	Peters, Floyd - T
Fichtner, Ross - B	Renfro, Ray - B
Fiss, Galen - LB	Ryan, Frank - Q
Fleming, Don - B	Scales, Charley - B
Franklin, Bob - B	Schafrath, Dick - T
Furman, John - Q	Shofner, Jim - B
Gain, Bob - T	Shorter, Jim - B
Glass, Bill - E	Smith, Jim Ray - G
Green, Ernie - B	Tidmore, Sam - LB
Groza, Lou - K	Wiggin, Paul - E
Hickerson, Gene - G	Wilson, Tom - B
Houston, Jim - LB	Wooten, John - G
Kreitling, Rich - E	

Impossible? He did it. R. C. Owens blocks a Redskin field goal attempt by leaping higher than the 10-foot high crossbar at Baltimore Stadium in 1962. (AP Wirephoto.)

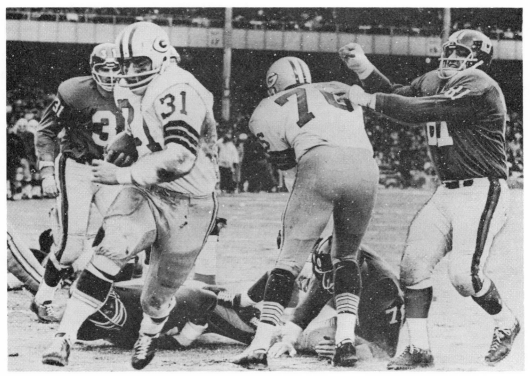

Jim Taylor slams through for a TD against the New York Giants in the title game of 1962. Green Bay won, 16-7. (UPI Photo.)

1962 DALLAS COWBOYS
COACH = Tom Landry
5th 5-8-1

Andrie, George - E
Baker, "Sam" - K
Bishop, Don - B
Brock, Clyde - T
Bullocks, Amos - B
Clark, Monte - T
Clarke, Frank - E
Connelly, Mike - C
Cvercko, Andy - G
Davis, Don - B
Dowdle, Mike - LB
Folkins, Lee - E
Frost, Ken - T
Fry, Bob - T
Gaechter, Mike - B
Green, Cornell - B
Gregory, Glynn - E
Howley, Chuck - LB
Howton, Bill - E

Hoyem, Lynn - G & C
Humphrey, "Buddy" - Q
Isbell, Joe Bob - G
LeBaron, Ed - Q
Lilly, Bob - E
Livingston, Warren - B
Lockett, J. W. - B
Long, Bob - LB
Marsh, Amos - B
Memmelaar, Dale - G
Meredith, Don - Q
Meyers, John - T
Nolan, Dick - B
Norman, Pettis - E
Norton, Gerry - B
Perkins, Don - B
Reese, Guy - T
Talbert, Don - LB
Tubbs, Gerry - LB

1962 DETROIT LIONS
COACH - George Wilson
2nd 11-3-0

Barr, Terry - B
Brettschneider, Carl - LB

Brown, Roger - T
Bundra, Mike - T

Cogdill, Gail - E
Compton, Dick - B
Gibbons, Jim - E
Gonzaga, John - G
Gordy, John - G & T
Hall, Tom - B
Hill, Harlon - E
Karras, Alex - T
Lane, Dick - B
LaRose, Dan - T
Lary, Yale - B
LeBeau, Dick - B
Lewis, Dan - B
Lloyd, Dave - LB & C
Lomakoski, John - T
Lowe, Gary - B
McCord, Darris - E
Maher, Bruce - B

Messner, Max - LB
Mills, Dick - G
Morrall, Earl - Q
Pietrosante, Nick - B
Plum, Milt - Q
Schmidt, Joe - LB
Scholtz, Bob - C & T
Sewell, Harley - G
Studstill, Pat - B
Sugar, Leo - E
Vargo, Larry - E
Walker, Wayne - LB
Ward, Paul - T
Watkins, Tom - B
Webb, Ken - B
Whitlow, Bob - C
Williams, Sam - E

1962 GREEN BAY PACKERS
COACH - Vince Lombardi
1st 13-1-0
(Best New York for title, 16-7)

Adderley, Herb - B
Barnes, Gary - E
Blaine, Ed - G
Carpenter, Lew - B
Currie, Dan - LB
Davis, Willie - E
Dowler, Boyd - E
Forester, "Bill" - LB

Gassert, Ron - T
Gregg, Forrest - T
Gremminger, Hank - B
Gros, Earl - B
Hanner, "Dave" - T
Hornung, Paul - B
Iman, Ken - C
Jordan, Henry - T & E

Knafelc, Gary - E
Kostelnik, Ron - E & T
Kramer, Gerry - G
Kramer, Ron - E
McGee, Max - E
Masters, Norm - T
Moore, Tom - B
Nitschke, Ray - LB
Pitts, Elijah - B
Quinlan, Bill - E
Ringo, Jim - C

Roach, John - Q
Skoronski, Bob - T
Starr, Bart - Q
Symank, John - B
Taylor, Jim - B
Thurston, Fred - G
Toburen, Nelson - LB
Whittenton, "Jess" - B
Williams, Howie - B
Wood, Willie - B

Janarette, Chuck - T
Katcavage, Jim - E
King, Phil - B
Larson, Greg - G
Lasse, Dick - LB
Lynch, Dick - B
Modzelewski, Dick - T
Morrison, Joe - B
Patton, Jim - B
Pesonen, Dick - B
Robustelli, Andy - E
Scott, Tom - LB

Shofner, Del - E
Simms, Bob - LB
Stroud, Jack - T & G
Thomas, Aaron - E
Tittle, Y. A. - Q
Walker, "Mickey" - LB
Walton, Joe - E
Webb, Allen - B
Webster, Alex - B
Wietecha, Ray - C
Winter, Bill - LB

1962 LOS ANGELES RAMS
COACHES - Bob Waterfield
& Harland Svare
7th 1-12-1

Allen, Duane - E
Arnett, Jon - B
Atkins, Pervis - B
Bass, Dick - B
Boeke, Jim - T
Bratkowski, "Zeke" - Q
Britt, Charley - B
Carollo, Joe - T
Cordileone, Lou - E
Cowan, Charley - G
Crow, Lindon - B
Dale, Carroll - E
Finch, Karl - E
Gabriel, Roman - Q
Hall, Alvin - B
Hayes, Larry - LB
Henry, Mike - LB
Hord, Roy - G
Hunter, Art - C
Jobko, Bill - LB & C

Jones, Dave - E
Lovetere, John - T
Lundy, Lamar - T
McKeever, Marlin - LB
Matson, Ollie - B
Meador, Ed - B
Miller, Ron - Q
Olsen, Merlin - T
Pardee, John - LB
Perkins, Art - B
Phillips, Jim - E
Putnam, Duane - G
Richter, Les - LB
Scibelli, Joe - G
Shannon, Carver - B
Shaw, Glenn - B
Smith, Bobby - B
Stephens, Larry - E
Varrichione, Frank - T
Villanueva, Dan - K

1962 PHILADELPHIA EAGLES
COACH - Nick Skorich
7th 3-10-1

Baker, John - E
Baughan, Max - LB
Beaver, Jim - T
Bednarik, "Chuck" - LB & C
Brown, Tim - B
Budd, Frank - B
Burroughs, Don - B
Butler, Bob - G
Carr, Jim - B
Case, "Pete" - G
Cassady, Howard - B
Cross, Irv - B
Dean, Ted - B
Douglas, Merrill - B
Gossage, "Gene" - E
Gregory, Ken - E
Gunnels, "Riley" - T
Harrison, Bob - LB
Hill, King - Q
Hord, Roy - G
Jonas, Don - B
Jurgensen, "Sonny" - Q

Kapele, John - T
Keys, Howie - C & G
Lewis, Joe - T
Lucas, Dick - E
McClellan, "Mike" - B
McCusker, Jim - T
McDonald, Tom - B
Nocera, John - LB
Oakes, Don - T
Peaks, Clarence - B
Retzlaff, "Pete" - E
Richards, Bob - E
Sapp, Theron - B
Schrader, Jim - C
Scotti, Ben - B
Smith, Jess - T
Smith, Ralph - E
Stafford, Dick - E
Walston, Bob - E
Wittenborn, John - G
Woulfe, Mike - LB

1962 MINNESOTA VIKINGS
COACH - Norm Van Brocklin
6th 2-11-1

Adams, Tom - E
Alderman, Grady - T
Bowie, Larry - G
Brown, Bill - B
Butler, Bill - B
Christopherson, Jim - LB
Denton, Bob - T
Derby, Dean - B
Dickson, Paul - T
Donahue, Oscar - E
Ferguson, Charley - E
Frankhauser, Tom - B
Hawkins, "Rip" - LB
Huth, Gerry - G
Lamson, Charley - B
Leo, Jim - E
Linden, Errol - T
Livingston, Cliff - LB
McCormick, John - Q

McElhenny, Hugh - B
Marshall, Jim - E
Mason, Tom - B
Mayberry, Doug - B
Mercer, Mike - K
Osborne, "Clancy" - LB
Prestel, Jim - T
Rabold, Mike - G
Reed, Bob - B
Reichow, Gerry - E
Sharockman, Ed - B
Smith, Gordon - E
Stonebreaker, Steve - E
Sumner, Charley - B
Tarkenton, Fran - Q
Tingelhoff, Mick - C
Triplett, Mel - B
Winston, Roy - LB
Youso, Frank - T

1962 PITTSBURGH STEELERS
COACH - "Buddy" Parker
2nd 9-5-0

Baker, John - E
Ballman, Gary - B
Bettis, Tom - LB
Bradshaw, Charley - T
Brown, Ed - Q
Burrell, John - E
Carpenter, Pres - E
Cordileone, Lou - T
Daniel, Bill - B
Dial, "Buddy" - E
Ferguson, Bob - B
Glass, Glenn - B
Haley, Dick - B
Hayes, Dick - LB
Hill, Harlon - E
Hoak, Dick - B
James, Dan - T
Johnson, John Henry - B
Kapele, John - E
Kenerson, John - T
Keys, Brady - B
Kirk, Ken - LB & C

Krupa, Joe - T
Layne, Bobby - Q
Lemek, Ray - G
Lipscomb, "Daddy" - T
Mack, "Red" - E
Michaels, Lou - E
Nofsinger, Terry - Q
Nutter, "Buzz" - C
Powers, John - E
Reger, John - LB
Sample, John - B
Sandusky, Mike - G
Schmitz, Bob - LB
Simms, Bob - LB
Simpson, Jackie - B
Stautner, Ernie - E
Stehouwer, Ron - G
Struger, George - T
Tarasovic, George - LB
Thomas, Clendon - B
Tracy, Tom - B
Womack, Joe - B

1962 NEW YORK GIANTS
COACH - "Allie" Sherman
1st 12-2-0
(Lost title to Green Bay, 16-7)

Barnes, Erich - B
Bohovich, Reed - T
Bolin, "Bookie" - G
Brown, Rosie - T
Byers, Ken - E
Chandler, Don - K
Collier, Jim - E
Counts, John - B

Dess, Darrell - G
Dudley, Paul - B
Gaiters, Bob - B
Gifford, Frank - B
Grier, Rosey - T
Guglielmi, Ralph - Q
Horner, Sam - B
Huff, "Sam" - LB

1962 ST. LOUIS CARDINALS
COACH - Wally Lemm
6th 4-9-1

Anderson, Taz - E
Bakken, Jim - K
Bates, Ted - LB
Beal, Norm - B

Boyette, Garland - LB
Bryant, Charles - E
Childress, Joe - B
Conrad, Bobby Joe - B

Cook, Ed - T
Crow, John David - B
DeMarco, Bob - C
Echols, Fate - T
Elwell, John - E
Etcheverry, Sam - Q
Fischer, Pat - B
Fuller, Frank - T
Gautt, Prentice - B
Goode, Irv - T
Gray, Ken - G
Hammack, Mal - B
Henke, Ed - E
Hill, Jim - B
Hultz, George - T
Jackson, Roland - B
Johnson, Charley - Q

Koman, Bill - LB
McGee, Mike - G
McInnis, Hugh - E
McMillan, Ernie - T
Meinert, Dale - LB
Owens, Don - T
Owens, Luke - E
Panfil, Ken - T
Perry, Gerry - T
Randle, "Sonny" - E
Redmond, Tom - G
Robb, Joe - E
Rushing, Marion - LB
Stacy, Bill - B
Triplett, Bill - B
Wilson, Larry - B

Felt, Dick - B
Garron, Larry - B
Graham, Milt - T
Hall, Ron - B
Hunt, Jim - E
Jacobs, Harry - LB
King, Claude - B
Klein, Dick - T
Leo, Charley - G
Long, Charley - T
Lott, Bill - B
Loudd, Rommie - LB
Moore, Leroy - E

Neighbors, Bill - G
O'Hanley, Ross - B
Parilli, "Babe" - Q
Richardson, Jess - T
Romeo, Tony - E
Rudolph, John - LB
Sardisco, Tony - G
Shonta, Chuck - B
Stephens, Tom - E
Webb, Don - B
Yates, Bob - C
Yewcic, Tom - Q

1962 SAN FRANCISCO 49ERS
COACH - "Red" Hickey
5th 6-8-0

Bosley, Bruce - G
Brodie, John - Q
Casey, Bernie - E
Colchico, Dan - E
Connor, Clyde - E
Connolly, Ted - G
Cooper, Bill - B
Davis, Tom - K
Donohue, Leon - T
Dove, Ed - B
Gaiters, Bob - B
Hazeltine, Matt - LB
Johnson, Jim - B
Kammerer, Carl - LB
Kilmer, Bill - Q
Kimbrough, Elbert - B
Krueger, Charley - T
Lakes, Roland - T
McFarland, Kay - B
Magac, Mike - G

Mellekas, John - C
Mertens, Jerry - B
Messer, Dale - B
Miller, Clark - E
Nomellini, Leo - T
Pine, Ed - LB
Ridlon, Jim - B
Roberts, Cornelius - B
Rohde, Len - E
Rubke, Karl - LB
St. Clair, Bob - T
Smith, J. D. - B
Stickles, Monty - E
Sutro, John - T
Thomas, Aaron - E
Thomas, John - LB
Vollenweider, Jim - B
Waters, Bob - Q
Winston, Lloyd - B
Woodson, Abe - B

1962 BUFFALO BILLS (AFL)
COACH - Lou Saban
3rd 7-6-1

Abruzzese, Ray - B
Baker, Art - B
Barber, Stu - T
Bass, Glenn - E
Bemiller, Al - C
Borden, Nate - E
Cannavino, Joe - B
Carlton, Wray - B
Charon, Carl - B
Crockett, Monte - E
Crotty, Jim - B
Crow, Wayne - B
Day, Tom - E
DeLucca, Gerry - T
Dorow, Al - Q
Dubenion, Elbert - B
Edgerson, Booker - B
Felton, Ralph - LB
Flint, George - T
Gilchrist, "Cookie" - B
Healey, Don - T
Henley, Carey - B
Jackunas, Frank - C
Jones, Willie - B

Kemp, Jack - Q
Louderback, Tom - LB
Matsos, Archie - LB
Matuszak, Marv - LB
Minter, Tom - B
Moore, Leroy - E
Olson, Hal - T
Rabb, Warren - Q
Rychlec, Tom - E
Saidock, Tom - T
Sestak, Tom - T
Shaw, Bill - G
Sorey, Jim - T
Stratton, Mike - LB
Taseff, Carl - B
Torczon, Laverne - E
Tracey, John - LB
Warlick, Ernie - E
West, Willie - B
Wheeler, Manch - Q
Yaccino, John - B
Yoho, Mack - E
Youngelman, Sid - T

1962 WASHINGTON REDSKINS
COACH - Bill McPeak
4th 5-7-2

Anderson, "Bill" - E
Barnes, Billy Ray - B
Bosseler, Don - B
Breedlove, Rod - LB
Crabb, Claude - B
Cronin, Gene - E
Cunningham, Jim - B
Davidson, Ben - T
Dugan, Fred - E
Elmore, Doug - B
Freeman, Bob - B
Hackbart, Dale - B
Hageman, Fred - C
Hall, Galen - Q
Hatcher, Ron - B
Izo, George - Q
Jackson, Leroy - B
James, Dick - B
Junker, Steve - E

Kelley, Gorden - LB
Kerr, Jim - B
Khayat, Ed - T
Khayat, Bob - K
Mattson, Riley - T
Miller, Allen - LB
Mitchell, Bob - B
Moore, Chuck - G
Nisby, John - G
O'Brien, Francis - T
Paluck, John - E
Pelligrini, Bob - LB
Promuto, Vince - G
Rutgens, Joe - T
Smith, Hugh - E
Snead, Norm - Q
Steffen, Jim - B
Stynchula, Andy - E
Toneff, Bob - T

1962 BOSTON PATRIOTS (AFL)
COACH - Mike Holovak
2nd 9-4-1

Addison, Tom - LB
Allard, Don - Q
Antwine, Houston - T
Bruney, Fred - B
Buoniconti, Nick - LB
Burton, Ron - B

Cappelletti, Gino - E
Colclough, Jim - E
Crawford, Jim - B
Cudzik, Walt - C
Dee, Bob - E
Eisenhauer, Larry - E

1962 DENVER BRONCOS (AFL)
COACH - Jack Faulkner

2nd 7-7-0

Adamson, Ken - G
Barton, Jim - C
Cash, John - E
Danenhauer, El - T
Denvir, John - G
Dickinson, "Bo" - B
Enis, Hunter - Q
Erlandson, Tom - LB
Fraser, Jim - LB
Frazier, Adolphus - B
Gavin, Chuck - E
Gonsoulin, "Goose" - B
Holz, Gordie - T
Jordan, Larry - E
Joyce, Don - E
Lassiter, Ike - E
McCullough, Bob - G
McDaniel, "Wahoo" - LB
McFadin, "Bud" - LB
McGeever, John - B
McMillin, Jim - B

Marshall, Charley - B
Mattox, John - T
Mingo, Gene - B
Minter, Tom - B
Olszewski, John - B
Perkins, Jim - T
Prebola, Gene - E
Roehnelt, Bill - LB
Rowland, Justin - B
Scarpitto, Bob - B
Shaw, George - Q
Stalcup, Jerry - LB
Stinnette, Jim - B
Stone, Don - B
Sturm, Jerry - T
Tarr, Gerry - B
Taylor, Lionel - E
Tripucka, Frank - Q
Wood, "Dick" - Q
Zeman, Bob - B

1962 HOUSTON OILERS (AFL)
COACH - "Pop" Ivy
1st 11-3-0
(Lost title to Dallas, 20-17, overtime)

Babb, Gene - LB	Jancik, Bob - B
Banfield, "Tony" - B	Johnston, Mark - B
Blanda, George - Q	Kelly, Bob - T
Cannon, Billy - B	Lanphear, Dan - E
Cline, Doug - LB	Lee, Jackie - Q
Culpepper, Ed - T	McDole, Roland - E
Cutsinger, Gary - E	McLeod, Bob - E
Dewveall, Will - E	Michael, Dick - T
Dukes, Mike - LB	Miller, Bill - T
Floyd, Don - E	Norton, Jim - B
Frazier, Charley - E	Onesti, Larry - LB
Frongillo, John - C & G	Schmidt, Bob - C
Glick, Fred - B	Smith, Dave - B
Goode, Tom - LB	Suci, Bob - B
Groman, Bill - E	Suggs, Walt - T
Hennigan, Charley - E	Talamini, Bob - G
Herchman, Bill - T	Tolar, Charley - B
Husmann, Ed - T	Wegener, Bill - G
Jamison, Al - T	Wharton, Hogan - G

1962 DALLAS TEXANS (AFL)
COACH - "Hank" Stram
1st 11-3-0
(Beat Houston for title, 20-17, overtime)

Arbanas, Fred - E	Jackson, Frank - B
Bishop, "Sonny" - G	Kelley, Ed - B
Branch, Mel - E	Larpenter, Carl - G
Brooker, Tom - E	McClinton, Curt - B
Burford, Chris - E	Mays, Gerry - T & E
Corey, Walt - LB	Merz, Curt - G
Cornelison, Jerry - T	Miller, Bill - E
Davidson, "Cotton" - Q	Pennington, Durwood - K
Davis, Dick - E	Ply, Bob - B
Dawson, Len - Q	Reynolds, Al - G
Diamond, Charley - T	Robinson, John - B
Gilliam, Jon - C	Rochester, Paul - T
Grayson, Dave - B	Saxton, Jim - B
Greene, Ted - LB	Spikes, Jack - B
Haynes, Abner - B	Stover, "Smokey" - LB
Headrick, Sherrill - LB	Terrell, Marv - G
Holub, Emil - LB & C	Tyrer, Jim - T
Hull, Bill - E	Wilson, Eddie - Q
Hunt, Bob - B	Wood, Duane - B

1962 NEW YORK TITANS (AFL)
COACH - "Bulldog" Turner
4th 5-9-0

Atkins, Bill - B	Klotz, John - T
Bobo, Hubert - LB	Kovac, Ed - B
Christy, Dick - B	Kroll, Alex - C & T
Cockrell, Gene - T	Look, Dean - Q
Cooke, Ed - LB	Mathis, Bill - B
Cooper, Thurlow - E	Maynard, Don - B
Ellis, Roger - LB	Mischak, Bob - G
Fields, Jerry - LB	Morelli, Frank - T
Flowers, Charley - B	Mumley, Nick - E
Fontes, Wayne - B	Paulson, Dainard - B
Fournet, Sid - G	Powell, Art - E
Fowler, Bob - B	Richards, Perry - E
Grantham, Larry - LB	Riley, Leon - B
Gray, Mose - T	Scrabis, Bob - Q
Green, John - Q	Shockley, Bill - B
Grosscup, Lee - Q	Songin, "Butch" - Q
Guesman, Dick - T	Stephens, "Hayseed" - Q
Hudock, Mike - C	Strugar, George - T
Hynes, Paul - B	Tiller, Jim - B
Jacobs, Proverb - T	Torczon, Laverne - E
Johnson, "Curley" - B	Watters, Bob - E
Kaimer, Karl - E	West, Mel - B
Kenerson, John - E	

1962 OAKLAND RAIDERS (AFL)
COACHES - Marty Feldman & "Red" Conkright
4th 1-13-0

Agajanian, Ben - K	McMurtry, Chuck - T
Allen, Dalva - E	Miller, Alan - B
Birdwell, Dan - E	Montalbo, Mel - B
Boydston, Max - E	Morris, Riley - E
Boynton, George - B	Morrow, Tom - B
Brown, Charley - T	Mostardi, Dick - B
Campbell, Stan - G	Nicklas, Pete - T
Craig, Dobie - B	Norris, Jim - T
Daniels, Clem - B	Novsek, Joe - E
Davidson, "Cotton" - Q	Otto, Jim - C
Dorsey, Dick - E	Reynolds, Mack - Q
Dougherty, Bob - LB	Rieves, Charley - LB
Enis, Hunter - Q	Rivera, "Hank" - B
Ficca, Dan - G	Roberson, "Bo" - B
Fuller, Charley - B	Shirkey, George - T
Gallegos, Chon - Q	Simpson, Jack - LB
Garner, Bob - B	Simpson, Willie - B
Hardy, Charley - E	Stone, Jack - T
Hawkins, Wayne - G	Trask, Orville - T
Heinrich, Don - Q	Valdez, Vernon - B
Jelacic, Jon - E	White, John - E
Lewis, Hal - B	Williamson, Fred - B

1962 SAN DIEGO CHARGERS (AFL)
COACH - Sid Gillman
3rd 4-10-0

Allen, Chuck - LB	Koltz, Jack - T
Alworth, Lance - B	Kocourek, Dave - E
Barnes, Ernie - G	Ladd, Ernie - T
Bethune, Bob - B	Lincoln, Keith - B
Blair, George - B	MacKinnon, Jacque - B
Braxton, Hezekiah - B	McDougall, Gerry - B
Buncom, Frank - LB	McNeil, Charley - B
Carolan, Reg - E	Maguire, Paul - LB
Coan, Bert - B	Miller, Paul - E
Faison, Earl - E	Mitinger, Bob - LB
Frazier, Wayne - C & LB	Mix, Ron - T
Gibson, Claude - B	Nery, Ron - E
Gillett, Fred - B	Norton, Don - E
Gruneisen, Sam - G	Plunkett, Sherman - T
Hadl, John - Q	Robinson, Jerry - E
Harris, Dick - B	Rogers, Don - C
Hudson, Bill - T	Schleicher, Maury - LB
Hudson, Dick - G	Schmidt, Henry - T & E
Jackson, Bob - B	Shea, Pat - G
Karas, Emil - LB	Whitehead, "Bud" - B
Keckin, Val - Q	Wood, "Dick" - Q
Kemp, Jack - Q	Wright, Ernie - T

1963

NATIONAL FOOTBALL LEAGUE
EASTERN CONFERENCE

New York	11	3	0	.786
Cleveland	10	4	0	.714
St. Louis	9	5	0	.643
Pittsburgh	7	4	3	.636
Dallas	4	10	0	.286
Washington	3	11	0	.214
Philadelphia	2	10	2	.167

WESTERN CONFERENCE

	W	L	T	Pct.
Chicago	11	1	2	.917
Green Bay	11	2	1	.846
Baltimore	8	6	0	.571
Detroit	5	8	1	.385
Minnesota	5	8	1	.385
Los Angeles	5	9	0	.357
San Francisco	2	12	0	.143

Chicago defeated New York, 14–10

AMERICAN FOOTBALL LEAGUE
EASTERN DIVISION

	W	L	T	Pct.
Boston	7	6	1	.538
Buffalo	7	6	1	.538
Houston	6	8	0	.429
New York	5	8	1	.385

Boston, 28; Buffalo, 7, in playoff

WESTERN DIVISION

	W	L	T	Pct.
San Diego	11	3	0	.786
Oakland	10	4	0	.714
Kansas City	5	7	2	.417
Denver	2	11	1	.154

Championship Game—
San Diego, 51; Boston, 10

TITLE: In the NFL, Chicago beat New York, 14-10 for the championship at Chicago, Dec. 29. Detroit beat Pittsburgh, 17-10 in the second place playoff at Miami. In the AFL, San Diego beat Boston, 51-10 at San Diego, Jan. 5, 1964.

NFL LEADERS: Individual leaders for the year: Scoring—Don Chandler (New York), 106; Rushing—Jim Brown (Cleveland), 1,863 yds. (new record); Passing—Y. A. Tittle (New York); Pass Receiving—Bobby Joe Conrad (St. Louis), 73; Field Goals—Jim Martin (Baltimore), 24; Punting—Yale Lary (Detroit), 48.9 yds.; Interceptions—Roosevelt Taylor (Chicago), Dick Lynch (New York), 9 (tie).

AFL LEADERS: Scoring—Gino Cappelletti (Boston), 113; Rushing—Clem Daniels (Oakland), 1,099 yds.; Passing—Tobin Rote (San Diego); Pass Receiving—Lionel Taylor (Denver), 79; Field Goals—Gino Cappelletti (Boston), 22; Punting—Jim Fraser (Denver), 44.4 yds.; Interceptions—Fred Glick (Houston), 12.

FIRST DRAFT: NFL—Terry Baker (Oregon State)—Qback—by Los Angeles. AFL —Kermit Alexander (UCLA)—Back—by Denver (signed with San Francisco, NFL).

COACHES: New coaches who took over before the season started were: Don Shula at Baltimore for "Weeb" Ewbank; Blanton Collier at Cleveland for Paul Brown; Jack Christiansen at San Francisco. Christiansen had finished the previous season as head coach after Howard Hickey resigned following the third league game. In the AFL, Weeb Ewbank replaced Bulldog Turner at New York; Al Davis replaced Red Conkright at Oakland.

NOTES: Alex Karras (Detroit) and Paul Hornung (Green Bay) suspended indefinitely April 17 for betting on NFL games; five other Detroit players were fined $2,000 each for betting; the Detroit management was fined $4,000 for failing to report information on gambling and permitting undesirables to mix with players on the sidelines. Detroit players were Joe Schmidt, Wayne Walker, John Gordy, Gary Lowe and Sam Williams.

Player limit raised one to 37.

Leo Nomellini, San Francisco tackle, retired after 14 years.

Ernie Stautner, Pittsburgh tackle, retired after 14 years.

Jim Brown, Cleveland, rushed 1,863 yards, breaking own record.

Jim Taylor, Green Bay, rushed 1,018 yards.

George Izo, Washington, passed 99 yards (TD) to Bobby Mitchell against Cleveland, Sept. 15.

Y. A. Tittle, New York, threw 36 touchdown passes, record.

Dallas franchise of AFL moved to Kansas City.

Ben Boynton, Rochester, Buffalo, qback (1921-24), died, Jan. 24.

Terry Dillon, Minnesota back (1962) drowned.

Clyde Ehrhardt, Washington center (1946, 48-49) died, Feb. 2.

Harold Erickson, Green Bay, Milwaukee, Minneapolis, Chi-Card back (1923-30) died, Jan. 28.

Don Fleming, Cleveland back (1960-62) electrocuted in construction accident, June 4.

Malcolm "Ike" Frankian, Boston, N. Y. Giants, L. A. Bulldogs end (1933-37) died, April 14.

Cecil Hare, Washington, N. Y. Giants back (1941-46) died, April 14.

Herb Joesting, Chi-Bear, Minneapolis, Frankford back (1929-32) died, Oct. 2.

Eugene "Big Daddy" Lipscomb, Los Angeles, Baltimore, Pittsburgh tackle (1953-62), died May 10.

Bernie Masterson, Chi-Bear qback (1934-40) died, May 16.

Century Milstead, New York Giant, Philadelphia Quaker tackle (1925-28 died, June 1.

Romanus Nadolney, Green Bay, Milwaukee guard (1922-25).

U. S. Fourth Circuit Court of Appeals turned down American Football League appeal to end 3½ years of litigation. AFL had charged NFL with monopoly and conspiracy in areas of expansion, television and player signings.

HALL OF FAME elected first group: Players—Sam Baugh, Earl "Dutch" Clark, "Red" Grange, George Halas, Mel Hein, Wilbur Henry, "Cal" Hubbard, Don Hutson, "Curly" Lambeau, John "Blood" McNally, Bronko Nagurski, Ernie Nevers, Jim Thorpe; Non-Players—DeBennville "Bert" Bell, Joe Carr, George P. Marshall.

NFL TITLE GAME

Weather frigid—less than 10 degrees. Field frozen but playable. New York scored first in the first quarter on a 14-yard pass from Y. A. Tittle to Frank Gifford and Don Chandler added the conversion. After Larry Morris intercepted Tittle's pass and ran 61 yards to the New York 5, Billy Wade banged over from the 2 and Bob Jencks converted to even the game.

In the second period, Chandler kicked a 13-yard field goal and New York led at halftime, 10-7.

Ed O'Bradovich intercepted another Tittle pass in the third period and ran it to the New York 4. Wade again smashed over, this time from the one. Jencks kicked the point and the Bears led, 14-10, which was the final score.

Tittle bombed the Chicago defenses through the final period but the Bears intercepted him five times during the game, the last, by Rich Petitbon, with 2 seconds left.

Chicago	7	0	7	0—14
New York	7	3	0	0—10

Touchdowns: Wade 2; Gifford
Field Goals: Chandler
Conversions: Jencks 2; Chandler

Attendance: 45,801.
Players' Share: Chicago $5,899.77; New York $4,218.15.

1963 AFL TITLE GAME

San Diego scored three touchdowns in the first period: Tobin Rote on a 2-yard drive, Keith Lincoln on a 67-yard run and Paul Lowe from 58 yards. George Blair added three conversion. For Boston, Larry Garron ran seven yards to score and Gino Cappelletti added the extra point.

Blair booted a 11-yard field goal in the second period and Cappelletti kicked one from the 15. Don Norton went over on a 14-yard pass from Rote and Blair added another point to give the Chargers a 31-10 halftime lead. Lance Alworth added six more points for San Diego in the third quarter on a pass from Rote and Blair again converted. In the final quarter, Keith Lincoln scored on a 25-yard pass from John Hadl and the 2-point conversion attempt failed. Hadl scored later on a 1-yard plunge and Blair converted.

San Diego	21	10	7	13	51
Boston	7	3	0	0	10

Touchdowns: Rote, Lincoln 2, Garron, Lowe, Norton, Alworth, Hadl.
Field Goals: Blair Cappelleti.
PAT's: Blair 6 Cappelletti.
Attendance: 30,127.
Players' Share: San Diego $2,498.89; Boston $1,596.52.

1963 BALTIMORE COLTS
COACH - Don Shula
3rd 8-6-0

Berry, Raymond - E
Bielski, Dick - E
Boyd, Bob - B
Braase, Ordell - E
Burkett, Walter - LB
Colvin, James - T
Craddock, Nat - B
Cuozzo, Gary - Q
Diehl, John - T
Gilburg, Tom - T
Harris, Wendell - B
Hawkins, Alex - B
Hill, Jerry - B
Lockett, J. W. - B
Logan, Jerry - B
Lyles, Lenny - B
McHan, Lamar - Q
Mackey, John - E
Maples, Jim - LB
Marchetti, Gino - E
Martin, Jim - K

Matte, Tom - B
Miller, Fred - T
Moore, Lenny - B
Nelson, Andy - B
Orr, Jim - E
Owens, Raleigh - E
Parker, Jim - G
Pellington, Bill - LB
Preas, George - T
Pyle, Palmer - G
Richardson, Willie - E
Sandusky, Alex - G
Saul, Bill - LB
Shinnick, Don - LB
Sullivan, Dan - T & G
Szymanski, Dick - C
Thompson, Don - E
Unitas, John - Q
Vogel, Bob - T
Welch, Jim - B
Wilson, George - E

1963 DALLAS COWBOYS
COACH - Tom Landry
5th 4-10-0

Andrie, George - E
Baker, "Sam" - K
Barnes, Gary - E
Bishop, Don - B
Brock, Clyde - T
Bullocks, Amos - B
Clarke, Frank - E
Connelly, Mike - C
Edwards, Dave - LB
Folkins, Lee - E
Fry, Bob - T
Gaechter, Mike - B
Gibbs, "Sonny" - Q
Green, Cornell - B
Hayes, Wendell - B
Hays, Hal - LB
Howley, Chuck - LB
Howton, Bill - E
Hoyem, Lynn - G & C
Isbell, Joe Bob - G
Jordan, Lee Roy - LB

LeBaron, Ed - Q
Lilly, Bob - E
Liscio, Tony - T
Livingston, Warren - B
Marsh, Amos - B
Memmelaar, Dale - G
Meredith, Don - Q
Meyers, John - T
Norman, Pettis - E
Nutting, John - T
Overton, Jerry - B
Perkins, Don - B
Poimbeouf, Lance - K
Reese, Guy - T
Ridlon, Jim - B
Schoenke, Ray - T
Smith, Jim Ray - G
Stephens, Larry - E
Stiger, Jim - B
Tubbs, Gerry - LB

1963 CHICAGO BEARS
COACH - George Halas
1st 11-1-2
(Beat New York for title, 14-10)

Atkins, Doug - E
Barnett, Steve - T
Bettis, Tom - LB
Bivins, Charley - B
Bukich, Rudy - Q
Bull, Ron - B
Cadile, Jim - G
Caroline, J. C. - B
Casares, Ric - B
Coia, Angie - E
Davis, Roger - G
Ditka, Mike - E
Farrington, "Bo" - E
Fortunato, Joe - LB
Galimore, Willie - B
George, Bill - LB
Glueck, Larry - B
Green, Bobby Joe - K
Jencks, Bob - E
Johnson, John - T

Jones, Stan - G
Karras, Ted - G
Kilcullen, Bob - E
LeClerc, Roger - LB
Lee, Herman - T
Leggett, Earl - T
McRae, Ben - B
Marconi, Joe - B
Martin, Bill - B
Morris, Johnny - B
Morris, Larry - LB
O'Bradovich, Ed - E
Petitbon, Rich - B
Pyle, Mike - C
Taylor, "Rosie" - B
Wade, Bill - Q
Wetoska, Bob - T
Whitsell, Dave - B
Williams, Fred - T

1963 DETROIT LIONS
COACH - George Wilson
4th 5-8-1

Barr, Terry - B
Brettschneider, Carl - LB
Brown, Roger - T
Bundra, Mike - T
Cassady, Howard - B
Clark, Ernie - LB
Cogdill, Gail - E
Compton, Dick - B
Ferguson, Larry - B
Gaubatz, Denny - LB
Gibbons, Jim - E
Gonzaga, John - G & T
Gordy, John - G
Greer, Al - E
Hall, Tom - B
Lane, Dick - B
LaRose, Dan - T & G
Lary, Yale - B
LeBeau, Dick - B
Lee, Monte - LB
Lewis, Dan - B

Lowe, Gary - B
McCord, Darris - E
Maher, Bruce - B
Matson, Ollie - B
Messner, Max - LB
Morrall, Earl - Q
Peters, Floyd - T
Pietrosante, Nick - B
Plum, Milt - Q
Reeberg, Lucian - T
Ryder, Nick - B
Sanders, Daryl - T
Schmidt, Joe - LB
Scholtz, Bob - C & T
Simon, Jim - LB & E & G
Vargo, Larry - E
Walker, Wayne - LB
Watkins, Tom - B
Whitlow, Bob - C
Williams, Sam - E

1963 CLEVELAND BROWNS
COACH - Blanton Collier
2nd 10-4-0

Beach, Walter - B
Benz, Larry - B
Brewer, John - E
Brown, Jim - B
Brown, John - T
Clark, Monte - T
Collins, Gary - E
Connolly, Ted - G
Costello, Vince - LB
Crespino, Bob - E
Cvercko, Andy - G
Fichtner, Ross - B
Fiss, Galen - LB
Franklin, Bob - B
Gain, Bob - T
Glass, Bill - E
Goosby, Tom - LB
Green, Ernie - B
Groza, Lou - K
Hickerson, Gene - G
Houston, Jim - LB
Hutchinson, Tom - E

Kanicki, Jim - T
Kreitling, Rich - E
Lucci, Mike - LB
McCusker, Jim - T
Morrow, John - C
Morze, Frank - C
Ninowski, Jim - Q
Parker, Frank - T
Parrish, Bernie - B
Renfro, Ray - B
Ryan, Frank - Q
Scales, Charley - B
Schafrath, Dick - T
Sczurek, Stan - LB
Shoals, Roger - T
Shofner, Jim - B
Shorter, Jim - B
Tidmore, Sam - LB
Webb, Ken - B
Wiggin, Paul - E
Wooten, John - G

1963 GREEN BAY PACKERS
COACH - Vince Lombardi
2nd 11-2-1

Adderley, Herb - B
Aldridge, Lionel - E
Barrett, Jan - E
Bratkowski, "Zeke" - Q
Carpenter, Lew - B
Currie, Dan - LB
Davis, Willie - E
Dowler, Boyd - B
Fleming, Marv - E
Forester, "Bill" - LB
Gregg, Forrest - T
Gremminger, Hank - B
Grimm, Dan - G
Gros, Earl - B
Hanner, "Dave" - T
Henry, Urban - E & T
Holler, Ed - LB
Iman, Ken - C
Jeter, Bob - B
Jordan, Henry - T & E

Kostelnik, Ron - E & T
Kramer, Gerry - G
Kramer, Ron - E
McGee, Max - E
Masters, Norm - T
Mestnik, Frank - B
Moore, Tom - B
Nitschke, Ray - LB
Norton, Gerry - B
Pitts, Elijah - B
Ringo, Jim - C
Roach, John - Q
Robinson, "Dave" - LB
Skoronski, Bob - T
Starr, Bart - Q
Taylor, Jim - B
Thurston, Fred - G
Whittenton, "Jess" - B
Williams, Howie - B
Wood, Willie - B

Chicago Bear QB Bill Wade (9) cocks arm amidst onrushing Giants as Bob Wetoska (63) blocks. Wade scored two TDs to lead Bears to 14-10 win over New York Giants and NFL title. (UPI Telephoto.)

1963 LOS ANGELES RAMS
COACH - Harland Svare
6th 5-9-0

Adams, John - E	Britt, Charley - B	Grier, Rosey - T	Pardee, John - LB
Allen, Duane - E	Carollo, Joe - T	Griffin, John - B	Perkins, Art - B
Arnett, Jon - B	Chuy, Don - G	Hall, Alvin - B	Phillips, Jim - E
Atkins, Pervis - B	Cowan, Charley - G	Hayes, Larry - LB & C	Scibelli, Joe - G
Baker, Terry - B	Crow, Lindon - B	Henry, Mike - LB	Sewell, Harley - G
Bass, Dick - B	Dale, Carroll - E	Hunter, Art - C	Shannon, Carver - B
Boeke, Jim - T	Fanning, Stan - E	Jones, Dave - E	Smith, Bobby - B
Bratkowski, "Zeke" - Q	Gabriel, Roman - Q	Kirk, Ken - LB & C	Swain, Bill - LB
		Livingston, Cliff - LB	Varrichione, Frank - T
		Lundy, Lamar - E	Villanueva, Dan - K
		McKeever, Marlin - E	Whitmyer, Nat - B
		Meador, Ed - B	Wilson, Ben - B
		Olsen, Merlin - T	

1963 MINNESOTA VIKINGS
COACH - Norm Van Brocklin
4th 5-8-1

Alderman, Grady - T
Battle, Jim - G
Bowie, Larry - G
Boylan, Jim - E
Brown, Bill - B
Butler, Bill - B
Calland, Lee - B
Campbell, John - LB
Clarke, Leon - E
Cox, Fred - K
Denton, Bob - T
Dickson, Paul - T
Dillon, Terry - B
Ferguson, Bob - B
Flatley, Paul - E
Frankhauser, Tom - B
Hawkins, "Rip" - LB
Hultz, Don - E
Huth, Gerry - G
Jobko, Bill - LB

Kassulke, Karl - B
Kosen, Terry - B
Lamson, Charley - B
Linden, Errol - T
Marshall, Jim - E
Mason, Tom - B
O'Brien, Dave - G & T
Poage, Ray - B
Prestel, Jim - T
Reed, Bob - B
Reichow, Gerry - E
Russ, Pat - T
Sharockman, Ed - B
Smith, Gordon - E
Stonebreaker, Steve - E
Tarkenton, Fran - Q
Tingelhoff, Mick - C
VanderKelen, Ron - Q
Wilson, Tom - B
Winston, Roy - LB

1963 NEW YORK GIANTS
COACH - "Allie" Sherman
1st 11-3-0
(Lost title to Chicago, 14-10)

Anderson, Bob - B
Barnes, Erich - B
Bolin, "Bookie" - G
Brown, Rosie - T
Byers, Ken - G & E
Chandler, Don - K
Counts, John - B
Dess, Darrell - G
Dove, Ed - B
Gifford, Frank - B
Griffing, Glynn - Q
Guglielmi, Ralph - Q
Gursky, Al - LB
Guy, Louis - B
Hillebrand, Jerry - LB
Howell, Lane - T
Huff, "Sam" - LB
Katcavage, Jim - E
Killett, Charles - B
King, Phil - B
Kirouac, Lou - T

Larson, Greg - C
Lovetere, John - T
Lynch, Dick - B
McElhenny, Hugh - B
Modzelewski, Dick - T
Morrison, Joe - B
Patton, Jim - B
Pesonen, Dick - B
Robustelli, Andy - E
Scott, Tom - LB
Shofner, Del - E
Stroud, Jack - T
Taylor, Bob - T
Thomas, Aaron - E
Tittle, Y. A. - Q
Walker, "Mickey" - LB
Walton, Joe - E
Webb, Allen - B
Webster, Alex - B
Winter, Bill - LB

1963 PHILADELPHIA EAGLES
COACH - Nick Skorich
7th 2-10-2

Baughan, Max - LB
Blaine, Ed - G
Brown, Tim - B
Burroughs, Don - B
Byrne, Bill - G
Caffey, Lee Roy - LB
Carr, Jim - B
Case, "Pete" - G
Clark, Mike - K
Cross, Irv - B
Dean, Ted - B
Dudley, Paul - B
Echols, Fate - T
Fuller, Frank - T
Goodwin, Ron - B
Graham, Dave - T
Guglielmi, Ralph - Q
Gunnels, "Riley" - T
Harrison, Bob - LB
Heck, Ralph - LB

Henson, Gary - E
Hill, King - Q
Jurgensen, "Sonny" - Q
Keys, Howie - T & C & G
Lloyd, Dave - LB
Lucas, Dick - E
McClellan, "Mike" - B
McDonald, Tom - B
Mansfield, Jim - T
Mazzanti, Jerry - E
Mellekas, John - T
Peaks, Clarence - B
Quinlan, Bill - E
Ramsey, Nate - B
Retzlaff, "Pete" - E
Richards, Bob - E
Sapp, Theron - B
Schrader, Jim - C
Scotti, Ben - B
Skaggs, Jim - G

Smith, Jess - T
Smith, Ralph - E
Stafford, Dick - E

1963 PITTSBURGH STEELERS
COACH - "Buddy" Parker
4th 7-4-3

Anderson, Art - T
Atkinson, Frank - T
Baker, John - E
Ballman, Gary - B
Bradshaw, Charley - T
Bradshaw, Jim - B
Brown, Ed - Q
Burrell, John - E
Carpenter, Pres - E
Cordileone, Lou - T
Curry, Roy - B
Daniel, Bill - B
Dial, "Buddy" - E
Ferguson, Bob - B
Glass, Glenn - B
Haley, Dick - B
Hoak, Dick - B
James, Dan - T
Johnson, John Henry - B
Keys, Brady - B

Tarasovic, George - E & LB
Woodeschick, Tom - B

Krupa, Joe - T
Lemek, Ray - G
Mack, "Red" - E
Michaels, Lou - E
Nelsen, Bill - Q
Nofsinger, Terry - Q
Nutter, "Buzz" - C
Pottios, Myron - LB
Powers, John - E
Reger, John - LB
Rowley, Bob - LB
Russell, Andy - LB
Sandusky, Mike - G
Sapp, Theron - B
Schmitz, Bob - LB
Stautner, Ernie - T
Stehouwer, Ron - G
Tarasovic, George - LB
Thomas, Clendon - B
Tracy, Tom - B

1963 ST. LOUIS CARDINALS
COACH - Wally Lemm
3rd 9-5-0

Anderson, Taz - E
Bakken, Jim - K
Boyette, Garland - LB
Brumm, Don - E
Burson, Jim - B
Childress, Joe - B
Conrad, Bobby Joe - B
Cook, Ed - T
Crow, John David - B
DeMarco, Bob - C
Echols, Fate - T
Fischer, Pat - B
Gambrell, Bill - E
Gautt, Prentice - B
Goode, Irv - T
Gray, Ken - G
Hammack, Mal - B
Henke, Ed - E
Hill, Jim - B
Houser, John - G
Humphrey, "Buddy" - Q
Johnson, Charley - Q

Koman, Bill - LB
McMillan, Ernie - T
Meggyesy, Dave - LB
Meinert, Dale - LB
Owens, Don - T
Owens, Luke - T
Paremore, Bob - B
Randle, "Sonny" - E
Redmond, Tom - G
Reynolds, Bob - T
Robb, Joe - E
Rushing, Marion - LB
Silas, Sam - T
Smith, Jackie - E
Stacy, Bill - B
Stallings, Larry - LB
Stovall, Jerry - B
Symank, John - B
Thornton, Bill - B
Triplett, Bill - B
Wilson, Larry - B

1963 SAN FRANCISCO 49ERS
COACHES - "Red" Hickey &
Jack Christiansen
7th 2-12-0

Alexander, Kermit - B
Bosley, Bruce - C
Brock, Clyde - T
Brodie, John - Q
Casey, Bernie - E
Colchico, Dan - E
Conner, Clyde - E
Cooper, Bill - LB
Davis, Tom - K
Donohue, Leon - G
Dove, Ed - B
Dowdle, Mike - LB
Hazeltine, Matt - LB
Johnson, Jim - B
Kimbrough, Elbert - B

Knafelc, Gary - E
Krueger, Charley - T
Lakes, Roland - T
Lind, "Mike" - B
Lisbon, Don - B
McFarland, Kay - B
McHan, Lamar - Q
Magac, Mike - G
Messer, Dale - B
Miller, Clark - E
Nomellini, Leo - T
Perry, Joe - B
Pine, Ed - LB
Rock, Walt - T
Rohde, Len - T

Rubke, Karl - E
St. Clair, Bob - T
Sieminski, Charley - T
Smith, J. D. - B
Stickles , Monty - E
Thomas, John - G

Vollenweider, Jim - B
Waters, Bob - Q
Williams, Howie -B
Williams, Roy - T
Winston, Lloyd - B
Woodson, Abe - B

Kochman, Roger - B
LaMonica, Daryle - Q
Leo, Charley - G
McDole, Roland - E
Matuszak, Marv - LB
Miller, Bill - E
Moore, Leroy - E
Murdock, Jesse - B
Paterra, Herb - LB
Rice, Ken - G
Rivera, "Hank" - B

Rutkowski, Ed - B
Saimes, George - B
Sestak, Tom - T
Shaw, Bill - B
Stratton, Mike - LB
Sykes, Gene - B
Tracey, John - LB
Warlick, Ernie - E
West, Willie - B
Yoho, Mack - E
Youngelman, Sid - T

1963 WASHINGTON REDSKINS
COACH - Bill McPeak
6th 3-11-0

Anderson, "Bill" - E
Barnes, Billy Ray - B
Bosseler, Don - B
Breedlove, Rod - LB
Budd, Frank - B
Butsko, Harry - LB
Collier, Jim - E
Crabb, Claude - B
Cunningham, Jim - B
Cvercko, Andy - G
Davidson, Ben - T
Dugan, Fred - E
Feagin, Tom - G
Francis, Dave - B
Hackbart, Dale - B
Hageman, Fred - C
Izo, George - Q
Jackson, Leroy - B
James, Dick - B
Kammerer, Carl - LB
Kelley, Gorden - LB

Khayat, Ed - T
Khayat, Bob - K
Mattson, Riley - T
Miller, Allen - LB
Mitchell, Bob - B
Nisby, John - G
O'Brien, Francis - T
Paluck, John - E
Pelligrini, Bob - LB
Promuto, Vince - G
Richter, "Pat" - E
Rutgens, Joe - T
Rzempoluch, Ted - B
Sample, John - B
Sanders, Lon - B
Snead, Norm - Q
Snidow, Ron - E
Steffen, Jim - B
Stynchula, Andy - E
Toneff, Bob - T
Tracy, Tom - B

1963 DENVER BRONCOS (AFL)
COACH - Jack Faulkner
4th 2-11-1

Barnes, Ernie - G
Breaux, Don - Q
Brown, Willie - B
Coffey, Don - B
Danenhauer, El - T
Dickinson, "Bo" - B
Dixon, Hewritt - B
Erlandson, Tom - LB
Fraser, Jim - LB
Frazier, Al - B
Gaiters, Bob - B
Gavin, Chuck - E
Gonsoulin, "Goose" - B
Groman, Bill - E
Holz, Gordie - T
Hopkins, Jerry - LB
Jackunas, Frank - C
Jacobs, Ray - E
Janik, Tom - B
Joe, Billy - B
Lassiter, Ike - E
McCormick, John - Q
McCullough, Bob - G
McDaniel, "Wahoo" - LB

McFadin, "Bud" - T
McGeever, John - B
Mingo, Gene - B
Mitchell, Charley -B
Nery, Ron - E
Nocera, John - LB
Nomina, Tom - G
Olson, Hal - T
Perkins, Jim - T
Peters, Anton - T
Prebola, Gene - E
Rychlec, Tom - E
Scarpitto, Bob - B
Simmons, Leon - LB
Sklopan, John - B
Slaughter, "Mickey" - Q
Starling, Bruce - B
Stone, Don - B
Sturm, Jerry - C
Taylor, Lionel - E
Tripucka, Frank - Q
Walker, Clarence - B
Zeman, Bob - B

1963 BOSTON PATRIOTS (AFL)
COACH - Mike Holovak
1st 7-6-1
(Beat Buffalo in division playoff,
28-7; lost title to San Diego,
51-10)

Addison, Tom - LB
Antwine, Houston - T
Buoncoati, Nick - LB
Burton, Ron - B
Cappelletti, Gino - E
Colclough, Jim - E
Crawford, Jim - B
Crump, Harry - B
Cudzik, Walt - C
Dee. Bob - E
DeLucca, Gerry - T
Eisenahuer, Larry - E
Felt, Dick - B
Garron, Larry - B
Graham, Art - E
Graham, Milt - T
Hall, Ron - B
Hudson, Bill - T

Hunt, Jim - E
Long, Charley - G
Lott, Bill - B
McKinnon, Don - LB
Neighbors, Bill - G
Neumann, Tom - B
Oakes, Don - T
O'Hanley, Ross - B
Parilli, "Babe" - Q
Richardson, Jess - T
Romeo, Tony - E
Rudolph, Jack - LB
Shonta, Chuck - B
Stephens, Tom - B & E
Suci, Bob - B
Watson, Dave - G
Yates, Bob - T
Yewcic, Tom - Q

1963 BUFFALO BILLS (AFL)
COACH - Lou Saban
1st 7-6-1 (tie)
(Lost playoff to Boston, 28-7)

Abruzzeze, Ray - B
Atkins, Bill - B
Barber, Stu - T
Bass, Glenn - E
Behrman, Dave - T
Bemiller, Al - C
Braxton, Hezekiah - B
Brown, Fred - B
Carlton, Wray - B
Charon, Carl - B
Crow, Wayne - B

Day, Tom - E
DeLucca, Gerry - T
Dubenion, Elbert - B
Dunaway, Jim - T
Edgerson, Booker - B
Ferguson, Charley - E
Flint, George - T
Gilchrist, "Cookie" - B
Hudson, Dick - G
Jacobs, Harry - LB
Kemp, Jack - Q

1963 HOUSTON OILERS (AFL)
COACH - "Pop" Ivy
3rd 6-8-0

Babb, Gene = LB
Baker, John - LB
Banfield, "Tony" - B
Blanda, George - Q
Brabham, Dan - LB
Brezina, Bob - B
Cannon, Billy - B
Cline, Doug - LB
Culpepper, Ed - T
Cutsinger, Gary - E
Dewveall, Will - E
Dickinson, "Bo" - B
Dukes, Mike - LB
Floyd, Don - E
Frazier, Charley - E
Frongillo, John - C
Glick, Fred - B
Goode, Tom - LB
Hennigan, Charley - E
Husmann, Ed - T

Jancik, Bob - B
Johnston, Mark - B
Kelly, Bob - T
Kerbow, Randy - B
Lee, Jackie - Q
McLeod, Bob - E
Meredith, Dud - T
Michael, Dick - T
Nery, Ron - E
Norton, Jim - B
Onesti, Larry - LB
Perkins, Will - E
Schmidt, Bob - C
Smith, Dave - B
Suggs, Walt - T
Talamini, Bob - G
Tobin, Bill - B
Tolar, Charley - B
Wegener, Bill - G
Wharton, Hogan - G

1963 KANSAS CITY CHIEFS (AFL)
COACH - "Hank" Stram
3rd 5-7-2

Arbanas, Fred - E
Bell, Bob - E & LB
Biodrowski, Denny - G
Branch, Mel - E

Brooker, Tom - E
Buchanan, "Buck" - T
Budde, Ed - G
Burford, Chris - E

Coan, Bert - B
Corey, Walt - LB
Dawson, Len - Q
Diamond, Charley - T
Diamond, Bill - G
Farrier, Curt - T
Gilliam, Jon - C
Grayson, Dave - B
Haynes, Abner - B
Headrick, Sherrill - LB
Hill, Dave - T
Holub, LB & C
Hunt, Bob - B
Jackson, Frank - B
Johnson, Dick - E

McClinton, Curt - B
Mays, Gerry - T
Merz, Curt - G & E
Ply, Bob - B
Reynolds, Al - G
Robinson, John - B
Rochester, Paul - T
Spikes, Jack - B
Stover, "Smokey" - LB
Terrell, Marv - G
Tyrer, Jim - T
Warner, Charley - B
Wilson, Eddie - Q
Wilson, Jerry - B & LB
Wood, Duane - B

1963 SAN DIEGO CHARGERS (AFL)
COACH - Sid Gillman
1st 11-3-0
(Beat Boston for title, 51-10)

Allen, Chuck - LB
Alworth, Lance - B
Blair, George - B
Buncom, Frank - LB
Carolan, Reg - E
DeLuca, Sam - G
Faison, Earl - E
Glick, Gary - B
Gross, George - T
Gruneisen, Sam - G
Hadl, John - Q
Harris, Dick - B
Jackson, Bob - B
Karas, Emil - LB
Kinderman, Keith - B
Kocourek, Dave - E
Ladd, Ernie - T
Lane, Bob - LB
Lincoln, Keith - B

Lowe, Paul - B
MacKinnon, Jacque - E
McDougall, Gerry - B
McNeil, Charley - B
Maguire, Paul - LB
Mitinger, Bob - LB
Mix, Ron - T
Norton, Don - E
Park, Ernie - T
Petrich, Bob - E
Robinson, Jerry - E
Rogers, Don - C
Rote, Tobin - Q
Schmidt, Henry - T
Shea, Pat - G
Sweeney, Walt - G
Westmoreland, Dick -
Whitehead, "Bud" - B
Wright, Ernie - T

1963 NEW YORK JETS (AFL)
COACH - "Weeb" Ewbank
4th 5-8-1

Atkins, Bill - B
Baird, Bill - B
Bates, Ted - LB
Butler, Bob - G
Chlebek, Ed -Q
Christy, Dick - B
Cooke, Ed - E & LB
Ellis, Roger - LB
Ficca, Dan - G
Fournet, Sid - G
Grantham, Larry - LB
Green, John - Q
Gregory, Ken - E
Guesman, Dick - T
Hall, Galen - Q
Heeter, Gene - E
Hill, Winston - T
Hord, Roy - G
Hudock, Mike - C
Janerette, Charley - T
Johnson, "Curley" - B
Klotz, John - T.
McAdams, Bob - T

Mackey, Dee - E
Mathis, Bill - B
Maynard, Don - B
Michaels, Walt - LB
Paulson, Dainard - B
Perkins, Bill - B
Perrault, Pete - G
Plunkett, Sherman - T
Price, Jim - LB
Rochester, Paul - T
Smolinski, Mark - B
Starks, Marshall - B
Stricker, Tony - B
Strugar, George - T
Torczon, Laverne - E
Turner, "Bake" - E
Washington, Clyde - B
Watters, Bob - E
West, Dave - B
Wood, "Dick" - Q
Wood, Bill - B
Yohn, Dave - LB

1964

NATIONAL FOOTBALL LEAGUE
EASTERN CONFERENCE

Cleveland	10	3	1	.769
St. Louis	9	3	2	.750
Washington	6	8	0	.429
Philadelphia	6	8	0	.429
Dallas	5	8	1	.385
Pittsburgh	5	9	0	.357
New York	2	10	2	.167

WESTERN CONFERENCE

Baltimore	12	2	0	.857
Green Bay	8	5	1	.615
Minnesota	8	5	1	.615
Detroit	7	5	2	.583
Los Angeles	5	7	2	.417
Chicago	5	9	0	.357
San Francisco	4	10	0	.286

AMERICAN FOOTBALL LEAGUE
EASTERN DIVISION

	W	L	T	Pct.
Buffalo	12	2	0	.857
Boston	10	3	1	.769
New York	5	8	1	.385
Houston	4	10	0	.286

WESTERN DIVISION

	W	L	T	Pct.
San Diego	8	5	1	.615
Kansas City	7	7	0	.500
Oakland	5	7	2	.417
Denver	2	11	1	.154

TITLE: In the NFL, Cleveland beat Baltimore, 27-0, for the championship at Cleveland. St. Louis beat Green Bay, 24-17, in the second place playoff at Miami. In the AFL, Buffalo beat San Diego, 20-7, at Buffalo, Dec. 26.

1963 OAKLAND RAIDERS (AFL)
COACH - Al Davis
2nd 10-4-0

Allen, Dalva - E
Barrett, Jan - E
Birdwell, Dan - E
Bishop, "Sonny" - G
Costa, Dave - T
Craig, Dobie - E
Daniels, Clem - B
Davidson, "Cotton" - Q
Dougherty, Bob - LB
Flores, Tom - Q
Garner, Bob - B
Gibson, Claude - B
Hawkins, Wayne - G
Herock, Ken - E
Jacobs, Proverb - T
Jelacic, Jon - E
Klein, Dick - T
Krakoski, Joe - B
McMillin, Jim - B
McMurtry, Chuck - T
Matson, Arch - LB

Mayberry, Doug - B
Mercer, Mike - K
Miller, Alan - B
Mischak, Bob - G
Morrow, Tom - B
Murdock, Jesse - B
Norris, Jim - T
Osborne, "Clancy" - LB
Otto, Jim - C
Powell, Art - E
Powers, Warren - B
Rieves, Charley - LB
Roberson, "Bo" - B
Shaw, Glenn - B
Simpson, Jack - LB
Sommer, Mike - B
Spencer, Ollie - G
Urenda, Herman - E & B
Williamson, Fred - B
Youso, Frank - T

NFL LEADERS: Individual leaders for the year: Scoring—Lenny Moore (Baltimore) 120 (20 TD's, new record); Rushing —Jim Brown (Cleveland), 1,446 yds.; Passing—Bart Starr (Green Bay); Pass Receiving—John Morris (Chicago), 93 (new record); Field Goals—Jim Bakken (St. Louis), 25; Punting—Bobby Walden (Minnesota), 46.4 yds.; Interceptions—Paul Krause (Washington), 12.

AFL LEADERS: Scoring—Gino Cappelletti (Boston), 155 (record); Rushing— "Cookie" Gilchrist (Buffalo), 981 yds.; Passing—Len Dawson (Kansas City); Pass Receiving—Charles Hennigan (Houston), 101 (record); Field Goals—Gino Cappelletti (Boston), 25; Punting—Jim Fraser (Denver), 44.2 yds.; Interceptions—Dainard Paulson (New York), 12.

FIRST DRAFT: NFL—David Parks (Texas Tech)—End—by San Francisco. AFL—Robert Brown (Nebraska)—Tackle— by Denver (signed with Philadelphia (NFL).

COACHES: Joe Kuharich signed as new coach of Philadelphia Eagles, replacing Nick Skorich. In the AFL, Mac Speedie replaced Jack Faulkner at Denver after four games; Sam Baugh replaced Pop Ivy at Houston.

HALL OF FAME added players Jim Conzelman, Ed Healey, Clark Hinkle, "Link" Lyman, "Mike" Michalske, George Trafton and owner Art Rooney.

NOTES: Player limit raised by three to 40.

Paul Hornung (Green Bay) and Alex Karras (Detroit), reinstated, March 16, after 11 months suspension for gambling.

Yelberton Abraham Tittle, San Francisco, Baltimore, New York Giants qback, retired after 15 years in NFL, two in AAFC.

Jim Martin, Cleveland, Detroit, Baltimore, Washington lineman-kicker, retired after 14 years.

Andy Robustelli, Los Angeles, New York Giants defensive end, retired after 14 years.

Jim Brown, Cleveland, tied Don Hutson's touchdown record at 105.

Lenny Moore, Baltimore back, scored 20 touchdowns, record.

Jim Bakken, St. Louis kicker, scored five field goals against Philadelphia, tying record, Dec. 13.

Jim Brown, Cleveland, rushed 1,446 yards.

Jim Taylor, Green Bay, rushed 1,169 yards.

John Henry Johnson, Pittsburgh, rushed 1,048 yards.

John Morris, Chi-Bear flanker, caught 93 passes, record.

Willie Galimore, back, and "Bo" Farrington, end, of Chi-Bears died in auto accident at training camp.

Harry Hopp, Detroit and AAFC qback, died Dec. 22.

Steve Juzwik Washington, Buffalo back (1942-48) died, June 6.

Kermit Laabs, Green Bay back (1929) died, May 24.

Paul Lipscomb, Green Bay, Washington, Chi-Bear tackle (1945-54) died Aug. 20.

Carlo Pignatelli, Cleveland back (1931) died June 14.

Lucien Reeberg, 308 pound Detroit tackle (1963) died of uremia at 21, Jan. 31.

Vic Morabito, San Francisco owner, died May 10.

Steve Owen, Kansas City, New York Giants tackle and head coach for 23 years, died May 17.

NFL TITLE GAME

Cleveland 27, Baltimore 0 (Dec. 17). Gary Collins, Cleveland flanker, caught three touchdown passes for a new title game record while Cleveland's defense stopped the Colts offense, which had scored 428 points in a 14-game season. Lou Groza added two field goals and three conversions.

Cleveland	0	0	17	10	27
Baltimore	0	0	0	0	0

Touchdowns: Collins 3.
Field Goals: Groza 2.
Conversions: Groza 3.
Attendance: 79,544.
Players' Share: Cleveland $8,052.82; Baltimore $5,570.40.

1964 AFL TITLE GAME

San Diego scored in the first period on a 26-yard touchdown pass from Tobin Rote to Dave Kocourek with Keith Lincoln adding the conversion. Also in the first quarter, Pete Gogolak kicked a 12-yard field goal for Buffalo. In the second quarter, Wray Carlton scored for the Bills on a 4-yard smash and Gogolak added the extra point and a 17 yard field goal for a 13-7 halftime lead.

Jack Kemp scored on a 1-yard plunge for a Buffalo touchdown in the final period and Gogolak's extra point made it 20-7, the final score.

Buffalo	3	10	0	7	20
San Diego	7	0	0	0	7

Touchdowns: Carlton, Kemp.
Field Goals: Gogolak 2.
PAT's: Gogolak 2.
Attendance: 40,242.
Players' Share: Buffalo $2,668.60; San Diego $1,738.63.

1964 BALTIMORE COLTS
COACH - Don Shula
1st 12-2-0
(Lost title to Cleveland, 27-0)

Berry, Raymond - E
Boyd, Bob - B
Braase, Ordell - E
Burkett, Walter - LB
Cuozzo, Gary - Q
Davis, "Ted" - LB
Diehl, John - T
Gilburg, Tom - T
Harris, Wendell - B
Hawkins, Alex - B & E
Haymond, Alvin - B
Hill, Jerry - B
Kirouac, Lou - T
Logan, Jerry - B
Looney, Joe Don - B
Lorick, Tony - B
Lyles, Lenny - B
Mackey, John - E
Marchetti, Gino - E
Matte, Tom - B

Michaels, Lou - E
Miller, Fred - T
Moore, Lenny - B
Orr, Jim - E
Parker, Jim - G
Pellington, Bill - LB
Petties, Neal - E
Preas, George - T
Reese, Guy - T
Richardson, Willie - E
Sandusky, Alex - G
Shinnick, Don - LB
Smith, Billy Ray - T
Stonebreaker, Steve - LB
Sullivan, Dan - T
Szymanski, Dick - C
Unitas, John - Q
Vogel, Bob - T
Welch, Jim - B
Wilson, George - E

1964 CHICAGO BEARS
COACH - George Halas
6th 5-9-0

Arnett, Jon - B
Atkins, Doug - E
Barnes, Gary - E
Bivins, Charley - B
Bukich, Rudy - Q
Bull, Ron - B
Burman, George - T & C
Cadile, Jim - G
Caroline, J. C. - B
Casares, Ric - B
Ditka, Mike - E
Evey, Dick - G & E
Fortunato, Joe - LB
George, Bill - LB
Glueck, Larry - B
Green, Bobby Joe - K
Jencks, Bob - E
Johnson, John - B
Jones, Stan - T
Karras, Ted - G
Kilcullen, Bob - E
Kreitling, Rich - E

LeClerc, Roger - LB
Lee, Herman - T
Leggett, Earl - T
Livingston, Andy - B
McRae, Ben - B
Marconi, Joe - B
Martin, Bill - B
Martin, Bill - E
Morris, Johnny - B
Morris, Larry - LB
O'Bradovich, Ed - E
Petitbon, Rich - B
Purnell, Jim - LB
Pyle, Mike - C
Rabold, Mike - G
Rakestraw, Larry - Q
Reilly, Mike - LB
Sisk, John - B
Taylor, "Rosie" - B
Wade, Bill - Q
Wetoska, Bob - T
Whitsell, Dave - B

1964 CLEVELAND BROWNS
COACH - Blanton Collier
1st 10-3-1
(Beat Baltimore for title, 27-0)

Beach, Walt - B
Benz, Larry - B
Bettridge, Ed - LB
Brewer, John - E
Brown, Jim - B
Brown, John - T
Bundra, Mike - T
Caylor, Lowell - B
Clark, Monte - T
Collins, Gary - E
Costello, Vince - LB
Fichtner, Ross - B
Fiss, Galen - LB
Franklin, Bob - B
Gain, Bob - T
Glass, Bill - E
Green, Ernie - B
Groza, Lou - K
Hickerson, Gene - G
Houston, Jim - LB
Hutchinson, Tom - E
Kanicki, Jim - T

Kelly, Leroy - B
Lucci, Mike - LB
McNeil, Clif - B
Memmelaar, Dale - G
Modzelewski, Dick - T
Morrow, John - C
Ninowski, Jim - Q
Parker, Frank - T
Parrish, Bernie - B
Raimey, Dave - B
Roberts, Walt - B
Ryan, Frank - Q
Scales, Charley - B
Schafrath, Dick - T
Sczurek, Stan - LB
Shoals, Roger - T
Warfield, Paul - E
Wiggin, Paul - E
Williams, Sid - E
Wooten, John - G

1964 DALLAS COWBOYS
COACH - Tom Landry
5th 5-8-1

Andrie, George - E
Bishop, Don - B
Boeke, Jim - T
Bullocks, Amos - B
Clarke, Frank - E
Colvin, Jim - T
Connelly, Mike - C
Dial, "Buddy" - E
Dunn, Perry Lee - B
Edwards, Dave - LB
Folkins, Lee - E
Frank, Bill - T
Fry, Bob - T
Gaechter, Mike - B
Gent, George - E
Green, Cornell - B
Hays, Hal - LB
Howley, Chuck - LB
Isbell, Joe Bob - G
Jordan, Lee Roy - LB
Kupp, Jake - G

Lilly, Bob - T
Liscio, Tony - T
Livingston, Warren - B
Lothridge, Bill - Q
McDonald, Tom - B
Manders, Dave - G & C
Marsh, Amos - B
Meredith, Don - Q
Norman, Pettis - E
Perkins, Don - B
Renfro, Mel - B
Ridlon, Jim - B
Roach, John - Q
Schoenke, Ray - T
Smith, Jim Ray - G
Stephens, Larry - E
Stiger, Jim - B
Tubbs, Gerry - LB
Van Raaphorst, Dick - K
Youmans, Maury - E

1964 DETROIT LIONS
COACH - George Wilson
4th 7-5-2

Barr, Terry - B
Batten, Pat - B
Brown, Roger - T
Clark, Ernie - LB
Cogdill, Gail - E
Compton, Dick - B
Gaubatz, Dennis - LB
Gibbons, Jim - E
Gibbs, "Sonny" - Q
Gonzaga, John - G
Gordy, John - G
Hilgenberg, Wally - LB
Karras, Alex - T
LaLonde, Roger - T
Lane, Dick - B
Lary, Yale - B
LeBeau, Dick - B
Lee, Monte - LB
Lewis, Dan - B
Lowe, Gary - B
McCord, Darris - E

McElhenny, Hugh - B
McInnis, Hugh - E
Maher, Bruce - B
Morrall, Earl - Q
Pietrosante, Nick - B
Plum, Milt - Q
Quinlan, Bill - E
Rasmussen, Wayne - B
Ryder, Nick - B
Sanders, Daryl - T
Schmidt, Joe - LB
Scholtz, Bob - G & T
Simon, Jim - G
Smith, Jess - T
Studstill, Pat - B
Thompson, Bob - B
Walker, Wayne - LB
Watkins, Tom - B
Wells, Warren - E
Whitlow, Bob - C
Williams, Sam - E

1964 GREEN BAY PACKERS
COACH - Vince Lombardi
2nd 8-5-1

Adderley, Herb - B
Aldridge, Lionel - E
Bowman, Ken - C
Bratkowski, "Zeke" - Q
Breen, Gene - LB
Brown, Tom - B
Caffey, Lee Roy - LB
Claridge, Dennie - Q
Crutcher, Tom - LB
Currie, Dan - LB
Davis, Willie - E
Dowler, Boyd - E
Fleming, Marv - E
Gregg, Forrest - T
Gremminger, Hank - B
Grimm, Dan -G
Hanner, "Dave" - T
Hart, Doug - B
Hornung, Paul - B
Jeter, Bob - B
Jordan, Henry - T

Kostelnik, Ron - E & T
Kramer, Gerry - G
Kramer, Ron - E
Long, Bob - B
McDowell, John - G
McGee, Max - E
Masters, Norm - T
Moore, Tom - B
Nitschke, Ray - LB
Norton, Gerry - B
Pitts, Elijah - B
Robinson, "Dave" - LB
Skoronski, Bob - T
Starr, Bart - Q
Taylor, Jim - B
Thurston, Fred - G
Voss, Lloyd - T
Whittenton, "Jess" - B
Wood, Willie - B
Wright, Steve - E

1964 LOS ANGELES RAMS
COACH - Harland Svare
5th - 5-7-2

Allen, Duane - E
Baker, Terry - B
Bass, Dick - B
Brown, Willie - B
Budka, Frank - B
Carollo, Joe - T
Chuy, Don - G
Cowan, Charley - T
Crow, Lindon - B
Dale, Carroll - E & B
Davis, Roger - G
Gabriel, Roman - Q
Gossett, Bruce - K
Grier, "Rosey" - T
Harris, Marv - LB
Henry, Mike - LB
Hunter, Art - C
Jones, Dave - E
Josephson, Les - B
Larsen, Gary - T
Livingston, Cliff - LB

Lundy, Lamar - E
McKeever, Marlin - E
Martin, Aaron - B
Meador, Ed - B
Munson, Bill - Q
Olsen, Merlin - T
Pardee, John - LB
Phillips, Jim - E & B
Pope, "Bucky" - E
Richardson, Gerry - B
Scibelli, Joe - G
Shannon, Carver - B
Smith, Bobby - B
Truax, Bill - E
Varrichione, Frank - T
Villanueva, Dan - K
Von Sonn, Andy - LB
Wendryhoski, Joe - C
Whittingham, Fred - G
Wilson, Ben - B

1964 MINNESOTA VIKINGS
COACH - Norm Van Brocklin
2nd 8-5-1

Alderman, Grady - T
Bedsole, Hal - E
Bowie, Larry - G
Britt, Charley - B
Brown, Bill - B
Bundra, Mike - T
Butler, Bill - B
Byers, Ken - G
Calland, Lee - B
Campbell, John - LB
Cox, Fred - K
Dean, Ted - B
Denton, Bob - T
Dickson, Paul - T
Eller, Carl - E
Flatley, Paul - E
Hall, Tom - B
Hawkins, "Rip" - LB
Jobko, Bill - LB
Kassulke, Karl - B
Kirby, John - LB
Lacey, Bob - E

Lester, Darrell - B
Linden, Errol - T
McWatters, Bill - B
Marshall, Jim - E
Mason, Tom - B
Michel, Tom - B
O'Brien, Dave - T
Prestel, Jim - T
Pyle, Palmer - G
Reichow, Gerry - E
Rose, George - B
Sharockman, Ed - B
Simpson, Howard - E
Smith, Gordon - E
Sunde, Milt - G
Swain, Bill - LB
Tarkenton, Fran - Q
Tingelhoff, Mick - C
VanderKelen, Ron - Q
Vargo, Larry - B
Walden, Bob - K
Winston, Roy - LB

1964 NEW YORK GIANTS
COACH - "Allie" Sherman
7th 2-12-0

Anderson, Roger - T
Barnes, Erich - B
Bolin, "Bookie" - G
Brown, Rosie - T
Byers, Ken - G
Chandler, Don - K
Childs, Clarence - B
Contoulis, John - T
Costello, Tom - LB
Crespino, Bob - E
Dess, Darrell - G
Gifford, Frank - B
Hillebrand, Jerry - LB
Howell, Lane - T
James, Dick - B
Jones, Homer - B
Katcavage, Jim - E
Larson, Greg - C
Lasky, Frank - T
Lovetere, John - T
Lynch, Dick - B
Messner, Max - LB
Moran, Jim - T

Morrison, Joe - B
Nelson, Andy - B
Owens, Raleigh - B
Patton, Jim - B
Pesonen, Dick - B
Robustelli, Andy - E
Schichtle, Henry - Q
Scott, Tom - LB
Shofner, Del - E
Slaby, Lou - LB
Stroud, Jack - T
Stynchula, Andy - E
Taylor, Bob - T & E
Thomas, Aaron - E
Thurlow, Steve - B
Tittle, Y. A. - Q
Walker, "Micky" - G & C
Webb, Allen - B
Webster, Alex - B
Wheelwright, Ernie - B
Winter, Bill - LB
Wood, Gary - Q

1964 PHILADELPHIA EAGLES
COACH - Joe Kuharich
3rd 6-8-0

Baker, "Sam" - K
Baughan, Max - LB
Blaine, Ed - G
Brown, Bob - T
Brown, Tim - B
Burroughs, Don - B
Case, "Pete" - G
Concannon, Jack - Q
Crabb, Claude - B
Cross, Irv - B
Gill, Roger - B
Glass, Glenn - B
Goodwin, Ron - B
Graham, Dave - T
Gros, Earl - B
Gunnels, "Riley" - E
Heck, Ralph - LB
Hill, King - Q
Hoyem, Lynn - G
Hultz, Don - E
Khayat, Ed - T

Lang, Israel - B
Lloyd, Dave - LB
Mack, "Red" - B
Matson, Ollie - B
Meyers, John - T
Morgan, Mike - LB
Peters, Floyd - T
Poage, Ray - E
Ramsey, Nate - B
Retzlaff, "Pete" - E
Richards, Bob - E
Ringo, Jim - C
Scarpati, Joe - B
Schrader, Jim - C
Skaggs, Jim - T
Smith, Ralph - E & B
Snead, Norm - Q
Tarasovic, George - LB & E
Thompson, Don - E
Woodeschick, Tom - B

1964 PITTSBURGH STEELERS
COACH - "Buddy" Parker
6th 5-9-0

Baker, John - E
Ballman, Gary - B
Bradshaw, Charley - T
Bradshaw, Jim - B
Brown, Ed - Q
Burrell, John - E
Clark, Mike - E & K
Daniel, Bill - B
Haley, Dick - B
Harrison, Bob - LB
Henry, Urban - T
Hinton, Chuck - T
Hoak, Dick - B
Holler, Ed - LB
James, Dan - T
Johnson, John Henry - B
Kelly, Jim - E

Keys, Brady - B
King, Phil - B
Krupa, Joe - T
LaRose, Dan - E
Lemek, Ray - G
Logan, Chuck - E
McGee, Ben - E
Mansfield, Jim - T
Martha, Paul - B
Messner, Max - LB
Nelsen, Bill - Q
Nofsinger, Terry - Q
Nutter, "Buzz" - C
Peaks, Clarence - B
Pottios, Myron - LB
Powers, John - E
Sandusky, Mike - G

Sapp, Theron - B
Saul, Bill - LB
Schmitz, Bob - LB
Sherman, Bob - B
Soleau, Bob - LB

Stehouwer, Ron - G
Thomas, Clendon - B
Wade, Tom - Q
Woodson, Marv - B

Promuto, Vince - G
Reger, John - LB
Richter, "Pat" - E
Rutgens, Joe - T
Sample, John - B
Sanders, Lon - B
Seals, George - G
Shiner, Dick - Q

Shorter, Jim - B
Snidow, Ron - E
Steffen, Jim - B
Taylor, Charley - B
Toneff, Bob - T
Tracy, Tom - B
Walters, Tom - B
Williams, Fred - T

1964 ST. LOUIS CARDINALS
COACH - Wally Lemm
2nd 9-3-2

Anderson, Taz - E
Bailey, "Monk" - B
Bakken, Jim - K
Brumm, Don - E
Burson, Jim - B
Childress, Joe - B
Conrad, Bobby Joe - B
Cook, Ed - T
Crenshaw, Willie - B
Crow, John David - B
DeMarco, Bob - C
Fischer, Pat - B
Gambrell, Billy - E
Gautt, Prentice - B
Goode, Irv - G
Gray, Ken - G
Hammack, Mal - E & B
Hill, Jim - B
Humphrey, "Buddy" - Q
Johnson, Charley - Q

Koman, Bill - LB
Kortas, Ken - T
McMillan, Ernie - T
Meggyesy, Dave - LB
Meinert, Dale - LB
Owens, Luke - T
Paremore, Bob - B
Randle, "Sonny" - E
Redmond, Tom - E
Reynolds, Bob - T
Robb, Joe - E
Rushing, Marion - LB
Silas, Sam - T
Smith, Jackie - E
Sortun, Rick - G
Stallings, Larry - LB
Stovall, Jerry - B
Thornton, Bill - B
Turner, Herschel - G
Walker, Charley - E
Wilson, Larry - B

1964 BOSTON PATRIOTS (AFL)
COACH - Mike Holovak
2nd 10-3-1

Addison, Tom - LB
Antwine, Houston - T
Buonoconti, Nick - LB
Burton, Ron - B
Cappelletti, Gino - E
Cloutier, Dave - B
Colclough, Jim - E
Crawford, Jim - E & B
Dee, Bob - E
DeLucca, Gerry - T
Dukes, Mike - LB
Eisenhauer, Larry - E
Farmer, Lonnie - LB
Felt, Dick - B
Garrett, John - B
Garron, Larry - B
Graham, Art - E
Hall, Ron - B
Hunt, Jim - E

Long, Charley - G
McKinnon, Don - LB
Morris, Jon - C
Neighbors, Bill - G
Oakes, Don - T
O'Hanley, Ross - B
Parilli, "Babe" - Q
Richardson, Jess - T
Romeo, Tony - E
Rudolph, Jack - B
St. Jean, Len - E
Schmidt, Bob - T
Shonta, Chuck - B
Snyder, Al - E
Stephens, Tom - B & E
Watson, Dave - G
Webb, Don - B
Yates, Bob - T
Yewcic, Tom - Q

1964 SAN FRANCISCO 49ERS
COACH - Jack Christiansen
7th 4-10-0

Alexander, Kermit - B
Bosley, Bruce - C
Britt, Charley - B
Brodie, John - Q
Casey, Bernie - E
Colchico, Dan - E
Cooper, Bill - LB
Davis, Tom - KK
Dean, Floyd - LB
Donohue, Leon - G
Dowdle, Mike - LB
Hazeltine, Matt - LB
Johnson, Jim - B
Johnson, Rudy - B
Kilmer, Bill - Q
Kimbrough, Elbert - B
Kopay, Dave - B
Krueger, Charley - T
Lakes, Roland - T
Lewis, Gary - B
Lind, "Mike" - B
Lisbon, Don - B

McFarland, Kay - B
Magac, Mike - G
Mertens, Jerry - B
Messer, Dale - B
Miller, Clark - E
Mira, George - Q
Morze, Frank - C
Mudd, Howard - G
Parks, Dave - E
Pine, Ed - LB
Poole, Bob - E
Rock, Walt - T
Rohde, Len - T
Rubke, Karl - E
Scotti, Ben - B
Sieminski, Charley - T
Smith, J. D. - B
Stickles, Monty - E
Thomas, John - G
Wilcox, Dave - LB
Woodson, Abe - B

1964 BUFFALO BILLS (AFL)
COACH - Lou Saban
1st 12-2-0
(Beat San Diego for title, 20-7)

Abrussese, Ray - B
Auer, Joe - B
Barber, Stu - T
Bass, Glenn - E
Bemiller, Al - G
Byrd, George - B
Carlton, Wray - B
Clarke, Hagood - B
Cudzik, Walt - C
Day, Tom - E
Dobbins, Ollie - B
Dubenion, Elbert - B
Dunaway, Jim - T
Edgerson, Booker - B
Flint, George - G
Gilchrist, "Cookie" - B
Gogolak, Pete - K
Hudson, Dick - T
Jacobs, Harry - LB

Keating, Tom - T
Kemp, Jack - Q
LaMonica, Daryle - Q
McDole, Roland - E
Maguire, Paul - LB
Meredith, Dud - T
O'Donnell, Joe - G
Rosdahl, "Hatch" - E
Ross, Bill - B
Rutkowski, Ed - B
Saimer, George - B
Sestak, Tom - T
Shaw, Bill - G
Smith, Bob - B
Stratton, Mike - LB
Sykes, Gene - B
Tracey, John - LB
Warlick, Ernie - E
Warner, Charley - B

1964 WASHINGTON REDSKINS
COACH - Bill McPeak
3rd (tie) 6-8-0

Atkins, Pervis - B
Barnett, Steve - T
Bosseler, Don - B
Breedlove, Rod - LB
Carpenter, Pres - E
Carr, Jim - LB
Clay, Ozzie - B
Coia, Angelo - E
Hageman, Fred - C
Hauss, Len - C
Hernandez, Joe - E
Huff, "Sam" - LB

Izo, George - Q
Jurgensen, "Sonny" - Q
Kammerer, Carl - E
Krause, Paul - B
Lockett, J. W. - B
Martin, Jim - K
Mattson, Riley - T
Mitchell, Bob - B
Nisby, John - G
O'Brien, Francis - T
Paluck, John - E
Pelligrini, Bob - LB

1964 DENVER BRONCOS (AFL)
COACH - Mac Speedie
4th 2-11-1

Atkins, Bill - B
Barnes, Ernie - G
Barry, Odell - B
Bass, Norm - B
Brown, Willie - B
Cooke, Ed - E
Danenhauer, El - T
Denson, Al - B
Dixon, Hewritt - E
Erlandson, Tom - LB
Fanning, Stan - E
Fraser, Jim - LB
Gonsoulin, "Goose" - B
Griffin, John - B

Guesman, Dick - T
Hopkins, Jerry - LB
Jacobs, Ray - T
Janarette, Charley - T
Janik, Tom - B
Joe, Billy - B
Jordan, Larry - LB
Kubala, Ray - C
Lassiter, Ike - E
Lee, Jackie - Q
McCullough, Bob - G
McGeever, John - B
McMillin, Jim - B

Gary Collins, Cleveland flanker, scoring one of his three touchdowns against the Baltimore Colts in the 1964 championship game. It was a record for Collins and a 27-0 upset of the Colts.

Matuszak, Marv - LB
Mingo, Gene - B & K
Mitchell, Charley - B
Moore, Leroy - E
Nomina, Tom - G
Olson, Hal - T
Perkins, Jim - T
Price, Jim - LB
Scarpitto, Bob - B

Shackleford, Don - G
Slaughter, "Mickey" - Q
Snorton, Matt - E
Stone, Don - B
Sturm, Jerry - C
Taylor, Lionel - E
West, Willie - B
Wright, Jim - B

1964 HOUSTON OILERS (AFL)
COACH - Sam Baugh
4th 4-10-0

Appleton, Scott - E
Baker, John - LB
Bishop, "Sonny" - G
Blanda, George - Q
Blanks, Sid - B
Brabham, Dan - LB
Burrell, Ode - B
Cline, Doug - LB
Cutsinger, Gary - E
Dewveall, Will - E
Fanning, Stan - E
Faulkner, Staley - T
Floyd, Don - E
Fowler, Jerry - T
Frazier, Charley - E
Frazier, Willie - E
Frongillo, John - G
Glick, Fred - B
Goode, Tom - C
Hennigan, Charley - E
Hicks, Wilmer - B

Hoffman, Dalton - B
Husmann, Ed - T
Jackson, Bob - B
Jancik, Bob - B
Jaquess, Pete - B
Kelly, Bob - T
Klotz, John - T
McFadin, "Bud" - T
McLeod, Bob - E
Nelson, Ben - B
Norton, Jim - B
Odom, Sam - LB
Onesti, Larry - LB
Rieves, Charley - LB
Smith, Dave - B
Suggs, Walt - T
Talamini, Bob - G
Tolar, Charley - B
Trull, Don - Q
Wittenborn, John - E

1964 KANSAS CITY CHIEFS (AFL)
COACH - "Hank" Stram
2nd 7-7-0

Arbanas, Fred - E
Beathard, Pete - Q
Bell, Bob - E & LB
Biodrowski, Denny - G
Branch, Mel - E
Brooker, Tom - E
Buchanan, "Buck" - T
Budde, Ed - G
Burford, Chris - E
Carolan, Reg - E
Coan, Bert - B
Cornelison, Jerry - T
Corey, Walt - LB
Dawson, Len - Q
Farrier, Curt - T
Gilliam, Jon - C
Grayson, Dave - B
Haynes, Abner - B
Headrick, Sherrill - LB
Hill, Dave - T
Hill, Mack Lee - B

Holub, Emil - LB
Hunt, Bob - B
Jackson, Frank - B
Lothamer, Ed - E
McClinton, Curt - B
Maczuzak, John - T
Mays, Gerry - T
Merz, Curt - G
Mitchell, Willie - B
Ply, Bob - B
Reynolds, Al - G
Robinson, John - B
Rosdahl, "Hatch" - E
Spikes, Jack - B
Stover, "Smokey" - LB
Tyrer, Jim - T
Warner, Charley - B
Wilson, Eddie - Q
Wilson, Jerry - B
Wood, Duane - B

1964 NEW YORK JETS (AFL)
COACH - "Weeb" Ewbank
3rd 5-8-1

Baird, Bill - B
Baker, Ralph - LB
Cummings, Ed - LB
DeLuca, Sam - G
Evans, Jim - B
Ficca, Dan - G
Grantham, Larry - LB
Heeter, Gene - E

Herman, Dave - G
Hill, Winston - T
Holz, Gordy - T
Hudock, Mike - C
Johnson, "Curley" - B
Johnston, Mark - B
Lawson, Al - B
Liske, Pete - Q

McAdams, Bob - T
McCusker, Jim - T
McDaniel, "Wahoo" - LB
Mackey, Dee - E
Mathis, Bill - B
Maynard, Don - B
Pashe, Bill - B
Paulson, Dainard - B
Perrault, Pete - G
Philbin, Gerry - E
Plunkett, Sherman - T
Rademacher, Bill - B
Rochester, Paul - T
Rowley, Bob - LB

Schmitt, John - C
Smolinski, Mark - B
Snell, Matt - B
Starks, Marshall - B
Taliaferro, Mike - Q
Torczon, Laverne - E
Turner, Jim - Q & K
Turner, "Bake" - E
Turner, Vince - B
Washington, Clyde - B
Watters, Bob - E
West, Willie - B
Wilder, Bert - E
Wood, "Dick" - Q

1964 OAKLAND RAIDERS (AFL)
COACH - Al Davis
3rd 5-7-2

Allen, Dalva - E
Barrett, Jan - E
Birdwell, Dan - T
Brown, Doug - T
Budness, Bill - LB
Cannon, Billy - B
Conners, Dan - LB
Costa, Dave - T
Daniels, Clem - B
Davidson, Ben - E
Davidson, "Cotton" - Q
Dickinson, "Bo" - B
Flores, Tom - Q
Gibson, Claude - B
Gillett, Fred - E
Guy, Lou - B
Hawkins, Wayne - G
Herock, Ken - E
Jackson, Bob - B
Jacobs, Proverb - T
Jelacic, Jon - E
Johnston, Mark - B
Klein, Dick - T

Krakoski, Joe - B
McMillin, Jim - B
Matsos, Arch - LB
Mercer, Mike - K
Miller, Bill - E
Mingo, Gene - B
Mirich, Rex - E
Mischak, Bob - G
Morrow, Tom - B
Norris, Jim - T
Osborne, "Clancy" - LB
Otto, Jim - C
Powell, Art - E
Powers, Warren - B
Rice, Ken - T
Roberson, "Bo" - E
Shaw, Glenn - B
Simpson, Jack - LB
Williams, Howie - B
Williamson, Fred - B
Williamson, John - LB
Youso, Frank - T

1964 SAN DIEGO CHARGERS (AFL)
COACH - Sid Gillman
1st 8-5-1
(Lost title to Buffalo, 20-7)

Agajanian, Ben - K
Allen, Chuck - LB
Alworth, Lance - B
Blair, George - B
Buncom, Frank - LB
Carpenter, Ron - LB
Duncan, Les - B
Faison, Earl - E
Graham, Ken - B
Gross, George - T
Gruneisen, Sam - G
Hadl, John - Q
Harris, Dick - B
Horton, Bob - LB
Karas, Emil - LB
Kinderman, Keith - B
Kirner, Gary - T
Kocourek, Dave - E
Ladd, Ernie - T
Lane, Bob - LB
Lincoln, Keith - B
Lowe, Paul - B

MacKinnon, Jacque - E
McCoy, Lloyd - G
McDougall, Gerry - B
McNeil, Charley - B
Mendez, Mario - B
Mitinger, Bob - E
Mix, Ron - T
Moore, Fred - T
Norton, Don - E
Park, Ernie - T
Petrich, Bob - E
Robinson, Jerry - E
Rogers, Don - C
Rote, Tobin - Q
Schmidt, Henry - T
Shea, Pat - G
Sweeney, Walt - G
Travenio, Herb - K
Warren, Jim - B
Westmoreland, Dick - B
Whitehead, "Bud" - B
Wright, Ernie - T

1965

NATIONAL FOOTBALL LEAGUE

EASTERN CONFERENCE

	Won	Lost	Tied	Pct.
Cleveland	11	3	0	.786
Dallas	7	7	0	.500
New York	7	7	0	.500
Washington	6	8	0	.429
Philadelphia	5	9	0	.357
St. Louis	5	9	0	.357
Pittsburgh	2	12	0	.143

WESTERN CONFERENCE

	Won	Lost	Tied	Pct.
†Green Bay	10	3	1	.769
Baltimore	10	3	1	.769
Chicago	9	5	0	.643
San Francisco	7	6	1	.538
Minnesota	7	7	0	.500
Detroit	6	7	1	.462
Los Angeles	4	10	0	.286

AMERICAN FOOTBALL LEAGUE

EASTERN CONFERENCE

	Won	Lost	Tied	Pct.
Buffalo	10	3	1	.769
New York	5	8	1	.385
Boston	4	8	2	.333
Houston	4	10	0	.286

WESTERN CONFERENCE

	Won	Lost	Tied	Pct.
San Diego	9	2	3	.818
Oakland	8	5	1	.615
Kansas City	7	5	2	.583
Denver	4	10	0	.286

TITLE: In the NFL Green Bay beat Cleveland, 23-12, for the championship at Green Bay, Jan. 2. The Packers got into the title game by beating Baltimore in a tie play-off in the Western Conference, a game that was ended by Don Chandler's field goal after 13 minutes of sudden-death overtime. In the AFL, Buffalo beat San Diego, 23-0, Dec. 26 in San Diego.

Baltimore beat Dallas, 35-3, in the second place playoff at Miami.

NFL LEADERS: Individual leaders for the year: Scoring—Gale Sayers (Chicago), 132 (22 TD's for new league record); Rushing—Jim Brown (Cleveland), 1,544 yds.; Passing—Rudy Bukich (Chicago); Pass Receiving—Dave Parks (San Francisco), 80; Field Goals—Fred Cox (Minnesota), 23;

Punting—Gary Collins (Cleveland), 46.7 yds.; Interceptions—Bob Boyd (Baltimore), 9.

AFL LEADERS: Scoring—Gino Cappelletti (Boston), 132; Rushing—Paul Lowe (San Diego), 1,121 yds. (record); Passing—John Hadl (San Diego); Pass Receiving—Lionel Taylor (Denver), 85; Field Goals—Pete Gogolak (Buffalo), 28 (record); Punting—Jerrel Wilson (Kansas City), 45.4 yds. (record); Interceptions—Wilmer Hicks (Houston), 9.

FIRST DRAFT: NFL—Ivan Frederickson (Auburn)—Back—by New York. AFL—Joe Namath (Alabama)—Qback—by New York.

COACHES: Harry Gilmer replaced George Wilson as head coach at Detroit and Mike Nixon replaced "Buddy" Parker at Pittsburgh. In the AFL, Hugh Taylor replaced Sam Baugh at Houston.

HALL OF FAME added players Guy Chamberlin, "Paddy" Driscoll, Dan Fortmann, Otto Graham, Sid Luckman, Steve Van Buren and Bob Waterfield.

NOTES: Gale Sayers, Chi-Bears, scored 22 touchdowns (record).

Jim Brown, Cleveland, scored 21 touchdowns, making 126 for career, topping Don Hutson (105) and Lennie Moore (106).

Four NFL head coaches were fired at the end of the season: Nixon (Pittsburgh), Svare (Los Angeles), McPeak (Washington) and Lemm (St. Louis).

Team rosters were held at 40 to prepare for stocking the new team at Atlanta and another to be added in 1967.

A sixth official was added by the NFL to keep time and check action at the line of scrimmage.

A new television contract was signed which would permit, for the first time, showing of other games in the area of a team playing at home.

Eugene Brito, Washington, Los Angeles end (1951-60) died, June 8.

Earl "Curly" Lambeau, player-founder-coach of Green Bay Packers (1921-49); head coach Chi-Cards (1950-51); head coach Washington Redskins (1952-53); Hall of Fame (1963); died May 31.

Wilbur Moore, Washington halfback (1939-47) shot dead by ex-wife August 9.

Dr. Boni Petcoff, Columbus tackle (1924-26) died Aug. 5.

Don Pierce, Chi-Card, Brooklyn center (1942-43) killed in auto accident Jan. 2.

Harry Stuhldreyer, Brooklyn qback (1926) died Jan. 25.

C. Leo DeOrsey, president Washington Redskins, died April 30.

Neilson Mathews, Hammond, Chi-Tiger back (1920) died July 17.

Jack Mara, president New York Giants, died June 29.

Mack Lee Hill, Kansas City back, died following knee surgery, Dec. 14.

Atlanta awarded 15th franchise in NFL

Miami awarded 9th franchise in AFL.

Second sudden-death overtime game in NFL when Baltimore, Green Bay played off tie in Western Conference. Backers defeated Baltimore, 13-10 after 13:39 of first extra period.

NFL TITLE GAME

Green Bay 23; Cleveland 12. Paul Hornung and Jim Taylor pounded enough yards in short smashes to give Green Bay control throughout the game on a snowy, muddy field. The Packer defense held Jim Brown to 50 yards in 12 attempts and smothered the Cleveland passing attack.

Green Bay scored first on a 47-yard pass play from Starr to Carroll Dale. Cleveland took the kickoff back for its only touchdown, Ryan throwing 17 yards to Collins to score. The conversion was fouled up on a bad pass from center. Groza booted a 24-yard field goal for the Browns in the first period, another from 28 in the second. Don Chandler kicked successfully from 15 and 23 yards in the second period and it was 13-12 at the half.

Hornung scored on a 13-yard run in the third period. Chandler converted and kicked a 29-yard goal in the last quarter.

| Green Bay | 7 | 6 | 7 | 3 | 23 |
| Cleveland | 9 | 3 | 0 | 0 | 12 |

Touchdowns: Dale, Hornung.

Field Goals: Chandler 3; Groza 2.

PAT's: Chandler 2; Groza 1.

Attendance: 50,852.

Players' Shares: Green Bay $7,819.91; Cleveland $5,288.83.

1965 AFL TITLE GAME

After a scoreless first period, Kemp passed 18 yards to Warlick for a touchdown and Gogolak added the extra point. Also in the second period, George Byrd, Buffalo defensive back returned a punt 74 yards for a TD and Gogolak converted for a 14-0 halftime lead.

Gogolak added 11 and 39 yard field goals in the third quarter and another from 32 in the final period to make it Buffalo 23, San Diego 0 at the end of the game.

| Buffalo | 0 | 14 | 6 | 3 | 23 |
| San Diego | 0 | 0 | 0 | 0 | 0 |

Touchdowns: Warlick, Byrd.

Field Goals: Gogolak 3.

PAT's: Gogolak 2.

Attendance: 30,361.

Players' Shares: Buffalo $5,189.92; San Diego $3,447.85.

1965 BALTIMORE COLTS
COACH - Don Shula
1st 10-3-1
(Tied - Lost playoff to Green Bay, 13-10, Overtime)

Allen, Duane - E
Berry, Ray - E
Boyd, Bob - B
Braase, Ordell - E
Brown, "Ed" - Q
Bundra, Mike - T
Burkett, Jackie - LB
Cuozzo, Gary - Q
Curtis, "Mike" - LB
Davis, "Ted" - LB
Feltz, Bob - B
Gaubatz, Denny - LB
Gilburg, Tom - T
Haffner, George - Q
Harris, Wendell - B
Hawkins, Alex - E & B
Haymond, Alvin - B
Hill, Jerry - B
Hilton, Roy - E
Lee, Monte - LB
Logan, Jerry - B
Lorick, Tony - B
Lyles, Len - B
Mackey, John - E

Matte, Tom - B
Michaels, Lou - E
Miller, Fred - T
Moore, Lenny - B
Nutter, "Buzz" - C
Orr, Jim - E
Parker, Jim - G
Petties, Neal - E
Preas, George - T
Reese, Guy - T
Ressler, Glen - T
Richardson, Willie - E
Sandusky, Alex - G
Shinnick, Don - LB
Smith, Billy Ray - E & T
Stonebreaker, Steve - LB
Strofolino, Mike - LB
Sullivan, Dan - G
Szymanski, Dick - C
Unitas, John - Q
Vogel, Bob - T
Welch, Jim - B
Wilson, George - E

1965 CHICAGO BEARS
COACH - George Hallas
3rd 9-5-0

Arnett, Jon - B
Atkins, Doug - E
Bivins, Charley - B
Bukich, Rudy - Q
Bull, Ron - B

Butkus, Dick - LB
Cadile, Jim - T
Caroline, J. C. - B
Ditka, Mike - E
Evey, Dick - E

Jim Taylor (31) Green Bay is stopped by "Little Mo" Modzelewski of Cleveland while Bart Starr (15) Green Bay quarterback watches. Taylor gained 96 yards as the Packers beat the Browns, 23-12, for the 1965 title, and was picked as Most Valuable player. (AP) Wirephoto.)

Fortunato, Joe - LB
George, Bill - LB
Glueck, Larry = B
Gordon, Dick - E
Green, Bobby Joe - K
Johnson, John - T
Jones, Jim - E
Jones, Stan - T
Kilcullen, Bob - T
Kurek, Ralph - B
LeClerc, Roger - LB
Lee, Herman - T
Leeuwenberg, Dick - T
Leggett, Earl - T
Livingston, Andy - B
McRae, Ben - B
Marconi, Joe - B

Martin, Bill - E
Morris, Johnny - B
Morris, Larry - LB
Murphy, Denny - T
O'Bradovich, Ed - E
Petitbon, Rich - B
Purnell, Jim - LB
Pyle, Mike - C
Rabold, Mike - G
Reilly, "Mike" - LB
Sayers, Gale - B
Seals, George - G
Smith, Ron - B
Taylor, "Rosey" - B
Wade, Bill - Q
Wetoska, Bob - T
Whitsell, Dave - B

Franklin, Bob - B
Garcia, Jim - E
Glass, Bill - E
Green, Ernie - B
Groza, Lou - K
Hickerson, Gene - G
Houston, Jim - LB
Howell, Mike - B
Hutchinson, Tom - E
Johnson, Walt - T
Kanicki, Jim - T
Kelly, Leroy - B
Lindsey, Dale - LB
McNeil, Clif - B
Memmelaar, Dale - G

Modzelewski, Dick - T
Morrow, John - C
Ninowski, Jim - Q
Parrish, Bernie - B
Roberts, Walt - B
Ryan, Frank - Q
Scales, Charley - B
Schafrath, Dick - T
Sczurek, Stan - LB
Smith, Ralph - E
Warfield, Paul - E
Wiggin, Paul - E
Williams, Sid - LB
Wooten, John - G

1965 CLEVELAND BROWNS
COACH - Blanton Collier
1st 11-3-0
(Lost title to Green Bay, 23-12)

Barnes, Erich - B
Beach, Walt - B
Benz, Larry - G
Brewer, John - E
Brown, Jim - B
Brown, John - T

Caleb, Jamie - B
Clark, Monte - T
Collins, Gary - E
Costello, Vince - LB
Fichtner, Ross - B
Fiss, Galen - LB

1965 DALLAS COWBOYS
COACH - Tom Landry
2nd 7-7-0

Andrie, George - E
Bishop, Don - B
Boeke, Jim - T
Clarke, Frank - E

Colvin, Jim - T
Connelly, Mike - G & C
Dial, "Buddy" - E
Diehl, John - T

Donohue, Leon - G
Dunn, Perry Lee - B
Edwards, Dave - LB
Gaechter, Mike - B
Gent, "Pete" - E
Green, Cornell - B
Hayes, Bob - E
Hays, Harold - LB
Howley, Chuck - LB
Isbell, Joe Bob - G
Johnson, Mitch - G
Jordan, Lee Roy - LB
Kupp, Jake - G
Lilly, Bob - T
Livingston, Warren - B
Logan, Obert - B
Manders, Dave - G & C
Meredith, Don - Q
Morton, Craig - Q

Neely, Ralph - T
Norman, Pettis - E
Perkins, Don - B
Porterfield, Garry - E
Pugh, Jethro - E
Reeves, Dan - B
Renfro, Mel - B
Rhome, Jerry - Q
Ridgway, Colin - K
Smith, J. D. - B
Stephens, Larry - E
Stiger, Jim - B
Talbert, Don - T
Tubbs, Jerry - LB
Villanueva, Danny - K
Wayt, Russ - LB
Whitfied, A. D. - B
Youmans, Maury - E

1965 LOS ANGELES RAMS
COACH - Harland Svare
7th 4-10-0

Baker, Terry - B
Bass, Dick - B
Brown, Fred - LB
Brown, Willie - B
Byrd, Mac - LB
Carollo, Joe - T
Chuy, Don - G
Cowan, Charley - T
Currie, Dan - LB
Gabriel, Roman - Q
Gossett, Bruce - K
Grier, "Rosey" - T
Guillory, Tony - LB
Heckard, Steve - E
Iman, Ken - C
Jones, Dave - E
Josephson, Les - B
Kilgore, Jon - K
Lamson, Chuck - B
Livingston, Cliff - LB
Lothridge, Billy - Q
Lundy, Lamar - E
McDonald, Tom - B

McIlhany, Dan - B
McKeever, Marlin - E
Marchlewski, Frank - C
Martin, Aaron - B
Meador, Ed - B
Molden, Frank - T
Munson, Bill - Q
Olsen, Merlin - T
Pillath, Roger - T
Powell, Tim - E
Richardson, Jerry - B
Scibelli, Joe - G
Smith, Bobby - B
Smith, Ron - Q
Snow, Jack - E
Stiger, Jim - B
Strofolino, Mike - LB
Truax, Bill - E
Varrichione, Frank - T
Wendryhoski, Joe - C
Williams, Clancy - B
Wilson, Ben - B
Woodlief, Doug - LB

1965 DETROIT LIONS
COACH - Harry Gilmer
6th 6-7-1

Barr, Terry - B
Brown, Roger - T
Clark, Ernie - LB
Cogdill, Gail - E
Felts, Bob - B
Flanagan, Ed - C
Gibbons, Jim - E
Gonzaga, John - G & T
Gordy, John - G
Hand, Larry - E
Henderson, John - E
Hilgenberg, Wally - LB
Hill, Jim - B
Izo, George - Q
Karras, Alex - T
Karras, Ted - G
Kearney, Jim - B
Kramer, Ron - E
Lane, Dick - B
LeBeau, Dick - B
Looney, Joe Don - B
Lucci, Mike - LB
McCord, Darris - E

Maher, Bruce - B
Marsh, Amos - B
Myers, Tom - Q
Nowatzke, Tom - B
Pietrosante, Nick - B
Plum, Milt - Q
Rasmussen, Wayne - B
Rush, Jerry - T
Sanders, Daryl - T
Schmidt, Joe - LB
Shoals, Roger - T
Simon, Jim - LB & G
Smith, Bobby - B
Studstill, Pat - B
Thompson, Bobby - B
Vaughn, Tom - B
Walker, Wayne - LB
Watkins, Tom - B
Wells, Warren - E
Whitlow, Bob - C
Williams, Sam   E

1965 MINNESOTA VIKINGS
COACH - Norm Van Brocklin
5th 7-7-0

Alderman, Grady - T
Barnes, Billy Ray - B
Bedsole, Hal - E
Berry, Bob - Q
Bowie, Larry - G
Brown, Bill - B
Byers, Ken - G
Calland, Lee - B
Cox, Fred - K
Dickson, Paul - T
Eller, Carl - E
Flatley, Paul - E
Hall, Tom - B
Hawkins, "Rip" - LB
Hill, Gary - B
James, Dick - B
Jobko, Bill - LB
Jordan, Jeff - B
Kassulke, Karl - B
King, Phil - B
Kirby, John - LB

Larsen, Gary - T
Mackabee, Earsell - B
Marshall, Jim - E
Mason, Tom - B
Osborn, Dave - B
Phillips, Jim - E
Prestel, Jim - T
Rentzel, Lance - E
Rose, George - B
Sharockman, Ed - B
Smith, Gordon - E
Sunde, Milt - G
Sutton, Archie - T
Tarkenton, Fran - Q
Tingelhoff, Mick - C
VanderKelen, Ron - Q
Vargo, Larry - B
Walden, Bob - K
Warwick, Lonnie - LB
Winston, Roy - LB
Young, Jim - B

1965 GREEN BAY PACKERS
COACH - Vince Lombardi
1st 10-3-1
(Beat Baltimore in playoff, 13-10,
overtime; beat Cleveland for
title, 23-12)

Adderley, Herb - B
Aldridge, Lionel - E
Anderson, "Bill" - E
Bowman, Ken - C
Bratkowski, "Zeke" - Q
Brown, Tom - B
Caffey, Lee Roy - LB
Chandler, Don - K
Claridge, Denny - Q
Coffey, Junior - B
Crutcher, Tom - LB
Curry, Bill - C
Dale, Carroll - E
Davis, Willie - E
Dowler, Boyd - E
Fleming, Marv - E
Gregg, Forrest - T
Gremminger, "Hank" - B
Grimm, Dan - G
Hart, Doug - B

Hornung, Paul - B
Jacobs, Al - B
Jeter, Bob - B
Jordan, Henry - T
Kostelnik, Ron - T
Kramer, Gerry - G
Long, Bob - B
McGee, Max - E
Marshall, Dick - T
Moore, Tom - B
Nitschke, Ray - LB
Pitts, Elijah - B
Robinson, "Dave" - LB
Skoronski, Bob - T
Starr, "Bart" - Q
Taylor, Jim - B
Thurston, Fred - G
Voss, Lloyd - T
Wood, Willie - B
Wright, Steve - T

1965 NEW YORK GIANTS
COACH - "Allie" Sherman
2nd 7-7-0

Adamchik, Ed - C
Anderson, Roger - T
Bolin, "Bookie" - G
Brown, Rosie - T
Bundra, Mike - T
Carr, Henry - B
Carroll, Jim - LB
Case, "Pete" - G
Childs, Clarence - B
Condren, Glen - E
Costello, Tom - LB
Crespino, Bob - E
Davis, Roger - G
Davis, "Rosey" - E
Frederickson, "Tucker" - B

Hillebrand, Jerry - LB
Jones, Homer - E
Katcavage, Jim - E
Koy, Ernie - B
Lacey, Bob - E
LaLonde, Roger - T
Larson, Greg - T & C
Lasky, Frank - T
Lockhart, "Spider" - B
Lovetere, John - T
Lynch, Dick - B
McDowell, John - T
Mercein, "Chuck" - B
Morrall, Earl - Q
Morrison, Joe - B

O' Brien, Dave - T
Patton, Jim - B
Reed, Smith - B
Scholtz, Bob - C
Shofner, Del - E
Slaby, Lou - LB
Stynchula, Andy - E
Swain, Bill - LB
Thomas, Aaron - E

Thurlow, Steve - B
Timberlake, Bob - Q
Underwood, Olen - LB
Walker, "Mickey" - G
Webb, Allen - B
Wheelwright, Ernie - B
Williams, Willie - B
Wood, Gary - Q

1965 PHILADELPHIA EAGLES
COACH - Joe Kuharich
5th 5-9-0

Baker, "Sam" - K
Baughan, Max - LB
Blaine, Ed - G
Brown, Bob - T
Brown, Tim - B
Concannon, Jack - Q
Crabb, Claude - B
Cronin, Bill - E
Cross, Irv - B
Gill, Roger - B
Glass, Glenn - B
Goodwin, Ron - E
Graham, Dave - T
Gros, Earl - B
Heck, Ralph - LB
Hill, Fred - E
Hill, King - Q
Howell, Lane - T
Hoyem, Lynn - G
Hultz, Don - LB & E
Kelly, Jim - E
Khayat, Ed - T

Lang, Israel - B
Lloyd, Dave - LB
Matson, Ollie - B
Meyers, John - T
Morgan, Mike - LB
Nelson, Ai - B
Nettles, Jim - B
Peters, Floyd - T
Poage, Ray - E
Ramsey. Nate - B
Recher, Dave - C
Retzlaff, "Pete" - E
Richards, Bob - E
Ringo, Jim - C
Scarpati, Joe - B
Shann, Bob - B
Skaggs, Jim - T
Snead, Norm = Q
Tarasovic, George LB & E
Wells, Hal - LB
Will, Erwin - T
Woodeschick, Tom - B

1965 PITTSBURGH STEELERS
COACH - Mike Nixon
7th 2-12-0

Adamchik, Ed - T
Allen, Duane - E
Baker, John - E
Ballman, Gary - B
Bradshaw, Charles - T
Bradshaw, Jim - B
Breedlove, Rod - LB
Breen, Gene - LB
Brown, Ed - Q
Butler, Jim - B
Campbell, John - LB
Clark, Mike - E & K
Daniel, Willie - B
Folkins, Lee - E
Gunnels, "Riley" - T
Henson, Ken - C
Hilton, John - E
Hinton, Chuck - T
Hoak, Don - B
Hohn, Bob - B
Hunter, Art - C
James, Dan - T
Jefferson, Roy - E
Johnson, John Henry - B
Keys, Brady - B

Kortas, Ken - T
Lambert, Frank - K
Lemek, Ray - T
Lind, "Mike" - B
McGee, Ben - E
Mack, "Red" - B
Magac, Mike - G
Mallick, Fran - T
Mansfield, Ray - T & C
Martha, Paul - B
Messner, Max - LB
Nelsen, Bill - Q
Nichols, Bob - T
Peaks, Clarence - B
Pine, Ed - LB
Pottios, Myron - LB
Powers, John - E
Sandusky, Mike - G
Sapp, Theron - B
Schmitz, Bob - LB
Sherman, Bob - B
Simmons, Jerry - B
Thomas, Clendon - B
Wade, Tom - Q
Woodson, Marv - B

1965 ST. LOUIS CARDINALS
COACH - Wally Lemm
5th 5-9-0

Alford, Mike - C
Bailey, "Monk" - B

Bakken, Jim - K
Brumm, Don - E

Burson, Jim - B
Childress, Joe - B
Conrad, Bobby Joe - B
Cook, Ed - T
Crenshaw, Willis - B
DeMarco, Bob - C
Fisher, Pat - E
Gambrell, Billy - E
Gautt, Prentice - B
Goode, Irv - G
Gray, Ken - G
Hammack, Mal - LB & E
Humphrey, "Buddy" - Q
Johnson, Charley - Q
Koman, Bill - LB
Logan, Chuck - E
McMillan, Ernie - T
McQuarters, Ed - T
Meggyesy, Dave - LB
Meinert, Dale - LB
Melinkovich, Mike - E

Nofsinger, Terry - Q
Ogden, Ray - B
Owens, Luke - T
Randle, "Sonny" - E
Redmond, Tom - E
Reynolds, Bob - T
Robb, Joe - E
Rushing, Marion - LB
Silas, Sam - T
Silvestri, Carl - B
Simmons, Dave - LB
Smith, Jackie - E
Sortun, Rick - G
Stallings, Larry - LB
Stovall, Jerry - B
Thornton, Bill - B
Triplett, Bill - B
Turner, Herschel - G
Walker, Charley - E
Wilson, Larry - B
Woodson, Abe - B

1965 SAN FRANCISCO 49ERS
COACH - Jack Christiansen
4th 7-6-1

Alexander, Kermit - B
Beard, Ed - T
Bosley, Bruce - C
Brodie, John - Q
Burke, Vern - E
Casey, Bernie - E
Cerne, Joe - C
Chapple, Jack - LB
Colchico, Dan - E
Crow, John David - B
Davis, Tom - K
Dean, Floyd - LB
Donnelly, George - B
Dowdle, Mike - LB
Harrison, Bob - LB
Hazeltine, Matt - LB
Johnson, Jim - B
Johnson, Rudy - B
Kimbrough, Elbert - B
Kopay, Dave - B
Krueger, Charley - T
Lakes, Roland - T

LaRose, Dan - E & T
Lewis, Gary - B
McFarland, Kay - B
Mertens, Jerry - B
Messer, Dale - B
Miller, Clark - E
Mira, George - Q
Mudd, Howard - G
Norton, Jim - B
Parks, Dave - E
Poole, Bob - E
Rock, Walt - T
Rohde, Len - T
Rubke, Karl - LB
Sieminski, Charley - T
Stickles, Monty - E
Swinford, Wayne - B
Thomas, John - G
Wilcox, Dave - LB
Willard, Ken - B
Wilson, Jim - G

1965 WASHINGTON REDSKINS
COACH - Bill McPeak
4th 6-8-0

Adams, Willie - LB
Atkins, Pervis - B
Briggs, Bob - B
Carpenter, Pres - E
Carr, Jim - LB
Casares, Ric - B
Coia, Angelo - E
Croftcheck, Don - G
Crossan, Dave - C
Dess, Darrell - G
Hanburger, Chris - LB
Harris, Rickie - B
Hauss, Len - C
Huff, "Sam" - LB
Hughley, George - B
Hunter, "Bill" - B
Jencks, Bob - K & E
Jurgensen, "Sonny" - Q
Kammerer, Carl - LB

Krause, Paul - B
Lewis, Dan - B
Mazurek, Fred - B
Mitchell, Bob - B
O'Brien, Francis - T
Paluck, John - E
Pelligrini, Bob - LB
Promuto, Vince - G
Quinlan, Bill - E
Reed, Bob - G
Reger, John - LB
Richter, "Pat" - E
Rutgens, Joe - T
Sample, John - B
Sanders, Lon - B
Seedborg, John - K
Shiner, Dick - Q
Shorter, Jim - B
Smith, Jerry - E

Snidow, Ron - E
Snowden, Jim - T
Steffen, Jim - B

Taylor, Charley - B
Walters, Tom - B
Williams, Fred - T

1965 BOSTON PATRIOTS (AFL)
COACH - Mike Holovak
3rd 4-8-2

Addison, Tom - LB
Antwine, Houston - T
Bellino, Joe - B
Buonoconti, Nick - LB
Burton, Ron - B
Canale, Justin - G
Cappelletti, Gino - E
Colclough, Jim - E
Cunningham, Jay - B
Dawson, Bill - E
Dee, Bob - E
Dukes, Mike - LB
Eisenauer, Larry - E
Farmer, Lonnie - LB
Felt, Dick - B
Garrett, John - B
Garron, Larry - B
Graham, Art - E
Graves, White - B
Hall, Ron - B
Hennessey, Tom - B

Hunt, Jim - E
Johnson, Ellis - B
Long, Charley - G
Meixler, Ed - LB
Morris, Jon - C
Nance, Jim - B
Neighbors, Bill - G
Neville, Tom - T
Oakes, Don - T
O'Hanley, Ross - B
Parilli, "Babe" - Q
Pyne, George - T
Romeo, Tony - E
Rudolph, John - LB
St. Jean, Len - E
Shonta, Chuck - B
Webb, Don - B
Whalen, Jim - E
Wilson, Ed - Q
Yates, Bob - T
Yewcic, Tom - Q

1965 BUFFALO BILLS (AFL)
COACH - Lou Saban
1st 10-3-1
(Beat San Diego for title, 23-0)

Auer, Joe - B
Barber, Stu - T
Bass, Glenn - E
Behrman, Dave - C
Bemiller, Al - G
Byrd, George - B
Carlton, Wray - B
Clarke, Hagood - B
Costa, Paul - E
Day, Tom - E
Dubenion, Elbert - B
Dunaway, Jim - T
Edgerson, Booker - B
Ferguson, Charley - E
Flint, George - G
Gogolak, Pete - K
Groman, Bill - E
Hudlow, Floyd - E
Hudson, Dick - T
Jacobs, Harry - LB
Janik, Tom - B
Joe, Billy - B
Keating, Tom - T

Kemp, Jack - Q
LaMonica, Daryle - Q
Laskey, Bill - LB
McDole, Roland - E
Maguire, Paul - LB
Meredith, Dud - T
Mills, "Pete" - B
O'Donnell, Joe - T
Roberson, "Bo" - B
Rutkowski, Ed - B
Saimes, George - B
Schmidt, Henry - T
Schottenheimer, Marty - LB
Sestak, Tom - T
Shaw, Bill - G
Smith, Bob - B
Stone, Don - B
Stratton, Mike - LB
Sykes, Gene - B
Tracey, John - LB
Warlick, Ernie - E
Warner, Charley - B

1965 DENVER BRONCOS (AFL)
COACH - Mac Speedie
4th 4-10-0

Barry, Odell - E
Bernet, Lee - T
Bramlett, John - LB
Breitenstein, Bob - T
Brown, Willie - B
Bussell, Gerry - B
Carmichael, Paul - B
Cooke, Ed - E

Cummings, Ed - LB
Danenhauer, El - T
Denson, Al - B
Dixon, Hewritt - E
Erlandson, Tom - LB
Farr, Miller - B
Gilchrist, "Cookie" - B
Gonsoulin, "Goose" - B

Griffin, John - B
Hayes, Wendell - B
Haynes, Abner - B
Hohman, Jon - G
Hopkins, Jerry - LB
Jacobs, Ray - T
Janarette, Charley - T
Jeter, Gene - LB
Kroner, Gary - K
Kubala, Ray - C
Lee, Jackie - Q
Leetzow, Max - E
Lester, Darrell - B
McCormick, John - Q

McCullough, Bob - G
McGeever, John - B
McMillin, Jim - B
Mitchell, Charley - B
Moore, Leroy - E
Nomina, Tom - T
Parker, Charley - G
Scarpitto, Bob - B
Slaughter, "Mickey" - Q
Sturm, Jerry - G
Taylor, Lionel - E
Thibert, Jim - LB
Thompson, Jim - T
Wilson, Nemiah - B

1965 HOUSTON OILERS (AFL)
COACH - Hugh Taylor
4th 4-10-0

Appleton, Scott - E
Baker, John - LB
Banfield, "Tony" - B
Bishop, "Sonny" - G
Blanda, George - Q
Brabham, Dan - LB
Burrell, Ode - B
Cheeks, B. W. - B
Cline, Doug - LB
Compton, Dick - B
Cutsinger, Gary - E
Evans, Norm - T
Evans, Bob - E
Floyd, Don - E
Frazier, Charley - E
Frazier, Wayne - C
Frazier, Willie - E
Frongillo, John - C
Glick, Fred - B
Goode, Tom - LB
Hayes, Jim - T
Hennigan, Charley - B
Hicks, Wilmer - B
Hoffman, Dalton - B

Hooligan, Henry - B
Husmann, Ed - T
Jackson, Bob - B
Jancik, Bob - B
Jaquess, Pete - B
Kinderman, Keith - B
Kinney, George - E
McFadin, "Bud" - T
McLeod, Bob - E
Maples, Bob - LB
Michael, Dick - T
Norton, Jim - B
Onesti, Larry - LB
Rieves, Charles - LB
Spikes, Jack - B
Strahan, Ray - E
Suggs, Walt - T
Talamini, Bob - G
Tolar, Charley - B
Trull, Don - Q
Weir, Sam - E
Williams, Maxie - T
Wittenborn, John - G

1965 KANSAS CITY CHIEFS (AFL)
COACH - "Hank" Stram
3rd 7-5-2

Arbanas, Fred - E
Beathard, Pete - Q
Bell, Bob - E & LB
Biodrowski, Denny - G
Branch, Mel - E
Brannan, Sol - B
Brooker, Tom - E
Buchanan, "Buck" - T
Budde, Ed - G
Burford, Chris - E
Carolan, Reg - E
Caveness, Ron - LB
Coan, Bert - B
Corey, Walt - LB
Cornelison, Jerry - T
Dawson, Len - Q
Dotson, Al - T
Farrier, Curt - T
Fraser, Jim - LB
Gilliam, Jon - C
Headrick, Sherrill - LB
Hill, Dave - T

Hill, Mack Lee - B
Holub, Emil - LB
Hunt, Bob - B
Hurston, Charley - E
Jackson, Frank - B
Lothamer, Ed - T
McClinton, Curt - B
Mays, Gerry - T
Merz, Curt - G
Mitchell, Willie - B
Pitts, Frank - E
Ply, Bob - B
Reynolds, Al - G
Robinson, John - B
Rosdahl, "Hatch" - T
Stover, "Smokey" - LB
Taylor, Otis - E
Tyrer, Jim - T
Williamson, Fred - B
Wilson, Jerry - B

1965 NEW YORK JETS (AFL)
COACH - "Webb" Ewbank
2nd 5-8-1

Abruzzeze, Ray - B
Atkinson, Al - LB
Baird, Bill - B
Baker, Ralph - LB
Biggs, Verlon - E
Browning, Charley - B
Carson, Kern - B
DeFelice, Nick - T
DeLuca, Sam - G
Dukes, Mike - LB
Evans, Jim - B
Ficca, Dan - G
Gordon, Cornell - B
Grantham, Larry - LB
Harris, Jim - T
Heeter, Gene - E
Herman, Dave - G
Hill, Winston - T
Hudock, Mike - C
Hudson, Jim - B
Iacavazzi, Cosmo - B
Johnson, "Curley" - B
McDaniel, "Wahoo" - LB
Mackey, Dee - E

Mathis, Bill - B
Maynard, Don - B
Namath, Joe - Q
O'Mahoney, Jim - LB
Paulson, Dainard - B
Perrault, Pete - G
Philbin, Gerry - E
Plunkett, Sherman - T
Rademacher, Bill - B
Robinson, Jerry - E
Rochester, Paul - T
Sauer, George - E
Schmitt, John - C
Schweickert, Bob - B
Simkus, Arnie - T
Smolinski, Mark - B
Snell, Matt - B
Taliaferro, Mike - Q
Torczon, Laverne - E
Turner, Jim - Q & K
Turner, "Bake" - B
Washington, Clyde - B
West, Willie - B
Wilder, Al - E

Kirner, Gary - T
Kocourek, Dave - E
Ladd, Ernie - T
Lincoln, Keith - B
Lowe, Paul - B
MacKinnon, Jacque - E
Mitchell, Ed - G
Mix, Ron - T
Moore, Fred - T
Norton, Don - E
Park, Ernie - G
Petrich, Bob - E

Redman, Rick - LB
Shea, Pat - G
Sweeney, Walt - G
Taylor, Sam - E
Tensi, Steve - Q
Travenio, Herb - K
Warren, Jim - B
Westmoreland, Dick - B
Whitehead, "Bud" - B
Wright, Ernie - T
Zeman, Bob - B

1965 OAKLAND RAIDERS (AFL)
COACH - Al Davis
2nd 8-5-1

Atkins, Pervis - E
Biletnikoff, Fred - E
Birdwell, Dan - T
Budness, Bill - LB
Cannon, Billy - E
Conners, Dan - T
Costa, Dave - LB
Daniels, Clem - B
Davidson, Ben - E
Davison, "Cotton" - Q
Diehl, John - T
Flores, Tom - Q
Gibson, Claude - B
Grayson, Dave - B
Hagberg, Roger - B
Hawkins, Wayne - G
Hermann, Dick - LB
Herock, Ken - E
Krakoski, Joe - B
Lassiter, Ike - E
McCloughan, Kent - B
Marinovich, Marv - G

Matsos, Arch - LB
Mercer, Mike - K
Miller, Al - B
Mingo, Gene - B
Mirich, Rex - T
Mischak, Bob - G
Oats, Carl - E
Otto, "Gus" - LB
Otto, Jim - C
Powell, Art - E
Powers, Warren - B
Rice, Ken -T
Roberson, "Bo" - B
Schuh, Harry - G
Svihus, Bob - T
Todd, Larry - B
Williams, Howie - B
Williamson, John - LB
Wood, "Dick" - Q
Youso, Frank - T
Zecher, Dick - T

1965 SAN DIEGO CHARGERS (AFL)
COACH - Sid Gillman
1st 9-2-3
(Lost title to Buffalo, 23-0)

Allen, Chuck - LB
Allison, Jim - B
Alworth, Lance - B
Breaux, Don - Q
Buncom, Frank - LB
Carpenter, Ron - LB
Carson, Kern - B
Degen, Dick - LB
DeLong, Steve - E
Duncan, Les - B
Faison, Earl - E

Farr, Miller - B
Farris, John - G
Foster, Gene - B
Graham, Ken - B
Gross, George - T
Gruneisen, Sam - C
Hadl, John - Q
Harris, Dick - B
Horton, Bob - LB
Jacobson, John - B
Kindig, Howard - E

1966

NATIONAL FOOTBALL LEAGUE

EASTERN DIVISION

	Won	Lost	Tied	Pct.
Dallas	10	3	1	.769
Cleveland	9	5	0	.643
Philadelphia	9	5	0	.643
St. Louis	8	5	1	.615
Washington	7	7	0	.500
Pittsburgh	5	8	1	.385
Atlanta	3	11	0	.214
New York	1	12	1	.077

WESTERN DIVISION

	Won	Lost	Tied	Pct.
Green Bay	12	2	0	.857
Baltimore	9	5	0	.643
Los Angeles	8	6	0	.571
San Francisco	6	6	2	.500
Chicago	5	7	2	.417
Detroit	4	9	1	.308
Minnesota	4	9	1	.308

CHAMPIONSHIP

Green Bay 34; Dallas 27

AMERICAN FOOTBALL LEAGUE

EASTERN DIVISION

	Won	Lost	Tied	Pct.
Buffalo	9	4	1	.692
Boston	8	4	2	.667
New York	6	6	2	.500
Houston	3	11	0	.214
Miami	3	11	0	.214

WESTERN DIVISION

	Won	Lost	Tied	Pct.
Kansas City	11	2	1	.846
Oakland	8	5	1	.615
San Diego	7	6	1	.538
Denver	4	10	0	.286

CHAMPIONSHIP

Kansas City 31, Buffalo 7
SUPER BOWL PLAYOFF
Green Bay (NFL) 35;
Kansas City (AFL) 10
1966 NFL CHAMPIONSHIP
(Cotton Bowl, Dallas, Jan. 1, 1967)
Attendance: 75,504.

Green Bay	14	14	7	6	34
Dallas	14	3	3	7	27

Touchdowns: Pitts, Grabowski, Reeves, Perkins, Dale, Dowler, McGee, Clarke.
Field Goals: Villanueva 2.
PAT's: Chandler 4, Villanueva 2.
Coaches: Vincent Lombardi (Green Bay), Tom Landry (Dallas).

THE GAME

Green Bay scored first, Elijah Pitts going over with a pass from Bart Starr from 17 yards. Chandler converted. On the following kickoff, Mel Renfro of Dallas fumbled when tackled on his 18 and Jim Grabowski picked it up and scored. Chandler again converted.

Dallas rallied to tie the game in the first quarter with Reeves scoring from the three, Perkins from the 23, plus two points by Villanueva.

Carroll Dale put Green Bay ahead for good in the second period on a 51-yard pass play from Starr and Chandler made it 21-14. Villanueva kicked a field goal for Dallas from the 11 and the half ended 21-17.

Villanueva kicked another from the 32 early in the second half for 21-20 but Starr's 16-yard pass to Dowler and Chandler's kick gave the Packers an eight point lead. In the final quarter, Green Bay scored another touchdown on Starr's fourth TD pass, a 28-yarder to Max McGee. Dallas blocked the conversion attempt by Chandler (They also blocked a field goal attempt by Chandler.) Dallas made it 34-27 late in the last period on Meredith's 68-yard pass play to Clarke and Villanueva's conversion.

In the final 2½ minutes, Dallas got the ball on Chandler's weak punt to the Green Bay 47. Meredith passed to Clarke for 21 yards, then to Clarke again near the goalline where he was fouled by Tom Brown of the Packers. Dallas failed to score in four plays, the last one ending in an interception of Meredith's pass by Tom Brown.

1966 AFL CHAMPIONSHIP

(War Memorial Stadium, Buffalo, Jan. 1, 1967)
Attendance: 42,080.

Kansas City 31; Buffalo 7

SCORING

First period: K.C.—Arbanas, 29, pass from Dawson (Mercer, kick). Buffalo—Dubenion, 69, pass from Kemp (Iusteg, kick).

Second period: K.C.—Taylor, 29, pass from Dawson (Mercer, kick). K. C. FG, Mercer, 43.

Third period—None.

Fourth period: K.C.—Garrett, 1 foot, run (Mercer, kick). KC.—Garrett, 18, run (Mercer, kick).

1966 INTERLEAGUE "SUPER BOWL"
(Los Angeles Coliseum, Jan. 15, 1967)
Attendance 63,036
Green Bay (35)

Green Bay	7	7	14	7	35
Kansas City	0	10	0	0	10

Touchdowns: McGee 2, Pitts 2, Taylor, McClinton.
Field Goals—Mercer.
PAT's: Chandler 5, Mercer.
Coaches: Vincent Lombardi (Green Bay), Henry Stram (Kansas City).

THE GAME

Green Bay's flanker, Boyd Dowler, was injured in the third play and replaced by Max McGee. McGee scored first on a 37 yard pass play from Bart Starr with Don Chandler adding the extra point. Kansas City tied the game in the second quarter when Len Dawson passed 7 yards to Curtis McClinton over the goal. Mike Mercer added the seventh point.

Green Bay went ahead to stay in the same period on Jim Taylor's 7 yard sweep and Chandler again converted. The Chiefs made in 14-10 at halftime on Mercer's 31-yard field goal.

On Kansas City's first series after the second half kickoff, Willie Wood of Green Bay intercepted Dawson's pass and took it to the Chief's five. Elijah Pitts scored on the next play and Chandler converted. McGee scored his second TD in the same period on a 13-yard pass from Starr.

Pitts scored again for the Packers in the final quarter on a one-yard smash and Chandler added his fifth extra point. Kansas City was stopped by the Packer defense in the second half and got into Green Bay country only once—to the 48 yard line.

The winning Green Bay players received a guaranteed $15,000 each, the losing Chiefs got $7,500.

Bart Starr, Green Bay quarterback was named the games most valuable player and was awarded a sports car. He had completed 16 of 24 passes with one intercepted.

NFL LEADERS: Rushing—Gale Sayers (Chicago), 1,231 yds.; Scoring—Bruce Gossett (Los Angeles), 113; Passing—Bryan Starr (Green Bay); Pass Receiving—Charles Taylor (Washington), 72; Field Goals—Bruce Gossett (Los Angeles), 28, new record; Punting—David Lee (Baltimore), 45.6 yds.; Interceptions—Lawrence Wilson (St. Louis), 10.

AFL LEADERS: Rushing—James Nance (Boston), 1,458 yds.; Scoring—Gino Cappelletti (Boston), 119; Passing—Leonard Dawson (Kansas City); Pass Receiving—Lance Alworth (San Diego), 73; Field Goals—Michael Mercer (Oakland-Kansas City), 21; Punting—Robert Scarpitto (Denver), 45.6 yds.; Interceptions—John Robinson (Kansas City), 10.

HALL OF FAME: New members—Players Charles Bednarik, Robert Layne, Kenneth Strong, Joseph Stydahar and Emlen Tunnell. Non-players Paul Brown (coach), Charles Bidwill (owner), Daniel Reeves (owner).

COACHES: In the NFL, Norbert Hecker was the first head coach of the new Atlanta Falcons. George Allen replaced Harland Svare at Los Angeles; William Austin replaced Michael Nixon at Pittsburgh; Charles Winner replaced Walter Lemm at St. Louis; Otto Graham replaced William McPeak at Washington. Thomas Fears was named first coach of the New Orleans Saints for 1967.

In the AFL, Joel Collier replaced Louis Saban at Buffalo; Walter Lemm replaced Hugh Taylor at Houston; Mac Speedie was replaced by Ray Malavasi in midseason at Denver and Malavasi was replaced by Louis Saban at the end of the season. George Wilson was the first coach of the new Miami Dolphins.

FIRST DRAFT PICK: NFL—Thomas Nobis, by Atlanta, signed with Atlanta. AFL—James Grabowski, by Miami; signed with Green Bay (NFL).

NOTES: On June 8, the NFL and AFL announced that a merger agreement had been completed leading to full integration with 28 teams for the 1970 season. The NFL would add one team for 1967 and this franchise was awarded to New Orleans.

The AFL would add one team for 1968 and two more before 1970.

An interleague championship game—soon called the "Super Bowl" would be played each year, starting with the 1966 winners of the NFL and AFL titles.

The NFL announced that it would divide its 16 teams into four divisions starting in 1967. Two divisions under both the Western and Eastern conferences would play for the conference titles at the end of the season, then the conference winners would play for the NFL championship and the right to meet the AFL champion.

The Western Conference was split into the Coastal Division (Atlanta, Baltimore, Los Angeles and San Francisco) and the Central Division (Chicago, Detroit, Green Bay, Minnesota) with these lineups assured for 1967 and 1968.

In the Eastern Conference for 1967 it would be the Federal Division (Cleveland,

New York, Pittsburgh and St. Louis) and the Capitol Division (Dallas, New Orleans, Philadelphia and Washington). In 1968, New Orleans and New York would switch divisions.

Bart Starr of Green Bay was intercepted only three times in 251 pass attempts during the regular season (new record) and was not intercepted at all in the title game with Dallas in 28 attempts. He threw one interception against Kansas City in the Super Bowl game in 24 attempts.

James Brown, Cleveland fullback, retired after leading the league in rushing eight times and in scoring once.

Garo Yepremian (Detroit) kicked six field goals (33, 26, 15, 17, 28, 32 yds.), new record, against Minnesota, Nov. 13.

Los Angeles Rams gained 38 first downs, new record, against New York, Nov. 13.

Henry Carr, New York back, ran 101 yards (TD) with intercepted pass against Los Angeles, Nov. 13.

Charles Gogolak, Washington, kicked nine extra points (tied record) against New York, Nov. 27.

Karl Sweetan, Detroit, passed 99 yards (TD) to Pat Studstill (tied record) against Baltimore, Oct. 16.

Washington (72) and New York (41) scored record number of points for two teams in one game, Nov. 27. Washington's 72 was also record for one team one game.

Herb Adderly, Green Bay back, tied record with fifth touchdown by interception in career, a 68 yarder, against Atlanta, Oct. 23.

Charles Howley, Dallas linebacker, scored 97-yard TD on fumble recovery against Atlanta, Oct. 2.

Timmy Brown, Philadelphia back, scored two TD's on kickoff returns (record) of 93 and 90 yards against Dallas, Nov. 6.

Dallas defense threw Pittsburgh passers 12 times (record), Nov. 20.

Deaths during the year included:

Charles Dressen, Chicago Staleys and Racine quarterback (1920-23), Aug. 10;

Richard Christy, Pittsburgh, Boston, New York (Jets) back, (1958-63) in car accident, Aug. 7;

Maurice Bray, Pittsburgh tackle (1935-36) shot dead by burglar, Dec. 9;

Joseph Bach, head coach Pittsburgh (1935-36 and 1952-53), Oct. 24;

Edward Erdelatz, head coach Oakland Raiders (AFL) (1960), Nov. 10;

Fred "Duke" Slater, Rock Island, Milwaukee, Chicago Cardinals tackle (1922-31), Aug. 14;

Samuel Stein, Newark, Staten Island, New York Giants, Brooklyn end (1929-32), March 31;

Dale Lee Gentry, Los Angeles Dons (AAFC) end (1946-48), Jan. 30;

Ray Krouse, New York Giants, Detroit, Baltimore, Washington tackle (1951-60), April 7.

Richard Barwegan, New York Yankees (AAFC), Baltimore (AAFC), Baltimore (NFL), Chicago Bears guard (1947-54).

Keith Molesworth, Portsmouth, Chicago Bears qback (1930-37); head coach Baltimore 1953.

1966 ATLANTA FALCONS
COACH - Norbert Hecker
7th 3-11-0

Anderson, Roger - T	Morris, Larry - LB
Anderson, Taz - E	Nobis, Tom - LB
Barnes, Gary - E	Rassas, Nick - B
Burke, Vern - E	Reaves, Ken - B
Calland, Lee - B	Rector, Ron - B
Claridge, Dennis - Q	Reese, Guy - T
Coffey, Junior - B	Richards, Bob - E
Coia, Angelo - E	Richardson, Jerry - B
Cook, Ed - T	Ridlehuber, Preston - B
Dunn, Perry Lee - B	Riggle, Bob - B
Glass, Glenn - B	Rubke, Karl - LB
Grimm, Dan - G	Rushing, Marion - LB
Hawkins, Alex - B	Scales, Charley - B
Heck, Ralph - LB	Sherlag, Bob - E
Hutchinson, Tom - E	Sieminski, Charley - T
Jobko, Bill - LB	Silvestri, Carl - B
Johnson, Randy - Q	Simon, Jim - LB
Johnson, Rudy - B	Sloan, Steve - Q
Jones, Jerry - T	Smith, Ron - B
Kirouac, Lou - T	Szczecko, Joe - T
Koeper, Dick - T	Talbert, Don - T
Linden, Errol - T	Tollefson, Tom - B
Lothridge, Bill - K	Traynham, Wade - K
McInnis, Hugh - E	Wheelwright, Ernie - B
Mack, "Red" - B	Whitlow, Bob - C
Marchlewski, Frank - C	Williams, Sam - E
Marshall, Rich - T	Wolski, Bill - B
Martin, Bill - E	

1966 BALTIMORE COLTS
COACH - Don Shula
2nd 9-5-0

Allen, Gerry - B
Baldwin, Bob - B
Ball, Sam - T
Berry, Raymond - E
Bleick, Tom - B
Boyd, Bob - B
Braase, Ordell - E
Brown, Barry - LB
Burkett, Jackie - LB
Cuozzo, Gary - Q
Curtis, "Mike" - LB
Davis, "Ted" - LB
Gaubatz, Dennis - LB
Harold, George - B
Haymond, Alvin - B
Hill, Jerry - B
Hilton, Roy - E
Lee, Dave - K
Logan, Jerry - B
Lorick, Tony - B
Lyles, Len - B
Mackey, John - E
Marchetti, Gino - E

Matte, Tom - B
Memmelaar, Dale - G
Michaels, Lou - E & K
Miller, Fred - T
Moore, Lenny - B
Orr, Jim - B
Parker, Jim - T
Petties, Neal - E
Ressler, Glenn - T
Richardson, Willie - E
Sandusky, Alex - G
Shinnick, Don - LB
Smith, Billy Ray - T
Snyder, Al - B
Stonebreaker, Steve - LB
Stynchula, Andy - E
Sullivan, Dan - G
Szymanski, Dick - C
Unitas, John - Q
Vogel, Bob - T
Welch, Jim - B
Wilson, "Butch" - E

Isbell, Joe Bob - G
Johnson, Walter - T
Kellerman, Ernie - B
Kelly, Leroy - B
Lane, Gary - B
Lindsey, Dale - LB
McNeil, Clif - B
Modzelewski, Dick - T
Morin, Milt - E
Morrow, John - C
Ninowski, Jim - Q
Parker, Frank - T

Parrish, Bernie - B
Pietrosante, Nick - B
Roberts, Walter - B
Ryan, Frank - Q
Schafrath, Dick - T
Schults, Randy - B
Smith, Ralph - E
Warfield, Paul - E
Wiggin, Paul - E
Williams, Sid - LB
Wooten, John - G

1966 CHICAGO BEARS
COACH - George Halas
5th 5-7-2

Allen, Duane - E
Arnett, Jon - B
Atkins, Doug - E
Bivins, Charley - B
Brown, Charley - B
Buffone, Doug - LB
Bukich, Rudy - Q
Bull, Ron - B
Butkus, Dick - LB
Cadile, Jim - T
Cornish, Frank - T
Ditka, Mike - E
Evey, Dick - E
Fortunato, Joe - LB
Gentry, Curtis - B
Gordon, Dick - E
Green, Bobby Joe - K
Johnson, John - T
Jones, Jim - E
Kilcullen, Bob - T
Kurek, Ralph - B

LeClerc, Roger - LB & K
Lee, Herman - T
McRae, Ben - B
Marconi, Joe - B
Mattson, Riley - T
Morris, John - B
O'Bradovich, Ed - E
Petitbon, Rich - B
Piccolo, Brian - B
Purnell, Jim - LB
Pyle, Mike - C
Rabold, Mike - G
Rakestraw, Larry - Q
Reilly, "Mike" - LB
Sayers, Gale - B
Schweda, Brian - E
Seals, George - G
Taylor, Rosey - B
Wade, Bill - Q
Wetoska, Bob - T
Whitsell, Dave - B

1966 DALLAS COWBOYS
COACH - Tom Landry
1st 10-3-1
(Lost title to Green Bay, 34-27)

Andrie, George - E
Boeke, Jim - T
Clarke, Frank - E
Colvin, Jim - T
Connelly, Mike - C
Daniels, Dick - B
Dial, Buddy - E
Donahue, Leon - T
Edwards, Dave - LB
Gaechter, Mike - B
Garrison, Walter - B
Gent, "Pete" - G
Green, Cornell - B
Hayes, Bob - E
Hays, Harold - LB
Howley, Chuck - LB
Johnson, Mike - B
Jordan, Lee Roy - LB
Lilly, Bob - T
Liscio, Tony - T
Livingston, Warren - B

Logan, Obert - B
Manders, Dave - G
Meredith, Don - Q
Morton, Craig - Q
Neely, Ralph - T
Niland, John - G
Norman, Pettis - E
Perkins, Don - B
Pugh, Jethro - E
Reeves, Dan - B
Renfro, Mel - B
Rhome, Gerry - Q
Sandeman, Bill - T
Shy, Les - B
Smith, J. D. - B
Stephens, Larry - E
Townes, Willie - T
Tubbs, Gerry - LB
Villanueva, Danny - K
Walker, Malcolm - C
Wilbur, John - T

1966 DETROIT LIONS
COACH - Harry Gilmer
6th 4-9-1
(Tied with Minnesota)

Alford, Mike - C
Brown, Roger - T
Clark, Ernie - LB
Cody, Bill - LB
Cogdill, Gail - E
Felts, Bobby - B
Flanagan, Ed - C
Gibbons, Jim - E
Gordy, John - G
Hand, Larry - E
Henderson, John - E
Hilgenberg, Walter - LB
Karras, Alex - T
Kearney, Jim - B
Kowalkowski, Bob - G
Kramer, Ron - E
LeBeau, Dick - B
Looney, Joe Don - B
Lucci, Mike - LB
McCord, Darris - E
McLenna, Bruce - B
Maher, Bruce - B
Malinchak, Bill - E

Marsh, Amos - B
Mazzanti, Jerry - E
Myers, Tom - Q
Nowatske, Tom - B
Plum, Milt - Q
Rasmussen, Wayne - B
Robinson, John - B
Rush, Gerry - T
Sanders, Daryl - T
Shoals, Roger - T
Slaby, Lou - LB
Smith, J. D. - T
Smith, Bob - B
Studstill, Pat - B
Sweetan, Karl - Q
Thompson, Bob - B
Todd, Jim - B
Van Horn, Doug - G
Vaughn, Tom - B
Walker, Wayne - LB
Walker, Willie - B
Yepremian, Garo - K

1966 CLEVELAND BROWNS
COACH - Blanton Collier
2nd 9-5-0
((Tied with Philadelphia)

Barnes, Erich - B
Battle, Jim - E
Beach, Walter - B
Brewer, John - LB
Brown, John - T
Clark, Monte - T
Collins, Gary - E
Costello, Vince - LB
Fichtner, Ross - B
Fiss, Galen - LB

Franklin, Bob - B
Glass, Bill - E
Green, Ernie - B
Groza, Lou - K
Harraway, Charley - B
Hickerson, Gene - G
Hoaglin, Fred - C
Houston, Jim - LB
Howell, Mike - B
Hutchinson, Tom - LB

1966 GREEN BAY PACKERS
COACH - Vince Lombardi
1st 12-2-0
(Beat Dallas for title, 34-27;
Beat Kansas City, 35-10)

Adderley, Herb - B
Aldridge, Lionel - E
Anderson, Donny - B
Anderson, Bill - E
Bowman, Ken - C
Bratkowski, Zeke - Q
Brown, Allen - E
Brown, Bob - E
Brown, Tom - B
Caffey, Lee Roy - LB
Chandler, Don - K
Crutcher, Tom - LB
Curry, Bill - C
Dale, Carroll - E
Davis, Willie - E
Dowler, Boyd - E
Fleming, Marv - E
Gillingham, Gale - G
Grabowski, Jim - B
Gregg, Forrest - T
Hart, Doug - B

Hathcock, Dave - B
Hornung, Paul - B
Jeter, Bob - B
Jordan, Henry - T
Kostelnik, Ron - T
Kramer, Gerry - G
Long, Bob - E
McGee, Max - E
Mack, "Red" - B
Nitschke, Ray - LB
Pitts, Elijah - B
Robinson, "Dave" - LB
Skoronski, Bob - T
Starr, Bart - Q
Taylor, Jim - B
Thurston, Fred - G
Vandersea, Phil - LB
Weatherwax, Jim - T
Wood, Willie - B
Wright, Steve - T

1966 LOS ANGELES RAMS
COACH - George Allen
3rd 8-6-0

Anderson, Bruce - T
Bass, Dick - B
Baughan, Maxie - LB
Carollo, Joe - G
Chuy, Don - G
Cowan, Charley - T
Crabb, Claude - B
Cross, Irv - B
Currie, Dan - LB
Dyer, Henry - B
Gabriel, Roman - Q
George, Bill - LB
Gossett, Bruce - K
Gremminger, Hank - B
Grier, Rosey - T
Heckard, Steve - E
Iman, Ken - C
Jones, Dave - E
Josephson, Les - B
Karras, Ted - G
Kilgore, Jon - K
Lamson, Chuck - B

Leggett, Earl - T
Lundy, Lamar - E
McDonald, Tom - B
McKeever, Marlin - E
Mack, Tom - G
Meador, Ed - B
Moore, Tom - B
Munson, Bill - Q
Nichols, Bob - T
Olsen, Merlin - T
Pardee, Jack - LB
Pivec, Dave - E
Pope, "Bucky" - E
Pottios, Myron - LB
Scibelli, Joe - T
Snow, Jack - E
Stiger, Jim - B
Truax, Bill - E
Wendryhoski, Joe - C
Williams, Clancy - B
Woodlief, Doug - LB
Youngblood, George - E

1966 MINNESOTA VIKINGS
COACH - Norm Van Brocklin
6th 4-9-1
(Tied with Detroit)

Alderman, Grady - G
Arrobio, Charley - T
Barnes, Billy Ray - B
Bedsole, Hal - E
Berry, Bob - Q
Bowie, Larry - G
Brown, Bill - B
Carpenter, Pres - E
Cox, Fred - K
Davis, Doug - T
Dickson, Paul - T
Eller, Carl - E
Fitzgerald, Mike - B
Flatley, Paul - E
Hackbart, Dale - B
Hall, Tom - B

Hansen, Don - LB
Jordan, Jeff - B
Kassulke, Karl - B
King, Phil - B
Kirby, John - LB
Larsen, Gary - T
Lindsey, Jim - B
Mackbee, Earsell - B
Marshall, Jim - E
Mason, Tom - B
Osborn, Dave - B
Phillips, Jim - E
Power s, John - E
Rentzel, Lance - B
Rose, George - B
Schmitz, Bob - LB

Sharockman, Ed - B
Shay, Jerry - T
Sunde, Milt - G
Sutton, Archie - T
Tarkenton, Fran - Q
Tilleman, Mike - T
Tingelhoff, Mick - C
Tobey, Dave - LB

VanderKelen, Ron - Q
Vellone, Jim - T
Walden, Bob - K
Warwick, Lonnie - LB
Williams, Jeff - B
Winston, Roy - LB
Young, Jim - B

1966 NEW YORK GIANTS
COACH - "Allie" Sherman
8th 1-12-1

Bolin, "Bookie" - G
Bowman, Steve - B
Carr, Henry - B
Carroll, Jim - LB
Case, "Pete" - G
Childs, Clarence - B
Ciccolella, Mike - LB
Condren, Glen - E
Crespino, Bob - E
Davis, Don - T
Davis, Roger - T
Davis, Rosey - E
Dess, Darrell - G
Garcia, Jim - E
Gogolak, Pete - K
Harper, Charley - G
Harris, Phil - B
Harris, Wendell - B
Hillebrand, Jerry - LB
Jacobs, Allen - B
Jones, Homer - E
Katcavage, Jim - E
Kennedy, Tom - Q
Koy, Ernie - B
Larson, Greg - C

Lewis, Dan - B
Lockhart, "Spider" - B
Lynch, Dick - B
Matan, Bill - E
Menefee, Hartwell - B
Mercein, Chuck - B
Moran, Jim - T
Morrall, Earl - Q
Morrison, Joe - B
Patton, Jim - B
Peay, Francis - T
Prestel, Jim - T
Reed, Smith - B
Scholtz, Bob - C
Sczurek, Stan - LB
Shofner, Del - E
Smith, Jeff - LB
Thomas, Aaron - E
Thurlow, Steve - B
Vargo, Larry - LB
Wellborn, Joe - C
White, Freeman - E & LB
Wood, Gary - Q
Young, Willie - T

1966 PHILADELPHIA EAGLES
COACH - Joe Kuharich
2nd 9-5-0
(Tied with Cleveland)

Baker, "Sam" - K
Beisler, Randy - E
Blaine, Ed - G
Brown, Bob - T
Brown, Timmie - B
Brown, Willie - B
Cahill, Davie - T
Concannon, Jack - Q
Goodwin, Ron - E
Graham, Dave - T
Gros, Earl - B
Hawkins, Ben - B
Hill, Fred - E
Hill, King - Q
Howel l, Lane - T
Hoyem, Lynn - G
Huitz, Don - E
Jackson, Trenton - B
Kelley, Dwight - LB
Lang, Izzy - B
Lince, Dave - E
Lloyd, Dave - LB

Martin, Aaron - B
Matson, Ollie - B
Medved, Ron - B
Meyers, John - T
Morgan, Mike - LB
Nelson, Al - B
Nettles, Jim - B
Peters, Floyd - E
Pettigrew, Gary - E
Ramsey, Nate - B
Recher, Dave - C
Retzlaff, "Pete" - E
Ringo, Jim - C
Rissmiller, Ray - T
Scarpati, Joe - B
Skaggs, Jim - G
Snead, Norm - Q
Van Dyke, Bruce - G
Vasys, Arunas - LB
Wells, Harold - LB
Whittingham, Fred - LB
Woodeschick, Tom - B

1966 PITTSBURGH STEELERS
COACH - Bill Austin
6th 5-8-1

Asbury, Willie - B
Baker, John - E
Ballman, Gary - E
Bradshaw, Charley - T
Bradshaw, Jim - B
Breen, Gene - LB
Breedlove, Rod - LB
Bullocks, Amos - B
Butler, Jim - B
Campbell, John - LB
Clark, Mike - K
Daniel, Willie - B
Gagner, Larry - G
Gunnels, Riley - T
Hilton, John - E
Hinton, Chuck - T
Hoak, Dick - B
Hohn, Bob - B
Izo, George - Q
James, Dan - T
Jefferson, Roy - E
Jeter, Tony - E
Keys, Brady - B
Killorin, Pat - C
Kortas, Ken - T

Lambert, Frank - K
Leftridge, Dick - B
Lind, "Mike" - B
McGee, Ben - E
Magac, Mike - G
Mansfield, Ray - T
Martha, Paul - B
Meyer, Ron - Q
Nelsen, Bill - Q
O'Brien, Fran - T
Pillath, Roger - T
Powell, Tim - E
Russell, Andy - LB
Saul, Bill - LB
Schmitz, Bob - LB
Simmons, Jerry - B
Smith, Bob - B
Smith, Ron - Q
Smith, Steve - E
Strand, Eli - G
Thomas, Clendon - B
Voss, Lloyd - E
Wenzel, Ralph - G
Wilburn, John - E
Woodson, Marv - B

1966 ST. LOUIS CARDINALS
COACH - Charley Winner
4th 8-5-1

Bakken, Jim - K
Brumm, Don - E
Bryant, Chuck - B
Burson, Jim - B
Conrad, Bobby Joe - B
Crenshaw, Willis - B
DeMarco, Bob - C
Fischer, Pat - B
Gambrell, Bill - E
Gautt, Prentice - B
Goode, Irv - G & C
Gray, Ken - G
Hammack, Mal - B
Hart, Jim - Q
Heidel, Jim - B
Heron, Fred - T
Johnson, Charley - Q
Kasperek, Dick - C
Koman, Bill - LB
Long, Dave - E
McDowell, John - T
McMillan, Ernie - T
Meggyesy, Dave - LB
Meinert, Dale - LB

Melinkovich, Mike - E
Nofsinger, Terry - Q
O'Brien, Dave - T
Ogden, Ray - B
Randle, "Sonny" - E
Reynolds, Bob - T
Robb, Joe - E
Roland, John - B
Roy, Frank   G
Shivers, Roy - B
Silas, Sam - T
Simmons, Dave - LB
Smith, Jackie - E
Sortun, Rickie - G
Stallings, Larry - LB
Stovall, Jerry - B
Strofolino, Mike - LB
Triplett, Bill - B
Turner, Herschel - G
Walker, Charley - T
Williams, Bob - B
Wilson, Larry - B
Woodson, Abe - B

1966 SAN FRANCISCO 49ERS
COACH - Jack Christiansen
4th 6-6-2

Alexander, Kermit - B
Beard, Ed - LB
Bosley, Bruce - C
Brodie, John - Q
Casey, Bernie - B
Cerne, Joe - C
Crow, John David - B
Daugherty, Bob - B
Davis, Tommy - K

Donnelly, George - B
Dowdle, Mike - LB
Harrison, Bob - LB
Hazeltine, Matt - LB
Hindman, Stan - E
Jackson, Jim - B
Johnson, Charles - T
Johnson, Jim - B
Kilmer, Bill - B

Kimbrough, Elbert - B
Kopay, Dave - B
Kramer, Kent - E
Krueger, Charley - T
Lakes, Roland - T
Lewis, Gary - B
McCormick, Dave - T
McFarland, Kay - B
Miller, Clark - E
Mira, George - Q
Mudd, Howard - G
Norton, Jim - E

Parks, Dave - F
Phillips, Mel - B
Randolph, Alvin - B
Rock, Walter - T
Rohde, Len - T
Stickles, Monty - F
Swinford, Wayne - B
Thomas, John - G
Wilcox, Dave - LB
Willard, Ken - B
Wilson, Jim - G
Witcher, Dick - B

1966 WASHINGTON REDSKINS
COACH - Otto Graham
5th 7-7-0

Adams, Willie - E
Avery, Jim - E
Barnes, Walter - T
Barrington, Tom - B
Briggs, Bill - E
Burrell, John - B
Carpenter, Pres - E
Carroll, Jim - LB
Clay, Billy - B
Croftcheck, Don - G
Crossan, Dave - C
Dess, Darrell - G
Gogolak, Charley - K
Goosby, Tom - G
Hanburger, Chris - LB
Harris, Rickie - B
Hauss, Len - C
Hodgson, Pat - E
Huff, "Sam" - LB
Jackson, Steve - LB
Johnson, Mitch - T
Jones, Stan - T
Jurgensen, "Sonny" - Q
Kammerer, Carl - E
Kantor, Joe - B

Kelly, John - T
Krause, Paul - B
Kupp, Jake - G
Looney, Joe Don - B
Marshall, Rich - T
Mazurek, Fred - B
Mitchell, Bob - B
O'Brien, Fran - T
Owens, Brig - B
Promuto, Vince - G
Rector, Ron - B
Reger, John - LB
Richter, "Pat" - E
Rutgens, Joe - T
Sanders, Lonnie - B
Schoenke, Ray - T
Shiner, Dick - Q
Shorter, Jim - B
Smith, Jerry - E
Snidow, Ron - T
Snowden, Jim - T
Taylor, Charley - B & E
Thurlow, Steve - B
Walters, Tom - B
Whitfield, A. D. - B

1966 BOSTON PATRIOTS (AFL)
COACH - Mike Holovak
2nd 8-4-2

Addison, Tom - LB
Antwine, Houston - T
Avezzano, Joe - C
Bellino, Joe - B
Boudreaux, Jim - E
Buoniconti, Nick - LB
Canale, Justin - G
Cappadonna, Bob - B
Cappelletti, Gino - E
Colclough, Jim - E
Cunningham, Jay - B
Dee, Bob - E
Eisenhauer, Larry - E
Farmer, Lonnie - LB
Felt, Dick - B
Fraser, Jim - LB
Garrett, John - B
Garron, Larry - B
Graham, Art - E
Graves, White - B
Hall, Ron - B
Hennessey, Tom - B

Huarte, John - Q
Hunt, Jim - E
Johnson, Ellis - B
Johnson, Bill - B
Khayat, Ed - T
Long, Charley - T
Mangum, John - T
Morris, Jon - C
Nance, Jim - B
Neville, Tom - T
Oakes, Don - T
Parilli, "Babe" - Q
Purvis, Vic - B
Romeo, Tony - E
St. Jean, Len - E
Satcher, Doug - LB
Shonta, Chuck - B
Singer, Karl - T
Webb, Don - B
Whalen, Jim - E
Yewcic, Tom - Q

1966 BUFFALO BILLS (AFL)
COACH - Joe Collier
1st 9-4-1
(Lost title to Kansas City, 31-7)

Barber, Stu - G
Bass, Glenn - E
Bemiller, Al - C
Burnett, Bob - B
Byrd, George - B
Carlton, Wray - B
Clarke, Hagood - B
Costa, Dave - LB
Costa, Paul - E
Crockett, Bob - E
Day, Tom - G
DeSutter, Wayne - T
Dubenion, Elbert - B
Dunaway, Jim - T
Edgerson, Booker - B
Ferguson, Charley - E
Goodwin, Doug - B
Guidry, Paul - LB
Hudson, Dick - G
Jacobs, Harry - LB
Janik, Tom - B

Kemp, John - Q
King, Charles - B
LaMonica, Daryl - Q
Lusteg, Booth - K
McDole, Roland - T
Maguire, Paul - LB
Meredith, Dud - T
Mills, Pete - B
O'Donnell, Joe - G
Prudhomme, Remi - G
Rutkowski, Ed - B
Saimes, George - B
Schmidt, Bob - T
Schottenheimer, Marty - LB
Sestak, Tom - T
Shaw, Bill - G
Smith, Allen - B
Spikes, Jack - B
Stratton, Mike - LB
Tracey, John - LB
Warner, Charles - B

Floyd, Don - E
Frazier, Charley - B
Frongillo, John - C
Glick, Fred - B
Granger, Hoyle - B
Hayes, Jim - T
Hennigan, Charley - B
Hicks, Wilmer - B
Hines, Glen Ray - T
Holmes, Pat - T
Humphrey, Buddy - Q
Jancik, Bob - B
Johnson, John Henry - B
Ladd, Ernie - T
Lee, Jackie - Q
McLeod, Bob - E
Maples, Bob - LB

Meyer, John - LB
Michael, Dick - T
Norton, Jim - B
Parrish, Bernie - B
Poole, Bob - E
Rice, George - T
Scrutchins, Ed - E
Stone, Don - B
Suggs, Walt - T
Sutton, Mickey - B
Talamini, Bob - G
Tolar, Charley - B
Trammell, Al - B
Trull, Don - Q
Underwood, Olen - LB
Viltz, Theo - B
Wittenborn, John - G

1966 KANSAS CITY CHIEFS (AFL)
COACH - "Hank" Stram

1st 11-2-1
(Beat Buffalo for title, 31-7; lost to Green Bay, 35-10)

1966 DENVER BRONCOS (AFL)
COACH - Mac Speedie & Ray Malavasi
4th 4-10-0

Bernet, Lee - T
Bramlett, John - LB
Breitenstein, Bob - T
Brown, Willie - B
Brunelli, Sam - G
Choboian, Max - Q
Cox, Larry - T
Crabtree, Eric - B
Davis, Marvin - E
Denson, Al - E
Fletcher, William - B
Franci, Jason - E
Glacken, "Scotty" - Q
Glass, Glenn - B
Gonsoulin, "Goose" - B
Gonzaga, John - G
Griffin, John - B
Gulseth, Don - LB
Hayes, Wendell - B
Haynes, Abner - B
Hohman, Jon - G
Hopkins, Jerry - B
Inman, Jerry - T
Jacobs, Ray - E
Jeter, Gene - LB
Kaminski, Larry - C

Keating, Bill - G
Kellogg, Mike - B
Kroner, Gary - K
Kubala, Ray - C
LaRose, Dan - E
Leetzow, Max - E
Lester, Darrell - B
McCormick, John - Q
Matson, Pat - G
Matsos, Arch - LB
Mitchell, Charley - B
Richardson, Bob - B
Rote, Tobin - Q
Sbranti, Ron - LB
Scarpitto, Bob - B
Scott, Lew - B
Sellers, Goldie - B
Slaughter, "Mickey" - Q
Sturm, Jerry - T
Tarasovic, George - LB
Taylor, Lionel - E
Wettstein, Max - E
Wilson, Nemiah - B
Wright, Lonnie - E
Young, Bob - T

Abell, "Bud" - LB
Arbanas, Fred - E
Beathard, Pete - Q
Bell, Bob - LB
Biodrowski, Dennis - G
Brannan, Sol - B
Brooker, Tom - K
Brown, Aaron - E
Buchanan, "Buck" - T
Budde, Ed - G
Burford, Chris - E
Carolan, Reg - E
Coan, Bert - B
Corey, Walt - LB
Dawson, Len - Q
DiMidio, Tony - T
Frazier, Wayne - C
Garrett, Mike - B
Gilliam, Jon - C
Headrick, Sherrill - LB
Hill, Dave - T
Hill, Jim - B
Holub, Emil - LB

Hunt, Bob - B
Hurston, Charles - E
Lothamer, Ed - E
McClinton, Curt - B
Mays, Jerry - T
Mercer, Mike - K
Merz, Curt - B
Mitchell, Willie - B
Pitts, Frank - E
Ply, Bob - B
Reynolds, Al - G
Rice, Andy - T
Robinson, John - B
Rosdahl, "Hatch" - E
Smith, Fletcher - B
Stover, Stewart - LB
Taylor, Otis - E
Thomas, Emmitt - B
Thomas, Gene - B
Tyrer, Jim - T
Williamson, Fred - B
Wilson, Jerry - B

1966 MIAMI DOLPHINS (AFL)
COACH - George Wilson
4th 3-11-0
(Tied with Houston)

Auer, Joe - B
Branch, Mel - E
Bruggers, Bob - LB
Canale, Whit - E
Casares, Ric - B
Chesser, George - B
Cooke, Ed - E
Cronin, Bill - E
Dotson, Al - T
Emanuel, Frank - LB
Erlandson, Tom - LB
Evans, Norman - T
Faison, Earl - E
Gilchrist, "Cookie" - B
Goode, Tom - LB
Higgins, Jim - G
Holmes, John - E
Hudock, Mike - C

Hunter, "Bill" - B
Jackson, Frank - B
Jaquess, Pete - B
Joe, Billy - B
Kocourek, Dave - E
McDaniel "Wahoo" - LB
McGeever, John - B
Matthews, Wes - E
Mingo, Gene - G
Mitchell, Stan - E
Moreau, Doug - E
Neff, Bob - B
Neighbors, Bill - T
Nomina, Tom - T
Noonan, Karl - E
Norton, Rich - Q
Park, Ernie - G
Petrella, Bob - B

1966 HOUSTON OILERS (AFL)
COACH - Wally Lemm
4th 3-11-0
(Tied with Miami)

Allen, George - T
Appleton, Scott - E
Baker, John - E
Bishop, "Sonny" - G
Blanda, George Q & K
Blanks, Sid - B
Boyette, Garland - LB

Brabham, Dan - LB
Burrell, Ode - B
Carrell, John - LB
Caveness, Ron - LB
Cline, Doug - LB
Cutsinger, Gary - B
Elkins, Larry - E

Price, Sam - B
Rice, Ken - T
Roberson, "Bo" - B
Roderick, John - E
Rudolph, John - LB
Stofa, John - Q
Thornton, John - LB
Torczon, Laverne - E
Twilley, Howard - E

Wantland, Harold - B
Warren, Jim - B
West, Willie - B
Westmoreland, Dick - B
Williams, Maxie - T
Wilson, George, Jr. - Q
Wood, "Dick" - Q
Zecher, Dick - T

1966 SAN DIEGO CHARGERS (AFL)
COACH - Sid Gillman
3rd 7-6-1

Allen, Chuck - LB
Allison, Jim - B
Alworth, Lance - E
Beauchamp, Joe - B
Buncom, Frank - LB
Cline, Doug - LB
Degen, Dick - LB
DeLong, Steve - E
Duncan, Les - B
Estes, Don - G
Faison, Earl - E
Farr, Miller - B
Farris, John - G
Foster, Gene - B
Frazier, Bill - E
Garrison, Gary - E
Good, Tom - LB
Graham, Ken - B
Griffin, Jim - E
Gross, George - T
Gruneisen, Sam - G
Hadl, John - Q
Hennings, Dan - Q
Karas, Emil - LB
Kindig, Howie - E
Kirner, Gary - T
Latzke, Paul - C

Lincoln, Keith - B
London, Mike - LB
Lowe, Paul - B
MacKinnon, Jacque - B
Martin, Larry - T
Matsos, Archie - LB
Milks, John - LB
Mitchell, Ed - G
Mitinger, Bob - LB
Mix, Ron - T
Moore, Fred - T
Norton, Don - E
Owens, Terry - T
Petrich, Bob - E
Plump, Dave - B
Redman, Dick - LB
Ridge, Houston - B
Sweeney, Walt - T
Tensi, Steve - Q
Tolbert, Jim - B
Travis, John - B
Van Raaphorst, Dick - K
Whitehead, "Bud" - B
Whitmyer, Nat - B
Wright, Ernie - T
Zeman, Bob - B

1966 NEW YORK JETS (AFL)
COACH - "Weeb" Ewbank
3rd 6-6-2

Abruzzese, Ray - B
Atkinson, Al - LB
Baird, Bill - B
Baker, Ralph - LB
Biggs, Verlon - E
Boozer, Emerson - B
Chomyszak, Steve - T
Christy, Earl - E
Crane, Paul - LB
DeFelice, Nick - T
DeLuca, Sam - G
Dudek, Mitch - T
Ficca, Dan - G
Gordon, Cornell - B
Grantham, Larry - LB
Gray, Jim - B
Gucciardo, Pat - B
Harris, Jim - T
Herman, Dave - G
Hill, Winston - T
Hudson, Jim - B
Johnson, Curley - B
Lammons, Pete - E
Lewis, Sherman - B
Mathis, Bill - B

Maynard, Don - B
Namath, Joe - Q
O'Mahoney, Jim - LB
Paulson, Dainard - B
Perreault, Pete - T
Philbin, Gerry - E
Plunkett, Sherman - T
Rademacher, Bill - B
Rochester, Paul - T
Sample, John - B
Sauer, George - E
Schmidt, Henry - T
Schmitt, John - C
Smith, Allen - B
Smolinski, Mark - B
Snell, Matt - B
Taliaferro, Mike - Q
Turner, Jim - Q & K
Turner, "Bake" - B
Waskiewicz, Jim - C
Weir, Sam - B
Werl, Bob - E
Wilder, Al - E
Yearby, Bill - E

1967

NATIONAL FOOTBALL LEAGUE

CENTURY DIVISION

	W.	L.	T.	Pc.
Cleveland	9	5	0	.643
New York	7	7	0	.500
St. Louis	6	7	1	.462
Pittsburgh	4	9	1	.308

CAPITOL DIVISION

Dallas	9	5	0	.643
Philadelphia	6	7	1	.462
Washington	5	6	3	.455
New Orleans	3	11	0	.214

CENTRAL DIVISION

Green Bay	9	4	1	.692
Chicago	7	6	1	.538
Detroit	5	7	2	.417
Minnesota	3	8	3	.273

COASTAL DIVISION

*Los Ang.	11	1	2	.917
Baltimore	11	1	2	.917
San Fran.	7	7	0	.500
Atlanta	1	12	1	.077

*Won division title on points vs. Baltimore.

1966 OAKLAND RAIDERS (AFL)
COACH - John Rauch
2nd 8-5-1

Atkins, Pervis - B
Banaszak, Pete - B
Biletnikoff, Fred - E
Bird, Rodger - B
Birdwell, Dan - E
Budness, Bill - LB
Cannon, Bill - E
Conners, Dan - LB
Daniels, Clem - B
Daniels, Dave - T
Davidson, Ben - E
Davidson, "Cotton" - Q
Dixon, Hewritt - B
Eischeid, Mike - K
Flores, Tom - Q
Grayson, Dave - B
Green, Charles - Q
Hagberg, Roger - B
Harvey, Jim - T
Hawkins, Wayne - G
Jackson, Dick - LB
Keating, Tom - T
Kent, Greg - T

Krakoski, Joe - B
Laskey, Bill - LB
Lassiter, Ike - T
McCloughan, Kent - B
Mercer, Mike - K
Miller, Bill - E
Mirich, Rex - T
Mitchell, Tom - E
Oats, Carl - E
Otto, Gus - LB
Otto, Jim - C
Powell, Art - E
Powers, Warren - B
Pyle, Palmer - G
Schmautz, Ray - LB
Schuh, Harry - G
Svihus, Bob - T
Todd, Larry - B
Tyson, Dick - G
Williams, Howie - B
Williams, Willie - B
Williamson, John - LB

AMERICAN FOOTBALL LEAGUE

EASTERN DIVISION

	W.	L.	T.	Pc.
Houston	9	4	1	.692
New York	8	5	1	.615
Buffalo	4	10	0	.286
Miami	4	10	0	.286
Boston	3	10	1	.231

WESTERN DIVISION

	W.	L.	T.	Pc.
Oakland	13	1	0	.929
Kans. City	9	5	0	.643
San Diego	8	5	1	.615
Denver	3	11	0	.214

TITLES: Green Bay beat Dallas, 21-17, for the NFL title. The Packers, who finished third in the Western conferences, gained the title game as the Central division winners, beating Los Angeles of the Coastal division, 28-7. Los Angeles, tied with Baltimore with 11-1-2 records, was eligible for the playoff by outscoring Baltimore in the two games against each other. Dallas of the Capitol division, beat Cleveland, winner of the Century division, 52-14, in the other semi-final match.

Los Angeles beat Cleveland, 30-6, in the second place playoff at Miami.

In the AFL, Oakland, Western division, beat Houston, Eastern division, 40-7, for the AFL title.

In the 1967 Interleague "Super Bowl," Green Bay beat Oakland, 33-14.

NFL LEADERS: Individual leaders for the year: Scoring—James Bakken (St. Louis), 117; Rushing—Leroy Kelly (Cleveland) 1,205 yds.; Passing—Christian "Sonny" Jurgensen (Washington); Pass Receiving—Charles Taylor (Washington) 70; Field Goals—James Bakken (St. Louis) 27; Punting—William Lothridge (Atlanta), 43.7 yds.; Interceptions—David Whitsell (New Orleans), Lemuel Barney (Cleveland) tied, 10.

AFL LEADERS: Scoring—George Blanda (Oakland) 116; Rushing—James Nance (Boston) 1,212 yds.; Passing—Daryle Lamonica (Oakland); Pass Receiving—George Sauer (New York)—75; Field Goals—Jan Stenerud (Kansas City)—21; Punting—Robert Scarpitto (Denver), 44.9 yds.; Interceptions—Miller Farr (Houston), Dick Westmoreland (Miami), Tom Janik (Buffalo) tied, 10.

FIRST DRAFT: NFL—Charles "Bubba" Smith, tackle, by Baltimore, signed with Baltimore, draft traded from New Orleans; AFL—Robert Griese, qback, by Miami, signed with Miami.

COACHES: In the NFL, Joseph Schmidt replaced Harry Gilmer at Detroit; Harry "Bud" Grant replaced Norman Van Brocklin at Minnesota; Thomas Fears was named first head coach at New Orleans. In the AFL, Lou Saban replaced Ray Malavasi at Denver.

Hall of Fame added players Charles Bednarik, Robert Layne, Kenneth Strong, Joseph Stydahar, Emlen Tunnell; also coach Paul Brown and owners Charles Bidwill and Daniel Reeves.

Running kickoffs back for TDs became an exciting new weapon in the NFL of 1967. John Love (Washington) and John Gilliam (New Orleans), both rookies, took the season's opening kicks all the way in their first 10 seconds of NFL action. Gale Sayers (Chicago) and Ron Smith (Atlanta) also scored with kickoffs the same day.

Travis Williams, Green Bay rookie, became the kickoff-return champion during the season with four for TDs a new record, including two against Cleveland to tie Timmy Brown's one-game record. Gale Sayers did it three times before the season ended. Others were scored by Walter Roberts (New Orleans) and Carl Ward of (Cleveland). In the AFL, Noland Smith (Kansas City) and "Zeke" Moore (Houston) scored with kickoff returns.

Jim Bakken (St. Louis) kicked seven field goals against Pittsburgh, Sept. 24, breaking Garabed Ypremian's record of six. Bakken scored from 18, 24, 33, 29, 24, 32 and 23 yards and missed from 50 and 45.

There were nine tied games in the NFL, a record.

Lou Michaels kicked 53-yard field goal against Dallas, Dec. 3.

Bill Kilmer (New Orleans) threw 96-yard TD pass to Walter Roberts vs Philadelphia, Nov. 19, longest of season in NFL.

Vito Parilli (Boston) threw 79-yard TD pass to Art Graham vs Denver, Sept. 3, longest of season in AFL.

Cincinnati was granted an AFL franchise, May 25, and, with Paul Brown as general manager and coach, was scheduled to play in 1968. Team was named Bengals, same name as the Cincinnati teams of 1940-41 who played in the AFL of that time.

Eppie Barney (Detroit) returned three interceptions for TDs, tying Lynch's record.

Leslie Duncan (San Diego) returned interception 100 yards for TD vs Kansas City, Oct. 15.

Jack Concannon (Chicago) threw 93-yard TD pass to Dick Gordon vs St. Louis, Nov. 19.

Rick Volk (Baltimore) returned interception 94 yards for TD vs Chicago, Oct. 8, longest in NFL for season.

Herb Adderley, Green Bay, scored his sixth TD with interception vs St. Louis, Oct. 31, to break career record held by several.

Jim Houston (Cleveland) returned interception 71 yards for TD vs New York, Dec. 3.

Loris "Sam" Baker (Philadelphia) scored 81 points during 1967. Lou Groza (Cleveland) scored 76. Groza now had career total of 1,349; Baker with 824 climbed to third place behind Bobby Walston (retired) who scored 881.

Bob Grim (Minnesota) returned punt 81 yards vs New York, Nov. 5, longest in NFL 1967.

Rodger Bird (Oakland) returned punt 78 yards vs San Diego, Oct. 29, longest in AFL for 1967.

Detroit set new record of fumbles in single game with 11 vs Minnesota, Nov. 12, losing ball five times.

John Unitas, Baltimore qback, took control of all lifetime passing records. At the end of 1967 he had completed 2,261 for 33,340 yards and 252 touchdowns.

Christian "Sonny" Jurgensen, Washington, was the top NFL passer for 1967, setting a one-season record of 288 completions in 508 attempts (56.7%) for 3,748 yards, also the record. Unitas, with 255 completions also topped the previous high of 254 held by Jurgensen.

Fran Tarkenton, New York qback, gained 3,088 yards passing, and with 17,667 for his 7-year career, had the best chance of catching Unitas.

The New York Giants were switched to the Capitol division and New Orleans to the Century division for 1968.

John Stofa, qback of the Miami Dolphins became the first member of the new Cincinnati Bengals roster in a pre-draft trade.

The NFL and AFL held the first combined player selection of college men, thus eliminating the competitive bidding of previous years.

Arthur Modell, president of the Cleveland Browns, was elected president of the NFL until Feb. 1968 (May 28).

Ric Casares, Chi-Bear, Miami Dolphin (AFL) fullback, retired after 12 years, sixth in all-time rushing with 5,662 yards.

Ollie Matson, Chi-Card, Los Angeles, Detroit, Philadelphia running back retired after 14 years, holding second best record in combined yardage, 12,844.

Paul Hornung, Green Bay running back retired after nine years, fourth in all-time scoring with 760 points.

Gino Marchetti, Dallas, Baltimore defensive end, retired after 14 years.

James Parker, Baltimore guard-tackle, retired late in season, his eleventh.

Palmer "Pete" Retzlaff, Philadelphia end, retired after 12 years, fifth in alltime pass receiving with 447 receptions for 7,412 yards.

DEATHS

The last two of the six Nesser brothers died, Alfred on March 12 and Fred on July 2. The brothers had been the stars of the Columbus Panhandles-Tigers for many years and with several other teams.

Richard McCann, first director of Hall of Fame at Canton, Ohio, died Nov. 5.

Dr. George McLaren, halfback 1919 Massillon Tigers, died Nov. 13.

Chester Gladchuk, center, 1941, 46-47 New York Giants, died Sept. 4.

Bruce Smith, back, 1945-48 Green Bay, Los Angeles, died Aug. 28.

Arthur Braman, tackle, 1923 Racine, died.

Larry Steinback, tackle, 1930-33 Chi-Bears Chicards, Philadelphia, died June 29.

Joseph Campanella, tackle, 1952-57 Dallas, Baltimore died Feb. 15.

Nicholas Susoeff, end, 1946-49 San Francisco (AAFC), died Jan. 31.

Berlin Guy Chamberlin, end-coach 1920-27, Decatur, Canton, Cleveland, Frankford, Chi-Cards; Hall of Fame 1965, died April 4.

Wayne Underwood, tackle, 1937 Cleveland, Cincinnati, died Oct. 26.

1967 NFL CHAMPIONSHIP

GREEN BAY 21; DALLAS 17

A one-yard smash for a touchdown by Bart Starr, Green Bay quarterback, with 13 seconds to play in the final quarter gave Green Bay its third consecutive NFL title. Temperature at Lambeau Stadium, Green Bay on Dec. 30, was —13 when the game started, lower when Starr's plunge wiped out the 17-14 lead which Dallas had taken earlier in the final period.

Following the script of a year before, the Packers gained a 14-0 lead on TD passes from Bart Starr to Boyd Dowler of eight and 46 yards, with Chandler converting. Dallas got seven back in the second period when Willie Townes, defensive end, smashed Starr down for a 19-yard loss and forced a fumble which was picked up and run in from the Green Bay seven by George Andrie.

Late in the second period, Willie Wood fumbled a punt, Dallas recovered and Villanueva kicked a 21-yard field goal to make it 14-10.

The third period was scoreless but Dallas was now taking charge and stopping the Packers' offense.

The Cowboys went ahead 17-14, early in the last quarter on a 50-yard pass from Dan Reeves to Lance Rentzel with Villanueva adding the 17th point. Green Bay made its final drive from 68-yards out with five minutes to play. Starr's gamble from the one-yard line on the icy field brought

memories of the finish of the 1965 game between the same teams when Dallas failed to score from the same distance.

Green Bay	7	7	0	7	21
Dallas	0	10	0	7	17

Touchdowns: Dowler (2), Starr, Rentzel
Field goals: Villanueva 1
PAT's: Chandler 3; Villanueva 2.
Attendance: 50,861

Players' shares: Green Bay $7,951; Dallas $5,879

1967 AFL CHAMPIONSHIP

OAKLAND 40; HOUSTON 7

Oakland, Western division leaders, slaughtered the Houston Oilers, 40-7 at Oakland, Dec. 30. The Oilers failed to score until late in the fourth period when Charlie Frazier took a 5-yard TD pass from Pete Beathard and John Wittenborn added their seventh point.

Throughout the game, the Raider defense stopped the Oilers with Hewritt Dixon romping for 144 yards and George Blanda kicking four field goals from 37,40,42 and 36 yards.

Pete Banaszak, Oakland halfback, added 114 yards rushing to Dixon's yardage.

Oakland	3	14	10	13	40
Houston	0	0	0	7	7

Touchdowns: Dixon, Kocourek, Lamonica, Miller, Frazier.
Field goals: Blanda 4.
PAT's: Blanda 3; Wittenborn 1.
Attendance: 53,330.
Players' shares: Oakland $6,321.77; Houston $4,996.45.

1967 SUPER BOWL PLAYOFF

GREEN BAY 33; OAKLAND 14

For the second straight year, the Packers exploded the dreams of AFL fans who had hoped that the eight-year-old AFL was getting close to the 47-year-old NFL. Once again, as in 1966 when Green Bay beat Kansas City, 35-10, the 1967 game developed as a controlled annihilation of the Raiders.

Bart Starr, Green Bay quarterback, picked the Oakland defense apart with a 62-yard touchdown pass to Boyd Dowler as one of 13 completions in 24 tries. Don Chandler added four field goals for Green Bay from 39,20,43 and 31 yards. Donny Anderson scored another TD on a five-yard smash and defensive back Herb Adderley added another on a 60-yard romp after intercepting one of Daryle Lamonica's 34 passes of which 15 were completed.

Green Bay's defense played its usual nearly flawless game, giving up two TDs on Lamonica passes to end Bill Miller, both from 23 yards out. Blanda scored both conversions.

Green Bay	3	13	10	7	33
Oakland	0	7	0	7	14

Touchdowns: Dowler, Anderson, Adderley, Miller 2.

Field Goals: Chandler 4.

PATs: Chandler 3, Blanda 2.

Attendance: 75,546

Players' shares: Green Bay $15,000; Oakland $7,500.

1967 ATLANTA FALCONS
COACH - Norb Hecker
8th 1-12-1

Absher, Dick - K
Anderson, Taz - E
Barnes, Gary - E
Bleick, Tom - B
Bowling, Andy - LB
Calland, Lee - B
Coffey, Junior - B
Cook, Ed - T
Dunn, Perry Lee - B
Fitzgerald, Mike - B
Grimm, Dan - G
Harmon, Tom - G
Hawkins, Alex - E
Heck, Ralph - LB
Hudlow, Floyd - E
Hughes, Bob - E
Johnson, Randy - Q
Kirouac, Lou - T
Kupp, Jake - G
Linden, Errol - T
Lothridge, Billy - K
McDonald, Tom - B
Mankins, Jim - B
Marchlewski, Frank - C
Martin, Billy - E
Moore, Tom - B
Nobis, Tom - LB

Nofsinger, Terry - Q
Norton, Jim - T
Ogden, Ray - B
Rassas, Nick - B
Reaves, Ken - B
Rector, Ron - B
Richards, Bob - E
Richardson, Jerry - B
Riggle, Bob - B
Rubke, Karl - LB
Rushing, Marion - LB
Sandeman, Bill - T
Sanders, Bob - LB
Sieminski, Clark - T
Simmons, Jerry - B
Simon, Jim - LB
Sloan, Steve - Q
Smith, Ron - B
Szczecko, Joe - T
Talbert, Don - T
Traynham, Wade - K
Wheelwright, Ernie - B
Williams, Sam - E
Wilson, Jim - G
Wood, "Bo" - E

1967 BALTIMORE COLTS
COACH - Don Shula
1st 11-1-2
(Tied with Los Angeles)

Alley, Don - B
Ball, Sam - T
Berry, Raymond - E
Boyd, Bob - B
Braase, Ordell - E
Brown, Barry - LB
Curry, Bill - C
Curtis, "Mike" - LB
Davis, Norman - G
Gaubatz, Dennis - LB
Harold, George - B
Hawkins, Alex - B
Haymond, Alvin - B
Hill, Jerry - B
Hilton, Roy - E
Lee, David - K
Logan, Jerry - B
Lorick, Tony - B
Lyles, Lenny - B
Mackey, John - E
Matte, Tom - B
Memmelaar, Dale - G
Michaels, Lou - E & K

Miller, Fred - T
Moore, Lenny - B
Orr, Jim - E
Parker, Jim - T
Pearson, Preston - B
Perkins, Ray - E
Porter, Ron - LB
Ressler, Glenn - T
Richardson, Willie - E
Shinnick, Don - LB
Smith, Billy Ray - T
Smith, "Bubba" - T
Stukes, Charles - B
Stynchula, Andy - E
Sullivan, Dan - G
Szymanski, Dick - C
Unitas, John - Q
Vogel, Bob - T
Volk, Dick - B
Ward, Jim - Q
Welch, Jim - B
Wilson, George - E

1967 CHICAGO BEARS
COACH - George Halas
4th 7-6-1

Allen, Duane - E
Amsler, Marty - E
Brown, Charles - B
Buffone, Doug - LB
Bukich, Rudy - Q
Bull, Ron - B
Butkus, Dick - LB
Cadile, Jim - T
Concannon, Jack - Q
Cornish, Frank - T
Croftcheck, Don - G
Denney, Austin - E
Dodd, Al - B
Evey, Dick - E
Gentry, Curtis - B
Gordon, Dick - E
Green, Bobby Joe - K
Jackson, Randy - T
James, Dan - T
Johnson, John - T
Jones, Jim - E
Jones, Bob - E
Kriewald, Doug - G

Kuechenberg, Rudy - LB
Kurek, Ralph - B
Livingston, Andy - B
McRae, Benny - B
McRae, Frank - T
Morris, John - B
O'Bradovich, Ed - E
Percival, Mac - K
Petitbon, Rich - B
Phillips, Loyd - E
Piccolo, Brian - B
Pickens, Bob - T
Purnell, Jim - LB
Pyle, Mike - C
Rakestraw, Larry - Q
Reilly, "Mike" - LB
Sayers, Gale - B
Seals, George - G
Stoepel, Terry - E
Taylor, Joe - B
Taylor, "Rosey" - B
Wetoska, Bob - T

1967 CLEVELAND BROWNS
COACH - Blanton Collier
1st 9-5-0
(Tied with Dallas; lost Eastern
Conference title to Dallas, 52-14)

Andrews, Bill - LB
Barnes, Erich - B
Barney, Eppie - B
Brewer, John - LB
Clark, Monte - T
Collins, Gary - E
Conjar, Larry - B
Copeland, Jim - G
Davis, Ben - B
Demarie, John - T
Devrow, Bill - B
Duncan, Ron - E
Fichtner, Ross - B
Glass, Bill - E

Green, Ernie - B
Green, Ron - B
Gregory, "Jack" - E
Groza, Lou - K
Harraway, Charles - B
Hickerson, Gene - G
Hoaglin, Fred - C
Houston, Jim - LB
Howell, Mike - B
Johnson, Walter - T
Kanicki, Jim - T
Kellerman, Ernie - B
Kelly, Leroy - B
Lane, Gary - Q

Lindsey, Dale - LB
McNeil, Clifton - E
Matheson, Bob - LB
Morin, Milt - E
Parker, Frank - T
Pietrosante, Nick - B
Ryan, Frank - Q
Schafrath, Dick - T

Shiner, Dick - Q
Smith, Ralph - E
Taffoni, Joe - G
Ward, Carl - B
Warfield, Paul - E
Wiggin, Paul - E
Wooten, John - G
Youngblood, George - B

1967 GREEN BAY PACKERS

COACH - Vincent Lombardi
3rd 9-4-1
(Beat Los Angeles, 28-7, for
Western Conference title;
beat Dallas, 21-17 for NFL
title; Beat Oakland 33-14,
for Interleague title)

Adderly, Herb - B
Aldridge, Lionel - E
Anderson, Donny - B
Bowman, Ken - C
Bratkowski, "Zeke" - Q
Brown, Allen - E
Brown, Bob - E
Brown, Tom - B
Caffey, Lee Roy - LB
Capp, Dick - E
Chandler, Don - K
Crutcher, Tom - LB
Dale, Carroll - E
Davis, Willie - E
Dowler, Boyd - E
Flanigan, Jim - LB
Fleming, Marv - E
Gillingham, Gale - G
Grabowski, Jim - B
Gregg, Forrest - T
Hart, Doug - B
Horn, Don - Q

Hyland, Bob - T
James, Claudis - B
Jeter, Bob - B
Jordan, Henry - T
Kostelnik, Ron - T
Kramer, Jerry - G
Long, Bob - E
McGee, Max - E
Mercein, Chuck - B
Nitschke, Ray - LB
Pitts, Elijah - B
Robinson, "Dave" - LB
Rowser, John - B
Skoronski, Bob - T
Starr, "Bart" - Q
Thurston, Fred - G
Weatherwax, Jim - T
Williams, Travis - B
Wilson, Ben - B
Wood, Willie - B
Wright, Steve - T

1967 DALLAS COWBOYS

COACH - Tom Landry
1st 9-5-0
(Tied with Cleveland; beat
Cleveland for Eastern Conf
title, 52-14; lost to Green Bay,
21-17 for NFL title)

Andrie, George - E
Baynham, Craig - B
Beeke, Jim - T
Clark, Phil - B
Clarke, Frank - E
Connelly, Mike - C
Daniels, Dick - B
Deters, Harold - K
Donahue, Leon - T
East, Ron - E
Edwards, Dave - LB
Gaechter, Mike - B
Garrison, Walter - B
Gent, "Pete" - E
Green, Cornell - B
Hayes, Bob - E
Hays, Harold - LB
Howley, "Chuck" - LB
Johnson, Mike - B
Jordan, Lee Roy - LB
Lilly, Bob - T

Liscio, Tony - T
Meredith, Don - Q
Morton, Craig - Q
Neely, Ralph - T
Niland, John - G
Norman, Pettis - E
Perkins, Don - B
Pugh, Jethro - T
Reeves, Dan - B
Renfro, Mel - B
Rentzel, Lance - E
Rhome, Gerry - Q
Shy, Les - B
Stephens, Larry - T
Stokes, Sims - E
Townes, Willie - E
Tubbs, Gerry - LB
Villanueva, Danny - K
Walker, Malcolm - C
Wilburn, John - T
Wright, Rayfield - E

1967 LOS ANGELES RAMS

COACH - George Allen
1st 11-1-2
(Tied with Baltimore; lost to
Green Bay, 28-7, in Western
Conference playoff)

Bass, Dick - B
Baughan, Maxie - LB
Breen, Gene - LB
Brown, Roger - T
Burman, George - T
Cahill, Dave - T
Carollo, Joe - T
Casey, Bernie - E
Chuy, Don - G
Cowan, Charles - T
Crabb, Claude - B
Cross, Irvin - B
Daniel, Willie - B
Ellison, Willie - B
Gabriel, Roman - Q
Gossett, Bruce - K
Guillory, Tony - LB
Iman, Ken - C
Jones, Dave - E
Josephson, Les - B
Kilgore, Jon - K
Lamson, Chuck - B

Lundy, Lamar - E
Mack, Tom - G
Mason, Tom - B
Meador, Ed - B
Munson, Bill - Q
Nichols, Bob - T
Olsen, Merlin - T
Pardee, John - LB
Pivec, Dave - E
Pope, "Bucky" - E
Pottios, Myron - LB
Schumacher, Gregg - E
Scibelli, Joe - T
Snow, Jack - E
Stiger, Jim - B
Talbert, Diron - T
Truax, Bill - E
Tucker, Wendell - E
Williams, Clarence - B
Winston, Kelton - B
Woodlief, Doug - LB

1967 DETROIT LIONS

COACH - Joe Schmidt
6th 5-7-2

Barney, Lem - B
Bass, Mike - B
Bradshaw, Charles - T
Clark, Ernie - LB
Cogdill, Gail - E
Cottrell, Bill - T
Farr, Mel - B
Felts, Bob - B
Flanagan, Ed - C
Gallagher, Frank - G
Gibbons, Jim - E
Goovert, Ron - LB
Gordy, John - T
Hand, Larry - E
Henderson, John - E
Kamanu, Lew - E
Karras, Alex - T
Kowalkowski, Bob - G
Kramer, Ron - E
LeBeau, Dick - B
Lucci, Mike - LB
McCambridge, John - E
McCord, Darris - E

Maher, Bruce - B
Malinchak, Bill - E
Marsh, Amos - B
Melinkovich, Mike - E
Moore, Denis - B
Naumoff, Paul - LB
Nowatzke, Tom - B
Plum, Milt - Q
Rasmussen, Wayne - B
Rush, Gerry - T
Shoals, Roger - T
Studstill, Pat - B
Sweetan, Karl - Q
Thompson, Bob - B
Vaughn, Tom - B
Walker, Wayne - LB
Walton, Charles - G
Watkins, Tom - B
Weger, Mike - B
Winkler, Randy - T
Yepremian, Garo - K
Zawadzkas, Gerry - E

1967 MINNESOTA VIKINGS

COACH - Howard Grant
7th 3-8-3

Alderman, Grady - G
Beasley, John - E
Berry, Bob - Q
Bowie, Larry - G
Breitenstein, Bob - T
Brown, Bill - B
Coleman, Alvin - B
Cox, Fred - K

Davis, Doug - T
Denny, Earl - B
Dickson, Paul - T
Eller, Carl - E
Faust, Paul - LB
Fitzgerald, Mike - B
Flatley, Paul - E
Grim, Bob - B

Hackbart, Dale - B
Hansen, Don - LB
Hargrove, Jim - LB
Jones, Clint - B
Jordon, Jeff - B
Kapp, Joe - Q
Kassulke, Karl - B
Keys, Brady - B
Kirby, John - LB
Larsen, Gary - T
Lindsey, Jim - B
McKeever, Marlin - E
Mackbee, Earsell - B
Marshall, Jim - E
Osborn, Dave - B
Page, Alan - T

Pentecost, John - G
Phillips, Jim - E
Sharockman, Ed - B
Shay, Jerry - T
Simkus, Arnold - T
Sunde, Milt - G
Sutton, Archie - T
Tatman, "Pete" - B
Tingelhoff, "Mick" - C
Tobey, Dave - LB
Vanderkelen, Ron - Q
Vellone, Jim - T
Walden, Bobby - K
Warwick, Lonnie - LB
Washington, Gene - E
Winston, Roy - LB

Murdock, Les - K
Peay, Francis - T
Post, Bob - B
Shofner, Del - E
Staten, Randy - E
Swain, Bill - LB
Tarkenton, Francis - Q

Thomas, Aaron - E
Triplett, Bill - B
Weisacosky, Ed - LB
White, Freeman - B
Williams, Willie - B
Young, Willie - T

1967 PHILADELPHIA EAGLES
COACH - Joe Kuharich
4th 6-7-1
(Tied with St. Louis)

Baker, "Sam" - K
Ballman, Gary - E
Beisler, Randy - E
Berry, Dan - B
Brown, Fred - LB
Brown, Bob - T
Brown, Timmy - B
Dial, Benjy - Q
Ditka, Mike - E
Emelianchik, Pete - E
Goodwin, Ron - E
Gray, Jim - B
Hart, Dick - G
Hawkins, Ben - B
Hill, Fred - E
Hill, King - Q
Howell, Lane - T
Hoyem, Lynn - G
Hughes, Charles - B
Hultz, Don - E
Jones, Harry - B
Kelley, "Ike" - LB
Kelly, Jim - E
Lang, Issy - B
Lince, Dave - E

Lloyd, Dave - LB
Martin, Aaron - B
Medved, Ron - B
Meyers, John - T
Morgan, Mike - LB
Nelson, Al - B
Nettles, Jim - B
Peters, Floyd - T
Pettigrew, Gary - E
Ramsey, Nate - B
Recher, Dave - C
Reed, Taft - B
Ringo, Jim - C
Scarpati, Joe - B
Shann, Bob - B
Skaggs, Jim - G
Snead, Norman - Q
Stetz, Bill - G
Tom, Mel - LB
Vasys, Arunas - LB
Wells, Harold - LB
Wilson, Harry - B
Wink, Dean - E
Woodeschick, Tom - B
Wright, Gordon - G

1967 NEW ORLEANS SAINTS
COACH - Tom Fears
8th 3-11-0

Abramowicz, Dave - E
Anderson, Dick - T
Atkins, Doug - E
Barrington, Tom - B
Brown, Charles - B
Burke, Vern - E
Burkett, "Jackie" - LB
Burris, "Bo" - B
Cody, Bill - LB
Cordileone, Lou - G
Cortez, Bruce - B
Cuozzo, Gary - Q
Davis, "Ted" - LB
Douglas, John - B
Durkee, Charles - K
Garcia, Jim - E
Gilliam, John - B
Hall, Tom - B
Hart, Ben - B
Harvey, George - T
Heidel, Jim - B
Hester, Jim - E
Jones, Jerry - T
Jordan, Jim - B
Kelley, Les - B
Kilmer, Bill - Q
Kramer, Kent - E
Kupp, Jake - G
Leggett, Earl - T
Logan, Obert - B

McCall, Don - B
McCormick, Dave - T
McNeil, Tom - K
Mingo, Gene - K
Nevett, Elijah - B
Ogden, Ray - B
Poage, Ray - E
Rissmiller, Ray - T
Roberts, Walt - B
Rose, George - B
Rowe, Dave - T
Sandeman, Bill - T
Schmidt, Roy - G
Schultz, Randy - B
Schweda, Brian - E
Simmons, Dave - LB
Simmons, Jerry - B
Stonebreaker, Steve - LB
Strand, Eli - G
Sturm, Jerry - T
Taylor, Jim - B
Tilleman, Mike - T
Vandersea, Phil - LB
Wndryhoski, Joe - C
Wheelwright, Ernie - B
Whitsell, Dave - B
Whittingham, Fred - G
Williams, Delano - G
Wood, Gary - Q
Youngblood, George - B

1967 PITTSBURGH STEELERS
COACH - Bill Austin
7th 4-9-1

Anderson, Chet - E
Arndt, Dick - T
Asbury, Willie - B
Badar, Dick - Q
Baker, John - E
Bivins, Charley - B
Bradshaw, Jim - B
Breedlove, Rod - LB
Brown, John - T
Butler, Jim - B
Campbell, John - LB
Clark, Michael - K
Compton, Dick - B
Cropper, Marshall - E
Davis, Sam - G
Elliott, Jim - K
Foruria, John - B
Gagner, Larry - G
Gros, Earl - B
Haggerty, Mike - G
Hilton, John - E
Hinton, Charles - T
Hoak, Dick - B

Hohn, Bob - B
Jefferson, Roy - E
Keys, Brady - B
Kortas, Ken - T
McGee, Ben - E
Mansfield, Ray - T
Marion, Jerry - B
Martha, Paul - B
May, Ray - LB
Mazzanti, Jerry - E
Morgan, Bob - B
Nelsen, Bill - Q
Nix, Kent - Q
O'Brien, Francis - T
Russell, Andy - LB
Saul, Bill - LB
Shy, Don - B
Thomas, Clendon - B
Van Dyke, Bruce - G
Voss, Lloyd - E
Wenzel, Ralph - G
Wilburn, John - E
Woodson, Marv - B

1967 NEW YORK GIANTS
COACH - Al Sherman
3rd 7-7-0

Anderson, Bruce - T
Anderson, Roger - T
Avery, Ken - LB
Bolin, "Bookie" - G
Carr, Henry - B
Case, "Pete" - G
Childs, Clarence - B
Ciccolella, Mike - LB
Colvin, Jim - T
Condren, Glen - E
Costello, Vince - LB
Crespino, Bob - E
Davis, "Rosey" - E
Dess, Darrell - G
Eaton, Scott - B
Fitzgerald, Mike - B
Frederickson, "Tucker" - B
Gogolak, Pete - K

Gross, Andy - G
Harper, Charles - T
Harris, Wendell - B
Hathcock, Dave - B
Hinton, Charles - T
Jacobs, Allen - B
Jones, Homer - E
Katcavage, Jim - E
Kotite, Dick - LB
Koy, Ernie - B
Larson, Greg - C
Lockhart, Carl - B
Lurtsema, Bob - T
Mercein, Chuck - B
Minniear, Randy - B
Moran, Jim - T
Morrall, Earl - Q
Morrison, Joe - B

1967 ST. LOUIS CARDINALS
COACH - Charles Winner
4th 6-7-1
(Tied with Philadelphia)

Bakken, Jim - K
Barnes, Mike - B

Brumm, Don - E
Bryant, Charles - B

Burson, Jim - B
Conrad, Bobby Joe - B
Crenshaw, Willis - B
DeMarco, Bob - C
Fischer, Pat - B
Gambrell, Billy - E
Gautt, Prentice - B
Goode, Irvin - T
Gray, Ken - G
Hart, Jim - Q
Heron, Fred - T
Hillebrand, Jerry - LB
Johnson, Charley - Q
Kasperek, Dick - C
Koman, Bill - LB
Latourette, Charles - K & B
Logan, Chuck - E
Long, Dave - T
McMillan, Ernie - T
Marcontell, Ed - G
Meggyesy, Dave - LB
Meinert, Dale - LB

O'Brien, Dave - T
Reynelds, Bob - T
Robb, "Joe" - E
Roland, John - B
Rowe, Bob - E
Shivers, Roy - E
Silas, Sam - T
Smith, Jackie - E
Sortun, Rick - G
Spiller, Phil - B
Stallings, Larry - LB
Stovall, Jerry - LB
Strofolino, Mike - LB
Thornton, Bill - B
Van Galder, Tim - C
Walker, Chuck - T
Wheeler, Ted - E
Williams, Clyde - T
Williams, Dave - E
Williams, Bob - B
Wilson, Larry - B

Smith, Dick - B
Snidow, Ron - E
Snowden, Jim - T
Taylor, Charley - E
Thurlow, Steve - B

Walters, Tom - B
Whitfield, A. D. - B
Williams, Sid - LB
Wingate, Heath - C

1967 BOSTON PATRIOTS
COACH - Mike Holovak
5th 3-10-1

Addison, Tom - LB
Antwine, Houston - G
Bellino, Joe - B
Boudreaux, Jim - E
Buoniconi, Nick - LB
Canale, Justin - G
Cappadonna, Bob - B
Cappelletti, Gino - E
Charles, John - B
Colclough, Jim - E
Cunningham, Jay - B
Dee, Bob - E
Eisenhauer, Larry - E
Fussell, Tom - E
Garrett, John - B
Garron, Larry - B
Graham, Art - E
Graves, White - B
Hall, Ron - B
Huarte, John - LB
Hunt, Jim - E
Ilg, Ray - LB

Johnson, Bill - B
Long, Charles - T
Mangum, John - T
Mitchell, Leroy - B
Morris, Jon - C
Nance, Jim - B
Neville, Tom - T
Nichols, Bob - E
Oakes, Don - T
Parilli, "Babe" - Q
Philpott, Ed - LB
Purvis, Vic - B
Romeo, Tony, - E
St. Jean, Len - G
Satcher, Doug - LB
Shonta, Chuck - B
Singer, Karl - T
Swanson, Terry - K
Toner, Ed - T
Trull, Don - LB
Webb, Don - B
Whalen, Jim - E

1967 SAN FRANCISCO 49ers
COACH - Jack Christiansen
5th 7-7-0

Alexander, Kermit - B
Beard, Ed - LB
Bosley, Bruce - C
Brodie, John - Q
Cerne, Joe - C
Collett, Elmer - G
Crow, John David - B
Cunningham, Doug - B
Davis, Tom - K
Donnelly, George - B
Gonsoulin, "Goose" - B
Harrison, Bob - LB
Hazeltine, Matt - LB
Hettema, Dave - T
Hindman, Stan - E
Holzer, Tom - E
Jackson, Jim - B
Johnson, Charles - T
Johnson, Jim - B
Johnson, Walt - E
Kopay, Dave - B
Krueger, Charles - T
Lakes, Roland - T
Lewis, Gary - B

Miller, Clark - E
Mira, George - Q
Mudd, Howard - G
Myers, "Chip" - B
Nunley, Frank - LB
Olerich, Dave - E
Parker, Don - G
Parks, Dave - E
Phillips, Mel - B
Randle, "Sonny" - E
Randolph, Alvin - B
Rock, Walter - E
Rohde, Len - T
Spurrier, Steve - Q
Stickles, Monty - E
Swinford, Wayne - B
Thomas, John - T
Trimble, Wayne - B
Tucker, Bill - B
Wilcox, Dave - LB
Willard, Ken - B
Windsor, Bob - E
Witcher, Dick - B

1967 BUFFALO BILLS (AFL)
COACH - Joel Collier
3rd 4-10-0
(Tied with Miami)

Bailey, Bill - B
Barber, Stu - G
Bemiller, Al - C
Bivins, Charley - B
Bugenhagen, Gary - T
Burnett, Bob - B
Byrd, George - B
Carlton, Wray - B
Clarke, Hagood - B
Costa, Paul - E
Cunningham, Dick - G
Donaldson, Gene - B
Dubenion, Elbert - E
Dunaway, Jim - T
Edgerson, Booker - B
Flores, Tom - QB
Frazier, Wayne - C
Guidry, Paul - LB
Hudson, Dick - G
Jacobs, Harry - LB
Janik, Tom - B
Kemp, Jack - QB
Kindig, Howard - E
King, Tony - B
King, Charles - B

Ledbetter, Monte - B
LeMoine, Jim - T
Lincoln, Keith - B
McDole, Roland - T
Maguire, Paul - LB
Masters, Bill - E
Mercer, Mike - K
Meredith, Dud - T
O'Donnell, Joe - G
Petrich, Bob - E
Pitts, John - B
Ply, Bobby - B
Powell, Art - E
Prudhomme, Remi - E
Rutkowski, Ed - B
Saimes, George - B
Schmidt, Bob - T
Schottenheimer, Marty - LB
Sestak, Tom - T
Shaw, Bill - G
Smith, Allen - B
Spikes, Jack - B
Stratton, Mike - LB
Tracey, John - LB
Zecher, Dick - T

1967 WASHINGTON REDSKINS
COACH - Otto Graham
6th 5-6-3

Absher, Dick - K
Alford, Bruce - K
Allen, Gerry - B
Bandy, Don - G
Barnes, Walt - T
Breding, Ed - LB
Briggs, Bill - E
Burrell, John - E
Carroll, Jim - LB
Crossan, Dave - C
Gogolak, Charles - K
Hanburger, Chris - LB
Harris, Rickie - B
Hauss, Len - C
Hendershot, Larry - LB
Huff, "Sam" - LB
Jackson, Steve - LB
Jackson, Trenton - B
Johnson, Mitch - G
Jurgensen, "Sonny" - Q

Kammerer, Carl - E
Kelly, John - T
Krause, Paul - B
Larson, "Pete" - B
Looney, Joe Don - B
Love, John - B
McDonald, Ray - B
Mingo, Gene - K
Mitchell, Bobby - B
Musgrove, Spain - T
Ninowski, Jim - Q
Owens, Brig - B
Prestel, Jim - T
Promuto, Vince - G
Richter, "Pat" - E & K
Rutgens, Joe - T
Sanders, Lonnie - B
Schoenke, Ray - T
Shorter, Jim - B
Smith, Jerry - E

1967 DENVER BRONCOS (AFL)

COACH - Louis Saban
4th 3-11-1

Andrus, Lou - E
Beer, Tom - E
Behrman, Dave - T
Breitenstein, Bob - T

Brunelli, Sam - G
Cassese, Tom - B
Cichowski, Tom - T
Costa, Dave - LB

Cox, Larry - T
Crabtree, Eric - B
Cunningham, Carl - LB
Current, Mike - T
Denson, Al - E
Duncan, Rick - K
Duranko, Pete - LB
Gilchrist, "Cookie" - B
Glacken, "Scotty" - Q
Goeddeke, George - G
Hayes, Wendell - B
Hickey, "Bo" - B
Huard, John - LB
Inman, Jerry - T
Humphries, Bob - K
Jackson, Dick - LB
Jaquess, "Pete" - B
Jeter, Gene - LB
Kaminski, Larry - C
Keating, Bill - G
Kellogg, Mike - B
Kroner, Gary - K
Kubala, Ray - C
LeClair, Jim - Q
LeClerc, Roger - LB

Lentz, "Jack" - B
Little, Floyd - B
Lynch, Francis - B
Matson, Pat - G
Mirich, Rex - T
Mitchell, Charles - B
Myrtle, Charles - LB
Park, Ernie - G
Ply, Bobby - B
Prisby, Errol - B
Richter, Frank - LB
Scarpitto, Bob - B
Sellers, Goldie - B
Smith, Donal - G
Sorrell, Harry - LB
Sommers, Jim - B
Sweeney, Neal - E
Sykes, Gene - B
Tensi, Steve - C
Tyson, Dick - G
White, Andre - E
Wilson, Nemiah - B
Wright, Larry - E
Young, Bob - T

Mays, Gerry - T
Merz, Curt - G
Mitchell, Willie - B
Pitts, Frank - E
Ply, Bobby - B
Reynolds, Al - G
Rice, Andy - T
Richardson, Gloster - B
Robinson, John - B
Smith, Fletcher - B

Smith, Noland - B
Stenerud, Jan - K
Taylor, Otis - E
Thomas, Emmitt - B
Thomas, Gene - B
Trosch, Gene - T
Tyrer, Jim - T
Walker, Wayne - K
Williamson, Fred - B
Wilson, Jerry - K

1967 HOUSTON OILERS (AFL)
COACH - Wally Lemm
1st 9-4-1

Anderson, Billy Guy - Q
Barnes, Pete - LB
Bass, Glenn - E
Beathard, Pete - Q
Bishop, "Sonny" - G
Blanks, Sid - B
Boyette, Garland - LB
Brabham, Dan - LB
Burrell, Ode - B
Campbell, "Woody" - B
Carwell, Larry - B
Caveness, Ron - LB
Davis, Bob - C
Elkins, Larry - E
Farr, Miller - B
Floyd, Don - E
Frazier, Charles - B
Granger, Hoyle - B
Hicks, Wilmer - B
Hines, Glen Ray - T
Holmes, "Pat" - T
Hopkins, Roy - B
Houston, Ken - B
Jancik, Bob - B

Johns, Pete - B
Jones, Willie - E
Ladd, Ernie - T
Ledbetter, Monte - B
Lee, Jackie - Q
Maples, Bob - LB
Marcontell, Ed - G
Marshall, Rich - T
Moore, "Zeke" - B
Norton, Jim - B
Parker, Willie - E
Poole, Bob - E
Reed, Alvin - E
Regner, Tom - G
Rice, Andy - T
Rice, George - T
Stith, Carl - T
Suggs, Walter - T
Talamini, Bob - G
Taylor, Lionel - E
Trull, Don - Q
Underwood, Olen - LB
Webster, George - LB
Wittenborn, John - G

1967 KANSAS CITY CHIEFS (AFL)
COACH - Henry Stram
2nd 9-5-0

Abell, Harry - LB
Arbanas, Fred - E
Beathard, Pete - Q
Bell, Bobby - LB
Biodrowski, Denny - G
Buchanan, "Buck" - T
Budde, Ed - G
Burford, Chris - E
Carolan, Reg - E
Coan, Bert - B
Dawson, Len - Q
DiMidio, Tony - T
Frazier, Wayne - C
Garrett, Mike - B
Gilliam, Jon - C

Headrick, Sherrill - LB
Hill, Dave - T
Holub, Emil - LB
Hudock, Mike - C
Hunt, Bob - B
Hurston, Charles - E
Kearney, Jim - B
Kelly, Bob - E
Ladd, Ernie - T
Lanier, Willie - LB
Lee, Jacky - Q
Longmire, Sam - B
Lothamer, Ed - E
Lynch, Jim - LB
McClinton, Curt - B

1967 MIAMI DOLPHINS (AFL)
COACH - George Wilson
3rd 4-10-0
(Tied with Buffalo)

Auer, Joe - B
Beier, Tom - B
Bramlett, John - LB
Branch, Mel - E
Brownlee, Claude - E
Bruggers, Bob - LB
Carpenter, Pres - E
Chesser, George - B
Clancy, Jack - B
Cooke, Ed - B
Emanuel, Frank - LB
Erlandson, Tom - LB
Evans, Norman - T
Fowler, Charles - T
Goode, Tom - LB
Griese, Bob - Q
Harper, Jack - B
Haynes, Abner - B
Hopkins, Jerry - B
Jackson, Frank - B
Jacobs, Ray - E
Jaquess, Pete - B
Keating, Bill - G
Lamb, Jack - B
Lusteg, Booth - K
McDaniel, "Wahoo" - LB

Mingo, Gene - K
Mitchell, Stan - E
Moreau, Doug - E
Neff, Bob - B
Neighbors, Billy - T
Nimona, Tom - T
Noonan, Karl - E
Norton, Rich - Q
Petrella, Bob - B
Price, Sam - B
Pyburn, Jack - T
Rice, Ken - T
Richardson, John - T
Riley, Jim - G
Roberts, Archie - Q
Roderick, John - E
Seiple, Larry - K
Stofa, John - Q
Twilley, Howard - E
Warren, Jim - B
West, Willie - B
Westmoreland, Dick - E
Williams, Maxie - T
Woodson, Fred - G
Zecher, Dick - T

1967 NEW YORK JETS (AFL)
COACH - Wilbur Ewbank
2nd 8-5-1

Atkinson, Al - LB
Baird, Bill - B
Baker, Ralph - LB
Beverly, Randy - B
Biggs, Verlon - E
Boozer, Emerson - B
Brannan, Solomon - B
Christy, Earl - E
Crane, Paul - LB
Elliott, John - LB
Gordon, Cornell - B
Grantham, Larry - LB
Harris, Jim - T
Haynes, Abner - B
Herman, Dave - G
Hill, Winston - T
Hudson, Jim - B
Joe, Billy - B
Johnson, Curley - B
King, Henry - B
Lammons, Pete - E
Lewis, Sherman - B
Lusteg, Booth - K
McAdams, Carl - LB

Mathis, Bill - B
Matlock, John - C
Maynard, Don - B
Namath, Joe Willie - Q
Perreault, Pete - T
Philbin, Gerry - E
Plunkett, Sherman - T
Rademacher, Bill - B
Randall, Dennis - E
Rasmussen, Randall - G
Richardson, Jeff - G
Rochester, Paul - T
Sample, John - B
Sauer, George - E
Schmitt, John - C
Schweichert, Bob - B
Seiler, Paul - T
Smolinski, Mark - B
Snell, Matt - B
Taliaferro, Mike - Q
Turner, Jim - K
Turner, "Bake" - B
Waskiewicz, Jim - C
Wilder, Albert - E

1967 OAKLAND RAIDERS (AFL)
COACH - John Rauch
1st 13-1-0

Archer, Dan - T	Keating, Tom - T
Banaszak, Pete - B	Kocourek, Dave - E
Banks, Estes - B	Kruse, Bob - G
Benson, Duane - LB	Lamonica, Daryle - Q
Biletnikoff, Fred - E	Laskey, Bill - LB
Bird, Rodger, - B	Lassiter, Ike - T
Birdwell, Dan - E	McCloughan, Kent - B
Blanda, George - Q & K	Miller, Bill - E
Brown, Willie - B	Oats, Carleton - E
Budness, Bill - LB	Otto, "Gus" - LB
Cannon, Billy - E	Otto, Jim - C
Conners, Dan - LB	Powers, Warren - B
Daniels, Clem - B	Schuh, Harry - G
Davidson, Ben - E	Sherman, Rod - B
Dixon, Hewritt - B	Slich, Dick - T
Eischeid, Mike - K	Svihus, Bob - T
Fairband, Bill - LB	Todd, Larry - B
Grayson, Dave - B	Upshaw, Gene - T
Hagberg, Roger - B	Wells, Warren - E
Harvey, Jim - T	Williams, Howard - B
Hawkins, Wayne - G	Williamson, John - LB
Herock, Ken - E	

1967 SAN DIEGO CHARGERS (AFL)
COACH - Sid Gillman
3rd 8-5-1

Akin, Harold - T	Hubbert, Brad - B
Allen, Charles - LB	Kindig, Howie - E
Allison, Jim - B	Kirner, Gary - T
Alworth, Lance - E	Latzke, Paul - C
Appleton, Scott - E	Little, Larry - T
Baker, John - E	Lowe, Paul - B
Beauchamp, Joe - B	MacKinnon, Jacque - B
Billingsley, Ron - E	Marsh, Frank - B
Brittenum, Jon - Q	Mitchell, Ed - G
Buncom, Frank - LB	Mix, Ron - T
Cordell, Ollie - E	Newell, Steve - E
Day, Tom - G	Owens, Terry - T
DeLong, Steve - E	Post, Dick - B
Duncan, Les - B	Print, Bob - LB
Erickson, Bernie - LB	Redman, Rich - LB
Foster, Gene - B	Ridge, Houston - B
Frazier, Bill - E	Smith, Russ - B
Garrison, Gary - E	Staggs, Jeff - LB
Graham, Kenny - B	Stephenson, Kay - Q
Griffin, Jim - E	Sweeney, Walt - T
Gross, George - T	Tolbert, Jim - B
Gruneisen, Sam - G	Van Raaphorst, Dick - K
Hadl, John - Q	Whitehead, "Bud" - B
Howard, Bob - B	Wright, Ernie - T

1968

NATIONAL FOOTBALL LEAGUE

WESTERN CONFERENCE

COASTAL DIVISION

	W.	L.	T.	Pc.
Baltimore	13	1	0	.929
Los Angeles	10	3	1	.769
San Francisco	7	6	1	.538
Atlanta	2	12	0	.143

CENTRAL DIVISION

	W.	L.	T.	Pc.
Minnesota	8	6	0	.571
Chicago	7	7	0	.500
Green Bay	6	7	1	.462
Detroit	4	8	2	.333

EASTERN CONFERENCE

CAPITAL DIVISION

	W.	L.	T.	Pc.
Dallas	12	2	0	.857
New York	7	7	0	.500
Washington	5	9	0	.357
Philadelphia	2	12	0	.143

CENTURY DIVISION

	W.	L.	T.	Pc.
Cleveland	10	4	0	.714
St. Louis	9	4	1	.692
New Orleans	4	9	1	.308
Pittsburgh	2	11	1	.154

AMERICAN FOOTBALL LEAGUE

EASTERN DIVISION

	W.	L.	T.	Pc.
New York	11	3	0	.786
Houston	7	7	0	.500
Miami	5	8	1	.385
Boston	4	10	0	.286
Buffalo	1	12	1	.077

WESTERN DIVISION

	W.	L.	T.	Pc.
*Oakland	12	2	0	.857
*Kansas City	12	2	0	.857
San Diego	9	5	0	.643
Denver	5	9	0	.357
Cincinnati	3	11	0	.214

*Oakland defeated Kansas City for Western Division title, 41–6.

TITLES: Baltimore beat Cleveland, 34-0, for the NFL title. The Baltimore Colts, of the Coastal Division, whipped the Minnesota Vikings, Central Division champions, 24-14, for the Western League title. The Cleveland Browns, Century Division champions, had upset the Dallas Cowboys, winner of the Capital Division, 31-20, for the Eastern Conference title. Dallas beat Minnesota, 17-13, in the second place playoff.

In the AFL championship, the New York Jets, Eastern Division champs, beat the Oakland Raiders, 27-23, for the league title after the Raiders routed the Kansas City Chiefs for the Western Division playoff, 41-6.

The third Interleague "Super Bowl" was won by the New York Jets, AFL, over the Baltimore Colts, NFL, 16-7.

NFL LEADERS: Individual leaders for the year: Scoring—Leroy Kelly (Cleveland) 120; Rushing—Leroy Kelly (Cleveland) 1,239 yds.; Passing—Earl Morrall (Baltimore); Pass Receiving—Clifton McNeil (San Francisco) 71; Field Goals—Mac Percival (Chicago) 25; Punting—William Lothridge (Atlanta) 44.3 yds.; Interceptions—Willie Williams (New York) 10.

AFL LEADERS: Scoring—Jim Turner (New York) 145; Rushing—Paul Robinson (Cincinnati) 1,023 yds.; Passing—Len Dawson (Kansas City); Pass Receiving—Lance Alworth (San Diego) 68; Field Goals—Jim Turner (New York) 34; Punting—Jerrel Wilson (Kansas City) 45.1 yds.; Interceptions—David Grayson (Oakland) 10.

FIRST DRAFT: NFL—Ronald Yary (S. Cal.), tackle, by Minnesota, signed by Minnesota; AFL—Robert Johnson (Tenn.), center, by Cincinnati, signed by Cincinnati.

COACHES: In the NFL, Norman Van Brocklin replaced Norb Hecker of Atlanta, Oct. 1; Jim Dooley replaced George Halas at Chicago; Phil Bengston took over for Vince Lombardi at Green Bay; and Dick Nolan replaced Jack Christiansen at San Francisco. In the AFL, Harvey Johnson replaced Joe Collier at Buffalo; and Paul Brown became head coach at Cincinnati.

HALL OF FAME elected players Albert "Turk" Edwards, Leo Nomellini, Joe Perry.

Ernie Stautner, and coach Earl "Greasy" Neale. Richard Gallagher became new director of the Hall in March.

NOTES: Don Shinnick, 12-year Colts vet, reached career interception record for linebackers with 37.

Earl Morrall led NFL in passing after directing Baltimore to title. As a backup quarterback for most of his career, he won the NFL Most Valuable Player award.

Bobby Boyd has made 57 interceptions in 9 years, ranking third behind leaders Emlen Tunnell (79) and Dick Lane (68).

Leroy Kelly, Browns' back, led the NFL in rushing for the second year with 1239 yds. and scored 20 TDs for 120 points (16 rushing, 4 receiving), to lead that category. He became the third three-time 1,000-yard ground gainer in NFL history.

Roy Jefferson (Pittsburgh), on Nov. 3 against Atlanta, hauled in 11 passes, four for TDs, to equal an NFL record for scoring catches. He finished second in the league with 58 receptions.

Chuck Latourette, Cardinal safety, ran back 46 kickoffs for 1237 yards, breaking the season record of Abe Woodson set in 1962. On punts, he recorded another 345 yards giving him 1582 yards on kick returns. On Sept. 29, he returned three punts 143 yds. to set an NFL record for one game. He also handled punting chores for St. Louis, finishing third with 41.6 average.

Don Perkins, Cowboy back, gained 836 yds. to become NFL's number five all-time rusher with 6244 career yards over 8 years. (Ahead of him: Jim Brown, Jim Taylor, Joe Perry, John Henry Johnson).

Earl McCulloch received NFL Rookie of the Year honors with the Detroit Lions.

Sam Baker, Eagles star, kicked 19 field goals in 1968; became second highest scorer in NFL history with 898 points (Lou Groza leads with 1349 pts.). Also, as Eagles' punter, his 703 kicks over 14 years top career records.

Dallas' Bob Hayes topped all punt returners, with a 20.8 average on 15 returns for 312 yards. He had a 63-yard TD return against New York.

Sonny Jurgensen, Washington quarterback, threw a TD pass to Gerry Allen that covered 99 yards in a game vs Chicago.

Don Shula of the Baltimore Colts was named NFL Coach of the year for the third time in five years.

John Widby, Dallas Cowboy punter, kicked an 84-yard punt against New Orleans.

The Minnesota Vikings' defensive back, Charlie West, ran back a 98-yard punt TD against Washington to tie the all-time NFL record.

New York blocked 3 conversion tries vs Philadelphia.

Al Haymond, Philadelphia, ran a 98-yard kickoff return (TD) vs New York.

Paul Robinson (Cincinnati) gained 1,023 yards in 238 carries in his first pro season and became the first rookie in the nine-year AFL history to surpass 1,000 yards. He was also named AFL Rookie of the Year.

Lance Alworth, San Diego, led the AFL for the sixth straight year with 68 catches for 1312 yards.

Daryle Lamonica and George Blanda, Oakland QBs, rang up 469 passing yards against Kansas City, Nov. 3, to set an AFL one-game record. They broke the old record of 464 yds. set in 1961 by Blanda, at that time Houston's QB.

Marlin Briscoe, opening the season on Denver's roster as rookie defensive back, became QB after many Bronco injuries; became the first Black to play regularly at quarterback in the pros.

Tom Janik ran back six interceptions for TDs. Janik's sixth was for 100 yds. against the Jets, Sept. 24, tying the AFL record for distance.

Bob Scarpitto, Boston Patriot, kicked an 87-yard punt to top the old AFL record of 82 set in 1961 by Paul Maguire of San Diego.

Miller Farr, Houston back, picked off two pass interceptions against Buffalo and ran them back for 52 and 40-yard touchdowns, an AFL record.

Don Maynard, N.Y. Jets flanker, caught 10 passes for 228 yds. against Oakland to set a record.

Jim Turner, New York kicker, hit 34 of 46 field goals (74%) for a new AFL record.

George "Papa Bear" Halas retired after coaching the Chicago club for 46 years.

Vince Lombardi, Green Bay's head coach, retired to the front office after 10 years.

An unusual number of talented players retired this year. Among them were;

Raymond Berry, Baltimore end, 12 years, two years #1 pass receiver, all-time leading pass receiver;

Don Chandler, New York-Green Bay kicker, 10 years; two years #1 punter;

Joe Fortunato, Chicago linebacker, 11 years;

Rosey Grier, New York-Los Angeles tackle, 10 years;

Lou Groza, Cleveland tackle-kicker, 15 years; five years #1 field goals, one year #1 scoring;

Sam Huff, New York-Washington linebacker, 10 years;

Darris McCord, Detroit end, 12 years;

Max McGee, Green Bay end, 11 years;

Dale Meinert, Chicago Cardinals-St. Louis linebacker, 8 years;

Len Moore, Baltimore back, 11 years, one year #1 scoring;

John Morris, Chicago back, one year #1 pass receiver;

Jim Ringo, Green Bay-Philadelphia center, 13 years;

Del Shofner, Los Angeles-New York end, 9 years;

Jim Taylor, Green Bay-New Orleans back, 9 years. One year #1 scoring, one year #1 ground gainer;

Fred Thurston, Baltimore-Green Bay guard, 9 years.

Deaths of former players included:

Calac, Peter—Back—1919-20, 25-26 Canton Bulldogs; 1921 Cleveland Indians 1922-23 Oorang Indians; 1924 Buffalo Bisons.

Christensen, George—Tackle—1931-33 Portsmouth Spartans; 1934-38 Detroit Lions

Driscoll, John "Paddy"—Back—1920 Decatur Staleys; 1920-25 Chicago Cardinals; 1926-29 Chicago Bears; 1956-57 head coach of Bears; 1965 Hall of Fame.

Gentry, Dale—End—1946-48 Los Angeles Dons (AAFC)

Grigg, Cecil—Qback—1919-23 Canton Bulldogs; 1924-25 Rochester Jeffersons; 1926 New York Giants; 1927 Frankford

Yellowjackets.

Handler, Philip—Guard—1930-36 Chicago Cardinals, veteran coach Cardinals and Bears.

Harris, Elmore—Back—1947 Brooklyn Dodgers (AAFC)

Jagade, Harry—Back—1949 Baltimore Colts (AAFC) ; 1951-53 Cleveland Browns; 1954-55 Chicago Bears.

Kenneally, George—End—1926-28 Pottsville Maroons; 1929, 32 Boston Braves; 1930 Chicago Cardinals; 1933-35 Philadelphia Eagles.

McLenna, Bruce—Back—1966 Detroit Lions. Car accident.

Morrissey, Frank—Tackle—1921 Rochester Jeffersons; 1922-23 Buffalo All Americans; 1924 Buffalo Bisons; 1924 Milwaukee Badgers.

Niemi, Laurie—Tackle—1949-53 Washington Redskins.

Rector, Ronald—Back—1966 Washington Redskins; 1966-67 Atlanta Falcons. Cycle accident.

Roehnelt, William—LB—1958-59 Chicago Bears; 1960 Washington Redskins; 1961-62 Denver Broncos (AFL).

Sheeks, Paul—Qback—1919 Toledo Maroons; 1921-22 Akron Pros.

Shellogg, Alec—Tackle—1939 Brooklyn Dodgers; 1939 Chicago Bears; 1940 Buffalo Indians (AFL) ; 1941 Buffalo Tigers (AFL).

Weaver, James—Center—1923 Columbus Tigers; 1926 Cleveland Panthers (AFL).

Zimmerman, Gifford—Back—1924 Akron Pros; 1925 Canton Bulldogs.

1968 NFL Championship
Baltimore 34; Cleveland 0

The Baltimore Colts completed their sensational season by shutting out the strong Cleveland team to win the National Football League championship. Tom Matte, Baltimore back, scored three touchdowns for the winners.

This was the final happy hour for Earl Morrall who had done a magnificent job of filling in for the injured John Unitas as the Baltimore quarterback.

There was no scoring in the first quarter. The Colts began to roll in the second with Lou Michaels kicking his first field goal from 28 yards, and Matte scoring his first T.D.s from 1 and 12 yards. Matte

scored again from 2 yards out in the third period, and the Colts completed the murder in the last quarter with Michaels' 10-yard field goal and a 4-yard touchdown run by Timmy Brown.

Baltimore	0	17	7	10	34
Cleveland	0	0	0	0	0

Touchdowns: Matte 3, Brown
Field Goals: Michaels 2.
PATs: Michaels 4.
Attendance: 80,628
Players' share: Baltimore $9,265.58

1968 AFL Championship
New York 27; Oakland 23

The New York Jets won the American Football League championship and an invitation to the Super Bowl by beating the Oakland Raiders with a late comeback in the final period.

They had lost the lead minutes earlier when Oakland scored a touchdown after intercepting a pass by Joe Namath and returning it to the New York 5-yard line. Namath drove the Jets to the go-ahead touchdown with a final 6-yard pass to his flanker, Don Maynard.

The same pair had scored from the 14-yard line in the first period and Namath threw a TD to end Pete Lammons in the third. Jim Turner scored field goals from 33 and 36 yards and all three conversions.

The Oakland Raiders, never able to organize a sound attack, scored on a 29-yard pass from Daryle Lamonica to Fred Biletnikoff, a 5-yard run from Pete Banaszak, three field goals by George Blanda and Blanda's two conversions.

New York	10	3	7	7	27
Oakland	0	10	3	10	23

Touchdowns: Maynard 2, Lammons, Biletnikoff, Banaszak.
Field Goals: Turner 2; Blanda 3.
PATs: Turner 3; Blanda 2.
Attendance: 62,627
Players' share: New York $7,007.91

1968 SUPER BOWL
New York 16; Baltimore 7

The New York Jets of the American Football League shocked the football world by beating the Baltimore Colts of the National Football League, 16 to 7, in the 3rd annual Super Bowl.

The Jets, supposedly outclassed by 17 to 20 points before the game, turned in one of the historic upsets in sports history against a Baltimore team which seemed unbeatable.

The three field goals scored by Jim Turner would have been enough to win; and Matt Snell of the Jets also scored on a 4-yard touchdown run.

Baltimore, obviously overconfident and flat, went into scoring territory five times and came out scoreless each time. Not until late in the 4th quarter did Jerry Hill, fullback, put 6 points on the scoreboard for the Colts.

It was a disastrous afternoon for Earl Morrall who had become a national hero throughout the season, winning many honors including the N.F.L. Most Valuable Player award.

Late in the game the crippled John Unitas, Baltimore quarterback, came off the bench to lead the only effective drives which the Colts could produce.

Joe Namath, Jets quarterback, although not directly involved in any scoring, kept the Baltimore defense off balance with his accurate passing, 16 completions—28 attempts.

New York	0	7	6	3	16
Baltimore	0	0	0	7	7

Touchdowns: Snell, Hill.

Field Goals: Turner 3.

PATs: Turner, Michaels

Attendance: 75,377

Players' share: New York $15,000; Baltimore $7,500.

Lee, Dwight - B
Lemmerman, Bruce - Q
Linden, Errol - T
Long, Bob - E
Lothridge, Billy - K
McCarthy, Brendan - B
Marchlewski, Frank - C
Nobis, Tom - LB
Norton, Jim - T
Ogden, Ray - B
Rassas, Nick - B
Reaves, Ken - B
Rushing, Marion - LB

Sandeman, Bill - T
Shay, Jerry - T
Simmons, Jerry - B
Simon, Jim - LB
Sobocinski, Phil - C
Spiller, Phil - B
Strahan, Art - T
Suchy, Larry - B
Szczecko, Joe - T
Talbert, Don - T
Wages, Harmon - B
Winkler, Randy - T
Wright, John - E

1968 BALTIMORE COLTS
COACH - Donald Shula
1st   13-1-0

(Won Western Conference, 24-14, over Minnesota; beat Cleveland, 34-0, for NFL Championship; lost to New York Jets, 16-7, in AFL-NFL Game.)

Austin, Ocie - B
Ball, Sam - T
Boyd, Bob - B
Braase, Ordell - E
Brown, Tim - B
Cogdill, Gail - E
Cole, Terry - B
Curry, Bill - C
Curtis, "Mike" - LB
Gaubatz, Dennis - LB
Grant, Bob - LB
Hawkins, Alex - E
Hill, Jerry - B
Hilton, Roy - E
Johnson, Charlie - T
Johnson, Cornelius - G
Lee, David - K
Logan, Jerry - B
Lorick, Tony - B
Lyles, Len - B
Mackey, John - E
Matte, Tom - B

Michaels. Lou - K, E
Miller, Fred - T
Mitchell, Tom - E
Morrall, Earl - Q
Orr, Jim - E
Pearson, Preston - B
Perkins, Ray - E
Porter, Ron - LB
Ressler, Glen - T
Richardson, Willie - E
Shinnick, Don - LB
Smith, Billy Ray - T
Smith, "Bubba" - E
Stukes, Charles - B
Sullivan, Dan - G
Szymanski, Dick - C
Unitas, John - Q
Vogel, Bob - T
Volk, Dick - B
Ward, Jim - Q
Williams, Sid - LB

1968 BOSTON PATRIOTS (AFL)
COACH Michael Holovak
4th   4-10-0

Antwine, Houston - G
Buoniconti, Nick - LB
Byrd, Dennis - E
Canale, Justin - G
Canale, "Whit" - E
Cappelletti, Gino - E
Charles, John - B
Cheyunski, Jim - LB
Colclough, Jim - E
Corcoran, Jim - Q
Eisenhauer, Larry - E
Feldhausen, Paul - C,T
Funches, Tom - T
Gamble, R. C. - B
Garron, Larry - B
Graham, Art - E
Hunt, Jim - E
Ilg, Ray - LB
Johnson, Daryl - B
Johnson, Preston - B
Johnson, Bill - B
Koontz, Ed - LB
Leo, Bob - B
Long, Charles - T

McMahon, Art - B
Marsh, Aaron - E
Mitchell, Leroy - B
Morris, Jon - C
Murphy, Bill - E
Nance, Jim - B
Neville, Tom - T
Nichols, Bob - E
Oakes, Don - T
Philpott, Ed - LB
Porter, Willie - B
St. Jean, Len - G
Satcher, Doug - LB
Scarpitto, Bob - B, K
Sherman, Tom - Q
Singer, Karl - T
Swanson, Terry - K
Taliaferro, Mike - Q
Thomas, Gene - B
Toner, Ed - T
Webb, Don - B
Whalen, Jim - E
Williamson, John - LB
Witt, Melvin - E

1968 ATLANTA FALCONS
COACH - Norbert Hecker to
Norman Van Brocklin
4th   2-12-0

Absher, Dick - K
Acks, Ron - LB
Allen, Grady - LB
Auer, Joe - B
Berry, Bob - Q
Brezina, Greg - LB
Bryant, Charles - B
Burson, Jim - B
Butler, Jim - B
Calland, Lee - B
Cash, Dick - T
Cerne, Joe - C
Cordill, Ollie - E
Dabney, Carlton - T
Donohoe, Mike - E

Duich, Steve - T
Dunaway, Dave - E
Dunn, Perry Lee - B
Eber, Rich - B
Etter, Bob - K
Flatley, Paul - E
Freeman, Mike - B
Garcia, Jim - E
Goodwin, Doug - B
Grimm, Dan - G
Harris, Bill - B
Heck, Ralph - LB
Hudlow, Floyd - E
Humphrey, Claude - E
Johnson, Randy - Q

1968 BUFFALO BILLS (AFL)
COACH - Joe Collier
Harvey Johnson

5th   1-12-1

Alford, Bruce - K
Anderson, Max - B
Barber, Stew - G
Bemiller, Al - C
Brown, Charles - B
Byrd, George - B
Cappadonna, Bob - B
Chandler, Ed - G
Clarke, Hagood - B
Costa, Paul - E
Crockett, Bob - E
Cunningham, Dick - G
Darragh, Dan - Q
Day, Tom - G
Dubenion, Elbert - E
Dunaway, Jim - T
Edgerson, Booker - B
Flint, George - T
Flores, Tom - Q
Frantz, John - LB
Gregory, Bennett - B
Guidry, Paul - LB
Jacobs, Harry - LB
Janik, Tom - B
Kalsu, Bob - G
Kindig, Howard - E

Lanson, Jerry - B
Ledbetter, Monte - B
Lincoln, Keith - B
McBath, Michael - T
McDermott, Gary - B
McDole, Roland - T
Maguire, Paul - LB
Masters, Bill - E
Mercer, Mike - K
Meredith, Dud - T
Mitchell, Charles - B
Moses, Haven - E
Patrick, Wayne - B
Pitts, John - B
Rissmiller, Ray - T
Russell, Ben - Q
Rutkowski, Ed - Q
Saimes, George - B
Schottenheimer, Martin - LB
Sestak, Tom - T
Shaw, Bill - G
Stephenson, Kay - Q
Tatarek, Bob - E
Trapp, Dick - E

1968 CHICAGO BEARS
COACH - James Dooley

2nd   7-7-0

Buffone, Doug - LB
Bukich, Rudy - Q
Bull, Ron - B
Butkus, Dick - LB
Cadile, Jim - T
Carter, Virgil - Q
Childs, Clarence - B
Concannon, Jack - Q
Cornish, Frank - T
Denney, Austin - E
Evey, Dick - E
Gentry, Curtis - B
Gordon, Dick - E
Green, Bobby Joe - K
Hazelton, Major - B
Holman, Willie - E
Hull, Mike - E
Jackson, Randall - T
Johnson, John - T
Jones, Bob - E
Kilgore, Jon - K
Kriewald, Doug - G
Kuechenberg, Rudy - LB
Kurek, Ralph - B

Livingston, Andy - B
Lyle, Garry - B
McRae, Benny - B
Mass, Wayne - T
O'Bradovich, Ed - E
Percival, Mac - K
Petitbon, Richie - B
Phillips, Loyd - E
Piccolo, Brian - B
Pickens, Bob - T
Pride, Dan - LB
Purnell, Jim - LB
Pyle, Mike - C
Rakestraw, Larry - Q
Reilly, "Mike" - LB
Sayers, Gale - B
Seals, George - G
Taylor, Joe - B
Taylor, Rosey - B
Turner, Cecil - E
Vallez, Emilio - E
Wallace, Bob - E
Wetoska, Bob - T

1968 CINCINNATI BENGALS
COACH - Paul Brown

5th   3-11-0

Archer, Dan - T
Baccaglio, Martin - E
Banks, Estes - B
Beauchamp, Al - LB
Brabham, Dan - LB
Buncom, Frank - LB
Chomyszak, Steve - T
Elzey, Paul - LB
Erickson, Bernie - LB
Fest, Howard - T
Frazier, Curt - B
Graves, White - B
Griffin, Jim - E
Gunner, Harry - E
Headrick, Sherrill - LB
Herock, Ken - E
Hibler, Mike - LB
Hunt, Bob - B
Johnson, Essex - B
Johnson, Bob - C

Keeling, Rex - K
Kelly, Bob - E
Kindricks, Bill - T
King, Charles - B
Lamb, Ron - B
Livingstom, Dale - K
McCall, Ed - B
McClure, Wayne - LB
McVea, Warren - E
Matlock, John - C
Matson, Pat - G
Middendorf, Dave - G
Neidert, John - LB
Perreault, Pete - T
Peterson, Bill - E
Phillips, Jesse - B
Randall, Dennis - E
Rice, Andy - T
Robinson, Paul - B
Saffold, Saint - E

Scott, Bill - B
Sherman, Rod - B
Smiley, Tom - B
Smith, Fletcher - B
Spiller, Phil - B
Staley, Bill - T
Stofa, John - Q

Trumpy, Bob - E
Warren, Dewey - Q
Washington, Teddy - B
White, Andre - B
Williams, "Monk" - B
Williams, Jim - B
Wright, Ernie - T
Wyche, Sam - Q

1968 CLEVELAND BROWNS
COACH - Blanton Collier
1st 10-4-0
(Beat Dallas, 31-20, for Eastern
Conference title; lost, 34-0 to
Baltimore for NFL championship.)

Andrews, Bill - LB
Barnes, Erich - B
Barney, Eppie - B
Clark, Monte - T
Cockroft, Don - K
Collins, Gary - E
Copeland, Jim - G
Davis, Ben - B
Demarie, John - G
Garlington, John - LB
Glass, Bill - E
Gregory, "Jack" - E
Green, Ernie - B
Harraway, Charles - B
Hickerson, Gene - G
Hoaglin, Fred - C
Howell, Mike - B
James, Nate - B
Johnson, Walter - T
Kanicki, Jim - T

Kellerman, Ernie - B
Kelly, Leroy - B
Leigh, Charles - B
Lindsey, Dale - LB
McDonald, Tom - E
Matheson, Bob - LB
Meylan, Wayne - LB
Mitchell, Alvin - B
Morin, Milt - E
Morrison, Reece - B
Nelsen, Bill - Q
Ryan, Frank - Q
Sabatino, Bill - T
Schafrath, Dick - T
Smith, Ralph - E
Snidow, Ron - E
Taffoni, Joe - G
Upshaw, Marv - T
Ward, Carl - B
Warfield, Paul - E
Whitlow, Bob - C

1968 DALLAS COWBOYS
COACH - Tom Landry
1st 12-2-0
(Lost Eastern conference
playoff to Cleveland, 31-20)

Andrie, George - E
Baynham, Craig - B
Burkett, Jackie - LB
Clark, Mike - K
Clark, Phil - B
Cole, Larry - E
Daniels, Dick - B
Donohue, Leon - T
East, Ron - E
Edwards, Dave - LB
Gaechter, Mike - B
Garrison, Walt - B
Gent, "Pete" - B
Green, Cornell - B
Hayes, Bob - E
Homan, Dennis - E
Howley, Chuck - LB
Johnson, Mike - B
Jordan, Lee Roy - LB
Lewis, Dwight - LB
Lilly, Bob - T
Liscio, Tony - T
McDaniels, Dave - E

Manders, Dave - G
Meredith, Don - Q
Morton, Craig - Q
Neely, Ralph - T
Niland, John - G
Norman, Pettis - E
Nye, Blaine - T
Perkins, Don - B
Pugh, Jethro - T
Randle, "Sonny" - E
Reeves, Dan - B
Renfro, Mel - B
Rentzel, Lance - B
Shy, Les - B
Simmons, Dave - LB
Sterling, Ernie - E
Stynchula, Andy - T
Townes, Willie - T
Walker, Mal - T
Widby, Ron - G
Wilburn, John - T
Wright, Rayfield - E

1968 DENVER BRONCOS
COACH - Lou Saban

4th   5-9-0

Bachman, Jay - T
Beer, Tom - E
Briscoe, Marlin - Q
Brunelli, Sam - G
Cichowski, Tom - T

Costa, Dave - LB
Cox, Larry - T
Crabtree, Eric - B
Cunningham, Carl - LB
Current, Mike - T

Denson, Al - E
Dickey, Wallace - T
DiVito, Joe - Q
Duranko, Peter - LB
Erwin, Terry - B
Ford, Garrett - B
Forsberg, Fred - LB
Gaiser, George - T
Garrett, Drake - B
Goeddeke, George - G
Greer, Charles - B
Haffner, Mike - E
Highsmith, Walter - C
Hollomon, Gus - B
Howfield, Bob - K
Huard, John - LB
Humphries, Bob - K
Inman, Jerry - T
Jackson, Dick - LB
Jaquess, Pete - B
Jones, Jim - B
Kaminski, Larry - C
Lamb, Ron - B

Lambert, Gordon - E
LeClair, Jim - Q
Lentz, Jack - B
Lewis, Harold - B
Lewis, Herman - E
Lindsey, Hubert - B
Little, Floyd - B
Luke, Tom - B
Lynch, Francis - B
McCormick, John - Q
Mirich, Rex - T
Moore, Alex - B
Moten, Bob - E
Myrtle, Charles - LB
Oberg, Tom - E
Richter, Frank - LB
Smith, Paul - LB
Tensi, Steve - Q
Tobey, Dave - LB
Van Heusen, Bill - E,K
Vaughn, Bob - G
Washington, David - E
Young, Bob - T

1968 DETROIT LIONS
COACH - Joe Schmidt
4th   4-8-2

Baker, John - E
Barney, Lem - B
Bradshaw, Charles - T
Campbell, Mike - B
Cogdill, Gail - E
Cottrell, Bill - T
DeFoyster, Gerry - K
Eddy, Nick - B
Farr, Mel - B
Flanagan, Ed - C
Freitas, Rockne - T
Gallagher, Frank - G
Gambrell, Billy - E
Gibbons, Jim - E
Hand, Larry - E
Kamanu, Lew - E
Karras, Alex - T
Kent, Greg - T
Kopay, Dave - B
Kowalkowski, Bob - G
Landry, Greg - Q
LeBeau, Dick - B
Lucci, Mike - LB

McCullouch, Earl - E
Malinchak, Bill - E
Mooney, Ed - LB
Moore, Denis - T
Munson, Bill - Q
Naumoff, Paul - LB
Nowatzki, Tom - B
Odle, Phil - E
Rasmussen, Wayne - B
Robb, Joe - E
Rush, Gerry - T
Sanders, Charles - E
Shoals, Roger - T
Sieminski, Clark - T
Swain, Bill - LB
Thompson, Bob - B
Triplett, Bill - B
Vaughn, Tom - B
Walker, Wayne - LB
Walton, Charles - G
Weger, Mike - B
Welch, Jim - B

1968 HOUSTON OILERS (AFL)
COACH - Wally Lemm
2nd   7-7-0

Barnes, Pete - LB
Bass, Glenn - E
Beathard, Pete - Q
Beirne, Jim - E
Bethea, Elvin - T
Bishop, "Sonny" - G
Blanks, Sid - B
Boyette, Garland - LB
Campbell, Woody - B
Carwell, Lawrence - B
Caveness, Ron - LB
Cutsinger, Gary - B
Davis, Bob - Q
Domres, Tom - E
Farr, Miller - B
Frazier, Charles - B
Granger, Hoyle - B
Haik, Joseph - B
Halley, Bill - E
Hicks, Wilmer - B
Hines, Glen Ray - T
Holmes, "Pat" - T
Hopkins, Roy - B
Houston, Ken - B

Johns, Pete - B
Lemoine, Jim - T
Maples, Bob - LB
Marshall, Rich - T
Meredith, Dud - T
Moore, "Zeke" - B
Norton, Jim - B
Parker, Willie - T
Quinn, Steve - C
Reed, Alvin - E
Regner, Tom - G
Rice, George - T
Robertson, Bob - C,T
Rushing, Marion - LB
Smith, Bob - B
Smith, Carel - T
Stotter, Dick - LB
Suggs, Walt - T
Swatland, Bob - G
Taylor, Lionel - E
Trull, Don - Q
Underwood, Olen - LB
Weler, Wayne - K
Wittenborn, John - G,K

1968 KANSAS CITY CHIEFS (AFL)
COACH - Henry Stram
1st   12-2-0
(Tied with Oakland; lost to Oakland, 41-6, in Western
Conference playoff.)

Abell, Harry - LB
Arbanas, Fred - E
Bell, Bobby - LB
Belser, Ceaser - B
Brown, Aaron - E
Buchanan, "Buck" - T
Budde, Ed - G
Carolan, Reg - E
Coan, Bert - B
Culp, Curley - T
Daney, George - G
Dawson, Ln - Q
Garrett, Mike - B
Gehrke, Hohn - B
Hayes, Wendell - B
Hill, David - T
Holmes, Bob - B
Holub, Emil - C
Kearney, Jim - B
Ladd, Ernie - T
Lanier, Willie - LB
Lee, Jack - Q

Livingston, Mike - Q
Longmire, Sam - B
Lothamer, Ed - E
Lowe, Paul - B
Lynch, Jim - LB
McClinton, Curt - B
Martin, David - B
Mays, Gerry - T
Merz, Curt - G
Mitchell, Willie - B
Moorman, "Mo" - G
Pitts, Frank - E
Prudhomme, Remi - E
Richardson, Gloster - B
Robinson, John - B
Sellers, Goldie - B
Smith, Noland - B
Stenerud, Jan - K
Taylor, Otis - E
Thomas, Emmitt - B
Tyrer, Jim - T
Wilson, Jerry - K

1968 GREEN BAY PACKERS
COACH - Phil Bengtson
3rd   6-7-1

Adderley, Herb - B
Aldridge, Lionel - E
Anderson, Donny - B
Bowman, Ken - C
Bratkowski, "Zeke" - Q
Brown, Bob - E
Brown, Tom - B
Caffey, Lee Roy - LB
Carr, Fred - LB
Carroll, Leo - E
Crenshaw, Leon - T
Dale, Carroll - E
Davis, Willie - E
Dowler, Boyd - E
Dunaway, Dave - E
Flanigan, Jim - LB
Fleming, Marv - E
Gillingham, Gale - G
Grabowski, Jim - B
Gregg, Forrest - T
Hart, Doug - B
Hines, Dick - T
Hyland, Bob - T

James, Claudis - B
Jeter, Bob - B
Jordan, Henry - T
Kostelnick, Ron - T
Kramer, Gerry - G
Lueck, Bill - G
Mann, Errol - K
Mercein, Chuck - B
Mercer, Mike - K
Nitschke, Ray - B
Peay, Francis - T
Pitts, Elijah - B
Pope, "Bucky" - E
Robinson, "Dave" - LB
Rowser, John - B
Rule, Gordon - B
Skoronski, Bob - T
Starr, Bart - Q
Stevens, Bill - Q
Vandersea, Phil - LB
Williams, Travis - B
Winkler, Francis - E
Wood, Willie - B

1968 LOS ANGELES RAMS
COACH - George Allen
2nd   10-3-1

Bacon, Coy - E
Bass, Dick - B
Baughan, Max - LB
Breen, Gene - LB
Brown, Roger - T
Burman, George - T
Carollo, Joe - T
Casey, Bernie - E
Chuy, Don - G
Cowan, Charles - T
Crabb, Claude - B
Cross, Irvin - B
Daniel, Willie - B
Dennis, "Mike" - B
Dyer, Henry - B
Ellison, Willie - B
Ezerins, Vilnis - B
Gabriel, Roman - Q
Gossett, Bruce - K
Guillory, Tony - LB
Halverson, Dean - LB
Iman, Ken - B
Jackson, Harold - B

Jones, Davied - E
Lundy, Lamar - E
Mack, Tom - G
Marchlewski, Frank - C
Mason, Tom - B
Meador, Ed - B
Olsen, Merlin - T
Pardee, John - LB
Pivec, David - E
Plum, Milt - Q
Pottios, Myron - LB
Schumacher, Gregg - E
Scibelli, Joe - T
Smith, Ron - B
Snow, Jack - E
Studstill, Pat - B
Talbert, Diron - T
Truax, Bill - E
Tucker, Wendell - E
Williams, Clarence - B
Wilson, Jim - G
Winston, Kelton - B
Woodloef, Doug - LB

1968 MIAMI DOLPHINS (AFL)
COACH - George Wilson
3rd   5-8-1

Anderson, Dick - B, K
Barber, Rudy - LB
Bramlett, John - LB
Branch, Mel - E
Bruggers, Bob - LB
Cox, Jim - E
Crusan, Doug - T
Csonka, Larry - B
Darnall, Bill - E, B
Edmunds, Randy - LB
Emanuel, Frank - LB
Evans, Norman - T
Fernandez, Manuel - T
Fowler, Charles - T
Goode, Tom - LB
Griese, Bob - Q
Hammond, Kim - Q
Harper, Jack - B
Jacobs, Ray - E
Joswick, Bob - T
Keyes, Jim - LB, K
Kiick, Jim - B
Lamb, Mack - B
McDaniel, "Wahoo" - LB

Milton, Gene - E
Mitchell, Stan - E
Moreau, Doug - E
Neff, Bob - B
Neighbors, Bill - T
Nomina, Tom - T
Noonan, Karl - E
Norton, Rick - Q
Petrella, Bob - B
Pyburn, Jack - T
Price, Sam - B
Richardson, John - T
Riley, Jim - G
Seiple, Larry - B, K
Tucker, Gary - B
Twilley, Howard - E
Urbanek, Jim - E
Warren, Jim - B
Washington, Dick - B
Weisacosky, Ed - LB
West, Willie - B
Westmoreland, Dick - B
Williams, Maxie - T
Woodson, Fred - G

1968 MINNESOTA VIKINGS
COACH - "Bud" Grant
1st   8-6-0

Alderman, Grady - G
Beasley, John - E
Bolin, Bookie - G
Bowie, Larry - G
Brown, Bill - B
Bryant, Bob - B
Cox, Fred - K
Cuozzo, Gary - Q
Davis, Doug - T
Denny, Earl - B
Dickson, Paul - T
Eller, Carl - E
Goodridge, Bob - E
Grim, Bob - B
Hackbart, Dale - B
Hall, Tom - B
Henderson, John - E
Hilgenberg, Wally - LB
Hill, King - K
Jones, Clint - B
Kapp, Joe - Q
Kassulke, Karl - B

Kirby, John - LB
Krause, Paul - B
Larsen, Gary - T
Lindsey, Jim - B
McGill, Mike - LB
Mackbee, Earsell - B
Marshall, Jim - E
Martin, Billy - E
Osborn, Dave - B
Page, Alan - T
Powell, Art - E
Reed, Oscar - B
Sharockman, Ed - B
Smith, Steve - E
Sunde, Milt - G
Tingelhoff, Mick - C
Vellone, Jim - T
Warwick, Lonnie - LB
Washington, Gene - E
West, Charles - B
Winston, Roy - LB
Yary, Ron - T

1968 NEW ORLEANS SAINTS
COACH - Tom Fears
3rd   4-9-1

Baker, "Tony" - B
Barrington, Tom - B
Boeke, Jim - T
Brewer, John - LB
Brown, Charles - B
Burris, "Bo" - B
Carr, Tom - E
Cody, Bill - LB
Cordileone, Lou - G
Davis, "Ted" - LB
Douglas, John - B
Durkee, Charles - K
Ferguson, Jim - C
Fichtner, Ross - B
Fraser, Jim - K
Gilliam, John - E
Gwinn, Ross - G
Hester, Jim - E
Howard, Gene - B
Jones, Jerry - T
Kelley, Les - B
Kilmer, Bill - Q
Kimbrough, Elbert - B
Kupp, Jake - G
Leggett, Earl - T

Lorick, Tony - B
McCall, Don - B
McCormick, Dave - T
McNeil, Tom - K
Nevett, Elijah - B
Parks, Dave - E
Poage, Ray - E
Rowe, Dave - T
Schmidt, Roy - G
Schultz, Randy - B
Schweda, Brian - E
South, Ron - Q
Stickles, Monty - E
Stonebreaker, Steve - LB
Sturm, Jerry - T
Sweetan, Karl - Q
Szymakowski, Dave - E
Tilleman, Mike - T
Wendryhoski, Joe - C
Wheelwright, Ernie - B
Whitsell, Dave - B
Whittingham, Fred - LB
Williams, Delano - G
Youngblood, George - B

1968 NEW YORK GIANTS
COACH - Allie Sherman
2nd   7-7-0

Anderson, Bruce - E
Anderson, Roger - T
Avery, Ken - LB
Blye, Ron - B
Boston, McKinley - E
Brown, Barry - LB
Buzin, Dick - T
Case, "Pete" - G
Ciccolella, Mike - LB
Costello, Vince - LB
Crespino, Bob - E
Crutcher, Tommy - LB
Davis, Henry - LB
Dess, Darrell - C
Duhon, Bob - B
Eaton, Scott - B
Frederickson, "Tucker" - B
Gogolak, Peter - K
Gross, Andy - G
Harper, Charles - G
Hinton, Charles - C
Holifield, Jim - B

Jacobs, Allen - B
Jones, Homer - E
Katcavage, Jim - E
Koontz, Joe - E
Koy, Ernie - B
Lane, Gary - Q
Larson, Greg - C
Lockhart, Carl - B
Lurtsema, Bob - T
Maher, Bruce - B
Minniear, Randy - B
Morrison, Joe - B
Silas, Sam - T
Tarkenton, Francis - Q
Thomas, Aaron - E
Van Horn, Doug - G
White, Freeman - E
Williams, Willie - B
Wilson, "Butch" - E
Wood, Gary - Q
Wright, Steve - T
Young, Willie - T

1968 NEW YORK JETS (AFL)
COACH "Weeb" Ewbank
1st   11-3-0
(Beat Oakland, 27-23, for AFL Championship; won AFL-NFL Championship, 16-7, over Baltimore.)

Atkinson, Al - LB
Baird, Bill - B
Baker, Ralph - LB
Beverly, Randy - B
Biggs, Verlon - E
Boozer, Emerson - B
Christy, Earl - E
Crane, Paul - LB
D'Amato, Mike - B
Dockery, John - B
Elliott, John - LB
Gordon, Cornell - B
Grantham, Larry - LB
Hayes, Ray - T
Henke, Karl - E
Herman, Dave - G
Hill, Winston - T
Hudson, Jim - B
Joe, Billy - B
Johnson, "Curley" - B, K
Lammons, Pete - E
McAdams, Carl - LB
Mathis, Bill - B

Maynard, Don - B
Nairn, Harvey - E
Namath, Joe - Q
Neidert, John - LB
Parilli, "Babe" - Q
Philbin, Gerry - E
Rademacher, Bill - B
Rasmussen, Randy - G
Richards, Jim - B
Richardson, Jeff - G
Rochester, Paul - T
Sample, John - B
Sauer, George - E
Schmitt, John - C
Smolinski, Mark - B
Snell, Matt - B
Stromberg, Mike - LB
Talamini, Bob - G
Thompson, Steve - E
Turner, Jim - K, G
Turner, "Bake" - B
Walton, Sam - T
White, Lee - B

1968 OAKLAND RAIDERS (AFL)
COACH - John Rauch
1st   12-2-0
(Tied with Kansas City; beat Kansas City, 41-6, in Western Conference playoff; lost to New York, 27-23, in AFL Championship.)

Atkinson, George - B
Banaszak, Pete - B
Benson, Duane - LB
Biletnikoff, Fred - E
Bird, Rodger - B
Birdwell, Dan - E
Blanda, George - K, Q
Brown, Willie - B
Budness, Bill - LB
Cannon, Billy - E, B
Conners, Dan - LB
Daniels, Clem - B
Davidson, Ben - E
Davidson, "Cotton" - Q
Dickey, Eldridge - E
Dixon, Hewritt - B
Dotson, Al - T
Eason, John - E
Eischeid, Mike - K
Fairband, Bill - LB
Grayson, Dave - B
Hagberg, Roger - B
Harvey, Jim - T
Hawkins, Wayne - G
Hopkins, Jerry - B
Kocourek, Dave - E

Kruse, Bob - G
Lamonica, Daryle - Q
Lassiter, Ike - E
McCloughan, Kent - B
Miller, Bill - E
Oats, Carleton - E
Ogas, Dave - G
Oliver, Ralph - LB
Otto, Gus - LB
Otto, Jim - C
Powers, Warren - B
Ridlehuber, Preston - B
Roderick, John - E
Rukbe, Karl - LB
Schuh, Harry - G
Shell, Art - T
Smith, Charles - B
Svihus, Bob - T
Thomas, Gene - B
Todd, Larry - B
Upshaw, Gene - T
Wells, Warren - E
Williams, Howie - B
Wilson, Nemiah - B

1968 PHILADELPHIA EAGLES
COACH - Joe Kuharich
4th   2-12-0

Baker, "Sam" - K	Lang, Issy - B
Ballman, Gary - B	Lloyd, Dave - LB
Beisler, Randy - E	Mallory, John - B
Brown, Fred - LB	Medved, Ron - B
Brown, Bob - T	Molden, Frank - T
Ceppetelli, Gene - C	Nelson, Al - B
Colman, Wayne - LB	Nettles, Jim - B
Conjar, Larry - B	Nordquist, Mark - T
Dirks, Marion - G	Norton, Jim - T
Ditka, Mike - E	Peters, Floyd - T
Duncan, Dick - K	Pettigrew, Gary - E
Evans, "Mike" - C	Pinder, Cyril - B
Goodwin, Ron - E	Ramsey, Nate - B
Graham, Dave - T	Recher, Dave - C
Hart, Dick - G	Rossovich, Tim - E
Hawkins, Ben - B	Scarpati, Joe - B
Haymond, Alvin - B	Snead, Norman - Q
Hill, Fred - E	Tom, Mel - LB
Hill, King - Q, K	Vasys, Arunas - LB
Howell, Lane - T	Wells, Harold - LB
Huarte, John - Q	Wink, Dean - E
Hughes, Charles - B	Woodeschick, Tom - B
Hultz, Don - E	Young, Adrian - LB
Jones, Harry - B	

1968 SAN FRANCISCO 49ERS
COACH - Dick Nolan
3rd   7-6-1

Alexander, Kermit - B	Lewis, Gary - B
Banaszek, Cas - LB	McFarland, Kay - B
Beard, Ed - LB	McNeil, Clif - B
Belk, Bill - E	Miller, Clark - T
Blue, Forrest - T	Mira, George - Q
Bosley, Bruce - C	Mudd, Howard - G
Brodie, John - Q	Nunley, Frank - LB
Collett, Elmer - G	Olerich, Dave - E
Crow, John David - E	Olssen, Lance - T
Cunningham, Doug - B	Patera, Dennis - K
Daniels, Clem - B	Peoples, Woodie - G
Davis, Tom - K	Phillips, Mel - B
Fuller, John - B	Randle, "Sonny" - E
Hardy, Kevin - E	Randolph, Alvin - B
Hart, Tom - LB	Rohde, Len - T
Hays, Harold - LB	Spurrier, Steve - K
Hazeltine, Matt - LB	Tucker, Bill - B
Hindman, Stan - E	Wilcox, Dave - LB
Johnson, Charles - T	Willard, Ken - B
Johnson, Jim - B	Windsor, Bob - E
Krueger, Charles - T	Witcher, Dick - B
Lakes, Roland - T	Woitt, John - B
Lee, Dwight - B	

1968 PITTSBURGH STEELERS
COACH - Bill Austin
4th   2-11-1

Arndt, Dick - T	Kotite, Dick - LB
Asbury, Bill - B	Lusteg, Booth - K
Bleier, Bob - B	McGee, Ben - E
Brown, John - T	Mansfield, Ray - T
Campbell, John - LB	Martha, Paul - B
Capp, Dick - E	May, Ray - LB
Compton, Dick - B	Nix, Kent - Q
Connelly, Mike - C	O'Brien, Francis - T
Cropper, Marsh - E	Parker, Frank - T
Davis, Sam - G	Rupley, Ernie - T
Foruria, John - B	Russell, Andy - LB
Gagner, Larry - G	Saul, Bill - LB
Gros, Earl - B	Shiner, Dick - Q
Haggerty, Mike - G	Shockley, Bill - K
Harris, Lou - B	Shy, Don - B
Hebert, Ken - E, K	Taylor, Mike - T
Henderson, Jon - B	Thomas, Clendon - B
Hillebrand, Jerry - LB	Van Dyke, Bruce - G
Hilton, John - E	Voss, Lloyd - E
Hinton, Charles - T	Wade, Bob - B
Hoak, Dick - B	Walden, Bob - K
Hohn, Bob - B	Watkins, Tom - B
Holman, Dan - Q	Wenzel, Ralph - G
Jefferson, Roy - E	Wilburn, John - E
Jeter, Tony - E	Woodson, Marv - B
Kortas, Ken - T	

1968 ST. LOUIS CARDINALS
COACH - Charles Winner
2nd   9-4-1

Atkins, Bob - B	Long, Dave - E, T
Bakken, Jim - K	McMillan, Ernie - T
Barnes, Mike - B	Meggyesy, Dave - LB
Brumm, Don - E	Reynolds, Bob - T
Clark, Ernie - LB	Rivers, Jamie - LB
Conrad, Bobby - B	Roland, John - B
Crenshaw, Willis - B	Rosema, Roger - LB
Daanen, Jerry - E	Rowe, Bob - E
DeMarco, Bob - C	Sanders, Lonnie - B
Duncum, Bob - T	Sauls, Kirby - B
Edwards, "Cid" - B	Schmiesing, Joe - E
Goode, Irv - T	Shivers, Roy - B
Gray, Ken - G	Smith, Jackie - E
Hart, Jim - Q	Sortum, "Rick" - G
Heron, Fred - T	Stallings, Larry - LB
Hyatt, Fred - E	Stovall, Jerry - B
Johnson, Charles - Q	Strofolino, Mike - LB
Kasperek, Dick - C	Walker, Charles - T
Kays, Brady - B	Wheeler, Ted - E
Lane, MacArthur - B	Williams, Clyde - T
Latourette, Chuck - K, B	Williams, Dave - T
Lee, Bob - E	Wilson, Larry - B
Logan, Charles - E	

1968 SAN DIEGO CHARGERS (AFL)
COACH - Sid Gillman
3rd   9-5-0

Akin, Harold - T	Hubbert, Brad - B
Allen, Chuck - LB	Jones, Curtis - G
Allison, Jim - B	Kirner, Gary - T
Alworth, Lance - E	Latzke, Paul - C
Appleton, Scott - E	Lenkaitis, Bill - C
Baccaglio, Marty - E	Leslie, "Speedy" - B
Beauchamp, Joe - B	Lincoln, Keith - B
Billingsley, Ron - E	Little, Larry - T
Briggs, Bob - T	Lowe, Paul - B
Brittenum, Jon - Q	MacKinnon, Jacque - B
Bruggers, Bob - LB	McCall, Ron - LB
DeLong, Steve - E	McDougall, Gerry - B
Dyer, Ken - B	Mitinger, Bob - LB
Erickson, Bernie - LB	Mix, Ron - T
Erlandson, Tom - LB	Owens, Terry - T
Farley, Dick - B	Partee, Dennis - K
Fenner, Lane - E	Post, Dick - B
Fetherston, Jim - LB	Print, Bob - LB
Foster, Gene - B	Ridge, Houston - B
Frazier, Willie - E	Schmedding, Jim - G
Garrison, Gary - E	Smith, Russ - B
Graham, Kenny - B	Speights, Dick - B
Gruneisen, Sam - G	Staggs, Jeff - LB
Hadl, John - Q	Sweeney, Walt - T
Howard, Bob - B	

1968 WASHINGTON REDSKINS
COACH - Otto Graham
3rd   5-9-0

Allen, Gerry - B	McKeever, Marlin - E
Bandy, Don - G	Martin, Aaron - B
Banks, Willie - G	Mitchell, Bobby - B
Barefoot, Ken - E	Morgan, Mike - LB
Barnes, Walt - T	Musgrove, Spain - T
Beban, Gary - Q	Ninowski, Jim - Q
Bosch, Frank - T	Owens, Brig - B
Bragg, Mike - K	Promuto, Vince - G
Breding, Ed - LB	Richter, Hugh - E, K
Brunet, Bob - B	Rock, Walter - T
Carroll, Jim - LB	Roussel, Tom - LB
Crane, Dennis - T	Rutgens, Joe - T
Crossan, Dave - C	Schoenke, Ray - T
Fischer, Pat - B	Smith, Jim - B
Gogolak, Charles - K	Smith, Jerry - E
Hanburger, Chris - LB	Smith, Dick - B
Harold, George - B	Snowden, Jim - T
Harris, Rick - B	Taylor, Charles - E
Hauss, Len - C	Theofiledes, Harry - Q
Jurgensen, "Sonny" - Q	Thurlow, Steve - B
Kammerer, Carl - E	Washington, Fred - T
Larson, "Pete" - B	Whitfield, A. D. - B
McDonald, Ray - B	Wooten, John - G

1969

NATIONAL FOOTBALL LEAGUE

WESTERN CONFERENCE
COASTAL DIVISION

	W.	L.	T.	Pc.
Los Angeles	11	3	0	.785
Baltimore	8	5	1	.615
Atlanta	6	8	0	.429
San Francisco	4	8	2	.333

CENTRAL DIVISION

	W.	L.	T.	Pc.
Minnesota	12	2	0	.857
Detroit	9	4	1	.692
Green Bay	8	6	0	.571
Chicago	1	13	0	.071

EASTERN CONFERENCE
CAPITAL DIVISION

	W.	L.	T.	Pc.
Dallas	11	2	1	.846
Washington	7	5	2	.583
New Orleans	5	9	0	.357
Philadelphia	4	9	1	.308

CENTURY DIVISION

	W.	L.	T.	Pc.
Cleveland	10	3	1	.769
New York	6	8	0	.429
St. Louis	4	9	1	.308
Pittsburgh	1	13	0	.071

AMERICAN FOOTBALL LEAGUE
EASTERN DIVISION

	W.	L.	T.	Pc.
New York	10	4	0	.714
Houston	6	6	2	.500
Boston	4	10	0	.286
Buffalo	4	10	0	.286
Miami	3	10	1	.231

WESTERN DIVISION

	W.	L.	T.	Pc.
Oakland	12	1	1	.923
Kansas City	11	3	0	.786
San Diego	8	6	0	.571
Denver	5	8	1	.385
Cincinnati	4	9	1	.308

TITLES: Minnesota beat Cleveland, 27-7, for the NFL title. Central Division champions, Minnesota Vikings, defeated the Coastal Los Angeles Rams, 23-20, for the Western Conference. Cleveland Browns, of the Century Division, beat the Dallas Cowboys, 38-14, of the Capital Division, for the Eastern Conference championship. Los Angeles whipped the Cowboys, 31-0, in the second place playoff.

Kansas City scrambled to beat Oakland, 17-7, for the AFL title. In the Inter-divisional playoffs, second place Kansas City Chiefs defeated Eastern Division champs, New York Jets, 13-6, to be eligible for the AFL title game. Western Division titlist Oakland Raiders clobbered second place Eastern Division Houston Oilers, 56-7, to qualify for the league title.

The fourth AFL-NFL Interleague "Super Bowl" was won by Kansas City, AFL, 23-7, over Minnesota, NFL titlists.

NFL LEADERS: Scoring—Fred Cox (Minn.) 121; Rushing—Gale Sayers (Chi.) 1,032 yds.; Passing—Sonny Jurgensen (Wash.); Pass Receiving—Dan Abramowicz (N. O.) 73; Field Goals—Fred Cox (Minn.) 26; Punting—David Lee (Balt.) 45.3 yds.; Interceptions—Mel Renfro (Dal.) 10.

AFL LEADERS: Scoring—Jim Turner (N. Y.) 129; Rushing—Dick Post (San Diego) 873 yds.; Passing—Greg Cook (Cin.); Pass Receiving—Lance Alworth (San Diego) 64; Field Goals—Jim Turner (N. Y.) 32; Punting—Dennis Partee (San Diego) 44.6 yds.; Interceptions—Emmitt Thomas (Kansas City) 9.

FIRST DRAFT: NFL—George Kunz (Notre Dame), tackle, by Atlanta, signed by Atlanta; AFL—O. J. Simpson (So. California), back, by Buffalo, signed by Buffalo.

COACHES: In the NFL, Alex Webster replaced New York Giants' coach Allie Sherman; Jerry Williams took over for Joseph Kuharich at Philadelphia; Charles Noll replaced William Austin at Pittsburgh; and Vince Lombardi took over coaching duties at Washington from Otto Graham. In the AFL, Clive Rush took over in Boston; John Rauch replaced Buffalo's Harvey Johnson; while in Oakland, John Madden took over for John Rauch; and Charles Waller took over Sid Gillman's duties at San Diego when he retired.

HALL OF FAME: There were four new members elected this year—John Christiansen, Tom Fears, Hugh McElhenny, and Peter Pihos.

NOTES: The merging of the NFL and the AFL into one league will take place in the 1970-71 season. The 26 teams have been divided into two 13-team conferences: the American Football Conference and the National Football Conference.

The two conferences have been realigned into six divisions as follows: AFC: Central Division—Cincinnati, Cleveland, Houston, Pittsburgh. Eastern Division—Baltimore, Boston, Buffalo, Miami, N.Y. Jets. Western Division—Denver, Kansas City, Oakland, San Diego. NFC: Central Division—Chicago, Detroit, Green Bay, Minnesota. Eastern Division—Dallas, N.Y. Giants, Philadelphia, St. Louis, Washington. Western Division—Atlanta, Los Angeles, New Orleans, San Francisco.

George Halas has been named president of the National Conference and Lamar Hunt is president of the American Conference.

John Unitas named Player of the Decade. Calvin Hill of Dallas named NFL Rookie of the Year and Carl Garrett, Boston, AFL Rookie of the Year.

George Halas celebrated his 50th year in Pro football.

The Cincinnati Bengals will have a new stadium in 1971. While the Philadelphia Eagles have a new 65,000 seat Veterans Stadium using Astroturf.

Greg Cook, Cincinnati quarterback, first rookie passer to win Passing title.

George Blanda, oldest player in the AFL, has played every game since league started with a record 154 regular season successive extra-points.

Joe Kapp threw a record-tying 7 TD passes as Minnesota beat Baltimore, 52-14.

Bill Kilmer, New Orleans, and Charlie Johnson, St. Louis, both threw 6 TDs in one game with the Saints winning 51-42.

Steve O'Neal, New York Jets kicker, set an AFL league mark with a 98-yd. kick against the Broncos.

John Mackey, retired Baltimore Colt tight end, assumed control of the merged NFL Players' Association on January 1st.

In the NFL there were 3 punt returns for TDs, while in the AFL there were none.

The Baltimore Colts will receive the Miami Dolphins' No. 1 draft choice in 1971 as compensation for the loss of head coach Don Shula, as Commissioner Pete Rozelle found Miami guilty of the NFL tampering rule.

Retired players:
Bobby Boyd, Baltimore cornerback, 9 years, one year #1 intercepter;
Ordell, Braase, Baltimore defensive end, 12 years;
Charlie Bradshaw, Los Angeles-Pittsburgh-Detroit tackle, 11 years;
Zeke Bratkowski, Chicago-Los Angeles-Green Bay quarterback, 13 years;
Tim Brown, Green Bay-Philadelphia-Baltimore back, 10 years;
Rudy Bukich, Los Angeles-Washington-Pittsburgh-Chicago quarterback, 16 years, one year #1 Passing;
Vince Costello, Cleveland-New York linebacker, 12 years;
John David Crow, Chicago-St. Louis-San Francisco running back, 11 years;
Jim Gibbons, Detroit end, 11 years;
Bill Glass, Detroit-Cleveland end, 11 years;
Ernie Green, Cleveland running back, 7 years;

Alex Hawkins, Baltimore-Atlanta end, 10 years;

Matt Hazeltine, San Francisco linebacker, 14 years;

Brady Keys, Pittsburgh-Minnesota-St. Louis, 8 years;

Jerry Kramer, Green Bay guard, 11 years;

Earl Leggett, Chicago-Los Angeles-New Orleans defensive tackle, 12 years;

Tommy McDonald, Philadelphia-Dallas-Los Angeles-Atlanta-Cleveland wide receiver, 12 years;

Don Meredith, Dallas quarterback, 9 years;

Bobby Mitchell, Cleveland-Washington back, 10 years, one year #1 Pass Receiver.

Don Perkins, Dallas running back, 9 years.

Sonny Randle, Chicago-St. Louis-San Francisco-Dallas end, 9 years.

Bob Skoronski, Green Bay tackle, 11 years.

Andy Stynchula, Washington-New York-Baltimore-Dallas tackle, 9 years.

Dick Szymanski, Baltimore center, 13 years.

Lionel Taylor, Chicago-Denver-Houston, wide receiver, 10 years.

Willie West, St. Louis-Buffalo-Denver-New York-Miami safety, 9 years.

DEATHS

Adams, John W. (Tree), a tackle for the Washington Redskins from 1945-49.

Barbee, Joseph, Tackle, played for the 1960 Oakland Raiders (AFL).

Brumbaugh, Carl, quarterback for the Chicago Bears from 1930-34, 36, 38, and for the Cleveland Rams in 1937.

Buncom, Frank, linebacker for the San Diego Chargers (AFL) from 1962-67 and for the Cincinnati Bengals (AFL) in 1968, died on opening day of the 1969 season.

Busler, Raymond, Tackle, 1940-41, 45 Chicago Cardinals.

Earpe, Francis, a guard with 1921-22, 24 Rock Island Independents; 1922-32 Green Bay Packers; 1927 New York Yankees.

Harman, Harvey, died Dec. 17, 1969, was executive director of the National Football Foundation and the Hall of Fame.

Herber, Arnold, quarterback Hall of Fame member, played from 1930-40 for the Green Bay Packers, and from 1944-45 for the New York Giants, with #1 passing honors in 1932, 34, and 36.

Ingwerson, Burton, played tackle for the old 1920 Decatur Staleys and the 1921 Chicago Staleys.

Joy, William, was a back with the 1919 Akron Pros.

Karilivacz, Carl, played from 1953-57 with the Detroit Lions; 1958 New York Giants; 1959-60 Los Angeles Rams as a back.

Kraehe, Oliver R., guard for the 1922 Rock Island Independents and 1923 St. Louis Browns.

Lahr, Warren, played back for the 1949 Cleveland Browns (AAFC), and with the Cleveland Browns from 1950-59.

Lantz, Montgomery (Mose), a 1933 Pittsburgh Pirate center.

Lazetich, Milan, guard for the Cleveland Rams in 1945, and from 1946-50 for the Los Angeles Rams.

Marshall, George P., one-time owner of the Washington Redskins.

Matisi, Anthony F., tackle for the 1938 Detroit Lions.

Strauss, Arthur, a back for the 1923 Toledo Maroons and the 1924 Kansas City Cowboys.

Treat, Roger, author of the Encyclopedia of Football.

Young, George, played end for the Cleveland Browns (AAFC) from 1946-49, and from 1950-53 for the Cleveland Browns.

1969 NFL Championship

Minnesota 27; Cleveland 7

It was the first NFL title for the Minnesota Vikings in their nine year history.

The Western Conference champions began to roll on the opening kickoff and didn't let up until they had bowled Cleveland over with a final, 27-7, score. The first TD came on a broken play with Viking quarterback Joe Kapp scrambling over friend and foe from the seven-yard line. The second came within minutes on a 75-yard bomb to Gene Washington. By half-time the scoreboard read, 24-0, on a Fred Cox field goal and Dave Osborn 20-yard run.

Cleveland's only score came in the last quarter with a pass from Bill Nelson to Gary Collins.

Minnesota	14	10	3	0	27
Cleveland	0	0	0	7	7

Touchdowns: Kapp, Washington, Osborn and Collins
Field Goals: Cox 2
PATs: Cox 3, Cockroft
Attendance: 47,900
Players' share: Minnesota $7,929.77

1969 AFL Championship

Kansas City 17; Oakland 7

The Kansas City Chiefs upset the Oakland Raiders for a return trip to the Super Bowl. Defense was the name of the game as the Chiefs dumped Daryl Lamonica four times and intercepted three of his passes. Oakland scored first on a Charlie Smith run in the first quarter and although there were several chances to score, the turnover from interceptions and two missed field goals by George Blanda kept the Raiders from further scoring.

Kansas City was able to tie the score, 7-7, just before the half on a Wendell Hayes one-yard run. It wasn't until late in the third quarter that the Chiefs were able to get the go-ahead TD.

George Blanda was forced to take over as quarterback when Lamonica injured his throwing hand. Emmitt Thomas, cornerback for the Chiefs, intercepted a Blanda pass in the end zone, bringing it out to the six-yard line. A second interception by Thomas set up a field goal by Jan Stenerud in the final quarter for Kansas City. Even though three times in the fourth quarter the Chiefs fumbled the ball, their defense returned it.

Kansas City	0	7	7	3	17
Oakland	7	0	0	0	7

Touchdowns: Smith, Hayes, Holmes
Field Goals: Stenerud
PATs: Blanda, Stenerud 2
Attendance: 54,544

1969 SUPER BOWL

Kansas City 23; Minnesota 7

In the 4th annual Super Bowl, the American League Kansas City Chiefs, 13-point underdogs, upended the National League champion Minnesota Vikings by a score of 23-7.

The formidable "Purple People Eaters" were unable to contain Lennie Dawson's ball carriers, while in the first half the Kansas City defense held Minnesota to four first downs. Minnesota's defense was unable to cope with Dawson's varied attack, with at least 15 different formations in as many plays. The Vikings only successful drive came in the third period with Joe Kapp, passing four times, advancing 69 yards to a TD by Dave Osborn.

Three field goals by Jan Stenerud and a Mike Garrett TD in the first half forced Minnesota's Joe Kapp into the air sooner than expected. Otis Taylor put the icing on the cake in the third quarter for the Chiefs with a 47-yard pass from Dawson.

Minnesota had possession of the ball three times in the final quarter and lost it three times by interceptions. It was a game filled with Minnesota errors—67 yards on six fouls and five turnovers (3 interceptions and 2 fumbles.)

Kansas City	3	13	7	0	23
Minnesota	0	0	7	0	7

Touchdowns: Garrett, Taylor, Osborn
Field Goals: Stenerud 3
PATs: Stenerud 2, Cox
Attendance: 80,998
Players' share: Kansas City $15,000; Minnesota $7,500.

1969 ATLANTA FALCONS
COACH - Norman Van Brocklin
3rd 6-8-0

Acks, Ron - LB
Allen, Grady - LB
Berry, Bob - Q
Bosley, Bruce - C
Breitenstein, Bob - T
Brezina, Greg - LB
Bryant, Charles - B
Butler, Jim - B
Cahill, Dave - T
Coffey, Junior - B
Cogdill, Gail - E
Condren, Glen - E & T
Cottrell, Ted - LB
Enderle, Dick - G
Etter, Bob - K
Ferguson, Jim - C
Flatley, Paul - E
Freeman, Mike - B
Gipson, Paul - B
Hansen, Don - LB
Hughes, Bob - E
Humphrey, Claude - E
Johnson, Randy - Q
Kelly, Bob - T
Kunz, George - T
Lavan, Al - B

Ledbetter, Monte - B & E
Lee, Bob - E
Lemmerman, Bruce - Q
Lothridge, Billy - K & B
McCauley, Tom - E
McDermott, Gary - B
Mallory, John - B
Mitchell, James - E
Nobis, Tom - LB
Reaves, Ken - B
Redmond, Rudy - B
Sabatino, Bill - T
Sandeman, Bill - T
Schmidt, Roy - G
Shay, Jerry - T
Simmons, Jerry - B
Smith, Ralph - E
Snider, Mal - G
Stanceil, Jeff - B
Van Note, Jeff - LB & C
Wages, Harmon - B
Waskiewicz, Jim - LB
Weatherford, Jim - B
Wright, Nate - B
Zook, John - E

1969 BALTIMORE COLTS
COACH - Don Shula
2nd 8-5-1

Austin, Ocie - B
Ball, Sam - T
Campbell, John - LB
Cole, Terry - B
Conjar, Larry - B
Curry, Bill - C
Curtis, "Mike" - LB
Duncan, Jim - B
Dunn, Perry Lee - B
Gaubatz, Dennis - LB
Grant, Bob - LB
Grimm, Dan - G
Havrilak, Sam - B
Hendricks, Ted - LB
Hill, Jerry - B
Hilton, Roy - E
Hinton, Ed - E
Johnson, Cornelius - G
Kostelnik, Ron - T
Lee, David - K
Logan, Jerry - B
Lyles, Len - B
Mackey, John - E
Matte, Tom - B

Mauck, Carl - LB
Maxwell, Tom - B
Michaels, Lou - K
Miller, Fred - T
Mitchell, Tom - E
Morrall, Earl - Q
Moss, Roland - E
Orr, Jim - E
Pearson, Preston - B
Perkins, Ray - E
Porter, Ron - LB
Ressler, Glenn - T & G
Richardson, Willie - E
Riley, "Butch" - LB
Shinnick, Don - LB
Smith, Billy Ray - T
Smith, "Bubba" - E
Stukes, Charles - B
Sullivan, Dan - G
Unitas, John - Q
Vogel, Bob - T
Volk, Dick - B
Williams, John - G

1969 BOSTON PATRIOTS (AFL)
COACH - Clive Rush
3rd 4-10-0
(Tied with Buffalo)

Antwine, Houston - T
Bailey, Bill - B
Berger, Ronald - E
Blanks, Sid - B
Bramlett, John - LB
Brown, Barry - LB
Cagle, John - E
Cappelletti, Gino - E & K
Carwell, Larry - B
Charles, John - B
Cheyunski, Jim - LB
Eisenhauer, Larry - E
Frazier, Charles - E
Funchess, Tom - T & E
Gamble, R. C. - B
Garrett, Carl - B
Gladieux, Bob - B
Hammond, Kim - Q
Henke, Karl - E & T
Herock, Ken - LB & E
Hunt, Jim - T
Jacobs, Ray - T
Janik, Tom - B
Johnson, Daryl - B

Jones, Ezell - T
Long, Charles - G
McMahon, Art - B
Marsh, Aaron - E
Montler, Mike - G & C
Morris, Jon - C
Nance, Jim - B
Neville, Tom - T
Outlaw, John - B
Philpott, Ed - LB
Rademacher, Bill - E
Richardson, Thomas - E
St. Jean, Len - G
Schottenheimer, Martin - LB
Scott, Clarence - B
Seller, Ron - E
Sherman, Tom - Q
Taliaferro, "Mike" - Q
Toner, Ed - T
Webb, Don - B
Whalen, Jim - E
Williamson, John - LB & C
Witt, Mel - E

1969 BUFFALO BILLS (AFL)
COACH - John Rauch
3rd 4-10-0
(Tied with Boston)

Alford, Bruce - K
Anderson, Max - B
Barber, Stew - G
Bemiller, Al - G
Briscoe, Marlin - E
Byrd, George - B
Chandler, Edgar - LB
Collins, Jerald - LB
Costa, Paul - T
Crawford, Hilton - B
Crockett, Bobby - E
Darragh, Dan - Q
DeVleigher, Charles - E
Dunaway, Jim - T
Edgerson, Booker - B
Enyart, Bill - B
Ferguson, Charley - E
Flores, Tom - Q
Grate, Willie - E
Guidry, Paul - LB

Harris, James - Q
Harvey, "Waddey" - T
Jacobs, Harry - LB
James, Robert - B
Kemp, Jack - Q
Kindig, Howard - C
Kruse, Robert - G
Ledbetter, Monte - E
Loukas, Angelo - G
McBath, Mike - T
McDole, Ron - E
Maguire, Paul - LB & K
Masters, Bill - E
Moses, Haven - E
Nunamaker, Julian - G
O'Donnell, Joe - G
Ogas, David - LB
Patrick, Wayne - B
Pitts, John - B
Reeves, Roy - B

Richardson, Pete - B
Richey, Mike - T
Ridlehuber, Preston - B
Saimes, George - B
Shaw, Billy - G

Sherman, Tom - Q
Simpson, O. J. - B
Stratton, Mike - LB
Tatarek, Bob - T
Thornton, Bubba - E

1969 CHICAGO BEARS
COACH - Jim Dooley
4th 1-13-0

Amsler, Marty - E
Buffone, Doug - LB
Bull, Ron - B
Butkus, Dick - LB
Cadile, Jim - G
Calland, Lee - B
Carter, Virgil - Q
Casey, Tim - LB
Concannon, Jack - Q
Copeland, Ron - E
Cornish, Frank - T
Daniels, Dick - B
Denney, Austin - E
Douglass, Bobby - Q
Evey, Dick - E & T
Ferguson, Jim - C
Gordon, Dick - E
Green, "Bobby Joe" - K
Hale, David - E
Hazelton, Major - B
Holman, Willie - E
Hull, Mike - E & B
Jackson, Randy - T
Jones, Bob - E
Kortas, Ken - T
Kuechenberg, Rudy - LB

Kurek, Ralph - B
Lyle, Garry - B
McRae, Benny - B
Martin, Dave - B
Mass, Wayne - T
Mayes, Rufus - T
Montgomery, Ross - B
Mudd, Howard - G
O'Bradovich, Ed - E
Ogden, Ray - E
Percival, Mac - K
Phillips, Loyd - E
Piccolo, Brian - B
Pickens, Bob - T
Pride, Dan - LB
Pyle, Mike - C
Sayers, Gale - B
Seals, George - G
Simmons, Jerry - E
Taylor, Joe - B
Taylor, Rosey - B
Turner, Cecil - E
Vallez, Emilio - E
Wallace, Bob - E
Wetoska, Bob - T & C
Youngblood, George - B

1969 CINCINNATI BENGALS (AFL)
COACH - Paul Brown
5th 4-9-1

Avery, Ken - LB
Baccaglio, Martin - E
Beauchamp, Al - LB
Bergey, Bill - LB
Berry, Royce - E & LB
Buchanan, Tim - LB
Canale, Justin - G
Chomyszak, Steve - T
Coleman, Alvin - B
Cook, Greg - Q
Coslet, Bruce - E
Crabtree, Eric - E
Dennis, Guy - G
Dyer, Ken - B
Fest, Howard - T
Gehrke, John - E
Guillory, John - B
Gunner, Harry - E
Harmon, Edward - LB
Hunt, Bobby - B
Johnson, Essex - B
Johnson, Robert - C
King, Charley - B
Lamb, Ron - B

Livingston, Dale - K
Matson, Pat - G
Middendorf, Dave - G
Muhlmann, Horst - K
Myers, "Chip" - E
Park, Ernie - T & G
Peters, Frank - T & C
Peterson, Bill - LB
Phillips, Jesse - B
Rice, Andy - T
Riley, Ken - B
Robinson, Paul - B
Smith, Fletcher - B
Smith, Thomas - E
Staley, Bill - T
Stofa, John - Q
Swanson, Terry - K
Thomas, "Speedy" - E
Trumpy, Bob - E
Turner, Clem - B
Wilson, Mike - B
Wright, Ernie - T
Wyche, Sam - Q

1969 CLEVELAND BROWNS
COACH - Blanton Collier
1st 10-3-1
(Beat Dallas, 38-14, for the Eastern
Conference; Lost, 27-7, to Minnesota
for NFL title)

Andrews, Bill - LB
Barnes, Erich - B
Brown, Dean - B
Clark, Monte - T
Cockroft, Don - K
Collins, Gary - E
Copeland, Jim - G
Demarie, John - G
Garlington, John - LB

Glass, "Chip" - E
Gregory, "Jack" - E
Hickerson, Gene - G
Hoaglin, Fred - C
Hooker, Fair - E
Houston, Jim - LB
Howell, Mike - B
Jenkins, Al - T
Johnson, Ron - B

Johnson, Walter - T
Jones, David - E
Kanicki, Jim - T
Kellerman, Ernie - B
Kelly, Leroy - B
Leigh, Charles - B
Lindsey, Dale - LB
Matheson, Bob - LB
Meylan, Wayne - LB
Mitchell, Alvin - B
Morin, Milt - E
Morrison, Reece - B
Nelsen, Bill - Q

Oliver, Bob - E
Reynolds, Chuck - C
Rhome, Gerry - Q
Righetti, Joe - T
Schafrath, Dick - T
Scott, "Bo" - B
Snidow, Ron - E
Summers, Fred - B
Sumner, Walter - B
Taffoni, Joe - T
Upshaw, Marv - E & T
Warfield, Paul - E

1969 DALLAS COWBOYS
COACH - Tom Landry
1st 11-2-1
(Lost to Cleveland, 38-14,
for Eastern Conference
title; lost to Los Angeles,
31-0, in Playoff Bowl)

Andrie, George - E
Baynham, Craig - B
Brown, Otto - B
Burkett, Jackie - LB
Clark, Mike - K
Clark, Phil - B
Cole, Larry - E
Conrad, "Bobby Joe" - B
Ditka, Mike - E
East, Ron - T
Edwards, Dave - LB
Flowers, Richmond - E
Gaechter, Mike - B
Garrison, Walt - B
Green, Cornell - B
Hagen, Halvor - E
Hayes, Bob - E
Hill, Calvin - B
Homan, Denis - E
Howley, Chuck - LB
Johnson, Mike - B
Jordan, Lee Roy - LB

Lilly, Bob - T
Liscio, Tony - T
Manders, Dave - C
Morton, Craig - Q
Neely, Ralph - T
Niland, John - G
Norman, Pettis - E
Nye, Blaine - G
Pugh, Jethro - T
Reeves, Dan - B
Renfro, Mel - B
Rentzel, Lance - E
Shy, Les - B
Staubach, Roger - Q
Stincic, Tom - LB
Walker, Malcolm - C
Welch, Claxton - B
Whittingham, Fred - LB
Widby, Ron - K
Wilbur, John - G
Wright, Rayfield - T

1969 DENVER BRONCOS (AFL)
COACH - Lou Saban
4th 5-8-1

Alflen, Ted - B
Bachman, Jay - C
Barnes, Walter - T
Beer, Tom - E
Brady, Phil - B
Brunelli, Sam - T
Buckman, Thomas - E
Burnett, Bobby - B
Burrell, George - B
Casey, Tim - LB
Cavness, Grady - B
Costa, Dave - T
Crane, Gary - E
Criter, Kenneth - LB
Cunningham, Carl - LB
Current, Mike - T
Denson, Al - E
Dickey, Wallace - T
Duranko, Pete - E
Embree, John - E
Goeddeke, George - G
Greer, Charlie - B
Haffner, Mike - E
Highsmith, Walter - G
Hollomon, Gus - B
Howfield, Bobby - K
Huard, John - LB

Inman, Jerry - T
Jackson, Richard - E
Jaquess, "Pete" - B
Jones, Henry - B
Kaminski, Larry - C
Lambert, Gordon - LB
Liske, Pete - Q
Little, Floyd - B
Lynch, Fran - B
McCarthy, Brendan - B
Mirich, Rex - T
Myrtle, "Chip" - LB
Oberg, Tom - B
Pastrana, Alan - Q
Pivec, David - E
Quayle, Frank - B
Richter, Frank - LB
Schnitker, Mike - LB
Smiley, Tom - B
Smith, James - T
Smith, Paul - E
Tensi, Steve - Q
Thompson, Bill - B
Van Heusen, Billy - E
Williams, Wandy - B
Young, Bobb - G

1969 DETROIT LIONS
COACH - Joe Schmidt
2nd 9-4-1

Barney, Lem - B & K
Barton, Greg - Q
Cotton, Craig - E
Cottrell, Bill - C
Duncan, Dick - K
Eddy, Nick - B
Farr, Mel - B
Flanagan, Ed - C
Freitas, Rockne - T
Gallagher, Frank - G
Goich, Dan - T
Hand, Larry - E
Karras, Alex - T
Kowalkowski, Bob - G
Landry, Greg - Q
LeBeau, Dick - B
Lucci, Mike - LB
McCullouch, Earl - E
Malinchak, Bill - E
Mann, Errol - K
Mooney, Ed - LB
Moore, Denis - E

Munson, Bill - Q
Naumoff, Paul - LB
Nowatzke, Tom - B
Odle, Phil - E
Rasley, "Rocky" - G
Rasmussen, Wayne - B
Robb, Joe - E
Rush, Jerry - T
Sanders, Charlie - E
Shoals, Roger - T
Swain, Bill - LB
Taylor, Altie - B
Triplett, Bill - B
Vaughn, Tom - B
Walker, Wayne - LB
Walton, Chuck - G
Walton, Larry - E
Watkins, Larry - B
Weger, Mike - B
Williams, Bobby - B
Wright, John - E
Yarbrough, Jim - T

1969 GREEN BAY PACKERS
COACH - Phil Bengtson
3rd 8-6-0

Adderley, Herb - B
Aldridge, Lionel - E
Anderson, Donny - B & K
Bowman, Ken - C
Bradley, Dave - T
Brown, Bob - T
Caffey, Lee Roy - LB
Carr, Fred - LB
Dale, Carroll - E
Davis, Willie - E
Dowler, Boyd - E
Flanigan, Jim - LB
Fleming, Marv - E
Gillingham, Gale - G
Grabowski, Jim - B
Gregg, Forrest - T
Hampton, Dave - B
Hart, Doug - B
Hayhoe, Bill - T
Himes, Dick - T
Horn, Don - Q
Hyland, Bob - G & C

Jeter, Bob - B
Jones, Ron - E
Jordan, Henry - T
Lueck, Bill - G
Lusteg, Booth - K
Mercer, Mike - K
Moore, Rich - T
Nitschke, Ray - LB
Peay, Francis - T
Pitts, Elijah - B
Robinson, Dave - LB
Rowser, John - B
Rule, Gordon - B
Spilis, John - E
Starr, "Bart" - Q
Stevens, Bill - Q
Vandersea, Phil - E
Weatherwax, Jim - T
Williams, Perry - B
Williams, Travis - B
Winkler, Francis - E
Wood, Willie - B

1969 HOUSTON OILERS (AFL)
COACH - Wally Lemm
2nd 6-6-2
(Lost to Oakland, 56-7,
in AFL Playoffs.)

Autry, Melvin - C
Beathard, Pete - Q
Beirne, Jim - E
Bethea, Elvin - E
Bishop, "Sonny" - G
Boyette, Garland - LB
Burrell, Ode - B
Campbell, Woody - B
Carrington, Ed - E
Davis, Bob - Q
Domres, Tom - T
Douglas, John - B
Drungo, Elbert - T
Farr, Miller - B
Gerela, Roy - K
Granger, Hoyle - B
Haik, "Mac" - E
Hicks, W. K. - B
Hines, Glen Ray - T
Holmes, "Pat" - E

Hopkins, Roy - B
Houston, Ken - B
Johnson, Richard - B
Joiner, Charlie - B & E
LeMoine, Jim - G
LeVias, Jerry - E
Maples, Bobby - C
Mayes, Ben - E
Moore, Ezekiel - B
Parker, Willie - T
Peacock, John - B
Pritchard, Ron - LB
Reed, Alvin - E
Regner, Tom - G
Rice, George - T
Richardson, Mike - B
Stith, Carel - T
Suggs, Walt - T
Trull, Don - Q
Underwood, Olen - LB

Wainscott, Loyd - LB
Watson, Ed - LB
Webster, George - LB

Woods, Glenn - E
Zaeske, Paul - E

1969 KANSAS CITY CHIEFS (AFL)
COACH - Hank Stram
2nd 11-3-0
(Beat New York, 13-6, in AFL
Playoffs; defeated Oakland, 17-7,
for AFL title; won Interleague
title, 23-7, over Minnesota)

Arbanas, Fred - E
Bell, Bobby - LB
Belser, Ceaser - B
Brown, Aaron - E
Buchanan, "Buck" - T
Budde, Ed - G
Culp, Curley - T
Daney, George - G
Dawson, Len - Q
Flores, Tom - Q
Garrett, Mike - B
Hayes, Wendell - B
Hill, Dave - T
Holmes, Robert - B
Holub, Emil - C
Hurston, Chuck - E
Kearney, Jim - B
Lanier, Willie - LB
Lee, Jack - Q
Livingston, Mike - Q
Lothamer, Ed - T
Lowe, Paul - B
Lynch, Jim - LB

McCarthy, Mickey - E
McClinton, Curtis - E
McVea, Warren - B
Marsalis, James - B
Mays, Jerry - E
Mitchell, Willie - B
Moorman, "Mo" - G
Pitts, Frank - E
Podolak, Ed - B
Prudhomme, Remi - C
Richardson, Gloster - E
Robinson, John - B
Sellers, Goldie - B
Smith, Noland - B
Stein, Bob - LB
Stenerud, Jan - K
Stroud, Morris - E
Taylor, Otis - E
Thomas, Emmitt - B
Trosch, Gene - E
Tyrer, Jim - T
Wilson, Jerrel - K

1969 LOS ANGELES RAMS
COACH - George Allen
1st 11-3-0
(Lost to Minnesota, 23-20, for
Western Conference; beat Dallas,
31-0, in Playoff Bowl.)

Bacon, Coy - T & E
Bass, Dick - B
Baughan, Maxie - LB
Brown, Bob - T
Brown, Roger - T
Burman, George - C & G
Cash, Rick - E
Cowan, Charlie - T
Curran, Pat - E
Daniel, Willie - B
Dennis, "Mike" - B
Ellison, Willie - B
Gabriel, Roman - Q
Gossett, Bruce - K
Haymond, Alvin - B
Iman, Ken - C
Johnson, Mitch - T
Jones, David - E
Josephson, Les - B
Klein, Bob - E
LaHood, Mike - G
Lang, Israel - B
Lundy, Lamar - E
Mack, Tom - G

Marchlewski, Frank - C
Mason, Tommy - B & E
Meador, Ed - B
Nettles, Jim - B
Olsen, Merlin - T
Pardee, Jack - LB
Pergine, John - LB
Petitbon, Richie - B
Pottios, Myron - LB
Purnell, Jim - LB
Ray, David - E & K
Scibelli, Joe - G
Shaw, Nate - B
Smith, Larry - B
Smith, Ron - B
Snow, Jack - E
Studstill, Pat - E & K
Sweetan, Karl - Q
Talbert, Diron - T & E
Truax, Billy - E
Tucker, Wendell - E
Williams, Clarence - B
Woodlief, Doug - LB

1969 MIAMI DOLPHINS (AFL)
COACH - George Wilson
5th 3-10-1

Anderson, Dick - B & K
Beier, Tom - B
Boutwell, Thomas - Q
Boynton, John - T
Buoniconti, Nick - LB
Clancy, John - E
Crusan, Doug - T
Csonka, Larry - B
Darnall, Bill - E
Edmunds, Randall - LB

Emanuel, Frank - LB
Evans, Norm - T
Fernandez, Manuel - E
Goode, Tom - C
Grady, Garry - B
Griese, Bob - Q
Heinz, Bob - T
Hines, Jimmy - E
Joswick, Bob - E
Keyes, Jim - LB & K

Kiick, Jim - B
Kremser, Karl - K
Little, Larry - G
McBride, Norman - LB
McCullers, Dale - LB

Mertens, Jim - E
Milton, Eugene - E
Mitchell, Stan - B
Moreau, Doug - E & K
Morris, "Mercury" - B
Mumphord, Lloyd - B
Neighbors, Billy - G

Noonan, Karl - E
Norton, Rick - Q
Pearson, Willie - B

Petrella, Bob - B
Powell, Jesse - LB
Pryor, Barry - B
Richardson, Jeff - T & C
Richardson, John - T
Riley, Jim - E
Seiple, Larry - B & K
Stanfill, Bill - E
Stofa, John - Q
Twilley, Howard - E
Warren, Jimmy - B
Weisacosky, Ed - LB
Westmoreland, Dick - B
Williams, Maxie - G
Woodson, Freddie - E

1969 MINNESOTA VIKINGS
COACH - "Bud" Grant
1st 12-2-0
(Beat Los Angeles, 23-20,
for Western Conference;
defeated Cleveland, 27-7,
for NFL title; lost to
Kansas City, 23-7, in
Interleague title.)

Alderman, Grady - T
Beasley, John - E
Bolin, "Bookie" - G
Brown, Bill - B
Bryant, Bob - B
Cox, Fred - K
Cuozzo, Gary - Q
Davis, Doug - T
Dickson, Paul - T
Eller, Carl - E
Grim, Bob - E
Hackbart, Dale - B
Hall, Tom - E
Hargrove, Jim - LB
Harris, Bill - B
Henderson, John - E
Hilgenberg, Wally - LB
Jones, Clinton - B
Kapp, Joe - Q
Kassulke, Karl - B
Kirby, John - LB
Kramer, Kent - E

Krause, Paul - B
Larsen, Gary - T
Lee, Bob - Q & K
Lindsey, Jim - B
McGill, Mike - LB
Mackbee, Earsell - B
Marshall, Jim - E
Osborn, Dave - B
Page, Alan - T
Reed, Oscar - B
Reilly, "Mike" - LB
Sharockman, Ed - B
Smith, Steve - E
Sunde, Milt - G
Tingelhoff, Mick - C
Vellone, Jim - G
Warwick, Lonnie - LB
Washington, Gene - E
West, Charlie - B
White, Ed - G
Winston, Roy - LB
Yary, Ron - T

1969 NEW ORLEANS SAINTS
COACH - Tom Fears
3rd 5-9-0

Abramowicz, Dan - E
Absher, Dick - LB
Atkins, Doug - E
Baker, "Tony" - B
Barrington, Tom - B
Brewer, John - LB
Burris, "Bo" - B
Cody, Bill - LB
Colchico, Dan - E
Colman, Wayne - LB
Cordill, Olie - B & K
Davis, Norman - G
Davis, "Ted" - LB
Dempsey, Tom - K
Dodd, Al - B
Hargett, Edd - Q
Hester, Jim - E
Howard, Gene - B
Jones, Jerry - T
Kelley, Les - LB
Kilmer, Bill - Q
Kupp, Jake - G
Linden, Errol - T
Livingston, Andy - B
Long, Dave - E

Looney, Joe Don - B & K
Lorick, Tony - B
McNeill, Tom - K
Morgan, Mike - LB
Neal, Richard - E
Nevett, Elijah - B
Ninowski, Jim - Q
Parks, Dave - E
Poage, Ray - E
Preece, Steve - B
Rengel, Mike - T
Rowe, David - T
Saul, Bill - LB
Shinners, John - G
Shy, Don - E
Sturm, Jerry - C
Talbert, Don - T
Taylor, Mike - T
Thompson, Bob - B
Tilleman, Mike - T
Ward, Carl - B
Wheelwright, Ernie - B
Whitsell, Dave - B
Williams, Del - G
Woodson, Marv - B

1969 NEW YORK GIANTS
COACH - Allie Sherman
to Alex Webster
2nd 6-8-0

Anderson, Bruce - E
Boston, McKinley - LB & E
Brenner, Al - B
Buzin, Rich - T
Case, "Pete" - G
Ceppetelli, Gene - C
Coffey, Junior - B
Crutcher, Tommy - LB
Davis, Henry - LB
Dess, Darrell - G
Dryer, Fred - E
Dunaway, Dave - E
Eaton, Scott - B
Frederickson, "Tucker" - B
Fuqua, John - B
Gogolak, Pete - K
Harper, Charlie - G
Heck, Ralph - LB
Herrmann, Don - E
Hickl, Ray - LB
Hinton, Chuck - C
Holifield, Jimmy - B
Houston, Rich - E
Johnson, "Curley" - K & E
Johnson, John - T
Jones, Homer - B
Kirby, John - LB
Kotite, Dick - E
Koy, Ernie - B & K
Larson, Greg - C
Lockhart, Carl - B
Longo, Tom - B
Lurtsema, Bob - T
McCann, Tim - T
Maher, Bruce - B
Minniear, Randy - B
Molden, Frank - T
Morrison, Joe - B & E
Parker, Frank - T
Plum, Milt - Q
Szczecko, Joe - T
Tarkenton, Fran - Q
Thomas, Aaron - E
Van Horn, Doug - G
Wells, Harold - LB
White, Freeman - E
Williams, Willie - B
Wilson, "Butch" - E
Wright, Steve - T
Young - Willie - T

1969 NEW YORK JETS (AFL)
COACH - "Weeb" Ewbank
1st 10-4-0
(Lost to Kansas City, 13-6, in the AFL Playoffs)

Atkinson, Al - LB
Baird, Bill - B
Baker, Ralph - LB
Battle, Mike - B
Beverly, Randy - B
Biggs, Verlon - E
Boozer, Emerson - B
Carroll, Jim - LB
Crane, Paul - C & LB
Dockery, John - B & E
Elliott, John - T
Finnie, Roger - E
Gordon, Cornell - B
Grantham, Larry - LB
Herman, Dave - G
Hill, Winston - T
Hudson, Jim - B
Jones, James - E & LB
Lammons, Pete - E
Leonard, Cecil - B
McAdams, Carl - LB
Mathis, Bill - B
Maynard, Don - E
Namath, Joe - Q
Neidert, John - LB
Nock, George - B
O'Neal, Steve - K
Parilli, "Babe" - Q
Perreault, Pete - G
Philbin, Gerry - E
Rasmussen, Randy -G
Richards, Jim - B
Rochester, Paul - T
Schmitt, John - C
Seiler, Paul - T
Snell, Matt - B
Stewart, Wayne - E
Thompson, Steve - T & E
Turner, Jim - Q & K
Turner, "Bake" - E
Walton, Sam - T
White, Lee - B
Woodall, "Al" - Q
Wright, Gordon - G

1969 OAKLAND RAIDERS (AFL)
COACH - John Madden
1st 12-1-1
(Beat Houston, 56-7, in AFL Playoffs; lost to Kansas City, 17-7, for AFL Title.)

Allen, Jack - B
Atkinson, George - B
Banaszak, Pete - B
Benson, Duane - LB
Biletnikoff, Fred - E
Birdwell, Dan - T
Blanda, George - Q & K
Brown, Willie - B
Budness, Bill - LB
Buehler, George - G
Buie, Drew - E
Cannon, Billy - E
Conners, Dan - LB
Davidson, Ben - E
Dixon, Jewritt - B
Dotson, Al - T
Edwards, Lloyd - E
Eischeid, Mike - K
Grayson, Dave - B
Hagberg, Roger - B
Harvey, Jim - T & G
Hawkins, Wayne - G
Hubbard, Marv - B
Keating, Tom - T
Lamonica, Daryle - Q
Laskey, Bill - LB
Lassiter, Ike - E
McCloughan, Kent - B
Oats, Carleton - E
Oliver, Ralph - LB
Otto, Gus - LB
Otto, Jim - C
Schuh, Harry - T
Shell, Art - T
Sherman, Rod - E
Smith, Clarles - B
Svihus, Bob - T
Thoms, Art - T
Todd, Larry - B
Upshaw, Gene - G
Wells, Warren - E
Williams, Howie - B
Wilson, Nemiah - B

1969 PHILADELPHIA EAGLES
COACH - Jerry Williams
4th 4-9-1

Baker, Sam - K
Ballman, Gary - E
Blye, Ron - B
Bradley, Bill - B & K
Brown, Fred - E
Calloway, Ernest - T
Carollo, Joe - T
Ceppetelli, Gene - C
Chuy, Don - G
Colman, Wayne - LB
Cross, Irvin - B
Dirks, "Mike" - T & G
Evans, "Mike" - C
Graham, Dave - T
Guillory, Tony - LB
Hart, Dick - G
Hawkins, Ben - E
Hill, Fred - E
Hobbs, William - LB
Howell, Lane - T
Hughes, Chuck - E
Hultz, Don - E
Jackson, Harold - E
Johnson, Oliver - LB
Jones, Harry - B
Kelley, "Ike" - LB
Keyes, Leroy - B
Lawrence, Kent - E
Lloyd, Dave - LB
Medved, Ron - B
Mira, George - Q
Nelson, Al - B
Nordquist, Mark - C & G
Peters, Floyd - T
Pettigrew, Gary - T
Pinder, Cyril - B
Porter, Ron - LB
Ramsey, Nate - B
Raye, Jimmy - B
Rossovich, Tim - E
Scarpati, Joe - B
Skaggs, Jim - G
Snead, Norman - Q
Tom, Mel - E
Wilson, Harry - B
Woodeschick, Tom - B
Young, Adrian - LB

1969 PITTSBURGH STEELERS
COACH - Chuck Noll
4th 1-13-0

Adams, Bob - E
Alley, Don - E
Arndt, Dick - T
Bankston, Warren - B
Beatty, Charles - B
Brown, John - T
Calland, Lee - B
Campbell, John - LB
Campbell, Robert - B
Cropper, Marshall - E
Davis, Sam - G
Fisher, Doug - LB
Gagner, Lawrence - G
Greene, Joe - T
Greenwood, L. C. - E
Gros, Earl - B
Haggerty, Mike - T
Hanratty, Terry - Q
Henderson, Jon - B
Hillebrand, Jerry - LB
Hilton, John - E
Hinton, Chuck - T
Hoak, Dick - B
Hohn, Bob - B
Jefferson, Roy - E
Kolb, Jon - C
McCall, Don - B
McGee, Ben - E
Mansfield, Ray - C
Martha, Paul - B
May, Ray - LB
Mingo, Gene - K
Nix, Kent - Q
Oliver, Clarence - B
Russell, Andy - LB
Shiner, Dick - Q
Shorter, Jim - B
Stenger, Brian - LB
Taylor, Mike - T
Van Dyke, Bruce - G
Voss, Lloyd - E
Walden, Bobby - K
Washington, Clarence - T
Wenzel, Ralph - G
Wilburn, J. R. - E
Williams, Erwin - E
Williams, Sidney - LB
Woodson, Marv - B

1969 ST. LOUIS CARDINALS
COACH - Charley Winner
3rd 4-9-1

Atkins, Robert - B
Bakken, Jim - K
Brown, Robert - E
Brown, Terry - B
Brumm, Don - E
Crenshaw, Willis - B
Daanen, Jerry - E
DeMarco, Bob - C
Edwards, "Cid" - B
Emerson, Vernon - T
Giliam, John - E
Goode, Irv - G
Gray, Ken - G
Hart, Jim - Q
Healy, "Chip" - LB
Heron, Fred - T
Hill, King - Q & K
Hyatt, Fred - E

Johnson, Charley - Q
Krueger, Rolf - E
Lane, MacArthur - B
McMillan, Ernie - T
Meggyesy, Dave - LB
Mulligan, Wayne - C
Olerich, Dave - E & LB
Reynolds, Bob - T
Rivers, Jamie - LB
Roland, John - B
Rosema, Roger, - LB
Rowe, Bob - T
Sanders, Lonnie - B
Sauls, "Mac" - B

Schmiesing, Joe - E
Shivers, Roy - B
Smith, Jackie - E
Snowden, Calvin - E
Sortun, Henrik - G
Stallings, Larry - LB
Stovall, Jerry - B
Walker, Chuck - E
Wehrli, Roger - B
Williams, Clyde - T
Williams, Dave - E
Wilson, Larry - B
Wilson, Mike - B
Wright, Nate - B

1969 SAN DIEGO CHARGERS (AFL)
COACH - Sid Gillman
to Charles Waller
3rd 8-6-0

Allen, Chuck - LB
Alworth, Lance - E
Barnes, Pete - LB
Beauchamp, Joe - B
Billingsley, Ron - T
Briggs, Bob - T
Bruggers, Bob - LB
Carr, Levert - T
DeLong, Steve - E
Domres, Marty - Q
Duncan, Leslie - B
Eber, Rick - E
Farley, Dick - B
Ferguson, Gene - T
Fetherston, Jim - LB
Foster, Gene - B
Frazier, Willie - E
Garrison, Gary - E
Graham, Kenny - B
Gruneisen, Sam - C
Hadl, John - Q
Hill, Jim - B
Howard, Bob - B

Hubbert, Brad - B
Huey, Eugene - E
Kirner, Gary - G
Lenkaitis, Bill - C
MacKinnon, Jacque - E
Mix, Ron - T
Owens, Terry - T
Partee, Dennis - K
Post, Dick - B
Queen, Jeff - B
Redman, Rick - LB
Rentz, Larry - E
Ridge, Houston - E
Sartin, Dan - T
Sayers, Ron - B
Schmedding, Jim - G
Smith, Russ - B
Staggs, Jeff - LB
Sweeney, Walt - G
Tolbert, Jim - B
Trapp, Richard - E
Washington, Russ - T
Wells, Robert - T

1969 SAN FRANCISCO 49ERS
COACH - Dick Nolan
4th 4-8-2

Alexander, Kermit - B
Banaszek, Cas - T
Beard, Ed - LB
Beisler, Randy - T
Belk, Bill - E
Blue, Forrest - C
Brodie, John - Q
Collett, Elmer - G
Cunningham, Doug - B
Davis, Tommy - K
Edwards, Earl - E
Fuller, John - B
Gavric, Momcilo - K
Greenlee, Fritz - LB
Hart, Tom - E
Hays, Harold - LB
Hindman, Stan - E
Johnson, Jim - B
Johnson, Leo - E
Kilgore, Jon - K
Krueger, Charlie - T
Kwalick, "Ted" - E
Lakes, Roland - T
Lewis, Gary - B

McNeil, Clifton - E
Moore, Gene - B
Mudd, Howard - G
Nunley, Frank - LB
Olsson, Lance - T
Peoples, Woody - G
Phillips, Mel - B
Randolph, Al - B
Rohde, Len - T
Silas, Sam - T
Smith, Noland - E
Sniadecki, Jim - LB
Spurrier, Steve - Q & K
Taylor, Rosey - B
Thomas, Jim - B
Tucker, Bill - B
Vanderbundt, "Skip" - LB
Washington, Gene - E
Wilcox, Dave - LB
Willard, Ken - B
Windsor, Bob - E
Witcher, Dick - E
Woitt, John - B
Wondolowski, Bill - E

1969 WASHINGTON REDSKINS
COACH - Vince Lombardi
2nd 7-5-2

Allen, Gerry - B
Banks, Willie - G
Bass, Mike - B
Beban, Gary - B
Bosch, Frank - T
Bragg, Mike - K
Brown, Larry - B
Brown, Tom - B
Carroll, Leo - E
Crane, Dennis - T
Crossan, Dave - C
Didion, John - LB
Duich, Steve - G
Dyer, Henry - B
Fischer, Pat - B
Grimm, Dan - C
Hanburger, Chris - LB
Harraway, Charley - B
Harris, Rickie - B
Hauss, Len - C
Hoffman, John - E
Huff, "Sam" - LB
Jurgensen, "Sonny" - Q
Kammerer, Carl - E

Knight, Curt - K
Kopay, Dave - B
Long, Bob - E
McKeever, Marlin - LB
McLinton, Harold - LB
Mercein, Chuck - B
Miller, Clark - E
Musgrove, Spain - T
Norton, Jim - T
Owens, Brig - B
Promuto, Vince - G
Richter, "Pat" - E
Roberts, Walt - E
Rock, Walter - T
Roussel, Tom - LB
Rutgens, Joe - T
Ryan, Frank - Q
Schoenke, Ray - G
Smith, Jerry - E
Snowden, Jim - T
Taylor, Charley - E
Vactor, Ted - B
Wade, Bob - B

1970

NATIONAL FOOTBALL LEAGUE
NATIONAL CONFERENCE
WESTERN DIVISION

	W.	L.	T.	Pc.
San Francisco	10	3	1	.769
Los Angeles	9	4	1	.692
Atlanta	4	8	2	.333
New Orleans	2	11	1	.154

EASTERN DIVISION

	W.	L.	T.	Pc.
Dallas	10	4	0	.714
N. Y. Giants	9	5	0	.643
St. Louis	8	5	1	.615
Washington	6	8	0	.429
Philadelphia	3	10	1	.231

CENTRAL DIVISION

	W.	L.	T.	Pc.
Minnesota	12	2	0	.857
Detroit	10	4	0	.714
Chicago	6	8	0	.429
Green Bay	6	8	0	.429

AMERICAN CONFERENCE
WESTERN DIVISION

	W.	L.	T.	Pc.
Oakland	8	4	2	.667
Kansas City	7	5	2	.583

	W.	L.	T.	Pc.
San Diego	5	6	3	.455
Denver	5	8	1	.357

EASTERN DIVISION

	W.	L.	T.	Pc.
Baltimore	11	2	1	.846
Miami	10	4	0	.714
N. Y. Jets	4	10	0	.286
Buffalo	3	10	1	.231
Boston	2	12	0	.143

CENTRAL DIVISION

	W.	L.	T.	Pc.
Cincinnati	8	6	0	.571
Cleveland	7	7	0	.500
Pittsburgh	5	9	0	.357
Houston	3	10	1	.231

TITLES: The Dallas Cowboys won their first National Football Conference title by beating San Francisco, 17-10, at Kezar Stadium. In the Divisional Playoffs to determine who would play for the championship, Dallas, the Eastern Division leader, beat Detroit, fourth qualifier, 5-0. Western Division leader, San Francisco, won over Central Division Minnesota, 17-14.

The American Football Conference winner was Baltimore, who defeated Oakland, 27-17, at Baltimore's Memorial Stadium. The Eastern Division champs shut out Cincinnati, Central Division leader, 17-0, in a divisional playoff game. Oakland, Western Division champ, won over Eastern Division qualifier Miami, 21-14, in their divisional playoff game. The fourth qualifier in each conference is the team with the best won-lost percentage.

The fifth "Super Bowl" between AFC winner Baltimore and NFC winner Dallas was won by Baltimore, 16-13, at the Orange Bowl in Miami.

NFC LEADERS: Scoring—Fred Cox (Minn.) 125; Rushing—Larry Brown (Wash.) 1,125 yds; Passing—John Brodie (S.F.); Pass Receiving—Dick Gordon (Chi.) 71; Field Goals—Fred Cox (Minn.) 30; Punting—Julian Fagan (N.O.) 42.5 average; Interceptions—Dick LeBeau (Det.) 9.

AFC LEADERS: Scoring—Jan Stenerud (K.C.) 116; Rushing—Floyd Little (Den.) 901 yds; Passing—Daryle Lamonica (Oak.); Pass Receiving—Marlin Briscoe (Buff.) 57; Field Goals—Jan Stenerud (K.C.) 30; Punting—Dave Lewis (Cin.) 46.2 average; Interceptions—Johnny Robinson (K.C.) 10.

FIRST DRAFT: AFC—Terry Bradshaw (Louisiana Tech), quarterback, by Pittsburgh, signed by Pittsburgh. NFC—Mike McCoy (Notre Dame), defensive tackle, selected by Green Bay, signed by Green Bay.

COACHES: In the NFC, Tom Fears was replaced by J. D. Roberts on Nov. 3, 1970 at New Orleans; Bill Austin took over for the late Vince Lombardi at Washington at the beginning of the season after Lombardi's fatal illness. In the AFC, John Mazur replaced Clive Rush on Nov. 4, 1970, at Boston.

HALL OF FAME: Seven members to be enshrined at Canton, Ohio in the fall of 1971—Vince Lombardi, Jimmy Brown, Andy Robustelli, Y. A. Tittle, Norm Van Brocklin, Bill Hewitt, and Frank "Bruiser" Kinard.

NOTES: Under the new NFL realignment, each team in a four-team division will play six games within its division (home and home), five games with the teams of the two other divisions in its conference, and three games with teams from the other conference. Each team in a five-team division will play eight games within its division (home and home), three games with teams in the other two divisions and three games with teams in the other conference, with one team in each conference in exception, playing a "fourth" inter-conference game. A total of 182 games being played: 88 are played within divisions, 54 are games played between divisions, and 40 inter-conference.

On Sept. 3, 1970, the football world was greatly saddened with the loss of Vincent Lombardi. As head coach for the Green Bay Packers, he led them from a 1-10-1 record in 1958, to a division championship in two years. In the next seven years, Green Bay won five NFL titles and the first two Super Bowls. After the 1967 season, Vince Lombardi quit coaching to become general manager of the Packers, but found himself pulled back to his first love, coaching. He took over the Washington Redskins in 1969 and took them to their first winning season in 14 years.

Beginning with Super Bowl V, the trophy presented for the permanent possession of the winning team will be known as the Vince Lombardi Trophy.

The Dallas Cowboys are getting a new stadium called Texas Stadium at Irving, Tex., to be ready for the 1971 season. Philadelphia is to move into Philadelphia Veterans Stadium, one year later than scheduled. San Francisco is moving into Candlestick Park for the 1971 season.

With their new stadium at Foxboro, Mass., the Boston Patriots have acquired a new name—the New England Patriots.

John Brodie, San Francisco quarterback, named Most Valuable Player of the Year. Bruce Taylor, cornerback and punt returner for the S.F. 49ers, named Defensive Rookie of the Year, and Dennis Shaw, Buffalo Bills quarterback, named Offensive Rookie of the Year.

Rookie Duane Thomas of the Dallas Cowboys had the best Rushing average with 5.3 for 803 yards on 151 attempts. First-year man Julian Fagan of the New Orleans Saints was Punting leader for the NFC with 42.5 average.

On Nov. 1, 1970, Tom Dempsey, kicker for the New Orleans Saints, pumped a record 63-yard field goal against Detroit.

George Blanda, oldest player in the league with 21 playing years, kicked a 52-yard field goal in the final three seconds of the game for Oakland, defeating Cleveland, 23-20, on Nov. 8th.

RETIRED PLAYERS:

Doug Atkins, Cleveland-Chicago-New Orleans defensive end, 17 years;

Sam Baker, Washington-Cleveland-Dallas-Philadelphia kicker, 15 years;

Dick Bass, Los Angeles running back, 10 years;

Bruce Bosley, San Francisco-Atlanta center, 14 years;

Roger Brown, Detroit-Los Angeles tackle, 10 years;

Monte Clark, San Francisco-Dallas-Cleveland tackle, 11 years;

Bobby Joe Conrad, Chicago-St. Louis-Dallas flanker, 12 years;

Tommy Davis, San Francisco kicker, 11 years;

Willie Davis, Cleveland-Green Bay defensive end, 12 years;

Darrell Dess, Pittsburgh-New York-Washington guard, 12 years;

Boyd Dowler, Green Bay end, 11 years;

Wayne Hawkins, Oakland (AFL), 10 years;

Stuart King Hill, Chicago-St. Louis-Philadelphia-Minnesota-St. Louis quarterback and kicker, 12 years;

Sam Huff, New York-Washington linebacker, 13 years;

John "Curley" Johnson, Dallas (AFL)-New York (AFL)-New York back and kicker, 10 years;

Henry Jordan, Cleveland-Green Bay tackle, 13 years;

John Kemp, Pittsburgh-Los Angeles (AFL)-San Diego (AFL)-Buffalo (AFL) quarterback, 10 years;

Jack Lee, Houston (AFL)-Denver (AFL)-Kansas City (AFL) quarterback, 10 years;

Lamar Lundy, Los Angeles defensive end, 13 years;

Leonard Lyles, Baltimore-San Francisco defensive back, 12 years;

Bruce Maher, Detroit defensive back, 10 years;

Bill Mathis, New York (AFL) running back, 10 years;

Lou Michaels, Los Angeles-Pittsburgh-Baltimore defensive end, kicker, 12 years;

Ronald Mix, Los Angeles (AFL)-San Diego (AFL) tackle, 10 years;

Jim Ninowski, Cleveland-Detroit-Washington-New Orleans quarterback, 12 years;

Babe Parilli, Green Bay-Cleveland-Oakland (AFL)-Boston (AFL)-New York (AFL), quarterback, 15 years;

Milt Plum, Cleveland-Detroit-Los Angeles-New York quarterback, 13 years;

Paul Rochester, Dallas (AFL)-Kansas City (AFL)-New York (AFL) defensive tackle, 10 years;

Don Shinnick, Baltimore linebacker, 12 years;

Beb Wetoska, Chicago defensive tackle and center, 10 years;

Dave Whitsell, Detroit-Chicago-New Orleans defensive back, 12 years;

DEATHS

Bingaman, Lester, guard, 1948-54 Detroit Lions, died Nov. 20, 1970.

Bruder, Henry (Hank), Qback, 1931-39 Green Bay Packers; 1940 Pittsburgh Steelers; died June 29, 1970.

Burgner, Dr. Earl, back for the 1923 Dayton Triangles, on Jan. 11, 1970.

Carr, Harlan (Gotch), played quarterback in 1927 for Buffalo Bisons and Pottsville Maroons, died Nov. 24, 1970.

Chesbro, Marcel, guard, 1938 Cleveland Rams, on Apr. 10, 1970.

Christman, Paul, quarterback, 1945-49 Chicago Cardinals, 1950 Green Bay Packers, died Mar. 2, 1970.

Conzelman, James, quarterback, 1920 Decatur Staleys; 1921-22 Rock Island Independents; 1923-24 Milwaukee Badgers; 1925-26 Detroit Panthers; 1927-29 Providence Steamrollers; 1964 Hall of Fame; coached Chicago Cardinals (1946-48); died July 31, 1970.

DeGroot, Dudley S., coach of the Washington Redskins, 1944-45, and Los Angeles Dons, 1946-47, died on May 5, 1970.

Dubofsky, Maurice, guard for the 1932 New York Giants, on Jan. 25, 1970.

Hagberg, Rudolph, center, 1929 Buffalo Bisons; 1930 Brooklyn Dodgers; died on Apr. 15, 1970.

Hanley, Richard E., coach of the 1946 Chicago Rockets, died Dec. 16, 1970.

Hanson, Thomas, back, 1931 Brooklyn Dodgers; 1932 Staten Island Stapletons; 1933-37 Philadelphia Eagles; 1938 Pittsburgh Pirates; died on Aug. 5, 1970.

Kalsu, Robert, guard, 1968 Buffalo Bills (AFL), in July, 1970.

Kempton, Herbert (Fido), back for the 1921 Canton Bulldogs, died Sept. 23, 1970.

Levey, James, back for the Pittsburgh Pirates (1934-36), died Mar. 14, 1970.

Lombardi, Vincent, coach for the Green Bay Packers from 1959 to 1967, and for the Washington Redskins in 1969, died Sept. 3, 1970.

McEwan, John J., coach of the Brooklyn Dodgers in 1933-34, died Aug. 9, 1970.

Nowaskey, Robert, end, 1940-42 Chicago Bears; 1946-47 Los Angeles Dons (AAFC); 1948-49 Baltimore Colts (AAFC); 1950 Baltimore Colts, died on Mar. 21, 1971.

Piccolo, Louis Brian, back, 1966-69 Chicago Bears, died June 16, 1970.

Rabold, Michael, guard, 1959 Detroit Lions; 1960 St. Louis Cardinals; 1961-62 Minnesota Vikings; 1964-67 Chicago Bears; died on Oct. 13, 1970.

Shaughnessy, Clark, coach of the Los Angeles Rams, 1948-49, on May 16, 1970.

Smith, Houston Allen, end, 1947-48 Chicago Bears, died Oct. 18, 1970.

Smukler, David, back, 1936-39 Philadelphia Eagles; 1944 Boston Yanks; died on Feb. 22, 1971.

Stahlman, Richard F., tackle, 1924 Hammond Pros; 1924 Kenosha Maroons; 1924-25 Akron Pros; 1926 Rock Island Independents (AFL); 1926 Chicago Bills (AFL); 1927-28, 30 New York Giants; 1931-32 Green Bay Packers; 1933 Chicago Bears; died on May 11, 1970.

Stein, Russell F., tackle, 1922 Toledo Maroons; 1924 Frankfort Yellowjackets; 1925 Pottsville Maroons; 1926 Canton Bulldogs; died in June, 1970.

Welch, Gustavos (Gus), back, 1916-17 Canton Bulldogs, died Jan. 29, 1970.

1970 NFC Championship

Dallas 17; San Francisco 10

The Eastern Division winners scored their first NFC championship win at Kezar Stadium in San Francisco over the 49ers.

It was a defensive first half with the Western Division leader scoring first on a Bruce Gossett field goal from the 16-yard line. Dallas evened the score in the second period with a 21-yard Mike Clark field goal.

Duane Thomas scored a 3rd quarter Cowboy TD on a 13-yard run, making the score, 10-3, after an intercepted John Brodie pass by Dallas linebacker Lee Roy Jordan.

It was all over for San Francisco when Dallas intercepted again the next time the 49ers had the ball. Mel Renfro grabbed a pass aimed at Gene Washington and returned it to the Dallas 38-yard line. Craig Morton threw a 5-yard Walt Garrison TD after pass interference was called against Mel Phillips, who knocked Bob Hayes, the intended Cowboy receiver.

Moving the ball for 73 yards, John

Brodie passed to Dick Witcher late in the 3rd quarter for a TD but was unable to score again after that.

The Dallas defense was able to get to Brodie for losses three times on pass attempts although he was sacked only eight times during regular season play.

| Dallas | 0 | 3 | 14 | 0 | 17 |
| San Francisco | 3 | 0 | 7 | 0 | 10 |

Touchdowns: Thomas, Garrison, Witcher.
Field Goals: Gossett, Clark.
PATs: Clark 2, Gossett.
Attendance: 59,364.
Players' share: Dallas $8,500; San Francisco $5,500.

1970 AFC Championship

Baltimore 27; Oakland 17

Baltimore's starring quarterback, John Unitas, took his squad off to a flying start with a 10-0 lead on a Jim O'Brien field goal and a Norm Bulaich 2-yard TD before Oakland scored a point.

Daryle Lamonica, who started as Oakland's quarterback, was replaced early in the 2nd quarter after Baltimore's Bubba Smith dumped him for a 14-yard loss. He was unable to get a prolonged drive going except for a George Blanda field goal from the 48-yard line before leaving due to a pulled leg muscle.

At the beginning of the 3rd quarter, with George Blanda calling the signals, the Raiders advanced 80 yards for a Blanda to Fred Biletnikoff touchdown. But the Colts put another ten points on the scoreboard with a 23-yard O'Brien field goal and the old Statue of Liberty play, with Bulaich making the score 20-10.

Oakland charged down the field again with Warren Wells snagging a TD pass to put the Raiders just 3 points behind with plenty of time left to put more points on the scoreboard. But Unitas put the damper on their aspirations by connecting with Ray Perkins who carried it 68 yards to make the final score 27-17.

| Baltimore | 3 | 7 | 10 | 7 | 27 |
| Oakland | 0 | 3 | 7 | 7 | 17 |

Touchdowns: Bulaich 2, Biletnikoff, Wells, Perkins.
Field Goals: O'Brien 2, Blanda.
PATs: O'Brien 3, Blanda 2.

Attendance: 54,799.
Players' shares: Baltimore $8,500; Oakland $5,500.

1970 Super Bowl

Baltimore 16; Dallas 13

This fifth Super Bowl game was a classic example of bumble and fumble for both teams. Baltimore, AFC champion, turned over the ball seven times by losing 4 of 5 fumbles and throwing 3 interceptions. Dallas turned it over four times on 3 interceptions and 1 fumble. Every point occurred after some kind of mistake.

The NFC champs would have had the game sewed up if they could have just played it conservative and not made any mistakes, but with three interceptions in the last seven minutes, they threw the game away.

The Cowboys scored first on a 14-yd. field goal by Mike Clark in the first quarter and again in the second with a 30-yarder before Baltimore managed to score with a 75-yard unintentional pass to John Mackey.

Colt quarterback, John Unitas, threw to Ed Hinton, who got a hand on it as Mel Renfro, Dallas defender, tried to steal it. Officials ruled Renfro touched it last as it bobbled off another Cowboy defender and landed in Mackey's lap. A blocked extra-point evened the score.

Dallas' first and only TD came after a Unitas fumble on the Baltimore 29, with Duane Thomas going over on a 7-yard Craig Morton pass. Earl Morrall came in during the second quarter after Unitas injured his ribs getting dumped by the Doomsday Defense.

In the second half, Dallas had their best drive of the day. Baltimore's Jim Duncan fumbled the kickoff with Dallas taking advantage of short drives, managing to get it to the Baltimore 1-foot line. Now it was Dallas' turn to fumble.

With only eight minutes to go, Craig Morton tried a 3rd down pass on his own 23-yard line to Walt Garrison who bobbled the ball right into the hands of Colt defender Rick Volk who returned it to the Dallas 3. Tom Nowatzke plowed to a 13-13 tie from the 2.

It looked like sudden death overtime was in the picture until Dallas decided it was their turn to booboo again. With only a little over a minute left, Morton tried to pass to Dan Reeves. It bounced off the Dallas receiver into the arms of Colt linebacker Mike Curtis who galloped to the Cowboy 28-yard line. On third down, Jim O'Brien made the 3-pointer from the 32-yd. line to make each Colt player $15,000 richer.

Baltimore	0	6	0	10	16
Dallas	3	10	0	0	13

Touchdowns: Mackey, Thomas, Nowatzke.

Field Goals: Clark 2, O'Brien.

PATs: Clark, O'Brien.

Attendance: 79,204.

Player's share: Baltimore, $15,000; Dallas, $7,500.

1970 ATLANTA FALCONS
COACH - Norm Van Brocklin
3rd - Western Div., 4-8-2

Acks, Ronald - LB
Allen, Grady - LB
Berry, Robert - Q
Breitenstein, Robert - T & G
Brunson, Michael - E
Butler, James - B
Campbell, Sonny - B
Cavness, Grady - B
Cogdill, Gail - E
Condren, Glen - E & T
Cottrell, Ted - LB
Donohoe, Mike - E
Enderle, Dick - G
Flatley, Paul - E
Freeman, Mike - B
Gipson, Paul - B
Halverson, Dean - LB
Hansen, Don - LB
Hettema, Dave - T
Humphrey, Claude - E
Johnson, Randy - Q
Kunz, George - T
Lavan, Al - B

Lawrence, Kent - E
Lens, Greg - T
Lothridge, Billy - K & B
McCauley, Tom - B
Mallory, John - B
Malone, Art - B
Marshall, Randy - E
Matlock, John - C
Mauer, Andy - G
Mitchell, Jim - E
Nobis, Tommy - LB
Reaves, Ken - B
Hedmond, Rudy - B
Roberts, Gary - G
Sandeman, Bill - T
Small, John - T
Snider, Malcolm - G & T
Snyder, Todd - E
Sullivan, Jim - T
Van Note, Jeff - LB & C
Vinyard, Kenny - K
Wages, Harmon - B
Zook, John - E

1970 BALTIMORE COLTS (AFC)
COACH - Don McCafferty
1st - Eastern Div., 11-2-1
(Beat Cincinnati, 17-0, in AFC
Divisional Playoff; defeated Oakland,
27-17, for AFC Championship; beat
Dallas, 16-13, in the Super Bowl)

Bailey, James - T
Ball, Sam - T
Bulaich, Norm - B
Conjar, Larry - B
Curry, Bill - C
Curtis, Mike - LB
Curtis, Tom - B
Duncan, Jim - B
Gardin, Ron - B
Goode, Tom - C
Grant, Bob - LB
Havrilak, Sam - B & Q
Hendricks, Ted - LB
Hill, Jerry - B
Hilton, Roy - E
Hinton, Ed - E
Jefferson, Roy - E
Johnson, Cornelius - G
Lee, David - K

Logan, Jerry - B
Mackey, John - E
Maitland, Jack - B
Matte, Tom - B
Maxwell, Tom - B
May, Ray - LB
Miller, Fred - T
Mitchell, Tom - E
Morrall, Earl - Q
Nelson, Dennis - T
Newsome, Billy - E
Nichols, Robbie - LB
Nowatzke, Tom - B
O'Brien, Jim - K & E
Orr, Jimmy - E
Perkins, Ray - E
Ressler, Glenn - G
Smith, Billy Ray - T
Smith, Bubba - E

Stukes, Charlie - B
Sullivan, Dan - G
Unitas, John - Q
Vogel, Bob - T

Volk, Rick - B
Williams, John - G
Wright, George - T

1970 BOSTON PATRIOTS (AFC)
COACH - Clive Rush to John Mazur
5th - Eastern Div., 2-12-0

Antwine, Houston - T
Ballou, Mike - LB
Beer, Tom - E
Berger, Ron - E
Beverly, Randy - B
Blanks, Sid - B
Bramlett, John - LB
Brown, Barry - LB
Bugenhagen, Gary - T & G
Cappelletti, Gino - K & E
Carwell, Larry - B
Cheyunski, Jim - LB
Frazier, Charles - E
Funchess, Tom - T
Garrett, Carl - B
Gladieux, Bob - B
Gogolak, Charlie - K
Hunt, Jim - T
Janik, Tom - K & B
Johnson, Daryl - B
Jones, Ezell - T
Kapp, Joe - Q
Knief, Gayle - E
Lassiter, Ike - E & T

Lawson, Odell - B
Loukas, Angelo - G
McMahon, Art - B
Mirich, Rex - T
Montler, Mike - G & C
Morris, Jon - C
Nance, Jim - B
Neville, Tom - T
Outlaw, John - B
Philpott, Ed - LB
Rademacher, Bill - E
Ray, Eddie - B & K
Richardson, Thomas - E
St. Jean, Len - G
Schottenheimer, Marty - LB
Scott, Clarence - B
Sellers, Ron - E
Taliaferro, Mike - Q
Turner, Bake - E
Webb, Don - B
Whittingham, Fred - LB
Williamson, J. R. - LB & C
Wirgowski, Dennis - E
Witt, Mel - E

1970 BUFFALO BILLS (AFC)
COACH - John Rauch
4th - Eastern Div., 3-10-1

Alexander, Glenn - E
Allen, Jackie - B
Andrews, Al - LB
Briscoe, Marlin - E
Byrd, George - B
Carr, Levert - T
Chandler, Edgar - LB
Cheek, Richard - G
Collins, Jerry - LB
Costa, Paul - T
Cowlings, Al - E
Cunningham, Dick - E
Darragh, Dan - Q
Denney, Austin - E
Dunaway, Jim - T
Enyart, Bill - B
Fowler, Wayne - T
Gantt, Jerome - T
Gladieux, Bob—B
Glosson, Clyde - E
Grate, Willie - E
Guidry, Paul - LB
Guthrie, Grant - K
Harris, Jim - Q
Harvey, Waddey - T

Hill, Ike - B
James, Robert - B
Jones, Greg - B
Kindig, Howard - T & C
Laster, Art - T
McBath, Mike - E
McCaffrey, Mike - LB
McDole, Ron - E
Maguire, Paul - K
Marchlewski, Frank - C
Moses, Haven - E
Moss, Roland - E
Nunamaker, Julian - G
O'Donnell, Joe - G
Pate, Lloyd - B
Patrick, Wayne - B
Pharr, Tommy - B
Pitts, John - B
Reilly, Jim - G
Richardson, Pete - B
Shaw, Dennis - Q
Simpson, O. J. - B
Stratton, Mike - LB
Tatarek, Bob - T

1970 CHICAGO BEARS
COACH - Jim Dooley
3rd - Central Div., 6-8-0
(tied with Green Bay)

Baynham, Craig - B
Brupbacher, Ross - LB
Buffone, Doug - LB
Bull, Ron - B
Butkus, Dick - LB
Cadile, James - G
Caffey, Lee Roy - LB
Clark, Phil - B
Coady, Rich - C
Cole, Linzy - E
Concannon, Jack - Q
Cornish, Frank—T
Curchin, Jeff - T
Daniels, Dick - B
Davis, "Butch" - B
Douglass, Bobby - Q
Farmer, George - E
Gordon, Dick - E

Green, Bobby Joe - K
Gunn, Jimmy - LB
Gunner, Harry - E
Hale, Dave - T
Hester, Jim - E
Holloway, Glenn - G
Holman, Willie - E
Hull, Mike - B
Hyland, Bob - C & T
Jackson, Randy - T
Kurek, Ralph - B
Lyle, Garry - B
McRae, Bennie - B
Mass, Wayne - T
Montgomery, Ross - B
Mudd, Howard - G
Neidert, John - LB

Nix, Kent - Q
O'Bradovich, Ed - E
Ogden, Ray - E
Percival, Max - K
Sayers, Gale - B
Seals, George - T
Seymour, Jim - E

Shy, Don - E
Smith, Ron - B
Staley, Bill - T
Taylor, Joe - B
Turner, Cecil - E
Wallace, Bob - E
Wheeler, Ted - G

Kiner, Steve - LB
Lewis, Dwight - LB
Lilly, Bob - T
Liscio, Tony - T
Manders, Dave - C
Morton, Craig - Q
Neely, Ralph - G & T
Niland, John - G
Norman, Pettis - E
Nye, Blaine - G
Pugh, Jethro - T
Reeves, Dan - B

Renfro, Mel - B
Rentzel, Lance - E
Rucker, Reggie - E
Staubach, Roger - Q
Stincic, Tom - LB
Thomas, Duane - B
Toomay, Pat - E
Washington, Mark - B
Waters, Charley - B
Welch, Claxton - B
Widby, Ron - K
Wright, Rayfield - T

1970 CINCINNATI BENGALS (AFC)
COACH - Paul Brown
1st - Central Div., 8-6-0
(Lost to Baltimore, 17-0,
in AFC Divisional Playoff)

Amsler, Marty - E
Avery, Ken - LB
Baccaglio, Martin - T
Beauchamp, Al - LB
Bergey, Bill - LB
Berry, Royce - E
Carpenter, Ron - E
Carter, Virgil - Q
Chomyszak, Steve - T
Coleman, Alvin - B
Coslet, Bruce - E
Crabtree, Eric - E
Dennis, Guy - G
Dressler, Doug - B
Dunn, Paul - E
Durko, Sandy - B
Dyer, Ken - B
Ely, Larry - LB
Fest, Howard - T
Graham, Kenny - B
Guillory, John - B
Johnson, Bob - C
Johnson, Essex - B

Kelly, Mike - E
Jones, Willie Lee - E
Lamb, Ron - B
Lewis, Dave - K & Q
McClure, Wayne - LB
Matson, Pat - G
Mayes, Rufus - G
Muhlmann, Horst - K
Myers, Chip - E
Parrish, Lemar - B
Peterson, Bill - LB
Phillips, Jess - B
Reid, Mike - T
Riley, Ken - B
Robinson, Paul - B
Roman, Nick - E
Smith, Fletcher - B
Thomas, Speedy - E
Trumpy, Bob - E
Wilson, Mike - T
Wright, Ernie - T
Wyche, Sam - Q

1970 CLEVELAND BROWNS (AFC)
COACH - Blanton Collier
2nd - Central Div., 7-7-0

Andrews, Bill - LB
Barnes, Erich - B
Beutler, Tom - LB
Brown, Ken - B
Cockroft, Don - K
Collins, Gary - B
Copeland, Jim - G
Davis, Ben - B
Demarie, John - G
Engel, Steve - B
Garlington, John - LB
Gault, Don - Q
Glass, Chip - E
Gregory, Jack - E
Hickerson, Gene - G
Hoaglin, Fred - C
Hooker, Fair - E
Houston, Jim - LB
Howell, Mike - B
Jenkins, Al - T
Johnson, Walter - T
Jones, Dave - E
Jones, Homer - B
Jones, Joe - E

Kellerman, Ernie - B
Kelly, Leroy - B
Kuechenberg, Rudy - LB
Lindsey, Dale - LB
McKay, Bob - T
Matheson, Bob - E
Minniear, Randy - B
Morin, Milt - E
Morrison, Reece - B
Nelsen, Bill - Q
Phipps, Mike - Q
Reynolds, Chuck - G
Righetti, Joe - T
Schafrath, Dick - T
Schoen, Tom - B
Scott, Bo - B
Sherk, Jerry - T
Snidow, Ron - E
Stevenson, Rickey - B
Summers, Freddie - B
Sumner, Walt - B
Taffoni, Joe - T
Yanchar, Bill - T

1970 DALLAS COWBOYS
COACH - Tom Landry
1st - Eastern Div., 10-4-0
(Beat Detroit, 5-0, for NFC Divisional
playoff; defeated San Francisco, 17-10,
in NFC Championship; lost to Baltimore
AFC, 16-13, in Super Bowl)

Adderley, Herb - B
Adkins, Margene - E
Andrie, George - E
Asher, Bob - T
Belden, Bob - Q
Clark, Mike - K
Cole, Larry - E
Ditka, Mike - E
East, Ron - T
Edwards, Dave - LB

Flowers, Richmond - B
Garrison, Walt - B
Green, Cornell - B
Hagen, Halvor - E
Harris, Cliff - B
Hayes, Bob - E
Hill, Calvin - B
Homan, Dennis - E
Howley, Chuck - LB
Jordan, Lee Roy - LB

1970 DENVER BRONCOS (AFC)
COACH - Lou Saban
4th - Western Div., 5-8-1

Alexakos, Steve - G
Anderson, Bob - B
Bachman, Jay - T
Barnes, Walt - E
Brunelli, Sam - T
Butler, Bill - LB
Costa, Dave - T
Crenshaw, Willis - B
Criter, Ken - LB
Cunningham, Carl - LB
Current, Mike - T
Davis, Dick - B
Denson, Al - E
Duranko, Pete - E
Edgerson, Booker - B
Embree, John - E
Forsberg, Fred - LB
Garrett, Drake - B
Goeddeke, George - G
Gordon, Cornell - B
Greer, Charlie - B
Haffner, Mike - E
Hendren, Jerry - E
Howfield, Bobby - K
Inman, Jerry - T

Jackson, Rich - E
Jaquess, Pete - B
Kaminski, Larry - C
Liske, Pete - Q
Little, Floyd - B
Lynch, Fran - B
McKoy, Bill - LB
Martha, Paul - B
Masters, Billy - E
Mitchell, Alvin - B
Myrtle, Chip - LB
Pastrana, Al - Q
Roche, Alden - E
Saimes, George - B
Schnitker, Mike - G
Smith, Paul - T
Tensi, Steve - Q
Thompson, Bill - B
Turner, Clem - B
Van Heusen, Bill - E & K
Wade, Bobby - B
Washington, Dave - LB
Whalen, Jim - E
Williams, Wandy - B
Young, Bob - G

1970 DETROIT LIONS
COACH - Joe Schmidt
2nd - Central Div., 10-4-0
(Lost to Dallas, 5-0, in
NFC Divisional Playoff)

Barney, Lem - B
Brown, Charlie - E
Cotton, Craig - E
Cottrell, Bill - C & G
Eddy, Nick - B
Farr, Mel - B
Flanagan, Ed - C
Freitas, Rocky - T
Gallagher, Frank - G
Goich, Dan - T
Hand, Larry - E
Haverdick, Dave - E
Hughes, Chuck - E
Karras, Alex - T
Kowalkowski, Bob - G
Landry, Greg - Q
Le Beau, Dick - B
Lucci, Mike - LB
McCullouch, Earl - E
Mann, Errol - K
Maxwell, Bruce - B
Mitchell, Jim - E

Mooney, Ed - LB
Munson, Bill - Q
Naumoff, Paul - LB
Odle, Phil - E
Owens, Steve - B
Rasmussen, Wayne - B
Rasley, Rocky - G
Robb, Joe - E
Rush, Jerry - T
Sanders, Charlie - E
Saul, Bill - LB
Shoals, Roger - T
Taylor, Altie - B
Triplett, Bill - B
Vaughn, Tom - B
Walker, Wayne - LB
Walton, Chuck - G
Walton, Larry - E
Weaver, Herman - K
Weger, Mike - B
Williams, Bobby - B
Yarbrough, Jim - T

1970 GREEN BAY PACKERS
COACH - Phil Bengston
3rd - Central Div., 6-8-0
(tied with Chicago)

Aldridge, Lionel - E
Amsler, Marty - E
Anderson, Donny - B & K
Bowman, Ken - C
Bradley, Dave - T
Brown, Bob - E
Carr, Fred - LB
Carter, Jim - LB
Carter, Mike - E

Clancy, Jack - E
Dale, Carroll - E
Ellis, Ken - B
Flanigan, Jim - LB
Gillingham, Gale - G
Grabowski, Jim - B
Gregg, Forrest - T
Hampton, Dave - B
Harden, Leon - B

Hardy, Kevin - E & T
Hart, Doug - B
Hayhoe, Bill - T
Hilton, John - E
Himes, Dick - T
Horn, Don - Q
Hunt, Ervin - B
Jeter, Bob - B
Krause, Larry - B
Kuechenberg, Randy - LB
Livingston, Dale - K
Lueck, Bill - G
McCoy, Mike - T
McGeorge, Rich - E
Matthews, Al - B

Moore, Rich - T
Nitschke, Ray - LB
Norton, Rick - Q
Patrick, Frank - Q
Peay, Francis - T
Robinson, Dave - LB
Spilis, John - E
Starr, Bart - Q
Walker, Cleo - LB & C
Walker, Malcolm - C
Williams, Clarence - E
Williams, Perry - B
Williams, Travis - B
Wood, Willie - B

Klein, Bob - E
Long, Bob - E
Mack, Tom - G
Mason, Tommy - B
Meador, Ed - B
Miller, Clark - E
Nettles, Jim - B
Olsen, Merlin - T
Pardee, Jack - LB
Pergine, John - LB
Petitbon, Richie - B
Pitts, Elijah - B
Pottios, Myron - LB
Purnell, Jim - LB
Ray, David - E & K

Reynolds, Jack - LB
Saul, Rich - C
Scibelli, Joe - G
Shaw, Nate - B
Smith, Larry - B
Snow, Jack - E
Studstill, Pat - E & K
Sweetan, Karl - Q
Talbert, Diron - E
Truax, Billy - E
Tucker, Wendell - E
Wilbur, John - G
Williams, Charlie - E
Williams, Clarence - B

1970 HOUSTON OILERS (AFC)
COACH - Wally Lemm
4th - Central Div., 3-10-1

Atkins, Bob - B
Autry, Hank - C
Beirne, Jim - E
Bethea, Elvin - E
Boyette, Garland - LB
Brooks, Leo - T
Campbell - Woody - B
Davis, Donnie - E
Dawkins, Joe - B
Domres, Tom - T
Drungo, Elbert - T
Gerela, Roy - K
Granger, Hoyle - B
Gray, Ken - G
Haik, Mac - E
Harvey, Claude - LB
Hines, Glen Ray - T
Holmes, Pat - E
Hopkins, Roy - B
Houston, Ken - B
Johnson, Benny - B
Johnson, Charley - Q
Joiner, Charlie - E
Jones, Spike - K

LeVias, Jerry - E
Lewis, Jess - LB
Maples, Bobby - C
Mitchell, Leroy - B
Moore, Zeke - B
Musgrove, Spain - T
Naponic, Bob - Q
Parker, Willie - T
Peacock, Johnny - B
Pritchard, Ron - LB
Reed, Alvin - E
Regner, Tom - G
Rhome, Jerry - Q
Richardson, Mike - B
Saul, Ron - G
Smiley, Tom - B
Stoepel, Terry - E
Suggs, Walt - T
Underwood, Olen - LB
Wainscott, Loyd - LB
Webster, George - LB
Wilkerson, Doug - E
Zaeske, Paul - E

1970 MIAMI DOLPHINS (AFC)
COACH - Don Shula
2nd - Eastern Div., 10-4-0
(Lost to Oakland, 21-14, in AFC
Divisional Playoff)

Anderson, Dick - B
Brown, Dean - B
Buoniconti, Nick - LB
Cornich, Frank - T
Crusan, Doug - T
Csonka, Larry - B
Davis, Ted - LB
DeMarco, Bob - C
Evans, Norm - T
Fernandez, Manny - T
Fleming, Marv - E
Foley, Tim - B
Ginn, Hubert - B
Griese, Bob - Q
Heinz, Bob - T
Johnson, Curtis - B
Kiick, Jim - B
Kolen, Mike - LB
Kremser, Karl - K
Kuechenberg, Bob - G
Langer, James - G
Little, Larry - G
McBride, Norm - E
Mandich, Jim - E

Mauck, Carl - C
Mitchell, Stan - B
Moore, Wayne - T
Morris, Mercury - B
Mumphord, Lloyd - B
Noonan, Karl - E
Palmer, Dick - LB
Petrella, Bob - B
Powell, Jesse - LB
Pryor, Barry - B
Richardson, John - T
Richardson, Willie - E
Riley, Jim - E
Scott, Jake - B
Seiple, Larry - E
Stanfill, Bill - E
Stofa, John - Q
Swift, Doug - LB
Twilley, Howard - E
Warfield, Paul - E
Weisacosky, Ed - LB
Williams, Maxie - G
Yepremian, Garo - K

1970 KANSAS CITY CHIEFS (AFC)
COACH - Hank Stram
2nd - Western Div., 7-5-2

Arbanas, Fred - E
Bell, Bobby - LB
Belser, Ceaser - B
Brown, Aaron - E
Buchanan, Buck - T
Budde, Ed - G
Cannon, Billy - E
Culp, Curley - T
Daney, George - G
Dawson, Len - Q
Garrett, Mike - B
Hadley, David - B
Hayes, Wendell - B
Hill, Dave - T
Holmes, Robert - B
Holub, E. J. - C
Huarte, John - Q
Hurston, Chuck - B
Kearney, Jim - B
Lanier, Willie - LB
Liggett, Bob - T
Livingston, Mike - Q
Lynch, Jim - LB

McVea, Warren - B
Marsalis, James - B
Mays, Jerry - E
Mitchell, Willie - B
Moorman, Mo - G
Oriad, Mike-C
Pitts, Frank - E
Podolak, Ed - B
Porter, Louis - B
Richardson, Gloster - E
Robinson, Johnny - B
Rudnay, Jack - C
Smith, Sid - T
Stein, Bob - LB
Stenerud, Jan - K
Stroud, Morris - E
Taylor, Otis - E
Thomas, Emmitt - B
Tyrer, Jim - T
Upshaw, Marvin - T
Werner, Clyde - LB
Wilson, Jerrell - K

1970 MINNESOTA VIKINGS
COACH - Bud Grant
1st - Central Div., 12-2-0
(Lost to San Francisco, 17-14,
in NFC Divisional Playoff)

Alderman, Grady - T
Beasley, John - E
Brown, Bill - B
Bryant, Bobbie - B
Cappleman, Bill - Q
Charles, John - B
Cox, Fred - K
Cuozzo, Gary - Q
Davis, Doug - T
Dickson, Paul - T
Eller, Carl - E
Farber, Hap - LB
Grim, Bob - E
Hackbart, Dale - LB
Hargrove, Jim - LB
Henderson, John - E
Hilgenberg, Wally - LB
Jones, Clinton - B
Kassulke, Karl - B
Kramer, Kent - E
Krause, Paul - B
Larsen, Gary - T
Lee, Bob - Q & K

Lindsey, Jim - B
McGill, Mike - LB
McNeill, Tom - K
Marshall, Jim - E
Meylan, Wayne - LB
Osborn, Dave - B
Page, Alan - T
Provost, Ted - B
Reed, Oscar - B
Sharockman, Ed - B
Smith, Steve - E
Sunde, Milt - G
Tingelhoff, Mick - C
Vellone, Jim - G
Voight, Stuart - E
Ward, John - T
Warwick, Lonnie - LB
Washington, Gene - E
West, Charlie - B
White, Ed - G
Winston, Roy - LB
Yary, Ron - T

1970 LOS ANGELES RAMS
COACH - George Allen
2nd - Western Div., 9-4-1

Alexander, Kermit - B
Bacon, Coy - T
Baughan, Maxie - LB
Brown, Bob - T
Burman, George - C & G
Cash, Rick - E
Cowan, Charlie - T
Curran, Pat - E
Ellison, Willie - B

Evey, Dick - T
Gabriel, Roman - Q
Haymond, Alvin - B
Iman, Ken - C
Johnson, Mitch - T
Jones, Deacon - E
Jordan, Jeff - B
Josephson, Les - B

1970 NEW ORLEANS SAINTS
COACH - Tom Fears to J. D. Roberts
4th - Western Div., 2-11-1

Abramowicz, Dan - E
Absher, Dick - LB & K
Baker, Tony - B
Barrington, Tom - B

Brewer, John - LB
Burkett, Jackie - LB
Burrough, Ken - E
Cody, Bill - LB

Colman, Wayne - LB
Davis, Dick - B
Dempsey, Tom - K
Dodd, Al - B
Dusenbery, Bill - B
Emanuel, Frank - LB
Estes, Lawrence - E
Fagan, Julian - K
Farber, Hap - LB
Gros, Earl - B
Hargett, Edd - Q
Hazelton, Major - B
Hollas, Hugo - B
Howard, Gene - B
Howell, Delles - B
Jacobs, Harry - LB
Kilmer, Bill - Q
Kupp, Jake - G
Lewis, Gary - B
Linden, Errol - T
Livingston, Andy - B
Long, Dave - E
Lyons, Dickie - B
McCall, Don - B
Morgan, Mike - LB

Neal, Richard - E
Nevett, Elijah - B
Nyvall, Vic - B
Otis, Jim - B
Parks, Dave - E
Pitts, Elijah - B
Poage, Ray - E
Ramsey, Steve - Q
Richey, Mike - T
Rowe, Dave - T
Scarpati, Joe - B
Shaw, Bob - E
Shinners, John - G
Sturm, Jerry - C
Sutherland, Doug - E
Swinney, Clovis - E
Talbert, Don - T
Taylor, Mike - T
Tilleman, Mike - T
Townes, Willie - E
Wheelwright, Ernie - B
Williams, Del - G
Wyatt, Doug - B

1970 OAKLAND RAIDERS (AFC)
COACH - John Madden
1st - Western Div., 8-4-2
(Beat Miami, 21-14, in AFC Divisional Playoff; lost to Baltimore, 27-17, for AFC Championship)

Atkinson, George - B
Banaszak, Pete - B
Benson, Duane - LB
Biletnikoff, Fred - E
Blanda, George - Q & K
Brown, Willie - B
Budness, Bill - LB
Buehler, George - G
Buie, Drew - E
Chester, Raymond - E
Cline, Tony - E
Conners, Dan - LB
Davidson, Ben - E
Dixon, Hewritt - B
Dotson, Al - T
Eischeid, Mike - K
Grayson, Dave - B
Harvey, Jim - G
Highsmith, Don - B
Hubbard, Marv - B
Irons, Gerald - LB
Keating, Tom - T

Koy, Ted - B
Lamonica, Daryle - Q
Laskey, Bill - LB
MacKinnon, Jacque - E
McCloughan, Kent - B
Oats, Carleton - E
Otto, Gus - LB
Otto, Jim - C
Schuh, Harry - T
Shell, Art - T
Sherman, Rod - E
Smith, Charlie - B
Stabler, Ken - Q
Svihus, Bob - T
Thoms, Art - T
Todd, Larry - B
Upshaw, Gene - G
Warren, Jim - B
Weathers, Carl - LB
Wells, Warren - E
Wilson, Nemiah - B
Wyatt, Alvin - B

1970 NEW YORK GIANTS
COACH - Alex Webster
2nd - Eastern Div., 9-5-0

Baker, John - E
Banks, Willie - G
Brenner, Al - B
Brown, Otto - B
Buzin, Rich - T
Case, Pete - G
Crane, Dennis - T
Douglas, John - LB
Dryer, Fred - E
Duhon, Bobby - B
Eaton, Scott - B
Files, Jim - LB
Frederickson, Tucker - B
Gogolak, Pete - K
Green, Joe - B
Harper, Charlie - G & T
Hazeltine, Matt - LB
Heck, Ralph - LB
Herrmann, Don - E
Hickl, Ray - LB
Houston, Rich - E
Hughes, Pat - C
Johnson, Len - G & C

Johnson, Ron - B
Johnson, Bill - K
Kanicki, Jim - T
Kirby, John - LB
Koy, Ernie - B & K
Larson, Greg - C
Lockhart, Carl - B
Longo, Tom - B
Lurtsema, Bob - T & E
McNeil, Clifton - E
Morrison, Joe - B
Norton, Jim - T
Parker, Ken - B
Shay, Jerry - T
Shiner, Dick - Q
Shy, Les - B
Tarkenton, Fran - Q
Thomas, Aaron - E
Tucker, Bob - E
Van Horn, Doug - G
Williams, Willie - B
Young, Willie - T

1970 PHILADELPHIA EAGLES
COACH - Jerry Williams
5th - Eastern Div., 3-10-1

Arrington, Rick - Q
Ballman, Gary - E
Bouggess, Lee - B
Bradley, Bill - B & K
Brumm, Don - E
Calloway, Ernie - T
Carollo, Joe - T
Davis, Norman - G
Dirks, Mike - T
Evans, Mike - C
Gersbach, Carl - LB
Hart, Dick - G
Harvey, Richard - B
Hawkins, Ben - E
Hayes, Ed - B
Hill, Fred - E
Hobbs, Bill - LB
Hultz, Don - E
Hunt, Calvin - C
Jackson, Harold - E
Johnson, Jay - LB
Jones, Harry - B
Jones, Raymond - B
Kelley, Ike - LB

Key, Wade - T
Keyes, Leroy - B
Lloyd, Dave - LB
Medved, Ron - B
Moseley, Mark - K
Nelson, Al - B
Nordquist, Mark - C & G
Pettigrew, Gary - T
Pinder, Cyril - B
Porter, Ron - LB
Preece, Steve - B
Ramsey, Nate - B
Rossovich, Tim - E
Skaggs, Jim - G
Snead, Norm - Q
Stevens, Richard - T
Thrower, Jim - B
Tom, Mel - E
Walik, Billy - E
Watkins, Larry - B
Woodeschick, Tom - B
Young, Adrian - LB
Zabel, Steve - E

1970 NEW YORK JETS (AFC)
COACH - Weeb Ewbank
3rd - Eastern Div., 4-10-0

Arthur, Gary - E & T
Atkinson, Al - LB
Baker, Ralph - LB
Battle, Mike - B
Bayless, Tom - G
Bell, Ed - E
Biggs, Verlon - E
Boozer, Emerson - B
Caster, Rich - E
Crane, Paul - LB
Davis, Bob - Q
Dockery, John - B
Ebersole, John - LB
Elliott, John - T
Finnie, Roger - T
Foley, Dave - T
Grantham, Larry - LB
Herman, Dave - G
Hicks, W. K. - B
Hill, Winston - T
Hollomon, Gus - B
Hudson, Jim - B
Jones, Jimmie - E
Lammons, Pete - E

Leonard, Cecil - B
Little, John - E & T
Lomas, Mark - E
McClain, Clifford - B
Maynard, Don - E
Mercein, Chuck - B
Middendorf, Dave - G
Namath, Joe - Q
Nock, George - B
O'Neal, Steve - K & E
Onkotz, Dennis - LB
Perreault, Pete - G
Philbin, Gerry - E
Rasmussen, Randy - G
Sauer, George - E
Schmitt, John - C
Snell, Matt - B
Stewart, Wayne - E
Tannen, Steve - B
Thomas, Earlie - B
Thompson, Steve - T
Turner, Jim - K & Q
White, Lee - B
Woodall, Al - Q

1970 PITTSBURGH STEELERS (AFC)
COACH - Chuck Noll
3rd - Central Div., 5-9-0

Adams, Bob - E
Allen, Chuck - LB
Arndt, Dick - T
Austin, Ocie - B
Bankston, Warren - B
Barry, Fred - B
Beatty, Charles - B
Blount, Melvin - B
Bradshaw, Terry - Q & K
Brown, John - T
Bryant, Hubie - E
Calland, Lee - B
Cole, Terry - B
Crennel, Carl - LB
Davis, Henry - LB
Davis, Sam - G
Fisher, Doug - LB
Fuqua, John - B
Graham, Kenny - B
Greene, Joe - T
Greenwood, L. C. - E
Haggerty, Mike - T
Hanratty, Terry - Q
Hillebrand, Jerry - LB
Hinton, Chuck - T

Hoak, Dick - B
Hughes, Dennis - E
Kalina, Dave—E
Kolb, Jon - C
McGee, Ben - E
Mansfield, Ray - C
Mingo, Gene - K
Oliver, Clarence - B
Pearson, Preston - B
Rowser, John - B
Russell, Andy - LB
Shanklin, Ron - E
Sharp, Rick - T
Smith, Dave - E
Sodaski, John - B
Staggers, Jon - E
Stenger, Brian - LB
Van Dyke, Bruce - G
Voss, Lloyd - E
Walden, Bob - K
Washington, Clarence - T
Watson, Allen - K
Wenzel, Ralph - G
Wilburn, J. R. - E

1970 ST. LOUIS CARDINALS
COACH - Charley Winner
3rd - Eastern Div., 8-5-1

Bakken, Jim - K	Parish, Don - LB
Beathard, Pete - Q	Pittman, Charlie - B
Brown, Bob - E	Plummer, Tony-B
Brown, Terry - B	Reynolds, Bob - T
Daanen, Jerry - E	Rivers, Jamie - LB
Edwards, Cid - B	Roland, John - B
Emerson, Vernon - T	Rosema, Rocky - LB
Farr, Miller - B	Rowe, Bob - T
Gilliam, John - E	Schmiesing, Joe - E
Goode, Irv - G & C	Shivers, Roy - B
Hart, Jim - Q	Siwek, Mike - T
Healy, Chip - LB	Smith, Jackie - E
Heron, Fred - T	Snowden, Cal - E
Hutchison, Charles - G	Stallings, Larry - LB
Hyatt, Fred - E	Stovall, Jerry - B
Krueger, Rolf - E	Walker, Chuck - E
LaHood, Mike - G	Wehrli, Roger - B
Lane, MacArthur - B	White, Paul - B
Latourette, Chuck - K & B & E	Williams, Clyde - T
McFarland, Jim - E	Williams, Dave - E
McMillan, Ernie - T	Wilson, Larry - B
Mulligan, Wayne - C	Wright, Nate - B
Olerich, Dave - LB	

1970 WASHINGTON REDSKINS
COACH - Bill Austin
4th - Eastern Div., 6-8-0

Alston, Mack - E	Kopay, Dave - B
Anderson, Bruce - E	Laaveg, Paul - T
Bass, Mike - B	McKeever, Marlin - LB
Bosch, Frank - T	McLinton, Harold - LB
Bragg, Mike - K	Malinchak, Bill - E
Brown, Larry - B	Owens, Brig - B
Brundige, Bill - T & E	Peters, Floyd - T
Brunet, Bob - B	Pierce, Danny - Q & B
Carroll, Leo - E	Promuto, Vince - G
Didion, John - C & LB	Richter, Pat - E
Dyer, Henry - B	Roberts, Walt - E
Fischer, Pat - B	Rock, Walter - T
Hamlin, Gene - C	Roussel, Tom - LB
Hanburger, Chris - LB	Ryan, Frank - Q
Harraway, Charley - B	Schmidt, Roy - G
Harris, Jim - B	Schoenke, Ray - G
Harris, Rickie - B	Sistrunk, Manuel - T
Hauss, Len - C	Smith, Jerry - E
Henderson, Jon - E	Snowden, Jim - T
Hermeling, Jerry - T	Taylor, Charley - E
Hoffman, John - E	Tillman, Russell - LB
Jaqua, Jon - B	Vactor, Ted - B
Jurgensen, Sonny - Q	Wright, Steve - T
Knight, Curt - K	

1970 SAN DIEGO CHARGERS (AFC)
COACH - Charlie Waller
3rd - Western Div., 5-6-3

Alworth, Lance - E	Howard, Bob - B
Babich, Bob - LB	Hubbert, Brad - B
Barnes, Pete - LB	Lenkaitis, Bill - G
Beauchamp, Joe - B	Mercer, Mike - K
Billingsley, Ron - T	Moss, Roland - B
Briggs, Bob - E	Owens, Joe - E
Bruggers, Bob - LB	Owens, Terry - T
Clark, Wayne - Q	Partee, Dennis - K
DeLong, Steve - E	Post, Dick - B
Detwiler, Chuck - B	Protz, John - LB
Domres, Marty - Q	Queen, Jeff - E
Duncan, Speedy - B	Redman, Rick - LB
Eber, Rick - E	Rice, Andy - T
Ferguson, Gene - T	Schmedding, Jim - G
Fletcher, Chris - B	Smith, Dave - B
Foster, Gene - B	Smith, Russ - B
Frazier, Willie - E	Staggs, Jeff - LB
Garrett, Mike - B	Strozier, Art - E
Garrison, Gary - E	Sweeney, Walt - G
Gillette, Walker - E	Tolbert, Jim - B
Gordon, Ira - G	Washington, Russ - T
Gruneisen, Sam - C	Wells, Bob - T
Hadl, John - Q	Williams, Tom - T
Hill, Jim - B	Withrow, Cal - C

1970 SAN FRANCISCO 49ERS
COACH - Dick Nolan
1st - Western Div., 10-3-1
(Beat Minnesota, 17-14, in NFC
Divisional Playoff; lost to Dallas,
17-10, for the NFC Championship)

Banaszek, Cas - T	Nunley, Frank - LB
Beard, Ed - LB	Peoples, Woody - G
Beisler, Randy - T	Phillips, Mel - B
Belk, Bill - E	Randolph, Al - B
Blue, Forrest - C	Riley, Preston - E
Brodie, John - Q	Rohde, Len - T
Campbell, Carter - LB	Silas, Sam - T & E
Collett, Elmer - G	Simpson, Mike - B
Cunningham, Doug - B	Sniadecki, Jim - LB
Edwards, Earl - E & T	Spurrier, Steve - Q & K
Fuller, Johnny - B	Strong, Jim - B
Gossett, Bruck - K	Taylor, Bruce - B
Hardman, Cedrick - E	Taylor, Rosey - B
Hart, Tommy - E	Thomas, Jimmy - B
Hindman, Stan - E	Tucker, Bill - B
Hoskins, Bob - G	Vanderbundt, Skip - LB
Isenbarger, John - B	Washington, Gene - E
Johnson, Jimmy - B	Wilcox, Dave - LB
Johnson, Leo - E	Willard, Ken - B
Krueger, Charlie - T	Windsor, Bob - E
Kwalick, Ted - E	Witcher, Dick - E
Lakes, Roland - T	

1971

NATIONAL FOOTBALL LEAGUE

NATIONAL CONFERENCE
WESTERN DIVISION

	W.	L.	T.	Pct.
San Francisco	9	5	0	.643
Los Angeles	8	5	1	.615
Atlanta	7	6	1	.538
New Orleans	4	8	2	.333

EASTERN DIVISION

	W.	L.	T.	Pct.
Dallas	11	3	0	.786
Washington*	9	4	1	.692
Philadelphia	6	7	1	.462
St. Louis	4	9	1	.308
N. Y. Giants	4	10	0	.286

CENTRAL DIVISION

	W.	L.	T.	Pct.
Minnesota	11	3	0	.786
Detroit	7	6	1	.538
Chicago	6	8	0	.429
Green Bay	4	8	2	.333

*Fourth Qualifier for Playoffs.

AMERICAN CONFERENCE
WESTERN DIVISION

	W.	L.	T.	Pct.
Kansas City	10	3	1	.769
Oakland	8	4	2	.667
San Diego	6	8	0	.429
Denver	4	9	1	.308

EASTERN DIVISION

	W.	L.	T.	Pct.
Miami	10	3	1	.769
Baltimore*	10	4	0	.714
New England	6	8	0	.429
N. Y. Jets	6	8	0	.429
Buffalo	1	13	0	.071

CENTRAL DIVISION

	W.	L.	T.	Pct.
Cleveland	9	5	0	.643
Pittsburgh	6	8	0	.429
Houston	4	9	1	.308
Cincinnati	4	10	0	.286

*Fourth Qualifier for Playoffs.

1971 AFC Championship

Miami 21, Baltimore 0

Miami, who defeated Kansas City in double overtime in the Divisional Playoffs, shut out the Baltimore Colts, 21-0, to head for the Super Bowl. It was the first time in 97 games the Colts were blanked.

While using an all around team effort and a strong running game, Dolphin QB Bob Griese also threw a 75-yd. TD pass to Paul Warfield in the second quarter and set up a Larry Csonka TD in the fourth.

Baltimore's John Unitas, unable to generate a satisfactory running attack with injuries sidelining his two key backs, took to the air only to have Dolphin safety Dick Anderson intercept and romp 62 yards for a third-quarter touchdown. The Miami defense also intercepted Unitas passes two other times, caused a missed field goal, and held the Colt defense on a 4th-down situation.

Miami	0	7	7	7	21
Baltimore	0	0	0	0	0

Touchdowns: Warfield, Anderson, Csonka.
PATs: Yepremian 3
Attendance: 76,622
Players' shares: Miami $8,500; Baltimore $5,500.

1971 NFC Championship

Dallas 14, San Francisco 3

Defense was the name of the game. Dallas defense, #1 in the NFC against rushing this year, was pitted against San Francisco's defense, which had allowed only four touchdowns rushing. Mistakes would win the game.

It started in the second quarter when the Dallas blitz caused a John Brodie pass to Ken Willard to be intercepted by end George Andrie, setting up the first Cowboy TD by Calvin Hill. Two other Brodie passes were intercepted but no scoring resulted while Dallas's only mistake was a fumble on the last play before the half.

San Francisco's only score was a Bruce Gossett 49-yd. field goal in the third quarter after Dallas held the 49ers to a single first down the entire first half.

San Francisco's defense forced Staubach to scramble a total of 55 yards after doubling up on the Cowboy wide receivers and forcing him out of the pocket. Duane Thomas took over the last Cowboy touchdown in an 80-yard, 14-play drive.

Dallas	0	7	0	7	14
San Francisco	0	0	3	0	3

Touchdowns: Hill, D. Thomas.
Field Goals: Gossett.
PATs: Clark 2
Attendance: 63,409.
Players' shares: Dallas $8,500; San Francisco $5,500.

1971 Super Bowl

Dallas 24, Miami 3

Dallas was finally able to "win the big one" after playing bridesmaid in the 1966, 1967 NFL title games and the 1970 Super Bowl.

By controlling the ball for 40 minutes of the 60-minute game time, the NFC champs were able to set S.B. records for most rushing plays, 48, and total yards rushing, 252. It also brought their game-winning streak to ten.

Their defense held Miami to only 80 yards on the ground while forcing a fumble on the Dolphin's second possession of the game, resulting in a Mike Clark field goal from the 9-yd. line.

Roger Staubach's first TD was a 7-yd. pass to Lance Alworth making the score 10-0 before Miami was able to get on the scoreboard. A 31-yard field goal by Dolphin kicker Garo Yepremian in the second period was the second time this season the AFC champions failed to get a touchdown.

A pitchout to Duane Thomas in the third quarter put another seven points on the scoreboard for Dallas. The icing on the cake came when Chuck Howley intercepted a Bob Griese pass in the 4th quarter setting up Staubach's second TD pass to Mike Ditka from the nine.

Dallas	3	7	7	7	24
Miami	0	3	0	0	3

Touchdowns: Alworth, Thomas, Ditka.
Field Goals: Clark, Yepremian.
PATs: Clark 3.
Attendance: 81,023.
Players' shares: Dallas $15,000; Miami $7,500.

RETIRED PLAYERS:

Gino Cappelletti, Boston Patriots end, kicker, 11 years;

Jim Hunt, Boston Patriots end, tackle, 11 years;

Alex Karras, Detroit Lions tackle, 12 years;

Frank Ryan, Los Angeles Rams-Cleveland Browns-Washington Redskins quarterback, 13 years;

Billy Ray Smith, Los Angeles Rams-Pittsburgh Steelers-Baltimore Colts tackle, 13 years.

DEATHS

Davies, Thomas J., back, 1922 Hammond Pros, on Feb. 29, 1972.

Ford, Leonard, end, 1948-49 Los Angeles Dons (AAFC); 1950-57 Cleveland Browns; 1958 Green Bay Packers, on Mar. 13, 1972.

Golding, Joseph G., back, 1947-48 Boston Yanks; 1949 New York Bulldogs; 1950-51 New York Yanks, on Dec. 26, 1971.

Guyon, Joseph, back, 1919-20 Canton Bulldogs; 1921 Cleveland Indians; 1922-23 Oorang Indians; 1924 Rock Island Independents; 1924-25 Kansas City Cowboys; 1927 New York Giants; 1966 Hall of Fame, on Nov. 27, 1971.

Hughes, Charles, back-end, 1967-69 Philadelphia Eagles; 1970-71 Detroit Lions (NFC), on Oct. 24, 1971.

Kellison, John, tackle, 1919-21 Canton Bulldogs; 1922 Toledo Maroons, on May 7, 1971.

Keys, Howard, tackle, 1960-63 Philadelphia Eagles, on Oct. 21, 1971.

Lester, Harold, end, 1926 Providence Steamrollers, on Jan. 1, 1972.

McAuliffe, John, back, 1926 Green Bay Packers, in 1971.

McDonald, Lester, end, 1937-39 Chicago Bears; 1940 Philadelphia Eagles; 1940 Detroit Lions, July 26, 1971.

Method, Russell, back, 1923-25 Duluth Kelleys; 1926-27 Duluth Eskimos; 1929 Chicago Cardinals, on Sept. 17, 1971.

O'Hanley, Ross, back, 1960-65 Boston Patriots (AFL), on Apr. 2, 1972.

Padlow, Max, end, 1935-36 Philadelphia Eagles; 1936 Cleveland Rams (AFL); 1937 Cincinnati Bengals (AFL), in Aug., 1971.

Reeves, Daniel, owner of Los Angeles Rams, on Apr. 15, 1971.

Renn, Robert, back, 1961 New York Titans (AFL), on Oct. 21, 1971.

Saenz, Edward, back, 1946-51 Washington Redskins, on Apr. 27, 1971.

Schrader, James, center, 1954, 56-61 Washington Redskins; 1962-64 Philadelphia Eagles, 1971.

Seibold, Champ, tackle, 1934-38, 40 Green Bay Packers; 1942 Chicago Cardinals, Nov. 2, 1971.

Sorenson, Glen, guard, 1943-45 Green Bay Packers on Feb. 26, 1972.

Taylor, John L., tackle, 1920 Decatur Staleys; 1921 Chicago Staleys; 1922 Canton Bulldogs; 1926 Brooklyn Lions; 1926 Brooklyn Horsemen (AFL), on May 1, 1971.

Trafton, George, center, 1920 Decatur Staleys; 1921 Chicago Staleys; 1922-32 Chicago Bears; 1964 Hall of Fame, on Sept. 5, 1971.

Washington, Kenneth S., back, 1946-48 Los Angeles Rams, on June 24, 1971.

1971 ATLANTA FALCONS (NFC)
Coach – Norm Van Brocklin
3rd – Western Div., 7–6–1

Acks, Ronald – LB	McCauley, Tom – B
Allen, Grady – LB	Mallory, John – B
Bell, William – K	Malone, Art – B
Belton, Willie – B	Marshall, Randy – E
Berry, Bob – Q	Matlock, John – C
Bramlett, John – LB	Mauer, Andy – G
Brezina, Greg – LB	Miller, Jim – G
Brown, Ray – B	Mitchell, Jim – E
Burrow, Ken – E	Nobis, Tommy – LB
Butler, Jim – B	Plummer, Tony – B
Campbell, Sonny – B	Poage, Ray – E
Chesson, Wes – E	Profit, Joe – B
Condren, Glen – T	Reaves, Ken – B
Donohoe, Mike – E	Redmond, Rudy – B
Enderle, Dick – G	Sandeman, Bill – T
Hansen, Don – LB	Shears, Larry – B
Hart, Leo – Q	Shiner, Dick – Q
Hayes, Tom – B	Small, John – T, LB
Humphrey, Claude – E	Snider, Malcolm – G, T
Jarvis, Ray – E	Snyder, Todd – E
Kuechenberg, Rudy – LB	Van Note, Jeff – C
Kunz, George – T	Wages, Harmon – B
Lens, Greg – T	Walker, Cleo – C
Lewis, Mike – E	Zook, John – E
Lothridge, Billy – K	

1971 BALTIMORE COLTS (AFC)
Coach – Don McCafferty
2nd – Eastern Div., 10–4–0
(Beat Cleveland, 20–3, in AFC
Divisional Playoffs; lost to Miami,
21 0, in AFC Championship Game)

Bailey, Jim – T
Beutler, Tom – LB
Bulaich, Norm – B
Curry, Bill – C
Curtis, Mike – LB
Curtis, Tom – B
Duncan, Jim – B
Dunlap, Leonard – B
Ganas, Rusty – T
Gardin, Ron – E
Havrilak, Sam – B,E
Hendricks, Ted – LB
Hepburn, Lonnie – B
Hilton, Roy – E
Hinton, Ed – E
Johnson, Cornelius – G
Kern, Rex – B
Larson, Lynn – T
Laskey, Bill – LB
Lee, David – K
Logan, Jerry – B
McCauley, Don – B
Mackey, John – E
Matte, Tom – B

May, Ray – LB
Mendenhall, Ken – C
Miller, Fred – T
Mitchell, Tom – E
Morrall, Earl – Q
Nelson, Dennis – T
Newsome, Billy – E
Nichols, Robbie – LB
Nottingham, Don – B
Nowatzke, Tom – B
O'Brien, Jim – K,E
Perkins, Ray – E
Pittman, Charlie – B
Ressler, Glenn – G
Richardson, Willie – E
Smith, Bubba – E
Stukes, Charlie – B
Sullivan, Dan – G,T
Unitas, John – Q
Vogel, Bob – T
Volk, Rick – B
Williams, John – G
Wright, George – T

1971 BUFFALO BILLS (AFC)
Coach – Harvey Johnson
5th – Eastern Div., 1–13–0

Allen, Jackie – B
Andrews, Al – LB
Beamer, Tim – B
Briscoe, Marlin – E
Braxton, Jim – B
Carr, Levert – T,G
Chandler, Edgar – LB
Chandler, Bob – E
Chapple, Dave – K
Collins, Jerald – LB
Costa, Paul – T
Cowlings, Al – E
Cunningham, Dick – LB
Denney, Austin – E
Dunaway, Jim – T
Grant, Wes – E
Green, Don – T
Greene, Tony – B
Guidry, Paul – LB
Guthrie, Grant – K
Harris, Jim – Q
Hews, Robert – E
Hill, Ike – B
Hill, J. D. – E
Hurston, Chuck – LB

James, Robert – B
Jarvis, Bruce – C
Jones, Greg – B
Jones, Spike – K
Kindig, Howard – T,C
Koy, Ted – B
Leypoldt, John – K
McBath, Mike – E
McKinley, Bill – E,LB
Moses, Haven – E
O'Donnell, Joe – G
Patrick, Wayne – B
Pitts, John – B
Reilly, Jim – G
Richardson, Pete – B
Ross, Louis – E
Shaw, Dennis – Q
Simpson, O. J. – B
Snowden, Cal – E
Stratton, Mike – LB
Tatarek, Bob – T
White, Jan – E
Wilson, Mike – G
Wyatt, Alvin – B
Young, Willie – T

1971 CHICAGO BEARS (NFC)
Coach – Jim Dooley
3rd – Central Div., 6–8–0

Brupbacher, Ross – LB
Buffone, Doug – LB
Butkus, Dick – LB
Cadile, Jim – G
Coady, Rich – C
Concannon, John – Q
Curchin, Jeff – T
Douglass, Bobby – Q
Farmer, George – E
Ford, Charlie – B
Gordon, Dick – E
Grabowski, Jim – B
Green, Bobby Joe – K
Gunn, Jimmy – LB

Hale, Dave – T
Hamlin, Gene – C
Hardy, Cliff – B
Harrison, Jim – B
Hoffman, John – E
Holloway, Glen – G
Holman, Willie – E
Jackson, Randy – T
Jeter, Bob – B
Lyle, Garry – B
McGee, Tony – E
Moore, Jerry – B
Moore, Joe – B
Newton, Bob – T

Nix, Kent – Q
O'Bradovich, Ed – E
Ogden, Ray – E
Percival, Mac – K
Pinder, Cyril – B
Rowden, Larry – LB
Sayers, Gale – B
Seals, George – T
Seymour, Jim – E

Shy, Don – B
Smith, Ron – B
Staley, Bill – T
Taylor, Joe – B
Thomas, Earl – E
Tucker, Bill – B
Turner, Cecil – E
Wallace, Bob – E
Wright, Steve – T

1971 CINCINNATI BENGALS (AFC)
Coach – Paul Brown
4th – Central Div., 4–10–0

Adams, Doug – LB
Anderson, Ken – Q
Avery, Ken – LB
Beauchamp, Al – LB
Bergey, Bill – LB
Berry, Royce – E
Carpenter, Ron – E
Carter, Virgil – Q
Chomyszak, Steve – T
Coleman, Al – B
Coslet, Bruce – E
Crabtree, Eric – E
Craig, Neal – B
Dennis, Guy – G
Dressler, Doug – B
Durko, Sandy – B
Dyer, Ken – B
Ely, Larry – LB
Fest, Howard – T
Haffner, Mike – E
Holland, Vernon – T
Johnson, Essex – B
Johnson, Ken – E

Johnson, Bob – C
Jones, Willie Lee – E,T
Kelly, Mike – E
Lamb, Ron – B
Lawson, Stephen – G
Lewis, Dave – K,Q
Marshall, Ed – E
Matson, Pat – G
Mayes, Rufus – T
Muhlmann, Horst – K
Myers, Chip – E
Parrish, Lemar – B
Peterson, Bill – LB
Phillips, Jess – B
Reid, Mike – T
Riley, Ken – B
Robinson, Paul – B
Roman, Nick – E
Smith, Fletcher – B
Thomas, Speedy – E
Trumpy, Bob – E
Willis, Fred – B
Wright, Ernie – T

1971 CLEVELAND BROWNS (AFC)
Coach – Nick Skorich
1st – Central Div., 9–5–0
(Lost to Baltimore, 20–3, in AFC
Divisional Playoffs)

Andrews, Bill – LB
Barnes, Erich – B
Briggs, Bob – E,T
Brown, Ken – B
Brown, Stanley – E
Cockroft, Don – K
Collins, Gary – E
Copeland, Jim – G,C
Cornell, Bo – B
Davis, Ben – B
Demarie, John – G
Dieken, Doug – T
Garlington, John – LB
Glass, Chip – E
Gregory, Jack – E
Hall, Charles – LB
Hickerson, Gene – G
Hoaglin, Fred – C
Hooker, Fair – E
Houston, Jim – LB
Howell, Mike – B
Johnson, Mitch – T

Johnson, Walter – T
Jones, Dave – E
Jones, Joe – E
Kellerman, Ernie – B
Kelly, Leroy – B
Kingrea, Rick – LB
Lindsey, Dale – LB
McKay, Bob – T
Morin, Milt – E
Morrison, Reece – B
Nelsen, Bill – Q
Phipps, Mike – Q
Pitts, Frank – E
Schafrath, Dick – T
Scott, Bo – B
Scott, Clarence – B
Sherk, Jerry – T
Sikich, Mike – G
Snidow, Ron – E
Summers, Freddie – B
Sumner, Walt – B

1971 DALLAS COWBOYS (NFC)
Coach – Tom Landry
1st – Eastern Div., 11–3–0
(Beat Minnesota, 20–12, in NFC
Divisional Playoff; defeated San
Francisco, 14–3, for NFC Champion-
ship; beat Miami, 24–3, in the
Super Bowl)

Adderley, Herb – B
Adkins, Margene – E
Alworth, Lance – E
Andrie, George – E

Caffey, Lee Roy – LB
Clark, Mike – K
Cole, Larry – E
Ditka, Mike – E

Edwards, Dave – LB
Fitzgerald, John – C
Flowers, Richmond – B
Fritsch, Toni – K
Garrison, Walt – B
Green, Cornell – B
Gregg, Forrest – T,G
Gregory, Bill – T
Harris, Cliff – B
Hayes, Bob – E
Hill, Calvin – B
Howley, Chuck – LB
Jordan, Lee Roy – LB
Lewis, D. D. – LB
Lilly, Bob – T
Liscio, Tony – T
Manders, Dave – C
Morton, Craig – Q
Neely, Ralph – T
Niland, John – G
Nye, Blaine – G

Pugh, Jethro – T
Reeves, Dan – B
Renfro, Mel – B
Richardson, Gloster – E
Rucker, Reggie – E
Smith, Tody – E
Staubach, Roger – Q
Stincic, Tom – LB
Talbert, Don – T
Thomas, Duane – B
Thomas, Isaac – B
Toomay, Pat – E
Truax, Billy – E
Washington, Mark – B
Waters, Charley – B
Welch, Claxton – B
Widby, Ron – K
Wallace, Rodney – G
Williams, Joe – B
Wright, Rayfield – T

1971 DENVER BRONCOS (AFC)
Coach – Lou Saban & Jerry Smith
4th – Western Div., 4-9-1

Alzado, Lyle – E
Anderson, Bob – B
Bachman, Jay – C
Barnes, Walt – E
Bowdell, Gordon – E
Brunelli, Sam – G
Byrd, Butch – B
Campbell, Carter – LB,E
Costa, Dave – T
Criter, Ken – LB
Current, Mike – T
Dawkins, Joe – B
Domres, Tom – T
Forsberg, Fred – LB
Gehrke, Jack – E
Goeddeke, George – G
Gordon, Cornell – B
Greer, Charlie – B
Harrison, Dwight – E
Horn, Don – Q
Inman, Jerry – T
Jackson, Larron – G,T
Jackson, Rich – E
Kaminski, Larry – C

Little, Floyd – B
Lynch, Fran – B
Lyons, Tommy – C
McKoy, Bill – LB
Masters, Billy – E
Mitchell, Leroy – B
Montgomery, Marv – T
Montgomery, Randy – B
Mosier, John – E
Myrtle, Chip – LB
Post, Dick – B
Ramsey, Steve – Q
Saimes, George – B
Schnitker, Mike – G
Shoals, Roger – T
Simmons, Jerry – E
Smith, Paul – T
Thompson, Bill – B
Turner, Clem – B
Turner, Jim – K
Underwood, Olen – LB
Van Heusen, Bill – E,K
Washington, Dave – LB
Whalen, Jim – E

1971 DETROIT LIONS (NFC)
Coach – Joe Schmidt
2nd – Central Div., 7-6-1

Barney, Lem – B
Bell, Bob – T
Clark, Al – B
Cotton, Craig – E
Evey, Dick – T
Farr, Mel – B
Flanagan, Ed – C
Freitas, Rocky – T
Gallagher, Frank – G
Gipson, Paul – B
Hand, Larry – E
Hughes, Chuck – E
Jessie, Ron – E
Kowalkowski, Bob – G
Landry, Greg – Q
LeBeau, Dick – B
Lee, Ken – LB
Lucci, Mike – LB
McCullouch, Earl – E
Mann, Errol – K
Mitchell, Jim – E
Mooney, Ed – LB

Munson, Bill – Q
Naumoff, Paul – LB
Owens, Steve – B
Parson, Ray – T
Rasmussen, Wayne – B
Robb, Joe – E
Rush, Jerry – T
Sanders, Charlie – E
Taylor, Altie – B
Thompson, Dave – G,C
Triplett, Bill – B
Vaughn, Tom – B
Walker, Wayne – LB
Walton, Chuck – G
Walton, Larry – E
Weaver, Charlie – LB
Weaver, Herman – K
Weger, Mike – B
Williams, Bobby Ray – B
Woods, Larry – T
Yarbrough, Jim – T
Zofko, Mickey – B

1971 GREEN BAY PACKERS (NFC)
Coach – Dan Devine
4th – Central Div., 4-8-2

Aldridge, Lionel – E
Anderson, Donny – B,K
Bowman, Ken – C
Bradley, Dave – G
Bratkowski, Zeke – Q
Brockington, John – B
Brown, Bob – E,T
Carr, Fred – LB
Carter, Jim – LB
Conway, Dave – K
Crutcher, Tommy – LB
Dale, Carroll – E
Davis, Dave – E
DeLisle, Jim – T
Duncan, Ken – K
Ellis, Ken – B
Garrett, Leonard – E
Gillingham, Gale – G
Hall, Charles – B
Hampton, Dave – B
Hart, Doug – B
Hayhoe, Bill – T
Himes, Dick – T
Hunter, Scott – Q

Krause, Larry – B
Lueck, Bill – G
McCoy, Mike – T
McGeorge, Rich – E
Matthews, Al – B
Michaels, Lou – K
Nitschke, Ray – LB
Patrick, Frank – Q
Peay, Francis – T
Pitts, Elijah – B
Randolph, Al – B
Robinson, Dave – LB
Roche, Alden – E
Smith, Donnell – E
Spilis, John – E
Starr, Bart – Q
Webster, Tim – K
Williams, Clarence – E
Williams, Perry – B
Winkler, Randy – G
Winther, Wimpy – C
Withrow, Cal – C
Wood, Willie – B

1971 HOUSTON OILERS (AFC)
Coach – Ed Hughes
3rd – Central Div., 4-9-1

Aldridge, Allen – E
Alexander, Willie – B
Atkins, Bob – B
Beck, Braden – K
Beirne, Jim – E
Bethea, Elvin – E
Billingsley, Ron – T
Boyette, Garland – LB
Brooks, Leo – T
Burrough, Ken – E
Campbell, Woody – B
Charles, John – B
Cole, Linzy – E
Croyle, Phil – LB
Dawkins, Joe – B
Dickey, Lynn – Q
Domres, Tom – T
Drungo, Elbert – T
Ferguson, Gene – T
Frazier, Willie – E
Funchess, Tom – T
Haik, Mac – E
Holmes, Pat – E
Holmes, Robert – B
Hopkins, Andy – B

Houston, Ken – B
Howard, Leroy – B
Johnson, Benny – B
Johnson, Charley – Q
Joiner, Charlie – E
Lewis, Scott – E
Moore, Zeke – B
Moseley, Mark – K
Olerich, Dave – LB
Pastorini, Dan – Q,K
Post, Dick – B
Pritchard, Ron – LB
Reed, Alvin – E
Regner, Tom – G,T
Rice, Floyd – E
Richardson, Mike – B
Saul, Ron – G
Sledge, Leroy – B
Sturm, Jerry – G,C
Suggs, Walt – T,C
Tilleman, Mike – T
Walsh, Ward – B
Walton, Sam – T
Webster, George – LB
Young, Bob – G

1971 KANSAS CITY CHIEFS (AFC)
Coach – Hank Stram
1st – Western Div., 10-3-1
(Lost to Miami, 27-24, in second
sudden death overtime period in
AFC Divisional Playoffs)

Adamle, Mike – B
Allen, Nathaniel – B
Bell, Bobby – LB
Belser, Ceaser – LB
Bergey, Bruce – E
Brown, Aaron – E
Buchanan, Buck – T
Budde, Ed – G
Culp, Curley – T
Daney, George – G
Dawson, Len – Q
Frazier, Willie – E
Hadley, David – B
Hayes, Wendell – B
Hill, Dave – T

Holmes, Bob – B
Homan, Dennis – E
Huarte, John – Q
Jankowski, Bruce – E
Kearney, Jim – B
Lanier, Willie – LB
Livingston, Mike – Q
Lothamer, Ed – T
Lynch, Jim – LB
McVea, Warren – B
Marsalis, James – B
Moorman, Mo – G
Oriard, Mike – C
Otis, Jim – B
Podolak, Ed – B

Reardon, Kenny – B
Robinson, Johnny – B
Rudnay, Jack – C
Sensibaugh, Mike – B
Smith, Sid – T
Stein, Bob – LB,E
Stenerud, Jan – K
Stroud, Morris – E

Taylor, Otis – E
Thomas, Emmitt – B
Tyrer, Jim – T
Upshaw, Marvin – T
Wilson, Jerrel – K
Wright, Elmo – E
Young, Wilbur – T,E

Eller, Carl – E
Gersbach, Carl – LB
Grim, Bob – E
Hayden, Leo – B
Henderson, John – E
Hilgenberg, Wally – LB
Hilton, John – E
Jenke, Noel – LB
Jones, Clint – B
Kassulke, Karl – B
Krause, Paul – B
Larsen, Gary – T
Lee, Bob – Q
Lindsey, Jim – B
Marshall, Jim – E
Osborn, Dave – B
Page, Alan – T
Perreault, Pete – G,T
Reed, Oscar – B

Schmidt, Roy – G
Sharockman, Ed – B
Snead, Norm – Q
Sunde, Milt – G
Sutherland, Doug – G
Tingelhoff, Mick – C
Voight, Stu – E
Ward, John – T
Warwick, Lonnie – LB
Washington, Gene – E
West, Charlie – B
White, Ed – G
Winfrey, Carl – LB
Winston, Roy – LB
Wright, Jeff – B
Wright, Nate – B
Yary, Ron – T
Zaunbrecher, Godfrey – C

1971 LOS ANGELES RAMS (NFC)
Coach – Tom Prothro
2nd – Western Div., 8-5-1

Alexander, Kermit – B
Bacon, Coy – E,T
Buzin, Rich – T
Carollo, Joe – T,G
Cowan, Charlie – T
Curran, Pat – E
Ellison, Willie – B
Elmendorf, Dave – B
Gabriel, Roman – Q
Geddes, Ken – LB
Halverson, Dean – LB
Haymond, Alvin – B
Howard, Gene – B
Iman, Ken – C
Jones, Deacon – E
Josephson, Les – B
Klein, Bob – E
LaHood, Mike – G
McKeever, Marlin – LB
Mack, Tom – G
Maslowski, Matt – E
Nelson, Bill – T
Nettles, Jim – B

Olsen, Merlin – T
Olsen, Phil – T
Parish, Don – LB
Pergine, John – LB
Purnell, Jim – LB
Ray, David – E,K
Rentzel, Lance – E
Reynolds, Jack – LB
Rhome, Jerry – Q
Robertson, Isiah – LB
Saul, Rich – G,C
Schuh, Harry – T
Scibelli, Joe – G
Smith, Larry – B
Snow, Jack – E
Studstill, Pat – E,K
Thomas, Bob – B
White, Lee – B
Williams, Clarence – B
Williams, Roger – E
Williams, Travis – B
Wojcik, Greg – T
Youngblood, Jack – E

1971 NEW ENGLAND PATRIOTS (AFC)
Coach – John Mazur
3rd – Eastern Div., 6-8-0

Adams, Julius – T,E
Antwine, Houston – T
Atessis, Bill – T,E
Beer, Tom – G,E
Berger, Ron – T,E
Beverly, Randy – B
Bryant, Hubie – E
Carwell, Larry – B
Cheyunski, Jim – LB
Clark, Phil – B
Coleman, Dennis – LB
Crabtree, Eric – E
Edmunds, Randy – LB
Gardin, Ron – B,E
Garrett, Carl – B
Gladieux, Bob – B
Gogolak, Charlie – K
Hagen, Halvor, C,G
Haggerty, Mike – T
Harris, Rickie – B
Janik, Thomas – K,B
Kiner, Steve – LB
Lassiter, Ike – E
Lawson, Odell – B

Lenkaitis, Bill – G,C
Maitland, Jack – B
Mallory, Irvin – B
May, Art – E
Montler, Mike – T,G
Morris, Jon – C
Moss, Roland – E,B
Nance, Jim – B
Neville, Tom – T
Outlaw, John – B
Philpott, Ed – LB
Plunkett, Jim – Q
Pruett, Perry – B
Rowe, Dave – T
Rucker, Reggie – E
St. Jean, Len – G
Scott, Clarence – B
Sellers, Ron – E
Sykes, Alfred – E
Vataha, Randy – E
Webb, Don – B
Weisacosky, Ed – LB
Wirgowski, Dennis – E

1971 MIAMI DOLPHINS (AFC)
Coach – Don Shula
1st – Eastern Div., 10-3-1
(Beat Kansas City, 27-24, in second
sudden death overtime period in AFC
Divisional Playoffs; defeated Baltimore, 21-0, for AFC Championship;
lost to Dallas, 24-3, in Super Bowl)

Anderson, Dick – B
Buoniconti, Nick – LB
Cole, Terry – B
Cornish, Frank – T
Crusan, Doug – T
Csonka, Larry – B
DeMarco, Bob – C
Den Herder, Vern – E
Evans, Norm – T
Farley, Dale – LB
Fernandez, Manny – T
Fleming, Marv – E
Foley, Tim – B
Ginn, Hubert – B
Griese, Bob – Q
Heinz, Bob – T
Johnson, Curtis – B
Jones, Ray – B
Kiick, Jim – B
Kolen, Mike – LB
Kuechenberg, Bob – G
Langer, Jim – G

Leigh, Charles – B
Little, Larry – G
Mandich, Jim – E
Mass, Wayne – T
Matheson, Bob – LB
Mira, George – Q
Moore, Wayne – T
Morris, Mercury – B
Mumphord, Lloyd – B
Noonan, Karl – E
Petrella, Bob – B
Powell, Jesse – LB
Richardson, John – T
Riley, Jim – E
Scott, Jake – B
Seiple, Larry – E,K
Stanfill, Bill – E
Stowe, Otto – E
Swift, Doug – LB
Twilley, Howard – E
Warfield, Paul – E
Yepremian, Garo – K

1971 NEW ORLEANS SAINTS (NFC)
Coach – J. D. Roberts
4th – Western Div., 4-8-2

Abramowicz, Dan – E
Absher, Dick – LB
Baker, Tony – B
Bell, Carlos – B
Burchfield, Don – E
Butler, Skip – K
Colman, Wayne – LB
Cunningham, Carl – LB
Didion, John – C
Dodd, Al – E
Durkee, Charlie – K
Estes, Lawrence – E
Fagan, Julian – K
Flanigan, Jim – LB
Ford, James – B
Goich, Dan – T
Granger, Hoyle – B
Gresham, Bob – B
Hargett, Edd – Q
Harris, Bill – B
Harvey, Richard – B
Hester, Ray – LB
Hines, Glen Ray – T
Holden, Sam – T
Hollas, Hugo – B

Howell, Delles – B
Huard, John – LB
Kopay, Dave – B
Kupp, Jake – G
Lee, Bivian – B
Long, Dave – T
Manning, Archie – Q
Martin, D'Artagnan – B
Mooers, Doug – E
Moore, Reynaud – B
Morrison, Don – T
Neal, Richard – E
Newland, Bob – E
Owens, Joe – E
Parks, Dave – E
Pollard, Bob – T
Prudhomme, Remi – C,G
Robinson, Virgil – B
Roussel, Tom – LB
Shinners, John – B
Strong, Jim – B
Walker, Mike – E
Williams, Del – G
Wyatt, Doug – B

1971 MINNESOTA VIKINGS (NFC)
Coach – Bud Grant
1st – Central Div., 11-3-0
(Lost to Dallas, 20-12, in the
NFC Divisional Playoffs)

Alderman, Grady – T
Brown, Bill – B
Brown, Bob – E
Bryant, Bob – B

Cox, Fred – K
Cuozzo, Gary – Q
Davis, Doug – T
Denson, Al – E

1971 NEW YORK GIANTS (NFC)
Coach – Alex Webster
5th – Eastern Div., 4-10-0

Alexakos, Steve – G	Johnson, Ron – B
Athas, Pete – B	Kanicki, Jim – T
Blanchard, Tom – K	Kotite, Dick – E
Brown, Otto – B	Lakes, Roland – T
Butler, Skip – K	Larson, Greg – C
Coffey, Junior – B	Lockhart, Carl – B
Douglas, John – LB	Lurtsema, Bob – E,T
Dryer, Fred – E	McNeil, Clifton – E
Duhon, Bobby – B	McRae, Bennie – B
Eaton, Scott – B	Morrison, Joe – B
Evans, Charlie – B	Reed, Henry – E
Files, Jim – LB	Roller, Dave – T
Flowers, Richmond – B	Rucker, Reggie – E
Frederickson, Tucker – B	Shay, Jerry – T
Gogolak, Pete – K	Tarkenton, Fran – Q
Green, Joe – B	Thompson, Rocky – B
Hanson, Dick – T	Tipton, Dave – E
Harper, Charlie – G,T	Tucker, Bob – E
Heck, Ralph – LB	Van Horn, Doug – G
Herrmann, Don – E	Vanoy, Vernon – T
Hornsby, Ron – LB	Walton, Wayne – G
Houston, Rich – E	Williams, Willie – B
Hughes, Pat – LB	Young, Willie – T
Hyland, Bob – T	Zeno, Coleman – E
Johnson, Randy – Q	

1971 NEW YORK JETS (AFC)
Coach – Weeb Ewbank
4th – Eastern Div., 6-8-0

Arthur, Gary – E	Little, John – E,T
Atkinson, Al – LB	Lomas, Mark – E,T
Baker, Ralph – LB	McClain, Clifford – B
Bell, Ed – E	Maynard, Don – E
Boozer, Emerson – B	Mooring, John – T
Caster, Rich – E	Namath, Joe – Q
Crane, Paul – LB,C	Nock, George – B
Davis, Bob – Q	O'Neal, Steve – K,E
Dockery, John – B	Palmer, Scott – T
Ebersole, John – LB	Philbin, Gerry – E
Elliott, John – T	Rasmussen, Randy – G
Farasopoulos, Chris – B	Riggins, John – B
Finnie, Roger – T	Schmitt, John – C
Foley, Dave – T,C	Snell, Matt – B
Grantham, Larry – LB	Sowells, Rich – B
Harkey, Steve – B	Stewart, Wayne – E
Herman, Dave – G	Studdard, Vern – E
Hicks, W. K. – B	Svihus, Bob – T
Hill, Winston – T	Swinney, Clovis – T
Hinton, Chuck – T	Tannen, Steve – B
Hollomon, Gus – B	Thomas, Earlie – B
Howfield, Bobby – K	Wise, Phil – B
Kirksey, Roy – G	Woodall, Al – Q
Lammons, Pete – E	Zapalac, Bill – LB,E

1971 OAKLAND RAIDERS (AFC)
COACH – John Madden
2nd – Western Div., 8-4-2

Atkinson, George – B	Enyart, Bill – LB
Banaszak, Pete – B	Gipson, Tom – T
Benson, Duane – LB	Harvey, Jim – G
Biletnikoff, Fred – E	Highsmith, Don – B
Blanda, George – Q, K	Hubbard, Marv – B
Brown, Bob – T	Irons, Gerald – LB
Brown, Willie – B	Jones, Horace – E
Buehler, George – G	Keating, Tom – T
Buie, Drew – E	Koegel, Warren – C
Chester, Raymond – E	Lamonica, Daryle – Q
Cline, Tony – E	Maxwell, Tom – B
Conners, Dan – LB	Mendenhall, Terry – LB
Davidson, Ben – E	Mix, Ron – T
Davis, Calerence – B	Moore, Bob – E
DePoyster, Jerry – K	Oats, Carlton – T
Dickey, Eldridge – E	Otto, Gus – LB
Eischeid, Mike – K	Otto, Jim – C
Ellison, Glenn –	

Rice, Harold – E	Tatum, Jack – B
Seiler, Paul – T	Thoms, Art – T
Shell, Art – T	Upshaw, Gene – G
Sherman, Rod – E	Villapiano, Phil – LB
Slough, Greg – LB	Warren, Jimmy – B
Smith, Charlie – B	Weathers, Carl – LB
Stabler, Ken – Q	Wilson, Nemiah – B

1971 PHILADELPHIA EAGLES (NFC)
COACH – Jerry Williams & Eddie Khyat
3rd – Eastern Div., 6-7-1

Allison, Henry – G	Keyes, Leroy – B
Arrington, Rick – Q	Kramer, Kent – E
Bailey, Tom – B	Liske, Pete – Q
Baker, Tony – B	McNeill, Tom – K
Ballman, Gary – E	Nelson, Al – B
Bouggess, Lee – B	Nordquist, Mark – G, C
Bradley, Bill – B	Pettigrew, Gary – T
Brumm, Don – E	Porter, Ron – LB
Bull, Ron – B	Preece, Steve – B
Calloway, Ernie – T, E	Ramsey, Nate – B
Carmichael, Harold – E	Rossovich, Tim – E
Creech, Bob – LB	Skaggs, Jim – G
Davis, Albert – B	Smith, Jack – B
Davis, Vern – B	Smith, Steve – T
Dempsey, Tom – K	Stevens, Richard – T
Dirks, Mike – T	Thrower, Jim – B
Evans, Mike – C	Tom, Mel – E
Feller, Happy – K	Uperesa, Tuufuli – G, T
Harris, Richard – E	Walik, Bill – E
Hawkins, Ben – E	Ward, Jim – Q
Hill, Fred – E	Watkins, Larry – B
Hobbs, Bill – LB	Whalen, Jim – E
Hultz, Don – T	Whittingham, Fred – LB
Jackson, Harold – E	Woodeschick, Tom – B
Kelley, Ike – LB	Young, Adrian – LB
Key, Wade – T	Zabel, Steve – E, LB

1971 PITTSBURGH STEELERS (AFC)
COACH – Chuck Noll
2nd – Central Div., 6-8-0

Adams, Bob – E	Hinton, Chuck – T
Allen, Chuck – LB	Holmes, Mel – G
Anderson, Ralph – B	Hughes, Dennis – E
Askson, Bert – E	Kolb, Jon – T, C
Austin, Ocie – B	Leahy, Robert – Q
Bankston, Warren – B	Lewis, Frank – E
Beatty, Chuck – B	McGee, Ben – E
Bleier, Rocky – B	Mansfield, Ray – C
Blount, Mel – B	Maples, Bobby – C
Bradshaw, Terry – Q	Mullins, Gerry – E
Brown, John – T	Pearson, Preston – B
Brown, Larry – E	Rowser, John – B
Brumfield, Jim – B	Russell, Andy – LB
Calland, Lee – B	Shanklin, Ron – E
Clack, Jim – C	Sharp, Rick – T
Davis, Henry – LB	Smith, Dave – E
Davis, Sam – G	Staggers, Jon – E
Edwards, Glen – E	Stenger, Brian – LB
Fuqua, John – B	Van Dyke, Bruce – G
Gerela, Roy – K	Voss, Lloyd – E
Greene, Joe – T	Wagner, Mike – B
Greenwood, L. C. – E	Walden, Bob – K
Ham, Jack – LB	White, Dwight – E
Hanratty, Terry – Q	Young, Al – E

1971 ST. LOUIS CARDINALS (NFC)
COACH – Bob Hollway
4th – Eastern Div., 4-9-1

Allen, Jeff – B	Farr, Miller – B
Bakken, Jim – K	Gilliam, John – E
Banks, Tom – C	Goode, Irv – G
Beathard, Pete – Q	Gray, Mel – E
Dickson, Paul – T	Hackbart, Dale – B
Dierdorf, Dan – G, T	Hargrove, Jim – LB
Edwards, Cid – B	Hart, Jim – Q
Emerson, Vern – T	Heron, Fred – T

Hoey, George – B
Hutchison, Chuck - G
Hyatt, Fred – E
Krueger, Rolf – E
Lane, MacArthur – B
Latourette, Chuck – E, K
Longo, Tom – B
McFarland, Jim – E
McGill, Mike – LB
McMillan, Ernie – T
Miller, Terry – LB
Mulligan, Wayne – C
Ogle, Rick – LB
Parish, Don – LB
Provost, Ted – B
Reynolds, Bob – T
Rivers, Jamie – LB
Roland, John – B

Rosema, Rocky – LB
Rowe, Bob – T
Schmiesing, Joe – E
Shivers, Roy – B
Smith, Jackie – E
Stallings, Larry – LB
Stegent, Larry – B
Stovall, Jerry – B
Thompson, Norm – B
Walker, Chuck – E
Wehrli, Roger – B
White, Paul – B
Williams, Clyde – G
Williams, Dave – E
Willingham, Larry – B
Wilson, Larry – B
Yankowski, Ron – E

1971 SAN DIEGO CHARGERS (AFC)
COACH – Sid Gillman & Harland Svare
3rd – Western Div., 6–8–0

Babick, Bob – LB
Barnes, Pete – LB
Beauchamp, Joe – B
Bruggers, Bob – LB
Burns, Leon – B
DeLong, Steve – T
Detwiler, Chuck – B
Dicus, Chuck – E
Domres, Marty – Q
East, Ron – T
Fletcher, Chris – B
Garrett, Mike – B
Garrison, Gary – E
Gillette, Walker – E
Gordon, Ira – G
Grant, Wes – E
Gruneisen, Sam – C
Hadl, John – Q
Hardy, Kevin – T
Hill, Jim – B
Howard, Bob – B
Jones, Harris – G
LeVias, Jerry – E

Mauck, Carl – C
Montgomery, Mike – B
Norman, Pettis – E
Nowak, Gary – E
Owens, Terry – T
Parks, William – E
Partee, Dennis – K
Queen, Jeff – B
Ray, Eddie – B, K
Redman, Rick – LB
Rice, Andy – T
Rogers, Mel – LB
Salter, Bryant – B
Staggs, Jeff – LB
Strozier, Art – E
Sweeney, Walt – G
Tanner, John – E
Tolbert, Jim – B
Thomas, Lee – E
Washington, Russ – T
White, Ray – LB
Wilkerson, Doug – G
Williams, Tom – T

1971 SAN FRANCISCO 49ERS (NFC)
COACH – Dick Nolan
1st – Western Div., 9–5–0
(Beat Washington, 24–20, in NFC
Divisional Playoffs; Lost to Dallas,
14–3, in NFC Championship Game)

Banaszek, Cas – T
Beard, Ed – LB
Beisler, Randy – G
Belk, Bill – E
Blue, Forrest – C
Brodie, John – Q
Collett, Elmer – G
Cunningham, Doug – B
Edwards, Earl – T
Fuller, Johnny – B
Gossett, Bruce – K
Hardman, Cedrick – E
Harris, Tony – B
Hart, Tommy – E
Hindman, Stan – T, E
Hoskins, Bob – G
Isenbarger, John – B
Johnson, Jimmy – B
Krueger, Charlie – T
Kwalick, Ted – E
McCann, Jim – K

Nunley, Frank – LB
Peoples, Woody – G
Phillips, Mel – B
Riley, Preston – E
Rohde, Len – T
Schreiber, Larry – B
Simpson, Mike – B
Sniadecki, Jim – LB
Spurrier, Steve – Q
Taylor, Bruce – B
Taylor, Rosey – B
Thomas, Jimmy – E, B
Vanderbundt, Skip – LB
Washington, Gene – E
Washington, Vic – B
Watson, John – T
Wilcox, Dave – LB
Willard, Ken – B
Windsor, Bob – E
Witcher, Dick – E

1971 WASHINGTON REDSKINS (NFC)
COACH – George Allen
2nd – Eastern Div., 9–4–1
(Lost to San Francisco, 24–20, in
NFC Divisional Playoffs)

—

Alston, Mack – E
Bass, Mike – B
Biggs, Verlon – E
Bragg, Mike – K
Brown, Larry – B
Brundige, Bill – T
Brunet, Bob – B
Burman, George – C, G
Dowler, Boyd – E
Duncan, Speedy – B
Fischer, Pat – B
Grant, Bob – LB
Hanburger, Chris – LB
Harraway, Charley – B
Hauss, Len – C
Hermeling, Terry – T
Hull, Mike – B
Jaqua, Jon – B
Jefferson, Roy – E
Jones, Jimmy – E
Jordan, Jeff – B
Jurgensen, Sonny – Q
Kilmer, Bill – Q

Knight, Curt – K
Laaveg, Paul – G
McDole, Ron – E
McLinton, Harold – LB
McNeil, Clifton – E
Malinchak, Bill – E
Mason, Tommy – B
Owens, Brig – B
Pardee, Jack – LB
Petitbon, Richie – B
Pottios, Myron – LB
Rock, Walter – T
Schoenke, Ray – G
Sistrunk, Manuel – T
Smith, Jerry – E
Snowden, Jim – T
Talbert, Diron – T
Taylor, Charley – E
Taylor, Mike – T
Tillman, Russell – LB
Vactor, Ted – B
Wilbur, John – G
Wyche, Sam – Q

TITLES: It was Dallas all the way after defeating Minnesota, 20–12, in one Divisional Playoff and beating San Francisco, 14–3, for the NFC Championship. San Francisco had beaten Washington, 24–20, in the other NFC Divisional Playoff to qualify for the championship game.

The AFC Divisional Playoffs pitted Miami against Kansas City and Baltimore against Cleveland. Baltimore easily trounced Cleveland, 20–3, while Miami had to go into 22:40 overtime to finally defeat Kansas City, 27–24, in their Divisional Playoff. The AFC Championship found Miami shutting out Baltimore, 21–0, for the coveted award.

Super Bowl VI between Dallas and Miami on January 16th, at New Orleans, was won for the first time by Dallas, 24–3.

NFC LEADERS: Scoring—Curt Knight (Wash.) 114 points; Rushing—John Brockington (Green Bay) 1,105 yds.; Passing—Roger Staubach (Dallas); Pass Receiving—Bob Tucker (N.Y. Giants) 59; Field Goals—Curt Knight (Wash.) 29; Punting—Tom McNeill (Phil.) 42.0 average; Interceptions—Bill Bradley (Phil.) 11.

AFC LEADERS: Scoring—Garo Yepremian (Miami) 117 points; Rushing—Floyd Little (Den.) 1,133 yds.; Passing—Bob Griese (Miami); Pass Receiving—Fred Biletnikoff (Oak.) 61; Field Goals—Garo Yepremian (Miami) 28; Punting—Dave Lewis (Cin.) 44.8 average; Interceptions—Ken Houston (Hou.) 9.

FIRST DRAFT: AFC—Jim Plunkett (Stanford), quarterback, by New England, signed by New England. NFC—Archie Manning (Mississippi), quarterback, by New Orleans, signed by New Orleans.

COACHES: In the AFC, Denver's Lou Saban resigned in Nov., 1971, to be replaced by Jerry Smith; Sid Gillman resigned Nov. 22, 1971, with Harland Svare taking over at San Diego: In the NFC, Ed Khayat took over the Philadelphia Eagles on Oct. 6, 1971, from Jerry Williams.

HALL OF FAME: Inductees to the Hall of Fame in 1972 at Canton, Ohio, are Lamar Hunt, Gino Marchetti, Ollie Matson, and Clarence "Ace" Parker.

NOTES: Green Bay's John Brockington won Offensive Rookie of the Year and this year's rushing title, having gained the highest total yardage, 1,105, for a first-year runner. He is the fourth rookie to achieve 1,000 yds. rushing.

Isiah Robertson of L.A. won Defensive Rookie of the Year; Roger Staubach, Player of the Year; Washington's George Allen won top coaching honors.

Bob Tucker, N.Y. Giants, is the first tight end ever to win a pass receiving title. Ken Willard, San Francisco rusher, became the 16th NFL player to reach the 5,000-yard mark.

Willie Ellison, L.A. back, established a new one-game rushing record of 247 yds. on 26 attempts. Ken Houston, Houston's defensive back, intercepted 9 passes to run back a record 4 TDs.

The NFC had zero punt returns for TDs. Baltimore equaled their 1968 season record of 3 shutouts. Dallas was highest scoring team while Minnesota was lowest point-yielding team.

NEW STADIUMS: Texas Stadium for Dallas; Veterans Stadium for Philadelphia. Not new stadiums but new locations this year for Chicago, at Soldier Field, and San Francisco, at Candlestick Park.

Two antitrust conspiracy suits have been filed this year. In claiming they were barred from participation, Joe Kapp filed against all 26 teams and Commissioner Pete Rozelle, while Bob Cappadona filed suit against 10 teams.

1972

NATIONAL FOOTBALL LEAGUE

NATIONAL CONFERENCE
EASTERN DIVISION

	W.	L.	T.	Pct.
Washington	11	3	0	.786
Dallas*	10	4	0	.714
New York Giants	8	6	0	.571
St. Louis	4	9	1	.321
Philadelphia	2	11	1	.179

CENTRAL DIVISION

	W.	L.	T.	Pct.
Green Bay	10	4	0	.714
Detroit	8	5	1	.607
Minnesota	7	7	0	.500
Chicago	4	9	1	.321

WESTERN DIVISION

	W.	L.	T.	Pct.
San Francisco	8	5	1	.607
Atlanta	7	7	0	.500
Los Angeles	6	7	1	.464
New Orleans	2	11	1	.179

* Fourth Qualifier for Playoffs

AMERICAN CONFERENCE
EASTERN DIVISION

	W.	L.	T.	Pct.
Miami	14	0	0	1.000
New York Jets	7	7	0	.500
Baltimore	5	9	0	.429
Buffalo	4	9	1	.321
New England	3	11	0	.214

CENTRAL DIVISION

	W.	L.	T.	Pct.
Pittsburgh	11	3	0	.786
Cleveland*	10	4	0	.714
Cincinnati	8	6	0	.571
Houston	1	13	0	.071

WESTERN DIVISION

	W.	L.	T.	Pct.
Oakland	10	3	1	.750
Kansas City	8	6	0	.571
Denver	5	9	0	.429
San Diego	4	9	1	.321

* Fourth Qualifier for Playoffs

1972 AFC Championship
Miami 21; Pittsburgh 17

The Eastern Division Miami Dolphins capitalized on Central Division Pittsburgh's mistakes to gain the AFC title, 21-17.

Pittsburgh quarterback Terry Bradshaw

was injured in the first quarter, fumbling the ball on the 2-yd. line. Although teammate Gerry Mullins recovered it in the end zone for a TD, Bradshaw was sidelined for over half the game. Misfortune number one.

Misfortune number two occurred when Miami kicker Larry Seiple romped to the Pittsburgh 12-yard line on a faked punt from the 49. This set up Miami's first score: a 9-yard pass from Earl Morrall to Larry Csonka.

The Steelers were ahead, 10-7, on a 3rd quarter field goal when misfortune number three occurred. An offside infraction nullified the interception by linebacker Jack Ham of a Bob Griese-to-Paul Warfield pass, thus positioning Miami for a 2-yd TD run by Jim Kiick. Kiick scored again on a 3-yarder in the 4th quarter to put the Dolphins ahead to stay.

| Miami | 0 | 7 | 7 | 7 | 21 |
| Pittsburgh | 7 | 0 | 3 | 7 | 17 |

Touchdowns: Miami, Csonka, Kiick 2; Pitts. Mullins
Field Goals: Gerela
PATs: Miami, Yepremian 3; Pitt. Gerela 2
Attendance: 50,845
Players' shares: Miami $8,500; Pittsburgh $5,500

1972 NFC Championship

Washington 26; Dallas 3

The Eastern Division Champs overwhelmed the Dallas Cowboys, 26-3, for the NFC title. By using a strong defense, diversified plays, and reading their opponent's offense, Washington was able to contain the explosive Cowboys.

Wide receiver Charley Taylor accounted for both Redskin TDs on passes from Bill Kilmer. The first came after Taylor outmaneuvered Cowboy cornerback Charlie Waters for a 15-yard touchdown in the 2nd quarter; the second after he galloped for 45 yards in the fourth after Mark Washington replaced the injured Waters.

Curt Knight added to the score by connecting on four-for-four field goals, three in the last quarter while Dallas kicker, Toni Fritsch, accounted for the Cowboys' only score.

| Dallas | 0 | 3 | 0 | 0 | 3 |
| Washington | 0 | 10 | 0 | 16 | 26 |

Touchdowns: Taylor 2
Field Goals: Wash. Knight 4; Dallas Fritsch
PATs: Knight 2
Attendance: 53,129
Players' shares: Washington $8,500; Dallas $5,500

1972 Super Bowl

Miami 14; Washington 7

Miami's second consecutive Super Bowl appearance was highlighted by an unprecedented 14-0 regular season record plus gaining an unpretentious nickname: "No Names Defense."

The Dolphins scored first on a Bob Griese to Howard Twilley 28-yard pass. Jim Kiick bulldozed his way over from the 1-yd. line to give Miami a 14-0 halftime lead after an illegal procedure penalty nullified Dolphin receiver Paul Warfield's 47-yard touchdown earlier in the period.

Washington's offensive drive was sporadic with three of Bill Kilmer's passes intercepted and a missed field goal by Curt Knight. Their only score came in the 4th quarter when Dolphin kicker Garo Yepremian's field goal attempt was blocked. Yepremian picked up the rebounding ball and hurriedly attempted a pass only to have it batted in the air and picked off by cornerback Mike Bass for a 49-yard romp.

Miami's win gave the AFC the edge of Super Bowl victories: four wins to the NFC's three.

| Miami | 7 | 7 | 0 | 0 | 14 |
| Washington | 0 | 0 | 0 | 7 | 7 |

Touchdowns: Miami, Twilley, Kiick; Wash. Bass
PATs: Miami, Yepremian 2; Wash. Knight
Attendance: 90,182
Players shares: Miami $15,000; Washington $7,500

RETIRED PLAYERS:

Erich Barnes, back for Chicago Bears, New York Giants, and Cleveland Browns (AFL) & (AFC) —14 years.
Tony Liscio, tackle for Dallas Cowboys— 8 years.
Ray Perkins, end for the Baltimore Colts (NFL) & (AFC) —5 years.
Elijah Pitts, back for Green Bay Packers,

Los Angeles Rams, New Orleans Saints—11 years.

Johnny Robinson, defensive back for the Dallas Texans (AFL); Kansas City Chiefs (AFL) & (AFC)—12 years.

Gale Sayers, back for Chicago Bears—7 years.

Bart Starr, quarterback for Green Bay Packers—16 years.

Olen Underwood, linebacker for New York Giants, Houston Oilers (AFL) & (AFC), and Denver Broncos (AFC)—7 years.

Willie Wood, back for Green Bay Packers—12 years.

DEATHS

Benkert, Henry (Heinie), back, 1925 New York Giants; 1926 Pottsville Maroons; 1929 Orange Tornadoes; 1930 Newark Tornadoes, on July 15, 1972.

Bergman, Arthur J. (Dutch), head coach of the 1943 Washington Redskins, on Aug. 18, 1972.

Berry, Charles F., end, 1925-26 Pottsville Maroons and NFL official, Sept. 6, 1972.

Bryant, James G., back, 1919 Akron Pros; 1920 Cleveland Panthers, on Apr. 18, 1972.

Buivid, Raymond (Buzz), back, 1937-38 Chicago Bears; 1937 New York Yanks (AFL), on July 5, 1972.

Clark, George (Potsy), coach for Detroit Spartans-Lions during 1930-36, 1940, died Nov. 8, 1972.

Doehring, John N. (Bull), back, 1932-34, 36-37 Chicago Bears; 1935 Pittsburgh Pirates; 1940 Milwaukee Chiefs (AFL), on Nov. 18, 1972.

Drulis, Charles, guard, 1942, 45-49 Chicago Bears; 1950 Green Bay Packers, on Aug. 23, 1972.

Duncan, James, back, 1969 Baltimore Colts; 1970-71 Baltimore Colts (AFC), on Oct. 20, 1972.

Edwards, Albert Glen, tackle, 1932 Boston Braves; 1933-36 Boston Redskins; 1937-40 Washington Redskins; 1969 Hall of Fame, on Jan. 10, 1973.

Farrar, Venice (Vinnie), back, 1936 New York Yanks (AFL); 1937 Rochester Tigers (AFL); 1939 Pittsburgh Steelers, on Jan. 1, 1973.

Fencil, Richard J., end, 1933 Philadelphia Eagles, on June 25, 1972.

Kessel, Harry, an AFL official, on Oct. 9, 1972.

King, Philip (Chief), back, 1958-63 New York Giants; 1964 Pittsburgh Steelers; 1965-66 Minnesota Vikings, on Jan. 18, 1973.

Koslowski, Stanley J., back, 1946 Miami Seahawks (AAFC), on Aug. 23, 1972.

Lyman, William Roy (Link), tackle, 1922-23, 25 Canton Bulldogs; 1924 Cleveland Bulldogs; 1925 Frankford Yellow-jackets; 1926-28, 30-31, 33-34 Chicago Bears; 1964 Hall of Fame, on Dec. 28, 1972.

Nash, Thomas, Sr., end, 1928-32 Green Bay Packers; 1933-34 Brooklyn Dodgers, on Aug. 24, 1972.

Olsson, Carl Lester (Swede), guard, 1934-36 Boston Redskins; 1937-38 Washington Redskins, on July 3, 1972.

Patton, James (Jimmy), back, 1955-66 New York Giants, on Dec. 22, 1972.

Reagan, Francis X. (Frank), back, 1941, 46-48 New York Giants; 1949-51 Philadelphia Eagles, on Nov. 20, 1972.

Vest, Jack D., NFL referee, on June 2, 1972.

1972 ATLANTA FALCONS (NFC)
Coach – Norm Van Brocklin
2nd – Western Div., 7–7–0

Allen, Grady – LB	Kunz, George – T
Bell, Bill – K	Lamb, Ron – B
Belton, Willie – B	Lewis, Mike, – E
Benson, Duane – LB	Malone, Art – B
Berry, Bob –	Manning, Rosie – T
Brezina, Gregory – LB	Mauer, Andy – G
Brown, Ray – B	Mialik, Larry – E
Burrow, Ken – E	Miller, Jim – G
Chesson, Wes – E	Mitchell, Jim – E
Condren, Glen – E, T	Nobis, Tommy – LB
Easterling, Ray – B	Plummer, Tony – B
Ellis, Clarence – B	Profit, Joe, – B
Fritsch, Ted – C	Ray, Eddie – B
Germany, Willie – B	Reaves, Ken – B
Gotshalk, Len – T	Sandeman, Bill – T
Hampton, Dave – B	Shears, Larry – B
Hansen, Don – LB	Small, John – T
Havig, Dennis – G	Snyder, Todd – E
Hayes, Tom – B	Sullivan, Pat – Q
Humphrey, Claude – E	Van Note, Jeff – C
James, John – K	Walker, Chuck – E, T
Jarvis, Ray – E	Zook, John – E
Jenke, Noel – LB	

1972 BALTIMORE COLTS (AFC)
Coach – Don McCafferty to John Sandusky
3rd – Eastern Div., 5–9–0

Amman, Richard – E	Hepburn, Lonnie – B
Bailey, Jim – T	Hilton, Roy – E
Bulaich, Norm – B	Hinton, Chuck – T
Curry, Bill – C	Hinton, Eddie – E
Curtis, Mike – LB	Johnson, Corny – G
Domres, Marty – Q	Kern, Rex – B
Doughty, Glenn – E	Laird, Bruce – B
Drougas, Tom – T	Laskey, Bill – LB
Edmunds, Randy – LB	Lee, David – K
Franklin, Willie – E	Logan, Jerry – B
Havrilak, Sam – E	McCauley, Don – B
Hendricks, Ted – LB	Matte, Tom – B

May, Ray – LB
Mendenhall, Ken – C
Mildren, Jack – B
Miller, Fred – T
Mitchell, Lydell – B
Mitchell, Tom – E
Mosier, John – E
Munsey, Nelson – B
Nelson, Dennis – T
Newsome, Billy – E
Nottingham, Don – B
Nowatzke, Tom – B

O'Brien, Jim – E, K
Ressler, Glenn – G
Shinners, John – G
Shlapak, Boris – K
Speyrer, Cotton – E
Stukee, Charlie – B
Sullivan, Dan – G
Unitas, John – Q
Vogel, Bob – T
Volk, Rick – B
White, Stan – LB

1972 BUFFALO BILLS (AFC)
Coach – Lou Saban
4th – Eastern Div., 4–9–1

Adams, Bill – G
Beard, Tom – C
Braxton, Jim – B
Chandler, Bob – E
Chandler, Edgar – LB
Christiansen, Bob – E
Cole, Linzy – E
Cornish, Frank – T
Costa, Paul – T
Cowlings, Al – E
Croft, Don – T
Cunningham, Dick – LB
Curchin, Jeff – T
Farley, Dale – LB
Foley, Dave – T, C
Garror, Leon – B
Green, Donnie – T
Greene, Tony – B
Guidry, Paul – LB
Harrison, Dwight – E
Hart, Leo – Q
Hart, Dick – G
Hill, J. D. – E
Jackson, Randy – B
James, Robert – B
Jarvis, Bruce – C
Jones, Spike – K
Koy, Ted – B

Lee, Kenneth – LB
Leypoldt, John – K
Lyman, Jeff – LB
McBath, Mike – T
McKenzie, Reggie – G
Matlock, John – C
Moses, Haven – E
Okoniewski, Steve – T
Palmer, Dick – LB
Patrick, Wayne – B
Patton, Jerry – T
Patulski, Walter – E
Penchion, Robert – G
Pitts, John – B
Prudhomme, Remi – C, G
Ross, Louis – E
Saunders, John – B
Selfridge, Andy – LB
Shaw, Dennis – Q
Simpson, O. J. – B
Stratton, Mike – LB
Taliaferro, Mike – Q
Tatarek, Bob – T
Tyler, Maurice – B
Washington, Dave – E,LB
White, Jan – E
Wyatt, Alvin – B

1972 CHICAGO BEARS (NFC)
Coach – Abe Gibron
4th – Central Div., 4–9–1

Antoine, Lionel – T
Asher, Bob – T
Brupbacher, Ross – LB
Buffone, Doug – LB
Butkus, Dick – LB
Buzin, Rich – T
Cadile, Jim – G
Clemons, Craig – B
Coady, Rich – C
DeLong, Steve – E
Douglass, Bobby – Q
Farmer, George – E
Ford, Charlie – B
Green, Bobby Joe – K
Gunn, Jimmy – LB
Harrison, Jim – B
Holloway, Glen – G
Holman, Willie – E
Horton, Larry – E
Huarte, John – Q
Jackson, Randy – T
Janet, Ernie – G, C
Jeter, Bob – B
Kosins, Gary – B

Lawson, Roger – B
Line, Bill – T
Lyle, Garry – B
McGee, Tony – T
McKinney, Bill – LB
Maslowski, Matt – E
Moore, Jerry – B
Newton, Bob – G
Osborne, Jim – T
Parsons, Bob – E
Percival, Mac – K
Pifferini, Bob – LB
Pinder, Cyril – B
Rice, Andy – T
Rowden, Larry – LB
Seymour, Jim – E
Shy, Don – B
Smith, Ron – B
Staley, Bill – T
Taylor, Joe – B
Thomas, Earl – E
Turner, Cecil – E
Wallace, Bob – E

1972 CINCINNATI BENGALS (AFC)
Coach – Paul Brown
3rd – Central Div., 8–6–0

Adams, Doug – LB
Anderson, Ken – Q
Avery, Ken – LB
Beauchamp, Al – LB

Bergey, Bill – LB
Berry, Royce – E
Buie, Drew – E
Carpenter, Ron – E

Carter, Virgil – Q
Casanova, Tom – B
Chomyszak, Steve – T
Conley, Steve – LB, B
Coslet, Bruce – E
Craig, Neal – B
DeLeone, Tom – C
Dennis, Guy – G
Dressler, Doug – B
Fest, Howard – T
Holland, Vernon – T
Jackson, Bernard – B
Johnson, Essex – B
Johnson, Ken – T
Johnson, Bob – C
Joiner, Charlie – E
Kearney, Tim – LB
Kellerman, Ernie – B
Kelly, Mike – E
Lawson, Steve – G
LeClair, Jim – LB

Lewis, Dave – K, Q
Matson, Pat – G
Mayes, Rufus – T
Morrison, Reece – B
Muhlmann, Horst – K
Myers, Chip – E
Parrish, Lemar – B
Peterson, Bill – LB
Phillips, Jess – B
Pritchard, Ron – LB
Randolph, Al – B
Reid, Mike – T
Riley, Ken – B
Robinson, Paul – B
Thomas, Speedy – E
Trumpy, Bob – E
Walters, Stan – T
Watson, Pete – E
White, Sherman
Willis, Fred – B

1972 CLEVELAND BROWNS (AFC)
Coach – Nick Skorich
2nd – Central Div., 10–4–0
(Lost to Miami, 20–14, in AFC Divisional Playoff)

Andrews, Bill – LB
Briggs, Bob – E, T
Brooks, Clifford – B
Brown, Ken – B
Carollo, Joe – T
Cockroft, Don – K
Copeland, Jim – C, G
Cornell, Bo – B
Darden, Tom – B
Davis, Ben – B
DeMarco, Bob – C
Demarie, John – G
Dieken, Doug – T
Garlington, John – LB
Glass, Chip – E
Grant, Wes – E
Hall, Charlie – LB
Hickerson, Gene – G
Hoaglin, Fred – C
Hooker, Fair – E
Houston, Jim – LB, E
Howell, Mike – B
Jackson, Rich – E
Johnson, Walter – T

Kelly, Leroy – B
Kingrea, Rick – LB
LeFear, Billy – E
Lindsey, Dale – LB
Long, Mel – LB
McKay, Bob – T
Majors, Bobby – B
Morin, Milt – E
Morris, Chris – T
Morrison, Reece – B
Nelson, Bill – Q
Pena, Bubba – G
Phipps, Mike – Q
Pitts, Frank – E
Richardson, Gloster, E
Roman, Nick – E
Scott, Clarence – B
Scott, Bo – B
Sherk, Jerry – T
Snidow, Ron – E
Staroba, Paul – E
Sumner, Walt – B
Wright, George – T
Wycinsky, Craig – G

1972 DALLAS COWBOYS (NFC)
Coach – Tom Landry
2nd – Eastern Div., 10–4–0
(Defeated San Francisco, 30–28, in NFC Divisional Playoffs; lost to Washington, 26–3, for the NFC Championship)

Adderley, Herb – B
Alworth, Lance – E
Andrie, George – E
Babinecz, John – LB
Barnes, Benny – B
Bateman, Marv – K
Cole, Larry – E
Coleman, Ralph – LB
Ditka, Mike – E
Edwards, Dave – LB
Fitzgerald, John – C
Fritsch, Toni – K
Fugett, Jean – E
Garrison, Walt – B
Green, Cornell – B
Gregory, Bill – T
Harris, Cliff – B
Hayes, Bob – E
Hill, Calvin – B
Howley, Chuck – LB
Jordan, Lee Roy – LB
Keller, Mike – LB
Lewis, D. D. – LB

Lilly, Bob – T
Manders, Dave – C
Montgomery, Mike – B
Morton, Craig – Q
Neely, Ralph – T
Newhouse, Robert – B
Niland, John – G
Nye, Blaine – G
Parks, Billy – E
Pugh, Jethro – T
Reeves, Dan – B
Renfro, Mel – B
Sellers, Ron – E
Smith, Tody – E
Staubach, Roger – Q
Thomas, Bill – B
Toomay, Pat – E
Truax, Billy – E
Wallace, Rodney – G
Washington, Mark – B
Waters, Charley – B
Wright, Rayfield – T

1972 DENVER BRONCOS (AFC)
Coach – John Ralston
3rd   Western Div., 5-9-0

Alzado, Lyle – E	McKoy, Bill – LB
Anderson, Bob – B	Maples, Bobby – C
Cottrell, Bill – C, G	Masters, Billy – E
Criter, Ken – LB	Mitchell, Leroy – B
Current, Mike – T	Montgomery, Marv – T
Dawkins, Joe – B	Montgomery, Randy – B
Domres, Tom – T	Moses, Haven, – E
Duranko, Pete – E	Myrtle, Chip – LB
Ernst, Mike – Q	Odoms, Riley – E
Forsberg, Fred – LB	Parish, Don – LB
Geddes, Bob – LB	Preece, Steve – B
Goeddeke, George – C, G	Ramsey, Steve – Q
Gordon, Cornell – B	Saimes, George – B
Graham, Tom – LB	Schnitker, Mike – G
Greer, Charlie – B	Sharp, Rick – T
Harrison, Dwight – E	Sherman, Rod – E
Hoffman, John – E	Simmons, Jerry – E
Horn, Don – Q	Simone, Mike – LB
Jackson, Larron – G	Smith, Paul – T
Jackson, Richard – E	Thompson, Bill – B
Johnson, Charley – Q	Turner, Clem – B
Kaminski, Larry – C	Turner, Jim – K
Krieg, Jim – E	Van Heusen, Bill – E, K
Little, Floyd, – B	Voss, Lloyd – E, T
Lynch, Fran – B	West, Bill – B
Lyons, Tommy – G	

1972 DETROIT LIONS (NFC)
Coach – Joe Schmidt
2nd – Central Div., 8-5-1

Barnes, Al – E	Ogle, Rick – LB
Barney, Lem – B	Orvis, Herb – E
Bell, Bob – T	Owens, Steve – B
Cotton, Craig – E	Potts, Charles – B
Eddy, Nick – B	Randolph, Al – B
Farr, Mel – B	Rasley, Rocky – G
Flanagan, Ed – C	Rasmussen, Wayne – B
Freitas, Rocky – T	Redmond, Rudy – B
Gallagher, Frank – G	Sanders, Charlie – E
Gordon, John – T	Sanders, Ken – E
Hamlin, Gene – C	Schmiesing, Joe – T
Hand, Larry – E	Tatarek, Bob – T
Hilton, John – E	Taylor, Altie – B
Jenkins, Leon – B	Thompson, Dave – C,G,T
Jessie, Ron – E	Triplett, Bill – B
Jolley, Gordon – T	Walker, Wayne – LB
Kowalkowski, Bob – G	Walton, Chuck – G
Landry, Greg – Q	Walton, Larry – E
LeBeau, Dick – B	Weaver, Charlie – LB
Lucci, Mike – LB	Weaver, Herman – K
McCullouch, Earl – E	Weger, Mike – B
Mann, Errol – K	Woods, Larry – T
Mitchell, Jim – E	Yarbrough, Jim – T
Munson, Bill – Q	Young, Adrian – LB
Naumoff, Paul – LB	Zofko, Mickey – B

1972 GREEN BAY PACKERS (NFC)
Coach – Dan Devine
1st – Central Div., 10-4-0
(Defeated by Washington, 16-3, in NFC Divisional
Playoff)

Bowman, Ken – C	Hefner, Larry – LB
Brockington, John – B	Hill, Jim – B
Brown, Bob – T	Himes, Dick – T
Buchanon, Willie – B	Hudson, Robert – B
Carr, Fred – LB	Hunt, Kevin – T
Carter, Jim – LB	Hunter, Scott – Q
Crutcher, Tommy Joe-LB	Kopay, Dave – B
Dale, Carroll – E	Kroll, Bob – B
Davis, Dave – E	Lammons, Pete – E
Ellis, Ken – B	Lane, MacArthur – B
Garrett, Len – E	Lueck, Bill – G
Gibson, Paul – B	McCoy, Mike – T
Gillingham, Gale – G	McGeorge, Rich – E
Glass, Leland – E	Marcol, Chester – K
Hall, Charlie – B	Matthews, Al – B
Hayhoe, Bill – T	Nitschke, Ray – LB

Patrick, Frank – Q	Thomas, Ike – B
Peay, Francis – T	Vanoy, Vernon – T, E
Pureifory, Dave – E	Walsh, Ward – B
Robinson, Dave – LB	Widby, Ron – K
Roche, Alden – E, T	Williams, Clarence – E
Snider, Malcolm – G	Williams, Perry – B
Staggers, Jon – E	Withrow, Cal – C
Tagge, Jerry – Q	Wortman, Keith – G

1972 HOUSTON OILERS (AFC)
Coach – Bill Peterson
4th – Central Div., 1-13-0

Aldridge, Allen – E	Johnson, Benny – B
Alexander, Willie – B	Joiner, Charlie – E
Atkins, Bob – B	Jolley, Lewis – B
Baker, Ed – Q	Lewis, Richard – LB
Beirne, Jim – E	Miller, Ralph – G
Bethea, Elvin – E	Moore, Zeke – B
Billingsley, Ron – T	Moseley, Mark – K
Boyette, Garland – LB	Murdock, Guy – C
Brooks, Leo – T	Nix, Kent – Q
Burrough, Ken – E	Pastorini, Dan – Q
Butler, Jimmy – E	Pritchard, Ron – LB
Butler, Skip – K	Reed, Alvin – E
Carr, Levert – G	Regner, Tom – G
Charles, John – B	Rice, Floyd, LB
Cole, Linzy – E	Roberts, Guy – LB
Croyle, Phil – LB	Robinson, Paul – B
Dawson, Rhett – E	Rodgers, Willie – B
Ferguson, Gene – T	Rudolph, Council – E
Freelon, Solomon – G	Sampson, Greg – E
Funchess, Tom – T	Saul, Ron – G
Granger, Hoyle – B	Smith, Dave – E
Highsmith, Walter – T, G	Tilleman, Mike – T
Holmes, Pat – E	Tolbert, Jim – B
Holmes, Robert – B	Walsh, Ward – B
Houston, Ken – B	Webster, George – LB
Hunt, Calvin – C	Willis, Fred – B
Johnson, Al – B	

1972 KANSAS CITY CHIEFS (AFC)
Coach – Hank Stram
2nd – Western Div., 8-6-0

Adamle, Mike – B	Marshall, Larry – B
Allen, Nate – B	Moorman, Mo – G
Bell, Bobby – LB	Oriard, Mike – C
Best, Keith – LB	Otis, Jim – B
Brown, Aaron – E	Podolak, Ed – B
Buchanan, Buck – T	Reardon, Kerry – B
Budde, Ed – G	Rudnay, Jack – C
Culp, Curley – T	Seals, George – T
Daney, George – G	Sensibaugh, Mike – B
Dawson, Len – Q	Smith, Sid – T
Frazier, Willie – E	Stein, Bob – LB
Gagner, Larry – G	Stenerud, Jan – K
Hayes, Wendell – B	Stroud, Morris – E
Hill, Dave – T	Taylor, Otis – E
Homan, Dennis – E	Thomas, Emmitt – B
Jankowski, Bruce – E	Tyrer, Jim – T
Kearney, Jim – B	Upshaw, Marvin – E
Kinney, Jeff – B	Werner, Clyde – LB
Lanier, Willie – LB	West, Robert – E
Livingston, Mike – Q	Wilson, Jerrel – K
Lothamer, Ed – T	Wright, Elmo – E
Lynch, Jim – LB	Young, Wilbur – T
Marsalis, Jim – B	

1972 LOS ANGELES RAMS (NFC)
Coach – Tommy Prothro
3rd – Western Div., 6-7-1

Bacon, Coy – E	Geddes, Ken – LB
Beathard, Pete – Q	Gordon, Dick – E
Bertelsen, Jim – B	Halverson, Dean – LB
Brooks, Larry – T	Howard, Gene – B
Chapple, Dave – K	Iman, Ken – C
Clark, Al – B	Josephson, Les – B
Cowan, Charlie – T	Klein, Bob – E
Curran, Pat – E	LaHood, Mike – G
Dryer, Fred – E	Love, John – E
Ellison, Willie – B	McCutcheon, Larry – B
Elmendorf, Dave – B	McKeever, Marlin – LB
Gabriel, Roman – Q	Mack, Tom – G

Nelson, Bill – T
Nettles, Jim – B
Olsen, Merlin – T
Olsen, Phil – T
Pergine, John – LB
Purnell, Jim – LB
Ray, David – E, K
Rentzel, Lance – E
Reynolds, Jack – LB
Robertson, Isiah – LB
Saul, Rich – T, C, G, E

Schuh, Harry – T
Scibelli, Joe – G
Smith, Larry – B
Snow, Jack – E
Sweet, Joe – E
Thomas, Bob – B
Williams, Clarence – B
Williams, John – G, T
Williams, Roger – B
Youngblood, Jack – E

1972 MIAMI DOLPHINS (AFC)
Coach – Don Shula
1st – Eastern Div., 14–0–0
(Defeated Cleveland, 20–14, in AFC Divisional Play-off; beat Pittsburgh, 21–17, for AFC Championship; defeated Washington (NFC), 14–7, in the Super Bowl)

Anderson, Dick – B, K
Babb, Charles – B
Ball, Larry – LB
Briscoe, Marlin – E
Buoniconti, Nick – LB
Crusan, Doug – T
Csonka, Larry – B
Del Gaizo, Jim – Q
Den Herder, Vern – E
Dunaway, Jim – T
Evans, Norm – T
Fernandez, Manny – T
Fleming, Marv – E
Foley, Tim – B
Ginn, Hubert – B
Griese, Bob – Q
Heinz, Bob – T
Howell, Mike – B
Jenkins, Al – T
Jenkins, Ed – E
Johnson, Curtis – B
Kiick, Jim – B
Kindig, Howard – T, C

Kolen, Mike – LB
Kuechenberg, Bob – G
Langer, Jim – C, G
Leigh, Charles – B
Little, Larry – G
Lothridge, Billy – K
Mandich, Jim – E
Matheson, Bob – LB
Moore, Maulty – T
Moore, Wayne – T
Morrall, Earl – Q
Morris, Mercury – B
Mumphord, Lloyd – B
Powell, Jesse – LB
Scott, Jake – B
Seiple, Larry – E, K
Stanfill, Bill – E
Stowe, Otto – E
Swift, Doug – LB
Twilley, Howard – E
Warfield, Paul – E
Yepremian, Garo – K

1972 MINNESOTA VIKINGS (NFC)
Coach – Bud Grant
3rd – Central Div., 7–7–0

Alderman, Grady – T
Beasley, John – E
Brown, Terry – B
Brown, Bill – B
Bryant, Bobbie Lee – B
Cox, Fred – K
Davis, Doug – T
Demery, Calvin – E
Eischeid, Mike – K
Eller, Carl – E
Gersbach, Carl – LB
Gilliam, John – E
Henderson, John – E
Hilgenberg, Wally – LB
Jones, Clinton – B
Kassulke, Karl – B
Krause, Paul – B
Larsen, Gary – T
Lee, Bob – Q
Lindsey, Jim – B
Lurtsema, Bob – E
Marinaro, Ed – B

Marshall, Jim – E
Martin, Amos – LB
Osborn, Dave – B
Page, Alan – T
Reed, Oscar – B
Sharockman, Ed – B
Siemon, Jeff – LB
Sunde, Milt – G
Sutherland, Doug – E
Tarkenton, Fran – Q
Tingelhoff, Mick – C
Voight, Stu – E
Ward, John – G
Warwick, Lonnis – LB
Washington, Gene – E
West, Charlie – B
White, Ed – G
Winston, Roy – LB
Wright, Jeff – B
Wright, Nate – B
Yary, Ron – T
Zaunbrecher, Godfrey – C

1972 NEW ENGLAND PATRIOTS (AFC)
Coach – John Mazur to Phil Bengtson
5th – Eastern Div., 3–11–0

Acks, Ron – LB
Adams, Julius – E
Adams, Sam – G
Ashton, Josh – B
Beer, Tom – E
Berger, Ron – E
Blanchard, Dick – LB

Bolton, Ron – B, K
Bryant, Hubie – E
Carwell, Larry – B
Cash, Rick – T
Chepunski, Jim – LB
Cindrich, Ralph – LB
Dowling, Brian – Q

Garrett, Carl – B
Gladieux, Bob – B
Gogolak, Charlie – K
Hagen, Halvor – G, E
Harris, Rickie – B
Hoey, George – LB, B
Jackson, Honor – B
Kadziel, Ron – LB
Lenkaitis, Bill – G
McMahon, Art – B
Maitland, Jack – B
Mass, Wayne – T
Matthews, Henry – B
Montler, Mike – T
Morris, Jon – C
Neville, Tom – T

Outlaw, John – B
Plunkett, Jim – Q
Reynolds, Bob – T
Reynolds, Tom – E
Rowe, Dave – T
Rucker, Reggie – E
St. Jean, Len – G
Scott, Clarence – B
Studstill, Pat – K, E
Tarver, John – B
Vataha, Randy – E
Walker, Mike – K
Weisacosky, Ed – LB
White, Jim – E
Windsor, Bob – E
Wirgowski, Dennis – T

1972 NEW ORLEANS SAINTS (NFC)
Coach – J. D. Roberts
4th – Western Div., 2–11–1

Abramowicz, Dan – E
Adkins, Margene – E
Brown, Bob – E
Butler, Bill – B
Colman, Wayne – LB
Crangle, Mike – E
Didion, John – C
Durkee, Charlie – K
Fagan, Julian – K
Federspiel, Joe – LB
Feller, Happy – K
Ford, Jim – B
Green, Arthur – B
Gresham, Bob – B
Hall, Willie – LB
Hargett, Edd – Q
Hayes, Billie – B
Hester, Ray – LB
Hines, Glen Ray – T
Hobbs, Bill – LB
Hollas, Hugo – B
Howell, Delles – B
Jackson, Ernie – B
Johnson, Carl – T, G
Kupp, Jake – G
Kuziel, Bob – C
Lee, Bivian – B

Linhart, Toni – K
Long, Dave – T
Manning, Archie – Q
Mooers, Doug – T
Morrison, Don – T
Myers, Tom – B
Neal, Richard – E
Newland, Bob – E
Owens, Joe – E
Palmer, Dick – LB
Parks, Dave – E
Pollard, Bob – T
Prudhomme, Remi – C, G
Robinson, Craig – T
Robinson, Virgil – B
Roussel, Tom – LB
Smith, Royce – G
Stincic, Tom – LB
Strong, Jim – B
Tillman, Faddie – T
Weatherspoon, Cephus – E
Whitaker, Creston – E
Williams, Del – G
Williams, Joe – B
Winther, Wimpy – C
Wyatt, Doug – B

1972 NEW YORK GIANTS (NFC)
Coach – Alex Webster
3rd – Eastern Div., 8–6–0

Athas, Pete – B
Blanchard, Tom – K
Brown, Otto – B
Campbell, Carter – LB
Clements, Vince – B
Crist, Charlie – B
Douglas, John – LB
Duhon, Bobby – B
Ellison, Mark – G
Enderle, Dick – G
Evans, Charlie – B
Files, Jim – LB
Flowers, Richmond – B
Gatewood, Tom – E
Goich, Dan – T
Gogolak, Pete – K
Gregory, Jack – E
Grim, Bob – E
Harper, Charlie – G, T
Herrmann, Don – E
Hill, John – C
Hornsby, Ron – LB

Houston, Rich – E
Hughes, Pat – LB
Hyland, Bob – C, G
Jacobson, Larry – E
Johnson, Randy – Q
Johnson, Ron – B
Kotite, Dick – E
Larson, Greg – C
Lockhart, Carl – B
Mendenhall, John – T
Morrison, Joe – B
Orduna, Joe – B
Reed, Henry – E
Small, Eldridge – B
Snead, Norm – Q
Taffoni, Joe – T
Thompson, Rocky – B
Tipton, Dave – E
Tucker, Bob – E
Van Horn, Doug – G
Williams, Willie – B
Young, Willie – T

1972 NEW YORK JETS – (AFC)
Coach – Weeb Ewbank
2nd · Eastern Div., 7–7–0

Atkinson, Al – LB
Baker, Ralph – LB
Barkum, Jerome – E
Bell, Ed – E
Bjorklund, Hank – B

Boozer, Emerson – B
Caster, Rich – E
Crane, Paul – LB, C
Davis, Bob – Q
Ebersole, John – LB

Elliott, John – T
Farasopoulos, Chris – B
Finnie, Roger – G, E
Galigher, Ed – E, T
Grantham, Larry – LB
Harkey, Steve – B
Herman, Dave – G
Hicks, W. K. – B
Hill, Winston – T
Hollomon, Gus – B
Howfield, Bobby – K
Jackson, Joey – E
Kirksey, Roy – G
Little, John – T
Lomas, Mark – E
McClain, Clifford – B
Maynard, Don – E
Mooring, John – G, T

Namath, Joe – Q
O'Neal, Steve – K
Philbin, Gerry – E
Rasmussen, Randy – G
Riggins, John – B
Schmitt, John – C
Snell, Matt – B
Sowells, Rich – B
Stewart, Wayne – E
Svihus, Bob – T
Tannen, Steve – B
Taylor, Mike – LB
Thomas, Earlie – B
Thompson, Steve – T
Turner, Rocky – E
Wise, Phil – B
Zapalac, Bill – LB

1972 OAKLAND RAIDERS (AFC)
Coach – John Madden
1st – Western Div., 10-3-1
(Lost to Pittsburgh, 13-7, in AFC Divisional Play-off)

Atkinson, George – B
Banaszak, Pete – B
Biletnikoff, Fred – E
Blanda, George – Q, K
Branch, Cliff – E
Brown, Bob – T
Brown, Willie – B
Buehler, George – G
Carroll, Joe – LB
Chester, Raymond – E
Cline, Tony – E
Conners, Dan – LB
Dalby, Dave – G, C
Davis, Clarence – B
DePoyster, Jerry – K
Highsmith, Don – B
Hubbard, Marv – B
Irons, Gerald – LB
Jones, Horace – E
Keating, Tom – T
Lamonica, Daryle – Q
Maxwell, Tom – B

Mendenhall, Terry – LB
Moore, Bob – E
Oats, Carleton – T
Otto, Gus – LB
Otto, Jim – C
Queen, Jeff – B
Seiler, Paul – C, T
Shell, Art – T
Siani, Mike – E
Sistrunk, Otis – E, T
Slough, Greg – LB
Smith, Charlie – B
Stabler, Ken – Q
Tatum, Jack – B
Thomas, Alonzo – B
Thoms, Art – T
Upshaw, Gene – G
Vella, John – G
Villapiano, Phil – LB
Warren, Jimmy – B
Wilson, Nemiah – B

1972 PHILADELPHIA EAGLES (NFC)
Coach – Ed Khayat
5th – Eastern Div., 2-11-1

Absher, Dick – LB
Alexander, Kermit – B
Allen, Chuck – LB
Allen, Jackie – B
Allison Henry – G
Antwine, Houston – T
Arrington, Rick – Q
Bailey, Tom – B
Baker, Tony – B
Ballman, Gary – E
Bradley, Bill – B, K
Bunting, John – LB
Calloway, Ernie – T, E
Carmichael, Harold – E
Cody, Bill – LB
Coleman, Al – B
Creech, Bob – LB
Crowe, Larry – B
Dempsey, Tom – K
Estes, Larry – E
Evans, Mike – C
Gibbs, Pat – B
Harris, Richard – E
Hawkins, Ben – E
Hoss, Clark – E
Hultz, Don – T
Jackson, Harold – E
James, Po – B

Key, Wade – T
Keyes, Leroy – B
Kramer, Kent – E
Liske, Pete – Q
Luken, Tom – G
McNeill, Tom – K
Mass, Wayne – T
Nelson, Al – B
Nordquist, Mark – G, C
Overmyer, Bill – LB
Pettigrew, Gary – T
Porter, Ron – LB
Preece, Steve – B
Ramsey, Nate – B
Reaves, John – Q
Skaggs, Jim – G
Smith, Steve – T
Sodaski, John – LB
Stevens, Richard – T
Sturm, Jerry – C
Sullivan, Tom – B
Thrower, Jim – B
Tom, Mel – E
Walik, Billy – E
Watkins, Larry – B
Winfield, Vern – G
Young, Adrian – LB
Zabel, Steve – LB

1972 PITTSBURGH STEELERS (AFC)
Coach – Chuck Noll
1st – Central Div., 11-3-0
(Beat Oakland, 13-7, in AFC Divisional Playoff;
lost to Miami, 21-17, for AFC Championship)

Anderson, Ralph – B
Bankston, Warren – B
Beatty, Chuck – B
Bleier, Rocky – B
Blount, Mel – B
Bradley, Ed – LB
Bradshaw, Terry – Q
Brown, Larry – E
Calland, Lee – B
Clack, Jim – C
Davis, Henry – LB
Davis, Sam – G
Davis, Steve – B
Dockery, John – B
Edwards, Glen – E
Furness, Steve – E
Fuqua, John – B
Gerela, Roy – K
Gilliam, Joe – Q
Gravelle, Gordon – T
Greene, Joe – T
Greenwood, L. C. – E
Ham, Jack – LB
Hanneman, Craig – T

Hanratty, Terry – Q
Harris, Franco – B
Holmes, Ernie – T
Holmes, Mel – T, G
Kolb, Jon – T
Lewis, Frank – E
McGee, Ben – T
McMakin, John – E
Mansfield, Ray – C
Mullins, Gerry – G
Pearson, Barry – E
Pearson, Preston – B
Rowser, John – B
Russell, Andy – LB
Shanklin, Ron – E
Smith, Dave – E
Stenger, Brian – LB
Van Dyke, Bruce – G
Wagner, Mike – B
Walden, Bobby – K
Webster, George – LB
White, Dwight – E
Winfrey, Carl – LB
Young, Al – E

1972 ST. LOUIS CARDINALS (NFC)
Coach – Bob Holloway
4th – Eastern Div., 4-9-1

Anderson, Donny – B
Arneson, Mark – LB
Bakken, Jim – K
Banks, Tom – C, G
Baynham, Craig – B
Beatty, Chuck – B
Beckman, Tom – E
Bradley, Dave – T, G
Brumm, Don – E
Burns, Leon – B
Butler, Jim – B
Conley, Steve – LB, B
Cuozzo, Gary – Q
Dierdorf, Dan – G
Dobler, Conrad – G
Farr, Miller – B
Gillette, Walker – E
Gray, Mel – E
Hackbart, Dale – B
Hargrove, Jim – LB
Hart, Jim – Q
Hayden, Leo – B
Heater, Don – B
Heron, Fred – T
Hoffman, John – E
Hutchinson, Chuck – G
Hyatt, Fred – E
Imhof, Martin – E
Lyman, Jeff – LB

McFarland, Jim – E
McGill, Mike – LB
McMillan, Ernie – T
Miller, Terry – LB
Moore, Bobby – E
Mulligan, Wayne – C
Palmer, Scott – T
Parish, Don – LB
Person, Ara – E
Richardson, John – T
Rivers, Jamie – LB
Roland, John – B
Rowe, Bob – T
Shivers, Roy – B
Smith, Jackie – E
Staggs, Jeff, LB
Stallings, Larry – LB
Thompson, Norm – B
Van Glader, Tim – Q
Walker, Chuck – E
Washington, Eric – B
Wehrli, Roger – B
Wicks, Bob – E
Willingham, Larry – B
Wilson, Larry – B
Woodeschick, Tom – B
Wright, Steve – T
Yankowski, Ron – E
Young, Bob – G

1972 SAN DIEGO CHARGERS (AFC)
Coach – Harland Svare
4th – Western Div., 4-9-1

Aldridge, Lionel – E
Andrews, John – E
Babich, Bob – LB
Barnes, Pete – LB
Beauchamp, Joe – B
Berry, Reggie – B
Caffey, Lee Roy – LB
Carter, Mike – E
Clark, Wayne – Q
Costa, Dave – T
Detwiler, Chuck – B
Dicus, Chuck – E
Dragon, Oscar – B
Dunlap, Leonard – B
East, Ron – T

Edwards, Cid – B
Fletcher, Chris – B
Garrett, Mike – B
Garrison, Gary – E
Gordon, Ira – T
Gruneisen, Sam – C
Hadl, John – Q
Hardy, Kevin – T
Howard, Bob – B
Jones, Deacon – E
Jones, Ray – B
Lazetich, Pete – LB
LeVias, Jerry – E
McClard, Bill – K
Mackey, John – E

Mauck, Carl – C
Norman, Pettis – E
Owens, Terry – T
Partee, Dennis – K
Redman, Rick – LB
Rossovich, Tim – E
Salter, Bryant – B
Snowden, Cal – E
Sweeney, Walt – G
Sykes, John – B

Taylor, Jesse – B
Thomas, Lee – E
Washington, Russ – T
Wenzel, Ralph – G
White, Lee – B
White, Ray – LB
Wilkerson, Doug – G
Williams, Dave – E
Wojcik, Greg – T
Wright, Ernie – T

1972 SAN FRANCISCO 49ers (NFC)
Coach – Dick Nolan
1st – Western Div., 8-5-1
(Lost to Dallas, 30-28, in the NFC Divisional Play-off)

Banaszek, Cas – T
Beard, Ed – LB
Beasley, Terry – E
Beisler, Randy – G
Belk, Bill – E
Blue, Forrest – C
Brodie, John – Q
Collett, Elmer – G
Cunningham, Doug – B
Edwards, Earl – T
Fuller, Johnny – B
Gossett, Bruce – K
Hall, Windlan – B
Hardman, Cedrick – E
Hart, Tommy – E
Hoskins, Bob – T
Huff, Marty – LB
Isenbarger, John – E
Johnson, Jimmy – B
Krueger, Charlie – T
Krueger, Rolf – E
Kwalick, Ted – E

McCann – Jim – K
McGill, Ralph – B
Nunley, Frank – LB
Olerich, Dave – LB
Peoples, Woody – G
Phillips, Mel – B
Reed, Joe – Q
Riley, Preston – E
Rohde, Len – T
Schreiber, Larry – B
Simpson, Mike – B
Sniadecki, Jim – LB
Spurrier, Steve – Q
Taylor, Bruce – B
Thomas, Jimmy – B
Vanderbundt, Skip – LB
Washington, Gene – E
Washington, Vic – B
Watson, John – T
Wilcox, Dave – LB
Willard, Ken – B
Witcher, Dick – E

1972 WASHINGTON REDSKINS (NFC)
Coach – George Allen
1st – Eastern Div., 11-3-0
(Beat Green Bay, 16-3, in NFC Divisional Playoff; defeated Dallas, 26-3, for the NFC Championship; lost to Miami (AFC), 14-7, in the Super Bowl)

Alston, Mack – E
Bass, Mike – B
Biggs, Verlon – E
Bragg, Mike – K
Brown, Larry – B
Brundige, Bill – E
Brunet, Bob – B
Burman, George – C, G
Duncan, Speedy – B
Fanucci, Mike – E
Fischer, Pat – B
Hanburger, Chris – LB
Harraway, Charley – B
Hauss, Len – C
Haymond, Alvin – B
Hermeling, Terry – T
Hull, Mike – B
Jaqua, Jon – B
Jefferson, Roy – E
Johnson, Mitchell – T
Jones, Jimmie – E
Jordan, Jeff – B
Jurgensen, Sonny – Q
Kilmer, Billy – Q

Knight, Curt – K
Laaveg, Paul – G
McDole, Ron – E
McLinton, Harold – LB
McNeil, Clifton – E
Malinchak, Bill – E
Mul-Key, Herb – B
Nock, George – B
Owens, Brig – B
Pardee, Jack – LB
Petitbon, Richie – B
Pottios, Myron – LB
Rock, Walter – T
Schoenke, Ray – G, T
Severson, Jeff – B
Sistrunk, Manuel – T
Smith, Jerry – E
Talbot, Diron – T
Taylor, Charley – E
Toylar, Rosey – B
Tillman, Rusty – LB
Vactor, Ted – B
Wilbur, John – G
Wyche, Sam – Q

TITLES: Miami won the American Football Conference Championship by defeating Pittsburgh, 21-17. In the Divisional Playoffs, Pittsburgh had defeated Oakland, 13-7, for the chance to play in the Championship Game. The Fourth Qualifier,

Cleveland, fell to Miami, 20-14, in their bid for the championship.

Washington became National Football Conference Champs after defeating the Dallas Cowboys, 26-3. Dallas was the Fourth Qualifier to be in the Divisional Playoffs and defeated San Francisco, 30-28, for another shot at the Super Bowl. Washington was in contention also by defeating Green Bay, 16-3.

The Super Bowl, played in Los Angeles, was won by AFC Champion Miami Dolphins over NFC Washington Redskins, 14-7.

AFC LEADERS: Scoring—Bobby Howfield (N.Y. Jets) 121; Rushing—O. J. Simpson (Buff.) 1,251 yds; Passing—Earl Morrall (Mia.); Pass Receiving—Fred Biletnikoff (Oak.) 58; Field Goals—Roy Gerela (Pitt.) 28; Punting—Jerrel Wilson (K.C.) 44.8 ave.; Interceptions—Mike Sensibaugh (K. C.) 8.

NFC LEADERS: Scoring—Rookie Chester Marcol (G.B.) 128; Rushing—Larry Brown (Wash.) 1,216 yds.; Passing—Norm Snead (N.Y.); Pass Receiving—Harold Jackson (Phil.) 62; Field Goals—Chester Marcol (G.B.) 33; Punting—Dave Chapple (L.A.) 44.2 ave.; Interceptions—Bill Bradley (Phil.) 9

FIRST DRAFT: AFC—Walt Patulski (Notre Dame), defensive end, by Buffalo, signed by Buffalo. NFC—Lionel Antoine (Sou. Ill.), tackle, by Chicago, signed by Chicago.

COACHES: In the AFC, John Sandusky replaced Don McCafferty on Oct. 16, 1972, at Baltimore. The New England Patriots hired Phil Bengtson to finish the season after John Mazur resigned on No. 13, 1972.

HALL OF FAME: The new members inducted into the Hall of Fame were: Lamar Hunt, Gino Marchetti, Ollie Matson, and Ace Parker.

NOTES: The Hashmark rule was introduced this year, moving field markings closer to the center of field so only 18'6" separated the two to help out offense.

Tie games count a half-game won and a half-game lost.

System of rating passers changed. Qualified passers to be rated in the following four categories: percentage of completions, percentage of TD passes per attempt, average yards gained per pass attempt, percentage of interceptions (rather than total TD passes, as in the past).

New stadium for Kansas City Chiefs—Arrowhead. Buffalo scheduled to have new stadium for next year.

Miami Dolphins became only NFL team to ever have two 1,000-yard rushers in one season—Larry Csonka and Mercury Morris. Dolphin coach, Don Shula, was first coach in NFL history to win 100 games in his first ten years.

Larry Brown, Washington running back, only player in NFL history to pass 1,000 yards total offense for four consecutive years; the third player to reach 1,000 yards rushing for four consecutive years.

CENTRAL DIVISION

	W.	L.	T.	Pct.
Cincinnati	10	4	0	.714
Pittsburgh*	10	4	0	.714
Cleveland	7	5	2	.571
Houston	1	13	0	.071

EASTERN DIVISION

	W.	L.	T.	Pct.
Miami	12	2	0	.857
Buffalo	9	5	0	.643
New England	5	9	0	.357
Baltimore	4	10	0	.286
New York Jets	4	10	0	.286

* Fourth Qualifier for Playoffs

1973

NATIONAL FOOTBALL LEAGUE

NATIONAL CONFERENCE

WESTERN DIVISION

	W.	L.	T.	Pct.
Los Angeles	12	2	0	.857
Atlanta	9	5	0	.643
New Orleans	5	9	0	.357
San Francisco	5	9	0	.357

CENTRAL DIVISION

	W.	L.	T.	Pct.
Minnesota	12	2	0	.857
Detroit	6	7	1	.464
Green Bay	5	7	2	.429
Chicago	3	11	0	.214

EASTERN DIVISION

	W.	L.	T.	Pct.
Dallas	10	4	0	.714
Washington*	10	4	0	.714
Philadelphia	5	8	1	.393
St. Louis	4	9	1	.321
New York Giants	2	11	1	.179

* Fourth Qualifier for Playoffs

AMERICAN CONFERENCE

WESTERN DIVISION

	W.	L.	T.	Pct.
Oakland	9	4	1	.679
Denver	7	5	2	.571
Kansas City	7	5	2	.571
San Diego	2	11	1	.179

1973 AFC Championship

Miami 27; Oakland 10

Miami captured its third straight AFC crown by defeating the Oakland Raiders, 27-10, using the pass only six times.

The Dolphins scored on their first possession in a 64-yard drive with running back Larry Csonka taking it in for the score from the 11. Csonka's second TD occurred late in the half from the 2 to make a half-time score of 14-0.

Oakland's kicker, George Blanda, scored a 21-yard field goal in the third quarter after missing a previous 41-yarder before the half. The Dolphins marched right back to set up Garo Yepremian's 42-yard field goal, keeping their 14-point edge.

Oakland's only successful offense came when a mixup in the Miami secondary enabled a 25-yard TD pass from Ken Stabler to Mike Siani. Miami retained control in the fourth quarter, adding ten points more on a 26-yard field goal by Yepremian and another TD by Csonka from the 2.

Miami's rushing yardage of 266 and Larry Csonka's three touchdowns became NFL Playoff records.

Oakland	0	0	10	0	10
Miami	7	7	3	10	27

Touchdowns: Miami, Csonka 3; Oakland, Siani

Field Goals: Miami, Yepremian 3; Oakland, Blanda

PATs: Miami, Yepremian 3; Oakland, Blanda

Attendance: 79,325

Players' shares: Miami $8,500; Oakland $5,500

1973 NFC Championship

Minnesota 27; Dallas 10

The Minnesota Vikings triumphed over the Dallas Cowboys, 27-10, to take the National Football Conference championship.

Minnesota dominated the first half with varied ground and air attacks to gain a half-time lead of 10-0 on Fred Cox's 44-yard field and rookie running back Chuck Foreman's 5-yard TD.

Dallas's hopes were revived when a 63-yard punt return touchdown by rookie wide receiver Golden Richards brought the Cowboys to a 10-7 score only to have Viking quarterback, Fran Tarkenton, come right back with a 54-yard bomb to end John Gilliam. The Cowboys were only able to score three more points on a Toni Fritsch 17-yard field goal while Minnesota added ten on an interception by cornerback Bobby Bryant for a 63-yard romp, and a Fred Cox field goal from the 34.

There were ten turnovers in the second half. Minnesota had 1 pass intercepted and lost 3 fumbles; Dallas had 4 passes intercepted and lost 2 fumbles.

Dallas	0	0	10	0	10
Minnesota	3	7	7	10	27

Touchdowns: Minnesota, Foreman, Gilliam, Bryant; Dallas, Richards

Field Goals: Minnesota, Cox 2; Dallas, Fritsch

PATs: Minnesota, Cox 3; Dallas, Fritsch

Attendance: 64,422

Players' shares: Minnesota $8,500; Dallas $5,500

1973 Super Bowl

Miami 24, Minnesota 7

In their third time around, the American Football Conference Miami Dolphins annihilated the NFC's Minnesota Vikings, 24-7, for a second consecutive Super Bowl victory. Dolphin coach Don Shula made his fourth S.B. appearance in eight years.

Using its one-two punch of running backs, Larry Csonka and Jim Kiick, Miami proceeded to control the scoreboard until the fourth quarter when Minnesota's Scramblin' Fran Tarkenton scampered across from the 4 yard line.

Two records were set on this eighth World Championship battle. Miami's Larry Csonka carried the ball 33 times for 145 yards, scoring 2 TDs; and Minnesota's general, Fran Tarkenton, set a passing record for 18 pass completions on 28 attempts for 182 yards.

Miami, using a ground game, was able to score on three of its first four possessions. A 62-yard opening game march brought Larry Csonka's first TD from the 5. Jim Kiick took in Miami's second TD from the 1. A 28-yard field goal by Garo Yepremian in the second quarter along with Csonka's second touchdown (a 2-yard plunge) in the third, gave the Dolphin a 24-0 lead that left Minnesota reeling and unable to recover.

The Vikings' chances flickered and died when their only sustained drive was fumbled away on Miami's 15 yard line late in the 2nd quarter. A clipping penalty against end Stu Voight nullified Minnesota teammate John Gilliam's 65-yard romp on the 2nd half kickoff.

Miami (AFC)	14	3	7	0	24
Minnesota (NFC)	0	0	0	7	7

Touchdowns: Miami, Csonka 2, Kiick; Minnesota, Tarkenton

Field Goals: Miami, Yepremian

PATs: Miami, Yepremian 3; Minnesota, Cox

Attendance: 71,882

Players' shares: Miami $15,000; Minnesota $7,500

RETIRED PLAYERS

Lance Alworth, end for the San Diego Chargers (AFL-AFC) and Dallas Cowboys (NFC)—11 years.

Ed Beard, linebacker for the San Francisco 49ers (NFL-NFC)—7 years.

Mike Ditka, end for the Chicago Bears, Philadelphia Eagles, and Dallas Cowboys (NFL-NFC)—12 years.

Bobby Duhon, back for the New York Giants (NFL-NFC)—4 years.

Larry Grantham, linebacker for the New York Titans (AFL), New York Jets (AFL-AFC)—13 years.

Charlie Harper, guard and tackle for the New York Giants (NFL-NFC)—7 years.

Dick LeBeau, back for the Detroit Lions (NFL-NFC)—14 years.

Ben McGee, end and tackle for the Pittsburgh Steelers (NFL-AFC)—9 years.

Marlin McKeever, end and linebacker for the Los Angeles Rams, Minnesota Vikings, Washington Redskins (NFL-NFC) and L.A. Rams (NFC)—12 years.

John Mackey, end for the Baltimore Colts (NFL-AFC) and San Diego Chargers (AFC)—10 years.

Ron Mix, tackle for the Los Angeles Chargers (AFL), San Diego Chargers

(AFL), and Oakland Raiders (AFC) —11 years.

Joe Morrison, back and end for the New York Giants (NFL-NFC) —14 years.

Bill Nelsen, quarterback for the Pittsburgh Steelers and Cleveland Browns (NFL-AFC) —10 years.

Rap Nitschke, Linebacker for the Green Bay Packers (NFL-NFC) —15 years.

August "Gus" Otto, linebacker for the Oakland Raiders (AFL-AFC) —8 years.

John "Jack" Pardee, linebacker for the Los Angeles Rams (NFL-NFC) and Washington Redskins (NFC) —15 years.

Wayne Walker, linebacker for the Detroit Lions (NFL-NFC) —15 years.

Larry Wilson, back for the St. Louis Cardinals (NFL-NFC) —13 years.

Ernie Wright, tackle for the Los Angeles Chargers (AFL), San Diego Chargers (AFL), Cincinnati Bengals (AFL-AFC), and again to the San Diego Chargers (AFC) —13 years.

DEATHS

Barrett, Jan, end, 1963 Green Bay Packers; 1963-64 Oakland Raiders (AFL), on October 7, 1973.

Basrak, Michael, center, 1937-38, Pittsburg Pirates, on December 18, 1973.

Bova, Anthony J. (Tony), end, 1942, 45-47 Pittsburgh Steelers; 1943 Phil-Pitt; 1944 Card-Pitt, on Oct. 16, 1973.

Campbell, Glenn R. (Slim), end, 1929-33 New York Giants; 1935 Pittsburgh Pirates, on September 16, 1973.

Crawford, Frederick, tackle, 1935 Chicago Bears, on March 5, 1974.

Gauer, Charles, end, 1943 Phil-Pitt; 1944-45 Philadelphia Eagles, on October 22, 1973.

Harris, Welton W. (Jack), back, 1925-26 Green Bay Packers, in January, 1974.

Jacobs, Jack, quarterback, back, punter, 1942, 45 Cleveland Rams; 1946 Washington Redskins; 1947-49 Green Bay Packers, on January 12, 1974.

Johnston, James E., back, 1939-40 Washington Redskins; 1946 Chicago Cardinals, on November 27, 1973.

Karcis, John, back, 1932-35 Brooklyn Dodgers; 1936-38 Pittsburgh Pirates; 1938-39, 43 New York Giants; interim coach for the Detroit Lions in 1942, on September 4, 1973.

Madarik, Elmer (Tippy), back, 1945-47 Detroit Lions; 1948 Washington Redskins, on March 3, 1974.

Morris, Glen E., end, 1940 Detroit Lions, on January 31, 1974.

Neale, Alfred Earle (Greasey), coach, 1941-42, 44-50 Philadelphia Eagles; co-coach, 1943 Phil-Pitt, on Novmeber 2, 1973.

Savoldi, Joseph A., back, 1930 Chicago Bears, on January 25, 1974.

Senn, William F., back, 1926-31 Chicago Bears; 1931 Brooklyn Dodgers; 1933 Cincinnati Reds; 1935 St. Louis Gunners, on September 5, 1973.

Simonetti, Leonard, tackle, 1947-48 Cleveland Browns (AAFC), on August 14, 1973.

Sitko, Emil, back, 1950 San Francisco 49ers; 1951-52 Chicago Cardinals, on December 15, 1973.

Stinchcomb, Gaylord, quarterback, 1921 Chicago Staleys; 1922 Chicago Bears; 1923 Columbus Tigers; 1923 Cleveland Indians; 1926 Louisville Colonels, on August 24, 1973.

Suffridge, Robert Lee, guard, 1941, 45 Philadelphia Eagles, on March 3, 1974.

West, D. Belford, tackle, 1921 Canton Bulldogs, on September 11, 1973.

Yablonski, Joseph, quarterback, 1940 Boston Bears (AFL), on February 19, 1974.

1973 ATLANTA FALCCNS (NFC)
Coach – Norm Van Brocklin
2nd – Western Div., 9–5–0

Bebout, Nick – T	Marx, Greg – E
Benson, Duane – LB	Matthews, Henry – B
Brezina, Gregory – LB	Maurer, Andy – G
Brown, Ray – B	Mialik, Larry – E
Burrow, Ken – E	Mike-Mayer, Nick – K
Chesson, Wes – E	Mitchell, Jim – E
Dodd, Al – E	Mitchell, Ken – LB
Easterling, Ray – B	Neal, Louis – E
Ellis, Clarence – B	Nobis, Tommy – LB
Fritsch, Ted – C	Plummer, Tony – B
Gallagher, Frank – G	Profit, Joe – B
Geredine, Tom – E	Ray, Eddie – B
Gotshalk, Len – T	Reaves, Ken – B
Hampton, Dave – B	Sandeman, Bill – T
Hansen, Don – LB	Shiner, Dick – Q
Havig, Dennis – G	Sovio, Henry – E
Hayes, Tom – B	Sullivan, Pat – Q
Humphrey, Claude – E	Tilleman, Mike – T
James, John – K	Van Note, Jeff – C
Kunz, George – T	Wages, Harmon – B
Lawrence, Rolland – B	Walker, Chick – T
Lee, Bob – Q	Warwick, Lonnie – LB
Lewis, Mike – T	Washington, Joe – B
Malone, Art – B	Zook, John – E
Manning, Rosie – T	

1973 BALTIMORE COLTS (AFC)
Coach – Howard Schnellenberger
4th – Eastern Div., 4–10–0

Amman, Richard – E, T	Curtis, Mike – LB
Andrews, John – E, B	Domres, Marty – Q
Bailey, Jim – T	Doughty, Glenn – E
Barnes, Mike – E	Drougas, Tom – T
Cherry, Stan – LB	Ehrmann, Joe – T
Chester, Raymond – E	Ginn, Hubert – B
Collett, Elmer – G	Havrilak, Sam – E

Hendricks, Ted – LB
Herosian, Brian – B
Hilton, Roy – E
Hoaglin, Fred – C
Hunt, George – K
Johnson, Cornelius – G
Jones, Bert – Q
Kaczmarek, Mike – LB
Kern, Rex – B
Laird, Bruce – B
Lee, David – K
McCauley, Don – B
May, Ray – LB
Mendenhall, Ken – C
Mildren, Jack – B
Mitchell, Lydell – B

Mitchell, Tom – E
Mooney, Ed – LB
Munsey, Nelson – B
Neal, Dan – C
Nelson, Dennis – T
Nottingham, Don – B
Oldham, Ray – B
Olds, Bill – B
Ressler, Glenn – G
Schmiesing, Joe – T, E
Smith, Ollie – E
Speyrer, "Cotton" – E
Taylor, David – T
Volk, Rick – B
White, Stan – LB
Windauer, Bill – T

1973 BUFFALO BILLS (AFC)
Coach – Lou Saban
2nd – Eastern Div., 9–5–0

Braxton, Jim – B
Cahill, Bill – B
Chandler, Bob – E
Cheyunski, Jim – LB
Cornell, "Bo" – B
Croyle, Phil – LB
DeLamielleure, Joe – G
Edwards, Earl – T, E
Farley, Dale – LB
Ferguson, Joe – Q
Foley, Dave – T
Forsberg, Fred – LB
Francis, Wallace – E
Garror, Leon – B
Green, Donnie – T
Greene, Tony – B
Hagen, Halvor – E
Harrison, Dwight – E, B
Hill, J. D. – E
James, Robert – B
Jarvis, Bruce – C
Jarvis, Ray – E
Jones, "Spike" – K
Jones, Steve – B
Kadish, Mike – T
Kampa, Bob – E

Kellerman, Ernie – B
Kingrea, Rick – LB
Koy, Ted – B, E, LB
Krakau, Merv – LB
Lewis, Richard – LB
Leypoldt, John – K
McConnell, Brian – E
McKenzie, Reggie – G
Montler, Mike – G, T, C
Okoniewski, Steve – E, T
Parker, Willie – C, G
Patton, Jerry – T
Patulski, Walter – E
Penchion, Robert – G
Pitts, John – B
Seymour, Paul – E
Shaw, Dennis – Q
Simpson, O. J. – B
Skorupan, John – LB
Stone, Ken – B
Van Valkenberg, Pete – B
Walker, Donnie – B
Washington, Dave – LB
Watkins, Larry – B
Winans, Jeff – T

1973 CHICAGO BEARS (NFC)
Coach – Abe Gibron
4th – Central Div., 3–11–0

Antoine, Lionel – T
Asher, Bob – T
Buffone, Doug – LB
Butkus, Dick – LB
Chambers, Wally – T, E
Clark, Gail – LB
Clemons, Craig – B
Coady, Rich – C
Cotton, Craig – E
Douglass, Bobby – Q
Ellis, Alan – B
Farmer, George – E
Ford, Charlie – B
Garrett, Carl – B
Green, Bobby Joe – K
Gunn, Jimmy – LB
Hale, Dave – T
Harrison, Jim – B
Hill, Ike – E
Holloway, Glen – G
Holman, Willie – E
Hrivnak, Gary – T, E
Huff, Gary – Q
Jackson, Randy – T
Janet, Ernie – G

Jeter, Bob – B
Juenger, Dave – E
Kinney, Steve – T
Kosins, Gary – B
Lawson, Roger – B
Lyle, Garry – B
McGee, Tony – E
Moore, Joe – B
Newton, Bob – G
Osborne, Jim – T
Parsons, Bob – E
Percival, Mac – K
Pifferini, Bob – LB
Reppond, Mike – E
Reynolds, Tom – E
Rice, Andy – T
Rives, Don – LB
Roberts, Willie – B
Roder, Mirro – K
Sanderson, Reggie – B
Taylor, Joe – B
Thomas, Earl – E
Tom, Mel – E
Turner, Cecil – E
Young, Adrian – LB

1973 CINCINNATI BENGALS (AFC)
Coach – Paul Brown
1st – Central Div., 10–4–0
(Lost to Miami, 34–16, in AFC Playoffs)

Adams, Douglas – LB
Anderson, Ken – Q
Avery, Ken – LB
Beauchamp, Al – LB
Bergey, Bill – LB
Berry, Royce – E
Blackwood, Lyle – B
Carpenter, Ron – E
Casanova, Tom – B
Chandler, Al – E
Chomyszak, Steve – T
Clark, "Booby" – B
Cook, Greg — Q
Coslet, Bruce – E
Craig, Neal – B
Curtis, "Ike" – E
DeLeone, Tom – C, G
Elliott, Lenvil – B
Ernst, Mike – Q
Fest, Howard – T, G
George, Tim – E
Green, Dave – K
Holland, Vernon – T
Jackson, Bernard – B

Johnson, Bob – C
Johnson, Essex – B
Johnson, Ken – T, E
Joiner, Charlie – E
Jones, Bob – B
Kearney, Tim – LB
LeClair, Jim – LB
Lewis, Dave, B, K
Matson, Pat – G
Mayes, Rufus – T
Morrison, Reece – B
Muhlmann, Horst – K
Myers, "Chip" – E
Parrish, Lemar – B
Pritchard, Ron – LB
Reid, Mike – T
Riley, Ken – B
Shinners, John – G
Thomas, Lee – E
Trumpy, Bob – E
Walters, Stan – T
White, Sherman – E
Wilson, Joe – B

1973 CLEVELAND BROWNS (AFC)
Coach – Nick Skorich
3rd – Central Div., 7–5–2

Andrews, Bill – LB
Babich, Bob – LB
Barisich, Carl – T
Briggs, Bob – E, T
Brooks, Clifford – B
Brown, Ken – B
Carollo, Joe – T
Cockroft, Don – K
Copeland, Jim – C, G
Darden, Tom – B
Davis, Ben – B
DeMarco, Bob – C
Demarie, John – G
Dieken, Doug – T
Garlington, John – LB
Glass, "Chip" – E
Green, Van – B
Hall, Charlie – LB
Hickerson, Gene – G
Holden, Steve – E
Hooker, Fair – E
Horn, Don – Q
Hutchison, Chuck – G

Johnson, Walter – T
Jones, Joe – E
Kelly, Leroy – B
Lefear, Billy – B
Lindsey, Dale – LB
Long, Mel – LB
McKay, Bob – T
McKinnis, Hugh – B
Morin, Milt – E
Morris, Chris – T
Phipps, Mike – Q
Pitts, Frank – E
Pruitt, Greg – B
Richardson, Gloster – E
Roman, Nick – E
Romaniszyn, Jim – LB
Scott, Clarence – B
Scott, "Bo" – B
Sherk, Jerry – T
Sims, Lester – E
Stienke, Jim – B
Sullivan, Dave – E
Sumner, Walt – B

1973 DALLAS COWBOYS (NFC)
Coach – Tom Landry
1st – Eastern Div., 10–4–0
(Beat Los Angeles, 27–16, in NFC Divisional Playoffs;
lost to Minnesota, 27–10, for the NFC Championship)

Arneson, Jim – G, T, C
Babinecz, John – LB
Barnes, Benny – B
Barnes, Rodrigo – LB
Bateman, Marv – K
Clark, Mike – K
Cole, Larry – E
Concannon, Jack – Q
DuPree, Billy Joe – E
Edwards, Dave – LB
Fitzgerald, John – C
Fritsch, Toni – K
Fugett, Jean – E
Garrison, Walt – B
Green, Cornell – B
Gregory, Bill – T

Harris, Cliff – B
Hayes, Bob – E
Hill, Calvin – B
Howley, Chuck – LB
Jordon, Lee Roy – LB
Lewis, D. D. – LB
Lilly, Bob – T
Manders, Dave – C
Martin, Harvey – T, E
Montgomery, Mike – E, K
Morton, Craig – Q
Neely, Ralph – T
Newhouse, Robert – B
Niland, John – G
Nye, Blaine – G

Pearson, Drew – E
Pinder, Cyril – B
Pugh, Jethro – T
Renfro, Mel – B
Richards, Golden – E
Robinson, Larry – B
Staubach, Roger – Q
Stowe, Otto – E

Strayhorn, Les – B
Toomay, Pat – E
Truax, Billy – E
Wallace, Rodney – G, T
Walton, Bruce – G, T, C
Washington, Mark – B
Waters, Charley – B
Wright, Rayfield – T

1973 DENVER BRONCOS (AFC)
Coach – John Ralston
2nd – Western Div., 7–5–2

Alzado, Lyle – E
Anderson, Bob – B
Armstrong, Otis – B
Askea, Mike – T
Chavous, Barney – E
Criter, Ken – LB
Current, Mike – T
Dawkins, Joe – B
Duranko, Pete – T
Forsberg, Fred – LB
Graham, Tom – LB
Grant, John – T, E
Greer, Charlie – B
Hackbart, Dale – B
Howard, Parl – G
Inman, Jerry – T
Jackson, Larron – G, T
Jackson, Tom – LB
Johnson, Charley – Q
Jones, Calvin – B
Kaminski, Larry – C
Laskey, Bill – LB
Little, Floyd – B
Lynch, Fran – B

Lyons, Tommy – G
Maples, Bobby – C
Masters, Billy – E
May, Ray – LB
Mitchell, Leroy – B
Montgomery, Marv – T
Montgomery, Randy – B
Moses, Haven – E
Odoms, Riley – E
O'Malley, Jim – LB
Pitts, John – B
Ramsey, Steve – Q
Ross, Oliver – B
Schnitker, Mike – G
Simmons, Jerry – E
Simone, Mike – LB
Smith, Ed – E
Smith, Paul – T
Thompson, Bill – B
Turner, Jim – K
Tyler, Maurice – B
Van Heusen, Bill – K, E
Washington, Gene – E

1973 DETROIT LIONS (NFC)
Coach – Don McCafferty
2nd – Central Div., 6–7–1

Barnes, Al – E
Barney, Lem – B
Bell, Bob – T
Cappleman, Bill – Q
Crosswhite, Leon – B
Dennis, Guy – G
Farr, Mel – B
Farr, Miller – B
Flanagan, Ed – C
Freitas, Rocky – T
Germany, Willie – B
Haggerty, Mike – T
Hand, Larry – E
Hennigan, Mike – LB
Hilton, John – E
Hooks, Jim – B
Jauron, Dick – B
Jessie, Ron – E
Johnson, Levi – B
Jolley, Gordon – T
Kowalkowski, Bob – G
Landry, Greg – Q
Laslavic, Jim – LB
Lucci, Mike – LB
McCullouch, Earl – E

Mann, Errol – K
Mitchell, Jim – E
Munson, Bill – Q
Naumoff, Paul – LB
O'Brien, Jim – E, K
Orvis, Herb – T, E
Owens, Steve – B
Price, Ernest – T, E
Rasley, Rocky – G
Sanders, Charlie – E
Sanders, Ken – E
Small, John – T, E
Taylor, Altie – B
Teal, Jim – LB
Thompson, Dave – C, G, T
Thrower, Jim – B
Walton, Chuck – G
Walton, Larry – E
Weaver, Charlie – LB
Weaver, Herman – K
Weger, Mike – B
Wyatt, Doug – B
Yarbrough, Jim – T
Zofko, Mickey – B

1973 GREEN BAY PACKERS (NFC)
Coach – Dan Devine
3rd – Central Div., 5–7–2

Austin, Hise – B
Bowman, Ken – C
Branstetter, Kent – T
Brockington, John – B
Brown, Aaron – E

Brown, Bob – E
Buchanon, Willie – B
Carr, Fred – LB
Carter, Jim – LB
Del Gaizo, Jim – Q

Donohoe, Mike – E
Ellis, Ken – B
Garrett, Len – E
Gillingham, Gale – G
Glass, Leland – E
Goodman, Les – B
Gordon, Dick – E
Hall, Charlie – B
Hayhoe, Bill – T
Hefner, Larry – LB
Highsmith, Don – B
Hill, Jim – B
Himes, Dick – T
Hunter, Scott – Q
Jenke, Noel – LB
Krause, Larry – B
Lane, MacArthur – B
Lueck, Bill – G
MacLeod, Tom – LB
McBride, Ron – B
McCarren, Larry – C

McCoy, Mike – T
McGeorge, Rich – E
Marcol, Chester – K
Matthews, Al – B
Nystrom, Lee – T
Oats, Carleton – T
Pureifory, Dave – E
Roche, Alden – T, E
Smith, Barry – E
Smith, Perry – B
Snider, Malcolm – G, T
Staggers, Jon – E
Staroba, Paul – E, K
Tagge, Jerry – Q
Thomas, Ike – B
Toner, Tom – LB
Widby, Ron – K
Williams, Clarence – E
Williams, Perry – B
Withrow, Cal – C
Wortman, Keith – G

1973 HOUSTON OILERS (AFC)
Coach – Bill Peterson to Sid Gillman
4th – Central Div., 1–13–0

Alexander, Willie – B
Alston, Mack – E
Amundson, George – B
Atkins, Bob – B, E
Beirne, Jim – E
Bethea, Elvin – E
Bingham, Gregg – LB
Blahak, Joe – B
Burrough, Ken – E
Butler, "Skip" – K
Carr, Levert – G, T
Charles, John – B
Cindrich, Ralph – LB
Cowlings, Al – T
Croyle, Phil – LB
Cunningham, Dick – LB
Curry, Bill – C
Dickey, Lynn – Q
Drungo, Elbert – T, G
Eaglin, Larry – B
Fanucci, Mike – E
Freelon, Solomon – G
Funchess, Tom – T
Goodman, Brian – G
Grant, Wes – E, T
Green, Dave – K
Gresham, Bob – B
Gruneisen, Sam – C
Guidry, Paul – LB
Haymond, Al – B

Hinton, Eddie – E
Hunt, Calvin – C
Hunt, Kevin – T
Jenkins, Al – G
Johnson, Al – B
Johnson, Benny – B
Jolley, Lewis – B
Jones, Harris – G
Lou, Ron – C
McConnell, Brian – E
McNeil, Clifton – E
Matuszak, John – T
Mayo, Ron – E
Miller, Ralph – G
Moore, Zeke – B
Parks, Dave – E
Parks, Billy – E
Pastorini, Dan – Q
Rice, Floyd, – LB
Roberts, Guy – LB
Robinson, Paul – B
Sampson, Greg – E, T
Saul, Ron – G
Severson, Jeff – B
Smith, Tody – E
Thomas, Bill – B
Vanoy, Vernon – T
Washington, Ted – LB
Willis, Fred – B
Wyatt, Alvin – B

1973 KANSAS CITY CHIEFS (AFC)
Coach – Hank Stram
3rd – Western Div., – 7–5–2

Allen, Nate – B
Beathard, Pete – Q
Bell, Bobby – LB
Buchanan, "Buck" – T
Budde, Ed – G
Butler, Gary – E
Culp, Curley – T
Daney, George – G
Dawson, Len – Q
Ellison, Willie – B
Hamilton, Andy – E
Hayes, Wendell – B
Hill, Dave – T
Holmes, Pat – E
Jones, Doug – B
Kearney, Jim – B
Keyes, Leroy – B
Kinney, Jeff – B
Kratzer, Dan – E

Lanier, Willie – LB
Livingston, Mike – Q
Lohmeyer, John – E
Lynch, Jim – LB
McVea, Warren – B
Marsalis, Jim – B
Marshall, Larry – B
Moorman, "Mo" – G
Oriard, Mike – C
Palewicz, Al – LB
Peay, Francis – T
Podolak, Ed – B
Reardon, Kerry – B
Rudnay, Jack – C
Seals, George – T
Sensibaugh, Mike – B
Smith, Dave – E
Stenerud, Jan – K
Stroud, Morris – E

Taylor, Otis – E
Thomas, Emmitt – B
Tyrer, Jim – T
Upshaw, Marvin – E
Walton, Wayne – G

Werner, Clyde – LB
West, Robert – E
Wilson, Jerrel – K
Wright, Elmo – E
Young, Wilbur – E

1973 LOS ANGELES RAMS (NFC)
Coach – Chuck Knox
1st – Western Div., 12–2–0
(Lost to Dallas, 27–16, in NFC Divisional Playoff)

Baker, Tony – B
Bertelsen, Jim – B
Brooks, Larry – T
Bryant, Cullen – B
Chapple, Dave – K
Clark, Al – B
Cowan, Charlie – T
Curran, Pat – E
Drake, Bill – B, E
Dryer, Fred – E
Elmendorf, Dave – B
Geddes, Ken – LB
Gordon, Dick – E
Hadl, John – Q
Harris, Jim – B
Iman, Ken – C
Jackson, Harold – E
Josephson, Les – B
Kay, Rick – LB
Klein, Bob – E
McCutcheon, Larry – B
McMillan, Eddie – B
Mack, Tom – G

Nelson, Bill – T
Nelson, Terry – E
Olsen, Merlin – T
Olsen, Phil – T
Preece, Steve – B
Ray, David – K
Reynolds, Jack – LB
Robertson, Isiah – LB
Saul, Rich – C, G
Schuh, Harry – T
Scibelli, Joe – G
Scribner, Bob – B
Sherman, Rod – E
Smith, Larry – B
Snow, Jack – E
Stein, Bob – LB
Stukes, Charlie – B
Sweet, Joe – E
Williams, John – G, T
Youngblood, Jack – E
Youngblood, Jim – LB

1973 MIAMI DOLPHINS (AFC)
Coach – Don Shula
1st – Eastern Div., 12–2–0
(Beat Cincinnati, 34–16, in AFC Playoffs; defeated Oakland, 27–10, for AFC Championship; beat Minnesota (NFC), 24–7, in the Super Bowl)

Anderson, Dick – B
Babb, Charles – B
Ball, Larry – LB
Bannon, Bruce – LB
Briscoe, Marlin – E
Buoniconti, Nick – LB
Crusan, Doug – T
Csonka, Larry – B
Den Herder, Vern – E
Evans, Norm – T
Fernandez, Manny – T
Fleming, Marv – E
Foley, Tim – B
Ginn, Hubert – B
Goode, Irv – G, C
Griese, Bob – Q
Heinz, Bob – T, E
Johnson, Curtis – B
Kiick, Jim – B
Kolen, Mike – LB
Kuechenberg, Bob – G
Langer, Jim – C
Leigh, Charles – B
Little, Larry – G

Mandich, Jim – E
Matheson, Bob – LB
Moore, Maulty – T
Moore, Wayne – T
Morrall, Earl – Q
Morris, "Mercury" – B
Mumphord, Lloyd – B
Newman, Ed – G
Nottingham, Don – B
Powell, Jesse – LB
Rather, "Bo" – E
Scott, Jake – B
Seiple, Larry – E, K
Sellers, Ron – E
Smith, Tom – B
Stanfill, Bill – E
Stuckey, Henry – B
Swift, Doug – LB
Twilley, Howard – E
Warfield, Paul – E
Woods, Larry – T
Yepremian, "Garo" – K
Young, Willie – T

1973 MINNESOTA VIKINGS (NFC)
Coach – Bud Grant
1st – Central Div., 12–2–0
(Beat Washington, 27–20, in NFC Divisional Playoffs; beat Dallas, 27–10, for NFC Championship; lost to Miami (AFC), 24–7, in Super Bowl)

Alderman, Grady – T
Ballman, Gary – E
Beasley, John – E

Berry, Bob – Q
Brown, Bill – B
Brown, Terry – B

Bryant, Bobbie Lee – B
Cox, Fred – K
Dale, Carroll – E
Dawson, Rhett – E
Eischeid, Mike – K
Eller, Carl – E
Foreman, Chuck – B
Gallagher, Frank – G
Gilliam, John – E
Goodrum, Charles – T, G
Hilgenberg, Wally – LB
Kingsriter, Doug – E
Krause, Paul – B
Larsen, Gary – T
Lash, Jim – E
Lawson, Steve – G
Lurtsema, Bob – E, T
McClanahan, Brent – B
Marinaro, Ed – B
Marshall, Jim – E

Martin, Amos – LB
Osborn, Dave – B
Page, Alan – T
Porter, Ron – LB
Randolph, Al – B
Reed, Oscar – B
Siemon, Jeff – LB
Sunde, Milt – G
Sutherland, Doug – T
Tarkenton, Fran – Q
Tinglehoff, Mick – C
Voigt, Stu – E
Ward, John – G
West, Charlie – B
White, Ed – G
Winston, Roy – LB
Wright, Jeff – B
Wright, Nate – B
Yary, Ron – T
Zaunbrecher, Godfrey – C

1973 NEW ENGLAND PATRIOTS (AFC)
Coach – Chuck Fairbanks
3rd – Eastern Div., 5–9–0

Acks, Ron – LB
Adams, Julius – E
Adams, Bob – E
Adams, Sam – G, T
Anderson, Ralph – B
Ashton, Josh – B
Banks, Willie – G
Barnes, Bruce – K
Bell, Bill – K
Bolton, Rin – B
Boyd, Greg – B
Cash, Rick – T
Chandler, Edgar – LB
Cunningham, Sam – B
Dorsey, Nate – E
Dowling, Brian – Q
Dumler, Doug – C
Durko, Sandy – B
Foster, Will – LB
Geddes, Bob – LB
Gipson, Paul – B
Gray, Leon – T
Hamilton, Ray – E
Hannah, John – G
Herron, Mack – B
Hoey, George – B
Hunt, Kevin – T

Jackson, Honor – B
Kiner, Steve – LB
King, Steve – LB
Lenkaitis, Bill – G
Lunsford, Mel – E, T
McCall, Bob – B
Martin, Don – B
Mason, Dave – B
Moore, Arthur – T
Morris, Jon – C
Mosier, John – E
Neville, Tom – T
Plunkett, Jim – Q
Reynolds, Bob – T
Rowe, Dave – T
Rucker, Reggie – E
St. Jean, Len – G
Shiner, Dick – Q
Smith, Donnell – E
Stenger, Brian – LB
Stingley, Darryl – E
Tanner, John – LB
Tarver, John – B
Vataha, Randy – E
Welch, Claxton – B
White, Jeff – K
Windsor, Bob – E

1973 NEW ORLEANS SAINTS (NFC)
Coach – John North
3rd – Western Div., 5–9–0

Abramowicz, Dan – E
Askson, Bert – E
Baumgartner, Steve – E
Beasley, John – E
Brown, Bob – E
Butler, Bill – B
Colman, Wayne – LB
Creech, Bob – LB
Davis, Bob – Q
Didion, John – C
Dorris, Andy – E, LB
Dunbar, Jubilee – E
Federspiel, Joe – LB
Feller, Happy – K
Fersen, Paul – T
Fink, Mike – B
Fuller, Johnny – B
Garrett, Len – E
Hall, Willie – LB
Hester, Ray – LB

Hyatt, Fred – E
Jackson, Ernie – B
Johnson, Carl – T
Jones, Ray – B
Kelly, Mike – E
Kingrea, Rick – LB
Kupp, Jake – G
Lawson, Odell – B
Lee, Bivian – B
Lindsey, Dale – LB
McClard, Bill – K
Manning, Archie – Q
Matthews, Henry – B
Merlo, Jim – LB
Minor, Lincoln – B
Moore, Derland – T
Moore, Jerry – B
Morrison, Don – T
Myers, Tom – B
Newland, Bob – E

Newsome, Billy – E
O'Neal, Steve – K
Owens, Joe – E
Palmer, Dick – LB
Philipps, Jess – B
Pollard, Bob – T
Price, Elex – T
Profit, Joe – B
Ramsey, Nate – B

Riley, Preston – E
Robinson, Craig – T
Scott, Bobby – Q
Smith, Royce – G
Stevens, Howard – B
Thomas, Speedy – E
Williams, Del – G, T, C
Winslow, Doug – E

1973 NEW YORK GIANTS (NFC)
Coach – Alex Webster
5th – Eastern Div., 2–11–1

Athas, Pete – B
Ballman, Gary – E
Blanchard, Tom – K
Brown, Otto – B
Buetow, Bart – T
Campbell, Carter – E
Clements, Vince – B
Crist, Chuck – B
Douglas, John – LB
Ellison, Mark – G
Enderle, Dick – G
Evans, Charlie – B
Files, Jim – LB
Flowers, Richmond – B
Gatewood, Tom – E
Glover, Rich – T
Gogolak, Pete – K
Goich, Dan – T
Gregory, Jack – E
Grim, Bob – E
Herrmann, Don – E
Hill, John – T
Hornsby, Ron – LB
Houston, Rich – E
Hughes, Pat – LB
Hyland, Bob – C, G

Jackson, Honor – B
Jacobson, Larry – T
Johnson, Randy – Q
Johnson, Ron – B
Kelley, Brian – LB
Larson, Greg – C
Lockhart, "Spider" – B
Love, Walter – E
Lumpkin, Ron – B
McCann, Jim – K
Mendenhall, John – T
Orduna, Joe – B
Reed, Henry – LB
Rizzo, Jack – B
Roland, John – B
Small, Eldridge – B
Snead, Norm – Q
Taffoni, Joe – T
Thompson, "Rocky" – B
Tipton, Dave – T
Tucker, Bob – E
Van Horn, Doug – G, T
Van Pelt, Brad – LB
Williams, Willie – B
Young, Willie – T

1973 NEW YORK JETS (AFC)
Coach – Weeb Ewbank
5th – Eastern Div., 4–10–0

Adamle, Mike – B
Adkins, Margene – E
Atkinson, Al – LB
Baker, Ralph – LB
Barkum, Jerome – E
Bell, Ed – E
Bjorklund, Hank – B
Boozer, Emerson – B
Cambal, Dennis – E, B
Caster, Rich – E
Demory, Bill – Q
Ebersole, John – E, LB
Elliott, John – T, E
Fagan, Julian – K
Farasopoulos, Chris – B
Ferguson, Bill – LB
Galigher, Ed – E
Harrell, Rick – C
Herman, Dave – G
Hill, Winston – T
Howell, Delles – B
Howfield, Bobby – K
Jackson, Joey – E, T
Knight, David – E

Little, John – T
Lomas, Mark – E
McClain, Clifford – B
Mooring, John – G, T, C
Namath, Joe – Q
Nance, Jim – B
Neal, Richard – E, T
Owens, Burgess – B
Puetz, Garry – T, G
Rasmussen, Randy – G
Riggins, John – B
Schmitt, John – C
Sowells, Rich – B
Spicer, Rob – LB
Svihus, Bob – T, G
Tannen, Steve – B
Taylor, Mike – LB
Thomas, Earlie – B
Thompson, Steve – E, T
Turner, "Rocky" – B, E
Wise, Phil – B
Woodall, Al – Q
Woods, Robert – T
Zapalac, Bill – LB

1973 OAKLAND RAIDERS (AFC)
Coach – John Madden
1st – Western Div., 9–4–1
(Beat Pittsburgh, 33–14, in AFC Divisional
Playoffs; lost to Miami, 27–10, for AFC
Championship)

Atkinson, George – B
Banaszak, Pete – B

Bankston, Warren – B, E
Biletnikoff, Fred – E

Blanda, George – K
Branch, Cliff – E
Brown, Bob – T
Brown, Willie – B
Buehler, George – G
Carroll, Joe – LB
Cline, Tony – E, LB
Conners, Dan – LB
Dalby, Dave – C, G, T
Davis, Clarence – B
Guy, Ray – K
Hubbard, Marv – B
Hudson, Bob – B
Irons, Gerald – LB
Johnson, Monte – T
Jones, Horace – E
Korver, Kelvin – T
Lamonica, Daryle – Q
Maxwell, Tom – E, B
Medlin, Dan – G

Moore, Bob – E
Otto, Jim – C
Queen, Jeff – B, E
Seiler, Paul – C, T
Shell, Art – T
Siani, Mike – E
Sistrunk, Otis – T
Smith, "Bubba" – E
Smith, Charlie – B
Stabler, Ken – Q
Sweeney, Steve – E
Tatum, Jack – B
Thomas, "Skip" – B
Thoms, Art – T
Upshaw, Gene – G
Vella, John – T, G
Villapiano, Phil – LB
Warren, Jimmy – B
Weaver, Gary – LB
Wilson, Nemiah – B

1973 PHILADELPHIA EAGLES (NFC)
Coach – Mike McCormack
3rd – Eastern Div., 5–8–1

Alexander, Kermit – B
Bailey, Tom – B
Bouggess, Lee – B
Bradley, Bill – B, K
Bulaich, Norm – B
Bunting, John – LB
Carmichael, Harold – E
Chesson, Wes – E
Coleman, Al – B
Cunningham, Dick – LB
Davis, Stan – E
Dempsey, Tom – K
Dunstan, Bill – E, T
Evans, Mike – C
Gabriel, Roman – Q
Halverson, Dean – LB
Harris, Richard – T
Hawkins, Ben – E
Hultz, Don – T
James, "Po" – B
Key, Wade – T
Kirksey, Roy – G
Kramer, Kent – E
Lavender, Joe – B
Logan, Randy – B
Luken, Tom – G

McKeever, Marlin – LB
McNeill, Tom – K
Morriss, Guy – G, C
Nelson, Al – B
Nordquist, Mark – G
Oliver, Greg – B
Outlaw, John – B
Pettigrew, Gary – T
Philbin, Gerry – E
Picard, Bob – E
Reaves, John – Q
Reilly, Kevin – LB
Roussel, Tom – LB
Sisemore, Jerry – T
Smith, Steve – T
Sodaski, John – LB
Stevens, Richard – T, G
Sullivan, Tom – B
Tom, Mel – E
Winfield, Vern – G
Wirgowski, Dennis – E
Wynn, William – E
Young, Charles – E
Zabel, Steve – LB
Zimmerman, Don – E

1973 PITTSBURGH STEELERS (AFC)
Coach – Chuck Noll
2nd – Central Div., 10–4–0
(Lost to Oakland, 33–14, in AFC Divisional
Playoffs)

Bleier, "Rocky" – B
Blount, Mel – B
Bradley, Ed – LB
Bradshaw, Terry – Q
Brown, Larry – E
Clack, Jim – C
Davis, Dave – E
Davis, Henry – B
Davis, Sam – G
Davis, Steve – B
Dockery, John – B
Edwards, Glen – B
Fuqua, "Frenchy" – B
Furness, Steve – T, E
Gerela, Roy – K
Gilliam, Joe – Q
Gravelle, Gordon – T
Greene, Joe – T
Greenwood, L. C. – E

Ham, Jack – LB
Hanneman, Craig – E
Hanratty, Terry – Q
Harris, Franco – B
Hines, Glen Ray – T
Holmes, Ernie – T
Holmes, Mel – T
Keating, Tom – T
Kolb, Jon – T
Lewis, Frank – E
McMakin, John – E
Mansfield, Ray – C
Meyer, Dennis – B
Mullins, Gerry – T, G
Pearson, Barry – E
Pearson, Preston – B, E
Rowser, John – B
Russell, Andy – LB

Scolnick, Glen – E
Shanklin, Ron – E
Thomas, James – B
Toews, Loren – LB
Van Dyke, Bruce – G

Wagner, Mike – B
Walden, Bob – K
Webster, George – LB
White, Dwight – E
Williams, Dave – E

1973 ST. LOUIS CARDINALS (NFC)
Coach – Don Coryell
4th – Eastern Div., 4–9–1

Anderson, Donny – B
Arneson, Mark – LB
Bakken, Jim – K
Banks, Tom – C, G
Barnes, Pete – LB
Belton, Willie – B
Brahaney, Tom – C
Brooks, Leo – E, T
Butz, Dave – E, T
Crump, Dwane – B
Davis, Ron – T
Detwiler, Chuck – B
Dierdorf, Dan – G, T
Dobler, Conrad – G
Dorris, Andy – E
Duren, Clarence – B
Finnie, Roger – G, T
Gillette, Walker – E
Gray, Mel – E
Hammond, Gary – B, E
Hart, Jim – Q
Hayden, Leo – B
Keithley, Gary – Q
Koegel, Warren – C
LeVeck, Jack – LB
McFarland, Jim – E
McMillan, Ernie – T

Maynard, Don – E
Metcalf, Terry – B
Miller, Terry – LB
Moss, Eddie – B
Mulligan, Wayne – C
Oliver, Clarence – B
Otis, Jim – B
Owens, Marv – E
Rashad, Ahmad – E
Reynolds, Bob – T
Richardson, John – T
Rivers, Jamie – LB
Rowe, Bob – T
Rudolph, Council – E
Shy, Don – B
Sloane, Bonnie – T
Smith, Jackie – E
Staggs, Jeff – LB
Stallings, Larry – LB
Taylor, Mike – T
Thompson, Norm – B
Tolbert, Jim – B
Washington, Eric – B
Wehrli, Roger – B
Yankowski, Ron – E
Young, Bob – G

1973 SAN DIEGO CHARGERS (AFC)
Coach – Harland Svare to Ron Waller
4th – Western Div., 2–11–1

Aldridge, Lionel – E
Bacon, Coy – T
Beauchamp, Joe – B
Berry, Reggie – B
Clark, Wayne – Q
Costa, Dave – T
Dennis, Al – G
Douglas, Jay – C
Dunlap, Leonard – B
East, Ron – T
Edwards, "Cid" – B
Fletcher, Chris – B
Fouts, Dan – Q
Garrett, Mike – B
Garrison, Gary – E
Gersbach, Carl – LB
Gordon, Ira – T
Holliday, Ron – E
Holmes, Robert – B
Howard, Bob – B
Jones, Clint – B
Jones, "Deacon" – E
Lazetich, Pete – E, LB
LeVias, Jerry – E

McGee, Willie – B, E
Mauck, Carl – C
Norman, Pettis – E
Owens, Terry – T
Parris, Gary – E
Partee, Dennis – K
Redman, Rick – LB
Rice, Floyd – LB
Rogers, Mel – LB
Rossovich, Tim – LB
Salter, Bryant – B
Smith, Ron – B
Snowden, Cal – E
Stratton, Mike – LB
Sweeney, Walt – G
Thaxton, Jim – E
Thomas, Bob – B
Unitas, John – Q
Washington, Russ – T
Wenzel, Ralph – G
Wersching, Ray – K
Wilkerson, Doug – G
Williams, Dave – E
Wojcik, Greg – T

1973 SAN FRANCISCO 49ERS (NFC)
Coach – Dick Nolan
4th – Western Div., 5–9–0

Abramowicz, Dan – E
Atkins, Dave – B
Banaszek, Cas – T
Barrett, Jean – T

Beisler, Randy – G
Belk, Bill – E
Bettiga, Mike – E
Beverly, Ed – E

Blue, Forrest – C
Brodie, John – Q
Cunningham, Doug – B
Gossett, Bruce – K
Hall, Windlan – B
Hardman, Cedrick – E
Hardy, Ed – G
Harper, Willie – LB
Hart, Tommy – E
Hoskins, Bob – T
Hunt, Charlie – LB
Isenbarger, John – E
Jackson, Randy – B
Johnson, Jimmy – B
Krueger, Charlie – T
Krueger, Rolf – E, T
Kwalick, Ted – E
McGill, Ralph – B
Nunley, Frank – LB

Olerich, Dave – LB
Peoples, Woody – G
Phillips, Mel – B
Reed, Joe – Q
Rohde, Len – T
Schreiber, Larry – B
Simpson, Mike – B
Sniadecki, Jim – LB
Spurrier, Steve – Q
Taylor, Bruce – B
Thomas, Jimmy – B
Vanderbundt, "Skip" – LB
Washington, Gene – E
Washington, Vic – B
Watson, John – G, T
Wilcox, Dave – LB
Willard, Ken – B
Witcher, Dick – E
Wittum, Tom – K

1973 WASHINGTON REDSKINS (NFC)
Coach – George Allen
2nd – Eastern Div., 10–4–0
(Lost to Minnesota, 27–20, in NFC Playoffs)

Bass, Mike – B
Biggs, Verlon – E
Bragg, Mike – K
Brown, Larry – B
Brundige, Bill – T
Brunet, Bob – B
Duncan, "Speedy" – B
Fischer, Pat – B
Grant, Frank – E
Hanburger, Chris – LB
Hancock, Mike – E
Harraway, Charley – B
Hauss, Len – C
Hermeling, Terry – T
Holman, Willie – E
Houston, Ken – B
Hull, Mike – B
Hyatt, Fred – E
Jefferson, Roy – E
Jones, Jimmie – E
Jurgensen, "Sonny" – Q
Kilmer, Billy – Q
Knight, Curt – K
Laaveg, Paul – G

McDole, Ron – E
McLinton, Harold – LB
Malinchak, Bill – E
Mul-Key, Herb – B
Owens, Brig – B
Pergine, John – LB
Pottios, Myron – LB
Reed, Alvin – E
Robinson, Dave – LB
Rock, Walter – T
Ryczek, Dan – C
Schoenke, Ray – G, T
Sistrunk, Manuel – T
Smith, Jerry – E
Starke, George – T
Stone, Ken – B
Talbert, Diron – T
Taylor, Charley – E
Thomas, Duane – B
Tillman, "Rusty" – LB
Vactor, Ted – B
Wilbur, John – G
Willis, Larry – B

TITLES: Miami defeated the Oakland Raiders, 27-10, for the American Football Conference Championship. The Divisional Playoffs saw Miami beating Cincinnati, 34-16, while Oakland defeated the fourth qualifier, Pittsburgh, by a score of 33-14.

The National Football Conference Championship game was won by Minnesota, 27-10, over the Dallas Cowboys. In the Playoffs, Minnesota defeated Washington, the fourth qualifier, by a score of 27-20. Dallas beat Los Angeles, 27-16, for a shot at the title.

Super Bowl Eight was won for the second straight year by the Miami Dolphins over Minnesota, 24-7.

AFC LEADERS: Scoring—Roy Gerela (Pittsburgh Steelers) 123; Rushing—O. J. Simpson (Buffalo) 2,003 yds.; Passing—Ken Stabler (Oakland); Pass Receiving—Fred Willis (Houston) 57; Field Goals—Roy Gerela (Pittsburgh) 29; Punting—Jerrel Wilson (Kansas City) 45.5 yds. ave.; Interceptions—Dick Anderson (Miami) 8.

NFC LEADERS: Scoring—David Ray (Los Angeles) 130; Rushing—John Brockington (Green Bay) 1,144 yds.; Passing—Roger Staubach (Dallas); Pass Receiving—Harold Carmichael (Philadelphia) 67; Field Goals—David Ray (Los Angeles) 30; Punting—Tom Wittum (San Francisco) 43.7 yds. ave.; Interceptions—Bob Bryant (Minnesota) 7.

FIRST DRAFT: AFC—John Matuszak (Tampa), defensive end, by Houston, signed by Houston. NFC—Bert Jones (LSU), quarterback, draft choice to AFC Baltimore from New Orleans, signed by Baltimore.

COACHES: Two AFC teams replaced coaches. Sid Gillman took over for Bill Peterson in Houston on Oct. 15, 1973. Ron Waller replaced Harland Svare on Nov. 5, 1973, for San Diego.

HALL OF FAME: This year's inductees into the Hall of Fame are: Raymond Berry, Jim Parker, and Joe Schmidt.

NOTES: Buffalo's O. J. Simpson set one season rushing records of: 2,003 yards, first player to go over 2,000 yards and exceeding Jim Brown's record of 1,863 yds. accomplished in 1963; most rushes, 332; most games 100 or more yards, 11; most games 200 or more yards, 3.

John Brockington, Green Bay, has broken 1,000 yards rushing in each of his 3 years in NFL, only player to do so.

New League ruling permitting "unlimited moves in 1973" for active and inactive members.

Jim Thorpe Trophy to O. J. Simpson, Buffalo, plus AFC Player of the Year. John Hadl of Los Angeles took NFC Player of the Year honors. Rookie of the Year won by Charles "Booby" Clark, Cin. (AFC) and Chuck Foreman, Minn. (NFC), both offense.

Weeb Ewbank, New York Jets head coach, plans to retire after this season— 20 years.

New Stadium for Buffalo Bills—Rich Stadium at Orchard Park, N. Y., 80,000 seats.

New York Giants divided their season between Yankee Stadium and Yale Bowl, New Haven, Conn., while new stadium being built.

1974

NATIONAL FOOTBALL LEAGUE

NATIONAL CONFERENCE

WESTERN DIVISION

	W.	L.	T.	Pct.
Los Angeles	10	4	0	.714
San Francisco	6	8	0	.429
New Orleans	5	9	0	.357
Atlanta	3	11	0	.214

CENTRAL DIVISION

	W.	L.	T.	Pct.
Minnesota	10	4	0	.714
Detroit	7	7	0	.500
Green Bay	6	8	0	.429
Chicago	4	10	0	.286

EASTERN DIVISION

	W.	L.	T.	Pct.
St. Louis	10	4	0	.714
Washington*	10	4	0	.714
Dallas	8	6	0	.571
Philadelphia	7	7	0	.500
New York Giants	2	12	0	.143

* Washington was beaten twice by St. Louis during the regular season, so St. Louis was awarded the division championship. However, Washington gained the wild card or fourth playoff spot.

AMERICAN CONFERENCE

WESTERN DIVISION

	W.	L.	T.	Pct.
Oakland	12	2	0	.857
Denver	7	6	1	.536
Kansas City	5	9	0	.357
San Diego	5	9	0	.357

CENTRAL DIVISION

	W.	L.	T.	Pct.
Pittsburgh	10	3	1	.750
Cincinnati	7	7	0	.500
Houston	7	7	0	.500
Cleveland	4	10	0	.286

EASTERN DIVISION

	W.	L.	T.	Pct.
Miami	11	3	0	.786
Buffalo*	9	5	0	.643
New England	7	7	0	.500
New York Jets	7	7	0	.500
Baltimore	2	12	0	.143

* Buffalo was awarded the fourth playoff spot.

1974 AFC Championship

Pittsburgh 24; Oakland 13

The Pittsburgh front four of Joe Greene, L. C. Greenwood, Ernie Holmes and Dwight White held Oakland to record low 29 yards rushing, while Franco Harris (111 yards and 2 TD's) and Rocky Bleier (98 yards) gave the Steelers a solid running attack. The Raiders were forced to pass, leading to inevitable interceptions. Defenders Jack Ham and J. T. Thomas each brought back passes for long returns which were followed by Pittsburgh touchdowns. Cliff Branch was the offensive standout for the losers, catching 9 passes for 186 yards and one score.

The first half ended in a tie, thanks to Steeler errors. A fumble and a long pass to Branch resulted in a 40-yard George Blanda field goal, while three Pittsburgh thrusts deep into Oakland territory produced only one three-pointer by Roy Gerela.

Oakland went ahead in the third quarter on a 38-yard Ken Stabler to Branch scoring pass, but Pittsburgh matched the 60-yard drive with one of their own, as Harris went over from 8 yards out. Ham's interception and 25-yard return to the Oakland nine was quickly followed by a fine TD pass from Terry Bradshaw to Lynn Swann. Oakland's next drive of 85 yards came up short and they had to settle for another Blanda field goal. Then Thomas's steal and 37-yard return was capped by a 21-yard score by Harris.

Pittsburgh	0	3	0	21	24
Oakland	3	0	7	3	13

Touchdowns: Pittsburgh, Harris 2, Swann; Oakland, Branch
Field Goals: Pittsburgh, Gerela; Oakland, Blanda 2
PATs: Pittsburgh, Gerela 3; Oakland, Blanda
Attendance: 53,515
Players' shares: Pittsburgh $8,500; Oakland $5,500

1974 NFC Championship

Minnesota 14; Los Angeles 10

Minnesota came out on top over Los Angeles in a game dominated by turnovers. The Rams lost three fumbles and suffered two interceptions, while the Vikings were intercepted once and fumbled five times, losing two.

Minnesota scored first in a 60-yard drive that featured three long passes by Fran Tarkenton. An 18-yarder to John Gilliam was sandwiched between two to Jim Lash, the second for 29 yards and a touchdown. Los Angeles came back with a 27-yard field goal by David Ray to trail at halftime 7-3.

The Rams lost a golden opportunity to go ahead in the third quarter. A 73-yard pass from James Harris to Harold Jackson gave Los Angeles a first and goal on the two, but a penalty on second and inches followed by an interception in the end zone stopped the Ram threat. The Vikings then drove the length of the field, scoring from inches away on a fourth down dive by Dave Osborn. Los Angeles came back with another long pass from Harris to Jackson, this time for a TD from 44 yards out. The Rams got the ball back with plenty of time left, but the Minnesota defense twice threw them for losses and L. A. was forced to punt. The Vikings were then able to run out the final five minutes to preserve their victory.

Los Angeles	0	3	0	7	10
Minnesota	0	7	0	7	14

Touchdowns: Minnesota, Lash, Osborn; Los Angeles, Jackson
Field Goal: Los Angeles, Ray
PAT's: Minnesota, Cox 2; Los Angeles, Ray
Attendance: 47,404
Players' shares: Minnesota $8,500; Los Angeles $5,500

1974 Super Bowl

Pittsburgh 16; Minnesota 6

After 42 years as owner of the Steelers, Art Rooney was rewarded with his first championship. The Steelers, led by Franco Harris, crushed the Vikings, with a 333 to 119 mark in total offense. Harris set Super Bowl records of 158 yards rushing and 34 attempts, and tied the mark for playoff touchdowns in a season with his sixth. The Pittsburgh defense held Minnesota to an incredible 17 yards rushing. Still, Minnesota stayed close throughout the game, and might have won except for glaring mistakes by its veteran offense.

The Steelers clung to a slim 2-0 lead after the first half, even though they clearly dominated the statistics. Pittsburgh's safety came when Fran Tarkenton recovered his own botched handoff in the end zone to prevent a Steeler TD. Near the end of the half, a Viking drive seemed headed for a score when Tarkenton hit John Gilliam with a pass close to the goal line. But Glen Edwards popped the ball out of Gilliam's hands with a vicious block just as he made the catch and Mel Blount intercepted.

There was more bad news for Minnesota as the second half began. Roy Gerela slipped as he hit the kickoff and the ball dribbled down the field. But Viking veteran Bill Brown was unable to find the handle and Pittsburgh recovered. Harris scored four plays later, a 9-yard run, to put the Steelers on top 9-0. The Vikings came back with the aid of a fumble and pass interference penalty to have a first and goal on the Steeler five, but Chuck Foreman promptly fumbled and Joe Greene recovered. Minnesota scored anyway, though, as Pittsburgh was unable to move and was forced to punt. The Vikings stormed Bobby Walden, with Matt Blair's block of the punt caught for an easy TD by Terry Brown. But then Fred Cox missed the conversion attempt.

The Steelers wrapped up the game with a 66-yard scoring drive which involved a controversial play. Pittsburgh quarterback Terry Bradshaw, who played a fine game, completed a crucial third-down pass for 30 yards to Larry Brown. Brown's apparent fumble, that was recovered by Minnesota, was ruled to be after the whistle. The Steelers went on to score with another Bradshaw-to-Brown pass, this one for four yards. The final two Viking drives were stopped by an interception and the second half gun.

Pittsburgh	0	2	7	7	16
Minnesota	0	0	0	6	6

Touchdowns: Pittsburgh, Harris, L. Brown; Minnesota, T. Brown
PAT's: Pittsburgh, Gerela 2
Attendance: 80,997
Players' shares: Pittsburgh $15,000; Minnesota $7,500

RETIRED PLAYERS

Lionel Aldridge, defensive end, Green Bay Packers and San Diego Chargers—11 years.

John Brodie, quarterback, San Francisco 49ers—17 years.

Dick Butkus, middle linebacker, Chicago Bears—9 years.

Dave Herman, guard, New York Jets—10 years.

Gene Hickerson, guard, Cleveland Browns —16 years.

Charlie Krueger, defensive tackle, San Francisco 49ers—15 years.

Greg Larsen, offensive lineman, New York Giants—13 years.

Mike Lucci, middle linebacker, Cleveland Browns and Detroit Lions—12 years.

Johnny Roland, running back, St. Louis Cardinals and New York Giants—8 years.

Johnny Unitas, quarterback, Baltimore Colts and San Diego Chargers—18 years.

DEATHS

Anderson, Dr. Edward N., end, 1922-26 Rochester, Chicago Cardinals, Bears and Bulls and longtime college coach, on April 26, 1974.

Cabrelli, Lawrence, end, 1941-47 Philadelphia Eagles, on June 5, 1974.

Celeri, Robert L., back, 1951-52 New York Yanks and Dallas Texans, on March 9, 1975.

Duggan, Gilford R., tackle, 1940-47 New York Giants, Chicago Cardinals, Los Angeles Dons (AAFC) and Buffalo Bills (AAFC), on October 18, 1974.

Feldhaus, William T., tackle 1937-40 Detroit Lions, on June 2, 1974.

Filipowicz, Stephen C., back, 1945-46 New York Giants, also played major league baseball, on February 21, 1975.

Flanagan, Dr. William, back, 1925-26 Pottsville, on February 3, 1975.

Gedman, Eugene, back, 1953-58 Detroit Lions, on August 19, 1974.

Geyer, Donald W., back, 1937 Cincinnati (AFL) on December 20, 1974.

Gillies, Frederick M., tackle, 1920-28 Chicago Cardinals, on May 8, 1974.

Harley, Charles W., back, 1921 Chicago Staleys on April 21, 1974.

Karas, Emil, linebacker, 1959-66 Washington Redskins and San Diego Chargers, on November 25, 1974.

Kuffel, Dr. Raymond, end, 1947-49 Buffalo and Chicago (AAFC), on December 22, 1974.

MacKinnon, Jacque, back, 1961-70 San

Diego Chargers and Oakland Raiders, on March 6, 1975.

Marone, Salvatore J., guard, 1943 New York Giants, on January 12, 1975.

McCafferty, Donald, end, 1946 New York Giants and coach Baltimore Colts and at the time of his death, Detroit Lions, on July 28, 1974.

McKeever, Edward C., coach, 1948 Chicago Rockets (AAFC), on September 12, 1974.

Meadows, Edward A., end, 1954-59 Chicago Bears, Pittsburgh Steelers, Philadelphia Eagles and Washington Redskins, on October 22, 1974.

Mishel, David, back, 1927 Providence Steamrollers, 1931 Cleveland Indians, on March 12, 1974.

Palm, Myron "Mike," quarterback, 1925–26 New York Giants, player-coach 1933 Cincinnati Reds, also coach of St. Louis 1934 and Brooklyn and Rochester (AFL) in 1936–37, on April 8, 1974.

Pearce, Walter, quarterback, 1920–25 Decatur and Chicago Staleys, Chicago Bears, Kenosha and Providence, on May 24, 1974.

Phelan, James, coach, 1948–49 Los Angeles Dons (AAFC) and 1952 Dallas Texans, on November 14, 1974.

Roderick, Benjamin, back 1923-27 Canton and Buffalo, in January 1975.

Rykovich, Julius, back 1947-53 Buffalo and Chicago (AAFC), Chicago Bears and Washington Redskins, on December 22, 1974.

Washington, Clyde, back, 1960-65 Boston Patriots and New York Jets (AFL), on December 29, 1974.

White, Paul G., back, 1947 Pittsburgh Steelers, on June 3, 1974.

Wycoff, Lee, tackle, 1923 St. Louis Browns, on April 30, 1974.

Wyland, Guido B., guard 1919–20 Rock Island Independents, on December 8, 1974.

TEAM ROSTERS

For each team, all players who were active at any time during the season are shown. Regular players at the 22 offensive and defensive positions are indicated by an asterisk. Players enclosed in parentheses did not appear in any games. Detailed position data is given, using the following abbreviations:

WR — Wide receiver
TE   — Tight end

OT   — Offensive tackle
G   — Guard
C   — Center
Q   — Quarterback
RB   — Running back

DE   — Defensive end
DT   — Defensive tackle
LB   — Linebacker
CB   — Cornerback
S   — Safety

K   — Placekicker
P   — Punter
KO   — Kickoff man

PR   — Punt return man
KR   — Kickoff return man
PKR — Punt and kickoff return man

1974 ATLANTA FALCONS (NFC)
Coach – Norm Van Brocklin, Marion Campbell (November 5th)
4th – Western Division, 3–11–0

Bailey, Larry – DT	*Malone, Art – RB
Bebout, Nick – OT	Manning, Rosie – DT
*Brezina, Greg – LB	McGee, Molly – RB
*Brown, Ray – S	McQuilken, Kim – QB
*Burrow, Ken – WR	Mailik, Larry – TE
Byas, Rick – CB	Mike-Mayer, Nick – K
Childs, Henry – TE	Miller, Jim – G
*Dodd, Al – WR, PR	*Mitchell, Jim – TE
Easterling, Ray – S	Mitchell, Ken – LB
*Ellis, Clarence – S	Neal, Louis – WR
Fritsch, Ted – C	*Nobis, Tommy – LB
Geredine, Tom – WR	Palmer, Dick – LB
*Gotshalk, Len – OT	Ray, Eddie – RB
*Hampton, Dave – RB	Ryczek, Paul – C
*Hansen, Don – LB	*Smith, Royce – G
*Havig, Dennis – G	Stanback, Haskel – RB
*Hayes, Tom – CB	Sullivan, Pat – QB
Holmes, Rudy – CB	*Tilleman, Mike – DT
*Humphrey, Claude – DE	Tinker, Gerald, WR, PKR
James, John – P	*Van Note, Jeff – C
Kendrick, Vince – RB	Walker, Chuck – DT
*Kunz, George – OT	Warwick, Lonnie – LB
*Lawrence, Rolland – CB	*Zook, John – DE
*Lee, Bob – QB	
*Lewis, Mike – DT	

1974 BALTIMORE COLTS (AFC)
Coach – Howard Schnellenberger, Joe Thomas (September 29th)
5th – Eastern Division, 2–12–0

Andrews, John – TE,RB	*Jones, Bert – QB
Bailey, Jim – DT	*Laird, Bruce – S,PKR
Barnes, Mike – DE	Lee, David – P
Berra, Tim – WR,PKR	Linhart, Toni – K
Bertuca, Tony – LB	*MacLeod, Tom – LB
*Carr, Roger – WR	Mayo, Ron – TE
*Chester, Raymond – TE	McCauley, Don – RB
*Collett, Elmer – G	*Mendenhall, Ken – C
*Cook; Fred – DE	*Mitchell, Lydell – RB
*Curtis, Mike – LB	*Munsey, Nelson – CB
Dickel, Dan – LB	Neal, Dan – C
Domres, Marty – QB	*Nelson, Dennis – OT
Doughty, Glenn – WR	Nettles, Doug – CB
*Dutton, John – DE	*Oldham, Ray – CB
*Ehrmann, Joe – DT	*Olds, Bill – RB
Hall, Randy – CB	Orduna, Joe – RB

Pratt, Robert – G
*Ressler, Glenn – G
Rhodes, Danny – LB
Rudnick, Tim – S
*Scott, Freddie – WR
Simonson, Dave – OT
Smith, Ollie – WR
Speyrer, Cotton – WR,
   PKR

*Taylor, David – OT
Troup, Bill – QB
Van Duyne, Bob – G
*Volk, Rick – S
*White, Stan – LB
Williams, Steve – DE
*Windauer, Bill – DT

*Wade, Charley – WR
Wheeler, Wayne – WR

*Williams, Perry – RB

1974 CINCINNATI BENGALS (AFC)
Coach – Paul Brown
2nd (tied) – Central Division, 7-7-0

Adams, Doug – LB
*Anderson, Ken – QB
*Avery, Ken – LB
*Beauchamp, Al – LB
Berry, Royce – DE
*Blackwood, Lyle – S
*Carpenter, Ron – DT
*Casanova, Tom – S, PR
Chandler, Al – TE
*Clark, Booby –RB
Clark, Wayne – QB
Coslet, Bruce – TE
*Curtis, Issac – WR
Davis, Charles – RB
Dressler, Doug – RB
*Elliott, Lenvil – RB
(Ernst, Mike – QB)
*Fest, Howard – G,C
Green, Dave – P,KO
Holland, Vern – OT
Jackson, Bernard, CB,S,
   KR
*Johnson, Bob – C
Johnson, Essex – RB
*Johnson, Ken –DE

*Joiner, Charlie – WR
Jolitz, Evan – LB
Jones, Bob – S
Kearney, Tim – LB
Kollar, Bill – DT
Koegel, Vic – LB
Lapham, Dave – OT
LeClair, Jim – LB
Maddox, Bob – DE
Matson, Pat – G
*Mayes, Rufus – OT
McDaniel, John – WR
Muhlmann, Horst – K
Myers, Chip – WR
*Parrish, Lemar – CB,
   PR
*Pritchard, Ron – LB
*Reid, Mike – DT
*Riley, Ken – CB
Sawyer, Ken – S
*Shinners, John – G
*Trumpy, Bob – TE
*Walters, Stan – OT
*White, Sherman – DE
Williams, Ed – RB

1974 BUFFALO BILLS (AFC)
Coach – Lou Saban
2nd – Eastern Division, 9-5-0
(Won wild card spot with best record of second-place AFC teams but lost to Pittsburgh 32-14 in first round of playoffs)

Adams, Bill – G
*Allen, Doug – LB
Bateman, Marv – P
*Braxton, Jim – RB
Cahill, Bill – S
Calhoun, Don – RB
Chandler, Bob – WR
*Cheyunski, Jim – LB
*Cornell, Bo – LB
Costa, Dave – DT
*Craig, Neal – S
Croft, Don – DE
*DeLamielleure, Joe – G
*Edwards, Earl – DE,DT
Fairley, Leonard – CB
*Ferguson, Joe – QB
*Foley, Dave – OT
Francis, Wallace – WR,
   KR
Gant, Reuben – TE
*Green, Don – OT
*Greene, Tony – S,CB
Hagen, Halvor – OT
*Harrison, Dwight – CB
Hayman, Gary – RB
*Hill, J. D. – WR
Hunter, Scott – QB
*James, Robert – CB

Jarvis, Bruce – C
Jenkins, Ed – RB
Jones, Spike – P
*Kadish, Mike – DT
Kampa, Bob – DE
Kern, Rex – S
Koy, Ted – TE
Krakau, Marv – LB
Leypoldt, John – K
Lewis, Rich – LB
Marangi, Gary – QB
*McKenzie, Reggie – G
Means, Dave – DE
*Montler, Mike – C,OT
Mosley, Wayne – RB
Nighswander, Nick – C
Parker, Willie – C,G
*Patulski, Walt – DE
Randolph, Al – CB
*Rashad, Ahmad – WR
*Seymour, Paul – TE
Skorupan, John – LB
Walker, Donnie – CB,PR
*Washington, Dave – LB
Watkins, Larry – RB
Yeats, Jeff – DT

Note – Buffalo used 3 linemen and 4 linebackers on
   defense

1974 CHICAGO BEARS (NFC)
Coach – Abe Gibron
4th – Central Division, 4-10-0

*Antoine, Lionel – OT
*Asher, Bob –OT
Barnes, Joe – QB
*Bryant, Waymond – LB
*Buffone, Doug – LB
*Chambers, Wally – DT
*Clemons, Craig – S
*Coady, Rich – C
Douglass, Bobby – QB
*Ellis, Allan – CB
Farmer, George – WR
Forrest, Tom – G
Gagnon, Dave – RB
Gallagher, Dave – DE
Garrett, Carl – RB
*Grandberry, Ken – RB,
   KR
*Gunn, Jimmy – LB
*Harris, Rich – DE
Harrison, Jim – RB
Haslerig, Clint – WR
Hill, Ike – WR,PR
Hoban, Mike – G,C
Hodgins, Norm – S
Hrivnak, Gary – DT
*Huff, Gary – QB

Hultz, Don – DT
Jackson, Randy – C,OT
*Janet, Ernie – G
*Kelly, Jim – TE
Kinney, Steve – OT
Knox, Bill – CB
Kosins, Gary – RB
*Lyle, Gary – S
Montgomery, Randy –
   CB
*Newton, Bob – G
*Osborne, Jim – DT
*Pagac, Fred – TE
Parsons, Bob – P,TE
Pifferini, Bob – LB
*Rather, Bo – WR
(Reynolds, Tom – WR)
Rives, Don – LB
Roder, Mirro – K
Scales, Hurles – CB
Taylor, Clifton – RB,
   KR
*Taylor, Joe – CB
*Tom, Mel – DE
Van Valkenburg, Pete –
   RB

1974 CLEVELAND BROWNS (AFC)
Coach – Nick Skorich
4th – Central Division, 4-10-0

*Adams, Pete – G
Aldridge, Allen – DE
Anderson, Preston – S
Andrews, Billy – LB
*Babich, Bob – LB
Barisich, Carl – DT
Brooks, Clifford – CB
Brown, Eddie – S
*Brown, Ken – RB
Cockroft, Don – K,P
Copeland, Jim – C
(Cureton, Will – QB)
*Darden, Tom – S,PR
Darrow, Barry – OT
DeLeone, Tom – C,G
*DeMarco, Bob – C
*Demarie, John – G
*Dieken, Doug – OT
Dunbar, Jubilee – WR
*Garlington, John – LB
Gartner, Chris – KO
George, Tim – WR
*Green, Van – CB
*Hall, Charles – LB
Hawkins, Ben – WR
*Holden, Steve – WR
Holloway, Glen – G

Hooker, Fair – WR
Hunt, Bob – RB
Hutchison, Chuck – G
Ilgenfritz, Mark – DE
*Johnson, Walter – DT
Lefear, Billy – RB, KR
Long, Mel – LB
McKay, Bob – OT
McKinnis, Hugh – RB
*Morin, Milt – TE
*Phipps, Mike – QB
*Pruitt, Greg – RB,PKR
(Richardson, Ernie –
   TE)
Richardson, Gloster –
   WR
*Roman, Nick – DE
Romaniszyn, Jim – LB
*Scott, Clarence – CB
Scott, Bo – RB
*Seifert, Mike – DE
*Sherk, Jerry – DT
Sipe, Brian – QB
*Sullivan, Dave – WR
*Sullivan, Gerry – OT
*Sumner, Walt – S
Thaxton, Jim – TE

1974 DALLAS COWBOYS (NFC)
Coach – Tom Landry
3rd – Eastern Division, 8-6-0

Arneson, Jim – G
*Barnes, Benny – CB,S
Barnes, Rodrigo – LB
Bateman, Marv – P
Carrell, Duane – P
*Cole, Larry – DE
Dennison, Doug – RB
*DuPree, Billy Joe – TE
*Edwards, Dave – LB
*FitzGerald, John – C

Fugett, Jean – TE
*Garrison, Walt – RB
*Green, Cornell – S
Gregory, Bill – DT
*Harris, Cliff – S,PR
Hayes, Bob – WR
Herrera, Efren – K
*Hill, Calvin – RB
Houston, William – WR
Howard, Ron – TE

Hutcherson, Ken – LB
Jones, Ed – DE
*Jordan, Lee Roy – LB
Killian, Gene – G
*Lewis, D. D. – LB
*Lilly, Bob – DT
Longley, Clint – QB
Manders, Dave – C
Martin, Harvey – DE
Morgan, Dennis – RB, PKR
Morton, Craig – QB
*Neely, Ralph – OT
Newhouse, Robert – RB
*Neiland, John – G
*Nye, Blaine – G

*Pearson, Drew – WR
Percival, Mac – K
Peterson, Cal – LB
*Pugh, Jethro – DT
*Renfro, Mel – CB
*Richards, Golden – WR
*Staubach, Roger – QB
Strayhorn, Les – RB
*Toomay, Pat – DE
Walker, Louie – LB
Walton, Bruce – OT
Washington, Mark – CB
Waters, Charlie – CB
*Wright, Rayfield – OT
Young, Charlie – RB

1974 DENVER BRONCOS (AFC)
Coach – John Ralston
2nd – Western Division, 7-6-1

*Alzado, Lyle – DE
*Armstrong, Otis – RB, KR
Arnold, LeFrancis – G
Brown, Boyd – TE
*Chavous, Barney – DE
Cindrich, Ralph – LB
Coleman, Steve – DE
Criter, Ken – LB
*Current, Mike – OT
Drougas, Tom – OT
*Duranko, Pete – DE
Goich, Dan – DT
Gradishar, Randy – LB
Graham, Tom – LB
*Grant, John – DT,DE
Greer, Charles – S,PR
*Hepburn, Lonnie – CB
*Howard, Paul – G
Hufnagel, John – QB
Jackson, Larron – G
*Jackson, Tom – LB
*Johnson, Charley – QB
Jones, Calvin – CB
Kampa, Bob – DT
*Keyworth, Jon – RB
Laskey, Bill – LB
Little, Floyd – RB

Lynch, Fran – RB
*Lyons, Tom – G
*Maples, Bobby – C
Masters, Billy – TE
*May, Ray – LB
*Minor, Claudie – OT
Montgomery, Marv – OT
*Moses, Haven – WR
*O'Malley, Jim – LB
*Odoms, Riley – TE
*Pitts, John – S
Ramsey, Steve – QB
Rizzo, Joe – LB
Ross, Oliver – RB
*Rowser, John – CB
Schnitker, Mike – G
Simmons, Jerry – WR
Simone, Mike – LB
Smith, Ed – DE
Smith, Paul – DT
Steele, Larry – P
Stowe, Otto – WR
*Thompson, Billy – S, KPR
Turner, Jim – K
Tyler, Maurice – S
*Van Heusen, Billy – WR,P

1974 DETROIT LIONS (NFC)
Coach – Rick Forzano
2nd – Central Division, 7-7-0

*Barney, Lem – CB
Blair, T. C. – TE
Bussey, Dexter – RB
Capria, Carl – S
Crosswhite, Leon – RB
Davis, Ben – CB
Dennis, Guy – G,C
*Flanagan, Ed – C
*Fretias, Rochne – OT
Frohbose, Bill – S
*Hand, Larry – DE
Hennigan, Mike – LB
Hooks, Jim – RB
Howard, Billy – DT
Jarvis, Ray – WR
*Jauron, Dick – S,PR
*Jessie, Ron – WR
*Johnson, Levi – CB
Jolley, Gordon – OT
Jones, Jimmie – RB,KR
*Kowalkowski, Bob – G
Landry, Greg – QB
*Laslavic, Jim – LB
Mann, Errol – K
*Mitchell, Jim – DT

*Munson, Bill – QB
*Naumoff, Paul – LB
O'Neil, Ed – LB
*Orvis, Herb – DT
*Owens, Steve – RB
Pickard, Bob – WR
Price, Ernie – DE
(Reed, Joe – QB)
Rothwell, Fred – C
*Sanders, Charlie – TE
*Sanders, Ken – DE
Small, John – LB,TE
*Taylor, Altie – RB
Thrower, Jim – S,CB
(Wakefield, Mark – WR)
*Walton, Chuck – G
*Walton, Larry – WR
*Weaver, Charlie – LB
Weaver, Herman – P
*West, Charlie – S,CB
White, Daryl – G
Wyatt, Doug – S
Wyche, Sam – QB
*Yarbrough, Jim – OT
Zofko, Mickey – RB

1974 GREEN BAY PACKERS (NFC)
Coach – Dan Devine
3rd – Central Division, 6-8-0

Acks, Ron – LB
Basinger, Mike – DT
*Brockington, John – RB
Brown, Aaron – DE
*Buchanon, Willie – CB
Carlson, Dean – QB
*Carr, Freddie – LB
*Carter, Jim – LB
Concannon, Jack – QB
Cooney, Mark – LB
Donohue, Mike – TE
*Ellis, Ken – CB
Fanucci, Mike – DE
*Gillingham, Gale – G
Goodman, Les – RB
*Hadl, John – QB
Hall, Charley – S,CB
Hayhoe, Bill – OT
Hefner, Larry – LB
*Hendricks, Ted – LB
*Hill, Jim – S
*Himes, Dick – OT
Jenke, Noel – LB
Krause, Larry – RB
*Lane, MacArthur – RB
Leigh, Charles – RB
Lueck, Bill – G
Marcol, Chester – K

Mason, Dave – S
*Matthews, Al – S
*McCarren, Larry – C
*McCoy, Mike – DT
*McGeorge, Rich – TE
Nystrom, Lee – OT
Odom, Steve – WR,PKR
*Okoniewski, Steve – DT
Payne, Ken – WR
Pureifory, Dave – DT
*Roche, Alden – DE
Schmitt, John – C
Schuh, Harry – OT
*Smith, Barry – WR
Smith, Barty – RB
Smith, Perry – CB
*Snider, Malcolm – G,OT
*Staggers, Jon – WR,PR
Tagge, Jerry – QB
Torkelson, Eric – RB
Van Dyke, Bruce – G
Van Valkenburg, Pete – RB
Wafer, Carl – DT,DE
Walker, Randy – P
Wicks, Bob – WR
*Williams, Clarence – DE
*Wortman, Keith – OT,G

1974 HOUSTON OILERS (AFC)
Coach – Sid Gillman
2nd (tied) – Central Division, 7-7-0

*Alexander, Willie – CB
*Alston, Mack – TE
Amundson, George – RB
*Atkins, Bob – S
*Benson, Duane – LB
*Bethea, Elvin – DE
Beverly, David – P
*Bingham, Greg – LB
Broadnax, Jerry – TE
*Burrough, Ken – WR
Butler, Skip – K
Carroll, Ronnie – DT
Charles, John – S
Cindrich, Ralph – LB
Coleman, Ronnie – RB
Cowlings, Al – LB
*Culp, Curley – DT
Davis, Marvin – LB
Dickey, Lynn – QB
*Drungo, Elbert – OT
Fairley, Leonard – CB
Fisher, Ed – DT
(Foote, James – QB)
Freelon, Solomon – G
*Goodman, Brian – G
Gresham, Bob – RB
Hoaglin, Fred – C

Hunt, Kevin – OT
Johnson, Al – S
*Johnson, Billy – WR, PKR
Jones, Harris – G
*Kiner, Steve – LB
Kirk, Ernie – DT
*Maxwell, Tom – S
McCollum, Jim – DT
Montgomery, Mike – WR
*Moore, Zeke – CB
Parks, Billy – WR
*Pastorini, Don – QB
Queen, Jeff – RB
Roberts, Guy – LB
*Rodgers, Willie – RB
*Sampson, Greg – OT
*Saul, Ron – G
Severson, Jeff – CB
*Smith, Sid – C
*Smith, Tody – DE
*Washington, Ted – LB
*Washington, Vic – RB
Wells, Terry – RB
White, Jim – DE
Whittington, C. L. – RB
Willis, Fred – RB

Note – Houston used 3 linemen and 4 linebackers on defense

1974 KANSAS CITY CHIEFS (AFC)
Coach – Hank Stram
3rd (tied) – Western Division, 5-9-0

*Allen, Nate – CB
*Bell, Bobby – LB
Briggs, Robert – DE
Brunson, Larry – WR, PR

*Buchanan, Buck – DT
*Budde, Ed – G
Butler, Gary – TE
Carlson, Dean – QB
Condon, Tom – G

Culp, Curley – DT
*Daney, George – G
*Dawson, Len – QB
DeBernardi, Fred – DE
Drougas, Tom – OT
Ellison, Willie – RB
*Getty, Charlie – OT
Graham, Tom – LB
*Green, Woody – RB
Hamilton, Andy – WR
Hayes, Wendell – RB
Hill, Dave – OT
Humphrey, Tom – C,OT
Jaynes, Dave – QB
Jones, Doug – S
*Kearney, Jim – S
Keating, Tom – DT
Kinney, Jeff – RB
*Lanier, Willie – LB
Livingston, Mike – QB
*Lynch, Jim – LB
Marsalis, Jim – CB
*Matuszak, John – DT
Miller, Cleophus – RB, KR

Morris, Donnie Joe – RB
*Nicholson, Jim – OT
Osley, Willie – CB
Palewicz, Al – LB
Pearson, Barry – WR
Peay, Francis – OT
*Podolak, Ed – RB,PR
Reardon, Kerry – CB,S
*Rudnay, Jack – C
*Sensibaugh, Mike – S
Stenerud, Jan – K
Strada, John – DE
*Stroud, Morris – TE
*Taylor, Otis – WR
*Thomas, Bill – RB,KR
*Thomas, Emmitt – CB
Thornbladh, Bob – LB
*Upshaw, Marvin – DE
Walton, Wayne – G,OT
Werner, Clyde – LB
Wilson, Jerrel – P
*Wright, Elmo – WR
*Young, Wilbur – DE

Leigh, Charles – RB
*Little, Larry – G
*Malone, Benny – RB
*Mandich, Jim – TE
*Matheson, Bob – LB
Moore, Maulty – DT
*Moore, Nat – WR,KR
Moore, Wayne – OT
Morrall, Earl – QB
Morris, Mercury – RB
Mumphord, Lloyd – CB
*Newman, Ed – G
Nottingham, Don – RB

Reese, Don – DE,DT
*Scott, Jake – S,PR
Seiple, Larry – P,TE
*Stanfill, Bill – DE
Strock, Don – QB
Stuckey, Henry – CB
Swift, Doug – LB
Twilley, Howard – WR
*Warfield, Paul – WR
White, Jeris – DB
Wickert, Tom – OT
Yepremian, Garo – K

1974 MINNESOTA VIKINGS (NFC)
Coach – Bud Grant
1st – Central Division, 10–4–0
(Beat St. Louis 30–14 in first round of NFC play-offs and beat Los Angeles 14–10 in NFC Championship Game, but lost to Pittsburgh (AFC) 16–6 in Super Bowl)

1974 LOS ANGELES RAMS (NFC)
Coach – Chuck Knox
1st – Western Division, 10–4–0
(Beat Washington 19–10 in first round of NFC playoffs and lost to Minnesota 14–10 in NFC Championship Game)

Baker, Tony – RB
*Bertelsen, Jim – RB
*Brooks, Larry – DT
Bryant, Cullen – RB, KPR
Burke, Mike – P
Cappelletti, John – RB
Chapple, Dave – P
*Clark, Al – CB
*Cowan, Charlie – OT
Curran, Pat – TE
Curry, Bill – C
Drake, Bill – S, CB
*Dryer, Fred – DE
*Elmendorf, Dave – S,PR
*Geddes, Ken – LB
Hadl, John – QB
*Harris, James – QB
Horton, Greg – G
*Iman, Ken – C
*Jackson, Harold – WR
Jaworski, Ron – QB
Jones, Cody – DE, DT
Josephson, Les – RB
*Klein, Bob – TE
*Mack, Tom – G
*McCutcheon, Lawrence – RB

McGee, Willie – WR,KR
McMillan, Eddie – CB
Milan, Don – QB
Nelson, Bill – DT
Nelson, Terry – TE
*Olsen, Merlin – DT
Olsen, Phil – DT
Peterson, Jim – LB
Plummer, Tony – S
Preece, Steve – S
Ray, David – K
Rentzel, Lance – WR
*Reynolds, Jack – LB
*Robertson, Isiah – LB
Saul, Rich – C,G
*Scibelli, Joe – G
Scribner, Rob – RB
*Simpson, Bill – S
*Snow, Jack – WR
Spencer, Maurice – S
Stein, Bob – LB
Stokes, Tim – OT
*Stukes, Charlie – CB
*Williams, John – OT
*Youngblood, Jack – DE
Youngblood, Jim – LB

Alderman, Grady, – OT
Anderson, Scott – C
Berry, Bob – QB
Blahak, Joe – CB
Blair, Matt – LB
Boone, David – DE
Brown, Bill – RB
Brown, Terry – S
Bryant, Bob – CB
Chealander, Hal – QB
Cox, Fred – K
Craig, Steve – TE
Eischeid, Mike – P
*Eller, Carl – DE
*Foreman, Chuck – RB
*Gilliam, John – WR
*Goodrum, Charles – OT
*Hilgenberg, Wally – LB
Holland, John – WR
Kingsriter, Doug – TE
*Krause, Paul – S
Larsen, Gary – DT
*Lash, Jim – WR
Lawson, Steve – G
Lurtsema, Bob – DE,DT
Marinaro, Ed – RB
*Marshall, Jim – DE

Marshall, Larry – S
Martin, Amos – LB
*Maurer, Andy – G
McClanahan, Brent – RB,KR
McCullum, Sam – WR, KPR
McNeill, Fred – LB
*Osborn, Dave – RB
*Page, Allen – DT
Poltl, Randy – S
Reed, Oscar – RB
Riley, Steve – OT
*Siemon, Jeff – LB
Sunde, Milt – G
*Sutherland, Doug – DT
*Tarkenton, Fran – QB
*Tingelhoff, Mick – C
*Voight, Stu – TE
*Wallace, Jackie – CB, PR
*White, Ed – G
*Winston, Roy – LB
*Wright, Jeff – S,CB
*Wright, Nate – CB
*Yary, Ron – OT

1974 NEW ENGLAND PATRIOTS (AFC)
Coach – Chuck Fairbanks
3rd (tied) – Eastern Division, 7–7–0

1974 MIAMI DOLPHINS (AFC)
Coach – Don Shula
1st – Eastern Division, 11–3–0
(Lost to Oakland 28–26, in first round of AFC playoffs)

*Anderson, Dick – S
Babb, Charlie – S
Baker, Melvin – WR
Ball, Larry – LB
Bannon, Bruce – LB
Briscoe, Marlin – WR
*Buoniconti, Nick – LB
Crowder, Randy – DT
Crusan, Doug – OT
*Csonka, Larry – RB
*Den Herder, Vern – DE
*Evans, Norm – OT
*Fernandez, Manny – DT

Fleming, Marv – TE
*Foley, Tim – CB
Funchess, Tom – OT
Ginn, Hubert – RB,KR
Goode, Irv – C,G
*Griese, Bob – QB
*Heinz, Bob – DT
*Johnson, Curtis – CB
Kiick, Jim – RB
Kolen, Mike – LB
*Kuechenberg, Bob – OT, G
*Langer, Jim – C

Adams, Bob – TE
*Adams, Julius – DE
*Adams, Sam – G
Ashton, Josh – RB
Barnes, Bruce – P
Barnes, Rodrigo – LB
*Bolton, Ron – CB
Carter, Kent – LB
Chapple, Dave – P
Clark, Gail – LB
*Cunningham, Sam – RB
Damkroger, Maury – LB
Dulac, Bill – G
Dumler, Doug – C
Durko, Sandy – S
Foster, Will – LB
Gallaher, Allen – OT
Geddes, Bob – LB
Gonzales, Noe – RB
Graff, Neil – QB
*Gray, Leon – OT
*Hamilton, Ray – DT
*Hannah, John – G
Hanneman, Craig – DE

*Herron, Mack – RB, PKR
Hinton, Eddie – WR
*Hunt, Sam – LB
Jenkins, Ed – RB
Johnson, Andy – WR, RB,KR
*King, Steve – LB
*Lenkatis, Bill – C
*Lunsford, Mel – DE
Marshall, Al – WR
Massey, Jim – CB
*McCray, Prentice – S
McCurry, Dave – S
McGee, Tony – DE
*Mildren, Jack – S
Moore, Arthur – DT
Morris, Jon – C
*Nelson, Steve – LB
*Neville, Tom – OT
Osley, Willie – CB
*Plunkett, Jim – QB
Pope, Ken – CB
*Rucker, Reggie – WR

*Sanders, John – CB,S
Schubert, Steve – WR
Shiner, Dick – QB
Smith, Donnell – DE
Smith, John – K
Stingley, Darryl – WR
Sweet, Joe – WR

Tanner, John – LB
Tarver, John – RB
*Vataha, Randy – WR
*Webster, George – LB
Wilson, Joe – RB
*Windsor, Bob – TE

Note – New England used 3 linemen and 4 line-backers on defense

1974 NEW ORLEANS SAINTS (NFC)
Coach – John North
3rd – Western Division, 5-9-0

Baumgartner, Steve – DE
Beasley, John – TE
Blanchard, Tom – P
Boyd, Greg – S
Butler, Bill – RB
Childs, Henry – TE
Cipa, Larry – QB
Coleman, Don – LB
*Colman, Wayne – LB
Davis, Dave – WR
DeGrenier, Jack – RB
*Didion, John – C
Dorris, Andy – DE
Farasopoulos, Chris – S
*Federspiel, Joe – LB
Fersen, Paul – OT
*Fuller, Johnny – S
Garrett, Len – TE
Gibbs, Donnie – P
Havrilak, Sam – WR
*Jackson, Ernie – CB
Kingrea, Rick – LB
*Kupp, Jake – G
Laporta, Phil – OT
Lawson, Odell – RB
Lee, Bivian – CB
*Manning, Archie – QB
Maurer, Andy – G
*Maxson, Alvin – RB
McClard, Bill – K

McCullouch, Earl – WR
McNeill, Rod – RB
*Merlo, Jim – LB
Middleton, Richard – LB
*Moore, Derland – DT
Moore, Jerry – S
Mooring, John – OT
*Morrison, Don – OT
*Myers, Tom – S
*Newland, Bob – WR
*Newsome, Billy – DE
Owens, Joe – DE
*Parker, Joel – WR
*Phillips, Jess – RB
*Pollard, Bob – DT
*Price, Elex – DT
Rasley, Rocky – G
Reaves, Ken – CB
*Schmidt, Terry – CB
Scott, Bobby – QB
*Seal, Paul – TE
Spencer, Maurice – S
Stevens, Howard – RB, PKR
Thomas, Speedy – WR
*Thompson, Dave – OT,G
Wicks, Bob – WR
Williams, Richard – WR
*Zanders, Emanuel – G

1974 NEW YORK GIANTS (NFC)
Coach – Bill Arnsparger
5th – Eastern Division, 2-12-0

*Athas, Pete – CB,PR
Brooks, Bobby – CB
Chandler, Karl – C
Clune, Don – WR
Crist, Chuck – S
Crosby, Steve – RB
*Dawkins, Joe – RB
Del Gaizo, Jim – QB
Dvorak, Rick – DE
Enderle, Dick – G
*Gillette, Walker – WR
Glass, Chip – TE
Gogolak, Pete – K
*Gregory, Jack – DE
*Grim, Bob – WR
Hasenohrl, George – DT
Herrmann, Don – WR
*Hicks, John – G
Hill, John – OT
*Hilton, Roy – DE
Hornsby, Ron – LB
*Hughes, Pat – LB
*Hyland, Bob – C
Jackson, Honor – CB
Jacobson, Larry – DT
Jenkins, Ed – RB
Jennings, Dave – P

*Johnson, Ron – RB
*Kelley, Brian – LB
Kotar, Doug – RB,KR
*Lockhart, Spider – S
McQuay, Leon – RB,KR
*Mendenhall, John – DT
*Morton, Craig – QB
*Mullen, Tom – G
Pettigrew, Gary – DT
*Pietrzak, Jim – DT
*Powers, Clyde – S
Reed, Henry – LB
Rhodes, Ray – WR
(Rice, Andy – DT)
Selfridge, Andy – LB
Singletary, Bill – LB
Small, Eldridge – CB
Snead, Norm – QB
*Stienke, Jim – CB
Strada, John – TE
Summerell, Carl – QB
*Tucker, Bob – TE
*Van Horn, Doug – OT
*Van Pelt, Brad – LB
Wafer, Carl – DT
*Young, Willie – OT
Zofko, Mickey – RB

1974 NEW YORK JETS (AFC)
Coach – Charley Winner
3rd (tied) – Eastern Division, 7-7-0

Adamle, Mike – RB
Atkinson, Al – LB
*Baker, Ralph – LB
*Barkum, Jerome – WR
*Barzilauskas, Carl – DT
Bell, Ed – WR
Bernhardt, Roger – G
Bjorklund, Hank – RB
*Boozer, Emerson – RB
Brister, Willie – TE
Browne, Gordie – OT
Burns, Bob – RB
*Caster, Richard – TE
Demory, Bill – QB
*Ebersole, John – LB
Ferguson, Bill – LB
*Galigher, Ed – DE
Gantt, Greg – P
*Hill, Winston – OT
Howell, Delles – CB
Howfield, Bobby – K
Jackson, Clarence – RB
Kindig, Howard – C
*Knight, David – WR
Koegel, Warren – C
Leahy, Pat – K

Lewis, Rich – LB
Little, John – DE,DT
*Lomas, Mark – DE
*Mulligan, Wayne – C
*Namath, Joe – QB
*Neal, Richard – DT,DE
*Owens, Burgess – S
Owens, Marv – WR
Piccone, Lou – WR,KR
*Puetz, Garry – G
*Rasmussen, Randy – G
Reese, Steve – LB
*Riggins, John – RB
*Rivers, Jamie – LB
Roach, Travis – G
Schmiesing, Joe – DE, DT
*Sowells, Rich – CB
Tannen, Steve – S,CB
Thomas, Earlie – CB
(Turk, Godwin – LB)
*Wise, Phil – S
Woodall, Al – QB
Woods, Larry – DT
*Woods, Robert – OT
*Word, Roscoe, CB,PR

1974 OAKLAND RAIDERS (AFC)
Coach – John Madden
1st – Western Division, 12-2-0
(Beat Miami 28-26 in first round of AFC playoffs, and lost to Pittsburgh 24-13 in AFC Championship Game)

*Atkinson, George – S
Banaszak, Pete – RB
Bankston, Warren – RB, TE
*Biletnikoff, Fred – WR
Blanda, George – K
Bradshaw, Morris – WR
*Branch, Cliff – WR
Brown, Willie – CB
*Buehler, George – G
Casper, Dave – TE
Cline, Tony – DE
*Conners, Dan – LB
Dalby, Dave – C,G
*Davis, Clarence – RB
Dennery, Mike – LB
Guy, Ray – P
Hart, Harold – RB,KR
*Hubbard, Marv – RB
Hudson, Bob – RB
*Irons, Gerald – LB
Jakowenko, George – KO
Johnson, Monte – LB
*Jones, Horace – DE
Korver, Kelvin – DT

Lamonica, Daryle – QB
Lawrence, Henry – OT
Lawrence, Larry – QB
Medlin, Dan – G
*Moore, Bob – TE
*Otto, Jim – C
Pitts, Frank – WR
Prout, Bob – S
*Shell, Art – OT
Siani, Mike – WR
*Sistrunk, Otis – DT
*Smith, Bubba – DE
Smith, Charlie – RB
Smith, Ron – S,PKR
*Stabler, Ken – QB
*Tatum, Jack – S
*Thomas, Skip – CB
*Thoms, Art – DT
*Upshaw, Gene – G
vanEeghen, Mark – RB
*Vella, John – OT
*Villapiano, Phil – LB
Warren, Jimmy – S
Weaver, Gary – LB
*Wilson, Nemiah – CB

1974 PHILADELPHIA EAGLES (NFC)
Coach – Mike McCormack
4th – Eastern Division, 7-7-0

Bailey, Tom – RB
*Bergey, Bill – LB
Boryla, Mike – QB
*Bradley, Bill – S,PR,P
Bulaich, Norm – RB
*Bunting, John – LB
Cagle, Jim – DT
*Carmichael, Harold – WR
Chesson, Wes – WR

Cullars, Willie – DE
Dempsey, Tom – K
Dobbins, Herb – OT
*Dunstan, Bill – DT
Ford, Charlie – CB
*Gabriel, Roman – QB
Halverson, Dean – LB
Jackson, Randy – RB, KR
*James, Ron – RB,KR

*Jones, Joe – DE
Kersey, Merritt – P,RB
*Key, Wade – G
Kirksey, Roy – G
Kramer, Kent – TE
*Lavender, Joe – CB
LeMaster, Frank – LB
*Logan, Randy – S
Luken, Tom – G
Marshall, Larry – S, KR
*Morriss, Guy – C
*Nordquist, Mark – G
Oliver, Greg – RB
*Outlaw, John – CB
Parker, Artimus – S
*Patton, Jerry – DT

Pettigrew, Gary – DT
Picard, Bob – WR
Reaves, John – QB
Reeves, Marion – CB
Reilly, Kevin – LB
*Sisemore, Jerry – OT
Smith, Charles – WR
*Smith, Steve, OT
Stevens, Richard – OT
*Sullivan, Tom – RB
Sutton, Mitch – DT
*Wynn, Will – DE
*Young, Charles – TE
*Zabel, Steve – LB
*Zimmerman, Don – WR

Scales, Hurles – CB
Shaw, Dennis – QB
*Smith, Jackie – TE
Spencer, Maurice – S
*Stallings, Larry – LB
Stringer, Scott – CB
*Thomas, Earl – WR
*Thompson, Norm – CB

*Tolbert, Jim – S,CB
*Wehrli, Roger – CB
(Wenzel, Ralph – G)
Willard, Ken – RB
Withrow, Cal – C
*Yankowski, Ron – DE
*Young, Bob – G

1974 PITTSBURGH STEELERS (AFC)
Coach – Chuck Noll
1st – Central Division, 10–3–1
(Beat Buffalo 32–14 in first round of AFC playoffs,
beat Oakland 24–13 for AFC Championship and
beat Minnesota (NFC) 16–6 in Super Bowl)

Allen, Jim – CB
*Bleier, Rocky – RB
*Blount, Mel – CB
Bradley, Ed – LB
*Bradshaw, Terry – QB
*Brown, Larry – TE
*Clack, Jim – G,C
Conn, Richard – S
Davis, Charlie – DT
*Davis, Sam – G
Davis, Steve – RB,KR
Druschel, Rick – G,OT
*Edwards, Glen – S,PR
Fuqua, John – RB
Furness, Steve – DT,DE
Garrett, Reggie – WR
Gerela, Roy – K
Gilliam, Joe – QB
*Gravelle, Gordon – OT
*Greene, Joe – DT
*Greenwood, L. C. – DE
Grossman, Randy – TE
*Ham, Jack – LB
Hanratty, Terry – QB
*Harris, Franco – RB

Harrison, Reggie – RB
*Holmes, Ernie – DT
Kellum, Marv – LB
*Kolb, Jon – OT
*Lambert, Jack – LB
*Lewis, Frank – WR
*Mansfield, Ray – C
McMakin, John – TE
Mullins, Gerry – G,OT,
  TE
Pearson, Preston – RB,
  KR
Reavis, Dave – OT
*Russell, Andy – LB
*Shanklin, Ron – WR
Shell, Donnie – S,CB
Stallworth, John – WR
Swann, Lynn – WR,PR
*Thomas, J. T. – CB
Toews, Loren – LB
*Wagner, Mike – S
Walden, Bobby – P
Webster, Mike – C,G
*White, Dwight – DE
Wolf, Jim – DE

1974 ST. LOUIS CARDINALS (NFC)
Coach – Don Coryell
1st – Eastern Division, 10–4–0
(Cardinals had beaten Washington twice in regular
season games, thus breaking first place tie)
(Lost to Minnesota 30–14, in first round of NFC
playoffs)

Albert, Sergio – KO
Anderson, Donny – RB,
  P
*Arneson, Mark – LB
Bakken, Jim – K
Banks, Tom – C
*Barnes, Pete – LB
Bell, Bob – DT
Belton, Willie – RB
*Brahaney, Tom – C
*Brooks, Leo – DT
Butz, Dave – DT
Cain, J. V. – WR
Crum, Bob – DE
Crump, Dwayne – CB
*Dierdorf, Dan – OT
*Dobler, Conrad – G
Duren, Clarence – S
Finney, Roger – G,OT
George, Steve – DT
*Gray, Mel – WR

Hammond, Gary – WR,
  PKR
Harrison, Reggie – RB
*Hart, Jim – QB
Hartle, Greg – LB
Jones, Steve – RB
(Keithley, Gary – QB)
Kindle, Greg – OT
LeVeck, Jack – LB
McFarland, Jim – TE
*McMillan, Ernie – OT
*Metcalf, Terry – RB,
  PKR
Miller, Terry – LB
Moss, Eddie – RB
Neils, Steve – LB
*Otis, Jim – RB
Reaves, Ken – S
Roberts, Hal – P
*Rowe, Bob – DT
*Rudolph, Council – DE

1974 SAN DIEGO CHARGERS (AFC)
Coach – Tommy Prothro
3rd (tied) – Western Division, 5–9–0

*Anthony, Charles – LB
*Bacon, Coy – DE
Baylor, Raymond – DE
*Beauchamp, Joe – S
Beirne, Jim – WR
Berry, Reggie – S
Boatwright, Bon – DT
Bonner, Glen – RB
*Brown, Bob – DT
(Carr, Raymond – DT,
  DE)
Colbert, Danny – CB,
  PKR
*Davis, Harrison – WR
Douglas, Jay – C
Dunlap, Len – S,CB
Edwards, Cid – RB
*Fletcher, Chris – S
Forsberg, Fred – LB
*Fouts, Dan – QB
Fretias, Jesse – QB
*Garrison, Gary – WR
Gay, Blenda – DE
Gersnach, Carl – LB
*Goode, Dan – LB
Gordon, Dick – WR,PKR
*Gordon, Ira – G
Grannell, Dave – TE
Hoey, George – S, CB
Horn, Don – QB

*Howard, Bob – CB
*Lazetich, Pete – DE
Lee, Mike – LB
LeVias, Jerry – WR
Markovich, Mark – G
*Matthews, Bo – RB
*Mauck, Carl – C
Myrtle, Chip – LB
*Owens, Terry – OT
Parris, Gary – TE
Partee, Dennis – K
Paul, Harold – OT,G
*Rice, Floyd – LB
Rogers, Mel – LB
*Rowe, Dave – DT
Staggs, Jeff – LB
*Stewart, Wayne – TE
Teerlinck, John – DT,
  DE
Thaxton, Jim – TE
Thomas, Bob – RB
Thompson, Tommy –
  RB,KR
Tipton, Dave – DE
Vertfeuille, Brian – OT
*Washington, Russ – OT
Wersching, Ray – K
*Wilkerson, Doug – G
*Williams, Sam – CB
*Woods, Don – RB

1974 SAN FRANCISCO 49ERS (NFC)
Coach – Dick Nolan
2nd – Western Division, 6–8–0

*Abramowicz, Danny –
  WR
Atkins, Dave – RB
*Banaszek, Cas – OT
Barrett, Jean – C,OT
Beasley, Terry – WR
Beisler, Randy – G
*Belk, Bill – DT,DE
Belser, Caeser – LB
Bettiga, Mike – WR
*Blue, Forrest – C
Bragonier, Dennis – S
Fahnhorst Keith – OT
Gossett, Bruce – K
*Hall, Windlan – S
*Hardman, Cedrick – DE
*Harper, Willie – LB
*Hart, Tommy – DE
Hindman, Stan – DT
Hollas, Hugo – S
Holmes, Mike – CB,KR
*Hoskins, Bob – DT
Hull, Tom – LB
*Jackson, Wilbur – RB
*Johnson, Jimmy – CB
Johnson, Sammy – RB
Krueger, Rolf – DE,DT
Kwalick, Ted – TE

*McGill, Ralph – CB, PR
McKoy, Billy – LB
*Mitchell, Tom – TE
Moore, Manfred – RB,
  KR
Morrison, Dennis – QB
*Nunley, Frank – LB
*Owen, Tom – QB
Penchion, Bob – G,OT
*Peoples, Woody – G
Phillips, Mel – S
Raines, Mike – DE,DT
Randolph, Al – S
Reed, Joe – QB
*Rohde, Len – OT
Sandifer, Bill – DT
Saunders, John – S
*Schreiber, Larry – RB
Snead, Norm – QB
Spurrier, Steve – QB
*Taylor, Bruce – CB
Vanderbundt, Skip – LB
*Washington, Gene – WR
*Watson, John – G,OT
West, Robert – WR
*Wilcos, Dave – LB
Williams, Delvin – RB
Wittum, Tom – P,K

1974 WASHINGTON REDSKINS (NFC)
Coach – George Allen
2nd – Eastern Division, 10–4–0
(Redskins were beaten twice by St. Louis during regular season, so St. Louis was awarded the division championship. However, Washington qualified for the wild card playoff spot because of their best record of any NFC second-place team. Lost to Los Angeles 19–10 in first round of NFC playoffs)

*Bass, Mike – CB
Baughan, Maxie – LB
*Biggs, Verlon – DE
Bragg, Mike – P,K
*Brown, Larry – RB
*Brundige, Bill – DT
Cunningham, Doug – RB
*Denson, Moses – RB,KR
Duncan, Speedy – S
Dusek, Brad – LB
Evans, Charlie – RB
*Fischer, Pat – CB
Grant, Frank – WR
*Hanburger, Chris – LB
Hancock, Mike – TE
*Hauss, Len – C
*Houston, Ken – S
Hull, Mike – RB
Imhoff, Martin – DE
*Jefferson, Roy – WR
Johnson, Dennis – DT
Jones, Deacon – DE
Jones, Larry – CB,KR
Jurgensen, Sonny – QB
*Kilmer, Billy – QB
*Laaveg, Paul – G
Malinchak, Bill – WR
*McDole, Ron – DE

*McLinton, Harold – LB
Moseley, Mark – K
Mul-Key, Herb – RB, PKR
O'Dell, Stu – LB
*Owens, Brig – S
Pergine, John – LB
Reed, Alvin – TE
*Robinson, Dave – LB
Ryczek, Dan – C
Salter, Bryant – S
*Schoenke, Ray – OT,G
Sistrunk, Manny – DT
*Smith, Jerry – TE
Smith, Larry – RB
*Starke, George – OT
Stone, Ken – S
Sturt, Fred – G
*Sweeney, Walt – G
*Talbert, Diron – DT
*Taylor, Charley – WR
Theismann, Joe – QB, PR
Thomas, Duane – RB
Tillman, Russell – LB
Tyrer, Jim – OT
Varty, Mike – LB
Wilbur, John – G

TITLES: Pittsburgh defeated Oakland, 24–13, for the American Conference Championship. The Divisional Playoffs resulted in Pittsburgh beating Buffalo, 32–14 and Oakland topping Miami, 28–26. Thus Miami failed in its bid to win three straight Super Bowls, although the game with Oakland was the best of all the post-season games and could have easily gone to either team.

Minnesota repeated as National Conference Champions, edging Los Angeles, 14–10. Minnesota had earlier whipped St. Louis, 30–14, while Los Angeles had beaten Washington, 19–10.

Pittsburgh went on to defeat Minnesota in the Super Bowl, 16–6.

AFC LEADERS: Scoring—Roy Gerela (Pittsburgh Steelers) 93 points; Rushing—Otis Armstrong (Denver) 1,407 yards; Passing—Ken Anderson (Cincinnati Bengals); Pass Receiving—Lydell Mitchell (Baltimore Colts) 72 catches; Field Goals—Roy Gerela (Pittsburgh Steelers) 20; Punting—Ray Guy (Oakland Raiders) 42.2 yards average; Interceptions — Emmitt Thomas (Kansas City Chiefs) 12.

NFC LEADERS: Scoring—Chester Marcol (Green Bay Packers) 94 points; Rushing—Lawrence McCutcheon (Los Angeles Rams) 1,109 yards; Passing—Sonny Jurgensen (Washington Redskins); Pass Receiving—Charles Young (Philadelphia Eagles) 63 catches; Field Goals—Chester Marcol (Green Bay Packers) 25; Punting—Tom Blanchard (New Orleans Saints) 42.1 yards average; Interceptions—Ray Brown (Atlanta Falcons) 8.

FIRST DRAFT: Ed "Too Tall" Jones (Tennessee State), defensive end, drafted and signed by Dallas NFC (choice obtained from Houston AFC).

COACHES: Rick Forzano, assistant coach, was named to the Detroit Lions position after the death of Don McCafferty during training. For the Baltimore Colts, Howard Schnellenberger was fired on September 29, with General Manager Joe Thomas taking the spot. Norm Van Brocklin was fired as Atlanta Falcons head coach on November 5th, being replaced by assistant coach Marion Campbell.

HALL OF FAME: Selected in 1974 were Tony Canadeo, Bill George, Lou Groza, and Dick "Night Train" Lane.

NOTES: A number of major rules changes were made to increase scoring. The kickoff was moved back to the 35-yard line, the goal posts were moved to the back of the end zone, a missed field goal was returned to the line of scrimmage if beyond the 20, punt or field goal team members except for two ends could not go down field until the ball was kicked plus a number of other changes were made. The main result of these changes was to sharply lower the number of field goals. Scoring was virtually unchanged and punt returns were up slightly.

The maximum number of players on each roster during the season was increased to 47 for 1974 only. This was a result of the player strike, which forced cancellation of the College All-Star game and caused many veterans to miss most of the training period.

Ken Stabler of Oakland won the Jim Thorpe Trophy as Most Valuable Player. Jim Hart of St. Louis was named NFC Player of the Year. Don Woods of San Diego and Jack Lambert of Pittsburgh were named as top rookies.

3 The Players

HALL OF FAME

The **Pro Football Hall of Fame** represents America's most popular sport in a great number of colorful and exciting ways. Included in the modern three-building complex are three eye-catching exhibition areas, a football action movie theater, a research library, a bustling and popular gift shop, plus the twin enshrinement halls, where the greats of pro football are permanently honored. The Hall is located on Interstate 77 in Ganton and is open every day of the year.

1963 — Front row, left to right: "Dutch" Clark, "Curly" Lambeau, Mel Hein, John "Blood" McNally, Don Hutson; back row: Sam Baugh, "Cal" Hubbard, Bronko Nagurski, George Halas, "Red" Grange, Ernie Nevers. (AP Wirephoto.)

1964 — Front row, left to right: Clarke Hinkle, Ed Healey, "Mike" Michalske; back row: Art Rooney, Jim Conzelman, "Link" Lyman, George Trafton. (UPI Telephoto.)

1965 — Left to Right: Bob Waterfield, Guy Chamberlin, Dr. Daniel J. Fortmann, Sid Luckman, Otto Graham, Steve Van Buren, Paddy Driscoll.

1966 — Front Row (l. to r.) Hugh Ray, Jr., representing his father Hugh "Shorty" Ray, George McAfee, Bill Dudley, Joe Guyon.
Back Row (l. to r.) Arnie Herber, John Blood McNally representing Walt Kiesling, Clyde "Bulldog" Turner, Jim Lee Howell representing Steve Owen.

1967—Front row, left to right: Bobby Layne, Ken Strong, Paul Brown, Dan Reeves; back row: Chuck Bednarik, Emlen Tunnell, Joe Stydahar.

1968—FRONT ROW (l to r) Art Donovan, Marion Motley, Cliff Battles, Charles Trippi; Back Row Elroy Hirsch, Wayne Millner, Alex Wojciechowski.

1969—Left to right: Albert Glen "Turk" Edwards, Ernest Stautner, Leo Nomellini, Fletcher "Joe" Perry, and Earle "Greasy" Neale.

1970—Left to right: Hugh McElhenny, Jack Christiansen, Tom Fears, and Pete Pihos.

1971—Front row, left to right: Andy Robustelli, Y. A. Tittle, Norm Van Brocklin; back row: Vince Lombardi, held by Vince, Jr., Frank "Bruiser" Kinard, Bill Hewitt, held by his daughter, Mrs. Mary Ellen Cocozza, and Jimmy Brown.

1972—Left to right: Ace Parker, Ollie Matson, Gino Marchetti, and Lamar Hunt.

1973—Left to right: Raymond Berry, Jim Parker, and Joe Schmidt.

1974—Left to right: Tony Canadeo, Bill George, Lou Groza and Night Train Lane.

Named to the Hall of Fame:

PLAYERS

Clifford Battles (1968) Boston Braves 1932; Boston Redskins 1933-36; Washington Redskins 1937; #1 Rushing 1933 and 1937.

Samuel Baugh (1963). Quarterback, Back, Washington Redskins, 1937-52; Led league in passing, 1937, '40, '43, '45, '49; led league in punting 1940, '41-42, '43; led league in interceptions, 1943; led Redskins to five division titles, 1937, '40, '42, '43, '45; and to two world titles, 1937, '42; passed for six TDs one game (twice).

Charles Bednarik (1967). Center, linebacker, Philadelphia Eagles 1949-62.

Raymond Berry (1973). End for the Baltimore Colts from 1955-67. Led league in pass receiving from 1958-60. Tied with P. Retzlaff in 1958.

James "Jimmy" Brown (1971). Back for the Cleveland Browns from 1957-65. Led the league #1 Rushing, 1957-61, 63-65. Also #1 Scoring in 1958. An all-league player for eight years.

Roosevelt "Rosey" Brown (1975). Offensive tackle New York Giants 1953-65; Assistant Coach for the Giants 1966-70 and scout 1971-date. Named to the all-league team 8 years in a row 1956-63.

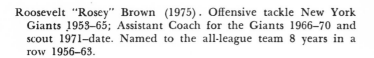

Anthony "Tony" Canadeo (1974). Back for the Green Bay
Packers from 1941 to 1952 except 1945 in military service.
Triple-threat single-wing tailback and then T-formation halfback. Used on punt and kickoff returns and also played
defensive back for first half of his career. Named to all-
league teams on two occasions.

Guy Chamberlin (1965). End Canton, 1921-23; Chicago Bears,
1921; Cleveland Bulldogs, 1924; Frankford Yellowjackets, 1925-
26; Chicago Cardinals, 1927-28. Player-coach on several teams.

John "Jack" Christiansen (1970). Defensive back, Detroit Lions,
1951-58. 1957 #1 Interceptions (tied with J. Butler & M. Davis)
Head coach San Francisco, 1963-67.

Earl "Dutch" Clark (1963). Quarterback Portsmouth Spartans,
1931-33, Detroit Lions, 1934-38; led league in scoring, 1932,
'35, '36; led league in field goals (dropkicks), 1932; head coach
of Cleveland Rams, 1939-42.

George Connor (1975). Offensive tackle and defensive linebacker Chicago Bears 1948–55. Named to all-league teams
for 5 years, including both offensive and defensive squads
in 1951 and 1952. One of the last of the two-way players.

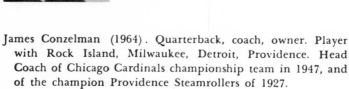

James Conzelman (1964). Quarterback, coach, owner. Player
with Rock Island, Milwaukee, Detroit, Providence. Head
Coach of Chicago Cardinals championship team in 1947, and
of the champion Providence Steamrollers of 1927.

Arthur Donovan (1968) Defensive tackle Baltimore Colts 1950, 53-61; New York Yanks 1951; Dallas Texans 1952.

John Driscoll (1965). Halfback, dropkicker, punter, Chicago Cardinals, 1921-25; Chicago Bears, 1926-29. Bears coach, including head coach, 1956-57.

William Dudley (1966). Halfback, Pittsburgh Steelers, 1942, 45-46; Detroit Lions, 1947-49; Washington Redskins, 1950-51, 53; #1 Rushing 1942, 46; #1 Interceptions 1946.

Albert Glen "Turk" Edwards (1969). Tackle, Boston-Washington Redskins, 1932–40; head coach Washington, 1946–48.

Tom Fears (1970). End, Los Angeles, 1948-56; 1948, 49, 50 #1 Pass Receiver. Assistant coach at Green Bay. Los Angeles & Atlanta. Head Coach New Orleans, 1967.

Daniel Fortmann (1965). Guard, Chicago Bears, 1936-43.

William "Bill" George (1974). Linebacker for the Chicago Bears from 1952 to 1965. Also played offensive guard first three seasons and was used as kicking specialist in 1954. Named to all-league teams 8 times.

Otto Graham (1965). Quarterback, Cleveland Browns, 1950-55. No. 1 Passing 1953.

Harold "Red" Grange (1963). Halfback, Chicago Bears 1925, '29-34; New York Yankees (AFL), 1926; New York Yankees (NFL), 1927.

Louis "Lou" Groza (1974). Offensive tackle and kicker for the Cleveland Browns 1946–49 (AAFC) and 1950–67 (NFL) except 1960 when injured. Knicknamed "The Toe" for his kicking feats, he was also named to the all-league team as an offensive tackle 6 times and played there regularly through 1959. Led league in field goals 1946, 1950, 1952–54 and 1957 and in scoring 1946 and 1957. Second all-time in scoring. A member of 8 champion teams, he kicked many dramatic field goals, including the game-winner in 1950 title contest.

Joseph Guyon (1966). Halfback, tackle, Cleveland Indians, 1921; Oorang Indians, 1922-23; Rock Island Independents, 1924; Kansas City Cowboys, 1924-25; New York Giants, 1927.

George Halas (1963). End, owner, coach, Decatur Staleys, 1920-21; Chicago Bears, 1922-63; active player, 1920-30; one of original founders of the NFL; top candidate for all-time "Mr. Pro Football."

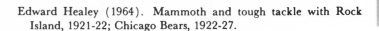

Edward Healey (1964). Mammoth and tough tackle with Rock Island, 1921-22; Chicago Bears, 1922-27.

Melvin Hein (1963). Center-line backer, New York Giants, 1931-45; several times all-league in days of 60-minute football.

Wilbur Henry (1963). Tackle-dropkicker, Canton Bulldogs, 1920-23, '25-26; New York Giants, 1927; Pottsville Maroons, 1927-28; 49 consecutive scoring dropkicks; 94-yard punt for Canton against Akron in 1923.

Arnold Herber (1966). Quarterback, Green Bay Packers, 1930-40; New York Giants, 1944-45; #1 Passing 1932, 34, 36.

William Hewitt (1971). An End, 1932-36 Chicago Bears; 1937-39 Philadelphia Eagles; 1943 Phil-Pitt.

Clarke Hinkle (1964). Fullback, Green Bay Packers, 1932-41; led league in scoring, 1938; led league in field goals, 1940 and 1941.

Elroy Hirsch (1968) Back-end Chicago Rockets (AAFC) 1946-48; Los Angeles Rams 1949-57; #1 Pass Receiving (NFL) 1951.

Robert "Cal" Hubbard (1963). Tackle-end, New York Giants, 1927-28, '36; Green Bay Packers, 1929-35; Pittsburgh Pirates, 1936. All-league offensive and defensive giant in days on two-way football. Played on four championship teams (New York, 1927; Green Bay, 1929-31).

Donald Hutson (1963). End-safety, Green Bay Packers, 1935-45; led league scoring, 1940, '41, '42, '43, '44; led league pass receiving, 1936, '37, '39, '41, '42, '43, '44, '45; led league field goals, 1943; caught 99 touchdown passes; gained 8,010 yards on passes; scored 825 points including 29 in one quarter.

Walter Kiesling (1966). Guard, Duluth Eskimos, 1926-27; Pottsville Maroons, 1928; Boston Braves, 1929; Chicago Cardinals, 1929-33; Chicago Bears, 1934; Green Bay Packers, 1935-36; Pittsburgh Steelers, 1937-38; head coach Pittsburgh 1939-42, 44, 54-56.

Frank "Bruiser" Kinard (1971). Tackle, 1938-44 Brooklyn Dodgers; 1946-47 New York Yankees (AAFC).

Earl "Curly" Lambeau (1963). Halfback-coach, Green Bay Packers, 1921-30; head coach, Packers, to 1949, including six championship teams; head coach, Chicago Cardinals, 1950-51, Washington Redskins, 1952-53; one of founders of NFL.

Richard "Night Train" Lane (1974). Defensive halfback for Los Angeles Rams 1952–53, Chicago Cardinals 1954–59 and Detroit Lions 1960–65. Set all-time record for interceptions with 14 in 1952 and also led in 1954. Second lifetime in interceptions. Named to all league teams five times.

Robert Layne (1967). Quarterback, Chicago Bears, 1948; New York Bulldogs, 1949; Detroit Lions, 1950-58; Pittsburgh Steelers, 1958-62; #1 Scoring 1956.

Dante Lavelli (1975). Offensive end Cleveland Browns 1946–49 (AAFC) and 1950–56 (NFL). Named to all-league teams 4 times. Led AAFC in pass-receiving 1946. Scored 4 touchdowns on October 14, 1949. A member of 7 champion teams and caught the winning TD pass in the 1946 title game.

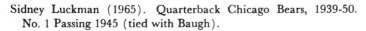

Sidney Luckman (1965). Quarterback Chicago Bears, 1939-50. No. 1 Passing 1945 (tied with Baugh).

William Roy "Link" Lyman (1964). Tackle, Canton Bulldogs 1922; Cleveland Indians, 1923-24; Canton, 1925; Chicago Bears, 1926-34.

George McAfee (1966). Halfback, Chicago Bears, 1940-41, 45-50.

Hugh McElhenny (1970). Back, San Francisco 49ers, 1952-60; Minnesota, 1961-62; New York Giants, 1963; Detroit, 1964.

John "Blood" McNally (1963). Halfback, Milwaukee Badgers, 1925-27; Duluth Eskimos, 1926-27; Pottsville Maroons, 1928; Green Bay Packers, 1928-36; Pittsburgh Steelers, 1937-39; All-league back for most of his 15 years; player-coach Pittsburgh, 1937-39.

Gino Marchetti (1972). End, 1952 Dallas Texans; 1953-64, 66 Baltimore Colts.

Oliver "Ollie" Matson (1972). Back, 1952, 54-58 Chicago Cardinals; 1959-62 Los Angeles Rams; 1963 Detroit Lions; 1964-66 Philadelphia Eagles.

August Michalske (1964). Guard, New York Yanks (AFL), 1926; New York Yankees (NFL), 1927-28; Green Bay, 1929-37.

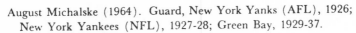

Wayne Millner (1968) End Boston Redskins 1936; Washington Redskins 1937-41, 45.

Leonard "Lenny" Moore (1975). Halfback Baltimore Colts 1956–67. Named to the all-league team 5 times. Second all-time in touchdowns with 113. Scored touchdowns in 18 consecutive games. Led league in yards rushing per attempt four times. A star of the Colts 1958–59 champion teams.

Marion Motley (1968) Fullback Cleveland Browns (AAFC) 1946-49; Cleveland Browns (NFL) 1950-53; Pittsburgh Steelers 1955; #1 Rushing (NFL) 1950.

Bronko Nagurski (1963). Fullback, Chicago Bears, 1930-37, '43; All-league player many years; big man of championship teams in 1932, '33, '43.

Ernest Nevers (1963). Fullback, Duluth Eskimos, 1926-27; Chicago Cardinals, 1929-31; scored 40 points in single game against Bears, 1929.

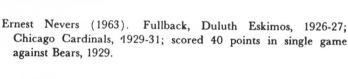

Leo Nomellini (1969). Tackle, San Francisco 49ers for 14 years, 1950–63, many times All-pro.

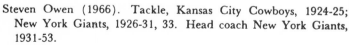

Steven Owen (1966). Tackle, Kansas City Cowboys, 1924-25; New York Giants, 1926-31, 33. Head coach New York Giants, 1931-53.

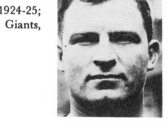

Clarence "Ace" Parker (1972). QBack, 1937-41 Brooklyn Dodgers; 1945 Boston Redskins; 1946 New York Yankees (AAFC).

James Parker (1973). Guard for the Baltimore Colts, 1957-67

Fletcher "Joe" Perry (1969). Fullback, 1948–49 San Francisco 49ers (AAFC); 1950-60, 63 San Francisco 49ers (NFL); 1961-62 Baltimore Colts; 1953, 54 #1 Rushing (NFL).

Peter Pihos (1970). End, Philadelphia Eagles, 1947-55; 1953, 54, 55 #1 Pass Receiver; 1955 (tied with W. Wilson).

Andrew Robustelli (1971). End, from 1951-55 Los Angeles Rams; 1956-64 New York Giants. An all-NFL player seven times and played seven Pro Bowl games.

Joseph Schmidt (1973). Linebacker for the Detroit Lions, 1953-65. Head coach for Detroit from 1967-72.

Ernest Stautner (1969). Defensive tackle, 14 years Pittsburgh Steelers, 1950–63 many times all-pro. Coach several teams since retiring.

Kenneth Strong (1967). Halfback, Staten Island Stapletons, 1929-32; New York Giants, 1933-35, 39, 44-47; New York Yanks (AFL), 1936-37; #1 Scoring 1933; #1 Field Goals 1944.

Joseph Stydahar (1967). Tackle, Chicago Bears, 1936-42, 45-46.

James Thorpe (1963). Halfback, pro player before start of the National Football League, beginning in about 1915. Played official NFL seasons with Cleveland, 1921; Canton, 1922, '26; Oorang Indians (Marion, Ohio), 1922-23; Toledo, 1923; Rock Island, 1924-25; New York, 1925.

Yelberton "Y. A." Tittle (1971). Quarterback, 1948-49 Baltimore Colts (AAFC); 1950 Baltimore Colts; 1951-60 San Francisco 49ers; 1961-64 New York Giants. Led league in Passing in 1963. Led New York to three championships and was all-NFL player three times.

George Trafton (1964). Center, Chicago Bears, 1921-32.

Charles Trippi (1968) Halfback-quarterback Chicago Cardinals 1947-55.

Emlen Tunnell (1967) Defensive back New York Giants 1948-58; Green Bay Packers 1959-61. Alltime interception leader (79 for career)

Clyde Turner (1966). Center, Chicago Bears, 1940-52; #1 Interceptions 1942.

Norman Van Brocklin (1971). Quarterback, 1949-57 Los Angeles Rams; 1958-60 Philadelphia Eagles. Led league in Passing in 1950, 1952, 1954. Also #1 Punting in 1955 and 1956. Led Philadelphia in an NFL championship. Head coach for the Minnesota Vikings, 1961-66, and the Atlanta Falcons from 1968 to 1974.

Steven Van Buren (1965). Halfback, Philadelphia Eagles, 1944-51. No. 1 scoring 1945, No. 1 Rushing 1945, 47, 48, 49.

Robert Waterfield (1965). Quarterback, Cleveland-Los Angeles Rams, 1945-52. No. 1 Passing 1946, 51. No. 1 Field Goals 1949, 51.

Alexander Wojciechowicz (1968) Center-defensive end Detroit Lions 1938-49; Philadelphia Eagles 1946-50.

NON-PLAYERS

De Bennville "Bert" Bell (1963). Founder-coach of Philadelphia Eagles through purchase of Frankfort Yellow-jackets franchise; commissioner of NFL from 1946 to his death in 1959; strong, intelligent, fair man who guided the NFL through the turbulent years of the war with the All-America Football Conference, the growth through television, and the shuffling of franchises in the search for prosperity. Bell was tough, humorous, and respected by everyone.

Charles Bidwill (1967). Owner of Chicago Cardinals, 1933-47. Died in April, 1947, a few months before his team won its first league championship.

Paul Brown (1967). Coach 1946–49 (AAFC) and 1950–62 (NFL) Cleveland Browns, 1968–69 (AFL) and 1970–present (NFL) Cincinnati Bengals. Won four AAFC titles, six straight NFL conference titles and three world (NFL) titles.

Joseph Carr (1963). First president of the league, 1921 until his death in 1939. Guided organization from the first attempt in 1920; instituted policy of pro football not negotiating with college players until their class has graduated; made many courageous decisions to eliminate abuses during the formative years.

Lamar Hunt (1972). Owner of Kansas City Chiefs (AFL-AFC). Founder of American Football League, 1960.

Vincent Lombardi (1971). Head coach, for the Green Bay Packers from 1959-67. General Manager for the Packers in 1968. Head coach for the Washington Redskins in 1969. Green Bay won five NFL titles and two Super Bowl games under his generalship.

Tim Mara (1963). Founder, New York Giants, 1925.

George P. Marshall (1963). Owner, Boston-Washington Redskins, 1932-63; instigator of many important rules changes to open up the excitement of the game, including the split into two divisions, the annual championship playoff, the Pro Bowl game. Great showman and dynamic force for football. His Redskin band and halftime shows admired all over the football world.

Hugh Ray (1966). Supervisor of NFL officials and technical adviser to league, 1938-56.

Earle "Greasy" Neale (1969). Head coach Philadelphia Eagles 1941–50; Eastern title 1947, 1948 and 1949 and NFL championships 1948 and 1949. Also played several years of pro ball before 1919 organization.

Daniel Reeves (1967). Owner of Cleveland-Los Angeles Rams, 1941-67 and still active at time of enshrinement. Moved team to Los Angeles in 1947, opening west coast for NFL football.

Arthur Rooney (1964). Owner of Pittsburgh Steelers since 1933. Pioneer enthusiast and faithful official of the league for 30 years at the time of his selection.

NFL/NFC INDIVIDUAL
DEPARTMENTAL CHAMPIONS

*First year in League/Conference

RUSHING

			Yds.	Atts.
1974	Lawrence McCutcheon	Los Angeles (NFC)	1,109	236
1973	John Brockington	Green Bay (NFC)	1,144	265
1972	Lawrence Brown	Washington (NFC)	1,216	285
1971	John Brockington	Green Bay (NFC) *	1,105	216
1970	Lawrence Brown	Washington (NFC)	1,125	237
1969	Gale Sayers	Chicago	1,032	236
1968	LeRoy Kelly	Cleveland	1,239	248
1967	LeRoy Kelly	Cleveland	1,205	235
1966	Gale Sayers	Chicago	1,231	229
1965	James Brown	Cleveland	1,544	289
1964	James Brown	Cleveland	1,446	280
1963	James Brown	Cleveland	1,863	291
1962	James Taylor	Green Bay	1,474	272
1961	James Brown	Cleveland	1,408	305
1960	James Brown	Cleveland	1,257	215
1959	James Brown	Cleveland	1,329	290
1958	James Brown	Cleveland	1,527	257
1957	James Brown	Cleveland*	942	202
1956	Rick Casares	Chicago Bears	1,126	234
1955	Alan Ameche	Baltimore*	961	213
1954	Fletcher Perry	San Francisco	1,049	173
1953	Fletcher Perry	San Francisco	1,018	192
1952	Dan Towler	Los Angeles	894	156
1951	Edward Price	New York Giants	971	271
1950	Marion Motley	Cleveland	810	140
1949	Steven Van Buren	Philadelphia	1,146	263
1948	Steven Van Buren	Philadelphia	945	201
1947	Steven Van Buren	Philadelphia	1,008	217
1946	William Dudley	Pittsburgh	604	146
1945	Steven Van Buren	Philadelphia	832	143
1944	William Paschal	New York	737	196
1943	William Paschal	New York*	572	147
1942	William Dudley	Pittsburgh*	696	162
1941	Clarence Manders	Brooklyn	486	111
1940	Byron White	Detroit	514	146
1939	William Osmanski	Chicago Bears*	699	121
1938	Byron White	Pittsburgh*	567	152
1937	Clifford Battles	Washington	874	216
1936	Alphonse Leemans	New York*	830	206
1935	Douglas Russell	Cardinals	499	140
1934	Beattie Feathers	Chicago Bears*	1,004	101
1933	James Musick	Boston	809	173
1932	Clifford Battles	Boston	576	148

SCORING

			Tds.	X Pt.	FG	Total
1974	Chester Marcol	Green Bay (NFC)	0	19	30	130
1973	David Ray	Los Angeles (NFC)	0	40	30	130
1972	Chester Marcol	Green Bay (NFC) *	0	29	33	128

			Tds.	X Pt.	FG	Total
1971	L. Curtis Knight	Washington (NFC)	0	27	29	114
1970	Frederick Cox	Minnesota (NFC)	0	35	30	125
1969	Frederick Cox	Minnesota	0	43	26	121
1968	LeRoy Kelly	Cleveland	20	0	0	120
1967	James Bakken	St. Louis	0	36	27	117
1966	Bruce Gossett	Los Angeles	0	29	28	113
1965	Gale Sayers	Chicago*	22	0	0	132
1964	Leonard Moore	Baltimore	20	0	0	120
1963	Donald Chandler	New York	0	52	18	106
1962	James Taylor	Green Bay	19	0	0	114
1961	Paul Hornung	Green Bay	10	41	15	146
1960	Paul Hornung	Green Bay	15	41	15	176
1959	Paul Hornung	Green Bay	7	31	7	94
1958	James Brown	Cleveland	18	0	0	108
1957	Loras Baker	Washington	1	29	14	77
	Lou Groza	Cleveland	0	32	15	77
1956	Robert Layne	Detroit	5	33	12	99
1955	Ewell Doak Walker	Detroit	7	27	9	96
1954	Robert Walston	Philadelphia	11	36	4	114
1953	Gordon Soltau	San Francisco	6	48	10	114
1952	Gordon Soltau	San Francisco	7	34	6	94
1951	Elroy Hirsch	Los Angeles Rams	17	0	0	102
1950	Ewell Doak Walker	Detroit*	11	38	8	128
1949	Marlin Harder	Cardinals	8	45	3	102
	Eugene Roberts	Giants	17	0	0	102
1948	Marlin Harder	Cardinals	6	53	7	110
1947	Marlin Harder	Cardinals	7	39	7	102
1946	Ted Fritsch	Green Bay	10	13	9	100
1945	Steven Van Buren	Philadelphia	18	2	0	110
1944	Don Hutson	Green Bay	9	31	0	85
1943	Don Hutson	Green Bay	12	36	3	117
1942	Don Hutson	Green Bay	17	33	1	138
1941	Don Hutson	Green Bay	12	20	1	95
1940	Don Hutson	Green Bay	7	15	0	57
1939	Andy Farkas	Washington	11	2	0	68
1938	Clark Hinkle	Green Bay	7	7	3	58
1937	Jack Manders	Chicago Bears	5	15	8	69
1936	Earl Clark	Detroit	7	19	4	73
1935	Earl Clark	Detroit	6	16	1	55
1934	Jack Manders	Chicago Bears	3	31	10	79
1933	Ken Strong	Giants	6	13	5	64
	Glenn Presnell	Portsmouth	6	10	6	64
1932	Earl Clark	Detroit	6	10	3	55

FIELD GOALS

1974	Chester Marcol	Green Bay (NFC)	25
1973	David Ray	Los Angeles (NFC)	30
1972	Chester Marcol	Green Bay (NFC) *	33
1971	L. Curtis Knight	Washington (NFC)	29
1970	Frederick Cox	Minnesota (NFC)	30
1969	Frederick Cox	Minnesota	26
1968	Mac Percival	Chicago	25
1967	James Bakken	St. Louis	27
1966	Bruce Gossett	Los Angeles	28
1965	Frederick Cox	Minnesota	23
1964	James Bakken	St. Louis	25
1963	James Martin	Baltimore	24
1962	Louis Michaels	Pittsburgh	26

1961	Steven Myhra	Baltimore	21
1960	Thomas Davis	San Francisco	19
1959	George Summerall	New York	20
1958	Paige Cothren	Los Angeles	14
	Thomas Miner*	Pittsburgh	14
1957	Lou Groza	Cleveland	15
1956	Loras Baker	Washington	17
1955	Fred Cone	Green Bay	16
1954	Lou Groza	Cleveland	16
1953	Lou Groza	Cleveland	23
1952	Lou Groza	Cleveland	19
1951	Robert Waterfield	Los Angeles	13
1950	Louis Groza	Cleveland	13
1949	John Patton	Philadelphia	9
	Robert Waterfield	Los Angeles	9
1948	John Patton	Philadelphia	8
1947	Marlin Harder	Cardinals	7
	Ward Cuff	Green Bay	7
	Robert Waterfield	Los Angeles	7
1946	Ted Fritsch	Green Bay	9
1945	Joseph Aguirre	Washington	7
1944	Kenneth Strong	New York	6
1943	Don Hutson	Green Bay	3
	Ward Cuff	New York	3
1942	William Daddio	Cardinals	5
1941	Clarke Hinkle	Green Bay	6
1940	Clarke Hinkle	Green Bay	9
1939	Ward Cuff	New York	7
1938	Ward Cuff	New York	5
	Ralph Kercheval	Brooklyn	5
1937	Jack Manders	Chicago Bears	8
1936	Jack Manders	Chicago Bears	7
	Armand Niccolai	Pittsburgh	7
1935	Armand Niccolai	Pittsburgh	6
	William Smith	Cardinals	6
1934	Jack Manders	Chicago Bears	10
1933	Jack Manders*	Chicago Bears	6
	Glenn Presnell	Portsmouth	6
1932	Earl Clark	Portsmouth	3

FORWARD PASSING

			Passes	Comp.	Yds.	Tds.	Inter.
1974	Christian Jurgensen	Wash'gton (NFC)	167	107	1,185	11	5
1973	Roger Staubach	Dallas (NFC)	286	179	2,428	23	15
1972	Norman Snead	New York (NFC)	325	196	2,307	17	12
1971	Roger Staubach	Dallas (NFC)	211	126	1,882	15	4
1970	John Brodie	San Fran. (NFC)	378	223	2,941	24	10
1969	Christian Jurgenson	Washington	442	274	3,102	22	15
1968	Earl Morrall	Baltimore	317	182	2,909	26	17
1967	Christian Jurgenson	Washington	508	288	3,747	31	16
1966	Bryan Starr	Green Bay	251	156	2,257	14	3
1965	Rudolph Bukich	Chicago	312	176	2,641	20	9
1964	Bryan Starr	Green Bay	272	163	2,144	15	4
1963	Yelberton Tittle	New York	367	221	3,145	36	14
1962	Bryan Starr	Green Bay	285	178	2,438	12	9
1961	Milton Plum	Cleveland	302	177	2,416	18	10
1960	Milton Plum	Cleveland	250	151	2,297	21	5
1959	Charles Conerly	New York	194	113	1,706	14	4
1958	Edward LeBaron	Washington	145	79	1,365	11	10
1957	Thomas O'Connell	Cleveland	110	63	1,229	9	8

			Passes	Comp.	Yds.	Tds.	Inter.
1956	Charles Brown	Chicago Bears	168	96	1,667	11	12
1955	Otto Graham	Cleveland	185	98	1,721	15	8
1954	Norman Van Brocklin	Los Angeles	260	139	2,637	13	21
1953	Otto Graham	Cleveland	258	167	2,722	11	9
1952	Norman Van Brocklin	Los Angeles	205	113	1,736	14	17
1951	Robert Waterfield	Los Angeles	176	88	1,566	13	10
1950	Norman Van Brocklin	Los Angeles	233	127	2,061	18	14
1949	Samuel Baugh	Washington	255	145	1,903	18	14
1948	Lurtis Thompson	Philadelphia	246	141	1.965	25	11
1947	Samuel Baugh	Washington	354	210	2,938	25	15
1946	Robert Waterfield	Los Angeles	251	127	1,747	18	17
1945	Sidney Luckman	Chicago Bears	217	117	1,725	14	10
1944	Frank Filchock	Washington	147	84	1,139	13	9
1943	Samuel Baugh	Washington	239	133	1,754	23	19
1942	Cecil Isbell	Green Bay	268	146	2,021	24	14
1941	Cecil Isbell	Green Bay	206	117	1,479	15	11
1940	Samuel Baugh	Washington	177	111	1,367	12	10
1939	Parker Hall	Cleveland*	208	106	1,227	9	13
1938	Ed Danowski	New York	129	70	848	7	8
1937	Samuel Baugh	Washington*	171	81	1,127	8	14
1936	Arnold Herber	Green Bay	173	77	1,239	11	13
1935	Ed Danowski	New York	113	57	794	10	9
1934	Arnold Herber	Green Bay	115	42	799	8	12
1933	Harry Newman	New York*	136	53	973	11	17
1932	Arnold Herber	Green Bay	101	37	639	9	9

NOTE: In 1972, system for rating passers changed. Qualifiers rated in four categories: Percentage of completions, average yards gained per pass attempt, percentage of interceptions, and percentage of touchdown passes per attempt (rather than total touchdown passes, as in the past).

PASS RECEIVING

			Caught	Yards	Tds.
1974	Charles Young	Philadelphia (NFC)	63	696	3
1973	Harold Carmichael	Philadelphia (NFC)	67	1,116	9
1972	Harold Jackson	Philadelphia (NFC)	62	1,048	4
1971	Robert Tucker	New York (NFC)	59	791	4
1970	Richard Gordon	Chicago (NFC)	71	1,026	13
1969	Daniel Abramowicz	New Orleans	73	1,015	7
1968	Clifton McNeil	San Francisco	71	994	7
1967	Charles Taylor	Washington	70	990	9
1966	Charles Taylor	Washington	72	1,119	12
1965	David Parks	San Francisco	80	1,344	12
1964	John Morris	Chicago	93	1,200	10
1963	Robert Conrad	St. Louis	73	967	10
1962	Robert Mitchell	Washington	72	1,384	11
1961	James Phillips	Los Angeles	78	1,092	5
1960	Raymond Berry	Baltimore	74	1,298	10
1959	Raymond Berry	Baltimore	66	959	14
1958	Raymond Berry	Baltimore	56	794	9
	Palmer Retzlaff	Philadelphia	56	766	2
1957	William Wilson	San Francisco	52	757	6
1956	William Wilson	San Francisco	60	889	5
1955	Peter Pihos	Philadelphia	62	864	7
1954	Peter Pihos	Philadelphia	60	872	10
	William Wilson	San Francisco	60	830	5
1953	Peter Pihos	Philadelphia	63	1,049	10
1952	Mac Speedie	Cleveland	62	911	5
1951	Elroy Hirsch	Los Angeles	66	1,495	17
1950	Tom Fears	Los Angeles	84	1,116	7

			Caught	Yards	Tds.
1949	Tom Fears	Los Angeles	77	1,013	9
1948	Tom Fears	Los Angeles*	51	698	4
1947	James Keane	Chicago Bears	64	910	10
1946	James Benton	Los Angeles	63	981	6
1945	Don Hutson	Green Bay	47	834	9
1944	Don Hutson	Green Bay	58	866	9
1943	Don Hutson	Green Bay	47	776	11
1942	Don Hutson	Green Bay	74	1,211	17
1941	Don Hutson	Green Bay	58	738	10
1940	Don Looney	Philadelphia*	58	707	4
1939	Don Hutson	Green Bay	34	846	6
1938	Gaynell Tinsley	Cardinals	41	516	1
1937	Don Hutson	Green Bay	41	552	7
1936	Don Hutson	Green Bay	34	536	8
1935	Charles Goodwin	New York*	26	432	4
1934	Joseph Carter	Philadelphia	16	238	4
	Morris Badgro	New York	16	206	1
1933	John Kelley	Brooklyn	22	246	3
1932	Ray Flaherty	New York	21	350	3

INTERCEPTIONS

			No.	Yards	Longest
1974	Raymond Brown	Atlanta (NFC)	8	164	59
1973	Bobby Bryant	Minnesota (NFC)	7	105	46
1972	William Bradley	Philadelphia (NFC)	9	73	21
1971	William Bradley	Philadelphia (NFC)	11	248	51
1970	Richard LeBeau	Detroit (NFC)	9	96	57
1969	Melvin Renfro	Dallas	10	118	41
1968	Willie Williams	New York	10	103	24
1967	James Whitsell	New Orleans	10	178	41
	Lemuel Barney	Detroit	10	232	71
1966	Lawrence Wilson	St. Louis	10	180	91
1965	Robert Boyd	Baltimore	9	78	24
1964 1963	Paul Krause	Washington*	12	140	35
	Roosevelt Taylor	Chicago	9	172	46
	Richard Lynch	New York	9	251	82
1962	William Wood	Green Bay	9	132	37
1961	Richard Lynch	New York	9	60	36
1960	Gerald Norton	St. Louis	10	96	26
	David Baker	San Francisco	10	96	28
1959	Dean Derby	Pittsburgh	7	127	24
	Milton Davis	Baltimore	7	119	57
	Donald Shinnick	Baltimore	7	70	57
1958	James Patton	New York	11	181	42
1957	Milton Davis	Baltimore*	10	219	65
	John Christiansen	Detroit	10	137	52
	John Butler	Pittsburgh	10	85	20
1956	Lindon Crow	Cardinals	11	170	42
1955	Willard Sherman	Los Angeles	11	101	36
1954	Richard Lane	Cardinals	10	181	64
1953	John Christiansen	Detroit	12	238	92
1952	Richard Lane	Los Angeles*	14	298	80
1951	Otto Schnellbacher	New York Giants	11	194	46
1950	Orban Sanders	New York Yanks	13	199	29
1949	Robert Nussbaumer	Cardinals	12	157	68
1948	Daniel Sandifer	Washington*	13	258	54
1947	Francis Reagan	New York Giants	10	203	71
	Frank Seno	Boston	10	100	
1946	William Dudley	Pittsburgh	10	242	80
1945	Leroy Zimmerman	Philadelphia	7	90	23

			No.	Yards	Longest
1944	**Howard Livingston**	New York Giants*	9	172	40
1943	**Samuel Baugh**	**Washington**	11	112	23
1942	**Clyde Turner**	**Chicago Bears**	8	96	42
1941	**Marshall Goldberg**	**Cardinals**	7	54	16
	Arthur Jones	Pittsburgh*	7	35	
1940	Clarence Parker	Brooklyn	6	146	
	Kent Ryan	Detroit	6	65	
	Don Hutson	Green Bay	6	24	

PUNTING

			Number	Average	Longest
1974	Thomas Blanchard	New Orleans (NFC)	88	42.1	71
1973	Thomas Wittum	San Francisco (NFC) *	79	43.7	62
1972	David Chapple	Los Angeles (NFC)	53	44.2	70
1971	Thomas McNeill	Philadelphia (NFC)	73	42.0	64
1970	Julian Fagan	New Orleans (NFC) *	77	42.5	64
1969	David Lee	Baltimore	57	45.3	66
1968	William Lothridge	Atlanta	75	44.3	70
1967	William Lothridge	Atlanta	87	43.7	62
1966	David Lee	Baltimore	49	45.6	64
1965	Gary Collins	Cleveland	65	46.7	71
1964	Robert Walden	Minnesota	72	46.4	73
1963	Robert Yale Lary	Detroit	35	48.9	73
1962	Thomas Davis	San Francisco	48	45.6	82
1961	Robert Yale Lary	Detroit	52	48.4	71
1960	Gerald Norton	St. Louis	39	45.6	62
1959	Robert Yale Lary	Detroit	45	47.1	67
1958	Loris Baker	Washington	48	45.4	64
1957	Donald Chandler	New York	60	44.6	61
1956	Norman Van Brocklin	Los Angeles	48	43.1	72
1955	Norman Van Brocklin	Los Angeles	60	44.6	61
1954	Patrick Brady	Pittsburgh	66	43.2	72
1953	Patrick Brady	Pittsburgh	80	46.9	64
1952	Horace Gillom	Cleveland Browns	61	45.7	73
1951	Horace Gillom	Cleveland Browns	73	45.5	66
1950	Fred Morrison	Chicago Bears*	57	43.3	65
1949	Michael Boyda	New York Bulldogs*	56	44.2	61
1948	Joseph Muha	Philadelphia	57	47.2	82
1947	Jack Jacobs	Green Bay	57	43.5	74
1946	Roy McKay	Green Bay	64	42.7	64
1945	Roy McKay	Green Bay	44	41.2	73
1944	Frank Sinkwich	Detroit	45	41.0	73
1943	Samuel Baugh	Washington	50	45.9	81
1942	Samuel Baugh	Washington	37	48.2	74
1941	Samuel Baugh	Washington	30	48.7	75
1940	Samuel Baugh	Washington	35	51.4	85
1939	Parker Hall	Cleveland Rams*	58	40.8	80

AFL/AFC INDIVIDUAL DEPARTMENTAL CHAMPIONS

	RUSHING	Yds.	Atts.
1974	Otis Armstrong, Denver (AFC)	1,407	263
1973	O. J. Simpson, Buffalo (AFC)	2,003	332

		Yds.	Atts.
1972	O. J. Simpson, Buffalo (AFC)	1,251	292
1971	Floyd Little, Denver (AFC)	1,133	284
1970	Floyd Little, Denver (AFC)	901	209
1969	Richard Post, San Diego	873	182
1968	Paul Robinson, Cincinnati*	1,023	238
1967	James Nance, Boston	1,216	269
1966	James Nance, Boston	1,458	299
1965	Paul Lowe, San Diego	1,121	222
1964	Carlton Gilchrist, Buffalo	981	230
1963	Clemon Daniels, Oakland	1,098	215
1962	Carlton Gilchrist, Buffalo	1,096	214
1961	William Cannon, Houston	948	200
1960	Abner Haynes, Dallas*	875	156

SCORING

		TDs	FGs	XPTs	Total
1974	Roy Gerela, Pittsburgh (AFC)	0	20	33	93
1973	Roy Gerela, Pittsburgh (AFC)	0	29	36	123
1972	Robert Howfield, N.Y. (AFC)	0	27	40	121
1971	Garabed Yepremian, Miami (AFC)	0	28	33	117
1970	Jan Stenerud, K.C. (AFC)	0	30	26	116
1969	James Turner, New York	0	32	33	129
1968	James Turner, New York	0	34	43	145
1967	George Blanda, Oakland	0	20	56	116
1966	Gino Cappelletti, Boston	6	16	35	119
1965	Gino Cappelletti, Boston	9	17	27	132
1964	Gino Cappelletti, Boston†	7	25	36	155
1963	Gino Cappelletti, Boston	2	22	35	113
1962	Eugene Mingo, Denver	4	27	32	137
1961	Gino Cappelletti, Boston	8	17	48	147
1960	Eugene Mingo, Denver*	6	18	33	123

† also 1 two-point conversion

FORWARD PASSING

		Atts.	Comp.	Yds.	Tds.	Inter.
1974	Kenneth Anderson, Cincinnati (AFC)	328	213	2,667	18	10
1973	Ken Stabler, Oakland (AFC)	260	163	1,997	14	10
1972	Earl Morrall, Miami (AFC)	150	83	1,360	11	7
1971	Robert Griese, Miami (AFC)	263	145	2,089	19	9
1970	Daryle Lamonica, Oakland (AFC)	356	179	2,516	22	15
1969	Gregory Cook, Cincinnati*	197	106	1,854	15	11
1968	Leonard Dawson, Kansas City	224	131	2,109	17	9
1967	Daryle Lamonica, Oakland	425	220	3,228	30	20
1966	Leonard Dawson, Kansas City	284	159	2,527	26	10
1965	John Hadl, San Diego	348	174	2,798	20	21
1964	Leonard Dawson, Kansas City	354	199	2,879	30	18
1963	Tobin Rote, San Diego	286	170	2,510	20	17
1962	Leonard Dawson, Dallas	310	189	2,759	29	17
1961	George Blanda, Houston	362	187	3,330	36	22
1960	Jack Kemp, Los Angeles	406	211	3,018	20	25

PASS RECEIVING

		Comp.	Yds.	Tds.
1974	Lydell Mitchell, Baltimore (AFC)	72	544	2
1973	Frederick Willis, Houston (AFC)	57	371	1
1972	Frederick Biletnikoff, Oakland (AFC)	58	802	7
1971	Frederick Biletnikoff, Oakland (AFC)	61	929	9
1970	Marlin Briscoe, Buffalo (AFC)	57	1,036	8

		Comp.	Yards	Tds.
1969	Lance Alworth, San Diego	64	1,003	4
1968	Lance Alworth, San Diego	68	1,312	10
1967	George Sauer, New York	75	1,189	6
1966	Lance Alworth, San Diego	73	1,383	13
1965	Lionel Taylor, Denver	85	1,131	6
1964	Charles Hennigan, Houston	101	1,546	8
1963	Lionel Taylor, Denver	78	1,101	10
1962	Lionel Taylor, Denver	77	908	4
1961	Lionel Taylor, Denver	100	1,176	4
1960	Lionel Taylor, Denver	92	1,235	12

FIELD GOALS

1974	Roy Gerela, Pittsburgh (AFC)	20
1973	Roy Gerela, Pittsburgh (AFC)	29
1972	Roy Gerela, Pittsburgh (AFC)	28
1971	Garabed Yepremian, Miami (AFC)	28
1970	Jan Stenerud, Kansas City (AFC)	30
1969	James Turner, New York	32
1968	James Turner, New York	34
1967	Jan Stenerod, K.C.	21
1966	Michael Mercer, Oakland-K.C.	21
1965	Peter Gogolak, Buffalo	28
1964	Gino Cappelletti, Boston	25
1963	Gino Cappelletti, Boston	22
1962	Eugene Mingo, Denver	27
1961	Gino Cappelletti, Boston	17
1960	Eugene Mingo, Denver*	18

PUNTING

		Atts.	Ave. Yds.
1974	Ray Guy, Oakland (AFC)	74	42.2
1973	Jerrel Wilson, Kansas City (AFC)	80	45.5
1972	Jerrel Wilson, Kansas City (AFC)	66	44.8
1971	David Lewis, Cincinnati (AFC)	72	44.8
1970	David Lewis, Cincinnati (AFC) *	79	46.2
1971	Dave Lewis, Cincinnati (AFC)	72	44.8
1970	Dave Lewis, Cincinnati (AFC)	79	46.2
1969	Dennis Partee, San Diego	71	44.6
1968	Jerrel Wilson, Kansas City	63	45.1
1967	Robert Scarpitto, Denver	105	44.9
1966	Robert Scarpitto, Denver	76	45.8
1965	Jerrel Wilson, Kansas City	69	45.4
1964	James Fraser, Denver	73	44.2
1963	James Fraser, Denver	81	44.4
1962	James Fraser, Denver	55	43.6
1961	William Atkins, Buffalo	85	44.5
1960	Paul Maguire, Los Angeles*	43	40.5

INTERCEPTIONS

		No.	Yards
1974	Emmitt Thomas, Kansas City (AFC)	12	214
1973	Richard Anderson, Miami (AFC)	8	163
1972	J. Michael Sensibaugh, Kansas City (AFC)	8	65
1971	Kenneth Houston, Houston (AFC)	9	220

		No.	Yards
1970	John Robinson, Kansas City (AFC)	10	155
1969	Emmitt Thomas, Kansas City	9	146
1968	David Grayson, Oakland	10	195
1967	Miller Farr, Houston	10	264
	Tom Janik, Buffalo	10	222
	Dick Westmoreland, Miami	10	127
1966	John Robinson, Kansas City	10	136
1965	Wilmer Hicks, Houston	9	156
1964	Dainard Paulson, New York	12	157
1963	Frederick Glick, Houston	12	180
1962	Leon Riley, New York	11	122
1961	William Atkins, Buffalo	10	158
1960	Austin Gonsoulin, Denver*	11	98

OUTSTANDING RUSHERS

200 YARDS OR MORE IN A GAME

Year	Date	Player and Opponent	Yards
1973	Sept. 16	O. J. Simpson, Buff. (AFC) vs. N. E. (AFC)	250 (29)
	Dec. 9	O. J. Simpson, Buff. (AFC) vs. N. E. (AFC)	219 (22)
	Dec. 16	O. J. Simpson, Buff. (AFC) vs. N. Y. (AFC)	200 (34)
1971	Dec. 5	Willie Ellison, L. A. (NFC) vs. N. O. (NFC)	247 (26)
1970	Dec. 20	John Fuqua, Pitt. (AFC) vs. Phil. (NFC)	218 (20)
1968	Nov. 3	Gale Sayers, Chi. vs G.B.	205 (24)
1966	Oct. 30	James Nance, Bos. vs. Oak., (AFL)	208 (38)
1964	Oct. 10	John Henry Johnson, Pitt. vs Clev.	200 (30)
1963	Sept. 22	Jim Brown, Clev. vs Dall.	232 (20)
	Oct. 20	Clem Daniels, Oak vs N.Y. (AFL)	200 (27)
	Nov. 3	Jim Brown, Clev. vs Phil.	223 (28)
	Dec. 8	Carlton Gilchrist, Buff. vs. N.Y., (AFL)	243 (36)
1961	Nov. 19	Jim Brown, Clev. vs Phil.	237 (34)
	Dec. 10	William Cannon, Hou. vs. N.Y., (AFL)	216 (25)
1960	Dec. 18	John David Crow, St. L. vs Pitt.	203 (24)
1959	Nov. 15	Bobby Mitchell, Clev. vs Wash.	232 (14)
1957	Nov. 24	Jim Brown, Clev. vs L. A.	237 (31)
1956	Dec. 16	Tom Wilson, L. A. vs G. B.	223 (23)
1953	Nov. 22	Dan Towler, L. A. vs Balt.	205 (14)
1950	Nov. 12	Gene Roberts, N. Y. Giants vs Chi. Cards	218 (26)
1949	Nov. 27	Steve Van Buren, Phil. vs Pitt.	205 (27)
1933	Oct. 8	Cliff Battles, Bos. vs N. Y.	215 (16)

1,000 YARDS OR MORE IN A SEASON

Year	Player	Team	Yards
1974	Otis Armstrong	Denver (AFC)	1,407
	Don Woods	San Diego (AFC)	1,162
	O. J. Simpson	Buffalo (AFC)	1,125
	Lawrence McCutcheon	Los Angeles (NFC)	1,109
	Franco Harris	Pittsburgh (AFC)	1,006

Year	Player	Team	Yards
1973	O. J. Simpson	Buffalo (AFC)	2,003
	John Brockington	Green Bay (NFC)	1,144
	Calvin Hill	Dallas (NFC)	1,142
	Lawrence McCutcheon	Los Angeles (NFC)	1,097
	Larry Csonka	Miami (AFC)	1,003
1972	O. J. Simpson	Buffalo (AFC)	1,251
	Larry Brown	Washington (NFC)	1,216
	Ron Johnson	N. Y. Giants (NFC)	1,182
	Larry Csonka	Miami (AFC)	1,117
	Marv Hubbard	Oakland (AFC)	1,100
	Franco Harris	Pittsburgh (AFC)	1,055
	Calvin Hill	Dallas (NFC)	1,036
	Mike Garrett	San Diego (AFC)	1,031
	John Brockington	Green Bay (NFC)	1,027
	Mercury Morris	Miami (AFC)	1,000
1971	Floyd Little	Denver (AFC)	1,133
	John Brockington	Green Bay (NFC)	1,105
	Larry Csonka	Miami (AFC)	1,051
	Steve Owens	Detroit (NFC)	1,035
	Willie Ellison	Los Angeles (NFC)	1,000
1970	Larry Brown	Washington (NFC)	1,125
	Ron Johnson	New York (NFC)	1,027
1969	Gale Sayers	Chicago	1,032
1968	LeRoy Kelly	Cleveland	1,239
	Paul Robinson	Cincinnati (AFL)	1,023
1967	James Nance	Boston (AFL)	1,216
	LeRoy Kelly	Cleveland	1,205
	Hoyle Granger	Houston (AFL)	1,194
	Michael Garrett	Kansas City (AFL)	1,087
1966	James Nance	Boston (AFL)	1,458
	Gale Sayers	Chicago	1,231
	Leroy Kelly	Cleveland	1,141
	Dick Bass	Los Angeles	1,090
1965	Jim Brown	Cleveland	1,544
	Paul Lowe	San Diego (AFL)	1,121
1964	Jim Brown	Cleveland	1,446
	Jim Taylor	Green Bay	1,169
	John Henry Johnson	Pittsburgh	1,048
1963	Jim Brown	Cleveland	1,863
	Clem Daniels	Oakland (AFL)	1,099
	Jim Taylor	Green Bay	1,018
	Paul Lowe	San Diego (AFL)	1,010
1962	Jim Taylor	Green Bay	1,474
	John Henry Johnson	Pittsburgh	1,141
	Carlton Gilchrist	Buffalo (AFL)	1,096
	Abner Haynes	Dallas (AFL)	1,049
	Dick Bass	Los Angeles	1,033
	Charlie Tolar	Houston (AFL)	1,012
1961	Jim Brown	Cleveland	1,408
	Jim Taylor	Green Bay	1,307
1960	Jim Brown	Cleveland	1,257
	Jim Taylor	Green Bay	1,101
	John Crow	St. Louis	1,071
1959	Jim Brown	Cleveland	1,329
	J. D. Smith	San Francisco	1,036
1958	Jim Brown	Cleveland	1,527
1956	Rick Casares	Chicago Bears	1,126
1954	Joe Perry	San Francisco	1,049
1953	Joe Perry	San Francisco	1,018

Year	Player	Team	Yards
1949	Steve Van Buren	Philadelphia	1,146
	Tony Canadeo	Green Bay	1,052
1947	Steve Van Buren	Philadelphia	1,008
1934	Beattie Feathers	Chicago Bears	1,004

NFL/NFC ALL-LEAGUE SELECTIONS

1931
L.E.–Dilweg–Green Bay
L.T.–Hubbard–Green Bay
L.G.–Michalske–Green Bay
C.–McNally–Cardinals
R.G.–Gibson–New York
R.T.–Christensen–Portsmouth
R.E.–Badgro–New York
Q.B.–Clark–Portsmouth
L.H.–Blood–Green Bay
R.H.–Grange–Bears
F.B.–Nevers–Cardinals

1932
L.E.–Flaherty–New York
L.T.–Hubbard–Green Bay
L.G.–Carlson–Bears
C.–Barrager–Green Bay
R.G.–Kiesling–Cardinals
R.T.–Edwards–Boston
R.E.–Johnsos–Bears
Q.B.–Clark–Portsmouth
L.H.–Herber–Green Bay
R.H.–Lumpkin–Portsmouth
F.B.–Nagurski–Bears

1933
L.E.–Hewitt–Bears
L.T.–Hubbard–Green Bay
L.G.–Hickman–Brooklyn
C.–Hein–New York
R.G.–Kopcha–Bears
R.T.–Edwards–Boston
R.E.–Badgro–New York
Q.B.–Newman–New York
L.H.–Presnell–Portsmouth
R.H.–Battles–Boston
F.B.–Nagurski–Bears

1934
L.E.–Hewitt–Bears
L.T.–Christensen–Detroit
L.G.–Gibson–New York
C.–Hein–New York
R.G.–Kopcha–Bears
R.T.–Morgan–New York
R.E.–Badgro–New York
Q.B.–Clark–Detroit
L.H.–Feathers–Bears
R.H.–Strong–New York
F.B.–Nagurski–Bears

1935
L.E.–Smith–Cardinals
L.T.–Morgan–New York
L.G.–Kopcha–Bears
C.–Hein–New York
R.G.–Michalske–Green Bay
R.T.–Musso–Bears
R.E.–Karr–Bears
Q.B.–Clark–Detroit
L.H.–Danowski–New York
R.H.–Caddel–Detroit
F.B.–Mikaluk–Cardinals

1936
L.E.–Hewitt–Philadelphia
L.T.–Smith, E.–Green Bay
L.G.–Evans–Green Bay
C.–Hein–New York
R.G.–Emerson–Detroit
R.T.–Edwards–Boston
R.E.–Hutson–Green Bay
Q.B.–Clark–Detroit
L.H.–Battles–Boston
R.H.–Leemans–New York
F.B.–Hinkle–Green Bay

1937
L.E.–Hewitt–Philadelphia
L.T.–Stydahar–Bears
L.G.–Evans–Green Bay
C.–Hein–New York
R.G.–Musso–Bears
R.T.–Edwards–Washington
R.E.–Tinsley–Cardinals
Q.B.–Clark–Detroit
L.H.–Battles–Washington
R.H.–Baugh–Washington
F.B.–Hinkle–Green Bay

1938
L.E.–Hutson–Green Bay
L.T.–Widseth–New York
L.G.–Fortmann–Bears
C.–Hein–New York
R.G.–Letlow–Green Bay
R.T.–Stydahar–Bears
R.E.–Tinsley–Cardinals
Q.B.–Parker–Brooklyn
L.H.–Danowski–New York
R.H.–Cardwell–Detroit
F.B.–Hinkle–Green Bay

1939

L.E.—Hutson—Green Bay
L.T.—Stydahar—Bears
L.G.—Fortmann—Bears
C.—Hein—New York
R.G.—Dell Isola—New York
R.T.—Barber—Washington
R.E.—Poole—New York
Q.B.—O'Brien—Philadelphia
L.H.—Leemans—New York
R.H.—Farkas—Washington
F.B.—Osmanski, W.—Bears

1940

L.E.—Hutson—Green Bay
L.T.—Stydahar—Bears
L.G.—Fortmann—Bears
C.—Hein—New York
R.G.—Wiethe—Detroit
R.T.—Kinard—Brooklyn
R.E.—Schwartz—Brooklyn
Q.B.—Parker—Brooklyn
L.H.—Baugh—Washington
R.H.—White—Detroit
F.B.—Drake—Cleveland

1941

L.E.—Hutson—Green Bay
L.T.—Kinard, F.—Brooklyn
L.G.—Fortmann—Bears
C.—Turner—Bears
R.G.—Kuharich—Cardinals
R.T.—Wilkin—Washington
R.E.—Schwartz—Brooklyn
Q.B.—Luckman—Bears
L.H.—Isbell—Green Bay
R.H.—McAfee—Bears
F.B.—Hinkle—Green Bay

1942

L.E.—Hutson—Green Bay
L.T.—Wilkin—Washington
L.G.—Fortmann—Bears
C.—Turner—Bears
R.G.—Edwards—New York
R.T.—Artoe—Bears
R.E.—Masterson—Washington
Q.B.—Luckman—Bears
L.H.—Isbell—Green Bay
R.H.—Dudley—Pittsburgh
F.B.—Famiglietti—Bears

Official selection discontinued in 1943.

Beginning in 1943, All-League Selections
have been made by the news services. A.P.
—Associated Press; U.P.—United Press; I.N.S.
International News Service; U.P.I.—United
Press International.)

1943

L.E.—Hutson—Green Bay (A.P., U.P.)
L.T.—Kinard, E.—Brooklyn (A.P.)
        Sears—Phil-Pitt (U.P.)
L.G.—Farman—Washington (A.P., U.P.)
C.—Turner—Chicago Bears (A.P., U.P.)
R.G.—Fortman—Chicago Bears (A.P., U.P.)
R.T.—Blozis—New York (A.P., U.P.)
R.E.—Rucinski—Cardinals (AP., U.P.)
Q.B.—Luckman—Chicago Bears (A.P., U.P.)
L.H.—Baugh—Washington (A.P., U.P.)
R.H.—Clark—Chicago Bears (A.P., U.P.)
F.B.—Canadeo—Green Bay (A.P.)
        Cuff—New York (U.P.)

1944

L.E.—Hutson—Green Bay (A.P., U.P.)
L.T.—Wistert—Philadelphia (A.P., U.P.)
L.G.—Younce—New York (A.P., U.P.)
C.—Turner—Chicago Bears (A.P., U.P.)
R.G.—Matheson—Cleveland (A.P., U.P.)
R.T.—Kinard, F.—Brooklyn (A.P.)
        Cope—New York (U.P.)
R.E.—Aguirre—Washington (A.P., U.P.)
Q.B.—Luckman—Chicago Bears (A.P.)
        Zimmerman—Philadelphia (U.P.)
L.H.—Sinkwich—Detroit (A.P., U.P.)
R.H.—Van Buren, S.—Philadelphia (A.P.)
        Cuff—New York (U.P.)
F.B.—Paschal—New York (A.P., U.P.)

1945

L.E.—Hutson—Green Bay (A.P., U.P.)
L.T.—Wistert—Philadelphia (A.P., U.P.)
L.G.—Matheson—Cleveland (A.P., U.P.)
C.—Brock—Green Bay (A.P., U.P.)
R.G.—Radovich, Detroit (A.P., U.P.)
R.T.—Cope—New York (A.P.)
        Uremovich, Detroit (U.P.)
R.E.—Benton—Cleveland (A.P.)
        Pritko—Cleveland (U.P.)
Q.B.—Waterfield—Cleveland (A.P.)
        Baugh—Washington (U.P.)
L.H.—Van Buren, S.—Phila. (A.P., U.P.)
R.H.—Bagarus—Washington (A.P.)
        Waterfield—Cleveland (U.P.)
F.B.—Westfall—Detroit (A.P.)
        Fritsch—Green Bay (U.P.)

1946
UNITED PRESS

L.E.—Benton, J.—Los Angeles
L.T.—Wistert—Philadelphia
L.G.—Lio—Philadelphia
C.—Turner—Bears
R.G.—Matheson—Los Angeles
R.T.—White—New York
R.E.—Kavanaugh—Bears
Q.B.—Waterfield—Los Angeles
L.H.—Dudley—Pittsburgh
R.H.—Filchock—New York
F.B.—Fritsch—Green Bay

1947
UNITED PRESS
L.E.—Kavanaugh—Bears
L.T.—Wistert—Philadelphia
L.G.—Younce—New York
C.—Banonis—Cardinals
R.G.—Moore, Wm.—Pittsburgh
R.T.—Davis, F.—Bears
R.E.—Kutner—Cardinals
Q.B.—Luckman—Bears
L.H.—Van Buren, S.—Philadelphia
R.H.—Baugh—Washington
F.B.—Harder—Cardinals

1948
UNITED PRESS
L.E.—Pihos—Philadelphia
L.T.—Wistert—Philadelphia
L.G.—Bray—Bears
C.—Turner—Bears
R.G.—Ramsey, G.—Cardinals
R.T.—Huffman—Los Angeles
R.E.—Kutner—Cardinals
Q.B.—Baugh—Washington
L.H.—Van Buren, S.—Philadelphia
R.H.—Trippi—Cardinals
F.B.—Harder—Cardinals

1949
UNITED PRESS
L.E.—Pihos—Philadelphia
L.T.—Sears—Philadelphia
L.G.—Bray—Bears
C.—Naumetz—Los Angeles
R.G.—Ramsey, G.—Cardinals
R.T.—Huffman—Los Angeles
R.E.—Fears—Los Angeles
Q.B.—Waterfield—Los Angeles
L.H.—Van Buren, S.—Philadelphia
R.H.—Canadeo—Green Bay
F.B.—Harder—Cardinals

1950
L.E.—Fears—Los Angeles (A.P., U.P.)
L.T.—Connor—Chicago Bears (A.P., U.P.)
L.G.—Barwegan—Bears (A.P., U.P.)
C.—Bednarik—Philadelphia (A.P.)
Tonnemaker,—Green Bay (U.P.)
R.G.—Signaigo—New York Yanks (A.P.)
Willis—Cleveland (U.P.)
R.T.—Weinmeister—Giants (A.P., U.P.)
R.E.—Edwards, New York Yanks (A.P.)
Speedie—Cleveland (U.P.)
Q.B.—Lujack—Chicago Bears (A.P., U.P.)
L.H.—Walker—Detroit (A.P., U.P.)
R.H.—Geri—Pittsburgh (A.P., U.P.)
F.B.—Motley—Cleveland (A.P., U.P.)

1951
OFFENSE

Hirsch, Los Angeles (A.P., U.P.)	end
Hart, Detroit (A.P.)	end
Lavelli, Cleveland (U.P.)	end
Connor, Chicago Bears (A.P.)	tackle
Groza, Cleveland (U.P.)	tackle
Nomellini, San Francisco (A.P.)	tackle
Coulter, New York Giants (U.P.)	tackle
Creekmur, Detroit (A.P., U.P.)	guard
Barwegan, Chicago Bears (A.P., U.P.)	guard
Lindskog, Philadelphia (A.P.)	center
Gatski, Cleveland (U.P.)	center
Graham, Cleveland (A.P., U.P.)	quarterback
Walker, Detroit (A.P., U.P.)	halfback
Jones, W., Cleveland (A.P., U.P.)	halfback
Price, New York Giants (A.P.)	fullback
Towler, Los Angeles (U.P.)	fullback

DEFENSE

Brink, Los Angeles (A.P.)	end
Hart, Detroit (U.P.)	end
Ford, Cleveland (A.P., U.P.)	end
Weinmeister, New York Giants (A.P., U.P.)	tackle
DeRogatis, New York Giants (A.P.)	tackle
Connor, Chicago Bears (U.P.)	tackle
Willis, Cleveland (A.P., U.P.)	guard
Bingaman, Detroit (A.P.)	guard
Baker, New York Giants (U.P.)	guard
Bednarik, Philadelphia (A.P., U.P.)	linebacker
Younger, Los Angeles (A.P.)	linebacker
Adamle, Cleveland (U.P.)	linebacker
Schnellbacher, New York Giants (A.P., U.P.)	halfback
Shipkey, Pittsburgh (A.P.)	halfback
Lahr, Cleveland (U.P.)	halfback
Tunnell, New York Giants (A.P., U.P.)	safety

1952
OFFENSE

Box, Detroit (A.P.)	end
Speedie, Cleveland (U.P.)	end
Soltau, San Francisco (A.P., U.P.)	end
Connor, Chicago Bears (A.P.)	tackle
Groza, Cleveland (U.P.)	tackle
Nomellini, San Francisco (A.P., U.P.)	tackle
Creekmur, Detroit (A.P., U.P.)	guard
Groza, Cleveland (A.P.)	guard
Fischer, Chicago Cardinals (U.P.)	guard
Gatski, Cleveland (A.P.)	center
Walsh, Pittsburgh (U.P.)	center
Layne, Detroit (A.P.)	quarterback
Graham, Cleveland (U.P.)	quarterback
McElhenny, San Francisco (A.P., U.P.)	halfback
Towler, Los Angeles (A.P., U.P.)	halfback
Price, New York Giants (A.P., U.P.)	fullback

DEFENSE

Brink, Los Angeles (U.P.)	end
Ford, Cleveland (A.P., U.P.)	end
Pihos, Philadelphia (A.P.)	end
Weinmeister, New York Giants (A.P., U.P.)	tackle
McGraw, Detroit (A.P., U.P.)	tackle
West, Los Angeles (A.P., U.P.)	guard
Willis, Cleveland (A.P.)	guard
Bingaman, Detroit (U.P.)	guard
Bednarik, Philadelphia (A.P., U.P.)	linebacker
Shipkey, Pittsburgh (A.P.)	linebacker
Connor, Chicago Bears (U.P.)	linebacker
Christiansen, Detroit (A.P.)	halfback
Matson, Chicago Cardinals (A.P.)	halfback
Smith, R., Detroit (U.P.)	halfback
Rich, Los Angeles (U.P.)	halfback
Tunnell, New York Giants (A.P., U.P.)	safety

1953
OFFENSE

Pihos, Philadelphia (A.P., U.P.)	end
Lavelli, Cleveland (U.P.)	end
Hirsch, Los Angeles (A.P.)	end
Connor, Chicago Bears (A.P.)	tackle
Groza, Cleveland (A.P., U.P.)	tackle
Creekmur, Detroit (U.P.)	tackle
Stanfel, Detroit (A.P., U.P.)	guard
Creekmur, Detroit (A.P.)	guard
Banducci, San Francisco (U.P.)	guard
Gatski, Cleveland (A.P., U.P.)	center
Graham, Cleveland (A.P., U.P.)	quarterback
McElhenny, San Francisco (A.P., U.P.)	halfback
Walker, Detroit (A.P.)	halfback
Towler, Los Angeles (U.P.)	halfback
Perry, San Francisco (A.P., U.P.)	fullback

DEFENSE

Ford, Cleveland (A.P., U.P.)	end
Robustelli, Los Angeles (A.P.)	end
Willey, Philadelphia (U.P.)	end
Weinmeister, New York (A.P., U.P.)	tackle
Nomellini, San Francisco (A.P., U.P.)	tackle
Bingaman, Detroit (A.P., U.P.)	guard
Willis, Cleveland (A.P.)	guard

Dodrill, Pittsburgh (U.P.)   guard
Bednarik, Philadelphia (A.P.)   linebacker
Paul, Los Angeles (A.P.)   linebacker
Connor, Chicago Bears (U.P.)   linebacker
Thompson, Cleveland (U.P.)   linebacker
Keane, T., Baltimore (A.P., U.P.)   halfback
Thompson, Cleveland (A.P.)   halfback
Christiansen, Detroit (U.P.)   halfback
Gorgal, Cleveland (U.P.)   safety
Christiansen, Detroit (A.P.)   safety

1954
OFFENSE

Pihos, Philadelphia (A.P., U.P.)   end
Boyd, Los Angeles (A.P.)   end
Hill, Chicago Bears (U.P.)   end
Creekmur, Detroit (A.P., U.P.)   tackle
Groza, Cleveland (A.P., U.P.)   tackle
Stanfel, Detroit (A.P., U.P.)   guard
Banducci, San Francisco (A.P., U.P.)   guard
Walsh, Pittsburgh (A.P., U.P.)   center
Graham, Cleveland (A.P., U.P.)   quarterback
Walker, Detroit (A.P., U.P.)   halfback
Matson, Chicago Cardinals (A.P., U.P.)   halfback
Perry, San Francisco (A.P., U.P.)   fullback

DEFENSE

Ford, Cleveland (A.P., U.P.)   end
Willey, Philadelphia (A.P., U.P.)   end
Nomellini, San Francisco (A.P., U.P.)   tackle
Donovan, Baltimore (A.P., U.P.)   tackle
Bingaman, Detroit (A.P., U.P.)   guard
Dodrill, Pittsburgh (A.P.)   guard
Kilroy, Philadelphia (U.P.)   guard
Bednarik, Philadelphia (A.P., U.P.)   linebacker
Schmidt, Detroit (A.P.)   linebacker
Zatkoff, Green Bay (U.P.)   linebacker
Landry, New York (A.P., U.P.)   halfback

Dillon, Green Bay (A.P.)   halfback
David, Detroit (U.P.)   halfback
Christiansen, Detroit (A.P., U.P.)   safety

1955
OFFENSE

Hill, Chicago Bears (A.P., U.P.)   end
Wilson, San Francisco (U.P.)   end
Pihos, Philadelphia (A.P.)   end
Groza, Cleveland (A.P., U.P.)   tackle
Wightkin, Chicago Bears (A.P.)   tackle
St. Clair, San Francisco (U.P.)   tackle
Jones, Chicago Bears (A.P.)   guard
Putnam, Los Angeles (A.P.)   guard
Gibron, Cleveland (U.P.)   guard
Austin, New York (U.P.)   guard
Gatski, Cleveland (A.P., U.P.)   center
Graham, Cleveland (A.P., U.P.)   quarterback
Matson, Chicago Cardinals (A.P., U.P.)   halfback
Gifford, New York (A.P.)   halfback
Waller, Los Angeles (U.P.)   halfback
Ameche, Baltimore (A.P., U.P.)   fullback

DEFENSE

Brito, Washington (A.P., U.P.)	end
Ford, Cleveland (U.P.)	end
Robustelli, Los Angeles (A.P.)	end
Donovan, Baltimore (A.P., U.P.)	tackle
Toneff, San Francisco (A.P.)	tackle
Colo, Cleveland (U.P.)	tackle
George, Chicago Bears (A.P.)	middle guard
Dodrill, Pittsburgh (U.P.)	middle guard
Bednarik, Philadelphia (U.P.)	linebacker
Connor, Chicago Bears (U.P.)	linebacker
Zatkoff, Green Bay (A.P.)	linebacker
Schmidt, Detroit (A.P.)	linebacker
Dillon, Green Bay (A.P.)	halfback
Sherman, Los Angeles (A.P., U.P.)	halfback
Paul, Cleveland (U.P.)	halfback
Christiansen, Detroit (A.P., U.P.)	safety
Dillon, Green Bay (U.P.)	safety
Tunnell, New York (A.P.)	safety

1956

OFFENSE

Hill, Chicago Bears (A.P., U.P.)	end
Howton, Green Bay (A.P., U.P.)	end
Creekmur, Detroit (A.P., U.P.)	tackle
Brown, New York (A.P., U.P.)	tackle
Jones, Chicago Bears (A.P., U.P.)	guard
Stanfel, Washington (A.P., U.P.)	guard
Strickland, Chicago Bears (A.P.)	center
Ane, Detroit (U.P.)	center
Layne, Detroit (A.P., U.P.)	quarterback
Gifford, New York (A.P., U.P.)	halfback
Matson, Chicago Cardinals (A.P., U.P.)	halfback
Casares, Chicago Bears (A.P., U.P.)	fullback

DEFENSE

Robustelli, New York (A.P., U.P.)	end
Brito, Washington (A.P., U.P.)	end
Grier, New York (A.P., U.P.)	tackle
Donovan, Baltimore (A.P.)	tackle
Stautner, Pittsburgh (U.P.)	tackle
George, Chicago Bears (A.P., U.P.)	middle guard
Schmidt, Detroit (A.P., U.P.)	linebacker
Bednarik, Philadelphia (U.P.)	linebacker
Richter, Los Angeles (A.P.)	linebacker
Lane, Chicago Cardinals (A.P., U.P.)	halfback
Tunnell, New York (U.P.)	halfback
Christiansen, Detroit (A.P.)	halfback
Lary, Detroit (A.P.)	safety
Tunnell, New York (A.P.)	safety
Christiansen, Detroit (U.P.)	safety
Dillon, Green Bay (U.P.)	safety

1957

OFFENSE

Wilson, San Francisco (A.P., U.P.)	end
Howton, Green Bay (A.P., U.P.)	end
Brown, New York (A.P., U.P.)	tackle
Creekmur, Detroit (A.P.)	tackle
Groza, Cleveland (U.P.)	tackle
Putnam, Los Angeles (A.P., U.P.)	guard
Stanfel, Washington (A.P., U.P.)	guard
Ringo, Green Bay (A.P.)	center

Strickland, Chicago Bears (U.P.)	center
Tittle, San Francisco (A.P., U.P.)	quarterback
Gifford, New York (A.P., U.P.)	halfback
Matson, Chicago Cardinals (A.P., U.P.)	halfback
Brown, Cleveland (A.P., U.P.)	fullback

DEFENSE

Marchetti, Baltimore (A.P., U.P.)	end
Robustelli, New York (U.P.)	end
Brito, Washington (A.P.)	end
Nomellini, San Francisco (A.P., U.P.)	tackle
Donovan, Baltimore (A.P., U.P.)	tackle
Schmidt, Detroit (A.P., U.P.)	linebacker
Matuszak, San Francisco (A.P., U.P.)	linebacker
George, Chicago Bears (A.P., U.P.)	linebacker
Christiansen, Detroit (A.P.)	halfback
Dillon, Green Bay (A.P.)	halfback
Butler, Pittsburgh (U.P.)	halfback
Lary, Detroit (U.P.)	halfback
Butler, Pittsburgh (A.P.)	safety
Davis, M., Baltimore (A.P.)	safety
Dillon, Green Bay (U.P.)	safety
Christiansen, Detroit (U.P.)	safety

1958
OFFENSE

Berry, Baltimore (A.P., U.P.I.)	end
Shofner, Los Angeles (A.P., U.P.I.)	end
Brown, New York (A.P., U.P.I.)	tackle
Parker, Baltimore (A.P., U.P.I.)	tackle
Stanfel, Washington (A.P., U.P.I.)	guard
Putnam, Los Angeles (A.P., U.P.I.)	guard
Wietecha, New York (A.P., U.P.I.)	center
Unitas, Baltimore (A.P., U.P.I.)	quarterback
Moore, Baltimore (A.P., U.P.I.)	halfback
Arnett, Los Angeles (A.P., U.P.I.)	halfback
Brown, Cleveland (A.P., U.P.I.)	fullback

DEFENSE

Marchetti, Baltimore (A.P., U.P.I.)	end
Robustelli, New York (A.P.)	end
Brito, Washington (U.P.I.)	end
Lipscomb, Baltimore (A.P., U.P.I.)	tackle
Stautner, Pittsburgh (A.P., U.P.I.)	tackle
Schmidt, Detroit (A.P., U.P.I.)	linebacker
Huff, New York (A.P., U.P.I.)	linebacker
George, Chicago Bears (A.P., U.P.I.)	linebacker
Butler, Pittsburgh (A.P., U.P.I.)	halfback
Lary, Detroit (A.P., U.P.I.)	halfback
Patton, New York (A.P., U.P.I.)	safety
Dillon, Green Bay (A.P., U.P.I.)	safety

1959
OFFENSE

Berry, Baltimore (A.P., U.P.I.)	end
Shofner, Los Angeles (A.P., U.P.I.)	end
Brown, New York (A.P., U.P.I.)	tackle
Parker, Baltimore (A.P., U.P.I.)	tackle
Smith, Cleveland (A.P., U.P.I.)	guard
Jones, Chicago Bears (A.P.)	guard
Spinney, Baltimore (U.P.I.)	guard
Ringo, Green Bay (A.P., U.P.I.)	center
Unitas, Baltimore (A.P., U.P.I.)	quarterback

Gifford, New York (A.P., U.P.I.)	halfback
Moore, Baltimore (A.P.)	halfback
J. D. Smith, San Francisco (U.P.I.)	halfback
Brown, Cleveland (A.P., U.P.I.)	fullback

DEFENSE

Marchetti, Baltimore (A.P., U.P.I.)	end
Robustelli, New York (A.P., U.P.I.)	end
Lipscomb, Baltimore (A.P., U.P.I.)	tackle
Nomellini, San Francisco (A.P., U.P.I.)	tackle
Huff, New York (A.P., U.P.I.)	linebacker
George, Chicago Bears (A.P., U.P.I.)	linebacker
Schmidt, Detroit (A.P., U.P.I.)	linebacker
Woodson, San Francisco (A.P., U.P.I.)	halfback
Butler, Pittsburgh, (A.P., U.P.I.)	halfback
Derby, Pittsburgh (U.P.I.)	safety
Patton, New York (A.P., U.P.I.)	safety
Nelson, Baltimore (A.P.)	safety

1960
OFFENSE

Berry, Baltimore (A.P., U.P.I.)	end
Randle, St. Louis (A.P., U.P.I.)	end
Parker, Baltimore (A.P., U.P.I.)	tackle
Gregg, Green Bay (A.P.)	tackle
Brown, New York (U.P.I.)	tackle
Smith, Cleveland (A.P., U.P.I.)	guard
Kramer, Green Bay (A.P.)	guard
Jones, Chicago (U.P.I.)	guard
Ringo, Green Bay (A.P., U.P.I.)	center
Van Brocklin, Philadelphia (A.P., U.P.I.)	quarterback
Hornung, Green Bay (A.P., U.P.I.)	halfback
Moore, Baltimore (A.P., U.P.I.)	halfback
Brown, Cleveland (A.P., U.P.I.)	fullback

DEFENSE

Marchetti, Baltimore (A.P., U.P.I.)	end
Robustelli, New York (A.P.)	end
Atkins, Chicago (U.P.I.)	end
Jordan, Green Bay (A.P., U.P.I.)	tackle
Karras, Detroit (A.P., U.P.I.)	tackle
Bednarik, Philadelphia (A.P., U.P.I.)	linebacker
George, Chicago (A.P., U.P.I.)	linebacker
Forester, Green Bay (A.P., U.P.I.)	linebacker
Brookshier, Philadelphia (A.P., U.P.I.)	halfback
Lane, Detroit (U.P.I.)	halfback
Woodson, (A.P.)	halfback
Norton, St. Louis (A.P., U.P.I.)	safety
Patton, New York (A.P., U.P.I.)	safety

1961
OFFENSE

Shofner, New York (A.P, U.P.I.)	end
Phillips, Los Angeles (A.P., U.P.I.)	end
Brown, New York (A.P., U.P.I.)	tackle
Gregg, Green Bay (U.P.I.)	tackle
Parker, Baltimore (A.P.)	tackle
Thurston, Green Bay (A.P., U.P.I.)	guard
Smith, Cleveland (A.P., U.P.I.)	guard
Ringo, Green Bay (A.P., U.P.I.)	center
Jurgenson, Philadelphia (A.P., U.P.I.)	quarterback
Hornung, Green Bay (A.P., U.P.I.)	halfback

Moore, Baltimore (A.P., U.P.I.)	halfback
Brown, Cleveland (A.P., U.P.I.)	fullback

DEFENSE

Marchetti, Baltimore (A.P., U.P.I.)	end
Katcavage, New York (A.P., U.P.I.)	end
Jordan, Green Bay (A.P., U.P.I.)	tackle
A. Karras, Detroit (A.P., U.P.I.)	tackle
Schmidt, Detroit (A.P., U.P.I.)	linebacker
Forester, Green Bay (A.P., U.P.I.)	linebacker
George, Chicago (A.P.)	linebacker
Currie, Green Bay (U.P.I.)	linebacker
E. Barnes, New York (A.P., U.P.I.)	halfback
Whittenton, Green Bay (A.P., U.P.I.)	halfback
Patton, New York (A.P., U.P.I.)	safety
Lane, Detroit (A.P.)	safety
Sample, Pittsburgh (U.P.I.)	safety

1962
OFFENSE

Shofner, New York (A.P., U.P.I.)	end
P. Kramer, Green Bay (A.P.)	end
Ditka, Chicago (U.P.I.)	end
R. Brown, New York (A.P., U.P.I.)	tackle
Gregg, Green Bay (A.P., U.P.I.)	tackle
J. Kramer, Green Bay (A.P., U.P.I.)	guard
Parker, Baltimore (A.P.)	guard
Thurston, Green Bay (U.P.I.)	guard
Ringo, Green Bay (U.P.I.)	center
Tittle, New York (A.P., U.P.I.)	quarterback
Mitchell, Washington (A.P., U.P.I.)	halfback
Perkins, Dallas (A.P.)	halfback
Bass, Los Angeles (U.P.I.)	halfback
Taylor, Green Bay (A.P., U.P.I.)	fullback

DEFENSE

Marchetti, Baltimore (A.P., U.P.I.)	end
W. Davis, Green Bay (A.P.)	end
Katcavage, New York (U.P.I.)	end
R. Brown, Detroit (A.P., U.P.I.)	tackle
Jordan, Green Bay (A.P.)	tackle
A. Karras, Detroit (U.P.I.)	tackle
Schmidt, Detroit (A.P., U.P.I.)	linebacker
Currie, Green Bay (A.P., U.P.I.)	linebacker
Forester, Green Bay (A.P., U.P.I.)	linebacker
Lane, Detroit (A.P., U.P.I.)	halfback
Adderley, Green Bay (A.P., U.P.I.)	halfback
Patton, New York (A.P., U.P.I.)	safety
Lary, Detroit (A.P., U.P.I.)	safety

1963
OFFENSE

Shofner, New York (A.P., U.P.I.)	end
Ditka, Chicago (A.P., U.P.I.)	end
Brown, Roosevelt, New York (U.P.I.)	tackle
Gregg, Green Bay (A.P., U.P.I.)	tackle
Schafrath, Cleveland (A.P.)	tackle
Kramer, J., Green Bay (A.P., U.P.I.)	guard
Parker, Baltimore (A.P.)	guard
Gray, St. Louis (U.P.I.)	guard
Ringo, Green Bay (A.P., U.P.I.)	center

Tittle, New York (A.P., U.P.I.)   quarterback
Mason, Minnesota (A.P., U.P.I.)   halfback
Conrad, St. Louis (A.P., U.P.I.)   halfback
Brown, James, Cleveland (A.P., U.P.I.)   fullback

DEFENSE

Atkins, Chicago (A.P., U.P.I.)   end
Katcavage, New York (A.P., U.P.I.)   end
Jordan, Green Bay (A.P., U.P.I.)   tackle
Brown, Roger, Detroit (A.P., U.P.I.)   tackle
George, Chicago (A.P., U.P.I.)   linebacker
Fortunato, Chicago (A.P., U.P.I.)   linebacker
Forester, Green Bay (A.P.)   linebacker
Pardee, Los Angeles (U.P.I.)   linebacker
Lynch, New York (A.P., U.P.I.)   halfback
Lane, Detroit (U.P.I.)   halfback
Adderley, Green Bay (A.P.)   halfback
Petitbon, Chicago (A.P., U.P.I.)   safety
Wilson, St. Louis (U.P.I.)   safety
Taylor, Chicago (A.P.)   safety

1964
OFFENSE

Clarke, Dallas (A.P.)   end
Ditka, Chicago (A.P., U.P.I.)   end
Mitchell, Washington (U.P.I.)   end
Gregg, Green Bay (A.P., U.P.I.)   tackle
Schafrath, Cleveland (A.P., U.P.I.)   tackle
Parker, Baltimore (A.P., U.P.I.)   guard
Gray, St. Louis (A.P., U.P.I.)   guard
Tinglehoff, Minnesota (A.P., U.P.I.)   center
Unitas, Baltimore (A.P., U.P.I.)   quarterback
Moore, Balimore (A.P., U.P.I.)   halfback
Morris, Chicago (A.P., U.P.I.)   halfback
Brown, Cleveland (A.P., U.P.I.)   fullback

DEFENSE

Marchetti, Baltimore (A.P., U.P.I.)   end
Davis, Green Bay (A.P., U.P.I.)   end
Jordan, Green Bay (A.P., U.P.I.)   tackle
Lilly, Dallas (A.P., U.P.I.)   tackle
Nitschke, Green Bay (A.P., U.P.I.)   linebacker
Fortunato, Chicago (A.P., U.P.I.)   linebacker
Baughan, Philadelphia (A.P.)   linebacker
Walker, Detroit (U.P.I.)   linebacker
Fischer, St. Louis (A.P., U.P.I.)   halfback
Boyd, Baltimore (A.P., U.P.I.)   halfback
Krause, Washington (A.P., U.P.I.)   safety
Wood, Green Bay (A.P., U.P.I.)   safety

1965

OFFENSE

Parks, San Francisco (A.P., U.P.I.)   end
Retzlaff, Philadelphia (A.P., U.P.I.)   end
Schafrath, Cleveland (A.P., U.P.I.)   tackle
Brown, Philadelphia (A.P.)   tackle
Gregg, Green Bay (U.P.I.)   tackle
Parker, Baltimore (A.P., U.P.I.)   guard
Gregg, Green Bay (A.P.)   guard
Gray, St. Louis (U.P.I.)   guard
Tingelhoff, Minnesota (A.P., U.P.I.)   center
Unitas, Baltimore (A.P., U.P.I.)   quarterback

Sayers, Chicago (A.P., U.P.I.)   halfback
Orr, Baltimore (A.P.)   halfback
Collins, Cleveland (U.P.I.)   halfback
Brown, Cleveland (A.P., U.P.I.)   fullback

DEFENSE

Davis, Green Bay (A.P., U.P.I.).   end
Jones, Los Angeles (A.P., U.P.I.)   end
Lilly, Dallas (A.P., U.P.I.)   tackle
Karras, Detroit (A.P., U.P.I.)   tackle
Walker, Detroit (A.P., U.P.I.)   linebacker
Butkus, Chicago (A.P.)   linebacker
Fortunato, Chicago (A.P.)   linebacker
Nitschke, Green Bay (U.P.I.)   linebacker
Houston, Cleveland (U.P.I)   linebacker
Adderley, Green Bay (A.P., U.P.I.)   halfback
Boyd, Baltimore (A.P., U.P.I.)   halfback
Wood, Green Bay (A.P., U.P.I.)   safety
Krause, Washington (A.P., U.P.I.)   safety

1966
OFFENSE

Hayes, Dallas (A.P., U.P.I)   end
Mackey, Baltimore (A.P., U.P.I.)   end
Brown, R., Philadelphia (A.P., U.P.I.)   tackle
Gregg, Green Bay (A.P., U.P.I.)   tackle
Kramer, Green Bay (A.P., U.P.I.)   guard
Thomas, San Francisco (A.P.)   guard
Gordy, Detroit (U.P.I.)   guard
Tingelhoff, Minnesota (A.P., U.P.I.)   center
Starr, Green Bay (A.P., U.P.I.)   quarterback
Sayers, Chicago (A.P., U.P.I.)   halfback
Studstill, Detroit (A.P., U.P.I.)   halfback
Kelly, Cleveland (A.P., U.P.I.)   fullback

DEFENSE

Davis, Green Bay (A.P., U.P.I.)   end
Jones, Los Angeles (A.P., U.P.I.)   end
Lilly, Dallas (A.P., U.P.I.)   tackle
Olson, Los Angeles (A.P., U.P.I.)   tackle
Howley, Dallas (A.P., U.P.I.)   linebacker
Nitschke, Green Bay (A.P., U.P.I.)   linebacker
Caffey, Green Bay (A.P., U.P.I.)   linebacker
Adderly, Green Bay (A.P., U.P.I.)   halfback
Boyd, Baltimore (U.P.I.)   halfback
Green, Dallas (A.P.)   halfback
Wood, Green Bay (A.P., U.P.I.)   safety
Wilson, St. Louis (A.P., U.P.I.)   safety

1967
OFFENSE

Taylor, Washington (A.P., U.P.I.)   end
Smith, St. Louis (U.P.I)   end
Mackey, Baltimore (A.P.)   end
Neely, Dallas (A.P., U.P.I.)   tackle
Gregg, Green Bay (A.P., U.P.I.)   tackle
Kramer, Green Bay (A.P., U.P.I.)   guard
Hickerson, Cleveland (A.P., U.P.I.)   guard

Tingelhoff, Minnesota (U.P.I.)	center
DeMarco, St. Louis (A.P.)	center
Unitas, Baltimore (A.P., U.P.I.)	qback
Kelly, Cleveland (A.P., U.P.I.)	back
Sayers, Chicago (A.P., U.P.I.)	back
Jones, New York (U.P.I.)	back
Richardson, Baltimore (A.P.)	back

DEFENSE

Jones, Los Angeles (A.P., U.P.I.)	end
Davis, Green Bay (A.P., U.P.I.)	end
Olsen, Los Angeles (A.P., U.P.I.)	tackle
Lilly, Dallas (A.P., U.P.I.)	tackle
Robinson, Green Bay (A.P., U.P.I.)	linebacker
Butkus, Chicago (U.P.I.)	linebacker
Baughan, Los Angeles (U.P.I.)	linebacker
Nobis, Atlanta (A.P.)	linebacker
Howley, Dallas (A.P.)	linebacker
Jeter, Green Bay (A.P., U.P.I.)	halfback
Green, Dallas (A.P., U.P.I.)	halfback
Wood, Green Bay (A.P., U.P.I.)	safety
Meador, Los Angeles (U.P.I.)	safety
Wilson, St. Louis (A.P.)	safety

1968
OFFENSE

Hayes, Dallas (A.P.)	end
Mackey, Baltimore (A.P., U.P.I.)	end
Warfield, Cleveland (U.P.I.)	end
Neely, Dallas (A.P., U.P.I.)	tackle
Brown, Philadelphia (A.P.)	tackle
Vogel, Baltimore (U.P.I.)	tackle
Hickerson, Cleveland (A.P., U.P.I.)	guard
Mudd, San Francisco (A.P., U.P.I.)	guard
Tingelhoff, Minnesota (A.P., U.P.I.)	center
Morrall, Baltimore (A.P., U.P.I.)	Qback
Kelly, Cleveland (A.P., U.P.I.)	back
Sayers, Chicago (A.P., U.P.I.)	back
McNeil, San Francisco (A.P., U.P.I.)	back

DEFENSE

Eller, Minnesota (A.P., U.P.I.)	end
Jones, Los Angeles (A.P., U.P.I.)	end
Olsen, Los Angeles (A.P., U.P.I.)	tackle
Lilly, Dallas (A.P., U.P.I.)	tackle
Butkus, Chicago (A.P., U.P.I.)	linebacker
Curtis, Baltimore (A.P., U.P.I.)	linebacker
Howley, Dallas (A.P.)	linebacker
Robinson, Green Bay (U.P.I.)	linebacker
Barney, Detroit (A.P., U.P.I.)	halfback
Boyd, Baltimore (A.P., U.P.I.)	halfback
Wilson, St. Louis (A.P., U.P.I.)	safety
Meador, Los Angeles (A.P.)	safety
Wood, Green Bay (U.P.I.)	safety

1969

OFFENSE

Jefferson, Pittsburgh (A.P., U.P.I.)	end

Collins, Cleveland (A.P., U.P.I.)   end
Abramowicz, New Orleans (A.P.)   end
Smith, Washington (A.P., U.P.I.)   end
Brown, Los Angeles (A.P., U.P.I.)   tackle
Neely, Dallas (A.P., U.P.I.)   tackle
Hickerson, Cleveland (A.P., U.P.I.)   guard
Mack, Los Angeles (U.P.I.)   guard
Niland, Dallas (A.P.)   guard
Tingelhoff, Minnesota (A.P., U.P.I.)   center
Gabriel, Los Angeles (A.P., U.P.I.)   Qback
Sayers, Chicago (A.P., U.P.I.)   back
Hill, Dallas (A.P., U.P.I.)   back

DEFENSE

Jones, Los Angeles (A.P., U.P.I.)   end
Eller, Minnesota (A.P., U.P.I.)   end
Olsen, Los Angeles (A.P., U.P.I.)   tackle
Lilly, Dallas (A.P.)   tackle
Page, Minnesota (U.P.I.)   tackle
Butkus, Chicago (A.P., U.P.I.)   linebacker
Howley, Dallas (A.P., U.P.I.)   linebacker
Robinson, Green Bay (A.P., U.P.I.)   linebacker
Barney, Detroit (A.P., U.P.I.)   cornerback
Adderley, Green Bay (A.P.)   cornerback
Green, Dallas (U.P.I.)   cornerback
Wilson, St. Louis (A.P., U.P.I.)   safety
Meador, Los Angeles (A.P., U.P.I.)   safety

1970
OFFENSE (NFC)

Washington, San Francisco (A.P., U.P.I., S.N.)   end
Gordon, Chicago (A.P., U.P.I., S.N.)   end
Sanders, Detroit (A.P., U.P.I., S.N.)   end
Brown, Los Angeles (A.P., U.P.I.)   tackle
McMillan, St. Louis (U.P.I., S.N.)   tackle
Banaszek, San Francisco (A.P.)   tackle
Yary, Minnesota (S.N.)   tackle
Gillingham, Green Bay (A.P., U.P.I., S.N.)   guard
Mack, Los Angeles (A.P., S.N.)   guard
Niland, Dallas (U.P.I.)   guard
Flanagan, Detroit (U.P.I., S.N.)   center
Tingelhoff, Minnesota (A.P.)   center
Brodie, San Francisco (A.P., U.P.I., S.N.)   qback
Brown, Washington (A.P., U.P.I., S.N.)   back
Lane, St Louis (U.P.I., S.N.)   back
Johnson, New York (A.P.)   back
Cox, Minnesota (S.N.)   kicker

DEFENSE (NFC)

Eller, Minnesota (A.P., U.P.I., S.N.)   end
Jones, Los Angeles (U.P.I., S.N.)   end
Humphrey, Atlanta (A.P.)   end
Olsen, Los Angeles (A.P., U.P.I., S.N.)   tackle
Page, Minnesota (A.P., U.P.I., S.N.)   tackle
Howley, Dallas (AP., U.P.I., S.N.)   linebacker
Butkus, Chicago (A.P., U.P.I., S.N.)   linebacker
Naumoff, Detroit (A.P.)   linebacker
Stallings, St. Louis (U.P.I.)   linebacker
Hanburger, Washington (S.N.)   linebacker
Johnson, San Francisco (A.P., U.P.I., S.N.)   cornerback
Wehrli, St. Louis (U.P.I., S.N.)   cornerback
Renfro, Dallas (A.P.)   cornerback

Wilson, St. Louis (A.P., U.P.I., S.N.)	safety
Lockhart, New York Giants (A.P.)	safety
Krause, Minnesota (U.P.I.)	safety
Wood, Green Bay (S.N.)	safety
Fagan, New Orleans (S.N.)	punter

Note—The Sporting News did not select an all-league team
before 1970.

1971
OFFENSE (NFC)

Washington, San Francisco (A.P., U.P.I., S.N.)	end
Grim, Minnesota (U.P.I., S.N.)	end
Jefferson, Washington (A.P.)	end
Sanders, Detroit (A.P., U.P.I., S.N.)	end
Yary, Minnesota (A.P., U.P.I., S.N.)	tackle
Wright, Dallas (AP.)	tackle
McMillan, St. Louis (U.P.I.)	tackle
Cowan, Los Angeles (S.N.)	tackle
Mack, Los Angeles (A.P., U.P.I.)	guard
Niland, Dallas (A.P., S.N.)	guard
Gillingham, Green Bay (U.P.I., S.N.)	guard
Blue, San Francisco (A.P., U.P.I.)	center
Flanagan, Detroit (S.N.)	center
Hauss, Washington (S.N.)	center
Staubach, Dallas (A.P., S.N.)	qback
Landry, Detroit (U.P.I.)	qback
Brockington, Green Bay (A.P., U.P.I., S.N.)	back
Brown, Washington (U.P.I., S.N.)	back
Owens, Detroit (A.P.)	back
Knight, Washington (S.N.)	kicker

DEFENSE (NFC)

Eller, Minnesota (A.P., U.P.I., S.N.)	end
Humphrey, Atlanta (A.P., U.P.I., S.N.)	end
Lilly, Dallas (AP., U.P.I., S.N.)	tackle
Page, Minnesota (A.P., U.P.I., S.N.)	tackle
Wilcox, San Francisco (A.P., U.P.I., S.N.)	linebacker
Pardee, Washington (AP., U.P.I.)	linebacker
Robertson, Los Angeles (S.N.)	linebacker
Butkus, Chicago (A.P., U.P.I.)	linebacker
Lucci, Detroit (S.N.)	linebacker
Johnson, San Francisco (A.P., U.P.I., S.N.)	cornerback
Wehrli, St. Louis (U.P.I., S.N.)	cornerback
Renfro, Dallas (A.P.)	cornerback
Bradley, Philadelphia (A.P., U.P.I., S.N.)	safety
Krause, Minnesota (U.P.I., S.N.)	safety
Green, Dallas (A.P.)	safety
Wood, Green Bay (S.N.)	safety
Widby, Dallas (S.N.)	punter

Note—Flanagan and Hauss plus Bradley and Wood were tied
in the Sporting News poll.

1972
OFFENSE (NFC)

Washington, San Francisco (A.P., U.P.I., S.N.)	end
Jackson, Philadelphia (A.P., U.P.I., S.N.)	end

Kwalick, San Francisco (A.P., U.P.I.)	end
Tucker, New York Giants (S.N.)	end
Wright, Dallas (A.P., U.P.I., S.N.)	tackle
Yary, Minnesota (A.P., U.P.I., S.N.)	tackle
Niland, Dallas (AP., U.P.I., S.N.)	guard
Mack, Los Angeles (A.P., U.P.I., S.N.)	guard
Blue, San Francisco (A.P., U.P.I., S.N.)	center
Tarkenton, Minnesota (U.P.I, S.N.)	qback
Kilmer, Washington (A.P.)	qback
Brockington, Green Bay (A.P., U.P.I., S.N.)	back
Brown, Washington (A.P., U.P.I., S.N.)	back
Marcol, Green Bay (SN.)	kicker

DEFENSE (NFC)

Humphrey, Atlanta (A.P., U.P.I., S.N.)	end
Gregory, Dallas (A.P., U.P.I.)	end
Eller, Minnesota (S.N.)	end
Lilly, Dallas (A.P., U.P.I., S.N.)	tackle
Page, Minnesota (A.P., U.P.I., S.N.)	tackle
Butkus, Chicago (AP., U.P.I., S.N.)	linebacker
Hanburger, Washington (A.P., U.P.I., S.N.)	linebacker
Wilcox, San Francisco (A.P., U.P.I., S.N.)	linebacker
Ellis, Green Bay (A.P., U.P.I.)	cornerback
Johnson, San Francisco (A.P., S.N.)	cornerback
Barney, Detroit (U.P.I., S.N.)	cornerback
Bradley, Philadelphia (A.P., U.P.I., S.N.)	safety
Krause, Minnesota (A.P., U.P.I., S.N.)	safety
Chapple, Los Angeles (SN.)	punter

1973
OFFENSE (NFC)

Jackson, Los Angeles (A.P., U.P.I., S.N.)	end
Gilliam, Minnesota (U.P.I., S.N.)	end
Carmichael, Philadelphia (A.P.)	end
Kwalick, San Francisco (U.P.I., S.N.)	end
Young, Philadelphia (A.P.)	end
Wright, Dallas (A.P., U.P.I., S.N.)	tackle
Yary, Minnesota (A.P., U.P.I., S.N.)	tackle
Mack, Los Angeles (AP., U.P.I., S.N.)	guard
Niland, Dallas (A.P., U.P.I., S.N.)	guard
Blue, San Francisco (A.P., U.P.I., S.N.)	center
Hadl, Los Angeles (A.P., U.P.I., S.N.)	qback
Brockington, Green Bay (A.P., U.P.I., S.N.)	back
Hill, Dallas (A.P., U.P.I., S.N.)	back
Mike-Mayer, Atlanta (AP., S.N.)	kicker
Gossett, San Francisco (S.N.)	kicker

DEFENSE (NFC)

Humphrey, Atlanta (A.P., U.P.I., S.N.)	end
Eller, Minnesota (A.P., U.P.I., S.N.)	end
Olsen, Los Angeles (AP., U.P.I., S.N.)	tackle
Page, Minnesota (A.P., U.P.I., S.N.)	tackle
Hanburger, Washington (A.P., U.P.I., S.N.)	linebacker
Jordan, Dallas (AP., U.P.I., S.N.)	linebacker
Wilcox, San Francisco (A.P., U.P.I., S.N.)	linebacker
Ellis, Green Bay (A.P., U.P.I., S.N.)	cornerback
Renfro, Dallas (A.P., U.P.I., S.N.)	cornerback
Houston, Washington (A.P., U.P.I., S.N.)	safety

Krause, Minnesota (A.P., U.P.I., S.N.)	safety
Wittum, San Francisco (SN.)	punter

Note—Mike-Mayer and Gossett tied in the Sporting News poll.

1974
OFFENSE (NFC)

Pearson, Dallas (A.P., U.P.I., S.N.)	end
Taylor, Washington (A.P., U.P.I., S.N.)	end
Young, Philadelphia (AP., U.P.I., S.N.)	end
Wright, Dallas (A.P., U.P.I., S.N.)	tackle
Yary, Minnesota (A.P., U.P.I., S.N.)	tackle
Gillingham, Green Bay (AP., U.P.I., S.N.)	guard
Mack, Los Angeles (A.P., U.P.I., S.N.)	guard
Hauss, Washington (A.P., S.N.)	center
Blue, San Francisco (U.P.I., S.N.)	center
Hart, St. Louis (A.P., U.P.I., S.N.)	qback
Foreman, Minnesota (A.P., U.P.I., S.N)	back
McCutcheon, Los Angeles (AP., U.P.I., S.N.)	back
Marcol, Green Bay (A.P., U.P.I., S.N.)	kicker

DEFENSE (NFC)

Humphrey, Atlanta (A.P., U.P.I., S.N.)	end
Youngblood, Los Angeles (A.P., U.P.I., S.N.)	end
Page, Minnesota (A.P., U.P.I., S.N.)	tackle
Chambers, Chicago (AP., S.N.)	tackle
Mendenhall, New York Giants (U.P.I.)	tackle
Bergey, Philadelphia (A.P., U.P.I., S.N.)	linebacker
Hanburger, Washington (A.P., U.P.I., S.N.)	linebacker
Hendricks, Green Bay (A.P., U.P.I., S.N.)	linebacker
Bass, Washington (A.P., U.P.I., S.N.)	cornerback
Wehrli, St Louis (A.P., U.P.I., S.N.)	cornerback
Houston, Washington (AP., U.P.I., S.N.)	safety
Harris, Dallas (U.P.I., S.N.)	safety
Elmendorf, Los Angeles (A.P.)	safety
Wittum, San Francisco (U.P.I., S.N.)	punter

Note—Blue and Hauss tied in the Sporting News poll.

AFL/AFC ALL-LEAGUE SELECTIONS
1960*
OFFENSE

Groman, Houston	end
Taylor, Denver	end
Michael, Houston	tackle
Mix, Los Angeles	tackle
Krisher, Dallas	guard
Mischak, New York	guard
Otto, Oakland	center
Kemp, Los Angeles	qback
Lowe, Los Angeles	back
Haynes, Dallas	back
Smith, Houston	back

DEFENSE

Torczon, Buffalo	end
Branch, Dallas	end
McFadin, Denver	tackle
Peters, Los Angeles	tackle
Matsos, Buffalo	linebacker
Headrick, Dallas	linebacker
Addison, Boston	linebacker
McCabe, Buffalo	back
Harris, Los Angeles	back
O'Hanley, Boston	back
Gonsoulin, Denver	back

* Selected by AFL team members

1961*
OFFENSE

Taylor, Denver	end
Hennigan, Houston	end
Mix, San Diego	tackle
Jamison, Houston	tackle
Mischak, New York	guard
Leo, Boston	guard
Otto, Oakland	center
Blanda, Houston	qback
Haynes, Dallas	back
Cannon, Houston	back
Mathis, New York	back

DEFENSE

Faison, San Diego	end
Floyd, Houston	end
McFadin, Denver	tackle
McMurty, Buffalo	tackle
Headrick, Dallas	linebacker
Matsos, Buffalo	linebacker
Allen, San Diego	linebacker
Banfield, Houston	back
Harris, San Diego	back
Webster, Dallas	back
McNeil, San Diego	back

* Selected by AFL coaches

1962*
OFFENSE

Kocourek, San Diego	ena
Hennigan, Houston	end
Burford, Dallas	flanker
Danenhauer, Denver	tackle
Tyrer, Dallas	tackle
Mix, San Diego	guard
Talamini, Houston	guard
Otto, Oakland	center
Dawson, Dallas	qback
Haynes, Dallas	back
Gilchrist, Buffalo	back

DEFENSE

Floyd, Houston	end
Branch, Dallas	end
McFadin, Denver	tackle
Mays, Dallas	tackle
Headrick, Dallas	linebacker
Grantham, New York	linebacker
Holub, Dallas	linebacker
Banfield, Houston	cornerback
Williamson, Oakland	cornerback

Gonsoulin, Denver   safety
Zeman, Denver   safety
* Selected by AFL team members

1963*
OFFENSE

Arbanas, Kansas City   end
Powell, Oakland   end
Alworth, San Diego   flanker
Mix, San Diego   tackle
Tyrer, Kansas City   tackle
Shaw, Buffalo   guard
Talamini, Houston   guard
Otto, Oakland   center
Rote, San Diego   qback
Daniels, Oakland   back
Lincoln, San Diego   back

DEFENSE

Eisenhauer, Boston   end
Faison, San Diego   end
Sestak, Buffalo   tackle
Antwine, Boston   tackle
Matsos, Oakland   linebacker
Holub, Kansas City   linebacker
Addison, Boston   linebacker
Grayson, Kansas City   cornerback
Williamson, Oakland   cornerback
Glick, Houston   safety
Gonsoulin, Denver   safety
* Selected by AFL team members

1964
OFFENSE
Hennigan, Houston (A.P., U.P.I.)   end
Arbanas, Kansas City (A.P., U.P.I.)   end
Mix, San Diego (A.P., U.P.I.)   tackle
Barber, Buffalo (A.P., U.P.I.)   tackle
Shaw, Buffalo (A.P., U.P.I.)   guard
Neighbors, Boston (A.P., U.P.I.)   guard
Otto, Oakland (A.P., U.P.I.)   center
Parilli, Boston (A.P., U.P.I.)   qback
Alworth, San Diego (A.P., U.P.I.)   back
Lincoln, San Diego (A.P., U.P.I.)   back
Gilchrist, Buffalo (A.P., U.P.I.)   back
DEFENSE
Faison, San Diego (A.P., U.P.I.)   end
Eisenhauer, Boston (A.P.)   end
Bell, Kansas City (U.P.I.)   end
Sestak, Buffalo (A.P., U.P.I.)   tackle
Ladd, San Diego (A.P., U.P.I.)   tackle
Buoniconti, Boston (A.P., U.P.I.)   linebacker
Grantham, New York (A.P., U.P.I.)   linebacker
Stratton, Buffalo (A.P., U.P.I.)   linebacker
Grayson, Kansas City (A.P.)   cornerback
Williamson, Oakland (U.P.I.)   cornerback
Brown, Denver (A.P., U.P.I.)   cornerback
Hall, Boston (A.P., U.P.I.)   safety
Saimes, Buffalo (A.P.)   safety
Paulson, New York (U.P.I.)   safety

1965
OFFENSE
Taylor, Denver (A.P., U.P.I.)   end

Frazier, Houston (A.P., U.P.I.)	end
Mix, San Diego (A.P., U.P.I.)	tackle
Tyrer, Kansas City (A.P., U.P.I.)	tackle
Shaw, Buffalo (A.P., U.P.I.)	guard
Talamini, Houston (A.P., U.P.I.)	guard
Otto, Oakland (A.P., U.P.I.)	center
Kemp, Buffalo (A.P., U.P.I.)	qback
Alworth, San Diego (A.P., U.P.I.)	back
Lowe, San Diego (A.P., U.P.I.)	back
Gilchrist, Denver (A.P., U.P.I.)	back

DEFENSE

Faison, San Diego (A.P., U.P.I.)	end
Mays, Kansas City (A.P.)	end
McDole, Buffalo (U.P.I.)	end
Ladd, San Diego (A.P., U.P.I.)	tackle
Sestak, Buffalo (A.P., U.P.I.)	tackle
Buoniconti, Boston (A.P., U.P.I.)	linebacker
Bell, Kansas City (A.P., U.P.I.)	linebacker
Grayson, Oakland (A.P., U.P.I.)	cornerback
Byrd, Buffalo (A.P.)	cornerback
Williamson, Kansas City (U.P.I.)	cornerback
Saimes, Buffalo (A.P., U.P.I.)	safety
Robinson, Kansas City (A.P.)	safety
Paulson, New York (U.P.I.)	safety

1966
OFFENSE

Taylor, Kansas City (A.P., U.P.I.)	end
Arbanas, Kansas City (A.P., U.P.I.)	end
Tyrer, Kansas City (A.P.. U.P.I.)	tackle
Mix, San Diego (A.P., U.P.I.)	tackle
Shaw, Buffalo (A.P., U.P.I.)	guard
Budde, Kansas City (A.P.)	guard
Hawkins, Oakland (U.P.I.)	guard
Morris, Boston (A.P.)	center
Otto, Oakland (U.P.I.)	center
Dawson, Kansas City (A.P., U.P.I.)	qback
Alworth, San Diego (A.P., U.P.I.)	back
Daniels, Oakland (A.P., U.P.I.)	back
Nance, Boston (A.P., U.P.I.)	back

DEFENSE

Mays, Kansas City (A.P., U.P.I.)	end
McDole, Buffalo (A.P.)	end
Biggs, New York (U.P.I.)	end
Buchanan, Kansas City (A.P., U.P.I.)	tackle
Dunaway, Buffalo (A.P.)	tackle
Antwine, Boston (U.P.I.)	tackle
Buoniconti, Boston (A.P., U.P.I.)	linebacker
Bell, Kansas City (A.P., U.P.I.)	linebacker
Stratton, Buffalo (A.P., U.P.I.)	linebacker
Byrd, Buffalo (A.P., U.P.I.)	cornerback
McCloughan, Oakland (A.P., U.P.I.)	cornerback
Robinson, Kansas City (A.P., U.P.I.)	safety
Graham, San Diego (A.P., U.P.I.)	safety

1967
OFFENSE

Sauer, New York (A.P., U.P.I.)	end
Cannon, Oakland (A.P., U.P.I.)	end
Mix, San Diego (A.P., U.P.I.)	tackle
Tyrer, Kansas City (A.P.)	tackle
Schuh, Oakland (U.P.I.)	tackle
Sweeney, San Diego (A.P., U.P.I.)	guard
Talamini, Houston (A.P., U.P.I.)	guard
Otto, Oakland (A.P., U.P.I.)	center

Lamonica, Oakland (A.P., U.P.I.)	qback
Garrett, Kansas City (A.P., U.P.I.)	back
Nance, Boston (A.P., U.P.I.)	back
Alworth, San Diego (A.P., U.P.I.)	back

DEFENSE

Holmes, Houston (A.P., U.P.I.)	end
Davidson, Oakland (A.P., U.P.I.)	end
Keating, Oakland (A.P., U.P.I.)	tackle
Buchanan, Kansas City (A.P., U.P.I.)	tackle
Buoniconti, Boston (A.P., U.P.I.)	linebacker
Webster, Houston (A.P., U.P.I.)	linebacker
Bell, Kansas City (A.P., U.P.I.)	linebacker
Farr, Houston (A.P., U.P.I.)	cornerback
McCloughan, Oakland (A.P., U.P.I.)	cornerback
Saimes, Buffalo (A.P., U.P.I.)	safety
Robinson, Kansas City (A.P., U.P.I.)	safety

1968
OFFENSE

Sauer, New York (A.P., U.P.I.)	end
Whalen, Boston (A.P., U.P.I.)	end
Mix, San Diego (A.P., U.P.I.)	tackle
Tyrer, Kansas City (A.P., U.P.I.)	tackle
Sweeney, San Diego (A.P., U.P.I.)	guard
Upshaw, Oakland (A.P., U.P.I.)	guard
Otto, Oakland (A.P., U.P.I.)	center
Namath, New York (A.P., U.P.I.)	qback
Robinson, Cincinnati (A.P., U.P.I.)	back
Dixon, Oakland (A.P., U.P.I.)	back
Alworth, San Diego (A.P., U.P.I.)	back

DEFENSE

Philbin, New York (A.P., U.P.I.)	end
Jackson, Denver (A.P., U.P.I.)	end
Buchanan, Kansas City (A.P., U.P.I.)	tackle
Birdwell, Oakland (A.P., U.P.I.)	tackle
Lanier, Kansas City (A.P.)	linebacker
Conners, Oakland (U.P.I.)	linebacker
Webster, Houston (A.P., U.P.I.)	linebacker
Bell, Kansas City (A.P., U.P.I.)	linebacker
Farr, Houston (A.P., U.P.I.)	cornerback
Brown, Oakland (A.P., U.P.I.)	cornerback
Robinson, Kansas City (A.P., U.P.I.)	safety
Grayson, Oakland (A.P., U.P.I.)	safety

1969
OFFENSE

Biletnikoff, Oakland (A.P.)	end
Alworth, San Diego (U.P.I.)	end
Maynard, New York (A.P.)	end
Wells, Oakland (U.P.I.)	end
Trumpy, Cincinnati (A.P., U.P.I.)·	end
Tyrer, Kansas City (A.P., U.P.I.)	tackle
Schuh, Oakland (A.P., U.P.I.)	tackle
Budde, Kansas City (A.P.)	guard
Upshaw, Oakland (A.P., U.P.I.)	guard
Sweeney, San Diego (U.P.I.)	guard
Otto, Oakland (A.P., U.P.I.)	center
Lamonica, Oakland (A.P., U.P.I.)	qback
Little, Denver (A.P., U.P.I.)	back
Snell, New York (A.P., U.P.I.)	back

DEFENSE

Jackson, Denver (A.P., U.P.I.)	end
Philbin, New York (A.P., U.P.I.)	end

Elliott, New York (A.P., U.P.I.)	tackle
Buchanan, Kansas City (A.P., U.P.I.)	tackle
Buoniconti, Miami (A.P., U.P.I.)	linebacker
Webster, Houston (A.P., U.P.I.)	linebacker
Bell, Kansas City (A.P., U.P.I.)	linebacker
Brown, Oakland (A.P., U.P.I.)	cornerback
Byrd, Buffalo (A.P., U.P.I.)	cornerback
Grayson, Oakland (A.P., U.P.I.)	safety
Robinson, Kansas City (A.P., U.P.I.)	safety

1970
OFFENSE (AFC)

Briscoe, Buffalo (A.P., U.P.I., S.N.)	end
Wells, Oakland (U.P.I., S.N.)	end
Biletnikoff, Oakland (A.P.)	end
Warfield, Miami (S.N.)	end
Trumpy, Cincinnati (A.P., S.N.)	end
Reed, Houston (U.P.I.)	end
Hill, New York Jets (A.P., U.P.I., S.N.)	tackle
Tyrer, Kansas City (A.P., U.P.I., S.N.)	tackle
Upshaw, Oakland (A.P., S.N.)	guard
Budde, Kansas City (U.P.I., S.N.)	guard
Sweeney, San Diego (A.P.)	guard
Hickerson, Cleveland (U.P.I.)	guard
Otto, Oakland (A.P., U.P.I., S.N.)	center
Lamonica, Oakland (A.P., U.P.I.)	qback
Griese, Miami (S.N.)	qback
Little, Denver (A.P., U.P.I., S.N.)	back
Dixon, Oakland (A.P., U.P.I.)	back
Phillips, Cincinnati (S.N.)	back
Stenerud, Kansas City (S.N.)	kicker

DEFENSE (AFC)

Jackson, Denver (A.P., U.P.I., S.N.)	end
Smith, Baltimore (U.P.I., S.N.)	end
Brown, Kansas City (A.P.)	end
Elliott, New York Jets (A.P., U.P.I.)	tackle
Greene, Pittsburgh (U.P.I., S.N.)	tackle
Buchanan, Kansas City (A.P.)	tackle
Keating, Oakland (S.N.)	tackle
Bell, Kansas City (A.P., U.P.I., S.N.)	linebacker
Lanier, Kansas City (A.P., U.P.I., S.N.)	linebacker
Russell, Pittsburgh (AP., U.P.I., S.N.)	linebacker
Brown, Oakland (A.P., U.P.I., S.N.)	cornerback
Marsalis, Kansas City (A.P., U.P.I., S.N.)	cornerback
Robinson, Kansas City (AP., U.P.I., S.N.)	safety
Logan, Baltimore (A.P., U.P.I.)	safety
Volk, Baltimore (S.N.)	safety
Lee, Baltimore (S.N.)	punter

1971
OFFENSE (AFC)

Taylor, Kansas City (A.P., U.P.I., S.N.)	end
Warfield, Miami (A.P., U.P.I., S.N.)	end
Morin, Cleveland (AP., U.P.I.)	end
Chester, Oakland (S.N.)	end
Tyrer, Kansas City (A.P., U.P.I., S.N.)	tackle

Brown, Oakland (A.P., S.N.)   tackle
Hill, New York Jets (U.P.I.,)   tackle
Little, Miami (A.P., U.P.I., S.N.)   guard
Sweeney, San Diego (A.P., U.P.I.)   guard
Upshaw, Oakland (S.N.)   guard
Curry, Baltimore (A.P., U.P.I.)   center
Otto, Oakland (S.N.)   center
Griese, Miami (A.P., U.P.I., S.N.)   qback
Csonka, Miami (A.P., U.P.I., S.N.)   back
Little, Denver (AP., U.P.I., S.N.)   back
Yepremian, Miami (A.P., S.N.)   kicker

DEFENSE (AFC)

Smith, Baltimore (A.P., U.P.I., S.N.)   end
Brown, Kansas City (A.P.)   end
Stanfill, Miami (U.P.I.)   end
Jackson, Denver (S.N.)   end
Greene, Pittsburgh (A.P., U.P.I., S.N.)   tackle
Reid, Cincinnati (A.P., U.P.I., S.N.)   tackle
Fernandez, Miami (S.N.)   tackle
Bell, Kansas City (A.P., U.P.I., S.N.)   linebacker
Hendricks, Baltimore (A.P., U.P.I., S.N.)   linebacker
Lanier, Kansas City (A.P., U.P.I., S.N.)   linebacker
Brown, Oakland (A.P., U.P.I., S.N.)   cornerback
Marsalis, Kansas City (UP.I., S.N.)   cornerback
Thomas, Kansas City (A.P.)   cornerback
Scott, Miami (A.P., U.P.I.)   safety
Houston, Houston (U.P.I., S.N.)   safety
Volk, Baltimore, (A.P.).   safety
Logan, Baltimore (S.N.)   safety
Robinson, Kansas City (S.N.)   safety
Wilson, Kansas City (S.N.)   punter

Note—Reid and Fernandez plus Houston and Logan tied in
    Sporting News poll.

1972
OFFENSE (AFC)

Biletnikoff, Oakland (A.P., U.P.I., S.N.)   end
Warfield, Miami (A.P., S.N.)   end
Taylor, Kansas City (U.P.I.)   end
Chester, Oakland (A.P., U.P.I., S.N.)   end
Brown, Oakland (A.P., U.P.I., S.N.)   tackle
Hill, New York Jets (A.P., U.P.I., S.N.)   tackle
Little, Miami (A.P., U.P.I., S.N.)   guard
Upshaw, Oakland (AP., U.P.I.)   guard
Van Dyke, Pittsburgh (S.N.)   guard
Otto, Oakland (A.P., S.N.)   center
Johnson, Cincinnati (U.P.I.)   center
Namath, New York Jets (U.P.I., S.N.)   qback
Morrall, Miami (A.P.)   qback
Csonka, Miami (A.P., U.P.I., S.N.)   back
Simpson, Buffalo (A.P., U.P.I., S.N.)   back
Harris, Pittsburgh (S.N.)   back
Gerela, Pittsburgh (S.N.)   kicker

DEFENSE (AFC)

Stanfill, Miami (A.P., U.P.I., S.N.)	end
Den Herder, Miami (A.P.)	end
White, Pittsburgh (U.P.I.)	end
Bethea, Houston (S.N.)	end
Greene, Pittsburgh (A.P., U.P.I., S.N.)	tackle
Reid, Cincinnati (A.P., U.P.I., S.N.)	tackle
Russell, Pittsburgh (AP., U.P.I., S.N.)	linebacker
Hendricks, Baltimore (A.P., U.P.I.)	linebacker
Lanier, Kansas City (U.P.I., S.N.)	linebacker
Buoniconti, Miami (A.P.)	linebacker
Bell, Kansas City (S.N.)	linebacker
Brown, Oakland (A.P., U.P.I., S.N.)	cornerback
James, Buffalo (A.P., U.P.I.)	cornerback
Parrish, Cincinnati (S.N.)	cornerback
Anderson, Miami (A.P., U.P.I., S.N.)	safety
Scott, Miami (A.P., U.P.I., S.N.)	safety
Wilson, Kansas City (SN.)	punter

1973
OFFENSE (AFC)

Warfield, Miami (A.P., U.P.I., S.N.)	end
Biletnikoff, Oakland (A.P., S.N.)	end
Shanklin, Pittsburgh (U.P.I.)	end
Odoms, Denver (A.P., U.P.I., S.N.)	end
Shell, Oakland (A.P., U.P.I.)	tackle
Hill, New York Jets (U.P.I., S.N.)	tackle
Evans, Miami (A.P.)	tackle
Washington, San Diego (S.N.)	tackle
Little, Miami (A.P., U.P.I., S.N.)	guard
McKenzie, Buffalo (A.P., U.P.I., S.N.)	guard
Langer, Miami (U.P.I., S.N.)	center
Rudnay, Kansas City (A.P.)	center
Stabler, Oakland (A.P.)	qback
Johnson, Denver (U.P.I.)	qback
Griese, Miami (S.N.)	qback
Csonka, Miami (A.P., U.P.I., S.N.)	back
Simpson, Buffalo (A.P., U.P.I., S.N.)	back
Yepremian, Miami (AP., S.N.)	kicker
Blanda, Oakland (S.N.)	kicker

DEFENSE (AFC)

Stanfill, Miami (A.P., U.P.I., S.N.)	end
White, Pittsburgh (A.P., U.P.I., S.N.)	end
Greene, Pittsburgh (AP., U.P.I., S.N.)	tackle
Reid, Cincinnati (A.P., U.P.I., S.N.)	tackle
Ham, Pittsburgh (A.P., U.P.I., S.N.)	linebacker
Lanier, Kansas City (AP., U.P.I., S.N.)	linebacker
Russell, Pittsburgh (U.P.I., S.N.)	linebacker
Hendricks, Baltimore (A.P.)	linebacker
James, Buffalo (A.P., U.P.I., S.N.)	cornerback
Brown, Oakland (A.P., S.N.)	cornerback
Scott, Cleveland (U.P.I.) •	cornerback
Anderson, Miami, (A.P., U.P.I., S.N.)	safety
Scott, Miami (A.P., U.P.I., S.N.)	safety
Guy, Oakland (S.N.)	punter

Note—Yepremian and Blanda tied in Sporting News poll.

1974
OFFENSE (AFC)

Branch, Oakland (A.P., U.P.I., S.N.)	end
Curtis, Cincinnati (A.P., U.P.I., S.N.)	end
Odoms, Denver (A.P., U.P.I., S.N.)	end
Shell, Oakland (AP., U.P.I., S.N.)	tackle
Washington, San Diego (A.P., S.N.)	tackle
Hill, New York Jets (U.P.I.)	tackle
Evans, Miami (S.N.)	tackle
Little, Miami (A.P., U.P.I., S.N.)	guard
McKenzie, Buffalo (U.P.I., S.N.)	guard
Upshaw, Oakland (A.P.)	guard
Hannah, New England (S.N.)	guard
Langer, Miami (A.P., U.P.I., S.N.)	center
Stabler, Oakland (A.P., U.P.I., S.N.)	qback
Armstrong, Denver (AP., U.P.I., S.N.)	back
Simpson, Buffalo (A.P., U.P.I., S.N.)	back
Gerela, Pittsburgh (A.P., U.P.I., S.N.)	kicker

DEFENSE (AFC)

Greenwood, Pittsburgh (A.P., U.P.I., S.N.)	end
Stanfill, Miami (A.P., U.P.I., S.N.)	end
Greene, Pittsburgh (AP., U.P.I., S.N.)	tackle
Sistrunk, Oakland (A.P., U.P.I.)	tackle
Thoms, Oakland (S.N.)	tackle
Ham, Pittsburgh (A.P., U.P.I., S.N.)	linebacker
Lanier, Kansas City (A.P., U.P.I., S.N.)	linebacker
Villapiano, Oakland (AP., U.P.I., S.N.)	linebacker
James, Buffalo (A.P., U.P.I., S.N.)	cornerback
Thomas, Kansas City (A.P., U.P.I., S.N.)	cornerback
Greene, Buffalo (A.P., U.P.I., S.N.)	safety
Anderson, Miami (S.N.)	safety
Scott, Miami, (A.P.)	safety
Tatum, Oakland (U.P.I.)	safety
Guy, Oakland (U.P.I., S.N.)	punter

Note—Washington and Evans plus Little and Hannah tied in the Sporting News poll.

PLAYER HONORS

JIM THORPE TROPHY (Most Valuable Player)

(Annual winners selected by ballot of all players in league)

1974—Ken Stabler
1973—O. J. Simpson
1972—Larry Brown
1971—Bob Griese
1970—John Brodie
1969—Roman Gabriel
1968—Earl Morrall
1967—John Unitas
1966—Bryan Starr
1965—Jim Brown
1964—Leonard Moore
1963—Jim Brown and Y. A. Tittle

1962—Jim Taylor
1961—Y. A. Tittle
1960—Norman Van Brocklin
1959—Charles Conerly
1958—James Brown
1957—John Unitas
1956—Frank Gifford
1955—Harlon Hill

PLAYER OF THE YEAR (DEFENSE)

(selected by news services)

1974—Joe Greene
1973—Dick Andreson
       Alan Page
1972—Joe Greene
1971—Alan Page
1970—Dick Butkus

PLAYER OF YEAR (AFL/AFC)

(Selected by news services)

1974—Ken Stabler, Oakland (AFC)
1973—O. J. Simpson, Buffalo (AFC)
1972—Earl Morrall, Miami (AFC)
       O. J. Simpson, Buffalo (AFC)
1971—Otis Taylor, Kansas City (AFC)
       Bob Griese, Miami (AFC)
1970—George Blanda, Oakland (AFC)
1969—Daryle Lamonica, Oak.
1968—Joe Namath, N.Y.
1967—Daryle Lamonica, Oak.
1966—Jim Nance, Bos.
1965—Paul Lowe, S.D.
1964—Gino Cappelletti, Bos.
1963—Clem Daniels, Oak.
1962—Len Dawson, K.C.
1961—George Blanda, Hou.
1960—Abner Haynes, Dal.

PLAYER OF YEAR (NFL/NFC)

(Selected by news services)

1974—Jim Hart, St. Louis (NFC)
1973—John Hadl, Los Angeles (NFC)
1972—Larry Brown, Washington (NFC)
1971—Alan Page, Minnesota (NFC)
1970—John Brodie, San Francisco (NFC)
1969—Roman Gabriel, Los Angeles

1968—Earl Morrall, Baltimore
1967—John Unitas, Baltimore
1966—Bart Starr, Green Bay
1965—Jim Brown, Cleveland
1964—John Unitas, Baltimore
1963—Jim Brown, Cleveland
1962—Y. A. Tittle, New York
1961—Paul Hornung, Green Bay
1960—Norm Van Brocklin, Philadelphia
1959—John Unitas, Baltimore
1958—Jim Brown, Cleveland
1957—Y. A. Tittle, San Francisco
1956—Frank Gifford, New York
1955—Otto Graham, Cleveland
1954—Joe Perry, San Francisco
1953—Otto Graham, Cleveland

JOE F. CARR TROPHY, League Most Valuable Player

1946—Bill Dudley, Pittsburgh
1945—Bob Waterfield, Los Angeles
1944—Frank Sinkwich, Detroit
1943—Sid Luckman, Chicago Bears
1942—Don Hutson, Green Bay
1941—Don Hutson, Green Bay
1940—Ace Parker, Brooklyn
1939—Parker Hall, Cleveland Rams
1938—Mel Hein, New York

ROOKIE OF YEAR (NFL/NFC-AFL/AFC)
(Selected by news services)

1974—Don Woods, San Diego (AFC)
    Jack Lambert, Pittsburgh (AFC)
1973—Chuck Foreman, Minnesota (NFC)
    Booby Clark, Cincinnati (AFC)
    Wally Chambers, Chicago (NFC)
    Charles Young, Philadelphia (NFC)
1972—Franco Harris, Pittsburgh (AFC)
    Willie Buchanon, Green Bay (NFC)
    Chester Marcol, Green Bay (NFC)
1971—John Brockington, Green Bay (NFC)
    Jim Plunkett, New England (AFC)
    Isiah Robertson, Los Angeles (NFC)
1970—Dennis Shaw, Buffalo (AFC)
    Bruce Taylor, San Francisco (NFC)
    Ray Chester, Oakland (AFC)
1969—Calvin Hill, Dal.
    Carl Garrett, Bos. (AFL)
1968—Earl McCullouch, Det.
    Paul Robinson, Cin. (AFL)

1967—Mel Farr, Det.
    George Webster, Hou. (AFL)
1966—John Roland, St. L.
    Bobby Burnett, Buff. (AFL)
1965—Gale Sayers, Chi.
    Joe Namath, N.Y. (AFL)
1964—Charlie Taylor, Wash.
    Matt Snell, N.Y. (AFL)
1963—Paul Flatley, Minn.
    Billy Joe, Den. (AFL)
1962—Ronnie Bull, Chi.
    Curtis McClinton, K.C. (AFL)
1961—Mike Ditka, Chi.
    Earl Faison, S.D. (AFL)
1960—Gail Cogdill, Det.
    Abner Haynes, Dal. (AFL)
1959—Nick Pietrosante, Det.
1958—Bobby Mitchell, Clev.

ALL-TIME INDIVIDUAL RECORDS

(Courtesy National Football League, Compiled by Elias Sports Bureau)

(Includes NFL/NFC, AFL/AFC, not AAFC)

SERVICE

Most Seasons, Active Player

25 George Blanda, Chicago Bears 1949-58; Balt. 1950; Hou. (AFL) 1960-66; Oak. (AFL-AFC) 1967-74

19 Earl Morrall, S. F. 1956; Pitt. 1957-58; Det. 1958-64; N. Y. Giants 1965-67; Balt. 1968-69; Balt. (AFC) 1970-71; Mia. (AFC) 1972-74

18 John Unitas, Balt. 1956-1969; Balt. (AFC) 1970-72; San Diego (AFC) 1973
Sonny Jurgensen, Phil. 1957-63; Wash. 1964-69; Wash. (NFC) 1970-74
Lennie Dawson, Pitt. 1957-59; Clev. 1960-61; Dal. (AFL) 1962; K.C. (AFL) 1968-69; K.C. (AFC) 1970-74

17 Lou Groza, Clev. 1950-59, 61-67
Doug Atkins, Clev. 1953-54; Chi. 1955-56; N. O. 1967-69
John Brodie, S. F. 1957-69; S. F. (NFC) 1970-73

16 Sammy Baugh, Wash. 1937-52
Bart Starr, Green Bay 1956-69; Green Bay (NFC) 1970-71

15 Johnny (Blood) McNally, Mil. 1925; Duluth 1926-27; Pottsville 1928; G. B. 1929-36; Pitt. 1937-39
Mel Hein, N. Y. 1931-45
Bobby Layne, Chi. Bears 1948; N. Y. Bulldogs 1949; Det. 1950-58; Pitt. 1958-62
Y. A. Tittle, Balt. 1950; S. F. 1951-60; N. Y. 1961-64
Bill George, Chi. Bears 1952-65; L. A. 1966
Jim Ringo, Green Bay 1953-63; Philadelphia, 1964-67
Sam Baker, Wash. 1953, 56-59; Clev. 1960-61; Dal. 1962-63; Phil. 1964-69
Babe Parilli, G. B. 1952-53; Clev. 1956; G. B. 1957-58; Oak. (AFL) 1960; Bos. (AFL) 1961-67; N. Y. Jets (AFL) 1968-69
Ray Nitschke, G. B. 1958-72 (NFL-NFC)
Jack Pardee, L. A. 1957-71; Wash. 1972 (NFL-NFC)
Wayne Walker, Det. 1958-72 (NFL-NFC)
Gene Hickerson, Clev. 1958-60, 62-69; Clev. (AFC) 1970-73

Don Maynard, N. Y. Giants 1958; N. Y. Titans (AFL) 1960-62; N. Y. Jets (AFL) 1963-69; N. Y. Jets (AFC) 1970-72; St. L. (NFC) 1973
Charlie Krueger, S. F. 1959-69; S. F. (NFC) 1970-73

Jim Otto, Oak. (AFL-AFC) 1960-74
Jim Marshall, Cle. 1960, Minn. (NFL-NFC) 1961-74
Grady Alderman, Det. 1960, Minn. (NFL-NFC) 1961-74
Len Rohde, S. F. (NFL-NFC) 1960-1974

14 Several

Most Games Played, Lifetime

326 George Blanda (NFL-AFL-AFC)
228 Earl Morrall (NFL-AFC)
218 Sonny Jurgensen (NFL-NFC)
216 Lou Groza
211 John Unitas (NFL-AFC)
210 Jim Otto (AFL-AFC)
208 Jim Marshall (NFL-NFC)
Len Rohde (NFL-NFC)
205 Doug Atkins
204 Grady Alderman (NFL-NFC)
202 Gene Hickerson (NFL-AFC)
200 Wayne Walker (NFL-NFC)
198 Charley Krueger (NFL-NFC)
197 Len Dawson (NFL-AFL-AFC)
196 Bart Starr (NFL-NFC)
Jack Pardee (NFL-NFC)
195 Sam Baker
194 John Brodie (NFL-NFC)
Fran Tarkenton (NFL-NFC)
Bill Brown (NFL-NFC)
Ken Iman (NFL-NFC)

Most Consecutive Games Played, Lifetime

210 George Blanda (AFL-AFC)
Jim Otto (AFL-AFC)
208 Jim Marshall (NFL-NFC)
Len Rohde (NFL-NFC)

Most Seasons, Head Coach

40 George Halas, Chi. Bears 1920-29, 33-42, 46-55; 58-67

32 Earl (Curly) Lambeau, G. B. 1921-49; Chi. Cards 1950-51; Wash. 1952-53

24 Paul Brown, Clev. (AAFC) 1946-49; Clev. 1950-62; Cin. (AFL) 1968-69; Cin. (AFC) 1970-74

22 Steve Owen, N. Y. 1931-52
20 Wilbur "Weeb" Ewbank, Balt. 1954-62; N. Y. (AFL) 1963-69; N. Y. (AFC) 1970-73
18 Sidney Gillman, L. A. 1955-59; L. A. (AFL) 1960; S. D. (AFL) 1961-69; S. D. (AFC) 1971; Houston (AFC) 1973-74
15 Tom Landry, Dal. 1960-69; Dal. (NFC) 1970-74
    Hank Stram, Dal. (AFL) 1960-62; K. C. (AFL) 1963-69; K. C. (AFC) 1970-74
14 Lou Saban, Bos. (AFL) 1960-61 Buff. (AFL) 1962-65; Den. (AFL) 1967-69; Den. (AFC) 1970-71; Buff. (AFC) 1972-74
13 Norm Van Brocklin, Minn. 1961-66; Atl. 1968-69; Atl. (NFC) 1970-74
12 Don Shula, Balt. 1963-69; Mia. (AFC) 1970-74
10 Vince Lombardi, Green Bay 1959-67; Wash. 1969
    Walter Lemm, Hou. (AFL) 1961 66-69; St. L. 1962-65; Hou. (AFC) 1970

SCORING

Most Seasons Leading League—Conference
5 Don Hutson, G. B. 1940-44
    Gino Cappelletti, Bos. 1961, 63-66 (AFL)
3 Earl (Dutch) Clark, Det. 1932, 35-36
    Marlin (Pat) Harder, Chi. Cards 1947-49
    Paul Hornung, G. B. 1959-61
2 Jack Manders, Chi. Bears 1934, 37
    Doak Walker, Det. 1950, 55
    Gordy Soltau, S. F. 1952-53
    Gene Mingo, Den. 1960, 62 (AFL)
    Jim Turner, N. Y. 1968-69 (AFL)
    Fred Cox, Minn. 1969-70 (NFC)
    Chester Marcol, G. B. 1972, 74 (NFC)
    Roy Gerela, Pitt. 1973-74 (AFC)

TOTAL POINTS

Most Points, Lifetime
1,919 George Blanda, Chi. Bears 1949-58; Balt. 1950; Hou. (AFL) 1960-66; Oak. (AFL) 1967-69; Oak. (AFC) 1970-74 (9-td, 899-pat, 322 fg)
1,349 Lou Groza, Clev. 1950-59, 61-67 (1-td, 641-pat, 234-fg)
1,142 Fred Cox, Minn. 1963-69; Minn. (NFC) 1970-74 (0-td, 416-pat, 242-fg)

1,130 Gino Cappelletti, Bos. (AFL) 1960-69; Bos. (AFC) 1970 (42-td, 350-pat, 176-fg)
1,074 Jim Bakken, St. L. 1962-69; St. L. (NFC) 1970-74 (0-td, 399-pat, 225-fg)
1,061 Jim Turner, N. Y. (AFL) 1964-69; N. Y. (AFC) 1970; Denver (AFC) 1971-74 (0-td, 368-pat, 231-fg)
1,031 Bruce Gossett, L. A. 1964-69; S. F. (NFC) 1970-74 (0-td, 374-pat, 219-fg)
977 Loris Baker, Wash. 1953, 56-58; Clev. 1960-61; Dall. 1962-63; Phil. 1964-69 (2-td, 428-pat, 179-fg)
955 Lou Michaels, L. A. 1958-60; Pit. 1961-63; Balt. 1964-69; G. B. (NFC) 1971 (1-td, 386-pat, 187-fg, 1-sfty)
881 Bobby Walston, Phil. 1951-62 (46-td, 365-pat, 80-fg)

Most Points, Season
176 Paul Hornung, G. B. 1960 (15-td, 41-pat, 15-fg)
155 Gino Cappelletti, Bos. (AFL) 1964 (7-td, 38-pat, 25-fg)
147 Gino Cappelletti, Bos. (AFL) 1961 (8-td, 48-pat, 17-fg)
146 Paul Hornung, G. B. 1961 (10-td, 41-pat, 15-fg)
145 Jim Turner, N. Y. Jets (AFL) 1968 (0-td, 43-pat, 34-fg)
138 Don Hutson, G. B. 1942 (17-td, 33-pat, 1-fg)

Most Points, Game
40 Ernie Nevers, Chi. Cards. vs. Chi. Bears, Nov. 28, 1929 (6-td, 4-pat)
36 William (Dub) Jones, Clev. vs. Chi. Bears, Nov. 25, 1951 (6-td)
    Gale Sayers, Chi. vs. S. F., Dec. 12, 1965 (6-td)
33 Paul Hornung, G. B. vs. Balt., Oct. 8, 1961 (3-td, 6-pat, 3-fg)
30 Abner Haynes, Dall. vs. Oak., Nov. 26, 1961 (5-td) (AFL)
    Billy Cannon, Hou. vs. N. Y., Dec. 10, 1961 (5-td) (AFL)
    Carlton (Cookie) Gilchrist, Buff. vs. N. Y., Dec. 8, 1963 (5-td) (AFL)

Most Consecutive Games Scoring
165 Fred Cox, Minn. 1963-69; Minn. (NFC) 1970-74
110 Loris (Sam) Baker, Dall. 1962-63; Phil. 1964-69
107 Lou Groza, Clev. 1950-59
99 George Blanda, Hou. (AFL) 1966; Oak. (AFL) 1967-69; Oak. (AFC) 1970-74
87 Tom Davis, S. F. 1961-67

83 George Blanda, Chi. Bears 1951-58
82 George Blanda, Hou. (AFL) 1966
56 Gordy Soltau, S. F. 1950-55

TOUCHDOWNS

Most Seasons Leading League—Conference
8 Don Hutson
3 Jim Brown
  Lance Alworth (AFL)
2 Several

Most Touchdowns, Lifetime
126 Jim Brown
113 Lenny Moore
105 Don Hutson
93 Jim Taylor
91 Bobby Mitchell
90 Leroy Kelly (NFL-AFC)
88 Don Maynard (NFL-AFL-AFC NFC)
87 Lance Alworth (AFL-AFC-NFC)
85 Tommy McDonald
   Charley Taylor (NFL-NFC)
82 Art Powell (AFL)
78 Frank Gifford
   Paul Warfield (NFL-AFC)
77 Steve Van Buren

Most Touchdowns, Season
22 Gale Sayers
21 Jim Brown
20 Lenny Moore
   LeRoy Kelly
19 Jim Taylor
   Abner Haynes (AFL)
18 Steve Van Buren
   Bill Groman (AFL)

Most Touchdowns, Game
6 Ernie Nevers, Chi. Cards vs. Chi. Bears, Nov. 28, 1929
  William (Dub) Jones, Clev. vs. Chi. Bears, Nov. 25, 1951
  Gale Sayers, Chi. Bears vs. S. F., Dec. 12, 1965
5 Bob Shaw, Chi. Cards vs. Balt. Oct. 2, 1950
  Jim Brown, Clev. vs. Balt., Nov, 1, 1959
  Paul Hornung, G. B. vs. Balt., Dec. 12, 1965
  Abner Haynes, Dall. vs. Oak., Nov. 26, 1961 (AFL)
  Billy Cannon, Hou. vs. N. Y., Dec. 10, 1961 (AFL)
  Carlton (Cookie) Gilchrist, Buff. vs. N. Y., Dec. 8, 1963 (AFL)
4 By many players

POINTS AFTER TOUCHDOWN

Most Seasons Leading League—Conference

8 George Blanda, Chi. Bears 1956; Hou. (AFL) 1961-62; Oak. (AFL) 1967-69; Oak. (AFC) 1972, 74
4 Bob Waterfield, Clev. 1945; L. A. 1946, 50, 52
3 Don Hutson, G. B. 1941-42, 45

Most Points After Touchdown, Lifetime
899 George Blanda, Chi. Bears 1949-58; Balt. 1950; Hou. (AFL) 1960-66; Oak. (AFL) 1967-69; Oak. (AFC) 1970-74
641 Lou Groza, Clev. 1950-59; 61-67
428 Loris "Sam" Baker, Wash. 1953, 56-59; Clev. 1960-61; Dall. 1962-63; Phila. 1964-69
416 Fred Cox, Minn. 1963-69; Minn. (NFC) 1970-74
399 Jim Bakken, St. L. 1962-69; St. L. (NFC) 1970-74
386 Lou Michaels, L. A. 1958-60; Pitt. 1961-63; Balt. 1964-69; G. B. (NFC) 1971
374 Bruce Gossett, L. A. 1964-69; S. F. (NFC) 1970-74
368 Jim Turner, N. Y. (AFL) 1964-69; N. Y. (AFC) 1970; Den. (AFC) 1971-74
365 Bobby Walston, Phil., 1951-62
348 Tommy Davis, S. F. 1959-69

Most Points After Touchdowns, Season
64 George Blanda, Hou. 1961 (AFL)
56 Danny Villanueva, Dall. 1966
   George Blanda, Oak. 1967 (AFL)
54 Bob Waterfield, L. A. 1950
   Mike Clark, Dall. 1968
   George Blanda, Oak. 1968 (AFL)
53 Marlin (Pat) Harder, Chi. Cards, 1948
52 Don Chandler, N. Y., 1963
   Roger LeClerc, Chicago, 1965
   Tom Davis, San Fran., 1965
50 John (Cliff) Patton, Phil., 1948
   Steve Myhra, Balt., 1959
   Loris (Sam) Baker, Dall., 1962

Most Points After Touchdown, Game
9 Marlin (Pat) Harder, Chi. Cards vs. N. Y., Oct. 17, 1948
  Bob Waterfield, L. A. vs. Balt., Oct. 22, 1950
  Charlie Gogolak, Wash, vs. N. Y. Giants, Nov. 27, 1966
8 By many, both leagues/conferences

Most Consecutive Points After Touchdown
234 Tommy Davis, S. F., 1959-65
220 Jim Turner, N. Y. (AFL) 1967-69; N. Y. (AFC) 1970; Den. (AFC) 1971-74

201 George Blanda, Oak. (AFL) 1967-69; Oak. (AFC) 1970-71

199 Fred Cox, Minn. 1968-69; Minn. (NFC) 1970-74

171 Bruce Gossett, L. A. 1965-69; S. F. (NFC) 1970

156 George Blanda, Chi. Bears, 1949-56

153 Jan Stenerud, K. C. (AFL) 1968-69; K. C. (AFC) 1970-73

149 Tom Brooker, K. C., 1962-66 (AFL)

138 Lou Groza, Clev., 1963-66

133 Pete Gogolak, N. Y. Giants (NFL-NFC) 1968-72

126 George (Pat) Summerall, N. Y., 1958-61

FIELD GOALS

Most Seasons, Leading League—Conference

5 Lou Groza, Clev., 1950, 52-54, 57

4 Jack Manders, Chi. Bears, 1933-34, 36-37

Ward Cuff, N. Y., 1938-39, 43; G. B. 1947

3 Bob Waterfield, L. A., 1947, 49, 51

Gino Cappelletti, Bos. 1961, 63-64 (AFL)

Fred Cox, Minn., 1965, 69-70 (NFL-NFC)

Roy Gerela, Pitt. (AFC) 1972-74

2 Armand Niccolai, Pitt., 1935-36

Clark Hinkle, G. B., 1940-41

John (Cliff) Patton, Phila., 1948-49

Gene Mingo, Den,, 1960, 62 (AFL)

Jim Turner, N. Y., 1968-69 (AFL)

Jan Stenerud, K. C., 1967 (AFL), 1970 (AFC)

Chester Marcol, G. B. (NFC) 1972, 74

Most Field Goals, Lifetime

322 George Blanda, Chi. Bears 1949-58; Balt. 1950; Hou. (AFL) 1960-66; Oak. (AFL) 1967-69; Oak. (AFC) 1970-74

242 Fred Cox, Minn. 1963-69; Minn. (NFC) 1970-74

234 Lou Groza, Clev. 1950-59, 61-67

231 Jim Turner, N. Y. (AFL) 1964-69; N. Y. (AFC) 1970; Den. (AFC) 1971-74

225 Jim Bakken, St. L. 1962-69; St. L. (NFC) 1970-74

219 Bruce Gossett, L. A. 1964-69; S. F. (NFC) 1970-74

196 Jan Stenerud, K. C. (AFL) 1967-69; K. C. (AFC) 1970-74

187 Lou Michaels, L. A. 1958-60; Pit. 1961-63; Balt. 1964-69; G. B. (NFC) 1971

179 Sam Baker, Wash. 1953, 56-59; Clev. 1960-61; Dal. 1962-63; Phil. 1964-69

176 Gino Cappelletti, Bos. (AFL) 1960-69; Bos. (AFC) 1970

Most Field Goals, Season

34 Jim Turner, N. Y. 1968 (AFL)

33 Chester Marcol, G. B. 1972 (NFC)

32 Jim Turner, N. Y. 1969 (AFL)

30 Jan Stenerud, K. C. 1968 (AFL)

Fred Cox, Minn. 1970 (NFC)

Jan Stenerud, K. C. 1970 (AFC)

David Ray, L. A. 1973 (NFC)

29 Curt Knight, Wash. 1971 (NFC)

Roy Gerela, Pitt. 1973 (AFC)

28 Bruce Gossett, L. A. 1966

Garo Yepremian, Miami, 1971 (AFC)

Roy Gerela, Pitt. 1972 (AFC)

Most Field Goals, Game

7 Jim Bakken, St. L. vs. Pitt., Sept. 24, 1967

6 Gino Cappelletti, Bos. vs. Den. Oct. 4, 1964 (AFL)

Garo Yepremian, Det. vs. Minn., Nov. 13, 1966

Jim Turner, N. Y. vs. Buff., Nov. 3, 1968 (AFL)

Tom Dempsey, Phil. (NFC) vs. Hou. (AFC), Nov. 12, 1972

Bobby Howfield, N. Y. (AFC) vs. N. O. (NFC), Dec. 3, 1972

Jim Bakken, St. L. vs. Atl.; Dec. 9, 1973 (NFC)

*5 By many (AFL-NFL)

Longest Field Goal

63 Tom Dempsey, N. O. vs. Det., Nov. 1, 1970 (NFC)

57 Don Crockroft, Clev. vs. Den., Oct. 29, 1972 (AFC)

56 Bert Rechichar, Balt. vs. Chi. Bears Sept. 27, 1953

55 George Blanda, Hou. vs. S. D., Dec. 1961 (AFL)

Tom Dempsey, N. O. vs. L. A., Oct. 5, 1969

Jan Stenerud, K. C. vs. Den., Oct. 4, 1970 (AFC)

---

* Field Goals credited to Ernie Nevers (Dul. vs. Hartford 1926) by NFL appear to be error. Score of game was 16-0 Nevers scoring 3 FG, 1 TD, 1 PAT. Date was 11-27 not 11-28.

SAFETIES

Most Safeties, Lifetime
3   Bill McPeak, Pitt., 1954, 56, 57
     Charlie Krueger, S. F., 1959, 60, 61
     Ernie Stautner, Pitt., 1950, 58, 62
     Jim Katcavage, N. Y. 1958, 61, 65
     Roger Brown, Det., 1962 (2), 65
     Bruce Maher, Det. 1960, 63, 67

Most Safeties, Season
2   Tom Nash, G. B., 1932
     Roger Brown, Det., 1962
     Ron McDole, Buff. (AFL), 1964
     Alan Page, Minn. (NFC), 1971
     Fred Dryer, L. A. (NFC), 1973

Most Safeties, Game
2   Fred Dryer, L. A. vs. G. B., Oct. 21, 1973 (NFC)
1   By many players

RUSHING

Most Seasons Leading League
8   Jim Brown, Clev., 1957-61, 63-65
4   Steve Van Buren, Phil., 1945, 47-49
2   By many players (NFL-AFL)

YARDAGE

Most Yards Gained, Lifetime
12,312   Jim Brown, Clev., 1957-65
8,597   Jim Taylor, G. B., 1958-66; N. O., 1967
8,378   Fletcher (Joe) Perry, S. F., 1950-60; Balt., 1961-62
7,274   Leroy Kelly, Clev. 1964-69; Clev. (AFC) 1970-73
6,803   John Henry Johnson, S. F., 1954-56; Det. 1957-59; Pitt. 1960-65
6,306   O. J. Simpson, Buff. (AFL-AFC) 1969-74
6,217   Don Perkins, Dall., 1961-68
6,105   Ken Willard, S. F. 1965-69; S. F. (NFC) 1970-73; St. L. (NFC) 1974
5,900   Larry Csonka, Miami (AFL-AFC) 1968-74
5,878   Floyd Little, Den. (AFL) 1967-69; Den. (AFC) 1970-74
5,838   Bill Brown, Chi. 1961; Minn. 1962-69; Minn. (NFC) 1970-74

Most Yards Gained, Season
2,003   O. J. Simpson, Buff. (AFC) 1973
1,863   Jim Brown, Clev., 1963
1,544   Jim Brown, Clev., 1965
1,527   Jim Brown, Clev., 1958
1,474   Jim Taylor, G. B., 1962
1,458   Jim Nance, Bos. (AFL) 1966
1,408   Jim Brown, Clev., 1961

Most Yards Gained, Game
250   O. J. Simpson, Buff. vs. N. E., Sept. 16, 1973 (AFC) (29 attempts)
247   Willie Ellison, L. A. vs. N. O., Dec. 4, 1971 (NFC) (26 attempts)
243   Carlton (Cookie) Gilchrist, Buff. vs. N. Y., Dec. 8, 1963 (AFL)
237   Jim Brown, Clev. vs. L. A., Nov. 24, 1957 (31 attempts)
       Jim Brown, Clev., vs. Phil., Nov. 19, 1961 (34 attempts)
232   Bobby Mitchell, Clev. vs. Wash., Nov. 15, 1959 (21 attempts)
       Jim Brown, Clev. vs. Dall., Sept. 22, 1963 (20 attempts)
223   Tom Wilson, L. A. vs. G. B., Dec. 16, 1956 (23 attempts)
       Jim Brown, Clev. vs. Phil., Nov. 3, 1963 (28 attempts)

Longest Run from Scrimmage
97   Andy Uram, G. B. vs. Chi. Cards, Oct. 8, 1939 (td)
      Bob Gage, Pitt. vs. Chi. Bears, Dec. 4, 1949 (td)
96   Bob Hoernschemeyer, Det. vs. N.Y. Yanks, Nov. 23, 1950 (td)
      Jim Spavital, Balt. vs. G. B., Nov. 5, 1950 (td)
94   O. J. Simpson, Buff. vs. Pitt., Oct. 29, 1972 (td) (AFC)
92   Kenny Washington, L. A. vs. Chi. Cards, Nov. 2, 1947 (td)
91   Sid Blanks, Hou. vs. N. Y., Dec. 13, 1964 (td) (AFL)

PASSING

Most Seasons Leading League
6   Sammy Baugh, Wash., 1937, 40, 43, 45, 47, 49
4   Len Dawson, Dall., 1962; K. C. 1964, 66, 68 (AFL)
3   Arnie Herber, G. B., 1932, 34, 36
     Norm Van Brocklin, L. A., 1950, 52, 54
     Bart Starr, G. B., 1962, 64, 66
     Sonny Jurgensen, Wash. 1967, 69 (NFL) 1973 (NFC)

COMPLETIONS

Most Passes Completed, Lifetime
2,830   John Unitas (NFL-AFC)
2,658   Fran Tarkenton (NFL-NFC)
2,469   John Brodie (NFL-NFC)
2,433   Sonny Jurgensen (NFL-NFC)
2,168   Roman Gabriel (NFL-NFC)
2,146   Norm Snead (NFL-NFC)

2,118   Y. A. Tittle (NFL)
2,109   John Hadl (AFL-AFC-NFC)
2,043   Len Dawson (NFL-AFL-AFC)
1,910   George Blanda (NFL-AFL-AFC)
1,814   Bobby Layne (NFL)
1,808   Bart Starr (NFL-NFC)

Most Passes Completed, Season
288   C. A. "Sonny" Jurgensen, Wash., 1967 (508 attempts)
274   C. A. "Sonny" Jurgensen, Wash., 1969 (442 attempts)
270   Roman Gabriel, Phil., 1973 (NFC) (460 attempts)
262   George Blanda, Hou., 1964 (AFL) (505 attempts)
258   Joe Namath, N. Y., 1967 (AFL) (491 attempts)
255   John Unitas, Balt., 1967 (436 attempts)
254   C. A. "Sonny" Jurgensen, Wash., 1966 (436 attempts)
248   Frank Tripucka, Den., 1960 (AFL) (478 attempts)
242   John Brodie, S. F., 1965 (391 attempts)

Most Passes Completed, Game
37   George Blanda, Hou. vs. Buff., Nov. 1, 1964 (AFL)
36   Charlie Conerly, N. Y. vs. Pitt., 1948
34   Mickey Slaughter, Den. vs. Hou., Dec. 20, 1964 (AFL)
     Joe Namath, N. Y. vs. Balt., Oct. 18, 1970 (AFC)
33   Robert (Davey) O'Brien, Phil. vs. Wash., 1940
     C. A. (Sonny) Jurgensen, Phil. vs. N. Y., 1962
     Bill Wade, Chi. vs. L. A., 1964
32   C. A. (Sonny) Jurgensen, Wash. vs. Clev., Nov. 26, 1967, (50 attempts)

EFFICIENCY

Passing Efficiency, Lifetime (1,500 att.)
57.4   Bart Starr, G. B., 1956-69; G. B. (NFC) 1970-71 (3,149-1,808)
57.1   Sonny Jurgensen, Phil. 1957-63; Wash., 1964-69; Wash. (NFC) 1970-74 (4,262-2,433)
56.7   Len Dawson, Pitt. 1957-59; Clev. 1960-61; Dal. (AFL) 1962; K. C. (AFL) 1963-69; K. C. (AFC) 1970-74 (3,601-2,043)
56.5   Sammy Baugh, Wash., 1937-52 (2,995-1,693)
55.7   Otto Graham, Clev., 1950-55 (1,565-872)

Passing Efficiency, Season (100 att.)
70.3   Sammy Baugh, Wash., 1945 (182-128)
64.9   Ken Anderson, Cinn., 1974 (AFC) (328-213)
64.7   Otto Graham, Clev., 1953 (258-167)
64.1   Sonny Jurgensen, Wash., 1974 (NFC) (167-107)
63.7   Bryan (Bart) Starr, G. B. (171-109)
63.6   John Brodie, S. F., 1972 (NFC) (110-70)
63.1   Y. A. Tittle, S. F., 1957 (279-176)
62.7   Ken Stabler, Oak. (AFC) 1973 (260-163)

YARDAGE

Most Yards Gained, Lifetime
40,239   John Unitas (NFL-AFC)
35,846   Fran Tarkenton (NFL-NFC)
32,224   Sonny Jurgensen (NFL-NFC)
31,548   John Brodie (NFL-NFC)
30,698   John Hadl (AFL-AFC-NFC)
29,221   Norm Snead (NFL-NFC)
28,339   Y. A. Tittle (NFL)
27,616   Len Dawson (NFL-AFL-AFC)
27,309   Roman Gabriel (NFL-NFC)
26,909   George Blanda (NFL-AFL-AFC)

Most Yards Gained, Season
4,007   Joe Namath, N. Y., 1967 (AFL)
3,747   C. A. (Sonny) Jurgensen, Wash., 1967
3,723   C. A. (Sonny) Jurgensen, Phil., 1961
3,481   John Unitas, Balt., 1963
3,473   John Hadl, S. D., 1968 (AFL)
3,465   Vito (Babe) Parilli, Bos., 1964 (AFL)
3,280   Charles Johnson, St. L., 1963
3,261   C. A. (Sonny) Jurgensen, Phil., 1962
3,224   Y. A. Tittle, N. Y., 1962

Most Yards Gained, Game
554   Norm Van Brocklin, L. A. vs. N. Y. Yanks, Sept. 28, 1951 (41-27)
505   Y. A. Tittle, N. Y. vs. Wash., Oct. 28, 1962 (39-27)
496   Joe Namath, N. Y. vs. Balt., Sept. 24, 1972 (AFC)
468   John Lujack, Chi. Bears vs. Chi. Cards, Dec. 11, 1949 (39-24)
464   George Blanda, Hou. vs. Buff., Oct. 29, 1961 (AFL)
457   Jackie Lee, Hou. vs. Bos., Oct. 13, 1961 (AFL)

Longest Pass Completion (all TDs)
99 C. A. Jurgensen (to Allen), Wash. vs. Chi., Sept. 15, 1968
      Karl Sweetan (to Studstill), Det. vs. Balt., Oct. 16, 1966
      George Izo (to Mitchell), Wash. vs. Clev., Sept. 15, 1963
      Frank Filchock (to Farkas), Wash. vs. Pitt., Oct. 15, 1939
98 Doug Russell (to Tinsley), Chi Cards vs. Clev., Nov. 27, 1938
      Ogden Compton (to Lane), Chi. Cards vs. G. B., Nov. 13, 1955
      Bill Wade (to Farrington), Chi. Bears vs. Det., Oct. 8, 1961
      Jack Lee (to Dewveall), Hou. vs. S. D., Nov. 25, 1962 (AFL)
      Earl Morrall (to Jones), N. Y. vs. Pitt., Sept. 11, 1966
97 James (Pat) Coffee (to Tinsley), Chi. Cards vs. Chi. Bears, Dec. 5, 1937
      Bobby Layne (to Box), Det. vs. G. B., Nov. 26, 1953
      George Shaw (to Tarr), Den. vs. Bos., Sept. 21, 1962 (AFL)

Shortest Pass Completion for Touchdown
2" Eddie LeBaron (to Bielski), Dall. vs. Wash., Oct. 9, 1960
4" Cecil Isbell (to Hutson), G. B. vs. Clev., Oct. 18, 1942

TOUCHDOWN PASSES

Most Touchdown Passes, Lifetime
290 John Unitas (NFL-AFC)
266 Fran Tarkenton (NFL-NFC)
255 Sonny Jurgensen (NFL-NFC)
236 George Blanda (NFL-AFL-AFC)
234 Len Dawson (NFL-AFL-AFC)
231 John Hadl (AFL-AFC-NFC)
214 John Brodie (NFL-NFC)
212 Y. A. Tittle (NFL)

Most Touchdown Passes, Season
36 George Blanda, Hou. 1961 (AFL)
34 Daryle Lamonica, Oak. 1969 (AFL)
33 Y. A. Tittle, N. Y. 1962

Most Touchdown Passes, Game
7 Sid Luckman, Chi. Bears vs N. Y., Nov. 14, 1943
    Adrian Burk, Phil. vs Wash., Oct. 17, 1954
    George Blanda, Hou. vs N. Y., Nov. 19, 1961 (AFL)
    Y. A. Tittle, N. Y. vs Wash., Oct. 28, 1962

Joe Kapp, Minn. vs Balt., Sept. 29, 1969
6 By many players (NFL-AFL)

HAD INTERCEPTED

Lowest Percentage Passes Had Intercepted, Lifetime (1,500 att.)
3.30 Roman Gabriel, L. A. (NFL-NFC) 1962-72; Philadelphia (NFC) 1973-74 (4111-136)
4.10 Bill Munson, L. A. 1964-67; Detroit (NFL-NFC) 1968-74 (1755-72)
4.15 Fran Tarkenton, Minn. (NFL-NFC) 1961-66, 72-74; New York Giants (NFL-NFC) 1967-71 (4800-199)

Fewest Passes Had Intercepted, Season (100 att.)
1 Bill Nelsen, Pitt., 1966 (112 attempts)
2 Roman Gabriel, L. A., 1962 (101 attempts)
   Robert Berry, Atl., 1969 (124 attempts)
3 Dwight Sloan, Det., 1939 (102 attempts)
   Y. A. Tittle, S. F., 1960 (127 attempts)
   Gary Wood, N. Y., 1964 (143 attempts)
   Bryan Starr, G. B., 1966 (251 attempts)
   Joe Kapp, Bos., 1970 (AFC) (219 attempts)

PASS RECEPTIONS

Most Seasons Leading League
8 Don Hutson
5 Lionel Taylor, Den. 1960-63, 65 (AFL)
3 Tom Fears
   Pete Pihos
   Billy Wilson
   Raymond Berry
   Lance Alworth, S. D., 1966, 68-69 (AFL)

Most Pass Receptions, Lifetime
633 Don Maynard (NFL-AFL-AFC-NFC)
631 Raymond Berry (NFL)
582 Charley Taylor (NFL-NFC)
567 Lionel Taylor (AFL)
542 Lance Alworth (AFL-AFC-NFC)
521 Bobby Mitchell (NFL)
503 Billy Howton (NFL)
495 Tommy McDonald (NFL)

488 Don Hutson (NFL)
479 Art Powell (NFL-AFL-NFC)
474 Boyd Dowler (NFL-AFC)

Most Pass Receptions, Season
101 Charley Hennigan, Hou. 1964 (AFL)
100 Lionel Taylor, Den. 1961 (AFL)
93 Johnny Morris, Chi. 1964
92 Lionel Taylor, Den. 1960 (AFL)

Most Pass Receptions, Game
18 Tom Fears, L. A. vs G. B., Dec. 3, 1950 (189 yds.)
16 Ulmo (Sonny) Randle, St. L. vs N. Y., Nov. 4, 1962 (256 yds.)

YARDAGE

Most Yards Gained, Lifetime
11,834 Don Maynard (NFL-AFL-AFC-NFC)
10,266 Lance Alworth (AFL-AFC-NFC)
9,275 Raymond Berry (NFL)
8,459 Billy Howton (NFL)
8,410 Tommy McDonald (NFL)
8,277 Carroll Dale (NFL-NFC)
8,208 Charley Taylor (NFL-NFC)
8,046 Art Powell (NFL-AFL-NFL)

Most Yards Gained, Season
1,746 Charley Hennigan, Hou. 1961 (AFL) (82 receptions)
1,602 Lance Alworth, S. D., 1965 (AFL) (69)
1,546 Charley Hennigan, Hou. 1964 (AFL) (101)
1,495 Elroy Hirsch, L. A. 1951 (66)
1,436 Bobby Mitchell, Wash. 1963 (69)
1,384 Bobby Mitchell, Wash. 1962 (72)
1,298 Raymond Berry, Balt. 1960 (74)

Most Yards Gained, Game
303 Jim Benton, Clev. Rams vs Det., Nov. 22, 1945 (10)
302 Cloyce Box, Det. vs Balt., Dec. 3, 1950
272 Charley Hennigan, Hou. vs Bos., Oct. 13, 1961 (AFL)
269 Del Shofner, N. Y. vs Wash., Oct. 26, 1962 (11)

Longest Pass Reception (all TDs)
99 Andy Farkas (Filchok), Wash. vs Pitt., Oct. 15, 1939
   Robert Mitchell (Izo), Wash. vs Clev., Sept. 15, 1963
   Pat Studstill (Sweetan), Det. vs Balt., Oct. 16, 1966
   Gerry Allen (Jurgensen), Wash. vs Chi., Sept. 15, 1968
98 Gaynell Tinsley (Russell), Chi. Cards vs Clev., Nov. 17, 1938

Richard (Night Train) Lane (Compton), Chi. Cards vs G. B., Nov. 13, 1955
John Farrington (Wade), Chi. Bears vs Det., Oct. 8, 1961
Willard Dewveall (Lee), Hou. vs S. D., Nov. 25, 1962 (AFL)
Homer Jones (Morrall), N. Y. vs Pitt., Sept. 11, 1966
97 Gaynell Tinsley (Coffee), Chi. Cards vs Chi. Bears, Dec. 5, 1937
   Cloyce Box (Layne), Det. vs G. B. Nov. 26, 1953
   Jerry Tarr (Shaw), Den. vs Bos., Sept. 21, 1962 (AFL)

TOUCHDOWNS

Most Touchdown Passes, Lifetime
99 Don Hutson (NFL)
88 Don Maynard (NFL-AFL-AFC)
85 Lance Alworth (AFL-AFC-NFC)
84 Tommy McDonald (NFL)
81 Art Powell (AFL)
77 Paul Warfield (NFL-AFC)
73 Charley Taylor (NFL-NFC)
71 Bob Hayes (NFL-NFC)
70 Gary Collins (NFL-AFC)

Most Touchdown Passes, Season
17 Don Hutson, G. B. 1942
   Elroy Hirsch, L. A. 1951
   Bill Groman, Hou. 1961 (AFL)
16 Art Powell, Oak. 1963 (AFL)
15 Cloyce Box, Det. 1952
   Ulmo (Sonny) Randle, St. L. 1960

Most Touchdown Passes, Game
5 Bob Shaw, Chi. Cards vs Balt., Oct. 2, 1950
4 By many players

INTERCEPTIONS BY

Most Seasons Leading League
2 Richard Lane
  Jack Christiansen
  Milt Davis
  Richard Lynch
  Johnny Robinson
  Bill Bradley (NFC)
  Emmitt Thomas (AFL-NFC)

Most Interceptions by Lifetime
79 Emlen Tunnell
68 Richard Lane
64 Paul Krause (NFL-NFC)
62 Dick LeBeau (NFL-NFC)
57 Johnny Robinson (AFL-AFC)
   Bob Boyd

52 Bob Dillon
Jack Butler
Jim Patton
Larry Wilson (NFL-NFC)

Most Interceptions by, Season
14 Richard Lane, L. A., 1952
13 Dan Sandifer ,Wash., 1948
Orban (Red) Sanders, N. Y. Yanks, 1950

Most Interceptions by, Game
4 By several

YARDAGE

Most Yards Gained, Lifetime
1,282 Emlen Tunnell
1,207 Richard Lane
1,046 Herb Adderley (NFL-NFC)
994 Bob Boyd
976 Bob Dillon
965 Lem Barney (NFL-NFC)

Most Yards Gained, Season
349 Charley McNeil, S. D. (AFL) 1961
301 Don Doll, Det. 1949
298 Richard Lane, L. A. 1952
275 Woodley Lewis, L. A. 1950

Most Yards Gained, Game
177 Charley McNeil, S. D. vs Hou., Sept. 24, 1961 (AFL)
162 Dick Jauron, Det. vs Chi., Nov. 18, 1973 (NFC)
137 Tom Janik, Buff. vs N. Y., Sept. 29, 1968 (AFL)
128 Miller Farr, Hou. vs N. Y., Oct. 15, 1967 (AFL)
121 Milt Davis, Balt. vs Chi. Bears, Nov. 17, 1957
Mike Gaechter, Dall. vs Wash., Nov. 3, 1963
115 Bernie Parrish, Clev. vs Chi. Bears, Dec. 11, 1960
Larry Wilson, St. L. vs Clev., Dec. 19, 1965

Longest Gain (all TDs)
102 Bob Smith, Det. vs Chi. Bears, Nov. 24, 1949
Erich Barnes, N. Y. vs Dall., Oct. 22, 1961
101 Ritchie Petibon, Chi. Bears vs L. A., Dec. 9, 1962
Henry Carr, N. Y. vs L. A., Nov. 13, 1966
100 Vern Huffman, Det. vs Brk., Oct. 17, 1937
Mike Gaechter, Dall. vs Phil., Oct. 14, 1962
Les Duncan, S. D. vs K. C., Oct. 15, 1967 (AFL)

Tom Janik, Buff. vs N. Y., Sept. 29, 1968 (AFL)

TOUCHDOWNS

Most Touchdowns, Lifetime
9 Ken Houston, Hou. (AFL) 1967-69; Hou. (AFC) 1970-72; Wash. (NFC) 1973-74
7 Herb Adderley, G. B. 1961-69; Dal. 1970-72 (NFC)
Erich Barnes, Chi. 1958-60; N. Y. 1961-64; Clev. 1965-69; Clev. (AFC) 1970-71
6 Tom Janik, Den. 1963-64; Buff. 1965-68; Bos. 1969, (AFL) ; Bos. (AFC) 1970
Miller Farr, Den. (AFL) 1965; S. D. (AFL) 1965-66; Hou. (AFL) 1967-69; St. L. (NFC) 1970-72; Det. (NFC) 1973
Lem Barney, Det. 1967-69; Det. (NFC) 1970-74
5 By many players (NFL/NFC-AFL/AFC)

Most Touchdowns, Season
4 Ken Houston, Hou., 1971 (AFC)
Jim Kearney, K. C., 1972 (AFC)
3 Dick Harris, S. D. 1961 (AFL)
Dick Lynch, N. Y. 1963
Herb Adderley, G. B. 1965
Lem Barney, Det. 1967
Miller Farr, Hou. 1967 (AFL)
2 By many players (NFL/NFC-AFL/AFC)

PUNTING

Most Seasons Leading League
4 Sammy Baugh, Wash. 1940-43
Jerrel Wilson, K. C. 1965-68, 72-73 (AFL-AFC)
3 Yale Lary, Det. 1959, 61, 63
Jim Fraser, Den. 1962-64 (AFL)
2 By many players (NFL-AFL)

Most Punts, Lifetime
970 Bobby Joe Green (NFL-NFC)
811 Jerrel Wilson (AFL-AFC)
795 Paul Maguire (AFL-NFC)
762 Bobby Walden (NFL-AFC)
703 Loris "Sam" Baker
660 Don Chandler

Most Punts, Season
105 Bob Scarpitto, Den. 1967 (AFL)
100 Paul Maguire, Buff. 1968 (AFL)
92 Howard Maley, Bos. 1947
91 Hugh Richter 1964

Most Punts, Game
14 Sammy Baugh, Wash. vs Phil., Nov. 5, 1939
    John Kinscherf, N. Y. vs Det., Nov. 7, 1943
    George Taliaferro, N. Y. Yanks vs L. A., Sept. 28, 1951
12 Parker Hall, Clev. vs G. B., Nov. 26, 1939
    Beryl Clark, Chi. Cards vs Det., Sept. 15, 1940
    Horace Gillom, Clev. vs Phil., Dec. 3, 1950
    Bob Scarpitto, Den. vs Oak., Sept. 10, 1967 (AFL)
    Bill Van Heusen, Den. vs Cin., Oct. 6, 1968 (AFL)

Longest Punt
98 Steve O'Neal, N. Y. vs Den., Sept. 21, 1969 (AFL)
*95 Joe Guyon, Canton vs Chicago Tigers, Nov. 4, 1920
94 Wilbur Henry, Canton vs Akron, Oct. 28, 1923
90 Don Chandler, G. B. vs S. F., Oct. 10, 1965
88 Bob Waterfield, L. A. vs G. B., Oct. 17, 1948
87 Bob Scarpitto, Bos. vs Oak., Oct. 6, 1968 (AFL)
               *Not recognized by NFL.

AVERAGE YARDAGE

Highest Punting Average Lifetime (300 punts)
45.10 Sammy Baugh
44.68 Tommy Davis
44.33 Jerrel Wilson (AFL-AFC)
44.30 R. Yale Lary

Highest Punting Average, Season (20 punts)
51.3 Sammy Baugh, Wash. 1940
48.9 Yale Lary, Det. 1963
48.7 Sammy Baugh, Wash. 1941
46.2 Dave Lewis, Cin. 1970 (AFC)
45.5 Jerrel Wilson, K. C. 1973 (AFC)
45.4 Jerrel Wilson, K. C. 1965 (AFL)
45.3 Ray Guy, Oak. 1973 (AFC)
45.2 Bob Walden, Pitt. 1970 (AFC)
45.1 Bill Van Heusen, Den. 1973 (AFC)

Highest Punting Average Game (4 punts)
59.4 Sammy Baugh, Wash. vs Det. Oct. 27, 1940 (5)
57.4 Steve O'Neal, N. Y. Jets vs Den., Sept. 21, 1969 (AFL)
56.8 Sammy Baugh, Wash. vs Clev., Oct. 26, 1941 (8)

55.8 Sammy Baugh, Wash. vs Chi. Bears, Nov. 17, 1940 (6)
55.3 Mike Mercer, Oak. vs S. D., Sept. 19, 1965 (AFL)

PUNT RETURNS

Most Punt Returns, Lifetime
258 Emlen Tunnell
253 Alvin Haymond (NFL-NFC-AFC)
235 Ron Smith (NFL-NFC-AFC)
199 Les (Speedy) Duncan (AFL-AFC-NFC)
187 Willie Wood (NFL-NFC)

Most Punt Returns, Season
53 Alvin Haymond, 1970 (NFC)
46 Rodger Bird, 1967 (AFL)
43 Donnie Walker, 1974 (AFC)
    Bruce Taylor, 1970 (NFC)
41 Alvin Haymond, 1965
    George Atkinson, 1973 (AFC)
    Lynn Swann, 1974 (AFC)
    Mack Herron, 1974 (AFC)
40 Ray Brown, 1973 (NFC)
    Alvin Haymond, 1966

YARDAGE

Most Yards Gained, Lifetime
2,209 Emlen Tunnell
2,182 Les (Speedy) Duncan (AFL-AFC-NFC)
2,148 Alvin Haymond (NFL-NFC-AFC)
1,788 Ron Smith (NFL-NFC-AFL)
1,599 Bill Thompson (AFL-AFC)
1,515 Bill Dudley
1,431 George McAfee
1,391 Willie Wood (NFL-NFC)

Most Yards Gained, Season
612 Rodger Bird, Oak., 1967 (AFL)
577 Lynn Swann, 1974 (AFC)
555 Bill Grimes, G. B., 1950
517 Mack Herron, 1974 (AFC)
516 Bruce Taylor, S. F., 1970 (NFC)
490 George Atkinson, Oak., 1968 (AFL)
489 Emlen Tunnell, N. Y. Giants 1951

Most Yards Gained, Game
205 George Atkinson, Oak. vs Buff., Sept. 15, 1968 (AFL)
184 Tom Watkins, Det. vs S. F., 1963
175 Jack Christiansen, Det. vs G. B., Nov. 22, 1951 (4 returns)
148 Carl Taseff, Balt. vs G. B., Oct. 14, 1956 (4)

143 Rodger Bird, Oak. vs Den., Sept. 10, 1967 (AFL)

Longest Punt Return (all TDs)
98 Gil LeFebvre, Cin. vs Brk., Dec. 3, 1933
    Dennis Morgan, Dall. vs St. L., Oct. 13, 1974 (NFC)
    Charles West, Minn. vs Wash., Nov. 3, 1968
96 Bill Dudley, Wash. vs Pitt., Dec. 3, 1950
95 Frank Bernardi, Chi. Cards vs Wash., Oct. 14, 1956
    Les (Speedy) Duncan, S. D. vs N. Y., Nov. 24, 1968 (AFL)

AVERAGE YARDAGE

Highest Average, Lifetime (75 returns)
12.8 George McAfee
      Jack Christiansen
12.6 Claude Gibson
12.2 Bill Dudley

Highest Average, Season (15 returns)
21.5 Jack Christiansen, Det. 1952 (15)
21.3 Dick Christy, N. Y. 1961 (AFL)
20.9 John Cochran, Chi. Cards 1949 (15)
20.8 Jerry Davis, Chi. Cards 1948 (16)

TOUCHDOWNS

Most Touchdowns, Lifetime
8 Jack Christiansen
5 Emlen Tunnell
4 Dick Christy
   Les (Speedy) Duncan (AFL-AFC-NFC)
   Lamar Parrish (AFC)
3 By several (NFL-AFL)

Most Touchdowns, Season
4 Jack Christiansen, Det. 1951
3 Emlen Tunnell, N. Y. Giants 1951
2 By many players (NFL-AFL)

Most Touchdowns, Game
2 Jack Christiansen, Det. 1951: vs L. A. Oct. 14; vs G. B. Nov. 22
   Dick Christy, N. Y. vs Den., Sept. 24, 1961 (AFL)

KICKOFF RETURNS

Most Kickoff Returns, Lifetime
275 Ron Smith (NFL-NFC-AFC)
193 Abe Woodson
191 Al Carmichael
189 Dick James
184 Tim Brown

182 Les (Speedy) Duncan (AFL-AFC-NFC)
170 Alvin Haymond (NFL-NFC-AFC)
158 Bobby Jancik (AFL)
145 Woodley Lewis

Most Kickoff Returns, Season
47 Odell Barry, Den. 1964 (AFL)
46 Charles Latourette, St. L. 1968
46 Dave Hampton, G. B. 1971 (NFC)
45 Bobby Jancik, Hou. 1963 (AFL)
43 Ron Smith, Atl. 1966
    Margene Adkins, N. O. 1972 (NFC)
41 Mack Herron, N. E. 1973 (AFC)
40 Mel Renfro, Dall. 1964
    Mike Battle, N. Y. 1970 (AFC)

Most Kickoff Returns, Game
9 Noland Smith, K. C. vs Oak., Nov. 23, 1967 (AFL)
8 George Taliaferro, N. Y. Yanks vs N. Y. Giants, Dec. 3, 1950
   Bobby Jancik, Hou. vs Bos., Dec. 8; vs Oak., Dec. 22, 1963 (AFL)
   Mel Renfro, Dal. vs G. B., Nov. 29, 1964
   Willie Porter, Bos. vs N. Y., Sept. 22, 1968 (AFL)
7 By many players (NFL-AFL)

AVERAGE YARDAGE

Highest Average, Lifetime (75 returns)
30.6 Gale Sayers
29.6 Lynn Chandnois
28.7 Abe Woodson
27.9 Claude (Buddy) Young
      Irv Cross
27.5 Travis Williams (NFL-NFC)

YARDAGE

Most Yards Gained, Lifetime
6,922 Ron Smith, Chi. 1965; Atl. 1966-67; L. A. 1968-69; Chi. (NFC) 1970-72; S. D. (AFC) 1973; Oak. (AFC) 1974
5,538 Abe Woodson, S. F. 1958-66
4,798 Al Carmichael, G. B. 1953-58; Den. (AFL) 1960-61
4,781 Tim Brown, G. B. 1959; ¯Phil. 1960-67
4,676 Dick James, Wash. 1956-63, N. Y. 1964; Minn. 1965
4,599 Les (Speedy) Duncan, S. D. (AFL) 1964-69; S. D. (AFC) 1970; Wash. (NFC) 1971-73
4,438 Alvin Haymond, Balt. 1964-67; Phil. 1968; L. A. 1969; L. A. (NFC) 1970-72; Hou. (AFC) 1973
3,907 Al Carmichael, G. B. 1953-58

3,798   Joe Arenas, S. F. 1951-57
3,480   Woodley Lewis, L. A. 1950-55;
         Chi. Cards 1956-59; Dall. 1960

Most Yards Gained, Season
1,317   Bobby Jancik, Hou. 1963 (AFL)
1,314   Dave Hampton, G. B. 1971 (NFC)
1,245   Odell Barry, Den. 1964 (AFL)
1,237   Charles Latourette, St. L. 1968
1,157   Abe Woodson, S. F. 1962
1,092   Mack Herron, N. E. 1973 (AFC)
1,022   Alvin Haymond, L. A. 1970 (NFC)
1,020   Margene Adkins, N. O. 1972
         (NFL)
1,017   Mel Renfro, Dall. 1964
1,013   Ron Smith, Atl. 1966
1,011   Herb Mul-Key, Wash. 1973 (NFC)

Most Yards Gained, Game
294   Wally Triplett, Det. vs L. A., Oct.
       29, 1950
247   Tim Brown, Phil. vs Dall., Nov.
       1966
244   Noland Smith, K. C. vs S. D., Oct.
       15, 1967 (AFL)
240   Bobby Jancik, Hou. vs Oak., Dec.
       22, 1963 (AFL)
221   Bobby Jancik, Hou. vs Bos., Dec.
       3, 1963 (AFL)
210   Abe Woodson, S. F. vs Det., Nov.
       11, 1962

Longest Kickoff Return (all TDs)
106   Al Carmichael, G. B. vs Chi. Bears,
       Oct. 7, 1956
       Noland Smith, K. C. vs Den., Dec.
       17, 1967 (AFL)
105   Frank Seno, Chi. Cards vs N. Y.,
       Oct. 20, 1946
       Ollie Matson, Chi. Cards vs Wash.,
       Oct. 14, 1956
       Abe Woodson, S. F. vs L. A., Nov.
       8, 1959
       Thomas (Tim) Brown, Phil. vs
       Clev., Sept. 17, 1961
       Jon Arnett, L. A. vs Det., Oct. 29,
       1961
       Eugene Morris, Mia. vs Cin., Sept.
       14, 1969 (AFL)
       Travis Williams, L. A. vs N. O.,
       Dec. 5, 1971 (NFC)
104   By many players (NFL-AFL)

Highest Average, Season (15 returns)
41.1   Travis Williams, G. B. 1967
37.7   Gale Sayers, Chi. 1967
35.5   Ollie Matson, Chi. Cards 1957
35.4   Les (Speedy) Duncan, Balt. 1970
        (AFC)
35.2   Lynn Chandnois, Pitt. 1952
34.4   Joe Arenas, S. F. 1953
        Tom Watkins, Det. 1965
33.7   Verda (Vitamin) Smith, L. A. 1950

TOUCHDOWNS

Most Touchdowns, Lifetime
6   Ollie Matson
     Gale Sayers
     Travis Williams
5   Bobby Mitchell
     Abe Woodson
     Tim Brown
4   Cecil Turner
3   By several (NFL-AFL)

Most Touchdowns, Season
4   Travis Willims, G. B. 1967
     Cecil Turner, Chi. 1970 (NFC)
3   Verda (Vitamin) Smith, L. A. 1950
     Abe Woodson, S. F. 1963
     Gale Sayers, Chi., 1967
2   By many players (NFL-AFL)

Most Touchdowns, Game
2   Tim Brown, Phil. vs Dal., Nov. 6,
     1966
     Travis Williams, G. B. vs Clev.,
     Nov. 12, 1967
1   By many players (NFL/NFC-
     AFL/AFC)

FUMBLES

Most Fumbles, Lifetime
95   John Unitas (NFL-AFC)

Most Fumbles, Season
17   Don Pastorini, Hou. 1973 (AFC)
16   Don Meredith, Dall. 1964
15   Paul Christman, Chi. Cards 1946
      Sammy Baugh, Wash. 1947
      Sam Etcheverry, St. L. 1961
      Len Dawson, K. C. 1964 (AFL)
14   Bill Wade, L. A. 1958
      John Crow, St. L. 1962
      Tom Mason, Minn. 1963
      Jack Kemp, Buff. 1967 (AFL)

OWN RECOVERIES

Most Own Fumbles Recovered, Lifetime
38   Jack Kemp (NFL-AFL)
29   John Unitas (NFL-AFC)
      Len Dawson (NFL-AFC)
      Fran Tarkenton (NFL-NFC)
      Roman Gabriel (NFL-NFC)
28   Vito (Babe) Parilli (NFL-AFL)
27   Bobby Layne

Most Own Fumbles Recovered, Season
8   Paul Christman, Chi. Cards 1945

Bill Butler, Minn. 1963
7 Sammy Baugh, Wash. 1947
Tommy Thompson, Phil. 1947
John Roach, St. L. 1960
Jack Larschied, Oak. 1960 (AFL)
6 By many players (NFL-AFL)

OPPONENTS' RECORDS

Most Opponents' Fumbles Recovered,
Lifetime
25 Dick Butkus (NFL-NFC)
24 Jim Marshall (NFL-NFC)
22 Andy Robustelli
Joe Fortunato
21 Ernie Stautner
Willie Davis
20 John Reger
Len Ford
Bill Koman
Ray Nitschke (NFL-NFC)
18 Jerry Norton

Most Opponents' Fumbles Recovered,
Season
9 Donald Hultz, Minn. 1963
8 Joe Schmidt, Det. 1955
7 Alan Page, Minn. 1970 (NFC)
6 G. Barney Poole, Balt. 1953
Gene Brito, Wash. 1955
Dick Butkus, Chi. 1965
5 Bob Dee, Bos. 1961 (AFL)
Ron McDole, Buff. 1965 (AFL)

YARDAGE

Longest Fumble Run (all TDs)
104 Jack Tatum, Oak. (AFC) vs G. B.
(NFC), Sept. 24, 1972
98 George Halas, Chi. Bears vs
Thorpe Indians, Nov. 4, 1923
97 Charles Howley, Dall. vs Atl., Oct.
2, 1966
92 Joe Carter, Phil. vs N. Y., Sept. 25,
1938
89 Don Paul, Clev. vs Pitt., Nov. 10,
1957
69 Lewis (Bud) McFadin, Den. vs
N. Y., Nov. 22, 1962 (AFL)

TOUCHDOWNS

Most Touchdowns, Lifetime
3 Ralph Heywood
Leo Sugar
Lewis (Bud) McFadin (NFL-AFL)
Charles Cline (AFL)
Bob Lilly (NFL-NFC)

Most Touchdowns, Season
·2 By several

Most Touchdowns (Opponents' Fumbles),
Lifetime
3 Leo Sugar, Chi. Cards 1954, 57
Lewis (Bud) McFadin, L. A. 1956;
Den. (AFL) 1962-63
Charles Cline, Hou. 1961, 66
(AFL)
Bob Lilly, Dal. 1963, 69, 71
(NFL-NFC)
2 By many players (NFL-AFL)

COMBINED NET YARDS GAINED

(Includes rushes, pass receptions and run
back of pass interceptions, punts, kickoffs,
and fumbles.)

YARDAGE

Most Yards Gained, Lifetime
15,459 Jim Brown
14,078 Bob Mitchell
12,844 Ollie Matson
12,379 Don Maynard (AFL-AFC-NFC)
12,319 Leroy Kelly (NFL-AFC)
12,065 Abner Haynes (AFL)
11,375 Hugh McElhenny
10,346 Fletcher (Joe) Perry

Most Yards Gained, Season
2,444 Mack Herron, N. E. 1974 (AFC)
2,440 Gale Sayers, Chi. 1966
2,428 Tim Brown, Phil. 1963
2,306 Tim Brown, Phil. 1962
2,147 Dick Christy, N. Y. 1962 (AFL)
2,131 Jim Brown, Clev. 1963

MISCELLANEOUS

SCORING

Most Drop Kick Field Goals, Game
4 John (Paddy) Driscoll, Chi. Cards
vs Columbus, Oct. 11, 1925
(23, 18, 50, 35 yds.)
Elbert Bloodgood, Kansas City vs
Duluth, Dec. 12, 1926 (35, 32, 20,
25 yds.)

Longest Drop Kick Field Goal
50 Wilbur (Pete) Henry, Canton vs
Toledo, Nov. 13, 1922
John (Paddy) Driscoll, Chi. Cards
vs Milwaukee, Sept. 28, 1924; vs
Columbus, Oct. 11, 1925

Most Touchdowns, Runbacks of Punts &
Kickoffs, Game
2 By many players (NFL-AFL)

Most Touchdowns, Blocked Punts, Season
  2 Tim Moynihan, Chi. Cards, 1932
     Tim Foley, Miami 1973 (AFC)

Most Touchdowns, Blocked Punts, Game
  2 Tim Foley, Mia. vs Balt., Nov. 11,
     1973 (AFC)

RUNNING

Most Yards Returned Missed Field Goal
  101 Al Nelson, Phil. vs Dal., Sept. 26,
      1971 (NFC)
  100 Al Nelson, Phil. vs Clev., Dec. 11,
      1966 (td)
      Ken Ellis, G. B. vs N. Y., Sept. 19,
      1971 (NFC)
   99 Jerry Williams, L. A. vs G. B., Dec.
      16, 1951 (td)
      Carl Taseff, Balt. vs L. A., Dec. 12,
      1959 (td)
      Thomas (Tim) Brown, Phil. vs St.
      L., Sept. 16, 1962 (td)

  97 Marshall Starks, N. Y. vs Hou.,
     Sept. 22, 1963 (AFL)

PASSING

Passer Catching Own Pass
     By ten players (NFL-AFL)

INTERCEPTIONS BY

Most Yards Intercepted Pass Plus Lateral
  99 George Buksar (18 yds with inter-
     ception, lateral to) Ernie Zalejski,
     81 yds for td, Balt. vs Wash., Nov.
     26, 1950

Most Yards Intercepted Lateral
  93 Dick Poillon, Wash. vs Phil., Nov.
     21, 1948 (td)

INDIVIDUAL
CHAMPIONSHIP GAME RECORDS

(Courtesy of NFL and Elias Sports Bureau)

SERVICE

GAMES—PLAYER

Most Games Played
10 George Blanda (QB,K) Chi. 1956; Hou. (AFL) 1960-62; Oak. (AFL) 1967-69; Oak. (AFC) 1970, 73-74.
9 Lou Groza (T-K), Clev. Browns 1950-55, 57, 64-65
Don Chandler (K) N.Y. 1956, 58-59, 61-63, G.B., 1965-67
8 Andy Robustelli (E), L. A., 1951, 55; N. Y. 1956, 58-59, 61-63
Dick Modzelewski (T), N.Y. 1956, 58-59, 61-63; Clev. 1964-65
Herb Adderley (B), G. B.1961-62, 65-67; Dal. (NFC) 1970-72
Daryle Lamonica (QB) Buff. (AFL) 1964-66; Oak. (AFL) 1967-69; Oak. (AFC) 1970, 73
7 George Musso (G), Chi. Bears 1933-34, 37, 40-43
Mel Hein (C), N. Y., 1933-35, 41, 44
Frank Gatski (C), Clev. Browns, 1950-55; Det. 1957
Henry Jordan (T) Clev. 1957; G. B. 1960-62, 65-67
Fred Thurston (G) Balt. 1958; G. B. 1960-62, 65-67
Dave Kocourek (E), L. A. 1960; S. D. (AFL) 1961, 63-65; Oak. (AFL) 1967-68
Forrest Gregg (T), G. B.1960-62, 65-67; Dal. (NFC) 1971
Paul Warfield (E) Clev. 1964-65, 68-69; Mia. (AFC) 1971-73

Most Different Teams Played On
3 Lew Carpenter (HB), Det. 1953-54; Clev. 1957; G. B. 1960-62
George Blanda (QB,K), Chi. 1956; Hou. (AFL) 1960-62; Oak. (AFL) 1967-69; Oak. (AFC) 1970, 73-74

GAMES—COACH

Most Games, Head Coach
8 Steve Owen, N. Y., 1933-35, 38-39, 41, 44, 46
7 Paul Brown, Clev. 1950-55, 57
George Halas, Chi. Bears 1933-34, 37, 40-41, 46, 63

Most Games Won
5 George Halas, Chi. Bears 1933, 40-41, 46, 63
Vince Lombardi, G. B. 1961-62, 65-66
3 Hank Stram, Dal. 1962; K.C. 1966 69 (AFL)
Don Shula, Miami 1971-73
Bud Grant, Minn. 1969, 73-74

SCORING

Most Points Scored
60 George Blanda (NFL-AFL-AFC)
55 Lou Groza
36 Ken Strong
33 Jack Manders

Most Points Scored (one game)
19 Paul Hornung
18 Gary Collins
Otto Graham
Boyd Dowler
Tom Matte
Larry Csonka (AFC)
17 Ken Strong
16 George Blanda (AFL)

Most Touchdowns
5 Otto Graham, Clev. (played in 6 games)
Gary Collins, Clev. (played in 4 games)
Larry Csonka (AFC) (played in 3 games)
4 Ken Strong, N. Y. (played in 5 games)
Harry Clark, Chi. Bears (played in 4 games)
Boyd Dowler, G. B. (played in 6 games)

Most Touchdowns (one game)
3 Otto Graham, Clev. vs Det., Dec. 26, 1954
Gary Collins, Clev. vs Balt., Dec. 27, 1964
Tom Matte, Balt. vs Clev., 1968
Larry Csonka, Mia. vs Oak., 1973 (AFC)

Most Extra Points
25 Lou Groza, Clev. (played in 9 games)

18   George Blanda, Chi.; Hou. (AFL);
Oak. (AFL-AFC) (played in 10
games)
11   Don Chandler (played in 9 games)
9   Ken Strong, N. Y. (played in 5
games)
Garo Yepremian, Mia. (played in
3 games)
8   Robert Waterfield, Clev. and L. A.
(played in 4 games)
Jim Martin, Det. (played in 4
games)
Bob Snyder, Chi. Bears (played in
3 games)

Most Extra Points (one game)
8   Lou Groza, Clev. vs Det., Dec. 26,
1954
Jim Martin, Det. vs Clev., Dec. 29,
1957
6   George Blair, S. D. vs Bos. 1963
(AFL)
5   Bob Snyder, Chi. Bears vs Wash.,
Dec. 26, 1943
Lou Groza, Clev. vs L. A., Dec. 26,
1955
Ben Agajanian, N. Y. vs Chi.
Bears, Dec. 30, 1956

Most Field Goals
14   George Blanda, Chi.; Hou. (AFL);
Oak. (AFL-AFC) (played in 10
games)
10   Lou Groza, Clev. (played in 9
games)
5   Jack Manders, Chi. Bears (played
in 4 games)
Paul Hornung, G. B. (played in 3
games)
Pete Gogolak, Buff. (AFL)
(played in 2 games)

Most Field goals (one game)
4   George Blanda, Oak. vs Hou.
1967 (AFL)
Curt Knight, Wash. vs Dal. 1972
(NFC)
3   By several (NFL-AFL)

Longest Field Goal
52 yds Lou Groza, Clev. vs L. A., Dec.
23, 1951
48 yds George Blanda, Oak. vs Balt.,
Jan. 3, 1971 (AFC)
46 yds George Blanda, Hou. vs S. D.,
Dec. 24, 1961 (AFL)
Curt Knight, Wash. vs Dal., Dec
31, 1972 (NFC)
45 yds Curt Knight, Wash. vs Dal., Dec.
31, 1972 (NFC)

44 yds Fred Cox, Minn. vs Dal., Dec. 30,
1973 (NFC)
43 yds Lou Groza, Clev. vs Det., Dec.
27, 1953
Ben Agajanian, N.Y. vs Chi. Bears,
Dec. 30, 1956

RUSHING

Most Yards Gained Rushing
392   James Taylor, G.B. (106 attempts;
played in 5 games)
380   Paul Lowe, L.A.-S.D. (57 attempts;
played in 5 games) (AFL)
320   Steven Van Buren, Phil. (75 attempts; played in 3 games)
276   Keith Lincoln, S.D. (23 attempts;
played in 4 games)
248   Larry Csonka, Mia. (68 attempts;
played in 3 games)
222   Otto Graham, Clev. (47 attempts;
played in 6 games)
214   Bronko Nagurski, Chi. Bears (57
attempts; played in 4 games)
211   Dave Osborn, Minn. (42 attempts;
played in 3 games)
206   Harry Jagade, Clev. (30 attempts;
played in 3 games)

Most Yards Gained Rushing (one game)
206   Keith Lincoln, S.D. vs Bos. Jan. 5,
1964 (13 attempts) (AFL)
196   Steve Van Buren, Phil. vs L. A.,
Dec. 18, 1949 (31 attempts)
165   Paul Lowe, L. A. vs Hou., Jan. 1,
1961 (21 attempts) (AFL)
159   Elmer Angsman, Jr., Chi. Cards
vs Phil., Dec. 28, 1947 (10 attempts)
143   Duane Thomas, Dal. vs S.F., Jan.
3, 1971 (27 attempts) (NFC)
117   Larry Csonka, Mia. vs Oak., Dec.
30, 1973 (29 attempts) (AFC)
111   Franco Harris, Pitt. vs Oak., Dec.
29, 1974 (29 attempts)
109   William Osmanski, Chi. Bears vs
Wash., Dec. 8, 1940 (10 attempts)
108   David Osborn, Minn. vs Clev.,
Jan. 4, 1970 (18 attempts)
105   James Taylor, G.B. vs Phil., Dec.
26, 1960 (24 attempts)

Longest Run from Scrimmage
70   Elmer Angsman, Jr. (made two of
70 yards each), Chi. Cards vs Phil.,
Dec. 28, 1947
69   Hewritt Dixon, Oak. vs Hou.
Dec. 31, 1967 (AFL)
68   William Osmanski, Chi. Bears vs
Wash., Dec. 8, 1940
67   Doak Walter, Det. vs Clev., Dec.
28, 1952

Keith Lincoln, S.D. vs Bos., Jan. 5, 1964 (AFL)

FORWARD PASSING

Most Passes Completed

87   John Unitas, Balt. (NFL-AFC) (154 attempts; played in 5 games)
86   Otto Graham, Clev. (attempted 159; played in 6 games)
83   Bryan Starr, G.B. (attempted 142; played in 6 games)
76   George Blanda, Chi., Hou. (AFL); Oak. (AFL/AFC) (156 attempts; played in 7 games)
68   Jack Kemp, L.A. (AFL); S.D. (AFL); Buff. (AFL) (139 attempts; played in 5 games)
46   Bob Waterfield, L.A. (attempted 95; played in 4 games)

Most Passes Completed (one game)

27   Tommy Thompson, Phil. vs Chi. Cards, Dec. 28, 1947 (attempted 44)
26   John Unitas, Balt. vs N. Y., Dec. 28, 1958 (attempted 40)
23   George Blanda, Hou. vs Dal., Dec. 23, 1962 (46 attempts) (AFL)
22   Otto Graham, Clev. vs L.A., Dec. 24, 1950 (attempted 32)
21   Bart Starr, G.B. vs Phil., Dec. 26, 1960 (attempted 34)
     Jack Kemp, L.A. vs Hou., Dec. 24, 1961 (41 attempts) (AFL)

Most Yards Gained Passing

1,177   John Unitas, Balt. (NFL-AFC) (87 completions; played in 5 games)
1,161   Otto Graham, Clev. (86 completions; played in 6 games)
1,069   Bryan Starr, G. B. (83 completions; played in 6 games)
1,017   George Blanda, Chi.; Hou. (AFL); Oak. (AFL); Oak. (AFC) (76 completions; played in 7 games)
993   Jack Kemp, L.A./S.D.; Buff., (AFL) (68 completions; played in 5 games)
672   Bob Waterfield, Clev. and L. A. (46 completions; played in 4 games)
670   Sid Luckman, Chi. Bears (41 completions; played in 5 games)

Most Yards Gained Passing (one game)

401   Daryle Lamonica, Oak. vs N. Y., Dec. 29, 1968 (19 completions) (AFL)
349   John Unitas, Balt. vs N. Y., Dec. 28, 1958 (26 completions)
335   Sammy Baugh, Wash. vs Chi. Bears, Dec. 12, 1937 (18 completions)
312   Bob Waterfield, L.A. vs Clev. Dec. 24, 1950 (18 completions)

Longest Completed Pass (all TDs)

88 yds   George Blanda, Hou., to Bill Cannon, vs L.A., Jan. 1, 1961 (AFL)
82 yds   Bob Waterfield, L. A., to Glenn Davis, vs Clev., Dec. 24, 1950
78 yds   Tobin Rote, Det., to Jim Doran, vs Clev., Dec. 29, 1957
77 yds   Sammy Baugh, Wash., to Wayne Millner, vs Chi. Bears, Dec. 12, 1937
75 yds   Bob Griese, Mia., to Paul Warfield, vs Balt., Jan. 2, 1972

Most Passes Had Intercepted

14   George Blanda, Chi.; Hou. (AFL); Oak. (AFL); Oak. (AFC) (played in 7 games)
13   Frank Filchock, Wash., and N. Y. (played in 3 games)
12   Otto Graham, Clev. (played in 3 games)
10   Y. A. Tittle, N. Y. (played in 3 games)
9   Bob Waterfield, Clev. and L. A. (played in 4 games)
     Jack Kemp, L.A./S.D.; Buff. (AFL) (played in 5 games)

Most Passes Had Intercepted (one game)

6   Frank Filchock, N. Y. vs Chi. Bears, Dec. 15, 1946 (attempted 26, completed 9)
    Bobby Layne, Det. vs Clev., Dec. 26, 1954 (attempted 42, completed 18)
    Norman Van Brocklin, L. A. vs Clev., Dec. 26, 1955 (attempted 25, completed 11)

Most Touchdown Passes

11   Bryan Starr, G. B. (played in 6 games)
10   Otto Graham, Clev. (played in 6 games)
7   Sid Luckman, Chi. Bears (played in 5 games)
     George Blanda, Chi.; Hou. (AFL); Oak. (AFL); Oak. (AFC) (played in 7 games)
6   Sammy Baugh, Wash. (played in 5 games)

Most Touchdown Passes (one game)

  5 Sid Luckman, Chi. Bears vs Wash., Dec. 26, 1943

  4 Otto Graham, Clev. vs L. A., Dec. 24, 1950

      Tobin Rote, Det. vs Clev., Dec. 19, 1957

      Bryan Starr, G. B. vs Dall., 1966

  3 George Blanda, Hou. vs L. A., 1960 (AFL)

      Joe Namath, N. Y. vs Oak., 1968 (AFL)

PASS RECEIVING

Most Passes Caught

  24 Dante Lavelli, Clev. (played in 6 games)

  22 Billy Cannon, Hou.; Oak. (AFL) (played in 6 games)

  20 Raymond Berry, Balt. (played in 3 games)

  19 Fred Biletnikoff, Oak. (AFL-AFC) (played in 5 games)

      Boyd Dowler, G. B. (played in 6 games)

  16 Wayne Millner, Boston Redskins and Wash. (played in 4 games)

      Tom Fears, L.A./S.D.; Buff. (AFL) (played in 4 games)

      Dave Kocourek, L.A., S.D., Oak. (AFL) (played in 7 games)

Most Passes Caught (one game)

  12 Raymond Berry, Balt. vs N. Y., Dec. 28, 1958

  11 Dante Lavelli, Clev. vs L. A., Dec. 24, 1950

  9 Wayne Millner, Wash. vs Chi. Bears, Dec. 12, 1937

      Jim Benton, Clev. vs Wash., Dec. 16, 1945

      Tom Fears, L. A. vs Clev., Dec. 24, 1950

      Robert Schnelker, N. Y. vs Balt., Dec. 27, 1959

      Cliff Branch, Oak. vs Pitt., Dec. 29, 1974

  8 Charles Smith, Oak. vs K.C., Jan. 4, 1970 (AFL)

Most Yards Gained

  361 Fred Biletnikoff, Oak. (AFL-AFC) (19 receptions; played in 5 games)

  357 Billy Cannon, Hou.; Oak. (AFL) (22 receptions; played in 6 games)

  340 Dante Lavelli, Clev. (24 receptions; played in 6 games)

  335 Paul Warfield, Clev.; Mia. (AFC) (14 receptions; played in 7 games)

  313 Tom Fears, L.A./S.D.; Buff. (AFL) (16 receptions; played in 4 games)

Most Yards Gained (one game)

  190 Fred Biletnikoff, Oak. vs N. Y., Dec. 29, 1968 (AFL) (7 receptions)

  186 Cliff Branch, Oak. vs Pitt., Dec. 29, 1974

  178 Raymond Berry, Balt. vs N. Y., Dec. 28, 1958 (12 receptions)

  175 Bob Schnelker, N. Y. vs Balt., Dec. 27, 1959 (9 receptions)

  160 Wayne Millner, Wash. vs Chi Bears, Dec. 12, 1937 (9 receptions)

  146 Tom Fears, L. A. vs Clev., Dec. 23, 1951 (4 receptions)

      Charley Taylor, Wash. vs Dal., Dec. 31, 1972 (7 receptions)

Most Touchdown Passes

  5 Gary Collins, Clev. (played in 3 games)

  4 Boyd Dowler, G. B. (played in 6 games)

  3 Dante Lavelli, Clev. (played in 6 games)

      Ray Renfro, Clev. (played in 5 games)

      Frank Gifford, N. Y. (played in 5 games)

  2 By several players (NFL-AFL)

Most Touchdown Passes (one game)

  3 Gary Collins, Clev. vs Balt., Dec. 27, 1964

  2 William Karr, Chi. Bears vs N. Y., Dec. 17, 1933

      Wayne Millner, Wash. vs Chi. Bears, Dec. 12, 1937

      Dante Magnani, Chi Bears vs Wash., Dec. 26, 1943

      Harry Clark, Chi. Bears vs Wash., Dec. 26, 1943

      Dante Lavelli, Clev. vs L. A., Dec. 24, 1950

      Ray Renfro, Clev. vs Det., Dec. 26, 1954

      Steve Junker, Det. vs Clev., Dec. 29, 1957

      Ron Kramer, G. B. vs N. Y., Dec. 31, 1961

      Boyd Dowler, G. B. vs Dall. 1967

      Don Maynard, N. Y. vs Oak., Dec. 29, 1968 (AFL)

Longest Completed Pass (all TDs)

  88 Billy Cannon, from Blanda, vs L. A., Jan. 1, 1961 (AFL)

  82 Glenn Davis, L. A., from Bob Waterfield, vs Clev., Dec. 24, 1950

  78 Jim Doran, Det., from Tobin Rote, vs Clev., Dec. 29, 1957

  77 Wayne Millner, Wash., from Sammy Baugh, vs Chi. Bears, Dec. 12, 1937

PASSES INTERCEPTED
Most Passes Intercepted By
4   Ken Konz, Clev. (played in 3 games)
Joe Laws, G. B. (played in 4 games)
Clyde Turner, Chi. Bears (played in 5 games)
3   By several (NFL-AFL)

Most Passes Intercepted by (one game)
3   Joe Laws, G. B. vs N. Y., Dec. 17, 1944
2   By several (NFL-AFL)

Most Yards Interceptions Returned
122   Johnny Robinson, Dal.; K. C. (AFL) (3 interceptions; 3 games)
97   Don Paul, Clev. (2 interceptions; 3 games)
95   Emmitt Thomas, K. C. (AFL) (3 interceptions; 2 games)
83   Larry Morris L.A., Chi. Bears (2 interceptions; 2 games)
76   John Sample, Balt. (2 interceptions; 1 game)

Most Yards Interception Returned (one game)
72   Johnny Robinson, K. C. vs. Buff., Jan. 1, 1967 (AFL) (1 interception)
69   Emmitt Thomas, K. C. vs Oak., Jan. 4, 1970 (AFL) (2 interceptions)
66   John Sample, Balt., vs N. Y., Dec. 27, 1959 (1 interception for Touchdown)
65   Don Paul, Clev. vs L. A., Dec. 26, 1955 (1 interception for Touchdown)
63   Bob Bryant, Minn. vs Dal., Dec. 30, 1973 (NFC) (2 interceptions; 1 for touchdown)
62   Dick Anderson, Miami vs Balt., Jan. 2, 1972 (AFC) (1 interception for touchdown)
61   Lawrence Morris, Chi., vs N. Y., Dec. 29, 1963

Longest Return of Intercepted Pass
72 yds Johnny Robinson, K. C. vs. Buff., Jan. 1, 1967 (AFL)
65 yds Don Paul, Clev. vs L. A., Dec. 26, 1955 (touchdown)
63 yds Bob Bryant, Minn. vs Dal., Dec. 30, 1973 (NFC) (Touchdown)
62 yds Emmitt Thomas, K. C. vs. Oak., Jan. 4, 1970 (AFL)
Dick Anderson, Miami vs Balt., Jan. 2, 1972 (AFC)
61 yds Lawrence Morris, Chi. vs N. Y., Dec. 29, 1963

45 yds Leonard Ford, Clev. vs Det., Dec. 26, 1954
52 yds John Sample, Balt. vs N. Y., Dec. 27, 1959 (Touchdown)
41 yds Garrard Ramsey, Chi. Cards vs Phil., Dec. 28, 1947

KICK-OFF RETURNS

Most Kick-Off Returns
9   Ken Carpenter, Clev. (played in 5 games)
Bobby Jancik, Hou. (AFL) (played in 2 games)
George Atkinson, Oak. (AFL) (AFC) (played in 4 games)
7   Don Bingham, Chi. Bears (played in 1 game)
Charley Warner, Buff. (AFL) (played in 3 games)
6   William Reynolds, Clev. (played in 3 games)

Most Kick-Off Returns (one game)
7   Don Bingham, Chi. Bears vs N. Y., Dec. 30, 1956
5   Ken Carpenter, Clev. vs. L. A., Dec. 23, 1951
Joel Wells, N. Y. vs G. B., Dec. 31, 1961
Mel Renfro, Dall. vs G. B., 1966
Bobby Jancik, Hou. vs Dal., Dec. 23, 1962 (AFL)
Charley Warner, Buff. vs K. C., Jan. 1, 1967 (AFL)

Longest Kick-Off Return
72 yds Les (Speedy) Duncan, S. D. vs Buff., Dec. 26, 1964 (AFL)
62 yds Max Krause, Wash. vs. Chi. Bears, Dec. 8, 1940
58 yds Ted Dean, Phil. vs G. B., Dec. 26, 1960
52 yds George Atkinson, Oak. vs K. C., Jan. 4, 1970 (AFL)
50 yds James Brown, Clev. vs Det., Dec. 20, 1957
47 yds Hugh McElhenny, N. Y. vs Chi., Dec. 29, 1963
46 yds Boris Dimancheff, Chi. Cards vs Phil., Dec. 28, 1947
William Reynolds, Clev. vs. Det., Dec. 26, 1954

Most Yards Gained on Kick-Off Returns
244 yds George Atkinson, Oak. (AFL) (AFC) (played in 4 games)
239 yds Bobby Janick, Hou. (AFL) (played in 2 games)
209 yds Les (Speedy) Duncan, S. D. (AFL) (played in 2 games)
208 yds Ken Carpenter, Clev. (played in 5 games)

143 yds William Reynolds, Clev. (played in 3 games)

PUNTING

Most Punts
- 38 Don Chandler, N. Y. (played in 9 games)
- 31 Mike Eischeid, Oak. (AFL-AFC); Minn. (NFC) (played in 6 games)
- 26 Bob Waterfield, Clev. and L. A. played in 4 games)
- 25 Paul Maguire, S. D.; Buff. (AFL) (played in 5 games)
- 24 Horace Gillom, Clev. (played in 6 games
- 19 Joe Muha, Phil. (played in 3 games)

Most Punts (one game)
- 11 Ken Strong, N. Y. vs Chi. Bears, Dec. 17, 1933
  Jim Norton, Hou. vs Oak., Dec. 31, 1967 (AFL)
- 10 By several (NFL-AFL)

Best Punting Average (one game)
- 52.5 yds Sam Baugh, Wash. vs Chi. Bears, Dec. 13, 1942 (6 punts)
- 51.4 yds John Hadl, S.D. vs Buff., Dec. 26, 1965 (AFL) (5 punts)
- 51.3 yds Bobby Walden, Pitt. vs Mia., Dec. 31, 1972 (AFC) (4 punts)
- 50.8 yds Bob Waterfield, L. A. vs Clev., Dec. 24, 1950 (4 punts)
  Ray Brown, Balt. vs N. Y., Dec. 28, 1958 (4 punts)

Longest Punt
- 72 yds Yale Lary, Det. vs Clev., Dec. 27, 1953
- 69 yds Joseph Muha, Phil. vs Chi. Cards, Dec. 28, 1947
- 68 yds Tom Yewcic, Bos. vs S. D., Jan. 5, 1964 (AFL)

PUNT RETURNS

Most Punt Returns
- 8 Willie Wood, G. B. (played in 5 games)
  Keith Molesworth, Chi. Bears (played in 3 games)
- 7 William Reynolds, Clev. (played in 3 games)
  Rodger Bird, Oak. (AFL) (played in 2 games)
  Mike Garrett, K. C. (AFL) (played in 2 games)

Most Punt Returns (one game)
- 5 Rodger Bird, Oak. vs. Hou., Dec. 31, 1967 (AFL)
  Rick Volk, Balt. vs Mia., Jan. 2, 1972 (AFC)
  Keith Moleworth, Chi. Bears vs N. Y., Dec. 9, 1934
  Irv Comp, G. B. vs N. Y., Dec. 17, 1944
  Steve Bagarus, Wash. vs Clev., Dec. 16, 1945
  Ray Renfro, Clev. vs Det., Dec. 28, 1952
  Carl Taseff, Balt. vs N. Y., Dec. 28, 1958
  Willie Wood, G. B. vs Dall., 1967
  Mike Garrett, K. C. vs Oak., Jan. 4, 1970 (AFL)
  Alvin Haymond, Wash. vs Dal., Dec. 31, 1972 (NFC)
- 3 By several players (NFL-AFL)

Longest Punt Return
- 75 yds Charles Trippi, Chi. Cards vs Phil., Dec. 28, 1947 (Touchdown)
- 74 yds George Byrd, Buff. vs S. D., Dec. 26, 1965 (AFL)
- 63 yds Golden Richards, Dal. vs Minn., Dec. 30, 1973 (NFC)
- 42 yds William Reynolds, Clev. vs Det. Dec. 26, 1954
  Ken Strong, N. Y. vs Chi. Bears, Dec. 9, 1934

SUPER BOWL GAME RECORDS

(Courtesy of N.F.L., Compiled by Elias Sports Bureau)

INDIVIDUAL RECORDS

SCORING

Most Points, Game
- 15 Don Chandler, G.B. 1968 (3-pat, 4-fg) (NFL)

Most Touchdowns, Game
- 2 Max McGee, G.B. 1967 (NFL)
  Elijah Pitts, G.B. 1967 (NFL)
  Bill Miller, Oak. 1968 (AFL)
  Larry Csonka, Mia. 1974 (AFC)

Most Points After Touchdown, Game
    5 Don Chandler, G.B. 1967 (NFL)

Most Field Goals Attempted, Game
    5 Jim Turner, N.Y. 1969 (AFL)

Most Field Goals, Game
    4 Don Chandler, G.B. 1968 (NFL)

Longest Field Goal
    48 Jan Stenerud, K.C. 1970 (AFL)

RUSHING

Most Attempts, Game
    34 Franco Harris, Pitt. 1975 (AFC)
    33 Larry Csonka, Mia. 1974 (AFC)

Most Yards Gained, Game
    158 Franco Harris, Pitt. 1975 (AFC)
    145 Larry Csonka, Mia. 1974 (AFC)

Longest Gain
    58 Tom Matte, Balt. 1969 (NFL)

Most Touchdowns, Game
    2 Elijah Pitts, G.B. 1967 (NFL)
        Larry Csonka, Mia. 1974 (AFC)

PASSING

Most Attempts, Game
    34 Daryle Lamonica, Oak. 1968 (15-comp) (AFL)

Most Completions, Game
    18 Fran Tarkenton, Minn. 1974 (28 att.) (NFC)
    17 Joe Namath, N.Y. 1969 (28-att) (AFL)

Most Yards Gained, Game
    250 Bart Starr, G.B. 1967 (NFL)

Longest Completion
    75 John Unitas (to Mackey), Balt. 1971 (TD) (AFC)

Most Touchdowns, Game
    2 Bart Starr, G.B. 1967 (NFL)
        Daryle Lamonica, Oak. 1968 (AFL)
        Roger Staubach, Dal. 1972 (NFC)

PASS RECEPTIONS

Most Receptions, Game
    8 George Sauer, N.Y. 1969 (133 yds) (AFL)

Most Yards Gained, Game
    138 Max McGee, G.B. 1967 (NFL)

Longest Reception
    75 John Mackey, Balt. 1971 (TD) (AFC)

Most Touchdowns, Game
    2 Max McGee, G.B. 1967 (NFL)
        Bill Miller, Oak. 1968 (AFL)

INTERCEPTIONS BY

Most Interceptions By, Game
    2 Randy Beverly, N.Y. 1969 (AFL)
        Chuck Howley, Dall. 1971 (NFC)
        Jake Scott, Mia. 1973 (AFC)

Most Yards Gained, Game
    63 Jake Scott, Mia. 1973 (AFC) (2 interceptions)
    60 Herb Adderley, G.B. 1968 (1) (NFL)

Longest Gain
    60 Herb Adderley, G.B. 1968 (TD) (NFL)

Most Touchdowns, Game
    1 Herb Adderley, G.B. 1968 (NFL)

PUNTING

Most Punts, Game
    9 Ron Widby, Dall. 1971 (NFC)

Longest Punt
    61 Jerrel Wilson, K.C. 1967 (AFL)

PUNT RETURNS

Most Punt Returns, Game
    5 Willie Wood, G.B. 1968 (NFL)

Most Yards Gained, Game
    35 Willie Wood, G.B. 1968 (5) (NFL)

Longest Punt Return
    31 Willie Wood, G.B. 1968 (NFL)

Highest Average, Game (3 Min.)
    11.3 Lynn Swann, Pitt. 1975 (3) (AFC)

Most Touchdowns, Game
None

KICKOFF RETURNS

Most Kickoff Returns, Game
    4 Bert Coan, K.C. 1967 (87 yds) (AFL)
       Jim Duncan, Balt. 1971 (90 yds) (AFC)
       Mercury Morris, Mia. 1972 (AFC)

Most Yards Gained, Game
    90 Jim Duncan, Balt. 1971 (4) (AFC
       Mercury Morris, Mia. 1972 (4) (AFC)

TEAM RECORDS

SCORING

Most Points, Game
    35 Green Bay 1967 (NFL)

Fewest Points, Game
    3 Miami 1972 (AFC)

Most Points, Both Teams, Game
    47 Green Bay (33) vs Oak. (14) 1968

Fewest Points, Both Teams, Game
    21 Miami (14) vs Wash. (7) 1973

Most Touchdowns, Game
    5 Green Bay 1967 (NFL)

Fewest Touchdowns, Game
    0 Miami 1972 (AFC)

Most Touchdowns, Both Teams, Game
    6 Green Bay (5) vs K.C. (1) 1967

Fewest Touchdowns, Both Teams, Game
    2 Baltimore (1) vs N.Y. (1) 1969

Most Points After Touchdown, Game
    5 Green Bay 1967 (NFL)

Most Points After Touchdown, Both Teams, Game
    6 Green Bay (5) vs K.C. (1) 1967

Most Field Goals Attempted, Game
    5 New York 1969 (AFL)

Most Field Goals Attempted, Both Team. Game
    7 New York (5) vs Balt. (2) 1969

Most Field Goals, Game
    4 Green Bay 1968 (NFL)

Most Field Goals, Both Teams, Game
    4 Green Bay (4) vs Oak. (0) 1968

NET YARDS GAINED

Most Yards Gained, Game
    358 Green Bay 1967 (NFC)

Fewest Yards Gained, Game
    119 Minnesota 1975 (NFC)

Most Yards Gained, Both Teams, Game
    661 New York (337) vs Balt. (324) 1969

Fewest Yards Gained, Both Teams, Game
    452 Pittsburgh (333) vs Minnesota (119) 1975

RUSHING

Most Attempts, Game
    57 Pittsburgh 1975 (AFC)

Fewest Attempts, Game
    19 Kansas City 1967 (AFL)
       Minnesota 1970 (NFL)

Most Attempts, Both Teams, Game
    78 Pitt. (57) vs Minn. (21) 1975

Fewest Attempts, Both Teams, Game
    52 Kansas City (19) vs G.B. (33) 1967

Most Yards Gained, Game
    252 Dallas 1972 (NFC)

Fewest Yards Gained, Game
    17 Minnesota 1975 (NFC)

Most Yards Gained, Both Teams, Game
    332 Dal. (252) vs Mia. (80) 1972

Fewest Yards Gained, Both Teams, Game
    171 Baltimore (69) vs Dall. (102) 1971

Most Touchdowns, Game
    3 Green Bay 1967 (NFL)
       Miami 1974 (AFC)

Fewest Touchdowns, Game
   0 Kansas City 1967 (AFL)
      Oakland 1968 (AFL)
      Miami 1972 (AFC)
      Wash. 1973 (NFC)
      Minnesota 1975 (NFC)

Most Touchdowns, Both Teams, Game
   4 Miami (3) vs Minn. (1) 1974

Fewest Touchdowns, Both Teams, Game
   1 Oakland (0) vs G.B. (1) 1968
      Dallas (0) vs Balt. (1) 1971
      Miami (0) vs Dallas (1) 1972
      Wash. (0) vs Mia. (1) 1973
      Minn. (0) vs Pitt. (1) 1975

PASSING

Most Passes Attempted, Game
  41 Baltimore 1969 (NFL)

Fewest Passes Attempted, Game
   7 Miami 1974 (AFC)

Most Passes Attempted, Both Teams, Game
  70 Baltimore (41) vs N.Y. (29) 1969

Fewest Passes Attempted, Both Teams, Game
  35 Mia. (7) vs Minn. (28) 1974

Most Passes Completed, Game
  18 Minnesota 1974 (NFC)

Fewest Passes Completed, Game
   6 Miami 1974 (AFC)

Most Passes Completed, Both Teams, Game
  34 Baltimore (17) vs N.Y. (17) 1969

Fewest Passes Completed, Both Teams, Game
  20 Pitt. (9) vs Minn. (11) 1975

Most Yards Gained, Game
 260 Baltimore 1971 (AFC)

Fewest Yards Gained, Game
  63 Miami 1974 (AFC)

Most Yards Gained, Both Teams, Game
 395 Green Bay (228) vs K.C. (167) 1967

Fewest Yards Gained, Both Teams, Game
 156 Mia. (69) vs Wash. (87) 1973

Most Touchdowns, Game
   2 Green Bay 1967 (NFL)
      Oakland 1968 (AFL)
      Dallas 1972 (NFC)

Fewest Touchdowns, Game
   0 Baltimore 1969 (NFL)
      New York 1969 (AFL)
      Minnesota 1970 (NFL)
      Miami 1972 (AFC)
      Washington 1973 (NFC)
      Miami 1974 (AFC)
      Minnesota 1974 (NFC)
      Minnesota 1975 (NFC)

Most Touchdowns, Both Teams, Game
   3 Green Bay (2) vs K.C. (1) 1967
      Oakland (2) vs G.B. (1) 1968

INTERCEPTIONS BY

Most Interceptions By, Game
   4 New York 1969 (AFL)

Most Yards Gained, Game
  95 Miami 1973 (AFC)

Most Interceptions By, Both Teams, Game
   6 Baltimore (3) vs Dall. (3) 1971

Most Touchdowns, Game
   1 Green Bay 1968 (NFL)

PUNTING

Most Punts, Game
   9 Dallas 1971 (NFC)

Fewest Punts, Game
   3 Baltimore 1969 (NFL)
      Minnesota 1970 (NFL)
      Miami 1974 (AFC)

Most Punts, Both Teams, Game
  13 Dallas (9) vs Balt. (4) 1971
      Pitt. (7) vs Minn. (6) 1975

Fewest Punts, Both Teams, Game
   7 Baltimore (3) vs N.Y. (4) 1969
      Minnesota (3) vs K.C. (4) 1970

PUNT RETURNS

Most Punt Returns, Game
   5 Green Bay 1968 (NFL)
      Baltimore 1971 (AFC)

Pittsburgh 1975 (AFC)

Fewest Punt Returns, Game
  1 New York 1969 (AFL)
     Kansas City 1970 (AFL)
     Dallas 1972 (NFC)
     Miami 1972 (AFC)

Most Punt Returns, Both Teams, Game
  9 Pitt. (5) vs Minn. (4) 1975

Fewest Punt Returns, Both Teams, Game
  2 Dall. (1) vs Mia. (1) 1972

Most Yards Gained, Game
  36 Pittsburgh 1975

Fewest Yards Gained, Game
—1 yd. Dallas 1972 (NFC) (1)

Most Yards Gained, Both Teams, Game
  48 Pitt. (36) vs Minn. (12) 1975

Fewest Yards Gained, Both Teams, Game
  13 Mia. (4) vs Wash. (9) 1973

Most Touchdowns, Game
  None

KICKOFF RETURNS

Most Kickoff Returns, Game
  7 Oakland 1968 (AFL)

Fewest Kickoff Returns, Game
  1 New York 1969 (AFL)
     Miami 1974 (AFC)

Most Kickoff Returns, Both Teams, Game
  10 Oakland (7) vs G.B. (3) 1968

Fewest Kickoff Returns, Both Teams, Game
  5 New York (1) vs Balt. (4) 1969
     Miami (2) vs Wash. (3) 1973
     Miami (4) vs Minn. (1) 1974

Most Yards Gained, Game
  130 Kansas City 1967

Fewest Yards Gained, Game
  25 New York 1969 (1)

Most Yards Gained, Both Teams, Game
  195 Kansas City (130) vs G.B. (65) 1967

Fewest Yards Gained, Both Teams, Game
  78 Miami (33) vs Wash. (45) 1973

Most Touchdowns, Game
  None

ALL TIME LEADERS

ALL-TIME NFL-NFC, AFL-AFC RUSHING
(Ranked on Yards Gained)

NO.	NAME	LEAGUE		YR.	ATT.	YDS.	AVE.	TD.
1	JIM BROWN		N	1957-1965	9	2359	12312	5.2	106
2	JOE PERRY	AA	N	1948-1963	16	1929	9723	5.0	71
3	JIM TAYLOR		N	1958-1967	10	1941	8597	4.4	83
4	LEROY KELLY		N	1964-1973	10	1727	7274	4.2	74
5	JOHN HENRY JOHNSON		N A	1954-1966	13	1571	6803	4.3	48
6	O. J. SIMPSON		N A	1969-1974	6	1378	6306	4.6	33
7	DON PERKINS		N	1961-1968	8	1500	6217	4.1	42
8	KEN WILLARD		N	1965-1974	10	1622	6105	3.8	45
9	LARRY CSONKA		N A	1968-1974	7	1286	5900	4.6	41
10	FLOYD LITTLE		N A	1967-1974	8	1516	5878	3.9	41
11	STEVE VAN BUREN		N	1944-1951	8	1320	5860	4.4	69
12	BILL BROWN		N	1961-1974	14	1649	5838	3.5	52
13	RICK CASARES		N A	1955-1966	12	1431	5797	4.1	49
14	MIKE GARRETT		N A	1966-1973	8	1308	5481	4.2	35
15	LARRY BROWN		N	1969-1974	6	1413	5467	3.9	32
16	DICK BASS		N	1960-1969	10	1218	5417	4.4	34
17	JIM NANCE		N A	1965-1973	8	1341	5401	4.0	45
18	HUGH MC ELHENNY		N	1952-1964	13	1124	5281	4.7	38
19	LENNY MOORE		N	1956-1967	12	1069	5174	4.8	63
20	OLLIE MATSON		N	1952-1966	14	1170	5173	4.4	40
21	CLEM DANIELS		N A	1960-1968	9	1146	5138	4.5	30
22	EMERSON BOOZER		N A	1966-1974	9	1271	5084	4.0	52
23	CALVIN HILL		N	1969-1974	6	1166	5009	4.3	39
24	PAUL LOWE		A	1960-1969	9	1026	4995	4.9	40
25	JOHN DAVID CROW		N	1958-1968	11	1157	4963	4.3	38
26	GALE SAYERS		N	1965-1971	7	991	4956	5.0	39
27	MARION MOTLEY	AA	N	1946-1955	9	828	4720	5.7	31
28	DONNY ANDERSON		N	1966-1974	9	1197	4696	3.9	41
29	J. D. SMITH		N	1956-1966	11	1100	4672	4.2	40
30	TOM MATTE		N	1961-1972	12	1200	4646	3.9	45
31	ALEX WEBSTER		N	1955-1964	10	1196	4638	3.9	39
32	ABNER HAYNES		A	1960-1967	8	1036	4630	4.5	46
33	BOB HOERNSCHEMEYER	AA	N	1946-1955	10	1059	4548	4.3	27
34	COOKIE GILCHRIST		A	1962-1967	6	1010	4293	4.3	37
35	MATT SNELL		N A	1964-1972	9	1057	4285	4.1	24
36	DAVE OSBORN		N	1965-1974	10	1141	4226	3.7	28
37	TOMMY MASON		N	1961-1971	11	1040	4203	4.0	32
38	TONY CANADEO		N	1941-1952	11	1025	4197	4.1	26
39	JOHN BROCKINGTON		N	1971-1974	4	1021	4159	4.1	20
40	MARV HUBBARD		N A	1969-1974	6	853	4100	4.8	20
41	ALAN AMECHE		N	1955-1960	6	964	4045	4.2	40
42	BRONKO NAGURSKI		N	1930-1943	9	873	4031	4.6	18
43	NICK PIETROSANTE		N	1959-1967	9	955	4026	4.2	28
44	DICK HOAK		N	1961-1970	10	1132	3965	3.5	25
45	RON JOHNSON		N	1969-1974	6	1087	3956	3.6	35
46	WALT GARRISON		N	1966-1974	9	899	3886	4.3	30
47	TIM BROWN		N	1959-1968	10	889	3862	4.3	31
48	CLARK HINKLE		N	1932-1941	10	1171	3860	3.3	43
49	JON ARNETT		N	1957-1966	10	964	3833	4.0	26
50	WENDELL HAYES		N A	1963-1974	11	988	3758	3.8	28
51	JOHNNY ROLAND		N	1966-1973	8	1015	3750	3.7	28
52	PAUL HORNUNG		N	1957-1966	9	893	3711	4.2	50
53	CLARENCE PEAKS		N	1957-1965	9	951	3660	3.8	21
54	ALTIE TAYLOR		N	1969-1974	6	970	3659	3.8	20
55	HOYLE GRANGER		N A	1966-1972	7	805	3653	4.5	19

NO.	NAME	LEAGUE			YR.	ATT.	YDS.	AVE.	TD.
56	JIM KIICK		N	A	1968-1974	7	997	3644	3.7	28
57	TANK YOUNGER		N		1949-1958	10	770	3640	4.7	34
58	FRANK GIFFORD		N		1952-1964	12	840	3609	4.3	34
59	BILL MATHIS			A	1960-1969	10	1044	3589	3.4	37
60	TOM WODDESCHICK		N		1963-1972	10	836	3577	4.3	21
61	FRAN TARKENTON		N		1961-1974	14	593	3521	5.1	23
62	CHARLEY TRIPPI		N		1947-1955	9	687	3506	5.1	23
63	DAN TOWLER		N		1950-1955	6	672	3493	5.2	43
64	MAC ARTHUR LANE		N		1968-1974	7	888	3447	3.9	22
65	WILLIE ELLISON		N		1967-1974	8	801	3426	4.3	24
66	BILL BARNES		N		1957-1966	9	994	3421	3.4	29
67	JOHN STRZYKALSKI	AA	N		1946-1952	7	662	3415	5.2	19
68	LES JOSEPHSON		N		1964-1974	10	797	3407	4.3	17
69	CLIFF BATTLES		N		1932-1937	6	832	3403	4.1	20
70	KEITH LINCOLN			A	1961-1968	8	758	3383	4.5	19
71	WRAY CARLTON			A	1960-1967	8	819	3368	4.1	29
72	CHARLIE SMITH		N	A	1968-1974	7	858	3351	3.9	24
73	JOHNNY OLSZEWSKI		N	A	1953-1962	10	837	3320	4.0	16
74	EDDIE PRICE		N		1950-1955	6	846	3292	3.9	20
75	ACE GUTOWSKY		N		1932-1939	8	917	3278	3.6	16
76	CHARLEY TOLAR			A	1960-1966	7	907	3277	3.6	21
77	FRANK ROGEL		N		1950-1957	8	900	3271	3.6	17
78	DAVE HAMPTON		N		1969-1974	6	815	3243	4.0	19
79	CARL GARRETT		N	A	1969-1974	6	808	3236	4.0	21
80	RON BULL		N		1962-1971	10	881	3222	3.7	9
81	AMOS MARSH		N		1961-1967	7	750	3222	4.3	25
82	DAN LEWIS		N		1958-1966	9	800	3205	4.0	19
83	ERNIE GREEN		N		1962-1968	7	668	3204	4.8	16
84	ED PODOLAK		N	A	1969-1974	6	834	3179	3.8	21
85	EARL GROS		N		1962-1970	9	821	3157	3.8	28
86	TOBIN ROTE		N	A	1950-1966	13	635	3128	4.9	37
87	CURTIS MC CLINTON			A	1962-1969	8	762	3124	4.1	18
88	TUFFY LEEMANS		N		1936-1943	8	926	3117	3.4	19
89	DON BOSSELER		N		1957-1964	8	775	3112	4.0	22
90	HEWRITT DIXON		N	A	1963-1970	8	772	3090	4.0	15
91	JESS PHILLIPS		N	A	1968-1974	7	796	3079	3.9	10
92	MEL FARR		N		1967-1973	7	739	3072	4.2	26
93	BILL DUDLEY		N		1942-1953	9	765	3057	4.0	23
94	CHET MUTRYN	AA	N		1946-1950	5	583	3031	5.2	27
95	CHARLIE HARRAWAY		N		1966-1973	8	822	3019	3.7	20
96	PAT HARDER		N		1946-1953	8	740	3016	4.1	33

TOUCHDOWN DATA INCOMPLETE FOR BATTLES AND GUTOWSKY

ALL-TIME NFL-NFC, AFL-AFC PASS RECEIVING
(Ranked on number received)

NO.	NAME	LEAGUE		YR.	RCV.	YDS.	AVE.	TD.
1	DON MAYNARD	N	A	1958-1973	15	633	11834	18.7	88
2	RAYMOND BERRY	N		1955-1967	13	631	9275	14.7	68
3	CHARLIE TAYLOR	N		1964-1974	11	582	8208	14.1	73
4	LIONEL TAYLOR		A	1959-1968	10	567	7195	12.7	45
5	LANCE ALWORTH	N	A	1962-1972	11	542	10266	18.9	85
6	BOBBY MITCHELL	N		1958-1968	11	521	7954	15.3	65
7	BILLY HOWTON	N		1952-1963	12	503	8459	16.8	61
8	TOMMY MC DONALD	N		1957-1968	12	495	8410	17.0	84
9	DON HUTSON	N		1935-1945	11	488	7991	16.4	99
10	ART POWELL	N	A	1959-1968	10	479	8046	16.8	81
11	BOYD DOWLER	N		1959-1971	12	474	7270	15.3	40
12	JACKIE SMITH	N		1963-1974	12	459	7601	16.6	37
13	FRED BILETNIKOFF	N	A	1965-1974	10	450	7105	15.8	60
14	PETE RETZLAFF	N		1956-1966	11	452	7412	16.4	47
15	CARROLL DALE	N		1960-1973	14	438	8277	18.9	52
16	MIKE DITKA	N		1961-1972	12	427	5812	13.6	43
17	BOBBY JOE CONRAD	N		1958-1969	12	422	5902	14.0	38
18	OTIS TAYLOR	N	A	1965-1974	10	410	7306	17.8	57
19	CHARLEY HENNIGAN		A	1960-1966	7	410	6823	16.6	51
20	ROY JEFFERSON	N		1965-1974	10	409	6920	16.9	48
21	BILLY WILSON	N		1951-1960	10	407	5902	14.5	49
22	JIM PHILLIPS	N		1958-1967	10	401	6044	15.1	34
23	JIMMY ORR	N		1958-1970	13	400	7914	19.8	66
24	TOM FEARS	N		1948-1956	9	400	5397	13.5	38
25	JOE MORRISON	N		1959-1972	14	395	4993	12.6	47
26	CHRIS BURFORD		A	1960-1967	8	391	5505	14.1	55
27	ELROY HIRSCH	AA	N	1946-1957	12	387	7029	18.2	60
28	DANTE LAVELLI	AA	N	1946-1956	11	386	6488	16.8	62
29	JERRY SMITH		N	1965-1974	10	382	5024	13.2	55
30	GARY GARRISON	N	A	1966-1974	9	375	7037	18.8	55
31	PETE PIHOS	N		1947-1955	9	373	5619	15.1	61
32	PAUL WARFIELD	N		1964-1974	11	371	7701	20.8	77
33	DAN ABRAMOWICZ	N		1967-1974	8	369	5686	15.4	39
34	FRANK GIFFORD	N		1952-1964	12	367	5434	14.8	43
35	BOB HAYES	N		1965-1974	10	365	7295	20.0	71
36	SONNY RANDLE	N		1959-1968	10	365	5996	16.4	65
37	LENNY MOORE	N		1956-1967	12	363	6039	16.6	48
38	DAVE PARKS	N		1964-1973	10	360	5619	15.6	44
39	BERNIE CASEY	N		1961-1968	8	359	5444	15.2	40
40	GAIL COGDILL	N		1960-1970	11	356	5696	16.0	34
41	JOHNNY MORRIS	N		1958-1967	10	356	5059	14.2	31
42	DEL SHOFNER	N		1957-1967	11	349	6470	18.5	51
43	MAC SPEEDIE	AA	N	1946-1952	7	349	5602	16.1	33
44	MAX MC GEE	N		1954-1967	12	345	6346	18.4	50
45	JACK SNOW	N		1965-1974	10	336	5926	17.6	44
46	GARY COLLINS	N		1962-1971	10	331	5299	16.0	70
47	JOHN MACKEY	N		1963-1972	10	331	5236	15.8	38
48	ELBIE NICKEL	N		1947-1957	11	329	5131	15.6	37
49	GARY BALLMAN	N		1962-1973	12	323	5366	16.6	37
50	BOBBY WALSTON	N		1951-1962	12	311	5363	17.2	46
51	GEORGE SAUER	N	A	1965-1970	6	309	4965	16.1	28
52	PAUL FLATLEY	N		1963-1970	8	306	4905	16.0	24
53	PRESTON CARPENTER	N	A	1955-1967	12	305	4457	14.6	23
54	JOHN GILLIAM	N		1967-1974	8	300	5854	19.5	38
55	KYLE ROTE	N		1951-1961	11	300	4797	16.0	48
56	ELBERT DUBENION		A	1960-1968	9	294	5294	18.0	35
57	GINO CAPPELLETTI	N	A	1960-1970	11	292	4589	15.7	42
58	FRANK CLARKE	N		1957-1967	11	291	5426	18.6	50
59	JIM BENTON	N		1938-1947	9	288	4801	16.7	45
60	JIM GIBBONS	N		1958-1968	11	287	3561	12.4	20
61	ABNER HAYNES		A	1960-1967	8	287	3535	12.3	20

NO.	NAME	LEAGUE		YR.	RCV.	YDS.	AVE.	TD.
62	BILL BROWN	N		1961-1974	14	286	3183	11.1	23
63	HAROLD JACKSON	N		1968-1974	7	285	4881	17.1	39
64	JIM COLCLOUGH		A	1960-1968	9	283	5001	17.7	39
65	RAY RENFRO	N		1952-1963	12	281	5508	19.6	50
66	KEN WILLARD	N		1965-1974	10	277	2184	7.9	17
67	HUGH TAYLOR	N		1947-1954	8	272	5233	19.2	58
68	MILT MORIN	N		1966-1974	9	270	4189	15.5	16
69	LANCE RENTZEL	N		1965-1974	9	268	4826	18.0	38
70	HUGH MC ELHENNY	N		1952-1964	13	264	3247	12.3	20
71	HEWRITT DIXON	N	A	1963-1970	8	263	2819	10.7	13
72	JIMMY BROWN	N		1957-1965	9	262	2499	9.5	20
73	GENE WASHINGTON	N		1969-1974	6	262	4834	18.5	39
74	AARON THOMAS	N		1961-1970	10	262	4554	17.4	37
75	BUDDY DIAL	N		1959-1966	8	261	5436	20.8	44
76	BEN HAWKINS	N		1966-1974	9	261	4764	18.3	32
77	AL DENSON	N	A	1964-1971	8	260	4275	16.4	32
78	JOE PERRY	AA N		1948-1963	16	260	2021	7.8	12
79	JOHN DAVID CROW	N		1958-1968	11	258	3699	14.3	35
80	CHARLEY SANDERS	N		1968-1974	7	250	3616	14.5	22

ALL-TIME NFL-NFC, AFL-AFC PASSING

NO.	NAME	LEAGUE		YR.	ATT.	COMP.	PCT.	YDS.	TD.	PCT.	INT.	PCT.	AVG. GAIN
1	JOHNNY UNITAS		N	1956-1973	18	5186	2830	54.6	40239	290	5.6	253	4.9	7.76
2	FRAN TARKENTON		N	1961-1974	14	4800	2658	55.4	35846	266	5.5	199	4.1	7.47
3	Y. A. TITTLE	AA	N	1948-1964	17	4395	2427	55.2	33070	242	5.5	248	5.6	7.52
4	SONNY JURGENSEN		N	1957-1974	18	4262	2433	57.1	32224	255	6.0	189	4.4	7.56
5	JOHN BRODIE		N	1957-1973	17	4491	2469	55.0	31548	214	4.8	224	5.0	7.02
6	JOHN HADL		N A	1962-1974	13	4197	2101	50.1	30698	231	5.5	235	5.6	7.31
7	NORM SNEAD		N	1961-1974	14	4122	2146	52.1	29221	187	4.5	243	5.9	7.09
8	LEN DAWSON		N A	1957-1974	18	3601	2043	56.7	27616	234	6.5	179	5.0	7.67
9	ROMAN GABRIEL		N	1962-1974	13	4111	2168	52.7	27309	186	4.5	136	3.3	6.64
10	GEORGE BLANDA		N A	1949-1974	25	4004	1910	47.7	26909	236	5.9	276	6.9	6.72
11	BOBBY LAYNE		N	1948-1962	15	3700	1814	49.0	26768	196	5.3	243	6.6	7.23
12	BART STARR		N	1956-1971	16	3149	1808	57.4	24718	152	4.8	138	4.4	7.85
13	JOE NAMATH		N A	1965-1974	10	3099	1565	50.5	23681	151	4.9	171	5.5	7.64
14	NORM VAN BROCKLIN		N	1949-1960	12	2895	1553	53.6	23611	173	6.0	178	6.1	8.16
15	OTTO GRAHAM	AA	N	1946-1955	10	2626	1464	55.8	23584	174	6.6	135	5.1	8.98
16	CHARLEY JOHNSON		N	1961-1974	14	3250	1672	51.4	23389	165	5.1	169	5.2	7.20
17	BABE PARILLI		N A	1952-1969	15	3330	1552	46.6	22681	178	5.3	220	6.6	6.81
18	SAMMY BAUGH		N	1937-1952	16	2995	1693	56.5	21886	186	6.2	203	6.8	7.31
19	JACKIE KEMP		N A	1957-1969	10	3073	1436	46.7	21218	114	3.7	183	6.0	6.90
20	EARL MORRALL		N	1956-1974	19	2620	1343	51.3	20388	157	6.0	145	5.5	7.78
21	CHARLEY CONERLY		N	1948-1961	14	2833	1418	50.1	19488	173	6.1	167	5.9	6.88
22	DARYLE LAMONICA		N A	1963-1974	12	2601	1288	49.5	19154	164	6.3	138	5.3	7.36
23	TOBIN ROTE		N A	1950-1966	13	2907	1329	45.7	18850	148	5.1	191	6.6	6.48
24	BILLY WADE		N	1954-1966	13	2523	1370	54.3	18530	124	4.9	134	5.3	7.34
25	MILT PLUM		N	1957-1969	13	2419	1306	54.0	17536	122	5.0	127	5.3	7.25
26	DON MEREDITH		N	1960-1968	9	2308	1170	50.7	17199	135	5.8	111	4.8	7.45
27	FRANK RYAN		N	1958-1970	13	2133	1090	51.1	16042	149	7.0	111	5.2	7.52
28	JIM HART		N	1966-1974	9	2336	1139	48.8	15874	102	4.4	115	4.9	6.80
29	ED BROWN		N	1954-1965	12	1987	949	47.8	15600	102	5.1	138	6.9	7.85
30	BILLY KILMER		N	1961-1974	12	2185	1177	53.9	15300	105	4.8	110	5.0	7.00
31	SID LUCKMAN		N	1939-1950	12	1744	904	51.8	14686	139	8.0	131	7.5	8.42
32	BOB GRIESE		N A	1967-1974	8	2014	1081	53.7	14309	114	5.7	103	5.1	7.10
33	BILL NELSEN		N	1963-1972	10	1905	963	50.6	14165	98	5.1	101	5.3	7.44
34	EDDIE LE BARON		N	1952-1963	11	1796	897	49.9	13399	104	5.8	141	7.9	7.46
35	TOM FLORES		A	1960-1969	9	1715	838	48.9	11959	93	5.4	92	5.4	6.97
36	BOB WATERFIELD		N	1945-1952	8	1617	813	50.3	11849	98	6.1	127	7.9	7.33
37	CRAIG MORTON		N	1965-1974	10	1545	807	52.2	11789	89	5.8	86	5.6	7.63
38	COTTON DAVIDSON		N A	1954-1968	10	1752	770	43.9	11760	73	4.2	108	6.2	6.71
39	BILL MUNSON		N	1964-1974	11	1755	938	53.4	11391	73	4.2	72	4.1	6.49
40	FRANK ALBERT	AA	N	1946-1952	7	1564	831	53.1	10795	115	7.4	98	6.3	6.90
41	GEORGE RATTERMAN	AA	N	1947-1956	10	1396	737	52.8	10473	91	6.5	96	6.9	7.50
42	TOMMY THOMPSON		N	1940-1950	9	1424	732	51.4	10400	90	6.3	103	7.2	7.30
43	ZEKE BRATOWSKI		N	1954-1971	14	1484	762	51.3	10345	65	4.4	122	8.2	6.97
44	FRANK TRIPUCKA		N A	1949-1963	8	1745	879	50.4	10282	59	3.4	114	6.5	5.89
45	BOBBY THOMASON		N	1949-1957	8	1346	687	51.0	9480	68	5.1	90	6.7	7.04
46	LAMAR MC HAN		N	1954-1963	10	1351	610	45.2	9449	73	5.4	108	8.0	6.99
47	JIM PLUNKETT		N	1971-1974	4	1411	693	49.1	9361	59	4.2	80	5.7	6.63
48	BOB BERRY		N	1965-1974	10	1167	658	56.4	9173	64	5.5	64	5.5	7.86
49	JIM FINKS		N	1949-1955	7	1382	661	47.8	8622	55	4.0	88	6.4	6.24
50	RUDY BUKICH		N	1953-1968	14	1190	626	52.6	8433	61	5.1	74	6.2	7.09
51	PETE BEATHARD		N A	1964-1973	10	1282	575	44.9	8176	43	3.4	84	6.6	6.38
52	GREG LANDRY		N	1968-1974	7	1083	575	53.1	8046	55	5.1	65	6.0	7.43
53	ARNIE HERBER		N	1932-1945	11	1177	481	40.9	8033	66	5.6	98	8.3	6.82
54	ROGER STAUBACH		N	1969-1974	6	1006	571	56.8	7923	52	5.2	46	4.6	7.88
55	KEN ANDERSON		N	1971-1974	4	1089	635	58.3	7790	48	4.4	33	3.0	7.15
56	AL DOROW		N A	1954-1962	7	1207	572	47.4	7708	64	5.3	93	7.7	6.39
57	RANDY JOHNSON		N	1966-1973	8	1172	585	49.9	7524	47	4.0	79	6.7	6.42
58	TERRY BRADSHAW		N	1970-1974	5	1227	589	48.0	7524	48	3.9	81	6.6	6.13
59	GARY CUOZZO		N	1963-1972	10	1182	584	49.4	7402	43	3.6	55	4.7	6.26
60	PAUL CHRISTMAN		N	1945-1950	6	1140	504	44.2	7294	58	5.1	76	6.7	6.40
61	DICK WOOD		A	1962-1966	5	1193	522	43.8	7151	50	4.2	70	5.9	5.99
62	JIM NINOWSKI		N	1958-1969	12	1048	513	49.0	7133	34	3.2	67	6.4	6.81
63	ARCHIE MANNING		N	1971-1974	4	1153	590	51.2	7016	40	3.5	58	5.0	6.08
64	ADRIAN BURK		N	1950-1956	7	1079	500	46.3	7001	61	5.7	89	8.2	6.49

ALL-TIME NFL-NFC, AFL-AFC SCORING

NO.	NAME	LEAGUE	YR.	TOUCHDOWNS				PAT		FIELD GOALS		PT
				RUSH	RETN	PASS	TOTL	MADE	ATT.	MADE	ATT.	
1	GEORGE BLANDA	N A	1949-1974	25	9	0	0	9	899	911	322	617	191
2	LOU GROZA	AA N	1946-1967	21	0	0	1	1	810	834	264	481	160
3	FRED COX	N	1963-1974	12	0	0	0	0	416	426	242	390	114
4	GINO CAPPELLETTI	N A	1960-1970	11	0	0	42	42	342	353	176	333	113
5	JIM BAKKEN	N	1962-1974	13	0	0	0	0	399	411	225	358	107
6	JIM TURNER	N A	1964-1974	11	0	0	0	0	368	375	231	377	106
7	BRUCE GOSSETT	N	1964-1974	11	0	0	0	0	374	383	219	360	103
8	SAM BAKER	N	1953-1969	15	2	0	0	2	428	444	179	316	97
9	LOU MICHAELS	N	1958-1971	13	1	0	0	1	386	402	187	341	95
10	BOBBY WALSTON	N	1951-1962	12	0	0	46	46	365	384	80	157	88
11	PETE GOGOLAK	N A	1964-1974	11	0	0	0	0	344	354	173	294	86
12	JAN STENERED	N A	1967-1974	8	0	0	0	0	257	262	196	295	84
13	DON HUTSON	N	1935-1945	11	4	2	99	105	172	184	7	17	82
14	PAUL HORNUNG	N	1957-1966	9	50	0	12	62	190	194	66	140	76
15	JIM BROWN	N	1957-1965	9	106	0	20	126	0	0	0	0	75
16	TOMMY DAVIS	N	1959-1969	11	0	0	0	0	348	350	130	276	73
17	MIKE CLARK	N	1963-1973	10	0	0	0	0	325	338	133	232	72
18	LENNY MOORE	N	1956-1967	12	63	2	48	113	0	0	0	0	67
19	BEN AGAJANIAN	N A	1945-1964	13	0	0	0	0	343	351	104	199	65
20	GORDY SOLTAU	N	1950-1958	9	0	0	25	25	284	302	70	138	64
21	GENE MINGO	N A	1960-1970	10	9	0	4	13	215	223	112	219	62
22	MIKE MERCER	N A	1961-1970	10	0	0	0	0	288	295	102	193	59
23	GARO YEPREMIAN	N	1966-1974	7	0	0	0	0	221	224	122	186	58
24	DON COCKROFT	N	1968-1974	7	0	0	0	0	240	245	115	171	58
25	ROY GERELA	N A	1969-1974	6	0	0	0	0	183	187	131	212	57
26	BOB WATERFIELD	N	1945-1952	8	13	0	0	13	315	336	60	109	57
27	PAT SUMMERALL	N	1952-1961	10	1	0	0	1	257	265	100	212	56
28	JIM TAYLOR	N	1958-1967	10	83	0	10	93	0	0	0	0	55
29	ERROL MANN	N	1968-1974	7	0	0	0	0	183	187	123	186	55
30	HORST MUHLMANN	N A	1969-1974	6	0	0	0	0	189	195	120	186	54
31	BOBBY MITCHELL	N	1958-1968	11	18	8	65	91	0	0	0	0	54
32	LEROY KELLY	N	1964-1973	10	74	3	13	90	0	0	0	0	54
33	DOAK WALKER	N	1950-1955	6	12	1	21	34	183	191	49	87	53
34	DON MAYNARD	N A	1958-1973	15	0	0	88	88	0	0	0	0	53
35	PAT HARDER	N	1946-1953	8	33	0	5	38	198	204	35	69	53
36	DON CHANDLER	N	1956-1967	12	0	0	0	0	248	258	94	161	53
37	LANCE ALWORTH	N A	1962-1972	11	2	0	85	87	0	0	0	0	52
38	JOE PERRY	AA N	1948-1963	16	71	1	12	84	6	7	1	6	51
39	TOMMY MC DONALD	N	1957-1968	12	0	1	84	85	0	0	0	0	51
40	CHARLEY TAYLOR	N	1964-1974	11	11	0	73	84	0	0	0	0	50
41	DAVID RAY	N	1969-1974	6	0	0	0	0	167	175	110	178	49
42	FRED CONE	N	1951-1960	8	12	0	4	16	221	237	59	102	49
43	ART POWELL	N A	1959-1968	10	0	1	81	82	0	0	0	0	49
44	DANNY VILLANUEVA	N	1960-1967	8	0	0	0	0	236	241	85	160	49
45	BOBBY HOWFIELD	N A	1968-1974	7	0	0	0	0	193	201	98	166	48
46	BILL DUDLEY	N	1942-1953	9	23	3	18	44	121	127	33	66	48
47	FRANK GIFFORD	N	1952-1964	12	34	1	43	78	10	11	2	7	48
48	KEN STRONG	N	1929-1947	12	***	***	***	33	167	***	38	***	47
49	CURT KNIGHT	N	1969-1973	5	0	0	0	0	172	175	101	175	47
50	PAUL WARFIELD	N	1964-1974	11	0	1	77	78	0	0	0	0	46
51	MAC PERCIVAL	N	1967-1974	8	0	0	0	0	163	167	101	190	46
52	STEVE VAN BUREN	N	1944-1951	8	69	5	3	77	2	2	0	0	46
53	BILL BROWN	N	1961-1974	14	52	1	23	76	0	0	0	0	45
54	BOB HAYES	N	1965-1974	10	2	3	71	76	0	0	0	0	45
55	TOM DEMPSEY	N	1969-1974	6	0	0	0	0	133	142	106	183	45
56	JOHN DAVID CROW	N	1958-1968	11	38	1	35	74	0	0	0	0	44
57	OLLIE MATSON	N	1952-1966	14	40	10	23	73	0	0	0	0	43
58	JIM MARTIN	N	1950-1964	14	0	0	0	0	158	169	92	191	43
59	GARY COLLINS	N	1962-1971	10	0	0	70	70	0	0	0	0	42
60	ABNER HAYNES	A	1960-1967	8	46	3	20	69	0	0	0	0	41
61	RAYMOND BERRY	N	1955-1967	13	0	0	68	68	0	0	0	0	40
62	ELROY HIRSCH	AA N	1946-1957	12	4	2	60	66	9	12	0	0	40
63	JIMMY ORR	N	1958-1970	13	0	0	66	66	0	0	0	0	39
64	BILLY CANNON	N A	1960-1970	11	17	1	47	65	0	0	0	0	39
65	PADDY DRISCOLL	N	1921-1929	9	***	***	***	29	63	***	51	***	39
66	SONNY RANDLE	N	1959-1968	10	0	0	65	65	0	0	0	0	39
67	JOE MORRISON	N	1959-1972	14	18	0	47	65	0	0	0	0	39
68	BOBBY JOE CONRAD	N	1958-1969	12	2	2	38	42	95	99	14	33	38
69	TIMMY BROWN	N	1959-1968	10	31	7	26	64	0	0	0	0	38
70	EMERSON BOOZER	N A	1966-1974	9	52	1	11	64	0	0	0	0	38

NO.	NAME	LEAGUE	YR.	TOUCHDOWNS RUSH	RETN	PASS	TOTL	PAT MADE	ATT.	FIELD GOALS MADE	ATT.	PTS.
1	ROGER LE CLERC	N A	1960-1967	8	0	0	0	0	154	160	76	152	382
2	TED FRITSCH	N	1942-1950	9	34	0	1	35	62	70	36	98	380
3	PETE PIHOS	N	1947-1955	9	0	2	61	63	0	0	0	0	378
4	DENNIS PARTEE	N A	1968-1974	7	0	0	0	0	165	173	71	121	378
5	BOBBY LAYNE	N	1948-1962	15	25	0	0	25	120	124	34	50	372
6	DANTE LAVELLI	AA N	1946-1956	11	0	0	62	62	0	0	0	0	372
7	KEN WILLARD	N	1965-1974	10	45	0	17	62	0	0	0	0	372
8	CLARK HINKLE	N	1932-1941	10	34	0	9	43	31	***	27	***	370
9	JACK MANDERS	N	1933-1940	8	11	2	6	19	137	154	40	***	368
10	DUTCH CLARK	N	1931-1938	7	***	***	***	42	71	***	15	***	368
11	BILLY HOWTON	N	1952-1963	12	0	0	61	61	0	0	0	0	366
12	FRED BILETNIKOFF	N A	1965-1974	10	0	1	60	61	0	0	0	0	366
13	HUGH MC ELHENNY	N	1952-1964	13	38	2	20	60	0	0	0	0	360
14	RICK CASARES	N	1955-1966	12	49	0	11	60	0	0	0	0	360
15	OTIS TAYLOR	N A	1965-1974	10	3	0	57	60	0	0	0	0	360

POINT CONVERSIONS - CAPPELLETTI 4, MAYNARD 2, CANNON, ALWORTH
SAFETY - MICHAELS
ASTERISKS INDICATE NO DATA AVAILABLE

ALL-TIME NFL-NFC, AFL-AFC INTERCEPTIONS

NO.	NAME	LEAGUE		YR.	INT.	YDS.	AVE.	TD.
1	EMLEN TUNNELL		N	1948-1961	14	79	1282	16.2	4
2	DICK LANE		N	1952-1965	14	68	1207	17.8	5
3	PAUL KRAUSE		N	1964-1974	11	64	889	13.9	3
4	DICK LE BEAU		N	1959-1972	14	62	762	12.3	3
5	BOB BOYD		N	1960-1968	9	57	994	17.4	4
6	JOHNNY ROBINSON		N A	1960-1971	12	57	741	13.0	1
7	BOB DILLON		N	1952-1959	8	52	976	18.8	5
8	JACK BUTLER		N	1951-1959	9	52	827	15.9	4
9	LARRY WILSON		N	1960-1972	13	52	800	15.4	5
10	JIM PATTON		N	1955-1966	12	52	712	13.7	2
11	YALE LARY		N	1952-1964	11	50	787	15.7	2
12	DON BURROUGHS		N	1955-1964	10	50	564	11.3	0
13	HERB ADDERLY		N	1961-1972	12	48	1046	21.8	7
14	DAVE GRAYSON		N A	1961-1970	10	48	933	19.4	5
15	PAT FISCHER		N	1961-1974	14	48	899	18.7	4
16	RICHIE PETIBON		N	1959-1973	15	48	801	16.7	3
17	WILLIE WOOD		N	1960-1971	12	48	699	14.6	2
18	EMMITT THOMAS		N A	1966-1974	9	47	788	16.8	5
19	LEM BARNEY		N	1967-1974	8	46	965	21.0	6
20	JACK CHRISTIANSEN		N	1951-1958	8	46	717	15.6	3
21	DAVE WHITSELL		N	1958-1969	12	46	668	14.5	4
22	AUSTIN GONSOULIN		N A	1960-1967	8	46	551	12.0	2
23	ED MEADOR		N	1959-1970	12	46	547	11.9	5
24	ERICH BARNES		N	1958-1971	14	45	853	19.0	7
25	JIM NORTON		A	1960-1968	9	45	592	13.2	1
26	JIMMY JOHNSON		N	1961-1974	14	44	598	13.6	2
27	WARREN LAHR	AA	N	1949-1959	11	44	590	13.4	5
28	KERMIT ALEXANDER		N	1963-1973	11	43	668	15.5	3
29	MEL RENFRO		N	1964-1974	11	43	505	11.7	3
30	BOBBY HUNT		A	1962-1969	8	42	755	18.0	1
31	WILLIE BROWN		N A	1963-1974	12	42	424	10.1	2
32	DON DOLL		N	1949-1954	6	41	617	15.0	3
33	JOHNNY SAMPLE		N A	1958-1968	11	41	460	11.2	4
34	ED SHAROCKMAN		N	1962-1972	11	40	804	20.1	3
35	BUTCH BYRD		N A	1964-1971	8	40	666	16.6	5
36	W. K. HICKS		N A	1964-1972	9	40	645	16.1	0
37	CARL LOCKHART		N	1965-1974	10	40	475	11.9	3
38	TOM KEANE		N	1948-1955	8	40	349	8.7	1
39	LINDON CROW		N	1955-1964	10	38	518	13.6	2
40	DICK LYNCH		N	1958-1966	9	37	600	16.2	4
41	DON SHINNICK		N	1957-1969	13	37	252	6.8	0
42	FRED WILLIAMSON		N A	1960-1967	8	36	477	13.3	2
43	JIM DAVID		N	1952-1959	8	36	259	7.2	0
44	RAY RAMSEY	AA	N	1947-1953	7	35	663	18.9	1
45	BRIG OWENS		N	1966-1974	9	35	661	18.9	3
46	MILLER FARR		N	1965-1973	9	35	578	16.5	6
47	WILLIE WILLIAMS		N A	1965-1973	9	35	462	13.2	0

THE ALL-TIME ROSTER

ABBEY, JOSEPH (NORTH TEXAS STATE) - END - 1948-49 CHICAGO BEARS; 1949
   NEW YORK BULLDOGS
ABBOTT, LAFAYETTE (SYRACUSE) - BACK - 1921-29 DAYTON TRIANGLES
ABBOTT - END - 1919 WHEELING
ABBRUZZI, LOUIS (RHODE ISLAND STATE) - BACK - 1946 BOSTON YANKS
ABEE, WILLIAM (NEW YORK UNIV.) - BACK - 1936-37 NEW YORK YANKS (AFL)
ABEL, FREDERICK (WASHINGTON) - BACK - 1926 MILWAUKEE BADGERS
ABELL, HARRY (MISSOURI) - LB - 1966-68 KANSAS CITY CHIEFS (AFL)
ABERSON, CLIFFORD - BACK - 1946 GREEN BAY PACKERS
ABRAMOWICZ, DANIEL (XAVIER-OHIO) - END - 1967-69 NEW ORLEANS SAINTS;
   1970-73 NEW ORLEANS SAINTS (NFC); 1973-74 SAN FRANCISCO 49ERS
   (NFC); 1969 PASS RECEIVING LEADER (NFC)
ABRAMS, NATHAN - END - 1921 GREEN BAY PACKERS
ABRAMSON, GEORGE (MINNESOTA) - TACKLE - 1925-26 GREEN BAY PACKERS
ABRELL, RICHARD (PURDUE) - BACK - 1919-20 DAYTON TRIANGLES
ABRUZZESE, RAYMOND (ALABAMA) - BACK - 1962-64 BUFFALO BILLS (AFL)
ABRUZZINO, FRANK (COLGATE) - END - 1931 BROOKLYN DODGERS; 1933
   CINCINNATI REDS
ABSHER, RICHARD (MARYLAND) - LB, KICKER - 1967 WASHINGTON REDSKINS;
   1967-68 ATLANTA FALCONS; 1969 NEW ORLEANS SAINTS; 1970-71 NEW
   ORLEANS SAINTS (NFC); 1972 PHILADELPHIA EAGLES (NFC)
ACHUI, WALTER (DAYTON) - BACK - 1927-28 DAYTON TRIANGLES
ACKS, RONALD (ILLINOIS) - LB - 1968-69 ATLANTA FALCONS; 1970-71
   ATLANTA FALCONS (NFC); 1972-73 NEW ENGLAND PATRIOTS (AFC); 1974
   GREEN BAY PACKERS (NFC)
ADAMCHIK, EDWARD (PITTSBURGH) - CENTER - 1965 NEW YORK GIANTS; 1965
   PITTSBURGH STEELERS
ADAMLE, ANTHONY (OHIO STATE) - BACK - 1947-49 CLEVELAND BROWNS
   (AAFC); 1950-51, 54 CLEVELAND BROWNS
ADAMLE, MICHAEL (NORTHWESTERN) - BACK - 1971-72 KANSAS CITY CHIEFS
   (AFC); 1973-74 NEW YORK JETS (AFC)
ADAMS, CHESTER (OHIO) - TACKLE - 1939-42 CLEVELAND RAMS; 1943 GREEN
   BAY PACKERS; 1946-48 CLEVELAND BROWNS (AAFC); 1949 BUFFALO BILLS
   (AAFC); 1950 NEW YORK YANKS
ADAMS, DOUGLAS (OHIO STATE) - LB - 1971-74 CINCINNATI BENGALS (AFC)
ADAMS, HENRY (PITTSBURGH) - CENTER - 1939 CHICAGO CARDINALS
ADAMS, HOWARD O'NEAL (ARKANSAS) - END - 1942-44 NEW YORK GIANTS;
   1946-47 BROOKLYN DODGERS (AAFC)
ADAMS, JOHN (NOTRE DAME) - TACKLE - 1945-49 WASHINGTON REDSKINS
ADAMS, JOHN (LOS ANGELES STATE) - BACK - 1959-62 CHICAGO BEARS; 1963
   LOS ANGELES RAMS
ADAMS, JOSEPH (DEPAUL) - TACKLE - 1924 ROCHESTER JEFFERSONS
ADAMS, JULIUS (TEXAS SOUTHERN) - TACKLE, END - 1971-74 NEW ENGLAND
   PATRIOTS (AFC)
ADAMS, PETER (USC) - GUARD, TACKLE - 1974 CLEVELAND BROWNS (AFC)
ADAMS, ROBERT (PACIFIC) - END - 1969 PITTSBURGH STEELERS; 1970-71
   PITTSBURGH STEELERS (AFC); 1973-74 NEW ENGLAND PATRIOTS (AFC)
ADAMS, SAMUEL (PRAIRIE VIEW) - GUARD, TACKLE - 1972-74 NEW ENGLAND
   PATRIOTS (AFC)
ADAMS, THOMAS (MINNESOTA AT DULUTH) - END - 1962 MINNESOTA VIKINGS
ADAMS, VERLIN (MORRIS HARVEY) - END - 1943-45 NEW YORK GIANTS
ADAMS, WILLIAM (HOLY CROSS) - GUARD - 1972, 74 BUFFALO BILLS (AFC)
ADAMS, WILLIE (NEW MEXICO STATE) - LB - 1965-66 WASHINGTON REDSKINS
ADAMSON, KENNETH (NOTRE DAME) - GUARD - 1960-62 DENVER BRONCOS (AFL)
ADDAMS, ABRAHAM (INDIANA) - END - 1949 DETROIT LIONS
ADDERLY, HERBERT (MICHIGAN STATE) - BACK - 1961-69 GREEN BAY PACKERS;
   1970-72 DALLAS COWBOYS (NFC)
ADDISON, THOMAS (SOUTH CAROLINA) - LB - 1960-67 BOSTON PATRIOTS (AFL)
ADDUCCI, NICHOLAS (NEBRASKA) - BACK - 1954-55 WASHINGTON REDSKINS
ADKINS, MARGENE (HENDERSON JUNIOR) - END - 1970-71 DALLAS COWBOYS
   (NFC); 1972 NEW ORLEANS SAINTS (NFC); 1973 NEW YORK JETS (AFC)
ADKINS, ROBERT (MARSHALL) - END - 1940-41, 45 GREEN BAY PACKERS
ADKINS, ROY (MILLIKIN) - GUARD - 1920 DECATUR STALEYS; 1921 CHICAGO
   STALEYS
AFFLIS, WILLIAM "DICK" (NEVADA) - GUARD - 1951-54 GREEN BAY PACKERS

AGAJANIAN, BENJAMIN (NEW MEXICO) - KICKER - 1945 PITTSBURGH STEELERS;
     1945 PHILADELPHIA EAGLES; 1947-48 LOS ANGELES DONS (AAFC); 1949
     NEW YORK GIANTS; 1953 LOS ANGELES RAMS; 1954-57 NEW YORK GIANTS;
     1960 LOS ANGELES CHARGERS (AFL); 1961 DALLAS TEXANS (AFL); 1961
     GREEN BAY PACKERS; 1962 OAKLAND RAIDERS (AFL); 1964 SAN DIEGO
     CHARGERS (AFL)
AGASE, ALEXANDER (ILLINOIS) - GUARD - 1947 LOS ANGELES DONS (AAFC);
     1947 CHICAGO ROCKETS (AAFC); 1948-49 CLEVELAND BROWNS (AAFC);
     1950-51 CLEVELAND BROWNS; 1953 BALTIMORE COLTS
AGEE, SAMUEL (VANDERBILT) - BACK - 1938-39 CHICAGO CARDINALS
AGLER, ROBERT (OTTERBEIN) - BACK - 1948-49 LOS ANGELES RAMS
AGUIRRE, JOSEPH (ST.MARY'S OF CAL.) - END - 1941, 43-45 WASHINGTON
     REDSKINS; 1946-49 LOS ANGELES DONS (AAFC); 1945 FIELD GOAL LEADER
AIELLO, ANTHONY (YOUNGSTOWN) - BACK - 1944 DETROIT LIONS; 1944
     BROOKLYN TIGERS
AILINGER, JAMES (BUFFALO) - GUARD - 1924 BUFFALO BISONS
AKIN, HAROLD (OKLAHOMA STATE) - TACKLE - 1967-68 SAN DIEGO CHARGERS
     (AFL)
AKIN, LEONARD (BAYLOR) - GUARD - 1940-41 MILWAUKEE CHIEFS (AFL); 1942
     CHICAGO BEARS
AKINS, ALBERT (WASHINGTON & WASH. STATE) - BACK - 1946 CLEVELAND
     BROWNS (AAFC); 1947-48 BROOKLYN DODGERS (AAFC); 1948 BUFFALO
     BILLS (AAFC)
AKINS, FRANK (WASHINGTON STATE) - BACK - 1943-46 WASHINGTON REDSKINS
ALBAN, RICHARD (NORTHWESTERN) - BACK - 1952-55 WASHINGTON REDSKINS;
     1956-59 PITTSBURGH STEELERS
ALBANESE, DONALD - END - 1925 COLUMBUS TIGERS
ALBANESE, VINCENT (SYRACUSE) - BACK - 1937-38 BROOKLYN DODGERS; 1940
     NEW YORK AMERICANS (AFL)
ALBERGHINI, THOMAS (HOLY CROSS) - GUARD - 1945 PITTSBURGH STEELERS
ALBERT, FRANK (STANFORD) - QBACK - 1946-49 SAN FRANCISCO 49ERS
     (AAFC); 1950-52 SAN FRANCISCO 49ERS
ALBERT, SERGIO (U.S.INTERNATIONAL) - KICKER - 1974 ST. LOUIS
     CARDINALS (NFC)
ALBRECHT, ARTHUR (WISCONSIN) - TACKLE - 1942 PITTSBURGH STEELERS;
     1943 CHICAGO CARDINALS; 1944 BOSTON YANKS
ALBRIGHT, WILLIAM (WISCONSIN) - GUARD - 1951-54 NEW YORK GIANTS
ALDERMAN, GRADY (DETROIT) - GUARD, TACKLE - 1960 DETROIT LIONS;
     1961-69 MINNESOTA VIKINGS; 1970-74 MINNESOTA VIKINGS (NFC)
ALDERTON, JOHN (MARYLAND) - END - 1953 PITTSBURGH STEELERS
ALDRICH, CHARLES "KI" (TCU) - CENTER - 1939-40 CHICAGO CARDINALS;
     1941-42, 45-47 WASHINGTON REDSKINS
ALDRIDGE, ALLEN (PRAIRIE VIEW) - END - 1971-72 HOUSTON OILERS (AFC);
     1974 CLEVELAND BROWNS (AFC)
ALDRIDGE, BENJAMIN (OKLAHOMA A&M) - BACK - 1950-51 NEW YORK YANKS;
     1952 SAN FRANCISCO 49ERS; 1953 GREEN BAY PACKERS
ALDRIDGE, LIONEL (UTAH STATE) - END - 1963-69 GREEN BAY PACKERS;
     1970-71 GREEN BAY PACKERS (NFC); 1972-73 SAN DIEGO CHARGERS (AFC)
ALESKUS, JOSEPH (OHIO STATE) - CENTER - 1940-41 COLUMBUS BULLIES (AFL)
ALEXAKOS, STEVE (SAN DIEGO STATE) - GUARD - 1970 DENVER BRONCOS
     (AFC); 1971 NEW YORK GIANTS (NFC)
ALEXANDER, GLENN (GRAMBLING) - END - 1970 BUFFALO BILLS (AFC)
ALEXANDER, KERMIT (UCLA) - BACK - 1963-69 SAN FRANCISCO 49ERS;
     1970-71 LOS ANGELES RAMS (NFC); 1972-73 PHILADELPHIA EAGLES (NFC)
ALEXANDER, JOHN (RUTGERS) - TACKLE - 1926 NEW YORK GIANTS
ALEXANDER, JOSEPH (SYRACUSE) - CENTER - 1921-22 ROCHESTER JEFFERSONS;
     1922 MILWAUKEE BADGERS; 1925-27 NEW YORK GIANTS
ALEXANDER, WILLIE (ALCORN A&M) - BACK - 1971-74 HOUSTON OILERS (AFC)
ALFLEN, THEODORE (SPRINGFIELD) - BACK - 1969 DENVER BRONCOS (AFL)
ALFONSE, JULES (MINNESOTA) - QBACK - 1937-38 CLEVELAND RAMS; 1940-41
     COLUMBUS BULLIES (AFL)
ALFORD, BRUCE (TCU) - KICKER - 1967 WASHINGTON REDSKINS; 1968-69
     BUFFALO BILLS (AFL)
ALFORD, EUGENE (TEXAS TECH) - BACK - 1931-33 PORTSMOUTH SPARTANS;
     1934 CINCINNATI REDS; 1934 ST. LOUIS GUNNERS
ALFORD, HERBERT BRUCE (TCU) - END - 1946-49 NEW YORK YANKEES (AAFC);
     1950-51 NEW YORK YANKS
ALFORD, MICHAEL (AUBURN) - CENTER - 1965 ST. LOUIS CARDINALS; 1966
     DETROIT LIONS
ALFSON, WARREN (NEBRASKA) - GUARD - 1941 BROOKLYN DODGERS

Top row (from left to right): Herb Adderly, Joe Alexander, Kermit Alexander and Jon Arnett. *Second Row:* Ben Agajanian, Joe Aguirre, Frank Albert and "Ki" Aldrich. *Third row:* Alan Ameche, "Hunk" Anderson, Dave Ariail and Lee Artoe. *Bottom row:* Doug Atkins, Steve Bagarus, John Baker and Jim Bakken.

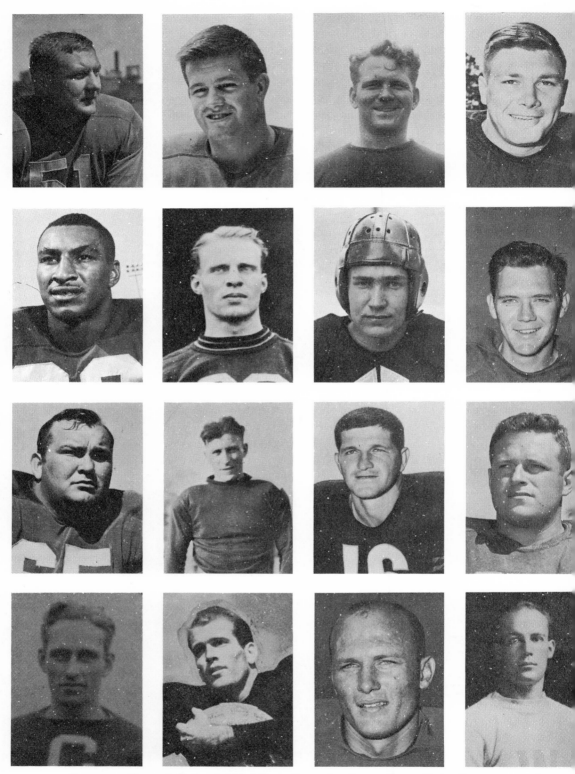

Top row (from left to right): **Vince Banonis, Terry Barr, Nate Barrager and Dick Barwegan.** *Second row:* **Dick Bass, Cliff Battles, Gil Berry and Raymond Berry.** *Third row:* **Les Bingaman, Ed Black, George Blanda and Gil Bouley.** *Bottom row:* **Arda Bowser, Cloyce Box, Bob Boyd and Ben Boynton.**

ALLARD, DONALD (BOSTON COLLEGE) - QBACK - 1961 NEW YORK TITANS (AFL);
    1962 BOSTON PATRIOTS (AFL)
ALLEN, CARL (OUACHITA) - BACK - 1948 BROOKLYN DODGERS (AAFC)
ALLEN, CHARLES (WASHINGTON) - LB - 1961-69 SAN DIEGO CHARGERS (AFL);
    1970-71 PITTSBURGH STEELERS (AFC); 1972 PHILADELPHIA EAGLES (NFC)
ALLEN, DALVA (HOUSTON) - END - 1960-61 HOUSTON OILERS (AFL); 1962-64
    OAKLAND RAIDERS (AFL)
ALLEN, DONALD (TEXAS) - BACK - 1960 DENVER BRONCOS (AFL)
ALLEN, DOUG (PENN STATE) - LB - 1974 BUFFALO BILLS (AFC)
ALLEN, DUANE (SANTA ANA) - END - 1961-64 LOS ANGELES RAMS; 1965
    PITTSBURGH STEELERS; 1965 BALTIMORE COLTS; 1966-67 CHICAGO BEARS
ALLEN, EDMUND (CREIGHTON) - END - 1928 CHICAGO CARDINALS
ALLEN, EDWARD (PENNSYLVANIA) - BACK - 1947 CHICAGO BEARS
ALLEN, ELIHU (UTAH STATE) - BACK - 1961 DENVER BRONCOS (AFL)
ALLEN, ERMAL (KENTUCKY) - QBACK - 1947 CLEVELAND BROWNS (AAFC)
ALLEN, FRANK (INDIANA) - END - 1921 MUNCIE FLYERS
ALLEN, GEORGE (WEST TEXAS STATE) - TACKLE - 1966 HOUSTON OILERS (AFL)
ALLEN, GERALD (OMAHA) - BACK - 1966 BALTIMORE COLTS; 1967-69
    WASHINGTON REDSKINS
ALLEN, GRADY (TEXAS A&M) - LB - 1968-69 ATLANTA FALCONS; 1970-72
    ATLANTA FALCONS (NFC)
ALLEN, JACK (BAYLOR) - BACK - 1969 OAKLAND RAIDERS (AFL); 1970-71
    BUFFALO BILLS (AFC); 1972 PHILADELPHIA EAGLES (NFC)
ALLEN, JEFFREY (IOWA STATE) - BACK - 1971 ST. LOUIS CARDINALS (NFC)
ALLEN, JIMMY (UCLA) - BACK - 1974 PITTSBURGH STEELERS (AFC)
ALLEN, JOHN (PURDUE) - CENTER - 1955-58 WASHINGTON REDSKINS
ALLEN, LOUIS (DUKE) - TACKLE - 1950-51 PITTSBURGH STEELERS
ALLEN, NATHANIEL (TEXAS SOUTHERN) - BACK - 1971-74 KANSAS CITY CHIEFS
    (AFC)
ALLEY, DONALD (ADAMS STATE) - END - 1967 BALTIMORE COLTS; 1969
    PITTSBURGH STEELERS
ALLISON, HENRY (SAN DIEGO STATE) - GUARD - 1971-72 PHILADELPHIA
    EAGLES (NFC)
ALLISON, JAMES (TEXAS A&M) - END - 1926 BUFFALO RANGERS; 1927 BUFFALO
    BISONS; 1928 NEW YORK GIANTS
ALLISON, JAMES (SAN DIEGO STATE) - BACK - 1965-68 SAN DIEGO CHARGERS
    (AFL)
ALLISTON, VAUGHAN (MISSISSIPPI) - LB - 1960 DENVER BRONCOS (AFL)
ALLMAN, ROBERT (MICHIGAN STATE) - END - 1936 CHICAGO BEARS
ALLMEN, STANLEY (CASE) - GUARD - 1936 CLEVELAND RAMS (AFL)
ALLSHOUSE, CHARLES (PITTSBURGH) - END - 1919 CLEVELAND INDIANS
ALLSHOUSE, GEORGE (PITTSBURGH) - GUARD - 1919 CLEVELAND INDIANS
ALLTON, JOSEPH (OKLAHOMA) - TACKLE - 1942 CHICAGO CARDINALS
ALOIA, HENRY (NIAGARA) - BACK - 1941 CINCINNATI BENGALS (AFL)
ALSTON, MACK (MARYLAND STATE) - END - 1970-72 WASHINGTON REDSKINS
    (NFC); 1973-74 HOUSTON OILERS (AFC)
ALWORTH, LANCE (ARKANSAS) - END - 1962-69 SAN DIEGO CHARGERS (AFL);
    1970 SAN DIEGO CHARGERS (AFC); 1971-72 DALLAS COWBOYS (NFC);
    1966, 68-69 PASS RECEIVING LEADER (AFL)
ALZADO, LYLE (YANKTON-SOUTH DAKOTA) - END - 1971-74 DENVER BRONCOS
    (AFC)
AMBERG, JOHN (KANSAS) - BACK - 1951-52 NEW YORK GIANTS
AMBROSE, JOHN (CATHOLIC) - CENTER - 1932 BROOKLYN DODGERS
AMBROSE, WALTER (CARROLL) - GUARD - 1930 PORTSMOUTH SPARTANS
AMECHE, ALAN (WISCONSIN) - BACK - 1955-60 BALTIMORE COLTS; 1955
    RUSHING LEADER
AMERSON, GLEN (TEXAS TECH) - BACK - 1961 PHILADELPHIA EAGLES
AMES, DAVID (RICHMOND) - BACK - 1961 NEW YORK TITANS (AFL); 1961
    DENVER BRONCOS (AFL)
AMMAN, RICHARD (FLORIDA STATE) - END, TACKLE - 1972-73 BALTIMORE
    COLTS (AFC)
AMSLER, C. MARTIN (INDIANA & EVANSVILLE ST.) - END - 1967, 69 CHICAGO
    BEARS; 1970 CINCINNATI BENGALS (AFC); 1970 GREEN BAY PACKERS
    (NFC)
AMSTUTZ, JOSEPH (INDIANA) - CENTER - 1957 CLEVELAND BROWNS
AMUNDSON, GEORGE (IOWA STATE) - BACK - 1973-74 HOUSTON OILERS (AFC)
AMUNDSEN, NORMAN (WISCONSIN) - GUARD - 1957 GREEN BAY PACKERS
ANANIS, VITO (BOSTON COLLEGE) - BACK - 1940 BOSTON BEARS (AFL); 1945
    WASHINGTON REDSKINS
ANDABAKER, RUDOLPH (PITTSBURGH) - GUARD - 1952, 54 PITTSBURGH STEELERS

ANDERSEN, STANLEY (STANFORD) - TACKLE - 1940-41 CLEVELAND RAMS; 1941
    DETROIT LIONS
ANDERSON, ARTHUR (IDAHO) - TACKLE - 1961-62 CHICAGO BEARS; 1963
    PITTSBURGH STEELERS
ANDERSON, BILLY GUY (TULSA) - QBACK - 1967 HOUSTON OILERS (AFL)
ANDERSON, BRUCE (WILLIAMETTE) - END - 1966 LOS ANGELES RAMS; 1967-69
    NEW YORK GIANTS; 1970 WASHINGTON REDSKINS (NFC)
ANDERSON, CHARLES (LOUISIANA TECH) - END - 1956 CHICAGO CARDINALS
ANDERSON, CHESTER - TACKLE - 1923 LOUISVILLE BRECKS
ANDERSON, CHESTER (MINNESOTA) - END - 1967 PITTSBURGH STEELERS
ANDERSON, CLIFTON (INDIANA) - END - 1952-53 CHICAGO CARDINALS; 1953
    NEW YORK GIANTS
ANDERSON, DONALD SCOTT (MISSOURI) - CENTER - 1974 MINNESOTA VIKINGS
    (NFC)
ANDERSON, EDWARD (NOTRE DAME) - END - 1922 ROCHESTER JEFFERSONS;
    1922-25 CHICAGO CARDINALS; 1923 CHICAGO BEARS; 1926 CHICAGO
    BULLS (AFL)
ANDERSON, EZZRET (KENTUCKY STATE) - END - 1947 LOS ANGELES DONS (AAFC)
ANDERSON, GARRY DON (TEXAS TECH) - BACK, KICKER - 1966-69 GREEN BAY
    PACKERS; 1970-71 GREEN BAY PACKERS (NFC); 1972-74 ST. LOUIS
    CARDINALS (NFC)
ANDERSON, HEARTLEY (NOTRE DAME) - GUARD - 1922-25 CHICAGO BEARS
ANDERSON, KENNETH (AUGUSTANA-ILLINOIS) - QBACK - 1971-74 CINCINNATI
    BENGALS (AFC); 1974 PASSING LEADER (AFC)
ANDERSON, MAX (ARIZONA STATE) - BACK - 1968-69 BUFFALO BILLS (AFL)
ANDERSON, OSCAR (COLGATE) - BACK - 1920-22 BUFFALO ALL-AMERICANS
ANDERSON, PRESTON (RICE) - BACK - 1974 CLEVELAND BROWNS (AFC)
ANDERSON, RALPH (LOS ANGELES STATE) - END - 1958 CHICAGO BEARS; 1960
    LOS ANGELES CHARGERS (AFL)
ANDERSON, RALPH (WEST TEXAS STATE) - BACK - 1971-72 PITTSBURGH
    STEELERS (AFC); 1973 NEW ENGLAND PATRIOTS (AFC)
ANDERSON, RICHARD (OHIO STATE) - TACKLE - 1967 NEW ORLEANS SAINTS
ANDERSON, RICHARD P. (COLORADO) - BACK, KICKER - 1968-69 MIAMI
    DOLPHINS (AFL); 1970-74 MIAMI DOLPHINS (AFC); 1973 INTERCEPTION
    LEADER (AFC)
ANDERSON, ROBERT (WEST POINT) - BACK - 1963 NEW YORK GIANTS
ANDERSON, ROBERT CONRAD (COLORADO) - BACK - 1970-73 DENVER BRONCOS
    (AFC)
ANDERSON, ROGER (VIRGINIA UNION) - TACKLE - 1964-65, 67-68 NEW YORK
    GIANTS; 1966 ATLANTA FALCONS
ANDERSON, TAZWELL (GEORGIA TECH) - END - 1961-64 ST. LOUIS CARDINALS;
    1966-67 ATLANTA FALCONS
ANDERSON, THOMAS (HASKELL) - BACK - 1924 KANSAS CITY COWBOYS
ANDERSON, WALTER "BILL" (TENNESSEE) - END - 1958-63 WASHINGTON
    REDSKINS; 1965-66 GREEN BAY PACKERS
ANDERSON, WILLARD (SYRACUSE) - BACK - 1923 CLEVELAND INDIANS; 1924
    ROCHESTER JEFFERSONS
ANDERSON, WILLIAM (COMPTON JUNIOR) - BACK - 1953-54 CHICAGO BEARS
ANDERSON, WILLIAM (WEST VIRGINIA) - END - 1945 BOSTON YANKS
ANDERSON, WINSTON (COLGATE) - END - 1936 NEW YORK GIANTS
ANDORKA, DELBERT (LOYOLA OF LOS ANGELES) - TACKLE - 1936 ROCHESTER
    TIGERS (AFL)
ANDRAKO, STEPHEN (OHIO STATE) - CENTER - 1940 WASHINGTON REDSKINS
ANDREWS, AL (NEW MEXICO STATE) - LB - 1970-71 BUFFALO BILLS (AFC)
ANDREWS, J. - BACK - 1934 ST. LOUIS GUNNERS
ANDREWS, JOHN (INDIANA) - END, BACK - 1972 SAN DIEGO CHARGERS (AFC);
    1973-74 BALTIMORE COLTS (AFC)
ANDREWS, LEROY (PITTSBURG STATE-KANSAS) - BACK - 1923 ST. LOUIS
    BROWNS; 1924-26 KANSAS CITY COWBOYS; 1927 CLEVELAND BULLDOGS;
    1928 DETROIT WOLVERINES
ANDREWS, WILLIAM (SOUTHEAST LOUISIANA) - LB - 1967-69 CLEVELAND
    BROWNS; 1970-74 CLEVELAND BROWNS (AFC)
ANDRIE, GEORGE (MARQUETTE) - END - 1962-69 DALLAS COWBOYS; 1970-72
    DALLAS COWBOYS (NFC)
ANDRULEWICZ, THEODORE (VILLANOVA) - BACK - 1930 NEWARK TORNADOS
ANDRUS, LOUIS (BRIGHAM YOUNG) - END - 1967 DENVER BRONCOS (AFL)
ANDRUSKING, SIGMUND (DETROIT) - GUARD - 1936 CLEVELAND RAMS (AFL);
    1937 NEW YORK YANKS (AFL); 1937 BROOKLYN DODGERS
ANDROS, PLATO (OKLAHOMA) - GUARD - 1947-50 CHICAGO CARDINALS
ANE, CHARLES (USC) - CENTER - 1953-59 DETROIT LIONS
ANGLE, ROBERT (IOWA STATE) - BACK - 1950 CHICAGO CARDINALS

ANGSMAN, ELMER (NOTRE DAME) - BACK - 1946-52 CHICAGO CARDINALS
ANNAN, DUNCAN (BROWN & CHICAGO) - QBACK - 1920 CHICAGO TIGERS; 1922
    TOLEDO MAROONS; 1923-25 HAMMOND PROS; 1925-26 AKRON PROS; 1926
    HAMMOND PROS
ANTHONY, CHARLES (USC) - LB - 1974 SAN DIEGO CHARGERS (AFC)
ANTOINE, LIONEL (SOUTHERN ILLINOIS) - TACKLE - 1972-74 CHICAGO BEARS
    (NFC)
ANTONINI, ETTORE (INDIANA) - END - 1937 CINCINNATI BENGALS (AFL)
ANTWINE, HOUSTON (SOUTHERN ILLINOIS) - GUARD, TACKLE - 1961-69 BOSTON
    PATRIOTS (AFL); 1970 BOSTON PATRIOTS (AFC); 1971 NEW ENGLAND
    PATRIOTS (AFC); 1972 PHILADELPHIA EAGLES (NFC)
APOLSKIS, CHARLES (DEPAUL) - END - 1938-39 CHICAGO BEARS; 1941 NEW
    YORK AMERICANS (AFL)
APOLSKIS, RAYMOND (MARQUETTE) - GUARD - 1941-42, 45-50 CHICAGO
    CARDINALS
APPLE, JAMES (UPSALA) - BACK - 1961 NEW YORK TITANS (AFL)
APPLEGRAN, CLARENCE (ILLINOIS) - GUARD - 1920 DETROIT HERALDS
APPLETON, GORDON SCOTT (TEXAS) - END - 1964-66 HOUSTON OILERS (AFL);
    1967-68 SAN DIEGO CHARGERS (AFL)
APSIT, MARGER (USC) - BACK - 1931 FRANKFORD YELLOWJACKETS; 1931
    BROOKLYN DODGERS; 1932 GREEN BAY PACKERS; 1933 BOSTON REDSKINS
ARBANAS, FREDERICK (MICHIGAN STATE) - END - 1962 DALLAS TEXANS (AFL);
    1963-69 KANSAS CITY CHIEFS (AFL); 1970 KANSAS CITY CHIEFS (AFC)
ARCHER, DANIEL (OREGON) - TACKLE - 1967 OAKLAND RAIDERS (AFL); 1968
    CINCINNATI BENGALS (AFL)
ARCHOSKA, JULIUS (SYRACUSE) - END - 1930 STATEN ISLAND STAPELTONS
ARENA, ANTHONY (MICHIGAN STATE) - CENTER - 1942 DETROIT LIONS
ARENAS, JOSEPH (OMAHA UNIV.) - BACK - 1951-57 SAN FRANCISCO 49ERS
ARENZ, ARNOLD (ST.LOUIS) - QBACK - 1934 BOSTON REDSKINS
ARGUS, ROBERT - BACK - 1919-25 ROCHESTER JEFFERSONS
ARIAIL, DAVID (AUBURN) - END - 1934 BROOKLYN DODGERS; 1934 CINCINNATI
    REDS
ARMS, LLOYD (OKLAHOMA A&M) - GUARD - 1946-48 CHICAGO CARDINALS
ARMSTRONG, CHARLES (MISSISSIPPI COLLEGE) - BACK - 1941 NEW YORK
    AMERICANS (AFL); 1946 BROOKLYN DODGERS (AAFC)
ARMSTRONG, ELLSWORTH (DARTMOUTH) - TACKLE - 1936 NEW YORK YANKS (AFL)
ARMSTRONG, GRAHAM (JOHN CARROLL) - TACKLE - 1941, 45 CLEVELAND RAMS;
    1947-48 BUFFALO BILLS (AAFC)
ARMSTRONG, JOHN (DUBUQUE) - QBACK - 1923-25 ROCK ISLAND INDEPENDENTS;
    1926 ROCK ISLAND INDEPENDENTS (AFL)
ARMSTRONG, NEIL (OKLAHOMA A&M) - END - 1947-51 PHILADELPHIA EAGLES
ARMSTRONG, OTIS (PURDUE) - BACK - 1973-74 DENVER BRONCOS (AFC); 1974
    RUSHING LEADER (AFC)
ARMSTRONG, P. NORRIS (CENTRE) - BACK - 1922 MILWAUKEE BADGERS
ARMSTRONG, RAMON (TCU) - GUARD - 1960 OAKLAND RAIDERS (AFL)
ARMSTRONG, ROBERT (MISSOURI) - TACKLE - 1931-32 PORTSMOUTH SPARTANS
ARMSTRONG, WILLIAM (UCLA) - GUARD - 1943 BROOKLYN DODGERS
ARNDT, ALFRED (SOUTH DAKOTA STATE) - GUARD - 1935 PITTSBURGH PIRATES
ARNDT, RICHARD (IDAHO) - TACKLE - 1967-69 PITTSBURGH STEELERS; 1970
    PITTSBURGH STEELERS (AFC)
ARNESON, JAMES (ARIZONA) - GUARD,TACKLE,CENTER - 1973-74 DALLAS
    COWBOYS (NFC)
ARNESON, MARK (ARIZONA) - LB - 1972-74 ST. LOUIS CARDINALS (NFC)
ARNETT, JON (USC) - BACK - 1957-63 LOS ANGELES RAMS; 1964-66 CHICAGO
    BEARS
ARNOLD, JAY (TEXAS) - QBACK - 1937-40 PHILADELPHIA EAGLES; 1940
    COLUMBUS BULLIES (AFL); 1941 PITTSBURGH STEELERS
ARNOLD, LEFRANCIS (OREGON) - GUARD - 1974 DENVER BRONCOS (AFC)
ARRINGTON, RICHARD (TULSA) - QBACK - 1970-72 PHILADELPHIA EAGLES (NFC)
ARROWHEAD - END - 1922-23 OORANG INDIANS
ARTERBURN, ELMER (TEXAS TECH) - BACK - 1954 CHICAGO CARDINALS
ARTHUR, GARY PATRICK (MIAMI-OHIO) - END, TACKLE - 1970-71 NEW YORK
    JETS (AFC)
ARTMAN, CORWAN (STANFORD) - TACKLE - 1931 NEW YORK GIANTS; 1932
    BOSTON BRAVES; 1933 PITTSBURGH PIRATES
ARTOE, LEE (SANTA CLARA & CALIFORNIA) - TACKLE - 1940-42, 45 CHICAGO
    BEARS; 1946-47 LOS ANGELES DONS (AAFC); 1948 BALTIMORE COLTS
    (AAFC)
ASAD, DOUGLAS (NORTHWESTERN) - END - 1960-61 OAKLAND RAIDERS (AFL)
ASBURY, WILLIE (KENT STATE) - BACK - 1966-68 PITTSBURGH STEELERS
ASCHBACHER, DARRELL (OREGON) - GUARD - 1959 PHILADELPHIA EAGLES.

ASCHENBRENNER, FRANK (NORTHWESTERN) - BACK - 1949 CHICAGO HORNETS
    (AAFC)
ASH, JULIAN (OREGON STATE) - GUARD - 1926 LOS ANGELES BUCCANEERS
ASHBAUGH, WILLIAM (PITTSBURGH) - BACK - 1924 ROCK ISLAND
    INDEPENDENTS; 1924-25 KANSAS CITY COWBOYS
ASHBURN, CLIFFORD (NEBRASKA) - GUARD - 1929 NEW YORK GIANTS; 1930
    CHICAGO BEARS
ASHER, ROBERT (VANDERBILT) - TACKLE - 1970 DALLAS COWBOYS (NFC);
    1972-74 CHICAGO BEARS (NFC)
ASHMORE, MARION (GONZAGA) - TACKLE - 1926 MILWAUKEE BADGERS; 1927
    DULUTH ESKIMOS; 1927 CHICAGO BEARS; 1928-29 GREEN BAY PACKERS
ASHTON, JOSH (TULSA) - BACK - 1972-74 NEW ENGLAND PATRIOTS (AFC)
ASKEA, MICHAEL (STANFORD) - TACKLE - 1973 DENVER BRONCOS (AFC)
ASKON, BERT (TEXAS SOUTHERN) - END - 1971 PITTSBURGH STEELERS (AFC);
    1973 NEW ORLEANS SAINTS (NFC)
ASPATORE, EDWARD (MARQUETTE) - TACKLE - 1934 CINCINNATI REDS; 1934
    CHICAGO BEARS
ASPLUNDH, LESTER (SWARTHMORE) - BACK - 1926 PHILADELPHIA QUAKERS (AFL)
ATCHASON, JACK (ILLINOIS WESTERN) - END - 1960 BOSTON PATRIOTS (AFL);
    1960 HOUSTON OILERS (AFL)
ATCHERSON - END - 1922 COLUMBUS PANHANDLES
ATESSIS, WILLIAM (TEXAS) - TACKLE, END - 1971 NEW ENGLAND PATRIOTS
    (AFC)
ATHAS, PETER (TENNESSEE) - BACK - 1971-74 NEW YORK GIANTS (NFC)
ATKESON, DALE - BACK - 1954-56 WASHINGTON REDSKINS
ATKINS, DAVID CHARLES (TEXAS-EL PASO) - BACK - 1973-74 SAN FRANCISCO
    49ERS (NFC)
ATKINS, DOUGLAS (TENNESSEE) - END - 1953-54 CLEVELAND BROWNS; 1955-66
    CHICAGO BEARS; 1967-69 NEW ORLEANS SAINTS
ATKINS, GEORGE (AUBURN) - GUARD - 1955 DETROIT LIONS
ATKINS, PERVIS (NEW MEXICO STATE) - BACK - 1961-63 LOS ANGELES RAMS;
    1964-65 WASHINGTON REDSKINS; 1965-66 OAKLAND RAIDERS (AFL)
ATKINS, ROBERT (GRAMBLING) - BACK, END - 1968-69 ST. LOUIS CARDINALS;
    1970-74 HOUSTON OILERS (AFC)
ATKINS, WILLIAM (AUBURN) - BACK - 1958-59 SAN FRANCISCO 49ERS;
    1960-61, 63 BUFFALO BILLS (AFL); 1962 NEW YORK TITANS (AFL);
    1963 NEW YORK JETS (AFL); 1964 DENVER BRONCOS (AFL); 1961
    PUNTING LEADER (AFL); 1961 INTERCEPTION LEADER (AFL)
ATKINSON, ALAN (VILLANOVA) - LB - 1965-69 NEW YORK JETS (AFL);
    1970-74 NEW YORK JETS (AFC)
ATKINSON, FRANK (STANFORD) - TACKLE - 1963 PITTSBURGH STEELERS; 1964
    DENVER BRONCOS (AFL)
ATKINSON, GEORGE (MORRIS BROWN) - BACK - 1968-69 OAKLAND RAIDERS
    (AFL); 1970-74 OAKLAND RAIDERS (AFC)
ATTACHE, REGINALD - BACK - 1922 OORANG INDIANS
ATTY, ALEXANDER (WEST VIRGINIA) - GUARD - 1939 CLEVELAND RAMS
ATWOOD, JOHN (WISCONSIN) - BACK - 1948 NEW YORK GIANTS
AUDET, EARL (USC) - TACKLE - 1945 WASHINGTON REDSKINS; 1946-48 LOS
    ANGELES DONS (AAFC)
AUER, HAROLD (MICHIGAN) - TACKLE - 1933 CHICAGO CARDINALS; 1933
    PHILADELPHIA EAGLES
AUER, JOSEPH (GEORGIA TECH) - BACK - 1964-65 BUFFALO BILLS (AFL);
    1966-67 MIAMI DOLPHINS (AFL); 1968 ATLANTA FALCONS
AUGUST, EDWARD (VILLANOVA) - BACK - 1931 PROVIDENCE STEAMROLLERS
AUGUSTERFER, EUGENE (CATHOLIC UNIV.) - BACK - 1935 PITTSBURGH PIRATES
AULT, CHALMERS (WEST VIRGINIA WESLEYAN) - GUARD - 1924-25 CLEVELAND
    BULLDOGS
AUSTIN, HISE (PRAIRE VIEW) - BACK - 1973 GREEN BAY PACKERS (NFC)
AUSTIN, JAMES (ST. MARY'S OF CALIFORNIA) - END - 1937 LOS ANGELES
    BULLDOGS (AFL); 1937-38 BROOKLYN DODGERS; 1939 DETROIT LIONS
AUSTIN, OCIE (UTAH STATE) - BACK - 1968-69 BALTIMORE COLTS; 1970-71
    PITTSBURGH STEELERS (AFC)
AUSTIN, WILLIAM (OREGON STATE) - GUARD - 1949-50, 53-57 NEW YORK
    GIANTS
AUTREY, WILLIAM (S. F. AUSTIN) - CENTER - 1953 CHICAGO BEARS
AUTRY, MELVIN "HANK" (SOUTHERN MISSISSIPPI) - CENTER - 1969 HOUSTON
    OILERS (AFL); 1970 HOUSTON OILERS (AFC)
AVEDISIAN, CHARLES (PROVIDENCE) - GUARD - 1942-44 NEW YORK GIANTS
AVENI, JOHN (INDIANA) - END - 1959-60 CHICAGO BEARS; 1961 WASHINGTON
    REDSKINS

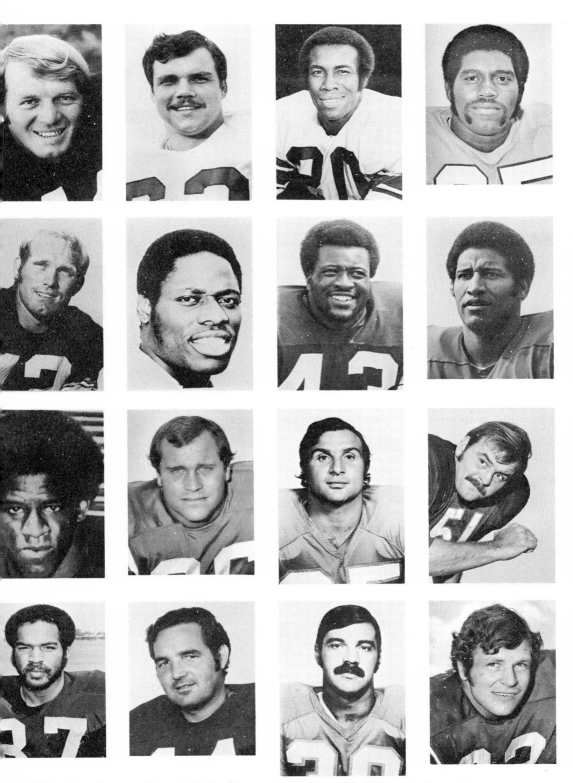

Top row (from left to right): Donny Anderson, Al Atkinson, Lem Barney and Elvin Bethea. Second row: Terry Bradshaw, John Brockington, Larry Brown and Buck Buchanan. Third row: Willie Buchanon, Norm Bulaich, Nick Buoniconti and Dick Butkus. Bottom row: Ray Chester, Fred Cox, Larry Csonka and Mike Curtis.

AVERNO, SISTO (MUHLENBERG) - GUARD - 1950 BALTIMORE COLTS; 1951 NEW
     YORK YANKS; 1952 DALLAS TEXANS; 1953-54 BALTIMORE COLTS
AVERY, DONALD (USC) - TACKLE - 1946-47 WASHINGTON REDSKINS; 1948 LOS
     ANGELES DONS (AAFC)
AVERY, JAMES (NORTHERN ILLINOIS) - END - 1966 WASHINGTON REDSKINS
AVERY, KENNETH (SOUTHERN MISSISSIPPI) - LB - 1967-68 NEW YORK GIANTS;
     1969 CINCINNATI BENGALS (AFL); 1970-74 CINCINNATI BENGALS (AFC)
AVEZZANO, JOSEPH (FLORIDA STATE) - CENTER - 1966 BOSTON PATRIOTS (AFL)
AVINGER, CLARENCE (ALABAMA) - BACK - 1953 NEW YORK GIANTS
BABARTSKY, ALBERT (FORDHAM) - TACKLE - 1938-39, 41-42 CHICAGO
     CARDINALS; 1943-45 CHICAGO BEARS
BABB, CHARLES (MEMPHIS STATE) - BACK - 1972-74 MIAMI DOLPHINS (AFC)
BABB, EUGENE (AUSTIN) - BACK - 1957-58 SAN FRANCISCO 49ERS; 1960-61
     DALLAS COWBOYS; 1962-63 HOUSTON OILERS (AFL)
BABCOCK, HARRY (GEORGIA) - END - 1953-55 SAN FRANCISCO 49ERS
BABCOCK, SAMUEL (MICHIGAN) - BACK - 1926 CHICAGO BULLS (AFL)
BABICH, ROBERT (MIAMI-OHIO) - LB - 1970-72 SAN DIEGO CHARGERS (AFC);
     1973-74 CLEVELAND BROWNS (AFC)
BABINECZ, JOHN (VILLANOVA) - LB - 1972-73 DALLAS COWBOYS (NFC)
BACCAGLIO, MARTIN (SAN JOSE STATE) - END, TACKLE - 1968 SAN DIEGO
     CHARGERS (AFL); 1968-69 CINCINNATI BENGALS (AFL); 1970
     CINCINNATI BENGALS (AFC)
BACCHUS, CARL (MISSOURI) - END - 1927 CLEVELAND BULLDOGS; 1928
     DETROIT WOLVERINES
BACHMAIER, JOSEPH - GUARD - 1919-24 ROCHESTER JEFFERSONS
BACHMAN, JAY (CINCINNATI) - CENTER, TACKLE - 1968-69 DENVER BRONCOS
     (AFL); 1970-71 DENVER BRONCOS (AFC)
BACHOR, LUDWIG (DETROIT) - TACKLE - 1928 DETROIT WOLVERINES
BACON, FRANCIS (WABASH) - BACK - 1919-26 DAYTON TRIANGLES
BACON, LANDER MC COY (JACKSON STATE) - TACKLE, END - 1968-69 LOS
     ANGELES RAMS; 1970-72 LOS ANGELES RAMS (NFC); 1973-74 SAN DIEGO
     CHARGERS (AFC)
BADACZEWSKI, JOHN (WESTERN RESERVE) - GUARD - 1946-48 BOSTON YANKS;
     1948 CHICAGO CARDINALS; 1949-51 WASHINGTON REDSKINS; 1953
     CHICAGO BEARS
BADAR, RICHARD (INDIANA) - QBACK - 1967 PITTSBURGH STEELERS
BADGRO, MORRIS (USC) - END - 1927 NEW YORK YANKEES; 1930-35 NEW YORK
     GIANTS; 1936 BROOKLYN DODGERS; 1936 ROCHESTER TIGERS (AFL); 1934
     PASS RECEIVING LEADER; (TIED WITH CARTER)
BAGARUS, STEPHEN (NOTRE DAME) - BACK - 1945-46, 48 WASHINGTON
     REDSKINS; 1947 LOS ANGELES RAMS
BAGBY, HERMAN (ARKANSAS) - BACK - 1926 BROOKLYN LIONS; 1926 KANSAS
     CITY COWBOYS; 1927 CLEVELAND BULLDOGS
BAGDON, EDWARD (MICHIGAN STATE) - GUARD - 1950-51 CHICAGO CARDINALS;
     1952 WASHINGTON REDSKINS
BAGGETT, WILLIAM (LSU) - BACK - 1952 DALLAS TEXANS
BAHAN, LEONARD (NOTRE DAME) - BACK - 1923 CLEVELAND INDIANS
BAHNSEN, KENNETH (NORTH TEXAS STATE) - BACK - 1953 SAN FRANCISCO 49ERS
BAILEY, BYRON (WASHINGTON STATE) - BACK - 1952-53 DETROIT LIONS; 1953
     GREEN BAY PACKERS
BAILEY, CLARON (UTAH) - BACK - 1964-65 ST. LOUIS CARDINALS
BAILEY, EDGAR (DUKE) - END - 1940-41 BROOKLYN DODGERS
BAILEY, GEORGE THOMAS (FLORIDA STATE) - BACK - 1971-74 PHILADELPHIA
     EAGLES (NFC)
BAILEY, HOWARD (TENNESSEE) - TACKLE - 1935 PHILADELPHIA EAGLES
BAILEY, JAMES (KANSAS) - TACKLE - 1970-74 BALTIMORE COLTS (AFC)
BAILEY, JAMES (WEST VIRGINIA STATE) - GUARD - 1949 CHICAGO HORNETS
     (AAFC)
BAILEY, LARRY (PACIFIC) - TACKLE - 1974 ATLANTA FALCONS (NFC)
BAILEY, RUSSELL (WEST VIRGINIA) - CENTER - 1920-21 AKRON PROS
BAILEY, SAMUEL (GEORGIA) - END - 1946 BOSTON YANKS
BAILEY, WILLIAM (CINCINNATI) - BACK - 1967 BUFFALO BILLS (AFL); 1969
     BOSTON PATRIOTS (AFL)
BAIRD, WILLIAM (SAN FRANCISCO STATE) - BACK - 1963-69 NEW YORK JETS
     (AFL)
BAISI, ALBERT (WEST VIRGINIA) - GUARD - 1940-41, 46 CHICAGO BEARS;
     1947 PHILADELPHIA EAGLES
BAKER, ARTHUR (SYRACUSE) - BACK - 1961-62 BUFFALO BILLS (AFL)
BAKER, CHARLES (SMU) - GUARD - 1936 BROOKLYN TIGERS (AFL)

BAKER, CONWAY (CENTENARY) - TACKLE - 1936-43, 45 CHICAGO CARDINALS;
    1944 CARD-PITT
BAKER, DAVID (OKLAHOMA) - BACK - 1959-61 SAN FRANCISCO 49ERS; 1960
    INTERCEPTION LEADER (TIED WITH NORTON)
BAKER, EDWARD (LAFAYETTE) - QBACK - 1972 HOUSTON OILERS (AFC)
BAKER, FRANK (NORTHWESTERN) - END - 1931 GREEN BAY PACKERS
BAKER, JOHN (MISSISSIPPI STATE) - LB - 1963-66 HOUSTON OILERS (AFL);
    1967 SAN DIEGO CHARGERS (AFL)
BAKER, JOHN (NORTH CAROLINA COLLEGE) - END - 1958-61 LOS ANGELES
    RAMS; 1962 PHILADELPHIA EAGLES; 1963-67 PITTSBURGH STEELERS;
    1968 DETROIT LIONS
BAKER, JOHN (NORFOLK STATE) - END - 1970 NEW YORK GIANTS (NFC)
BAKER, JON (CALIFORNIA) - GUARD - 1949-52 NEW YORK GIANTS
BAKER, LAWRENCE (BOWLING GREEN) - TACKLE - 1960 NEW YORK TITANS (AFL)
BAKER, LORIS "SAM" (OREGON STATE) - LB - 1953, 56-59 WASHINGTON
    REDSKINS; 1960-61 CLEVELAND BROWNS; 1962-63 DALLAS COWBOYS;
    1964-69 PHILADELPHIA EAGLES; 1956, 58 PUNTING LEADER; 1957
    SCORING LEADER; (TIED WITH GROZA)
BAKER, MELVIN (TEXAS SOUTHERN) - END - 1974 MIAMI DOLPHINS (AFC)
BAKER, RALPH (PENN STATE) - LB - 1964-69 NEW YORK JETS (AFL); 1970-74
    NEW YORK JETS (AFC)
BAKER, ROY (USC) - QBACK - 1926 NEW YORK YANKEES (AFL); 1927 NEW YORK
    YANKEES; 1928-29 GREEN BAY PACKERS; 1929-30 CHICAGO CARDINALS;
    1931 STATEN ISLAND STAPLETONS
BAKER, TERRY (OREGON STATE) - BACK - 1963-65 LOS ANGELES RAMS
BAKER, VERNON "TONY" (IOWA STATE) - BACK - 1968-69 NEW ORLEANS
    SAINTS; 1970-71 NEW ORLEANS SAINTS (NFC); 1971-72 PHILADELPHIA
    EAGLES (NFC); 1973-74 LOS ANGELES RAMS (NFC)
BAKKEN, JAMES (WISCONSIN) - KICKER - 1962-69 ST. LOUIS CARDINALS;
    1970-74 ST. LOUIS CARDINALS (NFC); 1964, 67 FIELD GOAL LEADER;
    1967 SCORING LEADER
BALATTI, EDWARD - END - 1946-48 SAN FRANCISCO 49ERS (AAFC); 1948 NEW
    YORK YANKEES (AAFC); 1948 BUFFALO BILLS (AAFC)
BALAZ, FRANK (IOWA) - BACK - 1939-41 GREEN BAY PACKERS; 1941, 45
    CHICAGO CARDINALS
BALDACCI, LOUIS (MICHIGAN) - BACK - 1956 PITTSBURGH STEELERS
BALDWIN, ALTON (ARKANSAS) - END - 1947-49 BUFFALO BILLS (AAFC); 1950
    GREEN BAY PACKERS
BALDWIN, BURR (UCLA) - END - 1947-49 LOS ANGELES DONS (AAFC)
BALDWIN, CLIFFORD - BACK - 1921 MUNCIE FLYERS
BALDWIN, GEORGE (VIRGINIA) - END - 1925 CLEVELAND BULLDOGS; 1926
    BROOKLYN HORSEMEN (AFL)
BALDWIN, JOHN (CENTENARY) - CENTER - 1946-47 NEW YORK YANKEES (AAFC);
    1947 SAN FRANCISCO 49ERS (AAFC); 1948 BUFFALO BILLS (AAFC)
BALDWIN, ROBERT (CLEMSON) - BACK - 1966 BALTIMORE COLTS
BALESTRERI, JOHN (EARLHAM) - END - 1940 CINCINNATI BENGALS (AFL);
    1940 COLUMBUS BULLIES (AFL)
BALL, LARRY (LOUISVILLE) - LB - 1972-74 MIAMI DOLPHINS (AFC)
BALL, SAMUEL (KENTUCKY) - TACKLE - 1966-69 BALTIMORE COLTS; 1970
    BALTIMORE COLTS (AFC)
BALLMAN, GARY (MICHIGAN STATE) - BACK, END - 1962-66 PITTSBURGH
    STEELERS; 1967-69 PHILADELPHIA EAGLES; 1970-72 PHILADELPHIA
    EAGLES (NFC); 1973 NEW YORK GIANTS (NFC); 1973 MINNESOTA VIKINGS
    (NFC)
BALLOU, MIKEL (UCLA) - LB - 1970 BOSTON PATRIOTS (AFC)
BALOG, ROBERT (DENVER) - CENTER - 1949-50 PITTSBURGH STEELERS
BALTZELL, VICTOR (SOUTHWESTERN KANSAS) - BACK - 1935 BOSTON REDSKINS;
    1936 NEW YORK YANKS (AFL)
BANAS, STEVEN (NOTRE DAME) - QBACK - 1935 DETROIT LIONS; 1935
    PHILADELPHIA EAGLES; 1940 BUFFALO INDIANS (AFL); 1941 BUFFALO
    TIGERS (AFL)
BANASZAK, PETER (MIAMI) - BACK - 1966-69 OAKLAND RAIDERS (AFL);
    1970-74 OAKLAND RAIDERS (AFC)
BANASZEK, CASMIR (NORTHWESTERN) - TACKLE - 1968-69 SAN FRANCISCO
    49ERS; 1970-74 SAN FRANCISCO 49ERS (NFC)
BANCROFT, HUGH (ALFRED) - END - 1923 ROCHESTER JEFFERSONS
BANDUCCI, BRUNO (STANFORD) - GUARD - 1944-45 PHILADELPHIA EAGLES;
    1946-49 SAN FRANCISCO 49ERS (AAFC); 1950-54 SAN FRANCISCO 49ERS
BANDURA, JOHN (SOUTHWESTERN LOUISIANA) - END - 1943 BROOKLYN DODGERS
BANDY, DONALD (TULSA) - GUARD - 1967-68 WASHINGTON REDSKINS
BANET, HERBERT (MANCHESTER) - BACK - 1937 GREEN BAY PACKERS

BANFIELD, JAMES (OKLAHOMA STATE) - BACK - 1960-63, 65 HOUSTON OILERS
    (AFL)
BANGS, BENTON (WASHINGTON STATE) - BACK - 1926 LOS ANGELES BUCCANEERS
BANJAVCIC, EMIL (ARIZONA) - BACK - 1942 DETROIT LIONS
BANKS, ESTES (COLORADO) - BACK - 1967 OAKLAND RAIDERS (AFL); 1968
    CINCINNATI BENGALS (AFL)
BANKS, THOMAS (AUBURN) - CENTER, GUARD - 1971-74 ST. LOUIS CARDINALS
    (NFC)
BANKS, WILLIE (ALCORN A&M) - GUARD - 1968-69 WASHINGTON REDSKINS;
    1970 NEW YORK GIANTS (NFC); 1973 NEW ENGLAND PATRIOTS (AFC)
BANKSTON, WARREN (TULANE) - BACK, END - 1969 PITTSBURGH STEELERS;
    1970-72 PITTSBURGH STEELERS (AFC); 1973-74 OAKLAND RAIDERS (AFC)
BANNON, BRUCE (PENN STATE) - LB - 1973-74 MIAMI DOLPHINS (AFC)
BANONIS, VINCENT (DETROIT) - CENTER - 1942, 46-50 CHICAGO CARDINALS;
    1944 CARD-PITT; 1951-53 DETROIT LIONS
BANSAVAGE, ALBERT (USC) - LB - 1960 LOS ANGELES CHARGERS (AFL); 1961
    OAKLAND RAIDERS (AFL)
BANTA, HERBERT JACK (USC) - BACK - 1941 WASHINGTON REDSKINS; 1941,
    44-45 PHILADELPHIA EAGLES; 1946-48 LOS ANGELES RAMS
BARBEE, JOSEPH (KENT STATE) - TACKLE - 1960 OAKLAND RAIDERS (AFL)
BARBER, BENJAMIN (VIRGINIA MILITARY INST.) - TACKLE - 1925 BUFFALO
    BISONS
BARBER, ERNEST (SAN FRANCISCO UNIV.) - CENTER - 1945 WASHINGTON
    REDSKINS
BARBER, JAMES (SAN FRANCISCO UNIV.) - TACKLE - 1935-36 BOSTON
    REDSKINS; 1937-41 WASHINGTON REDSKINS
BARBER, MARK (SOUTH DAKOTA STATE) - BACK - 1937 CLEVELAND RAMS
BARBER, RUDOLPH (BETHUNE-COOKMAN) - LB - 1968 MIAMI DOLPHINS (AFL)
BARBER, STEWART (PENN STATE) - TACKLE - 1961-69 BUFFALO BILLS (AFL)
BARBOLAK, PETER (PURDUE) - TACKLE - 1949 PITTSBURGH STEELERS
BARBOUR, ELMER (WAKE FOREST) - BACK - 1945 NEW YORK GIANTS
BARDES, HOWARD (NORTH CAROLINA) - QBACK - 1937 PITTSBURGH AMERICANS
    (AFL)
BAREFOOT, KENNETH (VPI) - END - 1968 WASHINGTON REDSKINS
BARFIELD, KENNETH (MISSISSIPPI) - GUARD - 1954 WASHINGTON REDSKINS
BARIL, ADRIAN (ST. THOMAS OF MINNESOTA) - TACKLE - 1923-24
    MINNEAPOLIS MARINES; 1925 MILWAUKEE BADGERS
BARISICH, CARL (PRINCETON) - TACKLE - 1973-74 CLEVELAND BROWNS (AFC)
BARKER, EDWARD (WASHINGTON STATE) - END - 1953 PITTSBURGH STEELERS;
    1954 WASHINGTON REDSKINS
BARKER, HUBERT (ARKANSAS) - BACK - 1943-45 NEW YORK GIANTS
BARKER, RICHARD (IOWA STATE) - GUARD - 1921 CHICAGO STALEYS; 1921
    ROCK ISLAND INDEPENDENTS
BARKMAN, RALPH (SCHUYLKILL) - QBACK - 1929 ORANGE TORNADOS; 1930
    NEWARK TORNADOS
BARKUM, JEROME (JACKSON STATE) - END - 1972-74 NEW YORK JETS (AFC)
BARLE, LOUIS - QBACK - 1938 DETROIT LIONS; 1939 CLEVELAND RAMS
BARNA, GEORGE (HOBART) - END - 1929 FRANKFORD YELLOWJACKETS
BARNARD, CHARLES (CENTRAL OKLAHOMA STATE) - END - 1938 NEW YORK GIANTS
BARNES, AL (NEW MEXICO STATE) - END - 1972-73 DETROIT LIONS (NFC)
BARNES, BENJAMIN (STANFORD) - BACK - 1972-74 DALLAS COWBOYS (NFC)
BARNES, BRUCE (UCLA) - KICKER - 1973-74 NEW ENGLAND PATRIOTS (AFC)
BARNES, CHARLES (NORTHEAST LOUISIANA STATE) - END - 1961 DALLAS
    TEXANS (AFL)
BARNES, EMERY (OREGON) - END - 1956 GREEN BAY PACKERS
BARNES, ERICH (PURDUE) - BACK - 1958-60 CHICAGO BEARS; 1961-64 NEW
    YORK GIANTS; 1965-69 CLEVELAND BROWNS; 1970-71 CLEVELAND BROWNS
    (AFC)
BARNES, ERNEST (NORTH CAROLINA COLLEGE) - GUARD - 1960 NEW YORK
    TITANS (AFL); 1961-62 SAN DIEGO CHARGERS (AFL); 1963-64 DENVER
    BRONCOS (AFL)
BARNES, GARY (CLEMSON) - END - 1962 GREEN BAY PACKERS; 1963 DALLAS
    COWBOYS; 1964 CHICAGO BEARS; 1966-67 ATLANTA FALCONS
BARNES, JOSEPH (TEXAS TECH) - BACK - 1974 CHICAGO BEARS (NFC)
BARNES, LAWRENCE (COLORADO A&M) - BACK - 1957 SAN FRANCISCO 49ERS;
    1960 OAKLAND RAIDERS (AFL)
BARNES, MICHAEL (MIAMI) - END - 1973-74 BALTIMORE COLTS (AFC)
BARNES, MICHAEL HOWARD (ARLINGTON STATE) - BACK - 1967-68 ST. LOUIS
    CARDINALS

BARNES, PETER (SOUTHERN) - LB - 1967-68 HOUSTON OILERS (AFL); 1969
     SAN DIEGO CHARGERS (AFL); 1970-72 SAN DIEGO CHARGERS (AFC);
     1973-74 ST. LOUIS CARDINALS (NFC)
BARNES, RODRIGO (RICE) - LB - 1973-74 DALLAS COWBOYS (NFC); 1974 NEW
     ENGLAND PATRIOTS (AFC)
BARNES, SHERMAN (BAYLOR) - END - 1940 MILWAUKEE CHIEFS (AFL); 1941
     BUFFALO TIGERS (AFL)
BARNES, WALTER (LSU) - GUARD - 1948-51 PHILADELPHIA EAGLES
BARNES, WALTER (NEBRASKA) - TACKLE, END - 1966-68 WASHINGTON
     REDSKINS; 1969 DENVER BRONCOS (AFL); 1970-71 DENVER BRONCOS (AFC)
BARNES, WILLIAM (WAKE FOREST) - BACK - 1957-61 PHILADELPHIA EAGLES;
     1962-63 WASHINGTON REDSKINS; 1965-66 MINNESOTA VIKINGS
BARNETT, SOLON (BAYLOR) - TACKLE - 1945-46 GREEN BAY PACKERS
BARNETT, JERRY STEPHEN (OREGON) - TACKLE - 1963 CHICAGO BEARS; 1964
     WASHINGTON REDSKINS
BARNETT, THOMAS (PURDUE) - BACK - 1959-60 PITTSBURGH STEELERS
BARNEY, EPPIE (IOWA STATE) - BACK, END - 1967-68 CLEVELAND BROWNS
BARNEY, LEMUEL (JACKSON STATE) - BACK, KICKER - 1967-69 DETROIT
     LIONS; 1970-74 DETROIT LIONS (NFC); 1967 INTERCEPTION LEADER;
     (TIED WITH WHITSELL)
BARNHART, DANIEL (CENTENARY) - BACK - 1934 PHILADELPHIA EAGLES; 1937
     LOS ANGELES BULLDOGS (AFL)
BARNI, ROY (SAN FRANCISCO) - BACK - 1952-53 CHICAGO CARDINALS;
     1954-55 PHILADELPHIA EAGLES; 1955-56 WASHINGTON REDSKINS
BARNIKOW, EDWARD - BACK - 1926 HARTFORD BLUES
BARNUM, LEONARD (WEST VIRGINIA WESLEYAN) - BACK - 1938-40 NEW YORK
     GIANTS; 1941-42 PHILADELPHIA EAGLES
BARNUM, ROBERT (WEST VIRGINIA) - BACK - 1926 COLUMBUS TIGERS
BARR, TERRY (MICHIGAN) - BACK - 1957-65 DETROIT LIONS
BARR, WALLACE (WISCONSIN) - BACK - 1923-24, 26 RACINE LEGION; 1925
     MILWAUKEE BADGERS
BARRABEE, ROBERT (NEW YORK UNIV.) - END - 1931 STATEN ISLAND
     STAPELTONS
BARRAGER, NATHAN (USC) - CENTER - 1930 MINNEAPOLIS REDJACKETS;
     1930-31 FRANKFORD YELLOWJACKETS; 1931-32, 34-35 GREEN BAY PACKERS
BARREL (CARLISLE) - CENTER - 1922-23 OORANG INDIANS
BARRETT, CHARLES (CORNELL) - BACK - 1919 MASSILLON TIGERS
BARRETT, EMMETT (PORTLAND) - CENTER - 1942 NEW YORK GIANTS
BARRETT, JAN (FRESNO STATE) - END - 1963 GREEN BAY PACKERS; 1963-64
     OAKLAND RAIDERS (AFL)
BARRETT, JEAN (TULSA) - TACKLE - 1973-74 SAN FRANCISCO 49ERS (NFC)
BARRETT, JEFFREY (LSU) - END - 1936-38 BROOKLYN DODGERS
BARRETT, JOHN (DETROIT) - TACKLE - 1924-25 AKRON PROS; 1926 DETROIT
     PANTHERS; 1927 POTTSVILLE MAROONS; 1928 DETROIT WOLVERINES
BARRETT, JOHN (WASHINGTON&LEE) - BACK - 1919, 22-23 HAMMOND PROS;
     1920 CHICAGO TIGERS
BARRETT, ROBERT (BALDWIN-WALLACE) - END - 1960 BUFFALO BILLS (AFL)
BARRINGTON, GEORGE THOMAS (OHIO STATE) - BACK - 1966 WASHINGTON
     REDSKINS; 1967-69 NEW ORLEANS SAINTS; 1970 NEW ORLEANS SAINTS
     (NFC)
BARRON, JAMES (GEORGETOWN) - TACKLE - 1919 CANTON BULLDOGS; 1921
     ROCHESTER JEFFERSONS
BARRY, ALLEN (USC) - GUARD - 1954, 57 GREEN BAY PACKERS; 1958-59 NEW
     YORK GIANTS; 1960 LOS ANGELES CHARGERS (AFL)
BARRY, FRED (BOSTON UNIV.) - BACK - 1970 PITTSBURGH STEELERS (AFC)
BARRY, NORMAN (NOTRE DAME) - QBACK - 1921 CHICAGO CARDINALS; 1921
     GREEN BAY PACKERS
BARRY, ODELL (FINDLAY) - END - 1964-65 DENVER BRONCOS (AFL)
BARRY, PAUL (TULSA) - BACK - 1950, 52 LOS ANGELES RAMS; 1953
     WASHINGTON REDSKINS; 1954 CHICAGO CARDINALS
BARSHA, JOHN (SYRACUSE) - BACK - 1919-20 ROCHESTER JEFFERSONS; 1920
     HAMMOND PROS
BARTHOLOMEW, SAMUEL (TENNESSEE) - BACK - 1941 PHILADELPHIA EAGLES
BARTLETT, EARL (CENTRE) - BACK - 1936-37 BOSTON SHAMROCKS (AFL); 1939
     PITTSBURGH STEELERS
BARTON, GREGORY (LONG BEACH STATE & TULSA) - QBACK - 1969 DETROIT
     LIONS
BARTON, DONALD (TEXAS) - BACK - 1953 GREEN BAY PACKERS
BARTON, JAMES (MARSHALL) - CENTER - 1960 DALLAS TEXANS (AFL); 1961-62
     DENVER BRONCOS (AFL)
BARTOS, HENRY (NORTH CAROLINA) - GUARD - 1938 WASHINGTON REDSKINS

BARTOS, JOSEPH (ANNAPOLIS) - BACK - 1950 WASHINGTON REDSKINS
BARWEGAN, RICHARD (PURDUE) - GUARD - 1947 NEW YORK YANKEES (AAFC);
    1948-49 BALTIMORE COLTS (AAFC); 1950-52 CHICAGO BEARS; 1953-54
    BALTIMORE COLTS
BARZILAUSKAS, CARL (INDIANA) - TACKLE - 1974 NEW YORK JETS (AFC)
BARZILAUSKAS, FRANCIS (YALE) - GUARD - 1947-48 BOSTON YANKS; 1949 NEW
    YORK BULLDOGS; 1951 NEW YORK GIANTS
BASCA, MICHAEL (VILLANOVA) - BACK - 1941 PHILADELPHIA EAGLES
BASING, MYRTON (LAWRENCE) - BACK - 1923-27 GREEN BAY PACKERS
BASINGER, MIKE (CALIFORNIA-RIVERSIDE) - TACKLE - 1974 GREEN BAY
    PACKERS (NFC)
BASRAK, MICHAEL (DUQUESNE) - CENTER - 1937-38 PITTSBURGH PIRATES
BASS, GLENN (EAST CAROLINA) - END - 1961-66 BUFFALO BILLS (AFL);
    1967-68 HOUSTON OILERS (AFL)
BASS, MICHAEL (MICHIGAN) - BACK - 1967 DETROIT LIONS; 1969 WASHINGTON
    REDSKINS; 1970-74 WASHINGTON REDSKINS (NFC)
BASS, NORMAN (PACIFIC) - BACK - 1964 DENVER BRONCOS (AFL)
BASS, RICHARD (PACIFIC) - BACK - 1960-69 LOS ANGELES RAMS
BASS, WILLIAM (NEVADA) - BACK - 1947 CHICAGO ROCKETS (AAFC)
BASSETT, HENRY (NEBRASKA) - TACKLE - 1924 KANSAS CITY COWBOYS
BASSETT, MAURICE (LANGSTON) - BACK - 1954-56 CLEVELAND BROWNS
BASSI, RICHARD (SANTA CLARA) - GUARD - 1937 WASHINGTON REDSKINS;
    1938-39 CHICAGO BEARS; 1940 PHILADELPHIA EAGLES; 1941 PITTSBURGH
    STEELERS; 1946-47 SAN FRANCISCO 49ERS (AAFC)
BASSMAN, HERMAN (URSINUS) - BACK - 1936 PHILADELPHIA EAGLES
BASTON, ALBERT (MINNESOTA) - END - 1919 HAMMOND PROS; 1920 BUFFALO
    ALL-AMERICANS; 1920 CLEVELAND PANTHERS; 1921 CLEVELAND INDIANS
BATCHELLOR, DONALD (GROVE CITY) - TACKLE - 1922 CANTON BULLDOGS; 1923
    TOLEDO MAROONS
BATEMAN, MARVIN (UTAH) - LB - 1972-74 DALLAS COWBOYS (NFC); 1974
    BUFFALO BILLS (AFC)
BATES, THEODORE (OREGON STATE) - LB - 1959 CHICAGO CARDINALS; 1960-62
    ST. LOUIS CARDINALS; 1963 NEW YORK JETS (AFL)
BATINSKI, STANLEY (TEMPLE) - GUARD - 1941, 43-47 DETROIT LIONS; 1948
    BOSTON YANKS; 1949 NEW YORK BULLDOGS
BATORSKI, JOHN (COLGATE) - END - 1946 BUFFALO BISONS (AAFC)
BATTEN, PATRICK (HARDIN-SIMMONS) - BACK - 1964 DETROIT LIONS
BATTLE, JAMES (SOUTHERN) - TACKLE - 1966 CLEVELAND BROWNS
BATTLE, JAMES (SOUTHERN ILLINOIS) - GUARD - 1963 MINNESOTA VIKINGS
BATTLE, MICHAEL (USC) - BACK - 1969 NEW YORK JETS (AFL); 1970 NEW
    YORK JETS (AFC)
BATTLES, CLIFFORD (WEST VIRGINIA WESLEYAN) - BACK - 1932 BOSTON
    BRAVES; 1933-36 BOSTON REDSKINS; 1937 WASHINGTON REDSKINS; 1932,
    37 RUSHING LEADER; 1968 HALL OF FAME
BAUER, HERBERT (BALDWIN-WALLACE) - TACKLE - 1925 CLEVELAND BULLDOGS
BAUER, JOHN (ILLINOIS) - GUARD - 1954 NEW YORK GIANTS
BAUGH, SAMUEL (TCU) - QBACK - 1937-52 WASHINGTON REDSKINS; 1937, 40,
    43, 45, 47, 49 PASSING LEADER; (1945 TIED WITH LUCKMAN); 1940-43
    PUNTING LEADER; 1943 INTERCEPTION LEADER; 1963 HALL OF FAME
BAUGHAN, MAXIE (GEORGIA TECH) - LB - 1960-65 PHILADELPHIA EAGLES;
    1966-69 LOS ANGELES RAMS; 1970 LOS ANGELES RAMS (NFC); 1974
    WASHINGTON REDSKINS (NFC)
BAUJAN, HARRY (NOTRE DAME) - END - 1919 MASSILLON TIGERS; 1920
    CLEVELAND PANTHERS; 1921 CLEVELAND INDIANS
BAUMANN, ALFRED (NORTHWESTERN) - TACKLE - 1947 CHICAGO ROCKETS
    (AAFC); 1947 PHILADELPHIA EAGLES; 1948-50 CHICAGO BEARS
BAUMGARDNER, MAX (TEXAS) - END - 1948 DETROIT LIONS
BAUMGARTNER, STEVEN (PURDUE) - END - 1973-74 NEW ORLEANS SAINTS (NFC)
BAUMGARTNER, WILLIAM (MINNESOTA) - END - 1947 BALTIMORE COLTS (AAFC)
BAUSCH, FRANK (KANSAS) - CENTER - 1934-36 BOSTON REDSKINS; 1937-40
    CHICAGO BEARS; 1941 PHILADELPHIA EAGLES
BAUSCH, JAMES (KANSAS) - BACK - 1933 CINCINNATI REDS; 1933 CHICAGO
    CARDINALS
BAWEL, EDWARD (EVANSVILLE) - BACK - 1952, 55-56 PHILADELPHIA EAGLES
BAXTER, ERNEST (CENTRE) - BACK - 1923 RACINE LEGION; 1924 KENOSHA
    MAROONS
BAXTER, JAMES - END - 1919 TOLEDO MAROONS
BAXTER, LLOYD (SMU) - CENTER - 1948 GREEN BAY PACKERS
BAYLESS, THOMAS (PURDUE) - GUARD - 1970 NEW YORK JETS (AFC)
BAYLEY, JOHN (SYRACUSE) - TACKLE - 1927 NEW YORK YANKEES
BAYLOR, RAYMOND (TEXAS SOUTHERN) - END - 1974 SAN DIEGO CHARGERS (AFC)

BAYNHAM, GORDON CRAIG (GEORGIA TECH) - BACK - 1967-69 DALLAS COWBOYS;
    1970 CHICAGO BEARS (NFC); 1972 ST. LOUIS CARDINALS (NFC)
BAYSINGER, REEVES (SYRACUSE) - TACKLE - 1924 ROCHESTER JEFFERSONS
BAZE, WINFORD (TEXAS TECH) - BACK - 1937 PHILADELPHIA EAGLES
BEACH, FREDERICK (CALIFORNIA) - GUARD - 1926 LOS ANGELES BUCCANEERS
BEACH, WALTER (MICHIGAN CENTRAL) - BACK - 1960-61 BOSTON PATRIOTS
    (AFL); 1963-66 CLEVELAND BROWNS
BEAL, NORMAN (MISSOURI) - BACK - 1962 ST. LOUIS CARDINALS
BEALS, ALYN (SANTA CLARA) - END - 1946-49 SAN FRANCISCO 49ERS (AAFC);
    1950-51 SAN FRANCISCO 49ERS
BEAMER, TIM (JOHNSON C. SMITH) - BACK - 1971 BUFFALO BILLS (AFC)
BEAMS, BYRON (NOTRE DAME) - TACKLE - 1959-60 PITTSBURGH STEELERS;
    1961 HOUSTON OILERS (AFL)
BEARD, EDWARD (TENNESSEE) - LB - 1965-69 SAN FRANCISCO 49ERS; 1970-72
    SAN FRANCISCO 49ERS (NFC)
BEARD, THOMAS (MICHIGAN STATE) - CENTER - 1972 BUFFALO BILLS (AFC)
BEASEY, JOHN - BACK - 1924 GREEN BAY PACKERS
BEASLEY, JOHN (CALIFORNIA) - END - 1967-69 MINNESOTA VIKINGS; 1970,
    72-73 MINNESOTA VIKINGS (NFC); 1973-74 NEW ORLEANS SAINTS (NFC)
BEASLEY, JOHN (FARIHAM) - GUARD - 1923 DAYTON TRIANGLES
BEASLEY, TERRY (AUBURN) - END - 1972, 74 SAN FRANCISCO 49ERS (NFC)
BEATHARD, PETER (USC) - QBACK - 1964-67 KANSAS CITY CHIEFS (AFL);
    1967-69 HOUSTON OILERS (AFL); 1970-71 ST. LOUIS CARDINALS (NFC);
    1972 LOS ANGELES RAMS (NFC); 1973 KANSAS CITY CHIEFS (AFC)
BEATTIE, ROBERT (PRINCETON) - TACKLE - 1926 PHILADELPHIA QUAKERS
    (AFL); 1927 NEW YORK YANKEES; 1929 ORANGE TORNADOS; 1930 NEWARK
    TORNADOS
BEATTY, CHARLES (NORTH TEXAS STATE) - BACK - 1969 PITTSBURGH
    STEELERS; 1970-72 PITTSBURGH STEELERS (AFC); 1972 ST. LOUIS
    CARDINALS (NFC)
BEATTY, EDWARD (MISSISSIPPI) - CENTER - 1955-56 SAN FRANCISCO 49ERS;
    1957-61 PITTSBURGH STEELERS; 1961 WASHINGTON REDSKINS
BEATTY, HOMER (USC) - BACK - 1937 LOS ANGELES BULLDOGS (AFL)
BEAUCHAMP, ALFRED (SOUTHERN) - LB - 1968-69 CINCINNATI BENGALS (AFL);
    1970-74 CINCINNATI BENGALS (AFC)
BEAUCHAMP, JOSEPH (IOWA STATE) - BACK - 1966-69 SAN DIEGO CHARGERS
    (AFL); 1970-74 SAN DIEGO CHARGERS (AFC)
BEAUREGARD, RICHARD (GONZAGA) - BACK - 1940 MILWAUKEE CHIEFS (AFL)
BEAVER, JAMES (FLORIDA) - TACKLE - 1962 PHILADELPHIA EAGLES
BEBAN, GARY (UCLA) - QBACK, END - 1968-69 WASHINGTON REDSKINS
BEBOUT, NICK (WYOMING) - TACKLE - 1973-74 ATLANTA FALCONS (NFC)
BECHTOL, HUBERT (TEXAS) - END - 1947-49 BALTIMORE COLTS (AAFC)
BECK, BRADEN (STANFORD) - LB - 1971 HOUSTON OILERS (AFC)
BECK, CARL (WEST VIRGINIA) - BACK - 1921 BUFFALO ALL-AMERICANS; 1925
    POTTSVILLE MAROONS
BECK, CLARENCE (PENN STATE) - TACKLE - 1925 POTTSVILLE MAROONS
BECK, KENNETH (TEXAS A&M) - TACKLE - 1959-60 GREEN BAY PACKERS
BECK, MARTIN - BACK - 1921-22, 24, 26 AKRON PROS
BECK, RAYMOND (GEORGIA TECH) - GUARD - 1952, 55-57 NEW YORK GIANTS
BECKER, JOHN (DENISON) - TACKLE - 1926-29 DAYTON TRIANGLES
BECKER, WAYLAND (MARQUETTE) - END - 1934 CHICAGO BEARS; 1934-35
    BROOKLYN DODGERS; 1936-38 GREEN BAY PACKERS; 1939 PITTSBURGH
    STEELERS; 1941 COLUMBUS BULLIES (AFL)
BECKER - END - 1919 WHEELING
BECKETT, WARREN (STEVENS POINT-WISCONSIN) - BACK - 1940 MILWAUKEE
    CHIEFS (AFL)
BECKLEY, ARTHUR (MICHIGAN STATE) - BACK - 1926 DAYTON TRIANGLES
BECKMAN, THOMAS (MICHIGAN) - END - 1972 ST. LOUIS CARDINALS (NFC)
BECKWITH - GUARD - 1919 COLUMBUS PANHANDLES
BEDFORD, WILLIAM (SMU) - END - 1925 ROCHESTER JEFFERSONS
BEDNAR, ALBERT (LAFAYETTE) - GUARD - 1924-25 FRANKFORD YELLOWJACKETS;
    1925-26 NEW YORK GIANTS
BEDNARIK, CHARLES (PENNSYLVANIA) - CENTER - 1949-62 PHILADELPHIA
    EAGLES; 1967 HALL OF FAME
BEDORE, THOMAS - GUARD - 1944 WASHINGTON REDSKINS
BEDSOLE, HAROLD (USC) - END - 1964-66 MINNESOTA VIKINGS
BEEBE, KEITH (OCCIDENTAL) - BACK - 1944 NEW YORK GIANTS
BEEKLEY, FERRIS E. (MIAMI-OHIO) - GUARD - 1921 CINCINNATI CELTS
BEEMING - GUARD - 1924 DAYTON TRIANGLES

BEER, THOMAS (HOUSTON) - END, GUARD - 1967-69 DENVER BRONCOS (AFL);
    1970 BOSTON PATRIOTS (AFC); 1971-72 NEW ENGLAND PATRIOTS (AFC)
BEGELMAN, JOHN (NEW YORK UNIV.) - BACK - 1936 BROOKLYN TIGERS (AFL)
BEHAN, CHARLES (NORTHERN ILLINOIS) - END - 1942 DETROIT LIONS
BEHAN, LEE (STEVENS POINT-WISCONSIN) - END - 1940 MILWAUKEE CHIEFS
    (AFL); 1940 BOSTON BEARS (AFL)
BEHM, NORTON (IOWA STATE) - BACK - 1926 CLEVELAND PANTHERS (AFL)
BEHMAN, RUSSELL (DICKINSON) - TACKLE - 1924-25, 27-31 FRANKFORD
    YELLOWJACKETS; 1926 PHILADELPHIA QUAKERS (AFL)
BEHRMAN, DAVID (MICHIGAN STATE) - TACKLE - 1963, 65 BUFFALO BILLS
    (AFL); 1967 DENVER BRONCOS (AFL)
BEIER, THOMAS (MIAMI) - BACK - 1967, 69 MIAMI DOLPHINS (AFL)
BEIL, LAWRENCE (PORTLAND) - TACKLE - 1948 NEW YORK GIANTS
BEINOR, J. EDWARD (NOTRE DAME) - TACKLE - 1940-41 CHICAGO CARDINALS;
    1941-42 WASHINGTON REDSKINS
BEIRNE, JAMES (PURDUE) - END - 1968-69 HOUSTON OILERS (AFL); 1970-73
    HOUSTON OILERS (AFC); 1974 SAN DIEGO CHARGERS (AFC)
BEISLER, RANDALL (INDIANA) - END, TACKLE, GUARD - 1966-68
    PHILADELPHIA EAGLES; 1969 SAN FRANCISCO 49ERS; 1970-74 SAN
    FRANCISCO 49ERS (NFC)
BELANICH, WILLIAM (DAYTON) - TACKLE - 1927-29 DAYTON TRIANGLES
BELDEN, CHARLES - BACK - 1927 DULUTH ESKIMOS; 1929-31 CHICAGO
    CARDINALS
BELDEN, ROBERT (NOTRE DAME) - QBACK - 1969 DALLAS COWBOYS; 1970
    DALLAS COWBOYS (NFC)
BELDING, LESTER (IOWA) - END - 1925 ROCK ISLAND INDEPENDENTS
BELICHICK, STEPHEN (WESTERN RESERVE) - BACK - 1941 DETROIT LIONS
BELK, WILLIAM (MARYLAND STATE) - END, TACKLE - 1968-69 SAN FRANCISCO
    49ERS; 1970-74 SAN FRANCISCO 49ERS (NFC)
BELL, CARLOS (HOUSTON) - BACK - 1971 NEW ORLEANS SAINTS (NFC)
BELL, EDWARD (IDAHO STATE) - END - 1970-74 NEW YORK JETS (AFC)
BELL, EDWARD (INDIANA) - GUARD - 1946 MIAMI SEAHAWKS (AAFC); 1947-49
    GREEN BAY PACKERS
BELL, EDWARD (PENNSYLVANIA) - BACK - 1955-58 PHILADELPHIA EAGLES;
    1960 NEW YORK TITANS (AFL)
BELL, HENRY - BACK - 1960 DENVER BRONCOS (AFL)
BELL, KAY (WASHINGTON STATE) - TACKLE - 1937 CHICAGO BEARS; 1940-41
    COLUMBUS BULLIES (AFL); 1942 NEW YORK GIANTS
BELL, ROBERT FRANCIS (CINCINNATI) - TACKLE - 1971-73 DETROIT LIONS
    (NFC); 1974 ST. LOUIS CARDINALS (NFC)
BELL, ROBERT LEE (MINNESOTA) - LB - 1963-69 KANSAS CITY CHIEFS (AFL);
    1970-74 KANSAS CITY CHIEFS (AFC)
BELL, WILLIAM (KANSAS) - KICKER - 1971-72 ATLANTA FALCONS (NFC); 1973
    NEW ENGLAND PATRIOTS (AFC)
BELLINO, JOSEPH (ANNAPOLIS) - BACK - 1965-67 BOSTON PATRIOTS (AFL)
BELLINGER, ROBERT (GONZAGA) - GUARD - 1934-35 NEW YORK GIANTS
BELOTTI, GEORGE (USC) - CENTER - 1960-61 HOUSTON OILERS (AFL); 1961
    SAN DIEGO CHARGERS (AFL)
BELSER, CEASER (ARKANSAS AM&N) - BACK, LB - 1968-69 KANSAS CITY
    CHIEFS (AFL); 1970-71 KANSAS CITY CHIEFS (AFC); 1974 SAN
    FRANCISCO 49ERS (NFC)
BELTON, WILLIE (MARYLAND STATE) - BACK - 1971-72 ATLANTA FALCONS
    (NFC); 1973-74 ST. LOUIS CARDINALS (NFC)
BELTZ, RICHARD (OHIO STATE) - BACK - 1936 PITTSBURGH AMERICANS (AFL)
BEMILLER, ALBERT (SYRACUSE) - CENTER - 1961-69 BUFFALO BILLS (AFL)
BENDER, EDWARD (FORT HAYS-KANSAS) - TACKLE - 1936-37 PITTSBURGH
    AMERICANS (AFL)
BENKERT, HENRY (RUTGERS) - BACK - 1925 NEW YORK GIANTS; 1926
    POTTSVILLE MAROONS; 1929 ORANGE TORNADOS; 1930 NEWARK TORNADOS
BENNERS, FRED (SMU) - QBACK - 1952 NEW YORK GIANTS
BENNETT, CHARLES (INDIANA) - BACK - 1930 PORTSMOUTH SPARTANS; 1933
    CHICAGO CARDINALS
BENNETT, EARL (HARDIN-SIMMONS) - GUARD - 1946 GREEN BAY PACKERS
BENNETT, JOSEPH (MARQUETTE) - TACKLE - 1920 CHICAGO TIGERS; 1922
    MILWAUKEE BADGERS
BENNETT, PHILIP (MIAMI) - LB - 1960 BOSTON PATRIOTS (AFL)
BENSON, DUANE (HAMLINE) - LB - 1967-69 OAKLAND RAIDERS (AFL); 1970-71
    OAKLAND RAIDERS (AFC); 1972-73 ATLANTA FALCONS (NFC); 1974
    HOUSTON OILERS (AFC)
BENSON, GEORGE (NORTHWESTERN) - BACK - 1947 BROOKLYN DODGERS (AAFC)
BENSON, HARRY (WESTERN MARYLAND) - GUARD - 1935 PHILADELPHIA EAGLES

BENSON, LEO (ILLINOIS WESLEYAN) - CENTER - 1941 CINCINNATI BENGALS
     (AFL)
BENTON, JAMES (ARKANSAS) - END - 1938-40, 42, 44-45 CLEVELAND RAMS;
     1943 CHICAGO BEARS; 1946-47 LOS ANGELES RAMS; 1946 PASS
     RECEIVING LEADER
BENTZ, EDWARD - END - 1922 ROCHESTER JEFFERSONS
BENTZ, ROMAN (TULANE) - TACKLE - 1946-48 NEW YORK YANKEES (AAFC);
     1948 SAN FRANCISCO 49ERS (AAFC)
BENTZIEN, ALFRED (MARQUETTE) - GUARD - 1924 RACINE LEGION
BENZ, LAWRENCE (NORTHWESTERN) - BACK - 1963-65 CLEVELAND BROWNS
BERCICH, ROBERT (MICHIGAN STATE) - BACK - 1960-61 DALLAS COWBOYS
BEREZNEY, PAUL (FORDHAM) - TACKLE - 1942-44 GREEN BAY PACKERS; 1946
     MIAMI SEAHAWKS (AAFC)
BEREZNEY, PETER (NOTRE DAME) - TACKLE - 1947 LOS ANGELES DONS (AAFC);
     1948 BALTIMORE COLTS (AAFC)
BERGEN, WILLIAM (MARQUETTE) - BACK - 1926 MILWAUKEE BADGERS
BERGER, RONALD (WAYNE STATE) - END, TACKLE - 1969 BOSTON PATRIOTS
     (AFL); 1970 BOSTON PATRIOTS (AFC); 1971-72 NEW ENGLAND PATRIOTS
     (AFC)
BERGER, WALTER (IOWA STATE) - TACKLE - 1924 MILWAUKEE BADGERS
BERGERSON, GILBERT (OREGON STATE) - TACKLE - 1932-33 CHICAGO BEARS;
     1933 CHICAGO CARDINALS; 1935-36 BROOKLYN DODGERS
BERGEY, BRUCE (UCLA) - END - 1971 KANSAS CITY CHIEFS (AFC)
BERGEY, WILLIAM (ARKANSAS STATE) - LB - 1969 CINCINNATI BENGALS
     (AFL); 1970-73 CINCINNATI BENGALS (AFC); 1974 PHILADELPHIA
     EAGLES (NFC)
BERGMAN, ALFRED (NOTRE DAME) - QBACK - 1919 HAMMOND PROS
BERNARD, CHARLES (MICHIGAN) - CENTER - 1934 DETROIT LIONS
BERNARD, DAVID (MISSISSIPPI) - QBACK - 1940-41 CINCINNATI BENGALS
     (AFL); 1944-45 CLEVELAND RAMS
BERNARD, GEORGE (DEPAUW) - GUARD - 1926 RACINE LEGION
BERNARDI, FRANK (COLORADO) - BACK - 1955-57 CHICAGO CARDINALS; 1960
     DENVER BRONCOS (AFL)
BERNER, MILFORD (SYRACUSE) - CENTER - 1933 CINCINNATI REDS
BERNET, EDWARD (SMU) - END - 1955 PITTSBURGH STEELERS; 1960 DALLAS
     TEXANS (AFL)
BERNET, LEE (WISCONSIN) - TACKLE - 1965-66 DENVER BRONCOS (AFL)
BERNHARDT, GEORGE (ILLINOIS) - GUARD - 1946-48 BROOKLYN DODGERS
     (AAFC); 1948 CHICAGO ROCKETS (AAFC)
BERNHARDT, ROGER (KANSAS) - GUARD - 1974 NEW YORK JETS (AFC)
BERNOSKE, DANIEL (INDIANA) - GUARD - 1926 LOUISVILLE COLONELS
BERNS, WILLIAM (PURDUE) - GUARD - 1922-24 DAYTON TRIANGLES
BERNSTEIN, JOSEPH (TULSA) - GUARD - 1923-24 ROCK ISLAND INDEPENDENTS;
     1924 HAMMOND PROS
BERQUIST, JAY (NEBRASKA) - GUARD - 1924, 26 KANSAS CITY COWBOYS; 1927
     CHICAGO CARDINALS
BERRA, TIM (MASSACHUSETTS) - END - 1974 BALTIMORE COLTS (AFC)
BERRANG, EDWARD (VILLANOVA) - END - 1949-52 WASHINGTON REDSKINS; 1951
     DETROIT LIONS
BERREHSEN, WILLIAM (WASHINGTON&JEFFERSON) - TACKLE - 1926 COLUMBUS
     TIGERS
BERRY, CHARLES (LAFAYETTE) - END - 1925-26 POTTSVILLE MAROONS
BERRY, CORNELIUS (NORTH CAROLINA STATE) - END - 1939 DETROIT LIONS;
     1940 CLEVELAND RAMS; 1940 NEW YORK AMERICANS (AFL); 1941
     MILWAUKEE CHIEFS (AFL); 1942-46 CHICAGO BEARS; 1947 CHICAGO
     ROCKETS (AAFC)
BERRY, DANIEL (CALIFORNIA) - BACK - 1967 PHILADELPHIA EAGLES
BERRY, GEORGE (BELOIT) - GUARD - 1922 RACINE LEGION; 1922-24, 26
     HAMMOND PROS; 1924-26 AKRON PROS
BERRY, GILBERT (ILLINOIS) - BACK - 1935 CHICAGO CARDINALS
BERRY, J. HOWARD (PENNSYLVANIA) - BACK - 1921-22 ROCHESTER JEFFERSONS
BERRY, RAYMOND (SMU) - END - 1955-67 BALTIMORE COLTS; 1958-60 PASS
     RECEIVING LEADER; (TIED WITH RETZLAFF 1958); 1973 HALL OF FAME
BERRY, REGGIE (LONG BEACH STATE) - BACK - 1972-74 SAN DIEGO CHARGERS
     (AFC)
BERRY, REX (BRIGHAM YOUNG) - BACK - 1951-56 SAN FRANCISCO 49ERS
BERRY, ROBERT (OREGON) - QBACK - 1965-67 MINNESOTA VIKINGS; 1968-69
     ATLANTA FALCONS; 1970-72 ATLANTA FALCONS (NFC); 1973-74
     MINNESOTA VIKINGS (NFC)
BERRY, ROYCE (HOUSTON) - END, LB - 1969 CINCINNATI BENGALS (AFL);
     1970-74 CINCINNATI BENGALS (AFC)
BERRY, WAYNE (WASHINGTON STATE) - BACK - 1954 NEW YORK GIANTS

BERRYMAN, ROBERT (PENN STATE) - BACK - 1924 FRANKFORD YELLOWJACKETS
BERSCHET, MARVIN (ILLINOIS) - GUARD - 1954-55 WASHINGTON REDSKINS
BERTAGNOLLI, LIBERO (WASHINGTON OF MISSOURI) - GUARD - 1942, 45
     CHICAGO CARDINALS
BERTELLI, ANGELO (NOTRE DAME) - QBACK - 1946 LOS ANGELES DONS (AAFC);
     1947-48 CHICAGO ROCKETS (AAFC)
BERTELSEN, JAMES (TEXAS) - BACK - 1972-74 LOS ANGELES RAMS (NFC)
BERTOGLIO, JAMES (CREIGHTON) - BACK - 1926 COLUMBUS TIGERS
BERTUCA, TONY (CHICO STATE) - LB - 1974 BALTIMORE COLTS (AFC)
BERWICK, EDWARD (LOYOLA OF CHICAGO) - CENTER - 1926 LOUISVILLE
     COLONELS
BERZINSKI, WILLIAM (LACROSSE STATE-WIS.) - BACK - 1956 PHILADELPHIA
     EAGLES
BESON, WARREN (MINNESOTA) - CENTER - 1949 BALTIMORE COLTS (AAFC)
BEST, KEITH (KANSAS STATE) - LB - 1972 KANSAS CITY CHIEFS (AFC)
BETHEA, ELVIN (NORTH CAROLINA A&T) - END - 1968-69 HOUSTON OILERS
     (AFL); 1970-74 HOUSTON OILERS (AFC)
BETHUNE, ROBERT (MISSISSIPPI STATE) - BACK - 1962 SAN DIEGO CHARGERS
     (AFL)
BETTENCOURT, LAWRENCE (ST. MARY'S OF CAL.) - CENTER - 1933 GREEN BAY
     PACKERS
BETTIGA, MICHAEL JOHN (HUMBOLDT STATE) - END - 1973-74 SAN FRANCISCO
     49ERS (NFC)
BETTIS, THOMAS (PURDUE) - LB - 1955-61 GREEN BAY PACKERS; 1962
     PITTSBURGH STEELERS; 1963 CHICAGO BEARS
BETTRIDGE, EDWARD (BOWLING GREEN) - LB - 1964 CLEVELAND BROWNS
BETTRIDGE, JOHN (OHIO STATE) - BACK - 1937 CLEVELAND RAMS; 1937
     CHICAGO BEARS
BEUTHEL, LLOYD (COLGATE) - GUARD - 1927 BUFFALO BISONS
BEUTLER, THOMAS (TOLEDO) - LB - 1970 CLEVELAND BROWNS (AFC); 1971
     BALTIMORE COLTS (AFC)
BEVERLY, DAVID (AUBURN) - KICKER - 1974 HOUSTON OILERS (AFC)
BEVERLY, EDWARD (ARIZONA STATE) - END - 1973 SAN FRANCISCO 49ERS (NFC)
BEVERLY, RANDOLPH (COLORADO STATE) - BACK - 1967-69 NEW YORK JETS
     (AFL); 1970 BOSTON PATRIOTS (AFC); 1971 NEW ENGLAND PATRIOTS
     (AFC)
BIANCONE, JOHN (OREGON STATE) - QBACK - 1936 BROOKLYN DODGERS
BIEBERSTEIN, ADOLPH (WISCONSIN) - GUARD - 1926 RACINE LEGION
BIELSKI, RICHARD (MARYLAND) - BACK - 1955-59 PHILADELPHIA EAGLES;
     1960-61 DALLAS COWBOYS; 1962-63 BALTIMORE COLTS
BIENEMANN, THOMAS (DRAKE) - END - 1951-56 CHICAGO CARDINALS
BIERCE, BRUCE (AKRON) - END - 1920-22, 25 AKRON PROS; 1923 CLEVELAND
     INDIANS; 1924 CLEVELAND BULLDOGS
BIG BEAR - TACKLE - 1923 OORANG INDIANS
BIG TWIG - GUARD - 1929 BUFFALO BISONS; (ALSO PLAYED AS NAT MC COMBS)
BIGGS, RILEY (BAYLOR) - CENTER - 1926 ROCK ISLAND INDEPENDENTS (AFL);
     1926-27 NEW YORK GIANTS
BIGGS, VERLON (JACKSON STATE) - END - 1965-69 NEW YORK JETS (AFL);
     1970 NEW YORK JETS (AFC); 1971-74 WASHINGTON REDSKINS (NFC)
BIGHEAD, JACK (PEPPERDINE) - END - 1954 BALTIMORE COLTS; 1955 LOS
     ANGELES RAMS
BIHL, VICTOR (BUCKNELL) - TACKLE - 1925 POTTSVILLE MAROONS
BILBO, JONATHAN (MISSISSIPPI) - TACKLE - 1938-39 CHICAGO CARDINALS
BILDA, RICHARD (MARQUETTE) - BACK - 1944 GREEN BAY PACKERS
BILETNIKOFF, FREDERICK (FLORIDA STATE) - END - 1965-69 OAKLAND
     RAIDERS (AFL); 1970-74 OAKLAND RAIDERS (AFC); 1971-72 PASS
     RECEIVING LEADER (AFC)
BILLINGSLEY, RONALD (WYOMING) - TACKLE - 1967-69 SAN DIEGO CHARGERS
     (AFL); 1970 SAN DIEGO CHARGERS (AFC); 1971-72 HOUSTON OILERS
     (AFC)
BILLMAN, JOHN (MINNESOTA) - GUARD - 1946 BROOKLYN DODGERS (AAFC);
     1947 CHICAGO ROCKETS (AAFC)
BILLOCK, FRANK (ST. MARY'S OF CAL.) - GUARD - 1937 PITTSBURGH PIRATES
BINGAMAN, LESTER (ILLINOIS) - GUARD - 1948-54 DETROIT LIONS
BINGHAM, DONALD (SUL ROSS STATE) - BACK - 1956 CHICAGO BEARS
BINGHAM, GREGG (PURDUE) - LB - 1973-74 HOUSTON OILERS (AFC)
BINGHAM, JOHN (YALE) - END - 1926 BROOKLYN HORSEMEN (AFL)
BINOTTO, JOHN (DUQUESNE) - BACK - 1942 PITTSBURGH STEELERS; 1942
     PHILADELPHIA EAGLES

BIODROWSKI, DENNIS (MEMPHIS STATE) - GUARD - 1963-67 KANSAS CITY
    CHIEFS (AFL)
BIRD, RODGER (KENTUCKY) - BACK - 1966-68 OAKLAND RAIDERS (AFL)
BIRDWELL, DANIEL (HOUSTON) - TACKLE - 1962-69 OAKLAND RAIDERS (AFL)
BIRK, FERDINAND (PURDUE) - BACK - 1922 HAMMOND PROS
BIRLEM, KEITH (SAN JOSE STATE) - BACK - 1939 CHICAGO CARDINALS; 1939
    WASHINGTON REDSKINS
BISBEE, BERTIN (MINNESOTA) - END - 1922 MILWAUKEE BADGERS
BISCAHA, JOSEPH (RICHMOND) - END - 1959 NEW YORK GIANTS; 1960 BOSTON
    PATRIOTS (AFL)
BISHOP, DONALD (LOS ANGELES COLLEGE) - BACK - 1958-59 PITTSBURGH
    STEELERS; 1959 CHICAGO BEARS; 1960-65 DALLAS COWBOYS
BISHOP, ERWIN "SONNY" (FRESNO STATE) - GUARD - 1962 DALLAS COWBOYS;
    1963 OAKLAND RAIDERS (AFL); 1964-69 HOUSTON OILERS (AFL)
BISHOP, WILLIAM (NORTH TEXAS STATE) - TACKLE - 1952-60 CHICAGO BEARS;
    1961 MINNESOTA VIKINGS
BISSELL, FREDERICK (FORDHAM) - END - 1925-26 AKRON PROS
BIVINS, CHARLES (MORRIS-BROWN) - BACK - 1960-66 CHICAGO BEARS; 1967
    PITTSBURGH STEELERS; 1967 BUFFALO BILLS (AFL)
BIZER, HERBERT (CARROLL-WISCONSIN) - BACK - 1929 BUFFALO BISONS
BJORK, DELBERT (OREGON) - TACKLE - 1937-38 CHICAGO BEARS
BJORKLUND, JOHN HENRY "HANK" (PRINCETON) - BACK - 1972-74 NEW YORK
    JETS (AFC)
BJORKLUND, ROBERT (MINNESOTA) - CENTER - 1941 PHILADELPHIA EAGLES
BLACK, CHARLES (KANSAS) - END - 1925 DULUTH KELLEYS
BLACK, EDWARD (MUHLENBERG) - END - 1926 NEWARK BEARS (AFL)
BLACK, JOHN (MISSISSIPPI STATE) - BACK - 1946 BUFFALO BISONS (AAFC);
    1947 BALTIMORE COLTS (AAFC)
BLACK BEAR - END - 1922-23 OORANG INDIANS
BLACKABY, INMAN (BUTLER) - BACK - 1940 CINCINNATI BENGALS (AFL)
BLACKBURN, WILLIAM (RICE) - CENTER - 1946-50 CHICAGO CARDINALS
BLACKLOCK, HUGH (MICHIGAN STATE) - TACKLE - 1919 HAMMOND PROS; 1920
    DECATUR STALEYS; 1921 CHICAGO STALEYS; 1922-25 CHICAGO BEARS;
    1926 BROOKLYN LIONS
BLACKMAN, E. LENNON (TULSA) - BACK - 1930 CHICAGO BEARS
BLACKWELL, HAROLD (SOUTH CAROLINA) - BACK - 1945 CHICAGO CARDINALS
BLACKWOOD, HOWARD (NORTHWESTERN) - GUARD - 1926 CHICAGO BULLS (AFL)
BLACKWOOD, LYLE (TCU) - BACK - 1973-74 CINCINNATI BENGALS (AFC)
BLAHA, ARTHUR (DUBUQUE) - BACK - 1940 MILWAUKEE CHIEFS (AFL)
BLAHAK, JOSEPH (NEBRASKA) - BACK - 1973 HOUSTON OILERS (AFC); 1974
    MINNESOTA VIKINGS (NFC)
BLAILOCK, W. RUSSELL (BAYLOR) - TACKLE - 1923 MILWAUKEE BADGERS; 1925
    AKRON PROS
BLAINE, EDWARD (MISSOURI) - GUARD - 1962 GREEN BAY PACKERS; 1963-66
    PHILADELPHIA EAGLES
BLAIR, ALBERT MATTHEW (IOWA STATE) - LB - 1974 MINNESOTA VIKINGS (NFC)
BLAIR, GEORGE (MISSISSIPPI) - BACK - 1961-64 SAN DIEGO CHARGERS (AFL)
BLAKE, THOMAS (CINCINNATI) - TACKLE - 1949 NEW YORK BULLDOGS
BLAIR, THOMAS "T.C." (TULSA) - END - 1974 DETROIT LIONS (NFC)
BLANCHARD, DONALD (VILLANOVA) - BACK - 1936-37 BOSTON SHAMROCKS (AFL)
BLANCHARD, RICHARD (TULSA) - LB - 1972 NEW ENGLAND PATRIOTS (AFC)
BLANCHARD, THOMAS (OREGON) - KICKER, QBACK - 1971-73 NEW YORK GIANTS
    (NFC); 1974 NEW ORLEANS SAINTS (NFC); 1974 PUNTING LEADER (NFC)
BLANDA, GEORGE (KENTUCKY) - QBACK, KICKER - 1949-58 CHICAGO BEARS;
    1960-66 HOUSTON OILERS (AFL); 1967-69 OAKLAND RAIDERS (AFL);
    1970-74 OAKLAND RAIDERS (AFC); 1961 PASSING LEADER (AFL); 1967
    SCORING LEADER (AFL)
BLANDIN, ERNEST (TULANE) - TACKLE - 1946-47 CLEVELAND BROWNS (AAFC);
    1948-49 BALTIMORE COLTS (AAFC); 1950, 53 BALTIMORE COLTS
BLANKS, SIDNEY (TEXAS A&I) - BACK - 1964, 66-68 HOUSTON OILERS (AFL);
    1969 BOSTON PATRIOTS (AFL); 1970 BOSTON PATRIOTS (AFC)
BLAZER, PHILIP (NORTH CAROLINA) - GUARD - 1960 BUFFALO BILLS (AFL)
BLAZINE, ANTHONY (ILLINOIS WESLEYAN) - TACKLE - 1935-40 CHICAGO
    CARDINALS; 1941 NEW YORK GIANTS
BLEEKER, MALCOLM (COLUMBIA) - GUARD - 1930 BROOKLYN DODGERS
BLEEKER, MELVIN (USC) - BACK - 1944-46 PHILADELPHIA EAGLES; 1947 LOS
    ANGELES RAMS
BLEICK, THOMAS (GEORGIA TECH) - BACK - 1966 BALTIMORE COLTS; 1967
    ATLANTA FALCONS

BLEIER, ROBERT "ROCKY" (NOTRE DAME) - BACK - 1968 PITTSBURGH
    STEELERS; 1971-74 PITTSBURGH STEELERS (AFC)
BLESSING, PAUL (KEARNEY STATE-NEB.) - END - 1944 DETROIT LIONS
BLISS, HARRY (OHIO STATE) - BACK - 1921 COLUMBUS PANHANDLES
BLISS, HOMER (WASHINGTON&JEFFERSON) - GUARD - 1928 CHICAGO CARDINALS
BLOCKER, FRANK (PURDUE) - CENTER - 1920 HAMMOND PROS
BLODINSKI, EDWARD (CANISIUS) - GUARD - 1941 BUFFALO TIGERS (AFL)
BLONDIN, THOMAS (WEST VIRGINIA WESLEYAN) - GUARD - 1933 CINCINNATI
    REDS
BLOODGOOD, ELBERT (NEBRASKA) - QBACK - 1925-26 KANSAS CITY COWBOYS;
    1927 CLEVELAND BULLDOGS; 1928 NEW YORK GIANTS; 1930 GREEN BAY
    PACKERS
BLOUNT, LAMAR (MISSISSIPPI STATE) - END - 1946 MIAMI SEAHAWKS (AAFC);
    1947 BUFFALO BILLS (AAFC); 1947 BALTIMORE COLTS (AAFC)
BLOUNT, MELVIN (SOUTHERN) - BACK - 1970-74 PITTSBURGH STEELERS (AFC)
BLOZIS, ALBERT (GEORGETOWN) - TACKLE - 1942-44 NEW YORK GIANTS
BLUE, FORREST (AUBURN) - CENTER, TACKLE - 1968-69 SAN FRANCISCO
    49ERS; 1970-74 SAN FRANCISCO 49ERS (NFC)
BLUMENSTOCK, JAMES (FORDHAM) - BACK - 1947 NEW YORK GIANTS
BLUMENTHAL, MORRIS (NORTHWESTERN) - BACK - 1925 CHICAGO CARDINALS
BLUMER, HERBERT (MISSOURI) - TACKLE - 1925-30, 33 CHICAGO CARDINALS
BLYE, RONALD (NOTRE DAME & FLORIDA A&M) - BACK - 1968 NEW YORK
    GIANTS; 1969 PHILADELPHIA EAGLES
BOATWRIGHT, BON (OKLAHOMA STATE) - TACKLE - 1974 SAN DIEGO CHARGERS
    (AFC)
BOBO, HUBERT (OHIO STATE) - LB - 1960 LOS ANGELES CHARGERS (AFL);
    1961-62 NEW YORK TITANS (AFL)
BOBROWSKY, PETER (NEW YORK UNIV.) - END - 1937 NEW YORK YANKS (AFL)
BOCK, WAYNE (ILLINOIS) - TACKLE - 1957 CHICAGO CARDINALS
BODENGER, MORRIS (TULANE) - GUARD - 1931-33 PORTSMOUTH SPARTANS; 1934
    DETROIT LIONS; 1936 NEW YORK YANKS (AFL)
BOEKE, JAMES (HEIDELBERG) - TACKLE - 1960-63 LOS ANGELES RAMS;
    1964-67 DALLAS COWBOYS; 1968 NEW ORLEANS SAINTS
BOEDECKER, WILLIAM (DEPAUL) - BACK - 1946 CHICAGO ROCKETS (AAFC);
    1947-49 CLEVELAND BROWNS (AAFC); 1950 GREEN BAY PACKERS; 1950
    PHILADELPHIA EAGLES
BOENSCH, FREDERICK (STANFORD) - GUARD - 1947-48 WASHINGTON REDSKINS
BOETTCHER, RAYMOND (LAWRENCE) - BACK - 1926 RACINE LEGION
BOGACKI, HENRY (CANISIUS) - CENTER - 1936 NEW YORK YANKS (AFL); 1936
    ROCHESTER TIGERS (AFL); 1940 BUFFALO INDIANS (AFL); 1941 BUFFALO
    TIGERS (AFL)
BOGDEN, PETER (UTAH) - END - 1940 COLUMBUS BULLIES (AFL)
BOGGAN, REX (MISSISSIPPI) - TACKLE - 1955 NEW YORK GIANTS
BOGUE, GEORGE (STANFORD) - BACK - 1930 CHICAGO CARDINALS; 1930 NEWARK
    TORNADOS
BOHLING, DEWEY (HARDIN-SIMMONS) - BACK - 1960-61 NEW YORK TITANS
    (AFL); 1961 BUFFALO BILLS (AFL)
BOHLMANN, FRANK (MARQUETTE) - GUARD - 1940 NEW YORK AMERICANS (AFL);
    1941 MILWAUKEE CHIEFS (AFL); 1942 CHICAGO CARDINALS
BOHNERT - BACK - 1921 LOUISVILLE BRECKS
BOHOVICH, GEORGE REED (LEHIGH) - GUARD - 1962 NEW YORK GIANTS
BOHREN, KARL (PITTSBURGH) - BACK - 1927 BUFFALO BISONS
BOHRER, ROBERT (CINCINNATI) - CENTER - 1940 CINCINNATI BENGALS (AFL)
BOLAN, GEORGE (PURDUE) - BACK - 1921 CHICAGO STALEYS; 1922-24 CHICAGO
    BEARS
BOLAN, JOSEPH (PURDUE) - TACKLE - 1926 LOUISVILLE COLONELS
BOLDEN, LEROY (MICHIGAN STATE) - BACK - 1958-59 CLEVELAND BROWNS
BOLDT, S. CHASE - END - 1921-23 LOUISVILLE BRECKS
BOLEN, CHARLES (OHIO STATE) - END - 1919 CANTON BULLDOGS
BOLGER, JAMES (ST. MARY'S OF CAL.) - BACK - 1926 BROOKLYN HORSEMEN
    (AFL)
BOLIN, TREVA "BOOKIE" (MISSISSIPPI) - GUARD - 1962-67 NEW YORK
    GIANTS; 1968-69 MINNESOTA VIKINGS
BOLKOVAC, NICHOLAS (PITTSBURGH) - TACKLE - 1953-54 PITTSBURGH STEELERS
BOLL, DONALD (NEBRASKA) - TACKLE - 1953-59 WASHINGTON REDSKINS; 1960
    NEW YORK GIANTS
BOLLINGER, EDWARD (BUCKNELL) - GUARD - 1930 FRANKFORD YELLOWJACKETS
BOLTON, RONALD (NORFOLK STATE) - BACK, KICKER - 1972-74 NEW ENGLAND
    PATRIOTS (AFC)
BOMAR, LYNN (VANDERBILT) - END - 1925-26 NEW YORK GIANTS
BONADIES, JOHN - GUARD - 1926 HARTFORD BLUES

BOND, CHARLES (WASHINGTON) - TACKLE - 1937-38 WASHINGTON REDSKINS
BOND, JAMES (PITTSBURGH) - GUARD - 1926 BROOKLYN LIONS
BOND, RANDALL (WASHINGTON) - BACK - 1938 WASHINGTON REDSKINS; 1939
     PITTSBURGH STEELERS
BONDURANT, J. BOURBON (DEPAUW) - GUARD - 1921 MUNCIE FLYERS; 1921-22
     EVANSVILLE CRIMSON GIANTS; 1922 CHICAGO BEARS
BONELLI, ERNEST (PITTSBURGH) - BACK - 1945 CHICAGO CARDINALS; 1946
     PITTSBURGH STEELERS
BONNER, GLEN (WASHINGTON) - BACK - 1974 SAN DIEGO CHARGERS (AFC)
BONOWITZ, ELLIOTT (WILMINGTON) - GUARD - 1922 COLUMBUS PANHANDLES;
     1923 COLUMBUS TIGERS; 1924-26 DAYTON TRIANGLES
BOOKER, PETER (BOWLING GREEN) - BACK - 1936 BOSTON SHAMROCKS (AFL)
BOOKMAN, JOHN (MIAMI) - BACK - 1957 NEW YORK GIANTS; 1960 DALLAS
     TEXANS (AFL); 1961 NEW YORK TITANS (AFL)
BOOKOUT, WILLIAM (AUSTIN) - BACK - 1955-56 GREEN BAY PACKERS
BOOKS, ROBERT (DICKINSON) - BACK - 1926 FRANKFORD YELLOWJACKETS
BOONE, DAVID (EASTERN MICHIGAN) - END - 1974 MINNESOTA VIKINGS (NFC)
BOONE, J. R. (TULSA) - BACK - 1948-51 CHICAGO BEARS; 1952 SAN
     FRANCISCO 49ERS; 1953 GREEN BAY PACKERS
BOONE, ROBERT (ELON) - BACK - 1942 CLEVELAND RAMS
BOOTH, CLARENCE (SMU) - TACKLE - 1943 CHICAGO CARDINALS; 1944
     CARD-PITT
BOOTH, RICHARD (WESTERN RESERVE) - BACK - 1941, 45 DETROIT LIONS
BOOZER, EMERSON (MARYLAND STATE) - BACK - 1966-69 NEW YORK JETS
     (AFL); 1970-74 NEW YORK JETS (AFC)
BORAK, ANTHONY (CREIGHTON) - END - 1938 GREEN BAY PACKERS
BORDEN, LESTER (FORDHAM) - END - 1935 NEW YORK GIANTS; 1936 NEW YORK
     YANKS (AFL)
BORDEN, NATHANIEL (INDIANA) - END - 1955-59 GREEN BAY PACKERS;
     1960-61 DALLAS COWBOYS; 1962 BUFFALO BILLS (AFL)
BORNTRAEGER, WILLIAM - QBACK - 1923 LOUISVILLE BRECKS
BORRELLI, NICHOLAS (MUHLENBERG) - BACK - 1930 NEWARK TORNADOS
BORTON, JOHN (OHIO STATE) - QBACK - 1957 CLEVELAND BROWNS
BORYLA, MICHAEL (STANFORD) - QBACK - 1974 PHILADELPHIA EAGLES (NFC)
BOSCH, FRANK (COLORADO) - TACKLE - 1968-69 WASHINGTON REDSKINS; 1970
     WASHINGTON REDSKINS (NFC)
BOSDETT, JOHN - END - 1920 CHICAGO TIGERS
BOSLEY, BRUCE (WEST VIRGINIA) - CENTER - 1956-68 SAN FRANCISCO 49ERS;
     1969 ATLANTA FALCONS
BOSSELER, DONALD (MIAMI) - BACK - 1957-64 WASHINGTON REDSKINS
BOSTICK, LEWIS (ALABAMA) - GUARD - 1939 CLEVELAND RAMS
BOSTON, MC KINLEY (MINNESOTA) - END, LB - 1968-69 NEW YORK GIANTS
BOSWELL, BENJAMIN (TCU) - TACKLE - 1933 PORTSMOUTH SPARTANS; 1934
     BOSTON REDSKINS
BOTCHAN, RONALD (OCCIDENTAL) - LB - 1960 LOS ANGELES CHARGERS (AFL);
     1962 HOUSTON OILERS (AFL)
BOUDREAUX, JAMES (LOUISIANA TECH) - END - 1966-68 BOSTON PATRIOTS
     (AFL)
BOUGGESS, LEE (LOUISVILLE) - BACK - 1970-71, 73 PHILADELPHIA EAGLES
     (NFC)
BOULDIN, FREDERICK (MISSOURI) - TACKLE - 1944 DETROIT LIONS
BOULEY, GILBERT (BOSTON COLLEGE) - TACKLE - 1945 CLEVELAND RAMS;
     1946-50 LOS ANGELES RAMS
BOUTWELL, LEON (CARLISLE) - QBACK - 1922-23 OORANG INDIANS
BOUTWELL, THOMAS (SOUTHERN MISSISSIPPI) - QBACK - 1969 MIAMI DOLPHINS
     (AFL)
BOVA, ANTHONY (ST. FRANCIS) - END - 1942, 45-47 PITTSBURGH STEELERS;
     1943 PHIL-PITT; 1944 CARD-PITT
BOVE, PETER (HOLY CROSS) - GUARD - 1930 NEWARK TORNADOS
BOWDELL, GORDON (MICHIGAN) - END - 1971 DENVER BRONCOS (AFC)
BOWDOIN, JAMES (ALABAMA) - GUARD - 1928-31 GREEN BAY PACKERS; 1932
     NEW YORK GIANTS; 1932, 34 BROOKLYN DODGERS; 1933 PORTSMOUTH
     SPARTANS
BOWER, J. PHILIP (DARTMOUTH) - BACK - 1921 CLEVELAND INDIANS
BOWERS, WILLIAM (USC) - BACK - 1954 LOS ANGELES RAMS
BOWIE, LAWRENCE (PURDUE) - GUARD - 1962-68 MINNESOTA VIKINGS
BOWLING, ANDREW (VIRGINIA TECH) - LB - 1967 ATLANTA FALCONS
BOWMAN, KENNETH (WISCONSIN) - CENTER - 1964-69 GREEN BAY PACKERS;
     1970-73 GREEN BAY PACKERS (NFC)
BOWMAN, STEVEN (ALABAMA) - BACK - 1966 NEW YORK GIANTS

BOWMAN, WILLIAM (WILLIAM&MARY) - BACK - 1954, 56 DETROIT LIONS; 1957
     PITTSBURGH STEELERS
BOWSER, ARDA (BUCKNELL) - BACK - 1922 CANTON BULLDOGS; 1923 CLEVELAND
     INDIANS
BOX, CLOYCE (WEST TEXAS STATE) - END - 1949-50, 52-54 DETROIT LIONS
BOYD, GREGORY (ARIZONA) - BACK - 1973 NEW ENGLAND PATRIOTS (AFC);
     1974 NEW ORLEANS SAINTS (NFC)
BOYD, ROBERT (LOYOLA OF L.A.) - END - 1950-51, 53-57 LOS ANGELES RAMS
BOYD, ROBERT (OKLAHOMA) - BACK - 1960-68 BALTIMORE COLTS; 1965
     INTERCEPTION LEADER
BOYD, SAMUEL (BAYLOR) - END - 1939-40 PITTSBURGH STEELERS
BOYD, WILLIAM (WESTMINSTER OF MO.) - BACK - 1930-31 CHICAGO CARDINALS
BOYDA, MICHAEL (WASHINGTON&LEE) - BACK - 1949 NEW YORK BULLDOGS; 1949
     PUNTING LEADER
BOYDSTON, MAX (OKLAHOMA) - END - 1955-58 CHICAGO CARDINALS; 1960-61
     DALLAS TEXANS (AFL); 1962 OAKLAND RAIDERS (AFL)
BOYER, VERDI (UCLA) - GUARD - 1936 BROOKLYN DODGERS; 1937 LOS ANGELES
     BULLDOGS (AFL)
BOYETTE, GARLAND (GRAMBLING) - LB - 1962-63 ST. LOUIS CARDINALS;
     1966-69 HOUSTON OILERS (AFL); 1970-72 HOUSTON OILERS (AFC)
BOYLAND, JAMES (WASHINGTON STATE) - END - 1963 MINNESOTA VIKINGS
BOYLE, JOHN (COLUMBIA COLLEGE) - END - 1926 CHICAGO BULLS (AFL)
BOYLE, WILLIAM - TACKLE - 1934 NEW YORK GIANTS
BOYNTON, BEN LEE (WILLIAMS) - QBACK - 1921-22 ROCHESTER JEFFERSONS;
     1924 BUFFALO BISONS
BOYNTON, GEORGE (EAST TEXAS STATE) - BACK - 1962 OAKLAND RAIDERS (AFL)
BOYNTON, JOHN (TENNESSEE) - TACKLE - 1969 MIAMI DOLPHINS (AFL)
BRAASE, ORDELL (SOUTH DAKOTA) - END - 1957-68 BALTIMORE COLTS
BRAATZ, THOMAS (MARQUETTE) - END - 1957 WASHINGTON REDSKINS; 1958 LOS
     ANGELES RAMS; 1958-59 WASHINGTON REDSKINS; 1960 DALLAS COWBOYS
BRABHAM, DANIEL (ARKANSAS) - LB - 1963-67 HOUSTON OILERS (AFL); 1968
     CINCINNATI BENGALS (AFL)
BRACE, WILLIAM (BROWN) - GUARD - 1920-22 BUFFALO ALL-AMERICANS
BRACKETT, MARTIN LUTHER (AUBURN) - TACKLE - 1956-57 CHICAGO BEARS;
     1958 NEW YORK GIANTS
BRACKINS, CHARLES (PRAIRE VIEW) - QBACK - 1955 GREEN BAY PACKERS
BRADEN, DAVID (MARQUETTE) - GUARD - 1945 CHICAGO CARDINALS
BRADEN - TACKLE - 1919 DETROIT HERALDS
BRADFUTE, BYRON (MISSISSIPPI SOUTHERN) - TACKLE - 1960-61 DALLAS
     COWBOYS
BRADLEY, DAVID (PENN STATE) - TACKLE, GUARD - 1969 GREEN BAY PACKERS;
     1970-71 GREEN BAY PACKERS (NFC); 1972 ST. LOUIS CARDINALS (NFC)
BRADLEY, EDWARD (WAKE FOREST) - END - 1950, 52 CHICAGO BEARS
BRADLEY, EDWARD (WAKE FOREST) - LB - 1972-74 PITTSBURGH STEELERS (AFC)
BRADLEY, GERALD (WITTENBERG) - BACK - 1928 DAYTON TRIANGLES
BRADLEY, HAROLD (IOWA) - GUARD - 1954-56 CLEVELAND BROWNS; 1958
     PHILADELPHIA EAGLES
BRADLEY, HAROLD (ELON) - END - 1938 CHICAGO CARDINALS; 1938-39
     WASHINGTON REDSKINS; 1939 CHICAGO CARDINALS
BRADLEY, ROBERT (OHIO STATE) - GUARD - 1928 CHICAGO CARDINALS
BRADLEY, WILLIAM (TEXAS) - BACK, KICKER - 1969 PHILADELPHIA EAGLES;
     1970-74 PHILADELPHIA EAGLES (NFC); 1971-72 INTERCEPTION LEADER
     (NFC)
BRADSHAW, CHARLES (BAYLOR) - TACKLE - 1958-60 LOS ANGELES RAMS;
     1961-66 PITTSBURGH STEELERS; 1967-68 DETROIT LIONS
BRADSHAW, JAMES (CHATTANOOGA) - BACK - 1963-67 PITTSBURGH STEELERS
BRADSHAW, JAMES (NEVADA) - QBACK - 1924 KANSAS CITY COWBOYS; 1926 LOS
     ANGELES WILDCATS (AFL)
BRADSHAW, MORRIS (OHIO STATE) - END - 1974 OAKLAND RAIDERS (AFC)
BRADSHAW, TERRY (LOUISIANA TECH) - QBACK, KICKER - 1970-74 PITTSBURGH
     STEELERS (AFC)
BRADSHAW, WESLEY (BAYLOR) - QBACK - 1924 ROCK ISLAND INDEPENDENTS;
     1926 ROCK ISLAND INDEPENDENTS (AFL); 1926 BUFFALO RANGERS
BRADY, PATRICK (NEVADA) - BACK - 1952-54 PITTSBURGH STEELERS; 1953-54
     PUNTING LEADER
BRADY, PHILIP (BRIGHAM YOUNG) - BACK - 1969 DENVER BRONCOS (AFL)
BRAGG, MICHAEL (RICHMOND) - LB - 1968-69 WASHINGTON REDSKINS; 1970-74
     WASHINGTON REDSKINS (NFC)
BRAGONIER, DENNIS (STANFORD) - BACK - 1974 SAN FRANCISCO 49ERS (NFC)

Top row (from left to right): Ordell Braase, Charles Bradshaw, "Zeke" Bratkowski and Ray Bray. *Second row:* Carl Brettschneider, Gene Brito, John Brodie and Ed Brown. *Third row:* Jim Brown, Jack Brown, Roger Brown and "Rosey" Brown. *Bottom row:* "Tim" Brown, Bill Brown, Don Burroughs and Ernie Caddel.

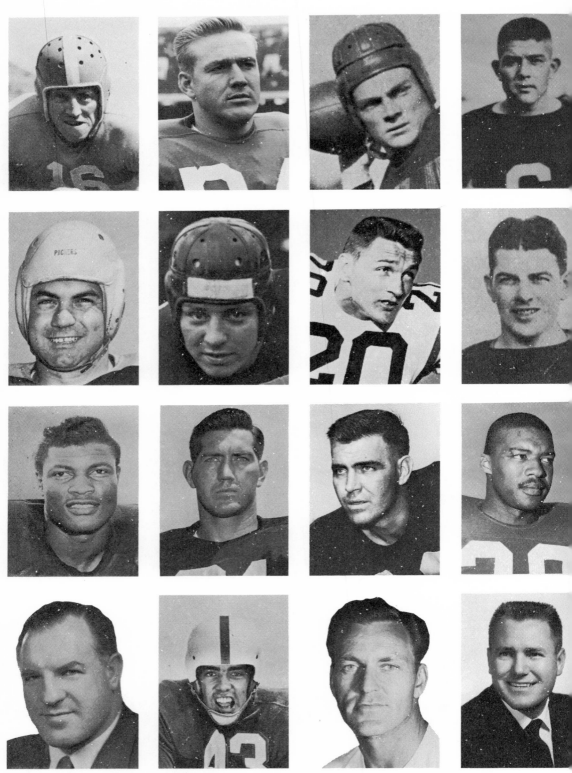

Top row (from left to right): George Cafego, Lee Roy Caffey, Chris Cagle and Pete Calac. *Second row:* Tony Canadeo, John Cannady, Billy Cannon and Art Carney. *Third row:* J. C. Caroline, Lew Carpenter, Preston Carpenter and Bernie Casey. *Bottom row:* Jim Castiglia, Don Chandler, Lynn Chandnois and Jack Christiansen.

BRAHANEY, THOMAS (OKLAHOMA) - CENTER - 1973-74 ST. LOUIS CARDINALS (NFC)

BRAHM, LAWRENCE (TEMPLE) - GUARD - 1942 CLEVELAND RAMS

BRAIDWOOD, CHARLES (CHATTANOOGA) - END - 1930 PORTSMOUTH SPARTANS; 1931 CLEVELAND INDIANS; 1932 CHICAGO CARDINALS; 1933 CINCINNATI REDS

BRAMAN, ARTHUR - TACKLE - 1923 RACINE LEGION

BRAMLETT, JOHN (MEMPHIS STATE) - LB - 1965-66 DENVER BRONCOS (AFL); 1967-68 MIAMI DOLPHINS (AFL); 1969 BOSTON PATRIOTS (AFL); 1970 BOSTON PATRIOTS (AFC); 1971 ATLANTA FALCONS (NFC)

BRANCATO, GEORGE (LSU) - BACK - 1954 CHICAGO CARDINALS

BRANCH, CLIFFORD (COLORADO) - END - 1972-74 OAKLAND RAIDERS (AFC)

BRANCH, MELVIN (LSU) - END - 1960-62 DALLAS TEXANS (AFL); 1963-65 KANSAS CITY CHIEFS (AFL); 1966-68 MIAMI DOLPHINS (AFL)

BRANDAU, ARTHUR (TENNESSEE) - CENTER - 1945-46 PITTSBURGH STEELERS

BRANDAU - BACK - 1921 DETROIT PANTHERS

BRANDT, JAMES (ST. THOMAS) - BACK - 1952-54 PITTSBURGH STEELERS

BRANEY, JOHN (SYRACUSE) - GUARD - 1925-26 PROVIDENCE STEAMROLLERS

BRANNAN, SOLOMON (MORRIS-BROWN) - BACK - 1965-66 KANSAS CITY CHIEFS (AFL)

BRANNON, PHILIP (HOLY CROSS) - END - 1925 CLEVELAND BULLDOGS

BRANSTETTER, KENT (HOUSTON) - TACKLE - 1973 GREEN BAY PACKERS (NFC)

BRATKOWSKI, EDMUND "ZEKE" (GEORGIA) - QBACK - 1954, 57-60 CHICAGO BEARS; 1961-63 LOS ANGELES RAMS; 1963-68 GREEN BAY PACKERS; 1971 GREEN BAY PACKERS (NFC)

BRATT, JOSEPH (SUPERIOR STATE-WIS.) - END - 1924 DULUTH KELLEYS

BRAVO, ALEXANDER (CAL. POLY) - BACK - 1957-58 LOS ANGELES RAMS; 1960-61 OAKLAND RAIDERS (AFL)

BRAWLEY, EDWARD (HOLY CROSS) - GUARD - 1921 CLEVELAND INDIANS

BRAXTON, HEZEKIAH (VIRGINIA UNION) - BACK - 1962 SAN DIEGO CHARGERS (AFL); 1963 BUFFALO BILLS (AFL)

BRAXTON, JAMES (WEST VIRGINIA) - BACK - 1971-74 BUFFALO BILLS (AFC)

BRAY, MAURICE (SMU) - TACKLE - 1935-36 PITTSBURGH PIRATES

BRAY, RAYMOND (WESTERN MICHIGAN) - GUARD - 1939-42, 46-51 CHICAGO BEARS; 1952 GREEN BAY PACKERS

BRAZELL, CARL (BAYLOR) - QBACK - 1938 CLEVELAND RAMS

BRAZINSKY, SAMUEL (VILLANOVA) - CENTER - 1946 BUFFALO BISONS (AAFC)

BREAUX, DONALD (MCNEESE STATE) - QBACK - 1963 DENVER BRONCOS (AFL); 1965 SAN DIEGO CHARGERS (AFL)

BREDDE, WILLIAM (OKLAHOMA A&M) - BACK - 1954 CHICAGO CARDINALS

BREDICE, JOHN (BOSTON UNIV.) - END - 1956 PHILADELPHIA EAGLES

BREEDING, EDWARD (TEXAS A&M) - LB - 1967-68 WASHINGTON REDSKINS

BREEDLOVE, RODNEY (MARYLAND) - LB - 1960-64 WASHINGTON REDSKINS; 1965-67 PITTSBURGH STEELERS

BREEDON, WILLIAM (OKLAHOMA) - BACK - 1937 PITTSBURGH PIRATES

BREEN, JOSEPH EUGENE (VIRGINIA TECH) - LB - 1964 GREEN BAY PACKERS; 1965-66 PITTSBURGH STEELERS; 1967-68 LOS ANGELES RAMS

BREITENSTEIN, ROBERT (TULSA) - TACKLE, GUARD - 1965-67 DENVER BRONCOS (AFL); 1967 MINNESOTA VIKINGS; 1969 ATLANTA FALCONS; 1970 ATLANTA FALCONS (NFC)

BRENKERT, WAYNE (WASHINGTON&JEFFERSON) - BACK - 1923-24 AKRON PROS

BRENNAN, JOHN (MICHIGAN) - GUARD - 1939 GREEN BAY PACKERS

BRENNAN, LEO (HOLY CROSS) - TACKLE - 1942 PHILADELPHIA EAGLES

BRENNAN, MATTHEW (LAFAYETTE) - BACK - 1925 NEW YORK GIANTS; 1926 BROOKLYN LIONS

BRENNAN, PAUL (FORDHAM) - TACKLE - 1926 BROOKLYN HORSEMEN (AFL)

BRENNAN, PHILIP (LOYOLA OF ILLINOIS) - END - 1930 NEWARK TORNADOS

BRENNAN, WILLIS - GUARD - 1920-27 CHICAGO CARDINALS

BRENNER, ALLEN (MICHIGAN STATE) - BACK - 1969 NEW YORK GIANTS; 1970 NEW YORK GIANTS (NFC)

BRENNER, RAYMOND - BACK - 1925 CANTON BULLDOGS

BRETHAUER, MONTE (OREGON) - END - 1953, 55 BALTIMORE COLTS

BRETT, EDWIN (WASHINGTON STATE) - END - 1936 CHICAGO CARDINALS; 1936-37 PITTSBURGH PIRATES

BRETTSCHNEIDER, CARL (IOWA STATE) - LB - 1956-59 CHICAGO CARDINALS; 1960-63 DETROIT LIONS

BREWER, BROOKE (MARYLAND) - BACK - 1921 CLEVELAND INDIANS; 1922 AKRON PROS

BREWER, HOMER (MISSISSIPPI) - BACK - 1960 WASHINGTON REDSKINS

BREWER, JOHN (GEORGIA TECH) - BACK - 1929 DAYTON TRIANGLES

BREWER, JOHN (LOUISVILLE) - BACK - 1952-53 PHILADELPHIA EAGLES

BREWER, JOHN (MISSISSIPPI) - LB - 1961-67 CLEVELAND BROWNS; 1968-69
    NEW ORLEANS SAINTS; 1970 NEW ORLEANS SAINTS (NFC)
BREWIN, JOHN (ST. BONAVENTURE) - END - 1937 BOSTON SHAMROCKS (AFL)
BREWINGTON, JAMES (NORTH CAROLINA COLLEGE) - TACKLE - 1961 OAKLAND
    RAIDERS (AFL)
BREWSTER, DARRELL (PURDUE) - END - 1952-58 CLEVELAND BROWNS; 1959-60
    PITTSBURGH STEELERS
BREWSTER, JAMES (GEORGIA TECH) - QBACK - 1926 NEWARK BEARS (AFL)
BREWSTER, WALTER (WEST VIRGINIA) - TACKLE - 1929 BUFFALO BISONS
BREZINA, GREGORY (HOUSTON) - LB - 1968-69 ATLANTA FALCONS; 1971-74
    ATLANTA FALCONS (NFC)
BREZINA, ROBERT (HOUSTON) - BACK - 1963 HOUSTON OILERS (AFL)
BRIAN, HARRY (GROVE CITY) - BACK - 1926 HARTFORD BLUES
BRIAN, WILLIAM (GONZAGA) - TACKLE - 1935-36 PHILADELPHIA EAGLES
BRIANTE, FRANK (NEW YORK UNIV.) - BACK - 1929 STATEN ISLAND
    STAPELTONS; 1930 NEWARK TORNADOS
BRICK, SHIRLEY (RICE) - END - 1920 BUFFALO ALL-AMERICANS
BRICKLEY, GEORGE (TRINITY OF CONN.) - BACK - 1919 CLEVELAND INDIANS;
    1919 HAMMOND PROS; 1920 CLEVELAND PANTHERS
BRIDGEFORD, LANE (KNOX) - BACK - 1921-22 ROCK ISLAND INDEPENDENTS
BRIGGS, PAUL (COLORADO) - TACKLE - 1948 DETROIT LIONS
BRIGGS, ROBERT (CENTRAL STATE-OKLA.) - BACK - 1965 WASHINGTON REDSKINS
BRIGGS, ROBERT (HEIDELBERG) - TACKLE, END - 1968-69 SAN DIEGO
    CHARGERS (AFL); 1970 SAN DIEGO CHARGERS (AFC); 1971-73 CLEVELAND
    BROWNS (AFC); 1974 KANSAS CITY CHIEFS (AFC)
BRIGGS, WILLIAM (IOWA) - END - 1966-67 WASHINGTON REDSKINS
BRIGHAM, HIRAM (OHIO STATE) - CENTER - 1919-20 COLUMBUS PANHANDLES
BRILL, HAROLD (WICHITA) - BACK - 1939 DETROIT LIONS
BRINDLEY, WALTER (DRAKE) - BACK - 1921-22 ROCK ISLAND INDEPENDENTS
BRINK, LAWRENCE (NORTHERN ILLINOIS) - END - 1948-53 LOS ANGELES RAMS;
    1954 CHICAGO BEARS
BRISCOE, MARLIN (OMAHA) - END, BACK - 1968 DENVER BRONCOS (AFL); 1969
    BUFFALO BILLS (AFL); 1970-71 BUFFALO BILLS (AFC); 1972-74 MIAMI
    DOLPHINS (AFC); 1970 PASS RECEIVING LEADER (AFC)
BRISTER, WILLIE (SOUTHERN) - END - 1974 NEW YORK JETS (AFC)
BRISTOW, GEORGE (NEBRASKA) - BACK - 1925 PROVIDENCE STEAMROLLERS
BRISTOW, OBIE - BACK - 1924-26 KANSAS CITY COWBOYS
BRITO, EUGENE (LOYOLA OF L.A.) - END - 1951-53, 55-58 WASHINGTON
    REDSKINS; 1959-60 LOS ANGELES RAMS
BRITT, CHARLES (GEORGIA) - BACK - 1960-63 LOS ANGELES RAMS; 1964
    MINNESOTA VIKINGS; 1964 SAN FRANCISCO 49ERS
BRITT, EDWARD (HOLY CROSS) - BACK - 1936 BOSTON REDSKINS; 1937
    WASHINGTON REDSKINS; 1938 BROOKLYN DODGERS; 1941 NEW YORK
    AMERICANS (AFL)
BRITT, MAURICE (ARKANSAS) - END - 1941 DETROIT LIONS
BRITT, OSCAR (MISSISSIPPI) - GUARD - 1946 WASHINGTON REDSKINS
BRITT, RANKIN (TEXAS A&M) - END - 1939 PHILADELPHIA EAGLES
BRITTENUM, JON (ARKANSAS) - QBACK - 1967-68 SAN DIEGO CHARGERS (AFL)
BRITTON, EARL (ILLINOIS) - BACK - 1925 CHICAGO BEARS; 1926 BROOKLYN
    LIONS; 1927 FRANKFORD YELLOWJACKETS; 1927-28 DAYTON TRIANGLES;
    1929 CHICAGO CARDINALS
BROADLEY, KARL (BETHANY-WEST VIRGINIA) - GUARD - 1925 CLEVELAND
    BULLDOGS
BROADNAX, JERRY (SOUTHERN) - END - 1974 HOUSTON OILERS (AFC)
BROADSTONE, MARION (NEBRASKA) - TACKLE - 1931 NEW YORK GIANTS
BROCHMAN, ARTHUR (PACIFIC) - TACKLE - 1937 ROCHESTER TIGERS (AFL)
BROCK, CHARLES (NEBRASKA) - CENTER - 1939-47 GREEN BAY PACKERS
BROCK, CLYDE (UTAH STATE) - TACKLE - 1962-63 DALLAS COWBOYS; 1963 SAN
    FRANCISCO 49ERS
BROCK, J. LOUIS (PURDUE) - QBACK - 1940-45 GREEN BAY PACKERS
BROCKINGTON, JOHN (OHIO STATE) - BACK - 1971-74 GREEN BAY PACKERS
    (NFC); 1971, 73 RUSHING LEADER (NFC)
BRODA, HAROLD (BROWN) - END - 1927 CLEVELAND BULLDOGS
BRODERICK, TED - BACK - 1923 LOUISVILLE BRECKS
BRODHEAD, ROBERT (DUKE) - QBACK - 1960 BUFFALO BILLS (AFL)
BRODIE, JOHN (STANFORD) - QBACK - 1957-69 SAN FRANCISCO 49ERS;
    1970-73 SAN FRANCISCO 49ERS (NFC); 1970 PASSING LEADER (NFC)
BRODNAX, JOHN (LSU) - BACK - 1960 DENVER BRONCOS (AFL)
BRODNICKI, CHARLES (VILLANOVA) - CENTER - 1934 PHILADELPHIA EAGLES;
    1934 BROOKLYN DODGERS
BROKER, EDWARD (CARLISLE) - TACKLE - 1922 OORANG INDIANS

BROKER, HIPPO (CARLISLE) - QBACK - 1922 OORANG INDIANS
BROOKER, WILLIAM THOMAS (ALABAMA) - END - 1962 DALLAS TEXANS (AFL);
    1963-66 KANSAS CITY CHIEFS (AFL)
BROOKS, BOBBY (BISHOP) - BACK - 1974 NEW YORK GIANTS (NFC)
BROOKS, CLIFFORD (TENNESSEE STATE) - BACK - 1972-74 CLEVELAND BROWNS
    (AFC)
BROOKS, LAWRENCE (VIRGINIA STATE-PETERSBURG) - TACKLE - 1972-74 LOS
    ANGELES RAMS (NFC)
BROOKS, LEONARD LEO (TEXAS) - TACKLE, END - 1970-72 HOUSTON OILERS
    (AFC); 1973-74 ST. LOUIS CARDINALS (NFC)
BROOKS, ROBERT (OHIO UNIV.) - BACK - 1961 NEW YORK TITANS (AFL)
BROOKSHIER, THOMAS (COLORADO) - BACK - 1953, 56-61 PHILADELPHIA EAGLES
BROSKY, ALBERT (ILLINOIS) - BACK - 1954 CHICAGO CARDINALS
BROSS, MALCOLM (GONZAGA) - QBACK - 1926 LOS ANGELES WILDCATS (AFL)
BROUSSARD, FREDERICK (TEXAS A&M-N.W.LA.) - CENTER - 1955 PITTSBURGH
    STEELERS; 1955 NEW YORK GIANTS
BROVELLI, ANGELO (ST.MARY'S OF CAL.) - QBACK - 1933-34 PITTSBURGH
    PIRATES
BROWN, AARON (MINNESOTA) - END - 1966, 68-69 KANSAS CITY CHIEFS
    (AFL); 1970-72 KANSAS CITY CHIEFS (AFC); 1973-74 GREEN BAY
    PACKERS (NFC)
BROWN, ALLEN (MISSISSIPPI) - END - 1966-67 GREEN BAY PACKERS
BROWN, BARRY (FLORIDA) - LB - 1966-67 BALTIMORE COLTS; 1968 NEW YORK
    GIANTS; 1969 BOSTON PATRIOTS (AFL); 1970 BOSTON PATRIOTS (AFC)
BROWN, BOYD (ALCORN A&M) - END - 1974 DENVER BRONCOS (AFC)
BROWN, CHARLES (HOUSTON) - TACKLE - 1962 OAKLAND RAIDERS (AFL)
BROWN, CHARLES (MISSOURI) - BACK - 1967-68 NEW ORLEANS SAINTS
BROWN, CHARLES (SYRACUSE) - BACK - 1966-67 CHICAGO BEARS; 1968
    BUFFALO BILLS (AFL)
BROWN, CHARLES EDWARD (SAN FRANCISCO) - QBACK - 1954-61 CHICAGO
    BEARS; 1962-65 PITTSBURGH STEELERS; 1965 BALTIMORE COLTS; 1956
    PASSING LEADER
BROWN, CHARLES KELLY (NORTHERN ARIZONA) - END - 1970 DETROIT LIONS
    (NFC)
BROWN, DANIEL (VILLANOVA) - END - 1950 WASHINGTON REDSKINS
BROWN, DAVID (ALABAMA) - BACK - 1943, 46-47 NEW YORK GIANTS
BROWN, DEAN (FORT VALLEY STATE) - BACK - 1969 CLEVELAND BROWNS; 1970
    MIAMI DOLPHINS (AFC)
BROWN, DONALD (HOUSTON) - BACK - 1960 HOUSTON OILERS (AFL)
BROWN, DOUGLAS (FRESNO STATE) - TACKLE - 1964 OAKLAND RAIDERS (AFL)
BROWN, EDDIE (TENNESSEE) - BACK - 1974 CLEVELAND BROWNS (AFC)
BROWN, EDWIN (SYRACUSE) - BACK - 1922 MILWAUKEE BADGERS
BROWN, FREDERICK (GEORGIA) - BACK - 1961, 63 BUFFALO BILLS (AFL)
BROWN, FREDERICK (MIAMI) - LB, END - 1965 LOS ANGELES RAMS; 1967-69
    PHILADELPHIA EAGLES
BROWN, FREDERICK (NEW YORK UNIV.) - GUARD - 1930 STATEN ISLAND
    STAPELTONS
BROWN, GEORGE (CARNEGIE TECH) - GUARD - 1919-20, 23 AKRON PROS
BROWN, GEORGE (TCU) - GUARD - 1949 NEW YORK YANKEES (AAFC); 1950 NEW
    YORK YANKS
BROWNE, GORDON (BOSTON COLLEGE) - TACKLE - 1974 NEW YORK JETS (AFC)
BROWN, HARDY (TULSA) - LB - 1948 BROOKLYN DODGERS (AAFC); 1949
    CHICAGO HORNETS (AAFC); 1950 BALTIMORE COLTS; 1950 WASHINGTON
    REDSKINS; 1951-56 SAN FRANCISCO 49ERS; 1956 CHICAGO CARDINALS;
    1960 DENVER BRONCOS (AFL)
BROWN, HOWARD (INDIANA) - GUARD - 1948-50 DETROIT LIONS
BROWN, JACK R. (DAYTON) - CENTER - 1926-29 DAYTON TRIANGLES
BROWN, JAMES (SYRACUSE) - BACK - 1957-65 CLEVELAND BROWNS; 1957-61,
    63-65 RUSHING LEADER; 1958 SCORING LEADER; 1971 HALL OF FAME
BROWN, JESSE (PITTSBURGH) - BACK - 1926 POTTSVILLE MAROONS
BROWN, JOHN (NORTH CAROLINA COLLEGE) - CENTER - 1947-49 LOS ANGELES
    DONS (AAFC)
BROWN, JOHN (SYRACUSE) - TACKLE - 1962-66 CLEVELAND BROWNS; 1967-69
    PITTSBURGH STEELERS; 1970-71 PITTSBURGH STEELERS (AFC)
BROWN, KENNETH - BACK - 1970-74 CLEVELAND BROWNS (AFC)
BROWN, LARRY (KANSAS) - END - 1971-74 PITTSBURGH STEELERS (AFC)
BROWN, LAWRENCE (KANSAS STATE) - BACK - 1969 WASHINGTON REDSKINS;
    1970-74 WASHINGTON REDSKINS (NFC); 1970, 72 RUSHING LEADER (NFC)
BROWN, MARVIN (EAST TEXAS STATE) - BACK - 1957 DETROIT LIONS
BROWN, MATTHEW (SYRACUSE) - BACK - 1919 CLEVELAND INDIANS

BROWN, OTTO (PRAIRIE VIEW) - BACK - 1969 DALLAS COWBOYS; 1970-73 NEW
     YORK GIANTS (NFC)
BROWN, PETER (GEORGIA TECH) - CENTER - 1953-54 SAN FRANCISCO 49ERS
BROWN, RAY (WEST TEXAS STATE) - BACK - 1971-74 ATLANTA FALCONS (NFC);
     1974 INTERCEPTION LEADER (NFC)
BROWN, RAYMOND - BACK - 1919-20 ROCHESTER JEFFERSONS
BROWN, RAYMOND (MISSISSIPPI) - BACK - 1958-60 BALTIMORE COLTS
BROWN, RICHARD (IOWA) - GUARD - 1930 PORTSMOUTH SPARTANS
BROWN, ROBERT EARL (ALCORN A&M) - END - 1969 ST. LOUIS CARDINALS;
     1970 ST. LOUIS CARDINALS (NFC); 1971 MINNESOTA VIKINGS (NFC);
     1972-73 NEW ORLEANS SAINTS (NFC)
BROWN, ROBERT EDDIE (ARKANSAS AM&N) - END, TACKLE - 1966-69 GREEN BAY
     PACKERS; 1970-73 GREEN BAY PACKERS (NFC); 1974 SAN DIEGO
     CHARGERS (AFC)
BROWN, ROBERT STANFORD (NEBRASKA) - TACKLE - 1964-68 PHILADELPHIA
     EAGLES; 1969 LOS ANGELES RAMS; 1970 LOS ANGELES RAMS (NFC);
     1971-73 OAKLAND RAIDERS (AFC)
BROWN, ROGER (MARYLAND STATE) - TACKLE - 1960-66 DETROIT LIONS;
     1967-69 LOS ANGELES RAMS
BROWN, ROOSEVELT (MORGAN STATE) - TACKLE - 1953-65 NEW YORK GIANTS;
     1975 HALL OF FAME
BROWN, STANLEY (PURDUE) - END - 1971 CLEVELAND BROWNS (AFC)
BROWN, TERRY (OKLAHOMA STATE) - BACK - 1969 ST. LOUIS CARDINALS; 1970
     ST. LOUIS CARDINALS (NFC); 1972-74 MINNESOTA VIKINGS (NFC)
BROWN, THOMAS "TIM" (BALL STATE-INDIANA) - BACK - 1959 GREEN BAY
     PACKERS; 1960-67 PHILADELPHIA EAGLES; 1968 BALTIMORE COLTS
BROWN, THOMAS (MARYLAND) - BACK - 1964-68 GREEN BAY PACKERS; 1969
     WASHINGTON REDSKINS
BROWN, THOMAS (WILLIAM&MARY) - END - 1942 PITTSBURGH STEELERS
BROWN, THOMAS - TACKLE - 1919 TOLEDO MAROONS
BROWN, WILLIAM (ARKANSAS) - GUARD - 1951-52 WASHINGTON REDSKINS;
     1953-56 GREEN BAY PACKERS
BROWN, WILLIAM FERDIE (GRAMBLING) - BACK - 1963-66 DENVER BRONCOS
     (AFL); 1967-69 OAKLAND RAIDERS (AFL); 1970-74 OAKLAND RAIDERS
     (AFC)
BROWN, WILLIAM DORSEY (ILLINOIS) - BACK - 1961 CHICAGO BEARS; 1962-69
     MINNESOTA VIKINGS; 1970-74 MINNESOTA VIKINGS (NFC)
BROWN, WILLIAM (SYRACUSE) - LB - 1960 BOSTON PATRIOTS (AFL)
BROWN, WILLIAM (TEXAS TECH) - QBACK - 1943 BROOKLYN DODGERS; 1944
     BROOKLYN TIGERS; 1945 PITTSBURGH STEELERS
BROWN, WILLIE (USC) - BACK - 1964-65 LOS ANGELES RAMS; 1966
     PHILADELPHIA EAGLES
BROWNING, CHARLES (WASHINGTON) - BACK - 1965 NEW YORK JETS (AFL)
BROWNING, GREGORY (DENVER) - END - 1947 NEW YORK GIANTS
BROWNING, ROBERT (WILLIAM JEWELL-MO.) - QBACK - 1925 KANSAS CITY
     COWBOYS
BROWNLEE, CLAUDE (BENEDICT) - END - 1967 MIAMI DOLPHINS (AFL)
BRUBAKER, RICHARD (OHIO STATE) - END - 1955, 57 CHICAGO CARDINALS;
     1960 BUFFALO BILLS (AFL)
BRUCE, GAIL (WASHINGTON) - END - 1948-49 SAN FRANCISCO 49ERS (AAFC);
     1950-51 SAN FRANCISCO 49ERS
BRUCKNER, LESLIE (MICHIGAN STATE) - BACK - 1945 CHICAGO CARDINALS
BRUDER, HENRY (NORTHWESTERN) - QBACK - 1931-39 GREEN BAY PACKERS;
     1940 PITTSBURGH STEELERS
BRUDER, WOODRUFF (WEST VIRGINIA) - BACK - 1925 BUFFALO BISONS;
     1925-26 FRANKFORD YELLOWJACKETS
BRUECKMAN, CHARLES (PITTSBURGH) - CENTER - 1958 WASHINGTON REDSKINS;
     1960 LOS ANGELES CHARGERS (AFL)
BRUGGERS, ROBERT (MINNESOTA) - LB - 1967-68 MIAMI DOLPHINS (AFL);
     1968-69 SAN DIEGO CHARGERS (AFL); 1970-71 SAN DIEGO CHARGERS
     (AFC)
BRUMBAUGH, BOYD (DUQUESNE) - BACK - 1937-39 BROOKLYN DODGERS; 1939-41
     PITTSBURGH STEELERS
BRUMBAUGH, CARL (FLORIDA) - QBACK - 1930-34, 36 CHICAGO BEARS; 1937
     CLEVELAND RAMS; 1938 CHICAGO BEARS
BRUMBAUGH, JUSTIN (BUCKNELL) - BACK - 1931 FRANKFORD YELLOWJACKETS
BRUMFIELD, JACKSON (MISSISSIPPI SOUTHERN) - END - 1954 SAN FRANCISCO
     49ERS
BRUMFIELD, JAMES (INDIANA STATE) - BACK - 1971 PITTSBURGH STEELERS
     (AFC)
BRUMLEY, ROBERT (RICE) - BACK - 1945 DETROIT LIONS

BRUMM, DONALD (PURDUE) - END - 1963-69 ST. LOUIS CARDINALS; 1970-71
     PHILADELPHIA EAGLES (NFC); 1972 ST. LOUIS CARDINALS (NFC)
BRUMM, ROMAN (WISCONSIN) - GUARD - 1922, 24 RACINE LEGION; 1925
     MILWAUKEE BADGERS; 1926 RACINE LEGION
BRUNDAGE, DEWEY (BRIGHAM YOUNG) - END - 1954 PITTSBURGH STEELERS
BRUNDIGE, WILLIAM (COLORADO) - TACKLE, END - 1970-74 WASHINGTON
     REDSKINS (NFC)
BRUNELLI, SAMUEL (COLORADO STATE COLLEGE) - TACKLE - 1966-69 DENVER
     BRONCOS (AFL); 1970-71 DENVER BRONCOS (AFC)
BRUNET, ROBERT (LOUISIANA TECH) - BACK - 1968 WASHINGTON REDSKINS;
     1970-73 WASHINGTON REDSKINS (NFC)
BRUNEY, FRED (OHIO STATE) - END - 1953, 56 SAN FRANCISCO 49ERS;
     1956-57 PITTSBURGH STEELERS; 1958 LOS ANGELES RAMS; 1960-62
     BOSTON PATRIOTS (AFL)
BRUNKLACHER, AUSTIN - GUARD - 1921-23 LOUISVILLE BRECKS
BRUNSON, LARRY (COLORADO) - END - 1974 KANSAS CITY CHIEFS (AFC)
BRUNSON, MICHAEL (ARIZONA STATE) - END - 1970 ATLANTA FALCONS (NFC)
BRUPBACHER, ROSS (TEXAS A&M) - LB - 1970-72 CHICAGO BEARS (NFC)
BRUTZ, JAMES (NOTRE DAME) - TACKLE - 1946, 48 CHICAGO ROCKETS (AAFC)
BRYAN, JOHN (CHICAGO) - BACK - 1922 CHICAGO CARDINALS; 1923-25
     CHICAGO BEARS; 1925-26 MILWAUKEE BADGERS; 1926 CHICAGO CARDINALS
BRYANT, BOBBY (SOUTH CAROLINA) - BACK - 1968-69 MINNESOTA VIKINGS;
     1970-74 MINNESOTA VIKINGS (NFC); 1973 INTERCEPTION LEADER (NFC)
BRYANT, CHARLES (ALLEN) - BACK - 1966-67 ST. LOUIS CARDINALS; 1968-69
     ATLANTA FALCONS
BRYANT, CHARLES (OHIO STATE) - END - 1962 ST. LOUIS CARDINALS
BRYANT, HUBIE (MINNESOTA) - END - 1970 PITTSBURGH STEELERS (AFC);
     1971-72 NEW ENGLAND PATRIOTS (AFC)
BRYANT, JAMES (PENNSYLVANIA) - BACK - 1919 AKRON PROS; 1920 CLEVELAND
     PANTHERS
BRYANT, ROBERT (TEXAS) - END - 1960 DALLAS TEXANS (AFL)
BRYANT, ROBERT (TEXAS TECH) - TACKLE - 1946-49 SAN FRANCISCO 49ERS
     (AAFC)
BRYANT, WALTER (TEXAS TECH) - BACK - 1955 BALTIMORE COLTS
BRYANT, WILLIAM CULLEN (COLORADO) - BACK - 1973-74 LOS ANGELES RAMS
     (NFC)
BRYANT, WAYMOND (TENNESSEE STATE) - LB - 1974 CHICAGO BEARS (NFC)
BUCCHIANERI, AMADEO (INDIANA) - GUARD - 1941, 44-45 GREEN BAY PACKERS
BUCEK, FELIX (TEXAS A&M) - GUARD - 1946 PITTSBURGH STEELERS
BUCHANAN, JUNIOUS "BUCK" (GRAMBLING) - TACKLE - 1963-69 KANSAS CITY
     CHIEFS (AFL); 1970-74 KANSAS CITY CHIEFS (AFC)
BUCHANAN, STEPHEN (MIAMI-OHIO) - QBACK - 1929 DAYTON TRIANGLES
BUCHANAN, TIMOTHY (HAWAII) - LB - 1969 CINCINNATI BENGALS (AFL)
BUCHANON, WILLIE (SAN DIEGO STATE) - BACK - 1972-74 GREEN BAY PACKERS
     (NFC)
BUCHER, FRANK (DETROIT) - END - 1925 DETROIT PANTHERS; 1925-26
     POTTSVILLE MAROONS
BUCK, HOWARD (WISCONSIN) - TACKLE - 1919-20 CANTON BULLDOGS; 1921-25
     GREEN BAY PACKERS
BUCKEYE, GARLAND - GUARD - 1920 CHICAGO TIGERS; 1920-24 CHICAGO
     CARDINALS; 1926 CHICAGO BULLS (AFL)
BUCKLER, WILLIAM (ALABAMA) - GUARD - 1926-28, 31-33 CHICAGO BEARS
BUCKLEW, PHILIP (XAVIER) - END - 1937 CLEVELAND RAMS; 1940-41
     COLUMBUS BULLIES (AFL)
BUCKLEY, EDWARD (NEW YORK UNIV.) - QBACK - 1930 STATEN ISLAND
     STAPELTONS
BUCKLEY, RUSSELL (GUSTAVOS-ADOLPHUS) - BACK - 1940-41 COLUMBUS
     BULLIES (AFL)
BUCKLIN, THOMAS (IDAHO) - BACK - 1926 LOS ANGELES WILDCATS (AFL);
     1927 CHICAGO CARDINALS; 1931 NEW YORK GIANTS
BUCKMAN, THOMAS (TEXAS A&M) - END - 1969 DENVER BRONCOS (AFL)
BUDA, CARL (TULSA) - GUARD - 1945 PITTSBURGH STEELERS
BUDD, FRANK (VILLANOVA) - BACK - 1962 PHILADELPHIA EAGLES; 1963
     WASHINGTON REDSKINS
BUDD, JOHN (LAFAYETTE) - TACKLE - 1926 FRANKFORD YELLOWJACKETS;
     1927-28 POTTSVILLE MAROONS
BUDDE, EDWARD (MICHIGAN STATE) - GUARD - 1963-69 KANSAS CITY CHIEFS
     (AFL); 1970-74 KANSAS CITY CHIEFS (AFC)
BUDKA, FRANK (NOTRE DAME) - BACK - 1964 LOS ANGELES RAMS

BUDNESS, WILLIAM (BOSTON UNIV.) - LB - 1964-69 OAKLAND RAIDERS (AFL);
     1970 OAKLAND RAIDERS (AFC)
BUDREWICZ, THOMAS (BROWN) - GUARD - 1961 NEW YORK TITANS (AFL)
BUEHLER, GEORGE (STANFORD) - GUARD - 1969 OAKLAND RAIDERS (AFL);
     1970-74 OAKLAND RAIDERS (AFC)
BUETOW, BART (MINNESOTA) - TACKLE - 1973 NEW YORK GIANTS (NFC)
BUFFALO - GUARD - 1922-23 OORANG INDIANS
BUFFINGTON, HARRY (OKLAHOMA A&M) - GUARD - 1942 NEW YORK GIANTS;
     1946-48 BROOKLYN DODGERS (AAFC)
BUFFONE, DOUGLAS (LOUISVILLE) - LB - 1966-69 CHICAGO BEARS; 1970-74
     CHICAGO BEARS (NFC)
BUGENHAGEN, GARY (SYRACUSE) - TACKLE, GUARD - 1967 BUFFALO BILLS
     (AFL); 1970 BOSTON PATRIOTS (AFC)
BUHLER, LAWRENCE (MINNESOTA) - BACK - 1939-41 GREEN BAY PACKERS
BUIE, L. DREW (CATAWBA) - END - 1969 OAKLAND RAIDERS (AFL); 1970-71
     OAKLAND RAIDERS (AFC); 1972 CINCINNATI BENGALS (AFC)
BUIVID, RAYMOND (MARQUETTE) - BACK - 1937 NEW YORK YANKS (AFL);
     1937-38 CHICAGO BEARS
BUKANT, JOSEPH (WASHINGTON-MO.) - BACK - 1938-40 PHILADELPHIA EAGLES;
     1942-43 CHICAGO CARDINALS
BUKATY, FREDERICK (KANSAS) - BACK - 1961 DENVER BRONCOS (AFL)
BUKICH, RUDOLPH (USC) - QBACK - 1953, 56 LOS ANGELES RAMS; 1957-58
     WASHINGTON REDSKINS; 1958-59, 62-68 CHICAGO BEARS; 1960-61
     PITTSBURGH STEELERS; 1965 PASSING LEADER
BUKOVICH, DANIEL (TOLEDO) - GUARD - 1940 BUFFALO INDIANS (AFL)
BUKSAR, GEORGE (PURDUE) - BACK - 1949 CHICAGO HORNETS (AAFC); 1950
     BALTIMORE COLTS; 1951-52 WASHINGTON REDSKINS
BULAICH, NORMAN (TCU) - BACK - 1970-72 BALTIMORE COLTS (AFC); 1973-74
     PHILADELPHIA EAGLES (NFC)
BULAND, WALTER - TACKLE - 1919-21, 24 ROCK ISLAND INDEPENDENTS; 1924
     GREEN BAY PACKERS; 1926 DULUTH ESKIMOS
BULGER, CHESTER (AUBURN) - TACKLE - 1942-43, 45-49 CHICAGO CARDINALS;
     1944 CARD-PITT; 1950 DETROIT LIONS
BULL, RONALD (BAYLOR) - BACK - 1962-69 CHICAGO BEARS; 1970 CHICAGO
     BEARS (NFC); 1971 PHILADELPHIA EAGLES (NFC)
BULLMAN, GALE (WEST VIRGINIA WESLEYAN) - END - 1925 COLUMBUS TIGERS
BULLOCKS, AMOS (SOUTHERN ILLINOIS) - BACK - 1962-64 DALLAS COWBOYS;
     1966 PITTSBURGH STEELERS
BULLOUGH, HENRY (MICHIGAN STATE) - GUARD - 1955, 58 GREEN BAY PACKERS
BULTMAN, ARTHUR (MARQUETTE) - CENTER - 1931 BROOKLYN DODGERS; 1932-34
     GREEN BAY PACKERS
BUMGARDNER, REX (WEST VIRGINIA) - BACK - 1948-49 BUFFALO BILLS
     (AAFC); 1950-52 CLEVELAND BROWNS
BUNCOM, FRANK (USC) - LB - 1962-67 SAN DIEGO CHARGERS (AFL); 1968
     CINCINNATI BENGALS (AFL)
BUNDRA, MICHAEL (USC) - TACKLE - 1962-63 DETROIT LIONS; 1964
     MINNESOTA VIKINGS; 1964 CLEVELAND BROWNS; 1965 NEW YORK GIANTS;
     1965 BALTIMORE COLTS
BUNTING, JOHN (NORTH CAROLINA) - LB - 1972-74 PHILADELPHIA EAGLES
     (NFC)
BUNYAN, JOHN (NEW YORK UNIV.) - GUARD - 1929-30, 32 STATEN ISLAND
     STAPELTONS; 1932 BROOKLYN DODGERS
BUONICONTI, NICHOLAS (NOTRE DAME) - LB - 1962-68 BOSTON PATRIOTS
     (AFL); 1969 MIAMI DOLPHINS (AFL); 1970-74 MIAMI DOLPHINS (AFC)
BURCH, GERALD (GEORGIA TECH) - END - 1961 OAKLAND RAIDERS (AFL)
BURCH, WILLIAM (CENTENARY) - BACK - 1937 CINCINNATI BENGALS (AFL)
BURCHFIELD, DONALD (BALL STATE-INDIANA) - END - 1971 NEW ORLEANS
     SAINTS (NFC)
BURDICK, LLOYD (ILLINOIS) - TACKLE - 1931-32 CHICAGO BEARS; 1933
     CINCINNATI REDS
BURFORD, CHRISTOPHER (STANFORD) - END - 1960-62 DALLAS TEXANS (AFL);
     1963-67 KANSAS CITY CHIEFS (AFL)
BURGEIS, GLEN (TULSA) - TACKLE - 1945 CHICAGO BEARS
BURGIN, ALBERT - GUARD - 1922 TOLEDO MAROONS
BURGNER, EARL (WITTENBERG) - BACK - 1923 DAYTON TRIANGLES
BURK, ADRIAN (BAYLOR) - QBACK - 1950 BALTIMORE COLTS; 1951-56
     PHILADELPHIA EAGLES
BURKE, CHARLES (DARTMOUTH) - BACK - 1925-26 PROVIDENCE STEAMROLLERS
BURKE, DONALD (USC) - LB - 1950-54 SAN FRANCISCO 49ERS
BURKE, MICHAEL (MIAMI) - KICKER - 1974 LOS ANGELES RAMS (NFC)
BURKE, ROBERT - TACKLE - 1927 DULUTH ESKIMOS

BURKE, VERNON (OREGON STATE) - END - 1965 SAN FRANCISCO 49ERS; 1966
    ATLANTA FALCONS; 1967 NEW ORLEANS SAINTS
BURKETT, JEFFERSON (LSU) - END - 1947 CHICAGO CARDINALS
BURKETT, WALTER JACKSON "JACKIE" (AUBURN) - LB - 1961-66 BALTIMORE
    COLTS; 1967 NEW ORLEANS SAINTS; 1968-69 DALLAS COWBOYS; 1970 NEW
    ORLEANS SAINTS (NFC)
BURKS, JOSEPH (WASHINGTON STATE) - CENTER - 1926 MILWAUKEE BADGERS
BURL, ALEX (COLORADO A&M) - BACK - 1956 CHICAGO CARDINALS
BURLESON, JOHN (SMU) - GUARD - 1933 PITTSBURGH PIRATES; 1933
    CINCINNATI REDS; 1933 PORTSMOUTH SPARTANS
BURMAN, GEORGE (NORTHWESTERN) - CENTER, GUARD - 1964 CHICAGO BEARS;
    1967-69 LOS ANGELES RAMS; 1970 LOS ANGELES RAMS (NFC); 1971-72
    WASHINGTON REDSKINS (NFC)
BURMEISTER, FORREST (PURDUE) - GUARD - 1937 CLEVELAND RAMS
BURNELL, HERMAN "MAX" (NOTRE DAME) - BACK - 1944 CHICAGO BEARS
BURNETT, DALE (EMPORIA-KANSAS) - BACK - 1930-39 NEW YORK GIANTS
BURNETT, LEONARD (OREGON) - END - 1961 PITTSBURGH STEELERS
BURNETT, ROBERT (ARKANSAS) - BACK - 1966-67 BUFFALO BILLS (AFL); 1969
    DENVER BRONCOS (AFL)
BURNETT, RAYMOND - BACK - 1938 CHICAGO CARDINALS
BURNETTE, THOMAS (NORTH CAROLINA) - BACK - 1938 PITTSBURGH PIRATES;
    1938 PHILADELPHIA EAGLES
BURNHAM, STANLEY (HARVARD) - BACK - 1925 FRANKFORD YELLOWJACKETS
BURNINE, HAROLD (MISSOURI) - END - 1956 NEW YORK GIANTS; 1956-57
    PHILADELPHIA EAGLES
BURNS, LEON (LONG BEACH STATE) - BACK - 1971 SAN DIEGO CHARGERS (AFC)
BURNS, ROBERT (GEORGIA) - BACK - 1974 NEW YORK JETS (AFC)
BURNSIDE, GEORGE (WISCONSIN & SOUTH DAKOTA) - QBACK - 1926 RACINE
    LEGION
BURRELL, GEORGE (PENNSYLVANIA) - BACK - 1969 DENVER BRONCOS (AFL)
BURRELL, JOHN (RICE) - END - 1962-64 PITTSBURGH STEELERS; 1966-67
    WASHINGTON REDSKINS
BURRELL, ODE (MISSISSIPPI STATE) - BACK - 1964-69 HOUSTON OILERS (AFL)
BURRIS, JAMES "BO" (HOUSTON) - BACK - 1967-69 NEW ORLEANS SAINTS
BURRIS, PAUL (OKLAHOMA) - GUARD - 1949-51 GREEN BAY PACKERS
BURROUGH, KENNETH (TEXAS SOUTHERN) - END - 1970 NEW ORLEANS SAINTS
    (NFC); 1971-74 HOUSTON OILERS (AFC)
BURROUGHS, DONALD (COLORADO A&M) - BACK - 1955-59 LOS ANGELES RAMS;
    1960-64 PHILADELPHIA EAGLES
BURROW, KENNETH (SAN DIEGO STATE) - END - 1971-74 ATLANTA FALCONS
    (NFC)
BURRUS, HARRY (HARDIN-SIMMONS) - END - 1946-47 NEW YORK YANKEES
    (AAFC); 1948 BROOKLYN DODGERS (AAFC); 1948 CHICAGO ROCKETS (AAFC)
BURSON, JAMES (AUBURN) - BACK - 1963-67 ST. LOUIS CARDINALS; 1968
    ATLANTA FALCONS
BURT, HAROLD (KANSAS) - GUARD - 1925 CLEVELAND BULLDOGS; 1925 CANTON
    BULLDOGS
BURT, RUSSELL (CANISIUS) - BACK - 1925 BUFFALO BISONS
BURTON, LEON (ARIZONA STATE) - BACK - 1960 NEW YORK TITANS (AFL)
BURTON, LYLE (DEPAUW) - GUARD - 1924-25 ROCK ISLAND INDEPENDENTS
BURTON, RONALD (NORTHWESTERN) - BACK - 1960-65 BOSTON PATRIOTS (AFL)
BUSBY, SHERRILL (TROY STATE-ALABAMA) - END - 1940 BROOKLYN DODGERS
BUSSEY, DEXTER (TEXAS-ARLINGTON) - BACK - 1974 DETROIT LIONS (NFC)
BUSCH, ELMER (CARLISLE) - GUARD - 1922-23 OORANG INDIANS
BUSCH, NICHOLAS (GONZAGA) - GUARD - 1926 LOS ANGELES BUCCANEERS
BUSH, RAYMOND (LOYOLA OF CHICAGO) - END - 1926 LOUISVILLE COLONELS
BUSHBY, THOMAS (KANSAS STATE) - BACK - 1934 CINCINNATI REDS; 1935
    PHILADELPHIA EAGLES
BUSICH, SAMUEL (OHIO STATE) - END - 1926 BOSTON BULLDOGS (AFL); 1937
    CLEVELAND RAMS; 1943 DETROIT LIONS
BUSLER, RAYMOND (MARQUETTE) - TACKLE - 1940-41, 45 CHICAGO CARDINALS
BUSS, ARTHUR (MICHIGAN STATE) - TACKLE - 1934-35 CHICAGO BEARS;
    1936-37 PHILADELPHIA EAGLES
BUSSE, ELLIS (CHICAGO) - BACK - 1929 CHICAGO CARDINALS
BUSSELL, GERALD (GEORGIA TECH) - BACK - 1965 DENVER BRONCOS (AFL)
BUSSEY, YOUNG (LSU) - QBACK - 1940-41 CHICAGO BEARS
BUTCHER, WENDELL (GUSTAVUS-ADOLPHUS) - BACK - 1939-42 BROOKLYN DODGERS
BUTKUS, CARL (GEORGE WASHINGTON) - TACKLE - 1948 WASHINGTON REDSKINS;
    1948 NEW YORK YANKEES (AAFC); 1949 NEW YORK GIANTS

BUTKUS, RICHARD (ILLINOIS) - LB - 1965-69 CHICAGO BEARS; 1970-73
     CHICAGO BEARS (NFC)
BUTLER, EDWARD "SOL" (DUBUQUE) - BACK - 1923 ROCK ISLAND
     INDEPENDENTS; 1923-24, 26 HAMMOND PROS; 1924 AKRON PROS; 1926
     CANTON BULLDOGS
BUTLER, FRANK (MICHIGAN STATE) - CENTER - 1934-36, 38 GREEN BAY
     PACKERS
BUTLER, GARY (RICE) - END - 1973-74 KANSAS CITY CHIEFS (AFC)
BUTLER, JAMES (EDWARD WATERS) - BACK - 1965-67 PITTSBURGH STEELERS;
     1968-69 ATLANTA FALCONS; 1970-71 ATLANTA FALCONS (NFC); 1972 ST.
     LOUIS CARDINALS (NFC)
BUTLER, JAMES A. (TULSA) - END - 1972 HOUSTON OILERS (AFC)
BUTLER, JOHN (ST.BONAVENTURE) - BACK - 1951-59 PITTSBURGH STEELERS;
     1957 INTERCEPTION LEADER; (TIED WITH M. DAVIS AND CHRISTIANSEN)
BUTLER, JOHN (TENNESSEE) - BACK - 1943 PHIL-PITT; 1944 CARD-PITT;
     1944 BROOKLYN TIGERS; 1945 PHILADELPHIA EAGLES
BUTLER, ROBERT (KENTUCKY) - GUARD - 1962 PHILADELPHIA EAGLES; 1963
     NEW YORK JETS (AFL)
BUTLER, WILLIAM (CHATTANOOGA) - BACK - 1959 GREEN BAY PACKERS; 1960
     DALLAS COWBOYS; 1961 PITTSBURGH STEELERS; 1962-64 MINNESOTA
     VIKINGS
BUTLER, WILLIAM (KANSAS STATE) - BACK - 1972-74 NEW ORLEANS SAINTS
     (NFC)
BUTLER, WILLIAM (SAN FERNANDO VALLEY) - LB - 1970 DENVER BRONCOS (AFC)
BUTLER WILLIAM "SKIP" (TEXAS-ARLINGTON) - KICKER - 1971 NEW ORLEANS
     SAINTS (NFC); 1971 NEW YORK GIANTS (NFC); 1972-74 HOUSTON OILERS
     (AFC)
BUTSKO, HARRY (MARYLAND) - LB - 1963 WASHINGTON REDSKINS
BUTTS, EDWARD (CHICO STATE) - BACK - 1929 CHICAGO CARDINALS
BUTZ, DAVID (PURDUE) - END, TACKLE - 1973-74 ST. LOUIS CARDINALS (NFC)
BUZIN, RICHARD (PENN STATE) - TACKLE - 1968-69 NEW YORK GIANTS; 1970
     NEW YORK GIANTS (NFC); 1971 LOS ANGELES RAMS (NFC); 1972 CHICAGO
     BEARS (NFC)
BUZYNSKI, BERNARD (HOLY CROSS) - LB - 1960 BUFFALO BILLS (AFL)
BYAS, RICK (WAYNE STATE) - BACK - 1974 ATLANTA FALCONS (NFC)
BYERS, KENNETH (CINCINNATI) - GUARD - 1962-64 NEW YORK GIANTS;
     1964-65 MINNESOTA VIKINGS
BYKOWSKI, FRANK (PURDUE) - GUARD - 1940 PITTSBURGH STEELERS; 1940-41
     MILWAUKEE CHIEFS (AFL)
BYLER, JOSEPH (NEBRASKA) - TACKLE - 1946 NEW YORK GIANTS
BYRD, DENNIS (NORTH CAROLINA STATE) - END - 1968 BOSTON PATRIOTS (AFL)
BYRD, GEORGE "BUTCH" (BOSTON UNIV.) - BACK - 1964-69 BUFFALO BILLS
     (AFL); 1970 BUFFALO BILLS (AFC); 1971 DENVER BRONCOS (AFC)
BYRD, MACARTHUR (USC) - LB - 1965 LOS ANGELES RAMS
BYRD, THOMAS (KENTUCKY STATE) - GUARD - 1941 NEW YORK AMERICANS (AFL)
BYRNE, WILLIAM (BOSTON COLLEGE) - GUARD - 1963 PHILADELPHIA EAGLES
CABRELLI, LAWRENCE (COLGATE) - END - 1941-42 PHILADELPHIA EAGLES;
     1943 PHIL-PITT; 1944-47 PHILADELPHIA EAGLES
CABRINHA, AUGUST (DAYTON) - BACK - 1927 DAYTON TRIANGLES
CADDEL, ERNEST (STANFORD) - BACK - 1933 PORTSMOUTH SPARTANS; 1934-38
     DETROIT LIONS
CADILE, JAMES (SAN JOSE STATE) - GUARD, CENTER - 1962-69 CHICAGO
     BEARS; 1970-72 CHICAGO BEARS (NFC)
CADWELL, JOHN (OREGON STATE) - GUARD - 1961 DALLAS TEXANS (AFL)
CAFEGO, GEORGE (TENNESSEE) - QBACK - 1940, 43 BROOKLYN DODGERS; 1943
     WASHINGTON REDSKINS; 1944-45 BOSTON YANKS
CAFFEY, LEE ROY (TEXAS A&M) - LB - 1963 PHILADELPHIA EAGLES; 1964-69
     GREEN BAY PACKERS; 1970 CHICAGO BEARS (NFC); 1971 DALLAS COWBOYS
     (NFC); 1972 SAN DIEGO CHARGERS (AFC)
CAGLE, CHRISTIAN (WEST POINT & S.W.LA.) - BACK - 1930-32 NEW YORK
     GIANTS; 1933-34 BROOKLYN DODGERS
CAGLE, JAMES (GEORGIA) - TACKLE - 1974 PHILADELPHIA EAGLES (NFC)
CAGLE, JOHN (CLEMSON) - END - 1969 BOSTON PATRIOTS (AFL)
CAHILL, DAVID (ARIZONA STATE) - TACKLE - 1966 PHILADELPHIA EAGLES;
     1967 LOS ANGELES RAMS; 1969 ATLANTA FALCONS
CAHILL, RONALD (HOLY CROSS) - BACK - 1943 CHICAGO CARDINALS
CAHILL, WILLIAM (WASHINGTON) - BACK - 1973-74 BUFFALO BILLS (AFC)
CAHILL (NOTRE DAME) - TACKLE - 1920 CHICAGO TIGERS
CAHOON, IVAN (GONZAGA) - TACKLE - 1926-29 GREEN BAY PACKERS

CAIN, JAMES (ALABAMA) - END - 1949 CHICAGO CARDINALS; 1950, 53-55
    DETROIT LIONS
CAIN, JAMES "J.V." (COLORADO) - END - 1974 ST. LOUIS CARDINALS (NFC)
CALAC, PETER (CARLISLE) - BACK - 1919-20, 25-26 CANTON BULLDOGS; 1921
    CLEVELAND INDIANS; 1922-23 OORANG INDIANS; 1924 BUFFALO BISONS
CALAHAN, JAMES (TEXAS) - BACK - 1946 DETROIT LIONS
CALCAGNI, CLEO RALPH (PENNSYLVANIA) - TACKLE - 1946 BOSTON YANKS;
    1947 PITTSBURGH STEELERS
CALDWELL, BRUCE (YALE) - BACK - 1928 NEW YORK GIANTS
CALDWELL, CYRIL (BALDWIN-WALLACE & WABASH) - TACKLE - 1925-26 AKRON
    PROS
CALEB, JAMIE (GRAMBLING) - BACK - 1960 CLEVELAND BROWNS; 1961
    MINNESOTA VIKINGS; 1965 CLEVELAND BROWNS
CALHOUN, DON (KANSAS STATE) - BACK - 1974 BUFFALO BILLS (AFC)
CALHOUN, ERIC (DENISON) - TACKLE - 1926 DAYTON TRIANGLES
CALLAND, LEE (LOUISVILLE) - BACK - 1963-65 MINNESOTA VIKINGS; 1966-68
    ATLANTA FALCONS; 1969 CHICAGO BEARS; 1969 PITTSBURGH STEELERS;
    1970-72 PITTSBURGH STEELERS (AFC)
CALL, JOHN (COLGATE) - BACK - 1957-58 BALTIMORE COLTS; 1959
    PITTSBURGH STEELERS
CALLAHAN, DANIEL (WOOSTER) - GUARD - 1960 NEW YORK TITANS (AFL)
CALLAHAN, ROBERT (MICHIGAN) - CENTER - 1948 BUFFALO BILLS (AAFC)
CALLIGARO, LEONARD (WISCONSIN) - QBACK - 1944 NEW YORK GIANTS
CALLIHAN, WILLIAM (NEBRASKA) - QBACK - 1940-45 DETROIT LIONS
CALLOWAY, ERNEST (TEXAS SOUTHERN) - TACKLE, END - 1969 PHILADELPHIA
    EAGLES; 1970-72 PHILADELPHIA EAGLES (NFC)
CALVELLI, ANTHONY (STANFORD) - CENTER - 1939-40 DETROIT LIONS; 1947
    SAN FRANCISCO 49ERS (AAFC)
CALVIN, THOMAS (ALABAMA) - BACK - 1952-54 PITTSBURGH STEELERS
CAMBAL, DENNIS (WILLIAM&MARY) - BACK, END - 1973 NEW YORK JETS (AFC)
CAMERON, EDMUND (WASHINGTON&LEE) - GUARD - 1926 DETROIT PANTHERS
CAMERON, PAUL (UCLA) - BACK - 1954 PITTSBURGH STEELERS
CAMP, JAMES (NORTH CAROLINA) - BACK - 1948 BROOKLYN DODGERS (AAFC)
CAMPANA, ALBERT (YOUNGSTOWN) - BACK - 1950-52 CHICAGO BEARS; 1953
    CHICAGO CARDINALS
CAMPANELLA, JOSEPH (OHIO STATE) - TACKLE - 1952 DALLAS TEXANS;
    1953-57 BALTIMORE COLTS
CAMPBELL, CARTER (WEBER STATE) - LB, END - 1970 SAN FRANCISCO 49ERS
    (NFC); 1971 DENVER BRONCOS (AFC); 1972-73 NEW YORK GIANTS (NFC)
CAMPBELL, DONALD (CARNEGIE TECH) - TACKLE - 1939-40 PITTSBURGH
    STEELERS
CAMPBELL, FRANCIS MARION (GEORGIA) - TACKLE - 1954-55 SAN FRANCISCO
    49ERS; 1956-61 PHILADELPHIA EAGLES
CAMPBELL, FREEMAN (KNOX) - END - 1926 CLEVELAND PANTHERS (AFL)
CAMPBELL, GLENN (EMPORIA STATE-KANSAS) - END - 1929-33 NEW YORK
    GIANTS; 1935 PITTSBURGH PIRATES
CAMPBELL, JIMMY RAY (WEST TEXAS STATE) - LB - 1969 SAN DIEGO CHARGERS
    (AFL)
CAMPBELL, JOHN (MINNESOTA) - LB - 1963-64 MINNESOTA VIKINGS; 1965-69
    PITTSBURGH STEELERS; 1969 BALTIMORE COLTS
CAMPBELL, KENNETH (WEST CHESTER STATE) - END - 1960 NEW YORK TITANS
    (AFL)
CAMPBELL, LEON (ARKANSAS) - BACK - 1950 BALTIMORE COLTS; 1952-54
    CHICAGO BEARS; 1955 PITTSBURGH STEELERS
CAMPBELL, MICHAEL (LENIOR RHYNE) - BACK - 1968 DETROIT LIONS
CAMPBELL, MILTON (INDIANA) - BACK - 1957 CLEVELAND BROWNS
CAMPBELL, RAYMOND (MARQUETTE) - LB - 1958-60 PITTSBURGH STEELERS
CAMPBELL, ROBERT (PENN STATE) - BACK - 1969 PITTSBURGH STEELERS
CAMPBELL, SONNY (NORTHERN ARIZONA) - BACK - 1970-71 ATLANTA FALCONS
    (NFC)
CAMPBELL, STANLEY (IOWA STATE) - GUARD - 1952, 55-58 DETROIT LIONS;
    1959-61 PHILADELPHIA EAGLES; 1962 OAKLAND RAIDERS (AFL)
CAMPBELL, WILLIAM (OKLAHOMA) - GUARD - 1945-49 CHICAGO CARDINALS;
    1949 NEW YORK BULLDOGS
CAMPBELL, WOODROW (NORTHWESTERN) - BACK - 1967-69 HOUSTON OILERS
    (AFL); 1970-71 HOUSTON OILERS (AFC)
CAMPIGLIO, ROBERT (WEST LIBERTY STATE) - BACK - 1932 STATEN ISLAND
    STAPELTONS; 1933 BOSTON REDSKINS
CAMPION, THOMAS (SOUTHEASTERN LOUISIANA) - TACKLE - 1947 PHILADELPHIA
    EAGLES

CAMPOFREDA, NICHOLAS (SOUTHWESTERN MARYLAND) - CENTER - 1944
     WASHINGTON REDSKINS
CAMPORA, DONALD (COLLEGE OF THE PACIFIC) - TACKLE - 1950, 52 SAN
     FRANCISCO 49ERS; 1953 WASHINGTON REDSKINS
CANADEO, ANTHONY (GONZAGA) - BACK - 1941-44, 46-52 GREEN BAY PACKERS;
     1974 HALL OF FAME
CANADY, JAMES (TEXAS) - BACK - 1948-49 CHICAGO BEARS; 1949 NEW YORK
     BULLDOGS
CANALE, JOHN (TENNESSEE) - END - 1966 MIAMI DOLPHINS (AFL); 1968
     BOSTON PATRIOTS (AFL)
CANALE, JUSTIN (MISSISSIPPI STATE) - GUARD - 1965-68 BOSTON PATRIOTS
     (AFL); 1969 CINCINNATI BENGALS (AFL)
CANALE, ROCCO (BOSTON COLLEGE) - GUARD - 1943 PHIL-PITT; 1944-45
     PHILADELPHIA EAGLES; 1946-47 BOSTON YANKS
CANNADY, JOHN (INDIANA) - LB - 1947-54 NEW YORK GIANTS
CANNAMELA, PATRICK (USC) - GUARD - 1952 DALLAS TEXANS
CANNAVA, ANTHONY (BOSTON COLLEGE) - BACK - 1950 GREEN BAY PACKERS
CANNAVINO, JOSEPH (OHIO STATE) - BACK - 1960-61 OAKLAND RAIDERS
     (AFL); 1962 BUFFALO BILLS (AFL)
CANNELLA, JOHN (FORDHAM) - TACKLE - 1933-34 NEW YORK GIANTS; 1934
     BROOKLYN DODGERS
CANNON, WILLIAM (LSU) - BACK, END - 1960-63 HOUSTON OILERS (AFL);
     1964-69 OAKLAND RAIDERS (AFL); 1970 KANSAS CITY CHIEFS (AFC);
     1961 RUSHING LEADER (AFL)
CANTOR, LEO (UCLA) - BACK - 1942 NEW YORK GIANTS; 1945 CHICAGO
     CARDINALS
CAPATELLI, JERRY (IOWA) - GUARD - 1937 PITTSBURGH PIRATES; 1937
     ROCHESTER TIGERS (AFL)
CAPP, RICHARD (BOSTON COLLEGE) - END - 1967 GREEN BAY PACKERS; 1968
     PITTSBURGH STEELERS
CAPPADONNA, ROBERT (NORTHEASTERN) - BACK - 1966-67 BOSTON PATRIOTS
     (AFL); 1968 BUFFALO BILLS (AFL)
CAPPELLETTI, GINO (MINNESOTA) - END, KICKER - 1960-69 BOSTON PATRIOTS
     (AFL); 1970 BOSTON PATRIOTS (AFC); 1961, 63-66 SCORING LEADER
     (AFL); 1961, 63-64 FIELD GOAL LEADER (AFL)
CAPPELLETTI, JOHN (PENN STATE) - BACK - 1974 LOS ANGELES RAMS (NFC)
CAPPELMAN, GEORGE WILLIAM (FLORIDA STATE) - QBACK - 1970 MINNESOTA
     VIKINGS (NFC); 1973 DETROIT LIONS (NFC)
CAPPS, WILBUR (EAST CENTRAL OKLAHOMA) - TACKLE - 1929-30 FRANKFORD
     YELLOWJACKETS; 1930 MINNEAPOLIS REDJACKETS
CAPRIA, CARL (PURDUE) - BACK - 1974 DETROIT LIONS (NFC)
CAPUZZI, JAMES (CINCINNATI) - QBACK - 1955-56 GREEN BAY PACKERS
CARA, DOMINIC (NORTH CAROLINA STATE) - END - 1937-38 PITTSBURGH
     PIRATES
CARANCI, ROLAND (COLORADO) - TACKLE - 1944 NEW YORK GIANTS
CARAPELLA, ALBERT (MIAMI) - TACKLE - 1951-55 SAN FRANCISCO 49ERS
CARBERRY, GLENN (NOTRE DAME) - END - 1923 BUFFALO ALL-AMERICANS; 1924
     BUFFALO BISONS; 1925 CLEVELAND BULLDOGS
CARD, J. HARPER - TACKLE - 1921-22 LOUISVILLE BRECKS
CARDARELLI, CARL - CENTER - 1924 AKRON PROS; 1925 CLEVELAND BULLDOGS
CARDINAL, FRED (BALDWIN-WALLACE) - BACK - 1947 NEW YORK YANKEES (AAFC)
CARDWELL, JOHN - BACK - 1923 ST. LOUIS BROWNS
CARDWELL, JOSEPH (DUKE) - TACKLE - 1937-38 PITTSBURGH PIRATES
CARDWELL, LLOYD (NEBRASKA) - BACK - 1937-43 DETROIT LIONS
CAREY, DANA (CALIFORNIA) - GUARD - 1926 LOS ANGELES WILDCATS (AFL)
CAREY, JOSEPH - GUARD - 1920 CHICAGO CARDINALS; 1921 GREEN BAY PACKERS
CAREY, ROBERT (MICHIGAN STATE) - END - 1952, 54, 56 LOS ANGELES RAMS;
     1958 CHICAGO BEARS
CARL, HARLAND (WISCONSIN) - BACK - 1956 CHICAGO BEARS
CARLETON, ARTHUR (TUFTS) - GUARD - 1919 DETROIT HERALDS
CARLSON, CLARENCE (BELOIT) - END - 1926 LOUISVILLE COLONELS
CARLSON, DEAN (IOWA STATE) - QBACK - 1974 GREEN BAY PACKERS (NFC);
     1974 KANSAS CITY CHIEFS (AFC)
CARLSON, HAROLD (DEPAUL) - TACKLE - 1937 NEW YORK YANKS (AFL); 1937
     CHICAGO CARDINALS
CARLSON, HENRY (PITTSBURGH) - END - 1919 CLEVELAND INDIANS
CARLSON, IRVIN (ST. JOHNS) - GUARD - 1924 KENOSHA MAROONS
CARLSON, JULES (OREGON STATE) - GUARD - 1929-36 CHICAGO BEARS; 1937
     CHICAGO CARDINALS

CARLSON, OKE EUGENE (IOWA STATE) - GUARD - 1924-25 DULUTH KELLEYS;
    1926-27 DULUTH ESKIMOS
CARLSON, ROY (BRADLEY) - END - 1928 CHICAGO BEARS; 1929 DAYTON
    TRIANGLES
CARLSON, WESLEY (DETROIT) - GUARD - 1926 GREEN BAY PACKERS; 1926
    DETROIT PANTHERS
CARLTON, LINWOOD WRAY (DUKE) - BACK - 1960-67 BUFFALO BILLS (AFL)
CARMAN, W. CHARLES (VANDERBILT) - TACKLE - 1919 DETROIT HERALDS; 1921
    DETROIT PANTHERS
CARMAN, EDMUND (PURDUE) - TACKLE - 1922, 25 HAMMOND PROS; 1925
    BUFFALO BISONS
CARMICHAEL, ALBERT (USC) - BACK - 1953-58 GREEN BAY PACKERS; 1960-61
    DENVER BRONCOS (AFL)
CARMICHAEL, LEE HAROLD (SOUTHERN) - END - 1971-74 PHILADELPHIA EAGLES
    (NFC); 1973 PASS RECEIVING LEADER (NFC)
CARMICHAEL, PAUL (EL CAMINO JUNIOR COLLEGE) - BACK - 1965 DENVER
    BRONCOS (AFL)
CARNELLY, RAYMOND (CARNEGIE TECH) - QBACK - 1939 BROOKLYN DODGERS
CARNES, WILCE (KENTUCKY) - BACK - 1940 CINCINNATI BENGALS (AFL)
CARNEY, ARTHUR (ANNAPOLIS) - GUARD - 1925-26 NEW YORK GIANTS
CAROLAN, REGINALD (IDAHO) - END - 1962-63 SAN DIEGO CHARGERS (AFL);
    1964-68 KANSAS CITY CHIEFS (AFL)
CAROLINE, JAMES C. (ILLINOIS) - BACK - 1956-65 CHICAGO BEARS
CAROLLO, JOSEPH (NOTRE DAME) - TACKLE, GUARD - 1962-68 LOS ANGELES
    RAMS; 1969 PHILADELPHIA EAGLES; 1970 PHILADELPHIA EAGLES (NFC);
    1971 LOS ANGELES RAMS (NFC); 1972-73 CLEVELAND BROWNS (AFC)
CAROTHERS, DONALD (BRADLEY) - END - 1960 DENVER BRONCOS (AFL)
CARPE, JOSEPH (MILLIKIN) - TACKLE - 1926-27 FRANKFORD YELLOWJACKETS;
    1928 POTTSVILLE MAROONS; 1929 BOSTON BRAVES; 1933 PHILADELPHIA
    EAGLES
CARPENTER, JOHN (MISSOURI & MICHIGAN) - TACKLE - 1947-49 BUFFALO
    BILLS (AAFC); 1949 SAN FRANCISCO 49ERS (AAFC)
CARPENTER, KENNETH (OREGON STATE) - BACK - 1950-53 CLEVELAND BROWNS;
    1960 DENVER BRONCOS (AFL)
CARPENTER, LEWIS (ARKANSAS) - BACK - 1953-55 DETROIT LIONS; 1957-58
    CLEVELAND BROWNS; 1959-63 GREEN BAY PACKERS
CARPENTER, RONALD (NORTH CAROLINA STATE) - END - 1970-74 CINCINNATI
    BENGALS (AFC)
CARPENTER, RONALD (TEXAS A&M) - LB - 1964-65 SAN DIEGO CHARGERS (AFL)
CARPENTER, VERDA PRESTON (ARKANSAS) - END - 1956-59 CLEVELAND BROWNS;
    1960-63 PITTSBURGH STEELERS; 1964-66 WASHINGTON REDSKINS; 1966
    MINNESOTA VIKINGS; 1967 MIAMI DOLPHINS (AFL)
CARPENTER, WALKER (GEORGIA TECH) - TACKLE - 1919 DETROIT HERALDS
CARR, EDWIN - BACK - 1947-49 SAN FRANCISCO 49ERS (AAFC)
CARR, FREDERICK (TEXAS-EL PASO) - LB - 1968-69 GREEN BAY PACKERS;
    1970-74 GREEN BAY PACKERS (NFC)
CARR, HARLAN (SYRACUSE) - QBACK - 1927 BUFFALO BISONS; 1927
    POTTSVILLE MAROONS
CARR, HENRY (ARIZONA STATE) - BACK - 1965-67 NEW YORK GIANTS
CARR, JAMES (MORRIS HARVEY) - BACK - 1955, 57 CHICAGO CARDINALS;
    1959-63 PHILADELPHIA EAGLES; 1964-65 WASHINGTON REDSKINS
CARR, LEE - BACK - 1926 HAMMOND PROS
CARR, LEVERT (NORTH CENTRAL STATE) - TACKLE, GUARD - 1969 SAN DIEGO
    CHARGERS (AFL); 1970-71 BUFFALO BILLS (AFC); 1972-73 HOUSTON
    OILERS (AFC)
CARR, PAUL (HOUSTON) - LB - 1955-57 SAN FRANCISCO 49ERS
CARR, ROGER (LOUISIANA TECH) - END - 1974 BALTIMORE COLTS (AFC)
CARRELL, JOHN (TEXAS TECH) - LB - 1966 HOUSTON OILERS (AFL)
CARRELL, DUANE (FLORIDA STATE) - KICKER - 1974 DALLAS COWBOYS (NFC)
CARRINGTON, EDWARD (VIRGINIA) - END - 1969 HOUSTON OILERS (AFL)
CARROCCIO, RUSSELL (VIRGINIA) - GUARD - 1954-55 NEW YORK GIANTS; 1955
    PHILADELPHIA EAGLES
CARROLL, BART (COLGATE) - CENTER - 1920, 23 ROCHESTER JEFFERSONS
CARROLL, ELMER (WASHINGTON&JEFFERSON) - END - 1921 CANTON BULLDOGS;
    1922 COLUMBUS PANHANDLES; 1922-23, 25 CANTON BULLDOGS
CARROLL, JAMES (NOTRE DAME) - LB - 1965-66 NEW YORK GIANTS; 1966-68
    WASHINGTON REDSKINS; 1969 NEW YORK JETS (AFL)
CARROLL, JOSEPH (PITTSBURGH) - LB - 1972-73 OAKLAND RAIDERS (AFC)
CARROLL, LEO (SAN DIEGO STATE) - END - 1968 GREEN BAY PACKERS; 1969
    WASHINGTON REDSKINS; 1970 WASHINGTON REDSKINS (NFC)

CARROLL, RONALD (SAM HOUSTON STATE) - TACKLE - 1974 HOUSTON OILERS
     (AFC)
CARROLL, VICTOR (NEVADA) - TACKLE - 1936 BOSTON REDSKINS; 1937-42
     WASHINGTON REDSKINS; 1943-47 NEW YORK GIANTS
CARSON, JOHN (GEORGIA) - END - 1954-59 WASHINGTON REDSKINS; 1960
     HOUSTON OILERS (AFL)
CARSON, KERN (SAN DIEGO STATE) - BACK - 1965 SAN DIEGO CHARGERS
     (AFL); 1965 NEW YORK JETS (AFL)
CARSON, W. HOWARD (ILLINOIS) - BACK - 1940-41 MILWAUKEE CHIEFS (AFL);
     1944 CLEVELAND RAMS
CARTER, JAMES C. (MINNESOTA) - LB - 1970-74 GREEN BAY PACKERS (NFC)
CARTER, JOSEPH (SMU) - END - 1933-40 PHILADELPHIA EAGLES; 1942 GREEN
     BAY PACKERS; 1944 BROOKLYN TIGERS; 1945 CHICAGO CARDINALS; 1934
     PASS RECEIVING LEADER; (TIED WITH BADGRO)
CARTER, KENT (USC) - LB - 1974 NEW ENGLAND PATRIOTS (AFC)
CARTER, MICHAEL (SACRAMENTO STATE) - BACK - 1970 GREEN BAY PACKERS
     (NFC); 1972 SAN DIEGO CHARGERS (AFC)
CARTER, ROSS (OREGON) - GUARD - 1936-39 CHICAGO CARDINALS
CARTER, VIRGIL (BRIGHAM YOUNG) - QBACK - 1968-69 CHICAGO BEARS;
     1970-72 CINCINNATI BENGALS (AFC)
CARTER, WILLIE (TENNESSEE STATE) - BACK - 1953 CHICAGO CARDINALS
CARTIN, CHARLES (HOLY CROSS) - TACKLE - 1925 FRANKFORD YELLOWJACKETS;
     1926 PHILADELPHIA QUAKERS (AFL)
CARTWRIGHT - BACK - 1919 CLEVELAND INDIANS
CARWELL, LAWRENCE (IOWA STATE) - BACK - 1967-68 HOUSTON OILERS (AFL);
     1969 BOSTON PATRIOTS (AFL); 1970 BOSTON PATRIOTS (AFC); 1971-72
     NEW ENGLAND PATRIOTS (AFC)
CASANEGA, KENNETH (SANTA CLARA) - BACK - 1946, 48 SAN FRANCISCO 49ERS
     (AAFC)
CASANOVA, THOMAS (LSU) - BACK - 1972-74 CINCINNATI BENGALS (AFC)
CASARES, RICARDO (FLORIDA) - BACK - 1955-64 CHICAGO BEARS; 1965
     WASHINGTON REDSKINS; 1966 MIAMI DOLPHINS (AFL); 1956 RUSHING
     LEADER
CASE, ERNEST (UCLA) - BACK - 1947 BALTIMORE COLTS (AAFC)
CASE, RONALD "PETE" (GEORGIA) - GUARD - 1962-64 PHILADELPHIA EAGLES;
     1965-69 NEW YORK GIANTS; 1970 NEW YORK GIANTS (NFC)
CASEY, ALBERT (ARKANSAS) - BACK - 1923 ST. LOUIS BROWNS
CASEY, BERNARD (BOWLING GREEN) - END - 1961-66 SAN FRANCISCO 49ERS;
     1967-68 LOS ANGELES RAMS
CASEY, EDWARD (HARVARD) - BACK - 1920 BUFFALO ALL-AMERICANS
CASEY, H. - (SEE RUNNING WOLF)
CASEY, THOMAS (HAMPTON INST.) - BACK - 1948 NEW YORK YANKEES (AAFC)
CASEY, TIMOTHY (OREGON) - LB - 1969 CHICAGO BEARS; 1969 DENVER
     BRONCOS (AFL)
CASH, JOHN (ALLEN) - END - 1961-62 DENVER BRONCOS (AFL)
CASH, RICHARD (NORTHEAST MISSOURI) - END, TACKLE - 1968 ATLANTA
     FALCONS; 1969 LOS ANGELES RAMS; 1970 LOS ANGELES RAMS (NFC);
     1972-73 NEW ENGLAND PATRIOTS (AFC)
CASNER, KENNETH (BAYLOR) - TACKLE - 1952 LOS ANGELES RAMS
CASON, JAMES (LSU) - BACK - 1948-49 SAN FRANCISCO 49ERS (AAFC);
     1950-52, 54 SAN FRANCISCO 49ERS; 1955-56 LOS ANGELES RAMS
CASPER, CHARLES (TCU) - QBACK - 1934 ST. LOUIS GUNNERS; 1934 GREEN
     BAY PACKERS; 1935 PITTSBURGH PIRATES
CASPER, DAVID (NOTRE DAME) - END - 1974 OAKLAND RAIDERS (AFC)
CASSADY, HOWARD "HOPALONG" (OHIO STATE) - BACK - 1956-61, 63 DETROIT
     LIONS; 1962 CLEVELAND BROWNS; 1962 PHILADELPHIA EAGLES
CASSARA, FRANK (ST. MARY'S OF CAL.) - BACK - 1954 SAN FRANCISCO 49ERS
CASSESE, THOMAS (C.W.POST) - BACK - 1967 DENVER BRONCOS (AFL)
CASSIANO, RICHARD (PITTSBURGH) - BACK - 1940 BROOKLYN DODGERS
CASSIDY, JOSEPH (ST. MARY'S OF CAL.) - BACK - 1937 PITTSBURGH PIRATES
CASSIDY, WILLIAM (DETROIT) - END - 1924 KENOSHA MAROONS
CASTEEL, MILES (KALAMAZOO) - BACK - 1922 ROCK ISLAND INDEPENDENTS
CASTER, RICHARD (JACKSON STATE) - END - 1970-74 NEW YORK JETS (AFC)
CASTETE, JESSE (MCNEESE STATE) - BACK - 1956 CHICAGO BEARS; 1956-57
     LOS ANGELES RAMS
CASTIGLIA, JAMES (GEORGETOWN) - BACK - 1941, 45-46 PHILADELPHIA
     EAGLES; 1947 BALTIMORE COLTS (AAFC); 1947-48 WASHINGTON REDSKINS
CATHCART, ROYAL (SANTA BARBARA) - BACK - 1950 SAN FRANCISCO 49ERS
CATHCART, SAMUEL (SANTA BARBARA) - BACK - 1949 SAN FRANCISCO 49ERS
     (AAFC); 1950, 52 SAN FRANCISCO 49ERS

CATLIN, THOMAS (OKLAHOMA) - LB - 1953-54, 57-58 CLEVELAND BROWNS;
    1959 PHILADELPHIA EAGLES
CATO, DARYL (ARKANSAS) - CENTER - 1946 MIAMI SEAHAWKS (AAFC)
CAVALLI, CARMEN (RICHMOND) - END - 1960 OAKLAND RAIDERS (AFL)
CAVENESS, RONALD (ARKANSAS) - LB - 1965 KANSAS CITY CHIEFS (AFL);
    1966-68 HOUSTON OILERS (AFL)
CAVNESS, GRADY (TEXAS-EL PASO) - BACK - 1969 DENVER BRONCOS (AFL);
    1970 ATLANTA FALCONS (NFC)
CAVOSIE, JOHN (BUTLER) - BACK - 1931-33 PORTSMOUTH SPARTANS
CAVOSIE, JOSEPH - BACK - 1936 CLEVELAND RAMS (AFL); 1937 CINCINNATI
    BENGALS (AFL)
CAYLOR, LOWELL (MIAMI OF OHIO) - BACK - 1964 CLEVELAND BROWNS
CAYWOOD, LESTER (ST.JOHN'S) - GUARD - 1926 KANSAS CITY COWBOYS; 1926
    BUFFALO RANGERS; 1927, 29-32 NEW YORK GIANTS; 1927 CLEVELAND
    BULLDOGS; 1927 POTTSVILLE MAROONS; 1928 DETROIT WOLVERINES; 1931
    CHICAGO CARDINALS; 1932 BROOKLYN DODGERS; 1933-34 CINCINNATI REDS
CEARING, LLOYD (VALPARAISO) - BACK - 1922-23 HAMMOND PROS
CELERI, ROBERT (CALIFORNIA) - QBACK - 1951 NEW YORK YANKS; 1952
    DALLAS TEXANS
CEMORE, ANTHONY (CREIGHTON) - GUARD - 1941 PHILADELPHIA EAGLES
CENCI, JOHN (PITTSBURGH) - CENTER - 1956 PITTSBURGH STEELERS
CEPPETELLI, EUGENE (VILLANOVA) - CENTER - 1968-69 PHILADELPHIA
    EAGLES; 1969 NEW YORK GIANTS
CERNE, JOSEPH (NORTHWESTERN) - CENTER - 1965-67 SAN FRANCISCO 49ERS;
    1968 ATLANTA FALCONS
CHALMERS, GEORGE (NEW YORK UNIV.) - GUARD - 1933 BROOKLYN DODGERS
CHAMBERLAIN, DANIEL (SACRAMENTO STATE) - END - 1960-61 BUFFALO BILLS
    (AFL)
CHAMBERLAIN, GARTH (BRIGHAM YOUNG) - GUARD - 1945 PITTSBURGH STEELERS
CHAMBERLIN, BERLIN GUY (NEBRASKA) - END - 1920 DECATUR STALEYS; 1921
    CHICAGO STALEYS; 1922-23 CANTON BULLDOGS; 1924 CLEVELAND
    BULLDOGS; 1925-26 FRANKFORD YELLOWJACKETS; 1927 CHICAGO
    CARDINALS; 1965 HALL OF FAME
CHAMBERS, WALLY (EASTERN KENTUCKY) - TACKLE, END - 1973-74 CHICAGO
    BEARS (NFC)
CHAMBERS, WILLIAM (UCLA) - TACKLE - 1948-49 NEW YORK YANKEES (AAFC)
CHAMPAGNE, EDWARD (LSU) - TACKLE - 1947-50 LOS ANGELES RAMS
CHAMPION, JAMES (MISSISSIPPI STATE) - GUARD - 1950-51 NEW YORK YANKS
CHANDLER, ALBERT (OKLAHOMA) - END - 1973-74 CINCINNATI BENGALS (AFC)
CHANDLER, DONALD (FLORIDA) - KICKER - 1956-64 NEW YORK GIANTS;
    1965-67 GREEN BAY PACKERS; 1957 PUNTING LEADER; 1963 SCORING
    LEADER
CHANDLER, EDGAR (GEORGIA) - LB, GUARD - 1968-69 BUFFALO BILLS (AFL);
    1970-72 BUFFALO BILLS (AFC); 1973 NEW ENGLAND PATRIOTS (AFC)
CHANDLER, KARL (PRINCETON) - CENTER - 1974 NEW YORK GIANTS (NFC)
CHANDLER, ROBERT (USC) - END - 1971-74 BUFFALO BILLS (AFC)
CHANDNOIS, LYNN (MICHIGAN STATE) - BACK - 1950-56 PITTSBURGH STEELERS
CHAPPLE, DAVID (CAL.-SANTA BARBARA) - LB - 1971 BUFFALO BILLS (AFC);
    1972-74 LOS ANGELES RAMS (NFC); 1974 NEW ENGLAND PATRIOTS (AFC);
    1972 PUNTING LEADER (NFC)
CHAPMAN, THOMAS (MOUNT. ST. MARY'S) - TACKLE - 1925 POTTSVILLE MAROONS
CHAPPIE, JOHN (STANFORD) - LB - 1965 SAN FRANCISCO 49ERS
CHAPPIUS, ROBERT (MICHIGAN) - BACK - 1948 BROOKLYN DODGERS (AAFC);
    1949 CHICAGO HORNETS (AAFC)
CHARLES, JOHN (PURDUE) - BACK - 1967-69 BOSTON PATRIOTS (AFL); 1970
    MINNESOTA VIKINGS (NFC); 1971-74 HOUSTON OILERS (AFC)
CHARLES, WINSTON (WILLIAM&MARY) - BACK - 1928 DAYTON TRIANGLES
CHARON, CARL (MICHIGAN STATE) - BACK - 1962-63 BUFFALO BILLS (AFL)
CHARPIER, LEONARD (ILLINOIS) - BACK - 1921 CHICAGO CARDINALS
CHASE, BENJAMIN (ANNAPOLIS) - GUARD - 1947 DETROIT LIONS
CHASE, RALPH (PITTSBURGH) - TACKLE - 1926 AKRON PROS
CHAVOUS, BARNEY (SOUTH CAROLINA STATE) - END - 1973-74 DENVER BRONCOS
    (AFC)
CHEALANDER, HAL (MISSISSIPPI STATE) - QBACK - 1974 MINNESOTA VIKINGS
    (NFC)
CHEATHAM, ERNEST (LOYOLA) - TACKLE - 1954 PITTSBURGH STEELERS; 1954
    BALTIMORE COLTS
CHEATHAM, LLOYD (AUBURN) - QBACK - 1942 CHICAGO CARDINALS; 1946-48
    NEW YORK YANKEES (AAFC)
CHECKAYE, SEVERIN - QBACK - 1921 MUNCIE FLYERS
CHEEK, RICHARD (AUBURN) - GUARD - 1970 BUFFALO BILLS (AFC)

CHEEKS, B. W. (TEXAS SOUTHERN) - BACK - 1965 HOUSTON OILERS (AFL)
CHEETAH, JAMES (OKLAHOMA) - TACKLE - 1919 MASSILLON TIGERS
CHELF, DONALD (IOWA) - GUARD - 1960-61 BUFFALO BILLS (AFL)
CHENOWETH, GEORGE - BACK - 1921 LOUISVILLE BRECKS
CHERNE, HAROLD (DEPAUL) - TACKLE - 1933 BOSTON REDSKINS
CHEROKE, GEORGE (OHIO STATE) - GUARD - 1946 CLEVELAND BROWNS (AAFC)
CHERRY, EDGAR (HARDIN-SIMMONS) - BACK - 1938-39 CHICAGO CARDINALS;
    1939 PITTSBURGH STEELERS
CHERRY, STANLEY (MORGAN STATE) - LB - 1973 BALTIMORE COLTS (AFC)
CHERUNDOLO, CHARLES (PENN STATE) - CENTER - 1937-39 CLEVELAND RAMS;
    1940 PHILADELPHIA EAGLES; 1941-42, 45-48 PITTSBURGH STEELERS
CHESBRO, MARCEL (COLGATE) - GUARD - 1938 CLEVELAND RAMS
CHESNEY, CHESTER (DEPAUL) - CENTER - 1939-40 CHICAGO BEARS
CHESSER, GEORGE (DELTA STATE) - BACK - 1966-67 MIAMI DOLPHINS (AFL)
CHESSON, WESLEY (DUKE) - END - 1971-73 ATLANTA FALCONS (NFC); 1973-74
    PHILADELPHIA EAGLES (NFC)
CHESTER, RAYMOND (MORGAN STATE) - END - 1970-72 OAKLAND RAIDERS
    (AFC); 1973-74 BALTIMORE COLTS (AFC)
CHEVERKO, GEORGE (FORDHAM) - BACK - 1947-48 NEW YORK GIANTS; 1948
    WASHINGTON REDSKINS
CHEYUNSKI, JAMES (SYRACUSE) - LB - 1968-69 BOSTON PATRIOTS (AFL);
    1970 BOSTON PATRIOTS (AFC); 1971-72 NEW ENGLAND PATRIOTS (AFC);
    1973-74 BUFFALO BILLS (AFC)
CHICKEN, FRED - BACK - 1919-21 ROCK ISLAND INDEPENDENTS; 1922-24
    MINNEAPOLIS MARINES
CHICKERNEO, JOHN (PITTSBURGH) - BACK - 1942 NEW YORK GIANTS
CHICKILLO, NICHOLAS (MIAMI) - GUARD - 1953 CHICAGO CARDINALS
CHILDRESS, JOSEPH (AUBURN) - BACK - 1956-59 CHICAGO CARDINALS; 1960,
    62-65 ST. LOUIS CARDINALS
CHILDS, CLARENCE (FLORIDA A&M) - BACK - 1964-67 NEW YORK GIANTS; 1968
    CHICAGO BEARS
CHILDS, HENRY (KANSAS STATE) - END - 1974 ATLANTA FALCONS (NFC); 1974
    NEW ORLEANS SAINTS (NFC)
CHIPLEY, WILLIAM (WASHINGTON&LEE) - END - 1947-48 BOSTON YANKS; 1949
    NEW YORK BULLDOGS
CHISICK, ANDREW (VILLANOVA) - CENTER - 1940-41 CHICAGO CARDINALS
CHLEBEK, EDWARD (WESTERN MICHIGAN) - QBACK - 1963 NEW YORK JETS (AFL)
CHOATE - GUARD - 1924 KANSAS CITY COWBOYS
CHOBOIAN, MAX (SAN FERNANDO STATE) - QBACK - 1966 DENVER BRONCOS (AFL)
CHOMYSZAK, STEVEN (SYRACUSE) - TACKLE - 1966 NEW YORK JETS (AFL);
    1968-69 CINCINNATI BENGALS (AFL); 1970-73 CINCINNATI BENGALS
    (AFC)
CHOROVICH, RICHARD (MIAMI OF OHIO) - TACKLE - 1955-56 BALTIMORE
    COLTS; 1960 LOS ANGELES CHARGERS (AFL)
CHRAPE, JOSEPH (HIBBING JUNIOR COLLEGE) - GUARD - 1929 MINNEAPOLIS
    REDJACKETS
CHRISTENSEN, ERIK (RICHMOND) - END - 1956 WASHINGTON REDSKINS
CHRISTENSEN, FRANK (UTAH) - BACK - 1934-37 DETROIT LIONS
CHRISTENSEN, GEORGE (OREGON) - TACKLE - 1931-33 PORTSMOUTH SPARTANS;
    1934-38 DETROIT LIONS
CHRISTENSEN, KOESTER (MICHIGAN STATE) - END - 1930 PORTSMOUTH SPARTANS
CHRISTENSON, MARTIN (MINNESOTA) - BACK - 1940 CHICAGO CARDINALS
CHRISTIANSEN, JOHN (COLORADA A&M) - BACK - 1951-58 DETROIT LIONS;
    1953, 57 INTERCEPTION LEADER; (1957 TIED WITH BUTLER AND M.
    DAVIS); 1970 HALL OF FAME
CHRISTIANSEN, ROBERT (UCLA) - END - 1972 BUFFALO BILLS (AFC)
CHRISTIANSON, OSCAR - END - 1921-24 MINNEAPOLIS MARINES
CHRISTMAN, FLOYD (THEIL) - BACK - 1925 BUFFALO BISONS
CHRISTMAN, PAUL (MISSOURI) - QBACK - 1945-49 CHICAGO CARDINALS; 1950
    GREEN BAY PACKERS
CHRISTOPHERSON, JAMES (CONCORDIA-MINNESOTA) - LB - 1962 MINNESOTA
    VIKINGS
CHRISTY, EARL (MARYLAND STATE) - BACK - 1966-68 NEW YORK JETS (AFL)
CHRISTY, RICHARD (NORTH CAROLINA STATE) - BACK - 1958 PITTSBURGH
    STEELERS; 1960 BOSTON PATRIOTS (AFL); 1961-62 NEW YORK TITANS
    (AFL); 1963 NEW YORK JETS (AFL)
CHURCHMAN, CHARLES (VIRGINIA) - BACK - 1925 COLUMBUS TIGERS
CHURCHWELL, DONNIS (MISSISSIPPI) - GUARD - 1959 WASHINGTON REDSKINS;
    1960 OAKLAND RAIDERS (AFL)

CHUY, DONALD (CLEMSON) - GUARD - 1963-68 LOS ANGELES RAMS; 1969
PHILADELPHIA EAGLES
CIBULAS, JOSEPH (DUQUESNE) - TACKLE - 1945 PITTSBURGH STEELERS
CICCOLELLA, MICHAEL (DAYTON) - LB - 1966-68 NEW YORK GIANTS
CICCONE, BENJAMIN (DUQUESNE) - CENTER - 1934-35 PITTSBURGH PIRATES;
1936 CLEVELAND RAMS (AFL); 1937 CINCINNATI BENGALS (AFL); 1942
CHICAGO CARDINALS
CICCONE, WILLIAM (WEST VIRGINIA WESLEYAN) - GUARD - 1941 COLUMBUS
BULLIES (AFL)
CICHOWSKI, EUGENE (INDIANA) - BACK - 1957 PITTSBURGH STEELERS;
1958-59 WASHINGTON REDSKINS
CICHOWSKI, THOMAS (MARYLAND) - TACKLE - 1967-68 DENVER BRONCOS (AFL)
CIFELLI, AUGUST (NOTRE DAME) - TACKLE - 1950-52 DETROIT LIONS; 1953
GREEN BAY PACKERS; 1954 PHILADELPHIA EAGLES; 1954 PITTSBURGH
STEELERS
CIFERS, EDWARD (TENNESSEE) - END - 1941-42, 46 WASHINGTON REDSKINS;
1947-48 CHICAGO BEARS
CIFERS, ROBERT (TENNESSEE) - QBACK - 1946 DETROIT LIONS; 1947-48
PITTSBURGH STEELERS; 1949 GREEN BAY PACKERS
CINDRICH, RALPH (PITTSBURGH) - LB - 1972 NEW ENGLAND PATRIOTS (AFC);
1973-74 HOUSTON OILERS (AFC); 1974 DENVER BRONCOS (AFC)
CIPA, LARRY (MICHIGAN) - QBACK - 1974 NEW ORLEANS SAINTS (NFC)
CIPRA, ERNEST (EMPORIA OF KANSAS) - CENTER - 1936-37 BOSTON SHAMROCKS
(AFL)
CIVILETTO, FRANK (SPRINGFIELD) - BACK - 1923 CLEVELAND INDIANS
CLACK, JAMES (WAKE FOREST) - CENTER, GUARD - 1971-74 PITTSBURGH
STEELERS (AFC)
CLAGO, WALTER (DETROIT) - END - 1921 DETROIT PANTHERS; 1922 ROCK
ISLAND INDEPENDENTS
CLAIR, FRANK (OHIO STATE) - END - 1941 WASHINGTON REDSKINS
CLANCY, JOHN "JACK" (MICHIGAN) - END - 1967-69 MIAMI DOLPHINS (AFL);
1970 GREEN BAY PACKERS (NFC)
CLANCY, PAUL (NIAGARA) - END - 1936 ROCHESTER TIGERS (AFL)
CLANCY, STUART (HOLY CROSS) - QBACK - 1930 NEWARK TORNADOS; 1931-32
STATEN ISLAND STAPELTONS; 1932-35 NEW YORK GIANTS; 1936 NEW YORK
YANKS (AFL)
CLARIDGE, DENNIS (NEBRASKA) - QBACK - 1964-65 GREEN BAY PACKERS; 1966
ATLANTA FALCONS
CLARK, AL (EASTERN MICHIGAN) - BACK - 1971 DETROIT LIONS (NFC);
1972-74 LOS ANGELES RAMS (NFC)
CLARK, ARTHUR (NEVADA) - BACK - 1927 FRANKFORD YELLOWJACKETS; 1927
DULUTH ESKIMOS
CLARK, BERYL (OKLAHOMA) - BACK - 1940 CHICAGO CARDINALS
CLARK, CHARLES "BOOBY" (BETHUNE-COOKMAN) - BACK - 1973-74 CINCINNATI
BENGALS (AFC)
CLARK, CHARLES (HARVARD) - GUARD - 1924 CHICAGO CARDINALS
CLARK, DONALD (USC) - GUARD - 1948-49 SAN FRANCISCO 49ERS (AAFC)
CLARK, EARL "DUTCH" (COLORADO COLLEGE) - QBACK - 1931-32 PORTSMOUTH
SPARTANS; 1934-38 DETROIT LIONS; 1932, 35-36 SCORING LEADER;
1932 FIELD GOAL LEADER; 1963 HALL OF FAME
CLARK, ERNEST (MICHIGAN STATE) - LB - 1963-67 DETROIT LIONS; 1968 ST.
LOUIS CARDINALS
CLARK, GAIL (MICHIGAN STATE) - LB - 1973 CHICAGO BEARS (NFC); 1974
NEW ENGLAND PATRIOTS (AFC)
CLARK, HAROLD (CATHEDRAL) - END - 1919-20 DAYTON TRIANGLES; 1920-25
ROCHESTER JEFFERSONS
CLARK, HARRY (WEST VIRGINIA) - BACK - 1940-43 CHICAGO BEARS; 1946-48
LOS ANGELES DONS (AAFC); 1948 CHICAGO ROCKETS (AAFC)
CLARK, HERMAN (OREGON STATE) - GUARD - 1952, 54-57 CHICAGO BEARS
CLARK, HOWARD (CHATTANOOGA) - END - 1960 LOS ANGELES CHARGERS (AFL);
1961 SAN DIEGO CHARGERS (AFL)
CLARK, JAMES (MONTANA) - END - 1926 LOS ANGELES WILDCATS (AFL)
CLARK, JAMES (OREGON STATE) - TACKLE - 1952-53 WASHINGTON REDSKINS
CLARK, JAMES (PITTSBURGH) - BACK - 1933-34 PITTSBURGH PIRATES; 1936
ROCHESTER TIGERS (AFL)
CLARK, LESLIE (BROWN) - BACK - 1919 CLEVELAND INDIANS
CLARK, MICHAEL (TEXAS A&M) - LB - 1963 PHILADELPHIA EAGLES; 1964-67
PITTSBURGH STEELERS; 1968-69 DALLAS COWBOYS; 1970-71, 73 DALLAS
COWBOYS (NFC)

CLARK, MONTE (USC) - TACKLE - 1959-61 SAN FRANCISCO 49ERS; 1962
    DALLAS COWBOYS; 1963-69 CLEVELAND BROWNS
CLARK, MYERS (OHIO STATE) - QBACK - 1930 BROOKLYN DODGERS; 1931
    CLEVELAND INDIANS; 1932 BOSTON BRAVES; 1933-34 CINCINNATI REDS;
    1934 PHILADELPHIA EAGLES
CLARK, PHILIP (NORTHWESTERN) - BACK - 1967-69 DALLAS COWBOYS; 1970
    CHICAGO BEARS (NFC); 1971 NEW ENGLAND PATRIOTS (AFC)
CLARK, RUSSELL (MUHLENBERG) - TACKLE - 1926 NEWARK BEARS (AFL)
CLARK, WAYNE (INTERNATIONAL-CALIFORNIA) - QBACK - 1970, 72-73 SAN
    DIEGO CHARGERS (AFC); 1974 CINCINNATI BENGALS (AFC)
CLARK, WAYNE (UTAH) - END - 1944 DETROIT LIONS
CLARK, WILLIAM - GUARD - 1920 DECATUR STALEYS; 1920 CHICAGO CARDINALS
CLARKE, FRANKLIN (COLORADO) - END - 1957-59 CLEVELAND BROWNS; 1960-67
    DALLAS COWBOYS
CLARKE, HAGOOD (FLORIDA) - BACK - 1964-68 BUFFALO BILLS (AFL)
CLARKE, LEON (USC) - END - 1956-59 LOS ANGELES RAMS; 1960-62
    CLEVELAND BROWNS; 1963 MINNESOTA VIKINGS
CLARKE, PEARL - BACK - 1922 OORANG INDIANS
CLARKIN, WILLIAM - TACKLE - 1929 ORANGE TORNADOS
CLARKSON, STUART (TEXAS A&I) - CENTER - 1942, 46-51 CHICAGO BEARS
CLATT, CORWIN (NOTRE DAME) - BACK - 1948-49 CHICAGO CARDINALS
CLATTERBUCK, ROBERT (HOUSTON) - QBACK - 1954-57 NEW YORK GIANTS; 1960
    LOS ANGELES CHARGERS (AFL)
CLAY, BOYD (TENNESSEE) - TACKLE - 1940-42, 44 CLEVELAND RAMS
CLAY, OZZIE (IOWA STATE) - BACK - 1964 WASHINGTON REDSKINS
CLAY, RANDALL (TEXAS) - BACK - 1950, 53 NEW YORK GIANTS
CLAY, ROY (COLORADO A&M) - BACK - 1944 NEW YORK GIANTS
CLAY, WALTER (COLORADO) - BACK - 1946-47 CHICAGO ROCKETS (AAFC);
    1947-49 LOS ANGELES DONS (AAFC)
CLAY, WILLIAM (MISSISSIPPI) - BACK - 1966 WASHINGTON REDSKINS
CLAYPOOL, RALPH (PURDUE) - CENTER - 1925-26, 28 CHICAGO CARDINALS
CLEARY, PAUL (USC) - END - 1948 NEW YORK YANKEES (AAFC); 1949 CHICAGO
    HORNETS (AAFC)
CLEMENS, CALVIN (USC) - QBACK - 1936 GREEN BAY PACKERS; 1937 LOS
    ANGELES BULLDOGS (AFL)
CLEMENS, ROBERT (PITTSBURGH) - BACK - 1962 BALTIMORE COLTS
CLEMENS, ROBERT (GEORGIA) - BACK - 1955 GREEN BAY PACKERS
CLEMENT, ALEX (WILLIAMS) - BACK - 1925 FRANKFORD YELLOWJACKETS
CLEMENT, HENRY (NORTH CAROLINA) - END - 1961 PITTSBURGH STEELERS
CLEMENT, JOHN (SMU) - BACK - 1941 CHICAGO CARDINALS; 1946-48
    PITTSBURGH STEELERS; 1949 CHICAGO HORNETS (AAFC)
CLEMENTS, CHASE (WASHINGTON&JEFFERSON) - TACKLE - 1925 AKRON PROS
CLEMENTS, VINCENT (CONNECTICUT) - BACK - 1972-73 NEW YORK GIANTS (NFC)
CLEMONS, CRAIG (IOWA) - BACK - 1972-74 CHICAGO BEARS (NFC)
CLEMONS, RAYMOND (ST. MARY'S OF CAL.) - GUARD - 1947 GREEN BAY PACKERS
CLEMONS, RAYMOND (CENTRAL OKLAHOMA STATE) - GUARD - 1937 LOS ANGELES
    BULLDOGS (AFL); 1939 DETROIT LIONS
CLEVE, EINAR (ST. OLAF) - BACK - 1922-24 MINNEAPOLIS MARINES
CLIME, BENJAMIN (SWARTHMORE) - TACKLE - 1920 ROCHESTER JEFFERSONS
CLINE, ANTHONY (MIAMI) - END, LB - 1970-74 OAKLAND RAIDERS (AFC)
CLINE, CHARLES DOUGLAS (CLEMSON) - LB - 1960-66 HOUSTON OILERS (AFL);
    1966 SAN DIEGO CHARGERS (AFL)
CLINE, OLIVER (OHIO STATE) - BACK - 1948 CLEVELAND BROWNS (AAFC);
    1949 BUFFALO BILLS (AAFC); 1950-53 DETROIT LIONS
CLOUD, JOHN (WILLIAM&MARY) - BACK - 1950-51 GREEN BAY PACKERS;
    1952-53 WASHINGTON REDSKINS
CLOUTIER, DAVID (MAINE) - BACK - 1964 BOSTON PATRIOTS (AFL)
CLOW, HERBERT - BACK - 1924 DULUTH KELLEYS
CLOWES, JOHN (WILLIAM&MARY) - TACKLE - 1948 BROOKLYN DODGERS (AAFC);
    1949 CHICAGO HORNETS (AAFC); 1950-51 NEW YORK YANKS; 1951
    DETROIT LIONS
CLUNE, DON (PENNSYLVANIA) - END - 1974 NEW YORK GIANTS (NFC)
COADY, RICH (MEMPHIS STATE) - CENTER - 1970-74 CHICAGO BEARS (NFC)
COAKER, JOHN - TACKLE - 1924 ROCHESTER JEFFERSONS
COAN, ELROY BERT (KANSAS) - BACK - 1962 SAN DIEGO CHARGERS (AFL);
    1963-68 KANSAS CITY CHIEFS (AFL)
COATES, RAYMOND (LSU) - BACK - 1948-49 NEW YORK GIANTS
COBB, ALFRED (SYRACUSE) - GUARD - 1919-22 AKRON PROS; 1923 CLEVELAND
    INDIANS; 1924-25 CLEVELAND BULLDOGS

COBB, THOMAS (ARKANSAS) - TACKLE - 1926 KANSAS CITY COWBOYS; 1927
    CLEVELAND BULLDOGS; 1928 DETROIT WOLVERINES; 1931 CHICAGO
    CARDINALS
COBB, WILLIAM (KANSAS STATE) - TACKLE - 1924-25 DULUTH KELLEYS; 1926
    DULUTH ESKIMOS
COCHRAN, JOHN (WAKE FOREST) - BACK - 1947-50 CHICAGO CARDINALS
COCHRAN, THOMAS (AUBURN) - BACK - 1949 WASHINGTON REDSKINS
COCKRELL, EUGENE (HARDIN-SIMMONS) - TACKLE - 1960-62 NEW YORK TITANS
    (AFL)
COCKROFT, DONALD (ADAMS STATE) - KICKER - 1968-69 CLEVELAND BROWNS;
    1970-74 CLEVELAND BROWNS (AFC)
CODY, EDWARD (PURDUE) - BACK - 1947-48 GREEN BAY PACKERS; 1949-50
    CHICAGO BEARS
CODY, LEO (GEORGETOWN) - BACK - 1919 CLEVELAND INDIANS
CODY, WILLIAM (AUBURN) - LB - 1966 DETROIT LIONS; 1967-69 NEW ORLEANS
    SAINTS; 1970 NEW ORLEANS SAINTS (NFC); 1972 PHILADELPHIA EAGLES
    (NFC)
COFALL, STANLEY (NOTRE DAME) - BACK - 1919 MASSILLON TIGERS; 1920
    CLEVELAND PANTHERS
COFFEE, JAMES (LSU) - BACK - 1937-38 CHICAGO CARDINALS
COFFEY, DONALD (MEMPHIS STATE) - BACK - 1963 DENVER BRONCOS (AFL)
COFFEY, JUNIOR (WASHINGTON) - BACK - 1965 GREEN BAY PACKERS; 1966-67,
    69 ATLANTA FALCONS; 1969 NEW YORK GIANTS; 1971 NEW YORK GIANTS
    (NFC)
COGDILL, GAIL (WASHINGTON STATE) - END - 1960-68 DETROIT LIONS; 1968
    BALTIMORE COLTS; 1969 ATLANTA FALCONS; 1970 ATLANTA FALCONS (NFC)
COGLIZER, ARTHUR (MISSOURI) - END - 1926 NEW YORK YANKEES (AFL)
COHEN, ABRAHAM (CHATTANOOGA) - GUARD - 1960 BOSTON PATRIOTS (AFL)
COIA, ANGELO (USC) - END - 1960-63 CHICAGO BEARS; 1964-65 WASHINGTON
    REDSKINS; 1966 ATLANTA FALCONS
COLAHAN, JOHN - GUARD - 1928 NEW YORK YANKEES
COLBERT, DANNY (TULSA) - BACK - 1974 SAN DIEGO CHARGERS (AFC)
COLCHICO, DANIEL (SAN JOSE STATE) - END - 1960-65 SAN FRANCISCO
    49ERS; 1969 NEW ORLEANS SAINTS
COLCLOUGH, JAMES (BOSTON COLLEGE) - END - 1960-68 BOSTON PATRIOTS
    (AFL)
COLE, EMERSON (TOLEDO) - BACK - 1950-52 CLEVELAND BROWNS; 1952
    CHICAGO BEARS
COLE, FREDERICK (MARYLAND) - GUARD - 1960 LOS ANGELES CHARGERS (AFL)
COLE, JOHN (ST. JOSEPH'S OF PA.) - BACK - 1938, 40 PHILADELPHIA EAGLES
COLE, LAWRENCE (HAWAII) - END - 1968-69 DALLAS COWBOYS; 1970-74
    DALLAS COWBOYS (NFC)
COLE, LINZY (TCU) - END - 1970 CHICAGO BEARS (NFC); 1971-72 HOUSTON
    OILERS (AFC); 1972 BUFFALO BILLS (AFC)
COLE, M. - END - 1920, 22 HAMMOND PROS
COLE, PETER (TRINITY OF TEXAS) - GUARD - 1937-40 NEW YORK GIANTS
COLE, RAYMOND (ARKANSAS) - QBACK - 1940 MILWAUKEE CHIEFS (AFL)
COLE, TERRY (INDIANA) - BACK - 1968-69 BALTIMORE COLTS; 1970
    PITTSBURGH STEELERS (AFC); 1971 MIAMI DOLPHINS (AFC)
COLELLA, THOMAS (CANISIUS) - BACK - 1942-43 DETROIT LIONS; 1944-45
    CLEVELAND RAMS; 1946-48 CLEVELAND BROWNS (AAFC); 1949 BUFFALO
    BILLS (AAFC)
COLEMAN, ALVIN (TENNESSEE STATE) - BACK - 1967 MINNESOTA VIKINGS;
    1969 CINCINNATI BENGALS (AFL); 1970-71 CINCINNATI BENGALS (AFC);
    1972-73 PHILADELPHIA EAGLES (NFC)
COLEMAN, DENNIS (MISSISSIPPI) - LB - 1971 NEW ENGLAND PATRIOTS (AFC)
COLEMAN, DON (MICHIGAN) - LB - 1974 NEW ORLEANS SAINTS (NFC)
COLEMAN, EDWARD (HOLY CROSS) - END - 1926 BOSTON BULLDOGS (AFL); 1926
    PHILADELPHIA QUAKERS (AFL)
COLEMAN, HERBERT (NOTRE DAME) - CENTER - 1946-48 CHICAGO ROCKETS
    (AAFC); 1948 BALTIMORE COLTS (AAFC)
COLEMAN, JAMES (XAVIER) - GUARD - 1937 CINCINNATI BENGALS (AFL)
COLEMAN, RALPH (NORTH CAROLINA A&T) - LB - 1972 DALLAS COWBOYS (NFC)
COLEMAN, RONNIE (ALABAMA A&M) - BACK - 1974 HOUSTON OILERS (AFC)
COLEMAN, STEVE (DELAWARE STATE) - END - 1974 DENVER BRONCOS (AFC)
COLHOUER, JACOB (OKLAHOMA A&M) - GUARD - 1946-48 CHICAGO CARDINALS;
    1949 NEW YORK GIANTS
COLLETT, CHARLES ELMER (SAN FRANCISCO STATE) - GUARD - 1967-69 SAN
    FRANCISCO 49ERS; 1970-72 SAN FRANCISCO 49ERS (NFC); 1973-74
    BALTIMORE COLTS (AFC)

COLLIER, FLOYD (SAN JOSE STATE) - TACKLE - 1948 SAN FRANCISCO 49ERS
   (AAFC)
COLLIER, JAMES (ARKANSAS) - END - 1962 NEW YORK GIANTS; 1963
   WASHINGTON REDSKINS
COLLIER, ROBERT (SMU) - TACKLE - 1951 LOS ANGELES RAMS
COLLINS, ALBIN (LSU) - BACK - 1949 CHICAGO HORNETS (AAFC); 1950
   BALTIMORE COLTS; 1951 GREEN BAY PACKERS
COLLINS, GARY (MARYLAND) - END, KICKER - 1962-69 CLEVELAND BROWNS;
   1970-71 CLEVELAND BROWNS (AFC); 1965 PUNTING LEADER
COLLINS, HARRY (CANISIUS) - GUARD - 1924 BUFFALO BISONS
COLLINS, JERALD (WESTERN MICHIGAN) - LB - 1969 BUFFALO BILLS (AFL);
   1970-71 BUFFALO BILLS (AFC)
COLLINS, PAUL (PITTSBURGH) - END - 1932 BOSTON BRAVES; 1933-35 BOSTON
   REDSKINS
COLLINS, PAUL (MISSOURI) - BACK - 1945 CHICAGO CARDINALS
COLLINS, RAYMOND (LSU) - TACKLE - 1950-52 SAN FRANCISCO 49ERS; 1954
   NEW YORK GIANTS; 1960-61 DALLAS TEXANS (AFL)
COLLINS, WILLIAM (TEXAS) - GUARD - 1947 BOSTON YANKS
COLMAN, WAYNE (TEMPLE) - LB - 1968-69 PHILADELPHIA EAGLES; 1969 NEW
   ORLEANS SAINTS; 1970-74 NEW ORLEANS SAINTS (NFC)
COLMER, JOHN (MIRAMONTE JUNIOR COLLEGE) - BACK - 1946-48 BROOKLYN
   DODGERS (AAFC); 1949 NEW YORK YANKEES (AAFC)
COLO, DONALD (BROWN) - TACKLE - 1950 BALTIMORE COLTS; 1951 NEW YORK
   YANKS; 1952 DALLAS TEXANS; 1953-58 CLEVELAND BROWNS
COLTERYAHN, LLOYD (MARYLAND) - END - 1954-56 BALTIMORE COLTS
COLVIN, JAMES (HOUSTON) - TACKLE - 1960-63 BALTIMORE COLTS; 1964-66
   DALLAS COWBOYS; 1967 NEW YORK GIANTS
COMBER, JOHN - BACK - 1926 CANTON BULLDOGS
COMBS, L. WILLIAM (PURDUE) - END - 1942 PHILADELPHIA EAGLES
COMER, MARTIN (TULANE) - END - 1946 BUFFALO BISONS (AAFC); 1947-48
   BUFFALO BILLS (AAFC)
COMMISA, VINCENT (NOTRE DAME) - GUARD - 1944 BOSTON YANKS
COMP, H. IRVIN (ST. BENEDICT'S OF KANSAS) - BACK - 1943-49 GREEN BAY
   PACKERS
COMPAGNO, ANTHONY (ST. MARY'S OF CAL.) - BACK - 1946-48 PITTSBURGH
   STEELERS
COMPTON, OGDEN (HARDIN-SIMMONS) - QBACK - 1955 CHICAGO CARDINALS
COMPTON, RICHARD (MCMURRAY-TEXAS) - BACK - 1962-64 DETROIT LIONS;
   1965 HOUSTON OILERS (AFL); 1967-68 PITTSBURGH STEELERS
COMSTOCK, EDWIN (WASHINGTON-MO.) - GUARD - 1929 BUFFALO BISONS; 1930
   BROOKLYN DODGERS; 1931 STATEN ISLAND STAPELTONS
COMSTOCK, RUDOLPH (GEORGETOWN) - GUARD - 1923, 25 CANTON BULLDOGS;
   1924 CLEVELAND BULLDOGS; 1926-29 FRANKFORD YELLOWJACKETS; 1930
   NEW YORK GIANTS; 1931-33 GREEN BAY PACKERS
CONCANNON, ERNEST (NEW YORK UNIV.) - GUARD - 1932 STATEN ISLAND
   STAPELTONS; 1934-36 BOSTON REDSKINS; 1936 NEW YORK YANKS (AFL);
   1937 BOSTON SHAMROCKS (AFL)
CONCANNON, JOHN (BOSTON COLLEGE) - QBACK - 1964-66 PHILADELPHIA
   EAGLES; 1967-69 CHICAGO BEARS; 1970-71 CHICAGO BEARS (NFC); 1973
   DALLAS COWBOYS (NFC); 1974 GREEN BAY PACKERS (NFC)
CONDIT, MERLYN (CARNEGIE TECH) - BACK - 1940 PITTSBURGH STEELERS;
   1941-43 BROOKLYN DODGERS; 1945 WASHINGTON REDSKINS; 1946
   PITTSBURGH STEELERS
CONDON, TOM (BOSTON COLLEGE) - GUARD - 1974 KANSAS CITY CHIEFS (AFC)
CONDREN, GLEN (OKLAHOMA) - TACKLE, END - 1965-67 NEW YORK GIANTS;
   1969 ATLANTA FALCONS; 1970-72 ATLANTA FALCONS (NFC)
CONE, FRED (CLEMSON) - BACK - 1951-57 GREEN BAY PACKERS; 1960 DALLAS
   COWBOYS; 1955 FIELD GOAL LEADER
CONERLY, CHARLES (MISSISSIPPI) - QBACK - 1948-61 NEW YORK GIANTS;
   1959 PASSING LEADER
CONGER, MELVIN (GEORGIA) - END - 1946 NEW YORK YANKEES (AAFC); 1947
   BROOKLYN DODGERS (AAFC)
CONJAR, LAWRENCE (NOTRE DAME) - BACK - 1967 CLEVELAND BROWNS; 1968
   PHILADELPHIA EAGLES; 1969 BALTIMORE COLTS; 1970 BALTIMORE COLTS
   (AFC)
CONKRIGHT, WILLIAM (OKLAHOMA) - CENTER - 1937-38 CHICAGO BEARS;
   1939-42, 44 CLEVELAND RAMS; 1943 WASHINGTON REDSKINS; 1943
   BROOKLYN DODGERS
CONLEE, GERALD (ST. MARY'S OF CAL.) - CENTER - 1938 CLEVELAND RAMS;
   1943 DETROIT LIONS; 1946-47 SAN FRANCISCO 49ERS (AAFC)

CONLEY, JOHN (NORTHERN OHIO) - TACKLE - 1922 COLUMBUS PANHANDLES;
     1926 COLUMBUS TIGERS
CONLEY, STEVE (KANSAS) - BACK, L - 1972 CINCINNATI BENGALS (AFC);
     1972 ST. LOUIS CARDINALS (NFC)
CONN, GEORGE (OREGON STATE) - BACK - 1919 MASSILLON TIGERS; 1920
     AKRON PROS; 1920 CLEVELAND PANTHERS
CONN, RICHARD (GEORGIA) - BACK - 1974 PITTSBURGH STEELERS (AFC)
CONNAUGHTON, HARRY (GEORGETOWN) - GUARD - 1927 FRANKFORD YELLOWJACKETS
CONNELL, JACKSON (DARTMOUTH) - BACK - 1919 CLEVELAND INDIANS
CONNELL, WARD (NOTRE DAME) - BACK - 1926 CHICAGO BULLS (AFL)
CONNELLEY, VINCENT (GEORGIA TECH) - BACK - 1926 NEWARK BEARS (AFL)
CONNELLY, MICHAEL (UTAH STATE) - CENTER - 1960-67 DALLAS COWBOYS;
     1968 PITTSBURGH STEELERS
CONNER, CLYDE (PACIFIC) - END - 1956-63 SAN FRANCISCO 49ERS
CONNERS, DANIEL (MIAMI) - LB - 1964-69 OAKLAND RAIDERS (AFL); 1970-74
     OAKLAND RAIDERS (AFC)
CONNOLLY, HARRY (BOSTON COLLEGE) - BACK - 1946 BROOKLYN DODGERS (AAFC)
CONNOLLY, THEODORE (SANTA CLARA) - GUARD - 1954, 56-62 SAN FRANCISCO
     49ERS; 1963 CLEVELAND BROWNS
CONNOR, GEORGE (NOTRE DAME) - TACKLE - 1948-55 CHICAGO BEARS; 1975
     HALL OF FAME
CONNOR, WILLIAM (CATHOLIC UNIV.) - TACKLE - 1929 BOSTON BRAVES; 1930
     NEWARK TORNADOS
CONNORS, HAMILTON - END - 1919-25 ROCHESTER JEFFERSONS
CONNORS, STAFFORD (NEW HAMPSHIRE) - BACK - 1925 PROVIDENCE
     STEAMROLLERS; 1926 BROOKLYN LIONS
CONOLY, WILLIAM (TEXAS) - GUARD - 1946 CHICAGO CARDINALS
CONOVER, LAWRENCE (PENN STATE) - CENTER - 1921-23 CANTON BULLDOGS;
     1925 CLEVELAND BULLDOGS; 1926 FRANKFORD YELLOWJACKETS
CONRAD, MARTIN (KALAMAZOO) - CENTER - 1922-23 TOLEDO MAROONS; 1924
     KENOSHA MAROONS; 1925 AKRON PROS
CONRAD, ROBERT (TEXAS A&M) - BACK - 1958-59 CHICAGO CARDINALS;
     1960-68 ST. LOUIS CARDINALS; 1969 DALLAS COWBOYS; 1963 PASS
     RECEIVING LEADER
CONSTANTINE, IRVING (SYRACUSE) - BACK - 1931 STATEN ISLAND STAPELTONS
CONTI, ENIO (BUCKNELL) - GUARD - 1941-42 PHILADELPHIA EAGLES; 1943
     PHIL-PITT; 1944-45 PHILADELPHIA EAGLES
CONTOULIS, JOHN (CONNECTICUT) - TACKLE - 1964 NEW YORK GIANTS
CONWAY, DAVID (TEXAS) - KICKER - 1971 GREEN BAY PACKERS (NFC)
CONZELMAN, JAMES (WASHINGTON-MO.) - QBACK - 1920 DECATUR STALEYS;
     1921-22 ROCK ISLAND INDEPENDENTS; 1923-24 MILWAUKEE BADGERS;
     1925-26 DETROIT PANTHERS; 1927-29 PROVIDENCE STEAMROLLERS; 1964
     HALL OF FAME
COOK, CLAIR - BACK - 1928 DAYTON TRIANGLES
COOK, DAVID (ILLINOIS) - BACK - 1934-36 CHICAGO CARDINALS; 1936
     BROOKLYN DODGERS
COOK, EDWARD (NOTRE DAME) - TACKLE - 1958-59 CHICAGO CARDINALS;
     1960-65 ST. LOUIS CARDINALS; 1966-67 ATLANTA FALCONS
COOK, EUGENE (TOLEDO) - END - 1959 DETROIT LIONS
COOK, FRED (SOUTHERN MISSISSIPPI) - END - 1974 BALTIMORE COLTS (AFC)
COOK, GREGORY (CINCINNATI) - QBACK - 1969 CINCINNATI BENGALS (AFL);
     1973 CINCINNATI BENGALS (AFC); 1969 PASSING LEADER (AFL)
COOK, JAMES - GUARD - 1921 GREEN BAY PACKERS
COOK, LEON (NORTHWESTERN) - TACKLE - 1942 PHILADELPHIA EAGLES
COOK, THEODORE (ALABAMA) - END - 1947 DETROIT LIONS; 1948-50 GREEN
     BAY PACKERS
COOKE, EDWARD (MARYLAND) - END - 1958 CHICAGO BEARS; 1958
     PHILADELPHIA EAGLES; 1959 BALTIMORE COLTS; 1960-62 NEW YORK
     TITANS (AFL); 1963 NEW YORK JETS (AFL); 1964-65 DENVER BRONCOS
     (AFL); 1966-67 MIAMI DOLPHINS (AFL)
COOLBAUGH, ROBERT (RICHMOND) - END - 1961 OAKLAND RAIDERS (AFL)
COOMER, JOSEPH (AUSTIN) - TACKLE - 1941, 45-46 PITTSBURGH STEELERS;
     1947-49 CHICAGO CARDINALS
COON, EDWARD (NORTH CAROLINA STATE) - GUARD - 1940 BROOKLYN DODGERS
COONEY, MARK (COLORADO) - LB - 1974 GREEN BAY PACKERS (NFC)
COOPER, HAROLD (DETROIT) - GUARD - 1937 DETROIT LIONS
COOPER, JAMES (NORTH TEXAS STATE) - CENTER - 1948 BROOKLYN DODGERS
     (AAFC)
COOPER, KENNETH (VANDERBILT) - GUARD - 1949 BALTIMORE COLTS (AAFC);
     1950 BALTIMORE COLTS
COOPER, NORMAN (HOWARD) - CENTER - 1937-38 BROOKLYN DODGERS

COOPER, SAMUEL (GENEVA) - TACKLE - 1933 PITTSBURGH PIRATES
COOPER, TAYLOR - CENTER - 1921 MUNCIE FLYERS
COOPER, THURLOW (MAINE) - END - 1960-62 NEW YORK TITANS (AFL)
COOPER, WILLIAM (PENN STATE) - QBACK - 1936 CLEVELAND RAMS (AFL);
     1937 CLEVELAND RAMS; 1937 CINCINNATI BENGALS (AFL)
COOPER, WILLIAM (MUSKINGUM) - LB - 1961-64 SAN FRANCISCO 49ERS
COPE, FRANK (SANTA CLARA) - TACKLE - 1938-47 NEW YORK GIANTS
COPELAND, RONALD (UCLA) - END - 1969 CHICAGO BEARS
COPELAND, WYATTE JAMES (VIRGINIA) - GUARD, CENTER - 1967-69 CLEVELAND
     BROWNS; 1970-74 CLEVELAND BROWNS (AFC)
COPLEY, CHARLES (MISSOURI MINES) - TACKLE - 1919-22 AKRON PROS; 1922
     MILWAUKEE BADGERS
COPPAGE, ALTON (OKLAHOMA) - END - 1940-42 CHICAGO CARDINALS; 1946
     CLEVELAND BROWNS (AAFC); 1947 BUFFALO BILLS (AAFC)
CORBETT, GEORGE (MILLIKIN) - QBACK - 1932-38 CHICAGO BEARS
CORBITT, DONALD (ARIZONA) - CENTER - 1948 WASHINGTON REDSKINS
CORBO, THOMAS (DUQUESNE) - GUARD - 1944 CLEVELAND RAMS
CORCORAN, ARTHUR (GEORGETOWN) - END - 1919-20 CANTON BULLDOGS; 1921
     CLEVELAND INDIANS; 1922 AKRON PROS; 1922 MILWAUKEE BADGERS; 1923
     BUFFALO ALL-AMERICANS
CORCORAN, JAMES (MARYLAND) - QBACK - 1968 BOSTON PATRIOTS (AFL)
CORCORAN, JOHN (ST. LOUIS) - CENTER - 1930 MINNEAPOLIS REDJACKETS
CORDILEONE, LOUIS (CLEMSON) - GUARD - 1960 NEW YORK GIANTS; 1961 SAN
     FRANCISCO 49ERS; 1962 LOS ANGELES RAMS; 1962-63 PITTSBURGH
     STEELERS; 1967-68 NEW ORLEANS SAINTS
CORDILL, OLIVER (MEMPHIS STATE) - BACK, KICKER - 1967 SAN DIEGO
     CHARGERS (AFL); 1968 ATLANTA FALCONS; 1969 NEW ORLEANS SAINTS
CORDILL, OLIVER (RICE) - BACK - 1940 CLEVELAND RAMS
CORDOVANO, SAMUEL (GEORGETOWN) - GUARD - 1930 NEWARK TORNADOS
COREY, WALTER (MIAMI) - LB - 1960, 62 DALLAS TEXANS (AFL); 1963-66
     KANSAS CITY CHIEFS (AFL)
CORGAN, CHARLES (ARKANSAS) - END - 1924-26 KANSAS CITY COWBOYS; 1926
     HARTFORD BLUES; 1927 NEW YORK GIANTS
CORGAN, MICHAEL (NOTRE DAME) - BACK - 1943 DETROIT LIONS
CORLEY, ELBERT (MISSISSIPPI STATE) - CENTER - 1947 BUFFALO BILLS
     (AAFC); 1948 BALTIMORE COLTS (AAFC)
CORN, JOSEPH - BACK - 1948 LOS ANGELES RAMS
CORNELISON, JERRY (SMU) - TACKLE - 1960-62 DALLAS TEXANS (AFL);
     1964-65 KANSAS CITY CHIEFS (AFL)
CORNELL, ROBERT "BO" (WASHINGTON) - BACK - 1971-72 CLEVELAND BROWNS
     (AFC); 1973-74 BUFFALO BILLS (AFC)
CORNISH, FRANK (GRAMBLING) - TACKLE - 1966-69 CHICAGO BEARS; 1970
     CHICAGO BEARS (NFC); 1970-71 MIAMI DOLPHINS (AFC); 1972 BUFFALO
     BILLS (AFC)
CORNSWEET, ALBERT (BROWN) - BACK - 1931 CLEVELAND INDIANS
CORONADO, ROBERT (PACIFIC) - END - 1961 PITTSBURGH STEELERS
CORRIGAN, PHILIP (BOSTON COLLEGE) - QBACK - 1926 BOSTON BULLDOGS (AFL)
CORTEMEGLIA, CHRISTOPHER (SMU) - BACK - 1927 FRANKFORD YELLOWJACKETS
CORTEZ, BRUCE (PARSONS-IOWA) - BACK - 1967 NEW ORLEANS SAINTS
CORY, THOMAS (UTAH) - END - 1940 BOSTON BEARS (AFL); 1940 COLUMBUS
     BULLIES (AFL)
CORZINE, LESTER (DAVIS&ELKINS) - BACK - 1933-34 CINCINNATI REDS; 1934
     ST. LOUIS GUNNERS; 1935-37 NEW YORK GIANTS; 1938 CHICAGO BEARS
COSLET, BRUCE (PACIFIC) - END - 1969 CINCINNATI BENGALS (AFL);
     1970-74 CINCINNATI BENGALS (AFC)
COSNER, DONALD (MONTANA STATE) - BACK - 1939 CHICAGO CARDINALS
COSTA, DAVID (UTAH) - LB, TACKLE - 1963-65 OAKLAND RAIDERS (AFL);
     1966 BUFFALO BILLS (AFL); 1967-69 DENVER BRONCOS (AFL); 1970-71
     DENVER BRONCOS (AFC); 1972-73 SAN DIEGO CHARGERS (AFC); 1974
     BUFFALO BILLS (AFC)
COSTA, SEBASTIAN PAUL (NOTRE DAME) - END, TACKLE - 1965-69 BUFFALO
     BILLS (AFL); 1970-72 BUFFALO BILLS (AFC)
COSTELL, CARL (DAYTON) - END - 1941 COLUMBUS BULLIES (AFL)
COSTELLO, HARRY (GEORGETOWN) - BACK - 1919 DETROIT HERALDS; 1921
     CINCINNATI CELTS
COSTELLO, RORY - CENTER - 1921 CINCINNATI CELTS
COSTELLO, THOMAS (DAYTON) - LB - 1964-65 NEW YORK GIANTS
COSTELLO, VINCENT (OHIO) - LB - 1957-66 CLEVELAND BROWNS; 1967-68 NEW
     YORK GIANTS
COSTON, FREDERICK (TEXAS A&M) - CENTER - 1939 PHILADELPHIA EAGLES

COTHERN, PAIGE (MISSISSIPPI) - BACK - 1957-58 LOS ANGELES RAMS; 1959
     PHILADELPHIA EAGLES; 1958 FIELD GOAL LEADER; (TIED WITH MINER)
COTTON, CRAIG (YOUNGSTOWN) - END - 1969 DETROIT LIONS; 1970-72
     DETROIT LIONS (NFC); 1973 CHICAGO BEARS (NFC)
COTTON, FORREST (NOTRE DAME) - TACKLE - 1923-25 ROCK ISLAND
     INDEPENDENTS
COTTON, RUSSELL (TEXAS MINES) - BACK - 1941 BROOKLYN DODGERS; 1942
     PITTSBURGH STEELERS
COTTRELL, THEODORE (DELAWARE VALLEY) - LB - 1969 ATLANTA FALCONS;
     1970 ATLANTA FALCONS (NFC)
COTTRELL, WILLIAM (DELAWARE VALLEY) - GUARD,CENTER,TACKLE - 1967-69
     DETROIT LIONS; 1970 DETROIT LIONS (NFC); 1972 DENVER BRONCOS
     (AFC)
COUGHLIN, FRANK (NOTRE DAME) - TACKLE - 1921 DETROIT PANTHERS; 1921
     GREEN BAY PACKERS; 1921 ROCK ISLAND INDEPENDENTS; 1923
     MINNEAPOLIS MARINES
COULTER, DEWITT "TEX" (WEST POINT) - TACKLE - 1946-49, 51-52 NEW YORK
     GIANTS
COUMIER, ULYSSES (LOUISIANA COLLEGE) - BACK - 1929 BUFFALO BISONS
COUNTS, JOHN (ILLINOIS) - BACK - 1962-63 NEW YORK GIANTS
COUPPEE, ALBERT (IOWA) - BACK - 1946 WASHINGTON REDSKINS
COURTNEY, GERARD (SYRACUSE) - BACK - 1942 BROOKLYN DODGERS
COUTRE, LAWRENCE (NOTRE DAME) - BACK - 1950, 53 GREEN BAY PACKERS;
     1953 BALTIMORE COLTS
COWAN, CHARLES (NEW MEXICO HIGHLANDS) - TACKLE - 1961-69 LOS ANGELES
     RAMS; 1970-74 LOS ANGELES RAMS (NFC)
COWAN, LESLIE (MCMURRY) - TACKLE - 1951 CHICAGO BEARS
COWAN, ROBERT (INDIANA) - BACK - 1947-48 CLEVELAND BROWNS (AAFC);
     1949 BALTIMORE COLTS (AAFC)
COWHIG, GERARD (NOTRE DAME) - BACK - 1947-49 LOS ANGELES RAMS; 1950
     CHICAGO CARDINALS; 1951 PHILADELPHIA EAGLES
COWLINGS, ALLEN (USC) - LB, END, TACKLE - 1970-72 BUFFALO BILLS
     (AFC); 1973-74 HOUSTON OILERS (AFC)
COX, BUDD (OHIO STATE) - END - 1936 CLEVELAND RAMS (AFL)
COX, FREDERICK (PITTSBURGH) - KICKER - 1963-69 MINNESOTA VIKINGS;
     1970-74 MINNESOTA VIKINGS (NFC); 1965, 69 FIELD GOAL LEADER;
     1970 FIELD GOAL LEADER (NFC); 1969 SCORING LEADER; 1970 SCORING
     LEADER (NFC)
COX, JAMES (MIAMI) - END - 1968 MIAMI DOLPHINS (AFL)
COX, JAMES (STANFORD) - GUARD - 1948 SAN FRANCISCO 49ERS (AAFC)
COX, LAWRENCE (ABILENE CHRISTIAN) - TACKLE - 1966-68 DENVER BRONCOS
     (AFL)
COX, NORMAN (TCU) - BACK - 1946-47 CHICAGO ROCKETS (AAFC)
COX, ROBERT (MUSKINGUM) - END - 1936 CLEVELAND RAMS (AFL)
COX, WILLIAM (DUKE) - END - 1951-52, 55 WASHINGTON REDSKINS
COX - END - 1940 COLUMBUS BULLIES (AFL)
COYLE, FRANK (DETROIT) - END - 1924 MILWAUKEE BADGERS; 1924-25 ROCK
     ISLAND INDEPENDENTS; 1926 ROCK ISLAND INDEPENDENTS (AFL)
COYLE, ROSS (OKLAHOMA) - BACK - 1961 LOS ANGELES RAMS
CRABB, CLAUDE (COLORADO) - BACK - 1962-63 WASHINGTON REDSKINS;
     1964-65 PHILADELPHIA EAGLES; 1966-68 LOS ANGELES RAMS
CRABTREE, CLEMENT (WAKE FOREST) - TACKLE - 1940-41 DETROIT LIONS
CRABTREE, CLYDE (FLORIDA) - QBACK - 1930 FRANKFORD YELLOWJACKETS;
     1930 MINNEAPOLIS REDJACKETS
CRABTREE, ERIC (PITTSBURGH) - BACK, END - 1966-68 DENVER BRONCOS
     (AFL); 1969 CINCINNATI BENGALS (AFL); 1970-71 CINCINNATI BENGALS
     (AFC); 1971 NEW ENGLAND PATRIOTS (AFC)
CRAIG, CORNELIUS "NEAL" (FISK) - BACK - 1971-73 CINCINNATI BENGALS
     (AFC); 1974 BUFFALO BILLS (AFC)
CRADDOCK, NATHANIEL (PARSONS) - BACK - 1963 BALTIMORE COLTS
CRAFT, RUSSELL (ALABAMA) - BACK - 1946-53 PHILADELPHIA EAGLES; 1954
     PITTSBURGH STEELERS
CRAIG, CLARK (PENNSYLVANIA) - END - 1925 FRANKFORD YELLOWJACKETS
CRAIG, DOBIE (HOWARD PAYNE) - BACK - 1962-63 OAKLAND RAIDERS (AFL);
     1964 HOUSTON OILERS (AFL)
CRAIG, LAWRENCE (SOUTH CAROLINA) - QBACK - 1939-49 GREEN BAY PACKERS
CRAIG, STEVE (NORTHWESTERN) - END - 1974 MINNESOTA VIKINGS (NFC)
CRAIN, MILTON (BAYLOR) - BACK - 1944 BOSTON YANKS
CRAKES, JOSEPH (SOUTH DAKOTA) - END - 1933 CINCINNATI REDS

CRAMER, CARL (HAMLINE) - BACK - 1920 CLEVELAND PANTHERS; 1921-26
AKRON PROS
CRANE, DENNIS (USC) - TACKLE - 1968-69 WASHINGTON REDSKINS; 1970 NEW
YORK GIANTS (NFC)
CRANE, GARY (ARKANSAS STATE) - END - 1969 DENVER BRONCOS (AFL)
CRANE, PAUL (ALABAMA) - LB, CENTER - 1966-69 NEW YORK JETS (AFL);
1970-72 NEW YORK JETS (AFC)
CRANGLE, JOHN (ILLINOIS) - BACK - 1923 CHICAGO CARDINALS
CRANGLE, MICHAEL (TENNESSE-MARTIN) - END - 1972 NEW ORLEANS SAINTS
(NFC)
CRASS, WILLIAM (LSU) - BACK - 1937 CHICAGO CARDINALS
CRAWFORD, DENVER (TENNESSEE) - TACKLE - 1948 NEW YORK YANKEES (AAFC)
CRAWFORD, EDWARD (MISSISSIPPI) - BACK - 1957 NEW YORK GIANTS
CRAWFORD, FREDERICK (DUKE) - TACKLE - 1935 CHICAGO BEARS
CRAWFORD, HILTON (GRAMBLING) - BACK - 1969 BUFFALO BILLS (AFL)
CRAWFORD, JAMES (WYOMING) - BACK - 1960-64 BOSTON PATRIOTS (AFL)
CRAWFORD, KENNETH (MIAMI OF OHIO) - GUARD - 1919-20 AKRON PROS; 1921
CINCINNATI CELTS; 1923 DAYTON TRIANGLES; 1925 HAMMOND PROS
CRAWFORD, WALTER (ILLINOIS) - TACKLE - 1925 CHICAGO BEARS; 1926
CHICAGO BULLS (AFL); 1927 NEW YORK YANKEES
CRAWFORD, WILLIAM (BRITISH COLUMBIA) - GUARD - 1960 NEW YORK GIANTS
CRANE, RICHARD (IOWA) - BACK - 1936-37 BROOKLYN DODGERS
CREECH, ROBERT (TCU) - LB - 1971-72 PHILADELPHIA EAGLES (NFC); 1973
NEW ORLEANS SAINTS (NFC)
CREEKMUR, LOUIS (WILLIAM&MARY) - GUARD - 1950-59 DETROIT LIONS
CREGAR, WILLIAM (HOLY CROSS) - GUARD - 1947-48 PITTSBURGH STEELERS
CREIGHTON, MILAN (ARKANSAS) - END - 1931-37 CHICAGO CARDINALS
CREMER, THEODORE (AUBURN) - END - 1946-47 DETROIT LIONS; 1948 GREEN
BAY PACKERS
CRENNEL, CARL (WEST VIRGINIA) - LB - 1970 PITTSBURGH STEELERS (AFC)
CRENSHAW, LEON (TUSKEGEE) - TACKLE - 1968 GREEN BAY PACKERS
CRENSHAW, WILLIS (KANSAS STATE) - BACK - 1964-69 ST. LOUIS CARDINALS;
1970 DENVER BRONCOS (AFC)
CRESPINO, ROBERT (MISSISSIPPI) - END - 1961-63 CLEVELAND BROWNS;
1964-68 NEW YORK GIANTS
CRIMMINS, BERNARD (NOTRE DAME) - GUARD - 1945 GREEN BAY PACKERS
CRISLER, HAROLD (SAN JOSE STATE) - END - 1946-47 BOSTON YANKS;
1948-49 WASHINGTON REDSKINS; 1950 BALTIMORE COLTS
CRISP, PARK (AKRON) - GUARD - 1919 AKRON PROS
CRIST, CHARLES (PENN STATE) - BACK - 1972-74 NEW YORK GIANTS (NFC)
CRITCHFIELD, HENRY (WOOSTER) - CENTER - 1931 CLEVELAND INDIANS
CRITCHFIELD, LAWRENCE (GROVE CITY) - GUARD - 1933 PITTSBURGH PIRATES
CRITER, KENNETH (WISCONSIN) - LB - 1969 DENVER BRONCOS (AFL); 1970-74
DENVER BRONCOS (AFC)
CRITTENDON, JOHN (WAYNE) - END - 1954 CHICAGO CARDINALS
CROCKETT, MONTE (HIGHLANDS) - END - 1960-62 BUFFALO BILLS (AFL)
CROCKETT, ROBERT (ARKANSAS) - END - 1966, 68-69 BUFFALO BILLS (AFL)
CROFT, ABRAHAM (SMU) - END - 1944-45 CHICAGO BEARS
CROFT, DONALD (TEXAS-EL PASO) - END, TACKLE - 1972, 74 BUFFALO BILLS
(AFC)
CROFT, JACK (UTAH STATE) - GUARD - 1924 RACINE LEGION
CROFT, MILBURN (RIPON) - TACKLE - 1942-47 GREEN BAY PACKERS
CROFT, WINFIELD (UTAH) - GUARD - 1935 BROOKLYN DODGERS; 1936
PITTSBURGH PIRATES
CROFTCHECK, DONALD (INDIANA) - GUARD - 1965-66 WASHINGTON REDSKINS;
1967 CHICAGO BEARS
CRONIN, EUGENE (PACIFIC) - END - 1956-59 DETROIT LIONS; 1960 DALLAS
COWBOYS; 1961-62 WASHINGTON REDSKINS
CRONIN, FRANCIS (ST. MARY'S OF MINN.) - END - 1927 DULUTH ESKIMOS
CRONIN, GERALD (RUTGERS) - END - 1932 BROOKLYN DODGERS
CRONIN, JOHN (BOSTON COLLEGE) - BACK - 1927-30 PROVIDENCE STEAMROLLERS
CRONIN, THOMAS (MARQUETTE) - BACK - 1922 GREEN BAY PACKERS
CRONIN, WILLIAM (BOSTON COLLEGE) - BACK - 1926 BOSTON BULLDOGS (AFL);
1927-29 PROVIDENCE STEAMROLLERS
CRONIN, WILLIAM (BOSTON COLLEGE) - END - 1965 PHILADELPHIA EAGLES;
1966 MIAMI DOLPHINS (AFL)
CRONKHITE, HENRY (KANSAS STATE) - END - 1934 BROOKLYN DODGERS
CROOK, ALBERT (WASHINGTON&JEFFERSON) - CENTER - 1925-26 DETROIT
PANTHERS; 1926 KANSAS CITY COWBOYS

CROOS, ROBERT (S.F.AUSTIN STATE) - TACKLE - 1952 CHICAGO BEARS;
    1954-55 LOS ANGELES RAMS; 1956-57 SAN FRANCISCO 49FRS; 1958-59
    CHICAGO CARDINALS; 1960 BOSTON PATRIOTS (AFL)
CROPPER, MARSHALL (MARYLAND STATE) - END - 1967-69 PITTSBURGH STEELERS
CROSBY, STEVEN (FORT HAYS STATE) - BACK - 1974 NEW YORK GIANTS (NFC)
CROSS, IRVIN (NORTHWESTERN) - BACK - 1961-65 PHILADELPHIA EAGLES;
    1966-68 LOS ANGELES RAMS; 1969 PHILADELPHIA EAGLES
CROSS, WILLIAM (WEST TEXAS STATE) - BACK - 1951-53 CHICAGO CARDINALS
CROSSAN, DAVID (MARYLAND) - CENTER - 1965-69 WASHINGTON REDSKINS
CROSSWHITE, LEON (OKLAHOMA) - BACK - 1973-74 DETROIT LIONS (NFC)
CROTTY, DAVID (DETROIT) - GUARD - 1937 ROCHESTER TIGERS (AFL)
CROTTY, JAMES (NOTRE DAME) - BACK - 1960-61 WASHINGTON REDSKINS;
    1961-62 BUFFALO BILLS (AFL)
CROUTHAMEL, JOHN JACOB (DARTMOUTH) - BACK - 1960 BOSTON PATRIOTS (AFL)
CROW, ALBERT (WILLIAM&MARY) - TACKLE - 1960 BOSTON PATRIOTS (AFL)
CROW, JOHN DAVID (TEXAS A&M) - BACK, END - 1958-59 CHICAGO CARDINALS;
    1960-64 ST. LOUIS CARDINALS; 1965-68 SAN FRANCISCO 49ERS
CROW, LINDON (USC) - BACK - 1955-57 CHICAGO CARDINALS; 1958-60 NEW
    YORK GIANTS; 1961-64 LOS ANGELES RAMS; 1956 INTERCEPTION LEADER
CROW, ORIEN (HASKELL) - CENTER - 1933-34 BOSTON REDSKINS
CROW, WAYNE (CALIFORNIA) - BACK - 1960-61 OAKLAND RAIDERS (AFL);
    1962-63 BUFFALO BILLS (AFL)
CROWDER, EARL (OKLAHOMA) - QBACK - 1939 CHICAGO CARDINALS; 1940
    CLEVELAND RAMS
CROWDER, RANDY (PENN STATE) - TACKLE - 1974 MIAMI DOLPHINS (AFC)
CROWE, LARRY (TEXAS SOUTHERN) - BACK - 1972 PHILADELPHIA EAGLES (NFC)
CROWE, PAUL (ST. MARY'S OF CAL.) - BACK - 1948-49 SAN FRANCISCO 49ERS
    (AAFC); 1949 LOS ANGELES DONS (AAFC); 1951 NEW YORK YANKS
CROWELL, ODIS (HARDIN-SIMMONS) - TACKLE - 1947 SAN FRANCISCO 49ERS
    (AAFC)
CROWL, RICHARD (RUTGERS) - CENTER - 1930 BROOKLYN DODGERS
CROWLEY, JAMES (NOTRE DAME) - BACK - 1925 GREEN BAY PACKERS; 1925
    PROVIDENCE STEAMROLLERS
CROWLEY, JOSEPH (DARTMOUTH) - END - 1944-45 BOSTON YANKS
CROWTHER, RAE (COLGATE) - END - 1925-26 FRANKFORD YELLOWJACKETS
CROWTHER, SAVILIE (COLGATE) - GUARD - 1925 FRANKFORD YELLOWJACKETS;
    1926 PHILADELPHIA QUAKERS (AFL)
CROYLE, PHILIP (CALIFORNIA) - LB - 1971-73 HOUSTON OILERS (AFC); 1973
    BUFFALO BILLS (AFC)
CRUM, ROBERT (ARIZONA) - END - 1974 ST. LOUIS CARDINALS (NFC)
CRUMP, DWAYNE (FRESNO STATE) - BACK - 1973-74 ST. LOUIS CARDINALS
    (NFC)
CRUMP, HARRY (BOSTON COLLEGE) - BACK - 1963 BOSTON PATRIOTS (AFL)
CRUSAN, DOUGLAS (INDIANA) - TACKLE - 1968-69 MIAMI DOLPHINS (AFL);
    1970-74 MIAMI DOLPHINS (AFC)
CRUTCHER, THOMAS (TCU) - LB - 1964-67 GREEN BAY PACKERS; 1968-69 NEW
    YORK GIANTS; 1971-72 GREEN BAY PACKERS (NFC)
CSONKA, LAWRENCE (SYRACUSE) - BACK - 1968-69 MIAMI DOLPHINS (AFL);
    1970-74 MIAMI DOLPHINS (AFC)
CUBA, PAUL (PITTSBURGH) - TACKLE - 1933-35 PHILADELPHIA EAGLES
CUBBAGE, BENJAMIN (PENN STATE) - GUARD - 1919 MASSILLON TIGERS
CUDZIK, WALTER (PURDUE) - CENTER - 1954 WASHINGTON REDSKINS; 1960-63
    BOSTON PATRIOTS (AFL); 1964 BUFFALO BILLS (AFL)
CUFF, WARD (MARQUETTE) - BACK - 1937-45 NEW YORK GIANTS; 1946 CHICAGO
    CARDINALS; 1947 GREEN BAY PACKERS; 1938-39, 43, 47 FIELD GOAL
    LEADER; (TIED - 1938 - KERCHEVAL, 1943 - HUTSON AND WATERFIELD,
    1947 - HARDER)
CULLARS, WILLIE (TEXAS) - END - 1974 PHILADELPHIA EAGLES (NFC)
CULLEN, DAVID (GENEVA) - GUARD - 1931 CLEVELAND INDIANS
CULLEN, RONALD (OKLAHOMA) - TACKLE - 1922 MILWAUKEE BADGERS
CULLOM, JAMES (CALIFORNIA) - GUARD - 1951 NEW YORK YANKS
CULP, CURLEY (ARIZONA STATE) - TACKLE - 1968-69 KANSAS CITY CHIEFS
    (AFL); 1970-74 KANSAS CITY CHIEFS (AFC); 1974 HOUSTON OILERS
    (AFC)
CULPEPPER, EDWARD (ALABAMA) - TACKLE - 1958-59 CHICAGO CARDINALS;
    1960 ST. LOUIS CARDINALS; 1961 MINNESOTA VIKINGS; 1962-63
    HOUSTON OILERS (AFL)
CULVER, ALVIN (NOTRE DAME) - TACKLE - 1932 CHICAGO BEARS; 1932 GREEN
    BAY PACKERS

CULVER, FRANK (SYRACUSE) - CENTER - 1923 BUFFALO ALL-AMERICANS; 1923, 25 CANTON BULLDOGS; 1924 BUFFALO BISONS; 1924 ROCHESTER JEFFERSONS

CUMISKEY, FRANK (OHIO STATE) - END - 1937 BROOKLYN DODGERS

CUMMINGS, EDWARD (STANFORD) - LB - 1964 NEW YORK JETS (AFL); 1965 DENVER BRONCOS (AFL)

CUNEO, EDWARD (COLUMBIA) - GUARD - 1929 ORANGE TORNADOS; 1930 BROOKLYN DODGERS

CUNNINGHAM, CARL (HOUSTON) - LB - 1967-69 DENVER BRONCOS (AFL); 1970 DENVER BRONCOS (AFC); 1971 NEW ORLEANS SAINTS (NFC)

CUNNINGHAM, HAROLD (OHIO STATE) - END - 1926 CLEVELAND PANTHERS (AFL); 1926 ROCK ISLAND INDEPENDENTS (AFL); 1927 CLEVELAND BULLDOGS; 1929 CHICAGO BEARS; 1931 STATEN ISLAND STAPELTONS

CUNNINGHAM, JAMES (PITTSBURGH) - BACK - 1961-63 WASHINGTON REDSKINS

CUNNINGHAM, JAY (BOWLING GREEN) - BACK - 1965-67 BOSTON PATRIOTS (AFL)

CUNNINGHAM, JULIAN DOUGLAS (MISSISSIPPI) - BACK - 1967-69 SAN FRANCISCO 49ERS; 1970-73 SAN FRANCISCO 49ERS (NFC); 1974 WASHINGTON REDSKINS (NFC)

CUNNINGHAM, LEON (SOUTH CAROLINA) - CENTER - 1955 DETROIT LIONS

CUNNINGHAM, RICHARD (ARKANSAS) - GUARD, LB - 1967-68 BUFFALO BILLS (AFL); 1970-72 BUFFALO BILLS (AFC); 1973 PHILADELPHIA EAGLES (NFC); 1973 HOUSTON OILERS (AFC)

CUNNINGHAM, SAMUEL (USC) - BACK - 1973-74 NEW ENGLAND PATRIOTS (AFC)

CUOZZO, GARY (VIRGINIA) - QBACK - 1963-66 BALTIMORE COLTS; 1967 NEW ORLEANS SAINTS; 1968-69 MINNESOTA VIKINGS; 1970-71 MINNESOTA VIKINGS (NFC); 1972 ST. LOUIS CARDINALS (NFC)

CUPPOLETTE, BREE (OREGON) - GUARD - 1934-38 CHICAGO CARDINALS; 1939 PHILADELPHIA EAGLES

CURCHIN, JEFF (FLORIDA STATE) - TACKLE - 1970-71 CHICAGO BEARS (NFC); 1972 BUFFALO BILLS (AFC)

CURCILLO, ANTHONY (OHIO STATE) - BACK - 1953 CHICAGO CARDINALS

CURE, ARMAND (RHODE SILAND STATE) - BACK - 1947 BALTIMORE COLTS (AAFC)

CURRAN, HARRY (BOSTON COLLEGE) - BACK - 1920-21 CHICAGO CARDINALS

CURRAN, PATRICK (LAKELAND) - END - 1969 LOS ANGELES RAMS; 1970-74 LOS ANGELES RAMS (NFC)

CURRENT, MICHAEL (OHIO STATE) - TACKLE - 1967 MIAMI DOLPHINS (AFL); 1967-69 DENVER BRONCOS (AFL); 1970-74 DENVER BRONCOS (AFC)

CURRIE, DANIEL (MICHIGAN STATE) - LB - 1958-64 GREEN BAY PACKERS; 1965-66 LOS ANGELES RAMS

CURRIVAN, DONALD (BOSTON COLLEGE) - END - 1943 CHICAGO CARDINALS; 1944 CARD-PITT; 1945-48 BOSTON YANKS; 1948-49 LOS ANGELES RAMS

CUFFY, WILLIAM (GEORGIA TECH) - CENTER - 1965-66 GREEN BAY PACKERS; 1967-69 BALTIMORE COLTS; 1970-72 BALTIMORE COLTS (AFC); 1973 HOUSTON OILERS (AFC); 1974 LOS ANGELES RAMS (NFC)

CURTIN, DONALD (MARQUETTE) - BACK - 1926 RACINE LEGION; 1926 MILWAUKEE BADGERS

CURTIS, ISAAC "IKE" (SAN DIEGO STATE) - END - 1973-74 CINCINNATI BENGALS (AFC)

CURTIS, JAMES MICHAEL (DUKE) - LB - 1965-69 BALTIMORE COLTS; 1970-74 BALTIMORE COLTS (AFC)

CURTIS, THOMAS (MICHIGAN) - BACK - 1970-71 BALTIMORE COLTS (AFC)

CURZON, HARRY - END - 1925 BUFFALO BISONS; 1925-26 HAMMOND PROS; 1926 LOUISVILLE COLONELS; 1928 CHICAGO CARDINALS

CUSACK, WILLIAM (GEORGETOWN) - END - 1919 AKRON PROS

CUTLER, HARRY - TACKLE - 1919-20 DAYTON TRIANGLES

CUTSINGER, GARY (OKLAHOMA STATE) - END - 1962-68 HOUSTON OILERS (AFL)

CVERCKO, ANDREW (NORTHWESTERN) - GUARD - 1960 GREEN BAY PACKERS; 1961-62 DALLAS COWBOYS; 1963 CLEVELAND BROWNS; 1963 WASHINGTON REDSKINS

CYRE, HECTOR (GONZAGA) - TACKLE - 1926-27 GREEN BAY PACKERS; 1928 NEW YORK YANKEES

CZAROBSKI, ZYGMONT (NOTRE DAME) - GUARD - 1948 CHICAGO ROCKETS (AAFC); 1949 CHICAGO HORNETS (AAFC)

DAANEN, JEROME (MIAMI) - END - 1968-69 ST. LOUIS CARDINALS; 1970 ST. LOUIS CARDINALS (NFC)

DABNEY, CARLTON (MORGAN STATE) - TACKLE - 1968 ATLANTA FALCONS

DADDIO, LOUIS "BILL" (PITTSBURGH) - END - 1941-42 CHICAGO CARDINALS; 1946 BUFFALO BISONS (AAFC); 1942 FIELD GOAL LEADER

DADMUN, HARRIE (HARVARD) - GUARD - 1920 CANTON BULLDOGS

DAFFER, TERRELL (TENNESSEE) - END - 1954 CHICAGO BEARS

DAGATA, FREDERICK (PROVIDENCE COLLEGE) - BACK - 1931 PROVIDENCE
    STEAMROLLERS
D'AGOSTINO, FRANK (AUBURN) - GUARD - 1956 PHILADELPHIA EAGLES; 1960
    NEW YORK TITANS (AFL)
DAHL, LEVANT (CANISIUS) - END - 1941 BUFFALO TIGERS (AFL)
DAHLGREN, GEORGE (BELOIT) - GUARD - 1924 KENOSHA MAROONS; 1925-26
    HAMMOND PROS
DAHMS, THOMAS (SAN DIEGO STATE) - TACKLE - 1951-54 LOS ANGELES RAMS;
    1955 GREEN BAY PACKERS; 1956 CHICAGO CARDINALS; 1957 SAN
    FRANCISCO 49ERS
DAILEY, DONALD (ST. STEPHENS) - END - 1936 BROOKLYN TIGERS (AFL)
DAILEY, THEODORE (PITTSBURGH) - END - 1933 PITTSBURGH PIRATES
DALBY, DAVID (UCLA) - GUARD,CENTER,TACKLE - 1972-74 OAKLAND RAIDERS
    (AFC)
DALE, CARROLL (VPI) - END - 1960-64 LOS ANGELES RAMS; 1965-69 GREEN
    BAY PACKERS; 1970-72 GREEN BAY PACKERS (NFC); 1973 MINNESOTA
    VIKINGS (NFC)
DALE, ROLAND (MISSISSIPPI) - END - 1950 WASHINGTON REDSKINS
DALEY, WILLIAM (MINNESOTA & MICHIGAN) - BACK - 1946 MIAMI SEAHAWKS
    (AAFC); 1946 BROOKLYN DODGERS (AAFC); 1947 CHICAGO ROCKETS
    (AAFC); 1948 NEW YORK YANKEES (AAFC)
DALLY - GUARD - 1926 HARTFORD BLUES
D'ALONZO, PETER (VILLANOVA) - BACK - 1951-52 DETROIT LIONS
DALRYMPLE, ROBERT (WABASH) - CENTER - 1922 EVANSVILLE CRIMSON GIANTS
DALTON, LEATHER (CARROLL) - BACK - 1922 RACINE LEGION
D'AMATO, MICHAEL (HOFSTRA) - BACK - 1968 NEW YORK JETS (AFL)
DAMIANI, FRANCIS (MANHATTAN) - TACKLE - 1944 NEW YORK GIANTS
DAMKROGER, MAURICE (NEBRASKA) - LB - 1974 NEW ENGLAND PATRIOTS (AFC)
DAMORE, JOHN (NORTHWESTERN) - GUARD - 1957, 59 CHICAGO BEARS
DANAHE, RICHARD (USC) - TACKLE - 1947-48 LOS ANGELES DONS (AAFC)
DANCEWICZ, FRANCIS (NOTRE DAME) - QBACK - 1946-48 BOSTON YANKS
DANENHAUER, ELDON (PITTSBURG STATE - KANSAS) - TACKLE - 1960-65
    DENVER BRONCOS (AFL)
DANENHAUER, WILLIAM (EMPORIA STATE - KANSAS) - END - 1960 DENVER
    BRONCOS (AFL); 1960 BOSTON PATRIOTS (AFL)
DANEY, GEORGE (TEXAS-EL PASO) - GUARD - 1968-69 KANSAS CITY CHIEFS
    (AFL); 1970-74 KANSAS CITY CHIEFS (AFC)
DANIEL, WILLIE (MISSISSIPPI STATE) - BACK - 1961-66 PITTSBURGH
    STEELERS; 1967-69 LOS ANGELES RAMS
DANIELL, AVERELL (PITTSBURGH) - TACKLE - 1937 GREEN BAY PACKERS; 1937
    BROOKLYN DODGERS
DANIELL, JAMES (OHIO STATE) - TACKLE - 1945 CHICAGO BEARS; 1946
    CLEVELAND BROWNS (AAFC)
DANIELS, CLEMON (PRAIRIE VIEW) - BACK - 1960 DALLAS TEXANS (AFL);
    1961-67 OAKLAND RAIDERS (AFL); 1968 SAN FRANCISCO 49ERS; 1963
    RUSHING LEADER (AFL)
DANIELS, DAVID (FLORIDA A&M) - TACKLE - 1966 OAKLAND RAIDERS (AFL)
DANIELS, RICHARD (PACIFIC) - BACK - 1966-68 DALLAS COWBOYS; 1969
    CHICAGO BEARS; 1970 CHICAGO BEARS (NFC)
DANJEAN, ERNEST (AUBURN) - GUARD - 1957 GREEN BAY PACKERS
DANOWSKI, EDWARD (FORDHAM) - QBACK - 1934-39, 41 NEW YORK GIANTS;
    1935, 38 PASSING LEADER
DANZIGER, FREDERICK (MICHIGAN STATE) - BACK - 1931 CLEVELAND INDIANS
DA PRATO, NENO (MICHIGAN STATE) - BACK - 1921 DETROIT PANTHERS
DARDEN, THOMAS (MICHIGAN) - BACK - 1972-74 CLEVELAND BROWNS (AFC)
DARLING, BERNARD (BELOIT) - CENTER - 1927-31 GREEN BAY PACKERS
DARNAIL, WILLIAM (NORTH CAROLINA) - END, BACK - 1968-69 MIAMI
    DOLPHINS (AFL)
DARNELL, LAWRENCE (KANSAS STATE) - GUARD - 1937 PITTSBURGH AMERICANS
    (AFL)
DARRAGH, DANIEL (WILLIAM&MARY) - QBACK - 1968-69 BUFFALO BILLS (AFL);
    1970 BUFFALO BILLS (AFC)
DARRE, BERNARD (TULANE) - GUARD - 1961 WASHINGTON REDSKINS
DARROW, BARRY (MONTANA) - TACKLE - 1974 CLEVELAND BROWNS (AFC)
DASSTLING, DANE (MARIETTA) - TACKLE - 1921 CINCINNATI CELTS
DAUGHERTY, RICHARD (OREGON) - GUARD - 1951-53, 56-58 LOS ANGELES RAMS
DAUGHERTY, ROBERT (TULSA) - BACK - 1966 SAN FRANCISCO 49ERS
DAUGHERTY, RUSSELL (ILLINOIS) - BACK - 1927 FRANKFORD YELLOWJACKETS
DAUKAS, LOUIS (CORNELL) - CENTER - 1947 BROOKLYN DODGERS (AAFC)

DAUKAS, NICHOLAS (DARTMOUTH) - TACKLE - 1946-47 BROOKLYN DODGERS
    (AAFC)
DAUM, CARL (AKRON UNIV.) - END - 1922-26 AKRON PROS
DAVENPORT, WAYNE (HARDIN-SIMMONS) - BACK - 1931 GREEN BAY PACKERS
DAVID, JAMES (COLORADO A&M) - BACK - 1952-59 DETROIT LIONS
DAVID, MARVIN (SOUTHERN) - LB - 1974 HOUSTON OILERS (AFC)
DAVID, ROBERT (VILLANOVA) - GUARD - 1947-48 LOS ANGELES RAMS; 1948
    CHICAGO ROCKETS (AAFC)
DAVIDSON, BENJAMIN (WASHINGTON) - END - 1961 GREEN BAY PACKERS;
    1962-63 WASHINGTON REDSKINS; 1964-69 OAKLAND RAIDERS (AFL);
    1970-71 OAKLAND RAIDERS (AFC)
DAVIDSON, FRANK (BAYLOR) - QBACK - 1954, 57 BALTIMORE COLTS; 1960-62
    DALLAS TEXANS (AFL); 1962-66, 68 OAKLAND RAIDERS (AFL)
DAVIDSON, JOSEPH (COLGATE) - GUARD - 1928 CHICAGO CARDINALS; 1930
    NEWARK TORNADOS
DAVIDSON, PETER (CITADEL) - TACKLE - 1960 HOUSTON OILERS (AFL)
DAVIDSON, WILLIAM (TEMPLE) - BACK - 1937-38 PITTSBURGH PIRATES; 1939
    PITTSBURGH STEELERS
DAVIES, THOMAS (PITTSBURGH) - BACK - 1922 HAMMOND PROS
DAVIS, ALBERT (TENNESSEE STATE) - BACK - 1971 PHILADELPHIA EAGLES
    (NFC)
DAVIS, ANDREW (GEORGE WASHINGTON) - BACK - 1952 WASHINGTON REDSKINS
DAVIS, ARNOLD (BAYLOR) - LB - 1961 DALLAS COWBOYS
DAVIS, ARTHUR (ALABAMA STATE) - TACKLE - 1953 CHICAGO BEARS
DAVIS, ARTHUR (MISSISSIPPI STATE) - BACK - 1956 PITTSBURGH STEELERS
DAVIS, BENJAMIN (DEFIANCE) - BACK - 1967-68 CLEVELAND BROWNS; 1970-73
    CLEVELAND BROWNS (AFC); 1974 DETROIT LIONS (NFC)
DAVIS, CARL (WEST VIRGINIA) - TACKLE - 1926 NEWARK BEARS (AFL); 1926
    AKRON PROS; 1927 FRANKFORD YELLOWJACKETS
DAVIS, CHARLES (COLORADO) - BACK - 1974 CINCINNATI BENGALS (AFC)
DAVIS, CHARLIE (TEXAS CHRISTIAN) - TACKLE - 1974 PITTSBURGH STEELERS
    (AFC)
DAVIS, CLARENCE (USC) - BACK - 1971-74 OAKLAND RAIDERS (AFC)
DAVIS, CORBETT (INDIANA) - BACK - 1938-39, 41-42 CLEVELAND RAMS
DAVIS, DAVID (TENNESSEE STATE) - END - 1971-72 GREEN BAY PACKERS
    (NFC); 1973 PITTSBURGH STEELERS (AFC); 1974 NEW ORLEANS SAINTS
    (NFC)
DAVIS, DAVID (USC) - BACK - 1937 LOS ANGELES BULLDOGS (AFL)
DAVIS, DONALD (LOS ANGELES STATE) - TACKLE - 1966 NEW YORK GIANTS
DAVIS, DONALD (SOUTHERN) - END - 1962 DALLAS COWBOYS; 1970 HOUSTON
    OILERS (AFC)
DAVIS, DOUGLAS (KENTUCKY) - TACKLE - 1966-69 MINNESOTA VIKINGS;
    1970-72 MINNESOTA VIKINGS (NFC)
DAVIS, EDWARD (INDIANA) - GUARD - 1920 HAMMOND PROS; 1920-21 DAYTON
    TRIANGLES; 1921-22 COLUMBUS PANHANDLES
DAVIS, FREDERICK (ALABAMA) - TACKLE - 1941-42, 45 WASHINGTON
    REDSKINS; 1946-51 CHICAGO BEARS
DAVIS, GAINES (TEXAS TECH) - GUARD - 1936 NEW YORK GIANTS
DAVIS, GLENN (OHIO STATE) - END - 1960-61 DETROIT LIONS
DAVIS, GLENN (WEST POINT) - BACK - 1950-51 LOS ANGELES RAMS
DAVIS, HARPER (MISSISSIPPI STATE) - BACK - 1949 LOS ANGELES RAMS;
    1950 CHICAGO BEARS; 1951 GREEN BAY PACKERS
DAVIS, HARRISON (VIRGINIA) - END - 1974 SAN DIEGO CHARGERS (AFC)
DAVIS, HENRY (GRAMBLING) - LB - 1968-69 NEW YORK GIANTS; 1970-73
    PITTSBURGH STEELERS (AFC)
DAVIS, HERBERT (XAVIER) - BACK - 1925-26 COLUMBUS TIGERS
DAVIS, JACK (ARIZONA) - GUARD - 1960 DENVER BRONCOS (AFL)
DAVIS, JACK (MARYLAND) - GUARD - 1960 BOSTON PATRIOTS (AFL)
DAVIS, JEROME (SOUTHEASTERN LOUISIANA) - BACK - 1948-51 CHICAGO
    CARDINALS; 1952 DALLAS TEXANS
DAVIS, JOHN "BUTCH" (MISSOURI) - BACK - 1970 CHICAGO BEARS (NFC)
DAVIS, JOHN - BACK - 1919-20 COLUMBUS PANHANDLES
DAVIS, JOSEPH (USC) - END - 1946 BROOKLYN DODGERS (AAFC)
DAVIS, KERMIT (BIRMINGHAM-SOUTHERN) - END - 1936 NEW YORK YANKS
    (AFL); 1936 ROCHESTER TIGERS (AFL); 1937 BOSTON SHAMROCKS (AFL)
DAVIS, MARVIN (WICHITA STATE) - END - 1966 DENVER BRONCOS (AFL)
DAVIS, MILTON (UCLA) - BACK - 1957-60 BALTIMORE COLTS; 1957
    INTERCEPTION LEADER; (TIED WITH CHRISTIANSEN AND BUTLER); 1959
    INTERCEPTION LEADER; (TIED BY DERBY AND SHINNICK)

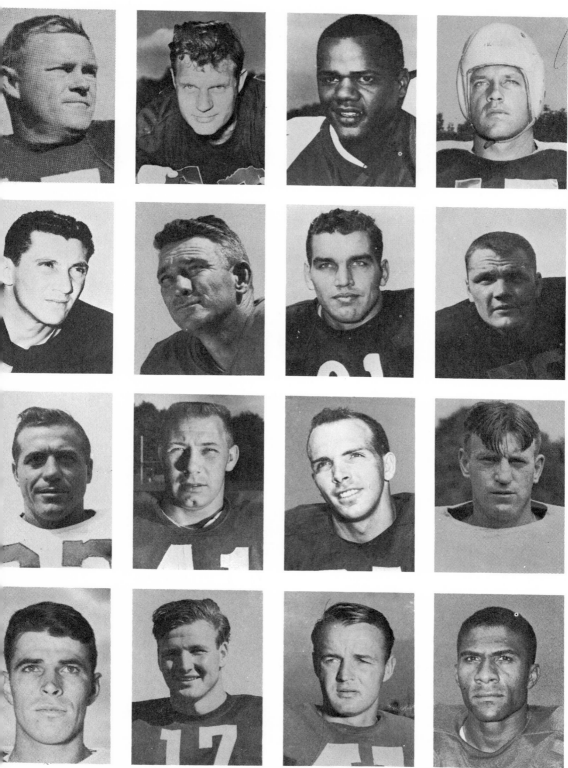

Top row (from left to right): Paul Christman, Ed Cifers, Frank Clarke and Ed Cody. *Second row:* Angelo Coia, Charley Conerly, George Connor and DeWitt Coulter. *Third row:* Russ Craft, Lindon Crow, Carroll Dale and Ed Danowski. *Bottom row:* Jim David, Fred Davis, Glenn Davis and Milt Davis.

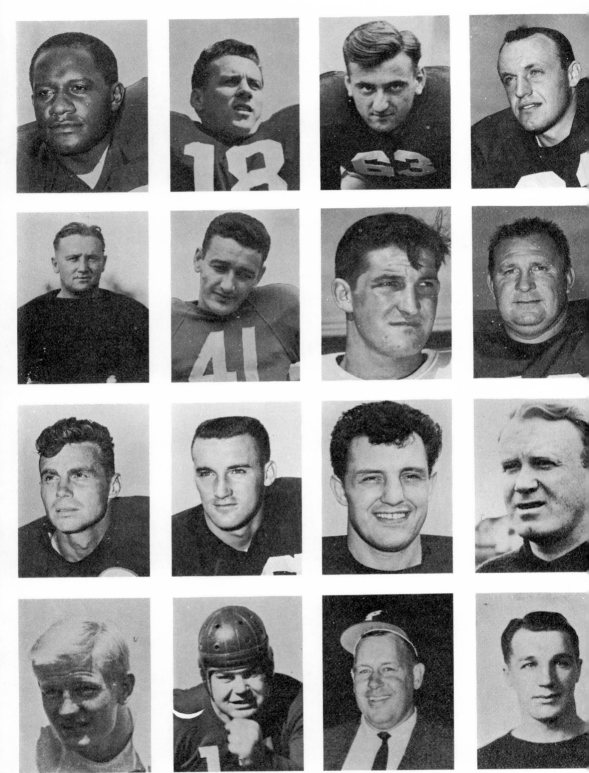

Top row (from left to right): Willie Davis, Len Dawson, Al DeMao and Bob DeMarco. *Second row:* John Depler, Bill Dewell, Dale Dodrill and Art Donovan. *Third row:* Jim Dooley, Boyd Dowler, Chuck Drazenovich and "Red" Dunn. *Bottom row:* Brad Ecklund, "Turk" Edwards, Clyde Ehrhardt and Jack Ernst.

DAVIS, NORMAN (GRAMBLING) - GUARD - 1967 BALTIMORE COLTS; 1969 NEW
    ORLEANS SAINTS; 1970 PHILADELPHIA EAGLES (NFC)
DAVIS, PAHL (MARQUETTE) - GUARD - 1922 GREEN BAY PACKERS
DAVIS, PAUL (OTTERBEIN) - QBACK - 1947-48 PITTSBURGH STEELERS
DAVIS, R. LAMAR (GEORGIA) - END - 1946 MIAMI SEAHAWKS (AAFC); 1947-49
    BALTIMORE COLTS (AAFC)
DAVIS, RALPH (WISCONSIN) - GUARD - 1947-48 GREEN BAY PACKERS
DAVIS, RAYMOND (HOWARD OF ALABAMA) - GUARD - 1932-33 PORTSMOUTH
    SPARTANS; 1935 CHICAGO CARDINALS; 1936 PITTSBURGH AMERICANS (AFL)
DAVIS, RICHARD "TED" (GEORGIA TECH) - LB - 1964-66 BALTIMORE COLTS;
    1967-69 NEW ORLEANS SAINTS; 1970 MIAMI DOLPHINS (AFC)
DAVIS, RICHARD (KANSAS) - TACKLE - 1962 DALLAS TEXANS (AFL)
DAVIS, RICHARD (NEBRASKA) - BACK - 1970 DENVER BRONCOS (AFC); 1970
    NEW ORLEANS SAINTS (NFC)
DAVIS, ROBERT (GEORGIA TECH) - TACKLE - 1948 BOSTON YANKS
DAVIS, ROBERT (KENTUCKY) - QBACK - 1938 CLEVELAND RAMS; 1940-41
    COLUMBUS BULLIES (AFL); 1942 PHILADELPHIA EAGLES; 1944-46 BOSTON
    YANKS
DAVIS, ROBERT (PENN STATE) - END - 1946-50 PITTSBURGH STEELERS
DAVIS, ROBERT (VIRGINIA) - QBACK - 1967-69 HOUSTON OILERS (AFL);
    1970-72 NEW YORK JETS (AFC); 1973 NEW ORLEANS SAINTS (NFC)
DAVIS, ROGER (SYRACUSE) - GUARD - 1960-63 CHICAGO BEARS; 1964 LOS
    ANGELES RAMS; 1965-66 NEW YORK GIANTS
DAVIS, RONALD (VIRGINIA STATE) - TACKLE - 1973 ST. LOUIS CARDINALS
    (NFC)
DAVIS, ROOSEVELT (TENNESSEE STATE) - END - 1965-67 NEW YORK GIANTS
DAVIS, SAMUEL (ALLEN-SOUTH CAROLINA) - GUARD - 1967-69 PITTSBURGH
    STEELERS; 1970-74 PITTSBURGH STEELERS (AFC)
DAVIS, STANLEY (MEMPHIS STATE) - END - 1973 PHILADELPHIA EAGLES (NFC)
DAVIS, STEVEN (DELAWARE STATE) - BACK - 1972-74 PITTSBURGH STEELERS
    (AFC)
DAVIS, SYLVESTER (GENEVA) - BACK - 1933 PORTSMOUTH SPARTANS; 1933
    PHILADELPHIA EAGLES
DAVIS, THOMAS (LSU) - KICKER - 1965-69 SAN FRANCISCO 49ERS; 1960
    FIELD GOAL LEADER; 1962 PUNTING LEADER
DAVIS, VAN (GEORGIA) - END - 1947-49 NEW YORK YANKEES (AAFC)
DAVIS, VERNON (WESTERN MICHIGAN) - BACK - 1971 PHILADELPHIA EAGLES
    (NFC)
DAVIS, WILLIAM (TEXAS TECH) - TACKLE - 1940-41 CHICAGO CARDINALS;
    1943 BROOKLYN DODGERS; 1946 MIAMI SEAHAWKS (AAFC)
DAVIS, WILLIE (GRAMBLING) - END - 1958-59 CLEVELAND BROWNS; 1960-69
    GREEN BAY PACKERS
DAVIS - END - 1919 COLUMBUS PANHANDLES
DAVLIN, MICHAEL (NOTRE DAME & SAN FRANCISCO) - TACKLE - 1955
    WASHINGTON REDSKINS
DAWKINS, JOE (WISCONSIN) - BACK - 1970-71 HOUSTON OILERS (AFC);
    1971-73 DENVER BRONCOS (AFC); 1974 NEW YORK GIANTS (NFC)
DAWLEY, FREDERICK (MICHIGAN) - BACK - 1944 DETROIT LIONS
DAWSON, GILBERT (TEXAS) - BACK - 1953 GREEN BAY PACKERS
DAWSON, LEONARD (PURDUE) - QBACK - 1957-59 PITTSBURGH STEELERS;
    1960-61 CLEVELAND BROWNS; 1962 DALLAS TEXANS (AFL); 1963-69
    KANSAS CITY CHIEFS (AFL); 1970-74 KANSAS CITY CHIEFS (AFC);
    1962, 64, 66, 68 PASSING LEADER (AFL)
DAWSON, RHETT (FLORIDA STATE) - END - 1972 HOUSTON OILERS (AFC); 1973
    MINNESOTA VIKINGS (NFC)
DAWSON, WILLIAM (FLORIDA STATE) - END - 1965 BOSTON PATRIOTS (AFL)
DAY, ALBERT (EASTERN MICHIGAN) - LB - 1960 DENVER BRONCOS (AFL)
DAY, HERMAN EAGLE (MISSISSIPPI) - QBACK - 1959-60 WASHINGTON REDSKINS
DAY, THOMAS (NORTH CAROLINA A&T) - END - 1960 ST. LOUIS CARDINALS;
    1961-66, 68 BUFFALO BILLS (AFL); 1967 SAN DIEGO CHARGERS (AFL)
DAYHOFF, HARRY (BUCKNELL) - BACK - 1924 FRANKFORD YELLOWJACKETS; 1925
    POTTSVILLE MAROONS
DEADRYE - TACKLE - 1922-23 OORANG INDIANS
DEAL, RUFUS (AUBURN) - BACK - 1942 WASHINGTON REDSKINS
DEAN, HAROLD (OHIO STATE) - GUARD - 1947-49 LOS ANGELES RAMS
DEAN, THEODORE (WICHITA) - BACK - 1960-63 PHILADELPHIA EAGLES; 1964
    MINNESOTA VIKINGS
DEAN, THOMAS (SMU) - TACKLE - 1946-47 BOSTON YANKS
DEAN, THOMAS FLOYD (FLORIDA) - LB - 1964-65 SAN FRANCISCO 49ERS
DEAN - TACKLE - 1926 CLEVELAND PANTHERS (AFL)

DE BERNARDI, FRANK FREDRICK (TEXAS-EL PASO) - END - 1974 KANSAS CITY
    CHIEFS (AFC)
DECARRO, NICHOLAS (DUQUESNE) - GUARD - 1933 PITTSBURGH PIRATES
DE CARLO, ARTHUR (GEORGIA) - BACK - 1953 PITTSBURGH STEELERS; 1956-57
    WASHINGTON REDSKINS; 1957-60 BALTIMORE COLTS
DE CLERK, FRANK (ST. AMBROSE) - CENTER - 1921-25 ROCK ISLAND
    INDEPENDENTS
DE CORREVONT, WILLIAM (NORTHWESTERN) - BACK - 1945 WASHINGTON
    REDSKINS; 1946 DETROIT LIONS; 1947-48 CHICAGO CARDINALS; 1948-49
    CHICAGO BEARS
DEE, ROBERT (HOLY CROSS) - END - 1957-58 WASHINGTON REDSKINS; 1960-67
    BOSTON PATRIOTS (AFL)
DEEKS, DONALD (WASHINGTON) - TACKLE - 1945-47 BOSTON YANKS; 1947
    WASHINGTON REDSKINS; 1948 GREEN BAY PACKERS
DEER SLAYER - END - 1922 OORANG INDIANS
DEES, ROBERT (SOUTHWEST MISSOURI STATE) - GUARD - 1952 GREEN BAY
    PACKERS
DE FELICE, NICHOLAS (SOUTHERN CONNECTICUT) - TACKLE - 1965-66 NEW
    YORK JETS (AFL)
DEFILIPPO, LOUIS (FORDHAM) - CENTER - 1941, 45-47 NEW YORK GIANTS
DE FRUITER, ROBERT (NEBRASKA) - BACK - 1945-47 WASHINGTON REDSKINS;
    1947 DETROIT LIONS; 1948 LOS ANGELES RAMS
DEGEN, RICHARD (LONG BEACH STATE) - LB - 1965-66 SAN DIEGO CHARGERS
    (AFL)
DE GREE, WALTER (NOTRE DAME) - GUARD - 1921 DETROIT PANTHERS
DE GRENIER, JACK (TEXAS-ARLINGTON) - BACK - 1974 NEW ORLEANS SAINTS
    (NFC)
DEIBEL, ARTHUR (LAFAYETTE) - TACKLE - 1919 AKRON PROS; 1926 CANTON
    BULLDOGS
DEKDERRUN, ALAN (CORNELL) - QBACK - 1946 BUFFALO BISONS (AAFC); 1947
    CHICAGO ROCKETS (AAFC); 1948 NEW YORK YANKEES (AAFC); 1948
    BOSTON YANKS
DEKKER, PAUL (MICHIGAN STATE) - END - 1953 WASHINGTON REDSKINS
DE LAMIELLEURE, JOSEPH (MICHIGAN STATE) - GUARD - 1973-74 BUFFALO
    BILLS (AFC)
DELAPORTE, DAROL - BACK - 1925 MILWAUKEE BADGERS
DE LAURR, ROBERT (USC) - CENTER - 1945 CLEVELAND RAMS; 1946 LOS
    ANGELES RAMS
DEL BELLO, JOHN (MIAMI) - BACK - 1953 BALTIMORE COLTS
DE LEONE, THOMAS (OHIO STATE) - CENTER, GUARD - 1972-73 CINCINNATI
    BENGALS (AFC); 1974 CLEVELAND BROWNS (AFC)
DELEVAN, BURTON (PACIFIC) - TACKLE - 1955-56 CHICAGO CARDINALS
DEL GAIZO, JAMES (TAMPA) - QBACK - 1972 MIAMI DOLPHINS (AFC); 1973
    GREEN BAY PACKERS (NFC); 1974 NEW YORK GIANTS (NFC)
DE LISLE, JAMES (WISCONSIN) - TACKLE - 1971 GREEN BAY PACKERS (NFC)
DELL ISOLA, JOHN (FORDHAM) - GUARD - 1934-40 NEW YORK GIANTS
DELLERBA, SPIRO (OHIO STATE) - BACK - 1947 CLEVELAND BROWNS (AAFC);
    1948-49 BALTIMORE COLTS (AAFC)
DELLINGER, LAWRENCE (ST. MARY'S OF OHIO) - GUARD - 1919-23 DAYTON
    TRIANGLES
DE LUCCA, GERALD (TENNESSEE) - TACKLE - 1959 PHILADELPHIA EAGLES;
    1960-61, 63-64 BOSTON PATRIOTS (AFL); 1962-63 BUFFALO BILLS (AFL)
DE LONG, STEVEN (TENNESSEE) - END, TACKLE - 1965-69 SAN DIEGO
    CHARGERS (AFL); 1970-71 SAN DIEGO CHARGERS (AFC); 1972 CHICAGO
    BEARS (NFC)
DE LUCA, SAMUEL (SOUTH CAROLINA) - TACKLE - 1960 LOS ANGELES CHARGERS
    (AFL); 1961, 63 SAN DIEGO CHARGERS (AFL); 1964-66 NEW YORK JETS
    (AFL)
DE MAO, ALBERT (DUQUESNE) - CENTER - 1945-53 WASHINGTON REDSKINS
DE MARCO, MARIO (MIAMI) - GUARD - 1949 DETROIT LIONS
DE MARCO, ROBERT (DAYTON) - CENTER - 1961-69 ST. LOUIS CARDINALS;
    1970-71 MIAMI DOLPHINS (AFC); 1972-74 CLEVELAND BROWNS (AFC)
DEMARIE, JOHN (LSU) - TACKLE, GUARD - 1967-69 CLEVELAND BROWNS;
    1970-74 CLEVELAND BROWNS (AFC)
DEMAS, GEORGE (WASHINGTON&JEFFERSON) - GUARD - 1932 STATEN ISLAND
    STAPELTONS; 1934 BROOKLYN DODGERS
DEMERY, CALVIN (ARIZONA STATE) - END - 1972 MINNESOTA VIKINGS (NFC)
DEMKO, GEORGE (APPALACHIAN STATE) - TACKLE - 1961 PITTSBURGH STEELERS
DE MOE, WILLIAM - END - 1921 GREEN BAY PACKERS
DEMORY, WILLIAM (ARIZONA) - QBACK - 1973-74 NEW YORK JETS (AFC)
DE MOSS, ROBERT (PURDUE) - BACK - 1949 NEW YORK BULLDOGS

DEMPSEY, FRANKLIN (FLRODIA) - TACKLE - 1950-53 CHICAGO BEARS
DEMPSEY, JOHN (BUCKNELL) - TACKLE - 1934 PITTSBURGH PIRATES; 1934, 37
    PHILADELPHIA EAGLES
DEMPSEY, THOMAS (PALOMAR JUNIOR) - KICKER - 1969 NEW ORLEANS SAINTS;
    1970 NEW ORLEANS SAINTS (NFC); 1971-74 PHILADELPHIA EAGLES (NFC)
DEMYANOVICH, JOHN - TACKLE - 1930-31 STATEN ISLAND STAPELTONS
DEMYANOVICH, JOSEPH (ALABAMA) - BACK - 1936 ROCHESTER TIGERS (AFL)
DENABLE, EDWARD (WESTERN RESERVE) - BACK - 1919 CLEVELAND INDIANS
DENFIELD, FREDERICK (ANNAPOLIS) - TACKLE - 1920 ROCK ISLAND
    INDEPENDENTS; 1925 DULUTH KELLEYS
DEN HERDER, VERNON (CENTRAL IOWA) - END - 1971-74 MIAMI DOLPHINS (AFC)
DENISCO, JERRY (NEW YORK UNIV.) - CENTER - 1940 NEW YORK AMERICANS
    (AFL)
DENNERLEIN, GERALD (ST. MARY'S OF CAL.) - TACKLE - 1937, 40 NEW YORK
    GIANTS
DENNERY, MICHAEL (SOUTHERN MISSISSIPPI) - LB - 1974 OAKLAND RAIDERS
    (AFC)
DENNERY, VINCENT (FORDHAM) - END - 1941 NEW YORK GIANTS
DENNEY, AUSTIN (TENNESSEE) - END - 1967-69 CHICAGO BEARS; 1970-71
    BUFFALO BILLS (AFC)
DENNIS, ALBERT (GRAMBLING) - GUARD - 1973 SAN DIEGO CHARGERS (AFC)
DENNIS, GUY (FLORIDA) - GUARD - 1969 CINCINNATI BENGALS (AFL);
    1970-72 CINCINNATI BENGALS (AFC); 1973-74 DETROIT LIONS (NFC)
DENNIS, WALTER "MIKE" (MISSISSIPPI) - BACK - 1968-69 LOS ANGELES RAMS
DENNISON, DOUG (KUTZTOWN STATE) - BACK - 1974 DALLAS COWBOYS (NFC)
DENNY, EARL (MISSOURI) - BACK - 1967-68 MINNESOTA VIKINGS
DENSON, ALFRED (FLORIDA A&M) - END - 1964-69 DENVER BRONCOS (AFL);
    1970 DENVER BRONCOS (AFC); 1971 MINNESOTA VIKINGS (NFC)
DENSON, MOSES (MARYLAND STATE) - BACK - 1974 WASHINGTON REDSKINS (NFC)
DENTON, ROBERT (PACIFIC) - TACKLE - 1960 CLEVELAND BROWNS; 1961-64
    MINNESOTA VIKINGS
DENVIR, JOHN (COLORADO) - GUARD - 1962 DENVER BRONCOS (AFL)
DE PASCAL, CARMINE (WICHITA) - END - 1945 PITTSBURGH STEELERS
DE PAUL, HENRY (DUQUESNE) - GUARD - 1945 PITTSBURGH STEELERS
DEPLER, JOHN (ILLINOIS) - CENTER - 1929 ORANGE TORNADOS; 1929 DAYTON
    TRIANGLES; 1930 NEWARK TORNADOS
DE POYSTER, JERRY DEAN (WYOMING) - KICKER - 1968 DETROIT LIONS;
    1971-72 OAKLAND RAIDERS (AFC)
DERBY, DEAN (WASHINGTON) - BACK - 1957-61 PITTSBURGH STEELERS;
    1961-62 MINNESOTA VIKINGS; 1959 INTERCEPTION LEADER; (TIED WITH
    M. DAVIS AND SHINNICK)
DEREMER, ARTHUR (NIAGARA) - CENTER - 1942 BROOKLYN DODGERS
DE FOGATIS, ALBERT (DUKE) - TACKLE - 1949-52 NEW YORK GIANTS
DERR, BENJAMIN (PENNSYLVANIA) - BACK - 1919 MASSILLON TIGERS; 1920
    CHICAGO TIGERS
DE SANTIS, DANIEL (NIAGARA) - BACK - 1941 PHILADELPHIA EAGLES
DESCHAINE, RICHARD - END - 1955-57 GREEN BAY PACKERS; 1958 CLEVELAND
    BROWNS
DE SHANE, CHARLES (ALABAMA) - BACK - 1945-49 DETROIT LIONS
DES JARDIEN, PAUL (CHICAGO) - GUARD - 1919 HAMMOND PROS; 1920 CHICAGO
    TIGERS; 1920 CHICAGO CARDINALS; 1921 ROCK ISLAND INDEPENDENTS
DESKIN, VERSIL (DRAKE) - END - 1935-39 CHICAGO CARDINALS
DESKINS, DONALD (MICHIGAN) - GUARD - 1960 OAKLAND RAIDERS (AFL)
DESS, DARRELL (NORTH CAROLINA STATE) - GUARD - 1958 PITTSBURGH
    STEELERS; 1959-64, 66-69 NEW YORK GIANTS; 1965-66 WASHINGTON
    REDSKINS
DE SUTTER, WAYNE (WESTERN ILLINOIS) - TACKLE - 1966 BUFFALO BILLS
    (AFL)
DE STEFANO, FREDERICK (NORTHWESTERN) - BACK - 1924-25 CHICAGO
    CARDINALS
DETERS, HAROLD (NORTH CAROLINA STATE) - KICKER - 1967 DALLAS COWBOYS
DETRAY - BACK - 1919 TOLEDO MAROONS
DETWILER, CHARLES (UTAH STATE) - BACK - 1970-72 SAN DIEGO CHARGERS
    (AFC); 1973 ST. LOUIS CARDINALS (NFC)
DETWILLER, JOHN (KANSAS) - BACK - 1923-24 HAMMOND PROS
DETZEL, ARTHUR (PITTSBURGH) - TACKLE - 1936 CLEVELAND RAMS (AFL)
DE VLEIGHER, CHARLES (MEMPHIS STATE) - END - 1969 BUFFALO BILLS (AFL)
DEVLIN, MARK (HOLY CROSS) - BACK - 1919-20 CANTON BULLDOGS; 1920
    CLEVELAND PANTHERS
DEVROW, WILLIAM (SOUTHERN MISSISSIPPI) - BACK - 1967 CLEVELAND BROWNS

DEWAR, JAMES (INDIANA) - BACK - 1947 CLEVELAND BROWNS (AAFC); 1948
    BROOKLYN DODGERS (AAFC)
DE WEESE, EVERETT - GUARD - 1927-28 DAYTON TRIANGLES; 1930 PORTSMOUTH
    SPARTANS
DEWELL, WILLIAM (SMU) - END - 1940-41, 45-49 CHICAGO CARDINALS
DEWVEALL, WILLARD (SMU) - END - 1959-60 CHICAGO BEARS; 1961-64
    HOUSTON OILERS (AFL)
DE WITZ, HERBERT (NEBRASKA) - BACK - 1927 CLEVELAND BULLDOGS
DE WITZ, RUFUS (NEBRASKA) - BACK - 1924-26 KANSAS CITY COWBOYS
DIAL, BENJAMIN (EASTERN NEW MEXICO) - QBACK - 1967 PHILADELPHIA EAGLES
DIAL, GILBERT "BUDDY" (RICE) - END - 1959-63 PITTSBURGH STEELERS;
    1964-66 DALLAS COWBOYS
DIAMOND, CHARLES (MIAMI) - TACKLE - 1960-62 DALLAS TEXANS (AFL); 1963
    KANSAS CITY CHIEFS (AFL)
DIAMOND, WILLIAM (MIAMI) - GUARD - 1963 KANSAS CITY CHIEFS (AFL)
DIBB, JOHN (WEST POINT) - TACKLE - 1930 NEWARK TORNADOS
DIBBLE, DORNE (MICHIGAN STATE) - END - 1951, 53-57 DETROIT LIONS
DICKEL, DANIEL (IOWA) - LB - 1974 BALTIMORE COLTS (AFC)
DICKEY, ELDRIDGE (TENNESSEE A&I) - END - 1968 OAKLAND RAIDERS (AFL);
    1971 OAKLAND RAIDERS (AFC)
DICKEY, LYNN (KANSAS STATE) - QBACK - 1971, 73-74 HOUSTON OILERS (AFC)
DICKEY, WALLACE (SOUTHWEST TEXAS STATE) - TACKLE - 1968-69 DENVER
    BRONCOS (AFL)
DICKINSON, RICHARD (MISSISSIPPI SOUTHERN) - BACK - 1960-61 DALLAS
    TEXANS (AFL); 1962-63 DENVER BRONCOS (AFL); 1963 HOUSTON OILERS
    (AFL); 1964 OAKLAND RAIDERS (AFL)
DICKSON, PAUL (BAYLOR) - TACKLE - 1959 LOS ANGELES RAMS; 1960 DALLAS
    COWBOYS; 1961-69 MINNESOTA VIKINGS; 1970 MINNESOTA VIKINGS
    (NFC); 1971 ST. LOUIS CARDINALS (NFC)
DICUS, CHARLES (ARKANSAS) - END - 1971-72 SAN DIEGO CHARGERS (AFC)
DIDION, JOHN (OREGON STATE) - LB, CENTER - 1969 WASHINGTON REDSKINS;
    1970 WASHINGTON REDSKINS (NFC); 1971-74 NEW ORLEANS SAINTS (NFC)
DIEHL, CHARLES (IDAHO) - GUARD - 1930-31 CHICAGO CARDINALS; 1934 ST.
    LOUIS GUNNERS
DIEHL, DAVID (MICHIGAN STATE) - END - 1939-40, 44-45 DETROIT LIONS
DIEHL, JOHN (VIRGINIA) - TACKLE - 1961-64 BALTIMORE COLTS; 1965
    DALLAS COWBOYS; 1965 OAKLAND RAIDERS (AFL)
DIEHL, WALTER (BUCKNELL) - BACK - 1928-30 FRANKFORD YELLOWJACKETS
DIEKEN, DOUGLAS (MICHIGAN) - TACKLE - 1971-74 CLEVELAND BROWNS (AFC)
DIERDORF, DANIEL (MICHIGAN) - GUARD, TACKLE - 1971-74 ST. LOUIS
    CARDINALS (NFC)
DIETER, HERBERT (PENNSYLVANIA) - GUARD - 1922 BUFFALO ALL-AMERICANS
DIETZ - GUARD - 1920 HAMMOND PROS
DIFILIPPO, DAVID (VILLANOVA) - GUARD - 1941 PHILADELPHIA EAGLES
DIGRIS, BERNARD (HOLY CROSS) - TACKLE - 1943 CHICAGO BEARS
DILLON, ROBERT (TEXAS) - BACK - 1952-59 GREEN BAY PACKERS
DILLON, TERRY (MONTANA) - BACK - 1963 MINNESOTA VIKINGS
DILWEG, LAVERN (MARQUETTE) - END - 1926 MILWAUKEE BADGERS; 1927-34
    GREEN BAY PACKERS
DIMANCHEFF, BORIS (PURDUE & BUTLER) - BACK - 1945-46 BOSTON YANKS;
    1947-50 CHICAGO CARDINALS; 1952 CHICAGO BEARS
DI MIDIO, ANTONIO (WEST CHESTER STATE) - TACKLE - 1966-67 KANSAS CITY
    CHIEFS (AFL)
DIMITROFF, THOMAS (MIAMI OF OHIO) - BACK - 1960 BOSTON PATRIOTS (AFL)
DIMMICK, DONALD (HOBART) - BACK - 1926 BUFFALO RANGERS; 1927 BUFFALO
    BISONS
DIMMICK, THOMAS (HOUSTON) - GUARD - 1956 PHILADELPHIA EAGLES; 1960
    DALLAS TEXANS (AFL)
DINSMORE, ROBERT (PRINCETON) - BACK - 1926 PHILADELPHIA QUAKERS (AFL)
DI PIERRO, RAYMOND (OHIO STATE) - GUARD - 1950-51 GREEN BAY PACKERS
DIRKS, MARION "MIKE" (WYOMING) - GUARD, TACKLE - 1968-69 PHILADELPHIA
    EAGLES; 1970-71 PHILADELPHIA EAGLES (NFC)
DISCENZO, ANTHONY (MICHIGAN STATE) - TACKLE - 1960 BOSTON PATRIOTS
    (AFL); 1960 BUFFALO BILLS (AFL)
DISEND, LEO (ALBRIGHT) - TACKLE - 1938-39 BROOKLYN DODGERS; 1940
    GREEN BAY PACKERS
DITKA, MICHAEL (PITTSBURGH) - END - 1961-66 CHICAGO BEARS; 1967-68
    PHILADELPHIA EAGLES; 1969 DALLAS COWBOYS; 1970-72 DALLAS COWBOYS
    (NFC)

Top row (from left to right): Vern Den Herder, Mike Ditka, Scott Eaton and John Elliott. Second row: Mel Farr, Miller Farr, Manny Fernandez and Marv Fleming. Third row: John Fuqua, Roman Gabriel, Carl Garrett and Mike Garrett. Bottom row: Gary Garrison, Walt Garrison, Roy Gerela and Pete Gogolak.

DITTRICH, JOHN (WISCONSIN) - GUARD - 1956 CHICAGO CARDINALS; 1959
     GREEN BAY PACKERS; 1960 OAKLAND RAIDERS (AFL); 1961 BUFFALO
     BILLS (AFL)
DI VITO, JOSEPH (BOSTON COLLEGE) - QBACK - 1968 DENVER BRONCOS (AFL)
DIXON, HEWRITT (FLORIDA A&M) - BACK - 1963-65 DENVER BRONCOS (AFL);
     1966-69 OAKLAND RAIDERS (AFL); 1970 OAKLAND RAIDERS (AFC)
DOANE, ERLING (TUFTS) - BACK - 1919 CLEVELAND INDIANS; 1920 CLEVELAND
     PANTHERS; 1922-24 MILWAUKEE BADGERS; 1925-26 DETROIT PANTHERS;
     1927 POTTSVILLE MAROONS; 1927 PROVIDENCE STEAMROLLERS
DOBBINS, HERBERT (SAN DIEGO STATE) - TACKLE - 1974 PHILADELPHIA
     EAGLES (NFC)
DOBBINS, JOHN (LEHIGH) - GUARD - 1919 AKRON PROS
DOBBINS, OLIVER (MORGAN STATE) - BACK - 1964 BUFFALO BILLS (AFL)
DOBBS, BEN (INDIANA & OHIO STATE) - END - 1937 NEW YORK YANKS (AFL);
     1937 PITTSBURGH AMERICANS (AFL)
DOBBS, GLENN (TULSA) - BACK - 1946-47 BROOKLYN DODGERS (AAFC);
     1948-49 LOS ANGELES DONS (AAFC)
DOBELEIT, RICHARD (OHIO STATE) - BACK - 1925-26 DAYTON TRIANGLES
DOBELSTEIN, ROBERT (TENNESSEE) - GUARD - 1946-48 NEW YORK GIANTS;
     1949 LOS ANGELES DONS (AAFC)
DOBLER, CONRAD (WYOMING) - GUARD - 1972-74 ST. LOUIS CARDINALS (NFC)
DOBRUS, PETER (CARNEGIE TECH) - TACKLE - 1941 BROOKLYN DODGERS
DOBYNS, ROBERT (MARQUETTE) - TACKLE - 1936 BROOKLYN TIGERS (AFL)
DOCKERY, JOHN (HARVARD) - BACK, END - 1968-69 NEW YORK JETS (AFL);
     1970-71 NEW YORK JETS (AFC); 1972-73 PITTSBURGH STEELERS (AFC)
DODD, ALVIN (NORTHWEST LOUISIANA) - BACK, END - 1967 CHICAGO BEARS;
     1969 NEW ORLEANS SAINTS; 1970-71 NEW ORLEANS SAINTS (NFC);
     1973-74 ATLANTA FALCONS (NFC)
DODRILL, DALE (COLORADO A&M) - GUARD - 1951-59 PITTSBURGH STEELERS
DODSON, LESLIE (MISSISSIPPI) - BACK - 1941 PITTSBURGH STEELERS
DOEHRING, JOHN - BACK - 1932-34, 36-37 CHICAGO BEARS; 1935 PITTSBURGH
     PIRATES; 1940 MILWAUKEE CHIEFS (AFL)
DOELL, WALTER (TEXAS) - TACKLE - 1933 CINCINNATI REDS
DOELLING, FREDERICK (PENNSYLVANIA) - BACK - 1960 DALLAS COWBOYS
DOHERTY, GEORGE (LOUISIANA TECH) - GUARD - 1944 BROOKLYN TIGERS; 1945
     BOSTON YANKS; 1946 NEW YORK YANKEES (AAFC); 1946 BUFFALO BISONS
     (AAFC); 1947 BUFFALO BILLS (AAFC)
DOHERTY, WILLIAM (MARIETTA) - CENTER - 1921 CINCINNATI CELTS
DOKAS, WILLIAM (FORDHAM) - END - 1940 NEW YORK AMERICANS (AFL)
DOLAN, JOHN (MONTANA) - END - 1941 BUFFALO TIGERS (AFL)
DOLL, DONALD (USC) - BACK - 1949-52 DETROIT LIONS; 1953 WASHINGTON
     REDSKINS; 1954 LOS ANGELES RAMS
DOLLY, RICHARD (WEST VIRGINIA) - END - 1941, 45 PITTSBURGH STEELERS
DOLOWAY, CLIFFORD (CARNEGIE TECH) - END - 1935 PITTSBURGH PIRATES
DOMBROWSKI, LEON (DELAWARE) - LB - 1960 NEW YORK TITANS (AFL)
DOMNANOVICH, JOSEPH (ALABAMA) - CENTER - 1946-48 BOSTON YANKS; 1949
     NEW YORK BULLDOGS; 1950-51 NEW YORK YANKS
DOMRES, MARTIN (COLUMBIA) - QBACK - 1969 SAN DIEGO CHARGERS (AFL);
     1970-71 SAN DIEGO CHARGERS (AFC); 1972-74 BALTIMORE COLTS (AFC)
DOMRES, THOMAS (WISCONSIN) - TACKLE - 1968-69 HOUSTON OILERS (AFL);
     1970-71 HOUSTON OILERS (AFC); 1971-72 DENVER BRONCOS (AFC)
DONAHUE, JOHN (BOSTON COLLEGE) - TACKLE - 1926-27 PROVIDENCE
     STEAMROLLERS
DONAHUE, OSCAR (SAN JOSE STATE) - END - 1962 MINNESOTA VIKINGS
DONALDSON, EUGENE (KENTUCKY) - GUARD - 1953 CLEVELAND BROWNS
DONALDSON, EUGENE (PURDUE) - BACK - 1967 BUFFALO BILLS (AFL)
DONALDSON, JOHN (GEORGIA) - BACK - 1949 CHICAGO HORNETS (AAFC); 1949
     LOS ANGELES DONS (AAFC)
DON CARLOS, WALDO (DRAKE) - CENTER - 1931 GREEN BAY PACKERS
DONELLI, ALLAN (DUQUESNE) - BACK - 1941-42 PITTSBURGH STEELERS; 1942
     PHILADELPHIA EAGLES
DONLAN, JAMES - GUARD - 1926 HAMMOND PROS
DONNAHOO, ROGER (MICHIGAN STATE) - BACK - 1960 NEW YORK TITANS (AFL)
DONNELL, BENJAMIN (VANDERBILT) - END - 1960 LOS ANGELES CHARGERS (AFL)
DONNEIL, JOHN (OREGON) - BACK - 1937 LOS ANGELES BULLDOGS (AFL); 1940
     BOSTON BEARS (AFL); 1940 COLUMBUS BULLIES (AFL)
DONNELLY, GEORGE (ILLINOIS) - BACK - 1965-67 SAN FRANCISCO 49ERS
DONOHUE, MICHAEL (SAN FRANCISCO) - END - 1968 ATLANTA FALCONS;
     1970-71 ATLANTA FALCONS (NFC); 1973-74 GREEN BAY PACKERS (NFC)

DONOHUE, LEON (SAN JOSE STATE) - TACKLE - 1962-64 SAN FRANCISCO
    49ERS; 1965-67 DALLAS COWBOYS
DONOHUE, WILLIAM (CARNEGIE TECH) - QBACK - 1927 FRANKFORD
    YELLOWJACKETS
DONOVAN, ARTHUR (BOSTON COLLEGE) - TACKLE - 1950, 53-61 BALTIMORE
    COLTS; 1951 NEW YORK YANKS; 1952 DALLAS TEXANS; 1968 HALL OF FAME
DOOLAN, GEORGE - CENTER - 1922 RACINE LEGION
DOOLAN, JOHN (GEORGETOWN) - BACK - 1945 WASHINGTON REDSKINS; 1945-46
    NEW YORK GIANTS; 1947-48 CHICAGO CARDINALS
DOOLEY, JAMES (MIAMI) - BACK - 1952-54, 56-57, 59-62 CHICAGO BEARS
DOOLEY, JOHN (SYRACUSE) - GUARD - 1922-25 ROCHESTER JEFFERSONS; 1923
    MILWAUKEE BADGERS
DORAIS, CHARLES "GUS" (NOTRE DAME) - QBACK - 1919 MASSILLON TIGERS
DORAN, JAMES (IOWA STATE) - END - 1951-59 DETROIT LIONS; 1960-62
    DALLAS COWBOYS
D'ORAZIO, JOSEPH (ITHACA COLLEGE) - TACKLE - 1944 DETROIT LIONS
DORFMAN, ARTHUR (BOSTON UNIV.) - GUARD - 1929 BUFFALO BISONS
DOROW, ALBERT (MICHIGAN STATE) - QBACK - 1954-56 WASHINGTON REDSKINS;
    1957 PHILADELPHIA EAGLES; 1960-61 NEW YORK TITANS (AFL); 1962
    BUFFALO BILLS (AFL)
DORRIS, ANDREW (NEW MEXICO STATE) - LB, END - 1973 ST. LOUIS
    CARDINALS (NFC); 1973-74 NEW ORLEANS SAINTS (NFC)
DORSEY, NATHANIEL (MISSISSIPPI VALLEY) - END - 1973 NEW ENGLAND
    PATRIOTS (AFC)
DORSEY, RICHARD (USC & OKLAHOMA) - BACK - 1962 OAKLAND RAIDERS (AFL)
DOSS, NOBLE (TEXAS) - BACK - 1947-48 PHILADELPHIA EAGLES; 1949 NEW
    YORK YANKEES (AAFC)
DOTSON, ALPHONSE (GRAMBLING) - TACKLE - 1965 KANSAS CITY CHIEFS
    (AFL); 1966 MIAMI DOLPHINS (AFL); 1968-69 OAKLAND RAIDERS (AFL);
    1970 OAKLAND RAIDERS (AFC)
DOTTLEY, JOHN (MISSISSIPPI) - BACK - 1951-53 CHICAGO BEARS
DOUDS, FORREST (WASHINGTON&JEFFERSON) - TACKLE - 1930 PROVIDENCE
    STEAMROLLERS; 1930-31 PORTSMOUTH SPARTANS; 1932 CHICAGO
    CARDINALS; 1933-34 PITTSBURGH PIRATES
DOUGHERTY, PHILIP (SANTA CLARA) - CENTER - 1938 CHICAGO CARDINALS
DOUGHERTY, ROBERT (KENTUCKY) - LB - 1957 LOS ANGELES RAMS; 1958
    PITTSBURGH STEELERS; 1960-63 OAKLAND RAIDERS (AFL)
DOUGHTY, GLENN (MICHIGAN) - END - 1972-74 BALTIMORE COLTS (AFC)
DOUGLAS, BENJAMIN (GRINNELL) - BACK - 1933 BROOKLYN DODGERS
DOUGLAS, EVERETT (FLORIDA) - TACKLE - 1953 NEW YORK GIANTS
DOUGLAS, GEORGE (MARQUETTE) - CENTER - 1921 GREEN BAY PACKERS
DOUGLAS, JAY (MEMPHIS STATE) - CENTER - 1973-74 SAN DIEGO CHARGERS
    (AFC)
DOUGLAS, JOHN (MISSOURI) - LB - 1970-73 NEW YORK GIANTS (NFC)
DOUGLAS, JOHN HENRY (TEXAS SOUTHERN) - BACK - 1967-68 NEW ORLEANS
    SAINTS; 1969 HOUSTON OILERS (AFL)
DOUGLAS, MERRILL (UTAH) - BACK - 1958-60 CHICAGO BEARS; 1961 DALLAS
    COWBOYS; 1962 PHILADELPHIA EAGLES
DOUGLAS, OTIS (WILLIAM&MARY) - TACKLE - 1946-49 PHILADELPHIA EAGLES
DOUGLAS, ROBERT (KANSAS STATE) - BACK - 1937 PITTSBURGH AMERICANS
    (AFL); 1937 NEW YORK YANKS (AFL); 1938 PITTSBURGH PIRATES
DOUGLASS, LEO (LEHIGH & VERMONT) - BACK - 1926 BROOKLYN LIONS; 1926
    FRANKFORD YELLOWJACKETS
DOUGLASS, ROBERT (KANSAS) - QBACK - 1969 CHICAGO BEARS; 1970-74
    CHICAGO BEARS (NFC)
DOVE, EDWARD (COLORADO) - BACK - 1959-63 SAN FRANCISCO 49ERS; 1963
    NEW YORK GIANTS
DOVE, ROBERT (NOTRE DAME) - END - 1946-47 CHICAGO ROCKETS (AAFC);
    1948-53 CHICAGO CARDINALS; 1953-54 DETROIT LIONS
DOW, HARLEY (SAN JOSE STATE) - GUARD - 1950 SAN FRANCISCO 49ERS
DOW, JESS ELWOOD (WEST TEXAS STATE) - QBACK - 1938-40 PHILADELPHIA
    EAGLES
DOW, KENNETH (OREGON STATE) - BACK - 1941 WASHINGTON REDSKINS
DOWD, GERALD (ST. MARY'S OF CAL.) - CENTER - 1939 CLEVELAND RAMS
DOWDA, HARRY (WAKE FOREST) - BACK - 1949-53 WASHINGTON REDSKINS;
    1954-55 PHILADELPHIA EAGLES
DOWDEN, STEPHAN (BAYLOR) - TACKLE - 1952 GREEN BAY PACKERS
DOWDLE, DON MICHAEL (TEXAS) - LB - 1960-62 DALLAS COWBOYS; 1963-66
    SAN FRANCISCO 49ERS
DOWELL, GWYN (TEXAS TECH) - BACK - 1935-36 CHICAGO CARDINALS

DOWLER, BOYD (COLORADO) - END - 1959-69 GREEN BAY PACKERS; 1971
     WASHINGTON REDSKINS (NFC)
DOWLER, THOMAS (COLGATE) - BACK - 1931 BROOKLYN DODGERS
DOWLING, BRIAN (YALE) - QBACK - 1972-73 NEW ENGLAND PATRIOTS (AFC)
DOWLING, PATRICK (DEPAUL) - END - 1929 CHICAGO CARDINALS
DOWNS, ROBERT (USC) - GUARD - 1951 SAN FRANCISCO 49ERS
DOWNWIND, XAVIER - BACK - 1922 OORANG INDIANS
DOYLE, EDWARD (WEST POINT) - END - 1924 FRANKFORD YELLOWJACKETS; 1925
     POTTSVILLE MAROONS
DOYLE, EDWARD (CANISIUS) - GUARD - 1927 BUFFALO BISONS
DOYLE, RICHARD (OHIO STATE) - BACK - 1955 PITTSBURGH STEELERS; 1960
     DENVER BRONCOS (AFL)
DOYLE, THEODORE (NEBRASKA) - TACKLE - 1938 PITTSBURGH PIRATES;
     1939-42, 45 PITTSBURGH STEELERS; 1943 PHIL-PITT; 1944 CARD-PITT
DRAGINIS, PETER (CATHOLIC UNIV.) - QBACK - 1936 PITTSBURGH AMERICANS
     (AFL); 1937 BOSTON SHAMROCKS (AFL)
DRAGON, OSCAR (ARIZONA STATE) - BACK - 1972 SAN DIEGO CHARGERS (AFC)
DRAHOS, NICHOLAS (CORNELL) - TACKLE - 1941 NEW YORK AMERICANS (AFL)
DRAKE, JOHN (PURDUE) - BACK - 1937-41 CLEVELAND RAMS
DRAKE, WILLIAM (OREGON) - BACK, END - 1973-74 LOS ANGELES RAMS (NFC)
DRAVELING, LEO (MICHIGAN) - TACKLE - 1933 CINCINNATI REDS
DRAYER, CLARENCE (ILLINOIS) - TACKLE - 1925-26 DAYTON TRIANGLES
DRAZENOVICH, CHARLES (PENN STATE) - LB - 1950-59 WASHINGTON REDSKINS
DREHER, FERDINAND (DENVER) - END - 1938 CHICAGO BEARS
DREILING, FRANK (FT. HAYS OF KANSAS) - GUARD - 1936-37 PITTSBURGH
     AMERICANS (AFL)
DRESSEN, CHARLES - QBACK - 1920 DECATUR STALEYS; 1922-23 RACINE LEGION
DRESSLER, DOUGLAS (CHICO STATE) - BACK - 1970-72, 74 CINCINNATI
     BENGALS (AFC)
DREWS, THEODORE (PRINCETON) - END - 1926 BROOKLYN HORSEMEN (AFL);
     1926 BROOKLYN LIONS; 1928 CHICAGO BEARS
DREYER, WALTER (WISCONSIN) - BACK - 1949 CHICAGO BEARS; 1950 GREEN
     BAY PACKERS
DRIESBACH, OLIVER (AKRON) - GUARD - 1919 AKRON PROS
DRISCOLL, JOHN "PADDY" (NORTHWESTERN) - BACK - 1920 DECATUR STALEYS;
     1920-25 CHICAGO CARDINALS; 1926-29 CHICAGO BEARS; 1965 HALL OF
     FAME
DRISKILL, JOSEPH (NORTHEAST LOUISIANA STATE) - BACK - 1960-61 ST.
     LOUIS CARDINALS
DROBNITCH, ALEX (DENVER) - GUARD - 1937 NEW YORK YANKS (AFL); 1940
     BUFFALO INDIANS (AFL); 1941 NEW YORK AMERICANS (AFL)
DROUGAS, THOMAS (OREGON) - TACKLE - 1972-73 BALTIMORE COLTS (AFC);
     1974 DENVER BRONCOS (AFC); 1974 KANSAS CITY CHIEFS (AFC)
DRUEHL, WILLIAM (COLBY) - BACK - 1929 BOSTON BRAVES
DRULIS, ALBERT (TEMPLE) - BACK - 1945-46 CHICAGO CARDINALS; 1947
     PITTSBURGH STEELERS
DRULIS, CHARLES (TEMPLE) - GUARD - 1942, 45-49 CHICAGO BEARS; 1950
     GREEN BAY PACKERS
DRUMMY, JAMES (TUFTS & BOSTON COLLEGE) - QBACK - 1919 CLEVELAND
     INDIANS
DRUNGO, ELBERT (TENNESSEE STATE) - TACKLE - 1969 HOUSTON OILERS
     (AFL); 1970-71, 73-74 HOUSTON OILERS (AFC)
DRURY, LYLE (ST. LOUIS UNIV.) - END - 1930-31 CHICAGO BEARS
DRUSCHEL, RICHARD (NORTH CAROLINA STATE) - GUARD, TACKLE - 1974
     PITTSBURGH STEELERS (AFC)
DRUZE, JOHN (FORDHAM) - END - 1938 BROOKLYN DODGERS
DRYDEN - BACK - 1930 STATEN ISLAND STAPELTONS
DRYER, JOHN FRED (SAN DIEGO STATE) - END - 1969 NEW YORK GIANTS;
     1970-71 NEW YORK GIANTS (NFC); 1972-74 LOS ANGELES RAMS (NFC)
DRZEWIECKI, RONALD (MARQUETTE) - BACK - 1955, 57 CHICAGO BEARS
DUBENION, ELBERT (BLUFFTON) - BACK - 1960-68 BUFFALO BILLS (AFL)
DUBILIER - CENTER - 1936 NEW YORK YANKS (AFL)
DUBLINSKI, THOMAS (UTAH) - QBACK - 1952-54 DETROIT LIONS; 1958 NEW
     YORK GIANTS; 1960 DENVER BRONCOS (AFL)
DUBOFSKY, MAURICE (GEORGETOWN) - GUARD - 1932 NEW YORK GIANTS
DUBZINSKI, WALTER (BOSTON COLLEGE) - GUARD - 1943 NEW YORK GIANTS;
     1944 BOSTON YANKS
DUCKWORTH, JOSEPH (COLGATE) - END - 1947 WASHINGTON REDSKINS
DUCOTE, RICHARD (AUBURN) - BACK - 1919 CLEVELAND INDIANS; 1920
     CLEVELAND PANTHERS
DUDEK, MITCHELL (XAVIER) - TACKLE - 1966 NEW YORK JETS (AFL)

DUDEN, RICHARD (ANNAPOLIS) - END - 1949 NEW YORK GIANTS

DUDISH, ANDREW (GEORGIA) - BACK - 1946 BUFFALO BISONS (AAFC); 1947
    BALTIMORE COLTS (AAFC); 1948 BROOKLYN DODGERS (AAFC); 1948
    DETROIT LIONS

DUDLEY, PAUL (ARKANSAS) - BACK - 1962 NEW YORK GIANTS; 1963
    PHILADELPHIA EAGLES

DUDLEY, WILLIAM (VIRGINIA) - BACK - 1942, 45-46 PITTSBURGH STEELERS;
    1947-49 DETROIT LIONS; 1950-51, 53 WASHINGTON REDSKINS; 1942, 46
    RUSHING LEADER; 1946 INTERCEPTION LEADER; 1966 HALL OF FAME

DUFFT, JAMES (RUTGERS) - GUARD - 1921 ROCHESTER JEFFERSONS; 1922
    MILWAUKEE BADGERS

DUFFY, PATRICK (DAYTON) - BACK - 1929 DAYTON TRIANGLES

DUFORD, WILFRED (MARQUETTE) - BACK - 1924 GREEN BAY PACKERS

DUGAN, FRED (DAYTON) - END - 1958-59 SAN FRANCISCO 49ERS; 1960 DALLAS
    COWBOYS; 1961-63 WASHINGTON REDSKINS

DUGAN, LEONARD (WICHITA) - CENTER - 1936 NEW YORK GIANTS; 1937-39
    CHICAGO CARDINALS; 1939 PITTSBURGH STEELERS

DUGGAN, EDWARD (NOTRE DAME) - BACK - 1921 ROCK ISLAND INDEPENDENTS

DUGGAN, GILFORD (OKLAHOMA) - TACKLE - 1940 NEW YORK GIANTS; 1942-43,
    45 CHICAGO CARDINALS; 1944 CARD-PITT; 1946 LOS ANGELES DONS
    (AAFC); 1947 BUFFALO BILLS (AAFC)

DUGGER, JOHN (OHIO STATE) - END - 1946 BUFFALO BISONS (AAFC); 1947-48
    DETROIT LIONS; 1949 CHICAGO BEARS

DUGGINS, GEORGE (PURDUE) - END - 1934 CHICAGO CARDINALS

DUHART, PAUL (FLORIDA) - BACK - 1944 GREEN BAY PACKERS; 1945
    PITTSBURGH STEELERS; 1945 BOSTON YANKS

DUHON, ROBERT (TULANE) - BACK - 1968 NEW YORK GIANTS; 1970-72 NEW
    YORK GIANTS (NFC)

DUICH, STEVEN (SAN DIEGO STATE) - TACKLE, GUARD - 1968 ATLANTA
    FALCONS; 1969 WASHINGTON REDSKINS

DUKE, PAUL (GEORGIA TECH) - CENTER - 1947 NEW YORK YANKEES (AAFC)

DUKES, MICHAEL (CLEMSON) - LB - 1960-63 HOUSTON OILERS (AFL); 1964-65
    BOSTON PATRIOTS (AFL); 1965 NEW YORK JETS (AFL)

DULAC, WILLIAM (EASTERN MICHIGAN) - GUARD - 1974 NEW ENGLAND PATRIOTS
    (AFC)

DULKIE, JOSEPH (FORDHAM) - BACK - 1937 BOSTON SHAMROCKS (AFL)

DUMLER, DOUGLAS (NEBRASKA) - CENTER - 1973-74 NEW ENGLAND PATRIOTS
    (AFC)

DUMOE, JOSEPH (SYRACUSE) - END - 1920-21 ROCHESTER JEFFERSONS

DUMOE, WILLIAM - BACK - 1919-20 ROCHESTER JEFFERSONS

DUNAWAY, DAVID (DUKE) - END - 1968 GREEN BAY PACKERS; 1968 ATLANTA
    FALCONS; 1969 NEW YORK GIANTS

DUNAWAY, JAMES (MISSISSIPPI) - TACKLE - 1963-69 BUFFALO BILLS (AFL);
    1970-71 BUFFALO BILLS (AFC); 1972 MIAMI DOLPHINS (AFC)

DUNBAR, ALLEN "JUBILEE" (SOUTHERN) - END - 1973 NEW ORLEANS SAINTS
    (NFC); 1974 CLEVELAND BROWNS (AFC)

DUNCAN, HEARST RANDOLPH (IOWA) - QBACK - 1961 DALLAS TEXANS (AFL)

DUNCAN, JAMES (DUKE & WAKE FOREST) - END - 1950-53 NEW YORK GIANTS

DUNCAN, JAMES (MARYLAND STATE) - BACK - 1969 BALTIMORE COLTS; 1970-71
    BALTIMORE COLTS (AFC)

DUNCAN, KENNETH (TULSA) - KICKER - 1971 GREEN BAY PACKERS (NFC)

DUNCAN, LESLIE "SPEEDY" (JACKSON STATE) - BACK - 1964-69 SAN DIEGO
    CHARGERS (AFL); 1970 SAN DIEGO CHARGERS (AFC); 1971-74
    WASHINGTON REDSKINS (NFC)

DUNCAN, MAURICE (SAN FRANCISCO STATE) - QBACK - 1954-55 SAN FRANCISCO
    49ERS

DUNCAN, RICHARD (EAST MONTANA STATE) - KICKER - 1967 DENVER BRONCOS
    (AFL); 1968 PHILADELPHIA EAGLES; 1969 DETROIT LIONS

DUNCAN, RONALD (WITTENBERG) - END - 1967 CLEVELAND BROWNS

DUNCUM, ROBERT (WEST TEXAS STATE) - TACKLE - 1968 ST. LOUIS CARDINALS

DUNLAP, LEONARD (NORTH TEXAS STATE) - BACK - 1971 BALTIMORE COLTS
    (AFC); 1972-74 SAN DIEGO CHARGERS (AFC)

DUNLAP, ROBERT (OKLAHOMA) - QBACK - 1935 CHICAGO BEARS; 1936 NEW YORK
    GIANTS

DUNN, COYE (USC) - BACK - 1943 WASHINGTON REDSKINS

DUNN, JOSEPH (MARQUETTE) - QBACK - 1924-25 MILWAUKEE BADGERS; 1925-26
    CHICAGO CARDINALS; 1927-31 GREEN BAY PACKERS

DUNN, PAUL (INTERNATIONAL-CALIFORNIA) - END - 1970 CINCINNATI BENGALS
    (AFC)

DUNN, PERRY LEE (MISSISSIPPI) - BACK - 1964-65 DALLAS COWBOYS;
    1966-68 ATLANTA FALCONS; 1969 BALTIMORE COLTS
DUNN, ROBERT (NEW YORK UNIV.) - CENTER - 1929 STATEN ISLAND STAPELTONS
DUNN, RODNEY - GUARD - 1923 DULUTH KELLEYS
DUNN, "PAT" - BACK - 1919-20 DETROIT HERALDS; 1921 DETROIT PANTHERS
DUNNIGAN, MERTON (MINNESOTA) - TACKLE - 1924 MINNEAPOLIS MARINES;
    1925-26 MILWAUKEE BADGERS
DUNNIGAM, WALTER (MINNESOTA) - END - 1922 GREEN BAY PACKERS
DUNNIGAN, WALTER (MINNESOTA) - END - 1922 GREEN BAY PACKERS
DUNSTAN, W. ELWYN (PORTLAND) - TACKLE - 1938-39 CHICAGO CARDINALS;
    1939-41 CLEVELAND RAMS
DUNSTAN, WILLIAM (UTAH STATE) - TACKLE, END - 1973-74 PHILADELPHIA
    EAGLES (NFC)
DUPRE, CHARLES (BAYLOR) - BACK - 1960 NEW YORK TITANS (AFL)
DUPRE, LOUIS (BAYLOR) - BACK - 1955-59 BALTIMORE COLTS; 1960-61
    DALLAS COWBOYS
DU PREE, BILLY JOE (MICHIGAN STATE) - END - 1973-74 DALLAS COWBOYS
    (NFC)
DURANKO, PETER (NOTRE DAME) - TACKLE, END, LB - 1967-69 DENVER
    BRONCOS (AFL); 1970, 72-74 DENVER BRONCOS (AFC)
DURDAN, DONALD (OREGON STATE) - BACK - 1946-47 SAN FRANCISCO 49ERS
    (AAFC)
DUREN, CLARENCE (CALIFORNIA) - BACK - 1973-74 ST. LOUIS CARDINALS
    (NFC)
DURISHAN, JOHN (PITTSBURGH) - TACKLE - 1947 NEW YORK YANKEES (AAFC)
DURKEE, CHARLES (OKLAHOMA STATE) - KICKER - 1967-68 NEW ORLEANS
    SAINTS; 1971-72 NEW ORLEANS SAINTS (NFC)
DURKO, JOHN (ALBRIGHT) - END - 1944 PHILADELPHIA EAGLES; 1945 CHICAGO
    CARDINALS
DURKO, SANDY (USC) - BACK - 1970-71 CINCINNATI BENGALS (AFC); 1973-74
    NEW ENGLAND PATRIOTS (AFC)
DURKOTA, JEFFREY (PENN STATE) - BACK - 1948 LOS ANGELES DONS (AAFC)
DUSEK, BRAD (TEXAS A&M) - LB - 1974 WASHINGTON REDSKINS (NFC)
DUSENBERY, WILLIAM (JOHNSON C. SMITH) - BACK - 1970 NEW ORLEANS
    SAINTS (NFC)
DUTTON, JOHN (NEBRASKA) - END - 1974 BALTIMORE COLTS (AFC)
DUTTON, WILLIAM (PITTSBURGH) - BACK - 1946 PITTSBURGH STEELERS
DUVALL, EARL (OHIO UNIV.) - GUARD - 1924-26 COLUMBUS TIGERS
DVORAK, BENJAMIN (MINNESOTA) - BACK - 1921-22 MINNEAPOLIS MARINES
DVORAK, RICHARD (WICHITA STATE) - END - 1974 NEW YORK GIANTS (NFC)
DWORSKY, DANIEL (MICHIGAN) - BACK - 1949 LOS ANGELES DONS (AAFC)
DWYER, JOHN (LOYOLA OF CAL.) - BACK - 1951 WASHINGTON REDSKINS;
    1952-54 LOS ANGELES RAMS
DWYER, ROBERT (GEORGETOWN) - BACK - 1929 ORANGE TORNADOS
DYE, LESTER (SYRACUSE) - END - 1944-45 WASHINGTON REDSKINS
DYE, WILLIAM (OHIO STATE) - BACK - 1937 CINCINNATI BENGALS (AFL)
DYER, HENRY (GRAMBLING) - BACK - 1966, 68 LOS ANGELES RAMS; 1969
    WASHINGTON REDSKINS; 1970 WASHINGTON REDSKINS (NFC)
DYER, KENNETH (ARIZONA STATE) - BACK - 1968 SAN DIEGO CHARGERS (AFL);
    1969 CINCINNATI BENGALS (AFL); 1970-71 CINCINNATI BENGALS (AFC)
EAGLE, ALEXANDER (OREGON) - TACKLE - 1935 BROOKLYN DODGERS
EAGLE FEATHER - BACK - 1923 OORANG INDIANS
EAGLIN, LARRY (STEPHEN F. AUSTIN) - BACK - 1973 HOUSTON OILERS (AFC)
EAKIN, OLIVER KAY (ARKANSAS) - BACK - 1940-41 NEW YORK GIANTS; 1946
    MIAMI SEAHAWKS (AAFC)
EARHART, RALPH (TEXAS TECH) - BACK - 1948-49 GREEN BAY PACKERS
EARLY, GUY (MIAMI-OHIO) - GUARD - 1920 DAYTON TRIANGLES; 1921
    CINCINNATI CELTS
EARON, BLAINE (DUKE) - END - 1952-53 DETROIT LIONS
EARPE, FRANCIS (MONMOUTH) - GUARD - 1921-22, 24 ROCK ISLAND
    INDEPENDENTS; 1922-32 GREEN BAY PACKERS; 1927 NEW YORK YANKEES
EASON, JOHN (FLORIDA A&M) - END - 1968 OAKLAND RAIDERS (AFL)
EASON, ROGER (OKLAHOMA) - TACKLE - 1945 CLEVELAND RAMS; 1946-48 LOS
    ANGELES RAMS; 1949 GREEN BAY PACKERS
EAST, RONALD (MONTANA STATE) - END, TACKLE - 1967-69 DALLAS COWBOYS;
    1970 DALLAS COWBOYS (NFC); 1971-73 SAN DIEGO CHARGERS (AFC)
EAST, VERNON (WASHBURN) - BACK - 1937 PITTSBURGH AMERICANS (AFL)
EASTERLING, CHARLES RAY (RICHMOND) - BACK - 1972-74 ATLANTA FALCONS
    (NFC)
EASTON, LOUIS (CALIFORNIA) - TACKLE - 1945 NEW YORK GIANTS

EATON, THOMAS SCOTT (OREGON STATE) - BACK - 1967-69 NEW YORK GIANTS;
      1970-71 NEW YORK GIANTS (NFC)
EATON, VICTOR (MISSOURI) - QBACK - 1955 PITTSBURGH STEELERS
EBDING, HARRY (ST. MARY'S OF CAL.) - END - 1931-33 PORTSMOUTH
      SPARTANS; 1934-37 DETROIT LIONS
EBER, RICHARD (TULSA) - BACK, END - 1968 ATLANTA FALCONS; 1969 SAN
      DIEGO CHARGERS (AFL); 1970 SAN DIEGO CHARGERS (AFC)
EBERDT, JESS (ALABAMA) - CENTER - 1932 BROOKLYN DODGERS
EBERSOLE, HAROLD (CORNELL) - GUARD - 1923 CLEVELAND INDIANS
EBERSOLE, JOHN (PENN STATE) - LB, END - 1970-74 NEW YORK JETS (AFC)
EBERTS, BERNARD (CATHOLIC) - GUARD - 1924 MINNEAPOLIS MARINES
EBLI, RAYMOND (NOTRE DAME) - END - 1942 CHICAGO CARDINALS; 1946
      BUFFALO BISONS (AAFC); 1947 CHICAGO ROCKETS (AAFC)
EBY, BYRON (OHIO STATE) - BACK - 1930 PORTSMOUTH SPARTANS
ECHOLS, FATE (NORTHWESTERN) - TACKLE - 1962-63 ST. LOUIS CARDINALS;
      1963 PHILADELPHIA EAGLES
ECKBERG, GUSTAVUS (WEST VIRGINIA) - BACK - 1925 CLEVELAND BULLDOGS
ECKER, ENRIQUE (JOHN CARROLL) - TACKLE - 1947 CHICAGO BEARS; 1948
      CHICAGO ROCKETS (AAFC); 1950-51 GREEN BAY PACKERS; 1952
      WASHINGTON REDSKINS
ECKHARDT, OSCAR (TEXAS) - BACK - 1928 NEW YORK GIANTS
ECKL, ROBERT (WISCONSIN) - TACKLE - 1940-41 MILWAUKEE CHIEFS (AFL);
      1941 CINCINNATI BENGALS (AFL); 1945 CHICAGO CARDINALS
ECKLUND, BRADLEY (OREGON) - CENTER - 1949 NEW YORK YANKEES (AAFC);
      1950-51 NEW YORK YANKS; 1952 DALLAS TEXANS; 1953 BALTIMORE COLTS
ECKSTEIN, ADOLPH (BROWN) - CENTER - 1925-26 PROVIDENCE STEAMROLLERS
EDDY, NICHOLAS (NOTRE DAME) - BACK - 1968-69 DETROIT LIONS; 1970, 72
      DETROIT LIONS (NFC)
EDGAR, ALEXANDER (PITTSBURGH & BUCKNELL) - BACK - 1923 BUFFALO
      ALL-AMERICANS; 1923 AKRON PROS
EDGERSON, BOOKER (WESTERN ILLINOIS) - BACK - 1962-69 BUFFALO BILLS
      (AFL); 1970 DENVER BRONCOS (AFC)
EDLER, ROBERT (OHIO WESLEYAN) - BACK - 1923 CLEVELAND INDIANS
EDMONDSON, VAN (OKLAHOMA) - CENTER - 1926 BUFFALO RANGERS
EDMUNDS, GEORGE RANDALL (GEORGIA TECH) - LB - 1968-69 MIAMI DOLPHINS
      (AFL); 1971 NEW ENGLAND PATRIOTS (AFC); 1972 BALTIMORE COLTS
      (AFC)
EDWARDS, ALBERT GLEN (WASHINGTON STATE) - TACKLE - 1932 BOSTON
      BRAVES; 1933-36 BOSTON REDSKINS; 1937-40 WASHINGTON REDSKINS;
      1969 HALL OF FAME
EDWARDS, CHARLES (BROWN) - BACK - 1930-31 PROVIDENCE STEAMROLLERS;
      1931 CHICAGO BEARS
EDWARDS, CLEOPHUS "CID" (TENNESSEE STATE) - BACK - 1968-69 ST. LOUIS
      CARDINALS; 1970-71 ST. LOUIS CARDINALS (NFC); 1972-74 SAN DIEGO
      CHARGERS (AFC)
EDWARDS, DANIEL (GEORGIA) - END - 1948 BROOKLYN DODGERS (AAFC); 1949
      CHICAGO HORNETS (AAFC); 1950-51 NEW YORK YANKS; 1952 DALLAS
      TEXANS; 1953-54 BALTIMORE COLTS
EDWARDS, DAVID (AUBURN) - LB - 1963-69 DALLAS COWBOYS; 1970-74 DALLAS
      COWBOYS (NFC)
EDWARDS, EARL (WICHITA STATE) - END, TACKLE - 1969 SAN FRANCISCO
      49ERS; 1970-72 SAN FRANCISCO 49ERS (NFC); 1973-74 BUFFALO BILLS
      (AFC)
EDWARDS, EUGENE (NOTRE DAME) - GUARD - 1919 CANTON BULLDOGS; 1922
      TOLEDO MAROONS; 1923 CLEVELAND INDIANS; 1924-25 CLEVELAND
      BULLDOGS
EDWARDS, GLEN (FLORIDA A&M) - BACK, END - 1971-74 PITTSBURGH STEELERS
      (AFC)
EDWARDS, LLOYD (SAN DIEGO STATE) - END - 1969 OAKLAND RAIDERS (AFL)
EDWARDS, MARSHALL (WAKE FOREST) - BACK - 1943 BROOKLYN DODGERS
EDWARDS, THOMAS (MICHIGAN) - TACKLE - 1926 DETROIT PANTHERS
EDWARDS, WELDON (TCU) - TACKLE - 1948 WASHINGTON REDSKINS
EDWARDS, WILLIAM (BAYLOR) - GUARD - 1940-42, 46 NEW YORK GIANTS
EDWARDS, WILLIAM - BACK - 1926 HARTFORD BLUES
EGAN, JOHN (TEMPLE) - QBACK - 1936 ROCHESTER TIGERS (AFL)
EGAN, RICHARD (WILMINGTON) - END - 1920-23 CHICAGO CARDINALS; 1924
      KENOSHA MAROONS; 1924 DAYTON TRIANGLES
EGGERS, DOUGLAS (SOUTH DAKOTA STATE) - LB - 1954-57 BALTIMORE COLTS;
      1958 CHICAGO CARDINALS
EHRHARDT, CLYDE (GEORGIA) - CENTER - 1946, 48-49 WASHINGTON REDSKINS
EHRMANN, JOSEPH (SYRACUSE) - TACKLE - 1973-74 BALTIMORE COLTS (AFC)

FIBNER, JOHN (KENTUCKY) - TACKLE - 1941-42, 46 PHILADELPHIA EAGLES
FICHENLAUB, RAY (NOTRE DAME) - BACK - 1925 COLUMBUS TIGERS; 1925
     CLEVELAND BULLDOGS
FIDEN, EDMUND (SCRANTON) - BACK - 1944 PHILADELPHIA EAGLES; 1944
     DETROIT LIONS
FIDEN, H. C. - TACKLE - 1926 LOUISVILLE COLONELS
FIFFIE, JAMES (COLORADO STATE) - LB - 1961 DENVER BRONCOS (AFL)
EIKENBERG, CHARLES (RICE) - BACK - 1948 CHICAGO CARDINALS
FISCHER, MICHAEL (UPPER IOWA) - KICKER - 1966-69 OAKLAND RAIDERS
     (AFL); 1970-71 OAKLAND RAIDERS (AFC); 1972-74 MINNESOTA VIKINGS
     (NFC)
EISELEE - BACK - 1920 CHICAGO TIGERS
EISENHAUER, LAWRENCE (BOSTON COLLEGE) - END - 1961-69 BOSTON PATRIOTS
     (AFL)
EKBERG, GUSTAV (MINNESOTA) - END - 1921 MINNEAPOLIS MARINES
ELDUAYAN, NERR (ST. MARY'S OF CAL.) - GUARD - 1936 CLEVELAND RAMS
     (AFL)
ELIASON, DONALD (HAMLINE) - END - 1942 BROOKLYN DODGERS; 1946 BOSTON
     YANKS
ELKINS, FAIT (HASKELL) - BACK - 1928-29 FRANKFORD YELLOWJACKETS; 1929
     CHICAGO CARDINALS; 1933 CINCINNATI REDS
ELKINS, LAWRENCE (BAYLOR) - END - 1966-67 HOUSTON OILERS (AFL)
ELLENA, JACK (UCLA) - GUARD - 1955-56 LOS ANGELES RAMS
ELLENSON, EUGENE (GEORGIA) - TACKLE - 1946 MIAMI SEAHAWKS (AAFC)
ELLER, CARL (MINNESOTA) - END - 1964-69 MINNESOTA VIKINGS; 1970-74
     MINNESOTA VIKINGS (NFC)
ELLERSICK, DONALD (WASHINGTON STATE) - BACK - 1960 LOS ANGELES RAMS
ELLIOTT, ALVAH (WISCONSIN) - BACK - 1922-24 RACINE LEGION; 1925 ROCK
     ISLAND INDEPENDENTS
ELLIOTT, BURTON - BACK - 1921 GREEN BAY PACKERS
ELLIOTT, CARLTON (VIRGINIA) - END - 1951-54 GREEN BAY PACKERS
ELLIOTT, CHARLES (OREGON) - TACKLE - 1947 NEW YORK YANKEES (AAFC);
     1948 CHICAGO ROCKETS (AAFC); 1948 SAN FRANCISCO 49ERS (AAFC)
ELLIOTT, DARRELL JOHN (TEXAS) - TACKLE, END - 1967-69 NEW YORK JETS
     (AFL); 1970-73 NEW YORK JETS (AFC)
ELLIOTT, JAMES (PRESBYTERIAN) - KICKER - 1967 PITTSBURGH STEELERS
ELLIOTT, LENVIL (NORTHEAST MISSOURI) - BACK - 1973-74 CINCINNATI
     BENGALS (AFC)
ELLIOTT, RALPH (WISCONSIN) - TACKLE - 1941 BUFFALO TIGERS (AFL); 1941
     MILWAUKEE CHIEFS (AFL)
ELLIOTT, WALLACE (LAFAYETTE) - BACK - 1922-23 CANTON BULLDOGS;
     1924-25 CLEVELAND BULLDOGS; 1926 PHILADELPHIA QUAKERS (AFL);
     1926 CLEVELAND PANTHERS (AFL); 1931 CLEVELAND INDIANS
ELLIS, ALAN (UCLA) - BACK - 1973-74 CHICAGO BEARS (NFC)
ELLIS, CLARENCE (NOTRE DAME) - BACK - 1972-74 ATLANTA FALCONS (NFC)
ELLIS, DREW (TCU) - TACKLE - 1938-39 PHILADELPHIA EAGLES
ELLIS, HERBERT (TEXAS A&M) - CENTER - 1949 NEW YORK BULLDOGS
ELLIS, JOHN (VANDERBILT) - GUARD - 1944 BROOKLYN TIGERS
ELLIS, KENNETH (SOUTHERN) - BACK - 1970-74 GREEN BAY PACKERS (NFC)
ELLIS, LAWRENCE (SYRACUSE) - BACK - 1948 DETROIT LIONS
ELLIS, ROGER (MAINE) - LB - 1960-62 NEW YORK TITANS (AFL); 1963 NEW
     YORK JETS (AFL)
ELLIS, VERNON (ST. NORBERT) - GUARD - 1941 MILWAUKEE CHIEFS (AFL)
ELLIS, WALTER (DETROIT) - TACKLE - 1924-25 COLUMBUS TIGERS; 1925-26
     DETROIT PANTHERS; 1926-27 CHICAGO CARDINALS
ELLISON, GLENN (ARKANSAS) - BACK - 1971 OAKLAND RAIDERS (AFC)
ELLISON, MARK (DAYTON) - GUARD - 1972-73 NEW YORK GIANTS (NFC)
ELLISON, WILLIAM "WILLIE" (TEXAS SOUTHERN) - BACK - 1967-69 LOS
     ANGELES RAMS; 1970-72 LOS ANGELES RAMS (NFC); 1973-74 KANSAS
     CITY CHIEFS (AFC)
ELLOR, ALBERT (BUCKNELL) - GUARD - 1930 NEWARK TORNADOS
ELLSTROM, MARVIN (OKLAHOMA) - BACK - 1934 BOSTON REDSKINS; 1934
     PHILADELPHIA EAGLES; 1935 PITTSBURGH PIRATES; 1936 CHICAGO
     CARDINALS; 1936 ROCHESTER TIGERS (AFL); 1936-37 BOSTON SHAMROCKS
     (AFL)
ELLZEY, CHARLES (MISSISSIPPI SOUTHERN) - LB - 1960-61 ST. LOUIS
     CARDINALS
ELMENDORF, DAVID (TEXAS A&M) - BACK - 1971-74 LOS ANGELES RAMS (NFC)
ELMORE, DOUGLAS (MISSISSIPPI) - BACK - 1962 WASHINGTON REDSKINS
ELNESS, LELAND (BRADLEY) - QBACK - 1929 CHICAGO BEARS
ELSER, DONALD (NOTRE DAME) - BACK - 1936 BOSTON SHAMROCKS (AFL)

ELSER, EARL (BUTLER) - TACKLE - 1933 PORTSMOUTH SPARTANS; 1934
        CINCINNATI REDS; 1934 ST. LOUIS GUNNERS; 1936 BOSTON SHAMROCKS
        (AFL)
ELSEY, EARL (LOYOLA OF CAL.) - BACK - 1946 LOS ANGELES DONS (AAFC)
ELSTON, ARTHUR (SOUTH CAROLINA) - QBACK - 1942 CLEVELAND RAMS;
        1946-48 SAN FRANCISCO 49ERS (AAFC)
ELTER, LEO (VILLANOVA & DUQUESNE) - BACK - 1953-54, 58-59 PITTSBURGH
        STEELERS; 1955-57 WASHINGTON REDSKINS
ELWELL, JOHN (PURDUE) - END - 1962 ST. LOUIS CARDINALS
ELY, HAROLD (IOWA) - TACKLE - 1932 CHICAGO BEARS; 1932-34 BROOKLYN
        DODGERS
ELY, LAWRENCE (IOWA) - LB - 1970-71 CINCINNATI BENGALS (AFC)
ELZEY, PAUL (TOLEDO) - LB - 1968 CINCINNATI BENGALS (AFL)
EMANUEL, THOMAS FRANK (TENNESSEE) - LB - 1966-69 MIAMI DOLPHINS
        (AFL); 1970 NEW ORLEANS SAINTS (NFC)
EMBREE, JOHN (COMPTON JUNIOR) - END - 1969 DENVER BRONCOS (AFL); 1970
        DENVER BRONCOS (AFC)
EMBREE, MELVIN (PEPPERDINE) - END - 1953 BALTIMORE COLTS; 1954
        CHICAGO CARDINALS
EMELIANCHIK, PETER (RICHMOND) - END - 1967 PHILADELPHIA EAGLES
EMERICK, ROBERT (MIAMI OF OHIO) - TACKLE - 1934 DETROIT LIONS; 1936
        NEW YORK YANKS (AFL); 1937 CLEVELAND RAMS
EMERSON, GROVER (TEXAS) - GUARD - 1931-33 PORTSMOUTH SPARTANS;
        1934-37 DETROIT LIONS; 1938 BROOKLYN DODGERS
EMERSON, RALPH (WASHINGTON) - GUARD - 1941 COLUMBUS BULLIES (AFL)
EMERSON, VERNON (MINNESOTA-DULUTH) - TACKLE - 1969 ST. LOUIS
        CARDINALS; 1970-71 ST. LOUIS CARDINALS (NFC)
EMMONS, FRANKLIN (OREGON) - BACK - 1940 PHILADELPHIA EAGLES
ENDERLE, RICHARD (MINNESOTA) - GUARD - 1969 ATLANTA FALCONS; 1970-71
        ATLANTA FALCONS (NFC); 1972-74 NEW YORK GIANTS (NFC)
ENGEL, STEVE (COLORADO) - BACK - 1970 CLEVELAND BROWNS (AFC)
ENDLER, HAROLD (BUCKNELL) - END - 1936 BROOKLYN TIGERS (AFL); 1937
        ROCHESTER TIGERS (AFL)
ENDRESS - BACK - 1922 EVANSVILLE CRIMSON GIANTS
ENDRISS, ALBERT (SAN FRANCISCO STATE) - END - 1952 SAN FRANCISCO 49ERS
ENGEBRETSEN, PAUL (NORTHWESTERN) - GUARD - 1932 CHICAGO BEARS; 1933
        PITTSBURGH PIRATES; 1933 CHICAGO CARDINALS; 1934 BROOKLYN
        DODGERS; 1934-41 GREEN BAY PACKERS
ENGELHARD, JOSEPH (ROSE POLY OF INDIANA) - BACK - 1921-22 LOUISVILLE
        BRECKS
ENGELMANN, WUERT (SOUTH DAKOTA STATE) - BACK - 1930-33 GREEN BAY
        PACKERS
ENGLUND, HARRY - END - 1920 DECATUR STALEYS; 1921 CHICAGO STALEYS;
        1922, 24 CHICAGO BEARS
ENGSTROM, GEORGE (SUPERIOR STATE OF WIS.) - GUARD - 1924 DULUTH
        KELLEYS
ENICH, STEPHEN (MARQUETTE) - GUARD - 1945 CHICAGO CARDINALS
ENIS, GEORGE HUNTER (TCU) - QBACK - 1960 DALLAS TEXANS (AFL); 1961
        SAN DIEGO CHARGERS (AFL); 1962 DENVER BRONCOS (AFL); 1962
        OAKLAND RAIDERS (AFL)
ENKE, FREDERICK (ARIZONA) - QBACK - 1948-51 DETROIT LIONS; 1952
        PHILADELPHIA EAGLES; 1953-54 BALTIMORE COLTS
ENRIGHT, REX (NOTRE DAME) - BACK - 1926-27 GREEN BAY PACKERS
ENYART, WILLIAM (OREGON STATE) - BACK - 1969 BUFFALO BILLS (AFL);
        1970 BUFFALO BILLS (AFC); 1971 OAKLAND RAIDERS (AFC)
EPPERSON, JOHN PATRICK (ADAMS STATE) - END - 1960 DENVER BRONCOS (AFL)
EPPS, ROBERT (PITTSBURGH) - BACK - 1954-55, 57 NEW YORK GIANTS
ERDLITZ, RICHARD (NORTHWESTERN) - BACK - 1942, 45 PHILADELPHIA
        EAGLES; 1946 MIAMI SEAHAWKS (AAFC)
EREHART, ARCH (INDIANA) - BACK - 1921 MUNCIE FLYERS
ERICKSON, CARLETON (WASHINGTON) - CENTER - 1938-39 WASHINGTON REDSKINS
ERICKSON, HAROLD (WASHINGTON&JEFFERSON) - BACK - 1923 GREEN BAY
        PACKERS; 1923-24 MILWAUKEE BADGERS; 1925-28 CHICAGO CARDINALS;
        1929-30 MINNEAPOLIS REDJACKETS
ERICKSON, HAROLD - END - 1921-22 MINNEAPOLIS MARINES
ERICKSON, JOHN BERNARD (ABILENE CHRISTIAN) - LB - 1967-68 SAN DIEGO
        CHARGERS (AFL); 1968 CINCINNATI BENGALS (AFL)
ERICKSON, MICHAEL (NORTHWESTERN) - CENTER - 1930-31 CHICAGO
        CARDINALS; 1932 BOSTON BRAVES

ERICKSON, WALDEN (WASHINGTON) - TACKLE - 1926 LOS ANGELES WILDCATS
    (AFL); 1927 POTTSVILLE MAROONS
ERICKSON, WILLIAM (MISSISSIPPI) - GUARD - 1948 NEW YORK GIANTS; 1949
    NEW YORK YANKEES (AAFC)
ERLANDSON, THOMAS (WASHINGTON STATE) - LB - 1962-65 DENVER BRONCOS
    (AFL); 1966-67 MIAMI DOLPHINS (AFL); 1968 SAN DIEGO CHARGERS
    (AFL)
ERNST, JOHN (LAFAYETTE) - QBACK - 1925, 30 FRANKFORD YELLOWJACKETS;
    1925-28 POTTSVILLE MAROONS; 1928 NEW YORK YANKEES; 1929 BOSTON
    BRAVES
ERNST, MICHAEL (CALIFORNIA-FULLERTON) - QBACK - 1972 DENVER BRONCOS
    (AFC); 1973 CINCINNATI BENGALS (AFC)
ERWIG, WILLIAM (SYRACUSE) - BACK - 1919-21 ROCHESTER JEFFERSONS
ERWIN, TERRENCE (BOSTON COLLEGE) - BACK - 1968 DENVER BRONCOS (AFL)
ESCHBACH, HERBERT (PENN STATE) - CENTER - 1930-31 PROVIDENCE
    STEAMROLLERS
ESHMONT, LEONARD (FORDHAM) - BACK - 1941 NEW YORK GIANTS; 1946-49 SAN
    FRANCISCO 49ERS (AAFC)
ESPIE, ALLEN - TACKLE - 1923 LOUISVILLE BRECKS
ESSER, CLARENCE (WISCONSIN) - END - 1947 CHICAGO CARDINALS
ESTES, DONALD (LSU) - GUARD - 1966 SAN DIEGO CHARGERS (AFL)
ESTES, LAWRENCE (ALCORN A&M) - END - 1970-71 NEW ORLEANS SAINTS
    (NFC); 1972 PHILADELPHIA EAGLES (NFC)
ESTES, ROY (GEORGIA) - BACK - 1928 GREEN BAY PACKERS
ETCHEVERRY, SAMUEL (DENVER) - QBACK - 1961-62 ST. LOUIS CARDINALS
ETELMAN, CARL (TUFTS) - BACK - 1926 PROVIDENCE STEAMROLLERS; 1926
    BOSTON BULLDOGS (AFL)
ETHRIDGE, JOSEPH (SMU) - TACKLE - 1949 GREEN BAY PACKERS
ETTER, ROBERT (GEORGIA) - KICKER - 1968-69 ATLANTA FALCONS
ETTINGER, DONALD (KANSAS) - GUARD - 1948-50 NEW YORK GIANTS
EVANS, CHARLES (USC) - BACK - 1971-73 NEW YORK GIANTS (NFC); 1974
    WASHINGTON REDSKINS (NFC)
EVANS, EARL (HARVARD) - TACKLE - 1925 CHICAGO CARDINALS; 1926-29
    CHICAGO BEARS
EVANS, FREDERICK (NOTRE DAME) - BACK - 1946 CLEVELAND BROWNS (AAFC);
    1947 BUFFALO BILLS (AAFC); 1947-48 CHICAGO ROCKETS (AAFC); 1948
    CHICAGO BEARS
EVANS, JAMES (TEXAS WESTERN) - BACK - 1964-65 NEW YORK JETS (AFL)
EVANS, JAY DALE (KANSAS STATE) - BACK - 1961 DENVER BRONCOS (AFL)
EVANS, JOHN (CALIFORNIA) - BACK - 1929 GREEN BAY PACKERS
EVANS, JON (OKLAHOMA A&M) - END - 1958 PITTSBURGH STEELERS
EVANS, LON (TCU) - GUARD - 1933-37 GREEN BAY PACKERS
EVANS, MURRAY (HARDIN-SIMMONS) - QBACK - 1942-43 DETROIT LIONS
EVANS, MYLES (OHIO WESLEYAN) - TACKLE - 1926 CLEVELAND PANTHERS (AFL)
EVANS, NORMAN (TCU) - TACKLE - 1965 HOUSTON OILERS (AFL); 1966-69
    MIAMI DOLPHINS (AFL); 1970-74 MIAMI DOLPHINS (AFC)
EVANS, RAY (KANSAS) - QBACK - 1948 PITTSBURGH STEELERS
EVANS, RAYMOND (TEXAS MINES) - TACKLE - 1949 SAN FRANCISCO 49ERS
    (AAFC); 1950 SAN FRANCISCO 49ERS
EVANS, RICHARD (IOWA) - END - 1940 GREEN BAY PACKERS; 1941-42 CHICAGO
    CARDINALS; 1943 GREEN BAY PACKERS
EVANS, ROBERT (TEXAS A&M) - END - 1965 HOUSTON OILERS (AFL)
EVANS, WILLIAM MICHAEL (BOSTON COLLEGE) - CENTER - 1968-69
    PHILADELPHIA EAGLES; 1970-73 PHILADELPHIA EAGLES (NFC)
EVANSEN, PAUL (OREGON STATE) - GUARD - 1948 SAN FRANCISCO 49ERS (AAFC)
EVERLY - TACKLE - 1940 NEW YORK AMERICANS (AFL)
EVEY, RICHARD (TENNESSEE) - END, TACKLE - 1964-69 CHICAGO BEARS; 1970
    LOS ANGELES RAMS (NFC); 1971 DETROIT LIONS (NFC)
EWALD, GEORGE (LOUISVILLE) - BACK - 1921 LOUISVILLE BRECKS
EZERINS, VILNIS (WHITEWATER) - BACK - 1968 LOS ANGELES RAMS
FAGAN, JULIAN (MISSISSIPPI) - KICKER - 1970-72 NEW ORLEANS SAINTS
    (NFC); 1973 NEW YORK JETS (AFC); 1970 PUNTING LEADER (NFC)
FAGIOLO, CARL - GUARD - 1944 PHILADELPHIA EAGLES
FAHAY, JOHN (MARQUETTE) - END - 1926 RACINE LEGION; 1926 CHICAGO
    BEARS; 1929 MINNEAPOLIS REDJACKETS
FAHNHORST, KEITH (MINNESOTA) - TACKLE - 1974 SAN FRANCISCO 49ERS (NFC)
FAILING, FREDERICK (CENTRAL JUNIOR-KANSAS) - GUARD - 1930 CHICAGO
    CARDINALS
FAIRBAND, WILLIAM (COLORADO) - LB - 1967-68 OAKLAND RAIDERS (AFL)

FAIRCLOTH, ARTHUR (NORTH CAROLINA STATE) - BACK - 1947-48 NEW YORK
 GIANTS
FAIRLEY, LEONARD (ALCORN A&M) - BACK - 1974 HOUSTON OILERS (AFC);
 1974 BUFFALO BILLS (AFC)
FAISON, WILLIAM EARL (INDIANA) - END - 1961-66 SAN DIEGO CHARGERS
 (AFL); 1966 MIAMI DOLPHINS (AFL)
FALASCHI, NELLO (SANTA CLARA) - QBACK - 1938-41 NEW YORK GIANTS
FALCON, GILBERT (WABASH) - BACK - 1919-20, 24-25 HAMMOND PROS; 1920
 CHICAGO TIGERS; 1921 CANTON BULLDOGS; 1922-23 TOLEDO MAROONS;
 1925 AKRON PROS
FALCON, RICHARD - CENTER - 1919 HAMMOND PROS
FALKENSTEIN, ANTHONY (ST. MARY'S OF CAL.) - BACK - 1943 GREEN BAY
 PACKERS; 1944 BROOKLYN TIGERS; 1944 BOSTON YANKS
FALLON, MICHAEL (SYRACUSE) - GUARD - 1922 MILWAUKEE BADGERS
FALLS, MICHAEL (MINNESOTA) - GUARD - 1960-61 DALLAS COWBOYS
FAMIGLIETTI, GARY (BOSTON UNIV.) - BACK - 1938-45 CHICAGO BEARS; 1946
 BOSTON YANKS
FANNING, STANLEY (IDAHO) - TACKLE - 1960-62 CHICAGO BEARS; 1963 LOS
 ANGELES RAMS; 1964 HOUSTON OILERS (AFL); 1964 DENVER BRONCOS
 (AFL)
FANUCCHI, LEDIO (FRESNO STATE) - TACKLE - 1954 CHICAGO CARDINALS
FANUCCI, MICHAEL (ARIZONA STATE) - END - 1972 WASHINGTON REDSKINS
 (NFC); 1973 HOUSTON OILERS (AFC); 1974 GREEN BAY PACKERS (NFC)
FARASOPOULOS, CHRISTOPHER (BRIGHAM YOUNG) - BACK - 1971-73 NEW YORK
 JETS (AFC); 1974 NEW ORLEANS SAINTS (NFC)
FARBER, HAP (MISSISSIPPI) - LB - 1970 MINNESOTA VIKINGS (NFC); 1970
 NEW ORLEANS SAINTS (NFC)
FARINA, RALPH "NICK" (VILLANOVA) - CENTER - 1927 POTTSVILLE MAROONS
FARKAS, ANDREW (DETROIT) - BACK - 1938-44 WASHINGTON REDSKINS; 1945
 DETROIT LIONS; 1939 SCORING LEADER
FARLEY, DALE (WEST VIRGINIA) - LB, END - 1971 MIAMI DOLPHINS (AFC);
 1972-73 BUFFALO BILLS (AFC)
FARLEY, RICHARD (BOSTON UNIV.) - BACK - 1968-69 SAN DIEGO CHARGERS
 (AFL)
FARMAN, RICHARD (WASHINGTON STATE) - GUARD - 1939-43 WASHINGTON
 REDSKINS
FARMER, GEORGE (UCLA) - END - 1970-74 CHICAGO BEARS (NFC)
FARMER, LONNIE (CHATTANOOGA) - LB - 1964-66 BOSTON PATRIOTS (AFL)
FARMER, THOMAS (IOWA) - BACK - 1946 LOS ANGELES RAMS; 1947-48
 WASHINGTON REDSKINS
FARR, MELVIN (UCLA) - BACK - 1967-69 DETROIT LIONS; 1970-73 DETROIT
 LIONS (NFC)
FARR, MILLER (WICHITA STATE) - BACK - 1965 DENVER BRONCOS (AFL);
 1965-66 SAN DIEGO CHARGERS (AFL); 1967-69 HOUSTON OILERS (AFL);
 1970-72 ST. LOUIS CARDINALS (NFC); 1973 DETROIT LIONS (NFC);
 1967 INTERCEPTION LEADER; (TIED WITH WESTMORELAND AND JANIK)
FARRAGUT, KENNETH (MISSISSIPPI) - CENTER - 1951-54 PHILADELPHIA EAGLES
FARRAR, VENICE (NORTH CAROLINA STATE) - BACK - 1936 NEW YORK YANKS
 (AFL); 1937 ROCHESTER TIGERS (AFL); 1939 PITTSBURGH STEELERS
FARRELL, EDWARD (MUHLENBERG) - BACK - 1938 PITTSBURGH PIRATES;
 1938-39 BROOKLYN DODGERS
FARRIER, CURTIS (MONTANA STATE) - TACKLE - 1963-65 KANSAS CITY CHIEFS
 (AFL)
FARRINGTON, JOHN (PRAIRIE VIEW) - END - 1960-63 CHICAGO BEARS
FARRIS, JOHN (WYOMING) - BACK - 1940 BUFFALO INDIANS (AFL); 1940 NEW
 YORK AMERICANS (AFL)
FARRIS, JOHN (SAN DIEGO STATE) - GUARD - 1965-66 SAN DIEGO CHARGERS
 (AFL)
FARRIS, THOMAS (WISCONSIN) - QBACK - 1946-47 CHICAGO BEARS; 1948
 CHICAGO ROCKETS (AAFC)
FARROH, SHIPLEY (IOWA) - GUARD - 1938 PITTSBURGH PIRATES
FAULKNER, STALEY (TEXAS) - TACKLE - 1964 HOUSTON OILERS (AFL)
FAUSCH, FRANKLIN (KALAMAZOO) - BACK - 1919 WHEELING; 1921-22
 EVANSVILLE CRIMSON GIANTS
FAUST, GEORGE (MINNESOTA) - BACK - 1939 CHICAGO CARDINALS
FAUST, PAUL (MINNESOTA) - LB - 1967 MINNESOTA VIKINGS
FAUST, RICHARD (OTTERBEIN) - TACKLE - 1924, 28-29 DAYTON TRIANGLES
FAVERTY, HAROLD (WISCONSIN) - CENTER - 1952 GREEN BAY PACKERS
FAWCETT, JACOB (SMU) - TACKLE - 1942-44 CLEVELAND RAMS; 1943 BROOKLYN
 DODGERS; 1946 LOS ANGELES RAMS
FAY, JAMES (CANISIUS) - BACK - 1926 BUFFALO RANGERS

FAY, JERRY (GROVE CITY) - TACKLE - 1926 PHILADELPHIA QUAKERS (AFL)
FAYE, ALLEN (MARQUETTE) - END - 1922 GREEN BAY PACKERS
FEAGIN, THOMAS WILEY (HOUSTON) - GUARD - 1961-62 BALTIMORE COLTS;
     1963 WASHINGTON REDSKINS
FEAMSTER, THOMAS (FLORIDA STATE) - END - 1956 BALTIMORE COLTS
FEARS, THOMAS (UCLA) - END - 1948-56 LOS ANGELES RAMS; 1948-50 PASS
     RECEIVING LEADER; 1970 HALL OF FAME
FEATHER, ELVIN (KANSAS STATE) - BACK - 1927 CLEVELAND BULLDOGS; 1928
     DETROIT WOLVERINES; 1929-33 NEW YORK GIANTS; 1931 STATEN ISLAND
     STAPELTONS; 1934 CINCINNATI REDS
FEATHERS, BEATTIE (TENNESSEE) - BACK - 1934-37 CHICAGO BEARS; 1938-39
     BROOKLYN DODGERS; 1940 GREEN BAY PACKERS; 1934 RUSHING LEADER
FEDEROVICH, JOHN (DAVIS&ELKINS) - TACKLE - 1941, 46 CHICAGO BEARS
FEDERSPIEL, JOSEPH (KENTUCKY) - LB - 1972-74 NEW ORLEANS SAINTS (NFC)
FEDORA, WALTER (GEORGE WASHINGTON) - BACK - 1942 BROOKLYN DODGERS
FEDORCHAK, JOHN (DUQUESNE) - BACK - 1940 BUFFALO INDIANS (AFL)
FEENEY, ALBERT (NOTRE DAME) - CENTER - 1919-21 CANTON BULLDOGS
FEHER, NICHOLAS (GEORGIA) - GUARD - 1951-54 SAN FRANCISCO 49ERS; 1955
     PITTSBURGH STEELERS
FEIBISH, BERNARD (NEW YORK UNIV.) - CENTER - 1941 PHILADELPHIA EAGLES
FEICHTINGER, ANDREW - END - 1920 DECATUR STALEYS; 1921 CHICAGO STALEYS
FEIST, LOUIS (CANISIUS) - TACKLE - 1924-25 BUFFALO BISONS; 1926
     BUFFALO RANGERS
FEKETE, EUGENE (OHIO STATE) - BACK - 1946 CLEVELAND BROWNS (AAFC)
FEKETE, JOHN (OHIO UNIV.) - BACK - 1946 BUFFALO BISONS (AAFC)
FELBER, FREDERICK (NORTH DAKOTA) - END - 1932 BOSTON BRAVES
FELDHAUS, WILLIAM (CINCINNATI) - TACKLE - 1937-40 DETROIT LIONS
FELDHAUSEN, PAUL (NORTHLAND) - CENTER - 1968 BOSTON PATRIOTS (AFL)
FELKER, ARTHUR (MARQUETTE) - END - 1951 GREEN BAY PACKERS
FELKER, EUGENE (WISCONSIN) - END - 1952 DALLAS TEXANS
FELLER, JAMES "HAPPY" (TEXAS) - KICKER - 1971 PHILADELPHIA EAGLES
     (NFC); 1972-73 NEW ORLEANS SAINTS (NFC)
FELT, RICHARD (BRIGHAM YOUNG) - BACK - 1960-61 NEW YORK TITANS (AFL);
     1962-66 BOSTON PATRIOTS (AFL)
FELTON, RALPH (MARYLAND) - BACK - 1954-60 WASHINGTON REDSKINS;
     1961-62 BUFFALO BILLS (AFL)
FELTS, ROBERT (FLORIDA A&M) - BACK - 1965 BALTIMORE COLTS; 1965-67
     DETROIT LIONS
FENA, THOMAS (DENVER) - GUARD - 1937 DETROIT LIONS
FENCIL, RICHARD (NORTHWESTERN) - END - 1933 PHILADELPHIA EAGLES
FENENBOCK, CHARLES (UCLA) - BACK - 1943, 45 DETROIT LIONS; 1946-48
     LOS ANGELES DONS (AAFC); 1948 CHICAGO ROCKETS (AAFC)
FENIMORE, ROBERT (OKLAHOMA A&M) - BACK - 1947 CHICAGO BEARS
FENNEMA, CARL (WASHINGTON) - CENTER - 1948-49 NEW YORK GIANTS
FENNER, LANE (FLORIDA STATE) - END - 1968 SAN DIEGO CHARGERS (AFL)
FENNER, LEE (ST. MARY'S OF OHIO) - END - 1919-29 DAYTON TRIANGLES;
     1930 PORTSMOUTH SPARTANS
FERGUSON, CHARLES (TENNESSEE STATE) - END - 1961 CLEVELAND BROWNS;
     1962 MINNESOTA VIKINGS; 1963, 65-66, 69 BUFFALO BILLS (AFL)
FERGUSON, EUGENE (NORFOLK STATE) - TACKLE - 1969 SAN DIEGO CHARGERS
     (AFL); 1970 SAN DIEGO CHARGERS (AFC); 1971-72 HOUSTON OILERS
     (AFC)
FERGUSON, HOWARD - BACK - 1953-58 GREEN BAY PACKERS; 1960 LOS ANGELES
     CHARGERS (AFL)
FERGUSON, JAMES (USC) - CENTER - 1968 NEW ORLEANS SAINTS; 1969
     ATLANTA FALCONS; 1969 CHICAGO BEARS
FERGUSON, JOE (ARKANSAS) - QBACK - 1973-74 BUFFALO BILLS (AFC)
FERGUSON, LAWRENCE (IOWA) - BACK - 1963 DETROIT LIONS
FERGUSON, ROBERT (OHIO STATE) - BACK - 1962-63 PITTSBURGH STEELERS;
     1963 MINNESOTA VIKINGS
FERGUSON, T. - TACKLE - 1921 LOUISVILLE BRECKS
FERGUSON, WILLIAM (SAN DIEGO STATE) - LB - 1973-74 NEW YORK JETS (AFC)
FERKO, JOHN (WEST CHESTER STATE) - GUARD - 1937-38 PHILADELPHIA EAGLES
FERNANDEZ, MANUEL (UTAH) - TACKLE, END - 1968-69 MIAMI DOLPHINS
     (AFL); 1970-74 MIAMI DOLPHINS (AFC)
FERRANTE, JACK - END - 1941, 44-50 PHILADELPHIA EAGLES
FERRANTE, ORLANDO (USC) - GUARD - 1960 LOS ANGELES CHARGERS (AFL);
     1961 SAN DIEGO CHARGERS (AFL)
FERRIS, NEIL (LOYOLA OF CAL.) - BACK - 1951-52 WASHINGTON REDSKINS;
     1952 PHILADELPHIA EAGLES; 1953 LOS ANGELES RAMS

FERRY, LOUIS (VILLANOVA) - TACKLE - 1949 GREEN BAY PACKERS; 1951
     CHICAGO CARDINALS; 1952-55 PITTSBURGH STEELERS
FERSEN, PAUL (GEORGIA) - TACKLE - 1973-74 NEW ORLEANS SAINTS (NFC)
FESIT - CENTER - 1919 WHEELING
FEST, HOWARD (TEXAS) - GUARD,CENTER,TACKLE - 1968-69 CINCINNATI
     BENGALS (AFL); 1970-74 CINCINNATI BENGALS (AFC)
FETHERSTON, JAMES (CALIFORNIA) - LB - 1968-69 SAN DIEGO CHARGERS (AFL)
FETZ, GUSTAVE - BACK - 1923 CHICAGO BEARS
FICCA, DANIEL (USC) - GUARD - 1962 OAKLAND RAIDERS (AFL); 1963-66 NEW
     YORK JETS (AFL)
FICHMAN, LEON (ALABAMA) - TACKLE - 1946-47 DETROIT LIONS
FICHTNER, ROSS (PURDUE) - BACK - 1960-67 CLEVELAND BROWNS; 1968 NEW
     ORLEANS SAINTS
FIEDLER, WILLIAM (PENNSYLVANIA) - GUARD - 1938 PHILADELPHIA EAGLES
FIELD, HARRY (OREGON STATE) - TACKLE - 1934-36 CHICAGO CARDINALS;
     1937 LOS ANGELES BULLDOGS (AFL)
FIELDS, GEORGE (BAKERSFIELD) - END - 1960-61 OAKLAND RAIDERS (AFL)
FIELDS, JERRY (OHIO STATE) - LB - 1961-62 NEW YORK TITANS (AFL)
FIFE, JAMES (WASHINGTON&JEFFERSON) - END - 1936-37 PITTSBURGH
     AMERICANS (AFL)
FIFE, RALPH (PITTSBURGH) - GUARD - 1942, 45 CHICAGO CARDINALS; 1946
     PITTSBURGH STEELERS
FIGNER, GEORGE (COLORADO) - BACK - 1953 CHICAGO BEARS
FILAK, JOHN (PENN STATE) - TACKLE - 1927-29 FRANKFORD YELLOWJACKETS
FILCHOCK, FRANK (INDIANA) - QBACK - 1938 PITTSBURGH PIRATES; 1938-41,
     44-45 WASHINGTON REDSKINS; 1946 NEW YORK GIANTS; 1950 BALTIMORE
     COLTS; 1944 PASSING LEADER
FILES, JAMES (OKLAHOMA) - LB - 1970-73 NEW YORK GIANTS (NFC)
FILIPOWICZ, STEPHEN (FORDHAM) - BACK - 1945-46 NEW YORK GIANTS
FILIPSKI, EUGENE (WEST POINT & VILLANOVA) - BACK - 1956-57 NEW YORK
     GIANTS
FILLINGHAM - TACKLE - 1936 ROCHESTER TIGERS (AFL)
FINCH, KARL (CAL POLY) - END - 1962 LOS ANGELES RAMS
FINCH, OLIN (WHITTIER) - BACK - 1926 LOS ANGELES BUCCANEERS
FINK, PAUL MICHAEL (MISSOURI) - BACK - 1973 NEW ORLEANS SAINTS (NFC)
FINKS, JAMES (TULSA) - QBACK - 1949-55 PITTSBURGH STEELERS
FINLAY, JOHN (UCLA) - GUARD - 1947-51 LOS ANGELES RAMS
FINN, BERNARD (HOLY CROSS) - BACK - 1930 NEWARK TORNADOS; 1930, 32
     STATEN ISLAND STAPELTONS; 1932 CHICAGO CARDINALS
FINN, JOHN (VILLANOVA) - QBACK - 1924 FRANKFORD YELLOWJACKETS
FINNEGAN, JAMES (ST. LOUIS) - END - 1923 ST. LOUIS BROWNS
FINNERAN, GARY (USC) - TACKLE - 1960 LOS ANGELES CHARGERS (AFL); 1961
     OAKLAND RAIDERS (AFL)
FINNIE, ROGER (FLORIDA A&M) - GUARD, TACKLE, END - 1969 NEW YORK JETS
     (AFL); 1970-72 NEW YORK JETS (AFC); 1973-74 ST. LOUIS CARDINALS
     (NFC)
FINNIN, THOMAS (DETROIT) - TACKLE - 1953-56 BALTIMORE COLTS; 1957
     CHICAGO CARDINALS
FINSTERWALD, RUSSELL (SYRACUSE) - BACK - 1919 DETROIT HERALDS
FIORENTINO, ALBERT (BOSTON COLLEGE) - GUARD - 1943-44 WASHINGTON
     REDSKINS; 1945 BOSTON YANKS
FIORENTINO, EDWARD (BOSTON COLLEGE) - END - 1947 BOSTON YANKS
FISCHER, CLARK (CATHOLIC UNIV. & MARQUETTE) - BACK - 1926 MILWAUKEE
     BADGERS
FISCHER, CLETIS (NEBRASKA) - BACK - 1949 NEW YORK GIANTS
FISCHER, LESTER (NEW YORK UNIV.) - CENTER - 1940 NEW YORK AMERICANS
     (AFL)
FISCHER, PATRICK (NEBRASKA) - BACK - 1961-67 ST. LOUIS CARDINALS;
     1968-69 WASHINGTON REDSKINS; 1970-74 WASHINGTON REDSKINS (NFC)
FISCHER, WILLIAM (NOTRE DAME) - TACKLE - 1949-53 CHICAGO CARDINALS
FISHEL, RICHARD (SYRACUSE) - QBACK - 1933 BROOKLYN DODGERS
FISHER, DARRELL (IOWA) - BACK - 1925 BUFFALO BISONS
FISHER, DOUGLAS (SAN DIEGO STATE) - LB - 1969 PITTSBURGH STEELERS;
     1970 PITTSBURGH STEELERS (AFC)
FISHER, ED (ARIZONA STATE) - TACKLE - 1974 HOUSTON OILERS (AFC)
FISHER, EVERETT (SANTA CLARA) - BACK - 1938-39 CHICAGO CARDINALS;
     1940 PITTSBURGH STEELERS
FISHER, GEORGE (INDIANA) - TACKLE - 1926 HAMMOND PROS
FISHER, RAYMOND (EASTERN ILLINOIS) - TACKLE - 1959 PITTSBURGH STEELERS
FISHER, ROBERT (USC) - TACKLE - 1940 WASHINGTON REDSKINS
FISHER, ROBERT (OHIO NORTHERN) - BACK - 1925 CANTON BULLDOGS

FISHER, THEL (DRAKE) - BACK - 1940 BOSTON BEARS (AFL)

FISHMAN, ABRAHAM - GUARD - 1921-22 EVANSVILLE CRIMSON GIANTS

FISHMAN, ALEXANDER - TACKLE - 1921-22 EVANSVILLE CRIMSON GIANTS

FISK, WILLIAM (USC) - END - 1940-43 DETROIT LIONS; 1946-47 SAN
      FRANCISCO 49ERS (AAFC); 1948 LOS ANGELES DONS (AAFC)

FISKE, MAX (DEPAUL) - BACK - 1936 PITTSBURGH PIRATES; 1937 CHICAGO
      CARDINALS; 1937-38 PITTSBURGH PIRATES; 1939 PITTSBURGH STEELERS

FISS, GALEN (KANSAS) - LB - 1956-66 CLEVELAND BROWNS

FITZGERAL, CLARK - 1921 LOUISVILLE BRECKS

FITZGERALD, DONALD (HOLY CROSS) - CENTER - 1930-31 STATEN ISLAND
      STAPELTONS

FITZGERALD, FRANCIS (DETROIT) - BACK - 1923 TOLEDO MAROONS

FITZGERALD, FREEMAN (NOTRE DAME) - BACK - 1920 DETROIT HERALDS;
      1920-21 ROCK ISLAND INDEPENDENTS

FITZGERLAD, JOHN (BOSTON COLLEGE) - CENTER, GUARD - 1971-74 DALLAS
      COWBOYS (NFC)

FITZGERALD, JOHN (ST JOHN'S) - QBACK - 1926 BROOKLYN HORSEMEN (AFL)

FITZGERALD, MICHAEL (IOWA STATE) - BACK - 1966-67 MINNESOTA VIKINGS;
      1967 NEW YORK GIANTS; 1967 ATLANTA FALCONS

FITZGIBBON, PAUL (CREIGHTON) - QBACK - 1926 DULUTH ESKIMOS; 1927
      FRANKFORD YELLOWJACKETS; 1928 CHICAGO CARDINALS; 1930-32 GREEN
      BAY PACKERS

FITZKE, ROBERT (IDAHO) - BACK - 1925 FRANKFORD YELLOWJACKETS

FIVAZ, WILLIAM (SYRACUSE) - GUARD - 1925 ROCHESTER JEFFERSONS; 1925
      MILWAUKEE BADGERS

FLAGERMAN, JOHN (ST. MARY'S OF CAL.) - CENTER - 1948 LOS ANGELES DONS
      (AAFC)

FLAHERTY, JAMES (GEORGETOWN) - END - 1923 CHICAGO BEARS

FLAHERTY, RAY (GONZAGA) - END - 1926 LOS ANGELES WILDCATS (AFL);
      1927-28 NEW YORK YANKEES; 1928-29, 31-35 NEW YORK GIANTS; 1932
      PASS RECEIVING LEADER

FLAHERTY, RICHARD (MARQUETTE) - END - 1926 GREEN BAY PACKERS

FLANAGAN, EDWARD (PURDUE) - CENTER - 1965-69 DETROIT LIONS; 1970-74
      DETROIT LIONS (NFC)

FLANAGAN, LATHAM (CARNEGIE TECH) - END - 1931 CHICAGO BEARS; 1931
      CHICAGO CARDINALS

FLANAGAN, PHILIP (HOLY CROSS) - GUARD - 1936 BOSTON SHAMROCKS (AFL)

FLANAGAN, RICHARD (OHIO STATE) - GUARD - 1948-49 CHICAGO BEARS;
      1950-52 DETROIT LIONS; 1953-55 PITTSBURGH STEELERS

FLANAGAN, WILLIAM (PITTSBURGH) - BACK - 1925-26 POTTSVILLE MAROONS

FLANIGAN, JAMES (PITTSBURGH) - LB - 1967-69 GREEN BAY PACKERS; 1970
      GREEN BAY PACKERS (NFC); 1971 NEW ORLEANS SAINTS (NFC)

FLANNIGAN, WILLIAM - TACKLE - 1926 LOUISVILLE COLONELS

FLATLEY, PAUL (NORTHWESTERN) - END - 1963-67 MINNESOTA VIKINGS;
      1968-69 ATLANTA FALCONS; 1970 ATLANTA FALCONS (NFC)

FLATTERY, WILSON (WOOSTER) - GUARD - 1925-26 CANTON BULLDOGS

FLAVIN, JOHN (GEORGETOWN) - BACK - 1923 BUFFALO ALL-AMERICANS; 1924
      BUFFALO BISONS

FLECKENSTEIN, WILLIAM (IOWA) - CENTER - 1925-30 CHICAGO BEARS; 1930
      PORTSMOUTH SPARTANS; 1931 FRANKFORD YELLOWJACKETS; 1931 BROOKLYN
      DODGERS

FLEISCHMAN, GODFREY (PURDUE) - GUARD - 1925-26 DETROIT PANTHERS;
      1927-29 PROVIDENCE STEAMROLLERS

FLEISCHMAN - TACKLE - 1919 WHEELING

FLEMING, DONALD (FLORIDA) - BACK - 1960-62 CLEVELAND BROWNS

FLEMING, FRANCIS (CATHOLIC UNIV.) - END - 1936-37 BOSTON SHAMROCKS
      (AFL)

FLEMING, MARVIN (UTAH) - END - 1963-69 GREEN BAY PACKERS; 1970-74
      MIAMI DOLPHINS (AFC)

FLEMING, GEORGE (WASHINGTON) - BACK - 1961 OAKLAND RAIDERS (AFL)

FLEMING, WILMER (MT. UNION) - BACK - 1925 CANTON BULLDOGS

FLENNIKEN, MAX (GENEVA) - BACK - 1930 CHICAGO CARDINALS; 1931 NEW
      YORK GIANTS

FLENTHORPE, DONALD (KANSAS STATE) - GUARD - 1936 NEW YORK YANKS (AFL)

FLETCHER, ANDREW (MARYLAND) - BACK - 1920 BUFFALO ALL-AMERICANS; 1920
      DECATUR STALEYS

FLETCHER, CHRISTOPHER (TEMPLE) - BACK - 1970-74 SAN DIEGO CHARGERS
      (AFC)

FLETCHER, OLIVER (USC) - GUARD - 1949 LOS ANGELES DONS (AAFC); 1950
      BALTIMORE COLTS

FLETCHER, WILLIAM (MEMPHIS STATE) - BACK - 1966 DENVER BRONCOS (AFL)

FLINT, GEORGE (ARIZONA STATE) - TACKLE - 1962-65, 68-69 BUFFALO BILLS
     (AFL)
FLORES, THOMAS (PACIFIC) - QBACK - 1960-61, 63-66 OAKLAND RAIDERS
     (AFL); 1967-69 BUFFALO BILLS (AFL); 1969 KANSAS CITY CHIEFS (AFL)
FLOWER, JAMES (OHIO STATE) - TACKLE - 1921-24 AKRON PROS
FLOWERS, BERNARD (PURDUE) - END - 1956 BALTIMORE COLTS
FLOWERS, CHARLES (MISSISSIPPI) - BACK - 1960 LOS ANGELES CHARGERS
     (AFL); 1961 SAN DIEGO CHARGERS (AFL); 1962 NEW YORK TITANS (AFL)
FLOWERS, KEITH (TCU) - CENTER - 1952 DALLAS TEXANS
FLOWERS, RICHARD (NORTHWESTERN) - QBACK - 1953 BALTIMORE COLTS
FLOWERS, RICHMOND (TENNESSEE) - END, BACK - 1969 DALLAS COWBOYS;
     1970-71 DALLAS COWBOYS (NFC); 1971-73 NEW YORK GIANTS (NFC)
FLOWERS, ROBERT (TEXAS TECH) - CENTER - 1942-49 GREEN BAY PACKERS
FLOYD, ALBERT (SOUTHWESTERN OF KANSAS) - END - 1936 NEW YORK YANKS
     (AFL); 1936 ROCHESTER TIGERS (AFL)
FLOYD, BOBBY JACK (TCU) - BACK - 1952 GREEN BAY PACKERS; 1953 CHICAGO
     BEARS
FLOYD, DONALD (TCU) - END - 1960-67 HOUSTON OILERS (AFL)
FLINT, GEORGE (ARIZONA STATE) - TACKLE - 1962-65 BUFFALO BILLS (AFL)
FLOHR, LESTER (BETHANY OF KANSAS) - CENTER - 1927 CLEVELAND BULLDOGS
FLORA, WILLIAM (MICHIGAN) - BACK - 1928 CHICAGO CARDINALS
FLORENCE, PAUL (LOYOLA OF ILLINOIS) - END - 1920 CHICAGO CARDINALS
FLYNN, DONALD (HOUSTON) - BACK - 1960-61 DALLAS TEXANS (AFL); 1961
     NEW YORK TITANS (AFL)
FLYNN, FURLONG (CORNELL) - TACKLE - 1926 HARTFORD BLUES
FLYNN, PAUL (MINNESOTA) - END - 1922-23 MINNEAPOLIS MARINES
FOLDBERG, HENRY (WEST POINT) - END - 1948 BROOKLYN DODGERS (AAFC);
     1949 CHICAGO HORNETS (AAFC)
FOLEY, DAVID (OHIO STATE) - TACKLE, CENTER - 1970-71 NEW YORK JETS
     (AFC); 1972-74 BUFFALO BILLS (AFC)
FOLEY, JAMES (SYRACUSE) - BACK - 1926 HARTFORD BLUES
FOLEY, THOMAS "TIM" (PURDUE) - BACK - 1970-74 MIAMI DOLPHINS (AFC)
FOLK, RICHARD (ARK. STATE & ILL. WESLEYAN) - BACK - 1939 BROOKLYN
     DODGERS
FOLKINS, LEE (WASHINGTON) - END - 1961 GREEN BAY PACKERS; 1962-64
     DALLAS COWBOYS; 1965 PITTSBURGH STEELERS
FOLLET, BERYL (NEW YORK UNIV.) - QBACK - 1930-31 STATEN ISLAND
     STAPELTONS
FOLTZ, VERNON (ST. VINCENT'S) - CENTER - 1944 WASHINGTON REDSKINS;
     1945 PITTSBURGH STEELERS
FOLZ, ARTHUR - QBACK - 1923-25 CHICAGO CARDINALS
FONTES, WAYNE (MICHIGAN STATE) - BACK - 1962 NEW YORK TITANS (AFL)
FORD, ADRIAN (LAFAYETTE) - BACK - 1926 PHILADELPHIA QUAKERS (AFL);
     1927 FRANKFORD YELLOWJACKETS; 1927 POTTSVILLE MAROONS
FORD, CHARLES (HOUSTON) - BACK - 1971-73 CHICAGO BEARS (NFC); 1974
     PHILADELPHIA EAGLES (NFC)
FORD, DUANE (WICHITA) - GUARD - 1936 NEW YORK YANKS (AFL)
FORD, FREDERICK (CAL POLY) - BACK - 1960 BUFFALO BILLS (AFL); 1960
     LOS ANGELES CHARGERS (AFL)
FORD, GARRETT (WEST VIRGINIA) - BACK - 1968 DENVER BRONCOS (AFL)
FORD, HENRY (PITTSBURGH) - BACK - 1955 CLEVELAND BROWNS; 1956
     PITTSBURGH STEELERS
FORD, JAMES (TEXAS SOUTHERN) - BACK - 1971-72 NEW ORLEANS SAINTS (NFC)
FORD, LEONARD (MICHIGAN) - END - 1948-49 LOS ANGELES DONS (AAFC);
     1950-57 CLEVELAND BROWNS; 1958 GREEN BAY PACKERS
FORD, SALEM (LOUISVILLE) - BACK - 1922-23 LOUISVILLE BRECKS
FORDHAM, JAMES (GEORGIA) - BACK - 1944-45 CHICAGO BEARS
FOREMAN, WALTER "CHUCK" (MIAMI) - BACK - 1973-74 MINNESOTA VIKINGS
     (NFC)
FORESTER, GEORGE "BILL" (SMU) - LB - 1953-63 GREEN BAY PACKERS
FORESTER, HERSCHEL (SMU) - GUARD - 1954-57 CLEVELAND BROWNS
FORKOVITCH, NICHOLAS (WILLIAM&MARY) - BACK - 1948 BROOKLYN DODGERS
     (AAFC)
FORREST, EDWARD (SANTA CLARA) - CENTER - 1946-47 SAN FRANCISCO 49ERS
     (AAFC)
FORREST, THOMAS (CINCINNATI) - GUARD - 1974 CHICAGO BEARS (NFC)
FORSBERG, FREDERICK (WASHINGTON) - LB - 1968 DENVER BRONCOS (AFL);
     1970-73 DENVER BRONCOS (AFC); 1973 BUFFALO BILLS (AFC); 1974 SAN
     DIEGO CHARGERS (AFC)
FORST, ARTHUR (VILLANOVA) - BACK - 1926 PROVIDENCE STEAMROLLERS
FORSYTH, BENJAMIN (SYRACUSE) - CENTER - 1919-20 ROCHESTER JEFFERSONS

FORTE, ALDO (MONTANA) - GUARD - 1939-41, 46 CHICAGO BEARS; 1946
    DETROIT LIONS; 1947 GREEN BAY PACKERS
FORTE, ROBERT (ARKANSAS) - BACK - 1946-50, 52-53 GREEN BAY PACKERS
FORTMANN, DANIEL (COLGATE) - GUARD - 1936-43 CHICAGO BEARS; 1965 HALL
    OF FAME
FORTMEYER, ALBEN - BACK - 1921 CINCINNATI CELTS
FORTUNATO, JOSEPH (MISSISSIPPI STATE) - LB - 1955-66 CHICAGO BEARS
FORTUNE, BURNELL (DEPAUW) - GUARD - 1923 MINNEAPOLIS MARINES; 1924
    KENOSHA MAROONS; 1924-25 HAMMOND PROS
FORUPIA, JOHN (IDAHO) - BACK - 1967-68 PITTSBURGH STEELERS
FOSDICK, ROBERT (IOWA) - GUARD - 1919, 24 ROCK ISLAND INDEPENDENTS;
    1923-24 MINNEAPOLIS MARINES
FOSTER, FREDERICK (SYRACUSE) - BACK - 1923 BUFFALO ALL-AMERICANS;
    1923-24 ROCHESTER JEFFERSONS
FOSTER, IRVING EUGENE (ARIZONA STATE) - BACK - 1965-69 SAN DIEGO
    CHARGERS (AFL); 1970 SAN DIEGO CHARGERS (AFC)
FOSTER, JAMES (BUCKNELL) - QBACK - 1925 BUFFALO BISONS
FOSTER, RALPH (OKLAHOMA A&M) - TACKLE - 1945-46 CHICAGO CARDINALS
FOSTER, ROBERT - BACK - 1922-23 RACINE LEGION; 1924 MILWAUKEE BADGERS
FOSTER, WILL (EASTERN MICHIGAN) - LB - 1973-74 NEW ENGLAND PATRIOTS
    (AFC)
FOURNET, SIDNEY (LSU) - GUARD - 1955-56 LOS ANGELES RAMS; 1957
    PITTSBURGH STEELERS; 1960-61 DALLAS TEXANS (AFL); 1962 NEW YORK
    TITANS (AFL); 1963 NEW YORK JETS (AFL)
FOUTS, DANIEL (OREGON) - QBACK - 1973-74 SAN DIEGO CHARGERS (AFC)
FOWLER, AUBREY (ARKANSAS) - BACK - 1948 BALTIMORE COLTS (AAFC)
FOWLER, CHARLES (HOUSTON) - TACKLE - 1967-68 MIAMI DOLPHINS (AFL)
FOWLER, JERRY (NORTHWEST LOUISIANA) - TACKLE - 1964 HOUSTON OILERS
    (AFL)
FOWLER, ROBERT (MARTIN JUNIOR) - BACK - 1962 NEW YORK TITANS (AFL)
FOWLER, WAYNE (RICHMOND) - TACKLE - 1970 BUFFALO BILLS (AFC)
FOWLER, WILLMER (NORTHWESTERN) - BACK - 1960-61 BUFFALO BILLS (AFL)
FOX, SAMUEL (OHIO STATE) - END - 1945 NEW YORK GIANTS
FOX, TERRANCE (MIAMI) - BACK - 1941, 45 PHILADELPHIA EAGLES; 1946
    MIAMI SEAHAWKS (AAFC)
FRAHM, HERALD (NEBRASKA) - BACK - 1932 STATEN ISLAND STAPELTONS; 1935
    PHILADELPHIA EAGLES; 1936 BROOKLYN TIGERS (AFL)
FRALEY, JAMES (EMPORIA STATE-KANSAS) - BACK - 1936 NEW YORK YANKS
    (AFL)
FRANCHESI, PETER (SAN FRANCISCO) - BACK - 1946 SAN FRANCISCO 49ERS
    (AAFC)
FRANCI, JASON (SANTA BARBARA) - END - 1966 DENVER BRONCOS (AFL)
FRANCIS, DAVID (OHIO STATE) - BACK - 1963 WASHINGTON REDSKINS
FRANCIS, EUGENE (CHICAGO) - BACK - 1926 CHICAGO CARDINALS
FRANCIS, HARRISON "SAM" (NEBRASKA) - BACK - 1937-38 CHICAGO BEARS;
    1939 PITTSBURGH STEELERS; 1939-40 BROOKLYN DODGERS
FRANCIS, JOSEPH (OREGON STATE) - QBACK - 1958-59 GREEN BAY PACKERS
FRANCIS, WALLACE (ARKANSAS AM&N) - END - 1973-74 BUFFALO BILLS (AFC)
FRANCIS - GUARD - 1919 AKRON PROS
FRANCK, GEORGE (MINNESOTA) - BACK - 1941, 45-47 NEW YORK GIANTS
FRANCKHAUSER, THOMAS (PURDUE) - BACK - 1959 LOS ANGELES RAMS; 1960-61
    DALLAS COWBOYS; 1962-63 MINNESOTA VIKINGS
FRANCO, EDWARD (FORDHAM) - GUARD - 1944 BOSTON YANKS
FRANK, JOSEPH (GEORGETOWN) - TACKLE - 1941-42 PHILADELPHIA EAGLES;
    1943 PHIL-PITT
FRANK, PAUL (WAYNESBURG) - BACK - 1930 NEWARK TORNADOS
FRANK, WILLIAM (COLORADO) - TACKLE - 1964 DALLAS COWBOYS
FRANKIAN, MALCOLM (ST. MARY'S OF CAL.) - END - 1933 BOSTON REDSKINS;
    1934-35 NEW YORK GIANTS; 1937 LOS ANGELES BULLDOGS (AFL)
FRANKLIN, NORMAN (OREGON STATE) - BACK - 1935-37 BROOKLYN DODGERS
FRANKLIN, PAUL (FRANKLIN COLLEGE) - BACK - 1930-33 CHICAGO BEARS
FRANKLIN, ROBERT (MISSISSIPPI) - BACK - 1960-66 CLEVELAND BROWNS
FRANKLIN, WILLIE (OKLAHOMA) - END - 1972 BALTIMORE COLTS (AFC)
FRANKLYN - TACKLE - 1936 ROCHESTER TIGERS (AFL)
FRANKOWSKI, RAYMOND (WASHINGTON) - GUARD - 1945 GREEN BAY PACKERS;
    1946-48 LOS ANGELES DONS (AAFC)
FRANTA, HERBERT (ST. THOMAS OF MINN.) - TACKLE - 1929-30 MINNEAPOLIS
    REDJACKETS; 1930 GREEN BAY PACKERS
FRANTZ, JOHN (CALIFORNIA) - LB - 1968 BUFFALO BILLS (AFL)

FRASER, JAMES (WISCONSIN) - LB, KICKER - 1962-64 DENVER BRONCOS
     (AFL); 1965 KANSAS CITY CHIEFS (AFL); 1966 BOSTON PATRIOTS
     (AFL); 1968 NEW ORLEANS SAINTS; 1962-64 PUNTING LEADER (AFL)
FRAZIER, ADOLPHUS (FLORIDA A&M) - BACK - 1961-63 DENVER BRONCOS (AFL)
FRAZIER, CHARLES (TEXAS SOUTHERN) - END - 1962-68 HOUSTON OILERS
     (AFL); 1969 BOSTON PATRIOTS (AFL); 1970 BOSTON PATRIOTS (AFC)
FRAZIER, CURTIS (FRESNO STATE) - BACK - 1968 CINCINNATI BENGALS (AFL)
FRAZIER, WILLIAM WAYNE (AUBURN) - CENTER - 1962 SAN DIEGO CHARGERS
     (AFL); 1965 HOUSTON OILERS (AFL); 1966-67 KANSAS CITY CHIEFS
     (AFL); 1967 BUFFALO BILLS (AFL)
FRAZIER, WILLIE (ARKANSAS AM&N) - END - 1964-65 HOUSTON OILERS (AFL);
     1966-69 SAN DIEGO CHARGERS (AFL); 1970 SAN DIEGO CHARGERS (AFC);
     1971 HOUSTON OILERS (AFC); 1971-72 KANSAS CITY CHIEFS (AFC)
FREDERICKSON, IVAN "TUCKER" (AUBURN) - BACK - 1965, 67-69 NEW YORK
     GIANTS; 1970-71 NEW YORK GIANTS (NFC)
FREELON, SOLOMON (GRAMBLING) - GUARD - 1972-74 HOUSTON OILERS (AFC)
FREEMAN, JOHN (TEXAS) - GUARD - 1946 BROOKLYN DODGERS (AAFC)
FREEMAN, MICHAEL (FRESNO STATE) - BACK - 1968-69 ATLANTA FALCONS;
     1970 ATLANTA FALCONS (NFC)
FREEMAN, ROBERT (AUBURN) - BACK - 1957-58 CLEVELAND BROWNS; 1959
     GREEN BAY PACKERS; 1960-61 PHILADELPHIA EAGLES; 1962 WASHINGTON
     REDSKINS
FREITAS, JESSE (SANTA CLARA) - BACK - 1946-47 SAN FRANCISCO 49ERS
     (AAFC); 1948 CHICAGO ROCKETS (AAFC); 1949 BUFFALO BILLS (AAFC)
FREITAS, JESSE (SAN DIEGO STATE) - QBACK - 1974 SAN DIEGO CHARGERS
     (AFC)
FREITAS, ROCKNE (OREGON STATE) - TACKLE - 1968-69 DETROIT LIONS;
     1970-74 DETROIT LIONS (NFC)
FRENCH, BARRY (PURDUE) - GUARD - 1947-49 BALTIMORE COLTS (AAFC); 1950
     BALTIMORE COLTS; 1951 DETROIT LIONS
FRENCH, WALTER (WEST POINT) - BACK - 1922 ROCHESTER JEFFERSONS; 1925
     POTTSVILLE MAROONS
FREY, GLENN (TEMPLE) - BACK - 1936-37 PHILADELPHIA EAGLES
FREY, RICHARD (TEXAS A&M) - END - 1960 DALLAS TEXANS (AFL); 1961
     HOUSTON OILERS (AFL)
FRICK, RAYMOND (PENNSYLVANIA) - CENTER - 1941 BROOKLYN DODGERS
FRIEDLUND, ROBERT (MICHIGAN STATE) - END - 1946 PHILADELPHIA EAGLES
FRIEDMAN, BENJAMIN (MICHIGAN) - QBACK - 1927 CLEVELAND BULLDOGS; 1928
     DETROIT WOLVERINES; 1929-31 NEW YORK GIANTS; 1932-34 BROOKLYN
     DODGERS
FRIEDMAN, JACOB - END - 1926 HARTFORD BLUES
FRIEDMAN, ROBERT (WASHINGTON) - GUARD - 1944 PHILADELPHIA EAGLES
FRIEND, BENJAMIN (LSU) - TACKLE - 1939 CLEVELAND RAMS
FRIES, SHERWOOD (COLORADO A&M) - GUARD - 1943 GREEN BAY PACKERS
FRITSCH, ERNEST (DETROIT) - CENTER - 1960 ST. LOUIS CARDINALS
FRITSCH, LOUIS - BACK - 1921 EVANSVILLE CRIMSON GIANTS
FRITSCH, THEODORE (ST. NORBERT) - CENTER - 1972-74 ATLANTA FALCONS
     (NFC)
FRITSCH, THEODORE (STEVENS POINT-WISCONSIN) - BACK - 1942-50 GREEN
     BAY PACKERS; 1946 SCORING LEADER; 1946 FIELD GOAL LEADER
FRITSCH, TONI - KICKER - 1971-73 DALLAS COWBOYS (NFC)
FRITTS, GEORGE (CLEMSON) - TACKLE - 1945 PHILADELPHIA EAGLES
FRITZ, RALPH (MICHIGAN) - GUARD - 1941 PHILADELPHIA EAGLES
FRKETICH, LEONARD (PENN STATE) - TACKLE - 1945 PITTSBURGH STEELERS
FROHBOSE, BILL (MIAMI-FLORIDA) - BACK - 1974 DETROIT LIONS (NFC)
FRONCZEK, ANDREW (RICHMOND) - TACKLE - 1941 BROOKLYN DODGERS
FRONGILLO, JOHN (BAYLOR) - CENTER - 1962-66 HOUSTON OILERS (AFL)
FROST, KENNETH (TENNESSEE) - TACKLE - 1961-62 DALLAS COWBOYS
FRUGONE, JAMES (SYRACUSE) - BACK - 1925 NEW YORK GIANTS; 1926
     BROOKLYN HORSEMEN (AFL)
FRUMP, MILTON (OHIO WESLEYAN) - GUARD - 1930 CHICAGO BEARS
FRUTIG, EDWARD (MICHIGAN) - END - 1941, 45 GREEN BAY PACKERS; 1945-46
     DETROIT LIONS
FRY, HARRY (BUCKNELL) - END - 1932 STATEN ISLAND STAPELTONS
FRY, ROBERT (KENTUCKY) - TACKLE - 1953, 56-59 LOS ANGELES RAMS;
     1960-64 DALLAS COWBOYS
FRY, WELSEY (IOWA) - QBACK - 1926 NEW YORK YANKEES (AFL); 1927 NEW
     YORK YANKEES
FRYER, KENNETH (WEST VIRGINIA) - BACK - 1944 BROOKLYN TIGERS
FUCCI, DOMINIC (KENTUCKY) - BACK - 1955 DETROIT LIONS
FUGETT, JEAN (AMHERST) - END - 1972-74 DALLAS COWBOYS (NFC)

FUGLER, RICHARD (TULANE) - TACKLE - 1952 PITTSBURGH STEELERS; 1954
    CHICAGO CARDINALS
FULCHER, WILLIAM (GEORGIA TECH) - TACKLE - 1956-58 WASHINGTON REDSKINS
FULLER, CHARLES (SAN FRANCISCO STATE) - BACK - 1961-62 OAKLAND
    RAIDERS (AFL)
FULLER, FRANK (KENTUCKY) - TACKLE - 1953, 55, 57-58 LOS ANGELES RAMS;
    1959 CHICAGO CARDINALS; 1960-62 ST. LOUIS CARDINALS; 1963
    PHILADELPHIA EAGLES
FULLER, JOHN (LAMAR TECH) - BACK - 1968-69 SAN FRANCISCO 49ERS;
    1970-73 SAN FRANCISCO 49ERS (NFC); 1974 NEW ORLEANS SAINTS (NFC)
FULLER, LAWRENCE - BACK - 1944-45 WASHINGTON REDSKINS; 1945 CHICAGO
    CARDINALS
FULLERTON, EDWARD (MARYLAND) - BACK - 1953 PITTSBURGH STEELERS
FULTON, THEODORE (OGLETHORPE) - GUARD - 1931-32 BROOKLYN DODGERS
FUNCHESS, THOMAS (JACKSON STATE) - TACKLE, END - 1968-69 BOSTON
    PATRIOTS (AFL); 1970 BOSTON PATRIOTS (AFC); 1971-73 HOUSTON
    OILERS (AFC); 1974 MIAMI DOLPHINS (AFC)
FUNK, FREDERICK (UCLA) - BACK - 1937 NEW YORK YANKS (AFL)
FUQUA, JOHN "FRENCHY" (MORGAN STATE) - BACK - 1969 NEW YORK GIANTS;
    1970-74 PITTSBURGH STEELERS (AFC)
FUQUA, RAYMOND (SMU) - END - 1935-36 BROOKLYN DODGERS
FUREY, JOHN (TEXAS WESTERN) - QBACK - 1962 CLEVELAND BROWNS
FURNESS, STEPHEN (RHODE ISLAND) - END, TACKLE - 1972-74 PITTSBURGH
    STEELERS (AFC)
FURST, ANTHONY (DAYTON) - TACKLE - 1940-41, 44 DETROIT LIONS
FUSSELL, THOMAS (LSU) - END - 1967 BOSTON PATRIOTS (AFL)
GABLER, JOHN (WEST VIRGINIA WESLEYAN) - CENTER - 1925-26 DAYTON
    TRIANGLES
GABRIEL, ROMAN (NORTH CAROLINA STATE) - QBACK - 1962-69 LOS ANGELES
    RAMS; 1970-72 LOS ANGELES RAMS (NFC); 1973-74 PHILADELPHIA
    EAGLES (NFC)
GAECHTER, MICHAEL (OREGON) - BACK - 1962-69 DALLAS COWBOYS
GAFFNEY, JAMES (TENNESSEE) - BACK - 1945-46 WASHINGTON REDSKINS
GAFFNEY (BOSTON UNIV.) - TACKLE - 1919 CLEVELAND INDIANS
GAFFORD, ROY (AUBURN) - BACK - 1946 MIAMI SEAHAWKS (AAFC); 1946-48
    BROOKLYN DODGERS (AAFC)
GAGE, ROBERT (CLEMSON) - BACK - 1949-50 PITTSBURGH STEELERS
GAGNER, LAWRENCE (FLORIDA) - GUARD - 1966-69 PITTSBURGH STEELERS;
    1972 KANSAS CITY CHIEFS (AFC)
GAGNON, DAVE (FERRIS) - BACK - 1974 CHICAGO BEARS (NFC)
GAGNON, ROY (OREGON) - GUARD - 1935 DETROIT LIONS
GAIN, ROBERT (KENTUCKY) - TACKLE - 1952, 54-64 CLEVELAND BROWNS
GAINOR, CHARLES (NORTH DAKOTA) - END - 1939 CHICAGO CARDINALS
GAISER, GEORGE (SMU) - TACKLE - 1968 DENVER BRONCOS (AFL)
GAITERS, ROBERT (NEW MEXICO STATE) - BACK - 1961-62 NEW YORK GIANTS;
    1962 SAN FRANCISCO 49ERS; 1963 DENVER BRONCOS (AFL)
GALAZIN, STANLEY (VILLANOVA) - CENTER - 1937-39 NEW YORK GIANTS
GALIFFA, ARNOLD (WEST POINT) - QBACK - 1953 NEW YORK GIANTS; 1954 SAN
    FRANCISCO 49ERS
GALIGHER, ED (UCLA) - END, TACKLE - 1972-74 NEW YORK JETS (AFC)
GALIMORE, WILLIE (FLORIDA A&M) - BACK - 1957-63 CHICAGO BEARS
GALLAGHER, ALLEN (USC) - TACKLE - 1974 NEW ENGLAND PATRIOTS (AFC)
GALLAGHER, BERNARD (PENNSYLVANIA) - GUARD - 1947 LOS ANGELES DONS
    (AAFC)
GALLAGHER, DAVE (MICHIGAN) - END - 1974 CHICAGO BEARS (NFC)
GALLAGHER, EDWARD (WASHINGTON&JEFFERSON) - TACKLE - 1928 NEW YORK
    YANKEES
GALLAGHER, FRANK (NORTH CAROLINA) - GUARD - 1967-69 DETROIT LIONS;
    1970-72 DETROIT LIONS (NFC); 1973 ATLANTA FALCONS (NFC); 1973
    MINNESOTA VIKINGS (NFC)
GALLAGHER, WILLIAM (IOWA STATE) - BACK - 1941 NEW YORK AMERICANS (AFL)
GALLARNEAU, HUGH (STANFORD) - BACK - 1941-42, 45-47 CHICAGO BEARS
GALLEGOS, CHON (SAN JOSE STATE) - QBACK - 1962 OAKLAND RAIDERS (AFL)
GALLOVICH, ANTHONY (WAKE FOREST) - BACK - 1941 CLEVELAND RAMS
GALVIN, JOHN (PURDUE) - BACK - 1947 BALTIMORE COLTS (AAFC)
GAMBINO, LUCIEN (MARYLAND) - BACK - 1948-49 BALTIMORE COLTS (AAFC)
GAMBLE, R. C. (SOUTH CAROLINA STATE) - BACK - 1968-69 BOSTON PATRIOTS
    (AFL)
GAMBOLD, ROBERT (WASHINGTON STATE) - BACK - 1953 PHILADELPHIA EAGLES

Top row (from left to right): Carl Etelman, Ray Evans, Andy Farkas, and Dick Farman. **Second row:** Tom Fears, Howie Ferguson, Frank Filchock and Pat Fischer. **Third row:** Ray Flaherty, Len Ford, "Bill" Forester and Joe Fortunato. **Bottom row:** Frank Fuller, Willie Galimore, Hugh Gallarneau and "Hec" Garvey.

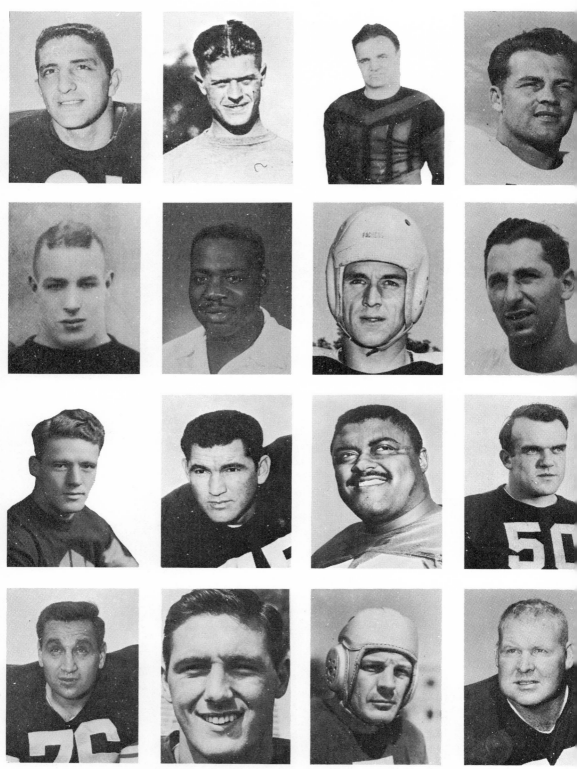

Top row (from left to right): **Bill George, Milton Ghee, Bill Giaver and Frank Gifford.** *Second row:* **Fred Gillies, Horace Gillom, "Jug" Girard and Marshall Goldberg.** *Third row:* **Garland Grange, Forrest Gregg, "Rosey" Grier and John Grigas.** *Bottom row:* **Lou Groza, Ralph Guglielmi, "Ace" Gutowsky and Joel Hanner.**

GAMBRELL, WILLIAM (SOUTH CAROLINA) - END - 1963-67 ST. LOUIS
        CARDINALS; 1968 DETROIT LIONS
GANAPOWSKI, EDWARD (ST. BONAVENTURE) - CENTER - 1937 ROCHESTER TIGERS
        (AFL)
GANAS, RUSTY (SOUTH CAROLINA) - TACKLE - 1971 BALTIMORE COLTS (AFC)
GANDEE, SHERWIN (OHIO STATE) - END - 1952 DALLAS TEXANS; 1952-56
        DETROIT LIONS
GANSBERG, ALFRED (MIAMI-OHIO) - TACKLE - 1926 LOUISVILLE COLONELS
GANT, REUBEN (OKLAHOMA STATE) - END - 1974 BUFFALO BILLS (AFC)
GANTENBEIN, MILTON (WISCONSIN) - END - 1931-40 GREEN BAY PACKERS
GANTT, GREG (ALABAMA) - KICKER - 1974 NEW YORK JETS (AFC)
GANTT, JEROME (NORTH CAROLINA CENTRAL) - TACKLE - 1970 BUFFALO BILLS
        (AFC)
GAONA, ROBERT (WAKE FOREST) - TACKLE - 1953-56 PITTSBURGH STEELERS;
        1957 PHILADELPHIA EAGLES
GARCIA, JAMES (PURDUE) - END - 1965 CLEVELAND BROWNS; 1966 NEW YORK
        GIANTS; 1967 NEW ORLEANS SAINTS; 1968 ATLANTA FALCONS
GARDELLA, AUGUSTUA (HOLY CROSS) - BACK - 1922 GREEN BAY PACKERS
GARDIN, RON (ARIZONA) - BACK, END - 1970-71 BALTIMORE COLTS (AFC);
        1971 NEW ENGLAND PATRIOTS (AFC)
GARDNER, GEORGE (CARLISLE) - END - 1923 CLEVELAND INDIANS
GARDNER, MILTON (WISCONSIN) - GUARD - 1919 DETROIT HERALDS; 1921
        DETROIT PANTHERS; 1921 BUFFALO ALL-AMERICANS; 1922-26 GREEN BAY
        PACKERS; 1924 KENOSHA MAROONS
GARLAND, EDWARD (CATAWBA) - TACKLE - 1936 ROCHESTER TIGERS (AFL)
GARLIN, DONALD (USC) - BACK - 1949 SAN FRANCISCO 49ERS (AAFC); 1950
        SAN FRANCISCO 49ERS
GARLINGTON, JOHN (LSU) - LB - 1968-69 CLEVELAND BROWNS; 1970-74
        CLEVELAND BROWNS (AFC)
GARNAAS, WILFORD (MINNESOTA) - BACK - 1946-48 PITTSBURGH STEELERS
GARNER, ROBERT - GUARD - 1945 NEW YORK GIANTS
GARNER, ROBERT (FRESNO STATE) - BACK - 1960 LOS ANGELES CHARGERS
        (AFL); 1961-63 OAKLAND RAIDERS (AFL)
GARNJOST, DONALD - GUARD - 1921 EVANSVILLE CRIMSON GIANTS
GARRETT, ALFRED (RUTGERS) - END - 1919 MASSILLON TIGERS; 1920 AKRON
        PROS; 1920 CLEVELAND PANTHERS; 1922 MILWAUKEE BADGERS
GARRETT, CARL (NEW MEXICO HIGHLANDS) - BACK - 1969 BOSTON PATRIOTS
        (AFL); 1970 BOSTON PATRIOTS (AFC); 1971-72 NEW ENGLAND PATRIOTS
        (AFC); 1973-74 CHICAGO BEARS (NFC)
GARRETT, DRAKE (MICHIGAN STATE) - BACK - 1968 DENVER BRONCOS (AFL);
        1970 DENVER BRONCOS (AFC)
GARRETT, JOHN (GRAMBLING) - BACK - 1964-67 BOSTON PATRIOTS (AFL)
GARRETT, LEONARD (NEW MEXICO HIGHLANDS) - END - 1971-73 GREEN BAY
        PACKERS (NFC); 1973-74 NEW ORLEANS SAINTS (NFC)
GARRETT, MICHAEL (USC) - BACK - 1966-69 KANSAS CITY CHIEFS (AFL);
        1970 KANSAS CITY CHIEFS (AFC); 1970-73 SAN DIEGO CHARGERS (AFC)
GARRETT, REGINALD (EASTERN MICHIGAN) - BACK - 1974 PITTSBURGH
        STEELERS (AFC)
GARRETT, ROBERT (STANFORD) - QBACK - 1954 GREEN BAY PACKERS
GARRETT, THURMAN (OKLAHOMA A&M) - CENTER - 1947-48 CHICAGO BEARS
GARRETT, WILLIAM (MISSISSIPPI STATE) - GUARD - 1948-49 BALTIMORE
        COLTS (AAFC); 1950 CHICAGO BEARS
GARRISON, GARY (SAN DIEGO STATE) - END - 1966-69 SAN DIEGO CHARGERS
        (AFL); 1970-74 SAN DIEGO CHARGERS (AFC)
GARRISON, WALTER (OKLAHOMA STATE) - BACK - 1966-69 DALLAS COWBOYS;
        1970-74 DALLAS COWBOYS (NFC)
GARRON, LAWRENCE (WESTERN ILLINOIS) - BACK - 1960-68 BOSTON PATRIOTS
        (AFL)
GARROR, LEON (ALCORN A&M) - BACK - 1972-73 BUFFALO BILLS (AFC)
GARTNER, CHRIS (INDIANA) - KICKER - 1974 CLEVELAND BROWNS (AFC)
GARVEY, ARTHUR "HEC" (NOTRE DAME) - TACKLE - 1922-25 CHICAGO BEARS;
        1926 HARTFORD BLUES; 1926 BROOKLYN LIONS; 1926 BROOKLYN HORSEMEN
        (AFL); 1926 NEW YORK YANKEES (AFL); 1927-28 NEW YORK GIANTS;
        1929 PROVIDENCE STEAMROLLERS; 1930 BROOKLYN DODGERS; 1931 STATEN
        ISLAND STAPELTONS
GARVEY, FRANCIS (HOLY CROSS) - END - 1925-26 PROVIDENCE STEAMROLLERS
GARVEY, JAMES (COLGATE) - TACKLE - 1941 CINCINNATI BENGALS (AFL)
GARZA, DANIEL (OREGON) - END - 1949 NEW YORK YANKEES (AAFC); 1951 NEW
        YORK YANKS

GARZONI, MICHAEL (USC) - GUARD - 1947 WASHINGTON REDSKINS; 1948 NEW
     YORK GIANTS; 1948 NEW YORK YANKEES (AAFC)
GASKEEN, HARRY (SYRACUSE) - END - 1919 AKRON PROS
GASPARELLA, JOSEPH (NOTRE DAME) - QBACK - 1948, 50-51 PITTSBURGH
     STEELERS; 1951 CHICAGO CARDINALS
GASTEEN - END - 1919 WHEELING
GASSERT, RONALD (VIRGINIA) - TACKLE - 1962 GREEN BAY PACKERS
GATEWOOD, LESTER (BAYLOR) - CENTER - 1946-47 GREEN BAY PACKERS
GATEWOOD, THOMAS (NOTRE DAME) - END - 1972-73 NEW YORK GIANTS (NFC)
GATSKI, FRANK (MARSHALL) - CENTER - 1946-49 CLEVELAND BROWNS (AAFC);
     1950-56 CLEVELAND BROWNS; 1957 DETROIT LIONS
GAUBATZ, DENNIS (LSU) - LB - 1963-64 DETROIT LIONS; 1965-69 BALTIMORE
     COLTS
GAUDIO, ROBERT (OHIO STATE) - GUARD - 1947-49 CLEVELAND BROWNS
     (AAFC); 1951 CLEVELAND BROWNS
GAUER, CHARLES (COLGATE) - END - 1943 PHIL-PITT; 1944-45 PHILADELPHIA
     EAGLES
GAUL, FRANCIS (NOTRE DAME) - BACK - 1936 CLEVELAND RAMS (AFL)
GAUL, FRANK (NOTRE DAME) - TACKLE - 1949 NEW YORK BULLDOGS
GAULKE, HAROLD - BACK - 1919-22 COLUMBUS PANHANDLES
GAULT, DONALD (HOFSTRA) - QBACK - 1970 CLEVELAND BROWNS (AFC)
GAULT, WILLIAM (TCU) - BACK - 1961 MINNESOTA VIKINGS
GAUSTAD, ARTHUR - GUARD - 1921-23 MINNEAPOLIS MARINES
GAUTT, PRENTICE (OKLAHOMA) - BACK - 1960 CLEVELAND BROWNS; 1961-67
     ST. LOUIS CARDINALS
GAVIGAN, MICHAEL (ST. BONAVENTURE) - BACK - 1923 ROCHESTER JEFFERSONS
GAVIN, CHARLES (TENNESSEE STATE) - END - 1960-63 DENVER BRONCOS (AFL)
GAVIN, FRANCIS (CANISIUS) - END - 1936 ROCHESTER TIGERS (AFL)
GAVIN, FRITZ - END - 1921, 23 GREEN BAY PACKERS
GAVIN, PATRICK "BUCK" - BACK - 1920 BUFFALO ALL-AMERICANS; 1921
     DETROIT PANTHERS; 1921-22, 24-25 ROCK ISLAND INDEPENDENTS; 1922
     BUFFALO ALL-AMERICANS; 1926 HAMMOND PROS
GAVRIC, MOMCILO - KICKER - 1969 SAN FRANCISCO 49ERS
GAY, BLENDA (FAYETTEVILLE STATE) - END - 1974 SAN DIEGO CHARGERS (AFC)
GAY, CHESTER (MINNESOTA) - TACKLE - 1925 BUFFALO BISONS; 1926 RACINE
     LEGION; 1926 MILWAUKEE BADGERS
GAY, WILLIAM (NOTRE DAME) - BACK - 1951-52 CHICAGO CARDINALS
GAYER, WALTER (CREIGHTON) - TACKLE - 1926 DULUTH ESKIMOS
GAZIANO, FRANK (HOLY CROSS) - GUARD - 1944 BOSTON YANKS
GEBHARD, LOUIS (LAFAYETTE) - BACK - 1926 PHILADELPHIA QUAKERS (AFL)
GEDDES, KENNETH (NEBRASKA) - LB - 1971-74 LOS ANGELES RAMS (NFC)
GEDDES, ROBERT (UCLA) - LB - 1972 DENVER BRONCOS (AFC); 1973-74 NEW
     ENGLAND PATRIOTS (AFC)
GEDMAN, EUGENE (INDIANA) - BACK - 1953, 56-58 DETROIT LIONS
GEHRKE, BRUCE (COLUMBIA) - END - 1948 NEW YORK GIANTS
GEHRKE, CLARENCE FRED (UTAH) - BACK - 1940, 45 CLEVELAND RAMS;
     1946-49 LOS ANGELES RAMS; 1950 SAN FRANCISCO 49ERS; 1950 CHICAGO
     CARDINALS
GEHRKE, ERWIN (HARVARD) - BACK - 1926 BOSTON BULLDOGS (AFL)
GEHRKE, JOHN (UTAH) - END - 1968 KANSAS CITY CHIEFS (AFL); 1969
     CINCINNATI BENGALS (AFL); 1971 DENVER BRONCOS (AFC)
GELATKA, CHARLES (MISSISSIPPI STATE) - END - 1937-40 NEW YORK GIANTS
GENT, GEORGE "PETE" (MICHIGAN STATE) - BACK - 1964-68 DALLAS COWBOYS
GENTRY, BYRON (USC) - GUARD - 1937 LOS ANGELES BULLDOGS (AFL);
     1937-38 PITTSBURGH PIRATES; 1939 PITTSBURGH STEELERS
GENTRY, CURTIS (MARYLAND STATE) - BACK - 1966-68 CHICAGO BEARS
GENTRY, DALE (WASHINGTON STATE) - END - 1946-48 LOS ANGELES DONS
     (AAFC)
GENTRY, LEE (TULSA) - BACK - 1941 WASHINGTON REDSKINS
GENTRY, WELDON (OKLAHOMA) - GUARD - 1930-31 PROVIDENCE STEAMROLLERS
GEORGE, KARL (CARROLL) - CENTER - 1922 RACINE LEGION
GEORGE, RAYMOND (USC) - TACKLE - 1939 DETROIT LIONS; 1940
     PHILADELPHIA EAGLES
GEORGE, STEPHEN (HOUSTON) - TACKLE - 1974 ST. LOUIS CARDINALS (NFC)
GEORGE, TIMOTHY (CARSON-NEWMAN) - END - 1973 CINCINNATI BENGALS
     (AFC); 1974 CLEVELAND BROWNS (AFC)
GEORGE, WILLIAM (WAKE FOREST) - LB - 1952-65 CHICAGO BEARS; 1966 LOS
     ANGELES RAMS; 1974 HALL OF FAME
GEPFORD, SIDNEY (MILLIKIN & BETHANY) - BACK - 1920 DECATUR STALEYS
GERBER, ELWOOD (ALABAMA) - GUARD - 1941-42 PHILADELPHIA EAGLES

GERDES, WILLIAM (KEARNEY STATE) - TACKLE - 1940-41 CINCINNATI BENGALS
      (AFL)
GEREDINE, THOMAS (NORTHEAST MISSOURI) - END - 1973-74 ATLANTA FALCONS
      (NFC)
GERELA, ROY (NEW MEXICO STATE) - KICKER - 1969 HOUSTON OILERS (AFL);
      1970 HOUSTON OILERS (AFC); 1971-74 PITTSBURGH STEELERS (AFC);
      1972-74 FIELD GOAL LEADER (AFC); 1973-74 SCORING LEADER (AFC)
GERI, JOSEPH (GEORGIA) - BACK - 1949-51 PITTSBURGH STEELERS; 1952
      CHICAGO CARDINALS
GERMAN, JAMES (CENTRE) - BACK - 1939 WASHINGTON REDSKINS; 1940
      CHICAGO CARDINALS
GERMANY, WILLIE (MORGAN STATE) - BACK - 1972 ATLANTA FALCONS (NFC);
      1973 DETROIT LIONS (NFC)
GERSBACH, CARL (WEST CHESTER STATE) - LB - 1970 PHILADELPHIA EAGLES
      (NFC); 1971-72 MINNESOTA VIKINGS (NFC); 1973-74 SAN DIEGO
      CHARGERS (AFC)
GETCHELL, GORHAM (TEMPLE) - END - 1947 BALTIMORE COLTS (AAFC)
GETTY, CHARLES (PENN STATE) - TACKLE - 1974 KANSAS CITY CHIEFS (AFC)
GETZ, FREDERICK (CHATTANOOGA) - END - 1930 BROOKLYN DODGERS
GEYER, DONALD (NORTHWESTERN) - BACK - 1937 CINCINNATI BENGALS (AFL)
GEYER, WILLIAM (COLGATE) - BACK - 1942-43, 46 CHICAGO BEARS
GHECAS, LOUIS (GEORGETOWN) - BACK - 1941 PHILADELPHIA EAGLES
GHEE, MILTON (DARTMOUTH) - QBACK - 1919, 22-23 HAMMOND PROS; 1920
      CHICAGO TIGERS; 1920 CLEVELAND PANTHERS; 1921 CLEVELAND INDIANS
GHERSANICH, VERNON (AUBURN) - GUARD - 1943 CHICAGO CARDINALS
GIANCANELLI, HAROLD (LOYOLA OF CAL.) - BACK - 1953-56 PHILADELPHIA
      EAGLES
GIANNELII, MARIO (BOSTON COLLEGE) - GUARD - 1948-51 PHILADELPHIA
      EAGLES
GIANNONI, JOHN (ST. MARY'S OF CAL.) - END - 1938 CLEVELAND RAMS
GIAVER, EINAR "BILL" (GEORGIA TECH) - BACK - 1922, 25 HAMMOND PROS;
      1923 ROCK ISLAND INDEPENDENTS; 1924 RACINE LEGION; 1926
      LOUISVILLE COLONELS; 1926 CHICAGO BULLS (AFL)
GIBBONS, AUSTIN (DEPAUL) - CENTER - 1929 CHICAGO CARDINALS
GIBBONS, JAMES (IOWA) - END - 1958-68 DETROIT LIONS
GIBBS, DONNIE (TCU) - KICKER - 1974 NEW ORLEANS SAINTS (NFC)
GIBBS, GUY (TCU) - QBACK - 1963 DALLAS COWBOYS; 1964 DETROIT LIONS
GIBBS, PATRICK (LAMAR) - BACK - 1972 PHILADELPHIA EAGLES (NFC)
GIBRON, ABRAHAM (PURDUE) - GUARD - 1949 BUFFALO BILLS (AAFC); 1950-56
      CLEVELAND BROWNS; 1956-57 PHILADELPHIA EAGLES; 1958-59 CHICAGO
      BEARS
GIBSON, BILLY JOE (TULSA) - BACK - 1942, 44 CLEVELAND RAMS; 1943
      WASHINGTON REDSKINS; 1946-47 BROOKLYN DODGERS (AAFC)
GIBSON, CLAUDE (NORTH CAROLINA STATE) - BACK - 1961-62 SAN DIEGO
      CHARGERS (AFL); 1963-65 OAKLAND RAIDERS (AFL)
GIBSON, DENVER (GROVE CITY) - GUARD - 1930 NEWARK TORNADOS; 1930-34
      NEW YORK GIANTS
GIBSON, GEORGE (MINNESOTA) - GUARD - 1930 FRANKFORD YELLOWJACKETS;
      1930 MINNEAPOLIS REDJACKETS
GIBSON, PAUL (NORTH CAROLINA STATE) - END - 1947-49 BUFFALO BILLS
      (AAFC)
GIBSON, PAUL (TEXAS-EL PASO) - BACK - 1972 GREEN BAY PACKERS (NFC)
GIBSON, RICHARD (CENTRE) - GUARD - 1922-23 LOUISVILLE BRECKS
GIDDENS, HERSCHEL (LOUISIANA TECH) - TACKLE - 1938 PHILADELPHIA
      EAGLES; 1944 BOSTON YANKS
GIFFORD, FRANCIS (USC) - BACK - 1952-60, 62-64 NEW YORK GIANTS
GIFFORD, ROBERT (DENVER) - BACK - 1942 BROOKLYN DODGERS
GIFT, L. WAYNE (PURDUE) - BACK - 1937 CLEVELAND RAMS
GILBERT, HOMER (ALBRIGHT) - TACKLE - 1936 PITTSBURGH AMERICANS (AFL)
GILBERT, KLINE (MISSISSIPPI) - TACKLE - 1953-57 CHICAGO BEARS
GILBERT, STEVEN (ST. BONAVENTURE) - END - 1940 BUFFALO INDIANS (AFL)
GILBERT, WALTER (VALPARAISO) - BACK - 1923-25 DULUTH KELLEYS; 1926-27
      DULUTH ESKIMOS
GILBURG, THOMAS (SYRACUSE) - TACKLE - 1961-65 BALTIMORE COLTS
GILCHRIST, CARLTON "COOKIE" - BACK - 1962-64 BUFFALO BILLS (AFL);
      1965, 67 DENVER BRONCOS (AFL); 1966 MIAMI DOLPHINS (AFL); 1962,
      64 RUSHING LEADER (AFL)
GILCHRIST, GEORGE (TENNESSEE STATE) - TACKLE - 1953 CHICAGO CARDINALS
GILDEA, DENNIS (HOLY CROSS) - CENTER - 1926 HARTFORD BLUES

GILDEA, JOHN (ST. BONAVENTURE) - QBACK - 1935-37 PITTSBURGH PIRATES;
       1938 NEW YORK GIANTS
GILL, ROGER (TEXAS TECH) - BACK - 1964-65 PHILADELPHIA EAGLES
GILL, SLOKO (YOUNGSTOWN) - GUARD - 1942 DETROIT LIONS
GILLETT, FREDERICK (LOS ANGELES STATE) - LB - 1962 SAN DIEGO CHARGERS
       (AFL); 1964 OAKLAND RAIDERS (AFL)
GILLETTE, JAMES (VIRGINIA) - BACK - 1940, 44-45 CLEVELAND RAMS; 1946
       BOSTON YANKS; 1947 WASHINGTON REDSKINS; 1947 GREEN BAY PACKERS;
       1948 DETROIT LIONS
GILLETTE, WALKER (RICHMOND) - END - 1970-71 SAN DIEGO CHARGERS (AFC);
       1972-73 ST. LOUIS CARDINALS (NFC); 1974 NEW YORK GIANTS (NFC)
GILLETTE - BACK - 1919 AKRON PROS
GILLIAM, JOHN RALLY (SOUTH CAROLINA STATE) - END - 1967-68 NEW
       ORLEANS SAINTS; 1969 ST. LOUIS CARDINALS; 1970-71 ST. LOUIS
       CARDINALS (NFC); 1972-74 MINNESOTA VIKINGS (NFC)
GILLIAM, JON (EAST TEXAS STATE) - CENTER - 1961-62 DALLAS TEXANS
       (AFL); 1963-67 KANSAS CITY CHIEFS (AFL)
GILLIAM, JOSEPH (TENNESSEE STATE) - QBACK - 1972-74 PITTSBURGH
       STEELERS (AFC)
GILLIES, FREDERICK (CORNELL) - TACKLE - 1920-28 CHICAGO CARDINALS
GILLINGHAM, GALE (MINNESOTA) - GUARD - 1966-69 GREEN BAY PACKERS;
       1970-74 GREEN BAY PACKERS (NFC)
GILLIS, DONALD (RICE) - CENTER - 1958-59 CHICAGO CARDINALS; 1960-61
       ST. LOUIS CARDINALS
GILLIS, JOSEPH (DETROIT) - TACKLE - 1923 TOLEDO MAROONS
GILLMAN, SIDNEY (OHIO STATE) - END - 1936 CLEVELAND RAMS (AFL)
GILLO, HENRY (COLGATE) - BACK - 1920 BUFFALO ALL-AMERICANS; 1920-21
       HAMMOND PROS; 1922-24, 26 RACINE LEGION; 1925 MILWAUKEE BADGERS
GILLOM, HORACE (NEVADA) - END - 1947-49 CLEVELAND BROWNS (AAFC);
       1950-56 CLEVELAND BROWNS; 1951-52 PUNTING LEADER
GILLSON, ROBERT (COLGATE) - GUARD - 1930-31 BROOKLYN DODGERS
GILMER, HARRY (ALABAMA) - QBACK - 1948-52, 54 WASHINGTON REDSKINS;
       1955-56 DETROIT LIONS
GILROY, JOHN (GEORGETOWN) - BACK - 1920 CANTON BULLDOGS; 1920
       CLEVELAND PANTHERS; 1926 BOSTON BULLDOGS (AFL)
GILFOY, RALPH (PRINCETON) - BACK - 1926 BOSTON BULLDOGS (AFL)
GINN, HUBERT (FLORIDA A&M) - BACK - 1970-74 MIAMI DOLPHINS (AFC);
       1973 BALTIMORE COLTS (AFC)
GINNEY, JERRY (SANTA CLARA) - GUARD - 1940 PHILADELPHIA EAGLES
GINSBERG, ISRAEL (SOUTH DAKOTA STATE) - END - 1936 ROCHESTER TIGERS
       (AFL)
GIPSON, PAUL (HOUSTON) - BACK - 1969 ATLANTA FALCONS; 1970 ATLANTA
       FALCONS (NFC); 1971 DETROIT LIONS (NFC); 1973 NEW ENGLAND
       PATRIOTS (AFC)
GIPSON, THOMAS (TEXAS-EL PASO) - TACKLE - 1971 OAKLAND RAIDERS (AFC)
GIRARD, EARL "JUG" (WISCONSIN) - BACK - 1948-51 GREEN BAY PACKERS;
       1952-56 DETROIT LIONS; 1957 PITTSBURGH STEELERS
GLACKEN, EDWARD SCOTT (DUKE) - QBACK - 1966-67 DENVER BRONCOS (AFL)
GLADCHUK, CHESTER (BOSTON COLLEGE) - CENTER - 1941, 46-47 NEW YORK
       GIANTS
GLADDEN, JAMES MACK (MISSOURI) - END - 1934 ST. LOUIS GUNNERS; 1936
       BROOKLYN TIGERS (AFL)
GLADIEUX, ROBERT (NOTRE DAME) - BACK - 1969 BOSTON PATRIOTS (AFL);
       1970 BOSTON PATRIOTS (AFC); 1970 BUFFALO BILLS (AFC); 1971-72
       NEW ENGLAND PATRIOTS (AFC)
GLADSTONE - GUARD - 1922 EVANSVILLE CRIMSON GIANTS
GLAMP, JOSEPH (LSU) - BACK - 1947-49 PITTSBURGH STEELERS
GLASS, CHARLES "CHIP" (FLORIDA STATE) - END - 1969 CLEVELAND BROWNS;
       1970-73 CLEVELAND BROWNS (AFC); 1974 NEW YORK GIANTS (NFC)
GLASS, GLENN (TENNESSEE) - BACK - 1962-63 PITTSBURGH STEELERS;
       1964-65 PHILADELPHIA EAGLES; 1966 ATLANTA FALCONS; 1966 DENVER
       BRONCOS (AFL)
GLASS, LELAND (OREGON) - END - 1972-73 GREEN BAY PACKERS (NFC)
GLASS, WILLIAM (BAYLOR) - END - 1958-61 DETROIT LIONS; 1962-68
       CLEVELAND BROWNS
GLASSFORD, J. WILLIAM (PITTSBURGH) - GUARD - 1937 CINCINNATI BENGALS
       (AFL)
GLASSGOW, WILLIS (IOWA) - BACK - 1930 PORTSMOUTH SPARTANS; 1931
       CHICAGO CARDINALS
GLASSMAN, FRANK (WILMINGTON) - GUARD - 1929 BUFFALO BISONS
GLASSMAN, MORRIS - END - 1921-22 COLUMBUS PANHANDLES

GLATZ, FRED (PITTSBURGH) - END - 1956 PITTSBURGH STEELERS
GLENN, HOWARD (LINFIELD) - GUARD - 1960 NEW YORK TITANS (AFL)
GLENN, WILLIAM (EASTERN ILLINOIS) - BACK - 1944 CHICAGO BEARS
GLENNIE, GEORGE (COLGATE) - GUARD - 1926 RACINE LEGION
GLICK, EDWARD - BACK - 1921-22 GREEN BAY PACKERS
GLICK, FREDERICK (COLORADO STATE) - BACK - 1959 CHICAGO CARDINALS;
    1960 ST. LOUIS CARDINALS; 1961-66 HOUSTON OILERS (AFL); 1963
    INTERCEPTION LEADER (AFL)
GLICK, GARY (COLORADO A&M) - BACK - 1956-59 PITTSBURGH STEELERS;
    1959-61 WASHINGTON REDSKINS; 1961 BALTIMORE COLTS; 1963 SAN
    DIEGO CHARGERS (AFL)
GLODEN, FREDERICK (TULANE) - BACK - 1941 PHILADELPHIA EAGLES; 1946
    MIAMI SEAHAWKS (AAFC)
GLOSSON, CLYDE (TEXAS-EL PASO) - END - 1970 BUFFALO BILLS (AFC)
GLOVER, RICHARD (NEBRASKA) - TACKLE - 1973 NEW YORK GIANTS (NFC)
GLUECK, LAWRENCE (VILLANOVA) - BACK - 1963-65 CHICAGO BEARS
GOAD, PAUL (ABILENE CHRISTIAN) - BACK - 1956 SAN FRANCISCO 49ERS
GOB, ARTHUR (PITTSBURGH) - END - 1959-60 WASHINGTON REDSKINS; 1960
    LOS ANGELES CHARGERS (AFL)
GOBLE, LESTER (ALFRED) - BACK - 1954-55 CHICAGO CARDINALS
GODDARD, EDWIN (WASHINGTON STATE) - QBACK - 1937 BROOKLYN DODGERS;
    1937-38 CLEVELAND RAMS
GODFREY, HERBERT (WASHINGTON STATE) - END - 1942 CLEVELAND RAMS
GODWIN, WALTER (GEORGIA TECH) - GUARD - 1929 STATEN ISLAND STAPELTONS
GODWIN, WILLIAM (GEORGIA) - CENTER - 1947-48 BOSTON YANKS
GOEBEL, PAUL (MICHIGAN) - END - 1923-25 COLUMBUS TIGERS; 1926 NEW
    YORK YANKEES (AFL)
GOEDDEKE, GEORGE (NOTRE DAME) - GUARD, CENTER - 1967-69 DENVER
    BRONCOS (AFL); 1970-72 DENVER BRONCOS (AFC)
GOETZ, ANGUS (MICHIGAN) - TACKLE - 1920, 22 BUFFALO ALL-AMERICANS;
    1923 COLUMBUS TIGERS; 1926 NEW YORK YANKEES (AFL)
GOFF, CLARK (FLORIDA) - TACKLE - 1940 PITTSBURGH STEELERS
GOGOLAK, CHARLES (PRINCETON) - KICKER - 1966-68 WASHINGTON REDSKINS;
    1970 BOSTON PATRIOTS (AFC); 1971-72 NEW ENGLAND PATRIOTS (AFC)
GOGOLAK, PETER (CORNELL) - KICKER - 1964-65 BUFFALO BILLS (AFL);
    1966-69 NEW YORK GIANTS; 1970-74 NEW YORK GIANTS (NFC); 1965
    FIELD GOAL LEADER (AFL)
GOICH, DANIEL (CALIFORNIA) - TACKLE - 1969 DETROIT LIONS; 1970
    DETROIT LIONS (NFC); 1971 NEW ORLEANS SAINTS (NFC); 1972-73 NEW
    YORK GIANTS (NFC); 1974 DENVER BRONCOS (AFC)
GOLDBERG, MARSHALL (PITTSBURGH) - BACK - 1939-43, 46-48 CHICAGO
    CARDINALS; 1941 INTERCEPTION LEADER; (TIED WITH A. JONES)
GOLDENBERG, CHARLES (WISCONSIN) - GUARD - 1933-45 GREEN BAY PACKERS
GOLDFEIN, JERSEY (SUPERIOR STATE-WISCONSIN) - BACK - 1927 DULUTH
    ESKIMOS
GOLDING, JOSEPH (OKLAHOMA) - BACK - 1947-48 BOSTON YANKS; 1949 NEW
    YORK BULLDOGS; 1950-51 NEW YORK YANKS
GOLDMAN, SAMUEL (HOWARD) - END - 1944, 46-47 BOSTON YANKS; 1948
    CHICAGO CARDINALS; 1949 DETROIT LIONS
GOLDSBERRY, JOHN (INDIANA) - TACKLE - 1949-50 CHICAGO CARDINALS
GOLDSMITH - END - 1921-22 EVANSVILLE CRIMSON GIANTS
GOLDSMITH, WENDELL (EMPORIA STATE-KANSAS) - CENTER - 1940 NEW YORK
    GIANTS
GOLDSTEIN, ALAN (NORTH CAROLINA) - END - 1960 OAKLAND RAIDERS (AFL)
GOLDSTEIN, ISRAEL (FLORIDA) - GUARD - 1926 NEWARK BEARS (AFL)
GOLDSTON, RALPH (YOUNGSTOWN) - BACK - 1952, 54-55 PHILADELPHIA EAGLES
GOLEMBESKI, ANTHONY (HOLY CROSS) - END - 1925-26, 29 PROVIDENCE
    STEAMROLLERS
GOLEMGESKE, JOHN (WISCONSIN) - TACKLE - 1937-40 BROOKLYN DODGERS
GOLOMB, RUDOLPH (CARROLL) - GUARD - 1936 PHILADELPHIA EAGLES
GOLSEN, EUGENE (GEORGETOWN) - BACK - 1926 LOUISVILLE COLONELS
GOLSEN, THOMAS (GEORGETOWN) - GUARD - 1926 LOUISVILLE COLONELS
GOMPERS, WILLIAM (NOTRE DAME) - BACK - 1948 BUFFALO BILLS (AAFC)
GONDA, GEORGE (DUQUESNE) - BACK - 1942 PITTSBURGH STEELERS
GONSOULIN, AUSTIN "GOOSE" (BAYLOR) - BACK - 1960-66 DENVER BRONCOS
    (AFL); 1967 SAN FRANCISCO 49ERS; 1960 INTERCEPTION LEADER (AFL)
GONYA, ROBERT (NORTHWESTERN) - TACKLE - 1933-34 PHILADELPHIA EAGLES
GONZAGA, JOHN - TACKLE - 1956-59 SAN FRANCISCO 49ERS; 1960 DALLAS
    COWBOYS; 1961-65 DETROIT LIONS; 1966 DENVER BRONCOS (AFL)

GONZALEZ, NOE (SOUTHWEST TEXAS STATE) - BACK - 1974 NEW ENGLAND
    PATRIOTS (AFC)
GOOD, THOMAS (MARSHALL) - LB - 1966 SAN DIEGO CHARGERS (AFL)
GOODBREAD, ROYCE (FLORIDA) - BACK - 1930 FRANKFORD YELLOWJACKETS;
    1930 MINNEAPOLIS REDJACKETS; 1931 PROVIDENCE STEAMROLLERS
GOODE, DONALD (KANSAS) - LB - 1974 SAN DIEGO CHARGERS (AFC)
GOODE, IRVIN (KENTUCKY) - GUARD, CENTER - 1962-69 ST. LOUIS
    CARDINALS; 1970-71 ST. LOUIS CARDINALS (NFC); 1973-74 MIAMI
    DOLPHINS (AFC)
GOODE, ROBERT (TEXAS A&M) - BACK - 1949-51, 54-55 WASHINGTON
    REDSKINS; 1955 PHILADELPHIA EAGLES
GOODE, THOMAS (MISSISSIPPI) - LB, CENTER - 1962-65 HOUSTON OILERS
    (AFL); 1966-69 MIAMI DOLPHINS (AFL); 1970 BALTIMORE COLTS (AFC)
GOODMAN, AUBREY (CHICAGO) - TACKLE - 1926 CHICAGO BULLS (AFL); 1927
    CHICAGO CARDINALS
GOODMAN, BRIAN (UCLA) - GUARD - 1973-74 HOUSTON OILERS (AFC)
GOODMAN, HENRY (WEST VIRGINIA) - TACKLE - 1942 DETROIT LIONS
GOODMAN, LESLIE (YANKTON-SOUTH DAKOTA) - BACK - 1973-74 GREEN BAY
    PACKERS (NFC)
GOODMAN, ROBERT (DUQUESNE) - GUARD - 1940 NEW YORK AMERICANS (AFL)
GOODNIGHT, CLYDE (TULSA) - END - 1945-48 GREEN BAY PACKERS; 1949-50
    WASHINGTON REDSKINS
GOODNIGHT, OWEN (HARDIN-SIMMONS) - BACK - 1941 CLEVELAND RAMS
GOODRIDGE, ROBERT (VANDERBILT) - END - 1968 MINNESOTA VIKINGS
GOODRUM, CHARLES LEO (FLORIDA A&M) - TACKLE, GUARD - 1973-74
    MINNESOTA VIKINGS (NFC)
GOODWIN, CHARLES "TOD" (WEST VIRGINIA) - END - 1935-36 NEW YORK
    GIANTS; 1935 PASS RECEIVING LEADER
GOODWIN, DOUGLAS (MARYLAND STATE) - BACK - 1966 BUFFALO BILLS (AFL);
    1968 ATLANTA FALCONS
GOODWIN, EARL (BUCKNELL) - END - 1928 POTTSVILLE MAROONS
GOODWIN, MYRL (BUCKNELL) - BACK - 1928 POTTSVILLE MAROONS
GOODWIN, RONALD (BAYLOR) - END - 1963-68 PHILADELPHIA EAGLES
GOODYEAR, JOHN (MARQUETTE) - BACK - 1942 WASHINGTON REDSKINS
GOOLSBY, JAMES (MISSISSIPPI STATE) - CENTER - 1940 CLEVELAND RAMS
GOOSBY, THOMAS (BALDWIN-WALLACE) - GUARD - 1963 CLEVELAND BROWNS;
    1966 WASHINGTON REDSKINS
GOOVERT, RONALD (MICHIGAN STATE) - LB - 1967 DETROIT LIONS
GORDON, CORNELL (NORTH CAROLINA A&T) - BACK - 1965-69 NEW YORK JETS
    (AFL); 1970-72 DENVER BRONCOS (AFC)
GORDON, IRA (KANSAS STATE) - GUARD, TACKLE - 1970-74 SAN DIEGO
    CHARGERS (AFC)
GORDON, JOHN (HAWAII) - TACKLE - 1972 DETROIT LIONS (NFC)
GORDON, LOUIS (ILLINOIS) - TACKLE - 1930-31 CHICAGO CARDINALS; 1931
    BROOKLYN DODGERS; 1932-35 CHICAGO CARDINALS; 1936-37 GREEN BAY
    PACKERS; 1938 CHICAGO BEARS
GORDON, RALPH - BACK - 1919 CLEVELAND INDIANS; 1920 CLEVELAND PANTHERS
GORDON, RICHARD (MICHIGAN STATE) - END - 1965-69 CHICAGO BEARS;
    1970-71 CHICAGO BEARS (NFC); 1972-73 LOS ANGELES RAMS (NFC);
    1973 GREEN BAY PACKERS (NFC); 1974 SAN DIEGO CHARGERS (AFC);
    1970 PASS RECEIVING LEADER (NFC)
GORDON, ROBERT (TENNESSEE) - BACK - 1958 CHICAGO CARDINALS; 1960
    HOUSTON OILERS (AFL)
GORDY, JOHN (TENNESSEE) - TACKLE - 1957, 59-67 DETROIT LIONS
GORE, GORDON (SOUTHWEST OKLAHOMA STATE) - BACK - 1937 LOS ANGELES
    BULLDOGS (AFL); 1939 DETROIT LIONS
GORGAL, ALEX - BACK - 1923 ROCK ISLAND INDEPENDENTS
GORGAL, KENNETH (PURDUE) - BACK - 1950, 53-54 CLEVELAND BROWNS;
    1955-56 CHICAGO BEARS; 1956 GREEN BAY PACKERS
GORGONE, PETER (MUHLENBERG) - BACK - 1946 NEW YORK GIANTS
GORINSKI, WALTER (LSU) - BACK - 1946 PITTSBURGH STEELERS
GORMAN, EARL - GUARD - 1921-22 EVANSVILLE CRIMSON GIANTS; 1922-23
    RACINE LEGION; 1924 KENOSHA MAROONS
GORMLEY, THOMAS (GEORGETOWN) - TACKLE - 1919-20 CANTON BULLDOGS; 1920
    BUFFALO ALL-AMERICANS; 1920 CLEVELAND PANTHERS
GORRILL, CHARLES (OHIO STATE) - END - 1926 COLUMBUS TIGERS
GOSS, DONALD (SMU) - TACKLE - 1956 CLEVELAND BROWNS
GOSSAGE, EZRA EUGENE (NORTHWESTERN) - TACKLE - 1960-62 PHILADELPHIA
    EAGLES

GOSSETT, DANIEL BRUCE (RICHMOND) - KICKER - 1964-69 LOS ANGELES RAMS;
      1970-74 SAN FRANCISCO 49ERS (NFC); 1966 SCORING LEADER; 1966
      FIELD GOAL LEADER
GOTSHALK, LEONARD (HUMBOLDT STATE) - TACKLE, GUARD - 1972-74 ATLANTA
      FALCONS (NFC)
GOTTLIEB, ARTHUR (RUTGERS) - BACK - 1940 BUFFALO INDIANS (AFL)
GOUGLER, ROSCOE (PITTSBURGH) - BACK - 1919 MASSILLON TIGERS
GOULD, GEORGE (MINNESOTA) - BACK - 1940 MILWAUKEE CHIEFS (AFL)
GOVERNALI, PAUL (COLUMBIA) - QBACK - 1946-47 BOSTON YANKS; 1947-48
      NEW YORK GIANTS
GOZDOWSKI, CASIMIR - BACK - 1922 TOLEDO MAROONS
GRABFELDER, EARL (KENTUCKY) - BACK - 1923 LOUISVILLE BRECKS
GRABINSKI, THADDEUS (DUQUESNE) - CENTER - 1939-40 PITTSBURGH STEELERS
GRABOSKY, EUGENE (SYRACUSE) - TACKLE - 1960 BUFFALO BILLS (AFL)
GRABOWSKI, JAMES (ILLINOIS) - BACK - 1966-69 GREEN BAY PACKERS; 1970
      GREEN BAY PACKERS (NFC); 1971 CHICAGO BEARS (NFC)
GRACE, LESLIE (TEMPLE) - END - 1930 NEWARK TORNADOS
GRADISHAR, RANDY (OHIO STATE) - LB - 1974 DENVER BRONCOS (AFC)
GRADY, GARRY (EASTERN MICHIGAN) - BACK - 1969 MIAMI DOLPHINS (AFL)
GRAFF, NEIL (WISCONSIN) - QBACK - 1974 NEW ENGLAND PATRIOTS (AFC)
GRAHAM, ALFRED - GUARD - 1925-29 DAYTON TRIANGLES; 1930 PORTSMOUTH
      SPARTANS; 1930-31 PROVIDENCE STEAMROLLERS; 1932-33 CHICAGO
      CARDINALS
GRAHAM, ARTHUR (BOSTON COLLEGE) - END - 1963-68 BOSTON PATRIOTS (AFL)
GRAHAM, CLARENCE - BACK - 1928 DAYTON TRIANGLES
GRAHAM, DAVID (VIRGINIA) - TACKLE - 1963-66, 68-69 PHILADELPHIA EAGLES
GRAHAM, FREDERICK (WEST VIRGINIA) - END - 1926 FRANKFORD
      YELLOWJACKETS; 1926 CHICAGO BULLS (AFL)
GRAHAM, JAMES "KENNY" (WASHINGTON STATE) - BACK - 1964-69 SAN DIEGO
      CHARGERS (AFL); 1970 CINCINNATI BENGALS (AFC); 1970 PITTSBURGH
      STEELERS (AFC)
GRAHAM, LESTER (TULSA) - GUARD - 1938 DETROIT LIONS
GRAHAM, MICHAEL (CINCINNATI) - BACK - 1948 LOS ANGELES DONS (AAFC)
GRAHAM, MILTON (COLGATE) - TACKLE - 1961-63 BOSTON PATRIOTS (AFL)
GRAHAM, OTTO (NORTHWESTERN) - QBACK - 1946-49 CLEVELAND BROWNS
      (AAFC); 1950-55 CLEVELAND BROWNS; 1953, 55 PASSING LEADER; 1965
      HALL OF FAME
GRAHAM, S. LYLE (RICHMOND) - CENTER - 1941 PHILADELPHIA EAGLES
GRAHAM, SAMUEL (WASHINGTON&LEE) - TACKLE - 1919 CLEVELAND INDIANS
GRAHAM, THOMAS (OREGON) - LB - 1972-74 DENVER BRONCOS (AFC); 1974
      KANSAS CITY CHIEFS (AFC)
GRAHAM, THOMAS (TEMPLE) - GUARD - 1935 PHILADELPHIA EAGLES
GRAIN, EDWIN (PENNSYLVANIA) - GUARD - 1947 NEW YORK YANKEES (AAFC);
      1947-48 BALTIMORE COLTS (AAFC)
GRANDBERRY, KEN (WASHINGTON STATE) - BACK - 1974 CHICAGO BEARS (NFC)
GRANDELIUS, EVERETT (MICHIGAN STATE) - BACK - 1953 NEW YORK GIANTS
GRANDERSON, RUFUS (PRAIRIE VIEW) - TACKLE - 1960 DALLAS TEXANS (AFL)
GRANDINETTE, GEORGE (FORDHAM) - GUARD - 1943 BROOKLYN DODGERS
GRANGE, GARLAND (ILLINOIS) - END - 1929-31 CHICAGO BEARS
GRANGE, HAROLD "RED" (ILLINOIS) - BACK - 1925, 29-34 CHICAGO BEARS;
      1926 NEW YORK YANKEES (AFL); 1927 NEW YORK YANKEES; 1963 HALL OF
      FAME
GRANGER, CHARLES (SOUTHERN UNIV.) - TACKLE - 1961 DALLAS COWBOYS;
      1961 ST. LOUIS CARDINALS
GRANGER, HOYLE (MISSISSIPPI STATE) - BACK - 1966-69 HOUSTON OILERS
      (AFL); 1970, 72 HOUSTON OILERS (AFC); 1971 NEW ORLEANS SAINTS
      (NFC)
GRANNELL, DAVID (ARIZONA STATE) - END - 1974 SAN DIEGO CHARGERS (AFC)
GRANT, AARON (CHATTANOOGA) - CENTER - 1930 PORTSMOUTH SPARTANS
GRANT, FRANK (SOUTH COLORADO STATE) - END - 1973-74 WASHINGTON
      REDSKINS (NFC)
GRANT, HARRY (MINNESOTA) - END - 1951-52 PHILADELPHIA EAGLES
GRANT, HUGH (ST. MARY'S OF CAL.) - BACK - 1928 CHICAGO CARDINALS
GRANT, JOHN (USC) - TACKLE, END - 1973-74 DENVER BRONCOS (AFC)
GRANT, LEONARD (NEW YORK UNIV.) - TACKLE - 1930-37 NEW YORK GIANTS
GRANT, ROBERT (WAKE FOREST) - LB - 1968-69 BALTIMORE COLTS; 1970
      BALTIMORE COLTS (AFC); 1971 WASHINGTON REDSKINS (NFC)
GRANT, ROSS (NEW YORK UNIV.) - GUARD - 1932 STATEN ISLAND STAPELTONS;
      1933-34 CINCINNATI REDS

GRANT, WESLEY (UCLA) - END, TACKLE - 1971 BUFFALO BILLS (AFC); 1971
    SAN DIEGO CHARGERS (AFC); 1972 CLEVELAND BROWNS (AFC); 1973
    HOUSTON OILERS (AFC)
GRANTHAM, JAMES LARRY (MISSISSIPPI) - LB - 1960-62 NEW YORK TITANS
    (AFL); 1963-69 NEW YORK JETS (AFL); 1970-72 NEW YORK JETS (AFC)
GRATE, CARL (GEORGIA) - GUARD - 1945 NEW YORK GIANTS
GRATE, WILLIE (SOUTH CAROLINA STATE) - END - 1969 BUFFALO BILLS
    (AFL); 1970 BUFFALO BILLS (AFC)
GRAVELLE, GORDON (BRIGHAM YOUNG) - TACKLE - 1972-74 PITTSBURGH
    STEELERS (AFC)
GRAVES, RAYMOND (TENNESSEE) - CENTER - 1942, 46 PHILADELPHIA EAGLES;
    1943 PHIL-PITT
GRAVES, WHITE (LSU) - BACK - 1965-67 BOSTON PATRIOTS (AFL); 1968
    CINCINNATI BENGALS (AFL)
GRAY, D. - END - 1923 GREEN BAY PACKERS; 1923 ST. LOUIS BROWNS
GRAY, JAMES (TOLEDO) - BACK - 1966 NEW YORK JETS (AFL); 1967
    PHILADELPHIA EAGLES
GRAY, KENNETH (HOWARD PAYNE) - GUARD - 1958-59 CHICAGO CARDINALS;
    1960-69 ST. LOUIS CARDINALS; 1970 HOUSTON OILERS (AFC)
GRAY, LEON (JACKSON STATE) - TACKLE - 1973-74 NEW ENGLAND PATRIOTS
    (AFC)
GRAY, MELVIN (MISSOURI) - END - 1971-74 ST. LOUIS CARDINALS (NFC)
GRAY, MOSES (INDIANA) - TACKLE - 1961-62 NEW YORK TITANS (AFL)
GRAY, SAMUEL (TULSA) - END - 1946-47 PITTSBURGH STEELERS
GRAY, WILLIAM (OREGON STATE) - GUARD - 1947-48 WASHINGTON REDSKINS
GRAY HORSE - BACK - 1923 OORANG INDIANS
GRAYSON, DAVID (OREGON) - BACK - 1961-62 DALLAS TEXANS (AFL); 1963-64
    KANSAS CITY CHIEFS (AFL); 1965-69 OAKLAND RAIDERS (AFL); 1970
    OAKLAND RAIDERS (AFC); 1968 INTERCEPTION LEADER (AFL)
GREAVES, GARY (MIAMI-FLORIDA) - GUARD - 1960 HOUSTON OILERS (AFL)
GRECNI, RICHARD (OHIO) - LB - 1961 MINNESOTA VIKINGS
GREEN, ALLEN (MISSISSIPPI) - KICKER - 1961 DALLAS COWBOYS
GREEN, ARTHUR (ALBANY STATE) - BACK - 1972 NEW ORLEANS SAINTS (NFC)
GREEN, CHARLES (WITTENBERG) - QBACK - 1966 OAKLAND RAIDERS (AFL)
GREEN, CORNELL (UTAH STATE) - BACK - 1962-69 DALLAS COWBOYS; 1970-74
    DALLAS COWBOYS (NFC)
GREEN, DAVID (OHIO) - KICKER - 1973 HOUSTON OILERS (AFC); 1973-74
    CINCINNATI BENGALS (AFC)
GREEN, DONALD (PURDUE) - TACKLE - 1971-74 BUFFALO BILLS (AFC)
GREEN, ERNEST (LOUISVILLE) - BACK - 1962-68 CLEVELAND BROWNS
GREEN, J. B. H. - TACKLE - 1926 LOUISVILLE COLONELS
GREEN, JEROME (GEORGIA TECH) - END - 1960 BOSTON PATRIOTS (AFL)
GREEN, JOE (BOWLING GREEN) - BACK - 1970-71 NEW YORK GIANTS (NFC)
GREEN, JOHN (CHATTANOOGA) - QBACK - 1960-61 BUFFALO BILLS (AFL); 1962
    NEW YORK TITANS (AFL); 1963 NEW YORK JETS (AFL)
GREEN, JOHN (TULSA) - END - 1947-51 PHILADELPHIA EAGLES
GREEN, LAWRENCE (GEORGETOWN) - END - 1920 CANTON BULLDOGS
GREEN, NELSON (TULSA) - TACKLE - 1948 NEW YORK YANKEES (AAFC)
GREEN, ROBERT "BOBBY JOE" (FLORIDA) - LB - 1960-61 PITTSBURGH
    STEELERS; 1963-69 CHICAGO BEARS; 1970-73 CHICAGO BEARS (NFC)
GREEN, RONALD (NORTH DAKOTA) - BACK - 1967 CLEVELAND BROWNS
GREEN, VAN (SHAW) - BACK - 1973-74 CLEVELAND BROWNS (AFC)
GREEN, WOODROW (ARIZONA STATE) - BACK - 1974 KANSAS CITY CHIEFS (AFC)
GREENBERG, BENJAMIN (RUTGERS) - BACK - 1930 BROOKLYN DODGERS
GREENE, ANTHONY (MARYLAND) - BACK - 1971-74 BUFFALO BILLS (AFC)
GREENE, EDWARD (LOYOLA OF ILLINOIS) - END - 1926-27 CHICAGO CARDINALS
GREENE, FRANK (TULSA) - QBACK - 1934 CHICAGO CARDINALS
GREENE, JOHN (MICHIGAN) - END - 1944-50 DETROIT LIONS
GREENE, JOSEPH "MEAN JOE" (NORTH TEXAS ST.) - TACKLE - 1969
    PITTSBURGH STEELERS; 1970-74 PITTSBURGH STEELERS (AFC)
GREENE, THEODORE (TAMPA) - LB - 1960-62 DALLAS TEXANS (AFL)
GREENE, THOMAS (HOLY CROSS) - QBACK - 1960 BOSTON PATRIOTS (AFL);
    1961 DALLAS TEXANS (AFL)
GREENEY, NORMAN (NOTRE DAME) - GUARD - 1933 GREEN BAY PACKERS;
    1934-35 PITTSBURGH PIRATES
GREENFIELD, THOMAS (ARIZONA) - CENTER - 1939-41 GREEN BAY PACKERS
GREENHALGH, ROBERT (SAN FRANCISCO) - BACK - 1949 NEW YORK GIANTS
GREENICH, HARLEY (MISSISSIPPI) - BACK - 1944 CHICAGO BEARS
GREENLEE, FRITZ (ARIZONA STATE) - LB - 1969 SAN FRANCISCO 49ERS
GREENSHIELDS, DONN (PENN STATE) - TACKLE - 1932-33 BROOKLYN DODGERS

GREENWOOD, DONALD (MISSOURI & ILLINOIS) - BACK - 1945 CLEVELAND RAMS;
    1946-47 CLEVELAND BROWNS (AAFC)
GREENWOOD, GLENN (IOWA) - BACK - 1924 CHICAGO BEARS
GREENWOOD, H. - BACK - 1926 LOUISVILLE COLONELS
GREENWOOD, L. C. (ARKANSAS AM&N) - END - 1969 PITTSBURGH STEELERS;
    1970-74 PITTSBURGH STEELERS (AFC)
GREER, ALBERT (JACKSON STATE) - END - 1963 DETROIT LIONS
GREER, CHARLES (COLORADO) - BACK - 1968-69 DENVER BRONCOS (AFL);
    1970-74 DENVER BRONCOS (AFC)
GREER, JAMES (ELIZABETH CITY STATE-N.C.) - END - 1960 DENVER BRONCOS
    (AFL)
GREFE, THEODORE (NORTHWESTERN) - END - 1945 DETROIT LIONS
GREGG, ALVIN FORREST (SMU) - TACKLE, GUARD - 1956, 58-69 GREEN BAY
    PACKERS; 1970 GREEN BAY PACKERS (NFC); 1971 DALLAS COWBOYS (NFC)
GREGG, EDWARD (KENTUCKY) - END - 1922 LOUISVILLE BRECKS
GREGORY, BENNETT (NEBRASKA) - BACK - 1968 BUFFALO BILLS (AFL)
GREGORY, BRUCE (MICHIGAN) - BACK - 1926 DETROIT PANTHERS
GREGORY, EARL "JACK" (CHATTANOOGA&DELTA ST.) - END - 1967-69
    CLEVELAND BROWNS; 1970-71 CLEVELAND BROWNS (AFC); 1972-74 NEW
    YORK GIANTS (NFC)
GREGORY, FRANK (WILLIAMS) - BACK - 1923 BUFFALO ALL-AMERICANS; 1924
    BUFFALO BISONS
GREGORY, GARLAND (LOUISIANA TECH) - GUARD - 1946-47 SAN FRANCISCO
    49ERS (AAFC)
GREGORY, GLYNN (SMU) - END - 1961-62 DALLAS COWBOYS
GREGORY, JOHN (CHATTANOOGA) - GUARD - 1941 CLEVELAND RAMS
GREGORY, KENNETH (WHITTIER) - END - 1961 BALTIMORE COLTS; 1962
    PHILADELPHIA EAGLES; 1963 NEW YORK JETS (AFL)
GREGORY, MICHAEL (DENISON) - GUARD - 1931 CLEVELAND INDIANS
GREGORY, WILLIAM (WISCONSIN) - TACKLE, END - 1971-74 DALLAS COWBOYS
    (NFC)
GREMMINGER, HENRY (BAYLOR) - BACK - 1956-65 GREEN BAY PACKERS; 1966
    LOS ANGELES RAMS
GRESHAM, ROBERT (WEST VIRGINIA) - BACK - 1971-72 NEW ORLEANS SAINTS
    (NFC); 1973-74 HOUSTON OILERS (AFC)
GRGICH, VISCO (SANTA CLARA) - GUARD - 1946-49 SAN FRANCISCO 49ERS
    (AAFC); 1950-52 SAN FRANCISCO 49ERS
GRIBBEN, WILLIAM (CASE) - BACK - 1926 CLEVELAND PANTHERS (AFL)
GRIER, ROOSEVELT (PENN STATE) - TACKLE - 1955-56, 58-62 NEW YORK
    GIANTS; 1963-66 LOS ANGELES RAMS
GRIESE, ROBERT (PURDUE) - QBACK - 1967-69 MIAMI DOLPHINS (AFL);
    1970-74 MIAMI DOLPHINS (AFC); 1971 PASSING LEADER (AFC)
GRIFFEN, HAROLD (IOWA) - CENTER - 1926 NEW YORK YANKEES (AFL); 1928
    GREEN BAY PACKERS; 1930, 32 PORTSMOUTH SPARTANS
GRIFFIN, DONALD (ILLINOIS) - BACK - 1946 CHICAGO ROCKETS (AAFC)
GRIFFIN, JAMES (GRAMBLING) - END - 1966-67 SAN DIEGO CHARGERS (AFL);
    1968 CINCINNATI BENGALS (AFL)
GRIFFIN, JOHN (MEMPHIS STATE) - BACK - 1963 LOS ANGELES RAMS; 1964-66
    DENVER BRONCOS (AFL)
GRIFFIN, ROBERT (BAYLOR) - BACK - 1951 NEW YORK YANKS
GRIFFIN, ROBERT (ARKANSAS) - GUARD - 1953-57 LOS ANGELES RAMS; 1961
    DENVER BRONCOS (AFL); 1961 ST. LOUIS CARDINALS
GRIFFING, GLYNN (MISSISSIPPI) - QBACK - 1963 NEW YORK GIANTS
GRIFFITH, FORREST (KANSAS) - BACK - 1950-51 NEW YORK GIANTS
GRIFFITH, HOMER (USC) - BACK - 1934 CHICAGO CARDINALS
GRIFFITHS, PAUL (PENN STATE) - GUARD - 1921 CANTON BULLDOGS
GRIGAS, JOHN (HOLY CROSS) - BACK - 1943 CHICAGO CARDINALS; 1944
    CARD-PITT; 1945-47 BOSTON YANKS
GRIGG, CECIL (AUSTIN) - QBACK - 1919-23 CANTON BULLDOGS; 1924-25
    ROCHESTER JEFFERSONS; 1926 NEW YORK GIANTS; 1927 FRANKFORD
    YELLOWJACKETS
GRIGG, FORREST (TULSA) - TACKLE - 1946 BUFFALO BISONS (AAFC); 1947
    CHICAGO ROCKETS (AAFC); 1948-49 CLEVELAND BROWNS (AAFC); 1950-51
    CLEVELAND BROWNS; 1952 DALLAS TEXANS
GRIGGS, HALDANE (BUTLER) - BACK - 1926 AKRON PROS
GRIGONIS, FRANK (CHATTANOOGA) - BACK - 1942 DETROIT LIONS
GRILLO, ALBERT (IDAHO) - TACKLE - 1937 NEW YORK YANKS (AFL); 1941 NEW
    YORK AMERICANS (AFL)
GRIM, ROBERT (OREGON) - END, BACK - 1967-69 MINNESOTA VIKINGS;
    1970-71 MINNESOTA VIKINGS (NFC); 1972-74 NEW YORK GIANTS (NFC)

GRIMES, GEORGE (VIRGINIA) - BACK - 1948 DETROIT LIONS
GRIMES, WILLIAM (OKLAHOMA A&M) - BACK - 1949 LOS ANGELES DONS (AAFC);
    1950-52 GREEN BAY PACKERS
GRIMM, DANIEL (COLORADO) - GUARD, CENTER - 1963, 65 GREEN BAY
    PACKERS; 1966-68 ATLANTA FALCONS; 1969 BALTIMORE COLTS; 1969
    WASHINGTON REDSKINS
GROOME, JEROME (NOTRE DAME) - CENTER - 1951-55 CHICAGO CARDINALS
GROOMES, MELVIN (INDIANA) - BACK - 1948-49 DETROIT LIONS
GROS, EARL (LSU) - BACK - 1962-63 GREEN BAY PACKERS; 1964-66
    PHILADELPHIA EAGLES; 1967-69 PITTSBURGH STEELERS; 1970 NEW
    ORLEANS SAINTS (NFC)
GROSS, ANDREW (AUBURN) - GUARD - 1967-68 NEW YORK GIANTS
GROSS, GEORGE (AUBURN) - TACKLE - 1963-67 SAN DIEGO CHARGERS (AFL)
GROSSCUP, CLYDE LEE (UTAH) - QBACK - 1960-61 NEW YORK GIANTS; 1962
    NEW YORK TITANS (AFL)
GROSSMAN, JOHN (RUTGERS) - BACK - 1932, 34-36 BROOKLYN DODGERS
GROSSMAN, RANDY (TEMPLE) - END - 1974 PITTSBURGH STEELERS (AFC)
GROSSMAN, REX (INDIANA) - BACK - 1948-49 BALTIMORE COLTS (AAFC); 1950
    BALTIMORE COLTS; 1950 DETROIT LIONS
GROSVENOR, GEORGE (COLORADO) - BACK - 1935-36 CHICAGO BEARS; 1936-37
    CHICAGO CARDINALS
GROTTKAU, ROBERT (OREGON) - GUARD - 1959-60 DETROIT LIONS; 1961
    DALLAS COWBOYS
GROVE, ROGER (MICHIGAN STATE) - BACK - 1931-35 GREEN BAY PACKERS
GROVES, GEORGE (MARQUETTE) - GUARD - 1947 BUFFALO BILLS (AAFC); 1948
    BALTIMORE COLTS (AAFC)
GROZA, LOUIS (OHIO STATE) - TACKLE, KICKER - 1946-49 CLEVELAND BROWNS
    (AAFC); 1950-59, 61-67 CLEVELAND BROWNS; 1950, 52-54, 57 FIELD
    GOAL LEADER; 1957 SCORING LEADER; (TIED WITH BAKER); 1974 HALL
    OF FAME
GRUBE, CHARLES (MICHIGAN) - END - 1926 DETROIT PANTHERS
GRUBE, FRANKLIN (LAFAYETTE) - END - 1928 NEW YORK YANKEES
GRUBER, HERBERT - END - 1921-23 LOUISVILLE BRECKS
GRUNEISEN, SAMUEL (VILLANOVA) - CENTER - 1962-69 SAN DIEGO CHARGERS
    (AFL); 1970-72 SAN DIEGO CHARGERS (AFC); 1973 HOUSTON OILERS
    (AFC)
GRUVER, GROVER (FT. HAYS STATE-KANSAS) - END - 1936 PITTSBURGH
    AMERICANS (AFL)
GRYGO, ALBERT (SOUTH CAROLINA) - BACK - 1944-45 CHICAGO BEARS
GUARNIERI, ALBERT (CANISIUS) - END - 1924 BUFFALO BISONS; 1925 CANTON
    BULLDOGS
GUCCIARDO, PASQUALE (KENT STATE) - BACK - 1966 NEW YORK JETS (AFL)
GUDAUSKAS, PETER (MURRAY STATE-KENTUCKY) - GUARD - 1940 CLEVELAND
    RAMS; 1941 CINCINNATI BENGALS (AFL); 1943-45 CHICAGO BEARS
GUDE, HENRY (VANDERBILT) - CENTER - 1946 PHILADELPHIA EAGLES
GUDMUNDSON, SCOTT (GEORGE WASHINGTON) - QBACK - 1944-45 BOSTON YANKS
GUESMAN, RICHARD (WEST VIRGINIA) - TACKLE - 1960-62 NEW YORK TITANS
    (AFL); 1963 NEW YORK JETS (AFL); 1964 DENVER BRONCOS (AFL)
GUFFEY, ROY (OKLAHOMA) - END - 1926 BUFFALO RANGERS
GUGLIEMI, RALPH (NOTRE DAME) - QBACK - 1955, 58-60 WASHINGTON
    REDSKINS; 1961 ST. LOUIS CARDINALS; 1962-63 NEW YORK GIANTS;
    1963 PHILADELPHIA EAGLES
GUIDRY, PAUL (MCNEESE STATE) - LB - 1966-69 BUFFALO BILLS (AFL);
    1970-72 BUFFALO BILLS (AFC); 1973 HOUSTON OILERS (AFC)
GUIGLIANO, PASQUALE - BACK - 1923 LOUISVILLE BRECKS
GUILLORY, ANTHONY (NEBRASKA & LAMAR TECH) - LB - 1965, 67-69 LOS
    ANGELES RAMS
GUILLORY, JOHN (STANFORD) - BACK - 1969 CINCINNATI BENGALS (AFL);
    1970 CINCINNATI BENGALS (AFC)
GULIAN, MICHAEL (BROWN) - TACKLE - 1923 BUFFALO ALL-AMERICANS; 1924
    FRANKFORD YELLOWJACKETS; 1925-27 PROVIDENCE STEAMROLLERS
GULSETH, DONALD (NORTH DAKOTA) - LB - 1966 DENVER BRONCOS (AFL)
GULYANICS, GEORGE (ELLISVILLE JUNIOR) - BACK - 1947-52 CHICAGO BEARS
GUNDERMAN, ROBERT (VIRGINIA) - BACK - 1957 PITTSBURGH STEELERS
GUNDERSON, HARRY - CENTER - 1920-21 ROCK ISLAND INDEPENDENTS; 1921-23
    MINNEAPOLIS MARINES
GUNN, JIMMY (USC) - LB - 1970-74 ST. LOUIS CARDINALS (NFC)
GUNNELS, JOHN RILEY (GEORGIA) - TACKLE - 1960-64 PHILADELPHIA EAGLES;
    1965-66 PITTSBURGH STEELERS

GUNNER, HARRY (OREGON STATE) - END - 1968-69 CINCINNATI BENGALS
 (AFL); 1970 CHICAGO BEARS (NFC)
GURSKY, ALBERT (PENN STATE) - LB - 1963 NEW YORK GIANTS
GUSSIE, MICHAEL (WEST VIRGINIA) - GUARD - 1940 BROOKLYN DODGERS
GUSTAFSON, EDSEL (GEORGE WASHINGTON) - CENTER - 1947-48 BROOKLYN
 DODGERS (AAFC)
GUSTAFSON, HARLAN (PENNSYLVANIA) - END - 1940 NEW YORK AMERICANS (AFL)
GUTHRIE, GRANT (FLORIDA STATE) - KICKER - 1970-71 BUFFALO BILLS (AFC)
GUTKNECHT, ALBERT (NIAGARA) - GUARD - 1943 BROOKLYN DODGERS; 1944
 CLEVELAND RAMS
GUTOWSKY, LEROY (OKLAHOMA CITY UNIV.) - BACK - 1932-33 PORTSMOUTH
 SPARTANS; 1934-38 DETROIT LIONS; 1939 BROOKLYN DODGERS
GUTTERON, WILLIAM (NEVADA) - BACK - 1926 LOS ANGELES BUCCANEERS
GUY, CHARLES (WASHINGTON&JEFFERSON) - CENTER - 1919-20 DETROIT
 HERALDS; 1921 DETROIT PANTHERS; 1921-22 BUFFALO ALL-AMERICANS;
 1923 CLEVELAND INDIANS; 1925 COLUMBUS TIGERS; 1925-26 DAYTON
 TRIANGLES
GUY, LOUIS (MISSISSIPPI) - BACK - 1963 NEW YORK GIANTS; 1964 OAKLAND
 RAIDERS (AFL)
GUY, MELWOOD (DUKE) - TACKLE - 1958-59 NEW YORK GIANTS; 1960 DALLAS
 COWBOYS; 1961 HOUSTON OILERS (AFL); 1961 DENVER BRONCOS (AFL)
GUY, WILLIAM RAY (SOUTHERN MISSISSIPPI) - KICKER - 1973-74 OAKLAND
 RAIDERS (AFC); 1974 PUNTING LEADER (AFC)
GUYON, JOSEPH (CARLISLE & GEORGIA TECH) - BACK - 1919-20 CANTON
 BULLDOGS; 1921 CLEVELAND INDIANS; 1922-23 OORANG INDIANS; 1924
 ROCK ISLAND INDEPENDENTS; 1924-25 KANSAS CITY COWBOYS; 1927 NEW
 YORK GIANTS; 1966 HALL OF FAME
GUZIK, JOHN (PITTSBURGH) - LB - 1959-60 LOS ANGELES RAMS; 1961
 HOUSTON OILERS (AFL)
GWINN, ROSS (NORTHWEST LOUISIANA) - GUARD - 1968 NEW ORLEANS SAINTS
GWOSDEN, MILO (PITTSBURGH) - END - 1925 BUFFALO BISONS
HAAK, ROBERT (INDIANA) - TACKLE - 1939 BROOKLYN DODGERS
HAAS, BRUNO (WORCESTER STATE-MASS.) - BACK - 1921 CLEVELAND INDIANS
HAAS, ROBERT - BACK - 1929 DAYTON TRIANGLES
HACHTEN, WILLIAM (STANFORD) - GUARD - 1947 NEW YORK GIANTS
HACKBART, DALE (WISCONSIN) - LB, BAC - 1960 GREEN BAY PACKERS;
 1961-63 WASHINGTON REDSKINS; 1966-69 MINNESOTA VIKINGS; 1970
 MINNESOTA VIKINGS (NFC); 1971-72 ST. LOUIS CARDINALS (NFC); 1973
 DENVER BRONCOS (AFC)
HACKENBRUCK, JOHN (OREGON STATE) - TACKLE - 1940 DETROIT LIONS
HACKETT, HUGH - END - 1919 TOLEDO MAROONS
HACKNEY, ELMER (KANSAS STATE) - BACK - 1940 PHILADELPHIA EAGLES; 1941
 PITTSBURGH STEELERS; 1942-46 DETROIT LIONS
HADDEN, ALDOUS (WASHINGTON&JEFFERSON) - BACK - 1925 CLEVELAND
 BULLDOGS; 1925-26 DETROIT PANTHERS; 1926 CLEVELAND PANTHERS
 (AFL); 1927-28 PROVIDENCE STEAMROLLERS; 1928 CHICAGO BEARS;
 1929-30 PROVIDENCE STEAMROLLERS
HADEN, JOHN (ARKANSAS) - TACKLE - 1936-38 NEW YORK GIANTS
HADL, JOHN (KANSAS) - QBACK - 1962-69 SAN DIEGO CHARGERS (AFL);
 1970-72 SAN DIEGO CHARGERS (AFC); 1973-74 LOS ANGELES RAMS
 (NFC); 1974 GREEN BAY PACKERS (NFC); 1965 PASSING LEADER (AFL)
HADLEY, DAVID (ALCORN A&M) - BACK - 1970-71 KANSAS CITY CHIEFS (AFC)
HAFEN, BARNARD (UTAH) - END - 1949-50 DETROIT LIONS
HAFFNER, GEORGE (MCNEESE STATE) - QBACK - 1965 BALTIMORE COLTS
HAFFNER, MICHAEL (UCLA) - END - 1968-69 DENVER BRONCOS (AFL); 1970
 DENVER BRONCOS (AFC); 1971 CINCINNATI BENGALS (AFC)
HAGBERG, ROGER (MINNESOTA) - BACK - 1965-69 OAKLAND RAIDERS (AFL)
HAGBERG, RUDOLPH (WEST VIRGINIA) - CENTER - 1929 BUFFALO BISONS; 1930
 BROOKLYN DODGERS
HAGEMAN, FREDERICK (KANSAS) - CENTER - 1961-64 WASHINGTON REDSKINS
HAGEN, HALVOR (WEBER STATE) - END, CENTER, GUARD - 1969 DALLAS
 COWBOYS; 1970 DALLAS COWBOYS (NFC); 1971-72 NEW ENGLAND PATRIOTS
 (AFC); 1973-74 BUFFALO BILLS (AFC)
HAGENBUCKLE, VERNON (DARTMOUTH) - END - 1926 PROVIDENCE STEAMROLLERS;
 1926 BOSTON BULLDOGS (AFL)
HAGERTY, LORIS (IOWA) - BACK - 1930 BROOKLYN DODGERS
HAGERTY, JOHN (GEORGETOWN) - BACK - 1926-30, 32 NEW YORK GIANTS
HAGGERTY, JOHN (TUFTS) - GUARD - 1919 CLEVELAND INDIANS; 1920
 CLEVELAND PANTHERS; 1920 CANTON BULLDOGS

HAGGERTY, MICHAEL (MIAMI) - TACKLE, GUARD - 1967-69 PITTSBURGH
    STEELERS; 1970 PITTSBURGH STEELERS (AFC); 1971 NEW ENGLAND
    PATRIOTS (AFC); 1973 DETROIT LIONS (NFC)
HAHN, RAYMOND (KANSAS STATE) - END - 1926 HAMMOND PROS
HAIK, JOSEPH "MAC" (MISSISSIPPI) - END - 1968-69 HOUSTON CILERS
    (AFL); 1970-71 HOUSTON OILERS (AFC)
HAINES, BYRON (WASHINGTON) - BACK - 1937 PITTSBURGH PIRATES
HAINES, HARRY (COLGATE) - TACKLE - 1930-31 BROOKLYN DODGERS; 1931
    STATEN ISLAND STAPELTONS
HAINES, HENRY (PENN STATE) - QBACK - 1925-28 NEW YORK GIANTS; 1929,
    31 STATEN ISLAND STAPELTONS
HAJEK, CHARLES (NORTHWESTERN) - CENTER - 1934 PHILADELPHIA EAGLES
HALAS, GEORGE (ILLINOIS) - END - 1919 HAMMOND PROS; 1920 DECATUR
    STALEYS; 1921 CHICAGO STALEYS; 1922-29 CHICAGO BEARS; 1963 HALL
    OF FAME
HALE, DAVID (OTTAWA-KANSAS) - END, TACKLE - 1969 CHICAGO BEARS;
    1970-71 CHICAGO BEARS (NFC)
HALE, RUSSELL (GONZAGA) - CENTER - 1936 ROCHESTER TIGERS (AFL)
HALEY, ARTHUR (AKRON) - BACK - 1920 CANTON BULLDOGS; 1923 AKRON PROS
HALEY, DONALD (BAYLOR) - GUARD - 1941 MILWAUKEE CHIEFS (AFL)
HALEY, GEORGE RICHARD (PITTSBURGH) - BACK - 1959-60 WASHINGTON
    REDSKINS; 1961 MINNESOTA VIKINGS; 1961-64 PITTSBURGH STEELERS
HALICKI, EDWARD (BUCKNELL) - BACK - 1929-30 FRANKFORD YELLOWJACKETS;
    1930 MINNEAPOLIS REDJACKETS
HALL, ALVIN - BACK - 1961-63 LOS ANGELES RAMS
HALL, CHARLES LESLIE (HOUSTON) - LB - 1971-74 CLEVELAND BROWNS (AFC)
HALL, CHARLES VAL "TIM" (PITTSBURGH) - BACK - 1971-74 GREEN BAY
    PACKERS (NFC)
HALL, FORREST (DUQUESNE & SAN FRANCISCO) - BACK - 1948 SAN FRANCISCO
    49ERS (AAFC)
HALL, GALEN (PENN STATE) - QBACK - 1962 WASHINGTON REDSKINS; 1963 NEW
    YORK JETS (AFL)
HALL, HAROLD (SPRINGFIELD) - CENTER - 1942 NEW YORK GIANTS
HALL, HARRY (ILLINOIS) - QBACK - 1926 CHICAGO BULLS (AFL)
HALL, IRVING (BROWN) - BACK - 1942 PHILADELPHIA EAGLES
HALL, JOHN (IOWA) - END - 1955 NEW YORK GIANTS
HALL, JOHN (TCU) - BACK - 1940-41, 43 CHICAGO CARDINALS; 1942 DETROIT
    LIONS
HALL, KENNETH (TEXAS A&M) - BACK - 1959 CHICAGO CARDINALS; 1960-61
    HOUSTON OILERS (AFL); 1961 ST. LOUIS CARDINALS
HALL, LINUS PARKER (MISSISSIPPI) - QBACK - 1939-42 CLEVELAND RAMS;
    1946 SAN FRANCISCO 49ERS (AAFC); 1939 PASSING LEADER; 1939
    PUNTING LEADER
HALL, PETER (MARQUETTE) - END - 1961 NEW YORK GIANTS
HALL, RANDY (IDAHO) - BACK - 1974 BALTIMORE COLTS (AFC)
HALL, RAYMOND (ILLINOIS) - TACKLE - 1926 NEW YORK YANKEES (AFL); 1927
    NEW YORK YANKEES
HALL, RONALD (MISSOURI VALLEY) - BACK - 1959 PITTSBURGH STEELERS;
    1961-67 BOSTON PATRIOTS (AFL)
HALL, THOMAS (MINNESOTA) - BACK, END - 1962-63 DETROIT LIONS;
    1964-66, 68-69 MINNESOTA VIKINGS; 1967 NEW ORLEANS SAINTS
HALL, WILLIE (USC) - LB - 1972-73 NEW ORLEANS SAINTS (NFC)
HALL, WINDLAN (ARIZONA STATE) - BACK - 1972-74 SAN FRANCISCO 49ERS
    (NFC)
HALLADAY, RICHARD (CHICAGO) - END - 1922-24 RACINE LEGION
HALLECK, NEIL - BACK - 1924 COLUMBUS TIGERS
HALLECK, PAUL (OHIO) - END - 1937 CLEVELAND RAMS
HALLEY, WILLIAM (LAVERNE) - END - 1968 HOUSTON OILERS (AFL)
HALLIDAY, JOHN (SMU) - TACKLE - 1951 LOS ANGELES RAMS
HALLORAN, CLARENCE (BOSTON C. & FORDHAM) - BACK - 1926 HARTFORD BLUES
HALLQUIST, STONE (MIDDLEBURY) - BACK - 1926 MILWAUKEE BADGERS
HALPERIN, ROBERT (NOTRE DAME) - BACK - 1932 BROOKLYN DODGERS
HALPERN, ROBERT (CCNY) - GUARD - 1930 STATEN ISLAND STAPELTONS
HALSTROM, BERNARD (ILLINOIS) - BACK - 1920-21 CHICAGO CARDINALS
HALUSKA, JAMES (WISCONSIN) - BACK - 1956 CHICAGO BEARS
HALVERSON, DEAN (WASHINGTON) - LB - 1968 LOS ANGELES RAMS; 1970
    ATLANTA FALCONS (NFC); 1971-72 LOS ANGELES RAMS (NFC); 1973-74
    PHILADELPHIA EAGLES (NFC)
HALVERSON, WILLIAM (OREGON STATE) - TACKLE - 1942 PHILADELPHIA EAGLES
HAM, JACK (PENN STATE) - LB - 1971-74 PITTSBURGH STEELERS (AFC)
HAMAN, JOHN (NORTHWESTERN) - CENTER - 1940-41 CLEVELAND RAMS

HAMAS, STEVEN (PENN STATE) - BACK - 1929 ORANGE TORNADOS
HAMBACHER, ERNEST (BUCKNELL) - BACK - 1929 ORANGE TORNADOS
HAMBRIGHT, FREDERICK (SOUTH CAROLINA) - BACK - 1937 NEW YORK YANKS
     (AFL)
HAMER, ERNEST (PENNSYLVANIA) - BACK - 1924-28 FRANKFORD YELLOWJACKETS
HAMILTON, ANDREW (LSU) - END - 1973-74 KANSAS CITY CHIEFS (AFC)
HAMILTON, RAYMOND (OKLAHOMA) - TACKLE, END - 1973-74 NEW ENGLAND
     PATRIOTS (AFC)
HAMILTON, RAYMOND (ARKANSAS) - END - 1938, 44-45 CLEVELAND RAMS; 1939
     DETROIT LIONS; 1946-47 LOS ANGELES RAMS
HAMLIN, EUGENE (WESTERN MICHIGAN) - CENTER - 1970 WASHINGTON REDSKINS
     (NFC); 1971 CHICAGO BEARS (NFC); 1972 DETROIT LIONS (NFC)
HAMMACK, MALCOLM (FLORIDA) - BACK - 1955, 57-59 CHICAGO CARDINALS;
     1960-66 ST. LOUIS CARDINALS
HAMMOND, GARY (SMU) - BACK, END - 1973-74 ST. LOUIS CARDINALS (NFC)
HAMMOND, HENRY (SOUTHWESTERN AT MEMPHIS) - END - 1937 CHICAGO BEARS
HAMMOND, KIM (FLORIDA STATE) - QBACK - 1968 MIAMI DOLPHINS (AFL);
     1969 BOSTON PATRIOTS (AFL)
HAMPTON, DAVID (WYOMING) - BACK - 1969 GREEN BAY PACKERS; 1970-71
     GREEN BAY PACKERS (NFC); 1972-74 ATLANTA FALCONS (NFC)
HANBURGER, CHRISTIAN (NORTH CAROLINA) - LB - 1965-69 WASHINGTON
     REDSKINS; 1970-74 WASHINGTON REDSKINS (NFC)
HANCOCK, MICHAEL (IDAHO STATE) - END - 1973-74 WASHINGTON REDSKINS
     (NFC)
HAND, LAWRENCE (APPALACHIAN STATE) - END - 1965-69 DETROIT LIONS;
     1970-74 DETROIT LIONS (NFC)
HANDLER, PHILIP (TCU) - GUARD - 1930-36 CHICAGO CARDINALS
HANDLEY, RICHARD (FRESNO STATE) - CENTER - 1947 BALTIMORE COLTS (AAFC)
HANKE, CARL (MINNESOTA) - END - 1921-22 HAMMOND PROS; 1922 CHICAGO
     BEARS; 1923 HAMMOND PROS; 1924 CHICAGO CARDINALS
HANKEN, RAYMOND (GEORGE WASHINGTON) - END - 1937-38 NEW YORK GIANTS
HANLEY, EDWARD (PITTSBURGH&WESTERN RESERVE) - BACK - 1919 CLEVELAND
     INDIANS; 1920 DETROIT HERALDS
HANLEY, RICHARD (WASHINGTON STATE) - BACK - 1924 RACINE LEGION
HANLON, ROBERT (LORAS) - BACK - 1948 CHICAGO CARDINALS; 1949
     PITTSBURGH STEELERS
HANNA, ELZAPHAN (SOUTH CAROLINA) - GUARD - 1945 WASHINGTON REDSKINS
HANNAH, HERBERT (ALABAMA) - TACKLE - 1951 NEW YORK GIANTS
HANNAH, JOHN (ALABAMA) - GUARD - 1973-74 NEW ENGLAND PATRIOTS (AFC)
HANNEMAN, CHARLES (MICHIGAN STATE NORMAL) - END - 1937-41 DETROIT
     LIONS; 1941 CLEVELAND RAMS
HANNEMAN, CRAIG (OREGON STATE) - TACKLE, END - 1972-73 PITTSBURGH
     STEELERS (AFC); 1974 NEW ENGLAND PATRIOTS (AFC)
HANNER, JOEL "DAVE" (ARKANSAS) - TACKLE - 1952-64 GREEN BAY PACKERS
HANNY, FRANK (INDIANA) - END - 1923-27 CHICAGO BEARS; 1928-29
     PROVIDENCE STEAMROLLERS; 1930 PORTSMOUTH SPARTANS; 1930 GREEN
     BAY PACKERS
HANRATTY, TERRENCE (NOTRE DAME) - QBACK - 1969 PITTSBURGH STEELERS;
     1970-74 PITTSBURGH STEELERS (AFC)
HANRICUS, RALPH - BACK - 1922 ROCHESTER JEFFERSONS
HANSEN, CLIFFORD (LUTHER) - BACK - 1933 CHICAGO CARDINALS
HANSEN, DONALD (ILLINOIS) - LB - 1966-67 MINNESOTA VIKINGS; 1969
     ATLANTA FALCONS; 1970-74 ATLANTA FALCONS (NFC)
HANSEN, HAROLD (MINNESOTA) - GUARD - 1926 NEWARK BEARS (AFL)
HANSEN, RONALD (MINNESOTA) - GUARD - 1954 WASHINGTON REDSKINS
HANSEN, ROSCOE (NORTH CAROLINA) - TACKLE - 1951 PHILADELPHIA EAGLES
HANSEN, W. DALE (MICHIGAN STATE) - TACKLE - 1944, 48 DETROIT LIONS
HANSEN, WAYNE (TEXAS WESTERN) - GUARD - 1950-58 CHICAGO BEARS; 1960
     DALLAS COWBOYS
HANSON, HAROLD (MINNESOTA) - GUARD - 1928-30 FRANKFORD YELLOWJACKETS;
     1930 MINNEAPOLIS REDJACKETS
HANSON, HOMER (KANSAS STATE) - GUARD - 1934 CINCINNATI REDS; 1935
     PHILADELPHIA EAGLES; 1935-36 CHICAGO CARDINALS
HANSON, RAYMOND (OHIO WESLEYAN) - BACK - 1923-24 COLUMBUS TIGERS
HANSON, RICHARD (NORTH DAKOTA STATE) - TACKLE - 1971 NEW YORK GIANTS
     (NFC)
HANSON, ROY - BACK - 1921 ROCK ISLAND INDEPENDENTS; 1923 MINNEAPOLIS
     MARINES; 1923 GREEN BAY PACKERS
HANSON, STEVEN - END - 1925 KANSAS CITY COWBOYS; 1926 LOUISVILLE
     COLONELS

HANSON, THOMAS (TEMPLE) - BACK - 1931 BROOKLYN DODGERS; 1932 STATEN
    ISLAND STAPELTONS; 1933-37 PHILADELPHIA EAGLES; 1938 PITTSBURGH
    PIRATES
HANTLA, ROBERT (KANSAS) - GUARD - 1954-55 SAN FRANCISCO 49ERS
HANULAK, CHESTER (MARYLAND) - BACK - 1954, 57 CLEVELAND BROWNS
HAPES, MERLE (MISSISSIPPI) - BACK - 1942, 46 NEW YORK GIANTS
HARDEN, LEON (TEXAS-EL PASO) - BACK - 1970 GREEN BAY PACKERS (NFC)
HARDER, MARLIN "PAT" (WISCONSIN) - BACK - 1946-50 CHICAGO CARDINALS;
    1951-53 DETROIT LIONS; 1947 FIELD GOAL LEADER; (TIED WITH CUFF
    AND WATERFIELD); 1947-49 SCORING LEADER; (1949 TIED WITH ROBERTS)
HARDHAM, CEDRICK (NORTH TEXAS STATE) - END - 1970-74 SAN FRANCISCO
    49ERS (NFC)
HARDING, ROGER (CALIFORNIA) - CENTER - 1945 CLEVELAND RAMS; 1946 LOS
    ANGELES RAMS; 1947 PHILADELPHIA EAGLES; 1948 DETROIT LIONS; 1949
    GREEN BAY PACKERS; 1949 NEW YORK BULLDOGS
HARDY, CARROLL (COLORADO) - BACK - 1955 SAN FRANCISCO 49ERS
HARDY, CHARLES (SAN JOSE STATE) - END - 1960-62 OAKLAND RAIDERS (AFL)
HARDY, EDGAR (JACKSON STATE) - GUARD - 1973 SAN FRANCISCO 49ERS (NFC)
HARDY, ISHAM (WILLIAM&MARY) - GUARD - 1923 AKRON PROS
HARDY, JAMES (USC) - BACK - 1946-48 LOS ANGELES RAMS; 1949-51 CHICAGO
    CARDINALS; 1952 DETROIT LIONS
HARDY, KEVIN (NOTRE DAME) - TACKLE, END - 1968 SAN FRANCISCO 49ERS;
    1970 GREEN BAY PACKERS (NFC); 1971-72 SAN DIEGO CHARGERS (AFC)
HARDY, RICHARD (BOSTON COLLEGE) - GUARD - 1926 RACINE LEGION
HARE, CECIL (GONZAGA) - BACK - 1941-42, 45 WASHINGTON REDSKINS; 1946
    NEW YORK GIANTS
HARE, RAYMOND (GONZAGA) - QBACK - 1940-43 WASHINGTON REDSKINS; 1944
    BROOKLYN TIGERS; 1946 NEW YORK YANKEES (AAFC)
HARGETT, EDWARD (TEXAS A&M) - QBACK - 1969 NEW ORLEANS SAINTS;
    1970-72 NEW ORLEANS SAINTS (NFC)
HARGROVE, JAMES (HOWARD PAYNE) - LB - 1967, 69 MINNESOTA VIKINGS;
    1970 MINNESOTA VIKINGS (NFC); 1971-72 ST. LOUIS CARDINALS (NFC)
HARKEY, LEMUEL (COLLEGE OF EMPORIA) - BACK - 1955 PITTSBURGH
    STEELERS; 1955 SAN FRANCISCO 49ERS
HARKEY, STEVEN (GEORGIA TECH) - BACK - 1971-72 NEW YORK JETS (AFC)
HARLAN, JULIAN (GEORGIA TECH) - BACK - 1922 HAMMOND PROS
HARLEY, CHARLES (OHIO STATE) - BACK - 1921 CHICAGO STALEYS
HARMON, EDWARD (LOUISVILLE) - LB - 1969 CINCINNATI BENGALS (AFL)
HARMON, HAMILTON (TULSA) - CENTER - 1937 CHICAGO CARDINALS
HARMON, THOMAS (MICHIGAN) - BACK - 1941 NEW YORK AMERICANS (AFL);
    1946-47 LOS ANGELES RAMS
HARMON, THOMAS (GUSTAVUS ADOLPHUS) - GUARD - 1967 ATLANTA FALCONS
HARMS, ARTHUR (VERMONT) - TACKLE - 1925 FRANKFORD YELLOWJACKETS; 1926
    NEW YORK GIANTS
HARNESS, JAMES (MISSISSIPPI STATE) - BACK - 1956 BALTIMORE COLTS
HAROLD, GEORGE (ALLEN) - BACK - 1966-67 BALTIMORE COLTS; 1968
    WASHINGTON REDSKINS
HARPER, CHARLES (OKLAHOMA STATE) - GUARD, TACKLE - 1966-69 NEW YORK
    GIANTS; 1970-72 NEW YORK GIANTS (NFC)
HARPER, DARRELL (MICHIGAN) - BACK - 1960 BUFFALO BILLS (AFL)
HARPER, JACK (FLORIDA) - BACK - 1967-68 MIAMI DOLPHINS (AFL)
HARPER, MAURICE (AUSTIN COLLEGE) - CENTER - 1937-40 PHILADELPHIA
    EAGLES; 1941 PITTSBURGH STEELERS
HARPER, RAYMOND (INDIANA) - BACK - 1921 LOUISVILLE BRECKS
HARPER, WILLIE (NEBRASKA) - LB - 1973-74 SAN FRANCISCO 49ERS (NFC)
HARRAWAY, CHARLES (SAN JOSE STATE) - BACK - 1966-68 CLEVELAND BROWNS;
    1969 WASHINGTON REDSKINS; 1970-73 WASHINGTON REDSKINS (NFC)
HARRE, GILBERT (OHIO STATE) - TACKLE - 1936 CLEVELAND RAMS (AFL)
HARRELL, RICK (CLEMSON) - CENTER - 1973 NEW YORK JETS (AFC)
HARRINGTON, JOHN (MARQUETTE) - END - 1946 CLEVELAND BROWNS (AAFC);
    1947 CHICAGO ROCKETS (AAFC)
HARRIS, AMOS (MISSISSIPPI STATE) - GUARD - 1947-48 BROOKLYN DODGERS
    (AAFC)
HARRIS, ANTHONY (TOLEDO) - BACK - 1971 SAN FRANCISCO 49ERS (NFC)
HARRIS, CLIFFORD (OUACHITA) - BACK - 1970-74 DALLAS COWBOYS (NFC)
HARRIS, DUDLEY (MARIETTA) - TACKLE - 1930 PORTSMOUTH SPARTANS; 1930
    BROOKLYN DODGERS
HARRIS, ELMORE (MORGAN STATE) - BACK - 1947 BROOKLYN DODGERS (AAFC)
HARRIS, FRANCO (PENN STATE) - BACK - 1972-74 PITTSBURGH STEELERS (AFC)
HARRIS, FREDERICK (SMU) - TACKLE - 1941 NEW YORK AMERICANS (AFL)
HARRIS, GEORGE (LOUISVILLE) - TACKLE - 1921 LOUISVILLE BRECKS

Top row (from left to right): Jack Gregory, Bob Griese, Bob Grim and John Hadl. Second row: Chris Hanburger, Franco Harris, Bob Hayes and Wendell Hayes. Third row: Marv Hubbard, Gerald Irons, Ron Johnson and Deacon Jones. Bottom row: Lee Roy Jordan, Leroy Kelly, Jim Kiick and Bill Kilmer.

HARRIS, HARRY (WEST VIRGINIA) - QBACK - 1920 AKRON PROS
HARRIS, HENRY (TEXAS) - GUARD - 1947-48 WASHINGTON REDSKINS
HARRIS, JAMES (HOWARD PAYNE) - BACK - 1970 WASHINGTON REDSKINS (NFC)
HARRIS, JAMES (OKLAHOMA) - BACK - 1957 PHILADELPHIA EAGLES; 1958 LOS
     ANGELES RAMS; 1960 DALLAS TEXANS (AFL); 1961 DALLAS COWBOYS
HARRIS, JAMES (UTAH STATE) - TACKLE - 1965-67 NEW YORK JETS (AFL)
HARRIS, JAMES L. (GRAMBLING) - QBACK - 1969 BUFFALO BILLS (AFL);
     1970-71 BUFFALO BILLS (AFC); 1973-74 LOS ANGELES RAMS (NFC)
HARRIS, JOHN (SANTA MONICA) - BACK - 1960-61 OAKLAND RAIDERS (AFL)
HARRIS, JOHN - BACK - 1926 HARTFORD BLUES
HARRIS, KENNETH (SYRACUSE) - BACK - 1923-24 DULUTH KELLEYS
HARRIS, LOUIS (KENT STATE) - BACK - 1968 PITTSBURGH STEELERS
HARRIS, MARVIN (STANFORD) - LB - 1964 LOS ANGELES RAMS
HARRIS, OLIVER (GENEVA) - END - 1926 NEW YORK GIANTS
HARRIS, PHILIP (TEXAS) - BACK - 1966 NEW YORK GIANTS
HARRIS, RICHARD (MCNEESE STATE-LOUISIANA) - BACK - 1960 LOS ANGELES
     CHARGERS (AFL); 1961-65 SAN DIEGO CHARGERS (AFL)
HARRIS, RICHARD D. (GRAMBLING) - END - 1971-73 PHILADELPHIA EAGLES
     (NFC); 1974 CHICAGO BEARS (NFC)
HARRIS, RICKIE (ARIZONA) - BACK - 1965-69 WASHINGTON REDSKINS; 1970
     WASHINGTON REDSKINS (NFC); 1971-72 NEW ENGLAND PATRIOTS (AFC)
HARRIS, WELTON (WISCONSIN) - BACK - 1925-26 GREEN BAY PACKERS
HARRIS, WENDELL (LSU) - BACK - 1962-65 BALTIMORE COLTS; 1966-67 NEW
     YORK GIANTS
HARRIS, WILLIAM (COLORADO) - BACK - 1968 ATLANTA FALCONS; 1969
     MINNESOTA VIKINGS; 1971 NEW ORLEANS SAINTS (NFC)
HARRIS, WILLIAM (HARDIN-SIMMONS) - END - 1937 PITTSBURGH PIRATES;
     1937 BOSTON SHAMROCKS (AFL)
HARRISON, DWIGHT (TEXAS A&I) - END, BACK - 1971-72 DENVER BRONCOS
     (AFC); 1972-74 BUFFALO BILLS (AFC)
HARRISON, EDWARD (BOSTON COLLEGE) - END - 1926 BROOKLYN LIONS; 1926
     BROOKLYN HORSEMEN (AFL)
HARRISON, GRANVILLE (MISSISSIPPI STATE) - END - 1941 PHILADELPHIA
     EAGLES; 1942 DETROIT LIONS
HARRISON, JAMES (MISSOURI) - BACK - 1971-74 CHICAGO BEARS (NFC)
HARRISON, MAXWELL (AUBURN) - END - 1940 NEW YORK GIANTS
HARRISON, PATRICK (HOWARD OF ALABAMA) - TACKLE - 1936 BROOKLYN TIGERS
     (AFL); 1937 BROOKLYN DODGERS; 1937 ROCHESTER TIGERS (AFL); 1937
     CINCINNATI BENGALS (AFL)
HARRISON, REGINALD (CINCINNATI) - BACK - 1974 ST. LOUIS CARDINALS
     (NFC); 1974 PITTSBURGH STEELERS (AFC)
HARRISON, RICHARD (BOSTON COLLEGE) - END - 1944 BOSTON YANKS
HARRISON, ROBERT (OHIO) - BACK - 1961 BALTIMORE COLTS
HARRISON, ROBERT (OKLAHOMA) - LB - 1959-61 SAN FRANCISCO 49ERS;
     1962-63 PHILADELPHIA EAGLES; 1964 PITTSBURGH STEELERS; 1965-67
     SAN FRANCISCO 49ERS
HART, BENJAMIN (OKLAHOMA) - BACK - 1967 NEW ORLEANS SAINTS
HART, DEE "PETE" (HARDIN-SIMMONS) - BACK - 1960 NEW YORK TITANS (AFL)
HART, DOUGLAS (ARLINGTON STATE) - BACK - 1964-69 GREEN BAY PACKERS;
     1970-71 GREEN BAY PACKERS (NFC)
HART, HAROLD (TEXAS SOUTHERN) - BACK - 1974 OAKLAND RAIDERS (AFC)
HART, J. LESLIE (COLGATE) - QBACK - 1931 STATEN ISLAND STAPLETONS
HART, JAMES (SOUTHERN ILLINOIS) - QBACK - 1966-69 ST. LOUIS
     CARDINALS; 1970-74 ST. LOUIS CARDINALS (NFC)
HART, LEON (NOTRE DAME) - END - 1950-57 DETROIT LIONS
HART, LEONARD (DUKE) - QBACK - 1971 ATLANTA FALCONS (NFC); 1972
     BUFFALO BILLS (AFC)
HART, RICHARD - GUARD - 1967-69 PHILADELPHIA EAGLES; 1970
     PHILADELPHIA EAGLES (NFC); 1972 BUFFALO BILLS (AFC)
HART, THOMAS (MORRIS BROWN) - END - 1968-69 SAN FRANCISCO 49ERS;
     1970-74 SAN FRANCISCO 49ERS (NFC)
HARTE, CHARLES (SCRANTON) - GUARD - 1940 NEW YORK AMERICANS (AFL)
HARTLE, GREGORY (NEWBERRY) - LB - 1974 ST. LOUIS CARDINALS (NFC)
HARTLEY, HOWARD (DUKE) - BACK - 1948 WASHINGTON REDSKINS; 1949-52
     PITTSBURGH STEELERS
HARTMAN, FREDERICK (RICE) - TACKLE - 1947 CHICAGO BEARS; 1948
     PHILADELPHIA EAGLES
HARTMAN, JAMES (COLORADO A&M) - END - 1936 BROOKLYN DODGERS
HARTMAN, WILLIAM (GEORGIA) - QBACK - 1938 WASHINGTON REDSKINS

HARTONG, GEORGE (CHICAGO) - GUARD - 1922-24 RACINE LEGION; 1924
    CHICAGO CARDINALS
HARTSHORN, LAWRENCE (KANSAS STATE) - GUARD - 1955 CHICAGO CARDINALS
HARTZOG, HOWARD (BAYLOR) - TACKLE - 1926 ROCK ISLAND INDEPENDENTS
    (AFL); 1928 NEW YORK GIANTS
HARVEY, CLAUDE (PRAIRIE VIEW) - LB - 1970 HOUSTON OILERS (AFC)
HARVEY, GEORGE (KANSAS) - TACKLE - 1967 NEW ORLEANS SAINTS
HARVEY, JAMES (MISSISSIPPI) - TACKLE, GUARD - 1966-69 OAKLAND RAIDERS
    (AFL); 1970-71 OAKLAND RAIDERS (AFC)
HARVEY, JAMES "WADDY" (VPI) - TACKLE - 1969 BUFFALO BILLS (AFL); 1970
    BUFFALO BILLS (AFC)
HARVEY, NORMAN (DETROIT) - TACKLE - 1925 BUFFALO BISONS; 1926 DETROIT
    PANTHERS; 1927 NEW YORK YANKEES; 1927 BUFFALO BISONS; 1928-29
    PROVIDENCE STEAMROLLERS
HARVEY, RICHARD (JACKSON STATE) - BACK - 1970 PHILADELPHIA EAGLES
    (NFC); 1971 NEW ORLEANS SAINTS (NFC)
HASBROUCK, JOHN (RUTGERS) - BACK - 1921 ROCK ISLAND INDEPENDENTS;
    1921 ROCHESTER JEFFERSONS
HASENOHRL, GEORGE (OHIO STATE) - TACKLE - 1974 NEW YORK GIANTS (NFC)
HASLERIG, CLINTON (MICHIGAN) - END - 1974 CHICAGO BEARS (NFC)
HASTINGS, CHARLES (PITTSBURGH) - BACK - 1920 CLEVELAND PANTHERS
HASTINGS, GEORGE (OHIO) - TACKLE - 1930-31 PORTSMOUTH SPARTANS
HATCHER, RONALD (MICHIGAN STATE) - BACK - 1962 WASHINGTON REDSKINS
HATHAWAY, RUSSELL (INDIANA) - TACKLE - 1920-24 DAYTON TRIANGLES; 1922
    CANTON BULLDOGS; 1925-26 POTTSVILLE MAROONS; 1927 BUFFALO BISONS
HATHCOCK, DAVID (MEMPHIS STATE) - BACK - 1966 GREEN BAY PACKERS; 1967
    NEW YORK GIANTS
HATLEY, JOHN (SUL ROSS STATE) - GUARD - 1953 CHICAGO BEARS; 1954-55
    CHICAGO CARDINALS; 1960 DENVER BRONCOS (AFL)
HAUPTLY, JOSEPH - GUARD - 1925 POTTSVILLE MAROONS
HAUSER, ARTHUR (XAVIER) - GUARD - 1954-57 LOS ANGELES RAMS; 1959
    CHICAGO CARDINALS; 1959 NEW YORK GIANTS; 1960 BOSTON PATRIOTS
    (AFL); 1961 DENVER BRONCOS (AFL)
HAUSER, EARL (MIAMI OF OHIO) - END - 1919-20 DAYTON TRIANGLES; 1921
    CINCINNATI CELTS; 1921 LOUISVILLE BRECKS
HAUSER, KENNETH - BACK - 1927 BUFFALO BISONS; 1930 NEWARK TORNADOS
HAUSS, LEONARD (GEORGIA) - CENTER - 1964-69 WASHINGTON REDSKINS;
    1970-74 WASHINGTON REDSKINS (NFC)
HAVEN, JOHN (HAMLINE) - END - 1923 DULUTH KELLEYS
HAVENS, CHARLES (WESTERN MARYLAND) - CENTER - 1930 FRANKFORD
    YELLOWJACKETS
HAVERDICK, DAVID (MOREHEAD STATE) - END - 1970 DETROIT LIONS (NFC)
HAVIG, DENNIS (COLORADO) - GUARD - 1972-74 ATLANTA FALCONS (NFC)
HAVRILAK, SAMUEL (BUCKNELL) - BACK, QBACK, END - 1969 BALTIMORE
    COLTS; 1970-73 BALTIMORE COLTS (AFC); 1974 NEW ORLEANS SAINTS
    (NFC)
HAWK - GUARD - 1920 COLUMBUS PANHANDLES
HAWKINS, BENJAMIN (ARIZONA STATE) - BACK, END - 1966-69 PHILADELPHIA
    EAGLES; 1970-73 PHILADELPHIA EAGLES (NFC); 1974 CLEVELAND BROWNS
    (AFC)
HAWKINS, CHILTON ALEX (SOUTH CAROLINA) - BACK - 1956-65, 67-68
    BALTIMORE COLTS; 1966-67 ATLANTA FALCONS
HAWKINS, JOHN (USC) - TACKLE - 1926 LOS ANGELES BUCCANEERS
HAWKINS, ROSS (NORTH CAROLINA) - LB - 1961-65 MINNESOTA VIKINGS
HAWKINS, WAYNE (PACIFIC) - GUARD - 1960-69 OAKLAND RAIDERS (AFL)
HAWS, HARVEY (DARTMOUTH) - QBACK - 1924-25 FRANKFORD YELLOWJACKETS
HAYCRAFT, KENNETH (MINNESOTA) - END - 1929-30 MINNEAPOLIS REDJACKETS;
    1930 GREEN BAY PACKERS
HAYDEN, KENNETH (ARKANSAS) - CENTER - 1942 PHILADELPHIA EAGLES; 1943
    WASHINGTON REDSKINS
HAYDEN, LEOPHUS (OHIO STATE) - BACK - 1971 MINNESOTA VIKINGS (NFC);
    1972-73 ST. LOUIS CARDINALS (NFC)
HAYDUK, HENRY (WASHINGTON STATE) - GUARD - 1935 PITTSBURGH PIRATES;
    1935 BROOKLYN DODGERS
HAYES, BILLIE (SAN DIEGO STATE) - BACK - 1972 NEW ORLEANS SAINTS (NFC)
HAYES, DAVID (NOTRE DAME) - END - 1921-22 GREEN BAY PACKERS
HAYES, EDWARD (MORGAN STATE) - BACK - 1970 PHILADELPHIA EAGLES (NFC)
HAYES, GERALD (NOTRE DAME) - END - 1921 ROCK ISLAND INDEPENDENTS
HAYES, JAMES (JACKSON STATE) - TACKLE - 1965-66 HOUSTON OILERS (AFL)

HAYES, LAWRENCE (VANDERBILT) - LB - 1961 NEW YORK GIANTS; 1962-63 LOS
    ANGELES RAMS
HAYES, LUTHER (USC) - END - 1961 SAN DIEGO CHARGERS (AFL)
HAYES, NORBERT (MARQUETTE) - END - 1922 RACINE LEGION; 1923 GREEN BAY
    PACKERS
HAYES, RAYMOND (CENTRAL OKLAHOMA STATE) - BACK - 1961 MINNESOTA
    VIKINGS
HAYES, RAYMOND (TOLEDO) - TACKLE - 1968 NEW YORK JETS (AFL)
HAYES, RICHARD (CLEMSON) - LB - 1959-60, 62 PITTSBURGH STEELERS
HAYES, ROBERT (FLORIDA A&M) - END - 1965-69 DALLAS COWBOYS; 1970-74
    DALLAS COWBOYS (NFC)
HAYES, THOMAS (SAN DIEGO STATE) - BACK - 1971-74 ATLANTA FALCONS (NFC)
HAYES, WENDELL (HUMBOLDT STATE) - BACK - 1963 DALLAS COWBOYS; 1965-67
    DENVER BRONCOS (AFL); 1968-69 KANSAS CITY CHIEFS (AFL); 1970-74
    KANSAS CITY CHIEFS (AFC)
HAYHOE, WILLIAM (USC) - TACKLE - 1969 GREEN BAY PACKERS; 1970-74
    GREEN BAY PACKERS (NFC)
HAYMAN, GARY (PENN STATE) - BACK - 1974 BUFFALO BILLS (AFC)
HAYMOND, ALVIN (SOUTHERN) - BACK - 1964-67 BALTIMORE COLTS; 1968
    PHILADELPHIA EAGLES; 1969 LOS ANGELES RAMS; 1970-71 LOS ANGELES
    RAMS (NFC); 1972 WASHINGTON REDSKINS (NFC); 1973 HOUSTON OILERS
    (AFC)
HAYNES, ABNER (NORTH TEXAS STATE) - BACK - 1960-62 DALLAS TEXANS
    (AFL); 1963-64 KANSAS CITY CHIEFS (AFL); 1965-66 DENVER BRONCOS
    (AFL); 1967 MIAMI DOLPHINS (AFL); 1967 NEW YORK JETS (AFL); 1960
    RUSHING LEADER (AFL)
HAYNES, HALL (SANTA CLARA) - BACK - 1950, 53 WASHINGTON REDSKINS;
    1954-55 LOS ANGELES RAMS
HAYNES, JOSEPH (TULSA) - GUARD - 1947 BUFFALO BILLS (AAFC)
HAYS, GEORGE (ST. BONAVENTURE) - END - 1950-52 PITTSBURGH STEELERS;
    1953 GREEN BAY PACKERS
HAYS, LEO HAROLD (MISSISSIPPI SOUTHERN) - LB - 1963-67 DALLAS
    COWBOYS; 1968-69 SAN FRANCISCO 49ERS
HAYS - BACK - 1919 DETROIT HERALDS
HAZELHURST, ROBERT (DENVER) - BACK - 1948 BOSTON YANKS
HAZELTINE, MATTHEW (CALIFORNIA) - LB - 1955-68 SAN FRANCISCO 49ERS;
    1970 NEW YORK GIANTS (NFC)
HAZELTON, MAJOR (FLORIDA A&M) - BACK - 1968-69 CHICAGO BEARS; 1970
    NEW ORLEANS SAINTS (NFC)
HAZELWOOD, THEODORE (NORTH CAROLINA) - TACKLE - 1949 CHICAGO HORNETS
    (AAFC); 1953 WASHINGTON REDSKINS
HEADRICK, SHERRILL (TCU) - LB - 1960-62 DALLAS TEXANS (AFL); 1963-67
    KANSAS CITY CHIEFS (AFL); 1968 CINCINNATI BENGALS (AFL)
HEALEY, EDWARD (DARTMOUTH) - TACKLE - 1920-22 ROCK ISLAND
    INDEPENDENTS; 1922-27 CHICAGO BEARS; 1964 HALL OF FAME
HEALY, MICHAEL DONALD (MARYLAND) - TACKLE - 1958-59 CHICAGO BEARS;
    1960-61 DALLAS COWBOYS; 1962 BUFFALO BILLS (AFL)
HEALY, WILLIAM "CHIP" (VANDERBILT) - LB - 1969 ST. LOUIS CARDINALS;
    1970 ST. LOUIS CARDINALS (NFC)
HEAP, JOSEPH (NOTRE DAME) - BACK - 1955 NEW YORK GIANTS
HEAP, WALTER (TEXAS) - BACK - 1947-48 LOS ANGELES DONS (AAFC)
HEARDEN, LEONARD (RIPON) - END - 1924 GREEN BAY PACKERS
HEARDEN, THOMAS (NOTRE DAME) - BACK - 1927-28 GREEN BAY PACKERS; 1929
    CHICAGO BEARS
HEATER, DONALD (MONTANA TECH) - BACK - 1972 ST. LOUIS CARDINALS (NFC)
HEATER, WILLIAM (SYRACUSE) - TACKLE - 1940 BROOKLYN DODGERS
HEATH, HERMAN LEON (OKLAHOMA) - BACK - 1951-53 WASHINGTON REDSKINS
HEATH, STANLEY (NEVADA) - QBACK - 1949 GREEN BAY PACKERS
HEBERT, KENNETH (HOUSTON) - KICKER - 1968 PITTSBURGH STEELERS
HECHT, ALFRED (ALABAMA) - GUARD - 1947 CHICAGO ROCKETS (AAFC)
HECK, RALPH (COLORADO) - LB - 1963-65 PHILADELPHIA EAGLES; 1966-68
    ATLANTA FALCONS; 1969 NEW YORK GIANTS; 1970-71 NEW YORK GIANTS
    (NFC)
HECK, ROBERT (PURDUE) - END - 1949 CHICAGO HORNETS (AAFC)
HECKARD, ROBERT "STEVE" (DAVIDSON) - END - 1965-66 LOS ANGELES RAMS
HECKER, NORBERT (BALDWIN-WALLACE) - END - 1951-53 LOS ANGELES RAMS;
    1955-57 WASHINGTON REDSKINS
HECTOR, WILLIAM (PACIFIC) - TACKLE - 1961 LOS ANGELES RAMS
HEENAN, PATRICK (NOTRE DAME) - END - 1960 WASHINGTON REDSKINS
HEETER, EUGENE (WEST VIRGINIA) - END - 1963-65 NEW YORK JETS (AFL)
HEFNER, LAWRENCE (CLEMSON) - LB - 1972-74 GREEN BAY PACKERS (NFC)

EGARTY, WILLIAM (VILLANOVA) - TACKLE - 1953 PITTSBURGH STEELERS;
    1953 WASHINGTON REDSKINS
EIDEL, JAMES (MISSISSIPPI) - BACK - 1966 ST. LOUIS CARDINALS; 1967
    NEW ORLEANS SAINTS
EIKKENEN, RALPH (MICHIGAN) - GUARD - 1939 BROOKLYN DODGERS
EILEMAN, CHARLES (IOWA STATE) - END - 1939 CHICAGO BEARS
EIMSCH, JOHN (MARQUETTE) - BACK - 1926 MILWAUKEE BADGERS
EIN, FLOYD (WASHINGTON STATE) - BACK - 1936 ROCHESTER TIGERS (AFL)
EIN, MELVIN (WASHINGTON STATE) - CENTER - 1931-45 NEW YORK GIANTS;
    1963 HALL OF FAME
EIN, ROBERT (KENT STATE) - END - 1947 BROOKLYN DODGERS (AAFC)
EINEMAN, KENNETH (TEXAS MINES) - BACK - 1940 CLEVELAND RAMS; 1943
    BROOKLYN DODGERS
EINISCH, FRED (LORAS) - BACK - 1923-24, 26 RACINE LEGION; 1924
    KENOSHA MAROONS; 1926 DULUTH ESKIMOS
EINRICH, DONALD (WASHINGTON) - QBACK - 1954-59 NEW YORK GIANTS; 1960
    DALLAS COWBOYS; 1962 OAKLAND RAIDERS (AFL)
EINZ, ROBERT (PACIFIC) - TACKLE, END - 1969 MIAMI DOLPHINS (AFL);
    1970-74 MIAMI DOLPHINS (AFC)
EKKERS, GEORGE (WISCONSIN) - TACKLE - 1946 MIAMI SEAHAWKS (AAFC);
    1947 BALTIMORE COLTS (AAFC); 1947-49 DETROIT LIONS
ELD, PAUL (SAN JOSE STATE) - QBACK - 1954 PITTSBURGH STEELERS; 1955
    GREEN BAY PACKERS
ELDT, CARL (PURDUE) - TACKLE - 1935-36 BROOKLYN DODGERS
ELDT, JOHN (IOWA) - CENTER - 1923, 26 COLUMBUS TIGERS
ELLER, WARREN (PITTSBURGH) - BACK - 1934-36 PITTSBURGH PIRATES
ELLUIN, FRANCIS (TULANE) - TACKLE - 1952-53 CLEVELAND BROWNS;
    1954-57 GREEN BAY PACKERS; 1960 HOUSTON OILERS (AFL)
ELMER, CLARE (PURDUE & DETROIT) - TACKLE - 1936 BROOKLYN TIGERS (AFL)
ELMS, JOHN (GEORGIA TECH) - END - 1946 DETROIT LIONS
ELVIE, CHARLES (PURDUE) - END - 1920 DAYTON TRIANGLES; 1921 MUNCIE
    FLYERS
ELWIG, JOHN (NOTRE DAME) - GUARD - 1953-56 CHICAGO BEARS
EMPEL, WILLIAM (CARROLI COLLEGE) - TACKLE - 1942 CHICAGO BEARS
ENDERSON, HERBERT (OHIO STATE) - BACK - 1921-22 EVANSVILLE CRIMSON
    GIANTS
ENDERSHOT, LAWRENCE (ARIZONA STATE) - LB - 1967 WASHINGTON REDSKINS
ENDERSON, JOHN (MICHIGAN) - END - 1965-67 DETROIT LIONS; 1968-69
    MINNESOTA VIKINGS; 1970-72 MINNESOTA VIKINGS (NFC)
ENDERSON, JON (COLORADO STATE) - BACK, END - 1968-69 PITTSBURGH
    STEELERS; 1970 WASHINGTON REDSKINS (NFC)
ENDLEY, RICHARD (CLEMSON) - QBACK - 1951 PITTSBURGH STEELERS
ENDREN, JERRY (IDAHO) - END - 1970 DENVER BRONCOS (AFC)
ENDREN, JOHN (BUCKNELL) - BACK - 1920 CANTON BULLDOGS; 1921
    CLEVELAND INDIANS
ENDREN, ROBERT (USC) - TACKLE - 1949-51 WASHINGTON REDSKINS
ENDRIAN, OSCAR (DEPAUW & DETROIT) - QBACK - 1922-23 CANTON BULLDOGS;
    1923 AKRON PROS; 1924 GREEN BAY PACKERS; 1925 ROCK ISLAND
    INDEPENDENTS; 1925 NEW YORK GIANTS
ENDPICKS, THEODORE (MIAMI) - LB - 1969 BALTIMORE COLTS; 1970-73
    BALTIMORE COLTS (AFC); 1974 GREEN BAY PACKERS (NFC)
ENKE, EDGAR (USC) - END - 1949 LOS ANGELES DONS (AAFC); 1951-52,
    56-60 SAN FRANCISCO 49ERS; 1961-63 ST. LOUIS CARDINALS
ENKE, KARL (TULSA) - TACKLE - 1968 NEW YORK JETS (AFL); 1969 BOSTON
    PATRIOTS (AFL)
ENLEY, CAREY (CHATTANOOGA) - BACK - 1962 BUFFALO BILLS (AFL)
ENNESSEY, JEROME (SANTA CLARA) - END - 1950-51 CHICAGO CARDINALS;
    1952-53 WASHINGTON REDSKINS
ENNESSEY, THOMAS (HOLY CROSS) - BACK - 1965-66 BOSTON PATRIOTS (AFL)
ENNIGAN, CHARLES (NORTHWEST STATE-LA.) - END - 1960-66 HOUSTON
    OILERS (AFL); 1964 PASS RECEIVING LEADER (AFL)
ENNIGAN, MICHAEL (TENNESSEE TECH) - LB - 1973-74 DETROIT LIONS (NFC)
ENNINGS, DANIEL (WILLIAM&MARY) - QBACK - 1966 SAN DIEGO CHARGERS
    (AFL)
ENRY, FRITZ - GUARD - 1925 AKRON PROS
ENRY, MICHAEL (USC) - LB - 1959-61 PITTSBURGH STEELERS; 1962-64 LOS
    ANGELES RAMS
ENRY, THOMAS (LSU) - BACK - 1919 ROCK ISLAND INDEPENDENTS
ENRY, URBAN (GEORGIA TECH) - TACKLE - 1961 LOS ANGELES RAMS; 1963
    GREEN BAY PACKERS; 1964 PITTSBURGH STEELERS

HENRY, WILBUR (WASHINGTON&JEFFERSON) - TACKLE - 1920-23, 25-26 CANTON
     BULLDOGS; 1927 NEW YORK GIANTS; 1927-28 POTTSVILLE MAROONS; 1963
     HALL OF FAME
HENRY - TACKLE - 1932 STATEN ISLAND STAPELTONS
HENSLEY, RICHARD (KENTUCKY) - END - 1949 NEW YORK GIANTS; 1952
     PITTSBURGH STEELERS; 1953 CHICAGO BEARS
HENSON, GARY (COLORADO) - END - 1963 PHILADELPHIA EAGLES
HENSON, KENNETH (TCU) - CENTER - 1965 PITTSBURGH STEELERS
HEPBURN, LONNIE (TEXAS SOUTHERN) - BACK - 1971-72 BALTIMORE COLTS
     (AFC); 1974 DENVER BRONCOS (AFC)
HERBER, ARNOLD (REGIS) - QBACK - 1930-40 GREEN BAY PACKERS; 1944-45
     NEW YORK GIANTS; 1932, 34, 36 PASSING LEADER; 1966 HALL OF FAME
HERCHMAN, WILLIAM (TEXAS TECH) - TACKLE - 1956-59 SAN FRANCISCO
     49ERS; 1960-61 DALLAS COWBOYS; 1962 HOUSTON OILERS (AFL)
HERGERT, JOSEPH (FLORIDA) - LB - 1960-61 BUFFALO BILLS (AFL)
HERMAN, DAVID (MICHIGAN STATE) - GUARD - 1964-69 NEW YORK JETS (AFL);
     1970-73 NEW YORK JETS (AFC)
HERMAN, EDWARD (NORTHWESTERN) - END - 1925 ROCK ISLAND INDEPENDENTS
HERMAN, RICHARD (FLORIDA STATE) - LB - 1965 OAKLAND RAIDERS (AFL)
HERMANN, JOHN (UCLA) - BACK - 1956 NEW YORK GIANTS; 1956 BALTIMORE
     COLTS
HERMELING, TERRY (NEVADA) - TACKLE - 1970-73 WASHINGTON REDSKINS (NFC)
HERNANDEZ, JOSE (ARIZONA) - END - 1964 WASHINGTON REDSKINS
HERNDON, DONALD (TAMPA) - BACK - 1960 NEW YORK TITANS (AFL)
HEROCK, KENNETH (WEST VIRGINIA) - END, LB - 1963-67 OAKLAND RAIDERS
     (AFL); 1968 CINCINNATI BENGALS (AFL); 1969 BOSTON PATRIOTS (AFL)
HERON, FREDERICK (SAN JOSE STATE) - TACKLE - 1966-69 ST. LOUIS
     CARDINALS; 1970-72 ST. LOUIS CARDINALS (NFC)
HEROSIAN, BRIAN (CONNECTICUT) - BACK - 1973 BALTIMORE COLTS (AFC)
HERRERA, EFREN (UCLA) - KICKER - 1974 DALLAS COWBOYS (NFC)
HERRIN, HOUSTON (ST. MARY'S OF CAL.) - GUARD - 1931 CLEVELAND INDIANS
HERRING, GEORGE (MISSISSIPPI SOUTHERN) - QBACK - 1960-61 DENVER
     BRONCOS (AFL)
HERRING, HAROLD (AUBURN) - CENTER - 1949 BUFFALO BILLS (AAFC);
     1950-52 CLEVELAND BROWNS
HERRMANN, DONALD (WAYNESBURG) - END - 1969 NEW YORK GIANTS; 1970-74
     NEW YORK GIANTS (NFC)
HERRON, JAMES "PAT" (PITTSBURGH) - END - 1919 MASSILLON TIGERS; 1920
     CLEVELAND PANTHERS
HERRON, MACK (KANSAS) - BACK - 1973-74 NEW ENGLAND PATRIOTS (AFC)
HERSHEY, KIRK (CORNELL) - END - 1941 PHILADELPHIA EAGLES; 1941
     CLEVELAND RAMS
HERTZ, FRANK (CARROLL-WISCONSIN) - END - 1926 MILWAUKEE BADGERS; 1926
     ROCK ISLAND INDEPENDENTS (AFL)
HESS, WALTER (INDIANA) - BACK - 1919 MASSILLON TIGERS; 1921-24
     HAMMOND PROS; 1924 KENOSHA MAROONS; 1925 HAMMOND PROS
HESTER, JAMES (NORTH DAKOTA) - END - 1967-69 NEW ORLEANS SAINTS; 1970
     CHICAGO BEARS (NFC)
HESTER, RAYMOND (TULANE) - LB - 1971-73 NEW ORLEANS SAINTS (NFC)
HETTEMA, DAVID (NEW MEXICO) - TACKLE - 1967 SAN FRANCISCO 49ERS; 1970
     ATLANTA FALCONS (NFC)
HEWITT, WILLIAM (MICHIGAN) - END - 1932-36 CHICAGO BEARS; 1937-39
     PHILADELPHIA EAGLES; 1943 PHIL-PITT; 1971 HALL OF FAME
HEWS, ROBERT (PRINCETON) - END - 1971 BUFFALO BILLS (AFC)
HEYWOOD, RALPH (USC) - END - 1946 CHICAGO ROCKETS (AAFC); 1947
     DETROIT LIONS; 1948 BOSTON YANKS; 1949 NEW YORK BULLDOGS
HIBBS, JESSE (USC) - TACKLE - 1931 CHICAGO BEARS
HIBLER, MICHAEL (STANFORD) - LB - 1968 CINCINNATI BENGALS (AFL)
HICKERSON, ROBERT EUGENE (MISSISSIPPI) - GUARD - 1958-60, 62-69
     CLEVELAND BROWNS; 1970-73 CLEVELAND BROWNS (AFC)
HICKEY, HOWARD (ARKANSAS) - END - 1941 PITTSBURGH STEELERS; 1942, 45
     CLEVELAND RAMS; 1946-48 LOS ANGELES RAMS
HICKEY, THOMAS (MARYLAND) - BACK - 1967 DENVER BRONCOS (AFL)
HICKEY, WILLIAM (ST. NORBERT) - BACK - 1940-41 MILWAUKEE CHIEFS (AFL)
HICKL, RAYMOND (TEXAS A&I) - LB - 1969 NEW YORK GIANTS; 1970 NEW YORK
     GIANTS (NFC)
HICKMAN, HERMAN (TENNESSEE) - GUARD - 1932-34 BROOKLYN DODGERS
HICKMAN, LAWRENCE (BAYLOR) - BACK - 1959 CHICAGO CARDINALS; 1960
     GREEN BAY PACKERS
HICKS, JOHN (OHIO STATE) - GUARD - 1974 NEW YORK GIANTS (NFC)

HICKS, WILMER "W.K." (TEXAS SOUTHERN) - BACK - 1964-69 HOUSTON OILERS
      (AFL); 1970-72 NEW YORK JETS (AFC); 1965 INTERCEPTION LEADER
      (AFL)
HICKS (INDIANA) - BACK - 1919 CLEVELAND INDIANS
HIEMSTRA, EDWARD (STERLING) - GUARD - 1942 NEW YORK GIANTS
HIGGINS, AUSTIN - CENTER - 1921-23 LOUISVILLE BRECKS
HIGGINS, JAMES (XAVIER) - GUARD - 1966 MIAMI DOLPHINS (AFL)
HIGGINS, JOHN (TRINITY-TEXAS) - GUARD - 1941 CHICAGO CARDINALS
HIGGINS, LUKE (NOTRE DAME) - GUARD - 1947 BALTIMORE COLTS (AAFC)
HIGGINS, PAUL (BROWN) - BACK - 1925 PROVIDENCE STEAMROLLERS
HIGGINS, ROBERT (PENN STATE) - END - 1920-21 CANTON BULLDOGS
HIGGINS, THOMAS (NORTH CAROLINA) - TACKLE - 1953 CHICAGO CARDINALS;
      1954-55 PHILADELPHIA EAGLES
HIGH, LEONARD - BACK - 1920 DECATUR STALEYS
HIGHSMITH, DONALD (MICHIGAN STATE) - BACK - 1970-72 OAKLAND RAIDERS
      (AFC); 1973 GREEN BAY PACKERS (NFC)
HIGHSMITH, WALTER (FLORIDA A&M) - GUARD, TACKLE - 1968-69 DENVER
      BRONCOS (AFL); 1972 HOUSTON OILERS (AFC)
HIGHTOWER, JOHN (SAM HOUSTON) - END - 1942 CLEVELAND RAMS; 1943
      DETROIT LIONS
HILGENBERG, WALTER (IOWA) - LB - 1964-66 DETROIT LIONS; 1968-69
      MINNESOTA VIKINGS; 1970-74 MINNESOTA VIKINGS (NFC)
HILL, CALVIN (YALE) - BACK - 1969 DALLAS COWBOYS; 1970-74 DALLAS
      COWBOYS (NFC)
HILL, CHARLES (BAKER) - BACK - 1924-26 KANSAS CITY COWBOYS
HILL, DAVID (AUBURN) - TACKLE - 1963-69 KANSAS CITY CHIEFS (AFL);
      1970-74 KANSAS CITY CHIEFS (AFC)
HILL, DONALD (STANFORD) - BACK - 1929 GREEN BAY PACKERS; 1929 CHICAGO
      CARDINALS
HILL, FREDERICK (USC) - END - 1965-69 PHILADELPHIA EAGLES; 1970-71
      PHILADELPHIA EAGLES (NFC)
HILL, GARY (USC) - BACK - 1965 MINNESOTA VIKINGS
HILL, GERALD (WYOMING) - BACK - 1961, 63-69 BALTIMORE COLTS; 1970
      BALTIMORE COLTS (AFC)
HILL, HARLON (FLORENCE STATE-ALABAMA) - END - 1954-61 CHICAGO BEARS;
      1962 PITTSBURGH STEELERS; 1962 DETROIT LIONS
HILL, HAROLD (HOWARD) - END - 1938-40 BROOKLYN DODGERS
HILL, HARRY (OKLAHOMA) - BACK - 1923 TOLEDO MAROONS; 1924-26 KANSAS
      CITY COWBOYS; 1926 NEW YORK GIANTS; 1926 ROCK ISLAND
      INDEPENDENTS (AFL)
HILL, IRVIN (TRINITY-TEXAS) - QBACK - 1931-32 CHICAGO CARDINALS
HILL, J. D. (ARIZONA STATE) - END - 1971-74 BUFFALO BILLS (AFC)
HILL, JACK (UTAH STATE) - BACK - 1961 DENVER BRONCOS (AFL)
HILL, JAMES (SAM HOUSTON) - BACK - 1955-57, 59 CHICAGO CARDINALS;
      1960-64 ST. LOUIS CARDINALS; 1965 DETROIT LIONS; 1966 KANSAS
      CITY CHIEFS (AFL)
HILL, JAMES (TENNESSEE) - BACK - 1951-52 DETROIT LIONS; 1955
      PITTSBURGH STEELERS
HILL, JAMES WEBSTER (TEXAS A&I) - BACK - 1969 SAN DIEGO CHARGERS
      (AFL); 1970-71 SAN DIEGO CHARGERS (AFC); 1972-74 GREEN BAY
      PACKERS (NFC)
HILL, JOHN "KID" (AMHERST) - BACK - 1926 NEW YORK GIANTS
HILL, JOHN (LEHIGH) - CENTER, TACKLE - 1972-74 NEW YORK GIANTS (NFC)
HILL, MACK LEE (SOUTHERN) - BACK - 1964-65 KANSAS CITY CHIEFS (AFL)
HILL, ROBERT (HASKELL) - GUARD - 1922 OORANG INDIANS
HILL, STUART KING (RICE) - QBACK, KICKER - 1958-59 CHICAGO CARDINALS;
      1960, 69 ST. LOUIS CARDINALS; 1961-68 PHILADELPHIA EAGLES; 1968
      MINNESOTA VIKINGS
HILL, TALMADGE "IKE" (CATAWBA) - END, BACK - 1970-71 BUFFALO BILLS
      (AFC); 1973-74 BUFFALO BILLS (AFC)
HILL, WINSTON (TEXAS SOUTHERN) - TACKLE - 1963-69 NEW YORK JETS
      (AFL); 1970-74 NEW YORK JETS (AFC)
HILLEBRAND, GERALD (COLORADO) - LB - 1963-66 NEW YORK GIANTS; 1967
      ST. LOUIS CARDINALS; 1968-69 PITTSBURGH STEELERS; 1970
      PITTSBURGH STEELERS (AFC)
HILLENBRAND, WILLIAM (INDIANA) - BACK - 1946 CHICAGO ROCKETS (AAFC);
      1947-48 BALTIMORE COLTS (AAFC)
HILLHOUSE, ANDREW (BROWN) - BACK - 1920-21 BUFFALO ALL-AMERICANS
HILLMAN, WILLIAM (TENNESSEE) - BACK - 1947 DETROIT LIONS

HILPERT, HAROLD (OKLAHOMA CITY UNIV.) - BACK - 1930 NEW YORK GIANTS;
    1933 CINCINNATI REDS
HILTON, JOHN (RICHMOND) - END - 1965-69 PITTSBURGH STEELERS; 1970
    GREEN BAY PACKERS (NFC); 1971 MINNESOTA VIKINGS (NFC); 1972-73
    DETROIT LIONS (NFC)
HILTON, ROY (JACKSON STATE) - END - 1965-69 BALTIMORE COLTS; 1970-73
    BALTIMORE COLTS (AFC); 1974 NEW YORK GIANTS (NFC)
HIMES, RICHARD (OHIO STATE) - TACKLE - 1968-69 GREEN BAY PACKERS;
    1970-74 GREEN BAY PACKERS (NFC)
HINCHMAN, HUBERT (BUTLER) - BACK - 1933-34 CHICAGO CARDINALS; 1934
    DETROIT LIONS
HINDMAN, STANLEY (MISSISSIPPI) - END, TACKLE - 1966-69 SAN FRANCISCO
    49ERS; 1970-71, 74 SAN FRANCISCO 49ERS (NFC)
HINES, GLEN RAY (ARKANSAS) - TACKLE - 1966-69 HOUSTON OILERS (AFL);
    1970 HOUSTON OILERS (AFC); 1971-72 NEW ORLEANS SAINTS (NFC);
    1973 PITTSBURGH STEELERS (AFC)
HINES, JAMES (TEXAS SOUTHERN) - END - 1969 MIAMI DOLPHINS (AFL)
HINKLE, BERNARD (EMPORIA STATE-KANSAS) - QBACK - 1936-37 BOSTON
    SHAMROCKS (AFL)
HINKLE, JOHN (SYRACUSE) - BACK - 1940 NEW YORK GIANTS; 1941 NEW YORK
    AMERICANS (AFL); 1943 PHIL-PITT; 1944-47 PHILADELPHIA EAGLES
HINKLE, W. CLARKE (BUCKNELL) - BACK - 1932-41 GREEN BAY PACKERS; 1938
    SCORING LEADER; 1940-41 FIELD GOAL LEADER; 1964 HALL OF FAME
HINTE, HALE (PITTSBURGH) - END - 1942 GREEN BAY PACKERS; 1942
    PITTSBURGH STEELERS
HINTON, CHARLES DUDLEY (N. CAROLINA COLLEGE) - TACKLE - 1964-69
    PITTSBURGH STEELERS; 1970-71 PITTSBURGH STEELERS (AFC); 1971 NEW
    YORK JETS (AFC); 1972 BALTIMORE COLTS (AFC)
HINTON, CHARLES RICHARD (MISSISSIPPI) - CENTER - 1967-69 NEW YORK
    GIANTS
HINTON, EDWARD (OKLAHOMA) - END - 1969 BALTIMORE COLTS; 1970-72
    BALTIMORE COLTS (AFC); 1973 HOUSTON OILERS (AFC); 1974 NEW
    ENGLAND PATRIOTS (AFC)
HINTON, J. W. (TCU) - QBACK - 1932 STATEN ISLAND STAPELTONS
HIPPA, SAMUEL (DAYTON) - END - 1927-28 DAYTON TRIANGLES
HIPPS, CLAUDE (GEORGIA) - BACK - 1952-53 PITTSBURGH STEELERS
HIRSCH, EDWARD (NORTHWESTERN) - LB - 1947-49 BUFFALO BILLS (AAFC)
HIRSCH, ELROY "CRAZYLEGS" (WISCONSIN) - END, BACK - 1946-48 CHICAGO
    ROCKETS (AAFC); 1949-57 LOS ANGELES RAMS; 1951 PASS RECEIVING
    LEADER; 1951 SCORING LEADER; 1968 HALL OF FAME
HITT, JOEL (MISSISSIPPI COLLEGE) - END - 1939 CLEVELAND RAMS
HIX, WILLIAM (ARKANSAS) - END - 1950 PHILADELPHIA EAGLES
HOAGUE, JOSEPH (COLGATE) - BACK - 1941-42 PITTSBURGH STEELERS; 1946
    BOSTON YANKS
HOAGLIN, GEORGE FREDERICK (PITTSBURGH) - CENTER - 1966-69 CLEVELAND
    BROWNS; 1970-72 CLEVELAND BROWNS (AFC); 1973 BALTIMORE COLTS
    (AFC); 1974 HOUSTON OILERS (AFC)
HOAK, RICHARD (PENN STATE) - BACK - 1961-69 PITTSBURGH STEELERS; 1970
    PITTSBURGH STEELERS (AFC)
HOBAN, MIKE (MICHIGAN) - GUARD, CENTER - 1974 CHICAGO BEARS (NFC)
HOBBS, HOMER (GEORGIA) - GUARD - 1949 SAN FRANCISCO 49ERS (AAFC);
    1950 SAN FRANCISCO 49ERS
HOBBS, WILLIAM (TEXAS A&M) - LB - 1969 PHILADELPHIA EAGLES; 1970-71
    PHILADELPHIA EAGLES (NFC); 1972 NEW ORLEANS SAINTS (NFC)
HOBSCHEID, FRANK (CHICAGO) - GUARD - 1926 RACINE LEGION; 1927 CHICAGO
    BEARS
HOBSON, BENJAMIN (ST. LOUIS UNIV.) - BACK - 1926 BUFFALO RANGERS;
    1927 BUFFALO BISONS
HOCK, JOHN (SANTA CLARA) - TACKLE - 1950 CHICAGO CARDINALS; 1953,
    55-57 LOS ANGELES RAMS
HOCTOR, JOSEPH (JOHN CARROLL) - BACK - 1940 NEW YORK AMERICANS (AFL)
HODEL, MERWIN (COLORADO) - BACK - 1953 NEW YORK GIANTS
HODGES, HERMAN (HOWARD) - END - 1939-42 BROOKLYN DODGERS
HODGINS, NORMAN (LSU) - BACK - 1974 CHICAGO BEARS (NFC)
HODGSON, PATRICK (GEORGIA) - END - 1966 WASHINGTON REDSKINS
HOEL, ROBERT (MINNESOTA) - GUARD - 1940-41 MILWAUKEE CHIEFS (AFL)
HOEL, ROBERT (PITTSBURGH)   GUARD - 1935 PITTSBURGH PIRATES; 1937-38
    CHICAGO CARDINALS
HOERNER, RICHARD (IOWA) - BACK - 1947-51 LOS ANGELES RAMS; 1952
    DALLAS TEXANS

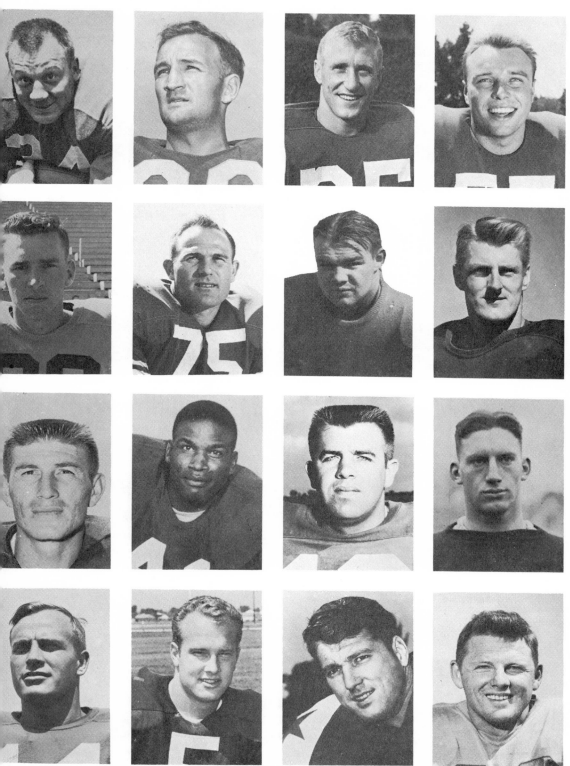

Top row (from left to right): "Pat" Harder, Tom Harmon, Alex Hawkins and Matt Hazeltine. *Second row:* Norb Hecker, Ed Henke, Herman Hickman and Elroy Hirsch. *Third row:* Harlon Hill, Jimmy Hill, King Hill and Andy Hillhouse. *Bottom row:* Bob Hoernschemeyer, Paul Hornung, Chuck Howley and Bill Howton.

Top row (from left to right): "Sam" Huff, Burt Ingwerson, Cecil Isbell and Jack Jacobs. *Second row:* Dick James, Vic Janowicz, Mike Jarmoluk and Bob Jeter. *Third row:* Charley Johnson, John Henry Johnson, Nate Johnson and Luke Johnsos. *Bottom row:* Dave Jones, Stan Jones, "Dub" Jones and Henry Jordan.

HOERNSCHEMEYER, ROBERT (INDIANA) - BACK - 1946-47 CHICAGO ROCKETS
     (AAFC); 1947-48 BROOKLYN DODGERS (AAFC); 1949 CHICAGO HORNETS
     (AAFC); 1950-55 DETROIT LIONS
HOEY, GEORGE (MICHIGAN) - BACK, LB - 1971 ST. LOUIS CARDINALS (NFC);
     1972-73 NEW ENGLAND PATRIOTS (AFC); 1974 SAN DIEGO CHARGERS (AFC)
HOFFMAN, ARNOLD (SYRACUSE) - BACK - 1925 ROCHESTER JEFFERSONS
HOFFMAN, DALTON (BAYLOR) - BACK - 1964-65 HOUSTON OILERS (AFL)
HOFFMAN, JACK (XAVIER) - END - 1952, 55-58 CHICAGO BEARS
HOFFMAN, JOHN (ARKANSAS) - BACK - 1949-56 CHICAGO BEARS
HOFFMAN, JOHN (HAWAII) - END - 1969 WASHINGTON REDSKINS; 1970
     WASHINGTON REDSKINS (NFC); 1971 CHICAGO BEARS (NFC); 1972 ST.
     LOUIS CARDINALS (NFC); 1972 DENVER BRONCOS (AFC)
HOFFMAN, WAYNE ROBERT (USC) - BACK - 1940-41 WASHINGTON REDSKINS;
     1946-48 LOS ANGELES RAMS; 1949 LOS ANGELES DONS (AAFC)
HOFFMAN, WILLIAM (LEHIGH) - GUARD - 1924-26 FRANKFORD YELLOWJACKETS;
     1927 POTTSVILLE MAROONS
HOGAN, DARRELL (TRINITY-TEXAS) - GUARD - 1949-53 PITTSBURGH STEELERS
HOGAN, PAUL (WASHINGTON&JEFFERSON & DETROIT) - BACK - 1924 AKRON
     PROS; 1925 CANTON BULLDOGS; 1926 NEW YORK GIANTS; 1926 FRANKFORD
     YELLOWJACKETS
HOGAN, THOMAS (DETROIT) - TACKLE - 1925-26 DETROIT PANTHERS; 1926
     CHICAGO CARDINALS; 1928 DETROIT WOLVERINES
HOGLAND, DOUGLAS (OREGON STATE) - GUARD - 1953-55 SAN FRANCISCO
     49ERS; 1956-58 CHICAGO CARDINALS; 1958 DETROIT LIONS
HOGUE, FRANK - BACK - 1924 AKRON PROS
HOGUE, MURRELL (CENTENARY) - GUARD - 1928 NEW YORK YANKEES; 1929-30
     CHICAGO CARDINALS; 1930 MINNEAPOLIS REDJACKETS
HOISINGTON, ALLAN (PASADENA) - END - 1960 OAKLAND RAIDERS (AFL); 1960
     BUFFALO BILLS (AFL)
HOHMAN, JON (WISCONSIN) - GUARD - 1965-66 DENVER BRONCOS (AFL)
HOHN, ROBERT (NEBRASKA) - BACK - 1965-69 PITTSBURGH STEELERS
HOKUF, STEPHEN (NEBRASKA) - QBACK - 1933-35 BOSTON REDSKINS
HOLCOMB, WILLIAM (TEXAS TECH) - TACKLE - 1937 PITTSBURGH PIRATES;
     1937 PHILADELPHIA EAGLES
HOLDEN, SAMUEL (GRAMBLING) - TACKLE - 1971 NEW ORLEANS SAINTS (NFC)
HOLDEN, STEVE (ARIZONA STATE) - END - 1973-74 CLEVELAND BROWNS (AFC)
HOLDEN - TACKLE - 1919 DETROIT HERALDS
HOLDER, LEWIS (TEXAS) - END - 1949 LOS ANGELES DONS (AAFC)
HOLE, ERNEST - TACKLE - 1921 MUNCIE FLYERS
HOLE, MICHAEL - BACK - 1921 MUNCIE FLYERS
HOLIFIELD, JAMES (JACKSON STATE) - BACK - 1968-69 NEW YORK GIANTS
HOLLADAY, ROBERT (TULSA) - BACK - 1956 LOS ANGELES RAMS; 1956-57 SAN
     FRANCISCO 49ERS
HOLLAND, JOHN (TENNESSEE STATE) - END - 1974 MINNESOTA VIKINGS (NFC)
HOLLAND, VERNON (TENNESSEE STATE) - TACKLE - 1971-74 CINCINNATI
     BENGALS (AFC)
HOLLAR, JOHN (APPALACHIAN STATE) - BACK - 1948-49 WASHINGTON
     REDSKINS; 1949 DETROIT LIONS
HOLLAS, HUGO (RICE) - BACK - 1970-72 NEW ORLEANS SAINTS (NFC); 1974
     SAN FRANCISCO 49ERS (NFC)
HOLLENBECK, OSCAR (COLGATE) - GUARD - 1919 AKRON PROS
HOLLER, EDWARD (SOUTH CAROLINA) - LB - 1963 GREEN BAY PACKERS; 1964
     PITTSBURGH STEELERS
HOLLERAN, THOMAS (PITTSBURGH) - BACK - 1923 BUFFALO ALL-AMERICANS
HOLLEY, KENNETH (HOLY CROSS) - BACK - 1946 MIAMI SEAHAWKS (AAFC)
HOLLIDAY, RON (PITTSBURGH) - END - 1973 SAN DIEGO CHARGERS (AFC)
HOLLINGSWORTH, JOSEPH (EAST KENTUCKY STATE) - BACK - 1949-51
     PITTSBURGH STEELERS
HOLLOMON, GUS (HOUSTON) - BACK - 1968-69 DENVER BRONCOS (AFL);
     1970-72 NEW YORK JETS (AFC)
HOLLOWAY, GLEN (NORTH TEXAS STATE) - GUARD - 1970-73 CHICAGO BEARS
     (NFC); 1974 CLEVELAND BROWNS (AFC)
HOLM, BERNARD (ALABAMA) - BACK - 1930 PROVIDENCE STEAMROLLERS; 1931
     PORTSMOUTH SPARTANS; 1932 CHICAGO CARDINALS; 1933 PITTSBURGH
     PIRATES
HOLMAN, DANIEL (MONTERREY & SAN JOSE STATE) - QBACK - 1968 PITTSBURGH
     STEELERS
HOLMAN, WILLIE (SOUTH CAROLINA STATE) - END - 1968-69 CHICAGO BEARS;
     1970-73 CHICAGO BEARS (NFC); 1973 WASHINGTON REDSKINS (NFC)

HOLMER, WALTER (NORTHWESTERN) - BACK - 1929-30 CHICAGO BEARS; 1931-32
    CHICAGO CARDINALS; 1933 BOSTON REDSKINS; 1933 PITTSBURGH PIRATES
HOLMES, ERNEST (TEXAS SOUTHERN) - TACKLE - 1972-74 PITTSBURGH
    STEELERS (AFC)
HOLMES, JAMES "PAT" (TEXAS TECH) - TACKLE, END - 1966-69 HOUSTON
    OILERS (AFL); 1970-72 HOUSTON OILERS (AFC); 1973 KANSAS CITY
    CHIEFS (AFC)
HOLMES, JOHN (FLORIDA A&M) - END - 1966 MIAMI DOLPHINS (AFL)
HOLMES, MELVIN (NORTH CAROLINA A&T) - GUARD, TACKLE - 1971-73
    PITTSBURGH STEELERS (AFC)
HOLMES, MICHAEL (TEXAS SOUTHERN) - BACK - 1974 SAN FRANCISCO 49ERS
    (NFC)
HOLMES, ROBERT (SOUTHERN) - BACK - 1968-69 KANSAS CITY CHIEFS (AFL);
    1970-71 KANSAS CITY CHIEFS (AFC); 1971-72 HOUSTON OILERS (AFC);
    1973 SAN DIEGO CHARGERS (AFC)
HOLMES, RUDY (DRAKE) - BACK - 1974 ATLANTA FALCONS (NFC)
HOLOVAK, MICHAEL (BOSTON COLLEGE) - BACK - 1946 LOS ANGELES RAMS;
    1947-48 CHICAGO BEARS
HOLSTROM, ROBERT (DETROIT TECH) - BACK - 1940 BOSTON BEARS (AFL);
    1940 MILWAUKEE CHIEFS (AFL); 1941 BUFFALO TIGERS (AFL)
HOLTZMAN, GLEN (NORTH TEXAS STATE) - TACKLE - 1955-58 LOS ANGELES RAMS
HOLUB, E. J. (TEXAS TECH) - LB - 1961-62 DALLAS TEXANS (AFL); 1963-69
    KANSAS CITY CHIEFS (AFL); 1970 KANSAS CITY CHIEFS (AFC)
HOLZ, GORDON (MINNESOTA) - TACKLE - 1960-63 DENVER BRONCOS (AFL);
    1964 NEW YORK JETS (AFL)
HOLZER, THOMAS (LOUISVILLE) - END - 1967 SAN FRANCISCO 49ERS
HOMAN, DENNIS (ALABAMA) - END - 1968-69 DALLAS COWBOYS; 1970 DALLAS
    COWBOYS (NFC); 1971-72 KANSAS CITY CHIEFS (AFC)
HOMAN, HENRY (LEBANON VALLEY) - QBACK - 1925-30 FRANKFORD
    YELLOWJACKETS
HONAKER, CHARLES (OHIO STATE) - END - 1924 CLEVELAND BULLDOGS
HOOD, FRANKLIN (PITTSBURGH) - BACK - 1933 PITTSBURGH PIRATES
HOOKER, FAIR (ARIZONA STATE) - END - 1969 CLEVELAND BROWNS; 1970-74
    CLEVELAND BROWNS (AFC)
HOOKS, JAMES (CENTRAL STATE) - BACK - 1973-74 DETROIT LIONS (NFC)
HOOLIGAN, HENRY (BISHOP) - BACK - 1965 HOUSTON OILERS (AFL)
HOPKINS, ANDY (S. F. AUSTIN) - BACK - 1971 HOUSTON OILERS (AFC)
HOPKINS, JERRELL (TEXAS A&M) - LB - 1963-66 DENVER BRONCOS (AFL);
    1967 MIAMI DOLPHINS (AFL); 1968 OAKLAND RAIDERS (AFL)
HOPKINS, ROY (TEXAS SOUTHERN) - BACK - 1967-69 HOUSTON OILERS (AFL);
    1970 HOUSTON OILERS (AFC)
HOPKINS, THEODORE - END - 1921-22 COLUMBUS PANHANDLES
HOPP, HARRY (NEBRASKA) - BACK - 1941-43 DETROIT LIONS; 1946 MIAMI
    SEAHAWKS (AAFC); 1946 BUFFALO BISONS (AAFC); 1947 LOS ANGELES
    DONS (AAFC)
HOPTOWIT, ALBERT (WASHINGTON STATE) - TACKLE - 1942-45 CHICAGO BEARS
HORD, AMBROSE ROY (DUKE) - GUARD - 1960-62 LOS ANGELES RAMS; 1962
    PHILADELPHIA EAGLES; 1963 NEW YORK JETS (AFL)
HORKEY, ROLAND (RIPON) - BACK - 1940 MILWAUKEE CHIEFS (AFL)
HORN, DONALD (SAN DIEGO STATE) - QBACK - 1967-69 GREEN BAY PACKERS;
    1970 GREEN BAY PACKERS (NFC); 1971-72 DENVER BRONCOS (AFC); 1973
    CLEVELAND BROWNS (AFC); 1974 SAN DIEGO CHARGERS (AFC)
HORN, RICHARD (STANFORD) - BACK - 1958 BALTIMORE COLTS
HORNBEAK, JAY (WASHINGTON) - BACK - 1935 BROOKLYN DODGERS
HORNE, RICHARD (OREGON) - END - 1941 NEW YORK GIANTS; 1946 MIAMI
    SEAHAWKS (AAFC); 1947 SAN FRANCISCO 49ERS (AAFC)
HORNER, SAMUEL (VMI) - BACK - 1960-61 WASHINGTON REDSKINS; 1962 NEW
    YORK GIANTS
HORNICK, WILLIAM (TULANE) - TACKLE - 1947 PITTSBURGH STEELERS
HORNING, CLARENCE (COLGATE) - TACKLE - 1919 DETROIT HERALDS; 1920-21
    BUFFALO ALL-AMERICANS; 1920-21 ROCHESTER JEFFERSONS; 1921
    DETROIT PANTHERS; 1922-23 TOLEDO MAROONS
HORNSBY, RONALD (SOUTHEAST LOUISIANA) - LB - 1971-74 NEW YORK GIANTS
    (NFC)
HORNUNG, PAUL (NOTRE DAME) - BACK - 1957-62, 64-66 GREEN BAY PACKERS;
    1959-61 SCORING LEADER
HORRELL, WILLIAM (MICHIGAN STATE) - GUARD - 1952 PHILADELPHIA EAGLES
HORSTMANN, ROY (PURDUE) - BACK - 1933 BOSTON REDSKINS; 1934 CHICAGO
    CARDINALS
HORTON, GREG (COLORADO) - GUARD - 1974 LOS ANGELES RAMS (NFC)
HORTON, LAWRENCE (IOWA) - END, TACKLE - 1972 CHICAGO BEARS (NFC)

HORTON, LESTER (RUTGERS) - BACK - 1930 NEWARK TORNADOS
HORTON, ROBERT (BOSTON UNIV.) - LB - 1964-65 SAN DIEGO CHARGERS (AFL)
HORVATH, LESLIE (OHIO STATE) - BACK - 1947-48 LOS ANGELES RAMS; 1949
     CLEVELAND BROWNS (AAFC)
HORWEEN, ARNOLD (HARVARD) - BACK - 1921-24 CHICAGO CARDINALS
HORWEEN, RALPH (HARVARD) - BACK - 1921-23 CHICAGO CARDINALS
HOSKINS, ROBERT (WICHITA STATE) - GUARD, TACKLE - 1970-74 SAN
     FRANCISCO 49ERS (NFC)
HOSS, CLARK (OREGON STATE) - END - 1972 PHILADELPHIA EAGLES (NFC)
HOUCK, JOSEPH - GUARD - 1921 COLUMBUS PANHANDLES
HOUGHTON, JERRY (WASHINGTON STATE) - TACKLE - 1950 WASHINGTON
     REDSKINS; 1951 CHICAGO CARDINALS
HOULE, WILFRED (ST. THOMAS-MINNESOTA) - BACK - 1924 MINNEAPOLIS
     MARINES
HOUSER, JOHN (REDLANDS) - GUARD - 1957-59 LOS ANGELES RAMS; 1960-61
     DALLAS COWBOYS; 1963 ST. LOUIS CARDINALS
HOUSTON, JAMES (OHIO STATE) - LB - 1960-69 CLEVELAND BROWNS; 1970-72
     CLEVELAND BROWNS (AFC)
HOUSTON, KENNETH (PRAIRIE VIEW) - BACK - 1967-69 HOUSTON OILERS
     (AFL); 1970-72 HOUSTON OILERS (AFC); 1973-74 WASHINGTON REDSKINS
     (NFC); 1971 INTERCEPTION LEADER (AFC)
HOUSTON, LINDELL (OHIO STATE) - GUARD - 1946-49 CLEVELAND BROWNS
     (AAFC); 1950-53 CLEVELAND BROWNS
HOUSTON, RICHARD (EAST TEXAS STATE) - END - 1969 NEW YORK GIANTS;
     1970-73 NEW YORK GIANTS (NFC)
HOUSTON, WALTER (PURDUE) - GUARD - 1955 WASHINGTON REDSKINS
HOUSTON, WILLIAM (JACKSON STATE) - END - 1974 DALLAS COWBOYS (NFC)
HOVIOUS, JOHN (MISSISSIPPI) - BACK - 1945 NEW YORK GIANTS
HOWARD, ALBERT (PRINCETON) - GUARD - 1926 BROOKLYN HORSEMEN (AFL);
     1926 BROOKLYN LIONS; 1927 NEW YORK GIANTS
HOWARD, BILLY (ALCORN A&M) - TACKLE - 1974 DETROIT LIONS (NFC)
HOWARD, EUGENE (LANGSTON-OKLAHOMA) - BACK - 1968-69 NEW ORLEANS
     SAINTS; 1970 NEW ORLEANS SAINTS (NFC); 1971-72 LOS ANGELES RAMS
     (NFC)
HOWARD, LEROY (BISHOP) - BACK - 1971 HOUSTON OILERS (AFC)
HOWARD, LYNN (INDIANA) - BACK - 1919 HAMMOND PROS; 1921-22 GREEN BAY
     PACKERS
HOWARD, PAUL (BRIGHAM YOUNG) - GUARD - 1973-74 DENVER BRONCOS (AFC)
HOWARD, ROBERT (MARIETTA) - GUARD - 1924-26 KANSAS CITY COWBOYS; 1927
     CLEVELAND BULLDOGS; 1928 DETROIT WOLVERINES; 1929-30 NEW YORK
     GIANTS
HOWARD, ROBERT (SAN DIEGO STATE) - BACK - 1967-69 SAN DIEGO CHARGERS
     (AFL); 1970-74 SAN DIEGO CHARGERS (AFC)
HOWARD, RON (SEATTLE) - END - 1974 DALLAS COWBOYS (NFC)
HOWARD, SHERMAN (NEVADA) - BACK - 1949 NEW YORK YANKEES (AAFC);
     1950-51 NEW YORK YANKS; 1952-53 CLEVELAND BROWNS
HOWARD, WILLIAM (USC) - BACK - 1937 LOS ANGELES BULLDOGS (AFL)
HOWELL, AUBREY LANE (GRAMBLING) - TACKLE - 1963-64 NEW YORK GIANTS;
     1965-69 PHILADELPHIA EAGLES
HOWELL, CLARENCE (TEXAS A&M) - END - 1948 SAN FRANCISCO 49ERS (AAFC)
HOWELL, DELLES (GRAMBLING) - BACK - 1970-72 NEW ORLEANS SAINTS (NFC);
     1973-74 NEW YORK JETS (AFC)
HOWELL, EARL (MISSISSIPPI) - BACK - 1949 LOS ANGELES DONS (AAFC)
HOWELL, FOSTER (TCU) - TACKLE - 1934 CINCINNATI REDS
HOWELL, JAMES LEE (ARKANSAS) - END - 1937-42, 46-48 NEW YORK GIANTS
HOWELL, JOHN (NEBRASKA) - QBACK - 1938 GREEN BAY PACKERS
HOWELL, MICHAEL (GRAMBLING) - BACK - 1965-69 CLEVELAND BROWNS;
     1970-72 CLEVELAND BROWNS (AFC); 1972 MIAMI DOLPHINS (AFC)
HOWELL, MILLARD (ALABAMA) - BACK - 1937 WASHINGTON REDSKINS
HOWELL, WILFRED (CATHOLIC UNIV.) - END - 1929 BOSTON BRAVES
HOWER - BACK - 1921 LOUISVILLE BRECKS
HOWFIELD, ROBERT - KICKER - 1968-69 DENVER BRONCOS (AFL); 1970 DENVER
     BRONCOS (AFC); 1971-74 NEW YORK JETS (AFC); 1972 SCORING LEADER
     (AFC)
HOWLEY, CHARLES (WEST VIRGINIA) - LB - 1958-59 CHICAGO BEARS; 1961-69
     DALLAS COWBOYS; 1970-73 DALLAS COWBOYS (NFC)
HOWTON, WILLIAM (RICE) - END - 1952-58 GREEN BAY PACKERS; 1959
     CLEVELAND BROWNS; 1960-63 DALLAS COWBOYS
HOYEM, LYNN (LONG BEACH STATE) - GUARD - 1962-63 DALLAS COWBOYS;
     1964-67 PHILADELPHIA EAGLES

HRABETIN, FRANK (LOYOLA OF CALIFORNIA) - TACKLE - 1942 PHILADELPHIA
     EAGLES; 1946 MIAMI SEAHAWKS (AAFC); 1946 BROOKLYN DODGERS (AAFC)
HRIVNAK, GARY (PURDUE) - TACKLE, END - 1973-74 CHICAGO BEARS (NFC)
HRYCYSZYN, STEVEN (ST. BONAVENTURE) - QBACK - 1940 BUFFALO INDIANS
     (AFL); 1941 BUFFALO TIGERS (AFL)
HUARD, JOHN (MAINE) - LB - 1967-69 DENVER BRONCOS (AFL); 1971 NEW
     ORLEANS SAINTS (NFC)
HUARTE, JOHN (NOTRE DAME) - QBACK - 1966-67 BOSTON PATRIOTS (AFL);
     1968 PHILADELPHIA EAGLES; 1970-71 KANSAS CITY CHIEFS (AFC); 1972
     CHICAGO BEARS (NFC)
HUBBARD, ROBERT "CAL" (GENEVA & CENTENARY) - TACKLE - 1927-28, 36 NEW
     YORK GIANTS; 1929-33, 35 GREEN BAY PACKERS; 1936 PITTSBURGH
     PIRATES; 1963 HALL OF FAME
HUBBARD, MARVIN (COLGATE) - BACK - 1969 OAKLAND RAIDERS (AFL);
     1970-74 OAKLAND RAIDERS (AFC)
HUBBARD, WESLEY (SAN JOSE STATE) - END - 1935 BROOKLYN DODGERS
HUBBELL, FRANKLIN (TENNESSEE) - END - 1947-49 LOS ANGELES RAMS
HUBBERT, BRADLEY (ARIZONA) - BACK - 1967-69 SAN DIEGO CHARGERS (AFL);
     1970 SAN DIEGO CHARGERS (AFC)
HUBERT, ALLISON (ALABAMA) - QBACK - 1926 NEW YORK YANKEES (AFL)
HUBKA, EUGENE (BUCKNELL) - BACK - 1947 PITTSBURGH STEELERS
HUDLOW, FLOYD (ARIZONA) - END - 1965 BUFFALO BILLS (AFL); 1967-68
     ATLANTA FALCONS
HUDOCK, MICHAEL (MIAMI) - CENTER - 1960-62 NEW YORK TITANS (AFL);
     1963-65 NEW YORK JETS (AFL); 1966 MIAMI DOLPHINS (AFL); 1967
     KANSAS CITY CHIEFS (AFL)
HUDSON, JAMES (TEXAS) - BACK - 1965-69 NEW YORK JETS (AFL); 1970 NEW
     YORK JETS (AFC)
HUDSON, RICHARD (MEMPHIS STATE) - GUARD - 1962 SAN DIEGO CHARGERS
     (AFL); 1963-67 BUFFALO BILLS (AFL)
HUDSON, RICHARD - BACK - 1923 MINNEAPOLIS MARINES; 1925-26 HAMMOND
     PROS
HUDSON, ROBERT (CLEMSON) - END - 1951-52 NEW YORK GIANTS; 1953-55,
     57-58 PHILADELPHIA EAGLES; 1959 WASHINGTON REDSKINS; 1960 DALLAS
     TEXANS (AFL); 1960-61 DENVER BRONCOS (AFL)
HUDSON, ROBERT (NORTHEASTERN OKLAHOMA) - BACK - 1972 GREEN BAY
     PACKERS (NFC); 1973-74 OAKLAND RAIDERS (AFC)
HUDSON, WILLIAM (CLEMSON) - TACKLE - 1961-62 SAN DIEGO CHARGERS
     (AFL); 1963 BOSTON PATRIOTS (AFL)
HUELLER, JOHN - GUARD - 1922-24 RACINE LEGION
HUEY, EUGENE (WYOMING) - END - 1969 SAN DIEGO CHARGERS (AFL)
HUFF, GARY (FLORIDA STATE) - QBACK - 1973-74 CHICAGO BEARS (NFC)
HUFF, MARTIN (MICHIGAN) - LB - 1972 SAN FRANCISCO 49ERS (NFC)
HUFF, ROBERT "SAM" (WEST VIRGINIA) - LB - 1956-63 NEW YORK GIANTS;
     1964-67, 69 WASHINGTON REDSKINS
HUFFINE, KENNETH (PURDUE) - BACK - 1921 MUNCIE FLYERS; 1921 CHICAGO
     STALEYS; 1922-26 DAYTON TRIANGLES
HUFFMAN, FRANK (MARSHALL) - GUARD - 1939-41 CHICAGO CARDINALS
HUFFMAN, IOLAS (OHIO STATE) - TACKLE - 1923 CLEVELAND INDIANS; 1924
     BUFFALO BISONS
HUFFMAN, RICHARD (TENNESSEE) - TACKLE - 1947-50 LOS ANGELES RAMS
HUFFMAN, VERNON (INDIANA) - QBACK - 1937-38 DETROIT LIONS
HUFNAGEL, JOHN (PENN STATE) - QBACK - 1974 DENVER BRONCOS (AFC)
HUFFORD, DARRELL (CALIFORNIA) - END - 1926 LOS ANGELES BUCCANEERS
HUGASIAN, HARRY (STANFORD) - BACK - 1955 CHICAGO BEARS; 1955
     BALTIMORE COLTS
HUGGINS, ROY (VANDERBILT) - BACK - 1944 CLEVELAND RAMS
HUGHES, BERNARD (OREGON) - CENTER - 1934-36 CHICAGO CARDINALS; 1937
     LOS ANGELES BULLDOGS (AFL)
HUGHES, CHARLES (TEXAS-EL PASO) - BACK, END - 1967-69 PHILADELPHIA
     EAGLES; 1970-71 DETROIT LIONS (NFC)
HUGHES, DENNIS (GEORGE WASHINGTON) - CENTER - 1925 POTTSVILLE MAROONS
HUGHES, DENNIS (GEORGIA) - END - 1970-71 PITTSBURGH STEELERS (AFC)
HUGHES, EDWARD (LACROSSE-WISCONSIN) - END - 1941 BUFFALO TIGERS
     (AFL); 1941 MILWAUKEE CHIEFS (AFL)
HUGHES, EDWARD (TULSA) - BACK - 1954-55 LOS ANGELES RAMS; 1956-58 NEW
     YORK GIANTS
HUGHES, FRANK (BOSTON UNIV.) - END - 1936 BROOKLYN TIGERS (AFL); 1936
     ROCHESTER TIGERS (AFL)
HUGHES, GEORGE (WILLIAM&MARY) - GUARD - 1950-54 PITTSBURGH STEELERS
HUGHES, HENRY (OREGON STATE) - BACK - 1932 BOSTON BRAVES

HUGHES, RICHARD (TULSA) - BACK - 1957 PITTSBURGH STEELERS
HUGHES, ROBERT (JACKSON STATE) - END - 1967, 69 ATLANTA FALCONS
HUGHES, WILLIAM (TEXAS) - CENTER - 1937-40 PHILADELPHIA EAGLES; 1941
    CHICAGO BEARS
HUGHES, WILLIAM PATRICK (BOSTON UNIV.) - LB, CENTER - 1970-74 NEW
    YORK GIANTS (NFC)
HUGHITT, ERNEST "TOMMY" (MICHIGAN) - QBACK - 1920-23 BUFFALO
    ALL-AMERICANS; 1924 BUFFALO BISONS
HUGHLEY, GEORGE (CENTRAL OKLAHOMA STATE) - BACK - 1965 WASHINGTON
    REDSKINS
HUGRET, JOSEPH (NEW YORK UNIV.) - END - 1934 BROOKLYN DODGERS
HULL, MICHAEL (USC) - END, BACK - 1968-69 CHICAGO BEARS; 1970 CHICAGO
    BEARS (NFC); 1971-74 WASHINGTON REDSKINS (NFC)
HULL, THOMAS (PENN STATE) - LB - 1974 SAN FRANCISCO 49ERS (NFC)
HULL, WILLIAM (WAKE FOREST) - END - 1962 DALLAS TEXANS (AFL)
HULTMAN, VIVIAN (MICHIGAN STATE) - END - 1925-26 DETROIT PANTHERS;
    1927 POTTSVILLE MAROONS
HULTZ, GEORGE (SOUTHERN MISSISSIPPI) - TACKLE - 1962 ST. LOUIS
    CARDINALS
HULTZ, WILLIAM DONALD (SOUTHERN MISSISSIPPI) - END, TACKLE - 1963
    MINNESOTA VIKINGS; 1964-69 PHILADELPHIA EAGLES; 1970-73
    PHILADELPHIA EAGLES (NFC); 1974 CHICAGO BEARS (NFC)
HUMBERT, RICHARD (RICHMOND) - END - 1941, 45-49 PHILADELPHIA EAGLES
HUMBLE, WELDON (RICE) - GUARD - 1947-49 CLEVELAND BROWNS (AAFC); 1950
    CLEVELAND BROWNS; 1952 DALLAS TEXANS
HUMMEL, ARNOLD (LOMBARD) - BACK - 1926 KANSAS CITY COWBOYS; 1927
    CHICAGO CARDINALS
HUMMEL - BACK - 1926 PROVIDENCE STEAMROLLERS
HUMMON, JOHN (WITTENBERG) - END - 1926-28 DAYTON TRIANGLES
HUMPHREY, CLAUDE (TENNESSEE STATE) - END - 1968-69 ATLANTA FALCONS;
    1970-74 ATLANTA FALCONS (NFC)
HUMPHREY, LOYIE (BAYLOR) - QBACK - 1959-60 LOS ANGELES RAMS; 1961-62
    DALLAS COWBOYS; 1963-65 ST. LOUIS CARDINALS; 1966 HOUSTON OILERS
    (AFL)
HUMPHREY, PAUL (PURDUE) - CENTER - 1939 BROOKLYN DODGERS; 1940-41
    MILWAUKEE CHIEFS (AFL)
HUMPHREY, TOMMY (ABILENE CHRISTIAN) - CENTER - 1974 KANSAS CITY
    CHIEFS (AFC)
HUMPHREIS, ROBERT (WICHITA STATE) - LB - 1967-68 DENVER BRONCOS (AFL)
HUNEKE, CHARLES (ST. BENEDICT'S) - TACKLE - 1946-47 CHICAGO ROCKETS
    (AAFC); 1947-48 BROOKLYN DODGERS (AAFC)
HUNSINGER, CHARLES (FLORIDA) - BACK - 1950-52 CHICAGO BEARS
HUNSINGER, EDWARD (NOTRE DAME) - END - 1926 BROOKLYN HORSEMEN (AFL)
HUNT, BEN (ALABAMA) - TACKLE - 1923 TOLEDO MAROONS
HUNT, CALVIN (BAYLOR) - CENTER - 1970 PHILADELPHIA EAGLES (NFC);
    1972-73 HOUSTON OILERS (AFC)
HUNT, CHARLES (FLORIDA STATE) - LB - 1973 SAN FRANCISCO 49ERS (NFC)
HUNT, ERVIN (FRESNO STATE) - BACK - 1970 GREEN BAY PACKERS (NFC)
HUNT, GEORGE (TENNESSEE) - KICKER - 1973 BALTIMORE COLTS (AFC)
HUNT, ISAAC "ZEKE" (BRADLEY) - CENTER - 1937 NEW YORK YANKS (AFL)
HUNT, JAMES (PRAIRIE VIEW) - END, TACKLE - 1960-69 BOSTON PATRIOTS
    (AFL); 1970 BOSTON PATRIOTS (AFC)
HUNT, JOHN (MARSHALL) - BACK - 1945 CHICAGO BEARS
HUNT, KEVIN (DOANE-NEBRASKA) - TACKLE - 1972 GREEN BAY PACKERS (NFC);
    1973-74 HOUSTON OILERS (AFC)
HUNT, ROBERT (AUBURN) - BACK - 1962 DALLAS TEXANS (AFL); 1963-67
    KANSAS CITY CHIEFS (AFL); 1968-69 CINCINNATI BENGALS (AFL)
HUNT, ROBERT (HEIDELBERG) - BACK - 1974 CLEVELAND BROWNS (AFC)
HUNT, SAMUEL (S.F.AUSTIN) - LB - 1974 NEW ENGLAND PATRIOTS (AFC)
HUNTER, ARTHUR (NOTRE DAME) - CENTER - 1954 GREEN BAY PACKERS;
    1956-59 CLEVELAND BROWNS; 1960-64 LOS ANGELES RAMS; 1965
    PITTSBURGH STEELERS
HUNTER, GEORGE "BILL" (SYRACUSE) - BACK - 1965 WASHINGTON REDSKINS;
    1966 MIAMI DOLPHINS (AFL)
HUNTER, JAMES SCOTT (ALABAMA) - QBACK - 1971-73 GREEN BAY PACKERS
    (NFC); 1974 BUFFALO BILLS (AFC)
HUNTER, MERLE (ASHLAND) - GUARD - 1925-26 HAMMOND PROS
HUNTER, ROMNEY (MARSHALL) - END - 1933 PORTSMOUTH SPARTANS
HUNZELMAN, HARRY (IOWA) - GUARD - 1919 ROCK ISLAND INDEPENDENTS

HUPKE, THOMAS (ALABAMA) - GUARD - 1934-37 DETROIT LIONS; 1938-39
    CLEVELAND RAMS
HURLBURT, JOHN (CHICAGO) - BACK - 1924-25 CHICAGO CARDINALS
HURLEY, GEORGE (WASHINGTON STATE) - GUARD - 1932 BOSTON BRAVES; 1933
    BOSTON REDSKINS
HURLEY, JOHN (WASHINGTON STATE) - END - 1931 CLEVELAND INDIANS
HURST, WILLIAM (OREGON) - GUARD - 1924 CHICAGO BEARS; 1924 KENOSHA
    MAROONS
HURSTON, CHARLES (AUBURN) - END, LB - 1965-69 KANSAS CITY CHIEFS
    (AFL); 1970 KANSAS CITY CHIEFS (AFC); 1971 BUFFALO BILLS (AFC)
HUSMANN, EDWARD (NEBRASKA) - TACKLE - 1953, 56-59 CHICAGO CARDINALS;
    1960 DALLAS COWBOYS; 1961-65 HOUSTON OILERS (AFL)
HUST, ALBERT (TENNESSEE) - END - 1946 CHICAGO CARDINALS
HUTCHERSON, KEN (LIVINGSTON STATE) - LB - 1974 DALLAS COWBOYS (NFC)
HUTCHINSON, ELVIN (WHITTIER) - BACK - 1939 DETROIT LIONS
HUTCHINSON, RALPH (CHATTANOOGA) - TACKLE - 1949 NEW YORK GIANTS
HUTCHINSON, THOMAS (KENTUCKY) - END - 1963-65 CLEVELAND BROWNS; 1966
    ATLANTA FALCONS
HUTCHINSON, WILLIAM (DARTMOUTH) - BACK - 1940 NEW YORK AMERICANS
    (AFL); 1941 NEW YORK AMERICANS (AFL); 1942 NEW YORK GIANTS
HUTCHISON, CHARLES (OHIO STATE) - GUARD - 1970-72 ST. LOUIS CARDINALS
    (NFC); 1973-74 CLEVELAND BROWNS (AFC)
HUTH, GERALD (WAKE FOREST) - GUARD - 1956 NEW YORK GIANTS; 1959-60
    PHILADELPHIA EAGLES; 1961-63 MINNESOTA VIKINGS
HUTSON, DONALD (ALABAMA) - END - 1935-45 GREEN BAY PACKERS; 1940-44
    SCORING LEADER; 1936-37, 39, 41-45 PASS RECEIVING LEADER; 1940
    INTERCEPTION LEADER; (TIED WITH PARKER AND RYAN); 1943 FIELD
    GOAL LEADER; 1963 HALL OF FAME
HUTSON, MERLE (HEIDELBERG) - GUARD - 1931 CLEVELAND INDIANS
HUTTON, LEON (PURDUE) - BACK - 1930 FRANKFORD YELLOWJACKETS
HUXHOLD, KENNETH (WISCONSIN) - GUARD - 1954-58 PHILADELPHIA EAGLES
HUZVAR, JOHN (N.CAROLINA STATE & PITTSBURGH) - BACK - 1952
    PHILADELPHIA EAGLES; 1953-54 BALTIMORE COLTS
HYATT, FREDERICK (AUBURN) - END - 1968-69 ST. LOUIS CARDINALS;
    1970-72 ST. LOUIS CARDINALS (NFC); 1973 NEW ORLEANS SAINTS
    (NFC); 1973 WASHINGTON REDSKINS (NFC)
HYLAND, ROBERT (BOSTON COLLEGE) - GUARD,CENTER,TACKLE - 1967-69 GREEN
    BAY PACKERS; 1970 CHICAGO BEARS (NFC); 1971-74 NEW YORK GIANTS
    (NFC)
HYNES, PAUL (LOUISIANA TECH) - BACK - 1961 DALLAS TEXANS (AFL);
    1961-62 NEW YORK TITANS (AFL)
IACAVAZZI, COSMO (PRINCETON) - BACK - 1965 NEW YORK JETS (AFL)
ICKES, LLOYD (PENN STATE) - BACK - 1940 NEW YORK AMERICANS (AFL)
IGLEHART, FLOYD (WILEY-TEXAS) - BACK - 1958 LOS ANGELES RAMS
ILG, RAYMOND (COLGATE) - LB - 1967-68 BOSTON PATRIOTS (AFL)
ILGENFRITZ, MARK (VANDERBILT) - END - 1974 CLEVELAND BROWNS (AFC)
ILLMAN, EDWARD (MONTANA) - QBACK - 1926 LOS ANGELES WILDCATS (AFL);
    1928 CHICAGO CARDINALS
ILLOWIT, ROY (CCNY) - TACKLE - 1937 BROOKLYN DODGERS
IMAN, KENNETH (SOUTHEAST MISSOURI STATE) - CENTER - 1960-63 GREEN BAY
    PACKERS; 1965-69 LOS ANGELES RAMS; 1970-74 LOS ANGELES RAMS (NFC)
IMHOF, MARTIN (SAN DIEGO STATE) - END - 1972 ST. LOUIS CARDINALS
    (NFC); 1974 WASHINGTON REDSKINS (NFC)
IMLAY, TALMA (CALIFORNIA) - BACK - 1926 LOS ANGELES BUCCANEERS; 1927
    NEW YORK GIANTS
INABINET, CLARENCE (CLEMSON) - GUARD - 1936 ROCHESTER TIGERS (AFL)
INGALLS, ROBERT (MICHIGAN) - CENTER - 1942 GREEN BAY PACKERS
INGLE - BACK - 1921 EVANSVILLE CRIMSON GIANTS
INGWERSON, BURTON (ILLINOIS) - TACKLE - 1920 DECATUR STALEYS; 1921
    CHICAGO STALEYS
INMAN, JERALD (OREGON) - TACKLE - 1966-69 DENVER BRONCOS (AFL);
    1970-71, 73 DENVER BRONCOS (AFC)
INTRIERI, MARNE (LOYOLA OF MARYLAND) - GUARD - 1932 STATEN ISLAND
    STAPELTONS; 1933-34 BOSTON REDSKINS
IPPOLITO, ANTHONY (PURDUE) - GUARD - 1943 CHICAGO BEARS
IRGENS, EINAR - END - 1921-24 MINNEAPOLIS MARINES
IRGENS, NEWMAN - BACK - 1922 MINNEAPOLIS MARINES
IRONS, GERALD (MARYLAND-EASTERN SHORE) - LB - 1970-74 OAKLAND RAIDERS
    (AFC)

IRVIN, BARLOW (TEXAS A&M) - GUARD - 1926 BUFFALO RANGERS; 1927
    BUFFALO BISONS
IRVIN, CECIL (DAVIS&ELKINS) - TACKLE - 1931 PROVIDENCE STEAMROLLERS;
    1932-35 NEW YORK GIANTS
IRWIN, WILLIAM (FLORIDA A&M) - END - 1953 PHILADELPHIA EAGLES
IRWIN, DONALD (COLGATE) - BACK - 1936 ROCHESTER TIGERS (AFL); 1936
    NEW YORK YANKS (AFL); 1936 BOSTON REDSKINS; 1937-39 WASHINGTON
    REDSKINS
IRWIN, JAMES - BACK - 1920 ROCHESTER JEFFERSONS; 1921-23 LOUISVILLE
    BRECKS
ISAACSON, THEODORE (WASHINGTON) - TACKLE - 1934-35 CHICAGO CARDINALS
ISABEL, WILMER (OHIO STATE) - BACK - 1923-24 COLUMBUS TIGERS
ISBELL, CECIL (PURDUE) - QBACK - 1938-42 GREEN BAY PACKERS; 1941-42
    PASSING LEADER
ISBELL, JOSEPH (HOUSTON) - GUARD - 1962-64 DALLAS COWBOYS; 1966
    CLEVELAND BROWNS
ISENBARGER, JOHN (INDIANA) - BACK, END - 1970-73 SAN FRANCISCO 49ERS
    (NFC)
ISSELHARDT, RALPH (FRANKLIN) - GUARD - 1937 DETROIT LIONS; 1937
    CLEVELAND RAMS
ITZEL, JOHN (PITTSBURGH) - BACK - 1945 PITTSBURGH STEELERS
IVERSON, CHRISTOPHER (OREGON) - BACK - 1947 NEW YORK GIANTS; 1948-49
    NEW YORK YANKEES (AAFC); 1950-51 NEW YORK YANKS
IVORY, ROBERT (DETROIT) - GUARD - 1947 DETROIT LIONS
IVY, FRANK (OKLAHOMA) - END - 1940 PITTSBURGH STEELERS; 1940-42,
    45-47 CHICAGO CARDINALS
IZO, GEORGE (NOTRE DAME) - QBACK - 1960 ST. LOUIS CARDINALS; 1961-64
    WASHINGTON REDSKINS; 1965 DETROIT LIONS; 1966 PITTSBURGH STEELERS
JACKSON, BERNARD (WASHINGTON STATE) - BACK - 1972-74 CINCINNATI
    BENGALS (AFC)
JACKSON, CHARLES (SMU) - BACK - 1958 CHICAGO CARDINALS; 1960 DALLAS
    TEXANS (AFL)
JACKSON, CLARENCE (WESTERN KENTUCKY) - BACK - 1974 NEW YORK JETS (AFC)
JACKSON, COLVILLE (CHICAGO) - END - 1921 EVANSVILLE CRIMSON GIANTS;
    1922 HAMMOND PROS
JACKSON, DONALD (NORTH CAROLINA) - BACK - 1936 PHILADELPHIA EAGLES
JACKSON, ERNEST (DUKE) - BACK - 1972-74 NEW ORLEANS SAINTS (NFC)
JACKSON, FRANK (SMU) - BACK - 1961-62 DALLAS TEXANS (AFL); 1963-65
    KANSAS CITY CHIEFS (AFL); 1966-67 MIAMI DOLPHINS (AFL)
JACKSON, HAROLD (JACKSON STATE) - END - 1968 LOS ANGELES RAMS; 1969
    PHILADELPHIA EAGLES; 1970-72 PHILADELPHIA EAGLES (NFC); 1973-74
    LOS ANGELES RAMS (NFC); 1972 PASS RECEIVING LEADER (NFC)
JACKSON, HENRY (MISSOURI) - BACK - 1928 DETROIT WOLVERINES
JACKSON, HONOR (PACIFIC) - BACK - 1972-73 NEW ENGLAND PATRIOTS (AFC);
    1973-74 NEW YORK GIANTS (NFC)
JACKSON, JAMES (WESTERN ILLINOIS) - BACK - 1966-67 SAN FRANCISCO 49ERS
JACKSON, JOEY (NEW MEXICO STATE) - END, TACKLE - 1972-73 NEW YORK
    JETS (AFC)
JACKSON, KENNETH (TEXAS) - TACKLE - 1952 DALLAS TEXANS; 1953-57
    BALTIMORE COLTS
JACKSON, LARRON (MISSOURI) - GUARD, TACKLE - 1971-74 DENVER BRONCOS
    (AFC)
JACKSON, LAWRENCE (LOYOLA OF ILLINOIS) - CENTER - 1926 LOUISVILLE
    COLONELS
JACKSON, LEROY (WESTERN ILLINOIS) - BACK - 1962-63 WASHINGTON REDSKINS
JACKSON, PERRY (SOUTHWEST OKLAHOMA STATE) - TACKLE - 1928-30
    PROVIDENCE STEAMROLLERS
JACKSON, RANDALL (FLORIDA) - TACKLE - 1967-69 CHICAGO BEARS; 1970-74
    CHICAGO BEARS (NFC)
JACKSON, RANDY (WICHITA STATE) - BACK - 1972 BUFFALO BILLS (AFC);
    1973 SAN FRANCISCO 49ERS (NFC); 1974 PHILADELPHIA EAGLES (NFC)
JACKSON, RICHARD (SOUTHERN) - LB, END - 1966 OAKLAND RAIDERS (AFL);
    1967-69 DENVER BRONCOS (AFL); 1970-72 DENVER BRONCOS (AFC); 1972
    CLEVELAND BROWNS (AFC)
JACKSON, ROBERT (ALABAMA) - BACK - 1960 PHILADELPHIA EAGLES; 1961
    CHICAGO BEARS
JACKSON, ROBERT (NEW MEXICO STATE) - BACK - 1962-63 SAN DIEGO
    CHARGERS (AFL); 1964 HOUSTON OILERS (AFL); 1964 OAKLAND RAIDERS
    (AFL); 1965 HOUSTON OILERS (AFL)
JACKSON, ROBERT (NORTH CAROLINA A&T) - BACK - 1950-51 NEW YORK GIANTS
JACKSON, ROLAND (RICE) - BACK - 1962 ST. LOUIS CARDINALS

JACKSON, STEPHEN (ARLINGTON STATE) - LB - 1966-67 WASHINGTON REDSKINS
JACKSON, THOMAS (LOUISVILLE) - LB - 1973-74 DENVER BRONCOS (AFC)
JACKSON, TRENTON (ILLINOIS) - BACK - 1966 PHILADELPHIA EAGLES; 1967
     WASHINGTON REDSKINS
JACKSON, WILBUR (ALABAMA) - BACK - 1974 SAN FRANCISCO 49ERS (NFC)
JACKSON - BACK - 1919 CANTON BULLDOGS
JACKUNAS, FRANK (DETROIT) - CENTER - 1962 BUFFALO BILLS (AFL); 1963
     DENVER BRONCOS (AFL)
JACOBS, ALLEN (UTAH) - BACK - 1965 GREEN BAY PACKERS; 1966-67 NEW
     YORK GIANTS
JACOBS, HARRY (BRADLEY) - LB - 1960-62 BOSTON PATRIOTS (AFL); 1963-69
     BUFFALO BILLS (AFL); 1970 NEW ORLEANS SAINTS (NFC)
JACOBS, HERSHELL RAY (HOWARD PAYNE) - TACKLE - 1963-66 DENVER BRONCOS
     (AFL); 1967-68 MIAMI DOLPHINS (AFL); 1969 BOSTON PATRIOTS (AFL)
JACOBS, JACK (OKLAHOMA) - QBACK - 1942, 45 CLEVELAND RAMS; 1946
     WASHINGTON REDSKINS; 1947-49 GREEN BAY PACKERS; 1947 PUNTING
     LEADER
JACOBS, MARVIN - TACKLE - 1948 CHICAGO CARDINALS
JACOBS, PROVERB (CALIFORNIA) - TACKLE - 1958 PHILADELPHIA EAGLES;
     1960 NEW YORK GIANTS; 1961-62 NEW YORK TITANS (AFL); 1963-64
     OAKLAND RAIDERS (AFL)
JACOBS - BACK - 1920 DETROIT HERALDS
JACOBSON, JOHN (OKLAHOMA STATE) - BACK - 1965 SAN DIEGO CHARGERS (AFL)
JACOBSON, LARRY (NEBRASKA) - END, TACKLE - 1972-74 NEW YORK GIANTS
     (NFC)
JACQUITH, JAMES - QBACK - 1926 KANSAS CITY COWBOYS; 1926 ROCK ISLAND
     INDEPENDENTS (AFL)
JACUNSKI, HARRY (FORDHAM) - END - 1939-44 GREEN BAY PACKERS
JAFFURS, JOHN (PENN STATE) - GUARD - 1946 WASHINGTON REDSKINS
JAGADE, HERRY (INDIANA) - BACK - 1949 BALTIMORE COLTS (AAFC); 1951-53
     CLEVELAND BROWNS; 1954-55 CHICAGO BEARS
JAGIELSKI, HARRY (INDIANA) - GUARD - 1956 CHICAGO CARDINALS; 1956
     WASHINGTON REDSKINS; 1960-61 BOSTON PATRIOTS (AFL); 1961 OAKLAND
     RAIDERS (AFL)
JAKOWENKO, GEORGE (SYRACUSE) - KICKER - 1974 OAKLAND RAIDERS (AFC)
JAMERSON, CHARLES (ARKANSAS) - END - 1926 HARTFORD BLUES
JAMES, CLAUDIS (JACKSON STATE) - BACK - 1967-68 GREEN BAY PACKERS
JAMES, DANIEL (OHIO STATE) - TACKLE - 1960-66 PITTSBURGH STEELERS;
     1967 CHICAGO BEARS
JAMES, JOHN (FLORIDA) - KICKER - 1972-74 ATLANTA FALCONS (NFC)
JAMES, NATHANIEL (FLORIDA A&M) - BACK - 1968 CLEVELAND BROWNS
JAMES, RICHARD (OREGON) - BACK - 1956-63 WASHINGTON REDSKINS; 1964
     NEW YORK GIANTS; 1965 MINNESOTA VIKINGS
JAMES, ROBERT (FISK) - BACK - 1969 BUFFALO BILLS (AFL); 1970-74
     BUFFALO BILLS (AFC)
JAMES, RON "PO" (NEW MEXICO STATE) - BACK - 1972-74 PHILADELPHIA
     EAGLES (NFC)
JANCIK, ROBERT (LAMAR TECH) - BACK - 1962-67 HOUSTON OILERS (AFL)
JAMES, THEODORE (NEBRASKA) - GUARD - 1929 FRANKFORD YELLOWJACKETS
JAMES, THOMAS (OHIO STATE) - BACK - 1947 DETROIT LIONS; 1948-49
     CLEVELAND BROWNS (AAFC); 1950-55 CLEVELAND BROWNS; 1956
     BALTIMORE COLTS
JAMIESON, RICHARD (BRADLEY) - QBACK - 1960-61 NEW YORK TITANS (AFL)
JAMIESON, ROBERT (FRANKLIN&MARSHALL) - CENTER - 1924 FRANKFORD
     YELLOWJACKETS
JAMISON, ALFRED (COLGATE) - TACKLE - 1960-62 HOUSTON OILERS (AFL)
JANECEK, CLARENCE (PURDUE) - GUARD - 1933 PITTSBURGH PIRATES
JANERETTE, CHARLES (PENN STATE) - GUARD - 1960 LOS ANGELES RAMS;
     1961-62 NEW YORK GIANTS; 1963 NEW YORK JETS (AFL); 1964-65
     DENVER BRONCOS (AFL)
JANET, ERNIE (WASHINGTON) - GUARD, CENTER - 1972-74 CHICAGO BEARS
     (NFC)
JANIAK, LEONARD (OHIO) - BACK - 1939 BROOKLYN DODGERS; 1940-42
     CLEVELAND RAMS
JANIK, THOMAS (TEXAS A&I) - - 1963-64 DENVER BRONCOS (AFL); 1965-68
     BUFFALO BILLS (AFL); 1969 BOSTON PATRIOTS (AFL); 1970 BOSTON
     PATRIOTS (AFC); 1971 NEW ENGLAND PATRIOTS (AFC); 1967
     INTERCEPTION LEADER (AFL); (TIED WITH WESTMORELAND AND FARR)
JANKOVICH, KEEVER (COLLEGE OF PACIFIC) - CENTER - 1952 DALLAS TEXANS;
     1953 CHICAGO CARDINALS
JANKOWSKI, BRUCE (OHIO STATE) - END - 1971-72 KANSAS CITY CHIEFS (AFC)

JANKOWSKI, EDWARD (WISCONSIN) - BACK - 1937-41 GREEN BAY PACKERS
JANOWICZ, VICTOR (OHIO STATE) - BACK - 1954-55 WASHINGTON REDSKINS
JANSANTE, VALERIO (DUQUESNE) - END - 1946-51 PITTSBURGH STEELERS;
    1951 GREEN BAY PACKERS
JANSIN, LOUIS - END - 1922 LOUISVILLE BRECKS
JAPPE, PAUL (SYRACUSE) - END - 1925, 27-28 NEW YORK GIANTS; 1926
    BROOKLYN LIONS
JAQUA, JON (LEWIS&CLARK) - BACK - 1970-72 WASHINGTON REDSKINS (NFC)
JAQUESS, LINDEL "PETE" (EASTERN NEW MEXICO) - BACK - 1964-65 HOUSTON
    OILERS (AFL); 1966-67 MIAMI DOLPHINS (AFL); 1967-69 DENVER
    BRONCOS (AFL); 1970 DENVER BRONCOS (AFC)
JARMOLUK, MICHAEL (TEMPLE) - TACKLE - 1946-47 CHICAGO BEARS; 1948
    BOSTON YANKS; 1949 NEW YORK BULLDOGS; 1949-55 PHILADELPHIA EAGLES
JARVI, TOIMI (NORTHERN ILLINOIS) - BACK - 1944 PHILADELPHIA EAGLES;
    1945 PITTSBURGH STEELERS
JARVIS, J. BRUCE (WASHINGTON) - CENTER - 1971-74 BUFFALO BILLS (AFC)
JARVIS, LEON RAFMINTON "RAY" (NORFOLK ST.) - END - 1971-72 ATLANTA
    FALCONS (NFC); 1973 BUFFALO BILLS (AFC); 1974 DETROIT LIONS (NFC)
JASZEWSKI, FLOYD (MINNESOTA) - TACKLE - 1950-51 DETROIT LIONS
JAURON, RICHARD (YALE) - BACK - 1973-74 DETROIT LIONS (NFC)
JAWISH, HENRY (GEORGETOWN) - GUARD - 1926 POTTSVILLE MAROONS
JAWORSKI, RON (YOUNGSTOWN STATE) - QBACK - 1974 LOS ANGELES RAMS (NFC)
JAYNES, DAVID (KANSAS) - QBACK - 1974 KANSAS CITY CHIEFS (AFC)
JEAN, WALTER - (PLAYED UNDER NAME OF WALTER LE JEUNE)
JECHA, RALPH (NORTHWESTERN) - GUARD - 1955 CHICAGO BEARS; 1956
    PITTSBURGH STEELERS
JEFFERS, W. EDWARD (OKLAHOMA A&M) - GUARD - 1947 BROOKLYN DODGERS
    (AAFC)
JEFFERSON, ROY (UTAH) - END - 1965-69 PITTSBURGH STEELERS; 1970
    BALTIMORE COLTS (AFC); 1971-74 WASHINGTON REDSKINS (NFC)
JEFFERSON, WILLIAM (MISSISSIPPI STATE) - BACK - 1941 DETROIT LIONS;
    1942 BROOKLYN DODGERS; 1942 PHILADELPHIA EAGLES
JEFFRIES, ROBERT (MISSOURI) - GUARD - 1942 BROOKLYN DODGERS
JELACIC, JON (MINNESOTA) - END - 1958 NEW YORK GIANTS; 1961-64
    OAKLAND RAIDERS (AFL)
JELLEY, THOMAS (MIAMI-FLORIDA) - END - 1951 PITTSBURGH STEELERS
JENCKS, ROBERT (MIAMI-OHIO) - END - 1963-64 CHICAGO BEARS; 1965
    WASHINGTON REDSKINS
JENISON, RAYMOND (SOUTH DAKOTA STATE) - TACKLE - 1931 GREEN BAY
    PACKERS
JENKE, NOEL (MINNESOTA) - LB - 1971 MINNESOTA VIKINGS (NFC); 1972
    ATLANTA FALCONS (NFC); 1973-74 GREEN BAY PACKERS (NFC)
JENKINS, ALFRED (TULSA) - TACKLE, GUARD - 1969 CLEVELAND BROWNS; 1970
    CLEVELAND BROWNS (AFC); 1972 MIAMI DOLPHINS (AFC); 1973 HOUSTON
    OILERS (AFC)
JENKINS, ED (HOLY CROSS) - BACK - 1972 MIAMI DOLPHINS (AFC); 1974 NEW
    YORK GIANTS (NFC); 1974 BUFFALO BILLS (AFC); 1974 NEW ENGLAND
    PATRIOTS (AFC)
JENKINS, JACQUE (VANDERBILT) - BACK - 1943, 46-47 WASHINGTON REDSKINS
JENKINS, JONATHAN (DARTMOUTH) - TACKLE - 1949 BALTIMORE COLTS (AAFC);
    1950 BALTIMORE COLTS; 1950 NEW YORK YANKS
JENKINS, LEON (WEST VIRGINIA) - BACK - 1972 DETROIT LIONS (NFC)
JENKINS, WALTER (WAYNE) - END - 1955 DETROIT LIONS
JENNINGS, DAVE (ST. LAWRENCE) - KICKER - 1974 NEW YORK GIANTS (NFC)
JENNINGS, JAMES (MISSOURI) - END - 1955 GREEN BAY PACKERS
JENNINGS, JOHN (OHIO STATE) - TACKLE - 1950-57 CHICAGO CARDINALS
JENNINGS, LOUIS (HASKELL) - END - 1929 PROVIDENCE STEAMROLLERS; 1930
    PORTSMOUTH SPARTANS
JENSEN, ROBERT (IOWA STATE) - END - 1948 CHICAGO ROCKETS (AAFC); 1949
    CHICAGO HORNETS (AAFC); 1950 BALTIMORE COLTS
JENSVOLD, LEO (IOWA) - QBACK - 1931 CHICAGO BEARS; 1931 CLEVELAND
    INDIANS
JERALDS, LUTHER (NORTH CAROLINA COLLEGE) - END - 1961 DALLAS TEXANS
    (AFL)
JESSEN, ERNEST (IOWA) - TACKLE - 1931 CLEVELAND INDIANS
JESSIE, RONALD (KANSAS) - END - 1971-74 DETROIT LIONS (NFC)
JESSUP, WILLIAM (USC) - END - 1951-52, 54, 56-58 SAN FRANCISCO 49ERS;
    1960 DENVER BRONCOS (AFL)
JETER, ANTHONY (NEBRASKA) - END - 1966, 68 PITTSBURGH STEELERS
JETER, EUGENE (ARKANSAS AM&N) - LB - 1965-67 DENVER BRONCOS (AFL)

JETER, ROBERT (IOWA) - BACK - 1963-69 GREEN BAY PACKERS; 1970 GREEN
    BAY PACKERS (NFC); 1971-73 CHICAGO BEARS (NFC)
JETT, JOHN (WAKE FOREST) - END - 1941 DETROIT LIONS
JEWETT, ROBERT (MICHIGAN STATE) - END - 1958 CHICAGO BEARS
JETER, PERRY (CALIFORNIA POLYTECH) - BACK - 1956-57 CHICAGO BEARS
JOBKO, WILLIAM (OHIO STATE) - LB - 1958-62 LOS ANGELES RAMS; 1963-65
    MINNESOTA VIKINGS; 1966 ATLANTA FALCONS
JOCHER, ARTHUR (MANHATTAN) - GUARD - 1940, 42 BROOKLYN DODGERS
JOE, BILLY (VILLANOVA) - BACK - 1963-64 DENVER BRONCOS (AFL); 1965
    BUFFALO BILLS (AFL); 1966 MIAMI DOLPHINS (AFL); 1967-68 NEW YORK
    JETS (AFL)
JOE, LAWRENCE (PENN STATE) - BACK - 1949 BUFFALO BILLS (AAFC)
JOESTING, HERBERT (MINNESOTA) - BACK - 1929-30 MINNEAPOLIS
    REDJACKETS; 1930-31 FRANKFORD YELLOWJACKETS; 1931-32 CHICAGO
    BEARS
JOHNS, JAMES (MICHIGAN) - GUARD - 1923 CLEVELAND INDIANS; 1924
    CLEVELAND BULLDOGS; 1924 MINNEAPOLIS MARINES
JOHNS, PETER (TULANE) - BACK - 1967-68 HOUSTON OILERS (AFL)
JOHNSON, ALBERT (CINCINNATI) - BACK - 1972-74 HOUSTON OILERS (AFC)
JOHNSON, ALBERT (KENTUCKY) - BACK - 1937 BROOKLYN DODGERS; 1938-39
    CHICAGO BEARS; 1939-41 CHICAGO CARDINALS; 1942 PHILADELPHIA
    EAGLES
JOHNSON, ALVIN (HARDIN-SIMMONS) - BACK - 1948 PHILADELPHIA EAGLES
JOHNSON, ANDERSON "ANDY" (GEORGIA) - BACK, END - 1974 NEW ENGLAND
    PATRIOTS (AFC)
JOHNSON, ARTHUR (FORDHAM) - TACKLE - 1923-25 DULUTH KELLEYS; 1926-27
    DULUTH ESKIMOS
JOHNSON, BENNY (JOHNSON C. SMITH) - BACK - 1970-73 HOUSTON OILERS
    (AFC)
JOHNSON, BILLY (WIDENER) - END - 1974 HOUSTON OILERS (AFC)
JOHNSON, CARL (NEBRASKA) - TACKLE, GUARD - 1972-73 NEW ORLEANS SAINTS
    (NFC)
JOHNSON, CARL (TENNESSEE) - LB - 1973 NEW ENGLAND PATRIOTS (AFC)
JOHNSON, CECIL (EAST TEXAS STATE) - BACK - 1943 BROOKLYN DODGERS;
    1944 BROOKLYN TIGERS
JOHNSON, CHARLES (LOUISVILLE) - TACKLE - 1966-68 SAN FRANCISCO 49ERS
JOHNSON, CHARLES LANE (NEW MEXICO STATE) - QBACK - 1961-69 ST. LOUIS
    CARDINALS; 1970-71 HOUSTON OILERS (AFC); 1972-74 DENVER BRONCOS
    (AFC)
JOHNSON, CLYDE (KENTUCKY) - TACKLE - 1946-47 LOS ANGELES RAMS; 1948
    LOS ANGELES DONS (AAFC)
JOHNSON, CORNELIUS (VIRGINIA UNION) - GUARD - 1968-69 BALTIMORE
    COLTS; 1970-73 BALTIMORE COLTS (AFC)
JOHNSON, CURTIS (TOLEDO) - BACK - 1970-74 MIAMI DOLPHINS (AFC)
JOHNSON, DARYL (MORGAN STATE) - BACK - 1968-69 BOSTON PATRIOTS (AFL);
    1970 BOSTON PATRIOTS (AFC)
JOHNSON, DENNIS (DELAWARE) - TACKLE - 1974 WASHINGTON REDSKINS (NFC)
JOHNSON, DONALD (CALIFORNIA) - BACK - 1953-55 PHILADELPHIA EAGLES
JOHNSON, DONALD (NORTHWESTERN) - CENTER - 1942 CLEVELAND RAMS
JOHNSON, ELLIS (SOUTHEASTERN LOUISIANA) - BACK - 1965-66 BOSTON
    PATRIOTS (AFL)
JOHNSON, ESSEX (GRAMBLING) - BACK - 1968-69 CINCINNATI BENGALS (AFL);
    1970-74 CINCINNATI BENGALS (AFC)
JOHNSON, EUGENE (CINCINNATI) - BACK - 1959-60 PHILADELPHIA EAGLES;
    1961 MINNESOTA VIKINGS; 1961 NEW YORK GIANTS
JOHNSON, FARNHAM (WISCONSIN & MICHIGAN) - END - 1948 CHICAGO ROCKETS
    (AAFC)
JOHNSON, FRANK (WASHINGTON&LEE) - TACKLE - 1919 MASSILLON TIGERS;
    1919-21 AKRON PROS; 1920 HAMMOND PROS
JOHNSON, GEORGE (DRAKE) - BACK - 1922 RACINE LEGION
JOHNSON, GILBERT (SMU) - BACK - 1949 NEW YORK YANKEES (AAFC)
JOHNSON, GLENN (ARIZONA STATE) - TACKLE - 1948 NEW YORK YANKEES
    (AAFC); 1949 GREEN BAY PACKERS
JOHNSON, HARVEY (WILLIAM&MARY) - BACK - 1946-49 NEW YORK YANKEES
    (AAFC); 1951 NEW YORK YANKS
JOHNSON, HERBERT (WASHINGTON) - BACK - 1954 NEW YORK GIANTS
JOHNSON, HOWARD (GEORGIA) - GUARD - 1940-41 GREEN BAY PACKERS
JOHNSON, JACK (MIAMI) - BACK - 1957-59 CHICAGO BEARS; 1960-61 BUFFALO
    BILLS (AFL); 1961 DALLAS TEXANS (AFL)

JOHNSON, JAMES (UCLA) - BACK - 1961-69 SAN FRANCISCO 49ERS; 1970-74
     SAN FRANCISCO 49ERS (NFC)
JOHNSON, JERRY (MORNINGSIDE) - BACK - 1922 ROCK ISLAND INDEPENDENTS
JOHNSON, JOHN (INDIANA) - TACKLE - 1963-68 CHICAGO BEARS
JOHNSON, JOHN (UTAH) - TACKLE - 1934-40 DETROIT LIONS
JOHNSON, JOHN CURLEY (HOUSTON) - BACK - 1960 DALLAS TEXANS (AFL);
     1961-62 NEW YORK TITANS (AFL); 1963-68 NEW YORK JETS (AFL); 1969
     NEW YORK GIANTS
JOHNSON, JOHN HENRY (ST.MARY'S & ARIZONA ST) - BACK - 1954-56 SAN
     FRANCISCO 49ERS; 1957-59 DETROIT LIONS; 1960-65 PITTSBURGH
     STEELERS; 1966 HOUSTON OILERS (AFL)
JOHNSON, JOSEPH (BOSTON COLLEGE) - BACK - 1954-58 GREEN BAY PACKERS;
     1960-61 BOSTON PATRIOTS (AFL)
JOHNSON, JOSEPH (MISSISSIPPI) - BACK - 1948 NEW YORK GIANTS
JOHNSON, KENNETH (INDIANA) - END, TACKLE - 1971-74 CINCINNATI BENGALS
     (AFC)
JOHNSON, KNUTE (MUHLENBERG) - END - 1926 PHILADELPHIA QUAKERS (AFL);
     1926 NEWARK BEARS (AFL)
JOHNSON, LAWRENCE (HASKELL) - CENTER - 1933-35 BOSTON REDSKINS; 1936
     NEW YORK YANKS (AFL); 1936-39 NEW YORK GIANTS; 1944 WASHINGTON
     REDSKINS
JOHNSON, LEN (ST. CLOUD-WISCONSIN) - CENTER, GUARD - 1970 NEW YORK
     GIANTS (NFC)
JOHNSON, LEO (COLUMBIA) - END - 1929 ORANGE TORNADOS
JOHNSON, LEO (MILLIKIN) - BACK - 1920 DECATUR STALEYS
JOHNSON, LEO (TENNESSEE STATE) - END - 1969 SAN FRANCISCO 49ERS; 1970
     SAN FRANCISCO 49ERS (NFC)
JOHNSON, LEVI (TEXAS A&I) - BACK - 1973-74 DETROIT LIONS (NFC)
JOHNSON, LORNE (TEMPLE) - BACK - 1934 PHILADELPHIA EAGLES
JOHNSON, MARVIN (SAN JOSE STATE) - BACK - 1951-52 LOS ANGELES RAMS;
     1952-53 GREEN BAY PACKERS
JOHNSON, MICHAEL (KANSAS) - BACK - 1966-69 DALLAS COWBOYS
JOHNSON, MITCHELL (UCLA) - GUARD, TACKLE - 1965 DALLAS COWBOYS;
     1966-67 WASHINGTON REDSKINS; 1969 LOS ANGELES RAMS; 1970 LOS
     ANGELES RAMS (NFC); 1971 CLEVELAND BROWNS (AFC); 1972 WASHINGTON
     REDSKINS (NFC)
JOHNSON, MONTE (NEBRASKA) - LB - 1973-74 OAKLAND RAIDERS (AFC)
JOHNSON, NATHAN (ILLINOIS) - TACKLE - 1946-47 NEW YORK YANKEES
     (AAFC); 1948 CHICAGO ROCKETS (AAFC); 1949 CHICAGO HORNETS
     (AAFC); 1950 NEW YORK YANKS
JOHNSON, O. G. - BACK - 1924 CHICAGO BEARS
JOHNSON, OLIVER "JAY" (EAST TEXAS STATE) - LB - 1969 PHILADELPHIA
     EAGLES; 1970 PHILADELPHIA EAGLES (NFC)
JOHNSON, OSCAR (VERMONT) - BACK - 1926 BOSTON BULLDOGS (AFL); 1929
     BOSTON BRAVES
JOHNSON, PETER (VMI) - BACK - 1959 CHICAGO BEARS
JOHNSON, PRESTON (FLORIDA A&M) - BACK - 1968 BOSTON PATRIOTS (AFL)
JOHNSON, RANDOLPH (TEXAS A&I) - QBACK - 1966-69 ATLANTA FALCONS; 1970
     ATLANTA FALCONS (NFC); 1971-73 NEW YORK GIANTS (NFC)
JOHNSON, RAYMOND (DENVER) - BACK - 1937-38 CLEVELAND RAMS; 1940
     COLUMBUS BULLIES (AFL); 1940 CHICAGO CARDINALS
JOHNSON, RICHARD (ILLINOIS) - BACK - 1969 HOUSTON OILERS (AFL)
JOHNSON, RICHARD (MINNESOTA) - END - 1963 KANSAS CITY CHIEFS (AFL)
JOHNSON, ROBERT (CHATTANOOGA) - TACKLE - 1930 PORTSMOUTH SPARTANS
JOHNSON, ROBERT (TENNESSEE) - CENTER - 1968-69 CINCINNATI BENGALS
     (AFL); 1970-74 CINCINNATI BENGALS (AFC)
JOHNSON, RONALD (MICHIGAN) - BACK - 1969 CLEVELAND BROWNS; 1970-74
     NEW YORK GIANTS (NFC)
JOHNSON, RUDOLPH (NEBRASKA) - BACK - 1964-65 SAN FRANCISCO 49ERS;
     1966 ATLANTA FALCONS
JOHNSON, SAMUEL (NORTH CAROLINA) - BACK - 1974 SAN FRANCISCO 49ERS
     (NFC)
JOHNSON, THOMAS (MICHIGAN) - TACKLE - 1952 GREEN BAY PACKERS
JOHNSON, WALTER (LOS ANGELES STATE) - TACKLE - 1965-69 CLEVELAND
     BROWNS; 1970-74 CLEVELAND BROWNS (AFC)
JOHNSON, WALTER CLARK (TUSKEGEE) - END - 1967 SAN FRANCISCO 49ERS
JOHNSON, WILLIAM (LIVINGSTON) - KICKER - 1970 NEW YORK GIANTS (NFC)
JOHNSON, WILLIAM (MINNESOTA) - END - 1941 GREEN BAY PACKERS
JOHNSON, WILLIAM (SMU) - GUARD - 1947 CHICAGO BEARS

JOHNSON, WILLIAM (TYLER JUNIOR COLLEGE-TEX.) - CENTER - 1948-49 SAN
     FRANCISCO 49ERS (AAFC); 1950-56 SAN FRANCISCO 49ERS
JOHNSON, WILLIAM WALTER (NEBRASKA) - BACK - 1966-68 BOSTON PATRIOTS
     (AFL)
JOHNSON - BACK - 1933 CHICAGO CARDINALS
JOHNSOS, LUKE (NORTHWESTERN) - END - 1929-36, 38 CHICAGO BEARS
JOHNSTON, ARTHUR (LAWRENCE) - BACK - 1931 GREEN BAY PACKERS
JOHNSTON, CHARLES (STANFORD) - TACKLE - 1926 LOS ANGELES WILDCATS
     (AFL)
JOHNSTON, CHESTER (ELMHURST & MARQUETTE) - BACK - 1934 ST. LOUIS
     GUNNERS; 1934-38 GREEN BAY PACKERS; 1939-40 PITTSBURGH STEELERS
JOHNSTON, JAMES (WASHINGTON) - BACK - 1939-40 WASHINGTON REDSKINS;
     1946 CHICAGO CARDINALS
JOHNSTON, MARK (NORTHWESTERN) - BACK - 1960-63 HOUSTON OILERS (AFL);
     1964 OAKLAND RAIDERS (AFL); 1964 NEW YORK JETS (AFL)
JOHNSTON, PRESTON (SMU) - BACK - 1946 MIAMI SEAHAWKS (AAFC); 1946
     BUFFALO BISONS (AAFC)
JOHNSTON, REX (USC) - BACK - 1960 PITTSBURGH STEELERS
JOINER, CHARLES (GRAMBLING) - END, BACK - 1969 HOUSTON OILERS (AFL);
     1970-72 HOUSTON OILERS (AFC); 1972-74 CINCINNATI BENGALS (AFC)
JOLITZ, EVAN (CINCINNATI) - LB - 1974 CINCINNATI BENGALS (AFC)
JOLLEY, ALVIN (MARIETTA & KANSAS STATE) - TACKLE - 1922 AKRON PROS;
     1923 DAYTON TRIANGLES; 1929 BUFFALO BISONS; 1930 BROOKLYN
     DODGERS; 1931 CLEVELAND INDIANS
JOLLEY, GORDON (UTAH) - TACKLE - 1972-74 DETROIT LIONS (NFC)
JOLLEY, LEWIS (NORTH CAROLINA) - BACK - 1972-73 HOUSTON OILERS (AFC)
JONAS, DONALD (PENN STATE) - BACK - 1962 PHILADELPHIA EAGLES
JONAS, MARVIN (UTAH) - CENTER - 1931 BROOKLYN DODGERS
JONASEN, CHARLES - BACK - 1921-23 MINNEAPOLIS MARINES
JONES, ARTHUR (RICHMOND) - BACK - 1941, 45 PITTSBURGH STEELERS; 1941
     INTERCEPTION LEADER; (TIED WITH GOLDBERG)
JONES, BEN (GROVE CITY) - BACK - 1923, 25 CANTON BULLDOGS; 1924
     DAYTON TRIANGLES; 1924-25 CLEVELAND BULLDOGS; 1925-26 FRANKFORD
     YELLOWJACKETS; 1927-28 CHICAGO CARDINALS
JONES, BERTRAM (LSU) - QBACK - 1973-74 BALTIMORE COLTS (AFC)
JONES, BUCK - TACKLE - 1922 OORANG INDIANS
JONES, CALVIN (WASHINGTON) - BACK - 1973-74 DENVER BRONCOS (AFC)
JONES, CHARLES (GEORGE WASHINGTON) - END - 1955 WASHINGTON REDSKINS
JONES, CLINTON (MICHIGAN STATE) - BACK - 1967-69 MINNESOTA VIKINGS;
     1970-72 MINNESOTA VIKINGS (NFC); 1973 SAN DIEGO CHARGERS (AFC)
JONES, CODY (SAN JOSE STATE) - END, TACKLE - 1974 LOS ANGELES RAMS
     (NFC)
JONES, CURTIS (MISSOURI) - GUARD - 1968 SAN DIEGO CHARGERS (AFL)
JONES, DAVID (KANSAS STATE) - END - 1969 CLEVELAND BROWNS; 1970-71
     CLEVELAND BROWNS (AFC)
JONES, DAVID "DEACON" (S.CAP.ST. & MISS.VOC) - END - 1961-69 LOS
     ANGELES RAMS; 1970-71 LOS ANGELES RAMS (NFC); 1972-73 SAN DIEGO
     CHARGERS (AFC); 1974 WASHINGTON REDSKINS (NFC)
JONES, DOUGLAS (SAN FERNANDO VALLEY) - BACK - 1973-74 KANSAS CITY
     CHIEFS (AFC)
JONES, EDGAR (PITTSBURGH) - BACK - 1945 CHICAGO BEARS; 1946-49
     CLEVELAND BROWNS (AAFC)
JONES, EDWARD "TOO TALL" (TENNESSEE STATE) - END - 1974 DALLAS
     COWBOYS (NFC)
JONES, ELLIS (TULSA) - GUARD - 1945 BOSTON YANKS
JONES, ELMER (WAKE FOREST) - GUARD - 1946 BUFFALO BISONS (AAFC);
     1947-48 DETROIT LIONS
JONES, EUGENE (RICE) - BACK - 1961 HOUSTON OILERS (AFL)
JONES, EZELL (MINNESOTA) - TACKLE - 1969 BOSTON PATRIOTS (AFL); 1970
     BOSTON PATRIOTS (AFC)
JONES, GERALD (BOWLING GREEN) - TACKLE, END - 1966 ATLANTA FALCONS;
     1967-69 NEW ORLEANS SAINTS
JONES, GOMER (OHIO STATE) - CENTER - 1936 CLEVELAND RAMS (AFL)
JONES, GREGORY (UCLA) - BACK - 1970-71 BUFFALO BILLS (AFC)
JONES, HARRIS (JOHNSON C. SMITH) - GUARD - 1971 SAN DIEGO CHARGERS
     (AFC); 1973-74 HOUSTON OILERS (AFC)
JONES, HARRY (ARKANSAS) - BACK - 1967-69 PHILADELPHIA EAGLES; 1970
     PHILADELPHIA EAGLES (NFC)
JONES, HARVEY (BAYLOR) - BACK - 1944-45 CLEVELAND RAMS; 1947
     WASHINGTON REDSKINS
JONES, HENRY (GRAMBLING) - BACK - 1969 DENVER BRONCOS (AFL)

JONES, HOMER (TEXAS SOUTHERN) - END - 1964-69 NEW YORK GIANTS; 1970
    CLEVELAND BROWNS (AFC)
JONES, HORACE (LOUISVILLE) - END - 1971-74 OAKLAND RAIDERS (AFC)
JONES, JAMES "CASEY" (UNION-TENNESSEE) - BACK - 1946 DETROIT LIONS
JONES, JAMES (WASHINGTON) - BACK - 1958 LOS ANGELES RAMS; 1961
    OAKLAND RAIDERS (AFL)
JONES, JAMES (WICHITA STATE) - END, LB - 1969 NEW YORK JETS (AFL);
    1970 NEW YORK JETS (AFC); 1971-73 WASHINGTON REDSKINS (NFC)
JONES, JAMES CLYDE (WISCONSIN) - END - 1965-67 CHICAGO BEARS; 1968
    DENVER BRONCOS (AFL)
JONES, JERRY (NOTRE DAME) - TACKLE - 1919 HAMMOND PROS; 1920 DECATUR
    STALEYS; 1921 CHICAGO STALEYS; 1922 ROCK ISLAND INDEPENDENTS;
    1922-23 TOLEDO MARCONS; 1924 CLEVELAND BULLDOGS
JONES, JIMMIE (UCLA) - BACK - 1974 DETROIT LIONS (NFC)
JONES, JOE (TENNESSEE STATE) - END - 1970-71, 73 CLEVELAND BROWNS
    (AFC); 1974 PHILADELPHIA EAGLES (NFC)
JONES, JOHN "SPIKE" (GEORGIA) - KICKER - 1970 HOUSTON OILERS (AFC);
    1971-74 BUFFALO BILLS (AFC)
JONES, KENNETH (FRANKLIN&MARSHALL) - BACK - 1924 BUFFALO BISONS
JONES, LARANCE (NORTHEAST MISSOURI STATE) - BACK - 1974 WASHINGTON
    REDSKINS (NFC)
JONES, LEWIS (WEATHERFORD) - GUARD - 1943 BROOKLYN DODGERS
JONES, MARCHALL (NORTH DAKOTA) - BACK - 1921 AKRON PROS
KELLUM, MARVIN (WICHITA STATE) - LB - 1974 PITTSBURGH STEELERS (AFC)
JONES, RALPH (ALABAMA) - END - 1946 DETROIT LIONS; 1947 BALTIMORE
    COLTS (AAFC)
JONES, RAYMOND (SOUTHERN) - BACK - 1970 PHILADELPHIA EAGLES (NFC);
    1971 MIAMI DOLPHINS (AFC); 1972 SAN DIEGO CHARGERS (AFC); 1973
    NEW ORLEANS SAINTS (NFC)
JONES, ROBERT (INDIANA) - GUARD - 1934 GREEN BAY PACKERS
JONES, ROBERT (VIRGINIA UNION) - BACK - 1973-74 CINCINNATI BENGALS
    (AFC)
JONES, ROBERT DEAN (SAN DIEGO STATE) - END - 1967-69 CHICAGO BEARS
JONES, RONALD (TEXAS-EL PASO) - END - 1969 GREEN BAY PACKERS
JONES, STANLEY (MARYLAND) - TACKLE - 1954-65 CHICAGO BEARS; 1966
    WASHINGTON REDSKINS
JONES, STEVE (DUKE) - BACK - 1973-74 BUFFALO BILLS (AFC); 1974 ST.
    LOUIS CARDINALS (NFC)
JONES, THOMAS (BUCKNELL) - GUARD - 1930 MINNEAPOLIS REDJACKETS;
    1930-31 FRANKFORD YELLOWJACKETS; 1932-36 NEW YORK GIANTS; 1937
    NEW YORK YANKS (AFL); 1938 GREEN BAY PACKERS
JONES, THOMAS (MIAMI-OHIO) - TACKLE - 1955 CLEVELAND BROWNS
JONES, THURMAN (ABILENE CHRISTIAN) - BACK - 1941-42 BROOKLYN DODGERS
JONES, WILLIAM (PURDUE) - BACK - 1962 BUFFALO BILLS (AFL)
JONES, WILLIAM "DUB" (TULANE & LSU) - BACK - 1946 MIAMI SEAHAWKS
    (AAFC); 1946-47 BROOKLYN DODGERS (AAFC); 1948-49 CLEVELAND
    BROWNS (AAFC); 1950-55 CLEVELAND BROWNS
JONES, WILLIAM (WEST VIRGINIA WESLEYAN) - GUARD - 1947 BROOKLYN
    DODGERS (AAFC)
JONES, WILLIE LEE (KANSAS STATE) - END - 1967 HOUSTON OILERS (AFL);
    1970-71 CINCINNATI BENGALS (AFC)
JORDAN, HENRY (VIRGINIA) - TACKLE - 1957-58 CLEVELAND BROWNS; 1959-69
    GREEN BAY PACKERS
JORDAN, JAMES (FLORIDA) - BACK - 1967 NEW ORLEANS SAINTS
JORDAN, JEFFERSON (TULSA) - BACK - 1965-67 MINNESOTA VIKINGS
JORDAN, JEFFREY (WASHINGTON) - BACK - 1970 LOS ANGELES RAMS (NFC);
    1971-72 WASHINGTON REDSKINS (NFC)
JORDAN, LAWRENCE (YOUNGSTOWN) - END - 1962, 64 DENVER BRONCOS (AFL)
JORDAN, LEE ROY (ALABAMA) - LB - 1963-69 DALLAS COWBOYS; 1970-74
    DALLAS COWBOYS (NFC)
JORGENSEN, CARL (ST. MARY'S OF CAL.) - TACKLE - 1934 GREEN BAY
    PACKERS; 1935 PHILADELPHIA EAGLES
JORGENSEN, WAGNER (ST. MARY'S OF CAL.) - CENTER - 1936-37 BROOKLYN
    DODGERS
JOSEPH, CHALMERS (MIAMI-OHIO) - END - 1927 DAYTON TRIANGLES; 1930
    PORTSMOUTH SPARTANS; 1931 CLEVELAND INDIANS
JOSEPH, ZERN (MIAMI-OHIO) - TACKLE - 1925, 27 DAYTON TRIANGLES
JOSEPHSON, LESTER (AUGUSTANA-SOUTH DAKOTA) - BACK - 1964-67, 69 LOS
    ANGELES RAMS; 1970-74 LOS ANGELES RAMS (NFC)
JOSWICK, ROBERT (TULSA) - END - 1968-69 MIAMI DOLPHINS (AFL)
JOY, WILLIAM (HOLY CROSS) - BACK - 1919 AKRON PROS

JOYCE, DONALD (TULANE) - TACKLE - 1951-53 CHICAGO CARDINALS; 1954-60
    BALTIMORE COLTS; 1961 MINNESOTA VIKINGS; 1962 DENVER BRONCOS
    (AFL)
JOYCE, EMMETT (NORTH CAROLINA) - GUARD - 1936 CLEVELAND RAMS (AFL)
JOYNER, L. C. - BACK - 1960 OAKLAND RAIDERS (AFL)
JUDD, SAXON (TULSA) - END - 1946-48 BROOKLYN DODGERS (AAFC)
JUENGER, DAVID (OHIO) - END - 1973 CHICAGO BEARS (NFC)
JULIAN, FREDERICK (MICHIGAN) - BACK - 1960 NEW YORK TITANS (AFL)
JUNGMICHEL, HAROLD (TEXAS) - GUARD - 1946 MIAMI SEAHAWKS (AAFC)
JUNKER, STEVEN (XAVIER) - END - 1957, 59-60 DETROIT LIONS; 1961-62
    WASHINGTON REDSKINS
JURGENSEN, CHRISTIAN "SONNY" (DUKE) - QBACK - 1957-63 PHILADELPHIA
    EAGLES; 1964-69 WASHINGTON REDSKINS; 1970-74 WASHINGTON REDSKINS
    (NFC); 1967, 69 PASSING LEADER; 1974 PASSING LEADER (NFC)
JURICH, MICHAEL (DENVER) - TACKLE - 1941-42 BROOKLYN DODGERS
JURKIEWICZ, WALTER (INDIANA) - CENTER - 1946 DETROIT LIONS
JUSTER, RUBIN (MINNESOTA) - TACKLE - 1946 BOSTON YANKS
JUSTICE, CHARLES "CHOO-CHOO" (N. CAROLINA) - BACK - 1950, 52-54
    WASHINGTON REDSKINS
JUZWIK, STEPHEN (NOTRE DAME) - BACK - 1942 WASHINGTON REDSKINS; 1946
    BUFFALO BISONS (AAFC); 1947 BUFFALO BILLS (AAFC); 1948 CHICAGO
    ROCKETS (AAFC)
KABEALO, MICHAEL (OHIO STATE) - BACK - 1944 CLEVELAND RAMS
KACZMAREK, MICHAEL (SOUTHERN ILLINOIS) - LB - 1973 BALTIMORE COLTS
    (AFC)
KADESKY, MAX (IOWA) - END - 1923 ROCK ISLAND INDEPENDENTS
KADISH, MICHAEL (NOTRE DAME) - TACKLE - 1973-74 BUFFALO BILLS (AFC)
KADZIEL, RONALD (STANFORD) - LB - 1972 NEW ENGLAND PATRIOTS (AFC)
KAER, MORTON (USC) - QBACK - 1931 FRANKFORD YELLOWJACKETS
KAHL, CYRUS (NORTH DAKOTA) - QBACK - 1930-31 PORTSMOUTH SPARTANS
KAHLER, ROBERT (NEBRASKA) - BACK - 1942-44 GREEN BAY PACKERS
KAHLER, ROYAL (NEBRASKA) - TACKLE - 1941 PITTSBURGH STEELERS; 1942
    GREEN BAY PACKERS
KAHN, EDWARD (NORTH CAROLINA) - GUARD - 1935-36 BOSTON REDSKINS; 1937
    WASHINGTON REDSKINS
KAIMER, KARL (BOSTON UNIV.) - END - 1962 NEW YORK TITANS (AFL)
KAKASIC, GEORGE (DUQUESNE) - GUARD - 1936-38 PITTSBURGH PIRATES; 1939
    PITTSBURGH STEELERS
KAKELA, WAYNE (MINNESOTA) - CENTER - 1930 MINNEAPOLIS REDJACKETS
KALINA, DAVID (MIAMI-FLORIDA) - END - 1970 PITTSBURGH STEELERS (AFC)
KALMANIR, THOMAS (NEVADA) - BACK - 1949-51 LOS ANGELES RAMS; 1953
    BALTIMORE COLTS
KALSU, ROBERT (OKLAHOMA) - GUARD - 1968 BUFFALO BILLS (AFL)
KAMANU, LEWIS (WEBER STATE) - END - 1967-68 DETROIT LIONS
KAMINSKI, LAWRENCE (PURDUE) - CENTER - 1966-69 DENVER BRONCOS (AFL);
    1970-73 DENVER BRONCOS (AFC)
KAMMERER, CARLTON (PACIFIC) - END - 1961-62 SAN FRANCISCO 49ERS;
    1963-69 WASHINGTON REDSKINS
KAMP, JAMES (OKLAHOMA CITY UNIV.) - TACKLE - 1932 STATEN ISLAND
    STAPELTONS; 1933 BOSTON REDSKINS
KAMPA, ROBERT (CALIFORNIA) - END - 1973-74 BUFFALO BILLS (AFC); 1974
    DENVER BRONCOS (AFC)
KANE, CARL (ST. LOUIS UNIV.) - BACK - 1936 PHILADELPHIA EAGLES
KANE, HERBERT (EAST CENTRAL OKLAHOMA STATE) - TACKLE - 1944-45 NEW
    YORK GIANTS
KANE - TACKLE - 1919 CLEVELAND INDIANS
KANICKI, JAMES (MICHIGAN STATE) - TACKLE - 1963-69 CLEVELAND BROWNS;
    1970-71 NEW YORK GIANTS (NFC)
KANTOR, JOSEPH (NOTRE DAME) - BACK - 1966 WASHINGTON REDSKINS
KANYA, ALBERT (SYRACUSE) - TACKLE - 1931-32 STATEN ISLAND STAPELTONS
KAPELE, JOHN (BRIGHAM YOUNG) - TACKLE - 1960-62 PITTSBURGH STEELERS;
    1962 PHILADELPHIA EAGLES
KAPITANSKY, BERNARD (LONG ISLAND UNIV.) - GUARD - 1942 BROOKLYN
    DODGERS
KAPLAN, BERNARD (WESTERN MARYLAND) - GUARD - 1935-36 NEW YORK GIANTS;
    1942 PHILADELPHIA EAGLES
KAPLAN, LOUIS (WESTERN MARYLAND) - GUARD - 1936 BROOKLYN TIGERS
    (AFL); 1937 ROCHESTER TIGERS (AFL)
KAPLAN, SIDNEY (HAMLINE) - BACK - 1923 MINNEAPOLIS MARINES; 1926 ROCK
    ISLAND INDEPENDENTS (AFL)

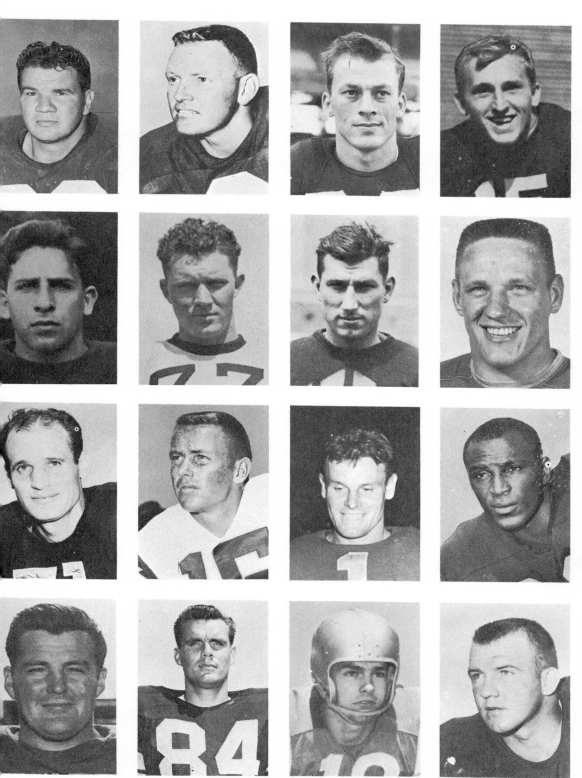

Top row (from left to right): Don Joyce, "Sonny" Jurgensen, Charley Justice and Steve Juzwik. *Second row:* Eddie Kahn, Ed Karpowich, Charles Kassel and Jim Katcavage. *Third row:* Ken Kavanaugh, Jack Kemp, Ralph Kercheval and Brady Keys. *Bottom row:* Frank Kilroy, Gary Knafelc, Ronnie Knox and Bill Koman.

Top row (from left to right): Walter Koppisch, Ron Kostelnik, Jerry Kramer and Ron Kramer. *Second row:* Joe Krupa, Irv Kupcinet, Lou Kusserow and Zvonimir Kvaternik. *Third row:* Joe LaBissoniere, Tom Landry, Dick Lane and Greg Larson. *Bottom row:* Yale Lary, "Hank" Lauricella, Dante Lavelli and Eddie LeBaron.

KAPLANOFF, KARL (OHIO STATE) - TACKLE - 1939 BROOKLYN DODGERS; 19
BOSTON BEARS (AFL)
KAPOPCH, ALBERT (ST. BONAVENTURE) - TACKLE - 1943-45 DETROIT LIONS
KAPP, JOSEPH (CALIFORNIA) - QBACK - 1967-69 MINNESOTA VIKINGS; 197
BOSTON PATRIOTS (AFC)
KAPTER, ALEXANDER (NORTHWESTERN) - GUARD - 1946-47 CLEVELAND BROWNS
(AAFC)
KARAMATIC, GEORGE (GONZAGA) - BACK - 1938 WASHINGTON REDSKINS; 1940
MILWAUKEE CHIEFS (AFL)
KARAS, EMIL (DAYTON) - LB, END - 1959 WASHINGTON REDSKINS; 1960 LOS
ANGELES CHARGERS (AFL); 1961-64, 66 SAN DIEGO CHARGERS (AFL)
KARCH, ROBERT (OHIO STATE) - TACKLE - 1921-22 COLUMBUS PANHANDLES;
1923 LOUISVILLE BRECKS
KARCHER, JAMES (OHIO STATE) - GUARD - 1936 BOSTON REDSKINS; 1937-39
WASHINGTON REDSKINS; 1940 COLUMBUS BULLIES (AFL)
KARCIS, JOHN (CARNEGIE TECH) - BACK - 1932-35 BROOKLYN DODGERS;
1936-38 PITTSBURGH PIRATES; 1938-39, 43 NEW YORK GIANTS
KARILIVACZ, CARL (SYRACUSE) - BACK - 1953-57 DETROIT LIONS; 1958 NEW
YORK GIANTS; 1959-60 LOS ANGELES RAMS
KARMAZIN, MICHAEL (DUKE) - GUARD - 1946 NEW YORK YANKEES (AAFC)
KARNOFSKY, ABRAHAM (ARIZONA) - BACK - 1945 PHILADELPHIA EAGLES; 1946
BOSTON YANKS
KARPOWICH, EDWARD (CATHOLIC UNIV.) - TACKLE - 1936-38 PITTSBURGH
PIRATES; 1939 PITTSBURGH STEELERS; 1940 BUFFALO INDIANS (AFL);
1941 BUFFALO TIGERS (AFL); 1941 NEW YORK AMERICANS (AFL)
KARPUS, ANDREW (DETROIT) - BACK - 1937 NEW YORK YANKS (AFL); 1937 LOS
ANGELES BULLDOGS (AFL); 1940 BOSTON BEARS (AFL)
KARR, WILLIAM (WEST VIRGINIA) - END - 1933-38 CHICAGO BEARS
KARRAS, ALEXANDER (IOWA) - TACKLE - 1958-62, 64-69 DETROIT LIONS;
1970 DETROIT LIONS (NFC)
KARRAS, JOHN (ILLINOIS) - BACK - 1952 CHICAGO CARDINALS
KARRAS, LOUIS (PURDUE) - TACKLE - 1950-51 WASHINGTON REDSKINS
KARRAS, THEODORE (INDIANA) - TACKLE - 1958-59 PITTSBURGH STEELERS;
1960-64 CHICAGO BEARS; 1965 DETROIT LIONS; 1966 LOS ANGELES RAMS
KASPEREK, RICHARD (IOWA STATE) - CENTER - 1966-68 ST. LOUIS CARDINALS
KARPS, JOHN (DUQUESNE) - QBACK - 1944 CLEVELAND RAMS
KARSTENS, GEORGE (INDIANA) - CENTER - 1949 DETROIT LIONS
KARWALES, JOHN (MICHIGAN) - END - 1947 CHICAGO CARDINALS
KASAP, MICHAEL (ILLINOIS & PURDUE) - TACKLE - 1947 BALTIMORE COLTS
(AAFC)
KASKA, ANTHONY (ILLINOIS WESLEYAN) - BACK - 1935 DETROIT LIONS;
1936-38 BROOKLYN DODGERS
KASKY, EDWARD (VILLANOVA) - TACKLE - 1942 PHILADELPHIA EAGLES
KASPER, THOMAS (NOTRE DAME) - BACK - 1923 ROCHESTER JEFFERSONS
KASSELL, CHARLES (ILLINOIS) - END - 1927 CHICAGO BEARS; 1927-28
FRANKFORD YELLOWJACKETS; 1929-33 CHICAGO CARDINALS
KASSULKE, KARL (DRAKE) - BACK - 1963-69 MINNESOTA VIKINGS; 1970-72
MINNESOTA VIKINGS (NFC)
KATALINAS, LEO (CATHOLIC UNIV.) - TACKLE - 1938 GREEN BAY PACKERS
KATCAVAGE, JAMES (DAYTON) - END - 1956-68 NEW YORK GIANTS
KATCIK, JOSEPH (NOTRE DAME) - TACKLE - 1960 NEW YORK TITANS (AFL)
KATRISHEN, MICHAEL (MISSISSIPPI SOUTHERN) - TACKLE - 1948-49
WASHINGTON REDSKINS
KAUFFMAN, JOHN - TACKLE - 1929 DAYTON TRIANGLES
KAUFMAN, LESTER (PRINCETON) - BACK - 1936 NEW YORK YANKS (AFL)
KAVANAUGH, KENNETH (LSU) - END - 1940-41, 45-50 CHICAGO BEARS
KAVEL, GEORGE (CARNEGIE TECH) - BACK - 1934 PHILADELPHIA EAGLES; 1934
PITTSBURGH PIRATES
KAW, EDGAR (CORNELL) - BACK - 1924 BUFFALO BISONS
KAWAL, EDWARD (ILLINOIS) - CENTER - 1931, 34-36 CHICAGO BEARS; 1937
WASHINGTON REDSKINS
KAY, RICHARD (COLORADO) - LB - 1973 LOS ANGELES RAMS (NFC)
KEADY, JAMES (LEHIGH) - BACK - 1919 CANTON BULLDOGS; 1919 MASSILLON
TIGERS
KEAHEY, EULIS (GEORGE WASHINGTON) - TACKLE - 1941 NEW YORK AMERICANS
(AFL); 1942 NEW YORK GIANTS; 1942 BROOKLYN DODGERS
KEANE, JAMES (IOWA) - END - 1946-51 CHICAGO BEARS; 1952 GREEN BAY
PACKERS; 1947 PASS RECEIVING LEADER
KEANE, THOMAS (WEST VIRGINIA) - BACK - 1948-51 LOS ANGELES RAMS; 1952
DALLAS TEXANS; 1953-54 BALTIMORE COLTS; 1955 CHICAGO CARDINALS
KEARNEY, FRANCIS (CORNELL) - TACKLE - 1926 NEW YORK YANKEES (AFL)

KEARNEY, JAMES (PRAIRIE VIEW) - BACK - 1965-66 DETROIT LIONS; 1967-69
    KANSAS CITY CHIEFS (AFL); 1970-74 KANSAS CITY CHIEFS (AFC)
KEARNEY, TIMOTHY (NORTHERN MICHIGAN) - LB - 1972-74 CINCINNATI
    BENGALS (AFC)
KEARNS, THOMAS (MIAMI) - TACKLE - 1945 NEW YORK GIANTS; 1946 CHICAGO
    CARDINALS
KEATING, THOMAS (MICHIGAN) - TACKLE - 1964-65 BUFFALO BILLS (AFL);
    1966-67, 69 OAKLAND RAIDERS (AFL); 1970-72 OAKLAND RAIDERS
    (AFC); 1973 PITTSBURGH STEELERS (AFC); 1974 KANSAS CITY CHIEFS
    (AFC)
KEATING, WILLIAM (MICHIGAN) - GUARD - 1966-67 DENVER BRONCOS (AFL);
    1967 MIAMI DOLPHINS (AFL)
KECK, J. STANTON (PRINCETON) - TACKLE - 1923 CLEVELAND INDIANS; 1923
    ROCHESTER JEFFERSONS
KECKIN, VALDEMAR (MISSISSIPPI SOUTHERN) - QBACK - 1962 SAN DIEGO
    CHARGERS (AFL)
KEEBLE, JOSEPH (UCLA) - QBACK - 1936 PITTSBURGH PIRATES; 1937 NEW
    YORK YANKS (AFL); 1937 CLEVELAND RAMS
KEEFE, EMMETT (NOTRE DAME) - GUARD - 1919 HAMMOND PROS; 1920 CHICAGO
    TIGERS; 1921 GREEN BAY PACKERS; 1921-22 ROCK ISLAND
    INDEPENDENTS; 1922 MILWAUKEE BADGERS
KEEFE, JERRY - GUARD - 1920 DECATUR STALEYS
KEEFER, JACKSON (BROWN) - BACK - 1926 PROVIDENCE STEAMROLLERS; 1928
    DAYTON TRIANGLES
KEELING, RAYMOND (TEXAS) - TACKLE - 1938-39 PHILADELPHIA EAGLES
KEELING, REX (SAMFORD-ALABAMA) - KICKER - 1968 CINCINNATI BENGALS
    (AFL)
KEEN, ALLEN (ARKANSAS) - BACK - 1937-38 PHILADELPHIA EAGLES
KEENAN, EDWARD (WASHINGTON COLLEGE-MARYLAND) - GUARD - 1926 HARTFORD
    BLUES
KEENAN, JOHN (SOUTH CAROLINA) - GUARD - 1944-45 WASHINGTON REDSKINS
KEENE, ROBERT (DETROIT) - BACK - 1943-45 DETROIT LIONS
KEITHLEY, GARY (TEXAS-EL PASO) - QBACK - 1973 ST. LOUIS CARDINALS
    (NFC)
KEKERIS, JAMES (MISSOURI) - TACKLE - 1947 PHILADELPHIA EAGLES; 1948
    GREEN BAY PACKERS
KELL, PAUL (NOTRE DAME) - TACKLE - 1939-40 GREEN BAY PACKERS
KELLAGHER, WILLIAM (FORDHAM) - BACK - 1946-48 CHICAGO ROCKETS (AAFC)
KELLER, KENNETH (NORTH CAROLINA) - BACK - 1956-57 PHILADELPHIA EAGLES
KELLER, MICHAEL (MICHIGAN) - LB - 1972 DALLAS COWBOYS (NFC)
KELLERMAN, ERNEST (MIAMI-OHIO) - BACK - 1966-69 CLEVELAND BROWNS;
    1970-71 CLEVELAND BROWNS (AFC); 1972 CINCINNATI BENGALS (AFC);
    1973 BUFFALO BILLS (AFC)
KELLEY, BRIAN (CALIFORNIA LUTHERAN) - LB - 1973-74 NEW YORK GIANTS
    (NFC)
KELLEY, DWIGHT "IKE" (OHIO STATE) - LB - 1966-67, 69 PHILADELPHIA
    EAGLES; 1970-71 PHILADELPHIA EAGLES (NFC)
KELLEY, EDWARD (TEXAS) - TACKLE - 1949 LOS ANGELES DONS (AAFC)
KELLEY, EDWARD (TEXAS) - BACK - 1961-62 DALLAS TEXANS (AFL)
KELLEY, FRANK (SOUTH DAKOTA STATE) - BACK - 1927 CLEVELAND BULLDOGS
KELLEY, GORDON (GEORGIA) - LB - 1960-61 SAN FRANCISCO 49ERS; 1962-63
    WASHINGTON REDSKINS
KELLEY, LAWRENCE (YALE) - END - 1937 BOSTON SHAMROCKS (AFL)
KELLEY, LESLIE (ALABAMA) - BACK - 1967-69 NEW ORLEANS SAINTS
KELLEY, ROBERT (WEST TEXAS STATE) - CENTER - 1955-56 PHILADELPHIA
    EAGLES
KELLEY, VINCENT (CENTENARY) - GUARD - 1940 COLUMBUS BULLIES (AFL)
KELLEY, WILLIAM (TEXAS TECH) - END - 1949 GREEN BAY PACKERS
KELLISON, JOHN (WEST VIRGINIA WESLEYAN) - TACKLE - 1919-21 CANTON
    BULLDOGS; 1922 TOLEDO MAROONS
KELLOGG, CLARENCE (ST. MARY'S OF CAL.) - BACK - 1936 CHICAGO CARDINALS
KELLOGG, MICHAEL (SANTA CLARA) - BACK - 1966-67 DENVER BRONCOS (AFL)
KELLOGG, ROBERT (TULANE) - BACK - 1940 CHICAGO CARDINALS
KELLOGG, WILLIAM (SYRACUSE) - BACK - 1924 FRANKFORD YELLOWJACKETS;
    1925 ROCHESTER JEFFERSONS; 1926 CHICAGO CARDINALS
KELLY, CHARLES (NORTHWESTERN) - BACK - 1923-25 DULUTH KELLEYS; 1926
    DULUTH ESKIMOS
KELLY, CLARENCE (OLYMPIA) - GUARD - 1922 TOLEDO MAROONS; 1923 BUFFALO
    ALL-AMERICANS; 1924-25 ROCHESTER JEFFERSONS
KELLY, ELLISON (MICHIGAN STATE) - GUARD - 1959 NEW YORK GIANTS
KELLY, ELMO (WICHITA) - END - 1944 CHICAGO BEARS

KELLY, JAMES (DETROIT) - BACK - 1919 DETROIT HERALDS
KELLY, JAMES (NOTRE DAME) - END - 1963 PITTSBURGH STEELERS; 1965, 67
 PHILADELPHIA EAGLES
KELLY, JIM (TENNESSEE STATE) - END - 1974 CHICAGO BEARS (NFC)
KELLY, JOHN (FLORIDA A&M) - TACKLE - 1966-67 WASHINGTON REDSKINS
KELLY, JOHN SIMMS (KENTUCKY) - BACK - 1932 NEW YORK GIANTS; 1933-34,
 37 BROOKLYN DODGERS
KELLY, LEROY (MORGAN STATE) - BACK - 1964-69 CLEVELAND BROWNS;
 1970-73 CLEVELAND BROWNS (AFC); 1967-68 RUSHING LEADER; 1968
 SCORING LEADER
KELLY, MICHAEL (DAVIDSON) - END - 1970-72 CINCINNATI BENGALS (AFC);
 1973 NEW ORLEANS SAINTS (NFC)
KELLY, ROBERT (NEW MEXICO STATE) - TACKLE - 1961-64 HOUSTON OILERS
 (AFL); 1967 KANSAS CITY CHIEFS (AFL); 1968 CINCINNATI BENGALS
 (AFL); 1969 ATLANTA FALCONS
KELLY, ROBERT (NOTRE DAME) - BACK - 1947-48 LOS ANGELES DONS (AAFC);
 1949 BALTIMORE COLTS (AAFC)
KELLY, WILLIAM (MONTANA) - QBACK - 1927-28 NEW YORK YANKEES; 1929
 FRANKFORD YELLOWJACKETS; 1930 BROOKLYN DODGERS
KELLY - GUARD - 1929 ORANGE TORNADOS
KELSCH, CHRISTIAN - BACK - 1933-34 PITTSBURGH PIRATES
KELSCH, MATTHEW (IOWA) - END - 1930 BROOKLYN DODGERS
KEMP, JOHN (OCCIDENTAL) - QBACK - 1957 PITTSBURGH STEELERS; 1960 LOS
 ANGELES CHARGERS (AFL); 1961-62 SAN DIEGO CHARGERS (AFL);
 1962-67, 69 BUFFALO BILLS (AFL); 1960 PASSING LEADER (AFL)
KEMP, RAYMOND (DUQUESNE) - TACKLE - 1933 PITTSBURGH PIRATES
KEMPINSKI, CHARLES (MISSISSIPPI) - GUARD - 1960 LOS ANGELES CHARGERS
 (AFL)
KEMPTON, HERBERT (YALE) - BACK - 1921 CANTON BULLDOGS
KENDALL, CHARLES (UCLA) - BACK - 1960 HOUSTON OILERS (AFL)
KENDRICK, JAMES (TEXAS A&M) - BACK - 1922 TOLEDO MAROONS; 1922 CANTON
 BULLDOGS; 1923 LOUISVILLE BRECKS; 1924 CHICAGO BEARS; 1925
 HAMMOND PROS; 1925 BUFFALO BISONS; 1926 BUFFALO RANGERS; 1927
 NEW YORK GIANTS
KENDRICK, VINCENT (FLORIDA) - BACK - 1974 ATLANTA FALCONS (NFC)
KENERSON, JOHN (KENTUCKY STATE) - GUARD - 1960 LOS ANGELES RAMS; 1962
 PITTSBURGH STEELERS; 1962 NEW YORK TITANS (AFL)
KENNARD, GEORGE (KANSAS) - GUARD - 1952-55 NEW YORK GIANTS
KENNEALLY, GEORGE (ST.BONAVENTURE) - END - 1926-28 POTTSVILLE
 MAROONS; 1929, 32 BOSTON BRAVES; 1930 CHICAGO CARDINALS; 1933-35
 PHILADELPHIA EAGLES
KENNEDY, JOSEPH (COLUMBIA) - BACK - 1925 BUFFALO BISONS
KENNEDY, ROBERT (WASHINGTON STATE) - BACK - 1946-49 NEW YORK YANKEES
 (AAFC); 1950 NEW YORK YANKS
KENNEDY, ROBERT (NORTH CAROLINA) - BACK - 1949 LOS ANGELES DONS (AAFC)
KENNEDY, THOMAS (LOS ANGELES STATE) - QBACK - 1966 NEW YORK GIANTS
KENNEDY, THOMAS (WAYNE STATE) - TACKLE - 1944 DETROIT LIONS
KENNEDY, WILLIAM (MICHIGAN STATE) - END - 1942 DETROIT LIONS; 1947
 BOSTON YANKS
KENT, EDWARD GREG (UTAH) - TACKLE - 1966 OAKLAND RAIDERS (AFL); 1968
 DETROIT LIONS
KENYON, CROWELL (RIPON) - GUARD - 1923 GREEN BAY PACKERS
KENYON, WILLIAM (GEORGETOWN) - BACK - 1925 NEW YORK GIANTS
KEPLER, ROBERT (OHIO UNIV.) - BACK - 1936 CLEVELAND RAMS (AFL); 1936
 BOSTON SHAMROCKS (AFL)
KERBOW, RANDOLPH (RICE) - BACK - 1963 HOUSTON OILERS (AFL)
KERCHER, RICHARD (TULSA) - BACK - 1954 DETROIT LIONS
KERCHER, ROBERT (GEORGETOWN) - END - 1944 GREEN BAY PACKERS
KERCHEVAL, RALPH (KENTUCKY) - BACK - 1934-40 BROOKLYN DODGERS; 1938
 FIELD GOAL LEADER; (TIED WITH CUFF)
KERIASOTIS, NICHOLAS (ST. AMBROSE) - GUARD - 1941 COLUMBUS BULLIES
 (AFL); 1942, 45 CHICAGO BEARS
KERKORIAN, GARY (STANFORD) - QBACK - 1952 PITTSBURGH STEELERS;
 1954-56 BALTIMORE COLTS
KERN, REX (OHIO STATE) - BACK - 1971-73 BALTIMORE COLTS (AFC); 1974
 BUFFALO BILLS (AFC)
KERN, WILLIAM (PITTSBURGH) - TACKLE - 1929-30 GREEN BAY PACKERS
KERNS, JOHN (OHIO UNIV.) - TACKLE - 1947-49 BUFFALO BILLS (AAFC)
KERNWEIN, GRAHAM (CHICAGO) - BACK - 1926 RACINE LEGION

KERR, GEORGE (CATHOLIC) - TACKLE - 1919 CLEVELAND INDIANS; 1920
     CLEVELAND PANTHERS
KERR, JAMES (PENN STATE) - BACK - 1961-62 WASHINGTON REDSKINS
KERR, WILLIAM (NOTRE DAME) - END - 1946 LOS ANGELES DONS (AAFC)
KERR - GUARD - 1926 NEWARK BEARS (AFL)
KERRIGAN, THOMAS (COLUMBIA) - GUARD - 1929 ORANGE TORNADOS; 1930
     NEWARK TORNADOS
KERSEY, MERRITT (WEST CHESTER STATE) - KICKER, BACK - 1974
     PHILADELPHIA EAGLES (NFC)
KERSHAW, GEORGE (COLGATE) - END - 1949 NEW YORK GIANTS
KESNER, JAMES (CARNEGIE TECH) - QBACK - 1919 CLEVELAND INDIANS
KESTER, WALTER (MOUNT UNION) - GUARD - 1919 AKRON PROS; 1919
     MASSILLON TIGERS
KETZKO, ALEXANDER (MICHIGAN STATE) - TACKLE - 1943 DETROIT LIONS
KEUPER, KENNETH (GEORGIA) - BACK - 1945-47 GREEN BAY PACKERS; 1948
     NEW YORK GIANTS
KEY, ALLAN WADE (SOUTHWEST TEXAS STATE) - GUARD - 1970-74
     PHILADELPHIA EAGLES (NFC)
KEYES, JAMES (MISSISSIPPI) - LB, KICKER - 1968-69 MIAMI DOLPHINS (AFL)
KEYES, LEROY (PURDUE) - BACK - 1969 PHILADELPHIA EAGLES; 1970-72
     PHILADELPHIA EAGLES (NFC); 1973 KANSAS CITY CHIEFS (AFC)
KEYES, ROBERT (SAN DIEGO UNIV.) - BACK - 1960 OAKLAND RAIDERS (AFL)
KEYS, BRADY (COLORADO STATE) - BACK - 1961-67 PITTSBURGH STEELERS;
     1967 MINNESOTA VIKINGS; 1968 ST. LOUIS CARDINALS
KEYS, HOWARD (OKLAHOMA STATE) - TACKLE - 1960-63 PHILADELPHIA EAGLES
KEYWORTH, JON (COLORADO) - BACK - 1974 DENVER BRONCOS (AFC)
KHAYAT, EDWARD (TULANE) - TACKLE - 1957, 62-63 WASHINGTON REDSKINS;
     1958-61, 64-65 PHILADELPHIA EAGLES; 1966 BOSTON PATRIOTS (AFL)
KHAYAT, ROBERT (MISSISSIPPI) - LB - 1960, 62-63 WASHINGTON REDSKINS
KIBLER, WILLIAM - BACK - 1922 BUFFALO ALL-AMERICANS
KICHEFSKI, WALTER (MIAMI) - END - 1940-42 PITTSBURGH STEELERS; 1944
     CARD-PITT
KIELBASA, MAX (DUQUESNE) - BACK - 1946 PITTSBURGH STEELERS
KIELEY, HOWARD - TACKLE - 1923-25 DULUTH KELLEYS; 1926 CHICAGO
     CARDINALS
KIESLING, WALTER (ST. THOMAS-MINNESOTA) - GUARD - 1926-27 DULUTH
     ESKIMOS; 1928 POTTSVILLE MAROONS; 1929-33 CHICAGO CARDINALS;
     1934 CHICAGO BEARS; 1935-36 GREEN BAY PACKERS; 1937-38
     PITTSBURGH PIRATES; 1966 HALL OF FAME
KIICK, GEORGE (BUCKNELL) - BACK - 1940, 45 PITTSBURGH STEELERS
KIICK, JAMES (WYOMING) - BACK - 1968-69 MIAMI DOLPHINS (AFL); 1970-74
     MIAMI DOLPHINS (AFC)
KILBOURNE, WARREN (MINNESOTA) - TACKLE - 1939 GREEN BAY PACKERS; 1940
     NEW YORK AMERICANS (AFL)
KILCULLEN, ROBERT (TEXAS TECH) - TACKLE - 1957-58, 60-66 CHICAGO BEARS
KILGORE, JOHN (AUBURN) - KICKER - 1965-67 LOS ANGELES RAMS; 1968
     CHICAGO BEARS; 1969 SAN FRANCISCO 49ERS
KILEY, ROGER (NOTRE DAME) - END - 1923 CHICAGO CARDINALS
KILLETT, CHARLES (MEMPHIS STATE) - BACK - 1963 NEW YORK GIANTS
KILLIAN, GENE (TENNESSEE) - GUARD - 1974 DALLAS COWBOYS (NFC)
KILLIHER, L. - GUARD - 1928 CHICAGO CARDINALS
KILLINGER, GLENN (PENN STATE) - BACK - 1926 NEW YORK GIANTS
KILLORIN, PATRICK (SYRACUSE) - CENTER - 1966 PITTSBURGH STEELERS
KILMER, WILLIAM (UCLA) - QBACK - 1961-62, 64, 66 SAN FRANCISCO 49ERS;
     1967-69 NEW ORLEANS SAINTS; 1970 NEW ORLEANS SAINTS (NFC);
     1971-74 WASHINGTON REDSKINS (NFC)
KILROY, FRANK "BUCKO" (TEMPLE) - TACKLE - 1943 PHIL-PITT; 1944-55
     PHILADELPHIA EAGLES
KIMBER, WILLIAM (FLORIDA STATE) - END - 1959-60 NEW YORK GIANTS; 1961
     BOSTON PATRIOTS (AFL)
KIMBLE, FRANK (WEST VIRGINIA) - END - 1945 PITTSBURGH STEELERS
KIMBROUGH, ELBERT (NORTHWESTERN) - BACK - 1961 LOS ANGELES RAMS;
     1962-66 SAN FRANCISCO 49ERS; 1968 NEW ORLEANS SAINTS
KIMBROUGH, JOHN (TEXAS A&M) - BACK - 1941 NEW YORK AMERICANS (AFL);
     1946-48 LOS ANGELES DONS (AAFC)
KIMMEL, J. D. (HOUSTON) - TACKLE - 1955-56 WASHINGTON REDSKINS
KINARD, FRANK "BRUISER" (MISSISSIPPI) - TACKLE - 1938-43 BROOKLYN
     DODGERS; 1944 BROOKLYN TIGERS; 1946-47 NEW YORK YANKEES (AAFC);
     1971 HALL OF FAME

KINARD, GEORGE (MISSISSIPPI) - GUARD - 1941-42 BROOKLYN DODGERS; 1946
    NEW YORK YANKEES (AAFC)
KINARD, WILLIAM (MISSISSIPPI) - BACK - 1956 CLEVELAND BROWNS; 1957-58
    GREEN BAY PACKERS; 1960 BUFFALO BILLS (AFL)
KINCAID, JAMES (SOUTH CAROLINA) - BACK - 1954 WASHINGTON REDSKINS
KINDERDINE, GEORGE - CENTER - 1920-29 DAYTON TRIANGLES
KINDERDINE, JAMES - GUARD - 1924 DAYTON TRIANGLES
KINDERDINE, WALTER - BACK - 1923-25 DAYTON TRIANGLES
KINDERMAN, KEITH (FLORIDA STATE) - BACK - 1963-64 SAN DIEGO CHARGERS
    (AFL); 1965 HOUSTON OILERS (AFL)
KINDIG, HOWARD (CAL.STATE-L.A.) - CENTER, TACKLE, END - 1965-67 SAN
    DIEGO CHARGERS (AFL); 1967-69 BUFFALO BILLS (AFL); 1970-71
    BUFFALO BILLS (AFC); 1972 MIAMI DOLPHINS (AFC); 1974 NEW YORK
    JETS (AFC)
KINDLE, GREGORY (TENNESSEE STATE) - TACKLE - 1974 ST. LOUIS CARDINALS
    (NFC)
KINDRICKS, WILLIAM (ALABAMA A&M) - TACKLE - 1968 CINCINNATI BENGALS
    (AFL)
KINDT, DONALD (WISCONSIN) - BACK - 1947-55 CHICAGO BEARS
KINEK, GEORGE (TULANE) - BACK - 1954 CHICAGO CARDINALS
KINEK, MICHAEL (MICHIGAN STATE) - END - 1940 CLEVELAND RAMS
KINER, STEVEN (TENNESSEE) - LB - 1970 DALLAS COWBOYS (NFC); 1971, 73
    NEW ENGLAND PATRIOTS (AFC); 1974 HOUSTON OILERS (AFC)
KING, ANDREW (WEST VIRGINIA) - BACK - 1920-22 AKRON PROS; 1922
    MILWAUKEE BADGERS; 1923-24 CHICAGO CARDINALS; 1925 HAMMOND PROS
KING, CHARLES (PURDUE) - BACK - 1966-67 BUFFALO BILLS (AFL); 1968-69
    CINCINNATI BENGALS (AFL)
KING, CLAUDE (HOUSTON) - BACK - 1961 HOUSTON OILERS (AFL); 1962
    BOSTON PATRIOTS (AFL)
KING, DONALD (KENTUCKY) - TACKLE - 1954 CLEVELAND BROWNS; 1956
    PHILADELPHIA EAGLES; 1956 GREEN BAY PACKERS; 1960 DENVER BRONCOS
    (AFL)
KING, EDWARD (BOSTON COLLEGE) - GUARD - 1948-49 BUFFALO BILLS (AAFC);
    1950 BALTIMORE COLTS
KING, EMMETT - BACK - 1954 CHICAGO CARDINALS
KING, GEORGE STEPHEN (TULSA) - LB - 1973-74 NEW ENGLAND PATRIOTS (AFC)
KING, HENRY (UTAH STATE) - BACK - 1967 NEW YORK JETS (AFL)
KING, KENNETH (KENTUCKY) - END - 1926 NEWARK BEARS (AFL)
KING, PAUL (CENTRE) - BACK - 1921 DAYTON TRIANGLES; 1921 CINCINNATI
    CELTS; 1922 TOLEDO MAROONS
KING, FREDERICK (HOBART) - BACK - 1937 BROOKLYN DODGERS
KING, H. LAFAYETTE (GEORGIA) - END - 1946 BUFFALO BISONS (AAFC); 1947
    BUFFALO BILLS (AAFC); 1948 CHICAGO ROCKETS (AAFC); 1949 CHICAGO
    HORNETS (AAFC)
KING, PHILIP (VANDERBILT) - BACK - 1958-63 NEW YORK GIANTS; 1964
    PITTSBURGH STEELERS; 1965-66 MINNESOTA VIKINGS
KING, RALPH (CHICAGO) - TACKLE - 1924 RACINE LEGION; 1925 CHICAGO
    BEARS
KING, RICHARD (HARVARD) - BACK - 1919, 21 HAMMOND PROS; 1920-21
    ROCHESTER JEFFERSONS; 1923 ST. LOUIS BROWNS
KING, TONY (FINDLAY) - BACK - 1967 BUFFALO BILLS (AFL)
KINGERY, ELLSWORTH (TULANE) - BACK - 1954 CHICAGO CARDINALS
KINGERY, WAYNE (LSU) - BACK - 1949 BALTIMORE COLTS (AAFC)
KINGREA, RICHARD (TULANE) - LB - 1971-72 CLEVELAND BROWNS (AFC); 1973
    BUFFALO BILLS (AFC); 1973-74 NEW ORLEANS SAINTS (NFC)
KINGSRITER, DOUGLAS (MINNESOTA) - END - 1973-74 MINNESOTA VIKINGS
    (NFC)
KINNEY, GEORGE (WILEY) - END - 1965 HOUSTON OILERS (AFL)
KINNEY, JEFFREY (NEBRASKA) - BACK - 1972-74 KANSAS CITY CHIEFS (AFC)
KINNEY, STEVE (UTAH STATE) - TACKLE - 1973-74 CHICAGO BEARS (NFC)
KINSCHERF, CARL (COLGATE) - BACK - 1943-44 NEW YORK GIANTS
KIRBY, JOHN (NEBRASKA) - LB - 1964-69 MINNESOTA VIKINGS; 1969 NEW
    YORK GIANTS; 1970 NEW YORK GIANTS (NFC)
KIRCHIRO, WILLIAM (MARYLAND) - GUARD - 1962 BALTIMORE COLTS
KIRCHNER, ADOLPH - TACKLE - 1926 LOUISVILLE COLONELS
KIRK, ERNIE (HOWARD PAYNE) - TACKLE - 1974 HOUSTON OILERS (AFC)
KIRK, GEORGE (BAYLOR) - CENTER - 1926 BUFFALO RANGERS
KIRK, KENNETH (MISSISSIPPI) - LB - 1960-61 CHICAGO BEARS; 1962
    PITTSBURGH STEELERS; 1963 LOS ANGELES RAMS
KIRKGARD (WAYNESBURG) - BACK - 1923 TOLEDO MAROONS
KIRKLAND, B'HO (ALABAMA) - GUARD - 1935-36 BROOKLYN DODGERS

KIRKSEY, ROY (MARYLAND-EASTERN SHORE) - GUARD, TACKLE - 1971-72 NEW
    YORK JETS (AFC); 1973-74 PHILADELPHIA EAGLES (NFC)
KIRLESKI, FRANK (LAFAYETTE) - BACK - 1927-28 POTTSVILLE MAROONS; 1929
    ORANGE TORNADOS; 1930 NEWARK TORNADOS; 1931 BROOKLYN DODGERS
KIRKMAN, ROGER (WASHINGTON&JEFFERSON) - QBACK - 1933-35 PHILADELPHIA
    EAGLES
KIRNER, GARY (USC) - TACKLE - 1964-69 SAN DIEGO CHARGERS (AFL)
KIROUAC, LOUIS (BOSTON COLLEGE) - END - 1963 NEW YORK GIANTS; 1964
    BALTIMORE COLTS; 1966-67 ATLANTA FALCONS
KIRSCHNER, HERBERT (NORTH CAROLINA STATE) - GUARD - 1940 NEW YORK
    AMERICANS (AFL)
KISH, BENJAMIN (PITTSBURGH) - BACK - 1940-41 BROOKLYN DODGERS; 1943
    PHIL-PITT; 1944-49 PHILADELPHIA EAGLES
KISIDAY, GEORGE (DUQUESNE & COLUMBIA) - END - 1948 BUFFALO BILLS
    (AAFC)
KISSELL, ADOLPH (BOSTON COLLEGE) - BACK - 1942 CHICAGO BEARS
KISSELL, EDWARD (WAKE FOREST) - BACK - 1952, 54 PITTSBURGH STEELERS
KISSELL, JOHN (BOSTON COLLEGE) - TACKLE - 1948-49 BUFFALO BILLS
    (AAFC); 1950-52, 54-56 CLEVELAND BROWNS
KISSELL, VITO (HOLY CROSS) - BACK - 1948 BUFFALO BILLS (AAFC); 1950
    BALTIMORE COLTS; 1951 NEW YORK YANKS
KITTREDGE, PAUL (HOLY CROSS) - BACK - 1929 BOSTON BRAVES
KITZMILLER, JOHN (OREGON) - BACK - 1931 NEW YORK GIANTS
KIZZIRE, LEE (WYOMING) - BACK - 1937 DETROIT LIONS
KLAPSTEIN, EARL (PACIFIC) - TACKLE - 1946 PITTSBURGH STEELERS
KLASNIC, JOHN - BACK - 1948 BROOKLYN DODGERS (AAFC)
KLAUS, FEE - CENTER - 1921 GREEN BAY PACKERS
KLAWITTER, RICHARD (SOUTH DAKOTA STATE) - CENTER - 1956 CHICAGO BEARS
KLEIN, IRVING (NEW YORK UNIV.) - END - 1936-37 NEW YORK YANKS (AFL)
KLEIN, RICHARD (IOWA) - TACKLE - 1958-59 CHICAGO BEARS; 1960 DALLAS
    COWBOYS; 1961 PITTSBURGH STEELERS; 1961-62 BOSTON PATRIOTS
    (AFL); 1963-64 OAKLAND RAIDERS (AFL)
KLEIN, ROBERT (USC) - END - 1969 LOS ANGELES RAMS; 1970-74 LOS
    ANGELES RAMS (NFC)
KLENK, QUENTIN (USC) - END - 1946 BUFFALO BISONS (AAFC); 1946 CHICAGO
    ROCKETS (AAFC)
KLEWICKI, EDWARD (MICHIGAN STATE) - END - 1935-38 DETROIT LIONS
KLIEBAN, ROGER (MILWAUKEE TEACHERS) - BACK - 1921 GREEN BAY PACKERS
KLIMEK, ANTHONY (ILLINOIS) - END - 1951-52 CHICAGO CARDINALS
KLINE, HARRY (EMPORIA STATE-KANSAS) - END - 1939-40, 42 NEW YORK
    GIANTS
KLOPPENBERG, HARRY (FORDHAM) - END - 1930 STATEN ISLAND STAPELTONS;
    1931, 33-34 BROOKLYN DODGERS
KLOSTERMAN, DONALD (LOYOLA OF CALIFORNIA) - QBACK - 1952 LOS ANGELES
    RAMS
KLOTOVICH, MICHAEL (ST. MARY'S OF CAL.) - BACK - 1945 NEW YORK GIANTS
KLOTZ, JOHN (PENN STATE) - TACKLE - 1960-62 NEW YORK TITANS (AFL);
    1962 SAN DIEGO CHARGERS (AFL); 1963 NEW YORK JETS (AFL); 1964
    HOUSTON OILERS (AFL)
KLUG, ALFRED (MARQUETTE) - TACKLE - 1946 BUFFALO BISONS (AAFC);
    1947-48 BALTIMORE COLTS (AAFC)
KLUMB, JOHN (WASHINGTON STATE) - END - 1939-40 CHICAGO CARDINALS;
    1940 PITTSBURGH STEELERS
KLUTKA, NICHOLAS (FLORIDA) - END - 1946 BUFFALO BISONS (AAFC)
KMETOVIC, PETER (STANFORD) - BACK - 1946 PHILADELPHIA EAGLES; 1947
    DETROIT LIONS
KNABB, CHESTER - BACK - 1921 CINCINNATI CELTS
KNAFELC, GARY (COLORADO) - END - 1954 CHICAGO CARDINALS; 1954-62
    GREEN BAY PACKERS; 1963 SAN FRANCISCO 49ERS
KNAPPER, JOSEPH (OTTAWA-KANSAS) - BACK - 1934 PHILADELPHIA EAGLES
KNECHT, WILLIAM (XAVIER-OHIO) - TACKLE - 1925-26 DAYTON TRIANGLES
KNIEF, GAYLE (MORNINGSIDE) - END - 1970 BOSTON PATRIOTS (AFC)
KNIGHT, CHARLES - CENTER - 1920 CHICAGO TIGERS; 1920-21 CHICAGO
    CARDINALS
KNIGHT, DAVID (WILLIAM&MARY) - END - 1973-74 NEW YORK JETS (AFC)
KNIGHT, LUTHER CURTIS (COAST GUARD) - KICKER - 1969 WASHINGTON
    REDSKINS; 1970-73 WASHINGTON REDSKINS (NFC); 1971 SCORING LEADER
    (NFC); 1971 FIELD GOAL LEADER (NFC)
KNIGHT, PATRICK (SMU) - BACK - 1952, 54-55 NEW YORK GIANTS
KNOLLA, JOHN (CREIGHTON) - BACK - 1942, 45 CHICAGO CARDINALS

KNOP, OSCAR (ILLINOIS) - BACK - 1920 CHICAGO TIGERS; 1922-23 HAMMOND
     PROS; 1923-28 CHICAGO BEARS
KNORR, LAWRENCE (DAYTON) - END - 1942, 45 DETROIT LIONS
KNOX, BILL (PURDUE) - BACK - 1974 CHICAGO BEARS (NFC)
KNOX, CHARLES (ST. EDMONDS) - TACKLE - 1937 PHILADELPHIA EAGLES
KNOX, FRANK SAMUEL (NEW HAMPSHIRE) - GUARD - 1934-36 DETROIT LIONS
KNOX, RONALD (UCLA) - QBACK - 1957 CHICAGO BEARS
KNUTSON, EUGENE (MICHIGAN) - END - 1954, 56 GREEN BAY PACKERS
KOBER, MATTHEW (VILLANOVA) - GUARD - 1940 BROOKLYN DODGERS
KOBOLINSKI, STANLEY (BOSTON COLLEGE) - CENTER - 1926 BROOKLYN LIONS;
     1926 POTTSVILLE MAROONS
KOBROSKY, MILTON (TRINITY-CONNECTICUT) - BACK - 1937 NEW YORK GIANTS
KOCH, GEORGE (BAYLOR & ST. MARY'S OF TEXAS) - BACK - 1945 CLEVELAND
     RAMS; 1947 BUFFALO BILLS (AAFC)
KOCHEL, MICHAEL (FORDHAM) - GUARD - 1939 CHICAGO CARDINALS
KOCHMAN, ROGER (PENN STATE) - BACK - 1963 BUFFALO BILLS (AFL)
KOCOUREK, DAVID (WISCONSIN) - END - 1960 LOS ANGELES CHARGERS (AFL);
     1961-65 SAN DIEGO CHARGERS (AFL); 1966 MIAMI DOLPHINS (AFL);
     1967-68 OAKLAND RAIDERS (AFL)
KODBA, JOSEPH (PURDUE) - CENTER - 1947 BALTIMORE COLTS (AAFC)
KOEGEL, VICTOR (OHIO STATE) - LB - 1974 CINCINNATI BENGALS (AFC)
KOEGEL, WARREN (PENN STATE) - CENTER - 1971 OAKLAND RAIDERS (AFC);
     1973 ST. LOUIS CARDINALS (NFC); 1974 NEW YORK JETS (AFC)
KOEHLER, ROBERT (NORTHWESTERN) - BACK - 1920 DECATUR STALEYS; 1921
     CHICAGO STALEYS; 1921-26 CHICAGO CARDINALS
KOENINGER, ARTHUR (CHATTANOOGA) - CENTER - 1931 FRANKFORD
     YELLOWJACKETS; 1932 STATEN ISLAND STAPELTONS; 1933 PHILADELPHIA
     EAGLES
KOEPER, RICHARD (OREGON STATE) - TACKLE - 1966 ATLANTA FALCONS
KOEPFER, KARL (BOWLING GREEN) - GUARD - 1958 DETROIT LIONS
KOEPSELL, WILLIAM (PENNSYLVANIA) - BACK - 1940 BUFFALO INDIANS (AFL)
KOHLER, MORRIS (OREGON STATE) - BACK - 1940 BOSTON BEARS (AFL); 1940
     COLUMBUS BULLIES (AFL); 1941 NEW YORK AMERICANS (AFL)
KOKEN, MICHAEL (NOTRE DAME) - BACK - 1933 CHICAGO CARDINALS
KOLB, JON (OKLAHOMA STATE) - CENTER, TACKLE - 1969 PITTSBURGH
     STEELERS; 1970-74 PITTSBURGH STEELERS (AFC)
KOLBERG, ELMER (OREGON STATE) - END - 1939-40 PHILADELPHIA EAGLES;
     1941 PITTSBURGH STEELERS
KOLEN, MICHAEL (AUBURN) - LB - 1970-74 MIAMI DOLPHINS (AFC)
KOLESAR, ROBERT (MICHIGAN) - GUARD - 1946 CLEVELAND BROWNS (AAFC)
KOLLAR, WILLIAM (MONTANA STATE) - TACKLE - 1974 CINCINNATI BENGALS
     (AFC)
KOLLS, LOUIS (ST. AMBROSE) - CENTER - 1920 HAMMOND PROS; 1921-25 ROCK
     ISLAND INDEPENDENTS; 1926 ROCK ISLAND INDEPENDENTS (AFL); 1927
     NEW YORK YANKEES
KOLMAN, EDWARD (TEMPLE) - TACKLE - 1940-42, 46-47 CHICAGO BEARS; 1949
     NEW YORK GIANTS
KOMAN, WILLIAM (NORTH CAROLINA) - LB - 1956 BALTIMORE COLTS; 1957-58
     PHILADELPHIA EAGLES; 1959 CHICAGO CARDINALS; 1960-67 ST. LOUIS
     CARDINALS
KOMPARA, JOHN (SOUTH CAROLINA) - TACKLE - 1960 LOS ANGELES CHARGERS
     (AFL)
KONDRLA, JOHN (ST. VINCENT'S) - TACKLE - 1945 PITTSBURGH STEELERS
KONETSKY, FLOYD (FLORIDA) - END - 1944-45 CLEVELAND RAMS; 1947
     BALTIMORE COLTS (AAFC)
KONISZEWSKI, JOHN (GEORGE WASHINGTON) - TACKLE - 1945-46, 48
     WASHINGTON REDSKINS
KONOVSKY, ROBERT (WISCONSIN) - GUARD - 1956-58 CHICAGO CARDINALS;
     1960 CHICAGO BEARS; 1961 DENVER BRONCOS (AFL)
KONZ, KENNETH (LSU) - BACK - 1953-59 CLEVELAND BROWNS
KOONS, JOSEPH (SCRANTON) - CENTER - 1941 BROOKLYN DODGERS
KOONTZ, EDWARD (CATAWBA) - LB - 1968 BOSTON PATRIOTS (AFL)
KOONTZ, JOSEPH (SAN FRANCISCO STATE) - END - 1968 NEW YORK GIANTS
KOPAY, DAVID (WASHINGTON) - BACK - 1964-67 SAN FRANCISCO 49ERS; 1968
     DETROIT LIONS; 1969 WASHINGTON REDSKINS; 1970 WASHINGTON
     REDSKINS (NFC); 1971 NEW ORLEANS SAINTS (NFC); 1972 GREEN BAY
     PACKERS (NFC)
KOPCHA, JOSEPH (CHATTANOOGA) - GUARD - 1929, 32-35 CHICAGO BEARS;
     1936 DETROIT LIONS
KOPCHA, MICHAEL (CHATTANOOGA) - CENTER - 1941 NEW YORK AMERICANS (AFL)
KOPP, WILLIAM (XAVIER-OHIO) - GUARD - 1941 CINCINNATI BENGALS (AFL)

KOPLOW, JOSEPH (BOSTON UNIV.) - TACKLE - 1926 PROVIDENCE
    STEAMROLLERS; 1929 BOSTON BRAVES
KOPPISCH, WALTER (COLUMBIA) - BACK - 1925 BUFFALO BISONS; 1926 NEW
    YORK GIANTS
KOPROWSKI, JOHN (XAVIER-OHIO) - BACK - 1941 CINCINNATI BENGALS (AFL)
KORISKY, EDWARD (VILLANOVA) - CENTER - 1944 BOSTON YANKS
KORTAS, KENNETH (LOUISVILLE) - TACKLE - 1964 ST. LOUIS CARDINALS;
    1965-68 PITTSBURGH STEELERS; 1969 CHICAGO BEARS
KORVER, KELVIN (NORTHWESTERN-IOWA) - TACKLE - 1973-74 OAKLAND RAIDERS
    (AFC)
KOSEL, STANLEY (ALBRIGHT) - BACK - 1938-39 BROOKLYN DODGERS
KOSENS, TERRY (HOFSTRA) - BACK - 1963 MINNESOTA VIKINGS
KOSHLAP, JULES (GEORGETOWN) - BACK - 1945 PITTSBURGH STEELERS
KOSIKOWSKI, FRANK (MARQUETTE & NOTRE DAME) - END - 1948 CLEVELAND
    BROWNS (AAFC); 1948 BUFFALO BILLS (AAFC)
KOSINS, GARY (DAYTON) - BACK - 1972-74 CHICAGO BEARS (NFC)
KOSLOWSKI, STANLEY (HOLY CROSS) - BACK - 1946 MIAMI SEAHAWKS (AAFC)
KOSTELNIK, RONALD (CINCINNATI) - TACKLE - 1961-68 GREEN BAY PACKERS;
    1969 BALTIMORE COLTS
KOSTIUK, MICHAEL (DETROIT TECH) - TACKLE - 1941 CLEVELAND RAMS; 1945
    DETROIT LIONS; 1946 BUFFALO BISONS (AAFC)
KOSTKA, STANLEY (MINNESOTA) - BACK - 1935 BROOKLYN DODGERS
KOSTOS, ANTHONY (BUCKNELL) - END - 1927-30 FRANKFORD YELLOWJACKETS;
    1930 MINNEAPOLIS REDJACKETS; 1931 FRANKFORD YELLOWJACKETS
KOSTOS, JOSEPH (BUCKNELL) - END - 1926 PHILADELPHIA QUAKERS (AFL)
KOSTOS, MARTIN (SCHUYLKILL) - END - 1929 FRANKFORD YELLOWJACKETS
KOTAL, EDWARD (LAWRENCE) - BACK - 1925-29 GREEN BAY PACKERS
KOTAR, DOUG (KENTUCKY) - BACK - 1974 NEW YORK GIANTS (NFC)
KOTITE, RICHARD (WAGNER) - LB, END - 1967, 69 NEW YORK GIANTS; 1968
    PITTSBURGH STEELERS; 1971-72 NEW YORK GIANTS (NFC)
KOTTLER, MARTIN (CENTRE) - BACK - 1933 PITTSBURGH PIRATES
KOVAC, EDWARD (CINCINNATI) - BACK - 1960 BALTIMORE COLTS; 1962 NEW
    YORK TITANS (AFL)
KOVASCY, WILLIAM (ILLINOIS) - TACKLE - 1923 HAMMOND PROS
KOVATCH, JOHN (NOTRE DAME) - END - 1942, 46 WASHINGTON REDSKINS; 1947
    GREEN BAY PACKERS
KOVATCH, JOHN (NORTHWESTERN) - END - 1938 CLEVELAND RAMS
KOWALCZYK, WALTER (MICHIGAN STATE) - BACK - 1958-59 PHILADELPHIA
    EAGLES; 1960 DALLAS COWBOYS; 1961 OAKLAND RAIDERS (AFL)
KOWALKOWSKI, ROBERT (VIRGINIA) - GUARD - 1966-69 DETROIT LIONS;
    1970-74 DETROIT LIONS (NFC)
KOWALSKI, ADOLPH (TULSA) - BACK - 1947 BROOKLYN DODGERS (AAFC)
KOWALSKI, ANDREW (MISSISSIPPI STATE) - END - 1943 BROOKLYN DODGERS;
    1944 BROOKLYN TIGERS; 1945 BOSTON YANKS; 1946 MIAMI SEAHAWKS
    (AAFC)
KOY, ERNEST (TEXAS) - BACK, KICKER - 1965-69 NEW YORK GIANTS; 1970
    NEW YORK GIANTS (NFC)
KOY, JAMES THEO "TED" (TEXAS) - BACK, END, LB - 1970 OAKLAND RAIDERS
    (AFC); 1971-74 BUFFALO BILLS (AFC)
KRAKAU, MERVIN (IOWA STATE) - LB - 1973-74 BUFFALO BILLS (AFC)
KOZEL, CHESTER (MISSISSIPPI) - TACKLE - 1947-48 BUFFALO BILLS (AAFC);
    1948 CHICAGO ROCKETS (AAFC)
KOZIAK, MICHAEL (NOTRE DAME) - GUARD - 1924-25 DULUTH KELLEYS
KOSLOCK - TACKLE - 1926 BROOKLYN HORSEMEN (AFL)
KOZLOWSKY, JOSEPH (BOSTON COLLEGE) - TACKLE - 1925-27, 30 PROVIDENCE
    STEAMROLLERS; 1929 BOSTON BRAVES
KRACUM, GEORGE (PITTSBURGH) - BACK - 1941 BROOKLYN DODGERS
KRAEHE, OLIVER (WASHINGTON-MISSOURI) - GUARD - 1922 ROCK ISLAND
    INDEPENDENTS; 1923 ST. LOUIS BROWNS
KRAEMER, ELDRED (PITTSBURGH) - GUARD - 1955 SAN FRANCISCO 49ERS
KRAFT, REYNOLD (ILLINOIS) - END - 1922 MINNEAPOLIS MARINES
KRAKER, JOSEPH (SASKATCHEWAN) - TACKLE - 1924 ROCK ISLAND INDEPENDENTS
KRAKOWSKI, JOSEPH (ILLINOIS) - BACK - 1961 WASHINGTON REDSKINS;
    1963-66 OAKLAND RAIDERS (AFL)
KRALL, GERALD (OHIO STATE) - BACK - 1950 DETROIT LIONS
KRAMER, FREDERICK (WASHINGTON STATE) - GUARD - 1927 NEW YORK YANKEES
KRAMER, GEORGE - GUARD - 1921-24 MINNEAPOLIS MARINES
KRAMER, GERALD (IDAHO) - GUARD, KICKER - 1958-68 GREEN BAY PACKERS
KRAMER, JOHN (MARQUETTE) - TACKLE - 1946 BUFFALO BISONS (AAFC)

KRAMER, KENT (MINNESOTA) - END - 1966 SAN FRANCISCO 49ERS; 1967 NEW
     ORLEANS SAINTS; 1969 MINNESOTA VIKINGS; 1970 MINNESOTA VIKINGS
     (NFC); 1971-74 PHILADELPHIA EAGLES (NFC)
KRAMER, RONALD (MICHIGAN) - END - 1957, 59-65 GREEN BAY PACKERS;
     1965-67 DETROIT LIONS
KRAMER, SOLOMON (SOUTH DAKOTA STATE) - QBACK - 1936 ROCHESTER TIGERS
     (AFL)
KRANZ, KENNETH (MILWAUKEE STATE) - BACK - 1949 GREEN BAY PACKERS
KRATZER, DANIEL (MISSOURI VALLEY) - END - 1973 KANSAS CITY CHIEFS
     (AFC)
KRAUS, FRANCIS (HOBART) - TACKLE - 1924 BUFFALO BISONS
KRAUSE, HENRY (ST. LOUIS UNIV.) - CENTER - 1936-37 BROOKLYN DODGERS;
     1937-38 WASHINGTON REDSKINS
KRAUSE, LARRY (ST.NORBERT) - BACK - 1970-71, 73-74 GREEN BAY PACKERS
     (NFC)
KRAUSE, MAX (GONZAGA) - BACK - 1933-36 NEW YORK GIANTS; 1937-40
     WASHINGTON REDSKINS
KRAUSE, PAUL (IOWA) - BACK - 1964-67 WASHINGTON REDSKINS; 1968-69
     MINNESOTA VIKINGS; 1970-74 MINNESOTA VIKINGS (NFC); 1964
     INTERCEPTION LEADER
KARUSE, WILLIAM (BALDWIN-WALLACE) - GUARD - 1938 CLEVELAND RAMS
KRAYENBUHL, CRAIG - BACK - 1922 LOUISVILLE BRECKS
KREAMCHECK, JOHN (WILLIAM&MARY) - GUARD - 1953-55 CHICAGO BEARS
KREGENOW, EDWARD (AKRON) - END - 1926 CLEVELAND PANTHERS (AFL)
KREINHEDER, WALTER (MICHIGAN) - GUARD - 1922 AKRON PROS; 1923 ST.
     LOUIS BROWNS; 1925 CLEVELAND BULLDOGS
KREITLING, RICHARD (ILLINOIS) - END - 1959-63 CLEVELAND BROWNS; 1964
     CHICAGO BEARS
KREJCI, JOSEPH (PERU STATE-NEBRASKA) - END - 1934 CHICAGO CARDINALS
KREMSER, KARL (TENNESSEE) - KICKER - 1969 MIAMI DOLPHINS (AFL); 1970
     MIAMI DOLPHINS (AFC)
KRENTLER, T. (DETROIT) - BACK - 1920 DETROIT HERALDS
KRESKY, JOSEPH (WISCONSIN) - GUARD - 1932 BOSTON BRAVES; 1933-35
     PHILADELPHIA EAGLES; 1935 PITTSBURGH PIRATES
KREUZ, ALBERT (PENNSYLVANIA) - BACK - 1926 PHILADELPHIA QUAKERS (AFL)
KREUZ, LOUIS (WISCONSIN) - QBACK - 1919 DETROIT HERALDS
KRIEG, JAMES (WASHINGTON) - END - 1972 DENVER BRONCOS (AFC)
KRIEGER, EARL (OHIO) - BACK - 1921 DETROIT PANTHERS; 1922 COLUMBUS
     PANHANDLES
KRIEGER, ROBERT (DARTMOUTH) - END - 1941, 46 PHILADELPHIA EAGLES
KRIEL, EMMETT (BAYLOR) - GUARD - 1939 PHILADELPHIA EAGLES
KRIEWALD, DOUGLAS (WEST TEXAS STATE) - GUARD - 1967-68 CHICAGO BEARS
KRING, FRANK (TCU) - BACK - 1945 DETROIT LIONS
KRISHER, WILLIAM (OKLAHOMA) - GUARD - 1958 PITTSBURGH STEELERS;
     1960-61 DALLAS TEXANS (AFL)
KRISS, HOWARD (OHIO STATE) - BACK - 1931 CLEVELAND INDIANS
KRISTUFEK, FRANK (PITTSBURGH) - TACKLE - 1940-41 BROOKLYN DODGERS
KRIVONAK, JOSEPH (SOUTH CAROLINA) - GUARD - 1946 MIAMI SEAHAWKS (AAFC)
KRIZ, LEO (IOWA) - TACKLE - 1926 NEW YORK YANKEES (AFL)
KROL, JOSEPH (WEST ONTARIO) - BACK - 1945 DETROIT LIONS
KROLL, ALEXANDER (YALE & RUTGERS) - CENTER - 1962 NEW YORK TITANS
     (AFL)
KROLL, ROBERT (NORTHERN MICHIGAN) - BACK - 1972 GREEN BAY PACKERS
     (NFC)
KRONER, GARY (WISCONSIN) - BACK - 1965-67 DENVER BRONCOS (AFL)
KROUSE, RAYMOND (MARYLAND) - TACKLE - 1951-55 NEW YORK GIANTS;
     1956-57 DETROIT LIONS; 1958-59 BALTIMORE COLTS; 1960 WASHINGTON
     REDSKINS
KRUECK, EDWARD (INDIANAPOLIS NORMAL) - END - 1921 CINCINNATI CELTS
KRUEGER, ALBERT (DRAKE) - TACKLE - 1924 KANSAS CITY COWBOYS
KRUEGER, ALVIN (USC) - END - 1941-42 WASHINGTON REDSKINS; 1946 LOS
     ANGELES DONS (AAFC)
KRUEGER, CHARLES (TEXAS S&M) - TACKLE - 1959-69 SAN FRANCISCO 49ERS;
     1970-73 SAN FRANCISCO 49ERS (NFC)
KRUEGER, ROLF (TEXAS A&M) - END, TACKLE - 1969 ST. LOUIS CARDINALS;
     1970-71 ST. LOUIS CARDINALS (NFC); 1972-74 SAN FRANCISCO 49ERS
     (NFC)
KRUMENACHER, PAUL (SALEM) - END - 1937 PITTSBURGH AMERICANS (AFL)
KRUPA, JOSEPH (PURDUE) - GUARD - 1956-64 PITTSBURGH STEELERS
KRUSE, JOSEPH (XAVIER-OHIO) - END - 1941 CINCINNATI BENGALS (AFL)

KRUSE, ROBERT (WAYNE STATE) - GUARD - 1967-68 OAKLAND RAIDERS (AFL);
     1969 BUFFALO BILLS (AFL)
KRUTKO, LAWRENCE (WEST VIRGINIA) - BACK - 1959-60 PITTSBURGH STEELERS
KRYSL, JERRY (KANSAS STATE) - TACKLE - 1927 CLEVELAND BULLDOGS
KSIONZYK, JOHN (ST. BONAVENTURE) - BACK - 1947 LOS ANGELES RAMS
KUBULA, RAYMOND (TEXAS A&M) - CENTER - 1964-67 DENVER BRONCOS (AFL)
KUCHARSKI, THEODORE (HOLY CROSS) - END - 1930 PROVIDENCE STEAMROLLERS
KUCHTA, FRANK (NOTRE DAME) - CENTER - 1958-59 WASHINGTON REDSKINS;
     1960 DENVER BRONCOS (AFL)
KUCZINSKI, BERNARD (PENNSYLVANIA) - END - 1943 DETROIT LIONS; 1946
     PHILADELPHIA EAGLES
KUCZO, PAUL (VILLANOVA) - BACK - 1929 STATEN ISLAND STAPELTONS
KUECHENBERG, ROBERT (NOTRE DAME) - TACKLE, GUARD - 1970-74 MIAMI
     DOLPHINS (AFC)
KUECHENBERG, RUDY (INDIANA) - LB - 1967-69 CHICAGO BEARS; 1970
     CLEVELAND BROWNS (AFC); 1970 GREEN BAY PACKERS (NFC); 1971
     ATLANTA FALCONS (NFC)
KUEHL, WALTER (DUBUQUE) - BACK - 1920, 23 ROCK ISLAND INDEPENDENTS;
     1921 DETROIT PANTHERS; 1921-22 BUFFALO ALL-AMERICANS; 1924
     DAYTON TRIANGLES
KUEHNRE, OSCAR - GUARD - 1919-21 COLUMBUS PANHANDLES
KUFFEL, RAYMOND (MARQUETTE) - END - 1947 BUFFALO BILLS (AAFC); 1948
     CHICAGO ROCKETS (AAFC); 1949 CHICAGO HORNETS (AAFC)
KUHARICH, JOSEPH (NOTRE DAME) - GUARD - 1940-41, 45 CHICAGO CARDINALS
KUHN, GILBERT (USC) - CENTER - 1937 NEW YORK YANKS (AFL)
KUICK, STANLEY (BELOIT) - GUARD - 1926 GREEN BAY PACKERS; 1926
     MILWAUKEE BADGERS
KULBACKI, JOSEPH (PURDUE) - BACK - 1960 BUFFALO BILLS (AFL)
KULBITSKI, VICTOR (MINNESOTA & NOTRE DAME) - BACK - 1946 BUFFALO
     BISONS (AAFC); 1947-48 BUFFALO BILLS (AAFC)
KUNZ, GEORGE (NOTRE DAME) - TACKLE - 1969 ATLANTA FALCONS; 1970-74
     ATLANTA FALCONS (NFC)
KUPCINET, IRVING (NORTH DAKOTA) - QBACK - 1935 PHILADELPHIA EAGLES
KUPP, JACOB (WASHINGTON) - - 1964-65 DALLAS COWBOYS; 1966 WASHINGTON
     REDSKINS; 1967 ATLANTA FALCONS
KUREK, RALPH (WISCONSIN) - BACK - 1965-69 CHICAGO BEARS; 1970 CHICAGO
     BEARS (NFC)
KURRASCH, ROY (UCLA) - END - 1947 NEW YORK YANKEES (AAFC); 1948
     PITTSBURGH STEELERS
KURTH, JOSEPH (NOTRE DAME) - TACKLE - 1933-34 GREEN BAY PACKERS
KUSKO, JOHN (TEMPLE) - BACK - 1936-38 PHILADELPHIA EAGLES
KUSSEROW, LOUIS (COLUMBIA) - BACK - 1949 NEW YORK YANKEES (AAFC);
     1950 NEW YORK YANKS
KUTLER, RUDOLPH (OHIO STATE) - END - 1925 CLEVELAND BULLDOGS
KUTNER, MALCOLM (TEXAS) - END - 1946-50 CHICAGO CARDINALS
KUUSISTO, WILLIAM (MINNESOTA) - GUARD - 1941-46 GREEN BAY PACKERS
KUZIEL, ROBERT (PITTSBURGH) - CENTER - 1972 NEW ORLEANS SAINTS (NFC)
KUZMAN, JOHN (FORDHAM) - TACKLE - 1941 CHICAGO CARDINALS; 1946 SAN
     FRANCISCO 49ERS (AAFC); 1947 CHICAGO ROCKETS (AAFC)
KVATERNICK, ZVONIMIR (KANSAS) - GUARD - 1934 PITTSBURGH PIRATES
KWALICK, THADDEUS "TED" (PENN STATE) - END - 1969 SAN FRANCISCO
     49ERS; 1970-74 SAN FRANCISCO 49ERS (NFC)
KYLE, JAMES (GETTYSBURG) - GUARD - 1925-26 CANTON BULLDOGS
KYLE, JOHN (INDIANA) - BACK - 1923 CLEVELAND INDIANS
LAABS, KERMIT (BELOIT) - BACK - 1929 GREEN BAY PACKERS
LAACK, GALEN (PACIFIC) - GUARD - 1958 PHILADELPHIA EAGLES
LAAVEG, PAUL (IOWA) - TACKLE, GUARD - 1970-74 WASHINGTON REDSKINS
     (NFC)
LA BISSONIERE, JOSEPH (ST. THOMAS) - CENTER - 1922 HAMMOND PROS
LACEY, ROBERT (NORTH CAROLINA) - END - 1964 MINNESOTA VIKINGS; 1965
     NEW YORK GIANTS
LACH, STEPHEN (DUKE) - BACK - 1942 CHICAGO CARDINALS; 1946-47
     PITTSBURGH STEELERS
LACHMAN, RICHARD - BACK - 1933-35 PHILADELPHIA EAGLES
LADD, ERNEST (GRAMBLING) - TACKLE - 1961-65 SAN DIEGO CHARGERS (AFL);
     1966-67 HOUSTON OILERS (AFL); 1967-68 KANSAS CITY CHIEFS (AFL)
LADD, JAMES (BOWLING GREEN) - END - 1954 CHICAGO CARDINALS
LADROW, WALTER - GUARD - 1921 GREEN BAY PACKERS
LADYGO, PETER (MARYLAND) - GUARD - 1952, 54 PITTSBURGH STEELERS
LA FITTE, WILLIAM (OUACHITA) - END - 1944 BROOKLYN TIGERS
LA FLEUR, JOSEPH - GUARD - 1922-24 CHICAGO BEARS

LA FOREST, W. - BACK - 1920 DECATUR STALEYS
LAGE, RICHARD (LENOIR RHYNE) - END - 1961 ST. LOUIS CARDINALS
LAGOD, CHESTER (CHATTANOOGA) - GUARD - 1953 NEW YORK GIANTS
LAHAR, HAROLD (OKLAHOMA) - GUARD - 1941 CHICAGO BEARS; 1946 BUFFALO
    BISONS (AAFC); 1947-48 BUFFALO BILLS (AAFC)
LAHEY, THOMAS (JOHN CARROLL) - END - 1946-47 CHICAGO ROCKETS (AAFC)
LA HOOD, MICHAEL (WYOMING) - GUARD - 1969 LOS ANGELES RAMS; 1970 ST.
    LOUIS CARDINALS (NFC); 1971-72 LOS ANGELES RAMS (NFC)
LAHR, WARREN (WESTERN RESERVE) - BACK - 1949 CLEVELAND BROWNS (AAFC);
    1950-59 CLEVELAND BROWNS
LAINHART, PORTER (WASHINGTON STATE) - BACK - 1933 CHICAGO CARDINALS;
    1933 PHILADELPHIA EAGLES
LAIRD, BRUCE (AMERICAN INTERNATIONAL) - BACK - 1972-74 BALTIMORE
    COLTS (AFC)
LAIRD, JAMES (COLGATE) - GUARD - 1920-21 ROCHESTER JEFFERSONS;
    1920-22 BUFFALO ALL-AMERICANS; 1925-28 PROVIDENCE STEAMROLLERS;
    1931 STATEN ISLAND STAPELTONS
LAJOUSKY, WILLIAM (CATHOLIC UNIV.) - GUARD - 1936 PITTSBURGH PIRATES
LAKES, ROLAND (WICHITA STATE) - TACKLE - 1961-69 SAN FRANCISCO 49ERS;
    1970 SAN FRANCISCO 49ERS (NFC); 1971 NEW YORK GIANTS (NFC)
LA LONDE, ROGER (MUSKINGUM) - TACKLE - 1964 DETROIT LIONS; 1965 NEW
    YORK GIANTS
LAMANA, PETER (BOSTON UNIV.) - CENTER - 1946-48 CHICAGO ROCKETS (AAFC)
LAMAS, JOSEPH (MOUNT ST. MARY'S) - GUARD - 1942 PITTSBURGH STEELERS
LAMB, MACK (TENNESSEE STATE) - BACK - 1967-68 MIAMI DOLPHINS (AFL)
LAMB, RONALD (SOUTH CAROLINA) - BACK - 1968 DENVER BRONCOS (AFL);
    1968-69 CINCINNATI BENGALS (AFL); 1970-71 CINCINNATI BENGALS
    (AFC); 1972 ATLANTA FALCONS (NFC)
LAMB, ROY (LOMBARD) - BACK - 1925 ROCK ISLAND INDEPENDENTS; 1926-27,
    33 CHICAGO CARDINALS
LAMB, WALTER (OKLAHOMA) - END - 1946 CHICAGO BEARS
LAMBEAU, EARL "CURLY" (NOTRE DAME) - BACK - 1921-29 GREEN BAY
    PACKERS; 1963 HALL OF FAME
LAMBERT, FRANK (MISSISSIPPI) - KICKER - 1965-66 PITTSBURGH STEELERS
LAMBERT, GORDON (TENNESSEE-MARTIN) - LB - 1968-69 DENVER BRONCOS (AFL)
LAMBERT, JACK (KENT STATE) - LB - 1974 PITTSBURGH STEELERS (AFC)
LAMBERTI, PASQUALE (RICHMOND) - LB - 1961 NEW YORK TITANS (AFL); 1961
    DENVER BRONCOS (AFL)
LAMME, EMERALD (OHIO WESLEYAN) - END - 1931 CLEVELAND INDIANS
LAMMONS, PETER (TEXAS) - END - 1966-69 NEW YORK JETS (AFL); 1970-71
    NEW YORK JETS (AFC); 1972 GREEN BAY PACKERS (NFC)
LAMONICA, DARYLE (NOTRE DAME) - QBACK - 1963-66 BUFFALO BILLS (AFL);
    1967-69 OAKLAND RAIDERS (AFL); 1970-74 OAKLAND RAIDERS (AFC);
    1967 PASSING LEADER (AFL); 1970 PASSING LEADER (AFC)
LAMSON, CHARLES (WYOMING) - BACK - 1962-63 MINNESOTA VIKINGS; 1965-67
    LOS ANGELES RAMS
LAND, FREDERICK (LSU) - TACKLE - 1948 SAN FRANCISCO 49ERS (AAFC)
LANDE, CLIFFORD (CARROLL-WISCONSIN) - END - 1921 GREEN BAY PACKERS
LANDER, LOWELL (WESTMINSTER-PA.) - BACK - 1958 CHICAGO CARDINALS
LANDRIGAN, JAMES (HOLY CROSS & DARTMOUTH) - TACKLE - 1947 BALTIMORE
    COLTS (AAFC)
LANDRY, GREGORY (MASSACHUSETTS) - QBACK - 1968-69 DETROIT LIONS;
    1970-74 DETROIT LIONS (NFC)
LANDRY, THOMAS (TEXAS) - BACK - 1949 NEW YORK YANKEES (AAFC); 1950-55
    NEW YORK GIANTS
LANDSBERG, MORTIMER (CORNELL) - BACK - 1941 PHILADELPHIA EAGLES; 1947
    LOS ANGELES DONS (AAFC)
LANE, CLAYTON (NEW HAMPSHIRE) - TACKLE - 1948 NEW YORK YANKEES (AAFC)
LANE, FRANCIS (MARQUETTE) - TACKLE - 1926 MILWAUKEE BADGERS
LANE, FRANK - GUARD - 1921 CINCINNATI CELTS
LANE, GARY (MISSOURI) - QBACK - 1966-67 CLEVELAND BROWNS; 1968 NEW
    YORK GIANTS
LANE, LESLIE (SOUTH DAKOTA UNIV.) - TACKLE - 1939 BROOKLYN DODGERS;
    1940 BOSTON BEARS (AFL)
LANE, LEWIS (ST. MARY'S OF KANSAS) - QBACK - 1924 KANSAS CITY COWBOYS
LANE, MAC ARTHUR (UTAH STATE) - BACK - 1968-69 ST. LOUIS CARDINALS;
    1970-71 ST. LOUIS CARDINALS (NFC); 1972-74 GREEN BAY PACKERS
    (NFC)

LANE, RICHARD "NIGHT TRAIN" (SCOTTSBLUFF) - BACK - 1952-53 LOS
      ANGELES RAMS; 1954-59 CHICAGO CARDINALS; 1960-65 DETROIT LIONS;
      1952, 54 INTERCEPTION LEADER; 1974 HALL OF FAME
LANE, ROBERT (BAYLOR) - LB - 1963-64 SAN DIEGO CHARGERS (AFL)
LANG, ISRAEL (TENNESSEE STATE) - BACK - 1964-68 PHILADELPHIA EAGLES;
      1969 LOS ANGELES RAMS
LANG, "TEX" - TACKLE - 1927 DULUTH ESKIMOS
LANGAS, ROBERT (WAYNE) - END - 1954 BALTIMORE COLTS
LANGE, JAMES (MONTANA STATE) - END - 1929 CHICAGO CARDINALS
LANGE, WILLIAM (DAYTON) - GUARD - 1951-52 LOS ANGELES RAMS; 1953
      BALTIMORE COLTS; 1954-55 CHICAGO CARDINALS
LANGER, JAMES (SOUTH DAKOTA STATE) - CENTER, GUARD - 1970-74 MIAMI
      DOLPHINS (AFC)
LANGHOFF, IRVING (MARQUETTE) - BACK - 1922-23 RACINE LEGION
LANHAM, CHARLES - TACKLE - 1922-23 LOUISVILLE BRECKS
LANIER, WILLIE (MORGAN STATE) - LB - 1967-69 KANSAS CITY CHIEFS
      (AFL); 1970-74 KANSAS CITY CHIEFS (AFC)
LANKAS, JAMES (ST. MARY'S OF CAL.) - BACK - 1942 PHILADELPHIA EAGLES;
      1943 GREEN BAY PACKERS
LAPHAM, DAVID (SYRACUSE) - TACKLE - 1974 CINCINNATI BENGALS (AFC)
LANDSELL, GRANVILLE (USC) - BACK - 1940 NEW YORK GIANTS
LANPHEAR, DANIEL (WISCONSIN) - END - 1960, 62 HOUSTON OILERS (AFL)
LANSFORD, ALEX (TEXAS) - TACKLE - 1955-57 PHILADELPHIA EAGLES;
      1958-60 LOS ANGELES RAMS
LANSFORD, JAMES (TEXAS) - TACKLE - 1952 DALLAS TEXANS
LANTZ, MONTGOMERY (GROVE CITY) - CENTER - 1933 PITTSBURGH PIRATES
LANUM, RALPH (ILLINOIS) - BACK - 1920 DAYTON TRIANGLES; 1921 CHICAGO
      STALEYS; 1922-24 CHICAGO BEARS
LAPHAM, WILLIAM (IOWA) - CENTER - 1960 PHILADELPHIA EAGLES; 1961
      MINNESOTA VIKINGS
LAPKA, THEODORE (ST. AMBROSE) - END - 1943-44, 46 WASHINGTON REDSKINS
LA PORTA, PHIL (PENN STATE) - TACKLE - 1974 NEW ORLEANS SAINTS (NFC)
LA PRESTA, BENJAMIN (ST. LOUIS UNIV.) - QBACK - 1933 BOSTON REDSKINS;
      1934 ST. LOUIS GUNNERS
LARABA, ROBERT (TEXAS WESTERN) - LB - 1960 LOS ANGELES CHARGERS
      (AFL); 1961 SAN DIEGO CHARGERS (AFL)
LARAWAY, JACK (PURDUE) - LB - 1960 BUFFALO BILLS (AFL); 1961 HOUSTON
      OILERS (AFL)
LA ROSA, PAUL - END - 1920-21 CHICAGO CARDINALS
LA ROSE, MARVIN DANIEL (MISSOURI) - TACKLE - 1961-63 DETROIT LIONS;
      1964 PITTSBURGH STEELERS; 1965 SAN FRANCISCO 49ERS; 1966 DENVER
      BRONCOS (AFL)
LARPENTER, CARL (TEXAS) - TACKLE - 1960-61 DENVER BRONCOS (AFL); 1962
      DALLAS TEXANS (AFL)
LARSCHEID, JACK (PACIFIC) - BACK - 1960-61 OAKLAND RAIDERS (AFL)
LARSEN, GARY (CONCORDIA-MINNESOTA) - TACKLE - 1964 LOS ANGELES RAMS;
      1965-69 MINNESOTA VIKINGS; 1970-74 MINNESOTA VIKINGS (NFC)
LARSEN, MERLE (MINNESOTA) - GUARD - 1940-41 MILWAUKEE CHIEFS (AFL)
LARSEN - BACK - 1923 HAMMOND PROS
LARSON, FREDERIC (NOTRE DAME) - CENTER - 1922 CHICAGO BEARS; 1923-24
      MILWAUKEE BADGERS; 1925 GREEN BAY PACKERS; 1926 CHICAGO BULLS
      (AFL); 1929 CHICAGO CARDINALS
LARSON, GREGORY (MINNESOTA) - CENTER,TACKLE,GUARD - 1961-69 NEW YORK
      GIANTS; 1970-73 NEW YORK GIANTS (NFC)
LARSON, HARRY "PETE" (CORNELL) - BACK - 1967-68 WASHINGTON REDSKINS
LARSON, LOUIS - BACK - 1926 DULUTH ESKIMOS; 1929 CHICAGO CARDINALS
LARSON, LYNDON (KANSAS STATE) - TACKLE - 1971 BALTIMORE COLTS (AFC)
LARSON, PAUL (CALIFORNIA) - QBACK - 1957 CHICAGO CARDINALS; 1960
      OAKLAND RAIDERS (AFL)
LARSON, WILLIAM (ILLINOIS WESLEYAN) - BACK - 1960 BOSTON PATRIOTS
      (AFL)
LARY, ROBERT YALE (TEXAS A&M) - BACK - 1952-53, 56-64 DETROIT LIONS;
      1959, 61, 63 PUNTING LEADER
LASCARI, JOHN (GEORGETOWN) - END - 1942 NEW YORK GIANTS
LASH, JAMES (NORTHWESTERN) - END - 1973-74 MINNESOTA VIKINGS (NFC)
LASKEY, WILLIAM (MICHIGAN) - LB - 1965 BUFFALO BILLS (AFL); 1966-67
      69 OAKLAND RAIDERS (AFL); 1970 OAKLAND RAIDERS (AFC); 1971-72
      BALTIMORE COLTS (AFC); 1973-74 DENVER BRONCOS (AFC)
LASKY, FRANCIS (FLORIDA) - TACKLE - 1964-65 NEW YORK GIANTS
LASLAVIC, JAMES (PENN STATE) - LB - 1973-74 DETROIT LIONS (NFC)

Top row (from left to right): Daryle Lamonica, Greg Landry, MacArthur Lane and Willie Lanier. **Second row:** Pete Liske, Larry Little, Mike Lucci and Don Maynard. **Third row:** Mercury Morris, Craig Morton, Haven Moses and Bill Munson. **Bottom row:** Joe Namath, Don Nottingham, Carleton Oats and Jim Otto.

LASS, RICHARD (LACROSSE) - BACK - 1941 CINCINNATI BENGALS (AFL); 1941
    MILWAUKEE CHIEFS (AFL)
LASSA, NICHOLAS (CARLISLE) - TACKLE - 1922-23 OORANG INDIANS; (ALSO
    KNOWN AS LONG TIME SLEEP)
LASSAHN, LOUIS (WESTERN MARYLAND) - END - 1938 PITTSBURGH PIRATES
LASSE, RICHARD (SYRACUSE) - LB - 1958-59 PITTSBURGH STEELERS; 1960-61
    WASHINGTON REDSKINS; 1962 NEW YORK GIANTS
LASSITER, ISSAC (ST. AUGUSTINE) - END, TACKLE - 1962-64 DENVER
    BRONCOS (AFL); 1965-69 OAKLAND RAIDERS (AFL); 1970 BOSTON
    PATRIOTS (AFC)
LASTER, ARTHUR (MARYLAND STATE) - TACKLE - 1970 BUFFALO BILLS (AFC);
    1971 NEW ENGLAND PATRIOTS (AFC)
LATONE, ANTHONY - BACK - 1925-28 POTTSVILLE MAROONS; 1929 BOSTON
    BRAVES; 1930 PROVIDENCE STEAMROLLERS
LATOURETTE, CHARLES (RICE) - BACK, KICKER, END - 1967-68 ST. LOUIS
    CARDINALS; 1970-71 ST. LOUIS CARDINALS (NFC)
LATTNER, JOHN (NOTRE DAME) - BACK - 1954 PITTSBURGH STEELERS
LATZKE, PAUL (PACIFIC) - CENTER - 1966-68 SAN DIEGO CHARGERS (AFL)
LAUER, ALFRED (IOWA) - BACK - 1921-22 EVANSVILLE CRIMSON GIANTS
LAUER, HAROLD (DETROIT) - BACK - 1922 ROCK ISLAND INDEPENDENTS; 1922
    GREEN BAY PACKERS; 1923 TOLEDO MAROONS; 1923 DAYTON TRIANGLES;
    1925-26 DETROIT PANTHERS
LAUER, LAWRENCE (ALABAMA) - CENTER - 1956-57 GREEN BAY PACKERS
LAUGHING GAS - BACK - 1922 OORANG INDIANS
LAUGHLIN, HENRY (KANSAS) - BACK - 1955 SAN FRANCISCO 49ERS
LAURICELLA, HENRY (TENNESSE) - BACK - 1952 DALLAS TEXANS
LAURINAITIS, FRANCIS (RICHMOND) - CENTER - 1947 BROOKLYN DODGERS
    (AAFC)
LAURO, LINDELL (PITTSBURGH) - BACK - 1951 CHICAGO CARDINALS
LAUX, THEODORE (ST. JOSEPH'S OF PA.) - BACK - 1943 PHIL-PITT; 1944
    PHILADELPHIA EAGLES
LAVAN, ALTON (COLORADO STATE) - BACK - 1969 ATLANTA FALCONS; 1970
    ATLANTA FALCONS (NFC)
LAVELLI, DANTE (OHIO STATE) - END - 1946-49 CLEVELAND BROWNS (AAFC);
    1950-56 CLEVELAND BROWNS; 1975 HALL OF FAME
LAVENDER, JOSEPH (SAN DIEGO STATE) - BACK - 1973-74 PHILADELPHIA
    EAGLES (NFC)
LAW, HUBBARD (SAM HOUSTON) - GUARD - 1942, 45 PITTSBURGH STEELERS
LAW, JOHN (NOTRE DAME) - TACKLE - 1930 NEWARK TORNADOS
LAWLER, ALLEN (TEXAS) - BACK - 1948 CHICAGO BEARS
LAWRENCE, DONALD (NOTRE DAME) - TACKLE - 1959-61 WASHINGTON REDSKINS
LAWRENCE, EDWARD (BROWN) - BACK - 1929 BOSTON BRAVES; 1930 STATEN
    ISLAND STAPELTONS
LAWRENCE, HENRY (FLORIDA A&M) - TACKLE - 1974 OAKLAND RAIDERS (AFC)
LAWRENCE, JAMES (TCU) - BACK - 1936-39 CHICAGO CARDINALS; 1939 GREEN
    BAY PACKERS
LAWRENCE, LARRY (IOWA) - QBACK - 1974 OAKLAND RAIDERS (AFC)
LAWRENCE, NORMAN KENT (GEORGIA) - END - 1969 PHILADELPHIA EAGLES;
    1970 ATLANTA FALCONS (NFC)
LAWRENCE, ROLLAND (TABOR) - BACK - 1973-74 ATLANTA FALCONS (NFC)
LAWS, JOSEPH (IOWA) - BACK - 1934-45 GREEN BAY PACKERS
LAWSON, ALPHONSE (DELAWARE STATE) - BACK - 1964 NEW YORK JETS (AFL)
LAWSON, JAMES (STANFORD) - END - 1926 LOS ANGELES WILDCATS (AFL);
    1927 NEW YORK YANKEES
LAWSON, JEROME (UTAH) - BACK - 1968 BUFFALO BILLS (AFL)
LAWSON, ODELL (LANGSTON-OKLAHOMA) - BACK - 1970 BOSTON PATRIOTS
    (AFC); 1971 NEW ENGLAND PATRIOTS (AFC); 1973-74 NEW ORLEANS
    SAINTS (NFC)
LAWSON, ROGER (WESTERN MICHIGAN) - BACK - 1972-73 CHICAGO BEARS (NFC)
LAWSON, STEPHEN (KANSAS) - GUARD - 1971-72 CINCINNATI BENGALS (AFC);
    1973-74 MINNESOTA VIKINGS (NFC)
LAY, RUSSELL (MICHIGAN STATE) - GUARD - 1934 DETROIT LIONS; 1934 ST.
    LOUIS GUNNERS; 1934 CINCINNATI REDS
LAYDEN, ELMER (NOTRE DAME) - BACK - 1926 BROOKLYN HORSEMEN (AFL)
LAYDEN, PETER (TEXAS) - BACK - 1948-49 NEW YORK YANKEES (AAFC); 1950
    NEW YORK YANKS
LAYDEN, ROBERT (SOUTHWESTERN-KANSAS) - END - 1943 DETROIT LIONS
LAYNE, ROBERT (TEXAS) - QBACK - 1948 CHICAGO BEARS; 1949 NEW YORK
    BULLDOGS; 1950-58 DETROIT LIONS; 1958-62 PITTSBURGH STEELERS;
    1956 SCORING LEADER; 1967 HALL OF FAME

LAYPORT, JOHN (WOOSTER) - GUARD - 1924 COLUMBUS TIGERS; 1925-26
    DAYTON TRIANGLES
LAZETICH, MILAN (MICHIGAN) - GUARD - 1945 CLEVELAND RAMS; 1946-50 LOS
    ANGELES RAMS
LAZETICH, PETER (STANFORD) - LB - 1972-74 SAN DIEGO CHARGERS (AFC)
LAZETICH, WILLIAM (MONTANA) - BACK - 1939, 42 CLEVELAND RAMS
LEA, PAUL (TULANE) - TACKLE - 1951 PITTSBURGH STEELERS
LEAF, GARFIELD (SYRACUSE) - TACKLE - 1926 LOUISVILLE COLONELS
LEAHY, BERNARD (NOTRE DAME) - BACK - 1932 CHICAGO BEARS
LEAHY, GERALD (COLORADO) - TACKLE - 1957 PITTSBURGH STEELERS
LEAHY, PATRICK (ST. LOUIS UNIV.) - KICKER - 1974 NEW YORK JETS (AFC)
LEAHY, ROBERT (EMPORIA) - QBACK - 1971 PITTSBURGH STEELERS (AFC)
LEAPER, WESLEY (WISCONSIN) - END - 1921, 23 GREEN BAY PACKERS
LEAR, LESLIE (MANITOBA UNIV.) - GUARD - 1944-45 CLEVELAND RAMS; 1946
    LOS ANGELES RAMS; 1947 DETROIT LIONS
LEARY, THOMAS (FORDHAM) - END - 1927-28, 31 FRANKFORD YELLOWJACKETS;
    1929 STATEN ISLAND STAPELTONS; 1930 NEWARK TORNADOS
LEATHERMAN, PAUL - END - 1922 HAMMOND PROS
LEATHERS, MILTON (GEORGIA) - GUARD - 1933 PHILADELPHIA EAGLES
LE BARON, EDWARD (PACIFIC) - QBACK - 1952-53, 55-59 WASHINGTON
    REDSKINS; 1960-63 DALLAS COWBOYS; 1958 PASSING LEADER
LE BAY, JOHN (WEST VIRGINIA WESLEYAN) - QBACK - 1940-41 COLUMBUS
    BULLIES (AFL)
LE BEAU, CHARLES RICHARD (OHIO STATE) - BACK - 1959-69 DETROIT LIONS;
    1970-72 DETROIT LIONS (NFC); 1970 INTERCEPTION LEADER (NFC)
LEBENGOOD, HOWARD (VILLANOVA) - BACK - 1925 POTTSVILLE MAROONS
LEBERMAN, ROBERT (SYRACUSE) - BACK - 1954 BALTIMORE COLTS
LECHNER, EDGAR (MINNESOTA) - TACKLE - 1942 NEW YORK GIANTS
LECHTHALER, ROY (LEBANON VALLEY) - GUARD - 1933 PHILADELPHIA EAGLES
LECKONBY, WILLIAM (ST. LAWRENCE) - BACK - 1939-41 BROOKLYN DODGERS
LE CLAIR, JAMES (C.W.POST) - QBACK - 1967-68 DENVER BRONCOS (AFL)
LE CLAIR, JAMES MICHAEL (NORTH DAKOTA) - LB - 1972-74 CINCINNATI
    BENGALS (AFC)
LE CLERC, ROGER (TRINITY-CONNECTICUT) - LB - 1960-66 CHICAGO BEARS;
    1967 DENVER BRONCOS (AFL)
LECTURE, JAMES (NORTHWESTERN) - GUARD - 1946 BUFFALO BISONS (AAFC)
LEDBETTER, HOMER (ARKANSAS) - BACK - 1932 STATEN ISLAND STAPELTONS;
    1932-33 CHICAGO CARDINALS
LEDBETTER, MONTE (NORTHWEST LOUISIANA) - - 1967 HOUSTON OILERS
    (AFL); 1967-69 BUFFALO BILLS (AFL); 1969 ATLANTA FALCONS
LEDYARD, HAROLD (CHATTANOOGA) - QBACK - 1953 SAN FRANCISCO 49ERS
LEE, BERNARD (VILLANOVA) - BACK - 1938 PHILADELPHIA EAGLES; 1938
    PITTSBURGH PIRATES
LEE, BIVIAN (PRAIRIE VIEW) - BACK - 1971-74 NEW ORLEANS SAINTS (NFC)
LEE, BOBBY (MINNESOTA) - END - 1969 ST. LOUIS CARDINALS; 1969 ATLANTA
    FALCONS
LEE, COBBIE (MURRAY STATE) - BACK - 1941 CINCINNATI BENGALS (AFL)
LEE, DAVID (LOUISIANA TECH) - LB - 1966-69 BALTIMORE COLTS; 1970-74
    BALTIMORE COLTS (AFC); 1966, 69 PUNTING LEADER
LEE, DWIGHT (MICHIGAN STATE) - BACK - 1968 SAN FRANCISCO 49ERS; 1968
    ATLANTA FALCONS
LEE, EUGENE (FLORDIA) - CENTER - 1946 BOSTON YANKS
LEE, HERMAN (FLORIDA A&M) - TACKLE - 1957 PITTSBURGH STEELERS;
    1958-66 CHICAGO BEARS
LEE, HILARY (OKLAHOMA) - GUARD - 1931 CLEVELAND INDIANS; 1931
    PORTSMOUTH SPARTANS; 1933-34 CINCINNATI REDS
LEE, JACK (CINCINNATI) - QBACK - 1960-63, 66-67 HOUSTON OILERS (AFL);
    1964-65 DENVER BRONCOS (AFL); 1967-69 KANSAS CITY CHIEFS (AFL)
LEE, JOHN (CARNEGIE TECH) - BACK - 1939 PITTSBURGH STEELERS
LEE, KENNETH (WASHINGTON) - LB - 1971 DETROIT LIONS (NFC); 1972
    BUFFALO BILLS (AFC)
LEE, MIKE (NEVADA) - LB - 1974 SAN DIEGO CHARGERS (AFC)
LEE, MONTE (TEXAS) - LB - 1961 ST. LOUIS CARDINALS; 1963-64 DETROIT
    LIONS; 1965 BALTIMORE COLTS
LEE, ROBERT (MISSOURI) - TACKLE - 1960 BOSTON PATRIOTS (AFL)
LEE, ROBERT (PACIFIC) - QBACK, KICKER - 1969 MINNESOTA VIKINGS;
    1970-72 MINNESOTA VIKINGS (NFC); 1973-74 ATLANTA FALCONS (NFC)
LEE, WILLIAM (ALABAMA) - TACKLE - 1935-37 BROOKLYN DODGERS; 1937-42,
    46 GREEN BAY PACKERS

LEEMANS, ALPHONSE "TUFFY" (GEO. WASHINGTON) - BACK - 1936-43 NEW YORK
    GIANTS; 1936 RUSHING LEADER
LEETZOW, MAX (IDAHO) - END - 1965-66 DENVER BRONCOS (AFL)
LEEUWENBERG, RICHARD (STANFORD) - TACKLE - 1965 CHICAGO BEARS
LEFEAR, BILLY (HENDERSON STATE) - BACK, END - 1972-74 CLEVELAND
    BROWNS (AFC)
LE FEBVRE, GILBERT - BACK - 1933-34 CINCINNATI REDS; 1935 DETROIT
    LIONS; 1937 ROCHESTER TIGERS (AFL)
LE FORCE, CLYDE (TULSA) - QBACK - 1947-49 DETROIT LIONS
LEFTRIDGE, RICHARD (WEST VIRGINIA) - BACK - 1966 PITTSBURGH STEELERS
LEGGETT, EARL (LSU) - TACKLE - 1957-60, 62-65 CHICAGO BEARS; 1966 LOS
    ANGELES RAMS; 1967-68 NEW ORLEANS SAINTS
LEGGETT, WILLIAM (OHIO STATE) - QBACK - 1955 CHICAGO CARDINALS
LEHRER, CHRISTOPHER (AUBURN) - BACK - 1922 ROCHESTER JEFFERSONS; 1926
    CLEVELAND PANTHERS (AFL)
LEICHT, JACOB (OREGON) - BACK - 1948-49 BALTIMORE COLTS (AAFC)
LEIGH, CHARLES - BACK - 1968-69 CLEVELAND BROWNS; 1971-74 MIAMI
    DOLPHINS (AFC); 1974 GREEN BAY PACKERS (NFC)
LEISK, WARDELL (LSU) - GUARD - 1937 BROOKLYN DODGERS
LEITH, ALBERT (PENNSYLVANIA) - BACK - 1926 BROOKLYN LIONS
LE JEUNE, WALTER (BETHANY-KANSAS) - GUARD - 1922-23 AKRON PROS; 1924
    MILWAUKEE BADGERS; 1925-26 GREEN BAY PACKERS; 1927 POTTSVILLE
    MAROONS; (REAL NAME WALTER JEAN)
LE MASTER, FRANK (KENTUCKY) - LB - 1974 PHILADELPHIA EAGLES (NFC)
LEMEK, RAYMOND (NOTRE DAME) - GUARD - 1957-61 WASHINGTON REDSKINS;
    1962-65 PITTSBURGH STEELERS
LEMMERMAN, BRUCE (SAN FERNANDO VALLEY) - QBACK - 1968-69 ATLANTA
    FALCONS
LE MOINE, JAMES (UTAH STATE) - TACKLE, GUARD - 1967 BUFFALO BILLS
    (AFL); 1968-69 HOUSTON OILERS (AFL)
LEMON, CLIFFORD (CENTRE) - TACKLE - 1926 CHICAGO BEARS
LENAHAN - BACK - 1919 DETROIT HERALDS
LENC, GEORGE (AUGUSTANA) - END - 1939 BROOKLYN DODGERS; 1940 NEW YORK
    AMERICANS (AFL)
LENICH, WILLIAM (ILLINOIS) - CENTER - 1940-41 MILWAUKEE CHIEFS (AFL)
LENKAITS, WILLIAM (PENN STATE) - CENTER, GUARD - 1968-69 SAN DIEGO
    CHARGERS (AFL); 1970 SAN DIEGO CHARGERS (AFC); 1971-74 NEW
    ENGLAND PATRIOTS (AFC)
LENNAN, BURGESS REID - GUARD - 1945 WASHINGTON REDSKINS; 1947 LOS
    ANGELES DONS (AAFC)
LENS, GREGORY (TRINITY-TEXAS) - TACKLE - 1970-71 ATLANTA FALCONS (NFC)
LENSING, VINCENT (NOTRE DAME) - GUARD - 1921 EVANSVILLE CRIMSON GIANTS
LENTZ, HARRY "JACK" (HOLY CROSS) - BACK - 1967-68 DENVER BRONCOS (AFL)
LEO, CHARLES (INDIANA) - GUARD - 1960-62 BOSTON PATRIOTS (AFL); 1963
    BUFFALO BILLS (AFL)
LEO, JAMES (CINCINNATI) - LB - 1960 NEW YORK GIANTS; 1961-62
    MINNESOTA VIKINGS
LEO, ROBERT (HARVARD) - BACK - 1967-68 BOSTON PATRIOTS (AFL)
LEON, ANTHONY (ALABAMA) - GUARD - 1943 WASHINGTON REDSKINS; 1944
    BROOKLYN TIGERS; 1945-46 BOSTON YANKS
LEONARD, CECIL (TUSKEGEE) - BACK - 1969 NEW YORK JETS (AFL); 1970 NEW
    YORK JETS (AFC)
LEONARD, JAMES (COLGATE) - GUARD - 1924 CHICAGO BEARS
LEONARD, JAMES (NOTRE DAME) - QBACK - 1934-37 PHILADELPHIA EAGLES
LEONARD, JOHN (INDIANA) - GUARD - 1922-23 CHICAGO CARDINALS
LEONARD, WILLIAM (NOTRE DAME) - END - 1949 BALTIMORE COLTS (AAFC)
LEONETTI, ROBERT (WAKE FOREST) - GUARD - 1948 BUFFALO BILLS (AAFC);
    1948 BROOKLYN DODGERS (AAFC)
LEPPER, BERNARD - TACKLE - 1920 BUFFALO ALL-AMERICANS
LEROY, EUGENE (DENISON) - BACK - 1940 CINCINNATI BENGALS (AFL)
LESANE, JAMES (VIRGINIA) - BACK - 1952, 54 CHICAGO BEARS; 1954
    BALTIMORE COLTS
LESTER, DARRELL (TCU) - CENTER - 1937-38 GREEN BAY PACKERS
LESTER, HAROLD - END - 1926 PROVIDENCE STEAMROLLERS
LESTER, MARCUS DARRELL (MCNEESE STATE) - BACK - 1964 MINNESOTA
    VIKINGS; 1965-66 DENVER BRONCOS (AFL)
LETLOW, RUSSELL (SAN FRANCISCO) - GUARD - 1936-42, 46 GREEN BAY
    PACKERS
LETNER, ROBERT (TENNESSEE) - BACK - 1961 BUFFALO BILLS (AFL)
LETSINGER, JAMES (PURDUE) - GUARD - 1933 PITTSBURGH PIRATES

LEVANITIS, STEPHEN (BOSTON COLLEGE) - TACKLE - 1942 PHILADELPHIA
     EAGLES
LEVANTI, LOUIS (ILLINOIS) - GUARD - 1951-52 PITTSBURGH STEELERS
LE VECK, JACK (OHIO) - LB - 1973-74 ST. LOUIS CARDINALS (NFC)
LEVEY, JAMES - BACK - 1934-36 PITTSBURGH PIRATES
LE VIAS, JERRY (SMU) - END - 1969 HOUSTON OILERS (AFL); 1970 HOUSTON
     OILERS (AFC); 1971-74 SAN DIEGO CHARGERS (AFC)
LEVY, HARVEY (SYRACUSE) - GUARD - 1928 NEW YORK YANKEES
LEVY, LEONARD (MINNESOTA) - GUARD - 1945 CLEVELAND RAMS; 1946 LOS
     ANGELES RAMS; 1947-48 LOS ANGELES DONS (AAFC)
LEWELLEN, VERNE (NEBRASKA) - BACK - 1924-27 GREEN BAY PACKERS; 1927
     NEW YORK YANKEES; 1928-32 GREEN BAY PACKERS
LEWIS, ARTHUR (OHIO) - TACKLE - 1936 NEW YORK GIANTS; 1938-39
     CLEVELAND RAMS
LEWIS, ARTHUR (WEST VIRGINIA) - TACKLE - 1921 CINCINNATI CELTS
LEWIS, CHARLES (IOWA) - TACKLE - 1959 CHICAGO CARDINALS
LEWSI, CLIFFORD (DUKE) - QBACK - 1946-49 CLEVELAND BROWNS (AAFC);
     1950-51 CLEVELAND BROWNS
LEWIS, DANIEL (WISCONSIN) - BACK - 1958-64 DETROIT LIONS; 1965
     WASHINGTON REDSKINS; 1966 NEW YORK GIANTS
LEWIS, DAVID (STANFORD) - KICKER, QBACK - 1970-73 CINCINNATI BENGALS
     (AFC); 1970-71 PUNTING LEADER (AFC)
LEWIS, DWIGHT "D.D." (MISSISSIPPI STATE) - LB - 1968 DALLAS COWBOYS;
     1970-74 DALLAS COWBOYS (NFC)
LEWIS, ERNEST (COLORADO) - BACK - 1946-48 CHICAGO ROCKETS (AAFC);
     1949 CHICAGO HORNETS (AAFC)
LEWIS, FRANK (GRAMBLING) - END - 1971-74 PITTSBURGH STEELERS (AFC)
LEWIS, GARY (ARIZONA STATE) - BACK - 1964-69 SAN FRANCISCO 49ERS;
     1970 NEW ORLEANS SAINTS (NFC)
LEWIS, HAROLD (ARIZONA STATE) - BACK - 1968 DENVER BRONCOS (AFL)
LEWIS, HAROLD (HOUSTON) - BACK - 1959 BALTIMORE COLTS; 1960 BUFFALO
     BILLS (AFL); 1962 OAKLAND RAIDERS (AFL)
LEWIS, HERMAN (VIRGINIA UNION) - END - 1968 DENVER BRONCOS (AFL)
LEWIS, JESS (OREGON STATE) - LB - 1970 HOUSTON OILERS (AFC)
LEWIS, JOSEPH (COMPTON JUNIOR) - TACKLE - 1959-60 PITTSBURGH
     STEELERS; 1961 BALTIMORE COLTS; 1962 PHILADELPHIA EAGLES
LEWIS, LELAND (NORTHWESTERN, - BACK - 1930 PORTSMOUTH SPARTANS; 1931
     CLEVELAND INDIANS
LEWIS, MICHAEL (ARKANSAS AM&N) - TACKLE, END - 1971-74 ATLANTA
     FALCONS (NFC)
LEWIS, R. - GUARD - 1921 LOUISVILLE BRECKS
LEWIS, RICHARD (PORTLAND STATE) - LB - 1972 HOUSTON OILERS (AFC);
     1973-74 BUFFALO BILLS (AFC); 1974 NEW YORK JETS (AFC)
LEWIS, SCOTT (GRAMBLING) - END - 1971 HOUSTON OILERS (AFC)
LEWIS, SHERMAN (MICHIGAN STATE) - BACK - 1966-67 NEW YORK JETS (AFL)
LEWIS, WILTON (TCU) - BACK - 1934 CINCINNATI REDS
LEWIS, WOODLEY (OREGON) - BACK - 1950-55 LOS ANGELES RAMS; 1956-59
     CHICAGO CARDINALS; 1960 DALLAS COWBOYS
LEYPOLDT, JOHN - KICKER - 1971-74 BUFFALO BILLS (AFC)
LIDBERG, CARL (MINNESOTA) - BACK - 1926-30 GREEN BAY PACKERS
LIDDICK, DAVID (GEORGE WASHINGTON) - TACKLE - 1957 PITTSBURGH STEELERS
LIEBEL, FRANK (NORWICH) - END - 1942-47 NEW YORK GIANTS; 1948 CHICAGO
     CARDINALS
LIEBERUM, DONALD (MANCHESTER-INDIANA) - BACK - 1942 NEW YORK GIANTS
LIGGETT, ROBERT (NEBRASKA) - TACKLE - 1970 KANSAS CITY CHIEFS (AFC)
LIGHTNER, HARRY (CINCINNATI) - CENTER - 1937 CINCINNATI BENGALS (AFL)
LILES, ELVIN (OKLAHOMA A&M) - GUARD - 1943-45 DETROIT LIONS; 1945
     CLEVELAND RAMS
LILLARD, JOSEPH (OREGON STATE) - BACK - 1932-33 CHICAGO CARDINALS
LILLY, ROBERT (TCU) - TACKLE - 1961-69 DALLAS COWBOYS; 1970-74 DALLAS
     COWBOYS (NFC)
LILLYWHITE, VERL (USC) - BACK - 1948-49 SAN FRANCISCO 49ERS (AAFC);
     1950-51 SAN FRANCISCO 49ERS
LINCE, DAVID (NORTH DAKOTA) - END - 1966-67 PHILADELPHIA EAGLES
LINCOLN, KEITH (WASHINGTON STATE) - BACK - 1961-66, 68 SAN FRANCISCO
     49ERS; 1967-68 BUFFALO BILLS (AFL)
LIND, ALBERT (NORTHWESTERN) - CENTER - 1936 CHICAGO CARDINALS
LIND, HARRY "MIKE" (NOTRE DAME) - BACK - 1963-64 SAN FRANCISCO 49ERS;
     1965-66 PITTSBURGH STEELERS
LINDAHL, VIRGIL (WAYNE STATE-NEBRASKA) - GUARD - 1945 NEW YORK GIANTS

LINDEN, ERROL (HOUSTON) - TACKLE - 1961 CLEVELAND BROWNS; 1962-65
    MINNESOTA VIKINGS; 1966-68 ATLANTA FALCONS; 1969 NEW ORLEANS
    SAINTS; 1970 NEW ORLEANS SAINTS (NFC)
LINDON, LUTHER (KENTUCKY) - TACKLE - 1940 BOSTON BEARS (AFL); 1940
    COLUMBUS BULLIES (AFL); 1944-45 DETROIT LIONS
LINDOW, ALLEN (WASHINGTON-MISSOURI) - BACK - 1945 CHICAGO CARDINALS
LINDQUIST, PAUL (NEW HAMPSHIRE) - TACKLE - 1961 BOSTON PATRIOTS (AFL)
LINDSEY, HUBERT (WYOMING) - BACK - 1968 DENVER BRONCOS (AFL)
LINDSEY, JAMES (ARKANSAS) - BACK - 1966-69 MINNESOTA VIKINGS; 1970-72
    MINNESOTA VIKINGS (NFC)
LINDSEY, MENZIES (WABASH) - BACK - 1921-22 EVANSVILLE CRIMSON GIANTS
LINDSEY, PHILIP DALE (WESTERN KENTUCKY) - LB - 1965-69 CLEVELAND
    BROWNS; 1970-73 CLEVELAND BROWNS (AFC); 1973 NEW ORLEANS SAINTS
    (NFC)
LINDSKOG, VICTOR (STANFORD) - CENTER - 1944-51 PHILADELPHIA EAGLES
LINE, WILLIAM (SMU) - TACKLE - 1972 CHICAGO BEARS (NFC)
LINGRELL, RAYMOND - BACK - 1919 MASSILLON TIGERS
LINHART, ANTON "TONI" - KICKER - 1972 NEW ORLEANS SAINTS (NFC); 1974
    BALTIMORE COLTS (AFC)
LININGER, RAYMOND (OHIO STATE) - CENTER - 1950-51 DETROIT LIONS
LINNAN, FRANCIS (MARQUETTE) - TACKLE - 1922, 26 RACINE LEGION
LINNE, AUBREY (TCU) - END - 1961 BALTIMORE COLTS
LINTZENICH, JOSEPH (ST. LOUIS UNIV.) - BACK - 1930-31 CHICAGO BEARS
LIO, AUGUSTINO (GEORGETOWN) - GUARD - 1941-43 DETROIT LIONS; 1944-45
    BOSTON YANKS; 1946 PHILADELPHIA EAGLES; 1947 BALTIMORE COLTS
    (AAFC)
LIPINSKI, JAMES (FAIRMONT STATE) - TACKLE - 1950 CHICAGO CARDINALS
LIPOSTAD, EDWARD (WAKE FOREST) - GUARD - 1952 CHICAGO CARDINALS
LIPSCOMB, EUGENE "BIG DADDY" - TACKLE - 1953-55 LOS ANGELES RAMS;
    1956-60 BALTIMORE COLTS; 1961-62 PITTSBURGH STEELERS
LIPSCOMB, PAUL (TENNESSEE) - TACKLE - 1945-49 GREEN BAY PACKERS;
    1950-54 WASHINGTON REDSKINS; 1954 CHICAGO BEARS
LIPSKI, JOHN (TEMPLE) - CENTER - 1933-34 PHILADELPHIA EAGLES
LISBON, DONALD (BOWLING GREEN) - BACK - 1963-64 SAN FRANCISCO 49ERS
LISCIO, ANTHONY (TULSA) - TACKLE - 1963-64, 66-69 DALLAS COWBOYS;
    1970-71 DALLAS COWBOYS (NFC)
LISKE, PETE (PENN STATE) - QBACK - 1964 NEW YORK JETS (AFL); 1969
    DENVER BRONCOS (AFL); 1970 DENVER BRONCOS (AFC); 1971-72
    PHILADELPHIA EAGLES (NFC)
LISTON, PAUL (GEORGETOWN) - TACKLE - 1930 NEWARK TORNADOS
LITTLE, FLOYD (SYRACUSE) - BACK - 1967-69 DENVER BRONCOS (AFL);
    1970-74 DENVER BRONCOS (AFC); 1970-71 RUSHING LEADER (AFC)
LITTLE, JACK (TEXAS A&M) - TACKLE - 1953-54 BALTIMORE COLTS
LITTLE, JAMES (KENTUCKY) - TACKLE - 1945 NEW YORK GIANTS
LITTLE, JOHN (OKLAHOMA) - END, TACKLE - 1970-74 NEW YORK JETS (AFC)
LITTLE, LAWRENCE (BETHUNE-COOKMAN) - GUARD, TACKLE - 1967-68 SAN
    DIEGO CHARGERS (AFL); 1969 MIAMI DOLPHINS (AFL); 1970-74 MIAMI
    DOLPHINS (AFC)
LITTLE, LOUIS (PENNSYLVANIA) - TACKLE - 1919 MASSILLON TIGERS;
    1920-21 BUFFALO ALL-AMERICANS
LITTLE BOY (CARLISLE) - BACK - 1920 COLUMBUS PANHANDLES
LITTLEFIELD, CARL (WASHINGTON STATE) - BACK - 1938 CLEVELAND RAMS;
    1939 PITTSBURGH STEELERS; 1940 BUFFALO INDIANS (AFL)
LITTLE TWIG, JOSEPH (CARLISLE) - END - 1922, 26 AKRON PROS; 1922-23
    OORANG INDIANS; 1924-25 ROCK ISLAND INDEPENDENTS; 1926 CANTON
    BULLDOGS; 1926 COLUMBUS TIGERS
LIVINGSTON, ANDREW - BACK - 1964-65, 67-68 CHICAGO BEARS; 1969 NEW
    ORLEANS SAINTS; 1970 NEW ORLEANS SAINTS (NFC)
LIVINGSTON, CLIFFORD (UCLA) - LB - 1954-61 NEW YORK GIANTS; 1962
    MINNESOTA VIKINGS; 1963-65 LOS ANGELES RAMS
LIVINGSTON, DALE (WESTERN MICHIGAN) - KICKER - 1968-69 CINCINNATI
    BENGALS (AFL); 1970 GREEN BAY PACKERS (NFC)
LIVINGSTON, HOWARD (FULLERTON JUNIOR) - BACK - 1944-47 NEW YORK
    GIANTS; 1948-50 WASHINGTON REDSKINS; 1950 SAN FRANCISCO 49ERS;
    1953 CHICAGO BEARS; 1944 INTERCEPTION LEADER
LIVINGSTON, MICHAEL (SMU) - QBACK - 1968-69 KANSAS CITY CHIEFS (AFL);
    1970-74 KANSAS CITY CHIEFS (AFC)
LIVINGSTON, ROBERT (NOTRE DAME) - BACK - 1948 CHICAGO ROCKETS (AAFC);
    1949 CHICAGO HORNETS (AAFC); 1949 BUFFALO BILLS (AAFC); 1950
    BALTIMORE COLTS

LIVINGSTON, THEODORE (INDIANA) - TACKLE - 1937-40 CLEVELAND RAMS;
     1941 COLUMBUS BULLIES (AFL)
LIVINGSTON, WALTER (HEIDELBERG) - BACK - 1960 BOSTON PATRIOTS (AFL)
LIVINGSTON, WARREN (ARIZONA) - BACK - 1961-66 DALLAS COWBOYS
LLOYD, DAVID (GEORGIA) - LB - 1959-61 CLEVELAND BROWNS; 1962 DETROIT
     LIONS; 1963-69 PHILADELPHIA EAGLES; 1970 PHILADELPHIA EAGLES
     (NFC)
LOCHINER, ARTHUR (MISSOURI) - BACK - 1936 BROOKLYN TIGERS (AFL); 1937
     ROCHESTER TIGERS (AFL)
LOCKETT, J. W. (CENTRAL STATE-OKLAHOMA) - BACK - 1961-62 DALLAS
     COWBOYS; 1963 BALTIMORE COLTS; 1964 WASHINGTON REDSKINS
LOCKHART, CARL "SPIDER" (NORTH TEXAS STATE) - BACK - 1965-69 NEW YORK
     GIANTS; 1970-74 NEW YORK GIANTS (NFC)
LOCKLIN, WILLIAM (NEW MEXICO STATE) - LB - 1960 OAKLAND RAIDERS (AFL)
LOEFFE, RICHARD (WISCONSIN) - TACKLE - 1948-49 CHICAGO CARDINALS
LOFTON, OSCAR (SOUTHEASTERN LOUISIANA) - END - 1960 BOSTON PATRIOTS
     (AFL)
LOGAN, ANDREW (WESTERN RESERVE) - TACKLE - 1941 DETROIT LIONS
LOGAN, CHARLES (NORTHWESTERN) - END - 1964 PITTSBURGH STEELERS; 1965,
     67-68 ST. LOUIS CARDINALS
LOGAN, JAMES (INDIANA) - GUARD - 1942 CHICAGO BEARS
LOGAN, JERRY (WEST TEXAS STATE) - BACK - 1963-69 BALTIMORE COLTS;
     1970-72 BALTIMORE COLTS (AFC)
LOGAN, OBERT (TRINITY-TEXAS) - BACK - 1965-66 DALLAS COWBOYS; 1967
     NEW ORLEANS SAINTS
LOGAN, RANDALL (MICHIGAN) - BACK - 1973-74 PHILADELPHIA EAGLES (NFC)
LOGAN, RICHARD (OHIO STATE) - GUARD - 1952-53 GREEN BAY PACKERS
LOGEL, ROBERT - END - 1949 BUFFALO BILLS (AAFC)
LOHMEYER, JOHN (EMPORIA STATE-KANSAS) - END - 1973 KANSAS CITY CHIEFS
     (AFC)
LOKANC, JOSEPH (NORTHWESTERN) - GUARD - 1941 CHICAGO CARDINALS
LOLLAR, GEORGE (HOWARD) - BACK - 1928 GREEN BAY PACKERS
LOLOTAI, ALBERT (WEBER STATE) - GUARD - 1945 WASHINGTON REDSKINS;
     1946-49 LOS ANGELES DONS (AAFC)
LOMAKOSKI, JOHN (WESTERN MICHIGAN) - TACKLE - 1962 DETROIT LIONS
LOMAS, MARK (NORTHERN ARIZONA) - END, TACKLE - 1970-74 NEW YORK JETS
     (AFC)
LOMASKEY, THOMAS (VILLANOVA) - END - 1929 STATEN ISLAND STAPELTONS
LONDON, MICHAEL (WISCONSIN) - LB - 1966 SAN DIEGO CHARGERS (AFL)
LONE STAR (CARLISLE) - TACKLE - 1920 COLUMBUS PANHANDLES
LONE WOLF (CARLISLE) - GUARD - 1922-23 OORANG INDIANS
LONG, BUFORD (FLORIDA) - BACK - 1953-55 NEW YORK GIANTS
LONG, CHARLES (CHATTANOOGA) - GUARD - 1961-69 BOSTON PATRIOTS (AFL)
LONG, DAVID (IOWA) - END - 1966-68 ST. LOUIS CARDINALS; 1969 NEW
     ORLEANS SAINTS; 1970-72 NEW ORLEANS SAINTS (NFC)
LONG, HARVEY (DETROIT) - TACKLE - 1929 CHICAGO BEARS; 1930 FRANKFORD
     YELLOWJACKETS
LONG, JOHN (COLGATE) - QBACK - 1944-45 CHICAGO BEARS
LONG, LEON (ALABAMA) - BACK - 1936 PITTSBURGH AMERICANS (AFL)
LONG, LOUIS (SMU) - END - 1931 PORTSMOUTH SPARTANS
LONG, MEL (TOLEDO) - LB - 1972-74 CLEVELAND BROWNS (AFC)
LONG, MICHAEL (BRANDEIS) - END - 1960 BOSTON PATRIOTS (AFL)
LONG, ROBERT (TENNESSEE) - BACK - 1947 BOSTON YANKS
LONG, ROBERT (UCLA) - LB - 1955-59 DETROIT LIONS; 1960-61 LOS ANGELES
     RAMS; 1962 DALLAS COWBOYS
LONG, ROBERT (WICHITA) - END - 1964-67 GREEN BAY PACKERS; 1968
     ATLANTA FALCONS; 1969 WASHINGTON REDSKINS; 1970 LOS ANGELES RAMS
     (NFC)
LONG, THOMAS (OHIO STATE) - GUARD - 1925 COLUMBUS TIGERS
LONG TIME SLEEP - (PLAYED UNDER NAME OF NICHOLAS LASSA)
LONG, WILLIAM (OKLAHOMA A&M) - END - 1949-50 PITTSBURGH STEELERS
LONG - GUARD - 1923 RACINE LEGION
LONGENECKER, KENNETH (LEBANON VALLEY) - TACKLE - 1960 PITTSBURGH
     STEELERS
LONGLEY, CLINT (ABILENE CHRISTIAN) - QBACK - 1974 DALLAS COWBOYS (NFC)
LONGMIRE, SAMUEL (PURDUE) - BACK - 1967-68 KANSAS CITY CHIEFS (AFL)
LONGO, ANTONIO (CONNECTICUT) - GUARD - 1928 PROVIDENCE STEAMROLLERS
LONGO, THOMAS (NOTRE DAME) - BACK - 1969 NEW YORK GIANTS; 1970 NEW
     YORK GIANTS (NFC); 1971 ST. LOUIS CARDINALS (NFC)
LONGSTREET, ROY (IOWA STATE) - CENTER - 1926 RACINE LEGION

LONGUA, PAUL (VILLANOVA) - END - 1929 ORANGE TORNADOS; 1930 NEWARK
        TORNADOS
LOOK, DEAN (MICHIGAN STATE) - QBACK - 1962 NEW YORK TITANS (AFL)
LOOKABAUGH, JOHN (MARYLAND) - END - 1946-47 WASHINGTON REDSKINS
LOOMIS, ACE (LACROSSE-WISCONSIN) - BACK - 1951-53 GREEN BAY PACKERS
LOONEY, J. DONALD (TCU) - END - 1940 PHILADELPHIA EAGLES; 1941-42
        PITTSBURGH STEELERS; 1940 PASS RECEIVING LEADER
LOONEY, JOE DON (OKLAHOMA) - BACK, KICKER - 1964 BALTIMORE COLTS;
        1965-66 DETROIT LIONS; 1966-67 WASHINGTON REDSKINS; 1969 NEW
        ORLEANS SAINTS
LOPASKY, WILLIAM (WEST VIRGINIA) - TACKLE - 1961 SAN FRANCISCO 49ERS
LORD, JACK (RUTGERS) - GUARD - 1929 STATEN ISLAND STAPELTONS
LORICK, WILLIAM ANTHONY (ARIZONA STATE) - BACK - 1964-67 BALTIMORE
        COLTS; 1968-69 NEW ORLEANS SAINTS
LOSCH, JOHN (MIAMI) - BACK - 1956 GREEN BAY PACKERS
LOSEY, LEON - BACK - 1941 BUFFALO TIGERS (AFL)
LOTHAMER, EDWARD (MICHIGAN STATE) - TACKLE - 1964-69 KANSAS CITY
        CHIEFS (AFL); 1971-72 KANSAS CITY CHIEFS (AFC)
LOTHRIDGE, WILLIAM (GEORGIA TECH) - BACK, KICKER - 1964 DALLAS
        COWBOYS; 1965 LOS ANGELES RAMS; 1966-69 ATLANTA FALCONS; 1970-71
        ATLANTA FALCONS (NFC); 1972 MIAMI DOLPHINS (AFC); 1967-68
        PUNTING LEADER
LOTT, JOHN - TACKLE - 1929 ORANGE TORNADOS; 1930 BROOKLYN DODGERS
LOTT, WILLIAM (MISSISSIPPI) - BACK - 1958 NEW YORK GIANTS; 1960
        OAKLAND RAIDERS (AFL); 1961-63 BOSTON PATRIOTS (AFL)
LOU, RONALD (ARIZONA STATE) - CENTER - 1973 HOUSTON OILERS (AFC)
LOUCKS, EDWIN (WASHINGTON&JEFFERSON) - END - 1925 CLEVELAND BULLDOGS
LOUDD, ROMMIE (UCLA) - LB - 1960 LOS ANGELES CHARGERS (AFL); 1961-62
        BOSTON PATRIOTS (AFL)
LOUDERBACK, THOMAS (SAN JOSE STATE) - LB - 1958-59 PHILADELPHIA
        EAGLES; 1960-61 OAKLAND RAIDERS (AFL); 1962 BUFFALO BILLS (AFL)
LOUGHLIN - QBACK - 1922 EVANSVILLE CRIMSON GIANTS
LOUKAS, ANGELO (NORTHWESTERN) - GUARD - 1969 BUFFALO BILLS (AFL);
        1970 BOSTON PATRIOTS (AFC)
LOVE, JOHN (NORTH TEXAS STATE) - BACK, END - 1967 WASHINGTON
        REDSKINS; 1972 LOS ANGELES RAMS (NFC)
LOVE, WALTER (WESTMINSTER) - END - 1973 NEW YORK GIANTS (NFC)
LOVETERE, JOHN (COMPTON) - TACKLE - 1959-62 LOS ANGELES RAMS; 1963-65
        NEW YORK GIANTS
LOVIN, FRITZ - GUARD - 1929 MINNEAPOLIS REDJACKETS
LOVUOLO, FRANK (ST. BONAVENTURE) - END - 1949 NEW YORK GIANTS
LOWE, GARY (MICHIGAN STATE) - BACK - 1956-57 WASHINGTON REDSKINS;
        1957-64 DETROIT LIONS
LOWE, GEORGE (FORDHAM & LAFAYETTE) - END - 1919 CLEVELAND INDIANS;
        1920 CANTON BULLDOGS; 1921 CLEVELAND INDIANS; 1922 BUFFALO
        ALL-AMERICANS; 1923 ROCK ISLAND INDEPENDENTS; 1924-26 FRANKFORD
        YELLOWJACKETS; 1925, 27 PROVIDENCE STEAMROLLERS; 1926 BOSTON
        BULLDOGS (AFL)
LOWE, LLOYD (NORTH TEXAS STATE) - BACK - 1953-54 CHICAGO BEARS
LOWE, PAUL (OREGON STATE) - BACK - 1960 LOS ANGELES CHARGERS (AFL);
        1961, 63-68 SAN DIEGO CHARGERS (AFL); 1968-69 KANSAS CITY CHIEFS
        (AFL); 1965 RUSHING LEADER (AFL)
LOWERY, DARBY (URSINUS) - TACKLE - 1920 DETROIT HERALDS; 1920-25
        ROCHESTER JEFFERSONS
LOWTHER, RUSSELL (DETROIT) - BACK - 1944 DETROIT LIONS; 1945
        PITTSBURGH STEELERS
LOYD, EDGAR ALEX (OKLAHOMA A&M) - END - 1950 SAN FRANCISCO 49ERS
LUBRATOVICH, MILO (WISCONSIN) - TACKLE - 1931-37 BROOKLYN DODGERS
LUCAS, RICHARD (PENN STATE) - QBACK - 1960-61 BUFFALO BILLS (AFL)
LUCAS, RICHARD (BOSTON COLLEGE) - END - 1960-63 PHILADELPHIA EAGLES
LUCCI, MICHAEL (TENNESSEE) - LB - 1962-64 CLEVELAND BROWNS; 1965-69
        DETROIT LIONS; 1970-73 DETROIT LIONS (NFC)
LUCE, LLEWELLYN (PENN STATE) - BACK - 1961 WASHINGTON REDSKINS
LUCENTE, JOHN (WEST VIRGINIA) - BACK - 1945 PITTSBURGH STEELERS
LUCKMAN, SIDNEY (COLUMBIA) - QBACK - 1939-50 CHICAGO BEARS; 1945
        PASSING LEADER; (TIED WITH BAUGH); 1965 HALL OF FAME
LUCKY, WILLIAM (BAYLOR) - TACKLE - 1955 GREEN BAY PACKERS
LUDTKE, NORMAN (CARROLL-WISCONSIN) - GUARD - 1924 GREEN BAY PACKERS
LUEBCKE, HENRY (IOWA) - TACKLE - 1941 BUFFALO TIGERS (AFL)

Top row (from left to right): "Tuffy" Leemans, Harvey Levy, Bob Lilly and Vic Lindskog. *Second row:* "Big Daddy" Lipscomb, Paul Lipscomb, Lou Little and Cliff Livingston. *Third row:* Paul Lowe, John Lujack, Lamar Lundy and Lenny Lyles. *Bottom row:* Dick Lynch, Mike McCormack, Tom McDonald and Hugh McElhenny.

Top row (from left to right): Banks McFadden, ''Max'' McGee, Thurman McGraw and Jim McMillen. *Second row:* Bill McPeak, ''Red'' Mack, Lloyd Madden and Lou Mahrt. *Third row:* Charley Malone, Jack Manders, Bob Mann and Gino Marchetti. *Bottom row:* Jim Marshall, Tom Mason, Norm Masters and Bob Masterson.

LUECK, WILLIAM (ARIZONA) - GUARD - 1968-69 GREEN BAY PACKERS; 1970-74
    GREEN BAY PACKERS (NFC)
LUFT, DONALD (INDIANA) - END - 1954 PHILADELPHIA EAGLES
LUHN, NOLAN (TULSA) - END - 1945-49 GREEN BAY PACKERS
LUJACK, JOHN (NOTRE DAME) - QBACK - 1948-51 CHICAGO BEARS
LUKE, THOMAS (MISSISSIPPI) - BACK - 1968 DENVER BRONCOS (AFL)
LUKEN, THOMAS (PURDUE) - GUARD - 1972-74 PHILADELPHIA EAGLES (NFC)
LUKENS, JAMES (WASHINGTON&LEE) - END - 1949 BUFFALO BILLS (AAFC)
LUMMUS, JOHN (BAYLOR) - END - 1941 NEW YORK GIANTS
LUMPKIN, RON (ARIZONA STATE) - BACK - 1973 NEW YORK GIANTS (NFC)
LUMPKIN, ROY (GEORGIA TECH) - QBACK - 1930-33 PORTSMOUTH SPARTANS;
    1934 DETROIT LIONS; 1935-37 BROOKLYN DODGERS
LUNA, ROBERT (ALABAMA) - BACK - 1955 SAN FRANCISCO 49ERS; 1959
    PITTSBURGH STEELERS
LUNCEFORD, DAVID (BAYLOR) - TACKLE - 1957 CHICAGO CARDINALS
LUND, WILLIAM (CASE) - BACK - 1946-47 CLEVELAND BROWNS (AAFC)
LUNDAY, KENNETH (ARKANSAS) - CENTER - 1937-41, 46-47 NEW YORK GIANTS
LUNDE, LESTER (RIPON) - GUARD - 1922-24 RACINE LEGION
LUNDELL, ROBERT (GUSTAVUS-ADOLPHUS) - END - 1929-30 MINNEAPOLIS
    REDJACKETS; 1930 STATEN ISLAND STAPELTONS
LUNDY, LAMAR (PURDUE) - END - 1957-69 LOS ANGELES RAMS
LUNGREN, CHARLES (SWARTHMORE) - BACK - 1923 ROCK ISLAND INDEPENDENTS
LUNSFORD, MELVIN (CENTRAL STATE) - END, TACKLE - 1973-74 NEW ENGLAND
    PATRIOTS (AFC)
LUNZ, GERALD (MARQUETTE) - GUARD - 1925-26 CHICAGO CARDINALS; 1930
    FRANKFORD YELLOWJACKETS
LURTSEMA, ROBERT (WESTERN MICHIGAN) - TACKLE, END - 1967-69 NEW YORK
    GIANTS; 1970-71 NEW YORK GIANTS (NFC); 1972-74 MINNESOTA VIKINGS
    (NFC)
LUSK, ROBERT (WILLIAM&MARY) - CENTER - 1956 DETROIT LIONS
LUSTEG, BOOTH (CONNECTICUT) - KICKER - 1966 BUFFALO BILLS (AFL); 1967
    MIAMI DOLPHINS (AFL); 1967 NEW YORK JETS (AFL); 1968 PITTSBURGH
    STEELERS; 1969 GREEN BAY PACKERS
LUTZ, RUDOLPH - END - 1919 TOLEDO MAROONS
LYLE, DEWEY - GUARD - 1919-22, 24-25 ROCK ISLAND INDEPENDENTS;
    1922-23 GREEN BAY PACKERS
LYLE, GARRY (GEORGE WASHINGTON) - BACK - 1968-69 CHICAGO BEARS;
    1970-74 CHICAGO BEARS (NFC)
LYLES, LEONARD (LOUISVILLE) - BACK - 1958, 61-69 BALTIMORE COLTS;
    1959-60 SAN FRANCISCO 49ERS
LYMAN, DELBERT (UCLA) - TACKLE - 1941 GREEN BAY PACKERS; 1941, 44
    CLEVELAND RAMS
LYMAN, JEFFREY (BRIGHAM YOUNG) - LB - 1972 ST. LOUIS CARDINALS (NFC);
    1972 BUFFALO BILLS (AFC)
LYMAN, WILLIAM ROY (NEBRASKA) - TACKLE - 1922-23, 25 CANTON BULLDOGS;
    1924 CLEVELAND BULLDOGS; 1925 FRANKFORD YELLOWJACKETS; 1926-28,
    30-31, 33-34 CHICAGO BEARS; 1964 HALL OF FAME
LYNCH, EDWARD (CATHOLIC) - END - 1925 ROCHESTER JEFFERSONS; 1926
    DETROIT PANTHERS; 1926 HARTFORD BLUES; 1927 PROVIDENCE
    STEAMROLLERS
LYNCH, FRANCIS (HOFSTRA) - BACK - 1967-69 DENVER BRONCOS (AFL);
    1970-74 DENVER BRONCOS (AFC)
LYNCH, JAMES (NOTRE DAME) - LB - 1967-69 KANSAS CITY CHIEFS (AFL);
    1970-74 KANSAS CITY CHIEFS (AFC)
LYNCH, LYNN (ILLINOIS) - GUARD - 1951 CHICAGO CARDINALS
LYNCH, PAUL (OHIO NORTHERN) - BACK - 1925 COLUMBUS TIGERS
LYNCH, RICHARD (NOTRE DAME) - BACK - 1958 WASHINGTON REDSKINS;
    1959-66 NEW YORK GIANTS; 1961, 63 INTERCEPTION LEADER; (1963
    TIED WITH R. TAYLOR)
LYON, GEORGE (KANSAS STATE) - TACKLE - 1929 NEW YORK GIANTS; 1930
    PORTSMOUTH SPARTANS; 1931 CHICAGO BEARS; 1931 CLEVELAND INDIANS;
    1932 BROOKLYN DODGERS; 1934 ST. LOUIS GUNNERS; 1936 BROOKLYN
    TIGERS (AFL)
LYONS, JOHN (TULSA) - END - 1933 BROOKLYN DODGERS
LYONS, LEO - END - 1919-20 ROCHESTER JEFFERSONS
LYONS, RICHARD (KENTUCKY) - BACK - 1970 NEW ORLEANS SAINTS (NFC)
LYONS, TOMMY (GEORGIA) - CENTER, GUARD - 1971-74 DENVER BRONCOS (AFC)
LYONS - GUARD - 1919 CLEVELAND INDIANS
MAACK, HERBERT (COLUMBIA) - TACKLE - 1946 BROOKLYN DODGERS (AAFC)
MAAS, WAYNE (CLEMSON) - TACKLE - 1968 CHICAGO BEARS

MAC AFEE, KENNETH (ALABAMA) - END - 1954-58 NEW YORK GIANTS; 1959
    PHILADELPHIA EAGLES; 1959 WASHINGTON REDSKINS
MAC AULIFFE, JOHN (BELOIT) - BACK - 1926 GREEN BAY PACKERS
MAC COLLUM, MAXWELL (CENTRE) - END - 1922 LOUISVILLE BRECKS
MAC DOWELL, JAY (WASHINGTON) - TACKLE - 1946-51 PHILADELPHIA EAGLES
MACEAU, MELVIN (MARQUETTE) - CENTER - 1946-48 CLEVELAND BROWNS (AAFC)
MACEFELLI, JOHN (ST.VINCENT'S) - GUARD - 1956 CLEVELAND BROWNS
MACHLOWITZ, NATHAN (NEW YORK UNIV.) - BACK - 1936 BROOKLYN TIGERS
    (AFL)
MACIOSZCZYK, ARTHUR (WESTERN MICHIGAN) - BACK - 1944, 47 PHILADELPHIA
    EAGLES; 1948 WASHINGTON REDSKINS
MACK, THOMAS (MICHIGAN) - GUARD - 1966-69 LOS ANGELES RAMS; 1970-74
    LOS ANGELES RAMS (NFC)
MACK, WILLIAM (NOTRE DAME) - BACK - 1961-63, 65 PITTSBURGH STEELERS;
    1964 PHILADELPHIA EAGLES; 1966 ATLANTA FALCONS; 1966 GREEN BAY
    PACKERS
MACKBEE, JAMES EARSELL (UTAH ST. & VALLEJO) - BACK - 1965-69
    MINNESOTA VIKINGS
MACKENROTH, JOHN (NORTH DAKOTA) - CENTER - 1938 DETROIT LIONS
MACKERT, ROBERT (LEBANON VALLEY) - GUARD - 1919 MASSILLON TIGERS
MACKERT, ROBERT (WEST VIRGINIA) - TACKLE - 1925 ROCHESTER JEFFERSONS
MACKEY, DEE (EAST TEXAS STATE) - END - 1960 SAN FRANCISCO 49ERS;
    1961-62 BALTIMORE COLTS; 1963-65 NEW YORK JETS (AFL)
MACKEY, JOHN (SYRACUSE) - END - 1963-69 BALTIMORE COLTS; 1970-71
    BALTIMORE COLTS (AFC); 1972 SAN DIEGO CHARGERS (AFC)
MAC KINNON, JACQUE (COLGATE) - BACK, END - 1961-69 SAN DIEGO CHARGERS
    (AFL); 1970 OAKLAND RAIDERS (AFC)
MACKORELL, JOHN (DAVIDSON) - BACK - 1935 NEW YORK GIANTS
MACKRIDES, WILLIAM (NEVADA) - QBACK - 1948-51 PHILADELPHIA EAGLES;
    1953 PITTSBURGH STEELERS; 1953 NEW YORK GIANTS
MAC LEAN, STUART (INDIANA) - BACK - 1921 LOUISVILLE BRECKS
MAC LEOD, ROBERT (DARTMOUTH) - BACK - 1939 CHICAGO BEARS
MAC LEOD, THOMAS (MINNESOTA) - LB - 1973 GREEN BAY PACKERS (NFC);
    1974 BALTIMORE COLTS (AFC)
MAC MILLAN, STEWART (NORTH DAKOTA) - CENTER - 1931 CLEVELAND INDIANS
MAC MURDO, JAMES (PITTSBURGH) - TACKLE - 1932 BOSTON BRAVES; 1933
    BOSTON REDSKINS; 1934-37 PHILADELPHIA EAGLES
MACON, EDWARD (PACIFIC) - BACK - 1952-53 CHICAGO BEARS; 1960 OAKLAND
    RAIDERS (AFL)
MAC PHEE, WALTER (PRINCETON) - BACK - 1925-26 PROVIDENCE STEAMROLLERS
MACZUZAK, JOHN (PITTSBURGH) - TACKLE - 1964 KANSAS CITY CHIEFS (AFL)
MADAR, ELMER (MICHIGAN) - END - 1947 BALTIMORE COLTS (AAFC)
MADARIK, ELMER (DETROIT) - BACK - 1945-47 DETROIT LIONS; 1948
    WASHINGTON REDSKINS
MADDEN, LLOYD (COLORADO MINES) - BACK - 1940 CHICAGO CARDINALS
MADDOCK, ROBERT (NOTRE DAME) - GUARD - 1942, 46 CHICAGO CARDINALS
MADDOX, GEORGE (KANSAS STATE) - TACKLE - 1935 GREEN BAY PACKERS
MADDOX, ROBERT (FROSTBURG STATE) - END - 1974 CINCINNATI BENGALS (AFC)
MADEROS, GEORGE (CHICO STATE) - BACK - 1955-56 SAN FRANCISCO 49ERS
MADIGAN, JOHN (ST. MARY'S OF MINNESOTA) - CENTER - 1922, 24
    MINNEAPOLIS MARINES; 1923 DULUTH KELLEYS
MAEDA, CHESTER (COLORADO A&M) - BACK - 1945 CHICAGO CARDINALS
MAEDER, ALBERT (MINNESOTA) - TACKLE - 1929 MINNEAPOLIS REDJACKETS
MAGAC, MICHAEL (MISSOURI) - GUARD - 1960-64 SAN FRANCISCO 49ERS;
    1965-66 PITTSBURGH STEELERS
MAGEE, JAMES (VILLANOVA) - CENTER - 1944-46 BOSTON YANKS
MAGEE, JOHN (RICE) - GUARD - 1948-55 PHILADELPHIA EAGLES
MAGGIOLO, ACHILLE (ILLINOIS & NOTRE DAME) - BACK - 1948 BUFFALO BILLS
    (AAFC); 1949 DETROIT LIONS; 1950 BALTIMORE COLTS
MAGINNES, W. DAVID (LEHIGH) - BACK - 1919 MASSILLON TIGERS
MAGLIOLO, JOSEPH (TEXAS) - BACK - 1948 NEW YORK YANKEES (AAFC)
MAGLISCEAU, ALBERT (GENEVA) - TACKLE - 1929 FRANKFORD YELLOWJACKETS
MAGNANI, DANTE (ST. MARY'S OF CAL.) - BACK - 1940-42 CLEVELAND RAMS;
    1943, 46, 49 CHICAGO BEARS; 1947-48 LOS ANGELES RAMS; 1950
    DETROIT LIONS
MAGNER, JAMES (NORTH CAROLINA) - BACK - 1931 FRANKFORD YELLOWJACKETS
MAGNUSSON, GLEN (NORTHWESTERN) - CENTER - 1925 HAMMOND PROS
MAGUIRE, PAUL (CITADEL) - LB, KICKER - 1960 LOS ANGELES CHARGERS
    (AFL); 1961-63 SAN DIEGO CHARGERS (AFL); 1964-69 BUFFALO BILLS
    (AFL); 1970 BUFFALO BILLS (AFC); 1960 PUNTING LEADER (AFL)
MAGULICK, GEORGE (ST. FRANCIS) - BACK - 1944 CARD-PITT

MAHAN, ROBERT (WASHINGTON-MISSOURI) - BACK - 1929 BUFFALO BISONS;
     1930 BROOKLYN DODGERS
MAHAN, WALTER (WEST VIRGINIA) - GUARD - 1926 FRANKFORD YELLOWJACKETS;
     1926 CHICAGO BULLS (AFL)
MAHER, BRUCE (DETROIT) - BACK - 1960-67 DETROIT LIONS; 1968-69 NEW
     YORK GIANTS
MAHER, FRANCIS (TOLEDO) - BACK - 1941 PITTSBURGH STEELERS; 1941
     CLEVELAND RAMS
MAHER - END - 1920 DETROIT HERALDS
MAHONEY, FRANK "IKE" (CREIGHTON) - BACK - 1925-28, 31 CHICAGO
     CARDINALS
MAHONEY, JOHN (CANISIUS) - BACK - 1923 BUFFALO ALL-AMERICANS
MAHONEY, ROGER (PENN STATE) - CENTER - 1928-30 FRANKFORD
     YELLOWJACKETS; 1930 MINNEAPOLIS REDJACKETS
MAHRT, ALPHONSE (ST. MARY'S OF OHIO) - QBACK - 1919-23 DAYTON
     TRIANGLES
MAHRT, ARMIN (WEST VIRGINIA) - BACK - 1924-25 DAYTON TRIANGLES
MAHRT, JOHN (DAYTON) - END - 1925 DAYTON TRIANGLES
MAHRT, LOUIS (DAYTON) - BACK - 1926-27 DAYTON TRIANGLES
MAILLARD, RALPH (CREIGHTON) - TACKLE - 1929 CHICAGO BEARS
MAINS, GILBERT (MURRAY STATE) - TACKLE - 1954-61 DETROIT LIONS
MAITLAND, JOHN "JACK" (WILLIAMS) - BACK - 1970 BALTIMORE COLTS (AFC);
     1971-72 NEW ENGLAND PATRIOTS (AFC)
MAJORS, ROBERT (TENNESSEE) - BACK - 1972 CLEVELAND BROWNS (AFC)
MAJORS, WILLIAM (TENNESSEE) - BACK - 1961 BUFFALO BILLS (AFL)
MALCOLM, HARRY (WASHINGTON&JEFFERSON) - TACKLE - 1929 FRANKFORD
     YELLOWJACKETS
MALESEVICH, BRONISLAW "BRONKO" (WISCONSIN) - QBACK - 1941 CINCINNATI
     BENGALS (AFL); 1941 MILWAUKEE CHIEFS (AFL)
MALEY, HOWARD (SMU) - BACK - 1946-47 BOSTON YANKS
MALINCHAK, WILLIAM (INDIANA) - END - 1966-69 DETROIT LIONS; 1970-74
     WASHINGTON REDSKINS (NFC)
MALINOWSKI, EUGENE (DETROIT) - BACK - 1948 BOSTON YANKS
MALKOVICH, JOSEPH (DUQUESNE) - CENTER - 1935 PITTSBURGH PIRATES
MALLANEY - QBACK - 1919 WHEELING
MALLICK, FRANCIS - TACKLE - 1965 PITTSBURGH STEELERS
MALLOUF, RAYMOND (SMU) - QBACK - 1941, 46-48 CHICAGO CARDINALS; 1949
     NEW YORK GIANTS
MALLORY, IRVIN (VIRGINIA UNION) - BACK - 1971 NEW ENGLAND PATRIOTS
     (AFC)
MALLORY, JOHN (WEST VIRGINIA) - BACK - 1968 PHILADELPHIA EAGLES; 1969
     ATLANTA FALCONS; 1970-71 ATLANTA FALCONS (NFC)
MALLOY, LESTER (LOYOLA OF ILLINOIS) - QBACK - 1931-33 CHICAGO
     CARDINALS
MALONE, ARTHUR (ARIZONA STATE) - BACK - 1970-74 ATLANTA FALCONS (NFC)
MALONE, BEN (ARIZONA STATE) - BACK - 1974 MIAMI DOLPHINS (AFC)
MALONE, CHARLES (TEXAS A&M) - END - 1934-36 BOSTON REDSKINS; 1937-40,
     42 WASHINGTON REDSKINS
MALONE, GROVER (NOTRE DAME) - BACK - 1920 CHICAGO TIGERS; 1921 GREEN
     BAY PACKERS; 1921 ROCK ISLAND INDEPENDENTS; 1923 AKRON PROS
MALONEY, GERALD (DARTMOUTH) - END - 1925 PROVIDENCE STEAMROLLERS;
     1926 NEW YORK YANKEES (AFL); 1927 NEW YORK YANKEES; 1929 BOSTON
     BRAVES
MALONEY, JOHN (GEORGETOWN) - CENTER - 1919 AKRON PROS
MALONEY, NORMAN (PURDUE) - END - 1948-49 SAN FRANCISCO 49ERS (AAFC)
MALTSCH, JOHN (MARQUETTE) - BACK - 1940-41 MILWAUKEE CHIEFS (AFL)
MANCHA, VAUGHN (ALABAMA) - CENTER - 1948 BOSTON YANKS
MANDARINO, MICHAEL (LASALLE) - CENTER - 1944-45 PHILADELPHIA EAGLES
MANDERS, CLARENCE (DRAKE) - BACK - 1939-43 BROOKLYN DODGERS; 1944
     BROOKLYN TIGERS; 1945 BOSTON YANKS; 1946 NEW YORK YANKEES
     (AAFC); 1947 BUFFALO BILLS (AAFC); 1941 RUSHING LEADER
MANDERS, DAVID (MICHIGAN STATE) - CENTER, GUARD - 1964-66, 68-69
     DALLAS COWBOYS; 1970-74 DALLAS COWBOYS (NFC)
MANDERS, JOHN (MINNESOTA) - BACK - 1933-40 CHICAGO BEARS; 1934, 37
     SCORING LEADER; 1933-34, 36-37 FIELD GOAL LEADER; (1933 TIED
     WITH PRESNELL, 1936 TIED WITH NICCOLAI)
MANDERS, PHILIP (DRAKE) - BACK - 1941 MILWAUKEE CHIEFS (AFL)
MANDICH, JAMES (MICHIGAN) - END - 1970-74 MIAMI DOLPHINS (AFC)
MANELLA, DONALD - GUARD - 1926 NEWARK BEARS (AFL)
MANFREDA, ANTHONY (HOLY CROSS) - BACK - 1930 NEWARK TORNADOS

MANGUM, ERNEST "PETE" (MISSISSIPPI) - LB - 1954 NEW YORK GIANTS; 1960
    DENVER BRONCOS (AFL)
MANGUM, JOHN (SOUTHERN MISSISSIPPI) - TACKLE - 1966-67 BOSTON
    PATRIOTS (AFL)
MANIACI, JOSEPH (FORDHAM) - BACK - 1936-38 BROOKLYN DODGERS; 1938-41
    CHICAGO BEARS
MANION, JAMES (ST. THOMAS OF MINNESOTA) - GUARD - 1926-27 DULUTH
    ESKIMOS
MANKAT, CARL (COLGATE) - TACKLE - 1928-29 DAYTON TRIANGLES
MANKINS, JAMES (FLORIDA STATE) - BACK - 1967 ATLANTA FALCONS
MANLEY, JOSEPH (MISSISSIPPI STATE) - CENTER - 1953 SAN FRANCISCO 49ERS
MANLEY, WILLIAM (OKLAHOMA) - GUARD - 1950-52 GREEN BAY PACKERS
MANN, DAVID (OREGON STATE) - BACK - 1955-57 CHICAGO CARDINALS
MANN, ERROL (NORTH DAKOTA) - KICKER - 1968 GREEN BAY PACKERS; 1969
    DETROIT LIONS; 1970-74 DETROIT LIONS (NFC)
MANN, ROBERT (MICHIGAN) - END - 1948-49 DETROIT LIONS; 1950-53 GREEN
    BAY PACKERS
MANNING, ELISHA ARCHIE (MISSISSIPPI) - QBACK - 1971-74 NEW ORLEANS
    SAINTS (NFC)
MANNING, JAMES (FORDHAM) - BACK - 1926 HARTFORD BLUES; 1926
    PROVIDENCE STEAMROLLERS
MANNING, PETER (WAKE FOREST) - END - 1960-61 CHICAGO BEARS
MANNING, ROOSEVELT "ROSIE" (NORTHEAST OKLA.) - TACKLE - 1972-74
    ATLANTA FALCONS (NFC)
MANOUKIAN, DONALD (STANFORD) - GUARD - 1960 OAKLAND RAIDERS (AFL)
MANRODT, SPENCER (BROWN) - GUARD - 1940 NEW YORK AMERICANS (AFL)
MANSFIELD, JAMES RAYMOND (WASHINGTON) - CENTER - 1963 PHILADELPHIA
    EAGLES; 1964-69 PITTSBURGH STEELERS; 1970-74 PITTSBURGH STEELERS
    (AFC)
MANSFIELD, JERRY - BACK - 1919-21 ROCK ISLAND INDEPENDENTS
MANSKE, EDGAR (NORTHWESTERN) - END - 1935-36 PHILADELPHIA EAGLES;
    1937-40 CHICAGO BEARS; 1938 PITTSBURGH PIRATES
MANTELL, JOSEPH - GUARD - 1924 COLUMBUS TIGERS
MANTON, TALDON (TCU) - BACK - 1936-38 NEW YORK GIANTS; 1938
    WASHINGTON REDSKINS; 1943 BROOKLYN DODGERS
MANZINI, BAPTISTE (ST. VINCENT'S) - CENTER - 1944-45, 48 PHILADELPHIA
    EAGLES
MANZO, JOSEPH (BOSTON COLLEGE) - TACKLE - 1945 DETROIT LIONS
MAPLE, HOWARD (OREGON STATE) - BACK - 1930 CHICAGO CARDINALS
MAPLES, BOBBY (BAYLOR) - CENTER - 1965-69 HOUSTON OILERS (AFL); 1970
    HOUSTON OILERS (AFC); 1971 PITTSBURGH STEELERS (AFC); 1972-74
    DENVER BRONCOS (AFC)
MAPLES, JAMES (BAYLOR) - LB - 1963 BALTIMORE COLTS
MAPLES, TALMADGE (TENNESSEE) - CENTER - 1934 CINCINNATI REDS
MARANGI, GARY (BOSTON COLLEGE) - QBACK - 1974 BUFFALO BILLS (AFC)
MARAS, JOSEPH (DUQUESNE) - CENTER - 1938 PITTSBURGH PIRATES; 1939-40
    PITTSBURGH STEELERS
MARCHETTI, GINO (SAN FRANCISCO) - END - 1952 DALLAS TEXANS; 1953-64,
    66 BALTIMORE COLTS; 1972 HALL OF FAME
MARCHI, BASILO (NEW YORK UNIV.) - CENTER - 1934 PITTSBURGH PIRATES;
    1942 PHILADELPHIA EAGLES
MARICHIBRODA, THEO. (ST.BONA'TURE & DETROIT) - QBACK - 1953, 55-56
    PITTSBURGH STEELERS; 1957 CHICAGO CARDINALS
MARCHLEWSKI, FRANK (MINNESOTA) - CENTER - 1965, 68-69 LOS ANGELES
    RAMS; 1966-68 ATLANTA FALCONS; 1970 BUFFALO BILLS (AFC)
MARCINIAK, RONALD (KANSAS STATE) - GUARD - 1955 WASHINGTON REDSKINS
MARCOL, CHESTER (HILLSDALE) - KICKER - 1972-74 GREEN BAY PACKERS
    (NFC); 1972, 74 SCORING LEADER (NFC); 1972, 74 FIELD GOAL LEADER
    (NFC)
MARCOLINI, HUGO (ST. BONAVENTURE) - BACK - 1948 BROOKLYN DODGERS
    (AAFC)
MARCONI, JOSEPH (WEST VIRGINIA) - BACK - 1956-61 LOS ANGELES RAMS;
    1962-66 CHICAGO BEARS
MARCONTELLI, EDMON (LAMAR TECH) - GUARD - 1967 ST. LOUIS CARDINALS;
    1967 HOUSTON OILERS (AFL)
MARCUS, PETER (KENTUCKY) - END - 1944 WASHINGTON REDSKINS
MAREFOS, ANDREW (ST. MARY'S OF CAL.) - BACK - 1941-42 NEW YORK
    GIANTS; 1946 LOS ANGELES DONS (AAFC)
MAREK, JOSEPH (TEXAS TECH) - BACK - 1943 BROOKLYN DODGERS
MARELLI, RAY (NOTRE DAME) - GUARD - 1928 CHICAGO CARDINALS
MARGARITA, HENRY (BROWN) - BACK - 1944-46 CHICAGO BEARS

MARGUCCI, JOSEPH (USC) - BACK - 1947-48 DETROIT LIONS
MARHEFKA, JOSEPH (LAFAYETTE) - BACK - 1926 PHILADELPHIA QUAKERS (AFL)
MARINARO, ED (CORNELL) - BACK - 1972-74 MINNESOTA VIKINGS (NFC)
MARINO, VICTOR (OHIO STATE) - GUARD - 1940 BOSTON BEARS (AFL); 1947
    BALTIMORE COLTS (AAFC)
MARINOVICH, MARVIN (USC) - GUARD - 1965 OAKLAND RAIDERS (AFL)
MARION, JERRY (WYOMING) - BACK - 1967 PITTSBURGH STEELERS
MARION, PHILIP (MICHIGAN) - BACK - 1925-26 DETROIT PANTHERS
MARK, LOUIS (NORTH CAROLINA STATE) - END - 1938-40 BROOKLYN DODGERS;
    1945 BOSTON YANKS
MARKER, CLIFFORD (WASHINGTON STATE) - BACK - 1926 CANTON BULLDOGS;
    1927 FRANKFORD YELLOWJACKETS; 1927 NEW YORK GIANTS
MARKER, HENRY (WEST VIRGINIA) - BACK - 1934 PITTSBURGH PIRATES
MARKO, STEPHEN - BACK - 1944 BROOKLYN TIGERS; 1945 BOSTON YANKS
MARKOV, VICTOR (WASHINGTON) - TACKLE - 1938 CLEVELAND RAMS
MARKOVICH, MARK (PENN STATE) - GUARD - 1974 SAN DIEGO CHARGERS (AFC)
MARKS, LAWRENCE (INDIANA) - QBACK - 1926 AKRON PROS; 1926 NEW YORK
    YANKEES (AFL); 1927 NEW YORK YANKEES; 1928 GREEN BAY PACKERS
MARONE, SALVATORE (MANHATTAN) - GUARD - 1943 NEW YORK GIANTS
MARONIC, DUSAN - GUARD - 1944-50 PHILADELPHIA EAGLES; 1951 NEW YORK
    GIANTS
MARONIC, STEPHEN (NORTH CAROLINA) - TACKLE - 1939-40 DETROIT LIONS
MAROTTI, LOUIS (TOLEDO) - GUARD - 1940 CINCINNATI BENGALS (AFL);
    1943, 45 CHICAGO CARDINALS; 1944 CARD-PITT
MARQUARDT, JOHN (ILLINOIS) - END - 1921 CHICAGO CARDINALS
MARQUES, ROBERT (BOSTON UNIV.) - LB - 1960 NEW YORK TITANS (AFL)
MARSALIS, JAMES (TENNESSEE STATE) - BACK - 1969 KANSAS CITY CHIEFS
    (AFL); 1970-74 KANSAS CITY CHIEFS (AFC)
MARSH, AARON (EASTERN KENTUCKY) - END - 1968-69 BOSTON PATRIOTS (AFL)
MARSH, AMOS (OREGON STATE) - BACK - 1961-64 DALLAS COWBOYS; 1965-67
    DETROIT LIONS
MARSH, FRANK (OREGON STATE) - BACK - 1967 SAN DIEGO CHARGERS (AFL)
MARSHALL, ALBERT (BOISE STATE) - END - 1974 NEW ENGLAND PATRIOTS (AFC)
MARSHALL, CHARLES (OREGON STATE) - BACK - 1962 DENVER BRONCOS (AFL)
MARSHALL, CLOYD (NEW YORK UNIV.) - END - 1931-32 STATEN ISLAND
    STAPELTONS
MARSHALL, EDWARD (CAMERON STATE-OKLAHOMA) - END - 1971 CINCINNATI
    BENGALS (AFC)
MARSHALL, JAMES (OHIO STATE) - END - 1960 CLEVELAND BROWNS; 1961-69
    MINNESOTA VIKINGS; 1970-74 MINNESOTA VIKINGS (NFC)
MARSHALL, LARRY (MARYLAND) - BACK - 1972-73 KANSAS CITY CHIEFS (AFC);
    1974 MINNESOTA VIKINGS (NFC); 1974 PHILADELPHIA EAGLES (NFC)
MARSHALL, RANDALL (LINFIELD-OREGON) - END - 1970-71 ATLANTA FALCONS
    (NFC)
MARSHALL, RICHARD (S.F.AUSTIN) - TACKLE - 1965 GREEN BAY PACKERS;
    1966 WASHINGTON REDSKINS; 1966 ATLANTA FALCONS; 1967-68 HOUSTON
    OILERS (AFL)
MARSHALL, ROBERT (MINNESOTA) - END - 1919-21 ROCK ISLAND
    INDEPENDENTS; 1920 CLEVELAND PANTHERS; 1922-24 MINNEAPOLIS
    MARINES; 1923-25 DULUTH KELLEYS; 1926-27 DULUTH ESKIMOS
MARSHALL, WILLIAM - QBACK - 1919 TOLEDO MAROONS
MARSTON, RALPH (BOSTON UNIV.) - BACK - 1929 BOSTON BRAVES
MARTELL, HERMAN - END - 1921 GREEN BAY PACKERS
MARTHA, JOHN PAUL (PITTSBURGH) - BACK - 1964-69 PITTSBURGH STEELERS;
    1970 DENVER BRONCOS (AFC)
MARTIN, AARON (NORTH CAROLINA COLLEGE) - BACK - 1964-65 LOS ANGELES
    RAMS; 1966-67 PHILADELPHIA EAGLES; 1968 WASHINGTON REDSKINS
MARTIN, ANTHONY "AMOS" (LOUISVILLE) - LB - 1972-74 MINNESOTA VIKINGS
    (NFC)
MARTIN, BLANCHE (MICHIGAN STATE) - BACK - 1960 NEW YORK TITANS (AFL);
    1960 LOS ANGELES CHARGERS (AFL)
MARTIN, CALEB (LOUISIANA TECH) - TACKLE - 1947 CHICAGO CARDINALS
MARTIN, D'ARTAGNAN (KENTUCKY STATE) - BACK - 1971 NEW ORLEANS SAINTS
    (NFC)
MARTIN, DAVID (NOTRE DAME) - BACK - 1968 KANSAS CITY CHIEFS (AFL);
    1969 CHICAGO BEARS
MARTIN, DONALD (YALE) - BACK - 1973 NEW ENGLAND PATRIOTS (AFC)
MARTIN, FRANK (ALABAMA) - BACK - 1943 BROOKLYN DODGERS; 1944 BROOKLYN
    TIGERS; 1945 NEW YORK GIANTS; 1945 BOSTON YANKS
MARTIN, GLEN (SOUTHERN ILLINOIS) - BACK - 1932 CHICAGO CARDINALS

MARTIN, HARVEY (EAST TEXAS STATE) - END, TACKLE - 1973-74 DALLAS
     COWBOYS (NFC)
MARTIN, HERSCHEL (MISSOURI) - BACK - 1929 STATEN ISLAND STAPELTONS;
     1930 NEWARK TORNADOS
MARTIN, JAKE WILLIAM (GEORGIA TECH) - END - 1964-65 CHICAGO BEARS;
     1966-67 ATLANTA FALCONS; 1969 MINNESOTA VIKINGS
MARTIN, JAMES (NOTRE DAME) - LB - 1950 CLEVELAND BROWNS; 1951-61
     DETROIT LIONS; 1963 BALTIMORE COLTS; 1964 WASHINGTON REDSKINS;
     1963 FIELD GOAL LEADER
MARTIN, JOHN (OKLAHOMA) - BACK - 1941-43 CHICAGO CARDINALS; 1944
     CARD-PITT; 1944-45 BOSTON YANKS
MARTIN, JOHN (ANNAPOLIS) - CENTER - 1947-49 LOS ANGELES RAMS
MARTIN, JOSEPH - BACK - 1921 LOUISVILLE BRECKS
MARTIN, LAWRENCE (SAN DIEGO STATE) - TACKLE - 1966 SAN DIEGO CHARGERS
     (AFL)
MARTIN, ROY (WILLIAM JEWELL-MISSOURI) - BACK - 1919 AKRON PROS;
     1919-20 CANTON BULLDOGS
MARTIN, VERNON (TEXAS) - BACK - 1942 PITTSBURGH STEELERS
MARTIN, WILLIAM (GEORGIA TECH) - END - 1964 CHICAGO BEARS
MARTIN, WILLIAM (MINNESOTA) - BACK - 1962-64 CHICAGO BEARS
MARTINEAU, ROY (SYRACUSE) - GUARD - 1922-25 ROCHESTER JEFFERSONS;
     1923 BUFFALO ALL-AMERICANS
MARTINELLI, JAMES (SCRANTON) - CENTER - 1946 BUFFALO BISONS (AAFC)
MARTINKOVIC, JOHN (XAVIER) - END - 1951-56 GREEN BAY PACKERS; 1957
     NEW YORK GIANTS
MARTINOVICH, PHILIP (PACIFIC) - GUARD - 1939 DETROIT LIONS; 1940
     CHICAGO BEARS; 1941 NEW YORK AMERICANS (AFL); 1946-47 BROOKLYN
     DODGERS (AAFC)
MARX, GREGORY (NOTRE DAME) - END - 1973 ATLANTA FALCONS (NFC)
MASINI, LEONARD (FRESNO STATE) - BACK - 1947-48 SAN FRANCISCO 49ERS
     (AAFC); 1948 LOS ANGELES DONS (AAFC)
MASKAS, JOHN (VIRGINIA POLYTECH) - GUARD - 1947, 49 BUFFALO BILLS
     (AAFC)
MASLOWSKI, MATHEW (SAN DIEGO STATE) - END - 1971 LOS ANGELES RAMS
     (NFC); 1972 CHICAGO BEARS (NFC)
MASON, DAVID (NEBRASKA) - BACK - 1973 NEW ENGLAND PATRIOTS (AFC);
     1974 GREEN BAY PACKERS (NFC)
MASON, JOEL (WESTERN MICHIGAN) - END - 1939 CHICAGO CARDINALS; 1940
     BOSTON BEARS (AFL); 1941 NEW YORK AMERICANS (AFL); 1942-45 GREEN
     BAY PACKERS
MASON, SAMUEL (VMI) - BACK - 1922 MINNEAPOLIS MARINES; 1925 MILWAUKEE
     BADGERS
MASON, THOMAS (TULANE) - BACK, END - 1961-66 MINNESOTA VIKINGS;
     1967-69 LOS ANGELES RAMS; 1970 LOS ANGELES RAMS (NFC); 1971
     WASHINGTON REDSKINS (NFC)
MASS, WAYNE (CLEMSON) - TACKLE - 1968-69 CHICAGO BEARS; 1970 CHICAGO
     BEARS (NFC); 1971 MIAMI DOLPHINS (AFC); 1972 NEW ENGLAND
     PATRIOTS (AFC); 1972 PHILADELPHIA EAGLES (NFC)
MASSEY, CARLTON (TEXAS) - END - 1954-56 CLEVELAND BROWNS; 1957-58
     GREEN BAY PACKERS
MASSEY, JIM (LINFIELD) - BACK - 1974 NEW ENGLAND PATRIOTS (AFC)
MASTERS, NORMAN (MICHIGAN STATE) - TACKLE - 1957-64 GREEN BAY PACKERS
MASTERS, ROBERT (BAYLOR) - BACK - 1937-38, 42 PHILADELPHIA EAGLES;
     1939 PITTSBURGH STEELERS; 1943 PHIL-PITT; 1943-44 CHICAGO BEARS
MASTERS, WALTER (PENNSYLVANIA) - BACK - 1936 PHILADELPHIA EAGLES;
     1943 CHICAGO CARDINALS; 1944 CARD-PITT
MASTERS, WILLIAM (LSU) - END - 1967-69 BUFFALO BILLS (AFL); 1970-74
     DENVER BRONCOS (AFC)
MASTERSON, BERNARD (NEBRASKA) - QBACK - 1934-40 CHICAGO BEARS
MASTERSON, FOREST (IOWA) - CENTER - 1945 CHICAGO BEARS
MASTERSON, ROBERT (MIAMI) - END - 1938-43 WASHINGTON REDSKINS; 1944
     BROOKLYN TIGERS; 1945 BOSTON YANKS; 1946 NEW YORK YANKEES (AAFC)
MASTRANGELO, JOHN (NOTRE DAME) - GUARD - 1947-48 PITTSBURGH STEELERS;
     1949 NEW YORK YANKEES (AAFC); 1950 NEW YORK GIANTS
MASTRIOLA, FREDERICK (NORTH CAROLINA STATE) - GUARD - 1940 BOSTON
     BEARS (AFL); 1941 BUFFALO TIGERS (AFL)
MASTROGANY, AUGUST (IOWA) - END - 1931 CHICAGO BEARS
MATAN, WILLIAM (KANSAS STATE) - END - 1966 NEW YORK GIANTS
MATESIC, EDWARD (PITTSBURGH) - BACK - 1934-35 PHILADELPHIA EAGLES;
     1936 PITTSBURGH PIRATES; 1937 PITTSBURGH AMERICANS (AFL)
MATESIC, JOSEPH (ARIZONA STATE) - TACKLE - 1954 PITTSBURGH STEELERS

MATHENY, WILLIAM (MINNESOTA) - BACK - 1941 COLUMBUS BULLIES (AFL)

MATHESON, JOHN (WESTERN MICHIGAN) - END - 1943-46 DETROIT LIONS; 1947
     CHICAGO BEARS

MATHESON, RILEY (TEXAS MINES) - GUARD - 1939-42, 44-45 CLEVELAND
     RAMS; 1943 DETROIT LIONS; 1946-47 LOS ANGELES RAMS; 1948 SAN
     FRANCISCO 49ERS (AAFC)

MATHESON, ROBERT (DUKE) - LB, END - 1967-69 CLEVELAND BROWNS; 1970
     CLEVELAND BROWNS (AFC); 1971-74 MIAMI DOLPHINS (AFC)

MATHEWS, EDWARD (UCLA) - BACK - 1941-43 DETROIT LIONS; 1945 BOSTON
     YANKS; 1946 CHICAGO ROCKETS (AAFC); 1946-47 SAN FRANCISCO 49ERS
     (AAFC)

MATHEWS, FRANK (NORTHWESTERN) - END - 1926 RACINE LEGION

MATHEWS, NEILSON (PENNSYLVANIA) - TACKLE - 1920 CHICAGO TIGERS; 1920
     HAMMOND PROS

MATHEWS, RAYMOND (CLEMSON) - BACK - 1951-59 PITTSBURGH STEELERS; 1960
     DALLAS COWBOYS

MATHIS, WILLIAM (CLEMSON) - BACK - 1960-62 NEW YORK TITANS (AFL);
     1963-69 NEW YORK JETS (AFL)

MATHYS, CHARLES (INDIANA) - BACK - 1921 HAMMOND PROS; 1922-26 GREEN
     BAY PACKERS

MATISI, ANTHONY (PITTSBURGH) - TACKLE - 1938 DETROIT LIONS

MATISI, JOHN (DUQUESNE) - TACKLE - 1943 BROOKLYN DODGERS; 1946
     BUFFALO BISONS (AAFC)

MATLOCK, JOHN (MIAMI) - CENTER - 1967 NEW YORK JETS (AFL); 1968
     CINCINNATI BENGALS (AFL); 1970-71 ATLANTA FALCONS (NFC); 1972
     BUFFALO BILLS (AFC)

MATSON, OLIVER "OLLIE" (SAN FRANCISCO) - BACK - 1952, 54-58 CHICAGO
     CARDINALS; 1959-62 LOS ANGELES RAMS; 1963 DETROIT LIONS; 1964-66
     PHILADELPHIA EAGLES; 1972 HALL OF FAME

MATSON, PATRICK (OREGON) - GUARD - 1966-67 DENVER BRONCOS (AFL);
     1968-69 CINCINNATI BENGALS (AFL); 1970-74 CINCINNATI BENGALS
     (AFC)

MATSOS, ARCHIBALD (MICHIGAN STATE) - LB - 1960-62 BUFFALO BILLS
     (AFL); 1963-65 OAKLAND RAIDERS (AFL); 1966 DENVER BRONCOS (AFL);
     1966 SAN DIEGO CHARGERS (AFL)

MATSU, ARTHUR (WILLIAM&MARY) - BACK - 1928 DAYTON TRIANGLES

MATTE, THOMAS (OHIO STATE) - BACK - 1961-69 BALTIMORE COLTS; 1970-72
     BALTIMORE COLTS (AFC)

MATTEO, FRANCIS (SYRACUSE) - TACKLE - 1922-25 ROCHESTER JEFFERSONS

MATTERN, JOSEPH (MINNESOTA) - BACK - 1919 CLEVELAND INDIANS; 1920
     DETROIT HERALDS; 1920 CLEVELAND PANTHERS

MATTHEWS, ALVIN (TEXAS A&I) - BACK - 1970-74 GREEN BAY PACKERS (NFC)

MATTHEWS, CLAY (GEORGIA TECH) - END - 1950, 53-55 SAN FRANCISCO 49ERS

MATTHEWS, HENRY (MICHIGAN STATE) - BACK - 1972 NEW ENGLAND PATRIOTS
     (AFC); 1973 NEW ORLEANS SAINTS (NFC); 1973 ATLANTA FALCONS (NFC)

MATTHEWS, WESLEY (NORTHEAST STATE-OKLAHOMA) - END - 1966 MIAMI
     DOLPHINS (AFL)

MATTHEWS, WILLIAM "BO" (COLORADO) - BACK - 1974 SAN DIEGO CHARGERS
     (AFC)

MATTIFORD, JOHN (MARSHALL) - GUARD - 1941 DETROIT LIONS

MATTINGLY, FRANCIS (TEXAS A&I) - GUARD - 1947 CHICAGO ROCKETS (AAFC)

MATTIOLI, FRANCIS (PITTSBURGH) - GUARD - 1946 PITTSBURGH STEELERS

MATTISON, RALPH (DAVIS&ELKINS) - GUARD - 1930 BROOKLYN DODGERS

MATTOS, HARRY (ST. MARY'S OF CAL.) - BACK - 1936 GREEN BAY PACKERS;
     1936 CLEVELAND RAMS (AFL); 1937 CINCINNATI BENGALS (AFL); 1937
     CLEVELAND RAMS

MATTOX, JOHN (FRESNO STATE) - TACKLE - 1961-62 DENVER BRONCOS (AFL)

MATTOX, MARVIN (WASHINGTON&LEE) - BACK - 1923 MILWAUKEE BADGERS

MATTSON, RILEY (OREGON) - TACKLE - 1961-64 WASHINGTON REDSKINS; 1966
     CHICAGO BEARS

MATUSZAK, JOHN (TAMPA) - TACKLE - 1973 HOUSTON OILERS (AFC); 1974
     KANSAS CITY CHIEFS (AFC)

MATUSZAK, MARVIN (TULSA) - LB - 1953, 55-56 PITTSBURGH STEELERS;
     1957-58 SAN FRANCISCO 49ERS; 1958 GREEN BAY PACKERS; 1959-61
     BALTIMORE COLTS; 1962-63 BUFFALO BILLS (AFL); 1964 DENVER
     BRONCOS (AFL)

MATUZA, ALBERT (GEORGETOWN) - CENTER - 1941-43 CHICAGO BEARS

MAUCK, CARL (SOUTHERN ILLINOIS) - CENTER, LB - 1969 BALTIMORE COLTS;
     1970 MIAMI DOLPHINS (AFC); 1971-74 SAN DIEGO CHARGERS (AFC)

MAUDER, LOUIS - GUARD - 1919 TOLEDO MAROONS

MAUER, JACOB - GUARD - 1923 RACINE LEGION

MAUL, ELMO (ST. MARY'S OF CAL.) - BACK - 1926 LOS ANGELES BUCCANEERS
MAULDIN, STANLEY (TEXAS) - TACKLE - 1946-48 CHICAGO CARDINALS
MAUREF, ANDREW (OREGON) - GUARD - 1970-73 ATLANTA FALCONS (NFC); 1974
    NEW ORLEANS SAINTS (NFC); 1974 MINNESOTA VIKINGS (NFC)
MAUREF, ADRIAN (OGLETHORPE) - BACK - 1926 NEWARK BEARS (AFL)
MAVES, EARL (WISCONSIN) - BACK - 1948 DETROIT LIONS; 1948 BALTIMORE
    COLTS (AAFC)
MAVRAIDES, MENIL (NOTRE DAME) - GUARD - 1954, 57 PHILADELPHIA EAGLES
MAXSON, ALVIN (SMU) - BACK - 1974 NEW ORLEANS SAINTS (NFC)
MAXWELL, BRUCE (ARKANSAS) - BACK - 1970 DETROIT LIONS (NFC)
MAXWELL, JOSEPH (NOTRE DAME) - END - 1927-29 FRANKFORD YELLOWJACKETS
MAXWELL, THOMAS (TEXAS A&M) - BACK, END - 1969 BALTIMORE COLTS; 1970
    BALTIMORE COLTS (AFC); 1971-73 OAKLAND RAIDERS (AFC); 1974
    HOUSTON OILERS (AFC)
MAY, ART (TUSKEGEE) - END, TACKLE - 1971 NEW ENGLAND PATRIOTS (AFC)
MAY, FRANCIS (CENTENARY) - CENTER - 1938 CLEVELAND RAMS
MAY, RAYMOND (USC) - LB - 1967-69 PITTSBURGH STEELERS; 1970-73
    BALTIMORE COLTS (AFC); 1973-74 DENVER BRONCOS (AFC)
MAY, WALTER - GUARD - 1920 DECATUR STALEYS
MAY, WILLIAM (LSU) - QBACK - 1937-38 CHICAGO CARDINALS
MAYBERRY, DOUGLAS (UTAH STATE) - BACK - 1961-62 MINNESOTA VIKINGS;
    1963 OAKLAND RAIDERS (AFL)
MAYER, EMIL (CATHOLIC UNIV.) - END - 1927 POTTSVILLE MAROONS; 1930
    PORTSMOUTH SPARTANS
MAYER, FRANK (NOTRE DAME) - GUARD - 1927 GREEN BAY PACKERS
MAYES, BENJAMIN (DRAKE) - TACKLE, END - 1969 HOUSTON OILERS (AFL)
MAYES, CARL (TEXAS) - BACK - 1952 LOS ANGELES RAMS
MAYES, RUFUS (OHIO STATE) - TACKLE, GUARD - 1969 CHICAGO BEARS;
    1970-74 CINCINNATI BENGALS (AFC)
MAYHEW, HAYDEN (TEXAS MINES) - GUARD - 1936-38 PITTSBURGH PIRATES
MAYL, EUGENE (NOTRE DAME) - END - 1925-26 DAYTON TRIANGLES
MAYNARD, DONALD (TEXAS-EL PASO) - END, BACK - 1958 NEW YORK GIANTS;
    1960-62 NEW YORK TITANS (AFL); 1963-69 NEW YORK JETS (AFL);
    1970-72 NEW YORK JETS (AFC); 1973 ST. LOUIS CARDINALS (NFC)
MAYNARD, LESTER (RIDER) - BACK - 1932 STATEN ISLAND STAPELTONS; 1933
    PHILADELPHIA EAGLES
MAYNAUGH, ROLAND (ST. THOMAS OF MINNESOTA) - GUARD - 1924 MINNEAPOLIS
    MARINES
MAYNE, LEWIS (TEXAS) - BACK - 1946 BROOKLYN DODGERS (AAFC); 1947
    CLEVELAND BROWNS (AAFC); 1948 BALTIMORE COLTS (AAFC)
MAYO, RONALD (MORGAN STATE) - END - 1973 HOUSTON OILERS (AFC); 1974
    BALTIMORE COLTS (AFC)
MAYS, GERALD (SMU) - TACKLE, END - 1961-62 DALLAS TEXANS (AFL);
    1963-69 KANSAS CITY CHIEFS (AFL); 1970 KANSAS CITY CHIEFS (AFC)
MAZNICKI, FRANK (BOSTON COLLEGE) - BACK - 1942, 46 CHICAGO BEARS;
    1947 BOSTON YANKS
MAZUREK, EDWARD (XAVIER-OHIO) - TACKLE - 1960 NEW YORK GIANTS
MAZUREK, FREDERICK (PITTSBURGH) - BACK - 1965-66 WASHINGTON REDSKINS
MAZZA, VINCENT - END - 1945-46 DETROIT LIONS; 1947-49 BUFFALO BILLS
    (AAFC)
MAZZANTI, GINO (ARKANSAS) - BACK - 1950 BALTIMORE COLTS
MAZZANTI, JERRY (ARKANSAS) - END - 1963 PHILADELPHIA EAGLES; 1966
    DETROIT LIONS; 1967 PITTSBURGH STEELERS
MC ADAMS, CARL (OKLAHOMA) - LB - 1967-69 NEW YORK JETS (AFL)
MC ADAMS, DEAN (WASHINGTON) - BACK - 1941-43 BROOKLYN DODGERS
MC ADAMS, ROBERT (NORTH CAROLINA COLLEGE) - END - 1963-64 NEW YORK
    JETS (AFL)
MC AFEE, GEORGE (DUKE) - BACK - 1940-41, 45-50 CHICAGO BEARS; 1966
    HALL OF FAME
MC AFEE, JOHN (OHIO STATE) - BACK - 1937 CINCINNATI BENGALS (AFL)
MC AFEE, WESLEY (DUKE) - BACK - 1941 PHILADELPHIA EAGLES
MC ARTHUR, JOHN (SANTA CLARA) - CENTER - 1926 LOS ANGELES BUCCANEERS;
    1927 BUFFALO BISONS; 1927-28 NEW YORK YANKEES; 1929 ORANGE
    TORNADOS; 1930 NEWARK TORNADOS; 1930 BROOKLYN DODGERS; 1930
    FRANKFORD YELLOWJACKETS; 1930-31 PROVIDENCE STEAMROLLERS
MC BATH, MICHAEL (PENN STATE) - TACKLE, END - 1968-69 BUFFALO BILLS
    (AFL); 1970-72 BUFFALO BILLS (AFC)
MC BRIDE, CHARLES (WASHINGTON STATE) - BACK - 1936 ROCHESTER TIGERS
    (AFL); 1936 CHICAGO CARDINALS

MC BRIDE, JOHN (SYRACUSE) - BACK - 1925-28, 32-34 NEW YORK GIANTS;
    1929 PROVIDENCE STEAMROLLERS; 1930-32 BROOKLYN DODGERS
MC BRIDE, NORMAN (UTAH) - LB, END - 1969 MIAMI DOLPHINS (AFL); 1970
    MIAMI DOLPHINS (AFC)
MC BRIDE, RON (MISSOURI) - BACK - 1973 GREEN BAY PACKERS (NFC)
MC CABE, RICHARD (PITTSBURGH) - BACK - 1955, 57-58 PITTSBURGH
    STEELERS; 1959 WASHINGTON REDSKINS; 1960-61 BUFFALO BILLS (AFL)
MC CAFFERTY, DONALD (OHIO STATE) - END - 1946 NEW YORK GIANTS
MC CAFFRAY, ARTHUR (PACIFIC) - TACKLE - 1946 PITTSBURGH STEELERS
MC CAFFREY, MICHAEL (CALIFORNIA) - LB - 1970 BUFFALO BILLS (AFC)
MC CAIN, ROBERT (MISSISSIPPI) - END - 1946 BROOKLYN DODGERS (AAFC)
MC CALL, DONALD (USC) - BACK - 1967-68 NEW ORLEANS SAINTS; 1969
    PITTSBURGH STEELERS; 1970 NEW ORLEANS SAINTS (NFC)
MC CALL, EDWARD (MILES) - BACK - 1968 CINCINNATI BENGALS (AFL)
MC CALL, ROBERT (ARIZONA) - BACK - 1973 NEW ENGLAND PATRIOTS (AFC)
MC CALL, RONALD (WEBER STATE) - LB - 1967-68 SAN DIEGO CHARGERS (AFL)
MC CAMBRIDGE, JOHN (NORTHWESTERN) - END - 1967 DETROIT LIONS
MC CANN, ERNEST (PENN STATE) - TACKLE - 1926 HARTFORD BLUES
MC CANN, JAMES (ARIZONA STATE) - KICKER - 1971-72 SAN FRANCISCO 49ERS
    (NFC); 1973 NEW YORK GIANTS (NFC)
MC CANN, TIMOTHY (PRINCETON) - TACKLE - 1969 NEW YORK GIANTS
MC CARREN, LAURENCE (ILLINOIS) - CENTER - 1973-74 GREEN BAY PACKERS
    (NFC)
MC CARTHY, BRENDAN (BOSTON COLLEGE) - BACK - 1968 ATLANTA FALCONS;
    1968-69 DENVER BRONCOS (AFL)
MC CARTHY, JAMES (CALIFORNIA) - TACKLE - 1927 DULUTH ESKIMOS
MC CARTHY, JAMES (ILLINOIS) - END - 1946-47 BROOKLYN DODGERS (AAFC);
    1948 CHICAGO ROCKETS (AAFC); 1949 CHICAGO HORNETS (AAFC)
MC CARTHY, JOHN (ST. FRANCIS) - BACK - 1944 CARD-PITT
MC CARTHY, VINCENT (ST. VIATOR) - QBACK - 1924-25 ROCK ISLAND
    INDEPENDENTS; 1926 ROCK ISLAND INDEPENDENTS (AFL)
MC CARTHY, WILLIAM (NOTRE DAME) - END - 1937 NEW YORK YANKS (AFL)
MC CARTY, ROBERT MICKEY (TCU) - END - 1969 KANSAS CITY CHIEFS (AFL)
MC CAULEY, DONALD (NORTH CAROLINA) - BACK - 1971-74 BALTIMORE COLTS
    (AFC)
MC CAULEY, THOMAS (WISCONSIN) - END, BACK - 1969 ATLANTA FALCONS;
    1970-71 ATLANTA FALCONS (NFC)
MC CAUSLAND, LEO (DETROIT) - CENTER - 1922 AKRON PROS
MC CAW, WILLIAM (INDIANA) - END - 1923 RACINE LEGION
MC CAW, WILLIAM (LOYOLA) - GUARD - 1926 LOUISVILLE COLONELS
MC CHESNEY, ROBERT (HARDIN-SIMMONS) - END - 1950-52 NEW YORK GIANTS
MC CHESNEY, ROBERT (UCLA) - END - 1936 BOSTON REDSKINS; 1937-42
    WASHINGTON REDSKINS
MC CLAIN, CLIFFORD (SOUTH CAROLINA STATE) - BACK - 1970-73 NEW YORK
    JETS (AFC)
MC CLAIN, CLINTON (SMU) - BACK - 1941 NEW YORK GIANTS
MC CLAIN, JOSEPH (ST. JOHN'S-NEW YORK) - GUARD - 1928 NEW YORK YANKEES
MC CLAIN, MALEDIN (SAN BERNADINO JUNIOR) - BACK - 1941 MILWAUKEE
    CHIEFS (AFL)
MC CLAIREN, JACK (BETHUNE-COOKMAN) - END - 1955-60 PITTSBURGH STEELERS
MC CLANAHAN, BRENT (ARIZONA STATE) - BACK - 1973-74 MINNESOTA VIKINGS
    (NFC)
MC CLARD, WILLIAM (ARKANSAS) - KICKER - 1972 SAN DIEGO CHARGERS
    (AFC); 1973-74 NEW ORLEANS SAINTS (NFC)
MC CLELLAN, WILLIAM MIKE (OKLAHOMA) - BACK - 1962-63 PHILADELPHIA
    EAGLES
MC CLELLAND, WILLIAM (PITTSBURGH) - QBACK - 1919 CANTON BULLDOGS
MC CLINTON, CURTIS (KANSAS) - BACK, END - 1962 DALLAS TEXANS (AFL);
    1963-69 KANSAS CITY CHIEFS (AFL)
MC CLOUGHAN, KENT (NEBRASKA) - BACK - 1965-69 OAKLAND RAIDERS (AFL);
    1970 OAKLAND RAIDERS (AFC)
MC CLUNG, WILLIE (FLORIDA A&M) - TACKLE - 1955-57 PITTSBURGH
    STEELERS; 1958-59 CLEVELAND BROWNS; 1960-61 DETROIT LIONS
MC CLURE, ROBERT (NEVADA) - GUARD - 1947-48 BOSTON YANKS
MC CLURE, WAYNE (MISSISSIPPI) - LB - 1968 CINCINNATI BENGALS (AFL);
    1970 CINCINNATI BENGALS (AFC)
MC COLL, WILLIAM (STANFORD) - END - 1952-59 CHICAGO BEARS
MC COLLUM, HARLEY (TULANE) - TACKLE - 1946 NEW YORK YANKEES (AAFC);
    1947 CHICAGO ROCKETS (AAFC)
MC COLLUM, JAMES (KENTUCKY) - TACKLE - 1974 HOUSTON OILERS (AFC)
MC COMB, DONALD (VILLANOVA) - END - 1960 BOSTON PATRIOTS (AFL)

MC COMBS, NATHANIEL (HASKELL) - TACKLE - 1926 AKRON PROS; 1929
    BUFFALO BISONS
MC CONNELL, BRIAN (MICHIGAN STATE) - LB - 1973 BUFFALO BILLS (AFC);
    1973 HOUSTON OILERS (AFC)
MC CONNELL, DEWEY (WYOMING) - END - 1954 PITTSBURGH STEELERS
MC CONNELL, FELTON (GEORGIA TECH) - GUARD - 1927 BUFFALO BISONS
MC CORD, DARRIS (TENNESSEE) - END - 1955-67 DETROIT LIONS
MC CORMICK, DAVID (LSU) - TACKLE - 1966 SAN FRANCISCO 49ERS; 1967-68
    NEW ORLEANS SAINTS
MC CORMACK, MICHAEL (KANSAS) - TACKLE - 1951 NEW YORK YANKS; 1954-62
    CLEVELAND BROWNS
MC CORMICK, FELIX (BUCKNELL) - BACK - 1929 ORANGE TORNADOS; 1930
    NEWARK TORNADOS
MC CORMICK, FRANK (SOUTH DAKOTA) - BACK - 1920-21 AKRON PROS
MC CORMICK, JOHN (MASSACHUSETTS) - QBACK - 1962 MINNESOTA VIKINGS;
    1963, 65-66, 68 DENVER BRONCOS (AFL)
MC CORMICK, LEONARD (BAYLOR) - CENTER - 1948 BALTIMORE COLTS (AAFC)
MC CORMICK, THOMAS (PACIFIC) - BACK - 1953-55 LOS ANGELES RAMS; 1956
    SAN FRANCISCO 49ERS
MC CORMICK, WALTER (USC) - CENTER - 1948 SAN FRANCISCO 49ERS (AAFC)
MC COY, JOEL (ALABAMA) - BACK - 1946 DETROIT LIONS
MC COY, LLOYD (SAN DIEGO STATE) - GUARD - 1964 SAN DIEGO CHARGERS
    (AFL)
MC COY, MICHAEL (NOTRE DAME) - TACKLE - 1970-74 GREEN BAY PACKERS
    (NFC)
MC CRARY, HURDIS (GEORGIA) - BACK - 1929-33 GREEN BAY PACKERS
MC CRAY, PRENTICE (ARIZONA STATE) - BACK - 1974 NEW ENGLAND PATRIOTS
    (AFC)
MC CREARY, ROBERT (WAKE FOREST) - TACKLE - 1961 DALLAS COWBOYS
MC CRILLIS, EDWARD (BROWN) - GUARD - 1926 PROVIDENCE STEAMROLLERS;
    1929 BOSTON BRAVES
MC CROHAN, JOHN (PRINCETON) - TACKLE - 1920 ROCHESTER JEFFERSONS
MC CULLERS, DALE (FLORIDA STATE) - LB - 1969 MIAMI DOLPHINS (AFL)
MC CULLOUCH, EARL (USC) - END - 1968-69 DETROIT LIONS; 1970-73
    DETROIT LIONS (NFC)
MC CULLOCH, JAMES (HOLY CROSS) - GUARD - 1926 BROOKLYN LIONS
MC CULLOUGH, HAROLD (CORNELL) - BACK - 1942 BROOKLYN DODGERS
MC CULLOUGH, HUGH (OKLAHOMA) - BACK - 1939 PITTSBURGH STEELERS;
    1940-41 CHICAGO CARDINALS; 1943 PHIL-PITT; 1945 BOSTON YANKS
MC CULLOUGH, ROBERT (COLORADO) - GUARD - 1962-65 DENVER BRONCOS (AFL)
MC CULLUM, SAMUEL (MONTANA STATE) - END - 1974 MINNESOTA VIKINGS (NFC)
MC CURRY, DAVID (IOWA STATE) - BACK - 1974 NEW ENGLAND PATRIOTS (AFC)
MC CUSKER, JAMES (PITTSBURGH) - TACKLE - 1958 CHICAGO CARDINALS;
    1959-62 PHILADELPHIA EAGLES; 1963 CLEVELAND BROWNS; 1964 NEW
    YORK JETS (AFL)
MC CUTCHEON, LAWRENCE (COLORADO STATE) - BACK - 1972-74 LOS ANGELES
    RAMS (NFC); 1974 RUSHING LEADER (NFC)
MC DADE, KARL (PORTLAND) - CENTER - 1938 PITTSBURGH PIRATES
MC DANIEL, EDWARD WAHOO (OKLAHOMA) - LB - 1960 HOUSTON OILERS (AFL);
    1961-63 DENVER BRONCOS (AFL); 1964-65 NEW YORK JETS (AFL);
    1966-68 MIAMI DOLPHINS (AFL)
MC DANIEL, JOHN (LINCOLN) - END - 1974 CINCINNATI BENGALS (AFC)
MC DANIELS, DAVID (MISSISSIPPI VALLEY) - END - 1968 DALLAS COWBOYS
MC DERMOTT, GARY (TULSA) - BACK - 1968 BUFFALO BILLS (AFL); 1969
    ATLANTA FALCONS
MC DERMOTT, LLOYD (KENTUCKY) - TACKLE - 1950 DETROIT LIONS; 1950-51
    CHICAGO CARDINALS
MC DOLE, ROLAND "RON" (NEBRASKA) - END - 1961 ST. LOUIS CARDINALS;
    1962 HOUSTON OILERS (AFL); 1963-69 BUFFALO BILLS (AFL); 1970
    BUFFALO BILLS (AFC); 1971-74 WASHINGTON REDSKINS (NFC)
MC DONALD, DONALD (OKLAHOMA) - END - 1944 BROOKLYN TIGERS; 1944-46
    PHILADELPHIA EAGLES; 1948 NEW YORK YANKEES (AAFC)
MC DONALD, EDWARD (DUQUESNE) - BACK - 1936 PITTSBURGH PIRATES
MC DONALD, JAMES (OHIO STATE) - QBACK - 1938-39 DETROIT LIONS
MC DONALD, JOHN - TACKLE - 1921 EVANSVILLE CRIMSON GIANTS; 1926
    LOUISVILLE COLONELS
MC DONALD, LESTER (NEBRASKA) - END - 1937-39 CHICAGO BEARS; 1940
    PHILADELPHIA EAGLES; 1940 DETROIT LIONS
MC DONALD, RAYMOND (IDAHO) - BACK - 1967-68 WASHINGTON REDSKINS

MC DONALD, THOMAS (OKLAHOMA) - END, BACK - 1957-63 PHILADELPHIA
    EAGLES; 1964 DALLAS COWBOYS; 1965-66 LOS ANGELES RAMS; 1967
    ATLANTA FALCONS; 1968 CLEVELAND BROWNS
MC DONALD, WALTER (UTAH) - CENTER - 1935 BROOKLYN DODGERS
MC DONALD, WALTER (TULANE) - BACK - 1946 MIAMI SEAHAWKS (AAFC);
    1946-48 BROOKLYN DODGERS (AAFC); 1949 CHICAGO HORNETS (AAFC)
MC DONNELL, JOHN "MICKEY" - BACK - 1923-25 DULUTH KELLEYS; 1925
    HAMMOND PROS; 1925-30 CHICAGO CARDINALS; 1926 DETROIT PANTHERS;
    1931 FRANKFORD YELLOWJACKETS
MC DONOUGH, COLEY (DAYTON) - QBACK - 1939 CHICAGO CARDINALS; 1939-41
    PITTSBURGH STEELERS; 1944 CARD-PITT
MC DONOUGH, PAUL (UTAH) - END - 1938 PITTSBURGH PIRATES; 1939-41
    CLEVELAND RAMS
MC DONOUGH, ROBERT (DUKE) - GUARD - 1946 PHILADELPHIA EAGLES
MC DOUGALL, GERALD (UCLA) - BACK - 1962-64, 68 SAN DIEGO CHARGERS
    (AFL)
MC DOWELL, JOHN (ST. JOHN'S) - TACKLE - 1964 GREEN BAY PACKERS; 1965
    NEW YORK GIANTS; 1966 ST. LOUIS CARDINALS
MC ELHENNY, HUGH (WASHINGTON) - BACK - 1952-60 SAN FRANCISCO 49ERS;
    1961-62 MINNESOTA VIKINGS; 1963 NEW YORK GIANTS; 1964 DETROIT
    LIONS; 1970 HALL OF FAME
MC ELROY, WILLIAM (MISSISSIPPI SOUTHERN) - BACK - 1954 CHICAGO BEARS
MC ELWAIN, WILLIAM (NORTHWESTERN) - BACK - 1924 CHICAGO CARDINALS;
    1925 CHICAGO BEARS; 1926 CHICAGO CARDINALS
MC ENULTY, DOUGLAS (WICHITA) - BACK - 1943-44 CHICAGO BEARS
MC EVOY, EDWARD (SPRING HILL) - BACK - 1926 HARTFORD BLUES
MC FADDEN, JAMES BANKS (CLEMSON) - BACK - 1940 BROOKLYN DODGERS
MC FADDEN, MARVIN (MICHIGAN STATE) - GUARD - 1953, 56 PITTSBURGH
    STEELERS
MC FADIN, LEWIS (TEXAS) - GUARD - 1952-56 LOS ANGELES RAMS; 1960-63
    DENVER BRONCOS (AFL); 1964-65 HOUSTON OILERS (AFL)
MC FARLAND, JAMES (NEBRASKA) - END - 1970-74 ST. LOUIS CARDINALS (NFC)
MC FARLAND, RUSSELL KAY (COLORADO STATE) - BACK - 1962-66, 68 SAN
    FRANCISCO 49ERS
MC FARLANE, NYLE (BRIGHAM YOUNG) - BACK - 1960 OAKLAND RAIDERS (AFL)
MC GANNON, WILLIAM (NOTRE DAME) - BACK - 1941 CINCINNATI BENGALS
    (AFL); 1941 COLUMBUS BULLIES (AFL)
MC GARRY, BERNARD (UTAH) - GUARD - 1939-42 CLEVELAND RAMS
MC GAW, WALTER (BELOIT) - GUARD - 1926 GREEN BAY PACKERS
MC GEARY, CLARENCE (NORTH DAKOTA STATE) - TACKLE - 1950 GREEN BAY
    PACKERS
MC GEE, ANTHONY (BISHOP-TEXAS) - END, TACKLE - 1971-73 CHICAGO BEARS
    (NFC); 1974 NEW ENGLAND PATRIOTS (AFC)
MC GEE, BENJAMIN (JACKSON STATE) - END, TACKLE - 1964-69 PITTSBURGH
    STEELERS; 1970-72 PITTSBURGH STEELERS (AFC)
MC GEE, EDWARD (TEMPLE) - TACKLE - 1940 NEW YORK AMERICANS (AFL);
    1940 NEW YORK GIANTS; 1944-46 BOSTON YANKS
MC GEE, GEORGE (SOUTHERN) - TACKLE - 1960 BOSTON PATRIOTS (AFL)
MC GEE, HARRY (KANSAS STATE) - CENTER - 1927 CLEVELAND BULLDOGS;
    1929, 32 STATEN ISLAND STAPELTONS; 1930 NEWARK TORNADOS
MC GEE, MICHAEL (DUKE) - GUARD - 1960-62 ST. LOUIS CARDINALS
MC GEE, ROBERT (SANTA CLARA) - TACKLE - 1938 CHICAGO CARDINALS
MC GEE, SYLVESTER "MOLLY" (RHODE ISLAND) - BACK - 1974 ATLANTA
    FALCONS (NFC)
MC GEE, WILLIAM MAX (TULANE) - END - 1954, 57-67 GREEN BAY PACKERS
MC GEE, WILLIE (ALCORN A&M) - END, BACK - 1973 SAN DIEGO CHARGERS
    (AFC); 1974 LOS ANGELES RAMS (NFC)
MC GEHEAN, ROBERT - BACK - 1923 LOUISVILLE BRECKS
MC GEORGE, RICHARD (ELON) - END - 1970-74 GREEN BAY PACKERS (NFC)
MC GIBBONY, CHARLES (ARKANSAS STATE) - BACK - 1944 BROOKLYN TIGERS
MC GILBRA, SANFORD (REDLANDS) - TACKLE - 1926 BUFFALO RANGERS
MC GILL, GEORGE - CENTER - 1922 RACINE LEGION
MC GILL, MICHAEL (NOTRE DAME) - LB - 1968-69 MINNESOTA VIKINGS; 1970
    MINNESOTA VIKINGS (NFC); 1971-72 ST. LOUIS CARDINALS (NFC)
MC GILL, RALPH LOUIS (TULSA) - BACK - 1972-74 SAN FRANCISCO 49ERS
    (NFC)
MC GINLEY, EDWARD (PENNSYLVANIA) - TACKLE - 1925 NEW YORK GIANTS
MC GINNIS, LAWRENCE (MARQUETTE) - END - 1923-24 MILWAUKEE BADGERS
MC GIRL, LEONARD (MISSOURI) - GUARD - 1934 ST. LOUIS GUNNERS

MC GLONE, JOSEPH (HARVARD) - QBACK - 1926 PROVIDENCE STEAMROLLERS;
     1926 BOSTON BULLDOGS (AFL)
MC GOLDRICK, HUGH (LEHIGH) - TACKLE - 1925 PROVIDENCE STEAMROLLERS
MC GRATH, BRIAN (NEW YORK UNIV.) - GUARD - 1922 LOUISVILLE BRECKS
MC GRATH, FRANK (GEORGETOWN) - END - 1927 FRANKFORD YELLOWJACKETS;
     1928 NEW YORK YANKEES
MC GRATH, MAURICE (NIAGARA) - TACKLE - 1940 BUFFALO INDIANS (AFL)
MC GRATH, RICHARD (HOLY CROSS) - TACKLE - 1926 BROOKLYN LIONS
MC GRAW, THURMAN (COLORADO A&M) - TACKLE - 1950-54 DETROIT LIONS
MC GREGOR, JOHN (ILLINOIS) - CENTER - 1919 CANTON BULLDOGS
MC GREW, DANIEL (PURDUE) - CENTER - 1960 BUFFALO BILLS (AFL)
MC GUIRK, WARREN (BOSTON COLLEGE) - TACKLE - 1929-30 PROVIDENCE
     STEAMROLLERS
MC HAN, LAMAR (ARKANSAS) - QBACK - 1954-58 CHICAGO CARDINALS; 1959-60
     GREEN BAY PACKERS; 1961-63 BALTIMORE COLTS; 1963 SAN FRANCISCO
     49ERS
MC HUGH, WILLIAM "PAT" (GEORGIA TECH) - BACK - 1947-51 PHILADELPHIA
     EAGLES
MC ILHANY, JOSEPH DANIEL (TEXAS A&M) - BACK - 1965 LOS ANGELES RAMS
MC ILHENNY, DONALD (SMU) - BACK - 1956 DETROIT LIONS; 1957-59 GREEN
     BAY PACKERS; 1960 DALLAS COWBOYS; 1961 SAN FRANCISCO 49ERS
MC ILWAIN, WALLACE (ILLINOIS) - BACK - 1926 RACINE LEGION
MC INERNY, ARNOLD (NOTRE DAME) - CENTER - 1920-27 CHICAGO CARDINALS
MC INNIS, HUGH (MISSISSIPPI SOUTHERN) - END - 1960-62 ST. LOUIS
     CARDINALS; 1964 DETROIT LIONS; 1966 ATLANTA FALCONS
MC INTOSH, IRA (RHODE ISLAND STATE) - BACK - 1925-26 PROVIDENCE
     STEAMROLLERS
MC INTOSH, JAY ANGUS (PURDUE) - BACK - 1936 CLEVELAND RAMS (AFL)
MC KALIP, WILLIAM (OREGON STATE) - END - 1931-32 PORTSMOUTH SPARTANS;
     1934, 36 DETROIT LIONS
MC KAY, ROBERT (TEXAS) - TACKLE - 1970-74 CLEVELAND BROWNS (AFC)
MC KAY, ROY (TEXAS) - BACK - 1944-47 GREEN BAY PACKERS; 1945-46
     PUNTING LEADER
MC KEE, PAUL (SYRACUSE) - END - 1947-48 WASHINGTON REDSKINS
MC KEEVER, MARLIN (USC) - END, LB - 1961-66 LOS ANGELES RAMS; 1967
     MINNESOTA VIKINGS; 1968-69 WASHINGTON REDSKINS; 1970 WASHINGTON
     REDSKINS; 1971-72 LOS ANGELES RAMS (NFC); 1973
     PHILADELPHIA EAGLES (NFC)
MC KENZIE, REGGIE (MICHIGAN) - GUARD - 1972-74 BUFFALO BILLS (AFC)
MC KETES - BACK - 1926 HAMMOND PROS
MC KINLEY, WILLIAM (ARIZONA) - END, LB - 1971 BUFFALO BILLS (AFC)
MC KINNEY, WILLIAM (WEST TEXAS STATE) - LB - 1972 CHICAGO BEARS (NFC)
MC KINNIS, HUGH (ARIZONA STATE) - BACK - 1973-74 CLEVELAND BROWNS
     (AFC)
MC KINNON, DONALD (DARTMOUTH) - LB - 1963-64 BOSTON PATRIOTS (AFL)
MC KISSACK, RICHARD (SMU) - BACK - 1952 DALLAS TEXANS
MC KOY, WILLIAM (PURDUE) - LB - 1970-72 DENVER BRONCOS (AFC); 1974
     SAN FRANCISCO 49ERS (NFC)
MC LAIN, MALCOLM (TULANE) - BACK - 1941 BUFFALO TIGERS (AFL)
MC LAIN, MAYES (HASKELL & IOWA) - BACK - 1930-31 PORTSMOUTH SPARTANS;
     1931 STATEN ISLAND STAPELTONS
MC LAREN, GEORGE (PITTSBURGH) - BACK - 1919 MASSILLON TIGERS
MC LAUGHLIN, CHARLES (WICHITA) - BACK - 1934 ST. LOUIS GUNNERS
MC LAUGHLIN, EUGENE (NORTHWESTERN) - TACKLE - 1919 HAMMOND PROS
MC LAUGHLIN, LEE (VIRGINIA) - GUARD - 1941 GREEN BAY PACKERS
MC LAUGHLIN, LEON (UCLA) - CENTER - 1951-55 LOS ANGELES RAMS
MC LAUGHRY, JOHN (BROWN) - BACK - 1940 NEW YORK GIANTS
MC LEAN, RAYMOND - BACK - 1919 TOLEDO MAROONS; 1921 GREEN BAY PACKERS
MC LEAN, RAYMOND (ST. ANSELM'S) - BACK - 1940-47 CHICAGO BEARS
MC LEMORE, EMMETT (HASKELL) - BACK - 1922-23 OORANG INDIANS; 1924
     KANSAS CITY COWBOYS
MC LENNA, BRUCE (HILLSDALE) - BACK - 1966 DETROIT LIONS
MC LEOD, ROBERT (ABILENE CHRISTIAN) - END - 1961-66 HOUSTON OILERS
     (AFL)
MC LEOD, RUSSELL (ST. LOUIS UNIV.) - CENTER - 1934 ST. LOUIS GUNNERS
MC LINTON, HAROLD (SOUTHERN) - LB - 1969 WASHINGTON REDSKINS; 1970-74
     WASHINGTON REDSKINS (NFC)
MC MAHAN (HEIDELBERG) - BACK - 1921 CINCINNATI CELTS

MC MAHON, ARTHUR (NORTH CAROLINA STATE) - END - 1968-69 BOSTON
    PATRIOTS (AFL); 1970 BOSTON PATRIOTS (AFC); 1972 NEW ENGLAND
    PATRIOTS (AFC)
MC MAHON, BYRON (CORNELL) - GUARD - 1923 CHICAGO CARDINALS
MC MAHON, HARRY (HOLY CROSS) - BACK - 1926 HARTFORD BLUES
MC MAKIN, JOHN (CLEMSON) - END - 1972-74 PITTSBURGH STEELERS (AFC)
MC MANUS, ARTHUR (BOSTON COLLEGE) - TACKLE - 1926 BOSTON BULLDOGS
    (AFL); 1926 NEWARK BEARS (AFL)
MC MICHAELS, JOHN (BIRMINGHAM SOUTHERN) - BACK - 1944 BROOKLYN TIGERS
MC MILLAN, CHARLES (JOHN CARROLL) - BACK - 1954 BALTIMORE COLTS
MC MILLAN, EDWARD (FLORIDA STATE) - BACK - 1973-74 LOS ANGELES RAMS
    (NFC)
MC MILLAN, ERNEST (ILLINOIS) - TACKLE - 1961-69 ST. LOUIS CARDINALS;
    1970-74 ST. LOUIS CARDINALS (NFC)
MC MILLEN, JAMES (ILLINOIS) - GUARD - 1924-28 CHICAGO BEARS
MC MILLIN, ALVIN "BO" (CENTRE) - QBACK - 1922-23 MILWAUKEE BADGERS;
    1923 CLEVELAND INDIANS
MC MILLIN, JAMES (COLORADO STATE) - BACK - 1961-62 DENVER BRONCOS
    (AFL); 1963-64 OAKLAND RAIDERS (AFL); 1964-65 DENVER BRONCOS
    (AFL)
MC MULLAN, JOHN (NOTRE DAME) - GUARD - 1960-61 NEW YORK TITANS (AFL)
MC MULLAN, JOHN (NOTRE DAME) - TACKLE - 1926 CHICAGO BULLS (AFL)
MC MULLEN, DANIEL (NEBRASKA) - GUARD - 1929 NEW YORK GIANTS; 1930-31
    CHICAGO BEARS; 1932 PORTSMOUTH SPARTANS
MC MURTRY, CHARLES (WHITTIER) - TACKLE - 1960-61 BUFFALO BILLS (AFL);
    1962-63 OAKLAND RAIDERS (AFL)
MC NALLY, FRANK (ST. MARY'S OF CAL.) - CENTER - 1931-34 CHICAGO
    CARDINALS
MC NALLY, JOHN "BLOOD" (ST. JOHN OF MINN.) - BACK - 1925-26 MILWAUKEE
    BADGERS; 1926-27 DULUTH ESKIMOS; 1928 POTTSVILLE MAROONS;
    1929-33, 35-36 GREEN BAY PACKERS; 1934, 37-38 PITTSBURGH
    PIRATES; 1939 PITTSBURGH STEELERS; 1963 HALL OF FAME
MC NAMARA, EDMUND (HOLY CROSS) - TACKLE - 1945 PITTSBURGH STEELERS
MC NAMARA, ROBERT (NEW YORK UNIV.) - END - 1934 BOSTON REDSKINS
MC NAMARA, ROBERT (MINNESOTA) - BACK - 1960-61 DENVER BRONCOS (AFL)
MC NAMARA, THOMAS (DETROIT) - GUARD - 1923 TOLEDO MAROONS; 1925-26
    DETROIT PANTHERS
MC NEESE, THOMAS (GONZAGA) - BACK - 1936 ROCHESTER TIGERS (AFL); 1937
    BOSTON SHAMROCKS (AFL)
MC NEIL, CHARLES (COMPTON JUNIOR) - BACK - 1960 LOS ANGELES CHARGERS
    (AFL); 1961-64 SAN DIEGO CHARGERS (AFL)
MC NEIL, CLIFTON (GRAMBLING) - END, BACK - 1964-67 CLEVELAND BROWNS;
    1968-69 SAN FRANCISCO 49ERS; 1970-71 NEW YORK GIANTS (NFC);
    1971-72 WASHINGTON REDSKINS (NFC); 1973 HOUSTON OILERS (AFC);
    1968 PASS RECEIVING LEADER
MC NEIL, FRANCIS (WASHINGTON&JEFFERSON) - END - 1932 BROOKLYN DODGERS
MC NEILL, FREDERICK (UCLA) - LB - 1974 MINNESOTA VIKINGS (NFC)
MC NEILL, RODNEY (USC) - BACK - 1974 NEW ORLEANS SAINTS (NFC)
MC NEILL, THOMAS (S.F.AUSTIN) - KICKER - 1967-69 NEW ORLEANS SAINTS;
    1970 MINNESOTA VIKINGS (NFC); 1971-73 PHILADELPHIA EAGLES (NFC);
    1971 PUNTING LEADER (NFC)
MC NELLIS, WILLIAM (ST. MARY'S OF MINNESOTA) - BACK - 1927 DULUTH
    ESKIMOS
MC NULTY, PAUL (NOTRE DAME) - END - 1924-25 CHICAGO CARDINALS
MC PEAK, WILLIAM (PITTSBURGH) - END - 1949-57 PITTSBURGH STEELERS
MC PHAIL, HAROLD (XAVIER) - BACK - 1934-35 BOSTON REDSKINS; 1937
    CINCINNATI BENGALS (AFL)
MC PHAIL, HOWARD (OKLAHOMA) - BACK - 1953 BALTIMORE COLTS
MC PHEE, FRANK (PRINCETON) - END - 1955 CHICAGO CARDINALS
MC PHERSON, FORREST (NEBRASKA) - TACKLE - 1935 CHICAGO BEARS; 1935-37
    PHILADELPHIA EAGLES; 1943-45 GREEN BAY PACKERS
MC QUADE, JOHN (GEORGETOWN) - BACK - 1922 CANTON BULLDOGS
MC QUARTERS, EDWARD (OKLAHOMA) - TACKLE - 1965 ST. LOUIS CARDINALS
MC QUAY, LEON (TAMPA) - BACK - 1974 NEW YORK GIANTS (NFC)
MC QUILKEN, KIM (LEHIGH) - QBACK - 1974 ATLANTA FALCONS (NFC)
MC RAE, BENJAMIN (MICHIGAN) - BACK - 1962-69 CHICAGO BEARS; 1970
    CHICAGO BEARS (NFC); 1971 NEW YORK GIANTS (NFC)
MC RAE, EDWARD (WASHINGTON) - GUARD - 1926 LOS ANGELES WILDCATS (AFL)
MC RAE, FRANKLIN (TENNESSEE STATE) - TACKLE - 1967 CHICAGO BEARS

MC RAVEN, WILLIAM (MURRAY STATE) - BACK - 1939 CLEVELAND RAMS; 1940
    CINCINNATI BENGALS (AFL)
MC ROBERTS, ROBERT (STOUT STATE-WISCONSIN) - BACK - 1944 BOSTON YANKS
MC ROBERTS, WADE (WESTMINSTER-PA.) - CENTER - 1925-26 CANTON BULLDOGS
MC SHEA, JOSEPH (ROCHESTER) - GUARD - 1923 ROCHESTER JEFFERSONS
MC VEA, WARREN (HOUSTON) - BACK, END - 1968 CINCINNATI BENGALS (AFL);
    1969 KANSAS CITY CHIEFS (AFL); 1970-71, 73 KANSAS CITY CHIEFS
    (AFC)
MC WATTERS, WILLIAM (NORTH TEXAS STATE) - BACK - 1964 MINNESOTA
    VIKINGS
MC WHERTER, KYLE (MILLIKIN & BETHANY) - BACK - 1920 DECATUR STALEYS
MC WILLIAMS, THOMAS (MISSISSIPPI STATE) - BACK - 1949 LOS ANGELES
    DONS (AAFC); 1950 PITTSBURGH STEELERS
MC WILLIAMS, WILLIAM (JORDAN COLLEGE) - BACK - 1934 DETROIT LIONS
MEAD, JOHN (WISCONSIN) - END - 1946-47 NEW YORK GIANTS
MEADE, JAMES (MARYLAND) - BACK - 1939-40 WASHINGTON REDSKINS
MEADOR, EDWARD (ARKANSAS TECH) - BACK - 1959-69 LOS ANGELES RAMS;
    1970 LOS ANGELES RAMS (NFC)
MEADOWS, EDWARD (DUKE) - END - 1954, 56-57 CHICAGO BEARS; 1955
    PITTSBURGH STEELERS; 1958 PHILADELPHIA EAGLES; 1959 WASHINGTON
    REDSKINS
MEADOWS, ERIC (PITTSBURGH) - BACK - 1923 MILWAUKEE BADGERS
MEADOWS - END - 1920 CANTON BULLDOGS
MEAGHER, JOHN (NOTRE DAME) - END - 1920 CHICAGO TIGERS
MEANS, DAVID (SOUTHWEST MISSOURI STATE) - END - 1974 BUFFALO BILLS
    (AFC)
MECHAM, CURTIS (OREGON) - BACK - 1942 BROOKLYN DODGERS
MEDLIN, DANIEL (NORTH CAROLINA STATE) - GUARD - 1974 OAKLAND RAIDERS
    (AFC)
MEDVED, DONALD (WASHINGTON) - BACK - 1966-69 PHILADELPHIA EAGLES;
    1970 PHILADELPHIA EAGLES (NFC)
MEEKER, HERBERT (WASHINGTON STATE) - BACK - 1930-31 PROVIDENCE
    STEAMROLLERS
MEEKS, BRYANT (SOUTH CAROLINA) - CENTER - 1947-48 PITTSBURGH STEELERS
MEEKS, EDWARD (LOUISVILLE) - BACK - 1922 LOUISVILLE BRECKS
MEESE, WARD (WABASH) - END - 1922 EVANSVILLE CRIMSON GIANTS; 1922
    MILWAUKEE BADGERS; 1923 ST. LOUIS BROWNS; 1924 KENOSHA MAROONS;
    1925 HAMMOND PROS
MEGGYESY, DAVID (SYRACUSE) - LB - 1963-69 ST. LOUIS CARDINALS
MEHELICH, CHARLES (DUQUESNE) - END - 1946-51 PITTSBURGH STEELERS
MEHELICH, THOMAS (ST. THOMAS OF MINNESOTA) - GUARD - 1929 MINNEAPOLIS
    REDJACKETS
MEHRE, HARRY (NOTRE DAME) - CENTER - 1923-24 MINNEAPOLIS MARINES
MEHRINGER, PETER (KANSAS) - TACKLE - 1934-36 CHICAGO CARDINALS; 1937
    LOS ANGELES BULLDOGS (AFL)
MEILINGER, STEVEN (KENTUCKY) - END - 1956-57 WASHINGTON REDSKINS;
    1958, 60 GREEN BAY PACKERS; 1961 PITTSBURGH STEELERS; 1961 ST.
    LOUIS CARDINALS
MEINERT, DALE (OKLAHOMA STATE) - LB - 1958-59 CHICAGO CARDINALS;
    1960-67 ST. LOUIS CARDINALS
MEINHARDT, GEORGE (ST. LOUIS UNIV.) - GUARD - 1923 ST. LOUIS BROWNS
MEISENHEIMER, DARRELL (OKLAHOMA A&M) - BACK - 1951 NEW YORK YANKS
MEIXLER, EDWARD (BOSTON UNIV.) - LB - 1965 BOSTON PATRIOTS (AFL)
MELINKOVICH, MICHAEL (GRAY HARBOR-WASH.) - END - 1965-66 ST. LOUIS
    CARDINALS; 1967 DETROIT LIONS
MELLEKAS, JOHN (ARIZONA) - TACKLE - 1956, 58-61 CHICAGO BEARS; 1962
    SAN FRANCISCO 49ERS; 1963 PHILADELPHIA EAGLES
MELLO, JAMES (NOTRE DAME) - BACK - 1947 BOSTON YANKS; 1948 LOS
    ANGELES RAMS; 1948 CHICAGO ROCKETS (AAFC); 1949 DETROIT LIONS
MELLUS, JOHN (VILLANOVA) - TACKLE - 1938-41 NEW YORK GIANTS; 1946 SAN
    FRANCISCO 49ERS (AAFC); 1947-49 BALTIMORE COLTS (AAFC)
MELVIN (MARIETTA) - END - 1921 CINCINNATI CELTS
MEMMELAAR, DALE (WYOMING) - GUARD - 1959 CHICAGO CARDINALS; 1960-61
    ST. LOUIS CARDINALS; 1962-63 DALLAS COWBOYS; 1964-65 CLEVELAND
    BROWNS; 1966-67 BALTIMORE COLTS
MENASCO, DONALD (TEXAS) - BACK - 1952-53 NEW YORK GIANTS; 1954
    WASHINGTON REDSKINS
MENDENHALL, JOHN (GRAMBLING) - TACKLE - 1972-74 NEW YORK GIANTS (NFC)
MENDENHALL, KENNETH (OKLAHOMA) - CENTER - 1971-74 BALTIMORE COLTS
    (AFC)

MENDENHALL, TERRY (SAN DIEGO STATE) - LB - 1971-72 OAKLAND RAIDERS
    (AFC)
MENDEZ, MARIO (SAN DIEGO STATE) - BACK - 1964 SAN DIEGO CHARGERS (AFL)
MENEFEE, HARTWELL (NEW MEXICO STATE) - BACK - 1966 NEW YORK GIANTS
MENEFEE, VICTOR (MORNINGSIDE) - END - 1921 ROCK ISLAND INDEPENDENTS
MERCEIN, CHARLES (YALE) - BACK - 1965-67 NEW YORK GIANTS; 1967-68
    GREEN BAY PACKERS; 1969 WASHINGTON REDSKINS; 1970 NEW YORK JETS
    (AFC)
MERCER, KENNETH (SIMPSON) - QBACK - 1927-29 FRANKFORD YELLOWJACKETS
MERCER, MICHAEL (ARIZONA STATE) - KICKER - 1961-62 MINNESOTA VIKINGS;
    1963-66 OAKLAND RAIDERS (AFL); 1966 KANSAS CITY CHIEFS (AFL);
    1967-68 BUFFALO BILLS (AFL); 1968-69 GREEN BAY PACKERS; 1970 SAN
    DIEGO CHARGERS (AFC); 1966 FIELD GOAL LEADER (AFL)
MEREDITH, CECIL DUDLEY (LAMAR TECH) - TACKLE - 1963, 68 HOUSTON
    OILERS (AFL); 1964-68 BUFFALO BILLS (AFL)
MEREDITH, JOE DON (SMU) - QBACK - 1960-68 DALLAS COWBOYS
MEREDITH, RUSSELL (WEST VIRGINIA) - GUARD - 1923 LOUISVILLE BRECKS;
    1925 CLEVELAND BULLDOGS
MERGEN, MICHAEL (SAN FRANCISCO) - TACKLE - 1952 CHICAGO CARDINALS
MERGENTHAL, ARTHUR (NOTRE DAME) - GUARD - 1940 CINCINNATI BENGALS
    (AFL); 1945 CLEVELAND RAMS; 1946 LOS ANGELES RAMS
MERILLAT, LOUIS (WEST POINT) - END - 1925 CANTON BULLDOGS
MERKA, MILTON (BAYLOR) - BACK - 1941 MILWAUKEE CHIEFS (AFL)
MERKEL, MONTE (KANSAS) - GUARD - 1943 CHICAGO BEARS
MERKLE, EDWARD (OKLAHOMA A&M) - GUARD - 1944 WASHINGTON REDSKINS
MERKOVSKY, ELMER (PITTSBURGH) - TACKLE - 1944 CARD-PITT; 1945-46
    PITTSBURGH STEELERS
MERLIN, EDWARD (VANDERBILT) - GUARD - 1938-39 BROOKLYN DODGERS; 1940
    MILWAUKEE CHIEFS (AFL)
MERLO, JAMES (STANFORD) - LB - 1973-74 NEW ORLEANS SAINTS (NFC)
MERRILL, WALTER (ALABAMA) - TACKLE - 1940-42 BROOKLYN DODGERS
MERTENS, JAMES (FAIRMONT STATE) - END - 1969 MIAMI DOLPHINS (AFL)
MERTENS, JEROME (DRAKE) - BACK - 1958-62, 64-65 SAN FRANCISCO 49ERS
MERZ, CURTIS (IOWA) - GUARD - 1962 DALLAS TEXANS (AFL); 1963-68
    KANSAS CITY CHIEFS (AFL)
MESAK, RICHARD (ST. MARY'S OF CAL.) - TACKLE - 1945 DETROIT LIONS
MESEC, IGNATIUS (NORTHWESTERN) - BACK - 1941 MILWAUKEE CHIEFS (AFL)
MESSER, LYNDY DALE (FRESNO STATE) - BACK - 1961-65 SAN FRANCISCO 49ERS
MESSNER, MAX (CINCINNATI) - LB - 1960-63 DETROIT LIONS; 1964 NEW YORK
    GIANTS; 1964-65 PITTSBURGH STEELERS
MESTNIK, FRANK (MARQUETTE) - BACK - 1960-61 ST. LOUIS CARDINALS; 1963
    GREEN BAY PACKERS
METCALF, TERRANCE (LONG BEACH STATE) - BACK - 1973-74 ST. LOUIS
    CARDINALS (NFC)
METHOD, RUSSELL - BACK - 1923-25 DULUTH KELLEYS; 1926-27 DULUTH
    ESKIMOS; 1929 CHICAGO CARDINALS
METZGER, CHARLES (MIAMI-OHIO) - BACK - 1940 CINCINNATI BENGALS (AFL)
METZGER, LOUIS (GEORGETOWN) - BACK - 1926 LOUISVILLE COLONELS
MEYER, DENNIS (ARKANSAS STATE) - BACK - 1973 PITTSBURGH STEELERS (AFC)
MEYER, EDWARD (WEST TEXAS STATE) - TACKLE - 1960 BUFFALO BILLS (AFL)
MEYER, ERNEST (GENEVA) - GUARD - 1930 PORTSMOUTH SPARTANS
MEYER, FREDERICK (STANFORD) - END - 1942, 45 PHILADELPHIA EAGLES
MEYER, GILBERT (WAKE FOREST) - END - 1947 BALTIMORE COLTS (AAFC)
MEYER, JOHN (NOTRE DAME) - LB - 1966 HOUSTON OILERS (AFL)
MEYER, RONALD (SOUTH DAKOTA STATE) - QBACK - 1966 PITTSBURGH STEELERS
MEYERS, JOHN (WASHINGTON) - TACKLE - 1962-63 DALLAS COWBOYS; 1964-67
    PHILADELPHIA EAGLES
MEYERS, PAUL (WISCONSIN) - END - 1920 HAMMOND PROS; 1923 RACINE LEGION
MEYERS, ROBERT (STANFORD) - BACK - 1952 SAN FRANCISCO 49ERS
MEYLAN, WAYNE (NEBRASKA) - LB - 1968-69 CLEVELAND BROWNS; 1970
    MINNESOTA VIKINGS (NFC)
MIALIK, LARRY (NEBRASKA) - LB - 1972-74 ATLANTA FALCONS (NFC)
MICHAEL, WILLIAM (OHIO STATE) - GUARD - 1957 PITTSBURGH STEELERS
MICHAELS, ALTON (HEIDELBERG & OHIO STATE) - BACK - 1923-25 AKRON
    PROS; 1925 CLEVELAND BULLDOGS; 1926 CLEVELAND PANTHERS (AFL)
MICHAELS, EDWARD (VILLANOVA) - GUARD - 1936 CHICAGO BEARS; 1937
    WASHINGTON REDSKINS; 1943 PHIL-PITT; 1944-46 PHILADELPHIA EAGLES
MICHAELS, RICHARD (OHIO STATE) - TACKLE - 1960-63, 65-66 HOUSTON
    OILERS (AFL)

MICHAELS, LOUIS (KENTUCKY) - END, KICKER - 1958-60 LOS ANGELES RAMS;
     1961-63 PITTSBURGH STEELERS; 1964-69 BALTIMORE COLTS; 1971 GREEN
     BAY PACKERS (NFC); 1962 FIELD GOAL LEADER
MICHAELS, WALTER (WASHINGTON&LEE) - GUARD - 1951 GREEN BAY PACKERS;
     1952-61 CLEVELAND BROWNS; 1963 NEW YORK JETS (AFL)
MICHALIK, ARTHUR (ST. AMBROSE) - GUARD - 1953-54 SAN FRANCISCO 49ERS;
     1955-56 PITTSBURGH STEELERS
MICHALSKE, AUGUST (PENN STATE) - GUARD - 1926 NEW YORK YANKEES (AFL);
     1927-28 NEW YORK YANKEES; 1929-35, 37 GREEN BAY PACKERS; 1964
     HALL OF FAME
MICHEL, WILLIAM "TOM" (EAST CAROLINA) - BACK - 1964 MINNESOTA VIKINGS
MICHELS, JOHN (TENNESSEE) - GUARD - 1953 PHILADELPHIA EAGLES
MICKA, MICHAEL (COLGATE) - BACK - 1944-45 WASHINGTON REDSKINS;
     1945-48 BOSTON YANKS
MIDDENDORF, DAVID (WASHINGTON STATE) - GUARD - 1968-69 CINCINNATI
     BENGALS (AFL); 1970 NEW YORK JETS (AFC)
MIDDLETON, DAVID (AUBURN) - END - 1955-60 DETROIT LIONS; 1961
     MINNESOTA VIKINGS
MIDDLETON, RICHARD (OHIO STATE) - LB - 1974 NEW ORLEANS SAINTS (NFC)
MIDLER, LOUIS (MINNESOTA) - GUARD - 1939 PITTSBURGH STEELERS; 1940
     GREEN BAY PACKERS
MIELZINER, SAUL (CARNEGIE TECH) - CENTER - 1929-30 NEW YORK GIANTS;
     1931-34 BROOKLYN DODGERS
MIESZKOWSKI, EDWARD (NOTRE DAME) - TACKLE - 1946-47 BROOKLYN DODGERS
     (AAFC)
MIGDAL, JOSEPH (MANHATTAN) - BACK - 1940 NEW YORK AMERICANS (AFL)
MIHAJLOVICH, LOUIS (INDIANA) - END - 1948 LOS ANGELES DONS (AAFC)
MIHAL, JOSEPH (PURDUE) - TACKLE - 1940-41 CHICAGO BEARS; 1946 LOS
     ANGELES DONS (AAFC); 1947 CHICAGO ROCKETS (AAFC)
MIKE, ROBERT (UCLA) - TACKLE - 1948-49 SAN FRANCISCO 49ERS (AAFC)
MIKE-MAYER, NICK (TEMPLE) - KICKER - 1973-74 ATLANTA FALCONS (NFC)
MIKETA, ANDREW (NORTH CAROLINA) - CENTER - 1954-55 DETROIT LIONS
MIKLICH, WILLIAM (IDAHO) - BACK - 1947-48 NEW YORK GIANTS; 1948
     DETROIT LIONS
MIKULA, THOMAS (WILLIAM&MARY) - BACK - 1948 BROOKLYN DODGERS (AAFC)
MIKULAK, MICHAEL (OREGON) - BACK - 1934-36 CHICAGO CARDINALS
MILAM, BARNES (AUSTIN) - GUARD - 1934 PHILADELPHIA EAGLES
MILAN, DONALD (CALIFORNIA POLYTECH) - QBACK - 1974 LOS ANGELES RAMS
     (NFC)
MILAN, JOSEPH (PHILLIPS) - END - 1924-25 KANSAS CITY COWBOYS
MILANO, ARCH (ST. FRANCIS) - END - 1945 DETROIT LIONS
MILDREN, LARRY JACK (OKLAHOMA) - BACK - 1972-73 BALTIMORE COLTS
     (AFC); 1974 NEW ENGLAND PATRIOTS (AFC)
MILES, LEO (VIRGINIA STATE) - BACK - 1953 NEW YORK GIANTS
MILES, MARK (WASHINGTON&LEE) - TACKLE - 1919 CLEVELAND INDIANS; 1920
     CLEVELAND PANTHERS; 1920 AKRON PROS
MILKS, JOHN (SAN DIEGO STATE) - LB - 1966 SAN DIEGO CHARGERS (AFL)
MILLER, ALAN (BOSTON COLLEGE) - BACK - 1960 BOSTON PATRIOTS (AFL);
     1961-63, 65 OAKLAND RAIDERS (AFL)
MILLER, ALFRED (HARVARD) - QBACK - 1929 BOSTON BRAVES
MILLER, ALLEN (OHIO UNIV.) - LB - 1962-63 WASHINGTON REDSKINS
MILLER, CHARLES (PURDUE) - CENTER - 1932-36 CHICAGO BEARS; 1937
     CLEVELAND RAMS; 1938 GREEN BAY PACKERS
MILLER, CLEOPHUS (ARKANSAS) - BACK - 1974 KANSAS CITY CHIEFS (AFC)
MILLER, DONALD (NOTRE DAME) - BACK - 1925 PROVIDENCE STEAMROLLERS
MILLER, DONALD (SMU) - BACK - 1954 GREEN BAY PACKERS; 1954
     PHILADELPHIA EAGLES
MILLER, EDWARD (NEW MEXICO A&M) - BACK - 1939-40 NEW YORK GIANTS
MILLER, EDWARD (PENN STATE) - QBACK - 1919 MASSILLON TIGERS
MILLER, FRANKLIN CLARK (UTAH STATE) - END - 1962-68 SAN FRANCISCO
     49ERS; 1969 WASHINGTON REDSKINS; 1970 LOS ANGELES RAMS (NFC)
MILLER, FREDERICK (LSU) - TACKLE - 1963-69 BALTIMORE COLTS; 1970-72
     BALTIMORE COLTS (AFC)
MILLER, FREDERICK (PACIFIC) - TACKLE - 1955 WASHINGTON REDSKINS
MILLER, HAROLD (GEORGIA TECH) - TACKLE - 1953 SAN FRANCISCO 49ERS
MILLER, HENRY (WEST VIRGINIA WESLEYAN) - BACK - 1930 BROOKLYN DODGERS
MILLER, HENRY (PENNSYLVANIA) - END - 1919 DETROIT HERALDS; 1919
     MASSILLON TIGERS; 1920-21 BUFFALO ALL-AMERICANS; 1924 FRANKFORD
     YELLOWJACKETS; 1925 MILWAUKEE BADGERS
MILLER, J. ROBERT (WITTENBERG) - CENTER - 1931 PORTSMOUTH SPARTANS
MILLER, JAMES (IOWA) - GUARD - 1971-72, 74 ATLANTA FALCONS (NFC)

Top row (from left to right): Riley Matheson, Ray Mathews, Ollie Matson and Tom Matte. *Second row:* Marv Matuszak, Dale Meinert, Joe Don Meredith and Lou Michaels. *Third row:* Dave Middleton, Mike Mikulak, Wayne Millner and Century Milstead. *Bottom row:* Bob Mitchell, Ed Modzelewski, Dick Modzelewski and Bow Tipp Mooney.

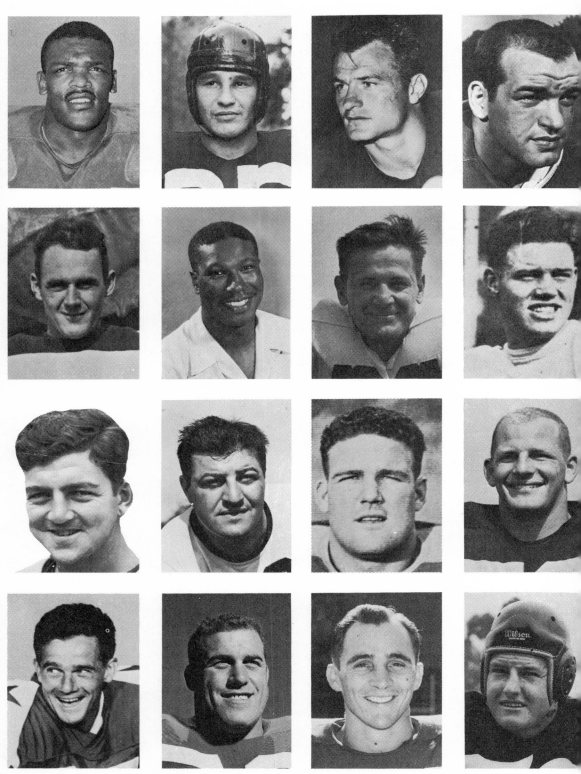

Top row (from left to right): Lenny Moore, Wilbur Moore, Larry Morris and Joe Morrison. *Second row:* Cliff Montgomery, Marion Motley, Joe Muha and "Brick" Muller. *Third row:* George Mulligan, George Musso, Ed Neal and Ray Nitschke. *Bottom row:* Dick Nolan, Leo Nomellini, Jerry Norton and Bob Nussbaumer.

MILLER, JOHN (BOSTON COLLEGE) - TACKLE - 1956, 58-59 WASHINGTON
    REDSKINS; 1960 GREEN BAY PACKERS
MILLER, JOHN (NEW YORK UNIV.) - TACKLE - 1929-31 STATEN ISLAND
    STAPELTONS
MILLER, JOHN (NOTRE DAME) - QBACK - 1919 MASSILLON TIGERS
MILLER, LLOYD (DARTMOUTH) - TACKLE - 1921-23 LOUISVILLE BRECKS
MILLER, MILFORD (CHADRON STATE-NEBRASKA) - GUARD - 1935 CHICAGO
    BEARS; 1936-37 CHICAGO CARDINALS
MILLER, PAUL (LSU) - END - 1954-57 LOS ANGELES RAMS; 1960-61 DALLAS
    TEXANS (AFL); 1962 SAN DIEGO CHARGERS (AFL)
MILLER, PAUL (SOUTH DAKOTA STATE) - BACK - 1936-38 GREEN BAY PACKERS
MILLER, RALPH (ALABAMA STATE) - GUARD - 1972-73 HOUSTON OILERS (AFC)
MILLER, RALPH (RICE) - TACKLE - 1937-38 CLEVELAND RAMS
MILLER, RAYMOND (PURDUE) - END - 1922 CANTON BULLDOGS; 1922-23 RACINE
    LEGION
MILLER, ROBERT TERRY (ILLINOIS) - LB - 1970 DETROIT LIONS (NFC);
    1971-74 ST. LOUIS CARDINALS (NFC)
MILLER, ROBERT (VIRGINIA) - TACKLE - 1952-58 DETROIT LIONS
MILLER, ROBERT "POI" - QBACK - 1937 LOS ANGELES BULLDOGS (AFL)
MILLER, RONALD (USC) - END - 1956 LOS ANGELES RAMS
MILLER, RONALD (WISCONSIN) - QBACK - 1962 LOS ANGELES RAMS
MILLER, THOMAS (HAMPTON-SYDNEY) - END - 1943 PHIL-PITT; 1944
    PHILADELPHIA EAGLES; 1945 WASHINGTON REDSKINS; 1946 GREEN BAY
    PACKERS
MILLER, VERNE (ST. MARY'S OF MINNESOTA) - BACK - 1930 MINNEAPOLIS
    REDJACKETS
MILLER, W. BLAKE (MICHIGAN STATE) - END - 1921 DETROIT PANTHERS
MILLER, WILLIAM (MIAMI) - END - 1962 DALLAS TEXANS (AFL); 1963
    BUFFALO BILLS (AFL); 1964, 66-68 OAKLAND RAIDERS (AFL)
MILLER, WILLIAM (NEW MEXICO HIGHLANDS) - TACKLE - 1962 HOUSTON OILERS
    (AFL)
MILLING, ALBERT (RICHMOND) - GUARD - 1942 PHILADELPHIA EAGLES
MILLMAN, ROBERT (LAFAYETTE) - BACK - 1926-27 POTTSVILLE MAROONS
MILLNER, WAYNE (NOTRE DAME) - END - 1936 BOSTON REDSKINS; 1937-41, 45
    WASHINGTON REDSKINS; 1968 HALL OF FAME
MILLNOVICH, JOSEPH (MINNESOTA) - BACK - 1941 CINCINNATI BENGALS (AFL)
MILLS, JOSEPH (CARNEGIE TECH) - CENTER - 1922-26 AKRON PROS
MILLS, RICHARD (PITTSBURGH) - GUARD - 1961-62 DETROIT LIONS
MILLS, STANLEY A. (MARYLAND) - BACK, END - 1920 BUFFALO
    ALL-AMERICANS; 1922-23 GREEN BAY PACKERS; 1924 AKRON PROS;
    (PLAYED UNDER CHARLES IN 1920, THOMAS IN 1922-23)
MILLS, SULLIVAN (WICHITA STATE) - BACK - 1965-66 BUFFALO BILLS (AFL)
MILNER, CHARLES "BILL" (DUKE) - GUARD - 1947-49 CHICAGO BEARS; 1950
    NEW YORK GIANTS
MILSTEAD, CENTURY (YALE) - TACKLE - 1925, 27-28 NEW YORK GIANTS; 1926
    PHILADELPHIA QUAKERS (AFL)
MILSTEAD, CHARLES (TEXAS A&M) - QBACK - 1960-61 HOUSTON OILERS (AFL)
MILTON, EUGENE (FLORIDA A&M) - END - 1968-69 MIAMI DOLPHINS (AFL)
MILTON, JOHN (USC) - END - 1924 KANSAS CITY COWBOYS
MILTON, THOMAS (LAKE FOREST) - END - 1923 MILWAUKEE BADGERS; 1923 ST.
    LOUIS BROWNS; 1924 GREEN BAY PACKERS
MINARIK, HENRY (MICHIGAN STATE) - END - 1951 PITTSBURGH STEELERS
MINER, THOMAS (TULSA) - END - 1958 PITTSBURGH STEELERS; 1958 FIELD
    GOAL LEADER; (TIED WITH COTHREN)
MINGO, EUGENE - KICKER, BACK - 1960-64 DENVER BRONCOS (AFL); 1964-65
    OAKLAND RAIDERS (AFL); 1966-67 MIAMI DOLPHINS (AFL); 1967
    WASHINGTON REDSKINS; 1967 NEW ORLEANS SAINTS; 1969 PITTSBURGH
    STEELERS; 1970 PITTSBURGH STEELERS (AFC); 1960, 62 SCORING
    LEADER (AFL); 1960, 62 FIELD GOAL LEADER (AFL)
MINICK, PAUL (IOWA) - GUARD - 1926 NEW YORK YANKEES (AFL); 1927
    BUFFALO BISONS; 1928-29 GREEN BAY PACKERS
MININI, FRANK (SAN JOSE STATE) - BACK - 1947-48 CHICAGO BEARS; 1949
    PITTSBURGH STEELERS
MINISI, ANTHONY (PENNSYLVANIA) - BACK - 1948 NEW YORK GIANTS
MINNIEAR, RANDOLPH (PURDUE) - BACK - 1967-69 NEW YORK GIANTS; 1970
    CLEVELAND BROWNS (AFC)
MINOR, CLAUDIE (SAN DIEGO STATE) - TACKLE - 1974 DENVER BRONCOS (AFC)
MINOR, LINCOLN (NEW MEXICO STATE) - BACK - 1973 NEW ORLEANS SAINTS
    (NFC)

MINTER, THOMAS (BAYLOR) - BACK - 1962 DENVER BRONCOS (AFL); 1962
    BUFFALO BILLS (AFL)
MINTUN, JOHN - CENTER - 1920 DECATUR STALEYS; 1921 CHICAGO STALEYS;
    1922 CHICAGO BEARS; 1922-24, 26 RACINE LEGION; 1924-25 KANSAS
    CITY COWBOYS
MIODUSZEWSKI, EDWARD (WILLIAM&MARY) - BACK - 1953 BALTIMORE COLTS
MIRA, GEORGE (MIAMI) - QBACK - 1964-68 SAN FRANCISCO 49ERS; 1969
    PHILADELPHIA EAGLES; 1971 MIAMI DOLPHINS (AFC)
MIRICH, REX (ARIZONA STATE) - TACKLE - 1964-66 OAKLAND RAIDERS (AFL);
    1967-69 DENVER BRONCOS (AFL); 1970 BOSTON PATRIOTS (AFC)
MISCHAK, ROBERT (WEST POINT) - GUARD - 1958 NEW YORK GIANTS; 1960-62
    NEW YORK TITANS (AFL); 1963-65 OAKLAND RAIDERS (AFL)
MISHEL, DAVID (BROWN) - BACK - 1927 PROVIDENCE STEAMROLLERS; 1931
    CLEVELAND INDIANS
MITCHAM, EUGENE (ARIZONA STATE) - END - 1958 PHILADELPHIA EAGLES
MITCHELL, ALBERT (THIEL) - TACKLE - 1924 BUFFALO BISONS
MITCHELL, ALVIN (MORGAN STATE) - BACK - 1968-69 CLEVELAND BROWNS;
    1970 DENVER BRONCOS (AFC)
MITCHELL, CHARLES (TULSA) - BACK - 1945 CHICAGO BEARS; 1946 GREEN BAY
    PACKERS
MITCHELL, CHARLES (WASHINGTON) - BACK - 1963-67 DENVER BRONCOS (AFL);
    1968 BUFFALO BILLS (AFL)
MITCHELL, EDWARD (SOUTHERN) - GUARD - 1965-67 SAN DIEGO CHARGERS (AFL)
MITCHELL, FONDREN (FLORIDA) - BACK - 1946 MIAMI SEAHAWKS (AAFC)
MITCHELL, FREDERICK (BUCKNELL) - CENTER - 1929 ORANGE TORNADOS; 1930
    NEWARK TORNADOS
MITCHELL, GRANVILLE (DAVIS&ELKINS) - END - 1931-33 PORTSMOUTH
    SPARTANS; 1934-35 DETROIT LIONS; 1935-36 NEW YORK GIANTS; 1937
    BROOKLYN DODGERS
MITCHELL, HAROLD (UCLA) - TACKLE - 1952 NEW YORK GIANTS
MITCHELL, JAMES HALCOT (VIRGINIA STATE) - TACKLE, END - 1970-74
    DETROIT LIONS (NFC)
MITCHELL, JAMES ROBERT (PRAIRIE VIEW) - END - 1969 ATLANTA FALCONS;
    1970-74 ATLANTA FALCONS (NFC)
MITCHELL, KENNETH (NEVADA-LAS VEGAS) - LB - 1973-74 ATLANTA FALCONS
    (NFC)
MITCHELL, LEROY (TEXAS SOUTHERN) - BACK - 1967-68 BOSTON PATRIOTS
    (AFL); 1970 HOUSTON OILERS (AFC); 1971-73 DENVER BRONCOS (AFC)
MITCHELL, LYDELL (PENN STATE) - BACK - 1972-74 BALTIMORE COLTS (AFC);
    1974 PASS RECEIVING LEADER (AFC)
MITCHELL, PAUL (MINNESOTA) - TACKLE - 1946-48 LOS ANGELES DONS
    (AAFC); 1948-49 NEW YORK YANKEES (AAFC); 1950-51 NEW YORK YANKS
MITCHELL, ROBERT (ILLINOIS) - BACK - 1958-61 CLEVELAND BROWNS;
    1962-68 WASHINGTON REDSKINS; 1962 PASS RECEIVING LEADER
MITCHELL, ROBERT (STANFORD) - BACK - 1946-48 LOS ANGELES DONS (AAFC)
MITCHELL, STANTON (TENNESSEE) - END, BACK - 1966-69 MIAMI DOLPHINS
    (AFL); 1970 MIAMI DOLPHINS (AFC)
MITCHELL, THOMAS (BUCKNELL) - END - 1966 OAKLAND RAIDERS (AFL);
    1968-69 BALTIMORE COLTS; 1970-73 BALTIMORE COLTS (AFC); 1974 SAN
    FRANCISCO 49ERS (NFC)
MITCHELL, WILLIE (TENNESSEE A&I) - BACK - 1964-69 KANSAS CITY CHIEFS
    (AFL); 1970 KANSAS CITY CHIEFS (AFC)
MITINGER, ROBERT (PENN STATE) - LB - 1962-64, 66, 68 SAN DIEGO
    CHARGERS (AFL)
MITRICK, JAMES (OGLETHORPE) - BACK - 1937 BOSTON SHAMROCKS (AFL)
MIX, RONALD (USC) - TACKLE - 1960 LOS ANGELES CHARGERS (AFL); 1961-69
    SAN DIEGO CHARGERS (AFL); 1971 OAKLAND RAIDERS (AFC)
MIXON, WILLIAM (GEORGIA) - BACK - 1953-54 SAN FRANCISCO 49ERS
MIZELL, WARNER (GEORGIA TECH) - BACK - 1931 BROOKLYN DODGERS; 1931
    FRANKFORD YELLOWJACKETS
MOAN, EMMETT (WEST VIRGINIA) - BACK - 1939 CLEVELAND RAMS
MOBLEY, RUDOLPH (HARDIN-SIMMONS) - BACK - 1947 BALTIMORE COLTS (AAFC)
MOCKMORE, CHARLES (IOWA) - GUARD - 1920 ROCK ISLAND INDEPENDENTS
MODZELEWSKI, EDWARD (MARYLAND) - BACK - 1952 PITTSBURGH STEELERS;
    1955-59 CLEVELAND BROWNS
MODZELEWSKI, RICHARD (MARYLAND) - TACKLE - 1953-54 WASHINGTON
    REDSKINS; 1955 PITTSBURGH STEELERS; 1956-63 NEW YORK GIANTS;
    1964-66 CLEVELAND BROWNS
MOE, HAROLD (OREGON STATE) - BACK - 1933 CHICAGO CARDINALS
MOEGLE, EDGAR (DETROIT) - BACK - 1921 DETROIT PANTHERS

MOEGLE, RICHARD (RICE) - BACK - 1955-59 SAN FRANCISCO 49ERS; 1960
    PITTSBURGH STEELERS; 1961 DALLAS COWBOYS
MOHARDT, JOHN (NOTRE DAME) - BACK - 1921 DAYTON TRIANGLES; 1922-23
    CHICAGO CARDINALS; 1924 RACINE LEGION; 1925 CHICAGO BEARS; 1926
    CHICAGO BULLS (AFL)
MOHS, LOUIS (ST. THOMAS OF MINNESOTA) - END - 1923-24 MINNEAPOLIS
    MARINES
MOJE, RICHARD (LOYOLA OF CALIFORNIA) - END - 1951 GREEN BAY PACKERS
MOLDEN, FRANK (JACKSON STATE) - TACKLE - 1965 LOS ANGELES RAMS; 1968
    PHILADELPHIA EAGLES; 1969 NEW YORK GIANTS
MOLENDA, JOHN (MICHIGAN) - BACK - 1927-28 NEW YORK YANKEES; 1929-32
    GREEN BAY PACKERS; 1932-35 NEW YORK GIANTS
MOLESWORTH, KEITH (MONMOUTH) - QBACK - 1931-37 CHICAGO BEARS
MOLINET, LOUIS (CORNELL) - BACK - 1927 FRANKFORD YELLOWJACKETS
MOMSEN, ANTHONY (MICHIGAN) - CENTER - 1951 PITTSBURGH STEELERS; 1952
    WASHINGTON REDSKINS
MOMSEN, ROBERT (OHIO STATE) - GUARD - 1951 DETROIT LIONS; 1952 SAN
    FRANCISCO 49ERS
MONACHINO, JAMES (CALIFORNIA) - BACK - 1951, 53 SAN FRANCISCO 49ERS;
    1955 WASHINGTON REDSKINS
MONACO, RAYMOND (HOLY CROSS) - GUARD - 1944 WASHINGTON REDSKINS; 1945
    CLEVELAND RAMS
MONAHAN, J. REGIS (OHIO STATE) - GUARD - 1935-38 DETROIT LIONS; 1939
    CHICAGO CARDINALS
MONDAY, OSCAR (CARSON-NEWMAN) - TACKLE - 1940 COLUMBUS BULLIES (AFL);
    1940 CINCINNATI BENGALS (AFL)
MONELIE, WILLIAM (ST. MARY'S OF MINN.) - BACK - 1927 DULUTH ESKIMOS
MONFORT, AVERY (NEW MEXICO) - BACK - 1941 CHICAGO CARDINALS
MONNETT, ROBERT (MICHIGAN STATE) - BACK - 1933-38 GREEN BAY PACKERS
MONT, THOMAS (MARYLAND) - QBACK - 1947-49 WASHINGTON REDSKINS
MONTALBO, MELVIN (UTAH STATE) - BACK - 1962 OAKLAND RAIDERS (AFL)
MONTGOMERY, CLIFFORD (COLUMBIA) - QBACK - 1934 BROOKLYN DODGERS
MONTGOMERY, JAMES (TEXAS A&M) - TACKLE - 1946 DETROIT LIONS
MONTGOMERY, JAMES MICHAEL (KANSAS STATE) - END, BACK, KICKER - 1971
    SAN DIEGO CHARGERS (AFC); 1972-73 DALLAS COWBOYS (NFC); 1974 NEW
    ORLEANS SAINTS (NFC)
MONTGOMERY, MARVIN (USC) - TACKLE - 1971-74 DENVER BRONCOS (AFC)
MONTGOMERY, RALPH (CENTRE) - TACKLE - 1923 CHICAGO CARDINALS; 1927
    FRANKFORD YELLOWJACKETS
MONTGOMERY, RANDY (WEBER STATE) - BACK - 1971-73 DENVER BRONCOS
    (AFC); 1974 CHICAGO BEARS (NFC)
MONTGOMERY, ROSS (TCU) - BACK - 1969 CHICAGO BEARS; 1970 CHICAGO
    BEARS (NFC)
MONTGOMERY, WILLIAM (ST. LOUIS UNIV.) - TACKLE - 1934 ST. LOUIS
    GUNNERS
MONTGOMERY, WILLIAM (LSU) - BACK - 1946 CHICAGO CARDINALS
MONTLER, MICHAEL (COLORADO) - TACKLE,GUARD,CENTER - 1969 BOSTON
    PATRIOTS (AFL); 1970 BOSTON PATRIOTS (AFC); 1971-72 NEW ENGLAND
    PATRIOTS (AFC); 1973-74 BUFFALO BILLS (AFC)
MOODY, WILKIE (DENISON) - BACK - 1920 COLUMBUS PANHANDLES; 1924-25
    COLUMBUS TIGERS
MOOERS, DOUGLAS (WHITTIER) - END, TACKLE - 1971-72 NEW ORLEANS SAINTS
    (NFC)
MOONEY, BOW TIPP (ABILENE CHRISTIAN) - BACK - 1944-45 CHICAGO BEARS
MOONEY, EDWARD (TEXAS TECH) - LB - 1968-69 DETROIT LIONS; 1970-71
    DETROIT LIONS (NFC); 1973 BALTIMORE COLTS (AFC)
MOONEY, GEORGE - BACK - 1922-24 MILWAUKEE BADGERS
MOONEY, JAMES (GEORGETOWN) - END - 1930 NEWARK TORNADOS; 1930-31
    BROOKLYN DODGERS; 1933-34 CINCINNATI REDS; 1935 CHICAGO
    CARDINALS; 1935 CHICAGO BEARS; 1936-37 NEW YORK YANKS (AFL)
MOONEY, TEX (WEST TEXAS STATE) - TACKLE - 1942 CLEVELAND RAMS; 1943
    BROOKLYN DODGERS; (REAL NAME O. T. SCHUPBACH)
MOORE, ALEXANDER (NORFOLK STATE) - BACK - 1968 DENVER BRONCOS (AFL)
MOORE, ALLEN (NORTHWESTERN) - BACK - 1932 CHICAGO BEARS
MOORE, ALLEN (TEXAS A&M) - END - 1939 GREEN BAY PACKERS
MOORE, ARTHUR (TULSA) - TACKLE - 1973-74 NEW ENGLAND PATRIOTS (AFC)
MOORE, CHARLES (ARKANSAS) - GUARD - 1962 WASHINGTON REDSKINS
MOORE, CLIFFORD (PENN STATE) - BACK - 1934 CINCINNATI REDS
MOORE, DERLAND (OKLAHOMA) - TACKLE - 1973-74 NEW ORLEANS SAINTS (NFC)
MOORE, EUGENE (COLORADO) - CENTER - 1938 BROOKLYN DODGERS
MOORE, EUGENE (OCCIDENTAL) - BACK - 1969 SAN FRANCISCO 49ERS

MOORE, EZEKIEL (LINCOLN) - BACK - 1967-69 HOUSTON OILERS (AFL);
    1970-74 HOUSTON OILERS (AFC)
MOORE, FREDERICK (MEMPHIS STATE) - TACKLE - 1964-66 SAN DIEGO
    CHARGERS (AFL)
MOORE, HENRY (ARKANSAS) - BACK - 1956 NEW YORK GIANTS; 1957 BALTIMORE
    COLTS
MOORE, JAMES DENIS (USC) - TACKLE, END - 1967-69 DETROIT LIONS
MOORE, JERRY (ARKANSAS) - BACK - 1971-72 CHICAGO BEARS (NFC); 1973-74
    NEW ORLEANS SAINTS (NFC)
MOORE, JOSEPH (MISSOURI) - BACK - 1971, 73 CHICAGO BEARS (NFC)
MOORE, KENNETH (WEST VIRGINIA WESLEYAN) - GUARD - 1940 NEW YORK GIANTS
MOORE, LEONARD (PENN STATE) - BACK - 1956-67 BALTIMORE COLTS; 1964
    SCORING LEADER; 1975 HALL OF FAME
MOORE, LEROY (FORT VALLEY STATE) - END - 1960, 62-63 BUFFALO BILLS
    (AFL); 1961-62 BOSTON PATRIOTS (AFL); 1964-65 DENVER BRONCOS
    (AFL)
MOORE, MANFRED (USC) - BACK - 1974 SAN FRANCISCO 49ERS (NFC)
MOORE, MAULTY (BETHUNE-COCKMAN) - TACKLE - 1972-74 MIAMI DOLPHINS
    (AFC)
MOORE, MC NEIL (SAM HOUSTON) - BACK - 1954, 56-57 CHICAGO BEARS
MOORE, NATHANIEL (FLORIDA) - END - 1974 MIAMI DOLPHINS (AFC)
MOORE, PAUL (PRESBYTERIAN) - BACK - 1940-41 DETROIT LIONS
MOORE, REYNAUD (UCLA) - BACK - 1971 NEW ORLEANS SAINTS (NFC)
MOORE, RICHARD (VILLANOVA) - TACKLE - 1969 GREEN BAY PACKERS; 1970
    GREEN BAY PACKERS (NFC)
MOORE, ROBERT (STANFORD) - END - 1971-74 OAKLAND RAIDERS (AFC)
MOORE, ROBERT EARL - (NAME CHANGED TO AHMAD RASHAD)
MOORE, SOLOMON WAYNE (LAMAR TECH) - TACKLE - 1970-74 MIAMI DOLPHINS
    (AFC)
MOORE, THOMAS (VANDERBILT) - BACK - 1960-65 GREEN BAY PACKERS; 1966
    LOS ANGELES RAMS; 1967 ATLANTA FALCONS
MOORE, WALTER (LAFAYETTE) - BACK - 1927 POTTSVILLE MAROONS
MOORE, WILBUR (MINNESOTA) - BACK - 1939-46 WASHINGTON REDSKINS
MOORE, WILLIAM (LOYOLA OF NEW ORLEANS) - BACK - 1932 CHICAGO
    CARDINALS; 1933 PITTSBURGH PIRATES
MOORE, WILLIAM (NORTH CAROLINA) - END - 1937 LOS ANGELES BULLDOGS
    (AFL); 1939 DETROIT LIONS
MOORE, WILLIAM (PENN STATE) - GUARD - 1947-49 PITTSBURGH STEELERS
MOORING, JOHN (TAMPA) - TACKLE, GUARD, CENTER - 1971-73 NEW YORK JETS
    (AFC); 1974 NEW ORLEANS SAINTS (NFC)
MOORMAN, MAURICE "MO" (TEXAS A&M) - GUARD - 1968-69 KANSAS CITY
    CHIEFS (AFL); 1970-73 KANSAS CITY CHIEFS (AFC)
MOOTY, JAMES (ARKANSAS) - BACK - 1960 DALLAS COWBOYS
MORABITO, DANIEL (MICHIGAN STATE) - TACKLE - 1941 BUFFALO TIGERS (AFL)
MORALES, GONZALES (ST. MARY'S OF CAL.) - BACK - 1947-48 PITTSBURGH
    STEELERS
MORAN, ARTHUR (MARQUETTE) - TACKLE - 1926 MILWAUKEE BADGERS
MORAN, FRANCIS (CARNEGIE TECH & GRINNELL) - BACK - 1925-27 FRANKFORD
    YELLOWJACKETS; 1927 CHICAGO CARDINALS; 1928 POTTSVILLE MAROONS;
    1928-33 NEW YORK GIANTS
MORAN, FRANK - GUARD - 1920 AKRON PROS
MORAN, JAMES (HOLY CROSS) - GUARD - 1935-36 BOSTON REDSKINS
MORAN, JAMES (IDAHO) - TACKLE - 1964, 66-67 NEW YORK GIANTS
MORAN, THOMAS (CENTRE) - BACK - 1925 NEW YORK GIANTS
MORANDOS, ANTHONY (HOLY CROSS) - CENTER - 1936-37 BOSTON SHAMROCKS
    (AFL)
MOREAU, DOUGLAS (LSU) - END, KICKER - 1966-69 MIAMI DOLPHINS (AFL)
MORELLI, FRANCIS (COLGATE) - TACKLE - 1962 NEW YORK TITANS (AFL)
MORELLI, JOHN (GEORGETOWN) - GUARD - 1944-45 BOSTON YANKS
MORGAN, BOYD (USC) - BACK - 1939-40 WASHINGTON REDSKINS
MORGAN, DENNIS (WESTERN ILLINOIS) - BACK - 1974 DALLAS COWBOYS (NFC)
MORGAN, JOSEPH (MISSISSIPPI SOUTHERN) - TACKLE - 1949 SAN FRANCISCO
    49ERS (AAFC)
MORGAN, MICHAEL (LSU) - LB - 1964-67 PHILADELPHIA EAGLES; 1968
    WASHINGTON REDSKINS; 1969 NEW ORLEANS SAINTS; 1970 NEW ORLEANS
    SAINTS (NFC)
MORGAN, ROBERT (MARYLAND) - TACKLE - 1954 CHICAGO CARDINALS; 1954
    WASHINGTON REDSKINS
MORGAN, ROBERT (NEW MEXICO) - BACK - 1967 PITTSBURGH STEELERS
MORGAN, WILLIAM (OREGON) - TACKLE - 1933-36 NEW YORK GIANTS

MORIN, MILTON (MASSACHUSETTS) - END - 1966-69 CLEVELAND BROWNS;
    1970-74 CLEVELAND BROWNS (AFC)
MORLEY, SAMUEL (STANFORD) - END - 1954 WASHINGTON REDSKINS
MORLOCK, JOHN (MARSHALL) - BACK - 1940 DETROIT LIONS
MORRALL, EARL (MICHIGAN STATE) - QBACK - 1956 SAN FRANCISCO 49ERS;
    1957-58 PITTSBURGH STEELERS; 1958-64 DETROIT LIONS; 1965-67 NEW
    YORK GIANTS; 1968-69 BALTIMORE COLTS; 1970-71 BALTIMORE COLTS
    (AFC); 1972-74 MIAMI DOLPHINS (AFC); 1968 PASSING LEADER; 1972
    PASSING LEADER (AFC)
MORRIS, CHRISTOPHER (INDIANA) - TACKLE - 1972-73 CLEVELAND BROWNS
    (AFC)
MORRIS, DENNIT (OKLAHOMA) - LB - 1958 SAN FRANCISCO 49ERS; 1960-61
    HOUSTON OILERS (AFL)
MORRIS, DONNIE JOE (NORTH TEXAS STATE) - BACK - 1974 KANSAS CITY
    CHIEFS (AFC)
MORRIS, EUGENE "MERCURY" (WEST TEXAS STATE) - BACK - 1969 MIAMI
    DOLPHINS (AFL); 1970-74 MIAMI DOLPHINS (AFC)
MORRIS, FRANCIS (BOSTON UNIV.) - BACK - 1942 CHICAGO BEARS
MORRIS, GEORGE (BALDWIN-WALLACE) - BACK - 1941-42 CLEVELAND RAMS
MORRIS, GEORGE (GEORGIA TECH) - CENTER - 1956 SAN FRANCISCO 49ERS
MORRIS, GLEN (COLORADO A&M) - END - 1940 DETROIT LIONS
MORRIS, HERMAN (MURRAY STATE) - GUARD - 1941 CINCINNATI BENGALS (AFL)
MORRIS, JOHN (OREGON) - BACK - 1958-60 LOS ANGELES RAMS; 1960
    PITTSBURGH STEELERS; 1961 MINNESOTA VIKINGS
MORRIS, JOHN (SANTA BARBARA) - BACK - 1958-67 CHICAGO BEARS; 1964
    PASS RECEIVING LEADER
MORRIS, JON (HOLY CROSS) - CENTER - 1964-69 BOSTON PATRIOTS (AFL);
    1970 BOSTON PATRIOTS (AFC); 1971-74 NEW ENGLAND PATRIOTS (AFC)
MORRIS, LAWRENCE (GEORGIA TECH) - LB - 1955-57 LOS ANGELES RAMS;
    1959-65 CHICAGO BEARS; 1966 ATLANTA FALCONS
MORRIS, NICHOLAS (HOLY CROSS) - BACK - 1936-37 BOSTON SHAMROCKS (AFL)
MORRIS, RILEY (FLORIDA A&M) - LB - 1960-62 OAKLAND RAIDERS (AFL)
MORRIS, ROBERT (CORNELL) - GUARD - 1926 BROOKLYN LIONS
MORRISON, CHARLES - END - 1926 BOSTON BULLDOGS (AFL)
MORRISON, CLARENCE (OKLAHOMA) - BACK - 1926 LOS ANGELES WILDCATS (AFL)
MORRISON, DENNIS (KANSAS STATE) - QBACK - 1974 SAN FRANCISCO 49ERS
    (NFC)
MORRISON, DONALD (TEXAS-ARLINGTON) - TACKLE - 1971-74 NEW ORLEANS
    SAINTS (NFC)
MORRISON, EDWARD (WEST VIRGINIA) - BACK - 1927 FRANKFORD YELLOWJACKETS
MORRISON, FRED (OHIO STATE) - BACK - 1950-53 CHICAGO BEARS; 1954-56
    CLEVELAND BROWNS; 1950 PUNTING LEADER
MORRISON, JESSE (CALIFORNIA) - BACK - 1926 LOS ANGELES WILDCATS (AFL)
MORRISON, JOSEPH (CINCINNATI) - BACK, END - 1959-69 NEW YORK GIANTS;
    1970-72 NEW YORK GIANTS (NFC)
MORRISON, MAYNARD (MICHIGAN) - CENTER - 1933-34 BROOKLYN DODGERS
MORRISON, REECE (SOUTHWEST TEXAS STATE) - BACK - 1968-69 CLEVELAND
    BROWNS; 1970-72 CLEVELAND BROWNS (AFC); 1972-73 CINCINNATI
    BENGALS (AFC)
MORRISON - BACK - 1921 EVANSVILLE CRIMSON GIANTS
MORRISS, GUY (TCU) - CENTER, GUARD - 1973-74 PHILADELPHIA EAGLES (NFC)
MORRISSEY, FRANK (BOSTON COLLEGE) - TACKLE - 1921 ROCHESTER
    JEFFERSONS; 1922-23 BUFFALO ALL-AMERICANS; 1924 BUFFALO BISONS;
    1924 MILWAUKEE BADGERS
MORROW, JAMES (PITTSBURGH) - BACK - 1921 CANTON BULLDOGS; 1922
    BUFFALO ALL-AMERICANS
MORROW, JOHN (KEARNEY STATE-NEBRASKA) - GUARD - 1937-38 CHICAGO
    CARDINALS
MORROW, ROBERT (ILLINOIS WESLEYAN) - BACK - 1941-43 CHICAGO
    CARDINALS; 1945 NEW YORK GIANTS; 1946 NEW YORK YANKEES (AAFC)
MORROW, RUSSELL (TENNESSEE) - CENTER - 1946-47 BROOKLYN DODGERS (AAFC)
MORROW, THOMAS (MISSISSIPPI SOUTHERN) - BACK - 1962-64 OAKLAND
    RAIDERS (AFL)
MORSE, RAYMOND (OREGON) - END - 1935-38, 40 DETROIT LIONS
MORSE, W. "RED" - GUARD - 1923 DULUTH KELLEYS
MORTELL, EMMETT (WISCONSIN) - QBACK - 1937-39 PHILADELPHIA EAGLES
MORTON, CRAIG (CALIFORNIA) - QBACK - 1965-69 DALLAS COWBOYS; 1970-74
    DALLAS COWBOYS (NFC); 1974 NEW YORK GIANTS (NFC)
MORTON, JOHN (TCU) - BACK - 1953 SAN FRANCISCO 49ERS

MORTON, JOHN (MISSOURI & PURDUE) - END - 1945 CHICAGO BEARS; 1946 LOS
    ANGELES DONS (AAFC); 1947 BUFFALO BILLS (AAFC)
MORZE, FRANK (BOSTON COLLEGE) - CENTER - 1957-61, 64 SAN FRANCISCO
    49ERS; 1962-63 CLEVELAND BROWNS
MOSCRIP, JAMES (STANFORD) - END - 1938-39 DETROIT LIONS
MOSELEY, MARK (S.F.AUSTIN) - KICKER - 1970 PHILADELPHIA EAGLES (NFC);
    1971-72 HOUSTON OILERS (AFC); 1974 WASHINGTON REDSKINS (NFC)
MOSELLE, DONALD (SUPERIOR STATE-WISCONSIN) - BACK - 1950 CLEVELAND
    BROWNS; 1951-52 GREEN BAY PACKERS; 1954 PHILADELPHIA EAGLES
MOSER, ROBERT (PACIFIC) - CENTER - 1951-53 CHICAGO BEARS
MOSER, TED - GUARD - 1921 LOUISVILLE BRECKS
MOSES, DONALD (USC) - BACK - 1933 CINCINNATI REDS
MOSES, HAVEN (SAN DIEGO STATE) - END - 1968-69 BUFFALO BILLS (AFL);
    1970-72 BUFFALO BILLS (AFC); 1972-74 DENVER BRONCOS (AFC)
MOSHER, CLURE (LOUISVILLE) - CENTER - 1942 PITTSBURGH STEELERS
MOSIER, JOHN (KANSAS) - END - 1971 DENVER BRONCOS (AFC); 1972
    BALTIMORE COLTS (AFC); 1973 NEW ENGLAND PATRIOTS (AFC)
MOSLEY, HENRY (MORRIS-BROWN) - BACK - 1955 CHICAGO BEARS
MOSLEY, NORMAN (ALABAMA) - BACK - 1948 PITTSBURGH STEELERS
MOSLEY, RUSSELL (ALABAMA) - BACK - 1945-46 GREEN BAY PACKERS
MOSLEY, WAYNE (ALABAMA A&M) - BACK - 1974 BUFFALO BILLS (AFC)
MOSS, EDWARD (SOUTHEAST MISSOURI STATE) - BACK - 1973-74 ST. LOUIS
    CARDINALS (NFC)
MOSS, JOSEPH (MARYLAND) - TACKLE - 1952 WASHINGTON REDSKINS
MOSS, PAUL (PURDUE) - END - 1933 PITTSBURGH PIRATES; 1934 ST. LOUIS
    GUNNERS
MOSS, PERRY (ILLINOIS) - QBACK - 1948 GREEN BAY PACKERS
MOSS, ROLAND (TOLEDO) - END, BACK - 1969 BALTIMORE COLTS; 1970 SAN
    DIEGO CHARGERS (AFC); 1970 BUFFALO BILLS (AFC); 1971 NEW ENGLAND
    PATRIOTS (AFC)
MOSTARDI, RICHARD (KENT STATE) - BACK - 1960 CLEVELAND BROWNS; 1961
    MINNESOTA VIKINGS; 1962 OAKLAND RAIDERS (AFL)
MOTE, KELLY (DUKE) - END - 1947-49 DETROIT LIONS; 1950-52 NEW YORK
    GIANTS
MOTEN, ROBERT (BISHOP) - END - 1968 DENVER BRONCOS (AFL)
MOTL, ROBERT (NORTHWESTERN) - END - 1946 CHICAGO ROCKETS (AAFC)
MOTLEY, MARION (NEVADA) - BACK - 1946-49 CLEVELAND BROWNS (AAFC);
    1950-53 CLEVELAND BROWNS; 1955 PITTSBURGH STEELERS; 1950 RUSHING
    LEADER; 1968 HALL OF FAME
MOTT, NORMAN (GEORGIA) - BACK - 1933 GREEN BAY PACKERS; 1934,
    CINCINNATI REDS; 1934 PITTSBURGH PIRATES
MOYNIHAN, RICHARD (VILLANOVA) - BACK - 1927 FRANKFORD YELLOWJACKETS
MOYNIHAN, TIMOTHY (NOTRE DAME) - CENTER - 1932-33 CHICAGO CARDINALS
MRKONIC, GEORGE (KANSAS) - GUARD - 1953 PHILADELPHIA EAGLES
MUCHA, RUDOLPH (WASHINGTON) - BACK - 1941, 45 CLEVELAND RAMS; 1945-46
    CHICAGO BEARS
MUDD, HOWARD (HILLSDALE) - GUARD - 1964-69 SAN FRANCISCO 49ERS; 1969
    CHICAGO BEARS; 1970 CHICAGO BEARS (NFC)
MUEHLHEUSER, FRANK (COLGATE) - BACK - 1948 BOSTON YANKS; 1949 NEW
    YORK BULLDOGS
MUELHAUPT, EDWARD (IOWA STATE) - GUARD - 1960-61 BUFFALO BILLS (AFL)
MUEILNER, WILLIAM (DEPAUL) - END - 1937 CHICAGO CARDINALS; 1937 LOS
    ANGELES BULLDOGS (AFL); 1937 NEW YORK YANKS (AFL); 1937
    CINCINNATI BENGALS (AFL)
MUGG, GARVIN (NORTH TEXAS STATE) - TACKLE - 1945 DETROIT LIONS
MUHA, JOSEPH (VMI) - BACK - 1946-50 PHILADELPHIA EAGLES; 1948 PUNTING
    LEADER
MUHLMANN, HORST - KICKER - 1969 CINCINNATI BENGALS (AFL); 1970-74
    CINCINNATI BENGALS (AFC)
MUIRHEAD, STANLEY (MICHIGAN) - GUARD - 1924 DAYTON TRIANGLES; 1924
    CLEVELAND BULLDOGS
MULBARGER, JOSEPH (BROADDUS) - TACKLE - 1919-22 COLUMBUS PANHANDLES;
    1923-26 COLUMBUS TIGERS
MULDOON, MATTHEW (ST. MARY'S OF CAL.) - TACKLE - 1922 ROCHESTER
    JEFFERSONS
MUL-KEY, HERBERT - BACK - 1972-74 WASHINGTON REDSKINS (NFC)
MULLEN, THOMAS (SOUTHEAST MISSOURI STATE) - GUARD - 1974 NEW YORK
    GIANTS (NFC)

MULLEN, VERNE (ILLINOIS) - END - 1922 EVANSVILLE CRIMSON GIANTS; 1923
    CANTON BULLDOGS; 1924-26 CHICAGO BEARS; 1927 CHICAGO CARDINALS;
    1927-28 POTTSVILLE MAROONS
MULLENEAUX, CARL (UTAH STATE) - END - 1938-41, 45-46 GREEN BAY PACKERS
MULLENEAUX, LEE (ARIZONA) - CENTER - 1932 NEW YORK GIANTS; 1933-34
    CINCINNATI REDS; 1934 ST. LOUIS GUNNERS; 1935-36 PITTSBURGH
    PIRATES; 1937 CINCINNATI BENGALS (AFL); 1938 GREEN BAY PACKERS;
    1938 CHICAGO CARDINALS; 1940-41 COLUMBUS BULLIES (AFL)
MULLER, HAROLD (CALIFORNIA) - END - 1926 LOS ANGELES BUCCANEERS
MULLIGAN, GEORGE (CATHOLIC) - END - 1936 PHILADELPHIA EAGLES; 1936
    BOSTON SHAMROCKS (AFL)
MULLIGAN, WAYNE (CLEMSON) - CENTER - 1969 ST. LOUIS CARDINALS;
    1970-73 ST. LOUIS CARDINALS (NFC); 1974 NEW YORK JETS (AFC)
MULLIN - BACK - 1940 BUFFALO INDIANS (AFL)
MULLINS, DON RAY (HOUSTON) - BACK - 1961-62 CHICAGO BEARS
MULLINS, GERRY (USC) - GUARD, TACKLE, END - 1971-74 PITTSBURGH
    STEELERS (AFC)
MULLINS, NOAH (KENTUCKY) - BACK - 1946-48 CHICAGO BEARS; 1949 NEW
    YORK GIANTS
MULREADY, GERALD (NORTH DAKOTA STATE) - END - 1947 CHICAGO ROCKETS
    (AAFC)
MULVEY, VINCENT (SYRACUSE) - BACK - 1923 BUFFALO ALL-AMERICANS
MUMGAVIN (WISCONSIN) - TACKLE - 1920 CHICAGO TIGERS
MUMLEY, NICHOLAS (PURDUE) - END - 1960-62 NEW YORK TITANS (AFL)
MUMPHORD, LLOYD (TEXAS SOUTHERN) - BACK - 1969 MIAMI DOLPHINS (AFL);
    1970-74 MIAMI DOLPHINS (AFC)
MUNDAY, GEORGE (EMPORIA STATE) - TACKLE - 1931 CLEVELAND INDIANS;
    1931-32 NEW YORK GIANTS; 1933-34 CINCINNATI REDS; 1934 ST. LOUIS
    GUNNERS; 1936 BROOKLYN TIGERS (AFL)
MUNDEE, FREDERICK (NOTRE DAME) - CENTER - 1943-45 CHICAGO BEARS
MUNN, LYLE (KANSAS STATE) - END - 1925-26 KANSAS CITY COWBOYS; 1927
    CLEVELAND BULLDOGS; 1928 DETROIT WOLVERINES; 1929 NEW YORK GIANTS
MUNNS, GEORGE (MIAMI-OHIO) - BACK - 1919 AKRON PROS; 1921 CINCINNATI
    CELTS
MUNSEY, NELSON (WYOMING) - BACK - 1972-74 BALTIMORE COLTS (AFC)
MUNSON, WILLIAM (UTAH STATE) - QBACK - 1964-67 LOS ANGELES RAMS;
    1968-69 DETROIT LIONS; 1970-74 DETROIT LIONS (NFC)
MUNSON - BACK - 1919 WHEELING
MURAKOWSKI, ARTHUR (NORTHWESTERN) - BACK - 1951 DETROIT LIONS
MURCHISON, OLA LEE (PACIFIC) - END - 1961 DALLAS COWBOYS
MURDOCK, GUY (MICHIGAN) - CENTER - 1972 HOUSTON OILERS (AFC)
MURDOCK, JESSE (CALIFORNIA WESTERN) - BACK - 1963 OAKLAND RAIDERS
    (AFL); 1963 BUFFALO BILLS (AFL)
MURDOCK, LESTER (FLORIDA STATE) - KICKER - 1967 NEW YORK GIANTS
MURLEY, RICHARD (PURDUE) - TACKLE - 1956 PITTSBURGH STEELERS; 1956
    PHILADELPHIA EAGLES
MURPHY, DENNIS (FLORIDA) - TACKLE - 1965 CHICAGO BEARS
MURPHY, FREDERICK (GEORGIA TECH) - END - 1960 CLEVELAND BROWNS; 1961
    MINNESOTA VIKINGS
MURPHY, GEORGE (USC) - BACK - 1949 LOS ANGELES DONS (AAFC)
MURPHY, HARVEY (MISSISSIPPI) - END - 1940 CLEVELAND RAMS
MURPHY, JAMES (ST. THOMAS OF MINNESOTA) - BACK - 1926 RACINE LEGION;
    1928 CHICAGO CARDINALS
MURPHY, JOSEPH (DARTMOUTH) - GUARD - 1919 CLEVELAND INDIANS; 1921
    CLEVELAND INDIANS
MURPHY, PHILIP (MARQUETTE) - CENTER - 1926 DULUTH ESKIMOS
MURPHY, THOMAS (ARKANSAS) - BACK - 1934 CHICAGO CARDINALS
MURPHY, THOMAS (ST. MARY'S OF KANSAS) - BACK - 1926 KANSAS CITY
    COWBOYS; 1926 COLUMBUS TIGERS
MURPHY, THOMAS (SUPERIOR STATE-WISCONSIN) - BACK - 1926 MILWAUKEE
    BADGERS
MURPHY, WILLIAM (BOSTON UNIV.) - END - 1926 BOSTON BULLDOGS (AFL)
MURPHY, WILLIAM (CORNELL) - END - 1968 BOSTON PATRIOTS (AFL)
MURPHY, WILLIAM (WASHINGTON-MISSOURI) - GUARD - 1940-41 CHICAGO
    CARDINALS
MURPHY - BACK - 1922 HAMMOND PROS
MURRAH, WILLIAM (TEXAS A&M) - TACKLE - 1922 CANTON BULLDOGS; 1923 ST.
    LOUIS BROWNS
MURRAY, EARL (PURDUE) - GUARD - 1950 BALTIMORE COLTS; 1951 NEW YORK
    GIANTS; 1952 PITTSBURGH STEELERS
MURRAY, FRANCIS (PENNSYLVANIA) - BACK - 1939-40 PHILADELPHIA EAGLES

MURRAY, JOHN (GEORGIA TECH) - CENTER - 1926 NEWARK BEARS (AFL)
MURRAY, JOHN (ST. THOMAS OF MINNESOTA) - END - 1926 DULUTH ESKIMOS
MURRAY, JOSEPH (PORTLAND) - END - 1940 MILWAUKEE CHIEFS (AFL)
MURRAY, RICHARD (MARQUETTE) - TACKLE - 1921-24 GREEN BAY PACKERS;
     1924 CHICAGO BEARS
MURRY, DONALD (WISCONSIN) - TACKLE - 1922-24 RACINE LEGION; 1925-32
     CHICAGO BEARS
MURTAGH, GEORGE (GEORGETOWN) - CENTER - 1926-32 NEW YORK GIANTS
MURTHA, PAUL - BACK - 1921 COLUMBUS PANHANDLES
MUSGROVE, SPAIN (UTAH STATE) - TACKLE - 1967-69 WASHINGTON REDSKINS;
     1970 HOUSTON OILERS (AFC)
MUSICK, JAMES (USC) - BACK - 1932 BOSTON BRAVES; 1933, 35-36 BOSTON
     REDSKINS; 1933 RUSHING LEADER
MUSSO, GEORGE (MILLIKIN) - GUARD - 1933-34 CHICAGO BEARS
MUTRYN, CHESTER (XAVIER) - BACK - 1946 BUFFALO BISONS (AAFC); 1947-49
     BUFFALO BILLS (AAFC); 1950 BALTIMORE COLTS
MUTSCHELLER, JAMES (NOTRE DAME) - END - 1954-61 BALTIMORE COLTS
MYERS, BRADFORD (BUCKNELL) - BACK - 1953, 56 LOS ANGELES RAMS; 1958
     PHILADELPHIA EAGLES
MYERS, CYRIL (OHIO STATE) - END - 1922 TOLEDO MAROONS; 1923 CLEVELAND
     INDIANS; 1925 CLEVELAND BULLDOGS
MYERS, DAVID (NEW YORK UNIV.) - GUARD - 1930 STATEN ISLAND STAPELTONS
MYERS, DENNIS (IOWA) - GUARD - 1931 BROOKLYN DODGERS; 1931 CHICAGO
     BEARS
MYERS, GLENN (SOUTH CAROLINA) - END - 1940 COLUMBUS BULLIES (AFL)
MYERS, JOHN (UCLA) - BACK - 1948-50 PHILADELPHIA EAGLES; 1952 LOS
     ANGELES RAMS
MYERS, PHILIP "CHIP" (NORTHWEST STATE-OKLA.) - END - 1967 SAN
     FRANCISCO 49ERS; 1969 CINCINNATI BENGALS (AFL); 1970-74
     CINCINNATI BENGALS (AFC)
MYERS, ROBERT (OHIO STATE) - TACKLE - 1955 BALTIMORE COLTS
MYERS, THOMAS (FORDHAM) - BACK - 1925 NEW YORK GIANTS; 1926 BROOKLYN
     LIONS
MYERS, THOMAS (NORTHWESTERN) - QBACK - 1965-66 DETROIT LIONS
MYERS, THOMAS (SYRACUSE) - BACK - 1972-74 NEW ORLEANS SAINTS (NFC)
MYHRA, STEVEN (NORTH DAKOTA) - GUARD - 1957-61 BALTIMORE COLTS; 1961
     FIELD GOAL LEADER
MYLES, HARRY (WEST VIRGINIA) - END - 1929 BUFFALO BISONS
MYLES, HENRY (HAMPDEN-SIDNEY) - END - 1930 NEWARK TORNADOS
MYRE, CHARLES (MINNESOTA) - BACK - 1940 MILWAUKEE CHIEFS (AFL)
MYRTLE, CHARLES "CHIP" (MARYLAND) - LB - 1967-69 DENVER BRONCOS
     (AFL); 1970-72 DENVER BRONCOS (AFC); 1974 SAN DIEGO CHARGERS
     (AFC)
NABORS, ROLAND (TEXAS TECH) - CENTER - 1948 NEW YORK YANKEES (AAFC)
NACRELLI, ANDREW (FORDHAM) - END - 1958 PHILADELPHIA EAGLES
NADOLNEY, ROMANUS (NOTRE DAME) - GUARD - 1922 GREEN BAY PACKERS;
     1923-25 MILWAUKEE BADGERS
NAGEL, RAYMOND (UCLA) - BACK - 1953 CHICAGO CARDINALS
NAGEL, ROSS (ST. LOUIS UNIV.) - TACKLE - 1942 CHICAGO CARDINALS; 1951
     NEW YORK YANKS
NAGIDA - BACK - 1926 HAMMOND PROS
NAGLER, GERN (SANTA CLARA) - END - 1953, 55-58 CHICAGO CARDINALS;
     1959 PITTSBURGH STEELERS; 1960-61 CLEVELAND BROWNS
NAGURSKI, BRONISLAW "BRONKO" (MINNESOTA) - BACK - 1930-37, 43 CHICAGO
     CARDINALS; 1963 HALL OF FAME
NAIOTA, JOHN (ST. FRANCIS) - BACK - 1942, 45 PITTSBURGH STEELERS
NAIPPAN, RALPH (TRINITY-TEXAS) - END - 1926 BUFFALO RANGERS
NAPIER, WALTER (PAUL QUINN) - TACKLE - 1960-61 DALLAS TEXANS (AFL)
NAIRN, HARVEY (SOUTHERN) - END - 1968 NEW YORK JETS (AFL)
NAMATH, JOSEPH (ALABAMA) - QBACK - 1965-69 NEW YORK JETS (AFL);
     1970-74 NEW YORK JETS (AFC)
NANCE, JAMES (SYRACUSE) - BACK - 1965-69 BOSTON PATRIOTS (AFL); 1970
     BOSTON PATRIOTS (AFC); 1971 NEW ENGLAND PATRIOTS (AFC); 1973 NEW
     YORK JETS (AFC); 1966-67 RUSHING LEADER (AFL)
NAPONIC, ROBERT (ILLINOIS) - QBACK - 1970 HOUSTON OILERS (AFC)
NARDACCI, NICHOLAS (WEST VIRGINIA) - BACK - 1925 CLEVELAND BULLDOGS
NARDI, RICHARD (OHIO STATE) - BACK - 1938 DETROIT LIONS; 1939
     BROOKLYN DODGERS; 1939 PITTSBURGH STEELERS
NASH, ROBERT (RUTGERS) - TACKLE - 1919 MASSILLON TIGERS; 1920 AKRON
     PROS; 1920-23 BUFFALO ALL-AMERICANS; 1925 NEW YORK GIANTS

NASH, THOMAS (GEORGIA) - END - 1929-32 GREEN BAY PACKERS; 1933-34
     BROOKLYN DODGERS
NASH, THOMAS (BROWN) - END - 1940 BOSTON BEARS (AFL)
NASON, EDWARD - BACK - 1922 OORANG INDIANS
NATOWICH, ANDREW (HOLY CROSS) - BACK - 1944 WASHINGTON REDSKINS
NAUGHTON, CLEMENT (DEPAUL) - END - 1941 BUFFALO TIGERS (AFL)
NAUMETZ, FREDERICK (BOSTON COLLEGE) - CENTER - 1946-50 LOS ANGELES
     RAMS
NAUMOFF, PAUL (TENNESSEE) - LB - 1967-69 DETROIT LIONS; 1970-74
     DETROIT LIONS (NFC)
NAUMU, JOHN (USC) - BACK - 1948 LOS ANGELES DONS (AAFC)
NEACY, CLEMENT (COLGATE) - END - 1924-26 MILWAUKEE BADGERS; 1927
     DULUTH ESKIMOS; 1927 CHICAGO BEARS; 1928 CHICAGO CARDINALS
NEAL, LOUIS (PRAIRIE VIEW) - END - 1973-74 ATLANTA FALCONS (NFC)
NEAL, RICHARD (SOUTHERN) - END, TACKLE - 1969 NEW ORLEANS SAINTS;
     1970-72 NEW ORLEANS SAINTS (NFC); 1973-74 NEW YORK JETS (AFC)
NEAL, ROBERT (WASHINGTON&JEFFERSON) - GUARD - 1922 AKRON PROS;
     1924-26 HAMMOND PROS
NEAL, THOMAS DANIEL (KENTUCKY) - CENTER - 1973-74 BALTIMORE COLTS
     (AFC)
NEAL, WILLIAM "ED" (TULANE & LSU) - TACKLE - 1945-51 GREEN BAY
     PACKERS; 1951 CHICAGO BEARS
NECK, THOMAS (LSU) - BACK - 1962 CHICAGO BEARS
NEELY, RALPH (OKLAHOMA) - TACKLE, GUARD - 1965-69 DALLAS COWBOYS;
     1970-74 DALLAS COWBOYS (NFC)
NEFF, ROBERT (S.F.AUSTIN) - BACK - 1966-68 MIAMI DOLPHINS (AFL)
NEGRI, WARREN (VIRGINIA TECH) - GUARD - 1940 BOSTON BEARS (AFL); 1941
     NEW YORK AMERICANS (AFL)
NEGUS, FREDERICK (WISCONSIN) - CENTER - 1947-48 CHICAGO ROCKETS
     (AAFC); 1949 CHICAGO HORNETS (AAFC); 1950 CHICAGO BEARS
NEIDERT, JOHN (LOUISVILLE) - LB - 1968 CINCINNATI BENGALS (AFL);
     1968-69 NEW YORK JETS (AFL); 1970 CHICAGO BEARS (NFC)
NEIGHBORS, WILLIAM (ALABAMA) - GUARD - 1962-65 BOSTON PATRIOTS (AFL);
     1966-69 MIAMI DOLPHINS (AFL)
NEIHAUS, FRANCIS (WASHINGTON&JEFFERSON) - BACK - 1925 AKRON PROS;
     1926 POTTSVILLE MAROONS
NEIHAUS, RALPH (DAYTON) - TACKLE - 1939 CLEVELAND RAMS; 1940-41
     COLUMBUS BULLIES (AFL)
NEILL, JAMES (TEXAS TECH) - BACK - 1937 NEW YORK GIANTS; 1939 CHICAGO
     CARDINALS
NEILS, STEVEN (MINNESOTA) - LB - 1974 ST. LOUIS CARDINALS (NFC)
NEITSKI - BACK - 1919 TOLEDO MAROONS
NELSEN, WILLIAM (USC) - QBACK - 1963-67 PITTSBURGH STEELERS; 1968-69
     CLEVELAND BROWNS; 1970-72 CLEVELAND BROWNS (AFC)
NELSON, ALBERT (CINCINNATI) - BACK - 1965-69 PHILADELPHIA EAGLES;
     1970-73 PHILADELPHIA EAGLES (NFC)
NELSON, ANDREW (MEMPHIS STATE) - BACK - 1957-63 BALTIMORE COLTS; 1964
     NEW YORK GIANTS
NELSON, BENJAMIN (ALABAMA) - BACK - 1964 HOUSTON OILERS (AFL)
NELSON, DENNIS (ILLINOIS STATE) - TACKLE - 1970-74 BALTIMORE COLTS
     (AFC)
NELSON, DONALD (OHIO WESLEYAN) - CENTER - 1926 CANTON BULLDOGS
NELSON, DONALD (IOWA) - GUARD - 1937 BROOKLYN DODGERS
NELSON, EVERETT (ILLINOIS) - TACKLE - 1929 CHICAGO BEARS
NELSON, FRANK (UTAH) - BACK - 1948 BOSTON YANKS; 1949 NEW YORK
     BULLDOGS
NELSON, HERBERT (PENNSYLVANIA) - END - 1946 BUFFALO BISONS (AAFC);
     1947-48 BROOKLYN DODGERS (AAFC)
NELSON, JAMES (ALABAMA) - BACK - 1946 MIAMI SEAHAWKS (AAFC)
NELSON, REED (BRIGHAM YOUNG) - CENTER - 1947 DETROIT LIONS
NELSON, ROBERT (BAYLOR) - CENTER - 1941, 45 DETROIT LIONS; 1946-49
     LOS ANGELES DONS (AAFC); 1950 BALTIMORE COLTS
NELSON, STEVEN (NORTH DAKOTA STATE) - LB - 1974 NEW ENGLAND PATRIOTS
     (AFC)
NELSON, TERRY (ARKANSAS AM&N) - END - 1973-74 LOS ANGELES RAMS (NFC)
NELSON, WILLIAM (OREGON STATE) - TACKLE - 1971-74 LOS ANGELES RAMS
     (NFC)
MEMECEK, ANDREW (OHIO STATE) - GUARD - 1923-25 COLUMBUS TIGERS
NEMECEK, JERALD (NEW YORK UNIV.) - END - 1931 BROOKLYN DODGERS

NEMETH, STEPHEN (NOTRE DAME) - QBACK - 1945 CLEVELAND RAMS; 1946
        CHICAGO ROCKETS (AAFC); 1947 BALTIMORE COLTS (AAFC)
NEMZEK, TED (MOOREHEAD STATE-MINNESOTA) - GUARD - 1930 MINNEAPOLIS
        REDJACKETS
NERY, CARL (DUQUESNE) - GUARD - 1940-41 PITTSBURGH STEELERS
NERY, RONALD (KANSAS STATE) - END - 1960 LOS ANGELES CHARGERS (AFL);
        1961-62 SAN DIEGO CHARGERS (AFL); 1963 DENVER BRONCOS (AFL);
        1963 HOUSTON OILERS (AFL)
NESBITT, RICHARD (DRAKE) - BACK - 1930-33 CHICAGO BEARS; 1933 CHICAGO
        CARDINALS; 1934 BROOKLYN DODGERS
NESMITH, ORLANDO (KANSAS) - QBACK - 1936-37 NEW YORK YANKS (AFL);
        1940 BUFFALO INDIANS (AFL)
NESS, VAL - GUARD - 1922 MINNEAPOLIS MARINES
NESSER, ALFRED - GUARD - 1919-26 AKRON PROS; 1925 CLEVELAND BULLDOGS;
        1926 CLEVELAND PANTHERS (AFL); 1926-28 NEW YORK GIANTS; 1931
        CLEVELAND INDIANS
NESSER, FRANK - BACK - 1920-22 COLUMBUS PANHANDLES; 1925-26 COLUMBUS
        TIGERS
NESSER, FRED - GUARD - 1919-22 COLUMBUS PANHANDLES
NESSER, JOHN - BACK - 1919-21 COLUMBUS PANHANDLES
NESSER, PHILIP - GUARD - 1919-21 COLUMBUS PANHANDLES
NESSER, THEODORE - CENTER - 1919-21 COLUMBUS PANHANDLES
NETHERTON, WILLIAM - END - 1921-22 LOUISVILLE BRECKS
NETTLES, GORDON DOUGLAS (VANDERBILT) - BACK - 1974 BALTIMORE COLTS
        (AFC)
NETTLES, JAMES (WISCONSIN) - BACK - 1965-68 PHILADELPHIA EAGLES; 1969
        LOS ANGELES RAMS; 1970-72 LOS ANGELES RAMS (NFC)
NEUMAN, ROBERT (ILLINOIS WESLEYAN) - END - 1934-36 CHICAGO CARDINALS
NEUMANN, THOMAS (NORTHERN MICHIGAN) - BACK - 1960 BOSTON PATRIOTS
        (AFL)
NEVERS, ERNEST (STANFORD) - BACK - 1926-27 DULUTH ESKIMOS; 1929-31
        CHICAGO CARDINALS; 1963 HALL OF FAME
NEVETT, ELIJAH (CLARK COLLEGE-GEORGIA) - BACK - 1967-69 NEW ORLEANS
        SAINTS; 1970 NEW ORLEANS SAINTS (NFC)
NEVILLE, THOMAS (MISSISSIPPI STATE) - TACKLE - 1965-69 BOSTON
        PATRIOTS (AFL); 1970 BOSTON PATRIOTS (AFC); 1971-74 NEW ENGLAND
        PATRIOTS (AFC)
NEWASHE (CARLISLE) - TACKLE - 1922 ORANG INDIANS
NEWELL, STEPHEN (LONG BEACH STATE) - END - 1967 SAN DIEGO CHARGERS
        (AFL)
NEWHOUSE, ROBERT (HOUSTON) - BACK - 1972-74 DALLAS COWBOYS (NFC)
NEWLAND, HOWARD (DETROIT) - TACKLE - 1921 LOUISVILLE BRECKS
NEWLAND, ROBERT (OREGON) - END - 1971-74 NEW ORLEANS SAINTS (NFC)
NEWMAN, EDWARD (DUKE) - GUARD - 1973-74 MIAMI DOLPHINS (AFC)
NEWMAN, HARRY (MICHIGAN) - QBACK - 1933-35 NEW YORK GIANTS; 1936
        BROOKLYN TIGERS (AFL); 1936 NEW YORK YANKS (AFL); 1937 ROCHESTER
        TIGERS (AFL); 1933 PASSING LEADER
NEWMAN, HOWARD (OHIO UNIV.) - TACKLE - 1924 AKRON PROS; 1924
        CLEVELAND BULLDOGS
NEWMAN, OLIN (CARNEGIE TECH) - END - 1925-26 AKRON PROS
NEWMEYER, DONALD (CALIFORNIA) - TACKLE - 1926 LOS ANGELES BUCCANEERS
NEWSOME, WILLIAM (GRAMBLING) - END - 1970-72 BALTIMORE COLTS (AFC);
        1973-74 NEW ORLEANS SAINTS (NFC)
NEWTON, CHARLES (WASHINGTON) - BACK - 1939-40 PHILADELPHIA EAGLES
NEWTON, ROBERT (NEBRASKA) - GUARD, TACKLE - 1971-74 CHICAGO BEARS
        (NFC)
NEWTON, WILLIAM (FLORIDA) - BACK - 1926 NEWARK BEARS (AFL)
NICCOLAI, ARMAND (DUQUESNE) - TACKLE - 1934-38 PITTSBURGH PIRATES;
        1939-42 PITTSBURGH STEELERS; 1935-36 FIELD GOAL LEADER; 1935
        TIED WITH W. SMITH; 1936 TIED WITH MANDERS)
NICELY - TACKLE - 1930 STATEN ISLAND STAPELTONS
NICHELINI, ALLEN JAMES (ST. MARY'S OF CAL.) - BACK - 1935-36 CHICAGO
        CARDINALS; 1937 LOS ANGELES BULLDOGS (AFL)
NICHOLS, ALLEN (TEMPLE) - BACK - 1945 PITTSBURGH STEELERS
NICHOLS, CHARLES - BACK - 1919 TOLEDO MAROONS
NICHOLS, HAMILTON (RICE) - GUARD - 1947-49 CHICAGO CARDINALS; 1951
        GREEN BAY PACKERS
NICHOLS, JOHN (OHIO STATE) - GUARD - 1926 CANTON BULLDOGS
NICHOLS, LEE "MIKE" (ARKANSAS A&M) - CENTER - 1960-61 DENVER BRONCOS
        (AFL)
NICHOLS, RALPH (KANSAS STATE-MANHATTAN) - TACKLE - 1926 HARTFORD BLUES

NICHOLS, BOBBIE (TULSA) - LB - 1970-71 BALTIMORE COLTS (AFC)
NICHOLS, ROBERT (BOSTON UNIV.) - END - 1967-68 BOSTON PATRIOTS (AFL)
NICHOLS, ROBERT GORDON (STANFORD) - TACKLE - 1965 PITTSBURGH
      STEELERS; 1966-67 LOS ANGELES RAMS
NICHOLS, ROBERT (OGLETHORPE) - TACKLE - 1926 BROOKLYN HORSEMEN (AFL)
NICHOLS, SIDNEY (ILLINOIS) - QBACK - 1920-21 ROCK ISLAND INDEPENDENTS
NICHOLSON, JIM (MICHIGAN STATE) - TACKLE - 1974 KANSAS CITY CHIEFS
      (AFC)
NICKEL, ELBERT (CINCINNATI) - END - 1947-57 PITTSBURGH STEELERS
NICKLA, EDWARD (MARYLAND & TENNESSEE) - TACKLE - 1959 CHICAGO BEARS
NICKLAS, PETER (BAYLOR) - TACKLE - 1962 OAKLAND RAIDERS (AFL)
NICKSICH, GEORGE (ST. BONAVENTURE) - GUARD - 1950 PITTSBURGH STEELERS
NIEDZIELA, BRUNO (IOWA) - TACKLE - 1947 CHICAGO ROCKETS (AAFC)
NIELSEN, WALTER (ARIZONA) - BACK - 1940 NEW YORK GIANTS
NIEMANN, WALTER (MICHIGAN) - CENTER - 1922-24 GREEN BAY PACKERS
NIEMI, LAURIE (WASHINGTON STATE) - TACKLE - 1949-53 WASHINGTON
      REDSKINS
NIGHSWANDER, NICK (MOREHEAD STATE) - CENTER - 1974 BUFFALO BILLS (AFC)
NILAND, JOHN (IOWA) - GUARD - 1966-69 DALLAS COWBOYS; 1970-74 DALLAS
      COWBOYS (NFC)
NILES, JERRY (IOWA) - BACK - 1947 NEW YORK GIANTS
NINOWSKI, JAMES (MICHIGAN STATE) - QBACK - 1958-59, 62-66 CLEVELAND
      BROWNS; 1960-61 DETROIT LIONS; 1967-68 WASHINGTON REDSKINS; 1969
      NEW ORLEANS SAINTS
NIPP, MAURICE (LOYOLA OF CAL.) - GUARD - 1952-53, 56 PHILADELPHIA
      EAGLES
NISBET, DAVID (WASHINGTON) - END - 1933 CHICAGO CARDINALS
NISBY, JOHN (PACIFIC) - TACKLE - 1957-61 PITTSBURGH STEELERS; 1962-64
      WASHINGTON REDSKINS
NITSCHKE, RAYMOND (ILLINOIS) - LB - 1958-69 GREEN BAY PACKERS;
      1970-72 GREEN BAY PACKERS (NFC)
NIX, DOYLE (SMU) - BACK - 1955 GREEN BAY PACKERS; 1958-59 WASHINGTON
      REDSKINS; 1960 LOS ANGELES CHARGERS (AFL); 1961 DALLAS TEXANS
      (AFL)
NIX, EMERY (TCU) - BACK - 1943, 46 NEW YORK GIANTS
NIX, GEORGE (HASKELL) - TACKLE - 1926 BUFFALO RANGERS
NIX, JOHN (MISSISSIPPI STATE) - BACK - 1940 CLEVELAND RAMS
NIX, JOHN (USC) - END - 1950 SAN FRANCISCO 49ERS
NIX, KENT (TCU) - QBACK - 1967-69 PITTSBURGH STEELERS; 1970-71
      CHICAGO BEARS (NFC); 1972 HOUSTON OILERS (AFC)
NIXON, MICHAEL (PITTSBURGH) - BACK - 1935 PITTSBURGH PIRATES; 1942
      BROOKLYN DODGERS
NOBILE, LEO (PENN STATE) - GUARD - 1947 WASHINGTON REDSKINS; 1948-49
      PITTSBURGH STEELERS
NOBIS, THOMAS (TEXAS) - LB - 1966-69 ATLANTA FALCONS; 1970-74 ATLANTA
      FALCONS (NFC)
NOBLE, DAVID (NEBRASKA) - BACK - 1924-25 CLEVELAND BULLDOGS; 1926
      CLEVELAND PANTHERS (AFL)
NOBLE, JAMES (SYRACUSE) - END - 1925 BUFFALO BISONS
NOBLE, RICHARD (TRINITY-CONNECTICUT) - GUARD - 1926 HARTFORD BLUES
NOCERA, JOHN (IOWA) - LB - 1959-62 PHILADELPHIA EAGLES; 1963 DENVER
      BRONCOS (AFL)
NOCK, GEORGE (MORGAN STATE) - BACK - 1969 NEW YORK JETS (AFL);
      1970-71 NEW YORK JETS (AFC); 1972 WASHINGTON REDSKINS (NFC)
NOFSINGER, TERRY (UTAH) - QBACK - 1961-64 PITTSBURGH STEELERS;
      1965-66 ST. LOUIS CARDINALS; 1967 ATLANTA FALCONS
NOLAN, EARL (ARIZONA) - TACKLE - 1937-38 CHICAGO CARDINALS
NOLAN, JOHN (SANTA CLARA) - GUARD - 1926 LOS ANGELES BUCCANEERS
NOLAN, JOHN (PENN STATE) - TACKLE - 1948 BOSTON YANKS; 1949 NEW YORK
      BULLDOGS; 1950 NEW YORK YANKS
NOLAN, RICHARD (MARYLAND) - BACK - 1954-57, 59-61 NEW YORK GIANTS;
      1958 CHICAGO CARDINALS; 1962 DALLAS COWBOYS
NOLANDER, DONALD (MINNESOTA) - CENTER - 1946 LOS ANGELES DONS (AAFC)
NOLL, CHARLES (DAYTON) - GUARD - 1953-59 CLEVELAND BROWNS
NOLTING, RAY (CINCINNATI) - BACK - 1936-43 CHICAGO BEARS
NOMELLINI, LEO (MINNESOTA) - TACKLE - 1950-63 SAN FRANCISCO 49ERS;
      1969 HALL OF FAME
NOMINA, THOMAS (MIAMI-OHIO) - TACKLE - 1963-65 DENVER BRONCOS (AFL);
      1966-68 MIAMI DOLPHINS (AFL)
NONNEMAKER, GUSTAVUS (WITTENBERG) - END - 1926 COLUMBUS TIGERS

NOONAN, GERALD (FORDHAM) - BACK - 1921-24 ROCHESTER JEFFERSONS; 1923
    HAMMOND PROS
NOONAN, KARL (IOWA) - END - 1966-69 MIAMI DOLPHINS (AFL); 1970-71
    MIAMI DOLPHINS (AFC)
NOPPENBERG, JOHN (MIAMI) - BACK - 1940-41 PITTSBURGH STEELERS; 1941
    DETROIT LIONS
NORBECK - GUARD - 1921 MINNEAPOLIS MARINES
NORBERG, HENRY (STANFORD) - END - 1946-47 SAN FRANCISCO 49ERS (AAFC);
    1948 CHICAGO BEARS
NORBY, JOHN (IDAHO) - BACK - 1934 ST. LOUIS GUNNERS; 1934
    PHILADELPHIA EAGLES; 1934 NEW YORK GIANTS; 1935 BROOKLYN DODGERS
NORDQUIST, MARK (PACIFIC) - GUARD, CENTER - 1968-69 PHILADELPHIA
    EAGLES; 1970-74 PHILADELPHIA EAGLES (NFC)
NORDSTROM, HARRY (TRINITY-CONNECTICUT) - GUARD - 1925 NEW YORK
    GIANTS; 1926 BROOKLYN LIONS
NORFENE, OLAF (MINNESOTA) - BACK - 1921 EVANSVILLE CRIMSON GIANTS
NORGARD, ALVAR (STANFORD) - END - 1934 GREEN BAY PACKERS
NORI, REINO (NORTHERN ILLINOIS) - BACK - 1937 BROOKLYN DODGERS; 1938
    CHICAGO BEARS
NORMAN, JAMES - GUARD - 1955 WASHINGTON REDSKINS
NORMAN, PETTIS (J.C.SMITH) - END - 1962-69 DALLAS COWBOYS; 1970
    DALLAS COWBOYS (NFC); 1971-73 SAN DIEGO CHARGERS (AFC)
NORMAN, RICHARD (STANFORD) - QBACK - 1961 CHICAGO BEARS
NORMAN, ROBERT - CENTER - 1945 CHICAGO CARDINALS
NORMAN, WILLARD (WASHINGTON&JEFFERSON) - BACK - 1928 POTTSVILLE
    MAROONS; 1929 ORANGE TORNADOS
NORRIS, HAROLD (CALIFORNIA) - BACK - 1955-56 WASHINGTON REDSKINS
NORRIS, JAMES (HOUSTON) - TACKLE - 1962-64 OAKLAND RAIDERS (AFL)
NORRIS, JOHN (MARYLAND) - END - 1932 STATEN ISLAND STAPELTONS
NORRIS, TRUSSE (UCLA) - END - 1960 LOS ANGELES CHARGERS (AFL)
NORTH, JAMES (CENTRAL WASHINGTON) - TACKLE - 1944 WASHINGTON REDSKINS
NORTON, DONALD (IOWA) - END - 1960 LOS ANGELES CHARGERS (AFL);
    1961-66 SAN DIEGO CHARGERS (AFL)
NORTON, JAMES (IDAHO) - BACK - 1960-68 HOUSTON OILERS (AFL)
NORTH, JOHN (VANDERBILT) - END - 1948-49 BALTIMORE COLTS (AAFC); 1950
    BALTIMORE COLTS
NORTON, GERALD (SMU) - BACK - 1954-58 PHILADELPHIA EAGLES; 1959
    CHICAGO CARDINALS; 1960-61 ST. LOUIS CARDINALS; 1962 DALLAS
    COWBOYS; 1963-64 GREEN BAY PACKERS; 1960 PUNTING LEADER; 1960
    INTERCEPTION LEADER; (TIED WITH D. BAKER)
NORTON, JAMES (WASHINGTON) - TACKLE - 1965-66 SAN FRANCISCO 49ERS;
    1967-68 ATLANTA FALCONS; 1968 PHILADELPHIA EAGLES; 1968
    WASHINGTON REDSKINS; 1970 NEW YORK GIANTS (NFC)
NORTON, MARTIN (CARLETON) - BACK - 1922, 24 MINNEAPOLIS MARINES;
    1925-26 GREEN BAY PACKERS; 1926 ROCK ISLAND INDEPENDENTS (AFL);
    1927-28 GREEN BAY PACKERS
NORTON, RAY (SAN JOSE STATE) - BACK - 1960-61 SAN FRANCISCO 49ERS
NORTON, RAYMOND - BACK - 1925 CLEVELAND BULLDOGS
NORTON, RICHARD (KENTUCKY) - QBACK - 1966-69 MIAMI DOLPHINS (AFL);
    1970 GREEN BAY PACKERS (NFC)
NOSICH, JOHN (DUQUESNE) - TACKLE - 1938 PITTSBURGH PIRATES
NOTT, DOUGLAS (DETROIT) - QBACK - 1935 DETROIT LIONS; 1935 BOSTON
    REDSKINS
NOTTINGHAM, DONALD (KENT STATE) - BACK - 1971-73 BALTIMORE COLTS
    (AFC); 1973-74 MIAMI DOLPHINS (AFC)
NOVAK, EDWARD - BACK - 1919-22, 24-25 ROCK ISLAND INDEPENDENTS; 1924
    MINNEAPOLIS MARINES; 1926 ROCK ISLAND INDEPENDENTS (AFL)
NOVAKOFSKI, ALBERT (LAWRENCE) - BACK - 1940-41 MILWAUKEE CHIEFS (AFL)
NOVOTNY, HARRY (SYRACUSE) - GUARD - 1940 NEW YORK AMERICANS (AFL)
NOVOTNY, RAYMOND (ASHLAND) - BACK - 1930 PORTSMOUTH SPARTANS; 1931
    CLEVELAND INDIANS; 1932 BROOKLYN DODGERS; 1936 CLEVELAND RAMS
    (AFL)
NOVSEK, JOSEPH (TULSA) - END - 1962 OAKLAND RAIDERS (AFL)
NOWAK, GARY (MICHIGAN STATE) - END - 1971 SAN DIEGO CHARGERS (AFC)
NOWAK, WALTER (VILLANOVA) - END - 1944 PHILADELPHIA EAGLES
NOWASKEY, ROBERT (GEORGE WASHINGTON) - END - 1940-42 CHICAGO BEARS;
    1946-47 LOS ANGELES DONS (AAFC); 1948-49 BALTIMORE COLTS (AAFC);
    1950 BALTIMORE COLTS
NOWATZKE, THOMAS (INDIANA) - BACK - 1965-69 DETROIT LIONS; 1970-72
    BALTIMORE COLTS (AFC)
NOYES, LEONARD (MONTANA) - TACKLE - 1938 BROOKLYN DODGERS

NUGENT, CLEMENT (IOWA) - BACK - 1924 CLEVELAND BULLDOGS
NUGENT, PHILIP (TULANE) - BACK - 1961 DENVER BRONCOS (AFL)
NUNAMAKER, JULIAN (TENNESSEE-MARTIN) - GUARD - 1969 BUFFALO BILLS
     (AFL); 1970 BUFFALO BILLS (AFC)
NUNLEY, FRANK (MICHIGAN) - LB - 1967-69 SAN FRANCISCO 49ERS; 1970-74
     SAN FRANCISCO 49ERS (NFC)
NUNN, HAROLD (CORNELL) - END - 1936 BOSTON SHAMROCKS (AFL)
NUNNERY, ROBERT (LSU) - TACKLE - 1960 DALLAS TEXANS (AFL)
NUSSNAUMER, ROBERT (MICHIGAN) - BACK - 1946, 51 GREEN BAY PACKERS;
     1947-48 WASHINGTON REDSKINS; 1949-50 CHICAGO CARDINALS; 1949
     INTERCEPTION LEADER
NUTTER, MADISON "BUZZ" (VIRGINIA POLYTECH) - CENTER - 1954-60, 65
     BALTIMORE COLTS; 1961-64 PITTSBURGH STEELERS
NUTTING, JOHN (GEORGIA TECH) - TACKLE - 1961 CLEVELAND BROWNS; 1963
     DALLAS COWBOYS
NUZUM, GERALD (NEW MEXICO A&M) - BACK - 1948-51 PITTSBURGH STEELERS
NYDALL, MALVIN (MINNESOTA) - BACK - 1929-30 MINNEAPOLIS REDJACKETS;
     1930-31 FRANKFORD YELLOWJACKETS
NYE, BLAINE (STANFORD) - GUARD - 1968-69 DALLAS COWBOYS; 1970-74
     DALLAS COWBOYS (NFC)
NYERS, RICHARD (INDIANA CENTRAL) - BACK - 1956-57 BALTIMORE COLTS
NYGREN BERNARD (SAN JOSE STATE) - BACK - 1946 LOS ANGELES DONS
     (AAFC); 1947 BROOKLYN DODGERS (AAFC)
NYSTROM, LEE (MACALESTER COLLEGE) - TACKLE - 1973-74 GREEN BAY
     PACKERS (NFC)
NYVALL, VICTOR (NORTHWEST LOUISIANA) - BACK - 1970 NEW ORLEANS SAINTS
     (NFC)
OAKES, DONALD (VIRGINIA TECH) - TACKLE - 1961-62 PHILADELPHIA EAGLES;
     1963-68 BOSTON PATRIOTS (AFL)
OAKES, WILLIAM (HASKELL) - TACKLE - 1921 GREEN BAY PACKERS
OAKLEY, CHARLES (LSU) - BACK - 1954 CHICAGO CARDINALS
OAS, BENJAMIN (ST. MARY'S OF MINNESOTA) - CENTER - 1929-30
     MINNEAPOLIS REDJACKETS
OATS, CARLETON (FLORIDA A&M) - END, TACKLE - 1965-69 OAKLAND RAIDERS
     (AFL); 1970-72 OAKLAND RAIDERS (AFC); 1973 GREEN BAY PACKERS
     (NFC)
OBECK, VICTOR (SPRINGFIELD) - GUARD - 1940 BOSTON BEARS (AFL); 1945
     CHICAGO CARDINALS; 1946 BROOKLYN DODGERS (AAFC)
OBEE, DUNCAN (DAYTON) - CENTER - 1941 DETROIT LIONS
OBERBROEKLING, RAYMOND (COLUMBIA COLLEGE) - TACKLE - 1924 KENOSHA
     MAROONS
OBERG, THOMAS (PORTLAND STATE) - BACK - 1968-69 DENVER BRONCOS (AFL)
O'BOYLE, HARRY (NOTRE DAME) - BACK - 1928-29, 32 GREEN BAY PACKERS;
     1933 PHILADELPHIA EAGLES
O'BRADOVICH, EDWARD (ILLINOIS) - END - 1962-69 CHICAGO BEARS; 1970-71
     CHICAGO BEARS (NFC)
O'BRIEN, CHARLES (CARLETON) - END - 1926 DULUTH ESKIMOS
O'BRIEN, DAVID (BOSTON COLLEGE) - TACKLE - 1963-64 MINNESOTA VIKINGS;
     1965 NEW YORK GIANTS; 1966-67 ST. LOUIS CARDINALS
O'BRIEN, FRANCIS (MICHIGAN STATE) - TACKLE - 1959 CLEVELAND BROWNS;
     1960-66 WASHINGTON REDSKINS; 1966-68 PITTSBURGH STEELERS
O'BRIEN, GAIL (NEBRASKA) - TACKLE - 1934-36 BOSTON REDSKINS; 1937 LOS
     ANGELES BULLDOGS (AFL)
O'BRIEN, JAMES (CINCINNATI) - KICKER, END - 1970-72 BALTIMORE COLTS
     (AFC); 1973 DETROIT LIONS (NFC)
O'BRIEN, JOHN (FLORIDA) - END - 1954-56 PITTSBURGH STEELERS
O'BRIEN, JOHN (MINNESOTA) - BACK - 1929 MINNEAPOLIS REDJACKETS
O'BRIEN, ROBERT DAVID (TCU) - QBACK - 1939-40 PHILADELPHIA EAGLES
O'BRIEN, THOMAS (BOSTON COLLEGE) - GUARD - 1926 BOSTON BULLDOGS (AFL)
O'BRIEN, WILLIAM - BACK - 1947 DETROIT LIONS
OBST, HENRY (SYRACUSE) - GUARD - 1931 STATEN ISLAND STAPLETONS; 1933
     PHILADELPHIA EAGLES; 1936 NEW YORK YANKS (AFL)
O'CONNELL, GRATTAN (BOSTON COLLEGE) - END - 1926 HARTFORD BLUES; 1927
     PROVIDENCE STEAMROLLERS
O'CONNELL, HARRY - CENTER - 1924 CHICAGO BEARS
O'CONNELL, MILTON (LAFAYETTE) - END - 1924-25 FRANKFORD YELLOWJACKETS
O'CONNELL, THOMAS (ILLINOIS) - QBACK - 1953 CHICAGO BEARS; 1956-57
     CLEVELAND BROWNS; 1960-61 BUFFALO BILLS (AFL); 1957 PASSING
     LEADER
O'CONNELL - BACK - 1919 WHEELING

O'CONNOR, DANIEL (GEORGETOWN) - GUARD - 1919-20 CANTON BULLDOGS; 1920
     DAYTON TRIANGLES; 1920 CLEVELAND PANTHERS; 1920-24 CHICAGO
     CARDINALS; 1921 CLEVELAND INDIANS
O'CONNOR, FRANCIS (HOLY CROSS) - TACKLE - 1926 HARTFORD BLUES
O'CONNOR, ROBERT (STANFORD) - GUARD - 1935 GREEN BAY PACKERS
O'CONNOR, WILLIAM (NOTRE DAME) - END - 1948 BUFFALO BILLS (AAFC);
     1949 CLEVELAND BROWNS (AAFC); 1951 NEW YORK YANKS
O'DELL, STU (INDIANA) - LB - 1974 WASHINGTON REDSKINS (NFC)
O'DELLI, MELVIN (DUQUESNE) - BACK - 1945 PITTSBURGH STEELERS
ODEN, OLAF (BROWN) - QBACK - 1925-31 PROVIDENCE STEAMROLLERS; 1932
     BOSTON BRAVES
ODLE, PHILIP (BRIGHAM YOUNG) - END - 1968-69 DETROIT LIONS; 1970
     DETROIT LIONS (NFC)
ODOM, SAMUEL (NORTHWEST LOUISIANA) - LB - 1964 HOUSTON OILERS (AFL)
ODOM, STEVE (UTAH) - END - 1974 GREEN BAY PACKERS (NFC)
ODOMS, RILEY (HOUSTON) - END - 1972-74 DENVER BRONCOS (AFC)
O'DONAHUE, PATRICK (WISCONSIN) - END - 1952 SAN FRANCISCO 49ERS; 1955
     GREEN BAY PACKERS
O'DONNELL, JOSEPH (MICHIGAN) - GUARD - 1964-67, 69 BUFFALO BILLS
     (AFL); 1970-71 BUFFALO BILLS (AFC)
O'DONNELL, RICHARD (MINNESOTA) - END - 1923 DULUTH KELLEYS; 1924-30
     GREEN BAY PACKERS; 1931 BROOKLYN DODGERS
O'DONNELL, THOMAS (VILLANOVA) - END - 1936 BOSTON SHAMROCKS (AFL)
ODSON, URBAN (MINNESOTA) - TACKLE - 1946-49 GREEN BAY PACKERS
OECH, VERNE (MINNESOTA) - TACKLE - 1936 CHICAGO BEARS
OEHLER, JOHN (PURDUE) - CENTER - 1933-34 PITTSBURGH PIRATES; 1935-36
     BROOKLYN DODGERS
OEHLRICH, ARNOLD (NEBRASKA) - BACK - 1928-29 FRANKFORD YELLOWJACKETS
OELERICH, JOHN (ST. AMBROSE) - BACK - 1938 PITTSBURGH PIRATES; 1938
     CHICAGO BEARS
OGAS, DAVID (SAN DIEGO STATE) - LB - 1968 OAKLAND RAIDERS (AFL); 1969
     BUFFALO BILLS (AFL)
OGDEN, RAYMOND (ALABAMA) - END - 1965-66 ST. LOUIS CARDINALS; 1967
     NEW ORLEANS SAINTS; 1967-68 ATLANTA FALCONS; 1969 CHICAGO BEARS;
     1970-71 CHICAGO BEARS (NFC)
OGLE, RICK (COLORADO) - LB - 1971 ST. LOUIS CARDINALS (NFC); 1972
     DETROIT LIONS (NFC)
OGLESBY, PAUL (UCLA) - TACKLE - 1960 OAKLAND RAIDERS (AFL)
O'HANLEY, ROSS (BOSTON COLLEGE) - BACK - 1960-65 BOSTON PATRIOTS (AFL)
O'HEARN, JOHN (CORNELL) - BACK - 1920 CLEVELAND PANTHERS; 1921
     BUFFALO ALL-AMERICANS
OHLGREN, EARL (MINNESOTA) - END - 1940-41 MILWAUKEE CHIEFS (AFL);
     1942 GREEN BAY PACKERS
OHRT, JOHN (NEVADA) - BACK - 1937 ROCHESTER TIGERS (AFL)
O'KEEFE, DECLAN (FINDLAY) - TACKLE - 1936 CLEVELAND RAMS (AFL); 1937
     CINCINNATI BENGALS (AFL); 1940-41 COLUMBUS BULLIES (AFL)
OKONIEWSKI, JOHN STEPHEN (MONTANA) - TACKLE, END - 1972-73 BUFFALO
     BILLS (AFC); 1974 GREEN BAY PACKERS (NFC)
OLDERSHAW, DOUGLAS (SANTA BARBARA) - GUARD - 1939-41 NEW YORK GIANTS
OLDHAM, DONNIE RAY (MIDDLE TENNESSEE STATE) - BACK - 1973-74
     BALTIMORE COLTS (AFC)
OLDHAM, JAMES (ARIZONA) - END - 1926 RACINE LEGION
OLDS, WILLIAM (NEBRASKA) - BACK - 1973-74 BALTIMORE COLTS (AFC)
OLEJINICZAK, STANLEY (PITTSBURGH) - TACKLE - 1935 PITTSBURGH PIRATES
OLENSKI, MITCHELL (ALABAMA) - TACKLE - 1946 MIAMI SEAHAWKS (AAFC);
     1947 DETROIT LIONS
OLERICH, DAVID (SAN FRANCISCO) - LB, END - 1967-68 SAN FRANCISCO
     49ERS; 1969 ST. LOUIS CARDINALS; 1970 ST. LOUIS CARDINALS (NFC);
     1971 HOUSTON OILERS (AFC); 1972-73 SAN FRANCISCO 49ERS (NFC)
OLIKER, AARON (WEST VIRGINIA) - END - 1926 POTTSVILLE MAROONS
OLIPHANT, ELMER (WEST POINT) - BACK - 1920-21 BUFFALO ALL-AMERICANS;
     1920-21 ROCHESTER JEFFERSONS
OLIVER, CLARENCE "CLANCY" (SAN DIEGO STATE) - BACK - 1969 PITTSBURGH
     STEELERS; 1970 PITTSBURGH STEELERS (AFC)
OLIVER, GREGORY (TRINITY) - BACK - 1973-74 PHILADELPHIA EAGLES (NFC)
OLIVER, RALPH (USC) - LB - 1968-69 OAKLAND RAIDERS (AFL)
OLIVER, RICHARD (TCU) - BACK - 1936 BROOKLYN TIGERS (AFL)
OLIVER, ROBERT (ABILENE CHRISTIAN) - END - 1969 CLEVELAND BROWNS
OLIVER, VINCENT (INDIANA) - BACK - 1945 CHICAGO CARDINALS

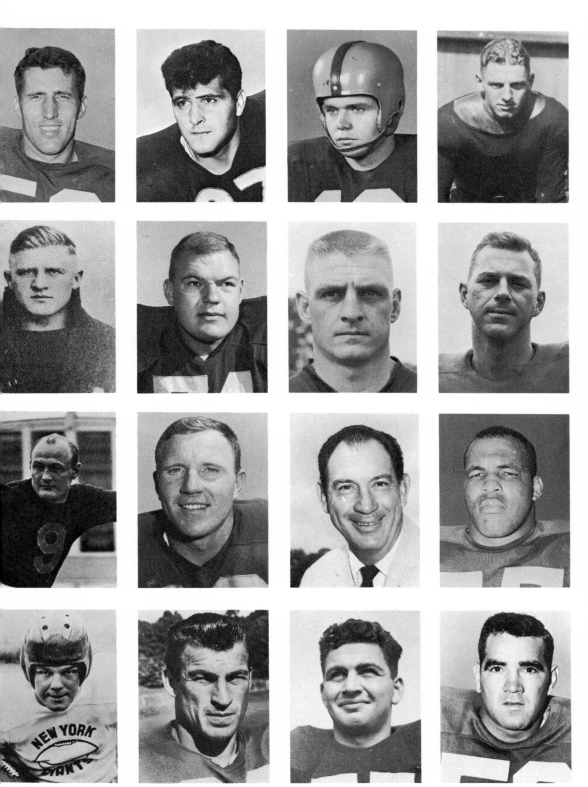

Top row (from left to right): "Buzz" Nutter, Ed O'Bradovich, Tom O'Connell and "Curly" Oden. *Second row:* Elmer Oliphant, Merlin Olsen, John Olszewski and Jimmy Orr. *Third row:* Bill Osmanski, Jack Pardee, "Ace" Parker, and Jim Parker. *Bottom row:* Bill Paschal, Jim Patton, Don Paul and Bob Pellegrini.

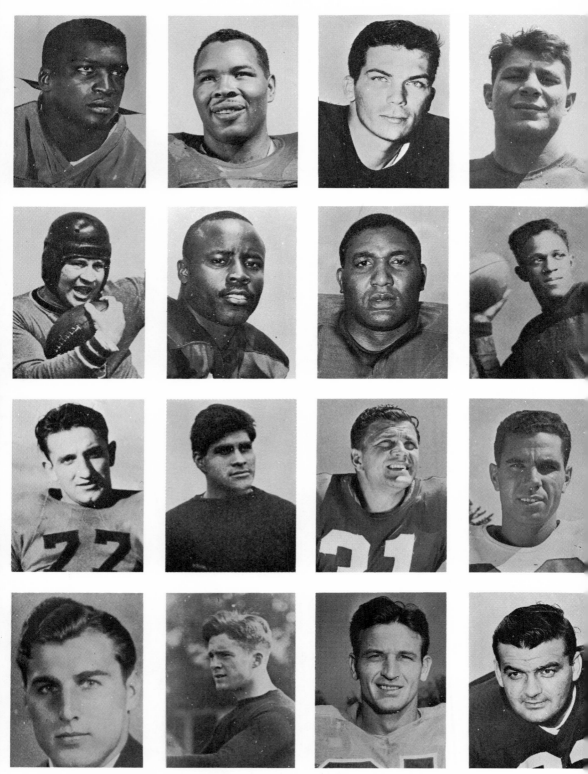

Top row (from left to right): **Don Perkins, Joe Perry, Rich Petitbon and Pete Pihos.** *Second row:* **Ernie Pinckert, Elijah Pitts, Sherman Plunkett and "Fritz" Pollard.** *Third row:* **Milt Popovich, Stancil Powell, Ed Price and "Bosh" Pritchard.** *Bottom row:* **Steve Pritko, Clair Purdy, Volney Quinlan and Bill Quinlan.**

OLIVER, WILLIAM (ALABAMA) - GUARD - 1926 NEW YORK YANKEES (AFL); 1927
     NEW YORK YANKEES
OLMSTEAD, LAWRENCE (PURDUE) - GUARD - 1922-23 LOUISVILLE BRECKS
OLSEN, MERLIN (UTAH STATE) - TACKLE - 1962-69 LOS ANGELES RAMS;
     1970-74 LOS ANGELES RAMS (NFC)
OLSEN, NORMAN (ALABAMA) - TACKLE - 1944 CLEVELAND RAMS
OLSEN, PHILIP (UTAH STATE) - TACKLE - 1971-74 LOS ANGELES RAMS (NFC)
OLSEN, RALPH (UTAH) - END - 1949 GREEN BAY PACKERS
OLSON, CARL (UCLA) - TACKLE - 1942 CHICAGO CARDINALS
OLSON, FORREST (IOWA) - GUARD - 1927 NEW YORK YANKEES
OLSON, GLENN (IOWA) - BACK - 1940 CLEVELAND RAMS; 1941 COLUMBUS
     BULLIES (AFL)
OLSON, HAROLD (CLEMSON) - TACKLE - 1960-62 BUFFALO BILLS (AFL);
     1963-64 DENVER BRONCOS (AFL)
OLSONOSKI, LAWRENCE (MINNESOTA) - GUARD - 1948-49 GREEN BAY PACKERS;
     1949 NEW YORK BULLDOGS
OLSSEN, LANCE (PURDUE) - TACKLE - 1968-69 SAN FRANCISCO 49ERS
OLSSON, LESTER (MERCER) - GUARD - 1934-36 BOSTON REDSKINS; 1937-38
     WASHINGTON REDSKINS
OLSZEWSKI, ALBERT (PENN STATE & PITTSBURGH) - END - 1945 PITTSBURGH
     STEELERS
OLSZEWSKI, JOHN (CALIFORNIA) - BACK - 1953-57 CHICAGO CARDINALS;
     1958-60 WASHINGTON REDSKINS; 1961 DETROIT LIONS; 1962 DENVER
     BRONCOS (AFL)
OLTZ, RUSSELL (WASHINGTON&JEFFERSON) - TACKLE - 1923-25 HAMMOND PROS;
     1924 RACINE LEGION
O'MAHONEY, JAMES (MIAMI) - LB - 1965-66 NEW YORK JETS (AFL)
O'MALLEY, JAMES (NOTRE DAME) - LB - 1973-74 DENVER BRONCOS (AFC)
O'MALLEY, JOSEPH (GEORGIA) - END - 1955-56 PITTSBURGH STEELERS
O'MALLEY, ROBERT (CINCINNATI) - BACK - 1950 GREEN BAY PACKERS
O'NEAL, JAMES (TCU) - GUARD - 1946-47 CHICAGO ROCKETS (AAFC)
O'NEAL, STEVE (TEXAS A&M) - KICKER, END - 1969 NEW YORK JETS (AFL);
     1970-72 NEW YORK JETS (AFC); 1973 NEW ORLEANS SAINTS (NFC)
O'NEIL, CHARLES (CONNECTICUT) - CENTER - 1926 HARTFORD BLUES
O'NEIL, EDWARD (PENN STATE) - LB - 1974 DETROIT LIONS (NFC)
O'NEIL, ROBERT (NOTRE DAME) - GUARD - 1956-57 PITTSBURGH STEELERS;
     1961 NEW YORK TITANS (AFL)
O'NEIL, WILLIAM (MARQUETTE) - END - 1921-22 EVANSVILLE CRIMSON GIANTS
O'NEIL, GERALD (DETROIT) - BACK - 1922 DAYTON TRIANGLES; 1922-23
     TOLEDO MAROONS
O'NEILL, THOMAS (ST. MARY'S OF MINNESOTA) - END - 1925 DULUTH KELLEYS
O'NEILL, WILLIAM (DETROIT) - BACK - 1935 DETROIT LIONS; 1936 BROOKLYN
     TIGERS (AFL); 1937 CLEVELAND RAMS; 1937 ROCHESTER TIGERS (AFL)
ONESTI, LAWRENCE (NORTHWESTERN) - LB - 1962-65 HOUSTON OILERS (AFL)
ONISKEY, RICHARD (CHATTANOOGA) - GUARD - 1955 PITTSBURGH STEELERS
ONKOTZ, DENNIS (PENN STATE) - LB - 1970 NEW YORK JETS (AFC)
OPALEWSKI, EDWARD (MICHIGAN NORMAL) - TACKLE - 1943-44 DETROIT LIONS
O'QUINN, JOHN (WAKE FOREST) - END - 1950-51 CHICAGO BEARS; 1951
     PHILADELPHIA EAGLES
ORDUNA, JOSEPH (NEBRASKA) - BACK - 1972-73 NEW YORK GIANTS (NFC);
     1974 BALTIMORE COLTS (AFC)
ORF, ROLAND (MISSOURI) - END - 1941 NEW YORK AMERICANS (AFL)
ORIARD, MICHAEL (NOTRE DAME) - CENTER - 1970-73 KANSAS CITY CHIEFS
     (AFC)
ORISTAGLIO, ROBERT (PENNSYLVANIA) - END - 1949 BUFFALO BILLS (AAFC);
     1950 BALTIMORE COLTS; 1951 CLEVELAND BROWNS; 1952 PHILADELPHIA
     EAGLES
ORLICH, DANIEL (NEVADA) - END - 1949-51 GREEN BAY PACKERS
ORMSBEE, ELLIOTT (BRADLEY TECH) - BACK - 1946 PHILADELPHIA EAGLES
O'ROURKE, CHARLES (BOSTON COLLEGE) - QBACK - 1942 CHICAGO BEARS;
     1946-47 LOS ANGELES DONS (AAFC); 1948-49 BALTIMORE COLTS (AAFC)
ORR, JAMES (GEORGIA) - END - 1958-60 PITTSBURGH STEELERS; 1961-69
     BALTIMORE COLTS; 1970 BALTIMORE COLTS (AFC)
ORTH, HENRY (MIAMI-OHIO) - GUARD - 1921 CINCINNATI CELTS
ORTMAN, CHARLES (MICHIGAN) - QBACK - 1951 PITTSBURGH STEELERS; 1952
     DALLAS TEXANS
ORVIS, HERBERT (COLORADO) - TACKLE, END - 1972-74 DETROIT LIONS (NFC)
ORWOLL, OSWALD (LUTHER) - BACK - 1926 MILWAUKEE BADGERS
OSBORN, DAVID (NORTH DAKOTA) - BACK - 1965-69 MINNESOTA VIKINGS;
     1970-74 MINNESOTA VIKINGS (NFC)

OSBORN, ROBERT (PENN STATE) - GUARD - 1921-23 CANTON BULLDOGS; 1924
    CLEVELAND BULLDOGS; 1925-28 POTTSVILLE MAROONS
OSBORNE, CLARENCE (ARIZONA STATE) - LB - 1959-60 SAN FRANCISCO 49ERS;
    1961-62 MINNESOTA VIKINGS; 1963-64 OAKLAND RAIDERS (AFL)
OSBORNE, JAMES (SOUTHERN) - TACKLE - 1972-74 CHICAGO BEARS (NFC)
OSBORNE, MERLE (IOWA STATE) - BACK - 1941 BUFFALO TIGERS (AFL)
OSBORNE, THOMAS (HASTINGS-NEBRASKA) - END - 1960-61 WASHINGTON
    REDSKINS
OSLEY, WILLIE (ILLINOIS) - BACK - 1974 NEW ENGLAND PATRIOTS (AFC);
    1974 KANSAS CITY CHIEFS (AFC)
OSMANSKI, JOSEPH (HOLY CROSS) - BACK - 1946-49 CHICAGO BEARS; 1949
    NEW YORK BULLDOGS
OSMANSKI, WILLIAM (HOLY CROSS) - BACK - 1939-43, 46-47 CHICAGO BEARS;
    1939 RUSHING LEADER
OSSOWSKI, MARTIN (SOUTHWESTERN-KANSAS) - TACKLE - 1936-37 NEW YORK
    YANKS (AFL)
OSSOWSKI, THEODORE (OREGON STATE) - TACKLE - 1947 NEW YORK YANKEES
    (AAFC)
OSTENDARP, JAMES (BUCKNELL) - BACK - 1950-51 NEW YORK GIANTS
OSTROWSKI, CHESTER (NOTRE DAME) - END - 1954-59 WASHINGTON REDSKINS
O'TOOLE, WILLIAM (ST. MARY'S OF MINNESOTA) - GUARD - 1924 DULUTH
    KELLEYS
OTTE, F. LOWELL (IOWA) - END - 1926 NEW YORK YANKEES (AFL); 1927
    BUFFALO BISONS
OTTELE, RICHARD (WASHINGTON) - BACK - 1948 LOS ANGELES DONS (AAFC)
OTTERBACHER - GUARD - 1926 CLEVELAND PANTHERS (AFL)
OTIS, JAMES (OHIO STATE) - BACK - 1970 NEW ORLEANS SAINTS (NFC);
    1971-72 KANSAS CITY CHIEFS (AFC); 1973-74 ST. LOUIS CARDINALS
    (NFC)
OTTO, ALVIN - TACKLE - 1922-23 LOUISVILLE BRECKS
OTTO, AUGUST (MISSOURI) - LB - 1965-69 OAKLAND RAIDERS (AFL); 1970-72
    OAKLAND RAIDERS (AFC)
OTTO, JAMES (MIAMI) - CENTER - 1960-69 OAKLAND RAIDERS (AFL); 1970-74
    OAKLAND RAIDERS (AFC)
OUTLAW, JAMES (JACKSON STATE) - BACK - 1969 BOSTON PATRIOTS (AFL);
    1970 BOSTON PATRIOTS (AFC); 1971-72 NEW ENGLAND PATRIOTS (AFC);
    1973-74 PHILADELPHIA EAGLES (NFC)
OVERMYER, WILLIAM (ASHLAND) - LB - 1972 PHILADELPHIA EAGLES (NFC)
OVERTON, JERRY (UTAH) - BACK - 1963 DALLAS COWBOYS
OWEN, ALTON (MERCER) - QBACK - 1939-40, 42 NEW YORK GIANTS; 1941 NEW
    YORK AMERICANS (AFL)
OWEN, STEVEN (PHILLIPS) - TACKLE - 1924-25 KANSAS CITY COWBOYS;
    1926-31, 33 NEW YORK GIANTS; 1966 HALL OF FAME
OWEN, WILLIAM (OKLAHOMA A&M) - TACKLE - 1925-26 KANSAS CITY COWBOYS;
    1927 CLEVELAND BULLDOGS; 1928 DETROIT WOLVERINES; 1929-36 NEW
    YORK GIANTS
OWEN, WILLIS THOMAS (WICHITA STATE) - QBACK - 1974 SAN FRANCISCO
    49ERS (NFC)
OWENS, BRIGMAN (CINCINNATI) - BACK - 1966-69 WASHINGTON REDSKINS;
    1970-74 WASHINGTON REDSKINS (NFC)
OWENS, BURGESS (MIAMI) - BACK - 1973-74 NEW YORK JETS (AFC)
OWENS, DONALD (MISSISSIPPI SOUTHERN) - TACKLE - 1957 WASHINGTON
    REDSKINS; 1958-60 PHILADELPHIA EAGLES; 1960-63 ST. LOUIS
    CARDINALS
OWENS, HARRY (WAKE FOREST) - GUARD - 1922 GREEN BAY PACKERS
OWENS, ISAIAH (ILLINOIS) - END - 1948 CHICAGO ROCKETS (AAFC)
OWENS, JAMES (OKLAHOMA) - END - 1950 BALTIMORE COLTS
OWENS, JOSEPH (ALCORN A&M) - END - 1970 SAN DIEGO CHARGERS (AFC);
    1971-74 NEW ORLEANS SAINTS (NFC)
OWENS, LUKE (KENT STATE) - TACKLE - 1957 BALTIMORE COLTS; 1958-59
    CHICAGO CARDINALS; 1960-65 ST. LOUIS CARDINALS
OWENS, MARVIN (SAN DIEGO STATE) - END - 1973 ST. LOUIS CARDINALS
    (NFC); 1974 NEW YORK JETS (AFC)
OWENS, RALEIGH (IDAHO COLLEGE) - END - 1957-61 SAN FRANCISCO 49ERS;
    1962-63 BALTIMORE COLTS; 1964 NEW YORK GIANTS
OWENS, STEVE (OKLAHOMA) - BACK - 1970-74 DETROIT LIONS (NFC)
OWENS, TERRY (JACKSONVILLE STATE) - TACKLE - 1966-69 SAN DIEGO
    CHARGERS (AFL); 1970-74 SAN DIEGO CHARGERS (AFC)
OWENS, TRUET (TEXAS TECH) - GUARD - 1943 BROOKLYN DODGERS

PACE, JAMES (MICHIGAN) - BACK - 1958 SAN FRANCISCO 49ERS; 1963 NEW
     YORK GIANTS
PACEWICZ, VINCENT (SAN FRANCISCO) - QBACK - 1947 WASHINGTON REDSKINS
PADAN, ROBERT (OHIO STATE) - BACK - 1922 LOUISVILLE BRECKS
PADGEN, NICHOLAS (CREIGHTON) - CENTER - 1940 BOSTON BEARS (AFL); 1941
     COLUMBUS BULLIES (AFL)
PADLOW, MAX (OHIO STATE) - END - 1935-36 PHILADELPHIA EAGLES; 1936
     CLEVELAND RAMS (AFL); 1937 CINCINNATI BENGALS (AFL)
PADOW, WALTER (DUQUESNE) - GUARD - 1940 BUFFALO INDIANS (AFL)
PAFFRATH, ROBERT (MINNESOTA) - BACK - 1946 MIAMI SEAHAWKS (AAFC);
     1946 BROOKLYN DODGERS (AAFC)
PAGAC, FRED (OHIO STATE) - END - 1974 CHICAGO BEARS (NFC)
PAGE, ALAN (NOTRE DAME) - TACKLE - 1967-69 MINNESOTA VIKINGS; 1970-74
     MINNESOTA VIKINGS (NFC)
PAGE, PAUL (SMU) - BACK - 1949 BALTIMORE COLTS (AAFC)
PAGLIEI, JOSEPH (CLEMSON) - BACK - 1959 PHILADELPHIA EAGLES; 1960 NEW
     YORK TITANS (AFL)
PAHL, LOUIS (ST. THOMAS OF MINNESOTA) - BACK - 1923-24 MINNEAPOLIS
     MARINES
PAINE, HOMER (OKLAHOMA) - TACKLE - 1949 CHICAGO HORNETS (AAFC)
PALATELLA, LOUIS (PITTSBURGH) - GUARD - 1955-58 SAN FRANCISCO 49ERS
PALAZZI, LOUIS (PENN STATE) - CENTER - 1946-47 NEW YORK GIANTS
PALEWICZ, ALBERT (MIAMI-FLORIDA) - LB - 1973-74 KANSAS CITY CHIEFS
     (AFC)
PALM, MYRON "MIKE" (PENN STATE) - QBACK - 1925-26 NEW YORK GIANTS;
     1933 CINCINNATI REDS
PALMER, CHARLES (NORTHWESTERN) - BACK - 1924 RACINE LEGION; 1926
     LOUISVILLE COLONELS
PALMER, DARRELL (TCU) - TACKLE - 1946-48 NEW YORK YANKEES (AAFC);
     1949 CLEVELAND BROWNS (AAFC); 1950-53 CLEVELAND BROWNS
PALMER, LESLIE (NORTH CAROLINA STATE) - BACK - 1948 PHILADELPHIA
     EAGLES
PALMER, MICHAEL - TACKLE - 1921 MINNEAPOLIS MARINES
PALMER, RICHARD (KENTUCKY) - LB - 1970 MIAMI DOLPHINS (AFC); 1972
     BUFFALO BILLS (AFC); 1972-73 NEW ORLEANS SAINTS (NFC); 1974
     ATLANTA FALCONS (NFC)
PALMER, SCOTT (TEXAS) - TACKLE - 1971 NEW YORK JETS (AFC); 1972 ST.
     LOUIS CARDINALS (NFC)
PALMER, THOMAS (WAKE FOREST) - TACKLE - 1953-54 PITTSBURGH STEELERS
PALUCK, JOHN (PITTSBURGH) - END - 1956, 59-65 WASHINGTON REDSKINS
PALUMBO, SAMUEL (NOTRE DAME) - CENTER - 1955-56 CLEVELAND BROWNS;
     1957 GREEN BAY PACKERS; 1960 BUFFALO BILLS (AFL)
PANACCION, VICTOR (PENN STATE) - TACKLE - 1930 FRANKFORD YELLOWJACKETS
PANCIERA, DONALD (SAN FRANCISCO) - BACK - 1949 NEW YORK YANKEES
     (AAFC); 1950 DETROIT LIONS; 1952 CHICAGO CARDINALS
PANELLI, JOHN (NOTRE DAME) - BACK - 1949-50 DETROIT LIONS; 1951-53
     CHICAGO CARDINALS
PANFIL, KENNETH (PURDUE) - TACKLE - 1956-58 LOS ANGELES RAMS; 1959
     CHICAGO CARDINALS; 1960-62 ST. LOUIS CARDINALS
PANGLE, HAROLD (OREGON STATE) - BACK - 1935-38 CHICAGO CARDINALS
PANNELL, ERNEST (TEXAS A&M) - TACKLE - 1941-42, 45 GREEN BAY PACKERS
PAOLUCCI, BEN (WAYNE STATE) - TACKLE - 1959 DETROIT LIONS
PAPAC, NICHOLAS (FRESNO STATE) - QBACK - 1961 OAKLAND RAIDERS (AFL)
PAPACH, GEORGE (PURDUE) - BACK - 1948-49 PITTSBURGH STEELERS
PAPE, ORAN (IOWA) - BACK - 1930 GREEN BAY PACKERS; 1930 MINNEAPOLIS
     REDJACKETS; 1931 PROVIDENCE STEAMROLLERS; 193_ BOSTON BRAVES;
     1932 STATEN ISLAND STAPELTONS
PAPIT, JOHN (VIRGINIA) - BACK - 1951-53 WASHINGTON REDSKINS; 1953
     GREEN BAY PACKERS
PAPPIO, JOSEPH (HASKELL) - END - 1930 CHICAGO CARDINALS
PAQUIN, LEO (FORDHAM) - END - 1937 NEW YORK YANKS (AFL)
PARDEE, JOHN (TEXAS A&M) - LB - 1957-64, 66-69 LOS ANGELES RAMS; 1970
     LOS ANGELES RAMS (NFC); 1971-72 WASHINGTON REDSKINS (NFC)
PARDONNER, PAUL (PURDUE) - QBACK - 1934-35 CHICAGO CARDINALS
PAREMORE, ROBERT (FLORIDA A&M) - BACK - 1963-64 ST. LOUIS CARDINALS
PARILLI, VITO "BABE" (KENTUCKY) - QBACK - 1952-53, 57-58 GREEN BAY
     PACKERS; 1956 CLEVELAND BROWNS; 1960 OAKLAND RAIDERS (AFL);
     1961-67 BOSTON PATRIOTS (AFL); 1968-69 NEW YORK JETS (AFL)
PARISH, DONALD (STANFORD) - LB - 1970-72 ST. LOUIS CARDINALS (NFC);
     1971 LOS ANGELES RAMS (NFC); 1972 DENVER BRONCOS (AFC)

PARK, ERNEST (MCMURRAY) - GUARD, TACKLE - 1963-65 SAN DIEGO CHARGERS
     (AFL); 1966 MIAMI DOLPHINS (AFL); 1967 DENVER BRONCOS (AFL);
     1969 CINCINNATI BENGALS (AFL)
PARKER, ARTIMUS (USC) - BACK - 1974 PHILADELPHIA EAGLES (NFC)
PARKER, BERNARD (SOUTHWESTERN-KANSAS) - END - 1937 NEW YORK YANKS
     (AFL)
PARKER, CHARLES (MISSISSIPPI SOUTHERN) - GUARD - 1965 DENVER BRONCOS
     (AFL)
PARKER, CLARENCE "ACE" (DUKE) - QBACK - 1937-41 BROOKLYN DODGERS;
     1945 BOSTON YANKS; 1946 NEW YORK YANKEES (AAFC); 1940
     INTERCEPTION LEADER; (TIED WITH HUTSON AND RYAN); 1972 HALL OF
     FAME
PARKER, DAVID (HARDIN-SIMMONS) - END - 1941 BROOKLYN DODGERS
PARKER, DONALD (VIRGINIA) - GUARD - 1967 SAN FRANCISCO 49ERS
PARKER, HOWARD (SMU) - BACK - 1948 NEW YORK YANKEES (AAFC)
PARKER, JAMES (OHIO STATE) - GUARD - 1957-67 BALTIMORE COLTS; 1973
     HALL OF FAME
PARKER, JOEL (FLORIDA) - END - 1974 NEW ORLEANS SAINTS (NFC)
PARKER, JOSEPH (TEXAS) - END - 1946-47 CHICAGO CARDINALS
PARKER, KENNETH (FORDHAM) - BACK - 1970 NEW YORK GIANTS (NFC)
PARKER, RAYMOND (CENTENARY) - BACK - 1935-36 DETROIT LIONS; 1937-43
     CHICAGO CARDINALS
PARKER, WILLIAM FRANK (OKLAHOMA STATE) - TACKLE - 1962-64, 66-67
     CLEVELAND BROWNS; 1968 PITTSBURGH STEELERS; 1969 NEW YORK GIANTS
PARKER, WILLIE (NORTH TEXAS STATE) - CENTER, GUARD - 1973-74 BUFFALO
     BILLS (AFC)
PARKER, WILLIE DAVID (ARKANSAS AM&N) - TACKLE - 1967-69 HOUSTON
     OILERS (AFL); 1970 HOUSTON OILERS (AFC)
PARKINSON, THOMAS (PITTSBURGH) - BACK - 1931 STATEN ISLAND STAPELTONS
PARKS, DAVID (TEXAS TECH) - END - 1964-67 SAN FRANCISCO 49ERS;
     1968-69 NEW ORLEANS SAINTS; 1970-72 NEW ORLEANS SAINTS (NFC);
     1965 PASS RECEIVING LEADER
PARKS, EDWARD (OKLAHOMA) - CENTER - 1938-40 WASHINGTON REDSKINS; 1946
     CHICAGO ROCKETS (AAFC)
PARKS, WILLIAM (LONG BEACH STATE) - END - 1971 SAN DIEGO CHARGERS
     (AFC); 1972 DALLAS COWBOYS (NFC); 1973-74 HOUSTON OILERS (AFC)
PARMER, JAMES (OKLAHOMA A&M) - BACK - 1948-56 PHILADELPHIA EAGLES
PARNELL, FREDERICK (COLGATE) - TACKLE - 1925-27 NEW YORK GIANTS
PARRIOTT, WILLIAM (WEST VIRGINIA) - BACK - 1934 CINCINNATI REDS
PARRIS, GARY (FLORIDA STATE) - END - 1973-74 SAN DIEGO CHARGERS (AFC)
PARRISH, BERNARD (FLORIDA) - BACK - 1959-66 CLEVELAND BROWNS; 1966
     HOUSTON OILERS (AFL)
PARRISH, LEMAR (LINCOLN-MISSOURI) - BACK - 1970-74 CINCINNATI BENGALS
     (AFC)
PARRY, OWEN (BAYLOR) - TACKLE - 1937-39 NEW YORK GIANTS
PARSEGHIAN, ARA (MIAMI-OHIO) - BACK - 1948-49 CLEVELAND BROWNS (AAFC)
PARSON, RAY (MINNESOTA) - TACKLE, END - 1971 DETROIT LIONS (NFC)
PARSONS, EARLE (USC) - BACK - 1946-47 SAN FRANCISCO 49ERS (AAFC)
PARSONS, LLOYD (GUSTAVUS-ADOLPHUS) - BACK - 1941 DETROIT LIONS
PARSONS, ROBERT (PENN STATE) - END - 1972-74 CHICAGO BEARS (NFC)
PARTEE, DENNIS (SMU) - KICKER - 1968-69 SAN DIEGO CHARGERS (AFL);
     1970-74 SAN DIEGO CHARGERS (AFC); 1969 PUNTING LEADER (AFL)
PARTLOW, LOUIS - BACK - 1919-29 DAYTON TRIANGLES; 1923 CLEVELAND
     INDIANS; 1924 CLEVELAND BULLDOGS
PASCHAL, WILLIAM (GEORGIA TECH) - BACK - 1943-47 NEW YORK GIANTS;
     1947-48 BOSTON YANKS; 1943-44 RUSHING LEADER
PASCHKA, GORDON (MINNESOTA) - GUARD - 1943 PHIL-PITT; 1947 NEW YORK
     GIANTS
PASHE, WILLIAM (GEORGE WASHINGTON) - BACK - 1964 NEW YORK JETS (AFL)
PASKVAN, GEORGE (WISCONSIN) - BACK - 1941 GREEN BAY PACKERS
PASQUA, JOSEPH (SMU) - TACKLE - 1942 CLEVELAND RAMS; 1943 WASHINGTON
     REDSKINS; 1946 LOS ANGELES RAMS
PASQUARIELLO, RALPH (VILLANOVA) - BACK - 1950 LOS ANGELES RAMS;
     1951-52 CHICAGO CARDINALS
PASQUESI, ANTHONY (NOTRE DAME) - TACKLE - 1955-57 CHICAGO CARDINALS
PASSUELO, WILLIAM - GUARD - 1923 COLUMBUS TIGERS
PASTIN, FRANK (WAYNESBURG) - GUARD - 1942 PITTSBURGH STEELERS
PASTORINI, DAN (SANTA CLARA) - QBACK, KICKER - 1971-74 HOUSTON OILERS
     (AFC)

PASTRANA, CHARLES ALAN (MARYLAND) - QBACK - 1969 DENVER BRONCOS
    (AFL); 1970 DENVER BRONCOS (AFC)
PATANELLI, MICHAEL (BALL STATE-INDIANA) - END - 1947 BROOKLYN DODGERS
    (AAFC)
PATE, LLOYD (CINCINNATI) - BACK - 1970 BUFFALO BILLS (AFC)
PATE, RUPERT (WAKE FOREST) - GUARD - 1940 CHICAGO CARDINALS; 1941 NEW
    YORK AMERICANS (AFL); 1942 PHILADELPHIA EAGLES
PATERA, DENNIS (BRIGHAM YOUNG) - KICKER - 1968 SAN FRANCISCO 49ERS
PATERA, JOHN (OREGON) - GUARD - 1955-57 BALTIMORE COLTS; 1958-59
    CHICAGO CARDINALS; 1960-61 DALLAS COWBOYS
PATERNOSTER, ANGELO (GEORGETOWN) - GUARD - 1943 WASHINGTON REDSKINS
PATERRA, HERBERT (MICHIGAN STATE) - LB - 1963 BUFFALO BILLS (AFL)
PATRICK, FRANK (NEBRASKA) - QBACK - 1970-72 GREEN BAY PACKERS (NFC)
PATRICK, FRANK (PITTSBURGH) - BACK - 1938-39 CHICAGO CARDINALS; 1940
    BOSTON BEARS (AFL); 1941 MILWAUKEE CHIEFS (AFL)
PATRICK, JOHN (PENN STATE) - BACK - 1941, 45-46 PITTSBURGH STEELERS
PATRICK, WAYNE (LOUISVILLE) - BACK - 1968-69 BUFFALO BILLS (AFL);
    1970-72 BUFFALO BILLS (AFC)
PATT, MAURICE (CARNEGIE TECH) - END - 1938 DETROIT LIONS; 1939-42
    CLEVELAND RAMS
PATTEN, STEVEN (BOSTON COLLEGE) - GUARD - 1926 BOSTON BULLDOGS (AFL)
PATTERSON, PAUL (ILLINOIS) - BACK - 1949 CHICAGO HORNETS (AAFC)
PATTERSON, WILLIAM (BAYLOR) - QBACK - 1939 CHICAGO BEARS; 1940
    PITTSBURGH STEELERS
PATTERSON - QBACK - 1921 CLEVELAND INDIANS
PATTISON, ROGER (MINNESOTA) - GUARD - 1924 KENOSHA MAROONS
PATTON, JAMES (MISSISSIPPI) - BACK - 1955-66 NEW YORK GIANTS; 1958
    INTERCEPTION LEADER
PATTON, JERRY (NEBRASKA) - TACKLE - 1972-73 BUFFALO BILLS (AFC); 1974
    PHILADELPHIA EAGLES (NFC)
PATTON, JOHN (TCU) - GUARD - 1946-50 PHILADELPHIA EAGLES; 1951
    CHICAGO CARDINALS; 1948-49 FIELD GOAL LEADER; (1949 TIED WITH
    WATERFIELD)
PATTON, ROBERT (CLEMSON) - TACKLE - 1952 NEW YORK GIANTS
PATULSKI, WALTER (NOTRE DAME) - END - 1972-74 BUFFALO BILLS (AFC)
PAUL, DON (UCLA) - LB - 1948-55 LOS ANGELES RAMS
PAUL, DON (WASHINGTON STATE) - BACK - 1950-53 CHICAGO CARDINALS;
    1954-58 CLEVELAND BROWNS
PAUL, HAROLD (OKLAHOMA) - GUARD, TACKLE - 1974 SAN DIEGO CHARGERS
    (AFC)
PAULEKAS, ANTHONY (WASHINGTON&JEFFERSON) - CENTER - 1936 GREEN BAY
    PACKERS
PAULEY, FRANK (WASHINGTON&JEFFERSON) - TACKLE - 1930 CHICAGO BEARS
PAULSON, DAINARD (OREGON STATE) - BACK - 1961-62 NEW YORK TITANS
    (AFL); 1963-66 NEW YORK JETS (AFL); 1964 INTERCEPTION LEADER
    (AFL)
PAUXTIS, SIMON (PENNSYLVANIA) - BACK - 1919 CLEVELAND INDIANS
PAVELEC, THEODORE (DETROIT) - GUARD - 1941-43 DETROIT LIONS
PAVKOV, STONKO (IDAHO) - GUARD - 1939-40 PITTSBURGH STEELERS
PAVLICH, CHARLES - GUARD - 1946 SAN FRANCISCO 49ERS (AAFC)
PAYN, MARSHALL (FRANKLIN&MARSHALL) - CENTER - 1925 ROCHESTER
    JEFFERSONS
PAYNE, CHARLES (DETROIT) - BACK - 1937 DETROIT LIONS
PAYNE, KENNETH (LANGSTON) - END - 1974 GREEN BAY PACKERS (NFC)
PEABODY, DWIGHT (OHIO STATE) - END - 1920 COLUMBUS PANHANDLES; 1922
    TOLEDO MAROONS
PEACE, LAWRENCE (PITTSBURGH) - BACK - 1940 BUFFALO INDIANS (AFL);
    1941 BROOKLYN DODGERS
PEACOCK, JOHN (HOUSTON) - BACK - 1969 HOUSTON OILERS (AFL); 1970
    HOUSTON OILERS (AFC)
PEAKS, CLARENCE (MICHIGAN STATE) - BACK - 1957-63 PHILADELPHIA
    EAGLES; 1964-65 PITTSBURGH STEELERS
PEARCE, HARLEY (OHIO WESLEYAN) - END - 1926 COLUMBUS TIGERS
PEARCE, WALTER (PENNSYLVANIA) - QBACK - 1920 DECATUR STALEYS; 1921
    CHICAGO STALEYS; 1922 CHICAGO BEARS; 1924 KENOSHA MAROONS; 1925
    PROVIDENCE STEAMROLLERS
PEARCY, JAMES (MARSHALL) - GUARD - 1946-48 CHICAGO ROCKETS (AAFC);
    1949 CHICAGO HORNETS (AAFC)
PEARSON, BARRY (NORTHWESTERN) - END - 1972-73 PITTSBURGH STEELERS
    (AFC)
PEARSON, DREW (TULSA) - END - 1973-74 DALLAS COWBOYS (NFC)

PEARSON, DUDLEY (NOTRE DAME) - BACK - 1922 RACINE LEGION
PEARSON, PRESTON (ILLINOIS) - BACK, END - 1967-69 BALTIMORE COLTS;
    1970-74 PITTSBURGH STEELERS (AFC)
PEARSON, LINDELL (OKLAHOMA) - BACK - 1950-52 DETROIT LIONS; 1952
    GREEN BAY PACKERS
PEARSON, MADISON "BERT" (KANSAS STATE) - CENTER - 1929-34 CHICAGO
    BEARS; 1935-36 CHICAGO CARDINALS; 1937 LOS ANGELES BULLDOGS (AFL)
PEARSON, WILLIE (NORTH CAROLINA A&T) - BACK - 1969 MIAMI DOLPHINS
    (AFL)
PEASE, GEORGE (COLUMBIA) - QBACK - 1926 NEW YORK YANKEES (AFL); 1929
    ORANGE TORNADOS
PEAY, FRANCIS (MISSOURI) - TACKLE - 1966-67 NEW YORK GIANTS; 1968-69
    GREEN BAY PACKERS; 1970-72 GREEN BAY PACKERS (NFC); 1973-74
    KANSAS CITY CHIEFS (AFC)
PECK, ROBERT (PITTSBURGH) - CENTER - 1919 MASSILLON TIGERS
PEDERSON, JAMES (AUGSBURG) - END - 1930 MINNEAPOLIS REDJACKETS;
    1930-31 FRANKFORD YELLOWJACKETS; 1932 CHICAGO BEARS
PEDERSON, WINFIELD (MINNESOTA) - TACKLE - 1940 MILWAUKEE CHIEFS
    (AFL); 1941, 45 NEW YORK GIANTS; 1946 BOSTON YANKS
PEEBLES, JAMES (VANDERBILT) - END - 1946-49, 51 WASHINGTON REDSKINS
PEERY, GORDON (OKLAHOMA A&M) - BACK - 1927 CLEVELAND BULLDOGS
PEGG, HAROLD (BUCKNELL) - CENTER - 1940 BUFFALO INDIANS (AFL)
PELFREY, RAYMOND (EASTER KENTUCKY STATE) - BACK - 1951 GREEN BAY
    PACKERS; 1952 DALLAS TEXANS; 1952 CHICAGO CARDINALS; 1953 NEW
    YORK GIANTS
PELLEGRINI, ROBERT (MARYLAND) - LB - 1956, 58-61 PHILADELPHIA EAGLES;
    1962-65 WASHINGTON REDSKINS
PELLINGTON, WILLIAM (RUTGERS) - LB - 1953-64 BALTIMORE COLTS
PENA, ROBERT "BUBBA" (MASSACHUSETTS) - GUARD - 1972 CLEVELAND BROWNS
    (AFC)
PENCHION, ROBERT (ALCORN A&M) - TACKLE, GUARD - 1972-73 BUFFALO BILLS
    (AFC); 1974 SAN FRANCISCO 49ERS (NFC)
PENDERGAST, WILLIAM (MANHATTAN) - BACK - 1937 BOSTON SHAMROCKS (AFL)
PENNINGTON, DURWOOD (GEORGIA) - KICKER - 1962 DALLAS TEXANS (AFL)
PENSE, LEON (ARKANSAS) - QBACK - 1945 PITTSBURGH STEELERS
PENTECOST, JOHN (UCLA) - GUARD - 1967 MINNESOTA VIKINGS
PEOPLES, WOODROW (GRAMBLING) - GUARD - 1968-69 SAN FRANCISCO 49ERS;
    1970-74 SAN FRANCISCO 49ERS (NFC)
PEPPER, EUGENE (MISSOURI) - GUARD - 1950-53 WASHINGTON REDSKINS; 1954
    BALTIMORE COLTS
PERANTONI, FRANCIS (PRINCETON) - CENTER - 1948-49 NEW YORK YANKEES
    (AAFC)
PERCIVAL, MAC (TEXAS TECH) - KICKER - 1967-69 CHICAGO BEARS; 1970-73
    CHICAGO BEARS (NFC); 1974 DALLAS COWBOYS (NFC); 1968 FIELD GOAL
    LEADER
PERDUE, WILLARD (DUKE) - END - 1940 NEW YORK GIANTS; 1946 BROOKLYN
    DODGERS (AAFC)
PEREZ, PETER (ILLINOIS) - GUARD - 1945 CHICAGO BEARS
PERGINE, JOHN (NOTRE DAME) - LB - 1969 LOS ANGELES RAMS; 1970-72 LOS
    ANGELES RAMS (NFC); 1973-74 WASHINGTON REDSKINS (NFC)
PERINA, ROBERT (PRINCETON) - BACK - 1946 NEW YORK YANKEES (AAFC);
    1947 BROOKLYN DODGERS (AAFC); 1948 CHICAGO ROCKETS (AAFC); 1949
    CHICAGO BEARS; 1950 BALTIMORE COLTS
PERINI, EVO (OHIO STATE) - BACK - 1954-55 CHICAGO BEARS; 1955
    CLEVELAND BROWNS
PERINO, MICHAEL (WICHITA) - TACKLE - 1940 MILWAUKEE CHIEFS (AFL)
PERKINS, ARTHUR (NORTH TEXAS STATE) - BACK - 1962-63 LOS ANGELES RAMS
PERKINS, DONALD (NEW MEXICO) - BACK - 1961-68 DALLAS COWBOYS
PERKINS, DONALD (PLATTEVILLE STATE-WIS.) - BACK - 1941 MILWAUKEE
    CHIEFS (AFL); 1943-45 GREEN BAY PACKERS; 1945-46 CHICAGO BEARS
PERKINS, JAMES (COLORADO) - TACKLE - 1962-64 DENVER BRONCOS (AFL)
PERKINS, WALTER RAY (ALABAMA) - END - 1967-69 BALTIMORE COLTS;
    1970-71 BALTIMORE COLTS (AFC)
PERKINS, WILLIAM (IOWA) - BACK - 1963 NEW YORK JETS (AFL)
PERKINS, WILLIS (TEXAS SOUTHERN) - GUARD - 1961-63 HOUSTON OILERS
    (AFL); 1961 BOSTON PATRIOTS (AFL)
PERKO, JOHN (DUQUESNE) - GUARD - 1937-38 PITTSBURGH PIRATES; 1939-40,
    45-47 PITTSBURGH STEELERS; 1944 CARD-PITT; 1945-47 PITTSBURGH
    STEELERS
PERKO, JOHN (MINNESOTA) - GUARD - 1946 BUFFALO BISONS (AAFC)

PERLMAN, LESTER (PITTSBURGH) - GUARD - 1919 CLEVELAND INDIANS; 1920
    CLEVELAND PANTHERS; 1921 CLEVELAND INDIANS; 1924 ROCHESTER
    JEFFERSONS
PERLO, PHILIP (MARYLAND) - LB - 1960 HOUSTON OILERS (AFL)
PERPICH, GEORGE (GEORGETOWN) - TACKLE - 1946 BROOKLYN DODGERS (AAFC);
    1947 BALTIMORE COLTS (AAFC)
PERREAULT, PETER (BOSTON UNIV.) - TACKLE, GUARD - 1963-67, 69 NEW
    YORK JETS (AFL); 1968 CINCINNATI BENGALS (AFL); 1970 NEW YORK
    JETS (AFC); 1971 MINNESOTA VIKINGS (NFC)
PERRIE, MICHAEL (ST. MARY'S OF CAL.) - BACK - 1939 CLEVELAND RAMS
PERRIN, JOHN - BACK - 1926 HARTFORD BLUES
PERROTTI, MICHAEL (CINCINNATI) - TACKLE - 1948-49 LOS ANGELES DONS
    (AAFC)
PERRY, CLAUDE (ALABAMA) - TACKLE - 1927-35 GREEN BAY PACKERS; 1931
    BROOKLYN DODGERS; 1936-37 PITTSBURGH AMERICANS (AFL)
PERRY, FLETCHER "JOE" (COMPTON JUNIOR) - BACK - 1948-49 SAN FRANCISCO
    49ERS (AAFC); 1950-60, 63 SAN FRANCISCO 49ERS; 1961-62 BALTIMORE
    COLTS; 1953-54 RUSHING LEADER; 1969 HALL OF FAME
PERRY, GERARD (CALIFORNIA) - TACKLE - 1954, 56-59 DETROIT LIONS;
    1960-62 ST. LOUIS CARDINALS
PERRY, LOWELL (MICHIGAN) - BACK - 1956 PITTSBURGH STEELERS
PERSON, ARA (MORGAN STATE) - END - 1972 ST. LOUIS CARDINALS (NFC)
PESHMALYAN, BARUYR (YALE) - END - 1920 CHICAGO TIGERS
PESONEN, RICHARD (MINNESOTA AT DULUTH) - BACK - 1960 GREEN BAY
    PACKERS; 1961 MINNESOTA VIKINGS; 1962-64 NEW YORK GIANTS
PESSALANO, LOUIS (VILLANOVA) - TACKLE - 1929 STATEN ISLAND STAPELTONS
PETCHEL, JOHN (DUQUESNE) - QBACK - 1942, 44 CLEVELAND RAMS; 1945
    PITTSBURGH STEELERS
PETCOGG, BONI (OHIO STATE) - TACKLE - 1924-26 COLUMBUS TIGERS
PETERS, ANTON (FLORIDA) - TACKLE - 1963 DENVER BRONCOS (AFL)
PETERS, FLOYD (SAN FRANCISCO STATE) - TACKLE - 1959-62 CLEVELAND
    BROWNS; 1963 DETROIT LIONS; 1964-69 PHILADELPHIA EAGLES; 1970
    WASHINGTON REDSKINS (NFC)
PETERS, FOREST (ILLINOIS) - BACK - 1930 PORTSMOUTH SPARTANS; 1930
    PROVIDENCE STEAMROLLERS; 1931 BROOKLYN DODGERS; 1932 CHICAGO
    CARDINALS
PETERS, FRANK (OHIO UNIV.) - TACKLE, CENTER - 1969 CINCINNATI BENGALS
    (AFL)
PETERS, VOLNEY (USC) - TACKLE - 1952-53 CHICAGO CARDINALS; 1954-57
    WASHINGTON REDSKINS; 1958 PHILADELPHIA EAGLES; 1960 LOS ANGELES
    CHARGERS (AFL); 1961 OAKLAND RAIDERS (AFL)
PETERSON, CALVIN (UCLA) - LB - 1974 DALLAS COWBOYS (NFC)
PETERSON, GERALD (TEXAS) - TACKLE - 1956 BALTIMORE COLTS
PETERSON, JIM (SAN DIEGO STATE) - LB - 1974 LOS ANGELES RAMS (NFC)
PETERSON, JOHN (KANSAS) - BACK - 1936 NEW YORK YANKS (AFL)
PETERSON, KENNETH (GONZAGA) - BACK - 1935 CHICAGO CARDINALS; 1936
    DETROIT LIONS
PETERSON, KENNETH (UTAH) - GUARD - 1961 MINNESOTA VIKINGS
PETERSON, LEONARD - END - 1924 KANSAS CITY COWBOYS
PETERSON, LESTER (TEXAS) - END - 1931 PORTSMOUTH SPARTANS; 1932
    STATEN ISLAND STAPELTONS; 1932-34 GREEN BAY PACKERS; 1933
    BROOKLYN DODGERS
PETERSON, NELSON (WEST VIRGINIA WESLEYAN) - BACK - 1937 WASHINGTON
    REDSKINS; 1938 CLEVELAND RAMS; 1940-41 COLUMBUS BULLIES (AFL)
PETERSON, PHILIP (WISCONSIN) - BACK - 1934 BROOKLYN DODGERS
PETERSON, RAYMOND (SAN FRANCISCO) - BACK - 1937 GREEN BAY PACKERS
PETERSON, RUSSELL (MONTANA) - BACK - 1952 DALLAS TEXANS; 1955-56
    CLEVELAND BROWNS; 1957 GREEN BAY PACKERS
PETERSON, WILLIAM (SAN JOSE STATE) - LB - 1968-69 CINCINNATI BENGALS
    (AFL); 1970-72 CINCINNATI BENGALS (AFC)
PETITBON, RICHARD (TULANE) - BACK - 1959-68 CHICAGO BEARS; 1969 LOS
    ANGELES RAMS; 1970 LOS ANGELES RAMS (NFC); 1971-72 WASHINGTON
    REDSKINS (NFC)
PETRELLA, JOHN (PENN STATE) - BACK - 1945 PITTSBURGH STEELERS
PETRELLA, ROBERT (TENNESSEE) - BACK - 1966-69 MIAMI DOLPHINS (AFL);
    1970-71 MIAMI DOLPHINS (AFC)
PETRICH, ROBERT (WEST TEXAS STATE) - END - 1963-66 SAN DIEGO CHARGERS
    (AFL); 1967 BUFFALO BILLS (AFL)
PETRIE, ELMER - BACK - 1920 CLEVELAND PANTHERS; 1922 TOLEDO MAROONS
PETRILAS, WILLIAM - BACK - 1944-45 NEW YORK GIANTS
PETRO, STEPHEN (PITTSBURGH) - GUARD - 1940-41 BROOKLYN DODGERS

PETROVICH, GEORGE (TEXAS) - TACKLE - 1949-50 CHICAGO CARDINALS
PETRY, BASIL (PURDUE) - CENTER - 1941 CINCINNATI BENGALS (AFL)
PETTIES, NEAL (SAN DIEGO STATE) - END - 1964-66 BALTIMORE COLTS
PETTIGREW, GARY (STANFORD) - TACKLE - 1966-69 PHILADELPHIA EAGLES;
    1970-74 PHILADELPHIA EAGLES (NFC); 1974 NEW YORK GIANTS (NFC)
PETTY, JOHN (PURDUE) - BACK - 1942 CHICAGO BEARS
PETTY, MANLEY ROSS (ILLINOIS) - GUARD - 1920 CANTON BULLDOGS; 1920
    DECATUR STALEYS
PEVIANA, ROBERT (USC) - GUARD - 1953 NEW YORK GIANTS
PEYTON, LEO (ST. LAWRENCE) - BACK - 1923-25 ROCHESTER JEFFERSONS
PFEFFER, HOWARD (ST. REGIS) - BACK - 1941 MILWAUKEE CHIEFS (AFL)
PFOHL, ROBERT (PURDUE) - BACK - 1948-49 BALTIMORE COLTS (AAFC)
PHARMER, ARTHUR (MINNESOTA) - BACK - 1930 MINNEAPOLIS REDJACKETS;
    1930-31 FRANKFORD YELLOWJACKETS
PHARR, TOMMY (MISSISSIPPI STATE) - BACK - 1970 BUFFALO BILLS (AFC)
PHELAN, ROBERT (NOTRE DAME) - BACK - 1922 TOLEDO MAROONS; 1923-24
    ROCK ISLAND INDEPENDENTS
PHELPS, DONALD (KENTUCKY) - BACK - 1950-52 CLEVELAND BROWNS
PHILBIN, GERALD (BUFFALO) - END - 1964-69 NEW YORK JETS (AFL);
    1970-72 NEW YORK JETS (AFC); 1973 PHILADELPHIA EAGLES (NFC)
PHILLIPS, EWELL (OKLAHOMA BAPTIST) - GUARD - 1936 NEW YORK GIANTS;
    1937 LOS ANGELES BULLDOGS (AFL)
PHILLIPS, GEORGE (UCLA) - BACK - 1945 CLEVELAND RAMS
PHILLIPS, JAMES "RED" (AUBURN) - END - 1958-64 LOS ANGELES RAMS;
    1965-67 MINNESOTA VIKINGS; 1961 PASS RECEIVING LEADER
PHILLIPS, JESSE (MICHIGAN STATE) - BACK - 1968-69 CINCINNATI BENGALS
    (AFL); 1970-73 CINCINNATI BENGALS (AFC); 1974 NEW ORLEANS SAINTS
    (NFC)
PHILLIPS, LOYD (ARKANSAS) - END - 1967-69 CHICAGO BEARS
PHILLIPS, MELVIN (NORTH CAROLINA A&T) - BACK - 1966-69 SAN FRANCISCO
    49ERS; 1970-74 SAN FRANCISCO 49ERS (NFC)
PHILLIPS, MICHAEL (WESTERN MARYLAND) - CENTER - 1947 BALTIMORE COLTS
    (AAFC)
PHILLIPS, WILLIAM - BACK - 1941 COLUMBUS BULLIES (AFL)
PHILPOTT, DEAN (FRESNO STATE) - BACK - 1958 CHICAGO CARDINALS
PHILPOTT, EDWARD (MIAMI-OHIO) - LB - 1967-69 BOSTON PATRIOTS (AFL);
    1970 BOSTON PATRIOTS (AFC); 1971 NEW ENGLAND PATRIOTS (AFC)
PHIPPS, MICHAEL (PURDUE) - QBACK - 1970-74 CLEVELAND BROWNS (AFC)
PIASECKY, ALEXANDER (DUKE) - END - 1943-45 WASHINGTON REDSKINS
PICARD, ROBERT (EASTERN WASHINGTON STATE) - END - 1973-74
    PHILADELPHIA EAGLES (NFC)
PICCOLO, LOUIS BRIAN (WAKE FOREST) - BACK - 1966-69 CHICAGO BEARS
PICCOLO, WILLIAM (CANISIUS) - CENTER - 1943-45 NEW YORK GIANTS
PICCONE, LOUIS (WEST LIBERTY STATE) - END - 1974 NEW YORK JETS (AFC)
PICKARD, BOB (XAVIER) - END - 1974 DETROIT LIONS (NFC)
PICKENS, ROBERT (NEBRASKA) - TACKLE - 1967-69 CHICAGO BEARS
PIEPUL, MILTON (NOTRE DAME) - BACK - 1941 DETROIT LIONS
PIERCE, BEMUS (CARLISLE) - BACK - 1920 AKRON PROS; 1922-23 OORANG
    INDIANS
PIERCE, DONALD (KANSAS) - CENTER - 1942 BROOKLYN DODGERS; 1943
    CHICAGO CARDINALS
PIERCE, GEORGE (MICHIGAN) - GUARD - 1919 CANTON BULLDOGS; 1920
    CHICAGO TIGERS
PIERCE, JOHN DANIEL (MEMPHIS STATE) - QBACK, BACK - 1970 WASHINGTON
    REDSKINS (NFC)
PIEROTTI, ALBERT (WASHINGTON&LEE) - CENTER - 1919 CLEVELAND INDIANS;
    1920 CLEVELAND PANTHERS; 1922-24 MILWAUKEE BADGERS; 1926 BOSTON
    BULLDOGS (AFL); 1927-28 PROVIDENCE STEAMROLLERS; 1929 BOSTON
    BRAVES
PIERRE, JOHN (PITTSBURGH) - END - 1945 PITTSBURGH STEELERS
PIETROSANTE, NICHOLAS (NOTRE DAME) - BACK - 1959-65 DETROIT LIONS;
    1966-67 CLEVELAND BROWNS
PIETRZAK, JAMES (EASTERN MICHIGAN) - TACKLE - 1974 NEW YORK GIANTS
    (NFC)
PIFFERINI, ROBERT (SAN JOSE STATE) - CENTER - 1949 DETROIT LIONS
PIFFERINI, ROBERT (UCLA) - LB - 1972-74 CHICAGO BEARS (NFC)
PIGGOTT, BERT (ILLINOIS) - BACK - 1947 LOS ANGELES DONS (AAFC)
PIGNATELLI, CARL (IOWA) - BACK - 1931 CLEVELAND INDIANS

Top row (from left to right): Steve Owens, Alan Page, Dan Pastorini and Walt Patulski. Second row: Gerry Philbin, Mike Phipps, Jim Plunkett and Ed Podolak. Third row: Myron Pottios, Jethro Pugh, Mel Renfro and Lance Rentzel. Bottom row: John Riggins, Isiah Robertson, Jake Scott and Robert Scott.

PIHOS, PETER (INDIANA) - END - 1947-55 PHILADELPHIA EAGLES; 1953-55
    PASS RECEIVING LEADER; (1955 TIED WITH W. WILSON); 1970 HALL OF
    FAME
PIKE, JOHN (DAVIS&ELKINS) - GUARD - 1936 NEW YORK YANKS (AFL)
PILCONIS, JOSEPH (TEMPLE) - END - 1934, 36-37 PHILADELPHIA EAGLES
PILLATH, ROGER (WISCONSIN) - TACKLE - 1965 LOS ANGELES RAMS; 1966
    PITTSBURGH STEELERS
PILLSBURY, GORDON (COLGATE) - CENTER - 1936 ROCHESTER TIGERS (AFL)
PINCKERT, ERNEST (USC) - BACK - 1932 BOSTON BRAVES; 1933-36 BOSTON
    REDSKINS; 1937-40 WASHINGTON REDSKINS
PINCURA, STANLEY (OHIO STATE) - QBACK - 1936 CLEVELAND RAMS (AFL);
    1937-38 CLEVELAND RAMS
PINCZAK, JOHN (AUGUSTANA) - GUARD - 1941 MILWAUKEE CHIEFS (AFL)
PINDER, CYRIL (ILLINOIS) - BACK - 1968-69 PHILADELPHIA EAGLES; 1970
    PHILADELPHIA EAGLES (NFC); 1971-72 CHICAGO BEARS (NFC); 1973
    DALLAS COWBOYS (NFC)
PINE, EDWARD (UTAH) - LB - 1962-64 SAN FRANCISCO 49ERS; 1965
    PITTSBURGH STEELERS
PINGEL, JOHN (MICHIGAN STATE) - BACK - 1939 DETROIT LIONS
PIPKIN, JOYCE (ARKANSAS) - END - 1948 NEW YORK GIANTS; 1949 LOS
    ANGELES DONS (AAFC)
PIRO, HENRY (SYRACUSE) - END - 1941 PHILADELPHIA EAGLES
PIRRO, ROCCO (CATHOLIC UNIV.) - GUARD - 1940-41 PITTSBURGH STEELERS;
    1946 BUFFALO BISONS (AAFC); 1947-49 BUFFALO BILLS (AAFC)
PISKOR, ROMAN (NIAGARA) - TACKLE -. 1946 NEW YORK YANKEES (AAFC); 1947
    CLEVELAND BROWNS (AAFC); 1948 CHICAGO ROCKETS (AAFC)
PITTMAN, CHARLES (PENN STATE) - BACK - 1970 ST. LOUIS CARDINALS
    (NFC); 1971 BALTIMORE COLTS (AFC)
PITTMAN, MELVIN (HARDIN-SIMMONS) - CENTER - 1935 PITTSBURGH PIRATES
PITTS, EDWIN "ALABAMA" - BACK - 1935 PHILADELPHIA EAGLES
PITTS, ELIJAH (PHILANDER SMITH) - BACK - 1961-69 GREEN BAY PACKERS;
    1970 LOS ANGELES RAMS (NFC); 1970 NEW ORLEANS SAINTS (NFC); 1971
    GREEN BAY PACKERS (NFC)
PITTS, FRANK (SOUTHERN) - END - 1965-69 KANSAS CITY CHIEFS (AFL);
    1970 KANSAS CITY CHIEFS (AFC); 1971-73 CLEVELAND BROWNS (AFC);
    1974 OAKLAND RAIDERS (AFC)
PITTS, HUGH (TCU) - LB - 1956 LOS ANGELES RAMS; 1960 HOUSTON OILERS
    (AFL)
PITTS, JOHN (ARIZONA STATE) - BACK - 1967-69 BUFFALO BILLS (AFL);
    1970-73 BUFFALO BILLS (AFC); 1973-74 DENVER BRONCOS (AFC)
PIVARNIK, JOSEPH (NOTRE DAME) - GUARD - 1936 PHILADELPHIA EAGLES
PIVEC, DAVID (NOTRE DAME) - END - 1966-68 LOS ANGELES RAMS; 1969
    DENVER BRONCOS (AFL)
PLANK, EARL - END - 1926 COLUMBUS TIGERS; 1929 BUFFALO BISONS; 1930
    BROOKLYN DODGERS
PLANSKY, ANTHONY (GEORGETOWN) - BACK - 1928-29 NEW YORK GIANTS; 1932
    BOSTON BRAVES
PLANUTIS, GERALD (MICHIGAN STATE) - BACK - 1956 WASHINGTON REDSKINS
PLASMAN, RICHARD (VANDERBILT) - END - 1937-41, 44 CHICAGO BEARS;
    1946-47 CHICAGO CARDINALS
PLATUKAS, GEORGE (DUQUESNE) - END - 1938 PITTSBURGH PIRATES; 1939-41
    PITTSBURGH STEELERS; 1942 CLEVELAND RAMS
PLATUKAS, VINCENT (ST. THOMAS) - BACK - 1936-37 PITTSBURGH AMERICANS
    (AFL)
PLISKA, JOSEPH (NOTRE DAME) - BACK - 1920 HAMMOND PROS
PLUM, MILTON (PENN STATE) - QBACK - 1957-61 CLEVELAND BROWNS; 1962-67
    DETROIT LIONS; 1968 LOS ANGELES RAMS; 1969 NEW YORK GIANTS;
    1960-61 PASSING LEADER
PLUMMER, TONY (PACIFIC) - BACK - 1970 ST. LOUIS CARDINALS (NFC);
    1971-73 ATLANTA FALCONS (NFC); 1974 LOS ANGELES RAMS (NFC)
PLUMP, DAVID (FRESNO STATE) - BACK - 1966 SAN DIEGO CHARGERS (AFL)
PLUMRIDGE, THEODORE (ST. JOHN'S OF NEW YORK) - CENTER - 1926 BROOKLYN
    LIONS; 1926 BROOKLYN HORSEMEN (AFL)
PLUNKETT, JAMES (STANFORD) - QBACK - 1971-74 NEW ENGLAND PATRIOTS
    (AFC)
PLUNKETT, SHERMAN (MARYLAND STATE) - TACKLE - 1958-60 BALTIMORE
    COLTS; 1961-62 NEW YORK TITANS (AFL); 1963-67 NEW YORK JETS (AFL)
PLUNKETT, WARREN (MINNESOTA) - BACK - 1942 CLEVELAND RAMS

PLY, ROBERT (BAYLOR) - BACK - 1962 DALLAS TEXANS (AFL); 1963-67
    KANSAS CITY CHIEFS (AFL); 1967 BUFFALO BILLS (AFL); 1967 DENVER
    BRONCOS (AFL)
POAGE, RAYMOND (TEXAS) - END - 1963 MINNESOTA VIKINGS; 1964-65
    PHILADELPHIA EAGLES; 1967-69 NEW ORLEANS SAINTS; 1970 NEW
    ORLEANS SAINTS (NFC); 1971 ATLANTA FALCONS (NFC)
PODMAJERSKI, PAUL (ILLINOIS) - GUARD - 1944 CHICAGO BEARS
PODOLAK, EDWARD (IOWA) - BACK - 1969 KANSAS CITY CHIEFS (AFL);
    1970-74 KANSAS CITY CHIEFS (AFC)
PODOLEY, JAMES (MICHIGAN CENTRAL) - BACK - 1957-60 WASHINGTON REDSKINS
POHLMAN, JOHN (BROWN) - BACK - 1925 PROVIDENCE STEAMROLLERS
POILEK, JOSEPH (WEST VIRGINIA) - BACK - 1936 PITTSBURGH AMERICANS
    (AFL)
POILLON, RICHARD (CANISIUS) - BACK - 1942, 46-49 WASHINGTON REDSKINS
POIMBEOUF, LANCE (SOUTHWEST LOUISIANA) - GUARD - 1963 DALLAS COWBOYS
POLANSKI, JOHN (WAKE FOREST) - BACK - 1942 DETROIT LIONS; 1946 LOS
    ANGELES DONS (AAFC)
POLISKY, JOHN (NOTRE DAME) - TACKLE - 1929 CHICAGO BEARS
POLLACK, MILTON (CALIFORNIA) - TACKLE - 1940 COLUMBUS BULLIES (AFL)
POLLARD, ALBERT (WEST POINT & LOYOLA-CAL.) - BACK - 1951 NEW YORK
    YANKS; 1951-53 PHILADELPHIA EAGLES
POLLARD, FREDERICK "FRITZ" (BROWN) - BACK - 1919-21, 25-26 AKRON
    PROS; 1922 MILWAUKEE BADGERS; 1923-25 HAMMOND PROS; 1925
    PROVIDENCE STEAMROLLERS
POLLARD, ROBERT (WEBER STATE) - TACKLE - 1971-74 NEW ORLEANS SAINTS
    (NFC)
POLLOCK, SHELDON (LAFAYETTE) - CENTER - 1926 BROOKLYN HORSEMEN (AFL)
POLLOCK, WILLIAM (PENN MILITARY ACADEMY) - BACK - 1935-36 CHICAGO
    BEARS
POLOFSKY, GORDON (TENNESSEE) - BACK - 1952-54 CHICAGO CARDINALS
POLSFOOT, FRANCIS (WASHINGTON STATE) - END - 1950-52 CHICAGO
    CARDINALS; 1953 WASHINGTON REDSKINS
POLTL, RANDALL (STANFORD) - BACK - 1974 MINNESOTA VIKINGS (NFC)
POOL, HAMPTON (STANFORD) - END - 1940-43 CHICAGO BEARS; 1946 MIAMI
    SEAHAWKS (AAFC)
POOLE, G. BARNEY (WEST POINT & MISSISSIPPI) - END - 1949 NEW YORK
    YANKEES (AAFC); 1950-51 NEW YORK YANKS; 1952 DALLAS TEXANS; 1953
    BALTIMORE COLTS; 1954 NEW YORK GIANTS
POOLE, JAMES (MISSISSIPPI) - END - 1937-41, 45-46 NEW YORK GIANTS;
    1945 CHICAGO CARDINALS
POOLE, OLIVER (MISSISSIPPI) - END - 1947 NEW YORK YANKEES (AAFC);
    1948 BALTIMORE COLTS (AAFC); 1949 DETROIT LIONS
POOLE, RAY (MISSISSIPPI) - END - 1947-52 NEW YORK GIANTS
POOLE, ROBERT (CLEMSON) - END - 1964-65 SAN FRANCISCO 49ERS; 1966-67
    HOUSTON OILERS (AFL)
POPA, ELI (ILLINOIS) - BACK - 1952 CHICAGO CARDINALS
POPADAK, JOHN (ST. BONAVENTURE) - TACKLE - 1937 ROCHESTER TIGERS (AFL)
POPE, FRANK (CATAWBA) - END - 1964, 66-67 LOS ANGELES RAMS; 1968
    GREEN BAY PACKERS
POPE, KENITH (OKLAHOMA) - BACK - 1974 NEW ENGLAND PATRIOTS (AFC)
POPE, LEWIS (PURDUE) - BACK - 1931 PROVIDENCE STEAMROLLERS; 1933-34
    CINCINNATI REDS
POPOV, JOHN (CINCINNATI) - BACK - 1940-41 CINCINNATI BENGALS (AFL)
POPOVICH, JOHN (ST. VINCENT'S) - BACK - 1944 CARD-PITT; 1945
    PITTSBURGH STEELERS
POPOVICH, MILTON (MONTANA) - BACK - 1938-42 CHICAGO CARDINALS
POPP, ANTHONY (TOLEDO) - END - 1940 CINCINNATI BENGALS (AFL)
PORTER, LOUIS (SOUTHERN) - BACK - 1970 KANSAS CITY CHIEFS (AFC)
PORTER, RONALD (IDAHO) - LB - 1967-69 BALTIMORE COLTS; 1969
    PHILADELPHIA EAGLES; 1970-72 PHILADELPHIA EAGLES (NFC); 1973
    MINNESOTA VIKINGS (NFC)
PORTER, WILLIE (TEXAS SOUTHERN) - BACK - 1968 BOSTON PATRIOTS (AFL)
PORTERFIELD, GARRY (TULSA) - END - 1965 DALLAS COWBOYS
POST, RICHARD (HOUSTON) - BACK - 1967-69 SAN DIEGO CHARGERS (AFL);
    1970 SAN DIEGO CHARGERS (AFC); 1971 DENVER BRONCOS (AFC); 1971
    HOUSTON OILERS (AFC); 1969 RUSHING LEADER (AFL)
POST, ROBERT (KINGS POINT) - BACK - 1967 NEW YORK GIANTS
POSTE, LESTER (NORTHEAST MISSOURI STATE) - QBACK - 1937 ROCHESTER
    TIGERS (AFL)
POSTUS, ALBERT (VILLANOVA) - BACK - 1945 PITTSBURGH STEELERS
POTH, PHILIP (GONZAGA) - GUARD - 1934 PHILADELPHIA EAGLES

POTO, JOHN - BACK - 1947-48 BOSTON YANKS

POTTEIGER, EARL (URSINUS) - QBACK - 1920 BUFFALO ALL-AMERICANS; 1921
    CHICAGO CARDINALS; 1922 MILWAUKEE BADGERS; 1924 KENOSHA MAROONS;
    1925-28 NEW YORK GIANTS

POTTER, CHARLES (WASHINGTON&JEFFERSON) - GUARD - 1926 CLEVELAND
    PANTHERS (AFL)

POTTER, LEXIE (KENTUCKY) - TACKLE - 1937 CINCINNATI BENGALS (AFL)

POTTIOS, MYRON (NOTRE DAME) - LB - 1961, 63-65 PITTSBURGH STEELERS;
    1966-69 LOS ANGELES RAMS; 1970 LOS ANGELES RAMS (NFC); 1971-74
    WASHINGTON REDSKINS (NFC)

POTTS, CHARLES (PURDUE) - BACK - 1972 DETROIT LIONS (NFC)

POTTS, ROBERT (CLEMSON) - TACKLE - 1926 FRANKFORD YELLOWJACKETS

POTTS, WILLIAM (VILLANOVA) - BACK - 1934 PITTSBURGH PIRATES; 1936
    PITTSBURGH AMERICANS (AFL)

POWELL, ARDEN "TIM" (NORTHWESTERN) - END - 1965 LOS ANGELES RAMS;
    1966 PITTSBURGH STEELERS

POWELL, ARTHUR (SAN JOSE STATE) - END, BACK - 1959 PHILADELPHIA
    EAGLES; 1960-62 NEW YORK TITANS (AFL); 1963-66 OAKLAND RAIDERS
    (AFL); 1967 BUFFALO BILLS (AFL); 1968 MINNESOTA VIKINGS

POWELL, CHARLES - END - 1952, 53, 55-57 SAN FRANCISCO 49ERS; 1960-61
    OAKLAND RAIDERS (AFL)

POWELL, JESSE (WEST TEXAS STATE) - LB - 1969 MIAMI DOLPHINS (AFL);
    1970-73 MIAMI DOLPHINS (AFC)

POWELL, PRESTON (GRAMBLING) - BACK - 1961 CLEVELAND BROWNS

POWELL, RICHARD (DAVIS&ELKINS) - END - 1932 NEW YORK GIANTS; 1933
    CINCINNATI REDS

POWELL, ROGER (TEXAS A&M) - END - 1926 BUFFALO RANGERS

POWELL, STANCIL (CARLISLE) - GUARD - 1923 OORANG INDIANS

POWERS, CLYDE (OKLAHOMA) - BACK - 1974 NEW YORK GIANTS (NFC)

POWERS, JAMES (USC) - QBACK - 1950-53 SAN FRANCISCO 49ERS

POWERS, JOHN (NOTRE DAME) - END - 1962-66 PITTSBURGH STEELERS

POWERS, SAMUEL (NORTHERN MICHIGAN) - GUARD - 1921 GREEN BAY PACKERS

POWERS, WARREN (NEBRASKA) - BACK - 1963-68 OAKLAND RAIDERS (AFL)

PRATHER, DALE (GEORGE WASHINGTON) - END - 1937 BOSTON SHAMROCKS
    (AFL); 1937-38 CLEVELAND RAMS

PRATT, ROBERT (NORTH CAROLINA) - GUARD - 1974 BALTIMORE COLTS (AFC)

PRCHLIK, JOHN (YALE) - TACKLE - 1949-53 DETROIT LIONS

PREAS, GEORGE (VIRGINIA POLYTECH) - TACKLE - 1955-65 BALTIMORE COLTS

PREBOLA, EUGENE (BOSTON UNIV.) - END - 1960 OAKLAND RAIDERS (AFL);
    1961-63 DENVER BRONCOS (AFL)

PREECE, STEVEN (OREGON STATE) - BACK - 1969 NEW ORLEANS SAINTS;
    1970-72 PHILADELPHIA EAGLES (NFC); 1972 DENVER BRONCOS (AFC);
    1973-74 LOS ANGELES RAMS (NFC)

PREGULMAN, MERVIN (MICHIGAN) - GUARD - 1946 GREEN BAY PACKERS;
    1947-48 DETROIT LIONS; 1949 NEW YORK BULLDOGS

PRENDERGADT, LEO (LAFAYETTE) - TACKLE - 1926 BROOKLYN HORSEMEN (AFL)

PRESCOTT, HAROLD (HARDIN-SIMMONS) - END - 1946 GREEN BAY PACKERS;
    1947-49 PHILADELPHIA EAGLES; 1949 NEW YORK BULLDOGS

PRESNELL, GLENN (NEBRASKA) - QBACK - 1931-33 PORTSMOUTH SPARTANS;
    1934-36 DETROIT LIONS; 1933 SCORING LEADER; (TIED WITH STRONG);
    1933 FIELD GOAL LEADER; (TIED WITH MANDERS)

PRESSLEY, LEE (OKLAHOMA) - CENTER - 1945 WASHINGTON REDSKINS

PRESTEL, JAMES (IDAHO) - TACKLE - 1960 CLEVELAND BROWNS; 1961-65
    MINNESOTA VIKINGS; 1966 NEW YORK GIANTS; 1967 WASHINGTON REDSKINS

PRESTON, PATTISON (WAKE FOREST) - GUARD - 1946-49 CHICAGO BEARS

PRESTON - TACKLE - 1920 AKRON PROS

PREWITT, FELTON (TULSA) - CENTER - 1946 BUFFALO BISONS (AAFC);
    1947-48 BUFFALO BILLS (AAFC); 1949 BALTIMORE COLTS (AAFC)

PRIATKO, WILLIAM (PITTSBURGH) - LB - 1957 PITTSBURGH STEELERS

PRICE, CHARLES (TEXAS A&M) - QBACK - 1940-41, 45 DETROIT LIONS; 1946
    MIAMI SEAHAWKS (AAFC)

PRICE, EDWARD (TULANE) - BACK - 1950-55 NEW YORK GIANTS; 1951 RUSHING
    LEADER

PRICE, ELEX (ALCORN A&M) - TACKLE - 1973-74 NEW ORLEANS SAINTS (NFC)

PRICE, ERNEST (TEXAS A&I) - END, TACKLE - 1973-74 DETROIT LIONS (NFC)

PRICE, JAMES (AUBURN) - LB - 1963 NEW YORK JETS (AFL); 1964 DENVER
    BRONCOS (AFL)

PRICE, SAMUEL (ILLINOIS) - BACK - 1966-68 MIAMI DOLPHINS (AFL)

PRICER, WILLIAM (OKLAHOMA) - BACK - 1957-60 BALTIMORE COLTS; 1961
    DALLAS TEXANS (AFL)

PRIDE, DANIEL (JACKSON STATE) - LB - 1968-69 CHICAGO BEARS

PRIESTLEY, ROBERT (BROWN) - END - 1942 PHILADELPHIA EAGLES
PRINCIPE, DOMINIC (FORDHAM) - BACK - 1940-42 NEW YORK GIANTS; 1946
    BROOKLYN DODGERS (AAFC)
PRINT, ROBERT (DAYTON) - LB - 1967-68 SAN DIEGO CHARGERS (AFL)
PRISBY, ERROL (CINCINNATI) - BACK - 1967 DENVER BRONCOS (AFL)
PRISCO, NICHOLAS (RUTGERS) - BACK - 1933 PHILADELPHIA EAGLES
PRITCHARD, ABISHA "BOSH" (VMI) - BACK - 1942 CLEVELAND RAMS; 1942,
    46-49, 51 PHILADELPHIA EAGLES; 1951 NEW YORK GIANTS
PRITCHARD, RONALD (ARIZONA STATE) - LB - 1969 HOUSTON OILERS (AFL);
    1970-72 HOUSTON OILERS (AFC); 1972-74 CINCINNATI BENGALS (AFC)
PRITCHARD, WILLIAM (PENN STATE) - BACK - 1927 PROVIDENCE
    STEAMROLLERS; 1928 NEW YORK YANKEES
PRITKO, STEPHEN (VILLANOVA) - END - 1943 NEW YORK GIANTS; 1944-45
    CLEVELAND RAMS; 1946-47 LOS ANGELES RAMS; 1948 BOSTON YANKS;
    1949 NEW YORK BULLDOGS; 1949-50 GREEN BAY PACKERS
PROCHASKA, RAYMOND (NEBRASKA) - END - 1941 CLEVELAND RAMS
PROCTOR, DEWEY (FURMAN) - BACK - 1946-47, 49 NEW YORK YANKEES (AAFC);
    1948 CHICAGO ROCKETS (AAFC)
PROCTOR, REX (RICE) - BACK - 1953 CHICAGO BEARS
PROFIT, JOSEPH (NORTHEAST LOUISIANA) - BACK - 1971-73 ATLANTA FALCONS
    (NFC); 1973 NEW ORLEANS SAINTS (NFC)
PROKOP, EDWARD (GEORGIA TECH) - BACK - 1946-47, 49 NEW YORK YANKEES
    (AAFC); 1948 CHICAGO ROCKETS (AAFC)
PROKOP, JOSEPH (BRADLEY) - BACK - 1948 CHICAGO ROCKETS (AAFC)
PROMUTO, VINCENT (HOLY CROSS) - GUARD - 1960-69 WASHINGTON REDSKINS;
    1970 WASHINGTON REDSKINS (NFC)
PROTZ, JOHN (SYRACUSE) - LB - 1970 SAN DIEGO CHARGERS (AFC)
PROUT, BOB (KNOX) - BACK - 1974 OAKLAND RAIDERS (AFC)
PROVO, FREDERICK (WASHINGTON) - BACK - 1948 GREEN BAY PACKERS
PROVOST, TED (OHIO STATE) - BACK - 1970 MINNESOTA VIKINGS (NFC); 1971
    ST. LOUIS CARDINALS (NFC)
PRUDHOMME, JOSEPH REMI (LSU) - GUARD, CENTER, END - 1966-67 BUFFALO
    BILLS (AFL); 1968-69 KANSAS CITY CHIEFS (AFL); 1971-72 NEW
    ORLEANS SAINTS (NFC); 1972 BUFFALO BILLS (AFC)
PRUETT, PERRY (NORTH TEXAS STATE) - BACK - 1971 NEW ENGLAND PATRIOTS
    (AFC)
PRUITT, GREGORY (OKLAHOMA) - BACK - 1973-74 CLEVELAND BROWNS (AFC)
PRYOR, BARRY (BOSTON UNIV.) - BACK - 1969 MIAMI DOLPHINS (AFL); 1970
    MIAMI DOLPHINS (AFC)
PSALTIS, JAMES (USC) - BACK - 1953-55 CHICAGO CARDINALS; 1954 GREEN
    BAY PACKERS
PTACEK, ROBERT (MICHIGAN) - QBACK - 1959 CLEVELAND BROWNS
PUCCI, BENITO - TACKLE - 1946 BUFFALO BISONS (AAFC); 1947 CHICAGO
    ROCKETS (AAFC); 1948 CLEVELAND BROWNS (AAFC)
PUDDY, HAROLD (OREGON STATE) - TACKLE - 1948 SAN FRANCISCO 49ERS
    (AAFC)
PUDLOSKI, CHESTER (VILLANOVA) - TACKLE - 1944 CLEVELAND RAMS
PUETZ, GARRY (VALPARAISO) - GUARD, TACKLE - 1973-74 NEW YORK JETS
    (AFC)
PUGH, JETHRO (ELIZABETH CITY STATE) - TACKLE - 1965-69 DALLAS
    COWBOYS; 1970-74 DALLAS COWBOYS (NFC)
PUGH, MARION (TEXAS A&M) - QBACK - 1941-45 NEW YORK GIANTS; 1946
    MIAMI SEAHAWKS (AAFC)
PUGH, W. HOWARD (TOLEDO) - TACKLE - 1922 MILWAUKEE BADGERS
PUPLIS, ANDREW (NOTRE DAME) - BACK - 1943 CHICAGO CARDINALS
PURDIN, CALVIN (TULSA) - BACK - 1943 CHICAGO CARDINALS; 1946 MIAMI
    SEAHAWKS (AAFC); 1946 BROOKLYN DODGERS (AAFC)
PURDY, CLAIR (BROWN) - QBACK - 1919 AKRON PROS; 1919-20 ROCHESTER
    JEFFERSONS; 1922 MILWAUKEE BADGERS
PURDY, EVERETTE (BELOIT) - BACK - 1926-27 GREEN BAY PACKERS
PUREIFORY, DAVID (EASTERN MICHIGAN) - TACKLE, END - 1972-74 GREEN BAY
    PACKERS (NFC)
PURNELL, FRANKLIN (ALCORN A&M) - BACK - 1957 GREEN BAY PACKERS
PURNELL, JAMES (WISCONSIN) - LB - 1964, 66-68 CHICAGO BEARS; 1969 LOS
    ANGELES RAMS; 1970-72 LOS ANGELES RAMS (NFC)
PURVIS, JAMES VICTOR (SOUTHERN MISSISSIPPI) - BACK - 1966-67 BOSTON
    PATRIOTS (AFL)
PUTMAN, EARL (ARIZONA STATE) - CENTER - 1957 CHICAGO CARDINALS
PUTNAM, DUANE (PACIFIC) - GUARD - 1952-59, 62 LOS ANGELES RAMS; 1960
    DALLAS COWBOYS; 1961 CLEVELAND BROWNS
PUTZIER, FREDERICK (ST. OLAF) - BACK - 1924 MINNEAPOLIS MARINES

PYBURN, JACK (TEXAS A&M) - TACKLE - 1967-68 MIAMI DOLPHINS (AFL)
PYEATT, JOHN - BACK - 1960-61 DENVER BRONCOS (AFL)
PYLE, MICHAEL (YALE) - CENTER - 1961-69 CHICAGO BEARS
PYLE, WILLIAM PALMER (MICHIGAN STATE) - GUARD - 1960-63 BALTIMORE
      COLTS; 1964 MINNESOTA VIKINGS; 1966 OAKLAND RAIDERS (AFL)
PYLMAN, ROBERT (SOUTH DAKOTA STATE) - TACKLE - 1938-39 PHILADELPHIA
      EAGLES
PYNE, GEORGE (HOLY CROSS) - TACKLE - 1931 PROVIDENCE STEAMROLLERS
PYNE, GEORGE (OLIVET) - TACKLE - 1965 BOSTON PATRIOTS (AFL)
QUAM, CHARLES - BACK - 1926 DULUTH ESKIMOS
QUAST, JOHN (PURDUE) - END - 1923 LOUISVILLE BRECKS
QUATSE, JESS (PITTSBURGH) - TACKLE - 1933 GREEN BAY PACKERS; 1933-34
      PITTSBURGH PIRATES; 1935 NEW YORK GIANTS; 1935 NEW YORK GIANTS;
      1936-37 PITTSBURGH AMERICANS (AFL)
QUAYLE, FRANK (VIRGINIA) - BACK - 1969 DENVER BRONCOS (AFL)
QUEEN, JEFFREY (MORGAN STATE) - BACK, END - 1969 SAN DIEGO CHARGERS
      (AFL); 1970-71 SAN DIEGO CHARGERS (AFC); 1972-73 OAKLAND RAIDERS
      (AFC); 1974 HOUSTON OILERS (AFC)
QUIGLEY, WILLIAM - QBACK - 1920 ROCHESTER JEFFERSONS
QUILLEN, FRANK (PENNSYLVANIA) - END - 1946-47 CHICAGO ROCKETS (AAFC)
QUILTER, CHARLES (TYLER JUNIOR) - TACKLE - 1949 SAN FRANCISCO 49ERS
      (AAFC); 1950 SAN FRANCISCO 49ERS
QUINLAN, VOLNEY (SAN DIEGO STATE) - BACK - 1952-56 LOS ANGELES RAMS;
      1956 CLEVELAND BROWNS
QUINLAN, WILLIAM (MICHIGAN) - END - 1957-58 CLEVELAND BROWNS; 1959-62
      GREEN BAY PACKERS; 1963 PHILADELPHIA EAGLES; 1964 DETROIT LIONS;
      1965 WASHINGTON REDSKINS
QUINN, GEORGE - BACK - 1919-21 ROCK ISLAND INDEPENDENTS
QUINN, IVAN (CARROLL) - GUARD - 1924 KANSAS CITY COWBOYS
QUIRK, EDWARD (MISSOURI) - BACK - 1948-51 WASHINGTON REDSKINS
RABB, S. WARREN (LSU) - QBACK - 1960 DETROIT LIONS; 1961-62 BUFFALO
      BILLS (AFL)
RABOLD, MICHAEL (INDIANA) - GUARD - 1959 DETROIT LIONS; 1960 ST.
      LOUIS CARDINALS; 1961-62 MINNESOTA VIKINGS; 1964-67 CHICAGO BEARS
RABORN, CARROLL (SMU) - CENTER - 1936-37 PITTSBURGH PIRATES
RACIS, FRANK - GUARD - 1925-28 POTTSVILLE MAROONS; 1928 NEW YORK
      YANKEES; 1929 BOSTON BRAVES; 1930 PROVIDENCE STEAMROLLERS; 1931
      FRANKFORD YELLOWJACKETS
RADEMACHER, WILLIAM (NORTHERN MICHIGAN) - END - 1964-68 NEW YORK JETS
      (AFL); 1969 BOSTON PATRIOTS (AFL); 1970 BOSTON PATRIOTS (AFC)
RADICK, KENNETH (MARQUETTE) - END - 1930-31 GREEN BAY PACKERS; 1931
      BROOKLYN DODGERS
RADO, ALEX (NEW RIVER STATE-WEST VIRGINIA) - BACK - 1934 PITTSBURGH
      PIRATES
RADO, GEORGE (DUQUESNE) - GUARD - 1935-37 PITTSBURGH PIRATES; 1937-38
      PHILADELPHIA EAGLES
RADOSEVICH, GEORGE (PITTSBURGH) - CENTER - 1954-56 BALTIMORE COLTS
RADOVICH, WILLIAM (USC) - GUARD - 1938-41, 45 DETROIT LIONS; 1946-47
      LOS ANGELES DONS (AAFC)
RADZIEVITCH, VICTOR (CONNECTICUT) - BACK - 1926 HARTFORD BLUES
RAFFEL, WILLIAM (PENNSYLVANIA) - END - 1932 BROOKLYN DODGERS
RAFTER, WILLIAM (SYRACUSE) - BACK - 1919-21, 24 ROCHESTER JEFFERSONS
RAGAZZO, PHILIP (WESTERN RESERVE) - TACKLE - 1938-40 CLEVELAND RAMS;
      1940-41 PHILADELPHIA EAGLES; 1945-46 NEW YORK GIANTS
RAGUNAS, VINCENT (VMI) - BACK - 1949 PITTSBURGH STEELERS
RAIFF, JAMES (DAYTON) - GUARD - 1954 BALTIMORE COLTS
RAIMEY, DAVID (MICHIGAN) - BACK - 1964 CLEVELAND BROWNS
RAIMONDI, BENJAMIN (INDIANA) - QBACK - 1947 NEW YORK YANKEES (AAFC)
RAINES, VAUGHN MICHAEL (ALABAMA) - END, TACKLE - 1974 SAN FRANCISCO
      49ERS (NFC)
RAJKOVICH, PETER (DETROIT) - BACK - 1934 PITTSBURGH PIRATES
RAKESTRAW, LAWRENCE (GEORGIA) - QBACK - 1964, 66-68 CHICAGO BEARS
RAMBAUD, CARL - TACKLE - 1919 MASSILLON TIGERS
RAMONA, JOSEPH (SANTA CLARA) - GUARD - 1953 NEW YORK GIANTS
RAMSEY, FRANK (OREGON STATE) - TACKLE - 1945 CHICAGO BEARS
RAMSEY, GARRARD (WILLIAM&MARY) - GUARD - 1946-51 CHICAGO CARDINALS
RAMSEY, HERSCHEL (TEXAS TECH) - END - 1938-40, 45 PHILADELPHIA EAGLES
RAMSEY, KNOX (WILLIAM&MARY) - GUARD - 1948-49 LOS ANGELES DONS
      (AAFC); 1950-51 CHICAGO CARDINALS; 1952 PHILADELPHIA EAGLES;
      1952-53 WASHINGTON REDSKINS

RAMSEY, NATHAN (INDIANA) - BACK - 1963-69 PHILADELPHIA EAGLES;
     1970-72 PHILADELPHIA EAGLES (NFC); 1973 NEW ORLEANS SAINTS (NFC)
RAMSEY, RAY (BRADLEY) - BACK - 1947 CHICAGO ROCKETS (AAFC); 1948
     BROOKLYN DODGERS (AAFC); 1949 CHICAGO HORNETS (AAFC); 1950-53
     CHICAGO CARDINALS
RAMSEY, STEPHEN (NORTH TEXAS STATE) - QBACK - 1970 NEW ORLEANS SAINTS
     (NFC); 1971-74 DENVER BRONCOS (AFC)
RANDALL, DENNIS (OKLAHOMA STATE) - END - 1967 NEW YORK JETS (AFL);
     1968 CINCINNATI BENGALS (AFL)
RANDELS, HORACE (KANSAS STATE) - END - 1926 KANSAS CITY COWBOYS; 1927
     CLEVELAND BULLDOGS; 1928 DETROIT WOLVERINES
RANDLE, ULMO "SONNY" (VIRGINIA) - END - 1959 CHICAGO CARDINALS;
     1960-66 ST. LOUIS CARDINALS; 1967-68 SAN FRANCISCO 49ERS; 1968
     DALLAS COWBOYS
RANDOLPH, ALVIN (IOWA) - BACK - 1966-69 SAN FRANCISCO 49ERS; 1970 SAN
     FRANCISCO 49ERS (NFC); 1971 GREEN BAY PACKERS (NFC); 1972
     CINCINNATI BENGALS (AFC); 1972 DETROIT LIONS (NFC); 1973
     MINNESOTA VIKINGS (NFC); 1974 SAN FRANCISCO 49ERS (NFC); 1974
     BUFFALO BILLS (AFC)
RANDOLPH, CLARE (INDIANA) - CENTER - 1930 CHICAGO CARDINALS; 1931-33
     PORTSMOUTH SPARTANS; 1934-36 DETROIT LIONS
RANDOLPH, HARRY (BETHANY-WEST VIRGINIA) - BACK - 1923 COLUMBUS TIGERS
RANKIN, WALTER (TEXAS TECH) - BACK - 1941, 43, 45-47 CHICAGO
     CARDINALS; 1944 CARD-PITT
RANSPOT, KEITH (SMU) - END - 1940 CHICAGO CARDINALS; 1940 BOSTON
     BEARS (AFL); 1941 NEW YORK AMERICANS (AFL); 1942 GREEN BAY
     PACKERS; 1942 DETROIT LIONS; 1943 BROOKLYN DODGERS; 1944-45
     BOSTON YANKS
RAPACZ, JOHN (OKLAHOMA) - CENTER - 1948 CHICAGO ROCKETS (AAFC); 1949
     CHICAGO HORNETS (AAFC); 1950-54 NEW YORK GIANTS
RAPP, HERBERT (XAVIER) - CENTER - 1930-31 STATEN ISLAND STAPELTONS
RAPP, MANUEL (ST. LOUIS UNIV.) - BACK - 1934 ST. LOUIS GUNNERS
RAPP, ROBERT - BACK - 1922 COLUMBUS PANHANDLES; 1923-26 COLUMBUS
     TIGERS; 1929 BUFFALO BISONS
RASCHER, AMBROSE (INDIANA) - TACKLE - 1932 PORTSMOUTH SPARTANS
RASHAD, AHMAD (OREGON) - END - 1972-73 ST. LOUIS CARDINALS (NFC);
     1974 BUFFALO BILLS (AFC); (NAME CHANGED FROM ROBERT EARL "BOBBY"
     MOORE)
RASKOWSKI, LEO (OHIO STATE) - TACKLE - 1932 STATEN ISLAND STAPELTONS;
     1933 BROOKLYN DODGERS; 1933 PITTSBURGH PIRATES; 1935
     PHILADELPHIA EAGLES
RASLEY, ROCKY (OREGON STATE) - GUARD - 1969 DETROIT LIONS; 1970,
     72-73 DETROIT LIONS (NFC); 1974 NEW ORLEANS SAINTS (NFC)
RASMUSSEN, RANDALL (KEARNEY STATE) - GUARD - 1967-69 NEW YORK JETS
     (AFL); 1970-74 NEW YORK JETS (AFC)
RASMUSSEN, WAYNE (SOUTH DAKOTA STATE) - BACK - 1964-69 DETROIT LIONS;
     1970-72 DETROIT LIONS (NFC)
RASSAS, NICHOLAS (NOTRE DAME) - BACK - 1966-68 ATLANTA FALCONS
RATE, EDWIN (PURDUE) - BACK - 1923 MILWAUKEE BADGERS
RATEKIN, ROY (COLORADO A&M) - TACKLE - 1921 AKRON PROS
RATHER, DAVID "BO" (MICHIGAN) - END - 1973 MIAMI DOLPHINS (AFC); 1974
     CHICAGO BEARS (NFC)
RATICA, JOSEPH (ST. VINCENT'S) - CENTER - 1939 BROOKLYN DODGERS; 1940
     BOSTON BEARS (AFL); 1941 BUFFALO TIGERS (AFL)
RATKOWSKI, RAYMOND (NOTRE DAME) - BACK - 1961 BOSTON PATRIOTS (AFL)
RATTERMAN, GEORGE (NOTRE DAME) - QBACK - 1947-49 BUFFALO BILLS
     (AAFC); 1950-51 NEW YORK YANKS; 1952-56 CLEVELAND BROWNS
RAUCH, JOHN (GEORGIA) - QBACK - 1949 NEW YORK BULLDOGS; 1950-51 NEW
     YORK YANKS; 1951 PHILADELPHIA EAGLES
RAUCH, RICHARD (PENN STATE) - GUARD - 1921 COLUMBUS PANHANDLES; 1922
     TOLEDO MAROONS; 1925 POTTSVILLE MAROONS; 1928 NEW YORK YANKEES;
     1929 BOSTON BRAVES
RAVENSBURG, ROBERT (INDIANA) - END - 1948-49 CHICAGO CARDINALS
RAWLINGS, ROBERT (GEORGETOWN) - BACK - 1922 BUFFALO ALL-AMERICANS
RAY, ARTHUR (HOLY CROSS) - GUARD - 1926 BUFFALO RANGERS
RAY, BUFORD (VANDERBILT) - TACKLE - 1938-48 GREEN BAY PACKERS
RAY, DAVID (ALABAMA) - KICKER, END - 1969 LOS ANGELES RAMS; 1970-74
     LOS ANGELES RAMS (NFC); 1973 SCORING LEADER (NFC); 1973 FIELD
     GOAL LEADER (NFC)

RAY, EDWARD (LSU) - BACK - 1970 BOSTON PATRIOTS (AFC); 1971 SAN DIEGO
      CHARGERS (AFC); 1972-74 ATLANTA FALCONS (NFC)
RAYBURN, VIRGIL (TENNESSEE) - END - 1933 BROOKLYN DODGERS
RAYE, JIMMY (MICHIGAN) - BACK - 1969 PHILADELPHIA EAGLES
READ - GUARD - 1921 AKRON PROS
READER, RUSSELL (MICHIGAN STATE) - BACK - 1947 CHICAGO BEARS
REAGAN, FRANK (PENNSYLVANIA) - BACK - 1941, 46-48 NEW YORK GIANTS;
      1949-51 PHILADELPHIA EAGLES; 1947 INTERCEPTION LEADER; (TIED
      WITH SENO)
REAGEN, EDWARD - TACKLE - 1926 BROOKLYN LIONS
REAM, CHARLES (OHIO STATE) - TACKLE - 1938 CLEVELAND RAMS
REARDON, KERRY (IOWA) - BACK - 1971-74 KANSAS CITY CHIEFS (AFC)
REAVES, THOMAS JOHNSON "JOHN" (FLORIDA) - QBACK - 1972-74
      PHILADELPHIA EAGLES (NFC)
REAVES, KENNETH (NORFOLK STATE) - BACK - 1966-69 ATLANTA FALCONS;
      1970-73 ATLANTA FALCONS (NFC); 1974 NEW ORLEANS SAINTS (NFC);
      1974 ST. LOUIS CARDINALS (NFC)
REAVIS, DAVE (ARKANSAS) - TACKLE - 1974 PITTSBURGH STEELERS (AFC)
REBOL, RAYMOND (OHIO WESLEYAN) - TACKLE - 1941 CINCINNATI BENGALS
      (AFL)
REBSEAMAN, PAUL (CENTENARY) - CENTER - 1927 POTTSVILLE MAROONS
RECHER, DAVID (IOWA) - CENTER - 1965-68 PHILADELPHIA EAGLES
RECHICHAR, ALBERT (TENNESSEE) - LB - 1952 CLEVELAND BROWNS; 1953-59
      BALTIMORE COLTS; 1960 PITTSBURGH STEELERS; 1961 NEW YORK TITANS
      (AFL)
RECKMACK, RAYMOND (SYRACUSE) - BACK - 1937 DETROIT LIONS; 1937
      BROOKLYN DODGERS
RECTOR, RONALD (NORTHWESTERN) - BACK - 1966 WASHINGTON REDSKINS;
      1966-67 ATLANTA FALCONS
RED FANG - TACKLE - 1922-23 OORANG INDIANS
RED FOOT - END - 1923 OORANG INDIANS
RED FOX - BACK - 1922-23 OORANG INDIANS; 1926 CLEVELAND PANTHERS (AFL)
REDINGER, OTIS (COLGATE & PENN STATE) - BACK - 1925 CANTON BULLDOGS
REDMAN, RICHARD (WASHINGTON) - LB - 1965-69 SAN DIEGO CHARGERS (AFL);
      1970-73 SAN DIEGO CHARGERS (AFC)
REDMOND, GUSTAVE - BACK - 1920-22, 24 DAYTON TRIANGLES
REDMOND, RUDOLPH (PACIFIC) - BACK - 1969 ATLANTA FALCONS; 1970-71
      ATLANTA FALCONS (NFC); 1972 DETROIT LIONS (NFC)
REDMOND, THOMAS (VANDERBILT) - END - 1960-65 ST. LOUIS CARDINALS
REEBERG, LUCIAN (HAMPTON INSTITUTE) - TACKLE - 1963 DETROIT LIONS
REECE, DONALD (MISSOURI) - TACKLE - 1946 MIAMI SEAHAWKS (AAFC)
REED, ALVIN (PRAIRIE VIEW) - END - 1967-69 HOUSTON OILERS (AFL);
      1970-72 HOUSTON OILERS (AFC); 1973-74 WASHINGTON REDSKINS (NFC)
REED, HENRY (WEBER STATE) - LB, END - 1971-74 NEW YORK GIANTS (NFC)
REED, J. MAXWELL (BUCKNELL) - CENTER - 1925 BUFFALO BISONS; 1926-27
      FRANKFORD YELLOWJACKETS; 1928 NEW YORK GIANTS
REED, JOSEPH (LSU) - BACK - 1937, 39 CHICAGO CARDINALS
REED, JOSEPH (MISSISSIPPI STATE) - QBACK - 1972-74 SAN FRANCISCO
      49ERS (NFC)
REED, LEO (COLORADO STATE) - GUARD - 1961 HOUSTON OILERS (AFL); 1961
      DENVER BRONCOS (AFL)
REED, OSCAR (COLORADO STATE) - BACK - 1968-69 MINNESOTA VIKINGS;
      1970-74 MINNESOTA VIKINGS (NFC)
REED, RICHARD (OREGON) - END - 1926 LOS ANGELES WILDCATS (AFL)
REED, ROBERT (TENNESSEE STATE) - GUARD - 1965 WASHINGTON REDSKINS
REED, SMITH (ALCORN A&M) - BACK - 1965-66 NEW YORK GIANTS
REED, TAFT (JACKSON STATE) - BACK - 1967 PHILADELPHIA EAGLES
REESE, DAVID (DENISON) - END - 1919-23 DAYTON TRIANGLES
REESE, DONALD (JACKSON STATE) - END TACKLE - 1974 MIAMI DOLPHINS
      (AFC)
REESE, GUY (SMU) - TACKLE - 1962-63 DALLAS COWBOYS; 1964-65 BALTIMORE
      COLTS; 1966 ATLANTA FALCONS
REESE, HENRY (TEMPLE) - CENTER - 1933-34 NEW YORK GIANTS; 1935-39
      PHILADELPHIA EAGLES; 1940 NEW YORK AMERICANS (AFL)
REESE, KENNETH (ALABAMA) - BACK - 1947 DETROIT LIONS
REESE, LLOYD (TENNESSEE) - BACK - 1946 CHICAGO BEARS
REESE, STEVE (LOUISVILLE) - LB - 1974 NEW YORK JETS (AFC)
REEVE, LEWIS (IOWA STATE) - TACKLE - 1920 CHICAGO TIGERS; 1921
      COLUMBUS PANHANDLES

REEVES, DANIEL (SOUTH CAROLINA) - BACK - 1965-69 DALLAS COWBOYS;
    1970-72 DALLAS COWBOYS (NFC)
REEVES, MARION (CLEMSON) - BACK - 1974 PHILADELPHIA EAGLES (NFC)
REEVES, ROY (SOUTH CAROLINA) - BACK - 1969 BUFFALO BILLS (AFL)
REGAN, JAMES (STILL) - BACK - 1925 COLUMBUS TIGERS
REGER, JOHN (PITTSBURGH) - LB - 1955-63 PITTSBURGH STEELERS; 1964-66
    WASHINGTON REDSKINS
REGNER, THOMAS (NOTRE DAME) - GUARD, TACKLE - 1967-69 HOUSTON OILERS
    (AFL); 1970-72 HOUSTON OILERS (AFC)
REGNIER, PETER (MINNESOTA) - BACK - 1921-22 MINNEAPOLIS MARINES; 1922
    GREEN BAY PACKERS
REHNQUIST, MILTON (BETHANY-KANSAS) - GUARD - 1924-26 KANSAS CITY
    COWBOYS; 1925, 27 CLEVELAND BULLDOGS; 1928-31 PROVIDENCE
    STEAMROLLERS; 1931 NEW YORK GIANTS; 1932 BOSTON BRAVES
REHOR, FREDERICK (MICHIGAN) - GUARD - 1919 CANTON BULLDOGS
REICHARDT, WILLIAM (IOWA) - BACK - 1952 GREEN BAY PACKERS
REICHLE, LOUIS (BUTLER) - CENTER - 1926 COLUMBUS TIGERS
REICHLE, RICHARD (ILLINOIS) - END - 1923 MILWAUKEE BADGERS
REICHOW, CHARLES (ST. THOMAS OF MINNESOTA) - BACK - 1926 RACINE LEGION
REICHOW, GARET "GERRY" (IOWA) - END - 1956-57, 59 DETROIT LIONS; 1960
    PHILADELPHIA EAGLES; 1961-64 MINNESOTA VIKINGS
REID, FLOYD (GEORGIA) - BACK - 1950 CHICAGO BEARS; 1950-56 GREEN BAY
    PACKERS
REID, JOSEPH (LSU) - CENTER - 1951 LOS ANGELES RAMS; 1952 DALLAS
    TEXANS
REID, MICHAEL (PENN STATE) - TACKLE - 1970-74 CINCINNATI BENGALS (AFC)
REIFSNYDER, ROBERT (ANNAPOLIS) - END - 1960-61 NEW YORK TITANS (AFL)
REILLY, CHARLES "MIKE" (IOWA) - LB - 1964-68 CHICAGO BEARS; 1969
    MINNESOTA VIKINGS
REILLY, JAMES (NOTRE DAME) - GUARD - 1970-71 BUFFALO BILLS (AFC)
REILLY, KEVIN (VILLANOVA) - LB - 1973-74 PHILADELPHIA EAGLES (NFC)
REINHARD, C. WILLIAM (CALIFORNIA) - BACK - 1947-48 LOS ANGELES DONS
    (AAFC)
REINHARD, ROBERT (CALIFORNIA) - TACKLE - 1946-49 LOS ANGELES DONS
    (AAFC); 1950 LOS ANGELES RAMS
REISER, EARL - END - 1923 LOUISVILLE BRECKS
REISSIG, WILLIAM (FT. HAYS STATE-KANSAS) - BACK - 1937 PITTSBURGH
    AMERICANS (AFL); 1938-39 BROOKLYN DODGERS
REISZ, ALBERT (SOUTHEASTERN LOUISIANA) - BACK - 1944-45 CLEVELAND
    RAMS; 1946 LOS ANGELES RAMS; 1947 BUFFALO BILLS (AAFC)
REITER, WILBUR (WEST VIRGINIA WESLEYAN) - GUARD - 1926-27 DAYTON
    TRIANGLES
REMINGTON, WILLIAM (WASHINGTON STATE) - CENTER - 1946 SAN FRANCISCO
    49ERS (AAFC)
REMMERT, DENNIS (IOWA STATE) - LB - 1960 BUFFALO BILLS (AFL)
RENDALL, KENNETH (RUTGERS) - BACK - 1920 AKRON PROS
RENFRO, DEAN (NORTH TEXAS STATE) - BACK - 1955 BALTIMORE COLTS
RENFRO, MELVIN (OREGON) - BACK - 1964-69 DALLAS COWBOYS; 1970-74
    DALLAS COWBOYS (NFC); 1969 INTERCEPTION LEADER
RENFRO, RAYMOND (NORTH TEXAS STATE) - BACK - 1952-63 CLEVELAND BROWNS
RENFRO, RICHARD (WASHINGTON STATE) - BACK - 1946 SAN FRANCISCO 49ERS
    (AAFC)
RENFROW WILLIAM (MEMPHIS STATE) - GUARD - 1957-59 WASHINGTON
    REDSKINS; 1960 PITTSBURGH STEELERS; 1961 PHILADELPHIA EAGLES
RENGEL, MICHAEL (HAWAII) - TACKLE - 1969 NEW ORLEANS SAINTS
RENGEL, NEIL (DAVIS&ELKINS) - BACK - 1930 FRANKFORD YELLOWJACKETS
RENN, ROBERT (FLORIDA STATE) - BACK - 1961 NEW YORK TITANS (AFL)
RENTNER, ERNEST (NORTHWESTERN) - BACK - 1934-36 BOSTON REDSKINS; 1937
    CHICAGO BEARS
RENTZ, RALPH LAWRENCE (FLORIDA) - END - 1969 SAN DIEGO CHARGERS (AFL)
RENTZEL, THOMAS LANCE (OKLAHOMA) - END, BACK - 1965-66 MINNESOTA
    VIKINGS; 1967-69 DALLAS COWBOYS; 1970 DALLAS COWBOYS (NFC);
    1971-72 LOS ANGELES RAMS (NFC)
REPKO, JOSEPH (BOSTON COLLEGE) - TACKLE - 1946-47 PITTSBURGH
    STEELERS; 1948-49 LOS ANGELES RAMS
REPPOND, MICHAEL (ARKANSAS) - END - 1973 CHICAGO BEARS (NFC)
RESSLER, GLENN (PENN STATE) - GUARD, TACKLE - 1965-69 BALTIMORE
    COLTS; 1970-74 BALTIMORE COLTS (AFC)
RESTIC, JOSEPH (VILLANOVA) - END - 1952 PHILADELPHIA EAGLES

PETZLAFF, PALMER "PETE" (SOUTH DAKOTA STATE) - END - 1956-66
     PHILADELPHIA EAGLES; 1958 PASS RECEIVING LEADER; (TIED WITH
     BERRY)
REUPKE, GORDON (IOWA STATE) - BACK - 1940 COLUMBUS BULLIES (AFL)
REUTER, VICTOR (LAFAYETTE) - CENTER - 1932 STATEN ISLAND STAPELTONS
REUTT, RAYMOND (VIRGINIA MILITARY INST.) - END - 1943 PHIL-PITT
REXER, FREEMAN (TULANE) - END - 1943, 45 CHICAGO CARDINALS; 1944
     DETROIT LIONS; 1944 BOSTON YANKS
REYNOLDS, ALLAN (TARKIO-MISSOURI) - GUARD - 1960-62 DALLAS COWBOYS;
     1963-67 KANSAS CITY CHIEFS (AFL)
REYNOLDS, CHARLES (TULSA) - CENTER, GUARD - 1969 CLEVELAND BROWNS;
     1970 CLEVELAND BROWNS (AFC)
REYNOLDS, HOMER (TULSA) - GUARD - 1934 ST. LOUIS GUNNERS; 1937
     CINCINNATI BENGALS (AFL)
REYNOLDS, JACK (TENNESSEE) - LB - 1970-74 LOS ANGELES RAMS (NFC)
REYNOLDS, JAMES (OKLAHOMA A&M) - BACK - 1946 PITTSBURGH STEELERS
REYNOLDS, JAMES (AUBURN) - BACK - 1946 MIAMI SEAHAWKS (AAFC)
REYNOLDS, JOHN (BAYLOR) - CENTER - 1937 CHICAGO CARDINALS
REYNOLDS, MACK CHARLES (LSU) - QBACK - 1958-59 CHICAGO CARDINALS;
     1960 WASHINGTON REDSKINS; 1961 BUFFALO BILLS (AFL); 1962 OAKLAND
     RAIDERS (AFL)
REYNOLDS, OWEN (GEORGIA) - END - 1925 NEW YORK GIANTS; 1926 BROOKLYN
     LIONS
REYNOLDS, QUENTIN (BROWN) - TACKLE - 1926 BROOKLYN LIONS
REYNOLDS, RAOUL THOMAS (SAN DIEGO STATE) - END - 1972 NEW ENGLAND
     PATRIOTS (AFC); 1973 CHICAGO BEARS (NFC)
REYNOLDS, ROBERT (BOWLING GREEN) - TACKLE - 1963-69 ST. LOUIS
     CARDINALS; 1970-71, 73 ST. LOUIS CARDINALS (NFC); 1972-73 NEW
     ENGLAND PATRIOTS (AFC)
REYNOLDS, ROBERT (STANFORD) - TACKLE - 1937-38 DETROIT LIONS
REYNOLDS, WILLIAM (MISSISSIPPI) - BACK - 1944 BROOKLYN TIGERS; 1945
     CHICAGO CARDINALS
REYNOLDS, WILLIAM (PITTSBURGH) - BACK - 1953-54, 57 CLEVELAND BROWNS;
     1958 PITTSBURGH STEELERS; 1960 OAKLAND RAIDERS (AFL)
RHEA, FLOYD (OREGON) - GUARD - 1943 CHICAGO CARDINALS; 1944 BROOKLYN
     TIGERS; 1945 BOSTON YANKS; 1947 DETROIT LIONS
RHEA, HUGH (NEBRASKA) - GUARD - 1933 BROOKLYN DODGERS; 1936 BROOKLYN
     TIGERS (AFL)
RHENSTROM, ELMER (BELOIT) - END - 1922 RACINE LEGION
RHODEMYRE, JAY (KENTUCKY) - CENTER - 1948-49, 51-52 GREEN BAY PACKERS
RHODES, DANNY (ARKANSAS) - LB - 1974 BALTIMORE COLTS (AFC)
RHODES, DONALD (WASHINGTON&JEFFERSON) - TACKLE - 1933 PITTSBURGH
     PIRATES; 1936 CLEVELAND RAMS (AFL)
RHOME, GERALD (TULSA) - QBACK - 1965-67 DALLAS COWBOYS; 1969
     CLEVELAND BROWNS; 1970 HOUSTON OILERS (AFC); 1971 LOS ANGELES
     RAMS (NFC)
RIBAR, FRANK (DUKE) - GUARD - 1943 WASHINGTON REDSKINS
RIBBLE, LORAN (HARDIN-SIMMONS) - GUARD - 1932 PORTSMOUTH SPARTANS;
     1933 CHICAGO CARDINALS; 1934-35 PITTSBURGH PIRATES; 1936-37
     PITTSBURGH AMERICANS (AFL)
RIBLETT, PAUL (PENNSYLVANIA) - END - 1932-36 BROOKLYN DODGERS
RICCA, JAMES (GEORGETOWN) - TACKLE - 1951-54 WASHINGTON REDSKINS;
     1955 DETROIT LIONS; 1955-56 PHILADELPHIA EAGLES
RICE, ANDREW (TEXAS SOUTHERN) - TACKLE - 1966-67 KANSAS CITY CHIEFS
     (AFL); 1967 HOUSTON OILERS (AFL); 1968-69 CINCINNATI BENGALS
     (AFL); 1970-71 SAN DIEGO CHARGERS (AFC); 1972-73 CHICAGO BEARS
     (NFC)
RICE, FLOYD (ALCORN A&M) - LB, END - 1971-73 HOUSTON OILERS (AFC);
     1973-74 SAN DIEGO CHARGERS (AFC)
RICE, GEORGE (LSU) - TACKLE - 1966-69 HOUSTON OILERS (AFL)
RICE, HAROLD (TENNESSEE STATE) - END - 1971 OAKLAND RAIDERS (AFC)
RICE, KENNETH (AUBURN) - TACKLE - 1961, 63 BUFFALO BILLS (AFL);
     1964-65 OAKLAND RAIDERS (AFL); 1966-67 MIAMI DOLPHINS (AFL)
RICE, ORIN (MUHLENBERG) - CENTER - 1926 NEWARK BEARS (AFL)
RICE, WILLIAM - CENTER - 1929 NEW YORK GIANTS
RICE - CENTER - 1940 CINCINNATI BENGALS (AFL)
RICH, HERBERT (VANDERBILT) - BACK - 1950 BALTIMORE COLTS; 1951-53 LOS
     ANGELES RAMS; 1954-56 NEW YORK GIANTS
RICHARDS, ELVIN (SIMPSON) - BACK - 1933-39 NEW YORK GIANTS
RICHARDS, JAMES (VIRGINIA TECH) - BACK - 1968-69 NEW YORK JETS (AFL)
RICHARDS, JOHN GOLDEN (HAWAII) - END - 1973-74 DALLAS COWBOYS (NFC)

RICHARDS, PERRY (DETROIT) - END - 1957 PITTSBURGH STEELERS; 1958
    DETROIT LIONS; 1959 CHICAGO CARDINALS; 1960 ST. LOUIS CARDINALS;
    1961 BUFFALO BILLS (AFL); 1962 NEW YORK TITANS (AFL)
RICHARDS, PETER (SWARTHMORE) - CENTER - 1927 FRANKFORD YELLOWJACKETS
RICHARDS, RAY (NEBRASKA) - GUARD - 1930 FRANKFORD YELLOWJACKETS;
    1933, 35 CHICAGO BEARS; 1934 DETROIT LIONS; 1937 LOS ANGELES
    BULLDOGS (AFL)
RICHARDS, RICHARD (KENTUCKY) - BACK - 1933 BROOKLYN DODGERS
RICHARDS, ROBERT (LSU) - END - 1962-65 PHILADELPHIA EAGLES; 1966-67
    ATLANTA FALCONS
RICHARDSON, ALVIN (GRAMBLING) - END - 1960 BOSTON PATRIOTS (AFL)
RICHARDSON, GERALD (WOFFORD) - END - 1959-60 BALTIMORE COLTS
RICHARDSON, GLOSTER (JACKSON STATE) - END - 1967-69 KANSAS CITY
    CHIEFS (AFL); 1970 KANSAS CITY CHIEFS (AFC); 1971 DALLAS COWBOYS
    (NFC); 1972-74 CLEVELAND BROWNS (AFC)
RICHARDSON, JEFFREY (MICHIGAN STATE) - TACKLE, CENTER - 1967-68 NEW
    YORK JETS (AFL); 1969 MIAMI DOLPHINS (AFL)
RICHARDSON, JERRY (WEST TEXAS STATE) - BACK - 1964-65 LOS ANGELES
    RAMS; 1966-67 ATLANTA FALCONS
RICHARDSON, JESS (ALABAMA) - TACKLE - 1953-56, 58-61 PHILADELPHIA
    EAGLES; 1962-64 BOSTON PATRIOTS (AFL)
RICHARDSON, JOHN (UCLA) - TACKLE - 1967-69 MIAMI DOLPHINS (AFL);
    1970-71 MIAMI DOLPHINS (AFC); 1972-73 ST. LOUIS CARDINALS (NFC)
RICHARDSON, MICHAEL (SMU) - BACK - 1969 HOUSTON OILERS (AFL); 1970-71
    HOUSTON OILERS (AFC)
RICHARDSON, PETER (DAYTON) - BACK - 1969 BUFFALO BILLS (AFL); 1970-71
    BUFFALO BILLS (AFC)
RICHARDSON, ROBERT (UCLA) - BACK - 1966 DENVER BRONCOS (AFL)
RICHARDSON, THOMAS (JACKSON STATE) - END - 1969 BOSTON PATRIOTS
    (AFL); 1970 BOSTON PATRIOTS (AFC)
RICHARDSON, WILLIE (JACKSON STATE) - END - 1963-69 BALTIMORE COLTS;
    1970 MIAMI DOLPHINS (AFC); 1971 BALTIMORE COLTS (AFC)
RICHESON, DOSS (MISSOURI) - GUARD - 1926 CHICAGO BULLS (AFL)
RICHESON, RAYMOND (ALABAMA) - GUARD - 1949 CHICAGO HORNETS (AAFC)
RICHEY, JAMES MICHAEL (NORTH CAROLINA) - TACKLE - 1969 BUFFALO BILLS
    (AFL); 1970 NEW ORLEANS SAINTS (NFC)
RICHINS, ALDO (UTAH) - BACK - 1935 DETROIT LIONS
RICHTER, FRANK (GEORGIA) - LB - 1967-69 DENVER BRONCOS (AFL)
RICHTER, HUGH "PAT" (WISCONSIN) - END - 1963-69 WASHINGTON REDSKINS;
    1970 WASHINGTON REDSKINS (NFC)
RICHTER, LESTER (CALIFORNIA) - LB - 1954-62 LOS ANGELES RAMS
RICHTER, NATHAN (OTTERBEIN) - TACKLE - 1926 LOUISVILLE COLONELS; 1926
    COLUMBUS TIGERS
RICKARDS, PAUL (PITTSBURGH) - BACK - 1948 LOS ANGELES RAMS
RIDDICK, RAYMOND (FORDHAM) - END - 1940-42, 46 GREEN BAY PACKERS
RIDGE, HOUSTON (SAN DIEGO STATE) - BACK, END - 1966-69 SAN DIEGO
    CHARGERS (AFL)
RIDGWAY, COLIN (LAMAR TECH) - KICKER - 1965 DALLAS COWBOYS
RIDLEHUBER, HOWARD PRESTON (GEORGIA) - BACK - 1966 ATLANTA FALCONS;
    1968 OAKLAND RAIDERS (AFL); 1969 BUFFALO BILLS (AFL)
RIDLER, DONALD (MICHIGAN STATE) - TACKLE - 1931 CLEVELAND INDIANS
RIDLON, JAMES (SYRACUSE) - BACK - 1957-62 SAN FRANCISCO 49ERS;
    1963-64 DALLAS COWBOYS
RIETH, WILLIAM (CARNEGIE TECH) - CENTER - 1941-42, 44-45 CLEVELAND
    RAMS
RIEVES, CHARLES (HOUSTON) - LB - 1962-63 OAKLAND RAIDERS (AFL);
    1964-65 HOUSTON OILERS (AFL)
RIFFENBURG, RICHARD (MICHIGAN) - END - 1950 DETROIT LIONS
RIFFLE, CHARLES (NOTRE DAME) - GUARD - 1944 CLEVELAND RAMS; 1946-48
    NEW YORK YANKEES (AAFC)
RIFFLE, RICHARD (ALBRIGHT) - BACK - 1938-40 PHILADELPHIA EAGLES;
    1941-42 PITTSBURGH STEELERS
RIGGINS, JOHN (KANSAS) - BACK - 1971-74 NEW YORK JETS (AFC)
RIGGLE, ROBERT (PENN STATE) - BACK - 1966-67 ATLANTA FALCONS
RIGGS, THEON (WASHINGTON UNIV.) - TACKLE - 1944 BOSTON YANKS
RIGHETTI, JOSEPH (WAYNESBURG) - TACKLE - 1969 CLEVELAND BROWNS; 1970
    CLEVELAND BROWNS (AFC)
RILEY, JAMES (OKLAHOMA) - END - 1967-69 MIAMI DOLPHINS (AFL); 1970-71
    MIAMI DOLPHINS (AFC)
RILEY, JOHN (NORTHWESTERN) - TACKLE - 1933 BOSTON REDSKINS

RILEY, KENNETH (FLORIDA A&M) - BACK - 1969 CINCINNATI BENGALS (AFL);
    1970-74 CINCINNATI BENGALS (AFC)
RILEY, LEON (DETROIT) - BACK - 1955 DETROIT LIONS; 1956, 58-59
    PHILADELPHIA EAGLES; 1960 NEW YORK GIANTS; 1961-62 NEW YORK
    TITANS (AFL); 1962 INTERCEPTION LEADER (AFL)
RILEY, PRESTON (MEMPHIS STATE) - END - 1970-72 SAN FRANCISCO 49ERS
    (NFC); 1973 NEW ORLEANS SAINTS (NFC)
RILEY, STEVE (USC) - TACKLE - 1974 MINNESOTA VIKINGS (NFC)
RILEY, THOMAS "BUTCH" (TEXAS A&I) - LB - 1969 BALTIMORE COLTS
RINGO, JAMES (SYRACUSE) - CENTER - 1953-63 GREEN BAY PACKERS; 1964-67
    PHILADELPHIA EAGLES
RINGWALT, CARROLL (INDIANA) - CENTER - 1930 PORTSMOUTH SPARTANS; 1931
    FRANKFORD YELLOWJACKETS
RIOPEL, ALBERT (HOLY CROSS) - BACK - 1925 PROVIDENCE STEAMROLLERS
RIORDAN, CHARLES (NEW YORK UNIV.) - END - 1929 STATEN ISLAND
    STAPELTONS
RISK, EDWARD (PURDUE) - BACK - 1932 CHICAGO CARDINALS
RISLEY, ELLIOTT (INDIANA) - TACKLE - 1921-23 HAMMOND PROS
RISSMILLER, RAYMOND (GEORGIA) - TACKLE - 1966 PHILADELPHIA EAGLES;
    1967 NEW ORLEANS SAINTS; 1968 BUFFALO BILLS (AFL)
RISVOLD, RAYMOND (ST. EDWARDS-TEXAS) - BACK - 1927-28 CHICAGO
    CARDINALS
RITCHHART, DELBERT (COLORADO) - CENTER - 1936-37 DETROIT LIONS
RIVERA, HENRY (OREGON STATE) - BACK - 1962 OAKLAND RAIDERS (AFL);
    1963 BUFFALO BILLS (AFL)
RIVERS, JAMES (BOWLING GREEN) - LB - 1968-69 ST. LOUIS CARDINALS;
    1970-73 ST. LOUIS CARDINALS (NFC); 1974 NEW YORK JETS (AFC)
RIVES, DONALD (TEXAS TECH) - LB - 1973-74 CHICAGO BEARS (NFC)
RIVES, ROBERT (VANDERBILT) - TACKLE - 1926 NEWARK BEARS (AFL)
RIZZO, JACK (LEHIGH) - BACK - 1973 NEW YORK GIANTS (NFC)
RIZZO, JOE (MERCHANT MARINE ACADEMY) - LB - 1974 DENVER BRONCOS (AFC)
ROACH, JOHN (SMU) - QBACK - 1956, 59 CHICAGO CARDINALS; 1960 ST.
    LOUIS CARDINALS; 1961-63 GREEN BAY PACKERS; 1964 DALLAS COWBOYS
ROACH, J. - GUARD - 1921 LOUISVILLE BRECKS
ROACH, ROLLIN (TCU) - BACK - 1927 CHICAGO CARDINALS
ROACH, TRAVIS (TEXAS) - GUARD - 1974 NEW YORK JETS (AFC)
ROBB, ALVIS "JOE" (TCU) - END - 1959-60 PHILADELPHIA EAGLES; 1961-67
    ST. LOUIS CARDINALS; 1968-69 DETROIT LIONS; 1970-71 DETROIT
    LIONS (NFC)
ROBB, HARRY (PENN STATE) - QBACK - 1921-23, 25-26 CANTON BULLDOGS
ROBB, LOYAL - BACK - 1919 ROCK ISLAND INDEPENDENTS
ROBB, STANLEY (CENTRE) - END - 1925-26 CANTON BULLDOGS
ROBBINS, JOHN (ARKANSAS) - QBACK - 1938-39 CHICAGO CARDINALS
ROBERSON, IRVIN "BO" (CORNELL) - BACK - 1961 SAN DIEGO CHARGERS
    (AFL); 1962-65 OAKLAND RAIDERS (AFL); 1965 BUFFALO BILLS (AFL);
    1966 MIAMI DOLPHINS (AFL)
ROBERSON, LAKE (MISSISSIPPI) - END - 1945 DETROIT LIONS
ROBERTS, ARCHIE (COLUMBIA) - QBACK - 1967 MIAMI DOLPHINS (AFL)
ROBERTS, CLIFFORD (ILLINOIS) - TACKLE - 1961 OAKLAND RAIDERS (AFL)
ROBERTS, CORNELIUS (USC) - BACK - 1959-62 SAN FRANCISCO 49ERS
ROBERTS, EUGENE (CHATTANOOGA) - BACK - 1947-50 NEW YORK GIANTS; 1949
    SCORING LEADER; (TIED WITH HARDER)
ROBERTS, FRED (IOWA) - TACKLE - 1930-32 PORTSMOUTH SPARTANS
ROBERTS, GARY (PURDUE) - GUARD - 1970 ATLANTA FALCONS (NFC)
ROBERTS, GUY (IOWA STATE) - BACK - 1926 CANTON BULLDOGS; 1926
    CLEVELAND PANTHERS (AFL); 1927 POTTSVILLE MAROONS
ROBERTS, GUY (MARYLAND) - LB - 1972-74 HOUSTON OILERS (AFC)
ROBERTS, HAL (HOUSTON) - KICKER - 1974 ST. LOUIS CARDINALS (NFC)
ROBERTS, JAMES (CENTRE) - END - 1922 TOLEDO MAROONS; 1923 AKRON PROS;
    1926 CLEVELAND PANTHERS (AFL)
ROBERTS, JOHN (GEORGIA) - BACK - 1932 BOSTON BRAVES; 1932 STATEN
    ISLAND STAPELTONS; 1933-34 PHILADELPHIA EAGLES; 1934 PITTSBURGH
    PIRATES
ROBERTS, MACE - BACK - 1920-22, 24 HAMMOND PROS
ROBERTS, THOMAS (DEPAUL) - TACKLE - 1943 NEW YORK GIANTS; 1944-45
    CHICAGO BEARS
ROBERTS, WALCOTT (ANNAPOLIS) - BACK - 1922-23 CANTON BULLDOGS;
    1924-25 CLEVELAND BULLDOGS; 1926 FRANKFORD YELLOWJACKETS
ROBERTS, WALTER "FLEA" (SAN JOSE STATE) - BACK, END - 1964-66
    CLEVELAND BROWNS; 1967 NEW ORLEANS SAINTS; 1969 WASHINGTON
    REDSKINS; 1970 WASHINGTON REDSKINS (NFC)

ROBERTS, WILLIAM (DARTMOUTH) - BACK - 1956 GREEN BAY PACKERS
ROBERTS, WILLIE (HOUSTON) - BACK - 1973 CHICAGO BEARS (NFC)
ROBERTSON, HARRY (SYRACUSE) - TACKLE - 1921-22 ROCHESTER JEFFERSONS;
    1922 MILWAUKEE BADGERS
ROBERTSON, ISIAH (SOUTHERN) - LB - 1971-74 LOS ANGELES RAMS (NFC)
ROBERTSON, JAMES (CARNEGIE TECH) - QBACK - 1924-25 AKRON PROS
ROBERTSON, ROBERT (ILLINOIS) - CENTER - 1968 HOUSTON OILERS (AFL)
ROBERTSON, ROBERT (USC) - BACK - 1942 BROOKLYN DODGERS
ROBERTSON, THOMAS (TULSA) - CENTER - 1941-42 BROOKLYN DODGERS; 1946
    NEW YORK YANKEES (AAFC)
ROBESON, PAUL (RUTGERS) - END - 1920 HAMMOND PROS; 1921 AKRON PROS;
    1922 MILWAUKEE BADGERS
ROBINSON, CHARLES (MORGAN STATE) - GUARD - 1954 BALTIMORE COLTS
ROBINSON, EDWARD - BACK - 1920, 23-25 HAMMOND PROS; 1926 LOUISVILLE
    COLONELS
ROBINSON, FREDERICK (WASHINGTON) - GUARD - 1957 CLEVELAND BROWNS
ROBINSON, GILBERT (CATAWBA) - END - 1933 PITTSBURGH PIRATES
ROBINSON, JACK (NORTHEAST MISSOURI STATE) - TACKLE - 1935-36 BROOKLYN
    DODGERS; 1936-37 CHICAGO CARDINALS; 1938 CLEVELAND RAMS; 1938
    PITTSBURGH PIRATES
ROBINSON, JERRY (GRAMBLING) - END - 1962-64 SAN DIEGO CHARGERS (AFL);
    1965 NEW YORK JETS (AFL)
ROBINSON, JOE CRAIG (HOUSTON) - TACKLE - 1972-73 NEW ORLEANS SAINTS
    (NFC)
ROBINSON, JOHN (TENNESSEE STATE) - BACK - 1966-67 DETROIT LIONS
ROBINSON, JOHN NOLAN (LSU) - BACK - 1960-62 DALLAS TEXANS (AFL);
    1963-69 KANSAS CITY CHIEFS (AFL); 1970-71 KANSAS CITY CHIEFS
    (AFC); 1966 INTERCEPTION LEADER (AFL); 1970 INTERCEPTION LEADER
    (AFC)
ROBINSON, KARL (PENNSYLVANIA) - CENTER - 1926 PHILADELPHIA QUAKERS
    (AFL)
ROBINSON, LARRY (TENNESSEE) - BACK - 1973 DALLAS COWBOYS (NFC)
ROBINSON, PAUL (ARIZONA) - BACK - 1968-69 CINCINNATI BENGALS (AFL);
    1970-72 CINCINNATI BENGALS (AFC); 1972-73 HOUSTON OILERS (AFC);
    1968 RUSHING LEADER (AFL)
ROBINSON, RICHARD DAVID (PENN STATE) - LB - 1963-69 GREEN BAY
    PACKERS; 1970-72 GREEN BAY PACKERS (NFC); 1973-74 WASHINGTON
    REDSKINS (NFC)
ROBINSON, VIRGIL (GRAMBLING) - BACK - 1971-72 NEW ORLEANS SAINTS (NFC)
ROBINSON, WAYNE (MINNESOTA) - LB - 1952-56 PHILADELPHIA EAGLES
ROBINSON, WILLIAM (LINCOLN) - BACK - 1952 GREEN BAY PACKERS
ROBISON, BURLE (BRIGHAM YOUNG) - END - 1935 PHILADELPHIA EAGLES
ROBISON, GEORGE (VMI) - GUARD - 1952 DALLAS TEXANS
ROBL, HAROLD (OSHKOSH STATE-WISCONSIN) - BACK - 1945 CHICAGO CARDINALS
ROBNETT, EDWARD (TEXAS TECH) - BACK - 1947 SAN FRANCISCO 49ERS (AAFC)
ROBNETT, MARSHALL (TEXAS A&M) - CENTER - 1943, 45 CHICAGO CARDINALS;
    1944 CARD-PITT
ROBOTTI, FRANK (BOSTON COLLEGE) - LB - 1961 BOSTON PATRIOTS (AFL)
ROBUSTELLI, ANDREW (ARNOLD) - END - 1951-55 LOS ANGELES RAMS; 1956-64
    NEW YORK GIANTS; 1971 HALL OF FAME
ROBY, DOUGLAS (MICHIGAN) - BACK - 1923 CLEVELAND INDIANS
ROCHE, ALDEN (SOUTHERN) - END, TACKLE - 1970 DENVER BRONCOS (AFC);
    1971-74 GREEN BAY PACKERS (NFC)
ROCHESTER, PAUL (MICHIGAN STATE) - TACKLE - 1960-62 DALLAS TEXANS
    (AFL); 1963 KANSAS CITY CHIEFS (AFL); 1963-69 NEW YORK JETS (AFL)
ROCK, WALTER (MARYLAND) - TACKLE - 1963-67 SAN FRANCISCO 49ERS;
    1968-69 WASHINGTON REDSKINS; 1970-73 WASHINGTON REDSKINS (NFC)
ROCKENBACH, LYLE (MICHIGAN STATE) - GUARD - 1943 DETROIT LIONS
ROCKNE, KNUTE (NOTRE DAME) - END - 1919 MASSILLON TIGERS
ROCKWELL, HENRY (ARIZONA STATE) - CENTER - 1940-42 CLEVELAND RAMS;
    1946-48 LOS ANGELES DONS (AAFC)
RODAK, MICHAEL (WESTERN RESERVE) - BACK - 1939-40 CLEVELAND RAMS;
    1942 PITTSBURGH STEELERS
RODER, MIRRO - KICKER - 1973-74 CHICAGO BEARS (NFC)
RODERICK, BENJAMIN (COLUMBIA & BOSTON COLL.) - BACK - 1923 BUFFALO
    ALL-AMERICANS; 1923, 25-26 CANTON BULLDOGS; 1927 BUFFALO BISONS

RODERICK, JOHN (SMU) - BACK - 1966-67 MIAMI DOLPHINS (AFL); 1968
     OAKLAND RAIDERS (AFL)
RODGERS, HOSEA (NORTH CAROLINA) - BACK - 1949 LOS ANGELES DONS (AAFC)
RODGERS, THOMAS (BUCKNELL) - TACKLE - 1947 BOSTON YANKS
RODGERS, WILLIE (KENTUCKY) - BACK - 1972, 74 HOUSTON OILERS (AFC)
RODRIGUEZ, JESS (SALEM) - BACK - 1929 BUFFALO BISONS
RODRIGUEZ, KELLY (WEST VIRGINIA WESLEYAN) - BACK - 1930 FRANKFORD
     YELLOWJACKETS; 1930 MINNEAPOLIS REDJACKETS
ROEDEL, HERBERT (MARQUETTE) - GUARD - 1961 OAKLAND RAIDERS (AFL)
ROEHNELT, WILLIAM (BRADLEY) - LB - 1958-59 CHICAGO BEARS; 1960
     WASHINGTON REDSKINS; 1961-62 DENVER BRONCOS (AFL)
ROEPKE, JOHN (PENN STATE) - BACK - 1928 FRANKFORD YELLOWJACKETS
ROESSLER, FRITZ (MARQUETTE) - END - 1922-24 RACINE LEGION; 1925
     MILWAUKEE BADGERS
ROEFFLER, WILLIAM (WASHINGTON STATE) - BACK - 1954 PHILADELPHIA EAGLES
ROGALLA, JOHN (SCRANTON) - BACK - 1945 PHILADELPHIA EAGLES
ROGAS, DANIEL (TULANE) - GUARD - 1951 DETROIT LIONS; 1952
     PHILADELPHIA EAGLES
ROGEL, FRANK (PENN STATE) - BACK - 1950-57 PITTSBURGH STEELERS
ROGERS, CHARLES (PENNSYLVANIA) - QBACK - 1927-29 FRANKFORD
     YELLOWJACKETS
ROGERS, CULLEN (TEXAS A&M) - BACK - 1946 PITTSBURGH STEELERS
ROGERS, DONALD (SOUTH CAROLINA) - CENTER - 1960 LOS ANGELES CHARGERS
     (AFL); 1961-64 SAN DIEGO CHARGERS (AFL)
ROGERS, GLYNN (TCU) - GUARD - 1939 CHICAGO CARDINALS
ROGERS, JOHN (DUQUESNE) - BACK - 1940-41 CINCINNATI BENGAIS (AFL)
ROGERS, JOHN (NOTRE DAME) - CENTER - 1933-34 CINCINNATI REDS; 1936
     BROOKLYN TIGERS (AFL)
ROGERS, MELVIN (FLORIDA A&M) - LB - 1971, 73-74 SAN DIEGO CHARGERS
     (AFC)
ROGERS, WALTER (OHIO UNIV.) - BACK - 1919, 22 COLUMBUS PANHANDLES
ROGERS, WILLIAM (VILLANOVA) - TACKLE - 1938-40, 44 DETROIT LIONS
ROGGE, GEORGE (IOWA) - END - 1931-33 CHICAGO CARDINALS; 1934 ST.
     LOUIS GUNNERS
ROGGEMAN, THOMAS (PURDUE) - TACKLE - 1956-57 CHICAGO BEARS
ROHDE, LEONARD (UTAH STATE) - TACKLE - 1960-69 SAN FRANCISCO 49ERS;
     1970-74 SAN FRANCISCO 49ERS (NFC)
ROHLEDER, GEORGE (WITTENBERG) - END - 1925 COLUMBUS TIGERS; 1926
     AKRON PROS
ROHRABAUGH, RAYMOND (FRANKLIN) - BACK - 1926 ROCK ISLAND INDEPENDENTS
     (AFL)
ROHRIG, HERMAN (NEBRASKA) - BACK - 1941, 46-47 GREEN BAY PACKERS
ROKISKY, JOHN (DUQUESNE) - END - 1946 CLEVELAND BROWNS (AAFC); 1947
     CHICAGO ROCKETS (AAFC); 1948 NEW YORK YANKEES (AAFC)
ROLAND, JOHN (MISSOURI) - BACK - 1966-69 ST. LOUIS CARDINALS; 1970-72
     ST. LOUIS CARDINALS (NFC); 1973 NEW YORK GIANTS (NFC)
ROLL, CLAYTON (MIAMI-OHIO) - END - 1927 DAYTON TRIANGLES
ROLLE, DAVID (OKLAHOMA) - BACK - 1960 DENVER BRONCOS (AFL)
ROLLER, DAVID (KENTUCKY) - TACKLE - 1971 NEW YORK GIANTS (NFC)
ROMAN, GEORGE (WESTERN RESERVE) - TACKLE - 1948 BOSTON YANKS; 1949
     NEW YORK BULLDOGS; 1950 NEW YORK GIANTS
ROMAN, NICHOLAS (OHIO STATE) - END - 1970-71 CINCINNATI BENGALS
     (AFC); 1973-74 CLEVELAND BROWNS (AFC)
ROMANIK, STEPHEN (VILLANOVA) - QBACK - 1950-53 CHICAGO BEARS; 1953-54
     CHICAGO CARDINALS
ROMANISZYN, JAMES (EDINBORO STATE) - LB - 1973-74 CLEVELAND BROWNS
     (AFC)
ROMBOLI, RUDOLPH - BACK - 1946-48 BOSTON YANKS
ROMEO, ANTHONY (FLORIDA STATE) - END - 1961 DALLAS TEXANS (AFL);
     1962-67 BOSTON PATRIOTS (AFL)
ROMERO, RAYMOND (KANSAS STATE) - GUARD - 1951 PHILADELPHIA EAGLES
ROMEY, RICHARD (IOWA UNIV.) - END - 1926 CHICAGO BULLS (AFL)
ROMINE, ALTON (FLORENCE STATE-ALABAMA) - BACK - 1955, 58 GREEN BAY
     PACKERS; 1960 DENVER BRONCOS (AFL); 1961 BOSTON PATRIOTS (AFL)
ROMNEY, MILTON (CHICAGO) - QBACK - 1923-24 RACINE LEGION; 1924-28
     CHICAGO BEARS
RONZANI, GENE (MARQUETTE) - QBACK - 1933-38, 44-45 CHICAGO BEARS
ROONEY, HARRY "COBBS" - QBACK - 1923-25 DULUTH KELLEYS; 1925 NEW YORK
     GIANTS; 1926-27 DULUTH ESKIMOS; 1928 NEW YORK YANKEES; 1929-30
     CHICAGO CARDINALS

ROONEY, JOSEPH - END - 1923-24 DULUTH KELLEYS; 1924-25 ROCK ISLAND
    INDEPENDENTS; 1926-27 DULUTH ESKIMOS; 1928 POTTSVILLE MAROONS
ROONEY, WILLIAM - BACK - 1923-25 DULUTH KELLEYS; 1926 BROOKLYN LIONS;
    1926-27 DULUTH ESKIMOS; 1929 CHICAGO CARDINALS
ROOT, JAMES (MIAMI-OHIO) - QBACK - 1953, 56 CHICAGO CARDINALS
RORISON, JAMES (USC) - TACKLE - 1938 PITTSBURGH PIRATES
ROSATO, SALVATORE (VILLANOVA) - BACK - 1945-47 WASHINGTON REDSKINS
ROSATTI, ROMAN (MICHIGAN) - TACKLE - 1923 CLEVELAND INDIANS; 1924,
    26-27 GREEN BAY PACKERS; 1928 NEW YORK GIANTS
ROSDAHL, HARRISON (PENN STATE) - TACKLE - 1964 BUFFALO BILLS (AFL);
    1964-66 KANSAS CITY CHIEFS (AFL)
ROSE, ALFRED (TEXAS) - END - 1930-31 PROVIDENCE STEAMROLLERS; 1932-36
    GREEN BAY PACKERS; 1936 NEW YORK YANKS (AFL)
ROSE, EUGENE (WISCONSIN) - BACK - 1929-32 CHICAGO CARDINALS
ROSE, GEORGE (AUBURN) - BACK - 1964-66 MINNESOTA VIKINGS; 1967 NEW
    ORLEANS SAINTS
ROSE, ROBERT (RIPON) - CENTER - 1926 GREEN BAY PACKERS
ROSE, ROY (TENNESSEE) - END - 1936 NEW YORK GIANTS
ROSEMA, ROGER "ROCKY" (MICHIGAN) - LB - 1968-69 ST. LOUIS CARDINALS;
    1970-71 ST. LOUIS CARDINALS (NFC)
ROSEN, STANLEY (RUTGERS) - BACK - 1929 BUFFALO BISONS
ROSENBERGER - TACKLE - 1921 EVANSVILLE CRIMSON GIANTS
ROSENOW, AUGUST (RIPON) - BACK - 1921 GREEN BAY PACKERS
ROSEQUIST, THEODORE (OHIO STATE) - TACKLE - 1934-36 CHICAGO BEARS;
    1937 CLEVELAND RAMS
ROSKIE, KENNETH (SOUTH CAROLINA) - BACK - 1946 SAN FRANCISCO 49ERS
    (AAFC); 1948 DETROIT LIONS; 1948 GREEN BAY PACKERS
ROSS, DAVID (LOS ANGELES STATE) - END - 1960 NEW YORK TITANS (AFL)
ROSS, LOUIS (SOUTH CAROLINA STATE) - END - 1971-72 BUFFALO BILLS (AFC)
ROSS, OLIVER (ALABAMA A&M) - BACK - 1973-74 DENVER BRONCOS (AFC)
ROSS, WILLIAM (NEBRASKA) - BACK - 1964 BUFFALO BILLS (AFL)
ROSSO, GEORGE (OHIO STATE) - BACK - 1954 WASHINGTON REDSKINS
ROSSOVICH, TIMOTHY (USC) - LB, END - 1968-69 PHILADELPHIA EAGLES;
    1970-71 PHILADELPHIA EAGLES (NFC); 1972-73 SAN DIEGO CHARGERS
    (AFC)
ROSTECK, ERNEST - CENTER - 1943-44 DETROIT LIONS
ROTE, KYLE (SMU) - END - 1951-61 NEW YORK GIANTS
ROTE, TOBIN (RICE) - QBACK - 1950-56 GREEN BAY PACKERS; 1957-59
    DETROIT LIONS; 1963-64 SAN DIEGO CHARGERS (AFL); 1966 DENVER
    BRONCOS (AFL); 1963 PASSING LEADER (AFL)
ROTHROCK, CLIFFORD (NORTH DAKOTA STATE) - CENTER - 1947 CHICAGO
    ROCKETS (AAFC)
ROTHWELL, FRED (KANSAS STATE) - CENTER - 1974 DETROIT LIONS (NFC)
ROTON, HERBERT (AUBURN) - END - 1937 PHILADELPHIA EAGLES
ROTUNNO, ANTHONY (ST. AMBROSE) - BACK - 1947 CHICAGO ROCKETS (AAFC)
ROUDEBUSH, GEORGE (DENISON) - BACK - 1919-21 DAYTON TRIANGLES
ROUSE, STILLMAN (MISSOURI) - END - 1940 DETROIT LIONS
ROUSSEL, THOMAS (SOUTHERN MISSISSIPPI) - LB - 1968-69 WASHINGTON
    REDSKINS; 1970 WASHINGTON REDSKINS (NFC); 1971-72 NEW ORLEANS
    SAINTS (NFC); 1973 PHILADELPHIA EAGLES (NFC)
ROUSSOS, MICHAEL (PITTSBURGH) - TACKLE - 1948-49 WASHINGTON REDSKINS;
    1949 DETROIT LIONS
ROVINSKI, ANTHONY (HOLY CROSS) - END - 1933 NEW YORK GIANTS
ROWAN, EVERETT (OHIO STATE) - END - 1930, 32 BROOKLYN DODGERS; 1933
    PHILADELPHIA EAGLES
ROWAN, JOHN (TENNESSEE) - BACK - 1923 LOUISVILLE BRECKS
ROWDEN, LARRY (HOUSTON) - LB - 1971-72 CHICAGO BEARS (NFC)
ROWE, DAVID (PENN STATE) - TACKLE, END - 1967-69 NEW ORLEANS SAINTS;
    1970 NEW ORLEANS SAINTS (NFC); 1971-73 NEW ENGLAND PATRIOTS (AFC)
ROWE, HARMON (SAN FRANCISCO) - BACK - 1947-49 NEW YORK YANKEES
    (AAFC); 1950-52 NEW YORK GIANTS
ROWE, ROBERT (COLGATE) - BACK - 1934 DETROIT LIONS; 1935 PHILADELPHIA
    EAGLES
ROWE, ROBERT (WESTERN MICHIGAN) - TACKLE - 1967-69 ST. LOUIS
    CARDINALS; 1970-74 ST. LOUIS CARDINALS (NFC)
ROWLAND, BRADLEY (MCMURRY) - BACK - 1951 CHICAGO BEARS
ROWLAND, JUSTIN (TCU) - BACK - 1960 CHICAGO BEARS; 1961 MINNESOTA
    VIKINGS; 1962 DENVER BRONCOS (AFL)
ROWLEY, ROBERT (VIRGINIA) - LB - 1963 PITTSBURGH STEELERS; 1964 NEW
    YORK JETS (AFL)

ROWSER, JOHN (MICHIGAN) - BACK - 1967-69 GREEN BAY PACKERS; 1970-73
     PITTSBURGH STEELERS (AFC); 1974 DENVER BRONCOS (AFC)
ROY, ELMER - END - 1921-25 ROCHESTER JEFFERSONS; 1927 BUFFALO BISONS
ROY, FRANK (UTAH) - GUARD - 1966 ST. LOUIS CARDINALS
ROYSTON, EDWARD (WAKE FOREST) - GUARD - 1948-49 NEW YORK GIANTS
ROZELLE, AUBREY (DELTA STATE) - LB - 1957 PITTSBURGH STEELERS
RUBINO, ANTHONY (WAKE FOREST) - GUARD - 1943, 46 DETROIT LIONS
RUBKE, KARL (USC) - LB - 1957-60, 62-65 SAN FRANCISCO 49ERS; 1961
     MINNESOTA VIKINGS; 1966-67 ATLANTA FALCONS; 1968 OAKLAND RAIDERS
     (AFL)
RUBY, MARTIN (TEXAS A&M) - TACKLE - 1946-48 BROOKLYN DODGERS (AAFC);
     1949 NEW YORK YANKEES (AAFC); 1950 NEW YORK YANKS
RUCINZKI, EDWARD (INDIANA) - END - 1941-42 BROOKLYN DODGERS; 1943,
     45-46 CHICAGO CARDINALS; 1944 CARD-PITT
RUCKA, LEO (RICE) - CENTER - 1956 SAN FRANCISCO 49ERS
RUCKER, REGINALD (BOSTON UNIV.) - END - 1970-71 DALLAS COWBOYS (NFC);
     1971 NEW YORK GIANTS (NFC); 1971-74 NEW ENGLAND PATRIOTS (AFC)
RUDNAY, JOHN "JACK" (NORTHWESTERN) - CENTER - 1970-74 KANSAS CITY
     CHIEFS (AFC)
RUDNICK, TIMOTHY (NOTRE DAME) - BACK - 1974 BALTIMORE COLTS (AFC)
RUDOLPH, COUNCIL (KENTUCKY STATE) - END - 1972 HOUSTON OILERS (AFC);
     1973-74 ST. LOUIS CARDINALS (NFC)
RUDOLPH, JOHN (GEORGIA TECH) - LB - 1960, 62-65 BOSTON PATRIOTS
     (AFL); 1966 MIAMI DOLPHINS (AFL)
RUETZ, HOWARD (LORAS) - TACKLE - 1951-53 GREEN BAY PACKERS
RUETZ, JOSEPH (NOTRE DAME) - GUARD - 1946, 48 CHICAGO ROCKETS (AAFC)
RUH, EMMETT (DAVIS&ELKINS) - BACK - 1919, 21-22 COLUMBUS PANHANDLES
RUH, HOMER - END - 1919-22 COLUMBUS PANHANDLES; 1923-25 COLUMBUS
     TIGERS
RUKAS, JUSTIN (LSU) - GUARD - 1936 BROOKLYN DODGERS
RULE, GORDON (DARTMOUTH) - BACK - 1968-69 GREEN BAY PACKERS
RUNDQUIST, ELMER (ILLINOIS) - TACKLE - 1922 CHICAGO CARDINALS
RUNDQUIST, HARRY - TACKLE - 1923-25 DULUTH KELLEYS; 1926 DULUTH
     ESKIMOS
RUNKLE, GILBERT - END - 1920 DETROIT HERALDS; 1925 COLUMBUS TIGERS
RUNNELS, THOMAS (NORTH TEXAS STATE) - BACK - 1956-57 WASHINGTON
     REDSKINS
RUNNING DEER - END - 1923 OORANG INDIANS
RUNNING WOLF (HASKELL) - TACKLE - 1926 AKRON PROS; (ALSO PLAYED AS H.
     CASEY)
RUNSEY, ROY - TACKLE - 1921 EVANSVILLE CRIMSON GIANTS
RUPLE, COY ERNEST (ARKANSAS) - TACKLE - 1968 PITTSBURGH STEELERS
RUPP, JOHN - GUARD - 1920 BUFFALO ALL-AMERICANS
RUPP, NELSON (DENISON) - QBACK - 1921 CHICAGO STALEYS; 1921 DAYTON
     TRIANGLES
RUSH, CLIVE (MIAMI-OHIO) - BACK - 1953 GREEN BAY PACKERS
RUSH, GERALD (MICHIGAN STATE) - TACKLE - 1965-69 DETROIT LIONS;
     1970-71 DETROIT LIONS (NFC)
RUSH, JAMES (MINNESOTA) - BACK - 1922 MINNEAPOLIS MARINES
RUSHING, MARION (SOUTHERN ILLINOIS) - LB - 1959 CHICAGO CARDINALS;
     1962-65 ST. LOUIS CARDINALS; 1966-68 ATLANTA FALCONS; 1968
     HOUSTON OILERS (AFL)
RUSKUSKY, RAYMOND (ST. MARY'S OF CAL.) - END - 1947 NEW YORK YANKEES
     (AAFC)
RUSS, PATRICK (PURDUE) - TACKLE - 1963 MINNESOTA VIKINGS
RUSSAS, ALBERT (TENNESSEE) - TACKLE - 1949 DETROIT LIONS
RUSSELL, BENJAMIN (LOUISVILLE) - QBACK - 1968 BUFFALO BILLS (AFL)
RUSSELL, CHARLES ANDREW (MISSOURI) - LB - 1963, 66-69 PITTSBURGH
     STEELERS; 1970-74 PITTSBURGH STEELERS (AFC)
RUSSELL, DOUGLAS (KANSAS STATE) - BACK - 1934-39 CHICAGO CARDINALS;
     1939 CLEVELAND RAMS; 1935 RUSHING LEADER
RUSSELL, JAMES (TEMPLE) - TACKLE - 1936-37 PHILADELPHIA EAGLES
RUSSELL, JOHN (BAYLOR) - END - 1946-49 NEW YORK YANKEES (AAFC); 1950
     NEW YORK YANKS
RUSSELL, KENNETH (BOWLING GREEN) - TACKLE - 1957-59 DETROIT LIONS
RUSSELL, LAFAYETTE (NORTHWESTERN) - BACK - 1933 NEW YORK GIANTS; 1933
     PHILADELPHIA EAGLES
RUSSELL, REGINALD - END - 1928 CHICAGO BEARS
RUSSELL, ROY (USC) - BACK - 1941 BUFFALO TIGERS (AFL)
RUSSELL, TORRANCE (AUBURN) - TACKLE - 1939-40 WASHINGTON REDSKINS
RUST, REGINALD (OREGON STATE) - BACK - 1932 BOSTON BRAVES

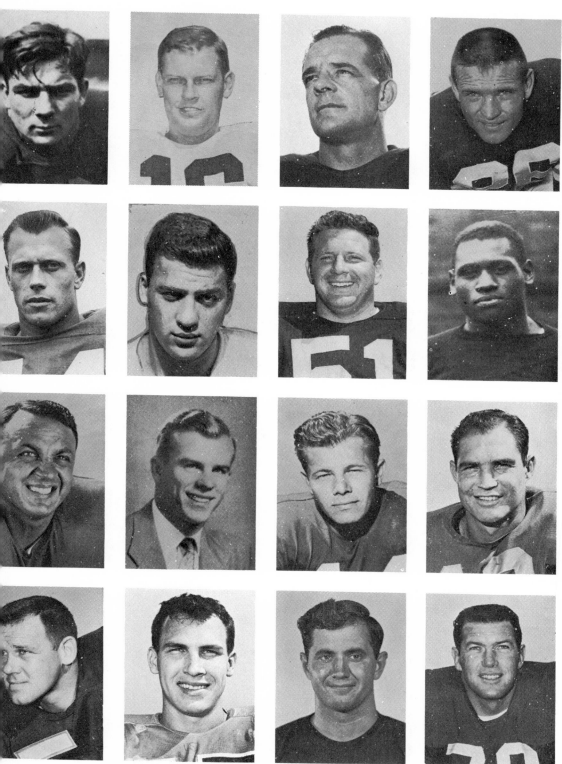

Top row (from left to right): George Rade, George Ratterman, Frank Reagan and Ray Renfro. *Second row:* "Pete" Retzlaff, Jim Ricca, Jim Ringo and Paul Robeson. *Third row:* Andy Robustelli, Steve Romanik, Kyle Rote and Tobin Rote. *Bottom row:* Karl Rubke, Frank Ryan, Julie Rykovich and Bob St. Clair.

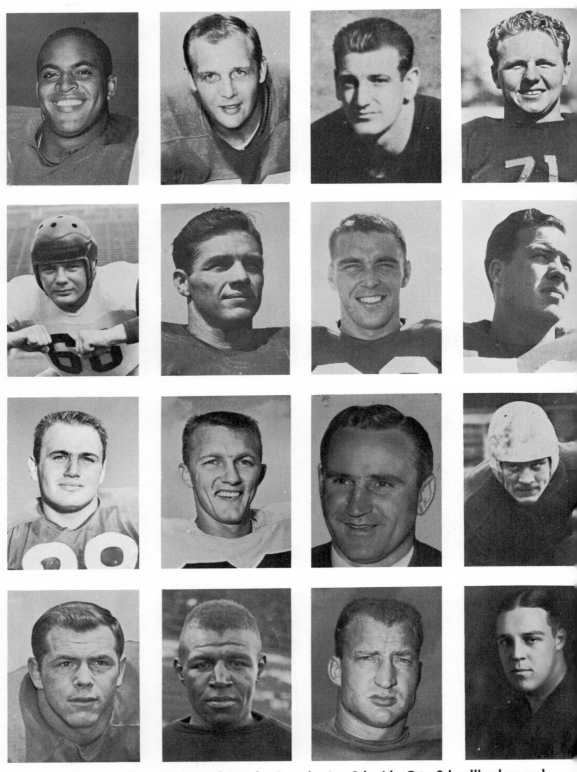

Top row (from left to right): John Sample, Joe Schmidt, Otto Schnellbacher and Perry Schwartz. *Second row:* John Schweder, Clyde Scott, Tom Scott and Vic Sears. *Third row:* Don Shinnick, Del Shofner, Don Shula and "Red" Sieck. *Bottom row:* Bob Skoronski, "Duke" Slater, Billy Ray Smith and Cedric "Pat" Smith.

RUSTICH, FRANK (CANISIUS) - BACK - 1936 BOSTON SHAMROCKS (AFL); 1936
    NEW YORK YANKS (AFL)
RUTGENS, JOSEPH (ILLINOIS) - TACKLE - 1961-69 WASHINGTON REDSKINS
RUTHERFORD - BACK - 1937 PITTSBURGH AMERICANS (AFL)
RUTHSTROM, RALPH (SMU) - BACK - 1945 CLEVELAND RAMS; 1946 LOS ANGELES
    RAMS; 1947 WASHINGTON REDSKINS; 1949 BALTIMORE COLTS (AAFC)
RUTKOWSKI, CHARLES (RIPON) - END - 1960 BUFFALO BILLS (AFL)
RUTKOWSKI, EDWARD (NOTRE DAME) - BACK - 1963-68 BUFFALO BILLS (AFL)
RUZICH, STEVEN (OHIO STATE) - GUARD - 1952-54 GREEN BAY PACKERS
RYAN, CLARENCE (WEST VIRGINIA) - BACK - 1929 BUFFALO BISONS
RYAN, DAVID (HARDIN-SIMMONS) - BACK - 1945-46 DETROIT LIONS; 1948
    BOSTON YANKS
RYAN, EDWARD (ST. MARY'S OF CAL.) - END - 1948 PITTSBURGH STEELERS
RYAN, FRANK (RICE) - QBACK - 1958-61 LOS ANGELES RAMS; 1962-68
    CLEVELAND BROWNS; 1969 WASHINGTON REDSKINS; 1970 WASHINGTON
    REDSKINS (NFC)
RYAN, JAMES (NOTRE DAME) - BACK - 1924 ROCK ISLAND INDEPENDENTS; 1924
    CHICAGO CARDINALS
RYAN, JOHN (DETROIT) - TACKLE - 1929 CHICAGO BEARS; 1930 PORTSMOUTH
    SPARTANS
RYAN, JOHN (ILLINOIS) - BACK - 1956-58 PHILADELPHIA EAGLES; 1958
    CHICAGO BEARS
RYAN, JOSEPH (VILLANOVA) - END - 1960 NEW YORK TITANS (AFL)
RYAN, KENT (UTAH STATE) - BACK - 1938-40 DETROIT LIONS; 1940
    INTERCEPTION LEADER; (TIED WITH HUTSON AND PARKER)
RYCHLEC, THOMAS (AMERICAN INTERNATIONAL) - END - 1958 DETROIT LIONS;
    1960-62 BUFFALO BILLS (AFL); 1963 DENVER BRONCOS (AFL)
RYCZEK, DANIEL (VIRGINIA) - CENTER - 1973-74 WASHINGTON REDSKINS (NFC)
RYCZEK, PAUL (VIRGINIA) - CENTER - 1974 ATLANTA FALCONS (NFC)
RYDER, NICHOLAS (MIAMI) - BACK - 1963-64 DETROIT LIONS
RYDZEWSKI, FRANK (NOTRE DAME) - TACKLE - 1919 MASSILLON TIGERS;
    1919-20, 22-26 HAMMOND PROS; 1920 CLEVELAND PANTHERS; 1921
    CHICAGO CARDINALS; 1923 CHICAGO BEARS; 1925 MILWAUKEE BADGERS
RYKOVICH, JULIUS (ILLINOIS & NOTRE DAME) - BACK - 1947-48 BUFFALO
    BILLS (AAFC); 1948 CHICAGO ROCKETS (AAFC); 1949-51 CHICAGO
    BEARS; 1952-53 WASHINGTON REDSKINS
RYMKUS, LOUIS (NOTRE DAME) - TACKLE - 1943 WASHINGTON REDSKINS;
    1946-49 CLEVELAND BROWNS (AAFC); 1950-51 CLEVELAND BROWNS
RZEMPOLUCH, THEODORE (VIRGINIA) - BACK - 1963 WASHINGTON REDSKINS
SABADOS, ANDREW (CITADEL) - GUARD - 1939-40 CHICAGO CARDINALS
SABAL, RONALD (PURDUE) - TACKLE - 1960-61 OAKLAND RAIDERS (AFL)
SABAN, LOUIS (INDIANA) - BACK - 1946-49 CLEVELAND BROWNS (AAFC)
SABASTEANSKI, JOSEPH (FORDHAM) - CENTER - 1947-48 BOSTON YANKS; 1949
    NEW YORK BULLDOGS
SABATINO, WILLIAM (COLORADO) - TACKLE - 1968 CLEVELAND BROWNS; 1969
    ATLANTA FALCONS
SABUCCO, TINO (SAN FRANCISCO) - CENTER - 1949 SAN FRANCISCO 49ERS
    (AAFC)
SACHS, LEONARD (LOYOLA-ILLINOIS) - END - 1920-23, 25 CHICAGO
    CARDINALS; 1923-24 MILWAUKEE BADGERS; 1924-25 HAMMOND PROS; 1926
    LOUISVILLE COLONELS
SACHESE, FRANCIS (TEXAS TECH) - BACK - 1943 BROOKLYN DODGERS; 1944
    BROOKLYN TIGERS; 1945 BOSTON YANKS
SACHESE, JOHN (TEXAS) - CENTER - 1945 BOSTON YANKS
SACK, JOHN (PITTSBURGH) - GUARD - 1923, 25 COLUMBUS TIGERS; 1926
    CANTON BULLDOGS; 1926 CLEVELAND PANTHERS (AFL)
SACKSTEDER, NORBERT (ST. MARY'S OF OHIO) - BACK - 1919 DETROIT
    HERALDS· 1920, 25 DAYTON TRIANGLES; 1921 DETROIT PANTHERS; 1922,
    25 CANTON BULLDOGS
SACRINTY, NICHOLAS (WAKE FOREST) - QBACK - 1947 CHICAGO BEARS
SADER, STEVEN - BACK - 1943 PHIL-PITT
SADOWSKY, LEONARD (OHIO) - BACK - 1936 CLEVELAND RAMS (AFL)
SAECKER, WELLINGTON - END - 1941 NEW YORK AMERICANS (AFL)
SAENZ, EDWARD (USC) - BACK - 1946-51 WASHINGTON REDSKINS
SAFFOLD, SAINT (SAN JOSE STATE) - END - 1968 CINCINNATI BENGALS (AFL)
SAGELY, FLOYD (ARKANSAS) - END - 1954, 56 SAN FRANCISCO 49ERS; 1957
    CHICAGO CARDINALS
SAIDOCK, THOMAS (MICHIGAN STATE) - TACKLE - 1957 PHILADELPHIA EAGLES;
    1960-61 NEW YORK TITANS (AFL); 1962 BUFFALO BILLS (AFL)

SAIMES, GEORGE (MICHIGAN STATE) - BACK - 1963-69 BUFFALO BILLS (AFL);
    1970-72 DENVER BRONCOS (AFC)
ST. CLAIR, ROBERT (TULSA & SAN FRANCISCO) - TACKLE - 1953-63 SAN
    FRANCISCO 49ERS
ST. GERMAINE, THOMAS (CARLISLE) - GUARD - 1922 OORANG INDIANS
ST. JEAN, LEONARD (NORTHERN MICHIGAN) - GUARD - 1964-69 BOSTON
    PATRIOTS (AFL); 1970 BOSTON PATRIOTS (AFC); 1971-73 NEW ENGLAND
    PATRIOTS (AFC)
ST. JOHN, HERBERT (GEORGIA) - GUARD - 1948 BROOKLYN DODGERS (AAFC);
    1949 CHICAGO HORNETS (AAFC)
SALATA, ANDREW (PITTSBURGH) - GUARD - 1929 ORANGE TORNADOS; 1930
    NEWARK TORNADOS
SALATA, PAUL (USC) - END - 1949 SAN FRANCISCO 49ERS (AAFC); 1950 SAN
    FRANCISCO 49ERS; 1950 BALTIMORE COLTS
SALEM, EDWARD (ALABAMA) - BACK - 1951 WASHINGTON REDSKINS
SALEMI, SAMUEL (ST. JOHN OF NEW YORK) - BACK - 1928 NEW YORK YANKEES
SALSBURY, JAMES (UCLA) - GUARD - 1955-56 DETROIT LIONS; 1957-58 GREEN
    BAY PACKERS
SALSCHNEIDER, JOHN (ST. THOMAS) - BACK - 1949 NEW YORK GIANTS
SALTER, BRYANT (PITTSBURGH) - BACK - 1971-73 SAN DIEGO CHARGERS
    (AFC); 1974 WASHINGTON REDSKINS (NFC)
SAMPLE, CHARLES (TOLEDO) - BACK - 1942, 45 GREEN BAY PACKERS
SAMPLE, JOHN (MARYLAND STATE) - BACK - 1958-60 BALTIMORE COLTS;
    1961-62 PITTSBURGH STEELERS; 1963-65 WASHINGTON REDSKINS;
    1966-68 NEW YORK JETS (AFL)
SAMPSON, ARTHUR - GUARD - 1921 DAYTON TRIANGLES
SAMPSON, RALPH GREGORY (STANFORD) - TACKLE, END - 1972-74 HOUSTON
    OILERS (AFC)
SAMPSON, SENECA (BROWN) - BACK - 1926 PROVIDENCE STEAMROLLERS
SAMUEL, DONALD (OREGON STATE) - BACK - 1949-50 PITTSBURGH STEELERS
SAMUELSON, CARL (NEBRASKA) - TACKLE - 1948-51 PITTSBURGH STEELERS
SANCHEZ, JOHN (SAN FRANCISCO) - TACKLE - 1947 CHICAGO ROCKETS (AAFC);
    1947 DETROIT LIONS; 1947-49 WASHINGTON REDSKINS; 1949-50 NEW
    YORK GIANTS
SANDBERG, CARL - BACK - 1929 MINNEAPOLIS REDJACKETS
SANDBERG, ARNOLD - BACK - 1926 LOS ANGELES BUCCANEERS
SANDBERG, SIGURD (IOWA WESLEYAN) - TACKLE - 1934 ST. LOUIS GUNNERS;
    1935-37 PITTSBURGH PIRATES; 1937 BROOKLYN DODGERS
SANDEFUR, WAYNE (PURDUE) - BACK - 1936-37 PITTSBURGH PIRATES; 1937
    ROCHESTER TIGERS (AFL)
SANDEMAN, WILLIAM (PACIFIC) - TACKLE - 1966 DALLAS COWBOYS; 1967 NEW
    ORLEANS SAINTS; 1967-69 ATLANTA FALCONS; 1970-73 ATLANTA FALCONS
    (NFC)
SANDERS, CHARLES (MINNESOTA) - END - 1968-69 DETROIT LIONS; 1970-74
    DETROIT LIONS (NFC)
SANDERS, DARYL (OHIO STATE) - TACKLE - 1963-66 DETROIT LIONS
SANDERS, JOHN (SOUTH DAKOTA) - BACK - 1974 NEW ENGLAND PATRIOTS (AFC)
SANDERS, JOHN (SMU) - GUARD - 1940-42 PITTSBURGH STEELERS; 1945
    PHILADELPHIA EAGLES
SANDERS, KENNETH (HOWARD PAYNE) - END - 1972-74 DETROIT LIONS (NFC)
SANDERS, LONNIE (MICHIGAN STATE) - BACK - 1963-67 WASHINGTON
    REDSKINS; 1968-69 ST. LOUIS CARDINALS
SANDERS, ORBAN "SPEC" (TEXAS) - BACK - 1946-48 NEW YORK YANKEES
    (AAFC); 1950 NEW YORK YANKS; 1950 INTERCEPTION LEADER
SANDERS, PAUL (UTAH STATE) - BACK - 1944 BOSTON YANKS
SANDERS, ROBERT (NORTH TEXAS STATE) - LB - 1967 ATLANTA FALCONS
SANDERSON, REGINALD (STANFORD) - BACK - 1973 CHICAGO BEARS (NFC)
SANDIFER, DANIEL (LSU) - BACK - 1948-49 WASHINGTON REDSKINS; 1950
    DETROIT LIONS; 1950 SAN FRANCISCO 49ERS; 1950-51 PHILADELPHIA
    EAGLES; 1952-53 GREEN BAY PACKERS; 1953 CHICAGO CARDINALS; 1948
    INTERCEPTION LEADER
SANDIFER, WILLIAM (UCLA) - TACKLE - 1974 SAN FRANCISCO 49ERS (NFC)
SANDIG, CURTIS (ST. MARY'S OF TEXAS) - BACK - 1942 PITTSBURGH
    STEELERS; 1946 BUFFALO BISONS (AAFC)
SANDUSKY, ALEXANDER (CLARION STATE-PA.) - GUARD - 1954-66 BALTIMORE
    COLTS
SANDUSKY, JOHN (VILLANOVA) - TACKLE - 1950-55 CLEVELAND BROWNS; 1956
    GREEN BAY PACKERS
SANDUSKY, MICHAEL (MARYLAND) - TACKLE - 1957-65 PITTSBURGH STEELERS
SANFORD, HAYWARD (ALABAMA) - END - 1940 WASHINGTON REDSKINS
SANFORD, JAMES (LEHIGH) - TACKLE - 1924 DULUTH KELLEYS

SANFORD, LEO OTIS (LOUISIANA TECH) - GUARD - 1951-57 CHICAGO
    CARDINALS; 1958 BALTIMORE COLTS
SANOOKE, STILWELL (CARLISLE) - END - 1922 OORANG INDIANS
SANSEN, OLIVER (IOWA) - BACK - 1932-35 BROOKLYN DODGERS
SANTONE, JOSEPH - GUARD - 1926 HARTFORD BLUES
SANTORA, FRANK - BACK - 1944 BOSTON YANKS
SANZOTTA, DOMINIC (WESTERN RESERVE) - BACK - 1942, 46 DETROIT LIONS
SAPIENZA, AMERICO (VILLANOVA) - BACK - 1960 NEW YORK TITANS (AFL)
SAPP, THERON (GEORGIA) - BACK - 1959-63 PHILADELPHIA EAGLES; 1963-65
    PITTSBURGH STEELERS
SARAFINY, ALBERT (ST. EDWARDS) - CENTER - 1933 GREEN BAY PACKERS
SARAUSKY, ANTHONY (FORDHAM) - BACK - 1935-37 NEW YORK GIANTS; 1938
    BROOKLYN DODGERS
SARBOE, PHILIP (WASHINGTON STATE) - BACK - 1934 BOSTON REDSKINS;
    1934-36 CHICAGO CARDINALS; 1936 BROOKLYN DODGERS
SARDISCO, ANTHONY (TULANE) - GUARD - 1956 WASHINGTON REDSKINS; 1956
    SAN FRANCISCO 49ERS; 1960-62 BOSTON PATRIOTS (AFL)
SARK, HARVEY (PHILLIPS) - GUARD - 1931 NEW YORK GIANTS; 1934
    CINCINNATI REDS
SARNO, AMERINO (FORDHAM) - TACKLE - 1936-37 BOSTON SHAMROCKS (AFL)
SARRATT, CHARLES (OKLAHOMA) - BACK - 1948 DETROIT LIONS
SARRINGHAUS, PAUL (OHIO STATE) - BACK - 1946 CHICAGO CARDINALS; 1948
    DETROIT LIONS
SARTIN, DANIEL (MISSISSIPPI) - TACKLE - 1969 SAN DIEGO CHARGERS (AFL)
SARTORI, LAWRENCE (FORDHAM) - GUARD - 1942, 45 DETROIT LIONS
SATCHER, DOUGLAS (SOUTHERN MISSISSIPPI) - LB - 1966-68 BOSTON
    PATRIOTS (AFL)
SATENSTEIN, BERNARD (NEW YORK UNIV.) - GUARD - 1929-32 STATEN ISLAND
    STAPELTONS; 1933 NEW YORK GIANTS
SATTERFIELD, ALFRED (VANDERBILT) - TACKLE - 1947 SAN FRANCISCO 49ERS
    (AAFC)
SAUER, GEORGE (NEBRASKA) - BACK - 1935-37 GREEN BAY PACKERS
SAUER, GEORGE, JR. (TEXAS) - END - 1965-69 NEW YORK JETS (AFL); 1970
    NEW YORK JETS (AFC); 1967 PASS RECEIVING LEADER (AFL)
SAUL, RICHARD (MICHIGAN STATE) - GUARD,CENTER,TACKLE - 1970-74 LOS
    ANGELES RAMS (NFC)
SAUL, RONALD (MICHIGAN STATE) - GUARD - 1970-74 HOUSTON OILERS (AFC)
SAUL, WILLIAM (PENN STATE) - LB - 1962-63 BALTIMORE COLTS; 1964,
    66-68 PITTSBURGH STEELERS; 1969 NEW ORLEANS SAINTS; 1970 DETROIT
    LIONS (NFC)
SAULIS, JOSEPH (MARSHALL) - BACK - 1937 PITTSBURGH AMERICANS (AFL)
SAULS, KIRBY "MAC" (SOUTHWEST TEXAS STATE) - BACK - 1968-69 ST. LOUIS
    CARDINALS
SAUMER, SYLVESTER (ST. CLAF) - BACK - 1934 CINCINNATI REDS; 1934
    PITTSBURGH PIRATES
SAUNDERS, JOHN (TOLEDO) - BACK - 1972 BUFFALO BILLS (AFC); 1974 SAN
    FRANCISCO 49ERS (NFC)
SAUNDERS, RUSSELL (USC) - BACK - 1931 GREEN BAY PACKERS
SAUNDERS - BACK - 1922 EVANSVILLE CRIMSON GIANTS; 1922 TOLEDO MAROONS
SAUSSELLE, THEODORE (WASHINGTON-MISSOURI) - BACK - 1936 ROCHESTER
    TIGERS (AFL)
SAVATSKY, OLIVER (MIAMI-OHIO) - END - 1937 CLEVELAND RAMS; 1937
    ROCHESTER TIGERS (AFL)
SAVITSKY, GEORGE (PENNSYLVANIA) - TACKLE - 1948-49 PHILADELPHIA EAGLES
SAVOLDI, JOSEPH (NOTRE DAME) - BACK - 1930 CHICAGO BEARS
SAWYER, HERMAN (SYRACUSE) - TACKLE - 1922 ROCHESTER JEFFERSONS
SAWYER, KENNETH (SYRACUSE) - BACK - 1974 CINCINNATI BENGALS (AFC)
SAXTON, JAMES (TEXAS) - BACK - 1962 DALLAS TEXANS (AFL)
SAYERS, GALE (KANSAS) - BACK - 1965-69 CHICAGO BEARS; 1970-71 CHICAGO
    BEARS (NFC); 1965 SCORING LEADER; 1966, 69 RUSHING LEADER
SAYERS, RONALD (OMAHA) - BACK - 1969 SAN DIEGO CHARGERS (AFL)
SAZIO, RALPH (WILLIAM&MARY) - TACKLE - 1948 BROOKLYN DODGERS (AAFC)
SBRANTI, RONALD (UTAH STATE) - LB - 1966 DENVER BRONCOS (AFL)
SCAFIDE, JOHN (TULANE) - TACKLE - 1933 BOSTON REDSKINS
SCAGLIONE - GUARD - 1926 CLEVELAND PANTHERS (AFL)
SCALES, CHARLES (INDIANA) - BACK - 1960-61 PITTSBURGH STEELERS;
    1962-65 CLEVELAND BROWNS; 1966 ATLANTA FALCONS
SCALES, HURLES (NORTH TEXAS STATE) - BACK - 1974 CHICAGO BEARS (NFC);
    1974 ST. LOUIS CARDINALS (NFC)
SCALISSI, THEODORE (RIPON) - BACK - 1947 CHICAGO ROCKETS (AAFC)
SCALZI, JOHN (GEORGETOWN) - BACK - 1931 BROOKLYN DODGERS

SCANLON, DEWEY (VALPARAISO) - BACK - 1926 DULUTH ESKIMOS
SCANLON, JOHN (DEPAUL) - BACK - 1921 CHICAGO CARDINALS; 1926
    LOUISVILLE COLONELS
SCARBATH, JOHN (MARYLAND) - QBACK - 1953-54 WASHINGTON REDSKINS; 1956
    PITTSBURGH STEELERS
SCARDINE, CARMEN - BACK - 1932 CHICAGO CARDINALS
SCARPATI, JOSEPH (NORTH CAROLINA STATE) - BACK - 1964-69 PHILADELPHIA
    EAGLES; 1970 NEW ORLEANS SAINTS (NFC)
SCARPITTO, ROBERT (NOTRE DAME) - BACK - 1961 SAN DIEGO CHARGERS
    (AFL); 1962-67 DENVER BRONCOS (AFL); 1968 BOSTON PATRIOTS (AFL);
    1966-67 PUNTING LEADER (AFL)
SCARPINO, WILLIAM (DRAKE) - END - 1926 ROCK ISLAND INDEPENDENTS (AFL)
SCARRY, MICHAEL (WAYNESBURG) - CENTER - 1944-45 CLEVELAND RAMS;
    1946-47 CLEVELAND BROWNS (AAFC)
SCHAAKE, ELMER (KANSAS) - BACK - 1933 PORTSMOUTH SPARTANS
SCHABARUM, PETER (CALIFORNIA) - BACK - 1951, 53-54 SAN FRANCISCO 49ERS
SCHAEFER, DONALD (NOTRE DAME) - BACK - 1956 PHILADELPHIA EAGLES
SCHAFFER, JOSEPH (TENNESSEE) - LB - 1960 BUFFALO BILLS (AFL)
SCHAFFNIT, PETER (CALIFORNIA) - END - 1926 LOS ANGELES BUCCANEERS
SCHAFRATH, RICHARD (OHIO STATE) - TACKLE - 1959-69 CLEVELAND BROWNS;
    1970-71 CLEVELAND BROWNS (AFC)
SCHAMMEL, FRANCIS (IOWA) - GUARD - 1937 GREEN BAY PACKERS
SCHARER, EDWARD (NOTRE DAME) - BACK - 1926 DETROIT PANTHERS; 1927
    POTTSVILLE MAROONS; 1928 DETROIT WOLVERINES
SCHEIN, JOSEPH (BROWN) - TACKLE - 1931 PROVIDENCE STEAMROLLERS
SCHELL, HERBERT - BACK - 1924 COLUMBUS TIGERS
SCHENKER, NATHAN (HOWARD) - TACKLE - 1939 CLEVELAND RAMS
SCHERER, BERNARD (NEBRASKA) - END - 1936-38 GREEN BAY PACKERS; 1939
    PITTSBURGH STEELERS
SCHEUER, ABRAHAM (NEW YORK UNIV.) - TACKLE - 1934 NEW YORK GIANTS
SCHEULE, NORMAN (WESTERN RESERVE) - BACK - 1919 CLEVELAND INDIANS
SCHIBANOFF, ALEXANDER (FRANKLIN&MARSHALL) - TACKLE - 1941-42 DETROIT
    LIONS
SCHICHTLE, HENRY (WICHITA) - QBACK - 1964 NEW YORK GIANTS
SCHICK, DOYLE (KANSAS) - BACK - 1961 WASHINGTON REDSKINS
SCHIEB, LEE (WASHINGTON-MISSOURI) - CENTER - 1930 BROOKLYN DODGERS
SCHIECHL, JOHN (SANTA CLARA) - CENTER - 1941-42 PITTSBURGH STEELERS;
    1942 DETROIT LIONS; 1945-46 CHICAGO BEARS; 1947 SAN FRANCISCO
    49ERS (AAFC)
SCHILLING, RALPH (OKLAHOMA CITY UNIV.) - END - 1946 WASHINGTON
    REDSKINS; 1946 BUFFALO BISONS (AAFC)
SCHIMITITSCH, STEVEN (COLUMBIA) - GUARD - 1926 NEW YORK YANKEES (AFL)
SCHIMMEL, JOHN - GUARD - 1919 TOLEDO MAROONS
SCHLEE, EDWARD - TACKLE - 1919 DETROIT HERALDS
SCHLEICH, VICTOR (NEBRASKA) - TACKLE - 1947 NEW YORK YANKEES (AAFC)
SCHLEICHER, MAURICE (PENN STATE) - LB - 1959 CHICAGO CARDINALS; 1960
    LOS ANGELES CHARGERS (AFL); 1961-62 SAN DIEGO CHARGERS (AFL)
SCHLFUSNER, VINCENT (IOWA) - TACKLE - 1930-31 PORTSMOUTH SPARTANS
SCHLINKMAN, WALTER (TEXAS TECH) - BACK - 1946-49 GREEN BAY PACKERS
SCHMAAR, HERMAN (CATHOLIC) - END - 1943 BROOKLYN DODGERS
SCHMAEHL, ARTHUR - BACK - 1921 GREEN BAY PACKERS
SCHMAUTZ, RAYMOND (SAN DIEGO STATE) - LB - 1966 OAKLAND RAIDERS (AFL)
SCHMEDDING, JAMES (WEBER STATE) - GUARD - 1968-69 SAN DIEGO CHARGERS
    (AFL); 1970 SAN DIEGO CHARGERS (AFC)
SCHMERGE, ALBERT (XAVIER) - GUARD - 1940 CINCINNATI BENGALS (AFL)
SCHMIDT, GEORGE (LEWIS) - CENTER - 1952 GREEN BAY PACKERS; 1953
    CHICAGO CARDINALS
SCHMIDT, HENRY (USC) - TACKLE - 1959-60 SAN FRANCISCO 49ERS; 1961-64
    SAN DIEGO CHARGERS (AFL); 1965 BUFFALO BILLS (AFL); 1966 NEW
    YORK JETS (AFL)
SCHMIDT, JOHN (CARNEGIE TECH) - CENTER - 1940 PITTSBURGH STEELERS
SCHMIDT, JOSEPH (PITTSBURGH) - LB - 1953-65 DETROIT LIONS; 1973 HALL
    OF FAME
SCHMIDT, KERMIT (CALIFORNIA POLYTECH) - END - 1932 BOSTON BRAVES;
    1933 CINCINNATI REDS
SCHMIDT, ROBERT (MINNESOTA) - TACKLE - 1959-60 NEW YORK GIANTS;
    1961-63 HOUSTON OILERS (AFL); 1964-65 BOSTON PATRIOTS (AFL);
    1966-67 BUFFALO BILLS (AFL)

SCHMIDT, ROY (LONG BEACH STATE) - GUARD - 1967-68 NEW ORLEANS SAINTS;
    1969 ATLANTA FALCONS; 1970 WASHINGTON REDSKINS (NFC); 1971
    MINNESOTA VIKINGS (NFC)
SCHMIDT, TERRY (BALL STATE-INDIANA) - BACK - 1974 NEW ORLEANS SAINTS
    (NFC)
SCHMIESING, JOSEPH (NEW MEXICO STATE) - END, TACKLE - 1968-69 ST.
    LOUIS CARDINALS; 1970-71 ST. LOUIS CARDINALS (NFC); 1972 DETROIT
    LIONS (NFC); 1973 BALTIMORE COLTS (AFC); 1974 NEW YORK JETS (AFC)
SCHMITT, JOHN (HOFSTRA) - CENTER - 1964-69 NEW YORK JETS (AFL);
    1970-73 NEW YORK JETS (AFC); 1974 GREEN BAY PACKERS (NFC)
SCHMITT, THEODORE (PITTSBURGH) - CENTER - 1938-40 PHILADELPHIA EAGLES
SCHMITZ, ROBERT (MONTANA STATE) - LB - 1961-66 PITTSBURGH STEELERS;
    1966 MINNESOTA VIKINGS
SCHNEIDER, DONALD (PENNSYLVANIA) - BACK - 1948 BUFFALO BILLS (AAFC)
SCHNEIDER, JOHN - BACK - 1920 COLUMBUS PANHANDLES
SCHNEIDER, LEROY (TULANE) - TACKLE - 1947 BROOKLYN DODGERS (AAFC)
SCHNEIDMAN, HERMAN (IOWA) - QBACK - 1935-38 GREEN BAY PACKERS; 1940
    CHICAGO CARDINALS
SCHNELKER, ROBERT (BOWLING GREEN) - END - 1953 PHILADELPHIA EAGLES;
    1954-60 NEW YORK GIANTS; 1961 MINNESOTA VIKINGS; 1961 PITTSBURGH
    STEELERS
SCHNELLBACHER, OTTO (KANSAS) - BACK - 1948-49 NEW YORK YANKEES
    (AAFC); 1950-51 NEW YORK GIANTS; 1951 INTERCEPTION LEADER
SCHNELLER, JOHN (WISCONSIN) - END - 1933 PORTSMOUTH SPARTANS; 1934-36
    DETROIT LIONS
SCHNITKER, JAMES MICHAEL (COLORADO) - GUARD, LB - 1969 DENVER BRONCOS
    (AFL); 1970-74 DENVER BRONCOS (AFC)
SCHOEMANN, LEROY (MARQUETTE) - CENTER - 1938 GREEN BAY PACKERS
SCHOEN, TOM (NOTRE DAME) - BACK - 1970 CLEVELAND BROWNS (AFC)
SCHOENKE, RAYMOND (SMU) - GUARD, TACKLE - 1963-64 DALLAS COWBOYS;
    1966-69 WASHINGTON REDSKINS; 1970-74 WASHINGTON REDSKINS (NFC)
SCHOLL, ROY (LEHIGH) - GUARD - 1929 BOSTON BRAVES
SCHOLTZ, ROBERT (NOTRE DAME) - CENTER - 1960-64 DETROIT LIONS;
    1965-66 NEW YORK GIANTS
SCHOTTEL, IVAN (NORTHWEST MISSOURI STATE) - BACK - 1946, 48 DETROIT
    LIONS
SCHOTTENHEIMER, MARTIN (PITTSBURGH) - LB - 1965-68 BUFFALO BILLS
    (AFL); 1969 BOSTON PATRIOTS (AFL); 1970 BOSTON PATRIOTS (AFC)
SCHRADER, JAMES (NOTRE DAME) - CENTER - 1954, 56-61 WASHINGTON
    REDSKINS; 1962-64 PHILADELPHIA EAGLES
SCHREIBER, LAWRENCE (TENNESSEE TECH) - BACK - 1971-74 SAN FRANCISCO
    49ERS (NFC)
SCHROEDER, EUGENE (VIRGINIA) - END - 1951-52, 54-57 CHICAGO BEARS
SCHROEDER, WILLIAM (WISCONSIN) - BACK - 1946-47 CHICAGO ROCKETS (AAFC)
SCHROLL, WILLIAM (LSU) - BACK - 1949 BUFFALO BILLS (AAFC); 1950
    DETROIT LIONS; 1951 GREEN BAY PACKERS
SCHUBER, JAMES (ANNAPOLIS) - BACK - 1930 BROOKLYN DODGERS
SCHUBERT, STEVE (MASSACHUSETTS) - END - 1974 NEW ENGLAND PATRIOTS
    (AFC)
SCHUEHLE, C. JACOB (RICE) - BACK - 1939 PHILADELPHIA EAGLES
SCHUELKE, KARL (WISCONSIN) - BACK - 1939 PITTSBURGH STEELERS
SCHUESSLER, ERWIN - TACKLE - 1921 CINCINNATI CELTS
SCHUETTE, CARL (MARQUETTE) - CENTER - 1948-49 BUFFALO BILLS (AAFC);
    1950-51 GREEN BAY PACKERS
SCHUETTE, PAUL (WISCONSIN) - GUARD - 1928 NEW YORK GIANTS; 1930-32
    CHICAGO BEARS; 1932 BOSTON BRAVES
SCHUH, HARRY (MEMPHIS STATE) - TACKLE, GUARD - 1965-69 OAKLAND
    RAIDERS (AFL); 1970 OAKLAND RAIDERS (AFC); 1971-73 LOS ANGELES
    RAMS (NFC); 1974 GREEN BAY PACKERS (NFC)
SCHULER, WILLIAM (YALE) - TACKLE - 1947-48 NEW YORK GIANTS
SCHULTZ, CHARLES (MINNESOTA) - TACKLE - 1939-41 GREEN BAY PACKERS
SCHULTZ, EBERLE (OREGON STATE) - GUARD - 1940 PHILADELPHIA EAGLES;
    1941-42 PITTSBURGH STEELERS; 1943 PHIL-PITT; 1944 CARD-PITT;
    1945 CLEVELAND RAMS; 1946-47 LOS ANGELES RAMS
SCHULTZ, RANDOLPH (IOWA STATE) - BACK - 1966 CLEVELAND BROWNS;
    1967-68 NEW ORLEANS SAINTS
SCHULTZ - CENTER - 1919 TOLEDO MAROONS
SCHUMACHER, GREGG (ILLINOIS) - END - 1967-68 LOS ANGELES RAMS
SCHUPBACH, O. T. - (PLAYED UNDER NAME OF "TEX" MOONEY)
SCHUPP, WALTER (MIAMI-OHIO) - TACKLE - 1921 CINCINNATI CELTS
SCHUSTER, RICHARD (PENN STATE) - END - 1925 CANTON BULLDOGS

SCHWAB, RAYMOND (OKLAHOMA CITY UNIV.) - BACK - 1931 NEW YORK GIANTS;
    1932 STATEN ISLAND STAPELTONS
SCHWALL, VICTOR (NORTHWESTERN) - BACK - 1947-50 CHICAGO CARDINALS
SCHWAMMEL, ADOLPH (OREGON STATE) - TACKLE - 1934-36, 43-44 GREEN BAY
    PACKERS
SCHWARTZ, ELMER (WASHINGTON STATE) - BACK - 1931 PORTSMOUTH SPARTANS;
    1932 CHICAGO CARDINALS; 1933 PITTSBURGH PIRATES
SCHWARTZ, PERRY (CALIFORNIA) - END - 1938-42 BROOKLYN DODGERS; 1946
    NEW YORK YANKEES (AAFC)
SCHWARZBERG, WILLIAM (CINCINNATI) - BACK - 1937 CINCINNATI BENGALS
    (AFL)
SCHWARZER, THEODORE (CENTENARY) - GUARD - 1926 BUFFALO RANGERS
SCHWEDA, BRIAN (KANSAS) - END - 1966 CHICAGO BEARS; 1967-68 NEW
    ORLEANS SAINTS
SCHWEDER, JOHN (PENNSYLVANIA) - GUARD - 1950 BALTIMORE COLTS; 1951-55
    PITTSBURGH STEELERS
SCHWEDES, GERHARD (SYRACUSE) - BACK - 1960-61 BOSTON PATRIOTS (AFL)
SCHWEICKERT, ROBERT (VIRGINIA TECH) - BACK - 1965, 67 NEW YORK JETS
    (AFL)
SCHWEIDLER, RICHARD (ST. LOUIS UNIV.) - BACK - 1938-39, 46 CHICAGO
    BEARS
SCHWENK, WILSON (WASHINGTON-MISSOURI) - QBACK - 1942 CHICAGO
    CARDINALS; 1946 CLEVELAND BROWNS (AAFC); 1947 BALTIMORE COLTS
    (AAFC); 1948 NEW YORK YANKEES (AAFC)
SCIBELLI, JOSEPH (NOTRE DAME) - GUARD, TACKLE - 1961-69 LOS ANGELES
    RAMS; 1970-74 LOS ANGELES RAMS (NFC)
SCOLLARD, NICHOLAS (ST. JOSEPHS-INDIANA) - END - 1946-48 BOSTON
    YANKS; 1949 NEW YORK BULLDOGS
SCOLNICK, GLEN (INDIANA) - END - 1973 PITTSBURGH STEELERS (AFC)
SCOTT, CHARLES (AUBURN) - TACKLE - 1926 PROVIDENCE STEAMROLLERS
SCOTT, CLARENCE (KANSAS STATE) - BACK - 1971-74 CLEVELAND BROWNS (AFC)
SCOTT, CLARENCE (MORGAN STATE) - BACK - 1969 BOSTON PATRIOTS (AFL);
    1970 BOSTON PATRIOTS (AFC); 1971-72 NEW ENGLAND PATRIOTS (AFC)
SCOTT, CLYDE (ARKANSA & ANNAPOLIS) - BACK - 1949-52 PHILADELPHIA
    EAGLES; 1952 DETROIT LIONS
SCOTT, EDWARD (MONMOUTH) - GUARD - 1924 ROCK ISLAND INDEPENDENTS
SCOTT, EUGENE (HAMLINE) - GUARD - 1923 AKRON PROS; 1924 MINNEAPOLIS
    MARINES
SCOTT, FREDDIE (AMHERST) - END - 1974 BALTIMORE COLTS (AFC)
SCOTT, GEORGE (MIAMI-OHIO) - BACK - 1959 NEW YORK GIANTS
SCOTT, JACOB (GEORGIA) - BACK - 1970-74 MIAMI DOLPHINS (AFC)
SCOTT, JAMES (PENNSYLVANIA) - END - 1919 CLEVELAND INDIANS; 1919
    MASSILLON TIGERS
SCOTT, JOHN (LAFAYETTE) - BACK - 1919 AKRON PROS; 1920-23 BUFFALO
    ALL-AMERICANS; 1924 FRANKFORD YELLOWJACKETS; 1926 PHILADELPHIA
    QUAKERS (AFL)
SCOTT, JOHN (OHIO STATE) - TACKLE - 1960-61 BUFFALO BILLS (AFL)
SCOTT, JOSEPH (SAN FRANCISCO) - BACK - 1948-53 NEW YORK GIANTS
SCOTT, L. PERRY (MUHLENBERG) - END - 1942 DETROIT LIONS
SCOTT, LEWIS (OREGON STATE) - BACK - 1966 DENVER BRONCOS (AFL)
SCOTT, PHILIP (NEBRASKA) - END - 1929 ORANGE TORNADOS
SCOTT, PRINCE (TEXAS TECH) - END - 1946 MIAMI SEAHAWKS (AAFC)
SCOTT, RALPH (WISCONSIN) - TACKLE - 1921 CHICAGO STALEYS; 1922-25
    CHICAGO BEARS; 1926 NEW YORK YANKEES (AFL); 1927 NEW YORK YANKEES
SCOTT, ROBERT "BO" (OHIO STATE) - BACK - 1969 CLEVELAND BROWNS;
    1970-74 CLEVELAND BROWNS (AFC)
SCOTT, ROBERT "BOBBY" (TENNESSEE) - QBACK - 1973-74 NEW ORLEANS
    SAINTS (NFC)
SCOTT, THOMAS (VIRGINIA) - LB - 1953-58 PHILADELPHIA EAGLES; 1959-64
    NEW YORK GIANTS
SCOTT, VINCENT (NOTRE DAME) - GUARD - 1947-48 BUFFALO BILLS (AAFC)
SCOTT, WILBERT (INDIANA) - LB - 1961 PITTSBURGH STEELERS
SCOTT, WILLIAM (IDAHO) - BACK - 1968 CINCINNATI BENGALS (AFL)
SCOTTI, BENJAMIN (MARYLAND) - BACK - 1959-61 WASHINGTON REDSKINS;
    1962-63 PHILADELPHIA EAGLES; 1964 SAN FRANCISCO 49ERS
SCRABIS, ROBERT (PENN STATE) - QBACK - 1960-62 NEW YORK TITANS (AFL)
SCRUGGS, EDWIN (RICE) - END - 1947-48 BROOKLYN DODGERS (AAFC)
SCRUTCHINS, EDWARD (TOLEDO) - END - 1966 HOUSTON OILERS (AFL)
SCRIBNER, ROBERT (UCLA) - BACK - 1973-74 LOS ANGELES RAMS (NFC)

SCUDERO, JOSEPH (SAN FRANCISCO) - BACK - 1954-58 WASHINGTON REDSKINS;
   1960 PITTSBURGH STEELERS
SCZUREK, STANLEY (PURDUE) - LB - 1963-65 CLEVELAND BROWNS; 1966 NEW
   YORK GIANTS
SEABRIGHT, CHARLES (WEST VIRGINIA) - QBACK - 1941 CLEVELAND RAMS;
   1946-50 PITTSBURGH STEELERS
SEABURY, GEORGE (YALE) - TACKLE - 1940 NEW YORK AMERICANS (AFL)
SEAL, PAUL (MICHIGAN) - END - 1974 NEW ORLEANS SAINTS (NFC)
SEALS, GEORGE (MISSOURI) - GUARD, TACKLE - 1964 WASHINGTON REDSKINS;
   1965-69 CHICAGO BEARS; 1970-71 CHICAGO BEARS (NFC); 1972-73
   KANSAS CITY CHIEFS (AFC)
SEARS, JAMES (USC) - BACK - 1954, 57-58 CHICAGO CARDINALS; 1960 LOS
   ANGELES CHARGERS (AFL); 1961 DENVER BRONCOS (AFL)
SEARS, RICHARD (KANSAS STATE) - BACK - 1924 KANSAS CITY COWBOYS
SEARS, VICTOR (OREGON STATE) - TACKLE - 1941-42, 45-53 PHILADELPHIA
   EAGLES; 1943 PHIL-PITT
SEASHOLTZ, GEORGE (LAFAYETTE) - BACK - 1922 MILWAUKEE BADGERS; 1924
   KENOSHA MAROONS
SEBASTIAN, MICHAEL (PITTSBURGH) - BACK - 1935 PHILADELPHIA EAGLES;
   1935 PITTSBURGH PIRATES; 1935 BOSTON REDSKINS; 1936 CLEVELAND
   RAMS (AFL); 1937 CLEVELAND RAMS; 1937 ROCHESTER TIGERS (AFL);
   1937 CINCINNATI BENGALS (AFL)
SEBEK, NICHOLAS (INDIANA) - QBACK - 1950 WASHINGTON REDSKINS
SEBO, SAMUEL (SYRACUSE) - BACK - 1930 NEWARK TORNADOS
SEBORG, HENRY (KALAMAZOO) - QBACK - 1930 MINNEAPOLIS REDJACKETS;
   1930-31 FRANKFORD YELLOWJACKETS
SECHRIST, WALTER (WEST VIRGINIA) - GUARD - 1924 AKRON PROS; 1925
   FRANKFORD YELLOWJACKETS; 1926 HAMMOND PROS; 1926 LOUISVILLE
   COLONELS; 1926 CLEVELAND PANTHERS (AFL); 1927 CLEVELAND BULLDOGS
SECORD, JOSEPH - CENTER - 1922 GREEN BAY PACKERS
SEDBROOK, LEONARD (PHILLIPS) - BACK - 1928 DETROIT WOLVERINES;
   1929-31 NEW YORK GIANTS
SEDLOCK, ROBERT (GEORGIA) - TACKLE - 1960 BUFFALO BILLS (AFL)
SEEDBORG, JOHN (ARIZONA STATE) - KICKER - 1965 WASHINGTON REDSKINS
SEEDS, FRANK - BACK - 1926 CANTON BULLDOGS
SEEMAN, GEORGE (NEBRASKA) - END - 1940 GREEN BAY PACKERS
SEFTON, FREDERICK (COLGATE) - END - 1919 AKRON PROS
SEGAL, MAURICE - END - 1925 CLEVELAND BULLDOGS
SEGRETTA, ROCCO - END - 1926 HARTFORD BLUES
SEHRES, DAVID (NEW YORK UNIV.) - BACK - 1926 BROOKLYN HORSEMEN (AFL)
SEIBERT, EDWARD (WEST VIRGINIA WESLEYAN) - GUARD - 1923 HAMMOND PROS
SEIBERT, EDWARD (OTTERBEIN) - GUARD - 1927-28 DAYTON TRIANGLES
SEIBERT, HARRY - BACK - 1919 TOLEDO MAROONS
SEIBOLD, CHAMP (WISCONSIN) - TACKLE - 1934-38, 40 GREEN BAY PACKERS;
   1942 CHICAGO CARDINALS
SEICK, EARL (MANHATTAN) - GUARD - 1936 BOSTON SHAMROCKS (AFL); 1937
   NEW YORK YANKS (AFL); 1940 BUFFALO INDIANS (AFL); 1941 NEW YORK
   AMERICANS (AFL); 1942 NEW YORK GIANTS
SEIDEL, FREDERICK (PITTSBURGH) - GUARD - 1919 CLEVELAND INDIANS;
   1919, 21 CANTON BULLDOGS
SEIDELSON, HARRY (PITTSBURGH) - GUARD - 1925 FRANKFORD YELLOWJACKETS;
   1926 AKRON PROS
SEIFERT, MIKE (WISCONSIN) - END - 1974 CLEVELAND BROWNS (AFC)
SEILER, PAUL (NOTRE DAME) - TACKLE, CENTER - 1967, 69 NEW YORK JETS
   (AFL); 1971-73 OAKLAND RAIDERS (AFC)
SEIPLE, LAWRENCE (KENTUCKY) - KICKER, BACK, END - 1967-69 MIAMI
   DOLPHINS (AFL); 1970-74 MIAMI DOLPHINS (AFC)
SELAWSKI, EUGENE (PURDUE) - TACKLE - 1959 LOS ANGELES RAMS; 1960
   CLEVELAND BROWNS; 1961 SAN DIEGO CHARGERS (AFL)
SELF, CLARENCE (WISCONSIN) - BACK - 1949 CHICAGO CARDINALS; 1950-51
   DETROIT LIONS; 1952, 54-55 GREEN BAY PACKERS
SELFRIDGE, ANDREW (VIRGINIA) - LB - 1972 BUFFALO BILLS (AFC); 1974
   NEW YORK GIANTS (NFC)
SELLERS, GOLDIE (GRAMBLING) - BACK - 1966-67 DENVER BRONCOS (AFL);
   1968-69 KANSAS CITY CHIEFS (AFL)
SELLERS, RONALD (FLORIDA STATE) - END - 1969 BOSTON PATRIOTS (AFL);
   1970 BOSTON PATRIOTS (AFC); 1971 NEW ENGLAND PATRIOTS (AFC);
   1972 DALLAS COWBOYS (NFC); 1973 MIAMI DOLPHINS (AFC)
SELTZER, HARRY (MORRIS-HARVEY) - BACK - 1942 DETROIT LIONS
SEMES, BERNARD (DUQUESNE) - BACK - 1944 CARD-PITT

SENN, WILLIAM (KNOX) - BACK - 1926-31 CHICAGO BEARS; 1931 BROOKLYN
    DODGERS; 1933 CINCINNATI REDS; 1934 ST. LOUIS GUNNERS
SENO, FRANK (GEORGE WASHINGTON) - BACK - 1943-44, 49 WASHINGTON
    REDSKINS; 1945-46 CHICAGO CARDINALS; 1946-48 BOSTON YANKS; 1947
    INTERCEPTION LEADER; (TIED WITH REAGAN)
SENSENBAUGHER, DEAN (OHIO STATE) - BACK - 1948 CLEVELAND BROWNS
    (AAFC); 1949 NEW YORK BULLDOGS
SENSIBAUGH, JAMES MICHAEL (OHIO STATE) - BACK - 1971-74 KANSAS CITY
    CHIEFS (AFC); 1972 INTERCEPTION LEADER (AFC)
SERGIENKO, GEORGE (AMERICAN INTERNATIONAL) - TACKLE - 1943 BROOKLYN
    DODGERS; 1944 BROOKLYN TIGERS; 1945 BOSTON YANKS; 1946 BROOKLYN
    DODGERS (AAFC)
SERINI, WASHINGTON (KENTUCKY) - GUARD - 1948-51 CHICAGO BEARS; 1952
    GREEN BAY PACKERS
SERMON, RAYMOND (CENTRAL STATE-MISSOURI) - BACK - 1925 KANSAS CITY
    COWBOYS
SESTAK, THOMAS (MCNEESE STATE) - TACKLE - 1962-68 BUFFALO BILLS (AFL)
SETCAVAGE, JOSEPH (DUQUESNE) - BACK - 1943 BROOKLYN DODGERS
SETRON, JOSEPH (WEST VIRGINIA) - GUARD - 1923 CLEVELAND INDIANS
SEVERSON, JEFFREY (CAL.STATE-LONG BEACH) - BACK - 1972 WASHINGTON
    REDSKINS (NFC); 1973-74 HOUSTON OILERS (AFC)
SEWELL, HARLEY (TEXAS) - GUARD - 1953-62 DETROIT LIONS; 1963 LOS
    ANGELES RAMS
SEXTON, LINWOOD (WICHITA) - BACK - 1948 LOS ANGELES DONS (AAFC)
SEYFRIT, MICHAEL (NOTRE DAME) - END - 1923 TOLEDO MAROONS; 1924
    HAMMOND PROS
SEYMOUR, JAMES (NOTRE DAME) - END - 1970-72 CINCINNATI BENGALS (AFC)
SEYMOUR, PAUL (MICHIGAN) - END - 1973-74 BUFFALO BILLS (AFC)
SEYMOUR, ROBERT (OKLAHOMA) - BACK - 1940-45 WASHINGTON REDSKINS; 1946
    LOS ANGELES DONS (AAFC)
SHACKLEFORD, DONALD (PACIFIC) - GUARD - 1964 DENVER BRONCOS (AFL)
SHAFFER, GEORGE (WASHINGTON&JEFFERSON) - BACK - 1933 PITTSBURGH
    PIRATES
SHAFFER, LELAND (KANSAS STATE) - QBACK - 1935-43, 45 NEW YORK GIANTS
SHAMIS, ANTHONY (MANHATTAN) - TACKLE - 1940 NEW YORK AMERICANS (AFL)
SHANK, HENRY - BACK - 1920 DECATUR STALEYS
SHANKLIN, RONNIE (NORTH TEXAS STATE) - END - 1970-74 PITTSBURGH
    STEELERS (AFC)
SHANLEY, JAMES (OREGON) - BACK - 1958 GREEN BAY PACKERS
SHANLEY - BACK - 1920 DETROIT HERALDS
SHANN, ROBERT (BOSTON COLLEGE) - BACK - 1965, 67 PHILADELPHIA EAGLES
SHANNON, CARVER (SOUTHERN ILLINOIS) - BACK - 1962-64 LOS ANGELES RAMS
SHAPIRO, JOHN (NEW YORK UNIV.) - BACK - 1929 STATEN ISLAND STAPELTONS
SHARE, NATHAN (TUFTS) - GUARD - 1925-26 PROVIDENCE STEAMROLLERS; 1926
    BROOKLYN HORSEMEN (AFL)
SHARKEY, EDWARD (NEVADA & DUKE) - GUARD - 1947-49 NEW YORK YANKEES
    (AAFC); 1950 NEW YORK YANKS; 1952 CLEVELAND BROWNS; 1953
    BALTIMORE COLTS; 1954-55 PHILADELPHIA EAGLES; 1955-56 SAN
    FRANCISCO 49ERS
SHAROCKMAN, EDWARD (PITTSBURGH) - BACK - 1962-69 MINNESOTA VIKINGS;
    1970-72 MINNESOTA VIKINGS (NFC)
SHARP, EVERETT (CALIFORNIA POLYTECH) - TACKLE - 1944-45 WASHINGTON
    REDSKINS
SHARP, RICK (WASHINGTON) - TACKLE - 1970-71 PITTSBURGH STEELERS
    (AFC); 1972 DENVER BRONCOS (AFC)
SHAUB, HARRY (CORNELL) - GUARD - 1935 PHILADELPHIA EAGLES; 1936
    ROCHESTER TIGERS (AFL)
SHAW, CHARLES (OKLAHOMA A&M) - GUARD - 1950 SAN FRANCISCO 49ERS
SHAW, DENNIS (SAN DIEGO STATE) - QBACK - 1970-73 BUFFALO BILLS (AFC);
    1974 ST. LOUIS CARDINALS (NFC)
SHAW, EDSON (NEBRASKA) - BACK - 1920 ROCK ISLAND INDEPENDENTS;
    1922-23 CANTON BULLDOGS; 1923 AKRON PROS
SHAW, GEORGE (OREGON) - QBACK - 1955-58 BALTIMORE COLTS; 1959-60 NEW
    YORK GIANTS; 1961 MINNESOTA VIKINGS; 1962 DENVER BRONCOS (AFL)
SHAW, GLEN (KENTUCKY) - BACK - 1960 CHICAGO BEARS; 1962 LOS ANGELES
    RAMS; 1963-64 OAKLAND RAIDERS (AFL)
SHAW, JESSE (USC) - GUARD - 1931 CHICAGO CARDINALS
SHAW, NATHANIEL (USC) - BACK - 1969 LOS ANGELES RAMS; 1970 LOS
    ANGELES RAMS (NFC)

Top row (from left to right): Dennis Shaw, O. J. Simpson, Manuel Sistrunk and Otis Sistrunk. Second row: Bubba Smith, Jan Stenerud, Diron Talbert and Altie Taylor. Third row: Charley Taylor, Otis Taylor, Emmitt Thomas and Marvin Upshaw. Bottom row: Paul Warfield, Gene Washington, Rayfield Wright and Garo Yepremian.

SHAW, ROBERT (OHIO STATE) - END - 1945 CLEVELAND RAMS; 1946, 49 LOS
        ANGELES RAMS; 1950 CHICAGO CARDINALS
SHAW, ROBERT (WINSTON-SALEM) - END - 1970 NEW ORLEANS SAINTS (NFC)
SHAW, WILLIAM (GEORGIA TECH) - GUARD - 1961-69 BUFFALO BILLS (AFL)
SHAY, JEROME (PURDUE) - TACKLE - 1966-67 MINNESOTA VIKINGS; 1968-69
        ATLANTA FALCONS; 1970-71 NEW YORK GIANTS (NFC)
SHEA, PATRICK (USC) - GUARD - 1962-65 SAN DIEGO CHARGERS (AFL)
SHEARD, ALFRED (ST. LAWRENCE) - BACK - 1923-25 ROCHESTER JEFFERSONS
SHEARER, RONALD (DRAKE) - TACKLE - 1930 PORTSMOUTH SPARTANS
SHEARS, LARRY (LINCOLN-MISSOURI) - BACK - 1971-72 ATLANTA FALCONS
        (NFC)
SHEDLOSKY, EDMOND (TULSA & FORDHAM) - BACK - 1945 NEW YORK GIANTS
SHEEHAN, JOHN (BOSTON COLLEGE) - GUARD - 1925 PROVIDENCE STEAMROLLERS
SHEEHY, JOHN (NEW YORK UNIV.) - CENTER - 1926 BROOKLYN HORSEMEN (AFL)
SHEEKS, PAUL (SOUTH DAKOTA) - QBACK - 1919 TOLEDO MAROONS; 1921-22
        AKRON PROS
SHEKLETON, VINCENT (MARQUETTE) - GUARD - 1922 RACINE LEGION
SHELBOURNE, JOHN (DARTMOUTH) - BACK - 1922 HAMMOND PROS
SHELDON, JAMES (BROWN) - END - 1926 BROOKLYN LIONS
SHELL, ARTHUR (MARYLAND-EASTERN SHORE) - TACKLE - 1968-69 OAKLAND
        RAIDERS (AFL); 1970-74 OAKLAND RAIDERS (AFC)
SHELL, DONNIE (SOUTH CAROLINA STATE) - BACK - 1974 PITTSBURGH
        STEELERS (AFC)
SHELLEY, DEXTER (TEXAS) - BACK - 1931 PROVIDENCE STEAMROLLERS; 1931
        PORTSMOUTH SPARTANS; 1932 CHICAGO CARDINALS; 1932 GREEN BAY
        PACKERS
SHELLOGG, ALEC (NOTRE DAME) - TACKLE - 1939 BROOKLYN DODGERS; 1939
        CHICAGO BEARS; 1940 BUFFALO INDIANS (AFL); 1941 BUFFALO TIGERS
        (AFL)
SHELTON, ALBERT (CINCINNATI) - END - 1937, 40-41 CINCINNATI BENGALS
        (AFL)
SHELTON, MURRAY (CORNELL) - END - 1920-22 BUFFALO ALL-AMERICANS
SHENEFELT, PAUL (MANCHESTER) - TACKLE - 1934-35 CHICAGO CARDINALS
SHEPARD, CHARLES (NORTH TEXAS STATE) - BACK - 1956 PITTSBURGH STEELERS
SHEPHERD, WILLIAM (WESTERN MARYLAND) - BACK - 1935 BOSTON REDSKINS;
        1935-40 DETROIT LIONS
SHERER, DAVID (SMU) - END - 1959 BALTIMORE COLTS; 1960 DALLAS COWBOYS
SHERIFF, STANLEY (CALIFORNIA POLYTECH) - LB - 1954 PITTSBURGH
        STEELERS; 1956-57 SAN FRANCISCO 49ERS; 1957 CLEVELAND BROWNS
SHERK, JERRY (OKLAHOMA STATE) - TACKLE - 1970-74 CLEVELAND BROWNS
        (AFC)
SHERLAG, ROBERT (MEMPHIS STATE) - END - 1966 ATLANTA FALCONS
SHERMAN, ALEX (BROOKLYN COLLEGE) - QBACK - 1943 PHIL-PITT; 1944-47
        PHILADELPHIA EAGLES
SHERMAN, ROBERT (IOWA) - BACK - 1964-65 PITTSBURGH STEELERS
SHERMAN, RODNEY (USC) - END - 1967, 69 OAKLAND RAIDERS (AFL); 1968
        CINCINNATI BENGALS (AFL); 1970-71 OAKLAND RAIDERS (AFC); 1972
        DENVER BRONCOS (AFC); 1973 LOS ANGELES RAMS (NFC)
SHERMAN, SAUL (CHICAGO) - QBACK - 1939-40 CHICAGO BEARS
SHERMAN, THOMAS (PENN STATE) - QBACK - 1968-69 BOSTON PATRIOTS (AFL);
        1969 BUFFALO BILLS (AFL)
SHERMAN, WILLARD (ST. MARY'S OF CAL.) - BACK - 1952 DALLAS TEXANS;
        1954-60 LOS ANGELES RAMS; 1961 MINNESOTA VIKINGS; 1955
        INTERCEPTION LEADER
SHERROD, HORACE (TENNESSEE) - END - 1952 NEW YORK GIANTS
SHIELDS, BURRELL (JOHN CARROLL) - BACK - 1954 PITTSBURGH STEELERS;
        1955 BALTIMORE COLTS
SHIELDS, LEBRON (TENNESSEE) - TACKLE - 1960 BALTIMORE COLTS; 1961
        MINNESOTA VIKINGS
SHINER, RICHARD (MARYLAND) - QBACK - 1964-66 WASHINGTON REDSKINS;
        1967 CLEVELAND BROWNS; 1968-69 PITTSBURGH STEELERS; 1970 NEW
        YORK GIANTS (NFC); 1971, 73 ATLANTA FALCONS (NFC); 1973-74 NEW
        ENGLAND PATRIOTS (AFC)
SHINNERS, JOHN (XAVIER) - GUARD - 1969 NEW ORLEANS SAINTS; 1970-71
        NEW ORLEANS SAINTS (NFC); 1972 BALTIMORE COLTS (AFC); 1973-74
        CINCINNATI BENGALS (AFC)
SHINNICK, DONALD (UCLA) - LB - 1957-68 BALTIMORE COLTS; 1959
        INTERCEPTION LEADER; (TIED WITH M. DAVIS AND DERBY)
SHIPKEY, GERALD (UCLA) - BACK - 1948-52 PITTSBURGH STEELERS; 1953
        CHICAGO BEARS
SHIPKEY, HARRY (STANFORD) - TACKLE - 1926 LOS ANGELES WILDCATS (AFL)

SHIPLA, STERLING (ST. NORBERTS) - GUARD - 1940 BOSTON BEARS (AFL);
     1940 MILWAUKEE CHIEFS (AFL)
SHIPP, WILLIAM (ALABAMA) - TACKLE - 1954 NEW YORK GIANTS
SHIRES, MARSHALL (TENNESSEE) - TACKLE - 1945 PHILADELPHIA EAGLES
SHIREY, FREDERICK (NEBRASKA) - TACKLE - 1940 GREEN BAY PACKERS;
     1940-41 CLEVELAND RAMS
SHIRK, JOHN (OKLAHOMA) - END - 1940 CHICAGO CARDINALS
SHIRKEY, GEORGE (S. F. AUSTIN STATE) - TACKLE - 1960-61 HOUSTON
     OILERS (AFL); 1962 OAKLAND RAIDERS (AFL)
SHIRLEY, MARION (OKLAHOMA CITY UNIV.) - TACKLE - 1948-49 NEW YORK
     YANKEES (AAFC)
SHIVER, RAYMOND (MIAMI) - BACK - 1956 LOS ANGELES RAMS
SHIVERS, ROY (UTAH STATE) - BACK - 1966-69 ST. LOUIS CARDINALS;
     1970-72 ST. LOUIS CARDINALS (NFC)
SHLAPAK, BORIS (MICHIGAN STATE) - KICKER - 1972 BALTIMORE COLTS (AFC)
SHOALS, ROGER (MARYLAND) - TACKLE - 1963-64 CLEVELAND BROWNS; 1965-69
     DETROIT LIONS; 1970 DETROIT LIONS (NFC); 1971 DENVER BRONCOS
     (AFC)
SHOCKLEY, ARNOLD (SOUTHWEST OKLAHOMA STATE) - GUARD - 1928-29
     PROVIDENCE STEAMROLLERS; 1929 BOSTON BRAVES
SHOCKLEY, WILLIAM (WEST CHESTER STATE) - KICKER - 1960-62 NEW YORK
     TITANS (AFL); 1961 BUFFALO BILLS (AFL); 1968 PITTSBURGH STEELERS
SHOEMAKE, C. HUBBARD (ILLINOIS) - GUARD - 1920 DECATUR STALEYS; 1921
     CHICAGO STALEYS
SHOENER, HAROLD (IOWA) - END - 1948-49 SAN FRANCISCO 49ERS (AAFC);
     1950 SAN FRANCISCO 49ERS
SHOENER, HERBERT (IOWA) - END - 1948-49 WASHINGTON REDSKINS
SHOFNER, DELBERT (BAYLOR) - END - 1957-60 LOS ANGELES RAMS; 1961-67
     NEW YORK GIANTS
SHOFNER, JAMES (TCU) - BACK - 1958-63 CLEVELAND BROWNS
SHONK, JOHN (WEST VIRGINIA) - END - 1941 PHILADELPHIA EAGLES
SHONTA, CHARLES (EASTERN MICHIGAN) - BACK - 1960-67 BOSTON PATRIOTS
     (AFL)
SHOOK, FREDERICK (TCU) - CENTER - 1941 CHICAGO CARDINALS
SHORTER, JAMES (DETROIT) - BACK - 1962-63 CLEVELAND BROWNS; 1964-67
     WASHINGTON REDSKINS; 1969 PITTSBURGH STEELERS
SHOULTS, PAUL (MIAMI-OHIO) - BACK - 1949 NEW YORK BULLDOGS
SHOWALTER, FRANK (NEVADA) - TACKLE - 1937 ROCHESTER TIGERS (AFL)
SHUGART, CLYDE (IOWA STATE) - GUARD - 1939-44 WASHINGTON REDSKINS
SHULA, DONALD (JOHN CARROLL) - BACK - 1951-52 CLEVELAND BROWNS;
     1953-56 BALTIMORE COLTS; 1957 WASHINGTON REDSKINS
SHULTZ, JOHN (TEMPLE) - BACK - 1930 FRANKFORD YELLOWJACKETS
SHURNAS, MARSHALL (MISSOURI) - END - 1947 CLEVELAND BROWNS (AAFC)
SHURTCLIFFE, CHARLES (MARIETTA) - BACK - 1929 BUFFALO BISONS
SHURTLEFF, BERTRAND (BROWN) - TACKLE - 1925-26 PROVIDENCE
     STEAMROLLERS; 1929 BOSTON BRAVES
SHURTZ, HUBERT (LSU) - TACKLE - 1948 PITTSBURGH STEELERS
SHY, DONALD (SAN DIEGO STATE) - BACK, END - 1967-68 PITTSBURGH
     STEELERS; 1969 NEW ORLEANS SAINTS; 1970-72 CHICAGO BEARS (NFC);
     1973 ST. LOUIS CARDINALS (NFC)
SHY, LESLIE (LONG BEACH STATE) - BACK - 1966-69 DALLAS COWBOYS; 1970
     NEW YORK GIANTS (NFC)
SIANI, MICHAEL (VILLANOVA) - END - 1972-74 OAKLAND RAIDERS (AFC)
SIANO, ANTHONY (FORDHAM) - CENTER - 1932 BOSTON BRAVES; 1934 BROOKLYN
     DODGERS
SIDLE, JAMES (AUBURN) - BACK - 1966 ATLANTA FALCONS
SIDORIK, ALEXANDER (MISSISSIPPI STATE) - TACKLE - 1947 BOSTON YANKS;
     1948-49 BALTIMORE COLTS (AAFC)
SIEB, WALTER (RIPON) - BACK - 1922 RACINE LEGION
SIEGAL, CHARLES (NEW YORK UNIV.) - BACK - 1936 NEW YORK YANKS (AFL)
SIEGAL, JOHN (COLUMBIA) - END - 1939-43 CHICAGO BEARS
SIEGERT, HERBERT (ILLINOIS) - GUARD - 1949-51 WASHINGTON REDSKINS
SIEGERT, WAYNE (ILLINOIS) - GUARD - 1951 NEW YORK YANKS
SIEGFRIED, ORVILLE (WASHINGTON&JEFFERSON) - BACK - 1923 ST. LOUIS
     BROWNS
SIEGLE, JULES (NORTHWESTERN) - BACK - 1948 NEW YORK GIANTS
SIEMERING, LAWRENCE (SAN FRANCISCO) - CENTER - 1935-36 BOSTON REDSKINS
SIEMINSKI, CLARK LEO (PENN STATE) - TACKLE - 1963-65 SAN FRANCISCO
     49ERS; 1966-67 ATLANTA FALCONS; 1968 DETROIT LIONS
SIEMON, JEFFREY (STANFORD) - LB - 1972-74 MINNESOTA VIKINGS (NFC)

SIERACKI, STANLEY (PENNSYLVANIA) - TACKLE - 1927 FRANKFORD
    YELLOWJACKETS
SIERADZKI, STEPHEN (MICHIGAN STATE) - BACK - 1948 NEW YORK YANKEES
    (AAFC); 1948 BROOKLYN DODGERS (AAFC)
SIEROCINSKI, STEPHEN - TACKLE - 1946 BOSTON YANKS
SIES, DALE (PITTSBURGH) - GUARD - 1919 MASSILLON TIGERS; 1920
    CLEVELAND PANTHERS; 1921-22, 24 DAYTON TRIANGLES; 1923 ROCK
    ISLAND INDEPENDENTS; 1924 KENOSHA MAROONS
SIGILLO, DOMINIC (XAVIER-OHIO) - TACKLE - 1937 CINCINNATI BENGALS
    (AFL); 1940-41 COLUMBUS BULLIES (AFL); 1943-44 CHICAGO BEARS;
    1945 DETROIT LIONS
SIGMUND, ARTHUR - GUARD - 1923 CHICAGO BEARS
SIGNAIGO, JOSEPH (NOTRE DAME) - GUARD - 1948-49 NEW YORK YANKEES
    (AAFC); 1950 NEW YORK YANKS
SIGURDSON, SIGURD (PACIFIC LUTHERAN) - END - 1947 BALTIMORE COLTS
    (AAFC)
SIKICH, MICHAEL (NORTHWESTERN) - GUARD - 1971 CLEVELAND BROWNS (AFC)
SIKICH, RUDOLPH (MINNESOTA) - TACKLE - 1945 CLEVELAND RAMS
SIKORA, MICHAEL (OREGON) - GUARD - 1952 CHICAGO CARDINALS
SILAS, SAMUEL (SOUTHERN ILLINOIS) - TACKLE, END - 1963-67 ST. LOUIS
    CARDINALS; 1968 NEW YORK GIANTS; 1969 SAN FRANCISCO 49ERS; 1970
    SAN FRANCISCO 49ERS (NFC)
SILLIN, FRANK (WESTERN MARYLAND) - BACK - 1927-29 DAYTON TRIANGLES
SILVESTRI, CARL (WISCONSIN) - BACK - 1965 ST. LOUIS CARDINALS; 1966
    ATLANTA FALCONS
SIMAS, WILLIAM (ST. MARY'S OF CAL.) - BACK - 1932-33 CHICAGO CARDINALS
SIMENDINGER, KENNETH (HOLY CROSS) - BACK - 1926 HARTFORD BLUES
SIMENSEN, DONALD (ST. THOMAS) - TACKLE - 1951-52 LOS ANGELES RAMS
SIMERSON, JOHN (PURDUE) - TACKLE - 1957-58 PHILADELPHIA EAGLES; 1958
    PITTSBURGH STEELERS; 1960 HOUSTON OILERS (AFL); 1961 BOSTON
    PATRIOTS (AFL)
SIMINGTON, MILTON (ARKANSAS) - GUARD - 1941 CLEVELAND RAMS; 1942
    PITTSBURGH STEELERS
SIMINSKI, EDWARD (BOWLING GREEN) - END - 1940 BUFFALO INDIANS (AFL)
SIMKUS, ARNOLD (MICHIGAN) - TACKLE - 1965 NEW YORK JETS (AFL); 1967
    MINNESOTA VIKINGS
SIMMONS, DAVID (GEORGIA TECH) - LB - 1965-66 ST. LOUIS CARDINALS;
    1967 NEW ORLEANS SAINTS; 1968 DALLAS COWBOYS
SIMMONS, FLOYD (NOTRE DAME) - BACK - 1948 CHICAGO ROCKETS (AAFC)
SIMMONS, JAMES (SOUTHWEST OKLAHOMA STATE) - BACK - 1927 CLEVELAND
    BULLDOGS; 1928 PROVIDENCE STEAMROLLERS
SIMMONS, JERRY (BETHUNE-COOKMAN) - END, BACK - 1965-66 PITTSBURGH
    STEELERS; 1967 NEW ORLEANS SAINTS; 1967-69 ATLANTA FALCONS; 1969
    CHICAGO BEARS; 1971-74 DENVER BRONCOS (AFC)
SIMMONS, JOHN (DETROIT) - CENTER - 1948 BALTIMORE COLTS (AAFC);
    1949-50 DETROIT LIONS; 1951-56 CHICAGO CARDINALS
SIMMONS, LEON (GRAMBLING) - LB - 1963 DENVER BRONCOS (AFL)
SIMMS, ROBERT (RUTGERS) - END - 1960-62 NEW YORK GIANTS; 1962
    PITTSBURGH STEELERS
SIMON, JAMES (MIAMI) - GUARD - 1963-65 DETROIT LIONS; 1966-68 ATLANTA
    FALCONS
SIMONE, MICHAEL (STANFORD) - LB - 1972-74 DENVER BRONCOS (AFC)
SIMONETTI, LEONARD (TENNESSEE) - TACKLE - 1947-48 CLEVELAND BROWNS
    (AAFC)
SIMONOVICH - TACKLE - 1940 NEW YORK AMERICANS (AFL)
SIMONS, JOHN (HAMLINE) - END - 1924 MINNEAPOLIS MARINES
SIMONSON, DAVE (MINNESOTA) - TACKLE - 1974 BALTIMORE COLTS (AFC)
SIMPSON, EBER (WISCONSIN) - BACK - 1921, 23-24 MINNEAPOLIS MARINES;
    1923 ST. LOUIS BROWNS
SIMPSON, HOWARD (AUBURN) - END - 1964 MINNESOTA VIKINGS
SIMPSON, J. FELIX (DETROIT) - BACK - 1922 TOLEDO MAROONS; 1924
    KENOSHA MAROONS
SIMPSON, JACK (MISSISSIPPI) - LB - 1961 DENVER BRONCOS (AFL); 1962-64
    OAKLAND RAIDERS (AFL)
SIMPSON, JACKIE (FLORIDA) - BACK - 1958-60 BALTIMORE COLTS; 1961-62
    PITTSBURGH STEELERS
SIMPSON, MICHAEL (HOUSTON) - BACK - 1970-73 SAN FRANCISCO 49ERS (NFC)
SIMPSON, ORENTHAL JAMES "O.J." (USC) - BACK - 1969 BUFFALO BILLS
    (AFL); 1970-74 BUFFALO BILLS (AFC); 1972-73 RUSHING LEADER (AFC)
SIMPSON, WILLIAM (MICHIGAN STATE) - BACK - 1974 LOS ANGELES RAMS (NFC)

SIMPSON, WILLIAM (SAN FRANCISCO STATE) - BACK - 1962 OAKLAND RAIDERS
     (AFL)
SIMS, GEORGE (BAYLOR) - BACK - 1949-50 LOS ANGELES RAMS
SINGER, KARL (PURDUE) - TACKLE - 1966-68 BOSTON PATRIOTS (AFL)
SINGER, WALTER (SYRACUSE) - END - 1935-36 NEW YORK GIANTS
SINGLETARY, WILLIAM (TEMPLE) - LB - 1974 NEW YORK GIANTS (NFC)
SINGLETON, JOHN - BACK - 1929 DAYTON TRIANGLES
SINGLETON, WILLIAM - GUARD - 1922 HAMMOND PROS
SINKO, STEPHEN (DUQUESNE) - TACKLE - 1934-36 BOSTON REDSKINS; 1937
     LOS ANGELES BULLDOGS (AFL)
SINKOVITZ, FRANK (DUKE) - CENTER - 1947-52 PITTSBURGH STEELERS
SINKWICH, FRANK (GEORGIA) - BACK - 1943-44 DETROIT LIONS; 1946-47 NEW
     YORK YANKEES (AAFC); 1947 BALTIMORE COLTS (AAFC); 1944 PUNTING
     LEADER
SIPE, BRIAN (SAN DIEGO STATE) - QBACK - 1974 CLEVELAND BROWNS (AFC)
SIROCHMAN, GEORGE (DUQUESNE) - GUARD - 1942 PITTSBURGH STEELERS; 1944
     DETROIT LIONS
SISEMORE, JERRY (TEXAS) - TACKLE - 1973-74 PHILADELPHIA EAGLES (NFC)
SISK, JOHN (MARQUETTE) - BACK - 1932-36 CHICAGO BEARS
SISK, JOHN, JR. (MIAMI) - BACK - 1964 CHICAGO BEARS
SISTRUNK, MANUEL (ARKANSAS AM&N) - TACKLE - 1970-74 WASHINGTON
     REDSKINS (NFC)
SISTRUNK, OTIS - TACKLE, END - 1972-74 OAKLAND RAIDERS (AFC)
SITES, VINCENT (PITTSBURGH) - END - 1936-37 PITTSBURGH PIRATES; 1937
     CINCINNATI BENGALS (AFL)
SITKO, EMIL (NOTRE DAME) - BACK - 1950 SAN FRANCISCO 49ERS; 1951-52
     CHICAGO CARDINALS
SIVELL, RALPH JAMES (AUBURN) - GUARD - 1938-42 BROOKLYN DODGERS; 1944
     BROOKLYN TIGERS; 1944-45 NEW YORK GIANTS; 1946 MIAMI SEAHAWKS
     (AAFC)
SIWEK, MIKE (WESTERN MICHIGAN) - TACKLE - 1970 ST. LOUIS CARDINALS
     (NFC)
SKAGGS, JAMES (WASHINGTON) - GUARD - 1963-67, 69 PHILADELPHIA EAGLES;
     1970-72 PHILADELPHIA EAGLES (NFC)
SKEATE, GILBERT (GONZAGA) - BACK - 1927 GREEN BAY PACKERS
SKIBINSKI, JOSEPH (PURDUE) - GUARD - 1952 CLEVELAND BROWNS; 1955-56
     GREEN BAY PACKERS
SKLADANY, JOSEPH (PITTSBURGH) - END - 1934 PITTSBURGH PIRATES
SKLADANY, LEO (PITTSBURGH) - END - 1949 PHILADELPHIA EAGLES; 1950 NEW
     YORK GIANTS
SKLOPAN, JOHN (MISSISSIPPI SOUTHERN) - BACK - 1963 DENVER BRONCOS
     (AFL)
SKOGLUND, ROBERT (NOTRE DAME) - END - 1947 GREEN BAY PACKERS
SKOOZEN, STANLEY (WESTERN RESERVE) - BACK - 1944 CLEVELAND RAMS
SKORICH, NICHOLAS (CINCINNATI) - GUARD - 1946-48 PITTSBURGH STEELERS
SKORONSKI, EDWARD (PURDUE) - END - 1935-36 PITTSBURGH PIRATES; 1937
     BROOKLYN DODGERS; 1937 CLEVELAND RAMS
SKORONSKI, ROBERT (INDIANA) - TACKLE - 1956, 59-68 GREEN BAY PACKERS
SKORUPAN, JOHN (PENN STATE) - LB - 1973-74 BUFFALO BILLS (AFC)
SKUDIN, DAVID (NEW YORK UNIV.) - GUARD - 1929 STATEN ISLAND STAPELTONS
SKULOS, MICHAEL (WASHINGTON&JEFFERSON) - GUARD - 1936-37 PITTSBURGH
     AMERICANS (AFL)
SLABY, LOUIS (PITTSBURGH) - LB - 1964-65 NEW YORK GIANTS; 1966
     DETROIT LIONS
SLACKFORD, FREDERICK (NOTRE DAME) - BACK - 1920 DAYTON TRIANGLES;
     1921 CANTON BULLDOGS
SLAGLE, CHARLES (NORTH CAROLINA) - GUARD - 1941 CINCINNATI BENGALS
     (AFL)
SLAGLE, GEORGE - TACKLE - 1926 LOUISVILLE COLONELS
SLATER, FRED "DUKE" (IOWA) - TACKLE - 1922 MILWAUKEE BADGERS; 1922-25
     ROCK ISLAND INDEPENDENTS; 1926 ROCK ISLAND INDEPENDENTS (AFL);
     1926-31 CHICAGO CARDINALS
SLATER, HOWARD (WASHINGTON STATE) - BACK - 1926 MILWAUKEE BADGERS
SLATER, WALTER (TENNESSEE) - BACK - 1947 PITTSBURGH STEELERS
SLAUGHTER, MILTON "MICKEY" (LOUISIANA TECH) - QBACK - 1963-66 DENVER
     BRONCOS (AFL)
SLEDGE, LEROY (BAKERSFIELD JUNIOR) - BACK - 1971 HOUSTON OILERS (AFC)
SLEIGHT, ELMER (PURDUE) - TACKLE - 1930-31 GREEN BAY PACKERS
SLIGH, RICHARD (NORTH CAROLINA COLLEGE) - TACKLE - 1967 OAKLAND
     RAIDERS (AFL)
SLIVINSKI, STEVEN (WASHINGTON) - GUARD - 1939-43 WASHINGTON REDSKINS

SLOAN, DWIGHT (ARKANSAS) - QBACK - 1938 CHICAGO CARDINALS; 1939-40
    DETROIT LIONS
SLOAN, STEPHEN (ALABAMA) - QBACK - 1966-67 ATLANTA FALCONS
SLOAN - TACKLE - 1919 WHEELING
SLOANE, BONNIE (AUSTIN PEAY) - TACKLE - 1973 ST. LOUIS CARDINALS (NFC)
SLOSBURG, PHILIP (TEMPLE) - BACK - 1948 BOSTON YANKS; 1949 NEW YORK
    BULLDOGS
SLOTNICK, LEO (NORTH CAROLINA) - BACK - 1940 BOSTON BEARS (AFL)
SLOUGH, ELMER (OKLAHOMA) - BACK - 1926 BUFFALO RANGERS
SLOUGH, GREGORY (USC) - LB - 1971-72 OAKLAND RAIDERS (AFC)
SLOVAK, MARTIN (TOLEDO) - BACK - 1939-41 CLEVELAND RAMS
SLYKER, WILLIAM (OHIO STATE) - END - 1922 EVANSVILLE CRIMSON GIANTS
SMALL, ELDRIDGE (TEXAS A&I) - BACK - 1972-74 NEW YORK GIANTS (NFC)
SMALL, JOHN (CITADEL) - TACKLE, CENTER, LB - 1970-72 ATLANTA FALCONS
    (NFC); 1973-74 DETROIT LIONS (NFC)
SMEJA, RUDOLPH (MICHIGAN) - END - 1944-45 CHICAGO BEARS; 1946
    PHILADELPHIA EAGLES
SMILANICH, BRONISLAW (ARIZONA) - BACK - 1939 CLEVELAND RAMS
SMILEY, THOMAS (LAMAR TECH) - BACK - 1968 CINCINNATI BENGALS (AFL);
    1969 DENVER BRONCOS (AFL); 1970 HOUSTON OILERS (AFC)
SMITH, ALLEN (FINDLAY) - BACK - 1966 NEW YORK JETS (AFL)
SMITH, ALLEN DUNCAN (FORT VALLEY STATE) - BACK - 1966-67 BUFFALO
    BILLS (AFL)
SMITH, BARRY (FLORIDA STATE) - END - 1973-74 GREEN BAY PACKERS (NFC)
SMITH, BARTON "BARTY" (RICHMOND) - BACK - 1974 GREEN BAY PACKERS (NFC)
SMITH, BEN (ALABAMA) - END - 1933 GREEN BAY PACKERS; 1934-35
    PITTSBURGH PIRATES; 1936 PITTSBURGH AMERICANS (AFL); 1937
    WASHINGTON REDSKINS
SMITH, BILLY RAY (ARKANSAS) - TACKLE - 1957 LOS ANGELES RAMS; 1958-60
    PITTSBURGH STEELERS; 1961-62, 64-69 BALTIMORE COLTS; 1970
    BALTIMORE COLTS (AFC)
SMITH, BRUCE (MINNESOTA) - BACK - 1945-48 GREEN BAY PACKERS; 1948 LOS
    ANGELES RAMS
SMITH, CARL (TENNESSEE) - BACK - 1960 BUFFALO BILLS (AFL)
SMITH, CEDRIC "PAT" (MICHIGAN) - BACK - 1919 MASSILLON TIGERS;
    1920-23 BUFFALO ALL-AMERICANS; 1924 FRANKFORD YELLOWJACKETS
SMITH, CHARLES (ABILENE CHRISTIAN) - END - 1956 SAN FRANCISCO 49ERS
SMITH, CHARLES (BOSTON COLLEGE) - END - 1966 BOSTON PATRIOTS (AFL)
SMITH, CHARLES (GEORGIA) - BACK - 1947 CHICAGO CARDINALS
SMITH, CHARLES (GRAMBLING) - END - 1974 PHILADELPHIA EAGLES (NFC)
SMITH, CHARLES "BUBBA" (MICHIGAN STATE) - END, TACKLE - 1967-69
    BALTIMORE COLTS; 1970-71 BALTIMORE COLTS (AFC); 1973-74 OAKLAND
    RAIDERS (AFC)
SMITH, CHARLES HENRY (UTAH) - BACK - 1968-69 OAKLAND RAIDERS (AFL);
    1970-74 OAKLAND RAIDERS (AFC)
SMITH, CLYDE (MISSOURI) - CENTER - 1926 KANSAS CITY COWBOYS; 1927
    CLEVELAND BULLDOGS; 1928-29 PROVIDENCE STEAMROLLERS
SMITH, DANIEL (NORTHEAST OKLAHOMA STATE) - BACK - 1961 DENVER BRONCOS
    (AFL)
SMITH, DAVID (INDIANA STATE-PA.) - END - 1970-72 PITTSBURGH STEELERS
    (AFC); 1972 HOUSTON OILERS (AFC); 1973 KANSAS CITY CHIEFS (AFC)
SMITH, DAVID (RIPON) - BACK - 1960-64 HOUSTON OILERS (AFL)
SMITH, DAVID (UTAH) - BACK - 1970 SAN DIEGO CHARGERS (AFC)
SMITH, DONALD - GUARD - 1929 ORANGE TORNADOS; 1930 NEWARK TORNADOS
SMITH, DONALD (FLORIDA A&M) - GUARD - 1967 DENVER BRONCOS (AFL)
SMITH, DONNELL (SOUTHERN) - END - 1971 GREEN BAY PACKERS (NFC);
    1973-74 NEW ENGLAND PATRIOTS (AFC)
SMITH, EALTHON PERRY (COLORADO STATE) - BACK - 1973-74 GREEN BAY
    PACKERS (NFC)
SMITH, EARL (RIPON) - TACKLE - 1922-23 GREEN BAY PACKERS; 1923 ROCK
    ISLAND INDEPENDENTS
SMITH, ED (COLORADO COLLEGE) - END - 1973-74 DENVER BRONCOS (AFC)
SMITH, EDWARD (NEW YORK UNIV.) - BACK - 1936 BOSTON REDSKINS; 1937
    GREEN BAY PACKERS
SMITH, ERNEST (COMPTON JUNIOR) - BACK - 1955-56 SAN FRANCISCO 49ERS
SMITH, ERNEST (USC) - TACKLE - 1935-37, 39 GREEN BAY PACKERS
SMITH, FLETCHER (TENNESSEE STATE) - BACK - 1966-67 KANSAS CITY CHIEFS
    (AFL); 1968-69 CINCINNATI BENGALS (AFL); 1970-71 CINCINNATI
    BENGALS (AFC)
SMITH, FRANCIS (HOLY CROSS) - CENTER - 1926 BOSTON BULLDOGS (AFL)
SMITH, FRANK - GUARD - 1919 ROCK ISLAND INDEPENDENTS

SMITH, GAYLON (SOUTHWESTERN-MEMPHIS) - BACK - 1939-42 CLEVELAND RAMS;
    1946 CLEVELAND BROWNS (AAFC)
SMITH, GEORGE (CALIFORNIA) - CENTER - 1937, 41-43 WASHINGTON
    REDSKINS; 1944 BROOKLYN TIGERS; 1945 BOSTON YANKS; 1947 SAN
    FRANCISCO 49ERS (AAFC)
SMITH, GEORGE (VILLANOVA) - BACK - 1943 CHICAGO CARDINALS
SMITH, GERALD (ARIZONA STATE) - END - 1965-69 WASHINGTON REDSKINS;
    1970-74 WASHINGTON REDSKINS (NFC)
SMITH, GORDON (MISSOURI) - END - 1961-65 MINNESOTA VIKINGS
SMITH, H. EUGENE (GEORGIA) - GUARD - 1930 PORTSMOUTH SPARTANS; 1930
    FRANKFORD YELLOWJACKETS
SMITH, HAROLD (UCLA) - TACKLE - 1960 BOSTON PATRIOTS (AFL); 1960
    DENVER BRONCOS (AFL); 1961 OAKLAND RAIDERS (AFL)
SMITH, HARRY (USC) - TACKLE - 1940 DETROIT LIONS
SMITH, HENRY - CENTER - 1920-25 ROCHESTER JEFFERSONS
SMITH, HOUSTON ALLEN (MISSISSIPPI) - END - 1947-48 CHICAGO BEARS
SMITH, HUGH (KANSAS) - END - 1962 WASHINGTON REDSKINS; 1962 DENVER
    BRONCOS (AFL)
SMITH, INWOOD (OHIO STATE) - GUARD - 1937 CINCINNATI BENGALS (AFL);
    1940 CINCINNATI BENGALS (AFL)
SMITH, J. D. (NORTH CAROLINA A&T) - BACK - 1956 CHICAGO BEARS;
    1956-64 SAN FRANCISCO 49ERS; 1965-66 DALLAS COWBOYS
SMITH, JACK (TROY STATE) - BACK - 1971 PHILADELPHIA EAGLES (NFC)
SMITH, JACKIE (NORTHWEST STATE-LOUISIANA) - END, KICKER - 1963-69 ST.
    LOUIS CARDINALS; 1970-74 ST. LOUIS CARDINALS (NFC)
SMITH, JAMES (COLORADO) - TACKLE - 1947 LOS ANGELES DONS (AAFC)
SMITH, JAMES "JETSTREAM" (COMPTON JUNIOR) - BACK - 1960 OAKLAND
    RAIDERS (AFL); 1961 CHICAGO BEARS
SMITH, JAMES (IOWA) - BACK - 1948 BROOKLYN DODGERS (AAFC); 1948
    BUFFALO BILLS (AAFC); 1949 CHICAGO HORNETS (AAFC); 1949-53
    DETROIT LIONS
SMITH, JAMES (OREGON) - BACK - 1968 WASHINGTON REDSKINS
SMITH, JAMES EARL (UTAH STATE) - BACK - 1969 DENVER BRONCOS (AFL)
SMITH, JAMES RAY (BAYLOR) - GUARD - 1956-62 CLEVELAND BROWNS; 1963-64
    DALLAS COWBOYS
SMITH, JEFFREY (USC) - LB - 1966 NEW YORK GIANTS
SMITH, JERALD (WISCONSIN) - GUARD - 1952-53, 56 SAN FRANCISCO 49ERS;
    1956 GREEN BAY PACKERS
SMITH, JESS (RICE) - TACKLE - 1959-63 PHILADELPHIA EAGLES; 1964, 66
    DETROIT LIONS
SMITH, JOHN - KICKER - 1974 NEW ENGLAND PATRIOTS (AFC)
SMITH, JOHN (FLORIDA) - TACKLE - 1945 PHILADELPHIA EAGLES
SMITH, JOHN (STANFORD) - END - 1942 PHILADELPHIA EAGLES; 1943
    WASHINGTON REDSKINS
SMITH, JOSEPH (TEXAS TECH) - END - 1948 BALTIMORE COLTS (AAFC)
SMITH, LAWRENCE (FLORIDA) - BACK - 1969 LOS ANGELES RAMS; 1970-73 LOS
    ANGELES RAMS (NFC); 1974 WASHINGTON REDSKINS (NFC)
SMITH, LAWRENCE EDWARD "TODY" (USC) - END - 1971-72 DALLAS COWBOYS
    (NFC); 1973-74 HOUSTON OILERS (AFC)
SMITH, LEO (PROVIDENCE) - END - 1928 PROVIDENCE STEAMROLLERS
SMITH, LEONARD (WISCONSIN) - TACKLE - 1923-24 RACINE LEGION
SMITH, MILTON (UCLA) - END - 1945 PHILADELPHIA EAGLES
SMITH, NOLAND (TENNESSEE STATE) - BACK, END - 1967-69 KANSAS CITY
    CHIEFS (AFL); 1969 SAN FRANCISCO 49ERS
SMITH, OKLA (DRAKE) - END - 1919-22 ROCK ISLAND INDEPENDENTS
SMITH, OLIN (OHIO WESLEYAN) - TACKLE - 1924 CLEVELAND BULLDOGS
SMITH, OLLIE (TENNESSEE STATE) - END - 1973-74 BALTIMORE COLTS (AFC)
SMITH, ORLAND (BROWN) - TACKLE - 1927-29 PROVIDENCE STEAMROLLERS
SMITH, OSCAR (TEXAS MINES) - BACK - 1948-49 GREEN BAY PACKERS; 1949
    NEW YORK BULLDOGS
SMITH, PAUL (NEW MEXICO) - TACKLE, END - 1968-69 DENVER BRONCOS
    (AFL); 1970-74 DENVER BRONCOS (AFC)
SMITH, RALPH (MISSISSIPPI) - END - 1962-64 PHILADELPHIA EAGLES;
    1965-68 CLEVELAND BROWNS; 1969 ATLANTA FALCONS
SMITH, RAY (MISSOURI) - CENTER - 1930 PORTSMOUTH SPARTANS; 1930-31
    PROVIDENCE STEAMROLLERS; 1933 PHILADELPHIA EAGLES
SMITH, RAYMOND (LEBANON VALLEY) - QBACK - 1926 BROOKLYN HORSEMEN (AFL)
SMITH, RAYMOND (MIDWESTERN) - BACK - 1954-57 CHICAGO BEARS
SMITH, REX (LACROSSE STATE-WISCONSIN) - END - 1922 GREEN BAY PACKERS
SMITH, RICHARD (NORTHWESTERN) - BACK - 1967-68 WASHINGTON REDSKINS

SMITH, RICHARD (NOTRE DAME) - BACK - 1927, 29 GREEN BAY PACKERS; 1928
    NEW YORK YANKEES; 1930 NEWARK TORNADOS; 1931 NEW YORK GIANTS
SMITH, RICHARD (OHIO STATE) - CENTER - 1933 PHILADELPHIA EAGLES; 1933
    CHICAGO BEARS
SMITH, RILEY (ALABAMA) - QBACK - 1936 BOSTON REDSKINS; 1937-38
    WASHINGTON REDSKINS
SMITH, ROBERT (NEBRASKA) - BACK - 1955-56 CLEVELAND BROWNS; 1956
    PHILADELPHIA EAGLES
SMITH, ROBERT (SOUTHERN) - TACKLE - 1948 BROOKLYN DODGERS (AAFC)
SMITH, ROBERT (TEXAS A&M) - BACK - 1953-54 DETROIT LIONS
SMITH, ROBERT BERT (MIAMI-OHIO) - BACK - 1968 HOUSTON OILERS (AFL)
SMITH, ROBERT LEE (NORTH TEXAS STATE) - BACK - 1964-65 BUFFALO BILLS
    (AFL); 1966 PITTSBURGH STEELERS
SMITH, ROBERT LEE (UCLA) - BACK - 1962-65 LOS ANGELES RAMS; 1965-66
    DETROIT LIONS
SMITH, ROGER "ZEKE" (AUBURN) - GUARD - 1960 BALTIMORE COLTS; 1961 NEW
    YORK GIANTS
SMITH, RONALD (WISCONSIN) - BACK - 1965 CHICAGO BEARS; 1966-67
    ATLANTA FALCONS; 1968-69 LOS ANGELES RAMS; 1970-72 CHICAGO BEARS
    (NFC); 1973 SAN DIEGO CHARGERS (AFC); 1974 OAKLAND RAIDERS (AFC)
SMITH, RONALD CHRISTOPHER (RICHMOND) - QBACK - 1965 LOS ANGELES RAMS;
    1966 PITTSBURGH STEELERS
SMITH, ROYCE (GEORGIA) - GUARD - 1972-73 NEW ORLEANS SAINTS (NFC);
    1974 ATLANTA FALCONS (NFC)
SMITH, RUSSELL (ILLINOIS) - CENTER - 1921 CHICAGO STALEYS; 1922, 25
    CHICAGO BEARS; 1923 CHICAGO CARDINALS; 1923 CANTON BULLDOGS;
    1923 MILWAUKEE BADGERS; 1924 CLEVELAND BULLDOGS; 1925 DETROIT
    PANTHERS; 1926 HAMMOND PROS
SMITH, RUSSELL (MIAMI) - BACK - 1967-69 SAN DIEGO CHARGERS (AFL);
    1970 SAN DIEGO CHARGERS (AFC)
SMITH, SIDNEY (USC) - TACKLE - 1970-72 KANSAS CITY CHIEFS (AFC); 1974
    HOUSTON OILERS (AFC)
SMITH, STEPHEN (MICHIGAN) - TACKLE, END - 1966 PITTSBURGH STEELERS;
    1968-69 MINNESOTA VIKINGS; 1970 MINNESOTA VIKINGS (NFC); 1971-73
    PHILADELPHIA EAGLES (NFC)
SMITH, STUART (BUCKNELL) - QBACK - 1937-38 PITTSBURGH PIRATES
SMITH, THOMAS (SAN JOSE STATE) - END - 1969 CINCINNATI BENGALS (AFL)
SMITH, TRUETT (WYOMING & MISSISSIPPI STATE) - QBACK - 1950-51
    PITTSBURGH STEELERS
SMITH, VERDA (ABILENE CHRISTIAN) - BACK - 1949-53 LOS ANGELES RAMS
SMITH, WARREN (CARLTON) - CENTER - 1921 GREEN BAY PACKERS
SMITH, WILFRED (DEPAUW) - END - 1922 HAMMOND PROS; 1922 LOUISVILLE
    BRECKS; 1923-25 CHICAGO CARDINALS
SMITH, WILLIAM (WASHINGTON) - END - 1934-39 CHICAGO CARDINALS; 1935
    FIELD GOAL LEADER; (TIED WITH NICCOLAI)
SMITH, WILLIAM (NORTH CAROLINA) - TACKLE - 1948 CHICAGO ROCKETS
    (AAFC); 1948 LOS ANGELES DONS (AAFC)
SMITH, WILLIE (MICHIGAN) - TACKLE - 1960 DENVER BRONCOS (AFL); 1961
    OAKLAND RAIDERS (AFL)
SMITH, WILLIS (IDAHO) - BACK - 1934 NEW YORK GIANTS
SMITH - GUARD - 1923 HAMMOND PROS
SMOLINSKI, MARK (WYOMING) - BACK - 1961-62 BALTIMORE COLTS; 1963-68
    NEW YORK JETS (AFL)
SMUKLER, DAVID (TEMPLE) - BACK - 1936-39 PHILADELPHIA EAGLES; 1944
    BOSTON YANKS
SMYTH, WILLIAM (CINCINNATI) - TACKLE - 1947-50 LOS ANGELES RAMS
SMYTHE, LOUIS (TEXAS) - BACK - 1920-23 CANTON BULLDOGS; 1924-25
    ROCHESTER JEFFERSONS; 1925-26 FRANKFORD YELLOWJACKETS; 1926
    PROVIDENCE STEAMROLLERS; 1926 HARTFORD BLUES
SNEAD, NORMAN (WAKE FOREST) - QBACK - 1961-63 WASHINGTON REDSKINS;
    1964-69 PHILADELPHIA EAGLES; 1970 PHILADELPHIA EAGLES (NFC);
    1971 MINNESOTA VIKINGS (NFC); 1972-74 NEW YORK GIANTS (NFC);
    1974 SAN FRANCISCO 49ERS (NFC); 1972 PASSING LEADER (NFC)
SNEDDON, ROBERT (ST. MARY'S OF CAL.) - BACK - 1944 WASHINGTON
    REDSKINS; 1945 DETROIT LIONS; 1946 LOS ANGELES DONS (AAFC)
SNELL, DANIEL (HOWARD) - END - 1940 BUFFALO INDIANS (AFL)
SNELL, GEORGE (PENN STATE) - BACK - 1926 BROOKLYN LIONS; 1927 BUFFALO
    BISONS
SNELL, MATHEWS (OHIO STATE) - BACK - 1964-69 NEW YORK JETS (AFL);
    1970-72 NEW YORK JETS (AFC)
SNELLING, KENNETH (UCLA) - BACK - 1945 GREEN BAY PACKERS

SNIADECKI, JAMES (INDIANA) - LB - 1969 SAN FRANCISCO 49ERS; 1970-73
SAN FRANCISCO 49ERS (NFC)
SNIDER, MALCOLM (STANFORD) - GUARD, TACKLE - 1969 ATLANTA FALCONS;
1970-71 ATLANTA FALCONS (NFC); 1972-74 GREEN BAY PACKERS (NFC)
SNIDOW, RONALD (OREGON) - END - 1963-67 WASHINGTON REDSKINS; 1968-69
CLEVELAND BROWNS; 1970-72 CLEVELAND BROWNS (AFC)
SNOOTS, J. LEE - BACK - 1919-22 COLUMBUS PANHANDLES; 1923-25 COLUMBUS
TIGERS
SNORTON, MATTHEW (MICHIGAN STATE) - END - 1964 DENVER BRONCOS (AFL)
SNOW, JACK (NOTRE DAME) - END - 1965-69 LOS ANGELES RAMS; 1970-74 LOS
ANGELES RAMS (NFC)
SNOWDEN, CALVIN (INDIANA) - END - 1969 ST. LOUIS CARDINALS; 1970 ST.
LOUIS CARDINALS (NFC); 1971 BUFFALO BILLS (AFC); 1972-73 SAN
DIEGO CHARGERS (AFC)
SNOWDEN, JAMES (NOTRE DAME) - TACKLE - 1965-69 WASHINGTON REDSKINS;
1970-71 WASHINGTON REDSKINS (NFC)
SNYDER, ALVIN (HOLY CROSS) - END - 1964 BOSTON PATRIOTS (AFL); 1966
BALTIMORE COLTS
SNYDER, GERALD (MARYLAND) - BACK - 1929 NEW YORK GIANTS; 1930 STATEN
ISLAND STAPELTONS
SNYDER, JAMES TODD (OHIO) - END - 1970-72 ATLANTA FALCONS (NFC)
SNYDER, KENNETH (GEORGIA TECH) - TACKLE - 1952-55, 58 PHILADELPHIA
EAGLES
SNYDER, ROBERT (OHIO) - QBACK - 1936 PITTSBURGH AMERICANS (AFL);
1937-38 CLEVELAND RAMS; 1939-41, 43 CHICAGO BEARS
SNYDER, WILLIAM (OHIO UNIV.) - GUARD - 1934-35 PITTSBURGH PIRATES
SOAR, ALBERT "HANK" (PROVIDENCE) - BACK - 1936 BOSTON SHAMROCKS
(AFL); 1937-44, 46 NEW YORK GIANTS
SOBOCINSKI, PHILIP (WISCONSIN) - CENTER - 1968 ATLANTA FALCONS
SOBOLESKI, JOSEPH (MICHIGAN) - TACKLE - 1949 CHICAGO HORNETS (AAFC);
1949 WASHINGTON REDSKINS; 1950 DETROIT LIONS; 1951 NEW YORK
YANKS; 1952 DALLAS TEXANS
SODASKI, JOHN (VILLANOVA) - LB, BACK - 1970 PITTSBURGH STEELERS
(AFC); 1972-73 PHILADELPHIA EAGLES (NFC)
SOFISH, ALEXANDER (GROVE CITY) - GUARD - 1931 PROVIDENCE STEAMROLLERS
SOHN, BENJAMIN (USC) - GUARD - 1941 NEW YORK GIANTS
SOHN, BENJAMIN (WASHINGTON) - BACK - 1934 CINCINNATI REDS
SOLEAU, ROBERT (WILLIAM&MARY) - LB - 1964 PITTSBURGH STEELERS
SOLON, LORIN - BACK - 1919 CLEVELAND INDIANS; 1920 CLEVELAND PANTHERS
SOLTAU, GORDON (MINNESOTA) - END - 1950-58 SAN FRANCISCO 49ERS;
1952-53 SCORING LEADER
SOLTIS, ROBERT (MINNESOTA) - BACK - 1960-61 BOSTON PATRIOTS (AFL)
SOMERS, GEORGE (LASALLE-PENNSYLVANIA) - TACKLE - 1939-40 PHILADELPHIA
EAGLES; 1941-42 PITTSBURGH STEELERS
SOMMER, MICHAEL (GEORGE WASHINGTON) - BACK - 1958-59, 61 WASHINGTON
REDSKINS; 1959-61 BALTIMORE COLTS; 1963 OAKLAND RAIDERS (AFL)
SONGIN, EDWARD "BUTCH" (BOSTON COLLEGE) - QBACK - 1960-61 BOSTON
PATRIOTS (AFL); 1962 NEW YORK TITANS (AFL)
SONNENBERG, GUSTAVE (DARTMOUTH & DETROIT) - GUARD - 1923 COLUMBUS
TIGERS; 1925-26 DETROIT PANTHERS; 1927-28, 30 PROVIDENCE
STEAMROLLERS
SORCE, ROSS (GEORGETOWN) - TACKLE - 1945 PITTSBURGH STEELERS
SORENSON, GLEN (UTAH STATE) - GUARD - 1943-45 GREEN BAY PACKERS
SOREY, JAMES (TEXAS SOUTHERN) - GUARD - 1960-62 BUFFALO BILLS (AFL)
SORRELL, HENRY (CHATTANOOGA) - LB - 1967 DENVER BRONCOS (AFL)
SORTET, WILBUR (WEST VIRGINIA) - END - 1933-38 PITTSBURGH PIRATES;
1939-40 PITTSBURGH STEELERS
SORTUN, HENRIK (WASHINGTON) - GUARD - 1964-69 ST. LOUIS CARDINALS
SOSSAMON, LOUIS (SOUTH CAROLINA) - CENTER - 1946-48 NEW YORK YANKEES
(AAFC)
SOUCHAK, FRANK (PITTSBURGH) - END - 1939 PITTSBURGH STEELERS
SOUDERS, CECIL (OHIO STATE) - END - 1947-49 DETROIT LIONS
SOUTH, RONALD (ARKANSAS) - QBACK - 1968 NEW ORLEANS SAINTS
SOVIO, HENRY (HAWAII) - END - 1973 ATLANTA FALCONS (NFC)
SOWELLS, RICHARD (ALCORN A&M) - BACK - 1971-74 NEW YORK JETS (AFC)
SPADACCINI, VICTOR (MINNESOTA) - QBACK - 1938-40 CLEVELAND RAMS; 1941
COLUMBUS BULLIES (AFL)
SPAGNA, JOSEPH (LEHIGH) - GUARD - 1919 MASSILLON TIGERS; 1920
CLEVELAND PANTHERS; 1920-21 BUFFALO ALL-AMERICANS; 1924-25
FRANKFORD YELLOWJACKETS; 1926 PHILADELPHIA QUAKERS (AFL)
SPAIN, RICHARD - GUARD - 1921-22 EVANSVILLE CRIMSON GIANTS

SPANGLER, EUGENE (TULSA) - BACK - 1946 DETROIT LIONS
SPANIEL, FRANK (NOTRE DAME) - BACK - 1950 BALTIMORE COLTS; 1950
     WASHINGTON REDSKINS
SPARKMAN, ALAN (TEXAS A&M) - TACKLE - 1948-49 LOS ANGELES RAMS
SPARKS, DAVID (SOUTH CAROLINA) - GUARD - 1951 SAN FRANCISCO 49ERS;
     1954 WASHINGTON REDSKINS
SPARLIS, ALBERT (UCLA) - GUARD - 1946 GREEN BAY PACKERS
SPAVITAL, JAMES (OKLAHOMA A&M) - BACK - 1949 LOS ANGELES DONS (AAFC);
     1950 BALTIMORE COLTS
SPEAR, GLEN (DRAKE) - BACK - 1926 KANSAS CITY COWBOYS
SPEARS, CLARENCE (DARTMOUTH) - TACKLE - 1919 CANTON BULLDOGS
SPECK, NORMAN "DUTCH" - GUARD - 1919-23, 25-26 CANTON BULLDOGS; 1920
     HAMMOND PROS; 1921 EVANSVILLE CRIMSON GIANTS; 1924 AKRON PROS
SPEEDIE, MAC (UTAH) - END - 1946-49 CLEVELAND BROWNS (AAFC); 1950-52
     CLEVELAND BROWNS; 1952 PASS RECEIVING LEADER
SPEEGLE, CLIFTON (OKLAHOMA) - CENTER - 1945 CHICAGO CARDINALS
SPEELMAN, HARRY (MICHIGAN STATE) - GUARD - 1940 DETROIT LIONS
SPEIGHTS, RICHARD (WYOMING) - BACK - 1968 SAN DIEGO CHARGERS (AFL)
SPELLACY - END - 1922 BUFFALO ALL-AMERICANS
SPELLMAN, JOHN (BROWN) - END - 1925-31 PROVIDENCE STEAMROLLERS; 1932
     BOSTON BRAVES
SPENCE, JULIAN (SAM HOUSTON) - BACK - 1956 CHICAGO CARDINALS; 1957
     SAN FRANCISCO 49ERS; 1960-61 HOUSTON OILERS (AFL)
SPENCER, JAMES (DAYTON) - GUARD - 1928-29 DAYTON TRIANGLES
SPENCER, JOSEPH (OKLAHOMA A&M) - TACKLE - 1948 BROOKLYN DODGERS
     (AAFC); 1949 CLEVELAND BROWNS (AAFC); 1950-51 GREEN BAY PACKERS
SPENCER, MAURICE (NORTH CAROLINA CENTRAL) - BACK - 1974 ST. LOUIS
     CARDINALS (NFC); 1974 LOS ANGELES RAMS (NFC); 1974 NEW ORLEANS
     SAINTS (NFC)
SPENCER, OLIVER (KANSAS) - TACKLE - 1953, 56, 59-61 DETROIT LIONS;
     1957-58 GREEN BAY PACKERS
SPETH, GEORGE (MURRAY STATE) - TACKLE - 1942 DETROIT LIONS
SPEYRER, CHARLES "COTTON" (TEXAS) - END - 1972-74 BALTIMORE COLTS
     (AFC)
SPICER, ROBERT (INDIANA) - LB - 1973 NEW YORK JETS (AFC)
SPIEGEL, CLARENCE (WISCONSIN) - BACK - 1921-22 EVANSVILLE CRIMSON
     GIANTS
SPIERS, ROBERT (OHIO STATE) - TACKLE - 1922 AKRON PROS; 1925
     CLEVELAND BULLDOGS; 1926 CLEVELAND PANTHERS (AFL)
SPIKES, JACK (TCU) - BACK - 1960-62 DALLAS COWBOYS; 1963-64 KANSAS
     CITY CHIEFS (AFL); 1964 SAN DIEGO CHARGERS (AFL); 1965 HOUSTON
     OILERS (AFL); 1966-67 BUFFALO BILLS (AFL)
SPILIS, JOHN (NORTHERN ILLINOIS) - END - 1969 GREEN BAY PACKERS;
     1970-71 GREEN BAY PACKERS (NFC)
SPILLER, PHILIP (CAL.STATE-LOS ANGELES) - BACK - 1967 ST. LOUIS
     CARDINALS; 1968 ATLANTA FALCONS; 1968 CINCINNATI BENGALS (AFL)
SPILLERS, RAYMOND (ARKANSAS) - TACKLE - 1937 PHILADELPHIA EAGLES
SPINKS, JACK (ALCORN A&M) - GUARD - 1952 PITTSBURGH STEELERS; 1953
     CHICAGO CARDINALS; 1955-56 GREEN BAY PACKERS; 1956-57 NEW YORK
     GIANTS
SPINNEY, ARTHUR (BOSTON COLLEGE) - GUARD - 1950, 53-60 BALTIMORE COLTS
SPINOSA, ALBERT (ST. VINCENT-PENNSYLVANIA) - CENTER - 1937 PITTSBURGH
     AMERICANS (AFL)
SPIRIDA, JOHN (ST. ANSELM'S) - END - 1939 WASHINGTON REDSKINS
SPLINTER, FRANCIS (PLATTEVILLE) - BACK - 1941 MILWAUKEE CHIEFS (AFL)
SPONAUGLE, ROBERT (PENNSYLVANIA) - END - 1949 NEW YORK BULLDOGS
SPRINGER, HAROLD (CENTRAL OKLAHOMA STATE) - END - 1945 NEW YORK GIANTS
SPRINGSTEEN, WILLIAM (LEHIGH) - CENTER - 1925-26 FRANKFORD
     YELLOWJACKETS; 1927-28 CHICAGO CARDINALS
SPRINKLE, EDWARD (HARDIN-SIMMONS) - END - 1944-55 CHICAGO BEARS
SPRINKLE, HUBERT (CARNEGIE TECH) - TACKLE - 1923-24 AKRON PROS; 1925
     CLEVELAND BULLDOGS
SPRUILL, JAMES (RICE) - TACKLE - 1948-49 BALTIMORE COLTS (AAFC)
SPURRIER, STEVEN (FLORIDA) - QBACK, KICKER - 1967-69 SAN FRANCISCO
     49ERS; 1970-74 SAN FRANCISCO 49ERS (NFC)
SQUYRES, SEAMAN (RICE) - BACK - 1933 CINCINNATI REDS
STABLER, KEN (ALABAMA) - QBACK - 1970-74 OAKLAND RAIDERS (AFC); 1973
     PASSING LEADER (AFC)
STACCO, EDWARD (COLGATE) - TACKLE - 1947 DETROIT LIONS; 1948
     WASHINGTON REDSKINS
STACY, JAMES (OKLAHOMA) - TACKLE - 1935-37 DETROIT LIONS

STACKPOOL, JOHN (WASHINGTON) - BACK - 1942 PHILADELPHIA EAGLES
STACY, WILLIAM (MISSISSIPPI STATE) - BACK - 1959 CHICAGO CARDINALS;
     1960-63 ST. LOUIS CARDINALS
STAFFORD, HARRISON (TEXAS) - BACK - 1934 NEW YORK GIANTS
STAFFORD, RICHARD (TEXAS TECH) - END - 1962-63 PHILADELPHIA EAGLES
STAGGERS, JONATHAN (MISSOURI) - END - 1970-71 PITTSBURGH STEELERS
     (AFC); 1972-74 GREEN BAY PACKERS (NFC)
STAGGS, JEFFREY (SAN DIEGO STATE) - LB - 1967-69 SAN DIEGO CHARGERS
     (AFL); 1970-71 SAN DIEGO CHARGERS (AFC); 1972-73 ST. LOUIS
     CARDINALS (NFC)
STAHL, EDWARD (PITTSBURGH) - TACKLE - 1919 CLEVELAND INDIANS; 1920
     CLEVELAND PANTHERS; 1921 DAYTON TRIANGLES
STAHLMAN, RICHARD (DEPAUL & NORTHWESTERN) - TACKLE - 1924 HAMMOND
     PROS; 1924 KENOSHA MAROONS; 1924-25 AKRON PROS; 1926 ROCK ISLAND
     INDEPENDENTS (AFL); 1926 CHICAGO BULLS (AFL); 1927-28, 30 NEW
     YORK GIANTS; 1931-32 GREEN BAY PACKERS; 1933 CHICAGO BEARS
STALCUP, GERALD (WISCONSIN) - LB - 1960 LOS ANGELES RAMS; 1961-62
     DENVER BRONCOS (AFL)
STALEY, WILLIAM (UTAH STATE) - TACKLE - 1968-69 CINCINNATI BENGALS
     (AFL); 1970 CHICAGO BEARS (NFC); 1971-72 CHICAGO BEARS (NFC)
STALLINGS, ALVA DONALD (NORTH CAROLINA) - TACKLE - 1960 WASHINGTON
     REDSKINS
STALLINGS, LAWRENCE (GEORGIA TECH) - LB - 1963-69 ST. LOUIS
     CARDINALS; 1970-74 ST. LOUIS CARDINALS (NFC)
STALLWORTH, JOHNNY (ALABAMA A&M) - END - 1974 PITTSBURGH STEELERS
     (AFC)
STANBACK, HASKEL (TENNESSEE) - BACK - 1974 ATLANTA FALCONS (NFC)
STANCIEL, JEFFREY (MISSISSIPPI VALLEY) - BACK - 1969 ATLANTA FALCONS
STANDLEE, NORMAN (STANFORD) - BACK - 1941 CHICAGO BEARS; 1946-49 SAN
     FRANCISCO 49ERS (AAFC); 1950-52 SAN FRANCISCO 49ERS
STANFEL, RICHARD (SAN FRANCISCO) - GUARD - 1952-55 DETROIT LIONS;
     1956-58 WASHINGTON REDSKINS
STANFILL, WILLIAM (GEORGIA) - END - 1969 MIAMI DOLPHINS (AFL);
     1970-74 MIAMI DOLPHINS (AFC)
STANLEY, C. E. (TULSA) - TACKLE - 1946 BUFFALO BISONS (AAFC)
STANSAUK, DONALD (DENVER) - TACKLE - 1950-51 GREEN BAY PACKERS
STANTON, HENRY (ARIZONA) - END - 1946-47 NEW YORK YANKEES (AAFC)
STANTON, JOHN (NORTH CAROLINA STATE) - BACK - 1961 PITTSBURGH STEELERS
STANTON, WILLIAM (NORTH CAROLINA STATE) - END - 1949 BUFFALO BILLS
     (AAFC)
STARK, EDWARD (OKLAHOMA BAPTIST) - BACK - 1937 LOS ANGELES BULLDOGS
     (AFL)
STARK, HOWARD (WISCONSIN) - TACKLE - 1923 RACINE LEGION
STARKE, GEORGE (COLUMBIA) - TACKLE - 1973-74 WASHINGTON REDSKINS (NFC)
STARKS, MARSHALL (ILLINOIS) - BACK - 1963-64 NEW YORK JETS (AFL)
STAPLING, BRUCE (FLORIDA) - BACK - 1963 DENVER BRONCOS (AFL)
STAROBA, PAUL (MICHIGAN) - END, KICKER - 1972 CLEVELAND BROWNS (AFC);
     1973 GREEN BAY PACKERS (NFC)
STARR, BRYAN "BART" (ALABAMA) - QBACK - 1956-69 GREEN BAY PACKERS;
     1970-71 GREEN BAY PACKERS (NFC); 1962, 64, 66 PASSING LEADER
STARR, DONALD (WESTERN RESERVE) - QBACK - 1940 NEW YORK AMERICANS
     (AFL)
STARRET, BENJAMIN (ST. MARY'S OF CAL.) - BACK - 1941 PITTSBURGH
     STEELERS; 1942-45 GREEN BAY PACKERS
STASICA, LEO (COLORADO) - BACK - 1941 BROOKLYN DODGERS; 1941
     PHILADELPHIA EAGLES; 1943 WASHINGTON REDSKINS; 1944 BOSTON YANKS
STASICA, STANLEY (SOUTH CAROLINA) - BACK - 1946 MIAMI SEAHAWKS (AAFC)
STATEN, RANDOLPH (MINNESOTA) - END - 1967 NEW YORK GIANTS
STATON, JAMES (WAKE FOREST) - TACKLE - 1951 WASHINGTON REDSKINS
STATUTO, ARTHUR (NOTRE DAME) - CENTER - 1948-49 BUFFALO BILLS (AAFC);
     1950 LOS ANGELES RAMS
STAUBACH, ROGER (ANNAPOLIS) - QBACK - 1969 DALLAS COWBOYS; 1970-74
     DALLAS COWBOYS (NFC); 1971, 73 PASSING LEADER (NFC)
STAUTBERG, GERALD (CINCINNATI) - GUARD - 1951 CHICAGO BEARS
STAUTNER, ERNEST (BOSTON COLLEGE) - TACKLE - 1950-63 PITTSBURGH
     STEELERS; 1969 HALL OF FAME
STAUTZENBERGER, ODELL (TEXAS A&M) - GUARD - 1949 BUFFALO BILLS (AAFC)
STEBER, JOHN (GEORGIA TECH) - GUARD - 1946-50 WASHINGTON REDSKINS
STEELE, CLIFFORD (SYRACUSE) - BACK - 1921-22 ROCHESTER JEFFERSONS;
     1922 AKRON PROS

STEELE, ERNEST (WASHINGTON) - BACK - 1942, 44-48 PHILADELPHIA EAGLES;
     1943 PHIL-PITT
STEELE, LARRY (SANTA ROSA) - KICKER - 1974 DENVER BRONCOS (AFC)
STEELE, PERCY (HARVARD) - END - 1921 CANTON BULLDOGS
STEEN, FRANK (RICE) - END - 1939 GREEN BAY PACKERS
STEEN, JAMES (SYRACUSE) - TACKLE - 1935-36 DETROIT LIONS
STEERE, RICHARD (DRAKE) - TACKLE - 1951 PHILADELPHIA EAGLES
STEFFEN, JAMES (UCLA) - BACK - 1959-61 DETROIT LIONS; 1961-65
     WASHINGTON REDSKINS
STEFIK, ROBERT (NIAGARA) - END - 1948 BUFFALO BILLS (AAFC)
STEGENT, LARRY (TEXAS A&M) - BACK - 1971 ST. LOUIS CARDINALS (NFC)
STEGER, PETER - BACK - 1921 CHICAGO CARDINALS
STEHOUWER, RONALD (COLORADO STATE) - GUARD - 1960-64 PITTSBURGH
     STEELERS
STEIN, HERBERT (PITTSBURGH) - CENTER - 1921 BUFFALO ALL-AMERICANS;
     1922 TOLEDO MAROONS; 1924 FRANKFORD YELLOWJACKETS; 1925-26, 28
     POTTSVILLE MAROONS
STEIN, ROBERT (MINNESOTA) - LB, END - 1969 KANSAS CITY CHIEFS (AFL);
     1970-72 KANSAS CITY CHIEFS (AFC); 1973-74 LOS ANGELES RAMS (NFC)
STEIN, RUSSELL (WASHINGTON&JEFFERSON) - TACKLE - 1922 TOLEDO MAROONS;
     1924 FRANKFORD YELLOWJACKETS; 1925 POTTSVILLE MAROONS; 1926
     CANTON BULLDOGS
STEIN, SAMUEL - END - 1926 NEWARK BEARS (AFL); 1929-30 STATEN ISLAND
     STAPELTONS; 1931 NEW YORK GIANTS; 1932 BROOKLYN DODGERS
STEIN, WILLIAM (FORDHAM) - GUARD - 1923-25 DULUTH KELLEYS; 1926-27
     DULUTH ESKIMOS; 1927-28 CHICAGO CARDINALS
STEINBACH, LAURENCE (ST. THOMAS) - TACKLE - 1930-31 CHICAGO BEARS;
     1931-33 CHICAGO CARDINALS; 1933 PHILADELPHIA EAGLES
STEINBRUNNER, DONALD (WASHINGTON STATE) - END - 1953 CLEVELAND BROWNS
STEINER, ROY (ALABAMA) - END - 1950-51 GREEN BAY PACKERS
STEINKE, GILBERT (TEXAS A&M) - BACK - 1945-48 PHILADELPHIA EAGLES
STEINKEMPER, WILLIAM (NOTRE DAME) - TACKLE - 1937 CINCINNATI BENGALS
     (AFL); 1943 CHICAGO BEARS
STEINMETZ, KENNETH - BACK - 1944-45 BOSTON YANKS
STENERUD, JAN (MONTANA STATE) - KICKER - 1967-69 KANSAS CITY CHIEFS
     (AFL); 1970-74 KANSAS CITY CHIEFS (AFC); 1967 FIELD GOAL LEADER
     (AFL); 1970 SCORING LEADER (AFC); 1970 FIELD GOAL LEADER (AFC)
STENGER, BRIAN (NOTRE DAME) - LB - 1969 PITTSBURGH STEELERS; 1970-72
     PITTSBURGH STEELERS (AFC); 1973 NEW ENGLAND PATRIOTS (AFC)
STENN, PAUL (VILLANOVA) - TACKLE - 1942 NEW YORK GIANTS; 1946
     WASHINGTON REDSKINS; 1947 PITTSBURGH STEELERS; 1948-51 CHICAGO
     BEARS
STENNETT, FRED (ST. MARY'S OF CAL.) - BACK - 1931 PORTSMOUTH
     SPARTANS; 1932 CHICAGO CARDINALS
STEPHENS, HAROLD (HARDIN-SIMMONS) - QBACK - 1962 NEW YORK TITANS (AFL)
STEPHENS, JOHN (MARSHALL) - END - 1938 CLEVELAND RAMS
STEPHENS, LAWRENCE (TEXAS) - END - 1960-61 CLEVELAND BROWNS; 1962 LOS
     ANGELES RAMS; 1963-67 DALLAS COWBOYS
STEPHENS, LESLIE (IDAHO) - CENTER - 1926 LOS ANGELES WILDCATS (AFL);
     1927 NEW YORK YANKEES
STEPHENS, LOUIS (SAN FRANCISCO) - GUARD - 1955-60 WASHINGTON REDSKINS
STEPHENS, ROBERT (MICHIGAN TECH) - BACK - 1941 MILWAUKEE CHIEFS (AFL)
STEPHENS, THOMAS (SYRACUSE) - END - 1960-64 BOSTON PATRIOTS (AFL)
STEPHENS, WILLIAM (BROWN) - CENTER - 1926 BROOKLYN LIONS; 1926 BOSTON
     BULLDOGS (AFL)
STEPHENSON, GEORGE KAY (FLORIDA) - QBACK - 1967 SAN DIEGO CHARGERS
     (AFL); 1968 BUFFALO BILLS (AFL)
STEPHENSON, J. DAVIDSON (WEST VIRGINIA) - GUARD - 1950 LOS ANGELES
     RAMS; 1951-55 GREEN BAY PACKERS
STEPONOVICH, ANTHONY (USC) - GUARD - 1930 MINNEAPOLIS REDJACKETS;
     1930 FRANKFORD YELLOWJACKETS
STEPONOVICH, MICHAEL (ST. MARY'S OF CAL.) - GUARD - 1933 BOSTON
     REDSKINS
STERLING, ERNEST (GRAMBLING) - END - 1968 DALLAS COWBOYS
STERNAMAN, EDWARD (ILLINOIS) - BACK - 1920 DECATUR STALEYS; 1921
     CHICAGO STALEYS; 1922-27 CHICAGO BEARS
STERNAMAN, JOSEPH (ILLINOIS) - QBACK - 1922-25, 27-30 CHICAGO BEARS;
     1923 DULUTH KELLEYS; 1926 CHICAGO BULLS (AFL)
STERR, GILBERT (CARROLL) - QBACK - 1926 RACINE LEGION
STETZ, WILLIAM (BOSTON COLLEGE) - GUARD - 1967 PHILADELPHIA EAGLES

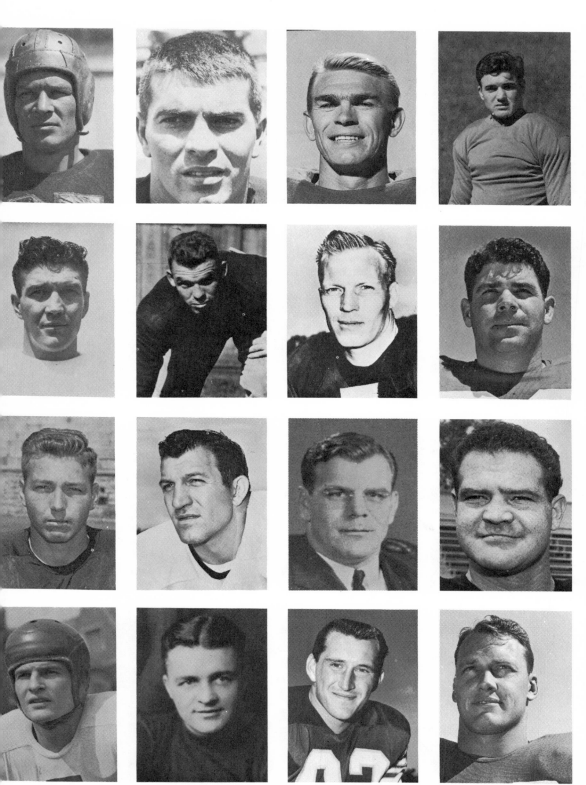

Top row (from left to right): Riley Smith, Norman Snead, Gordon Soltau and Vic Spadaccini. *Second row:* Mac Speedie, John Spellman, Ed Sprinkle and Norm Standlee. *Third row:* "Bart" Starr, Ernie Stautner, Paul Stenn and "Red" Stephens. *Bottom row:* Walter Stickles, Houston Stockton, Steve Stonebreaker and Jack Stroud.

Top row (from left to right): Lee Sugar, "Pat" Summerall, Harland Svare and Bill Svoboda. *Second row*: Bill Swiacki, Dick Szymanski, George Tarasovic and Fran Tarkenton. *Third row*: Hugh Taylor, Jim Taylor, Joe Tereshinski and Bob Thomason. *Bottom row*: Lurtis Thompson, Fred Thurston, "Mick" Tingelhoff and Bob Titchenal.

STEUBER, ROBERT (MISSOURI) - BACK - 1943 CHICAGO BEARS; 1946
    CLEVELAND BROWNS (AAFC); 1947 LOS ANGELES DONS (AAFC); 1948
    BUFFALO BILLS (AAFC)
STEVENS, DONALD (ILLINOIS) - BACK - 1952, 54 PHILADELPHIA EAGLES
STEVENS, HOWARD (LOUISVILLE) - BACK - 1973-74 NEW ORLEANS SAINTS (NFC)
STEVENS, PETER (TEMPLE) - CENTER - 1936 PHILADELPHIA EAGLES
STEVENS, RICHARD (BAYLOR) - TACKLE, GUARD - 1970-74 PHILADELPHIA
    EAGLES (NFC)
STEVENS, WILLIAM (TEXAS-EL PASO) - QBACK - 1968-69 GREEN BAY PACKERS
STEVENSON, ARTHUR (FORDHAM) - GUARD - 1926 NEW YORK GIANTS; 1926
    BROOKLYN LIONS; 1928 NEW YORK YANKEES
STEVENSON, MARTIN (NOTRE DAME) - GUARD - 1922 COLUMBUS PANHANDLES
STEVENSON, RALPH (OKLAHOMA) - GUARD - 1940 CLEVELAND RAMS
STEVENSON, RICKY (ARIZONA) - BACK - 1970 CLEVELAND BROWNS (AFC)
STEVERSON, NORRIS (ARIZONA STATE) - BACK - 1934 CINCINNATI REDS
STEWARD, DEAN (URSINUS) - BACK - 1943 PHIL-PITT
STEWART, CHARLES (COLGATE) - GUARD - 1923 AKRON PROS
STEWART, RALPH (MISSOURI & NOTRE DAME) - CENTER - 1947-48 NEW YORK
    YANKEES (AAFC); 1948 BALTIMORE COLTS (AAFC)
STEWART, VAUGHN (ALABAMA) - CENTER - 1943 CHICAGO CARDINALS; 1943
    BROOKLYN DODGERS; 1944 BROOKLYN TIGERS
STEWART, WAYNE (CALIFORNIA) - END - 1969 NEW YORK JETS (AFL); 1970-72
    NEW YORK JETS (AFC); 1974 SAN DIEGO CHARGERS (AFC)
STICKEL, WALTER (PENNSYLVANIA) - TACKLE - 1946-49 CHICAGO BEARS;
    1950-51 PHILADELPHIA EAGLES
STICKLES, MONTFORD (NOTRE DAME) - END - 1960-67 SAN FRANCISCO 49ERS;
    1968 NEW ORLEANS SAINTS
STIDHAM, ERNEST (HOWARD-LOUISIANA) - CENTER - 1937 ROCHESTER TIGERS
    (AFL)
STIENKE, JAMES (SOUTHWEST TEXAS STATE) - BACK - 1973 CLEVELAND BROWNS
    (AFC); 1974 NEW YORK GIANTS (NFC)
STIFLER, JAMES (BROWN) - END - 1926-27 PROVIDENCE STEAMROLLERS
STIGER, JAMES (WASHINGTON) - BACK - 1963-65 DALLAS COWBOYS; 1965-67
    LOS ANGELES RAMS
STILL, JAMES (GEORGIA TECH) - QBACK - 1948-49 BUFFALO BILLS (AAFC)
STINCHCOMB, GAYLORD (OHIO STATE) - QBACK - 1921 CHICAGO STALEYS; 1922
    CHICAGO BEARS; 1923 COLUMBUS TIGERS; 1923 CLEVELAND INDIANS;
    1926 LOUISVILLE COLONELS
STINIC, THOMAS (MICHIGAN) - LB - 1969 DALLAS COWBOYS; 1970-71 DALLAS
    COWBOYS (NFC); 1972 NEW ORLEANS SAINTS (NFC)
STINGLEY, DARRYL (PURDUE) - END - 1973-74 NEW ENGLAND PATRIOTS (AFC)
STINNETTE, JAMES (OREGON STATE) - BACK - 1961-62 DENVER BRONCOS (AFL)
STITH, CAREL (NEBRASKA) - TACKLE - 1967-69 HOUSTON OILERS (AFL)
STITH, HOWARD - GUARD - 1921 LOUISVILLE BRECKS
STITS, WILLIAM (UCLA) - BACK - 1954-56 DETROIT LIONS; 1957-58 SAN
    FRANCISCO 49ERS; 1959 WASHINGTON REDSKINS; 1959-61 NEW YORK
    GIANTS
STOBBS, WILLIAM (WASHINGTON&JEFFERSON) - BACK - 1921 DETROIT PANTHERS
STOCK, HERBERT (KENYON) - BACK - 1924-25 COLUMBUS TIGERS
STOCK, JOHN (PITTSBURGH) - END - 1956 PITTSBURGH STEELERS
STOCKTON, HERSCHEL (MCMURRY) - GUARD - 1937-38 PHILADELPHIA EAGLES
STOCKTON, HOUSTON (GONZAGA) - BACK - 1925-26, 28 FRANKFORD
    YELLOWJACKETS; 1929 PROVIDENCE STEAMROLLERS; 1929 BOSTON BRAVES
STOECKLIN, EARL - TACKLE - 1919-20 DAYTON TRIANGLES
STOEPEL, TERRY (TULSA) - END - 1967 CHICAGO BEARS; 1970 HOUSTON
    OILERS (AFC)
STOFA, JOHN (BUFFALO) - QBACK - 1966-67, 69 MIAMI DOLPHINS (AFL);
    1968-69 CINCINNATI BENGALS (AFL); 1970 MIAMI DOLPHINS (AFC)
STOFER, KENNETH (CORNELL) - QBACK - 1946 BUFFALO BISONS (AAFC)
STOFKO, EDWARD (ST. FRANCIS) - BACK - 1945 PITTSBURGH STEELERS
STOJACK, FRANK (WASHINGTON STATE) - GUARD - 1935-36 BROOKLYN DODGERS
STOKES, LEE (CENTENARY) - CENTER - 1937-39 DETROIT LIONS; 1943
    CHICAGO CARDINALS
STOKES, SIMS (NORTH ARIZONA STATE) - END - 1967 DALLAS COWBOYS
STOKES, TIM (OREGON) - TACKLE - 1974 LOS ANGELES RAMS (NFC)
STOLFA, ANTON (LUTHER) - BACK - 1939 CHICAGO BEARS
STOLHANDSKE, THOMAS (TEXAS) - END - 1955 SAN FRANCISCO 49ERS
STONE, AVATUS (SYRACUSE) - BACK - 1958 BALTIMORE COLTS
STONE, EDWARD DONALD (ARKANSAS) - BACK - 1961-64 DENVER BRONCOS
    (AFL); 1965 BUFFALO BILLS (AFL); 1966 HOUSTON OILERS (AFL)

STONE, JACK (OREGON) - TACKLE - 1960 DALLAS TEXANS (AFL); 1961-62
    OAKLAND RAIDERS (AFL)
STONE, KENNETH (VANDERBILT) - BACK - 1973 BUFFALO BILLS (AFC);
    1973-74 WASHINGTON REDSKINS (NFC)
STONE, WILLIAM (BRADLEY) - BACK - 1949 BALTIMORE COLTS (AAFC); 1950
    BALTIMORE COLTS; 1951-54 CHICAGO BEARS
STONE - BACK - 1919 WHEELING
STONEBRAKER, JOHN (USC) - END - 1942 GREEN BAY PACKERS
STONEBREAKER, THORNTON "STEVE" (DETROIT) - LB - 1962-63 MINNESOTA
    VIKINGS; 1964-66 BALTIMORE COLTS; 1967-68 NEW ORLEANS SAINTS
STONESIFER, DONALD (NORTHWESTERN) - END - 1951-56 CHICAGO CARDINALS
STORER, JOHN (LEHIGH) - BACK - 1924 FRANKFORD YELLOWJACKETS
STORM, EDWARD (SANTA CLARA) - BACK - 1934-35 PHILADELPHIA EAGLES
STOTSBERRY, HAROLD (XAVIER) - TACKLE - 1930 BROOKLYN DODGERS
STOTTER, RICHARD (HOUSTON) - LB - 1968 HOUSTON OILERS (AFL)
STOUGH, GLEN (DUKE) - TACKLE - 1945 PITTSBURGH STEELERS
STOUT, PETER (TCU) - BACK - 1949-50 WASHINGTON REDSKINS
STOVALL, JERRY (LSU) - BACK - 1963-69 ST. LOUIS CARDINALS; 1970-71
    ST. LOUIS CARDINALS (NFC)
STOVALL, RICHARD (ABILENE CHRISTIAN) - CENTER - 1947-48 DETROIT
    LIONS; 1949 WASHINGTON REDSKINS
STOVER, STEWART (NORTHEAST LOUISIANA STATE) - LB - 1960-62 DALLAS
    COWBOYS; 1963-66 KANSAS CITY CHIEFS (AFL)
STOWE, OTTO (IOWA STATE) - END - 1971-72 MIAMI DOLPHINS (AFC); 1973
    DALLAS COWBOYS (NFC); 1974 DENVER BRONCOS (AFC)
STRACK, CHARLES (COLGATE) - GUARD - 1928 CHICAGO CARDINALS
STRADA, JOHN (WILLIAM JEWELL) - END - 1974 NEW YORK GIANTS (NFC);
    1974 KANSAS CITY CHIEFS (AFC)
STRADER, NORMAN (ST. MARY'S OF CAL.) - BACK - 1926 CHICAGO BULLS
    (AFL); 1927 CHICAGO CARDINALS
STRAHAN, ARTHUR (TEXAS SOUTHERN) - TACKLE - 1968 ATLANTA FALCONS
STRAHAN, RAYMOND (TEXAS SOUTHERN) - END - 1965 HOUSTON OILERS (AFL)
STRAIGHT, HERBERT (MICHIGAN STATE) - GUARD - 1919 DETROIT HERALDS
STRALKA, CLEMENT (GEORGETOWN) - GUARD - 1938-42, 45-46 WASHINGTON
    REDSKINS
STRAMIELLO, MICHAEL (COLGATE) - END - 1930-32, 34 BROOKLYN DODGERS;
    1932 STATEN ISLAND STAPELTONS
STRAND, ELI (IOWA STATE) - GUARD - 1966 PITTSBURGH STEELERS; 1967 NEW
    ORLEANS SAINTS
STRAND, LIEF (FORDHAM) - CENTER - 1923-25 DULUTH KELLEYS; 1926-27
    DULUTH ESKIMOS
STRANSKY, ROBERT (COLORADO) - BACK - 1960 DENVER BRONCOS (AFL)
STRASSER, CLARENCE (FINDLAY) - END - 1925 CANTON BULLDOGS
STRATTON, DAVID MICHAEL (TENNESSEE) - LB - 1962-69 BUFFALO BILLS
    (AFL); 1970-72 BUFFALO BILLS (AFC); 1973 SAN DIEGO CHARGERS (AFC)
STRAUSBAUGH, JAMES (OHIO STATE) - BACK - 1941 COLUMBUS BULLIES (AFL);
    1946 CHICAGO CARDINALS
STRAUSS, ARTHUR (PHILLIPS) - BACK - 1923 TOLEDO MAROONS; 1924 KANSAS
    CITY COWBOYS
STRAYHORN, LES (EAST CAROLINA) - BACK - 1973-74 DALLAS COWBOYS (NFC)
STRIBLING, MAJURE (MISSISSIPPI) - END - 1951-53 NEW YORK GIANTS;
    1955-57 PHILADELPHIA EAGLES
STRICKER, ANTHONY (COLORADO) - BACK - 1963 NEW YORK JETS (AFL)
STRICKLAND, BISHOP (SOUTH CAROLINA) - BACK - 1951 SAN FRANCISCO 49ERS
STRICKLAND, DAVIS (MEMPHIS STATE) - GUARD - 1960 DENVER BRONCOS (AFL)
STRICKLAND, LAWRENCE (NORTH TEXAS STATE) - CENTER - 1954-59 CHICAGO
    BEARS
STRICKLAND, WILLIAM (LOMBARD) - GUARD - 1923 MILWAUKEE BADGERS; 1923
    RACINE LEGION
STRIEGEL, WILLIAM (PACIFIC) - GUARD - 1959 PHILADELPHIA EAGLES; 1960
    BOSTON PATRIOTS (AFL); 1960 OAKLAND RAIDERS (AFL)
STRINGER, EUGENE (JOHN CARROLL) - BACK - 1925 CLEVELAND BULLDOGS
STRINGER, ROBERT (TULSA) - BACK - 1952-53 PHILADELPHIA EAGLES
STRINGER, SCOTT (CALIFORNIA) - BACK - 1974 ST. LOUIS CARDINALS (NFC)
STRINGFELLOW, JOSEPH (MISSISSIPPI SOUTHERN) - END - 1942 DETROIT LIONS
STROBEL - END - 1919 WHEELING
STROCK, DONALD (VIRGINIA TECH) - QBACK - 1974 MIAMI DOLPHINS (AFC)
STRODE, WOODROW (UCLA) - END - 1946 LOS ANGELES RAMS
STROFOLINO, MICHAEL (VILLANOVA) - LB - 1965 LOS ANGELES RAMS; 1965
    BALTIMORE COLTS; 1966-68 ST. LOUIS CARDINALS

STROHMEYER, GEORGE (NOTRE DAME) - CENTER - 1948 BROOKLYN DODGERS
    (AAFC); 1949 CHICAGO HORNETS (AAFC)
STROM, FRANK (OKLAHOMA MILITARY ACADEMY) - TACKLE - 1944 BROOKLYN
    TIGERS
STROMBERG, MICHAEL (TEMPLE) - LB - 1968 NEW YORK JETS (AFL)
STRONG, DAVID (MICHIGAN) - BACK - 1940 MILWAUKEE CHIEFS (AFL)
STRONG, JAMES (HOUSTON) - BACK - 1970 SAN FRANCISCO 49ERS (NFC);
    1971-72 NEW ORLEANS SAINTS (NFC)
STRONG, KENNETH (NEW YORK UNIV.) - BACK - 1929-32 STATEN ISLAND
    STAPLETONS; 1933-35, 39, 44-47 NEW YORK GIANTS; 1936-37 NEW YORK
    YANKS (AFL); 1933 SCORING LEADER; (TIED WITH PRESNELL); 1944
    FIELD GOAL LEADER; 1967 HALL OF FAME
STROSCHEIN, BROCK (UCLA) - END - 1951 NEW YORK YANKS
STROSNIDER, AUBREY (DAYTON) - GUARD - 1928 DAYTON TRIANGLES
STROSSER, WALTER (ST. VINCENT) - BACK - 1940 NEW YORK AMERICANS (AFL)
STROUD, JACK (TENNESSEE) - GUARD - 1953-64 NEW YORK GIANTS
STROUD, MORRIS (CLARK) - END - 1969 KANSAS CITY CHIEFS (AFL); 1970-74
    KANSAS CITY CHIEFS (AFC)
STROZIER, ART (KANSAS STATE) - END - 1970-71 SAN DIEGO CHARGERS (AFC)
STRUGAR, GEORGE (WASHINGTON) - TACKLE - 1957-61 LOS ANGELES RAMS;
    1962 PITTSBURGH STEELERS; 1962 NEW YORK TITANS (AFL); 1963 NEW
    YORK JETS (AFL)
STRUTT, ARTHUR (DUQUESNE) - BACK - 1935-36 PITTSBURGH PIRATES
STRZYKALSKI, JOHN (MARQUETTE) - BACK - 1946-49 SAN FRANCISCO 49ERS
    (AAFC); 1950-52 SAN FRANCISCO 49ERS
STUART, JAMES (OREGON) - TACKLE - 1941 WASHINGTON REDSKINS
STUART, ROY (TULSA) - GUARD - 1942 CLEVELAND RAMS; 1943 DETROIT
    LIONS; 1946 BUFFALO BISONS (AAFC)
STUCKEY, HENRY (MISSOURI) - BACK - 1973-74 MIAMI DOLPHINS (AFC)
STUCKEY, WILLIAM (LOYOLA-ILLINOIS) - BACK - 1926 LOUISVILLE COLONELS
STUDDARD, VERNON (MISSISSIPPI) - END - 1971 NEW YORK JETS (AFC)
STUDSTILL, PATRICK (HOUSTON) - END, KICKER - 1961-62, 64-67 DETROIT
    LIONS; 1968-69 LOS ANGELES RAMS; 1970-71 LOS ANGELES RAMS (NFC);
    1972 NEW ENGLAND PATRIOTS (AFC)
STUESSY, MELVIN (ST. EDWARDS-TEXAS) - TACKLE - 1926 CHICAGO CARDINALS
STUHLDREHER, HARRY (NOTRE DAME) - QBACK - 1926 BROOKLYN LIONS; 1926
    BROOKLYN HORSEMEN (AFL)
STUKES, CHARLES (MARYLAND STATE) - BACK - 1967-69 BALTIMORE COLTS;
    1970-72 BALTIMORE COLTS (AFC); 1973-74 LOS ANGELES RAMS (NFC)
STULGATE, JERRY (ST. THOMAS-PENNSYLVANIA) - END - 1937 ROCHESTER
    TIGERS (AFL)
STUMP - TACKLE - 1919 WHEELING
STURGEON, CECIL (NORTH DAKOTA STATE) - TACKLE - 1941 PHILADELPHIA
    EAGLES
STURGEON, LYLE (NORTH DAKOTA STATE) - TACKLE - 1937 GREEN BAY PACKERS
STURM, JERRY (ILLINOIS) - GUARD, CENTER - 1961-66 DENVER BRONCOS
    (AFL); 1967-69 NEW ORLEANS SAINTS; 1970 NEW ORLEANS SAINTS
    (NFC); 1971 HOUSTON OILERS (AFC); 1972 PHILADELPHIA EAGLES (NFC)
STURT, FREDRICK (BOWLING GREEN) - GUARD - 1974 WASHINGTON REDSKINS
    (NFC)
STURTRIDGE, RICHARD (DEPAUW) - BACK - 1928-29 CHICAGO BEARS
STYDAHAR, JOSEPH (WEST VIRGINIA) - TACKLE - 1936-42, 45-46 CHICAGO
    BEARS; 1967 HALL OF FAME
STYLIANOS, JOHN (TEMPLE) - BACK - 1940 BUFFALO INDIANS (AFL)
STYNCHULA, ANDREW (PENN STATE) - END - 1960-63 WASHINGTON REDSKINS;
    1964-65 NEW YORK GIANTS; 1966-67 BALTIMORE COLTS; 1968 DALLAS
    COWBOYS
SUCHY, LAWRENCE (MISSISSIPPI COLLEGE) - BACK - 1968 ATLANTA FALCONS
SUCHY, PAUL - END - 1925 CLEVELAND BULLDOGS
SUCI, ROBERT (MICHIGAN STATE) - BACK - 1962 HOUSTON OILERS (AFL);
    1963 BOSTON PATRIOTS (AFL)
SUCIC, STEPHEN (ILLINOIS) - BACK - 1946 LOS ANGELES RAMS; 1947 BOSTON
    YANKS; 1947-48 DETROIT LIONS
SUESS, RAYMOND (VILLANOVA) - TACKLE - 1926-27 DULUTH ESKIMOS
SUFFRIDGE, ROBERT (TENNESSEE) - GUARD - 1941, 45 PHILADELPHIA EAGLES
SUGAR, LEO (PURDUE) - END - 1954-59 CHICAGO CARDINALS; 1960 ST. LOUIS
    CARDINALS; 1961 PHILADELPHIA EAGLES; 1962 DETROIT LIONS
SUGGS, WILLIAM WALTER (MISSISSIPPI STATE) - TACKLE, CENTER - 1962-69
    HOUSTON OILERS (AFL); 1970-71 HOUSTON OILERS (AFC)
SUHEY, STEPHEN (PENN STATE) - GUARD - 1948-49 PITTSBURGH STEELERS

SULATIS, JOSEPH - BACK - 1943-45, 47-53 NEW YORK GIANTS; 1946 BOSTON
     YANKS
SULIMA, GEORGE (BOSTON UNIV.) - END - 1952-54 PITTSBURGH STEELERS
SULLIVAN, DANIEL (BOSTON COLLEGE) - GUARD, TACKLE - 1962-69 BALTIMORE
     COLTS; 1970-72 BALTIMORE COLTS (AFC)
SULLIVAN, DAVID (VIRGINIA) - END - 1973-74 CLEVELAND BROWNS (AFC)
SULLIVAN, FRANK (LOYOLA-NEW ORLEANS) - CENTER - 1935-39 CHICAGO
     BEARS; 1940 PITTSBURGH STEELERS
SULLIVAN, GEORGE (NOTRE DAME) - END - 1948 BOSTON YANKS
SULLIVAN, GEORGE (PENNSYLVANIA) - BACK - 1924-25 FRANKFORD
     YELLOWJACKETS; 1926 PHILADELPHIA QUAKERS (AFL)
SULLIVAN, GERALD (ILLINOIS) - TACKLE - 1974 CLEVELAND BROWNS (AFC)
SULLIVAN, HEW - TACKLE - 1926 DULUTH ESKIMOS
SULLIVAN, JAMES (LINCOLN) - TACKLE - 1970 ATLANTA FALCONS (NFC)
SULLIVAN, JOHN - BACK - 1921 BUFFALO ALL-AMERICANS
SULLIVAN, PATRICK (AUBURN) - QBACK - 1972-74 ATLANTA FALCONS (NFC)
SULLIVAN, ROBERT (HOLY CROSS & IOWA) - BACK - 1947 PITTSBURGH
     STEELERS; 1948 SAN FRANCISCO 49ERS (AAFC); 1948 BROOKLYN DODGERS
     (AAFC)
SULLIVAN, STEVEN (MONTANA) - QBACK - 1922 EVANSVILLE CRIMSON GIANTS;
     1922-24 HAMMOND PROS
SULLIVAN, THOMAS (MIAMI) - BACK - 1972-74 PHILADELPHIA EAGLES (NFC)
SULLIVAN, WALTER - GUARD - 1921 GREEN BAY PACKERS; 1922 MILWAUKEE
     BADGERS
SUMINSKI, DAVID (WISCONSIN) - TACKLE - 1953 WASHINGTON REDSKINS; 1953
     CHICAGO CARDINALS
SUMMERALL, GEORGE "PAT" (ARKANSAS) - END - 1952 DETROIT LIONS;
     1953-57 CHICAGO CARDINALS; 1958-61 NEW YORK GIANTS; 1959 FIELD
     GOAL LEADER
SUMMERELL, CARL (EAST CAROLINA) - QBACK - 1974 NEW YORK GIANTS (NFC)
SUMMERHAYS, ROBERT (UTAH) - BACK - 1949-51 GREEN BAY PACKERS
SUMMERS, FREDERICK (WAKE FOREST) - BACK - 1969 CLEVELAND BROWNS;
     1970-71 CLEVELAND BROWNS (AFC)
SUMMERS, JAMES (MICHIGAN STATE) - BACK - 1967 DENVER BRONCOS (AFL)
SUMNER, CHARLES (WILLIAM&MARY) - BACK - 1955, 58-60 CHICAGO BEARS;
     1961-62 MINNESOTA VIKINGS
SUMNER, WALTER (FLORIDA STATE) - BACK - 1969 CLEVELAND BROWNS;
     1970-74 CLEVELAND BROWNS (AFC)
SUMPTER, ANTHONY (CAMERON STATE) - GUARD - 1946-47 CHICAGO ROCKETS
     (AAFC)
SUNDE, MILTON (MINNESOTA) - GUARD - 1964-69 MINNESOTA VIKINGS;
     1970-74 MINNESOTA VIKINGS (NFC)
SUPULSKI, LEONARD (DICKINSON) - END - 1942 PHILADELPHIA EAGLES
SURABIAN, ZAREH (WILLIAMS) - TACKLE - 1926 BOSTON BULLDOGS (AFL);
     1927 PROVIDENCE STEAMROLLERS; 1929 BOSTON BRAVES
SUSOEFF, NICHOLAS (WASHINGTON STATE) - END - 1946-49 SAN FRANCISCO
     49ERS (AAFC)
SUSTERIC, EDWARD (FINDLAY) - BACK - 1949 CLEVELAND BROWNS (AAFC)
SUTCH, GEORGE (TEMPLE) - BACK - 1946 CHICAGO CARDINALS
SUTHERIN, DONALD (OHIO STATE) - BACK - 1959 NEW YORK GIANTS; 1959-60
     PITTSBURGH STEELERS
SUTHERLAND, DOUGLAS (SUPERIOR STATE-WIS.) - TACKLE, END - 1970 NEW
     ORLEANS SAINTS (NFC); 1971-74 MINNESOTA VIKINGS (NFC)
SUTHERLAND, JOHN (PITTSBURGH) - GUARD - 1919 MASSILLON TIGERS
SUTRO, JOHN (SAN JOSE STATE) - GUARD - 1962 SAN FRANCISCO 49ERS
SUTTON, ARCHIE (ILLINOIS) - TACKLE - 1965-67 MINNESOTA VIKINGS
SUTTON, EDWARD (NORTH CAROLINA) - BACK - 1957-59 WASHINGTON REDSKINS;
     1960 NEW YORK GIANTS
SUTTON, JOSEPH (TEMPLE) - BACK - 1949 BUFFALO BILLS (AAFC); 1950-52
     PHILADELPHIA EAGLES
SUTTON, MICHAEL (AUBURN) - BACK - 1966 HOUSTON OILERS (AFL)
SUTTON, MITCHELL (KANSAS) - TACKLE - 1974 PHILADELPHIA EAGLES (NFC)
SVARE, HARLAND (WASHINGTON STATE) - LB - 1953-54 LOS ANGELES RAMS;
     1955-60 NEW YORK GIANTS
SVENDSEN, EARL (MINNESOTA) - GUARD - 1937, 39 GREEN BAY PACKERS;
     1940-43 BROOKLYN DODGERS
SVENDSEN, GEORGE (MINNESOTA) - CENTER - 1935-37, 40-41 GREEN BAY
     PACKERS
SVIHUS, ROBERT (USC) - TACKLE, GUARD - 1965-69 OAKLAND RAIDERS (AFL);
     1970 OAKLAND RAIDERS (AFC); 1971-73 NEW YORK JETS (AFC)

SVOBODA, WILLIAM (TULANE) - LB - 1950-53 CHICAGO CARDINALS; 1954-58 NEW YORK GIANTS

SWAIN, ALTON (TRINITY-TEXAS) - END - 1926 BUFFALO RANGERS

SWAIN, WILLIAM (OREGON) - LB - 1963 LOS ANGELES RAMS; 1964 MINNESOTA VIKINGS; 1965, 67 NEW YORK GIANTS; 1968-69 DETROIT LIONS

SWAN, JOSEPH (WAKE FOREST) - TACKLE - 1937 BOSTON SHAMROCKS (AFL)

SWAN, PATRICK (WAKE FOREST) - TACKLE - 1936-37 BOSTON SHAMROCKS (AFL)

SWANN, LYNN (USC) - END - 1974 PITTSBURGH STEELERS (AFC)

SWANSON, ERNEST EVAR (LOMBARD) - END - 1924 MILWAUKEE BADGERS; 1925 ROCK ISLAND INDEPENDENTS; 1926-27 CHICAGO CARDINALS

SWANSON, TERRY (MASSACHUSETTS) - KICKER - 1967-68 BOSTON PATRIOTS (AFL); 1969 CINCINNATI BENGALS (AFL)

SWATLAND, ROBERT (NOTRE DAME) - GUARD - 1968 HOUSTON OILERS (AFL)

SWEENEY, JAMES (CINCINNATI) - TACKLE - 1944 CHICAGO BEARS

SWEENEY, NEAL (TULSA) - END - 1967 DENVER BRONCOS (AFL)

SWEENEY, RUSSELL (XAVIER) - END - 1937 CINCINNATI BENGALS (AFL)

SWEENEY, STEVE (CALIFORNIA) - END - 1973 OAKLAND RAIDERS (AFC)

SWEENEY, WALTER (SYRACUSE) - GUARD, TACKLE - 1963-69 SAN DIEGO CHARGERS (AFL); 1970-73 SAN DIEGO CHARGERS (AFC); 1974 WASHINGTON REDSKINS (NFC)

SWEENEY, WILLIAM (PENNSYLVANIA) - GUARD - 1936 CLEVELAND RAMS (AFL)

SWEENEY (CALIFORNIA) - END - 1919 AKRON PROS

SWEET, FREDERICK (BROWN) - BACK - 1925-26 PROVIDENCE STEAMROLLERS

SWEET, JOSEPH (TENNESSEE STATE) - END - 1972-73 LOS ANGELES RAMS (NFC); 1974 NEW ENGLAND PATRIOTS (AFC)

SWEETAN, KARL (WAKE FOREST) - QBACK - 1966-67 DETROIT LIONS; 1968 NEW ORLEANS SAINTS; 1969 LOS ANGELES RAMS; 1970 LOS ANGELES RAMS (NFC)

SWEETLAND, FRED (WASHINGTON &LEE) - BACK - 1919 CLEVELAND INDIANS; 1920 CLEVELAND PANTHERS; 1920 AKRON PROS

SWEIGER, ROBERT (MINNESOTA) - BACK - 1946-48 NEW YORK YANKEES (AAFC); 1949 CHICAGO HORNETS (AAFC)

SWENSON, MERWIN (CHICAGO & DARTMOUTH) - CENTER - 1926 CHICAGO BULLS (AFL)

SWIACKI, WILLIAM (COLUMBIA) - END - 1948-50 NEW YORK GIANTS; 1951-52 DETROIT LIONS

SWIADON, PHILIP (NEW YORK UNIV.) - GUARD - 1943 BROOKLYN DODGERS

SWIFT, DOUGLAS (AMHERST) - LB - 1970-74 MIAMI DOLPHINS (AFC)

SWINFORD, LENIS WAYNE (GEORGIA) - BACK - 1965-67 SAN FRANCISCO 49ERS

SWINK, JAMES (TCU) - BACK - 1960 DALLAS TEXANS (AFL)

SWINNEY, CLOVIS (ARKANSAS STATE) - END, TACKLE - 1970 NEW ORLEANS SAINTS (NFC); 1971 NEW YORK JETS (AFC)

SWISHER, ROBERT (NORTHWESTERN) - BACK - 1938-41, 45 CHICAGO BEARS

SWISTOWICZ, MICHAEL (NOTRE DAME) - BACK - 1950 NEW YORK YANKS; 1950 CHICAGO CARDINALS

SWITZER, VERYL (KANSAS STATE) - BACK - 1954-55 GREEN BAY PACKERS

SYKES, ALFRED (FLORIDA A&M) - END - 1971 NEW ENGLAND PATRIOTS (AFC)

SYKES, EUGENE (LSU) - BACK - 1963-65 BUFFALO BILLS (AFL); 1967 DENVER BRONCOS (AFL)

SYKES, JOHN (MORGAN STATE) - BACK - 1972 SAN DIEGO CHARGERS (AFC)

SYKES, ROBERT (SAN JOSE STATE) - BACK - 1952 WASHINGTON REDSKINS

SYLVESTER, JOHN (TEMPLE) - BACK - 1947 NEW YORK YANKEES (AAFC); 1948 BALTIMORE COLTS (AAFC)

SYMANK, JOHN (FLORIDA) - BACK - 1957-62 GREEN BAY PACKERS; 1963 ST. LOUIS CARDINALS

SYMONDS-THOMPSON, RALPH GARY - (PLAYED UNDER NAME OF RALPH "ROCKY" THOMPSON)

SYNHORST, JOHN (IOWA UNIV.) - TACKLE - 1920 ROCK ISLAND INDEPENDENTS

SZAFARYN, LEONARD (NORTH CAROLINA) - TACKLE - 1949 WASHINGTON REDSKINS; 1950, 53-56 GREEN BAY PACKERS; 1957-58 PHILADELPHIA EAGLES

SZAKASH, PAUL (MONTANA) - BACK - 1938-39, 41-42 DETROIT LIONS

SZCZECKO, JOSEPH (NORTHWESTERN) - TACKLE - 1966-68 ATLANTA FALCONS; 1969 NEW YORK GIANTS

SZOT, WALTER (BUCKNELL) - TACKLE - 1946-48 CHICAGO CARDINALS; 1949-50 PITTSBURGH STEELERS

SZUR, JOSEPH (CANISIUS) - BACK - 1940 BUFFALO INDIANS (AFL)

SZYMAKOWSKI, DAVID (WEST TEXAS STATE) - END - 1968 NEW ORLEANS SAINTS

SZYMANSKI, FRANK (NOTRE DAME) - CENTER - 1945-47 DETROIT LIONS; 1948 PHILADELPHIA EAGLES; 1949 CHICAGO BEARS

SZYMANSKI, RICHARD (NOTRE DAME) - CENTER - 1955, 57-68 BALTIMORE COLTS

TACKETT, DOYLE - BACK - 1946-48 BROOKLYN DODGERS (AAFC)

TACKWELL, CHARLES (KANSAS STATE) - END - 1930 MINNEAPOLIS REDJACKETS;
    1930-31 FRANKFORD YELLOWJACKETS; 1931-33 CHICAGO BEARS; 1933-34
    CINCINNATI REDS

TAFFONI, JOSEPH (W.VIRGINIA & TENN.-MARTIN) - TACKLE, GUARD - 1967-69
    CLEVELAND BROWNS; 1970 CLEVELAND BROWNS (AFC); 1972-73 NEW YORK
    GIANTS (NFC)

TAFT, MERRILL (WISCONSIN) - BACK - 1924 CHICAGO BEARS

TAGGE, JERRY (NEBRASKA) - QBACK - 1972-74 GREEN BAY PACKERS (NFC)

TAIT, ARTHUR (MISSISSIPPI STATE) - END - 1951 NEW YORK YANKS; 1952
    DALLAS TEXANS; 1972 BUFFALO BILLS (AFC)

TALAMINI, ROBERT (KENTUCKY) - GUARD - 1960-67 HOUSTON OILERS (AFL);
    1968 NEW YORK JETS (AFL)

TALBERT, DIRON (TEXAS) - TACKLE, END - 1967-69 LOS ANGELES RAMS; 1970
    LOS ANGELES RAMS (NFC); 1971-74 WASHINGTON REDSKINS (NFC)

TALBERT, DONALD (TEXAS) - TACKLE - 1962-65 DALLAS COWBOYS; 1966-68
    ATLANTA FALCONS; 1969 NEW ORLEANS SAINTS; 1970 NEW ORLEANS
    SAINTS (NFC); 1971 DALLAS COWBOYS (NFC)

TALBOT, JOHN (BROWN) - END - 1926 PROVIDENCE STEAMROLLERS

TALCOTT, DONALD (NEVADA) - TACKLE - 1947 PHILADELPHIA EAGLES

TALIAFERRO, GEORGE (INDIANA) - BACK - 1949 LOS ANGELES DONS (AAFC);
    1950-51 NEW YORK YANKS; 1952 DALLAS TEXANS; 1953-54 BALTIMORE
    COLTS; 1955 PHILADELPHIA EAGLES

TALIAFERRO, MYRON "MIKE" (ILLINOIS) - QBACK - 1964-67 NEW YORK JETS
    (AFL); 1968-69 BOSTON PATRIOTS (AFL); 1970 BOSTON PATRIOTS (AFC)

TALLANT, DAVID (GROVE CITY) - TACKLE - 1921-25 HAMMOND PROS

TALLMAN, CHARLES (WEST VIRGINIA) - TACKLE - 1919 CLEVELAND INDIANS

TALMAN, HOWARD (RUTGERS) - TACKLE - 1919 DETROIT HERALDS; 1919
    MASSILLON TIGERS

TALLY - 1921 EVANSVILLE CRIMSON GIANTS

TAMBURO, SAMUEL (PENN STATE) - END - 1949 NEW YORK BULLDOGS

TANDY, GEORGE (NORTH CAROLINA) - CENTER - 1919 DETROIT HERALDS; 1921
    CLEVELAND INDIANS

TANGUAY, JAMES (NEW YORK UNIV.) - BACK - 1933 PITTSBURGH PIRATES

TANNEN, STEVE (FLORIDA) - BACK - 1970-74 NEW YORK JETS (AFC)

TANNER, HAMPTON (GEORGIA) - TACKLE - 1951 SAN FRANCISCO 49ERS; 1952
    DALLAS TEXANS

TANNER, JOHN (CENTRE) - END - 1922 TOLEDO MAROONS; 1923 CLEVELAND
    INDIANS; 1924 CLEVELAND BULLDOGS

TANNER, JOHN (TENNESSEE TECH) - LB, END - 1971 SAN DIEGO CHARGERS
    (AFC); 1973-74 NEW ENGLAND PATRIOTS (AFC)

TANNER, ROBERT (MINNESOTA) - END - 1930 FRANKFORD YELLOWJACKETS

TARASOVIC, GEORGE (LSU) - END - 1952-53, 56-63 PITTSBURGH STEELERS;
    1963-65 PHILADELPHIA EAGLES; 1966 DENVER BRONCOS (AFL)

TARBOX, BRUCE (SYRACUSE) - GUARD - 1961 LOS ANGELES RAMS

TARKENTON, FRANCIS (GEORGIA) - QBACK - 1961-66 MINNESOTA VIKINGS;
    1967-69 NEW YORK GIANTS; 1970-71 NEW YORK GIANTS (NFC); 1972-74
    MINNESOTA VIKINGS (NFC)

TARR, GERALD (OREGON) - BACK - 1962 DENVER BRONCOS (AFL)

TARR, JAMES (MISSOURI) - END - 1931 CLEVELAND INDIANS

TARRANT, JAMES (HOWARD & TENNESSEE) - BACK - 1946 MIAMI SEAHAWKS
    (AAFC)

TARRANT, ROBERT (PITTSBURG STATE-KANSAS) - END - 1936 NEW YORK
    GIANTS; 1936 BOSTON SHAMROCKS (AFL)

TARVER, JOHN (COLORADO) - BACK - 1972-74 NEW ENGLAND PATRIOTS (AFC)

TASEFF, CARL (JOHN CARROLL) - BACK - 1951 CLEVELAND BROWNS; 1953-61
    BALTIMORE COLTS; 1961 PHILADELPHIA EAGLES; 1962 BUFFALO BILLS
    (AFL)

TASSOS, DAMON (TEXAS A&M) - GUARD - 1945-46 DETROIT LIONS; 1947-49
    GREEN BAY PACKERS

TATAREK, ROBERT (MIAMI) - TACKLE - 1968-69 BUFFALO BILLS (AFL);
    1970-72 BUFFALO BILLS (AFC); 1972 DETROIT LIONS (NFC)

TATMAN, ALLEN (NEBRASKA) - BACK - 1967 MINNESOTA VIKINGS

TATUM, JACK (OHIO STATE) - BACK - 1971-74 OAKLAND RAIDERS (AFC)

TATUM, JESS (NORTH CAROLINA STATE) - END - 1938 PITTSBURGH PIRATES

TAUGHER, CLAUDE (MARQUETTE) - BACK - 1922 GREEN BAY PACKERS; 1924
    MILWAUKEE BADGERS

TAVENOR, JOHN (INDIANA) - CENTER - 1946 MIAMI SEAHAWKS (AAFC)

TAYLOR, ALTIE (UTAH STATE) - BACK - 1969 DETROIT LIONS; 1970-74
    DETROIT LIONS (NFC)

TAYLOR, BRUCE (BOSTON UNIV) - BACK - 1970-74 SAN FRANCISCO 49ERS (NFC)

TAYLOR, CECIL (KANSAS STATE) - BACK - 1955, 57 LOS ANGELES RAMS
TAYLOR, CHARLES (ARIZONA STATE) - END, BACK - 1964-69 WASHINGTON
    REDSKINS; 1970-74 WASHINGTON REDSKINS (NFC); 1966-67 PASS
    RECEIVING LEADER
TAYLOR, CHARLES (OUACHITA) - BACK - 1944 BROOKLYN TIGERS
TAYLOR, CHARLES (STANFORD) - GUARD - 1946 MIAMI SEAHAWKS (AAFC)
TAYLOR, CLIFTON (MEMPHIS STATE) - BACK - 1974 CHICAGO BEARS (NFC)
TAYLOR, DAVID (CATAWBA) - TACKLE - 1973-74 BALTIMORE COLTS (AFC)
TAYLOR, ERQUIET (AUBURN) - GUARD - 1931 STATEN ISLAND STAPELTONS
TAYLOR, HUGH (OAKLAND CITY UNIV.) - END - 1947-54 WASHINGTON REDSKINS
TAYLOR, JAMES (LSU) - BACK - 1958-66 GREEN BAY PACKERS; 1967 NEW
    ORLEANS SAINTS; 1962 SCORING LEADER; 1962 RUSHING LEADER
TAYLOR, JESSE (CINCINNATI) - BACK - 1972 SAN DIEGO CHARGERS (AFC)
TAYLOR, JOHN (OHIO STATE) - TACKLE - 1920 DECATUR STALEYS; 1921
    CHICAGO STALEYS; 1922 CANTON BULLDOGS; 1926 BROOKLYN LIONS; 1926
    BROOKLYN HORSEMEN (AFL)
TAYLOR, JOSEPH (NORTH CAROLINA A&T) - BACK - 1967-69 CHICAGO BEARS;
    1970-74 CHICAGO BEARS (NFC)
TAYLOR, LIONEL (NEW MEXICO HIGHLANDS) - END - 1959 CHICAGO BEARS;
    1960-66 DENVER BRONCOS (AFL); 1967-68 HOUSTON OILERS (AFL);
    1960-63, 65 PASS RECEIVING LEADER (AFL)
TAYLOR, MICHAEL (MICHIGAN) - LB - 1972-73 NEW YORK JETS (AFC)
TAYLOR, MICHAEL RAY (USC) - TACKLE - 1968-69 PITTSBURGH STEELERS;
    1969 NEW ORLEANS SAINTS; 1970 NEW ORLEANS SAINTS (NFC); 1971
    WASHINGTON REDSKINS (NFC); 1973 ST. LOUIS CARDINALS (NFC)
TAYLOR, OTIS (PRAIRIE VIEW) - END - 1965-69 KANSAS CITY CHIEFS (AFL);
    1970-74 KANSAS CITY CHIEFS (AFC)
TAYLOR, ROBERT (MARYLAND STATE) - TACKLE - 1963-64 NEW YORK GIANTS
TAYLOR, ROOSEVELT (GRAMBLING) - BACK - 1961-69 CHICAGO BEARS; 1969
    SAN DIEGO CHARGERS (AFL); 1970-71 SAN FRANCISCO 49ERS (NFC);
    1972 WASHINGTON REDSKINS (NFC); 1963 INTERCEPTION LEADER; (TIED
    WITH LYNCH)
TAYLOR, SAMUEL (GRAMBLING) - END - 1965 SAN DIEGO CHARGERS (AFL)
TAYS, JAMES (PENN STATE) - BACK - 1924 KANSAS CITY COWBOYS; 1925
    CHICAGO CARDINALS; 1926 CHICAGO BULLS (AFL); 1927 DAYTON
    TRIANGLES; 1930 NEWARK TORNADOS; 1930 STATEN ISLAND STAPELTONS
TEAL, JAMES (PURDUE) - LB - 1973 DETROIT LIONS (NFC)
TEBELL, GUSTAVUS (WISCONSIN) - END - 1923-24 COLUMBUS TIGERS
TEERLINCK, JOHN (WESTERN ILLINOIS) - TACKLE, END - 1974 SAN DIEGO
    CHARGERS (AFC)
TEETER, ALAN (MINNESOTA) - END - 1932 STATEN ISLAND STAPELTONS
TEEUWS, LEONARD (TULANE) - TACKLE - 1952-53 LOS ANGELES RAMS; 1954-57
    CHICAGO CARDINALS
TELFER, ALEXANDER (DARTMOUTH) - END - 1919 CANTON BULLDOGS; 1919
    CLEVELAND INDIANS
TEMP, JAMES (WISCONSIN) - END - 1957-60 GREEN BAY PACKERS
TEMPLE, HARRY (NEW YORK UNIV.) - BACK - 1936 NEW YORK YANKS (AFL)
TEMPLE, MARK (OREGON) - BACK - 1936 BROOKLYN DODGERS; 1936 BOSTON
    REDSKINS
TEMPLE, ROBERT (ARIZONA) - END - 1940-41 MILWAUKEE CHIEFS (AFL)
TENNER, ROBERT (MINNESOTA) - END - 1935 GREEN BAY PACKERS
TENSI, STEPHEN (FLORIDA STATE) - QBACK - 1965-66 SAN DIEGO CHARGERS
    (AFL); 1967-69 DENVER BRONCOS (AFL); 1970 DENVER BRONCOS (AFC)
TEPE, LOUIS (DUKE) - CENTER - 1953-55 PITTSBURGH STEELERS
TERESA, ANTHONY (SAN JOSE STATE) - BACK - 1958 SAN FRANCISCO 49ERS;
    1960 OAKLAND RAIDERS (AFL)
TERESHINSKI, JOSEPH (GEORGIA) - END - 1947-54 WASHINGTON REDSKINS
TERLEP, GEORGE (NOTRE DAME) - QBACK - 1946 BUFFALO BISONS (AAFC);
    1947-48 BUFFALO BILLS (AAFC); 1948 CLEVELAND BROWNS (AAFC)
TERRELL, MARVIN (MISSISSIPPI) - GUARD - 1960-62 DALLAS TEXANS (AFL);
    1963 KANSAS CITY CHIEFS (AFL)
TERRELL, RAYMOND (MISSISSIPPI) - BACK - 1946-47 CLEVELAND BROWNS
    (AAFC); 1947 BALTIMORE COLTS (AAFC)
TERSCH, RUDOLPH - TACKLE - 1921-24 MINNEAPOLIS MARINES
TESSER, RAYMOND (CARNEGIE TECH) - END - 1933-34 PITTSBURGH PIRATES
TETEAK, DARREL (WISCONSIN) - GUARD - 1952-56 GREEN BAY PACKERS
TEVIS, LEEK (MIAMI-OHIO & WASHINGTON-MO.) - BACK - 1947-48 BROOKLYN
    DODGERS (AAFC)
TEW, LOWELL (ALABAMA) - BACK - 1948-49 NEW YORK YANKEES (AAFC)
THACKER, ALVIN (MORRIS-HARVEY) - BACK - 1942 PHILADELPHIA EAGLES
THARP, THOMAS (ALABAMA) - BACK - 1960 NEW YORK TITANS (AFL)

THAXTON, JAMES (TENNESSEE STATE) - END - 1973-74 SAN DIEGO CHARGERS
    (AFC); 1974 CLEVELAND BROWNS (AFC)
THAYER, HARRY (TENNESSEE) - TACKLE - 1933 PORTSMOUTH SPARTANS
THEISMANN, JOSEPH (NOTRE DAME) - QBACK - 1974 WASHINGTON REDSKINS
    (NFC)
THEOFILEDES, HARRY (WAYNESBURG) - QBACK - 1968 WASHINGTON REDSKINS
THIBAUT, JAMES (TULANE) - BACK - 1946 BUFFALO BISONS (AAFC)
THIBERT, JAMES (TOLEDO) - LB - 1965 DENVER BRONCOS (AFL)
THIELE, CARL (DENISON) - END - 1919-23 DAYTON TRIANGLES
THIELSCHER, KARL (DARTMOUTH) - BACK - 1920 BUFFALO ALL-AMERICANS
THIESSEN, DONALD (REELEY JUNIOR) - END - 1967 BUFFALO BILLS (AFL)
THOM, LEONARD (OHIO STATE) - END - 1941 COLUMBUS BULLIES (AFL)
THOMAS, AARON (OREGON STATE) - END - 1961 SAN FRANCISCO 49ERS;
    1962-69 NEW YORK GIANTS; 1970 NEW YORK GIANTS (NFC)
THOMAS, ALONZO "SKIP" (USC) - BACK - 1972-74 OAKLAND RAIDERS (AFC)
THOMAS, CALVIN (TULSA) - GUARD - 1939-40 DETROIT LIONS
THOMAS, CARL (PENNSYLVANIA) - TACKLE - 1919 WHEELING; 1919 CLEVELAND
    INDIANS; 1920-21, 24 ROCHESTER JEFFERSONS; 1922 MILWAUKEE
    BADGERS; 1922-23 BUFFALO ALL-AMERICANS
THOMAS, DUANE (WEST TEXAS STATE) - BACK - 1970-71 DALLAS COWBOYS
    (NFC); 1973-74 WASHINGTON REDSKINS (NFC)
THOMAS, EARL (HOUSTON) - END - 1971-73 CHICAGO BEARS (NFC); 1974 ST.
    LOUIS CARDINALS (NFC)
THOMAS, EARLIE (COLORADO STATE) - BACK - 1970-74 NEW YORK JETS (AFC)
THOMAS, EMMITT (BISHOP) - BACK - 1966-69 KANSAS CITY CHIEFS (AFL);
    1970-74 KANSAS CITY CHIEFS (AFC); 1969 INTERCEPTION LEADER
    (AFL); 1974 INTERCEPTION LEADER (AFC)
THOMAS, ENID (PENNSYLVANIA) - BACK - 1926 HARTFORD BLUES
THOMAS, EUGENE (FLORIDA A&M) - BACK - 1966-67 KANSAS CITY CHIEFS
    (AFL); 1968 BOSTON PATRIOTS (AFL); 1968 OAKLAND RAIDERS (AFL)
THOMAS, GEORGE (OKLAHOMA) - BACK - 1950-51 WASHINGTON REDSKINS; 1952
    NEW YORK GIANTS
THOMAS, ISSAC (BISHOP) - BACK - 1971 DALLAS COWBOYS (NFC); 1972-73
    GREEN BAY PACKERS (NFC)
THOMAS, J. RUSSELL (OHIO STATE) - TACKLE - 1946-49 DETROIT LIONS
THOMAS, JAMES "J.T." (FLORIDA STATE) - BACK - 1973-74 PITTSBURGH
    STEELERS (AFC)
THOMAS, JAMES (OKLAHOMA) - GUARD - 1939 CHICAGO CARDINALS
THOMAS, JESSE (MICHIGAN STATE) - BACK - 1955-57 BALTIMORE COLTS; 1960
    LOS ANGELES CHARGERS (AFL)
THOMAS, JIMMY (TEXAS-ARLINGTON) - BACK, END - 1969 SAN FRANCISCO
    49ERS; 1970-73 SAN FRANCISCO 49ERS (NFC)
THOMAS, JOHN (PACIFIC) - GUARD - 1958-67 SAN FRANCISCO 49ERS
THOMAS, LEE (JACKSON STATE) - END - 1971-72 SAN DIEGO CHARGERS (AFC);
    1973 CINCINNATI BENGALS (AFC)
THOMAS, LOUIS "SPEEDY" (UTAH) - END - 1969 CINCINNATI BENGALS (AFL);
    1970-72 CINCINNATI BENGALS (AFC); 1973-74 NEW ORLEANS SAINTS
    (NFC)
THOMAS, RALPH (SAN FRANCISCO) - END - 1952 CHICAGO CARDINALS; 1955-56
    WASHINGTON REDSKINS
THOMAS, REX (ST. JOHN'S) - BACK - 1926 BROOKLYN LIONS; 1927 CLEVELAND
    BULLDOGS; 1928 DETROIT WOLVERINES; 1930-31 BROOKLYN DODGERS
THOMAS, ROBERT (ARIZONA STATE) - BACK - 1971-72 LOS ANGELES RAMS
    (NFC); 1973-74 SAN DIEGO CHARGERS (AFC)
THOMAS, ROBERT CLENDON (OKLAHOMA) - BACK - 1958-61 LOS ANGELES RAMS;
    1962-68 PITTSBURGH STEELERS
THOMAS, WILLIAM (BOSTON COLLEGE) - BACK - 1972 DALLAS COWBOYS (NFC);
    1973 HOUSTON OILERS (AFC); 1974 KANSAS CITY CHIEFS (AFC)
THOMAS, WILLIAM (PENN STATE) - BACK - 1924 FRANKFORD YELLOWJACKETS;
    1926 PHILADELPHIA QUAKERS (AFL)
THOMAS - BACK - 1925-26 PROVIDENCE STEAMROLLERS
THOMASON, JAMES (TEXAS A&M) - BACK - 1945 DETROIT LIONS
THOMASON, JOHN (GEORGIA TECH) - QBACK - 1930-35 BROOKLYN DODGERS;
    1935-36 PHILADELPHIA EAGLES
THOMASON, ROBERT (VMI) - QBACK - 1949 LOS ANGELES RAMS; 1951 GREEN
    BAY PACKERS; 1952-57 PHILADELPHIA EAGLES
THOMPSON, ALVIE (LOMBARD) - TACKLE - 1923 ROCK ISLAND INDEPENDENTS;
    1924-26 KANSAS CITY COWBOYS
THOMPSON, CLARENCE (MINNESOTA) - BACK - 1937-38 PITTSBURGH PIRATES;
    1939 GREEN BAY PACKERS

THOMPSON, DAVID (CLEMSON) - TACKLE,GUARD,CENTER - 1971-73 DETROIT
    LIONS (NFC); 1974 NEW ORLEANS SAINTS (NFC)
THOMPSON, DAVID (DENISON) - BACK - 1921 CINCINNATI CELTS
THOMPSON, DONALD (RICHMOND) - LB - 1962-63 BALTIMORE COLTS; 1964
    PHILADELPHIA EAGLES
THOMPSON, FREDERICK (NEBRASKA) - END - 1924 ROCK ISLAND INDEPENDENTS
THOMPSON, GEORGE (IOWA) - GUARD - 1923-25 ROCK ISLAND INDEPENDENTS
THOMPSON, GEORGE (SYRACUSE) - GUARD - 1922 ROCHESTER JEFFERSONS
THOMPSON, GILBERT (MARQUETTE) - END - 1941 MILWAUKEE CHIEFS (AFL)
THOMPSON, HAROLD (DELAWARE) - END - 1947-48 BROOKLYN DODGERS (AAFC)
THOMPSON, HARRY (UCLA) - GUARD - 1950-54 LOS ANGELES RAMS; 1955
    CHICAGO CARDINALS
THOMPSON, JAMES (SOUTHERN ILLINOIS) - TACKLE - 1965 DENVER BRONCOS
    (AFL)
THOMPSON, JOHN (LAFAYETTE) - TACKLE - 1929 FRANKFORD YELLOWJACKETS
THOMPSON, LURTIS "TOMMY" (TULSA) - QBACK - 1940 PITTSBURGH STEELERS;
    1941-42, 45-50 PHILADELPHIA EAGLES; 1948 PASSING LEADER
THOMPSON, NORMAN (UTAH) - BACK - 1971-74 ST. LOUIS CARDINALS (NFC)
THOMPSON, RALPH "ROCKY" (WEST TEXAS STATE) - BACK - 1971-73 NEW YORK
    GIANTS (NFC); (REAL NAME RALPH GARY SYMONDS-THOMPSON)
THOMPSON, ROBERT (ARIZONA) - BACK - 1964-68 DETROIT LIONS; 1969 NEW
    ORLEANS SAINTS
THOMPSON, ROBERT "DON" (REDLANDS) - GUARD - 1926 LOS ANGELES
    BUCCANEERS
THOMPSON, RUSSELL (NEBRASKA) - TACKLE - 1936-39 CHICAGO BEARS; 1940
    PHILADELPHIA EAGLES
THOMPSON STEVEN (WASHINGTON) - END, TACKLE - 1968-69 NEW YORK JETS
    (AFL); 1970, 72-73 NEW YORK JETS (AFC)
THOMPSON, THOMAS (SOUTHERN ILLINOIS) - BACK - 1974 SAN DIEGO CHARGERS
    (AFC)
THOMPSON, THOMAS (WILLIAM&MARY) - CENTER - 1949 CLEVELAND BROWNS
    (AAFC); 1950-53 CLEVELAND BROWNS
THOMPSON, WILLIAM (MARYLAND STATE) - BACK - 1969 DENVER BRONCOS
    (AFL); 1970-74 DENVER BRONCOS (AFC)
THOMPSON, WILLIAM (WASHBURN) - CENTER - 1936 NEW YORK YANKS (AFL);
    1936 BROOKLYN TIGERS (AFL)
THOMS, ARTHUR (SYRACUSE) - TACKLE - 1969 OAKLAND RAIDERS (AFL);
    1970-74 OAKLAND RAIDERS (AFC)
THORNBLADH, BOB (MICHIGAN) - LB - 1974 KANSAS CITY CHIEFS (AFC)
THORNBURG, ALVIN (IOWA STATE) - TACKLE - 1926 CLEVELAND PANTHERS (AFL)
THORNHILL, CLAUDE (PITTSBURGH) - TACKLE - 1919 MASSILLON TIGERS; 1920
    BUFFALO ALL-AMERICANS; 1920 CLEVELAND PANTHERS
THORNTON, CHARLES "BUBBA" (TCU) - END - 1969 BUFFALO BILLS (AFL)
THORNTON, LAWRENCE "JACK" (AUBURN) - LB - 1966 MIAMI DOLPHINS (AFL)
THORNTON, RICHARD (MISSOURI MINES) - BACK - 1933 PHILADELPHIA EAGLES
THORNTON, ROBERT (SANTA CLARA) - GUARD - 1946-47 SAN FRANCISCO 49ERS
    (AAFC)
THORNTON, WILLIAM (NEBRASKA) - BACK - 1963-65, 67 ST. LOUIS CARDINALS
THORPE, JACK - GUARD - 1922-23 OORANG INDIANS
THORPE, JAMES (CARLISLE) - BACK - 1919-20, 26 CANTON BULLDOGS; 1921
    CLEVELAND INDIANS; 1922-23 OORANG INDIANS; 1923 TOLEDO MAROONS;
    1924 ROCK ISLAND INDEPENDENTS; 1925 NEW YORK GIANTS; 1963 HALL
    OF FAME
THORPE, WILFRED (ARKANSAS) - GUARD - 1941-42 CLEVELAND RAMS
THROWER, JAMES (EAST TEXAS STATE) - BACK - 1970-72 PHILADELPHIA
    EAGLES (NFC); 1973-74 DETROIT LIONS (NFC)
THROWER, WILLIE (MICHIGAN STATE) - QBACK - 1953 CHICAGO BEARS
THUNDER, BAPTIST - GUARD - 1922 OORANG INDIANS
THURBON, ROBERT (PITTSBURGH) - BACK - 1943 PHIL-PITT; 1944 CARD-PITT;
    1946 BUFFALO BISONS (AAFC)
THURLOW, STEVEN (STANFORD) - BACK - 1964-66 NEW YORK GIANTS; 1966-68
    WASHINGTON REDSKINS
THURMAN, JOHN (PENNSYLVANIA) - TACKLE - 1926 LOS ANGELES BUCCANEERS
THURSTON, FRED "FUZZY" (VALPARAISO) - GUARD - 1958 BALTIMORE COLTS;
    1959-67 GREEN BAY PACKERS
TIDD, GLENN - TACKLE - 1919-24 DAYTON TRIANGLES
TIDMORE, SAMUEL (OHIO STATE) - LB - 1962-63 CLEVELAND BROWNS
TIDWELL, TRAVIS (AUBURN) - QBACK - 1950-51 NEW YORK GIANTS
TIDWELL, WILLIAM (TEXAS A&M) - BACK - 1954 SAN FRANCISCO 49ERS

TIERNEY, FESTUS (MINNESOTA) - GUARD - 1922 HAMMOND PROS; 1922 TOLEDO
        MAROONS; 1923-24 MINNEAPOLIS MARINES; 1925 MILWAUKEE BADGERS
TILLEMAN, MICHAEL (MONTANA) - TACKLE - 1966 MINNESOTA VIKINGS;
        1967-69 NEW ORLEANS SAINTS; 1970 NEW ORLEANS SAINTS (NFC);
        1971-72 HOUSTON OILERS (AFC); 1973-74 ATLANTA FALCONS (NFC)
TILLER, JAMES (PURDUE) - BACK - 1962 NEW YORK TITANS (AFL)
TILLER, MORGAN (DENVER) - END - 1944 BOSTON YANKS; 1945 PITTSBURGH
        STEELERS
TILLMAN, ALONZO (OKLAHOMA) - CENTER - 1949 BALTIMORE COLTS (AAFC)
TILLMAN, EDDIE (BOISE STATE) - TACKLE - 1972 NEW ORLEANS SAINTS (NFC)
TILLMAN, RUSSELL "RUSTY" (NORTHERN ARIZONA) - LB - 1970-74 WASHINGTON
        REDSKINS (NFC)
TIMBERLAKE, GEORGE (USC) - GUARD - 1955 GREEN BAY PACKERS
TIMBERLAKE, ROBERT (MICHIGAN) - QBACK - 1965 NEW YORK GIANTS
TIMMONS, CHARLES (CLEMSON) - BACK - 1946 BROOKLYN DODGERS (AAFC)
TINGELHOFF, HENRY "MICK" (NEBRASKA) - CENTER - 1962-69 MINNESOTA
        VIKINGS; 1970-74 MINNESOTA VIKINGS (NFC)
TINKER, GERALD (KENT STATE) - END - 1974 ATLANTA FALCONS (NFC)
TINSLEY, GAYNELL (LSU) - END - 1937-38, 40 CHICAGO CARDINALS; 1938
        PASS RECEIVING LEADER
TINSLEY, JESS (LSU) - TACKLE - 1929-33 CHICAGO CARDINALS
TINSLEY, PETER (GEORGIA) - GUARD - 1938-45 GREEN BAY PACKERS
TINSLEY, ROBERT (BAYLOR) - TACKLE - 1949 LOS ANGELES DONS (AAFC)
TINSLEY, SIDNEY (CLEMSON) - BACK - 1945 PITTSBURGH STEELERS
TIPTON, DAVID (STANFORD) - END - 1971-73 NEW YORK JETS (AFC); 1974
        SAN DIEGO CHARGERS (AFC)
TIPTON, HOWARD (USC) - QBACK - 1933-37 CHICAGO CARDINALS
TITCHENAL, ROBERT (SAN JOSE STATE) - END - 1940-42 WASHINGTON
        REDSKINS; 1946 SAN FRANCISCO 49ERS (AAFC); 1947 LOS ANGELES DONS
        (AAFC)
TITMAS, HERBERT (SYRACUSE) - BACK - 1931 PROVIDENCE STEAMROLLERS
TITTLE, YELBERTON "Y.A." (LSU) - QBACK - 1948-49 BALTIMORE COLTS
        (AAFC); 1950 BALTIMORE COLTS; 1951-60 SAN FRANCISCO 49ERS;
        1961-64 NEW YORK GIANTS; 1963 PASSING LEADER; 1971 HALL OF FAME
TITUS, GEORGE (HOLY CROSS) - CENTER - 1946 PITTSBURGH STEELERS
TITUS, SILAS (HOLY CROSS) - END - 1940-42 BROOKLYN DODGERS; 1945
        PITTSBURGH STEELERS
TOBEY, DAVID (OREGON) - LB - 1966-67 MINNESOTA VIKINGS; 1968 DENVER
        BRONCOS (AFL)
TOBIN, ELGIE (PENN STATE) - END - 1919-21 AKRON PROS
TOBIN, GEORGE (NOTRE DAME) - GUARD - 1947 NEW YORK GIANTS
TOBIN, LEO (GROVE CITY) - GUARD - 1921 AKRON PROS
TOBIN, REX (MINNESOTA) - END - 1925 DULUTH KELLEYS
TOBIN, WILLIAM (MISSOURI) - BACK - 1963 HOUSTON OILERS (AFL)
TOBUREN, NELSON (WICHITA) - LB - 1961-62 GREEN BAY PACKERS
TODD, JAMES (BALL STATE-INDIANA) - BACK - 1966 DETROIT LIONS
TODD, LAWRENCE (ARIZONA STATE) - BACK - 1965-69 OAKLAND RAIDERS
        (AFL); 1970 OAKLAND RAIDERS (AFC)
TODD, RICHARD (TEXAS A&M) - BACK - 1939-42, 45-48 WASHINGTON REDSKINS
TOEWS, LOREN (CALIFORNIA) - LB - 1973-74 PITTSBURGH STEELERS (AFC)
TOFIL, JOSEPH (INDIANA) - END - 1942 BROOKLYN DODGERS
TOLAR, CHARLES (NORTHWEST STATE-LOUISIANA) - BACK - 1960-66 HOUSTON
        OILERS (AFL)
TOLBERT, LOVE JAMES (LINCOLN) - BACK - 1966-69 SAN DIEGO CHARGERS
        (AFL); 1970-71 SAN DIEGO CHARGERS (AFC); 1972 HOUSTON OILERS
        (AFC); 1973-74 ST. LOUIS CARDINALS (NFC)
TOLLEFSON, CHARLES (IOWA) - GUARD - 1944-46 GREEN BAY PACKERS
TOLLESON, THOMAS (ALABAMA) - BACK - 1966 ATLANTA FALCONS
TOLLEY, EDWARD - GUARD - 1929 DAYTON TRIANGLES
TOM, MELVYN (SAN JOSE STATE) - END, LB - 1967-69 PHILADELPHIA EAGLES;
        1970-73 PHILADELPHIA EAGLES (NFC); 1973-74 CHICAGO BEARS (NFC)
TOMAHAWK (CARLISLE) - BACK - 1923 OORANG INDIANS
TOMAINI, ARMY (CATAWBA) - TACKLE - 1945 NEW YORK GIANTS
TOMAINI, JOHN (GEORGETOWN) - END - 1929 ORANGE TORNADOS; 1930 NEWARK
        TORNADOS; 1930-31 BROOKLYN DODGERS
TOMASELLI, CARL (SCRANTON) - END - 1940 NEW YORK GIANTS
TOMASETTI, LOUIS (BUCKNELL) - BACK - 1939-40 PITTSBURGH STEELERS;
        1941 DETROIT LIONS; 1941-42 PHILADELPHIA EAGLES; 1946 BUFFALO
        BISONS (AAFC); 1947-49 BUFFALO BILLS (AAFC)
TOMASIC, ANDREW (TEMPLE) - BACK - 1942, 46 PITTSBURGH STEELERS

TOMLIN, BRADLEY (SYRACUSE) - GUARD - 1920-21 AKRON PROS; 1921 HAMMOND
     PROS; 1922 MILWAUKEE BADGERS; 1925-26 NEW YORK GIANTS
TOMLINSON, RICHARD (KANSAS) - GUARD - 1950-51 PITTSBURGH STEELERS
TOMMERSON, CLARENCE (WISCONSIN) - BACK - 1938 PITTSBURGH PIRATES;
     1939 PITTSBURGH STEELERS
TONEFF, ROBERT (NOTRE DAME) - TACKLE - 1952, 54-58 SAN FRANCISCO
     49ERS; 1959-64 WASHINGTON REDSKINS
TONELLI, AMERIGO (USC) - CENTER - 1939 DETROIT LIONS
TONELLI, MARIO (NOTRE DAME) - BACK - 1940, 45 CHICAGO CARDINALS
TONER, EDWARD (MASSACHUSETTS) - TACKLE - 1967-69 BOSTON PATRIOTS (AFL)
TONER, THOMAS (IDAHO STATE) - LB - 1973 GREEN BAY PACKERS (NFC)
TONNEMAKER, CLAYTON (MINNESOTA) - CENTER - 1950, 53-54 GREEN BAY
     PACKERS
TOOGOOD, CHARLES (NEBRASKA) - TACKLE - 1951-56 LOS ANGELES RAMS; 1957
     CHICAGO CARDINALS
TOOMAY, PATRICK (VANDERBILT) - END - 1970-74 DALLAS COWBOYS (NFC)
TOPER, THEODORE (MICHIGAN) - LB - 1955 DETROIT LIONS
TOPP, ROBERT (MICHIGAN) - END - 1954 NEW YORK GIANTS
TORCZON, LAVERNE (NEBRASKA) - END - 1960-62 BUFFALO BILLS (AFL); 1962
     NEW YORK TITANS (AFL); 1963-65 NEW YORK JETS (AFL); 1966 MIAMI
     DOLPHINS (AFL)
TORGESON, LAVERN (WASHINGTON STATE) - LB - 1951-54 DETROIT LIONS;
     1955-57 WASHINGTON REDSKINS
TORKELSON, ERIC (CONNECTICUT) - BACK - 1974 GREEN BAY PACKERS (NFC)
TORNQUIST, EUGENE (CORNELL-IOWA) - BACK - 1941 CINCINNATI BENGALS
     (AFL)
TORRANCE, JOHN (LSU) - TACKLE - 1939-40 CHICAGO BEARS
TOSCANI, FRANCIS (ST. MARY'S OF CAL.) - BACK - 1932 BROOKLYN DODGERS;
     1932 CHICAGO CARDINALS
TOSI, FLAVIO (BOSTON COLLEGE) - END - 1934-36 BOSTON REDSKINS
TOSI, JOHN (NIAGARA) - GUARD - 1939 PITTSBURGH STEELERS; 1939
     BROOKLYN DODGERS
TOTH, NICHOLAS (CANISIUS) - GUARD - 1941 BUFFALO TIGERS (AFL)
TOTH, ZOLLIE (LSU) - BACK - 1950-51 NEW YORK YANKS; 1952 DALLAS
     TEXANS; 1954 BALTIMORE COLTS
TOWELL (CARLISLE) - BACK - 1922 OORANG INDIANS
TOWLE, THURSTON (BROWN) - END - 1929 BOSTON BRAVES
TOWLER, DANIEL (WASHINGTON&JEFFERSON) - BACK - 1950-55 LOS ANGELES
     RAMS; 1952 RUSHING LEADER
TOWNES, WILLIE (TULSA) - TACKLE, END - 1966-68 DALLAS COWBOYS; 1970
     NEW ORLEANS SAINTS (NFC)
TOWNS, ROBERT (GEORGIA) - BACK - 1960 ST. LOUIS CARDINALS; 1961
     BOSTON PATRIOTS (AFL)
TOWNSEND, OTTO - GUARD - 1922 MINNEAPOLIS MARINES
TRACEY, JOHN (TEXAS A&M) - LB - 1959 CHICAGO CARDINALS; 1960 ST.
     LOUIS CARDINALS; 1961 PHILADELPHIA EAGLES; 1962-67 BUFFALO BILLS
     (AFL)
TRACY, JOHN THOMAS (TENNESSEE) - BACK - 1956-57 DETROIT LIONS;
     1958-63 PITTSBURGH STEELERS; 1963-64 WASHINGTON REDSKINS
TRAFTON, GEORGE (NOTRE DAME) - CENTER - 1920 DECATUR STALEYS; 1921
     CHICAGO STALEYS; 1922-32 CHICAGO BEARS; 1964 HALL OF FAME
TRAMMEL, ALLEN (FLORIDA) - BACK - 1966 HOUSTON OILERS (AFL)
TRAPP, RICHARD (FLORIDA) - END - 1968 BUFFALO BILLS (AFL); 1969 SAN
     DIEGO CHARGERS (AFL)
TRASK, ORVILLE (RICE) - TACKLE - 1960-61 HOUSTON OILERS (AFL); 1962
     OAKLAND RAIDERS (AFL)
TRAVENIO, HERBERT - KICKER - 1964-65 SAN DIEGO CHARGERS (AFL)
TRAVIS, JOHN (SAN DIEGO STATE) - BACK - 1966 SAN DIEGO CHARGERS (AFL)
TRAYNHAM, WADE (FREDERICK) - KICKER - 1966-67 ATLANTA FALCONS
TRAYNOR, BERNARD (COLGATE) - CENTER - 1925 MILWAUKEE BADGERS
TRAYNOR, MICHAEL (CANISIUS) - BACK - 1923 BUFFALO ALL-AMERICANS; 1924
     BUFFALO BISONS
TREADWAY, JOHN (HARDIN-SIMMONS) - TACKLE - 1949 NEW YORK GIANTS; 1949
     DETROIT LIONS
TREAT, C. HERBERT (PRINCETON) - TACKLE - 1926 BOSTON BULLDOGS (AFL)
TREBBINS, JOHN (ST. OLAF-MINNESOTA) - BACK - 1941 MILWAUKEE CHIEFS
     (AFL)
TREBOTICH, IVAN (ST. MARY'S OF CAL.) - BACK - 1944-45 DETROIT LIONS;
     1947 BALTIMORE COLTS (AAFC)
TRESSELL, JOHN (WASHINGTON&JEFFERSON) - END - 1919 MASSILLON TIGERS
TRIGGS, JOHN (PROVIDENCE) - BACK - 1926 PROVIDENCE STEAMROLLERS

TRIGILIO, FRANK (ALFRED & VERMONT) - BACK - 1946 MIAMI SEAHAWKS
    (AAFC); 1946 LOS ANGELES DONS (AAFC)
TRIMBLE, WAYNE (ALABAMA) - BACK - 1967 SAN FRANCISCO 49ERS
TRIPLETT, MELVIN (TOLEDO) - BACK - 1955-60 NEW YORK GIANTS; 1961-62
    MINNESOTA VIKINGS
TRIPLETT, WALLACE (PENN STATE) - BACK - 1949-50 DETROIT LIONS;
    1952-53 CHICAGO CARDINALS
TRIPLETT, WILLIAM (MIAMI-OHIO) - BACK - 1962-63, 65-66 ST. LOUIS
    CARDINALS; 1967 NEW YORK GIANTS; 1968-69 DETROIT LIONS; 1970-72
    DETROIT LIONS (NFC)
TRIPPI, CHARLES (GEORGIA) - BACK - 1947-55 CHICAGO CARDINALS; 1968
    HALL OF FAME
TRIPSON, JOHN (MISSISSIPPI STATE) - TACKLE - 1941 DETROIT LIONS
TRIPUCKA, FRANK (NOTRE DAME) - QBACK - 1949 PHILADELPHIA EAGLES; 1949
    DETROIT LIONS; 1950-52 CHICAGO CARDINALS; 1952 DALLAS TEXANS;
    1960-63 DENVER BRONCOS (AFL)
TROCOLOR, ROBERT (ALABAMA) - BACK - 1942-43 NEW YORK GIANTS; 1944
    BROOKLYN TIGERS
TROSCH, EUGENE (MIAMI) - END, TACKLE - 1967, 69 KANSAS CITY CHIEFS
    (AFL)
TROST, MILTON (MARQUETTE) - TACKLE - 1935-39 CHICAGO BEARS; 1940
    PHILADELPHIA EAGLES; 1941 MILWAUKEE CHIEFS (AFL)
TROUP, BILL (SOUTH CAROLINA) - QBACK - 1974 BALTIMORE COLTS (AFC)
TROWBRIDGE, RAYMOND (BOSTON COLLEGE) - END - 1919 CLEVELAND INDIANS;
    1920 CLEVELAND PANTHERS
TRUAX, DALTON (TULANE) - TACKLE - 1960 OAKLAND RAIDERS (AFL)
TRUAX, WILLIAM (LSU) - END - 1964-69 LOS ANGELES RAMS; 1970 LOS
    ANGELES RAMS (NFC); 1971-73 DALLAS COWBOYS (NFC)
TRUCKENMILLER, KENNETH (CORNELL-IOWA) - GUARD - 1926 ROCK ISLAND
    INDEPENDENTS (AFL)
TRUESDELL, HAROLD (HAMLINE) - TACKLE - 1930 MINNEAPOLIS REDJACKETS
TRULL, DONALD (BAYLOR) - QBACK - 1964-69 HOUSTON OILERS (AFL); 1967
    BOSTON PATRIOTS (AFL)
TRUMPY, ROBERT (ILLINOIS & UTAH) - END - 1968-69 CINCINNATI BENGALS
    (AFL); 1970-74 CINCINNATI BENGALS (AFC)
TRYON, EDWARD (COLGATE) - BACK - 1926 NEW YORK YANKEES (AFL); 1927
    NEW YORK YANKEES
TSCHAPPATT, CHALMER (WEST VIRGINIA WESLEYAN) - TACKLE - 1921 DAYTON
    TRIANGLES
TSOUTSOUVAS, JOHN (OREGON STATE) - CENTER - 1940 DETROIT LIONS
TSOUTSOUVAS, LOUIS (STANFORD) - CENTER - 1938 PITTSBURGH PIRATES
TUBBS, GERALD (OKLAHOMA) - LB - 1957-58 CHICAGO CARDINALS; 1958-59
    SAN FRANCISCO 49ERS; 1960-67 DALLAS COWBOYS
TUCKER, GARY (CHATTANOOGA) - BACK - 1968 MIAMI DOLPHINS (AFL)
TUCKER, ROBERT (BLOOMSBURG STATE) - END - 1970-74 NEW YORK GIANTS
    (NFC); 1971 PASS RECEIVING LEADER (NFC)
TUCKER, WENDELL (SOUTH CAROLINA STATE) - END - 1967-69 LOS ANGELES
    RAMS; 1970 LOS ANGELES RAMS (NFC)
TUCKER, WILLIAM (TENNESSEE STATE) - BACK - 1967-69 SAN FRANCISCO
    49ERS; 1970 SAN FRANCISCO 49ERS (NFC); 1971 CHICAGO BEARS (NFC)
TUCKETT, PHILIP (WEBER STATE) - END - 1968 SAN DIEGO CHARGERS (AFL)
TUCKEY, RICHARD (MANHATTAN) - BACK - 1938 WASHINGTON REDSKINS; 1938
    CLEVELAND RAMS
TULLY, DARRELL (EAST TEXAS STATE) - BACK - 1939 DETROIT LIONS
TULLY, GEORGE (DARTMOUTH) - END - 1926 PHILADELPHIA QUAKERS (AFL);
    1927 FRANKFORD YELLOWJACKETS
TUNNELL, EMLEN (IOWA) - BACK - 1948-58 NEW YORK GIANTS; 1959-61 GREEN
    BAY PACKERS; 1967 HALL OF FAME
TURBERT, FRANCIS (MORRIS-HARVEY) - BACK - 1944 BOSTON YANKS
TURLEY, DOUGLAS (SCRANTON) - END - 1944-48 WASHINGTON REDSKINS
TURLEY, JOHN (OHIO WESLEYAN) - QBACK - 1935-36 PITTSBURGH PIRATES
TURNBOW, GUY (MISSISSIPPI) - TACKLE - 1933-34 PHILADELPHIA EAGLES
TURNER, CECIL (CALIFORNIA POLYTECH) - END - 1968-69 CHICAGO BEARS;
    1970-73 CHICAGO BEARS (NFC)
TURNER, CLEMENT (CINCINNATI) - BACK - 1969 CINCINNATI BENGALS (AFL);
    1970-72 DENVER BRONCOS (AFC)
TURNER, CLYDE "BULLDOG" (HARDIN-SIMMONS) - CENTER - 1940-52 CHICAGO
    BEARS; 1942 INTERCEPTION LEADER; 1966 HALL OF FAME
TURNER, HARLEY "ROCKY" (CHATTANOOGA) - END - 1972-73 NEW YORK JETS
    (AFC)
TURNER, HAROLD (TENNESSEE STATE) - END - 1954 DETROIT LIONS

TURNER, HERSCHEL (KENTUCKY) - GUARD - 1964-65 ST. LOUIS CARDINALS
TURNER, JAMES (NORTHWESTERN) - BACK - 1923 MILWAUKEE BADGERS
TURNER, JAMES (OKLAHOMA A&M) - CENTER - 1936 PITTSBURGH AMERICANS
    (AFL); 1937 CLEVELAND RAMS
TURNER, JAMES (UTAH STATE) - KICKER, QBACK - 1964-69 NEW YORK JETS
    (AFL); 1970 NEW YORK JETS (AFC); 1971-74 DENVER BRONCOS (AFC);
    1968-69 SCORING LEADER (AFL); 1968-69 FIELD GOAL LEADER (AFL)
TURNER, JAY LEWIS (GEORGE WASHINGTON) - BACK - 1938-39 WASHINGTON
    REDSKINS
TURNER, JOHN - GUARD - 1919 CANTON BULLDOGS; 1920 DAYTON TRIANGLES
TURNER, ROBERT "BAKE" (TEXAS TECH) - END, BACK - 1962 BALTIMORE
    COLTS; 1963-69 NEW YORK JETS (AFL); 1970 BOSTON PATRIOTS (AFC)
TURNER, VINCENT (MISSOURI) - BACK - 1964 NEW YORK JETS (AFL)
TURNQUIST - TACKLE - 1919 TOLEDO MAROONS
TURSI, SILVIO (MUHLENBERG) - END - 1926 NEWARK BEARS (AFL)
TUTTLE, GEORGE (MINNESOTA) - END - 1927 GREEN BAY PACKERS
TUTTLE, ORVILLE (OKLAHOMA CITY) - GUARD - 1937-41, 46 NEW YORK GIANTS
TWEDELL, FRANCIS (MINNESOTA) - GUARD - 1939 GREEN BAY PACKERS
TWILLEY, HOWARD (TULSA) - END - 1966-69 MIAMI DOLPHINS (AFL); 1970-74
    MIAMI DOLPHINS (AFC)
TYLER, MAURICE (MORGAN STATE) - BACK - 1972 BUFFALO BILLS (AFC);
    1973-74 DENVER BRONCOS (AFC)
TYLER, PETER (HARDIN-SIMMONS) - BACK - 1937-38 CHICAGO CARDINALS
TYNES, DAVID (TEXAS) - BACK - 1924-25 COLUMBUS TIGERS
TYRER, JAMES (OKLAHOMA) - END - 1948 BOSTON YANKS
TYRER, JAMES (OHIO STATE) - TACKLE - 1961-62 DALLAS TEXANS (AFL);
    1963-69 KANSAS CITY CHIEFS (AFL); 1970-73 KANSAS CITY CHIEFS
    (AFC); 1974 WASHINGTON REDSKINS (NFC)
TYRRELL, JOSEPH (TEMPLE) - GUARD - 1952 PHILADELPHIA EAGLES
TYSON, EDWARD - GUARD - 1936-37 PITTSBURGH AMERICANS (AFL)
TYSON, RICHARD (TULSA) - GUARD - 1966 OAKLAND RAIDERS (AFL); 1967
    DENVER BRONCOS (AFL)
UCOVICH, MITCHELL (SAN JOSE STATE) - TACKLE - 1944 WASHINGTON
    REDSKINS; 1945 CHICAGO CARDINALS
UGUCCIONI, ENRICO (MURRAY STATE) - END - 1944 BROOKLYN TIGERS
UHRINYAK, STEVEN (FRANKLIN & MARSHALL) - GUARD - 1939 WASHINGTON
    REDSKINS
ULINSKI, EDWARD (MARSHALL) - GUARD - 1946-49 CLEVELAND BROWNS (AAFC)
ULINSKI, HARRY (KENTUCKY) - CENTER - 1950-51, 53-56 WASHINGTON
    REDSKINS
ULLERY, WILLIAM (PENN STATE) - BACK - 1922 DAYTON TRIANGLES
ULRICH, CHARLES (ILLINOIS) - TACKLE - 1954-58 CHICAGO CARDINALS
ULRICH, HUBERT (KANSAS) - END - 1946 MIAMI SEAHAWKS (AAFC)
UMONT, FRANK - TACKLE - 1943-45 NEW YORK GIANTS
UNDERWOOD, JOHN - GUARD - 1924-25 DULUTH KELLEYS; 1926-27 DULUTH
    ESKIMOS; 1927 POTTSVILLE MAROONS; 1927 BUFFALO BISONS; 1929
    CHICAGO CARDINALS
UNDERWOOD, JOHN (RICE) - GUARD - 1923 MILWAUKEE BADGERS
UNDERWOOD, OLEN (TEXAS) - LB - 1965 NEW YORK GIANTS; 1966-69 HOUSTON
    OILERS (AFL); 1970 HOUSTON OILERS (AFC); 1971 DENVER BRONCOS
    (AFC)
UNDERWOOD, WAYNE (DAVIS&ELKINS) - TACKLE - 1937 CLEVELAND RAMS; 1937
    CINCINNATI BENGALS (AFL)
UNGERER, JOSEPH (FORDHAM) - TACKLE - 1944-45 WASHINGTON REDSKINS
UNITAS, JOHN (LOUISVILLE) - QBACK - 1956-69 BALTIMORE COLTS; 1970-72
    BALTIMORE COLTS (AFC); 1973 SAN DIEGO CHARGERS (AFC)
UPDIKE, HAROLD (RUTGERS) - TACKLE - 1936 NEW YORK YANKS (AFL)
UPERESA, TUUFULI (MONTANA) - GUARD, TACKLE - 1971 PHILADELPHIA EAGLES
    (NFC)
UPSHAW, EUGENE (TEXAS A&I) - GUARD - 1967-69 OAKLAND RAIDERS (AFL);
    1970-74 OAKLAND RAIDERS (AFC)
UPSHAW, MARVIN (TRINITY-TEXAS) - END, TACKLE - 1968-69 CLEVELAND
    BROWNS; 1970-74 KANSAS CITY CHIEFS (AFC)
URAM, ANDREW (MINNESOTA) - BACK - 1938-43 GREEN BAY PACKERS
URBAN, ALEXANDER (SOUTH CAROLINA) - END - 1941, 44-45 GREEN BAY
    PACKERS
URBAN, GASPER (NOTRE DAME) - GUARD - 1948 CHICAGO ROCKETS (AAFC)
URBAN, JOHN (PITTSBURGH) - BACK - 1940 NEW YORK AMERICANS (AFL)
URBAN, LOUIS (BOSTON COLLEGE) - END - 1921-23 BUFFALO ALL-AMERICANS;
    1924 BUFFALO BISONS; 1926 ROCK ISLAND INDEPENDENTS (AFL)
URBANEK, JAMES (MISSISSIPPI) - END - 1968 MIAMI DOLPHINS (AFL)

UREMOVICH, EMIL (INDIANA) - TACKLE - 1941-42, 45-46 DETROIT LIONS;
      1948 CHICAGO ROCKETS (AAFC)
URENDA, HERMAN (PACIFIC) - END - 1963 OAKLAND RAIDERS (AFL)
USHER, EDWARD (MICHIGAN) - BACK - 1921 BUFFALO ALL-AMERICANS; 1922
      ROCK ISLAND INDEPENDENTS; 1922 GREEN BAY PACKERS; 1924-25 KANSAS
      CITY COWBOYS
USHER, LOUIS (SYRACUSE) - TACKLE - 1920-21 ROCHESTER JEFFERSONS; 1921
      CHICAGO STALEYS; 1923 CHICAGO BEARS; 1923-24 MILWAUKEE BADGERS;
      1923-24, 26 HAMMOND PROS; 1924 KENOSHA MAROONS
UZDAVINIS, WALTER (FORDHAM) - END - 1936 BOSTON SHAMROCKS (AFL); 1937
      CLEVELAND RAMS
VACANTI, SAMUEL (NEBRASKA & IOWA) - QBACK - 1947-48 CHICAGO ROCKETS
      (AAFC); 1948-49 BALTIMORE COLTS (AAFC)
VACTOR, THEODORE (NEBRASKA) - BACK - 1969 WASHINGTON REDSKINS;
      1970-73 WASHINGTON REDSKINS (NFC)
VAESSEN, MATTHEW (GONZAGA) - GUARD - 1940 MILWAUKEE CHIEFS (AFL)
VAINOWSKI, PETER - GUARD - 1926 LOUISVILLE COLONELS
VAIRO, DOMINIC (NOTRE DAME) - END - 1935 GREEN BAY PACKERS
VALDEZ, VERNON (SAN DIEGO UNIV.) - BACK - 1960 LOS ANGELES RAMS; 1961
      BUFFALO BILLS (AFL); 1962 OAKLAND RAIDERS (AFL)
VALLEZ, EMILIO (NEW MEXICO) - END - 1968-69 CHICAGO BEARS
VAN BROCKLIN, NORMAN (OREGON) - QBACK - 1949-57 LOS ANGELES RAMS;
      1958-60 PHILADELPHIA EAGLES; 1950, 52, 54 PASSING LEADER;
      1955-56 PUNTING LEADER; 1971 HALL OF FAME
VAN BUREN, EBERT (LSU) - BACK - 1951-53 PHILADELPHIA EAGLES
VAN BUREN, STEPHEN (LSU) - BACK - 1944-51 PHILADELPHIA EAGLES; 1945,
      47-49 RUSHING LEADER; 1945 SCORING LEADER; 1965 HALL OF FAME
VANCE, JOSEPH (SOUTHWEST TEXAS STATE) - BACK - 1931 BROOKLYN DODGERS
VANCE, ROBERT (CCNY) - BACK - 1932 STATEN ISLAND STAPELTONS
VAN CLEFF - BACK - 1936 ROCHESTER TIGERS (AFL)
VANDERBUNDT, WILLIAM "SKIP" (OREGON STATE) - LB - 1969 SAN FRANCISCO
      49ERS; 1970-74 SAN FRANCISCO 49ERS (NFC)
VANDERKELEN, RONALD (WISCONSIN) - QBACK - 1963-67 MINNESOTA VIKINGS
VANDERLOO, VIVIAN (IOWA STATE) - BACK - 1921 ROCK ISLAND INDEPENDENTS
VANDERSEA, PHILIP (MASSACHUSETTS) - LB, END - 1966, 68-69 GREEN BAY
      PACKERS; 1967 NEW ORLEANS SAINTS
VANDEWEGHE, ALFRED (WILLIAM&MARY) - END - 1946 BUFFALO BISONS (AAFC)
VAN DOREN, ROBERT (USC) - END - 1953 SAN FRANCISCO 49ERS
VAN DUYNE, ROBERT (IDAHO) - GUARD - 1974 BALTIMORE COLTS (AFC)
VAN DYKE, BRUCE (MISSOURI) - GUARD - 1966 PHILADELPHIA EAGLES;
      1967-69 PITTSBURGH STEELERS; 1970-73 PITTSBURGH STEELERS (AFC);
      1974 GREEN BAY PACKERS (NFC)
VAN DYKE, JAMES - BACK - 1922-23 LOUISVILLE BRECKS
VAN DYNE, CHARLES (MISSOURI) - TACKLE - 1925 BUFFALO BISONS
VAN EEGHEN, MARK (COLGATE) - BACK - 1974 OAKLAND RAIDERS (AFC)
VAN EVERY, HAROLD (MINNESOTA) - BACK - 1940-41 GREEN BAY PACKERS
VAN GALDER, THOMAS "TIM" (IOWA STATE) - QBACK - 1972 ST. LOUIS
      CARDINALS (NFC)
VAN HEUSEN, WILLIAM (MARYLAND) - END, KICKER - 1968-69 DENVER BRONCOS
      (AFL); 1970-74 DENVER BRONCOS (AFC)
VAN HORN, DOUGLAS (OHIO STATE) - TACKLE, GUARD - 1966 DETROIT LIONS;
      1968-69 NEW YORK GIANTS; 1970-74 NEW YORK GIANTS (NFC)
VAN HORNE, CHARLES (WASHINGTON&LEE) - BACK - 1927 BUFFALO BISONS;
      1929 ORANGE TORNADOS
VAN NOTE, JEFFREY (KENTUCKY) - CENTER, LB - 1969 ATLANTA FALCONS;
      1970-74 ATLANTA FALCONS (NFC)
VANOY, VERNON (KANSAS) - END, TACKLE - 1971 NEW YORK GIANTS (NFC);
      1972 GREEN BAY PACKERS (NFC); 1973 HOUSTON OILERS (AFC)
VAN PELT, BRAD (MICHIGAN STATE) - LB - 1973-74 NEW YORK GIANTS (NFC)
VAN RAAPHORST, RICHARD (OHIO STATE) - KICKER - 1964 DALLAS COWBOYS;
      1966-67 SAN DIEGO CHARGERS (AFL)
VAN SICKLE, CLYDE (ARKANSAS) - TACKLE - 1930 FRANKFORD YELLOWJACKETS;
      1932-33 GREEN BAY PACKERS
VANT HULL, FREDERICK (MINNESOTA) - GUARD - 1942 GREEN BAY PACKERS
VAN TONE, ARTHUR (MISSISSIPPI SOUTHERN) - BACK - 1943-45 DETROIT
      LIONS; 1946 BROOKLYN DODGERS (AAFC)
VAN VALKENBERG, PETER (BRIGHAM YOUNG) - BACK - 1973 BUFFALO BILLS
      (AFC); 1974 GREEN BAY PACKERS (NFC); 1974 CHICAGO BEARS (NFC)
VANZO, FREDERICK (NORTHWESTERN) - QBACK - 1938-41 DETROIT LIONS; 1941
      CHICAGO CARDINALS

VARDIAN, JOHN - BACK - 1946 MIAMI SEAHAWKS (AAFC); 1947-48 BALTIMORE
    COLTS (AAFC)
VARGO, LAWRENCE (DETROIT) - LB - 1962-63 DETROIT LIONS; 1964-65
    MINNESOTA VIKINGS; 1966 NEW YORK GIANTS
VARRICHONE, FRANK (NOTRE DAME) - TACKLE - 1955-60 PITTSBURGH
    STEELERS; 1961-65 LOS ANGELES RAMS
VARTY, MIKE (NORTHWESTERN) - LB - 1974 WASHINGTON REDSKINS (NFC)
VASICEK, VICTOR (USC & TEXAS) - GUARD - 1949 BUFFALO BILLS (AAFC);
    1950 LOS ANGELES RAMS
VASSAU, ROY (ST. THOMAS OF MINNESOTA) - TACKLE - 1923 MILWAUKEE
    BADGERS
VASYS, ARUNAS (NOTRE DAME) - LB - 1966-68 PHILADELPHIA EAGLES
VATAHA, RANDEL (STANFORD) - END - 1971-74 NEW ENGLAND PATRIOTS (AFC)
VAUGHAN, CHARLES (TENNESSEE) - BACK - 1935 DETROIT LIONS; 1936
    CHICAGO CARDINALS
VAUGHAN, JOHN (INDIANA STATE-PENNSYLVANIA) - QBACK - 1933-34
    PITTSBURGH PIRATES
VAUGHN, ROBERT (MISSISSIPPI) - GUARD - 1968 DENVER BRONCOS (AFL)
VAUGHN, THOMAS (IOWA STATE) - BACK - 1965-69 DETROIT LIONS; 1970-71
    DETROIT LIONS (NFC)
VAUGHN, WILLIAM (SMU) - BACK - 1926 BUFFALO RANGERS
VAUGHT, THOMAS (TCU) - END - 1955 SAN FRANCISCO 49ERS
VEACH, WILLIAM WALTER - BACK - 1920 DECATUR STALEYS
VEDDER, NORTON - BACK - 1927 BUFFALO BISONS
VELLA, JOHN (USC) - TACKLE, GUARD - 1972-74 OAKLAND RAIDERS (AFC)
VELLONE, JAMES (USC) - TACKLE, GUARD - 1966-69 MINNESOTA VIKINGS;
    1970 MINNESOTA VIKINGS (NFC)
VENTURELLI, FRED - KICKER - 1948 CHICAGO BEARS
VENUTO, SAMUEL (GUILFORD) - BACK - 1952 WASHINGTON REDSKINS
VEREB, EDWARD (MARYLAND) - BACK - 1960 WASHINGTON REDSKINS
VEREEN, CARL (GEORGIA TECH) - TACKLE - 1957 GREEN BAY PACKERS
VERGARA, GEORGE (NOTRE DAME) - END - 1925 GREEN BAY PACKERS
VERRY, NORMAN (USC) - TACKLE - 1946-47 CHICAGO ROCKETS (AAFC)
VERTEFEUILLE, BRIAN (IDAHO STATE) - GUARD - 1974 SAN DIEGO CHARGERS
    (AFC)
VESSELS, WILLIAM (OKLAHOMA) - BACK - 1956 BALTIMORE COLTS
VESSER, JOHN (IDAHO) - END - 1926 LOS ANGELES WILDCATS (AFL); 1927,
    30-31 CHICAGO CARDINALS
VETRANO, JOSEPH (MISSISSIPPI SOUTHERN) - BACK - 1946-49 SAN FRANCISCO
    49ERS (AAFC)
VETTER, JOHN (MCPHERSON-KANSAS) - BACK - 1942 BROOKLYN DODGERS
VEXALL, ROY - BACK - 1923-25 DULUTH KELLEYS
VEZMAR, WALTER (MICHIGAN STATE) - GUARD - 1946-47 DETROIT LIONS
VICK, HENRY "ERNIE" (MICHIGAN) - CENTER - 1925 DETROIT PANTHERS;
    1927-28 CHICAGO BEARS; 1928 DETROIT WOLVERINES
VICK, RICHARD (WASHINGTON&JEFFERSON) - QBACK - 1924 KENOSHA MAROONS;
    1925-26 DETROIT PANTHERS; 1926 CANTON BULLDOGS
VIDONI, VICTOR (DUQUESNE) - END - 1935-36 PITTSBURGH PIRATES
VILLANUEVA, DANIEL (NEW MEXICO STATE) - KICKER - 1960-64 LOS ANGELES
    RAMS; 1965-67 DALLAS COWBOYS
VILLAPIANO, PHILIP (BOWLING GREEN) - LB - 1971-74 OAKLAND RAIDERS
    (AFC)
VILTZ, THEOPHILE (USC) - BACK - 1966 HOUSTON OILERS (AFL)
VINCE, RALPH (WASHINGTON&JEFFERSON) - GUARD - 1923 CLEVELAND INDIANS;
    1924-25 CLEVELAND BULLDOGS; 1926 CLEVELAND PANTHERS (AFL)
VINNOLA, PAUL (SANTA CLARA) - BACK - 1946 LOS ANGELES DONS (AAFC)
VINYARD, KENNY (TEXAS TECH) - KICKER - 1970 ATLANTA FALCONS (NFC)
VIRANT, LEO (DAYTON) - GUARD - 1926 CLEVELAND PANTHERS (AFL)
VISNIC, LAWRENCE (ST. BENEDICT'S-KANSAS) - GUARD - 1943-45 NEW YORK
    GIANTS
VODICKA, JOSEPH - BACK - 1943, 45 CHICAGO BEARS; 1945 CHICAGO
    CARDINALS
VOGDS, EVAN (WISCONSIN) - GUARD - 1946-47 CHICAGO ROCKETS (AAFC);
    1948-49 GREEN BAY PACKERS
VOGEL, ROBERT (OHIO STATE) - TACKLE - 1963-69 BALTIMORE COLTS;
    1970-72 BALTIMORE COLTS (AFC)
VOGELAAR, CARROLL (SAN FRANCISCO) - TACKLE - 1947-48 BOSTON YANKS;
    1949 NEW YORK BULLDOGS; 1950 NEW YORK YANKS
VOIGHT, ROBERT (LOS ANGELES STATE) - TACKLE - 1961 OAKLAND RAIDERS
    (AFL)
VOIGHT, STUART (WISCONSIN) - END - 1970-74 MINNESOTA VIKINGS (NFC)

VOKATY, OTTO (HEIDELBERG) - BACK - 1931 CLEVELAND INDIANS; 1932 NEW
    YORK GIANTS; 1933 CHICAGO CARDINALS; 1934 CINCINNATI REDS
VOLK, RICHARD (MICHIGAN) - BACK - 1967-69 BALTIMORE COLTS; 1970-74
    BALTIMORE COLTS (AFC)
VOLOK, WILLIAM (TULSA) - GUARD - 1934-39 CHICAGO CARDINALS
VOLLENWEIDER, JAMES (MIAMI) - BACK - 1962-63 SAN FRANCISCO 49ERS
VOLZ, PETER - END - 1920 CHICAGO TIGERS; 1921 CINCINNATI CELTS
VOLZ, WILBUR (MISSOURI) - BACK - 1949 BUFFALO BILLS (AAFC)
VON SOHN, ANDREW (UCLA) - LB - 1964 LOS ANGELES RAMS
VOSBERG, DONALD (MARQUETTE) - END - 1941 NEW YORK GIANTS
VOSS, LLOYD (NEBRASKA) - TACKLE, END - 1964-65 GREEN BAY PACKERS;
    1966-69 PITTSBURGH STEELERS; 1970-71 PITTSBURGH STEELERS (AFC);
    1972 DENVER BRONCOS (AFC)
VOSS, WALTER (DETROIT) - END - 1921 DETROIT PANTHERS; 1921 BUFFALO
    ALL-AMERICANS; 1922 ROCK ISLAND INDEPENDENTS; 1922 AKRON PROS;
    1923 TOLEDO MAROONS; 1924 GREEN BAY PACKERS; 1925 DETROIT
    PANTHERS; 1926 NEW YORK GIANTS; 1927-28 CHICAGO BEARS; 1929
    DAYTON TRIANGLES; 1929 BUFFALO BISONS
VOYTEK, EDWARD (PURDUE) - GUARD - 1957-58 WASHINGTON REDSKINS
VUCINICH, MILTON (STANFORD) - CENTER - 1945 CHICAGO BEARS
WADE, CHARLEY (TENNESSEE STATE) - END - 1974 CHICAGO BEARS (NFC)
WADE, JAMES (OKLAHOMA CITY UNIV.) - BACK - 1949 NEW YORK BULLDOGS
WADE, ROBERT (MORGAN STATE) - BACK - 1968 PITTSBURGH STEELERS; 1969
    WASHINGTON REDSKINS; 1970 DENVER BRONCOS (AFC)
WADE, THOMAS (TEXAS) - QBACK - 1964-65 PITTSBURGH STEELERS
WADE, WILLIAM (VANDERBILT) - QBACK - 1954-60 LOS ANGELES RAMS;
    1961-66 CHICAGO BEARS
WAFER, CARL (TENNESSEE STATE) - TACKLE, END - 1974 GREEN BAY PACKERS
    (NFC); 1974 NEW YORK GIANTS (NFC)
WAGER, CLINTON (ST. MARY'S OF MINNESOTA) - END - 1942 CHICAGO BEARS;
    1943, 45 CHICAGO CARDINALS; 1944 CARD-PITT
WAGER, JOHN (CARTHAGE) - CENTER - 1931-33 PORTSMOUTH SPARTANS
WAGES, HARMON (FLORIDA) - BACK - 1968-69 ATLANTA FALCONS; 1970-71, 73
    ATLANTA FALCONS (NFC)
WAGNER, BUFFTON (NORTHERN MICHIGAN) - BACK - 1921 GREEN BAY PACKERS
WAGNER, HARRY (PITTSBURGH) - BACK - 1937 PITTSBURGH AMERICANS (AFL)
WAGNER, LOWELL (USC) - BACK - 1946-48 NEW YORK YANKEES (AAFC); 1949
    SAN FRANCISCO 49ERS (AAFC); 1950-53, 55 SAN FRANCISCO 49ERS
WAGNER, MICHAEL (WESTERN ILLINOIS) - BACK - 1971-74 PITTSBURGH
    STEELERS (AFC)
WAGNER, RAYMOND (COLUMBIA) - END - 1930 NEWARK TORNADOS; 1931
    BROOKLYN DODGERS
WAGNER, SHELDON (KENTUCKY) - TACKLE - 1937 CINCINNATI BENGALS (AFL)
WAGNER, SIDNEY (MICHIGAN STATE) - GUARD - 1936-38 DETROIT LIONS
WAGSTAFF, JAMES (IDAHO STATE) - BACK - 1959 CHICAGO CARDINALS;
    1960-61 BUFFALO BILLS (AFL)
WAINSCOTT, LOYD (TEXAS-AUSTIN) - LB - 1969 HOUSTON OILERS (AFL); 1970
    HOUSTON OILERS (AFC)
WAITE, CARL (GEORGETOWN) - END - 1928 FRANKFORD YELLOWJACKETS; 1929
    ORANGE TORNADOS; 1930 NEWARK TORNADOS
WAITE, WILLARD - GUARD - 1919-21 COLUMBUS PANHANDLES
WAKEMAN, ARGYLE (CENTRAL MISSOURI STATE) - END - 1940 CINCINNATI
    BENGALS (AFL)
WALBRIDGE, LYMAN (FORDHAM) - CENTER - 1925 NEW YORK GIANTS
WALDEN, ROBERT (GEORGIA) - KICKER - 1964-67 MINNESOTA VIKINGS;
    1968-69 PITTSBURGH STEELERS; 1970-74 PITTSBURGH STEELERS (AFC);
    1964 PUNTING LEADER
WALDRON, AUSTIN (GONZAGA) - GUARD - 1927 CHICAGO CARDINALS
WALDSMITH, RALPH (AKRON) - GUARD - 1919 AKRON PROS; 1921 CLEVELAND
    INDIANS; 1922 CANTON BULLDOGS
WALESKI, STANLEY (ST. THOMAS-PENNSYLVANIA) - BACK - 1936 NEW YORK
    YANKS (AFL)
WALIK, WILLIAM (VILLANOVA) - END - 1970-72 PHILADELPHIA EAGLES (NFC)
WALKER, ASA - END - 1922 OORANG INDIANS
WALKER, CHARLES (DUKE) - TACKLE, END - 1964-69 ST. LOUIS CARDINALS;
    1970-72 ST. LOUIS CARDINALS (NFC); 1972-74 ATLANTA FALCONS (NFC)
WALKER, CLARENCE (SOUTHERN ILLINOIS) - BACK - 1963 DENVER BRONCOS
    (AFL)
WALKER, CLEO (LOUISVILLE) - LB, CENTER - 1970 GREEN BAY PACKERS
    (NFC); 1971 ATLANTA FALCONS (NFC)

WALKER, DONNIE (CENTRAL STATE-OHIO) - BACK - 1973-74 BUFFALO BILLS
    (AFC)
WALKER, EWELL DOAK (SMU) - BACK - 1950-55 DETROIT LIONS; 1950, 55
    SCORING LEADER
WALKER, GEORGE "MICKEY" (MICHIGAN STATE) - GUARD - 1961-65 NEW YORK
    GIANTS
WALKER, HOMER (BAYLOR) - END - 1926 ROCK ISLAND INDEPENDENTS (AFL)
WALKER, LOUIE (COLORADO STATE) - LB - 1974 DALLAS COWBOYS (NFC)
WALKER, MALCOLM (RICE) - CENTER - 1966-69 DALLAS COWBOYS; 1970 GREEN
    BAY PACKERS (NFC)
WALKER, MICHAEL - KICKER - 1972 NEW ENGLAND PATRIOTS (AFC)
WALKER, MICHAEL (TULANE) - END - 1971 NEW ORLEANS SAINTS (NFC)
WALKER, PAUL (YALE) - END - 1948 NEW YORK GIANTS
WALKER, RANDELL (NORTHWEST STATE-LOUISIANA) - KICKER - 1974 GREEN BAY
    PACKERS (NFC)
WALKER, VAL JOE (SMU) - BACK - 1953-56 GREEN BAY PACKERS; 1957 SAN
    FRANCISCO 49ERS
WALKER, WAYNE (NORTHWEST STATE-LOUISIANA) - LB - 1967 KANSAS CITY
    CHIEFS (AFL); 1968 HOUSTON OILERS (AFL)
WALKER, WAYNE HARRISON (IDAHO) - LB, KICKER - 1958-69 DETROIT LIONS;
    1970-72 DETROIT LIONS (NFC)
WALKER, WILLIAM (KENTUCKY) - GUARD - 1922 COLUMBUS PANHANDLES
WALKER, WILLIAM (VMI) - GUARD - 1944-45 BOSTON YANKS
WALKER, WILLIE (TENNESSEE STATE) - BACK - 1966 DETROIT LIONS
WALL, PETER (GEORGETOWN) - BACK - 1919 AKRON PROS
WALLACE, BEVERLY (COMPTON JUNIOR) - QBACK - 1947-49 SAN FRANCISCO
    49ERS (AAFC); 1951 NEW YORK YANKS
WALLACE, FRED - GUARD - 1923-24, 26 AKRON PROS; 1925 CLEVELAND
    BULLDOGS; 1926 CANTON BULLDOGS
WALLACE, GORDON (ROCHESTER) - BACK - 1923 ROCHESTER JEFFERSONS
WALLACE, HENRY (PACIFIC) - BACK - 1960 LOS ANGELES CHARGERS (AFL)
WALLACE, JACKIE (ARIZONA) - BACK - 1974 MINNESOTA VIKINGS (NFC)
WALLACE, JOHN (NOTRE DAME) - END - 1928 CHICAGO BEARS; 1929 DAYTON
    TRIANGLES
WALLACE, ROBERT (TEXAS-EL PASO) - END - 1968-69 CHICAGO BEARS;
    1970-72 CHICAGO BEARS (NFC)
WALLACE, RODNEY (NEW MEXICO) - GUARD, TACKLE - 1971-73 DALLAS COWBOYS
    (NFC)
WALLACE, STANLEY (ILLINOIS) - BACK - 1954, 56-58 CHICAGO BEARS
WALLER, RONALD (MARYLAND) - BACK - 1955-58 LOS ANGELES RAMS; 1960 LOS
    ANGELES CHARGERS (AFL)
WALLER, WILLIAM (ILLINOIS) - END - 1937 LOS ANGELES BULLDOGS (AFL);
    1938 BROOKLYN DODGERS
WALLIS, JAMES (HOLY CROSS) - BACK - 1926 BOSTON BULLDOGS (AFL)
WALLNER, FREDERICK (NOTRE DAME) - GUARD - 1951-52, 54-55 CHICAGO
    CARDINALS; 1960 HOUSTON OILERS (AFL)
WALLS, WILLIAM (TCU) - END - 1937-39, 41-43 NEW YORK GIANTS
WALQUIST, LAURIE (ILLINOIS) - QBACK - 1922-31 CHICAGO BEARS
WALSH, EDWARD (PENN MILITARY) - TACKLE - 1961 NEW YORK TITANS (AFL)
WALSH, WARD (COLORADO) - BACK - 1971-72 HOUSTON OILERS (AFC); 1972
    GREEN BAY PACKERS (NFC)
WALSH, WILLIAM (NOTRE DAME) - CENTER - 1949-54 PITTSBURGH STEELERS
WALSTON, ROBERT (GEORGIA) - END - 1951-62 PHILADELPHIA EAGLES; 1954
    SCORING LEADER
WALTERS, CHALMERS (WASHINGTON) - CENTER - 1926 LOS ANGELES WILDCATS
    (AFL)
WALTERS, LESTER (PENN STATE) - END - 1958 WASHINGTON REDSKINS
WALTERS, STANLEY (SYRACUSE) - TACKLE - 1972-74 CINCINNATI BENGALS
    (AFC)
WALTERS, THOMAS (MISSISSIPPI SOUTHERN) - BACK - 1964-67 WASHINGTON
    REDSKINS
WALTERS - BACK - 1919 COLUMBUS PANHANDLES; 1924 KENOSHA MAROONS
WALTON, BRUCE (UCLA) - TACKLE,GUARD,CENTER - 1973-74 DALLAS COWBOYS
    (NFC)
WALTON, CHARLES (IOWA) - GUARD - 1967-69 DETROIT LIONS; 1970-74
    DETROIT LIONS (NFC)
WALTON, FRANK (PITTSBURGH) - GUARD - 1934 BOSTON REDSKINS; 1944-45
    WASHINGTON REDSKINS
WALTON, GERALD WAYNE (ABILENE CHRISTIAN) - GUARD, TACKLE - 1971 NEW
    YORK GIANTS (NFC); 1973-74 KANSAS CITY CHIEFS (AFC)

WALTON, JOSEPH (PITTSBURGH) - END - 1957-60 WASHINGTON REDSKINS;
   1961-63 NEW YORK GIANTS
WALTON, LAWRENCE (ARIZONA STATE) - END - 1969 DETROIT LIONS; 1970-74
   DETROIT LIONS (NFC)
WALTON, SAMUEL (EAST TEXAS STATE) - TACKLE - 1968-69 NEW YORK JETS
   (AFL); 1971 HOUSTON OILERS (AFC)
WANLESS, GEORGE - BACK - 1921-23 LOUISVILLE BRECKS
WANTLAND, HOWELL "HAL" (TENNESSEE) - BACK - 1966 MIAMI DOLPHINS (AFL)
WARD, CARL (MICHIGAN) - BACK - 1967-68 CLEVELAND BROWNS; 1969 NEW
   ORLEANS SAINTS
WARD, DAVID (NEW MEXICO) - TACKLE - 1933 BOSTON REDSKINS
WARD, ELMER (UTAH STATE) - CENTER - 1935 DETROIT LIONS
WARD, GILBERT (NOTRE DAME) - TACKLE - 1923 DAYTON TRIANGLES
WARD, JAMES (GETTSBURG) - QBACK - 1967-68 BALTIMORE COLTS; 1971
   PHILADELPHIA EAGLES (NFC)
WARD, JOHN (OKLAHOMA STATE) - TACKLE, END, GUARD - 1970-73 MINNESOTA
   VIKINGS (NFC)
WARD, JOHN (USC) - TACKLE - 1930 FRANKFORD YELLOWJACKETS; 1930
   MINNEAPOLIS REDJACKETS
WARD, PAUL (WHITWORTH) - TACKLE - 1961-62 DETROIT LIONS
WARD, WILLIAM (PENNSYLVANIA) - TACKLE - 1921 BUFFALO ALL-AMERICANS
WARD, WILLIAM (WASHINGTON STATE) - GUARD - 1946-47 WASHINGTON
   REDSKINS; 1947-49 DETROIT LIONS
WARD - QBACK - 1920 HAMMOND PROS
WARDLOW, DUANE (WASHINGTON) - END - 1954, 56 LOS ANGELES RAMS
WARE, CHARLES (BIRMINGHAM-SOUTHERN) - TACKLE - 1944 BROOKLYN TIGERS
WARFIELD, PAUL (OHIO STATE) - END - 1964-69 CLEVELAND BROWNS; 1970-74
   MIAMI DOLPHINS (AFC)
WARLICK, ERNEST (NORTH CAROLINA COLLEGE) - END - 1962-65 BUFFALO
   BILLS (AFL)
WARNER, CHARLES (PRAIRIE VIEW) - BACK - 1963-64 KANSAS CITY CHIEFS
   (AFL); 1964-66 BUFFALO BILLS (AFL)
WARNER, ROBERT - BACK - 1927 DULUTH ESKIMOS
WARREN, BUSIT (TENNESSEE) - BACK - 1945 PHILADELPHIA EAGLES; 1945
   PITTSBURGH STEELERS
WARREN, JAMES (ILLINOIS) - BACK - 1964-65 SAN DIEGO CHARGERS (AFL);
   1966-69 MIAMI DOLPHINS (AFL); 1970-74 OAKLAND RAIDERS (AFC)
WARREN, MADISON DEWEY (TENNESSEE) - QBACK - 1968 CINCINNATI BENGALS
   (AFL)
WARREN, MORRISON (ARIZONA STATE) - BACK - 1948 BROOKLYN DODGERS (AAFC)
WARREN - BACK - 1920 HAMMOND PROS
WARRINGTON, CALEB (WILLIAM&MARY & AUBURN) - CENTER - 1946-48 BROOKLYN
   DODGERS (AAFC)
WARWEG, EARL - BACK - 1921 EVANSVILLE CRIMSON GIANTS
WARWICK, EDWARD (PENNSYLVANIA) - BACK - 1936-37 BOSTON SHAMROCKS (AFL)
WARWICK, LONNIE (TENNESSEE TECH) - LB - 1965-69 MINNESOTA VIKINGS;
   1970-72 MINNESOTA VIKINGS (NFC); 1973-74 ATLANTA FALCONS (NFC)
WARZEKA, RONALD (MONTANA STATE) - TACKLE - 1960 OAKLAND RAIDERS (AFL)
WASHINGTON, CLARENCE (ARKANSAS AM&N) - TACKLE - 1969 PITTSBURGH
   STEELERS; 1970 PITTSBURGH STEELERS (AFC)
WASHINGTON, CLYDE (PURDUE) - BACK - 1960-61 BOSTON PATRIOTS (AFL);
   1963-65 NEW YORK JETS (AFL)
WASHINGTON, DAVID (ALCORN A&M) - LB, END - 1970-71 DENVER BRONCOS
   (AFC); 1972-74 BUFFALO BILLS (AFC)
WASHINGTON, DAVID EUGENE (USC) - END - 1968 DENVER BRONCOS (AFL)
WASHINGTON, ERIC (TEXAS-EL PASO) - BACK - 1972-73 ST. LOUIS CARDINALS
   (NFC)
WASHINGTON, EUGENE (MICHIGAN STATE) - END - 1967-69 MINNESOTA
   VIKINGS; 1970-72 MINNESOTA VIKINGS (NFC); 1973 DENVER BRONCOS
   (AFC)
WASHINGTON, FREDERICK (NORTH TEXAS STATE) - TACKLE - 1968 WASHINGTON
   REDSKINS
WASHINGTON, GENE ALDEN (STANFORD) - END - 1969 SAN FRANCISCO 49ERS;
   1970-74 SAN FRANCISCO 49ERS (NFC)
WASHINGTON, JOSEPH (ILLINOIS STATE) - BACK - 1973 ATLANTA FALCONS
   (NFC)
WASHINGTON, KENNETH (UCLA) - BACK - 1946-48 LOS ANGELES RAMS
WASHINGTON, MARK (MORGAN STATE) - BACK - 1970-74 DALLAS COWBOYS (NFC)
WASHINGTON, RICHARD (BETHUNE-COOKMAN) - BACK - 1968 MIAMI DOLPHINS
   (AFL)

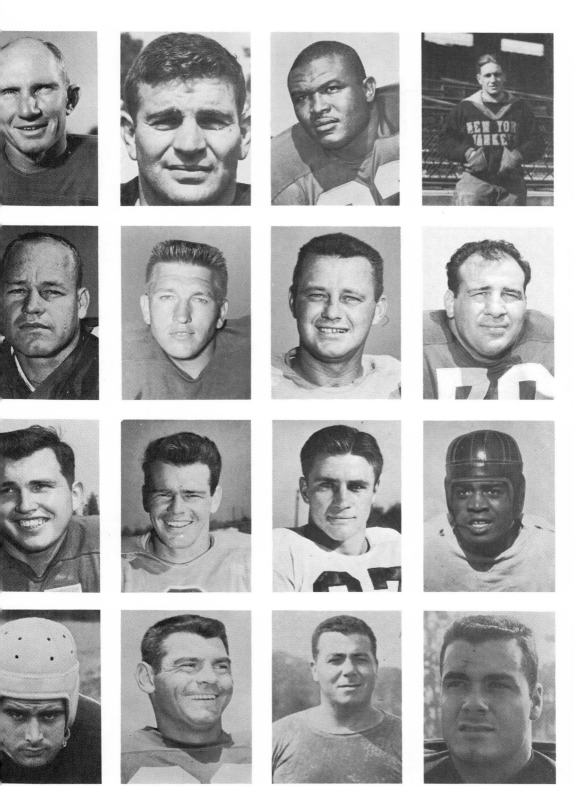

Top row (from left to right): Y. A. Tittle, Bob Toneff, Mel Triplett and Eddie Tryon. *Second row*: Jerry Tubbs, John Unitas, Norman Van Brocklin and Frank Varrichione. *Third row*: Danny Villanueva, Bill Wade, Doak Walker and Ken Washington. *Bottom row*: Bill Walsh, Bobby Walston, Frank Walton and Joe Walton.

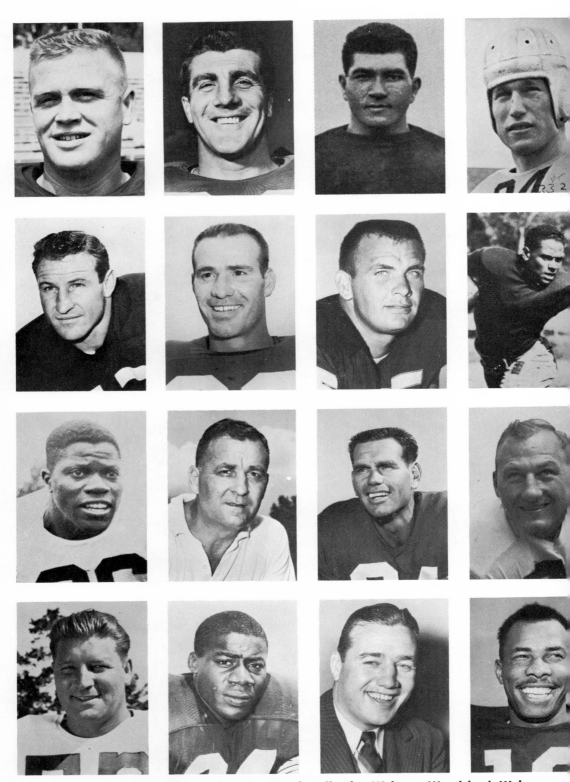

Top row (from left to right): Jim Weatherall, Alex Webster, Woodchuck Welmus and Byron White. *Second row:* Jess Whittenton, Norman Willey, Fred Williams and "Inky" Williams. *Third row:* Bill Willis, George Wilson, Bill Wilson and Al Wistert. *Bottom row:* Alex Wojciechewicz, Willie Wood, Doug Wycoff and "Tank" Younger.

WASHINGTON, RUSSELL (MISSOURI) - TACKLE - 1968-69 SAN DIEGO CHARGERS
    (AFL); 1970-74 SAN DIEGO CHARGERS (AFC)
WASHINGTON, TED (SAN DIEGO STATE) - BACK - 1968 CINCINNATI BENGALS
    (AFL)
WASHINGTON, VICTOR (WYOMING) - BACK - 1971-73 SAN FRANCISCO 49ERS
    (NFC); 1974 HOUSTON OILERS (AFC)
WASICEK, CHARLES (COLGATE) - TACKLE - 1936 ROCHESTER TIGERS (AFL)
WASKIEWICZ, JAMES (WICHITA STATE) - CENTER, LB - 1966-67 NEW YORK
    JETS (AFL); 1969 ATLANTA FALCONS
WASSERBACH, LLOYD (WISCONSIN) - TACKLE - 1946-47 CHICAGO ROCKETS
    (AAFC)
WATERFIELD, ROBERT (UCLA) - QBACK - 1945 CLEVELAND RAMS; 1946-52 LOS
    ANGELES RAMS; 1946, 51 PASSING LEADER; 1947, 49, 51 FIELD GOAL
    LEADER; (1947 TIED WITH CUFF AND HARDER, 1949 TIED WITH PATTON);
    1965 HALL OF FAME
WATERS, CHARLIE (CLEMSON) - BACK - 1970-74 DALLAS COWBOYS (NFC)
WATERS, DALE (FLORIDA) - END - 1931 CLEVELAND INDIANS; 1931
    PORTSMOUTH SPARTANS; 1932 BOSTON BRAVES; 1933 BOSTON REDSKINS
WATFORD, GERALD (ALABAMA) - END - 1953-54 CHICAGO CARDINALS
WATKINS, FORREST (WEST TEXAS STATE) - BACK - 1940-41 PHILADELPHIA
    EAGLES
WATKINS, GORDON (GEORGIA TECH) - TACKLE - 1930 MINNEAPOLIS
    REDJACKETS; 1930 FRANKFORD YELLOWJACKETS; 1931 BROOKLYN DODGERS
WATKINS, LAWRENCE (ALCORN A&M) - BACK - 1969 DETROIT LIONS; 1970-72
    PHILADELPHIA EAGLES (NFC); 1973-74 BUFFALO BILLS (AFC)
WATKINS, ROBERT (OHIO STATE) - BACK - 1955-57 CHICAGO BEARS; 1958
    CHICAGO CARDINALS
WATKINS, THOMAS (IOWA STATE) - BACK - 1961 CLEVELAND BROWNS; 1962-67
    DETROIT LIONS; 1968 PITTSBURGH STEELERS
WATSON, ALLEN (NEWPORT-WALES) - KICKER - 1970 PITTSBURGH STEELERS
    (AFC)
WATSON, DAVID (GEORGIA TECH) - GUARD - 1963-64 BOSTON PATRIOTS (AFL)
WATSON, EDWARD (GRAMBLING) - LB - 1969 HOUSTON OILERS (AFL)
WATSON, GRADY (TEXAS) - BACK - 1922-23 TOLEDO MAROONS; 1924 KENOSHA
    MAROONS; 1924-25 HAMMOND PROS; 1927 BUFFALO BISONS
WATSON, JAMES (PACIFIC) - CENTER - 1945 WASHINGTON REDSKINS
WATSON, JOHN (OKLAHOMA) - TACKLE, GUARD - 1971-74 SAN FRANCISCO 49ERS
    (NFC)
WATSON, JOSEPH (RICE) - CENTER - 1950 DETROIT LIONS
WATSON, PETER (TUFTS) - END - 1972 CINCINNATI BENGALS (AFC)
WATSON, SIDNEY (NORTHEASTERN) - BACK - 1955-57 PITTSBURGH STEELERS;
    1958 WASHINGTON REDSKINS
WATT, JOSEPH (SYRACUSE) - BACK - 1947 BOSTON YANKS; 1947-48 DETROIT
    LIONS; 1949 NEW YORK BULLDOGS
WATT, WALTER (MIAMI) - BACK - 1945 CHICAGO CARDINALS
WATTERS, LEONARD (SPRINGFIELD) - END - 1924 BUFFALO BISONS
WATTERS, ROBERT (LINCOLN-MISSOURI) - END - 1962 NEW YORK TITANS
    (AFL); 1963-64 NEW YORK JETS (AFL)
WATTS, GEORGE (APPLACHIAN STATE) - TACKLE - 1942 WASHINGTON REDSKINS
WAY, CHARLES (PENN STATE) - BACK - 1921 CANTON BULLDOGS; 1924
    FRANKFORD YELLOWJACKETS; 1926 PHILADELPHIA QUAKERS (AFL)
WAYT, RUSSELL (RICE) - LB - 1965 DALLAS COWBOYS
WEAR, ROBERT (PENN STATE) - CENTER - 1942 PHILADELPHIA EAGLES
WEATHERALL, JAMES (OKLAHOMA) - TACKLE - 1955-57 PHILADELPHIA EAGLES;
    1958 WASHINGTON REDSKINS; 1959-60 DETROIT LIONS
WEATHERFORD, JAMES (TENNESSEE) - BACK - 1969 ATLANTA FALCONS
WEATHERLY, GERALD (RICE) - CENTER - 1950, 52-54 CHICAGO BEARS
WEATHERS, CARL (SAN DIEGO STATE) - LB - 1970-71 OAKLAND RAIDERS (AFC)
WEATHERS, GUY (BAYLOR) - GUARD - 1926 BUFFALO RANGERS
WEATHERSPOON, CEPHUS (FORT LEWIS-COLORADO) - END - 1972 NEW ORLEANS
    SAINTS (NFC)
WEATHERWAX, JAMES (LOS ANGELES STATE) - TACKLE - 1966-67, 69 GREEN
    BAY PACKERS
WEAVER, CHARLES (CHICAGO) - GUARD - 1930 CHICAGO CARDINALS; 1930
    PORTSMOUTH SPARTANS
WEAVER, CHARLES (USC) - LB - 1971-74 DETROIT LIONS (NFC)
WEAVER, GARY (CALIFORNIA) - LB - 1973-74 OAKLAND RAIDERS (AFC)
WEAVER, JAMES (CENTRE) - CENTER - 1923 COLUMBUS TIGERS; 1926
    CLEVELAND PANTHERS (AFL)
WEAVER, JOHN (MIAMI-OHIO) - GUARD - 1949 NEW YORK BULLDOGS
WEAVER, LARRYE (FULLERTON JUNIOR) - BACK - 1955 NEW YORK GIANTS

WEAVER, WILLIAM HERMAN (TENNESSEE) - KICKER - 1970-74 DETROIT LIONS
    (NFC)
WEBB, ALLEN (ARNOLD) - BACK - 1961-65 NEW YORK GIANTS
WEBB, ARTHUR (GENESEO WESLEYAN) - TACKLE - 1920 ROCHESTER JEFFERSONS;
    1922 MILWAUKEE BADGERS
WEBB, DONALD (IOWA STATE) - BACK - 1961-62, 64-69 BOSTON PATRIOTS
    (AFL); 1970 BOSTON PATRIOTS (AFC); 1971 NEW ENGLAND PATRIOTS
    (AFC)
WEBB, GEORGE (TEXAS TECH) - END - 1943 BROOKLYN DODGERS
WEBB, KENNETH (PRESBYTERIAN) - BACK - 1958-62 DETROIT LIONS; 1963
    CLEVELAND BROWNS
WEBBER, HARRY (MORNINGSIDE) - END - 1922 ROCK ISLAND INDEPENDENTS
WEBBER, HOWARD (KANSAS STATE) - END - 1924-25 KANSAS CITY COWBOYS;
    1925, 27 CLEVELAND BULLDOGS; 1926 HARTFORD BLUES; 1926 NEW YORK
    GIANTS; 1928 GREEN BAY PACKERS; 1930 PROVIDENCE STEAMROLLERS;
    1930 NEWARK TORNADOS
WEBER, CHARLES (COLGATE) - GUARD - 1926 BROOKLYN LIONS
WEBER, CHARLES (WEST CHESTER STATE) - LB - 1955-56 CLEVELAND BROWNS;
    1956-58 CHICAGO CARDINALS; 1959-61 PHILADELPHIA EAGLES
WEBER, RICHARD (ST. LOUIS UNIV.) - BACK - 1945 DETROIT LIONS
WEBSTER, ALEX (NORTH CAROLINA STATE) - BACK - 1955-64 NEW YORK GIANTS
WEBSTER, DAVID (PRAIRIE VIEW) - BACK - 1960-61 DALLAS TEXANS (AFL)
WEBSTER, FREDERICK (COLGATE) - BACK - 1924 RACINE LEGION
WEBSTER, GEORGE (MICHIGAN STATE) - LB - 1967-69 HOUSTON OILERS (AFL);
    1970-72 HOUSTON OILERS (AFC); 1972-73 PITTSBURGH STEELERS (AFC);
    1974 NEW ENGLAND PATRIOTS (AFC)
WEBSTER, MIKE (WISCONSIN) - CENTER, GUARD - 1974 PITTSBURGH STEELERS
    (AFC)
WEBSTER, TIM (ARKANSAS) - KICKER - 1971 GREEN BAY PACKERS (NFC)
WEDEL, RICHARD (WAKE FOREST) - GUARD - 1948 CHICAGO CARDINALS
WEDEMEYER, HERMAN (ST. MARY'S OF CAL.) - BACK - 1948 LOS ANGELES DONS
    (AAFC); 1949 BALTIMORE COLTS (AAFC)
WEED, THURLOW (OHIO STATE) - KICKER - 1955 PITTSBURGH STEELERS
WEEDON, DONALD (TEXAS) - GUARD - 1947 PHILADELPHIA EAGLES
WEEKS, GEORGE (ALABAMA) - END - 1944 BROOKLYN TIGERS
WEGENER, WILLIAM (MISSOURI) - END - 1962-63 HOUSTON OILERS (AFL)
WEGER, MICHAEL (BOWLING GREEN) - BACK - 1967-69 DETROIT LIONS;
    1970-73 DETROIT LIONS (NFC)
WEGERT, THEODORE - BACK - 1955-56 PHILADELPHIA EAGLES; 1960 NEW YORK
    TITANS (AFL); 1960 DENVER BRONCOS (AFL); 1960 BUFFALO BILLS (AFL)
WEHBA, RAYMOND (USC) - END - 1943 BROOKLYN DODGERS; 1944 GREEN BAY
    PACKERS
WEHRLI, ROGER (MISSOURI) - BACK - 1969 ST. LOUIS CARDINALS; 1970-74
    ST. LOUIS CARDINALS (NFC)
WEIMER, HOWARD (WILMINGTON) - BACK - 1929 BUFFALO BISONS; 1930
    BROOKLYN DODGERS; 1931 CLEVELAND INDIANS
WEIMER - 1920 COLUMBUS PANHANDLES
WEINBERG, HENRY (DUQUESNE) - GUARD - 1934 PITTSBURGH PIRATES
WEINBERG, SAUL (WESTERN RESERVE) - TACKLE - 1923 CLEVELAND INDIANS
WEINER, ALBERT (MUHLENBERG) - BACK - 1934 PHILADELPHIA EAGLES
WEINER, ARTHUR (NORTH CAROLINA) - END - 1950 NEW YORK YANKS
WEINER, BERNARD (KANSAS STATE) - TACKLE - 1942 BROOKLYN DODGERS
WEINMEISTER, ARNOLD (WASHINGTON) - TACKLE - 1948-49 NEW YORK YANKEES
    (AAFC); 1950-53 NEW YORK GIANTS
WEINSTOCK, ISADORE (PITTSBURGH) - QBACK - 1935 PHILADELPHIA EAGLES;
    1937-38 PITTSBURGH PIRATES
WEIR, EDWARD (NEBRASKA) - TACKLE - 1926-28 FRANKFORD YELLOWJACKETS
WEIR, JOSEPH (NEBRASKA) - END - 1927 FRANKFORD YELLOWJACKETS
WEIR, SAMUEL (ARKANSAS STATE) - BACK - 1965 HOUSTON OILERS (AFL);
    1966 NEW YORK JETS (AFL)
WEISACOSKY, EDWARD (MIAMI) - LB - 1967 NEW YORK GIANTS; 1968-69 MIAMI
    DOLPHINS (AFL); 1970 MIAMI DOLPHINS (AFC); 1971-72 NEW ENGLAND
    PATRIOTS (AFC)
WEISENBAUGH, HENRY (PITTSBURGH) - BACK - 1935 PITTSBURGH PIRATES;
    1935-36 BOSTON REDSKINS
WEISGERBER, RICHARD (VILLANOVA) - QBACK - 1938-40, 42 GREEN BAY
    PACKERS
WEISS, HOWARD (WISCONSIN) - BACK - 1939-40 DETROIT LIONS; 1941
    MILWAUKEE CHIEFS (AFL)
WEISS, JOHN - END - 1944-47 NEW YORK GIANTS
WEISS, JULES - CENTER - 1919 TOLEDO MAROONS

WELCH, CLAXTON (OREGON) - BACK - 1969 DALLAS COWBOYS; 1970-71 DALLAS
    COWBOYS (NFC); 1973 NEW ENGLAND PATRIOTS (AFC)
WELCH, GILBERT (PITTSBURGH) - BACK - 1928 NEW YORK YANKEES; 1929
    PROVIDENCE STEAMROILERS
WELCH, HOWARD - END - 1919 AKRON PROS
WELCH, JAMES (SMU) - BACK - 1960-67 BALTIMORE COLTS; 1968 DETROIT
    LIONS
WELDIN, HAROLD (NORTHWESTERN) - CENTER - 1934 ST. LOUIS GUNNERS
WELDON, JOHN (LAFAYETTE) - BACK - 1920-22 BUFFALO ALL-AMERICANS
WELDON, LAWRENCE (PRESBYTERIAN) - BACK - 1944-45 WASHINGTON REDSKINS
WELLBORN, JOSEPH (TEXAS A&M) - CENTER - 1966 NEW YORK GIANTS
WELLER, LOUIS (HASKELL) - BACK - 1933 BOSTON REDSKINS
WELLER, RAYMOND (NEBRASKA) - TACKLE - 1923 ST. LOUIS BROWNS; 1924
    MILWAUKEE BADGERS; 1926-27 CHICAGO CARDINALS; 1928 FRANKFORD
    YELLOWJACKETS
WELLS, DONALD (GEORGIA) - END - 1946-49 GREEN BAY PACKERS
WELLS, HAROLD (PURDUE) - LB - 1965-68 PHILADELPHIA EAGLES; 1969 NEW
    YORK GIANTS
WELLS, JOEL (CLEMSON) - BACK - 1961 NEW YORK GIANTS
WELLS, ROBERT (J.C.SMITH) - TACKLE - 1968-69 SAN DIEGO CHARGERS
    (AFL); 1970 SAN DIEGO CHARGERS (AFC)
WELLS, TERRENCE (SOUTHERN MISSISSIPPI) - BACK - 1974 HOUSTON OILERS
    (AFC)
WELLS, WARREN (TEXAS SOUTHERN) - END - 1964 DETROIT LIONS; 1967-69
    OAKLAND RAIDERS (AFL); 1970 OAKLAND RAIDERS (AFC)
WELLS, WILLIAM (MICHIGAN STATE) - BACK - 1954, 56-57 WASHINGTON
    REDSKINS; 1957 PITTSBURGH STEELERS; 1958 PHILADELPHIA EAGLES;
    1960 BOSTON PATRIOTS (AFL)
WELMUS, WOODCHUCK (CARLISLE) - END - 1923 OORANG INDIANS
WELSH, JAMES (COLGATE) - GUARD - 1924-25 FRANKFORD YELLOWJACKETS;
    1926 POTTSVILLE MAROONS
WELTMAN, LAWRENCE (SYRACUSE) - BACK - 1922 ROCHESTER JEFFERSONS
WEMPLE, DONALD (COLGATE) - END - 1941 BROOKLYN DODGERS
WENDELL, MARTIN (NOTRE DAME) - GUARD - 1949 CHICAGO HORNETS (AAFC)
WENDLER, HAROLD (OHIO STATE) - BACK - 1926 AKRON PROS
WENDLICK, JOSEPH (OREGON STATE) - END - 1940 PHILADELPHIA EAGLES;
    1941 PITTSBURGH STEELERS
WENDRYHOSKI, JOSEPH (ILLINOIS) - CENTER - 1964-66 LOS ANGELES RAMS;
    1967-68 NEW ORLEANS SAINTS
WENDT, KENNETH (MARQUETTE) - GUARD - 1932 CHICAGO CARDINALS
WENIG, OBE (MORNINGSIDE) - END - 1920-22 ROCK ISLAND INDEPENDENTS
WENKE, ADOLPH (NEBRASKA) - TACKLE - 1923 MILWAUKEE BADGERS
WENTWORTH, SHIRLEY (NEW HAMPSHIRE) - BACK - 1925-26 PROVIDENCE
    STEAMROLLERS; 1929 BOSTON BRAVES
WENTZ, BRYON (PENN STATE) - BACK - 1925-28 POTTSVILLE MAROONS
WENZEL, RALPH (SAN DIEGO STATE) - GUARD - 1966-69 PITTSBURGH
    STEELERS; 1970 PITTSBURGH STEELERS (AFC); 1972-73 SAN DIEGO
    CHARGERS (AFC)
WENZEL, RALPH (TULANE) - END - 1942 PITTSBURGH STEELERS
WERDER, GERARD (PENN STATE) - BACK - 1920 BUFFALO ALL-AMERICANS
WERDER, RICHARD (GEORGETOWN) - GUARD - 1948 NEW YORK YANKEES (AAFC)
WERL, ROBERT (MIAMI) - END - 1966 NEW YORK JETS (AFL)
WERNER, CLYDE (WASHINGTON) - LB - 1970, 72-74 KANSAS CITY CHIEFS (AFC)
WERNER, SOX (CENTRAL MISSOURI STATE) - BACK - 1923 ST. LOUIS BROWNS
WERSCHING, RAIMOND (CALIFORNIA) - KICKER - 1973-74 SAN DIEGO CHARGERS
    (AFC)
WERWAISS, ELBERT (DEAN JUNIOR) - TACKLE - 1926 HARTFORD BLUES
WESBECHER, ALOYSIUS (WASHINGTON&JEFFERSON) - TACKLE - 1919 MASSILLON
    TIGERS; 1920 CLEVELAND PANTHERS
WESLEY, LECIL (ALABAMA) - CENTER - 1926-27 PROVIDENCE STEAMROLLERS;
    1928 NEW YORK GIANTS; 1930 PORTSMOUTH SPARTANS
WEST, CHARLES (TEXAS-EL PASO) - BACK - 1968-69 MINNESOTA VIKINGS;
    1970-73 MINNESOTA VIKINGS (NFC); 1974 DETROIT LIONS (NFC)
WEST, CHARLES (WASHINGTON&JEFFERSON) - BACK - 1924 AKRON PROS
WEST, D. BELFORD (COLGATE) - TACKLE - 1921 CANTON BULLDOGS
WEST, DAVID (CENTRAL STATE-OHIO) - BACK - 1963 NEW YORK JETS (AFL)
WEST, EDWARD (OHIO STATE) - END - 1940 COLUMBUS BULLIES (AFL); 1941
    CINCINNATI BENGALS (AFL)
WEST, HODGES (TENNESSEE) - TACKLE - 1941 PHILADELPHIA EAGLES
WEST, JOHN (IOWA STATE) - CENTER - 1940 MILWAUKEE CHIEFS (AFL)

WEST, MELVIN (MISSOURI) - BACK - 1961 BOSTON PATRIOTS (AFL); 1961-62
    NEW YORK TITANS (AFL)
WEST, PAT (USC) - BACK - 1945 CLEVELAND RAMS; 1946-48 LOS ANGELES
    RAMS; 1948 GREEN BAY PACKERS
WEST, ROBERT (SAN DIEGO STATE) - END - 1972-73 KANSAS CITY CHIEFS
    (AFC); 1974 SAN FRANCISCO 49ERS (NFC)
WEST, STANLEY (OKLAHOMA) - GUARD - 1950-54 LOS ANGELES RAMS; 1955 NEW
    YORK GIANTS; 1956-57 CHICAGO CARDINALS
WEST, WALTER (PITTSBURGH) - QBACK - 1944 CLEVELAND RAMS
WEST, WILLIAM (TENNESSEE STATE) - BACK - 1972 DENVER BRONCOS (AFC)
WEST, WILLIE (OREGON) - BACK - 1960-61 ST. LOUIS CARDINALS; 1962-63
    BUFFALO BILLS (AFL); 1964 DENVER BRONCOS (AFL); 1964-65 NEW YORK
    JETS (AFL); 1966-68 MIAMI DOLPHINS (AFL)
WESTFALL, EDGAR (OHIO WESLEYAN) - BACK - 1932 BOSTON BRAVES; 1933
    BOSTON REDSKINS; 1933 PITTSBURGH PIRATES
WESTFALL, ROBERT (MICHIGAN) - BACK - 1944-47 DETROIT LIONS
WESTMORELAND, RICHARD (NORTH CAROLINA A&T) - BACK - 1963-65 SAN DIEGO
    CHARGERS (AFL); 1966-69 MIAMI DOLPHINS (AFL); 1967 INTERCEPTION
    LEADER (AFL); (TIED WITH FARR AND JANIK)
WESTOUPAL, JOSEPH (NEBRASKA) - CENTER - 1926 KANSAS CITY COWBOYS;
    1928 DETROIT WOLVERINES; 1929-30 NEW YORK GIANTS
WETOSKA, ROBERT (NOTRE DAME) - TACKLE, CENTER - 1960-69 CHICAGO BEARS
WETTERLUND, CHESTER (ILLINOIS WESLEYAN) - BACK - 1942 DETROIT LIONS
WETTSTEIN, MAX (FLORIDA STATE) - END - 1966 DENVER BRONCOS (AFL)
WETZ, HARLAN (TEXAS) - TACKLE - 1947 BROOKLYN DODGERS (AAFC)
WETZEL, DAMON (OHIO STATE) - BACK - 1935 CHICAGO BEARS; 1935
    PITTSBURGH PIRATES; 1936 CLEVELAND RAMS (AFL)
WEXLER, WILLIAM (NEW YORK UNIV.) - CENTER - 1930 STATEN ISLAND
    STAPELTONS
WHALEN, JAMES (BOSTON COLLEGE) - END - 1965-69 BOSTON PATRIOTS (AFL);
    1970-71 DENVER BRONCOS (AFC); 1971 PHILADELPHIA EAGLES (NFC)
WHALEN, JERALD (CANISIUS) - CENTER - 1948 BUFFALO BILLS (AAFC)
WHALEN, THOMAS (CATHOLIC) - BACK - 1933 PITTSBURGH PIRATES
WHALEN, WILLIAM (LEHIGH) - BACK - 1919 MASSILLON TIGERS; 1919 TOLEDO
    MAROONS
WHALEN, WILLIAM - GUARD - 1920-24 CHICAGO CARDINALS
WHALEY, BENJAMIN (VIRGINIA STATE) - GUARD - 1949 LOS ANGELES DONS
    (AAFC)
WHAM, THOMAS (FURMAN) - END - 1949-51 CHICAGO CARDINALS
WHARTON, HOGAN (HOUSTON) - GUARD - 1960-63 HOUSTON OILERS (AFL)
WHATLEY, JAMES (ALABAMA) - TACKLE - 1936-38 BROOKLYN DODGERS
WHEELER, ERNEST (NORTH DAKOTA STATE) - BACK - 1939 PITTSBURGH
    STEELERS; 1939, 42 CHICAGO CARDINALS; 1940 BOSTON BEARS (AFL);
    1941 BUFFALO TIGERS (AFL)
WHEELER, KYLE (RIPON) - END - 1921-23 GREEN BAY PACKERS
WHEELER, MANCH (MAINE) - QBACK - 1962 BUFFALO BILLS (AFL)
WHEELER, TED (WEST TEXAS STATE) - END, GUARD - 1967-68 ST. LOUIS
    CARDINALS; 1970 CHICAGO BEARS (NFC)
WHEELER, WAYNE (ALABAMA) - END - 1974 CHICAGO BEARS (NFC)
WHEELRIGHT, ERNEST (SOUTHERN ILLINOIS) - BACK - 1964-65 NEW YORK
    GIANTS; 1966-67 ATLANTA FALCONS; 1967-69 NEW ORLEANS SAINTS;
    1970 NEW ORLEANS SAINTS (NFC)
WHELAN, THOMAS (GEORGETOWN) - CENTER - 1919 MASSILLON TIGERS; 1919-20
    CANTON BULLDOGS; 1921 CLEVELAND INDIANS
WHIPPLE, RAYMOND (NOTRE DAME) - END - 1919 DETROIT HERALDS
WHIRE, JOHN (GEORGIA) - BACK - 1933 PHILADELPHIA EAGLES
WHITAKER, CRESTON (NORTH TEXAS STATE) - END - 1972 NEW ORLEANS SAINTS
    (NFC)
WHITCOMB, FRANK (SYRACUSE) - GUARD - 1921 ROCHESTER JEFFERSONS
WHITE, ANDRE (FLORIDA A&M) - END - 1967 DENVER BRONCOS (AFL); 1968
    CINCINNATI BENGALS (AFL); 1968 SAN DIEGO CHARGERS (AFL)
WHITE, ARTHUR (ALABAMA) - GUARD - 1937-39, 45 NEW YORK GIANTS;
    1940-41 CHICAGO CARDINALS
WHITE, BYRON "WHIZZER" (COLORADO) - BACK - 1938 PITTSBURGH PIRATES;
    1940-41 DETROIT LIONS; 1938, 40 RUSHING LEADER
WHITE, DWIGHT (EAST TEXAS STATE) - END - 1971-74 PITTSBURGH STEELERS
    (AFC)
WHITE, EDWARD (CALIFORNIA) - GUARD - 1969 MINNESOTA VIKINGS; 1970-74
    MINNESOTA VIKINGS (NFC)
WHITE, ELLERY - BACK - 1926 LOS ANGELES BUCCANEERS
WHITE, EUGENE (FLORIDA A&M) - BACK - 1962 OAKLAND RAIDERS (AFL)

WHITE, EUGENE (GEORGIA) - END - 1954 GREEN BAY PACKERS
WHITE, EUGENE (INDIANA) - GUARD - 1946 BUFFALO BISONS (AAFC)
WHITE, FREEMAN (NEBRASKA) - END - 1966-69 NEW YORK GIANTS
WHITE, HAROLD (SYRACUSE) - GUARD - 1919 AKRON PROS
WHITE, HARVEY (CLEMSON) - QBACK - 1960 BOSTON PATRIOTS (AFL)
WHITE, JAMES (COLORADO STATE) - END - 1972 NEW ENGLAND PATRIOTS
     (AFC); 1974 HOUSTON OILERS (AFC)
WHITE, JAMES (NOTRE DAME) - TACKLE - 1946-50 NEW YORK GIANTS
WHITE, JAN (OHIO STATE) - END - 1971-72 BUFFALO BILLS (AFC)
WHITE, JEFFREY (TEXAS-EL PASO) - KICKER - 1973 NEW ENGLAND PATRIOTS
     (AFC)
WHITE, JERIS (HAWAII) - BACK - 1974 MIAMI DOLPHINS (AFC)
WHITE, JOHN (TEXAS SOUTHERN) - END - 1960-61 HOUSTON OILERS (AFL);
     1962 OAKLAND RAIDERS (AFL)
WHITE, LEE (WEBER STATE) - BACK - 1968-69 NEW YORK JETS (AFL); 1970
     NEW YORK JETS (AFC); 1971 LOS ANGELES RAMS (NFC); 1972 SAN DIEGO
     CHARGERS (AFC)
WHITE, LOREN ROBERT (OHIO STATE) - BACK - 1960 HOUSTON OILERS (AFL)
WHITE, PAUL (MICHIGAN) - BACK - 1947 PITTSBURGH STEELERS
WHITE, PAUL (TEXAS-EL PASO) - BACK - 1970-71 ST. LOUIS CARDINALS (NFC)
WHITE, PHILIP (OKLAHOMA) - BACK - 1924-25 KANSAS CITY COWBOYS; 1925,
     27 NEW YORK GIANTS; 1926 CHICAGO BULLS (AFL)
WHITE, ROBERT - END - 1923 LOUISVILLE BRECKS
WHITE, ROBERT (STANFORD) - BACK - 1951-52 SAN FRANCISCO 49ERS; 1955
     CLEVELAND BROWNS; 1955 BALTIMORE COLTS
WHITE, ROBERT DARYL (NEBRASKA) - GUARD - 1974 DETROIT LIONS (NFC)
WHITE, ROY (VALPARAISO & DANIEL BAKER-TEXAS) - BACK - 1924-25, 27-29
     CHICAGO BEARS; 1926 CHICAGO BULLS (AFL)
WHITE, ROY (NYU) - END - 1927 BUFFALO BISONS
WHITE, SHERMAN (CALIFORNIA) - END - 1972-74 CINCINNATI BENGALS (AFC)
WHITE, STANLEY (OHIO STATE) - LB - 1972-74 BALTIMORE COLTS (AFC)
WHITE, THOMAS "ALLIE" (TCU) - TACKLE - 1939 PHILADELPHIA EAGLES
WHITE, WILBUR (COLORADO A&M) - BACK - 1935 BROOKLYN DODGERS; 1936
     DETROIT LIONS
WHITE, WILBUR (MARIETTA) - END - 1922-23 TOLEDO MAROONS
WHITE, WILFORD (ARIZONA STATE) - BACK - 1951-52 CHICAGO BEARS
WHITED, MARVIN (OKLAHOMA) - BACK - 1942, 45 WASHINGTON REDSKINS
WHITEHEAD, RUBIN ANGUS (FLORIDA STATE) - BACK - 1961-68 SAN DIEGO
     CHARGERS (AFL)
WHITEHEAD, WALKER - BACK - 1921-22 EVANSVILLE CRIMSON GIANTS
WHITEMAN, SAMUEL (MISSOURI) - BACK - 1926 CHICAGO BULLS (AFL)
WHITFIELD, A. D. (NORTH TEXAS STATE) - BACK - 1965 DALLAS COWBOYS;
     1966-68 WASHINGTON REDSKINS
WHITLEY, HALL (TEXAS A&I) - LB - 1960 NEW YORK TITANS (AFL)
WHITLOW, KENNETH (RICE) - CENTER - 1946 MIAMI SEAHAWKS (AAFC)
WHITLOW, ROBERT (ARIZONA) - CENTER - 1960-61 WASHINGTON REDSKINS;
     1961-65 DETROIT LIONS; 1966 ATLANTA FALCONS; 1968 CLEVELAND
     BROWNS
WHITMAN, S. J. LAVERNE (TULSA) - BACK - 1951-53 CHICAGO CARDINALS;
     1953-54 CHICAGO BEARS
WHITMYER, NATHANIEL (WASHINGTON) - BACK - 1963 LOS ANGELES RAMS; 1966
     SAN DIEGO CHARGERS (AFL)
WHITSELL, DAVID (INDIANA) - BACK - 1958-60 DETROIT LIONS; 1961-66
     CHICAGO BEARS; 1967-69 NEW ORLEANS SAINTS; 1967 INTERCEPTION
     LEADER; (TIED WITH BARNEY)
WHITTENTON, URSHELL "JESS" (TEXAS WESTERN) - BACK - 1956-57 LOS
     ANGELES RAMS; 1958-64 GREEN BAY PACKERS
WHITTINGHAM, FREDERICK (CALIFORNIA POLYTECH) - LB - 1964 LOS ANGELES
     RAMS; 1966 PHILADELPHIA EAGLES; 1967-68 NEW ORLEANS SAINTS; 1969
     DALLAS COWBOYS; 1970 BOSTON PATRIOTS (AFC); 1971 PHILADELPHIA
     EAGLES (NFC)
WHITTINGTON, COLUMBUS "C.L." (PRAIRIE VIEW) - BACK - 1974 HOUSTON
     OILERS (AFC)
WIATRAK, JOHN (WASHINGTON) - CENTER - 1939 DETROIT LIONS
WIBERG, OSCAR (NEBRASKA WESLEYAN) - BACK - 1927 CLEVELAND BULLDOGS;
     1928 DETROIT WOLVERINES; 1930 NEW YORK GIANTS; 1932 BROOKLYN
     DODGERS; 1933 CINCINNATI REDS
WICKERSHAM, HAROLD (TULSA) - QBACK - 1937 LOS ANGELES BULLDOGS (AFL)
WICKERT, TOM (WASHINGTON STATE) - TACKLE - 1974 MIAMI DOLPHINS (AFC)
WICKETT, LLOYD (OREGON STATE) - TACKLE - 1943, 46 DETROIT LIONS

WICKS, ROBERT (UTAH STATE) - END - 1972 ST. LOUIS CARDINALS (NFC); 1974 GREEN BAY PACKERS (NFC); 1974 NEW ORLEANS SAINTS (NFC)
WIDBY, GEORGE RONALD (TENNESSEE) - KICKER - 1968-69 DALLAS COWBOYS; 1970-71 DALLAS COWBOYS (NFC); 1972-73 GREEN BAY PACKERS (NFC)
WIDERQUIST, CHESTER% (WASHINGTON&JEFFERSON) - TACKLE - 1923-24 MILWAUKEE BADGERS; 1925 ROCK ISLAND INDEPENDENTS; 1926 ROCK ISLAND INDEPENDENTS (AFL); 1926, 28 CHICAGO CARDINALS; 1928 DETROIT WOLVERINES; 1929 MINNEAPOLIS REDJACKETS
WIDSETH, EDWIN (MINNESOTA) - TACKLE - 1937-40 NEW YORK GIANTS
WIECZOREK, JOHN (DETROIT) - BACK - 1937 NEW YORK YANKS (AFL)
WIEDICH, RALPH (EMPORIA STATE-KANSAS) - TACKLE - 1924 KANSAS CITY COWBOYS; 1926 ROCK ISLAND INDEPENDENTS (AFL)
WIEHL, JOSEPH (DUQUESNE) - TACKLE - 1935 PITTSBURGH PIRATES
WIESE, ROBERT (MICHIGAN) - BACK - 1947-48 DETROIT LIONS
WIETECHA, RAYMOND (NORTHWESTERN) - CENTER - 1953-62 NEW YORK GIANTS
WIETHE, JOHN (XAVIER-OHIO) - GUARD - 1939-42 DETROIT LIONS
WIGGIN, PAUL (STANFORD) - END - 1957-67 CLEVELAND BROWNS
WIGGS, EUGENE - GUARD - 1921 LOUISVILLE BRECKS
WIGGS, HUBERT (VANDERBILT) - BACK - 1921-23 LOUISVILLE BRECKS
WIGHTKIN, WILLIAM (NOTRE DAME) - END - 1950-57 CHICAGO BEARS
WILCOX, EDWARD (SWARTHMORE) - BACK - 1926-27 FRANKFORD YELLOWJACKETS
WILBUR, JOHN (STANFORD) - GUARD - 1966-69 DALLAS COWBOYS; 1970 LOS ANGELES RAMS (NFC); 1971-74 WASHINGTON REDSKINS (NFC)
WILBURN, JOHN "J.R." (SOUTH CAROLINA) - END - 1966-69 PITTSBURGH STEELERS; 1970 PITTSBURGH STEELERS (AFC)
WILCOX, DAVID (OREGON) - LB - 1964-69 SAN FRANCISCO 49ERS; 1970-74 SAN FRANCISCO 49ERS (NFC)
WILCOX, JOHN (OKLAHOMA) - TACKLE - 1926 BUFFALO RANGERS; 1930 STATEN ISLAND STAPELTONS
WILCOX, JOHN (OREGON) - TACKLE - 1960 PHILADELPHIA EAGLES
WILDE, GEORGE (TEXAS A&M) - BACK - 1947 WASHINGTON REDSKINS
WILDER, ALBERT (NORTH CAROLINA STATE) - END - 1964-67 NEW YORK JETS (AFL)
WILDER, HAROLD (NEBRASKA) - GUARD - 1923 ST. LOUIS BROWNS
WILDER, NEWELL (COLUMBIA) - CENTER - 1936 NEW YORK YANKS (AFL)
WILDUNG, RICHARD (MINNESOTA) - GUARD - 1946-51, 53 GREEN BAY PACKERS
WILE, RUSSELL (MINNESOTA) - END - 1940 BUFFALO INDIANS (AFL)
WILEY, JOHN (WAYNESBURG) - TACKLE - 1946-50 PITTSBURGH STEELERS
WILGING, COLEMAN (XAVIER) - TACKLE - 1934 CINCINNATI REDS
WILKE, ROBERT (NOTRE DAME) - BACK - 1937 CINCINNATI BENGALS (AFL)
WILKERSON, BASIL (OKLAHOMA CITY UNIV.) - END - 1932 STATEN ISLAND STAPELTONS; 1932 BOSTON BRAVES; 1934 CINCINNATI REDS
WILKERSON, DOUGLAS (NORTH CAROLINA CENTRAL) - GUARD, END - 1970 HOUSTON OILERS (AFC); 1971-74 SAN DIEGO CHARGERS (AFC)
WILKIN, WILBUR (ST. MARY'S OF CAL.) - TACKLE - 1938-43 WASHINGTON REDSKINS; 1946 CHICAGO ROCKETS (AAFC)
WILKINS, RICHARD (OREGON) - END - 1949 LOS ANGELES DONS (AAFC); 1952 DALLAS TEXANS; 1954 NEW YORK GIANTS
WILKINS, ROY (GEORGIA) - END - 1958-59 LOS ANGELES RAMS; 1960-61 WASHINGTON REDSKINS
WILKINS, THEODORE (INDIANA) - END - 1925 GREEN BAY PACKERS
WILKINSON, ROBERT (UCLA) - END - 1951-52 NEW YORK GIANTS
WILL, ERWIN (DAYTON) - TACKLE - 1965 PHILADELPHIA EAGLES
WILLARD, KENNETH (NORTH CAROLINA) - BACK - 1965-69 SAN FRANCISCO 49ERS; 1970-73 SAN FRANCISCO 49ERS (NFC); 1974 ST. LOUIS CARDINALS (NFC)
WILLEGAILE, HENRY (CARLETON) - BACK - 1929 MINNEAPOLIS REDJACKETS
WILLERT - GUARD - 1922 HAMMOND PROS
WILLEY, NORMAN (MARSHALL) - END - 1950-57 PHILADELPHIA EAGLES
WILLIAMS, A. D. (PACIFIC) - END - 1959 GREEN BAY PACKERS; 1960 CLEVELAND BROWNS; 1961 MINNESOTA VIKINGS
WILLIAMS, ARTHUR (CONNECTICUT) - BACK - 1928-31 PROVIDENCE STEAMROLLERS; 1932 BROOKLYN DODGERS
WILLIAMS, BOBBY RAY (CENTRAL OKLAHOMA) - BACK - 1966-67 ST. LOUIS CARDINALS; 1969 DETROIT LIONS; 1970-71 DETROIT LIONS (NFC)
WILLIAMS, BOYD (SYRACUSE) - CENTER - 1947 PHILADELPHIA EAGLES
WILLIAMS, BURTON "CY" (FLORIDA) - GUARD - 1926 NEWARK BEARS (AFL); 1929-30 STATEN ISLAND STAPELTONS; 1932 BROOKLYN DODGERS
WILLIAMS, CHARLES (ARKANSAS A&M) - BACK - 1968 CINCINNATI BENGALS (AFL)

WILLIAMS, CHARLES DONELL (PRAIRIE VIEW) - END - 1970 LOS ANGELES RAMS
    (NFC)
WILLIAMS, CLARENCE "SWEENY" (PRAIRIE VIEW) - END - 1970-74 GREEN BAY
    PACKERS (NFC)
WILLIAMS, CLARENCE "CLANCY" (WASHINGTON ST.) - BACK - 1965-69 LOS
    ANGELES RAMS; 1970-72 LOS ANGELES RAMS (NFC)
WILLIAMS, CLYDE (GEORGIA TECH) - TACKLE - 1935 PHILADELPHIA EAGLES;
    1936 BROOKLYN TIGERS (AFL)
WILLIAMS, CLYDE (SOUTHERN) - TACKLE - 1967-69 ST. LOUIS CARDINALS;
    1970-71 ST. LOUIS CARDINALS (NFC)
WILLIAMS, DANIEL (ST. CLOUD STATE-MINNESOTA) - GUARD - 1923-25 DULUTH
    KELLEYS; 1926-27 DULUTH ESKIMOS
WILLIAMS, DAVID (WASHINGTON) - END - 1967-69 ST. LOUIS CARDINALS;
    1970-71 ST. LOUIS CARDINALS (NFC); 1972-73 SAN DIEGO CHARGERS
    (AFC); 1973 PITTSBURGH STEELERS (AFC)
WILLIAMS, DELANO (FLORIDA STATE) - GUARD,TACKLE,CENTER - 1967-69 NEW
    ORLEANS SAINTS; 1970-73 NEW ORLEANS SAINTS (NFC)
WILLIAMS, DELVIN (KANSAS) - BACK - 1974 SAN FRANCISCO 49ERS (NFC)
WILLIAMS, DONALD (TEXAS) - GUARD - 1941 PITTSBURGH STEELERS
WILLIAMS, ED (LANGSTON) - BACK - 1974 CINCINNATI BENGALS (AFC)
WILLIAMS, ELLERY (SANTA CLARA) - END - 1950 NEW YORK GIANTS
WILLIAMS, ERWIN (MARYLAND STATE) - END - 1969 PITTSBURGH STEELERS
WILLIAMS, FRANK (PEPPERDINE) - BACK - 1961 LOS ANGELES RAMS
WILLIAMS, FRANK (UTAH STATE) - BACK - 1948 NEW YORK GIANTS
WILLIAMS, FRED (ARKANSAS) - TACKLE - 1952-63 CHICAGO BEARS; 1964-65
    WASHINGTON REDSKINS
WILLIAMS, GARLAND (GEORGIA) - TACKLE - 1947-48 BROOKLYN DODGERS
    (AAFC); 1949 CHICAGO HORNETS (AAFC)
WILLIAMS, HOWARD (HOWARD-D.C.) - BACK - 1962-63 GREEN BAY PACKERS;
    1963 SAN FRANCISCO 49ERS; 1964-69 OAKLAND RAIDERS (AFL)
WILLIAMS, IVAN (GEORGIA TECH) - BACK - 1926 NEWARK BEARS (AFL); 1929
    STATEN ISLAND STAPELTONS
WILLIAMS, JACOB (TCU) - TACKLE - 1929-33 CHICAGO CARDINALS
WILLIAMS, JAMES (ALCORN A&M) - BACK - 1968 CINCINNATI BENGALS (AFL)
WILLIAMS, JAY "INKY" (BROWN) - END - 1921 CANTON BULLDOGS; 1921-26
    HAMMOND PROS; 1924 KENOSHA MAROONS; 1924 DAYTON TRIANGLES; 1925
    CLEVELAND BULLDOGS
WILLIAMS, JEFFREY (OKLAHOMA STATE) - BACK - 1966 MINNESOTA VIKINGS
WILLIAMS, JEROME (WASHINGTON STATE) - BACK - 1949-52 LOS ANGELES
    RAMS; 1953-54 PHILADELPHIA EAGLES
WILLIAMS, JOE (WYOMING) - BACK - 1971 DALLAS COWBOYS (NFC); 1972 NEW
    ORLEANS SAINTS (NFC)
WILLIAMS, JOEL (TEXAS) - CENTER - 1948 SAN FRANCISCO 49ERS (AAFC);
    1950 BALTIMORE COLTS
WILLIAMS, JOHN (AUBURN) - CENTER - 1942 PHILADELPHIA EAGLES; 1946
    MIAMI SEAHAWKS (AAFC)
WILLIAMS, JOHN (MINNESOTA) - TACKLE, GUARD - 1968-69 BALTIMORE COLTS;
    1970-71 BALTIMORE COLTS (AFC); 1972-74 LOS ANGELES RAMS (NFC)
WILLIAMS, JOHN (USC) - BACK - 1952-53 WASHINGTON REDSKINS; 1954 SAN
    FRANCISCO 49ERS
WILLIAMS, JOSEPH (LAFAYETTE) - GUARD - 1923 CANTON BULLDOGS; 1925-26
    NEW YORK GIANTS
WILLIAMS, JOSEPH (OHIO STATE) - BACK - 1937 CLEVELAND RAMS; 1939
    PITTSBURGH STEELERS; 1940 COLUMBUS BULLIES (AFL)
WILLIAMS, MAXIE (SOUTHEAST LOUISIANA) - TACKLE, GUARD - 1965 HOUSTON
    OILERS (AFL); 1966-69 MIAMI DOLPHINS (AFL); 1970 MIAMI DOLPHINS
    (AFC)
WILLIAMS, PERRY (PURDUE) - BACK - 1969 GREEN BAY PACKERS; 1970-73
    GREEN BAY PACKERS (NFC); 1974 CHICAGO BEARS (NFC)
WILLIAMS, REX (TEXAS TECH) - CENTER - 1940 CHICAGO CARDINALS; 1940
    NEW YORK AMERICANS (AFL); 1945 DETROIT LIONS
WILLIAMS, RICHARD (ABILENE CHRISTIAN) - END - 1974 NEW ORLEANS SAINTS
    (NFC)
WILLIAMS, ROBERT (NOTRE DAME) - QBACK - 1951-52, 55 CHICAGO BEARS
WILLIAMS, ROGER (GRAMBLING) - END, BACK - 1971-72 LOS ANGELES RAMS
    (NFC)
WILLIAMS, ROLLAND (WISCONSIN) - BACK - 1923 MINNEAPOLIS MARINES; 1923
    RACINE LEGION
WILLIAMS, ROY (PACIFIC) - TACKLE - 1963 SAN FRANCISCO 49ERS
WILLIAMS, SAM (CALIFORNIA) - BACK - 1974 SAN DIEGO CHARGERS (AFC)

WILLIAMS, SAMUEL (MICHIGAN STATE) - END - 1959 LOS ANGELES RAMS;
    1960-65 DETROIT LIONS; 1966-67 ATLANTA FALCONS
WILLIAMS, SIDNEY (SOUTHERN) - LB - 1964-66 CLEVELAND BROWNS; 1967
    WASHINGTON REDSKINS; 1968 BALTIMORE COLTS; 1969 PITTSBURGH
    STEELERS
WILLIAMS, STANLEY (BAYLOR) - END - 1952 DALLAS TEXANS
WILLIAMS, STEVE (WESTERN CAROLINA) - END - 1974 BALTIMORE COLTS (AFC)
WILLIAMS, THEODORE (BOSTON COLLEGE) - BACK - 1942 PHILADELPHIA
    EAGLES; 1944 BOSTON YANKS
WILLIAMS, TRAVIS (INDIANA) - BACK - 1921-22 EVANSVILLE CRIMSON GIANTS
WILLIAMS, WALTER (BOSTON UNIV.) - BACK - 1946 CHICAGO ROCKETS (AAFC);
    1947 BOSTON YANKS
WILLIAMS, WANQUALIN (HOFSTRA) - BACK - 1969 DENVER BRONCOS (AFL);
    1970 DENVER BRONCOS (AFC)
WILLIAMS, WILLIAM THOMAS (CALIFORNIA-DAVIS) - TACKLE - 1970-71 SAN
    DIEGO CHARGERS (AFC)
WILLIAMS, WILLIE (GRAMBLING) - BACK - 1965, 67-69 NEW YORK GIANTS;
    1966 OAKLAND RAIDERS (AFL); 1970-73 NEW YORK GIANTS (NFC); 1968
    INTERCEPTION LEADER
WILLIAMS, WINDELL (RICE) - END - 1948-49 BALTIMORE COLTS (AAFC)
WILLIAMSON, ERNEST (NORTH CAROLINA) - TACKLE - 1947 WASHINGTON
    REDSKINS; 1948 NEW YORK GIANTS; 1949 LOS ANGELES DONS (AAFC)
WILLIAMSON, FREDERICK"HAMMER" (NORTHWESTERN) - BACK - 1960 PITTSBURGH
    STEELERS; 1961-64 OAKLAND RAIDERS (AFL); 1965-67 KANSAS CITY
    CHIEFS (AFL)
WILLIAMSON, JOHN (LOUISIANA TECH) - LB, CENTER - 1964-67 OAKLAND
    RAIDERS (AFL); 1968-69 BOSTON PATRIOTS (AFL); 1970 BOSTON
    PATRIOTS (AFC)
WILLINGHAM, LARRY (AUBURN) - BACK - 1971-72 ST. LOUIS CARDINALS (NFC)
WILLIS, FRED (BOSTON COLLEGE) - BACK - 1971-72 CINCINNATI BENGALS
    (AFC); 1972-74 HOUSTON OILERS (AFC); 1973 PASS RECEIVING LEADER
    (AFC)
WILLIS, LARRY (TEXAS-EL PASO) - BACK - 1973 WASHINGTON REDSKINS (NFC)
WILLIS, WILLIAM (OHIO STATE) - GUARD - 1946-49 CLEVELAND BROWNS
    (AAFC); 1950-53 CLEVELAND BROWNS
WILLSON, JOSEPH (PENNSYLVANIA) - GUARD - 1926 BUFFALO RANGERS; 1927
    BUFFALO BISONS
WILLSON, OSBORNE (PENNSYLVANIA) - GUARD - 1933-35 PHILADELPHIA EAGLES
WILSBACH, FRANK (BUCKNELL) - GUARD - 1925 FRANKFORD YELLOWJACKETS
WILSON, ABRAHAM (WASHINGTON) - GUARD - 1926 LOS ANGELES WILDCATS
    (AFL); 1927-29 PROVIDENCE STEAMROLLERS
WILSON, BENJAMIN (USC) - BACK - 1963-65 LOS ANGELES RAMS; 1967 GREEN
    BAY PACKERS
WILSON, "DRIP" - CENTER - 1931 CLEVELAND INDIANS
WILSON, EDWARD (ARIZONA) - QBACK - 1962 DALLAS TEXANS (AFL); 1963-64
    KANSAS CITY CHIEFS (AFL); 1965 BOSTON PATRIOTS (AFL)
WILSON, EUGENE (SMU) - END - 1947-48 GREEN BAY PACKERS
WILSON, FAYE (TEXAS A&M) - BACK - 1926 BUFFALO RANGERS; 1926 KANSAS
    CITY COWBOYS; 1927-30 NEW YORK GIANTS; 1930 STATEN ISLAND
    STAPELTONS; 1930-31 GREEN BAY PACKERS; 1932-33 PORTSMOUTH
    SPARTANS
WILSON, GEORGE "BUTCH" (ALABAMA) - END - 1963-67 BALTIMORE COLTS;
    1968-69 NEW YORK GIANTS
WILSON, GEORGE (LAFAYETTE) - BACK - 1929 FRANKFORD YELLOWJACKETS
WILSON, GEORGE (NORTHWESTERN) - END - 1937-46 CHICAGO BEARS
WILSON, GEORGE (TEXAS MINES) - GUARD - 1941 COLUMBUS BULLIES (AFL);
    1941 CLEVELAND RAMS; 1942-43, 45 CHICAGO CARDINALS; 1944
    BROOKLYN TIGERS; 1944 BOSTON YANKS
WILSON, GEORGE (WASHINGTON) - BACK - 1926 LOS ANGELES WILDCATS (AFL);
    1927-29 PROVIDENCE STEAMROLLERS
WILSON, GEORGE, JR. (XAVIER) - QBACK - 1966 MIAMI DOLPHINS (AFL)
WILSON, HARRY (NEBRASKA) - BACK - 1967, 69 PHILADELPHIA EAGLES
WILSON, JAMES (GEORGIA) - GUARD - 1965-66 SAN FRANCISCO 49ERS; 1967
    ATLANTA FALCONS; 1968 LOS ANGELES RAMS
WILSON, JERREL (SOUTHERN MISSISSIPPI) - KICKER, BACK - 1963-69 KANSAS
    CITY CHIEFS (AFL); 1970-74 KANSAS CITY CHIEFS (AFC); 1965, 68
    PUNTING LEADER (AFL); 1972-73 PUNTING LEADER (AFC)
WILSON, JOHN (BAYLOR) - BACK - 1946-47 LOS ANGELES RAMS
WILSON, JOHN (WESTERN RESERVE) - END - 1939-42 CLEVELAND RAMS

WILSON, JOHN (WISCONSIN & DUBUQUE) - BACK - 1940 MILWAUKEE CHIEFS
    (AFL)
WILSON, JOSEPH (HOLY CROSS) - BACK - 1973 CINCINNATI BENGALS (AFC);
    1974 NEW ENGLAND PATRIOTS (AFC)
WILSON, LAWRENCE (UTAH) - BACK - 1960-69 ST. LOUIS CARDINALS; 1970-73
    ST. LOUIS CARDINALS (NFC); 1966 INTERCEPTION LEADER
WILSON, LELAND (CORNELL-IOWA) - END - 1929-30 MINNEAPOLIS REDJACKETS;
    1930-31 FRANKFORD YELLOWJACKETS
WILSON, MICHAEL (DAYTON) - GUARD, TACKLE - 1969 CINCINNATI BENGALS
    (AFL); 1970 CINCINNATI BENGALS (AFC); 1971 BUFFALO BILLS (AFC)
WILSON, MICHAEL S. (WESTERN ILLINOIS) - BACK - 1969 ST. LOUIS
    CARDINALS
WILSON, MILTON (OSHKOSH STATE-WISCONSIN) - TACKLE - 1921 GREEN BAY
    PACKERS; 1923-24 AKRON PROS
WILSON, NEMIAH (GRAMBLING) - BACK - 1965-67 DENVER BRONCOS (AFL);
    1968-69 OAKLAND RAIDERS (AFL); 1970-74 OAKLAND RAIDERS (AFC)
WILSON, ROBERT (SMU) - BACK - 1936 BROOKLYN DODGERS
WILSON, SAMUEL "MIKE" (LEHIGH) - END - 1923-25 ROCK ISLAND
    INDEPENDENTS; 1926 ROCK ISLAND INDEPENDENTS (AFL)
WILSON, STUART (WASHINGTON&JEFFERSON) - END - 1932 STATEN ISLAND
    STAPELTONS
WILSON, THOMAS - BACK - 1956-61 LOS ANGELES RAMS; 1962 CLEVELAND
    BROWNS; 1963 MINNESOTA VIKINGS
WILSON, WARREN CAMP (TULSA) - BACK - 1946-49 DETROIT LIONS
WILSON, WILLIAM (GONZAGA) - END - 1935-37 CHICAGO CARDINALS; 1938
    PITTSBURGH PIRATES; 1938 PHILADELPHIA EAGLES
WILSON, WILLIAM (SAN JOSE STATE) - END - 1951-60 SAN FRANCISCO 49ERS;
    1954, 56-57 PASS RECEIVING LEADER; (1954 TIED WITH PIHOS)
WILTON, EDWARD (GEORGIA TECH) - END - 1926 POTTSVILLE MAROONS
WIMBERLY, ABNER (LSU) - END - 1949 LOS ANGELES DONS (AAFC); 1950-52
    GREEN BAY PACKERS
WIMBERLY, BYRON (WASHINGTON&JEFFERSON) - GUARD - 1919 MASSILLON
    TIGERS; 1925 DETROIT PANTHERS
WINANS, JEFF (USC) - TACKLE - 1973 BUFFALO BILLS (AFC)
WINDAUER, WILLIAM (IOWA) - TACKLE - 1973-74 BALTIMORE COLTS (AFC)
WINDBIEL, JOSEPH - CENTER - 1921-22 EVANSVILLE CRIMSON GIANTS
WINDBURN, ERNEST (CENTRAL MISSOURI STATE) - END - 1923 ST. LOUIS
    BROWNS
WINDSOR, ROBERT (KENTUCKY) - END - 1967-69 SAN FRANCISCO 49ERS;
    1970-71 SAN FRANCISCO 49ERS (NFC); 1972-74 NEW ENGLAND PATRIOTS
    (AFC)
WINFIELD, VERNON (MINNESOTA) - GUARD - 1972-73 PHILADELPHIA EAGLES
    (NFC)
WINFREY, CARL (WISCONSIN) - LB - 1971 MINNESOTA VIKINGS (NFC); 1972
    PITTSBURGH STEELERS (AFC)
WINGATE, ELMER (MARYLAND) - END - 1953 BALTIMORE COLTS
WINGATE, HEATH (BOWLING GREEN) - CENTER - 1967 WASHINGTON REDSKINS
WINK, DEAN (YANKTON-SOUTH DAKOTA) - END - 1967-68 PHILADELPHIA EAGLES
WINKELMAN, BENJAMIN (ARKANSAS) - END - 1922-24 MILWAUKEE BADGERS
WINKER, FRANCIS (MEMPHIS STATE) - END - 1968-69 GREEN BAY PACKERS
WINKLER, BERNARD (TEXAS TECH) - TACKLE - 1948 LOS ANGELES DONS (AAFC)
WINKLER, JAMES (TEXAS A&M) - TACKLE - 1951-52 LOS ANGELES RAMS; 1953
    BALTIMORE COLTS
WINKLER, JOSEPH (PURDUE) - CENTER - 1945 CLEVELAND RAMS
WINKLER, RANDOLPH (TARLETON STATE-TEXAS) - TACKLE, GUARD - 1967
    DETROIT LIONS; 1968 ATLANTA FALCONS; 1971 GREEN BAY PACKERS (NFC)
WINNESHEK, WILLIAM (CARLISLE) - CENTER - 1922 OORANG INDIANS
WINSLOW, CHARLES DOUGLAS (DRAKE) - END - 1973 NEW ORLEANS SAINTS (NFC)
WINSLOW, PAUL (NORTH CAROLINA COLLEGE) - BACK - 1960 GREEN BAY PACKERS
WINSLOW, ROBERT (USC) - END - 1940 DETROIT LIONS; 1940 BROOKLYN
    DODGERS
WINSTON, CHARLES (PURDUE) - GUARD - 1919-20 DAYTON TRIANGLES
WINSTON, KELTON (WILEY) - BACK - 1967-68 LOS ANGELES RAMS
WINSTON, LLOYD (USC) - BACK - 1962-63 SAN FRANCISCO 49ERS
WINSTON, ROY (LSU) - LB - 1962-69 MINNESOTA VIKINGS; 1970-74
    MINNESOTA VIKINGS (NFC)
WINTER, WILLIAM (ST. OLAF) - LB - 1962-64 NEW YORK GIANTS
WINTERHEIMER, LEON - TACKLE - 1922 EVANSVILLE CRIMSON GIANTS
WINTERS, JAY (OHIO WESLEYAN) - BACK - 1926 CLEVELAND PANTHERS (AFL)
WINTERS, LINGREL (OHIO WESLEYAN) - BACK - 1923-24 COLUMBUS TIGERS

WINTHER, RICHARD "WIMPY" (MISSISSIPPI) - CENTER - 1971 GREEN BAY
    PACKERS (NFC); 1972 NEW ORLEANS SAINTS (NFC)
WIPER, DONALD (OHIO STATE) - BACK - 1922 COLUMBUS PANHANDLES
WIRGOWSKI, DENNIS (PURDUE) - END, TACKLE - 1970 BOSTON PATRIOTS
    (AFC); 1971-72 NEW ENGLAND PATRIOTS (AFC); 1973 PHILADELPHIA
    EAGLES (NFC)
WISE, PHILIP (NEBRASKA-OMAHA) - BACK - 1971-74 NEW YORK JETS (AFC)
WISENER, GARY (BAYLOR) - END - 1960 DALLAS COWBOYS; 1961 HOUSTON
    OILERS (AFL)
WISSMAN, PETER (ST. LOUIS UNIV.) - CENTER - 1949 SAN FRANCISCO 49ERS
    (AAFC); 1950-52, 54 SAN FRANCISCO 49ERS
WISSINGER, ZONAR (PITTSBURGH) - GUARD - 1926 POTTSVILLE MAROONS
WISTERT, ALBERT (MICHIGAN) - TACKLE - 1943 PHIL-PITT; 1944-51
    PHILADELPHIA EAGLES
WITCHER, RICHARD (UCLA) - END, BACK - 1966-69 SAN FRANCISCO 49ERS;
    1970-73 SAN FRANCISCO 49ERS (NFC)
WITCHER, THOMAS (BAYLOR) - END - 1960 HOUSTON OILERS (AFL)
WITHROW, JAMES CALVIN (KENTUCKY) - CENTER - 1970 SAN DIEGO CHARGERS
    (AFC); 1971-73 GREEN BAY PACKERS (NFC); 1974 ST. LOUIS CARDINALS
    (NFC)
WITT, MELVIN (ARLINGTON STATE) - END - 1967-69 BOSTON PATRIOTS (AFL);
    1970 BOSTON PATRIOTS (AFC)
WITTE, EARL (GUSTAVUS-ADOLPHUS) - BACK - 1934 GREEN BAY PACKERS
WITTENBORN, JOHN (SOUTHEAST MISSOURI STATE) - GUARD - 1958-60 SAN
    FRANCISCO 49ERS; 1960-62 PHILADELPHIA EAGLES; 1964-68 HOUSTON
    OILERS (AFL)
WITTER, RAYMOND (SYRACUSE) - BACK - 1919-21, 23 ROCHESTER JEFFERSONS
WITTER, ROBERT (ALFRED) - BACK - 1919-20 ROCHESTER JEFFERSONS
WITTUM, THOMAS (NORTHERN ILLINOIS) - KICKER - 1973-74 SAN FRANCISCO
    49ERS (NFC); 1973 PUNTING LEADER (NFC)
WITUCKI, CASIMIR (INDIANA) - GUARD - 1950-51, 53-56 WASHINGTON
    REDSKINS
WIZBICKI, ALEXANDER (HOLY CROSS) - BACK - 1947-49 BUFFALO BILLS
    (AAFC); 1950 GREEN BAY PACKERS
WOERNER, ERWIN (BUCKNELL) - TACKLE - 1930 NEWARK TORNADOS
WOIT, RICHARD (ARKANSAS STATE) - BACK - 1955 DETROIT LIONS
WOITT, JOHN (MISSISSIPPI STATE) - BACK - 1968-69 SAN FRANCISCO 49ERS
WOJCIECHOWICZ, ALEXANDER (FORDHAM) - CENTER - 1938-46 DETROIT LIONS;
    1946-50 PHILADELPHIA EAGLES; 1968 HALL OF FAME
WOJCIK, GREGORY (USC) - TACKLE - 1971 LOS ANGELES RAMS (NFC); 1972-73
    SAN DIEGO CHARGERS (AFC)
WOLCUFF, NICHOLAS (MIAMI) - TACKLE - 1937 NEW YORK YANKS (AFL)
WOLF, JAMES (PRAIRIE VIEW) - BACK - 1974 PITTSBURGH STEELERS (AFC)
WOLF, RICHARD (MIAMI-OHIO) - BACK - 1923 CLEVELAND INDIANS; 1924-25,
    27 CLEVELAND BULLDOGS; 1926 CLEVELAND PANTHERS (AFL)
WOLFE, HUGH (TEXAS) - BACK - 1938 NEW YORK GIANTS
WOLFENDALE, RALPH (FORDHAM) - GUARD - 1936 BOSTON SHAMROCKS (AFL)
WOLFF, WAYNE (WAKE FOREST) - GUARD - 1961 BUFFALO BILLS (AFL)
WOLFORD, OSCAR - GUARD - 1920-22 COLUMBUS PANHANDLES; 1924 COLUMBUS
    TIGERS
WOLSKI, WILLIAM (NOTRE DAME) - BACK - 1966 ATLANTA FALCONS
WOLTMAN, CLEMENT (PURDUE) - TACKLE - 1938-40 PHILADELPHIA EAGLES
WOMACK, BRUCE (WEST TEXAS STATE) - GUARD - 1951 DETROIT LIONS
WOMACK, JOSEPH (LOS ANGELES STATE) - BACK - 1962 PITTSBURGH STEELERS
WOMBLE, ROYCE (NORTH TEXAS STATE) - BACK - 1954-57 BALTIMORE COLTS;
    1960 LOS ANGELES CHARGERS (AFL)
WONDOLOWSKI, WILLIAM (EASTERN MONTANA) - END - 1969 SAN FRANCISCO
    49ERS
WOOD, CHARLES (NORTH CAROLINA) - END - 1967 ATLANTA FALCONS
WOOD, DUANE (OKLAHOMA STATE) - BACK - 1960-62 DALLAS TEXANS (AFL);
    1963-64 KANSAS CITY CHIEFS (AFL)
WOOD, GARY (CORNELL) - QBACK - 1964-66, 68 NEW YORK GIANTS; 1967 NEW
    ORLEANS SAINTS
WOOD, JAMES - GUARD - 1919-24 ROCHESTER JEFFERSONS
WOOD, MALCOLM "DICK" (AUBURN) - QBACK - 1962 SAN DIEGO CHARGERS
    (AFL); 1962 DENVER BRONCOS (AFL); 1963-64 NEW YORK JETS (AFL);
    1965 OAKLAND RAIDERS (AFL); 1966 MIAMI DOLPHINS (AFL)
WOOD, MARVIN (CALIFORNIA) - GUARD - 1924 KENOSHA MAROONS
WOOD, ROBERT (ALABAMA) - TACKLE - 1940 CHICAGO CARDINALS

WOOD, WILLIAM (USC) - BACK - 1960-69 GREEN BAY PACKERS; 1970-71 GREEN
    BAY PACKERS (NFC); 1962 INTERCEPTION LEADER
WOOD, WILLIAM (WEST VIRGINIAN WESLEYAN) - BACK - 1963 NEW YORK JETS
    (AFL)
WOODALL, FRANK ALLEY "AL" (DUKE) - QBACK - 1969 NEW YORK JETS (AFL);
    1970-74 NEW YORK JETS (AFC)
WOODESCHICK, THOMAS (WEST VIRGINA) - BACK - 1963-69 PHILADELPHIA
    EAGLES; 1970-71 PHILADELPHIA EAGLES (NFC); 1972 ST. LOUIS
    CARDINALS (NFC)
WOODIN, HOWARD (MARQUETTE) - GUARD - 1922 RACINE LEGION; 1922-31
    GREEN BAY PACKERS
WOODLIEF, DOUGLAS (MEMPHIS STATE) - LB - 1965-69 LOS ANGELES RAMS
WOODRUFF, JAMES (PITTSBURGH) - END - 1926 CHICAGO CARDINALS; 1929
    BUFFALO BISONS
WOODRUFF, LEE (MISSISSIPPI) - BACK - 1931 PROVIDENCE STEAMROLLERS;
    1932 BOSTON BRAVES; 1933 PHILADELPHIA EAGLES
WOODS, CLARENCE GLEN (PRAIRIE VIEW) - END - 1969 HOUSTON OILERS (AFL)
WOODS, DONALD (NEW MEXICO HIGHLANDS) - BACK - 1974 SAN DIEGO CHARGERS
    (AFC)
WOODS, GERALD (BUTLER) - BACK - 1926 COLUMBUS TIGERS
WOODS, LARRY (TENNESSEE STATE) - TACKLE - 1971-72 DETROIT LIONS
    (NFC); 1973 MIAMI DOLPHINS (AFC); 1974 NEW YORK JETS (AFC)
WOODS, ROBERT (TENNESSEE STATE) - TACKLE - 1973-74 NEW YORK JETS (AFC)
WOODSON, ABRAHAM (ILLINOIS) - BACK - 1958-64 SAN FRANCISCO 49ERS;
    1965-66 ST. LOUIS CARDINALS
WOODSON, FREDERICK (FLORIDA A&M) - END - 1967-69 MIAMI DOLPHINS (AFL)
WOODSON, MARVIN (INDIANA) - BACK - 1964-69 PITTSBURGH STEELERS; 1969
    NEW ORLEANS SAINTS
WOODWARD, RICHARD (IOWA) - CENTER - 1949 LOS ANGELES DONS (AAFC);
    1950-51, 53 NEW YORK GIANTS; 1952 WASHINGTON REDSKINS
WOOTEN, JOHN (COLORADO) - GUARD - 1959-67 CLEVELAND BROWNS; 1968
    WASHINGTON REDSKINS
WORD, ROSCOE (JACKSON STATE) - BACK - 1974 NEW YORK JETS (AFC)
WORDEN, JAMES (WAYNESBORO) - BACK - 1945 CLEVELAND RAMS
WORDEN, NEIL (NOTRE DAME) - BACK - 1954, 57 PHILADELPHIA EAGLES
WORDEN, STUART (HAMPDEN-SIDNEY) - GUARD - 1930, 32-34 BROOKLYN DODGERS
WORK, JOSEPH (MIAMI-OHIO) - BACK - 1923 CLEVELAND INDIANS; 1924-25
    CLEVELAND BULLDOGS
WORKMAN, BLAKE (TULSA) - BACK - 1933 CINCINNATI REDS; 1934 ST. LOUIS
    GUNNERS
WORKMAN, HARRY (OHIO STATE) - BACK - 1924-25 CLEVELAND BULLDOGS; 1931
    CLEVELAND INDIANS; 1932 NEW YORK GIANTS
WORTMAN, KEITH (NEBRASKA) - TACKLE, GUARD - 1972-74 GREEN BAY PACKERS
    (NFC)
WOUDENBERG, JOHN (DENVER) - TACKLE - 1940-42 PITTSBURGH STEELERS;
    1946-49 SAN FRANCISCO 49ERS (AAFC)
WOULFE, MICHAEL (COLORADO) - LB - 1962 PHILADELPHIA EAGLES
WOZNIAK, JOHN (ALABAMA) - GUARD - 1948 BROOKLYN DODGERS (AAFC); 1949
    NEW YORK YANKEES (AAFC); 1950-51 NEW YORK YANKS; 1952 DALLAS
    TEXANS
WRAY, LUDLOW (PENNSYLVANIA) - CENTER - 1919 MASSILLON TIGERS; 1920-21
    BUFFALO ALL-AMERICANS; 1922 ROCHESTER JEFFERSONS
WREN, LOWE (MISSOURI) - BACK - 1956-59 CLEVELAND BROWNS; 1960
    PITTSBURGH STEELERS; 1961 NEW YORK TITANS (AFL)
WRIGHT, ALBERT (OKLAHOMA A&M) - BACK - 1930 FRANKFORD YELLOWJACKETS
WRIGHT, ELMO (HOUSTON) - END - 1971-74 KANSAS CITY CHIEFS (AFC)
WRIGHT, ERNEST (OHIO STATE) - TACKLE - 1960 LOS ANGELES CHARGERS
    (AFL); 1961-67 SAN DIEGO CHARGERS (AFL); 1968-69 CINCINNATI
    BENGALS (AFL); 1970-71 CINCINNATI BENGALS (AFC); 1972 SAN DIEGO
    CHARGERS (AFC)
WRIGHT, GEORGE (SAM HOUSTON) - TACKLE - 1970-71 BALTIMORE COLTS
    (AFC); 1972 CLEVELAND BROWNS (AFC)
WRIGHT, GORDON (DELAWARE STATE) - GUARD - 1937 PHILADELPHIA EAGLES;
    1969 NEW YORK JETS (AFL)
WRIGHT, JAMES (MEMPHIS STATE) - BACK - 1964 DENVER BRONCOS (AFL)
WRIGHT, JAMES (SMU) - GUARD - 1947 BOSTON YANKS
WRIGHT, JEFFREY (MINNESOTA) - BACK - 1971-74 MINNESOTA VIKINGS (NFC)
WRIGHT, JOHN (ILLINOIS) - END - 1968 ATLANTA FALCONS; 1969 DETROIT
    LIONS
WRIGHT, JOHN (MARYLAND) - BACK - 1947 BALTIMORE COLTS (AAFC)

WRIGHT, LARRY PAYFIELD (FT. VALLEY STATE-GA) - TACKLE, END - 1967-69
    DALLAS COWBOYS; 1970-74 DALLAS COWBOYS (NFC)
WRIGHT, LAWRENCE (COLORADO STATE) - END - 1966-67 DENVER BRONCOS (AFL)
WRIGHT, NATE (SAN DIEGO STATE) - BACK - 1969 ATLANTA FALCONS; 1969
    ST. LOUIS CARDINALS; 1970 ST. LOUIS CARDINALS (NFC); 1971-74
    MINNESOTA VIKINGS (NFC)
WRIGHT, RALPH (KENTUCKY) - TACKLE - 1933 BROOKLYN DODGERS
WRIGHT, STEPHEN (ALABAMA) - TACKLE - 1964-67 GREEN BAY PACKERS;
    1968-69 NEW YORK GIANTS; 1970 WASHINGTON REDSKINS (NFC); 1971
    CHICAGO BEARS (NFC); 1972 ST. LOUIS CARDINALS (NFC)
WRIGHT, WELDON "TED" (DENTON TEACHERS-TEXAS) - BACK - 1934-35 BOSTON
    REDSKINS; 1935 BROOKLYN DODGERS
WRINKLE MEAT - GUARD - 1922 OORANG INDIANS
WUKITS, ALBERT (DUQUESNE) - CENTER - 1943 PHIL-PITT; 1944 CARD-PITT;
    1945 PITTSBURGH STEELERS; 1946 MIAMI SEAHAWKS (AAFC); 1946
    BUFFALO BISONS (AAFC)
WULFF, JAMES (MICHIGAN STATE) - BACK - 1960-61 WASHINGTON REDSKINS
WUNDERLICH, FREDERICK (XAVIER) - QBACK - 1937 CINCINNATI BENGALS
    (AFL); 1940 COLUMBUS BULLIES (AFL)
WUNSCH, HARRY (NOTRE DAME) - GUARD - 1934 GREEN BAY PACKERS
WYANT, FRED (WEST VIRGINIA) - QBACK - 1956 WASHINGTON REDSKINS
WYATT, ALVIN (BETHUNE-COOKMAN) - BACK - 1970 OAKLAND RAIDERS (AFC);
    1971-72 BUFFALO BILLS (AFC); 1973 HOUSTON OILERS (AFC)
WYATT, JOHN DOUGLAS (TULSA) - BACK - 1970-72 NEW ORLEANS SAINTS
    (NFC); 1973-74 DETROIT LIONS (NFC)
WYCHE, SAMUEL (FURMAN) - QBACK - 1968-69 CINCINNATI BENGALS (AFL);
    1970 CINCINNATI BENGALS (AFC); 1971-72 WASHINGTON REDSKINS
    (NFC); 1974 DETROIT LIONS (NFC)
WYCINSKI, CRAIG (MICHIGAN) - GUARD - 1972 CLEVELAND BROWNS (AFC)
WYCOFF, DOUGLAS (GEORGIA TECH) - QBACK - 1926 NEWARK BEARS (AFL);
    1927, 31 NEW YORK GIANTS; 1929-30, 32 STATEN ISLAND STAPELTONS;
    1934 BOSTON REDSKINS; 1936 NEW YORK YANKS (AFL)
WYCOFF, IRE (WASHBURN) - TACKLE - 1923 ST. LOUIS BROWNS
WYDO, FRANK (CORNELL) - TACKLE - 1947-51 PITTSBURGH STEELERS; 1952-57
    PHILADELPHIA EAGLES
WYHONIC, JOHN (ALABAMA) - GUARD - 1946-47 PHILADELPHIA EAGLES;
    1948-49 BUFFALO BILLS (AAFC)
WYLAND, GUIDO - GUARD - 1919-20 ROCK ISLAND INDEPENDENTS
WYMAN, ARNOLD (MINNESOTA) - BACK - 1919 DETROIT HERALDS; 1919 HAMMOND
    PROS; 1920-21 ROCK ISLAND INDEPENDENTS
WYNN, WILLIAM (TENNESSEE STATE) - END - 1973-74 PHILADELPHIA EAGLES
    (NFC)
WYNNE, CHESTER (NOTRE DAME) - BACK - 1922 ROCHESTER JEFFERSONS
WYNNE, ELMER (NOTRE DAME) - BACK - 1928 CHICAGO BEARS; 1929 DAYTON
    TRIANGLES
WYNNE, HARRY (ARKANSAS) - END - 1944 BOSTON YANKS; 1945 NEW YORK
    GIANTS
WYSONG - 1920 COLUMBUS PANHANDLES
YABLOK, JULIUS (COLGATE) - BACK - 1930-31 BROOKLYN DODGERS; 1931
    STATEN ISLAND STAPELTONS
YABLONSKI, JOSEPH (HOLY CROSS) - QBACK - 1940 BOSTON BEARS (AFL)
YABLONSKI, VENTAN (COLUMBIA) - BACK - 1948-51 CHICAGO CARDINALS
YACKANICH, JOSEPH (FORDHAM) - GUARD - 1946-48 NEW YORK YANKEES (AAFC)
YACCINO, JOHN (PITTSBURGH) - BACK - 1962 BUFFALO BILLS (AFL)
YAGIELLO, RAYMOND (CATAWBA) - GUARD - 1948-49 LOS ANGELES RAMS
YANCHAR, WILLIAM (PURDUE) - TACKLE - 1970 CLEVELAND BROWNS (AFC)
YANKOWSKI, RONALD (KANSAS STATE) - END - 1971-74 ST. LOUIS CARDINALS
    (NFC)
YARBROUGH, JAMES (FLORIDA) - TACKLE - 1969 DETROIT LIONS; 1970-74
    DETROIT LIONS (NFC)
YARR, THOMAS (NOTRE DAME) - CENTER - 1933 CHICAGO CARDINALS
YARY, ANTHONY RONALD (USC) - TACKLE - 1968-69 MINNESOTA VIKINGS;
    1970-74 MINNESOTA VIKINGS (NFC)
YATCHET, VINCENT (MOORHEAD STATE-MINNESOTA) - BACK - 1940 MILWAUKEE
    CHIEFS (AFL)
YATES, ROBERT (SYRACUSE) - TACKLE - 1960-65 BOSTON PATRIOTS (AFL)
YEAGER, HOWARD (SANTA BARBARA) - BACK - 1941 NEW YORK GIANTS
YEAGER, JAMES (LEHIGH) - TACKLE - 1926 BROOKLYN LIONS; 1929 ORANGE
    TORNADOS
YEARBY, WILLIAM (MICHIGAN) - END - 1966 NEW YORK JETS (AFL)
YEATES, JEFFREY (BOSTON COLLEGE) - TACKLE - 1974 BUFFALO BILLS (AFC)

YEISLEY, DONALD - END - 1927-28 CHICAGO CARDINALS
YELVERTON, WILLIAM (MISSISSIPPI) - END - 1960 DENVER BRONCOS (AFL)
YELVINGTON, RICHARD (GEORGIA) - TACKLE - 1952-57 NEW YORK GIANTS
YEPREMIAN, GARABED - KICKER - 1966-67 DETROIT LIONS; 1970-74 MIAMI
    DOLPHINS (AFC); 1971 SCORING LEADER (AFC); 1971 FIELD GOAL
    LEADER (AFC)
YERGER, HOWARD (PENN STATE) - BACK - 1919 DAYTON TRIANGLES; 1921
    LOUISVILLE BRECKS
YEWCIC, THOMAS (MICHIGAN STATE) - KICKER, QBACK - 1961-66 BOSTON
    PATRIOTS (AFL)
YEZERSKI, JOHN (ST. MARY'S) - TACKLE - 1936 BROOKLYN DODGERS
YOHN, JOHN DAVID (GETTSBURG) - LB - 1962 BALTIMORE COLTS; 1963 NEW
    YORK JETS (AFL)
YOHO, MACK (MIAMI-OHIO) - END - 1960-63 BUFFALO BILLS (AFL)
YOKAS, FRANK - GUARD - 1946 LOS ANGELES DONS (AAFC); 1947 BALTIMORE
    COLTS (AAFC)
YONAKER, JOHN (NOTRE DAME) - END - 1946-49 CLEVELAND BROWNS (AAFC);
    1950 NEW YORK YANKS; 1952 WASHINGTON REDSKINS
YONAMINE, WALLACE - BACK - 1947 SAN FRANCISCO 49ERS (AAFC)
YOUEL, JAMES (IOWA) - QBACK - 1946-48 WASHINGTON REDSKINS; 1948
    BOSTON YANKS
YOUMANS, MAURICE (SYRACUSE) - END - 1960-62 CHICAGO BEARS; 1964-65
    DALLAS COWBOYS
YOUNCE, LEONARD (OREGON STATE) - GUARD - 1941, 43-44, 46-48 NEW YORK
    GIANTS
YOUNG, ALFRED (SOUTH CAROLINA STATE) - END - 1971-72 PITTSBURGH
    STEELERS (AFC)
YOUNG, CHARLES (NORTH CAROLINA STATE) - BACK - 1974 DALLAS COWBOYS
    (NFC)
YOUNG, CHARLES (USC) - END - 1973-74 PHILADELPHIA EAGLES (NFC); 1974
    PASS RECEIVING LEADER (NFC)
YOUNG, CLAUDE "BUDDY" (ILLINOIS) - BACK - 1947-49 NEW YORK YANKEES
    (AAFC); 1950-51 NEW YORK YANKS; 1952 DALLAS TEXANS; 1953-55
    BALTIMORE COLTS
YOUNG, GEORGE (GEORGIA) - END - 1946-49 CLEVELAND BROWNS (AAFC);
    1950-53 CLEVELAND BROWNS
YOUNG, GLEN (PURDUE) - BACK - 1956 GREEN BAY PACKERS
YOUNG, HERMAN (DETROIT) - END - 1930 PROVIDENCE STEAMROLLERS
YOUNG, JAMES (QUEENS-ONTARIO) - BACK - 1965-66 MINNESOTA VIKINGS
YOUNG, JOHN (CALIFORNIA) - BACK - 1926 LOS ANGELES BUCCANEERS
YOUNG, JOSEPH (ARIZONA) - END - 1960-61 DENVER BRONCOS (AFL)
YOUNG, LESLIE (MACALESTER) - BACK - 1927 PROVIDENCE STEAMROLLERS
YOUNG, LLOYD "SAM" (BROWN) - TACKLE - 1925-27 PROVIDENCE
    STEAMROLLERS; 1929-30 MINNEAPOLIS REDJACKETS
YOUNG, MATTHEW ADRIAN (USC) - LB - 1968-69 PHILADELPHIA EAGLES;
    1970-72 PHILADELPHIA EAGLES (NFC); 1972 DETROIT LIONS (NFC);
    1973 CHICAGO BEARS (NFC)
YOUNG, PAUL (OKLAHOMA) - CENTER - 1933 GREEN BAY PACKERS
YOUNG, RANDOLPH (MILLIKIN) - TACKLE - 1920 CHICAGO TIGERS; 1920
    DECATUR STALEYS
YOUNG, RICHARD (CHATTANOOGA) - BACK - 1955-56 BALTIMORE COLTS; 1957
    PITTSBURGH STEELERS
YOUNG, ROBERT (HOWARD PAYNE) - GUARD, TACKLE - 1966-69 DENVER BRONCOS
    (AFL); 1970 DENVER BRONCOS (AFC); 1971 HOUSTON OILERS (AFC);
    1972-74 ST. LOUIS CARDINALS (NFC)
YOUNG, ROY (TEXAS A&M) - TACKLE - 1938 WASHINGTON REDSKINS
YOUNG, RUSSELL - BACK - 1925-26 DAYTON TRIANGLES
YOUNG, WALTER (OKLAHOMA) - END - 1939-40 BROOKLYN DODGERS
YOUNG, WILBUR (WILLIAM PENN) - END, TACKLE - 1971-74 KANSAS CITY
    CHIEFS (AFC)
YOUNG, WILLIAM (OHIO STATE) - GUARD - 1929 GREEN BAY PACKERS
YOUNG, WILLIAM (ALABAMA) - TACKLE - 1937-42, 46 WASHINGTON REDSKINS
YOUNG, WILLIAM (GRAMBLING) - TACKLE - 1966-69 NEW YORK GIANTS;
    1970-74 NEW YORK GIANTS (NFC)
YOUNG, WILLIE (ALCORN A&M) - TACKLE - 1971 BUFFALO BILLS (AFC); 1973
    MIAMI DOLPHINS (AFC)
YOUNGBLOOD, GEORGE (LOS ANGELES STATE) - BACK - 1966 LOS ANGELES
    RAMS; 1967 CLEVELAND BROWNS; 1967-68 NEW ORLEANS SAINTS; 1969
    CHICAGO BEARS

YOUNGBLOOD, HERBERT JOHN "JACK" (FLORIDA) - END - 1971-74 LOS ANGELES
        RAMS (NFC)
YOUNGBLOOD, JAMES (TENNESSEE TECH) - LB - 1973-74 LOS ANGELES RAMS
        (NFC)
YOUNGELMAN, SIDNEY (ALABAMA) - GUARD - 1955 SAN FRANCISCO 49ERS;
        1956-58 PHILADELPHIA EAGLES; 1959 CLEVELAND BROWNS; 1960-61 NEW
        YORK TITANS (AFL); 1962-63 BUFFALO BILLS (AFL)
YOUNGER, PAUL "TANK" (GRAMBLING) - BACK - 1949-57 LOS ANGELES RAMS;
        1958 PITTSBURGH STEELERS
YOUNGFLEISH, FRANCIS (VILLANOVA) - CENTER - 1926-27 POTTSVILLE MAROONS
YOUNGSTROM, ADOLPH (DARTMOUTH) - GUARD - 1920-23 BUFFALO
        ALL-AMERICANS; 1921 CANTON BULLDOGS; 1924-25 BUFFALO BISONS;
        1926-27 FRANKFORD YELLOWJACKETS
YOUSO, FRANK (MINNESOTA) - TACKLE - 1958-60 NEW YORK GIANTS; 1961-62
        MINNESOTA VIKINGS; 1963-65 OAKLAND RAIDERS (AFL)
YOVICSIN, JOHN (GETTYSBURG) - END - 1944 PHILADELPHIA EAGLES
YOWARSKY, WALTER (KENTUCKY) - END - 1951, 54 WASHINGTON REDSKINS;
        1955 DETROIT LIONS; 1955-57 NEW YORK GIANTS; 1958 SAN FRANCISCO
        49ERS
YURCHEY, JOHN (DUQUESNE) - BACK - 1940 PITTSBURGH STEELERS
YURKONIS, LAWRENCE (NIAGARA) - BACK - 1941 BUFFALO TIGERS (AFL)
ZABEL, STEVE (OKLAHOMA) - LB, END - 1970-74 PHILADELPHIA EAGLES (NFC)
ZADWORNEY, FRANK (OHIO STATE) - BACK - 1940 BROOKLYN DODGERS
ZAESKE, PAUL (NORTH PARK COLLEGE) - END - 1969 HOUSTON OILERS (AFL);
        1970 HOUSTON OILERS (AFC)
ZAGERS, ALBERT (MICHIGAN STATE) - BACK - 1955, 57-58 WASHINGTON
        REDSKINS
ZALEJSKI, ERNEST (NOTRE DAME) - BACK - 1950 BALTIMORE COLTS
ZANDERS, EMANUEL (JACKSON STATE) - GUARD - 1974 NEW ORLEANS SAINTS
        (NFC)
ZANINELLI, SILVIO (DUQUESNE) - BACK - 1934-37 PITTSBURGH PIRATES
ZAPALAC, WILLIAM (TEXAS) - LB, END - 1971-73 NEW YORK JETS (AFC)
ZAPUSTAS, JOSEPH (FORDHAM) - BACK - 1933 NEW YORK GIANTS; 1936-37
        BOSTON SHAMROCKS (AFL)
ZARNAS, AUGUSTUS (OHIO STATE) - GUARD - 1938 CHICAGO BEARS; 1939
        BROOKLYN DODGERS; 1939-40 GREEN BAY PACKERS
ZARUBA, CARROLL (NEBRASKA) - BACK - 1960 DALLAS TEXANS (AFL)
ZATKOFF, ROGER (MICHIGAN) - TACKLE - 1953-56 GREEN BAY PACKERS;
        1957-58 DETROIT LIONS
ZAUNBRECHER, GODFREY (LSU) - CENTER - 1971-73 MINNESOTA VIKINGS (NFC)
ZAWADZKAS, GERALD (COLUMBIA) - END - 1967 DETROIT LIONS
ZECHER, RICHARD (UTAH STATE) - TACKLE - 1965 OAKLAND RAIDERS (AFL);
        1966-67 MIAMI DOLPHINS (AFL); 1967 BUFFALO BILLS (AFL)
ZEHRER, HENRY - BACK - 1926 HARTFORD BLUES
ZELENICK, FRANK (OGLETHORPE) - TACKLE - 1939 CHICAGO CARDINALS
ZELLER, JEROME - BACK - 1921-22 EVANSVILLE CRIMSON GIANTS
ZELLER, JOSEPH (INDIANA) - GUARD - 1932 GREEN BAY PACKERS; 1933-38
        CHICAGO BEARS
ZEMAN, EDWARD "BOB" (WISCONSIN) - BACK - 1960 LOS ANGELES CHARGERS
        (AFL); 1961, 65-66 SAN DIEGO CHARGERS (AFL); 1962-63 DENVER
        BRONCOS (AFL)
ZEMEN, LADIMIR (CORNELL) - END - 1919 MASSILLON TIGERS
ZENO, COLEMAN (GRAMBLING) - END - 1971 NEW YORK GIANTS (NFC)
ZENO, JOSEPH (HOLY CROSS) - GUARD - 1942-44 WASHINGTON REDSKINS;
        1946-47 BOSTON YANKS
ZERBE, HAROLD - END - 1926 CANTON BULLDOGS
ZIEGLER, AUGUSTUS (PENNSYLVANIA) - GUARD - 1919 AKRON PROS; 1919
        CLEVELAND INDIANS
ZIEGLER, FRANK (GEORGIA TECH) - BACK - 1949-53 PHILADELPHIA EAGLES
ZIFF, DAVID (SYRACUSE) - END - 1925 ROCHESTER JEFFERSONS; 1926
        BROOKLYN LIONS
ZILLY, JOHN (NOTRE DAME) - END - 1947-51 LOS ANGELES RAMS; 1952
        PHILADELPHIA EAGLES
ZIMMERMAN, CARL (MOUNT UNION) - GUARD - 1927-29 DAYTON TRIANGLES
ZIMMERMAN, DONALD (NORTHEAST LOUISIANA) - END - 1973-74 PHILADELPHIA
        EAGLES (NFC)
ZIMMERMAN, GIFFORD (SYRACUSE) - BACK - 1924 AKRON PROS; 1925 CANTON
        BULLDOGS
ZIMMERMAN, JOSEPH (CENTENARY) - GUARD - 1940-41 COLUMBUS BULLIES (AFL)

ZIMMERMAN, LEROY (SAN JOSE STATE) - QBACK - 1940-42 WASHINGTON
    REDSKINS; 1943 PHIL-PITT; 1944-46 PHILADELPHIA EAGLES; 1947
    DETROIT LIONS; 1948 BOSTON YANKS; 1945 INTERCEPTION LEADER
ZIMNY, ROBERT (INDIANA) - TACKLE - 1945-49 CHICAGO CARDINALS
ZIRINSKY, WALTER (LAFAYETTE) - BACK - 1945 CLEVELAND RAMS
ZIZAK, VINCENT (VILLANOVA) - TACKLE - 1934 CHICAGO BEARS; 1934-37
    PHILADELPHIA EAGLES; 1937 ROCHESTER TIGERS (AFL)
ZOFKO, MICKEY (AUBURN) - BACK - 1971-74 DETROIT LIONS (NFC); 1974 NEW
    YORK GIANTS (NFC)
ZOIA, CLYDE (NOTRE DAME) - GUARD - 1920-23 CHICAGO CARDINALS
ZOLL, CARL - GUARD - 1921-22 GREEN BAY PACKERS
ZOLL, MARTIN - GUARD - 1921 GREEN BAY PACKERS
ZOLL, RICHARD (INDIANA) - GUARD - 1937-38 CLEVELAND RAMS
ZOMBEK, JOSEPH (PITTSBURGH) - END - 1954 PITTSBURGH STEELERS
ZONTINI, LOUIS (NOTRE DAME) - BACK - 1940-41 CHICAGO CARDINALS; 1944
    CLEVELAND RAMS; 1946 BUFFALO BISONS (AAFC)
ZOOK, JOHN (KANSAS) - END - 1969 ATLANTA FALCONS; 1970-74 ATLANTA
    FALCONS (NFC)
ZOPETTI, FRANK (DUQUESNE) - BACK - 1941 PITTSBURGH STEELERS
ZORICH, GEORGE (NORTHWESTERN) - GUARD - 1944-45 CHICAGO BEARS; 1946
    MIAMI SEAHAWKS (AAFC); 1947 BALTIMORE COLTS (AAFC)
ZUCCO, VICTOR (MICHIGAN STATE) - BACK - 1957-60 CHICAGO BEARS
ZUIDMULDER, DAVID (ST. AMBROSE) - BACK - 1929-31 GREEN BAY PACKERS
ZUK, STANLEY - BACK - 1936 BROOKLYN TIGERS (AFL)
ZUNKER, CHARLES (SOUTHWEST TEXAS STATE) - TACKLE - 1934 CINCINNATI
    REDS
ZUPEK, ALBERT (LAWRENCE) - BACK - 1946 GREEN BAY PACKERS
ZUVER, MERLE (NEBRASKA) - CENTER - 1930 GREEN BAY PACKERS
ZUZZIO, ANTHONY (MUHLENBERG) - GUARD - 1942 DETROIT LIONS
ZYNTELL, I. JAMES (HOLY CROSS) - GUARD - 1933 NEW YORK GIANTS;
    1933-35 PHILADELPHIA EAGLES; 1936-37 BOSTON SHAMROCKS (AFL)

4 The Coaches

Mr. National Football League

GEORGE S. HALAS

George Stanley Halas, aged twenty-two, his football career finished at the University of Illinois, sat at his team's banquet in the early winter of 1917 and listened to the farewell speech of Bob Zuppke, his coach, who was complaining bitterly about certain traditional patterns of life.

"Why is it," Zup demanded, "that just when you players are beginning to know something about football after three years, I lose you—and you stop playing? It makes no sense. Football is the only sport that ends a man's career just when it should be beginning."

That remark by Bob Zuppke might well be credited with starting a series of cosmic reactions which resulted, 50 years later, in more than five million rabid major league football fans scrambling into pro football parks to watch America's most thrilling sport. For the words made something click in the brain of Left End Halas, Navy-bound at the moment, but unhappy because he still had a lot of football left in his system and he didn't want it to rot there.

Halas had been an all-round athlete at Illinois, which he chose for an engineering course after graduating from Crane Tech in his native Chicago. He'd been so good at baseball that the New York Yankees wanted him as soon as the war was over. At basketball he had sparkled, becoming team captain in his senior year. But football was his own first choice, and he had become an end instead of a halfback as he had planned, because,

as Zuppke once said, "he ran so hard I was afraid he'd get killed as a halfback."

It was a happy surprise to George Halas when he reported to Great Lakes Naval Training Station to learn that the Navy was going to have football too, and that there were plenty of stars on hand to make it roll. Emmett Keefe, a guard from Notre Dame, was captain of the team. John "Paddy" Driscoll, a flashy back from Northwestern, was part of the backfield which included the versatile Jim Conzelman, Harold Erickson, Dutch Lauer and many others. Hugh Blacklock was a roadblock at tackle next to end George Halas, a neighborly pairing which was to endure long after the war was over.

Great Lakes was good enough to tie Notre Dame, to beat the Naval Academy at Annapolis, to be chosen to play in the Rose Bowl on New Year's Day, 1919, where they caused a sensation by upsetting the tremendous team from the base at Mare Island.

Halas was discharged as an ensign and soon reported to the Yankee baseball team in Florida, depressed once more because he still had lots of football left in his fuel-system and it seemed that now it must surely be over for him. He soon won a permanent job with the Yankees. Then he sustained a leg injury in a thundering slide into third base after belting one of Rube Marquard's slants through the outfield during an exhibition game. The injury sidelined him and eventually caused his release to St. Paul. He finished an impressive rookie season there and was headed back to the Yankees the next spring. But he was still restless for more football; he still remembered Bob Zuppke's remarks.

He managed to play a few football games that fall with the independent team of Hammond, Indiana, and then came the break which led the way to the Chicago Bears and the National Football League. Mr. A. E. Staley, owner of a corn products company in Decatur, Illinois, was a sports fan who wanted his firm to be represented by teams in all possible sports. Joe "Iron Man" McGinnity managed the strong Staley baseball team. Why shouldn't George Halas, the young firebrand who would play football twenty-four hours a day if he could arrange it, be the Staley football leader?

It was all right with Halas. He worked full hours at the plant, played on its baseball team and started recruiting football players with the same acumen and fervor he still employs. When the American Professional Football Association was organized in Ralph Hays's garage at Canton, Ohio, that fall, Halas was there, ready to go with a roster of players that scared the other owners half to death. He proposed to line up with Guy Chamberlain and himself at end; Hugh Blacklock and Bert Ingwerson at tackle; Hubbard Shoemaker and Jerry Jones at guard; George Trafton, center; and the backs would be Ed "Dutch" Sternaman, Jake Lanum, Bob Koehler, Walter "Pard" Pearce and Charlie Dressen. They were the cream of the college crop. His only disappointment was the fact that Paddy Driscoll had joined the Chicago Cardinals and it would be six years before Halas could sign him to a contract.

The Staleys were indeed loaded with talent and end-coach-manager George Halas was a clever field general. They won every game until the Cardinals dumped them, 7–6. Then they came back to whip the Cards, 10–0, to finish a glorious season.

Papa Bear was on his way.

During the ensuing five decades, Halas and his Monsters of the Midway dominated football. They won the most championships, 7; they won the most games, over 400; they scored the most points, more than 11,000; they gained the most yards, nearly 25 miles;

they scored the most touchdowns, nearly 1,600; played to most fans, nearly 15,000,000 They probably made the most money. And they were definitely penalized the most.

The list of Bear players shines brighter than all the rest in the honor rolls of football. They have been noted for team spirit and have won many games with inferior teams because of this spirit, which originates in the explosive violence and the competitive drive of their owner-coach. Since he retired as a player in 1932 ("When they began to run over me, under me, around me and through me"), Halas has prowled the sidelines through nearly every game, except during World War II when he served in the Navy as a commander. Every cell in his body is in every play, and his spectacular rages against officiating lapses have bemused hundreds of thousands of fans.

Halas made a habit of writing "first" into the record book from the start. The Bears were the first official champions of the reorganized league in 1921 when they moved to Chicago to play that season as the Staleys and to become the Bears a year later. They were the first professional team to practice daily; the first big league team to travel coast-to-coast (the Red Grange Unveiling Tour, which started in Chicago on Thanksgiving Day, 1925, ended three months later after playing in New York, Washington, Providence, Pittsburgh, Detroit, Chicago again, Tampa, Jacksonville, Miami, New Orleans, Los Angeles, San Diego, San Francisco, Portland and Seattle). Other minor firsts were a band and a team song, and a club newspaper; and they were the first to have their games broadcast on radio, and to take movies of games for study and strategy.

Nearly every team which plays football under the banner of T-formation in 1952, whether it be professional, college or grade school, will be using plays which were first diagrammed by the Chicago Bears, which means by George Halas and his Bear-trained staff, all former Bear stars, with occasional help from the brilliant theorist, Clark Shaughnessy. Halas added the man-in-motion to the ineffective T of older days and made it come alive. In 1937, he bet the future of his team on the ability of an awkward young halfback named Sidney Luckman to make it work. Luckman floundered for a few weeks, but suddenly, through unbeatable determination and endless hours of practice, he got it and a new era was born in football. Halas, Luckman and the T grew to maturity together.

Luckman went on to rank himself as the smartest field general of them all. His nickname, "Mr. Quarterback," was well earned. Today George Halas will testify under oath that Sid Luckman never called a wrong play during twelve years of action; that he was always thinking so far ahead of his opponents, his teammates and everyone else, that he drove most of them crazy, including George Halas himself.

It was inevitable that someday George Halas would come up with a performance that would live forever as the mark of perfection. It happened in Griffith Stadium, Washington, D.C. on December 8, 1940, and when it was over, Steve Owen, coach of the New York Giants, which team had finished third in the Eastern division behind the Redskins, had this to say, "Now I'm glad we didn't win the Eastern championship. In fact, I'm glad we didn't finish second. Even that would have been too close to the Bears today."

For the story of that spectacle, unparalleled in football history and unlikely to be repeated, this encyclopedia will borrow from that fine book, *The Chicago Bears*, written by Howard Roberts, pro football expert of the Chicago *Daily News*, and published by G. P. Putnam's Sons, the complete story of the cold-blooded, premeditated massacre of a sorrowful group of young men known as the Washington Redskins. It was a crime committed with well-planned malice aforethought. In sixty minutes of official play, George Halas made his team do everything lethal a football team can do a little better than it has ever been done before or since, to score a staggering 73–0 humiliation over one of the strongest teams Washington has ever had —and they have had some dandies; to annihilate a team which had beaten the Bears, 7–3, only three weeks before.

It was the masterpiece of football, fashioned by George Halas. This is the way Roberts saw it:

Sunday, December 8, 1940, was a beautiful day in Washington. The sun shone brilliantly and with a warmth surprisingly pleasant for the time of year. The sky was blue and cloudless. Scarcely a breeze rippled the flags over Griffith Stadium where 36,034 people clustered in quivering anticipation as their Redskins prepared to face the Bears for the championship.

Two hours later, although the sun still shone, it was the darkest day the nation's capital would know until another Sunday, 364 days later, when Jap bombs fell on Pearl Harbor to plunge the United States into war.

The events that filled those two hours are unparalleled in sports history. They were so beyond comprehension that even those who saw them or took part in them have difficulty believing it wasn't a dream. To all but a handful of those 36,034 the dream was a nightmare, yet they left the park content. They were disappointed, certainly, but not unhappy. After all, they could tell their grandchildren that they had witnessed the impossible; that they had looked on perfection.

The Bears were perfection that day. There is no other explanation for the score that reads like a misprint in the record books: Chicago Bears 73; Washington Redskins 0.

The score itself is a story, but back of it is another one, a tale of psychology, of emotional uplift, of planning so meticulous that almost nothing was left to chance— except the fervent hope the Redskins would employ the same defense that had kept their goal line inviolate three weeks before.

Halas and his board of strategy knew from bitter experience that Washington was not a team to be taken lightly, for with Slingin' Sammy Baugh pitching passes, the Redskins were almost certain to score against the best of defenses. The trick was to keep Baugh from passing, in so far as that could be achieved. And the best way to keep Sammy from throwing touchdowns was to keep his hands off the ball as much as possible. If the Bears could control the ball throughout most of the afternoon, they might be able to outscore the enemy.

With that in mind, the faculty of

Halas U. set about polishing their T until it shone. Movies of the Redskin defeat were studied over and over again. So were films of other Bear-Redskin games. From these showings and from the penciled notes in the coach's little black book were culled only the plays that had worked against Washington. These were perfected and refined; new variations were added; plays the Redskins had stopped were discarded and replaced by new ones calculated to take advantage of Ray Flaherty's defense.

The players saw the movies almost as many times as did the coaches. Every play was analyzed—why this one worked, why that one didn't, what this mistake cost, what that good block accomplished. The Bears, seeing their previous mistakes pointed out on the screen, vowed they wouldn't happen again. Morning practice on the field was followed by chalk talks, lectures, written examinations on individual assignments, more movies. Clark Shaughnessy was brought in to discuss strategy with the quarterbacks—Luckman, Masterson and Solly Sherman.

The greatest weapon Halas brought into play was psychology. The Redskins had made what Halas termed some "tactical vocal errors" after the earlier 7–3 victory, and now they were deftly turned against them. It seems that a club official with a careless disregard for the interpretation that might be placed on his words, had been quoted in the public prints as referring to the Bears by such uncomplimentary terms, as "front-runners" and a "first-half ball club." The Redskins themselves had called the Bears "crybabies" in the final minute of their earlier meeting.

When the Bears came to practice the Monday morning preceding the championship game, their eyes fell upon these disparagements of their courage and staying power plastering the walls of the clubhouse. The reaction was terrific. Mutterings grew to shouts of revenge. The boys were mad clean through. Halas kept them that way, reminding them that Washington regarded them as quitters a final time in his between-halves speech even though the score at that time was Bears 28; Washington 0.

Get one of the 1940 Bears into conversation today about that week of drill and

the game itself, and you'll find him turning slightly hysterical, his voice rising in excitement and his eyes flashing.

"I've never experienced anything like it," Luckman admits with a look almost of wonder. "There was a feeling of tension in the air as though something tremendous was about to happen."

That feeling was apparent on the train en route to Washington. Ball players customarily while away train rides by playing cards or sitting around swapping stories. There is laughing, joking, wisecracks, fun. But not this time. There was no laughter, no frolicking, not a single deck of cards in sight. The Bears sat huddled in their seats, notebooks on their laps, studying.

One bit of superstition crept in, too. For luck the Bears moved from their usual Washington hotel to another, a shift Secretary Frank Halas believes entitles him to a share of credit for the momentous events that were in store.

The opening whistle unleashed a Bear attack that was concentrated fury. The kick-off sailed into the arms of Nolting, who sprinted back twenty-two yards to the twenty-four yard line. In the huddle Luckman called a "feeler," the first of four Bear offensive plays having been charted long before to test the Redskin defense. Was it the same as before? Everything depended on the answer to that question.

Kavanaugh, at left end, went 18 yards out on the flank, and the Washington right halfback followed him out. Nolting, at left half, went in motion to the right, and the Redskin backerup trailed him out. That was all Luckman wanted to see. The Washington defense was unchanged. On the play McAfee bolted between guard and tackle for eight yards.

On the next play the left end went wide again, but McAfee, the right half, went in motion to his left. Luckman, making a reverse pivot, gave the ball to Osmanski on a run to the spread side.

"Bill was really driving when I handed off that ball to him," Luckman grins. "I knew he was going someplace in a hurry."

That someplace was sixty-eight yards to a touchdown.

Here, however, is a secret never before revealed about the play—it didn't go according to plan or blueprint. Actually it called for a straight slant off tackle, but McAfee's block hadn't flattened the Redskin right end.

"George had him blocked off," says Osmanski, "but he was reaching out with his hands, and I was afraid he could grab me, so I just made a sort of dip and went out wide around end." That dip, incidentally, is now a charted play in the Bears' book.

Osmanski, who was possessed of jet-propulsion acceleration, streaked away, as Musso, pulling out from right guard to join the interference, flattened the up man in the secondary. Near the Washington thirty-five yard line Osmanski was walking a tightrope down the south sideline, with Ed "Chug" Justice and Jimmy Johnston closing in on him. Osmanski saw them, but what neither he nor the two Redskins saw was George Wilson, cutting across from his position at right end, whizzing like a tornado into their path. Just as Justice set himself to tackle Osmanski, Wilson hurtled into him from the blind side with such force the impact could be felt in the stands.

"I've never seen a block like it," Halas maintains.

It knocked Justice into Johnston and both of them into a cartwheel that sent them rolling out of the field of play. Both had to be helped to their feet. As a parlay it was a knockout.

Osmanski, of course, simply kept running. As he flashed over the last white line and into the end zone with a touchdown, the big scoreboard clock showed just fifty-five seconds of playing time elapsed. Jack Manders kicked the extra point, but the parade wasn't on—not quite yet.

Max Krause, who is so much a Redskin at heart that he served as their water boy at times while he was in the Navy and too old and too busy to play football, took the next kickoff and promptly scared the Bears half to death. Straight down the field he raced for sixty-two yards before he was finally tackled on the Bear thirty-two yard line. Then came the play that turned the ball game and set the Bear adding machine in motion.

Baugh faded back and shot a long pass to Charlie Malone. The big end was in the clear with a touchdown and an almost certain tie score in his grasp—but he dropped the ball. And, as that pass trickled off his finger tips, Fate turned her back on the Redskins. Had Malone caught the ball the game might have been the nip-and-tuck, slam-bang affair a championship game is supposed to be. As it was, the Redskins never again were a factor.

No one suspected that such was the case when Bob Masterson missed a field goal attempt from the thirty-two yard line, but the handwriting soon became legible on the wall. The Bears put it there with a magnificent display of power football that swept eighty yards in seventeen plays and four first downs without the use of a pass. Luckman scored the touchdown on a sneak of about a foot under Bulldog Turner. Bob Snyder came in for Osmanski to add the point and make the score 14–0.

The Redskins, startled and shocked into desperation, tried three fruitless passes after receiving the kickoff, then were forced to punt, Luckman coming back to the Washington forty-two. Here Luckman called for almost the identical play on which Osmanski had made his great run. This time, however, Joe Maniaci was the fullback, and instead of taking the ball on a handoff, he got it on a shovel pass. Otherwise the pattern was almost identical, for Maniaci didn't stop running until he had touchdown number three. Phil Martinovich converted, making it three different Bears to add a point after each of three scores.

Twelve minutes and forty seconds had been ticked off on the clock, and the scoreboard read: Bears 21; Redskins 0.

Still another touchdown was added before the end of the half, Kavanaugh leaping in the corner of the end zone behind Frank Filchock and Andy Farkas to catch Luckman's thirty-yard pass. Bob Snyder kicked the twenty-eighth point.

The Redskins still refused to concede defeat and came out for the second half charged with new spirit. Wee Willie Wilkin, the gigantic blond tackle, in particular, was a heroic figure until he was led off the field late in the game, crying in anger and humiliation.

But if the Redskins were fired by the

half-time revival, so were the Bears. Halas' brief oration dwelt solely on the premise that Washington regarded the Bears strictly as a "first-half ball club" and "quitters."

They quickly proved this to be a myth. On the second play of the third period Baugh attempted a short pass to fullback Johnston in the flat, but Hampton Pool, the Bear end, sensed the play, batted the ball into the air, caught it, and sped fifteen yards to a touchdown. He had scored before most of the Redskins knew anything was amiss.

That was the coup de grace. The Redskins were done. You could see them wilt before your eyes as the fire and spark and spirit drained out of them like air from a punctured tire.

Three more Bear touchdowns clattered across in the third period. Nolting collected the first when he bolted through a quick-opening hole inside the Washington right tackle and scooted twenty-three yards. Two plays after the ensuing kickoff McAfee intercepted a pass by Roy Zimmerman and zigzagged thirty-four yards behind fine blocking to plant the ball in the end zone. Another Zimmerman pass boomeranged later, Turner intercepting this one and going twenty-one yards to score, aided by a furious block with which Pool removed the unhappy Zimmerman from the picture.

The fourth quarter brought more of the same as the "first-half ball club" made it seven touchdowns for the second half. Harry Clark started it with a forty-four-yard run in the course of which he powered his way right out of Filchock's tackle on the ten yard line.

The Redskins received once more, and immediately things went wrong for them again. A pass from center got away from Filchock and Turner recovered only two yards from the goal line. Famiglietti bridged this gap in one drive.

At just about this moment the public address loudspeakers boomed forth with what was probably the most ill-advised and poorly timed announcement ever made. "Those who wish to purchase season tickets for next year . . ." came the brassy voice, only to be lost in a cascade of boos and catcalls. Strangely enough those boos meant

nothing for the Redskins advance sale for the '41 season had set a new record high by Christmas.

Again the Bears kicked off, and this time the Redskins held possession of the ball for only one play. The second was a pass by Filchock, and Maniaci stepped into its path, returning twenty-one yards to Washington's forty-two yard line. From there the Bears turned on the power, with Clark picking up the final yard and the last points of an historic afternoon.

Dick Plasman and Joe Stydahar added extra points from placement in this half with Maniaci getting another on a pass from Sherman. By this time the Bears didn't care much whether they kicked extra points or not, while the officials and the Washington ball club were hoping they wouldn't. Every placement kick propelled by the strong and accurate toes of the Bears, sailed into the stands and didn't return. So it was that after the last two TDs officials asked the Bears please not to kick for points. Sherman, an obliging fellow, tried passing for two points, one of which scored.

In the course of compiling this astronomical score the Bears gained 372 yards rushing to Washington's 3. But this wasn't the only unusual phase of the statistics. The Redskins, the top offensive team in the league, had been held scoreless for the first time. The Bears divided their eleven touchdowns among ten men, Clark being the only repeater. In all, sixteen Bears shared in the point production, six having a hand (or toe) in conversions. Eight Washington passes were intercepted.

The Bears never let up. So tensely were they keyed for this game that even late in the fourth period players leaving the field would whack their substitutes on the seats of their silk pants and exhort: "Pour it on. Don't let up. Pour it on." They kept on pouring their T until the cup ran over.

Superlatives fairly drooled off the typewriters of the nation's top sports writers as they reached in vain for words to describe the game. Typical of the accolades was that given a Washington newspaper by "Dutch" Bergman, then coach at Catholic University.

"I saw the perfect football team in the Bears," Bergman wrote. "I have been associated with the game as player and coach for twenty-five years, but never in that time did I ever see a team that did everything perfectly, with such flawless execution, as did the Bears in humbling the Redskins."

Phil Handler, line coach of the Chicago Cardinals, shook his head and muttered, "I've never seen anything like it and never will again."

Halas, over the radio, came up with his second masterpiece of the afternoon, this time one of understatement. "My team played a great game," he told the armchair spectators. "I think they deserved to win."

The bark of the gun ending the massacre caused some pressbox wit to remark, "George Marshall (Redskin Owner) just shot himself." The Redskin man hadn't gone to such lengths, but he was heartbroken, shamefaced, and completely at a loss to account for the holocaust.

The next day as the Bears rode triumphantly home with bruises, a championship, and a few hangovers, a Pullman passenger looked with interest at the rainbow decorating Danny Fortmann's left eye.

"My, my," he clucked sympathetically. "That's a terrible black eye you have there."

"Yes," Fortmann agreed, "but it will disappear in a day or two. Think of the Redskins—that seventy-three-to-nothing score is in the record books for all time."

George Halas, independently wealthy now, has founded a dynasty of sport. His Bears stand for quality, spirit and a dramatic ability. They are entirely his creation. The National Football League can be credited more to him than to any other man. His innovations on the T-formation dominate football in every league.

It is with restraint, rather than over-enthusiasm, that the hungry Bohemian lad who listened, more than 50 years ago, to a querulous complaint by Bob Zuppke, is now called "Mr. Football" as often as he is "Papa Bear." For it was his dream alone that has grown into spectacular reality; his courage and determination that would not let it die.

NATIONAL LEAGUE/
CONFERENCE COACHES

(In 1970, the NFL became NFC after merger and expansion with AFL/AFC)

ATLANTA FALCONS

1966–68	Norb Hecker*
1968–74	Norm Van Brocklin**
1974	Marion Campbell

*Released Oct. 1, 1968
**Released Nov. 5, 1974

BALTIMORE COLTS

(Transferred to AFC in 1970)

1950	Clem Crowe
1953	Keith Molesworth
1954–62	Weeb Ewbank
1963–69	Don Shula

BOSTON REDSKINS

(Transferred to Washington 1937)

1932	Lud Ray
1933–34	Bill "Lone Star" Dietz
1935	Eddie Casey
1936	Ray Flaherty

CHICAGO BEARS

(Known as Decatur Staleys in 1920, Chicago Staleys in 1921)

1920–29	George Halas
1930–32	Ralph Jones

1933–42	George Halas*
1942–45	Luke Johnsos and Heartley "Hunk" Anderson**
1946–55	George Halas
1956–57	John "Paddy" Driscoll
1958–67	George Halas
1968–71	Jim Dooley
1972–74	Abe Gibron

*Re-entered Navy Oct. 25, 1942
**Co-coaches

CHICAGO CARDINALS

(Transferred to St. Louis 1960)

1920	Marshall Smith
1921–22	John "Paddy" Driscoll
1923–24	Arnold Horween
1925–26	Norm Barry
1927	Fred Gillies
1928	Guy Chamberlain
1929–30	Ernie Nevers
1931	Leroy Andrews*
1931	Ernie Nevers
1932	Jack Chevigny
1933–34	Paul Schissler
1935–38	Milan Creighton
1939	Ernie Nevers
1940–42	Jimmy Conzelman
1943–45	Phil Handler**
1946–48	Jimmy Conzelman
1949	Phil Handler and Buddy Parker***
1950–51	Curly Lambeau
1952	Joe Kuharich
1953–54	Joe Stydahar
1955–57	Ray Richards
1958–59	Frank "Pop" Ivy

*Resigned after 2 games 1931
**Merged with Pittsburgh 1944 Handler was co-coach with Kiesling
***Co-coaches

CLEVELAND BROWNS

(Transferred to AFC in 1970)

1950–62	Paul Brown
1963–69	Blanton Collier

CLEVELAND RAMS

(Transferred to Los Angeles 1946)

1937–38	Hugo Bezdek
1938	Art Lewis
1939–42	Dutch Clark
1943	(Suspended operation)
1944	Buff Donelli
1945	Adam Walsh

DALLAS COWBOYS

1960–74	Tom Landry

DETROIT LIONS

(Transferred from Portsmouth after 1933)

1934–36	Potsy Clark

1937–38	Dutch Clark
1939	Gus Henderson
1940	Potsy Clark
1941–42	Bill Edwards*
1942	John "Bull" Karcis
1943–47	Gus Dorais
1948–50	Bo McMillin
1951–56	Buddy Parker
1957–64	George Wilson
1965–66	Harry Gilmer
1967–72	Joe Schmidt
1973	Don McCafferty
1974	Rick Forzano

*Released Oct. 4, 1942

GREEN BAY PACKERS

1921–49	Curly Lambeau
1950–53	Gene Ronzani
1954–57	Lisle Blackbourn
1958	Ray McLean
1959–67	Vince Lombardi
1968–70	Phil Bengston
1971–74	Dan Devine

LOS ANGELES RAMS

(Transferred from Cleveland after 1945)

1946	Adam Walsh
1947	Bob Snyder
1948–49	Clark Shaughnessy
1950–52	Joe Stydahar*
1952–54	Hamp Pool
1955–59	Sid Gillman
1960–62	Bob Waterfield**
1962–65	Harland Svare
1966–70	George Allen
1971–72	Tommy Prothro
1973–74	Chuck Knox

*Resigned after 1 game 1952
**Resigned after 8 games 1962

MINNESOTA VIKINGS

1961–66	Norm Van Brocklin
1967–74	Bud Grant

NEW ORLEANS SAINTS

1967–70	Tom Fears*
1970–72	J. D. Roberts
1973–74	John North

*Released Nov. 3, 1970

NEW YORK GIANTS

1925	Bob Folwell
1926	Joe Alexander
1927–28	Earl Potteiger
1929–30	Leroy Andrews
1931–53	Steve Owen
1954–60	Jim Lee Howell
1961–68	Allie Sherman
1969–73	Alex Webster
1974	Bill Arnsparger

PHILADELPHIA EAGLES

1933–35	Lud Wray

1936–40	Bert Bell
1941–50	Greasy Neale*
1951	Bo McMillin**
1951	Wayne Millner
1952–55	Jim Trimble
1956–57	Hugh Devore
1958–60	Buck Shaw
1961–63	Nick Skorich
1964–68	Joe Kuharich
1969–71	Jerry Williams***
1971–72	Ed Khayat
1973–74	Mike McCormack

*Merged with Pittsburgh 1943, Neale was co-coach with Kiesling
**Resigned due to illness after 2 games
***Released Oct. 6, 1971

PITTSBURGH STEELERS

(Transferred to AFC in 1970)

1933	Jap Douds
1934	Luby DiMeolo
1935–36	Joe Bach
1937–39	John "Blood" McNally*
1939–40	Walt Kiesling
1941	Bert Bell**
1941	Buff Donelli
1941–44	Walt Kiesling***
1945	Jim Leonard
1946–47	Jock Sutherland
1948–51	John Michelosen
1952–53	Joe Bach
1954–56	Walt Kiesling
1957–64	Buddy Parker
1965	Mike Nixon
1966–68	Bill Austin
1969	Chuck Noll

*Resigned in mid-season
**Retired after 2 games
***Merged with Philadelphia 1943, Chicago Cardinals 1944

PORTSMOUTH SPARTANS

(Transferred to Detroit 1934)

1930–33	Potsy Clark

ST. LOUIS CARDINALS

(Transferred from Chicago after 1959)

1960–61	Frank "Pop" Ivy*
1961	Chuck Drulis, Ray Prochaska and Ray Willsey
1962–65	Wally Lemm
1966–70	Charley Winner
1971–72	Bob Hollway
1973–74	Don Coryell

*Resigned after 12 games 1961, three assistants served as co-coaches

SAN FRANCISCO 49ERS

1950–54	Buck Shaw
1955	Red Strader
1956–58	Frank Albert
1959–63	Red Hickey*
1963–67	Jack Christiansen
1968–74	Dick Nolan

*Resigned after 3rd game 1963

WASHINGTON REDSKINS

(Transferred from Boston after 1936)

1937–42	Ray Flaherty
1943	Dutch Bergman
1944–45	Dudley DeGroot
1946–48	Glenn "Turk" Edwards
1949	John Whelchel*
1949–51	Herman Ball**
1951	Dick Todd
1952–53	Curly Lambeau
1954–58	Joe Kuharich
1959–60	Mike Nixon
1961–65	Bill McPeak
1966–68	Otto Graham
1969	Vince Lombardi
1970	Bill Austin
1971–74	George Allen

*Resigned Nov. 7, 1949
**Resigned Oct. 18, 1951

AMERICAN LEAGUE/ CONFERENCE COACHES

(In 1970, the AFL became AFC after merger and expansion with NFL/NFC)

BALTIMORE COLTS

(Member of NFL 1950, 1953–1969)

1970–72 Don McCafferty*
1972 John Sandusky
1973–74 Howard Schnellenberger**
1974 Joe Thomas
*Released Oct. 16, 1972
**Released Sept. 29, 1974

BOSTON PATRIOTS

(See New England)

BUFFALO BILLS

1960–61 Buster Ramsey
1962–65 Lou Saban
1966–68 Joe Collier*
1968 Harvey Johnson
1969–70 John Rauch
1971 Harvey Johnson
1972–74 Lou Saban
*Released Sept. 15, 1968

CINCINNATI BENGALS

1968–74 Paul Brown

CLEVELAND BROWNS

(Member of NFL 1950–69)

1970 Blanton Collier
1971–74 Nick Skorich

DALLAS TEXANS

(Transferred to Kansas City 1963)

1960–62 Hank Stram

DENVER BRONCOS

1960–61 Frank Filchock
1962–64 Jack Faulkner*
1964–66 Mac Speedie**
1966 Ray Malavisi
1967–71 Lou Saban***
1971 Jerry Smith
1972–74 John Ralston
*Released Oct. 4, 1964
**Resigned Sept. 18, 1966
***Resigned Nov. 17, 1971

HOUSTON OILERS

1960–61 Lou Rymkus*
1961 Wally Lemm

1962–63 Frank "Pop" Ivy
1964 Sammy Baugh
1965 Hugh "Bones" Taylor
1966–70 Wally Lemm
1971 Ed Hughes
1972–73 Bill Peterson**
1973–74 Sid Gillman
*Released Oct. 16, 1961
**Released Oct. 16, 1973

KANSAS CITY CHIEFS

(Transferred from Dallas after 1962)

1963–74 Hank Stram

LOS ANGELES CHARGERS

(Transferred to San Diego 1961)

1960 Sid Gillman

MIAMI DOLPHINS

1966–69 George Wilson
1970–74 Don Shula

NEW ENGLAND PATRIOTS

(Played as Boston Patriots 1960–70)

1960–61 Lou Saban*
1961–68 Mike Holovak
1969–70 Clive Rush**
1970–72 John Mazur***
1972 Phil Bengston
1973–74 Chuck Fairbanks
*Released Oct. 19, 1961
**Released Nov. 4, 1970
***Resigned Nov. 13, 1972

NEW YORK JETS

(Played as New York Titans 1960–62)

1960–61 Sammy Baugh
1962 Clyde "Bulldog" Turner
1963–73 Weeb Ewbank
1974 Charley Winner

OAKLAND RAIDERS

1960 Eddie Erdalatz
1961–62 Marty Feldman
1962 Red Conkright
1963–65 Al Davis
1966–68 John Rauch
1969–74 John Madden

PITTSBURGH STEELERS

(Member of NFL 1933–69)

1970–74   Chuck Noll

SAN DIEGO CHARGERS

(Transferred from Los Angeles after 1960)

1961–69   Sid Gillman*

1969–70   Charlie Waller
1971   Sid Gillman**
1971–73   Harland Svare***
1973   Ron Waller
1974   Tommy Prothro
*Resigned Nov. 10, 1969
**Resigned Nov. 22, 1971
***Resigned Nov. 5, 1973

5 The Teams

In modern major league football, thirty-plus rather than eleven men make up the team. Limitless combinations of eleven can be made from thirty-plus. There is the kick-off team; the kick-off receiving team; the team for the plunge through the middle; the team for skirting the end; the team for forward-passing in endless patterns of deception; the teams for defense against all these and more expected thrusts by the enemy; the team to kick field goals and extra points; the team to defend against them; the punting team; the punt-receiving team. Within these named there are countless combinations of men who do each factor best, so that in a league game, which averages eighty offensive and eighty defensive plays, more than a hundred different line-ups could be found on the field.

The team is the final end product of all the players and coaches listed in previous pages. The headline names, the All-Time All-Stars, are forgotten for the moment. The muscular device made up of twenty-two legs, twenty-two arms and twenty-two eyes must start and accelerate and move as one gigantic creature.

The records of those who did this best will be found at, or near, the top of the ensuing categories and break-downs.

In 1970, the National Football League and the American Football League merged and expanded into two conferences under one major league, the National Football League. These two conferences, the NFC and AFC, with three divisions each, play divisional playoffs with a fourth qualifier to determine the conference winners. The World Championship Game is then played between the NFC and AFC.

TIE-BREAKING PROCEDURE FOR NFL POST-SEASON PLAYOFFS

Qualifiers for post-season playoffs: Four teams from each Conference, a total of eight. In each Conference, the three divisional champions enter the playoff and the fourth team is the remaining team with the best won-lost percentage. To break any tie within a division, these steps will be taken, in order:

DIVISION TIES

a) Best won-lost percentage in head-to-head competition
b) Best won-lost percentage in games within division
c) Best won-lost percentage in games within conference
d) Best point differential in head-to-head competition
e) Best point rating (offense and defense) applied to division games only
f) Best point rating (offense and defense) applied to full 14-game regular season schedule
g) Coin flip

If in selecting the fourth qualifier, there are two or more teams tied with the leading won-lost percentage, these steps will be taken, in order:

a) If there are more than two teams tied, and two are from the same division, the division tie will be broken first using the method for breaking division ties. The surviving ties then are broken through these steps:

CONFERENCE TIES

b) Best percentage in head-to-head competition, when applicable. Head-to-head is applicable when each team involved in the tie has had at least one opportunity to play one of the other teams involved. If A, B, and C are tied and team C has played neither A nor B, head-to-head cannot be applied.

c) Best won-lost percentage in games within conference

d) Best point differential in head-to-head competition, when applicable (see point "b" for applicability)

e) Best point rating (offense and defense) applied to conference games only

f) Best point rating (offense and defense) applied to full 14-game regular season schedule

g) Coin flip

Notes: —If there is a first place tie in a division, the loser under the tie-breaking system above becomes a candidate for fourth qualifier.

—The point rating system (steps 5 and 6 in Division Ties and steps 4 and 5 in Conference Ties) is based on points scored and points allowed by each team, with each of the 13 teams in each conference rated from 1 to 13 on offense and defense. The team with the lowest number of rating points is the winner. These would be computed on intra-division games, and if still tied, on all 14 games, to break a division tie; on intra-conference games, and if still tied, on all 14 games to break a conference tie.

WORLD CHAMPIONSHIP GAME (SUPER BOWL)

Year	Date	Winner—Share	Loser—Share	Score	Site	Attendance
1975	Jan. 12	Pit.-AFC ($15,000)	Minn.-NFC ($7,500)	16-6	N.O.	80,997
1974	Jan. 13	Mia.-AFC ($15,000)	Minn.-NFC ($7,500)	24-7	Hou.	71,882
1973	Jan. 14	Mia.-AFC ($15,000)	Wash.-NFC ($7,500)	14-7	L.A.	90,182
1972	Jan. 16	Dal.-NFC ($15,000)	Mia.-AFC ($7,500)	24-3	N.O.	81,023
1971	Jan. 17	Balt.-AFC ($15,000)	Dal.-NFC ($7,500)	16-13	Miami	79,204
1970	Jan. 11	K.C.-AFL ($15,000)	Minn.-NFL ($7,500)	23-7	N.O.	80,562
1969	Jan. 12	N.Y.-AFL ($15,000)	Balt.-NFL ($7,500)	16-7	Miami	75,389
1968	Jan. 14	G.B.-NFL ($15,000)	Oak.-AFL ($7,500)	33-14	Miami	75,546
1967	Jan. 15	G.B.-NFL ($15,000)	K.C.-AFL ($7,500)	35-10	L. A.	61,946

NFL/NFC CHAMPIONSHIP GAME

Year	Date	Winner—Share		Loser—Share		Score	Site	Attendance
1974*	Dec. 29	Vikings	($8,500)	Rams	($5,500)	14-10	Minnesota	47,404
1973*	Dec. 30	Vikings	($8,500)	Cowboys	($5,500)	27-10	Dallas	64,422
1972*	Dec. 31	Redskins	($8,500)	Cowboys	($5,500)	26-3	Washington	53,129
1971*	Jan. 2	Cowboys	($8,500)	49ers	($5,500)	14-3	Dallas	63,409
1970*	Jan. 3	Cowboys	($8,500)	49ers	($5,500)	17-10	San Francisco	59,364
1969	Jan. 4	Vikings	($7,930)	Browns	($5,118)	27-7	Minnesota	46,503
1968	Dec. 29	Colts	($9,306)	Browns	($5,963)	34-0	Cleveland	78,410
1967	Dec. 31	Packers	($7,950)	Cowboys	($5,299)	21-17	Green Bay	50,861
1966	Jan. 1	Packers	($9,813)	Cowboys	($6,527)	34-27	Dallas	74,152
1965	Jan. 2	Packers	($7,819)	Browns	($5,288)	23-12	Green Bay	50,777
1964	Dec. 27	Browns ($8,052)		Colts ($5,571)		27-0	Cleveland	79,544
1963	Dec. 29	Bears ($5,899)		Giants ($4,218)		14-10	Chicago	45,801
1962	Dec. 30	Packers ($5,888)		Giants ($4,166)		16-7	New York	64,892
1961	Dec. 31	Packers ($5,195)		Giants ($3,339)		37-0	Green Bay	39,029
1960	Dec. 26	Eagles ($5,116)		Packers ($3,105)		17-13	Philadelphia	67,325
1959	Dec. 27	Colts ($4,674)		Giants ($3,083)		31-16	Baltimore	57,545
1958	Dec. 28	Colts ($4,718)		Giants ($3,111)		23-17**	New York	64,185
1957	Dec. 29	Lions ($4,295)		Browns ($2,750)		59-14	Detroit	55,263
1956	Dec. 30	Giants ($3,779)		Bears ($2,485)		47-7	New York	56,836
1955	Dec. 26	Browns ($3,508)		Rams ($2,316)		38-14	Los Angeles	85,693
1954	Dec. 26	Browns ($2,478)		Lions ($1,585)		56-10	Cleveland	43,827
1953	Dec. 27	Lions ($2,424)		Browns ($1,654)		17-16	Detroit	54,577
1952	Dec. 28	Lions ($2,274)		Browns ($1,712)		17-7	Cleveland	50,934
1951	Dec. 23	Rams ($2,108)		Browns ($1,483)		24-17	Los Angeles	57,522
1950	Dec. 24	Browns ($1,113)		Rams ($686)		30-28	Cleveland	29,751
1949	Dec. 18	Eagles ($1,094)		Rams ($739)		14-0	Los Angeles	27,980
1948	Dec. 19	Eagles ($1,540)		Cardinals ($874)		7-0	Philadelphia	36,309
1947	Dec. 28	Cardinals ($1,132)		Eagles ($754)		28-21	Chicago	30,759
1946	Dec. 15	Bears ($1,975)		Giants ($1,295)		24-14	New York	58,346
1945	Dec. 16	Rams ($1,469)		Redskins ($902)		15-14	Cleveland	32,178
1944	Dec. 17	Packers ($1,449)		Giants ($814)		14-7	New York	46,016
1943	Dec. 26	Bears ($1,146)		Redskins ($765)		41-21	Chicago	34,320
1942	Dec. 13	Redskins ($965)		Bears ($637)		14-6	Washington	36,006
1941	Dec. 21	Bears ($430)		Giants ($288)		37-9	Chicago	13,341
1940	Dec. 8	Bears ($873)		Redskins ($606)		73-0	Washington	36,034
1939	Dec. 10	Packers ($850)		Giants ($650)		27-0	Milwaukee	32,279
1938	Dec. 11	Giants ($900)		Packers ($700)		23-17	New York	48,120
1937	Dec. 12	Redskins ($300)		Bears ($250)		28-21	Chicago	15,870
1936	Dec. 13	Packers ($540)		Redskins ($400)		21-6	New York	29,545
1935	Dec. 15	Lions ($300)		Giants ($200)		26-7	Detroit	15,000
1934	Dec. 9	Giants ($621)		Bears ($414)		30-13	New York	35,059
1933	Dec. 17	Bears ($210)		Giants ($140)		23-21	Chicago	26,000

* NFC, Starting 1970
** (Sudden death—8:15)

BERT BELL BENEFIT BOWL

(Miami Playoff Bowl)
Discontinued
(This game was played from 1960–69 and
was between the runners-up in each division
of the NFL)

1969—Los Angeles 31; Dallas 0
1968—Dallas 17; Minnesota 13
1967—Los Angeles 30; Cleveland 6

1966—Baltimore, 20; Philadelphia, 14
1965—Baltimore, 35; Dallas, 3
1964—St. Louis, 24; Green Bay, 17
1963—Green Bay, 40; Cleveland, 23
1962—Detroit, 17; Pittsburgh, 10
1961—Detroit, 38; Philadelphia, 10
1960— Detroit 17; Cleveland 16

NFC DIVISIONAL PLAYOFFS

1974 Minnesota (Cen.) 30, St. Louis (East) 14
      Los Angeles (West) 19, Washington (East) 10
1973 Minnesota (Cen.) 27, Washington (East) 20
      Dallas (East) 27, Los Angeles (West) 16
1972 Dallas (East) 30, San Francisco (West) 28
      Washington (East) 16, Green Bay (Cen.) 3
      San Francisco (West) 24, Washington (East) 20
1971 Dallas (East) 20, Minnesota (Cen.) 12
1970 Dallas (East) 5, Detroit (Cen.) 0
      San Francisco (West) 17, Minnesota (Cen.) 14
1969 Minnesota (Central) 23, Los Angeles (Coastal) 20
      Cleveland (Century) 38, Dallas (Capitol) 14
1968 Baltimore (Coastal) 24, Minnesota (Central) 14
      Cleveland (Century) 31, Dallas (Capitol) 20
1967 Green Bay (Central) 28, Los Angeles (Coastal) 7
      Dallas (Capitol) 52, Cleveland (Century) 14
1965* Green Bay 13, Baltimore 10
1958* N. Y. Giants 10, Cleveland 0
1957* Detroit 31, San Francisco 27
1952* Detroit 31, Los Angeles 21
1950* Cleveland 8, N. Y. Giants 3
      Los Angeles 24, Chi. Bears 14
1947* Philadelphia 21, Pittsburgh 0
1943* Washington 28, N. Y. Giants 0
1941* Chi. Bears 33, Green Bay 14
* Tie Playoff

AFL/AFC CHAMPIONSHIP GAMES

Year	Date	Winner—Share	Loser—Share	Score	Site	Attendance
1974*	Dec. 29	Pittsburgh ($8,500)	Oakland ($5,500)	24-13	Oakland	53,515
1973*	Dec. 30	Miami ($8,500)	Oakland ($5,500)	27-10	Miami	79,325
1972*	Dec. 31	Miami ($8,500)	Pitt. ($5,500)	21-17	Pitt	50,845
1971*	Jan. 2	Mia. ($8,500)	Balt. $5,500)	21-0	Miami	76,622
1970*	Jan. 3	Balt. ($8,500)	Oakland ($5,500)	27-17	Balt.	54,799
1969	Jan. 4	K. C. ($7,755)	Oakland ($6,252)	17-7	Oakland	53,564
1968	Dec. 29	N. Y. ($7,007)	Oakland ($5,349)	27-23	N. Y.	62,627
1967	Dec. 31	Oakland ($6,321)	Houston ($4,996)	40-7	Oakland	53,330
1966	Jan. 1	K. C. ($5,309)	Buffalo ($3,799)	31-7	Buffalo	42,080
1965	Dec. 26	Buffalo ($5,189)	S. D. ($3,447)	23-0	S. D.	30,361
1964	Dec. 26	Buffalo ($2,668)	S. D. ($1,738)	20-7	Buffalo	40,242
1963	Jan. 5	S. D. ($2,498)	Boston ($1,596)	51-10	S. D.	30,127
1962	Dec. 23	Dallas ($2,206)	Houston ($1,471)	20-17**	Hous.	37,981
1961	Dec. 24	Houston ($1,792)	S. D. ($1,111)	10-3	S. D.	29,556
1960	Jan. 1	Houston ($1,025)	L. A. ($718)	24-16	Hous.	32,183

* AFC, Starting 1970
** Sudden death—17:54

AFL/AFC DIVISIONAL PLAYOFFS

1974* Pittsburgh (Cent.) 32, Buffalo (East) 14
   Oakland (West) 28, Miami (East) 26
1973* Miami (East) 34, Cincinnati (Cen.) 16
   Oakland (West) 33. Pittsburgh (Cen.) 14
1972* Pittsburgh (Cen.) 13, Oakland (West) 7
   Miami (East) 20, Cleveland (Cen.) 14
1971* Miami (East) 27, Kansas City (West) 24**
   Baltimore (East) 20, Cleveland (Central) 3
1970* Baltimore (East) 17, Cincinnati (Cen.) 0
   Oakland (West) 21, Miami (East) 14
1969* Kansas City (West) 13, New York (East) 6
   Oakland (West) 56, Houston (East) 7
1968 Oakland (West) 41, Kansas City (West) 6
1963 Boston (East) 26, Buffalo (East) 8
* Interdivisional Playoff
** In 22:40 Overtime (6th Quarter)

PRO BOWL RESULTS

New York

1936—New York, 12; All-Stars, 2
1937—New York, 14; All-Stars, 7
1938—New York, 6; All-Stars, 0
1939—New York, 10; All-Stars, 0
1940—All Stars, 16; New York, 7
1941—New York, 23; All-Stars, 3
1942—Army, 16; New York, 0
1947—New York, 21; All-Stars, 0
1949—All-Stars, 28; New York, 13

Pro-Bowl

*1938—N. Y. Giants, 13; All-Stars, 10
*1939—Green Bay, 16; All-Stars, 7
*1940—Bears, 28; All-Stars, 14
†1941—Bears, 35; All-Stars, 24
‡1942—All-Stars, 17; Washington, 14
*1951—Am. Conf., 28; Nat. Conf., 27
*1952—Nat. Conf., 30; Am. Conf., 13
*1953—Nat Conf., 27; Am. Conf., 7
*1954—East. Conf., 20; West. Conf., 9
*1955—West. Conf., 26; East. Conf., 19
*1956—East Conf., 31; West. Conf., 30
*1957—West. Conf., 19; East. Conf., 10
*1958—West. Conf., 26; East. Conf., 7
*1959—East. Conf., 28; West. Conf., 21
*1960—West. Conf., 38; East Conf., 21
*1961—West Conf., 34; East Conf., 31
*1962—West Conf., 31; East Conf., 30
*1963—East Conf., 30; West Conf., 20
*1964—West Conf., 31; East Conf., 17
*1965—West Conf., 34; Eas Conf., 14

*1966—East Conf., 36; West Conf., 7
*1967—East Conf., 20; West Conf., 10

*1968—West Conf., 38. East Conf., 20
*1969—West. Conf., 10; East Conf., 7
*1970—West Conf., 16; East Conf., 13
*1971—Nat. Conf., 27; Am. Conf., 6
*1972—Am. Conf., 26; Nat. Conf., 13
** 1973—Am. Conf., 33; Nat. Conf., 28
††1974—Am. Conf., 15; Nat. Conf., 13
***1975 Nat. Conf., 17; Am. Conf., 10

•—Played in Los Angeles. †—Played in New York. ‡—Played in Philadelphia.
**Played in Texas   ††Played in Kansas City ***Played in Miami

CHICAGO ALL-STAR GAMES

1934	Chicago Bears	0	All-Stars	0
1935	Chicago Bears	5	All-Stars	0
1936	Detroit Lions	7	All-Stars	7
1937	All-Stars	6	Green Bay Packers	0
1938	All-Stars	28	Washington Redskins	16
1939	New York Giants	9	All-Stars	0
1940	Green Bay Packers	45	All-Stars	28
1941	Chicago Bears	37	All-Stars	13
1942	Chicago Bears	21	All-Stars	0
1943	All-Stars	27	Washington Redskins	7
1944	Chicago Bears	24	All-Stars	21
1945	Green Bay Packers	19	All-Stars	7
1946	All-Stars	16	Los Angeles Rams	0
1947	All-Stars	16	Chicago Bears	0
1948	Chicago Cardinals	28	All-Stars	0
1949	Philadelphia Eagles	38	All-Stars	0
1950	All-Stars	17	Philadelphia Eagles	7
1951	Cleveland Browns	33	All-Stars	0
1952	Los Angeles Rams	10	All-Stars	7
1953	Detroit	24	All-Stars	10
1954	Detroit	31	All-Stars	6
1955	All-Stars	30	Cleveland	27
1956	Cleveland	26	All-Stars	0
1957	New York	22	All-Stars	12
1958	All-Stars	35	Detroit	19
1959	Baltimore	29	All-Stars	0
1960	Baltimore	32	All-Stars	7
1961	Philadelphia	28	All-Stars	14
1962	Green Bay	42	All-Stars	20
1963	All-Stars	20	Green Bay	17
1964	Chicago	28	All-Stars	17
1965	Cleveland	24	All-Stars	16
1966	Green Bay	38	All-Stars	0
1967	Green Bay	27	All-Stars	0
1968	Green Bay	34	All-Stars	17
1969	New York (AFL)	26	All-Stars	24
1970	Kansas City (AFC)	24	All-Stars	3
1971	Baltimore (AFC)	24	All-Stars	17
1972	Dallas (NFC)	20	All-Stars	7
1973	Miami (AFC)	14	All-Stars	3

(1974 game was cancelled due to the NFL player strike)

AFL ALL-STAR GAMES

1962	West	47	East	27
1963	West	21	East	21
1964	West	27	East	24
1965	West	38	East	14
1966	All-Stars	30	Buffalo	19
1967	East	30	West	23
1968	East	25	West	24
1969	West	38	East	25
1970	West	26	East	3

Discontinued

ALL-TIME TEAM RECORDS–OFFENSE

(Includes NFL/NFC, AFL/AFC, not AAFC)

CHAMPIONSHIPS

Most Seasons League Champion
11   Green Bay 1929-31, 36, 39, 44, 61-62, 65-67
8   Chicago Bears 1921, 32-33, 40-41, 43, 46, 63
4   New York 1927, 34, 38, 56
   Detroit 1935, 52-53, 57
   Cleveland 1950, 54-55, 64
   Baltimore (NFL-AFC) 1958-59, 68, 70
3   Dallas/Kansas City (AFL) 1962, 66, 69
   Washington (NFL-NFC) 1937, 42, 72
   Philadelphia 1948-49, 60
   Miami (AFC) 1971-73
   Minnesota (NFL-NFC) 1969, 73-74
2   Houston (AFL) 1960-61
   Buffalo (AFL) 1964-65
   Dallas (NFC) 1970-71
   Clev./L.A. Rams 1945, 51

Most Consecutive Seasons League Champion
3   Green Bay 1929-31, 1965-67
   Canton 1922-23 (1924 as Cleveland Bulldogs)
   Miami (AFC) 1971-73
2   Chicago Bears 1932-33
   Chicago Bears 1940-41
   Philadelphia 1948-49
   Detroit 1952-53
   Cleveland 1954-55
   Baltimore 1958-59
   Houston (AFL) 1960-61
   Green Bay 1961-62
   Buffalo (AFL) 1964-65
   Dallas (NFC) 1970-71
   Minnesota (NFC) 1973-74

Most Seasons Leading Conference (Since 1933)
14   New York 1933-35, 38-39, 41, 44, 46, 56, 58-59, 61-62-63
11   Cleveland 1950-55, 57, 64-65, 68-69
10   Chicago Bears 1933-34, 37, 40-43, 46, 56, 63
   Green Bay 1936, 38-39, 44, 60-62, 65-67

GAMES

Most Consecutive Games Without Defeat
24   Chicago Bears, 1941-43 (won 23, tied 1)

   Canton 1922-23 (Won-21 Tied-3)
23   Green Bay 1928-30 (Won-21 Tied-2)
18   Miami (AFC) 1971-73
15   Los Angeles/San Diego (AFL), 1960-61
   Oakland (AFL) 1968-69
14   Oakland (AFL) 1967-68
11   Buffalo (AFL) 1963-64
   Houston (AFL) 1961-62 (incl. 1 tie)

Most Consecutive Victories
17   Chicago Bears 1933-34; 1941-42
16   Chicago Bears 1941-42
   Miami (AFC) 1972-73
15   Los Angeles/San Diego (AFL) 1960-61
14   Los Angeles 1967-68
13   Washington 1942-43
   Cleveland 1951-52

Most Consecutive Shutout Games Won
7   Detroit 1934

SCORING

Most Seasons Leading League/Conference
9   Chicago Bears 1934-35, 39, 41-43, 46-47, 56
6   Green Bay 1932, 36-38, 61-62
   Los Angeles (NFL-NFC) 1950-52, 57, 67, 73
4   San Francisco (NFL-NFC) 1953, 65, 70, 72
   Baltimore (NFL-AFC) 1958-59, 64, 70
   Oakland (AFL-AFC) 1967-69, 71

Most Points, Season
513   Houston (AFL) 1961
468   Oakland (AFL) 1967
466   Los Angeles 1950 (12 gs)
453   Oakland (AFL) 1968
448   New York 1963
445   Dallas 1966
428   Baltimore 1964

Most Points, Game
72   Washington vs N.Y., Nov. 27, 1966
70   Los Angeles vs Balt., Oct. 22, 1950
65   Chicago Cards vs N.Y. Bulldogs, Nov. 13, 1949
   Los Angeles vs Det., Oct. 29, 1950
64   Philadelphia vs Cin., Nov. 6, 1934
62   New York vs Phil (NFC) Nov. 26, 1972
   Atlanta vs N. O. (NFC) Sept. 16, 1973

61 Cincinnati vs Hou. (AFC) Dec. 17, 1972

59 Kansas City vs Den., (AFL) Sept. 7, 1963

58 San Diego vs Den., (AFL) Dec. 22, 1963
   Buffalo vs Mia., (AFL) Sept. 18, 1966

56 Houston vs N.Y., (AFL) Oct. 14, 1962
   Kansas City vs Den., (AFL) Oct. 23, 1966

Most Points, Both Teams, Game

113 Washington (72) vs N. Y. (41), Nov. 27, 1966

101 Oakland (52) vs Hou. (49), (AFL) Dec. 22, 1963

98 Chicago Cards (63) vs N.Y. (35), Oct. 17, 1948

97 Los Angeles (70) vs Balt. (27), Oct. 22, 1950

93 New Orleans (51) vs St. L. (42), Nov. 2, 1969
   Los Angeles (50) vs N. Y. (43), (AFL) Dec. 18, 1960

91 New York (46) vs Den. (45), (AFL) Nov. 22, 1962

89 Los Angeles (52) vs N. Y. (37), Nov. 14, 1948
   Los Angeles (65) vs Det. (24), Oct. 29, 1950
   Baltimore (51) vs Chi. Bears (38), Oct. 4, 1958

Most Points, One Quarter

41 Green Bay vs Det. (2d Q), Oct. 7, 1945
   Los Angeles vs Det. (3d Q), Oct. 29, 1950

35 Chicago Cards vs Bos. (3d Q), Oct. 24, 1948
   Green Bay vs Clev. (1st Q), Nov. 12, 1967

31 Chicago Cards vs Bulldogs (2d Q), Nov. 13, 1949
   Oakland vs Den. (4Q), Dec. 17, 1960 (AFL)
   Oakland vs S. D. (4Q), Dec. 8, 1963 (AFL)
   Buffalo vs K.C. (1Q), Sept. 13, 1964 (AFL)

28 By many teams

Most Touchdowns, Season

66 Houston 1961 (AFL)
64 Los Angeles 1950
58 Oakland 1967 (AFL)
57 New York 1963
56 Chicago Bears 1941
   Dallas 1966
55 Kansas City 1966 (AFL)
   Oakland 1968 (AFL)

Most Touchdowns, Game

10 Philadelphia vs Cin., Nov. 6, 1934
   Los Angeles vs Balt., Oct. 22, 1950
   Washington vs N.Y., Nov. 27, 1966

9 Chicago Cards vs Roch., Oct. 7, 1923
   Chicago Cards vs N. Y., Oct. 17, 1948
   Chicago Cards vs N. Y. Bulldogs, Nov. 13, 1949
   Los Angeles vs Det., Oct. 29, 1950
   Pittsburgh vs N. Y., Nov. 30, 1952
   Chicago vs S. F., Dec. 12, 1965

Most Touchdowns, Both Teams, Game

16 Washington (10) vs N. Y. (6), Nov. 27, 1966

14 Chicago Cards (9) vs N. Y. (5), Oct. 17, 1948
   Los Angeles (10) vs Balt. (4), Oct. 22, 1950
   Houston (7) vs Oakland (7), Dec. 22, 1963 (AFL)

13 New Orleans (7) vs St. L. (6), Nov. 2, 1969

12 New York (6) vs L. A. (6), Dec. 18, 1960 (AFL)

11 Several games

Most Points After Touchdown, Season

65 Houston 1961 (AFL)
59 Los Angeles 1950
56 Dallas 1966
   Oakland 1967 (AFL)
54 Dallas 1968
   Oakland 1968 (AFL)
53 Chicago Cards 1948
   Baltimore 1964
52 Green Bay 1962
   New York 1963

Most Points After Touchdown, Game

10 Los Angeles vs Balt., Oct. 22, 1950
9 Chicago Cards vs N. Y., Oct. 17, 1948
   Pittsburgh vs N. Y., Nov. 30, 1952
   Washington vs N.Y., Nov. 27, 1966
8 By many teams

Most Points After Touchdown, Both Teams, Game

14 Chicago Cards (9) vs N. Y. (5), Oct. 17, 1948
   Houston (7) vs Oak. (7), Dec. 22, 1963 (AFL)
   Washington vs N.Y., Nov. 27, 1966

13 Los Angeles (10) vs Balt. (3), Oct. 22, 1950

Most Field Goals, Season

34 New York 1968 (AFL)
33 Green Bay 1972 (NFC)
32 New York 1969 (AFL)

30 Kansas City 1968 (AFL)
Kansas City 1970 (AFC)
Minnesota 1970 (NFC)
Los Angeles 1973 (NFC)
29 Washington 1971 (NFC)
Pittsburgh 1973 (AFC)
28 Los Angeles 1966
Miami 1971 (AFC)
Pittsburgh 1972 (AFC)

Most Field Goals, Game
7 St. Louis vs Pitt, Sept. 24, 1967
6 Boston vs Den., Oct. 4, 1964
(AFL)
Detroit vs Minn., Nov. 13, 1966
New York vs Buff., Nov. 3, 1968
(AFL)
Philadelphia (NFC) vs Hou.
(AFC), Nov. 12, 1972
N. Y. Jets (AFC) vs N. O. (NFC),
Dec. 3, 1972
St. Louis vs Atl., Dec. 9, 1973
(NFC)
5 By many teams

FIRST DOWNS

Most First Downs, Season
297 Dallas 1968
Oakland 1972 (AFC)
294 Los Angeles 1973 (NFC)
293 Houston 1961 (AFL)
292 San Francisco 1965
291 Miami 1972 (AFC)

Fewest First Downs, Season
51 Cincinnati 1933
64 Pittsburgh 1935
68 Philadelphia 1937
Chicago Cards 1933
75 Pittsburgh 1941
159 Buffalo 1968 (AFL)
171 Denver 1966 (AFL)
Cincinnati 1968 (AFL)
172 Denver 1967 (AFL)

Most First Downs, Game
38 L. A. vs N. Y., Nov. 13, 1966
37 Green Bay vs Phil., Nov. 11, 1962
35 Pittsburgh vs Chi. Cards, Dec. 13, 1958
34 Los Angeles vs N. Y. Yanks, Sept. 28, 1951
33 Oakland vs Cin., Nov. 24, 1968
(AFL)
32 Kansas City vs Hou., Oct. 24, 1965
(AFL)
Atlanta vs N. O., Sept. 16, 1973
(NFC)

31 Los Angeles vs Oak., Nov. 27, 1960
(AFL)
Boston vs Hou., Dec. 11, 1966
(AFL)

Fewest First Downs, Game
0 Hammond vs Canton, Sept. 30, 1923
Racine vs Chi. Cards, Oct. 3, 1926
New York vs G. B., Oct. 1, 1933
Pittsburgh vs Bos., Oct. 29, 1933
Philadelphia vs Det., Sept. 20, 1935
New York vs Wash., Sept. 27, 1942
Denver vs Hou., Sept. 3, 1966
(AFL)

Most First Downs, Both Teams, Game
58 Los Angeles (30) vs Chi. Bears
(28), Oct. 24, 1954
Denver (34) vs Kansas City (24),
Nov. 18, 1974
57 Los Angeles (32) vs N. Y. Yanks
(25), Nov. 19, 1950
54 N. Y. Giants (31) vs Pitt. (23),
Dec. 5, 1948
Dallas (31) vs S. F. (23), Nov. 10,
1963
Washington (30) vs S. F. (24),
Nov. 12, 1967
53 Los Angeles (31) vs Oak. (22),
Nov. 27, 1960 (AFL)
Kansas City (32) vs Hou. (21),
Oct. 24, 1965 (AFL)

YARDS GAINED
(Rushes and Passes)

Most Seasons Leading League
12 Chicago Bears 1932, 34-35, 39, 41-44, 47, 49, 55-56
Los Angeles 1946, 50-51, 54, 57, 73 (NFL-NFC)
5 Baltimore 1958-60, 64, 67
Dallas 1966, 68-69, 71 (NFL-NFC)
4 Oakland 1968-70, 73-74 (AFL-AFC)

Most Yards Gained, Season
6,288 Houston 1961 (AFL)
5,696 Oakland 1967 (AFL)
5,506 Los Angeles 1951
5,420 Los Angeles 1950
5,388 San Diego 1968 (AFL)

5,270   San Francisco 1965
5,187   Los Angeles 1954

Most Yards Gained, Game
  735   Los Angeles vs N. Y. Yanks, Sept. 28, 1951 (181-r, 554-p)
  683   Pittsburgh vs Chi. Cards. Dec. 13, 1958 (211-r, 472-p)
  682   Chicago vs N. Y. Giants, Nov. 14, 1943
  626   Oakland vs Den., Oct. 25, 1964 (AFL)
  614   Kansas City vs Den., Oct. 23, 1966 (AFL)
  604   Oakland vs Cin., Nov. 24, 1968 (AFL)

Most Yards Gained, Both Teams, Game
1,133   Los Angeles (636) vs N. Y. Yanks (497), Nov. 19, 1950
1,087   Philadelphia (498) vs St. L. (589), Dec. 16, 1962
1,057   San Diego (581) vs Den. (476), Oct. 20, 1968 (AFL)
1,008   Oakland (540) vs Hou. (468), Dec. 22, 1963 (AFL)
  989   New York (528) vs Bos. (461), Dec. 17, 1966 (AFL)

RUSHING

Most Seasons Leading League
  11   Chicago Bears 1932, 34-35, 39-42, 51, 55-56, 68 (NFL)
   6   Cleveland 1958-59, 63, 65-67
   4   Green Bay 1946, 61-62, 64
      Dallas/Kansas City 1961, 66, 68-69 (AFL)

Most Attempts, Season
  659   Los Angeles 1973 (NFC)
  632   Philadelphia 1949
        Detroit 1934
  613   Miami 1972 (AFC)
  605   Buffalo 1973 (AFC)
  592   Detroit 1936
  581   Philadelphia 1950
  578   Pittsburgh 1963
  574   Chicago Bears 1950

Most Attempts, Game
  72   Chicago Bears vs Brk., Oct. 20, 1935
  70   Chicago Cards vs G. B., Dec. 5, 1948
  69   Chicago Cardinals vs G. B., Dec. 6, 1936
  65   Washington vs L.A., Nov. 25, 1951
  64   By five teams

Most Yards Gained, Season
3,088   Buffalo 1973 (AFC)

2,960   Miami 1972 (AFC)
2,925   Los Angeles 1973 (NFC)
2,885   Detroit 1936
2,835   Chicago Bears 1934
2,763   Detroit 1934
2,521   Miami 1973 (AFC)
2,520   Pittsburgh 1972 (AFC)

Fewest Yards Gained, Season
  298   Philadelphia 1940
  471   Boston 1944
  472   Detroit 1946
  978   New York 1963 (AFL)
1,040   Boston 1970 (AFC)
1,104   Denver 1961 (AFL)
1,106   Houston 1971 (AFC)
1,117   Boston 1963 (AFL)

Most Yards Gained, Game
  426   Detroit vs Pitt., Nov. 4, 1934
  423   New York Giants vs Balt., Nov. 19, 1950
  420   Boston vs N.Y. Giants, Oct. 8, 1933
  408   Chi. Bears vs Brk., Oct. 20, 1935
  398   Dallas vs Hou., Oct. 1, 1961 (AFL)
  380   Kansas City vs Den., Oct. 23, 1966 (AFL)
  360   Buffalo vs N. E., Sept. 16, 1973 (AFC)
  320   Dallas vs Buff., Sept. 30, 1962 (AFL)

Fewest Yards Gained, Game
 −36   Philadelphia vs Chi. Bears, Nov. 19, 1939
 −33   Phil/Pitt. vs Brk., Oct. 2, 1943
 −29   Cleveland Rams vs Wash., Oct. 11, 1942
   0   Kansas City vs Den., Dec. 19, 1965 (AFL)

Highest Average Gain, Season
 5.7   Cleveland 1963
 5.6   San Francisco 1954
 5.5   San Diego 1963 (AFL)
 5.3   Cleveland 1958
 5.2   Los Angeles 1951, 56
      Cleveland 1966
      Kansas City 1966 (AFL)
 5.1   Pittsburgh 1972 (AFC)
      Buffalo 1973 (AFC)
 5.0   Dallas 1962 (AFL)
      Miami 1971 (AFC)
      Miami 1973 (AFC)

Most Touchdowns, Season
  36   Green Bay 1962
  31   Chicago Bears 1941
  29   Green Bay 1960
      Baltimore 1964
  26   Miami 1972 (AFC)

25 Buffalo 1964 (AFL)
    Dallas 1971 (NFC)
24 Dallas 1960 (AFL)
    San Diego 1961 (AFL)

Most Touchdowns, Game
6 By many teams. Last:
   Green Bay vs Phil., Nov. 11, 1962
   New York vs Bos., Oct. 27, 1968
   (AFL)

PASSING

Most Seasons Leading League, Efficiency
10 Washington 1937, 39-40, 42-45, 47,
    67, 74
8 New York Giants 1932, 34-35, 38,
   48, 59, 62-63 (NFL)
6 Los Angeles 1946, 49-51, 54, 73
   (NFL-NFC)
5 Green Bay 1931, 36, 41, 52, 66
   Los Angeles 1946, 49-51, 54
4 Houston 1960-61, 63-64 (AFL)
   Cleveland 1953, 55, 57, 68 (NFL)

Most Passes Attempted, Season
592 Houston 1964 (AFL)
568 Denver 1961 (AFL)
559 Denver 1962 (AFL)
527 Washington 1967
500 San Francisco 1966
494 Chicago Bears 1964
479 Philadelphia 1973 (NFC)
478 Green Bay 1951
466 San Francisco 1973 (NFC)
462 N. Y. Giants 1971 (NFC)
461 Philadelphia 1974 (NFC)
453 Los Angeles 1950
450 San Diego 1971 (NFC)

Fewest Passes Attempted, Season
102 Cincinnati 1933
106 Boston 1933
120 Detroit 1937
125 New York 1944
127 Chicago Cards 1935
205 Chicago 1972 (NFC)
213 Buffalo 1973 (AFC)
270 Kansas City 1968 (AFL)

Most Passes Attempted, Game
68 Houston vs Buff., Nov. 1, 1964
    (AFL)
62 New York vs Den., Dec. 3, 1967
    (AFL)
    N. Y. Jets vs Balt., Oct. 18, 1970
    (AFC)
61 Houston vs Oak., Nov. 7, 1965
    (AFL)
60 Philadelphia vs Wash., Dec. 1,
    1940 (33-comp)
59 Chicago Bears vs N. Y. Giants,
    Oct. 23, 1949 (34-comp)

58 Chicago Bears vs Wash., Oct. 25,
    1964 (33-comp)
57 Philadelphia vs N. Y., Sept. 23,
    1962 (33-comp)

Fewest Passes Attempted, Game
0 Green Bay vs Port., Oct. 8, 1933
   Detroit vs Clev., Sept. 10, 1937
   Pittsburgh vs Brk., Nov. 16, 1941
   Green Bay vs Chi. Bears, Sept. 25,
   1949
   Pittsburgh vs L. A., Nov. 13, 1949
   Cleveland vs Phil., Dec. 3, 1950
3 Kansas City vs Oak., Oct. 20, 1968
   (AFL)

Most Passes Attempted, Both Teams, Game
98 Minnesota (56) vs Balt. (42),
    Sept. 28, 1969
97 Denver (53) vs Hou. (44), Dec.
    2, 1962 (AFL)
95 Los Angeles (48) vs Chi. (47)
    Oct. 11, 1964
94 Chicago Bears (50) vs S. F. (44),
    Nov. 1, 1953
    Pittsburgh (52) vs Chi. Cards
    (42), Dec. 13, 1958
    Buffalo (52) vs Den. (42), Sept.
    19, 1965 (AFL)
93 Houston (55) vs L. A. (38), Nov.
    13, 1960 (AFL)
    New York (53) vs Buff. (40),
    Oct. 30, 1966 (AFL)
91 Pittsburgh (48) vs L. A. (43),
    Dec. 14, 1952
89 Pittsburgh (48) vs Clev. (41),
    Nov. 16, 1952

Most Passes Completed, Season
301 Washington 1967
299 Houston 1964 (AFL)
292 Denver 1962 (AFL)
282 Chicago Bears 1964
278 San Francisco 1969
275 Washington 1969
     Philadelphia 1973 (NFC)
272 San Francisco 1965
268 N. Y. Giants 1971 (NFC)
261 San Francisco 1966
258 Philadelphia 1974 (NFC)
254 Washington 1974 (NFC)
253 Los Angeles 1950
248 Baltimore 1963

Fewest Passes Completed, Season
25 Cincinnati 1933
33 Boston 1933
34 Chicago Cards 1934
    Detroit 1934
39 Boston 1934
    Philadelphia 1936
78 Chicago 1972 (NFC)
96 Buffalo 1973 (AFC)
101 Green Bay 1972 (NFC)

119 N. Y. Jets 1971 (AFC)
     Green Bay 1973 (NFC)
121 Green Bay 1971 (NFC)
143 Houston 1967 (AFL)

Most Passes Completed, Game
37   Houston vs Buff., Nov. 1, 1964
     (AFL)
36   New York vs Pitt., Dec. 5, 1948
     Minnesota vs Balt., Sept. 28, 1969
35   Denver vs Hou., Dec. 20, 1964
     (AFL)
34   Chicago Bears vs N. Y. Giants, Oct.
     23, 1949 (59-att)
31   Denver vs Hou., Nov. 6, 1960
     (AFL)
     Houston vs L.A., Nov. 13, 1960
     (AFL)

Most Passes Completed, Both Teams, Game
56   Minnesota (36) vs. Balt. (20),
     Sept. 28, 1969
55   Chicago Bears (30) vs S. F. (25),
     Nov. 1, 1953
53   Denver (35) vs Hou. (18) Dec.
     20, 1964 (AFL)
51   Washington (26) vs Chi. Bears
     (25), Oct. 26, 1947
     Washington (26) vs Philadelphia
     (21), Dec. 3, 1967

Most Seasons Leading League, Yardage
8   Chicago Bears 1932, 39, 41, 43, 45,
     49, 54, 64
7   Washington 1938, 40, 44, 47-48,
     67, 74
5   Green Bay 1934-37, 42
     Philadelphia 1953, 55, 61, 62, 73
     (NFL-NFC)
4   Houston 1960-61, 63-64 (AFL)
     Philadelphia 1953, 55, 61, 62
     San Francisco 1965, 69, 70, 72
     (NFL-NFC)

Most Yards Gained, Season
4,392 Houston 1961 (AFL)
3,845 New York 1967 (AFL)
3,730 Washington 1967
3,709 Los Angeles 1950
3,623 San Diego 1968 (AFL)
3,605 Philadelphia 1961
       Baltimore 1963
3,487 San Francisco 1965

Fewest Yards Gained, Season
302   Chicago Cards 1934
357   Cincinnati 1933
577   Brooklyn 1934
652   Pittsburgh 1945
654   Pittsburgh 1941
997   Buffalo 1973 (AFC)
1,108 Chicago 1972 (NFC)
1,222 Chicago 1973 (NFC)
1,283 Green Bay 1973 (NFC)
1,343 Buffalo 1968 (AFL)

Most Yards Gained, Game
554   Los Angeles vs N. Y. Yanks, Sept.
       28, 1951
530   Minnesota vs Balt., Sept. 28, 1969
505   New York vs Wash., Oct. 28, 1962
501   Washington vs Bos., Oct. 31, 1948
469   Oakland vs K. C., Nov. 3, 1968
       (AFL)
464   Houston vs Buff., Oct. 29, 1961
       (AFL)

Fewest Yards Gained, Game
−53   Denver vs Oak., Sept. 10, 1967
       (AFL)
−52   Cincinnati vs Hou., Oct. 31, 1971
       (AFC)
−32   Washington vs Pitt., Nov. 27, 1955
−28   Washington vs Pitt., Dec. 7, 1958
−22   Kansas City vs Oak., Nov. 8, 1963
       (AFL)
−19   Buffalo vs Oak., Sept. 15, 1968
       (AFL)
−13   Washington vs Pitt., Oct. 18, 1959

Most Yards Gained, Both Teams, Game
851   New York (505) vs Wash. (346)
       Oct. 28, 1962
834   Philadelphia (419) vs St. L. (415),
       Dec. 16, 1962
822   New York Jets (490) vs Balt. (332),
       Sept. 24, 1972 (AFC)
753   Dallas (406) vs Wash. (347), Nov.
       13, 1966
748   Chi. Bears (468) vs Chi. Cards
       (280), Dec. 11, 1949
733   Oakland (378) vs Buff. (355),
       Sept. 15, 1963 (AFL)
726   Boston (405) vs Oak. (321), Oct.
       16, 1964 (AFL)

Most Touchdowns, Season
48   Houston 1961 (AFL)
39   New York 1963
36   Oakland 1969 (AFL)
35   New York 1962
     San Francisco 1965
34   Philadelphia 1961

Fewest Touchdowns, Season
0   Pittsburgh 1945
1   Detroit 1942
2   Chicago Cards 1935
     Brooklyn 1936
     Pittsburgh 1942
4   Buffalo 1973 (AFC)
7   Buffalo 1968 (AFL)
     Boston 1970 (AFC)
     Green Bay 1972 (NFC)
     Green Bay 1973 (NFC)

Most Touchdowns, Game
7   Chicago Bears vs N. Y., Nov. 14,
     1943

Philadelphia vs Wash., Oct. 17, 1954
Houston vs N. Y., Nov. 19, 1961 (AFL)
Houston vs N. Y., Oct. 14, 1962 (AFL)
New York vs Wash., Oct. 28, 1962
Minnesota vs Balt., Sept. 28, 1969
6   By many teams (NFL-AFL)

Most Touchdowns, Both Teams, Game
12   New Orleans (6) vs St. L. (6), Nov. 2, 1969
11   New York (7) vs Wash. (4), Oct. 28, 1962
     Oakland (6) vs Hou. (5), Dec. 22, 1963 (AFL)
10   Chicago Bears (6) vs Chi. Cards (4), Dec. 5, 1937

Most Passes Had Intercepted, Season
48   Houston 1962 (AFL)
45   Denver 1961 (AFL)
41   Card/Pitt 1944
40   Pittsburgh 1933
     Denver 1962 (AFL)
39   Chicago Cards 1943
37   Detroit 1943
     Houston 1971 (AFC)

Fewest Passes Had Intercepted, Season
5   Cleveland 1960
     Green Bay 1966
7   Los Angeles 1969
8   St. Louis 1974 (NFC)
9   Green Bay 1972 (NFC)
     Minnesota 1973 (NFC)
10   San Francisco 1970 (NFC)
     Washington 1970 (NFC)
     Miami 1971 (AFC)
11   Cincinnati 1968 (AFL)
     Kansas City 1968 (AFL)
     Cincinnati 1970 (AFC)
     Los Angeles 1971 (NFC)
     Cincinnati 1972 (AFC)

Most Passes Had Intercepted, Game
9   Detroit vs G. B., Oct. 24, 1943
     Pitt. vs Phil., Dec. 12, 1965
8   Green Bay vs N. Y., Nov. 2, 1948
     Chicago Cards vs Phil., Sept. 24, 1950
     New York Yanks vs N. Y. Giants, Dec. 16, 1951
     Denver vs Hou., Dec. 2, 1962 (AFL)
     Chicago Bears vs Det., Sept. 22, 1968
     New York Jets vs Balt., Sept. 23, 1973 (AFC)
7   By many teams (NFL-AFL)

Most Passes Had Intercepted, Both Teams, Game
13   Denver (8) vs Hou. (5), Dec. 2, 1962

11   Several

PUNTING

Most Punts, Season
113   Boston 1934
      Brooklyn 1934
112   Boston 1935
105   Denver 1967 (AFL)
100   Buffalo 1968 (AFL)

Fewest Punts, Season
32   Chicago Bears 1941
33   Washington 1945
38   Chicago Bears 1947
42   Detroit 1971 (NFC)
43   Detroit 1972 (NFC)
44   Miami 1972 (AFC)
45   San Diego 1972 (AFC)

Most Punts, Game
17   Chicago Bears vs G. B., Oct. 22, 1933
     Cincinnati vs Pitt., Oct. 22, 1933
16   Cincinnati vs Port., Sept. 17, 1933
     Chicago Cards vs Chi. Bears, Nov. 30, 1933
     Chicago Cards vs Det., Sept. 15, 1940

Fewest Punts, Game
0   Several

PUNT RETURNS

Most Punt Returns, Season
67   Pittsburgh 1974 (AFC)
63   Denver 1970 (AFC)
62   Dallas 1974 (NFC)
     Los Angeles 1970 (NFC)
61   Cleveland 1954
60   Chicago Bears 1950
58   Los Angeles 1969
57   Detroit 1963
55   Oakland 1968 (AFL)

Most Punt Returns, Game
12   Philadelphia vs Clev., Dec. 3, 1950
11   Chicago Bears vs Chi. Cards, Oct. 8, 1950
10   Philadelphia vs N. Y. Giants, Nov. 26, 1950
9   Buffalo vs Hou., Oct. 11, 1964 (AFL)
     Oakland vs Den., Sept. 10, 1967 (AFL)

Most Yards Gained, Season
781   Chicago Bears 1948
774   Pittsburgh 1974 (AFC)
729   Green Bay 1950

717   New York 1941
666   Oakland 1968 (AFL)
642   Oakland 1967 (AFL)

Most Yards Gained, Game
231   Det. vs S. F., Oct. 6, 1963
225   Oakland vs Buff., Sept. 15, 1968
      (AFL)
178   Bkn. vs Pitt., Nov. 29, 1942
175   Detroit vs G. B., Nov. 22, 1951
164   Chicago Cards vs N. Y., Nov. 22,
      1959
155   Chicago Cards vs Pitt., Nov. 1,
      1959
151   San Diego vs K. C., Sept. 26, 1965
      (AFL)

Most Touchdowns, Season
5   Chicago Cards 1959
4   Chicago Cards 1948
    Detroit 1951
    New York Giants 1951
3   By three teams

KICKOFF RETURNS

Most Kickoff Returns, Season
82   Atlanta 1966
80   New York 1966
78   Denver 1963 (AFL)
77   Houston 1965 (AFL)
76   Denver 1964 (AFL)
     Houston 1973 (AFC)
74   Buffalo 1971 (AFC)
72   New Orleans 1967
     Minnesota 1961
70   Los Angeles 1963
     San Diego 1973 (AFC)

Most Kickoff Returns, Game
12   New York vs Wash., Nov. 27, 1966
10   By many teams (NFL-AFL)

Most Yards Gained, Season
1,824   Houston 1963 (AFL)
1,801   Denver 1963 (AFL)
1,799   Houston 1973 (AFC)
1,758   Denver 1964 (AFL)
1,739   New Orleans 1967
        San Francisco 1962
1,737   Atlanta 1966
1,720   Washington 1962
1,718   Washington 1963

Most Yards Gained, Game
362   Detroit vs L. A., Oct. 29, 1950
304   Green Bay vs Chi. Bears, Nov. 9,
      1952

295   Denver vs Bos., Oct. 4, 1964 (AFL)
289   Denver vs K. C., Sept. 7, 1963
      (AFL)
282   Chicago Cards vs G. B., Nov. 1,
      1942
269   Houston vs Oak., Dec. 22, 1963
      (AFL)
263   New York vs L. A., Nov. 14, 1948

Most Touchdowns, Season
4   Green Bay 1969
    Chicago 1970 (NFC)
3   Los Angeles 1950
    Chicago Cards 1954
    San Francisco 1963
    Denver 1966 (AFL)
    Chicago Bears 1967
2   By many teams

Most Touchdowns, Game
2   Chicago Bears vs G. B., Nov. 9,
    1952
    Phil. vs Dall., Nov. 6, 1966
    Green Bay vs Clev., Nov. 12, 1967

FUMBLES

Most Fumbles, Season
56   Chicago Bears 1938
54   Philadelphia 1946
51   New England 1973 (AFC)
49   New York 1961
43   St. Louis 1972 (NFC)
     Houston 1973 (AFC)

Fewest Fumbles, Season
8   Cleveland 1959
11   Green Bay 1944
12   Brooklyn 1934
     Detroit 1943
15   New York 1964, 67 (AFL)
     Boston 1969 (AFL)
     Denver 1969 (AFL)

Most Fumbles, Game
10   Phil/Pitt vs N. Y., Oct. 9, 1943
     Detroit vs Minn., Nov. 12, 1967
     Kansas City vs Hou., Oct. 12, 1969
     (AFL)
9   Philadelphia vs G. B., Oct. 13, 1946
     Kansas City vs S. D., Nov. 15, 1964
     (AFL)
8   Several

Most Fumbles, Both Teams, Game
14   Chicago Bears (7) vs Clev. (7),
     Nov. 24, 1940
     St. Louis (8) vs N. Y. (6), Sept. 17,
     1961
     Kansas City (10) vs Hou. (4), Oct.
     12, 1969 (AFL)

Most Opponents' Fumbles Recovered Season

31	Minnesota 1963
29	Cleveland 1951
28	Green Bay 1946
26	Houston 1960 (AFL)
25	Dallas 1971 (NFC)
	New Orleans 1971 (NFC)
	Philadelphia 1971 (NFC)
24	Buffalo 1965 (AFL)

Fewest Opponents' Fumbles Recovered, Season

3	Los Angeles 1974 (NFC)
4	Philadelphia 1944
6	Brooklyn 1939
	Chicago Bears 1943
	Chicago Bears 1945
	Washington 1945
	New York 1967 (AFL)
	San Diego 1969 (AFL)
	Kansas City 1971 (AFC)

Most Opponents' Fumbles Recovered, Game

7	Buffalo vs Cin., Nov. 30, 1969 (AFL)
6	By many teams (NFL-AFL)

Most Own Fumbles Recovered, Season

27	Philadelphia 1946
	Minnesota 1963
26	Pittsburgh 1948
	Chicago 1973 (NFC)
25	Dallas 1961
	Houston 1973 (AFC)
	New England 1973 (AFC)
23	Oakland 1960 (AFL)

Fewest Own Fumbles Recovered, Season

2	Washington 1958
3	Detroit 1956
	Cleveland 1959
4	By many teams (NFL-AFL)

Most Fumbles (Opponents' and Own) Recovered, Season

58	Minnesota 1963
46	New York 1946
45	Philadelphia 1946
	Houston 1960 (AFL)

PENALTIES

Most Penalties, Season

122	Washington 1948
	Chicago Bears 1948
121	Chicago Bears 1944
118	Chicago Bears 1951
100	Oakland 1969 (AFL)
99	Buffalo 1970 (AFC)

Fewest Penalties, Season

19	Detroit 1937
21	Boston 1935
24	Philadelphia 1936
48	Denver 1967 (AFL)
	Miami 1968 (AFL)
	Detroit 1972 (NFC)

Most Penalties, Game

22	Brooklyn vs G. B., Sept. 17, 1944
	Chicago Bears vs Phil., Nov. 26, 1944
21	Cleveland vs Chi. Bears, Nov. 25, 1951
18	Chicago Bears vs L. A., Nov. 10, 1946
	Cleveland vs L. A., Oct. 7, 1951
17	Oakland vs Hou., Sept. 7, 1963

Fewest Yards Penalized, Season

139	Detroit 1937
146	Philadelphia 1937
159	Philadelphia 1936
416	Miami 1973 (AFC)
417	Detroit 1972 (NFC)
440	Minnesota 1972 (NFC)
456	Oakland 1961 (AFL)
	Boston 1962 (AFL)

Most Yards Penalized, Game

209	Cleveland vs Chi. Bears, Nov. 25, 1951
189	Houston vs Buff., Oct. 31, 1965 (AFL)
184	Green Bay vs Bos., Oct. 21, 1945
180	Oakland vs S. D., Oct. 26, 1969 (AFL)
177	New York Giants vs Wash., Oct. 9, 1949

Most Yards Penalized, Both Teams, Game

374	Cleveland (209) vs Chi. Bears (165), Nov. 25, 1951
309	Green Bay (184) vs Bos. (125), Oct. 21, 1945
281	Oakland (176) vs Bos. (105), Sept. 28, 1969 (AFL)

Most Yards Penalized, Season

1,274	Oakland 1969 (AFL)
1,194	Chicago Bears 1968
1,108	Buffalo 1970 (AFC)
1,107	Chicago Bears 1951
1,100	Washington 1948
1,075	Minnesota 1967
1,066	Chicago Bears 1948

ALL-TIME TEAM RECORDS—DEFENSE

SCORING

Fewest Points Allowed, Season
- *0   Akron 1920
- 15   Canton 1922
- 19   Canton 1923
- 20   New York 1927
- 24   Green Bay 1929
- 44   Chicago Bears 1932
- 54   Brooklyn 1933
- 59   Detroit 1934
- 75   New York 1944
- 139   Minnesota 1971 (NFC)
- 140   Baltimore 1971 (AFC)
- 143   Minnesota 1970 (NFC)
- 150   Miami 1973 (AFC)
- 168   Minnesota 1973 (NFC)
- 170   Kansas City 1968 (AFL)

* Not recognized by NFL.

Most Points Allowed, Season
- 501   New York 1966
- 473   Denver 1963 (AFL)
- 462   Baltimore 1950
- 458   Oakland 1961 (AFL)
- 447   Houston 1973 (AFC)
- 446   New England 1972 (AFC)

Fewest Touchdowns Allowed, Season
- 1   Canton 1923
- 2   Canton 1922
- 3   New York Giants 1927
     Green Bay 1929
- 7   Detroit 1934
- 9   New York 1944
- 14   Minnesota 1970 (NFC)
     Minnesota 1971 (NFC)
- 15   Miami 1973 (AFC)
     Minnesota 1973 (NFC)
- 17   Los Angeles 1973 (NFC)
- 18   Houston 1967 (AFL)
     Kansas City 1968 (AFL)
     Baltimore 1971 (AFC)
     Pittsburgh 1972 (AFC)

Most Touchdowns Allowed, Season
- 66   New York 1966
- 63   Baltimore 1950
- 61   Denver 1963 (AFL)
- 60   Oakland 1961 (AFL)

YARDS ALLOWED

(Rushing and Passing)

Fewest Yards Allowed, Season
- 1,578   Chicago Cards 1934

- 1,703   Chicago Bears 1942
- 2,803   Minnesota 1970 (NFC)
- 2,852   Baltimore 1971 (AFC)
- 2,951   Los Angeles 1973 (NFC)
- 3,160   Oakland 1973 (AFC)
- 3,163   Kansas City 1969 (AFL)

Most Yards Allowed, Season
- 5,593   Minnesota 1961
- 5,531   Atlanta 1967
- 5,447   San Francisco 1963
- 5,402   Baltimore 1950
- 5,337   Cincinnati 1969 (AFL)
- 5,250   New England 1972 (AFC)
- 5,241   Houston 1964 (AFL)
- 5,201   Denver 1967 (AFL)

RUSHING

Fewest Yards Allowed, Season
- 519   Chicago Bears 1942
- 558   Philadelphia 1944
- 793   Phil./Pitt. 1943
- 913   Buffalo 1964 (AFL)

Most Yards Allowed, Season
- 2,857   Baltimore 1950
- 2,850   New England 1973 (AFC)
- 2,717   New England 1972 (AFC)
- 2,699   Houston 1965 (AFL)
- 2,667   Minnesota 1961
- 2,651   Cincinnati 1969 (AFL)
- 2,619   Green Bay 1956

PASSING

Fewest Yards Allowed, Season
- 625   Chicago Cards 1934
- 928   Boston 1934
- 939   Pittsburgh 1946
- 1,290   Miami 1973 (AFC)
- 1,338   New England 1973 (AFC)
- 1,430   Atlanta 1973 (NFC)
- 1,438   Minnesota 1970 (NFC)
- 1,825   Buffalo 1967 (AFL)

Most Yards Allowed, Season
- 3,674   Dallas 1962
- 3,602   Washington 1962
- 3,532   St. Louis 1969
- 3,525   Houston 1960 (AFL)
- 3,493   Washington 1961
- 3,403   Washington 1967
- 3,365   Denver 1963 (AFL)
- 3,356   Boston 1966 (AFL)

INTERCEPTIONS BY

Fewest Passes Intercepted by, Season
- 6 Houston 1972 (AFC)
- 7 Los Angeles 1959
- 8 Pittsburgh 1940
   Boston 1970 (AFC)
- 9 San Diego 1970 (AFC)
- 10 Brooklyn 1944
   Pittsburgh 1955
   Chicago Bears 1960
   Cincinnati 1968 (AFL)
   Philadelphia 1970 (NFC)

Denver 1972 (AFC)
New England 1972 (AFC)
St. Louis 1973 (NFC)

Most Passes Intercepted by, Season
- 49 San Diego 1961 (AFL)
- 42 Green Bay 1943
- 41 New York Giants 1951
- 40 Green Bay 1940
   Baltimore 1959

NFL/NFC DEPARTMENTAL CHAMPIONS

TOTAL YARDS GAINED

1974—Dallas (NFC)	4.983
1973—Los Angeles (NFC)	4,906
1972—New York Giants (NFC)	4,483
1971—Dallas (NFC)	5,035
1970—San Francisco (NFC)	4,503
1969—Dallas	5,122
1968—Dallas	5,117
1967-Baltimore	5,008
1966—Dallas	5,145
1965—San Francisco	5,270
1964—Baltimore	4,779
1963—New York	5,024
1962—New York	5,005
1961—Philadelphia	5,112
1960—Baltimore	4,245
1959—Baltimore	4,458
1958—Baltimore	4,539
1957—Los Angeles	4,143
1956—Chicago Bears	4,537
1955—Chicago Bears	4,316
1954—Los Angeles	5,187
1953—Philadelphia	4,811
1952—Cleveland	4,352
1951—Los Angeles	5,506
1950—Los Angeles	5,420
1949—Chicago Bears	4,873
1948—Chicago Cards	4,694
1947—Chicago Bears	5,053
1946—Los Angeles	3,763
1945—Washington	3,549
1944—Chicago Bears	3,239
1943—Chicago Bears	4,045
1942—Chicago Bears	3,900
1941—Chicago Bears	4,265
1940—Green Bay	3,400
1939—Chicago Bears	3,988
1938—Green Bay	3,037
1937—Green Bay	3,201
1936—Detroit	3,703
1935—Chicago Bears	3,454
1934—Chicago Bears	3,750
1933—New York	2,970
1932—Chicago Bears	2,755

YARDS RUSHING

1974—Dallas (NFC)	2,454
1973—Los Angeles (NFC)	2,925
1972—Chicago (NFC)	2,360
1971—Detroit (NFC)	2,376
1970—Dallas (NFC)	2,300
1969—Dallas	2,276
1968—Chicago	2,377
1967—Cleveland	2,139
1966—Cleveland	2,166
1965—Cleveland	2,331
1964—Green Bay	2,276

1963—Cleveland	2,639
1962—Green Bay	2,460
1961—Green Bay	2,350
1960—St. Louis	2,356
1959—Cleveland	2,149
1958—Cleveland	2,526
1957—Los Angeles	2,142
1956—Chicago Bears	2,468
1955—Chicago Bears	2,388
1954—San Francisco	2,498
1953—San Francisco	2,230
1952—San Francisco	1,905
1951—Chicago Bears	2,408
1950—New York	2,336
1949—Philadelphia	2,607
1948—Chicago Cards	2,560
1947—Los Angeles	2,171
1946—Green Bay	1,765
1945—Cleveland Rams.	1,714
1944—Philadelphia	1,661
1943—Phil-Pitt	1,730
1942—Chicago Bears	1,881
1941—Chicago Bears	2,263
1940—Chicago Bears	1,818
1939—Chicago Bears	2,043
1938—Detroit	1,893
1937—Detroit	2,074
1936—Detroit	2,885
1935—Chicago Bears	2,096
1934—Chicago Bears	2,847
1933—Boston Redskins	2,260
1932—Chicago Bears	1,770

FORWARD PASSING

1974—Washington (NFC)	86.4 rating
1973—Los Angeles (NFC)	84.9 rating
1972—New York (NFC)	
1971—Dallas (NFC)	
1970—San Francisco (NFC)	
1969—Dallas	
1968—Cleveland	
1967—Washington	
1966—Green Bay	
1965—San Francisco	
1964—Minnesota	
1963—New York	
1962—New York	
1961—Philadelphia	
1960—Philadelphia	
1959—New York	8.37 yd/att
1958—Pittsburgh	8.19 yd/att
1957—Cleveland	8.80 yd/att
1956—Chicago Bears	8.28 yd/att
1955—Cleveland	8.30 yd/att
1954—Los Angeles	9.51 yd/att
1953—Cleveland	9.27 yd/att

1952—Green Bay	7.04 yd/att		1948—Washington	2,861
1951—Los Angeles	8.56 yd/att		1947—Washington	3,336
1950—Los Angeles	7.80 yd/att		1946—Los Angeles	2,080
1949—Los Angeles			1945—Chicago Bears	1,857
1948—New York			1944—Washington	2,021
1947—Washington			1943—Chicago Bears	2,310
1946—Los Angeles			1942—Green Bay	2,407
1945—Washington	64.4 % comp		1941—Chicago Bears	2,002
1944—Washington	56.8 % comp		1940—Washington	1,887
1943—Washington	54.7 % comp		1939—Chicago Bears	1,965
1942—Washington	53.3 % comp		1938—Washington	1,536
1941—Green Bay	52.6 % comp		1937—Green Bay	1,398
1940—Washington	59.0 % comp		1936—Green Bay	1,629
1939—Washington	58.2 % comp		1935—Green Bay	1,449
1938—New York	48.9 % comp		1934—Green Bay	1,165
1937—Washington	44.6 % comp		1933—New York Giants	1,348
1936—Green Bay	42.4 % comp		1932—Chicago Bears	1,013
1935—New York	44.8 % comp			
1934—New York	40.9 % comp			
1933—Brooklyn	46.7 % comp			
1932—New York	46.2 % comp			
1931—Green Bay	40.4 % comp			

Leadership based as follows:
  1931–45—Percent completion.
  1946–49—Percent completion, lowest percent interception, total yardage.
  1950–59—Net yards per attempt.
  1960–71—Percent completion, lowest percent interception, net yards per attempt, touchdowns passes.
  1972–date—Same as 1960–71 except percent TD used, not total TD.

YARDS PASSING
(Based on Net Yards Since 1949)

1974—Washington (NFC)	2,802
1973—Philadelphia (NFC)	2,998
1972—San Francisco (NFC)	2,735
1971—Dallas (NFC)	2,786
1970—San Francisco (NFC)	2,923
1969—San Francisco	3,158
1968—Dallas	3,026
1967—Washington	3,730
1966—Dallas	3,023
1965—San Francisco	3,487
1964—Chicago	2,841
1963—Baltimore	3,296
1962—Philadelphia	3,385
1961—Philadelphia	3,605
1960—Baltimore	2,956
1959—Baltimore	2,753
1958—Pittsburgh	2,752
1957—Baltimore	2,388
1956—Los Angeles	2,419
1955—Philadelphia	2,472
1954—Chicago Bears	3,104
1953—Philadelphia	3,089
1952—Cleveland	2,566
1951—Los Angeles	3,199
1950—Los Angeles	3,529
1949—Chicago Bears	2,930

POINTS SCORED

1974—Washington (NFC)	320
1973—Los Angeles (NFC)	388
1972—San Francisco (NFC)	353
1971—Dallas (NFC)	406
1970—San Francisco (NFC)	352
1969—Minnesota	379
1968—Dallas	431
1967—Los Angeles	398
1966—Dallas	445
1965—San Francisco	421
1964—Baltimore (14 games)	428
1963—New York (14 games)	448
1962—Green Bay (14 games)	415
1961—Green Bay (14 games)	391
1960—Cleveland	362
1959—Baltimore (12 games)	374
1958—Baltimore (12 games)	381
1957—Los Angeles (12 games)	307
1956—Chicago Bears (12 games)	363
1955—Cleveland (12 games)	349
1954—Detroit	337
1953—San Francisco	372
1952—Los Angeles	349
1951—Los Angeles	392
1950—Los Angeles	466
1949—Philadelphia	364
1948—Chicago Cardinals	395
1947—Chicago Bears	363
1946—Chicago Bears	289
1945—Philadelphia	272
1944—Philadelphia	267
1943—Chicago Bears	303
1942—Chicago Bears	376
1941—Chicago Bears	396
1940—Washington	245
1939—Chicago Bears	298

1938—Green Bay	223	1934—Chicago Bears	286
1937—Green Bay	220	1933—New York	244
1936—Green Bay	248	1932—Green Bay	152
1935—Chicago Bears	192		

AFL/AFC TEAM
DEPARTMENTAL CHAMPIONS

TOTAL YARDS GAINED

1974—Oakland (AFC)	4,718
1973—Oakland (AFC)	4,773
1972—Miami (AFC)	5,036
1971—San Diego (AFC)	4,738
1970—Oakland (AFC)	4,829
1969—Oakland	5,036
1968—Oakland	5,696
1967—New York	5,152
1966—Kansas City	5,114
1965—San Diego	5,188
1964—Buffalo	5,206
1963—San Diego	5,153
1962—Houston	4,971
1961—Houston	6,288
1960—Houston	4,936

1963—Houston	
1962—Denver	
1961—Houston	
1960—Houston	

YARDS PASSING (NET)

1974—Cincinnati (AFC)	2,511
1973—Denver (AFC)	2,519
1972—New York Jets (AFC)	2,777
1971—San Diego (AFC)	3,134
1970—Oakland (AFC)	2,865
1969—Oakland	3,271
1968—San Diego	3,623
1967—New York	3,845
1966—New York	3,464
1965—San Diego	3,103
1964—Houston	3,527
1963—Houston	3,222
1962—Denver	3,404
1961—Houston	4,392
1960—Houston	3,203

YARDS RUSHING

1974—Pittsburgh (AFC)	2,417
1973—Buffalo (AFC)	3,088
1972—Miami (AFC)	2,960
1971—Miami (AFC)	2,429
1970—Miami (AFC)	2,082
1969—Kansas City	2,220
1968—Kansas City	2,227
1967—Houston	2,122
1966—Kansas City	2,274
1965—San Diego	2,085
1964—Buffalo	2,040
1963—San Diego	2,203
1962—Buffalo	2,480
1961—Dallas	2,189
1960—Oakland	2,056

POINTS SCORED

1974—Oakland (AFC)	355
1973—Denver (AFC)	354
1972—Miami (AFC)	385
1971—Oakland (AFC)	344
1970—Baltimore (AFC)	321
1969—Oakland	377
1968—Oakland	453
1967—Oakland	468
1966—Kansas City	448
1965—San Diego	340
1964—Buffalo	400
1963—San Diego	399
1962—Dallas	389
1961—Houston	513
1960—New York	382

FORWARD PASSING

1974—Cincinnati (AFC)	83.4 rating
1973—Cincinnati (AFC)	79.6 rating
1972—Miami (AFC)	
1971—San Diego (AFC)	
Miami (AFC)	
1970—Oakland (AFC)	
1969—Cincinnati	
1968—Kansas City	
1967—Oakland	
1966—New York	
1965—San Diego	
1964—Houston	

6 Other Leagues

Starting in 1926, five other leagues made serious challenges against the National Football League.

The first of these, named the American Football League, was organized for the 1926 season by C. C. Pyle, a spectacular promoter, who was acting as manager of Harold "Red" Grange.

Grange, after turning pro with the Chicago Bears late in the 1925 season, had led them through a 19-game coast-to-coast tour which had been a financial lifesaver for all of pro football.

Pyle, believing that Grange's fan appeal could be strong enough to vitalize a 9-team league put a franchise into New York City with Grange as its star. Other teams were the Boston Bulldogs, Brooklyn Horsemen, Chicago Bulls, Cleveland Panthers, New York Yankees, Newark (N. J.) Bears, Philadelphia Quakers, Rock Island Independents and the Los Angeles West Coast Wildcats, a road team with no home field.

Not all teams finished the season although each had a good supply of the top professional players of the time. The Philadelphia Quakers, under the playing leadership and coaching of Century Milstead, former Yale All American and New York Giant, won the championship with a 7–2–0 record. Grange and his Yankees were second at 9–5–0.

The 1926 AFL disbanded after one season, with Grange's Yankees, and Grange, joining the NFL and playing there for two more years. Players from other squads returned to or were picked up by other NFL teams. Grange went back to the Bears in 1928 and played with them through 1934.

AMERICAN FOOTBALL LEAGUE
(1926)

	W	L	T	Pct.
Philadelphia	7	2	0	.778
New York	9	5	0	.643
Cleveland	3	2	0	.600
Los Angeles	6	6	2	.600
Chicago	5	6	3	.455
Boston	2	4	0	.333
Rock Island	2	5	1	.283
Brooklyn	1	3	0	.250
Newark	0	4	2	.000

In 1936 another league was formed, again calling itself the American Football League. Some of its teams lasted two years, the life span of the league as a whole. They were: Boston Shamrocks, played two years, champions in 1936; Brooklyn Tigers, 1936 only; Cleveland Rams, 1936 only; New York Yanks, two years; Los Angeles Bulldogs, 1937 only and were undefeated champions; Pittsburgh Americans, two years; Rochester Tigers, two years after originating as the Syracuse Braves and moving quickly to Rochester where the Brooklyn Tigers joined them early in 1936; Cincinnati Bengals, 1937 only.

AMERICAN FOOTBALL LEAGUE
(1936)

	W	L	T	Pct.
Boston	8	3	0	.727
Cleveland	5	2	2	.714
New York	5	3	2	.625
Pittsburgh	3	2	1	.600
Rochester	1	6	0	.143
Brooklyn	0	6	1	.000

AMERICAN FOOTBALL LEAGUE
(1937)

	W	L	T	Pct.
Los Angeles	8	0	0	1.000
Rochester	3	3	1	.500
New York	2	3	1	.400
Cincinnati	2	3	2	.400
Boston	2	5	0	.286
Pittsburgh	0	3	0	.000

In 1940, a third American Football League was formed. It gathered several top level players but survived only two years. Boston, Buffalo, Cincinnati, Columbus, Milwaukee and New York were represented. They had all tried it before and some would try it again.

AMERICAN FOOTBALL LEAGUE
(1940)

	W	L	T	Pct.
Columbus	8	1	1	.888
Milwaukee	7	2	0	.777
Boston	5	4	1	.555
New York	4	5	0	.445
Buffalo	2	8	0	.200
Cincinnati	1	7	0	.125

AMERICAN FOOTBALL LEAGUE
(1941)

	W	L	T	Pct.
Columbus	5	1	2	.833
New York	5	2	1	.714
Milwaukee	4	3	1	.591
Buffalo	2	6	0	.250
Cincinnati	1	5	2	.167

The All America Football Conference was created at the end of World War II. Its Eastern Division had teams in Brooklyn ("jumped" out of the NFL after the previous season by owner, Daniel Topping), Buffalo, New York and Miami. The Western group moved into Chicago, Cleveland (vacated by the Rams who had won the NFL championship there the previous fall and then moved to Los Angeles) Los Angeles and San Francisco.

Miami dropped out after one season and Baltimore was added. This line-up held through 1947 and 1948. In 1949, the end of the road for the AAFC, the Brooklyn franchise was merged with New York to make a seven-team league.

The Cleveland Browns won the AAFC championship four straight years, and, with San Francisco and Baltimore, joined the NFL in 1950. Players from other AAFC squads were put into a pool and chosen by the older NFL teams.

ROSTER OF COACHES
The All America Football Conference

BALTIMORE COLTS

1947	Cecil Isbell
1948	Cecil Isbell
1949	Cecil Isbell
	Walter Driskill

BUFFALO BILLS (BISONS)

1946	Lowell Dawson
1947	Lowell Dawson
1948	Lowell Dawson
1949	Lowell Dawson
	Clem Crowe

BROOKLYN DODGERS

1946	Dr. Malcolm Stevens
	Thomas Scott
	Cliff Battles
1947	Cliff Battles
1948	Carl Voyles
1949	Disbanded

BROOKLYN— NEW YORK YANKEES

1946	Ray Flaherty
1947	Ray Flaherty
1948	Ray Flaherty
	Norman Strader
1949	Norman Strader

LOS ANGELES DONS

1946	Dudley DeGroot
1947	Dudley DeGroot
	Mel Hein, and Ted Shipkey
1948	James M. Phelan
1949	James M. Phelan

CHICAGO HORNETS (ROCKETS)

1946	Richard Hanley
	Robert Dove, Ned Mathews, Wilbur
	Wilkin, Pat Boland
1947	James H. Crowley
	Hampton Pool
1948	Edward McKeever
1949	Ray Flaherty

CLEVELAND BROWNS

1946	Paul E. Brown
1947	Paul E. Brown
1948	Paul E. Brown
1949	Paul E. Brown

SAN FRANCISCO 49ers

1946	Lawrence T. Shaw
1947	Lawrence T. Shaw
1948	Lawrence T. Shaw
1949	Lawrence T. Shaw

MIAMI SEAHAWKS

1946	Jack Meagher
	Hampton Pool

FINAL STANDINGS

AAFC

1949

	W	L	T	Pct.
Cleveland	9	1	2	.900
San Francisco	9	3	0	.750
Bklyn-N.Y.	8	4	0	.667
Buffalo	5	5	2	.500
Chicago	4	8	0	.333
Los Angeles	4	8	0	.333
Baltimore	1	11	0	.083

Championship Game—
Cleveland 21, San Francisco 7

1948

WESTERN DIVISION

Cleveland	14	0	0	1.000
San Francisco	12	2	0	.857
Los Angeles	7	7	0	.500
Chicago	1	13	0	.071

EASTERN DIVISION

Buffalo	8*	7	0	.533
Baltimore	7	8*	0	.467
New York	6	8	0	.429
Brooklyn	2	12	0	.143

* Includes divisional play-off

Championship Game—
Cleveland 49, Buffalo 7

1947

WESTERN DIVISION

Cleveland	12	1	1	.923
San Francisco	8	4	2	.667
Los Angeles	7	7	0	.500
Chicago	1	13	0	.071

EASTERN DIVISION

New York	11	2	1	.846
Buffalo	8	4	2	.667
Brooklyn	3	10	1	.231
Baltimore	2	11	1	.154

Championship Game—
Cleveland 14, New York 3

1946

WESTERN DIVISION

Cleveland	12	2	0	.857
San Francisco	9	5	0	.643
Los Angeles	7	5	2	.583
Chicago	5	6	3	.455

EASTERN DIVISION

New York	10	3	1	.769
Brooklyn	3	10	1	.231
Buffalo	3	10	1	.231
Miami	3	11	0	.154

Championship Game—
Cleveland 14, New York 9

ALL-TIME LEADERS

ALL-TIME AAFC RUSHING
(Ranked on Yards Gained)

No.	Name	Yr.		Att.	Yds.	Td.
1	Marion Motley	1946-1949	4	489	3024	26
2	Spec Sanders	1946-1948	3	540	2900	34
3	Chet Mutryn	1946-1949	4	475	2676	25
4	John Strzykalski	1946-1949	4	429	2454	14
5	Bob Hoernschemeyer	1946-1949	4	506	2109	10
6	Norm Standlee	1946-1949	4	375	1734	17
7	Mickey Colmer	1946-1949	4	398	1537	15
8	Edgar Jones	1946-1949	4	289	1509	10
9	Buddy Young	1947-1949	3	262	1452	9
10	Lou Tomasetti	1946-1949	4	323	1430	12
11	Joe Perry	1948-1949	2	192	1345	18
12	John Kimbrough	1946-1948	3	329	1224	17
13	Len Eshmont	1946-1949	4	232	1181	7
14	Bus Mertes	1946-1949	4	301	1120	6
15	Glenn Dobbs	1946-1949	4	262	1039	12
16	Bob Kennedy	1946-1949	4	253	1017	9
17	Vic Kulbitski	1946-1948	3	193	1006	3
18	Eddie Prokop	1946-1949	4	226	935	8
19	Billy Hillenbrand	1946-1948	3	216	889	11
20	Julie Rykovich	1947-1948	2	188	839	10

ALL-TIME AAFC PASSING
(Ranked on Yards Gained)

No.	Name	Yr.	Att.	Yds.	Pct.	Yds.	Td.	In.	In. Pct.	Avg. G.
1	Otto Graham	1946-1949	4	1061	592	55.8	10085	86	41	4.0	9.51
2	Frankie Albert	1946-1949	4	963	515	53.5	6948	88	55	5.7	7.21
3	George Ratterman	1947-1949	3	831	438	52.7	6194	52	55	6.3	7.45
4	Glenn Dobbs	1946-1949	4	934	446	47.8	5876	45	52	5.6	6.29
5	Y. A. Tittle	1948-1949	2	578	309	53.5	4731	30	27	4.7	8.19
6	Bob Hoernschemeyer	1946-1949	4	688	308	44.8	4109	32	51	7.4	5.96
7	Charley O'Rourke	1946-1949	4	418	219	52.4	3088	28	35	8.4	7.39
8	Spec Sanders	1946-1948	3	418	204	48.8	2771	23	37	8.9	6.63
9	Bud Schwenk	1946-1948	3	367	189	51.5	2564	17	23	6.3	6.96
10	Sam Vacanti	1947-1948	2	368	154	41.8	2238	18	32	8.7	6.35
11	Tony Frietas	1946-1949	4	253	123	48.6	1884	21	27	10.7	7.44
12	Bob Chappuis	1948-1949	2	227	102	44.9	1442	8	17	7.5	6.35
13	Al Dekdebrun	1946-1948	3	161	83	51.6	1222	13	17	10.6	7.59
14	Angelo Bertelli	1946-1948	3	166	76	45.8	972	8	19	11.4	5.86
15	Johnny Clement	1949	1	114	58	50.9	906	6	13	11.4	7.95
16	Pete Layden	1948-1949	2	115	45	39.1	841	9	9	7.8	7.31
17	Don Panciera	1949	1	150	51	34.0	801	5	16	10.7	5.33
18	George Taliaferro	1949	1	124	45	36.3	790	4	14	11.3	6.37
19	Ace Parker	1946	1	115	62	53.9	763	8	3	2.6	6.63
20	George Terlep	1946-1948	3	150	54	36.0	652	9	19	12.7	4.35

ALL-TIME AAFC PASS RECEIVING
(Ranked on Number of Completions)

No.	Name		Yr.	No.	Yds.	Avg.	Td.
1	Mac Speedie	1946-1949	4	211	3554	16.8	24
2	Alyn Beals	1946-1949	4	177	2510	14.2	46
3	Lamar Davis	1946-1949	4	147	2103	14.3	12
4	Dante Lavelli	1946-1949	4	142	2580	14.8	29
5	Alton Baldwin	1947-1949	3	132	2103	15.9	22
6	Fay King	1946-1949	4	115	1583	13.8	20
7	Billy Hillenbrand	1946-1948	3	110	2053	18.7	18
8	Chet Mutryn	1946-1949	4	85	1471	11.3	10
9	Saxon Judd	1946-1948	3	84	997	11.9	7
10	Bruce Alford	1946-1949	4	76	1262	16.6	9
11	Dale Gentry	1946-1948	3	74	1001	13.5	5
12	Jack Russell	1946-1949	4	73	1154	15.8	13
13	Len Ford	1948-1949	2	67	1175	17.5	8
14	Ray Ramsey	1947-1949	3	65	1449	22.3	14
15	Dan Edwards	1948-1949	2	65	749	11.5	3
16	Joe Aguirre	1946-1949	4	63	1040	16.5	16
17	Mickey Colmer	1946-1949	4	63	899	14.3	6
18	Nick Susoeff	1946-1949	4	61	610	10.0	4
19	Buddy Young	1947-1949	3	60	733	12.2	8
20	Max Morris	1946-1948	3	53	677	12.8	2

ALL-TIME AAFC SCORING

No.	Name		Yr.	Td.	Xp.	Fg.	Pts.
1	Alyn Beals	1946-1949	4	46	2	0	278
2	Lou Groza	1946-1949	4	0	165	30	259
3	Joe Vetrano	1946-1949	4	2	187	16	247
4	Spec Sanders	1946-1948	3	40	0	0	240
5	Chet Mutryn	1946-1949	4	38	1	0	229
6	Harvey Johnson	1946-1949	4	0	147	22	213
7	Billy Hillenbrand	1946-1948	3	31	0	0	186
8	Marion Motley	1946-1949	4	31	0	0	186
9	Edgar Jones	1946-1949	4	29	0	0	174
10	Dante Lavelli	1946-1949	4	29	0	0	174
11	Mac Speedie	1946-1949	4	25	1	0	151
12	John Strzykalski	1946-1949	4	25	0	0	150
13	Joe Aquirre	1946-1949	4	16	33	5	141
14	Joe Perry	1948-1949	2	23	0	0	138
15	John Kimbrough	1946-1948	3	23	0	0	138
16	Alton Baldwin	1947-1949	3	22	0	0	132
17	Ben Agajanian	1947-1948	2	0	70	20	130
18	Frankie Albert	1946-1949	4	20	1	0	121
19	Mickey Colmer	1946-1949	4	20	0	0	120
20	Buddy Young	1947-1949	3	20	0	0	120
21	Fay King	1946-1949	4	20	0	0	120

STATISTICAL CHAMPIONS

AAFC

BALL CARRYING

1949	Fletcher Perry, San Francisco	783 yards
1948	Marion Motley, Cleveland	964 yards
1947	Orban Sanders, New York	1,432 yards
1946	Orban Sanders, New York	709 yards

FIELD GOALS

1949	Harvey Johnson, New York	7
1948	Rex Grossman, Baltimore	10
1947	Ben Agajanian, Los Angeles	15
1946	Louis Groza, Cleveland	13

FORWARD PASSING

		Atts.	Comp.	Yds.
1949	Otto Graham, Cleveland	285	161	2,785
1948	Otto Graham, Cleveland	333	173	2,713
1947	Otto Graham, Cleveland	269	163	2,753
1946	*Glenn Dobbs, Brooklyn	269	135	1,886
	*Otto Graham, Cleveland	174	95	1,834

* Co-Champions

PASS RECEIVING

		Comp.	Yds.
1949	Mac Speedie, Cleveland	40	843
1948	Mac Speedie, Cleveland	58	816
1947	Mac Speedie, Cleveland	67	1,146
1946	Dante Lavelli, Cleveland	40	843

PUNTING

		Atts.	Ave. Yds.
1949	Frankie Albert, San Francisco	31	48.2
1948	Glenn Dobbs, Los Angeles	68	49.1
1947	John Colmer, Brooklyn	56	44.7
1946	Glenn Dobbs	80	47.8

SCORING

		TDs	FG	XPTs	Total
1949	Alyn Beals, San Francisco	12	1	0	73
1948	Chester Mutryn, Buffalo	16	0	0	96
1947	Orban Sanders, New York	19	0	0	114
1946	Lou Groza, Cleveland	0	13	45	84

WORLD FOOTBALL LEAGUE

The first season of the World Football League could hardly be described as a success. There were many problems that were faced. Padded attendance figures, missed payrolls, franchise shifting and folding, confiscated equipment and uniforms in lieu of payment of debts were among these problems. The twelve teams averaged about 21,000 fans per game (revised to eliminate tickets given away) and lost a grand total of about twenty million dollars. These losses may have been largely artificial due to the special advantages related to income tax payments, however. Certainly among the high points for the league were the announced signings of Larry Csonka, Jim Kiick, and Paul Warfield of Miami by John Bassett of the Toronto team, that was later moved to Memphis before the season began because of restrictions imposed by the Canadian government. Since the players were already under contract for the 1974 season, they were not to join the WFL until 1975. The reported three million dollar price tag for the Miami trio encouraged a number of other NFL stars to sign with the WFL, but nearly all of these were for 1975 or beyond, and very few NFL regulars played in the new league in 1974. Also, World Football was not very successful in signing collegiate players, except for Southern California, which inked a number of UCLA and USC graduates. A major impact on the existing league by the WFL concerned rule changes designed to add more scoring to the game. Most of the changes were hurriedly adopted by the NFL for the 1974 season.

For 1975, the WFL is planning to operate with at least 11 clubs. Although only Memphis and Philadelphia are under the same management as last season, the cities represented are just about the same. San Antonio is being added, while Detroit and Florida were dropped. New league president Chris Hemmeter, a successful businessman from Hawaii, has established a number of strict financial ground rules designed to avoid the embarrassment of 1974. Some of the NFL stars who were going to go to the WFL were relieved of their obligations to the new league due to contract defaults by the clubs. However, a number of others, including Csonka, Kiick and Warfield, have indicated that they are going to play in the World Football League in the 1975 season.

Although none of the WFL clubs appear in the all-time roster included in this encyclopedia, many of the WFL players have appeared in games for NFL teams in previous seasons. Those players marked with asterisks have played in the NFL and their records can be found in the roster.

1974

WORLD FOOTBALL LEAGUE

WESTERN DIVISION

	W.	L.	T.	Pct.
Southern California	13	7	0	.650
Hawaii	9	11	0	.450
Portland	7	12	1	.375
Shreveport	7	12	1	.375

CENTRAL DIVISION

	W.	L.	T.	Pct.
Memphis	17	3	0	.850
Birmingham	15	5	0	.750
Chicago*	7	12	0	.368
Detroit*	1	13	0	.071

EASTERN DIVISION

	W.	L.	T.	Pct.
Florida	14	6	0	.700
Charlotte	10	10	0	.500
Philadelphia	8	11	0	.421
Jacksonville*	4	10	0	.286

*Team disbanded before close of season

WFL TITLE GAME

Birmingham 22; Florida 21

The Birmingham Americans won the World Bowl for the WFL Championship, as the Florida Blazers' fourth-quarter rally came up one point short. Each team scored three touchdowns, but only a single action point conversion was successful, giving Birmingham the narrow victory. George Mira led the victors to a 22–0 lead with one TD pass and Joe Profit topped the Americans in rushing and contributed the first score. The Florida rally was sparked by two long scoring passes by Bob Davis, one to the game's leading rusher—Tommy Reamon. Rod Foster made the final score on a 76-yard punt return. Florida, however, which had rallied from a 15–0 deficit the week before, was unable to repeat this time .

Florida	0	0	0	21	21
Birmingham	0	15	7	0	22

Touchdowns: Birmingham, Profit, Cantrelle, Brown; Florida, Reamon, Latta, Foster

Action point: Birmingham: Reed

Attendance: 32,376

LEADERS: Scoring—Ed Marshall (Memphis) 144; Rushing—Tommy Reamon (Florida) 1576 yds.; Passing—Tony Adams (Southern California) 3905 yds.; Pass Receiving—Tim Delaney (Hawaii) 89; Punting—Ken Clark (Portland) 41.8 yds.; Interceptions—David Thomas (Memphis) 10.

1974 BIRMINGHAM AMERICANS (WFL)
Coach – Jack Gotta
2nd – Central Division, 15-5-0
(Received bye in first round of playoffs, beat Hawaii 22-19 in second round and beat Florida 22-21 in championship World Bowl)

Andrews, John – DT
Arnold, Chris – CB
*Baker, John (Norfolk St) DT
Bartles, Carl – RB
Bishop, Jim – TE
Brezina, Butch – DE
*Brown, Bob (Alcorn A&M) TE
Brown, Buddy – OT
*Brupbacher, Ross – LB
Bryant, William – DB
*Butler, James (Waters) RB
Cantrelle, Art – RB
Capone, Warren – LB
Casey, Jay – C
Champagne, Gary – LB
*Chandler, Edgar – LB
Connally, Steve – TE
*Costa, Paul – OT
Cvitanich, Grant – DT
Duron, Denny – QB, WR
Edwards, Jimmy – RB
Engle, Phil – OT
*Estes, Larry – DE
Foxx, Ronald – LB
Gennerick, Gary – G
*Guthrie, Grant – K
*Harraway, Charley – RB
Haynes, George – DB
*Holmes, Mel – G
*Homan, Dennis – WR
Jenkins, Alfred – WR
Kregel, Jim – G
Lee, Randy – S
*Leonard, Cecil – DB
*Lyons, Dicky – S

Manstedt, Steve – LB
*Matlock, John – C
*Mira, George – QB
Mullen, Mike – LB
*O'Donnell, Joe – G
Owings, Jim – TE
Powell, Ted – TE
*Profit, Joe – RB
Reamon, Charles – CB
Reed, Matthew – QB
*Robinson, Paul – RB
Sark, Earl – K
Scrievener, Duane – CB
Sitterle, Al – G
Skladany, John – DT
Smith, Willie – DB
*Taterak, Bob – DT
*Teal, Jimmy – LB
Trower, Dick – DT
Truax, Mike – LB
Washington, Clarence – DT
Williams, Gerard – CB
Williams, Steve – CB
*Willingham, Larry – CB
*Winther, Wimpy – C
Wolf, Jessie – DT
Wolfe, Bob – OT

1974 CHARLOTTE HORNETS (WFL)
(New York Stars transferred to Charlotte after 12 games)
Coach – Babe Parilli
2nd – Eastern Division, 10-10-0

Askson, Bert – TE
*Barnes, Al – WR
Boston, Charles – CB
*Bouggess, Lee – RB
Brown, Jere – LB
Bunge, Darrel – G
Butler, Larry – G
*Campbell, Carter – DE
Carpenter, Dana – LB
Champagne, Larry – LB
Chandler, Tom – LB
Danielson, Gary – QB
DeFlavio, Bill – DT
Dennis, Steve – S
*Dockery, John – CB
*Dowling, Brian – QB
*Elliott, John – DT
Ellison, Jerry – DE
*Estes, Larry – DE
*Ford, Jim – RB
*Gladieux, Bob – RB
*Grant, Bob – LB
*Hart, Dick – G
Herkenhoff, Matt – OT
Hermann, Bob – WR
*Highsmith, Don – RB
Hoepner, Terry – S
Huff, Andy – LB
*Huff, Marty – LB
*Jackson, Joe – DT
Jannsen, Bill – C
*Jolley, Lewis – RB
Kapitan, Kreg – WR
King, John – RB
*Kuziel, Bob – C
*Lens, Greg – DT
Parson, Ray – TE
*Philbin, Gerry – DE
Rajecki, Pete – K
Reynolds, Art – LB
Reynolds, Robbie – P
Richards, Dave – WR
Richardson, Ernie – LB
*Sauer, George – WR
*St. Jean, Len – OG
*Sharp, Rick – OT
*Shears, Larry – CB
*Sherman, Tom – QB
Sims, James – S
*Thomas, Ike – DB
*Voss, Lloyd – DT
White, Bryan – CB
Wilson, Wendell – CB
Woodcock, Jeff – CB
Wolley, Dave – RB
*Young, Al – WR

1974 CHICAGO FIRE (WFL)
Coach – Jim Spavital
3rd – Central Division, 7-12-0
(Team declined to play final game with Philadelphia)

*Anderson, Ralph – DB
Armstrong, J. D. – LB
Bailey, Chuck – DT
Belgrave, Earl – OT
*Best, Keith – LB
Botts, Mike – C
*Bradley, Dave – G
Brewer, Richard – LB
*Burchfield, Don – TE
Calip, Jimmie – RB
*Cappleman, Bill – QB
Carter, Mike – CB
*Carter, Virgil – QB
Crittendon, Lon – WR
Daigneau, Maurie – QB
Damato, Glenn – WR
Dolbin, Jack – WR
*Evey, Dick – DE
Gleason, Dan – DE
*Hale, Dave – DT
*Hart, Leo – QB
Heath, Clayton – RB
Heinrich, Mike – DE
*Holman, Willie – DE
Howard, Harry – S
Hyde, Glen – OT
Jarmon, Sherwin – LB
*Jenkins, Al – OT
Kellar, Mark – RB
*Kelly, Leroy – RB
Kennedy, Jimmie – TE
Kiley, Kevin – LB

Kogut, Chuck – LB
*Kuechenberg, Rudy – LB
*McCarty, Mickey – TE
McCreight, Tom – G
Miller, Willie – WR
*Murdock, Guy – C
O'Sadnick, Craig – DB
Palmer, Luther – TE
Phillips, Hal – CB
*Pinder, Cyril – RB
*Porter, Ron – LB
Ramsey, Chuck, P, K
Reamon, Charlie – DB
Redmond, Tom – WR
Rhone, Walter – DB
*Rice, Andy – DT
Richardson, Randy – DB
*Roussel, Tom – LB

Rudder, Bill – RB
Ruffner, Barry – S
Sanderson, Reggie – RB
Sanduk, Ken – RB
Scott, James – WR
Scrievener, Duane – DB
*Seymour, Jim – WR
*Sikich, Mike – G
*Spicer, Rob – LB
Stemrick, Greg – DB
Taylor, Billy – RB
Troszakde, Doug – DB
*Watson, Allan – K
Whye, Wayne – DT
Womack, Joe – CB
*Wright, Steve – OT
Wyatt, Bob – RB
Wyche, Bubba – QB

*Johnson, Mitch – OT
*Kaczmarek, Mike – LB
Lachowicz, Ted – C
Latta, Greg – TE
Maree, Ron – OT
*Maslowski, Matt – WR
*McBath, Mike – DT
*McClain, Clifford – RB
Palazzo, Buddy – QB
Palmer, Luther – TE
Peiffer, Dan – C
Perry, Les – K
Ratliff, Don – DE
Reamon, Tommy – RB

Ricca, John – DE
Richardson, Eddie – WR
*Rock, Walter – DT
*Ross, Louis – DE
Rush, Bob – TE
Sheats, Eddie – LB
Strock, Dave – P, K
*Strong, Jim – RB
*Trapp, Richard – WR
*Turner, Cecil – WR
Vellano, Paul – DT
*Whitfield, A. D. – RB
*Williams, Del – G
*Willis, Larry – CB
Yoest, Billy – G

1974 THE HAWAIIANS (WFL)
Coach – Mike Giddings
2nd – Western Division, 9–11–0
(Beat Southern California 34–14 in first round of playoffs and lost to Birmingham 22–19 in second round of playoffs)

Andre, Phil – DB
Atkinson, Dave – DB
Baccus, Gary – LB
Boyer, Tim – WR
Brice, Larry – RB
*Brown, Otto – DB
Buchanan, Dave – RB
Burnham, Lem – DE
*Cadile, Jim – C, G
*Cheek, Richard – G
*Clements, Vin – RB
Cooch, Jim – DB
Coppedge, R. A. – K
Corey, Jay – LB
Davis, Al – RB
Delaney, Tim – WR
*Detwiler, Chuck – DB
Donckers, Bill – QB
*Douglas, John – LB
*Eaglin, Larry – DB
*East, Ron – DT
Fiatoa, Louis – LB
Gentry, Butch – K
*Hargett, Edd – QB
Heath, Clayton – RB
*Hester, Ray – LB
*Isenbarger, John – WR
*Johnson, Cornelius – G
Johnson, Frank – LB
*Johnson, Randy – QB
Kelsey, John – TE

*Line, Bill – OT
Lorch, Karl – DE
McGirr, Mike – OT
Moseley, John – DB
O'Leary, Ernie – RB
*Olerich, Dave – LB
Oliver, Al – OT
Poe, Tom – LB
Powell, Jerry – WR
Richards, Bob – G
Richardson, Grady – WR
Schultz, Jack – DB
Sevy, Jeff – G
*Slough, Greg – LB
*Sniadecki, Jim – LB
Solverson, Peder – C
Stanley, Levi – DT
Stringert, Hal – DB
Vella, Chris – TE
Viney, Willie – G
Watkins, Richard – DT, DE
Weber, Fred – DT, DE
Weese, Norris – QB
*Wilbur, John – G
Williams, Derrick – DB
*Williams, Willie – DB
*Wojcik, Greg – DT
*Young, Adrian – LB

1974 DETROIT WHEELS (WFL)
(Club folded after 14 games)
Coach – Dan Boisture
4th – Central Division, 1–13–0

Adolfi, Henry – LB
Battle, Charles – LB
*Blanchard, Dick – LB
*Bryant, Hubie – WR
Cook, Lewis – DB
Cooke, Jim – OT
*Davis, Norm – G
Edwards, Bennett – G
Engle, Phil – DT
Fernandes, Ron – DE
Fobbs, Lee – RB
Glosson, Clyde – WR
Guthrie, Eric – QB, K
Hayes, Charles – OT
Haynes, George – DB
Henderson, Jon – WR
Hoeppner, Terry – DB
Holmes, Reggie – DB
Hudson, Gary – DB
Joppru, Sheldon – TE
Kemp, Dennis – OT
Kuhn, Mike – LB
Levanti, John – G
Limebrook, Dave – C
Linter, Dan – DB
*Livingston, Dale – K
Long, Rocky – S
Martin, Rocky – LB

*McCarty, Micky – TE
McKee, Charles – WR
Mimms, Jesse – RB
Parks, Jesse – WR
Perkins, Renard – DT
Phillips, Terry – WR
Priester, Floyd – DB
Ramsey, Tom – DE
Ratcliff, Larry – RB
Ratliff, Don – DE
Rathje, Jim – RB
Sadler, Bill – RB
*Sartin, Dan – OT
Scales, Joe – TE
Scarber, Sam – RB
Shaw, Bruce – QB
*Stenger, Brian – LB
Taibi, Carl – DE
*Taylor, Mike – LB
*Trosch, Gene – DE
Walker, Dave – DB
*Walker, Mike – DE
*Wheeler, Ted – OT
Williams, Terry – TE
*Wilson, Mike – G
*Winther, Wimpy – C
Wyche, Bubba – QB

1974 FLORIDA BLAZERS (WFL)
Coach – Jack Pardee
1st – Eastern Division, 14–6–0
(Beat Philadelphia 18–3 in first round of playoffs, beat Memphis 18–15 in second round of playoffs and lost to Birmingham 22–21 in championship World Bowl)

*Amman, Richard – DE
*Anderson, Roger – DT
Anthony, Rick – OT
*Beatty, Charles – DB
Brannan, Tim – G
Brown, Henry – WR
*Bryant, Hubie – WR
*Buzin, Rich – G, OT
*Collins, Gary – WR
Crittendon, Lonnie – WR
Crone, Eric – QB

*Davis, Bob – QB
*Ely, Larry – LB
*Farr, Miller – DB
Foster, Rod – S
Gatti, Bill – RB
*Grantham, Larry – LB
*Harris, Rickie – S
*Hayes, Billie – CB
*Hicks, W. K. – S
Hilton, John – TE
*Hobbs, Billy – LB
James, Richard – RB

1974 JACKSONVILLE SHARKS (WFL)
(Club folded after 14 games)
Coach – Bud Asher, Charley Tate
4th – Eastern Division, 4–10–0

Abbott, Fred – LB
Baker, Sam – G
*Brannan, Solomon – DB
*Buie, Drew – WR
*Carrell, Duane – P
*Cherry, Stan – LB
*Cheek, Richard – G
Coppenbarger, Ron – DB
*Cornish, Frank – OT
Creaney, Mike – TE
Davis, Jeff – RB
Davis, Jerry – DB

*Dunaway, Jim – DT
Durrance, Tommy – RB
*Ellison, Glenn – LB
Foster, Eddie – G
*Gagner, Larry – G
Gaspard, Glen – LB
*Guthrie, Grant – K
*Haggerty, Mike – OT, G
Haywood, Alfred – RB
*Hughes, Dennis – TE
Johnson, Tom – C

*Kindig, Howard – C, G, OT
Krepfle, Keith – TE
Lake, Ricky – RB
*Lamb, Ron – RB
*Lassiter, Ike – DE
Lomak, Tony – WR
Mack, Johnny – LB
May, Art – DT
*Mayes, Benjamin – DE
Melby, Russ – DT
Mullen, Mike – LB
*Oats, Carleton – DE
Oliver, Reggie – QB
Osborne, John – DB
Parrish, Bob – TE

Scott, Edgar – RB
Simonton, Claud – LB
*Smith, Fletcher – DB
*Stephenson, Kay – QB
*Stofa, John – QB
Swierc, Carl – WR
*Taterak, Bob – DT
Thomann, Rich – LB
Townsend, Mike – DB
*Vanoy, Vernon – DE
Walker, Tom – DB
White, O. Z. – DT
Whittier, Tom – WR
*Wyatt, Alvin – DB

Laputka, Tom – DT
Lozzi, Dennis – OT
Mabra, Ron – DB
Mansfield, Mike – LB
Marshall, Bryan – S
McGuigan, Frank – RB
Mitchell, Walt – DE
Olson, Doug – DE
Papale, Vince – WR
Parmenter, Skip – DT
*Peterson, Bill – LB
Pettaway, Mark – DB
Pettigrew, Len – DE
Ratliff, Don – DE
Rickenbach, Bob – OT
Riley, Mike – LB
*Rossovich, Tim – LB
Schaukowitch, Carl – G

Scott, Ken – DT
Shanklin, Don – WR
Shaw, Mike – DB
Simcsak, Jack – K
Sixkiller, Sonny – QB
*Sodaski, John – LB
Sonntag, Ralph – OT
Steinberger, Jeff – LB
Thompson, Alan – RB
Vallery, Don – DB
Warren, Jerry – K
Watts, Claude – RB
Wilson, Mike – G
Wyche, Bubba – QB
Yancheff, Mike—QB
Yaralian, Zaven – DB

1974 MEMPHIS SOUTHMEN (WFL)
Coach – John McVay
1st – Central Division, 17–3–0
(Received bye in first round of playoffs and lost to Florida 18–15 in second round)

*Andrews, Al – LB
*Beamer, Tim – WR
*Beckman, Tom – DE
*Beutler, Tom – LB
Bonham, Bracy – G
Booras, Steve – DE
Boyd, Dave – DB
Bray, Charles – G
Bumpas, Dick – TE
Burkhardt, Jake – LB
*Canale, Justin – G
Code, Merl – DB
Cotton, Festus – DT
Dempsey, Wally – LB
Dever, Dan – LB
Ellegood, Ben – DE
*Etter, Bob – K
Ettinger, Jack – WR
Ettinger, Jim – QB
Gibbons, Mike – OT
Harvey, John – RB
Hicks, Emery – LB
Hicks, Sonny – DB
*Highsmith, Walter – OT
Hill, Ralph – C
Houmard, Bob – TE
*Huarte, John – QB
Jackson, Herman – LB

Jennings, J. J. – RB
Jones, Willie Lee – LB
Kruyer, Tom – G
Lally, Bob – DT
Leheup, John – DT
Longwell, Brent – TE
*Majors, Bobby – DB
*Marshall, Ed – WR
Mikolajczyk, Ron – OT
Miles, Paul – RB
Miller, Seth – DB
*Morris, Chris – OT
Powell, Gary – WR
Pryor, Cecil – DE
*Sartin, Dan – DT
Schmid, Anton – RB
Selmon, Lucious – DE
Shirk, Gary – TE
Smiley, Larry – DE
Spencer, Willie – RB
Stevenson, Bill – DT
Taylor, Billy – RB
Thomas, David – DB
Thornton, Dick – DB
Tiblom, Charles – C, G
Wallace, Roger – WR
White, Danny – QB, P

1974 PHILADELPHIA BELL (WFL)
Coach – Ron Waller
3rd – Eastern Division, 8–11–0
(Final game of season cancelled by Chicago. Lost to Florida 18–3 in first round of playoffs)

Bartek, Mike – WR
Bowens, Cecil – RB
Brinkley, Lorenzo – DB
*Carter, Mike – WR
*Cash, Rick – DE
Chatlos, George – LB
*Chomyszak, Steve – DT
Code, Merl – DB
Corcoran, Jim "King" – QB
Craven, Bill – CB
Dempsey, Wally – LB
DiMaggio, Frank – QB
*Dunn, Paul – TE
Ellenbogan, John – OT
*Franklin, Willie – WR

*Gallagher, Frank – G
*Germany, Willie – DB
*Grant, Bob – LB
Gray, Gary – C
Guthrie, Erik – K
*Hayes, Ed – DB
Hill, Levell – TE
*Holliday, Ron – WR
Horoszko, Pete – OT
Hughes, Walt – G
Izzo, Len – WR
Joe, Jimmy – RB
*Johnson, Benny – DB
Jornov, Ted – LB
Joyner, David – G
Kecman, Ron – C
Knoble, John – LB, P
Kral, Curt – LB
Land, John – RB

1974 PORTLAND STORM (WFL)
Coach – Dick Coury
3rd (tied) – Western Division, 7–12–1

*Askea, Mike – OT
*Austin, Hise – CB
Baker, Jeff – WR
*Barton, Greg – QB
*Beathard, Pete – QB
*Bergey, Bruce – DE
Bishop, Ed – DB
Borjas, Phil – S
Brazeau, Buzz – OT
Brock, Lee – DE
Brown, Dave – C
*Carr, Levert – OT
*Christiansen, Bob – TE
Ciufo, Lennie – LB
Clark, Ken – P, K
*Condren, Glenn – DT
*Cotton, Greg – TE
Crtalic, Don – LB
*Davidson, Ben – DE
Dickerson, Sam – WR
Ellis, Glen – DT
*Ferguson, Gene – OT
Ferguson, Rufus – RB
*Guidry, Paul – LB
Hinton, Charles – DB
*Holmes, Robert – RB
*Hoss, Clark – TE
*Inman, Jerry – DT
Jensen, Flemming – K
*Johnson, Carl – G
Johnson, Ken – QB
*Jones, Ray – DB
Kendricks, Marv – RB
*Krieg, Jim – WR

*Lusteg, Booth – K
McConnell, Mike – LB
*Meyer, Dennis – DB
Mitchell, Darrell – QB
*Mitchell, Leroy – DB
Muhlbeier, Ken – G
*Oberg, Tom – DB
*Oliver, Clancy – DB
*Patrick, Wayne – RB
*Prudhomme, Remi – G
*Redman, Rick – LB
Roberts, Marvin – G
Schmit, Bob – LB
*Schottenheimer, Marty – LB
Sherman, Ray – S
*Silas, Sam – DT
Sinclair, Robin – DB
Specht, Greg – WR
Stecher, Chris – DE
Taylor, Drew – DT
*Taylor, Mike – OT
Terry, Tony – DT
*Thompson, Steve – DE
*Turner, Clem – RB
Van Galder, Don – QB
Vella, Chris – TE
Washington, Ed – CB
Warehime, Clyde – LB
*Williams, Clancy – CB
Williams, Wallace – OT
Wylie, Joe – RB, WR

1974 SHREVEPORT STEAMER (WFL)
(Houston Texans transferred to Shreveport after 12 games)
Coach – Jim Garrett, Marshall Taylor
3rd (tied) – Western Division, 7–12–1

Bailey, Tom – OT
*Bishop, Sonny – C
Blackney, Harry – RB
*Blanks, Sid – RB
*Boyette, Garland – LB
Brown, Chad – DE
*Brumm, Don – DE

*Carroll, Joe – LB
*Creech, Bob – LB
*Davis, Don – TE
*Dotson, Al – DT
*Durkee, Charlie – K, S
*Eber, Rick – WR
*Flowers, Richmond – S

*Frazier, Willie – TE
*Gibbs, Pat – CB
*Gipson, Paul – RB
*Glover, Rich – DT
*Green, Joe – S
*Hines, Glen Ray – OT
 Holden, Sam – OT
*Jankowski, Bruce –
  WR
*Johnson, Daryl – CB
*Jones, Willie Lee – DE
*Kanicki, Jim – DT
 Kupp, Andy – G
*Latourette, Chuck – P,
  WR
*Mallory, John – S
 Mays, David – QB
 McConnell, Mike – LB
*McMahon, Art – RB
*McVea, Warren – RB
 Miller, Joe – OT
*Mooney, Ed – LB
*Nance, Jim – RB
 Nobles, D. C. – QB
 Odom, John – WR

*Parker, Willie – DT
 Pitts, Rex – G
 Price, Kenny – LB
*Regner, Tom – G
*Robb, Joe – DE
*Robinson, Virgil – RB
 Rydalch, Ron – DT
*Shorter, Jim – CB
*Taliaferro, Mike – QB
 Thompson, Durfey –
  LB
*Thompson, Rocky –
  RB
*Trull, Don – QB
 Villapiano, John –
  LB
*Wainscott, Loyd – LB
*Walik, Billy – WR
*Walker, Cleo – LB, C
*Walker, Mike – DE
*Wells, Robert – OT
*Williams, Clyde – G
*Winslow, Doug – WR
 Yoest, Billy – G
*Zaeske, Paul – WR

1974 SOUTHERN CALIFORNIA SUN (WFL)
Coach – Tom Fears
1st – Western Division, 13–7–0
(Lost to Hawaii 34–14 in first round of playoffs)

 Adams, Tony – QB
 Baker, James – LB
 Ballew, Mike – DE
 Bowman, Jim – CB
 Bradley, Charles – C
 Bright, James – S
 Brown, Booker – OT
 Buckmon, James – LB
*Carollo, Joe – OT
 Connors, Jack – DB
*Crane, Dennis – DT
 Cullen, Bruce – RB
 Dejurnett, Charles –
  DT
 Denimarck, Mike – LB
 Denson, Keith – WR
 Emery, Alonzo – RB
 Garcia, Rod – K
 Grady, Kevin – G
 Hainlen, Norm – K
 Harris, Ike – WR
 Herd, Greg – RB
*Hoffman, John – DE
*Howard, Eugene – DB
 Jeffries, Clay – RB
 Johnson, Eric – S
 Johnson, Kermit – RB
 Keeton, Durwood – DB

 Kezirian, Ed – OT
 Klippert, Younger – G
*Lee, Ken – LB
 Lindsey, Terry – WR,
  K
 Mason, Greg – CB
 McAlister, James –
  RB
*McCall, Don – RB
 McMichael, Al – TE
 Nelson, Ralph – RB
*Oats, Carleton – DE
*Parks, Dave – TE
 Patton, Eric – LB
*Philpott, Ed – LB
*Redman, Rudy – DB
*Roller, Dave – DT
 Ryan, Mike – C
 Schroder, Steve – K
 Seifert, Ted – C
*Seiler, Paul – C, OT
 Skarin, Neal – DT
 Valbuena, Gary – QB
 Vann, Cleveland – LB
*Williams, Dave – WR
*Witcher, Dick – TE,
  WR

7 The Commissioner's Office

The National Football League has been both wise and fortunate in its choice of Commissioners, and for more than 30 of its 50 years of existence, it was guided by two rare men, Joe F. Carr and Bert Bell.

Carr took control in 1921 after one year of confusion and birth pains under the presidency of Jim Thorpe, who was never more than a figurehead with publicity value. Carr ruled the league for 18 years until his death in 1939. His fearless justice and flawless faith in the future of professional football helped the league ride through its stormy adolescence until it was a strong organization ready for the tremendous race to prosperity at the end of World War II.

It was Carr who insisted in his first year of control that post-graduate football must keep faith with the colleges. He instituted the rule, always scrupulously followed, that the pro league must not negotiate with any college player until his class has graduated. Carr believed that an education was most important and that professional sports must not attempt for its own selfish reasons to disrupt the years of study.

The wisdom of this ruling was most apparent in the continued good relationships between the NFL and the colleges 40 years after Carr insisted on it in 1921. By contrast, professional baseball, which has had no such interest in education, was blundering down the slide to becoming a lesser sport while football was still climbing rapidly to the number one position on the American scene.

Carr showed his strength and courage many times during the league's formative years. In 1925 the Milwaukee team made the mistake of placing four high-school players in the line-up for a game against the Chicago Cardinals. Carr struck swiftly: Milwaukee was banished from the league; the man responsible for recruiting the players was banned from the league for life; the Cardinal owners were fined for permitting their team to take part in the game. At the same time the Pottsville Maroon team was censured for playing a game in the territory of the Frankford Yellowjackets, and the football world, in fact, the entire sports world, was applauding Joe Carr for being a Commissioner with spirit and courage.

After Carr's death in 1939, Carl L. Storck served as president until 1941, when he resigned to make way for Elmer Layden, one of the famed Four Horsemen of Notre Dame. The lull of the war years kept football operating on a restrained basis through the Storck and Layden eras, but in 1946 a new war was declared and again the NFL picked an outstanding leader to fight it. He was de Bennville "Bert" Bell, a former player, coach and owner, a man who had turned his back on his inherited life of wealth and high society, to devote all his energies to the game of football that he loved.

Bell passed his first test almost immediately. An attempt was made by New York nxers to tamper with the championship game between the Giants and the Chicago Bears in 1946. It was a moment when the integrity of pro football was at stake before public opinion, and Bell moved bravely, openly and decisively. He permitted one of the two players involved to play in the game and was rewarded by that player giving a little more than seemed possible in his performance to prove that there had never been any intention on his part of doing anything less than his best. Bell then barred both players from the league for an indefinite period.

He turned then to the "war" with the new All America Football Conference, which was shooting with its millions of dollars at the contracts of National League stars and was determined to defeat the NFL with the power of its almost unlimited funds. Four years later Bell and the NFL accepted the complete surrender of the AAFC and Bell's life contract as leader of the NFL was assured. He died at a pro football game in the fall of 1959.

The league then picked a much younger man, Alvin "Pete" Rozelle, at the time general manager of the Los Angeles Rams, and within his first year Rozelle faced a new problem, a "war" with another new league, the American Football League. The veterans who had chosen Rozelle were calm and sure that he, like Carr and Bell before him, would meet the unknown tests ahead.

In 1966, their confidence was rewarded when Rozelle brought about the merger of the NFL and AFL after a suicidal financial battle between the leagues. A year after Bert Bell's death, Tex Maule, pro football editor of *Sports Illustrated,* wrote these words about Bert Bell, in his fine book, *THE PROS.* They seemed to say everything that those who had known Bell best would have wanted to say:

He was a potbellied little man with a frog voice and he knew more about football than anyone. He played it and coached it and he was president of the National Football League and, a small man in a world of giants, he did very well. He died at a professional football game, and I guess that if you had asked Bert Bell the way he wanted to go, he would have said, "At a pro football game."

Death came for him at a game between the Philadelphia Eagles and the Pittsburgh Steelers in 1959 and the stands were full, which must have made him very happy. As much as any one man, he was responsible for the filled stands.

Bert came from a very posh Philadelphia family. They were society and politics and wealth, and Bert must have seemed a throwback to an earlier, lustier time. He went to the University of Pennsylvania and played football there, and later he coached the team. Back in the early Thirties, he bought the moribund Philadelphia Eagles and they remained moribund under his direction. Bert coached the team reasonably well, but you can't win without the horses and he didn't have horses. And he was involved in all the other myriad details of running a professional football team too. Once he stood on a downtown street corner in Philadelphia and hawked tickets to the Eagle games. He found very few takers. The nadir of his career as a pro football owner came at one game when there were more inhabitants of the press box than there were spectators in the stands.

Maybe Bert's trouble was that he was ahead of his time. He was elected Commissioner of the National Football League on January 11, 1946. At the time, he was a part owner of the Pittsburgh Steelers, and more than a few of the owners thought they were electing a figurehead. Bert changed their minds in a hurry.

He never took a step back from anyone, least of all the owners. In the frequent and bitter arguments between owner and owner, and owner and player,

Bert was always fair. It was Bell who designed and implemented the league policy on television, which made pro football the fastest-growing professional sport in the United States. It was this little, fat and stubborn man who introduced the player draft to pro football and so equalized the teams in the league that on any Sunday the lowest team can, with a break, beat the best.

None of that really makes any difference. Bert was a strong man and an intelligent one, and, above all, a fair man. You could call him at three o'clock in the morning and he would talk to you without resentment or anger, and in the last few years that took self-control because he was a sick man. His heart had begun to fail, but he overlooked that, as he overlooked anything which might have made him less of a Commissioner.

I talked to him for a long time one afternoon just a couple of weeks before he died. Our conversation was interrupted by phone calls from owners and players, and in one of these calls he told an owner he was a cheapskate for trying to avoid paying an injured player.

Then he turned to me and said, "Tex, the one thing we can't forget is that this game was built and made popular by the players. We owe them everything. I don't think that any group of athletes in the world can match pro football players for honesty and character and strength."

He was, of course, right.

The Office of the Commissioner of the National Football League is the clearing house through which passes all the business of the organization. It is the keystone of the arch around which the member teams have built their own business structures.

A recital of all that the league office does would fill many pages. A brief summary of its activities will give the reader some idea of its functions as the headquarters of the league.

The Commissioner must approve every contract made between a club and a player, also all trades and sales of players. A card bearing the complete playing record of each player is kept as part of the permanent records of the league office. The eligibility of every player, according to the Constitution and By-Laws, must be proved to the Commissioner's satisfaction.

All officials, referees, umpires, field judges, back judges and linesmen are appointed by the Commissioner and assigned by him to teams of officials. For pre-season and regular season games the officiating teams are assigned to games by the Commissioner.

The Commissioner must approve all contracts for pre-season games. This involves an investigation of promoters of proposed contests, the sites of the games and other matters directly related to the games.

Every employee of every club in the league must be approved by the Commissioner. This includes not only the coaches but those responsible for management, trainers and other personnel.

The Commissioner drafts a schedule of games for each season, a task that requires several hundred hours of work.

From the Commissioner's office are sent bulletins of information to each club: the list of players signed and those being waived by teams: facts about the sale of players, which must have the Commissioner's approval before being consummated. The office compiles a reserve list of players numbering about 1,500 names and sends master questionnaires to every player whose contract is approved.

The Commissioner presides at the annual business meeting of the league. He is also the final court of appeal in any dispute between club and player. He enforces the Constitution and By-Laws of the league. He has the power to suspend and/or fine any player or executive of the league who violates the Constitution and By-Laws. The Commissioner also has sole power over the World Championship football game played each year between the winners of the Conference championships.

The Office of the Commissioner includes a treasurer, a publicity director and such assistants as the Commissioner requires for the proper conduct of his office. A technical assistant who interprets rules and keeps records of officials is a member of the Commissioner's staff.

All the statistical records of the teams and individual players are kept by the Elias Sports Bureau, run by Seymour Siwoff. During the season they are released weekly to the press, radio and television. At the conclusion of the season the final statistics are compiled and released.

The annual *Record and Rules Manual* of the league, which contains the league's records, history, statistics, rules and other information, is edited in the office of the Commissioner.

PAID ATTENDANCE

Year	Regular Season		*Post-season	Super Bowl
1974	10,236,332 (182 games)		438,664 (7)	80,997
1973	10,730,933 (182 games)		453,551 (7)	71,882
1972	10,445,827 (182 games)		393,163 (7)	90,182
1971	10,076,035 (182 games)		402,868 (7)	81,023
1970	9,533,333 (182 games)		379,389 (7)	79,204
1969	6,096,127 (112 games)	NFL	162,279 (3)	80,562
	2,843,373 (70 games)	AFL	167,088 (3)	
1968	5,882,313 (112 games)	NFL	215,902 (3)	75,377
	2,635,004 (70 games)	AFL	114,438 (2)	
1967	5,938,924 (112 games)	NFL	166,208 (3)	75,546
	2,295,697 (63 games)	AFL	53,330 (1)	
1966	5,337,044 (105 games)	NFL	74,152 (1)	61,946
	2,160,369 (63 games)	AFL	42,080 (1)	
1965	4,634,021 (98 games)	NFL	100,304 (2)	
	1,782,384 (56 games)	AFL	30,361 (1)	
1964	4,563,049 (98 games)	NFL	79,544 (1)	
	1,447,875 (56 games)	AFL	40,242 (1)	
1963	4,163,643 (98 games)	NFL	45,801 (1)	
	1,208,697 (56 games)	AFL	63,171 (2)	
1962	4,003,421 (98 games)	NFL	64,892 (1)	
	1,147,302 (56 games)	AFL	37,981 (1)	
1961	3,986,159 (98 games)	NFL	39,029 (1)	
	1,002,657 (56 games)	AFL	29,556 (1)	
1960	3,128,296 (78 games)	NFL	67,325 (1)	
	926,156 (56 games)	AFL	32,183 (1)	
1959	3,140,000 (72 games)		57,545 (1)	
1958	3,006,124 (72 games)		123,659 (2)	
1957	2,836,318 (72 games)		119,579 (2)	
1956	2,551,263 (72 games)		56,836 (1)	
1955	2,521,836 (72 games)		85,693 (1)	
1954	2,190,571 (72 games)		43,827 (1)	
1953	2,164,585 (72 games)		54,577 (1)	
1952	2,052,126 (72 games)		97,507 (2)	
1951	1,913,019 (72 games)		57,522 (1)	
1950	1,977,753 (78 games)		136,647 (3)	
1949	1,391,735 (60 games)		27,980 (1)	
1948	1,525,243 (60 games)		36,309 (1)	
1947	1,837,437 (60 games)		66,268 (2)	
1946	1,732,135 (55 games)		58,346 (1)	

1945	1,270,401	(50 games)	32,178	(1)
1944	1,019,649	(50 games)	46,016	(1)
1943	969,128	(50 games)	71,315	(2)
1942	887,920	(55 games)	36,006	(1)
1941	1,108,615	(55 games)	55,870	(2)
1940	1,063,025	(55 games)	36,034	(1)
1939	1,071,200	(55 games)	32,279	(1)
1938	937,197	(55 games)	48,120	(1)
1937	963,039	(55 games)	15,878	(1)
1936	816,007	(54 games)	29,545	(1)
1935	638,178	(53 games)	15,000	(1)
1934	492,684	(60 games)	35,059	(1)

* Includes division, conference and league championship from 1934; number of post-season games in parentheses in 1970 and 1971 include division playoffs, conference championship games, and AFC-NFC Pro Bowl, but does not include Super Bowl.

STANDARD PLAYER CONTRACT
FOR
THE NATIONAL FOOTBALL LEAGUE

BETWEEN

. . . .

a . . . . Corporation, (a Limited Partnership), hereinafter called "Club," which Club operates under the name and style of . . . . .and which Club is presently a member of the National Football League, hereinafter called "League" and . . . . , hereinafter called "Player."

In consideration of the respective promises herein the parties agree as follows:

1. The term of this contract shall be from the date of execution hereof until the first day of May following the close of the football season commencing in the calendar year 19   , subject, however, to termination, extension or renewal as specified herein.

2. The Player agrees that during the term of this contract he will play football and engage in activities related to football only for the Club and as directed by the Club according to: this contract; the Constitution and By-Laws, Rules and Regulations of the League and of the Club; and the Club, subject to the provisions hereof, agrees during such term to employ the Player as a skilled football player. The Player agrees during the term of this contract to report promptly for the Club's training sessions and, at the Club's direction, to render his full time services during such training sessions and to participate in all practice sessions and in all League and other football games scheduled for or by the Club.

3. For: the Player's services as a skilled football player during the term of this contract: his agreement not to play football or engage in activities related to football for any other person, firm, corporation or institution during the term of this contract; the option hereinafter set forth giving the Club the right to renew this contract; and all other undertakings of the Player herein; the Club promises, subject to Paragraph 7 hereof, to pay the Player each football season during the term of this contract, unless the compensation is changed under Paragraph 10 hereof, the amount of $ . . . . to be payable as follows:

     . . . % of "said amount in equal semi-monthly installments commencing with the first regularly scheduled League game played by the Club during each season and continuing each semi-monthly period thereafter; the balance of . . . % of said amount shall be paid on the date of the last regularly scheduled League game.

In addition, the Club agrees to pay: the reasonable board and lodging expenses of the Player incurred in pre-season training and/or while playing pre-season and/or regularly scheduled League games for the Club in other than the Club's home city; and all proper and necessary traveling expenses of the Player en route to and from said games in other than the Club's home city. Any advances made to the Player shall be repaid promptly to the Club by means of deduction from payments coming due to the Player hereunder, the amounts of such deductions to be determined by the Club unless otherwise agreed by the parties. The Player hereby authorizes the Club to make such deductions.

If, either this agreement is executed, or the Player reports for play and thereafter is placed on the Active List of the Club after the Club has played one or more regularly scheduled games in the applicable season, the obligation of the Club to pay Player the salary prescribed in Paragraph 3 hereof shall be reduced in the proportion that the number of said games already played by the Club bears to the total number of regularly scheduled games to be played by the Club in the applicable season.

4. The Player agrees at all times to comply with and be bound by: the Constitution and By-Laws, Rules and Regulations of the League, of the Club, and the decisions of the Commissioner of the League (hereinafter called "Commissioner"), which shall be final, conclusive and unappealable. The enumerated Constitution, By-Laws, Rules and Regulations are intended to include the present Constitution, By-Laws, Rules and Regulations as well as all amendments thereto, all of which are by reference incorporated herein. If the Player fails to comply with said Constitution, By-Laws, Rules and Regulations, the Club shall have the right to terminate this contract as provided in Paragraph 6 hereof or to take such other action as may be specified in said Constitution, By-Laws, Rules and Regulations, or as may be directed by the Commissioner. The Player agrees to submit himself to the discipline of the League

and of the Club, for any violation of said Constitution, By-Laws, Rules and Regulations, subject, however, to the right to a hearing by the Commissioner. All matters in dispute between the Player and the Club shall be referred to the Commissioner and his decision shall be accepted as final, complete, conclusive, binding and unappealable, by the Player and by the Club. The Player, if involved or affected in any manner whatsoever by a decision of the Commissioner, whether the decision results from a dispute between the Player and the Club or otherwise, hereby releases and discharges the Commissioner, the League, each Club in the League, each Director, Officer, Stockholder, Owner or Partner of any Club in the League, each employee, agent, official or representative of the League or of any Club in the League, jointly and severally, individually and in their official capacities, of and from any and all claims, demands, damages, suits, actions and causes of action whatsoever, in law or in equity, arising out of or in connection with any decision of the Commissioner, except to the extent of awards made by the Commissioner to the Player. The Player hereby acknowledges that he has read the present said Constitution, By-Laws, Rules and Regulations, and that he understands their meaning.

5. The Player promises and agrees that during the term of this contract he will not play football or engage in activities related to football for any other person, firm, corporation or institution, or on his own behalf, except with the prior written consent of the Club and the Commissioner, and, that he will not, during the term of this contract, without the prior consent of the Club, engage in any other sport. The knowledge of the Club or the Commissioner of any of the foregoing activities by the Player shall not be deemed to be a consent thereto. Such activities if engaged in by the Player shall be at his own risk and any injury suffered therein shall not be deemed to be in the performance of his services under this contract. The Player likewise promises and agrees that, during the term of this contract, when, as and if he shall receive an invitation to participate in any All-Star football game which is sponsored by the League, he will play in said game in accordance with all of the terms and conditions relating thereto, including the player compensation therein set forth, as are agreed to between the League and the Sponsor of such game. The Player likewise promises and agrees that during the term of this contract, he will not participate in any other outside football game not sponsored by the League unless such game is first approved by the League; despite such approval by the League, the Player shall not be obligated to participate therein.

6. The Player represents and warrants that he is and will continue to be sufficiently highly skilled in all types of football team play, to play professional football of the caliber required by the League and by the Club, and that he is and will continue to be in excellent physical condition, and agrees to perform his services hereunder to the complete satisfaction of the Club and its Head Coach. Player shall undergo a complete physical examination by the Club physician at the start of each training session during the term hereof. If Player fails to establish his excellent physical condition to the satisfaction of the Club physician by the physical examination, or (after having so established his excellent physical condition) if, in the opinion of the Head Coach, Player does not maintain himself in such excellent physical condition or fails at any time during the football seasons included in the terms of this contract to demonstrate sufficient skill and capacity to play professional football of the caliber required by the League or by the Club, or if in the opinion of the Head Coach the Player's work or conduct in the performance of this contract is unsatisfactory as compared with the work and conduct of other members of the Club's squad of players, the Club shall have the right to terminate this contract.

7. Upon termination of this contract the Club shall pay the Player only the balance, if any, remaining due him for traveling, board and lodging expenses and for football seasons completed prior to termination, and if termination takes place during a football season, the balance, if any, remaining due him on that portion of his total compensation for that season as provided in ¶3 or ¶10 hereof, whichever is applicable, which the number of regularly scheduled League games already played by the Club during that season bears to the total number of League games scheduled for the Club for that season.

8. The Player hereby represents that he has special, exceptional and unique knowledge, skill and ability as a football player, the loss of which cannot be estimated with any certainty and cannot be fairly or adequately compensated by damages and therefore agrees that the Club shall have the right, in addition to any other rights which the Club may possess, to enjoin him by appropriate injunction proceedings against playing football or any other professional sport, without the consent of the Club, or engaging in activities related to football for any person, firm, corporation,

institution, or on his own behalf, and against any other breach of this contract.

9. It is mutually agreed that the Club shall have the right to sell, exchange, assign or transfer this contract and the Player's services hereunder to any other Club in the League. Player agrees to accept such assignment and to report promptly to the assignee Club and faithfully to perform and carry out this contract with the assignee Club as if it had been entered into by the Player with the assignee Club instead of with this Club.

10. The Club may, by sending notice in writing to the Player, on or before the first day of May following the football season referred to in ¶1 hereof, renew this contract for a further term of one (1) year on the same terms as are provided by this contract, except that (1) the Club may fix the rate of compensation to be paid by the Club to the Player during said further term, which rate of compensation shall not be less than ninety percent (90%) of the sum set forth in ¶3 hereof and shall be payable in installments during the football season in such further term as provided in ¶3; and (2) after such renewal this contract shall not include a further option to the Club to renew the contract. The phrase "rate of compensation" as above used shall not include bonus payments or payments of any nature whatsoever and shall be limited to the precise sum set forth in ¶3 hereof.

11. Player acknowledges the right and power of the Commissioner (a) to fine and suspend, (b) to fine and suspend for life or indefinitely, and/or (c) to cancel the contract of, any player who accepts a bribe or who agrees to throw or fix a game or who, having knowledge of the same, fails to report an offered bribe or an attempt to throw or fix a game, or who bets on a game, or who is guilty of any conduct detrimental to the welfare of the League or of professional football. The Player, if involved or affected in any manner whatsoever by a decision of the Commissioner in any of the aforesaid cases, hereby releases and discharges the Commissioner, the League, each Club in the League, each Director, Officer, Stockholder, Owner, Partner, employee, agent, official or representative of any Club in the League, jointly and severally, individually and in their official capacities, of and from any and all claims, demands, damages, suits, actions, and causes of action whatsoever, in law or in equity, arising out of or in connection with any such decision of the Commissioner.

12. Any payments made hereunder to the Player, for a period during which he is entitled to workmen's compensation benefits by reason of temporary total, permanent total, temporary partial, or permanent partial disability shall be deemed an advance payment of workmen's compensation benefits due the Player, and the Club shall be entitled to be reimbursed the amounts thereof out of any award of compensation.

13. Should Player become a member of the Armed Forces of the United States or any other country; or fail or refuse to perform his services as provided in this contract; or retire from professional football as a player prior to the expiration of this contract or any option renewal term hereof, and subsequently be released from the Armed Forces or return to professional football as a player, then, and in either event, the time elapsed between Player's induction into the Armed Forces and his discharge therefrom, or between the date of his failure or refusal to perform his services as provided in this contract, or between the date of his retirement from professional football as a player, and his return thereto, shall be tolled, and the term of this contract shall be for a period beginning with Player's failure or refusal to perform his services hereunder, release from the Armed Forces, or his return to professional football as a player, as the case may be, and ending after a period of time equal to the portion of the term of this contract which was unexpired at the time Player entered the Armed Forces, failed or refused to perform his services hereunder, or retired from professional football as a player. The renewal option contained herein shall be continuously in effect from the date of this contract until the end of such extended term. During the period of such services in the Armed Forces or such retirement, or while failing or refusing to perform his services hereunder, the Player shall not be entitled to any compensation, expenses or other payments under this contract.

14. In the event that Player is injured in the performance of his services under this contract, and if Player gives written notice to the Club Physician of such injury within thirty-six (36) hours of its occurrence, the Club will: (1) provide, during the term of this contract, such medical or hospital care as, in the opinion of the Club Physician, may be necessary; and (2) continue, during the term of this contract, to pay Player his salary as provided in ¶3 or ¶10 hereof, whichever is applicable if and so long as it is the opinion of the Club Physician that Player, because of such injury, is unable to perform the services required of him by this contract. Player, may, within seventy-two (72) hours after his examination by the Club Physician, submit

at his own expense to an examination by a physician of his choice. If the opinion of such physician with respect to Player's physical ability to render the services required of him by this contract is contrary to that of the Club Physician, the dispute shall be submitted to a disinterested physician to be selected by the Club Physician and Player's physician or, if they are unable to agree, by the Commissioner, and the opinion of such disinterested physician shall be conclusive and binding upon the Player and the Club. Except as provided in this paragraph, Player's failure for any reason whatsoever to perform this contract or the services required of him by this contract, or his failure to comply with: the Constitution and By-Laws, Rules and Regulations of the League, or of the Club, shall entitle the club, at its option, to terminate such contract, such termination to be effective when the Club sends to the Player written notice of such termination, or shall entitle the Club at its option to terminate Player's salary under this contract. The Player's death shall automatically terminate this contract. The rights of termination set forth in this paragraph shall be in addition to the rights of termination set forth in ¶6 hereof, and any other rights of termination allowed by law.

If Player is injured in the performance of his services under this contract, this contract shall remain in full force and effect despite the fact that Player, following injury, is either carried by the Club on its Reserve List or is waived out as an injured player while injured; when such Player is, in the opinion of the Club physician, again physically able to perform his services under this contract, the Club shall have the right to activate such Player, and Player shall be obligated to perform his services hereunder in accordance with the terms hereof.

15. Any notice, request, demand, approval or consent required or permitted under this contract to be given by one party to the other shall be deemed sufficiently given if delivered in person or mailed (registered or first-class) to such other party at his or its address set forth in this contract or to such other address as such other party may previously have furnished to the sender in writing.

16. This contract sets forth the entire agreement between the parties. The signing of this agreement by the parties constitutes their mutual recognition that no other contract or agreements, oral or written, except as attached hereto or specifically incorporated herein, exists between them, that, if any such oral or written contracts or agreements exist, such are hereby cancelled; each party hereby represents to the other that it will not rely upon any agreement or understanding not reduced to writing and incorporated in this agreement prior to the execution hereof.

17. This contract shall be valid and binding upon the parties hereto immediately upon its execution. A copy of such contract shall be filed by the Club with the Commissioner within ten (10) days after execution. The Commissioner shall have the right to terminate this contract by his disapproval thereof within ten (10) days after the filing thereof in his office; such action by the Commissioner shall be exercised in accordance with and pursuant to the power vested in the Commissioner by the Constitution and By-Laws of the League; in such event, the Commissioner shall give both parties written notice of such termination, and thereupon, both parties shall be relieved of their respective rights and liabilities hereunder.

18. This agreement has been made under and shall be governed by the laws of the State of . . . .

IN WITNESS WHEREOF the Player has hereunto set his hand and seal and the Club has caused this contract to be executed by its duly authorized officer on the date set opposite their respective names.

. . . .

Name of Club

By . . . .

Date

. . . .

Player   Date

. . . .

Player's Address

Telephone No. . . . .

CLUB RULES AND REGULATIONS

1. All players must be on time for all meetings, practice sessions, meals, and all types of transportation. The curfew must be observed. Players must keep all publicity appointments and be on time.

2. Drinking of intoxicants is forbidden.

3. Players must not frequent gambling resorts nor associate with gamblers or other notorious characters.

4. Players must report all injuries to a coach and the club physician or trainer immediately, and be prompt in keeping appointments.

5. Players must wear coats and neckties in hotel lobbies, public eating places, and on all public conveyances.

6. Players must familiarize themselves with their contract, especially paragraph 11 thereof.

7. Players shall not write or sponsor magazine or newspaper articles, or endorse any product or service or appear on or participate in any radio or television program without the consent of the club.

8 Football for Females

by ELINOR GRAHAM KAINE

(HOW TO MARRY OR KEEP THE MALE FOOTBALL MANIAC)

If you can't beat 'em, join 'em . . . that is, join HIM! You should sit by his side at all football games. It's silly to be OUT and left at home. Go gridiron—and become a real, dyed in the wool (or in mink) football fan.

A GIRL NEEDS A GAME PLAN

First Commandment: Pay Attention

Don't talk to a female friend about children, clothes and/or food during the game; Don't sit down during a kick-off, whispering to your pal behind HIS back.
If your mind must wander, remember to keep staring intently at the field.
ALWAYS stare intently at the field.

Second Commandment: Sound Interested

Looking interested is not enough. You must plan some game talk. But you must plan carefully; don't just talk about what's obvious. Don't just talk about the super stars. Don't just talk about the home team, or the local heroes. Instead talk about rookies, or newcomers, or linemen. Or talk about the visitors.

Third Commandment: Be Witty

Don't talk like a hard-nosed man fan. Use a soft-nosed approach. Smile a lot. After all, football is a game. It's supposed to be fun.

Last Commandment: Don't Forget What You Learn

Remember what happens from game to game. Remember, football is an investment. Pro football teams don't have a high turnover rate like high schools and colleges (where three years on the varsity is two years longer than usual). What you learn today can prove useful for years and years and years.

NOTE: Best example of longevity is George Blanda. He first played pro football in 1949. Suppose a lady had singled out a spot in her memory for Blanda back in 1949, learning his name, college, number, position, etc. For the last eighteen autumns she would have been able to chat confidently, first-hand, about old George. You could call Blanda a real blue chip investment in gridiron gamesmanship. You could also call him a bit daft.

After all, in a 15-game season a girl could learn about two home-team players per game and by Christmas she would be able to talk up a storm about the whole team. This is the learn-as-you-go school of the gridiron.

IN GENERAL A TEAM IS DIVIDED INTO SIX SECTIONS, PLUS KICKERS

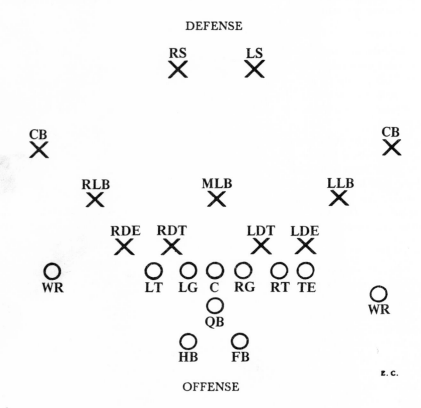

The team with the possession of the ball, trying to score, is the OFFENSE; the DEFENSE is trying to stop them. The offense is divided into three parts.

The Backs

The name of the game is QUARTERBACK. The quarterback (QB) is always in the lime-light; he's the star. He gets the most publicity and makes the most money. Actually he's the coach's deputy, to run the team on the field.

In a game, a QB does one of three things after he calls the signals and receives the ball from the center. He either passes . . . or hands the ball to a runner . . . or if something goes wrong he keeps it and runs himself.

There are usually two running backs with similar responsibilities—running, blocking, and sometimes pass-catching. The fullback (FB) is usually bigger and blocks more often than the halfback (HB).

On a running play the two backs stand behind the QB. He will either hand the ball to the runner immediately, or delay a moment and then hand-off or flip the ball sideways (pitch-out) to a running back. The other back either acts as a decoy or blocks, or both.

A decoy pretends to have the ball and runs, trying to draw the defense away from the real ball carrier. When a back moves ahead of the QB and tries to protect him from on-rushing defenders until he has time to throw the ball, the back is blocking (called pass protection).

Good backs are good fakers, and successfully fool the defense by making them think something is going to happen which doesn't. This is hard on spectators because good fakers can fool the spectators every time.

The Pass Catchers

Pass catchers are usually called ends. They stand in various positions. Once upon a time the ends were called ends because they stood at each end of the line of scrimmage. No longer. Today only the left end stands where he belongs. The right end has been re-named the tight end, and has been moved in tight near the right tackle. From this spot he catches passes, like an end, but occasionally he acts like a tackle and carries out block-ing assignments.

Out wide to the right where the end used to be is the FLANKER, the third end. The flanker is technically a back so he must stand a step behind the line of scrimmage, but the flanker is to the right side what the left end is to the left. These two are stationed out wide where they have a maximum amount of room to maneuver; they are very speedy, usually. But a few have everybody fooled; they aren't big but they're slow. The trick of talking about wide ends who can't run too fast is to talk about their hands instead of where the trouble lies, their feet.

The Line (Offensive)

No team can be better than its offensive line . . . which begins with the left tackle and continues through the guards and center to the right tackle. This fivesome is the anchor to windward of a football team.

No running back can make big gains if the line hasn't cleared the way. No QB can throw touchdown (TD) passes if he doesn't have TIME. A QB must wait for his ends to get down the field before he can throw, and without the protection of his offensive line a QB would be flat on his back much too soon.

The center is the odds-on choice to win a "least sexy football player" contest. He has to wear a dirty towel stuck in his pants for the quarterback to wipe his hands on, especially if the QB is high-strung and sweaty-palmed. I've always suspected that the New York Giants' new QB Fran Tarkenton made too much use of the towel; whether from nervousness or from the exercise of scrambling is still a moot question. Needless to say, the better the blocking of the offensive line, the dryer the towel.

Any girl who wants a sophisticated football fan to fall in love with her should talk about the offensive line. That is one line that is guaranteed.

For Every Offense There Is a Defense

It tries its best to prevent the best laid plans of the enemy from succeeding.

In front is the defensive line, four giant monsters who must be particularly adept at trying to flatten the quarterback. This foursome is the biggest in football and has an ad-vantage, besides size, over the offensive linemen they play against. Defensive linemen are allowed to USE THEIR HANDS when they go after a man; offensive linemen may not. (It is a penalty for an offensive lineman to use his hands when blocking, which is why he uses his shoulder and forearm.)

Defensive linemen can use their hands at will while tackling. (Tackling is the "with-hands" counterpart of the no-hands offensive maneuver, blocking). The biggest and best "front fours" are particularly good at rushing the passer. They figure the quicker they make him throw the worse his aim will be.

In back of the defensive line is a devastating trio, the linebackers (LB). Part of the time they act like linemen, so they must be big and strong for tackling and defending against running plays. Part of the time they must be fast and agile like defensive backs, dropping back on passing plays and helping the backs defend against the pass—particularly passes to either of the running backs. Good linebackers are persevering, fast and strong. In the usual pro set-up the left linebacker (LLB) often defends against the tight end, the middle linebacker against the fullback, and the right linebacker is the "floater" and goes to the ball—that is, forward on a run and backward on a pass.

The RLB doesn't have to worry much about the left end because behind the line-backers there are four defensive backs and the right one has the left end as his primary responsibility.

About linebackers, New York is dreamsville for them. Because it is "communications central" New York is the easiest place to start a fad. For this reason two linebackers, Sam Huff of the Giants and Wahoo McDaniel of the Jets, became household words more by word than by deed.

The Defensive Backs

The left defensive back (left cornerback) defends against the flanker and the two in the middle are called safeties. All four defensive backs are referred to as the secondary. The secondary is supposed to stop completed passes.

The left safety must worry about the tight end when he is a possible long receiver, but the right safety (RS) has no specific assignment. He is a trouble-shooter and is supposed to go where the ball is going. The right safety is the last man in the way to a touchdown.

The two cornerbacks' duties are difficult because they are continually engaged in man-to-man duels with the two wide ends. The offensive end always knows where he is going but the defensive back doesn't, and must always react, which is a definite dis-advantage.

When a cornerback makes a mistake it usually ends up a touchdown, and everyone knows the culprit. The isolated eye of the television has made the football public aware of the secondary; a few years ago it was rare to hear a cornerback or safety discussed by name. A cornerback who gets beaten on a long TD pass becomes a household word by the end of an afternoon after many videotape replays of the scoring play.

SCORING

Scoring in football is done in the air (by passing), on the ground (by running) or by kicking. A point-after-touchdown counts one point and a Field Goal counts 3. A TD by running or passing counts six points.

You can think of a touchdown as a pie; In the same way that a pie is made up of pieces, a touchdown is made up of DOWNS . . . actually FIRST DOWNS.

When the offense gets the ball the QB has four chances, or downs, to move forward at least ten yards. If successful, they make a first down and get four more chances . . . and so on until they either score or fail.

If a team fails to gain the necessary ten yards on three tries it figures it probably won't on the fourth. Instead of giving up the ball on the spot, on the fourth down a team will choose to kick (punt) instead . . . which puts the ball as far away as possible from its own goal line and makes the opposition's task as difficult as possible.

Punting is super conservative, but because it is so common the third down becomes the most important down of all. A punt means the third down play was a failure.

A girl who wants to sound like she knows what's going on should concentrate on third downs. They are an automatic occasion for some hard-nosed gab designed to make the man fan realize what a real fan you are.

"Third down situations are so crucial," you might say, or shake your curls and murmur philosophically, "Football is a game of third downs."

No one will ever argue that.

"In recent years, both offensive and defensive teams have changed their personnel based on the particular situation. Offensive teams routinely replace one wide receiver with a second tight end in short yardage situations, and occasionally replace the other wide receiver with another running back. But the major shifts have been on defense. In passing situations, various strategies have developed. The most common is to remove one linebacker and replace him with another defensive back. Some teams add an additional lineman in place of the linebacker to rush the passer. Simply changing the particular players at defensive end in these situations to those who are adept at pass rushing is also common. One team removes all three linebackers, inserting a lineman and two backs. Some teams insert an extra linebacker in place of a lineman in certain situations, and several teams have adopted this configuration for their standard defense.

Appendix

THE NATIONAL FOOTBALL LEAGUE DIGEST OF RULES*

FIELD

1. Side lines and end lines are out of bounds. Goal line is actually in the end zone. A player with the ball in his possession scores when the ball is on, above or over the goal line.
2. The field is 360 feet long and 160 feet wide. The end zones are 30 feet deep. The line used in try-for-point plays is 2 yards out from the goal line.
3. Inbound lines (hash marks) are 70 feet, 9 inches from each side line.
4. Goal posts must be single-standard type, offset from the end line and painted bright gold. The goal posts must be 18 feet, 6 inches wide and the top face of crossbar 10 feet above ground. Vertical goal posts extend 20 feet above crossbar. The goal is the vertical plane extending indefinitely above crossbar and between the lines indicated by the *outer edges* of the goal posts.
5. The playing field will be rimmed by a white border 6 feet wide along the sideline. All of this is out of bounds.

BALL

1. The home club must have 12 balls available for testing by the Referee one hour before game time. In case of bad weather, a playable ball is to be substituted on request of the offensive team captain.

NUMBERING

1. Offensive and defensive players must be numbered as follows: 1–19 quarterbacks and kickers; 20–49 running backs and defensive backs; 50–59 centers and line-backers; 60–79 defensive linemen and interior offensive linemen, except centers; 80–89 wide receivers and tight ends (Numbers in 90s will be permitted only in preseason.)

   Exception: All players who were in the NFL in 1972 or before may use old numbers.

COIN TOSS

1. Toss of coin will take place thirty minutes before scheduled game time in center of field.
   (a) Toss will be called by visiting team captain.
   (b) The winner of toss must choose one of two privileges, and the loser is given the other. The two choices are:
      1. Which team is to kick-off
      2. The goal his team is to defend
   (c) At the end of first half, the captains of both teams must immediately appear at center of field in order to inform Referee of their choices for the start of the second half. The loser of the toss gets first choice.
2. In case of inclement weather, toss may be made by the Referee and the two coaches.
3. Three minutes prior to game time, both captains are to appear at center of field at which time Referee will indicate which team is to kick-off, and goal receivers will defend. No toss simulated.

* See page 701 for rules changes.

TIMING

1. The stadium electric clock shall be the official time. The Line Judge shall be responsible for supervision of the timing and in case the stadium clock becomes inoperative, or for any other reason it is not being operated correctly, he shall take over the official timing on the field, or adjust the time remaining.

2. Each period is 15 minutes. The intermission between the periods is two minutes. Halftime is 15 minutes, unless otherwise specified.

3. On charged team timeouts, the Field Judge starts watch and blows whistle after 1 minute 30 seconds. However, Referee may allow two minutes for injured player and three minutes for equipment repair.

4. Each team allowed three time outs each half.

5. Offensive team has thirty seconds to put ball in play, timed by Field Judge. Failure to do so is delay of game. Penalty 5 yards.

6. Clock will start running when ball is snapped following all changes of team possession (previously, referee wound the clock if ball remained inbounds).

SUDDEN DEATH

1. The sudden death system of determining the winner shall prevail when score is tied at the end of the regulation playing time of all NFL games. The team scoring first during overtime play shall be the winner and the game automatically ends upon any score (by safety, field goal or touchdown) or when a score is awarded by Referee for a palpably unfair act.

2. At the end of regulation time the Referee will immediately toss coin at center of field in accordance with rules pertaining to the usual pregame toss. The captain of the visiting team will call the toss.

3. Following a 3-minute intermission after the end of the regulation game, play will be continued in 15-minute periods or until there is a score. There is a 2-minute intermission between subse-

quent periods. The teams change goals at the start of each period. Each team has 3 time outs and general provisions for play in the last 2 minutes of a half shall prevail. Disqualified players are not allowed to return.

Exception: In preseason and regular season games there shall be a maximum of 15 minutes of sudden death with 2 time outs instead of 3. General provisions for play in the last two minutes of a half will be in force.

TIMING CHANGES DURING LAST TWO MINUTES OF EACH HALF

1. On kick-off, clock does not start until the ball has been legally touched by a player of either team in the field of play. (In all other cases, clock starts with kick-off.)

2. During the last two minutes, a team cannot buy a fourth time-out for a penalty. A fourth time-out during the last two minutes will only be allowed for an injured player who must be immediately designated and removed. No penalty. Fifth or more are allowed only under the same condition, but are penalized 5 yards. (Time in with Referee's ready signal in both cases.)

3. During last two minutes of either half, if score is tied or team in possession is behind in score and has exhausted its legal time-outs, an additional time-out may be requested and granted under the same conditions as above. Clock shall start with Referee's whistle upon removal of injured player from field, and ball cannot be put in play until ten seconds have expired. Game can end before snap if less than ten seconds remain.

TRY-FOR-POINT

1. After a touchdown, the scoring team is allowed a try-for-point. This try is an attempt to score one additional point, whether by run, kick or pass.

2. The *defensive team never can score* on a try-for-point. As soon as defense gets possession, or kick is blocked, ball is dead.

SUBSTITUTIONS

1. Each team is permitted 11 men on the field at the same time.
2. Unlimited substitution. Players may enter the field only when ball is dead.
3. Players leaving field must clear field on their own side, *between end lines* before snap or free kick. If player crosses end line leaving field, 5-yard penalty for delay of game.

KICK-OFF (FREE-KICK)

1. The kick-off shall be from the kicking team's 35-yard line at the start of each half and after a field goal and following a try for point.
   (a) On the above situations a 3-inch kicking "T" may be used. Punt not allowed. The ball is put in play by a placekick or dropkick. (No tee permitted for field goal or try-for-point plays.)
2. If kickoff clears the opponent's goal posts it is *not a field goal.*
3. Kick-off is not a legal kick unless kick travels 10 yards or has been touched by receivers. Once ball touched by receiving team it is a free ball. Receivers may recover and advance, kicking team may recover, but not advance, unless receivers had possession of ball.
4. A kick-off which goes out of bounds between the goal lines without being touched by receiving team, must be re-kicked. (5-yard penalty) If touched last by receiving team it is their ball at out-of-bounds spot. The last touching is the important thing even though it may have been touched by both teams.
5. Free-kick situations also develop following fair catch and safety. In both cases, a dropkick, placekick or punt may be used. (A punt may not be used on a kickoff.)
   When receiving team fair catches ball, captain has option on how he wishes to put ball in play. (1) Free-kick (punt, drop-kick, or place-kick without "T") or (2) By snap. If place or drop-kick attempted and ball kicked between uprights, field goal is awarded for successful kick. (3 points) All other free-kick rules apply.

Following a safety the team scored upon must next put ball in play at their 20-yard line by free-kick. (Punt, drop-kick or place-kick—no "T") All free-kick rules apply. No score may be made on free-kick following safety, even though a series of penalties may place a team in position to do so. (A field goal can be scored only on a play from scrimmage or a freekick after a fair catch.)

FIELD GOAL

1. All field goals attempted and missed from scrimmage line beyond the 20-yard line will result in the defensive team taking possession of the ball at the scrimmage line. On any field goal attempted and missed from scrimmage line inside the 20-yard line, ball will revert to defensive team at the 20-yard line.

SAFETY

1. A safety is the situation in which ball is dead on or behind a team's goal line. Provided: The impetus came from a player of that team. (2 points)
   Examples:
   (a) Blocked punt which goes out of the kicking team's end zone. Impetus was put on ball by the punting team; the block only changes direction of ball and not the impetus. (2 points)
   (b) Ball carrier runs into his own end zone and is downed. Ball carrier responsible for ball being in the end zone. (2 points)
   (c) Safety by penalty: When offensive team commits a foul, and spot of enforcement is behind their goal line. (2 points)
2. Player on receiving team muffs punt and, trying to get ball, forces or illegally kicks it into end zone where he or a teammate recovers. He has given new impetus to the ball (Safety).
   Examples of non-safety:
   (a) Player intercepts a pass inside his own 5-yard line and his momentum carries him into his own end zone

(No safety). Ball is put in play at spot of interception.

(b) Player intercepts a pass *in his own end zone* and is downed. Impetus came from passing team, not from defense (Touchback, no safety).

(c) Player passes from *behind his own goal line*. Opponent bats down ball in end zone (Incomplete pass, no safety).

MEASURING

1. The forward point of the ball is used when measuring.

POSITION OF PLAYERS AT SNAP

1. Offensive team must have seven or more players on line of scrimmage at snap.

2. Offensive players, other than the snap receiver who are not on line of scrimmage, must be at least one yard behind line at snap.

3. No interior lineman may move after taking or simulating a three-point stance.

4. After neutral zone starts, no player of either team may encroach upon it, nor may he be off-side at snap.

5. From start of neutral zone until snap, no offensive player after assuming a set position shall charge or move in such a way as to lead defense to believe that the snap has started.

6. A player entering game wearing an illegal number for the position he takes, must report to the Referee. Referee in turn will report same to the defensive captain. (Specifically, player wearing ineligible pass receiver number, playing eligible pass receiving position)

7. All players of offensive team must be stationary at snap, except one back who may be in motion parallel to scrimmage line or backward (not forward).

8. After a shift or huddle all players on offensive team must come to an absolute stop for *at least one second* with no movement of hands, feet, head or swaying of body.

9. Lineman may lock legs with the snapper only.

USE OF HANDS, ARMS AND BODY

1. No player on offense may assist runner except by individually blocking opponents for him, and there shall be no interlocked interference.

2. Runner may ward off opponents with his hands and arms, but no other offensive player may use them to obstruct an opponent. That is, grasping with hands or using them to push, encircling with arm in any degree any part of body, during block.

3. Pass blocking is the obstructing of an opponent by use of that part of the blocker's body above his knees. During a legal block, the hand(s) must be cupped or closed and remain inside blocker's elbow(s) and must remain inside the frame of opponent as well as blocker's body. Arm(s) may be in a flexed position, but cannot be fully extended forward to create a push. By use of up and down action of flexed arm(s), blocker is permitted to ward off opponent's attempt to grasp jersey, arm(s) and prevent legal contact to head. Blocker is not permitted to push, clamp down on, hang on to or encircle opponent.

4. A defensive player may not tackle or hold any opponent other than a runner. He may use his hands and arms only:

   (1) To ward off an obstructing opponent

   (2) To push or pull him out of the way on line of scrimmage or to cross it

   (3) In an actual attempt to get at or tackle runner

   (4) To push or pull him out of the way in an actual legal attempt to recover a loose ball

   (5) During a legal block

   (6) When legally blocking an eligible pass receiver above the waist.

   Exception: Eligible receivers lined up within two yards of the tackle, whether on or immediately behind the line, may be blocked below the waist AT or behind the line of scrimmage. NO eligible receiver may be blocked below the waist after he goes beyond the line.

5. A defensive player shall not contact an opponent above shoulders with palm of his hands except during an initial charge or to ward him off on line, and then only if it is not a repeated act against the same opponent during any one contact. Otherwise they may be used on his head, neck, or face only to ward off or push him in an actual legal attempt to get at ball.

6. Any offensive player who pretends to possess the ball, and/or one to whom a teammate pretends to give the ball, may be tackled provided he is *crossing* his scrimmage line between the offensive ends of a normal tight offensive line.

7. A player of either team may block any time provided it is not pass interference, fair catch interference, or otherwise unnecessary roughness.

8. A player may not bat or punch:
   (a) A loose ball (in field of play) towards opponents' goal line, or in any direction if it is in either end zone.
   (b) A ball in player possession or attempt to do so.
   Exception: A pass in flight (forward or backward) may be batted in any direction, or at any time (including end zone), by (a) defense and (b) offense only to prevent an opponent from intercepting. (Penalty for illegal batting or punching of ball: loss of 15 yards)

9. No player may kick or kick at any ball except as a punt, drop-kick, or place-kick. (Illegal kicking with foot, loss of 15 yards)

10. Quarterbacks can be called for a false start penalty (5 yards) if their actions are judged to be an obvious attempt to draw an opponent offside.

11. An offensive player who lines up more than 2 yards outside his own tackle may not contact an opponent below the waist if the blocker is moving toward the ball and if contact is made within an area 3 yards on either side of the line.

FORWARD PASS

1. A forward pass may be touched or caught only by an eligible receiver. All members of the defensive team are eligible. Eligible receivers on the offensive team are players on either end of line (other than center, guard or tackle) or players at least one yard behind the line at the snap. A T-Formation quarterback is not eligible to receive a forward pass during a play from scrimmage.

2. An offensive team may make only one forward pass during each play from scrimmage (Loss of down).

3. The passer must be behind his line of scrimmage (Loss of down and 5 yards, enforced from the spot of pass).

4. Only one eligible offensive player may catch a forward pass. If pass is touched by one offensive player and touched or caught by a second eligible offensive player, it is a violation (Loss of down). However, if a forward pass is touched by a defensive player before, at same time or after touching by an eligible offensive receiver, all offensive players then become eligible.

5. The rules concerning a forward pass and ineligible receivers:
   (a) If ball is touched accidentally by an ineligible receiver on or behind his line (Loss of down).
   (b) If touched or caught intentionally by an ineligible receiver on or behind his line (Loss of down and 15 yards.
   (c) If touched or caught (intentionally or accidentally) by ineligible receiver beyond the line (Loss of down and 15 yards).
   (d) If ineligible receiver is illegally downfield (15 yards).

6. If a forward pass is caught simultaneously by eligible players on opposing teams, possession goes to passing team.

7. Any forward pass becomes incomplete and ball is dead if:
   (a) Pass hits the ground or goes out of bounds.
   (b) Hits the goal post or the cross bar of either team.
   (c) Is caught by offensive player after

touching ineligible receiver.

(d) Is caught by second eligible receiver before being touched by defensive player.

(e) An illegal pass is caught by the passer.

8. A forward pass is complete when a receiver touches the ground with both feet inbounds while in possession of the ball. If a receiver is carried out of bounds by an opponent while in possession in the air, pass is complete at the out-of-bounds spot.

9. If an eligible receiver goes out of bounds accidentally or is forced out by a defender and returns to catch a pass, the play is regarded as a pass caught out of bounds (Loss of down, no yardage).

10. On a fourth down pass—when the offensive team is inside the opposition's 20-yard-line—an incomplete pass is an automatic touchback (Opponent's ball, first and 10 on opponent's 20).

11. If a personal foul is committed by the defense prior to the completion of a pass, the penalty is 15 yards from the spot where ball becomes dead.

12. If a personal foul is committed by the offense prior to the completion of a pass, the penalty is 15 yards from the previous line of scrimmage.

INTENTIONAL GROUNDING OF A PASS

1. It is considered intentional incompletion of a forward pass under the following condition: When the ball strikes the ground after passer throws, tosses or lobs the ball with a *deliberate attempt to prevent loss of yards by his team.*

2. Intentional incompletion of a forward pass is a violation (Loss of down and 15 yards from previous spot).
Exception: If the spot of intentional incompletion is on or behind defensive team's goal line during fourth down, and previous spot was inside the opponent's 5-yard line, it is a touchback.

PROTECTION OF PASSER

1. No defensive player may run into a passer of a legal forward pass after the ball has left his hand (15 yards). The Referee must determine whether opponent had a reasonable chance to stop his momentum during an attempt to block the pass or tackle the passer while he still had the ball.

By interpretation, a pass begins when the passer—with possession of the ball—starts to bring his hand forward. If ball strikes ground after this action has begun, play is ruled as an incomplete pass. If passer loses control of ball prior to his bringing his hand forward, play is ruled a fumble.

PASS INTERFERENCE

1. There shall be no interference with a forward pass thrown from behind the line. The restriction for the passing team starts with the snap of the ball, and the restriction for the defensive team starts when the ball leaves the passer's hand, and ends when the ball is touched by anyone.

2. Defensive pass interference. (Penalty—automatic first down at the spot of foul.) If interference is in the end zone, it is first down for the offense on the defense's 1-yard line. If previous spot was inside the defense's 1-yard line, penalty is half the distance to the goal line.

3. Offensive pass interference including ineligible receiver downfield. (Penalty—15 yards from previous spot.)

4. It is interference by either offense or defense when any player movement beyond offensive team's line hinders the progress of an eligible opponent in his attempt to reach a pass.
Exception: Such incidental movement or contact when two or more eligible players make a *simultaneous and bona fide* attempt to catch or bat the ball is permitted. *"Simultaneous and bona fide"* means the contact of an eligible receiver and a defensive player when each is playing the ball and contact is unavoidable and incidental to the act of trying to catch or bat the ball.

5. During a forward pass, it must be remembered that defensive players have

as much right to the *path to ball* as eligible opponents. Any bodily contact, however severe, between players who are making a bona fide and simultaneous attempt to catch or bat ball, is not interference.

6. Pass interference by defense is independent of the direction in flight of pass, and as to whether or not offensive team might have completed it. This is not a judgment situation on the part of the official. Passer may have changed his pass to another receiver due to interference or a possible receiver being covered.

BACKWARD PASS

1. Any pass not a forward pass is regarded as a backward pass or lateral. A pass parallel to the line is a backward pass. A runner may pass backward at any time. Any player on either team may catch the pass or recover the ball after it touches the ground.

2. A backward pass that strikes the ground can be recovered and advanced by offensive team.

3. A backward pass that strikes the ground can be recovered but cannot be advanced by the defensive team.

4. A backward pass caught in the air can be advanced by the defensive team.

FUMBLE

1. The distinction between a fumble and a muff should be kept in mind in considering rules about fumbles. A fumble is the loss of possession of the ball. A muff is the touching of a loose ball by a player in an unsuccessful attempt to obtain possession.

2. A fumble may be advanced by any player on either team regardless of whether recovered before or after ball hits the ground.

3. On fourth down fumble (unintentional) inside the defense's 10-yard line during a play from scrimmage and not touched by any defensive player, only the offensive player fumbling may advance. If recovered by any other offensive player, the ball is dead at the

spot of fumble unless it is recovered behind the spot of fumble. In that case, ball is dead at spot of recovery.

PUNTS—KICKS FROM SCRIMMAGE

1. Any punt or attempted field goal that touches the receiver's end zone or goal post is dead. Automatic touchback.

2. During a kick from scrimmage, only the end men, as eligible receivers on the line of scrimmage at the time of the snap, are permitted to go beyond the line before the ball is kicked.

   Exception: An eligible receiver who, at the snap is aligned or in motion behind the line and more than one yard outside the end man on his side of the line, clearly making him the outside receiver, REPLACES that end man as the player eligible to go downfield after the snap. All other members of the kicking team must remain at the line of scrimmage until the ball has been kicked.

3. Any punt that is blocked and does not cross the line of scrimmage is not a kicked ball—both teams eligible to recover and advance. However, if offensive team recovers it must make the yardage necessary for its first down to retain possession if punt was on fourth down.

4. Kicking team may never advance its own kick even though legal recovery was made. Possession only.

5. A member of the receiving team may not run into or rough a kicker who kicks from behind his line unless contact is:
   (a) Incidental to and after he had touched ball in flight.
   (b) Caused by kicker's own motions.
   (c) Occurs during a quick kick or a kick made after a run or after kicker recovers a loose ball. Ball is loose when kicker muffs snap or snap hits ground.
   (The penalty for running into the kicker is 5 yards. For roughing the kicker 15 yards and disqualification if flagrant.)

6. If a member of the kicking team at-

tempting to down the ball on or inside opponent's 5-yard line carries the ball into the end zone, it is a touchback.

7. Fouls during a punt are enforced from the previous spot—line of scrimmage. Exception: Illegal touching, illegal fair catch, invalid fair catch signal, unsportsmanlike conduct after fair catch signal, and fouls by the receiving team during loose ball after ball is kicked (fouls against kicker not included).

8. While the ball is in the air or rolling on the ground following a punt or field goal attempt and receiving team commits a foul before gaining possession, receiving team will retain possession and will be penalized for its foul.

9. It will be illegal for a defensive player to jump on, stand on or be picked up by a teammate in an attempt to block a kick. (Penalty 15 yards, unsportsmanlike conduct).

10. A punted ball remains a kicked ball until it is declared dead or in possession of either team.

11. Any member of the punting team may *down* the ball anywhere in the field of play. However, it is *illegal touching* (Official's timeout and receiver's ball at spot of illegal touching). This foul does *not* offset any foul by receivers during the down.

12. Defensive team may advance all kicks from scrimmage (including unsuccessful field goal) whether or not ball crosses defensive team's goal line. Rules pertaining to kicks from scrimmage apply until defensive team gains possession.

FAIR CATCH

1. The member of the receiving team must raise one arm full length above his head while kick is in flight. (Failure to give proper sign, receivers' ball five yards behind spot of signal.)

2. No opponent may interfere with the fair catcher, the ball or his path to the ball (15 yards from spot of foul and fair catch is awarded).

3. A player who signals for a fair catch is not required to catch the ball. How-

ever, if a player signals for a fair catch, he may not block or initiate contact with any player on the kicking team until the ball touches a player. (Penalty, snap 15 yards behind spot of foul).

4. If ball hits ground or touches one of the kicking team in flight fair catch signal is off, and all rules for a kicked ball apply.

5. Any undue advance by a fair catch receiver is delay of game. No specific distance is specified for "undue advance" as ball is dead at spot of catch. If player comes to a reasonable stop no penalty (For violation, 5 yards).

6. If time expires while ball is in play and a fair catch has been awarded to a team, they may choose to extend period by one free-kick down. However, placekicker may not use tee.

FOUL ON LAST PLAY OF HALF OR GAME

1. Foul by defense on last play of half or game: Down will be replayed if penalty is accepted.

2. Foul by offense on last play of half or game: Down will not be replayed, and the play in which the foul is committed is nullified.
   Exception: Fair catch interference, foul following change of possession, illegal touching. No score by offense is counted.

3. Double foul on last play of half or game: The down is replayed.

SPOT OF ENFORCEMENT OF FOUL

There are four basic spots at which a penalty for a foul is enforced:

1. Spot of foul: The spot where the foul is committed.

2. Previous spot: The spot where the ball was put in play.

3. Spot of snap, pass, fumble, return kick or freekick; The spot where the act connected with the foul occurred.

4. Succeeding spot: The spot where the ball next would be put in play if no distance penalty were to be enforced. *Exception:* If foul occurs after a touchdown and before the whistle for a try-

for-point, succeeding spot is spot of next kickoff.

5. All fouls committed by *offensive* team *behind* the line of scrimmage and in the field of play shall be penalized from the *previous spot*.

DOUBLE FOUL

1. If there is a double foul *during* a down in which there is a change of possession, the team last gaining possession may keep the ball unless its foul was committed prior to the change of possession.
2. If double foul occurs *after* a change of possession, the defensive team retains the ball at the spot possession was gained.

PENALTY ENFORCED ON FOLLOWING KICKOFF:

1. When a team scores by touchdown, field goal, extra point or safety and either team commits a personal foul, unsportsmanlike conduct or obvious unfair act during the down, the penalty will be assessed on the following kickoff.

DEFINITIONS

1. *CLIPPING:* Throwing the body across the back of an opponent's leg or hitting him from the back while moving up from behind unless the opponent is a runner or the action is in close line play.
2. *CLOSE LINE PLAY:* The area between the positions normally occupied by the offensive tackles, extending three yards on each side of the line of scrimmage.
3. *DEAD BALL:* Ball not in play.
4. *DOUBLE FOUL:* A foul by each team during the same down.
5. *DOWN:* The period of action that starts when the ball is put in play and ends when it is dead.
6. *ENCROACHMENT:* When a player moves across the neutral zone (see below) and makes contact with an opponent *before* the ball is snapped.
7. *FAIR CATCH:* An unhindered catch of a kick by a member of the receiving team who must raise one arm full length above his head while the kick is in flight.

8. *FOUL:* Any violation of a playing rule.
9. *FREE KICK:* A kickoff, kick after a safety or kick after a fair catch. It may be a placekick, dropkick or punt except a punt may *not* be used on a kickoff.
10. *FUMBLE:* The loss of possession of the ball.
11. *IMPETUS:* The action of a player which gives momentum to the ball.
12. *LIVE BALL:* A ball legally free-kicked or snapped. It continues in play until the down ends.
13. *LOOSE BALL:* A live ball not in possession of any player.
14. *MUFF:* The touching of a loose ball by a player in an *unsuccessful* attempt to obtain possession.
15. *NEUTRAL ZONE:* The space the length of a ball between the two scrimmage lines. The offensive team and defensive team must remain behind their end of the ball.
    Exception: The offensive player who snaps the ball.
16. *OFFSIDE:* A player is offside when any part of his body is beyond his scrimmage or free kick line *when the ball is snapped*.
17. *OWN GOAL:* The goal a team is guarding.
18. *POSSESSION:* When a player holds the ball long enough to give him control to perform any act common to the game.
19. *PUNT:* A kick made when a player drops the ball and kicks it while in flight.
20. *SAFETY:* The situation in which the ball is dead on or behind a team's own goal if the *impetus* comes from a player on that team. Two points are scored for the opposing team.
21. *SHIFT:* The movement of two or more offensive players at the same time before the snap.
22. *TOUCHBACK:* When a ball is dead on or behind a team's own goal line, provided the impetus came from an opponent and provided it is not a touchdown.
23. *TOUCHDOWN:* When any part of the ball, legally in possession of a player

inbounds, is on, above or over the opponent's goal line, provided it is not a touchback.

24. *UNSPORTSMANLIKE CONDUCT:* Any act contrary to the generally understood principles of sportsmanship.

SUMMARY OF PENALTIES

AUTOMATIC FIRST DOWN

1. Awarded to offensive team on *all defensive fouls* with these exceptions:
   (a) Offsides
   (b) Encroachment
   (c) Delay of game
   (d) Illegal substitution
   (e) Excessive time outs

LOSS OF DOWN (No yardage)

1. Second forward pass *behind* the line.
2. Forward pass strikes ground, goal post or crossbar.
3. Forward pass goes out of bounds.
4. Forward pass is first touched by eligible receiver who has gone out of bounds and returned.
5. Forward pass touched or caught by second eligible receiver before touched by defense.
6. Forward pass accidentally touches ineligible receiver on or behind line.

FIVE YARDS

1. Crawling.
2. Defensive holding or illegal use of hands, including chucking an eligible receiver more than once after he is more than 3 yards downfield (automatic first down)
3. Delay of game (if at start of half, 15 yards)
4. Encroachment
5. Too many time outs.
6. False start.
7. Illegal formation.
8. Illegal shift.
9. Illegal motion.
10. Illegal substitution.
11. Kickoff out of bounds between goal lines and not touched.
12. Invalid fair catch signal.
13. More than 11 players on the field for either team.

14. Less than seven men on offensive line at snap.
15. Offsides.
16. Failure to pause one second after shift or huddle.
17. Running into kicker (automatic first down) .
18. More than one man in motion at snap.
19. Grasping face mask of opponent (automatic first down) (15 yards and disqualification if flagrant.)
20. Player out of bounds at snap.
21. Ineligible member (s) of kicking team going beyond line of scrimmage before ball is kicked.

FIFTEEN YARDS

1. Clipping.
2. Fair catch intereference.
3. Illegal batting, kicking or punching loose ball (if by defense, automatic first down) .
4. Illegal crackback block by offense.
5. Ineligible receiver downfield.
6. Offensive pass interference.
7. Piling on (automatic first down) .
8. Roughing the kicker (automatic first down) .
9. Roughing the passer (automatic first down) .
10. Unnecessary roughness (if by defense, automatic first down) .
11. Unsportsmanlike conduct.
12. Delay of game at start of either half.
13. Helping the runner.
14. Holding, illegal use of hands or tripping on offense.
    Exception: 10-yard penalty if enforced from a spot at or behind line of scrimmage or no deeper than 3 yards downfield.

FIVE YARDS AND LOSS OF DOWN

1. Forward pass thrown from *beyond* line of scrimmage.

FIFTEEN YARDS AND LOSS OF DOWN

1. Forward pass intentionally touched by ineligible receiver on or behind line.
2. Forward pass intentionally or accidentally touched by ineligible receiver beyond the line of scrimmage.

3. Intentional grounding of forward pass (cannot score a safety).

DISQUALIFICATION AND 15 YARDS

1. Striking opponent with fist.
2. Kicking or kneeing opponent.
3. Striking opponent on head or neck with forearm, elbow or hands.
4. Entering game a second time with illegal equipment.

DISQUALIFICATION AND 15 YARDS (IF FLAGRANT)

1. Roughing kicker.
2. Roughing passer.
3. Malicious unnecessary roughness.
4. Unsportsmanlike conduct.

5. Palpably unfair act (Distance penalty determined by the Referee after consultation with other officials).

SUSPENSION FROM GAME AND FIVE YARDS

1. Illegal equipment. (Player may return after one down when legally equipped).

TOUCHDOWN

1. When Referee determines a palpably unfair act deprived a team of a touchdown. (Example: Player comes off bench and tackles runner apparently enroute to touchdown.)

OFFICIALS' JURISDICTIONS, POSITIONS AND DUTIES

REFEREE—General oversight and control of game. Gives signals for all fouls and is final authority for rule interpretations. Takes a position in backfield 10 to 12 yards behind line of scrimmage, favors right side (if quarterback is right-handed passer). Determines legality of snap, observes deep back(s) for legal motion. On running play, observes quarterback during and after handoff, remains with him until action has cleared away, then proceeds downfield, checking on runner and contact behind him. When runner is downed, Referee determines forward progress from wing official and if necessary, adjusts final position of ball.

On pass plays, drops back as quarterback begins to fade back, picks up legality of blocks by near linemen. Changes to complete concentration on quarterback as defenders approach. Primarily responsible to rule on possible roughing action on passer and if ball becomes loose, rules whether ball is free on a fumble or dead on an incomplete pass.

During kicking situations, Referee has primary responsibility to rule on kicker's actions and whether or not any subsequent contact by a defender is legal.

UMPIRE—Primary responsibility to rule on players' equipment, as well as their conduct and actions on scrimmage line. Lines up approximately 4 to 5 yards downfield, varying position from in front of weakside tackle to strongside guard. Looks for possible false start by offensive linemen. Observes legality of contact by both offensive linemen while blocking and by defensive players while they attempt to ward off blockers. Is prepared to call rule infractions if they occur on offense or defense. Moves forward to line of scrimmage when pass play develops in order to insure that interior linemen do not move illegally downfield. If offensive linemen indicate screen pass is to be attempted, Umpire shifts his attention toward screen side, picks up potential receiver in order to insure that he will legally be permitted to run his pattern and continues to rule on action of blockers. Umpire is to assist in ruling on incomplete or trapped passes when ball is thrown overhead or short.

HEAD LINESMAN—Primarily responsible for ruling on offside, encroachment and actions pertaining to scrimmage line prior to or at snap. Keys on wide receiver on his side, observing his early and continuing movement after snap. Has full responsibility for ruling on sideline plays on his side, e.g.—pass receiver or runner in or out of bounds. Together with Referee, Linesman is responsible for keeping track of number of downs and is in charge of mechanics of his chain crew in connection with its duties.

Linesman must be prepared to assist in determining forward progress by a runner on play directed toward middle or into his side zone. He, in turn, is to signal Referee or Umpire what forward point ball has reached. Linesman is responsible to rule on legality of action involving wide receiver on his side as well as that of other receivers who approach his side zone. He is to call pass interference when the infraction occurs and is to rule on legality of blockers and defenders on plays involving ball carriers, whether it is entirely a running play, a combination pass and run or a play involving a kick.

LINE JUDGE—Straddles line of scrimmage on side of field opposite Linesman. Keeps time of game as a backup for clock operator. Along with Linesman is responsible for offside, encroachment and actions pertaining to scrimmage line prior to or at snap. Line Judge keys on wide receiver on his side observing his movements downfield after snap. When receiver clears area, Judge moves toward backfield side being especially alert to rule on flight of ball when pass is made (he must rule whether forward or backward). Line Judge has primary responsibility to rule whether or not passer is behind or beyond line of scrimmage when pass is made. He also assists in observing actions by blockers and defenders who are on his side of field. After pass is thrown, Line Judge directs attention toward activities which occur in back of Umpire. During punting situations, Line Judge remains at line of scrimmage, observes action on end closest to him and rules whether or not kick crossed line.

BACK JUDGE—Operates on same side of field as Line Judge 15 to 17 yards deep. Keys on tight end, if on his side, or near back, if tight end is on opposite side. Concentrates on path of end or back, observing legality of his potential block (s) or of actions taken against him. Is prepared to rule from *deep* position on holding or illegal use of hands by end or back or on defensive infractions committed by player guarding him. Has primary responsibility to make decisions involving sideline on his side of field—e.g., pass receiver or runner in or out of bounds.

Back Judge makes decisions involving catching, recovery or illegal touching of a loose ball beyond line of scrimmage; rules on plays involving pass receiver, including legality of catch or pass interference; assists in covering actions of runner, including blocks by teammates and that of defenders; calls clipping on punt returns and, together with Field Judge, rules whether or not field goal attempts are successful.

FIELD JUDGE—Takes a position between 22 to 25 yards downfield, favoring Head Linesman's side of field. Keys on tight end, if on his side, or on near back, if tight end is on opposite side. Concentrates on path of end or back, observing legality of his potential block (s) or of actions taken against him. Is prepared to rule from *deep* position on holding or illegal use of hands by end or back or on defensive infractions committed by player guarding him.

Field Judge times 30-second interval between plays and intermission between two periods of each half; makes decisions involving catching, recovery or illegal touching of a loose ball beyond line of scrimmage; is responsible to rule on plays involving end line, calls pass interference, fair catch infractions and clipping on kick returns and, together with Back Judge, rules whether or not field goal attempts are successful.

THE OFFICIALS' SIGNALS

Touchdown, Field Goal or Successful Try
Both arms extended above head

Safety
Palms together over head

Loss of Down
(Follows signal for foul)
Tapping both shoulders with finger tips

Penalty Refused, Incomplete Pass, Play Over, or Missed Goal
Shifting of hands in horizontal plane

First Down
Arm raised then pointed toward defensive team's goal

Dead Ball or Neutral Zone Established
One arm with hand
up for dead ball, fourth down

No Time-Out or Time-In With Whistle
Full arm circles to simulate winding clock

Time-Out
Hands criss-crossed over head
Referee's Time-Out Same signal followed by placing one hand on top of cap
Touchback Same signal followed by

Ineligible Receiver Downfield

Offside, Encroaching or Free Kick Violation

Crawling, Pushing or Helping Runner
Pushing movement of hands to front with arms downward.

Illegal Motion at Snap
Horizontal arc with either hand

Illegal Forward Pass
Waving hand behind back
Intentional Grounding of Pass
Same as above followed by raised hand hung downward

Unsportsmanlike Conduct
Arms outstretched, palms down
(Same signal means continuing action fouls are disregarded)

Interference With Fair Catch or Forward Pass
Pushing hands forward from shoulder with hands vertical

Holding or Illegal Use of Hands or Arms
Grasping of one wrist at chest level

Personal Foul
Striking of one wrist above head
Running into or Roughing Kicker — Followed by swinging leg.
Running into Passer — Followed by raised arm swung forward.
Tripping — Followed by hooking foot behind opposite ankle.
Clipping — (Below Waist) — Followed by striking back of calf with hand.
Clipping — (Above Waist) — Followed by striking back of thigh with hand

Delay of Game or Excess Time-Out
Folded arms
Illegal Formation — Same signal followed by half and half rotation of the arms in front of body.

SEATING DIAGRAMS

Atlanta Stadium, Atlanta, Georgia

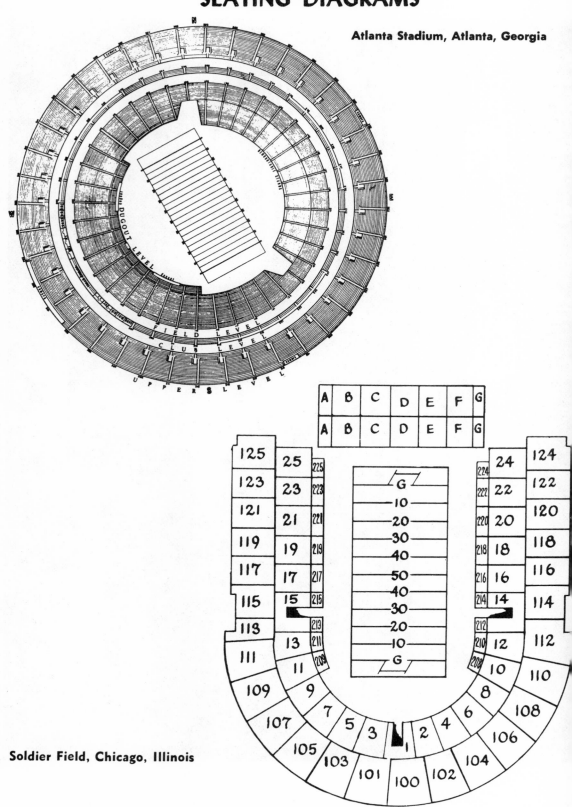

Soldier Field, Chicago, Illinois

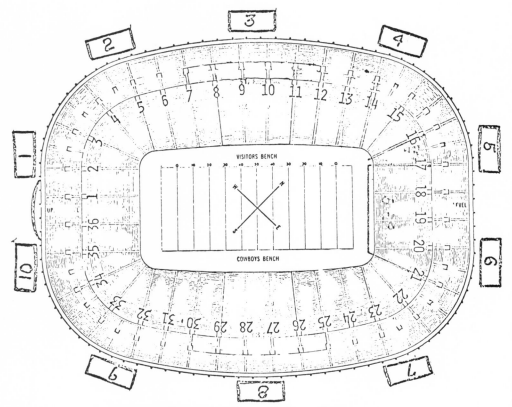

Texas Stadium, Dallas, Texas

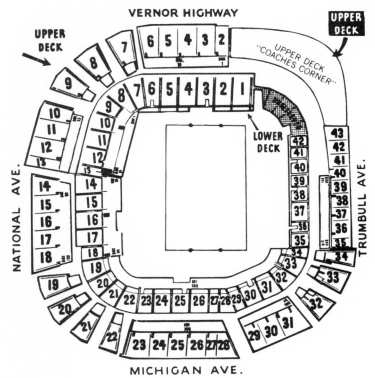

Tiger Stadium, Detroit, Michigan

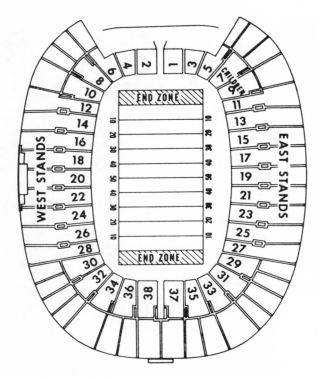

Lambeau Stadium, Green Bay, Wisconsin

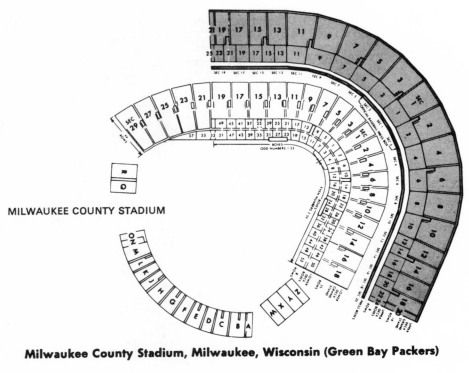

MILWAUKEE COUNTY STADIUM

Milwaukee County Stadium, Milwaukee, Wisconsin (Green Bay Packers)

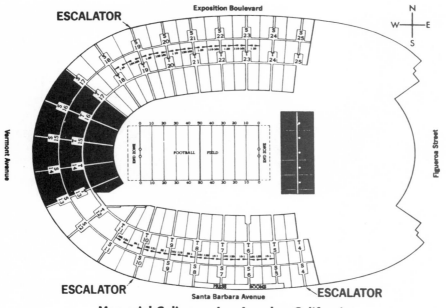

Memorial Coliseum, Los Angeles, California

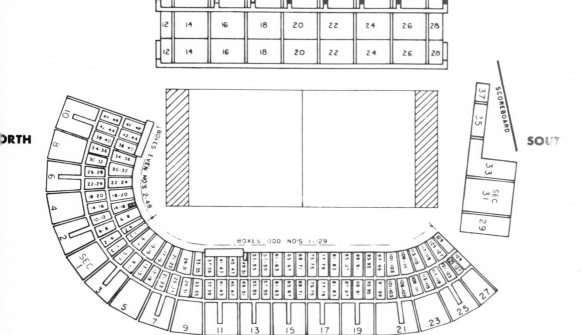

FIRST, SECOND, THIRD DECK (THIRD DECK THROUGH SECTION 11 ONLY)

WEST SIDELINES

Metropolitan Stadium, Bloomington, Minnesota

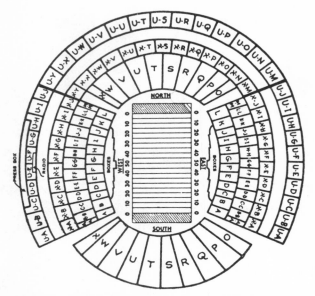

Tulane Stadium (Sugar Bowl), New Orleans, Louisiana

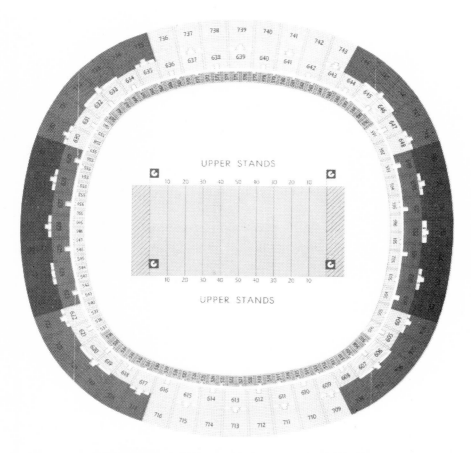

Veterans Stadium, Philadelphia, Pennsylvania

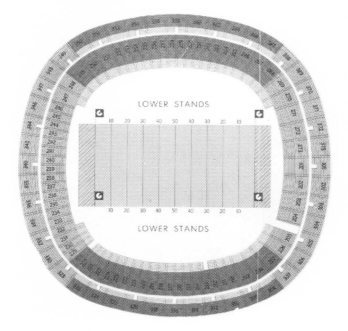

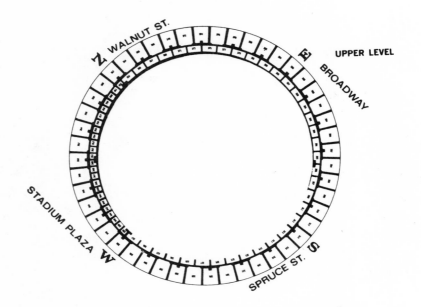

UPPER LEVEL

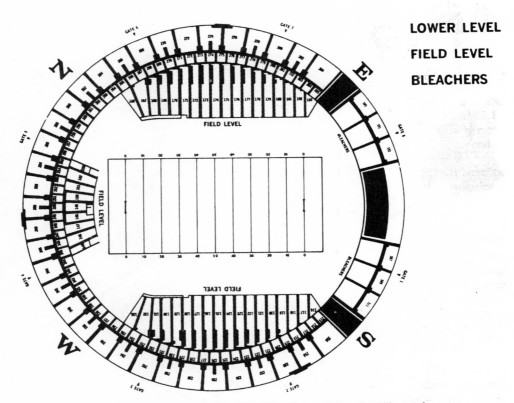

LOWER LEVEL

FIELD LEVEL

BLEACHERS

Civic Center Busch Memorial Stadium, St. Louis, Missouri

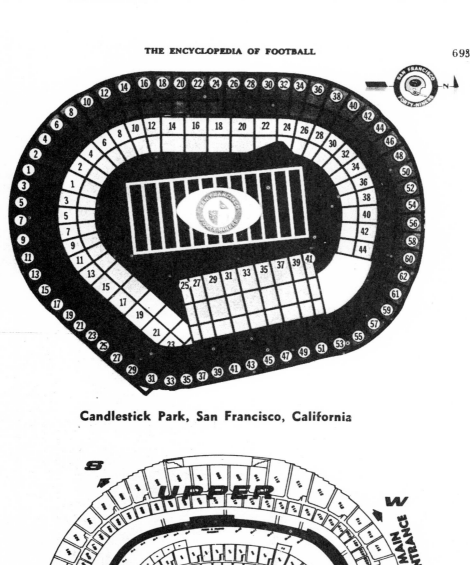

Candlestick Park, San Francisco, California

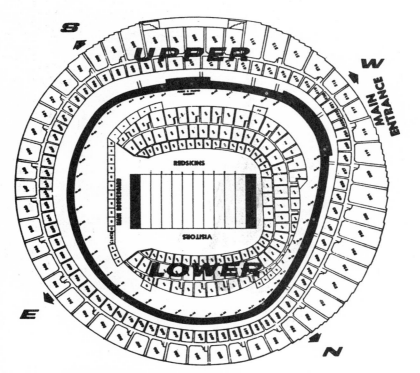

Robert F. Kennedy Stadium, Washington, D. C.

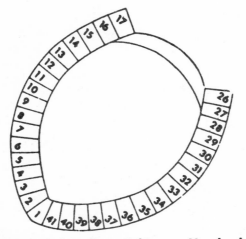

Memorial Stadium, Baltimore, Maryland

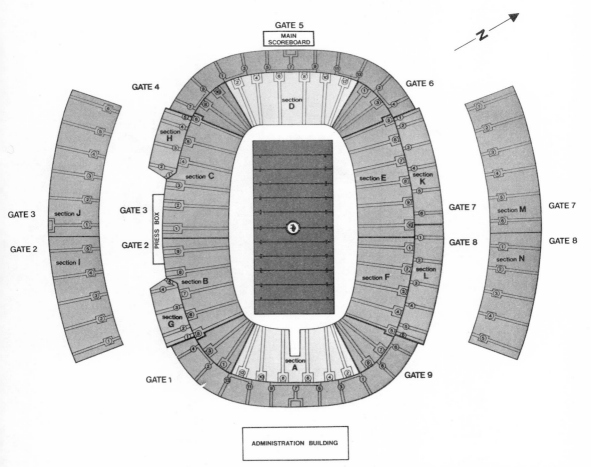

Rich Stadium, Orchard Park, New York
(Buffalo Bills)

(NORTH)

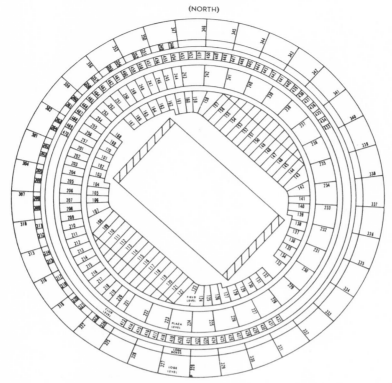

Riverfront Stadium, Cincinnati, Ohio

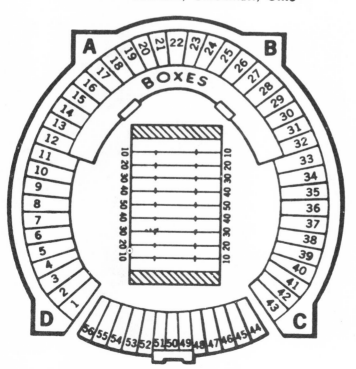

Municipal Stadium, Cleveland, Ohio

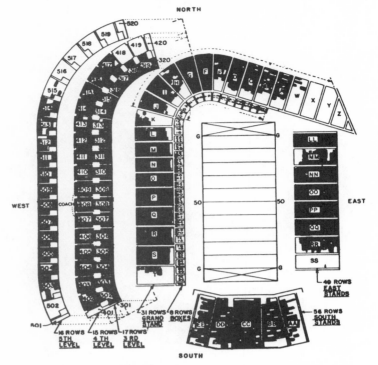

Mile High Stadium, Denver, Colorado

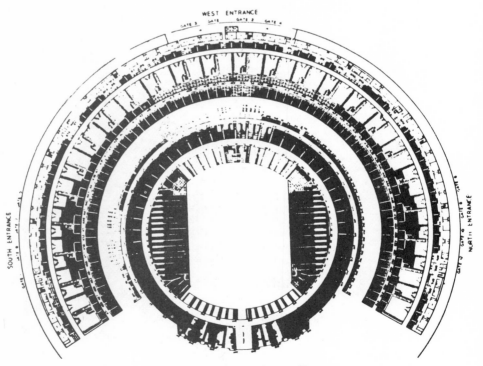

Astrodome, Houston, Texas

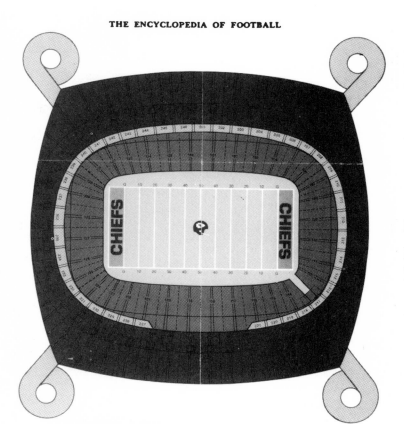

Arrowhead Stadium, Kansas City, Missouri

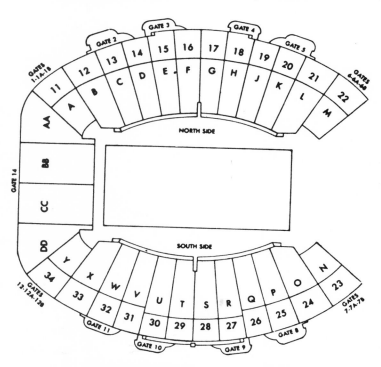

Orange Bowl Stadium, Miami, Florida

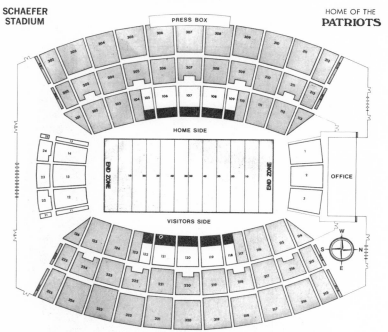

Schaefer Stadium, Foxboro, Massachusetts

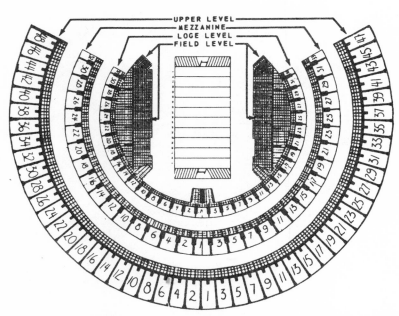

Shea Stadium, New York, New York (N. Y. Jets and N. Y. Giants)

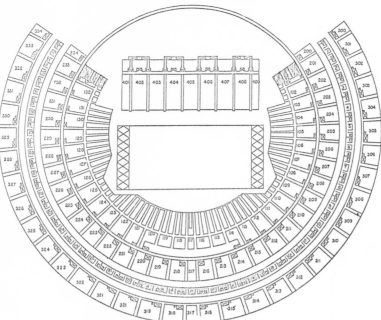

Oakland-Alameda County Coliseum, Oakland, California

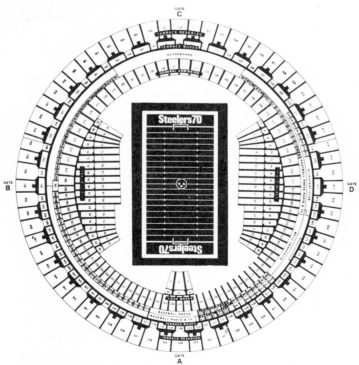

Three Rivers Stadium, Pittsburgh, Pennsylvania

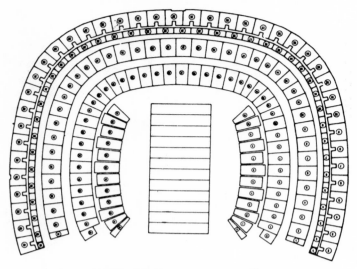

San Diego Stadium, San Diego, California

ADDENDUM TO RULES

The following rules changes were adopted in April, 1974, and may be subject to further modifications:

SUDDEN DEATH
For all games, but duration limited to 15-minute overtime in pre-season and regular season games.

THE KICKING GAME
1. Move goal posts to end line.
2. Kickoff from 35-yard line.
3. Missed field goals returned to line of scrimmage or 20-yard line whichever is farther from goal line.
4. Members of a team kicking from scrimmage (punt or field goal) cannot cross line of scrimmage until ball is kicked.

THE PASSING GAME
Afford wide receivers better opportunity to get downfield by:
1. Eliminating roll blocking and cutting of wide receivers.
2. Restricting extent of downfield contact defender permitted to have with eligible receivers.

PENALTY CHANGE
Penalty for offensive holding, illegal use of hands and tripping reduced to 10 yards from 15 yards, when infraction occurs in area of line of scrimmage and three yards beyond.

BLOCKING CHANGE
Wide receivers blocking back toward the ball three yards from the line of scrimmage cannot block below the waist.

NFL RULES CHANGES FOR 1975

1. On a fourth down pass—when the offensive team is inside the opposition's 20-yard line—an incomplete pass is no longer an automatic touchback. Now the opponents will have a first and ten at the original line of scrimmage, not the 20 yard line.
2. Two penalties reduced from 15 yards to 10 yards—offensive pass interference and illegal receiver downfield.
3. Any huddle containing more than 11 men is unsportsmanlike conduct, a 15-yard penalty. Previously there was no penalty if extra players were off the field before the play.
4. If defensive holding occurs when the passer is sacked, the penalty is marked off from the line for scrimmage, not the spot of the foul.